ANNUAL UPDATE
Strategic Management Theory

Business Ethics and Strategy

The annual update for *Strategic Management* offers an expanded treatment of business ethics and strategy. Although there has always been a section on ethics in the text, the corporate scandals of the last few years suggest that additional emphasis needs to be placed on this topic.

Between 2001 and 2004 accounting scandals unfolded at a number of major corporations, including Enron, WorldCom, Tyco, Computer Associates, Health South, Adelphia Communications and, most recently, the major Italian food company, Parmalat, where managers apparently "invented" some $8–$12 billion in assets.[1]

Beyond accounting scandals, there have been accusations of securities fraud at numerous companies and financial institutions. At the biotechnology firm ImClone, CEO Sam Waksal went to jail in June 2003 after admitting to insider trading. High-profile television personality Martha Stewart, a friend of Waksal, was indicted on similar charges. Frank Quattrone, a star investment banker at Credit Suisse First Boston, was accused of improperly allocating shares in the Initial Public Offerings (IPOs) of technology companies to movers and shakers in Silicon Valley, known as the "friends of Frank," with the understanding that his "friends" would push future IPOs to his unit at Credit Suisse.[2] In 2004, Quattrone faced a trial for obstruction of justice. In April 2003, ten major investment banks including Credit Suisse settled a class action lawsuit brought by investors alleging that the banks fraudulently painted a favorable picture of over 300 technology IPOs that they bought to market during the late 1990s and early 2000s, bilking ordinary investors of billions of dollars. The banks agreed to pay $1.4 billion in damages to investors.[3]

Other companies have been accused of illegal competitive tactics. Despite a 2001 settlement with the Justice Department, Microsoft continues to be dogged by accusations that it is violating antitrust law in both the United States and the European Union.[4] In 2003 Visa and MasterCard settled an antitrust suit for $3 billion brought against them by retailers who charged that the credit card issuers illegally forced them to take their debit cards as well and attached high merchant fees to those cards.[5]

Still another set of ethics violations concern corporations with significant government contracts. In mid-2003 the Air Force stripped Boeing of $1 billion in contracts to launch satellites when it was discovered that Boeing had obtained thousands of pages of proprietary information from rival Lockheed Martin to prepare its winning bid for the contract. This was followed by the revelation that Boeing's CFO, Mike Sears, had offered a government official, Darleen Druyun, a lucrative job at Boeing while Druyun was still involved in evaluating whether Boeing should be awarded a $17 billion contract to build tankers for the Air Force. Boeing won the contract against strong competition from Airbus, and Druyun was hired by Boeing. The job offer may have had an impact on the Air Force decision. Boeing fired the CFO and Druyun, and shortly afterwards Boeing CEO Phil Condit resigned in a tacit acknowledgement that he bore responsibility for the ethics violations that had occurred at Boeing during his tenure as leader.[6]

In December 2003 Halliburton, a major Texas-based oil service firm, announced that two of its employees had taken kickbacks worth $6 million for awarding a Kuwaiti-based company with lucrative work supplying U.S. troops in Iraq. Halliburton immediately fired the two individuals, but quickly found itself defending its billing practices when two other former employees came forward and told a U.S. congressman that the company "routinely overcharged" for work done for the U.S. government. Moreover, the company was simultaneously defending itself against charges that, along with other companies in a consortium, it made over $180 million in illegal payments to secure a $4.9 billion contract to build a liquefied natural gas plant in Nigeria.[7]

These examples suggest that a major ethical crisis swept through the business world in the late 1990s and early 2000s. This occurred despite the fact that business ethics, as a topic, has been actively taught at most business schools since the 1980s, and that managers at most corporations have long paid lip service to the need to behave in an ethical manner. Kenneth Lay, former CEO of Enron, which collapsed when a multi-billion-dollar accounting fraud was revealed, was fond of quoting the company's code of ethics during the period when it accumulated $27 billion in off-balance-sheet debt.[8] Given this apparent disconnect between lip service and practice, expanded treatment of this timely topic seems warranted.

The Law and Business Ethics

The term **ethics** refers to accepted principles of right or wrong that govern the conduct of a person, the members of a profession, or the actions of an organization. **Business ethics** are the accepted principles of right or wrong governing the conduct of business people. Ethical decisions are those that are in accordance with those accepted principles of right and wrong, whereas an unethical decision is one that violates accepted principles. Managers may be confronted with **ethical dilemmas,** which are situations where there is no agreement over what the accepted principles of right and wrong are, or where none of the available alternatives seems ethically acceptable.[9]

In our society many accepted principles of right and wrong are universally recognized and codified into law. In the business arena there are laws governing product liability (*tort laws*), contracts and breaches of contract (*contract law*), the protection of intellectual property (*intellectual property law*), competitive behavior (*antitrust law*), and the selling of securities (*securities law*). Not only is it unethical to break these laws, it is illegal.

In this book we argue that the preeminent goal of managers in a business should be to pursue strategies that maximize the long-run profitability of the enterprise, thereby boosting returns to stockholders. Strategies must be consistent with the laws that govern business behavior—managers must act legally while maximizing the profitability of the enterprise. Unfortunately, there are numerous examples of managers breaking the law and taking advantage of legal ambiguities and grey areas to pursue actions that are legally suspect and clearly unethical.

For example, tobacco has been linked to health problems in smokers since the 1960s, but for years tobacco companies questioned the scientific evidence, continued to promote smoking, and successfully fought any legal cases brought against them by smokers. They argued that smoking was a matter of individual choice and that government health warnings on packets of cigarettes made smokers aware of the dangers of the product. Eventually evidence was found that managers at these companies had deliberately suppressed internal research that concluded that tobacco products were indeed harmful—a clear example of unethical behavior. This allowed lawyers to claim that tobacco companies had intentionally broken tort law by promoting a product that they knew did serious harm to consumers. In 1999, the tobacco companies settled a lawsuit, brought by the states who sought to recover health care costs associated with tobacco-related illnesses, for $260 billion.[10]

It is important to realize, however, that behaving ethically goes beyond staying within the bounds of the law. There are many examples of strategies and actions that, while legal, do not seem to be ethical. In an attempt to reduce costs Nike, the athletic shoe company, has historically outsourced the manufacture of its shoes to suppliers based in developing nations where labor costs are considerably lower than in the United States. In the 1990s the company was dogged by repeated and persistent accusations that its products were made in "sweatshops" where workers, many of them children, slave away in hazardous conditions for wages that are below subsistence level.[11] Typical of the allegations were those detailed in the CBS news program *48 Hours*.[12] The program painted a picture of young women at a Vietnamese subcontractor who worked six days a week, in poor working conditions with toxic materials, for only 20 cents an hour. The report also stated that a living wage in Vietnam was at least $3 a day, an income that could not be achieved without working substantial overtime.

Nike and its subcontractors were not breaking any laws, but this report, and others like it, raised questions about the ethics of companies using "sweatshop labor" to make what are essentially fashion accessories. It may be legal, but is it ethical to use subcontractors who by Western standards clearly exploit their workforce? Nike's critics thought not, and the company found itself the focus of a wave of demonstrations and consumer boycotts. In response, Nike established a code of conduct for its suppliers that required them to adhere to minimum acceptable standards with regard to working conditions, hired an independent firm to audit the operations of its suppliers on a regular basis, and terminated business with suppliers who were found to be in persistent violation of the code. Thus, Nike's management took concrete steps to make sure that their actions were legal and ethical.

Ethical Issues in Strategy

Most of the ethical issues that strategic managers confront arise from a potential conflict between the goals of the enterprise, or the goals of individual managers, and the fundamental rights of important stakeholders such as stockholders, customers, employees, suppliers, competitors, communities, and the general public.[13] Stakeholders have basic rights that should be respected, and it is unethical to violate those rights.

Stockholders have the right to timely and accurate information about their investment. As providers of risk capital, they also have the right to expect managers to behave in their interests and take legal and ethical actions to maximize the value of their investments. Customers have the right to be fully informed about the products and services they purchase and how those products may cause harm to them or others. Employees have the right to safe working conditions, to fair compensation, and to be treated in a just manner by management. Suppliers have the right to expect that contracts will be respected, and that a firm will not take advantage of a power disparity to opportunistically rewrite a contract. Competitors have the right to expect that a firm will abide by the rules of competition and not violate the basic principles of antitrust laws. Communities and the general public, including their political representatives in government, have the right to expect that a firm will not violate the basic expectations that society places on enterprises—for example, by dumping toxic pollutants into the environment or overcharging for work performed on government contracts.

Those who take the stakeholder view of business ethics often argue that it is in the enlightened self-interest of managers to behave in an ethical manner that recognizes and respects the fundamental rights of stakeholders, because doing so will ensure the support of stakeholders and benefit the firm and its managers. Others go beyond this instrumental approach to ethics to say that, in many cases, acting ethically is simply the right thing to do.[14] They argue that in a business setting benevolent behavior is the moral responsibility of successful enterprises. Businesses need to give something back to the society that made their success possible.

Oftentimes, unethical behavior arises in a corporate setting when managers decide to put their own personal goals, or the goals of the enterprise, above the fundamental rights of one or more stakeholder groups. The most common examples of such behavior involve self-dealing, information manipulation, anticompetitive behavior, opportunistic exploitation of other players in the value chain in which the firm is embedded (including suppliers, complement providers, and distributors), the maintenance of substandard working conditions, environmental degradation, and corruption.

Self-dealing occurs when managers find a way to feather their own nests with corporate monies. Classical examples of this behavior include (1) senior managers who treat corporate funds as their own personal treasury and raid them to support a lavish lifestyle (as apparently happened at Tyco under former CEO Dennis Kozlowski); (2) senior managers who use their control over the compensation committee of the board of directors to award themselves pay increases or stock option grants that are out of proportion with their contribution to the corporation; and (3) instances where individual managers award business contracts to the supplier that provides the largest kickback (as occurred at Halliburton). In these cases, managers are not acting in the best interests of shareholders but are consuming funds that should legitimately go to stockholders. Some of this behavior, while technically legal, is unethical since it violates the basic right of stockholders to a fair return on their investment.

Information manipulation occurs when managers use their control over corporate data to distort or hide information in order to enhance their own financial situation, or the competitive position of the firm. Enron's practice of hiding significant debt from shareholders in off-balance-sheet partnerships is an example of this behavior. This practice misled investors and supported a much higher stock price than was justified. Not surprisingly, this higher stock price enabled managers to exercise stock option grants for considerable personal gain. When the scale of hidden debts was finally revealed the company quickly collapsed into bankruptcy, wiping out the value of shareholders' equity in the process. Again, such actions are unethical since they violate the right of investors to accurate and timely information.

Information manipulation can also occur with regard to nonfinancial data. As noted in chapter 11, John Manville, once the largest producer of asbestos in the world, violated the rights of both employees and customers by systematically suppressing internal data that linked asbestos to lung cancer. For decades Manville allowed its employees and customers to continue working with the substance, which ultimately resulted in asbestos-related deaths. This action kept Manville in business longer but caused considerable human and financial damage in the long run. Since the 1970s, U.S. companies have paid out $54 billion on more than 600,000 asbestos injury claims. Some sixty companies have sought bankruptcy protection to limit their losses from asbestos-related lawsuits, and estimates suggest that asbestos claims could ultimately cost as much as $210 billion.[15]

Anticompetitive behavior covers a range of actions aimed at harming actual or potential competitors, most often by using monopoly power, thereby enhancing the long-run prospects of the firm. For example, in the 1990s the Justice Department claimed that Microsoft used its monopoly power and threatened to withhold Windows unless PC makers bundled Microsoft's web browser, Internet Explorer, with Windows and displayed Internet Explorer prominently on the computer desktop. Since PC makers need Windows to sell their machines, this would be a powerful threat. The alleged aim of the action, which is an example of "tie-in sales" and illegal under antitrust laws, was to drive a competing browser maker, Netscape, out of business. The courts ruled that Microsoft was abusing its monopoly power in this case, and under a 2001 consent decree the company agreed to stop the practice.

Putting the legal issues aside, action such as that allegedly undertaken by Microsoft is unethical on at least three counts; first, it violates the rights of end consumers by unfairly limiting their choice; second, it violates the rights of downstream participants in the industry value chain, in this case PC makers, by forcing them to incorporate a particular product in their design; and third, it violates the rights of competitors to free and fair competition.

Opportunistic exploitation of other players in the value chain in which the firm is embedded is another example of unethical behavior. **Opportunistic exploitation** of this kind typically occurs when the managers of a firm seek to unilaterally rewrite the terms of a contract with suppliers, buyers, or complement providers in a way that is more favorable to the firm, often using their power to force the revision through. For example, in the late 1990s Boeing entered into a $2 billion contract with Titanium Metals Corporation to buy certain amounts of titanium for ten years. In 2000, after Titanium Metals had spent $100 million to expand its production capacity to fulfill the contract, Boeing demanded that the contract be renegotiated, asking for lower prices and an end to minimum purchase agreements. Managers at Boeing may have thought they could push this contract revision through since Titanium's investment meant that it would be unlikely to walk away from the deal. Titanium Metals promptly sued Boeing for breach of contract. The dispute was settled out of court; under a revised agreement Boeing agreed to pay monetary damages to Titanium Metals (reported to be in the $60 million range) and entered into an amended contract to purchase titanium.[16] Irrespective of the legality of this action, it is arguably unethical since it violates the rights of suppliers to buyers who deal with them in a fair and open way.

Substandard working conditions arise when managers underinvest in working conditions, or pay employees below market rates, in order to reduce their costs of production. The most extreme examples of this occur when a firm establishes operations in countries that lack the workplace regulations found in developed nations such as the United States. Nike falls into this category. In another recent example, The Ohio Art Company ran into an ethical storm when newspaper reports alleged that it had moved production of its popular Etch a Sketch toy to a supplier in Shenzhen Province in China where employees, mostly teenagers, worked long hours for 24 cents per hour, well below the legal minimum wage of 33 cents an hour. The reports also claimed that production started at 7:30 A.M. and continued until 10 P.M., seven days a week. Such hours would translate into an eighty-four-hour workweek, well above the standard forty-hour week set by authorities in Shenzhen, and clearly violate the rights of the workers, as specified by local regulations (which were poorly enforced). Would it be ethical for The Ohio Art Company to use such a supplier? Most would say not.[17]

Environmental degradation occurs when a firm takes actions that directly or indirectly result in pollution or other forms of environmental harm. Environmental degradation can violate the rights of local communities and the general public for clean air and water, land that is free from pollution by toxic chemicals and excessive deforestation that results in land erosion and floods (forests absorb rainfall and limit flooding), and so on.

Finally, **corruption** can arise in a business context when managers pay bribes to gain access to lucrative business contracts. Halliburton, mentioned earlier, is an example of this. Corruption is clearly unethical since it violates many rights, including the right of competitors to a level playing field when bidding for contracts. If government officials are involved, the rights of citizens to expect that government officials act in the best interest of the local community or nation are violated.

Roots of Unethical Behavior

Why do some managers behave unethically? What motivates them to engage in actions that violate accepted principles of right and wrong, trample on the rights of one or more stakeholder groups, or simply break the law? While there is no simple answer to this question, a few generalizations can be made.[18]

First, it is important to recognize that business ethics are not divorced from *personal ethics*—the generally accepted principles of right and wrong governing the conduct of individuals. As individuals we are taught that it is wrong to lie and cheat, and that it is right to behave with integrity and honor and stand up for what we believe in. The personal ethical code that guides our behavior comes from a number of sources, including our parents, our schools, our religion, and the media. An individual with a strong sense of personal ethics is less likely to behave in an unethical manner in a business setting, and in particular, is less likely to engage in self-dealing.

Second, many studies of unethical behavior in a business setting have found that businesspeople do not always realize that they are behaving unethically, simply because they fail to ask if a decision or action is ethical.[19] Instead of incorporating ethical considerations into business decision making, they apply a straightforward business calculus to what they perceive to be a business decision, and forget that the decision may also have an important ethical dimension. This may have been the case regarding the alleged subcontracting decisions made by Nike. Perhaps managers made decisions on the basis of business variables such as cost, delivery, and product quality, and failed to ask, "How does this subcontractor treat its workforce?" If they thought about the question at all, they may have reasoned that it was the subcontractor's concern, not theirs.

Unfortunately, the climate in some businesses does not encourage people to think through the ethical consequences of business decisions. This brings us to the third cause of unethical behavior in businesses—an organizational culture that deemphasizes business ethics, reducing all decisions to the purely economic. Author Robert Bryce has written how the organization culture at Enron was built on values that emphasized greed and deception.[20] According to Bryce, the tone was set by top managers who engaged in self-dealing to enrich themselves and their own families. Former CEO Kenneth Lay made sure that his own family benefited handsomely from Enron. Much of Enron's corporate travel business was handled by a travel agency partly owned by Lay's sister. In 1997 Enron acquired a company owed by Kenneth Lay's son, Mark Lay. At the time Mark Lay and another company he controlled were targets of a federal criminal investigation of bankruptcy fraud and embezzlement. Bryce also details how Lay's grown daughter used an Enron jet to transport her king-size bed to France. With Kenneth Lay as an example, it is not surprising that self-dealing soon became endemic at Enron.

A fourth cause of unethical behavior has already been hinted at above—pressure from top management to meet unrealistic performance goals that can only be attained by cutting corners or acting in an unethical manner. At Enron, Lay's successor as CEO, Jeff Skilling, put a performance evaluation system in place that weeded out 15 percent of underperformers every six months. This created a pressure-cooker culture with a myopic focus on short-run performance, and some executives and energy traders responded to that pressure by falsifying their performance.

The lesson that we learn from the Enron debacle is that an organizational culture can "legitimize" behavior that society would judge as unethical. In such circumstances there is a greater-than-average probability that managers will violate their own personal ethics and engage in behavior that is unethical. By the same token, an organizational culture can reinforce the need for ethical behavior. At Hewlett-Packard Bill Hewlett and David Packard, the company's founders, propagated a set of values known as The HP Way. These values, which shape the way business is conducted both within and by the corporation, have an important ethical component. Among other things, they stress the need for confidence in and respect for people, open communication, and concern for the individual employee.

The Enron and Hewlett-Packard examples suggest a fifth root cause of unethical behavior—*leadership*. Leaders help to establish the culture of an organization and set the example that others follow. Employees in a business often take their cue from business leaders. It is not what leaders say that matters, but what they do.

Philosophical Approaches to Ethics

Before we discuss what steps managers can take to make sure that that they and their co-workers act in an ethical manner, it is necessary to take a closer look at the philosophical underpinnings of business ethics. Ultimately it is this philosophy that can provide managers with a moral compass that will guide them through difficult ethical issues. We will start with the approach suggested by the Nobel Prize–winning economist Milton Friedman.

The Friedman Doctrine

Back in 1970, Milton Friedman wrote an article that has since become a classic straw man that business ethics scholars outline only to then tear down.[21] Friedman's basic position is that the only social responsibility of business is to increase profits, so long as the company stays within the rules of law. He explicitly rejects the idea that businesses should undertake social expenditures beyond those mandated by the law and required for the efficient running of a business. For example, he suggests that improving working conditions beyond the level required by the law *and* necessary to maximize employee productivity will reduce profits and is not appropriate. He believes that a firm should maximize its profits, since that is the way to maximize the returns that accrue to the owners of the firm, its stockholders. According to Friedman, if stockholders wish to use the proceeds to make social investments, that is their right, but managers of the firm should not make that decision for them.

Although Friedman is talking about social responsibility, most business ethics scholars equate social responsibility with ethical behavior, and thus believe Friedman is also arguing against business ethics. However, this assumption is not quite true, for Friedman does state that businesses should behave in an ethical manner:

> "There is one and only one social responsibility of business—to use its resources and engage in activities designed to increase its profits so long as it stays within the rules of the game, which is to say that it engages in open and free competition without deception or fraud."[22]

Nevertheless, Friedman's arguments do break down under closer examination. This is particularly true where the "rules of the game" are not well established, are ambiguous and open to different interpretations, or differ substantially from country to county. Using child labor may not be against the law in a developing nation, but it is still immoral because the practice conflicts with widely-held views about the right and proper way to treat children. Similarly, there may be no rules against pollution in a developed nation, but generalized notions of morality would hold that it is unethical to dump toxic pollutants into rivers, or foul the air with gas releases.

Utilitarian and Kantian Ethics

The utilitarian and Kantian approaches to business ethics were developed in the eighteenth and nineteenth centuries. Although they have been largely superseded by more modern approaches, they form part of the tradition upon which newer approaches have been constructed.

Utilitarian approaches to ethics hold that the moral worth of actions or practices is determined by their consequences.[23] An action is judged to be desirable if it leads to the best possible balance of good consequences over bad consequences. Utilitarianism is committed to the maximization of good and the minimization of harm. Utilitarianism recognizes that actions have multiple consequences, some of which are good in a social sense, and some of which are harmful. As a philosophy for business ethics, it focuses attention on the need to carefully weigh all of the social benefits and costs of a business action, and to pursue only those actions where the benefits outweigh the costs. The best decisions, from a utilitarian perspective, are those that produce the greatest good for the greatest number of people.

Many businesses have adopted specific tools, such as cost-benefit analysis and risk assessment, that are firmly rooted in a utilitarian philosophy. Managers often weigh the benefits and costs of a course of action before deciding whether to pursue it. For example, how does an oil company that wants to drill in an Alaskan wildlife preserve measure the economic benefits of increased oil production and job creation against the costs of environmental degradation in a fragile ecosystem? An agricultural biotechnology company such as Monsanto must decide whether the benefits of genetically modified crops that produce "natural pesticides" outweigh the risks. Do increased crop yields and a reduced need for chemical fertilizers outweigh the possibility that insects may develop a resistance to the "natural pesticides" engineered into Monsanto's plants, thus making the plants vulnerable to a new generation of "super bugs"? In general, utilitarian philosophers recognize that the measurement of benefits, costs, and risks is often not possible due to limited knowledge.

The second problem with utilitarianism is that the philosophy does not consider justice. The action that produces the greatest good for the greatest number of people may result in the unjustified treatment of a minority. Such action cannot be ethical, precisely because it is unjust. For example, in the interests of keeping health insurance costs down, the government screens people for the HIV virus and denies insurance coverage to those who are HIV positive. By reducing health costs, this action might produce significant benefits for a large number of people, but the action is unjust, because it discriminates unfairly against a minority.

Kantian ethics are based on the philosophy of Immanuel Kant (1724–1804). Kant argued that people should be treated as ends and never purely as *means* to the ends of others. According to Kantian philosophy, employing people in sweatshops and making them work long hours for low pay in poor working conditions is a violation of ethics. The people are treated as mere cogs in a machine and not as conscious moral beings that have dignity. Although contemporary moral philosophers tend to view Kant's ethical philosophy as incomplete—for example, his system has no place for moral emotions or sentiments such as sympathy or caring—the notion that people should be respected and treated with dignity still resonates in the modern world.

Rights Theories

Developed in the twentieth century, **rights theories** recognize that human beings have fundamental rights and privileges. Rights establish a minimum level of morally acceptable behavior. One well-known definition of a fundamental right construes it as something that takes precedence over or "trumps" a collective good. Thus we might say that the right to free speech is fundamental and takes precedence over all but the most compelling collective goals, and overrides, for example, the interest of the state in civil harmony or moral consensus.[24] Moral theorists argue that fundamental human rights form the basis of the *moral compass* managers should navigate by when making decisions that have an ethical component. In a business setting, stakeholder theory provides a useful way for managers to frame any discussion of rights.

It is important to note that along with *rights* come *obligations*. Because we have the right to free speech we are also obligated to make sure that we respect the free speech of others. Within the framework of a theory of rights, certain people or institutions are obligated to provide benefits or services that secure the rights of others. Such obligations also fall upon more than one class of moral agent (a moral agent is any person or institution, such as a government or corporation, that is capable of moral action).

For example, in the late 1980s several firms shipped their toxic waste to African nations in order to escape the high costs of toxic waste disposal in the West. In 1987 five European ships unloaded toxic waste containing dangerous poisons in Nigeria. Workers unloaded the barrels for $2.50 a day, and placed them in a dirt lot in a residential area. The workers and the residents were not told about the contents of the barrels.[25] Who bears the obligation for protecting the rights and safety of the workers and residents in a case like this? According to rights theorists, the obligation rests on the shoulders of all moral agents whose actions might harm or contribute to the harm of the workers and residents. Thus it was the obligation of the Nigerian government and the multinational firms to make sure the toxic waste did no harm to residents and workers. In this case, both the government and the multinationals apparently failed to recognize their basic obligation to protect the fundamental human rights of others.

Justice Theories

Justice theories focus on the attainment of a just distribution of economic goods and services. A **just distribution** is one that is considered fair and equitable. There is no one theory of justice, and several theories of justice conflict with each other in important ways.[26] Here we shall focus on one particular theory of justice, attributed to philosopher John Rawls, that is very influential and has important ethical implications.[27] Rawls' theory argues that all economic goods and services should be distributed equally except when an unequal distribution would work to everyone's advantage.

According to Rawls, valid principles of justice are those to which all persons would agree with if they could freely and impartially consider the situation. Impartiality is guaranteed by a conceptual device that Rawls calls the *veil of ignorance*. Under the veil of ignorance, everyone is imagined to be ignorant of all of his or her particular characteristics, for example, race, sex, intelligence, nationality, family background, and special talents. Rawls then asks, what system would people design under a veil of ignorance? His answer is that under these conditions people would unanimously agree on two fundamental principles of justice.

The first principle is that each person be permitted the maximum amount of basic liberty compatible with a similar liberty for others. Roughly speaking, Rawls takes these to be political liberty, freedom of speech and assembly, liberty of conscience and freedom of thought, the freedom and right to hold personal property, and freedom from arbitrary arrest and seizure. The second principle is that once equal basic liberty is assured, inequalities in basic social goods—such as income, wealth distribution, and opportunities—are to be allowed *only* if they benefit everyone. Rawls accepts that inequalities can be just so long as the system that produces inequalities is to the advantage of everyone. More precisely, he formulates what he calls the *difference principle*, which states that inequalities are justified if they benefit the position of the least advantaged person. For example, the wide variations in income and wealth that we see in the United States can be considered "just" if the market-based system that produces this unequal distribution also benefits the least advantaged members of society. One can argue that a well-regulated market-based economy, by promoting economic growth, benefits the least advantaged members of society. In principle at least, the inequalities inherent in such systems are therefore just. In the context of business ethics, Rawls' theory creates an interesting perspective. Is it "just," for example, to pay foreign workers less than workers in the firm's home country? Rawls' theory would suggest it is, so long as the inequality benefits the least advantaged members of the global society (which is what economic theory suggests). Alternatively, it is difficult to imagine that managers operating under a veil of ignorance would design a system where employees are paid subsistence wages, work long hours in sweatshop conditions, and are exposed to toxic materials. Such working conditions are clearly unjust in Rawls' framework, and therefore, it is unethical to adopt them. Rawls' veil of ignorance is a conceptual tool that contributes towards the moral compass that managers can use to help them navigate through difficult ethical dilemmas.

Behaving Ethically

What, then, is the best way for managers to make sure that ethical considerations are taken into account when making business decisions, especially when many of the most vexing ethical problems arise because there is no obvious right course of action? Here we focus on six things that a business and its managers can do to make sure that ethical issues are considered in business decisions.

1. Favor hiring and promoting people with a well-grounded sense of personal ethics.

2. Build an organizational culture that places a high value on ethical behavior.

3. Make sure that leaders within the business not only articulate the rhetoric of ethical behavior, but also act in a manner that is consistent with that rhetoric.

4. Put decision-making processes in place that require people to consider the ethical dimension of business decisions.

5. Put strong governance processes in place.

6. Act with moral courage.

Hiring and Promotion

It seems obvious that businesses should strive to hire and promote people with a strong sense of personal ethics who would not engage in unethical or illegal behavior, and to fire people whose behavior does not match generally accepted ethical standards. But doing so is actually very difficult.

How do you know that someone has a poor sense of personal ethics? Is there anything that businesses can do to make sure that they do not hire people who subsequently turn out to have poor personal ethics, particularly given that people have an incentive to hide this from public view? Indeed, the unethical person may well lie about his or her nature. Businesses can give potential employees psychological tests to try and discern their ethical predisposition. They can ask for letters of reference or talk to people who have worked with the prospective employee. The latter is certainly not uncommon and does indeed influence the hiring process. As for promoting people who have displayed poor ethics, that should not occur in a company where the organizational culture places a high value on the need for ethical behavior, and where leaders act accordingly.

It is also in the interests of prospective employees to find out as much as they can about the ethical climate in an organization. After all, who wants to end up working at a firm like Enron?

Organizational Culture and Leadership

To foster ethical behavior, businesses need to build an organizational culture that places a high value on ethical behavior. Three things are particularly important in building an organizational culture that emphasizes ethical behavior.

First, businesses must explicitly articulate values that place a strong emphasis on ethical behavior. Many companies now do this by drafting a **code of ethics,** which is a formal statement of the ethical priorities a business adheres to. Others have incorporated ethical statements into documents that articulate the values or mission of the business. For example, the food and consumer products giant Unilever has a code of ethics that states:

> "We will not use any form of forced, compulsory or child labor. . . No employee may offer, give or receive any gift or payment which is, or may be construed as being, a bribe. Any demand for, or offer of, a bribe must be rejected immediately and reported to management."[28]

Unilever's principles send a very clear message about the appropriate ethics to managers and employees within the organization.

Second, having articulated values in a code of ethics or some other document, it is important that leaders in the business give life and meaning to those words by *acting on them*. This means using every relevant opportunity to stress the importance of business ethics and making sure that key business decisions make good economic sense and are ethical. Many companies have gone a step further, hiring independent firms to audit the company and make sure that they are behaving in a manner consistent with their ethical code.

Finally, building an organizational culture that places a high value on ethical behavior requires incentives and a system that rewards people who engage in ethical behavior and sanctions those who do not. At General Electric, for example, former CEO Jack Welsh reviewed the performance of managers, dividing them into overperformers who displayed the right values and were singled out for advancement and bonuses, and overperformers who displayed the wrong values and were let go. Welsh was not willing to tolerate leaders within the company who did not act in accordance with the central values of the company, even if they were in all other respects skilled managers.[29]

Decision-Making Processes

In addition to establishing the right kind of ethical culture in an organization, businesspeople must be able to think through the ethical implications of decisions in a systematic way. Rights theories and Rawls' theory of justice can help them do so. Beyond these theories, some experts on ethics have proposed a straightforward practical guide—or ethical algorithm—to determine whether a decision is ethical.[30] As stated in Chapter 11, a decision is acceptable on ethical grounds if a businessperson can answer "yes" to each of these questions:

1. Does my decision fall within the accepted values or standards that typically apply in the organizational environment (as articulated in a code of ethics or some other corporate statement)?

2. Am I willing to see the decision communicated to all stakeholders affected by it—for example, by having it reported in newspapers or on television?

3. Would the people I have significant personal relationships with—family members, friends, or even managers in other businesses—approve of the decision?

As noted in Chapter 11, others have recommended a five-step process to think through ethical problems (see Chapter 11 for details).[31]

Ethics Officers

To make sure that a business behaves in an ethical manner, a number of firms now have ethics officers. These are individuals who are responsible for making sure that all employees are trained to be ethically aware, that ethical considerations enter the business decision-making process, and that the company's code of ethics is adhered to. Ethics officers may also be responsible for auditing decisions to make sure that they are consistent with this code. In many businesses, ethics officers act as an internal ombudsperson with responsibility for handling confidential inquiries from employees, investigating complaints from employees or others, reporting findings, and making recommendations for change.

United Technologies, a large aerospace company with worldwide revenues of over $28 billion, has had a formal code of ethics since 1990.[32] There are now some 160 business practice officers within United Technologies (this is the company's name for ethics officers) who are responsible for making sure that the code is adhered to. United Technologies also established an ombudsperson program in 1986 that lets employees inquire anonymously about ethics issues. The program has received some 56,000 inquiries since 1986 and 8,000 cases have been handled by an ombudsperson.

Strong Corporate Governance

Strong corporate governance procedures are needed to make sure that managers adhere to ethical norms, and, in particular, to make sure that senior managers do not engage in self-dealing or information manipulation.

There are five cornerstones of strong governance. The first is a board of directors that is composed of a majority of outside directors who have no management responsibilities in the firm, who are willing and able to hold top managers accountable, and who do not have business ties with important insiders. These outside directors should be individuals of high integrity whose reputation is based on their ability to act independently. The second cornerstone is a board where the position of CEO and chairman are held by separate individuals, and the chairman is an outside director. When the CEO is also chairman of the board of directors, he can further his own personal agenda or limit criticism against current corporate policies. The third cornerstone is a compensation committee of the board, composed entirely of outside directors, that sets the level of pay for top managers, including stock option grants and the like. By making sure that the compensation committee is independent of managers, the scope for self-dealing is reduced. Fourth, the audit committee of the board, which reviews the financial statements of the firm, should also be composed of outsiders, thereby encouraging vigorous independent questioning of the financial statements of the firm. Finally, the board should use outside auditors who are truly independent and do not have a conflict of interest. This was not the case in many recent accounting scandals, where outside auditors were also consultants to the corporation and less likely to ask questions that would jeopardize lucrative consulting contracts. The 2002 Sarbanes-Oxley Act has significantly strengthened corporate governance by legally requiring that accounting firms who audit the affairs of a corporation do not provide consulting services to the enterprise.

Moral Courage

It is important to recognize that, on occasion, managers may need significant *moral courage* to walk away from a decision that is profitable but unethical. It is moral courage that gives an employee the strength to say no to a superior that instructs her to pursue actions that are unethical or blow the whistle on persistent unethical behavior in a company. Moral courage does not come easily—there are well-known cases where individuals have lost their jobs because they exposed corporate behaviors they thought unethical.[33]

Companies can strengthen the moral courage of employees by giving them "permission" to exercise moral courage, say no to superiors, or otherwise complain about unethical actions. Consider the following extract from Unilever's code of ethics:

> "Any breaches of the Code must be reported in accordance with the procedures specified by the Joint Secretaries. The Board of Unilever will not criticize management for any loss of business resulting from adherence to these principles and other mandatory policies and instructions. The Board of Unilever expects employees to bring to their attention, or to that of senior management, any breach or suspected breach of these principles. Provision has been made for employees to be able to report in confidence and no employee will suffer as a consequence of doing so."[34]

This statement allows employees to exercise moral courage. Companies can also set up ethics hotlines, which allow employees to anonymously register a complaint with a corporate ethics officer.

Final Words

All of the steps discussed here can help make sure that when managers make business decisions they are fully cognizant of the ethical implications and do not violate basic ethical prescripts. At the same time, it must be recognized that not all ethical dilemmas have a clean and obvious solution. At the end of the day, there are clearly things that a business should and should not do, but there are also actions that present managers with true dilemmas. In these cases a premium is placed the ability of managers to make sense out of complex, messy situations and make balanced decisions that are as just as possible.

Endnotes

1. G. Edmondson and L. Cohn. "How Parmalat Went Sour," *Business Week*, January 12, 2004, pp. 46–50.

2. L. Himelstein, S. Hamm, and P. Burrows. "Inside Frank Quattrone's Money Machine," *Business Week*, October 13, 2003, pp. 104–109.

3. "Unsettling Wall Street," *The Economist*, May 30, 2003, p. 10.

4. J.R. Wilke. "U.S. Criticizes Microsoft Settlement," *Wall Street Journal*, January 19, 2004, p. B4.

5. R. Parloff. "Winning at Cards," *Fortune*, May 26, 2003, pp. 36–40.

6. A.L. Velocci, D.A. Fulghum, and R. Wall. "Damage Control," *Aviation Week*, December 1, 2003, pp. 26–27.

7. See: (1) N. King. "Halliburton Tells the Pentagon Workers Took Iraq Deal Kickbacks," *Wall Street Journal*, January 23, 2004, p. A1. (2) "Whistleblowers Say Company Routinely Overcharged," Reuters, February 12, 2004. (3) R. Gold and J.R. Wilke. "Data Sought in Halliburton Inquiry," *Wall Street Journal*, February 5, 2004, p. A6.

8. Robert Bryce. *Pipe Dreams: Greed, Ego and the Death of Enron*. Public Affairs, New York, 2002.

9. Richard T. De George. *Competing with Integrity in International Business*. Oxford: Oxford University Press, 1993.

10. Henry Weinstein, "Philip Morris Ordered to Pay $28 Billion to Smoker," *Los Angeles Times*, October 5, 2002, p. A1.

11. See (1) D. Jones. "Critics Tie Sweatshop Sneakers to 'Air Jordan,'" *USA Today*, June 6, 1996, p. 1B; (2) S. Greenhouse. "Nike Shoeplant in Vietnam Is Called Unsafe for Workers," *New York Times*, November 8, 1997; (3) V. Dobnik. "Chinese Workers Abused Making Nikes, Reeboks," *Seattle Times*, September 21, 1997, p. A4.

12. "Boycott Nike," CBS News, *48 Hours*, October 17, 1996.

13. For example, see R. Edward Freeman and Daniel Gilbert. *Corporate Strategy and the Search for Ethics*. Englewood Cliffs, N.J.: Prentice-Hall, 1988.

14. S.A. Waddock and S.B. Graves. "The Corporate Social Performance-Financial Performance Link," *Strategic Management Journal*, Vol. 8, 1997, pp. 303–319.

15. Steven Carroll et al. *Asbestos Litigation Costs and Compensation*. The Rand Institute, 2002.

16. "Timet, Boeing Settle Lawsuit," *Metal Center News*, June 2001, Vol. 41, pp. 38–39.

17. Joseph Kahn. "Ruse in Toyland: Chinese Workers' Hidden Woe," *New York Times*, December 7, 2003, pp. A1, A8.

18. Saul W. Gellerman, "Why Good Managers Make Bad Ethical Choices," *Ethics in Practice: Managing the Moral Corporation* (ed. Kenneth R. Andrews), Harvard Business School Press, 1989.

19. David Messick and Max H. Bazerman. "Ethical Leadership and the Psychology of Decision Making," *Sloan Management Review*, Winter 1996, Vol. 37, pp. 9–20.

20. Robert Bryce. *Pipe Dreams: Greed, Ego and the Death of Enron*. Public Affairs, New York, 2002.

21. Milton Friedman. "The Social Responsibility of Business Is to Increase Profits," *New York Times Magazine,* September 13, 1970. Reprinted in Tom L. Beauchamp and Norma E. Bowie, *Ethical Theory and Business,* Pearson, Prentice Hall, 2001 (Seventh edition).

22. *Ibid*, p. 55.

23. *Ibid*, pp. 17–23.

24. Thomas Donaldson. *The Ethics of International Business.* Oxford: Oxford University Press, 1989.

25. *Ibid.*

26. See Chapter 10 in Tom L. Beauchamp and Norman E. Bowie, *Ethical Theory and Business.* Pearson, Prentice Hall, 2001 (Seventh edition).

27. John Rawles. *A Theory of Justice: Revised Edition*. Belknap Press, 1999 (original edition 1971).

28. Can be found on Unilever's web site: **http://www.unilever.com/company/ourprinciples/.**

29. Joseph Bower and Jay Dial. "Jack Welsh: General Electrics Revolutionary," Harvard Business School Case, Case # 9-394-065, April 1994.

30. For example, see (1) R. Edward Freeman and Daniel Gilbert. *Corporate Strategy and the Search for Ethics*. Englewood Cliffs, N.J.: Prentice-Hall, 1988; (2) Thomas Jones. "Ethical Decision Making by Individuals in Organizations," *Academy of Management Review*, 16 (1991), 366–395; (3) J. R. Rest. *Moral Development: Advances in Research and Theory*. New York: Praeger, 1986.

31. For example, see (1) R. Edward Freeman and Daniel Gilbert. *Corporate Strategy and the Search for Ethics*. Englewood Cliffs, N.J.: Prentice-Hall, 1988; (2) Thomas Jones. "Ethical Decision Making by Individuals in Organizations," *Academy of Management Review*, 16 (1991), 366–395; (3) J. R. Rest. *Moral Development: Advances in Research and Theory*. New York: Praeger, 1986.

32. The code can be accessed at United Technologies web site: **http://www.utc.com/profile/ethics/index.htm.**

33. Colin Grant. "Whistle Blowers: Saints of Secular Culture," *Journal of Business Ethics,* September 2002, pp. 391–400.

34. Can be found on Unilever's web site: **http://www.unilever.com/company/ourprinciples/.**

Annual Update
Cases in Strategic Management

Since 2001, Toyota, under the leadership of new president Jujio Cho, has continued to find ways to improve its manufacturing and materials management systems to enhance efficiency, quality, and customer responsiveness. It has begun a series of programs to improve the way the company's design and production system operates.

One program involves strengthening its *kaizen* program using "pokayoke," or mistake-proofing. In this program employees are now required to double- and triple-check a particular stage of the assembly process that once led to customer complaints. Another program is "CCC21." Here Toyota has worked with suppliers and found ways to reduce the costs of the components going into its cars by 30 percent. This has resulted in billions of dollars of cost savings. Toyota is planning further programs to find new ways to reduce costs.

Toyota has also introduced a sophisticated new assembly process called GBL, which allows welding and assembly operations to be performed more accurately—resulting in a better quality vehicle. With GBL Toyota has been able to build factories that can assemble several different car models along the same production line with no loss in efficiency or quality. This gives Toyota a major competitive advantage; it can now move quickly to respond to increasing or decreasing customer demand for a certain type of vehicle.

These programs have focused on helping Toyota alter its car development and design process to respond to changing customer needs. Despite climbing global sales—over $146 billion in 2003—the average Toyota car buyer steadily aged in the 1990s, and the company was criticized for failing to understand changing customer needs. Analysts pointed to Toyota's centralized decision making and a culture dominated by the cautious and frugal values of its Japanese designers as the source of its problems. Designers put the need to reduce costs and increase quality ahead of designing innovative, flexible vehicles. The result was major car design errors. When Toyota's U.S. designers, for example, argued with Japanese designers in Tokyo that new kinds of vehicles were needed to compete in the United States. with those of GM and Ford, and to appeal to young customers, they were ignored. Slow sales of small pickups and compact cars soon showed that design changes were necessary.

To speed and improve the design process Cho championed two new techniques, PDCA and Obeya, to radically change the design process. Obeya is based on frequent brainstorming sessions between engineers, designers, production managers, and marketers that are designed to speed new car models to the market. PDCA, or plan, do, check, action, is a program designed to allow designers outside Japan to intervene in the development process and champion designs that meet the needs of local customers. The results of promoting a flexible, decentralized car design process were the speedy introduction of the Tundra pickup truck and the ScionxB compact in the United States, as well as the Yaris, Toyota's best-selling European car. The Yaris was designed in Europe, and its success there led to its subsequent introduction into Japan (where it also sold well).

In 2003, a vicious price war began in the U.S. market as car companies began to offer zero financing and other incentives to attract car buyers. Toyota, with its efficient manufacturing, has been able to withstand the effects of falling prices, and has managed to maintain profitability despite intense competition. Indeed, most of the cars it sells in the United States are now made in the United States, and profitability has soared past more inefficient U.S. competitors. In fact, with all its new manufacturing and materials management processes operating at full speed, Toyota replaced Ford as the world's second largest carmaker in 2004, and Cho has set his sights on Toyota replacing GM as the world's largest carmaker by 2010.

CASE 17
A New Era of Competition in Digital Devices

Since 2001, competition in the digital device arena has become intense in the kinds of functions and the different operating systems that are competing to be the dominant standard for PDAs and smartphones.

In terms of functions, competition has centered on the choice of which, and how many, functions to incorporate into the next generation of PDAs and smartphones. In 2002, PDAs became increasingly incorporated into web-enabled cell phones that allowed users access to email and Microsoft's suite of office products. Web-enabled cell phones have also found other uses. In 2001 Sony introduced the first color display screens on cell phones, which made them attractive to game players who could now download games from companies such as Sony and Nintendo.

Another major event was the decision by Sony and Samsung to embed digital cameras in cell phones. This development drove sales of cell phones to new heights. It also increased customers' demand for PDAs that linked directly to the Internet so customers could access email and send photographs to friends.

In 2003, Apple's iPod suggested how future generations of PDAs could incorporate MP3 players that downloaded and stored digital music files. At the same time, users demand for access to sophisticated word processing and other functions also increased. These developments caught Nokia and Motorola by surprise, and allowed Japanese companies to increase their share of the cell phone and PDA markets.

As cell phones and PDAs became increasingly integrated in new generations of smartphones that could work anywhere in the world using either the CDMA or GSM global operating system, competition became intense between Microsoft, Palm, and Symbian to make their operating systems the dominant standard. In 2003, Microsoft beat rivals Nokia and Symbian to the CDMA mobile phone market when Samsung launched the first CDMA smartphone using both the Windows and Palm operating systems. Palm, which has a 90 percent of the share of the CDMA market, announced that it would market two versions of its operating system for the CDMA mobile phone, one for the high-end market and one for the low-end market, and that both would be compatible with Microsoft's system.

To counter the threat from Palm and Microsoft, Nokia announced in 2004 that it was taking control of Symbian to make its GSM mobile phone operating system the global standard for new smartphones. Nokia also announced that it had entered into deals with Samsung and Sony to make versions of their mobile phones that would work on Symbian's GSM as well as Microsoft's CDMA system. However, Motorola, which had adopted the GSM standard, switched allegiance to Microsoft and brought out new generations of smartphones based on Microsoft's operating system.

Fighting back, Nokia introduced its new 6620 smartphone in 2004, which allows users to check email, send digital photos, and access the web twice as fast as its rivals. The phone also comes with the Real One video player, Mighty Phone synching software, and seventy Symbian-designed business applications.

To complicate matters further, in 2004 Intel announced that it intended to remake the global mobile phone industry by offering a new line of high-performance chips that would offer superior performance. For example, besides their ability to run Windows-type applications, the new chips would enable phones to play digital music files and act as a 1.3 megapixel camera, one much more powerful than those currently available. These chips would also make it easier to move data between PDAs and LANs and facilitate video transmissions. Finally, the chips would be compatible with both GSM and CDMA smartphone standards because Intel believes that no one standard will win the global battle.

CASE 19
New Developments in the Home Videogame Industry

The home videogame industry posted a record-breaking $9.4 billion in sales in 2001 as a number of new games were introduced to promote Microsoft's new X-Box, and to feed the appetites of Sony PlayStation and Nintendo users. Sales of Microsoft's X-Box were slower than expected in 2002, in part because of a lack of games. In a bid to boost sales Microsoft announced it would spend $1 billion to create an online videogame service called X-Box Live, which would allow users to play against each other online and sample Microsoft's new game offerings.

The X-Box's hard drive, growing availability of new games, and ability to connect to the Internet proved to be a major competitive advantage, and in 2003 X-Box sales began to take off. Microsoft also began to package games with the X-Box console, sometimes in conjunction with an extra hand console and the package necessary to use the X-Box as a DVD player. This boosted sales, and in 2004 Microsoft said that it was on track to reach its goal of 16 million X-Box players as well as 1 million X-Box Live subscribers by the summer of 2004.

Sony, with over 40 million PlayStation users, and Nintendo, with over 14 million users, realized that their game consoles needed to connect to the Internet and have a hard drive to stay competitive. Nintendo reduced the price of its new Game Cube from $149 to $99, which allowed it to regain sales from Microsoft. However, the X-Box gained the number two position in the industry. Meanwhile, Sony, the market leader, took the biggest hit as sales of its PlayStation dropped by 26 percent. Sony announced that its next generation PlayStation would connect to the Internet,

To protect its dominant position in the digital entertainment market, Sony also announced that it would offer a combined package consisting of a satellite TV tuner with DVD recorder, a PlayStation 2, and a hard disc that could function as a game player and record and store up to 250 hours of digital programming. In doing so, Sony hopes to further differentiate its products from Microsoft and keep its huge base of customers loyal.

Microsoft, unwilling to let Sony dominate the digital entertainment market, is championing the personal computer to integrate digital entertainment, including

TV, video, music, gaming, and photography. In 2004 it announced a new version of Windows XP Media that would allow users to perform all these functions seamlessly. Microsoft is working with companies like HP and Phillips to develop Windows-based computers and PDAs to compete with Sony's.

New competition is also emerging in the handheld game market. In 2002 Nintendo, long dominant in the industry, offered customers the Game Boy Advance, a rechargeable device that used a smaller game cartridge. This device is backwardly compatible and led to an increase of 56 percent in sales of handheld devices in 2003. Also in 2003, Sony announced that it would introduce its own handheld device in 2004. Code-named PSP, it will combine game capabilities with the ability to play movies and music. However, a lack of games for the new device has led Sony to delay its launch in the United States until 2005. In a somewhat surprising development, Nokia introduced a new range of cell phones in 2003 that are capable of playing sophisticated games, and it views the new generation of smartphones as a clear substitute for a separate handheld gaming console.

Sega, which stopped producing videogame consoles because it could not compete with its stronger rivals, is now licensing its games to be played on any company's operating system. Some analysts believe that Nintendo may also take this route in the future if online gaming becomes the most important source of competitive advantage. Sony, for example, has teamed up with AOL to offer its games online to compete with X-Box Live until its next generation console is ready.

CASE 20
The Windows-Linux Battle Intensifies

In 2003, the Gartner Consulting Group estimated that sales of servers running Linux were up by 60 percent from a year earlier, even though Windows had over 50 percent of the market compared to Linux's 20 percent. Nevertheless, Linux was gaining momentum in the server market, and the operating system was being increasingly used at other levels of computing. Companies such as IBM, HP, and Redhat, a Linux-only service provider, were now producing desktop computers, laptops, and even PDAs based on Linux and its software application package called "Lindows." Even Sun, long a leader in the server market with its Solaris platform, announced that it was partnering with chip maker Advanced Micro Devices to make new low-cost servers that would use its Star applications package but operate on Linux.

With the number of companies using Linux increasing, Microsoft began to take the offensive. It offered steep discounts on leasing its Windows system. It also funded research that claimed to show that the long-term cost of using Linux was greater than the cost of using Windows XP because of higher deployment and maintenance costs—although some critics charged that the study was flawed.

In another move to forestall Linux, a company called SCO claimed that it owned the copyright to large parts of the original Unix-based code from which Linux was originally developed. With funding from Microsoft, SCO sued IBM in 2003, charging that IBM had illegally used and adapted the Linux code without SCO's permission and without paying any licensing fees. Currently, this case is still in the courts and IBM is expected to win the suit. Nevertheless, pending litigation may have put off many IT managers who were afraid that a move to Linux might lead to hefty license fees in the future.

A boost to Linux was the decision by Asian countries, particularly China, to use Linux because it costs less than Windows and because its open source code allows users to control subsequent development and better protect vital information. China has since been joined by Korea and Japan to develop a version of Linux that is attuned to their character-based languages. If Asia gravitates to the Linux system this will have global implications for the use of Windows, since so much global commerce is electronic in nature. Microsoft is responding by arguing that Windows is less expensive to maintain and is backed by constant research to improve the system to meet the needs of its users—something that is not certain with the Linux system.

Inside the United States companies in all segments of the computer and digital products industries seem determined to prevent Microsoft from establishing its Pocket PC (and its suite of Windows media applications) as the standard operating system for mobile devices—something it had achieved with Windows on personal computers. While Sony uses Windows on its computers, for example, it refuses to use Microsoft's software in its PlayStation 2. Apple Computer does not use Windows on its iPod music player, and TiVo uses Linux on its video recorder. In the video-on-demand market, major film studios such as Disney and Viacom use software from both Microsoft and Real Networks to transmit movies over the Internet. In addition, HP has announced it will put Apple's music software in its machines, which will hurt Microsoft's attempts to make Windows Media the online music standard.

In fact, Apple software is based on a standard called Advanced Audio Coding that can be licensed by any company and could be incorporated into Linux as the need arises. Major global electronics companies such as Matsushita, Hitachi, Sony, NEC, Phillips, and Samsung have teamed up to promote the use of Linux in consumer devices, once again seeking to forestall Microsoft from establishing Pocket PC as the standard. These companies fear what Microsoft could do if it controls the operating standard and do not wish to be put under any threat by its future actions. Conditions in the computer and digital products industries are working together to promote the use of Linux at all levels of computing, something that will be necessary if Linux is to really pose a major threat to Windows in the years ahead.

CASE 22
SAP's New Moves

Throughout 2002 and 2003 companies worldwide continued to limit or reduce their IT expenditures. SAP, like all other computer hardware and software companies, found its revenues falling. While SAP's revenues fell by 5 percent in 2003 because of lower ERP and consulting sales, its net income almost doubled because its global cost structure was under control and it was making better use of its resources. Strict new controls on expenses had been implemented and a hiring freeze imposed, and the company was focusing on urgent problems. SAP also began to outsource its future programming development work to low-cost countries such as India. By 2003, SAP employed 750 software programmers in India, and announced that it planned to double that number by 2004. This would make the Indian group bigger than the research center in Waldorf, Germany, and save billions of euros a year, further boosting SAP's profitability.

To help increase revenues, SAP began to use its Indian research center to develop ERP modules to serve more markets. At the same time, SAP used its new army of low-cost Indian programmers to debug its SAP modules and increase their reliability. This prevented the embarrassing blowsups that sometimes happened when SAP's ERP was implemented for the first time. Fewer bugs also made it easier to install the modules in a new company, which reduced the need for consulting, lowered costs, and led to more satisfied customers.

In 2003, SAP changed the name of its software from mySAP.com to mySAP Business Suite; more and more customers were now buying software using a suite licensing arrangement. To increase sales revenues SAP began a major push into the small and medium business (SMB) segment of the ERP market. To accomplish this transition, it scaled down its modules for use by small companies and called the new ERP system "Business One."

In 2003 SAP formed a partnership with AMEX and IBM to perfect the design of its new Business One modules for SMB customers. AMEX provides the financial and credit support for thousands of small business customers, and SAP wanted to tap into this market. IBM's sales reps also visit thousands of small business customers. In targeting this market SAP came into increased competition with Microsoft, which has a huge base of small business customers using its Windows platform. PeopleSoft and Oracle were also striving to become major players in the SMB market.

In fact, increasing competition in the SMB segment of the ERP market led to a wave of consolidation in 2003, as PeopleSoft bought J.D. Edwards to expand its presence in the SMB segment. PeopleSoft then found itself the target of a hostile takeover by Oracle. Taking over PeopleSoft would give Oracle the resources and customers necessary to gain a large market share in the SMB segment at the expense of SAP and Microsoft. As PeopleSoft battled to prevent the takeover, SAP tried to take advantage of the confusion and poached their customers by offering them special low-cost licensing deals on its software and guaranteeing a smooth changeover. SAP's improving reputation for "less buggy" software aided it in this endeavor, and its share of the market has risen sharply at the cost of smaller companies such as PeopleSoft, Siebel Systems, and BEA.

In February 2004, the U.S Justice Department announced that it would attempt to block the merger and Oracle now faces a long court battle. This decision has helped SAP to attract SMB customers concerned about the eventual outcome. However, analysts pointed out that in 2004 SAP's reputation at the SMB level has not been good; it is perceived as a "big, scary, expensive option." SAP's U.S. managers have realized they need to make efforts to carefully position its Business One software to suit the needs of a business that has thirty rather than 30,000 employees. For example, in the U.S. and Canadian market it has been estimated that 90 percent of companies fall into the SMB category. While SAP might have the greatest product in the world, if it cannot customize and market it to suit its needs, these customers will not adopt it.

Finally, in 2003 it became clear that SAP was trying to lessen its reliance on Microsoft, which was now becoming a major competitor, by increasing its support for the Linux system. It made a deal with Sybase to use its database software to enable SAP's applications to run on both the UNIX and Linux systems. As Microsoft spent billions to enter the SMB segment of the market to become one of SAP's competitors, SAP sought to reach and serve the growing number of small companies that are choosing the Linux operating system.

In 2004, SAP's new 34-year-old chief technology officer, Shai Agassi, announced that as the $40 billion-dollar-a-year business-software industry heads for a shakeout, to protect its 35 percent global market share SAP must change its strategy. "Training people on computer systems is stupid. We need to train the systems to work with people," he stated. Clearly, new challenges for SAP lie ahead.

CASES 29 AND 30 Airborne Express and the Air Express Industry

In 2001 UPS sought to make better use of its ground and air delivery network by purchasing the franchise core of Mail Boxes Etc., now renamed UPS Stores, for $185 million. This move gave it direct access to customers of all 4,500 franchises. During 2001–2003, both UPS and FedEx began to play a leading role in global supply chain management by establishing huge warehouses throughout the world to handle the warehousing and shipping of components for global companies.

The major delivery companies felt that, in the future, competitive advantage depended on being a major player in both the domestic U.S. market and the global market. DHL decided to act. In 2003, DHL and Airborne Express announced that they would combine their operations. Under the terms of their agreement, Airborne Express sold its truck delivery system to DHL for $1.05 billion. Airborne's fleet of planes became an independent company called ABX Air, owned by Airborne's shareholders, and continued to serve DHL Worldwide Express. This arrangement overcame the U.S. law prohibiting foreign control of domestic airlines. In the meantime DHL spun its own fleet of U.S.-based planes into a U.S.-owned company called Astar, also to escape the charge that its U.S. airline was foreign-owned.

The merger created three major competitors in the U.S. and global delivery markets. By the fall of 2003 DHL had launched an ad campaign aimed at UPS and FedEx customers promoting the service and cost benefits from its merger with Airborne. DHL claimed to be number one in international markets, something important to many companies given the increasing importance of global commerce. In its ads DHL stated that "Current Airborne customers will be connected to DHL's extensive international delivery system in more than 200 countries."

UPS and FedEx went to court to block DHL's expansion, arguing that both ABX and Astar, despite appearances, were still foreign-owned and should be forced to stop flying. In late 2003, the courts ruled that DHL should be allowed to operate these airlines in the interest of competition in the industry. UPS and FedEx appealed this decision. The final outcome was not clear in the spring of 2004, although it seemed likely DHL would prevail. Clearly, UPS and FedEx do not want competition from a strong global player that could depress prices. Additional attempts to use regulatory or legal attacks to derail DHL in the U.S. market could generate charges that both companies are simply attempting to prevent new competitors from entering the market. A DHL spokesman said that the legal fight with Astar had taken an enormous toll on its managers, and called upon FedEx and UPS to "get on about competing and not trying to rely on a technical rationale for putting us out of business."

DHL's goal is to become a powerhouse in the U.S. cargo market. In 2003, FedEx and UPS carried nearly 75 percent of U.S. air and ground shipments. The U.S. Post Office carried 19 percent, while DHL had about a 6 percent share. However, in 2003 DHL was the leader in international air express with 41 percent of the market; UPS and FedEx controlled 40 percent. Package delivery was worth $48 billion in 2003; on any given day UPS alone transports more than 13 million packages (over 5 percent of U.S. total economic output). DHL wants a larger share and has positioned itself to achieve this.

Reflecting the new competitive climate in late 2003, UPS announced a rate increase of just 1.9 percent for ground-based deliveries and 2.9 percent for air, its lowest price increase since 1999. Analysts felt that growing pressure from DHL, now actively seeking to expand its share of the U.S. market, was the main reason for the small increase. Service gaps, in terms of delivery time, are closing between the three carriers. As they close customers are becoming increasingly price conscious, putting carriers under greater pressure to reduce costs.

To increase efficiency FedEx, UPS, and DHL began to invest heavily in new information technology. UPS spent $30 million for a new package-flow system, based on smart labels containing bar-coded delivery information, which will distribute packages more efficiently to its 70,000 U.S. truck drivers and allow them to make more stops with no loss of time. Formerly drivers had to physically examine packages and the way they were loaded into the truck to determine the best route. Now they will have a delivery manifest that provides a map that can be electronically transmitted to the handheld devices used by drivers.

Air carriers are expected to introduce radio frequency identification (RFID) technology, which allows package tags to contain much more information than bar codes and can be tracked through radio waves. Wal-Mart has required its top 100 suppliers to begin using this technology, which helps drive down inventory stocking costs but raises the costs for its suppliers and shippers.

Finally, as industry competition for customers continues to increase, FedEx announced in 2004 that it would buy privately held Kinko's for $2.1 billion. This will give FedEx a nationwide system of package stores similar to the UPS stores. Will DHL also embark on a similar strategy?

Deliverers forecasted that the U.S. market would increase by 4 percent in 2004. They also saw an upsurge in global business of 10 percent, suggesting that there would be few pressures to reduce prices. The stocks of all three carriers surged. Even with three players in the global market, conditions look good in the air express industry if the U.S. and global economy continue to recover.

CASE 31
Independence for Blockbuster

In the fall of 2002, the courts dismissed a lawsuit against Blockbuster by independent video rental retailers. Throughout 2002 and 2003 the decision to switch to DVD rentals paid huge dividends. While Blockbuster's earnings in 2003 increased by 42 percent, generating a free cash flow in excess of $400 million, a large part of these extra profits came from aggressive cost-cutting efforts and substantial reductions in advertising.

Although Blockbuster increased its share of DVD movie sales, DVD prices fell and low-cost competitors like Wal-Mart and Best Buy began to aggressively sell DVDs. In 2003 customers spent significantly more on purchasing DVDs and tapes than on movie rentals. Thus, while retail sales of movies rose 19 percent to $12.3 billion, movie rentals slipped 3 percent to $9.9 billion. Blockbuster, which had opened over 550 new stores, watched sales at stores opened for one year fall by 6 percent. However, John Antioco, Blockbuster's CEO, believed that the rental market would stabilize by 2005.

To encourage DVD rentals Blockbuster tested unlimited DVD rental for a monthly fee of $24.99 in some of its stores; the success of this program led to its national rollout in 2004. Moreover, to compete with Netflix, the online DVD rental company, Blockbuster announced it would launch an online DVD rental service by 2004. Blockbuster claimed that its program would be better because customers could return DVDs to its stores. Given that Blockbuster has 48 million members, accounts analysts believed that cost-effective online DVD rental might prove to be a lucrative activity.

On the other hand, analysts also believed that Blockbuster faced a growing threat from new technology to that would make video-on-demand through TV or computer a reality. With video-on-demand there are no late fees, which reportedly contribute to the majority of Blockbuster's profits. Netflix, which does not charge late fees, feels this gives it a substantial advantage over Blockbuster. Blockbuster's new unlimited rental program will reduce the impact of late fees, however.

On the home videogame front, Antioco's decision to offer videogame rentals also paid off handsomely. The company tested a new concept of a videogame store-in-store called Game Rush in 2003, attracting new customers who pay a monthly fee for unlimited videogame rental. Its success led to the decision to roll Game Rush out to half of its stores as quickly as possible in 2004. However, these new initiatives will cost between $80 to $100 million, and with the high costs of store maintenance could cause net income to fall by as much as 10 percent.

While Blockbuster's 2003 revenues proved a major boost to majority owner Viacom in 2002 and 2003, its new retail initiatives and uncertainty about home video and videogame rentals began to cause Viacom's chairman Sumner Redstone problems. The uncertainty of Blockbuster's future revenue stream impacted Viacom's stock price; throughout 2003 Redstone tried, but failed, to find a buyer for the remaining 82 percent of Blockbuster shares Viacom owned.

Believing that the two companies' business models were now too far apart, in 2004 Viacom announced that it would allow holders of Viacom shares to swap them for shares in Blockbuster. When completed, Blockbuster will once again become an independent company and will be free to pursue whatever business model Antioco believes will be most profitable. How will Blockbuster retain the loyalty of its customers? Is going to a video store a pleasant family event as some analysts believe? Will online rental of DVDs ultimately be as easy to use as a video-on-demand service?

CASE 33
The AOL Time Warner Merger Turns into a Debacle

By the end of 2001, falling advertising revenues were leading to the collapse of AOL's profitability. This dragged AOL Time Warner's stock down by 70 percent. The company finished 2002 with a historic loss of nearly $100 billion, the largest annual loss in U.S. corporate history. AOL also lost more than one million U.S. subscribers between 2002 and 2003 as they defected to broadband Internet service providers (ISPs), and online advertising revenues continued to fall. Moreover, the principal rationale for the merger—distribution of films and music over the Internet—had not been achieved by delivering Time Warner's content over AOL's pipeline. Apparently, Time Warner executives were deliberately trying to sabotage AOL, and there was also a tremendous culture clash between the two companies.

Irate shareholders demanded to know what had gone wrong, and analysts began to search for the reasons for the disastrous merger. The main culprit for the $100 billion merger debacle seemed to be the dot-com bubble, which had inflated AOL's stock price to ridiculous heights and enabled it to make a takeover bid for Time Warner. However, a darker side of the story began to emerge.

Some analysts argued that CEO Gerald Levin bears the greatest responsibility for the disastrous merger. Few Time Warner executives knew about the impending deal until hours before the announcement, and fewer actually supported the proposal. Levin decided that Time Warner should receive 45 percent of the merged company and AOL 55 percent; in making this decision he did not exercise due diligence towards Time Warner shareholders.

What of Steve Case's role in the merger? According to some sources, early in 2000 Case had already explained to top managers that AOL needed to acquire a content company like Time Warner while its stock price was still high, because he believed the Internet sector was already highly overvalued. A merger with Time Warner offered a way to protect AOL's assets and position.

Also, AOL may have entered into questionable deals before and during the merger process to inflate its advertising revenues in order to maintain its high stock price. These alleged deals helped to misrepresent AOL's financial position, inflate AOL's stock price, and make the merger possible. In one example AOL reportedly agreed to purchase $250 million in computer hardware from Sun Microsystems, provided Sun bought $37.5 million in ads on AOL. In reality, Sun paid nothing for the advertising, instead giving AOL a credit. AOL then booked the $37.5 million as revenue. The Justice Department is still investigating these charges.

Soon after the merger both companies' top managers sold large chunks of their stock, making hundreds of millions of dollars in profit. Case alone sold shares worth over $100 million. Some critics argue these sales indicate that even the managers were not sure about the company's future prospects.

Soon after Richard Parsons was named as the company's new CEO, copresident Bob Pitman resigned, and the company's continuing poor performance led to the removal of almost every AOL top executive. Power in the company returned to Time Warner executives. Aware of the rumors about the advertising deals, unhappy shareholders pressured Case, and he resigned as chairman in the summer of 2003.

In September 2003, AOL Time Warner announced it would remove AOL from its name and be known as Time Warner. Parsons announced that AOL would generate over $1 billion in free cash flow for the year and was having success with its new strategic plan. Indeed, AOL still has over 25 million U.S. subscribers and more than 6 million European subscribers, and will continue to be a strong generator of cash flow. What will happen to the combined company is still unclear, but Parsons is credited with paying down its debt and building its businesses. The company's stock price recovered somewhat in 2004 as its fortunes improved.

CASE 34
Viacom and Advertising Revenues

Since 2002 Viacom has made no major acquisitions. Both Sumner Redstone and Mel Karmazin feel that the company has all the right pieces of entertainment property in place and that the main issue is to realize profits Operating revenues from the entertainment division rose by 46 percent during 2003, and operating income was up 15 percent as a result of higher movie ticket sales and DVD sales. Blockbuster's Viacom Plus unit continued to aggressively market its "one stop shopping approach across all marketing channels" and, as the economy picked up in 2003, advertising revenues at the national level rebounded. In the spring of 2004, Viacom was happy to announce that the company's overall revenues were up 11 percent and that 46 percent of its 2003 revenues came from advertising.

While national advertising revenues on Viacom's cable channels rebounded, revenues from TV stations and radio stations lagged behind, and Viacom just met analysts' earnings expectations. Analysts thought local advertising had not kept pace with national advertising because fewer people were watching local channels, preferring to watch cable channels or surf the web, and that local revenues might not recover. Others pointed out that the forthcoming Olympic Games and presidential election would likely raise local advertising, especially if the economy continues to recover. Karmazin and Redstone announced that they expected revenue increases in 2004 of 5 to 7 percent and operating profits to increase by 12 to 14 percent.

As discussed in the Blockbuster case, Redstone and Karmazin also announced that business models of both companies had drifted so far apart that a split was best. Viacom's model is based on growing the value of its properties and the advertising revenues they generate; Blockbuster's model is based on increasing its presence in the retail market. In 2004 increasing competition in the home video retail market would likely result in falling revenues that would offset any increase in revenues Viacom might gain from advertising. However, divesting Blockbuster and losing retail revenues will make Viacom even more dependent on advertising revenues.

If the Blockbuster spin-off goes according to plan, Viacom will emerge as a much smaller company revenue-wise in 2004. After Comcast, the largest U.S. cable company, offered to purchase the Disney Company, analysts began to wonder if Viacom would make a counteroffer to secure Disney's range of entertainment assets. In response Viacom executives stated that while they would like to buy certain assets they had no desire to buy the whole corporation. Also, a whole host of new cable properties would only increase Viacom's dependency on advertising revenues.

Other analysts began to wonder if Comcast's offer and the decision by News-Corp (owner of the Fox movie studio and channels) to buy DirecTV meant that content providers, like Viacom, should once again be integrated with the companies that distribute that content. Such a move would reduce Viacom's dependence on advertising revenues. Redstone and Karmazin responded that Viacom made a deliberate decision *not* to enter the distribution business, and that its strong stable of entertainment assets meant it would always have power to negotiate with distributors. They also argued that because Viacom was not a provider, or allied to any particular provider, it had more power in its negotiating deals with distributors.

On a managerial level, the personal relationship between Redstone and Karmazin continued to deteriorate, although in 2003 it was announced that Karmazin's contract would be renewed for two more years. Reportedly, the two men hardly speak to one another anymore. This is unlikely to help Viacom in its search for future acquisitions to help build profitability.

CASES 35 AND 36 New Developments at Monsanto

Monsanto's success in selling its genetically engineered seeds globally continued as the news about higher crop yields and resistance to pests became known to farmers worldwide. In India, for example, available seeds sold out quickly. However, sales in the first half of 2002 fell because wet weather in the United States delayed corn and soybean planting and reduced demand for Roundup, Monsanto's weed killer.

In August 2002, Monsanto's stock, which had fallen heavily, soared after its final separation from Pharmacia. It also rose because the company announced that, despite losing worldwide patent protection for Roundup, it still had a 90 percent share of the glyphosate herbicide market; nearly half of its 2001 sales of $4.9 billion came from this source. Monsanto forecasted that its market share would slip to 60 percent by 2005 because of competition from generics, but said the lost profit from sales of Roundup would be offset by higher profit from its seeds and biotechnology "traits," the genes that transform ordinary seeds into new types of crops. It predicted profits from this business would rise from $800 million in 2002 to $1.3 billion by 2005, as its YeildGard rootworm corn and Roundup Ready Corn lead sales.

By 2003, Monsanto was the world's number two company in sales of agricultural seeds. However, its profitability had been lackluster due to the heavy spending necessary to develop new seeds and to convince the world, particularly Europe, that its genetically altered seeds were safe. Also, Monsanto's high-cost structure led to its low profitability, and a management shakeup occurred in 2003. Chief operating officer Hugh Grant succeeded Hendrik Verfaillie as CEO. Grant announced that for the first time, over half of Monsanto's profits would come from the non-chemical side of its business: "Fifteen years ago we were making nylon. We were a fibers company. Then we were a fine-chemicals company. Now we're a seeds and biotechnology company." Grant also reorganized the company to better target its new markets and give managers more control over costs.

Although Monsanto had a strong lead in the market, its biggest rivals—Dupont, Syngenta, and Bayer—were working to develop their own biotech crops. Analysts predicted that by 2005 Dupont and Syngenta would release products that go head-to-head with Monsanto, something that might pressure Monsanto to reduce its prices. Analysts also say that Monsanto's competitors are working on a new class of "output traits" or genes that could improve the quality or taste of crops like corn, soybeans, and tomatoes, and that this development will ignite the real biotech race.

Monsanto said it was planning to stack genetically altered traits in seeds, one on top of the other, so the seeds would possess both yield and taste advantages. It also said it was preparing to introduce "consumer traits" into its seeds, traits that are beneficial to human health. For example, it plans to incorporate a trait that will be fortified with omega–3, a fatty acid that benefits the heart, into its corn and canola seed. In 2003 Monsanto planned to devote nearly 80 percent of its annual R&D budget to develop seeds with both kinds of traits. However, such heavy spending will also hold down its profitability.

By the fall of 2003, Monsanto's earnings were being eroded by the escalating price of Roundup, its biggest product, although sales of its seeds were still increasing. It began a round of cost cutting to reduce R&D expenses. It also announced that it was abandoning efforts to produce pharmaceuticals in genetically engineered crops to focus on businesses that would pay off sooner. Finally, Monsanto said that it would cut 900–1200 jobs by the end of 2004, which will save about $100 million a year.

In February 2004, Monsanto forecasted that increased sales of corn seeds and next-generation biotech products would lead to profit growth of up to 10 percent in 2005 and 2006. Also in February 2004, Europe's top food agency was preparing to deliver a verdict on the safety of Monsanto's genetically engineered rapeseed. If the rapeseed receives a favorable opinion Monsanto hopes the intense opposition from European countries with strong anti-biotech sentiments will end and it will be allowed to sell its seeds in this important market. This would lead to major increase in sales and profits.

CASE 41
Kodak's New Moves

2002 proved to be a turning point in the photographic imaging business as sales of digital cameras and other products started to soar. Not only did sales of Kodak film start to fall but, as analysts feared, photographers were printing only a fraction of the pictures they had taken. Demand for Kodak paper also began to fall. In 2003, Kodak's film and paper revenues continued to fall as digital cameras became the camera of choice for photographers worldwide. Film and paper are Kodak's most profitable products and generate most of its cash. Kodak's fourth quarter net income in 2003 was only $19 million, compared with a net income of $113 million in 2002.

This huge fall in Kodak's profitability was somewhat ironic, given that Kodak's line of EasyShare digital cameras were the best-selling cameras in the United States in 2003. Sales rose by 87 percent in 2003, making Kodak the number two global seller with about 18 percent of the market. However, rising sales were not enough to offset losses in film. Profit margins are tight in digital products because of intense competition from companies such as Canon, Olympus, and Nikon. Also, since every new digital camera sold meant that less of its film would be sold, Kodak was "gaining on the swings it was losing on the roundabout."

In response to this situation, Kodak bought the remaining 44 percent of Chinon, the Japanese company that made its digital cameras. Also, in 2003 it announced that it was withdrawing from the Advanced Photo Systems camera business and stopping sales of reloadable film cameras in North America and Europe, where business was drying up the fastest.

In the fall of 2003, Kodak CEO Daniel Carp announced that Kodak's cash-cow yellow box business was in "irreversible decline." At the same time he announced a major change of strategy for Kodak. Kodak would stop investing in its traditional business, and instead pour all its resources into building digital products. Also, Kodak would try to grow its successful and highly profitable digital health imaging business. Finally, he announced Kodak would enter the inkjet printing business and try to make inroads in the digital commercial printing business.

Analysts and investors reacted badly to this news. Xerox had tried to enter the printing business years before with no success against Hewlett-Packard. Moreover, they wondered how new revenues from digital products could make up for the loss of Kodak's film and paper revenues. To fund this new strategy Carp announced that Kodak would reduce its hefty dividend by 72 percent to raise $1.3 billion for investment in digital products. Kodak's stock, which had been around $27, plunged to $22, its lowest price in decades.

Analysts argued that Kodak should have funded its new strategy by reducing operating costs to increase business efficiency, pointing out that a 5 percent increase in efficiency would have raised the $1.3 billion. Kodak's top management came under intense criticism and its stock price continued to fall. It became obvious the new strategy would do little to raise revenues, which had fallen by $1 billion from 2000 to 2002 and reduced Kodak's net income by half.

Finally, in the spring of 2004, Carp announced another strategy change for Kodak—a strategy that should have been implemented two decades earlier when competition from Fuji began to bite into its profits. Announcing it "was smart business in a business that's shrinking," Carp said Kodak will cut its workforce by 21 percent by the end of 2006 and take charges of $1.5 billion against revenues to cover the cost of this new round of layoffs. This means that another 12,000–15,000 Kodak employees will lose their jobs, and that operating costs will drop by about $1 billion a year. Jobs will be lost in film manufacturing at the support and corporate levels, and Kodak will reduce its total facilities worldwide by one third.

While this news sent Kodak's share price up by 20 percent, the question remains if Kodak will be able to take the profits from its streamlined film business and invest them successfully in new digital imaging technology ventures. Had Kodak taken this move years ago it could have built up distinctive competences in many digital research areas. Today, with so many competitors, this may be far more difficult to do because of the rapid growth of low-cost digital competitors in China and Taiwan.

CASE 43
Dial Is Bought by Henkel

At the end of 2002 Dial reported that it had turned an operating loss of $132 million in 2001 into a profit of $16 million. CEO Herbert Baum's turnaround strategy to build Dial's strengths in its core washing powder, soap, and foods brands was apparently working. The company's stock price shot up as investors either hoped for continued operating improvements or a takeover by another company. By the end of 2003, Dial's stock price had doubled since Baum became its CEO.

In 2003, however, it became clear that Dial's worries were not over. In the retail industry, many retailers who were struggling to compete with Wal-Mart began to demand lower prices for products from their suppliers. At the same time, sales of Dial's products to discount operations such as Sam's and Costco were accounting for an increasingly larger part of its sales. By 2003, Wal-Mart, which accounted for 28 percent of Dial's sales, was putting constant pressure on Dial for cost reductions in order to maintain its price advantage over retail competitors.

At the same time, Dial was struggling to compete with Procter & Gamble and Unilever in an industry increasingly dominated by a few global giants with broad product range and financial resources. Indeed, P&G had become the leading seller of liquid soap, putting Dial in second place. In addition, demand for bar soap had dropped significantly as customers turned to milder body wash products. P&G and Unilever had begun to dominate this market, although Baum fought back by introducing and promoting Dial's own line of body washes.

In this increasingly competitive industry environment Baum continued to search for a potential takeover partner, even as he strengthened the company's core products. In 2003, Baum succeeded in rejuvenating Armor and Armor Star, Dial's food products line, by manufacturing meat products for third parties under their own private brand labels. This accounted for 28 percent of their business in 2003; with Armor's 20 percent market share, Dial had close to half of the U.S. canned meats business.

In December 2003 Henkel—the German company in alliance with Dial to develop advanced washing powders and dry cleaning products—announced it would take over Dial in a deal worth $2.9 billion. This merger would combine two small global players who would still be dwarfed by P&G and Unilever. However, for Henkel the acquisition of Dial would bring it broader global reach and allow it to enter the profitable U.S. market. Despite the marketing mistakes Dial made with Advanced Purex, Henkel saw many opportunities for using its expertise in chemicals to innovate new and improved products.

To fund the acquisition, Henkel plans to sell its 29.7 percent stake in Clorox, the profitable U.S. maker of bleach and other household products. Clorox had no interest in purchasing Dial because of Dial's previously unprofitable meat operations. Some analysts speculate that the Henkel-Dial merger might be followed up by a merger with Clorox, uniting the three company's different product lines. Their combined strength could put the company on a footing to compete globally against P&G and Unilever. Other analysts point out that Dial's brands are aimed at low-cost segments of the market and that such a move might prove extremely risky.

In any event, in 2004, if the merger proceeds as planned, Dial will cease to exist as an independent operating company. Henkel has gained Herbert Baum's commitment to stay on as its CEO for the next two years to guide the transition of its new U.S. operations.

Endnotes

Case 15:
http://www.toyota.com/index3.html;
http://www.toyota.co.jp/en/news/04/index.html

Case 17:
http://sony.com/;
http://www.sony.net/SonyInfo/News/Press/;
http://www.apple.com/;
http://www.apple.com/pr/library/;
http://www.microsoft.com/;
http://www.microsoft.com/presspass/press/default.asp;
http://www.samsung.com/;
http://www.samsung.com/PressCenter/index.asp;
http://www.palmsource.com/;
http://www.palmsource.com/press/;
http://www.palmone.com/us/?siteRef=p1-xfer;
http://www.palmone.com/us/company/pr/?siteRef=p1-xfer-pr;
http://nokia.com/;
http://press.nokia.com/pressreleases.html;
http://www.motorola.com/;
http://www.motorola.com/mediacenter;
http://intel.com/;
http://appzone.intel.com/pressroom/PressReleases.asp

Case 19:
http://www.microsoft.com/;
http://www.microsoft.com/msft/press.mspx;
http://sony.com/;
http://www.sony.net/SonyInfo/News/Press/;
http://www.nintendo.com/home;
http://www.nintendo.com/newsmain;
http://www.sega.com/;
http://www.sega.com/corporate/corporate.php?item=
    corporate_pr

Case 20:
http://www.g2r.com/RecognizedUser;
http://www.g2r.com/1_researchanalysis/research_overview.html;
http://www.sun.com/;
http://www.sun.com/aboutsun/media/;
http://www.microsoft.com/;
http://www.microsoft.com/msft/default.mspx;
http://www.thescogroup.com/;
http://www.thescogroup.com/company/presskit/;
http://www.ibm.com/us/;
http://www-1.ibm.com/press/PressServletForm.wss;
http://www.hp.com/;
http://www.hp.com/hpinfo/newsroom/index.html?mtxs=
    corp&mtxb=3&mtxl=4

Case 22:
http://www.sap.com/;
http://www.sap.com/company/investor/;
http://www.peoplesoft.com/corp/en/public_index.jsp;

http://www.peoplesoft.com/corp/en/news_events/index
    .jsp?site=corp;
http://www.oracle.com/;
http://www.oracle.com/corporate/pressroom/

Cases 29 and 30:
http://ups.com/;
http://www.pressroom.ups.com/pressreleases/archives/
    frontpage/;
http://www.fedex.com/;
http://www.businesswire.com/fdx/;
http://www.dhl.com/index.jsp;
http://www.dhl-usa.com/Company/pressroom.asp?nav=
    AboutDHLUSA/CompanyInfo/PressRoom;
http://www.abxair.com/;
http://www.astaraircargo.us/;
http://www.astaraircargo.us/about/pressroom.html

Case 31:
http://www.blockbuster.com/;
http://www.blockbuster.com/bb/tpn/frameset/
    0,7868,NT-ABT,00.html?;
http://www.netflix.com/Default?mqso=60154315;
http://www.netflix.com/PressRoom?hnjr=8;
http://www.viacom.com/;
http://www.viacom.com/announce.tin?sUnitNickname=viacorp

Case 33:
http://www.timewarner.com/flash.adp;
http://www.corp.aol.com/;
http://media.aoltimewarner.com/media/press.cfm;
http://media.aoltimewarner.com/media/newmedia/
    cb_press.cfm;
http://www.sun.com/;
http://www.sun.com/realitycheck/haveyouheard/

Case 34:
http://viacom.com/;
http://viacom.com/announce.tin?sSegmentNickname=co;
http://www.comcast.com/;
http://www.cmcsk.com/phoenix.zhtml?c=147565&p=
    irol-irhome;
http://www.newscorp.com/index2.html;
http://www.newscorp.com/news/index.html

Cases 35 and 36:
http://monsanto.com/monsanto/layout/default.asp;
http://monsanto.com/monsanto/layout/investor/news&events/
    archive.asp;
http://www1.dupont.com/NASApp/dupontglobal/corp/
    index.jsp;
http://www1.dupont.com/NASApp/dupontglobal/corp/index
    .jsp?page=/content/US/en_US/news/index.html;
http://syngenta.com/en/index.aspx;

http://syngenta.com/en/media/index.aspx;
http://www.bayer.com/;
http://www.press.bayer.com/News/News.nsf/id/010005

Case 41:
http://www.kodak.com;
http://www.kodak.com/US/en/corp/pressCenter/pressCenter
   .shtml

Case 43:
http://www.dialcorp.com/;
http://investor.info.dialcorp.com/releases.cfm?companyid=DL;
http://www.pg.com/main.jhtml;
http://www.pg.com/news/sectionmain.jhtml;
http://www.unilever.com/home/;
http://www.unilever.com/news/;
http://henkel.com/int_henkel/company/index.cfm;
http://henkel.com/int_henkel/channelpress/index.cfm

Strategic Management

Strategic Management

An Integrated Approach

Charles W. L. Hill
University of Washington

Gareth R. Jones
Texas A&M University

Houghton Mifflin Company

Boston   New York

To my wife, Alexandra Hill, for her ever increasing support and affection
Charles W. L. Hill

For Nicholas and Julia and Morgan and Nia
Gareth R. Jones

Editor-in-Chief: George T. Hoffman
Associate Sponsoring Editor: Susan M. Kahn
Senior Project Editor: Rachel D'Angelo Wimberly
Editorial Assistant: May Jawdat
Senior Production/Design Coordinator: Jennifer Meyer Dare
Senior Manufacturing Coordinator: Marie Barnes
Marketing Manager: Steven W. Mikels
Marketing Associate: Lisa Boden

Cover image and design: © Ron Chapple/Getty Images

Library of Congress Control Number: 2002109474

Sixth Edition ISBN: 0-618-30953-5
Sixth Edition Update ISBN: 0-618-49771-4

3 4 5 6 7 8 9 — DOW — 07 06 05

Brief Contents

Contents

2

External Analysis:
The Identification of Industry Opportunities and Threats   35

PART II   **The Nature of Competitive Advantage**

3 Internal Analysis: Distinctive Competencies, Competitive Advantage, and Profitability   74

4 Building Competitive Advantage Through Functional-Level Strategy   109

7   Strategy in High-Technology Industries   224

8 Strategy in the Global Environment

259

9 Corporate Strategy: Horizontal Integration, Vertical Integration, and Strategic Outsourcing   297

10 Corporate Strategy: Diversification, Acquisitions, and Internal New Ventures   326

12 Implementing Strategy in Companies That Compete in a Single Industry 402

Cases

SECTION A: Small Business, Entrepreneurship, and Ethics Cases

Preface

In its fifth edition, *Strategic Management: An Integrated Approach* was the most widely used strategic management textbook on the market. In every edition we have attracted new users who share with us the concern for currency in text and examples to ensure that cutting edge issues and theories in strategic management are addressed. This revision of *Strategic Management* was fairly significant. The first edition of this book was written in the late 1980s. Although we have always endeavored to keep the book as up-to-date as possible, we felt that the structure of the book, and some of the key themes, still reflected strategic thinking as it was then and not as it is today. To make sure that the book was absolutely current in its content and coverage of material, we decided to embark upon a significant rewrite. The objective of the rewrite was to maintain all that was good about prior editions, while adding new material to the text when appropriate, and deleting materials that most professors now ignore. We believe that the result is a book that is much more focused on the realities of strategy and competitive advantage in the 2000s than any other textbook on the market, and is closely aligned with the needs of today's professors and students.

Comprehensive and Up-To-Date Coverage

The overall organization of this edition, as noted in Figure 1.3 on page 9, reflects that of previous editions and is designed so that the concepts build upon one another, with early chapters providing a strong foundation for later ones. Though the overall organization remains familiar, there have been significant changes in some of the chapters, and new chapters have been added to reflect current thinking in the field of strategic management.

Changes in Organization of the Book

- Chapter 7, **"Strategy in High-Technology Industries"** is new. This chapter was added to strengthen the book's coverage of strategy in markets driven by rapid technological change.

- Chapter 11, **"Corporate Performance, Governance, and Business Ethics"** is new. This Chapter was added to strengthen coverage of material on business ethics and corporate governance in light of numerous examples of unethical behavior by corporate managers, the failure of corporate governance mechanisms such as the board of directors to check unethical behavior, and the negative impact of such failures on corporate performance. For example, unethical behavior at WorldCom and Enron was unchecked by the boards of those companies, and contributed to the poor performance and bankruptcy of both enterprises in 2002.

- The material that appeared in Chapter 2 of the fifth edition, "Stakeholders and the Corporate Mission" has been merged into other chapters where appropriate. Material on mission and goals has been moved into Chapter 1, "The Strategic Management Process." Material on stakeholders, business ethics, and corporate governance has been moved to the new Chapter 11 where it has received expanded treatment.

- Chapters 11–14 in the fifth edition have been compressed into two chapters in the sixth edition, Chapters 12 and 13. Chapter 12 covers implementation issues that are relevant for firms that compete in a single industry including organizational structure, strategic control, and culture. It also addresses implementation issues of functional and generic business-level strategies, along with restructuring and reengineering. Chapter 13 provides information about implementation issues for firms competing in multiple businesses, and it specifically focuses on implementing global strategies and the impact of information technology on strategy implementation.

Major Content Changes Within Chapters

- In Chapter 1 there is a new section added on **performance and competitive advantage** to drive home the point that strategy is about attaining a sustainable competitive advantage.

- In Chapter 3 there is a new section on **analyzing sources of competitive advantage and profitability.** This section explains in detail how strategic choice impacts the profitability of a company as measured by the return on invested capital. This section shows how an analysis of financial statements can reveal the financial impact of major differences in strategic choices. It also explains how strategic managers must think through the impact of their decisions on the financial position of the company.

- In Chapter 5 a new section has been added on **business strategy and game theory.** This section shows how managers can make better strategic choices by drawing on principles derived from game theory.

- In Chapter 6 the section on **strategy in embryonic and growth industries** has been substantially revised to add more material, particularly on how the nature of competition changes as industries pass through different growth stages and how this impacts the choice of strategy. This section looks at why many companies that are successful in embryonic industries fail to cross the chasm that separates an embryonic industry from a growth industry.

- Chapter 7 is new to this edition. The chapter looks at the importance of technological standards in industries, the nature of "network economics," and strategies for winning "format wars" between companies that are promoting different, and incompatible, technical standards. Also discussed are the cost structure of high-technology firms and its strategic implications, strategies for managing intellectual property rights, and strategies for capturing a first-mover advantage. The chapter closes with a review of the strategic implications of technological paradigm shifts for both new entrants and incumbent firms in an industry.

- Chapter 9 contains a new section on **horizontal integration**. This section looks at why companies in the same industry acquire or merge with each other and the strategic implications of this. The chapter also contains an expanded treatment of strategic outsourcing and looks at how companies can outsource activities to attain a competitive advantage.

- Chapter 11 is a new chapter that looks at **corporate performance, governance, and business ethics.** The chapter explains how poor corporate performance can be caused by a combination of poor corporate governance systems and unethical behavior. The chapter reviews the strategic importance of managing stakeholders, putting strong corporate governance mechanisms in place, and making ethical decisions. Agency theory is used to explain failures of corporate governance and poor managerial ethics. The chapter draws heavily on recent examples of corporate fraud to illustrate the main points. The opening case features Enron, and discussions of recently discovered fraud/unethical behavior at WorldCom, Tyco, and Computer Associates are contained within the chapter.

Throughout the revision, we have been careful to preserve the *balanced and integrated* nature of our account of the strategic management process. Moreover, as we added new material, we deleted less current or less important concepts and information to ensure that students would concentrate on the core concepts and issues in the field. We have also paid close attention to retaining the book's readability.

Finally, it is important to emphasize that we have overhauled the case selection. There are 43 cases in this edition. Twenty-seven of these cases are new to this edition. The remaining cases have been updated and revised. For example, the home video game case has been revised to include material on X-Box and Sony PlayStation 2. The Air Express and Airborne Express cases have been revised and updated to 2002. The Kodak case has been substantially rewritten around the issue of digital imaging. As always, we have used a tight screen to weed out poor quality cases and we believe that the selection we offer is the best on the market.

Practicing Strategic Management: An Interactive Approach

We hope you are excited by the hands-on learning possibilities provided by the exercises/assignments in the end-of-chapter *Practicing Strategic Management* sections. Following the Chapter Summary and Discussion Questions, each chapter contains the following assignments/exercises:

■ *Small Group Exercise.* This short (20 minute) experiential exercise asks students to divide into groups and discuss a scenario concerning some aspect of strategic management. For example, the scenario in Chapter 11 asks students to identify the stakeholders of their educational institution and evaluate how stakeholders' claims are being and should be met.

■ *Exploring the Web.* The Internet exercise requires students to explore a particular web site and answer chapter-related questions. For example, the Chapter 8 assignment is to go to the web site of IBM and analyze its strategy for competing in the global marketplace. This section also asks students to explore the Web for relevant sites of their own choosing and answer questions.

■ *Article File.* As in the last edition, this exercise requires students to search business magazines to identify a company that is facing a particular strategic management problem. For instance, students are asked to locate and research a company pursuing a low-cost or a differentiation strategy, and to describe this company's strategy, its advantages and disadvantages, and the core competencies required to pursue it. Students' presentations of their findings lead to lively class discussions.

■ *Strategic Management Project.* Students, in small groups, choose a company to study for the whole semester and then analyze the company using the series of questions provided at the end of every chapter. For example, students might select Ford Motor Co. and, using the series of chapter questions, collect information on Ford's top managers, mission, ethical position, domestic and global strategy and structure, and so on. Eventually, students would write a case study of their company and present it to the class at the end of the semester. Normally, we also have students present one or more of the cases in the book early in the semester, but in our classes we now treat the students' own projects as the major class assignment and their case presentations as the climax of the semester's learning experience.

■ *Closing case study.* A short closing case provides an opportunity for a short class discussion of a chapter-related theme.

In creating these exercises it is not our intention to suggest that they should *all* be used for *every* chapter. For example, over a semester an instructor might combine a group Strategic Management Project with five to six Article File assignments and five to six Exploring the Web exercises, while doing eight to ten Small Group Exercises in class.

We have found that our interactive approach to teaching strategic management appeals to students. It also greatly improves the quality of their learning experience. Our approach is more fully discussed in the *Instructor's Resource Manual.*

Strategic Management Cases

The 43 cases that we have selected for this edition will appeal, we are certain, to students and professors alike, both because these cases are intrinsically interesting and because of the number of strategic management issues they illuminate. The organizations discussed in the cases range from large, well-known ones, for which students can do research in order to update the information, to small, entrepreneurial businesses that illustrate the uncertainty and challenge of the strategic management process. In addition, the selections include many international cases, and most of the other cases contain some element of global strategy. Refer to the table of contents for a complete listing of the cases with brief descriptions.

We feel that our entire selection is unrivaled in breadth and depth, and we are grateful to the other case authors who have contributed to this edition.

Larry D. Alexander, *Virginia Tech*
Simon Algar, *Thunderbird, The American Graduate School of International Management*
A. J. Almaney, *DePaul University*
Bharat Anand, *Harvard Business School*
Steven Angga-Prana, *New York University*
Frank C. Barnes, *University of North Carolina–Charlotte*
M. Edgar Barrett, *Thunderbird, The American Graduate School of International Management*
Chad Beaupierre, *New York University*
Scott Bevier, *New York University*
Herman L. Boschken, *San Jose State University*
James W. Camerius, *Northern Michigan University*
Jonathan Charlton, *Virginia Tech*
Joyce A. Claterbos, *University of Kansas*
Billy Cockrell, *Adrenaline Air Sports*
Gabriella Del Carro, *St. John's University*
Dorothy G. Dologite, *Baruch College, City University of New York*
John Dunkelberg, *Wake Forest University*
Harold Dyck, *California State University*
Roberto Ekesi, *New York University*
Joseph N. Fry, *Richard Ivey School of Business*
Marc E. Gartenfeld, *St. John's University*
Tim Goho, *Wake Forest University*
Sue Greenfeld, *California State University*
Myra Hart, *Harvard Business School*

Andrew C. Inkpen, *Thunderbird, The American Graduate School of International Management*
Lawrence R. Jauch, *University of Louisiana at Monroe*
Min Yee Ji, *New York University*
Andrew Kimbrough, *Thunderbird, The American Graduate School of International Management*
Suresh Kotha, *University of Washington*
David Lane, *Harvard Business School*
Vipon Kumar, *Thunderbird, The American Graduate School of International Management*
Vicken Librarikian, *New York University*
Meredith Martin, *Thunderbird, The American Graduate School of International Management*
Melissa V. Melancon, *University of Louisiana at Monroe*
Robert J. Mockler, *St. John's University*
Chiaki Moriguchi, *Harvard Business School*
Richard Moxon, *University of Washington*
Vincent Pawlowski, *St. John's University*
Elizabeth Petrovski, *St. John's University*
Sharon I. Peyus, *Harvard Business School*
Taz Pirmohamed, *Harvard Business School*
Steve Preziosi, *St. John's University*
Frank T. Rothaermel, *Michigan State University*
George C. Rubenson, *Salisbury University*
Melissa A. Schilling, *New York University*
Frank M. Shipper, *Salisbury University*
Damon Swaner, *St. John's University*
Norihito Tanaka, *Kanagawa University*
Marilyn L. Taylor, *University of Missouri at Kansas City*
Beverly B. Tyler, *North Carolina State University*
Roderick E. White, *Richard Ivey School of Business*

To help students learn how to effectively analyze and write a case study, we continue to include a special section on this subject. This section includes a checklist and explanation of areas to consider, suggested research tools, and tips on financial analysis.

Teaching and Learning Aids

Taken together, the teaching and learning features of *Strategic Management* provide a package that is unsurpassed in its coverage and that supports the integrated approach that we have taken throughout the book.

For the Instructor

■ The **Instructor's Resource Manual** has been completely revised. For each chapter we provide a clearly focused *synopsis*, a list of *teaching objectives,* a *comprehensive lecture outline* that includes references to the transparencies, and *answers to discussion questions.* Each of the chapter opening cases also has a corresponding teaching note to help guide class discussion. Furthermore, the lecture outlines include summaries and teaching notes for the *Strategy in Action* boxes. Finally, the manual includes comments on the Practicing Strategic Management sections and suggested answers to the Closing Case Discussion Questions.

■ The **Test Bank** (in the *Instructor's Resource Manual*) has been revised and offers a set of comprehensive true/false and multiple-choice questions, and new essay questions for each chapter in the book. The mix of questions has been adjusted to provide fewer fact-based or simple memorization items and to provide more items that rely on synthesis or application. Also, more items now reflect real or hypothetical situations in organizations. Every question is keyed to the teaching objectives in the *Instructor's Resource Manual* and includes an answer and page reference to the textbook.

■ The **Instructor's Resource Manual: Cases** includes a complete list of Case Discussion Questions as well as a *comprehensive teaching note* for each case, which gives a complete analysis of case issues.

■ New for this edition is the **HM ClassPrep with HMTesting CD**. This instructor CD provides a variety of teaching resources in electronic format allowing for easy customization to meet specific instructional needs. Included in ClassPrep are **Power-Point slides** for classroom presentation and Word files from the *Instructor's Resource Manuals* that can be easily edited.

   HMTesting, the computerized version of the *Test Bank,* allows instructors to select, edit, and add questions, or generate randomly selected questions to produce a test master for easy duplication. Online Testing and Gradebook functions allow instructors to administer tests via their local area network or the World Wide Web, set up classes, record grades from tests or assignments, analyze grades, and produce class and individual statistics.

■ A package of **color transparencies** is available for adopters. These include nearly all the figures found in the chapters.

■ New **Videos** from CNN's award-winning "CEO Exchange" series are available to adopters. This series uses in-depth interviews with internationally recognized and respected CEOs to shed light on those managerial, organizational, and technological issues that are shaping the marketplace of ideas. In addition, this series explores the personal side of commerce, as industry icons discuss the values and experiences that shape and influence their business philosophies, strategies, and decisions. The programs that accompany this book are "Jack Welch: Icon of Leadership," "Creating New Categories, Businesses, and Markets" (featuring Thomas Stemberg, chairman and CEO of Staples, and Carl Yankowski, former CEO of Palm, a market leader in handheld computers), "The Built to Order Revolution" (featuring Michael Dell, chairman and CEO of Dell Computer Corporation, and Frederick Smith, chairman, president, and CEO of FedEx Corporation), and "Innovators of Silicon Valley" (featuring Scott McNealy, chairman and CEO of Sun Microsystems, and Marc Andreessen, chairman of Loudcloud and co-founder of Netscape). Each program includes business students and faculty asking questions of the discussants. We are confident this video series will help highlight many issues of interest and can be used to spark class discussion.

■ An extensive **web site** contains many features to aid instructors including downloadable files for the text and case materials from the *Instructor's Resource Manuals,* the downloadable PowerPoint slides, the Video Guide, and sample syllabi. Additional materials on the student web site may also be of use to instructors.

For the Student

- A student **web site** provides help for students as they make their way through the course. The web site features links to the companies highlighted in each chapter's boxes and opening and closing cases as well as the full-length cases, links to other sites of general interest while studying strategic management, the Exploring the Web exercises with any updates as necessary to account for the inevitable changes that occur to the relevant sites, case discussion questions to guide students as they analyze the in-depth cases, ACE self-tests related to each chapter, and a glossary and flashcards of key terms.

- The **Real Deal UpGrade CD-ROM** includes a glossary of key terms, chapter learning objectives, brief chapter outlines, chapter summaries, and quizzes to test understanding of the major concepts.

Acknowledgments

This book is the product of far more than two authors. We are grateful to George Hoffman, our editor-in-chief, and Steve Mikels, our marketing manager, for their help in promoting and developing the book and for providing us with timely feedback and information from professors and reviewers that have allowed us to shape the book to meet the needs of its intended market. We are also grateful to Susan Kahn, associate sponsoring editor, for ably coordinating the planning of our book and for managing the creation of the ancillary materials; and grateful to Rachel D'Angelo Wimberly, senior project editor, and May Jawdat, editorial assistant, for their adept handling of production. We are also grateful to the case authors for allowing us to use their materials. We also want to thank the departments of management at the University of Washington and Texas A&M University for providing the setting and atmosphere in which the book could be written, and the students of these universities who reacted to and provided input for many of our ideas. In addition, the following reviewers of this and earlier editions gave us valuable suggestions for improving the manuscript from its original version to its current form:

Ken Armstrong, *Anderson University*
Kunal Banerji, *West Virginia University*
Glenn Bassett, *University of Bridgeport*
Thomas H. Berliner, *The University of Texas at Dallas*
Richard G. Brandenburg, *University of Vermont*
Steven Braund, *University of Hull*
Philip Bromiley, *University of Minnesota*
Geoffrey Brooks, *Western Oregon State College*
Lowell Busenitz, *University of Houston*
Gene R. Conaster, *Golden State University*
Steven W. Congden, *University of Hartford*
Catherine M. Daily, *Ohio State University*
Robert DeFillippi, *Suffolk University Sawyer School of Management*
Helen Deresky, *SUNY–Plattsburgh*
Gerald E. Evans, *The University of Montana*
John Fahy, *Trinity College, Dublin*
Patricia Feltes, *Southwest Missouri State University*
Mark Fiegener, *Oregon State University*
Isaac Fox, *Washington State University*

Craig Galbraith, *University of North Carolina at Wilmington*
Scott R. Gallagher, *Rutgers University*
Eliezer Geisler, *Northeastern Illinois University*
Gretchen Gemeinhardt, *University of Houston*
Lynn Godkin, *Lamar University*
Robert L. Goldberg, *Northeastern University*
Graham L. Hubbard, *University of Minnesota*
Tammy G. Hunt, *University of North Carolina at Wilmington*
James Gaius Ibe, *Morris College*
W. Grahm Irwin, *Miami University*
Jonathan L. Johnson, *University of Arkansas Walton College of Business Administration*
Marios Katsioloudes, *St. Joseph's University*
Robert Keating, *University of North Carolina at Wilmington*
Geoffrey King, *California State University–Fullerton*
Rico Lam, *University of Oregon*
Robert J. Litschert, *Virginia Polytechnic Institute and State University*
Franz T. Lohrke, *Louisiana State University*
Lance A. Masters, *California State University–San Bernardino*
Robert N. McGrath, *Embry-Riddle Aeronautical University*
Charles Mercer, *Drury College*
Van Miller, *University of Dayton*
Joanna Mulholland, *West Chester University of Pennsylvania*
Francine Newth, *Providence College*
Paul R. Reed, *Sam Houston State University*
Rhonda K. Reger, *Arizona State University*
Malika Richards, *Indiana University*
Ronald Sanchez, *University of Illinois*
Joseph A. Schenk, *University of Dayton*
Brian Shaffer, *University of Kentucky*
Pradip K. Shukla, *Chapman University*
Dennis L. Smart, *University of Nebraska at Omaha*
Barbara Spencer, *Clemson University*
Lawrence Steenberg, *University of Evansville*
Kim A. Stewart, *University of Denver*
Ted Takamura, *Warner Pacific College*
Bobby Vaught, *Southwest Missouri State*
Robert P. Vichas, *Florida Atlantic University*
Daniel L. White, *Drexel University*
Edgar L. Williams, Jr., *Norfolk State University*

Charles W. L. Hill
Gareth R. Jones

Strategic Management

The Strategic Management Process

1

Opening Case

Dell Computer

Dell Computer is one of the most extraordinary success stories in business history. Started in 1984 by Michael Dell in his dorm room when he was an undergraduate student at the University of Texas in Austin, Dell has become the world's largest producer of computer systems. The company sells notebook and desktop computers, network servers, storage products, workstations, and peripheral hardware. In 2002, its sales are projected to exceed $30 billion. Dell is a highly profitable company and is the highest performer in its industry. The figure shows that its profit rate has exceeded that of all its competitors in every year since 1995. This superior performance persisted through 2001, a difficult and dismal year for the computer industry: slumping demand from corporate customers led to excess productive capacity and substantial price competition. In 2001, Dell's return on invested capital was 26 percent compared to 1.5 percent at Compaq, and zero at Apple and Gateway. How did Dell achieve its high performance? What explains the company's persistently high profitability?

The answer can be found in Dell's business model: selling directly to customers. Michael Dell reasoned that by cutting out wholesalers and retailers, he would obtain the profit they

Profitability in the Personal Computer Industry, 1995–2001

Data Source: Value Line Investment Survey

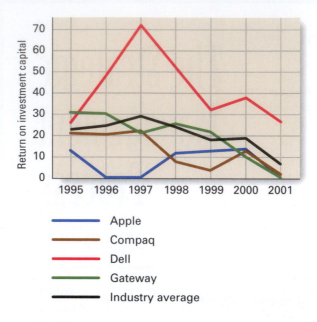

would otherwise receive and could give part of the profit back to customers in the form of lower prices. Initially, Dell did its direct selling through mailings and telephone contacts, but since the mid-1990s, most of its sales have been made through its web site. By 2001, 85 percent of Dell's sales were made through the Internet. Dell's sophisticated interactive web site allows customers to mix and match product features such as microprocessors, memory, monitors, internal hard drives, CD and DVD drives, keyboard and mouse format, and so on to customize their own computer system.

Another major reason for Dell's high performance is the way it manages its supply chain to minimize its cost structure, in particular, the costs of holding inventory yet with the ability build a computer to individual customer specifications within three days. Dell has about 200 suppliers, over half of them located outside the United States. Dell uses the Internet to feed real-time information about order flow to its suppliers so they have up-to-the-minute information about demand trends for the components they produce, along with volume expectations for the upcoming four to twelve weeks. Dell's suppliers use this information to adjust their own production schedules, manufacturing just enough components for Dell's needs and shipping them by the most appropriate mode so that they arrive just in time for production. This tight coordination is pushed back even further down the supply chain because Dell shares this information with its suppliers'

biggest suppliers. For example, Selectron builds motherboards for Dell that incorporate digital signal processing chips from Texas Instruments. To coordinate the supply chain, Dell passes information to both Texas Instruments and Selectron. Texas Instruments then adjusts its schedules to Selectron's needs, and Selectron adjusts its schedule to fit the order data it receives from Dell. All of this coordination results in lower costs along the supply chain.

Dell's ultimate goal is to drive all inventories out of the supply chain apart from those actually in transit between suppliers and Dell, effectively replacing inventory with information. Although it has not yet achieved this goal, it has succeeded in driving down inventory to the lowest level in the industry. Dell has about five days of inventory on hand, compared to thirty, forty-five, or even ninety days at competitors such as Compaq Computer and Gateway. This is a major source of competitive advantage in the computer industry, where component costs account for 75 percent of revenues and typically fall by 1 percent per week due to rapid obsolescence. Thus, lowering its cost structure by streamlining its inventory management systems is a critical reason for Dell's high profitability.

Sources: D. Hunter, "How Dell Keeps from Stumbling," *Business Week,* May 14, 2001, pp. 38–40; "Enter the Eco-System: From Supply Chain to Network," *Economist,* November 11, 2000; "Dell's Direct Initiative," *Country Monitor,* June 7, 2000, p. 5; Dell Computer Corporation 10K, 2001.

Overview

Why do some organizations succeed while others fail? Why has Dell Computer been able to do so well in the fiercely competitive personal computer industry, while others like Compaq, Gateway, and Apple have not had the same success in recent years? In the retail industry, what distinguishes successes such as Wal-Mart and Target from struggling rivals Sears and Kmart? In the market for database software, why have Oracle and Microsoft managed to build and retain strong market positions, while rivals such as Informix and Sybase have lost significant market share? In the airline industry, how is it that Southwest Airlines has managed to keep increasing its revenues and profits through both good times and bad, while rivals such as Delta and US Airways have struggled to avoid bankruptcy? How did Sony come to dominate the market for video games with its highly successful PlayStation, while former industry leader Sega saw its market share slump from 60 percent in the early 1990s to the low single digits by 2000, and finally pulled out of the market in 2001?

In this book, we argue that the strategies that an organization's managers pursue have a major impact on its performance relative to its peers. A **strategy** is an action that managers take to attain one or more of the organization's goals. For most, if not all organizations, an overriding goal is to achieve superior performance relative to rivals. If a company's strategy results in superior performance, it is said to have a *competitive advantage.* Dell's strategies produced superior performance from 1996 to 2001; Dell thus has had a competitive advantage over its rivals.

How did Dell attain this competitive advantage? In the early 1990s, Michael Dell hired a number of highly experienced managers from established companies such as IBM. Then Dell and these managers developed and pursued strategies that enabled the company to satisfy customers better than its competitors did while simultaneously giving it a cost structure that was the lowest in the industry. In 2001, Dell took advantage of its low cost structure to launch a price war in the personal computer industry. It took significant market share from its competitors while remaining profitable. In contrast, Dell's competitors saw their profitability slump, and some, like Gateway, had losses. (We will return to the example of Dell several times throughout this book in a *Running Case* that examines various aspects of Dell's strategy and performance.)

Much of strategic management is about identifying and describing the strategies that managers can pursue to attain superior performance and a competitive advantage for their organization. Many of these strategies are generic—that is, they apply to all organizations, large and small, manufacturing and service, and profit seeking and nonprofit. A central aim of this book is to give you a thorough understanding of the analytical techniques and skills necessary to identify and exploit strategies successfully. The first step toward achieving this objective is to explain in more detail what *superior performance* and *competitive advantage* mean. Then the nature of the **strategic management process**—the process by which managers choose a set of strategies for a company that will allow it to achieve superior performance—is described. By the end of this chapter, you will understand the processes managers use to choose strategies for their organization and have an appreciation for the strengths and weaknesses of these processes.

Superior Performance and Competitive Advantage

In the business world, superior performance is typically thought of in terms of one company's profitability relative to that of other companies in the same or a similar kind of business or industry. The **profitability** of a company can be measured by the return that it makes on the capital invested in the enterprise.[1] The return on invested capital that a company earns is defined as its profit over the capital invested in the firm (profit/capital invested). By *profit,* we mean before-tax profits. By *capital,* we mean the sum of money invested in the company, that is, stockholders' equity plus debt owed to creditors. This capital is used to buy the resources a company needs to produce and sell goods and services. A company that uses its resources efficiently makes a positive return on invested capital. The more efficient a company is, the higher are its profitability and return on invested capital.

Firm-Specific Performance and Profitability

A company's profitability—its return on invested capital—is determined by the strategies its managers adopt. For example, in the *Opening Case,* we saw that Michael Dell's direct selling strategy enabled his company to lower prices and increase its revenues over time. In addition, Dell's strategy for using the Web to manage its supply chain allowed it to lower costs by taking inventory out of its system. As a result, Dell has been more profitable than its competitors.

A company is said to have a **competitive advantage** over its rivals when its profitability is greater than the average profitability for all firms in its industry. The greater the extent to which a company's profitability exceeds the average profitability for its industry, the greater is its competitive advantage. A company is said to have a **sustained competitive advantage** when it is able to maintain above-average profitability for a number of years. Clearly, Dell Computer had a significant and sustained competitive advantage between 1996 and 2001.

Much of this book is devoted to examining the strategies that managers can use to gain and maintain a competitive advantage for their company, thereby enabling it to achieve above-average profitability over a sustained period of time. At the most basic level, strategy is concerned with understanding the relationship between *prices, customer demand, and cost structure* and manipulating these variables in a way that lead to higher profitability. It follows that to *think strategically* is to think about which actions to take to optimize prices, increase customer demand, and/or lower costs, and to do so in a manner that is consistent with boosting the *profitability* of the company. A company's **business model** is management's model of how the strategies they pursue will allow the company to gain a competitive advantage and achieve superior profitability. Business models are usually based on financial projections of the pricing structure, unit sales volume, revenues, cost structure, profit levels, and profitability that the company can attain if it successfully implements its strategies and meets its goals. Strategies are the actions that managers take to execute a business model. Dell's direct distribution business model, for example, is based on the central idea that prices for PCs can be lowered through bypassing distributors and selling directly to consumers. The business model also assumes that at lower prices, Dell will gain market share, increasing its revenues and allowing it to realize substantial scale economies and unit cost reductions that will make the company very profitable, even at lower price points. Dell's success in the PC industry is a testament to the fact that its business model is superior to the business model of rivals such as Gateway and Compaq.

Managers do not make strategic decisions in a vacuum. Strategic thinking and strategy making take place in a competitive arena where managers think not only about the strategies *their* firm is pursuing, but also about the strategies their *competitors* are pursuing and about how competitors might respond to any strategic initiative they decide to take. Firm performance and profitability are determined by the success of the strategies that its managers pursue relative to the strategies pursued by the managers of rival firms. The best-made plans and strategy will not be successful if they do not take into account what competitors are doing now and what they will do in the future.

Industry Structure and Profitability

A company's profitability is also determined by the characteristics of its industry. Different industries are characterized by different competitive conditions. In some, demand is growing rapidly, and in others it is contracting. Some might be beset by excess capacity and persistent price wars, and others by excess demand and rising prices. In some, technological change might be revolutionizing competition, and others might be characterized by a lack of technological change. In some industries, high profitability among incumbent firms might induce new firms to enter the industry, and these new entrants might depress prices and profits in the industry. In other industries, new entry might be difficult, and periods of high profitability might persist for a considerable time. Thus, the different competitive conditions prevailing in different industries might lead to different average profitability. The average profit rate might be higher in some industries and lower in other industries because competitive conditions vary from industry to industry.

Figure 1.1 shows the average return on invested capital earned by firms in several different industries between 1997 and 2001. The drug industry had a favorable competitive environment to operate in: demand for drugs was high, and competition was generally not based on price. Just the opposite was the case in the steel and air transport industries: both are extremely price competitive. In addition, the steel industry was characterized by declining demand, excess capacity, and price wars. Exactly how industries differ is discussed in detail in Chapter 2. For now, the important point to remember is that the profitability of a firm is determined by two main factors: its relative success in its industry and the overall performance of its industry relative to other industries.[2]

Performance in Nonprofit Enterprises

A final point concerns the concept of superior performance in the nonprofit sector. By definition, nonprofit enterprises such as government agencies, universities, and charities are not in "business" to make profits. Nevertheless, they are expected to use their resources efficiently and operate effectively, and their managers set goals to measure their performance. The performance goal for a business school might be to get its programs ranked among the best in the nation. The performance goal for a charity might be to prevent childhood illnesses in poor countries. The performance goal

FIGURE 1.1

Return on Invested Capital in Selected Industries, 1997–2001

Data Source: Value Line Investment Survey

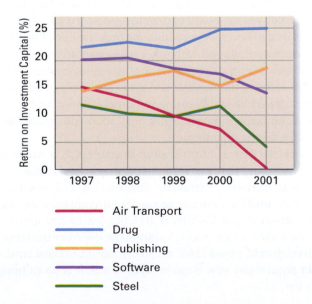

for a government agency might be to improve its services while not exceeding its budget. The managers of nonprofits need to map out strategies to attain these goals. They also need to understand that nonprofits compete with each other for scarce resources just as businesses do. For example, charities compete for scarce donations, and their managers must plan and develop strategies that lead to high performance and demonstrate a track record of meeting performance goals. A successful strategy gives potential donors a compelling message as to why they should contribute additional donations. Thus, planning and thinking strategically is as important for managers in the nonprofit sector as it is for managers in profit-seeking firms.

Strategic Managers

In most companies, there are two main types of managers: **general managers,** who bear responsibility for the overall performance of the company or for one of its major self-contained subunits or divisions, and **functional managers,** who are responsible for supervising a particular function, that is, a task, activity, or operation, like accounting, marketing, R&D, information technology, or materials management.

A company is a collection of functions or departments that work together to bring a particular product or service to the market. If a company provides several different kinds of products or services, it often duplicates these functions and creates a series of self-contained divisions (each of which contains its own set of functions) to manage each different product or service. The general managers of these divisions then become responsible for their particular product line. The overriding concern of general managers is for the health of the whole company or division under their direction; they are responsible for deciding how to create a competitive advantage and achieve high profitability with the resources and capital they have at their disposal. Figure 1.2 shows the organization of a **multidivisional company,** that is, a company that competes in several different businesses and has created a separate self-contained division to manage each of these. As you can see, there are three main levels of management: corporate, business, and functional. General managers are found at the first two of these levels, but their strategic roles differ depending on their sphere of responsibility.

Corporate-Level Managers

The corporate level of management consists of the chief executive officer (CEO), other senior executives, the board of directors, and corporate staff. These individuals occupy the apex of decision making within the organization. The CEO is the principal general manager. In consultation with other senior executives, the role of *corporate-level managers* is to oversee the development of strategies for the whole organization. This role includes defining the mission and goals of the organization, determining what businesses it should be in, allocating resources among the different businesses, formulating and implementing strategies that span individual businesses, and providing leadership for the organization.

Consider General Electric as an example. GE is active in a wide range of businesses, including lighting equipment, major appliances, motor and transportation equipment, turbine generators, construction and engineering services, industrial electronics, medical systems, aerospace, aircraft engines, and financial services. The main strategic responsibilities of its CEO, Jeffrey Immelt, are setting overall strategic objectives, allocating resources among the different business areas, deciding whether the firm should divest itself of any of its businesses, and determining whether it should acquire any new ones. In other words, it is up to Immelt to develop strategies

FIGURE 1.2

Levels of Strategic
Management

Corporate Level
CEO, other senior executives,
board of directors,
and corporate staff

Head Office

Business Level
Divisional managers
and staff

Division A   Division B   Division C

Functional Level
Functional managers

Business functions   Business functions   Business functions

Market A   Market B   Market C

that span individual businesses; his concern is with building and managing the corporate portfolio of businesses to maximize corporate profitability.

It is *not* his specific responsibility to develop strategies for competing in the individual business areas, such as financial services. The development of such strategies is the responsibility of the general managers in these different businesses or *business-level managers.* However, it is Immelt's responsibility to probe the strategic thinking of business-level managers to make sure that they are pursuing robust strategies that will contribute toward the maximization of GE's long-run profitability and to hold them into account for their performance.

Besides overseeing resource allocation and managing the divestment and acquisition processes, corporate-level managers provide a link between the people who oversee the strategic development of a firm and those who own it (the shareholders). Corporate-level managers, and particularly the CEO, can be viewed as the guardians of shareholder welfare. It is their responsibility to ensure that the corporate and business strategies that the company pursues are consistent with maximizing shareholder wealth. If they are not, then ultimately the CEO is likely to be called to account by the shareholders.

**Business-Level
Managers**

A business unit is a self-contained division (with its own functions—for example, finance, purchasing, production, and marketing departments) that provides a product or service for a particular market. The principal general manager at the business level, or the business-level manager, is the head of the division. The strategic role of these managers is to translate the general statements of direction and intent that come from the corporate level into concrete strategies for individual businesses. Thus, whereas corporate-level general managers are concerned with strategies that span individual businesses, business-level general managers are concerned with strategies that are specific to a particular business. At GE, a major corporate goal is to be first or second in every business in which the corporation competes. Then the general managers in each division work out for their business the details of a strategy that is consistent with this objective.

Functional-Level Managers

Functional-level managers are responsible for the specific business functions or operations (human resources, purchasing, product development, customer service, and so on) that constitute a company or one of its divisions. Thus, a functional manager's sphere of responsibility is generally confined to *one* organizational activity, whereas general managers oversee the operation of a *whole* company or division. Although they are not responsible for the overall performance of the organization, functional managers nevertheless have a major strategic role: to develop functional strategies in their area that help fulfill the strategic objectives set by business- and corporate-level general managers.

In GE's aerospace business, for instance, manufacturing managers are responsible for developing manufacturing strategies consistent with the corporate objective of being first or second in that industry. Moreover, functional managers provide most of the information that makes it possible for business- and corporate-level general managers to formulate realistic and attainable strategies. Indeed, because they are closer to the customer than the typical general manager is, functional managers themselves may generate important ideas that subsequently may become major strategies for the company. Thus, it is important for general managers to listen closely to the ideas of their functional managers. An equally great responsibility for managers at the operational level is strategy implementation: the execution of corporate- and business-level plans.

Strategic Planning

A number of business writers have emphasized that strategy is the outcome of a formal planning process and that top management plays the most important role in this process.[3] Although this view has some basis in reality, it is not the whole story. As we shall see later in the chapter, valuable strategies often emerge from deep within the organization without prior planning. Nevertheless, a consideration of formal, rational planning is a useful starting point for our journey into the world of strategy. Accordingly, we consider what might be described as a typical formal strategic planning model.

A Model of the Strategic Planning Process

The formal strategic planning process has five main steps:

1. Select the corporate mission and major corporate goals.

2. Analyze the organization's external competitive environment to identify *opportunities* and *threats*.

3. Analyze the organization's internal operating environment to identify the organization's *strengths* and *weaknesses*.

4. Select strategies that build on the organization's strengths and correct its weaknesses in order to take advantage of external opportunities and counter external threats.

5. Implement the strategy.

The task of analyzing the organization's external and internal environment and then selecting an appropriate strategy is normally referred to as **strategy formulation.** In contrast, **strategy implementation** typically involves designing appropriate organizational structures and control systems to put the organization's chosen strategy into action.

These steps are illustrated in Figure 1.3 as the plan of this book. Each step illustrated in the figure constitutes a *sequential* step in the strategic planning process. At

FIGURE 1.3

Main Components of
the Strategic Planning
Process

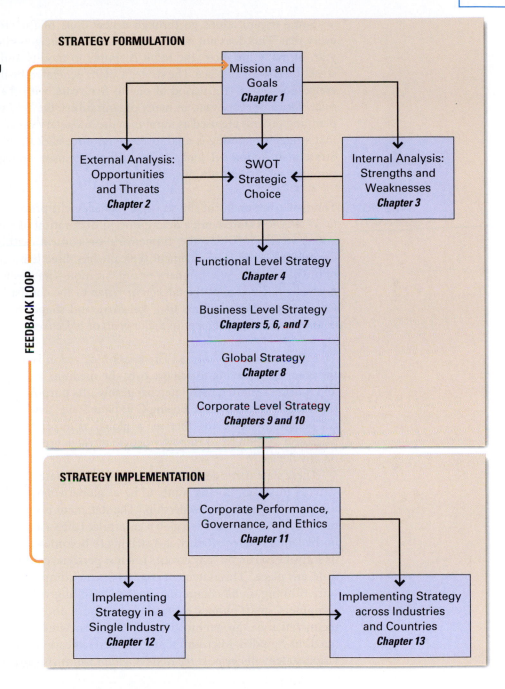

STRATEGY FORMULATION

Mission and
Goals
Chapter 1

External Analysis:
Opportunities
and Threats
Chapter 2

SWOT
Strategic
Choice

Internal Analysis:
Strengths and
Weaknesses
Chapter 3

Functional Level Strategy
Chapter 4

Business Level Strategy
Chapters 5, 6, and 7

Global Strategy
Chapter 8

Corporate Level Strategy
Chapters 9 and 10

FEEDBACK LOOP

STRATEGY IMPLEMENTATION

Corporate Performance,
Governance, and Ethics
Chapter 11

Implementing
Strategy in a
Single Industry
Chapter 12

Implementing Strategy
across Industries
and Countries
Chapter 13

step 1, each round or cycle of the planning process begins with a statement of the corporate mission and major corporate goals. The mission statement is followed by the foundation of strategic thinking: external analysis, internal analysis, and strategic choice, that is, the analysis and choice of which strategies to pursue. The strategy-making process ends with the design of the organizational structure and control systems necessary to implement the organization's chosen strategy. In this chapter the issue of how to select a corporate mission and choose major goals is discussed in detail. Detailed discussion of the other parts of strategic planning is reserved for later chapters.

Some organizations go through a new cycle of the strategic planning process every year. This does not necessarily mean that managers choose a new strategy each year. In many instances, the result is simply to modify and reaffirm a strategy and structure already in place. The strategic plans generated by the planning process generally look out over a period of one to five years, with the plan being updated, or *rolled forward,* every year. In many organizations, the results of the annual strategic planning process are used as input into the budgetary process for the coming year so that strategic planning is used to shape resource allocation within the organization. Strategy in Action 1.1 looks at how Microsoft uses strategic planning to drive its resource allocation decisions.

Mission Statement   The first component of the strategic management process is crafting the organization's **mission statement:** a description or declaration of *why* a company is in operation, which provides the framework or context within which strategies are formulated. A mission statement typically has three main components: a statement of the *raison d'être* of a company or organization—its reason for existence—which is normally referred to as the *mission* or *vision* of the company; a statement of the key *values* or *guiding standards* that will drive and shape the actions and behavior of employees; and a statement of *major goals* or *objectives.*

The Mission or Vision. The mission or vision is a formal declaration of what the company is trying to achieve over the medium to long term. (The terms *vision* and *mission* are often used interchangeably.) Its purpose is to provide a platform for thinking strategically. The Boeing Company states that its vision for Boeing in 2016 is "people working together as a global enterprise for aerospace leadership."[4] Microsoft's vision is "to empower people through great software, any time, any place, on any device."[5]

These statements declare some desired future state that a company's managers are striving to attain. Boeing wants to be a "global enterprise" in which people "work together" for "aerospace leadership." The statement is significant because Boeing currently does not see itself as a global enterprise (the vast majority of Boeing's assets are in the United States). Rather, it is striving to become one. Similarly, Microsoft wants its software to run on "any device," not just personal computers or servers, and at "any time, any place." This statement emphasizes the company's ambitions to have its software running on *all* computing devices, including videogame terminals, hand-held computers, smart phones, embedded processors, and set-top boxes. This vision statement, which has grown broader over time as new uses for software are being developed, has guided Microsoft's product diversification efforts because mission and vision statements *help set the context within which strategies are formulated.*

Formulating the Mission. An important first step in the process of formulating a mission statement is to come up with a definition of the organization's business. Essentially, the definition answers these questions: "What is our business? What will it be? What should it be?"[6] The responses guide the formulation of a mission statement.

To answer the question, "What is our business?" Derek Abell, a prominent business scholar, has suggested that a company should define its business in terms of three dimensions: who is being satisfied (what customer groups), what is being satisfied (what customer needs), and how customers' needs are being satisfied (by what skills, knowledge, or distinctive competencies).[7] Figure 1.4 (on p. 12) illustrates these dimensions. Abell's approach stresses the need for a *customer-oriented* rather than

Strategy in Action   1.1

Strategic Planning at Microsoft

There is a widespread belief that strategic planning does not apply to high-tech industries. "You can't plan for the unpredictable," the argument goes, "and technology markets are characterized by rapid and unpredictable change, so why bother with planning?" Nevertheless, the world's most successful high-tech company, Microsoft, has had a formal strategic planning process in place for many years. The genesis of Microsoft's planning process goes back to 1994 when the rapidly growing company hired Bob Herbold from Procter & Gamble as Microsoft's chief operations officer. Herbold was hired to bring some operating discipline to Microsoft's fluid, freewheeling culture, but without undermining the entrepreneurial values and passion for innovation that had made Microsoft so successful. Microsoft's top managers, Bill Gates and Steve Balmer, had been growing increasingly frustrated with the lack of operating efficiency and coherence at Microsoft, and they wanted to do something about it.

One area that Herbold focused on was strategic planning, almost nonexistent when he arrived. What did exist was "a rat's nest of incompatible planning approaches used by the different units and divisions. . . . Bill [Gates] wanted a more formal planning process because, as he said, 'We have no sense of where we will be in two years except for the product guys saying they have great new products coming along.'" At the very least, Gates felt that Microsoft needed some sense of its financial outlook for the next year or two that it could communicate to investors.

Herbold, Gates, and Balmer understood that any assumptions underlying a plan could be made invalid by unforeseen changes in the business environment, and such changes were commonplace in the software industry. At the same time, they acknowledged that Microsoft had some fairly traditional businesses with established revenue streams, such as Microsoft Office and Windows, and the company needed a plan for the future to craft a strategy for these businesses, focus product development efforts, and allocate resources to these businesses. Moreover, the company needed to plan for the future of its newer businesses, such as MSN, the video game business (X-Box), and its hand-held computer business.

What has emerged at Microsoft is a three-year planning process that compares the subsequent performance of divisions and units against the strategies and goals outlined in the plan to determine future resource alloca-

tion. The planning process is built on a standard format that makes it easy to compare the performance data obtained from each of Microsoft's different businesses or divisions. Planning data include projections for market share, revenues, and profits three years into the future, as well as a statement of major strategies and goals. These projections are updated every year in a rolling plan because the industry changes so much.

Unit strategies are hashed out over the year in strategic planning review meetings between top managers (Gates and Balmer) and division managers. Typically, the unit managers develop strategies, and the top managers probe the strategic thinking of unit managers, asking them to justify their assumptions and ultimately approving, amending, or not approving the unit strategy. Unit strategies are also debated at regular strategy conferences, which Gates and Balmer normally attend.

The strategies that result from these processes are the product of an intense dialogue between top management and unit managers. Unit managers are held accountable for any commitments made in the plan. Thus, the plan not only drives resource allocation, it is also used as a control mechanism. Gates and Balmer determine the overall strategy of Microsoft in consultation with the board of directors, although many of the ideas for new businesses, new products, and acquisitions do not come from the top. Instead, they are proposed by employees within the units and approved if they survive scrutiny.

The planning process is formal, decentralized, and flexible. It is formal insofar as it is a regular process that uses standard information to help drive resource allocation for the coming year and holds managers accountable for their performance. It is decentralized insofar as unit managers propose many of the strategies that make up the plan, and those plans are accepted only after scrutiny by the top managers. It is flexible in that top managers do not see the plan as a straitjacket, but as a document that helps to map out where Microsoft may be going over the next few years. All managers recognize that the assumptions contained in the plan may be invalidated by unforeseen events, and they are committed to rapidly changing strategies if the need arises, as it has often in the past.

Sources: Interviews by Charles Hill. R. J. Herbold, "Inside Microsoft: Balancing Creativity and Discipline," *Harvard Business Review* (January 2002): 72–79.

FIGURE 1.4

Abell's Framework for Defining the Business

Source: D. F. Abell, *Defining the Business: The Starting Point of Strategic Planning* (Englewood Cliffs, Prentice-Hall, 1980, page 7.

a *product-oriented* business definition. A product-oriented business definition focuses on the characteristics of the products sold and markets served, not on which kinds of customer needs the products are satisfying. Abell maintains that such an approach obscures the company's true mission because a product is only the physical manifestation of applying a particular skill to satisfy a particular need for a particular customer group. In practice, that need may be served in many different ways, and a broad customer-oriented business definition that identifies these ways can safeguard companies from being caught unaware by major shifts in demand. Indeed, by helping anticipate demand shifts, Abell's framework can assist companies in capitalizing on the changes in their environment. It can help answer the question, "What will our business be?" Recall that Microsoft's managers quickly realized they were not just offering software to satisfy only consumers' desktop computing needs; their mission was to offer software that would satisfy any form of customers' needs for complex information processing software for any kind of device.

The need to take a customer-oriented view of a company's business has often been ignored. History is littered with the wreckage of once-great corporations that did not define their business or defined it incorrectly so that ultimately they declined. Back in the 1950s and 1960s, there were many office equipment companies such as Smith Corona and Underwood that defined their businesses as being the production of typewriters. This product-oriented definition ignored the fact that they were really in the business of satisfying customers' information processing needs. Unfortunately for those companies, when a new technology came along that better served customer needs for information processing (computers), demand for typewriters plummeted. The last great typewriter company, Smith Corona, went bankrupt in 1996, a victim of the success of computer-based word processing technology.

In contrast, IBM correctly foresaw what its business would be. In the 1950s, IBM was a leader in the manufacture of typewriters and mechanical tabulating equipment using punch-card technology. However, unlike many of its competitors, IBM defined its business as *providing a means for information processing and storage,* rather than just supplying mechanical tabulating equipment and typewriters.[8] Given this definition, the company's subsequent moves into computers, software systems, office systems, and printers seem logical.

Values. The values of a company state how managers and employees should conduct themselves, how they should do business, and what kind of organization they should build to help a company achieve its mission. Insofar as they help drive and shape behavior within a company, values are commonly seen as the bedrock of a company's **organizational culture:** the set of values, norms, and standards that control how employees work to achieve an organization's mission and goals. An organization's culture is commonly seen as an important source of its competitive advantage.[9] (We discuss the issue of organization culture in depth in Chapter 12.) For example, Nucor Steel is one of the most productive and profitable steel firms in the world. Its competitive advantage is based in part on the extremely high productivity of its workforce, something, the company maintains, that is a direct result of its cultural values, which determine how it treats its employees. These values are as follow:

- "Management is obligated to manage Nucor in such a way that employees will have the opportunity to earn according to their productivity."

- "Employees should be able to feel confident that if they do their jobs properly, they will have a job tomorrow."

- "Employees have the right to be treated fairly and must believe that they will be."

- "Employees must have an avenue of appeal when they believe they are being treated unfairly."[10]

At Nucor, values emphasizing pay for performance, job security, and fair treatment for employees help to create an atmosphere within the company that leads to high employee productivity. In turn, this has helped to give Nucor one of the lowest cost structures in its industry, which helps to explain the company's profitability in a very price-competitive business.

Another example of how strong cultural values can help a company pursue its mission and create a competitive advantage is given in Table 1.1, which sets out the values emphasized at Texas Instruments. Note the explicit commitment to

TABLE 1.1

Values at Texas Instruments

Values	
TI has established shared values and beliefs that unite us as a company and guide our actions and decisions:	
Integrity	We respect and value people by treating others as we want to be treated. We are honest by representing ourselves and our intentions truthfully.
Innovation	We learn and create by understanding that impatience with the status quo drives business and personal growth. We act boldly by pioneering new business directions and opportunities.
Commitment	We take responsibility by being at our competitive best for TI. We commit to win by being personally dedicated to making TI a winner.

Source: http://www.ti.com/corp/docs/company/vision.shtml. Accessed October 25, 2002. Copyright © 1995–2002 Texas Instruments Incorporated. All rights reserved. Reprinted by permission.

innovation, integrity and commitment. These value statements send a strong message to employees about the kind of company that Texas Instruments wants to become. If reinforced by top managers through rewards and exemplary behavior, such values help to shape behavior within the company and thus the culture of the organization. Organizational culture is an important source of competitive advantage, so statements such as these should be seen as more than just public relations exercises.

In one study of organizational values, researchers identified a set of values associated with high-performing organizations that help companies achieve superior financial performance through their impact on employee behavior.[11] These values included respect for the interests of key organizational **stakeholders**: individuals or groups that have an interest, claim, or stake in the company, in what it does, and in how well it performs.[12] They include stockholders, bondholders, employees, customers, the communities in which the company does business, and the general public. The study found that deep respect for the interests of customers, employees, suppliers, and shareholders was associated with high performance. The study also noted that the encouragement of leadership and entrepreneurial behavior by mid- and lower-level managers and a willingness to support change efforts within the organization contributed to high performance. Companies found to emphasize such values consistently throughout their organization include Hewlett-Packard, Wal-Mart, and PepsiCo. The same study identified the values of poorly performing companies—values that, as might be expected, are *not* articulated in company mission statements: (1) arrogance, particularly to ideas from outside the company; (2) a lack of respect for key stakeholders; and (3) a history of resisting change efforts and "punishing" mid- and lower-level managers who showed "too much leadership." General Motors was held up as an example of one such organization. According to the authors, a mid- or lower-level manager who showed too much leadership and initiative there was not promoted!

Major Goals and Objectives. Having stated a **mission** or vision that is founded on a customer-oriented definition of the company's business, and having articulated some key values, strategic managers can take the next step in the formulation of a mission statement: establishing major goals and objectives. A **goal** is a desired future state or objective that a company attempts to realize. In this context, the purpose of goals is to specify with precision what must be done if the company is to attain its mission or vision.

Well-constructed goals have four main characteristics:[13]

1. They are *precise and measurable*. Measurable goals give managers a yardstick or standard against which they can judge their performance.

2. They *address crucial issues*. To maintain focus, managers should select a limited number of major goals to assess the performance of the company. The goals that are selected should be crucial or important ones.

3. They are *challenging but realistic*. They give all employees an incentive to look for ways of improving the operations of an organization. If a goal is unrealistic in the challenges it poses, employees may give up; a goal that is too easy may fail to motivate managers and other employees.[14]

4. They *specify a time period* in which they should be achieved when that is appropriate. Time constraints tell employees that success requires a goal to be attained

by a given date, not after that date. Deadlines can inject a sense of urgency into goal attainment and act as a motivator. However, not all goals require time constraints.

Well-constructed goals also provide a means by which the performance of managers can be evaluated.

Profitability: Maximizing Returns to Shareholders. Although most profit-seeking organizations operate with a variety of goals, a central goal of most corporations is to maximize shareholder returns, which means increasing the long-run returns earned by shareholders from owning shares in the corporation. A company's shareholders are its legal owners and the providers of risk capital—the source of the capital resources that allows it to pursue its mission and business. Shareholders receive their rewards or returns from assuming this risk in two ways: from dividend payments and from capital appreciation in the market value of a share (that is, by increases in stock market prices). *A company can best maximize shareholder returns by pursuing strategies that maximize its own profitability.* In general, the more efficient a company is, the higher its profitability will be, and the better its future prospects look to shareholders, and the greater is its ability to pay dividends in the future. Thus, higher profitability leads to greater demand for a company's shares. Demand bids up the share price and leads to capital appreciation.

It is important that top managers do not make the mistake of overemphasizing current profitability to the detriment of long-term profitability, however.[15] The overzealous pursuit of current profitability to maximize short-term returns can encourage such misguided managerial actions as cutting expenditures judged to be nonessential in the short run—for instance, expenditures for research and development, marketing, and new capital investments. Although cutting current expenditure increases current profitability, the resulting underinvestment, lack of innovation, and diminished marketing can jeopardize long-run profitability. These expenditures are vital if a company is to pursue its long-term mission and sustain its competitive advantage and profitability over time. Despite these negative consequences, managers may make such decisions because the adverse effects of a short-run orientation may not materialize and become apparent to shareholders for several years or because they are under extreme pressure to hit short-term profitability goals.[16] It is also worth noting that pressures to maximize short-term profitability may result in managers' acting in an unethical manner. This apparently occurred at Enron Corporation, where profits were systematically inflated by managers who manipulated the firm's financial accounts in a manner that misrepresented the true performance of the firm to shareholders. (Chapter 11 provides a detailed discussion of the issues.)

To guard against short-run behavior, managers need to ensure that they adopt goals whose attainment will increase the long-run performance and competitiveness of their enterprise. Long-term goals are related to such issues as product development, customer satisfaction, and employee productivity, and they emphasize specific objectives or targets concerning such things as efficiency, product quality, and innovation. Recall from the opening case how Dell's managers are continually striving to reduce inventory costs on an ongoing basis. The thinking here is that to achieve long-run goals, companies like Dell have to make continual investments in plant, equipment, R&D, information technology, and people. Only by paying constant attention to their processes and operations can companies improve their customer satisfaction, productivity, product quality, and innovation over the long run. Managers' ability to make the right decisions gives their companies a competitive advantage and boosts *long-term* profitability. Both analysts and shareholders watch how well a company makes these decisions and attains its goals, and its stock price fluctuates according to the perception of how well a company has succeeded. Positive shareholder perceptions boost stock price and help maximize the returns to be had from holding a company's stock.

External Analysis

The second component of the strategic management process is an analysis of the organization's external operating environment. The essential purpose of the external analysis is to identify strategic *opportunities* and *threats* in the organization's operating environment that will affect how it pursues its mission. Three interrelated environments should be examined at this stage: the immediate or *industry environment* in which the organization operates, the country or *national environment*, and the wider socioeconomic or *macroenvironment*.

Analyzing the industry environment requires an assessment of the competitive structure of the organization's industry, including the competitive position of the specific or focal organization and its major rivals. It also requires analysis of the nature, stage, dynamics, and history of the industry. Because many markets are now global markets, analyzing the industry environment also means assessing the impact of globalization on competition within an industry. Analyzing the national environment requires an assessment of whether the national context, that is, the particular configuration of country-specific forces within which a company operates, facilitates the attainment of a competitive advantage in the *global* marketplace. If it does not, then the company might have to consider shifting a significant part of its operations to countries where the national context does facilitate the attainment of a competitive advantage. Analyzing the macroenvironment consists of examining macroeconomic, social, government, legal, international, and technological factors that may affect the organization.

Internal Analysis

Internal analysis, the third component of the strategic management process, serves to pinpoint the *strengths* and *weaknesses* of the organization. Such issues as identifying the quantity and quality of a company's resources and capabilities and ways of building unique skills and company-specific or distinctive competencies are considered here when we probe the sources of competitive advantage. Building and sustaining a competitive advantage requires a company to achieve superior efficiency, quality, innovation, and responsiveness to its customers. Company strengths lead to superior performance in these areas, whereas company weaknesses translate into inferior performance.

SWOT Analysis and the Business Model

The next component of strategic thinking requires the generation of a series of strategic alternatives, or choices of future strategies to pursue, given the company's internal strengths and weaknesses and its external opportunities and threats. The comparison of **s**trengths, **w**eaknesses, **o**pportunities, and **t**hreats is normally referred to as a **SWOT analysis.**[17] Its central purpose is to identify the strategies that will create a firm-specific business model that will best *align, fit,* or *match* a company's resources and capabilities to the demands of the environment in which it operates. Strategic managers compare and contrast the various alternative possible strategies against each other with respect to their ability to achieve major goals and superior profitability. Thinking strategically requires managers to identify the set of *strategies* that will create and sustain a competitive advantage:

■ *Functional-level strategy,* directed at improving the effectiveness of operations within a company, such as manufacturing, marketing, materials management, product development, and customer service

■ *Business-level strategy,* which encompasses the business's overall competitive theme, the way it positions itself in the marketplace to gain a competitive advantage, and the different positioning strategies that can be used in different industry settings—for example, *cost leadership, differentiation, focusing on a particular niche or segment of the industry,* or some *combination* of these

■ *Global strategy,* addressing how to expand operations outside the home country to grow and prosper in a world where competitive advantage is determined at a global level

■ *Corporate-level strategy,* which answers the primary questions: What business or businesses should we be in to maximize the long-run profitability of the organization, and how should we enter and increase our presence in these businesses to gain a competitive advantage?

SWOT analysis helps managers to craft a business model (or models) that will allow a company to gain a competitive advantage in its industry (or industries). Competitive advantage leads to increased profitability, and this maximizes a company's chances of surviving in the fast-changing, global competitive environment that characterizes most industries today.

Strategy Implementation

Having chosen a set of strategies to achieve a competitive advantage and increase performance, managers must put that strategy into action: strategy has to be implemented. In this book, the subject of strategy implementation is broken down into three main components: (1) corporate performance, governance, and ethics; (2) implementing strategy in a single industry; and (3) implementing strategy across industries and across countries.

The Feedback Loop

The feedback loop in Figure 1.3 indicates that strategic planning is ongoing; it *never* ends. Once a strategy has been implemented, its execution must be monitored to determine the extent to which strategic goals and objectives are actually being achieved and to what degree competitive advantage is being created and sustained. This information and knowledge pass back up to the corporate level through feedback loops and become the input for the next round of strategy formulation and implementation. Top managers can then decide whether to reaffirm existing corporate goals and strategies or suggest changes for the future. For example, a strategic objective may prove to be too optimistic, and so the next time more conservative objectives are set. Or feedback may reveal that strategic objectives were attainable but implementation was poor. In that case, the next round in strategic planning may concentrate more on implementation.

Strategy as an Emergent Process

The basic planning model suggests that an organization's strategies are the result of a plan, that the strategic planning process itself is rational and highly structured, and that the process is orchestrated by top management. But recently, several scholars have criticized the formal planning model for three main reasons: the unpredictability of the real world, the role that lower-level managers can play in the strategic management process, and the fact that many successful strategies are often the result of serendipity, not rational strategizing. They have advocated an alternative view of strategy making.[18]

Strategy Making in an Unpredictable World

Critics of formal planning systems argue that we live in a world in which uncertainty, complexity, and ambiguity dominate, and in which small chance events can have a large and unpredictable impact on outcomes.[19] In such circumstances, they claim, even the most carefully thought-out strategic plans are prone to being rendered useless by rapid and unforeseen change. In an unpredictable world, there is a premium on being able to respond quickly to changing circumstances, altering the strategies of the organization accordingly.

A dramatic example of this occurred in 1994 and 1995 when Microsoft CEO Bill Gates shifted the company strategy after the unanticipated emergence of the World Wide Web (see Strategy in Action 1.2). According to critics of formal systems, such a flexible approach to strategy making is not possible within the framework of a traditional strategic planning process, with its implicit assumption that an organization's strategies need to be reviewed only during the annual strategic planning exercise.

Strategy Making by Lower-Level Managers

Another criticism leveled at the rational planning model of strategy is that too much importance is attached to the role of top management.[20] An alternative view now gaining wide acceptance is that individual managers deep within an organization can and often do exert a profound influence over the evolution of strategy.[21] Writing with Robert Burgelman of Stanford University, Andy Grove, the former CEO of Intel, noted that many important strategic decisions at Intel were initiated not by top managers but by the autonomous action of midlevel managers deep within Intel.[22] These strategic decisions included the decision to exit an important market (the DRAM memory chip market) and develop a certain class of microprocessors (RISC-based microprocessors) in direct contrast to the stated strategy of Intel's top managers. We saw in Strategy in Action 1.2 how autonomous action by two young employees drove the evolution of Microsoft's strategy toward the Internet. Another famous example of autonomous action example is given in Strategy in Action 1.3.

Serendipity and Strategy

Business history is replete with examples of accidental events that help to push companies in new and profitable directions. What these examples suggest is that many successful strategies are not the result of well-thought-out plans but of serendipity, that is, stumbling across good things unexpectedly. One such example occurred at 3M during the 1960s. At that time, 3M was producing fluorocarbons for sale as coolant liquid in air-conditioning equipment. One day, a researcher working with fluorocarbons in a 3M lab spilled some of the liquid on her shoes. Later that day when she spilled coffee over her shoes, she watched with interest as the coffee formed into little beads of liquid and then ran off her shoes without leaving a stain. Reflecting on this phenomenon, she realized that a fluorocarbon-based liquid might turn out to be useful for protecting fabrics from liquid stains, and so the idea for Scotch Guard was born. Subsequently, Scotch Guard became one of 3M's most profitable products and took the company into the fabric protection business, an area it had never planned to participate in.[23]

Serendipitous discoveries are often the unintended consequence of scientific endeavor, but this is not always the case. In the mid-1980s, an employee at a small software company, WRQ, wanted to access the company's Hewlett Packard computer from home by turning his personal computer into an HP terminal. No software existed to perform this task, so he wrote a program for his personal use that enabled his personal computer to emulate a Hewlett Packard terminal. Some of his colleagues thought that other companies might want to buy this software, so WRQ tried to sell

Strategy in Action   1.2

A Strategic Shift at Microsoft

The Internet has been around since the 1970s, but prior to the early 1990s, it was a drab place, lacking the color, content, and richness of today's environment. What changed the Internet from a scientific tool to a consumer-driven media environment was the invention of hypertext markup language (HTML) and the related invention of a browser for displaying graphics-rich web pages based on HTML. The combination of HTML and browsers effectively created the World Wide Web (WWW). This was a development that was unforeseen.

A young programmer at the University of Illinois in 1993, Mark Andreesen, had developed the first browser, known as Mosaic. In 1994, he left Illinois and joined a start-up company, Netscape, which produced an improved browser, the Netscape Navigator, along with software that enabled organizations to create web pages and host them on computer servers. These developments led to a dramatic and unexpected growth in the number of people connecting to the Internet. In 1990, the Internet had 1 million users. By early 1995, the number had exceeded 80 million and was growing exponentially.

Prior to the emergence of the Web, Microsoft did have a strategy for exploiting the Internet, but it was one that emphasized set-top boxes, video on demand, interactive TV, and an online service, MSN, modeled after AOL and based on proprietary standards. In early 1994, Gates received emails from two young employees, Jay Allard and Steve Sinofsky, who argued that Microsoft's current strategy was misguided and ignored the rapidly emerging Web. In companies with a more hierarchical culture, such action might have been ignored, but in Microsoft, which operates as a meritocracy in which good ideas trump hierarchical position, it produced a very different response. Gates convened a meeting of senior executives in April 1994, then wrote a memo to senior executives arguing that the Internet represented a sea change in computing and that Microsoft had to respond.

What ultimately emerged was a 180 degree shift in Microsoft's strategy. Interactive TV was placed on the backburner, and MSN was relaunched as a Web service based on HTML. Microsoft committed to developing its own browser technology and within a few months had issued Internet Explorer to compete with Netscape's Navigator (the underlying technology was gained by an acquisition). Microsoft licensed Java, a computer language designed to run programs on the Web, from a major competitor, Sun Microsystems. Internet protocols were built into Windows 95 and Windows NT, and Gates insisted that henceforth Microsoft's applications, such as the ubiquitous Office, embrace the WWW and have the ability to convert documents into an HTML format. The new strategy was given its final stamp on December 7, 1995, Pearl Harbor Day, when Gates gave a speech arguing that the Internet was now pervasive in everything Microsoft was doing. By then, Microsoft had been pursuing the new strategy for a year. In short, Microsoft quickly went from a proprietary standards approach to one that embraced the public standards on the WWW.

Source: Interviews by Charles Hill.

---

it as a product. To their surprise, they found that the demand was strong. Personal computers were starting to make their way onto the desks of many people in business, but these people still wanted to access data stored on mainframe computers and therefore needed software that would transform their personal computers into mainframe terminals. For the next fifteen years, the company generated sales of over $100 million from terminal emulation software.

The point is that serendipitous discoveries and events can open up all sorts of profitable avenues for a company. But some companies have missed out on profitable opportunities because serendipitous discoveries or events were inconsistent with their prior (planned) conception of what their strategy should be. In one of the classic examples of such myopia, a century ago the telegraph company Western Union turned down an opportunity to purchase the rights to an invention made by

Strategy in Action   1.3

The Genesis of Autonomous Action at 3M

In the 1920s, the Minnesota Mining and Manufacturing Company (3M) was a small manufacturer of sandpaper. Its best-selling product, wet-and-dry sandpaper, was introduced in 1921 and was sold primarily to automobile companies, which used it to sand auto bodies between paint coats and was valued for producing a smooth finish. A problem with wet and dry, however, was that the grit did not always stay bound to the sandpaper, and bits of grit that had detached from the paper could ruin an otherwise perfect paint job. To deal with this problem in the early 1920s, the CEO, a young William McKnight, hired 3M's first research scientist, Richard Drew. Drew himself was straight out of college; this was his first job. McKnight charged Drew with developing a stronger adhesive to bind the grit to paper backing better.

While experimenting with adhesives, Drew developed a weak adhesive that had an interesting quality: if placed on the back of a strip of paper and stuck to a surface, the strip of paper could be peeled off the surface it was adhered to without leaving any adhesive residue on that surface. This serendipitous discovery gave Drew an epiphany. He had been visiting auto body paint shops to see how 3M's sandpaper was used and noticed a problem with paint running. His epiphany was to cover the back of a strip of paper with his weak adhesive and use it as "masking tape" to cover parts of the auto body that were not to be painted. An excited Drew took his idea to McKnight and explained how masking tape might create an entirely new business for 3M. McKnight reminded Drew that he had been hired to fix a specific problem and pointedly suggested that he concentrate on doing that and not on dreaming up other business ideas.

Chastised, Drew went back to his lab but could not get the idea out of his mind, so he continued to work on it at night, long after everyone else had gone home. He succeeded in perfecting the masking tape product and then went to visit several auto body shops to show them his innovation. He quickly received several commitments for orders. Drew then went to McKnight again. He told him that he had continued to work on the masking tape idea on his own time, had perfected the product, and got several customers interested in purchasing it. This time it was McKnight's turn to be chastised. Realizing that he had almost killed a good business idea, McKnight reversed his original position and gave Drew the go-ahead to pursue the idea.

Sticky tape subsequently became a huge business for 3M. Moreover, McKnight went on to become a long-serving CEO and then chairman of 3M's board until 1966. Drew became the chief science officer and also served until the 1960s. Together they helped build 3M and shaped its organization culture. One of the main principles of that culture came out of the original incident between Drew and McKnight: top management should "delegate responsibility and encourage men and women to exercise their initiative." According to McKnight, as business grows, "It becomes increasingly necessary to delegate responsibility and to encourage men and women to exercise their initiative. . . . Mistakes will be made. But if a person is essentially right, the mistakes he or she makes are not as serious in the long run as the mistakes management will make if it undertakes to tell those in authority exactly how they must do their jobs. . . . Management that is destructively critical when mistakes are made kills initiative. And it's essential that we have many people with initiative if we are to continue to grow." Based on their own experience, McKnight and Drew established a culture at 3M that encourages autonomous action.

Source: M. Dickson, "Back to the Future," *Financial Times,* 1994, May 30, 1994, p. 7. http://www.3m.com/profile/looking/mcknight.jhtml.

Alexander Graham Bell. The invention was the telephone, a technology that subsequently made the telegraph obsolete.

Intended and Emergent Strategies

Henry Mintzberg's model of strategy development provides a more encompassing view of what strategy actually is. According to this model, illustrated in Figure 1.5, a company's *realized strategy* is the product of whatever planned, **intended strategies,** are actually put into action *and* of any unplanned, or **emergent, strategies.** In

FIGURE 1.5

Emergent and
Deliberate Strategies

Source: Adapted from H.
Mintzberg and A. McGugh,
Administrative Science
Quarterly, Vol. 30. No 2, June
1985.

Mintzberg's view, emergent strategies are the unplanned responses to unforeseen circumstances. They often arise from autonomous action by individual managers deep within the organization or from serendipitous discoveries or events. They are *not* the product of formal top-down planning mechanisms.

Mintzberg maintains that emergent strategies are often successful and may be more appropriate than intended strategies. Richard Pascale has described how this was the case for the entry of Honda Motor Co. into the U.S. motorcycle market.[24] When a number of Honda executives arrived in Los Angeles from Japan in 1959 to establish a U.S. operation, their original aim (intended strategy) was to focus on selling 250-cc and 350-cc machines to confirmed motorcycle enthusiasts rather than 50-cc Honda Cubs, which were a big hit in Japan. Their instinct told them that the Honda 50s were not suitable for the U.S. market, where everything was bigger and more luxurious than in Japan.

However, sales of the 250-cc and 350-cc bikes were sluggish, and the bikes themselves were plagued by mechanical failure. It looked as if Honda's strategy was going to fail. At the same time, the Japanese executives who were using the Honda 50s to run errands around Los Angeles were attracting a lot of attention. One day they got a call from a Sears, Roebuck buyer who wanted to sell the 50-cc bikes to a broad market of Americans who were not necessarily already motorcycle enthusiasts. The Honda executives were hesitant to sell the small bikes for fear of alienating serious bikers, who might then associate Honda with "wimpy" machines. In the end, they were pushed into doing so by the failure of the 250-cc and 350-cc models.

Honda had stumbled onto a previously untouched market segment that was to prove huge: the average American who had never owned a motorbike. Honda had also found an untried channel of distribution: general retailers rather than specialty motorbike stores. By 1964, nearly one out of every two motorcycles sold in the United States was a Honda.

The conventional explanation of Honda's success is that the company redefined the U.S. motorcycle industry with a brilliantly conceived *intended* strategy. The fact was that Honda's intended strategy was a near disaster. The strategy that *emerged* did so not through planning but through unplanned action in response to unforeseen circumstances. Nevertheless, credit should be given to the Japanese management for recognizing the strength of the emergent strategy and for pursuing it with vigor.

The critical point demonstrated by the Honda example is that successful strategies can emerge within an organization without prior planning often in response to unforeseen circumstances. As Mintzberg has noted, strategies can take root virtually wherever people have the capacity to learn and the resources to support that capacity.

In practice, the strategies of most organizations are probably a combination of the intended (planned) and the emergent. The message for management is that it needs to recognize the process of emergence and to intervene when appropriate, killing off bad emergent strategies but nurturing potentially good ones.[25] To make such decisions, managers must be able to judge the worth of emergent strategies. *They must be able to think strategically.* Although emergent strategies arise from within the organization without prior planning—that is, without going through the steps illustrated in Figure 1.3 in a *sequential* fashion—top management still has to evaluate emergent strategies. Such evaluation involves comparing each emergent strategy with the organization's goals, external environmental opportunities and threats, and internal strengths and weaknesses. The objective is to assess whether the emergent strategy fits the organization's needs and capabilities. In addition, Mintzberg stresses that an organization's capability to produce emergent strategies is a function of the kind of corporate culture that the organization's structure and control systems foster. In other words, the different components of the strategic management process are just as important from the perspective of emergent strategies as they are from the perspective of intended strategies.

Strategic Planning in Practice

Despite these criticisms, research suggests that formal planning systems do help managers make better strategic decisions. A study that analyzed the results of twenty-six previously published studies came to the conclusion that on average, strategic planning has a positive impact on company performance.[26] For strategic planning to work, it is important that top-level managers plan not just in the context of the *current* competitive environment but also try to find the strategy that will best allow them to achieve a competitive advantage in the *future* competitive environment. To try to forecast what that future will look like, managers can use scenario planning techniques to plan for different possible futures. They can also involve operating managers in the planning process and seek to shape the future competitive environment by emphasizing strategic intent.

Scenario Planning

One reason that strategic planning may fail over the long run is that strategic managers, in their initial enthusiasm for planning techniques, may forget that the future is inherently unpredictable. Even the best-laid plans can fall apart if unforeseen contingencies occur, and that happens all the time in the real world. The recognition that uncertainty makes it difficult to forecast the future accurately led planners at Royal Dutch Shell to pioneer the *scenario approach* to planning.

In the scenario approach, managers are given a set of possible future scenarios for the development of competition in their industry. Some scenarios are optimistic and some pessimistic, and then teams of managers are asked to develop specific strategies to cope with each different scenario. A set of industry-specific indicators is chosen and used as signposts to track the development of their industry and identify the probability that any particular scenario is coming to pass. The idea is to get managers to understand the dynamic and complex nature of their environment, think through problems in a strategic fashion, and generate a range of strategic options that might be pursued under different circumstances.[27]

The scenario approach to planning has spread rapidly among large companies. According to one survey, over 50 percent of the Fortune 500 companies use some form of scenario planning methods.[28] Strategy in Action 1.4 examines how managers at one of these companies, Duke Energy, use a scenario approach.

Involving Functional Managers

A serious mistake that some companies have made in constructing their strategic planning process has been to treat planning as an exclusively top management responsibility. This *ivory tower* approach can result in strategic plans formulated in a

Strategy in Action

Scenario Planning at Duke Energy

Duke Energy in 2002 was one of the top ten energy generators in the United States, the second largest marketer of natural gas in the country, and the third largest marketer of power. It operates in an industry that has become significantly more complex and unpredictable over the last decade. Substantial deregulation has changed the competitive landscape. The rise of the Internet is changing the way in which power is bought and sold in the United States. New electronic markets for energy contracts have been created, and major producers and customers now routinely buy and sell power on a daily basis on a spot market. These changes are increasing the level of competition and potentially depressing prices for power. The rate of growth in energy consumption is also highly sensitive to underlying economic growth. Errors in predicting future growth rates can result in over- or underinvestment in future production capacity, leaving a generator such as Duke with too much capacity or too little. Moreover, the lead times for bringing new capacity on stream are long, and Duke has to make investment decisions now based on its projection of what demand and supply conditions will look like in five years.

To deal with these uncertainties, Duke Energy has adopted a scenario planning methodology for testing strategy. In 2000, managers were working with three future scenarios for the next five years: Economic Treadmill, which imagines U.S. economic growth slipping to 1 percent per year; Market.com, in which the Internet revolutionizes the buying and selling of electricity and natural gas; and Flawed Competition, which assumes continuing, uneven deregulation of the energy industry and a U.S. economic growth rate of over 3 percent.

Duke has generated twenty to twenty-three signposts for each scenario to indicate that a scenario might be coming to pass. In mid-2000, three of twenty signposts of the Economic Treadmill were flashing, eleven of twenty for Flawed Competition, and three of twenty-three for Market.com. Duke assumed from this analysis that Flawed Competition was the most likely scenario and that the United States would grow at about 3 percent per annum. Based on this scenario, Duke has begun to invest in additional production capacity, building thousands of megawatts of new-generation capacity and hundreds of miles of natural gas pipeline, connecting supply from the Rockies, Gulf Coast, and eastern Canada to markets in the West, Midwest, Florida, and New England. By 2004, Duke Energy will have added more than 26,000 megawatts of new-generation capacity, enough electricity to light 26 million homes. In addition, it is planning to build more than 1,300 miles of natural gas pipeline that can deliver nearly 3.5 billion cubic feet per day.

Managers at Duke have also considered what they would do strategically if the other scenarios emerged. This exercise has led them to take some strategic steps—hedging their bets—in case another scenario should emerge. For example, if the Market.com scenario emerges, it becomes very important to be able to acquire customers over the Internet. Recognizing this, Duke created an e-commerce unit to explore the business possibilities. If the Economic Treadmill scenario starts to emerge, Duke is prepared to scale back on its capacity expansion plans midstream so that it does not have too much capacity, a situation that would depress prices and profits.

Source: B. Wysocki, "Power Grid: Soft Landing or Hard," *Wall Street Journal,* July 7, 2000, p. A1 (http://www.duke-energy.com/decorp/content/AboutUs/deip9.asp?RBU=1).

vacuum by top managers who have little understanding or appreciation of current operating realities. Consequently, top managers may formulate strategies that do more harm than good. For example, when demographic data indicated that houses and families were shrinking, planners at GE's appliance group concluded that smaller appliances were the wave of the future. Because they had little contact with homebuilders and retailers, they did not realize that kitchens and bathrooms were the two rooms that were *not* shrinking. Nor did they appreciate that working women wanted big refrigerators to cut down on trips to the supermarket. GE ended up wasting a lot of time designing small appliances with limited demand.

The ivory tower concept of planning can also lead to tensions between corporate-, business-, and functional-level managers. The experience of GE's appliance group is again illuminating. Many of the corporate managers in the planning group were recruited from consulting firms or top-flight business schools. Many of the functional managers took this pattern of recruitment to mean that corporate managers did not think they were smart enough to think through strategic problems for themselves. They felt shut out of the decision-making process, which they believed to be unfairly constituted. Out of this perceived lack of procedural justice grew an us-versus-them mindset that quickly escalated into hostility. As a result, even when the planners were right, operating managers would not listen to them. For example, the planners correctly recognized the importance of the globalization of the appliance market and the emerging Japanese threat. However, operating managers, who then saw Sears Roebuck as the competition, paid them little heed.

Correcting the ivory tower approach to planning requires recognizing that successful strategic planning encompasses managers at *all* levels of the corporation. Much of the best planning can and should be done by functional managers who are closest to the facts. The role of corporate-level planners should be that of *facilitators* who help functional managers do the planning by setting the broad strategic goals of the organization and providing the resources required to identify the strategies that might be required to attain those goals.

It is not enough to involve lower-level managers in the strategic planning process, however; they also need to perceive that the decision-making process is fair, a concept that Chan Kim and Renee Mauborgne refer to as **procedural justice.**[29] If people perceive the decision-making process to be unjust, they are less likely to be committed to any resulting decisions and to cooperate voluntarily in activities designed to implement those decisions. Consequently, the strategy chosen might fail for lack of support among those who must implement it at the operating level.

Strategic Intent

The formal strategic planning model has been characterized as the *fit model* of strategy making. This is because it attempts to achieve a fit between the internal resources and capabilities of an organization and external opportunities and threats in the industry environment. Gary Hamel and C. K. Prahalad have criticized the fit model because it can lead to a mindset in which management focuses too much on the degree of fit between the *existing* resources of a company and *current* environmental opportunities, and not enough on building *new* resources and capabilities to create and exploit *future* opportunities.[30] Strategies formulated with only the present in mind, argue Prahalad and Hamel, tend to be more concerned with today's problems than with tomorrow's opportunities. As a result, companies that rely exclusively on the fit approach to strategy formulation are unlikely to be able to build and maintain a competitive advantage. This is particularly true in a dynamic competitive environment, where new competitors are continually arising and new ways of doing business are constantly being invented.

As Prahalad and Hamel note, again and again, companies using the fit approach have been surprised by the ascent of competitors that initially seemed to lack the resources and capabilities needed to make them a real threat. This happened to Xerox, which ignored the rise of Canon and Ricoh in the photocopier market until they had become serious global competitors; to General Motors, which initially overlooked the threat posed by Toyota and Honda in the 1970s; and to Caterpillar, which ignored the danger Komatsu posed to its heavy earthmoving business until it was almost too late to respond.

The secret of the success of companies like Toyota, Canon, and Komatsu, according to Prahalad and Hamel, is that they all had bold ambitions that outstripped their existing resources and capabilities. All wanted to achieve global leadership, and they set out to build the resources and capabilities that would enable them to attain this goal. Consequently, top management created an obsession with winning at all levels of the organization that they sustained over a ten- to twenty-year quest for global leadership. It is this obsession that Prahalad and Hamel refer to as **strategic intent.** They stress that strategic intent is more than simply unfettered ambition. It encompasses an active management process, which includes "focusing the organization's attention on the essence of winning; motivating people by communicating the value of the target; leaving room for individual and team contributions; sustaining enthusiasm by providing new operational definitions as circumstances change; and using intent consistently to guide resource allocations."[31]

Thus, underlying the concept of strategic intent is the notion that strategic planning should be based on setting ambitious goals that stretch a company and then finding ways to build the resources and capabilities necessary to attain those goals. As Prahalad and Hamel note, in practice the two approaches to strategy formulation are not mutually exclusive. All the components of the strategic planning process that we discussed earlier (see Figure 1.3) are important.

In addition, say Prahalad and Hamel, the strategic management process should begin with challenging goals, such as attaining global leadership, that stretch the organization. And throughout the process, the emphasis should be on finding ways (strategies) to develop the resources and capabilities necessary to achieve these goals rather than on exploiting *existing* strengths to take advantage of *existing* opportunities. The difference between strategic fit and strategic intent, therefore, may just be one of emphasis. Strategic intent is more internally focused and is concerned with building new resources and capabilities. Strategic fit focuses more on matching existing resources and capabilities to the external environment.

Strategic Leadership and Decision Making

Even the best-designed strategic planning systems will fail to produce the desired results if managers do not use the information at their disposal effectively. Consequently, it is important that strategic managers learn to make better use of the information they have and understand the reasons that sometimes they make poor decisions. One important way in which managers can make better use of their knowledge and information is to understand how to become an effective or strategic leader and to learn how to understand and manage their emotions during the course of decision making.[32]

Strategic Leadership and Emotional Intelligence

One of the key strategic roles of both general and functional managers is to use all their knowledge, energy, and enthusiasm to provide strategic leadership for their subordinates and develop a high-performing organization. **Strategic leadership** refers to a manager's ability to articulate a strategic vision for the company, or a part of the company, and to motivate others to buy into that vision. Several authors have identified a few key characteristics of good strategic leaders that do lead to high performance: (1) vision, eloquence, and consistency, (2) commitment, (3) being well informed, (4) willingness to delegate and empower, (5) astute use of power, and (6) emotional intelligence.[33]

Vision, Eloquence, and Consistency.   One of the key tasks of leadership is to give an organization a sense of direction. Strong leaders seem to have a vision of where the organization should go, are eloquent enough to communicate this vision to others within the organization in terms that energize people, and consistently articulate their vision until it becomes part of the culture of the organization.[34] John F. Kennedy, Martin Luther King, Jr., and Margaret Thatcher have all been held up as examples of visionary leaders. Think of the impact of Kennedy's phrase, "Ask not what your country can do for you, ask what you can do for your country," and of King's "I have a dream" speech. Kennedy and Thatcher were also able to use their political office to push for governmental actions that were consistent with their vision, and King was able to pressure the government from outside to make changes in society. Strong business leaders include rivals Microsoft's Bill Gates and Sun Microsystems's Scott McNeally, Avon's Andrea Jung, and Jack Welch and Herb Kelleher, the former CEOs of General Electric and Southwest Airlines, respectively.

Commitment. Strong leaders demonstrate their commitment to their vision by actions and words, and they often lead by example. Consider Nucor's former CEO, Ken Iverson. Nucor is a very efficient steelmaker with perhaps the lowest cost structure in the steel industry. It has turned in thirty years of profitable performance in an industry where most other companies have lost money because of its relentless focus on cost minimization. In his tenure as CEO, Iverson set the example: he answered his own phone, employed only one secretary, drove an old car, flew coach class, and was proud of the fact that his base salary was the lowest in the Fortune 500 (Iverson made most of his money from performance-based pay bonuses). This commitment was a powerful signal to employees that Iverson was serious about doing everything possible to minimize costs. It earned him the respect of Nucor employees, which made them more willing to work hard. Although Iverson has retired, his legacy lives on in the cost-conscious organization culture that has been built at Nucor, and like all other great leaders, his impact will go beyond his tenure as a leader.

Being Well Informed. Effective strategic leaders develop a network of formal and informal sources who keep them well informed about what is going on within their company. Herb Kelleher at Southwest Airlines, for example, was able to find out a lot about the health of his company by dropping in unannounced on aircraft maintenance facilities and helping workers there to perform their tasks; McDonald's Ray Kroc and Wal-Mart's Sam Walton routinely dropped in unannounced to visit their restaurants and stores. Using informal and unconventional ways to gather information is wise because formal channels can be captured by special interests within the organization or by gatekeepers, managers who may misrepresent the true state of affairs within the company to the leader, such as may have happened at Enron (see Chapter 11). People like Kelleher who constantly interact with employees at all levels are better able to build informal information networks than leaders who closet themselves and never interact with lower-level employees.

Willingness to Delegate and Empower. High-performance leaders are skilled at delegation. They recognize that unless they learn how to delegate effectively, they can quickly become overloaded with responsibilities. They also recognize that empowering subordinates to make decisions is a good motivation tool. Delegating also makes sense when it results in decisions being made by those who must implement them. At the same time, astute leaders recognize that they need to maintain control over certain key decisions. Thus, although they will delegate many *important* decisions to lower-level employees, they will not delegate those that they judge to be of *critical importance* to the future success of the organization under their leadership.

The Astute Use of Power. In a now classic article on leadership, Edward Wrapp noted that effective leaders tend to be very astute in their use of power.[35] By this he meant three things. First, strategic leaders must play the power game with skill and attempt to build consensus for their ideas rather than use their authority to force ideas through; they act as members or democratic leaders of a coalition rather than as dictators. Second, good leaders often hesitate to commit themselves publicly to detailed strategic plans or precise objectives, since in all probability the emergence of unexpected contingencies will require adaptation. Thus, a successful leader might commit the organization to a particular vision, such as minimizing costs or boosting product quality, without stating precisely how or when this will be achieved. Good leaders often have precise private objectives and strategies that they would like to see the organization pursue. However, they recognize the futility of public commitment given the likelihood of change and the difficulties of implementation.

Third, Wrapp claimed that effective leaders possess the ability to push through programs in a piecemeal fashion. They recognize that on occasion, it may be futile to try to push total packages or strategic programs through an organization, since significant objections to at least part of such programs are likely to arise. Instead, the successful leader may be willing to take less than total acceptance in order to achieve modest progress toward a goal. The successful leader tries to push through ideas one piece at a time, so that they appear incidental to other ideas, though in fact they are part of a larger program or hidden agenda that moves the organization in the direction of the manager's objectives.

Jeffery Pfeffer has articulated a similar vision of the politically astute manager who gets things done in organizations by the intelligent use of power.[36] In Pfeffer's view, power comes from control over resources: budgets, capital, positions, information, and knowledge that is important to the organization. Politically astute managers use these resources to acquire another critical resource: critically placed allies who can help a manager attain preferred strategic objectives. Pfeffer stresses that one does not need to be a CEO to assemble power in an organization. Sometimes quite junior functional managers can build a surprisingly effective power base and use it to influence organizational outcomes.

Emotional Intelligence. Emotional intelligence is a term that Daniel Goldman coined to describe a bundle of psychological attributes that many strong and effective leaders exhibit:[37]

- Self-awareness—the ability to understand one's own moods, emotions, and drives, as well as their effect on others

- Self-regulation—the ability to control or redirect disruptive impulses or moods, that is, to think before acting

- Motivation—a passion for work that goes beyond money or status and a propensity to pursue goals with energy and persistence

- Empathy—understanding the feelings and viewpoints of subordinates, and taking those into account when making decisions

- Social skills—friendliness with a purpose

According to Goldman, leaders who possess these attributes—who exhibit a high degree of emotional intelligence—tend to be more effective than those who lack these attributes. Their self-awareness and self-regulation help to elicit the trust and confidence of subordinates. In Goldman's view, people respect leaders who, because they are self-aware, recognize their own limitations and because they are self-regulating consider decisions carefully. Goldman also argues that self-aware and self-regulating individuals tend to be more self-confident and therefore better able to cope with ambiguity and more open to change. A strong motivation exhibited in a passion for work can also be infectious, helping to persuade others to join together in pursuit of a common goal or organizational mission. Finally, strong empathy and social skills can help leaders earn the loyalty of subordinates. Empathetic and socially adept individuals tend to be skilled at managing disputes between managers, better able to find common ground and purpose among diverse constituencies, and better able to move people in a desired direction than leaders who lack these skills. In short, Goldman's arguments are that the psychological makeup of a leader matters.

Cognitive Biases and Strategic Decision Making

The rationality of human decision makers is bounded by our own cognitive capabilities.[38] We are not supercomputers, and it is difficult for us absorb and process large amounts of information effectively. As a result, when making decisions, we tend to fall back on certain rules of thumb, or heuristics, that help us to make sense out of a complex and uncertain world. However, sometimes they lead to severe and systematic errors in the decision-making process.[39] Systematic errors are those that appear time and time again. They seem to arise from a series of **cognitive biases** in the way that human decision makers process information and reach decisions. Because of cognitive biases, many managers end up making poor strategic decisions.

A number of biases have been verified repeatedly in laboratory settings, so we can be reasonably sure that they exist and that we are all prone to them.[40] The **prior hypothesis bias** refers to the fact that decision makers who have strong prior beliefs about the relationship between two variables tend to make decisions on the basis of these beliefs, even when presented with evidence that their beliefs are wrong. Moreover, they tend to seek and use information that is consistent with their prior beliefs, while ignoring information that contradicts these beliefs. To put this bias in a strategic context, it suggests that a CEO who has a strong prior belief that a certain strategy makes sense might continue to pursue that strategy, despite evidence that it is inappropriate or failing.

Another well-known cognitive bias, **escalating commitment,** occurs when decision makers, having already committed significant resources to a project, commit even more resources if they receive feedback that the project is failing.[41] This may be an irrational response; a more logical response would be to abandon the project and move on (that is, to cut your losses and run), rather than escalate commitment. Feelings of personal responsibility for a project apparently induce decision makers to stick with a project despite evidence that it is failing.

A third bias, **reasoning by analogy,** involves the use of simple analogies to make sense out of complex problems. The problem with this heuristic is that the analogy may not be valid. A fourth bias, **representativeness,** is rooted in the tendency to generalize from a small sample or even a single vivid anecdote. This bias violates the statistical law of large numbers, which says that it is inappropriate to generalize from a small sample, let alone from a single case. In many respects, the dot-com boom of the late 1990s was based on reasoning by analogy and representativeness. Prospective entrepreneurs saw some of the early dot-com companies such Amazon and Yahoo achieve rapid success, at least judged by some metrics. Reasoning by analogy from a very small sample, they assumed that any dot-com could achieve similar success. Many investors reached similar conclusions. The result was a massive wave of start-ups that jumped into the Internet space in an attempt to capitalize on the perceived opportunities. That the vast majority of these companies subsequently went bankrupt is testament to the fact that the analogy was wrong and the success of the small sample of early entrants was no guarantee that all dot-coms would succeed.

The final cognitive bias is referred to as the **illusion of control:** the tendency to overestimate one's ability to control events. General or top managers seem to be particularly prone to this bias: having risen to the top of an organization, they tend to be overconfident about their ability to succeed. According to Richard Roll, such overconfidence leads to what he has termed the **hubris hypothesis** of takeovers.[42] Roll argues that top managers are typically overconfident about their abilities to create value by acquiring another company. Hence, they end up making poor acquisition decisions, often paying far too much for the companies they acquire. Subsequently, servicing the debt taken on to finance such an acquisition makes it all but impossible to make money from the acquisition.

Groupthink and Strategic Decisions

Because most strategic decisions are made by groups, the group context within which decisions are made is clearly an important variable in determining whether cognitive biases will operate to adversely affect the strategic decision-making processes.

The psychologist Irvin Janis has argued that many groups are characterized by a process known as groupthink and as a result make poor strategic decisions.[43] **Groupthink** occurs when a group of decision makers embarks on a course of action without questioning underlying assumptions. Typically, a group coalesces around a person or policy. It ignores or filters out information that can be used to question the policy and develops after-the-fact rationalizations for its decision. Commitment to mission or goals becomes based on an emotional rather than an objective assessment of the "correct" course of action. The consequences can be poor decisions.

This phenomenon may explain, at least in part, why companies often make poor strategic decisions in spite of sophisticated strategic management. Janis traced many historical fiascoes to defective policymaking by government leaders who received social support from their in-group of advisers. For example, he suggested that President John F. Kennedy's inner circle suffered from groupthink when the members of this group supported the decision to launch the Bay of Pigs invasion of Cuba in 1961, even though available information showed that it would be an unsuccessful venture and would damage U.S. relations with other countries. Janis has observed that groupthink-dominated groups are characterized by strong pressures toward uniformity, which make their members avoid raising controversial issues, questioning weak arguments, or calling a halt to soft-headed thinking.

Techniques for Improving Decision Making

The existence of cognitive biases and groupthink raises the issue of how to bring critical information to bear on the decision mechanism so that a company's strategic decisions are realistic and based on thorough evaluation. Two techniques known to enhance strategic thinking and counteract groupthink and cognitive biases are devil's advocacy and dialectic inquiry (see Figure 1.6).[44] **Devil's advocacy** requires the generation of both a plan and a critical analysis of the plan. One member of the decision-making group acts as the devil's advocate, bringing out all the reasons that might make the proposal unacceptable. In this way, decision makers can become aware of the possible perils of recommended courses of action.

FIGURE 1.6

Processes for Improving Decision Making

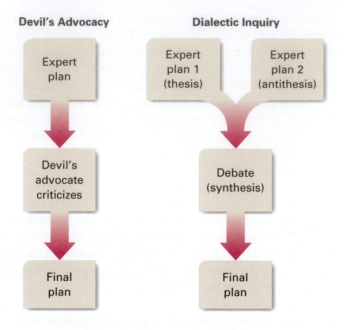

Dialectic Inquiry

Devil's Advocacy

Dialectic inquiry is more complex, for it requires the generation of a plan (a thesis) and a counter-plan (an antithesis) that reflect *plausible but conflicting* courses of action.[45] Strategic managers listen to a debate between advocates of the plan and counter-plan and then make a judgment of which plan will lead to the higher performance. The purpose of the debate is to reveal problems with definitions, recommended courses of action, and assumptions of both plans. As a result of this exercise, strategic managers are able to form a new and more encompassing conceptualization of the problem, which becomes the final plan (a synthesis). Dialectic inquiry can promote thinking strategically.

Summary of Chapter

1. A strategy is an action that a company takes to attain one or more of its goals.

2. The profitability of a company can be measured by the return that it makes on the capital invested in the enterprise. Profitability is determined by the strategies the company adopts.

3. A company has a competitive advantage over its rivals when it is more profitable than the average for all firms in its industry. It has a sustained competitive advantage when it is able to maintain an above-average profitability over a number of years.

4. General managers are responsible for the overall performance of the organization or for one of its major self-contained divisions. Their overriding strategic concern is for the health of the total organization under their direction.

5. Functional managers are responsible for a particular business function or operation. Although they lack general management responsibilities, they play a very important strategic role.

6. Formal strategic planning models stress that an organization's strategy is the outcome of a rational planning process.

7. The major components of the strategic management process are defining the mission and major goals of the organization; analyzing the external and internal environments of the organization; choosing a business model and strategies that align or fit an organization's strengths and weaknesses with external environmental opportunities and threats; and adopting organizational structures and control systems to implement the organization's chosen strategy.

8. A revision of the concept suggests that strategy can emerge from deep within an organization in the

absence of formal plans as lower-level managers respond to unpredicted situations.

9. Strategic planning often fails because executives do not plan for uncertainty and because ivory tower planners lose touch with operating realities.

10. The fit approach to strategic planning has been criticized for focusing too much on the degree of fit between existing resources and current opportunities, and not enough on building new resources and capabilities to create and exploit future opportunities.

11. Strategic intent refers to an obsession with achieving an objective that stretches the company and requires it to build new resources and capabilities.

12. Good leaders of the strategy-making process have a number of key attributes: vision, eloquence, and consistency; commitment; being well informed; a willingness to delegate and empower; political astuteness; and emotional intelligence.

13. In spite of systematic planning, companies may adopt poor strategies if their decision-making processes are vulnerable to groupthink and if individual cognitive biases are allowed to intrude into the decision-making process.

14. Devil's advocacy and dialectic inquiry are techniques for enhancing the effectiveness of strategic decision making.

Discussion Questions

1. What do we mean by *strategy*?
2. What do you think are the sources of sustained superior profitability?
3. What are the strengths of formal strategic planning? What are its weaknesses?
4. **Discuss the accuracy of this statement:** Formal strategic planning systems are irrelevant for firms competing in high-technology industries where the pace of change is so rapid that plans are routinely made obsolete by unforeseen events.
5. Evaluate President George W. Bush against the leadership characteristics discussed in the text. On the basis of this comparison, do you think that President Bush is a good strategic leader?

Practicing Strategic Management

SMALL-GROUP EXERCISE: DESIGNING A PLANNING SYSTEM

Break up into groups of three to five people each. Appoint one group member as a spokesperson for the group, who will communicate your findings to the class when called on to do so by the instructor.

You are a group of senior managers working for a fast-growing computer software company. Your product allows users to play interactive role-playing games over the Internet. In the past three years, your company has gone from being a start-up enterprise with 10 employees and no revenues to a company with 250 employees and revenues of $60 million. It has been growing so rapidly that you have not had time to create a strategic plan, but now your board of directors is telling you that they want to see a plan, and they want it to drive decision making and resource allocation at the company. They want you to design a planning process that will have the following attributes:

1. It will be democratic, involving as many key employees as possible in the process.
2. It will help to build a sense of shared vision within the company about how to continue to grow rapidly.

3. It will lead to the generation of three to five key strategies for the company.
4. It will drive the formulation of detailed action plans, and these plans will be subsequently linked to the company's annual operating budget.

Design a planning process to present to your board of directors. Think carefully about who should be included in this process. Be sure to outline the strengths and weaknesses of the approach you choose, and be prepared to justify why your approach might be superior to alternative approaches.

ARTICLE FILE 1

At the end of every chapter in this book is an article file task. The task requires you to search newspapers or magazines in the library for an example of a real company that satisfies the task question or issue.

Your first article file task is to find an example of a company that has recently changed its strategy. Identify whether this change was the outcome of a formal planning process or whether it was an emergent response to unforeseen events occurring in the company's environment.

STRATEGIC MANAGEMENT PROJECT: MODULE 1

To give you practical insight into the strategic management process, we provide a series of strategic modules; one is at the end of every chapter in this book. Each module asks you to collect and analyze information relating to the material discussed in that chapter. By completing these strategic modules, you will gain a clearer idea of the overall strategic management process.

The first step in this project is to pick a company to study. We recommend that you focus on the same company throughout the book. Remember also that we will be asking you for information about the corporate and international strategy of your company, as well as its structure. We strongly recommend that you pick a company for which such information is likely to be available.

There are two approaches that can be used to select a company to study, and your instructor will tell you which one to follow. The first approach is to pick a well-known company that has a lot of information written about it. For example, large publicly held companies such as IBM, Microsoft, and Southwest Airlines are routinely covered in the business and financial press. By going to the library at your university, you should be able to track down a great deal of information on such companies. Many libraries now have comprehensive web-based electronic data search facilities such as *ABI/Inform, The Wall Street Journal Index,* the *F&S Index,* and the *Nexis-Lexis* databases. These enable you to identify any article that has been written in the business press on the company of your choice within the past few years. A number of nonelectronic data sources are also available and useful. For example, *F&S Predicasts* publishes an annual list of articles relating to major companies that appeared in the national and international business press. *S&P Industry Surveys* is also a great source for basic industry data, and *Value Line Ratings and Reports* contain good summaries of a firm's financial position and future prospects. Collect full financial information on the company that you pick. This can be accessed from web-based electronic databases such as the Edgar database, which archives all forms that publicly quoted companies have to file with the Securities and Exchange Commission (SEC); for example, 10-K filings can be accessed from the SEC's Edgar database. Most SEC forms for public companies can now be accessed from Internet-based financial sites, such as Yahoo's finance site (**http://finance.yahoo.com/**).

A second approach is to pick a smaller company in your city or town to study. Although small companies are not routinely covered in the national business press, they may be covered in the local press. More important, this approach can work well if the management of the company will agree to talk to you at length about the strategy and structure of the company. If you happen to know somebody in such a company or if you have worked there at some point, this approach can be very worthwhile. However, we *do not* recommend this approach unless you can get a *substantial* amount of guaranteed access to the company of your choice. If in doubt, ask your instructor before making a decision. The key issue is to make sure that you have access to enough interesting information to complete a detailed and comprehensive analysis.

Your assignment for Module 1 is to choose a company to study and to obtain enough information about it to carry out the following instructions and answer the questions:

1. Give a short account of the history of the company, and trace the evolution of its strategy. Try to determine whether the strategic evolution of your company is the product of intended strategies, emergent strategies, or some combination of the two.

2. Identify the mission and major goals of the company.

3. Do a preliminary analysis of the internal strengths and weaknesses of the company and the opportunities and threats that it faces in its environment. On the basis of this analysis, identify the strategies that you think the company should pursue. (You will need to perform a much more detailed analysis later in the book.)

4. Who is the CEO of the company? Evaluate the CEO's leadership capabilities.

EXPLORING THE WEB
Visiting 3M

Go to the web site of 3M (**http://www.3m.com**) and visit the section that describes its history (**http://www.3m.com/profile/looking/index.jhtml**). Using the information contained here, map out the evolution of strategy at 3M from its establishment to the present day. To what degree do you think that this evolution was the result of detailed long-term strategic planning, and to what degree was it the result of unplanned actions taken in response to unpredictable circumstances?

General Task: Search the Web for a company site with sufficient information to map out the evolution of that company's strategy over a significant period of time. What drove this evolution? To what degree was it the result of detailed long-term strategic planning, and to what degree the result of unplanned actions taken in response to unpredictable circumstances?

Closing Case

The Evolution of Strategy at Yahoo

In 1993, Jerry Yang and David Filo were two graduate engineering students at Stanford University. Instead of writing their dissertations (which they probably should have been), the two were spending a lot of time surfing the Web and building lists of their favorite sites. On a whim, they decided to post their list on the Web, which they dubbed "Jerry's Guide to the World Wide Web." Almost by accident, they had created one of the first web directories and in the process had solved a pressing need: how to find things on the Web. In 1994, they changed the name of the directory to Yahoo (**http://www.yahoo.com**), which is supposed to stand for "Yet Another Hierarchical Officious Oracle," although Filo and Yang insist they selected the name because they considered themselves yahoos.

By late 1994, Yahoo was drawing over 100,000 people a day. The directory had outgrown the limited capacity of the Stanford site, and Yahoo was borrowing server space from nearby Netscape. Yang and Filo had decided to put their graduate studies on hold while they turned their attention to building Yahoo into a business. One of their first employees, Srinija Srinivasan, or "ontological yahoo" as she became known within the company, refined and developed the classification scheme that has become the hallmark of Yahoo's web directory. Yang and Filo's business model was to derive revenues from renting advertising space on the pages of the fast-growing directory.

To develop the business, they needed capital to fund investments in servers, software development, and classification personnel. A solution came in the form of an investment from Sequoia Capital, a Silicon Valley venture capital firm. As part of the investment package, Sequoia required Yang and Filo to hire an experienced CEO. The man chosen for the job was Andrew Koogle, a forty-five-year-old engineer with fifteen years of experience in the management of high-technology firms, including a stint as president of InterMec, a Seattle-based manufacturer of bar code scanning equipment.

By mid-1996, Koogle was heading a publicly traded company that listed 200,000 web sites under 20,000 different categories and was being used by 800,000 people daily. This was just the beginning. In conjunction with Yang, Filo, and another "gray-haired" hire, chief operating officer Jeffrey Mallett, Koogle crafted a vision of Yahoo as a global media company whose principal asset would be a major Internet gateway, or portal, that would enable any-

one to connect with anything or anybody. Koogle's ambition was to transform Yahoo's simple directory service into a conduit for bringing together buyers and sellers, thereby facilitating commercial transactions over the Web (e-commerce). In this vision, Yahoo would continue to generate revenues from the sale of advertising space on its directory pages, and it would also garner significant revenues from e-commerce transactions by taking a small slice of each transaction executed over its service. The service, Yahoo! Store (**http://store.yahoo.com**), enables businesses to quickly create, publish, and manage secure online stores to market and sell goods and services. After launching their store, merchants are included in searches on Yahoo! Shopping (**http://shopping.yahoo.com**), Yahoo's Internet shopping service.

To make this vision a reality, Yahoo had to become one of the most useful and well-known locations on the Web—in short, it had to become a mega-brand. A directory alone would not suffice, no matter how useful. In order to increase traffic, Yahoo began to add features that increased its appeal to users. One was to supplement the directory with compelling content. Another was to allow registered users to customize Yahoo pages to match their needs. For example, registered Yahoo users can customize a page in Yahoo's financial area so that they can track the value of their personal stock portfolio. The page provides links to message boards, where individual investors can discuss a company's prospects. Other links connect investors to valuable content pertaining to the companies in their stock portfolio, including news reports and commentary, research reports, detailed financial data, and each company's web site.

To build brand awareness, Yahoo spent heavily on advertising, using radio and television ads targeted at mainstream America. To expand the reach of the service, Yahoo embarked on a strategy of opening up Yahoo services around the world. It also began to work with content providers and merchants to build their online presence and, by extension, to increase the value of Yahoo's site to users who could access the content and merchants through Yahoo. Yahoo increased its value to advertisers by enabling them to target their advertising message to certain demographics better. For example, the online broker E*Trade advertises heavily on Yahoo's financial pages. Such targeted advertising increases the conversion rate or yield associated with advertisements.

By many measures, the results of this strategy were spectacular. In 2000, the company generated revenues of almost $900 million. By September 2001, Yahoo had more than 210 million unique users worldwide, up from 166 million in September 2000 and just 50 million in 1998. Traffic increased to a record 1.25 billion page views per day on average during September 2001, up from 167 million page views per day in December 1998. According to Nielsen//NetRatings, worldwide consumers spent an average of 147 minutes on the Yahoo network, up from 119 minutes in the previous quarter. Some 80 million active registered users logged onto one or more personalized Yahoo services during September 2001, up from 55 million in September 2000.

However, in the first nine months of 2001, sales slumped by 34 percent and the company registered a loss of $84 million versus a profit of $169 million in the previous period. The revenue and profit declines reflected slumping advertising revenues, which accounted for close to 80 percent of Yahoo's revenues in 2000. The problem, in the wake of a slowdown in business activity in the United States, had resulted in declining advertising revenues across the board. Moreover, many of the best advertisers on Yahoo had been other dot-com companies, and a large number of these had gone bankrupt in 2001.

In the wake of slumping revenues, CEO Koogle resigned and was replaced by Terry Semel, a former Warner Brothers executive. Semel's strategic goal for Yahoo was twofold: to reduce the company's dependence on advertising revenues and to increase the quality of advertising revenues by targeting well-established companies as opposed to dot-com enterprises. Semel's strategy

for boosting nonadvertising revenues was to introduce a range of subscription-based value-added or premium services, such as online music that would be broadcast by the Net to a subscriber's computer or digital device. In addition, Semel wanted the company to push more aggressively into the co-marketing business, helping established companies to sell their merchandise on the Web, and taking a cut of their revenues.

Discussion Questions

1. To what extent was the evolution of strategy at Yahoo planned? To what extent was it an emergent response to unforeseen events?

2. Could Yahoo have done a better job of anticipating the slowdown in advertising revenue that occurred in 2000–2001 and positioning itself for that slowdown? How? What might it have done differently from a strategic planning perspective?

3. Does Yahoo have a source of potential long-term competitive advantage? Where does this come from?

4. What does Koogle's resignation in May 2001 tell you about the role of a CEO in a public company?

Sources: S. G. Steinberg, "Seek and Ye Shall Find (Maybe)," *Wired* (May 1996). L. Himelstein, H. Green, and R. Siklos, "Yahoo! The Company, the Strategy, the Stock," *Business Week,* September 7, 1998, p. 66. S. Moran, "For Yahoo, GeoCities May Only Be the Start," *Internet World,* March 15, 1999. Yahoo 1998 and 2000 Annual Reports and www.yahoo.com. K. Swisher, "Time Runs Short for Terry Semel to Save Yahoo," *Wall Street Journal,* October 15, 2001, p. B1. N. Wingfield, "Yahoo Restructuring to Slash 400 Jobs," *Wall Street Journal,* November 16, 2001, p. B10.

External Analysis: The Identification of Industry Opportunities and Threats

2

Opening Case

Boom and Bust in Telecommunications

In the mid-1990s, the telecommunications services industry was beset by three significant changes. The first of these was the arrival of the World Wide Web as a prime-time phenomenon. As the volume of Web traffic grew at an exponential pace, so too did demand for the capacity to transmit the digital data on which the Web was based. In 1996, in an effort to foster greater competition among telecommunications service providers, the U.S. government deregulated the U.S. telecommunication service industry. Local and long-distance phone companies and cable TV companies were allowed to enter each other's markets. In addition, deregulation made it much easier for new entrants to get into the telecommunications service business. Similar moves to deregulate telecommunications services took place in other countries. Finally, wireless services made inroads in many developed nations, with market penetration rates for wireless phones reaching as high as 70 percent in Finland and 30 percent in the United States, where

35

demand was growing rapidly. By decade's end, the wireless industry was beginning to embrace the Web, with wireless companies planning to offer their customers Internet access through wireless phones.

Many analysts believed that demand for telecommunications services would expand exponentially for years to come. In the near future, some argued, vast amounts of data will flow around the world through fiber-optic cable as ever more companies, individuals, and organizations connect to the Internet by high-speed wire line and wireless networks, and as they used the Internet for a vast array of high-bandwidth services, including videoconferencing and the transmitting of music files. The possibilities seemed limitless. A host of companies were established to compete with incumbent telecommunications service providers and to exploit the expected bandwidth boom. They included PSINet, 360 Networks, Covad Communications, Global Crossing, Level 3 Communications, ICG Communications, RCN Corporation, XO Communications, and WinStar.

Driven by a desire to share in the coming boom for telecommunications services, these new entrants raised billions of dollars in equity and some $650 billion in debt from the capital markets. They used the funds to build out fiber-optic networks within cities, between cities, and between countries. They invested in optical technology that increased by a hundred-fold the amount of data that could be sent down a single strand of glass fiber. And they built out wireless networks. Telecom service providers in the United States alone boosted their capital spending by 25 percent each year from 1996 to 2000, when they invested $124 billion. Worldwide, a staggering $1.2 trillion was spent on telecommunications equipment in 2000.

Producers of telecommunications equipment such as switches, routers, fiber-optic cables, and optical gear were beneficiaries of this boom. Lucent, Cisco, Nortel Networks, JDS Uniphase, Corning, and other companies saw their sales and profits surge. Cisco, founded only in the mid-1980s, made an after-tax profit of $2.7 billion in 2000 on sales of $19 billion. To grab even more sales, these equipment companies started making loans to the telecom service start-ups to help them buy the equipment. It seemed like a sure thing, a perfect bet on a glittering future. But the glittering future didn't arrive as expected.

By 2000, it became clear that although the volume of data traffic was doubling every year, the capacity to transmit data along fiber-optic networks was increasing much faster than that as dozens of service providers rushed to grab a share of the projected boom in demand. The result was huge excess capacity and plummeting prices for data transmission services using fiber-optic networks. By 2001, it was estimated that there was ten times more fiber-optic capacity than needed. Suddenly the telecommunications service providers were in trouble, particularly the new ones that had borrowed heavily to finance their growth. They could not generate enough revenues to cover the interest payments on their debt. As 2000 turned into 2001, many started to go bankrupt. PSINet, 360 Networks, Covad Communications, ICG Communications, and WinStar are among the many that filed for bankruptcy protection. By early 2002, others such as Level 3 and Global Crossing were teetering on the brink. In the space of a year, shares in Level 3 fell from $132 a share to under $3. Global Crossing saw its shares fall from a high of $64 a share in 1999 to $0.50 by the end of 2001. And in 2002, it too went bankrupt.

As telecommunications service providers started to go bankrupt, demand for telecommunications equipment imploded. Lucent saw its sales drop by 30 percent and was forced to take some $15 billion in charges to write off the value of loans given to service providers that no longer existed and to close down excess capacity. Lucent's stock price fell from a high of $70 a share in May 2000 to under $2 a share by mid-2002. Cisco, long the darling of the industry, lost over $1 billion on falling sales, and its share price slumped from a high of $80 in May 2000 to around $16 by early 2002. JDS Uniphase took a record $50 billion charge against earnings in 2001 to write down the value of companies it had acquired during the boom.

In retrospect, what happened can be analyzed quite easily. Although demand for telecommunications capacity did increase markedly, demand projections got way ahead of reality. Moreover, each service company raised capital and made investments on the assumption that they would be the ones to capture a significant proportion of those inflated demand projections, while failing to appreciate that given the number of other competitors making similar investments, there would not be enough demand to go around. The result of this myopic behavior was excess capacity in the services business. This triggered a price war and ruined any hope that many new service providers had of becoming profitable. As the service providers started to lose money, they slashed their capital investment budgets, which caused the slump in the equipment market. What had been an extraordinary profitable sector turned into an economic disaster zone; an unprecedented boom and been replaced by an unprecedented bust.

Sources: J. Shinal, "Dead Dot.Coms Can Still Cause Havoc," *Business Week,* March 12, 2001, p. 50; S. Rosenbush and P. Elstrom, "Eight Lessons from the Telecom Mess," *Business Week,* August 13, 2001, pp. 60–67; S. Rosenbush and B. Einhorn, "Those Wires Sure Are Cold," *Business Week,* September 17, 2001, pp. 104–105; "Drowning in Glass," *Economist,* March 24, 2001, p. 76.

Overview

The process of thinking strategically requires that managers understand how the structure and competitive dynamics of their industry affect the performance and profitability of their companies. Armed with an appreciation of the forces in their industry that give rise to opportunities and threats, managers should be able to make better strategic decisions. One interpretation of what happened in the telecommunication markets during the 1990s is that the opportunities were exaggerated and the threats were ignored because managers viewed demand conditions through rose-colored lenses. Managers systematically misread the realities of the situation because their decision making was colored and distorted by the kinds of cognitive biases and errors discussed in Chapter 1 (and no scenario planning was taking place). The result was excessive investment in telecommunications equipment, excess network capacity, plunging prices for telecommunications services, the failure of significant service revenues to materialize, and a wave of disastrous bankruptcies that helped plunge the economy into recession.

This chapter examines the conceptual models that can prevent mistakes in strategic thinking. It discusses several models that provide managers with a rational or objective means to analyze the dynamics of the industries in which their companies compete and help to identify the opportunities and threats that are inherent in them. **Opportunities** arise when a company can take advantage of conditions in its environment to formulate and implement strategies that enable it to become more profitable. Surging demand for telecommunications services, when coupled with deregulation, was seen as an enormous opportunity for new companies to enter the telecom service industry and compete with existing companies for industry revenues. **Threats** arise when conditions in the external environment endanger the integrity and profitability of the company's business. The irony in the telecommunications industry was that the rapid entry of new companies to take advantage of growing demand and profits led to the excess industry capacity that created the threat that led to the price war and falling industry profits.

This chapter begins with an analysis of the industry environment. First, it examines concepts and tools for analyzing the competitive structure of an industry and identifying industry opportunities and threats. Second, it analyzes the competitive implications that arise when groups of companies *within* an industry pursue similar and different kinds of competitive strategies. Third, it explores the way an industry evolves over time and the accompanying changes in competitive conditions is examined. Fourth, it looks at the way in which forces in the macroenvironment affect industry structure and creates and shapes opportunities and threats. Finally, it discusses the way in which the national and global environment shapes the competitive forces at work both within and across industries is discussed.

By the end of the chapter, you will understand that to succeed, a company must either fit its strategy to the external environment in which it operates or must be able to reshape the environment to its advantage through its chosen strategy.

Defining an Industry

An **industry** can be defined as a group of companies offering products or services that are close substitutes for each other—that is, products or services that satisfy the same basic customer needs. A company's closest **competitors,** its rivals, are those that serve the same basic customer needs. For example, carbonated drinks, fruit punches, and bottled water can be viewed as close substitutes for each other because they serve the same basic customer needs for refreshing and cold nonalcoholic beverages. Thus, we can talk about the soft drink industry, whose major players are Coca-Cola, PepsiCo, and Cadbury Schweppes. Similarly, desktop computers and notebook computers satisfy the same basic need that customers have for computer hardware on which to run personal productivity software, browse the Internet, send email, play games, and store, display, and manipulate digital images. Thus, we can talk about the personal computer industry, whose major players are Dell, Compaq, Hewlett Packard, IBM, Gateway, and Apple Computer.

The starting point of external analysis is to identify the industry that a company competes in. To do this, managers must begin by looking at the basic customer needs their company is serving—that is, they must take a customer-oriented view of their business as opposed to a product-oriented view (see Chapter 1). An industry is the *supply side* of a market, and companies in the industry are the suppliers. Customers are the *demand side* of a market and are the buyers of the industry's products. *The basic customer needs that are served by a market define an industry's boundary.* It is very important for managers to realize this, for if they define industry boundaries incorrectly, they may be caught flat-footed by the rise of competitors that serve the same basic customer needs with different product offerings. For example, for a long time, Coca-Cola saw itself as being in the soda industry—meaning carbonated soft drinks—whereas in fact it was in the soft drink industry, which includes noncarbonated soft drinks. In the mid-1990s, Coca-Cola was caught by surprise by the rise of customer demand for bottled water and fruit drinks, which began to cut into the demand for sodas. Coca-Cola moved quickly to respond to these threats, introducing its own brand of water, Dasani, and acquiring orange juice maker Minute Maid. By defining its industry boundaries too narrowly, Coke almost missed the rapid rise of the noncarbonated soft drinks segment of the soft drinks market.

Industry and Sector

An important distinction that needs to be made is between an *industry* and the **sector,** that is, the group of closely related industries of which it is a part. For example, the telecommunications sector encompasses two industries: the telecommunications equipment industry and the telecommunications services industry. Similarly, as illustrated in Figure 2.1, the computer sector comprises several related industries: the computer component industries (e.g., the disk drive industry, the semiconductor industry, and the modem industry), the computer hardware industries (e.g., the personal computer industry, the handheld computer industry, and the mainframe computer industry), and the computer software industry. Industries within a sector may be involved with each other in many different ways. For example, companies in the telecommunications equipment industry are the *suppliers* of the telecommunications services industry, and companies in the computer component industries *supply* inputs to companies in the computer hardware industries. Companies in the computer software industry provide important *complements* to computer hardware: the software programs that customers purchase to run on their hardware. And companies in the personal, hand-held, and mainframe industries are in indirect *competition* with each other because all provide products that are *substitutes* for each other.

Industry and Market Segments

It is also important to recognize the difference between an *industry* and the *market segments* within that industry. **Market segments** are distinct groups of customers within a market that can be differentiated from each other on the basis of their distinct attributes and specific demands. In the soft drink industry, for example, although all customers demand refreshing and cold nonalcoholic beverages, there is a group within this market who in addition demand (need) sodas that do not contain caffeine. Coca-Cola has recognized the existence of this caffeine-free market segment and sought to satisfy the needs of customers within it by producing and

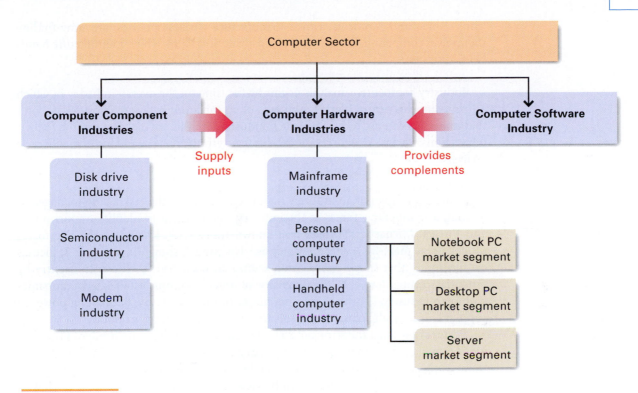

FIGURE 2.1

The Computer Sector: Industries and Segments

marketing noncaffeinated colas. Similarly, in the personal computer industry, there are different segments where customers desire desktop machines, lightweight portable machines, and servers that sit at the center of a network of personal computers (see Figure 2.1). Personal computer makers recognize the existence of these different segments by producing a range of product offerings that appeal to customers in different segments. Customers in all of these different segments, however, share a common need for PCs on which to run personal software applications.

Changing Industry Boundaries   Industry boundaries may change over time as customer needs evolve or new technologies emerge that enable companies in hitherto unrelated industries to satisfy established customer needs in new ways. We have noted that during the 1990s, as consumers of soft drinks began to develop a taste for bottled water and noncarbonated fruit-based drinks, Coca-Cola found itself in direct competition with the manufacturers of bottled water and fruit-based soft drinks: all were in the same industry.

For an example of how technological change can alter industry boundaries, consider the convergence that is currently taking place between the computer and telecommunications industries. Historically, the telecommunications equipment industry has been considered a distinct entity from the computer hardware industry. However, as telecommunications equipment has moved from traditional analogue technology to digital technology, so telecommunications equipment has increasingly come to resemble computers. The result is that the boundaries between these different industries is blurring. A digital wireless phone, for example, is nothing more than a small hand-held computer with a wireless connection, and small hand-held computers often now come with wireless capabilities, transforming them into phones.

Thus, Nokia and Motorola, which manufacture wireless phones, are now finding themselves competing directly with Handspring and Palm, which manufacture handheld computers.

Industry competitive analysis begins by focusing on the overall industry in which a firm competes before market segments or sector-level issues are considered. Tools that managers can use to perform such industry analysis are discussed in the following sections: Porter's five forces model, strategic group analysis, and industry life cycle analysis.

Porter's Five Forces Model

Once the boundaries of an industry have been identified, the task facing managers is to analyze competitive forces in the industry environment to identify opportunities and threats. Michael E. Porter's well-known framework, known as the five forces model, helps managers with this analysis.[1] His model, shown in Figure 2.2, focuses on five forces that shape competition within an industry: (1) the risk of entry by potential competitors, (2) the intensity of rivalry among established companies within an industry, (3) the bargaining power of buyers, (4) the bargaining power of suppliers, and (5) the closeness of substitutes to an industry's products.

Porter argues that the stronger each of these forces is, the more limited is the ability of established companies to raise prices and earn greater profits. Within Porter's framework, a *strong* competitive force can be regarded as a *threat* because it depresses profits. A *weak* competitive force can be viewed as an *opportunity* because it allows a company to earn greater profits. The strength of the five forces may change through time as industry conditions change, as illustrated by the opening telecommunications case. The task facing managers is to recognize how changes in the five forces give rise to new opportunities and threats and to formulate appropriate strategic responses. In addition, it is possible for a company, *through its choice of strategy,* to alter the strength of one or more of the five forces to its advantage. This is discussed in the following chapters.

Risk of Entry by Potential Competitors

Potential competitors are companies that are not currently competing in an industry but have the capability to do so if they choose. For example, electric utilities are potential competitors to telecommunications companies in the markets for phone

FIGURE 2.2

Porter's Five Forces Model

Adapted and reprinted by permission of *Harvard Business Review.* From "How Competitive Forces Shape Strategy," by Michael E. Porter, *Harvard Business Review,* March/April 1979. by the President and Fellows of Harvard College. All rights reserved.

service and Internet access. In order to be able to deliver electricity to residential and commercial property, many electric utilities have been granted rights of way by state and local governments for their electric cable. There is nothing to stop electric utilities from laying fiber-optic along these rights of way and offering high-bandwidth communications services to residential and commercial customers. In fact, a number of utilities have started to do this. For example, Tacoma City Light in Washington State used its rights of way to run fiber-optic lines to several commercial buildings in the city of Tacoma and has taken business away from the dominant telecommunications provider in the region, Verizon. Tacoma City Light is also laying coaxial cable to homes in its service region and offering cable TV service in direct competition to the local cable provider, AT&T Broadband.[2]

Established companies already operating in an industry often attempt to discourage potential competitors from entering the industry because the more companies that enter, the more difficult it becomes for established companies to protect their share of the market and generate profits. AT&T Broadband's response to Tacoma City Light was to threaten intense competition on price and service for cable TV. A high risk of entry by potential competitors represents a threat to the profitability of established companies. But if the risk of new entry is low, established companies can take advantage of this opportunity to raise prices and earn greater returns.

The risk of entry by potential competitors is in part a function of the height of **barriers to entry,** that is, factors that make it costly for companies to enter an industry. The greater the costs are that potential competitors must bear to enter an industry, the greater are the barriers to entry and the *weaker* is this competitive force. High entry barriers may keep potential competitors out of an industry even when industry profits are high. Economist Joe Bain, who did the classic work on barriers to entry, identified three main sources of barriers to new entry: brand loyalty, absolute cost advantages, and economies of scale.[3] Two more that are important in many situations can be added to Bain's list of entry barriers: customer switching costs and government regulation.

Brand Loyalty.   **Brand loyalty** is buyers' preference for the products of any established company. A company can create brand loyalty through continuous advertising of its brand-name products and company name, patent protection of products, product innovation achieved through company research and development programs, an emphasis on high product quality, and good after-sales service. Significant brand loyalty makes it difficult for new entrants to take market share away from established companies. Thus, it reduces the threat of entry by potential competitors since they may see the task of breaking down well-established customer preferences as too costly.

Absolute Cost Advantages.   Sometimes established companies have an **absolute cost advantage** relative to potential entrants, meaning that entrants cannot expect to match the established companies' lower cost structure. Absolute cost advantages arise from three main sources (1) superior production operations and processes due to experience, patents, or secret processes; (2) control of particular inputs required for production, such as labor, materials, equipment, or management skills; and (3) access to cheaper funds because existing companies represent lower risks than new entrants. If established companies have an absolute cost advantage, the threat of entry as a competitive force is weaker.

Economies of Scale. **Economies of scale** are the relative cost advantages associated with large volumes of production that lower a company's cost structure. Sources of scale economies include (1) cost reductions gained through mass producing a standardized output, (2) discounts on bulk purchases of raw material inputs and component parts, (3) the advantages gained by spreading fixed production costs over a large production volume, and (4) the cost savings associated with spreading marketing and advertising costs over a large as compared to a small volume of output. If these cost advantages are significant, a new company that enters the industry and produces on a small scale suffers a significant cost disadvantage relative to established companies. If the new company decides to enter on a large scale to obtain these economies of scale, it has to bear the high risks associated with a large investment. A further risk of large-scale entry is that the increased supply of products will depress prices and result in vigorous retaliation by established companies. For these reasons, the threat of entry is reduced when established companies have economies of scale.

Customer Switching Costs. **Switching costs** arise when it costs a customer time, energy, and money to switch from the products offered by one established company to the products offered by a new entrant. When switching costs are high, customers can be *locked in* to the product offerings of established companies, even if new entrants offer better products.[4] A familiar example of switching costs concerns the costs associated with switching from one computer operating system to another. If a person currently uses Microsoft's Windows operating system and has a library of related software applications (e.g., word processing software, spreadsheet, games) and document files, it is expensive for that person to switch to another computer operating system. To effect the change, this person would have to buy a new set of software applications and convert all existing document files to run with the new system. Faced with such an expense of money and time, most people are unwilling to make the switch *unless* the competing operating system offers a *substantial* leap forward in performance. Thus, the higher the switching costs are, the higher is the barrier to entry for a company attempting to promote a new computer operating system.

Government Regulation. Historically, government regulation has constituted a major entry barrier into many industries. For example, until the mid-1990s, U.S. government regulation prohibited providers of long-distance telephone service from competing for local telephone service and vice versa. Other potential providers of telephone service, including cable television service companies such as AOL Time Warner and Viacom (which could in theory use their cables to carry telephone traffic as well as TV signals), were prohibited from entering the market altogether. These regulatory barriers to entry significantly reduced the level of competition in both the local and long-distance telephone markets, enabling telephone companies to earn higher profits than might otherwise have been the case. As noted in the *Opening Case,* all this changed in 1996 when the government deregulated the industry significantly. In the months that followed this announcement, local, long-distance, and cable TV companies all announced their intention to enter each other's markets, and a host of new players entered the market. The five forces model predicts that falling entry barrier due to government deregulation would result in significant new entry, an increase in the intensity of industry competition, and lower industry profit rates.

In summary, if established companies have built brand loyalty for their products, have an absolute cost advantage with respect to potential competitors, have significant scale economies, are the beneficiaries of high switching costs, or enjoy regulatory protection, the risk of entry by potential competitors is greatly diminished; it is a weak competitive force. Consequently, established companies can charge higher prices, and industry profits are higher. Indeed, empirical evidence suggests that the height of barriers to entry is one of the most important determinants of profit rates in an industry.[5] Clearly, it is in the interest of established companies to pursue strategies consistent with raising entry barriers to secure these profits. A detailed example of entry barriers is given in Strategy in Action 2.1, which looks at the Japanese brewing industry.

Even when entry barriers are very high, new firms may still enter an industry if they perceive that the benefits outweigh the substantial costs of entry. This is what appears to have occurred in the telecommunications industry following deregulation in 1996. The new entrants had to undertake huge capital expenditure to build out their networks and match the scale advantages of established companies. However, they were able to raise the capital to do so from investors who shared management's euphoric vision of future demand in the industry. In time, this euphoric vision proved to be false, and many of the new entrants went bankrupt, but not before their investments had created excess capacity in the industry and sparked intense price competition that depressed the returns for all players, new entrants and established companies alike.

Rivalry Among Established Companies

The second of Porter's five competitive forces is the intensity of rivalry among established companies within an industry. **Rivalry** refers to the competitive struggle between companies in an industry to gain market share from each other. The competitive struggle can be fought using price, product design, advertising and promotion spending, direct selling efforts, and after-sales service and support. More intense rivalry implies lower prices or more spending on non-price-competitive weapons, or both. Because intense rivalry lowers prices and raises costs, it squeezes profits out of an industry. Thus, intense rivalry among established companies constitutes a strong threat to profitability. Alternatively, if rivalry is less intense, companies may have the opportunity to raise prices or reduce spending on non-price-competitive weapons, which leads to a higher level of industry profits. The intensity of rivalry among established companies within an industry is largely a function of three factors: (1) industry competitive structure, (2) demand conditions, and (3) the height of exit barriers in the industry.

Industry Competitive Structure. The *competitive structure* of an industry refers to the number and size distribution of companies in it, something that strategic managers determine at the beginning of an industry analysis. Industry structures vary, and different structures have different implications for the intensity of rivalry. A **fragmented industry** consists of a large number of small or medium-sized companies, none of which is in a position to determine industry price. A **consolidated industry** is dominated by a small number of large companies (an **oligopoly**), or in extreme cases, by just one company (a **monopoly**) and companies often are in a position to determine industry prices. Examples of fragmented industries are agriculture, dry cleaning, video rental, health clubs, real estate brokerage, and sun tanning parlors. Consolidated industries include the aerospace, automobile, pharmaceutical, and stockbrokerage industries.

Many fragmented industries are characterized by low entry barriers and commodity-type products that are hard to differentiate. The combination of these traits tends to result in boom-and-bust cycles as industry profits rise and fall. Low entry

Strategy in Action

2.1

Entry Barriers into the Japanese Brewing Industry

In 1565, an English visitor to Japan noted that the Japanese "feed moderately but drink largely." This is still the case today: the Japanese have one of the highest levels of beer consumption per capita in the world. In 1998, for example, 50 liters of beer were sold for every man, woman, and child in the country, making Japan's level of beer consumption per capita similar to that of big beer drinking nations such as Australia, Britain, and Germany.

The Japanese market is dominated by Kirin, Asahi, Sapporo, and Suntory, which have a combined market share of around 97 percent. Collectively, these companies enjoy one of the highest profit rates of any industry in Japan. Despite this high level of profitability, there has been very little entry into this industry over the last three decades. Suntory is the only successful new entrant in the past thirty years, and its market share stands at no more than 6 percent.

Normally, a lack of new entry into a profitable industry indicates the presence of high entry barriers, and that is certainly the case here. Like other large brewing companies all over the world, Japan's big four spend heavily on advertising and promotions. Moreover, Japan's big brewers have been aggressive in the area of product development. During the 1990s, Asahi gained significant share from its competitors by pushing its "Super Dry" beer. The resulting brand identification certainly helped to limit the potential for new entry. But some argue that there is more to it than this, and in fact Japan's brewing companies have also been the beneficiaries of significant regulatory barriers to entry. Brewers in Japan must have a license from the Ministry of Finance (MOF), and until 1994 the MOF would not issue a license to any brewer producing less than 2 million liters annually. This restriction represented an imposing hurdle to any potential new entrant: because a new company could not enter at a small scale of output, it would have to invest in very expensive brewing facilities. Why this regulation? Bureaucratic convenience. It is easier to collect tax from 4 companies than from 400.

Another significant barrier to entry has been Japan's distribution system. Roughly half the beer consumed in Japan is distributed and sold in bars and restaurants whose owners are loyal to the big brewers and are often reluctant to distribute competing brands that might alienate their main supplier. Small liquor stores are another main distribution outlet for beer, and they too were unwilling to sell the products of new entrants for fear that the big brewers might "punish" them by denying them access to adequate supplies.

It appears that some of the barriers to entering Japan's brewing industry are declining, however. As part of an economic liberalization plan, in 1994 the MOF reduced the production threshold required to gain a license from 2 million liters to 60,000 liters, low enough to allow for the entry of microbreweries using the same technology that is now found in many brew pubs in the United States and Britain. Moreover, regulatory changes also allowed for the establishment of large new discount stores in Japan. (Until 1994, small retailers could effectively block the opening of a large discount store in their region by appealing to the local authorities.) Unlike traditional small retailers, large discount retailers are motivated more by price and profit than by loyalties to an established supplier and are eager to sell the beer of foreign companies and microbreweries, in addition to that of Japan's big four.

Given the decline in barriers to entry associated with regulation and distribution channels, many observers thought that Japan's big four brewers would have to face up to new competitors after 1994. So far, however, this has not been the case. Japan's big four brewing companies continue to dominate the domestic market, a testament perhaps to the significance of advertising, promotions, and product differentiation as barriers to entry. However, Japan's brewers are facing indirect competition from an alternative alcoholic beverage, wine, which is starting to become fashionable among younger people.

Sources: "Only Here for the Biru," *Economist,* May 14, 1994, pp. 69–71; T. Craig, "The Japanese Beer Industry," in C. W. L. Hill and G. R. Jones, *Strategic Management: An Integrated Approach* (Boston: Houghton Mifflin, 1995); "Japan's Beer Wars," *Economist,* February 28, 1998, p. 68; A. Harney, "Japan's Favorite Beer Could Face Losing Its Sparkle," *Financial Times,* March 24, 1999, p. 27.

barriers imply that whenever demand is strong and profits are high, new entrants will flood the market, hoping to profit from the boom. The explosion in the number of video stores, health clubs, and sun tanning parlors during the 1980s and 1990s exemplifies this situation.

Often the flood of new entrants into a booming fragmented industry creates excess capacity, so companies start to cut prices in order to use their spare capacity. The difficulty companies face when trying to differentiate their products from those of competitors can exacerbate this tendency. The result is a price war, which depresses industry profits, forces some companies out of business, and deters potential new entrants. For example, after a decade of expansion and booming profits, many health clubs are now finding that they have to offer large discounts in order to hold onto their membership. In general, the more commodity-like an industry's product is, the more vicious will be the price war. This bust part of the cycle continues until overall industry capacity is brought into line with demand (through bankruptcies), at which point prices may stabilize again.

A fragmented industry structure, then, constitutes a threat rather than an opportunity. Most booms are relatively short-lived because of the ease of new entry and will be followed by price wars and bankruptcies. Because it is often difficult to differentiate products in these industries, the best strategy for a company is to try to minimize its costs so it will be profitable in a boom and survive any subsequent bust. Alternatively, companies might try to adopt strategies that change the underlying structure of fragmented industries and lead to a consolidated industry structure in which the level of industry profitability is increased. Exactly how companies can do this is something we shall consider in later chapters.

In consolidated industries, companies are interdependent, because one company's competitive actions or moves (with regard to price, quality, and so on) directly affect the market share of its rivals, and thus their profitability. When one company makes a move, this generally "forces" a response from its rivals, and the consequence of such competitive interdependence can be a dangerous competitive spiral. Rivalry increases as companies attempt to undercut each other's prices or offer customers more value in their products, pushing industry profits down in the process. The fare wars that have periodically created havoc in the airline industry provide a good illustration of this process.

When demand for airline travel fell during the recession of 2001, and particularly after the terrorist attacks of September 11, airlines started cutting prices to try to maintain their passenger loads in the face of declining demand. When one airline serving a particular route cut its prices, its competitors would follow. The result was a downward price spiral. In the fourth quarter of 2001, prices fell by 15 percent as airlines tried to induce people to fly. Despite this, passenger traffic fell by 19 percent, and revenue at major airlines fell by over 30 percent. U.S. Airlines alone lost some $4.2 billion in the last three months of 2001 and $6.4 billion for the entire year.[6] Clearly, high rivalry between companies in consolidated industries and the possibility of a price war constitute a major threat.

Companies in consolidated industries sometimes seek to reduce this threat by following the prices set by the dominant company in the industry.[7] However, companies must be careful, for explicit face-to-face price-fixing agreements are illegal. (Tacit, indirect agreements, arrived at without direct or intentional communication, are legal.) Instead, companies set prices by watching, interpreting, anticipating, and responding to each other's behavior (something discussed in detail in Chapter 5 when the competitive dynamics of game theory is examined). However, tacit price leadership agreements often break down under adverse economic conditions, as has occurred in the breakfast cereal industry, profiled in Strategy in Action 2.2.

Industry Demand. The level of industry demand is a second determinant of the intensity of rivalry among established companies. Growing demand from new customers or additional purchases by existing customers tend to moderate competition by providing greater scope for companies to compete for customers. Growing demand tends to reduce rivalry because all companies can sell more without taking market share away from other companies. High industry profits are often the result. Conversely, declining demand results in more rivalry as companies fight to maintain market share and revenues (as in the breakfast cereal industry). Demand declines when customers are leaving the marketplace or each customer is buying less. Now a company can grow only by taking market share away from other companies. Thus, declining demand constitutes a major threat, for it increases the extent of rivalry between established companies.

Exit Barriers. Exit barriers are economic, strategic, and emotional factors that prevent companies from leaving an industry. If exit barriers are high, companies become locked into an unprofitable industry where overall demand is static or declining. The result is often excess productive capacity, which leads to even more intense rivalry and price competition as companies cut prices in the attempt to obtain the customer orders needed to use their idle capacity and cover their costs.[8] Common exit barriers include the following:

■ Investments in assets such as specific machines, equipment, and operating facilities that are of little or no value in alternative uses or cannot be sold off. If the company wishes to leave the industry, it has to write off the book value of these assets.

■ High fixed costs of exit, such as the severance pay, health benefits, and pensions that have to be paid to workers who are being made redundant when a company ceases to operate.

■ Emotional attachments to an industry, as when a company's owners or employees are unwilling to exit from an industry for sentimental reasons or because of pride.

■ Economic dependence on the industry because a company relies on a single industry for its revenue and profit.

■ The need to maintain an expensive collection of assets at or above some minimum level in order to participate effectively in the industry.

As an example of the effect of exit barriers in practice, consider the express mail and parcel delivery industry. The key players in this industry such as Federal Express and UPS rely on the delivery business entirely for their revenues and profits. They have to be able to guarantee their customers that they will deliver packages to all major localities in the United States, and much of their investment is specific to this purpose. To meet this guarantee, they need a nationwide network of air routes and ground routes, an asset that is required in order to participate in the industry. If excess capacity develops in this industry, as it does from time to time, Federal Express cannot incrementally reduce or minimize its excess capacity by deciding not to fly to and deliver packages in, say, Miami because that proportion of its network is underused. If it did that, it would no longer be able to guarantee to its customers that it would be able to deliver packages to all major locations in the United States, and its customers would switch to some other carrier. Thus, the need to maintain a nation-

Strategy in Action   2.2

Price Wars in the Breakfast Cereal Industry

For decades, the breakfast cereal industry was one of the most profitable in the United States. The industry has a consolidated structure dominated by Kellogg, General Mills, and Kraft Foods with its Post brand. Strong brand loyalty, coupled with control over the allocation of supermarket shelf space, helped to limit the potential for new entry. Meanwhile, steady demand growth of around 3 percent per annum kept industry revenues expanding. For years, Kellogg, which accounted for over 40 percent of the market share, acted as the price leader in the industry. Every year Kellogg increased cereal prices, its rivals followed, and industry profits remained high.

This favorable industry structure started to change in the early 1990s when growth in demand slowed and then stagnated as a latte and bagel or muffin replaced cereal as the morning fare for many American adults. Then came the rise of powerful discounters such as Wal-Mart, which entered the grocery industry in the early 1990s and began to promote aggressively its own brand of cereal, priced significantly below the brand-name cereals. As the decade progressed, other grocery chains such as Kroger's started to follow suit, and brand loyalty in the industry began to decline as customers realized that a $2.50 bag of wheat flakes from Wal-Mart tasted about the same as a $3.50 box of Cornflakes from Kellogg. As sales of cheaper store brand cereals began to take off, supermarkets, no longer as dependent on brand names to bring traffic into their stores, began to demand lower prices from the branded cereal manufacturers.

For several years, the manufacturers of brand cereals tried to hold out against these adverse trends, but in the mid-1990s the dam broke. In 1996, Kraft (then owned by Philip Morris) aggressively cut prices by 20 percent for its Post brand in an attempt to gain market share. Kellogg soon followed with a 19 percent price cut on two-thirds of its brands, and General Mills quickly did the same. The decades of tacit price collusion were officially over.

If the breakfast cereal companies were hoping that the price cuts would stimulate demand, they were wrong. Instead, demand remained flat while revenues and margins followed prices down and Kellogg's operating margins dropped from 18 percent in 1995 to 10.2 percent in 1996, a trend experienced by the other brand cereal manufacturers.

By 2000, conditions had only worsened. Private label sales continued to make inroads, gaining over 10 percent of the market. Moreover, sales of breakfast cereals started to contract at 1 percent per annum. To cap it off, an aggressive General Mills continued to launch expensive price and promotion campaigns in an attempt to take share away from the market leader. Kellogg saw its market share slip to just over 30 percent in 2001, *behind* the 31 percent now held by General Mills. For the first time since 1906, Kellogg no longer led the market. Moreover, profits at all three major producers remained weak in the face of continued price discounting.

In mid-2001, General Mills finally blinked and raised prices a modest 2 percent in response to its own rising costs. Competitors followed, signaling perhaps that after a decade of costly price warfare, pricing discipline might once more emerge in the industry, only this time General Mills, not Kellogg, would be the price leader.

Sources: G. Morgenson, "Denial in Battle Creek," *Forbes,* October 7, 1996, p. 44; J. Muller, "Thinking out of the Cereal Box," *Business Week,* January 15, 2001, p. 54; A. Merrill, "General Mills Increases Prices," *Star Tribune,* June 5, 2001, p. 1D.

wide network is an exit barrier that can result in persistent excess capacity in the air express industry during periods of weak demand. Finally, both UPS and Federal Express managers and employees are emotionally tied to this industry because they both were first movers, in the ground and air segments of the industry, respectively, and because their employees are also major owners of their companies' stock and they are dependent financially on the fortunes of the delivery business.

The Bargaining Power of Buyers

The third of Porter's five competitive forces is the bargaining power of buyers. An industry's buyers may be the individual customers who ultimately consume its products (its end users) or the companies that distribute an industry's products to end users, such as retailers and wholesalers. For example, while soap powder made by Procter & Gamble and Unilever is consumed by end users, the principal buyers of soap powder are supermarket chains and discount stores, which resell the product to end users. The **bargaining power of buyers** refers to the ability of buyers to bargain down prices charged by companies in the industry or to raise the costs of companies in the industry by demanding better product quality and service. By lowering prices and raising costs, powerful buyers can squeeze profits out of an industry. Thus, powerful buyers should be viewed as a threat. Alternatively, when buyers are in a weak bargaining position, companies in an industry can raise prices, and perhaps reduce their costs by lowering product quality and service, and increase the level of industry profits. According to Porter, buyers are most powerful in the following circumstances:

- When the industry that is supplying a particular product or service is composed of many small companies and the buyers are large and few in number. These circumstances allow the buyers to dominate supplying companies.

- When the buyers purchase in large quantities. In such circumstances, buyers can use their purchasing power as leverage to bargain for price reductions.

- When the supply industry depends on the buyers for a large percentage of its total orders.

- When switching costs are low so that buyers can play off the supplying companies against each other to force down prices.

- When it is economically feasible for buyers to purchase an input from several companies at once so that buyers can play off one company in the industry against another.

- When buyers can threaten to enter the industry and produce the product themselves and thus supply their own needs, also a tactic for forcing down industry prices.

The auto component supply industry, whose buyers are large automobile manufacturers such as GM, Ford, and DaimlerChrysler, is a good example of an industry in which buyers have strong bargaining power and thus a strong competitive threat. Why? The suppliers of auto component are numerous and typically small in scale; their buyers, the auto manufacturers, are large in size and few in number. DaimlerChrysler, for example, does business with nearly 2,000 different component suppliers in the United States and normally contracts with a number of different companies to supply the same part. Additionally, to keep component prices down, both Ford and GM have used the threat of manufacturing a component themselves rather than buying it from auto component suppliers. The automakers have used their powerful position to play off suppliers against each other, forcing down the price they have to pay for component parts and demanding better quality. If a component supplier objects, the automaker uses the threat of switching to another supplier as a bargaining tool.

Another issue is that the relative power of buyers and suppliers tends to change in response to changing industry conditions. For example, due to changes now taking place in the pharmaceutical and health care industries, major buyers of pharmaceuticals (hospitals and health maintenance organizations) are gaining power over the suppliers of pharmaceuticals and have been able to demand lower prices.

The Bargaining Power of Suppliers

The fourth of Porter's five competitive forces is the bargaining power of suppliers—the organizations that provide inputs into the industry, such as materials, services, and labor (which may be individuals, organizations such as labor unions, or companies that supply contract labor). The **bargaining power of suppliers** refers to the ability of suppliers to raise input prices, or to raise the costs of the industry in other ways—for example, by providing poor-quality inputs or poor service. Powerful suppliers squeeze profits out of an industry by raising the costs of companies in the industry. Thus, powerful suppliers are a threat. Alternatively, if suppliers are weak, companies in the industry have the opportunity to force down input prices and demand higher-quality inputs (e.g., more productive labor). As with buyers, the ability of suppliers to make demands on a company depends on their power relative to that of the company. According to Porter, suppliers are most powerful in these situations:

- The product that suppliers sell has few substitutes and is vital to the companies in an industry.

- The profitability of suppliers is not significantly affected by the purchases of companies in a particular industry, in other words, when the industry is not an important customer to the suppliers.

- Companies in an industry would experience significant switching costs if they moved to the product of a different supplier because a particular supplier's products are unique or different. In such cases, the company depends on a particular supplier and cannot play suppliers off against each other to reduce price.

- Suppliers can threaten to enter their customers' industry and use their inputs to produce products that would compete directly with those of companies already in the industry.

- Companies in the industry cannot threaten to enter their suppliers' industry and make their own inputs as a tactic for lowering the price of inputs.

An example of an industry in which companies are dependent on a powerful supplier is the personal computer industry. They are heavily dependent on Intel, the world's largest supplier of microprocessors for PCs. The industry standard for personal computers runs on Intel's X86 microprocessor chips, such as its Pentium series. Intel's competitors, such as Advanced Micro Devices (AMD), must develop and supply chips that are compatible with Intel's standard. Although AMD has developed competing chips, Pentium still supplies about 85 percent of the chips used in PCs primarily because only Intel has the manufacturing capacity required to serve a large share of the market. It is beyond the financial resources of Intel's competitors, such as AMD, to match the scale and efficiency of Intel's manufacturing systems. This means that while PC manufacturers can buy some microprocessors from Intel's rivals, most notably AMD, they still have to turn to Intel for the bulk of their supply. Because Intel is in a powerful bargaining position, it can charge higher prices for its microprocessors than would be the case if its competitors were more numerous and stronger (i.e., if the microprocessor industry were fragmented).

Substitute Products

The final force in Porter's model is the threat of **substitute products**: the products of different businesses or industries that can satisfy similar customer needs. For example, companies in the coffee industry compete indirectly with those in the tea and soft drink industries because all three serve customer needs for nonalcoholic drinks. The existence of close substitutes is a strong competitive threat because this limits the price that companies in one industry can charge for their product, and thus industry profitability. If the price of coffee rises too much relative to that of tea or soft drinks, coffee drinkers may switch to those substitutes.

If an industry's products have few close substitutes, so that substitutes are a weak competitive force, then, other things being equal, companies in the industry have the opportunity to raise prices and earn additional profits. Thus, there is no close substitute for microprocessors, which gives companies like Intel and AMD the ability to charge higher prices than would be the case if there were a substitute for microprocessors.

A Sixth Force: Complementors

Andrew Grove, the former CEO of Intel, has argued that Porter's five forces model ignores a sixth force: the power, vigor, and competence of complementors.[9] **Complementors** are companies that sell products that add value to (complement) the products of companies in an industry because when used *together,* the products better satisfy customer demands. For example, the complementors to the personal computer industry are the companies that make software applications to run on those machines. The greater the supply of high-quality software applications to run on personal computers, the greater is the value of personal computers to customers, the greater the demand for PCs, and the greater the profitability of the personal computer industry.

Grove's argument has a strong foundation in economic theory, which has long argued that *both* substitutes and complements influence demand in an industry.[10] Moreover, recent research has emphasized the importance of complementary products in determining demand and profitability in many high-technology industries, such as the computer industry in which Grove made his mark.[11] The issue, therefore, is that when complements are an important determinant of demand for an industry's products, industry profits depend critically on there being an adequate supply of complementary products. When the number of complementors is increasing and they produce attractive complementary products, this boosts demand and profits in the industry and can open up many new opportunities for creating value. Conversely, if complementors are weak and are not producing attractive complementary products, this can be a threat that slows industry growth and limits profitability.

The systematic analysis of forces in the industry environment using the Porter framework is a powerful tool that helps managers to think strategically. It is important to recognize that one competitive force often affects the others, so that all forces need to be considered and thought about when performing industry analysis. Indeed, industry analysis leads managers to think systematically about the way their strategic choices will both be affected by the forces of industry competition and how their choices will affect the five forces and change conditions in the industry. Had managers or investors in the telecommunications service industry stopped to consider what would happen to the industry when new and existing companies simultaneously expanded capacity—intense rivalry and price competition—perhaps the huge boom and bust cycle could have been avoided. For an illustration of how important industry analysis is in driving strategy, consider the *Running Case* on Dell Computer, which looks at how the nature of rivalry in the personal computer industry has changed in recent years.

Strategic Groups Within Industries

Companies in an industry often differ significantly from each other with respect to the way they strategically position their products in the market in terms of such factors as the distribution channels they use, the market segments they serve, the quality of their products, technological leadership, customer service, pricing policy, advertising policy, and promotions. As a result of these differences, within most

Running Case

Dell—Changing Rivalry in the Personal Computer Industry

Throughout the 1990s, the personal computer industry was a good one to be in. New entry was limited by the brand loyalty and scale economies enjoyed by the established companies in the business. The most significant new entrant during the decade, Hewlett Packard, was able to enter because it already competed in the computer sector (it made midrange computers) and could leverage its brand loyalty and existing scale economies to reduce the costs of entry (something companies outside the computer sector could not do) into the personal computer market. Also, a robust supply of complementary products, including Microsoft's Office productivity suite, online service providers such as AOL and MSN, Internet browsers, email programs, personal finance software such as Quicken, digital imaging hardware and software, and PC games, helped to keep customer demand growing at 15 percent per annum compounded, giving all PC makers a chance to increase their revenues and profits. Nor were there any potential substitutes that might limit demand growth. In this growing industry, rivalry between companies, while vigorous, did not lead to major price wars, and this helped to keep industry profitability high.

The industry did have two strong suppliers that enjoyed substantial bargaining power: Intel, which provided the microprocessor for the majority of personal computers, and Microsoft, which provided the operating system. To sell their machines, personal computer companies had to include an Intel or Intel-compatible microprocessor and a Microsoft operating system. This enabled Intel and Microsoft to charge higher prices than would otherwise have been the case and thus reduced the profitability of the personal computer industry somewhat. However, this negative was not enough to offset the positive growth fundamentals, which were strong. Moreover, the buyers in the industry—individual customers, corporations, and distributors such as CompUSA—did not exercise significant bargaining power.

All of this changed in 2000 as the industry became consolidated. Dell now had a 14 percent share of worldwide PC shipments, Compaq 11 percent, Hewlett Packard 8 percent, IBM 6 percent, Fujitsu 5 percent, and Gateway 4 percent. With almost half of the world market in the hands of just six companies, there was now a substantial level of interdependence among industry companies. Moreover, these companies offered such similar products that analysts worried that PCs were fast becoming mere

"commodities" like corn or wheat and that price would become be the main competitive weapon. Since differentiating products on nonprice factors was becoming increasingly difficult, analysts postulated that it would be only a matter of time before one player cut prices, and the others would be forced to respond in kind in order to try to hold onto their market share, plunging the entire industry into a price war.

This scenario became more likely in 2001 when the growth rate in the industry began to slow to single digits. There were two reasons for the slowing growth. First, after two decades of robust growth, the market had become mature. By 2001, almost all businesses and 65 percent of homes in the United States had personal computers. Second, demand for personal computers was hurt by a lack of compelling complementary products that might persuade businesses and household customers to replace their existing equipment with more powerful machines. For the first time in two decades, worldwide unit shipments of personal computers fell to 130 million, down from 132 million in 2000. In the large U.S. market, demand fell by 13 percent in 2001.

The combination of a consolidated industry, a product that was increasingly difficult to differentiate, and slowing demand set the scene for a marked change in the intensity of rivalry in the industry. Dell, which had the lowest cost structure in the industry, launched a price war. Its rivals were forced to respond in kind in order to try to maintain their market share, and prices and profits in the industry plunged. During 2001, the average selling price in the industry fell from $1,850 a machine to $1,460. By late 2001, Dell was the only major personal computer company making money, and it was also gaining market share and increasing revenues. Industry observers believed that Dell's strategic goal was to drive some of its weaker competitors out of the market altogether, leading to a more consolidated industry in which Dell would be the dominant player.

By early 2002 it looked as if Dell might be getting closer to achieving this goal. Compaq and Hewlett Packard, the number two and three companies, had announced their intention to merge, partly in an attempt to rationalize their PC manufacturing operations, closing down some of their plants to take surplus capacity out of the industry. IBM announced its intention to exit the business of making PCs, selling its facilities to a contract manufacturer. Gateway was still hanging on, but its sales revenues had slumped by 35 percent during 2001 as prices plunged, and it was losing money. To many, it seemed as if Dell had analyzed the structure of its industry in late 2000 and decided that the time was ripe to launch a price war in which it would be the major beneficiary.

Sources: G. McWilliams, "Dell Boosts Estimates for Profits and Sales," *Wall Street Journal,* January 21, 2002, p. B4. W. M. Bulkeley, "As PC Industry Slumps, IBM Hands Off Manufacturing of Desktops," *Wall Street Journal,* January 9, 2002, p. B1. G. McWilliams, "Computer Trouble: As More Buyers Suffer from Upgrade Fatigue, PC Sales Are Falling," *Wall Street Journal,* August 24, 2001, p. A1. J. Pellet, "Who's Afraid of Michael Dell?" *Chief Executive* (July 2001): 28–35.

industries, it is possible to observe groups of companies in which each company follows the same basic product positioning strategy as the other companies in the group, but a strategy that is *different* from that followed by companies in other groups. These different groups of companies are known as **strategic groups.**[12]

Normally, the basic differences between the positioning strategies that companies in different strategic groups use can be captured by a relatively small number of strategic factors. For example, in the pharmaceutical industry, two main strategic groups stand out (see Figure 2.3).[13] One group, which includes such companies as Merck, Eli Lilly, and Pfizer, is characterized by competitive positioning based on heavy R&D spending and a focus on developing new, proprietary, blockbuster drugs. The companies in this *proprietary* strategic group are pursuing a high-risk, high-return strategy. It is a high-risk strategy because basic drug research is difficult and expensive. Bringing a new drug to market can cost up to $500 million in R&D money and a decade of research and clinical trials. The risks are high because the failure rate in new drug development is very high: only one out of every ten drugs entering clinical trials is ultimately approved by the U.S. Food and Drug Administration. However, the strategy is also a high-return one because a single successful drug can be patented, giving the innovator a twenty-year monopoly on its production and sale. This lets these proprietary companies charge a high price for the patented drug, allowing them to earn millions, if not billions, of dollars over the lifetime of the patent.

FIGURE 2.3

Strategic Groups in the Pharmaceutical Industry

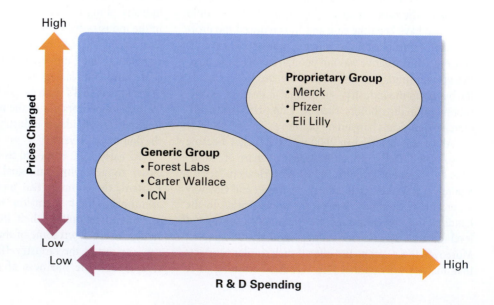

The second strategic group might be characterized as the *generic drug* strategic group. This group of companies, which includes Forest Labs, ICN, and Carter Wallace, focuses on the manufacture of generic drugs: low-cost copies of drugs that were developed by companies in the proprietary group whose patents have now expired. Low R&D spending and an emphasis on low prices characterize the competitive positioning of companies in this strategic group. They are pursuing a low-risk, low-return strategy. It is low risk because they are not investing millions of dollars in R&D. It is low return because they cannot charge high prices.

Implications of Strategic Groups

The concept of strategic groups has a number of implications for the identification of opportunities and threats within an industry. First, because all the companies in a strategic group are pursuing a similar positioning strategy, customers tend to view the products of such enterprises as *direct substitutes* for each other. Thus, a company's *closest* competitors are those in its strategic group, not those in other strategic groups in the industry. The most immediate threat to a company's profitability comes from rivals within its own strategic group. For example, in the retail industry, there is a group of companies that might be characterized as discounters. Included in this group are Wal-Mart, Kmart, Target, and Fred Meyer. These companies compete most vigorously with each other, as opposed to with other retailers in different groups, such as Nordstrom or The Gap. Kmart, for example, was driven into bankruptcy in late 2001, not because Nordstrom or The Gap took business from it, but because Wal-Mart and Target gained share in the discounting group by virtue of their superior strategies.

A second competitive implication is that different strategic groups can have a different standing with respect to each of the competitive forces; thus, *each strategic group may face a different set of opportunities and threats.* The risk of new entry by potential competitors, the degree of rivalry among companies within a group, the bargaining power of buyers, the bargaining power of suppliers, and the competitive force of substitute and complementary products can each be a relatively strong or weak competitive force depending on the competitive positioning approach adopted by each strategic group in the industry. For example, in the pharmaceutical industry, companies in the proprietary group have historically been in a very powerful position in relation to buyers because their products are patented and there are no substitutes. Also, rivalry within this group has been low because competition in the industry revolves around being the first to patent a new drug (so-called patent races), not around drug prices. Thus, companies in this group have been able to charge high prices and earn high profits. In contrast, companies in the generic group have been in a much weaker position because many companies are able to produce different versions of the same generic drug after patents expire. Thus, in this strategic group, products are close substitutes, rivalry has been high, and price competition has led to lower profits for this group as compared to companies in the proprietary group.

The Role of Mobility Barriers

It follows from these two issues that some strategic groups are more desirable than others because Porter's five forces open up greater opportunities and present fewer threats for those groups. Managers, after having analyzed their industry, might identify a strategic group where the five forces are weaker and higher profits can be made. Sensing an opportunity, they might contemplate changing their positioning approach and move to compete in that strategic group. However, taking advantage of this opportunity may be difficult because of mobility barriers between strategic groups.

Mobility barriers are within-industry factors that inhibit the movement of companies between strategic groups. They include the barriers to entry into a group and the barriers to exit from a company's existing group. For example, Forest Labs would encounter mobility barriers if it attempted to enter the proprietary group in the pharmaceutical industry because it lacks R&D skills, and building these skills would be an expensive proposition. Essentially, over time, companies in different groups develop different cost structures and skills and competencies that give them different pricing options and choices. A company contemplating entry into another strategic group must evaluate whether it has the ability to imitate, and indeed outperform, its potential competitors in that strategic group. Managers must determine if it is cost-effective to overcome mobility barriers before deciding whether the move is worthwhile.

In summary, an important task of industry analysis is to determine the sources of the similarities and differences among companies in an industry and to work out the broad themes that underlie competition in an industry. This analysis often reveals new opportunities to compete in an industry by developing new kinds of products to meet the needs of customers better. It can also reveal emerging threats that can be countered effectively by changing competitive strategy. This issue is taken up in Chapters 5, 6, and 7, which examine crafting competitive strategy in different kinds of markets to build a competitive advantage over rivals and best satisfy customer needs.

Industry Life Cycle Analysis

An important determinant of the strength of the competitive forces in an industry (and thus of the nature of opportunities and threats) is the changes that take place in it over time. The similarities and differences between companies in an industry often become more pronounced over time, and its strategic group structure frequently changes. The strength and nature of each of Porter's five competitive forces also change as an industry evolves, particularly the two forces of risk of entry by potential competitors and rivalry among existing firms.[14]

A useful tool for analyzing the effects of industry evolution on competitive forces is the **industry life cycle** model, which identifies five sequential stages in the evolution of an industry that lead to five distinct kinds of industry environment: embryonic, growth, shakeout, mature, and decline (see Figure 2.4). The task facing managers is to *anticipate* how the strength of competitive forces will change as the industry environment evolves and to formulate strategies that take advantage of opportunities as they arise and that counter emerging threats.

Embryonic Industries

An *embryonic* industry is just beginning to develop (for example, personal computers in 1976). Growth at this stage is slow because of such factors as buyers' unfamiliarity with the industry's product, high prices due to the inability of companies to reap any significant scale economies, and poorly developed distribution channels. Barriers to entry tend to be based on access to key technological know-how rather than cost economies or brand loyalty. If the core know-how required to compete in the industry is complex and difficult to grasp, barriers to entry can be quite high, and established companies will be protected from potential competitors. Rivalry in embryonic industries is based not so much on price as on educating customers, opening up distribution channels, and perfecting the design of the product. Such rivalry can be intense, and the company that is the first to solve design problems often

FIGURE 2.4

Stages in the Industry Life Cycle

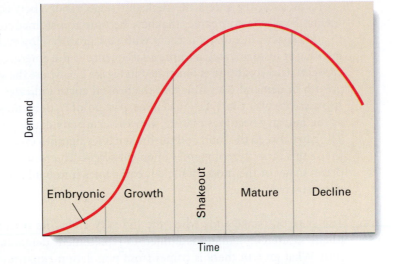

Growth
Industries

Once demand for the industry's product begins to take off, the industry develops the characteristics of a growth industry. In a *growth* industry, first-time demand is expanding rapidly as many new customers enter the market. Typically, an industry grows when customers become familiar with the product, prices fall because experience and scale economies have been attained, and distribution channels develop. The U.S. cellular telephone industry was in the growth stage for most of the 1990s. In 1990, there were only 5 million cellular subscribers in the nation. By 2002, this figure had increased to 88 million, and overall demand was still growing at a rate in excess of 25 percent per year.

Normally, the importance of control over technological knowledge as a barrier to entry has diminished by the time an industry enters its growth stage. Because few companies have yet achieved significant scale economies or built brand loyalty, other entry barriers tend to be relatively low as well, particularly early in the growth stage. Thus, the threat from potential competitors generally is highest at this point. Paradoxically, however, high growth usually means that new entrants can be absorbed into an industry without a marked increase in the intensity of rivalry. Thus, rivalry tends to be relatively low. Rapid growth in demand enables companies to expand their revenues and profits without taking market share away from competitors. A strategically aware company takes advantage of the relatively benign environment of the growth stage to prepare itself for the intense competition of the coming industry shakeout.

Industry
Shakeout

Explosive growth cannot be maintained indefinitely. Sooner or later, the rate of growth slows, and the industry enters the shakeout stage. This is now occurring in the personal computer industry (see the *Running Case* in this chapter). In the *shakeout* stage, demand approaches saturation levels: most of the demand is limited to replacement because there are few potential first-time buyers left.

has the opportunity to develop a significant market position. An embryonic industry may also be the creation of one company's innovative efforts, as happened with personal computers (Apple), vacuum cleaners (Hoover), and photocopiers (Xerox). In such circumstances, the company has a major opportunity to capitalize on the lack of rivalry and build a strong hold on the market.

As an industry enters the shakeout stage, rivalry between companies becomes intense. Typically, companies that have become accustomed to rapid growth continue to add capacity at rates consistent with past growth. However, demand is no longer growing at historic rates, and the consequence is the emergence of excess productive capacity. This condition is illustrated in Figure 2.5, where the solid curve indicates the growth in demand over time and the broken curve indicates the growth in productive capacity over time. As you can see, past point t_1, demand growth becomes slower as the industry becomes mature. However, capacity continues to grow until time t_2. The gap between the solid and the broken lines signifies excess capacity. In an attempt to use this capacity, companies often cut prices. The result can be a price war, which drives many of the most inefficient companies into bankruptcy, which is enough to deter any new entry.

Mature Industries

The shakeout stage ends when the industry enters its *mature* stage: the market is totally saturated, demand is limited to replacement demand, and growth is low or zero. What growth there is comes from population expansion that brings new customers into the market or an increase in replacement demand.

As an industry enters maturity, barriers to entry increase, and the threat of entry from potential competitors decreases. As growth slows during the shakeout, companies can no longer maintain historic growth rates merely by holding on to their market share. Competition for market share develops, driving down prices. Often the result is a price war, as happened in the airline and personal computer industries. To survive the shakeout, companies begin to focus on cost minimization and building brand loyalty. The airlines, for example, tried to cut operating costs by hiring nonunion labor and to build brand loyalty by introducing frequent-flyer programs. Personal computer companies have sought to build brand loyalty by providing excellent after-sales service and working to lower their cost structures. By the time an industry matures, the surviving companies are those that have brand loyalty and low-cost operations. Because both these factors constitute a significant barrier to entry, the threat of entry by potential competitors is greatly diminished. High entry barriers in mature industries give companies the opportunity to increase prices and profits.

As a result of the shakeout, most industries in the maturity stage have consolidated and become oligopolies. As you can see from the *Running Case* in this chapter, this process now seems to be unfolding in the personal computer industry, with the

FIGURE 2.5

Growth in Demand and Capacity

price war that Dell started leading some companies to exit the industry (IBM) or merge their operations (Compaq and Gateway). The end result will be a more consolidated industry structure. In mature industries, companies tend to recognize their interdependence and try to avoid price wars. Stable demand gives them the opportunity to enter into price leadership agreements. The net effect is to reduce the threat of intense rivalry among established companies, thereby allowing greater profitability. Nevertheless, the stability of a mature industry is always threatened by further price wars. A general slump in economic activity can depress industry demand. As companies fight to maintain their revenues in the face of declining demand, price leadership agreements break down, rivalry increases, and prices and profits fall. The periodic price wars that occur in the airline industry seem to follow this pattern.

Declining Industries   Eventually, most industries enter a *decline stage:* growth becomes negative for a variety of reasons, including technological substitution (for example, air travel for rail travel), social changes (greater health consciousness hitting tobacco sales), demographics (the declining birthrate hurting the market for baby and child products), and international competition (low-cost foreign competition pushing the U.S. steel industry into decline). Within a declining industry, the degree of rivalry among established companies usually increases. Depending on the speed of the decline and the height of exit barriers, competitive pressures can become as fierce as in the shakeout stage.[15] The main problem in a declining industry is that falling demand leads to the emergence of excess capacity. In trying to use this capacity, companies begin to cut prices, thus sparking a price war. The U.S. steel industry experienced these problems because steel companies tried to use their excess capacity despite falling demand. The same problem occurred in the airline industry in the 1990–1992 period and again in 2001–2002, as companies cut prices to ensure that they would not be flying with half-empty planes (that is, that they would not be operating with substantial excess capacity). Exit barriers play a part in adjusting excess capacity. The greater the exit barriers, the harder it is for companies to reduce capacity and the greater is the threat of severe price competition.

In summary, a third task of industry analysis is to identify the opportunities and threats that are characteristic of different kinds of industry environments in order to develop an effective business model and competitive strategy. Strategic managers have to tailor their strategies to changing industry conditions. And they have to learn to recognize the crucial points in an industry's development so that they can forecast when the shakeout stage of an industry might begin or when an industry might be moving into decline. This is also true at the level of strategic groups, for new embryonic groups may emerge because of shifts in customer needs and tastes or some groups may grow rapidly because of changes in technology and others will decline as their customers defect. Thus, for example, companies in the upscale retail group such as Macy's, Dillard's, and Nordstrom are facing declining sales as customers defect to discount retailers like Target and Wal-Mart and online companies like amazon.com and landsend.com.

Limitations of Models for Industry Analysis   The five forces, strategic groups, and life cycle models provide useful ways of thinking about and analyzing the nature of competition within an industry to identify opportunities and threats. However, each has its limitations, and managers need to be aware of their shortcomings.

Life Cycle Issues

It is important to remember that the industry life cycle model is a generalization. In practice, industry life cycles do not always follow the pattern illustrated in Figure 2.4. In some cases, growth is so rapid that the embryonic stage is skipped altogether. In others, industries fail to get past the embryonic stage. Industry growth can be revitalized after long periods of decline through innovation or social change. For example, the health boom brought the bicycle industry back to life after a long period of decline.

The time span of the stages can also vary significantly from industry to industry. Some industries can stay in maturity almost indefinitely if their products become basic necessities of life, as is the case for the car industry. Other industries skip the mature stage and go straight into decline, as in the case of the vacuum tube industry. Transistors replaced vacuum tubes as a major component in electronic products even though the vacuum tube industry was still in its growth stage. Still other industries may go through several shakeouts before they enter full maturity, as appears to be happening in the telecommunications industry.

Innovation and Change

Over any reasonable length of time, in many industries competition can be viewed as a process driven by innovation.[16] Indeed, innovation is frequently the major factor in industry evolution and causes the movement through the industry life cycle. Innovation is attractive because companies that pioneer new products, processes, or strategies can often earn enormous profits. Consider the explosive growth of Apple Computer, Toys "R" Us, Dell Computer, and Wal-Mart. In a variety of different ways, all of these companies were innovators. Apple pioneered the personal computer, Toys "R" Us pioneered a new way of selling toys (through large discount warehouse-type stores), Dell pioneered a whole new way of selling personal computers (by mail order), and Wal-Mart pioneered the low-price discount superstore concept.

Successful innovation can transform the nature of industry competition. In recent decades, one frequent consequence of innovation has been to lower the fixed costs of production, thereby reducing barriers to entry and allowing new, and smaller, enterprises to compete with large established organizations. For example, two decades ago, large integrated steel companies such as US Steel, LTV, and Bethlehem Steel dominated the steel industry. The industry was a typical oligopoly, dominated by a small number of large producers, in which tacit price collusion was practiced. Then along came a series of efficient mini-mill producers such as Nucor and Chaparral Steel, which used a new technology: electric arc furnaces. Over the past twenty years, they have revolutionized the structure of the industry. What was once a consolidated industry is now much more fragmented and price competitive. The successor company to US Steel, USX, now has only a 15 percent market share, down from 55 percent in the mid-1960s, and both Bethlehem and LTV have been through Chapter 11 bankruptcy proceedings. In contrast, the mini-mills as a group now hold over 40 percent of the market, up from 5 percent twenty years ago.[17] Thus, the mini-mill innovation has reshaped the nature of competition in the steel industry.[18] A five forces model applied to the industry in 1970 would look very different from a five forces model applied in 2002.

In his more recent work, Michael Porter, the originator of the five forces and strategic group concepts, has explicitly recognized the role of innovation in revolutionizing industry structure. Porter now talks of innovations as "unfreezing" and "reshaping" industry structure. He argues that after a period of turbulence triggered by innovation, the structure of an industry once more settles down into a fairly stable pattern, and the five forces and strategic group concepts can once more be applied.[19] This view of the evolution of industry structure is often referred to as *punctuated equilibrium*.[20] The punctuated equilibrium view holds that long periods of equilibrium, when an industry's structure is stable, are punctuated by periods of rapid change when industry structure is revolutionized by innovation; there is an unfreezing and refreezing process.

Figure 2.6 shows what punctuated equilibrium might look like for one key dimension of industry structure: competitive structure. From time t_0 to t_1, the competitive structure of the industry is a stable oligopoly, with a few companies sharing the market. At time t_1, a major new innovation is pioneered by either an existing company or a new entrant. The result is a period of turbulence between t_1 and t_2. After a while, the industry settles down into a new state of equilibrium, but now the competitive structure is far more fragmented. Note that the opposite could have happened: the industry could have become more consolidated, although this seems to be less common. In general, innovations seem to lower barriers to entry, allow more companies into the industry, and as a result lead to fragmentation rather than consolidation.

During a period of rapid change when industry structure is being revolutionized by innovation, value typically migrates to business models based on new positioning strategies.[21] In the stock brokerage industry, value has migrated away from the full-service broker model to the online trading model. In the steel industry, the introduction of electric arc technology led to a migration of value away from large, integrated enterprises and toward small mini-mills. In the book-selling industry, value has migrated away from small boutique "bricks and mortar" booksellers toward large bookstore chains like Barnes & Noble and online bookstores such as amazon.com.

Because the five forces and strategic group models are static, they cannot adequately capture what occurs during periods of rapid change in the industry environment when value is migrating. Similarly, a simple view of the industry life cycle does not allow for an industry to repeat a stage or even jump stages that technological upheavals can lead to. Nevertheless, they are useful tools for analyzing industry structure during periods of stability.

Some scholars question the validity of the punctuated equilibrium approach. Richard D'Avani has argued that many industries are **hypercompetitive,** meaning

FIGURE 2.6

Punctuated
Equilibrium and
Competitive Structure

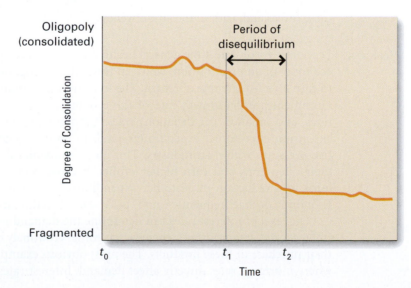

that they are characterized by permanent and ongoing innovation (the computer industry is often cited as an example of a hypercompetitive industry).[22] The structure of such industries is constantly being revolutionized by innovation, so there are no periods of equilibrium. When this is the case, some might argue that the five forces and strategic group models are of limited value because they represent no more than snapshots of a moving picture. Thus, managers must constantly repeat industry analysis and pay attention to changes in the forces of competition.

Company Differences   Another criticism of industry models is that they overemphasize the importance of industry structure as a determinant of company performance and underemphasize the importance of variations or differences among companies within an industry or a strategic group.[23] As we discuss in the next chapter, there can be enormous variance in the profit rates of individual companies within an industry. Research by Richard Rumelt and his associates, for example, suggests that industry structure explains only about 10 percent of the variance in profit rates across companies.[24] The implication is that individual company differences explain much of the remainder. Other studies have put the explained variance closer to 20 percent, which is still not a large figure.[25] Similarly, a growing number of studies have found only weak evidence of a link between strategic group membership and company profit rates, despite the fact that the strategic group model predicts a strong link.[26] Collectively, these studies suggest that the individual resources and capabilities of a company are far more important determinants of its profitability than is the industry or strategic group of which the company is a member. Although these findings do not make the five forces and strategic group models irrelevant, they do mean that the models have limited usefulness. A company will not be profitable just because it is based in an attractive industry or strategic group. As we discuss in Chapters 3 and 4, more is required.

The Macroenvironment

Just as the decisions and actions of strategic managers can often change an industry's competitive structure, so too can changing conditions or forces in the wider **macroenvironment,** that is, the broader economic, technological, demographic, social, and political context in which companies and industries are embedded (see Figure 2.7). Changes in the forces in the macroenvironment can have a direct impact on any or all of the forces in Porter's model, thereby altering the relative strength of these forces and, with it, the attractiveness of an industry.

Economic Forces   Economic forces affect the general health and well-being of a nation or the regional economy of an organization, which in turn affect companies' and industries' ability to earn an adequate rate of return. The four most important factors in the macroenvironment are the growth rate of the economy, interest rates, currency exchange rates, and inflation (or deflation) rates. Economic growth, because it leads to an expansion in customer expenditures, tends to produce a general easing of competitive pressures within an industry. This gives companies the opportunity to expand their operations and earn higher profits. Because economic decline (a recession) leads to a reduction in customer expenditures, it increases competitive pressures. Economic decline frequently causes price wars in mature industries.

The level of interest rates can determine the demand for a company's products. Interest rates are important whenever customers routinely borrow money to finance their purchase of these products. The most obvious example is the housing market, where mortgage rates directly affect demand. Interest rates also have an impact on

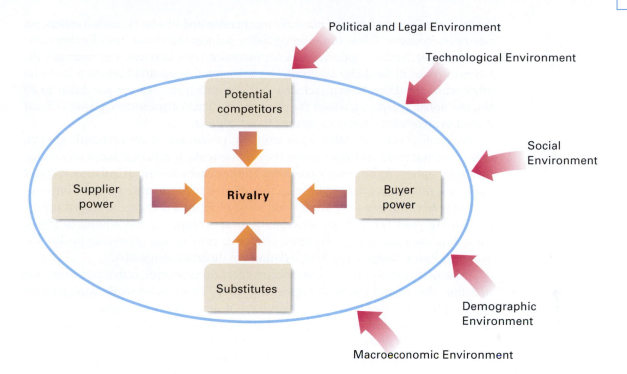

FIGURE 2.7

The Role of the Macroenvironment

the sale of autos, appliances, and capital equipment, to give just a few examples. For companies in such industries, rising interest rates are a threat and falling rates an opportunity.

Interest rates are also important insofar as they influence a company's cost of capital, and therefore its ability to raise funds and invest in new assets. The lower that interest rates are, the lower the cost of capital for companies will be, and the more investment there will be. This is not always a good thing. In the late 1990s, the very low cost of capital allowed dot-com and telecommunications companies with questionable business plans to raise large amounts of money and invest those funds in computers and telecommunications gear (the low cost of capital lowered barriers to entry by enabling start-ups to raise the capital required to circumvent entry barriers). This was initially good for the manufacturers of telecommunications equipment and computers, but the demand signal that was being sent was not sustainable: many of the dot-com and telecommunications start-ups of the 1990s went bankrupt between 2000 and 2002. Second-hand computers and telecommunications equipment from these bankrupt companies flooded the market, depressing first-time demand for that equipment and helping to plunge the computer and telecommunications equipment businesses into a deep slowdown. (For example, in January 2002, Internet auction house eBay listed more than 3,000 Cisco products that were being auctioned for much less than their initial prices.)

Currency exchange rates define the value of different national currencies against each other. Movement in currency exchange rates has a direct impact on the competitiveness of a company's products in the global marketplace. For example, when the value of the dollar is low compared with the value of other currencies, products made in the United States are relatively inexpensive and products made overseas are relatively expensive. A low or declining dollar reduces the threat from foreign competitors while creating opportunities for increased sales overseas. For example, the fall in the value of the dollar against the Japanese yen that occurred between 1985 and 1995, when the dollar-to-yen exchange rate declined from 240 yen per dollar to 85 yen per dollar, sharply increased the price of imported Japanese cars, giving U.S. car manufacturers some protection against those imports.

Price inflation can destabilize the economy, producing slower economic growth, higher interest rates, and volatile currency movements. If inflation keeps increasing, investment planning becomes hazardous. The key characteristic of inflation is that it makes the future less predictable. In an inflationary environment, it may be impossible to predict with any accuracy the real value of returns that can be earned from a project five years hence. Such uncertainty makes companies less willing to invest. Their holding back in turn depresses economic activity and ultimately pushes the economy into a slump. Thus, high inflation is a threat to companies.

Price deflation also has a destabilizing effect on economic activity. If prices are deflating, the real price of fixed payments goes up. This is particularly damaging for companies and individuals with a high level of debt who must make regular fixed payments on that debt. In a deflationary environment, the increase in the real value of debt consumes more of household and corporate cash flows, leaving less for other purchases and depressing the overall level of economic activity. Although significant deflation has not been seen since the 1930s, in the 1990s it started to take hold in Japan.

Technological Forces

Since World War II, the pace of technological change has accelerated.[27] This has unleashed a process that has been called a "perennial gale of creative destruction."[28] Technological change can make established products obsolete overnight and simultaneously create a host of new product possibilities. Thus, technological change is both creative and destructive—both an opportunity and a threat.

One of the most important impacts of technological change is that it can affect the height of barriers to entry and therefore radically reshape industry structure. The Internet, because it is so pervasive, has the potential for changing the competitive structure of many industries. It often lowers barriers to entry and reduces customer switching costs, changes that tend to increase the intensity of rivalry in an industry and lower both prices and profits.[29] For example, the Internet has lowered barriers to entry into the news industry. Providers of financial news now have to compete for advertising dollars and customer attention with new Internet-based media organizations that sprung up during the 1990s such as TheStreet.com, the Motley Fool, and Yahoo's financial section. The resulting increase in rivalry has given advertisers more choices, enabling them to bargain down the prices that they must pay to media companies. Similarly, in the automobile industry, the ability of customers to comparison-shop for cars online and purchase cars online from a number of distributors such as Auto Nation has increased the ability of customers to find the best value for money. Customers' increased bargaining power enables them to put downward pressure on car prices and squeeze profits out of the automobile industry.

Another example of how technology change is reshaping an established industry can be found by looking at the impact of biotechnology on the pharmaceutical industry. Although Merck, Pfizer, and Eli Lilly have long dominated the industry, a significant number of small biotechnology companies using recombinant DNA technology are threatening to change the competitive landscape. Between 1945 and 1990, only one new firm became a major player in the pharmaceutical industry: Syntex. Since 1990, a number of biotechnology companies have started to generate significant sales, including Amgen, Biogen, Genetech, and Chiron. Moreover, there are now over 300 publicly traded companies in the United States developing novel medicines using biotechnology. The chance is that some of these will develop into significant companies in their own right, illustrating once again that technological change lowers entry barriers and allows new players to challenge the dominance of established companies.

Demographic Forces

Demographic forces are outcomes of changes in the characteristics of a population, such as age, gender, ethnic origin, race, sexual orientation, and social class. Like the other forces in the general environment, demographic forces present managers with opportunities and threats and can have major implications for organizations. Over the past thirty years, for example, women have entered the work force in increasing numbers. Between 1973 and 2002, the percentage of women in the work force increased from 44 to 60 percent in the United States, 48 to 68 percent in Canada, and 51 to 68 percent in Britain.[30] This dramatic increase has brought issues such as equal pay for equal work and sexual harassment at work to the forefront of issues that managers must address if they are to attract and make full use of the talents of female workers.

Changes in the age distribution of a population are another example of a demographic force that affects managers and organizations. Currently, most industrialized nations are experiencing the aging of their populations as a consequence of falling birth and death rates and the aging of the baby boom generation. In Germany, for example, the percentage of the population over age sixty-five is expected to rise from 15.4 percent in 1990 to 20.7 percent in 2010. Comparable figures for Canada are 11.4 and 14.4 percent; for Japan, 11.7 and 19.5 percent; and for the United States, 12.6 and 13.5 percent.[31]

The aging of the population is increasing opportunities for organizations that cater to older people; the home health care and recreation industries, for example, are seeing an upswing in demand for their services. As the baby boom generation from the late 1950s to the early 1960s has aged, it has created a host of opportunities and threats. During the 1980s, many baby boomers were getting married and creating an upsurge in demand for the customer appliances normally bought by couples marrying for the first time. Companies such as Whirlpool Corporation and General Electric capitalized on the resulting upsurge in demand for washing machines, dishwashers, dryers, and the like. In the 1990s, many of these same baby boomers were starting to save for retirement, creating an inflow of money into mutual funds and creating a boom in the mutual fund industry. In the next twenty years, many of these same baby boomers will retire, creating a boom in retirement communities.

Social Forces

Social forces refer to the way in which changing social mores and values affect an industry. Like the other macroenvironmental forces discussed here, social change creates opportunities and threats. One of the major social movements of recent decades has been the trend toward greater health consciousness. Its impact has been immense, and companies that recognized the opportunities early have often reaped significant gains. Philip Morris, for example, capitalized on the growing health consciousness trend when it acquired Miller Brewing Company and then redefined competition in the beer industry with its introduction of low-calorie beer (Miller Lite). Similarly, PepsiCo was able to gain market share from its rival, Coca-Cola, by being the first to introduce diet colas and fruit-based soft drinks. At the same time, the health trend has created a threat for many industries. The tobacco industry, for example, is in decline as a direct result of greater customer awareness of the health implications of smoking.

Political and Legal Forces

Political and legal forces are outcomes of changes in laws and regulations. They result from political and legal developments within society and significantly affect managers and companies.

Political processes shape a society's laws, which constrain the operations of organizations and managers and thus create both opportunities and threats.[32] For example, throughout much of the industrialized world, there has been a strong trend toward deregulation of industries previously controlled by the state and privatization of organizations once owned by the state. In the United States, deregulation of the airline industry in 1979 allowed twenty-nine new airlines to enter the industry between 1979 and 1993. The increase in passenger carrying capacity after deregulation led to excess capacity on many routes, intense competition, and fare wars. To respond to this more competitive task environment, airlines have had to look for ways to reduce operating costs. The development of hub-and-spoke systems, the rise of nonunion airlines, and the introduction of no-frills discount service are all responses to increased competition in the airlines' task environment. Despite these innovations, the airline industry still experiences intense fare wars, which have lowered profits and caused numerous airline company bankruptcies. The global telecommunications service industry is now experiencing the same kind of turmoil following the deregulation of that industry in the United States and elsewhere (see the *Opening Case*).

In most countries, the interplay between political and legal forces, on the one hand, and industry competitive structure, on the other, is a two-way process in which the government sets regulations that influence competitive structure, and firms in an industry often seek to influence the regulations that governments enact by a number of means. First, when permitted, they may provide financial support to politicians or political parties that espouse views favorable to the industry and lobby government legislators directly to shape government regulations. For example, during the 1990s and early 2000s, the now-bankrupt energy trading company Enron lobbied government legislators to persuade them to deregulate energy markets in the United States, an action that Enron would benefit from. Second, companies and industries may lobby the government through industry associations. In 2002, the United States Steel Industry Association was a prime mover in persuading President Bush to enact a 30 percent tariff on imports of foreign steel into the United States. The purpose of the tariff was to protect American steel makers from foreign competitors, thereby reducing the intensity of rivalry in the United States steel markets.

The Global and National Environments

Many important processes operating at the level of the global and national environments directly and indirectly affect the competitive structure of an industry (Chapter 8 is devoted to describing strategy at the global level). Here we look at two of these: the globalization of production and markets and the effect of national or country-specific factors on home industries' competitive advantage.

The Globalization of Production and Markets

The past fifty years have seen a dramatic lowering of barriers to cross-border trade and investment. For example, the average tariff rate on manufactured goods traded between advanced nations has fallen from around 40 percent to under 4 percent. Similarly, in nation after nation, regulations prohibiting foreign companies from entering domestic markets and establishing production facilities, or acquiring domestic companies, have been removed. As a result of these two developments, there has been a surge in both the volume of international trade and the value of foreign direct investment. Between 1950 and 2000, the volume of world trade increased more than twenty-fold, while the inflation-adjusted value of world gross domestic product (GDP) increased a little over sixfold. Foreign direct investment increased from $60 billion in 1980, to $210 billion in 1990, and $1.4 trillion in 2001.[33] These two trends have led to the globalization of production and the globalization of markets.[34]

The globalization of production has been increasing as companies take advantage of lower barriers to cross-border trade and investment to disperse important parts of their production process around the globe. Doing so enables them to take advantage of national differences in the cost and quality of factors of production such as labor, energy, land, and capital, which allow them to lower their cost structures and boost profits. For example, the Boeing Company's commercial jet aircraft, the 777, uses 132,500 engineered parts that are produced around the world by 545 suppliers. Eight Japanese suppliers make parts of the fuselage, doors, and wings; a supplier in Singapore makes the doors for the nose landing gear; three suppliers in Italy manufacture wing flaps; and so on. Part of Boeing's rationale for outsourcing so much production to foreign suppliers is that these suppliers are the best in the world at performing their particular activity. Therefore, the result of having foreign suppliers build specific parts is a better final product.[35]

As for the globalization of markets, it has been argued that the world's economic system is moving from one in which national markets are distinct entities, isolated from each other by trade barriers and barriers of distance, time, and culture, toward a system in which national markets are merging into one huge global marketplace. Increasingly, customers around the world demand and use the same basic product offerings. Consequently, in many industries, it is no longer meaningful to talk about the German market, the U.S. market, or the Japanese market; there is only the global market. The global acceptance of Coca-Cola, Citigroup credit cards, blue jeans, the Sony PlayStation, McDonald's hamburgers, the Nokia wireless phone, and Microsoft's Windows operating system are examples of this trend.[36]

The trend toward the globalization of production and markets has several important implications for competition within an industry. First, industry boundaries do not stop at national borders. Because many industries are becoming global in scope, actual and potential competitors exist not only in a company's home market but also in other national markets. Managers who analyze only their home market can be caught unprepared by the entry of efficient foreign competitors. The globalization of markets and production implies that companies around the globe are finding their home markets under attack from foreign competitors. For example, in Japan, Merrill Lynch and Citicorp are making inroads against Japanese financial service institutions. In the United States, Fuji has been taking market share from Kodak, and Finland's Nokia has taken the lead from Motorola in the market for wireless phone handsets (see Strategy in Action 2.3). In the European Union, the once dominant Dutch company Philips has seen its market share in the customer electronics industry taken by Japan's JVC, Matsushita, and Sony.

Second, the shift from national to global markets during the past twenty years has intensified competitive rivalry in industry after industry. National markets that once were consolidated oligopolies, dominated by three or four companies and subjected to relatively little foreign competition, have been transformed into segments of fragmented global industries, where a large number of companies battle each

Strategy in Action

Finland's Nokia

The wireless phone market is one of the great growth stories of the last decade. Starting from a very low base in 1990, annual global sales of wireless phones surged to reach 400 million units in 2001. Two companies currently dominate the global market for wireless handsets: Motorola and Nokia. In 2001, the global market leader was Nokia, which had a 35 percent share, three times that of its nearest competitor, Motorola, which had around 13 percent, and way ahead of Ericsson and Siemens, each with around 6 to 8 percent.

Nokia's roots are in Finland, not normally a country that jumps to mind when we talk about leading-edge technology companies. In the 1980s, Nokia was a rambling Finnish conglomerate with activities that embraced tire manufacturing, paper production, customer electronics, and telecommunications equipment. Much of the answer to how this former conglomerate emerged to take a global leadership position in wireless handsets lies in the history, geography, and political economy of Finland and its Nordic neighbors.

The story starts in 1981 when the Nordic nations got together to create the world's first international wireless telephone network. Sparsely populated and inhospitably cold, they had good reason to become pioneers: it cost far too much to lay down a traditional wire line telephone service. Yet the same features that made it difficult make telecommunications all the more valuable there: people driving through the Arctic winter and owners of remote northern houses needed a telephone to summon help if things go wrong. As a result, Sweden, Norway, and Finland became the first nations in the world to take wireless telecommunications seriously. They found, for example, that although it cost up to $800 per subscriber to bring a traditional wireline service to remote locations, the same locations could be linked by wireless cellular for only $500 per person. As a consequence, 12 percent of people in Scandinavia owned cellular phones by 1994, compared with less than 6 percent in the United States, the world's second most developed market. This lead continued during the decade. By 2001, over 70 percent of Finland's phone users had a wireless phone, compared to 33 percent in the United States, and the figure for Finland may reach 100 percent by 2010.

Nokia, a long-time telecommunications equipment supplier, was well positioned to take advantage of this development from the start, but there were also other forces at work that helped Nokia develop its competitive edge. Unlike virtually every other developed nation, Finland has never had a national telephone monopoly. Instead, the country's telephone services have long been provided by about fifty or so autonomous local telephone companies whose elected boards set prices by referendum (which naturally means low prices). This army of independent and cost-conscious telephone service providers prevented Nokia from taking anything for granted in its home country. With typical Finnish pragmatism, its customers were willing to buy from the lowest-cost supplier, whether that was Nokia, Ericsson, Motorola, or some other company. This situation contrasted sharply with that prevailing in most developed nations until the late 1980s and early 1990s, where domestic telephone monopolies typically purchased equipment from a dominant local supplier or made it themselves. Nokia responded to this competitive pressure by doing everything possible to drive down its manufacturing costs while staying at the leading edge of wireless technology.

The consequences of these forces are clear: the once obscure Finnish firm is now a global leader in the wireless market. In no small part, Nokia has the lead because Scandinavia started switching over to digital technology five years before the rest of the world. In addition, spurred on by its cost-conscious customers, Nokia now has the lowest cost structure of any wireless handset equipment manufacturer in the world and is a more profitable enterprise than its global competitors.

Sources: "Lessons from the Frozen North," *Economist,* October 8, 1994, pp. 76–77. G. Edmondson, "Grabbing Markets from the Giants," *Business Week,* Special Issue: 21st Century Capitalism, 1995, p. 156. Q. Hardy, "Bypassing the Bells—A Wireless World," *Wall Street Journal,* September 21, 1998, p. R16. Q. Hardy and G. Naik, "Nokia Takes the Lead as Wireless Makers Sell 162.9 Million Phones in 1998," *Wall Street Journal,* February 8, 1999, p. A1. "A Finnish Fable," *Economist,* October 14, 2000. "Nokia Succumbs," *Economist,* June 16, 2001.

other for market share in country after country. This rivalry has driven down profit rates and made it all the more critical for companies to maximize their efficiency, quality, customer responsiveness, and innovative ability. The painful restructuring and downsizing that has been going on at companies such as Motorola and Kodak is as much a response to the increased intensity of global competition as it is to anything else. However, not all global industries are fragmented. Many remain consolidated oligopolies, except that now they are consolidated global, rather than national, oligopolies.

Third, as competitive intensity has increased, so has the rate of innovation. Companies strive to gain an advantage over their competitors by pioneering new products, processes, and ways of doing business. The result has been to compress product life cycles and make it vital for companies to stay on the leading edge of technology. In regard to highly competitive global industries, where the rate of innovation is accelerating, the criticism that Porter's five forces model is too static may be particularly relevant.

Finally, although globalization has increased both the threat of entry and the intensity of rivalry within many formerly protected national markets, it has also created enormous opportunities for companies based in those markets. The steady decline in barriers to cross-border trade and investment has opened up many once protected markets to companies based outside them. Thus, for example, in recent years, Western European, Japanese, and U.S. companies have accelerated their investments in the nations of Eastern Europe, Latin America, and Southeast Asia as they try to take advantage of growth opportunities in those areas.

National Competitive Advantage

Despite the globalization of production and markets, many of the most successful companies in certain industries are still clustered in a small number of countries. For example, many of the world's most successful biotechnology and computer companies are based in the United States, many of the world's most successful customer electronics companies are based in Japan, and many of the world's most successful chemical and engineering companies are based in Germany. This suggests that the nation-state within which a company is based may have an important bearing on the competitive position of that company in the global marketplace.

Companies need to understand how national factors can affect competitive advantage, for then they will be able to identify (1) where their most significant competitors are likely to come from and (2) where they might want to locate certain productive activities. Thus, seeking to take advantage of U.S. expertise in biotechnology, many foreign companies have set up research facilities in San Diego, Boston, and Seattle, where U.S. biotechnology companies tend to be clustered. Similarly, in an attempt to take advantage of Japanese success in customer electronics, many U.S. electronics companies have set up research and production facilities in Japan, often in conjunction with Japanese partners.

In a study of national competitive advantage, Michael Porter identified four attributes of a national or country-specific environment that have an important impact on the global competitiveness of companies located within that nation:[37]

■ *Factor endowments:* A nation's position in factors of production such as skilled labor or the infrastructure necessary to compete in a given industry

■ *Demand conditions:* The nature of home demand for the industry's product or service

■ *Relating and supporting industries:* The presence or absence in a nation of supplier industries and related industries that are internationally competitive

■ *Firm strategy, structure, and rivalry:* The conditions in the nation governing how companies are created, organized, and managed and the nature of domestic rivalry

Porter speaks of these four attributes as constituting the *diamond,* arguing that companies are most likely to succeed in industries or strategic groups where the four attributes are favorable (see Figure 2.8). He also argues that the diamond's attributes form a mutually reinforcing system in which the effect of one attribute is dependent on the state of others.

Factor Endowments. **Factor endowments**—the cost and quality of factors of production—are a prime determinant of the competitive advantage that certain countries might have in certain industries. Factors of production include **basic factors,** such as land, labor, capital, and raw materials, and **advanced factors,** such as technological know-how, managerial sophistication, and physical infrastructure (roads, railways, and ports). The competitive advantage that the United States enjoys in biotechnology might be explained by the presence of certain advanced factors of production—for example, technological know-how—in combination with some basic factors, which might be a pool of relatively low-cost venture capital that can be used to fund risky start-ups in industries such as biotechnology.

Local Demand Conditions. Home demand plays an important role in providing the impetus for "upgrading" competitive advantage. Companies are typically most sensitive to the needs of their closest customers. Thus, the characteristics of home demand are particularly important in shaping the attributes of domestically made products and creating pressures for innovation and quality. A nation's companies gain competitive advantage if their domestic customers are sophisticated and

FIGURE 2.8

National Competitive Advantage

Source: Adapted from M. E. Porter. The Competitive Advantage of Nations. *Harvard Business Review*, March–April, 1990, page 77.

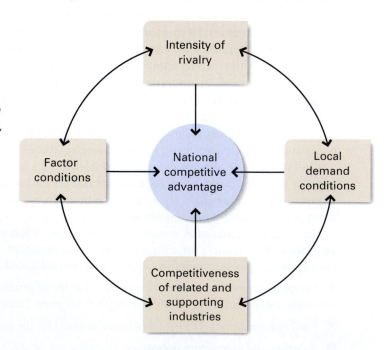

demanding and pressure local companies to meet high standards of product quality and produce innovative products. Japan's sophisticated and knowledgeable buyers of cameras helped stimulate the Japanese camera industry to improve product quality and introduce innovative models. A similar example can be found in the cellular phone equipment industry, where sophisticated and demanding local customers in Scandinavia helped push Nokia of Finland and Ericsson of Sweden to invest in cellular phone technology long before demand for cellular phones took off in other developed nations. As a result, Nokia and Ericsson, together with Motorola, are significant players in the global cellular telephone equipment industry. The case of Nokia is reviewed in more depth in Strategy in Action 2.3.

Competitiveness of Related and Supporting Industries. The third broad attribute of national advantage in an industry is the presence of internationally competitive suppliers or related industries. The benefits of investments in advanced factors of production by related and supporting industries can spill over into an industry, thereby helping it achieve a strong competitive position internationally. Swedish strength in fabricated steel products (such as ball bearings and cutting tools) has drawn on strengths in Sweden's specialty steel industry. Switzerland's success in pharmaceuticals is closely related to its previous international success in the technologically related dye industry. One consequence of this process is that successful industries within a country tend to be grouped into clusters of related industries. Indeed, this was one of the most pervasive findings of Porter's study. One such cluster is the German textile and apparel sector, which includes high-quality cotton, wool, synthetic fibers, sewing machine needles, and a wide range of textile machinery.

Intensity of Rivalry. The fourth broad attribute of national competitive advantage in Porter's model is the strategy, structure, and rivalry of companies within a nation. Different nations are characterized by different management ideologies that either help or do not help them to build national competitive advantage. For example, the predominance of engineers on the top management teams of German and Japanese companies can be attributed to an emphasis in these countries on improving manufacturing processes and product design. In contrast, people with finance backgrounds dominate the top management teams of many U.S. companies. This might lead to a lack of attention in U.S. companies to improving manufacturing processes and product design. Conversely, the dominance of finance may have led to a corresponding overemphasis on maximizing short-term financial returns. One consequence of these different management ideologies has been a relative loss of U.S. competitiveness in many engineering-based industries where manufacturing processes and product design issues are all important, such as automobiles. A second issue is a strong association between vigorous domestic rivalry and the creation and persistence of competitive advantage in an industry. Rivalry induces companies to look for ways to improve efficiency, which makes them better international competitors. Domestic rivalry creates pressures to innovate, improve quality, reduce costs, and invest in upgrading advanced factors. All this helps to create world-class competitors. The stimulating effects of strong domestic competition are clear in the story of the rise of Nokia of Finland in the market for wireless handsets and telephone equipment (see Strategy in Action 2.3).

Summary of Chapter

1. An industry can be defined as a group of companies offering products or services that are close substitutes for each other. Close substitutes are products or services that satisfy the same basic customer needs.

2. The main technique used to analyze competition in the industry environment is the five forces model. The five forces are (1) the risk of new entry by potential competitors, (2) the extent of rivalry among established firms, (3) the bargaining power of buyers, (4) the bargaining power of suppliers, and (5) the threat of substitute products. The stronger each force is, the more competitive the industry and the lower the rate of return that can be earned.

3. The risk of entry by potential competitors is a function of the height of barriers to entry. The higher the barriers to entry are, the lower is the risk of entry and the greater are the profits that can be earned in the industry.

4. The extent of rivalry among established companies is a function of an industry's competitive structure, demand conditions, and barriers to exit. Strong demand conditions moderate the competition among established companies and create opportunities for expansion. When demand is weak, intensive competition can develop, particularly in consolidated industries with high exit barriers.

5. Buyers are most powerful when a company depends on them for business but they themselves are not dependent on the company. In such circumstances, buyers are a threat.

6. Suppliers are most powerful when a company depends on them for business but they themselves are not dependent on the company. In such circumstances, suppliers are a threat.

7. Substitute products are the products of companies serving customer needs similar to the needs served by the industry being analyzed. The more similar the substitute products are to each other, the lower is the price that companies can charge without losing customers to the substitutes.

8. Some argue for a sixth competitive force of some significance: the power, vigor, and competence of complementors. Powerful and vigorous complementors may have a strong positive impact on demand in an industry.

9. Most industries are composed of strategic groups: groups of companies pursuing the same or a similar strategy. Companies in different strategic groups pursue different strategies.

10. The members of a company's strategic group constitute its immediate competitors. Because different strategic groups are characterized by different opportunities and threats, it may pay a company to switch strategic groups. The feasibility of doing so is a function of the height of mobility barriers.

11. Industries go through a well-defined life cycle: from an embryonic stage, through growth, shakeout, and maturity, and eventually decline. Each stage has different implications for the competitive structure of the industry, and each gives rise to its own set of opportunities and threats.

12. The five forces, strategic group, and industry life cycles models all have limitations. The five forces and strategic group models present a static picture of competition that deemphasizes the role of innovation. Yet innovation can revolutionize industry structure and completely change the strength of different competitive forces. The five forces and strategic group models have been criticized for deemphasizing the importance of individual company differences. A company will not be profitable just because it is based in an attractive industry or strategic group; much more is required. The industry life cycle model is a generalization that is not always followed, particularly when innovations revolutionize an industry.

13. The macroenvironment affects the intensity of rivalry within an industry. Included in the macroenvironment are the macroeconomic environment, the technological environment, the demographic and social environment, and the political and legal environment.

14. The global environment has been changing rapidly in recent years. A fundamental change is occurring in the world economy: the globalization of production and of markets. The consequences of this change include more intense rivalry, more rapid innovation, and shorter product life cycles.

15. There is a link between the national environment and the competitive advantage of a company in the global economy.

Discussion Questions

1. Under what environmental conditions are price wars most likely to occur in an industry? What are the implications of price wars for a company? How should a company try to deal with the threat of a price war?

2. Discuss Porter's five forces model with reference to what you know about the U.S. airline industry. What does the model tell you about the level of competition in this industry?

3. Identify a growth industry, a mature industry, and a declining industry. For each industry, identify the following: (a) the number and size distribution of companies, (b) the nature of barriers to entry, (c) the height of barriers to entry, and (d) the extent of product differentiation. What do these factors tell you about the nature of competition in each industry?

What are the implications for the company in terms of opportunities and threats?

4. Assess the impact of macroenvironmental factors on the likely level of enrollment at your university over the next decade. What are the implications of these factors for the job security and salary level of your professors?

Practicing Strategic Management

SMALL-GROUP EXERCISE: COMPETING WITH MICROSOFT

Break up into groups of three to five people, and appoint one group member as a spokesperson who will communicate your findings to the class.

You are a group of managers and software engineers at a small start-up. You have developed a revolutionary new operating system for personal computers that offers distinct advantages over Microsoft's Windows operating system: it takes up less memory space on the hard drive of a personal computer; it takes full advantage of the power of the personal computer's microprocessor, and in theory can run software applications much faster than Windows; it is much easier to install and use than Windows; and it responds to voice instructions with an accuracy of 99.9 percent, in addition to input from a keyboard or mouse. The operating system is the only product offering that your company has produced.

Complete the following exercises:

1. Analyze the competitive structure of the market for personal computer operating systems. On the basis of this analysis, identify what factors might inhibit adoption of your operating system by customers.

2. Can you think of a strategy that your company might pursue, either alone or in conjunction with other enterprises, in order to "beat Microsoft"? What will it take to execute that strategy successfully?

ARTICLE FILE 2

Find an example of an industry that has become more competitive in recent years. Identify the reasons for the increase in competitive pressure.

STRATEGIC MANAGEMENT PROJECT: MODULE 2

This module requires you to analyze the industry environment in which your company is based using the information you have already gathered:

1. Apply the five forces model to the industry in which your company is based. What does this model tell you about the nature of competition in the industry?

2. Are any changes taking place in the macroenvironment that might have an impact, positive or negative, on the industry in which your company is based? If so, what are these changes, and how might they affect the industry?

3. Identify any strategic groups that might exist in the industry. How does the intensity of competition differ across these strategic groups?

4. How dynamic is the industry in which your company is based? Is there any evidence that innovation is reshaping competition or has done so in the recent past?

5. In what stage of its life cycle is the industry in which your company is based? What are the implications of this for the intensity of competition both now and in the future?

6. Is your company based in an industry that is becoming more global? If so, what are the implications of this change for competitive intensity?

7. Analyze the impact of national context as it pertains to the industry in which your company is based. Does national context help or hinder your company in achieving a competitive advantage in the global marketplace?

EXPLORING THE WEB
Visiting Boeing and Airbus

Visit the web sites of the Boeing Corporation (**http://www.boeing.com**) and Airbus Industrie (**http://www.airbus.com**). Go to the news features of both sites, and read through the press releases issued by both companies. Also look at the annual reports and company profile (or history features) contained on both sites. With this material as your guide:

1. Use Porter's five forces model to analyze the nature of competition in the global commercial jet aircraft market.

2. Assess the likely outlook for competition over the next ten years in this market. Try to establish whether new entry into this industry is likely, whether demand will grow or shrink, how powerful buyers are likely to become, and what the implications of all this are for the nature of competition ten years out.

General Task: Search the Web for information that allows you to assess the current state of competition in the market for personal computers. Use that information to perform an analysis of the structure of the market in the United States. (Hint: Try visiting the web sites of personal computer companies. Also visit Electronic Business Today at **http://www.ebtmag.com**).

Closing Case

How the Internet Revolutionized the Stockbrokerage Industry

For years, only professional stockbrokers with expensive computer hardware could trade online. An individual investor who wanted to buy or sell a stock had to call a stockbroker and place an order, for which the stockbroker would charge a commission. At full-service stockbrokers such as Merrill Lynch, which offer clients detailed research reports, stock recommendations, and financial planning services, these commissions could run to 2.5 percent of the value of the order. Thus, an order worth $10,000 could generate $250 in commissions.

The situation began to change in 1994 when a small discount broker, K. Aufhauser & Co., took advantage of new technology to become the first to offer its clients the ability to trade online over the Internet, effectively bypassing stockbrokers. The offering allowed Aufhauser to operate with fewer personnel, and the cost saving was passed on to customers in the form of lower commissions. At first, online trading was nothing more than a curiosity, but several things changed this. First, the Internet started to make rapid inroads into the homes of individual Americans. Second, within a short space of time, a vast amount of investment information was being offered on the Internet. Individual investors soon found that they could go to sites such as the Motley Fool at America Online or Yahoo's finance site and get much of the information that they needed to make informed investment decisions. No longer did they have to call their stockbrokers to ask for information. Third, a number of small companies quickly followed Aufhauser's lead and took advantage of the Internet to offer their clients online trading for commissions that were significantly below those offered by full-service stockbrokers in the physical world. Finally, America's long bull market drew ever more individuals into the stock market, particularly among America's large baby boom generation, who were drawn to

investing in order to build up funds for retirement. Increasingly, these newcomers set up online trading accounts.

The effects of these trends were dramatic. By mid-2000, 150 firms were offering online trading over the Internet. Many of these companies did not even exist six years before. The arrival of the Internet had lowered barriers to entry and allowed these companies to enter the stockbrokerage industry and compete against established brokers. As the competition for the business of online investors started to heat up, commissions started to fall. By early 1999, online brokerages such as E*Trade were charging deep discount fees of $14.95 per market order for trades of up to 5,000 shares. Thus, whereas an order for 1,000 shares of a stock trading at $20 a share could cost the client of a full-service broker as much as $500 in commission, the same trade could be executed over E*Trade for $14.95! Attracted by such low prices, from little more than a trickle in 1994, the volume of online trades grew to account for 40 percent of all stock trades by individuals as of mid-2000. Discount broker Charles Schwab emerged as the leader of this new segment, with eight out of ten online trades in 2000 being executed by Schwab.

At first, full-service brokers derided online trading as dangerous and justified their high commissions by claiming that they offered their clients sound financial advice and proprietary research reports. However, with as many as 40 percent of all stockbrokers lacking much in the way of experience and with the rapid increase in the amount of investment information that could be accessed online, such arguments sounded increasingly shrill and self-serving. By early 1999, it was becoming apparent that full-service brokers needed to adapt to the new technology or risk seeing their client base evaporate.

The landmark event occurred in June 1999 when Merrill Lynch, the world's largest full-service broker, bowed to the inevitable and announced that it too would soon offer its clients the ability to trade online for a fee of $29.95 for trades of up to 1,000 shares. In addition, Merrill Lynch changed its pricing structure for many individual clients, replacing a fee structure that was based on the number of trades with a new flat fee that allowed unlimited numbers of trades. An internal Merrill report estimated that as a result, its army of 14,800 well-paid stockbrokers, who were paid chiefly in commissions, might initially see their incomes decline by 18 percent as a result of this move. Merrill knew that it faced a potential rebellion from its stockbrokers, but it also knew that it had no choice: forecasts suggested that more than 50 percent of stock trades by individuals would be online by 2001. The early results suggest that Merrill did the right thing. Soon after the introduction of Merrill's online trading service, account transfers to rival firms dried. Many of Merrill's clients realized that the combination of its research and online trading made it a better value proposition than discount online trading houses, such as E*Trade, which could not offer the same depth and breadth of research.

In late 2000, the online trading revolution appeared to stall when the NASDAQ stock market began what would prove to be a 60 percent decline in value over the next twelve months. As the stock market imploded, the volume of online trading dried up. Schwab saw online trading volumes drop over 50 percent in the first six months of 2001, which decimated the company's bottom line, leading to a 60 percent fall in net income. The same happened at other former high-flying Internet stockbro-kers, including E*Trade, which lost money in 2001 on a 40 percent decline in online trading volume and declining revenues. It remains to be seen whether this represents nothing more than a temporary setback in the rise of online trading, or the end of the boom.

Sources: C. Gasparino and R. Buckman, "Horning In: Facing Internet Threat Merrill to Offer Trading Online for Low Fee," *Wall Street Journal,* June 1, 1999, p. A1. "Bears or Bulls, More and More People Are Trading Shares Online," *Economist,* October 17, 1998. L. N. Spiro and E. C. Baig, "Who Needs a Broker?" *Business Week,* February 22, 1999, p. 113. "A Reluctant Success," *Economist,* June 9, 2001, pp. 79–80. M. J. Ybarra, "The Brokerage Blues," *Upside* (August 2001): 46–51.

Discussion Questions

1. How did the rise of the Internet alter competitive forces in the brokerage industry?

2. How does the rise of online brokers change the likely long-term profitability of the stockbrokerage industry?

3. How did the change in competitive forces in the brokerage industry change the strategies required for success in that industry?

4. Do you think the decline in online trading volumes observed in 2001 represents the highwater market for the rise of online trading, or is it simply a temporary setback?

5. What was Merrill Lynch's strategy for gaining the business of individual investors in the pre-Internet era? What is the strategy today? What should be the strategy in the future?

3

Internal Analysis: Distinctive Competencies, Competitive Advantage, and Profitability

Opening Case

BJ'S Wholesale-Competitive Advantage

BJ's Wholesale is a membership-based warehouse club that, like its main competitors, Costco and Wal-Mart's Sam's Club, offers fee-paying members a limited selection of low-priced products across a wide range of merchandise categories. The typical warehouse club carries 4,000 items compared to 40,000 to 60,000 items at discount retailers and supermarkets. The warehouse club business model is aimed at driving down operating costs to enable the club to charge lower prices than those found at other retail establishments and still be profitable. Warehouse clubs lower their cost structure by purchasing in large volumes, maximizing inventory turnover, achieving efficient distribution, and reduced handling of merchandise in no-frills, self-service warehouse facilities.

BJ's is currently the best performer in the highly competitive warehouse club segment of the U.S. retail industry. Founded in 1984, it has grown to over 120 stores, most of them concentrated in the northeastern United States (Costco and Sam's Club both have over 400 stores). In 2001, BJ's generated $5.3 billion in sales, an increase of 15 percent over 2000. Not only has the company grown rapidly, it has also done so profitably. In 2001, its return on invested capital (ROIC) was 19 percent compared to 13.5 percent for Wal-Mart, 11 percent for Costco, and an average for the retail industry of 10 percent. Moreover, this performance was not a one-time event: BJ's ROIC has outperformed that of the industry and its closest competitors every year since 1996.

How does BJ's achieve its superior profitability? By buying in bulk, BJ's is able to get deep price discounts from merchandise vendors, lowering its cost of goods sold. Moreover, because it also sells its own label products, it is able to use this as a lever to bargain down the prices it pays for branded merchandise. BJ's eliminates many of the merchandise handling costs associated with traditional multiple-step distribution channels by purchasing full truckloads of merchandise directly from manufacturers and storing merchandise on the sales floor rather than in central warehouses. In essence, BJ's devotes far less space to storing inventory than traditional retailers do, thereby driving down its investments in property, plant, and equipment relative to its sales base and driving up its ROIC. BJ's warehouses have minimal fixtures, which also reduces investments in property plant and equipment relative to sales and increases the company's return on capital. Moreover, because its high sales volume leads to rapid inventory turnover, it generates cash from the sale of a large portion of inventory before it is required to pay its merchandise vendors, thereby reducing its working capital and boosting its ROIC.

Although these strategies help explain its superior performance, Costco and Sam's Club operate with a similar business model. So what does BJ's do differently from competitors that explain its superior profitability? First, unlike Costco, BJ's pursues a clustering strategy and places its stores close to each other so that they *cannibalize* sales from each other. By doing this, BJ's can maximize the efficiency of its distribution system, and this increases profitability. BJ's strong presence in a locality also maximizes opportunities for word-of-mouth advertising, which reduces the need for costly advertising, which also increases profitability. Finally, it combines purchases for nearby clubs and ships them on a same-day basis, which results in higher volume discounts, reduced freight expenses, and lower receiving costs.

Second, BJ's focuses on only smaller towns and suburban locations outside cities, which tend to be less expensive than the larger urban locations favored by its competitors, thereby reducing BJ's investment in stores and increasing its profitability. The average BJ's location is 111,000 square feet, 20 percent less than Costco and 10 percent less than Sam's Club. Although the average Costco store racks up twice the sales of the average BJ's store ($100 million versus $43 million), due to differences in location and store size costs, the average breakeven sales figure for a Costco store is $45 million, or 45 percent of average sales, compared to $17 million at BJ's, or 39 percent of average sales. Lower breakeven sales figures translate into higher profitability.

Third, BJ's has tried to differentiate itself by focusing on and catering to the needs of individual retail customers. In contrast, its competitors focus on both small business and individuals. To do this, BJ's carries more merchandise items than its competitors do: 6,000 on average versus 4,000 each at Costco and Sam's Club. Thus, BJ's might carry four or five styles of TVs compared to one or two at Costco. BJ's believes that its wider selection appeals more to retail customers and allows it to charge slightly higher prices than Costco and Sam's Club. Whereas Costco operates with markups on goods in the 8 to 12 percent range, BJ's places markups as high as 15 percent of goods. This retail customer orientation also led BJ's to be the first warehouse store to accept credit cards and debit cards (to keep costs down, Costco and Sam's Club were long a cash- or check-only operation). The suburban location strategy also ties into BJ's focus on retail customers.

Finally, BJ's has been a leader in investments in information technology. It was the first warehouse club to introduce scanning devices that work in conjunction with electronic point of sale (EPOS) terminals, which have enabled it to streamline its reordering and payments systems. BJ's analyzes sales data daily for stock replenishment purposes. The efficiencies gained have allowed it to employ fewer people. The company has lowered its payroll as a percentage of sales in each of the past three years, which has translated into lower sales expenses and greater profitability. BJ's has also used its information systems to collect detailed purchasing data on individual members. This permits buying staff and store managers to track changes in members' buying behavior, altering stocking accordingly to meet customer needs better.

Thus, through its distinctive approach to doing business—its focus on providing a broader range of products for individual retail customers in suburban locations and its aggressive use of information systems—BJ's has been able to achieve higher profitability than its competitors in the sector.

Sources: BJ's Wholesale, 2000 10K Report. Costco Wholesale 2001 10K Report. K. Clark, "Two Strategies, One Popular Segment," *Chain Store Age* (November 2001): 56–58. M. Prior, "The Super Growth Leaders," *DSN Retailing*, December 10, 2001, pp. 29–30.

Overview

Why, within a particular industry or market, do some companies outperform others? What is the basis of their (sustained) competitive advantage?

The *Opening Case* provides some clues to the sources of competitive advantage. The conclusion from its description of how BJ's operates is that BJ's competitive advantage derives from the *distinctive way its managers have pursued the warehouse club business model and the way they have combined specific strategies to give BJ's superior efficiency, responsiveness to customers, and innovation.* As you will see in this chapter, three of the four main building blocks of competitive advantage are *efficiency, innovation,* and *responsiveness to customers;* the fourth is the *quality of product or service offering.*

This chapter focuses on internal analysis, which is concerned with identifying the *strengths* and *weaknesses* of the company. Together with an analysis of the company's external environment, internal analysis gives managers the information they need to choose the strategies and business model that will enable their company to attain a sustained competitive advantage. Internal analysis is a three-step process. First, managers must understand the process by which companies create value for customers and profit for themselves, and they need to understand the role of *resources, capabilities,* and *distinctive competencies* in this process. Second, they need to understand how important superior *efficiency, innovation, quality,* and *responsiveness to customers* are in creating value and generating high profitability. Third, they must be able to analyze the sources of their company's competitive advantage to identify what is driving the profitability of their enterprise and where opportunities for improvement might lie. In other words, they must be able to identify how the *strengths* of the enterprise boost its profitability and how any *weaknesses* lead to lower profitability.

Three more critical issues in internal analysis are addressed in this chapter. First, what factors influence the *durability* of competitive advantage? Second, why do successful companies often lose their competitive advantage? Third, how can companies avoid competitive failure and sustain their competitive advantage over time?

After reading this chapter, you will understand the nature of competitive advantage and why managers need to perform internal analysis, just as they must conduct industry analysis, to achieve superior performance and profitability.

Distinctive Competencies and Competitive Advantage

A company has a *competitive advantage* over its rivals when its profitability is greater than the average profitability for all companies in its industry. It has a *sustained competitive advantage* when it is able to maintain above-average profitability over a number of years. Figure 3.1 compares BJ's profitability (measured by return on invested capital, ROIC) against that of several other well-known retailers for the period 1996–2001. BJ's outperformed all of them, including Wal-Mart, the world's largest retailer, which also enjoys superior profitability. BJ's profitability was 50 percent higher than the average for the U.S. retail industry during this period: it had a competitive advantage. What are the sources of BJ's competitive advantage and superior profitability, or that of any other company? Moreover, what is the link between strategy, competitive advantage, and profitability?

Strategy, Distinctive Competencies, and Competitive Advantage

The primary objective of strategy is to achieve a competitive advantage because then superior profitability will follow. Thus, strategy is the driver of competitive advantage and profitability. All the levels of strategy identified in Chapter 1—functional, business, global, and corporate—are involved in creating a competitive advantage, and they are discussed in detail in the next chapters. No matter what the level, however,

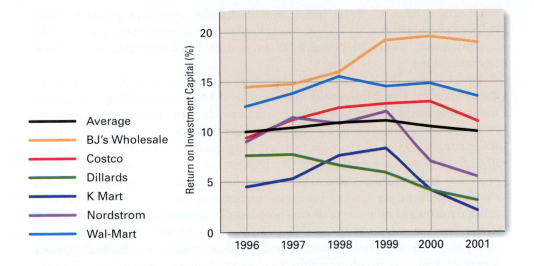

FIGURE 3.1

Profitability in the U. S. Retail Industry, 1996–2001

to use strategy to achieve a competitive advantage, a company must create distinctive competencies.

Distinctive competencies are firm-specific strengths that allow a company to *differentiate* its products and/or achieve substantially *lower costs* than its rivals and thus gain a competitive advantage. It can be argued, for example, that Toyota has distinctive competencies in the development and operation of manufacturing processes. Toyota pioneered a whole range of manufacturing techniques, such as just-in-time inventory systems, self-managing teams, and reduced setup times for complex equipment. These competencies, collectively known as the Toyota *lean production* system, helped it attain superior efficiency and product quality, which are the basis of its competitive advantage in the global automobile industry.[1] Distinctive competencies arise from two complementary sources: *resources* and *capabilities*.[2]

Resources. **Resources** are the capital or financial, physical, social or human, technological, and organizational factor endowments that allow a company to create value for its customers. Company resources can be divided into two types: tangible and intangible resources. **Tangible resources** are something physical, such as land, buildings, plant, equipment, inventory, and money. **Intangible resources** are nonphysical entities that are the creation of the company and its employees, such as brand names, the reputation of the company, the knowledge that employees have gained through experience, and the intellectual property of the company, including patents, copyrights, and trademarks.

The more *firm specific* and *difficult to imitate* is a resource, the more likely a company is to have a distinctive competency. For example, Polaroid's distinctive competency in instant photography was based on a firm-specific and valuable intangible resource: technological know-how in instant film processing that was protected from imitation by a thicket of patents. Once a process can be imitated, as when patents expire, or a superior technology, such as digital photography, comes along, the distinctive competency disappears, as has happened to Polaroid. Another important quality of a resource that leads to a distinctive competency is that it is *valuable:* in some way, it helps to create strong *demand* for the company's products. Thus, Polaroid's technological know-how was valuable while it created strong demand for its photographic products; it became far less valuable when superior digital technology came along.

Capabilities. **Capabilities** refer to a company's skills at coordinating its resources and putting them to productive use. These skills reside in an organization's rules, routines, and procedures, that is, the style or manner through which it makes decisions and manages its internal processes to achieve organizational objectives. More generally, a company's capabilities are the product of its organizational structure, processes, and control systems. They specify how and where decisions are made within a company, the kind of behaviors the company rewards, and the company's cultural norms and values. (We discuss how organizational structure and control systems help a company obtain capabilities in Chapters 12 and 13.) Capabilities are intangible. They reside not so much in individuals as in the way individuals interact, cooperate, and make decisions within the context of an organization.[3]

A Critical Distinction. The distinction between resources and capabilities is critical to understanding what generates a distinctive competency. A company may have firm-specific and valuable resources, but unless it has the capability to use those resources effectively, it may not be able to create a distinctive competency. It is also important to recognize that a company may not need firm-specific and valuable resources to establish a distinctive competency so long as it *does have* capabilities that no competitor possesses. For example, the steel mini-mill operator Nucor is widely acknowledged to be the most cost-efficient steel maker in the United States. Its distinctive competency in low-cost steel making does not come from any firm-specific and valuable resources. Nucor has the same resources (plant, equipment, skilled employees, know-how) as many other mini-mill operators. What distinguishes Nucor is its unique capability to manage its resources in a highly productive way. Specifically, Nucor's structure, control systems, and culture promote efficiency at all levels within the company.

In sum, for a company to have a distinctive competency it must at a minimum have either (1) a firm-specific and valuable resource and the capabilities (skills) necessary to take advantage of that resource (as illustrated by Polaroid) or (2) a firm-specific capability to manage resources (as exemplified by Nucor). A company's distinctive competency is strongest when it possesses *both* firm-specific and valuable resources and firm-specific capabilities to manage those resources.

Figure 3.2 illustrates the relationship of a company's strategies, distinctive competencies, and competitive advantage. Distinctive competencies shape the strategies that the company pursues, which lead to competitive advantage and superior profitability. However, it is also very important to realize that the strategies a company adopts can build new resources and capabilities or strengthen the existing resources and capabilities of the company, thereby enhancing the distinctive competencies of the enterprise. Thus, the relationship between distinctive competencies and strategies is not a linear one; rather, it is a reciprocal one in which distinctive competencies shape strategies, and strategies help to build and create distinctive competencies.[4] The history of The Walt Disney Company since the 1980s illustrates the way this process works.

In the early 1980s, Disney suffered a string of poor financial years that culminated in a 1984 management shakeup when Michael Eisner was appointed CEO. Four years

FIGURE 3.2

Strategy, Resources, Capabilities, and Competencies

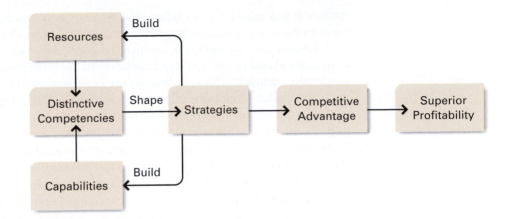

later, Disney's sales had increased from $1.66 billion to $3.75 billion, its net profits from $98 million to $570 million, and its stock market valuation from $1.8 billion to $10.3 billion. What brought about this transformation was the company's deliberate attempt to use its resources and capabilities more aggressively: Disney's enormous film library, its brand name, and its filmmaking skills, particularly in animation. Under Eisner, many old Disney classics were re-released, first in movie theaters and then on video, earning the company millions in the process. Then Eisner reintroduced the product that had originally made Disney famous: the full-length animated feature. Putting together its brand name and in-house animation capabilities, Disney produced a stream of major box office hits, including *The Little Mermaid, Beauty and the Beast, Aladdin, Pocahontas,* and *The Lion King.* Disney also started a cable television channel, the Disney Channel, to use this library and capitalize on the company's brand name. In other words, Disney's existing resources and capabilities shaped its strategies.

Through his choice of strategies, Eisner also developed new competencies in different parts of the business. In the filmmaking arm of Disney, for example, Eisner created a new low-cost film division under the Touchstone label, and the company had a string of low-budget box office hits. It entered into a long-term agreement with the computer animation company Pixar to develop a competency in computer-generated animated films. This strategic collaboration has produced several hits, including *Toy Story* and *Monsters Incorporated.* In sum, Disney's transformation was based not only on strategies that took advantage of the company's existing resources and capabilities, but also on strategies that built new resources and capabilities, such as those that underlie the company's competency in computer-generated animated films.

Competitive Advantage, Value Creation, and Profitability

Competitive advantage leads to superior profitability. At the most basic level, how profitable a company becomes depends on three factors: (1) the amount of *value* customers place on the company's products, (2) the *price* that a company charges for its products, and (3) the *costs* of creating that value. Note the important distinction between *value* and *price*. *Value* is something that customers assign to a product. It is a function of the attributes of the product, such as its performance, design, quality, and point-of-sale and after-sale service. For example, most customers would place a much higher value on a top-end Lexus car from Toyota than on a low-end basic economy car from General Motors, precisely because they perceive the Lexus to have better performance and superior design, quality, and service. A company that strengthens the value of its products in the eyes of customers gives it more *pricing options:* it can raise prices to reflect that value or hold prices lower, which induces more customers to purchase its product and expand unit sales volume.

Whatever pricing option a company chooses, however, the price a company charges for a good or service is typically less than the value placed on that good or service by the customer. This is so because the customer captures some of that value in the form of what economists call a *consumer surplus.*[5] The customer is able to do this because the company is competing with other companies for the customer's business, so the company must charge a lower price than it could were it a monopoly supplier. Moreover, it is normally impossible to segment the market to such a degree that the company can charge each customer a price that reflects that individual's unique assessment of the value of a product—what economists refer to as a customer's *reservation price.* For these reasons, the price that gets charged tends to be less than the value placed on the product by many customers. Nevertheless, remember the basic principle here: *the more value a company creates, the more pricing options it has.*

These concepts are illustrated in Figure 3.3: *V* is the average value per unit of a product to a customer, *P* is the average price per unit that the company decides to charge for that product, and *C* is the average unit costs of producing that product (including actual production costs and the cost of capital investments in production systems). The company's average profit per unit is equal to $P - C$, and the consumer surplus is equal to $V - P$. The company makes a profit so long as *P* is more than *C*, and its profitability will be greater the lower *C* is *relative* to *P*. Bear in mind that the difference between *V* and *P* is in part determined by the intensity of competitive pressure in the market place; the lower the intensity of competitive pressure is, the higher the price that can be charged relative to *V* is, but it is also determined by the company's pricing choice.[6] As we shall see, a company may choose to keep prices low relative to volume because lower prices enable the company to sell more products, attain scale economies, and boost its profit margin by lowering *C* relative to *P*.

Note also that the *value created* by a company is measured by the difference between perceived value (*V*) and costs of production (*C*), that is $V - C$. A company creates value by converting factors of production that cost *C* into a product on which customers place a value of *V*. A company can create more value for its customers by lowering *C* or making the product more attractive through superior design, performance, quality, service and the like. When customers place a greater value on the product (*V* increases), they are willing to pay a higher price (*P* increases). This discussion suggests that a company has a competitive advantage and high profitability when it creates more value for its customers than do rivals.[7]

FIGURE 3.3

Value Creation per Unit

V = **Value** to consumer
P = **Price**
C = **Costs** of production
$V - P$ = Consumer surplus
$P - C$ = **Profit** margin
$V - C$ = **Value** created

Includes **cost** of capital per unit

The company's pricing options are captured in Figure 3.4. Suppose a company's current pricing option is the one pictured in the middle column of Figure 3.4. Imagine that the company decides to pursue strategies to increase the perceived value of its product offering from V to V^* in order to boost its profitability. Increasing value initially raises production costs because the company has to spend money to increase product performance, quality, service, and other factors. Now there are two different pricing options that the company can pursue. Option 1 is to raise prices to reflect the higher value: the company raises prices more than its costs increase, and profit margins $(P - C)$ increase. Option 2 involves a very different set of choices: the company *lowers* prices in order to expand unit volume. Basically, what is happening here is that customers recognize that they are getting a great bargain because price is now much lower than value (the *consumer surplus* has increased) so they rush out to buy more (*demand* had increased). As unit volume expands due to increased demand, the company is able to realize scale economies and reduce its average unit costs. The net result is although prices are lowered and creating the extra value initially cost more, the average unit costs of production fall as volume increases and scale economies are attained, so profit margins widen.

Of course, there are more pricing options than those illustrated in Figure 3.4. For example, the company could have held prices constant, raised prices by less than illustrated in Option 1, or expanded profit margins by simultaneously raising prices and realizing some cost scale economies from a higher unit volume. What a company does depends on its industry environment and its business model, issues considered in the following chapters.

For now, the important point is that managers must understand the dynamic relationships among *value, pricing, demand,* and *costs* and make decisions on the basis of that understanding to maximize competitive advantage and profitability. Option 2 in Figure 3.4, for example, might not be a viable strategy if demand did not increase rapidly with lower prices or if there are few economies of scale to be had by increasing volume. Managers must understand the impact of value creation and pricing decisions on demand and how unit costs change with increases in volume. In other words, they must have a good grasp of the demand for the company's product and its

FIGURE 3.4

Value Creation and
Pricing Options

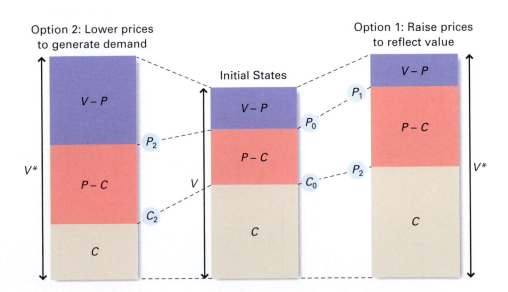

cost structure at different levels of output if they are to make decisions that maximize profitability.

Consider the automobile industry. According to a study by Harbour & Associates, in 2001 Toyota made $900 profit on every vehicle it manufactured in North America. General Motors, in contrast, made only $176 profit per vehicle. What accounts for the difference? First, Toyota has the best reputation for quality in the industry. According to annual surveys issued by J. D. Power, Toyota consistently tops the list in terms of quality, while GM cars are at best in the middle of the pack. The higher quality translates into a higher value and allows Toyota to charge 5 to 10 percent higher prices than General Motors for equivalent cars. Second, Toyota has a lower cost per vehicle than General Motors, due in part to superior labor productivity. For example, in Toyota's North American plants, it took an average of 31.06 employee hours to build a car in 2001, compared to 40.52 at GM plants in North America. That 9.5 hour productivity advantage translates into much lower labor costs for Toyota and, hence, a lower overall cost structure. Hence, as summarized in Figure 3.5, Toyota's advantage over GM derives from greater perceived value (V), which has allowed the company to charge a higher price (P) for its cars, and from a lower cost structure (C), which taken together implies significantly greater profitability per vehicle ($P - C$).

Toyota's decisions with regard to pricing are guided by its managers' understanding of the relationship of value, prices, demand, and costs. Given its ability to create more value, Toyota could have charged even higher prices than illustrated in Figure 3.5, but that might have led to lower sales volume, fewer scale economies, higher unit costs, and lower profit margins. Toyota's managers have sought to find the pricing option that enables the company to maximize its profitability given their assessment of demand for its products and its cost function. Thus, superior value creation does not necessarily require a company to have the lowest cost structure in an industry or to create the most valuable product in the eyes of customers. Rather, it requires that the gap between perceived value (V) and costs of production (C) be greater than the gap attained by competitors.

Differentiation and Cost Structure   Note that Toyota has *differentiated* itself from General Motors by its superior quality, which allows it to charge higher prices, and its *lower cost structure*. Thus, its competitive advantage over General Motors is the result of strategies that have led to distinctive competencies, resulting in greater *differentiation* and a lower *cost structure*.[8]

Indeed, at the heart of any company's business model is the combination of strategies aimed at creating distinctive competencies that (1) *differentiate* its products in some way so it creates more *value* for customers, which gives it more pricing

FIGURE 3.5

Comparing Toyota and General Motors

FIGURE 3.6

The Roots of Competitive Advantage

options, and (2) result in a *lower cost structure,* which also gives it a broader range of pricing choices.[9] Achieving a sustained competitive advantage and superior profitability requires the right choices with regard to value creation through differentiation and pricing given the demand conditions in the company's market, and the company's cost structure at different levels of output. This issue is addressed in detail in the following chapters and captured in Figure 3.6.

The Value Chain

All of the functions of a company—such as production, marketing, R&D, service, information systems, materials management, and human resources—have a role in lowering the cost structure and increasing the perceived value of the products through differentiation. As the first step in examining this concept, consider the value chain, which is illustrated in Figure 3.7.[10] The term **value chain** refers to the idea that a company is a chain of activities for transforming inputs into outputs that customers value. The process of transformation is composed of a number of primary activities and support activities that add value to the product.

FIGURE 3.7

The Value Chain

Primary Activities

Primary activities have to do with the design, creation, and delivery of the product, its marketing, and its support and after-sales service. In the value chain illustrated in Figure 3.7, the primary activities are broken down into four functions: research and development, production, marketing and sales, and customer service.

Research and Development. **Research and development** (R&D) is concerned with the design of products and production processes. Although we think of R&D as being associated with the design of physical products and production processes in manufacturing enterprises, many service companies also undertake R&D. For example, banks compete with each other by developing new financial products and new ways of delivering those products to customers. Online banking and smart debit cards are two recent examples of the fruits of new product development in the banking industry. Earlier examples of innovation in the banking industry were ATM machines, credit cards, and debit cards.

By superior product design, R&D can increase the functionality of products, which makes them more attractive to customers by raising value. Alternatively, the work of R&D may result in more efficient production processes, thereby lowering production costs. Either way, the R&D function can help to lower costs or permit a company to charge higher prices. At Intel, for example, R&D creates value by developing ever more powerful microprocessors and helping to pioneer ever more efficient manufacturing processes (in conjunction with equipment suppliers).

Production. **Production** is concerned with the creation of a good or service. For physical products, when we talk about production, we generally mean manufacturing. For services such as banking or retail operations, "production" typically takes place when the service is delivered to the customer, as when a bank makes a loan to a customer. By performing its activities efficiently, the production function of a company helps to lower its cost structure. For example, the efficient production operations of Honda and Toyota help those automobile companies achieve higher profitability relative to competitors such as General Motors. The production function can also perform its activities in a way that is consistent with high product quality, which leads to differentiation (and higher value) and lower costs.

Marketing and Sales. There are several ways in which the **marketing and sales** functions of a company can help to create value. Through brand positioning and advertising, the marketing function can increase the value that customers perceive to be contained in a company's product. Insofar as these help to create a favorable impression of the company's product in the minds of customers, they increase value. For example, in the 1980s, the French company Perrier persuaded U.S. customers that slightly carbonated bottled water was worth $1.50 per bottle rather than a price closer to the $0.50 that it cost to collect, bottle, and distribute the water. Perrier's marketing function essentially increased the perception of value that customers ascribed to the product.

Marketing and sales can also create value by discovering customer needs and communicating them back to the R&D function of the company, which can then design products that better match those needs. For another example of value creation by the marketing function of an enterprise, see Strategy in Action 3.1, which looks at how Pfizer's sales force increased the perception of the value associated with one of its main pharmaceuticals, Zoloft.

Strategy in Action   3.1

Value Creation at Pfizer

The antidepressant drug Prozac, introduced by Eli Lilly & Co. in 1988, was one of the most lucrative mental health drugs in history. In 1995, U.S. customers alone filled almost 19 million prescriptions for Prozac, used to mitigate the effects of a wide range of mental disorders, including chronic depression, bulimia, and obsessive disorders. Worldwide sales of the drug topped $2 billion in 1995, making it a gold mine for Lilly.

During the 1990s, Prozac's market position came under attack from an aggressive marketing and sales campaign by rival pharmaceutical company Pfizer. In 1992, Pfizer introduced its own antidepressant, Zoloft. According to medical experts, the differences between Prozac and Zoloft are slight at best. Both drugs function in the same basic manner, by boosting serotonin, a brain chemical believed to be in short supply in many depressed people. Both drugs also have a similar list of possible side effects. Prozac's label cites nausea, nervousness, anxiety, insomnia, and drowsiness as possible side effects. Zoloft's label lists nausea and other stomach problems, diarrhea, sexual dysfunction, and sleepiness. As one expert noted, "These drugs are so similar that you have to be kidding yourself if you think one drug is going to be consistently superior to the other in treating patients."

Despite the similarity between the two products, Pfizer gained share from Lilly in the antidepressant market. By 1998, Zoloft accounted for 40 percent of the market, up from little more than zero in 1992. The main reason for this success seems to have been Pfizer's aggressive marketing and sales campaign, which created an impression in the eyes of physicians that Zoloft is a safer drug. Pfizer sales representatives bill their product as just as effective as Prozac but without its occasional downside, anxiety. The reference to anxiety seems carefully designed to remind doctors of a spate of failed lawsuits alleging that Prozac caused suicides and other violent acts. Pfizer's sales force also logged more "face time" with physicians than Lilly's. According to Scott-Levin and Associates, in 1995 Zoloft sales representatives made 660,000 sales visits to doctors, 70,000 more than the Prozac sales force logged. About three-quarters of these were not to psychiatrists but to basic primary care physicians, who increasingly prescribe antidepressants but presumably are less familiar with their more subtle properties than psychiatrists are. Doctors also claim that Pfizer salespeople play up Prozac's clinical reputation for being more agitating than Zoloft. They also emphasize that unlike Zoloft, Prozac remains in the bloodstream for weeks after a patient stops taking it, raising the possibility of adverse drug interaction if a patient switches to other medications.

The important point here is that Pfizer's marketing and sales force altered physicians' perceptions of the relative value of Prozac and Zoloft. For Pfizer, the payoff came in terms of rapidly increasing revenues and market share and, of course, a greater return on the company's investment in developing Zoloft.

Source: R. Langreth, "High Anxiety: Rivals Threaten Prozac's Reign," *Wall Street Journal*, May 9, 1996, pp. B1–B2.

Customer Service. The role of the **service** function of an enterprise is to provide after-sales service and support. This function can create a perception of superior value in the minds of customers by solving customer problems and supporting customers after they have purchased the product. For example, Caterpillar, the U.S.-based manufacturer of heavy earthmoving equipment, can get spare parts to any point in the world within twenty-four hours, thereby minimizing the amount of downtime its customers have to face if their Caterpillar equipment malfunctions. This is an extremely valuable support capability in an industry where downtime is very expensive. It has helped to increase the value that customers associate with Caterpillar products, and thus the price that Caterpillar can charge for its products.

Support Activities

The **support activities** of the value chain provide inputs that allow the primary activities to take place. These activities are broken down into four functions: materials management, human resources, information systems, and company infrastructure (see Figure 3.7).

Materials Management. The **materials management** (or logistics) function controls the transmission of physical materials through the value chain, from procurement through production and into distribution. The efficiency with which this is carried out can significantly lower cost, thereby creating more value. Wal-Mart, the U.S. retailing giant, reportedly has the most efficient materials management setup in the retail industry. By tightly controlling the flow of goods from its suppliers through its stores and into the hands of customers, Wal-Mart has eliminated the need to hold large inventories of goods. Lower inventories mean lower costs, and hence greater value creation.

Human Resources. There are a number of ways in which the **human resource** function can help an enterprise to create more value. This function ensures that the company has the right mix of skilled people to perform its value-creation activities effectively. It is also the job of the human resource function to ensure that people are adequately trained, motivated, and compensated to perform their value-creation tasks. If the human resources are functioning well, employee productivity rises (which lowers costs) and customer service improves (which raises perceived value), thereby enabling the company to create more value.

Information Systems. **Information systems** refer to the largely electronic systems for managing inventory, tracking sales, pricing products, selling products, dealing with customer service inquiries, and so on. Information systems, when coupled with the communications features of the Internet, are holding out the promise of being able to improve the efficiency and effectiveness with which a company manages its other value-creation activities. For example, Wal-Mart uses information systems to alter the way it does business. By tracking the sale of individual items very closely, its materials management function has enabled it to optimize its product mix and pricing strategy. Wal-Mart is rarely left with unwanted merchandise on its hands, which saves on costs, and the company is able to provide the right mix of goods to customers, which increases the perception of value that customers associate with Wal-Mart.

Company Infrastructure. **Company infrastructure** is the companywide context within which all the other value creation activities take place: the organizational structure, control systems, and company culture. Because top management can exert considerable influence in shaping these aspects of a company, top management should also be viewed as part of the infrastructure of a company. Indeed, through strong leadership, top management can shape the infrastructure of a company and, through that, the performance of all other value-creation activities that take place within it.

The Generic Building Blocks of Competitive Advantage

The four factors that build and sustain competitive advantage—superior efficiency, quality, innovation, and customer responsiveness—are the product of the company's distinctive competencies. In turn, they allow a company to (1) differentiate its product offering, and hence create greater perceived customer value, and (2) lower its cost structure (see Figure 3.8). These factors are *generic* building blocks of competitive advantage: any company, regardless of its industry or the products or services it pro-

FIGURE 3.8

Generic Building Blocks of Competitive Advantage

duces, can pursue them. Although they are discussed sequentially below, they are highly interrelated, and the important ways they affect each other should be noted. For example, superior quality can lead to superior efficiency, and innovation can enhance efficiency, quality, and responsiveness to customers.

Efficiency   In one sense, a business is simply a device for transforming inputs into outputs. Inputs are basic factors of production such as labor, land, capital, management, and technological know-how. Outputs are the goods and services that the business produces. The simplest measure of efficiency is the quantity of inputs that it takes to produce a given output, that is, efficiency = outputs/inputs. The more efficient a company is, the fewer the inputs required to produce a given output. For example, if it takes General Motors thirty hours of employee time to assemble a car and it takes Ford twenty-five hours, we can say that Ford is more efficient than GM. And as long as other things are equal, such as wage rates, we can assume from this information that Ford will have a lower cost structure than GM. Thus, efficiency helps a company attain a competitive advantage through a lower cost structure. Similarly, an analysis of financial statements suggests that in 2000, BJ's Wholesale generated $7.47 of sales for every dollar of capital it invested in its business, whereas Costco generated $6.29 of sales for every dollar of capital it invested in its business. Clearly BJ's is more efficient in its use of capital: it needs less capital (the input) to generate a dollar of sales (the output) than Costco.

As these examples suggest, two of the most important components of efficiency for many companies are employee productivity and capital productivity. *Employee productivity* is usually measured by output per employee and *capital productivity* by output per unit of invested capital (this is discussed in depth in the next section). Holding all else constant, the company with the highest labor and capital productivity in an industry will typically have the lowest cost structure and therefore a cost-based competitive advantage. The concept of productivity is not limited to employee and capital productivity. Pharmaceutical companies, for example, often talk about the productivity of their R&D spending, by which they mean how many new drugs they develop from their investment in R&D. Other companies talk about their sales force productivity, which means how many sales they generate from every sales call, and so on. The important point to remember is that high productivity leads to greater efficiency and lower costs.

Strategy in Action 3.2 looks at how Southwest Airlines has attained its low-cost position in the U.S. airline industry. As you will see, its competitive advantage derives from its superior labor productivity.

Quality: Reliability and Other Attributes

A product can be thought of as a bundle of attributes.[11] For example, the attributes of many physical products include the form, features, performance, durability, reliability, style, and design of the product.[12] A product is said to have *superior quality* when customers perceive there to be greater value in the attributes of a specific product, compared to the same attributes in rival products. For example, a Rolex watch has attributes—such as design, styling, performance, and reliability—that customers perceive as being superior to the same attributes in many other watches. Thus, we can refer to a Rolex as a high-quality product: Rolex has *differentiated* its watches by these attributes.

Among the various attributes of products, one in particular has taken on special significance in the last two decades: *reliability*. A product can be said to be *reliable* when it consistently does the job it was designed for, does it well, and rarely, if ever, breaks down. As we shall see, increasing product reliability has been the central goal of an influential management philosophy that came out of Japan in the 1980s and is commonly referred to as **total quality management.** Because of its unique role in the overall perception of quality, in this book we separate out *reliability* from other attributes of a product when discussing product quality. Thus, we define **quality products** as goods and services that are *reliable* in the sense that they do the job they were designed for and do it well, which increases perceived value, but they are also differentiated by various *attributes* that customers perceive to have a higher value.

The position of a product against these two dimensions, reliability and other attributes, can be plotted on a figure similar to Figure 3.9. For example, a Lexus has attributes—such as design, styling, performance, and safety features—that customers perceive as being superior to those of most other cars. Lexus is also a very reliable car. Thus, the overall level of quality of the Lexus is very high, which creates an impression of value in the minds of customers and gives Toyota the option of charging a premium price for the Lexus. Toyota also produces another very reliable vehicle, the Toyota Corolla, but this is aimed at less wealthy customers and it lacks many of the superior attributes of the Lexus. Thus, although this is also a high-quality car in the sense of being reliable, it is not as high quality as a Lexus. At the other end of the spectrum, we can find poor-quality products that have both low reliability and inferior attributes, such as poor design, performance, and styling. An example is the Yugo, a car that was made in the former Yugoslavia in the 1980s. The Yugo was a boxy, low-powered vehicle aimed at the budget segment of the market, and it had a dismal reputation for styling, reliability, and safety. Thus, its overall quality was very low. A car (or any other product, for that matter) might also have a collection of superior attributes but nevertheless suffer from very poor reliability, which would damage its overall quality.

The concept of quality applies whether we are talking about Toyota automobiles, clothes designed and sold by the Gap, the customer service department of Citibank, or the ability of airlines to arrive on time. Quality is just as relevant to services as it is to goods.[13] The impact of high product quality on competitive advantage is twofold.[14] First, providing high-quality products increases the value of those products in the eyes of customers. This enhanced perception of value gives the company the option of charging a higher price for its products. In the automobile industry, for example, Toyota can charge a higher price for its cars because of the higher quality of

Strategy in Action

Southwest Airlines' Low Cost Structure

3.2

Southwest Airlines has long been one of the standout performers in the U.S. airline industry. It is famous for its low fares, generally some 30 percent below those of its rivals, which are balanced by an even lower cost structure, which has enabled it to record superior profitability even in bad years such as 2001, when the industry faced slumping demand. Southwest was the only airline among the top eight in the United States to show a profit for the quarter immediately following the September 11 terrorist attacks on the World Trade Center and the Pentagon.

A major source of Southwest's low cost structure seems to be its very high employee productivity. One way the airlines measure employee productivity is by the ratio of employees to passengers carried. According to figures from the Air Transport Association, in 2000 Southwest had an employee-to-passenger ratio of 1 to 2,424, followed by Alaska Airlines at 1,518 and Delta Airlines at 1,493. The worst performer among the major U.S. airlines, United, had an employee-to-passenger ratio of 1 to 938 in 2000. These figures suggest that holding size constant, Southwest runs its operation with far fewer people than any of its competitors. How does it do this?

First, Southwest devotes enormous attention to whom it hires. On average, the company hired only 3 percent of those interviewed in a year. When hiring, it places a big emphasis on teamwork and a positive attitude. Southwest rationalizes that skills can be taught, but a positive attitude and a willingness to pitch in cannot. Southwest also creates incentives for its employees to work hard. All employees are covered by a profit-sharing plan, and at least 25 percent of an employee's share of the profit-sharing plan has to be invested in Southwest Air-

lines stock. This gives rise to a simple formula: the harder employees work, the more profitable Southwest becomes, and the richer the employees get. The results are clear. At other airlines, one would never see a pilot helping to check passengers onto the plane. At Southwest, pilots and flight attendants have been known to help clean the aircraft and check in passengers at the gate. They do this to turn around an aircraft as quickly as possible and get it into the air again because an aircraft doesn't make money when it is sitting on the ground.

Southwest also reduces its costs by striving to keep its operations as simple as possible. By operating only one type of plane, the Boeing 737, it reduces training costs, maintenance costs, and inventory costs while increasing efficiency in crew and flight scheduling. The operation is nearly ticketless, which reduces cost and back-office accounting functions. There is no seat assignment, which again reduces costs. There are no meals or movies in flight, and the airline will not transfer baggage to other airlines, reducing the need for baggage handlers. Another major difference between Southwest and most other airlines is that Southwest flies point to point rather than operating from congested airport hubs. As a result, its costs are lower because there is no need for dozens of gates and thousands of employees needed to handle banks of flights that come in and then disperse within a two-hour window, leaving the hub empty until the next flights a few hours later.

Source: M. Brelis, "Simple Strategy Makes Southwest a Model for Success," *Boston Globe,* November 5, 2000, p. F1. Southwest Airlines 10K 2001.

its products. Thus, compared with General Motors, Toyota has had both lower costs and the ability to charge higher prices. As a result, historically it has operated with a bigger profit margin than GM.

The second impact of high quality on competitive advantage comes from the greater efficiency and the lower unit costs associated with *reliable* products. When products are reliable, less employee time is wasted making defective products or providing substandard services and less time has to be spent fixing mistakes, which translates into higher employee productivity and lower unit costs. Thus, high product quality not only enables a company to differentiate its product from that of rivals, but if the product is reliable, it also lowers costs.

FIGURE 3.9

A Quality Map for Automobiles

The importance of reliability in building competitive advantage has increased dramatically over the past decade. Indeed, so crucial is the emphasis placed on reliability by many companies that achieving high product reliability can no longer be viewed as just one way of gaining a competitive advantage. In many industries, it has become an absolute imperative for survival. Strategy in Action 3.3, which looks at the turnaround of Continental Airlines, illustrates the importance of quality in a service environment.

Innovation   **Innovation** refers to the act of creating new products or processes. There are two main types of innovation: product innovation and process innovation. **Product innovation** is the development of products that are new to the world or have superior attributes to existing products. Examples are Intel's invention of the microprocessor in the early 1970s, Cisco's development of the router for routing data over the Internet in the mid-1980s, and Palm's development of the PalmPilot, the first commercially successful hand-held computer, in the mid-1990s. **Process innovation** is the development of a new process for producing products and delivering them to customers. Examples include Toyota, which developed a range of new techniques collectively known as the Toyota *lean production system* for making automobiles: just-in-time inventory systems, self-managing teams, and reduced setup times for complex equipment. Wal-Mart pioneered efforts to use information systems to manage its logistics, product mix, and product pricing, and Staples applied the supermarket business model to the retail office supplies business.

Product innovation creates value by creating new products, or enhanced versions of existing products, that customers perceive as more desirable, thus increasing the company's pricing options. Process innovation often allows a company to create more value by lowering production costs. Toyota's lean production system, for example, helped to boost employee productivity, thus giving Toyota a cost-based competitive advantage.[15] Similarly, Staples' application of the supermarket business model to retail office supplies dramatically lowered the cost of selling office supplies. Staples passed on some of this cost saving to customers in the form of lower prices, which enabled the company to increase its market share rapidly.

Strategy in Action   3.3

Continental Airlines Goes from Worst to First

When Gordon Bethune left Boeing to become the CEO of Continental Airlines in 1994, the company was the worst performing and least profitable of all major U.S. airlines. One of its major problems was the lack of reliability. In 1994, Continental planes arrived on time only 61 percent of the time, placing it dead last in the influential Air Customer Satisfaction Study produced by J. D. Power & Associates. Worse, airline travelers ranked on-time performance the most important factor when deciding which airline to fly on. Reliability was the primary metric passengers used to determine an airline's quality.

Bethune soon came to the conclusion that the prior management had cut costs so far that service had suffered. In his words, "Our service was lousy and nobody knew when a plane might land. We were unpredictable and unreliable, and when you are an airline, where does that leave you? It leaves you with a lot of empty planes. We had a lousy product, and nobody particularly wanted to buy it." Bethune's solution? He told Continental employees that if the airline's on-time performance improved, every employee would receive a $65 bonus. The total cost to the airline was $2.6 million. Bethune was proposing to improve performance by spending more money, and it worked. When the program was launched in January 1995, 71 percent of the planes landed on time. By year end, the figure was up to 80 percent, and Continental had risen to fifth place in its on-time performance. For 1996,

Bethune announced that the airline had to finish third or higher for employees to get the bonus, which he increased to $100. The airline finished second. It has not dropped out of the top three since.

To support the drive to increase reliability, Bethune reorganized the way employees were managed. Out went the employee manual, to be replaced by a new set of guidelines for employees. Under these guidelines, front-line employees were given significant decision-making power to fix customer problems. For example, if a flight is canceled, a customer service agent might have to decide which passengers should receive priority to get on the next flight. Under the old system, the employee would have had to refer to the rule book, and if that did not provide an answer, ask a higher-level manager. This inflexible approach led to significant frustration among both passengers and employees. Under the new system, the customer service agent has been given the power to fix the problem as she sees fit. According to Bethune, concentrating decision-making power in the hands of employees has given them the ability to solve customer problems in creative ways, which has had a dramatic impact on customers' perception of the quality of service they get at Continental.

Source: G. Bethune, "From Worst to First," *Fortune*, May 25, 1998, pp. 185–190.

In the long run, innovation of products and processes is perhaps the most important building block of competitive advantage.[16] Competition can be viewed as a process driven by innovations. Although not all innovations succeed, those that do can be a major source of competitive advantage because, by definition, they give a company something **unique**—something its competitors lack (at least until they imitate the innovation). Uniqueness can allow a company to differentiate itself from its rivals and charge a premium price for its product or, in the case of many process innovations, reduce its unit costs far below those of competitors.

Responsiveness to Customers

To achieve superior responsiveness to customers, a company must be able to do a better job than competitors of identifying and satisfying its customers' needs. Customers will then place more value on its products, creating a differentiation based on competitive advantage. Improving the quality of a company's product offering is consistent with achieving responsiveness, as is developing new products with features that existing products lack. In other words, achieving superior quality and innovation is integral to achieving superior responsiveness to customers.

Another factor that stands out in any discussion of responsiveness to customers is the need to customize goods and services to the unique demands of individual customers or customer groups. For example, the proliferation of soft drinks and beers can be viewed partly as a response to this trend. Automobile companies have become more adept at customizing cars to the demands of individual customers. For instance, following the lead of Toyota, the Saturn division of General Motors builds cars to order for individual customers, letting them choose from a wide range of colors and options.

An aspect of responsiveness to customers that has drawn increasing attention is **customer response time:** the time that it takes for a good to be delivered or a service to be performed.[17] For a manufacturer of machinery, response time is the time it takes to fill customer orders. For a bank, it is the time it takes to process a loan or that a customer must stand in line to wait for a free teller. For a supermarket, it is the time that customers must stand in checkout lines. Customer survey after customer survey has shown slow response time to be a major source of customer dissatisfaction.[18]

Other sources of enhanced responsiveness to customers are superior design, superior service, and superior after-sales service and support. All of these factors enhance responsiveness to customers and allow a company to differentiate itself from its less responsive competitors. In turn, differentiation enables a company to build brand loyalty and charge a premium price for its products. Consider how much more people are prepared to pay for next-day delivery of express mail, as opposed to delivery in three to four days. In 1996, a two-page letter sent by overnight Express Mail within the United States cost about $10, compared with 32 cents for regular mail. Thus, the price premium for express delivery (reduced response time) was $9.68, or a premium of 3,025 percent over the regular price.

Analyzing Competitive Advantage and Profitability

If a company's managers are to perform a good internal analysis, they need to be able to analyze the financial performance of their company, identifying how its strategies contribute (or not) to profitability. To perform this crucial step of identifying strengths and weaknesses effectively, they need to be able to compare, or *benchmark,* the performance of their company against that of competitors and the historic performance of the company itself. This will help them to determine whether they are more or less profitable than competitors and whether the performance of the company has been improving or deteriorating through time; whether their strategies of the company are maximizing the value being created; whether their cost structure is out of line with those of competitors; and whether they are using the resources of the company to the greatest effect.

As we noted in Chapter 1, the key measure of a company's financial performance is its profitability, which captures the return that a company is generating on its investments. Although several different measures of profitability exist, such as return on assets and return on equity, many authorities on the measurement of profitability argue that return on invested capital (ROIC) is the best measure because "it focuses on the true operating performance of the company."[19] ROIC is defined as net profit over invested capital, or ROIC = Net profit/invested capital.

Net profit is calculated by subtracting the total costs of operating the company away from its total revenues (total revenues − total costs). *Net profit* is what is left over before the government takes its share in taxes. *Invested capital* is the amount that is invested in the operations of a company: property, plant, equipment, inventories, and other assets. Invested capital comes from two main sources: interest-bearing debt and shareholders' equity. Interest-bearing debt is money the company borrows from banks and those who purchase its bonds. Shareholders' equity is the money raised from selling shares to the public, *plus* earnings that the company has retained in prior years and are available to fund current investments. ROIC measures the effectiveness with which a company is using the capital funds that it has available for investment. As such, it is recognized to be an excellent measure of the value a company is creating.[20]

A company's ROIC can be algebraically decomposed into two major components: *return on sales* and *capital turnover:*[21] Specifically:

$$\text{ROIC} = \text{Net profits/invested capital}$$
$$= \text{Net profits/revenues} \times \text{revenues/invested capital,}$$

where net profits/revenues is the return on sales, and revenues/invested capital is capital turnover. Return on sales measures how effectively the company converts revenues into profits. Capital turnover measures how effectively the company employs its invested capital to generate revenues. These two ratios can be further decomposed into some basic accounting ratios, as shown in Figure 3.10 (these ratios are defined in Table 3.1).[22]

Figure 3.10 says that a company's managers can increase ROIC by pursuing strategies that increase the company's return on sales. To increase the company's return on sales, they can pursue strategies that reduce the cost of goods sold (COGS) for a given level of sales revenues (COGS/sales); reduce the level of spending on sales force, marketing, general, and administrative expenses (SG&A) for a given level of sales revenues (SG&A/sales); and reduce R&D spending for a given level of sales revenues

TABLE 3.1

Definitions of Basic Accounting Terms

Term	Definition	Source
Cost of goods sold (COGS)	Total costs of manufacturing products	Income statement
Sales, general, and administrative expenses (SG&A)	Costs associated with selling products and administering the company	Income statement
R&D expenses (R&D)	Research and development expenditure	Income statement
Working capital	The amount of money the company has to work with in the short term	Balance sheet
Property, plant, and equipment (PPE)	The value of investments in the property, plant, and equipment that the company uses to manufacture and sell its products; also known as *fixed capital*	Balance sheet
Return on sales (ROS)	Net profit expressed as a percentage of sales; measures how effectively the company converts revenues into profits	Ratio
Capital turnover	Revenues divided by invested capital; measures how effectively the company uses its capital to generate revenues	Ratio
Return on invested capital (ROIC)	Net profit divided by invested capital	Ratio
Net profit	Total revenues minus total costs before tax	Income statement
Invested capital	Interest-bearing debt plus shareholders' equity	Balance sheet

FIGURE 3.10

Drivers of Profitability
(ROIC)

(R&D/sales). Alternatively, they can increase return on sales by pursuing strategies that increase sales revenues more than they increase the costs of the business, as measured by COGS, SG&A, and R&D expenses. That is, they can increase the return on sales by pursuing strategies that *lower costs* or increase value through *differentiation*, and allow the company to increase its prices more than its costs.

Figure 3.10 also tells us that a company's managers can boost the profitability of their company by getting greater sales revenues from their invested capital, thereby increasing capital turnover). They do this by pursuing strategies that reduce the amount of *working capital*, such as the amount of capital invested in inventories, needed to generate a given level of sales (working capital/sales) and then pursuing strategies that reduce the amount of *fixed capital* that they have to invest in plant, property, and equipment (PPE) to generate a given level of sales (PPE/sales). That is, they pursue strategies that reduce the amount of capital that they need to generate every dollar of sales, and thus their cost of capital. Now recall that cost of capital is part of the cost structure of a company (see Figure 3.2), so strategies designed to increase capital turnover also *lower the cost structure*.

To see how these basic drivers of profitability help us to understand what is going on in a company and to identify its strengths and weaknesses, let us return to the *Opening Case* and the example of BJ's Wholesale. BJ's superior profitability can be understood in terms of the impact of its strategies on the various ratios identified in Figure 3.10. Recall first that BJ's is more profitable not only than many other retail establishments, but also than Costco, which has a similar business model and is a direct competitor. In 2000, BJ's ROIC was 19.7 percent, and Costco's was 12.9 percent. The first point to make is that BJ's superior profitability came in part from higher return on sales: 4.34 percent in 2000 versus 3.27 percent for Costco. But where did the higher return on sales come from? BJ's ratio of COGS/sales at 88.7 percent was actually not quite as good as Costco's, which stood at 88.1 percent, so it certainly was not from prices relative to the costs of goods sold. However, BJ's SG&A expenses as a percentage of sales were 6.9 percent, compared to 8.7 percent for Costco, suggesting that BJ's had higher return on sales, and thus higher ROIC, in part because it spent less on sales, marketing, general, and administrative expenses.

To understand why BJ's was spending significantly less than Costco on SG&A/sales, we have to we have to go back to BJ's strategy. Recall that BJ's was an innovator in using information systems to automate its point of sale terminals, inventory reordering systems, and payment systems. This enabled it to reduce its dependence on people to perform these functions, thereby reducing its payroll and SG&A expenses for a given level of sales. Moreover, BJ's strategy of entering small towns or basing stores close to each other in suburban areas means that the company has a visible presence in these areas, which reduces its need to advertise and also brings down its SG&A expenses. So in part, BJ's superior profitability relative to its closest competitor, Costco, comes from lower SG&A expenses, which are a direct result of the strategies its managers pursue with regard to information systems and location.

Superior profitability can also come from more efficient use of capital. A comparative analysis of BJ's and Costco shows that in 2000, Costco's capital turnover ratio (sales/invested capital) was 6.29 compared to 7.41 at BJ's. BJ's was getting significantly more sales from its capital investment than Costco. Costco generates $6.29 in revenues from every dollar invested and BJ's generates $7.41. The big difference is in the ratio of property plant and equipment to sales (PPE/sales). For Costco, this ratio was 0.16, and for BJ's it was 0.11. BJ's was getting more sales from its investment in property, plant, and equipment than Costco was. Again, the difference is the result of strategy. BJ's strategy of entering small towns or suburban areas has enabled it to buy or rent less expensive real estate than Costco. In sum, BJ's superior profitability relative to its close competitor, Costco, seems to derive from lower SG&A expenses and PPE expenses relative to sales, which are the result of the strategies that BJ's pursues.

For another example of the impact of strategy on profitability, see the *Running Case* for this chapter, which compares Dell Computer to Compaq Computer.

In sum, the methodology described in this section can be a very useful tool to analyze why and how well a company is achieving and sustaining a competitive advantage. It highlights a company's strengths and weaknesses, showing where there is room for improvement and where a company is excelling. As such, it can drive strategy formulation, as it apparently has at Dell Computer (see the *Running Case*).

The analysis can be taken a lot further than we have here. For example, consider just one element in Figure 3.10 and the figure in the *Running Case*: ratio of costs of goods sold to sales (COGS/sales). This ratio is an indicator of the production efficiency of an enterprise: the lower the value of the ratio is, the more efficient the company is in manufacturing products, other things being equal. However, the ratio hides a lot of detail. For example, it does not reveal whether the efficiency comes from high production employee productivity, low costs of raw material inputs, or some other source. Working this out would further decomposition of the ROIC tree shown in Figure 3.10 into more basic elements. Although such detailed analysis is generally beyond the scope of this book, you should bear in mind how important such work can be in identifying a company's strengths and weaknesses.[23]

The Durability of Competitive Advantage

The next question we must address is how long a competitive advantage will last once it has been created. In other words, what is the *durability* of competitive advantage given that other companies are also seeking to develop distinctive competencies that will give them a competitive advantage? The answer depends on three factors: barriers to imitation, the capability of competitors, and the general dynamism of the industry environment.

Running Case

Drivers of Profitability for Dell Computer and Compaq

In the *Opening Case* to Chapter 1, we noted that Dell has had a persistently higher profit rate than its competitors, such as Compaq (see Figure). And we suggested that Dell's superior profitability came from the pursuit of a different strategy that enabled it to attain a very low-cost structure relative to that of its rivals. The figure shown here compares the drivers of profitability, as measured by ROIC, for Dell and Compaq in 2000. The figures are given in percentages to aid comparison. What we see is that in 2000, Dell, with an ROIC of 38.1 percent, was significantly more profitable than Compaq, which had an ROIC of 13.3 percent.

The figure helps us to identify the source of Dell's superior profitability by detailing some of the drivers of profitability at Dell and Compaq. Dell's cost structure is lower not because its COGS is lower; in fact, it is higher than Compaq's as a percentage of revenues. However, Dell spends only 10 percent of revenues on SG&A compared to Compaq's 14 percent. The reason is that Dell sells direct via the Web, while Compaq sells through distributors and has a much bigger sales force as a result—hence the higher SG&A. Moreover, Dell spends less on R&D than Compaq (1.5 percent of sales as against 3.5 percent). In part, this difference reflects the fact that Dell has positioned itself as a low-cost producer of personal computers and servers, whereas Compaq tries to differentiate its product offering by producing leading-edge machines that incorporate proprietary technology developed in-house. In other words, different strategies lead to different cost structures.

What is also striking, and a major source of Dell's superior profitability, is that its capital turnover ratio is far superior to that of Compaq. This suggests that Dell is using its capital much more efficiently than Compaq. Dell's lower working capital to sales ratio reflects the more efficient management of inventory, which reduces the need to working capital to finance that inventory. What is particularly striking is Dell's PPE/sales ratio,

Comparing Dell
and Compaq

which is only 3 percent compared to 8.1 percent at Compaq. This means that Dell is using far less property, plant, and equipment to generate its sales than Compaq is. This is the direct consequence of Dell's business model in which a substantial proportion of the work that goes into making Dell computers is outsourced to suppliers. Dell adds value by using its web-based information systems to coordinate the entire supply chain in a very efficient manner. As a result of this strategy, it does not have to invest as much capital in factories to make computers. Thus, Dell's superior profitability comes from a low-cost operating structure and the efficient use of its capital, both of which are the consequences of Dell's basic strategy of direct marketing and managing the supply chain via web-based information systems.

Interestingly, Dell measures its own performance by ROIC. According to Michael Dell, ROIC "is a focusing device. We introduced it in 1995 with a companywide push to educate everyone about the benefits of a positive ROIC. . . . We explained specifically how everyone could contribute by reducing cycle times, eliminating scrap and waste, selling more, forecasting accurately, scaling operations effectively, increasing inventory turns, collecting accounts receivables efficiently, and doing things right the first time. And we made it the core of our incentive compensation program for all employees."

Source: Data taken from 2000 10K reports filed with the Securities and Exchange Commission by Dell and Compaq. Dell quote from Michael Dell, *Direct from Dell: Strategies That Revolutionized an Industry* (New York: HarperBusiness, 1999), p. 135.

Barriers to Imitation

A company with a competitive advantage will earn higher-than-average profits. These profits send a signal to rivals that the company has some valuable distinctive competency that allows it to create superior value. Naturally, its competitors will try to identify and imitate that competency, and insofar as they are successful, ultimately their increased success may whittle away the company's superior profits.[24]

How quickly rivals will imitate a company's distinctive competencies is an important issue, because the speed of imitation has a bearing on the durability of a company's competitive advantage. Other things being equal, the more rapidly competitors imitate a company's distinctive competencies, the less durable its competitive advantage will be, and the more important it is that the company endeavor to improve its competencies to stay one step ahead of the imitators. It is important to stress at the outset that ultimately almost any distinctive competency can be imitated by a competitor. The critical issue is *time:* the longer it takes competitors to imitate a distinctive competency, the greater the opportunity the company has to build a strong market position and reputation with customers, which is then more difficult for competitors to attack. Moreover, the longer it takes to achieve an imitation, the greater is the opportunity for the imitated company to improve on its competency or build other competencies, thereby staying one step ahead of the competition.

Barriers to imitation are a primary determinant of the speed of imitation. **Barriers to imitation** are factors that make it difficult for a competitor to copy a company's distinctive competencies; the greater the barriers to imitation, the more sustainable are a company's competitive advantage.[25] Barriers to imitation differ depending on whether a competitor is trying to imitate resources or capabilities.

Imitating Resources. In general, the easiest distinctive competencies for prospective rivals to imitate tend to be those based on possession of firm-specific and valuable tangible resources, such as buildings, plant, and equipment. Such resources are visible to competitors and can often be purchased on the open market. For example, if a company's competitive advantage is based on sole possession of efficient-scale manufacturing facilities, competitors may move fairly quickly to establish similar facilities. Although Ford gained a competitive advantage over General Motors in the 1920s by being the first to adopt an assembly line manufacturing technology to produce automobiles, General Motors quickly imitated that innovation, competing away Ford's distinctive competence in the process. A similar process is occurring in the auto industry now, as companies try to imitate Toyota's famous production system.

Intangible resources can be more difficult to imitate. This is particularly true of brand names, which are important because they symbolize a company's reputation. In the heavy earthmoving equipment industry, for example, the Caterpillar brand name is synonymous with high quality and superior after-sales service and support. Similarly, the St. Michael's brand name used by Marks & Spencer, Britain's largest retailer, symbolizes high-quality but reasonably priced clothing. Customers often display a preference for the products of such companies because the brand name is an important guarantee of high quality. Although competitors might like to imitate well-established brand names, the law prohibits them from doing so.

Marketing and technological know-how are also important intangible resources and can be relatively easy to imitate. The movement of skilled marketing personnel between companies may facilitate the general dissemination of marketing know-how. For example, in the 1970s, Ford was acknowledged as the best marketer among the big three U.S. auto companies. In 1979, it lost a lot of its marketing know-how to Chrysler when its most successful marketer, Lee Iacocca, joined Chrysler and subsequently hired many of Ford's top marketing people to work with him at Chrysler. More generally, successful marketing strategies are relatively easy to imitate because they are so visible to competitors. Thus, Coca-Cola quickly imitated PepsiCo's Diet Pepsi brand with the introduction of its own brand, Diet Coke.

With regard to technological know-how, the patent system in theory should make technological know-how relatively immune to imitation. Patents give the inventor of a new product a twenty-year exclusive production agreement. For example, the biotechnology company Immunex discovered and patented Enbrel, which is capable of halting the disease-causing mechanism that leads to rheumatoid arthritis. All prior treatments simply provided patients with some relief from the symptoms of rheumatoid arthritis. Approved by the Food and Drug Administration in 1998, Enbrel racked up sales of over $400 million in its first year on the market and may ultimately generate annual revenues of $2 billion for Immunex. (In 2002, Immunex was acquired by Amgen.) Despite the large market potential, Immunex's patent stops potential competitors from introducing their own version of Enbrel. However, whereas it is relatively easy to use the patent system to protect a biological product from imitation, this is not true of many other inventions. In electrical and computer engineering, for example, it is often possible to invent around patents. That is, produce a product that is functionally equivalent, but does not rely upon the patented technology. One study found that 60 percent of patented innovations were successfully invented around in four years.[26] This suggests that in general, distinctive competencies based on technological know-how can be relatively short-lived.

Imitating Capabilities. Imitating a company's capabilities tends to be more difficult than imitating its tangible and intangible resources, chiefly because capabilities are based on the way in which decisions are made and processes managed deep within a company. It is hard for outsiders to discern them.

On its own, the invisible nature of capabilities would not be enough to halt imitation; competitors could still gain insights into how a company operates by hiring people away from that company. However, a company's capabilities rarely reside in a single individual. Rather, they are the product of how numerous individuals interact within a unique organizational setting.[27] It is possible that no one individual within a company may be familiar with the totality of a company's internal operating routines and procedures. In such cases, hiring people away from a successful company in order to imitate its key capabilities may not be helpful.

Capability of Competitors

According to work by Pankaj Ghemawat, a major determinant of the capability of competitors to imitate a company's competitive advantage rapidly is the nature of the competitors' prior strategic commitments.[28] By **strategic commitment,** Ghemawat means a company's commitment to a particular way of doing business—that is, to developing a particular set of resources and capabilities. Ghemawat's point is that once a company has made a strategic commitment, it will have difficulty responding to new competition if doing so requires a break with this commitment. Therefore, when competitors have long-established commitments to a particular way of doing business, they may be slow to imitate an innovating company's competitive advantage. Its competitive advantage will thus be relatively durable.

The U.S. automobile industry again offers an example. From 1945 to 1975, the industry was dominated by the stable oligopoly of General Motors, Ford, and Chrysler, all of which geared their operations to the production of large cars, which American customers demanded at the time. When the market shifted from large cars to small, fuel-efficient ones during the late 1970s, U.S. companies lacked the resources and capabilities required to produce these cars. Their prior commitments had built the wrong kind of skills for this new environment. As a result, foreign producers, and particularly the Japanese, stepped into the market breach by providing compact, fuel-efficient, high-quality, and low-cost cars. The failure of U.S. auto manufacturers to react quickly to the distinctive competency of Japanese auto companies gave the latter time to build a strong market position and brand loyalty, which subsequently has proved difficult to attack.

Another determinant of the ability of competitors to respond to a company's competitive advantage is the absorptive capacity of competitors.[29] **Absorptive capacity** refers to the ability of an enterprise to identify, value, assimilate, and use new knowledge. For example, in the 1960s and 1970s, Toyota developed a competitive advantage based on its innovation of lean production systems. Competitors such as General Motors were slow to imitate this innovation, primarily because they lacked the necessary absorptive capacity. General Motors was such a bureaucratic and inward-looking organization that it was very difficult for the company to identify, value, assimilate, and use the knowledge that underlay lean production systems. Indeed, long after General Motors had identified and understood the importance of lean production systems, it was still struggling to assimilate and use that new knowledge. Put differently, internal inertia forces can make it difficult for established competitors to respond to a rival whose competitive advantage is based on new products or internal processes—that is, on innovation.

Taken together, factors such as existing strategic commitments and low absorptive capacity limit the ability of established competitors to imitate the competitive advantage of a rival, particularly when that competitive advantage is based on innovative products or processes. This is why when innovations reshape the rules of competition in an industry, value often migrates away from established competitors and toward new enterprises that are operating with new business models.

Industry Dynamism

A dynamic industry environment is one that is changing rapidly. We examined the factors that determine the dynamism and intensity of competition in an industry in

Chapter 2 when we discussed the external environment. The most dynamic industries tend to be those with a very high rate of product innovation—for instance, the customer electronics industry and the personal computer industry. In dynamic industries, the rapid rate of innovation means that product life cycles are shortening and that competitive advantage can be fleeting. A company that has a competitive advantage today may find its market position outflanked tomorrow by a rival's innovation.

In the personal computer industry, the rapid increase in computing power during the past two decades has contributed to a high degree of innovation and a turbulent environment. Reflecting the persistence of innovation, Apple Computer in the late 1970s and early 1980s had an industrywide competitive advantage due to its innovation. In 1981, IBM seized the advantage with its introduction of its first personal computer. By the mid-1980s, IBM had lost its competitive advantage to high-power "clone" manufacturers such as Compaq that had beaten IBM in the race to introduce a computer based on Intel's 386 chip. In turn, in the 1990s, Compaq subsequently lost its competitive advantage to Dell, which pioneered new low-cost ways of delivering computers to customers using the Internet as a direct selling device.

The durability of a company's competitive advantage depends on the height of barriers to imitation, the capability of competitors to imitate its innovation, and the general level of dynamism in the industry environment. When barriers to imitation are low, capable competitors abound, and the environment is dynamic, with innovations being developed all the time, then competitive advantage is likely to be transitory. But even within such industries, companies can build a more enduring competitive advantage if they are able to make investments that build barriers to imitation.

During the 1980s, Apple Computer built a competitive advantage based on the combination of a proprietary disk operating system and an intangible product image. The resulting brand loyalty enabled Apple to carve out a fairly secure niche in an industry where competitive advantage has otherwise proven to be very fleeting. However, by the mid-1990s, its strategy had been imitated, primarily due to the introduction of Microsoft's Windows operating system, which imitated most of the features that had enabled Apple to build brand loyalty. By 1996, Apple was in financial trouble, providing yet another example that no competitive advantage lasts forever. Ultimately, anything can be imitated. Interestingly enough though, Apple has shown remarkable resilience; in the late 1990s, it clawed its way back from the brink of bankruptcy to establish a viable position within its niche once again.

Avoiding Failure and Sustaining Competitive Advantage

How can a company avoid failure and escape the traps that have snared so many once successful companies? How can managers build a sustainable competitive advantage? Much of the remainder of this book deals with these issues. Here, we make a number of key points that set the scene for the coming discussion.

Why Companies Fail

When a company loses its competitive advantage, its profitability falls. The company does not necessarily fail; it may just have average or below-average profitability and can remain in this mode for a considerable time, although its resource and capital base is shrinking. Failure implies something more drastic. A failing company is one whose profitability is now substantially lower than the average profitability of its competitors; it has lost the ability to attract and generate resources so that its profit margins and invested capital are shrinking rapidly.

Why does a company lose its competitive advantage and fail? The question is particularly pertinent since some of the most successful companies of the twentieth century have seen their competitive position deteriorate at one time or another. IBM, General Motors, American Express, Digital Equipment, and Compaq Computer, among many others, all at one time held up as examples of managerial excellence, have gone through periods where their financial performance was poor and they clearly lacked any competitive advantage. We explore three related reasons for failure: inertia, prior strategic commitments, and the Icarus paradox.

Inertia. The inertia argument says that companies find it difficult to change their strategies and structures in order to adapt to changing competitive conditions.[30] IBM is a classic example of this problem. For thirty years, it was viewed as the world's most successful computer company. Then in the space of a few years, its success turned into a disaster: it lost $5 billion in 1992, leading to layoffs of more than 100,000 employees. IBM's troubles were caused by a dramatic decline in the cost of computing power as a result of innovations in microprocessors. With the advent of powerful low-cost microprocessors, the locus of the computer market shifted from mainframes to small, low-priced personal computers, leaving IBM's huge mainframe operations with a diminished market. Although IBM had, and still has, a significant presence in the personal computer market, it had failed to shift the focus of its efforts away from mainframes and toward personal computers. This failure meant deep trouble for one of the most successful companies of the twentieth century (although IBM has now executed a successful turnaround with a repositioning as a provider of e-commerce infrastructure and solutions).

One reason that companies find it so difficult to adapt to new environmental conditions seems to be the role of capabilities in causing inertia. Organizational capabilities—the way a company makes decisions and manages its processes—can be a source of competitive advantage, but they are difficult to change. IBM always emphasized close coordination among operating units and favored decision processes that stressed consensus among interdependent operating units as a prerequisite for a decision to go forward.[31] This capability was a source of advantage for IBM during the 1970s, when coordination among its worldwide operating units was necessary to develop, manufacture, and sell complex mainframes. But the slow-moving bureaucracy that it had spawned was a source of failure in the 1990s, when organizations had to adapt readily to rapid environmental change.

Capabilities are difficult to change because a certain distribution of power and influence is embedded within the established decision-making and management processes of an organization. Those who play key roles in a decision-making process clearly have more power. It follows that changing the established capabilities of an organization means changing its existing distribution of power and influence, and those whose power and influence would diminish resist such change. Proposals for change trigger turf battles. This power struggle and the political resistance associated with trying to alter the way in which an organization makes decisions and manages its process—that is, trying to change its capabilities—bring on inertia. This is not to say that companies cannot change. However, because change is so often resisted by those who feel threatened by it, change in most cases has to be induced by a crisis. By then, the company may already be failing, as happened at IBM.

Prior Strategic Commitments. Ghemawat has argued that a company's prior strategic commitments not only limit its ability to imitate rivals but may also cause competitive disadvantage.[32] IBM, for instance, had major investments in the mainframe computer business, so when the market shifted, it was stuck with significant resources specialized to that particular business: its manufacturing facilities were geared to the production of mainframes, its research organization was similarly specialized, and so was its sales force. Because these resources were not well suited to the newly emerging personal computer business, IBM's difficulties in the early 1990s were in a sense inevitable. Its prior strategic commitments locked it into a business that was shrinking. Shedding these resources was bound to cause hardship for all organization stakeholders.

The Icarus Paradox. Danny Miller has postulated that the roots of competitive failure can be found in what he termed the *Icarus paradox*.[33] Icarus is a figure in Greek mythology who used a pair of wings, made for him by his father, to escape from an island where he was being held prisoner. He flew so well that he went higher and higher, ever closer to the sun, until the heat of the sun melted the wax that held his wings together and he plunged to his death in the Aegean Sea. The paradox is that his greatest asset, his ability to fly, caused his demise. Miller argues that the same paradox applies to many once successful companies. According to Miller, many companies become so dazzled by their early success that they believe more of the same type of effort is the way to future success. As a result, they can become so specialized and inner directed that they lose sight of market realities and the fundamental requirements for achieving a competitive advantage. Sooner or later, this leads to failure.

Miller identifies four major categories among the rising and falling companies, which he labels "craftsmen," "builders," "pioneers," and "salesmen." The "craftsmen," such as Texas Instruments and Digital Equipment Corp. (DEC), achieved early success through engineering excellence. But then they became so obsessed with engineering details that they lost sight of market realities. (The story of DEC's demise is summarized in Strategy in Action 3.4.) Among the "builders" are Gulf & Western and ITT. Having built successful, moderately diversified companies, they then became so enchanted with diversification for its own sake that they continued to diversify far beyond the point at which it was profitable to do so. Miller's third group are the "pioneers" like Wang Labs. Enamored of their own originally brilliant innovations, they continued to search for additional brilliant innovations and ended up producing novel but completely useless products. The final category comprises the "salesmen," exemplified by Procter & Gamble and Chrysler. They became so convinced of their ability to sell anything that they paid scant attention to product development and manufacturing excellence and as a result spawned a proliferation of bland, inferior products.

Steps to Avoid Failure

Given that so many traps wait for companies, the question arises as to how strategic managers can use internal analysis to find them and escape them. We now look at several tactics that managers can use.

Focus on the Building Blocks of Competitive Advantage. Maintaining a competitive advantage requires a company to continue focusing on all four generic building blocks of competitive advantage—efficiency, quality, innovation, and responsiveness to customers—and to develop distinctive competencies that con-

Strategy in Action

The Road to Ruin at DEC

3.4

DEC's original success was founded on the minicomputer, a cheaper, more flexible version of its mainframe cousins that Ken Olson and his brilliant team of engineers invented in the 1960s. They then improved on their original minicomputers until they could not be beat for quality and reliability. In the 1970s, their VAX series of minicomputers was widely regarded as the most reliable computers ever produced, and DEC was rewarded by high profit rates and rapid growth. By 1990, it was number 27 on the Fortune 500 list of the largest corporations in America.

Buoyed by its success, DEC turned into an engineering monoculture: its engineers became idols; its marketing and accounting staff, however, were barely tolerated. Component specs and design standards were all that senior managers understood. Technological fine tuning became such an obsession that the needs of customers for smaller, more economical, user-friendly computers were ignored. DEC's personal computers, for example, bombed because they were out of touch with the needs of customers, and the company failed to respond to the threat to its core market presented by the rise of computer workstations and client-server architecture. Indeed, Ken Olson was known for dismissing such new products. He once said, "We always say that customers are right, but they are not always right." Perhaps. But DEC, blinded by its early success, failed to remain responsive to its customers and changing market conditions.

By the early 1990s, DEC was in deep trouble. Olson was forced out in July 1992, and the company lost billions of dollars between 1992 and 1995. It returned to profitability in 1996, primarily because of the success of a turnaround strategy aimed at reorientating the company to serve precisely those areas that Olson had dismissed. In 1998, the company was acquired by Compaq Computer.

Sources: D. Miller, *The Icarus Paradox* (New York: HarperBusiness, 1990). P. D. Llosa, "We Must Know What We Are Doing," *Fortune,* November 14, 1994, p. 68.

tribute to superior performance in these areas. One of the messages of Miller's Icarus paradox is that many successful companies become unbalanced in their pursuit of distinctive competencies. DEC, for example, focused on engineering quality at the expense of almost everything else including, most important, responsiveness to customers. Other companies forget to focus on any distinctive competency at all.

Institute Continuous Improvement and Learning. The only constant in the world is change. Today's source of competitive advantage may soon be rapidly imitated by capable competitors or made obsolete by the innovations of a rival. In such a dynamic and fast-paced environment, the only way that a company can maintain a competitive advantage over time is to continually improve its efficiency, quality, innovation, and responsiveness to customers. The way to do this is to recognize the importance of learning within the organization.[34] The most successful companies are not those that stand still, resting on their laurels. They are those that are always seeking out ways of improving their operations and in the process are constantly upgrading the value of their distinctive competencies or creating new competencies. Companies such as General Electric and Toyota have a reputation for being learning organizations. This means that they are continually analyzing the processes that underlie their efficiency, quality, innovation, and responsiveness to customers. Their objective is to learn from prior mistakes and to seek out ways to improve their processes over time. This has enabled Toyota, for example, to continually upgrade its employee productivity and product quality, allowing it to stay ahead of imitators.

Track Best Industrial Practice and Use Benchmarking. One of the best ways to develop distinctive competencies that contribute to superior efficiency, quality, innovation, and responsiveness to customers is to identify and adopt best industrial practice. Only in this way will a company be able to build and maintain the resources and capabilities that underpin excellence in efficiency, quality, innovation, and responsiveness to customers. (What constitutes best industrial practice is an issue we discuss in some depth in Chapter 4.) It requires tracking the practice of other companies, and perhaps the best way to do so is through **benchmarking:** the process of measuring the company against the products, practices, and services of some of its most efficient global competitors. For example, when Xerox was in trouble in the early 1980s, it decided to institute a policy of benchmarking as a means of identifying ways to improve the efficiency of its operations. Xerox benchmarked L. L. Bean for distribution procedures, Deere & Company for central computer operations, Procter & Gamble for marketing, and Florida Power & Light for total quality management processes. By the early 1990s, Xerox was benchmarking 240 functions against comparable areas in other companies. This process has been credited with helping it dramatically improve the efficiency of its operations.[35]

Overcome Inertia. Overcoming the internal forces that are a barrier to change within an organization is one of the key requirements for maintaining a competitive advantage, and an entire chapter, Chapter 14, is spent discussing this issue. Suffice it to say here that identifying barriers to change is an important first step. Once this step has been taken, implementing change requires good leadership, the judicious use of power, and appropriate changes in organizational structure and control systems.

The Role of Luck

A number of scholars have argued that luck plays a critical role in determining competitive success and failure.[36] In its most extreme version, the luck argument devalues the importance of strategy altogether. Instead, it states that in the face of uncertainty, some companies just happen to pick the correct strategy.

Although luck may be the reason for a company's success in particular cases, it is an unconvincing explanation for the persistent success of a company. Recall our argument that the generic building blocks of competitive advantage are superior efficiency, quality, innovation, and responsiveness to customers. Keep in mind also that competition is a process in which companies are continually trying to outdo each other in their ability to achieve high efficiency, superior quality, outstanding innovation, and quick responsiveness to customers. It is possible to imagine a company getting lucky and coming into possession of resources that allow it to achieve excellence on one or more of these dimensions. However, it is difficult to imagine how *sustained* excellence on any of these four dimensions could be produced by anything other than conscious effort, that is, by strategy. Luck may indeed play a role in success, and managers must always exploit a lucky break (Strategy in Action 3.5 discusses the role of luck in the early history of Microsoft and how Bill Gates exploited that luck). However, to argue that success is entirely a matter of luck is to strain credibility. As the great banker of the early twentieth century, J. P. Morgan, once said, "The harder I work, the luckier I seem to get." Managers who strive to formulate and implement strategies that lead to a competitive advantage are more likely to be lucky.

Strategy in Action   3.5

Bill Gates's Lucky Break

The product that launched Microsoft into its leadership position in the software industry was MS-DOS, the operating system for IBM and IBM-compatible PCs. The original DOS program, however, was developed not by Microsoft but by Seattle Computer, where it was known as Q-DOS (which stood for "quick and dirty operating system"). When IBM was looking for an operating system to run its original PC, it talked to a number of software companies, including Microsoft, asking whether they could develop such a system. Seattle Computer was not one of those companies. Bill Gates, already a player in the emerging Seattle computer community, knew that Seattle Computer had developed a disk operating system and took action: he borrowed $50,000 from his father, a senior partner in a prominent Seattle law firm, and then went to see the CEO of Seattle Computer and offered to purchase the rights to the company's Q-DOS system. He did not, of course, reveal that IBM was looking for a disk operating system. Seattle Computer, short of cash, quickly agreed. Gates then renamed the system MS-DOS, upgraded it somewhat, and licensed it to IBM. The rest, as they say, is history.

So was Gates lucky? Of course he was. It was lucky that Seattle Computer had not heard about IBM's request. It was lucky that IBM approached Microsoft. It was lucky that Gates knew about Seattle Computer's operating system. And it was lucky that Gates had a father wealthy enough to lend him $50,000 on short notice. Nevertheless, to attribute all of Microsoft's subsequent success to luck would be wrong. Although MS-DOS gave Microsoft a tremendous head start in the industry, it did not guarantee that Microsoft would continue to enjoy the kind of worldwide success that it has. To do that, Microsoft had to build the appropriate set of resources and capabilities required to produce a continual stream of innovative software, which is precisely what the company did with the cash generated from MS-DOS.

Source: Stephen Manes and Paul Andrews, *Gates* (New York: Simon & Schuster 1993).

Summary of Chapter

1. Distinctive competencies are the firm-specific strengths of a company. Valuable distinctive competencies enable a company to earn a profit rate that is above the industry average.

2. The distinctive competencies of an organization arise from its resources (its financial, physical, human, technological, and organizational assets) and capabilities (its skills at coordinating resources and putting them to productive use).

3. In order to achieve a competitive advantage, a company needs to pursue strategies that build on its existing resources and capabilities and formulate strategies that build additional resources and capabilities (develop new competencies).

4. The source of a competitive advantage is superior value creation.

5. To create superior value, a company must lower its costs or differentiate its product so that it creates more value and can charge a higher price, or do both simultaneously.

6. Managers must understand how value creation and pricing decisions affect demand and how costs change with increases in volume. They must have a good grasp of the demand conditions in the company's market and the cost structure of the company at different levels of output if they are to make decisions that maximize the profitability of their enterprise.

7. The four generic building blocks of competitive advantage are efficiency, quality, innovation, and responsiveness to customers. Superior efficiency enables a company to lower its costs; superior quality allows it to charge a higher price and lower its costs; and superior customer service lets it charge a higher price. Superior innovation can lead to higher prices, particularly in the case of product innovations, or lower unit costs, particularly in the case of process innovations.

8. If a company's managers are to perform a good internal analysis, they need to be able to analyze the financial performance of their company, identifying how

the strategies of the company relate to its profitability, as measured by the return on invested capital.

9. The durability of a company's competitive advantage depends on the height of barriers to imitation, the capability of competitors, and environmental dynamism.

10. Failing companies typically earn low or negative profits. Three factors seem to contribute to failure: organizational inertia in the face of environmental change, the nature of a company's prior strategic commitments, and the Icarus paradox.

11. Avoiding failure requires a constant focus on the basic building blocks of competitive advantage, continuous improvement, identification and adoption of best industrial practice, and victory over inertia.

Discussion Questions

1. What are the main implications of the material discussed in this chapter for strategy formulation?

2. When is a company's competitive advantage most likely to endure over time?

3. It is possible for a company to be the lowest-cost producer in its industry and simultaneously have an output that is the most valued by customers. Discuss this statement.

4. Why is it important to understand the drivers of profitability, as measured by the return on invested capital?

5. Which is more important in explaining the success and failure of companies: strategizing or luck?

Practicing Strategic Management

SMALL-GROUP EXERCISE: ANALYZING COMPETITIVE ADVANTAGE

Break into a group of three to five people. Drawing on the concepts introduced in this chapter, analyze the competitive position of your business school in the market for business education. Then answer the following questions:

1. Does your business school have a competitive advantage?

2. If so, on what is this advantage based, and is this advantage sustainable?

3. If your school does not have a competitive advantage in the market for business education, identify the inhibiting factors that are holding it back.

4. How might the Internet change the way in which business education is delivered?

5. Does the Internet pose a threat to the competitive position of your school in the market for business education, or is it an opportunity for your school to enhance its competitive position? (Note that it can be both.)

ARTICLE FILE 3

Find a company that has sustained its competitive advantage for more than ten years. Identify the source of the competitive advantage, and explain why it has lasted so long.

STRATEGIC MANAGEMENT PROJECT: MODULE 3

This module deals with the competitive position of your company. With the information you have at your disposal, perform the tasks and answer the questions listed:

1. Identify whether your company has a competitive advantage or disadvantage in its primary industry. (Its primary industry is the one in which it has the most sales.)

2. Evaluate your company against the four generic building blocks of competitive advantage: efficiency, quality, innovation, and responsiveness to customers. How does this exercise help you understand the performance of your company relative to its competitors?

3. What are the distinctive competencies of your company?

4. What role have prior strategies played in shaping the distinctive competencies of your company? What has been the role of luck?

5. Do the strategies your company is pursuing now build on its distinctive competencies? Are they an attempt to build new competencies?

6. What are the barriers to imitating the distinctive competencies of your company?

7. Is there any evidence that your company finds it difficult to adapt to changing industry conditions? If so, why do you think this is the case?

EXPLORING THE WEB
Visiting Johnson & Johnson

Visit the web site of Johnson and Johnson (**http://www.jnj.com**). Read through the material contained on the site, paying particular attention to the features on company history, Johnson & Johnson's credo, innovations, and company news. On the basis of the information contained here, answer the following questions:

1. Do you think that Johnson & Johnson has a distinctive competence?
2. What is the nature of this competence? How does it help the company to attain a competitive advantage?
3. What are the resources and capabilities that underlie this competence? Where do these resources and capabilities come from?
4. How imitable is Johnson & Johnson's distinctive competence?

General Task: Search the Web for a company site that goes into depth about the history, products, and com-

petitive position of that company. On the basis of the information you collect, answer the following questions:

1. Does the company have a distinctive competence?
2. What is the nature of this competence? How does it help the company to attain a competitive advantage?
3. What are the resources and capabilities that underlie this competence? Where do these resources and capabilities come from?
4. How imitable is the company's distinctive competence?

Closing Case

Cisco Systems

Cisco Systems is one of the great recent success stories. Two Stanford University computer scientists, Leonard Bosack and Sandra Lerner, founded the company in 1984. In the early 1980s, Stanford University had accumulated many separate computer networks, each using different machines and different electronic languages to communicate among themselves. The problem was that these networks could not talk to each other. Bosack and Lerner, who were married at the time, were the managers of separate networks and worked on the problem of hooking these networks together, partly, so legend has it, in order to be able to send each other email messages. Their solution was a specialized computer known as a router that was able to connect different computer systems. Realizing that this device might have commercial value, they established Cisco and shipped their first product in 1987. The company went public in 1990 with annual sales of around $70 million. Soon after, Cisco's sales started to increase exponentially as routers became a critical component of the rapidly expanding Internet. By 1999, Cisco had evolved into the dominant supplier of network equipment for the Internet—including routers, switches, and hubs—with annual sales in excess of $19 billion, no debt, and a return on invested capital of around 22 percent.

Cisco's rapid sales growth and high profitability owe much to its product innovation, which has continued at a rapid pace since the company went public, but it is also due to the company's aggressive adoption of an e-business infrastructure. Here too Cisco has been an innovator. This infrastructure has enabled the company to reap major efficiency gains, while providing its customers with superior point-of-sales service and after-sales service and

support. Cisco was one of the first companies to move much of its sales effort onto the Internet. The process began in 1996 when it realized that its traditional sales infrastructure could not keep up with increasing demand. Rather than hire additional personnel to manage customer accounts, the company began to experiment with online sales. It developed a computer program to walk customers through the process of ordering equipment online. A critical feature of this program helps customers to order exactly the right mix of equipment, thereby avoiding any ordering mistakes, such as ordering incompatible equipment. In 1997, the company sold $500 million worth of equipment online. By 1999, this figure had ballooned to $10 billion, or 80 percent of its total sales, making the company one of the most aggressive adopters of an online sales approach in the world.

Customers seem to love the automated order processing system, primarily because it minimizes ordering mistakes and allows for quicker execution of orders. For example, at Sprint, a major customer, it used to take sixty days from the signing of a contract to complete a networking project. Now it takes thirty-five to forty-five days, primarily due to the efficiency of Cisco's online ordering system. Moreover, Sprint has been able to cut its order processing staff from twenty-one to six, significantly saving costs. As for Cisco, the company has just 300 service agents handling all of its customer accounts, compared to the 900 it would need if sales were not handled online. The difference represents an annual saving of $20 million.

Cisco has also placed its customer support functions online. All routine customer service functions are now handled online by a computer program that can translate a customer's fuzzy inquiry into a standard description of a familiar problem; then it provides the four most likely explanations onscreen, allowing the customer to avoid blind alleys and time wasted. Since implementing the system in 1996, Cisco's sales have quadrupled, while its engineering support staff has merely doubled to 800. Without automated sales support, Cisco calculates that it would need at least 1,000 additional service engineers, which would cost around $75 million. Cisco has also moved to distributing all support software over the Internet rather than transferring it to disks and mailing it to customers. This has saved it another $250 million per year in annual operating costs.

Discussion Questions

1. What are the sources of competitive advantage at Cisco?

2. How does the implementation of an e-business infrastructure at Cisco help the company to create value?

3. How secure do you think Cisco's competitive advantage is?

4. In 2000–2002, the telecommunications equipment industry suffered a sharp contraction in demand. Although Cisco's sales continued to expand, hitting $22 billion in 2001, its return on invested capital fell to just 6.7 percent. In 2002, revenues fell to under $18.5 billion and profitability shrank to under 6 percent. On the basis of the case, do you think that Cisco did worse or better than its rivals? How successful do you think Cisco will be once demand revives? Why?

Sources: "Cisco@speed," *Economist,* June 26, 1999, p. 12. S. Tully, "How Cisco Mastered the Net," *Fortune,* August 17, 1997, pp. 207–210. C. Kano, "The Real King of the Internet," *Fortune,* September 7, 1998, pp. 82–93.

Building Competitive Advantage Through Functional-Level Strategy

4

Opening Case

CSX—Getting the Trains to Run on Time

CSX Corporation, whose business is the transportation of freight, is one of the largest U.S. railroads as the result of a 1996 merger with Conrail. The merger took place because managers expected to reap huge savings in costs from operating an expanded freight rail network: a 23,000-mile network in twenty-three states in the eastern half of the United States. However, these cost savings did not result, and a host of postmerger problems associated with trying to join together two previously independent networks emerged.

Following the merger, the operating efficiency of the railroad fell. Trains were often late or delayed because of poor track and congested terminals. The Federal Railroad Administration told CSX that a government audit of 4,000 miles of its track had found serious defects, including excessive space between rails that could lead to train derailments. Employee morale was poor in the merged company, and customers, who relied on CSX Corporation to deliver products on time, were dissatisfied with its service and defecting to other railroads. As a result of these problems, earnings took a hit. CSX's operating margins fell from 21.4 percent in 1997 to 15.2 percent in 1999, primarily due to rising costs. Its stock price tumbled from a 1998 high of $62 to just $19.50 by mid-2000.

In 2000, the company launched an efficiency campaign to try to correct the problems. First, management recognized that if they were to improve operations, they needed to focus on some key measures of operating efficiency. They picked fourteen critical operating metrics—including safety standards (train derailments and accidents), train velocity (average speed), cars on line (a measure of inventory), terminal dwell time (how much time a locomotive is sitting idle at a terminal), and on-time departures and arrivals—each of which was given a clear ninety-day target for improvement. Performance against each of these targets was measured daily and communicated immediately throughout the organization.

By the end of 2001, it was clear that CSX had made substantial improvement against these targets. Train derailments had fallen by 39 percent, from 10.6 per week in 2000 to 6.5 per week in 2001. Train velocity for merchandise improved from 18.7 miles per hour in 2000 to 21.7 miles per hour in 2001. Over the same period, terminal dwell time fell from 30.8 hours to 24.5 hours, on-time originations rose from 69.2 percent to 88.1 percent, on-time arrivals increased from 51.3 percent to 75.6 percent, and the number of cars on line fell from 258,000 to 240,000. All of these measures implied increased operating efficiency and reliability.

How did CSX achieve this? The company's managers refer to their new business model as "Railroad 101." First, CSX management focused on congested terminals in its troubled southern region, where trains often got backed up for days. CSX put in extra resources—people and locomotives—and gave them the authority to do whatever was necessary to solve the congestion. Among other things, they changed several long-standard practices, such as holding up locomotives from departure in order to maximize the number of freight cars and train length. Although this practice was meant to boost productivity by realizing scale economies, paradoxically it hurt productivity and raised costs because of its unintended consequences: poor on-time performance, which alienated customers, and poor on time performance of the locomotive and crew time. Second, CSX focused resources on fixing defective track, which reduced derailments and also reduced unproductive locomotive and crew downtime, while increasing on-time performance.

Simultaneously, CSX launched a major initiative to build a web-based customer interface as a way of improving customer service. This interface allows customers to perform several important functions online. For example, a new shipment tracking function enables customers to obtain train and car information, including origination, current location, and destination. Customers can create and send bills of lading online, order empty railcars for the coming week, change the status of orders, or retrieve the history of previous orders.

CSX soon found that as a result of its initiatives, its reputation with customers was improving. The increased reliability of service not only boosted productivity and lowered costs but also created more value for customers. In turn, CSX found that its customers were willing to pay more for its services, and the company pushed through modest price increases in 2001 and 2002, which its customers accepted.

Sources: W. C. Vantuono, "Turnaround Time at CSXT," *Railway Age* (August 2001): 29–30. D. Machalaba, "CSX Corp.'s Railroad Unit Gets Business Back on Track," *Wall Street Journal,* January 29, 2002, p. B4. CSX Corporation, earnings and productivity information www.csx.com.

Overview

In this chapter, we take a close look at **functional-level strategies:** those aimed at improving the effectiveness of a company's operations and thus its ability to attain superior efficiency, quality, innovation, and customer responsiveness.

It is important to keep in mind the relationships of functional strategies, distinctive competencies, differentiation, low cost, value creation, and profitability (see Figure 4.1). Note that distinctive competencies shape the functional-level strategies that a company can pursue and that through their choices with regard to functional-level strategies, managers can build resources and capabilities that enhance a company's distinctive competencies. Note also that the ability of a company to attain superior efficiency, quality, innovation, and customer responsiveness will determine if its product offering is *differentiated* from that of rivals and if it has a *low cost structure.* Recall that companies that increase value through differentiation, while simultane-

FIGURE 4.1

The Roots of Competitive Advantage

ously lowering their cost structure, create more value than their rivals, and this leads to a competitive advantage and superior profitability.

The *Opening Case* illustrates some of these relationships. CSX, a large railroad operator, pursued functional-level strategies to improve the efficiency, reliability (quality), and customer responsiveness of its service. By improving safety and removing congestion at terminals, CSX was able to get its trains to run on time. With more of its assets carrying goods, rather than sitting in terminals or on sidings waiting for track to be repaired, productivity went up, costs went down, and service reliability improved. As reliability improved, the railroad was able to differentiate itself better, which allowed it to raise prices and capture more business from customers, particularly in the area of time-sensitive and perishable goods where on-time arrival is critical. As a result of better differentiation and lower costs, CSX's profitability improved in 2001 over the prior two years, despite the fact that the U.S. economy was in recession. The case shows just how important operating efficiency and reliability can be. CSX described its approach as "Railroad 101" by which it meant doing the basics as efficiently as possible. Much of this chapter is devoted to looking at the basic changes that can be made at the operating level to improve competitive position. By the end of this chapter, you will understand how functional level strategies can be used to build a sustainable competitive advantage.

Achieving Superior Efficiency

A company is a device for transforming inputs (labor, land, capital, management, and technological know-how) into outputs (the goods and services produced). The simplest measure of efficiency is the quantity of inputs that it takes to produce a given output; that is, efficiency = outputs/inputs. The more efficient a company is, the fewer the inputs required to produce a given output and therefore the lower its cost structure will be. Put another way, an efficient company has higher productivity, and therefore lower costs, than its rivals. Here we review the steps that companies can take at the functional level to increase their efficiency and thereby lower their cost structure.

**Efficiency and
Economies of
Scale**

Economies of scale are unit cost reductions associated with a large scale of output. You will recall from the last chapter that it is very important for managers to understand how the cost structure of their enterprise varies with output because this understanding should help to drive strategy. For example, if unit costs fall significantly as output is expanded—that is, if there are significant economies of scale—a company may benefit by keeping prices down and increasing volume.

One source of economies of scale is the ability to spread fixed costs over a large production volume. *Fixed costs* are costs that must be incurred to produce a product whatever the level of output; examples are the costs of purchasing machinery, setting up machinery for individual production runs, building facilities, and advertising and R&D. For example, in 2001, Anheuser-Busch spent $500 million on advertising, about twice as much as Coors, the number three brewer in the United States. Because of its much larger output, Anheuser-Busch's advertising cost per barrel of beer was only $5 compared to $10 at Coors, and thus it enjoyed significant economies of scale in advertising. For another example, Microsoft spent approximately $1 billion to develop the latest version of its Windows operating system, Windows XP. It can realize substantial scale economies by spreading the fixed costs associated with developing the new operating system over the enormous unit sales volume it expects for this system (95 percent of the world's personal computers use a Microsoft operating system). These scale economies are significant because of the trivial incremental (or marginal) cost of producing additional copies of Windows XP: once the master copy has been produced, additional CDs containing the operating system can be produced for a few cents. The key to Microsoft's efficiency and profitability (and that of other companies with high fixed costs and trivial incremental or marginal costs) is to increase sales rapidly enough that fixed costs can be spread out over a large unit volume and substantial scale economies can be realized.

Another source of scale economies is the ability of companies producing in large volumes to achieve a greater division of labor and specialization. Specialization is said to have a favorable impact on productivity, mainly because it enables employees to become very skilled at performing a particular task. The classic example of such economies is Ford's Model T car. The world's first mass-produced car, the Model T Ford was introduced in 1923. Until then, Ford had made cars using an expensive hand-built craft production method. By introducing mass-production techniques, the company achieved greater division of labor (it split assembly into small, repeatable tasks) and specialization, which boosted employee productivity. Ford was also able to spread the fixed costs of developing a car and setting up production machinery over a large volume of output. As a result of these economies, the cost of manufacturing a car at Ford fell from $3,000 to less than $900 (in 1958 dollars).

Service companies also benefit from the realization of scale economies. In 1996 two of the world's largest banks, Chemical Banking and Chase Manhattan, both of New York, merged their operations, primarily to achieve cost savings, anticipated to be more than $1.7 billion per year, primarily through economies of scale. Economies of scale would come from combining the 600 retail branches of the original banks. By closing excess branches and consolidating its retail business into a smaller number of branches, the bank was able to increase the capacity utilization of its retail banking network significantly. The combined bank was able to generate the same volume of retail business from fewer branches. The fixed costs associated with retail branches—including rents, personnel, equipment, and utility costs—fell, which translated into a substantial reduction in the costs required to serve the average customer and the bank's cost structure.

These examples illustrate that economies of scale can boost profitability, as measured by return on invested capital (ROIC), in a number of ways. Economies of scale exist in production, sales and marketing, and R&D, and the overall effect of realizing scale economies is to reduce spending as a percentage of revenues on costs of goods sold (COGS), sales, general, and administrative expenses (SG&A), and R&D expenses, thereby boosting return on sales and, by extension, ROIC (see Figure 3.10). Moreover, by making more intensive use of existing capacity, a company can increase the amount of sales generated from its property, plant, and equipment (PPE), thereby reducing the amount of capital it needs to generate a dollar of sales, increasing its capital turnover and its ROIC.

The concept of scale economies is illustrated in Figure 4.2, which shows that as a company increases its output, unit costs fall. This process comes to an end at an output of Q^1, where all scale economies are exhausted. Indeed, at outputs of greater than Q^1, the company may encounter **diseconomies of scale,** which are the unit cost increases associated with a large scale of output. Diseconomies of scale occur primarily due to the increasing bureaucracy associated with large-scale enterprises and the managerial inefficiencies that can result.[1] Larger enterprises have a tendency to develop extensive managerial hierarchies in which dysfunctional political behavior is commonplace, information about operating matters is accidentally and deliberately distorted by the number of managerial layers through which it has to travel to reach top decision makers, and poor decisions are the result. As a result, past some point (such as $Q1$ in Figure 4.2), the inefficiencies that result from such developments outweigh any additional gains from economies of scale, and unit costs start to rise as output expands.

Managers must know not only the extent of economies of scale, but also where diseconomies of scale begin to occur. At Nucor Steel, for example, the realization that diseconomies of scale exist has led to a decision not to build plants that employ more than 300 individuals. The belief is that it is more efficient to build two plants, each employing 300 people, than one plant employing 600 people. Although the larger plant might theoretically be able to reap greater scale economies, Nucor's management believes that these would be swamped by the diseconomies of scale that come with larger organizational units.

FIGURE 4.2

Economies and
Diseconomies of
Scale

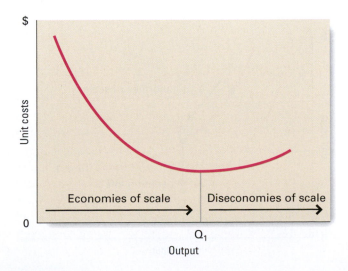

Efficiency and Learning Effects

Learning effects are cost savings that come from learning by doing. Labor, for example, learns by repetition how best to carry out a task. Therefore, labor productivity increases over time, and unit costs fall as individuals learn the most efficient way to perform a particular task. Equally important, management in new manufacturing facilities typically learns over time how best to run the new operation. Hence, production costs decline because of increasing labor productivity and management efficiency. Japanese companies like Toyota are noted for making learning a central part of their operating philosophy.

Learning effects tend to be more significant when a technologically complex task is repeated because there is more to learn. Thus, learning effects will be more significant in an assembly process that has 1,000 complex steps than in one with 100 simple steps. Although learning effects are normally associated with the manufacturing process, there is reason to believe that they are just as important in service industries. For example, one famous study of learning in the context of the health care industry found that more experienced medical providers posted significantly lower mortality rates for a number of common surgical procedures, suggesting that learning effects are at work in surgery.[2] The authors of this study used the evidence to argue for establishing regional referral centers for the provision of highly specialized medical care. These centers would perform many specific surgical procedures (such as heart surgery), replacing local facilities with lower volumes and presumably higher mortality rates.

In terms of the unit cost curve of a company, although economies of scale imply a movement along the curve (say, from A to B in Figure 4.3), the realization of learning effects implies a downward shift of the *entire* curve (B to C in Figure 4.3) as both labor and management become more efficient over time at performing their tasks at every level of output. In accounting terms, learning effects in a production setting will reduce the cost of goods sold as a percentage of revenues, enabling the company to earn a higher return on sales and return on invested capital.

No matter how complex the task is, however, learning effects typically die out after a limited period of time. Indeed, it has been suggested that they are really important only during the start-up period of a new process and cease after two or three years.[3] When changes occur to a company's production system—as a result of merger or the use of new information technology, for example—the learning process has to begin again.

FIGURE 4.3

The Impact of Learning and Scale Economies on Unit Costs

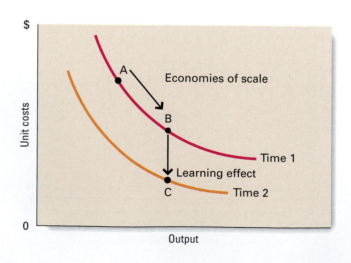

Efficiency and the Experience Curve

The experience curve refers to the systematic lowering of the cost structure, and consequent unit cost reductions, that have been observed to occur over the life of a product.[4] According to the experience curve concept, unit manufacturing costs for a product typically decline by some characteristic amount each time *accumulated* output of the product is doubled (accumulated output is the total output of a product since its introduction). This relationship was first observed in the aircraft industry, where it was found that each time accumulated output of airframes was doubled, unit costs declined to 80 percent of their previous level.[5] Thus, the fourth airframe typically cost only 80 percent of the second airframe to produce, the eighth airframe only 80 percent of the fourth, the sixteenth only 80 percent of the eighth, and so on. The outcome of this process is a relationship between unit manufacturing costs and accumulated output similar to that illustrated in Figure 4.4. Economies of scale and learning effects underlie the experience curve phenomenon. Put simply, as a company increases the accumulated volume of its output over time, it is able to realize both economies of scale (as volume increases) and learning effects. Consequently, unit costs and cost structure fall with increases in accumulated output.

The strategic significance of the experience curve is clear: increasing a company's product volume and market share will lower its cost structure relative to its rivals. Thus, company A in Figure 4.4, because it is farther down the experience curve, has a cost advantage over company B because of its lower cost structure. The concept is perhaps most important in industries that mass-produce a standardized output (for example, the manufacture of semiconductor chips). A company that wishes to become more efficient and lower its cost structure must try to ride down the experience curve as quickly as possible. This means constructing efficient scale manufacturing facilities even before it has generated demand for the product and aggressively pursuing cost reductions from learning effects. It might also need to adopt an aggressive marketing strategy, cutting prices to the bone and stressing heavy sales promotions and extensive advertising in order to build up demand, and hence accumulated volume, as quickly as possible. The need to be aware of the relationship of demand, price options, and costs noted in Chapter 4 is clear.

Once down the experience curve because of its superior efficiency, the company is likely to have a significant cost advantage over its competitors. For example, it has been argued that Intel uses such tactics to ride down the experience curve and gain a competitive advantage over its rivals in the market for microprocessors. Similarly, one

FIGURE 4.4

The Experience Curve

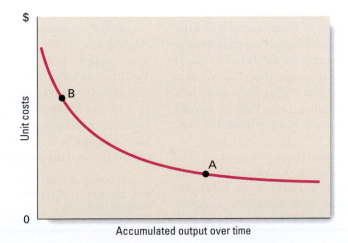

reason Matsushita came to dominate the global market for VHS videotape recorders is that it based its strategy on the experience curve.[6] The early success of Texas Instruments was also based on exploiting the experience curve, as Strategy in Action 4.1 details.

The company farthest down the experience curve cannot become complacent about its cost advantage. Strategy in Action 4.1 explains how obsession with the experience curve at Texas Instruments harmed the company. More generally, there are three reasons that managers should not become complacent about their efficiency-based cost advantages derived from experience effects. First, since neither learning effects nor economies of scale go on forever, the experience curve is likely to bottom out at some point; indeed, it must do so by definition. When this occurs, further unit cost reductions from learning effects and economies of scale will be hard to come by. Thus, in time, other companies can lower their cost structures and match the cost leader. Once this happens, a number of low-cost companies can have cost parity with each other. In such circumstances, a sustainable competitive advantage must rely on strategic factors besides the minimization of production costs by using existing technologies—factors such as better responsiveness to customers, product quality, or innovation.

Second, as noted in Chapter 2, changes that are always taking place in the external environment disrupt a company's business model, so cost advantages gained from experience effects can be made obsolete by the development of new technologies. The price of television picture tubes followed the experience curve pattern from the intro-

Strategy in Action

4.1

Too Much Experience at Texas Instruments

Texas Instruments (TI) was an early user of the experience curve concept. TI was a technological innovator, first in silicon transistors and then in semiconductors. The company discovered that with every doubling of accumulated production volume of a transistor or semiconductor, unit costs declined to 73 percent of their previous level. Building on this insight, when TI first produced a new transistor or semiconductor, it would slash the price of the product to stimulate demand. The goal was to drive up the accumulated volume of production and so drive down costs through the realization of experience curve economies. As a result, during the 1960s and 1970s, TI hammered its competitors in transistors and moved on to prevail in semiconductors and, ultimately, in hand-held calculators and digital watches. Until 1982, TI enjoyed rapid growth, with sales quadrupling between 1977 and 1981 alone.

After 1982, things began to go wrong for TI. The company's single-minded focus on cost reductions, an outgrowth of its strategic reliance on the experience curve, left it with a poor understanding of customer needs and market trends. Competitors such as Casio and Hewlett-Packard began to make major inroads into TI's hand-held calculator business by focusing on features in addition to cost and price that customers demanded. TI was slow to react to this trend and lost substantial market share as a result. In the late 1970s, it also decided to focus on semiconductors for watches and calculators, where it had gained substantial experience-curve-based cost economies, rather than developing metal oxide semiconductors for computer memories and advanced semiconductors. As it turned out, with the growth in minicomputers and personal computers in the early 1980s, the market shifted toward high-power metal oxide semiconductors. Consequently, TI found itself outflanked by Intel and Motorola. In sum, TI's focus on realizing experience curve economies initially benefited the company, but then it seems to have contributed toward a myopia that cost the company dearly.

Sources: G. Stalk and T. M. Hout, *Competing Against Time* (New York: Free Press, 1990). D. Miller, *The Icarus Paradox* (New York: HarperBusiness, 1990).

duction of television in the late 1940s until 1963. The average unit price dropped from $34 to $8 (in 1958 dollars) in that time. However, the advent of color TV interrupted the experience curve. To make picture tubes for color TVs, a new manufacturing technology was required, and the price of color TV tubes shot up to $51 by 1966. Then the experience curve reasserted itself. The price dropped to $48 in 1968, $37 in 1970, and $36 in 1972.[7] In short, technological change can alter the rules of the game, requiring that former low-cost companies take steps to reestablish their competitive edge.

A further reason for avoiding complacency is that producing a high volume of output does not necessarily give a company a lower cost structure. Different technologies have different cost structures. For example, the steel industry has two alternative manufacturing technologies: an integrated technology, which relies on the basic oxygen furnace, and a mini-mill technology, which depends on the electric arc furnace. As illustrated in Figure 4.5, mini-mills are cost efficient at relative low volume (Q^m), whereas the basic oxygen furnace requires high volumes to attain maximum efficiency (Q^i: $Q^i > Q^m$). Moreover, even when both technologies are producing at their most efficient output levels, steel companies with basic oxygen furnaces do not have a cost advantage over mini-mills.

Consequently, the pursuit of experience economies by an integrated company using basic oxygen technology may not bring the kind of cost advantages that a naive reading of the experience curve phenomenon would lead the company to expect. Indeed, there have been significant periods of time when integrated companies have not been able to get enough orders to run at optimum capacity (they have been producing at Q^i). Hence, their production costs have been considerably higher than those of minimills.[8] More generally, as we discuss next, in many industries, new flexible manufacturing technologies hold out the promise of allowing small manufacturers to produce at unit costs comparable to those of large assembly-line operations.

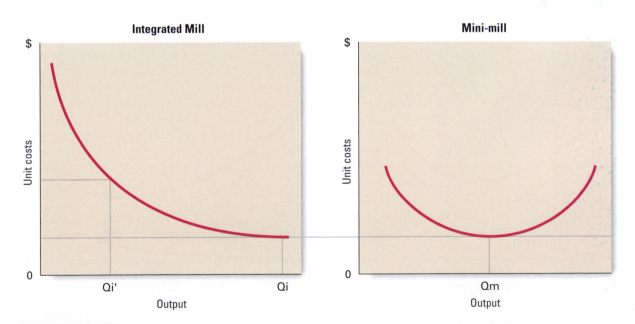

FIGURE 4.5

Unit Production Costs in an Integrated Mill and Mini-Mill

Efficiency, Flexible Manufacturing, and Mass Customization

Central to the concept of economies of scale is the idea that the best way to achieve high efficiency and a lower cost structure is through the mass production of a standardized output. The trade-off implicit in this idea is between unit costs and product variety. Producing greater product variety from a factory implies shorter production runs, which implies an inability to realize economies of scale and higher costs. That is, a wide product variety makes it difficult for a company to increase its production efficiency and thus reduce its unit costs. According to this logic, the way to increase efficiency and achieve a lower cost structure is to limit product variety and produce a standardized product in large volumes (see Figure 4.6a).

This view of production efficiency has been challenged by the rise of flexible manufacturing technologies. The term **flexible manufacturing technology**—or **lean production,** as it is often called—covers a range of manufacturing technologies designed to reduce setup times for complex equipment, increase the use of individual machines through better scheduling, and improve quality control at all stages of the manufacturing process.[9] Flexible manufacturing technologies allow the company to produce a wider variety of end products at a unit cost that at one time could be achieved only through the mass production of a standardized output (see Figure 4.6b). Indeed, research suggests that the adoption of flexible manufacturing technologies may increase efficiency and lower unit costs relative to what can be achieved by the mass production of a standardized output, while at the same time enabling the company to customize its product offering to a much greater extent than was once thought possible. The term **mass customization** has been coined to describe the ability of companies to use flexible manufacturing technology to reconcile two goals that were once thought to be incompatible: *low cost* and *differentiation through product customization.*[10]

Flexible manufacturing technologies vary in their sophistication and complexity. One of the most famous examples, Toyota's production system, is relatively unso-

FIGURE 4.6

Tradeoff Between Costs and Product Variety

phisticated, but it has been credited with making Toyota the most efficient auto company in the global industry. Toyota's flexible manufacturing system is profiled in Strategy in Action 4.2. **Flexible machine cells** are another common flexible manufacturing technology. A flexible machine cell is a grouping of various types of machinery, a common materials handler, and a centralized cell controller (a computer). Each cell normally contains four to six machines capable of performing a variety of operations but dedicated to producing a family of parts or products. The settings on machines are computer controlled, which allows each cell to switch quickly between the production of different parts or products.

Improved capacity utilization and reductions in work-in-progress (that is, stockpiles of partly finished products) and waste are major efficiency benefits of flexible machine cells. Improved capacity utilization arises from the reduction in setup times and from the computer-controlled coordination of production flow between machines, which eliminate bottlenecks. The tight coordination between machines also reduces work-in-progress. Reductions in waste are due to the ability of computer-controlled machinery to identify ways to transform inputs into outputs while producing a minimum of unusable waste material. Free-standing machines might be in use 50 percent of the time; the same machines when grouped into a cell can be used more than 80 percent of the time and produce the same end product with half the waste, thereby increasing efficiency and resulting in lower costs.

The effects of installing flexible manufacturing technology on a company's cost structure can be dramatic. W. L. Gore, a privately owned company that manufactures

Strategy in Action   4.2

Toyota's Lean Production System

Toyota's flexible manufacturing system was developed by one of the company's engineers, Ohno Taiichi. After working at Toyota for five years and visiting Ford's U.S. plants, Ohno became convinced that the mass production philosophy for making cars was flawed. He saw numerous problems, including three major drawbacks. First, long production runs created massive inventories, which had to be stored in large warehouses. This was expensive because of the cost of warehousing and because inventories tied up capital in unproductive uses. Second, if the initial machine settings were wrong, long production runs resulted in the production of a large number of defects (that is, waste). And third, the mass production system was unable to accommodate consumer preferences for product diversity.

In looking for ways to make shorter production runs economical, Ohno developed a number of techniques designed to reduce setup times for production equipment, a major source of fixed costs. By using a system of levers and pulleys, he was able to reduce the time required to change dies on stamping equipment from a full day in 1950 to three minutes by 1971. This advance made small production runs economical, which allowed Toyota to respond better to consumer demands for product diversity. Small production runs also eliminated the need to hold large inventories, thereby reducing warehousing costs. Furthermore, small product runs and the lack of inventory meant that defective parts were produced only in small numbers and entered the assembly process immediately. This reduced waste and made it easier to trace defects to their source and fix the problem. In sum, Ohno's innovations enabled Toyota to produce a more diverse product range at a lower unit cost than was possible with conventional mass production.

Sources: M. A. Cusumano, *The Japanese Automobile Industry* (Cambridge, Mass.: Harvard University Press, 1989). Ohno Taiichi, *Toyota Production System* (Cambridge, Mass.: Productivity Press, (1990). J. P. Womack, D. T. Jones, and D. Roos, *The Machine That Changed the World* (New York: Rawson Associates, 1990).

a wide range of products, from high-tech computer cables to its famous Gore-Tex fabric, has adopted flexible cells in several of its forty-six factories. In its cable-making facilities, the effect has been to cut the time taken to make computer cables by 50 percent, reduce stock by 33 percent, and shrink the space taken up by the plant by 25 percent.[11] More generally, in terms of the profitability framework developed in Chapter 3, flexible manufacturing technology should boost profitability (measured by ROIC) by reducing the cost of goods sold as a percentage of revenues, reducing the working capital needed to finance work in progress (because there is less of it), and reducing the amount of capital that needs to be invested in property plant and equipment to generate a dollar of sales (because less space is needed to store inventory).

Marketing and Efficiency

The marketing strategy that a company adopts can have a major impact on efficiency and cost structure. **Marketing strategy** refers to the position that a company takes with regard to pricing, promotion, advertising, product design, and distribution. Some of the steps leading to greater efficiency are fairly obvious. For example, riding down the experience curve to achieve a lower cost structure can be facilitated by aggressive pricing, promotions, and advertising, all of which are the task of the marketing function. Other aspects of marketing strategy have a less obvious but no less important impact on efficiency. One important aspect is the relationship of customer defection rates, cost structure, and unit costs.[12]

Customer defection rates are the percentage of a company's customers who defect every year to competitors. Defection rates are determined by customer loyalty, which in turn is a function of the ability of a company to satisfy its customers. Because acquiring a new customer entails certain one-time fixed costs for advertising, promotions, and the like, there is a direct relationship between defection rates and costs. The longer a company holds on to a customer, the greater is the volume of customer-generated unit sales that can be set against these fixed costs and the lower the average unit cost of each sale. Thus, lowering customer defection rates allows a company to achieve a lower cost structure.

One consequence of the defection-cost relationship depicted is illustrated in Figure 4.7. Because of the relatively high fixed costs of acquiring new customers, serving customers who stay with the company only for a short time before switching to competitors often leads to a loss on the investment made to acquire that customer. The longer a customer stays with the company, the more the fixed costs of acquiring that customer can be spread out over repeat purchases, boosting the profit per customer.

FIGURE 4.7

The Relationship Between Customer Loyalty and Profit per Customer

Thus, there is a positive relationship between the length of time that a customer stays with a company and profit per customer. So if a company can reduce customer defection rates, it can make a much better return on its investment in acquiring customers and thereby boost its profitability. In terms of the profitability framework developed in Chapter 3, reduced customer defection rates means that the company needs to spend less on sales, general, and administrative expenses to generate a dollar of sales revenue, which increases both return on sales and return on invested capital.

For an example, consider the credit card business.[13] Most credit card companies spend an average of $50 to recruit a customer and set up a new account. These costs come from the advertising required to attract new customers, credit checks required for each customer, and the mechanics of setting up an account and issuing a card. These one-time fixed costs can be recouped only if a customer stays with the company for at least two years. Moreover, when customers stay a second year, they tend to increase their use of the credit card, which raises the volume of revenues generated by each customer over time. As a result, although the credit card business loses $50 per customer in Year 1, it makes a profit of $44 in Year 3 and $55 in Year 6.

Another economic benefit of long-time customer loyalty is the free advertising that customers provide for a company. Loyal customers can dramatically increase the volume of business through referrals. A striking example is Britain's largest retailer, the clothing and food company Marks & Spencer, whose success is built on a well-earned reputation for providing its customers with high-quality goods at reasonable prices. The company has generated such customer loyalty that it does not need to advertise in Britain, a major source of cost saving.

The key message, then, is that reducing customer defection rates and building customer loyalty can be major sources of a lower cost structure. A 5 percent reduction in customer defection rates leads to the following increases in profits per customer over average customer life: 75 percent in the credit card business, 50 percent in the insurance brokerage industry, 45 percent in the industrial laundry business, and 35 percent in the computer software industry.[14]

A central component of developing a strategy to reduce defection rates is to identify customers who do defect, find out why they defected, and act on that information so that other customers do not defect for similar reasons in the future. To take these measures, the marketing function must have information systems capable of tracking customer defections.

Materials Management, Just-in-Time, and Efficiency

The contribution of materials management to boosting the efficiency of a company can be just as dramatic as the contribution of production and marketing. **Materials management** encompasses the activities necessary to get inputs and components to a production facility (including the costs of purchasing inputs), through the production process, and out through a distribution system to the end user.[15] Because there are so many sources of cost in this process, the potential for reducing costs through more efficient materials management strategies is enormous. For a typical manufacturing company, materials and transportation costs account for 50 to 70 percent of its revenues, so even a small reduction in these costs can have a substantial impact on profitability. According to one estimate, for a company with revenues of $1 million, a return on invested capital of 5 percent, and materials management costs that amount to 50 percent of sales revenues (including purchasing costs), increasing total profits by $15,000 would require either a 30 percent increase in sales revenues or a 3 percent reduction in materials costs.[16] In a typical competitive market, reducing materials costs by 3 percent is usually much easier than increasing sales revenues by 30 percent.

Improving the efficiency of the materials management function typically requires the adoption of a just-in-time (JIT) inventory system, designed to economize on inventory holding costs by having components arrive at a manufacturing plant just in time to enter the production process or goods at a retail store only when stock is depleted. The major cost saving comes from increasing inventory turnover, which reduces inventory holding costs, such as warehousing and storage costs, and the company's need for working capital. For example, Wal-Mart uses JIT systems to replenish the stock in its stores at least twice a week; many stores receive daily deliveries if they are needed. The typical competitor replenishes its stock every two weeks so that they have to carry a much higher inventory and need more working capital per dollar of sales. Compared to its competitors, Wal-Mart can maintain the same service levels with one-fourth the inventory investment, a major source of its lower cost structure. Thus, faster inventory turnover has helped Wal-Mart achieve an efficiency-based competitive advantage in the retailing industry.[17] More generally, in terms of the profitability model developed in Chapter 3, JIT inventory systems reduce the need for working capital (since there is less inventory to finance) and fixed capital to finance storage space (since there is less to store), which reduces capital needs, increases capital turnover, and, by extension, boosts the return on invested capital.

The drawback of JIT systems is that they leave a company without a buffer stock of inventory. Although buffer stocks are expensive to store, they can help tide a company over shortages on inputs brought about by disruption among suppliers (for instance, a labor dispute at a key supplier) and help a company respond quickly to increases in demand. However, there are ways around these limitations. For example, to reduce the risks linked to dependence on just one supplier for an important input, a company might decide to source inputs from multiple suppliers.

Recently, the efficient management of materials and inventory has been recast in terms of **supply chain management:** the task of managing the flow of inputs and components from suppliers into the company's production processes to minimize inventory holding and maximize inventory turnover. One of the exemplary companies in terms of supply chain management is Dell, whose goal is to streamline its supply chain to such an extent that it "replaces inventory with information" (See the *Running Case* in this section for details.) Strategy in Action 4.3 looks at how the three major office superstores—Office Depot, Staples, and Office Max—are competing against each other by trying to manage their supply chains more efficiently.

R&D Strategy and Efficiency

The role of superior research and development (R&D) in helping a company achieve a greater efficiency and a lower cost structure is twofold. First, the R&D function can boost efficiency by designing products that are easy to manufacture. By cutting down on the number of parts that make up a product, R&D can dramatically decrease the required assembly time, which translates into higher employee productivity, lower costs, and higher profitability. For example, after Texas Instruments redesigned an infrared sighting mechanism that it supplies to the Pentagon, it found that it had reduced the number of parts from 47 to 12, the number of assembly steps from 56 to 13, the time spent fabricating metal from 757 minutes per unit to 219 minutes per unit, and unit assembly time from 129 minutes to 20 minutes. The result was a substantial decline in production costs. Design for manufacturing requires close coordination between the production and R&D functions of the company, of course. Cross-functional teams that contain production and R&D personnel who work jointly on the problem best achieve this.

Strategy in Action

4.3

Supply Chain Management at Office Superstores

Over the past decade, Office Depot, Staples, and Office Max have been engaged in an intense race to dominate the office superstore business. Office superstores have adopted a supermarket approach to selling office supplies and equipment, which includes everything from paper and printer ink to computers and office furniture. Like all other supermarket-type retailers, their margins are razor thin. So to boost their profitability, all three have been looking at ways of managing their supply chains more efficiently. The goal is to coordinate the flow of materials from vendors to such a degree that inventory turns over more rapidly and so less store space needs to be devoted to storing inventory, which allows for smaller, less expensive stores. To the extent that they are successful, this strategy should produce higher sales per square foot, require less investment in store real estate, and tie up less working capital in inventory. All of this will boost profitability as measured by the return on invested capital.

Using inventory turnover as a metric, Office Depot is the clear leader, with a 7.1 inventory turn rate for 2001; its inventory turns over (i.e., is replaced) 7.1 times per year. Staples is next, with 4.2 inventory turns, followed by Office Max, with 3.2 inventory turns. Office Depot attributes its high inventory turnover to an early investment in information systems, which allow it to track the sales of individual items closely and link them to an optimal reordering cycle. In addition, these systems have helped it to identify slow-moving, low-margin items. Over the past few years, Office Depot has scaled back the number of products it keeps in stock—its stock keeping units (SKUs)—by about 20 percent by removing slow-moving, low-margin items from its stores. As a result, it can operate with slightly smaller stores and still generate comparable sales levels; its new stores are 25,000 square feet, compared to 30,000 square feet in older stores. As it has grown larger, Office Depot has also been able to use its buying power to persuade vendors to drop-ship supplies at Office Depot warehouses on a just-in-time basis, thereby removing the need to hold expensive inventory.

For its part, Staples announced in 2001 that more efficient supply chain management was one of its top priorities. Staples has put some thirty initiatives in place in recent years in an attempt to manage its inventory better. Among them is working closely with its top thirty suppliers to develop joint processes for streamlining the supply process. Regular meetings with Hewlett Packard, for example, has prompted the retailer to move ink cartridges, one of its major categories, to the front of the store to yield faster inventory turns. Staples credits this action with a $6 million to $8 million reduction in inventory. More generally, Staples maintains that between 1998, when it started work on these initiatives, and 2001, the average inventory per store has fallen by some 30 percent. One of the most dramatic steps Staples has taken has been to eliminate the in-store stock of personal computers from some 200 stores, replacing the product displays and on-floor inventory with a web-based display that allows Staples customers to enter a customized order for a PC, which a Staples vendor then builds.

Office Max too is investing aggressively in supply chain management initiatives in an attempt to take inventory out of its system. Like its competitors, it has invested in information systems to track the sale of individual items and link that to reordering cycles. It is in the process of rationalizing its SKUs, removing slow-selling, low-margin items from stores, and downscaling the size of its stores while planning to boost sales per square foot. As a result, the average size of a new Office Max store has fallen by 15 percent over the last few years.

Source: M. Prior, "Major Office Suppliers Hone Supply Chain Efficiencies," *DSN Retailing,* November 5, 2001, pp. 27–31.

The second way in which the R&D function can help a company achieve a lower cost structure is by pioneering process innovations. A *process innovation* is an innovation in the way production processes operate that improves their efficiency. Process innovations have often been a major source of competitive advantage. Toyota's competitive advantage is based partly on the company's invention of new flexible manufacturing processes that dramatically reduced setup times. This process innovation enabled it to obtain efficiency gains associated with flexible manufacturing systems years ahead of its competitors.

Human Resource Strategy and Efficiency

Employee productivity is one of the key determinants of an enterprise's efficiency, cost structure, and profitability.[18] Productive manufacturing employees can lower the cost of goods sold as a percentage of revenues, a productive sales force can increase sales revenues for a given level of expenses, and productive employees in the company's R&D function can boost the percentage of revenues generated from new products for a given level of R&D expenses. Thus, productive employees lower the costs of generating revenues, increase the return on sales, and by extension boost the company's return on invested capital. The challenge for a company's human resource function is to devise ways to increase employee productivity. Among the choices it has are hiring strategies, training employees, organizing the work force into self-managing teams, and linking pay to performance.

Hiring Strategy. Many companies well known for their productive employees devote considerable attention to hiring. Wal-Mart, for example, seeks employees who share the values that are central to the Wal-Mart culture, including frugality, a belief in good customer service, and an appreciation for the value of money. Southwest Airlines hires people who have a positive attitude and work well in teams because it believe that people who have a positive attitude will work hard and interact well with customers, therefore helping to create customer loyalty. Nucor hires people who are self-reliant and goal oriented, because its employees work in self-managing teams where they have to be self-reliant and goal oriented to perform well. As these examples suggest, it is important to make sure that the hiring strategy of the company is consistent with its own internal organization, culture, and strategic priorities. The people a company hires should have attributes that match the strategic objectives of the company.

Employee Training. Employees are a major input into the production process. Those who are highly skilled can perform tasks faster and more accurately and are more likely to learn the complex tasks associated with many modern production methods than individuals with lesser skills. Training upgrades employee skill levels, bringing the company productivity-related efficiency gains from learning and experimentation.[19]

Self-Managing Teams. The use of **self-managing teams,** whose members coordinate their own activities, including making their own hiring, training, work, and reward decisions, has been spreading rapidly. The typical team comprises five to fifteen employees who produce an entire product or undertake an entire task. Team members learn all team tasks and rotate from job to job. Because a more flexible work force is one result, team members can fill in for absent coworkers and take over managerial duties such as work and vacation scheduling, ordering materials, and hiring new members. The greater responsibility thrust on team members and the empowerment it implies are seen as motivators. (Empowerment is the process of giving lower-level employees decision-making power.) People often respond well to being given greater autonomy and responsibility. Performance bonuses linked to team production and quality targets work as an additional motivator.

The effect of introducing self-managing teams is reportedly an increase in productivity of 30 percent or more and a substantial increase in product quality. Further cost savings arise from eliminating supervisors and creating a flatter organizational hierarchy, which also lowers the cost structure of the company. In manufacturing companies, perhaps the most potent way to lower the cost structure is to combine self-managing teams with flexible manufacturing cells. For example, after the introduction of flexible manufacturing technology and work practices based on self-managing teams, a General Electric plant in Salisbury, North Carolina, increased productivity by 250 percent compared with GE plants that produced the same products four years earlier.[20]

Still, teams are no panacea; in manufacturing companies, self-managing teams may fail to live up to their potential unless they are integrated with flexible manufacturing technology. Also, teams put a lot of management responsibilities on team members, and helping team members to cope with these responsibilities often requires substantial training—a fact that many companies often forget in their rush to drive down costs, with the result that the teams don't work out as well as planned.[21]

Pay for Performance. It is hardly surprising that linking pay to performance can help increase employee productivity, but the issue is not quite so simple as just introducing incentive pay systems. It is also important to define what kind of job performance is to be rewarded and how. Some of the most efficient companies in the world, mindful that cooperation among employees is necessary to realize productivity gains, link pay to group or team (rather than individual) performance. Nucor divides its work force into teams of thirty or so, with bonus pay, which can amount to 30 percent of base pay, linked to the ability of the team to meet productivity and quality goals. This link creates a strong incentive for individuals to cooperate with each other in pursuit of team goals; that is, it facilitates teamwork.

Information Systems, the Internet, and Efficiency

With the rapid spread of computers, the explosive growth of the Internet and corporate intranets (internal corporate computer networks based on Internet standards), and the spread of high-bandwidth fiber optics and digital wireless technology, the information systems function is moving to center stage in the quest for operating efficiencies and a lower cost structure.[22] The impact of information systems on productivity is wide ranging and potentially affects all other activities of a company. For example, in the *Closing Case* to Chapter 3, we saw how Cisco Systems has been able to realize significant cost savings by moving its ordering and customer service functions online. The company has just 300 service agents handling all of its customer accounts, compared to the 900 it would need if sales were not handled online. The difference represents an annual saving of $20 million a year. Moreover, without automated customer service functions, Cisco calculates that it would need at least 1,000 additional service engineers, which would cost around $75 million.[23] Dell Computer also makes extensive use of the Internet to lower its cost structure and differentiate itself from rivals (see the *Running Case*).

More generally, companies like Cisco and Dell are using web-based information systems to reduce the costs of coordination between the company and its customers and the company and its suppliers. By using web-based programs to automate customer and supplier interactions, the number of people required to manage these interfaces can be substantially reduced, thereby reducing costs. This trend extends beyond high-tech companies. Banks and financial service companies are finding that they can substantially reduce costs by moving customer accounts and support functions online. Such a move reduces the need for customer service representatives, bank tellers, stockbrokers, insurance agents, and others. For example, it costs an average of about $1.07 to execute a transaction at a bank, such as shifting money from one account to another; executing the same transaction over the Internet costs $0.01.[24]

Running Case

Dell's Utilization of the Internet

By 2001, more than 85 percent of Dell's computers were sold online. According to Michael Dell, "As I saw it, the Internet offered a logical extension of the direct (selling) model, creating even stronger relationships with our customers. The Internet would augment conventional telephone, fax, and face-to-face encounters, and give our customers the information they wanted faster, cheaper, and more efficiently." Dell's web site allows customers to customize their orders to get the system that best suits their particular requirements. By allowing customers to configure their order, Dell increases its customer responsiveness, thereby differentiating itself from rivals. Dell has also put much of its customer service functions online, reducing the need for telephone calls to customer service representatives and saving costs in the process. Each week, some 200,000 people access Dell's troubleshooting tips online. Each of these visits to Dell's web site saves the company a potential $15, which is the average cost of a technical support call. If just 10 percent of these online visitors were to call Dell by telephone instead, it would cost the company $15.6 million per year.

Dell uses the Internet to manage its supply chain, feeding real-time information about order flow to its suppliers, which use this information to schedule their own production, providing components to Dell on a just-in-time basis, thereby taking inventory out of the system and reducing Dell's need for working capital and space to store the inventory. Dell's ultimate goal is to drive all inventories out of the supply chain apart from that in transit between suppliers and Dell, effectively replacing inventory with information. In that way, Dell can drive significant costs out of its system.

Internet-based customer ordering and procurement systems have also allowed the company to synchronize demand and supply to an extent that few other companies can. For example, if Dell sees that it is running out of a particular component, say 17-inch monitors from Sony, it can manipulate demand by offering a 19-inch model at a lower price until Sony delivers more 17-inch monitors. By taking such steps to fine-tune the balance between demand and supply, Dell can meet customers' expectations and maintain its differential advantage. Moreover, balancing supply and demand allows the company to minimize excess and obsolete inventory. Dell writes off between 0.05 percent and 0.1 percent of total materials costs in excess or obsolete inventory. Its competitors write off between 2 and 3 percent, which again gives Dell a significant cost advantage.

Sources: B. Gates, *Business @ the Speed of Thought* (New York: Warner Books, 1999). "Enter the Eco-System: From Supply Chain to Network," *Economist,* November 11, 2000. "Dell's Direct Initiative," *Country Monitor,* June 7, 2000, p. 5. Michael Dell, *Direct from Dell: Strategies That Revolutionized an Industry* (New York: HarperBusiness, 1999). (The Dell quote is from p. 91.)

Similarly, the theory behind Internet-based retailers such as Amazon.com is that by replacing physical stores and their supporting personnel with an online virtual store and automated ordering and checkout processes, significant costs can be taken out of the retailing system. Cost savings can also be realized by using web-based information systems to automate many internal company activities, from managing expense reimbursements to benefits planning and hiring processes, thereby reducing the need for internal support personnel.

For many years, skeptics questioned the impact that computer-based information systems were having on productivity, but recent data suggest that the gains are starting to appear. For the period 1996–2000, U.S. nonfarm productivity growth accelerated from a historic average of 1 percent per year to 2.8 percent per year. The productivity growth was greatest in the computer industry, which is not surprising given the efforts by companies like Cisco and Dell to implement web-based sales and service functions. Moreover, careful analysis has shown that productivity growth was greater in sectors of the economy that invested more in information technology during this period.[25]

Infrastructure and Efficiency

A company's infrastructure—that is, its structure, culture, style of strategic leadership, and control system—determines the context within which all other value creation activities take place. It follows that improving infrastructure can help a company increase efficiency and lower its cost structure. Above all, an appropriate infrastructure can help foster a companywide commitment to efficiency and promote cooperation among different functions in pursuit of efficiency goals. These issues are addressed at length in later chapters.

For now, it is important to note that strategic leadership is especially important in building a companywide commitment to efficiency. The leadership task is to articulate a vision that recognizes the need for *all* functions of a company to focus on improving efficiency. It is not enough to improve the efficiency of production, or of marketing, or of R&D in a piecemeal fashion. Achieving superior efficiency requires a companywide commitment to this goal that must be articulated by general and functional managers. A further leadership task is to facilitate cross-functional cooperation needed to achieve superior efficiency. For example, designing products that are easy to manufacture requires that production and R&D personnel communicate; integrating JIT systems with production scheduling requires close communication between material management and production; designing self-managing teams to perform production tasks requires close cooperation between human resources and production; and so on.

Table 4.1 summarizes the primary roles that various functions must take in order to achieve superior efficiency. Bear in mind that achieving superior efficiency is not something that can be tackled on a function-by-function basis. It requires an organization-wide commitment and an ability to ensure close cooperation among functions. Top management, by exercising leadership and influencing the infrastructure, plays a major role in this process.

TABLE 4.1

Primary Roles of Value Creation Functions in Achieving Superior Efficiency

Value Creation Function	Primary Roles
Infrastructure (leadership)	1. Provide companywide commitment to efficiency. 2. Facilitate cooperation among functions.
Production	1. Where appropriate, pursue economies of scale and learning economics. 2. Implement flexible manufacturing systems.
Marketing	1. Where appropriate, adopt aggressive marketing to ride down the experience curve. 2. Limit customer defection rates by building brand loyalty.
Materials management	1. Implement JIT systems.
R&D	1. Design products for ease of manufacture. 2. Seek process innovations.
Information systems	1. Use information systems to automate processes. 2. Use information systems to reduce costs of coordination.
Human resources	1. Institute training programs to build skills. 2. Implement self-managing teams. 3. Implement pay for performance.

Achieving Superior Quality

In Chapter 3, we noted that quality can be thought of in terms of two dimensions: product *reliability* and other product *attributes*. High-quality products are both reliable, in the sense that they do the job they were designed for and do it well, and are also perceived by consumers to have superior attributes. We also noted that superior quality gives a company two advantages. First, a strong reputation for quality allows a company to *differentiate* itself from rivals by creating more value in the eyes of customers, and this gives it the option of charging a premium price for its products. Second, eliminating defects or errors from the production process reduces waste, increases efficiency, and lowers the cost structure of the company and increases its profitability. For example, reducing the number of defects in a company's manufacturing process will lower the cost of goods sold as a percentage of revenues, thereby raising the company's return on sales and return on invested capital. In this section, we look in more depth at what managers can do to enhance the reliability and other attributes of the company's product offering.

Attaining Superior Reliability

The principal tool that managers use to increase the reliability of their product offering is total quality management, or some variation of that tool, such as the Six Sigma quality improvement methodology made famous by General Electric. **Total quality management** (TQM) stresses that all company operations should be oriented toward improving the reliability of a company's product offerings.[26] The TQM concept was developed by a number of American consultants, including W. Edwards Deming, Joseph Juran, and A. V. Feigenbaum.[27] Originally, these consultants won few converts in the United States. However, managers in Japan embraced their ideas enthusiastically and even named their premier annual prize for manufacturing excellence after Deming. The philosophy underlying TQM, as articulated by Deming, is based on the following five-step chain reaction:

1. Improved quality means that costs decrease because of less rework, fewer mistakes, fewer delays, and better use of time and materials.

2. As a result, productivity improves.

3. Better quality leads to higher market share and allows the company to raise prices.

4. This increases the company's profitability and allows it to stay in business.

5. Thus the company creates more jobs.[28]

   Deming identified a number of steps that should be part of any TQM program:

■ A company should have a clear business model to specify where it is going and how it is going to get there.

■ Management should embrace the philosophy that mistakes, defects, and poor-quality materials are not acceptable and should be eliminated.

■ Quality of supervision should be improved by allowing more time for supervisors to work with employees and giving them appropriate skills for the job.

■ Management should create an environment in which employees will not fear reporting problems or recommending improvements.

■ Work standards should be defined not only as numbers or quotas but should also include some notion of quality to promote the production of defect-free output.

■ Management is responsible for training employees in new skills to keep pace with changes in the workplace.

■ Achieving better quality requires the commitment of everyone in the company.

It took the rise of Japan to the top rank of economic powers in the 1980s to alert Western business to the importance of the TQM concept. Since then, TQM practices have spread rapidly throughout Western industry. Strategy in Action 4.4 describes one of the most successful implementations of a quality improvement process, General Electric's Six Sigma program.

Despite such instances of spectacular success, TQM practices are not universally accepted. A study by the American Quality Foundation found that only 20 percent of

Strategy in Action   4.4

General Electric's Six Sigma Quality Improvement Process

Six Sigma, a quality and efficiency program adopted by several major corporations, including Motorola, General Electric, and Allied Signal, aims to reduce defects, boost productivity, eliminate waste, and cut costs throughout a company. "Sigma" comes from the Greek letter that statisticians use to represent a standard deviation from a mean: the higher the number of sigmas, the smaller the number of errors. At 6 sigma, a production process would be 99.99966 percent accurate, creating just 3.4 defects per million units. Although it is almost impossible for a company to achieve such perfection, several companies strive toward that goal.

General Electric is perhaps the most fervent adopter of Six Sigma programs. Under the direction of long-serving CEO Jack Welch, GE spent nearly $1 billion between 1994 and 1998 to convert all of its divisions to the Six Sigma faith. Welch credits the program with raising GE's operating profit margins to 16.6 percent in 1998, up from 14.4 percent three years earlier.

One of the first products that was designed from start to finish using Six Sigma processes was a $1.25 million diagnostic computer tomography (CT) scanner, the Lightspeed, which produces rapid three-dimensional imagines of the human body. The new scanner captures multiple images simultaneously, requiring only twenty seconds to do full body scans that once took three minutes—important because patients must remain perfectly still during the scan. GE spent $50 million to run 250 separate Six Sigma analyses designed to improve the reliability and lower the manufacturing cost of the new scanner. Its efforts were rewarded when the Lightspeed's first customers soon noticed that it ran without downtime from the start, a testament to the reliability of the product.

Achieving that reliability took a lot of work. GE's engineers deconstructed the scanner into its basic components and tried to improve the reliability of each component through a detailed step-by-step analysis. For example, the most important part of CT scanners is vacuum tubes that focus X-ray waves. The tubes that GE used in previous scanners, which cost $60,000 each, suffered from low reliability. Hospitals and clinics wanted the tubes to operate for twelve hours a day for at least six months, but typically they lasted only half that long. Moreover, GE was scrapping some $20 million in tubes each year because they failed preshipping performance tests, and a disturbing number of faulty tubes were slipping past inspection, only to be pronounced dead on arrival.

To try to solve the reliability problem, the Six Sigma team took the tubes apart. They knew that one problem was a petroleum-based oil used in the tube to prevent short circuits by isolating the anode, which has a positive charge, from the negatively charged cathode. The oil often deteriorated after a few months, leading to short circuits, but the team did not know why. By using statistical "what-if" scenarios on all parts of the tube, the researchers learned that the lead-based paint on the inside of the tube was adulterating the oil. Acting on this information, the team developed a paint that would preserve the tube and protect the oil.

By pursuing this and other improvements, the Six Sigma team was able to extend the average life of a vacuum tube in the CT scanner from three months to over a year. Although the improvements increased the cost of the tube from $60,000 to $85,000, the increased cost was outweighed by the reduction in replacement costs, making it an attractive proposition for customers.

Sources: C. H. Deutsch, "Six-Sigma Enlightenment," *New York Times,* December 7, 1998, p. 1. J. J. Barshay, "The Six-Sigma Story," *Star Tribune,* June 14, 1999, p. 1. D. D. Bak, "Rethinking Industrial Drives," *Electrical/Electronics Technology,* November 30, 1998, p. 58.

U.S. companies regularly review the consequences of quality performance, compared with 70 percent of Japanese companies.[29] Another study, this one by Arthur D. Little, of 500 American companies using TQM found that only 36 percent believed that TQM was increasing their competitiveness.[30] A prime reason for this, according to the study, was that many companies had not fully understood or embraced the TQM concept. They were looking for a quick fix, whereas implementing a quality improvement program is a long-term commitment.

Implementing Reliability Improvement Methodologies

Among companies that have successfully adopted quality improvement methodologies, certain imperatives stand out. These are discussed below in the order in which they are usually tackled in companies implementing quality improvement programs. What needs to be stressed first, however, is that TQM is a cross-functional process. Its implementation requires close cooperation among all functions in the pursuit of the common goal of improving quality; it is a process that cuts across functions. The role played by the different functions in implementing TQM is summarized in Table 4.2.

Build Organizational Commitment to Quality. There is evidence that TQM will do little to improve the performance of a company unless everyone in the organization embraces it.[31] When Xerox launched its quality program, its first step was to educate the entire work force, from top management down, in the importance and operation of the TQM concept. It did so by forming groups, beginning with a group at the top of the organization that included the CEO. The top group was the first to receive basic TQM training. Each member of this group was then given the task of training a group at the next level in the hierarchy, and so on down throughout the organization until all 100,000 employees had received basic TQM training. Both top management and the human resource function of the company can play a major role in this process. Top management has the responsibility of exercising the

---

TABLE 4.2

The Role Played by Different Functions in Implementing TQM

Value Creation Function	Primary Roles
Infrastructure (leadership)	1. Provide leadership and commitment to quality. 2. Find ways to measure quality. 3. Set goals, and create incentives. 4. Solicit input from employees. 5. Encourage cooperation among functions.
Production	1. Shorten production runs. 2. Trace defects back to source.
Marketing	1. Focus on the customer. 2. Provide customers' feedback on quality.
Materials management	1. Rationalize suppliers. 2. Help suppliers implement TQM. 3. Trace defects back to suppliers.
R&D	1. Design products that are easy to manufacture.
Information systems	1. Use information systems to monitor defect rates.
Human resources	1. Institute TQM training programs. 2. Organize employees into quality teams.

leadership required to make a commitment to quality an organization-wide goal. The human resource function must take on responsibility for companywide training in TQM techniques.

Focus on the Customer. TQM practitioners see a focus on the customer as the starting point, and indeed, the raison d'être, of the whole quality philosophy.[32] The marketing function, because it provides the primary point of contact with the customer, should play a major role here. It needs to identify what customers want from the good or service that the company provides, what the company actually provides to customers, and the gap between what customers want and what they get, which could be called the quality gap. Then, together with the other functions of the company, it needs to formulate a plan for closing the quality gap.

Find Ways to Measure Quality. Another imperative of any TQM program is to create a metric that can be used to measure quality. This is relatively easy in manufacturing companies, where quality can be measured by criteria such as defects per million parts. It tends to be more difficult in service companies, but with a little creativity, suitable metrics can be devised. For example, one of the metrics Florida Power & Light uses to measure quality is meter-reading errors per month. Another is the frequency and duration of power outages. L. L. Bean, the Freeport, Maine, mail-order retailer of outdoor gear, uses the percentage of orders that are correctly filled as one of its quality measures. For some banks, the key measures are the number of customer defections per year and the number of statement errors per thousand customers. The common theme that runs through all these examples is identifying what quality means from a customer's perspective and devising a method to gauge this. Top management should take primary responsibility for formulating metrics to measure quality, but to succeed in this effort, it must receive input from the various functions of the company.

Set Goals and Create Incentives. Once a metric has been devised, the next step is to set a challenging quality goal and create incentives for reaching it. Xerox again provides an example. When it introduced its TQM program, its initial goal was to reduce defective parts from 25,000 per million to 1,000 per million. One way of creating incentives to attain such a goal is to link rewards, like bonus pay and promotional opportunities, to the goal. Thus, within many companies that have adopted self-managing teams, the bonus pay of team members is determined in part by their ability to attain quality goals. The task of setting goals and creating incentives is one of the key tasks of top management.

Solicit Input from Employees. Employees can be a vital source of information regarding the sources of poor quality. Therefore, a framework must be established for soliciting employee suggestions for improvements. Quality circles, which are meetings of groups of employees, have often been used to achieve this goal. Other companies have used self-managing teams as forums for discussing quality improvement ideas. Whatever forum is used, soliciting input from lower-level employees requires that management be open to receiving, and acting on, bad news and criticism from employees. According to Deming, one problem with U.S. management is that it has grown used to "killing the bearer of bad tidings." But, he argues, managers who are committed to the quality concept must recognize that bad news is a gold mine of information.[33]

Identify Defects and Trace Them to Source.

TQM preaches the need to identify defects during the work process, trace them to their source, find out what caused them, and make corrections so that they do not recur. Production and materials management typically have primary responsibility for this task.

To uncover defects, Deming advocates the use of statistical procedures to pinpoint variations in the quality of goods or services. Deming views variation as the enemy of quality.[34] Once variations have been identified, they must be traced to their source and eliminated. One technique that helps greatly in tracing defects to their source is reducing lot sizes for manufactured products. With short production runs, defects show up immediately. Consequently, they can be quickly traced to the source, and the problem can be addressed. Reducing lot sizes also means that when defective products are produced, their number will not be large, thus decreasing waste. Flexible manufacturing techniques, discussed earlier, can be used to reduce lot sizes without raising costs. Consequently, adopting flexible manufacturing techniques is an important aspect of a TQM program.

JIT inventory systems also play a part. Under a JIT system, defective parts enter the manufacturing process immediately; they are not warehoused for several months before use. Hence, defective inputs can be quickly spotted. The problem can then be traced to the supply source and corrected before more defective parts are produced. Under a more traditional system, the practice of warehousing parts for months before they are used may mean that large numbers of defects are produced by a supplier before they enter the production process.

Supplier Relations.

A major source of poor-quality finished goods is poor-quality component parts. To decrease product defects, a company has to work with its suppliers to improve the quality of the parts they supply. The primary responsibility in this area falls on the materials management function, which interacts with suppliers.

To implement JIT systems with suppliers and to get suppliers to adopt their own TQM programs, two steps are necessary. First, the number of suppliers has to be reduced to manageable proportions. Second, the company must commit to building a cooperative long-term relationship with the suppliers that remain. Asking suppliers to invest in JIT and TQM systems is asking them to make major investments that tie them to the company. For example, in order to implement a JIT system fully, the company may ask a supplier to relocate its manufacturing plant so that it is next door to the company's assembly plant. Suppliers are likely to be hesitant about making such investments unless they feel that the company is committed to an enduring, long-term relationship with them.

Design for Ease of Manufacture.

The more assembly steps a product requires, the more opportunities there are for making mistakes. Designing products with fewer parts should make assembly easier and result in fewer defects. Both R&D and manufacturing need to be involved in designing products that are easy to manufacture.

Break Down Barriers Among Functions.

Implementing TQM requires organization-wide commitment and substantial cooperation among functions. R&D has to cooperate with production to design products that are easy to manufacture, marketing has to cooperate with production and R&D so that customer problems identified by marketing can be acted on, human resource management has to cooperate with all the other functions of the company in order to devise suitable quality-training programs, and so on. The issue of achieving cooperation among subunits within a company is explored in Chapter 11. What needs stressing at this point is that ultimately it is the responsibility of top management to ensure that such cooperation occurs. Strategy in Action 4.5 describes the efforts of a service company to put TQM into practice and the benefits it has gained as a result.

Developing Superior Attributes

As we stated in Chapter 3, a product is a bundle of different attributes, and reliability is just one of them, albeit an important one. Products can also be *differentiated* by attributes such as their form, features, performance, durability, and styling. In addition, a company can differentiate itself by emphasizing attributes of the service

Strategy in Action   4.5

Improving Quality in Health Care

Following the lead of General Electric, a number of health care organizations have adopted the Six Sigma approach or similar quality improvement tools as a way of trying to improve the quality of their service offerings. One of them is Mount Carmel Health, a health care provider in Ohio. Mount Carmel Health implemented a Six Sigma program after suffering from poor financial performance in 2000. By early 2002, some fifty employees had been trained in Six Sigma principles, and they were leading some sixty projects in different phases of implementation.

One of the first projects focused on a simple and common problem among health care providers: timely and accurate reimbursement of costs. Mount Carmel discovered that it was writing off large amounts of potential revenues from the government-run Medicare programs as uncollectible because the charges were denied by Medicare administrators. Mount Carmel had low expectations for this business anyway so had never analyzed why the write-offs were so high. After careful analysis as part of a Six Sigma project, it discovered that a significant portion of the denials were due to the incorrect coding of reports submitted to Medicare. If the reports were coded correctly—that is, if fewer errors were made in the "production" of forms—the Six Sigma team estimated that annual income would be some $300,000 higher, so they devised improved processes for coding the forms to reduce the error rate. The result was that net income rose by over $800,000. It appeared that improving the coding process for this one parameter improved the reporting of many other parameters and led to a reimbursement rate much higher than anticipated.

In another case, Intermountain Health Care, a non-profit chain of twenty-four hospitals operating in Idaho, Utah, and Wyoming, adopted a quality improvement methodology to find and eliminate inappropriate variations in medical care—that is, to provide the patient with better health care and in the process reduce costs. The starting point was to identify variations in practice across physicians, particularly with regard to the cost and success rate of treatments. These data were then shared among physicians within the Intermountain system. The next step was for the physicians to use these data to eliminate poor practices and generally upgrade the quality of medical care. The results were quite striking. One early improvement was an attempt by Intermountain's hospital in Salt Lake City to lower the rate of postoperative wound infections. Before the effort began, the hospital's post-op infection rate was 1.8 percent, 0.2 point below the national average but still unacceptably high from a quality care perspective. By using a bedside computer system to make sure that antibiotics were given to patients two hours before surgery, the hospital dropped the infection rate in half, to 0.9 percent, within a year. Since then the post-op infection rate has dropped further still, to 0.4 percent compared to the current national average of 2 percent. Given that the average post-op infection adds $14,000 to a hospital bill, this constitutes not only a big improvement in patient outcomes but also a big cost saving.

Sources: I. R. Lazarus and K. Butler, "The Promise of Six-Sigma," *Managed Healthcare Executive* (October 2001): 22–26. D. Scalise, "Six-Sigma, the Quest for Quality," *Hospitals and Health Networks* (December 2001): 41–44. J. F. Siler and S. Atchison, "The Rx at Work in Utah," *Business Week*, October 25, 1991, p. 113.

associated with the product, such as ordering ease, prompt delivery, easy installation, the availability of customer training and consulting, and maintenance services. Dell Computer, for example, differentiates itself on ease of ordering (via the Web), prompt delivery, easy installation, and the ready availability of customer support and maintenance services. Differentiation can also be based on the attributes of the people in the company whom customers interact with when making a product purchase, such as their competence, courtesy, credibility, responsiveness, and communication. Singapore Airlines, for example, enjoys an excellent reputation for quality service, largely because passengers perceive their flight attendants as competent, courteous, and responsive to their needs. Thus, we can talk about the product attributes, service attributes, and personnel attributes associated with a company's product offering (see Table 4.3).

For a product to be regarded as high quality, a company's product offering must be seen as superior to that of rivals. Achieving a perception of high quality on any of these attributes requires specific actions by managers. First, it is important for managers to collect marketing intelligence indicating which of these attributes are most important to customers. For example, consumers of personal computers may place a low weight on durability because they expect their PC to be made obsolete by technological advances within three years, but they may place a high weight on features and performance. Similarly, ease of ordering and timely delivery may be very important attributes for customers of online booksellers (as they indeed are for customers of Amazon.com), whereas customer training and consulting may be very important attributes for customers who purchase complex business-to-business software to manage their relationships with suppliers.

Second, once the company has identified the attributes that are important to customers, it needs to design its products, and the associated services, so that those attributes are embodied in the product, and it needs to make sure that personnel in the company are appropriately trained so that the correct attributes are emphasized. This requires close coordination between marketing and product development (the topic of the next section), and the involvement of the human resource management function in employee selection and training.

Third, the company must decide which of the significant attributes to promote and how best to position those attributes in the minds of consumers, that is, how to tailor the marketing message so that it creates a consistent image in the minds of customers.[35] At this point, it is important to recognize that although a product might be

TABLE 4.3

Attributes Associated with a Product Offering

Product Attributes	Service Attributes	Associated Personnel Attributes
Form	Ordering ease	Competence
Features	Delivery	Courtesy
Performance	Installation	Credibility
Durability	Customer training	Reliability
Reliability	Customer consulting	Responsiveness
Style	Maintenance and repair	Communication

differentiated on the basis of six attributes, covering all of those attributes in the company's communication messages may lead to an unfocused message. Many marketing experts advocate promoting only one or two central attributes to customers. For example, Volvo consistently emphasizes the safety and durability of its vehicles in all marketing messages, creating the perception in the minds of consumers (backed by product design) that Volvo cars are safe and durable. Volvo cars are also very reliable and have high performance, but the company does not emphasize these attributes in its marketing messages. In contrast, Porsche emphasizes performance and styling in all of its marketing messages; thus, a Porsche is positioned differently in the minds of consumers than a Volvo is. Both are regarded as high-quality products because both have superior attributes, but the attributes that the two companies have chosen to emphasize are very different. They are differentiated from the average car in different ways.

Finally, it must be recognized that competition does not stand still, but instead produces continual improvement in product attributes and often the development of new product attributes. This is obvious in fast-moving high-tech industries where product features that were considered leading edge just a few years ago are now obsolete, but the same process is also at work in more stable industries. For example, the rapid diffusion of microwave ovens during the 1980s required food companies to build new attributes into their frozen food products: they had to maintain their texture and consistency while being microwaved. A product could not be considered high quality unless it could do that. This speaks to the importance of having a strong R&D function in the company that can work with marketing and manufacturing to continually upgrade the quality of the attributes that are designed into the company's product offerings. Exactly how to achieve this is covered in the next section.

Achieving Superior Innovation

In many ways, building distinctive competencies that result in innovation is the most important source of competitive advantage. This is because innovation can result in new products that better satisfy customer needs, can improve the quality (attributes) of existing products, or can reduce the costs of making products that customers want. Thus, the ability to develop innovative new products or processes gives a company a major competitive advantage that allows it to (1) *differentiate* its products and charge a premium price and/or (2) *lower its cost structure* below that of its rivals. Competitors, however, attempt to imitate successful innovations and often succeed. Therefore, maintaining a competitive advantage requires a continuing commitment to innovation.

Robert Cooper found that successful new product launches are major drivers of superior profitability. Cooper looked at more than 200 new product introductions and found that of those classified as successes, some 50 percent achieve a return on investment in excess of 33 percent, half have a payback period of two years or less, and half achieve a market share in excess of 35 percent.[36] Many companies have established a track record for successful innovation. Among them are Du Pont, which has produced a steady stream of successful innovations, such as cellophane, Nylon, Freon, and Teflon; Sony, whose successes include the Walkman, the Compact Disc, and the PlayStation; Nokia, which has been a leader in the development of wireless phones; Pfizer, a drug company that during the 1990s and early 2000s produced eight blockbuster new drugs; 3M, which has applied its core competency in tapes and adhesives to developing a wide range of new products; Intel, which has consistently managed to lead in the development of innovative new microprocessors to run personal computers; and Cisco Systems, whose innovations helped to pave the way for the rapid growth of the Internet.

The High Failure Rate of Innovation

Although promoting innovation can be a source of competitive advantage, the failure rate of innovative new products is high. One study of product development in the chemical, drug, petroleum, and electronics industries suggested that only about 20 percent of R&D projects ultimately result in a commercially successful products or process.[37] An in-depth case study of product development in three companies (one in chemicals and two in drugs) reported that about 60 percent of R&D projects reached technical completion, 30 percent were commercialized, and only 12 percent earned a profit that exceeded the company's cost of capital.[38] A famous study by the consulting division of Booz, Allen & Hamilton found that over one-third of 13,000 new customer and industrial products failed to meet company-specific financial and strategic performance criteria.[39] Another study found that 45 percent of new products introduced into the marketplace did not meet their profitability goals.[40]

This evidence suggests that many R&D projects do not result in a commercial product and that between 33 percent and 60 percent of all new products that do reach the marketplace fail to generate an adequate economic return. Two well-publicized product failures are Apple Computer's Newton, a personal digital assistant, and Sony's Betamax format in the video player and recorder market. While many reasons have been advanced to explain why so many new products fail to generate an economic return, five explanations for failure appear on most lists: uncertainty, poor commercialization, poor positioning strategy, technological myopia, and being slow to market.[41]

Uncertainty. New-product development is an inherently risky process. It requires testing a hypothesis whose answer is impossible to know prior to market introduction: Have we tapped an unmet customer need? Is there sufficient market demand for this new technology? Although good market research can reduce the uncertainty about likely future demand for a new technology, uncertainty cannot be eradicated, so a certain failure rate is to be expected.

The failure rate is higher for quantum product innovations than for incremental innovations. A **quantum innovation** represents a radical departure from existing technology—the introduction of something that is new to the world. The development of the World Wide Web can be considered a quantum innovation in communications technology. Other quantum innovations include the development of the first photocopier by Xerox, the first videocassette recorder by AMPEX, and the first contact lenses by Bausch and Lomb. **Incremental innovation** refers to an extension of existing technology. For example, Intel's Pentium Pro microprocessor is an incremental product innovation because it builds on the existing microprocessor architecture of Intel's X86 series. The uncertainty of future demand for a new product is much greater if that product represents a quantum innovation that is new to the world than if it is an incremental innovation designed to replace an established product whose demand profile is already well known. Consequently, the failure rate tends to be higher for quantum innovations.

Poor Commercialization. A second reason frequently cited to explain the high failure rate of new product introductions is **poor commercialization**—something that occurs when there is definite customer demand for a new product, but the product is not well adapted to customer needs because of factors such as poor design and poor quality. For instance, many of the early personal computers failed to sell because customers needed to understand computer programming to use them. Steve Jobs at Apple Computer understood that if the technology could be made user friendly (if it could be *commercialized*), there would be an enormous market for it. Hence, the original personal computers that Apple marketed incorporated little in the way of radically new technology, but they made existing technology accessible to the average person. Paradoxically, the failure of Apple Computer to establish a market for the Newton, the hand-held personal digital system that Apple introduced in the summer of 1993, can be traced to poor commercialization of a potentially attractive technology. Apple predicted a $1 billion market for the Newton, but sales failed to materialize when it became clear that the Newton's handwriting software, an attribute that Apple chose to emphasize in its marketing promotions, could not adequately recognize messages written on the Newton's message pad.

Poor Positioning Strategy. Poor positioning strategy arises when a company introduces a potentially attractive new product, but sales fail to materialize because it is poorly positioned in the marketplace. **Positioning strategy** is the specific set of options a company adopts for a product on four main dimensions of marketing: price, distribution, promotion and advertising, and product features. Apart from poor product quality, another reason for the failure of the Apple Newton was poor positioning strategy. The Newton was introduced at such a high initial price (close to $1,000) that there would probably have been few buyers even if the technology had been adequately commercialized.

Technological Myopia. Another reason that many new product introductions fail is that companies often make the mistake of marketing a technology for which there is not enough customer demand. **Technological myopia** occurs when a company gets blinded by the wizardry of a new technology and fails to examine whether there is customer demand for the product. This problem may have been a factor in the failure of the desktop computer introduced by NeXT in the late 1980s (NeXT was founded by Steve Jobs, the founder of Apple Computer). Technologically, the NeXT machines were clearly ahead of their time with advanced software and hardware features that would not be incorporated into most PCs for another decade. However, customer acceptance was very slow, primarily because of the complete lack of applications software such as spreadsheet and word processing programs to run on the machines. Management at NeXT was so enthused by the technology incorporated in their new computer that they ignored this basic market reality. After several years of slow sales, NeXT eventually withdrew the machines from the marketplace.

Slow to Market. Finally, companies fail when they are slow to get their products to market. The more time that elapses between initial development and final marketing—that is, the slower the "cycle time"—the more likely it is that someone else will beat the company to market and gain a first-mover advantage.[42] By and large, slow innovators update their products less frequently than fast innovators do. Consequently, they can be perceived as technical laggards relative to the fast innovators. In the car industry, General Motors has suffered from being a slow innovator. Its product development cycle has been about five years, compared with two to three years at Honda, Toyota, and Mazda and three to four years at Ford. Because they are based on five-year-old technology and design concepts, GM cars are already out of date when they reach the market.

Building Competencies in Innovation

Companies can take a number of steps to build a competency in innovation and avoid failure. Five of the most important steps seem to be (1) building skills in basic and applied scientific research, (2) developing a good process for project selection and project management, (3) cross-functional integration, (4) product development teams, and (5) partly parallel development processes.[43]

Building Skills in Basic and Applied Research. Building skills in basic and applied research requires the employment of research scientists and engineers and the establishment of a work environment that fosters creativity. A number of top companies try to achieve this by setting up university-style research facilities, where scientists and engineers are given time to work on their own research projects, in addition to projects that are linked directly to ongoing company research. At Hewlett-Packard, for example, company labs are open to engineers around the clock. Hewlett-Packard even encourages its corporate researchers to devote 10 percent of company time to exploring their own ideas and does not penalize them if they fail. 3M allows researchers to spend 15 percent of the workweek researching any topic that intrigues them, as long as there is the potential of a payoff for the company. The most famous outcome of this policy is the ubiquitous Post-its. The idea for them evolved from a researcher's desire to find a way to keep the bookmark from falling out of his hymnal. Post-its are now a major 3M business, with annual revenues of around $300 million.

Project Selection and Management. Project management is the overall management of the innovation process, from generation of the original concept, through development, and into final production and shipping. Project management requires three important skills: the ability to generate as many good ideas as possible, the ability to select among competing projects at an early stage of development so that the most promising receive funding and potential costly failures are killed off, and the ability to minimize time to market. The concept of the development funnel, divided into three phases, summarizes what is required to build these skills (see Figure 4.8).[44]

The objective in Phase I is to widen the mouth of the tunnel to encourage as much idea generation as possible. To this end, a company should solicit input from all its functions, as well as from customers, competitors, and suppliers. At Gate 1, the funnel narrows. Here ideas are reviewed by a cross-functional team of managers who

FIGURE 4.8

The Development Funnel

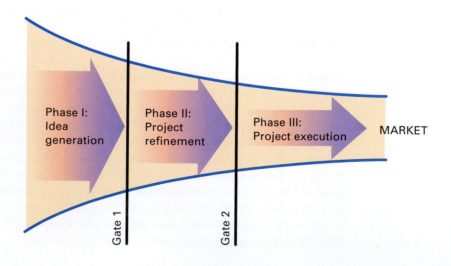

Phase I: Idea generation

Phase II: Project refinement

Phase III: Project execution

MARKET

Gate 1

Gate 2

did not participate in the original concept development. Concepts that are ready to proceed then move to Phase II, where the details of the project proposal are worked out. Note that Gate 1 is not a go/no-go evaluation point. At this screen, ideas may be sent back for further concept development and then resubmitted for evaluation.

During Phase II, which typically lasts only one or two months, the data and information from Phase I are put into a form that will enable senior management to evaluate proposed projects against competing projects. Normally, this requires the development of a careful project plan, complete with details of the proposed target market, attainable market share, likely revenues, development costs, production costs, key milestones, and the like. The next big selection point, Gate 2, is a go/no-go evaluation point. Senior managers review the projects under consideration and select those that seem likely winners and make most sense from a strategic perspective given the long-term goals of the company. The overriding objective is to select projects whose successful completion will help to maintain or build a competitive advantage for the company. A related objective is to ensure that the company does not spread its scarce capital and human resources too thinly over too many projects and instead concentrates resources on projects where the probability of success and potential returns are most attractive. Any project selected to go forward at this stage will be funded and staffed, the expectation being that it will be carried through to market introduction. In Phase III, the project development proposal is executed by a cross-functional product development team.

Cross-Functional Integration. Tight cross-functional integration between R&D, production, and marketing can help a company to ensure that:

1. Product development projects are driven by customer needs.

2. New products are designed for ease of manufacture.

3. Development costs are kept in check.

4. Time to market is minimized.

5. Close integration between R&D and marketing is achieved to ensure that product development projects are driven by the needs of customers.

A company's customers can be one of its primary sources of new product ideas. The identification of customer needs, and particularly unmet needs, can set the context within which successful product innovation takes place. As the point of contact with customers, the marketing function can provide valuable information. Moreover, integrating R&D and marketing is crucial if a new product is to be properly commercialized. Otherwise, a company runs the risk of developing products for which there is little or no demand.

The case of Techsonic Industries illustrates the benefits of integrating R&D and marketing. This company manufactures depth finders—electronic devices that fishermen use to measure the depth of water beneath a boat and to track their prey. Techsonic had weathered nine new-product failures in a row when the company decided to interview sportspeople across the country to identify what it was they needed. They discovered an unmet need for a depth finder with a gauge that could be read in bright sunlight, so that is what Techsonic developed. In the year after the $250 depth finder hit the market, Techsonic's sales tripled to $80 million, and its market share surged to 40 percent.[45]

Integration between R&D and production can help a company to ensure that products are designed with manufacturing requirements in mind. Design for manufacturing lowers manufacturing costs and leaves less room for mistakes and thus can lower costs and increase product quality. Integrating R&D and production can help lower development costs and speed products to market. If a new product is not designed with manufacturing capabilities in mind, it may prove too difficult to build, given existing manufacturing technology. In that case, the product will have to be redesigned, and both overall development costs and time to market may increase significantly. For example, making design changes during product planning could increase overall development costs by 50 percent and add 25 percent to the time it takes to bring the product to market.[46] Moreover, many quantum product innovations require new processes to manufacture them, which makes it all the more important to achieve close integration between R&D and production, since minimizing time to market and development costs may require the simultaneous development of new products and new processes.[47]

Product Development Teams. One of the best ways to achieve cross-functional integration is to establish cross-functional product development teams, composed of representatives from R&D, marketing, and production. The objective of a team should be to take a product development project from the initial concept development to market introduction. A number of attributes seem to be important in order for a product development team to function effectively and meet all its development milestones.[48]

First, a heavyweight project manager—one who has high status within the organization and the power and authority required to get the financial and human resources that the team needs to succeed—should lead the team and be dedicated primarily, if not entirely, to the project. The leader should believe in the project (a champion) and be skilled at integrating the perspectives of different functions and helping personnel from different functions work together for a common goal. The leader should also be able to act as an advocate of the team to senior management.

Second, the team should be composed of at least one member from each key function. The team members should have a number of attributes, including an ability to contribute functional expertise, high standing within their function, a willingness to share responsibility for team results, and an ability to put functional advocacy aside. It is generally preferable if core team members are 100 percent dedicated to the project for its duration. This makes sure that their focus is on the project, not on the ongoing work of their function.

Third, the team members should be physically co-located to create a sense of camaraderie and facilitate communication. Fourth, the team should have a clear plan and clear goals, particularly with regard to critical development milestones and development budgets. The team should have incentives to attain those goals; for example, pay bonuses when major development milestones are hit. Fifth, each team needs to develop its own processes for communication and conflict resolution. For example, one product development team at Quantum Corporation, a California-based manufacturer of disk drives for personal computers, instituted a rule that all major decisions would be made and conflicts resolved at meetings that were held every Monday afternoon. This simple rule helped the team to meet its development goals.[49]

Partly Parallel Development Processes. One way in which a product development team can compress the time it takes to develop a product and bring it to market is to use a partly parallel development process. Traditionally, product development processes have been organized on a sequential basis, as illustrated in Figure 4.9a. A problem with this kind of process is that product development proceeds without manufacturing issues in mind. Most significant, because the basic design of a product is completed prior to the design of a manufacturing process and full-scale commercial production, there is no early warning system to indicate manufacturability. As a consequence, the company may find that it cannot cost-efficiently manufacture the product and have to send it back to the design stage for redesign. The cycle time lengthens as the product bounces back and forth between stages.

To solve this problem, companies typically use a process similar to that illustrated in Figure 4.9b. In the partly parallel development process, development stages overlap so that, for example, work starts on the development of the production process before the product design is finalized. By reducing the need for expensive and time-consuming product redesigns, such a process can significantly reduce the time it takes to develop a new product and bring it to market.

For an example, consider what occurred after Intel Corporation introduced its 386 microprocessor in 1986. A number of companies, including IBM and Compaq, were racing to be the first to introduce a 386-based personal computer. Compaq beat IBM by six months and gained a major share of the high-power market mainly because it used a cross-functional team and a partly parallel process to develop the product. The team included engineers (R&D) and marketing, production, and finance people. Each function worked in parallel rather than sequentially. While engineers were designing the product, production people were setting up the manufacturing facilities, marketing people were working on distribution and planning marketing campaigns, and the finance people were working on project funding.

The primary role that the various functions play in achieving superior innovation is summarized in Table 4.4. The table makes two matters clear. First, top management must bear primary responsibility for overseeing the whole development process. This entails both managing the development funnel and facilitating cooperation among

FIGURE 4.9

Sequential and Partly Parallel Development Processes

TABLE 4.4

Function Roles for Achieving Superior Innovation

Value Creation Function	Primary Roles
Infrastructure (leadership)	1. Manage overall project (i.e., manage the development function). 2. Facilitate cross-functional cooperation.
Production	1. Cooperate with R&D on designing products that are easy to manufacture. 2. Work with R&D to develop process innovations.
Marketing	1. Provide market information to R&D. 2. Work with R&D to develop new products.
Materials management	No primary responsibility.
R&D	1. Develop new products and processes. 2. Cooperate with other functions, particularly marketing and manufacturing, in the development process.
Information Systems	1. Use information systems to coordinate cross-functional and cross-company product development work.
Human resources	1. Hire talented scientists and engineers.

the functions. Second, the effectiveness of R&D in developing new products and processes depends on its ability to cooperate with marketing and production.

Achieving Superior Responsiveness to Customers

To achieve superior responsiveness to customers, a company must give customers what they want, when they want it, and at a price they are willing to pay—so long as the company's long-term profitability is not compromised in the process. Customer responsiveness is an important *differentiating* attribute that can help to build brand loyalty. Strong product differentiation and brand loyalty give a company more pricing options; it can charge a premium price for its products or keep prices low to sell more goods and services to customers. Either way, the company that is more responsive to its customers' needs than rivals will have a competitive advantage, all else being equal.

Achieving superior responsiveness to customers means giving customers value for money, and steps taken to improve the efficiency of a company's production process and the quality of its products should be consistent with this aim. In addition, giving customers what they want may require the development of new products with new features. *In other words, achieving superior efficiency, quality, and innovation are all part of achieving superior responsiveness to customers.* There are two other prerequisites for attaining this goal. First, a company has to develop a competency in listening to and focusing on its customers and in investigating and identifying their needs. Second, it constantly needs to seek better ways to satisfy those needs.

Customer Focus

A company cannot be responsive to its customers' needs unless it knows what those needs are. Thus, the first step to building superior responsiveness to customers is to motivate the whole company to focus on the customer. The means to this end are demonstrating leadership, shaping employee attitudes, and using mechanisms for bringing customers into the company.

Leadership. Customer focus must start at the top of the organization. A commitment to superior responsiveness to customers brings attitudinal changes throughout a company that ultimately can be built only through strong leadership. A mission statement that puts customers first is one way to send a clear message to employees about the desired focus. Another avenue is top management's own actions. For example, Tom Monaghan, the founder of Domino's Pizza, stayed close to the customer by visiting as many stores as possible every week, running some deliveries himself, insisting that other top managers do the same, and eating Domino's pizza regularly.[50]

Employee Attitudes. Leadership alone is not enough to attain a superior customer focus. All employees must see the customer as the focus of their activity and be trained to focus on the customer, whether their function is marketing, manufacturing, R&D, or accounting. The objective should be to make employees think of themselves as customers—to put themselves in customers' shoes. At that point, employees will be better able to identify ways to improve the quality of a customer's experience with the company.

To reinforce this mindset, incentive systems within the company should reward employees for satisfying customers. For example, senior managers at the Four Seasons hotel chain, who pride themselves on their customer focus, like to tell the story of Roy Dyment, a doorman in Toronto who neglected to load a departing guest's briefcase into his taxi. The doorman called the guest, a lawyer, in Washington D.C., and found that he desperately needed the briefcase for a morning meeting. Dyment hopped on a plane to Washington and returned it—without first securing approval from his boss. Far from punishing Dyment for making a mistake and for not checking with management before going to Washington, the Four Seasons responded by naming Dyment Employee of the Year.[51] This action sent a powerful message to Four Seasons employees about the importance of satisfying customer needs.

Bringing Customers into the Company. "Know thy customer" is one of the keys to achieving superior responsiveness to customers. Knowing the customer not only requires that employees think like customers themselves; it also demands that they listen to what their customers have to say and, as much as possible, bring them into the company. Although this may not involve physically bringing customers into the company, it does mean bringing in customers' opinions by soliciting feedback from customers on the company's goods and services and by building information systems that communicate the feedback to the relevant people.

For an example, consider direct selling clothing retailer Lands' End. Through its catalog, the Internet, and customer service telephone operators, Lands' End actively solicits comments from its customers about the quality of its clothing and the kind of merchandise they want it to supply. Indeed, it was customers' insistence that initially prompted the company to move into the clothing segment. Lands' End used to supply equipment for sailboats through mail-order catalogs. However, it received so many requests from customers to include outdoor clothing in its offering that it responded by expanding the catalog to fill this need. Soon clothing became the main business, and Lands' End dropped the sailboat equipment. Today, the company still pays close attention to customer requests. Every month, a computer printout of customer requests and comments is given to managers. This feedback helps the company to fine-tune the merchandise it sells. Indeed, frequently new lines of merchandise are introduced in response to customer requests.[52]

Satisfying Customer Needs

Once a focus on the customer is an integral part of the company, the next requirement is to satisfy customer needs that have been identified. As already noted, efficiency, quality, and innovation are crucial competencies that help a company satisfy customer needs. Beyond that, companies can provide a higher level of satisfaction if they differentiate their products by (1) customizing them, where possible, to the requirements of individual customers and (2) reducing the time it takes to respond to or satisfy customer needs.

Customization. **Customization** is varying the features of a good or service to tailor it to the unique needs or tastes of groups of customers or, in the extreme case, individual customers. Although extensive customization can raise costs, the development of flexible manufacturing technologies has made it possible to customize products to a much greater extent than was feasible ten to fifteen years ago without experiencing a prohibitive rise in cost structure (particularly when flexible manufacturing technologies are linked with web-based information systems). For example, online retailers such as Amazon.com have used web-based technologies to develop a home page customized for each individual user. When a customer accesses Amazon.com, he or she is offered a list of recommendations for books or music to purchase based on an analysis of prior buying history, a powerful competency that gives Amazon.com a competitive advantage.

The trend toward customization has fragmented many markets, particularly customer markets, into ever smaller niches. An example of this fragmentation occurred in Japan in the early 1980s when Honda dominated the motorcycle market there. Second-place Yamaha decided to go after Honda's lead. It announced the opening of a new factory that, when operating at full capacity, would make Yamaha the world's largest manufacturer of motorcycles. Honda responded by proliferating its product line and stepping up its rate of new-product introduction. At the start of what became known as the "motorcycle wars," Honda had 60 motorcycles in its product line. Over the next eighteen months, it rapidly increased its range to 113 models, customizing them to ever smaller niches. Honda was able to accomplish this without bearing a prohibitive cost penalty because it has a competency in flexible manufacturing. The flood of Honda's customized models pushed Yamaha out of much of the market, effectively stalling its bid to overtake Honda.[53]

Response Time. Giving customers what they want when they want it requires speed of response to customer demands. To gain a competitive advantage, a company must often respond to customer demands very quickly, whether the transaction is a furniture manufacturer's delivery of a product once it has been ordered, a bank's processing of a loan application, an automobile manufacturer's delivery of a spare part for a car that broke down, or the wait in a supermarket checkout line. We live in a fast-paced society, where time is a valuable commodity. Companies that can satisfy customer demands for rapid response build brand loyalty, differentiate their products, and can charge higher prices for them.

Increased speed often lets a company choose a premium pricing option, as the mail delivery industry illustrates. The air express niche of the mail delivery industry is based on the notion that customers are often willing to pay considerably more for overnight express mail as opposed to regular mail. Another example of the value of rapid response is Caterpillar, the manufacturer of heavy earth-moving equipment, which can get a spare part to any point in the world within twenty-four hours. Downtime for heavy construction equipment is very costly, so Caterpillar's ability to

TABLE 4.5

The Primary Role of Different Functions in Achieving Superior Responsiveness to Customers

Value Creation Function	Primary Roles
Infrastructure (leadership)	1. Through leadership by example, build a companywide commitment to responsiveness to customers.
Production	1. Achieve customization through implementation of flexible manufacturing. 2. Achieve rapid response through flexible manufacturing.
Marketing	1. Know the customer. 2. Communicate customer feedback to appropriate functions.
Materials management	1. Develop logistics systems capable of responding quickly to unanticipated customer demands (JIT).
R&D	1. Bring customers into the product development process.
Information systems	1. Use web-based information systems to increase responsiveness to customers.
Human resources	1. Develop training programs that get employees to think like customers themselves.

respond quickly in the event of equipment malfunction is of prime importance to its customers. As a result, many of them have remained loyal to Caterpillar despite the aggressive low-price competition from Komatsu of Japan.

In general, reducing response time requires (1) a marketing function that can quickly communicate customer requests to production, (2) production and materials management functions that can quickly adjust production schedules in response to unanticipated customer demands, and (3) information systems that can help production and marketing in this process.

Table 4.5 summarizes the steps different functions must take if a company is to achieve superior responsiveness to customers. Although marketing plays the critical role in helping a company attain this goal, primarily because it represents the point of contact with the customer, Table 4.5 shows that the other functions also have major roles. Moreover, like achieving superior efficiency, quality, and innovation, achieving superior responsiveness to customers requires top management to lead in building a customer orientation within the company.

Summary of Chapter

1. A company can increase efficiency through a number of steps: exploiting economies of scale and learning effects, adopting flexible manufacturing technologies, reducing customer defection rates, implementing just-in-time systems, getting the R&D function to design products that are easy to manufacture, upgrading the skills of employees through training, introducing self-managing teams, linking pay to performance, building a companywide commitment to efficiency through strong leadership, and designing structures that facilitate cooperation among different functions in pursuit of efficiency goals.

2. Superior quality can help a company lower its costs and differentiate its product and charge a premium price.

3. Achieving superior quality demands an organization-wide commitment to quality and a clear focus on the customer. It also requires metrics to measure quality goals and incentives that emphasize quality, input from employees regarding ways in which quality can be improved, a methodology for tracing defects to their source and correcting the problems that produce

them, rationalization of the company's supply base, cooperation with the suppliers that remain to implement total quality management programs, products that are designed for ease of manufacturing, and substantial cooperation among functions.

4. The failure rate of new-product introductions is high due to factors such as uncertainty, poor commercialization, poor positioning strategy, slow cycle time, and technological myopia.

5. To achieve superior innovation, a company must build skills in basic and applied research; design good processes for managing development projects; and achieve close integration between the different functions of the company, primarily through the adoption of cross-functional product development teams and partly parallel development processes.

6. To achieve superior responsiveness to customers often requires that the company achieve superior efficiency, quality, and innovation.

7. To achieve superior responsiveness to customers, a company needs to give customers what they want when they want it. It must ensure a strong customer

focus, which can be attained through leadership; train employees to think like customers and bring customers into the company through superior market research; customize the product to the unique needs of individual customers or customer groups; and respond quickly to customer demands.

Discussion Questions

1. How are the four generic building blocks of competitive advantage related to each other?

2. What role can top management play in helping a company achieve superior efficiency, quality, innovation, and responsiveness to customers?

3. In the long run, will adoption of Six Sigma quality improvement processes give a company a competitive advantage, or will it be required just to achieve parity with competitors?

4. In what sense might innovation be called the single most important building block of competitive advantage?

Practicing Strategic Management

SMALL-GROUP EXERCISE: IDENTIFYING EXCELLENCE

Break up into groups of three to five people, and appoint one group member as a spokesperson who will communicate your findings to the class.

You are the management team of a start-up company that will produce disk drives for the personal computer industry. You will sell your product to manufacturers of personal computers (original equipment manufacturers). The disk drive market is characterized by rapid technological change, product life cycles of only six to nine months, intense price competition, high fixed costs for manufacturing equipment, and substantial manufacturing economies of scale. Your customers, the original equipment manufacturers, issue very demanding technological specification that your product has to comply with. They also pressure you to deliver your product on time so that it fits in with their own product introduction schedule.

1. In this industry, what functional competencies are the most important for you to build?

2. How will you design your internal processes to ensure that those competencies are built within the company?

ARTICLE FILE 4

Choose a company that is widely regarded as excellent. Identify the source of its excellence, and relate it to the material discussed in this chapter. Pay particular attention to the role played by the various functions in building excellence.

STRATEGIC MANAGEMENT PROJECT: MODULE 4

This module deals with the ability of your company to achieve superior efficiency, quality, innovation, and responsiveness to customers. With the information you have at your disposal, answer the questions and perform the tasks listed:

1. Is your company pursuing any of the efficiency-enhancing practices discussed in this chapter?

2. Is your company pursuing any of the quality-enhancing practices discussed in this chapter?

3. Is your company pursuing any of the practices designed to enhance innovation discussed in this chapter?

4. Is your company pursuing any of the practices designed to increase responsiveness to customers discussed in this chapter?

5. Evaluate the competitive position of your company in the light of your answers to questions 1–4. Explain what, if anything, the company needs to do to improve its competitive position.

EXPLORING THE WEB
Visiting Applied Materials

Visit the web site of Applied Materials, the world's largest manufacturer of semiconductor fabrication equipment (**http://www.appliedmaterials.com**). Go to the section titled "About" Applied Materials, and read the company's mission statement. What does this mission statement tell you about the kind of competitive advantage that Applied Materials is trying to build? How important are efficiency, quality, innovation, and responsiveness to customers to this company?

Now go to the sections of Applied's web site that detail the company's financial results, products, and press releases. Read through these sections and try to establish how successful Applied has been at meeting the objectives set down in its mission statement. What do you think the company has done at the functional level to increase its efficiency, responsiveness to customers, innovative ability, and product quality?

General Task: Search the Web for a company whose home page describes in some detail its approach to achieving one of the following: superior productivity, product quality, customer service, or innovation. Using this information, document the company's functional-level strategy and assess whether the strategy makes sense given what you have learned so far in this book?

Closing Case

Reinventing Levi's

Levi Strauss is an American icon. For two generations, it has dressed the world in its fabled blue jeans. In recent years, however, Levi's luster has begun to fade even more rapidly than the blue dye on an old pair of 501s. The fast-moving fashion world seems to be leaving it behind. After peaking in 1996 with sales of $7.1 billion, Levi's sales fell for the next five years, dropping to $4.1 billion in 2001. Levi's problems have several sources.

First, a combination of good design and savvy marketing has helped competitors such as The Gap take share from Levi's. The company badly missed the urban-inspired wide-legged jean trend. Levi's Dockers brand, which is suitable for casual dress, also seems to have become tired. Moreover, traditionally Levi has focused on jeans for men, where sales have been falling industry-wide, as opposed to women's jeans, where industry sales are at least stable. Second, some retailers say the company has had a take-it-or-leave-it sales attitude. "They were arrogant. They thought they were selling couture merchandise," complained the director of general merchandising for Fred Meyer, the Portland-based superstore unit of Kroger. Third, Levi's jeans were just too expensive. Unlike most of its competitors, which moved the bulk of their manufacturing to Asia or Central America long ago, Levi continued to have a significant manufacturing presence in the United States. But the high cost of labor in the United States means that it has to charge higher prices to recoup its costs, and customers didn't seem to be willing to pay a premium price for Levi jeans anymore.

Levi's solution to this problem has been threefold. First, the company closed all but eight of the twenty-two U.S. plants it operated in 1996, laying off 6,500 domestic employees, and moved manufacturing to low-cost foreign locations. Second, it is attempting to get ahead of fashion trends rather than follow them. Levi is now paying much more attention to women. It has recognized that women in junior, petite, and plus sizes call for special attention. New designs such as the Superlow line of jeans are meant to be feminine and sexy rather than retrofits of menswear.

Unlike prior designs that have mostly bubbled up in-house, the idea for the Superlows was adapted from the phenomenon of celebrities such as Mariah Carey cutting off the waistbands of Levi's mainstay 501s. After briefly testing the jeans in boutiques and mainstream stores such as J.C. Penney, the company began mass marketing of the Superlows for women within three months rather than the typical twelve months for past launches. The new look seems to have hit the spot. By late 2001, weekly sell-through rates (the fraction of an order that a retailer can move out the door) of Superlow jeans were ranging between 15 and 22 percent, well above the 5 percent typical for Levi's. Superlows now make up the largest portion of junior sales.

Third, the company announced that it would step up its Original Spin program to supply jeans that are custom made for individual customers. Levi's thinking is that if it can customize its jeans for each individual's body shape (no two people are identical), it will be able to charge a premium price and therefore cover the costs of continuing to have a substantial manufacturing presence in the United States. At the core of the Original Spin program is an attempt to use web-based technology and computer-controlled production equipment to implement a strategy of mass customization that has as its goal a desire to give each customer a better-fitting pair of jeans in their preferred style. The idea is that with the help of a sales associate, customers will create the jeans they want by picking from six colors, three basic models, five different leg openings, and two types of fly. Then their waist, rear, and inseam will be measured. The customer will try on a pair of plain "test-drive" jeans to make sure that they like the fit. If they do, the order will be punched into a web-based computer terminal linked to the stitching machines in a Levi Strauss factory. Customers can even give the jeans a name—for example, "Rebel" for a pair of black jeans. At the factory, computer-controlled tools precision-cut the jeans and stitch an individual bar code inside. The jeans are then sewn and washed, identified by the code, and shipped to the customer's home. The whole process takes no more than two to three weeks. The bar code tag stores the measurements for simple reordering.

Today, a fully stocked Levi's store carries approximately 130 pairs of ready-to-wear jeans. With the Original Spin program, the number of choices available will leap to 750. Sanjay Choudhuri, Levi's director of mass customization, feels that 750 is about the right number of choices. An unlimited amount of choice will create inefficiencies at the manufacturing plant. Levi's strategy is to offer a healthy number of choices that give the customer the illusion of infinite variety and can be produced with little or no additional cost penalty. Levi does hope to charge a premium price for this service of about 20 percent. However, in the company's view, the real benefit of the program is that it changes the nature of the relationship between Levi Strauss and its customers. Instead of an anonymous relationship in which the customer walks out of the store with a pair of off-the-shelf jeans, Levi Strauss aims to become each customer's personal "jeans adviser." If the program works, Levi might well extend it to embrace several other apparel offerings, such as its Dockers line of pants for men, in addition to rolling out the program in international markets.

Further down the road, Levi might use a device that will scan the entire body. The machine, which has been developed by an independent company, projects 300,000 pinpoints of light from head to toe, then photographs the body from six angles to produce a kind of three-dimensional portrait. Those data result in a custom pattern that can be transmitted to a production plant to manufacture jeans, shirts, or any other item of clothing. Within five years, body-scanning equipment may be found in Levi stores.

Case Discussion Questions

1. From a value creation perspective, what exactly is Levi trying to achieve by (a) moving manufacturing out of the United States, (b) refocusing its design efforts on women, and (c) introducing the Original Spin program?

2. How exactly might the Original Spin program change the nature of the relationship between Levi Strauss and its customers?

3. Do you think that the strategic actions Levi is taking will allow it to reverse its six-year decline and build a sustainable competitive advantage?

Sources: Erick Schonfeld, "The Customized, Digitized, Have It Your Way Economy," *Fortune,* September 28, 1998, p. 117. Molly Knight, "Levi's to Close 11 plants in Shift to Offshore Manufacturing," *Business and Industry,* February 24, 1999, p. 6. "The View from the Outside, Levi's Needs More Than a Patch," *New York Times,* February 28, 1999, p. 4. K. Barron, "Getting a Rise out of Levi's," *Fortune,* November 26, 2001, pp. 156–158.

Building Competitive Advantage Through Business-Level Strategy

5

Opening Case

Toyota's Goal? A High-Value Vehicle to Match Every Customer Need

The car industry has always been one of the most competitive in the world because of the huge revenues and profits that are at stake, with annual global car sales at over $250 billion. It is small wonder, then, that industry rivalry has been increasing as carmakers have been fighting to develop new kinds of car models that better satisfy the needs of particular groups of buyers. One company at the forefront of these endeavors is Toyota.

As the pioneer of lean production, Toyota has used its low-cost structure to produce efficiently an ever-increasing range of vehicles tailored to different segments of the car market. Its ability to go from the initial design stage to production stage in two to three years gives it the ability to bring out new models faster than its competitors and capitalize on the development of new market segments or niches. Low costs and fast time to market also allow it to correct mistakes quickly when it designs a car that subsequently proves to have little market appeal—and Toyota has made mistakes.

In 1999, for example, Toyota brought out the Echo, a subcompact car that featured state-of-the-art engineering to deliver exceptional fuel economy: around 50 to 60 miles per gallon.

Designed to be inexpensive to run and buy, Toyota targeted this vehicle at buyers in their twenties, expecting them to appreciate these qualities. Its designers were disappointed when they displayed little enthusiasm for the car; its styling did not appeal to this age group even if its performance did fit their budget. The Echo's buyers turned out to be individuals in their forties who appreciated its economy and found it a useful second car to get around in.

Recognizing their failure to position their product to hit the important market segment of young adults, the main car buyers of the future, Toyota's designers went back to the drawing board. Analyzing changing market trends and demographics, they sought to find the styling and features that would offer a car that was good looking, fun to drive for this market segment, and could be sold for $16,000 to $18,000. Toyota (and several other carmakers) realized that perhaps the time was right for the return to the hatchback, but an updated version of it. Hatchbacks had been very popular in the early 1980s; however, the cars then were small and often had an ungainly appearance. Sales of hatchbacks had dropped off quickly when carmakers began to offer new sports utility vehicles and updated small sedans; by 1995, relatively few were available.

Drawing on its design and manufacturing competencies, Toyota's engineers updated and shaped the hatchback to suit the needs of the young adults in their twenties: the result was the Toyota Matrix, introduced in 2002 at a price starting at $17,000. The Matrix features revolutionary body styling reflective of much more expensive, sporty cars. It is spacious inside and geared to the needs of its intended young buyers; for example, seats fold back to allow for carrying a large cargo volume, and many storage bins and two-prong plugs for power outlets allow for the use of VCRs, MP3 players, and other devices. The message is that the Matrix is designed to be functional, fun, and a sporty ride. To launch the car, Toyota partnered with Island Records and MP3.com to sponsor an eight-week Toyota Matrix "Fuel the Music" rock and roll tour featuring Island artists Sum41, Hoobastank, and American HiFi.

Toyota has also been a leader in positioning its whole range of vehicles to take advantage of emerging market segments. In the sports utility segment, its first offering was the expensive Toyota Land Cruiser, priced at over $35,000. Realizing the need for sports utility vehicles in other price ranges, it next introduced the 4Runner, priced at $20,000 and designed for the average sports utility customer; the RAV4, a small sports utility vehicle in the low $20,000 range followed; and then came the Sequoia, a bigger, more powerful version of the 4Runner in the upper $20,000 range. Finally, taking the technology from its Lexus R3000 vehicle, in 2001 it introduced the luxury Highlander sports utility in the low $30,000 range. It now offers six models of sports utility vehicles, each offering a combination of price, size, performance, styling, and luxury that appeals to different customer groups within the sports utility segment of the car market. Toyota also positions its sedans to appeal to different sets of buyers. For example, the Camry, one of the best-selling cars in the United States, is targeted toward the middle of the market, to customers who can afford to pay about $25,000 and want a balance of luxury, performance, safety, and reliability.

Toyota's strategy and business model on the demand side is to produce that range of vehicles that optimizes the amount of value it can create for different groups of customers. On the supply side, the number of models it makes is constrained by the need to keep its cost structure efficient and to choose the car pricing options that allows it to generate the sales revenue that result in the best return on invested capital.

The decision about how many kinds of vehicles to produce is also affected by the strategies of its rivals, for they are also trying to determine the optimum range of cars to produce. Toyota was not alone in its decision to produce a hatchback in 2002; other noticeable competitors included BMW, which introduced the redesigned Mini Cooper; Honda's new Civic hatchbacks; the already well-received PT Cruiser from DaimlerChrysler; and Ford's Focus. In fact, the number of hatchback models doubled between 2000 and 2002, as did the expected number of sales (to 650,000 vehicles). Competition in this market segment is now intense. Each car company needs to anticipate the actions of its rivals, and each hopes, like Toyota, that it has made the right choices to obtain a large share of customers in this important market segment.

Source: www.toyota.com, 2002.

Overview

As the *Opening Case* suggests, this chapter examines how companies can compete effectively in a market or industry and scrutinizes the potential strategies for maximizing competitive advantage and profitability. Its focus is on the most important level of strategy making that goes to make a company's business model: the choice of business-level strategies that a company can use to compete effectively in an industry and achieve superior performance.

By the end of this chapter, you will be able to identify and distinguish among the principal kinds of business-level strategies and tactics that managers can choose from to achieve a competitive advantage over their rivals. You will also understand why, and under what circumstances, strategic managers choose to pursue one rather than another of these strategies as the approach to create value and profit through their business model.

What Is Business-Level Strategy?

At the heart of **business-level strategy** is the objective of developing a firm-specific business model that will allow a company to gain a competitive advantage over its rivals in a market or industry. As we noted in Chapter 1, the way that strategic managers define their company's business is the first step in crafting business-level strategy. According to Abell, the process of business definition entails decisions about (1) customers' needs, or what is to be satisfied, (2) customer groups, or who is to be satisfied, and (3) distinctive competencies, or how customer needs are to be satisfied.[1] These three decisions are the basis of the choice of a business-level strategy because they determine where and how a company seeks to compete in a business or industry—essentially, how a company proposes to create *value* for customers. Consequently, the ways in which a company makes these three decisions to gain a competitive advantage over its rivals need to be considered.

Customer Needs and Product Differentiation

Customer needs are desires, wants, or cravings that can be satisfied by means of the attributes or characteristics of a product—a good or service. For example, a person's craving for something sweet can be satisfied by a box of Godiva chocolates, a carton of Ben & Jerry's ice cream, a Snickers bar, or a spoonful of sugar. Two factors determine which product a customer chooses to satisfy these needs: (1) the price of the product and (2) the way a product is differentiated from other products of its type.

Product differentiation is the process of designing products to satisfy customers' needs. A company obtains a competitive advantage when it creates, designs, and supplies a product in a way that better satisfies customer needs than its rivals do and chooses the correct pricing option—the one that results in the level of demand that optimizes profitability. Consider the luxury segment of the car market, where customers pay more than $35,000 to satisfy their needs for personal transportation. In this segment, Cadillac, Mercedes-Benz, Infiniti, BMW, Jaguar, Lexus, Lincoln, Audi, Volvo, Acura, and others are engaged in a continuing battle to design the "perfect" luxury car—the one that best meets the needs of those who have decided to purchase a personal luxury vehicle. Over time, the companies that attract the most luxury car buyers—because they have the distinctive competencies that allow them to produce the cars that possess the features or qualities these customers desire the most—are the ones that achieve a sustained competitive advantage over rivals.

There are many different luxury carmakers because even within this car market segment, customers have widely different kinds of needs. As a result, luxury carmakers can differentiate their product in a number of ways to satisfy a particular group of customers, just as Toyota did in the *Opening Case* in the sports utility segment. For example, some customers highly value a sporty ride and performance handling; Mercedes-Benz and BMW are on the cutting edge of technical design, which allows them to be able to offer this driving experience that no other maker has been able to match.

Toyota's Lexus division is well known for the smoothness and quietness of its cars and their exceptional reliability. Lexus cars consistently outrank all other cars in published reliability rankings, and this appeals to a large group of customers who appreciate these qualities. Volvo has a reputation for producing safe cars and Rolls Royce for the prestige that possessing such a car confers on its owner. Other luxury carmakers have not fared so well. Cadillac, Lincoln, Audi, Acura, and Infinity have found it more difficult to differentiate their cars, which sometimes compare unfavorably in terms of ride, comfort, safety, or reliability to their rivals. Although these less successful companies still sell many cars, customers often find their needs better satisfied by the attributes and qualities of their rivals' cars.

At every price range in the car market—cars under $15,000, from $15,000 to $25,000, $25,000 to $35,000, and the luxury segment above $35,000—many models of cars compete to attract customers. For each price range, a carmaker has to make a choice concerning how much to differentiate a particular car model. Typically, the more differentiated a product is, the more it will cost to design and produce, and differentiation leads to a higher cost structure. Thus, if a carmaker is to stay within the $15,000 to $25,000 price range, and yet design and produce a differentiated car that will give it a competitive advantage and allow it to outperform its competitors in the price range, strategic managers have to make crucial and difficult decisions. For example, they have to forecast what kind of features customers will most value: car styling, safety, performance, or something else; what size engine will be acceptable; and how much should be spent on air bags to make a car safe while making sure the car will not cost too much to produce—ensuring that they can make a good profit and still sell the car for less than $25,000.

Thus, the way that companies in a business or industry differentiate their products in order to attract customers is not a free choice. Strategic managers are constrained by the need to balance differentiation against cost, which is always reflected in the price of a product. In the under-$15,000 segment, carmakers compete by producing a car with a level of differentiation that offers customers the most value for their money in its price range while still allowing them to make an acceptable level of profit. If they succeed and the car sells well, then the higher perceived value translates into high demand and generates high sales revenues and profitability, even though the profit per vehicle sold might not be very high.

Differentiation has another important aspect. Companies that can create something distinct or different about their products and can satisfy customers' needs in ways that other products cannot can often charge a higher, or premium, price for their product. For example, superb design or technical sophistication allows companies to charge more for their products, and customers are often willing to pay those higher prices. For example, Mercedes-Benz buyers pay a high premium price to enjoy their vehicles, as do customers of Godiva chocolates, which retail for about $26 a pound—much more than, say, a Hershey bar.

Distinctness or distinctiveness can be achieved in countless different ways, which also explains why there may be so many companies competing in an industry. Distinctness may relate to the physical characteristics of the product, such as quality, reliability, or performance. Or it may lie in the product's appeal to customers' psychological needs, such as the body styling of a Porsche, Jaguar, or Corvette or a personal need for prestige or status.[2] Thus, a Lexus may be differentiated by its reputation for reliability and a Mercedes-Benz by its ability to satisfy customers' needs for power and status. Similarly, in the luxury segment, carmakers compete to offer customers a car with the ride, performance, and features that provide them with the most value (satisfies their needs) given the price of the car. Thus, Lexus cars are always several thousand dollars less than comparable cars from its rivals. For example, the Lexus ES300 introduced in 2001, at around $35,000, is $7,000 less than the BMW 5 series and $10,000 less than the Mercedes E Class, its nearest rivals. Most customers are discriminating and match price to differentiation even in the luxury car segment of the market. Of course, some customers simply want to purchase the absolute best technology there is and think nothing of spending $120,000 on the elegant Mercedes CL600 coupe because, among other qualities it possesses, it has an unmatched V12 engine.

In sum, product differentiation is a powerful competitive weapon. Companies that can differentiate their products more successfully than their rivals can increase the perceived value of those products. This gives them the opportunity to choose a higher price option and charge a premium price, and still generate the demand necessary to achieve above-average profitability. Successful differentiators obtain a competitive advantage, outperform their competitors, and can dominate the market or the market segment in which they compete.

Customer Groups and Market Segmentation

Market segmentation is the way a company decides to group customers, based on important differences in their needs or preferences, in order to gain a competitive advantage.[3] One principal way of grouping customers and segmenting the market is by what customers are able and willing to pay for a particular product. Once price has been taken into consideration, the other principal method of segmenting customers is according to the specific kinds of need that is being satisfied by a particular product. Managers, such as designers and engineers, have to think strategically about which segments they are going to compete in and then how they will differentiate their products for each segment. The result of this choice process determines a particular company's product range.

Market segmentation is an evolving, ongoing process that presents considerable opportunities for strategic managers. For example, in the car industry, savvy strategists often recognize opportunities to create a product for a new market segment that will attract a specific group of car buyers who before had to "satisfice," and buy a model that did not meet their needs exactly but was a reasonable compromise. This was the origin of the sports utility market segment. Many people wanted a more rugged and powerful vehicle capable of holding many people or towing heavy loads. They liked the comfort of a car but also the qualities of a pickup; by combining these two, carmakers created the SUV market segment. This process continues in the sports utility and other segments. Obviously, differentiation increases as new models are introduced and costs increase. However, if the right products are being made, the extra demand the new products generate results in sales revenues that more than make up for increasing costs and profitability increases. If managers make mistakes, however, and design products that have little appeal or price them too high, then the opposite occurs, and profitability will fall. In 2002, for example, Ford announced that it was ending production of its $52,000 luxury Lincoln truck after announcing that sales had been only in the hundreds, and not the 10,000 a year it had projected.

In general, a company can adopt three alternative strategies toward market segmentation.[4] First, it can choose not to recognize that different groups of customers have different needs and instead adopt the approach of serving the average customer. Second, it can choose to segment its market into different constituencies and develop a product to suit the needs of each. For example, Sony offers twenty-four different nineteen-inch color television sets, each targeted at a different market segment.

Third, a company can choose to recognize that the market is segmented but concentrate on serving only one of a few market segments or niches, such as the luxury car segment pursued by BMW.

The decision to provide many products for many market niches allows a company to satisfy a wider range of customer needs better. As a result, when it prices the product correctly, customer demand for the company's products rises and generates more revenue than would be the case if the company offered just one product for the whole market.[5]

Sometimes the nature of the product or the nature of the industry does not allow much differentiation, which is the case, for example, with bulk chemicals and cement.[6] In these industries, there may be little opportunity for obtaining a competitive advantage through product differentiation and market segmentation because there is little opportunity for serving customers' needs and customer groups in different ways. Instead, price is the main criterion that customers use to evaluate the product, and the competitive advantage lies with the company that has superior efficiency and the lowest cost structure, which allows it to charge the lowest prices.

Distinctive Competencies

The third issue in business-level strategy is to decide which distinctive competencies to create and build to achieve a competitive advantage in satisfying particular customers' needs and customer groups.[7] As Chapter 4 describes, there are four main ways companies can pursue a competitive advantage: superior efficiency, quality, innovation, and responsiveness to customers. In choosing a business-level strategy, strategic managers must decide which business model to follow that will best allow them to organize and combine their company's distinctive competencies to gain a competitive advantage.

The Dynamics of Business-Level Strategy

Companies pursue a business-level strategy to gain a competitive advantage that allows them to outperform rivals and achieve above-average profitability. In determining how to achieve a competitive advantage, strategic managers have to make a consistent or compatible set of choices concerning (1) how to differentiate and price their product, (2) when and how much to segment their market to maximize demand, and (3) and where and how to invest their capital to develop distinctive competencies that will create the most value while keeping their cost structures viable (because of the need to be price competitive). These three decisions determine which business-level strategy a company is pursuing. They also set in motion the specific set of functional-level strategies needed to create the differentiation and value and cost structure positions needed to pursue such a strategy. Business-level strategy is therefore the main determinant of a company's business model.

Figure 5.1 presents a way of thinking about the relationships of these variables in a company's business model.[8] The decision to differentiate a product increases the perceived value to the customer, so that market demand for the product increases. In turn, increased demand leads to economies of scale, which lowers the cost structure and unit costs. Thus, from this point of view, differentiation can lower unit costs.[9] Differentiation also requires additional expenditures on resources, for example, to improve product quality or support a higher level of service so that an increase in differentiation will also raise a company's cost structure and result in a higher unit cost.

To maximize profitability, managers must choose the pricing option that compensates for the extra costs of product differentiation but does not choke off an increase in expected demand. They must also search for other ways to reduce costs and therefore lower the company's cost structure but will not harm its level of differ-

FIGURE 5.1

The Dynamics of
Business-Level
Strategy

Source: Copyright © C. W. L.
Hill and G. R. Jones, "The
Dynamics of Business-Level
Strategy," (unpublished
manuscript, 2002).

entiation. There are many specific functional strategies a company can adopt to achieve this. For example, Nordstrom, the luxury department store retailer, differentiates itself in the retail clothing industry by providing a high-quality shopping experience with elegant store operations and a high level of customer service, all of which raise Nordstrom's cost structure. However, Nordstrom can still lower its cost structure by, for example, managing its inventories efficiently and increasing inventory turnover. Also, its strategy of being highly responsive to customers results in more customers and higher demand, which means that sales per square foot increase, and this enables it to make more intensive use of its facilities and salespeople, which leads to scale economies and lower costs. Thus, no matter what the level of differentiation is that a company chooses to pursue in its business model, it always has to recognize the way its cost structure will vary as a result of its choice of differentiation and the other specific strategies it adopts to lower its cost structure; differentiation and cost structure decisions affect one another.

The last main dynamic shown in Figure 5.1 concerns the impact of the industry's competitive structure on a company's differentiation, cost structure, and pricing choices. Recall that strategic thinking takes place in an environment where watchful and agile competitors and potential competitors exist, so one company's choices are always made with reference to those of its major competitors. Often, therefore, a company may be forced to increase its level of differentiation because its competitors start to offer products with new or improved features. If competitors also decide to develop products for new market segments, this will also force it to follow suit.

On the cost side of the equation, industry competition drives a company's cost structure because differentiation increases costs and competitors' pricing decisions affect a company's pricing options. For example, a company's ability to charge a high premium price depends on the other choices customers have and its competitors' pricing choices. Companies need to consider carefully whether they can recoup the extra costs of differentiation given the pricing choices of the other companies in the industry. For example, Dell's decision not to choose a high-price option for its state-of-the-art computers led to problems for its competitors because they lacked Dell's low cost structure. Because they were forced to match Dell's low prices to compete effectively, many started to see losses because they had higher costs and this helped Dell gain more market share.

In sum, the task facing strategic managers at the business level is to position a company with respect to both differentiation and cost structure. That is, the choice of business-level strategy revolves around (1) how to differentiate products to create more value for customers, which permits a broader range of pricing options and (2) how to invest in functional activities to achieve a cost structure that also gives it a broader range of pricing choices.[10] Maximizing profitability is about making the right choices with regard to value creation through differentiation, costs, and pricing given both the demand conditions in the company's market and the competitive conditions in the company's industry.

Choosing a Generic Business-Level Strategy

In developing a business-level strategy and business model, usually strategic managers emphasize one of five generic competitive strategies: cost leadership, differentiation, cost leadership *and* differentiation, focus differentiation, and focus cost leadership.[11] These strategies are called *generic* because all companies or businesses can pursue them regardless of whether they are manufacturing, service, or nonprofit enterprises. These strategies are also generic because they can be pursued in different kinds of industry environments. Each of the generic strategies results from a company's consistent choices on product, market, and distinctive competencies—choices that reinforce each other and result in a competitive business model (see Table 5.1).

Cost-Leadership Strategy

A company's business model in pursuing a cost-leadership strategy is based on the intent to outperform competitors by doing everything it can to establish a cost structure that allows it to produce or provide goods or services at a lower unit cost than they can. It is also about finding ways to lower the cost structure given its choice of differentiation because differentiation typically raises costs. In essence, a company pursuing a cost-leadership strategy seeks to achieve a competitive advantage and above-average profitability by developing a business model primarily aimed at lowering its cost structure.

Two advantages accrue from a cost-leadership strategy. First, if its closest rivals in an industry, for example, those that compete in the same price range or market seg-

TABLE 5.1

Product/Market/Distinctive-Competency Choices and Generic Competitive Strategies

	Cost Leadership	Differentiation	Focus
Product Differentiation	Low (principally by price)	High (principally by uniqueness)	Low to high (price or uniqueness)
Market Segmentation	Low (mass market)	High (many market segments)	Low (one or a few segments)
Distinctive Competency	Manufacturing and materials management	Research and development, sales and marketing	Any kind of distinctive competency

ment, charge similar prices for their products, the cost leader achieves superior profitability than its competitors because of its lower costs. Second, and more common, because of its lower cost structure, the cost leader is able to charge a lower price than its competitors, and this gives it a competitive advantage. As discussed earlier, offering customers the same kind of value from a product but at a lower price attracts many more customers, so that even though it has chosen the lower price option, the increased volume of its sales causes the company's profits to surge. If its competitors try to get lost customers back by reducing their prices and companies start to compete on price, the cost leader will still be able to withstand competition better than the other companies because of its lower costs. It is likely to win any competitive struggle. For these reasons, cost leaders are likely to earn above-average profits. How does a company become the cost leader? It achieves this position by means of the way strategic managers make compatible product, market, and distinctive competency choices to gain a low-cost competitive advantage (see Table 5.1).

Strategic Choices. The cost leader chooses a low to moderate level of product differentiation relative to its competitors. Differentiation is expensive; the more a company expends resources to make its products distinct, the more its costs rise.[12] The cost leader aims for a level of differentiation not markedly inferior to that of the differentiator (a company that competes by spending resources on product development), but a level obtainable at low cost.[13] The cost leader does not try to be the industry leader in differentiation; it waits until customers want a feature or service before providing it. For example, a cost leader does not introduce a theater-quality sound system in DVD sets; instead, it adds such sound quality only when it is obvious that customers want it. Wal-Mart, for example, does not spend hundreds of millions of dollars on store design to create an attractive shopping experience as chains like Macy's, Dillard's, or Saks Fifth Avenue have done. Nor does it follow Kmart's strategy and pay celebrities like Martha Stewart millions to promote the distinctness or quality of its products. As Wal-Mart puts it in its mission statement, "We think of ourselves as buyers for our customers and we apply our considerable strengths to get the best *value* for you."[14]

The cost leader also frequently ignores the many different market segments in an industry and positions its products to appeal to the "average" customer. The reason the cost leader makes this choice is that developing or selling many different products tailored to the needs of different market segments is an expensive proposition. A cost leader normally engages in only a limited amount of market segmentation. In targeting the average customer, strategic managers try to produce or provide the least or smallest number of products that will be desired by the highest number of customers, something at the heart of Wal-Mart's and BJ's approach discussed in Chapter 3. Thus, although a customer may not get exactly the product he or she wants, paying a lower price than at the cost leader's competitors attracts more customers to its products.

In developing distinctive competencies, the overriding goal of the cost leader must be to increase its efficiency and lower its cost structure compared with its rivals. The development of distinctive competencies in manufacturing, materials management, and information technology is central to achieving this goal. For example, manufacturing companies pursuing a low-cost strategy concentrate on doing all they can to ride down the experience curve so that they can keep lowering their costs. Achieving a low-cost position requires that the company develop skills in flexible manufacturing, adopt efficient materials management techniques, and do all it can to increase inventory turnover and reduce costs of good sold. (Table 4.1 outlined the ways in which a company's functions can be used to increase efficiency.) Consequently, the manufacturing and materials management functions are the center of attention for a company pursuing a cost-leadership strategy, and the other functions shape their distinctive competencies to meet the needs of manufacturing and materials management.[15]

The sales function, for example, may develop the competency of capturing large, stable sets of customers' orders. In turn, this allows manufacturing to make longer production runs and so achieve economies of scale and reduce costs. At Dell, for example, online customers are provided with a limited set of choices so that Dell can customize PCs to a customer's need at low cost. Finding ways to customize its products at low cost is an important task facing managers pursuing a cost-leadership strategy. The human resource function may focus on instituting training programs and compensation systems that lower costs by improving employees' productivity, and the research and development function may specialize in process improvements to lower the manufacturing costs. Wal-Mart has taken advantage of advances in information technology to lower the costs associated with getting goods from manufacturers to customers just as Dell, the cost leader in the personal computer industry, uses the Internet to lower the cost of selling its computers. Strategy implementation, another source of cost savings in pursuing cost leadership, is the design of the organizational structure to match this strategy, since structure is a major source of a company's costs. Thus, a low-cost strategy usually implies tight production or sales controls and rigorous use of budgets to control the production process.

Advantages and Disadvantages. The advantages of each generic strategy are best discussed in terms of Porter's five forces model, introduced in Chapter 2.[16] The five forces are threats from competitors, powerful suppliers, powerful buyers, substitute products, and new entrants. The cost leader is protected from industry competitors by its cost advantage. Its lower costs also mean that it will be less affected than its competitors by increases in the price of inputs if there are powerful suppliers and less affected by a fall in the price it can charge for its products if there are powerful buyers. Moreover, since cost leadership usually requires a big market share, the cost leader purchases in relatively large quantities, increasing its bargaining power over suppliers. If substitute products start to come onto the market, the cost leader can reduce its price to compete with them and retain its market share. Finally, the leader's cost advantage constitutes a barrier to entry, since other companies are unable to enter the industry and match the leader's costs or prices. The cost leader is therefore relatively safe as long as it can maintain its cost advantage, and price is the key for a significant number of buyers.

The principal dangers of the cost-leadership approach lurk in competitors' ability to find ways to lower *their* cost structures and beat the cost leader at its own game. For instance, if technological change makes experience curve economies obsolete, new companies may apply lower-cost technologies that give them a cost advantage over the cost leader. The steel mini-mills discussed in Chapter 4 gained this advantage. Competitors may also draw a cost advantage from labor-cost savings. Foreign competitors in the Third World have very low labor costs; for example, wage costs in the United States are roughly 600 percent more than they are in Malaysia, China, or Mexico. Most U.S. companies now assemble their products abroad as part of their low-cost strategy; many are forced to do so simply to compete and stay in business, as Strategy in Action 5.1 illustrates.

Strategy in Action   5.1

Levi Strauss's Big Challenge

Levi Strauss, the well-known jeans maker, was once a leading differentiator in the apparel industry. Its jeans commanded a premium price as customers the world over perceived the value or status of wearing Levi jeans was worth paying extra for. Indeed, in Europe and Asia, Levi jeans were often sold at double or triple their U.S. price. No more. Levi is now fighting to lower its costs to be able to pursue a cost-leadership strategy, which has become the principal way to compete in the fast changing jeans industry.

Levi's problems arose because of changes in the business models of other jeans makers and apparel companies. Early in the 1990s, other jeans makers such as VF Corp (which makes Wrangler jeans), Calvin Klein, and Polo moved most of their jeans production capacity abroad to countries where labor costs are lowest. With their lower cost structures, these companies then began to charge lower prices for their products so that customers began to consider carefully whether a pair of Levi's was worth a premium price. Then, in a significant move, apparel companies such as Wal-Mart and Sam's, J.C. Penney, Sears, and Dillard's began to wonder why they should pay Levi a premium price for selling its jeans when they could sell jeans under their own labels at a lower price and still make more profit than if they sold Levi's jeans. So they contracted with low-cost foreign producers to make jeans under their own in-house labels. The result was that

sales of Levi jeans plummeted as many customers began to buy jeans on the basis of their price and not a particular product's differentiated appeal.

Levi, because it still produced most of its jeans in the United States, was burdened with a high cost structure and could not reduce prices to compete. It started to suffer billions of dollars of losses in the 1990s as its sales fell from a peak of $7.1 billion in 1996 to just $4.6 billion in 2000. To survive in a market now driven by both competitors and buyers pursuing a low-cost strategy, Levi had to respond in kind. Since 1997, it has closed twenty-nine U.S. manufacturing facilities and laid off 20,000 employees. In 2002, it announced it would close six more plants and lay off 3,300 more employees, which will leave it with just two sewing and finishing facilities in San Antonio, which it will use to experiment with new kinds of jeans before it contracts with foreign manufacturers to produce these products in volume overseas. As Phillip Marineau, CEO of Levi, commented, "Outsourcing production supports a variable cost structure, helps us maintain strong margins, and enables us to invest more resources in product, marketing, and retail initiatives." Sometimes pursuing a low-cost strategy is the only way to survive in a market.

Sources: www.levistrauss.com (2002). T. Agins, "Levi Will Cut 20% of Work Force, Shut Six Plants in Restructuring," *Wall Street Journal,* April 9, 2002, p. B10.

Competitors' ability to imitate the cost leader's methods easily is another threat to the cost-leadership strategy. For example, companies in China routinely take apart the electronic products of Japanese companies like Sony and Panasonic to see how they are designed and assembled. Then, using Chinese-made components and a huge pool of inexpensive domestic labor, they manufacture clones of these products and flood the U.S. market with inexpensive tape players, radios, phones, and DVD players.

Finally, the cost-leadership strategy carries a risk that strategic managers in their single-minded desire to reduce costs might make decisions that decrease costs but then drastically affect demand for the product. This happened to Gateway Computer in 2001, when, to reduce the costs of customer service, customer support people were instructed not to help customers who were experiencing problems with their new Gateway computers if they had installed their own new software on the machines. New buyers, most of whom install, and Gateway's sales began to fall as word spread. Within six months, managers had reversed their decision, and once again Gateway began offering full customer support.

Implications. To pursue a full-blown cost-leadership strategy, strategic managers need to devote enormous efforts to incorporate all the latest information, materials management, and manufacturing technology into their operations to find new ways to reduce costs. Often, as we saw in Chapter 4, using new technology will also raise quality and increase responsiveness to customers as well. Pursuing a business model based on a low-cost approach is an ongoing endeavor that requires ongoing strategic thinking to make sure the business model is aligned to changing environmental opportunities and threats.

Strategic managers in companies throughout the industry are watching the cost leader and will move quickly to imitate its innovations because they also want to reduce their costs. A differentiator cannot let a cost leader get too great a cost advantage because the leader might then be able to use its high profits to invest more in product differentiation and beat the differentiator at its own competitive game! For example, Toyota and Honda began as cost leaders, manufacturing simple low-priced cars. Their cars sold well, and they then invested their profits to design and make new models of cars that became increasingly differentiated in features and quality. Today, Toyota and Honda, with cars in every market segment, are essentially pursuing a differentiation strategy, although Toyota remains the global cost leader as well. Its managers' ability to sustain both a low cost and a differentiation strategy has made it the most profitable car company in the world by far.

A cost leader must also respond to the strategic moves of its differentiated competitors and increase the quality and features of its products if it is to prosper in the long run. Even low-priced products, such as Timex watches and Bic razors, cannot be too inferior to the more expensive Seiko watches or Gillette razors if the low-cost, low-price policy is to succeed. All business-level strategy plays out with all rivals closely watching each other's strategic moves. If Seiko brings out a novel kind of liquid-crystal-illuminated watch dial or Gillette a three-bladed razor, managers at Timex and Bic will respond within months by incorporating these innovations in their low-priced products. This situation is very common in the high-priced women's fashion industry as well. As soon as the famous designers like Gucci and Dior have shown their spring and fall collections, their designs are copied and the plans transmitted to factories in Malaysia, where workers are ready to manufacture low-priced imitations that within months will reach low-price clothing retail stores around the world.

A generic strategy like cost leadership should be thought of as a specific plan of action that helps strategic managers keep focused on how to compete most effectively over time. It is all too easy for strategic managers, flush with the success of their cost-leadership strategy, to become less vigilant and lose sight of changes in the five forces of competition, and in the macroenvironment, that change the rules of the competitive game. McDonald's, long the cost leader in the fast food industry, was surprised when rivals like Taco Bell began to offer 99-cent daily specials. McDonald's had to learn how to make fast food more cheaply to compete, and the need to do so drove its managers to adopt new cooking techniques and food management practices that have ratcheted it down the experience curve. Today, 99-cent meals are a permanent fixture on most fast food menus.

Differentiation Strategy

The objective of the generic differentiation strategy is to achieve a competitive advantage by creating a product (good or service) that customers perceive as different or distinct in some important way. The differentiated company's ability to satisfy customers' needs in a way that its competitors cannot means that it can charge a premium price (one higher than that charged by its closest rivals). The ability to increase revenues by charging premium prices (rather than by reducing costs, as the cost leader does) allows the differentiator to outperform its competitors and achieve superior profitability. As noted earlier, customers pay a premium price when they believe the product's differentiated qualities are worth the extra money. Consequently, differentiated products are often priced on the basis of what the market will bear.[17]

Thus, Mercedes-Benz cars are more expensive than the cars of its closest rivals because customers believe they offer more features and confer more status on their owners. Similarly, a BMW is not a lot more expensive to produce than a Honda, but customers who perceive that the distinct sporty ride and prestige of owning a BMW is something worth paying a lot more for determine its high price. (In fact, in Japan, BMW prices its entry cars quite modestly to attract young, well-heeled Japanese customers from Honda.) Similarly, Rolex watches do not cost much to produce, their design has not changed very much for years, and their gold content represents only a small fraction of the price. Customers, however, buy a Rolex because of the distinct qualities they perceive in it: its look and its ability to confer status on its wearer.

Strategic Choices. As Table 5.1 shows, a differentiator chooses a high level of product differentiation to gain a competitive advantage. Product differentiation can be achieved in three principal ways (see Chapter 4): quality, innovation, and responsiveness to customer needs. For example, Procter & Gamble claims that its product quality is high and that Ivory soap is 99.44 percent pure. Maytag stresses reliability and the best repair record of any other washer on the market. IBM promotes the quality service provided by its well-trained sales force. Innovation is commonly the source of differentiation for technologically complex products, and many people pay a premium price for new and innovative products, such as a state-of-the-art computer, DVD player, or car.

When differentiation is based on responsiveness to customers, a company offers comprehensive after-sales service and product repair. This is an especially important consideration for complex products such as cars and domestic appliances, which are likely to break down periodically. Maytag, Dell Computer, and BMW all excel in responsiveness to customers. In service organizations, quality-of-service attributes are also very important. Neiman Marcus, Nordstrom, and FedEx can charge premium prices because they offer an exceptionally high level of service. Firms of lawyers, accountants, and consultants stress the service aspects of their operations to clients: their knowledge, professionalism, and reputation.

Finally, a product's appeal to customers' psychological desires is a source of differentiation. The appeal can be to prestige or status, as it is with BMWs and Rolex watches; to safety of home and family, as with Aetna or Prudential Insurance; or simply providing a superior shopping experience, as with Target and Macy's. Differentiation can also be tailored to age groups and to socioeconomic groups. Indeed, the bases of differentiation are endless.

A company that pursues a differentiation strategy strives to differentiate itself along as many dimensions as possible. The less it resembles its rivals, the more it is protected from competition and the wider is its market appeal. Thus, BMWs offer more than prestige; they also offer technological sophistication, luxury, reliability, and good, although very expensive, repair service. All these bases of differentiation help increase sales.

Generally, a differentiator chooses to segment its market into many segments and niches, just as Toyota did. Strategic managers recognize the revenue-enhancing ability of being able to attract more customers willing to pay a premium price in each market segment. Now and then, a company offers a product designed for most market segments and decides to be a broad differentiator, but a company might choose to serve just those segments in which it has a specific differentiation advantage. For example, Sony produces twenty-four models of television sets, filling all the niches from mid-priced to high-priced sets. However, its lowest-priced model is always priced about $60 above that of its competitors, bringing into play the premium-price factor. Consumers have to pay extra for a Sony. Similarly, although Mercedes-Benz has filled niches below its high-priced models with its S and C series, recently it has produced a car for the low-priced market segment. It sells this car only in Europe because it fears introducing it in the United States would dilute its exclusive image and affect its differentiated appeal.

Finally, in choosing which distinctive competency to pursue, a differentiated company concentrates on the organizational functions that provide the source of its differentiation advantage. Differentiation on the basis of innovation and technological competency depends on the R&D function, as discussed in Chapter 4. Efforts to improve service to customers depend on the quality of the sales function. Because developing the distinctive competency needed to provide a differentiation advantage is often expensive, a differentiator normally has a higher cost structure than the cost leader does.

Building new competencies in the functions that sustain its differentiated appeal does not mean neglecting cost control. As noted earlier, the differentiator studies how the cost leader operates and attempts to copy cost-saving innovations that will reduce its costs while preserving the source of its competitive advantage. The differentiator must control all costs that do not contribute to its differentiation advantage so that the price of the product does not exceed what customers are willing to pay, as noted in Nordstrom's case. Otherwise, it risks letting the cost leader go upmarket and steal its customers. Also, since superior profitability is the result of controlling costs as well as maximizing value and revenues, it pays to watch costs closely. The issue is not to minimize them to the point of losing the source of differentiation.[18] The owners of the famous Savoy Hotel in London, England, face just this problem. The Savoy's reputation has always been based on the incredibly high level of service it offers its customers. Three hotel employees serve the needs of each guest, and in every room, a guest can summon a waiter, maid, or valet by pressing a button at bedside. The cost of offering this level of service has been so high that the hotel makes less than 1 percent net profit every year.[19] Its owners try to find ways to reduce costs to increase profits, but if they reduce the number of hotel staff (the main source of the Savoy's high costs), they may destroy the main source of its differentiated appeal.

Advantages and Disadvantages. The advantages of the differentiation strategy can also be discussed in the context of the five forces model. Differentiation safeguards a company against competitors to the degree that customers develop brand loyalty for its products, a valuable asset that protects the company on all fronts. Powerful suppliers are rarely a problem because the differentiated company's strategy is geared more toward the price it can charge than toward costs. Also, differentiators can often pass on price increases to customers because they are willing to pay the premium price. Thus, a differentiator can tolerate moderate increases in the prices of its inputs better than the cost leader can. Differentiators are unlikely to experience problems with powerful buyers because the differentiator offers a distinct product. Only it can supply the product, and it commands brand loyalty. Differentiation and brand loyalty also create a barrier to entry for other companies seeking to enter the industry. New companies are forced to develop their own distinctive competency to be able to compete, an expensive undertaking.

Finally, the threat of substitute products depends on the ability of competitors' products to meet the same customers' needs as the differentiator's products and to break customers' brand loyalty. This can happen; phone companies are suffering as alternative ways of making phone calls through digital fiber-optic cable, satellite, and the Internet are becoming increasingly available. The issue is how much of a premium price a company can charge for distinctness before customers switch products. In the phone industry, the answer is "not much"; the large carriers were forced to reduce prices drastically so that 7 cents a minute is a common rate, down from 37 cents just a decade ago.

The main problems with a differentiation strategy center on strategic managers' long-term ability to maintain a product's perceived difference or distinctness in customers' eyes. What has become increasingly apparent is how quickly agile competitors move to imitate and copy successful differentiators. This has happened across many industries, such as retailing, computers, autos, home electronics, telecommunications, and pharmaceuticals. Patents and first-mover advantages (the advantages of being the first to market a product or service) last only so long, and as the overall quality of products produced by all companies goes up, brand loyalty declines. The story of the way American Express lost its competitive advantage, told in Strategy in Action 5.2, highlights many of the threats that face a differentiator.

Strategy in Action   5.2

Why So Many American Express Cards?

American Express's (AmEx) green, gold, and platinum charge cards (cards whose balance had to be paid off each month in full) used to be closely linked with high status and prestige. Obtaining an AmEx card required a high income, and obtaining a gold or platinum card required an even higher one. AmEx carefully differentiated its product by using famous people to advertise the virtues—exclusivity and distinctness—of possessing its card. Customers were willing to pay the high yearly fee to use the card. AmEx's cards were a premium product that allowed the company to charge both customers and merchants more because it offered quality service and conferred status on the user. For many years, its charge card operation was the money-spinner of AmEx's Travel Related Services (TRS) Division, and the company's stock price soared as its profits reached over $200 million by 1990.

AmEx's differentiated strategy suffered in the 1990s, however. Rival companies like MasterCard and Visa began to issue true credit cards whose balance did not have to be paid off monthly, although of course high interest is charged on the unpaid balance. They also advertised that their cards could be used at locations where AmEx's were not accepted (because of the high fees it charged). In addition, various companies banded together with MasterCard and Visa to offer customers many other benefits of using their particular credit cards. For example, airlines issued credit cards through MasterCard or Visa that allowed customers to accumulate miles toward the purchase of an airline's tickets. This strategy encourages high customer loyalty, and by 1995, thousands of other companies, such as AT&T, GM, Yahoo, and Dell, began issuing credit cards that offer customers savings on their products.

AmEx failed to respond to these developments. Its managers were so convinced that their card was the best and commanded the most loyalty that they spurned attempts to ally with airlines, hotels, or car companies to develop new kinds of cards. Moreover, they failed to see the potential of credit cards that allow customers to carry unpaid balances. This was a grave error. The emergence of all these new credit cards, which better satisfied the needs of millions of new customers, broke the loyalty of AmEx customers. Soon the AmEx card had lost its differentiated appeal; it was now just one more credit card in an overcrowded market. More than 2 million of its users deserted AmEx, which lost hundreds of millions of dollars by 1996.

Under new management, AmEx strove to fight back and develop a new business model to restore its profitability. Realizing its mistakes, it started its own airline mileage program to try to entice its previous cardholders back. It also decided to issue a true credit card, but its managers bungled the introduction, and it flopped. Desperate, AmEx lowered the fees it charged merchants to process card payments and tried to increase the number of outlets that accept the card. However, it found that MasterCard and Visa, anticipating such a move, had allied to develop a proprietary electronic system to process credit card payments and would not let AmEx participate so that merchants were reluctant to take its card since this increased their paperwork.

In 2001, AmEx was helped enormously in its efforts to capture back customers when the Monopolies and Exchange Commission ruled that MasterCard and Visa had unfairly locked AmEx out of the market with their electronic system. AmEx would be allowed to participate, and with this hurdle overcome, it launched new credit cards and began to issue new kinds of cards that targeted specific market segments. In 1999, for example, it announced a new electronic smart card intended to be the global standard for travel and entertainment transactions. Among other things, this card permits electronic ticketing and boarding passes, automated car rental check-in, Internet identification and access, and payment functions including an electronic purse. It also brought out cash-back AmEx cards that gave cardholders up to 2 percent back on their purchases, creating a product similar to the Discover Card, which offers a 1 percent rebate. And it allied with airlines and hotels and developed cards specifically for their users.

By 2002, it offered nine kinds of charge cards and fourteen kinds of credit cards in the attempt to expand its market reach. It also spent over $1 billion a year on marketing and promotion to rebuild its brand name. AmEx hopes these moves will restore its differentiated image so that once again it becomes the credit card of choice. However, the growing importance of the electronic marketplace has created new challenges for the company, and the success of its efforts is still uncertain.

Sources: www.americanexpress.com (2002). L. Nathans Spiro and M. Landler, "Less-Than-Fantastic Plastic," *Business Week,* November 9, 1992, pp. 100–101; Edward Baig, "Platinum Cards: Move Over, Amex," *Business Week,* August 19, 1996, p. 84; John N. Frank, "American Express's Attention Getter," *Credit Card Management* (August 1996): 36–37. L. Beyer, "Breaking Tradition," *Credit Card Management* (1999): 57–60. R. Rolfe, "The Smart Centurion." *Credit Card Management* 12:1 (1999): 132–136.

A strategy of differentiation, then, requires a company to develop a competitive advantage by making choices about its product, market, and distinctive competencies that reinforce each other and together increase the value of a good or service in the eyes of customers. When a product has distinctness in customers' eyes, differentiators can charge a premium price. The disadvantages of a differentiation strategy are the ease with which competitors can imitate a differentiator's product and the difficulty of maintaining a premium price. When differentiation stems from the design or physical features of the product, differentiators are at great risk because imitation is easy. The risk is that over time, products such as VCRs or stereos become commodity-like products, for which the importance of differentiation diminishes as customers become more price sensitive. When differentiation stems from quality of service or reliability or from any intangible source, such as FedEx's guarantee or the prestige of a Rolex, a company is much more secure. It is difficult to imitate intangibles, and the differentiator can reap the benefits of this strategy for a long time. Nevertheless, all differentiators must watch out for imitators and be careful that they do not charge a price higher than the market will bear.

Cost Leadership and Differentiation Strategy

Changes in technology—in particular, the development of flexible manufacturing technologies (discussed in Chapter 4) and new digital, electronic, and information technologies (examined in detail in Chapter 7)—have made the choice between cost-leadership and differentiation strategies less clear-cut. This is illustrated in Table 5.1, which shows that for many companies, the choice of how much to differentiate their products, segment their markets, and leverage their distinctive competencies is a matter of positioning relative to the cost leader or the leading differentiator. In essence, the goal is to find a way to pursue the business models of the cost leader and differentiator simultaneously.

New technologies provide many ways for companies pursuing a cost-leadership strategy to differentiate their goods and services increasingly while maintaining a low cost structure. Conversely, technological developments often provide many ways for a company that has traditionally pursued a differentiation strategy to find ways to do it at a significantly lower cost so that it can choose a lower pricing option and build demand. The result has been that companies pursuing the different strategies have been drawn into closer competition for customers; rivalry among competitors has increased as they jockey for position, and competitive advantage has become more fragile and short lived than ever before.

Companies like Dell, BMW, and Toyota are continuously experimenting with new ways to reduce costs and segment their markets. The use of robots and flexible manufacturing cells reduces the costs of retooling the production line, and the costs associated with small production runs make it much easier to produce a wide variety of vehicle models and maintain an efficient cost structure. Today, flexible manufacturing enables a company pursuing differentiation to manufacture a range of products at a cost comparable to that of the cost leader. BMW, for example, has taken advantage of flexible manufacturing technologies to reduce its costs, but it also chose to charge only a modest premium price to boost its sales revenues and obtain its profits that way. Its new strategy worked: its market share and profitability have increased in recent years. Indeed, a factor promoting the trend toward market fragmentation and niche marketing in many customer goods industries, such as mobile phones, computers, and appliances, is the substantial reduction of the costs of differentiation by flexible manufacturing.

Another way that a differentiated producer may be able to realize significant economies of scale is by standardizing many of the component parts used in its end products. Toyota's various models of sports utility vehicles are built on only three different car platforms. As a result, Toyota is able to realize significant economies of scale in the manufacture and bulk purchase of standardized component parts despite its high level of market segmentation. Indeed, Toyota is driving the simultaneous cost-leadership and differentiation strategy business model in the car industry, and companies like Ford and DaimlerChrysler are struggling to keep up.

A company can also reduce both production and marketing costs if it limits the number of options it allows customers to choose from for a particular model of car. Increasingly, carmakers, for example, offer a model with an economy, luxury, or sports package that appeal to the principal market segments. Package offerings substantially lower manufacturing costs because long production runs of the various packages are possible. Once again, the company is getting gains from differentiation and from low cost at the same time. Just-in-time inventory systems can also help reduce costs and improve the quality and reliability of a company's products. This benefit is important to differentiated companies, for which quality and reliability are essential ingredients of the product's appeal. Rolls Royces, for example, are never supposed to break down. Improved quality control enhances a company's reputation and thus allows it to charge a premium price.

The Internet and e-commerce also provide an inexpensive way of informing millions of potential customers about the nature and quality of a company's products. Similarly, when customers do their own work on the Internet, such as managing their own finances, stock trades, bill paying, travel booking, and purchasing, the company is no longer bearing these costs because they have been shifted to customers. Direct selling to the customer also avoids the need to use wholesalers and other intermediaries, which results in great cost savings. It has been estimated that 40 percent of the profit in a new car goes to the dealership that sells the car and for costs associated with marketing the car.

Finally, the costs of making low-cost and differentiated products are often not very different because both are produced in countries with low labor costs. For example, the work of sewing an inexpensive cotton shirt for Sears does not cost less than sewing an expensive silk designer shirt for Nordstrom. The raw materials may cost more, but here too companies in countries like Malaysia, India, and China are constantly experimenting with ways to reduce the costs of weaving and dying silk and linen and assembling the final product. Differentiators try to charge what the market will bear (the highest price they can get) so that the profits to be obtained from selling foreign-made differentiated products can be enormous. For example, a $100 pair of Nike shoes may cost less than $1 in labor costs.

Taking advantage of the many ways new technology allows them to manage their value chains more efficiently, many companies are reaping the gains that follow from positioning themselves competitively to obtain the benefits from both low-cost and differentiation strategies. Like Nike, these companies can charge a premium price for their products compared with the price charged by the cost leader—the sneaker sold in Wal-Mart, for example—and their attention to reducing costs probably means they have lower costs than the pure differentiator, which is still focused solely on providing distinct products with high perceived quality. As a result, they achieve at least an equal, and probably a higher, level of profitability than companies pursuing only one of the generic strategies. Hence, the combined strategy is the most profitable to pursue, which is why companies have moved rapidly to take advantage of the new manufacturing and information technologies.

Focus Strategies: Low Cost and Differentiation

The last generic competitive strategies, the *focus low-cost* and *focus differentiation* strategies, are directed toward serving the needs of a *particular or specific market segment or niche*. In general, focus strategies position a company to compete for customers in a particular market segment, which can be defined geographically, by type of customer, or by segment of the product line.[20] For example, a geographic niche can be defined by region or even by locality. Selecting a niche by type of customer might mean serving only the very rich, the very young, or the very adventurous. Concentrating on only a segment of the product line means focusing only on vegetarian foods or very fast automobiles or designer clothes or sunglasses. In following a focus strategy, a company is *specializing* in some way.

Once it has chosen its market segment, a focused company positions itself using either a differentiation or a low-cost approach. Figure 5.2 compares these with a pure cost-leadership or differentiation strategy.

In essence, a focused company is a specialized differentiator or a cost leader. If a company uses a focused low-cost approach, it competes against the cost leader in the

FIGURE 5.2

Why Focus Strategies
Are Different

	Offers products to only one group of customers	Offers products to many kinds of customers
Offers low-priced products to customers	Focused Cost-Leadership Strategy	Cost-Leadership Strategy
Offers unique or distinctive products to customers	Focused Differentiation Strategy	Differentiation Strategy

market segments in which it has no cost disadvantage. For example, in local lumber, cement, bookkeeping, or pizza delivery markets, the focuser may have lower materials or transportation costs than the low-cost national company. The focuser may also have a cost advantage because it is producing complex or custom-built products that do not lend themselves easily to economies of scale in production and therefore offer few experience curve advantages. With a focus strategy, a company concentrates on small-volume custom products, for which it has a cost advantage, and leaves the large-volume standardized market to the cost leader—low-priced Mexican food specials versus Big Macs, for example.

If a company uses a focused differentiation approach, then all the means of differentiation that are open to the differentiator are available to the focused company. The point is that the focused company positions itself to compete with the differentiator in just one or a few segments. For example, Porsche, a focused company, competes against GM only in the sports car segment of the car market. Focused companies are likely to develop differentiated product qualities successfully because of their knowledge of a small customer set (such as sports car buyers), knowledge of a region, or expertise in a particular field (such as corporate law, management consulting, or web site management for retail customers or restaurants).

Concentration on a small range of products sometimes allows a focuser to develop innovations faster than a large differentiator can. However, the focuser does not attempt to serve all market segments because that would bring it into direct competition with the differentiator. Instead, it concentrates on building market share in one market segment; if it is successful, it may begin to serve more and more market segments and chip away at the differentiator's competitive advantage. The way in which many small software companies have emerged to take advantage of specialized niches in the outsourcing market, discussed in Strategy in Action 5.3, illustrates how focused companies can obtain a competitive advantage.

Table 5.1 illustrates the specific product, market, and distinctive competency choices made by a focused company. Differentiation can be high or low because the company can pursue a low-cost or a differentiation approach. As for customer groups, a focused company chooses specific niches in which to compete rather than going for a whole market, as a cost leader does, or filling a large number of niches, as a broad differentiator does. The focused company can pursue any distinctive competency because it can seek any kind of differentiation or low-cost advantage. Thus, it might find a cost advantage and develop a superior efficiency in low-cost manufacturing or web site hosting within a particular region or industry. Alternatively, it might develop superior skills in responsiveness to customers, based on its ability to

Strategy in Action

5.3

Finding a Niche in the Outsourcing Market

Outsourcing occurs when one company contracts with another company to perform one of the value creation functions on its behalf. Increasingly, many companies are finding it very difficult to keep up with the pace of technological change in the computer software industry and are outsourcing their data-processing needs to specialized software companies. Others are also outsourcing their web site design and management needs. Electronic Data Systems (EDS), IBM, and Computer Associates are some of the industry giants that manage other companies' data-processing and web site operations using their own proprietary software.

Different kinds of organizations, such as universities, banks, insurance agencies, local governments, and utilities, have different kinds of data-processing and web site design needs and problems. Often, each kind of company requires a specialized kind of software system that can be customized to its specific needs. As a result, it is difficult for any one software company to service the needs of a wide range of different companies, and the outsourcing market in data processing and web site design is fragmented. Large companies such as EDS and IBM have only relatively small market shares; consequently, opportunities abound for new companies to position themselves to provide dedicated service to a particular kind of business or industry.

Increasingly, small, specialized software companies have been springing up to manage the needs of particular kinds of clients. An example is Systems & Computer Technology, based in Malvern, Pennsylvania, which went head-to-head with EDS to secure a seven-year $35 million outsourcing contract to service the data-processing needs

of Dallas County. The company has yearly revenues of only $200 million, compared with EDS's $15 billion, but it won the contract because it specializes in servicing the needs of local government and institutions of higher education. It could show Dallas County its twelve ongoing contracts with municipal clients, whereas EDS could offer its experience with only one, a hospital. The focused company won out over the differentiator.

Other focused companies are also springing up—for instance, the Bisys Group and Systematics Company, which serve the needs of banks and universities. It appears that in the data-processing industry, small, focused companies are strong competitors because of their ability to provide specialized, personal service to specific clients in a way that large differentiators cannot. Indeed, EDS ran into problems because of the emergence of agile, Internet-based competitors that can provide e-commerce solutions at a price much lower than EDS's. The collapse of the e-commerce environment in 2001 intensified competition between large and small rivals, and the small specialist companies have benefited from their lower cost structures and ability to respond quickly to the changing needs of their clients.

Sources: J. W. Verity, "They Make a Killing Minding Other People's Business," *Business Week,* November 30, 1992, p. 96. Mark Willis, "Outsourcing Benefits Administration: A Disciplined Process for Conducting a Thorough Cost-Benefit Analysis," *Compensation and Benefits Management* (Winter 1996): 45–53. Jane Gebhart, "Beyond the Information Systems Outsourcing Bandwagon: The Insourcing Response," *Sloan Business Review* (Winter 1996): 177. B. Caldwell and J. Mateyaschuk, "Reviving EDS," *Informationweek* 742 (1999): 18–19.

serve the particular needs of regional or industry customers in ways that a national differentiator would find very expensive.

The many avenues a focused company can take to develop a competitive advantage explain why there are so many small companies in relation to large ones. A focused company has enormous opportunity to develop its own niche and compete against companies pursuing low-cost and differentiated strategies. A focus strategy provides an opportunity for an entrepreneur to find and then exploit a gap in the market by developing an innovative product that customers cannot do without.[21] The steel mini-mills discussed in Chapter 4 are a good example of how focused companies specializing in one market can grow so efficient that they become the cost leaders. Many large companies started with a focus strategy, and, of course, one means by which companies can expand is to take over other focused companies. For example, Cisco Systems, the largest Internet router maker, grew by buying over fifty small specialist software and hardware companies. Its managers believed these companies possessed the products and knowledge that would allow it to become the leading differentiator in the industry, and despite the downturn in e-commerce Cisco remains the dominant industry competitor.

Advantages and Disadvantages. A focused company's competitive advantages stem from the source of its distinctive competency: efficiency, quality, innovation, or responsiveness to customers. The company is protected from rivals to the extent that it can provide a product or service they cannot. This ability also gives the focuser power over its buyers because they cannot get the same thing from anyone else. With regard to powerful suppliers, however, a focused company is at a disadvantage, because it buys in small volume and thus is in the suppliers' power. However, as long as it can pass on price increases to loyal customers, this disadvantage may not be a significant problem. Potential entrants have to overcome the loyalty from customers the focuser has generated, and the development of customer loyalty also lessens the threat from substitute products. This protection from the five forces allows the focuser to earn above-average returns on its investment. Another advantage of the focus strategy is that it permits a company to stay close to its customers and respond to their changing needs. The difficulty a large differentiator sometimes experiences in managing a large number of market segments is not an issue for a focuser.

Because a focuser produces a small volume, its cost structure may be higher than that of a low-cost company. Higher costs can reduce profitability if a focuser is forced to invest heavily in developing a distinctive competency, such as expensive product innovation, in order to compete with a differentiated company. However, once again, flexible manufacturing systems are opening up new opportunities for focused companies because small production runs become possible at a lower cost. Increasingly, small, specialized companies are competing with large companies in specific market segments in which their cost disadvantage is much reduced.

A second problem is that the focuser's niche can suddenly disappear because of technological change or changes in customers' tastes. Unlike the more generalist differentiator, a focuser cannot move easily to new niches, given its concentration of resources and competency in one or a few niches. For example, clothing store chain Brooks Brothers, whose focus was on providing formal business attire, ran into great difficulty in the 1990s when business casual became the clothing norm at most companies. It found it hard to adapt to the changing market and was bought out in 2001. Diners have become almost a thing of the past as they have become unable to compete with the low prices and speed of fast food chains like McDonald's and the upscale atmosphere of Starbuck's. The disappearance of niches is one reason that so many small companies fail.

Finally, there is the very real prospect that differentiators will compete for a focuser's niche by offering a product that can satisfy the demands of the focuser's customers; for example, GM's new midsize Cadillac and Ford's new midsized Jaguar are aimed at Lexus, BMW, and Mercedes-Benz buyers. A focuser is vulnerable and has to defend its niche constantly.

Stuck in the Middle   Successful competitive positioning requires that a company make consistent product, market, and distinctive competency choices. In other words, a company must achieve a fit among the three components of business-level strategy to create a business model that gives it a competitive advantage. Thus, a low-cost company cannot strive for a high level of market segmentation, as a differentiator does, and provide a wide range of products because those choices would raise its cost structure too much and the company would lose its low-cost advantage. Similarly, a differentiator with a competency in innovation that tries to reduce its expenditures on research and development or one with a competency in responsiveness to customers through after-sales service that seeks to economize on its sales force to decrease costs is asking for trouble because it will lose its competitive advantage as its distinctive competency disappears.

Pursuing a business-level strategy successfully means giving serious attention to all elements of the business model on an ongoing basis. Many companies, through ignorance or error, do not do the planning necessary for success in their chosen strategy. Such companies are said to be "stuck in the middle" because they have made product and market choices that they have been unable to obtain or sustain a competitive advantage.[22] As a result, they have no consistent business-level strategy, experience below-average profitability, and suffer when industry competition intensifies.

Some stuck-in-the-middle companies may have started out pursuing cost leadership or differentiation strategies but then made wrong resource allocation decisions or experienced a hostile, changing environment. It is very easy for strategic managers to lose control of a generic strategy unless they keep close track of the business and its environment, constantly adjusting product and market choices to suit changing conditions within the industry. This is why it is so important that managers think strategically. In Chapter 1, we defined *strategic intent* as the way managers think about where they want their organization to be in the future and what kinds of resources and capabilities they will need to achieve this vision. Strategic intent provides a company with a sense of direction and stretches managers at all levels to be more inventive or innovative and to think how to make better use of resources. Moreover, it "implies a competitive distinct point of view about the future; it holds out to employees the promise of exploring new competitive territory."[23] The experience of Holiday Inns described in Strategy in Action 5.4 shows how a company can become stuck in the middle but also how a company can change its business model to regain its competitive advantage.

As the experience of Holiday Inns suggests, there are many paths to being stuck in the middle. Quite commonly, a focuser can get stuck in the middle when it becomes overconfident and starts to act like a broad differentiator. People Express, the defunct airline, exemplified a company in this situation. It started out as a specialized air carrier serving a narrow market niche: low-priced travel on the eastern seaboard. In pursuing this focus strategy based on cost leadership, it was very successful, but when it tried to expand to other geographic regions and began taking over other airlines to gain a larger number of planes, it lost its niche. People Express became one more carrier in an increasingly competitive market in which it had no special competitive advantage against the other national carriers. The result was financial trouble. People Express was swallowed up by Texas Air and incorporated into Continental Airlines. By contrast, Southwest Airlines, the focused low-cost company, has continued to focus on this strategy and has grown successfully.

Differentiators too can fail in the market and end up stuck in the middle if competitors attack their markets with more specialized or low-cost products that blunt their competitive edge. This happened to IBM in the large-frame computer market as personal computers became more powerful and able to do the job of the much more expensive mainframes. The increasing movement toward flexible manufacturing systems aggravates the problems of cost leaders and differentiators. Many large

Strategy in Action

Holiday Inns on Six Continents

The history of the Holiday Inns motel chain is one of the great success stories in U.S. business. Its founder, Kemmons Wilson, vacationing in the early 1950s, found motels to be small, expensive, and of unpredictable quality. This discovery, along with the prospect of unprecedented highway travel that would come with the new interstate highway program, triggered a realization: there was an unmet customer need—a gap in the market for quality accommodations. Holiday Inns was founded to meet that need. From the beginning, Holiday Inns set the standard for offering motel features such as air-conditioning and icemakers while keeping room rates reasonable. These amenities enhanced the motels' popularity, and motel franchising, Wilson's invention, made rapid expansion possible. By 1960, Holiday Inns could be found in virtually every city and on every major highway. Before the 1960s ended, more than 1,000 of them were in full operation, and occupancy rates averaged 80 percent. The concept of mass accommodation had arrived.

The service it offered appealed to the average traveler, who wanted a standardized product (a room) at an average price—the middle of the hotel room market. But by the 1970s, travelers were beginning to make different demands on hotels and motels. Some wanted luxury and were willing to pay higher prices for better accommodations and service. Others sought low prices and accepted rock-bottom quality and service in exchange. As the market fragmented into different groups of customers with different needs, Holiday Inns was still offering an undifferentiated, average-cost, average-quality product.

Although Holiday Inns missed the change in the market and thus failed to respond appropriately to it, the competition did not. Companies such as Hyatt siphoned off the top end of the market, where quality and service sold rooms. Chains such as Motel 6 and Days Inns captured the basic-quality, low-price end of the market. In between were many specialty chains that appealed to business travelers, families, or self-caterers (people who want to be able to cook in their hotel rooms). Holiday Inns' position was attacked from all sides. As occupancy rates dropped drastically with increasing competition, profitability declined.

Wounded but not dead, Holiday Inns began a counterattack. The original chain was upgraded to suit quality-oriented travelers. Then to meet the needs of different kinds of travelers, Holiday Inns created new hotel and motel chains: the luxury Crowne Plazas; the Hampton Inns serving the low-priced end of the market; and the all-suite Embassy Suites. Holiday Inns attempted to meet the demands of the many niches, or segments, of the hotel market that have emerged as customers' needs have changed over time. These moves were successful in the early 1990s, and Holiday Inns grew to become one of the largest suppliers of hotel rooms in the industry. However, by the late 1990s, it became clear that with intense competition in the industry from other chains such as Marriott, Holiday Inns was once again losing its differentiated appeal as its revenues and profits fell.

In the fast-changing hotel and lodging market, positioning each hotel brand or chain to maximize customer demand is an ever-changing endeavor. In 2000, the pressure on all hotel chains to adapt to the challenges of global competition and become a globally differentiated brand led to the takeover of the company and its incorporation in the international Six Continents Hotel chain. Today, around the globe, more than 3,200 hotels flying the flags of Holiday Inn, Holiday Inn Express, Crowne Plaza, Staybridge Suites by Holiday Inn, and luxury Inter-Continental Hotels and Resorts are positioning themselves to offer the services, amenities, and lodging experiences that will cater to virtually every travel occasion and guest need. A massive modernization campaign is under way in the United States to take existing full-service Holiday Inns to their next evolution and the opening of the first "Holiday Inn of the Future" is planned for late 2002. Holiday Inns plans to have a room to meet the need of every segment of the lodging market.

Sources: "The Holiday Inns Trip; A Breeze for Decades, Bumpy Ride in the 1980s," *Wall Street Journal,* February 11, 1987, p. 1. Holiday Inns, *Annual Report* (1985). U.S. Bureau of Labor Statistics, *U.S. Industrial Output* (Washington, D.C.: U.S. Government Printing Office, 1986). Mark Gleason and Alan Salomon, "Fallon's Challenge: Make Holiday Inn More 'In,'" *Advertising Age,* September 2, 1996, p. 14. Julie Miller, "Amenities Range from Snacks to Technology," *Hotel and Motel Management,* July 3, 1996, pp. 38–40. www.sixcontinenthotels.com, 2002.

companies become stuck in the middle unless they make the investment needed to pursue both strategies simultaneously. No company is safe in the jungle of competition, and each must be constantly on the lookout to take advantage of competitive advantages as they arise and to defend the advantages it already has.

Successful management of a generic competitive strategy requires strategic managers to attend to two main matters. First, they need to ensure that the product, market, and distinctive competency decisions they make result in a business-level strategy that gives them a competitive advantage and a business model that results in superior profitability. Second, they need to monitor the environment and their competitors constantly so that they can keep the company's sources of competitive advantage in tune with changing opportunities and threats.

Competitive Positioning and Business-Level Strategy

Business-level strategy determines how a company will compete for customers in a particular market segment or industry. In every market segment or industry, typically several companies are competing for the same set of customers. This means that the actions of one company will have an impact on the others, and over time, companies competing for the same customers become rivals locked in a competitive struggle to be the ones that obtain a competitive advantage and achieve above-average profitability. How many companies might be expected to achieve above-average profitability in a particular market or industry? And how can managers increase their chances of being one of the fortunate few? Several tools are useful in helping managers to position their companies competitively with regard to both the customer and their competitors. Here, we examine three of these tools: strategic group analysis, investment analysis, and game theory.

Strategic Group Analysis

Strategic group analysis helps a company identify the strategies that its industry rivals are pursuing. Within most industries, strategic groups emerge, each composed of companies pursuing a similar generic strategy.[24] All the companies inside an industry pursuing a low-cost strategy form one strategic group, all those seeking to pursue a broad differentiation strategy constitute another strategic group, and all those pursuing a focus differentiation or low-cost strategy form yet other strategic groups.

The concept of strategic groups has a number of implications for business-level strategy. First, strategic managers can map their competitors according to their choice of generic strategy. They can identify the different ways rivals have decided what customers' needs to satisfy, which customer groups to serve, and which distinctive competencies to develop. They can then use this knowledge to position themselves closer to customers and differentiate themselves from their competitors. In other words, careful strategic group analysis allows managers to uncover the most important basis of competition in an industry and identify products and market segments where they can compete most successfully for customers. Such analysis also helps to reveal what competencies are likely to be most valuable in the future so that companies can make the right investment decision. For example, the need to develop new models of cars that can be sold across the world and are assembled reliably by low-cost labor has dominated competitive positioning in the global car industry. U.S. car companies have bought or formed alliances with almost every other foreign car manufacturer to obtain marketing, design, or manufacturing knowledge.

Second, a company's nearest competitors are those companies pursuing a similar strategy in its strategic group. Customers tend to view the products of such enterprises as being direct substitutes for each other. Thus, a major threat to a company's profitability may arise primarily from within its own strategic group, not necessarily from the other companies in the industry pursuing different generic business-level strategies. For example, the competition for Toyota comes from Honda, Ford, and Volkswagen, not from Hyundai or Rolls Royce.

Third, different strategic groups can have a different standing with respect to each of Porter's five competitive forces because these forces affect companies in different ways. In other words, the risk of new entry by potential competitors, the degree of rivalry among companies within a group, the bargaining power of buyers, the bargaining power of suppliers, and the competitive force of substitute products can all vary in intensity among different strategic groups within the same industry. In the global car industry, for example, the smaller, more focused companies pursuing both low-cost and differentiated luxury strategies were in big trouble in the 1990s. Their input costs were rising, and they could not afford billions of dollars to design new models and build new flexible manufacturing plants needed to produce them. Indeed, some European, Korean, and even Japanese companies started to lose billions of dollars, while the big differentiators such as Toyota, Volkswagen, and Ford were making record profits.

As discussed in Chapter 2, mobility barriers are factors that inhibit the movement of companies between groups in an industry. The relative height of mobility barriers determines how successfully companies in one group can compete with companies in another group. For example, can a company in the differentiation strategic group also pursue a low-cost strategy and thus achieve the low cost-differentiation strategy? To the degree that one or more companies in one group can develop or obtain the functional and financial resources they need to lower their costs or embark on a major R&D expansion, they may be able to compete successfully with companies in another strategic group. In effect, they have created yet another strategic group: a combined low-cost and differentiation strategic group, which has the strongest competitive advantage and the greatest ability to earn above-average profits. In fact, the need to pursue a simultaneous global low-cost and differentiation strategy has been the major driving force behind the wave of merger activities among the large car companies that has left just a handful of global giants to compete in the 2000s. For example, Daimler Benz took over Chrysler, GM took control of Isuzu, and Ford merged with Mazda to pursue a global low-cost/differentiation strategy. Thus, the strategic group map in the global car industry has changed dramatically as companies fight to survive in the rapidly consolidating global car industry. A few companies like BMW and Porsche still pursue a focus differentiated strategy. However, some analysts believe it is only a matter of time before they will be forced to join with one of the low-cost/differentiators.

Choosing an Investment Strategy at the Business Level

A second major choice to be made at the business level is which type of investment strategy to pursue in support of the competitive strategy. An investment strategy sets the amount and type of resources—human, functional, and financial—that must be invested to maximize a company's profitability over time.[25] Recall from Chapter 3 that a company's return on invested capital is a major indicator of its competitive advantage in an industry. Generic competitive strategies provide competitive advantages, but they are expensive to develop and maintain. For example, a simultaneous differentiation/cost-leadership strategy is the most expensive, because it requires that a company invest resources not only in functions such as R&D, sales, and marketing to develop distinctive competencies but also in functions such as manufacturing and materials management to find ways to reduce costs. A focus strategy is probably the least expensive because fewer resources are needed to serve one market segment than the whole market.

In deciding on an investment strategy, a company must evaluate the potential return (on invested capital) from investing in a generic competitive strategy against the cost. In this way, it can determine whether pursuing a certain strategy is likely to be profitable and how profitability will change as competition within the industry changes. Two factors are crucial in choosing an investment strategy: the strength of a company's position in an industry relative to its competitors and the stage of the industry's life cycle in which the company is competing.[26]

In determining the strength of a company's relative competitive position, market share and distinctive competencies become important. A large market share signals greater potential returns from future investment because it suggests a company has brand loyalty and is in a strong competitive position. Similarly, the more difficult it is to imitate a company's distinctive competencies, such as those in R&D or manufacturing and marketing, the stronger a company's relative competitive position becomes. These two attributes also reinforce one another; for example, a large market share may help a company to create and develop distinctive competencies because high demand allows it to ride down the experience curve and lower its cost structure. Also, a large market share can create a large cash flow, which may allow for more investment to develop competencies in R&D or elsewhere. In general, companies with the largest market share and the strongest distinctive competencies are in the best position to build and sustain their competitive advantage. Companies with a small market share and little potential for developing a distinctive competency are in a much weaker competitive position.[27]

The second main factor influencing the investment attractiveness of a generic strategy is the stage of the industry life cycle. A particular industry environment, presenting different opportunities and threats, accompanies each life cycle stage. Each stage therefore has different implications for the investment of resources needed to obtain a competitive advantage. Competition is strongest in the shakeout stage of the life cycle and least important in the embryonic stage, for example. The risks of pursuing a strategy change over time. The difference in risk explains why the potential returns from investing in a competitive strategy depend on the life cycle stage. Table 5.2 summarizes the relationship among the stage of the life cycle, the competitive position, and the investment strategy at the business level.

TABLE 5.2

Choosing an Investment Strategy at the Business Level

Stage of Industry Life Cycle	Strong Competitive Position	Weak Competitive Position
Embryonic	Share building	Share building
Growth	Growth	Market concentration
Shakeout	Share increasing	Market concentration or harvest/liquidation
Maturity	Hold-and-maintain or profit	Harvest or liquidation/divestiture
Decline	Market concentration or harvest (asset reduction)	Turnaround, liquidation, or divestiture

Embryonic Strategy. In the embryonic stage, all companies, weak and strong, emphasize the development of a distinctive competency and an associated business model. During this stage, investment needs are great because a company has to establish a competitive advantage. Many fledgling companies in the industry are seeking resources to develop a distinctive competency. Thus, the appropriate business-level investment strategy is a **share-building strategy.** The aim is to build market share by developing a stable and distinct competitive advantage to attract customers who have no knowledge of the company's products.

Companies require large amounts of capital to build research and development competencies or sales and service competencies. They cannot generate much of this capital internally. Thus, a company's success depends on its ability to demonstrate a distinct competency to attract outside investors, or venture capitalists. If a company gains the resources to develop a distinctive competency, it will be in a relatively stronger competitive position. If it fails, its only option may be to exit the industry. In fact, companies in weak competitive positions at all stages in the life cycle may choose to exit the industry to cut their losses.

Growth Strategies. At the growth stage, the task facing a company is to consolidate its position and provide the base it needs to survive the coming shakeout. Thus, the appropriate investment strategy is the **growth strategy.** The goal is to maintain its relative competitive position in a rapidly expanding market and, if possible, to increase it—in other words, to grow with the expanding market. However, other companies are entering the market and catching up with the industry's innovators. As a result, first movers—companies first into the market with a particular kind of good or service—often require successive waves of capital infusion to maintain the momentum generated by their success in the embryonic stage. For example, differentiators need to engage in extensive research and development to maintain their technological lead, and cost leaders need to invest in state-of-the-art machinery and computers to obtain new experience curve economies. All this investment is very expensive.

The growth stage is also the time when companies attempt to consolidate existing market niches and enter new ones so that they can increase their market share. Increasing the level of market segmentation to become a broad differentiator is expensive as well. A company has to invest resources to develop a new sales and marketing competency. Consequently, at the growth stage, companies fine-tune their competitive strategy (which we discuss at length in Chapter 7) and make business-level investment decisions about the relative advantages of a differentiation, low-cost, or focus strategy, given financial needs and relative competitive position. If one company has emerged as the cost leader, for example, some others may decide to compete head-to-head with it and enter this strategic group, but others will not and instead will pursue a growth strategy using a differentiation or focus approach and invest resources in developing other competencies. As a result, strategic groups start to develop in an industry as each company seeks the best way to invest its scarce resources to maximize its competitive advantage.

Companies must spend a lot of money just to keep up with growth in the market, and finding additional resources to develop new skills and competencies is a difficult task for strategic managers. Consequently, companies in a weak competitive position at this stage engage in a **market concentration** strategy to consolidate their position. They seek to specialize in some way and may adopt a focus strategy and move to a focused strategic group to reduce their investment needs. If they are very weak, they may also choose to exit the industry and sell out to a stronger competitor.

Shakeout Strategies. By the shakeout stage, demand is increasing slowly, and competition by price or product characteristics becomes intense. Companies in strong competitive positions need resources to invest in a **share-increasing strategy** to attract customers from weak companies exiting the market. In other words, companies attempt to maintain and increase market share despite fierce competition. The way companies invest their resources depends on their generic strategy.

For cost leaders, because of the price wars that can occur, investment in cost control is crucial if they are to survive the shakeout stage; they must do all they can to reduce costs. Differentiators in a strong competitive position choose to forge ahead and become broad differentiators. Their investment is likely to be oriented toward marketing, and they are likely to develop a sophisticated after-sales service network. They also widen the product range to match the range of customers' needs. Differentiators in a weak position reduce their investment burden by withdrawing to a focused strategy—the **market concentration strategy**—to specialize in a particular niche or product. Weak companies exiting the industry engage in a **harvest** or **liquidation** strategy, both of which are discussed later in this chapter.

Maturity Strategies. By the maturity stage, a relatively stable strategic group structure has emerged in the industry, and companies have learned how their competitors will probably react to their competitive moves. At this point, companies want to reap the rewards of their previous investments in developing a generic strategy. Until now, profits have been reinvested in the business, and dividends have been small. Investors in strong companies have obtained their rewards through the appreciation of the value of their stock, because the company has reinvested most of its capital to maintain and increase market share. As market growth slows in the maturity stage, a company's investment strategy depends on the level of competition in the industry and the source of the company's competitive advantage.

In environments in which competition is high because of technological change or low barriers to entry, companies need to defend their competitive position. Strategic managers need to continue to invest heavily in maintaining the company's competitive advantage. Both low-cost companies and differentiators adopt a **hold-and-maintain** strategy to support their generic strategies. They expend resources to develop their distinctive competency so as to remain the market leaders. For example, differentiated companies may invest in improved after-sales service, and low-cost companies may invest in the latest production technologies.

It is at this point, however, that companies realize they must begin to pursue both a low-cost and a differentiation strategy if they are to protect themselves from aggressive competitors (both at home and abroad) that are watching for any opportunity or perceived weakness to take the lead in the industry. Differentiators take advantage of their strong position to develop flexible manufacturing systems to reduce their production costs. Cost leaders move to start differentiating their products to expand their market share by serving more market segments. For example, Gallo moved from the bulk wine segment and began marketing premium wines and wine coolers to take advantage of its low production costs. Soon, Gallo's new premium brands, like Falling Leaf chardonnay, became the best-selling wines in the United States.

Historically, however, many companies have felt protected from competition within the industry in the maturity stage and decide to exploit their competitive advantage to the fullest by engaging in a **profit strategy:** they attempt to maximize their present returns, not their future profitability, from previous investments. Typically, they reinvest proportionally less in improving their functional resources and increased returns to shareholders. The profit strategy works well only as long as competitive forces remain relatively constant, so that a company can maintain the profit margins developed by its competitive strategy. However, it must be alert to threats from the environment and take care not to become complacent and unresponsive to changes. All too often, market leaders fail to exercise vigilance in managing the environment, imagining that they are impervious to competition. Kodak, which had profited for so long from its strengths in film processing, was slow to respond to the threat of electronic imaging techniques. Sears and Kmart woke up too late to the threat posed by Wal-Mart. Paradoxically, very successful companies often fail to sense changes in the market.

Decline Strategies. The decline stage of an industry's life cycle begins when demand for its product starts to fall. Among the many possible reasons for decline are foreign competition and the loss of a company's distinctive competency as its rivals enter with new or more efficient technologies. A company must now decide what investment strategy to adopt in order to deal with new circumstances within its industry.[28] The initial strategies that companies can adopt are market concentration and asset reduction.[29]

With a **market concentration strategy,** a company attempts to consolidate its product and market choices. It narrows its product range and exits marginal niches in an attempt to redeploy its resources more effectively and improve its competitive position. Reducing customer groups served may also allow it to pursue a focus strategy in order to survive the decline stage. An **asset reduction strategy** requires a company to limit or decrease its investment in a business and to extract, or milk, the investment as much as it can. This approach is sometimes called a **harvest strategy** because a company will exit the industry once it has "harvested" all the returns it can. It reduces to a minimum the assets it employs in the business and forgoes investment for the sake of immediate profits.[30] A market concentration strategy generally indicates that a company is trying to turn around its business so that it can survive in the long run. Low-cost companies are more likely to pursue a harvest strategy because a smaller market share means higher costs and they are unable to move to a focus strategy. Differentiators, in contrast, have a competitive advantage in this stage if they can move to a focus strategy.

At any stage of the life cycle, companies that are in weak competitive positions may apply **turnaround strategies.**[31] The questions that a company has to answer are whether it has the resources available to develop a viable business-level strategy to compete in the industry and how much it will cost. A company stuck in the middle, for example, must assess the investment costs of developing a low-cost or differentiation strategy. Perhaps a company pursuing a low-cost strategy has not made the right product or market choices, or perhaps a differentiation has been missing niche opportunities. In such cases, the company can redeploy resources and change its strategy.

If a company decides that turnaround is not possible for competitive or life cycle reasons, then the two remaining investment alternatives are liquidation and divestiture: exit the industry by liquidating assets or selling the whole business. Both are radical forms of harvesting strategy, because the company is seeking to get back as much as it can from its investment in the business. Often, however, it can exit only at a loss and take a tax write-off. Timing is important; the earlier a company senses that divestiture is necessary, the more it can get for its assets. There are many stories about companies that buy weak or declining companies, thinking they can turn them around, and as the new acquisitions become a drain on their resources they then realize their mistake.

Strategic managers must always consider the costs of pursuing a generic strategy when developing or refining their business models. The issue is how to invest a company's capital in resources that will result in the greatest potential future returns. Achieving superior performance and profitability requires constant attention to the bottom line—to understanding how to increase a company's return on invested capital through the investment strategy in its business model.

Business-Level Strategy and Game Theory

Companies are in a constant competitive struggle with rivals in their industry and strategic group to gain more business from customers. A useful way of viewing this struggle is as a competitive game between companies, where companies are continually using competitive moves and tactics to compete effectively in an industry. Companies that understand the nature of the competitive game they are playing can often make better strategic moves that increase the profitability of their business-level strategies. For example, they can find a better way to pursue a cost leadership or a differentiation strategy. A branch of work in the social sciences known as *game theory* can be used to model competition between a company and its rivals and help managers improve their business models and strategies.[32]

From a game theory perspective, companies in an industry can be viewed as players that are all simultaneously making choices about which generic strategies to pursue to maximize their profitability. The problem strategic managers face is that the potential profitability of each strategy is not some fixed amount; it varies depending on the strategy one company selects and also the strategies that its rivals select. There are two basic types of game: sequential move games and simultaneous move games. In a *sequential move game,* such as chess, players move in turn, and one player can select a strategy to pursue after considering its rival's choice of strategies. In a *simultaneous move game,* the players act at the same time, in ignorance of their rival's current actions. The classic game of rock-paper-scissors is a simultaneous move game.

In the business world, both sequential and simultaneous move games are commonplace as strategic managers jockey for competitive position in the industry. Indeed, game theory is particularly useful in analyzing situations where a company is competing against a limited number of rivals, and there is a considerable level of interdependence in the industry, as occurs in a consolidated industry. In such a setting, the profitability of a strategy depends critically on the strategy pursued by rival companies. Several of the basic principles that underlie game theory are examined below; these principles can be useful in determining which business-level strategies managers should pursue.

Look Forward and Reason Back. One of the most basic messages of game theory is that managers need to think strategically in two related ways: (1) look forward, think ahead, and anticipate how rivals will respond to whatever strategic moves they make, and (2) reason backward to determine which strategic moves to pursue today given their assessment of how the company's rivals will respond to various future strategic moves. Managers who do both of these things should be able to discover the specific competitive strategy that will lead to the greatest potential returns. This cardinal principle of game theory is known as *look forward and reason back.* To understand its importance consider this scenario.

Two large companies, UPS and FedEx, which specialize in next-day delivery of packages, dominate the U.S. air express industry. They have a very high fixed cost structure because they need to invest in a capital-intensive nationwide network of aircraft, trucks, and package sorting facilities. The key to their profitability is to increase volume sufficiently so that these fixed costs can be spread out over a large number of packages, reducing the unit cost of transporting each package.

Imagine that a bright young manager at UPS calculates that if UPS cuts prices for next-day delivery service by 15 percent, the volume of packages the company ships will grow by over 30 percent, and so will UPS's total revenues and profitability. Is this a smart move? The answer depends on whether the bright young manager has remembered to look forward and reason back and think through how FedEx would respond to UPS's price cuts.

Because UPS and FedEx are competing directly against each other, their strategies are interdependent. If UPS cuts prices, FedEx will lose market share, its volume of shipments will decline, and its profitability will suffer. Because FedEx is unlikely to accept this result, if UPS cuts prices by 15 percent, FedEx is likely to follow and cut its prices by 15 percent in order to hold onto market share. The net result is that the average level of prices in the industry will fall by 15 percent, as will revenues, and both players will see their profitability decline—a lose-lose situation. By looking forward and reasoning back, the new manager discovers that the strategy of cutting prices is not a good one.

Decision trees can be used to help in the process of looking forward and reasoning back. Figure 5.3 maps out the decision tree for the simple game analyzed above from the perspective of UPS. (Note that this is a sequential move game.) UPS moves first, and then FedEx must decide how to respond. Here, you see that UPS has to choose between two strategies: cutting prices by 15 percent or leaving them unchanged. If it leaves prices unchanged, it will continue to earn its current level of profitability, which is $100 million. If it cuts prices by 15 percent, one of two things can happen: FedEx matches the price cut, or FedEx leaves its prices unchanged. If FedEx matches UPS's price cut (FedEx decides to fight a price war), profits are competed away and UPS's profit will be $0. If FedEx does not respond and leaves its prices unaltered, UPS will gain market share and its profits will rise to $180 million. So the best pricing strategy for UPS to pursue depends on its assessment of FedEx's likely response.

FIGURE 5.3

A Decision Tree for
UPS's Pricing Strategy

Figure 5.3 assigns probabilities to the different responses from FedEx: specifically there is a 70 percent chance that FedEx will match UPS's price cut and a 30 percent chance that it will do nothing. These probabilities come from an assessment of how UPS's price cut will affect FedEx's sales volume and profitability. The bigger the negative impact of UPS's price cut is on FedEx's sales volume and profitability, the more likely it is that FedEx will match UPS's price cuts. This is another example of the principle of looking forward and reasoning backward. Assigning a 70 percent probability to the top branch in Figure 5.3 assumes that the price cut from UPS will have a significant negative impact on FedEx's business and will force the company to respond with a price cut of its own. The probabilities can also come from looking at the history of FedEx's responses to UPS's price moves. If FedEx has a long history of matching UPS's price cuts, the probability that it will do so this time is high. If FedEx does not have a history of matching UPS's price cuts, the probability will be lower.

Now let us revisit the question of what strategy UPS should pursue. If UPS does not cut prices, its profits are $100 million. If it cuts prices, its expected profits are $(.70) \times \$0 + (.30) \times \$180 = \$60$ million. Since $60 million is less than $100 million, UPS should not pursue the price cutting strategy. If it did, FedEx would probably respond, and the net effect would be to depress UPS's profitability. Another way of looking at this scenario is to ask under what assumptions about the probability of FedEx's responding it would be worthwhile for UPS to cut prices by 15 percent. For UPS to move forward with its price cuts, the expected profits from doing so must be greater than $100 million, which is the profit from doing nothing. The way to work this out is to find the probability for which UPS is indifferent between leaving prices unaltered or changing them. Signifying probability by p, $\$100m = p \times \$180m$, and solving for p, $p = \$100m/\$180m = 0.556$. In other words, for UPS to go ahead with the proposed price cut, the probability that FedEx will do nothing must be greater than 55.6 percent.

Know Thy Rival. At this juncture, the question of whether this example is rather contrived might arise. After all, could UPS managers *really* anticipate how FedEx's profits could be affected if UPS cut its prices by 15 percent? And could UPS really assign a probability to FedEx's likely response? The answer is that although UPS's managers cannot calculate exactly what the profit impact and probabilities would be, they can make an informed decision by collecting competitive information and thinking strategically. For example, they could estimate FedEx's cost structure by looking at FedEx's published financial accounts. And because they are in the same business as FedEx and use the same basic business model, they can assess the effect of falling demand on FedEx's cost structure and bottom line. Moreover, by looking at the history of FedEx's competitive behavior, they can assess how FedEx will respond to a price cut.

This illustrates a second basic principle of game theory: know thy rivals. In other words, in thinking strategically, managers put themselves in the position of a rival to answer the question of how that rival is likely to act in a particular situation. If a company's managers are to be effective at looking forward and reasoning back, they must have a good understanding of what their rival is likely to do under different scenarios, and they need to be able to extrapolate their rival's future behavior based on this understanding.

Find the Most Profitable Dominant Strategy. A **dominant strategy** is one that makes you better off than you would be if you played any other strategy, *no matter what strategy your opponent uses.* To grasp this concept, consider a simultaneous move game based on a situation that developed in the U.S. car industry in the early 1990s (so far we have been considering a sequential move game). Two car companies, Ford and GM, both differentiators, have to decide whether to introduce cash-back rebate programs in November to move unsold inventory that is building up on the lots of car dealers nationwide. Each company can make one of two moves: offer rebates or do not offer rebates. Because the advanced planning associated with launching such a strategy is fairly extensive, both companies must make a decision about what to do by mid-October, which is before they have had a chance to see what their rival is doing.

In each of the previous four years, both companies have introduced just such programs on November 1 and kept them in place until December 31. Customers have become conditioned to expect these programs and increasingly have held back their new car purchases in anticipation of the cash rebate programs beginning in November. This learned behavior by customers has increased the strategic importance of the rebate programs and made the rebate programs themselves increasingly expensive for the automobile companies. Figure 5.4 lays out a payoff matrix associated with each strategy.

The four cells in this matrix represent the four possible outcomes of pursuing or not pursuing a cash rebate strategy. The numbers in parentheses in the center of each cell represent the profit that General Motors and Ford, respectively, will get in each case (in millions of dollars). If both General Motors and Ford decide not to introduce cash rebates (Cell 1), each will get $800 million in profit for the November 1–December 31 period. If GM introduces a cash rebate program but Ford doesn't, GM will gain market share at Ford's expense, and GM will get $1,000 million in profit, while Ford gets just $200 million (Cell 2). The converse holds if Ford introduces a rebate program but GM doesn't (Cell 3). If both companies introduce rebate programs, both get $400 million (remember, the rebates are expensive and essentially represent deep price discounting to move unsold inventory)(Cell 4). Finally, the figures in parentheses in the lower-left-hand corner of each cell represent the joint profit associated with each outcome.

If you look at this payoff matrix, you will see that GM's dominant strategy is to offer cash rebates because whatever strategy Ford pursues, GM does better if it offers cash rebates than if it doesn't. If Ford's strategy is to offer no cash rebates, GM's best strategy is to offer rebates and capture a profit of $1,000 million. If Ford's strategy is

FIGURE 5.4

A Payoff Matrix for
GM and Ford

Ford's Strategy

	No cash rebates	Cash rebates
No cash rebates	(800, 800) (1600)	(200, 1000) (1200)
Cash rebates	(1000, 200) (1200)	(400, 400) (800)

GM's Strategy

to offer cash rebates, GM's best strategy is again to offer cash rebates and get a profit of $400 million. So whatever Ford does, GM's best strategy is to offer cash rebates.

An interesting aspect of this game is that Ford also goes through the same reasoning process. Indeed, the payoff matrix shows that Ford's dominant strategy is also to offer cash rebates. The net result is that while both players get $400 million profit, the combined payoff of $800 million is the lowest of any combination! Clearly, both automakers could have done better if they had cooperated and jointly decided not to offer cash rebates. Why didn't they do this? There are two reasons. First, cooperation to set prices is illegal under U.S. antitrust law. Second, even though neither party will gain from offering rebates, *it cannot trust the other party not to offer cash rebates since then it would be even worse off.* As the payoff matrix shows, if Ford does not offer cash rebates, GM has a very big incentive to do so, and vice versa. So both companies assume that the other will offer rebates, both end up doing so, and customers receive the value and are the winners!

The payoff structure in this game is very famous. It is known as the *prisoner's dilemma game* because it was first explained using an example of two suspects, or "prisoners," who are being interrogated for possible involvement in a crime. In the original exposition, the prisoners could confess to the crime and also implicate their partner in the crime to get a reduced sentence, or not confess or implicate the other. If the other prisoner also either doesn't confess or implicate the other, they both end up going free. The problem is that neither prisoner can trust the other not to implicate the other in order to get a reduced sentence. So to reduce their losses (length of jail time), both end up confessing and implicate the other, and both go to jail.

The prisoner's dilemma is thought to capture the essence of many situations where two or more companies are competing against each other and their dominant strategy is to fight a price war, even if they would collectively be better off by *not* doing so. In other words, the prisoner's dilemma can be used to explain the mutually destructive price competition that breaks out in many industries from time to time. It also raises the question of whether companies can do anything to extricate themselves from such a situation. This brings us to the final principle of game theory explored here.

Strategy Shapes the Payoff Structure of the Game. An important lesson of game theory is that through its choice of strategy, a company can alter the payoff structure of the competitive game being played in the industry. To understand this, consider once more the cash rebate game played by Ford and GM where both companies are compelled to choose a dominant strategy that depresses total payoffs. How can they extricate themselves from this predicament? By changing the behavior of customers.

Recall that rebates were necessary only because customers had come to expect them and held off purchasing a car until the rebates were introduced. In a self-fulfilling prophecy, this depresses demand and forces the companies to introduce rebates to move unsold inventory on the lots of car dealers. If these expectations could be changed, customers would not hold off their purchases in anticipation of the rebates being introduced in November of each year. Companies would no longer have to introduce rebates to move unsold inventory on the lots of car dealers. So how can a company change customer behavior? Through its choice of strategy.

This is what GM actually did. After several years of rebate wars, GM decided to issue a new credit card that allowed cardholders to apply 5 percent of their charges toward buying or leasing a new GM car, up to $500 a year with a maximum of $3,500.

The credit card launch was one of the most successful in history: within two years, there were 9 million GM credit card holders, and the card had replaced the other incentives that GM offered, principally the end-of-year cash rebates. Because of the card, price-sensitive customers who typically waited for the rebates could purchase a reduced price car any time of the year. Moreover, once they had the card, they were much more likely to buy from GM than Ford. This strategy changed customer behavior. Customers no longer waited for rebates at the end of the year before buying, an inventory of unsold cars did not build up on the lots of dealers, and GM was not forced into fighting a rebate war to clear inventory.

If this strategy was so successful what was to stop Ford from imitating it? Nothing! Ford began to offer its own credit card soon after GM. In this case, however, imitation of the strategy led to increased profitability because both GM and Ford had found a clever way to differentiate themselves from each other: by issuing credit cards that created stronger brand loyalty. With the new cards, a GM cardholder was more likely to buy a GM car and a Ford cardholder was more likely to buy a Ford car. By reducing the tendency of customers to play GM and Ford dealers off against each other, the card also had the effect of enabling both GM and Ford to raise their prices. Figure 5.5 illustrates how strategy can change the payoff matrix.

By issuing credit cards and strengthening the differentiation component of their strategy, both Ford and GM reduced the value of cash rebates and made it less likely that customers would switch to the company that offers rebates. The payoff structure of the game changed and so did the dominant strategy. Now that GM's dominant strategy is to not offer cash rebates, for whatever Ford does, GM is better off by not offering rebates. The same is true for Ford. In other words, by their choice of strategy, General Motors and Ford have changed their dominant strategy in a way that boosts their profitability.

More generally, this example suggests that the way out of mutually destructive price competition associated with a prisoner's dilemma type of game is for the players to change their business models and differentiate their product offerings in the minds of customers, thereby reducing their sensitivity to price competition. In other words, by their choice of strategy and business model (one principally based on differentiation), companies can alter the payoff structure associated with the game, alter their dominant strategy, and move it away from a prisoner's dilemma type of game structure.

FIGURE 5.5

Altered Payoff Matrix for GM and Ford

This insight also points to the need for companies to think through how their choice of business strategy might change the structure of the competitive game they are playing. Although we have looked at how strategy can transform the payoff structure of the game in a way that is more favorable, the opposite can and does occur. Companies often unintentionally change their business models and pursue strategies that change the payoff structure of the game in a way that is much less favorable to them, and comes to resemble a prisoner's dilemma, as the competitive dynamics between Coca-Cola and PepsiCo in the soft drinks industry suggest in Strategy in Action 5.5.

In retrospect, what happened was that the Pepsi challenge changed the long-established competitive rules in the industry. As the basis of competition shifted from differentiation by abstract lifestyle advertising to direct product comparisons, and then to price competition, the payoff structure associated with their game changed and became more of a prisoner's dilemma type of structure. Had Pepsi's managers looked ahead and reasoned back, they might have realized that price competition would be the outcome of its new aggressive strategy and might not have launched the Pepsi challenge, especially because the company was gaining market share from Coke, albeit slowly. However, because Pepsi's strategy changed the nature of differentiation in the industry, it led to a lose-lose situation.

Strategy in Action 5.5

Coca-Cola and PepsiCo Go Head to Head

For thirty years, until the late 1970s, the cola segment of the soft drink industry went through a golden age in which the main players, Coca-Cola and PepsiCo, were very profitable. These two companies competed against each other on the basis of advertising their products, Coke and Pepsi, based on abstract lifestyle product attributes. PepsiCo would introduce advertisements showing that it was cool to drink Pepsi, and Coca-Cola would produce advertisements with catchy jingles such as "Things go better with Coke." Neither company competed on price. Coke led the market throughout the period, although by the mid-1970s, Pepsi was closing in.

It was at this juncture that Pepsi launched a new and innovative strategy: the Pepsi challenge. The Pepsi challenge was a taste test in which customers were blindfolded and asked which drink they preferred, Pepsi or Coke. In the test, about 55 percent of customers consistently said they preferred Pepsi, a significant result given that Pepsi trailed Coke in market share. Pepsi test-marketed the Pepsi challenge in Dallas, and it was so successful that in the late 1970s, it rolled out the challenge nationally, a situation that presented a real dilemma for Coke. It could

not respond with its own blind taste test, because in the tests, the majority of people preferred Pepsi. Moreover, the Pepsi challenge had changed the nature of competition in the industry. After thirty years of competition through product differentiation based on lifestyle product attributes with no direct (and aggressive) product comparisons, Pepsi had shifted to a direct product comparison based on a real attribute of the product: taste.

PepsiCo had altered its business model and changed how it chose to differentiate its product from Coke. As Pepsi was now gaining market share, Coca-Cola's managers decided to make an aggressive response: deep price discounts for Coke in local markets where they controlled the Coke bottler and the local Pepsi bottler was weak. This was a successful move; in markets where price discounting was used, Coke started to gain its share back. PepsiCo then decided to respond in kind and cut prices too. Before long, price discounting was widespread in the industry. Customers were coming to expect price discounting, brand loyalty had been eroded, and the value associated with differentiation had been reduced. Both Coke and Pepsi experienced declining profitability.

So how did the soft drink manufacturers try to extricate themselves from this situation? Over the course of a few years, they once more shifted the way in which they differentiated their products. They introduced new products, such as Diet Coke and Cherry Coke, to rebuild brand loyalty, and they reemphasized abstract advertising by using celebrities to help create a brand image for their soda, thus differentiating it from their competitors' offerings and reducing customer price sensitivity. They are still doing this today, advertising Pepsi, for example, using the gyrations and music of Brittney Spears as a device for building a brand image that differentiates its offering from Coke. However, it took several years for Pepsi and Coke to do this, and in the interim they had to grapple with a payoff structure that reduced profitability in the industry; moreover, price discounting is still common today.

Summary of Chapter

1. Business-level strategy refers to the way strategic managers devise a plan of action to use a company's resources and distinctive competencies to gain a competitive advantage over rivals in a market or industry.

2. At the heart of developing a generic business-level strategy are choices concerning product differentiation, market segmentation, and distinctive competency. The combination of those three choices results in the specific form of generic business-level strategy employed by a company.

3. Cost leadership, differentiation, cost leadership and differentiation, focused low cost, and focused differentiation are generic competitive strategies. Each has advantages and disadvantages. A company must constantly manage its strategy; otherwise, it risks being stuck in the middle.

4. Most industries are composed of strategic groups: groups of companies pursuing the same or a similar business-level strategy. The members of a strategic group constitute its immediate competitors. Because different strategic groups are characterized by different opportunities and threats, it may pay a company to switch strategic groups. The feasibility of doing so is a function of the height of mobility barriers.

5. The choice of investment strategy for supporting the competitive strategy depends on the strength of a company's competitive position in the industry and the stage of the industry's life cycle. The main types of investment strategy are share building, growth, share increasing, hold-and-maintain, profit, market concentration, asset reduction, harvest, turnaround, liquidation, and divestiture.

6. Game theory offers a number of interesting insights into the kinds of competitive moves and tactics that companies can adopt to increase the returns from pursuing their business-level strategies. Some principles of game theory are look forward and reason back, know thy rival, find the most profitable dominant strategy, remember that strategy can alter the payoff structure of the game, and use strategy to change the payoff structure of the game.

Discussion Questions

1. Why does each generic competitive strategy require a different set of product, market, and distinctive competency choices? Give examples of pairs of companies in (a) the computer industry and (b) the auto industry that pursue different competitive strategies.

2. How can companies pursuing a cost-leadership, differentiation, or focus strategy become stuck in the middle? In what ways can they regain their competitive advantage?

3. Over an industry's life cycle, what investment strategy choices should be made by (a) differentiators in a strong competitive position and (b) differentiators in a weak competitive position?

4. How do technical developments affect the generic strategies that companies in an industry pursue? How might they do so in the future?

5. Why is it difficult for a company in one strategic group to change to a different strategic group?

6. What insights would game theory offer (a) a small pizza place operating in a crowded college market and (b) a detergent manufacturer seeking to bring out new products in established markets?

Practicing Strategic Management

SMALL-GROUP EXERCISE: FINDING A STRATEGY FOR A RESTAURANT

Break up into groups of three to five people. You are a group of partners contemplating opening a new restaurant in your city and trying to decide what business-level strategy can provide your restaurant with the best competitive advantage to make it as profitable as possible.

1. Create a strategic group of the restaurants in your city, and define their generic strategies.
2. Identify which restaurants you think are the most profitable and why.
3. On the basis of this analysis, decide what kind of restaurant you want to open and why.

ARTICLE FILE 5

Find an example (or several examples) of a company pursuing one of the generic business-level strategies. Which strategy is it? What product, market, or distinctive competency choices is it based on? What are its advantages and disadvantages?

STRATEGIC MANAGEMENT PROJECT: MODULE 5

This part of the project focuses on the nature of your company's business-level strategy. If your company operates in more than one business, concentrate on either its core, or most central, business or on its most important businesses. Using all the information you have collected on your company so far, answer the following questions:

1. How differentiated are the products or services of your company? What is the basis of their differentiated appeal?
2. What is your company's strategy toward market segmentation? If it segments its market, on what basis does it do so?
3. What distinctive competencies does your company have? (Use the information from the module on func-

tional-level strategy in the last chapter to answer this question.) Is efficiency, quality, innovation, responsiveness to customers, or a combination of these factors the main driving force in your company?

4. Based on these product, market, or distinctive competency choices, what generic business-level strategy is your company pursuing?
5. What are the advantages and disadvantages associated with your company's choice of business-level strategy?
6. Is your company a member of a strategic group in an industry? If so, which one?
7. What investment strategy is your company pursuing to support its generic strategy? How does this match the strength of its competitive position and the stage of its industry's life cycle?
8. How could you improve its business-level strategy to strengthen its competitive advantage?

EXPLORING THE WEB
Visiting the Luxury Car Market

Enter the web sites of three luxury car makers such as Lexus (**www.lexususa.com**), BMW (**www.bmw.com**), and Cadillac (**www.cadillac.com, www.gm.com**), all of which compete in the same strategic group. Scan the sites to determine the key features of each company's business-level strategy. In what ways are their strategies similar and different? Which of these companies do you think has a competitive advantage over the others? How could these companies use game theory in deciding how to compete?

General Task: Search the Web for a company pursuing a low-cost strategy, a differentiation strategy, or both. What product, market, or distinctive competency choices has it made to pursue this strategy? How successful has it been in its industry using this strategy?

Closing Case

How E*Trade Uses the Internet to Gain a Low-Cost Advantage

In many industries, new entrants have taken advantage of the opportunities opened up by the Internet to overcome barriers to entry and compete successfully against market leaders. Consider the situation of E*Trade, the online brokerage company. For many years, large, established brokerages like Merrill Lynch had dominated the industry

and used their protected positions to charge high brokerage fees. E*Trade's managers bought and developed software and hardware that allowed their customers to make their own trades and to do so at a price as low as $19.95.

The low-cost competition story in the brokerage industry did not stop here. By 1999, E*Trade itself came under pressure from a new generation of online brokerage houses such as Suretrade, Ameritrade, and DLJ, which began offering customers trades for only $9.95 and even $7.95, undercutting E*Trade's prices by 100 percent. How could E*Trade, which had made its reputation by being the low-cost leader in the industry, compete against companies boasting that *they* were the new cost leaders?

The answer for E*Trade was to enhance its differentiated appeal to its customers by offering a higher quality of service and a broader product line. E*Trade introduced a new software package that made it even easier for customers to use the Internet to trade shares. Very importantly, the new software was more reliable in that customers were able to make their trades when they wanted. Previously, E*Trade, like other brokerage companies, had experienced many problems when too many customers made trades at once; often the overloaded system simply crashed, and customers were unable to buy or sell shares. In addition, E*Trade's new package offered customers more financial research tools and gave them access to more information about specific companies to aid in their investment decisions. E*Trade also offered customers increased access to real-time stock quotes so that they could take advantage of second-to-second changes in stock prices to make money. Finally, it offered customers the opportunity to invest in initial public offerings of shares from new companies, where both potential risks and returns are high.

In 1999, E*Trade decided to merge with an online bank, Telebank, in order to offer its customers a broad range of online banking services such as bill paying online and thus become a one-stop online shopping site for all of a customer's financial needs. It also took over a variety of other insurance and financial service companies to offer its customers a broad financial service product line.

The realization that it could not just be a low-cost company but also had to create a differentiation advantage in the quickly evolving online financial services industry has paid off for E*Trade. Its customers did not switch to the new low-cost leaders because customers perceived that for the $19.95 price, they were receiving extra value for money in terms of service and reliability. E*Trade's customer accounts have increased steadily and its stock price rose as investors perceive that the company's competitive advantage is sustainable and that the company is likely to remain a dominant player in the changed industry environment. Indeed, E*Trade has shown the other companies in the industry that to remain viable, they must all pursue a simultaneous low-cost and differentiation strategy—something that has become possible only because of the emergence of the Internet, which has created external economies that companies can exploit to increase their performance and competitive advantage.

Case Discussion Questions

1. How has E*Trade's business-level strategy changed over time?

2. What is happening in the stock brokerage industry today? How has E*Trade been altering its business-level strategy to compete?

Sources: www.E*trade.com (1999). www.E*trade.com, Press Releases (1999).

6

Competitive Strategy and the Industry Environment

Opening Case

Information Technology, the Internet, and Changing Strategies in the Fashion World

Well-known fashion houses like Channel, Dior, Gucci, and Armani charge thousands of dollars for the fashionable collections of suits and dresses that they introduce twice yearly in the fall and in the spring. Only the very rich can afford such differentiated and expensive clothing, however, so to expand demand for its luxury products, most luxury designers produce less expensive lines of clothing and accessories that are sold in upscale fashion retailers such as Neiman Marcus, Nordstrom, and Saks Fifth Avenue.

Both fashion clothes designers and retailers have experienced enormous problems in the past decade. New kinds of competitors have taken advantage of the opportunities opened by the Internet and advances in information technology (IT) to enter the high fashion market segment and compete head-to-head with them by offering high-quality clothes at significantly lower prices. Essentially, all of these new competitors have developed capabilities in using IT that allow them to pursue a focused differentiation strategy but at a much lower cost than the luxury fashion houses. This has allowed them to circumvent barriers to entry into the high fashion segment and develop well-received brand names.

First, upscale department stores and retail chains like Dillard's and Macy's, which target the middle of the fashion clothing market, have developed their own store-specific prestigious clothing labels. These well-made clothes are often sold at a significant price discount from luxury brands and thus attract customers away. Second, many small, agile fashion designers such as England's Jaeger and Laura Ashley and Spain's Zara now produce fashionable clothes at lower prices and sell them in their own chains of clothing stores. Zara, in particular, has achieved significant success, and its sales have soared. It has managed to position itself as the low price and cost leader in the fashion segment of the clothing market because it has created innovative information systems that lower costs and speed time to market.

Zara uses IT to manage the interface between its design and manufacturing operations efficiently. Major fashion houses like Dior and Gucci can take six or more months to design their collections and then three to six more before their moderately priced lines become available in upscale retailers. Zara's designers closely watch the trends in the high fashion industry and the kinds of innovations that the major houses are introducing. Then using their information systems, which are linked to their suppliers and the low-cost manufacturers it uses abroad, its designers can create a new collection in only five weeks, and these clothes can then be made in a week and in its stores soon after. This short time to market gives Zara great flexibility and has allowed it to compete effectively in the rapidly changing fashion market, where customer tastes evolve quickly.

IT also gives it instantaneous feedback on which of its clothes are selling well and in which countries, which gives it a competitive advantage because Zara can engage in constant product development and remain at the cutting edge of fashion, a major source of differentiation advantage. For example, Zara can manufacture more of a particular kind of dress or suit to meet high customer demand and constantly change the mix of clothes it offers customers in its rapidly expanding network of global stores to keep up with fashion. Moreover, it can do this at relatively small output levels, part of a specialized, focused strategy.

Indeed, another important aspect of Zara's competitive strategy is that its use of IT allows it to minimize the inventory it has to carry—the major cost of goods sold of a clothing maker/retailer—and thus is a major driver of profitability. Because of the quick manufacturing-to-sales cycle and just-in-time fashion, Zara has been able to offer its collections at comparatively low prices and still make profits that are the envy of the fashion clothing industry. Indeed, pricing has become the major competitive tool for managing competition in the fashion industry. When Zara offered its shares to the public for the first time in 2001, its shares soared in price due to its high return on invested capital. Investors believe that there will soon be a chain of Zara stores in most major cities across the world as its name becomes as common to customers as those of well-known designers.

The other clothing design and retail companies have woken up to the threat posed by companies like Zara. Many retailers have pioneered their own proprietary lines of clothes (Dillard's Daniel Cremeaux line is one) and use a similar strategy to Zara's. Clothing designers like Ralph Lauren and Tommy Hilfiger have been forced to adopt similar approaches, bringing out new clothes collections several times a year and instituting price markdowns to sell inventory quickly. Even the major fashion houses have taken note of what is happening. Gucci, for example, which began to experience problems in the 1990s, brought in Thomas Ford, an American, as its chief designer and invested its resources to produce a new Ford-designed clothes line for both men and women to attract back Gucci's customers. Using IT, Gucci has also been able to design, manufacture, and distribute its clothing at a faster rate too.

Increasingly, these companies are realizing that maintaining a competitive advantage and superior profitability cannot be achieved by brand image alone; all clothing companies must learn to use competitive moves and tactics to defend their differentiated appeal, something that can be quickly lost in today's fast-changing global marketplace.

Sources: www.zara.com (2002). www.gucci.com (2002). C. Vitzthum, "Just-in-Time-Fashion," *Wall Street Journal*, May 18, 2001, pp. B1, B4.

Overview   If strategic managers do succeed in developing a successful generic business-level strategy, they still face another crucial issue: positioning their company to sustain its competitive advantage over time in different kinds of industry environments. Different industry environments present particular kinds of opportunities and threats for companies, and a company's business model has to adapt and change to meet the changing environment. Various kinds of competitive maneuvers, gambits, and tactics become appropriate in different kinds of environment.

This chapter begins by examining the way in which companies in fragmented industries try to develop competitive strategies that support their generic strategies. It then considers the challenges of developing and sustaining a competitive advantage in embryonic, growth, mature, and declining industries.

By the end of this chapter, you will understand how the successful pursuit of a generic strategy depends on the selection of the right competitive strategy to manage the industry environment.

Strategies in Fragmented Industries

A *fragmented industry* is one composed of a large number of small and medium-sized companies—for example, the dry cleaning, restaurant, health club, and the legal services industries. There are several reasons that an industry may consist of many small companies rather than a few large ones.[1]

First, fragmented industries are characterized by low barriers to entry because of the lack of economies of scale. Many home buyers, for example, have a preference for dealing with local real estate agents, whom they perceive as having better local knowledge than national chains. Second, in some industries, there may even be diseconomies of scale. In the restaurant business, for example, customers often prefer the unique food and style of a popular local restaurant rather than the standardized offerings of some national chain. Third, low entry barriers that permit constant entry by new companies also serve to keep an industry fragmented. The restaurant industry exemplifies this situation. The costs of opening a restaurant are moderate and can be borne by a single entrepreneur. High transportation costs, too, can keep an industry fragmented, and local or regional production may be the only efficient way to satisfy customers' needs, as in the cement business. Finally, an industry may be fragmented because customers' needs are so specialized that only small job lots of products are required, and thus there is no room for a large mass-production operation to satisfy the market.

For some fragmented industries, these factors dictate the competitive strategy to pursue, and the *focus strategy* stands out as a principal choice. Companies may specialize by customer group, customer need, or geographic region, so that many small specialty companies operate in local or regional market segments. All kinds of custom-made products—furniture, clothing, hats, boots, and so on—fall into this category, as do all small service operations that cater to particular customers' needs, such as laundries, restaurants, health clubs, and furniture rental stores. Indeed, service companies make up a large proportion of the enterprises in fragmented industries because they provide personalized service to clients and therefore need to be responsive to their needs.

Strategic managers are eager to gain the cost advantages of pursuing a low-cost strategy or the sales-revenue-enhancing advantages of differentiation by circumventing the problems of a fragmented industry and finding a way to consolidate it. Consolidated industries offer much higher potential returns, and during the past thirty years, many companies have developed competitive strategies to consolidate fragmented industries and obtain these returns. These companies include large retailers such as Wal-Mart and Target, fast food chains such as McDonald's and Burger King, video rental chains such as Blockbuster Video and Hollywood Video, chains of health clubs such as Bally's and President and First Lady, repair shops like Midas Muffler, and even lawyers, consultants, and tax preparers. To grow, consolidate their industries, and become the industry leaders, these companies have pioneered new business models and used several specific strategies such as chaining, franchising, horizontal merger, and also using the Internet and IT.

Many of these pioneered a new business model in an industry that lowers costs or confers a differentiation advantage (or both). The way that a company can do this is by competing in a very different way from established rivals. Managers in a fragmented industry must seek out cost or differentiation advantages that others have not recognized. Once a company has a cost or differential advantage, it can increase its revenues at the expense of competitors and consolidate the industry in the process. Moreover, as the company pioneering the new business model grows larger, it may be able to capture additional scale economies and so increase its competitive advantage. The pioneering company can then use its growing cost-based advantage to choose a low-price option, price aggressively, generate high demand, and drive its established rivals out of the industry.

Chaining   Companies such as Wal-Mart and Midas International pursue a **chaining** strategy to obtain the advantages of cost leadership. They establish networks of linked merchandising outlets that are so interconnected that they function as one large business entity. The consolidated buying power that these companies possess through their nationwide store chains allows them to negotiate large price reductions with their suppliers, which promotes their competitive advantage. They overcome the barrier of high transportation costs by establishing sophisticated regional distribution centers, which can economize on inventory costs and maximize responsiveness to the needs of stores and customers. (This is Wal-Mart's specialty.) They also realize economies of scale from sharing managerial skills across the chain and from placing nationwide, rather than local, advertising.

The U.S. food retail business during the 1950s, when supermarkets revolutionized the business model behind the selling of food products, is a good example of the advantages of the chaining business model. Prior to the development of supermarkets, the food retail industry was fragmented with many small mom-and-pop retailers selling a limited range of products and providing full service to customers, including home delivery. Mostly regionally based at first, with fewer than a hundred stores, the first supermarkets differentiated themselves by offering a much larger selection of items in a big store layout. At the same time, they lowered their costs by moving from a full-service to a self-service model (they needed far fewer employees to run a store), and they passed on those cost savings to customers in the form of lower prices. In other words, the supermarkets competed in a very different way from established food retailers: they adopted a new business model.

As the supermarkets started to grow, opening hundreds of more stores, they were able to capture scale economies that were not available to smaller retailers. For example, by clustering their stores around central distribution warehouses in different cities and eventually regions, they were able to gain distribution efficiencies and reduce the amount of inventory they had to hold in a store. Also, by buying from vendors in large quantities, they were able to demand deep price discounts that they passed on to customers in the form of lower prices, enabling them to gain even more market share from smaller retailers. In the 1970s and 1980s, the supermarkets were also the first to introduce information systems based on point-of-sale terminals that tracked the sale of individual items. The information provided enabled the supermarkets to optimize their stocking of items, quickly cutting back on items that were not selling and devoting more shelf space to items that were selling faster. This reducing the need to hold inventory took even more costs out of the systems and ensured a good match between customer demands and items in the supermarket, which further differentiated the supermarkets from smaller retailers. Although these information systems were expensive to implement, the supermarkets could spread the costs over a large volume of sales. The small mom-and-pop retailers could not afford such systems because their sales base was too small. As a consequence of these developments, the food retail industry was becoming consolidated by the 1980s, a trend that is accelerating today. The small mom-and-pop food retailer is now almost extinct.

The new supermarket business model that provided a cost and differentiation advantage over the old established mom-and-pop model has been applied to a wide range of retail industries, consolidating one after the other. Barnes & Noble and Borders applied the supermarket business model to book retailing, Staples applied it to office supplies, Best Buy to electronic retailing, Home Depot to building supplies, and so on. In each case, the company that introduced the new business model helped to change the underlying competitive structure of the industry to its advantage, consolidating the industry and weakening the five forces of competition in the process.

Franchising

For differentiated companies in fragmented industries, such as McDonald's or Century 21 Real Estate, the competitive advantage comes from a business model that employs franchise agreements. In franchising, the franchisor (parent) grants to its franchisees the right to use the parent's name, reputation, and business skills at a particular location or area. When franchisees also manage the business, they are strongly motivated to make the business model work effectively and make sure that quality and standards are consistently high so that customers' needs are always satisfied. Such motivation is particularly critical in a strategy of differentiation, where it is important for a company to maintain its distinctive edge. One reason that industries are fragmented is the difficulty of maintaining control over the many small outlets that must be operated while at the same time retaining their differentiated appeal. The franchising model solves this problem.[2] In addition, franchising lessens the financial burden of swift expansion and so permits rapid growth of the company. Finally, a nationwide franchised company can reap the advantages of large-scale advertising, as well as economies in purchasing, management, and distribution, as McDonald's does very efficiently. Indeed, McDonald's is able to pursue cost leadership and differentiation simultaneously only because franchising allows costs to be controlled locally and differentiation to be achieved by marketing on a national level.

Horizontal Merger

Companies such as Anheuser-Busch, Dillard's Department Stores, and Blockbuster Entertainment have been choosing a strategy of *horizontal merger* to consolidate their respective industries. For example, Dillard's arranged the merger of regional store chains in order to form a national company. By pursuing horizontal merger, companies are able to obtain economies of scale or secure a national market for their product. As a result, they are able to pursue a cost-leadership or a differentiation strategy, or both. The many important strategic implications of horizontal merger are discussed in detail in Chapter 9.

Using IT and the Internet

The arrival of new technology often gives a company the opportunity to develop new business models that can consolidate a fragmented industry. eBay and Amazon.com, for example, used the Internet to develop a new business model—auctions and bookselling—that is consolidating a fragmented industry. Before eBay, the auction business was extremely fragmented, with local auctions in cities being the principal way in which people could dispose of their antiques and collectibles. By harnessing the Internet, eBay can now assure sellers that they are getting wide visibility for their collectibles and are likely to receive a higher price for their product. Similarly, Amazon.com's success in the book market has accelerated the consolidation of the book retail industry, with many small bookstores closing because they cannot compete by price or selection. Clear Channel Communications, profiled in Strategy in Action 6.1, has used many of these methods simultaneously to create a business model that has made it the biggest radio broadcaster in the United States.

The challenge in a fragmented industry is to figure out the best strategy to overcome a fragmented market so that the competitive advantages associated with different generic business-level strategies can be realized. It is difficult to think of any major service activities—from consulting and accounting firms to businesses satisfying the smallest customer need, such as beauty parlors and car repair shops—that have not been consolidated by companies that developed new business models or used franchising and horizontal mergers.

Strategy in Action   6.1

Clear Channel Creates a National Chain of Local Radio Stations

In 2002, Clear Channel Communications, based in San Antonio, Texas, operated over 1,200 U.S. radio stations compared with its largest competitors: Viacom with 186 and Citadel with 205. The company started out with only one station in San Antonio in 1995, something that used to be typical of the radio broadcasting industry. Historically, the industry was fragmented because a federal law prevented any company from owning more than 40 stations nationwide; as a result, a large proportion of the local radio stations were independently owned and operated.

Clear Channel took advantage of the repeal of this law in 1996 to start to buy up radio stations and, most important, find a business model that would allow it to obtain the gains from consolidating this fragmented industry. Its strategic managers recognized from the beginning that the major way to increase the profitability of city and small town radio stations was to obtain economies of scale from operating and marketing on a national level. The issue was to find ways to raise the quality of its programming to increase its value to listeners, increase the number of listeners, and thus increase advertising revenues (because advertising rates are based on the number of listeners). At the same time, it needed to find ways to reduce each station's high operating costs and lower its cost structure. How to do both simultaneously was the challenge.

On the value side of the equation, an important issue that had to be addressed was how to achieve the economies of scale from having a national reach while maintaining the local ties of a station to its community. Many listeners like to feel they are listening to a local station that understands who they are and what their needs are. Yet if all programming and service is handled on a local level, how can economies of scale from a national base be achieved? Most cost savings come from standardization of service across stations, from broadcasting uniform content. Similarly, local listeners often become used to the glitzy, slick productions put on by national cable television broadcasting companies such as MTV and the main TV networks. Because they are national, these companies can afford to pay large sums to stars and celebrities and invest heavily in developing quality products. Such large expenditures are beyond most radio stations' budgets and simply increase the cost of goods sold too much. Moreover, advertising rates had to be kept at a level that both large national companies and small local ones would find acceptable; they could not simply be raised to cover higher costs.

Clear Channel's managers began to experiment with IT and the Internet and took advantage of emerging digital technology that allowed for the easy and rapid manipulation and transfer of large volumes of data. By the late 1990s, music and programming could easily be recorded, stored in digital format, and edited. Its managers hit on a strategy called "voice tracking." To obtain economies of scale, Clear Channel employed popular regional or national DJs to record its daily programs, and these same DJs customize their productions to suit the needs of local markets. For example, one technology allows DJs to isolate and listen to the end of one track and the beginning of the next; then they can insert whatever talk, news, or information that is appropriate between tracks as and when they like. The local stations supply this local information; after they have customized their program, the DJs send it over the Internet, where the local operators handle it. This practice has enormous advantages. On the cost side, the programming costs of a limited number of popular DJs are much lower than the cost of employing an army of local DJs. On the differentiation side, the quality of programming is much higher because Clear Channel can invest more in its programming and because the appeal of some DJs is much higher than others. Over time, higher-quality programming increases the number of listeners, and this attracts more national advertisers, whose digital advertisements can be easily inserted in the programming by local operators.

In addition, Clear Channel is developing its own proprietary brand name, KISS, across its radio stations so that when people travel, they will be attracted to its local stations wherever they are. It also hopes this will stimulate word-of-mouth advertising. As its brand becomes national, this widened scope will attract larger advertisers and boost its sales revenues. To speed this process, it is also now in the process of linking its different businesses—for example, it is the largest billboard and concert operator in the United States—to its KISS label. Through these means, it hopes that increased customer demand will drive up advertising revenues, which will allow it to start or buy more radio stations and expand its reach and thereby lower its cost structure and so increase its future profitability.

Sources: www.clearchannel.com (2002). A. W. Mathews, "From a Distance: A Giant Chain Is Perfecting the Art of Seeming Local," *Wall Street Journal,* February 25, 2002, pp. A1, A4.

Strategies in Embryonic and Growth Industries

As Chapter 2 discusses, an embryonic industry is one that is just beginning to develop, and a growth industry is one in which first-time demand is expanding rapidly as many new customers enter the market. Embryonic and growth industries pose special challenges in choosing and pursuing a business-level strategy because the attributes of customers change as market demand expands and new groups of customers who have new and evolving needs emerge. Also, other factors affect the rate at which a market grows and expands. Strategic managers have to be aware of the way competitive dynamics in embryonic and growth industries change over time because they commonly have to build and develop new kinds of competencies and refine their business models to compete effectively over time.

Most embryonic industries emerge when a technological innovation creates new product or market opportunities that companies start to take advantage of. For example, a century ago, the car industry was born following the development of a new technology, the internal combustion engine, which gave rise to many new products, including the motorcar and motorbus. In 1975, the PC industry was born after new microprocessor technology was developed to build the world's first commercially available PC, the Altair 8800, sold by MITS. Shortly afterward, the PC software industry was born when a Harvard dropout, Bill Gates, and his old school friend, Paul Allen, wrote a version of a popular computer language, BASIC, that would run on the Altair 8800.[3] In 1986, the Internet protocol (IP) network equipment industry was born following the development of the router, an IP switch, by an obscure California start-up, Cisco Systems.

Customer demand for the products of an embryonic industry is frequently limited at first for a variety of reasons. Strategic managers who understand how markets develop are in a much better position to build a business model and strategy that will lead to a sustained competitive advantage. Reasons for slow growth in market demand include (1) the limited performance and poor quality of the first products, (2) customer unfamiliarity with what the new product can do for them, (3) poorly developed distribution channels to get the product to customers, (4) a lack of complementary products to increase the value of the product for customer, and (5) high production costs because of small volumes of production. For example, demand for the first cars was limited by their poor performance (they were no faster than a horse, far noisier, and frequently broke down), a lack of important complementary products such as a network of paved roads and gas stations, and high production costs, which made them a luxury item. Similarly, demand for the first PCs was limited because buyers had to be able to program a computer to use it, and there were no software application programs that could be purchased to run on the PCs. Because of such problems, early demand for the products of embryonic industries comes from a small set of technologically sophisticated customers who are willing to put up with, and may even enjoy, imperfections in the product. Computer hobbyists, who got great joy out of tinkering with their imperfect machines and finding ways to make them work, bought the first PCs.

An industry moves from an embryonic to a growth stage when a *mass market* starts to develop for the industry's product (a mass market is one in which large numbers of customers enter the market). Mass markets typically start to develop when three things occur: (1) ongoing technological progress makes a product easier to use and increases the value of the product to the average customer, (2) key complementary products are developed that do the same, and (3) companies in the industry strive to find ways to reduce production costs so they can lower their cost structure and choose a low price option, and this stimulates high demand.[4] For example, a mass market for cars emerged when (1) technological progress increased the performance of cars, (2) a network of paved roads and gas stations was established (which meant a car could go more places and thus had more value), and (3) Henry Ford began to mass-produce cars, which dramatically lowered production costs and allowed him to reduce prices, causing the demand for cars to surge. Similarly, the mass market for PCs started to emerge when technological advances made them easier to use, a supply of complementary software such as spreadsheets and word processing programs was developed that increased the value of owning a PC, and companies in the industry started to use mass production to build PCs at low cost.

Strategic managers with knowledge about changing market demand can focus on how they must change their business models to build competencies in low-cost manufacturing and product development. For example, they need to share their knowledge with companies that can supply complementary products so that customers will be convinced the new product is worth buying. Another important factor they must understand is how customer groups and needs change over time.

The Changing Nature of Market Demand

The development of most markets follows an S-shaped growth curve similar to that illustrated in Figure 6.1. As the stage of market development moves from embryonic to growth, customer demand first accelerates and then decelerates as a market approaches saturation. As noted in Chapter 2, in a saturated market, most customers have already bought the product, and demand is limited to replacement demand; the market is mature. Figure 6.1 shows that different groups of customers who have different needs enter the market over time.[5]

The first group of customers to enter the market are referred to as the *innovators*. Innovators are "technocrats" who get great delight from being the first to purchase and experiment with products based on a new technology, even though that technology is imperfect and expensive. They often have an engineering mindset and want to own the technology for its own sake. In the PC industry, the first customers were software engineers and computer hobbyists who wanted to write computer code at home.[6]

The *early adopters* are the second group of customers to enter the market. Early adopters understand that the technology might have important future applications and are willing to experiment with it to see if they can pioneer uses for it, often by finding new ways to satisfy customer needs. Early adopters are often visionaries who appreciate how the technology may be used in the future and try to be the first to profit from its use. Jeff Bezos, the founder of Amazon.com, was an early adopter of the Internet and web-based technology, who saw in 1994 that the Internet could be used in innovative ways to sell books. He saw this possibility before anyone else and was one of the first dot-com pioneers to purchase web servers and related software and use it to sell products over the Internet. Amazon was thus an early adopter.

Both innovators and early adopters enter the market while the industry is in its embryonic stage. The next group of customers, the *early majority,* represents the leading wave or edge of the mass market; their entry signifies the beginning of the growth stage. Customers in the early majority are comfortable with the new technology and products. However, they are pragmatists: they weigh the benefits of adopting new products against their costs and wait to enter the market until they are confident that products will offer them tangible benefits. Once they start to enter the market, however, they do so in large numbers. This is what happened in the PC market after IBM's introduction of the PC in 1981. For the early majority, IBM's entry into the market legitimized the technology and signaled that the benefits of adoption would be worth the costs of purchasing and learning to use the product. The growth of the PC market was then given further impetus by the development of important applications that added value to it, such as new spreadsheet and word processing programs. These applications transformed the PC from a hobbyist's toy into a business productivity tool.

Once the mass market attains a critical mass, with something like 30 percent of the potential market penetrated, the next wave of customers enters the market. This wave is characterized as the *late majority:* the customers who purchase a new technology or product only when it is clear it will be around for a long time. A typical late majority customer group is the customers who started to enter the PC market in the mid-1990s who were older and somewhat intimidated by computers. However, watching others similar to themselves buying PCs to send email and browse the Web, they overcame their hesitancy and started to purchase PCs. By 2002, some 65 percent of homes in the United States had at least one PC, suggesting that the product was well into the late majority group and thus the market was approaching saturation. Indeed, the entry of the late majority signals the end of the growth stage.

Laggards, the last group of customers to enter the market, are inherently conservative and technophobic. They often refuse to adopt a new technology even if its benefits are obvious or unless they are forced by circumstances—to reply to a colleague's email, for example—to do so. People who stick to using typewriters rather than computers to write letters and books could be considered laggards today.

Figure 6.2 looks at the differences among these groups of consumers in a somewhat different way. The bell-shaped curve represents the total market, and the divisions in the curve show the percentage of customers who on average fall into each customer group. The early adopters are a very small percentage of the total customers who will ultimately buy the product. Thus, it illustrates a vital competitive fact: *Most market demand and industry profits arise when the early and late majority enters the market.* And research has found that although many of the early pioneering companies do well in attracting innovators and early adopters, many of these companies often *fail* to attract a significant share of early and late majority customers and ultimately go out of business.

Strategic Implications: Crossing the Chasm

Why are pioneering companies often unable to develop a business model that allows them to become the market leaders? Once again, the issue revolves around understanding the basic issues in business-level strategy: identifying customer needs, identifying customer groups, and choosing distinctive competencies. *Innovators and early adopters have very different customer needs from the early majority.* In an influential book, Geoffrey Moore argued that as a consequence of the differences in customer needs between these groups, the distinctive competencies required for companies to succeed in the emerging mass market are quite different from the distinctive competencies required to succeed in the embryonic market.[7] Therefore,

FIGURE 6.2

Market Share of Different Customer Groups

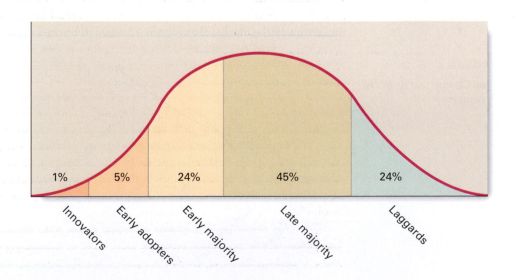

| 1% | 5% | 24% | 45% | 24% |

Innovators   Early adopters   Early majority   Late majority   Laggards different strategies and business models are often required as a market develops over time for these reasons:

■ Innovators and early adopters are technologically sophisticated individuals who are willing to tolerate engineering imperfections in the product. The early majority, however, value ease of use and reliability. Companies competing in an embryonic market typically pay more attention to increasing the performance of a product than to its ease of use and reliability. Those competing in a mass market need to make sure that the product is reliable and easy to use. Thus, the product development capabilities required for success are different as a market develops over time.

■ Innovators and early adopters are typically reached through specialized distribution channels, and the products are often sold by word of mouth or focused promotion campaigns. Reaching the early majority requires mass-market distribution channels and mass media advertising campaigns, which require a different set of marketing and sales capabilities.

■ Because innovators and the early majority are relatively few in number and are not particularly price sensitive, companies serving them do not need capabilities in mass production. To serve a rapidly growing mass market, large-scale manufacturing capabilities may be critical to ensure that a high-quality product can be produced reliably at a low price point.

In sum, the competencies (resources and capabilities) required to compete in an embryonic market populated by early adopters and innovators are very different from those required to compete in a high-growth mass market populated by the early majority. As a consequence, the transition between the embryonic market and the mass market is not a smooth, seamless one. Rather, it represents a *competitive chasm,* or gulf, that companies must cross. According to Moore, many companies do not or cannot develop the right business model; they fall into the chasm and go out of business. This insight is consistent with the observation that although embryonic markets are frequently populated by large numbers of small companies, once the mass market begins to develop, the number of companies in the marketplace drops off sharply.[8]

Figure 6.3 illustrates Moore's thesis by showing that a wide chasm exists between innovators and early majority, that is, between the embryonic market and the rapidly growing mass market. Note also that other smaller chasms exist between other sets of customers, and that these too represent important, although less dramatic, breaks in the nature of the market that require changes in business-level strategy (for example,

FIGURE 6.3

The Chasm: AOL and Prodigy

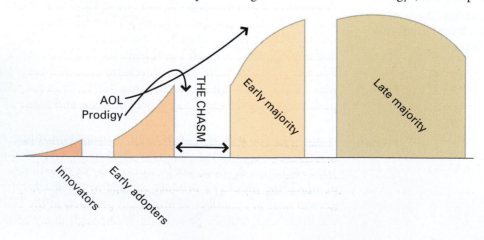

a different approach to market segmentation). The implication of Moore's thesis is that a company must often build new competencies if it is to cross the chasm: it must accumulate new resources and capabilities to build and sustain a competitive advantage. Strategy in Action 6.2 describes how the early leader in online services, Prodigy, fell into the chasm, while AOL successfully crossed it because AOL built competencies that were to be vital in the mass market and Prodigy did not.

To cross this chasm successfully, Moore argues, companies need to find a beachhead, a strategic opportunity, to compete for the mass market. By this, he means that managers must correctly identify the customer needs of the first wave of early majority users who are the leading edge of the mass market. Even in a market where the majority of customers are still innovators and early adopters, some members of the early majority will start to enter. Once companies have identified these customers' needs, they must alter their business model in response by developing new competencies and redesigning products. Strategic managers must also look to their company's value chains and develop distribution channels and marketing strategies for reaching the early majority. They must also design the product so that it matches the needs of the early majority, can be modified easily, and can be produced or provided at low cost. In this way, they will have ready a suitable product, at a reasonable price, that they can sell to the early majority as they start to enter the market in large numbers.

Equally important, industry pioneers must not become too focused on the needs of their early or initial customers because this may lead them to ignore the needs of the early majority, which can lead them to competitive disaster. In fact, anticipating the moves of their competitors by drawing on game theory principles is another useful tool they can use to help them choose the right business model, as the early history of Apple Computer illustrates. Apple stumbled across the leading edge of the early majority in 1979 when it noticed that business customers were beginning to purchase the Apple II in order to run VisiCalc, the first business spreadsheet program made for PCs. It soon became a best-seller and helped to drive sales of the Apple II. However, Apple failed to appreciate the real importance of this event—*that it revealed the needs of business customers*—and instead continued to focus its sales and marketing efforts on computer hobbyists and higher educational institutions, where many of its early adopters were to be found. In fact, Apple had a direct sales force that visited universities but no sales force visiting businesses! Although VisiCalc was helping to sell Apple computers, Apple made no effort to develop its own business applications or get other companies to do so.

Apple had found a beachhead—the developing needs of business customers—but squandered that advantage. It was left to IBM to recognize the importance of the business customer group and develop a business model to meet the needs of the early majority. It entered the market with its IBM PC in 1981, which was an instant success and the beginning of Apple's problems. IBM offered a version of VisiCalc for the IBM PC, along with an early word processing program, Easy Writer. This, together with IBM's established business-focused sales force, soon propelled IBM into a leadership position among the early majority of business and home office users.[9]

Strategic Implications of Market Growth Rates

A final important issue that strategic managers must understand in embryonic and growth industries is that different markets develop at different rates. The rate at which a market develops can be assessed by its growth rate, which measures the rate at which the industry's product spreads in the marketplace. Figure 6.4 charts the growth rates of a number of important products in the United States from their initial introduction to the present time. Although many of these products display the

Strategy in Action   6.2

How Prodigy Fell into the Chasm

Before America Online (AOL) became a household name, Prodigy was a market leader. Founded in 1984, Prodigy was a joint venture between Sears, IBM, and CBS. CBS soon dropped out, but IBM and Sears stuck with it, investing $500 million in developing the network and finally launching it in 1990. The goal was to build the largest proprietary online network whose focus was to be online shopping: the system would give its customers the ability to buy anything, even plane tickets, online. IBM knew about computers, and Sears knew about retail. It seemed like the perfect marriage.

Launched in the fall of 1990, the service quickly accumulated half a million users. There was little sense of competition at the time. The largest competitor, CompuServe, was conservatively managed, and its business model was focused on technical users and financial services (CompuServe was owned by H&R Block, America's largest tax return service). There was another small competitor, AOL, but in the words of one Prodigy executive, "It was just a little thing off to the side." Ten years later, the little thing had become the largest online service in the world, with 33 million members. Prodigy had exited the online business altogether after IBM and Sears had invested, and lost, some $1.2 billion on the venture.

Why did Prodigy fail? The company appeared to be focusing on the mass market. Its target customers were not computer-oriented early adopters but typical middle-class Americans. And its strategy to sell products online seemed correct; surely this ultimately had to become a major application of the Internet. The problem was that the long-term vision was right, but the business model was not. One of the surprise early drivers of customers signing up for online services and the creation of the mass market was email. AOL offered its members unlimited email, while Prodigy charged members a fee for sending more than thirty emails per month—a big difference in business models. Another important application of online service was chatrooms, a service that customers were increasingly embracing. AOL saw chatrooms as one of the unique possibilities of online service for satisfying customer needs and rushed to develop the software that would soon make chatrooms one of its most popular features.

The lawyers at Prodigy's corporate headquarters, however, feared that Prodigy might be held legally liable for comments made in chatrooms or events that arose from them and discouraged Prodigy from offering this service. The same problem hindered Prodigy's introduction of bulletin boards, also a popular feature at CompuServe and AOL. Prodigy introduced bulletin boards but censored them, removing the kind of posting that its lawyers thought might create legal problems. This censorship, lack of chatrooms, and charges for email rankled members, who soon started to switch in droves to AOL.

The nature of the software interface used to allow customers to connect to an online service also became a critical competitive issue as the market developed. When it was introduced, Prodigy's primitive graphical user interface was acceptable by the PC standards of the time, which were based on Microsoft's MS-DOS operating system. When Microsoft introduced its much more user-friendly Windows 3.0 systems in 1990, AOL moved quickly to redesign its software interface to be compatible with Windows, and this made AOL much easier to use. Prodigy, however, was part owned by IBM, which at that time was trying to promote its own new PC operating system—the ill-fated OS/2. So Prodigy dragged its feet. It waited to introduce a Windows version of its own interface until December 1993, by which time it had lost the majority of Windows users to AOL. Prodigy's software was also much more complicated for users to install and update. AOL could be installed on a computer in five minutes, and small updates were installed automatically when the user was online. Prodigy's users had to wait until there was a major revision of the service to obtain new features.

By 1996, it was effectively over. AOL was growing by leaps and bounds, and Prodigy was losing customers at a rapid pace. The combination of a clunky interface, failure to embrace two killer applications that drove online services into the mass market (chatrooms and email), censorship, and slow product development conspired to trip up Prodigy and send it tumbling into the chasm. Meanwhile, AOL, by correctly sensing the product attributes that mass-market customers desired in an online service, crossed the chasm with ease.

Sources: www.aoltimewarner.com (2002). Kara Swisher, *aol.com* (New York: Random House, 1998).

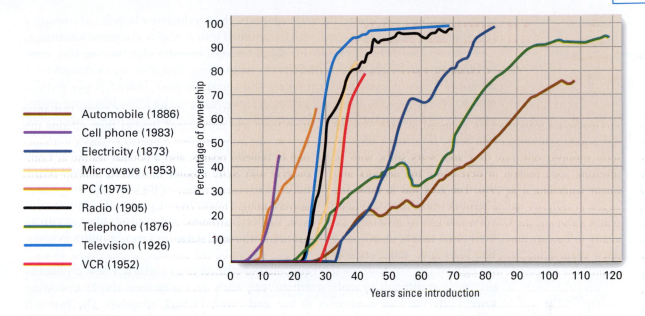

FIGURE 6.4

Differences in Diffusion Rates

Source: Peter Brimelow, "The Silent Boom," *Forbes,* July 7, 1997, pp. 170–171.
Reprinted by permission of Forbes Magazine © 2002 Forbes, Inc.

classic S-shaped growth curve, their markets have grown at different rates. For example, demand for TVs has grown more rapidly than demand for cars. The market growth rates for new kinds of products seem to have accelerated over time, probably because the increasing use of the mass media and low-cost mass production help to accelerate the demand for new products. However, there are also differences in the growth rate for new products introduced at around the same time. For example, the cell phone was introduced somewhat later than the PC, and yet market demand has grown more rapidly. Similarly, following the introduction of the PalmPilot in 1996, demand for hand-held computers has grown even more rapidly than demand for cell phones did.

Factors Affecting Market Growth Rates. A number of factors explain the variation in market growth rates for different products and thus the speed with which a particular industry develops. It is important for strategic managers to understand the source of these differences, for by their choice of strategy and business model, they can accelerate or retard the rate at which a particular market grows.[10] *In other words, business-level strategy is a major determinant of industry profitability.*

The first factor that accelerates customer demand is a new product's *relative advantage,* that is, the degree to which a new product is perceived as better at satisfying customer needs than the product it supersedes. The degree of relative advantage can be measured by the extra value it provides for customers, which can be economic or social in nature. For example, the early growth in demand for cell phones was partly driven by their economic benefits. Early studies showed that because business customers could always be reached by cell phone, they made better use of their time—for example, by not showing up at a meeting that had been canceled at the last minute—and saved two hours per week in time that would otherwise have been wasted. For busy executives, the early adopters, the productivity benefits of owning a cell phone outweighed the costs, which translated into a relative economic advantage. Cell phones also diffused rapidly for social reasons, in particular, because they conferred glamour or prestige on their users (something that also drives demand for advanced kinds of hand-held computers and smart phones). Indeed, it was considered so cool to be seen with a cell phone in Hong Kong in the 1980s that some entrepreneurs established thriving businesses selling fake cell phones to people who could not afford the real thing.

Another factor in driving growth in demand is *compatibility,* which refers to the degree to which a new product is perceived as being consistent with the current needs or existing values of potential adopters. Demand for cell phones grew rapidly because their operation was compatible with the prior experience of potential adopters who used traditional wire-line phones. In contrast, demand for contraceptive products has grown slowly in nations with strong Catholic and Muslim communities because they clash with religious values.

Complexity is a third factor. Complexity is the degree to which a new product is perceived as difficult to understand and use. Early PCs with their clunky operating system interfaces were complex to use, and this held back adoption. The first cell phones were very simple to use, and this accelerated adoption.

A fourth factor is *trialability,* which is the degree to which a new product can be experimented with on a hands-on trial basis. Many people first used cell phones by borrowing one from a colleague to make a call, and this positive experience helped to accelerate growth rates. In contrast, the original PCs were more difficult to obtain to experiment with and use because they were expensive and some training was involved, and this led to slower growth rates.

A fifth factor is *observability,* which refers to the degree to which the results of adopting a new product can be clearly seen and appreciated by other people. The PalmPilot diffused rapidly because it was easy to observe its users scheduling meetings, entering addresses, documenting expenses, and so on. The utility of the device was clear. The same was true of the cell phone and hence its rapid adoption. It was less easy to observe the benefits that many people got from using PCs because they were often used behind closed doors in a business setting.

A final factor that is very important in the growth of many new products is the *availability of complementary products.* Cell phone use grew rapidly because an important complement—a nationwide telecommunications network to route calls—was already in place; cell phone operators merely had to build out cell sites and connect them to that network.

Strategic Implications of Differences in Growth Rates. From a strategic perspective, companies can increase the demand for a new technology or product if they develop a business model that clearly shows its relative advantage, make it as compatible as possible with customers' prior needs and experiences, reduce its complexity, make it possible for customers to try and observe others using the technology or product, and make sure that the necessary complementary products are in place. These considerations must drive product development and a company's business-level strategy. Many companies that have paid attention to these factors have invested in developing the right kinds of distinctive competencies and gained a competitive advantage and market share as a result.

The early success of Apple was based on the fact that the less complex design of its Apple II PC made it easier to use than competing designs. The Apple II also had a relative economic advantage because some key complements (particularly VisiCalc, the first business spreadsheet) soon became available for the machine. As we noted earlier, however, Apple largely squandered its early advantage by not paying attention to the way customer needs were evolving. Similarly, the first Sony PlayStation was very popular because Sony pioneered the marketing strategy of setting up displays in retail stores where potential customers could try a PlayStation and others could observe them trying it.

Another important issue is that new products often spread in a way that is analogous to a viral model of infection. Lead adopters (the first customers who buy a product) in a community become "infected" with the product (enthused by it). Subsequently, they infect other people by telling them about its advantages, and after having observed the benefits of the product, these others also adopt it. A good example of this model of diffusion occurred with Hotmail, the free email service now owned by Microsoft. When it was established, its developers decided to add a tag line on the bottom of the email that read "get your free e-mail at Hotmail.com." This tag line proved remarkably efficient in recruiting new members. Someone would sign on at one institution, say the University of Washington, and send email via Hotmail to friends. Some of the recipients would also sign on. Within a few days, there would be ten members at the University of Washington, then one hundred, and within a month a thousand—all "infected" from the original user.

Companies promoting new products can take advantage of this viral diffusion phenomenon by identifying and aggressively courting potential opinion leaders—customers whose views command respect—in a community. For example, when the manufacturers of new high-tech medical equipment, such as an MRI scanner, start to sell a new product, they first try to get well-known doctors at major research and teaching hospitals to adopt the technology. They may give these opinion leaders free machines for their research purposes and work closely with them in developing the technology. Once these opinion leaders commit to the technology, and particularly if they give it their stamp of approval by using it for research and teaching purposes, doctors at many other hospitals often follow.

In sum, understanding competitive dynamics in embryonic and growth industries is an important strategic issue. The way in which different kinds of customer groups emerge and customer needs change are important determinants of business-level strategy. Similarly, understanding the factors that affect a market's growth rate allow managers to tailor their business model to a changing industry environment. (Much more is said about competition in dynamic, changing, high-tech industries in the next chapter.)

Strategy in Mature Industries

As a result of fierce competition in the shakeout stage, an industry becomes consolidated, and so a mature industry is often dominated by a small number of large companies. Although it may also contain many medium-sized companies and a host of small, specialized ones, the large companies determine the nature of competition in the industry because they can influence the five competitive forces. Indeed, these large companies owe their leading positions to the fact that they developed the most successful generic business-level strategies in the industry.

By the end of the shakeout stage, strategic groups of companies pursuing similar generic competitive strategies have normally emerged in an industry. As we discussed in Chapter 5, for example, companies pursuing a low-cost strategy can be viewed as composing one strategic group, all those pursuing differentiation constitute another, and other companies focusing on particular kinds of market niches form still other strategic groups. Finally, companies whose business models are responding to changing customer needs may be developing both low-cost and differentiation competencies, which will change strategic group structure and promote competition.

As Chapter 5 discusses, companies in an industry constantly analyze each other's business-level strategies, and they know that if they move to change their strategies, their actions are likely to stimulate a competitive response from rivals in their strategic group and other groups that may be threatened by the change in strategy. Industry companies are, in other words, playing a competitive game, and such games can be analyzed using game theory. For example, a differentiator that starts to lower its prices because it has adopted a more cost-efficient technology not only threatens other differentiators in its group, it also threatens low-cost companies, which see their competitive edge being eroded. These other companies may now change their strategies in response, most likely by reducing their prices, as is currently occurring in the PC industry.

Thus, the way one company changes its strategy and fine-tunes its business model over time affects the way the other companies in the industry pursue theirs. Hence, the high level of strategic interdependence that exists in mature, consolidated industries makes it very important for managers to look forward and reason back before launching a strategic initiative. They must think through how their rivals will respond to their actions and pursue a strategy that makes the most sense given this reasoning. In fact, the main issue facing a company in a mature industry is to adopt a competitive strategy that simultaneously enables it to maximize its profitability given the strategies that all other companies in the industry are likely to pursue. No generic strategy will generate above-average profits if competitive forces in an industry are so strong that companies are at the mercy of each other, potential entrants, powerful suppliers, powerful customers, and others. As a result, in mature industries, competitive strategy revolves around understanding how large companies *collectively* try to reduce the strength of industry competition to preserve both company and industry profitability.

Interdependent companies can help protect their competitive advantage and profitability by adopting competitive moves and tactics to reduce the threat of each competitive force. In the next sections, we examine the various price and nonprice competitive moves and tactics that companies use—first, to deter entry into an industry, and second, to reduce the level of rivalry within an industry. Many of these competitive moves and tactics were first understood by applying the principles of game theory to analyzing competitive interactions in a consolidated industry. We then discuss methods that companies can employ to gain more control over suppliers and buyers.

Strategies to Deter Entry: Product Proliferation, Pricing Games, and Maintaining Excess Capacity

Companies can use three main methods to deter entry by potential rivals and hence maintain and increase industry profitability: product proliferation, pricing games, and maintaining excess capacity (see Figure 6.5). Of course, *potential entrants* will try to circumvent such entry-deterring strategies by incumbent companies. Competition is rarely a one-way street.

Product Proliferation. Companies most commonly produce a range of products aimed at different market segments so that they have broad product lines. Sometimes, to reduce the threat of entry, they expand the range of products they make to

FIGURE 6.5

Strategies for
Deterring Entry of
Rivals

fill a wide variety of niches. This creates a barrier to entry because potential competitors now find it harder to break into an industry in which all the niches are filled.[11] This strategy of pursuing a broad product line to deter entry is known as **product proliferation.**

Because the large U.S. carmakers were so slow to fill the small-car niches (they did *not* pursue a product proliferation strategy), they were vulnerable to the entry of the Japanese into these market segments in the United States in the 1980s. Ford and GM really had no excuse for this situation, for in their European operations, they had a long history of small-car manufacturing. Managers should have seen the opening and filled it ten years earlier, but the (mistaken) view was that "small cars mean small profits." Better small profits than no profits! In the soap and detergent industry, on the other hand, competition is based on the production of new kinds of soaps and detergents to satisfy or create new desires by customers. Thus, the number of soaps and detergents, and especially the way they are packaged (powder, liquid, or tablets), proliferates, making it very difficult for prospective entrants to attack a new market segment.

Figure 6.6 indicates how product proliferation can deter entry. It depicts product space in the restaurant industry along two dimensions: atmosphere, which ranges from fast food to candlelight dining, and quality of food, which ranges from average to gourmet. The circles represent product spaces filled by restaurants located along the two dimensions. Thus, McDonald's is situated in the average quality/fast food area. A gap in the product space gives a potential entrant or an existing rival an opportunity to enter the market and make inroads. The shaded unoccupied product space represents areas where new restaurants can enter the market. When all the product spaces are filled, this barrier to entry makes it much more difficult for a new company to gain a foothold in the market and differentiate itself.

Pricing Games.   In some situations, pricing strategies can be used to deter entry by other companies, thus protecting the profit margins of companies already in an industry. One entry-deterring strategy is to cut prices every time a new company enters the industry or, even better, every time a potential entrant is *contemplating* entry, and then raise prices once the new or potential entrant has withdrawn. The goal here is to send a signal to potential entrants that new entry will be met with price cuts. If incumbent companies in an industry consistently pursue such a strategy, potential entrants will come to understand that their entry will spark off a price war, the threat of new entry will be reduced, average prices will be higher, and industry profitability will increase.

FIGURE 6.6

Product Proliferation in the Restaurant Industry

The pricing signal sent must be clear and credible. Put differently, it is important that established companies in the industry develop a reputation for responding to new entry by aggressively cutting prices. If they lack this reputation and do not always cut prices when a new firm enters their industry, the signal will lack credibility, and potential entrants will be more likely to try their luck and risk entry.[12]

Large airlines have been known to pursue such a selective price-cutting strategy to deter budget airlines from entering their most profitable markets. For example, if a budget airline were to try to enter a profitable market, say, flights from New York to Chicago, the response of the established airlines might be to increase the number of daily flights they run between those two cities. Increasing capacity in this manner has the effect of driving down prices and making the market less attractive for the new entrant, which subsequently withdraws from the market. Once the new entrant has gone, the airlines might reduce the number of flights they run per day, thereby raising prices. Companies must be very careful when they pursue such a pricing strategy, however, for it could be perceived as predatory pricing, that is, pricing to drive out competitors, which is illegal under U.S. antitrust law. **Predatory pricing** involves using revenue generated in one product market to support pricing below the company's costs of production in another to drive rivals out of the market.

A second entry deterring pricing strategy is known as limit pricing. **Limit pricing** is a strategy that can be used when the established companies in an industry enjoy scale economies, but those scale economies are not sufficient to deter entry. This is illustrated in Figure 6.7, where the average cost structure of potential new entrants is shown to be higher than the average cost structure of established companies.

The justification is that initially, new entrants will have a lower sales volume than established companies and will not enjoy the same scale economies. However, imagine that for established companies in the industry, the profit-maximizing output is Q_1 and the prevailing price for their product is P_1. This price is above the average cost

FIGURE 6.7

Limit Pricing Strategy

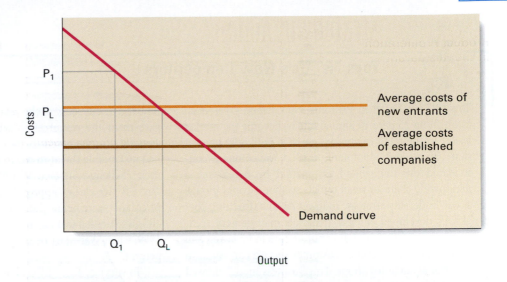

structure of potential new entrants, so although they will not be as profitable as established companies, the potential competitors still have an incentive to enter the market. Established companies can eliminate this incentive by charging a price that is *below* the average cost structure of new entrants, but still *above* their own average cost structure. In Figure 6.7, this price is P_L, which is known as the *limit price*. By adopting such a price, established companies can effectively deter entry and still be profitable. In fact, a limit-pricing strategy may well be consistent with maximizing the long-run profitability of an industry precisely because it reduces the incentive that potential entrants have to enter the market.

However, a limit-pricing strategy will not keep out an entrant that plans to adopt a new technology that will give it a cost advantage over established companies or that has pioneered a new business model that its managers expect will also give it a competitive advantage. In fact, many of the most successful entrants into mature industries are companies that have done just this. For example, the Japanese car companies were able to enter the U.S. market because they had pioneered new lean manufacturing technologies that gave them a cost and quality advantage over established U.S. companies. Today, Japanese car companies' share of the U.S. market is limited only by an informal trade agreement; it could easily double if they were allowed to import all the cars they wished and sell them at whatever price they chose, which might drive one or more U.S. car companies out of the market.

It is also important to note that selective price-cutting and limit-pricing strategies may not deter a strong potential competitor—for example, a leading company in another industry that is trying to find profitable investment opportunities in other industries. It is difficult, for example, to imagine 3M's being afraid to enter an industry because companies there threaten to drive down prices. 3M has the resources to withstand any short-term losses. Hewlett-Packard also had few worries about entering the highly competitive PC industry because of its powerful set of distinctive competencies. Hence, when faced with such a scenario, it may be in the interests of incumbent companies to accept new entry gracefully, giving up market share gradually to the new entrants to prevent price wars from developing and thus save their profits, if this is feasible. As Strategy in Action 6.3 details, Toys 'R' Us has been forced to give up market share in the toy market, and it has lost much of its prominence as a result.

Strategy in Action

6.3

Toys "R" Us's New Competitors

Toys "R" Us, based in Paramus, New Jersey, grew at an astonishing 25 percent annual rate to become the market leader in the retail toy market in 1990 with a 20 percent share. To reach its dominant position, the company consolidated the fragmented toy market by developing a nationwide chain of retail outlets so that it could pursue a cost-leadership strategy. To lower its cost structure, Toys "R" Us developed efficient materials management techniques for ordering and distributing toys to its stores, and it provided a low level of customer service compared to traditional small toy shops. This business model allowed it to achieve a low expense-to-sales ratio of 17 percent, and it then used this favorable cost structure to promote a philosophy of everyday low pricing. The company deliberately set out to undercut the prices of its rivals, and it succeeded: two of its largest competitors, Child World and Lionel went bankrupt.

With its dominant position in the industry established, Toys "R" Us continued to build its chain of toy stores, and it began stocking an ever larger and more complex array of products. This would raise its costs; nevertheless, its managers reasoned that they could afford to do so since they were in the driver's seat, and customers would find more value in a wider toy selection. Moreover, raising prices to customers could offset any cost increases, or perhaps the company could negotiate higher price discounts from toy makers like Mattel or Parker Bros.

The company received a shock in 1995 when its commanding position was threatened by the entry of a new set of rivals. Recognizing the high profits that Toys "R" Us was earning, rapidly expanding companies such as Wal-Mart, Kmart, and Target began to make toy selling a major part of their business model. What could Toys "R" do to stop them? Not much. Because of its failure to control costs, Toys "R" Us could not stop their entry into its business by reducing its prices; in other words, by failing to pursue its cost leadership strategy faithfully, it had lost its ability to play pricing games as it had done with its earlier rivals. The entry of these other companies also reduced its power over its suppliers, the toy makers, because they now had important new customers. Finally, some of the new entrants, Wal-Mart in particular, were now the cost leaders in the retail industry, and their size gave them the resources to withstand any problems if Toys "R" Us attempted to start a price war. Toys "R" Us had no credible threat to use to threaten them or fend off their challenge. In fact, Wal-Mart simply imitated the Toys "R" Us earlier approach and began selling toys at prices that were below those of Toys "R" Us! Indeed, Toys "R" Us's sales fell from 25 percent in 1990 to 17 percent by 1999, when Wal-Mart became the market leader with 18 percent.

To survive, Toys "R" Us has had to return to its low-cost strategy in its core toy business. It installed new IT to increase the efficiency of its purchasing and distribution operations. It reduced the number of items its stores carry by over 30 percent to slash its cost structure. At the same time, recognizing that it might never be able to match Wal-Mart's low costs, it changed its business model to try to create customer value by developing other kinds of stores for related market segments, such as Kids "R" Us and Babies "R" Us. In 2000, it introduced a new kind of store, Imaginarium, a premier specialty upscale toy retailer, and in this business it pursues a focus differentiation strategy. Each Imaginarium employs a knowledgeable team of "toyologists," expert salespeople extensively trained to provide parents and children with the highest level of one-on-one customer service. It also went online and attempted to develop a major web presence. However, faced with the high costs of online selling today, it subsequently partnered with Amazon.com; toys bought in its shop on Amazon's web site can be picked up at any Toys "R" Us store.

To date, these moves have halted the decline in its market share, and in 2002 it announced a gain of a few points. Its profitability has not increased in any significant way, however, and its new CEO, John Eyles, is striving to work on both the value and cost sides of the equation to find the business model that will work best in the highly competitive toy business.

Sources: M. Maremont and G. Bowens, "Brawls in Toyland," *Business Week,* December 21, 1992, pp. 36–37. S. Eads, "The Toys 'R' Us Empire Strikes Back," *Business Week,* June 7, 1999, pp. 55–59. www.toysrus.co (2002); amazon.com (2002).

Maintaining Excess Capacity. A third competitive technique that allows companies to deter entry involves maintaining excess capacity, that is, maintaining the physical capability to produce more of a product than customers currently demand. Existing industry companies may deliberately develop some limited amount of excess capacity to warn potential entrants that if they enter the industry, existing firms can retaliate by increasing output and forcing down prices until entry would become unprofitable. However, as with selective price cutting, the threat to increase output has to be *credible,* that is, companies in an industry must collectively be able to raise the level of production quickly if entry appears likely.

Strategies to Manage Rivalry

Beyond seeking to deter entry, companies also wish to develop a competitive strategy to manage their competitive interdependence and decrease price rivalry. Unrestricted competition over prices reduces both company and industry profitability. Several competitive tactics and gambits are available to companies to manage industry relations. The most important are price signaling, price leadership, nonprice competition, and capacity control.

Price Signaling. A company's ability to choose the price option that leads to superior performance is a function of several factors, including the strength of demand for a product and the intensity of competition between rivals. Price signaling is a first means by which companies attempt to control rivalry among competitors so as to allow the industry to choose the most favorable pricing option.[13] **Price signaling** is the process by which companies increase or decrease product prices to convey their intentions to other companies and so influence the way they price their products.[14] Companies use price signaling to improve industry profitability.

Companies may use price signaling to announce that they will respond vigorously to hostile competitive moves that threaten them. For example, they may signal that if one company starts to cut prices aggressively, they will respond in kind, a common game theory outcome. A **tit-for-tat strategy** is a well-known price signaling strategy that involves a company's doing exactly what its rivals do: if its rivals cut prices, the company follows; if its rivals raise prices, the company follows. By pursuing this strategy consistently over time, a company sends a clear signal to its rivals that it will match any pricing moves they make, the idea being that, sooner or later, rivals will learn that the company will always pursue a tit-for-tat strategy. Because rivals now know that the company will match any price reductions and cutting prices will only reduce profits, price cutting becomes less common in the industry. Moreover, a tit-for-tat strategy also signals to rivals that price increases will be followed, increasing the probability that rivals will initiate price increases to raise profits. Thus, a tit-for-tat strategy can be a useful way of shaping pricing behavior in an industry.[15]

The airline industry is a good example of the power of price signaling, where prices typically rise and fall depending on the current state of customer demand. If one carrier signals the intention to lower prices, a price war frequently ensues as other carriers copy each other's signals. If one carrier feels demand is strong, it might test the waters by signaling an intention to increase prices, and price signaling thus becomes a competitive tool to obtain uniform price increases. Nonrefundable tickets, another way of obtaining a more favorable pricing option, originated as a market signal by one company that was quickly copied by all other companies in the industry. Carriers recognized that they could stabilize their revenues and earn interest on customers' money if they collectively acted to force customers to assume the risk of buying airline tickets in advance. In essence, price signaling allows companies to give one another information that enables them to understand each other's competitive product or market strategy and make coordinated, price competitive moves.

Price Leadership. Price leadership—one company's assuming the responsibility for choosing the most favorable industry pricing option—is a second tactic used to reduce price rivalry and thus enhance the profitability of companies in a mature industry.[16] Formal price leadership, or price setting by companies jointly, is illegal under antitrust laws, so the process of price leadership is often very subtle. In the car industry, for example, prices are set by imitation. The price set by the weakest company—that is, the one with the highest cost structure—is often used as the basis for competitors' pricing. Thus, U.S. carmakers set their prices, and Japanese carmakers then set theirs with reference to the U.S. prices. The Japanese are happy to do this because they have lower costs than U.S. companies, so they make higher profits than U.S. carmakers without competing with them by price. Pricing is done by market segment. The prices of different auto models in the model range indicate the customer segments that the companies are aiming for and the price range they believe the market segment can tolerate. Each manufacturer prices a model in the segment with reference to the prices charged by its competitors, not by reference to competitors' costs. Price leadership also allows differentiators to charge a premium price and helps low-cost companies like Toyota by increasing their margins.

Although price leadership can stabilize industry relationships by preventing head-to-head competition and thus raise the level of profitability within an industry, it has its dangers. It helps companies with high cost structures, allowing them to survive without becoming more productive or more efficient. Thus, it may foster complacency as companies may keep harvesting profits without reinvesting much to improve their productivity. In the long term, such behavior makes them vulnerable to new entrants that have lower costs because they have developed new low-cost production techniques. That is what happened in the U.S. car industry after the Japanese entered the market. After years of tacit price fixing, with GM as the price leader, the carmakers were subjected to growing low-cost Japanese competition, to which they were unable to respond. Indeed, most U.S. carmakers survived only because the Japanese carmakers were foreign firms. Had the foreign firms been new U.S. entrants, the government would probably not have taken steps to protect Chrysler, Ford, or GM.

Nonprice Competition. A third very important aspect of product and market strategy in mature industries is the use of **nonprice competition** to manage rivalry within an industry. Using various tactics and maneuvers to try to prevent costly price cutting and price wars does not preclude competition by product differentiation. Indeed, in many industries, product differentiation is the principal tactic used to prevent competitors from obtaining access to a company's customers and attacking its market share. In other words, companies rely on product differentiation to deter potential entrants and manage rivalry within their industry. Product differentiation allows industry rivals to compete for market share by offering products with different or superior features or by applying different marketing techniques. In Figure 6.8, product and market segment dimensions are used to identify four nonprice competitive strategies based on product differentiation: market penetration, market development, product development, and product proliferation. (Notice that this model applies to new market segments, not new markets.)[17]

FIGURE 6.8

Four Nonprice Competitive Strategies

Market Penetration. When a company concentrates on expanding market share in its existing product markets, it is engaging in a strategy of **market penetration.**[18] Market penetration involves heavy advertising to promote and build product differentiation. In a mature industry, the thrust of advertising is to influence customers' brand choice and create a brand-name reputation for the company and its products. In this way, a company can increase its market share by attracting the customers of its rivals. Because brand-name products often command premium prices, building market share in this situation is very profitable.

In some mature industries—for example, soap and detergent, disposable diapers, and brewing—a market-penetration strategy becomes a way of life.[19] In these industries, all companies engage in intensive advertising and battle for market share. Each company fears that by not advertising, it will lose market share to rivals. Consequently, in the soap and detergent industry, Procter & Gamble spends more than 20 percent of sales revenues on advertising, with the aim of maintaining and perhaps building market share. These huge advertising outlays constitute a barrier to entry for prospective entrants.

Product Development. **Product development** is the creation of new or improved products to replace existing ones.[20] The wet-shaving industry depends on product replacement to create successive waves of customer demand, which then create new sources of revenue for companies in the industry. Gillette, for example, periodically comes out with a new and improved razor, such as the Sensor shaving system, which often gives a boost to its market share. Similarly, in the car industry, each major car company replaces its models every three to five years to encourage customers to trade in their old models and buy the new one.

Product development is crucial for maintaining product differentiation and building market share.[21] For instance, the laundry detergent Tide has gone through more than fifty changes in formulation during the past forty years to improve its performance. The product is always advertised as Tide, but it is a different product each year. Refining and improving products is an important competitive tactic in defending a company's generic competitive strategy in a mature industry, but this kind of competition can be as vicious as a price war because it is very expensive and raises costs dramatically.

Market signaling to competitors can also be an important part of a product development strategy. One company may let the others know that it is proceeding with product innovations that will provide a competitive advantage the others will be unable to imitate effectively because their entry into the market will be too late. For example, software companies such as Microsoft often announce new operating systems years in advance. The purpose of the announcement is to deter prospective competitors from making the huge investments needed to compete with the industry leaders and let its customers know that the company still has the competitive edge so important to retaining customers' loyalty. However, preemptive signaling can backfire, as IBM found out when it announced that its PS/2 operating system would not be compatible with the operating systems already standard in the industry. Other companies in the industry collectively signaled to IBM and IBM's customers that they would band together to protect the existing operation systems, thus preserving industry standards and preventing IBM from obtaining a competitive advantage from its new technology. IBM subsequently backed down. If a preemptive move is to succeed, competitors must believe that a company will act according to its signals and stick to its position. If the threat is not credible, the signaling company weakens its position.

Market Development. **Market development** finds new market segments for a company's products. A company pursuing this strategy wants to capitalize on the brand name it has developed in one market segment by locating new market segments in which to compete. In this way, it can exploit the product differentiation advantages of its brand name. The Japanese auto manufacturers provide an interesting example of the use of market development. When they entered the market, each Japanese manufacturer offered a car such as the Toyota Corolla and the Honda Accord aimed at the economy segment of the auto market. Then they upgraded each car over time, and now each is directed at a more expensive market segment. The Accord is a leading contender in the midsize car segment, and the Corolla fills the small-car segment that used to be occupied by the Celica, which is now aimed at a sportier market segment. By redefining their product offerings, Japanese manufacturers have profitably developed their market segments and successfully attacked their industry rivals, wresting market share from these companies. Although the Japanese used to compete primarily as low-cost producers, market development has allowed them to become differentiators as well. Toyota has used market development to pursue a simultaneous low-cost and differentiation strategy.

Product Proliferation. **Product proliferation** can be used to manage rivalry within an industry and to deter entry. The strategy of product proliferation generally means that large companies in an industry all have a product in each market segment or niche and compete head-to-head for customers. If a new niche develops, such as sports utility vehicles, designer sunglasses, or Internet web sites, then the leader gets a first-mover advantage, but soon all the other companies catch up. Once again, competition is stabilized, and rivalry within the industry is reduced. Product proliferation thus allows the development of stable industry competition based on product differentiation, not price—that is, nonprice competition based on the development of new products. The battle is over a product's perceived quality and uniqueness, not over its price.

The story of competition in the hamburger segment of the fast food industry told in Strategy in Action 6.4 illustrates how many of these strategies work in practice.

Capacity Control. Although nonprice competition helps mature industries avoid the cutthroat price cutting that reduces company and industry levels of profitability, price competition does periodically break out when excess capacity exists in an industry. Excess capacity arises when companies collectively produce too much output, and to dispose of it, they cut prices. When one company cuts prices, the

Strategy in Action   6.4

Fast Food Is a Ruthless Business

In the mature and saturated fast food industry, competition for customers by hamburger chains has been intense. McDonald's, the industry leader, has been under intense pressure to maintain its profit margins, because as the price of fast food has fallen, price wars have periodically broken out. Taco Bell started the first price war in the industry when it introduced its $.99 taco. Taken aback, McDonald's and other burger chains, such as Burger King and Wendy's, had to find ways to lower their costs and prices. As a result of price competition, all the burger chains were forced to learn how to lower their cost structures to make a cheaper hamburger. Today, constant innovation in food preparation is the name of the game, and companies have been able to lower their prices.

With most fast food restaurants now offering comparable prices, the focus of competition has shifted to other aspects of their products. First, the major chains competed by introducing bigger burger patties to increase market penetration. Burger King started the battle in an aggressive campaign to increase its market share at the expense of McDonald's. It added a full ounce of beef to its 1.8 ounce regular patty and followed this with an intense advertising campaign based on the slogan, "Get Your Burger's Worth," directed at McDonald's burger, which then was 40 percent lighter. The campaign worked for Burger King for a while, and its market share rose by 18 percent, but then in a nonprice tit-for-tat, McDonald's announced that it would enlarge its regular patty by 25 percent to beat back the challenge from Burger King and from Wendy's, which has always offered a larger burger (and whose "Where's the Beef?" slogan helped it gain market share).

Burger King and McDonald's have also pursued market penetration by opening up new kinds of restaurants to attract customers. Because all of the big chains have thousands of restaurants each, many analysts thought that the market was saturated, meaning that it would not be profitable to open more restaurants. However, McDonald's in particular has opened hundreds of restaurants in new locations, such as gas stations and large retail stores (for example, Wal-Mart), and new kinds of restaurants, such as small ones at airports and those that contain indoor playgrounds. These moves have helped it protect its market share and maintain its margins.

The main burger chains are also constantly experimenting with product development and introducing improved kinds of burgers to appeal to regular customers—burgers that add cheese, bacon, different kinds of vegetables, and exotic sauces, and new kinds of burgers, such as diet or low-fat burgers to attract new customers. They also all introduced whole-meal offerings, such as McDonald's "value meals," to provide a competitive package to attract customers. Individual restaurants are also allowed to customize their menus to suit the tastes of customers in the region in which they are located. For example, McDonald's restaurants in New England have lobster on the menu, and those in Japan serve sushi. Such product development is a major part of competitive strategy in the industry.

Recognizing the competition from other kinds of fast food chains such as those specializing in chicken or Mexican food, the burger chains have also moved to broaden their menus. McDonald's, for example, offers chicken dishes, pizza, and salads and increasingly tries to be a one-stop shop for all kinds of foods. This is a form of product proliferation designed to keep customers coming back. It makes it more difficult for a competitor or potential entrant to find a new food niche to take advantage of and attract away customers.

In the mature fast food industry, developing new competitive strategies to fend off attacks by other companies within the industry and to protect and enhance competitive advantage is a never-ending task for strategic managers. Indeed, recently, a franchisee in Orlando announced a new gourmet McDonald's restaurant. In a restaurant featuring gilded decor and sophisticated game and media rooms, they will serve white pizza, barbecue pizza, crème blur cheesecake with raspberry oculus, and cappuccino. Can this really be McDonald's?

Sources: R. Gibson, "Bigger Burger by McDonald's: A Two Ounce," *Wall Street Journal,* April 18 1996, p. B1. www.mcdonalds.com (2002). D. Leonhardt, "McDonald's: Can It Regain Its Golden Touch?" *Business Week,* February 28, 1998, pp. 22–27. D. Leonhardt and A. T. Palmer, "Getting off Their McButts," *Business Week,* February 22, 1999, pp. 65–66. "Gourmet McDonald's? Central Florida Has It," *Orlando Sentinel,* December 19, 2001, p. A4.

others quickly follow (a game theory prediction; see Chapter 5) because they fear that the price cutter will be able to sell its entire inventory while they will be left with unwanted goods. The result is that a price war develops.

Excess capacity may be caused by a shortfall in demand, as when a recession lowers the demand for cars and causes car companies to give customers price incentives to purchase a new car. In this situation, companies can do nothing except wait for better times. By and large, however, excess capacity results from companies within an industry simultaneously responding to favorable conditions: they all invest in new plants to be able to take advantage of the predicted upsurge in demand. Paradoxically, each individual company's effort to outperform the others means that collectively, the companies create industry overcapacity, which hurts them all, a game theory prediction. Although demand is rising, the consequence of each company's decision to increase capacity is a surge in industry capacity, which drives down prices. To prevent the accumulation of costly excess capacity, companies must devise strategies that let them control—or at least benefit from—capacity expansion programs. Before we examine these strategies, however, we need to consider in greater detail the factors that cause excess capacity.[22]

Factors Causing Excess Capacity. The problem of excess capacity often derives from technological developments. Sometimes new low-cost technology is the culprit because all companies invest in it simultaneously to prevent being left behind. Excess capacity occurs because the new technology can produce more than the old. In addition, new technology is often introduced in large increments, which generate overcapacity. For instance, an airline that needs more seats on a route must add another plane, thereby adding hundreds of seats even if only fifty are needed. To take another example, a new chemical process may operate efficiently only at the rate of a 1,000 gallons a day, whereas the previous process was efficient at 500 gallons a day. If all companies within an industry change technologies, industry capacity may double and enormous problems can result.

Overcapacity may also be caused by competitive factors within an industry. Entry into an industry is one such a factor. The entry of South Korean companies into the global semiconductor industry in the 1990s caused massive overcapacity and price declines. Similarly, the entry of steel producers from the former Soviet Union countries into the global steel market produced excess capacity and plunging prices in the world steel market in the late 1990s and early 2000s. Sometimes the age of a company's plant is the source of the problem. For example, in the hotel industry, given the rapidity with which the quality of hotel furnishings declines, customers are always attracted to new hotels. When new hotel chains are built alongside the old chains, excess capacity can result. Often companies are simply making simultaneous competitive moves based on industry trends, but those moves eventually lead to head-to-head competition. Most fast food chains, for instance, establish new outlets whenever demographic data show population increases. However, the companies seem to forget that all other chains use the same data (they are not fully anticipating their rivals' actions). Thus, a locality that has no fast food outlets may suddenly see several being built at the same time. Whether they can all survive depends on the growth rate of demand relative to the growth rate of the chains.

Choosing a Capacity-Control Strategy. Given the various ways in which capacity can expand, companies clearly need to find some means of controlling it. If they are always plagued by price cutting and price wars, they will be unable to recoup the investments in their generic strategies. Low profitability within an industry caused by overcapacity forces not just the weakest companies but also sometimes the major players as well to exit the industry. In general, companies have two strategic choices: either (1) each company individually must try to preempt its rivals and seize the initiative, or (2) the companies collectively must find indirect means of coordinating with each other so that they are all aware of the mutual effects of their actions.

To *preempt* rivals, a company must forecast a large increase in demand in the product market and then move rapidly to establish large-scale operations that will be able to satisfy the predicted demand. By achieving a first-mover advantage, the company may deter other firms from entering the market since the preemptor will usually be able to move down the experience curve, reduce its costs and therefore its prices as well, and threaten a price war if necessary.

This strategy, however, is extremely risky, for it involves investing resources in a generic strategy before the extent and profitability of the future market are clear. Wal-Mart, with its strategy of locating in small rural towns to tap an underexploited market for discount goods, preempted Sears and Kmart. Wal-Mart has been able to engage in market penetration and market expansion because of the secure base it established in its rural strongholds.

A preemptive strategy is also risky if it does not deter competitors and they decide to enter the market. If the competitors have a stronger generic strategy or more resources, such as Microsoft or Intel, they can make the preemptor suffer. Thus, for the strategy to succeed, the preemptor must generally be a credible company with enough resources to withstand a possible price war.

To *coordinate* with rivals as a capacity-control strategy, caution must be exercised since collusion on the timing of new investments is illegal under antitrust law. However, tacit coordination is practiced in many industries as companies attempt to understand and forecast the competitive moves of each other. Generally, companies use market signaling and engage in a kind of tit-for-tat strategy to secure coordination. They make announcements about their future investment decisions in trade journals and newspapers. In addition, they share information about their production levels and their forecasts of demand within an industry to bring supply and demand into equilibrium. Thus, a coordination strategy reduces the risks associated with investment in the industry. This is very common in the chemical refining and oil business, where new capacity investments frequently cost hundreds of millions of dollars.

Supply and Distribution Strategy

As you saw in Chapter 2, when an industry becomes consolidated and comprises a few large companies, it may gain strength over its suppliers and buyers. Suppliers can become dependent on the industry for buying their inputs, and buyers can become dependent on the industry as a source of important products. By the mature stage, to protect their market position, brand name, and product quality, many companies decide to take over more of the distribution of their products and control the source of inputs crucial to the production process. That is, sometimes strategic considerations move them to be more involved in the value chain. When they seek ownership of supply or distribution operations, they are pursuing a strategy of vertical integration. At the same time, to reduce costs, mature companies often outsource, or "deintegrate," their value chains if this will lead to competitive advantage. Both of these choices are considered in detail in Chapter 9.

There are many reasons that a mature company might decide to control its supplier and distributor relationships and protect its generic strategy. In this way, it can safeguard its ability to dispose of its outputs or acquire inputs in a timely, reliable manner, thereby reducing costs and improving product quality. One way to analyze the issues in choosing a distribution or supplier strategy is to contrast two kinds of relationship that can exist between a company and its suppliers and distributors.

The first relationship, which can be called the *anonymous approach,* is for a company and its suppliers and distributors to have an arms-length, short-term relationship in which each party simply tries to strike the best bargain to make the most profit, inputs are inspected as they arrive, and defective ones are sent back. Often purchasing and distribution personnel are routinely rotated to prevent kickbacks. In contrast, with a *relational approach,* a company and its suppliers and distributors cooperate and try to develop a long-term perspective and base their exchanges on trust. With a relational approach, suppliers are sensitive to the needs of the company, respond quickly to changes in the specification of inputs, and adjust supply to meet the requirements of a company's just-in-time inventory system. The results of this close relationship are lower costs and the ability to respond to unexpected changes in demand. Developing close supplier-distributor relationships supports both companies' generic strategies. Clearly, it pays a company to develop a long-term relationship with its suppliers and distributors, and more and more companies, such as Motorola, McDonald's, and Wal-Mart, have formed close linkages with their suppliers.

A company has many options to choose from in deciding on the appropriate way to distribute its products to gain a competitive advantage. It may distribute its products to an independent distributor, which in turn distributes them to retailers. Alternatively, it might distribute directly to retailers or even to the final customer. This option is being used more and more by companies as they use the Internet to market and sell their products, as the *Running Case* illustrates.

In general, the *complexity of a product and the amount of information* needed about its operation and maintenance determine the distribution strategy chosen. Car companies, for example, use franchisees rather than car supermarkets to control the distribution of their autos. The reason is the high level of after-sales service and support needed to satisfy customers. Carmakers are able to penalize franchisees by withholding cars from a dealership if customers' complaints rise, giving them effective control over franchisees' behavior.

Large electronics manufacturers and producers of customer durables such as appliances generally prefer to use a network of distributors to control distribution. To enhance market share and control the way products are sold and serviced, manufacturers choose five or six large distributors in each state to control distribution. The distributors are required to carry the full line of a company's products and invest in after-sales service facilities. The result is that the manufacturer receives good feedback on how its products are selling, and the distributor becomes knowledgeable about a company's products and thus helps the company maintain and increase its control over the market. The company is able to discipline its distributors if they start to discount prices or otherwise threaten the company's reputation or generic strategy.

Large manufacturers such as Johnson & Johnson, Procter & Gamble, and General Foods typically sell directly to a retailer and avoid giving profits to a distributor or wholesaler. They do so in part because they have lower profit margins than the makers of electronic equipment and customer durables. However, this strategy also allows them to influence a retailer's behavior directly. For example, they can refuse to supply a particular product that a retailer wants unless the retailer stocks the entire range of the company's products. In addition, the companies are assured of shelf space for new products. Coca-Cola and PepsiCo are able to influence retailers to reduce the

Running Case

Compaq and Dell Go Head-to-Head in Customer Service

As new developments in technology alter the nature of competition in the PC industry, the distribution strategies of its major players are also changing. These changes are evident in the struggle between Dell Computer and Compaq Computer for domination of the PC market.

Founded by a team of engineers, Compaq from the start emphasized the engineering and research side of the PC business. For example, it was the first company to bring out a computer using Intel's new 486 chip. Its differentiation strategy was to produce high-end PCs based on the newest technology, which would command a premium price. Compaq specialized in the business market, and it developed a sophisticated dealer network to distribute, sell, and service its expensive PCs. Dell, on the other hand, focused from the beginning on the marketing and distribution end of the PC business. Its low-cost strategy was to assemble a PC and then sell it directly to customers through mail order outlets, cutting out the dealer in order to offer a rock-bottom price. Its managers viewed the company primarily as a distribution or mail order company, not as an engineering one.

As computers increasingly became commodity products and prices fell drastically, Compaq realized that its strategy of selling only though high-priced dealers would mean disaster; it then changed its strategy to produce a low-cost computer and in the 1990s began its own mail order distribution, offering its machines directly to customers and, more recently, to businesses. However, Compaq has not been as successful as Dell in its online distribution strategy because Dell was first to do so and gained a first-mover advantage and because Dell established a more customer-friendly web site and until 2002 enjoyed the record for fewest customer complaints. Moreover, although each company offered next-day delivery and installation of computers, as well as extended warranties, Dell reached ahead in providing the best online customer service, and indeed made quality customer service, as well as price, a main focus of its competitive advantage.

In 2000, Compaq's new CEO, Michael Capellas, announced a bold new Internet distribution and sales strategy to catch up with Dell and make Compaq the leader in online selling to businesses and customers. He directed all of Compaq's business units to make the Internet a major focus of their business models. Apparently, Capellas's efforts have been rewarded: a report in April 2002 announced that Dell's customer service had slipped, with 40 percent more customer complaints, and it was now tied with Compaq for first place. Apparently, the combination of exceptionally strong Christmas sales in 2001 and an understaffed service department overtaxed Dell's service abilities. In 2002, Dell was scrambling to hire hundreds of new service reps to solve the problem. Compaq, because of its 2002 merger with Hewlett-Packard, will also have more resources and capabilities to upgrade its service capabilities. The battle between these companies is not over.

Sources: K. Pope, "Out for Blood: For Compaq and Dell Accent Is on Personal in the Computer Wars," *Wall Street Journal,* February 13, 1993, pp. A1, A6. M. Stepanek, "What Does No. 1 Do for an Encore?" *Business Week,* November 2, 1998, pp. 44–47. A. Taylor III, "Compaq Looks Inside for Salvation," *Fortune,* August 16, 1999, pp. 124–129. M. Kessler, "Dude, Dell's Service Has Slipped, But Company's Working on It," *USA Today,* April 29, 2002, p. B2. www.hp.com (2002).

shelf space given to competing products or even to exclude them because soft drinks have the highest profit margins of products sold in supermarkets. Gallo is one of the few winemakers that controls the distribution and retailing of its own products. This is one reason Gallo is so consistently profitable.

In sum, devising the appropriate strategy for acquiring inputs and disposing of outputs is a crucial part of competitive strategy in mature industries. Companies can gain a competitive advantage through the way they choose to control their relationships with distributors and suppliers. By choosing the right strategy, they are able to control their costs, their price and nonprice strategies, their reputation, and product quality. These critical issues are expanded on in Chapter 9.

Strategies in Declining Industries

Sooner or later, many industries enter into a decline stage, in which the size of the total market starts to shrink. Examples are the railroad industry, the tobacco industry, and the steel industry. Industries start declining for a number of reasons, including technological change, social trends, and demographic shifts. The railroad and steel industries began to decline when technological changes brought viable substitutes for their products. The advent of the internal combustion engine drove the railroad industry into decline, and the steel industry fell into decline with the rise of plastics and composite materials. As for the tobacco industry, changing social attitudes toward smoking, which are themselves a product of growing concerns about the health effects of smoking, have caused decline.

There are four main strategies that companies can adopt to deal with decline: (1) a **leadership strategy,** by which a company seeks to become the dominant player in a declining industry; (2) a **niche strategy,** which focuses on pockets of demand that are declining more slowly than the industry as a whole; (3) a **harvest strategy,** which optimizes cash flow; and (4) a **divestment strategy,** by which a company sells off the business to others. Before examining each of these strategies in detail, it is important to note that the choice of strategy depends in part on the *intensity* of the competition.

The Severity of Decline

When the size of the total market is shrinking, competition tends to intensify in a declining industry and profit rates tend to fall. The intensity of competition in a declining industry depends on four critical factors, which are indicated in Figure 6.9. First, the intensity of competition is greater in industries in which decline is rapid as opposed to industries, such as tobacco, in which decline is slow and gradual.

Second, the intensity of competition is greater in declining industries in which exit barriers are high. As you recall from Chapter 2, high exit barriers keep companies locked into an industry even when demand is falling. The result is the emergence of excess productive capacity and, hence, an increased probability of fierce price competition.

Third, and related to the previous point, the intensity of competition is greater in declining industries in which fixed costs are high (as in the steel industry). The reason is that the need to cover fixed costs, such as the costs of maintaining productive capacity, can make companies try to use any excess capacity they have by slashing prices, which can trigger a price war.

Finally, the intensity of competition is greater in declining industries in which the product is perceived as a commodity (as it is in the steel industry) in contrast to industries in which differentiation gives rise to significant brand loyalty, as was true until very recently of the declining tobacco industry.

FIGURE 6.9

Factors that Determine the Intensity of Competition in Declining Industries

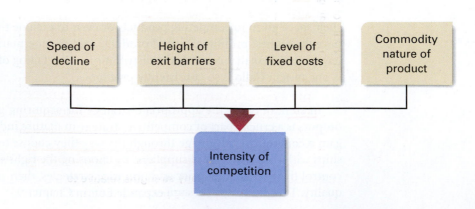

Not all segments of an industry typically decline at the same rate. In some segments, demand may remain reasonably strong despite decline elsewhere. The steel industry illustrates this situation. Although bulk steel products, such as sheet steel, have suffered a general decline, demand has actually risen for specialty steels, such as those used in high-speed machine tools. Vacuum tubes provide another example. Although demand for them collapsed when transistors replaced them as a key component in many electronics products, vacuum tubes still had some limited applications in radar equipment for years afterward. Consequently, demand in this vacuum tube segment remained strong despite the general decline in the demand for vacuum tubes. The point, then, is that there may be pockets of demand in an industry in which demand is declining more slowly than in the industry as a whole or not declining at all. Price competition thus may be far less intense among the companies serving such pockets of demand than within the industry as a whole.

Choosing a Strategy

Four main strategies are available to companies in a declining industry: a leadership strategy, a niche strategy, a harvest strategy, and a divestment strategy. Figure 6.10 provides a simple framework for guiding strategic choice. Note that the intensity of competition in the declining industry is measured on the vertical axis and that a company's strengths relative to remaining pockets of demand are measured on the horizontal axis.

Leadership Strategy. A leadership strategy aims at growing in a declining industry by picking up the market share of companies that are leaving the industry. A leadership strategy makes most sense (1) when the company has distinctive strengths that allow it to capture market share in a declining industry and (2) the speed of decline and the intensity of competition in the declining industry are moderate. Philip Morris has pursued such a strategy in the tobacco industry. By

FIGURE 6.10

Strategy Selection in a Declining Industry

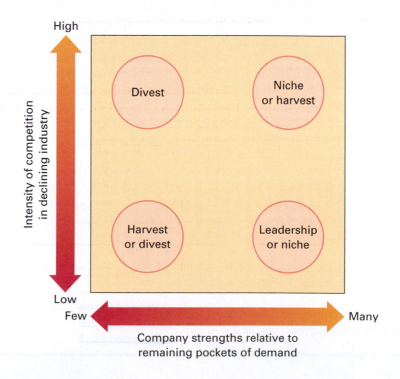

aggressive marketing, Philip Morris has increased its market share in a declining industry and earned enormous profits in the process.

The tactical steps companies might use to achieve a leadership position include aggressive pricing and marketing to build market share, acquiring established competitors to consolidate the industry, and raising the stakes for other competitors—for example, by making new investments in productive capacity. Such competitive tactics signal to other competitors that the company is willing and able to stay and compete in the declining industry. These signals may persuade other companies to exit the industry, which would further enhance the competitive position of the industry leader. Strategy in Action 6.5 offers an example of a company, Richardson Electronics, that has prospered by taking a leadership position in a declining industry. It is one of the last companies in the vacuum tube business.

Niche Strategy.   A niche strategy focuses on pockets of demand in the industry in which demand is stable or declining less rapidly than the industry as a whole. The strategy makes sense when the company has some unique strengths relative to those niches where demand remains relatively strong. As an example, consider Naval, a company that manufactures whaling harpoons and small guns to fire them and makes money doing so. This might be considered rather odd, since the world com-

Strategy in Action   6.5

How to Make Money in the Vacuum Tube Business

At its peak in the early 1950s, the vacuum tube business was a major industry in which companies such as Westinghouse, General Electric, RCA, and Western Electric had a large stake. Then along came the transistor, making most vacuum tubes obsolete, and one by one all the big companies exited the industry. One company, however, Richardson Electronics, not only stayed in the business but also demonstrated that high returns are possible in a declining industry. Primarily a distributor (although it does have some manufacturing capabilities), Richardson bought the remains of a dozen companies in the United States and Europe as they exited the vacuum tube industry. Richardson now has a warehouse that stocks more than 10,000 different types of vacuum tubes. The company is the world's only supplier of many of them, which helps explain why its gross margin is in the 35 to 40 percent range.

Richardson survives and prospers because vacuum tubes are vital parts of some older electronic equipment that would be costly to replace with solid-state equipment. In addition, vacuum tubes still outperform semiconductors in some limited applications, including radar and welding machines. The U.S. government and General Motors are big customers of Richardson.

Speed is the essence of Richardson's business. The company's Illinois warehouse offers overnight delivery to some 40,000 customers, processing 650 orders a day, whose average price is $550. Customers such as GM do not really care whether a vacuum tube costs $250 or $350; what they care about is the $40,000 to $50,000 downtime loss that they face when a key piece of welding equipment isn't working. By responding quickly to the demands of such customers and being the only major supplier of many types of vacuum tubes, Richardson has placed itself in a position that many companies in growing industries would envy: a monopoly position. In 1997, however, a new company, Westrex, was formed to take advantage of the growing popularity of vacuum tubes in high-end stereo systems, and by 1999 was competing head to head with Richardson in some market segments. Clearly, competition can be found even in a declining industry.

Source: P. Haynes, "Western Electric Redux," *Forbes,* January 26, 1998, pp. 46–47.

munity has outlawed whaling. However, Naval survived the terminal decline of the harpoon industry by focusing on the one group of people who are still allowed to hunt whales, although only in very limited numbers: North American Eskimos. Eskimos are permitted to hunt bowhead whales, provided that they do so only for food and not for commercial purposes. Naval is the sole supplier of small harpoon whaling guns to Eskimo communities, and its monopoly position allows it to earn a healthy return in this small market.[23]

Harvest Strategy. As we noted in Chapter 5, a harvest strategy is the best choice when a company wishes to get out of a declining industry and perhaps optimize cash flow in the process. This strategy makes the most sense when the company foresees a steep decline and intense future competition or lacks strengths relative to remaining pockets of demand in the industry. A harvest strategy requires the company to cut all new investments in capital equipment, advertising, R&D, and the like. The inevitable result is that it will lose market share, but because it is no longer investing in this business, initially its positive cash flow will increase. Essentially, the company is taking cash flow in exchange for market share. Ultimately, cash flows will start to decline, and at this stage it makes sense for the company to liquidate the business. Although this strategy is very appealing in theory, it can be somewhat difficult to put into practice. Employee morale in a business that is being run down may suffer. Furthermore, if customers catch on to what the company is doing, they may defect rapidly. Then market share may decline much faster than the company expected.

Divestment Strategy. A divestment strategy rests on the idea that a company can maximize its net investment recovery from a business by selling it early, before the industry has entered into a steep decline. This strategy is appropriate when the company has few strengths relative to whatever pockets of demand are likely to remain in the industry and when the competition in the declining industry is likely to be intense. The best option may be to sell out to a company that is pursuing a leadership strategy in the industry. The drawback of the divestment strategy is that it depends for its success on the ability of the company to spot its industry's decline before it becomes serious and to sell out while the company's assets are still valued by others.

Summary of Chapter

1. In fragmented industries composed of a large number of small and medium-sized companies, the principal forms of competitive strategy are chaining, franchising, and horizontal merger.

2. In embryonic and growth industries, the way in which different kinds of customer groups emerge over time, and customer needs change, are important determinants of business-level strategy. Similarly, understanding the factors that affect a market's growth rate allow managers to tailor their business model to a changing industry environment.

3. Mature industries are composed of a few large companies whose actions are so highly interdependent

that the success of one company's strategy depends on the responses of its rivals.

4. The principal competitive tactics and moves used by companies in mature industries to deter entry are product proliferation, pricing games, and maintaining excess capacity.

5. The principal competitive tactics and maneuvers used by companies in mature industries to manage rivalry are price signaling, price leadership, nonprice competition, and capacity control.

6. Companies in mature industries need to develop a supply-and-distribution strategy to protect the source of their competitive advantage.

7. In declining industries in which market demand has leveled off or is falling, companies must tailor their

price and nonprice strategies to the new competitive environment. They also need to manage industry capacity to prevent the emergence of capacity expansion problems.

8. There are four main strategies a company can pursue when demand is falling: leadership, niche, harvest, and divestment. The choice is determined by the severity of industry decline and the company's strengths relative to the remaining pockets of demand.

Discussion Questions

1. Why are industries fragmented? What are the main ways in which companies can turn a fragmented industry into a consolidated one?
2. What are the key problems in maintaining a competitive advantage in embryonic and growth industry environments? What are the dangers associated with being the leader?
3. Discuss how companies can use (a) product differentiation and (b) capacity control to manage rivalry and increase an industry's profitability.

Practicing Strategic Management

SMALL-GROUP EXERCISE: HOW TO KEEP THE HOT SAUCE HOT

Break up into groups of three to five people, and appoint one group member as a spokesperson who will communicate your findings to the class. You are the managers of a company that has pioneered a new kind of hot sauce for chicken that has taken the market by storm. The hot sauce's differentiated appeal has been based on a unique combination of spices and packaging that has allowed you to charge a premium price. Over the past three years, your hot sauce has achieved a national reputation, and now major food companies such as Kraft and Nabisco, seeing the potential of this market segment, are beginning to introduce hot sauces of their own, imitating your product.

1. Describe the generic business-level strategy you are pursuing.
2. Describe the industry's environment in which you are competing.
3. What kinds of competitive tactics and maneuvers could you adopt to protect your generic strategy in this kind of environment?
4. What do you think is the best strategy for you to pursue in this situation?

ARTICLE FILE 6

Find an example of the ways in which a company or group of companies in a particular industry environment has adopted a competitive strategy to protect or enhance its business-level strategy.

STRATEGIC MANAGEMENT PROJECT: MODULE 6

This part of the project continues the analysis of your company's business-level strategy and considers how conditions in the industry's environment affect the company's competitive strategy. With the information you have at your disposal, perform the tasks and answer the questions listed:

1. In what kind of industry environment (for example, embryonic, mature) does your company operate? Use the information from Strategic Management Project: Module 2 to answer this question.
2. Discuss how your company has attempted to develop a competitive strategy to protect its business-level strategy. For example, if your company is operating in an embryonic industry, discuss the ways it has attempted to increase its competitive advantage over time. If it operates in a mature industry, discuss how it has tried to manage the five forces of industry competition.
3. What new strategies would you advise your company to pursue to increase its competitive advantage? For example, what kinds of strategy toward buyers or suppliers should it adopt? How should it attempt to differentiate its products in the future?
4. Based on this analysis, do you think your company will be able to maintain its competitive advantage in the future? Why or why not?

EXPLORING THE WEB
Visiting Wal-Mart

Enter the web site of retailer Wal-Mart (**www.walmartstores.com**). Click on "About Wal-Mart," and then click on "Timeline." Study the events in Wal-Mart's timeline, and from them outline the way Wal-Mart's competitive strategy in the retailing industry has developed over time.

General Task: Search the Web for a company that has recently changed its competitive strategy in some way. What precipitated the change in its strategy? What were the strategy changes the company made?

Closing Case

How eBay Revolutionized the Auction Business

In the 1990s, many entrepreneurs attempted to use new information technologies and particularly the Internet to provide new or improved services to customers. Their goal was to use the potential of the new technology to find ways to obtain a competitive advantage over existing firms in a particular industry environment. Nowhere has this been more evident than in the auction industry.

Traditionally, auctions have been places where buyers and sellers meet face-to-face to determine the fair market value of a product. Auction houses range from the most prestigious ones, like Sotheby's and Christie's, which sell fine art and antiques, to small local auction companies that sell the contents of someone's house.

In the early 1990s, Pierre Omidyar had an idea for a new kind of auction company, an online auction company, which he believed would revolutionize the selling of all kinds of products—not just fine arts and antiques but any kind of collectible, from cars to Beanie Babies—by bringing buyers and sellers together by using the Internet. He left his job at Microsoft and began to write the software that would provide the platform for an online auction service. The result was eBay, which was launched on Labor Day in 1995.

On the eBay web site, sellers describe their product electronically, post a photograph, and set an initial price, which buyers can then bid up: the highest bidder wins. eBay charges a modest fee to list the product plus a low percentage of the final sales price. Sellers have the advantage that their product appears before buyers in every part of the United States and abroad—anywhere where someone has a computer and can log on to eBay's online auction site. Buyers enjoy access to a huge array of merchandise that can be quickly scanned by using the appropriate keywords on eBay's search engine. eBay thus provides a low-cost forum in which buyers and sellers can meet to buy and sell products. It makes its money from the sheer volume of products that it sells. Every day, millions of items are listed, so that even with low fees, it generates high profits.

As you can imagine, eBay's low-cost approach has generated many imitators; after all, it is relatively easy to write a software program and develop an online auction site. However, eBay's early start has also given it another major competitive advantage: being the first in the online auction business, it has attracted a loyal audience of buy-

ers and sellers who will not switch to other online auction companies, even when they provide the service for free. For example, by 1999, Yahoo and MSN, and hundreds of small, specialized companies had developed their own online auction businesses and decided to charge users nothing for their services. However, many of these, including Yahoo's auction site, have not attracted many buyers and sellers. The reason is that sellers know that eBay's site attracts many more buyers than does Yahoo's so that they are likely to obtain the highest price, and eBay buyers know that they will find the greatest selection on eBay and so focus their search there. Thus, eBay has not only developed a low-cost competency; it also has developed a substantial reputation that has given it a differentiation advantage as well.

Other online companies are not content to give away the lucrative online auction market to eBay, however, and are searching for ways to fight back. In June 1999, bookseller Amazon.com announced that it was forming an alliance with Sotheby's to create an upmarket online auction service, and other companies are also searching for partners. In October 1999, Yahoo, Amazon.com, and others announced that they were banding together to combine their auction businesses to offer a credible alternative to eBay.

After this announcement, eBay's price, which has soared several thousand percent because investors thought that its strategy had given it a sustainable competitive advantage over its rivals, fell back. Through his innovative use of new information technology, Omidyar has brought increased value for millions of buyers and sellers and in the meantime has created over a billion dollars of value for himself in his eBay stock. The question now is whether eBay can maintain the value it has created.

Case Discussion Questions

1. Describe the nature of competition and the industry environment of the online auction industry.

2. Go to eBay's web site, and analyze the strategies it has been pursuing to protect its competitive position (for example, different kinds of auction sites and services).

Sources: www.ebay.com (1999). www.amazon.com press releases (1999).

Strategy in High-Technology Industries

Opening Case

Extending the Wintel Monopoly to Wireless

Microsoft and Intel are co-owners of the dominant Wintel standard, based on the combination of a Microsoft operating system and an Intel microprocessor that is used in over 90 percent of the world's PCs. ("Wintel" was coined because Microsoft's Windows operating system is designed to run on an Intel microprocessor.) This fact has helped to make Microsoft and Intel the two most valuable companies in the global computer industry. Now the duo is trying to extend their standard and make it the dominant one in the wireless phone industry. The focus of their attention is next-generation wireless phones, or 3G phones, which will increasingly come to resemble computers. They will have color screens; a full range of personal information management applications such as address and date books; and the ability to browse the Internet, send and receive text-based email, and run a variety of applications, including pocket-sized versions of Microsoft's popular Office suite.

The strategy that Microsoft and Intel are pursuing is to create a reference design, or template, for making 3G wireless phones that they will license to electronics companies that wish to manufacture these devices. Microsoft will supply the operating system, which will be based on its Pocket PC operating system, a Windows-based operating system for small digital devices. Intel will supply key elements of the onboard microprocessor technology. Both companies will work together to produce the reference design, which is a set of standard specifications outlining how to build a handset using Microsoft and Intel technology. In creating this design, Microsoft and Intel claim that their main motive is to "demystify and democratize the wireless industry, so that more companies can break into the market. We want to enable one of them to become the next Nokia," said a Microsoft spokesman. (Nokia is the global leader in the market, with a 40 percent share of all wireless handset sales.) More generally, the idea is to try to accelerate the adoption of 3G wireless technology.

If all goes well, the Microsoft-Intel reference design will be licensed to a number of electronics companies that will use it to make wireless handsets. These companies will no longer have to invest in creating the design themselves, enabling them to cut R&D expenses and hence handset prices. As cheap handsets reach the market, probably in 2003–2004, demand will start to expand. As the installed base of Microsoft-Intel phones grows, more applications will be written to run on those phones. In addition, software companies will write web-based applications that reside on servers and can be accessed by consumers with a Microsoft-Intel phone over a wireless connection. These two developments will increase the value of owning a Microsoft-Intel phone, as opposed to a phone based on a different reference design. As the value increases, more consumers will buy phones based on the Microsoft-Intel design, as opposed to phones made by companies like Nokia, and the installed base of Microsoft-Intel phones will expand further, creating an incentive to develop more software for those phones, and so on. In other words, through the operation of a positive feedback loop, the reference design now being developed by Microsoft and Intel could become the de facto standard in the wireless handset market.

If this occurs, Microsoft and Intel will have extended their dominant position in PCs to the wireless handset market. They should be able to profit from this by charging a licensing fee for the reference design and by developing and selling complementary products, such as additional applications that run on a wireless handset or reside on servers that consumers with handsets can access via wireless connections to the Web.

The eventual outcome is less clear than the strategy. For one thing, several other companies are promoting alternative and potentially incompatible reference designs and operating systems for wireless handsets. These include Qualcomm, Nokia, Ericsson, and Motorola, all heavyweights in the wireless market. For another, it is still not clear that the wireless handset market has the same imperatives for standardization as the personal computer market does. If it does, however, the market will probably hone in on a single reference design. Whether that design is the one promoted by Microsoft and Intel or by another competitor depends in large part on the differential success of the strategies these different companies are pursuing as they try to win this emerging format war.

Sources: D. Pringle, "Wintel Duo Targets the Cellphone," *Wall Street Journal,* February 19, 2002, p. E2. A Doland, "Looking Beyond the Basic Cell Phone," *Columbian,* February 19, 2002, p. E2. B. McDonough, "Microsoft Jostles for Mobile Market Position," Wireless.Newsfactor.com, February 19, 2002.

Overview

In this chapter, we look at the nature of competition and strategy in high-technology industries. **Technology** refers to the body of scientific knowledge used in the production of goods or services. **High-technology (high-tech) industries** are those in which the underlying scientific knowledge that companies in the industry use is advancing rapidly, and by implication so are the attributes of the products and services that result from its application. The computer industry is often thought of as the quintessential example of a high-technology industry. Other industries often considered high tech are telecommunications, where new technologies based on wireless and the Internet have proliferated in recent years; consumer electronics, where the digital technology underlying products from DVD players to video game terminals and digital cameras is advancing rapidly; pharmaceuticals, where new technologies based on cell biology, recombinant DNA, and genomics are revolutionizing the process of drug discovery; power generation, where new technologies based on fuel cells and cogeneration may change the economics of the industry; and aerospace, where the combination of new composite materials, electronics, and more efficient jet engines may give birth to a new era of near-supersonic commercial aircraft, such as Boeing's planned sonic cruiser.

This chapter focuses on high-technology industries for a number of reasons. First, technology is accounting for an ever larger share of economic activity. Estimates suggest that roughly 15 percent of total economic activity in the United States is accounted for by information technology industries.[1] This figure actually underestimates the true impact of technology on the economy, because it ignores the other high-technology areas we just mentioned. Moreover, as technology advances, many low-technology industries are becoming more high tech. For example, the development of biotechnology and genetic engineering transformed the production of seed corn, long considered a low-technology business, into a high-technology business. Moreover, high-technology products are making their way into a wide range of businesses; today a Ford Taurus contains more computing power than the multimillion dollar mainframe computers used in the Apollo space program, and the competitive advantage of physical stores, such as Wal-Mart, is based on their use of information technology.[2] The circle of high-technology industries is both large and expanding, and even in industries not thought of as high tech, technology is revolutionizing aspects of the product or production system.

Although high-tech industries may produce very different products, when it comes to developing a business model and strategies that will lead to a competitive advantage and superior profitability, they face a similar situation. This chapter examines the competitive features found in many high-tech industries and the kinds of strategies that companies must adopt to build business models that will allow them to achieve superior performance and profitability.

By the time you have completed this chapter, you will have an understanding of the nature of competition in high-tech industries and strategies that companies can pursue to succeed in those industries.

Technical Standards and Format Wars

Especially in high-tech industries, ownership of **technical standards**—a set of technical specifications that producers adhere to when making the product or a component of it—can be an important source of competitive advantage.[3] *Indeed, the source of product differentiation is based on the technical standard.* Often, only one standard will come to dominate a market, so many battles in high-tech industries revolve around companies competing to be the one that sets the standard.

Battles to set and control technical standards in a market are referred to as **format wars;** they are essentially battles to control the source of differentiation and thus the value that such differentiation can create for the customer. Because differentiated products often command premium prices and are often expensive to develop, the competitive stakes are enormous. The profitability and very survival of a company may depend on the outcome of the battle, for example, the outcome of the battle now being waged over the establishment and ownership of the reference design for next-generation wireless handsets will help to determine which companies will be the leaders in the decades to come.

Examples of Standards

A familiar example of a standard is the layout of a computer keyboard. No matter what keyboard you buy, the letters are all in the same pattern.[4] The reason is quite obvious. Imagine if each computer maker changed the ways the keys were laid out—

if some started with QWERTY on the top row of letters (which is indeed the format used and is known as the QWERTY format), some with YUHGFD, and some with ACFRDS. If you learned to type on one layout, it would be irritating and time-consuming to have to relearn on a YUHGFD layout. So we have this standard format (QWERTY) because it makes it easy for people to move from computer to computer because the input medium, the keyboard, is set out in a standard way.

Another example of a technical standard concerns the dimensions of containers used to ship goods on trucks, railcars, and ships: all have the same basic dimensions—the same height, length, and width—and all make use of the same locking mechanisms to hold them onto a surface or to bolt against each other. Having a standard ensures that containers can easily be moved from one mode of transportation to another—from trucks, to railcars, to ships, and back to railcars. If containers lacked standard dimensions and locking mechanisms, it would suddenly become much more difficult to ship containers around the world. Shippers would have to make sure that they had the right kind of container to go on the ships and trucks and railcars scheduled to carry a particular container around the world—very complicated indeed.

Consider, finally, the personal computer. Most share a common set of features: an Intel or Intel-compatible microprocessor, random access memory (RAM), a Microsoft operating system, an internal hard drive, a floppy disk drive, a CD drive, a keyboard, a monitor, a mouse, a modem, and so on. We call this set of features the dominant design for personal computers (a **dominant design** refers to a common set of features or design characteristics). Embedded in this design are several technical standards (see Figure 7.1). For example, there is the Wintel technical standard based on an Intel microprocessor and a Microsoft operating system. Microsoft and Intel own that standard, which is central to the personal computer. Developers of software applications, component parts, and peripherals such as printers adhere to this standard when developing their own products because this guarantees that their products will work well with a personal computer based on the Wintel standard. Another technical standard for connecting peripherals to the PC is the Universal Serial Bus (or USB), established by an industry standards-setting board. No one owns it; the standard is in the public domain. A third technical standard is for communication between a PC and the Internet via a modem. Known as TCP/IP, this standard was also

FIGURE 7.1

Technical Standards for Personal Computers

set by an industry association and is in the public domain. Thus, as with many other products, the PC is actually based on several technical standards. It is also important to note that when a company owns a standard, as Microsoft and Intel do with the Wintel standard, it may be a source of competitive advantage and high profitability.

Benefits of Standards

Standards emerge because there are economic benefits associated with them. First, having a technical standard helps to guarantee *compatibility* between products and their complements, other products used with them. For example, containers are used with railcars, trucks, and ships, and PCs are used with software applications. Compatibility has tangible economic benefits of reducing the costs associated with making sure that products work well with each other.

Second, having a standard can help to *reduce confusion* in the minds of consumers. A few years ago, several consumer electronics companies were vying with each other to produce and market the first DVD players, and they were championing different variants of the basic DVD technology—different standards—that were incompatible with each other; a DVD disc designed to run on a DVD player made by Toshiba would not run on a player made by Sony, and vice versa. The companies feared that selling these incompatible versions of the same technology would produce confusion in the minds of consumers, who would not know which version to purchase and might decide to wait and see which technology ultimately dominated the marketplace. With lack of demand, the technology might fail to gain traction in the marketplace and would not be successful. To avoid this possibility, the developers of DVD equipment established a standard-setting body for the industry, the DVD Forum, which established a common technical standard for DVD players and discs that all companies adhered to. The result was that when DVDs were introduced, there was a common standard and no confusion in consumers' minds. This helped to boost demand for DVD players, making this one of the fastest-selling technologies of the late 1990s and early 2000s. First introduced in 1997, by 2001 some 13 million DVD players were sold in the United States, and they are now in one in four homes in the country.[5] However, so far the DVD Forum has not been able to agree on a common standard for the next version of DVDs, DVD recorders., which is slowing diffusion and adoption of the technology (see Strategy in Action 7.1).

Third, the emergence of a standard can help to *reduce production costs*. Once a standard emerges, products based on that standard design can be mass-produced, enabling the manufacturers to realize substantial economies of scale and lower their cost structures. The fact that there is a central standard for PCs (the Wintel standard) means that the component parts for a PC can be mass-produced. A manufacturer of internal hard drives, for example, can mass-produce drives for Wintel PCs, enabling it to realize substantial scale economies. If there were several competing and incompatible standards, each of which required a unique type of hard drive, production runs for hard drives would be shorter, unit costs would be higher, and the cost of PCs would go up.

Fourth, the emergence of standards can help to reduce the *risks associated with supplying complementary products* and thus increase the supply for those complements. Consider the risks associated with writing software applications to run on personal computers. This is a risky proposition, requiring the investment of considerable sums of money for developing the software before a single unit is sold. Imagine what would occur if there were ten different operating systems in use for PCs, each with only 10 percent of the market, rather than the current situation, where 95 percent of the world's PCs adhere to the Wintel standard. Software developers would be faced with the need to write ten different versions of the same software applica-

Strategy in Action   **7.1**

Where Is the Standard for DVD Recorders?

A few years ago, the 200-member DVD Forum achieved something of a coup when it managed to broker an agreement among some of its most important members on a common set of standards for DVD players. This common standard reduced consumer confusion and helped to propel DVD players into a mass market phenomenon, now replacing analog VHS video players in many living rooms. Nevertheless, current technology lacks one attribute of VHS technology: it cannot record. It's not that a technology for making DVD recorders does not exist; in fact, several do, and therein lies the problem. The DVD Forum has been unable to get some of its most powerful members to agree on a common technical standard for DVD recorders, primarily because different companies want to see their variant of the technology become the industry standard.

There are at least three versions of DVD recorders now on offer: Hewlett Packard is pushing one format, Sony and Philips are sponsoring another, and Matsushita yet another. And most important, DVD discs recorded using one format may not play on widely used DVD players or on computers that use another recording format.

First introduced in 1999, by 2001 some 350,000 DVD recorders had sold, many of them incorporated into new personal computers. But industry observers feel that sales could have been much higher had there been harmonization of standards. By way of comparison, some 40 million CD recorders were sold in 2001, making CD recording technology solidly mainstream (DVDs can hold ten times

as many data as CDs and are thus better suited to recording video). One reason for the slow takeup of DVD recorders has been the confusion over standards, and it's not just consumers who are confused. Many retailers are hesitant about stocking the technology until the battle over standards is resolved.

Another reason for the slow market growth has been the high price of DVD recorders. As of mid-2002, a stand-alone DVD recorder still cost around $1,500, putting the technology out of the reach of most people. However, DVD-recordable drives built into personal computers had fallen to $400 per unit, bringing them close to the price point at which a mass market develops. For the price to fall lower, producers need to be able to manufacture in high volume and realize significant scale economies. But here lies the catch: to generate significant demand to support mass production and bring prices down, it may first be necessary to harmonize standards and reduce consumer confusion—and that is something that the producers currently seem unwilling to do. For the time being, the different companies are continuing to push their own proprietary standard in the hope that they establish it as the leading standard in the industry and reap the associated gains.

Sources: E. Ramstad, "DVD Makers Battle over Tech Standard," *Wall Street Journal,* November 9, 2000, p. B6. B. Dudley, "Dueling DVD-Recorder Formats Make Playing Discs a Challenge," *Seattle Times,* January 9, 2002, p. C3.

tion, each for a much smaller market segment. This would change the economics of software development, increase its risks, and reduce potential profitability. Moreover, because of their higher cost structure and fewer economies of scale, the price of software programs would increase.

Thus, although many people complain about the consequences of Microsoft's near monopoly of PC operating systems, that monopoly does have at least one good effect: it substantially reduces the risks facing the makers of complementary products and the costs of those products. In fact, standards lead to both low-cost and differentiation advantages for individual companies and can help raise the level of industry profitability.

Establishment of Standards

Standards emerge in an industry in three main ways. First, recognizing the benefits of establishing a standard, companies in an industry might lobby the government to mandate an industry standard. In the United States, for example, the Federal

Communication Commission (FCC), after detailed discussions with broadcasters and consumer electronics companies, has mandated a single technical standard for digital television broadcast (DTV) and is requiring broadcasters to have capabilities in place for broadcasting digital signals based on this standard by 2006. The FCC took this step because it believed that without government action to set the standard, the rollout of DTV would be very slow. With a standard set by the government, consumer electronics companies can have greater confidence that a market will emerge, and this should encourage them to develop DTV products.

Second, technical standards are often set by cooperation among businesses, without government help, often through the medium of an industry forum, such as the DVD Forum. Companies cooperate in this way when they decide that competition among them to create a standard might be harmful because of the uncertainty that it would create in the minds of consumers.

When standards are set by the government or an industry association, they fall into the **public domain,** meaning that anyone can freely incorporate the knowledge and technology on which the standard is based into their products. For example, no one owns the QWERTY format, and therefore no one company can profit from it directly. Similarly, the language that underlies the presentation of text and graphics on the Web, hypertext markup language (HTML), is in the public domain; it is free for all to use. The same is true for TCP/IP, the communications standard used for transmitting data on the Internet.

Often, however, the industry standard is selected competitively by the purchasing patterns of customers in the marketplace—that is, by *market demand*. In this case, the strategy and business model a company has developed for promoting its technological standard is of critical importance because ownership of an industry standard that is protected from imitation by patents and copyrights is a valuable asset—a source of sustained competitive advantage and superior profitability. Microsoft and Intel, for example, both owe their competitive advantage to their ownership of Format wars, which exist between two or more companies competing against each other to get their designs adopted as the industry standard, are common in high-tech industries because of the high stakes. The Wintel standard became the dominant standard for PCs only after Microsoft and Intel won format wars against Apple Computer's proprietary system and later against IBM's OS/2 operating system. Microsoft and Real Networks are currently competing head to head in a format war to establish rival technologies—Windows Media Player and RealPlayer—as the standard for streaming video and audio technology on the Web. The *Opening Case* tells how Microsoft and Intel are also engaged in a format war in the wireless business as they try to get their standard for 3G wireless phones established as the industry standard.

Network Effects, Positive Feedback, and Lockout

There has been a growing realization that when standards are set by competition between companies promoting different formats, network effects are a primary determinant of how standards are established.[6] **Network effects** arise in industries where the size of the "network" of *complementary* products is a primary determinant of demand for an industry's product. For example, the demand for automobiles early in the twentieth century was an increasing function of the *network* of paved roads and gas stations. Similarly, the demand for telephones is an increasing function of the number of other numbers that can be called with that phone; that is, of the size of the telephone network (i.e., the telephone network is the complementary product). When the first telephone service was introduced in New York City, only a hundred numbers could be called. The network was very small because of the limited number of wires and telephone switches, which made the telephone a relatively useless piece of equipment. As more and more people got telephones and as the network of wires and switches expanded, the value of a telephone connection increased. This led to an increase in demand for telephone lines, which further increased the value of owning a telephone, setting up a positive feedback loop. The same type of positive feedback loop is now at work in the Internet.

To understand why network effects are important in the establishment of standards, consider the classic example of a format war: the battle between Sony and Matsushita to establish their respective technology for videocassette recorders (VCRs) as the standard in the marketplace. Sony was first to market with its Betamax technology, followed by Matsushita with its VHS technology. Both companies sold VCR recorder-players, and movie studios issued films prerecorded on VCR tapes for rental to consumers. Initially, all tapes were issued in Betamax format to play on Sony's machine. Sony *did not* license its Betamax technology, preferring to make all of the player-recorders itself. When Matsushita entered the market, it realized that to make its VHS format players valuable to consumers, it would have to encourage movie studios to issue movies for rental on VHS tapes. The only way to do that, Matsushita's managers reasoned, was to increase the installed base of VHS players as rapidly as possible. They believed that the greater the installed base of VHS players, the greater the incentive would be for movie studios to issue movies for rental on VHS format tapes. The more prerecorded VHS tapes were available for rental, the greater the value of a VHS player became to consumers, and therefore, the greater the demand would be VHS players (see Figure 7.2). Matsushita wanted to exploit a positive feedback loop.

To do this, Matsushita chose a licensing strategy under which any consumer electronics company was allowed to manufacture VHS format players under license. The strategy worked. A large number of companies signed on to manufacture VHS players, and soon far more VHS players were available for purchase in stores than Betamax players. As sales of VHS players started to grow, movie studios issued more films for rental in VHS format, and this stoked demand. Before long, it was clear to anyone who walked into a video rental store that there were more and more VHS tapes available for rent and fewer and fewer Betamax tapes. This served to reinforce the positive feedback loop, and ultimately Sony's Betamax technology was shut out of the market. The pivotal difference between the two companies was strategy: Matsushita chose a licensing strategy, and Sony did not. As a result, Matsushita's VHS technology became the de facto standard for VCRs, while Sony's Betamax technology was locked out.

FIGURE 7.2

Positive Feedback in the Market for VCRs

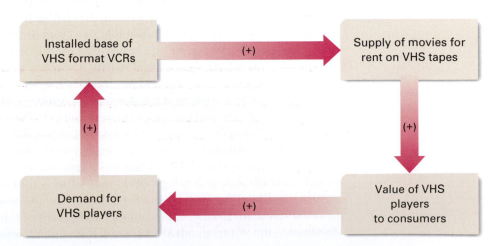

The general principle that emerges from this example is that when two or more companies are competing with each other to get their technology adopted as a standard in an industry, and when network effects and positive feedback loops are important, the company that wins the format war will be the one whose strategy best exploits positive feedback loops. It turns out that this is a very important strategic principle in many high-technology industries, particularly computer hardware, software, telecommunications, and consumer electronics. Microsoft is where it is today because it exploited a positive feedback loop. So did Dolby (see Strategy in Action 7.2).

An important implication of the positive feedback process is that as the market settles on a standard, companies promoting alternative standards can become **locked out** of the market when consumers are unwilling to bear the switching costs required for them to abandon the established standard and adopt the new standard. In this context, **switching costs** are the costs that consumers must bear to switch from a product based on one technological standard to a product based on another.

For illustration, imagine that a company developed an operating system for personal computers that was both faster and more stable (crashed less) than the current standard in the marketplace, Microsoft Windows. Would this company be able to gain significant market share from Microsoft? Only with great difficulty. Consumers buy personal computers not for their operating system but for the applications that run on that system. A new operating system would initially have a very small installed base, so few developers would be willing to take the risks in writing word processing programs, spreadsheets, games, and other applications for that operating system. Because there would be very few applications available, consumers who did make the switch would have to bear the switching costs associated with giving up some of their applications—something that they might be unwilling to do. Moreover, even if applications were available for the new operating system, consumers would have to bear the costs of purchasing those applications, another source of switching costs. In addition, they would have to bear the costs associated with learning to use the new operating system, yet another source of switching costs. Thus, many consumers would be unwilling to switch even if the new operating system performed better than Windows, and the company promoting the new operating system would be locked out of the market.

Consumers *will* bear switching costs if the benefits of adopting the new technology outweigh the costs of switching. For example, in the late 1980s and early 1990s, millions of people switched from analog record players to digital CD players even though the switching costs were significant: they had to purchase the new player technology, and many people purchased duplicate copies of their favorite music recordings. They nevertheless made the switch because for many people, the perceived benefit—the incredibly better sound quality associated with CDs—outweighed the costs of switching.

As this process started to get under way, a positive feedback started to develop, with the growing installed base of CD players leading to an increase in the number of music recordings issued on CDs, as opposed to or in addition to vinyl records. Past some point, the installed base of CD players got so big that music companies started to issue recordings only on CDs. Once this happened, even those who did not want to switch to the new technology were required to if they wished to purchase new music recordings. The industry standard had shifted: the new technology had locked in as the standard, and the old technology was locked out. It follows that despite its dominance, the Wintel standard for personal computers could one day be superseded

Strategy in Action

7.2

How Dolby Became the Standard in Sound Technology

Inventor Ray Dolby's name has become synonymous with superior sound in homes, movie theaters, and recording studios. The technology produced by his company, Dolby Laboratories, is part of nearly every music cassette and cassette recorder, prerecorded videotape, and, most recently, DVD movie disc and player. Since 1976, close to 1 billion audio products that use Dolby's technology have been sold worldwide. More than 29,000 movie theaters now show films in Dolby Digital Surround Sound, and some 10 million Dolby Digital home theater receivers have been sold since 1999. Dolby technology has become the industry standard for high-quality sound in the music and film industry. Any company that wants to promote its products as having superior technology licenses sound technology from Dolby. How did Dolby build this technology franchise?

The story goes back to 1965 when Dolby Laboratories was founded in London by Ray Dolby (the company's headquarters moved to San Francisco in 1976). Dolby, who had a Ph.D in physics from Cambridge University in England, had invented a technology for reducing the background hiss in professional tape recording without compromising the quality of the material being recorded. Dolby manufactured the sound systems incorporating his technology, but sales to professional recording studios were initially slow. Then in 1968 Dolby had a big break. He met Henry Kloss, whose company, KLH, was a highly regarded American producer of audio equipment (record players and tape decks) for the consumer market. Dolby reached an agreement to license his noise-reduction technology to KLH, and soon other manufacturers of consumer equipment started to approach Dolby to license the technology. Dolby briefly considered manufacturing record players and tape decks for the consumer market, but as he later commented, "I knew that if we entered that market and tried to make something like a cassette deck, we would be in competition with any licensee that we took on. . . . So we had to stay out of manufacturing in that area in order to license in that area."

Dolby adopted a licensing business model and then had to determine what licensing fee to charge. He knew his technology was valuable, but he also understood that charging a high licensing fee would encourage manufacturers to invest in developing their own noise-reduction technology. He decided to charge a modest fee to reduce the incentive that manufacturers would have to develop

their own technology. Then there was the question of which companies to license to. Dolby wanted the Dolby name associated with superior sound, so he needed to make sure that licensees adhered to quality standards. Therefore, the company set up a formal quality control program for its licensees' products. Licensees have to agree to have their products tested by Dolby, and the licensing agreement states that they cannot sell products that do not pass Dolby's quality tests. By preventing products with substandard performance from reaching the market, Dolby has maintained the quality image of products featuring Dolby technology and trademarks. Today, Dolby Laboratories tests samples of hundreds of licensed products every year under this program. By making sure that the Dolby name is associated with superior sound quality, Dolby's quality assurance strategy has increased the power of the Dolby brand, making it very valuable to license.

Another key aspect of Dolby's strategy was born in 1970 when Dolby began to promote the idea of releasing prerecorded cassettes encoded with Dolby noise-reduction technology so that they would have low noise when played on players equipped with Dolby noise-reduction technology. Dolby decided to license the technology on prerecorded tapes for free, instead collecting licensing fees just from the sales of tape players that used Dolby technology. This strategy was hugely successful and set up a positive feedback loop that helped to make Dolby technology ubiquitous. Growing sales of prerecorded tapes encoded with Dolby technology created a demand for players that contained Dolby technology, and as the installed base of players with Dolby technology grew, the proportion of prerecorded tapes that were encoded with Dolby technology surged, further boosting demand for players incorporating Dolby technology. By the mid-1970s, virtually all prerecorded tapes were encoded with Dolby noise-reduction technology. This strategy remains in effect today for all media recorded with Dolby technology and encompasses not only videocassettes but video games and DVD releases encoded with Dolby Surround or Dolby Digital.

As a result of its licensing and quality assurance strategies, Dolby has become the standard for high-quality sound in the music and film industries. Although the company is small—its revenues were around $125 million in 2001—its influence is large. It continues to push the boundaries of sound-reduction technology (it has been a leader in digital sound since the mid-1980s) and has successfully extended its noise-reduction franchise, first into films, then into DVD and video game technology, and most recently onto the Web, where it has licensed its digital technology to a wide range of media companies for digital music delivery and digital audio players, such as those built into personal computers and devices like Compaq's popular iPAQ hand-held computer.

Sources: M. Snider, "Ray Dolby, Audio Inventor," *USA Today,* December 28, 2000, p. D3. D. Dritas, "Dealerscope Hall of Fame: Ray Dolby," *Dealerscope* (January 2002): 74–76. J. Pinkerton, "At Dolby Laboratories: A Clean Audio Pipe," *Dealerscope* (December 2000): 33–34. Company history archived at www.dolby.com.

if a competitor finds a way of providing sufficient benefits that enough consumers are willing to bear the switching costs associated with moving to a new operating system.

Strategies for Winning a Format War

From the perspective of a company pioneering a new technological standard in a marketplace where network effects and positive feedback loops operate, the key question becomes, "What strategy should we pursue to establish our format as the dominant one?"

The various strategies that companies should adopt to win format wars revolve around *finding ways to make network effects work in their favor and against their competitors.* Winning a format war requires a company to build the installed base for its standard as rapidly as possible, thereby leveraging the positive feedback loop, inducing consumers to bear switching costs, and ultimately locking the market into its technology. It requires the company to jump-start and then accelerate demand for its technological standard or format such that it becomes established as quickly as possible as the industry standard, thereby locking out competing formats. There are a number of key strategies and tactics that can be adopted to try and achieve this.[7]

Ensure a Supply of Complements

It is important for the company to make sure that in addition to the product itself, there is an adequate supply of complements. For example, no one will buy the Sony PlayStation II unless there is an adequate supply of games to run on that machine. And no one will purchase a Palm hand-held computer unless there are enough software applications to run on it. Companies normally take two steps to ensure an adequate supply of complements.

First, they may diversify into the production of complements and seed the market with sufficient supply to help jump-start demand for their format. Before Sony produced the original PlayStation in the early 1990s, it established its own in-house unit to produce video games for the PlayStation. When it launched the PlayStation, Sony also simultaneously issued sixteen games to run on the machine, giving consumers a reason to purchase the format. Second, they may create incentives or make it easy for independent companies to produce complements. Sony also licensed the right to produce games to a number of independent game developers, charged the developers a lower royalty rate than they had to pay to competitors such as Nintendo and Sega, and provided them with software tools that made it easier for them to develop the games. Thus, the launch of the Sony PlayStation was accompanied by the simultaneous launch of thirty or so games, which quickly helped to stimulate demand for the machine.

Leverage Killer Applications

Killer applications are applications or uses of a new technology or product that are so compelling that they persuade customers to adopt the new format or technology in droves, thereby "killing" demand for competing formats. Killer applications often help to jump-start demand for the new standard. For example, in the late 1990s, hand-held computers based on the Palm operating system became the dominant format in the market for personal digital assistants (PDA). The killer applications that drove adoption of the Palm format were the personal information management functions and a pen-based input medium (based on **Graffiti**) that Palm bundled with its original PalmPilot, which it introduced in 1996. There had been PDAs before the PalmPilot, including Apple Computer's ill-fated Newton, but it was the applications and ease of use of the PalmPilot that persuaded many consumers to enter this market. Within eighteen months of its initial launch, more than 1 million PalmPilots had been launched, making for a faster demand ramp-up than the first cell phones and pagers. Similarly, the killer applications that induced consumers to sign up to online services such as AOL were email, chatroom, and the ability to browse the Web.

Ideally, the company promoting a technological standard will want to develop the killer applications itself—that is, develop the appropriate complementary products—as Palm did with the PalmPilot. However, it may also be able to leverage the applications that others develop. For example, the early sales of the IBM PC following its 1981 introduction were driven primarily by IBM's decision to license two important software programs for the PC, VisiCalc (a spreadsheet program) and Easy Writer (a word processing program), both developed by independent companies. IBM saw that they were driving rapid adoption of rival personal computers, such as the Apple II, so it quickly licensed them, produced versions that would run on the IBM PC, and sold them as complements to the IBM PC, a strategy that was to prove very successful.

Aggressively Price and Market   A common tactic to jump-start demand is to adopt a **razor and blade strategy:** pricing the product (razor) low in order to stimulate demand and increase the installed base, and then trying to make high profits on the sale of complements (razor blades), which are priced relatively high. This strategy owes its name to the fact that it was pioneered by Gillette to sell its razors and razor blades. Many other companies have followed this strategy—for example, Hewlett Packard typically sells its printers at cost but makes significant profits on the subsequent sale of its replacement cartridges. In this case, the printer is the "razor," and it is priced low to stimulate demand and induce consumers to switch from their existing printer, while the cartridges are the "blades," which are priced high to make profits. The inkjet printer represents a proprietary technological format because only Hewlett Packard cartridges can be used with the printers, and not cartridges designed for competing inkjet printers, such as those sold by Canon. A similar strategy is used in the video game industry: manufacturers price video game consoles at cost to induce consumers to adopt their technology, while making profits on the royalties they receive from the sales of games that run on their system.

Aggressive marketing is also a key factor in jump-starting demand to get an early lead in installed base. Substantial up-front marketing and point-of-sales promotion techniques are often used to try to get potential early adopters to bear the switching costs associated with adopting the format. If these efforts are successful, they can be the start of a positive feedback loop. Again, the Sony PlayStation provides a good example. Sony co-linked the introduction of the PlayStation with nationwide television advertising aimed at its primary demographic (eighteen to thirty-four-year-olds) and in-store displays that allowed potential buyers to play games on the machine before making a purchase. More recently, Microsoft earmarked $500 million for marketing its new X-Box in 2002. Successful marketing can set the ball rolling and create a positive feedback loop.

Cooperate with Competitors

Companies have been close to simultaneously introducing competing and incompatible technological standards a number of times. A good example is the compact disc. Initially four companies—Sony, Philips, JVC, and Telefunken—were developing CD players using different variations of the underlying laser technology. If this situation had persisted, they might have ultimately introduced incompatible technologies into the marketplace, so a CD made for a Philips CD player would not play on a Sony CD player. Understanding that the near-simultaneous introduction of such incompatible technologies can create significant confusion among consumers and often leads them to delay their purchases, Sony and Philips decided to join forces with each other and cooperate on developing the technology. Sony contributed its error correction technology, and Philips contributed its laser technology. The result of this cooperation was that momentum among other players in the industry shifted toward the Sony-Philips alliances; JVC and Telefunken were left with little support. Most important, recording labels announced that they would support the Sony-Philips format but not the Telefunken or JVC format. Telefunken and JVC subsequently decided to abandon their efforts to develop CD technology. The cooperation between Sony and Philips was important because it reduced confusion in the industry and allowed a single format to rise to the fore, which speeded up adoption of the technology. The cooperation was a win-win situation for both Philips and Sony, which eliminated the competitors and were able to share in the success of the format.

License the Format

Another strategy often adopted is to license the format to other enterprises so that they can produce products based on it. The company that pioneered the format gains from the licensing fees that flow back to it and from the enlarged supply of the product, which can stimulate demand and help accelerate market adoption. This was the strategy that Matsushita adopted with its VHS format for the videocassette recorder. In addition to producing VCRs at its own factory in Osaka, Matsushita let a number of other companies produce VHS format players under license (Sony decided not to license its competing Betamax format and produced all Betamax format players itself), and so VHS players were more widely available. More people purchased VHS players, which created an incentive for film companies to issue more films on VHS tapes (as opposed to Betamax tapes), which further increased demand for VHS players, and hence helped Matsushita to lock in VHS as the dominant format in the marketplace. Sony, ironically the first to market, saw its position marginalized by the reduced supply of the critical complement, prerecorded films, and ultimately withdrew Betamax players from the consumer marketplace.

Dolby, we saw in Strategy in Action 7.2, adopted a similar licensing strategy to get its noise-reduction technology adopted as the technological standard in the music and film industries. By charging a modest licensing fee for use of the technology in recording equipment and forgoing licensing fees on media recorded using Dolby technology, Dolby deliberately sought to reduce the financial incentive that potential competitors might have to develop their own, possibly superior, technology. Dolby calculated that its long-run profitability would be maximized by adopting a licensing strategy that limited the incentive of competitors to enter the market (this can be thought of as an example of limit pricing; see Chapter 6).

The correct strategy to pursue in a particular scenario requires that the company consider all of these different strategies and tactics and pursue those that seem most appropriate given the competitive circumstances prevailing in the industry and the likely strategy of rivals. Although there is no one best mix of strategies and tactics, of critical importance is keeping the goal of rapidly increasing the installed base of products based on its standard at the front of its mind. By helping to jump-start demand for its format, a company can induce consumers to bear the switching costs associated with adopting its technology and leverage any positive feedback process that might exist. Also important is not pursuing strategies that have the opposite effect. For example, pricing high to capture profits from early adopters, who tend not to be as price sensitive as later adopters, can have the unfortunate effect of slowing demand growth and letting a more aggressive competitor pick up share and establish its format as the industry standard.

Costs in High-Technology Industries

In many high-tech industries, the fixed costs of developing the product are very high, but the costs of producing one extra unit of the product are very low. This is most obvious in the case of software. For example, it reportedly cost Microsoft $1 billion to develop Windows XP, the latest version of its Windows operating system, but the costs of producing one more copy of Windows XP is virtually zero. Once Windows XP was completed, Microsoft produced master disks that it sent out to PC manufacturers, such as Dell Computer, which then loaded a copy of Windows XP onto every PC it sells. The cost to Microsoft was effectively zero, and yet it receives a significant licensing fee for each copy of Windows XP installed on a PC.[8] For Microsoft, the *marginal cost* of making one more copy of Windows XP is close to zero, although the *fixed costs* of developing the product are $1 billion.

Many other high-technology products have similar cost economics: very high fixed costs and very low marginal costs. Most software products share these features, although if the software is sold through stores, the costs of packaging and distribution will raise the marginal costs, and if it is sold by a sales force direct to end users, this too will raise the marginal costs. Many consumer electronics products have the same basic economics. The fixed costs of developing a DVD player or a video game console can be very expensive, but the costs of producing an incremental unit are very low. The costs of developing a new drug, such as Viagra, can run to over $500 million, but the marginal costs of producing each additional pill is at most a few cents.

Comparative Cost Economics

To grasp why this cost structure is strategically important, it must be understood that in many industries, marginal costs *rise* as a company tries to expand output (economist call this the *law of diminishing returns*). To produce more of a good, a company has to hire more labor and invest in more plant and machinery. At *the margin,* the additional resources used are not as productive, so this leads to increasing marginal costs. However, the law of diminishing returns often does not apply in many high-tech settings, such as the production of software or sending one more bit of data down a digital telecommunications network.

Consider two companies, α and β (see Figure 7.3). Company α is a conventional producer and faces diminishing returns, so as it tries to expand output, its marginal costs rise. Company β is a high-tech producer, and its marginal costs do not rise at all as output is increased. Note that in Figure 7.3, Company β's marginal cost curve is drawn as a straight line near to the horizontal axis, implying that marginal costs are close to zero and do not vary with output, whereas Company α's marginal costs rise as output is expanded, illustrating diminishing returns. Company β's flat and low marginal cost curve means that its average cost curve will fall continuously over all ranges of output as it spreads its fixed costs out over greater volume. In contrast, the

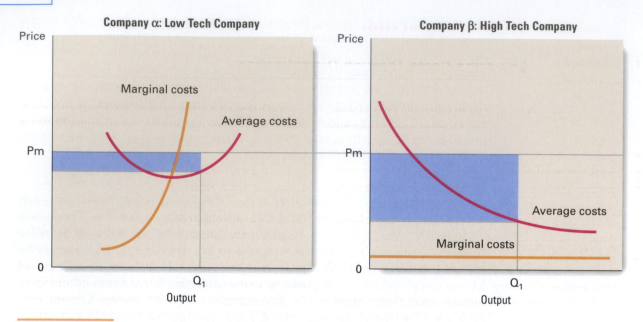

FIGURE 7.3

Cost Structures in High-Technology Industries

rising marginal costs encountered by Company α mean that its average cost curve is the **U**-shaped curve familiar from basic economics texts. For simplicity, assume that both companies sell their product at the same price, P_m, and both sell exactly the same quantity of output, $0 - Q_1$. You will see from Figure 7.3 that at an output of Q_1, Company β has much lower average costs than Company α and as a consequence is making far more profit (profit is the shaded area in Figure 7.3).

Strategic Significance   If a company can shift from a cost structure where it encounters increasing marginal costs to one where fixed costs may be high but marginal costs are much lower, its profitability may increase. In the consumer electronics industry, such a shift has been playing out for two decades. Music recordings used to be based on analog technology where marginal costs rose as output expanded due to diminishing returns (as in the case of Company α in Figure 7.3). Since the 1980s, digital systems such as CD players have replaced analog systems. Digital systems are software based, and this implies much lower marginal costs of producing one more copy of a recording. As a result, the music labels have been able to lower prices, expand demand, and see their profitability increase (their production system that has more in common with Company β in Figure 7.3).

This process is still unfolding. The latest technology for making copies of music recordings is based on distribution over the Internet (for example, by downloading onto an MP3 player). Here, the marginal costs of making one more copy of a recording are lower still. In fact, they are close to zero and do not increase with output. The only problem is that the low costs of copying and distributing music recordings have created a major copyright problem that the major music labels have yet to solve (we discuss this in more detail shortly when we consider intellectual property rights). The same shift is now beginning to affect other industries. Some companies are building their strategies around trying to exploit and profit from this shift. For an example, Strategy in Action 7.3 looks at SonoSite.

Strategy in Action   7.3

Lowering Costs Through Digitalization

The ultrasound unit has been an important piece of diagnostic equipment in hospitals for some time. Ultrasound units use the physics of sound to produce images of soft tissues in the human body. They can produce detailed three-dimensional color images of organs and, by using contrast agents, track the flow of fluids through an organ. A cardiologist, for example, can use an ultrasound in combination with contrast agents injected into the bloodstream to track the flow of blood through a beating heart. In additional to the visual diagnosis, ultrasound also produces an array of quantitative diagnostic information of great value to physicians.

Modern ultrasound units are sophisticated instruments that cost around $250,000 to $300,000 each for a top-line model. They are fairly bulky instruments, weighing some 300 pounds, and are wheeled around hospitals on carts.

A few years back, a group of researchers at ATL, one of the leading ultrasound companies, came up with an idea for reducing the size and cost of a basic unit. They theorized that it might be possible to replace up to 80 percent of the solid circuits in an ultrasound unit with software, in the process significantly shrinking the size and reducing the weight of machines and thereby producing portable ultrasound units. Moreover, by digitalizing much of the ultrasound, replacing hardware with software, they could considerably drive down the marginal costs of making additional units, allowing them to make a good profit at much lower price points.

They reasoned that a portable and inexpensive ultrasound unit would find market opportunities in totally new niches. For example, a small, inexpensive ultrasound unit could be placed in an ambulance or carried into battle by an army medic, or purchased by family physicians for use in their offices. Although they realized that it would be some time, perhaps decades, before such small, inexpensive machines could attain the image quality and diagnostic sophistication of top-of-the-line machines, they saw the opportunity in terms of creating market niches that previously could not be served by ultrasound companies due to the high costs and bulk of the product.

The researchers ultimately became a project team within ATL and were then spun out of ATL as an entirely new company, SonoSite. In late 1999, they introduced their first portable product, weighing just six pounds and costing around $25,000. SonoSite targeted niches that full-sized ultrasound products could not reach: ambulatory care and foreign markets that could not afford the more expensive equipment. In 2001, the company sold $46 million worth of its product. In the long run, SonoSite plans to build more features and greater image quality into the small hand-held machines, primarily by improving the software. This could allow the units to penetrate U.S. hospital markets that currently purchase the established technology, much as client-server systems based on PC technology came to replace mainframes for some functions in business corporations.

Sources: Interviews by Charles W. L. Hill. SonoSite 10K for 2001.

Another implication of its cost structure is that when a high-tech company faces high fixed costs and low marginal costs, its strategy should emphasize the low-cost option: deliberately drive prices down to drive volume up. Look again at Figure 7.3 and you will see that *the high-tech company's average costs fall rapidly as output expands.* This implies that prices can be reduced to stimulate demand, and so long as prices fall less rapidly than average costs, per unit profit margins will expand as prices fall. This is a consequence of the fact that the firm's marginal costs are low and do not rise with output. This strategy of pricing low to drive volume and reap wider profit margins is central to the business model of some very successful high-technology companies, including Microsoft. When Microsoft founder Bill Gates was called into a U.S. Senate hearing during the Microsoft antitrust investigation in 2000, he explained to the bemused senators that Microsoft did not behave like a classic monopolist, raising prices and restricting output to maximize profits. Rather, he said, Microsoft cut prices to stimulate sales and thus increase its profit margins. Gates claimed the strategy was good for consumers—they got cheaper software—and good for Microsoft's profit margins. It was clear from the questioning that the senators had trouble believing this explanation, but for Gates and his company, it has been a central aspect of their strategy since the early 1980s.

Managing Intellectual Property Rights

Ownership of a technology can be a source of sustained competitive advantage and superior profitability, particularly when the company owns a technology that is the standard in an industry, such as Microsoft and Intel's Wintel standard for personal computers and Dolby's ownership of the standard for noise-reduction technology in the music and film recording industries. Even if a technology is not standard but is valued by a sufficient numbers of consumers, ownership of that technology can still be very profitable. Apple's current personal computer technology is by no means the standard in the marketplace, much as Apple would like it to be. In fact, the company's iMac technology accounts for less than 10 percent of the personal computers sold every year. But that small slice of a very large market is still a valuable niche for Apple.

Intellectual Property Rights

Because new technology is the product of intellectual and creative effort, we call it intellectual property. The term **intellectual property** refers to the product of any intellectual and creative effort and includes not only new technology but also a wide range of intellectual creations, including music, films, books, and graphic art. As a society, we value the products of intellectual and creative activity. Intellectual property is seen as a very important driver of economic progress and social wealth.[9] But it is also often expensive, risky, and time-consuming to create intellectual property.

For example, a new drug to treat a dangerous medical condition such as cancer can take twelve to sixteen years to develop and cost $500 million. Moreover, only 20 percent of new drugs that are tested in humans actually make it to the market.[10] The remainder fail because they are found to be unsafe or ineffective. Given the costs, risks, and time involved in this activity, few companies would be willing to embark on the road required to develop a new drug and bring it to market unless they could be reasonably sure that if they were successful in developing the drug, their investment would be profitable. If the minute they introduced a successful cancer drug, their competitors produced imitations of that drug, no company would even consider making the initial investment.

To make sure that this does not happen, we grant the creators of intellectual property certain rights over their creation. These rights, which stop competitors from copying or imitating the creation for a number of years, take the legal forms of patents, copyrights, and trademarks, which all serve the same basic objective: to give individuals and companies an incentive to engage in the expensive and risky business of creating new intellectual property.

The creation of intellectual property is a central endeavor in high-technology industries, and the management of intellectual property rights has moved to center stage in many of these companies. Developing strategies to protect and enforce intellectual property rights can be an important aspect of competitive advantage. For many companies, this amounts to making sure that their patents and copyrights are respected. It is not uncommon, therefore, to see high-technology companies bringing lawsuits against their competitors for patent infringement. In general, companies often use such lawsuits not only to sanction those they suspect of violating the company's intellectual property rights, but also to signal to potential violators that the company will aggressively defend its property. Legal action alone suffices to protect intellectual property in many industries, but in others, such as software, the low costs of illegally copying and distributing intellectual property call for more creative strategies to manage intellectual property rights.

Digitalization and Piracy Rates

Protecting intellectual property has become more complicated in the past few decades because of **digitalization,** that is, the rendering of creative output in digital form. This can be done for music recordings, films, books, newspapers, magazines, and computer software. Digitalization has dramatically lowered the cost of copying and distributing digitalized intellectual property or digital media. As we have seen, the marginal cost of making one more copy of a software program is very low, and the same is true for any other intellectual property rendered in digital form. Moreover, digital media can be distributed at a very low cost (again, almost zero), for example, by distributing over the Internet. Reflecting on this, one commentator has described the Internet as a "giant out-of-control copying machine."[11] The low marginal costs of copying and distributing digital media have made it very easy to sell illegal copies of such property. In turn, this has helped to produce a high level of piracy (in this context, **piracy** refers to the theft of intellectual property).

In the software industry, estimates suggest that in 2000, some 37 percent of all software used around the world was pirated, costing software companies close to $12 billion in lost revenues. The piracy rate ranged from 94 percent in China to 24 percent in the United States. As a region, Asia had the highest piracy rate at 51 percent and North America had the lowest piracy rate at 25 percent. The piracy rate in Western Europe was 34 percent. Although North America had the lowest rate of software piracy, because of the size of the market, the loss to companies was still huge, amounting to almost $3 billion.[12] The problem of piracy is also endemic in the music industry. The International Federation of the Phonographic Industry estimates that in 2000, some 36 percent of all CDs around the globe were illegally produced and sold, costing the music recording industry some $4.1 billion in lost revenues.[13]

The scale of this problem is so large that simply resorting to legal tactics to enforce intellectual property rights has amounted to nothing more than a partial solution to the piracy problem. Many companies now build sophisticated encryption software into their digital products, which can make it more difficult for pirates to copy digital media and thereby raise the costs of stealing. But the pirates too are sophisticated and often seem to be able to find their way around encryption software. This raises the question of whether there are additional strategies that can be adopted to manage digital rights, and thereby limit piracy.

Strategies for Managing Digital Rights

One strategy is simply to recognize that while the low costs of copying and distributing digital media make some piracy inevitable, the same attributes can be used to the company's advantage. The basic strategy here represents yet another variation of the basic razor and razor blades principle: give something away for free in order to boost the sales of a complementary product. A familiar example concerns Adobe Acrobat Reader, the software program for reading documents formatted by Adobe Acrobat (i.e., PDF formatted documents). Adobe developed Adobe Acrobat to allow people to format documents in a manner that resembled a high-quality printed page and to display and distribute these documents over the Web. Moreover, Adobe documents are formatted in a read-only format, meaning that they cannot be altered by individuals nor can parts of those documents be copied and pasted to other documents. Its strategy has been to give away Adobe Acrobat Reader for free and then make money by selling its Acrobat software for formatting documents. The strategy has worked extremely well. Anyone can download a copy of Acrobat Reader from Adobe's web site. Because the marginal costs of copying and distributing this software over the Web are extremely low, the process is almost costless for both Adobe and its customers. The result is that the Acrobat Reader has diffused very rapidly and is now the dominant format for viewing high-quality documents distributed and downloaded over the Web. As the installed base of Acrobat Readers has grown, sales of Adobe Acrobat software have soared as more and more organizations and individuals realize that formatting their digital documents in Acrobat format makes sense.

Another strategy is to take advantage of the low costs of copying and distributing digital media to drive down the costs of purchasing those media, thereby reducing the incentive that consumers have to steal. When coupled with encryption software that makes piracy more difficult and vigorous legal actions to enforcement of intellectual property regulations, this can slow the piracy rate and generate incremental revenues that cost little to produce.

Several music companies are now experimenting with variants of this strategy. Roxio, a manufacturer of software for copying, or "burning," music onto CDs, has begun to partner with several music labels to develop just such a strategy.[14] In 2001, Roxio's Easy CD Creator and Toast software accounted for 70 percent of the CD burning software sold. The software is now preloaded onto most new personal computers. However, Roxio's sales growth has been hampered by opposition from music labels, which argue that Roxio's software is promoting music piracy and hurting CD sales. In response, Roxio has persuaded several music companies to start experimenting with a service that allows users to burn music onto CDs. In January 2002, Pressplay, a service backed by Sony, Universal Music, and EMI, began to allow users to download songs digitally and burn them onto CDs. Users pay $25 a month to burn twenty songs, although they can burn only two tracks from a single artist each month. This business model allows subscribers to customize a CD, which is what many do anyway when pirating CDs by burning them. However, in theory, the service saves customers money because they do not have to purchase the original CDs. Pressplay and Roxio hope that the strategy will reduce piracy rates, while generating incremental revenues that cost very little to produce due to the extremely low marginal costs of copying and distributing music in this manner.

Capturing First-Mover Advantages

In high-technology industries, companies often compete by striving to be the first to develop revolutionary new products, that is, to be a **first mover.** By definition, the first mover with regard to a revolutionary product is in a monopoly position. If the new product satisfies unmet consumer needs and demand is high, the first mover can capture significant revenues and profits. Such revenues and profits signal to potential rivals that there is money to be made by imitating the first mover. As illustrated in Figure 7.4, in the absence of strong barriers to imitation, this implies that imitators will rush into the market created by the first mover, competing away the first mover's monopoly profits and leaving all participants in the market with a much lower level of returns.

Despite imitation, some first movers have the ability to capitalize on and reap substantial **first-mover advantages**—the advantages of pioneering new technologies and products that lead to an enduring competitive advantage. Intel introduced the world's first microprocessor in 1971 and today still dominates the microprocessor

FIGURE 7.4

The Impact of
Imitation on Profits of
a First Mover

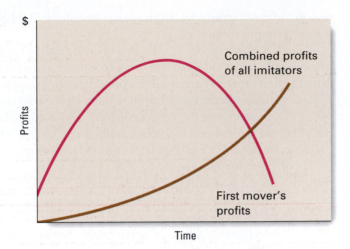

segment of the semiconductor industry. Xerox introduced the world's first photo-copier and for a long time enjoyed a leading position in the industry. Cisco intro-duced the first Internet protocol network router in 1986 and still dominates the market for that equipment today. Some first movers can reap substantial advantages from their pioneering activities that lead to an enduring competitive advantage. They can, in other words, limit or slow the rate of imitation.

But there are plenty of counterexamples suggesting that first-mover advantages might not be easy to capture and, in fact, that there might be **first mover disadvantages**—the competitive *disadvantages* associated with being first. For example, Apple Computer was the first company to introduce a hand-held computer, the Apple Newton, but the product failed; a second mover, Palm, succeeded where Apple had failed. In the market for commercial jet aircraft, DeHavilland was first to market with the Comet, but it was the second mover, Boeing, with its 707 jetliner, that went on to dominate the market.

Clearly being a first mover does not by itself guarantee success. As we shall see, the difference between innovating companies that capture first-mover advantages and those that fall victim to first-mover disadvantages in part turns on the strategy that the first mover pursues. Before considering the strategy issue, however, we need to take a closer look at the nature of first-mover advantages and disadvantages.[15]

First-Mover Advantages

There are five main sources of first-mover advantages.[16] First, the first mover has an opportunity to *exploit network effects* and positive feedback loops, locking consumers into its technology. In the VCR industry, Sony could have exploited network effects by licensing its technology, but instead the company ceded its first-mover advantage to the second mover, Matsushita.

Second, the first mover may be able to establish significant *brand loyalty,* which is expensive for later entrants to break down. Indeed, if the company is successful in this endeavor, its name may become closely associated with the entire class of products, including those produced by rivals. People still talk of "Xeroxing" when they are going to make a photocopy or "FedExing" when they are going to send a package by overnight mail.

Third, the first mover may be able to ramp up sales volume ahead of rivals and thus reap cost advantages associated with the realization of *scale economies and learning effects* (see Chapter 4). Once the first mover has these cost advantages, it can respond to new entrants by cutting prices in order to hold on to its market share and still earn significant profits.

Fourth, the first mover may be able to create *switching costs* for its customers that subsequently make it difficult for rivals to enter the market and take customers away from the first mover. Wireless service providers, for example, will give new customers a "free" wireless phone, but customers must sign a contract agreeing to pay for the phone if they terminate the service contract within a specified time period, such as a year. Because the real cost of a wireless phone may run $100 to $200, this represents a significant switching cost that later entrants have to overcome.

Finally, the first mover may be able to *accumulate valuable knowledge* related to customer needs, distribution channels, product technology, process technology, and so on. This accumulated knowledge gives it a knowledge advantage that later entrants might find difficult or expensive to match. Sharp, for example, was the first mover in the commercial manufacture of active matrix liquid crystal displays used in laptop computers. The process for manufacturing these displays is very difficult, with a high reject rate for flawed displays. Sharp has accumulated such an advantage with regard to production processes that it has been very difficult for later entrants to match it on product quality, and thus costs.

First-Mover Disadvantages

Balanced against these first-mover advantages are a number of disadvantages. First, the first mover has to bear significant *pioneering costs* that later entrants do not. The first mover has to pioneer the technology, develop distribution channels, and educate customers about the nature of the product. All of this can be expensive and time-consuming. Later entrants, by way of contrast, might be able to *free-ride* on the first mover's investments in pioneering the market and customer education.

Related to this, first movers are more prone to *make mistakes* because there are so many uncertainties in a new market. Later entrants may be able to learn from the mistakes made by first movers, improve on the product or the way in which it is sold, and come to market with a superior offering that captures significant market share from the first mover. For example, one of the reasons that the Apple Newton failed was that the handwriting software in the hand-held computer failed to recognize human handwriting. The second mover in this market, Palm, learned from Apple's error. When it introduced the PalmPilot, it used software that recognized letters written in a particular way, Graffiti, and then persuaded customers to learn this method of inputting data into the hand-held computer.

Third, first movers run the risk of *building the wrong resources and capabilities* because they are focusing on a customer set that is not going to be characteristic of the mass market. This is the *crossing the chasm* problem that we discussed in the previous chapter. You will recall that the customers in the early market—those we categorized as innovators and early adopters—have different characteristics from the first wave of the mass market, the early majority. The first mover runs the risk of gearing its resources and capabilities to the needs of innovators and early adopters and not being able to switch when the early majority enters the market. As a result, first movers run a greater risk of plunging into the chasm that separates the early market from the mass market.

Finally, the first mover may invest in *inferior or obsolete technology*. This can happen when its product innovation is based on underlying technology that is advancing rapidly. By basing its product on an early version of the technology, it may lock itself into something that rapidly becomes obsolete. In contrast, later entrants may be able to leapfrog the first mover and introduce products that are based on later versions of the underlying technology. This happened in France during the 1980s when, at the urging of the government, France Telecom introduced the world's first consumer online service, Minitel. France Telecom distributed crude terminals to consumers for free, which they could hook up to their phone line and use to browse phone directories. Other simple services were soon added, and before long the French could carry out online shopping, banking, travel, weather, and news—all years before the Web was invented. The problem was that by the standards of the Web, Minitel was very crude and inflexible, and France Telecom, as the first mover, suffered. The French were very slow to adopt personal computers and then the Internet primarily because Minitel had such a presence. As late as 1998, only a fifth of French households had a computer, compared with two-fifths in the United States, and only 2 percent of households were connected to the Internet compared to over 30 percent in the United States. As the result of a government decision, France Telecom, and indeed an entire nation, was slow to adopt a revolutionary new online medium, the Web, because they were the first to invest in a more primitive version of the technology.[17]

Strategies for Exploiting First-Mover Advantages

The task facing a first mover is how to exploit its lead in order to capitalize on first-mover advantages and build a sustainable long-term competitive advantage while simultaneously reducing the risks associated with first mover disadvantages, There are three basic strategies available: (1) develop and market the innovation itself, (2) develop and market the innovation jointly with other companies through a strategic alliance or joint venture, and (3) license the innovation to others and let them develop the market.

The optimal choice of strategy depends on the answers to three questions:

1. Does the innovating company have the *complementary assets* to exploit its innovation and capture first-mover advantages?

2. How difficult is it for imitators to copy the company's innovation? In other words, what is the *height of barriers to imitation?*

3. Are there *capable competitors* that could rapidly imitate the innovation?

Complementary Assets. **Complementary assets** are the assets required to exploit a new innovation and gain a competitive advantage.[18] Among the most important complementary assets are competitive manufacturing facilities capable of handling rapid growth in customer demand while maintaining high product quality. State-of-the-art manufacturing facilities enable the first mover to move quickly down the experience curve without encountering production bottlenecks or problems with the quality of the product. The inability to satisfy demand because of these problems, however, creates the opportunity for imitators to enter the marketplace. For example, in 1998, Immunex was the first company to introduce a revolutionary new biological treatment for rheumatoid arthritis. Sales for this product, Enbrel, ramped up very rapidly, hitting $750 million in 2001. However, Immunex had not invested in sufficient manufacturing capacity. In mid-2000, it announced that it lacked the capacity to satisfy demand and that bringing additional capacity on line would take at least two years. This manufacturing bottleneck gave the second mover in the market, Johnson & Johnson, the opportunity to expand demand for its product rapidly, which by early 2002 was outselling Enbrel. Immunex's first-mover advantage had been partly eroded because it lacked an important complementary asset, the manufacturing capability required to satisfy demand.

Complementary assets also include marketing know-how, an adequate sales force, access to distribution systems, and an after-sales service and support network. All of these assets can help an innovator build brand loyalty and help the innovator achieve market penetration more rapidly.[19] In turn, the resulting increases in volume facilitate more rapid movement down the experience curve and the attainment of a sustainable cost-based advantage due to scale economies and learning effects. One of the reasons that EMI, the first mover in the market for CT scanners, ultimately lost out to established medical equipment companies, such as GE Medical Systems, was that it lacked the marketing know-how, sales force, and distribution systems required to compete effectively in the world's largest market for medical equipment, the United States.

Developing complementary assets can be very expensive, and companies often need large infusions of capital for this purpose. That is the reason first movers often lose out to late movers that are large, successful companies, often established in other industries, with the resources to develop a presence in the new industry quickly. Microsoft and 3M exemplify companies that can move quickly to capitalize on the opportunities when other companies open up new product markets, such as compact discs or floppy disks. For example, although Netscape pioneered the market for Internet browsers with the Netscape Navigator, Microsoft's Internet Explorer ultimately dominated the market for Internet browsers.

Height of Barriers to Imitation.   Recall from Chapter 3 that **barriers to imitation** are factors that prevent rivals from imitating a company's distinctive competencies and innovations. Although ultimately any innovation can be copied, the higher the barriers are, the longer it takes for rivals to imitate, and the more time the first mover has to build an enduring competitive advantage.

Barriers to imitation give an innovator time to establish a competitive advantage and build more enduring barriers to entry in the newly created market. Patents, for example, are among the most widely used barriers to imitation. By protecting its photocopier technology with a thicket of patents, Xerox was able to delay any significant imitation of its product for seventeen years. However, patents are often easy to "invent around." For example, one study found that this happened to 60 percent of patented innovations within four years.[20] If patent protection is weak, a company might try to slow imitation by developing new products and processes in secret. The most famous example of this approach is Coca-Cola, which has kept the formula for Coke a secret for generations. But Coca-Cola's success in this regard is an exception. A study of 100 companies has estimated that proprietary information about a company's decision to develop a major new product or process is known to its rivals within about twelve to eighteen months of the original development decision.[21]

Capable Competitors.   **Capable competitors** are companies that can move quickly to imitate the pioneering company. Competitors' capability to imitate a pioneer's innovation depends primarily on two factors: (1) R&D skills and (2) access to complementary assets. In general, the greater the number of capable competitors with access to the R&D skills and complementary assets needed to imitate an innovation, the more rapid imitation is likely to be.

In this context, R&D skills refer to the ability of rivals to reverse-engineer an innovation in order to find out how it works and quickly develop a comparable product. As an example, consider the CT scanner. GE bought one of the first CT scanners produced by EMI, and its technical experts reverse-engineered it. Despite the product's technological complexity, GE developed its own version, which allowed it to imitate EMI quickly and ultimately to replace EMI as the major supplier of CT scanners.

With regard to complementary assets, the access that rivals have to marketing, sales know-how, or manufacturing capabilities is one of the key determinants of the rate of imitation. If would-be imitators lack critical complementary assets, not only do they have to imitate the innovation, they may also have to imitate the innovator's complementary assets. This is expensive, as AT&T discovered when it tried to enter the personal computer business in 1984. AT&T lacked the marketing assets (sales force and distribution systems) necessary to support personal computer products. The lack of these assets and the time it takes to build them partly explain why four years after it entered the market, AT&T had lost $2.5 billion and still had not emerged as a viable contender. It subsequently pulled out of this business.

Three Innovation Strategies. The way in which these three factors—complementary assets, height of barriers to imitation, and the capability of competitors—influence the choice of innovation strategy is summarized in Table 7.1. The competitive strategy of *developing and marketing the innovation alone* makes most sense when (1) the innovator has the complementary assets necessary to develop the innovation, (2) the barriers to imitating a new innovation are high, and (3) the number of capable competitors is limited. Complementary assets allow rapid development and promotion of the innovation. High barriers to imitation buy the innovator time to establish a competitive advantage and build enduring barriers to entry through brand loyalty or experience-based cost advantages. The fewer the capable competitors there are, the less likely it is that any one of them will succeed in circumventing barriers to imitation and quickly imitating the innovation.

The competitive strategy of *developing and marketing the innovation jointly with other companies through a strategic alliance or joint venture* makes most sense when (1) the innovator lacks complementary assets, (2) barriers to imitation are high, and (3) there are several capable competitors. In such circumstances, it makes sense to enter into an alliance with a company that already has the complementary assets—in other words, with a capable competitor. Theoretically, such an alliance should prove to be mutually beneficial, and each partner can share in high profits that neither could earn on its own. Moreover, such a strategy has the benefit of co-opting a potential rival. For example, had EMI teamed up with a capable competitor to develop the market for CT scanners, such as GE Medical Systems, instead of going it alone, the company might not only have been able to build a more enduring competitive advantage, it would also have co-opted a potentially powerful rival into its camp.

TABLE 7.1

Strategies for Profiting from Innovation

Strategy	Does the Innovator Have the Required Complementary Assets?	Likely Height of Barriers to Imitation	Number of Capable Competitors
Going it alone	Yes	High	Very few
Entering into an alliance	No	High	Moderate number
License the innovation	No	Low	Many

The third strategy, *licensing*, makes most sense when (1) the innovating company lacks the complementary assets, (2) barriers to imitation are low, and (3) there are many capable competitors. The combination of low barriers to imitation and many capable competitors makes rapid imitation almost certain. The innovator's lack of complementary assets further suggests that an imitator will soon capture the innovator's competitive advantage. Given these factors, because rapid diffusion of the innovator's technology through imitation is inevitable, the innovator can at least share in some of the benefits of this diffusion by licensing out its technology.[22] Moreover, by setting a relatively modest licensing fee, the innovator may be able to reduce the incentive that potential rivals have to develop their own competing, and possibly superior technology. This seems to have been the strategy Dolby adopted to get its technology established as the standard for noise reduction in the music and film businesses (see Strategy in Action 7.2).

Technological Paradigm Shifts

Technological paradigm shifts occur when new technologies come along that revolutionize the structure of the industry, dramatically alter the nature of competition, and require companies to adopt new strategies in order to survive. A good example of a paradigm shift that is currently unfolding is the shift from chemical to digital photography (another example of *digitalization*). For over half a century, the large incumbent enterprises in the photographic industry such as Kodak and Fuji film have generated most of their revenues from selling and processing film using traditional silver halide technology. The rise of digital photography is a huge threat to their business models. Digital cameras do not use film, the mainstay of Kodak's and Fuji's business. Moreover, these cameras are more like specialized computers than conventional cameras and are thus based on scientific knowledge that Kodak and Fuji have little knowledge of. Although both Kodak and Fuji are investing heavily in the development of digital cameras, they are facing intense competition from companies such as Sony, Canon, and Hewlett Packard, which have developed their own digital cameras, from software developers such as Adobe and Microsoft, which make the software for manipulating digital images, and from printer companies such as Hewlett Packard and Canon, which are making the printers that consumers can use to print out their own high-quality pictures at home. As digital substitution gathers speed in the photography industry, it is not clear that the traditional incumbents will be able to survive this shift; the new competitors might well rise to dominance in the new market.

If Kodak and Fuji do decline, they will not be the first large incumbents to be felled by a technological paradigm shift in their industry. In the early 1980s, the computer industry was revolutionized by the arrival of personal computer technology, which gave rise to client-server networks that replaced traditional mainframe and minicomputers for many business uses. Many incumbent companies in the mainframe era, such as Wang, Control Data, and DEC, ultimately did not survive, and even IBM went through a decade of wrenching changes and large losses before it reinvented itself as a provider of e-business solutions. In their place, new entrants such as Microsoft, Intel, Dell, and Compaq rose to dominance in this new computer industry.

Examples such as these raise four questions:

1. When do paradigm shifts occur, and how do they unfold?

2. Why do so many incumbents go into decline following a paradigm shift?

3. What strategies can incumbents adopt in order to increase the probability that they will survive a paradigm shift and emerge the other side of the market abyss created by the arrival of new technology as a profitable enterprise?

4. What strategies can new entrants into a market adopt in order to profit from a paradigm shift?

We shall answer each of these questions in the remainder of this chapter.

Paradigm Shifts and the Decline of Established Companies

Paradigm shifts appear to be more likely to occur in an industry when one, or both, of the following conditions are in place.[23] First, the established technology in the industry is mature and approaching or at its "natural limit," and second, a new "disruptive technology" has entered the marketplace and is taking root in niches that are poorly served by incumbent companies using the established technology.

The Natural Limits to Technology. Richard Foster has formalized the relationship between the performance of a technology and time in terms of what he calls the technology S-curve (see Figure 7.5).[24] This curve shows the relationship over time of *cumulative* investments in R&D and the performance (or functionality) of a given technology. Early in its evolution, R&D investments in a new technology tend to yield rapid improvements in performance as basic engineering problems are solved. After a time, diminishing returns to cumulative R&D begin to set in, the rate of improvement in performance slows, and the technology starts to approach its natural limit, where further advances are not possible. For example, one can argue that there was more improvement in the first fifty years of the commercial aerospace business following the pioneering flight by the Wright Brothers than there has been in the second fifty years. Indeed, the world's largest commercial jet aircraft, the Boeing 747, is based on a 1960s design, as is the world's fastest commercial jet aircraft, the Concorde. In commercial aerospace, therefore, we are now in the region of diminishing returns and may be approaching the natural limit to improvements in the technology of commercial aerospace.

Similarly, it can be argued that we are approaching the natural limit to technology in the performance of silicon-based semiconductor chips. Over the past two decades, the performance of semiconductor chips has been increased dramatically by packing ever more transistors onto a single small silicon chip. This process has helped to increase the power of computers, lower their cost, and shrink their size. But we are starting to approach limits to the ability to shrink the width of lines on a chip and therefore pack ever more transistors onto a single chip. The limit is imposed by the natural laws of physics. Light waves are used to help etch lines onto a chip, and one cannot etch a line that is smaller than the wavelength of light being used. Semiconductor companies are already using light with very small wavelengths, such as extreme ultraviolet, to etch lines onto a chip, but there are limits to how far this

FIGURE 7.5

The Technology S-Curve

technology can be pushed, and many believe that we will reach those limits within the decade. Does this mean that our ability to make smaller, faster, cheaper computers is coming to an end? Probably not. It is more likely that we will find another technology to replace silicon-based computing and enable us to continue building smaller, faster, cheaper computers. In fact, several exotic competing technologies are already being developed that may replace silicon-based computing. These include self-organizing molecular computers, three-dimensional microprocessor technology, quantum computing technology, and using DNA to perform computations.[25]

What does all of this have to do with paradigm shifts? According to Foster, when a technology approaches its natural limit, research attention turns to possible alternative technologies, and sooner or later one of those alternatives might be commercialized and replace the established technology. That is, the probability that a paradigm shift will occur increases. Thus, sometime in the next decade or two, another paradigm shift might shake the very foundations of the computer industry as exotic computing technology replaces silicon-based computing. If history is any guide, if and when this happens, many of the incumbents in today's computer industry will go into decline, and new enterprises will rise to dominance.

Foster pushes this point a little further, noting that initially, the contenders for the replacement technology are not as effective as the established technology in producing the attributes and features that consumers demand in a product. For example, in the early years of the twentieth century, automobiles were just starting to be produced. They were valued for their ability to move people from place to place, but so was the horse and cart (the established technology). When automobiles originally appeared, the horse and cart was still quite a bit better than the automobile at doing this (see Figure 7.6). After all, the first cars were slow, noisy, and prone to breakdown. Moreover, they needed a network of paved roads and gas stations to be really useful, and that network didn't exist, so for most applications, the horse and cart was still the preferred mode of transportation—to say nothing of the fact that it was cheaper.

However, this comparison ignored the fact that in the early twentieth century, automobile technology was at the very start of its S-curve and was about to experience dramatic improvements in performance as major engineering problems were solved (and those paved roads and gas stations were built). In contrast, after 3,000 years of continuous improvement and refinement, the horse and cart was almost definitely at the end of its technological S-curve. The result was that the rapidly improv-

FIGURE 7.6

Established and Successor Technologies

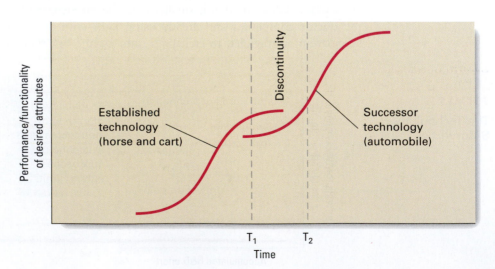

ing automobile soon replaced the horse and cart as the preferred mode of transportation. At time T_1 in Figure 7.6, the horse and cart was still superior to the automobile. By time T_2, the automobile had surpassed the horse and cart.

Foster notes that because the successor technology is initially less efficient than the established technology, established companies and their customers often make the mistake of dismissing it, only to be taken off-guard by its rapid performance improvement. A final point here is that often there is not one potential successor technologies but a swarm of potential successor technologies, only one of which might ultimately rise to the fore (see Figure 7.7). When this is the case, established companies are put at a disadvantage. Even if they recognize that a paradigm shift is imminent, they may not have the resources to invest in all the potential replacement technologies. If they invest in the wrong one, something that is easy to do given the uncertainty that surrounds the entire process, they may be locked out of subsequent development.

Disruptive Technology. Clayton Christensen has built on Foster's insights and his own research to develop a theory of disruptive technology that has become very influential in high-technology circles.[26] Christensen uses the term **disruptive technology** to refer to a new technology that gets its start away from the mainstream of a market and then, as its functionality improves over time, invades the main market. Such technologies are disruptive because they revolutionize industry structure and competition, often causing the decline of established companies. They cause a technological paradigm shift.

Christensen's greatest insight is that established companies are often aware of the new technology but do not invest in it because they listen to their customers, and their customers do not want it. Of course, this arises because the new technology is early in its development, and thus only at the beginning of the S-curve for that technology. Once the performance of the new technology improves, customers *do* want it, but by this time it is new entrants, as opposed to established companies, that have accumulated the knowledge required to bring the new technology into the mass market. Christensen supports his view by several detailed historical case studies, one of which is summarized in Strategy in Action 7.4.

FIGURE 7.7

Swarm of Successor
Technologies

Strategy in Action

7.4

Disruptive Technology in Mechanical Excavators

Excavators are used to dig out foundations for large buildings, trenches to lay large pipes for sewers and the like, and foundations and trenches for residential construction and farm work. Prior to the 1940s, the dominant technology used to manipulate the bucket on a mechanical excavator was based on a system of cables and pulleys. Although these mechanical systems could lift large buckets of earth, the excavators themselves were quite large, cumbersome, and expensive. Thus, they were rarely used to dig small trenches for house foundations, irrigation ditches for farmers, and the like. In most cases, these small trenches were dug by hand.

In the 1940s, a new technology made its appearance: hydraulics. In theory, hydraulic systems had certain advantages over the established cable and pulley systems. Most important, their energy efficiency was higher: for a given bucket size, a smaller engine would be required using a hydraulic system. However, the initial hydraulic systems also had drawbacks. The seals on hydraulic cylinders were prone to leak under high pressure, effectively limiting the size of bucket that could be lifted using hydraulics. Notwithstanding this drawback, when hydraulics first appeared, many of the incumbent firms in the mechanical excavation industry took the technology seriously enough to ask their primary customers whether they would be interested in products based on hydraulics. Since the primary customers of incumbents needed excavators with large buckets to dig out the foundations for buildings and large trenches, their reply was negative. For this customer set, the hydraulic systems of the 1940s were not reliable or powerful enough. Consequently, after consulting with their customers, these established companies in the industry made the strategic decision not to invest in hydraulics. Instead, they continued to produce excavation equipment based on the dominant cable and pulley technology.

It was left to a number of new entrants, which included J. I. Case, John Deere, J. C. Bamford, and Caterpillar, to pioneer hydraulic excavation equipment. Because of the limits on bucket size imposed by the seal problem, these companies initially focused on a poorly served niche in the market that could make use of small buckets: residential contractors and farmers. Over time, these new entrants were able to solve the engineering problems associated with weak hydraulic seals, and as they did this, they manufactured excavators with larger buckets. Ultimately, they invaded the market niches served by the old-line companies: general contractors that dug the foundations for large buildings, sewers, and so on. At this point, Case, Deere, Caterpillar, and their kin rose to dominance in the industry, while the majority of established companies from the prior era lost share. Of the thirty or so manufacturers of cable-actuated equipment in the United States in the late 1930s, only four survived to the 1950s.

Source: M. Christensen, *The Innovator's Dilemma* (Boston: Harvard Business School Press, 1997).

In addition to listening too closely to their customers, Christensen also identifies a number of other factors that make it very difficult for established companies to adopt a new disruptive technology. He notes that many established companies declined to invest in new disruptive technologies because initially they served such small market niches that it seemed unlikely that they would have an impact on the company's revenues and profits. As the new technology started to improve in functionality and invade the main market, their investment was often hindered by the fact that exploiting the new technology required a new business model totally different from the company's established model, and thus very difficult to implement.

Both of these points can be illustrated by reference to one more example: the rise of online discount stockbrokers during the 1990s such as Ameritrade and E*Trade, which made use of a new technology, the Internet, to allow individual investors to trade stocks for a very low commission fee, whereas full-service stockbrokers, such as

Merrill Lynch, where orders had to be placed through a stockbroker who earned a commission for performing the transaction, did not. (This story is told in more detail in the *Closing Case* in Chapter 5.)

Christensen also notes that a new network of suppliers and distributors typically grows up around the new entrants. Not only do established companies initially ignore disruptive technology, so do their suppliers and distributors. This creates an opportunity for new suppliers and distributors to enter the market to serve the new entrants. As the new entrants grow, so does the associated network. Ultimately, Christensen suggests, the new entrants and their network may replace not only established enterprises, but also the entire network of suppliers and distributors associated with established companies. Taken to its logical extreme, this view suggests that disruptive technologies may result in the demise of the entire network of enterprises associated with established companies in an industry.

The established companies in an industry that is being rocked by a technological paradigm shift often have to cope with internal inertia forces that limit their ability to adapt, but the new entrants do not and thereby have an advantage. They do not have to deal with an established and conservative customer set and an obsolete business model. Instead, they can focus on optimizing the new technology, improving its performance, and riding the wave of disruptive technology into new market segments until they invade the main market and challenge the established companies, by which time they may be well equipped to beat them.

Strategic Implications for Established Companies

Although Christensen has uncovered an important tendency, it is by no means written in stone that all established companies are doomed to fail when faced with disruptive technologies, as we have seen with IBM and Merrill Lynch. Established companies must meet the challenges created by the emergence of disruptive technologies.

First, having access to the knowledge about how disruptive technologies can revolutionize markets is itself a valuable strategic asset. Many of the established companies that Christensen examined failed because they took a myopic view of the new technology and asked their customers the wrong question. Instead of asking, "Are you interested in this new technology?" they should have recognized that the new technology was likely to improve rapidly over time and instead have asked, "Would you be interested in this new technology if it improves its functionality over time?" If they had done this, they may have made very different strategic decisions.

Second, it is clearly important for established enterprises to invest in newly emerging technologies that may ultimately become disruptive technologies. Companies have to hedge their bets about new technology. As we have noted, at any time, there may be a swarm of emerging technologies, any one of which might ultimately become a disruptive technology. Large, established companies that are generating significant cash flows can and often should establish and fund central R&D operations to invest in and develop such technologies. In addition, they may wish to acquire newly emerging companies that are pioneering potentially disruptive technologies or enter into alliances with them to develop the technology jointly. The strategy of acquiring companies that are developing potentially disruptive technology is one that Cisco Systems, a dominant provider of Internet network equipment, is famous for pursuing. At the heart of this strategy must be a recognition on the part of the incumbent enterprise that it is better for the company to develop disruptive technology and then cannibalize its established sales base than to have that sales base taken away by new entrants.

However, Christensen makes the very important point that even when established companies do undertake R&D investments in potentially disruptive technologies, they often fail to commercialize those technologies because of internal forces that suppress change. For example, managers in the parts of the business that are currently generating the most cash may claim that they need the greatest R&D investment to maintain their market position and may lobby top management to delay investment in a new technology. Early on in the S-curve, when it is very unclear what the long-term prospects of a new technology may be, this can be a powerful argument. The consequence, however, may be that the company fails to build a competence in the new technology and will suffer accordingly.

In addition, Christensen argues that the commercialization of new disruptive technology often requires a radically different value chain with a completely different cost structure—a new business model. For example, it may require a different manufacturing system, a different distribution system, and different pricing options and involve very different gross margins and operating margins. Christensen argues that it is almost impossible for two distinct business models to coexist within the same organization. When they try to do that, almost inevitably the established business model will suffocate the business model associated with the disruptive technology.

The solution to this problem is to separate out the disruptive technology and place it in its own autonomous operating division. For example, during the early 1980s Hewlett Packard (HP) built a very successful laser jet printer business. Then along came ink jet technology. Some in the company believed that ink jet printers would cannibalize sales of laser jets and consequently argued that HP should not produce ink jets. Fortunately for HP, senior management at the time saw ink jet technology for what it was: a potential disruptive technology. Far from not investing in it, they allocated significant R&D funds toward its commercialization. Furthermore, when the technology was ready for market introduction, they established an autonomous ink jet division at a different geographic location with its own manufacturing, marketing, and distribution activities. They accepted that the ink jet division might take sales away from the laser jet division and decided that it was better to have an HP division cannibalize the sales of another HP division than have those sales cannibalized by another company. Happily for HP, it turns out that ink jets cannibalize sales of laser jets only on the margin and that both have profitable market niches. This felicitous outcome, however, does not detract from the message of the story: if your company is developing a potentially disruptive technology, the chances of success will be enhanced if it is placed in a stand-alone product division and given its own mandate.

Strategic Implications for New Entrants

This stream of work also holds implications for new entrants. The new entrants, or attackers, have several advantages over established enterprises. Pressures to continue the existing out-of-date business model do not hamstring new entrants, which do not have to worry about product cannibalization issues. They do not have to worry about their established customer base or relationships with established suppliers and distributors. Instead, they can focus all their energies on the opportunities offered by the new disruptive technology, ride the S-curve of technology improvement, and grow rapidly with the market for that technology. This does not mean that the new entrants have no problems to solve. They may be constrained by a lack of capital or have to manage the organizational problems associated with rapid growth; most important, they may need to find a way to take their technology from a small out-of-the-way niche into the mass market.

Perhaps one of the most important issues facing new entrants is the choice of whether to partner with an established company or go it alone in their attempt to develop and profit from a new disruptive technology. Although a new entrant may enjoy all of the advantages of the attacker, it may lack the resources required to exploit them fully. In such a case, it might want to consider forming a strategic alliance with a larger, established company to gain access to those resources. The main issues here are the same as those that we discussed earlier when examining the three strategies that companies can pursue to capture first-mover advantages: go it alone, enter into a strategic alliance, or license its technology.

Summary of Chapter

1. Technical standards are important in many high-tech industries: they guarantee compatibility, reduce confusion in the minds of customers, allow for mass production and lower costs, and reduce the risks associated with supplying complementary products.

2. Network effects and positive feedback loops often determine which standard comes to dominate a market.

3. Owning a standard can be a source of sustained competitive advantage.

4. Establishing a proprietary standard as the industry standard may require the company to win a format war against a competing and incompatible standard. Strategies for doing this include producing complementary products, leveraging killer applications, aggressive pricing and marketing, licensing the technology, and cooperating with competitors.

5. Many high-tech products are characterized by high fixed costs of development but very low or zero marginal costs of producing one extra unit of output. These cost economics create a presumption in favor of strategies that emphasize aggressive pricing to increase volume and drive down average total costs.

6. Many digital products suffer from very high piracy rates due to the low marginal costs of copying and distributing such products. Piracy can be reduced by the appropriate combination of strategy, encryption software, and vigorous defense of intellectual property rights.

7. It is very important for a first mover to develop a strategy to capitalize on first-mover advantages. A company can choose from three strategies: develop and market the technology itself, to do so jointly with another company, and license the technology to existing companies. The choice depends on the complementary assets required to capture a first-mover advantage, the height of barriers to imitation, and the capability of competitors.

8. Technological paradigm shifts occur when new technologies come along that revolutionize the structure of the industry, dramatically alter the nature of competition, and require companies to adopt new strategies in order to survive.

9. Technological paradigm shifts are more likely to occur when progress in improving the established technology is slowing due to diminishing returns and a new disruptive technology is taking root in a market niche.

10. Established companies can deal with paradigm shifts by hedging their bets with regard to technology or setting up a stand-alone division to exploit the technology.

Discussion Questions

1. What is different about high-tech industries? Were all industries once high tech?

2. Why are standards so important in many high-tech industries? What are the competitive implications of this?

3. You work for a small company that has the leading position in an embryonic market. Your boss believes that the company's future is assured because it has a 60 percent share of the market, the lowest cost structure in the industry, and the most reliable and highest-valued product. Write a memo to him outlining why his assumptions might be incorrect.

4. You are working for a small company that has developed an operating system for PCs that is faster and more stable than Microsoft's Windows operating system. What strategies might the company pursue to unseat Windows and establish its new operating system as the dominant technical standard in the industry?

5. You are a manager for a major music record label. Last year, music sales declined by 10 percent, primarily due to very high piracy rates for CDs. Your boss has asked you to develop a strategy for reducing piracy rates. What would you suggest that the company do?

Practicing Strategic Management

SMALL-GROUP EXERCISE: BURNING DVDs

Break up into groups of three to five people, and appoint one group member as a spokesperson who will communicate your findings to the class.

You are a group of managers and software engineers at a small start-up that has developed software that enables customers with PCs to copy films from one DVD to another (i.e., to "burn" DVDs).

1. How do you think that the market for this software is likely to develop? What factors might inhibit adoption of software?

2. Can you think of a strategy that your company might pursue in combination with film studios that will enable your company to increase revenues and the film companies to reduce piracy rates?

ARTICLE FILE 7

Find an example of an industry that has undergone a technological paradigm shift in recent years. What happened to the established companies as that paradigm shift unfolded?

STRATEGIC MANAGEMENT PROJECT: MODULE 7

This module requires you to analyze the industry environment in which your company is based and determine if it is vulnerable to a technological paradigm shift. With the information you have at your disposal, answer the following questions:

1. What is the dominant product technology used in the industry in which your company is based?

2. Are technical standards important in your industry? If so, what are they?

3. What are the attributes of the majority of customers purchasing the product of your company (for example, early adopters, early majority, late majority)? What does this tell you about the strategic issues that the company is likely to face in the future?

4. Did the dominant technology in your industry diffuse rapidly or slowly? What drove the speed of diffusion?

5. Where is the dominant technology in your industry on its S-curve? Are alternative competing technologies being developed that might give rise to a paradigm shift in your industry?

6. Are intellectual property rights important to your company? If so, what strategies is it adopting to protect those rights? Is it doing enough?

EXPLORING THE WEB
Visiting Kodak

Visit the web site of Kodak (**http://www.kodak.com**), and search it to find out what Kodak is doing in the area of digital photography. Use this information to answer the following questions:

1. How important do you think digital photography is in Kodak's total revenues?

2. How is this likely to change over the next decade?

3. Where is digital photography on the S-curve? Where is traditional photography? What are the implications of this comparison for Kodak?

4. Identify Kodak's competitors in (a) its traditional film business and (b) the digital photography business. What are the implications of the change in the set of competitors confronting Kodak?

5. How does the switch from traditional to digital photography change the economics of the photography business?

6. Do you think that Kodak is pursuing the correct strategies to deal with digital substitution? What do you think is the long-term outlook for Kodak's business if it continues pursuing its current strategies? Do you think the company should make some changes? If so, what?

General Task: Search the Web for information that allows you to assess the current state of competition in the market for hand-held computers such as those produced by Palm, Handspring, and Compaq. Use that information to perform an analysis of the market in the United States. Answer the following questions:

1. What is the leading standard for operating systems in this market?

2. How did this standard emerge to become the market leader?

3. How secure is this standard? Could it be supplanted by another standard over the next few years?

Closing Case

The Evolution of IBM

IBM is in many ways a remarkable organization. Founded in 1911 from the merger of two companies, the early IBM sold mechanical clocks, scales, and punch-card tabulating equipment. By 2001, it was the largest technology company on the planet with earnings of $7.7 billion on revenues of $86 billion, almost twice as much as any other technology company. In its ninety-year history, IBM has survived several paradigm shifts in technology that led to the decline and bankruptcy of many of its peers.

During the 1930s, IBM was a leader in the production of mechanical tabulators using punch-card technology. When this technology was ultimately replaced by electronic calculators and computers, many manufacturers of mechanical tabulating equipment went the way of the dinosaur. IBM, however, had begun to build capabilities in electronics during the 1930s. In 1933, it acquired a producer of electric typewriters. This led to the 1935 introduction of IBM's first electric typewriter, a technology that was to transform the typewriter industry where most incumbent enterprises sold mechanical typewriters. More important, the acquisition gave IBM access to knowledge of electronics, which it ultimately put to use elsewhere in the company. In 1947, IBM introduced its first "electronic multiplier," a calculator with electronic, as opposed to mechanical, working elements. More significant, IBM's electronic knowledge underlay its introduction in 1952 of its first production computer, the IBM 701.

In the ensuing decades, IBM rode the wave of disruptive technology. Its revolutionary System 360 computer, introduced in 1964, began to replace mechanical and simple electronic systems for performing scientific and business calculations. Its System 370 computer, introduced in 1970, solidified this trend. By the mid-1980s, IBM had emerged as the largest manufacturer of mainframe computers in the world and at the time had the dominant computing technology, with a virtual lock on the market. But by this time, a new technology was taking root that was to threaten IBM's very survival: the personal computer.

Personal computer technology was developed in the mid-1970s by a number of small start-up enterprises, including MITS and Apple. In 1980, William Lowe, the lab director at IBM's Entry Level Systems (ELS) unit in Boca Raton, Florida, pushed IBM management to give him authorization to try and develop a personal computer. Top management was initially reluctant. Its two previous attempts to introduce a PC had ended in total failure. Lowe ultimately got permission to produce a PC but with an almost unrealistic deadline of one year to complete the job. He recruited another IBM insider, Don Estridge, to head the project team. Estridge was soon persuaded that the only way to meet the deadline was for IBM to purchase off-the-shelf components, such as an Intel microprocessor and a Microsoft operating system, and to adopt an open systems design, where technical specifications were published. This would allow developers to write software applications that would run on the PC. Strategically, this approach represented a radical departure for IBM, which had tended to make the majority of its own components and software in-house and had adopted a closed systems approach. The countercultural strategy was possible only because the ELS unit was outside IBM's business mainstream, geographically separated from the company's center of operations, staffed by a maverick group of engineers and managers, and protected from IBM's bureaucracy by its CEO, Frank Cary.

Introduced in August 1981, the IBM PC was a dramatic success. However, the use of open systems architecture and off-the-shelf components soon gave rise to a thriving industry of companies that made IBM-compatible machines, or clones, such as Compaq Computer. By the mid-1980s, these clone makers were starting to eat into IBM's market share. Moreover, PC architecture based on an Intel microprocessor and Microsoft operating system went on to revolutionize the computer industry. In many companies, client-server systems based on PC technology replaced mainframe and midrange computers. As this occurred, sales of IBM mainframes slumped, and by 1993 IBM was awash in red ink. It lost $8 billion on shrinking sales as the PC technology it had given birth to cannibalized its profitable mainframe computers. Many observers were already writing IBM's obituary.

At this juncture, Lou Gerstner became CEO. A former management consultant and CEO of the tobacco company R. J. Reynolds with no computer industry experience, most observers thought that Gerstner, who knew little about computing technology, was poorly equipped to be IBM's CEO. However, Gerstner soon realized that IBM's computer business was rapidly becoming commoditized. Having given up control over microprocessor technology to Intel and software to Microsoft, IBM had no proprietary advantage. His strategy was to take IBM out of the commoditization game by emphasizing its service business. He believed that if IBM could solve the information technology problems of large corporations, the company would win big sales with recurring sales revenues spread out over years and margins that were a lot better than those IBM could get by competing only at the product level.

Not only has this strategy been very successful, it has given IBM a way to exploit the latest disruptive technology, the Internet. As Internet-centric computing has grown in importance, IBM has reinvented itself as a dominant provider of e-business solutions and services. Now if a company wishes to establish an intranet or use the Internet to execute business transactions, IBM is one of the vendors it turns to first. Although IBM still produces and sells its own computer hardware, it will now recommend the hardware of other companies if it suits the clients' needs better. It has become an e-business solutions company, ideally positioning itself to profit from the spread of web-based technology into every nook and cranny of the modern business corporation.

Case Discussion Questions

1. How many paradigm shifts has IBM survived in its history?

2. Describe how IBM was able to survive each of these paradigm shifts.

3. What does the history of IBM tell you about the strategies that incumbent companies must pursue to survive paradigm shifts?

4. In many ways, the IBM PC launched the personal computer into the mass market. How was a large incumbent enterprise able to develop what was a revolutionary product?

5. With the benefit of hindsight, could IBM have done anything different in the development of the IBM PC that would have not allowed control over the dominant standard in the market to be captured by Microsoft and Intel?

Sources: D. Kirkpatrick, "The Future of IBM," *Fortune,* February 18, 2002, pp. 60–68. P. Freiberger and M. Swaine, *Fire in the Valley* (New York: McGraw-Hill, 2000). "Follow That," *Economist,* February 2, 2002, p. 64. History of IBM from www.ibm.com.

Strategy in the Global Environment

8

Opening Case

MTV Has to Sing a New Song as It Expands Globally

MTV Networks has become something of a symbol of globalization. Established in 1981, the U.S.-based music TV station has been expanding outside its North American base since 1987, when it opened MTV Europe. Now owned by media conglomerate Viacom, MTV Networks, which includes siblings Nickelodeon and VH1, the music station for the baby boomer set, generates over $1 billion in operating profit per year on annual revenues of $3 billion. Since 1987, MTV has become the most ubiquitous cable programmer in the world. By 2001, the network had 29 channels, or distinct feeds, that reached some 330 million households in 140 countries. Although the United States still leads with 70 million households, the most rapid growth is elsewhere, particularly in Asia, where nearly two-thirds of the region's 3 billion people are under thirty-five years old, the middle class is expanding fast, and TV ownership is spreading rapidly.

Despite its success, MTV's global expansion got off to a weak start. In 1987, it piped a single feed across Europe almost entirely composed of American programming with English-speaking veejays. Naively, the network's U.S. managers thought that Europeans would flock to the American programming. But while viewers in Europe shared a common interest in a handful of global superstars, who at the time included Madonna and Michael Jackson, their tastes turned out to be surprisingly local. What was popular in Germany might not be popular in Britain, and many staples of the American music scene left Europeans cold. MTV suffered as a result. Soon local copycat stations were springing up in Europe that focused on the music scene in individual countries and took viewers and advertisers away from MTV. As explained by Tom Freston, chairman of MTV Networks, "We were going for the most shallow layer of what united viewers and brought them together. It didn't go over too well."

In 1995, MTV changed its strategy and broke Europe into eight regional feeds: one for the United Kingdom and Ireland; another for Germany, Austria, and Switzerland; one for Scandinavia; one for Italy; one for France; one for Spain; one for Holland; and a feed for the other European nations, including Belgium and Greece. The network adopted the same localization strategy elsewhere in the world. For example, in Asia, it has an English-Hindi channel for India, separate Mandarin feeds for China and Taiwan, a Korean feed for South Korea, a Bahasa language feed for Indonesia, and a Japanese feed for Japan. Digital and satellite technology have made the localization of programming cheaper and easier. MTV Networks can now beam half a dozen feeds of one satellite transponder.

Although MTV Networks exercises creative control over these different feeds and all of the channels have the same familiar frenetic look and feel of MTV in the United States, an increasing share of the programming and content is local. When MTV opens a local station now, it begins with expatriates from elsewhere in the world to do a "gene transfer" of company culture and operating principles. But once these are established, the network switches over to local employees, and the expatriates move on. The idea is to produce programming that matches the tastes of the local population. Although as much as 60 percent of the programming still originates in the United States, with staples such as *The Real World* having equivalents in different countries, an increasing share of programming is local in conception. In Italy, *MTV Kitchen* combines cooking with a music

countdown. *Erotica* airs in Brazil and features a panel of youngsters discussing sex. The Indian channel produces twenty-one home-grown shows hosted by local veejays who speak "Hinglish," a city-bred breed of Hindi and English. Hit shows include *MTV Cricket in Control,* appropriate for a land where cricket is a national obsession; *MTV Housefull,* which hones in on Hindi film stars (India has the biggest film industry outside of Hollywood); and *MTV Bakra,* which is modeled on *Candid Camera.*

The same local variation is evident in the music videos aired by the different feeds. Although some music stars still have global appeal, 70 percent of the video content in most markets is now local. Indeed, in a direct countertrend to the notion that popular culture is becoming more global and homogeneous, William Roedy, president of MTV's international networks, observes, "People root for the home team, both culturally and musically. Local repertoire is a worldwide trend. There are fewer global megastars." Moreover, when music tastes do transcend borders, MTV has found that it is often in ways that would have been difficult to predict. Currently, Japanese pop music is all the range in Taiwan, and soul and hip-hop are big in Korea.

This localization push has reaped big benefits for MTV. It has helped MTV capture viewers back from local imitators. In India, ratings increased by more than 700 percent between 1996, when the localization push began, and 2000. In turn, localization helps MTV to capture more of those all-important advertising revenues, even from other multinationals such as Coca-Cola, whose own advertising budgets are often locally determined. In Europe, MTV's advertising revenues increased by 50 percent between 1995 and 2000. While the total market for pan-European advertising is valued at just $200 million, the total market for local advertising across Europe is a much bigger pie, valued at $12 billion. MTV now gets 70 percent of its European advertising revenue from local spots, up from 15 percent in 1995. Similar trends are evident elsewhere in the world.

Sources: B. Pulley and A. Tanzer, "Sumner's Gemstone," *Forbes,* February 21, 2000, pp. 107–111. K. Hoffman, "Youth TV's Old Hand Prepares for the Digital Challenge," *Financial Times,* February 18, 2000, p. 8. Presentation by Sumner M. Redstone, chairman and CEO, Viacom, delivered to Salomon Smith Barney Eleventh Annual Global Entertainment and Media Telecommunications Conference, Scottsdale, Arizona, January 8, 2001, archived at www.viacom.com.

Overview

As MTV found when it began to expand globally, it had to change its *business model* and develop a strategy of customizing its product to different national markets. It could not offer a standardized MTV channel worldwide.

This chapter outlines the global strategies that companies can pursue to gain a competitive advantage in the global marketplace and discusses the advantages and disadvantages of each. It also explores two related strategic issues: (1) how managers decide which foreign markets to enter, when to enter them, and on what scale and (2) what kind of vehicle or means a company should use to expand globally and enter a foreign country. Once a company has entered a foreign market, it becomes a **multinational company,** that is, a company that does business in two or more national markets. The vehicles that companies can employ to enter foreign markets and become multinationals include exporting, licensing, setting up a joint venture with a foreign company, and setting up a wholly owned subsidiary. The chapter closes with a discussion of the benefits and costs of entering into strategic alliances with other global companies.

By the time you have completed this chapter, you will have a good understanding of the various strategic issues that companies face when they decide to expand their operations abroad to achieve competitive advantage and superior profitability.

Increasing Profitability Through Global Expansion

Expanding globally allows companies to increase their profitability in ways not available to purely domestic enterprises. As we shall see, by producing goods and services in other countries, companies may be able to lower their cost structure or better differentiate their final product offering. In addition, a company may be able to increase its sales volume more rapidly and thus reap the cost advantages that flow from greater economies of scale.

Location Economies

Chapter 2 discussed how countries differ from each other along a number of dimensions, including differences in the cost and quality of factors of production. These differences imply that some locations are more suited than others for producing certain goods and services.[1] **Location economies** are the economic benefits that arise from performing a value creation activity in the optimal location for that activity, wherever in the world that might be (transportation costs and trade barriers permitting). Locating a value creation activity in the optimal location for that activity can have one of two effects: (1) it can lower the costs of value creation, helping the company achieve a low-cost position, or (2) it can enable a company to differentiate its product offering, which gives it the option of charging a premium price or keeping price low and using differentiation as a means of increasing sales volume. Thus, efforts to realize location economies are consistent with the business-level strategies of low cost and differentiation. In theory, a company that realizes location economies by dispersing each of its value creation activities to the optimal location for that activity should have a competitive advantage over a company that bases all of its value creation activities at a single location. It should be able to differentiate its product offering better and lower its cost structure more than its single-location competitor. In a world where competitive pressures are increasing, such a strategy may well become an imperative for survival.

For an example of location economies, consider Swan Optical, a U.S. manufacturer and distributor of eyewear. With sales revenues only in the $20 to $30 million range, Swan is hardly a giant, yet it manufactures its eyewear in low-cost factories in Hong Kong and China that it jointly owns with a Hong Kong–based partner. Swan also has a minority stake in eyewear design houses in Japan, France, and Italy. Thus, even small companies can disperse their value creation activities around the world to take advantage of the favorable skill base and cost structure found in other countries. Investments in Hong Kong and then China have helped Swan to lower its cost structure, and investments in Japan, France, and Italy have helped it to produce differentiated designer eyewear for which it can charge a premium price.[2]

For an example of a large company, consider GM's Pontiac Le Mans.[3] Marketed and sold primarily in the United States, the car was designed in Germany; key components were manufactured in Japan, Taiwan, and Singapore; the assembly operation was performed in South Korea; and the advertising strategy was formulated in Great Britain. The car was designed in Germany because GM believed the designers in its German subsidiary were the most capable of producing a car design that added value. Components were manufactured in Japan, Taiwan, and Singapore because favorable factor conditions there—relatively low-cost skilled labor—gave these locations a comparative advantage in the production of components. The car was assembled in South Korea because GM believed that the costs of assembly would be at a minimum there because of low labor costs. Finally, the advertising strategy was formulated in Great Britain because GM believed a particular advertising agency there had a distinct competency to produce an advertising campaign that would help differentiate and sell the car. The result of this kind of strategic thinking is clear: managers must create a global web of value chain activities in which each activity is located in the country where value added through differentiation can be maximized or where the costs of value creation are minimized.

Some Caveats. Introducing transportation costs and trade barriers complicates this picture somewhat. New Zealand might have a comparative advantage for low-cost car assembly operations, but high transportation costs make it an uneconomical location from which to serve global markets. Factoring transportation costs and trade barriers into the cost equation helps explain why many U.S. companies have been shifting their production from Asia to Mexico. Mexico has three distinct advantages over many Asian countries as a location for value creation activities: low labor costs; Mexico's proximity to the large U.S. market, which reduces transportation costs; and the North American Free Trade Agreement (NAFTA), which has removed many trade barriers between Mexico, the United States, and Canada, increasing Mexico's attractiveness as a production site for the North American market. Thus, although the relative costs of value creation are important, transportation costs and trade barriers also must be considered in location decisions.

Another caveat concerns the importance of assessing political and economic risks when making location decisions. Even if a country looks very attractive as a production location when measured against cost or differentiation criteria, if its government is unstable or totalitarian, companies are usually well advised not to base production there. Similarly, if a particular national government appears to be pursuing inappropriate social or economic policies, this might be another reason for not basing production in that location, even if other factors look favorable.

The Experience Curve   As you recall from Chapter 4, the experience curve refers to the systematic decrease in production costs that has been observed to occur over the life of a product. Learning effects and economies of scale underlie the experience curve, and moving down the experience curve allows a company to lower its cost structure and achieve a cost advantage in relation to its competitors.

Many of the underlying sources of experience-based cost economies are found at the level of individual plants. Thus, the key to riding down the experience curve as rapidly as possible is to increase the accumulated volume *produced by a plant* as quickly as possible. Because global markets are larger than domestic markets, companies that produce for a global market from one or a handful of locations are likely to build up accumulated volume faster than companies that focus primarily on serving their home market or on producing for multiple markets from many different production locations. Thus, serving a global market from one or a few plants is consistent with moving down the experience curve and establishing a low-cost position.

Another point to bear in mind is that the cost advantages of serving the world market from one or a few plants will be greater if those plants are based in the country or countries that are optimal for performing that value creation activity. Such a strategy will enable a company to realize cost economies from experience curve effects at the plant level and from location economies *simultaneously*. For an example of a company that excelled in doing just this, consider the history of Matsushita, which makes electronic products under the Panasonic and JVC labels.

In the 1970s, Matsushita, along with competitors Sony and Philips, was in a race to develop a commercially viable VCR. As discussed in Chapter 7, although Matsushita initially lagged behind both Philips and Sony, its strategy to get its VHS format accepted as the global industry standard ultimately allowed it to reap enormous experience curve cost economies. To ensure that it could accommodate the huge increase in worldwide demand for its VCRs once its format was accepted, Matsushita increased its VCR production capacity from 205,000 units in 1977 to 6.8 million units by 1984. Its strategy was to serve the world market from only a handful of large factories, and it took advantage of the highly skilled, low-cost Japanese labor. As a result, Matsushita was able to realize significant learning effects and economies of scale. This allowed it to reduce the prices of its VCRs by 50 percent within five years of selling its first one, a cost advantage that allowed it to become the world's largest VCR producer by 1983 with 45 percent of world sales.[4]

Today companies like Intel are the masters of this kind of strategy. Because the costs of building a state-of-the-art facility to manufacture microprocessors are easily in excess of $1 billion, to make this investment pay Intel *must* pursue experience curve effects—serving world markets from a few plants to maximize the cost economies that derive from scale and learning effects.

Transferring Distinctive Competencies

Distinctive competencies, introduced in Chapter 3, are the firm-specific resources and capabilities that allow a company to achieve superior efficiency, quality, innovation, or responsiveness to customers and thus gain a competitive advantage. Such strengths typically find their expression in new and improved goods and services that other companies find difficult to match or imitate. Thus, distinctive competencies form the bedrock of a company's competitive advantage. They enable a company to lower its cost structure or perform value creation activities in ways that lead to differentiation, premium pricing, and increased demand. For example, Toyota's distinctive competencies allow it to produce high-quality, well-designed cars at a lower delivered cost than any other company in the world.[5]

For such companies, global expansion is a way of further exploiting the value creation potential of their distinctive competencies. Companies with valuable distinctive competencies can often realize enormous returns by using those competencies and selling the products that result from them in overseas markets where indigenous competitors lack similar competencies and products. The *Opening Case* described how MTV has been able to build a vibrant global business by leveraging its competencies in the programming and delivery of music and related content and applying those skills to various national markets where local competitors lack equivalent skills. The network's success has raised the value that viewers ascribe to MTV and, by extension, the value that advertisers ascribe to an advertising slot on an MTV channel. In turn, this has enabled MTV to command a higher price for advertising slots than competitors. Another example is detailed in Strategy in Action 8.1, which describes how McDonald's has leveraged its distinctive competence in running fast food restaurants to overseas markets where indigenous competitors either did not exist or lacked similar skills.

Strategy in Action   8.1

McDonald's Is Here, There, and Everywhere

Established in 1955, by the early 1980s McDonald's faced a problem: after three decades of rapid growth, the U.S. fast food market was beginning to show signs of market saturation. McDonald's response to the slowdown was to expand rapidly abroad. In 1980, 28 percent of the chain's new restaurant openings were abroad; in 1986, the figure was 40 percent, in 1990, it was close to 60 percent; and in 2000, it was almost 90 percent. Since the early 1980s, the company's overseas revenues and profits have grown at 22 percent annually. By the end of 2000, McDonald's had 28,707 restaurants in 120 countries outside the United States, which generated $21 billion, or 53 percent of the company's $40 billion in revenues.

McDonald's shows no signs of slowing down. Management notes that there is still only one McDonald's restaurant for every 500,000 people in the overseas countries that it currently does business in, which compares to one McDonald's restaurant for every 25,000 people in the United States. Moreover, the company currently serves less than 1 percent of the world's population. Thus, the company's strategy is for this overseas expansion to continue at a rapid rate. In Europe, it opened more than 500 new restaurants in 1999 and in 2000, while the figure for Asia was around 600. A major expansion plan is for Latin America, where the company plans to invest $2 billion over the next few years.

McDonald's enters an overseas country only after careful preparation. In what is a fairly typical pattern, before McDonald's opened its first Polish restaurant in 1992, it spent eighteen months establishing essential contacts and getting to know the local culture. Locations, real estate, construction, supply, personnel, legal, and government relations were all worked out in advance. In June 1992, a team of fifty employees from the United States, Russia, Germany, and Britain went to Poland to help with the opening of the first four restaurants there. By mid-1994, all of these employees except one had returned to their home countries. They were no longer needed because Polish nationals had been trained to run an efficient McDonald's operation.

Indeed, another key to the company's global expansion strategy is the export of the business model that spurred its growth in the United States. McDonald's success was built on a formula of close relations with suppliers, nationwide marketing might, tight control over store-level operating procedures, and a franchising system that encourages entrepreneurial individual franchisees. Although this system has worked well in the United States, some modifications must be made in other countries. One of the company's biggest challenges had been to infuse each store with the same culture and standardized operating procedures that have been the hallmark of its success in the United States. To aid in this task, in many countries McDonald's has enlisted the help of large partners through joint venture arrangements. The partners play a key role in learning and transplanting the organization's values to local employees. Overseas partners have also played a key role in helping McDonald's adapt its marketing methods and menu to local conditions. Although U.S.-style fast food remains the staple fare on the menu, local products have been added. In Brazil, for example, McDonald's sells a soft drink made from the guarana, an Amazonian berry. Patrons of McDonald's in Malaysia, Singapore, and Thailand savor milkshakes flavored with durian, a fruit considered an aphrodisiac by the locals. In Arab countries, McDonald's restaurants maintain *halal* menus, which signify compliance with Islamic laws on food preparation, especially beef. In 1995, McDonald's opened the first kosher restaurant in suburban Jerusalem which does not serve dairy products. And in India, the big Mac is made with lamb and called the Maharaja Mac.

McDonald's biggest problem has been to replicate its U.S. supply chain in other countries. U.S. suppliers are fiercely loyal to McDonald's; they must be, because their fortunes are closely linked to those of McDonald's. McDonald's maintains rigorous specifications for all the raw ingredients it uses—the key to its consistency and quality control. Outside the United States, however, McDonald's has found suppliers far less willing to make the investments required to meet its specifications. In Great Britain, for example, McDonald's experienced quality problems with two local bakeries supplying hamburger buns, so it built its own bakery to supply its stores there. In a more extreme case, when McDonald's decided to open a store in Russia, it found that local suppliers lacked the capability to produce goods of the quality it required. The company was forced to integrate vertically through the local food industry on a heroic scale, importing potato seeds and bull semen and indirectly managing dairy farms, cattle ranches, and vegetable plots. It also had to construct the world's largest food-processing plant, at a cost of $40 million. The restaurant itself cost only $4.5 million.

Now that it has a successful overseas operation, McDonald's is experiencing benefits that go beyond the immediate financial ones. Increasingly, it is finding that its overseas franchisees are a source of valuable new ideas. The Dutch operation created a prefabricated modular store that can be moved over a weekend and is now widely used to set up temporary restaurants at big outdoor events. The Swedes came up with an enhanced meat freezer that is now used companywide. And the small satellite stores and low-overhead mini-McDonald's that are now appearing in hospitals and sports arenas in the United States originated in Singapore.

Sources: Kathleen Deveny, et al., "McWorld?" *Business Week,* October 13, 1986, pp. 78–86. "Slow Food," *Economist,* February 3, 1990, p. 64. Harlan S, Byrne. "Welcome to McWorld," *Barron's,* August 29, 1994, pp. 25–28. Andrew E. Serwer, "McDonald's Conquers the World," *Fortune,* October 17, 1994, pp. 103–116.

Leveraging the Skills of Global Subsidiaries

Initially, many multinational companies develop valuable competencies at home and then leverage them overseas. However, it is becoming increasingly apparent that for more mature multinationals that have already established a network of subsidiary operations in foreign markets, the development of valuable competencies can just as well take place in foreign subsidiaries.[6] Indeed, competencies can be created anywhere within a multinational's global network of operations, wherever people have the opportunity and incentive to try new ways of doing things. The competencies that help to lower the costs of production or to enhance perceived value and support higher product pricing are not the monopoly of the corporate center.

For the managers of a multinational company, this phenomenon creates important new challenges. First, they must recognize that the corporate center does not hold a monopoly on the creation of valuable competencies and have the humility to recognize that valuable skills can arise anywhere within the company's global network. Second, they must establish an incentive system that encourages local employees to engage in the business of acquiring new competencies. This is not as easy as it sounds. Creating new competencies is risky because not all new resources and capabilities add value. For every valuable idea created by a McDonald's subsidiary in an overseas country, there may be several failures. The management of the multinational must put incentives in place that encourage employees to take the necessary risks. They must reward people for successes and not sanction them unnecessarily for taking risks that did not pan out. Third, they must have processes in place for identifying when valuable new competencies have been created in a subsidiary, and, finally, they need to act as a facilitator, helping to transfer valuable competencies within the company. For example, after employees in Singapore distinguished themselves by finding ways to reduce production costs through better product design, Hewlett Packard decentralized the authority for the design and production of many of its leading-edge ink jet printers to its operation in Singapore (see Strategy in Action 8.2).

Strategy in Action   8.2

Hewlett Packard in Singapore

In the late 1960s, Hewlett Packard was looking around Asia for a low-cost location to produce electronic components that were to be manufactured using labor-intensive processes. It eventually settled on Singapore, opening its first factory there in 1970. Although Singapore did not have the lowest labor costs in the region, costs were low relative to North America, plus the Singapore location had several important benefits that could not be found at many other locations in Asia. The education level of the local work force was high; English was widely spoken; the government seemed stable and committed to economic development; and the city-state had one of the better-developed infrastructures in the region, including good communications and transportation networks and a rapidly developing industrial and commercial base. HP also extracted favorable terms from the Singapore government with regard to taxes, tariffs, and subsidies.

Initially, the plant manufactured only basic components. The combination of low labor costs and a favorable tax regime helped to make this plant profitable early. In 1973, HP transferred the manufacture of one of its basic hand-held calculators from the United States to Singapore in order to reduce manufacturing costs, which the Singapore factory was quickly able to do. Increasingly confident in the capability of the Singapore factory to handle entire products as opposed to just components, HP's management transferred other products to Singapore over the next few years, including keyboards, solid-state displays, and integrated circuits. However, all of these products were still designed, developed, and initially produced in the United States.

The plant's status shifted in the early 1980s when HP embarked on a worldwide campaign to boost product quality and reduce costs. HP transferred the production of its HP41C hand-held calculator to Singapore. The managers at the Singapore plant were given the goal of substantially reducing manufacturing costs. They argued that this could be achieved only if they were allowed to redesign the product so it could be manufactured at a lower overall cost. HP's central management agreed, and

twenty engineers from the Singapore facility were transferred to the United States for one year to learn how to design application-specific integrated circuits. They took this expertise back to Singapore and set about redesigning the HP41C.

The results were a huge success. By redesigning the product, the Singapore engineers reduced manufacturing costs for the HP41C by 50 percent. Using this newly acquired capability for product design, the Singapore facility then set about redesigning other products it produced. HP's corporate managers were so impressed with the progress made at the factory that they transferred production of the entire calculator line to Singapore in 1983. This was followed by the partial transfer of ink jet production to Singapore in 1984 and keyboard production in 1986. In all cases, the facility redesigned the products and often reduced unit manufacturing costs by more than 30 percent. The initial development and design of all these products, however, still occurred in the United States.

In the late 1980s and early 1990s, the Singapore plant started to take on added responsibilities, particularly in the ink jet printer business. In 1990, it was given the job of redesigning an HP ink jet printer for the Japanese market. Although the initial product redesign was a market failure, the managers at Singapore pushed to be allowed to try again, and in 1991 they were given the job of redesigning HP's DeskJet 505 printer for the Japanese market. This time the redesigned product was a success, garnering significant sales in Japan. Emboldened by this success, the plant has continued to take on additional design responsibilities. Today, it is viewed as a lead plant within HP's global network, with primary responsibility not just for manufacturing but also for the development and design of a family of small ink jet printers targeted at the Asian market.

Sources: K. Ferdows, "Making the Most of Foreign Factories," *Harvard Business Review* (March–April 1997): 73–88. "Hewlett-Packard: Singapore," Harvard Business School Case #694-035 (1996).

Pressures for Cost Reductions and Local Responsiveness

Companies that compete in the global marketplace typically face two types of competitive pressures: *pressures for cost reductions* and *pressures to be locally responsive* (see Figure 8.1).[7] These competitive pressures place conflicting demands on a company. Responding to pressures for cost reductions requires that a company try to minimize its unit costs. To attain this goal, it may have to base its productive activities at the most favorable low-cost location, wherever in the world that might be. It may also have to offer a standardized product to the global marketplace in order to ride down the experience curve as quickly as possible. On the other hand, responding to pressures to be locally responsive requires that a company differentiate its product offering and marketing strategy from country to country in an effort to accommodate the diverse demands arising from national differences in consumer tastes and preferences, business practices, distribution channels, competitive conditions, and government policies. Because differentiation across countries can involve significant duplication and a lack of product standardization, it may raise costs.

While some companies, such as Company A in Figure 8.1, face high pressures for cost reductions and low pressures for local responsiveness, and others, such as Company B, face low pressures for cost reductions and high pressures for local responsiveness, many companies are in the position of Company C. They face high pressures for *both* cost reductions and local responsiveness. Dealing with these conflicting and contradictory pressures is a difficult strategic challenge, primarily because being locally responsive tends to raise costs.

Pressures for Cost Reductions

Increasingly, multinational companies must cope with pressures for cost reductions, which can be particularly intense in industries producing commodity-type products, where meaningful differentiation on nonprice factors is difficult and price is the main competitive weapon. Products that serve universal needs tend to fall into this category. Universal needs exist when the tastes and preferences of consumers in different nations are similar, if not identical. This obviously applies to conventional

FIGURE 8.1

Pressures for Cost Reductions and Local Responsiveness

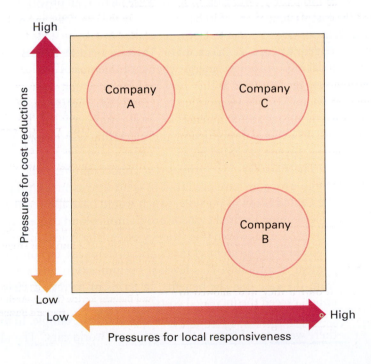

commodity products such as bulk chemicals, petroleum, steel, and sugar. It also tends to be true for many industrial and consumer products—for instance, hand-held calculators, semiconductor chips, and personal computers. Pressures for cost reductions are also intense in industries where major competitors are based in low-cost locations, where there is persistent excess capacity, and where consumers are powerful and face low switching costs. Many commentators have also argued that the liberalization of the world trade and investment environment has generally increased cost pressures by facilitating greater international competition.[8] For example, taking advantage of low barriers to direct investment, Wal-Mart is rapidly expanding globally using its cost-leadership strategy to penetrate new national markets. Its business model is threatening rivals at home and abroad.

Consider the history of the global tire industry, where pressures for cost reductions have been intense in recent years. Tires are essentially a commodity product for which differentiation is difficult and price is the main competitive weapon. The major buyers of tires, automobile companies, are powerful and face low switching costs, so they have been playing tire companies off against each other in an attempt to get lower prices. Moreover, a decline in global demand for automobiles in the early 1990s created serious excess capacity in the tire industry, with as much as 25 percent of world capacity standing idle. The result was a worldwide price war, with almost all tire companies suffering heavy losses in the early 1990s. In response to the cost pressures, most tire companies rationalized their operations in a way consistent with the attainment of a low-cost position. They moved production to low-cost facilities and offered globally standardized products in an attempt to realize experience curve economies.[9]

Pressures for Local Responsiveness

Pressures for local responsiveness arise from differences in consumer tastes and preferences, infrastructure and traditional practices, distribution channels, and host government demands. Recall that responding to pressures to be locally responsive requires that a company differentiate its products and marketing strategy from country to country to accommodate these factors, all of which tends to raise a company's cost structure.

Differences in Customer Tastes and Preferences.

Strong pressures for local responsiveness emerge when customer tastes and preferences differ significantly between countries, as they may for historic or cultural reasons. In such cases, a multinational company's products and marketing message have to be customized to appeal to the tastes and preferences of local customers. This typically creates pressures for the delegation of production and marketing responsibilities and functions to a company's overseas subsidiaries.

The *Opening Case* provided a good example. Other things being equal, MTV would probably have preferred to centralize as much programming and content in the United States as possible, which would have allowed it to realize scale economies by leveraging its fixed costs of programming and content development over a global viewer base. However, this strategy essentially failed. Instead, MTV has found that it needs to respond to local tastes and preferences, customizing its programming and content accordingly. This level of customization raises MTV's costs, but it is clear from the case that the benefits, in terms of increased viewers and advertising revenues, exceed the increased costs.

The automobile industry provides another example. In the 1980s and early 1990s, there was a trend toward the creation of "world cars." The idea was that global companies such as General Motors, Ford, and Toyota would be able to sell the same basic vehicle the world over, sourcing it from centralized production locations. If successful, the strategy would have enabled automobile companies to reap significant gains from global scale economies. However, this strategy has frequently run aground on the hard rocks of consumer reality. The fact is that consumers in different automobile markets do seem to have different tastes and preferences, and therefore they require different types of vehicles. There is a strong demand among North American consumers for pickup trucks, particularly in the South and West. In contrast, in European countries, pickup trucks are considered utility vehicles and are purchased primarily by firms rather than individuals.

As a counterpoint, some commentators have argued that customer demands for local customization are on the decline worldwide.[10] According to this argument, modern communications and transport technologies have created the conditions for a convergence of the tastes and preferences of customers from different nations. The result is the emergence of enormous global markets for standardized consumer products. The worldwide acceptance of McDonald's hamburgers, Coca-Cola, Gap clothes, Nokia cell phones, and Sony television sets, all of which are sold globally as standardized products, are often cited as evidence of the increasing homogeneity of the global marketplace.

This argument, however, has been characterized as extreme by others. For example, Christopher Bartlett and Sumantra Ghoshal have observed that in the consumer electronics industry, buyers reacted to an overdose of standardized global products by showing a renewed preference for products that are differentiated to local conditions.[11]

Differences in Infrastructure and Traditional Practices. Pressures for local responsiveness arise from differences in infrastructure or traditional practices among countries, creating a need to customize products accordingly. Fulfilling this need may require the delegation of manufacturing and production functions to foreign subsidiaries. For example, in North America, consumer electrical systems are based on 110 volts, whereas in some European countries, 240-volt systems are standard. Thus, domestic electrical appliances have to be customized to take this difference in infrastructure into account. Traditional practices also often vary across nations. For example, in Britain, people drive on the left-hand side of the road, creating a demand for right-hand-drive cars, whereas in France (and the rest of Europe), people drive on the right-hand side of the road and therefore want left-hand-drive cars. Obviously, automobiles have to be customized to take this difference in traditional practices into account.

Although many of the country differences in infrastructure are rooted in history, some are quite recent. For example, in the wireless telecommunications industry, different technical standards are found in different parts of the world. A technical standard known as GSM is common in Europe, and an alternative standard, CDMA, is more common in the United States and parts of Asia. The significance of these different standards is that equipment designed for GSM will not work on a CDMA network, and vice versa. Thus, companies such as Nokia, Motorola, and Ericsson, which manufacture wireless handsets and infrastructure such as switches, need to customize their product offering according to the technical standard prevailing in a given country.

Differences in Distribution Channels. A company's marketing strategies may have to be responsive to differences in distribution channels among countries, which may necessitate the delegation of marketing functions to national subsidiaries. In the pharmaceutical industry, for example, the British and Japanese distribution system is radically different from the U.S. system. British and Japanese doctors will not accept or respond favorably to a U.S.-style high-pressure sales force. Thus, pharmaceutical companies have to adopt different marketing practices in Britain and Japan compared with the United States—soft sell versus hard sell.

Host Government Demands. Economic and political demands imposed by host country governments may require local responsiveness. For example, the politics of health care around the world require that pharmaceutical companies manufacture in multiple locations. Pharmaceutical companies are subject to local clinical testing, registration procedures, and pricing restrictions, all of which make it necessary that the manufacturing and marketing of a drug should meet local requirements. Moreover, because governments and government agencies control a significant proportion of the health care budget in most countries, they are in a powerful position to demand a high level of local responsiveness.

More generally, threats of protectionism, economic nationalism, and local content rules (which require that a certain percentage of a product should be manufactured locally) dictate that international businesses manufacture locally. As an example, consider Bombardier, the Canadian-based manufacturer of railcars, aircraft, jet boats, and snowmobiles. Bombardier has twelve railcar factories across Europe. Critics of the company argue that the resulting duplication of manufacturing facilities leads to high costs and helps explain why Bombardier makes lower profit margins on its railcar operations than on its other business lines. In reply, managers at Bombardier argue that in Europe, informal rules with regard to local content favor people who use local workers. To sell railcars in Germany, they claim, you must manufacture in Germany. The same goes for Belgium, Austria, and France. To try and address its cost structure in Europe, Bombardier has centralized its engineering and purchasing functions, but it has no plans to centralize manufacturing.[12]

Choosing a Global Strategy

Pressures for local responsiveness imply that it may not be possible for a firm to realize the full benefits from experience curve and location economies. For example, it may not be possible to serve the global marketplace from a single low-cost location, producing a globally standardized product, and marketing it worldwide to achieve experience curve cost economies. In practice, the need to customize the product offering to local conditions may work against the implementation of such a strategy. For example, automobile firms have found that Japanese, American, and European consumers demand different kinds of cars, and this necessitates producing products that are customized for local markets. In response, firms like Honda, Ford, and Toyota are pursuing a strategy of establishing top-to-bottom design and production facilities in each of these regions so that they can better serve local demands. Although such customization brings benefits, it also limits the ability of a firm to realize significant experience curve cost economies and location economies.

In addition, pressures for local responsiveness imply that it may not be possible to leverage skills and products associated with a firm's distinctive competencies wholesale from one nation to another. Concessions often have to be made to local conditions. Despite being depicted as "poster boy" for the proliferation of standardized global products, even McDonald's has found that it has to customize its product offerings (i.e., its menu) in order to account for national differences in tastes and preferences.

Given the need to balance the cost and differentiation (value) sides of a company's business model, how do differences in the strength of pressures for cost reductions versus those for local responsiveness affect the choice of a company's strategy? Companies make a choice among four strategies to enter and compete in the global market: an international strategy, a multidomestic strategy, a global strategy, and a transnational strategy.[13] The appropriateness of each strategy varies given the extent of pressures for cost reductions and local responsiveness. Figure 8.2 illustrates the conditions under which each of these strategies is most appropriate.

International Strategy

Companies that pursue an **international strategy** try to create value by transferring valuable competencies and products to foreign markets where indigenous competitors lack those competencies and products. Most international companies have created value by transferring differentiated product offerings developed at home to foreign markets. Accordingly, they tend to centralize product development functions (for instance, R&D) at home. However, they also tend to establish manufacturing and marketing functions in each major country in which they do business. Although they may undertake some local customization of product offering and marketing strategy, this tends to be rather limited in scope. Ultimately, in most international companies, the head office retains tight control over marketing and product strategy.

International firms include Toys "R" Us, McDonald's, IBM, Kellogg, Procter & Gamble, Wal-Mart, and Microsoft. Microsoft, for example, develops the core architecture underlying its products at its Redmond campus in Washington State and also writes the bulk of the computer code there. However, it does allow national subsidiaries to develop their own marketing and distribution strategy and to customize aspects of the product to account for such basic local differences as language and

FIGURE 8.2

Four Basic Strategies

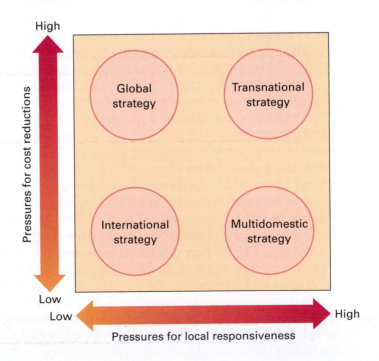

alphabet. For another example, see Strategy in Action 8.3, which profiles IKEA, the Swedish retailer. IKEA has traditionally pursued an international strategy, transferring the business model it developed in Sweden wholesale into other markets. However, this strategy did not work for IKEA once it started to open stores in the United States.

An international strategy makes sense if a company has a valuable competence that indigenous competitors in foreign markets lack and if it faces relatively weak pressures for local responsiveness and cost reductions (as is so with Microsoft). In such circumstances, an international strategy can be very profitable. However, when pressures for local responsiveness are high, companies pursuing this strategy lose out to those that place a greater emphasis on customizing the product offering and market strategy to local conditions. IKEA experienced this problem in the United States and subsequently shifted its strategy to accommodate local differences in tastes and preferences (see Strategy in Action 8.3). Similarly, when MTV originally expanded into Europe, it pursued an international strategy, but as we saw from the *Opening Case*, this strategy failed, given the high need for local responsiveness. In addition, because of duplication of manufacturing facilities, companies that pursue an international strategy tend to suffer from high operating costs. This makes the strategy inappropriate in manufacturing industries where cost pressures are high.

Multidomestic Strategy

Companies pursuing a **multidomestic strategy** develop a business model that allows them to achieve maximum local responsiveness. Because cost considerations often take a back seat to this, few companies are able to pursue this strategy in the intense competitive conditions of the 2000s, and it is mostly a thing of the past.

The key distinguishing feature of multidomestic companies is that they extensively customize both their product offering and their marketing strategy to match different national conditions. Consistent with this, they also have a tendency to establish a complete set of value creation activities, including production, marketing, and R&D, in each major national market in which they do business. As a consequence, they are generally unable to realize value from experience curve effects and location economies. Accordingly, many multidomestic firms have a high cost structure. They also tend to do a poor job of leveraging distinctive competencies within the firm.

A multidomestic strategy makes most sense when there are high pressures for local responsiveness and low pressures for cost reductions. The high cost structure associated with the duplication of production facilities makes this strategy inappropriate in industries where cost pressures are intense. Another weakness of this strategy is that many multidomestic companies have developed into decentralized federations in which each national subsidiary functions in a largely autonomous manner. Consequently, after a time, they begin to lose the ability to transfer the skills and products derived from distinctive competencies to their various national subsidiaries around the world. In a famous case that illustrates the problems this can cause, the failure of Philips NV to establish its V2000 VCR format as the dominant design in the VCR industry during the late 1970s, as opposed to Matsushita's VHS format, was due to the refusal of its U.S. subsidiary company to adopt the V2000 format. Instead, the subsidiary bought VCRs produced by Matsushita and put its own label on them, directly hurting Philips's attempts to establish its V2000 product as the global standard for VCRs.

Global Strategy

Companies that pursue a **global strategy** focus on increasing profitability by reaping the cost reductions that come from experience curve effects and location economies; that is, their business model is based on pursuing a low-cost strategy on a global scale.

Strategy in Action

IKEA's Swedish Ways

Established in the 1940s in Sweden by Ingvar Kamprad, IKEA has grown rapidly in recent years to become one of the world's largest retailers of home furnishings. In its initial push to expand globally, IKEA largely ignored the retailing rule that international success involves tailoring product lines closely to national tastes and preferences. Instead, it stuck with the vision articulated by founder Kamprad that the company should sell a basic product range that is "typically Swedish" wherever it ventures in the world. The company also remained primarily production oriented; the Swedish management and design group decided what it was going to sell and then presented it to the worldwide public, often with very little research as to what the public actually wanted. Moreover, the company emphasized its Swedish roots in its international advertising, even going as far as to insist on a Swedish blue and gold color scheme for its stores.

Despite breaking some key rules of international retailing, the formula of selling Swedish-designed products in the same manner everywhere seemed to work. Between 1974 and 2000, IKEA expanded from a company with 10 stores, only one of them outside Scandinavia, and annual revenues of $210 million to a group with 159 stores in 30 countries and sales of $8.6 billion. In 2000, only 8 percent of its sales were generated in Sweden. Of the balance, 21.6 percent of sales came from Germany, 49.5 percent from the rest of Europe, and 16 percent from North America. IKEA is now beginning to expand in Asia, which generated 3 percent of total sales in 2000.

The foundation of IKEA's success has been to offer customers good value for money. Its approach starts with a global network of suppliers, which now numbers 1,960 firms in 53 countries. An IKEA supplier gains long-term contracts, technical advice, and leased equipment from the company. In return, IKEA demands an exclusive contract and low prices. Its designers work closely with suppliers to build savings into the products from the outset by designing products that can be produced at a low cost. IKEA displays its enormous range of more than 10,000 products in cheap out-of-town stores. It sells most of its furniture as knocked-down kits for customers to take home and assemble themselves. The firm reaps huge economies of scale from the size of each store and the big production runs made possible by selling the same products all over the world. This strategy allows it to match its rivals on quality, while undercutting them by up to 30 percent on price and still maintaining a healthy after-tax return on sales of around 7 percent.

This strategy worked well until 1985, when IKEA decided to enter the North American market. Between 1985 and 1996, it opened six stores in North America, but unlike the company's experience across Europe, the stores did not quickly become profitable. Indeed, as early as 1990, it was clear that IKEA's North American operations were in trouble. Part of the problem was an adverse movement in exchange rates. In 1985, the exchange rate was $1 per 8.6 Swedish krona; by 1990, it was $1 per 5.8 krona. At this exchange rate, many products imported from Sweden did not look inexpensive to American consumers.

But there was more to IKEA's problems than adverse movements in exchange rates. IKEA's unapologetically Swedish products, which had sold so well across Europe, jarred with American tastes and sometimes physiques. Swedish beds were narrow and measured in centimeters. IKEA did not sell the matching bedroom suites that Americans like. Its kitchen cupboards were too narrow for the large dinner plates needed for pizza. Its glasses were too small for a nation that added ice to everything. The drawers in IKEA's bedroom chests were too shallow for American consumers, who tend to store sweaters in them. And the company made the mistake of selling European-sized curtains that did not fit American windows. As one senior IKEA manager joked later, "American's just wouldn't lower their ceilings to fit our curtains."

By 1991, the company's top management came to the realization that if it was going to succeed in North America, it would have to customize its product offering to North American tastes. The company set about redesigning its product range. The drawers on bedroom chests were designed to be two inches deeper, and sales immediately increased by 30 to 40 percent. IKEA now sells American-style king- and queen-sized beds, measured in inches, and it sells them as part of complete bedroom suites. It has redesigned its entire range of kitchen furniture and kitchenware to appeal to American tastes better. The company has also boosted the amount of products being sourced locally from 15 percent in 1990 to 45 percent in 1997, which makes it far less vulnerable to adverse movements in exchange rates. By 2000, about one-third of IKEA's total product offerings were designed exclusively for the U.S. market.

This break with IKEA's traditional strategy seems to be paying off. Between 1990 and 1994, IKEA's North American sales tripled to $480 million, and they nearly doubled again to around $900 million in 1997 and reached $1.38 billion in 2000. The company claims that it has been making a profit in North America since early 1993, although it does not release precise figures and does admit that its profit rate is lower in America than Europe. Still, the company is pushing ahead with plans for expansion in North America, including a goal of opening 15 new stores between 2000 and 2005, which will bring its total North American stores to 35.

Sources: "Furnishing the World," *Economist,* November 19, 1994, pp. 79–80. H. Carney, "Struggle to Save the Soul of IKEA," *Financial Times,* March 27, 1995, p. 12. J. Flynn and L. Bongiorno, "IKEA's New Game Plan," *Business Week,* October 6, 1997, pp. 99–102. IKEA's web site, www.ikea.com.

The production, marketing, and R&D activities of companies pursuing a global strategy are concentrated in a few favorable locations. Companies pursuing a global strategy try not to customize their product offering and marketing strategy to local conditions because customization, which involves shorter production runs and the duplication of functions, raises costs. Instead, they prefer to market a standardized product worldwide so that they can reap the maximum benefits from the economies of scale that underlie the experience curve. They also tend to use their cost advantage to support aggressive pricing in world markets.

This strategy makes most sense when there are strong pressures for cost reductions and demand for local responsiveness is minimal. Increasingly, these conditions prevail in many industrial goods industries. In the semiconductor industry, for example, global standards have emerged, creating enormous demands for standardized global products. Accordingly, companies such as Intel, Texas Instruments, and Motorola all pursue a global strategy. Similarly, Dell Computer pursues a global strategy and sells standardized products around the world (see the *Running Case* later in this chapter).

These conditions are not found in many consumer goods markets, where demands for local responsiveness remain high, as in the markets for automobiles and processed food products. The strategy is inappropriate when demands for local responsiveness are high.

Transnational Strategy

The strategies we have just looked at all have downsides. The multidomestic strategy is rarely profitable today. An international strategy can increase costs and put a company under threat if low-cost competitors emerge. A global strategy can give a company a low-cost advantage, but the strategy may not work if customers do not appreciate and value globally standardized products and instead turn to the more customized or differentiated products of rivals.

What strategy can a company pursue, then, to avoid these problems? This is one of the most complex questions that large global companies are grappling with today. Companies like Ford, Sony, and IBM have been trying for decades to come up with the "perfect" strategy that will give them a competitive advantage in the global arena. Ford has changed strategy repeatedly to try to raise its profitability; so far, it has not succeeded, announcing huge losses in 2001 from failed global ventures. Although the perfect strategy will be specific to each company and must be aligned to its particular business model, some researchers do offer guidelines for companies seeking to maximize their profitability in the global marketplace.

Two of these researchers, Christopher Bartlett and Sumantra Ghoshal, argue that in today's global environment, competitive conditions are so intense that to survive, companies must essentially do all they can to respond to pressures for cost reductions and local responsiveness. They must *simultaneously* exploit experience-based cost economies and location economies, transfer distinctive competencies within the company, and pay attention to pressures for local responsiveness.[14] Moreover, Bartlett and Ghoshal note that in the modern multinational enterprise, distinctive competencies do not reside just in the home country but can develop in any of the company's worldwide operations. Thus, they maintain that the flow of skills and product offerings should not be all one way, from home company to foreign subsidiary, as in the case of companies pursuing an international strategy. Rather, the flow should also be from foreign subsidiary to home country and from foreign subsidiary to foreign subsidiary, a process Bartlett and Ghoshal refer to as *global learning*. They use the term **transnational strategy** to describe the strategy of simultaneously seeking to lower costs, be locally responsive, and transfer competencies in a way that is consistent with global learning.

In essence, companies that pursue a transnational strategy are trying to develop a business model that simultaneously achieves low-cost and differentiation advantages. As attractive as this may sound, the strategy is not an easy one to pursue, as the failure of companies like Ford and ABB (one of the world's largest engineering conglomerates), which did try to pursue one, suggests. Pressures for local responsiveness and cost reductions place conflicting demands on a company; local responsiveness raises costs and makes cost reductions difficult to achieve. How, then, can a company effectively pursue a transnational strategy?

Some clues can be derived from the case of Caterpillar. The need to compete with low-cost competitors such as Komatsu of Japan forced Caterpillar to look for greater cost economies. However, variations in construction practices and government regulations across countries mean that Caterpillar also has to be responsive to local demands. Therefore, as illustrated in Figure 8.3, Caterpillar confronts significant pressures for cost reductions and for local responsiveness.

To deal with cost pressures, Caterpillar redesigned its products to use many identical components and invested in a few large-scale component manufacturing

FIGURE 8.3

Cost Pressures and Pressures for Local Responsiveness Facing Caterpillar

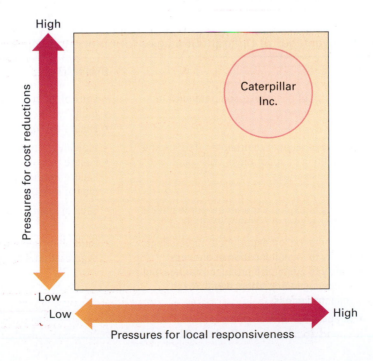

facilities, sited at favorable locations, to fill global demand and realize scale economies. At the same time the company augments the centralized manufacturing of components with assembly plants in each of its major global markets. At these plants, Caterpillar adds local product features, tailoring the finished product to local needs. Thus, Caterpillar is able to realize many of the benefits of global manufacturing while reacting to pressures for local responsiveness by differentiating its product among national markets.[15] Caterpillar started to pursue this strategy in 1979 and by 1997 had succeeded in doubling output per employee, significantly reducing its overall cost structure in the process. Meanwhile, Komatsu and Hitachi, which are still wedded to a Japan-centric global strategy, have seen their cost advantages evaporate and have been steadily losing market share to Caterpillar.

One might also argue that MTV Networks shifted from an international to a transnational strategy in the 1990s (see the *Opening Case*). Rather than creating everything in the United States, MTV now tries to strike a balance between the need to maintain uniformity in operating principles and the "frenetic look" of MTV programming across its global operations and the need to customize programming and content to local tastes and preferences.

Changing a company's business model to build an organization capable of supporting a transnational strategy is a complex and challenging task. Indeed, some would say it is too complex, because the strategy implementation problems of creating a viable organizational structure and control systems to manage this strategy are immense. Thus, a company might be better off focusing on tailoring or adjusting an international or global strategy to its particular needs by working on its business model to achieve the gains from both low cost and differentiation. After all, today, every business model is a matter of balancing pressures to lower a company's cost structure against pressures to provide customers with valuable differentiated products. Recognizing these caveats, the potential advantages and disadvantages of each of these four strategies are summarized in Table 8.1.

TABLE 8.1

The Advantages and Disadvantages of Different Strategies for Competing Globally

Strategy	Advantages	Disadvantages
International	• Transfer of distinctive competencies to foreign markets	• Lack of local responsiveness • Inability to realize location economies • Failure to exploit experience-curve effects
Multidomestic	• Ability to customize product offerings and marketing in accordance with local responsiveness	• Inability to realize location economies • Failure to exploit experience-curve effects • Failure to transfer distinctive competencies to foreign markets
Global	• Ability to exploit experience-curve effects • Ability to exploit location economies	• Lack of local responsiveness
Transnational	• Ability to exploit experience-curve effects • Ability to exploit location economies • Ability to customize product offerings and marketing in accordance with local responsiveness • Reaping benefits of global learning	• Difficulties in implementation because of organizational problems

Basic Entry Decisions

A company contemplating foreign expansion must make three basic decisions: which overseas markets to enter, when to enter those markets, and on what scale.

Which Overseas Markets to Enter

There are over 200 nation-states in the world, and they do not all hold out the same profit potential for a company contemplating foreign expansion. The choice of foreign markets must be made on an assessment of their long-run profit potential. The attractiveness of a country as a potential market for an international business depends on balancing the benefits, costs, and risks associated with doing business in that country. The long-run economic benefits of doing business in a country are a function of factors such as the size of a market (in terms of demographics), the existing wealth (purchasing power) of consumers in that market, and the likely future wealth of consumers. Some markets are very large when measured by numbers of consumers (e.g., China and India), but low living standards may imply limited purchasing power and therefore a relatively small market when measured in economic terms. The costs and risks associated with doing business in a foreign country are typically lower in economically advanced and politically stable democratic nations and greater in less developed and politically unstable nations.

By performing benefit-cost-risk calculations, a company can come up with a ranking of countries in terms of their attractiveness and long-run profit potential.[16] Obviously, preference is given to entering markets that rank highly. For an example, consider the case of the American financial services company Merrill Lynch, whose situation is profiled in Strategy in Action 8.4. During the past decade, Merrill Lynch greatly expanded its operations in the United Kingdom, Canada, and Japan. All three of these countries have a large pool of private savings and exhibit relatively low political and economic risks, so it makes sense that they would be attractive to Merrill Lynch. By offering its financial service products, such as mutual funds and investment advice, Merrill Lynch should be able to capture a large enough proportion of the private savings pool in each country to justify its investment in setting up business there. Of the three countries, Japan is probably the riskiest given the fragile state of its financial system, still suffering from a serious bad debt problem. However, the large size of the Japanese market and the fact that its government seems to be embarking on significant reform explains why Merrill has been attracted to this nation.

One other factor of importance is the value that a company's business model can create in a foreign market. This depends on the suitability of its business model to that market and the nature of indigenous competition.[17] Most important, if the company can offer a product that has not been widely available in that market and satisfies an unmet need, the value of that product to consumers is likely to be much greater than if the company simply offers the same type of product that indigenous competitors and other foreign entrants are already offering. Greater value translates into an ability to charge higher prices or build up unit sales volume more rapidly (or both). Again, on this count, Japan is clearly very attractive to Merrill Lynch.

Timing of Entry

Once a set of attractive national markets has been identified, it is important to consider the timing of entry: *early* (before other overseas companies) or *late* (after other international businesses have already established themselves in the market).

Several first-mover advantages are frequently associated with entering a market early.[18] One advantage is the ability to preempt rivals and capture demand by establishing a strong brand name. A second is the ability to build up demand, sales revenue, and market share in that country and ride down the experience curve ahead of

Strategy in Action

Merrill Lynch in Japan

8.4

Merrill Lynch, the U.S.-based financial services institution, is an investment banking titan. It is the world's largest underwriter of debt and equity and the third largest mergers and acquisitions adviser behind Morgan Stanley and Goldman Sachs. As one might expect, its investment banking operations have long had a global reach. The company has a dominant presence not only in New York but also in London and Tokyo. However, until recently, Merrill's international presence was limited to the investment banking side of its business. In contrast, its private client business, which offers banking, financial advice, and stock brokerage services to individuals, has historically been concentrated in the United States. This is now changing rapidly. In 1995, Merrill purchased Smith New Court, the largest stock brokerage firm in Britain and in 1997 acquired Mercury Asset Management, the U.K.'s leading manager of mutual funds. Then in 1998 Merrill acquired Midland Walwyn, Canada's last major independent stock brokerage firm. The company's boldest moves, however, have probably been in Japan.

Merrill started to establish a private client business in Japan in the 1980s but met with limited success. At the time, it was the first foreign firm to enter Japan's private client investment market, and it had great difficulty in attracting employee talent and customers away from Japan's big four stock brokerage firms, which traditionally had monopolized the Japanese market. Moreover, restrictive regulations made it almost impossible for Merrill to offer its Japanese private clients the range of services it offered clients in the United States. For example, foreign exchange regulations meant that it was very difficult for Merrill to sell non-Japanese stocks, bonds, and mutual funds to Japanese investors. In 1993, Merrill admitted defeat, closed down its six retail branches in Kobe and Kyoto, and withdrew from the private client market in Japan.

Over the next few years, however, things started to change. In the mid-1990s, Japan embarked on a wide-ranging deregulation of its financial services industry. Among other things, this led to the removal of many of the restrictions that had made it so difficult for Merrill to do business in Japan. For example, the relaxation of foreign exchange controls meant that by 1998, it was possible for Japanese citizens to purchase foreign stocks, bonds, and mutual funds. Meanwhile, Japan's big four stock brokerage firms continued to struggle with serious financial problems, the result of the 1991 crash of that country's stock market. In November 1997, in what was a dramatic shock to many Japanese, one of these firms, Yamaichi Securities, declared that it was bankrupt: it had $2.2 billion in accumulated "hidden losses" and would shut its doors. Recognizing the country's financial system was strained and in need of fresh capital, know-how, and the stimulus of greater competition, the Japanese government signaled that it would adopt a much more relaxed attitude to foreign entry into its financial services industry. This attitude underlay Japan's wholehearted endorsement of a 1997 deal brokered by the World Trade Organization (WTO) to liberalize global financial services. Among other things, the WTO deal made it much easier for foreign firms to sell financial service products to Japanese investors.

By 1997, it had become clear to Merrill Lynch that the climate in Japan had changed significantly. The big attraction of the market was still the same: the financial assets owned by Japanese households are huge, amounting to a staggering 1,220 trillion yen in late 1997, with only 3 percent invested in mutual funds (most are invested in low-yielding bank accounts and government bonds). However, attitudes were changing, and it looked as if it would be much easier to do business in Japan.

Accordingly, in mid-1997, Merrill started to consider reentering the Japanese private client market. Initially, it considered a joint venture with Sanwa Bank to sell Merrill's mutual fund products to Japanese consumers through Sanwa's 400 retail branches. The proposed alliance had the advantage of allowing Merrill to leverage Sanwa's existing distribution system rather than having to build a distribution system of its own from scratch. However, in the long run, the strategy would not have given Merrill the presence that it felt it needed to build a solid financial services business in Japan. Merrill's executives reasoned that it was important for them to make a major commitment to the Japanese market in order to establish its brand name as a premier provider of investment products and financial advice to individuals. This would enable the company to entrench itself as a major player before other foreign institutions entered the market—and before Japan's own stock brokerages rose to the challenge. At the same time, given their prior experience in Japan, Merrill's executives were hesitant to go down this road because of the huge costs and risks.

The problem of how best to enter the Japanese market was solved by the bankruptcy of Yamaichi Securities. Suddenly Yamaichi's nationwide network of offices and 7,000 employees were up for grabs. In late December 1997, Merrill announced that it would hire some 2,000 of Yamaichi's employees and acquire up to 50 of Yamaichi's branch offices. The deal, enthusiastically endorsed by the Japanese government, significantly lowered Merrill's costs of establishing a retail network in Japan. Merrill's goal for the new subsidiary was to have $20 billion under management by 2000 and break even by 2001. The company got off to a quick start. In February 1998, Merrill launched its first mutual fund in Japan and saw the value of its assets swell to $1 billion by April. By the beginning of 2001, Merrill Lynch announced that it had $26 billion under management in Japan, giving the company a significant head start over other foreign financial service

institutions in building a private client network in Japan. However, unfortunately for Merrill, Japan's economy weakened significantly in 2001 and it now seems unlikely that Merrill will break even on its Japanese investment until 2003. Still, Merrill's belief is that when the Japanese economy recovers and other foreign institutions enter, it will already have a commanding presence in Japan that will be difficult to challenge.

Sources: "Japan's Big Bang. Enter Merrill," *Economist,* January 3, 1998, p. 72. J. P. Donlon, "Merrill Cinch," *Chief Executive* (March 1998): 28–32. D. Holley, "Merrill Lynch to Open 31 Offices Throughout Japan," *Los Angeles Times,* February 13, 1998, p. D1. A. Rowley, "Merrill Thunders into Japan," *Banker* (March 1998): 6. Staff Reporter. "Hard Times: Foreign Brokers in Japan," *The Economist,* February 23rd, 2002, pp. 78–79. Merrill Lynch's web site, www.ml.com.

future rivals. Both factors give the early entrant a cost advantage over later entrants, which may enable it to respond to later entry by cutting prices below those of later entrants and drive them out of the market. A third advantage is the ability of early entrants to create switching costs that tie customers into their products or services. Such switching costs make it difficult for later entrants to win business.

The case of Merrill Lynch illustrates these ideas. By entering the private client market in Japan early, Merrill hoped to establish a brand name that later entrants would find difficult to match. Moreover, by entering early with a valuable product offering, Merrill hoped to build up its sales volume rapidly, which will enable it to realize scale economies from establishing a network of Japanese branches. In addition, as Merrill trains its Japanese staff, their productivity should rise, due to learning economies, which again translates into lower costs. Thus, Merrill should be able to ride down the experience curve and achieve a lower cost structure than later entrants.

Finally, Merrill's business model is based on establishing close relationships between its financial advisers (i.e., stockbrokers) and private clients. Merrill's financial advisers are taught to get to know the needs of their clients and help manage their finances more effectively. Once these relationships are established, people rarely change. In other words, due to switching costs, they are unlikely to shift their business to later entrants. This effect is likely to be particularly strong in a country like Japan, where long-term relationships have traditionally been very important in business and social settings. For all of these reasons, Merrill Lynch may be able to capture first-mover advantages that will enable it to enjoy a strong competitive position in Japan for years to come.

There can also be first-mover disadvantages associated with entering a foreign market before other global companies.[19] These disadvantages are associated with *pioneering costs*, which an early entrant has to bear that a later entrant can avoid. Pioneering costs arise when the business system in a foreign country is so different from that in a company's home market that a company has to devote considerable effort, time, and expense to learning the rules of the game. Pioneering costs also include the costs of business failure if the company, due to its ignorance of the overseas environment, makes major strategic mistakes. There is a liability associated with being a global company that is one of the first to enter a national market.[20] Research evidence suggests that the probability of survival increases if an international business enters a national market *after* several other overseas companies have already done so.[21] The late entrant, it would appear, benefits by observing and learning from the mistakes made by early entrants.

Pioneering costs also include the costs of promoting and establishing a product offering, including the costs of educating customers. These costs can be particularly significant when the product being promoted is one that local customers are unfamiliar with. In many ways, Merrill Lynch will have to bear such pioneering costs in Japan. Most Japanese are not familiar with the type of investment products and services that it intends to sell, so Merrill will have to invest significant resources in customer education. In contrast, later entrants may be able to free-ride on an early entrant's investments in learning and customer education by watching how the early entrant proceeded in the market, avoiding costly mistakes made by the early entrant, and exploiting the market potential created by the early entrant's investments in customer education.

Scale of Entry and Strategic Commitments

The final issue that a company needs to consider when contemplating market entry is the scale of entry. Entering a market on a large scale involves the commitment of significant resources to that venture. Not all companies have the resources necessary to enter on a large scale, and even some large companies prefer to enter overseas markets on a small scale and then build their presence slowly over time as they become more familiar with the market. The original entry by Merrill Lynch into the private client market in Japan was on a small scale, involving only a handful of branches. In contrast, Merrill's reentry into the Japanese market in 1997 was on a significant scale.

The consequences of entering on a significant scale are associated with the value of the resulting strategic commitments.[22] A *strategic commitment* is a decision that has a long-term impact and is difficult to reverse. Deciding to enter a foreign market on a significant scale is a major strategic commitment. Strategic commitments, such as large-scale market entry, can have an important influence on the nature of competition in a market. For example, by entering Japan's private client business on a significant scale, Merrill has signaled its commitment to the market. This will have several effects. On the positive side, it will make it easier for Merrill to attract clients. The scale of entry gives potential clients reason for believing that Merrill will remain in the market for the long run. It may also give other overseas institutions considering entry into Japan's market pause for thought, since now they will have to compete not only against Japan's indigenous institutions but also against an aggressive and successful U.S. institution. On the negative side, the move may wake up Japan's financial institutions and elicit a vigorous competitive response from them. Moreover, by committing itself heavily to Japan, Merrill may have fewer resources available to support expansion in other desirable markets. In other words, Merrill's commitment to Japan limits its strategic flexibility.

As this example suggests, significant strategic commitments are neither unambiguously good nor bad. Rather, they tend to change the competitive playing field and unleash a number of changes, some of which may be desirable and some of which will not. It is therefore important for a company to think through the implications of large-scale entry into a market and act accordingly. Of particular relevance is trying to identify how actual and potential competitors might react to large-scale entry into a market. It is also important to bear in mind a connection between large-scale entry and first-mover advantages. Specifically, the large-scale entrant is more likely than the small-scale entrant to be able to capture first-mover advantages associated with demand preemption, scale economies, and switching costs.

Balanced against the value and risks of the commitments associated with large-scale entry are the benefits of entering on a small scale. Small-scale entry has the advantage of allowing a company to learn about a foreign market while simultaneously limiting the company's exposure to that market. In this sense, small-scale entry can be seen as a way of gathering more information about a foreign market before deciding whether to enter on a significant scale and how best to enter that market. In other words, by giving the company time to collect information, small-scale entry reduces the risks associated with a subsequent large-scale entry. On the other hand, the lack of commitment associated with small-scale entry may make it more difficult for the small-scale entrant to build market share and capture first-mover or early-mover advantages. The risk-averse company that enters a foreign market on a small scale may limit its potential losses, but it may also lose the chance to capture first-mover advantages.

The Choice of Entry Mode

The issue of when and how to enter a new national market raises the question of how to determine the best mode or vehicle for such entry. There are five main choices of entry mode: exporting, licensing, franchising, entering into a joint venture with a host country company, and setting up a wholly owned subsidiary in the host country. Each entry mode has its advantages and disadvantages, and managers must weigh these carefully when deciding which mode to use.[23]

Exporting

Most manufacturing companies begin their global expansion as exporters and only later switch to one of the other modes for serving a foreign market. Exporting has two distinct advantages: it avoids the costs of establishing manufacturing operations in the host country, which are often substantial, and it may be consistent with realizing experience curve cost economies and location economies. By manufacturing the product in a centralized location and then exporting it to other national markets, the company may be able to realize substantial scale economies from its global sales volume. That is how Sony came to dominate the global television market, how Matsushita came to dominate the VCR market, and how many Japanese auto companies originally made inroads into the U.S. auto market.

There are also a number of drawbacks to exporting. First, exporting from the company's home base may not be appropriate if there are lower-cost locations for manufacturing the product abroad (that is, if the company can realize location economies by moving production elsewhere). Thus, particularly in the case of a company pursuing a global or transnational strategy, it may pay to manufacture in a location where conditions are most favorable from a value creation perspective and then export from that location to the rest of the globe. This is not so much an argument against exporting as an argument against exporting from the company's home country. For example, many U.S. electronics companies have moved some of their manufacturing to Asia because low-cost but highly skilled labor is available there. They export from that location to the rest of the globe, including the United States.

Another drawback is that high transport costs can make exporting uneconomical, particularly in the case of bulk products. One way of getting around this problem is to manufacture bulk products on a regional basis, realizing some economies from large-scale production while limiting transport costs. Many multinational chemical companies manufacture their products on a regional basis, serving several countries in a region from one facility.

Tariff barriers, too, can make exporting uneconomical, and a government's threat to impose tariff barriers can make the strategy very risky. Indeed, the implicit threat from the U.S. Congress to impose tariffs on Japanese cars imported into the United States led directly to the decision by many Japanese auto companies to set up manufacturing plants in the United States.

Finally, a common practice among companies that are just beginning to export also poses risks. A company may delegate marketing activities in each country in which it does business to a local agent, but there is no guarantee that the agent will act in the company's best interest. Often foreign agents also carry the products of competing companies and thus have divided loyalties. Consequently, they may not do as good a job as the company would if it managed marketing itself. One way to solve this problem is to set up a wholly owned subsidiary in the host country to handle local marketing. In this way, the company can reap the cost advantages that arise from manufacturing the product in a single location and exercise tight control over marketing strategy in the host country.

Licensing

International licensing is an arrangement whereby a foreign licensee buys the rights to produce a company's product in the licensee's country for a negotiated fee (normally, royalty payments on the number of units sold). The licensee then puts up most of the capital necessary to get the overseas operation going.[24] The advantage of licensing is that the company does not have to bear the development costs and risks associated with opening up a foreign market. Licensing therefore can be a very attractive option for companies that lack the capital to develop operations overseas. It can also be an attractive option for companies that are unwilling to commit substantial financial resources to an unfamiliar or politically volatile foreign market where political risks are particularly high.

Licensing has three serious drawbacks, however. First, it does not give a company the tight control over manufacturing, marketing, and strategic functions in foreign countries that it needs to have in order to realize experience curve cost economies and location economies—as companies pursuing both global and transnational strategies try to do. Typically, each licensee sets up its own manufacturing operations. Hence, the company stands little chance of realizing experience curve cost economies and location economies by manufacturing its product in a centralized location. When these economies are likely to be important, licensing may not be the best way of expanding overseas.

Second, competing in a global marketplace may make it necessary for a company to coordinate strategic moves across countries so that the profits earned in one country can be used to support competitive attacks in another. Licensing, by its very nature, severely limits a company's ability to coordinate strategy in this way. A licensee is unlikely to let a multinational company take its profits (beyond those due in the form of royalty payments) and use them to support an entirely different licensee operating in another country.

A third problem with licensing is the risk associated with licensing technological know-how to foreign companies. For many multinational companies, technological know-how forms the basis of their competitive advantage, and they would want to maintain control over the use to which it is put. By licensing its technology, a company can quickly lose control over it. RCA, for instance, once licensed its color television technology to a number of Japanese companies. The Japanese companies quickly assimilated RCA's technology and then used it to enter the U.S. market. Now the Japanese have a bigger share of the U.S. market than the RCA brand does.

There are ways of reducing this risk. One way is by entering into a cross-licensing agreement with a foreign firm. Under **a cross-licensing agreement,** a firm might license some valuable intangible property to a foreign partner, and in addition to a royalty payment, also request that the foreign partner license some of its valuable know-how to the firm. Such agreements are reckoned to reduce the risks associated with licensing technological know-how, since the licensee realizes that if it violates the spirit of a licensing contract (by using the knowledge obtained to compete directly with the licensor), the licensor can do the same to it. Put differently, cross-licensing agreements enable firms to hold each other hostage, which thereby reduces the probability that they will behave opportunistically toward each other.[25] Such cross-licensing agreements are increasingly common in high-technology industries. For example, the U.S. biotechnology firm Amgen has licensed one of its key drugs, Nuprogene, to Kirin, the Japanese pharmaceutical company. The license gives Kirin the right to sell Nuprogene in Japan. In return, Amgen receives a royalty payment, and through a licensing agreement it gained the right to sell certain of Kirin's products in the United States.

Franchising

In many respects, franchising is similar to licensing, although franchising tends to involve longer-term commitments than licensing. **Franchising** is basically a specialized form of licensing in which the franchiser not only sells intangible property to the franchisee (normally a trademark), but also insists that the franchisee agree to abide by strict rules as to how it does business. The franchiser will also often assist the franchisee to run the business on an ongoing basis. As with licensing, the franchiser typically receives a royalty payment, which amounts to some percentage of the franchisee revenues.

Whereas licensing is a strategy pursued primarily by manufacturing companies, franchising, which resembles it in some respects, is a strategy employed chiefly by service companies. McDonald's provides a good example of a firm that has grown by using a franchising strategy. McDonald's has set down strict rules as to how franchisees should operate a restaurant. These rules extend to control over the menu, cooking methods, staffing policies, and restaurant design and location. McDonald's also organizes the supply chain for its franchisees and provides management training and financial assistance.[26]

The advantages of franchising are similar to those of licensing. Specifically, the franchiser does not have to bear the development costs and risks of opening up a foreign market on its own, for the franchisee typically assumes those costs and risks. Thus, using a franchising strategy, a service company can build up a global presence quickly and at a low cost.

The disadvantages are less pronounced than in the case of licensing. Because franchising is a strategy used by service companies, a franchiser does not have to consider the need to coordinate manufacturing in order to achieve experience curve effects and location economies. Nevertheless, franchising may inhibit a company's ability to achieve global strategic coordination.

A more significant disadvantage of franchising is the lack of quality control. The foundation of franchising arrangements is the notion that the company's brand name conveys a message to consumers about the quality of the company's product. Thus, a traveler booking into a Hilton International hotel in Hong Kong can reasonably expect the same quality of room, food, and service as she would receive in New York; the Hilton brand name is a guarantee of the consistency of product quality. However, foreign franchisees may not be as concerned about quality as they should be, and poor quality may mean not only lost sales in the foreign market but also a decline in the company's worldwide reputation. For example, if the traveler has a bad experience at the Hilton in Hong Kong, she may never go to another Hilton hotel and steer her colleagues away as well. The geographic distance separating it from its foreign franchisees and the sheer number of individual franchisees—tens of thousands in the case of McDonald's—can make it difficult for the franchiser to detect poor quality. Consequently, quality problems may persist.

To reduce this problem, a company can set up a subsidiary in each country or region in which it is expanding. The subsidiary, which might be wholly owned by the company or a joint venture with a foreign company, then assumes the rights and obligations to establish franchises throughout that particular country or region. The combination of proximity and the limited number of independent franchisees that have to be monitored reduces the quality control problem. Besides, since the subsidiary is at least partly owned by the company, the company can place its own managers in the subsidiary to ensure the kind of quality monitoring it wants. This organizational arrangement has proved very popular in practice. It has been used by McDonald's, KFC, and Hilton Hotels Corp. to expand their international operations, to name just three examples.

Joint Ventures

Establishing a joint venture with a foreign company has long been a favored mode for entering a new market. One of the most famous long-term joint ventures is the Fuji-Xerox joint venture to produce photocopiers for the Japanese market. The most typical form of joint venture is a fifty-fifty venture, in which each party takes a 50 percent ownership stake and operating control is shared by a team of managers from both parent companies. Some companies have sought joint ventures in which they have a majority shareholding (for example, a 51 percent to 49 percent ownership split), which permits tighter control by the dominant partner.[27]

Joint ventures have a number of advantages. First, a company may feel that it can benefit from a local partner's knowledge of a host country's competitive conditions, culture, language, political systems, and business systems. Second, when the development costs and risks of opening up a foreign market are high, a company might gain by sharing these costs and risks with a local partner. Third, in some countries, political considerations make joint ventures the only feasible entry mode.[28] For example, historically many U.S. companies found it much easier to get permission to set up operations in Japan if they went in with a Japanese partner than if they tried to enter on their own. This is why Xerox originally teamed up with Fuji to sell photocopiers in Japan.

Despite these advantages, joint ventures can be difficult to establish and run because of two main drawbacks. First, as in the case of licensing, a company that enters into a joint venture risks losing control over its technology to its venture partner. To minimize this risk, it can seek a majority ownership stake in the joint venture, for as the dominant partner it would be able to exercise greater control over its technology. The trouble with this strategy is that it may be difficult to find a foreign partner willing to accept a minority ownership position.

The second disadvantage is that a joint venture does not give a company the tight control over its subsidiaries that it might need in order to realize experience curve effects or location economies—as both global and transnational companies try to do—or to engage in coordinated global attacks against its global rivals. Consider the entry of Texas Instruments (TI) into the Japanese semiconductor market. When TI established semiconductor facilities in Japan, part of its objective was to limit Japanese manufacturers' market share and the amount of cash available to them to invade TI's global market. In other words, TI was engaging in global strategic coordination. To implement this strategy, TI's Japanese subsidiary had to be prepared to take instructions from the TI corporate headquarters regarding competitive strategy. The strategy also required that the Japanese subsidiary be run at a loss if necessary. Clearly, a Japanese joint venture partner would have been unlikely to accept such conditions since they would have meant a negative return on investment. Thus, in order to implement this strategy, TI set up a wholly owned subsidiary in Japan instead of entering this market through a joint venture.

Wholly Owned Subsidiaries

A **wholly owned subsidiary** is one in which the parent company owns 100 percent of the subsidiary's stock. To establish a wholly owned subsidiary in a foreign market, a company can either set up a completely new operation in that country or acquire an established host country company and use it to promote its products in the host market (as Merrill Lynch did when it acquired various assets of Yamaichi Securities; see Strategy in Action 8.3).

Setting up a wholly owned subsidiary offers three advantages. First, when a company's competitive advantage is based on its control of a technological competency, a wholly owned subsidiary will normally be the preferred entry mode, since it reduces the company's risk of losing this control. Consequently, many high-tech companies prefer wholly owned subsidiaries to joint ventures or licensing arrangements. Wholly owned subsidiaries tend to be the favored entry mode in the semiconductor, computer, electronics, and pharmaceutical industries. Second, a wholly owned subsidiary gives a company the kind of tight control over operations in different countries that it needs if it is going to engage in global strategic coordination—taking profits from one country to support competitive attacks in another.

Third, a wholly owned subsidiary may be the best choice if a company wants to realize location economies and experience curve effects. When pressures on costs are intense, it may pay a company to configure its value chain in such a way that value added at each stage is maximized. Thus, a national subsidiary may specialize in manufacturing only part of the product line or certain components of the end product, exchanging parts and products with other subsidiaries in the company's global system. Establishing such a global production system requires a high degree of control over the operations of national affiliates. Different national operations have to be prepared to accept centrally determined decisions as to how they should produce, how much they should produce, and how their output should be priced for transfer between operations. A wholly owned subsidiary would have to comply with these mandates, whereas licensees or joint venture partners would most likely shun such a subservient role. This is one reason that Dell Computer has used wholly owned subsidiaries as its vehicle for expanding its global business (see the *Running Case* for Dell's global strategy).

On the other hand, establishing a wholly owned subsidiary is generally the most costly method of serving a foreign market. The parent company must bear all the costs and risks of setting up overseas operations—in contrast to joint ventures, where the costs and risks are shared, or licensing, where the licensee bears most of the costs and risks. But the risks of learning to do business in a new culture diminish if the company acquires an established host country enterprise. Acquisitions, though, raise a whole set of additional problems, such as trying to marry divergent corporate cultures, and these problems may more than offset the benefits. (The problems associated with acquisitions are discussed in Chapter 10.)

Choosing Among Entry Modes   The advantages and disadvantages of the various entry modes are summarized in Table 8.2. Inevitably, there are trade-offs in choosing one entry mode over another. For example, when considering entry into an unfamiliar country with a track record of nationalizing foreign-owned enterprises, a company might favor a joint venture

Running Case

Dell's Global Business

For more than a decade, Dell Computer has been expanding outside its U.S. base. In 2001, it generated revenues of $5.59 billion from Europe and $1.80 billion from the Asia-Pacific region. Although this level of sales is still small compared to the $17.88 billion it logged in North America, growth is now more rapid overseas, particularly in Asia. Dell's strategic goal is to be the low-cost player in the global industry. It does not alter its business model from country to country, but instead uses the same direct selling model and supply chain management process that have been the cornerstone of its success in North America. Dell is thus pursuing a global strategy.

Dell's basic approach to overseas expansion has been to serve foreign markets from a handful of regional manufacturing facilities, each established as a wholly owned subsidiary. To support its global business, it operates manufacturing facilities in and around Austin, Texas; Eldorado do Sul, Brazil; Nashville, Tennessee; Limerick, Ireland; Penang, Malaysia; and Xiamen, China. The plants in Austin and Tennessee serve North America, Eldorado do Sul serves South America, and Penang serves all of Asia-Pacific except China and Hong Kong, which are served from Xiamen. Europe is served from the Limerick facility.

Each of these manufacturing plants is large enough to attain significant scale economies, helping to underpin Dell's quest to be the low-cost player in the global industry. When demand in a region starts to get big enough, Dell considers opening up a second plant. It has two plants in Limerick. Its plant in Xiamen, China, was established to accommodate rapid demand growth in that country. Currently, one of Dell's fastest-growing Asian markets is India, and to accommodate demand there, it is looking at the possibility of establishing an Indian manufacturing operation.

Each plant uses exactly the same supply chain management processes that have made Dell famous. Taking advantage of its Internet-based supply chain management software, Dell schedules production of every line in every factory around the world every two hours. Every factory in the world is run with no more than six hours of inventory on hand, including work in progress. To serve Dell's global factories, many of its largest suppliers have also located facilities close to Dell's manufacturing plants so that they can better meet the company's demand for just-in-time inventory.

Dell has set up customer service centers at each of these plants to handle phone and online orders and to provide technical assistance. Each center serves an entire region, which Dell has found to be more efficient than locating a customer service center in each country where the company does business. Although online orders as a percentage of the total are lower outside the United States, they are growing rapidly. In Asia, for example, more than 40 percent of orders are now made online, up from 20 percent a few years ago.

For all of the similarities, however, Dell's customer mix is different overseas. In Asia, for example, Dell is seen primarily as a supplier of PCs and servers to businesses. It does not have the large consumer business that it has in the United States. However, this may be about to change. In 2001, Dell opened an overseas product development center in Beijing, China. Set up as a wholly owned subsidiary, the center has been charged with creating products geared toward the low end of the Chinese market. Apparently, even low-end PCs designed in the United States are too sophisticated and powerful for many Chinese consumers.

Sources: Dell Computer Corporation, 2001 Form 10K. K. James, "What Slowdown? Dell Asia-Pac's Going Great Guns," *Business Times,* January 15, 2001, p. 1. F. Balfour, "Penang's Secret," *Business Week,* November 6, 2000, p. 50.

TABLE 8.2

The Advantages and Disadvantages of Different Entry Modes

Entry Mode	Advantages	Disadvantages
Exporting	• Ability to realize location and experience-curve economies	• High transport costs • Trade barriers • Problems with local marketing agents
Licensing	• Low development costs and risks	• Inability to realize location and experience-curve economies • Inability to engage in global strategic coordination • Lack of control over technology
Franchising	• Low development costs and risks	• Inability to engage in global strategic coordination • Lack of control over quality
Joint ventures	• Access to local partner's knowledge • Shared development costs and risks • Political dependency	• Inability to engage in global strategic coordination • Inability to realize location and experience-curve economies • Lack of control over technology
Wholly owned subsidiaries	• Protection of technology • Ability to engage in global strategic coordination • Ability to realize location and experience-curve economies	• High costs and risks

with a local enterprise. Its rationale might be that the local partner will help it establish operations in an unfamiliar environment and speak out against nationalization should the possibility arise. But if the company's distinctive competency is based on proprietary technology, entering into a joint venture might mean risking loss of control over that technology to the joint venture partner, which would make this strategy unattractive. Despite such hazards, some generalizations can be offered about the optimal choice of entry mode.

Distinctive Competencies and Entry Mode. When companies expand internationally to earn greater returns from their distinctive competencies, transferring the skills and products derived from their competencies to foreign markets where indigenous competitors lack those skills, the companies are pursuing an international strategy. The optimal entry mode for such companies depends to some degree on the nature of their distinctive competency. In particular, we need to distinguish between companies with a distinctive competency in technological know-how and those with a distinctive competency in management know-how.

If a company's competitive advantage—its distinctive competency—derives from its control of proprietary *technological know-how,* licensing and joint venture arrangements should be avoided if possible in order to minimize the risk of losing control of that technology. Thus, if a high-tech company is considering setting up operations in a foreign country in order to profit from a distinctive competency in technological know-how, it should probably do so through a wholly owned subsidiary.

However, this rule should not be viewed as a hard and fast one. For instance, a licensing or joint venture arrangement might be structured in such a way as to reduce the risks that a company's technological know-how will be expropriated by licensees or joint venture partners. We consider this kind of arrangement in more detail later in the chapter when we discuss the issue of structuring strategic alliances. To take another exception to the rule, a company may perceive its technological advantage as being only transitory and expect rapid imitation of its core technology by competitors. In this situation, the company might want to license its technology as quickly as possible to foreign companies in order to gain global acceptance of its technology before imitation occurs.[29] Such a strategy has some advantages. By licensing its technology to competitors, the company may deter them from developing their own, possibly superior, technology. It also may be able to establish its technology as the dominant design in the industry (as Matsushita did with its VHS format for VCRs), ensuring a steady stream of royalty payments. Such situations apart, however, the attractions of licensing are probably outweighed by the risks of losing control of technology, and therefore licensing should be avoided.

The competitive advantage of many service companies, such as McDonald's or Hilton Hotels, is based on *management know-how*. For such companies, the risk of losing control of their management skills to franchisees or joint venture partners is not that great. The reason is that the valuable asset of such companies is their brand name, and brand names are generally well protected by international laws pertaining to trademarks. Given this fact, many of the issues that arise in the case of technological know-how do not arise in the case of management know-how. As a result, many service companies favor a combination of franchising and subsidiaries to control franchisees within a particular country or region. The subsidiary may be wholly owned or a joint venture. In most cases, however, service companies have found that entering into a joint venture with a local partner in order to set up a controlling subsidiary in a country or region works best because a joint venture is often politically more acceptable and brings a degree of local knowledge to the subsidiary.

Pressures for Cost Reduction and Entry Mode. The greater the pressures for cost reductions are, the more likely it is that a company will want to pursue some combination of exporting and wholly owned subsidiaries. By manufacturing in the locations where factor conditions are optimal and then exporting to the rest of the world, a company may be able to realize substantial location economies and experience curve effects. The company might then want to export the finished product to marketing subsidiaries based in various countries. Typically, these subsidiaries would be wholly owned and have the responsibility for overseeing distribution in a particular country. Setting up wholly owned marketing subsidiaries is preferable to a joint venture arrangement or using a foreign marketing agent because it gives the company the tight control over marketing that might be required to coordinate a globally dispersed value chain. In addition, tight control over a local operation enables the company to use the profits generated in one market to improve its competitive position in another market. Hence companies pursuing global or transnational strategies prefer to establish wholly owned subsidiaries.

Global Strategic Alliances

Global strategic alliances are cooperative agreements between companies from different countries that are actual or potential competitors. Strategic alliances run the range from formal joint ventures, in which two or more companies have an equity stake, to short-term contractual agreements, in which two companies may agree to cooperate on a particular problem (such as developing a new product).

Advantages of Strategic Alliances

Companies enter into strategic alliances with competitors to achieve a number of strategic objectives.[30] First, strategic alliances may be a way of *facilitating entry into a foreign market*. For example, Motorola initially found it very difficult to gain access to the Japanese cellular telephone market. In the mid-1980s, it complained loudly about formal and informal Japanese trade barriers. The turning point for Motorola came in 1987, when it formed its alliance with Toshiba to build microprocessors. As part of the deal, Toshiba provided Motorola with marketing help, including some of its best managers. This aided Motorola in the political game of winning government approval to enter the Japanese market and obtaining allocations of radio frequencies for its mobile communications systems. Since then, Motorola has played down the importance of Japan's informal trade barriers. Although privately the company still admits they exist, with Toshiba's help Motorola has become skilled at getting around them.[31]

Second, many companies enter into strategic alliances to share the *fixed costs and associated risks* that arise from the development of new products or processes. Motorola's alliance with Toshiba was partly motivated by a desire to share the high fixed costs associated with setting up an operation to manufacture microprocessors. The microprocessor business is so capital intensive (it cost Motorola and Toshiba close to $1 billion to set up their facility) that few companies can afford the costs and risks of going it alone.

Third, many alliances can be seen as a way of bringing together *complementary skills and assets* that neither company could easily develop on its own. For example, in 1990, AT&T struck a deal with NEC Corp. of Japan to trade technological skills. Under the agreement, AT&T transferred some of its computer-aided design technology to NEC. In return, NEC gave AT&T access to the technology underlying NEC advanced logic computer chips. Such equitable trading of distinctive competencies seems to underlie many of the most successful strategic alliances.

Finally, it may make sense to enter into an alliance if it helps the company *set technological standards for its industry* and if those standards benefit the company. For example, in 1992, the Dutch electronics company Philips entered into an alliance with its global competitor, Matsushita, to manufacture and market the digital compact cassette (DDC) system pioneered by Philips. Linking up with Matsushita would help Philips establish the DCC system as a new technological standard in the recording and customer electronics industries. The issue is an important one because Sony was developing a competing technology that it hoped to establish as the new technical standard. Thus, Philips saw the alliance with Matsushita as a tactic for winning the standard race, for it ties a potential major competitor into its standard.

Disadvantages of Strategic Alliances

The various advantages can be very significant. Nevertheless, some commentators have criticized strategic alliances on the grounds that they give competitors a low-cost route to gain new technology and market access.[32] For example, Robert Reich and Eric Mankin have argued that strategic alliances between U.S. and Japanese companies are part of an implicit Japanese strategy to keep higher-paying, higher-value-added jobs in Japan while gaining the project engineering and production process skills that underlie the competitive success of many U.S. companies.[33] They have viewed Japanese success in the machine tool and semiconductor industries as largely built on U.S. technology acquired through various strategic alliances. And they have asserted that increasingly, U.S. managers are aiding the Japanese in achieving their goals by entering into alliances that channel new inventions to Japan and provide a U.S. sales and distribution network for the resulting products. Although such deals may generate short-term profits, in the long run, according to Reich and Mankin, the result is to "hollow out" U.S. companies, leaving them with no competitive advantage in the global marketplace.

Reich and Mankin have a point: alliances do have risks. Unless it is careful, a company can give away more than it gets in return. Nevertheless, there are so many examples of apparently successful alliances between companies, including alliances between U.S. and Japanese companies, that Reich and Mankin's position seems more than a little extreme. It is difficult to see how the Motorola-Toshiba alliance or the long-standing alliance between Fuji Film and Xerox to manufacture photocopiers (Fuji-Xerox) fit their thesis. In all of these cases, both partners seemed to have gained from the alliance. Because Reich and Mankin undoubtedly do have a point, the question becomes, *Why do some alliances benefit the company, whereas in others, it can end up giving away technology and market access and get very little in return?* The next section provides an answer to this question.

Making Strategic Alliances Work

The failure rate for international strategic alliances is quite high. For example, one study of forty-nine international strategic alliances found that two-thirds run into serious managerial and financial troubles within two years of their formation, and that although many of these problems are ultimately solved, 33 percent are ultimately rated as failures by the parties involved.[34] The success of an alliance seems to be a function of three main factors: partner selection, alliance structure, and the manner in which the alliance is managed.

Partner Selection

One of the keys to making a strategic alliance work is to select the right kind of partner. A good partner has three principal characteristics. First, a good partner helps the company achieve strategic goals such as achieving market access, sharing the costs and risks of new-product development, or gaining access to critical core competencies. In other words, the partner must have capabilities that the company lacks and that it values. Second, a good partner shares the firm's vision for the purpose of the alliance. If two companies approach an alliance with radically different agendas, the chances are great that the relationship will not be harmonious and will end in divorce. This seems to have been the case with the alliance between GM and Daewoo. GM's agenda was to use Daewoo as a source of cheap labor to produce cars for the Korean and U.S. markets, whereas Daewoo wanted to use GM's know-how and distribution systems to increase its own business not just in Korea and the United States but also in Europe. Different perceptions over the strategic role of the venture ultimately contributed to the dissolution of the alliance.

Third, a good partner is unlikely to try to exploit the alliance opportunistically for its own ends—that is, to expropriate the company's technological know-how while giving away little in return. In this respect, firms with reputations for fair play to maintain probably make the best partners. For example, IBM is involved in so many strategic alliances that it would not pay the company to trample roughshod over individual alliance partners. Such actions would tarnish IBM's hard-won reputation of being a good partner and would make it more difficult for IBM to attract alliance partners in the future. Similarly, their reputations make it less likely that Japanese companies such as Sony, Toshiba, and Fuji, which have histories of alliances with non-Japanese firms, would opportunistically exploit an alliance partner.

To select a partner with these three characteristics, a company needs to conduct some comprehensive research on potential alliance candidates. To increase the probability of selecting a good partner, the company should collect as much pertinent publicly available information about potential allies as possible; collect data from informed third parties, including companies that have had alliances with the potential partners, investment bankers who have had dealings with them, and some of their former employees; and get to know potential partners as well as possible before committing to an alliance. This last step should include face-to-face meetings between senior managers (and perhaps middle-level managers) to ensure that the chemistry is right.

Alliance Structure

Having selected a partner, the alliance should be structured so that the company's risk of giving too much away to the partner is reduced to an acceptable level. Figure 8.4 depicts the four safeguards against opportunism by alliance partners that we discuss here. (**Opportunism** includes the "theft" of technology or markets that Reich and Mankin describe.) First, alliances can be designed to make it difficult (if not impossible) to transfer technology not meant to be transferred. Specifically, the design, development, manufacture, and service of a product manufactured by an alliance can be structured so as to "wall off" sensitive technologies to prevent their leakage to the other participant. In the alliance between General Electric and Snecma to build commercial aircraft engines, for example, GE reduced the risk of "excess transfer" by walling off certain sections of the production process. The modularization effectively cut off the transfer of what GE regarded as key competitive technology while permitting Snecma access to final assembly. Similarly, in the alliance between Boeing and the Japanese to build the 767, Boeing walled off research, design, and marketing functions considered central to its competitive position, while allowing the Japanese to share in production technology. Boeing also walled off new technologies not required for 767 production.[35]

Second, contractual safeguards can be written into an alliance agreement to guard against the risk of opportunism by a partner. For example, TRW has three strategic alliances with large Japanese auto component suppliers to produce seat belts, engine valves, and steering gears for sale to Japanese-owned auto assembly plants in the United States. TRW has clauses in each of its alliance contracts that bar the Japanese firms from competing with TRW to supply U.S.-owned auto companies with component parts. By doing this, TRW protects itself against the possibility that the Japanese companies are entering into the alliances merely as a means of gaining access to the North American market to compete with TRW in its home market.

FIGURE 8.4

Structuring Alliances to Reduce Opportunism

Third, both parties to an alliance can agree in advance to swap skills and technologies, thereby ensuring a chance for equitable gain. Cross-licensing agreements are one way to achieve this goal. For example, in the alliance between Motorola and Toshiba, Motorola has licensed some of its microprocessor technology to Toshiba, and in return Toshiba has licensed some of its memory chip technology to Motorola.

Fourth, the risk of opportunism by an alliance partner can be reduced if the firm extracts a significant credible commitment from its partner in advance. The long-term alliance between Xerox and Fuji to build photocopiers for the Asian market perhaps best illustrates this. Rather than enter into an informal agreement or some kind of licensing arrangement (which Fuji Photo initially wanted), Xerox insisted that Fuji invest in a fifty-fifty joint venture to serve Japan and East Asia. This venture constituted such a significant investment in people, equipment, and facilities that Fuji Photo was committed from the outset to making the alliance work in order to earn a return on its investment. By agreeing to the joint venture, Fuji essentially made a credible commitment to the alliance. Given this, Xerox felt secure in transferring its photocopier technology to Fuji.[36]

Managing the Alliance

Once a partner has been selected and an appropriate alliance structure agreed on, the task facing the company is to maximize the benefits from the alliance. One important ingredient of success appears to be sensitivity to cultural differences. Differences in management style can often be attributed to cultural differences. Managers need to make allowances for such differences when dealing with their partner.

In addition, managing an alliance successfully means building interpersonal relationships among managers from the different companies, a lesson that can be drawn from the successful strategic alliance between Ford and Mazda to jointly develop cars for the global auto industry. This partnership resulted in the development of such best-selling cars as the Ford Explorer and the Mazda Navajo. Ford and Mazda have set up a framework of meetings within which managers from Ford and Mazda not only discuss matters pertaining to the alliance but also have sufficient non-work-time to allow them to get to know each other better. The resulting personal friendships can help build trust and facilitate harmonious relations between the two companies.[37] Moreover, personal relationships can create an informal management network between the companies, and this network can then be used to help solve problems that arise in more formal contexts, such as joint committee meetings between personnel from both firms.

A major factor determining how much a company gains from an alliance is its ability to learn from alliance partners. Gary Hamel, Yves Doz, and C. K. Prahalad reached this conclusion after a five-year study of fifteen strategic alliances between major multinationals. They focused on a number of alliances between Japanese companies and Western (European or American) partners. In every case in which a Japanese company emerged from an alliance stronger than its Western partner, the Japanese company had made a greater effort to learn. Indeed, few Western companies seemed to want to learn from their Japanese partners. They tended to regard the alliance purely as a cost-sharing or risk-sharing device rather than as an opportunity to learn how a potential competitor does business.[38]

For an example of an alliance in which there was a clear learning asymmetry, consider the agreement between General Motors and Toyota Motor Corp. to build the Chevrolet Nova. This alliance is structured as a formal joint venture, New United Motor Manufacturing, in which both parties have a 50 percent equity stake. The venture owns an auto plant in Fremont, California. According to one of the Japanese managers, Toyota achieved most of its objectives from the alliance: "We learned about U.S. supply and transportation. And we got the confidence to manage U.S. workers." All that knowledge was then quickly transferred to Georgetown, Kentucky, where Toyota opened a plant of its own in 1988. By contrast, although General Motors got a new product, the Chevrolet Nova, some GM managers complained that their new knowledge was never put to good use inside GM. They say that they should have been kept together as a team to educate GM's engineers and workers about the Japanese system. Instead, they were dispersed to different GM subsidiaries.[39]

When entering an alliance, a company must take some measures to ensure that it learns from its alliance partner and then puts that knowledge to good use within its own organization. One suggested approach is to educate all operating employees about the partner's strengths and weaknesses and make clear to them how acquiring particular skills will bolster their company's competitive position. For such learning to be of value, the knowledge acquired from an alliance has to be diffused throughout the organization—as did not happen at GM. To spread this knowledge, the managers involved in an alliance should be used as a resource in familiarizing others within the company about the skills of an alliance partner.

Summary of Chapter

1. For some companies, international expansion represents a way of earning greater returns by transferring the skills and product offerings derived from their distinctive competencies to markets where indigenous competitors lack those skills.

2. Because of national differences, it pays a company to base each value creation activity it performs at the location where factor conditions are most conducive to the performance of that activity. This strategy is known as focusing on the attainment of location economies.

3. By building sales volume more rapidly, international expansion can assist a company in the process of moving down the experience curve.

4. The best strategy for a company to pursue may depend on the kind of pressures it must cope with: pressures for cost reductions or for local responsiveness. Pressures for cost reductions are greatest in industries producing commodity-type products, where price is the main competitive weapon. Pressures for local responsiveness arise from differences in consumer tastes and preferences, as well as from national infrastructure and traditional practices, distribution channels, and host government demands.

5. Companies pursuing an international strategy transfer the skills and products derived from distinctive competencies to foreign markets, while undertaking some limited local customization.

6. Companies pursuing a multidomestic strategy customize their product offering, marketing strategy, and business strategy to national conditions.

7. Companies pursuing a global strategy focus on reaping the cost reductions that come from experience curve effects and location economies.

8. Many industries are now so competitive that companies must adopt a transnational strategy. This involves a simultaneous focus on reducing costs, transferring skills and products, and local responsiveness. Implementing such a strategy may not be easy.

9. The most attractive foreign markets tend to be found in politically stable developed and developing nations that have free market systems and where there is not a dramatic upsurge in either inflation rates or private sector debt.

10. Several advantages are associated with entering a national market early, before other international businesses have established themselves. These advantages must be balanced against the pioneering costs that early entrants often have to bear, including the greater risk of business failure.

11. Large-scale entry into a national market constitutes a major strategic commitment that is likely to change the nature of competition in that market and limit the entrant's future strategic flexibility. The firm needs to think through the implications of such commitments before embarking on a large-scale entry. Although making major strategic commitments can yield many benefits, there are also risks associated with such a strategy.

12. There are five different ways of entering a foreign market: exporting, licensing, franchising, entering into a joint venture, and setting up a wholly owned subsidiary. The optimal choice among entry modes depends on the company's strategy.

13. Strategic alliances are cooperative agreements between actual or potential competitors. The advantages of alliances are that they facilitate entry into foreign markets, enable partners to share the fixed costs and risks associated with new products and processes, facilitate the transfer of complementary skills between companies, and help companies establish technical standards.

14. The drawbacks of a strategic alliance are that the company risks giving away technological know-how and market access to its alliance partner while getting very little in return.

15. The disadvantages associated with alliances can be reduced if the company selects partners carefully, paying close attention to reputation, and structures the alliance so as to avoid unintended transfers of know-how.

Discussion Questions

1. Plot the position of the following companies on Figure 8.1: Procter & Gamble, IBM, Coca-Cola, Dow Chemicals, AOL, and McDonald's. In each case, justify your answer.

2. Are the following global industries or multidomestic industries: bulk chemicals, pharmaceuticals, branded food products, moviemaking, television manufacture, personal computers, airline travel, and Internet online services such as AOL and MSN?

3. Discuss how the need for control over foreign operations varies with the strategy and distinctive competencies of a company. What are the implications of this relationship for the choice of entry mode?

4. Licensing proprietary technology to foreign competitors is the best way to give up a company's competitive advantage. Discuss.

5. What kind of companies stand to gain the most from entering into strategic alliances with potential competitors? Why?

Practicing Strategic Management

SMALL-GROUP EXERCISE: DEVELOPING A GLOBAL STRATEGY

Break into groups of three to five people, and appoint one group member as a spokesperson who will communicate your findings to the class. You work for a company in the soft drink industry that has developed a line of carbonated fruit-based drinks. You have already established a significant presence in your home market, and now you are planning the global strategy development of the company in the soft drink industry. You need to decide the following:

1. What overall strategy to pursue: a global strategy, multidomestic strategy, international strategy, or transnational strategy

2. Which markets to enter first

3. What entry strategy to pursue (e.g., franchising, joint venture, wholly owned subsidiary)

What information do you need in order to make this kind of decision? On the basis of what you do know, what strategy would you recommend?

ARTICLE FILE 8

Find an example of a multinational company that in recent years has switched its strategy from a multidomestic, international, or global strategy to a transnational strategy.

Identify why the company made the switch and any problems that the company may be encountering while it tries to change its strategic orientation.

STRATEGIC MANAGEMENT PROJECT: MODULE 8

This module requires you to identify how your company might profit from global expansion, the strategy that your company should pursue globally, and the entry mode that it might favor. With the information you have at your disposal, answer the questions regarding the following two situations:

Your company is already doing business in other countries

1. Is your company creating value or lowering the costs of value creation by realizing location economies, transferring distinctive competencies abroad, or realizing cost economies from the experience curve? If not, does it have the potential to?

2. How responsive is your company to differences among nations? Does it vary its product and marketing message from country to country? Should it?

3. What are the cost pressures and pressures for local responsiveness in the industry in which your company is based?

4. What strategy is your company pursuing to compete globally? In your opinion, is this the correct strategy, given cost pressures and pressures for local responsiveness?

5. What major foreign market does your company serve, and what mode has it used to enter this market? Why is your company active in these markets and not others? What are the advantages and disadvantages of using this mode? Might another mode be preferable?

Your company is not yet doing business in other countries

1. What potential does your company have to add value to its products or lower the costs of value creation by expanding internationally?

2. On the international level, what are the cost pressures and pressures for local responsiveness in the industry in which your company is based? What implications do these pressures have for the strategy that your company might pursue if it chose to expand globally?

3. What foreign market might your company enter, and what entry mode should it use to enter this market? Justify your answer.

EXPLORING THE WEB
Visiting IBM

IBM stands for International Business Machines. Using the significant resources located at IBM's corporate web site (**www.ibm.com**), including annual reports and company history, explain what the "International" means in IBM. Specifically, how many countries is IBM active in? How does IBM create value by expanding into foreign markets? What entry mode does IBM adopt in most markets? Can you find any exceptions to this? How would you characterize IBM's strategy for competing in the global marketplace? Is IBM pursuing a transnational, global, international, or multidomestic strategy?

General Task: Search the Web for a company site where there is a good description of that company's international operations. On the basis of this information, try to establish how the company enters foreign markets and what overall strategy it is pursuing (global, international, multidomestic, transnational).

Closing Case

Global Strategy at General Motors

In many respects, General Motors is one of the oldest multinational corporations in the world. Founded in 1908, it established its first international operations in the 1920s. GM is now the world's largest industrial corporation and full-line automobile manufacturer with annual revenues of over $100 billion. The company sells 8 million vehicles per year, 3.2 million of them produced and marketed outside its North American base. In 1997, GM had a 31 percent share of the North American market and an 8.9 percent share of the market in the rest of the world.

Historically, the bulk of GM's foreign operations have been concentrated in Western Europe. Local brand names such as Opel, Vauxhall, Saab, and Holden helped the company to sell 1.7 million vehicles in 1997 and gain an 11.3 percent market share, second only to that of Ford. Although GM has long had a presence in Latin America and Asia, until recently sales there accounted for only a relatively small fraction of the company's total international business. However, GM's plans call for this to change rapidly over the next few years. Sensing that Asia, Latin America, and Eastern Europe may be the automobile industry's growth markets early in this century, GM has embarked on ambitious plans to invest $2.2 billion in four new manufacturing facilities in Argentina, Poland, China, and Thailand. One of the most significant things about this expansion is that it is going hand in hand with a sea change in GM's philosophy toward the management of its international operations.

Traditionally, GM saw the developing world as a dumping ground for obsolete technology and outdated models. Just a few years ago, for example, GM's Brazilian factories were churning out U.S.-designed Chevy Chevettes that hadn't been produced in North America for years. GM's Detroit-based executives saw this as a way of trying to squeeze the maximum cash flow from the company's investments in aging technology. GM managers in the developing world, however, took it as an indication that the center did not view developing world operations as being of great significance. This feeling was exacerbated by the fact that most operations in the developing world were instructed to carry out manufacturing and marketing plans formulated in the company's Detroit headquarters rather than being trusted to develop their own.

In contrast, GM's European operations were traditionally managed on an arm's-length basis, with the company's national operations often being allowed to design their own cars and manufacturing facilities and formulate their own marketing strategies. This regional and national autonomy did allow GM's European operations to produce vehicles that were closely tailored to the needs of local customers. However, it also led to the costly duplication of effort in design and manufacturing operations and to a failure to share valuable technology, skills, and practices across different national subsidiaries. Thus, while General Motors exerted tight control over its operations in the developing world, its control over operations in Europe was perhaps too lax. The result was a company whose international operations lacked overall strategic coherence.

Now GM is trying to change this. It is switching from its Detroit-centric view of the world to a philosophy that centers of excellence may reside anywhere in the company's global operations. The company is consciously trying to tap these centers of excellence to provide its global operations with the very latest technology. The four new manufacturing plants being constructed in the developing world are an embodiment of this new approach. Each is identical, each incorporates state-of-the art technology, and each has been designed not by Americans but by a team of Brazilian and German engineers. By building identical plants, GM should be able to mimic Toyota, whose plants are so much alike that a change in a car in Japan can be quickly replicated around the world. The plants are modeled after GM's Eisenach facility in Germany, which is managed by the company's Opel subsidiary. It was at the Eisenach plant that GM figured out how to implement the lean production system pioneered by Toyota. The plant is now the most efficient auto manufacturing operation in Europe and the best within GM, with a productivity rate at least twice that of most North American assembly operations. When completed, each of these new plants will produce state-of-the-art vehicles for local consumption.

In order to realize scale economies, GM is also trying to design and build vehicles that share a common global platform. Engineering teams located in Germany, Detroit, South America, and Australia are designing these common vehicle platforms. The idea is that local plants will be allowed to customize certain features of these vehicles to match the tastes and preferences of local customers. At the same time, adhering to a common global platform will enable the company to spread its costs of designing a car over greater volume and realize scale economies in the manufacture of shared components, both of which should help it lower its overall cost structure. The first fruits of this effort include the 1998 Cadillac Seville, which was designed to be sold in more than forty countries. GM's family of front-wheel-drive minivans was also designed around a common platform that will allow the vehicles to be produced in multiple locations around the globe, as was the 1998 Opel Astra, GM's best-selling car in Europe.

Despite making bold moves in the direction of greater global integration, numerous problems can still be seen on GM's horizon. Compared to Ford, Toyota, or the new Mercedes-Chrysler combination, GM still suffers from high costs, low perceived quality, and a profusion of brands. Moreover, while its aggressive move into emerging markets may be based on the reasonable assumption that demand will grow strong in these areas, other automobile companies are also expanding their production facilities in the same markets, raising the specter of global excess capacity and price wars. Finally, and perhaps most significant, there are those within GM who argue that the push toward "global cars" is misconceived. In particular, the German-based engineering staff at Opel's Russelsheim design facility, which takes the lead on design of many key global models, has voiced concerns that distinctively European engineering features they deem essential to a car's local success may be left by the wayside in a drive to devise what they see as blander "global" cars.

Case Discussion Questions

1. How would you characterize the strategy that GM pursued prior to 1997 in the (a) developing world and (b) Europe?

2. What do you think were the likely competitive effects of the pre-1997 strategy?

3. How would you characterize the strategy that GM has been pursuing since 1997? How should this strategy affect GM's ability to create value in the global automobile market?

Sources: R. Blumenstein, "GM Is Building Plants in Developing Nations to Woo New Markets," *Wall Street Journal,* August 4, 1997, p. A1. Haig Simonian, "GM Hopes to Turn Corner with New Astra," *Financial Times,* November 29, 1997, p. 15. D. Howes, "GM, Ford Play for Keeps Abroad," *Detroit News,* March 8, 1998, p. D1.

Corporate Strategy: Horizontal Integration, Vertical Integration, and Strategic Outsourcing

9

Opening Case

The Rise of WorldCom

In 1983, WorldCom was a small reseller of long-distance telephone service. By 2001, the company generated sales of $40 billion, making it the second largest provider of telecommunications services in the industry, behind AT&T. WorldCom entered 2001 as the number two provider of long-distance phone service in the United States, with 19 percent of the market, the largest single carrier of Internet data in the country, with an estimated 37 percent of the market, and a dazzling array of strategic assets, including a 300,000-mile fiber-optic network that was global in its reach.

WorldCom was very much the creation of its swaggering cowboy CEO, Bernie Ebbers, whose strategy for growth was quite simple: acquire competitors. An apparently savvy dealmaker, over seventeen years Ebbers acquired some sixty other telecommunication service providers, capping off the spree with the acquisition of MCI Communications, which at the

297

time was larger than WorldCom and the number two long-distance telephone company in the nation. Ebbers's deal making was financed by a combination of World-Com stock and debt. As long as the stock continued to rise—and it increased by a staggering 7,000 percent during the 1990s—WorldCom could use its "currency" to buy other companies in the industry. In addition, World-Com borrowed large amounts of money from the debt markets, some $30 billion by late 2001. The debt markets proved only too willing to lend to WorldCom given the company's glittering growth prospects.

Driving the buying spree were two strategic objectives that were central to WorldCom's business model: (1) the desire to reap scale economies in order to drive down costs and (2) the desire to capture and retain customers by bundling together telecommunications services, such as long-distance service and Internet access, and selling them under a single contract. Ebbers reasoned that the scale economies would come from assembling a nationwide and international network to transmit data and voice traffic. The costs of assembling such a network are primarily fixed and include the costs of laying fiber-optic networks and installing switches. Once the network has been built, the costs of sending additional traffic down the network are virtually zero. This gives the company with the largest volume of traffic a huge cost advantage, because it can spread the fixed costs of building and maintaining its network over a very large volume, driving down the average costs of serving each customer. In addition, Ebbers believed that customers would want only one telecommunications service provider, and one bill, for all services they used, including long-distance and local phone service, Internet access, and wireless phone service. By assembling a company that could provide all of those services to consumers in a single bundle with a single bill, Ebbers believed that WorldCom would have a competitive advantage in the marketplace that would help it to increase volume more rapidly than rivals and thus better realize potential scale economies.

WorldCom grew through acquisition, as opposed to organically, because it was quicker to grow this way and cheaper to use a mix of WorldCom's high-flying stock and long-term debt to buy competitors than to build the network entirely on its own. Moreover, when WorldCom made an acquisition, it applied a fairly standard formula: cut the overhead, eliminate any duplication, and drive the traffic of the acquired customers through WorldCom's network to realize scale economies.

The strategy seemed to work well until 2000, when WorldCom made a bid to acquire Sprint for $115 billion. Sprint was the number three long-distance company in the United States with 8 percent of the market, operated

the second largest data network in the country with 16 percent of the market, and was one of the largest providers of wireless service in the United States. The acquisition made perfect strategic sense. It would enable WorldCom to reap additional scale economies and bundle wireless service with its long-distance and Internet access service. Unfortunately for WorldCom, antitrust authorities in both the United States and the European Union thought that it would also give WorldCom substantial monopoly power, and both indicated that they would oppose the acquisition. The U.S. Justice Department claimed that the acquisition would create an unacceptable level of concentration in the long-distance phone business, with AT&T and WorldCom controlling 80 percent of the market after the acquisition. The Department of Justice also claimed that the acquisition would result in the monopolization of high-speed Internet data lines, creating a company that controlled 53 percent of Internet traffic, giving the expanded WorldCom the ability to discriminate against rivals and "irrevocably tip the market" toward a monopoly outcome.

In mid-2000, WorldCom announced that in the face of opposition from antitrust authorities, it would abandon the acquisition. This proved to be a turning point in the company's fortunes. During the next two years the company's stock plummeted from over $50 a share to under $1. A number of factors contributed to the implosion in the stock price. First, a price war erupted in the long-distance telephone service business. A combination of slowing growth and the entry of new competitors, particularly the Baby Bells that had been allowed by the 1996 Telecommunications Act to start offering-long distance telephone service, conspired to drive down prices for long-distance service. Second, in the data area, many of WorldCom's largest customers were other telecommunications providers, particularly new companies that had entered the market in the aftermath of 1996 act. By mid-2001, many of these companies were in trouble. They had taken on too much debt to build out their own networks ahead of demand and now were unable to generate the cash flow to meet their debt obligations. As they crumbled into bankruptcy, WorldCom lost business that it had counted on to generate its own growth and service its debt commitments. It also started to lose customers who had come with the acquisition of other carriers, such as MCI, and complained that the quality of customer service had declined markedly under WorldCom.

The net result was that by 2002, WorldCom was looking at declining revenues and steep losses, a far cry from the double-digit earnings growth it had been predicting eighteen months earlier. Suddenly the company was struggling to generate the cash flow required to service its debt commitments. Moreover, a May 2002 financial audit ordered by WorldCom's board of directors discovered that the company had understated expenses by $3 billion during 2001 and inflated its income by $1.4 billion in the quarter ending March 31st, 2002. This revelation led to the resignation of several senior executives, including CEO Bernie Ebbers. The news of possible accounting fraud, taken together with WorldCom's sudden losses, led rating agencies to downgrade WorldCom's debt. This pushed up the interest rate on that debt, making it more expensive for WorldCom to serve. The company was now caught in a vice—on one side, due to unexpectedly poor business conditions its cash flow was plunging, and on the other, the price of serving its debt was surging. In July 2002, WorldCom bowed to the inevitable and declared bankruptcy. Bernie Ebbers' grand strategic vision lay in ruins.

Sources: S. N. Mehta, "Can Bernie Bounce Back?" *Fortune,* January 22, 2001. S. N. Mehta, "WorldCom's Bad Trip," *Fortune,* March 4, 2002. R. Blumenstein, J. R. Wilke, N. Harris, and D. Solomon, "Called Off?" *Wall Street Journal,* June 28, 2000, p. A1.

Overview

This chapter is the first of two that deal with the issue of corporate-level strategy. The principal concerns of corporate-level strategy are to identify the businesses in which a company should participate, the value creation activities it should perform in those businesses, and the best means for expanding or contracting in different businesses, including mergers, acquisitions, and spin-offs. As with all other strategies, the goal is to maximize the long-run profitability of the company. The focus of this chapter is on three corporate-level strategies: horizontal integration, vertical integration, and strategic outsourcing. In the next chapter, we look at a fourth corporate-level strategy, diversification, and discuss the different means that companies use to execute their corporate-level strategy, such as mergers and acquisitions.

Horizontal integration is the process of acquiring or merging with industry competitors in an effort to achieve the competitive advantages that come with large scale and scope. An **acquisition** occurs when one company uses its capital resources—such as stock, debt, or cash—to purchase the other, and a **merger** is an agreement between equals to pool their operations and create a new entity. The corporate strategy that WorldCom pursued between 1983 and 2001 is an example of horizontal integration. WorldCom acquired over sixty companies over this period in an effort to become one of the largest players in the telecommunications service industry. Although it stayed within the bounds of a single industry, its strategy was to enter different *businesses* within that industry: long-distance service, Internet access, and wireless service. Its goal was to reduce costs by realizing economies of scale and scope and increase its value to customers by bundling together different services, which would give the company more pricing options. The ultimate goal was to execute the business model that CEO Bernie Ebbers had mapped out for the company, thereby boosting WorldCom's profitability (return on invested capital). The story of WorldCom also illustrates some of the risks associated with this strategy.

By **vertical integration,** a company expands its operations either *backward* into an industry that produces inputs for the company's products or *forward* into an industry that uses or distributes the company's products. Traditionally, IBM has been a very vertically integrated corporation. It integrated backward into the disc drive industry to produce the disc drives that go into its computer hardware systems and forward into the computer consulting services industry.

Strategic outsourcing involves separating out some of a company's value creation activities *within a business* and letting them be performed by an independent entity or spinning off the part of the company that performs that activity as an independent entity. In early 2002, for example, IBM announced that it would no longer make personal computers, although it would continue to design and sell personal computers with the IBM brand name. Instead, it entered into an agreement with a contract manufacturer, Sanmina-SCI, under which Sanmina would manufacture all of IBM's PCs. As part of the agreement, IBM sold its PC manufacturing operations in the United States and Scotland to Sanmina for about $200 million. In taking this action, IBM's managers had decided that a value creation activity that was long an integral part of the company's PC business, manufacturing, could be performed more efficiently by a contract manufacturer. IBM would benefit from the lower prices it paid for PCs that it resold under its own brand name, boosting the company's profitability.

Throughout the chapter and the next, we repeatedly stress that to succeed, corporate-level strategies should increase profitability. To understand what this means, we have to go back to the concepts of profitability and the value chain, introduced in Chapter 3. To increase profitability, a corporate strategy should enable a company, or one or more of its business units, to perform one or more of the value-creation functions at a lower cost, or perform one or more of the value-creation functions in a way that allows for differentiation and gives a company pricing options. In addition, corporate-level strategy will boost profitability if it helps the company to manage industry rivalry better by reducing the threat of damaging price competition. Thus, a company's *corporate* strategy should help in the process of establishing a sustainable competitive advantage *at the business level,* and of course, it is that competitive advantage that leads to higher profitability. There is, therefore, a very important link between corporate-level strategy and competitive advantage and profitability at the business level.

By the end of the chapter, you should have a good understanding of how managers can use horizontal integration, vertical integration, and strategic outsourcing to execute their business model and boost their profitability and what the drawbacks associated with each strategy are.

Horizontal Integration

Horizontal integration has been a popular corporate strategy for a decade or so. In industry after industry, there have been numerous mergers and acquisitions. For example, in the automobile industry, Chrysler merged with Daimler Benz to create DaimlerChrysler; in the aerospace industry, Boeing merged with McDonald Douglass to create the world's largest aerospace company; in the pharmaceutical industry, Pfizer acquired Warner Lambert to become the largest pharmaceutical firm; in the financial services industry, Citicorp and Travelers merged to create Citigroup, the world's largest financial services company; and in the computer hardware industry, Compaq acquired Digital Equipment and then itself was acquired by Hewlett Packard. The most recent wave of mergers and acquisitions peaked in 2000, when U.S. firms spent some $1.6 trillion on 11,000 mergers and acquisitions, up from $300 billion in 1991. Although not all of these acquisitions and mergers involved horizontal integration (some entailed vertical integration or diversification), the vast majority appear to have been.[1] Moreover, many of these mergers and acquisitions were cross-border affairs as companies raced to acquire foreign companies in the same industry. In 2000, companies from all nations spent around $1.1 trillion on 7,900 cross-border mergers and acquisitions, over 70 percent of them horizontal mergers and acquisitions.[2] In 2001, the number and value of both domestic and international mergers and acquisitions fell by 20 to 30 percent, although the figure remained high by historic standards.

The net result of this wave of mergers and acquisitions has been to increase the level of concentration in a wide range of industries. Consolidated oligopolies have been replacing more fragmented industry structures. For example, twenty years ago, cable television was dominated by a patchwork of thousands of small, family-owned businesses, but by 2002, three companies controlled nearly two-thirds of the market. In 1990, the three big publishers of college textbooks accounted for 35 percent of the market; by 2002, they accounted for 62 percent. In 1996, there were eight Baby Bells offering regional telephone service in the United States; by 2002, there were four. In the manufacture of basic DRAM semiconductor chips, due to mergers and acquisitions the four largest firms accounted for 83 percent of the global market in early 2002, up from 45 percent in 1995.[3] Why is this happening? An answer can be found by looking at the economic benefits of horizontal integration.

Benefits of Horizontal Integration

Horizontal integration is a way of trying to increase the profitability of a company by (1) reducing costs, (2) increasing the value of the company's product offering through differentiation, (3) managing rivalry within the industry to reduce the risk of price warfare, and (4) increasing bargaining power over suppliers and buyers.

Reducing Costs. Horizontal integration is often seen as a way to capture the cost advantages associated with *economies of scale*. This was one of the motives behind WorldCom's acquisitions during the 1990s (see the *Opening Case*). Such a motive can be very important in industries that have a high fixed-cost structure. In these industries, large size allows companies to spread their fixed costs over a large volume, thereby driving down the average unit cost. As noted in the *Opening Case*, the fixed costs of building a telecommunications network are very high, and to make that investment pay, the company needs a large volume of customers. Thus, WorldCom often acquired other telecommunications companies in order to get their customers, who would then be switched to WorldCom's network, driving up its utilization and driving down the unit cost of serving each customer on the network. Similarly, mergers and acquisition in the pharmaceutical industry have in part been driven by a desire to realize scale economies. The fixed costs of building a nationwide pharmaceutical sales force are very high, and pharmaceutical companies need a good portfolio of products to use that sales force fully. Thus, Pfizer acquired Warner Lambert in part because it would give its sales force more products to talk about and sell when they visited physicians, thereby increasing sales force productivity and lowering costs.

In addition to scale economies, cost savings may also be had by *reducing duplication* between two companies, for example, by eliminating two sets of corporate head offices, duplicate sales forces, and so on. Thus, as part of the justification for acquiring rival computer maker Compaq, Hewlett Packard claimed that the acquisition would save the combined company $2.5 billion in annual expenses by eliminating redundant functions (see the *Running Case*).

Increasing Value. The value of a company's product offerings may be increased if horizontal integration allows the company to offer a wider range of products that can be bundled together. **Product bundling** entails offering a bundle of products to a customer and charging a single price. Because they have to pay only once and deal with one company for a set of products they may need, customers place a higher value on the bundle product offering. In other words, bundling is a source of *differential* advantage. WorldCom was pursuing this strategy. One goal of CEO Bernie Ebbers was to be able to offer customers a single provider and a single bill for a range of telecommunications services. One of the famous illustrations of the value of bundling concerns Microsoft Office, which is a bundle of different software programs, including a word processor, spreadsheet, and presentation program. In the early 1990s, Microsoft was number two or three in each of these product categories behind companies such as WordPerfect (which led in the word processing category), Lotus (which had the best-selling spreadsheet), and Harvard Graphics (which had the best-selling presentation software). By offering all three programs in a single package, Microsoft presented consumers with a superior value proposition, and its product bundle quickly gained market share, ultimately accounting for more than 90 percent of all sales of word processors, spreadsheets, and presentation software.

A variation on the bundling theme is providing a "total solution." Becoming a total solution provider is an important rationale for horizontal integration in the computer sector, where companies have tried to increase the value of their offerings by being able to provide all of the hardware and services needs of corporate customers (for an example, see the *Running Case* in this chapter). The argument is that this saves customers money (because they do not have to deal with several suppliers) and helps ensure that different parts of a customer's information technology system all work together. Both increase the value of the company's offering in the eyes of customers and enable the total solution provider to gain market share.

Another way of trying to increase value is to cross-sell. With **cross selling,** a company tries to leverage its relationship with its customers by acquiring additional product categories that can be sold to them. This has been a very popular strategy in the financial services industry and has driven significant horizontal integration. Here, the basic idea has been a belief that customers would prefer to purchase all of their financial service products from a single provider: their checking account, mortgage loans, insurance policies, and investment services in a sort of *financial services supermarket.* A big part of the rationale behind the creation of Citigroup from the merger of Citicorp and Travelers was to create a company that could sell insurance products directly to banking customers and banking services to insurance customers. The increase in value here comes from the idea that customers will prefer to do business with a single provider of such service and thus place a higher value on purchasing from a company that can provide such services.

Managing Industry Rivalry. Horizontal integration can help a company to manage industry rivalry in two ways. First, acquiring or merging with a competitor may be required in order to *eliminate excess capacity* in an industry. As discussed in Chapter 6, the need to use excess capacity often triggers price wars. By taking excess capacity out of an industry, horizontal integration can create a more manageable environment in which prices might stabilize or even increase.

In addition, by reducing the number of players in an industry, horizontal integration might make it easier to implement *tacit price coordination* between rivals (recall that tacit coordination refers to coordination reached without communication, and explicit communication to fix prices being illegal; see Chapter 6). As a general rule, the larger the number of players in an industry, the more difficult it is to establish pricing conventions, such as price leadership by a dominant firm, that reduce the possibility that a price war will erupt. By concentrating the industry and creating an oligopoly, horizontal integration can make tacit coordination between rivals easier to establish.

Both of these motives seem to have been behind the acquisition of Compaq by Hewlett Packard in 2002. The personal computer industry was suffering from significant excess capacity and a serious price war, triggered by Dell Computer's desire to gain market share. By acquiring Compaq, Hewlett Packard hoped to be able to remove excess capacity in the industry, and by reducing the number of large players, the company hoped to be able to impose some pricing discipline in the industry (see the *Running Case* for details).

Increasing Bargaining Power. A final important motive for horizontal integration is that it may help the company gain bargaining power over suppliers or buyers and thus increase the company's profitability at their expense. By consolidating the industry through horizontal industry, a company can account for more of a supplier's business and use this fact as leverage to bargain down the price it pays to

Running Case

Beating Dell: Why Hewlett Packard Wanted to Acquire Compaq

On September 4, 2001, Hewlett Packard's CEO, Carly Fiorina, shocked the business world by announcing that rival computer maker Compaq had agreed to be acquired by HP. The acquisition announcement came at the end of a year in which slumping demand and strong competition from Dell Computer had buffeted both companies. The merged company would have annual revenues of about $87.4 billion, putting it in the same league as IBM, from a range of products that span printers, personal computers, servers, storage, and information technology services. With the exception of printers, where HP is the clear market leader, there was significant product overlap between HP and Compaq.

To justify the acquisition, Fiorina claimed that it would yield a number of benefits. First, there would be significant cost savings. Some $2.5 billion a year would be taken out of annual expenses by eliminating redundant administrative functions and cutting 15,000 employees. By combining the personal computer businesses of HP and Compaq, Fiorina argued that the new HP would leapfrog Dell to seize the number one position in the PC business with a 21 percent share of the market. The expanded volume would enable HP to capture significant scale economies and thus compete more efficiently with Dell. The same would be true in the computer server and storage businesses, areas where Dell was gaining share. Here too the new HP would take the number one spot, with a 27 percent share of the market in servers and a 26 percent of the market in storage systems. Critics, however, were quick to point out that Dell's competitive advantage was based on its direct selling model and the efficient management of its supply chain, areas where both HP and Compaq lagged Dell. Economies of scale are all very well, they argued, but unless the new HP

could sell computers and servers the way Dell does and manage its supply chain efficiently, the new HP might just give Dell a bigger target to aim at.

In addition to the cost advantages of the merger, Fiorina argued that the acquisition would give the new HP a critical mass in the service area, where it lagged leaders IBM and EDS significantly. By being able to offer customers a total solution to their information technology needs, both hardware *and* services, Fiorina argued that HP could gain back market share among corporate customers from commodity box providers such as Dell and reap the benefits associated with the higher margin service business. Here too, though, critics were quick to perceive flaws. They argued that HP would still be a minnow in the information technology services area, with under 3 percent of the market share, well behind IBM and EDS. Moreover, they noted, Dell's success suggested that building a service business was not necessarily consistent with maximizing profitability.

The proposed acquisition turned into a long-running corporate saga when Walter Hewlett, son of one of the company's founders and an HP board member, came out and publicly opposed the deal, stating that it lacked strategic rationale. A proxy battle between backers of Fiorina and Hewlett ensued. A shareholder vote on March 20, 2002, gave Fiorina's plan a slim majority and in May 2002 the merger was formally completed. Meanwhile, Dell continued to gain share in the critical PC, server, and storage areas.

Sources: P. Burrows and A. Park, "Compaq and HP: What's an Investor to Do?" *Business Week,* March 18, 2002, pp. 62–64. "Carly v Walter," *Economist,* January 26, 2002. "Sheltering from the Storm," *Economist,* September 8, 2001.

suppliers for inputs, thereby lowering the company's costs. Similarly, through consolidation, a company can control a greater percentage of industry output, making buyers more dependent on the company for product. Other things being equal, the company gains power to raise prices and earn more profits, primarily because customers have less choice.

The better ability to raise prices to consumers or bargain down the price paid for inputs is known as **market power** or monopoly power. For an example of how the process of consolidation through horizontal integration can play out, see Strategy in Action 9.1, which looks at the way in which health care providers in eastern Massachusetts have pursued horizontal integration in order to gain bargaining power, and hence market power, over insurance providers.

Drawbacks and Limits of Horizontal Integration

Although horizontal integration has clear benefits, there are also several drawbacks and limitations associated with the strategy. One problem concerns the numerous pitfalls associated with mergers and acquisitions, which are the vehicles by which a horizontal integration strategy is executed. The pitfalls are a topic that we shall discuss in depth in Chapter 10. For now, the important point to note is that a wealth of data suggests that the majority of mergers and acquisitions *do not* create value and that many actually destroy value.[4] For example, a recent study by KPMG, a large accounting and management consulting company, looked at 700 large acquisitions between 1996 and 1998 and found that although some 30 percent of these created value for the acquiring company, 31 percent destroyed value, and the remainder had little impact.[5] Many of these acquisitions were made to execute a strategy of horizontal integration. The implication is that *implementing* a horizontal integration strategy is not easy.

As we shall see in Chapter 10, mergers and acquisitions often fail to produce the anticipated gains for a number of reasons: problems associated with merging very different company cultures, high management turnover in the acquired company when the acquisition was a hostile one, a tendency on the part of managers to underestimate the expenses associated with rationalizing operations to eliminate duplicate assets and realize scale economies, and a tendency of managers to overestimate the benefits to be had from a merger or acquisition and for an acquiring company to overpay for the assets of the acquired company. WorldCom, for example, may well have overpaid for the assets of long-distance telephone provider MCI when it acquired the company in 1999 (see the *Opening Case*). Since the acquisition, the price for long-distance service in the United States has fallen by over 30 percent, and revenues from this business have begun to decline. Similarly, much of the opposition to the merger between Hewlett Packard and Compaq was based on the belief that Carly Fiorina was glossing over the difficulties and costs associated with merging the operations of these two companies and eliminating duplicate operations and products (see the *Running Case*).

Another limitation of a horizontal integration strategy is that it can bring the company into conflict with the government agency responsible for enforcing antitrust law. Antitrust authorities are concerned about the potential for abuse of market power. They believe that in general, more competition (that is, more choice) is better for consumers than less competition. They worry that large companies that dominate their industry may be in a position to use their market power to raise prices to consumers above the level that would exist in more competitive situations. They also believe that dominant enterprises can use their market power to crush potential competitors by, for example, using their financial resources to cut prices selectively

Strategy in Action

9.1

Horizontal Integration in Health Care

In the United States, health maintenance organizations (HMO) have become a powerful force in the health care sector. HMOs are health insurance companies that people choose for their health care coverage. Often companies contract with HMOs on behalf of their employees for health insurance coverage. The HMOs then "supply" patients to health care providers. Thus, the HMOs can be viewed as the suppliers of the critical input—patients—to health care providers. In turn, the revenues of health care providers are dependent on the number of patients who pass through their system. Clearly, it is in the interests of HMOs to bargain down the price they must pay health care providers for coverage. They have gained bargaining power through horizontal integration, merging with each other until they have gotten large enough to control a large volume of patients. But now there are signs that this strategy is backfiring, for the health care providers are also resorting to horizontal integration.

For an example of how this process is being played out, consider how the relationship between HMOs and hospitals has evolved in eastern Massachusetts over the past decade. In the early 1990s, three big HMOs controlled 75 percent of the market for health insurance in eastern Massachusetts. In contrast, there were thirty-four separate hospital networks in the region. Thus, the insurance providers were consolidated, while the health care providers were fragmented, giving the insurance providers considerable bargaining power. The HMOs used their bargaining power to demand deep discounts from health care providers. If a hospital wouldn't offer discounts to an HMO, the HMO would threaten to remove it from its list of providers. Because losing all of those potential patients would severely damage the revenues that a hospital could earn, the hospitals had little chance but to comply with the request.

This began to change in 1994 when two of the most prestigious hospitals in the region, Massachusetts General and Brigham & Women's Hospital, merged with each other to form Partners HealthCare System. Since then, Partners has continued to pursue the strategy, acquiring other hospitals in order to gain power over HMOs. By 2002, it had seven hospitals and some 5,000 doctors in its system. Other regional hospitals pursued a similar strategy, and the number of independent hospital networks in the region fell from thirty-four in 1994 to twelve by 2002.

In 2000, Partners started to exercise its strengthened bargaining power by demanding that HMOs accept a fee increase for services offered by Partners hospitals. One of the biggest HMOs, Tufts, refused to accept the increase and informed nearly 200,000 of its 900,000 subscribers that they would no longer be able to use Partners hospitals or physicians affiliated with Partners. The uproar among subscribers was enormous. So many employers threatened to pull out of the HMO and switch to another if the policy was not changed that Tufts quickly realized it had little choice but to change its policy, and accept the fee increase. Tufts went back to Partners and agreed to a 30 percent fee increase over three years. Clearly, bargaining power in the system had shifted away from the HMOs and toward the hospital networks. However, in 2001, the Massachusetts attorney general received so many complaints from employers about rising health care premiums that he launched an investigation into market power and anticompetitive behavior among health care providers in eastern Massachusetts, although he has stated that he is not focusing on Partners.

Sources: Y. J. Dreazen, G. Ip, and N. Kulish, "Why the Sudden Rise in the Urge to Merge and Create Oligopolies?" *Wall Street Journal*, February 25, 2002, p. A1. L. Kowalczyk, "A Matter of Style," *Boston Globe*, February 22, 2002, p. C1.

whenever new competitors enter a market or market segment, forcing them out of business, and then raising prices again once the threat has been eliminated. Because of these concerns, any merger or acquisition that is perceived by the antitrust authorities as creating too much consolidation and the *potential* for future abuse of market power may be blocked. This is what happened when WorldCom tried to acquire Sprint. The Justice Department was concerned that the proposed acquisition would reduce the number of major long-distance providers in the United States from three to two, creating in their view an unacceptable level of market concentration and lack of competition. WorldCom was obliged to drop the acquisition bid.

In sum, horizontal integration can be a very attractive strategy for a company to pursue but clearly is not without risks and drawbacks. Horizontal integration can be a valid strategy for consolidating an industry and realizing all of the associated gains, but many acquisitions and mergers fail to realize the hoped-for gains, primarily because they are expensive and postacquisition integration may be problematic. Moreover, there are clearly limits to the degree to which a company can pursue this strategy, for sooner or later it will bring the company into direct conflict with the antitrust authorities.

Vertical Integration

Vertical integration means that a company is expanding its operations either *backward* into an industry that produces inputs for the company's products or *forward* into an industry that uses or distributes the company's products. A steel company that supplies its iron ore needs from company-owned iron ore mines exemplifies backward integration. A personal computer maker that sells its PCs through company-owned retail outlets illustrates forward integration. For example, in 2001, Apple Computer entered the retail industry when it decided to set up a chain of Apple Stores to sell its computers.

Figure 9.1 illustrates four *main* stages in a typical raw-material-to-consumer production chain. For a company based in the assembly stage, backward integration means moving into component parts manufacturing and raw material production. Forward integration means moves into distribution. At each stage in the chain, *value is added* to the product. This means that a company at that stage takes the product produced in the previous stage and transforms it in some way so that it is worth more to a company at the next stage in the chain and, ultimately, to the end user. It is important to note that each stage is in a separate industry, or industries, and that within each industry there is also a value chain that encompasses the basic value creation activities we discussed in Chapter 3 of R&D, production, marketing, and customer service. In other words, we can think of a value chain that runs *across* industries, and embedded within that are the value chains *within* each industry.

As an example of the value-added concept, consider the production chain in the personal computer industry, illustrated in Figure 9.2. Here, the raw materials companies include the manufacture of specialty ceramics, chemicals, and metal, such as Kyocera of Japan, which manufactures the ceramic substrate for semiconductors. These companies sell their output to the manufacturers of component products, such as Intel and Micron Technology, which transform the ceramics, chemicals, and metals

Upstream industries   Downstream industries

FIGURE 9.1

Stages in the Raw Material to Consumer Value Chain

Raw materials	Component part manufacturing	Final assembly	Retail	Customer

Examples:
  Dow Chemical
  Union Carbide
  Kyocera

Examples:
  Intel
  Micron–Technology

Examples:
  Dell
  Hewlett Packard
  Gateway

Examples:
  Office Max
  CompUSA

FIGURE 9.2

The Raw Material to Consumer Value Chain in the Personal Computer Industry

they purchase into computer components such as microprocessors, disk drives, and memory chips. In the process, they *add value* to the raw materials they purchase. These components are then sold to assembly companies such as Gateway, Apple, Dell, and Hewlett Packard, which take these components and transform them into personal computers—that is, *add value* to the components they purchase. Many of the completed personal computers are then sold to distributors such as OfficeMax and CompUSA or value-added resellers that sell them to final customers. (Recall that Dell sells direct, while both Apple and Gateway have established some retail stores to sell their products.) The distributors also *add value* to the product by making it accessible to customers and by providing service and support. Thus, companies add value at each stage in the raw-materials-to-consumer chain. Viewed in this way, vertical integration presents companies with a choice about which industries in the raw-material-to-consumer chain to compete in.

Finally, note that besides forward and backward integration, it is also possible to distinguish between **full integration** and **taper integration** (see Figure 9.3).[6] A company achieves full integration when it produces all of a particular input needed for its processes or disposes of all of its output through its own operations. Taper integration occurs when a company buys from independent suppliers in addition to company-owned suppliers or disposes of its output through independent outlets in

FIGURE 9.3

Full and Taper Integration

FULL INTEGRATION

| In house suppliers | In house manufacturing | In house distributors | → Customers |

TAPER INTEGRATION

| In house suppliers | In house manufacturing | In house distributors | → Customers |

Outside suppliers

Independent distributors

addition to company-owned outlets. The advantages of taper integration over full integration are discussed later in the chapter.

Increasing Profitability Through Vertical Integration

A company pursuing vertical integration is normally motivated by a desire to strengthen the competitive position of its original, or core, business.[7] There are four main arguments for pursuing a vertical integration strategy. Vertical integration (1) enables the company to build barriers to new competition, (2) facilitates investments in efficiency-enhancing specialized assets, (3) protects product quality, and (4) results in improved scheduling.

Building Barriers to Entry. By vertically integrating backward to gain control over the source of critical inputs or vertically integrating forward to gain control over distribution channels, a company can build barriers to new entry into its industry. To the extent that this strategy is effective, it limits competition in the company's industry, thereby enabling the company to charge a higher price and make greater profits than it could otherwise.[8] To grasp this argument, consider a famous example of this strategy from the 1930s.

At that time, commercial smelting of aluminum was pioneered by companies like Alcoa and Alcan. Aluminum is derived from smelting bauxite. Bauxite is a common mineral, but the percentage of aluminum in it is usually so low that it is not economical to mine and smelt. During the 1930s, only one large-scale deposit of bauxite had been discovered where the percentage of aluminum in the mineral made smelting economical. This deposit was on the Caribbean island of Jamaica. Alcoa and Alcan vertically integrated backward and acquired ownership over this deposit, thereby creating a barrier to entry into the aluminum industry. Potential competitors were deterred from entry because they could not get access to high-grade bauxite. Alcoa and Alcan owned it all. Those that did enter the industry found themselves at a cost disadvantage because they had to use lower-grade bauxite. This situation persisted until the 1950s, when new high-grade deposits were discovered in Australia and Indonesia.

During the 1970s and 1980s, a similar strategy was pursued by vertically integrated companies in the computer sector such as IBM and Digital Equipment. These companies manufactured the main components of computers such as microprocessors and memory chips, designed and assembled the computers, produced the software that ran the computers, and sold the final product directly to end users. The original rationale behind this strategy was that many of the key components and software used in computers contained proprietary elements. These companies reasoned that by producing the proprietary technology in-house, they could limit rivals' access to it, thereby building barriers to entry. Thus, when IBM introduced its PS/2 personal computer system in the mid-1980s, it announced that certain component parts incorporating proprietary technology would be manufactured in-house by IBM.

This strategy worked well from the 1960s until the early 1980s, but it has been failing since then, particularly in the personal computer industry. During the 1990s, the worst performers in the computer industry were precisely the companies that pursued the vertical integration strategy: IBM and Digital Equipment. The shift to open standards in computer hardware and software has nullified the advantages for computer companies of being extensively vertically integrated. In addition, companies such as Dell and Compaq found that they could quickly reverse-engineer and duplicate the proprietary components that companies such as IBM placed in their personal computers, effectively circumventing this barrier to entry.

Facilitating Investments in Specialized Assets. A specialized asset is one that is designed to perform a specific task and whose value is significantly reduced in its next best use.[9] It may be a piece of equipment that has specialized uses or the know-how or skills that an individual or company has acquired through training and experience. Companies (and individuals) invest in specialized assets because these assets allow them to *lower the costs* of value creation or to *differentiate* their product offering from that of competitors better, thereby facilitating premium pricing. A company might invest in specialized equipment because that enables it to lower its manufacturing costs, or it might invest in developing highly specialized technological knowledge because doing so lets it develop better-quality products than its rivals. Thus, specialization can be the basis for achieving a competitive advantage at the business level.

Here we will look at why a company may find it very difficult to persuade other companies in *adjacent* stages in the raw-material-to-consumer production chain to undertake investments in specialized assets. To realize the economic gains associated with such investments, the company may have to integrate vertically into such adjacent stages and make the investments itself. As an illustration, imagine that Ford has developed a new high-performance, high-quality, and uniquely designed fuel injection system that will increase fuel efficiency and thereby help differentiate Ford's cars from those of its rivals. In other words, it will give Ford a competitive advantage. Ford has to decide whether to make the system in-house (vertical integration) or contract out manufacturing to an independent supplier (outsourcing). Manufacturing these systems requires substantial investments in equipment that can be used for only this purpose. Because of its unique design, the equipment cannot be used to manufacture any other type of fuel injection system for Ford or any other automaker. Thus, the investment in this equipment constitutes an investment in specialized assets.

First consider this situation from the perspective of an independent supplier that Ford has asked to make this investment. The supplier might reason that once it has made the investment, it will become dependent on Ford for business *since Ford is the only possible customer for the output of this equipment.* The supplier perceives this as putting Ford in a strong bargaining position and worries that Ford might use this position to squeeze down prices for the carburetors that it makes. Given this risk, the supplier declines to make the investment in specialized equipment.

Now consider Ford's position. Ford might reason that if it contracts out production of these systems to an independent supplier, it might become too dependent on that supplier for a vital input. Because specialized equipment is required to produce the fuel injection systems, Ford cannot easily switch its orders to other suppliers that lack the equipment. Ford perceives this as increasing the bargaining power of the supplier and worries that the supplier might use its bargaining strength to demand higher prices.

The situation of *mutual dependence* that would be created by the investment in specialized assets makes Ford hesitant to contract out and makes any potential suppliers hesitant to undertake the investments. The real problem here is a lack of trust. Neither Ford nor the supplier completely trusts the other to play fair in this situation. The lack of trust arises from the **risk of holdup,** that is, of being taken advantage of by a trading partner after the investment in specialized assets has been made.[10] Because of this risk, Ford might reason that the only safe way to get the new fuel injection systems is to manufacture them itself.

To generalize from this example, when achieving a competitive advantage requires one company to make investments in specialized assets in order to trade with another, the risk of holdup may serve as a deterrent and the investment may not take place. Consequently, the potential for higher profitability from specialization would be lost. To prevent such loss, companies vertically integrate into adjacent stages in the value chain. Historically, this consideration has driven automobile companies to vertically integrate backward into the production of component parts, steel companies to vertically integrate backward into the production of iron, computer companies to vertically integrate backward into chip production, and aluminum companies to vertically integrate backward into bauxite mining. The rationale underlying vertical integration in the aluminum industry is explored in greater detail in Strategy in Action 9.2.

Protecting Product Quality. By protecting product quality, vertical integration enables a company to become a *differentiated* player in its core business, which, as we saw in Chapter 5, gives the company more pricing options. The banana industry illustrates this situation. Historically, a problem facing food companies that import bananas was the variable quality of delivered bananas, which often arrived on

Strategy in Action   9.2

Specialized Assets and Vertical Integration in the Aluminum Industry

The metal content and chemical composition of bauxite ore, used to produce aluminum, vary from deposit to deposit, so each type of ore requires a specialized refinery—that is, the refinery must be designed for a particular type of ore. Running one type of bauxite through a refinery designed for another type reportedly increases production costs by 20 percent to 100 percent. Thus, the value of an investment in a specialized aluminum refinery, and the cost of the output produced by that refinery, depends on receiving the right kind of bauxite ore.

Imagine that an aluminum company has to decide whether to invest in an aluminum refinery designed to refine a certain type of ore. Assume further that this ore is produced only by a bauxite company at a single bauxite mine. Using a different type of ore would raise production costs by 50 percent. Therefore, the value of the aluminum company's investment is dependent on the price it must pay the bauxite company for this bauxite. Recognizing this, once the aluminum company has made the investment in a new refinery, what is to stop the bauxite company from raising bauxite prices? Nothing. Once it has made the investment, the aluminum company is locked into its relationship with its bauxite supplier. The bauxite company can increase prices secure in the knowledge that as long as the increase in the total production

costs of the aluminum company is less than 50 percent, the aluminum company will continue to buy from it. Thus, once the aluminum company has made the investment, the bauxite company can hold up the aluminum company.

How can the aluminum company reduce the risk of holdup? The answer is by purchasing the bauxite company. If the aluminum company can purchase the bauxite company or that company's bauxite mine, it need no longer fear that bauxite prices will be increased after the investment in an aluminum refinery has been made. In other words, it makes economic sense for the aluminum company contemplating the investment to engage in vertical integration. Vertical integration, by eliminating the risk of holdup, makes the specialized investment worthwhile. In practice, it has been argued that these kinds of considerations have driven aluminum companies to pursue vertical integration to such a degree that, according to one study, 91 percent of the total volume of bauxite is transferred within vertically integrated aluminum companies.

Source: J-F. Hennart, "Upstream Vertical Integration in the Aluminum and Tin Industries," *Journal of Economic Behavior and Organization* 9 (1988): 281–299.

the shelves of American stores either too ripe or not ripe enough. To correct this problem, major U.S. food companies such as General Foods have integrated backward to gain control over supply sources. Consequently, they have been able to distribute bananas of a standard quality at the optimal time for consumption. Knowing they can rely on the quality of these brands, consumers are willing to pay more for them. Thus, by vertically integrating backward into plantation ownership, the banana companies have built consumer confidence, which enables them to charge a premium price for their product.

The same kind of considerations can result in forward integration. Ownership of retail outlets may be necessary if the required standards of after-sales service for complex products are to be maintained. For example, in the 1920s, Kodak owned retail outlets for distributing photographic equipment. The company felt that few established retail outlets had the skills necessary to sell and service its photographic equipment. By the 1930s, Kodak decided that it no longer needed to own its retail outlets because other retailers had begun to provide satisfactory distribution and service for Kodak products. It then withdrew from retailing.

Improved Scheduling. It is sometimes argued that strategic advantages arise from the easier planning, coordination, and scheduling of adjacent processes made possible in vertically integrated organizations.[11] Such advantages can be particularly important to companies trying to realize the benefits of just-in-time inventory systems, discussed in detail in Chapter 4. For example, in the 1920s, Ford profited from the tight coordination and scheduling that is possible with backward vertical integration. Ford integrated backward into steel foundries, iron ore shipping, and iron ore mining. Deliveries at Ford were coordinated to such an extent that iron ore unloaded at Ford's steel foundries on the Great Lakes was turned into engine blocks within twenty-four hours. Thus, Ford substantially lowered its cost structure by eliminating the need to hold excessive inventories.

The improved scheduling that vertical integration makes feasible may also enable a company to respond better to sudden changes in demand conditions or to get its product into the marketplace faster. A situation in the microprocessor industry of the early 1990s illustrates this point. Demand for microprocessors was at an all-time high, and most microprocessor manufacturing plants were operating at full capacity. At that time, several microprocessor companies that specialized in chip design but contracted out manufacturing found themselves at a strategic disadvantage. For example, in 1991 Chips & Technologies succeeded in designing a clone of Intel's 386 microprocessor. Chips & Technologies sent its clone design to Texas Instruments (TI) to be manufactured, only to find that it had to wait fourteen weeks until TI could schedule time to manufacture that item. In that short span, prices for 386 microprocessors fell from $112 to $50. By the time TI produced the 386 clone for Chips & Technologies, the company had missed the best part of the market. Had Chips & Technologies been vertically integrated into manufacturing, this loss would not have occurred.[12]

Arguments Against Vertical Integration   Vertical integration has its disadvantages. Most important among them are (1) cost disadvantages, (2) disadvantages that arise when technology is changing fast, and (3) disadvantages that arise when demand is unpredictable. These disadvantages imply that the benefits of vertical integration are not always as substantial as they might seem initially and that far from increasing profitability, vertical integration can actually reduce it.

Cost Disadvantages. Although vertical integration is often undertaken to gain a production cost advantage, it can raise costs if a company becomes committed to purchasing inputs from company-owned suppliers when low-cost external sources of supply exist. For example, during the early 1990s, General Motors made 68 percent of the component parts for its vehicles in-house, more than any other major automaker (at Chrysler, the figure was 30 percent, and at Toyota 28 percent). That vertical integration has caused GM to be the highest-cost producer among the world's major car companies. In 1992, it was paying $34.60 an hour in United Auto Workers wages and benefits to its employees at company-owned suppliers for work that rivals could get done by independent nonunionized suppliers at half these rates.[13] Thus, vertical integration can be a disadvantage when a company's own sources of supply have higher operating costs than those of independent suppliers.

Company-owned suppliers might have high operating costs compared with independent suppliers because those suppliers know that they can always sell their output to other parts of the company. Not having to compete for orders lessens the *incentive* to minimize operating costs. Indeed, the managers of the supply operation may be tempted to pass on any cost increases to other parts of the company in the form of higher transfer prices rather than looking for ways to lower those costs. Thus, the lack of incentive to reduce costs can raise operating costs and reduce profitability. The problem may be less serious when the company pursues taper, rather than full, integration, because the need to compete with independent suppliers can produce a downward pressure on the cost structure of company-owned suppliers.

Technological Change. When technology is changing fast, vertical integration poses the hazard of tying a company to an obsolescent technology.[14] Consider a radio manufacturer that in the 1950s integrated backward and acquired a manufacturer of vacuum tubes. When transistors replaced vacuum tubes as a major component in radios in the 1960s, this company found itself tied to a technologically obsolescent business. Switching to transistors would have meant writing off its investment in vacuum tubes. Therefore, the company was reluctant to change and instead continued to use vacuum tubes in its radios while its nonintegrated competitors were rapidly switching to the new technology. Because it kept making an outdated product, the company rapidly lost market share. Thus, vertical integration can inhibit a company's ability to change its suppliers or its distribution systems to match the requirements of changing technology.

Demand Unpredictablility. Vertical integration can also be risky in unstable or unpredictable demand conditions. When demand is stable, higher degrees of vertical integration might be managed with relative ease. Stable demand allows better scheduling and coordination of production flows among different activities. When demand conditions are unstable or unpredictable, achieving close coordination among vertically integrated activities may be difficult.

The problem is to balance capacity among process stages. For example, an auto manufacturer might vertically integrate backward to acquire a supplier of carburetors that has a capacity exactly matching the auto manufacturer's needs. However, if demand for autos subsequently falls, the automaker will find itself locked into a business running below capacity. Clearly, this would be uneconomical. The auto manufacturer could avoid this situation by continuing to buy carburetors on the open market rather than making them itself. If demand conditions are unpredictable, taper integration might be somewhat less risky than full integration. When a company obtains only part of its total input requirements from company-owned suppliers, it can keep its in-house suppliers running at full capacity in times of low demand by ordering exclusively from them.

Bureaucratic Costs and the Limits of Vertical Integration

Although vertical integration can create value, it may also result in substantial bureaucratic costs caused by a lack of incentive on the part of company-owned suppliers to reduce their operating costs, a possible lack of strategic flexibility in times of changing technology, or uncertain demand. In this context, **bureaucratic costs** are the cost increases that arise in large, complex organizations due to managerial inefficiencies, such as the incentive problems that arise in vertically integrated enterprises. Bureaucratic costs place a limit on the amount of vertical integration that can be profitably pursued: it makes sense for a company to integrate vertically only if the potential of the strategy for increasing profitability is not swamped by the bureaucratic costs associated with expanding the boundaries of the organization to incorporate additional upstream or downstream activities.

Commonsense reasoning suggests that not all vertical integration opportunities have the same potential for increasing profitability. Although vertical integration may initially have a favorable impact, the benefits from additional integration into areas more distant from a company's core business are likely to become increasingly marginal. The more marginal the economic value created by vertical integration move, the more likely it is that the bureaucratic costs associated with expanding the boundaries of the organization into new activities will outweigh the value created and captures by the company. Once this occurs, a limit to profitable vertical integration has been reached.[15]

However, it is worth bearing in mind that the pursuit of taper integration rather than full integration may decrease the bureaucratic costs of vertical integration. This occurs because taper integration creates an incentive for in-house suppliers to reduce their operating costs and increases the company's ability to respond to changing demand conditions. Hence, it reduces some of the organizational inefficiencies that raise bureaucratic costs.

Alternatives to Vertical Integration: Cooperative Relationships

Is it possible to reap the benefits of vertical integration without having to bear the same level of bureaucratic costs? Can the benefits associated with vertical integration be captured while letting other companies perform upstream and downstream activities? The answer seems to be a qualified yes. Under certain circumstances, companies can realize the gains associated with vertical integration without having to bear the bureaucratic costs if they enter into long-term cooperative relationships with their trading partners. Such long term-relationships are typically referred to as strategic alliances. However, companies will generally be unable to realize the gains associated with vertical integration if they enter into short-term contracts with their trading partners. To see why this is so, we first discuss the problems associated with short-term contracts. Then we look at strategic alliances and long-term contracts as an alternative to vertical integration and discuss how companies can build enduring long-term relationships with their trading partners.

Short-Term Contracts and Competitive Bidding

Many companies use short-term contracts, which last for a year or less, to structure the purchasing of their inputs or the sale of their outputs. A classic example is the automobile company that uses a **competitive bidding strategy** to negotiate the price for a particular part produced by component suppliers. For example, General Motors often solicits bids from a number of suppliers for producing a component part and awards a one-year contract to the supplier submitting the lowest bid. At the end of the year, the contract is put out for competitive bid again. There is no guarantee that the company that won the contract one year will hold on to it the next.

The benefit of this strategy is that it forces suppliers to keep down their prices. But GM's lack of long-term commitment to individual suppliers may make them very hesitant to undertake the type of investments in specialized assets that may be needed to improve the design or quality of component parts or to improve scheduling between GM and its suppliers. Indeed, with no guarantee that it would remain a GM supplier the following year, the supplier may refuse to undertake investments in specialized assets. GM then may have to vertically integrate backward in order to realize the gains associated with specialization.

In other words, the strategy of short-term contracting and competitive bidding, *because it signals a lack of long-term commitment to its suppliers on the part of a company,* will make it very difficult for that company to realize the gains associated with vertical integration. This is not a problem when there is minimal need for close cooperation between the company and its suppliers to facilitate investments in specialized assets, improve scheduling, or improve product quality. In such cases, competitive bidding may be optimal. However, when this need is significant, considerations arise. A competitive bidding strategy can be a serious drawback.

Interestingly enough, there are indications that in the past, GM placed itself at a competitive disadvantage by adopting a competitive bidding stance with regard to its suppliers. In 1992, the company instructed its parts suppliers to cut their prices by 10 percent, regardless of prior pricing agreements. In effect, GM tore up existing contracts and tried to force through its policy by threatening to weed out suppliers that did not agree to the price reduction. Although such action may yield short-term benefits for companies, there is a long-term cost: the loss of trust and the hostility created between the company and its suppliers. According to press reports, several suppliers claimed that they cut back on research for future GM parts. They also indicated that they would first impart new ideas to Chrysler (now DaimlerChrysler) or Ford, both of which took a more cooperative approach to forging long-term relationships with suppliers.[16]

Strategic Alliances and Long-Term Contracting

Long-term contracts are long-term cooperative relationships between two companies, often referred to in the popular press as **strategic alliances.** Typically, one company agrees to supply the other, and the other company agrees to continue purchasing from that supplier; both make a commitment to jointly seek ways of lowering the costs or raising the quality of inputs into the downstream company's value creation process. A stable long-term relationship lets the participating companies share the value that might be created by vertical integration while avoiding many of the bureaucratic costs linked with ownership of an adjacent stage in the raw-material-to-consumer production chain. Thus, long-term contracts can substitute for vertical integration.

Consider the cooperative relationships that many Japanese auto companies have with their component-parts suppliers (the *keiretsu* system), which exemplify successful long-term contracting. These relationships often go back decades. Together, the auto companies and their suppliers work out ways to increase value-added—for instance, by implementing just-in-time inventory systems or cooperating on component-parts designs to improve quality and lower assembly costs. As part of this process, the suppliers make substantial investments in specialized assets in order to serve the needs of the auto companies better. Thus, the Japanese automakers have been able to capture many of the benefits of vertical integration without having to bear the associated bureaucratic costs. The component-parts suppliers also benefit from these relationships, for they grow with the company they supply and share in its success.[17]

In contrast to their Japanese counterparts, U.S. auto companies historically tended to pursue formal vertical integration.[18] According to several studies, the increased bureaucratic costs of managing extensive vertical integration helped place GM and Ford at a disadvantage relative to their Japanese competition.[19] Moreover, when U.S. auto companies decided not to integrate vertically, they did not necessarily enter into cooperative long-term relationships with independent component suppliers. Instead, they tended to use their powerful position to pursue an aggressive competitive bidding strategy, playing off component suppliers against each other.[20] This mindset now seems to be changing. For details on how DaimlerChrysler has attempted to build long-term cooperative relationships with suppliers, see Strategy in Action 9.3.

Building Long-Term Cooperative Relationships

The interesting question raised by the preceding section is how a company can achieve a stable long-term strategic alliance with another, given the lack of trust and the fear of holdup that arises when one company has to invest in specialized assets in order to trade with another. How have companies like Toyota managed to develop such enduring relationships with their suppliers?

Companies can take some specific steps to ensure that a long-term cooperative relationship can work and to lessen the chances of a partner's reneging on an agreement. One of those steps is for the company making investments in specialized assets to demand a hostage from its partner. Another is to establish a credible commitment on both sides to build a trusting long-term relationship.[21]

Hostage Taking. Hostage taking is essentially a means of guaranteeing that a partner will keep its side of the bargain. The cooperative relationship between Boeing and Northrop illustrates this type of situation. Northrop is a major subcontractor for Boeing's commercial airline division, providing many component parts for the 747 and 767 aircraft. To serve Boeing's special needs, Northrop has had to make substantial investments in specialized assets. In theory, because of the sunk costs associated with such investments, Northrop is dependent on Boeing, and Boeing is in a position to renege on previous agreements and use the threat to switch orders to other suppliers as a way of driving down prices. However, in practice, Boeing is unlikely to do so since the company is also a major supplier to Northrop's defense division, providing many parts for the Stealth bomber. Boeing has had to make substantial investments in specialized assets in order to serve Northrop's needs. Thus, the companies are *mutually dependent*. Boeing is unlikely to renege on any pricing agreements with Northrop because it knows that Northrop could respond in kind. Each company holds a hostage that can be used as insurance against the other company's unilateral reneging on prior pricing agreements.

Credible Commitments. A credible commitment is a believable commitment to support the development of a long-term relationship between companies. To understand the concept of credibility in this context, consider the following relationship between General Electric and IBM. GE is one of the major suppliers of advanced semiconductor chips to IBM, and many of the chips are customized to IBM's requirements. To meet IBM's specific needs, GE has had to make substantial investments in

Strategy in Action

9.3

DaimlerChrysler's U.S. *Keiretsu*

Like many other long-established companies, Chrysler (now DaimlerChrysler) for most of its history managed suppliers through a competitive bidding process: suppliers were selected on the basis of their ability to supply components at the lowest possible cost to Chrysler. A supplier's track record on performance and quality was relatively unimportant in this process. Contracts were renegotiated every two years, with little or no commitment from Chrysler to continuing to do business with a particular supplier. As a result, the typical relationship between Chrysler and its suppliers was characterized by mutual distrust, suspicion, and a reluctance on the part of suppliers to invest too much in their relationship with Chrysler.

Since the early 1990s, Chrysler has systematically reorganized its dealings with suppliers in an attempt to build stable long-term relationships. The aim of this new approach has been to try and get suppliers to help Chrysler in the process of developing new products and improving its production processes. To encourage suppliers to cooperate and make investments specific to Chrysler's needs, the company has moved sharply away from its old adversarial approach. The average contract with suppliers has been lengthened from two years to over four and a half years. Furthermore, Chrysler has given 90 percent of its suppliers oral commitments that business will be extended for at least the life of a model, if not beyond that. The company has also committed itself to share with suppliers the benefits of any process improvements they might suggest. The basic thinking behind offering suppliers such credible commitments is to align incentives between Chrysler and its suppliers—to create a sense of shared destiny—that encourage mutual cooperation to increase the size of the financial pie available to both.

By 1996 the fruits of this new approach were beginning to appear. By involving suppliers early on in product development and giving them greater responsibility for design and manufacturing, DaimlerChrysler was able to compress its product development cycle and take a lot of cost out of the product development effort. DaimlerChrysler's U.S. operation also reduced the time it took to develop a new vehicle from 234 weeks during the mid-1980s to about 160 weeks by 1996. The total cost of developing a new vehicle also fell by 20 percent to 40 percent, depending on the model. With development costs in the automobile industry running at between $1 and $2 billion, that translates into a huge financial saving. Many of these savings were the direct result of engineering improvements suggested by suppliers or of improved coordination between the company and suppliers in the design process. To facilitate this process, the number of resident engineers from suppliers who work side by side with DaimlerChrysler engineers in cross-company design teams increased from 30 in 1989 to more than 300 by 1996.

In 1990, Chrysler began implementing a program known internally as the supplier cost reduction effort (SCORE), which focuses on cooperation between DaimlerChrysler and suppliers to identify opportunities for process improvements. In its first two years of operation, SCORE generated 875 ideas from suppliers that were worth $170.8 million in annual savings to suppliers. In 1994, suppliers submitted 3,786 ideas that produced $504 million in annual savings. By December 1995, Chrysler had implemented 5,300 ideas that have generated more than $1.7 billion in annual savings. One supplier alone, Magna International, submitted 214 proposals; Chrysler adopted 129 of them for a total cost saving of $75.5 million. Many of the ideas themselves have a relatively small financial impact; for example, a Magna suggestion to change the type of decorative wood grain used on minivans saved $0.5 million per year. But the cumulative impact of thousands of such ideas has had a significant impact on DaimlerChrysler's bottom line.

Source: J. H. Dyer, "How Chrysler Created an American Keiretsu," *Harvard Business Review* (July–August 1996): 42–56.

specialized assets that have little other value. As a consequence, GE is dependent on IBM and faces a risk that IBM will take advantage of this dependence to demand lower prices. Theoretically, IBM could back up its demand with the threat to switch to another supplier. However, GE reduced this risk by having IBM enter into a contractual agreement that committed IBM to purchase chips from GE for a ten-year period. In addition, IBM agreed to share in the costs of developing the customized chips, thereby reducing GE's investments in specialized assets. Thus, by publicly committing itself to a long-term contract and putting some money into the development of the customized chips, IBM has essentially made a *credible commitment* to continue purchasing those chips from GE.

Maintaining Market Discipline. A company that has entered into a long-term relationship can become too dependent on an inefficient partner. Because it does not have to compete with other organizations in the marketplace for the company's business, the partner may lack the incentive to be cost-efficient. Consequently, a company entering into a cooperative long-term relationship must be able to apply some kind of market discipline to its partner.

The company holds two strong cards. First, even long-term contracts are periodically renegotiated, generally every four to five years. Thus, a partner knows that if it fails to live up to its commitments, the company may refuse to renew the contract. Second, some companies engaged in long-term relationships with suppliers use a **parallel sourcing policy**—that is, they enter into a long-term contract with two suppliers for the same part (as is the practice at Toyota, for example).[22] This arrangement gives the company a hedge against a defiant partner, for each supplier knows that if it fails to comply with the agreement, the company can switch all its business to the other. This threat is rarely made explicit, because that would be against the spirit of building a cooperative long-term relationship. But the mere awareness of parallel sourcing serves to inject an element of market discipline into the relationship, signaling to suppliers that if the need arises, they can be replaced at short notice.

The growing importance of just-in-time inventory systems as a way of reducing costs and enhancing quality is increasing the pressure on companies to enter into long-term agreements in a wide range of industries. These agreements thus might become much more popular in the future. However, when such agreements cannot be reached, formal vertical integration may be called for.

Strategic Outsourcing

Strategic outsourcing involves separating out some of a company's value creation activities within a business and letting them be performed by a specialist in that activity (the specialist focuses on just this one activity). In other words, strategic outsourcing is concerned with reducing the boundaries of the company and focusing on *fewer* value creation functions. The activity to be outsourced may encompass an entire function, such as the manufacturing function, or it may entail an activity embedded within a function. For example, many companies outsource management of their pension systems, while keeping other human resource function activities within the company.

There has been a clear move among many enterprises to outsource activities designated as noncore or nonstrategic.[23] One survey found that some 54 percent of the companies polled had outsourced manufacturing processes or services in the past three years.[24] Another survey estimates that some 56 percent of all global product manufacturing is outsourced to manufacturing specialists.[25] Many high-technology companies, for example, outsource much, if not all, of their manufacturing activity to contract manufacturers, which specialize in the manufacturing function. Cisco, which is in the router and switch business, does not actually manufacture routers and switches. Rather, they are made by contract manufacturers such as Flextronics and

Jabil Circuit. What Cisco does is design the routers and switches, sell the routers and switches, and coordinate the supply chain to match demand for routers and switches with the supply of routers and switches (see Strategy in Action 9.4). Palm does not actually make the hand-held computers sold under the Palm brand name; they are made in Mexico by Solectron. It is not just high-technology companies that outsource manufacturing. Nike does not actually make running shoes and The Gap does not make jeans; they are made under contract at low-cost locations (on the other hand, Levi's still makes jeans, which may be a competitive disadvantage).

Nor is strategic outsourcing confined to manufacturing; many other activities are also outsourced. Microsoft has long outsourced its entire customer technical support operation to an independent company, as does Dell Computer. A few years ago, BP Amoco outsourced the bulk of its human resource functions to Exult, a San Antonio company, in a five-year deal worth $600 million. At the time, this was the largest deal of its kind, but a couple of years later, Exult won a $1.1 billion contract to handle personnel matters for all of Bank of America's 150,000 employees for a decade. In early 2002, American Express outsourced its entire information technology function to IBM in a seven-year deal worth $4 billion.[26] The Gartner Group, a market research company, estimates the information technology outsourcing market in North America was worth $101 billion in 2000 and will grow to $160 billion by 2005.[27]

Companies engage in strategic outsourcing because they believe they can better execute their business model by doing so and thus increase their profitability. The process of strategic outsourcing typically begins with a company's identifying the value creation activities that form the basis of its competitive advantage (its distinctive competencies). The idea is to keep performing these activities within the company. The remaining activities are then reviewed to see whether they can be performed more effectively and efficiently by independent companies that specialize in that activity—that is, by companies that can perform those activities at a lower cost or perform them in a way that leads to better differentiation. If they can, these activities are outsourced to those specialists. A possible result is illustrated in Figure 9.4, which shows the primary value creation activities and boundaries of a company before and after outsourcing. In this example, the company decided to outsource its production and customer service functions, leaving just R&D and marketing and sales within the company.

Once outsourcing has been executed, the relationships between the company and specialists are then often structured as long-term contractual relationships with rich information sharing between the company and the specialist organization to which it has contracted the activity. The term **virtual corporation** has been coined to describe companies that have pursued extensive strategic outsourcing.[28]

Benefits of Outsourcing

The trend toward strategic outsourcing is being driven by a realization that outsourcing can *lower the cost structure* of a company and help it to *differentiate* its product offerings in the marketplace better, thereby strengthening its business model and boosting its profitability.[29] In addition, strategic outsourcing of noncore activities helps the company to focus management attention on those activities that are most important for its long term competitive position: its distinctive competencies.

Reducing Costs Through Outsourcing. Outsourcing an activity will reduce costs when the price that must be paid to a specialist company to perform that activity is less than what it would cost the company to perform that activity internally. Specialists may be able to perform an activity at a lower cost because they are able to

Strategy in Action

9.4

Cisco's $2 Billion Blunder

During the late 1990s, Cisco Systems became famous for the way it focused on a few core activities while outsourcing the remainder to specialists. Cisco was known as the hardware maker that didn't make hardware. It dominated the market for Internet protocol (IP) routers and switches, critical components of IP networks, but these products were actually made by a number of contract manufacturers, while Cisco focused its efforts on just three main activities: product innovation, marketing and selling (primarily through Cisco's web site), and managing the supply chain. Cisco claimed that this strategy allowed it to focus on core competencies, while getting out of capital-intensive manufacturing activities, thereby reducing the company's need for capital resources and boosting its return on invested capital. Moreover, Cisco boasted that under its outsourcing strategy, it did not have to deal with the hassle and expense of maintaining inventory. Inventory was maintained at the contract manufacturer, which shipped finished products directly to customers.

Cisco's supply chain was structured like a four-tier pyramid, with Cisco at the pinnacle. The contract manufacturers responsible for final assembly of Cisco's products formed the second tier of the pyramid. These manufacturers were fed by a third tier that supplied components such as processor chips and optical gear. The third-tier companies drew on an even larger base of suppliers of commodity inputs. According to Cisco CEO John Chambers, the system was very responsive to shifts in demand, with Cisco immediately communicating orders it received through its web site back down the supply chain, allowing contract manufacturers and component producers to optimize their production schedules in real time. This dramatically reduced inventory in the supply chain, which reduced Cisco's working capital requirements (since the company did not have to finance extensive inventories) and further boosted the company's return on invested capital.

In May 2001, however, it became apparent that Cisco's vaunted outsourcing strategy had not been working as well as touted. The company announced that it would take a $2.2 billion charge against earnings to write down the value of inventory in the supply chain that had been ordered but could not be used. The problem was that demand for routers and switches had collapsed, but Cisco's systems had not detected this until it was too late.

How did this happen? Why did a system that has been praised for being very responsive to shifts in demand fail to detect a major shift in demand?

As it turns out, there was a flaw in the way in which Cisco managed its supply chain. During the boom years of the late 1990s and 2000, demand for routers and switches rocketed as a large number of companies from established and new telecommunications companies and dot-coms invested in IP networks. These customers could not get products from Cisco quickly enough, so by 2000 they were starting to double- and triple-book from Cisco and its competitors, knowing that they would ultimately make purchases from just one company. Cisco, however, did not detect this. As far as it knew, it couldn't produce products fast enough. Moreover, the problem was amplified as orders moved down the supply chain. Suppose Cisco ordered 10,000 units of a particular router. Each of the contract manufacturers would compete to fill the entire order, and to gain an edge they often tried to lock up supplies of scarce components. If three contract manufacturers were competing to build 10,000 routers, it would look like sudden demand for 30,000 machines, so component makers too would increase their output. But the demand signals were grossly misleading. They reflected double booking by Cisco's customers and, on top of that, double booking by the contract manufacturers. The result was a huge surge in inventory that far outstripped underlying demand. When the telecommunications and dot-com bubble burst in early 2001 and demand from these customers slumped, Cisco was left with a supply chain that was bloated with inventory that was no longer needed.

To reduce the risk of this problem occurring again, Cisco is reconfiguring the way it manages its supply chain. It has created a central Internet-based repository of information, known as eHub, that *all* participants in the supply chain can access. Now, if contract manufacturers get an order for 10,000 routers and all turn around and place orders for 10,000 chips each (for a total of 30,000) to try to tie up scarce components, the chip makers can access eHub and see that the true order is for just 10,000 routers, not 30,000, and plan accordingly.

Sources: S. N. Mehta, "Cisco Fractures Its Own Fairy Tale," *Fortune,* May 14, 2001, pp. 104–112. P. Kaihla, "Inside Cisco's $2 Billion Blunder," *Business 2.0* (March 2002). www.business2.com.

FIGURE 9.4

Strategic Outsourcing
of Primary Value
Creation Functions

realize scale economies or other efficiencies that are not available to the company. For example, performing basic personnel activities, such as managing pay and benefit systems, requires significant investments in information technology infrastructure (i.e., computers and software). Purchasing this technology represents a considerable fixed cost, but the average cost of performing a personnel transaction can be driven down if a large volume of transactions is handled by the infrastructure. By aggregating the demand from many different companies, vendors that specialize in this activity, such as Exult and Paycheck, can attain huge economies of scale that a company could not hope to achieve by itself. Some of these cost savings can then be passed on to clients in the form of lower prices, while still leaving the specialist with a decent return. A similar dynamic is at work in the contract manufacturing business, where manufacturing specialists like Solectron, Flextronics, and Jabil Circuit bear significant fixed costs to build efficient scale manufacturing facilities, but then are able to spread those fixed costs over a huge volume, driving down unit costs, by building equipment for a number of companies.

In addition to the gains from scale economies, the greater acceleration in *cumulative* volume handled by specialists means that they are likely to realize the cost savings associated with learning effects much more rapidly than the company that performs an activity just for itself (see Chapter 4 for a review of learning effects). For example, because a company like Flextronics is manufacturing similar products for several different companies, it is able to build up *cumulative* volume more rapidly, and thus learn how to manage and operate the manufacturing process more rapidly than any of its clients could. Thus, the specialists realize learning-based gains in employee and management productivity, which drives down their cost structure, allowing them to charge their customers a lower price for the activity than what it would cost the customer itself to perform that activity. In essence, the specialists gain distinctive competencies in the activity that they specialize in, which increases the benefit of outsourcing that activity for a company where the activity is not core.

The specialist may also be able to perform an activity at a lower cost than the company because the specialist is based in a low-cost location. Nike, for example, outsources the manufacture of its running shoe to companies based in China because the lower wage rate in China, for what is a very labor-intensive activity, means that the specialist will have a much lower cost than if Nike performed the same activity itself in the United States. In theory, Nike could set up its own operation in China to manufacture running shoes, but that would limit its ability to switch its production to another location later if costs in China start to rise and the costs of making running shoes can be further reduced by sourcing them from, say, India. So for Nike and many other apparel companies, the efficient choice is to outsource the manufacturing activity, because it gains both lower costs and the opportunity to switch to another more favorable location should the cost equation change.

Differentiation Through Outsourcing. A company may also be able to differentiate its final product offering better by outsourcing certain noncore activities to specialists. For this to occur, the *quality* of the activity performed by the specialists must be greater than if that same activity was performed by the company. On the reliability *dimension* of quality, for example, a specialist may be able to achieve a lower error rate in performing an activity, precisely because it focuses on that activity and has accumulated competencies in total quality management for that activity. Again, this is one advantage claimed for contract manufacturers. Companies like Flextronics have adopted Six Sigma methodologies (see Chapter 4) and driven down the defect rate associated with manufacturing a product. This means they can provide more reliable products to their clients, which in turn can differentiate their products on the basis of superior quality measured by reliability.

Companies can also outsource other differentiating activities to specialists. For example, the excellence of Dell Computer's customer service and maintenance is a differentiating factor. A customer that has a problem with a product purchased from Dell can call customer service and get excellent help over the phone. If it turns out that there is a defective part in the computer, a maintenance person will be dispatched and replace the part within twenty-four hours. The excellence of this service clearly differentiates Dell and helps to guarantee repeat purchases, but what most customers do not realize is that those activities are *not* performed by Dell: they are performed by the employees of specialist organizations. In the same manner, automobile companies outsource part of their vehicle design activities to specialist organizations that focus on this activity and have earned a reputation for design excellence.

Focus Through Outsourcing. A final advantage of strategic outsourcing is that it removes distractions and allows the management of the company to focus both their attention and company resources on performing those activities that are most important for value creation and competitive advantage. Other things being equal, this focus allows companies to enhance their competencies in their chosen areas. Cisco, for example, has developed competencies in product design, marketing and sales, and supply chain management. But Cisco does not physically make the routers and switches it designs and sells; it does not even touch them, for they are delivered straight from the contract manufacturer's factory to customers (see Strategy in Action 9.4). Of course, what really occurs here is that by focusing on just those activities that are essential for competitive advantage, companies like Cisco are better able to build competencies in those activities, and thus drive down the costs of performing those activities, and better differentiate their ultimate product offering.

Identifying and Managing the Risks of Outsourcing

Although outsourcing noncore activities can have considerable benefits, there are also significant risks associated with it—risks associated with holdup, the loss of direct control over the scheduling of activities, and a loss of important information when an activity is outsourced—that must be balanced against the benefits of outsourcing before deciding whether to outsource a particular activity. By taking the appropriate steps, these risks can be reduced.

Holdup. In the context of an outsourcing agreement, **holdup** refers to the risk that a company can become too dependent on the provider of an outsourced activity, and the provider can use that fact to raise prices beyond some previously agreed-on rate. We have already examined the problem of holdup in the discussion of vertical integration. As in the case of alternatives to vertical integration, the risk of holdup can be reduced by outsourcing from several suppliers and pursuing *a parallel sourcing* policy, as Cisco does (see Strategy in Action 9.4). Moreover, when a number of rivals are competing with each other to provide an outsourced activity and that activity can be performed well by any one of those companies, the threat that a contract will not be renewed in the future is normally sufficient to keep the chosen provider from trying to exercise bargaining power and hold up the company. For example, although IBM enters into long-term contracts to provide information technology services to a wide range of companies, it would be highly unlikely to try to raise prices after the contract has been signed because it knows full well that such action would reduce its chance of getting the contract renewed in the future. Moreover, the fact that IBM has many strong competitors in the information technology services business, such as EDS and Computer Sciences, gives it a very strong incentive to deliver significant value to its client and not to practice holdup.

Scheduling of Activities. The risks associated with loss of control with scheduling are clearly illustrated by the experience Cisco faced in 2001, which we reviewed in Strategy in Action 9.4. The essence of the problem is that if the company is not careful, the signals sent down a supply chain can be distorted by practices such as double booking when supplies of inputs are in short supply. This is a potential problem for any enterprise that has to manage demand and a long supply chain, and it is exacerbated when activities once considered core, such as manufacturing, are outsourced to a number of competing specialists. In times of strong demand, the specialists might try to capture a greater share of orders from the company by making sure that they have access to critical components needed in the manufacture the product, so they book orders for more components than they need. This creates a problem when the component suppliers to the specialists have no way of seeing the true demand from the company at the top of the supply chain, and they may produce excess inventory.

Loss of Information. A company that is not careful can lose important competitive information when it outsources an activity. For example, many computer hardware and software companies have outsourced their customer technical support function to specialists. Although this makes good sense from a cost and differentiation perspective, it may also mean that a critical point of contact with the customer, and a source of important feedback, is lost. Customer complaints can be a useful piece of information and a valuable input into future product design, but if those complaints are not clearly communicated to the company by the specialists performing the technical support activity, the company can lose that data. Again, this is not an argument against outsourcing. Rather, it is an argument for making sure that there is good communication flow between the outsourcing specialist and the company. At Dell, for example, a great deal of attention is paid to making sure that the specialist responsible for providing technical support and on-site maintenance collects and communicates all relevant data regarding product failures and other problems to Dell, so that Dell can design better products.

Summary of Chapter

1. A corporate strategy should enable a company, or one or more of its business units, to perform one or more of the value creation functions at a lower cost or in a way that allows for differentiation and a premium price.

2. Horizontal integration can be understood as a way of trying to increase the profitability of a company by (a) reducing costs, (b) increasing the value of the company's product offering through differentiation, (c) managing rivalry within the industry to reduce the risk of price warfare, and (d) increasing bargaining power over suppliers and buyers.

3. There are two drawbacks associated with horizontal integration: the numerous pitfalls associated with mergers and acquisitions and that the strategy can bring a company into direct conflict with the antitrust authorities.

4. Vertical integration can enable a company to achieve a competitive advantage by helping build barriers to entry, facilitating investments in specialized assets, protecting product quality, and helping to improve scheduling between adjacent stages in the value chain.

5. The disadvantages of vertical integration include cost disadvantages if a company's internal source of supply is a high-cost one and lack of flexibility when technology is changing fast or demand is uncertain.

6. Entering into a long-term contract can enable a company to realize many of the benefits associated with vertical integration without having to bear the same level of bureaucratic costs. However, to avoid the risks associated with becoming too dependent on its partner, it needs to seek a credible commitment from its partner or establish a mutual hostage-taking situation.

7. The strategic outsourcing of noncore value creation activities may allow a company to lower its costs, better differentiate its product offering, and make better use of scarce resources, while also enabling it to respond rapidly to changing market conditions. However, strategic outsourcing may have a detrimental effect if the company outsources important value creation activities or becomes too dependent on key suppliers of those activities.

Discussion Questions

1. Why was it profitable for General Motors and Ford to integrate backward into component-parts manufacturing in the past, and why are both companies now trying to buy more of their parts from outside?

2. Under what conditions might horizontal integration be inconsistent with the goal of maximizing profitability?

3. What value creation activities should a company outsource to independent suppliers? What are the risks involved in outsourcing these activities?

4. What steps would you recommend that a company take in order to build long-term cooperative relationships with its suppliers that are mutually beneficial?

Practicing Strategic Management

SMALL-GROUP EXERCISE: COMPARING VERTICAL INTEGRATION STRATEGIES

Break up into small groups of three to five people, and appoint one group member as a spokesperson who will communicate your findings to the class when called on to do so by the instructor. Then read the following description of the activities of Seagate Technologies and Quantum Corporation, both of which manufacture computer disk drives. On the basis of this description, outline the pros and cons of a vertical integration strategy? Which strategy do you think makes most sense in the context of the computer disk drive industry?

Quantum Corporation and Seagate Technologies are major producers of disk drives for personal computers and workstations. The disk drive industry is characterized by sharp fluctuations in the level of demand, intense price competition, rapid technological change, and product life cycles of no more than twelve to eighteen months. In recent years, Quantum and Seagate have pursued very different vertical integration strategies.

Seagate is a vertically integrated manufacturer of disk drives, both designing and manufacturing the bulk of its own disk drives. Quantum specializes in design, while outsourcing most of its manufacturing to a number of independent suppliers including, most importantly, Matsushita Kotobuki Electronics (MKE) of Japan. Quantum makes only its newest and most expensive products in-house. Once a new drive is perfected and ready for large-scale manufacturing, Quantum turns over manufacturing to MKE. MKE and Quantum have cemented their partnership over eight years. At each stage in designing a new product, Quantum's engineers send the newest drawings to a production team at MKE. MKE examines the drawings and is constantly proposing changes that make new disk drives easier to manufacture. When the product is ready for manufacture, eight to ten Quantum engineers travel to MKE's plant in Japan for at least a month to work on production ramp-up.

ARTICLE FILE 9

Find an example of a company whose vertical integration or diversification strategy appears to have dissipated rather than created value. Identify why this has been the case and what the company should do to rectify the situation.

STRATEGIC MANAGEMENT PROJECT: MODULE 9

This module requires you to assess the vertical integration and diversification strategy being pursued by your company. With the information you have at your disposal, answer the questions and perform the tasks listed:

1. Has your company ever pursued a horizontal integration strategy? What was the strategic reason for pursuing this strategy?
2. How vertically integrated is your company? If your company does have vertically integrated operations, is it pursuing a strategy of taper or full integration?
3. Assess the potential for your company to create value through vertical integration. In reaching your assessment, also consider the bureaucratic costs of managing vertical integration.
4. On the basis of your assessment in question 3, do you think your company should (a) outsource some operations that are currently performed in-house or (b) bring some operations in-house that are currently outsourced? Justify your recommendations.
5. Is your company involved in any long-term cooperative relationships with suppliers or buyers? If so, how are these relationships structured? Do you think that these relationships add value to the company? Why?
6. Is there any potential for your company to enter into (additional) long-term cooperative relationships with suppliers or buyers? If so, how might these relationships be structured?

EXPLORING THE WEB
Visiting Motorola

Visit Motorola's web site (**http://www.motorola.com**), and review its various business activities. Using this information, answer the following questions:

1. To what extent is Motorola vertically integrated?
2. Does vertical integration help Motorola establish a competitive advantage, or does it put the company at a competitive disadvantage?

General Task: Search the Web for an example of a company that has pursued a strategic outsourcing strategy. Describe that strategy, and assess whether the strategy has increased the profitability of the company?

Closing Case

AOL Time Warner: Horizontal and Vertical Integration

On January 11, 2001, one of the premier companies of the Internet era, AOL, merged with one of the dominant old media companies, Time Warner, to create AOL Time Warner. Founded in 1923, Time Warner had a vast array of magazine, TV broadcasting, film, music, and cable service properties. These include *Time* and *Life* magazines,

Warner's film and music properties, CNN, TNT, and HBO, and cable systems that serve 20 percent of the United States. AOL, founded only fifteen years ago, has just 20 percent of the revenue and 15 percent of the employees of Time Warner. However, most observers commented that in this "marriage of equals," it was the upstart that was in effect acquiring the older company. The merger had elements of both horizontal and vertical integration. Both were media companies active in content creation, and both had substantial interests in the distribution of content. AOL distributed its content and that of its media partners over the Internet, while Time Warner distributed some of its TV programming content over its cable TV system.

AOL believed that the merger would at a stroke help solve one of the company's biggest problems: how to offer high-speed Internet service to its 22 million subscribers. As many Internet users have found out, downloading graphics-intensive web content over telephone lines using 56k modems can be a very slow process, to say nothing of the wait required to download streaming video data. If the Internet is to fulfill its potential, the speed of Internet connections (the bandwidth) must be increased. There are three ways of increasing bandwidth: offering direct subscriber line service over existing telephone lines, offering Internet service via a satellite as with Direct TV, and making use of the existing cable TV infrastructure to allow consumers to access the Internet over cable systems. Of the three, upgrading cable TV infrastructure to allow it to facilitate access to the Internet seems to offer the most promise. With the addition of a cable modem, computer users would be able to cruise the Internet at speeds 1,000 times faster than that offered by conventional modems. In turn, this would allow for the streaming of high-resolution digital video and audio data. Until this merger was announced, AOL had little access to cable TV providers, many of which, like AT&T, had signed exclusive deals with AOL's competitors, such as Microsoft's MSN. The merger, it was argued, would give AOL access to Time Warner's cable TV system, with its 13 million subscribers. AOL could then offer these customers high-speed access to the Internet over Time Warner's cable TV systems. In effect, the merger allowed AOL to integrate forward into the distribution of its content.

A second benefit claimed for the merger is that AOL would be able to offer Time Warner's rich array of content to its subscribers, thereby enhancing the value of its service. AOL has always seen itself as a media company offering compelling content to its customers. If content is indeed king on the Internet, the combination of AOL's web savvy and Time Warner's magazine and broadcasting properties opens up the potential for delivering a wide range of innovative content over the Internet to AOL's subscriber base. In addition to existing Time Warner services, such as CNN.com, these might include an ability to access TNT's vast film library on demand (assuming a cable modem), archived CNN news clips, web versions of *Time* magazine, and a whole range of web properties that have yet to be imagined.

Before the merger was completed, however, a difficult antitrust issue had to be resolved. Regulators harbored fears that the new AOL would deny competing providers of Internet service, such as Earthlink, Juno, and Microsoft's MSN service, access to its cable TV subscribers. To guard against this, officials at the Federal Trade Commission (FTC) required that AOL Time Warner not only commit to opening up Time Warner's cable system to competing providers, but also sign a deal with a competing provider as a precondition for approval of the merger. The reason that the FTC gave for taking this hard-line stance is that its commissioners did not want the new AOL to offer its service first, before opening up the Time Warner cable system to competing providers. On November 20, 2000, Time Warner announced that it had struck a deal with Earthlink, which would allow this provider to offer Internet service to Time Warner's cable customers. The deal seemed to satisfy the concerns of the FTC, and the merger was approved.

Case Discussion Questions

1. What aspects of the AOL Time Warner merger can be considered horizontal integration? What can be considered vertical integration?

2. What are the benefits associated with this merger? How might it boost the profitability of the combined unit? Can you see any risks here?

3. Why do you think the FTC was concerned about the competitive implications of the merger? Were the FTC's concerns reasonable?

Sources: C. Yang et al., "Welcome to the 21st Century," *Business Week,* January 24, 2000, pp. 36–38. M. Peers, N. Wingfield, and L. Landro, "AOL, Time Warner, Leap Borders to Plan a Mammoth Merger," *Wall Street Journal,* January 11, 2000, p. A1. M. Peters and A. Petersen, "Time Warner Reaches Out to Earthlink," *Wall Street Journal,* November 21, 2000, p. A3.

10

Corporate Strategy— Diversification, Acquisitions, and Internal New Ventures

Opening Case

Tyco International

Tyco International has been one of the great growth stories of the past decade. Under the leadership of Dennis Kozlowski, who became CEO in 1992, Tyco's sales expanded from $3.1 billion in 1992 to $38 billion in 2001, when it earned some $5.12 billion in after-tax profits. Much of this growth was driven by acquisitions that took Tyco into a diverse range of businesses, including medical supplies, security equipment, electronic components, plastics, financial services, and telecommunications. Between 1996 and 2001, Tyco spent some $45 billion in cash (much of it raised from debt offerings) and stock to purchase more than 100 companies. With the acquisitions fueling growth, Tyco's earnings expanded by 35 percent each year between 1996 and 2001.

Tyco's success has been attributed to the consistent application of a business model that comprises a number of elements. First, although the company is diversified, it seeks to attain a critical mass in the industries in which it competes. Through acquisitions, it has become one of the largest providers of security systems, basic medical supplies, and electronic components in the United States. Indeed, it sees itself as using acquisitions to consolidate fragmented industries and attain economies of scale, which give it a cost-based advantage over smaller rivals. Second, the company *never* makes hostile acquisitions, which would be too expensive and could result in bad feelings among the managers of an acquired company. Third, Tyco deliberately seeks out companies that make basic products that have a strong market franchise but have been underperforming relative to their peers in recent years. Tyco's management believes that this indicates there is substantial room for improvement. Once it identifies a potential target, Tyco approaches management to see if they are interested in backing a sale of the company. If they express interest in supporting an acquisition, Tyco sends in teams of independent auditors to carefully go through the books of the target and identify the potential for improving performance. If the target company has potential, Tyco makes a formal bid. As a precondition of the bid, the top managers of the target company normally agree to step down (with a substantial severance package). Tyco typically replaces them with up-and-coming managers two or three layers below.

Once an acquisition has been completed, Tyco sets to work improving the performance of the acquired unit. Typically excess capacity is shut down, corporate overhead slashed, unprofitable product lines sold off or discontinued, plants and sales forces merged with those of similar operations within Tyco to attain scale economies, and head count reduced. For example, in 1999, Tyco acquired AMP, the world's largest manufacturer of electronic components, for $12 billion in Tyco stock. Within months, Tyco had identified close to $1 billion in cost savings that could be implemented by 2002 by closing unprofitable plants and reducing the work force by 8,000. On average, Tyco finds cost savings in an acquisition that amount to about 11 percent of the target company's revenues.

In addition to taking excess costs out of a newly acquired company, the employees of the acquired unit are given incentives to boost profitability. No bonuses are paid to anyone at Tyco unless annual net income growth exceeds 10 percent. However, bonuses quickly ramp up for each increment above that minimum and are unlimited for senior managers. In the best years, senior managers receive bonuses that are multiples of their salaries, super-visors at the plant level can receive cash or stock options worth as much as 40 percent of their salary, and hourly factor workers receive two to three weeks of extra pay.

Tyco's corporate structure is also very lean. There are only seventy employees at the head office, most of whom focus on tax and legal issues. Kozlowski ran operations on an arm's-length basis. Performance goals for the coming year are set by negotiation between top management and the management of operating units. Once targets are set, the policy is one of management by exception, with operating managers being given considerable autonomy so long as they hit or exceed their targets.

Despite Tyco's impressive track record, the stock price underperformed the general market during much of 1998–2001. The stock was given a "diversification discount" by investors, who were put off by the complexity of Tyco's financial accounts and the lack of transparency with regard to the profitability of individual operations. In 1999, Tyco was the target of criticism by analysts who accused the company of inappropriate accounting methods. However, a subsequent investigation by the Securities and Exchange Commission gave Tyco's accounting practices a clean bill of health. Despite this, the criticisms persisted, and in late 2001 the company came under renewed attack from critics who argued that it had systematically inflated its profitability to make its performance look better than it actually was. According to the critics, the management at several companies Tyco acquired all artificially depressed the profitability of their companies in the final months before the deals were completed. This was done by taking numerous charges, slowing sales, and pushing up expenses. Consequently, Tyco's operating results were "spring-loaded" for a quarter or two after the acquisition closed as sales and profit margins suddenly expanded. They also argued that the debt that Tyco had taken on to finance some of its acquisitions, which by early 2002 totaled some $23 billion, left the company excessively leveraged and potentially vulnerable should cash flow projections fall short.

Tyco dismissed the charges of accounting tricks and pointed out that it would generate over $4 billion in free cash flow during 2002, more than enough to cover all of its short-term debt commitments. Nevertheless, the attacks persisted, and the stock price slid to under $20 by May 2002. To try to halt the slide, Kozlowski floated a number of ideas, including splitting up the company into four independent units and selling off its plastics and financial services unit, then using the proceeds to pay down the company's debt. However, with none of these ideas seeming to help the stock price, Kozlowski ultimately stated that he would continue to run the company as a diversified entity and focus on generating cash flow to pay down the company's debt load. Tyco would sell off some of its acquired businesses, but only if it could get a decent price for them, and it would use the proceeds to pay down debt. Whatever the ultimate outcome, it seems clear that after a decade of success, investors had turned sour on Tyco's business model, recognizing, belatedly perhaps, that Tyco's growth had been bought at the price of accumulating tremendous debt.

To complicate matters, in June 2002 Kozlowski resigned after being charged with tax evasion. He was replaced by John Fort, Tyco's CEO between 1982 and 1992. One of Fort's first actions was to complete a spin-off of CIT Group, Tyco's finance arm, for $4.6 billion, significantly less than the $11 billion Tyco had paid to acquire CIT in 2000. With this cash in hand, however, Tyco appeared to have enough funds to service its debt commitments through until November 2003, and with the company continuing to generate positive cash flow, its survival seemed more certain.

Sources: J. R. Laing, "Tyco's Titan," *Barron's,* April 12, 1999, pp. 27–32. M. Maremont, "How Is Tyco Accounting for Cash Flow?" *Wall Street Journal,* March 5, 2002, p. C1. J. R. Laing, "Doubting Tyco," *Barron's,* January 28, 2002, pp. 19–20. Staff Reporter, "Tyco's Troubles," *Economist,* June 8th, 2002, p. 71.

Overview

This chapter continues with the theme of corporate-level strategy than we discussed in Chapter 9. It begins with a detailed look at the strategy of **diversification,** which is the process of adding new businesses to the company that are distinct from its established operations. A **diversified company** is thus one that is involved in two or more distinct businesses. After reviewing diversification, we turn to the different vehicles, or means, that companies use to execute a diversification strategy and establish new business areas. The basic choice here is among internal new ventures, acquisitions, and joint ventures. **Internal new venturing** is about starting a new business from scratch, **acquisitions** involve buying an existing business, and **joint ventures** typically establish a new business with the assistance of a partner. The chapter closes with a look at **restructuring,** which is the process of reducing the scope of the company's diversified operations by exiting from business areas. By the end of this chapter you will have a good grasp of the pros and cons of different diversification strategies, and of the relative merits of the different vehicles that can be used to execute a diversification strategy.

Expanding Beyond a Single Industry

The role of management in corporate-level strategy is to identify which industries a company should compete in to maximize its long-run profitability. For many companies, profitable growth and expansion often entails concentrating on a single industry or market. For example, McDonald's focuses on the global fast food restaurant business and Wal-Mart on global discount retailing.

One advantage of staying inside the industry is that it allows a company to focus its total managerial, financial, technological, and functional resources and capabilities on competing successfully in just one area. This is important in fast-growing and fast-changing industries, where demands on the company's resources and capabilities are likely to be substantial, but where the long-term profits that flow from establishing a competitive advantage are also likely to be very significant.

A second advantage of staying inside a single industry is that a company stays focused on what it knows and does best.[1] By doing so, it does not make the mistake of entering new industries where its existing resources and capabilities add little value or where it confronts a whole new set of competitive industry forces that present unanticipated threats. Both Sears and Coca-Cola, like many other companies, have committed this strategic error. Coca-Cola once decided to expand into the movie business, acquiring Columbia Pictures. It also acquired a large wine-producing business. Similarly, Sears, the clothing seller, once decided to become a one-stop shopping place and bought Allstate Insurance, Coldwell Banker (a real estate company), and Dean Witter (a financial services enterprise). Both Coca-Cola and Sears found that they not only lacked the competencies needed to compete successfully in their new industries but had not foreseen the different kinds of competitive forces that existed in these industries. They came to the conclusion that entry into these industries dissipated, rather than created, value and lowered their profitability, and they ultimately sold off the businesses they had acquired, at a loss.

As the previous chapter discussed, companies that stay inside one industry can pursue both horizontal integration and outsourcing to strengthen their competitive position. They can also pursue vertical integration and enter industries at adjacent stages of the value chain to strengthen their position in their core business. However, with all of these strategies, a company's fortunes are still mostly tied to the profitability of its original industry, which can be dangerous if that industry goes into decline. Moreover, companies that concentrate on just one industry may be missing out on opportunities to create value and increase their profitability by leveraging their resources and capabilities to other activities. There is compelling evidence to suggest that companies that rest on their laurels and do not engage in constant learning and force themselves to stretch can lose out to agile new competitors that come along with superior business models.[2] For these reasons, many argue that companies must leverage their resources and capabilities across market segments and industries if they are to survive and prosper.

A Company as a Portfolio of Distinctive Competencies

Gary Hamel and C. K. Prahalad have developed a model that can help managers assess how and when they should expand beyond their current market segments or industry. According to these authors, a fruitful approach to identifying the different product and market opportunities is to reconceptualize the company as a portfolio of distinctive competencies, as opposed to a portfolio of products, and then consider how those competencies might be leveraged to create business opportunities in new industries.[3] Recall from Chapter 4 that a distinctive competency is a value-creating company-specific resource or capability. For example, Canon, the Japanese company best known for its cameras and photocopiers, has distinctive competencies in precision mechanics, fine optics, microelectronics, and electronic imaging.

Hamel and Prahalad maintain that the identification of *current* distinctive competencies constitutes the first step for a company that is engaged in the process of deciding which diversification opportunities to pursue. Once a company has identified its competencies, Hamel and Prahalad advocate using a matrix similar to that illustrated in Figure 10.1 to establish an agenda for building and leveraging competencies to create new businesses. This matrix distinguishes between existing and new competencies, and between the existing industries in which a company participates and new industries. Each quadrant in the matrix has a title, the strategic implications of which are discussed in the text that follows.

Fill-in-the-Blanks. The lower-left quadrant of Figure 10.1 represents the company's existing portfolio of competencies and products. In the 1900s, for example, Canon had distinctive competencies in precision mechanics, fine optics, and microelectronics and was active in two basic industries: cameras and photocopiers. It used the competencies in precision mechanics and fine optics to produce basic mechanical cameras. These two competencies plus an additional competence in

Industry

	Existing	New
New (Competence)	**Premier plus 10** What new competencies will we need to build to protect and extend our franchise in current industries?	**Mega-opportunities** What new competencies will we need to build to participate in the most exciting industries of the future?
Existing (Competence)	**Fill in the blanks** What is the opportunity to improve our position in existing industries and better leverage our existing competencies?	**White spaces** What new products or services could we create by creatively redeploying or recombining our current competencies?

microelectronics were required to produce plain paper copiers. The term "fill-in-the-blanks" refers to the opportunity to improve the company's competitive position in existing industries by transferring existing competencies. Canon was able to improve the position of its camera business by transferring microelectronics skills from its copier business to support the development of cameras with electronic features, such as auto-focus capabilities.

Premier Plus 10. The upper-left quadrant in Figure 10.1 is referred to as *premier plus 10.* The wording is meant to suggest another important question: What new distinctive competencies must be built today to ensure that the company remains a *premier* provider of its existing products in *ten* years? Canon decided that in order to maintain a competitive edge in its copier business, it was going to have to build a new competence in electronic imaging (which refers to the ability to capture and store images in a digital format, as opposed to using more traditional chemical-based photographic processes). This new competence has subsequently helped it to extend its product range to include laser copiers, color copiers, and digital cameras.

White Spaces. The lower-right quadrant of Figure 10.1 is referred to as *white spaces* because the issue to be addressed is how best to fill the "white space" by creatively redeploying or recombining current distinctive competencies to enter new industries. Canon has been able to recombine its established competencies in precision mechanics, fine optics, and its recently acquired competence in electronic imaging to produce fax machines and laser jet printers, thereby entering the fax and printer industries. In other words, it has leveraged its competencies to exploit diversification opportunities.

Mega-Opportunities. Opportunities represented by the upper-right quadrant of Figure 10.1 do not overlap with the company's current industries or its current competencies. Rather, they imply entry into new industries where the company currently has none of the competencies required to succeed. Nevertheless, a company may choose to pursue such opportunities if they are seen to be particularly attractive, significant, or relevant to its existing business opportunities. For example, in 1979,

Monsanto was primarily a manufacturer of chemicals, including fertilizers. However, the company saw enormous opportunities in the emerging biotechnology industry. Senior research scientists felt that it might be possible to produce genetically engineered crop seeds that would produce their own "organic" pesticides. In that year, the company embarked on a massive investment that ultimately amounted to several hundred million dollars to build a world-class competence in biotechnology. This investment was funded by cash flows generated from Monsanto's operations in the chemical industry. The investment began to bear fruit in the mid-1990s when Monsanto introduced a series of genetically engineered crop seeds including Bollgard, a cotton seed that is resistant against many common pests, including the bollworm, and Roundup-resistant soybean seeds (Roundup is a herbicide produced by Monsanto).[4]

The Multibusiness Model

A focus on using or recombining existing competencies or building new competencies to enter new market segments and industries helps managers to think strategically about how industry boundaries might change over time and how this will affect their current business models. By thinking about how to transfer and leverage competencies across industries, Prahalad and Hamel's model can help managers to avoid the strategic mistake of entering new markets where their business model will fail to give them a competitive advantage, as both Coca-Cola and Sears did.

Once a decision has been reached to expand beyond one industry and enter others, a company confronts the need to construct its business model at two levels. First, it has to develop a business model for each industry in which it competes. Sometimes it may be able to take the core set of strategies employed in a business model developed in one industry and implant them in a business unit in a new industry. For example, General Electric has developed a business model that involves selling a piece of expensive capital equipment at a low price and then making significant profits from providing ongoing services for that equipment. Thus, it makes jet engines that it sells to airlines at a low price, and it bundles this sale with a contract to service those engines over their twenty-five-year life span. GE makes substantial profits not from the initial sale of the engines, which are priced at cost, but from the ongoing service contract (this is an example of the razor and razor blades strategy discussed in Chapter 7). Although this model was developed originally by its jet engine business, GE has applied it to several other businesses, including medical imaging, where it sells complex medical equipment to hospitals at cost and then makes profits from the service contracts bundled with the sale of equipment. In other cases, however, the company may have to develop an entirely distinct business model for different industries. Again, in the case of GE, the business model used in its jet engine and medical equipment businesses is not appropriate for its broadcasting business (NBC), where the profit comes primarily from advertising revenues.

In addition to developing a business model for each industry in which it competes, a diversified company has to develop a higher-level *multibusiness model* that justifies entry into different industries in terms of the way it will increase the company's profitability. From a distinctive competency perspective, a multibusiness model would explain how and why transferring and leveraging distinctive competencies across industries will increase a company's return on invested capital. A multibusiness model would also explain how a company is seeking to create value through its choice of corporate-level strategies. For example, Tyco's *multibusiness model* was based on strategies that included using acquisitions to consolidate fragmented industries, acquiring companies that were underperforming their peers, never making hostile acquisitions, identifying the potential for cost savings prior to the acquisition, moving rapidly to realize those cost savings after the acquisition had been completed, and making sure that the employees of acquired companies were given incentives to develop distinctive competencies to boost profitability.

Increasing Profitability Through Diversification

Diversification is the process of adding new businesses to the company that are distinct from its established operations. A diversified or multibusiness company is thus one that is involved in two or more distinct industries. To approach this issue, it is useful to restate the proposition put forward in the last chapter: To increase profitability, a diversification strategy should enable a company or one or more of its business units to (1) perform one or more of the value creation functions at a lower cost, (2) perform one or more of the value creation functions in a way that allows for differentiation and gives a company pricing options, or (3) help the company to manage industry rivalry better.

The managers of most companies first consider diversification when they are generating **free cash flow,** which is cash *in excess* of that required to fund investments in the company's existing business and to meet any debt commitments.[5] Put differently, free cash flow is cash in excess of that which can be profitably reinvested in an existing business. Thus, in the *Opening Case,* it was noted that Tyco was predicted to generate $4 billion of *free cash flow* in 2002, this being cash *in excess* of that required to fund all profitable investments in its existing businesses and to meet its short-term debt commitments. *Cash* is simply *capital* by another name. When a company is generating free cash flow, the question managers must tackle is whether to return that capital to shareholders in the form of higher dividend payouts or invest it in diversification. Technically, any free cash flow belongs to the company's owners—its shareholders. For diversification to make sense, the return on investing free cash flow in pursuit of diversification opportunities (the return on invested capital, ROIC) *must* exceed the return that stockholders could get by investing that capital in a diversified portfolio of stocks and bonds. If this were not the case, it would be in the best interests of shareholders for the company to return any excess cash to them through higher dividends rather than pursue a diversification strategy. Thus, a diversification strategy is not consistent with maximizing returns to shareholders unless management can create significant value by pursuing it and thereby generating a positive return on any capital invested in diversification that exceeds the return shareholders could gain by investing the same capital in a portfolio of stocks and bonds. The managers of a diversified company can boost profitability in five main ways: (1) transferring competencies among existing business, (2) leveraging competencies to create new businesses, (3) sharing resources to realize economies of scope, (4) using diversification as a means of managing rivalry in one or more industries, and (5) exploiting general organizational competencies that enhance the performance of all business units within a diversified company.

Transferring Competencies

Transferring competencies involves taking a distinctive competence developed in one industry and applying it to an *existing* business in another industry. For example, Philip Morris developed distinctive competencies in product development, consumer marketing, and brand positioning that took it to a leadership position in the tobacco industry. It then acquired Miller Brewing, at the time a relatively small player in the brewing industry. Philip Morris subsequently transferred some of its very best marketing people to Miller Brewing, where they applied the skills acquired at Philip Morris to Miller's lackluster brewing business (see Figure 10.2). The result was the creation of Miller Light, the first light beer, and a marketing campaign that helped to push Miller from number six to number two in the brewing industry in terms of market share.

Companies that base their diversification strategy on transferring competencies tend to acquire businesses *related* to their existing activities by one or more value creation functions—for example, manufacturing, marketing, materials management, or R&D. For example, Miller Brewing was related to Philip Morris's tobacco business by marketing commonalities; both beer and tobacco are mass market consumer goods where brand positioning, advertising, and product development skills are important. In general, such competency transfers can lower the costs of value creation in one or more of a company's diversified businesses or enable one or more of its diversified businesses to undertake their value creation functions in a way that leads to differentiation and gives that business unit pricing options.

For such a strategy to work, the competencies being transferred must involve activities that are important for establishing a competitive advantage. All too often companies assume that any commonality is sufficient for creating value. General Motors's acquisition of Hughes Aircraft, made simply because autos and auto manufacturing were going electronic and Hughes was an electronics concern, demonstrates the folly of overestimating the commonalities among businesses. The acquisition failed to realize any of the anticipated gains for GM, whose competitive position did not improve, and GM subsequently sold off Hughes.

Leveraging Competencies

Leveraging competencies involves taking a distinctive competency developed by a business in one industry and using it to create a *new* business in a different industry. The central idea here is that a distinctive competency that is the source of competitive advantage in one industry might also be applied to create a differentiation- or cost-based competitive advantage for a new business in a different industry. For example, Canon used its distinctive competencies in precision mechanics, fine optics, and electronic imaging to produce laser jet printers, which for Canon was a new business in a new industry. Its competitive advantage in laser printers came from the fact that its competencies enabled it to produce high-quality (differentiated) printers that could be manufactured at a low cost.

FIGURE 10.2

Transfer of Competencies at Philip Morris

The difference between leveraging competencies and transferring competencies is that in the case of leveraging competencies, an entirely *new* business is being created, whereas transferring competencies involves a transfer between *existing* businesses. Although the distinction may seem subtle, it is actually very important, because different managerial processes are involved. Companies that leverage competencies to establish new business tend to be technology-based enterprises that use their R&D competencies to create new business opportunities in diverse industries. In contrast, companies that transfer competencies typically enter new industries by acquiring established businesses. They then transfer competencies to the acquired businesses in order to enhance their profitability, as Philip Morris did with Miller Brewing.

A number of companies have based their diversification strategy on leveraging competencies and applying them to the creation of new businesses in different industries. Microsoft has leveraged its skills in software development and marketing to create two new businesses, its online network MSN and the X-Box video game business. It is important to emphasize that Microsoft's management decided to invest in these businesses, rather than return the free cash flow generated from its operating system and application software businesses to shareholders in the form of higher dividend payouts, primarily because they believed that the return on invested capital they could earn from those investments exceeded the return that Microsoft shareholders could reasonably be expected to earn by investing that same capital in a diversified portfolio of stocks and bonds. In other words, Microsoft's management believes that the company's diversification strategy is in the best interests of shareholders because they think that the company's competencies will enable it to attain a competitive advantage in the video game and online industries.

Another company that is famous for its ability to leverage competencies and create *new* businesses in diverse industries is 3M, which among other things leveraged its skills in adhesives to create new business opportunities (see Strategy in Action 10.1). From the humble beginning as a manufacturer of sandpaper, 3M has become one of the most diversified corporations in the United States. Most of this diversification was the result not of acquisitions but of the organic creation of new businesses.

Sharing Resources: Economies of Scope

When two or more business units in different industries share resources such as manufacturing facilities, distribution channels, advertising campaigns, or R&D costs, they may be able to realize **economies of scope:** the cost reductions associated with sharing resources across businesses.[6] These cost reductions have two major sources. First, companies that can share resources across businesses have to invest proportionately less in the shared resource than companies that cannot share. For example, Procter & Gamble makes both disposable diapers and paper towels, paper-based products valued for their ability to absorb liquid without disintegrating. Because both products need the same attribute—absorbency—Procter & Gamble can share the R&D costs associated with producing an absorbent paper-based product across the two businesses. Similarly, because both products are sold to the same customer set (supermarkets), it can use the same sales force to sell both products (see Figure 10.3). In contrast, competitors that make just paper towels or just disposable diapers cannot achieve the same economies and have to invest proportionately more in both R&D and maintaining a sales force. The net result is that other things being equal, P&G will have lower expenses and earn a higher return on invested capital than companies that lack the ability to share resources.

Second, resource sharing across businesses may enable a company to use the shared resource more intensively, thereby realizing *economies of scale* (i.e., economies

Strategy in Action   10.1

Diversification at 3M: Leveraging Technology

3M is a 100-year-old industrial colossus that in 2001 generated revenues of $16 billion and profits of $1.4 billion from a portfolio of more than 50,000 individual products ranging from sandpaper and sticky tape to medical devices, office supplies, and electronic components. The company has consistently created new businesses by leveraging its scientific knowledge to find new applications for its proprietary technology. Today the company is composed of more than forty discrete business units grouped into six major sectors: transportation, health care, industrial, consumer and office, electro and communications, and specialty materials. The company has consistently generated 30 percent of sales from products introduced within the prior five years and currently is operating with the goal of producing 40 percent of sales from products introduced within the previous four years. The goal is to attain revenues of $20 billion by 2004, some $8 billion of it expected to come from products that were not launched in 1999, many in new businesses that did not exist in any strategic plan.

The process of leveraging technology to create new businesses at 3M can be illustrated by the following quotation from William Coyne, head of R&D at 3M: "It began with sandpaper: mineral and glue on a substrate. After years as an abrasives company, it created a tape business. A researcher left off the mineral, and adapted the glue and substrate to create the first sticky tape. After creating many varieties of sticky tape—consumer, electrical, medical—researchers created the world's first audio and videotapes. In their search to create better tape backings, other researchers happened on multilayer films that, surprise, have remarkable light management qualities. This multiplayer film technology is being used in brightness enhancement films, which are incorporated in the displays of virtually all laptops and palm computers."

How does 3M do it? First, the company is a science-based enterprise with a strong tradition of innovation and risk taking. Risk taking is encouraged, and failure is not punished but seen as a natural part of the process of creating new products and business. Second, 3M's management is relentlessly focused on the company's customers and the problems they face. Many of 3M's products have come from helping customers to solve difficult problems. Third, managers set stretch goals that require the company to create new products and businesses at a rapid pace (e.g., the current goal that 40 percent of sales should come from products introduced within the last four years). Fourth, employees are given considerable autonomy to pursue their own ideas. An employee can spend 15 percent of his or her time working on a project of his or her own choosing without management approval. Many products have resulted from this autonomy, including the ubiquitous Post-it notes. Fifth, while products belong to business units and it is business units that are responsible for the profits they generate and are rewarded for maximizing profitability, the technologies belong to everyone within the company. Anyone at 3M is free to try to develop new applications for a technology developed within a business unit; they do not have to belong to that unit. Sixth, there are mechanisms for sharing technological knowledge within 3M so that opportunities can be identified, such as conferences where researchers from different business units are brought together to share the results of their work. And finally, 3M uses numerous mechanisms to recognize and reward those who develop new technologies, products, and businesses, including peer-nominated award programs, a corporate hall of fame, and of course, monetary rewards.

Sources: W. E. Coyne, "How 3M Innovates for Long-Term Growth," *Research Technology Management* (March–April 2001): 21–24. 3M's 2001 10K form.

of scale are a source of economies of scope). For example, one of the motives behind the 1998 merger of Citicorp and Travelers to form Citigroup was that the merger would allow Travelers to sell its insurance products and financial services through Citicorp's retail banking network. The merger allows the expanded group to better use an existing asset—its retail-banking network—thereby realizing economies of scale. Because economies of scale lower the cost structure of one or more businesses, the net result is to increase the profitability of the diversified company.

FIGURE 10.3

Sharing Resources at
Procter & Gamble

Diversification to attain economies of scope is possible only when there are significant commonalities between one or more of the value creation functions of a company's existing and new activities. Moreover, managers need to be aware that the bureaucratic costs of coordination necessary to achieve economies of scope within a company often outweigh the value that can be created by such a strategy.[7] Consequently, the strategy should be pursued only when sharing is likely to generate a *significant* competitive advantage in one or more of a company's business units.

Managing Rivalry: Multipoint Competition

Sometimes a company benefits by diversifying into an industry in order to hold a competitor in check that has either entered its industry or has the potential to do so. For example, if an aggressive enterprise based in another industry enters a company's market and tries to gain share by cutting prices, the company can respond in kind and diversify into the aggressor's home industry and also cut prices. In this way, the company sends a signal: "If you attack me, I'll respond in kind and make things tough for you." (This is an example of the strategy of tit-for-tat discussed in Chapter 5 under the heading of game theory.) The hope is that such a move will cause the aggressor to pull back from its attack, moderating rivalry in the company's home industry and allowing for higher prices and profits. Of course, for this to stick and the tit-for-tat strategy to have its desired effect, the company would then need to pull back from its competitive attack in the aggressor's home market.

An example of diversification to keep a potential competitor in check occurred in the late 1990s when Microsoft awoke to the fact that Sony might emerge as a rival. Although Sony was in a different industry (consumer electronics as opposed to software), Microsoft realized that the Sony PlayStation was in essence nothing more than a specialized computer and, moreover, one that did not use a Microsoft operating system. Microsoft's fear was that Sony might use the PlayStation II, which came equipped with web browsing potential, as a "Trojan horse" to gain control of web browsing and computing from the living room, ultimately taking customers away from PCs with Microsoft operating systems. The desire to keep Sony's ambitions in check was another part of the rationale for Microsoft's diversification into the video game industry with the launch of the X-Box.

There are other diversified companies that compete against each other in several different industries. Microsoft and Sony now compete directly against each other in the video game industry and the wireless handset industry. Canon and Kodak compete against each other in photocopiers and digital cameras. Unilever and Procter & Gamble compete against each other in laundry detergents, personal care products, and packaged foods. When companies compete against each other in different industries, we refer to it as **multipoint competition.** Companies that are engaged in multipoint competition might be better able to manage rivalry by signaling that competitive attacks in one industry will be met by retaliatory attacks in another industry. If successful, such signaling might lead to *mutual forbearance,* and thus less intense rivalry and higher profit in each industry where a company competes. It follows that the desire to manage rivalry better through multipoint competition might be a motive for diversification that increases profitability.

Exploiting General Organizational Competencies

By **general organizational competencies,** we mean competencies that transcend individual functions or businesses and reside at the corporate level in the multibusiness enterprise, typically in the skills of the company's top managers. These competencies help each business unit within the corporation to perform at a higher level than would be the case were they independent companies in their own right.[8] Such general organizational competencies can take on several forms, which include (1) entrepreneurial capabilities, (2) capabilities in developing effective organizational structures and control systems, and (3) superior strategic capabilities. The important point to recognize is that although any diversified company can develop these capabilities, few do because the required managerial skills are rare and difficult to develop and implement.

Entrepreneurial Capabilities. Some companies have a long history of developing new businesses internally; examples include 3M (see Strategy in Action 10.1), Hewlett Packard, IBM, Canon, Sony, and Matsushita.[9] They do this because they have management systems backed by an organization culture that stimulates managers to act entrepreneurially. The consequence is that these companies generate profitable new businesses at a much higher rate than most other enterprises, and their diversification is a result of this. We will highlight some of the systems required to generate profitable new businesses later in this chapter when we discuss internal new ventures. For now, note that the management systems of the company must (1) encourage managers to take risks, (2) give them the time and resources to pursue novel ideas, (3) not punish managers for taking risks that fail, but also (4) make sure that the company does not waste resources on too many risky ventures that have a low probability of generating a decent return on investment. Obviously, a difficult organizational balancing act is required here, for the company has to simultaneously encourage risk taking while limiting the amount of risk being undertaken.

Companies with entrepreneurial capabilities are able to achieve this balancing act. 3M's corporate goal of generating 40 percent of revenues from products introduced within the past four years focuses the organization's intention of the importance of developing new products and businesses. The company's famous 15 percent rule gives employees the time to pursue novel ideas. The company's long-standing commitment to helping customers solve problems helps ensure that ideas for new businesses are customer focused. The company's celebration of employees who created new businesses helps to reinforce the norm of entrepreneurship and risk taking. Similarly, there is a norm that failure should not be punished but viewed as a learning experience.

Effective Organization Structure and Controls. The organization structure and controls of a diversified company provide the context within which the managers of business units run. Effective organizational structure and controls can create a set of incentives that strongly encourage business unit (divisional) managers to maximize the efficiency and effectiveness of their units, which will increase the company's return on invested capital. We shall look closely at what constitutes effective organization structure and controls in the following chapters. For now, note that an examination of diversified corporations that are successful at boosting profitability through effective organization structure and controls suggests that a number of features are common across such companies.[10] First, the different business units of the company tend to be placed into self-contained divisions. Second, these divisions tend to be managed by senior executives in a decentralized fashion. Rather than get involved in the day-to-day operations of such divisions, they set challenging financial goals for each division, probe the general managers of each division about their strategy for attaining these goals, monitor divisional performance, and hold the general managers accountable for that performance. Third, these internal monitoring and control mechanisms are linked with progressive incentive pay systems that reward divisional personnel for attaining or surpassing performance goals. Although this sounds like a relatively easy strategy to pursue, in practice it seems to require very good senior executives to pull it off—that is, senior executives with superior strategic capabilities.

Superior Strategic Capabilities. For diversification to increase profitability, a company's top managers must have superior strategic capabilities. These capabilities give top managers the intangible governance skills that allow them to manage the different business units within the organization in a way that allows them to perform at a higher level than they would do if they were independent companies in their own right.[11] Simply put, in the context of a diversified company, governance skills determine how effective top managers are at managing business units and the managers who control those units. The business of top management in the diversified company is to manage the managers of business units. This is not an easy thing to do well; governance skills are a rare and valuable capability. However, certain senior executives seem to have developed a skill for managing businesses and pushing the heads of those business units to achieve superior performance. Examples include Jack Welch at General Electric, Bill Gates and Steve Ballmer at Microsoft, and, despite Tyco's recent troubles and his own personal shortcomings, Dennis Kozlowski (see the *Opening Case*).

A flair for entrepreneurship is often found in top managers who have developed superior strategic capabilities or governance skills. As important, if not more so, is the ability to recognize ways to enhance the performance of individual managers, functions, and business units. Jack Welch, for example, was a master in improving the skills of his managers across the board in GE. He created organization-wide management development programs focusing on change management and created procedures to make middle managers question top management actions. At the functional and business levels, he instituted many of the techniques discussed in Chapter 4 to promote superior efficiency and quality, such as the Six Sigma quality improvement methodology, and he pushed hard to make sure that business unit managers used these techniques to improve the efficiency of the operations under their control.

An especially important governance skill in the diversified company is the ability to diagnose the real source of performance problems in an underperforming business unit and take the appropriate steps to fix those problems, whether through pushing the top managers of the unit to take certain strategic actions or replacing top managers with individuals better able to fix the problems. Top managers who have such governance skills tend to be very good at probing business unit managers for information and helping them to think through strategic problems.

Related to this skill, an important way in which a diversified company can increase its profitability is by recognizing inefficient and poorly managed companies, acquiring them, and then restructuring them to improve their performance. The acquired company does not have to be in the same industry as the acquiring company for the strategy to work; thus, the strategy often leads to diversification. Improvements in the performance of the acquired company can come from a number of sources. First, the acquiring company usually replaces the top managers of the acquired company with a more aggressive management team. Second, the new managers of the acquired business are encouraged to sell off any unproductive assets, such as executive jets and elaborate corporate headquarters, and to reduce staffing levels. Third, the new management team is encouraged to intervene in the operations of the acquired business to seek out ways to improve the unit's efficiency, quality, innovativeness, and customer responsiveness. Fourth, to motivate the new management team and other employees of the acquired unit to undertake such actions, increases in their pay are typically linked to increases in the performance of the acquired unit. In addition, the acquiring company often establishes performance goals for the acquired company that cannot be met without significant improvements in operating efficiency. It also makes the new top management aware that failure to achieve performance improvements consistent with these goals within a given amount of time will probably result in their being replaced.

Thus, the system of rewards and sanctions established by the acquiring company gives the new managers of the acquired unit strong incentives to look for ways of improving the performance of the unit under their charge. The strategy of acquiring and restructuring underperforming companies was in fact what Tyco International pursued for most of the 1990s, apparently with considerable success, until Tyco's senior managers erred by getting too ambitious, acquiring too many companies in too short a space of time, and taking on too much debt (see the *Opening Case*). From time to time, General Electric also pursued a similar strategy under the leadership of Jack Welch, again with some success.

Types of Diversification

The two main types of diversification are related diversification and unrelated diversification.[12] **Related diversification** is diversification into a new business activity in a different industry that is *related* to a company's existing business activity, or activities, by commonalities between one or more components of each activity's value chain. Normally, these linkages are based on manufacturing, marketing, or technological commonalities. The diversification of Philip Morris into the brewing industry with the acquisition of Miller Brewing is an example of related diversification because there are marketing commonalities between the brewing and tobacco businesses: both are mass market consumer product businesses in which competitive success depends on brand-positioning skills. 3M is another example of a company that has long pursued a strategy of related diversification. In 3M's case, the commonality is in the development of core technology, which is then applied to a wide range of business areas. Another example of related diversification is given in Strategy in Action 10.2, which looks at Intel's recent diversification into the communications chip business.

Strategy in Action

10.2

Related Diversification at Intel

Although Intel has had a small presence in the communications chip business since the 1980s, for a long time it languished as the company focused all of its attention and resources on the booming business of making microprocessors for personal computers. According to managers at Intel, "feeding the processor monster" consumed all of the company's financial resources. Although Intel was generating high profits and significant positive cash flows, it took the strategic decision to reinvest those cash flows in the design of new generations of its highly successful X86 microprocessor architecture and in large-scale (and expensive) fabrication facilities to manufacture microprocessors in very high volumes. The decision seemed logical: Intel had the dominant position in the microprocessor market, its primary customers (personal computer makers) were growing by leaps and bounds, and demand for its microprocessors was soaring. Indeed, had Intel not made these investments, it may have opened the door to competitors in the microprocessor business, such as AMD.

All this changed at a contentious strategy meeting of Intel's top executives in September 1996. Intel's executives came away from that meeting with two important insights. First, the personal computer industry would approach market saturation in several developed markets by the early 2000s. This meant that the growth in demand for Intel's microprocessors would slow. Therefore, Intel needed to find a new growth driver. Second, the executives decided that with the advent of the Internet, "communications was going to be the driver for everything in the future, that all computing was connected computing, and that connectivity had as important and strategic a role to play as the microprocessor did." Moreover, it was clear that demand for products of the communications industry such as communications network gear, which needed advanced communications chips, was accelerating rapidly.

Intel's executives decided that they could probably boost the company's return on invested capital by diverting some cash flow away from the microprocessor industry and use it to build a strong position in the rapidly growing communications chip industry. This was seen as a different industry because the product technology was different, the production technology was different, the customers were different, and the competitors were different. Intel believed, however, that because the commu-

nications chip industry was closely related to the microprocessor industry, Intel could attain a competitive advantage by transferring its leading-edge technology, honed in the microprocessor industry, and manufacturing and marketing capabilities to the communications chip business.

Once the decision was made to enter the communications chip industry on a significant scale, Intel had to decide how best to execute the strategy. The company's managers decided that the only way they could get big enough fast enough to gain scale economies and establish a sustainable competitive advantage in this booming market was for the company to buy the required technology, fabrication facilities, and sales forces. It could then improve the performance of the acquired businesses by transferring its competencies to them. So Intel went on an acquisition binge. Between January 1997 and June 2001, it made eighteen major acquisitions of companies in the communications chip industry for a combined total of $8 billion. These acquisitions include the purchase of the communications chip business of Digital Equipment Corporation for $625 million, Level One Communications (which made high-speed networking and telecommunications chips) for $2.4 billion, DSP (a maker of chip sets for cell phones) for $1.6 billion, and Giga A/S of Denmark (a maker of optical networking chips) for $1.25 billion.

As a result of these acquisitions, by mid-2001 Intel became the fourth largest global company in the communications chip industry, behind only Lucent, Motorola, and Texas Instruments, with revenues of $2.5 billion. Unfortunately, Intel and all these other companies were hard hit by the slump in global demand for telecommunications equipment that began in 2000 and continued through 2001–2002. As of mid-2002, Intel was losing money in its communications chip business, and revenues were declining. In contrast, although revenues in its microprocessor business had also slipped by 20 percent, it was still making strong profits in that area. Only time will tell whether Intel's diversification move will have been a profitable use of the company's financial resources or an ill-timed entry into a difficult business where the company has no competitive advantage.

Sources: R. Arensman, "Intel's Second Try," *Electronic Business* (March 2001): 62–70. Intel 10K Report, 2001.

Companies that pursue a strategy of related diversification can increase profitability in all of the ways we have just discussed. In contrast, **unrelated diversification** is based on entry into industries that have *no* obvious connection to any of a company's value chain activities in its present industry (or industries). Companies pursuing a strategy of unrelated diversification lack the ability to transfer or leverage competencies and to realize economies of scope. Indeed, most companies that pursue a strategy of unrelated diversification focus on increasing profitability by exploiting general organizational competencies. This was certainly the prime rationale for Tyco's diversification strategy during the 1990s, much of which was unrelated diversification. Kozlowski's focus was on increasing Tyco's profitability by establishing an effective organization structure and set of controls at Tyco, and then acquiring and restructuring businesses that he thought were not performing to their full potential. These acquired businesses were in a wide range of industries with no obvious value chain connection, for example, plastics, security systems, and telecommunications, and medical supplies.

In short, Kozlowski's *multibusiness model* for Tyco, like that of all other companies that pursue an unrelated diversification strategy, was *founded on exploiting the gains from general organizational competencies in order to increase the profitability of the constituent businesses of the corporation*. By contrast, the *multibusiness model* for companies pursuing a strategy of related diversification is first and foremost to *achieve the gains from transferring and leveraging competencies and from sharing resources*. In addition, although both related and unrelated diversification might be associated in theory with managing rivalry through multipoint competition, as a practical matter, related diversified companies are far more likely to encounter each other in different industries than unrelated companies are. So this benefit too is more likely to be attained by companies pursuing a related diversification strategy than those pursuing an unrelated diversification strategy.

The Limits of Diversification

One issue a company must confront is whether to pursue related or unrelated diversification. Because related diversification can boost profitability in more ways than unrelated diversification can, this might lead one to believe that related diversification should be the preferred strategy. In addition, related diversification is sometimes perceived as involving fewer risks because the company is moving into industries about which top management usually has some knowledge. Probably because of these considerations, most diversified companies display a preference for related diversification.[13] However, research suggests that the average related company is at best only marginally more profitable than the average unrelated company.[14]

A large number of academic studies support the conclusion that *extensive* diversification tends to depress rather than improve company profitability.[15] For example, in a study that looked at the diversification of thirty-three major U.S. corporations over thirty-five years, Michael Porter observed that the track record of corporate diversification has been poor.[16] Porter found that most of the companies had divested many more diversified acquisitions than they had kept. He and others have concluded that the corporate diversification strategies pursued by most companies can dissipate value instead of creating it.[17]

Why is related diversification only marginally more profitable than unrelated, and why and how can diversification dissipate rather than create value? On the other hand, why are there many examples of individual companies that have performed spectacularly well using a strategy of related diversification? Two reasons are considered in the next sections: the bureaucratic costs of diversification and the possibility that many companies diversify for the wrong reasons.

Bureaucratic Costs and Diversification Strategy

Although diversification can create value for a company, it can end up doing just the opposite. One reason for the failure of diversification to achieve its aims is that often the *bureaucratic costs* of diversification exceed the value created by the strategy. You will recall from the Chapter 9 that **bureaucratic costs** are the cost increases that arise in large, complex organizations due to managerial inefficiencies. The level of bureaucratic costs in a diversified organization is a function of two factors: (1) the number of businesses in a company's portfolio and (2) the extent of coordination required among the different businesses of the company in order to realize value from a diversification strategy.

Number of Businesses. The greater the number of businesses there are in a company's portfolio, the more difficult it is for corporate management to remain informed about the complexities of each business. Management simply does not have the time to process all the information needed to assess the strategic plan of each business unit objectively. This problem began to occur at General Electric in the 1970s. As then CEO Reg Jones commented,

> I tried to review each plan in great detail. This effort took untold hours and placed a tremendous burden on the corporate executive office. After a while I began to realize that no matter how hard we would work, we could not achieve the necessary in-depth understanding of the 40-odd business unit plans.[18]

The information overload in extensively diversified companies may lead corporate-level management to base important resource allocation decisions on only the most superficial analysis of each business unit's competitive position. For example, a promising business unit may be starved of investment funds, while other business units receive far more cash than they can profitably reinvest in their operations. Furthermore, the lack of familiarity with operating affairs on the part of corporate-level management increases the chances that business-level managers might deceive corporate-level managers. For instance, business unit managers might blame poor performance on difficult competitive conditions, even when it is the consequence of poor management. Thus, information overload can result in substantial inefficiencies within extensively diversified companies that cancel out the value created by diversification. These inefficiencies include the suboptimal allocation of cash resources within the company and a failure by corporate management to encourage and reward aggressive profit-seeking behavior by business unit managers.

The inefficiencies arising from information overload can be viewed as one component of the bureaucratic costs of extensive diversification. Of course, these costs can be reduced to manageable proportions if a company limits the scope of its diversification. Indeed, a desire to decrease these costs lay behind the 1980s and 1990s divestments and strategic concentration strategies of highly diversified conglomerates created in the 1960s and 1970s, such as Esmark Corporation, General Electric, ITT, Textron, Tenneco, and United Technologies. For example, under the leadership of Jack Welch, GE switched its emphasis from forty main business units to sixteen contained within three clearly defined sectors.

Coordination Among Businesses. The coordination required to realize value from transferring competencies and sharing resources to realize economies of scope can also be a source of bureaucratic costs. In particular, the transfer of competencies and the achievement of economies of scope demand close coordination among business units. It is the bureaucratic mechanisms needed for this coordination that give rise to bureaucratic costs. (We discuss the mechanisms for achieving coordination in Chapter 12.)

A more serious matter is that substantial bureaucratic costs can result from a firm's inability to identify the unique profit contribution of a business unit that is sharing resources with another unit in an attempt to realize economies of scope. Consider a company that has two business units: one producing household products (such as liquid soap and laundry detergent) and the other producing packaged food products. The products of both units are sold through supermarkets. In order to lower the costs of value creation, the parent company decides to pool the marketing and sales functions of each business unit. Pooling allows the business units to share the costs of a sales force (one sales force can sell the products of both divisions) and gain cost economies from using the same physical distribution system. The organizational structure required to achieve this might be similar to that illustrated in Figure 10.4. The company is organized into three divisions: a household products division, a food products division, and a marketing division.

Although such an arrangement may create value, it can also give rise to substantial control problems and hence bureaucratic costs. For example, if the performance of the household products business begins to slip, identifying who is to be held accountable—the management of the household products division or of the marketing division—may prove difficult. Indeed, each may blame the other for poor performance. The management of the household products division might blame the marketing policies of the marketing division, and the management of the marketing division might blame the poor quality and high costs of products produced by the household products division. Although this kind of problem can be resolved if corporate management directly audits the affairs of both divisions, this effort is costly in terms of the time and the effort that corporate management must expend.

Now imagine the situation within a company that is trying to create value by sharing marketing, manufacturing, and R&D resources across ten businesses rather than just two. Clearly, the accountability problem could become far more severe in such a company. Indeed, the problem might become so acute that the effort in trying to tie down accountability might create serious information overload for corporate management. When this occurs, corporate management effectively loses control of the company. If accountability cannot be sorted out, the consequences may include

FIGURE 10.4

Coordination Among
Related Business
Units

poor resource allocation decisions, a generally high level of organizational slack, and an inability by corporate management to encourage and reward aggressive profit-seeking behavior by business unit managers. All these inefficiencies can be considered part of the bureaucratic costs of diversification to realize economies of scope.

Limits of Diversification. Thus, although diversification can create value for a company, it inevitably involves bureaucratic costs. As is the case with vertical integration, the existence of bureaucratic costs places a limit on the amount of diversification that can profitably be pursued. It makes sense for a company to diversify only as long as the value created by such a strategy exceeds the bureaucratic costs associated with expanding the boundaries of the organization to incorporate additional business activities.

Remember that the greater the number of business units within a company and the greater the need for coordination among those business units, the larger the bureaucratic costs are likely to be. Hence, a company that has twenty businesses, all of them trying to share resources, incurs much larger bureaucratic costs than a company that has ten businesses, none of them trying to share resources. The implications of this relationship are quite straightforward. Specifically, the greater the number of businesses already in a company's portfolio and the greater the need for coordination among those businesses, the more probable it is that the value created by a diversification move will be outweighed by the resulting increase in bureaucratic costs. Once this occurs, a profitable limit to the diversified scope of the enterprise will be reached. However, many companies continue to diversify past this limit, and their performance declines. To solve this problem, a company must reduce the scope of the enterprise through divestments.

Related or Unrelated Diversification? A related diversified company has more opportunities for boosting profitability than an unrelated company, and because of this, managers might think that related diversification should be the preferred strategy. But we also noted that research suggests that the average related company is no more profitable than the average unrelated company.[19] This presents us with a puzzle: If related diversification is associated with more benefits than unrelated diversification, why isn't the strategy consistently more profitable?

The answer has to do with bureaucratic costs and the limits to diversification. As we have seen, bureaucratic costs arise from (1) the number of businesses in a company's portfolio and (2) the extent of coordination required among the different businesses in order to realize value from a diversification strategy. An unrelated company does not have to achieve coordination between business units, and so it has to cope only with the bureaucratic costs that arise from the number of businesses in its portfolio. In contrast, a related diversified company has to achieve coordination among business units if it is to realize the value that comes from skill transfers and resource sharing. Consequently, it has to cope with the bureaucratic costs that arise from *both* the number of business units in its portfolio *and* from coordination among business units. Thus, although it is true that related diversified companies can create value in more ways than unrelated companies, they have to bear higher bureaucratic costs in order to do so. These higher costs may cancel out the higher benefits, making the strategy no more profitable than one of unrelated diversification.

How, then, is a company to choose between these strategies? The choice depends on a comparison of the relative value-added and the bureaucratic costs associated with each strategy. In making this comparison, note that the opportunities for creating value from related (and closely related) diversification are a function of the extent of commonalities between the skills required to compete in the company's core business and the skills required to compete in other industries. Some companies' skills are so specialized that they have few applications outside the core businesses. For example, since the commonalities between steel making and other industrial or commercial operations are few, most steel companies have diversified into unrelated industries (USX into oil and gas). When companies have more generalized skills, they can find many more related diversification opportunities outside the core business. Examples include chemical companies (such as Dow Chemical and Du Pont) and electrical engineering companies. Consequently, the opportunities available to them to create value from related diversification are much greater.

Thus, it pays a firm to concentrate on related diversification when (1) the company's core competencies are applicable to a wide variety of industrial and commercial situations and (2) the bureaucratic costs of implementation do not exceed the value that can be created through resource sharing or transferring competencies. The second condition is likely to hold only for companies that are moderately diversified. At high levels of related diversification, the bureaucratic costs of additional diversification are likely to outweigh the value created by that diversification, and the strategy may become unprofitable.

By the same logic, it may pay a company to concentrate on unrelated diversification when (1) its core functional skills are highly specialized and have few applications outside the company's core business; (2) its top management possess superior strategic capabilities and are able to manage businesses effectively and acquire and restructure poorly run businesses; and (3) the bureaucratic costs of implementation do not exceed the value that can be created by pursuing a restructuring strategy. However, the third condition is *unlikely* to hold for companies that are highly diversified. Thus, no matter whether a company pursues a related or an unrelated diversification strategy, the existence of bureaucratic costs suggests the very real limits to the profitable diversification of the company.

Diversification That Dissipates Value

Another reason so much diversification fails to create value is that many companies diversify for the wrong reasons. This is particularly true of diversification to pool risks or achieve greater growth, both of which are often given by company managers as reasons for diversification.

Consider diversification to pool risks. The benefits of risk pooling are said to come from merging imperfectly correlated income streams to create a more stable income stream. An example of risk pooling might be the diversification by U.S. Steel into the oil and gas industry in an attempt to offset the adverse effects of cyclical downturns in the steel industry. According to advocates of risk pooling, the more stable income stream reduces the risk of bankruptcy and is in the best interests of the company's stockholders.

This simple argument ignores two facts. First, stockholders can easily eliminate the risks inherent in holding an individual stock by diversifying their own portfolios, and they can do so at a much lower cost than the company can. Thus, far from being in the best interests of stockholders, attempts to pool risks through diversification represent an unproductive use of resources. Second, research on this topic suggests that corporate diversification is not a very effective way to pool risks.[20] The business cycles of different industries are not easy to predict and in any case tend to be less important in terms of their impact on profits than a general economic downturn, which hits all industries simultaneously.

Now consider diversification to achieve greater growth. Such diversification is not a coherent strategy because growth on its own does not create value. Growth should be the *byproduct,* not the objective, of a diversification strategy. However, companies sometimes diversify for reasons of growth alone rather than to gain any well-thought-out strategic advantage. The problems that Tyco encountered in 2002 may well be the result of the fact that by the late 1990s, the company's top managers lost sight of the need for diversification to increase profitability and instead became enamored with the pursuit of growth for its own sake. It was unclear to many observers how some of their later acquisitions would add value to Tyco or how Tyco would generate sufficient performance improvements to cover the cost of the acquisition and generate a decent return on invested capital. Moreover, to maintain its growth rate, Tyco had to make ever larger acquisitions (the bigger Tyco became, the larger each subsequent acquisition had to be to add significantly to the company's growth rate). It took on so much debt during the later stages of its expansion phase when it was acquiring large enterprises for billions of dollars at a time that it effectively hamstrung the company with a huge debt burden that would absorb much of the company's free cash flow for years to come.

Entry Strategy: Internal New Ventures

There are three vehicles that companies use to execute corporate-level strategies: internal new ventures, acquisitions, and joint ventures. In this section we look at pros and cons of using internal new ventures. In subsequent sections we look at acquisitions and joint ventures.

The Attractions of Internal New Venturing

Internal new venturing is typically used to execute corporate-level strategies when a company possesses a set of valuable competencies (resources and capabilities) in its existing businesses that can be leveraged or recombined to enter the new business area. As a rule, science-based companies that use their technology to create market opportunities in related business areas tend to favor internal new venturing as an entry strategy. That is, companies pursuing related or closely related diversification often use internal new venturing. Du Pont, for example, has created whole new markets with products such as cellophane, nylon, Freon, and Teflon—all internally generated innovations. 3M has a near-legendary knack for shaping new markets from internally generated ideas (see Strategy in Action 10.1). Similarly, Hewlett Packard moved into computers and peripherals by creating internal new ventures.

Even if it lacks the competencies required to compete in a new business area, a company may pursue an internal venturing strategy when it is entering a newly emerging or embryonic industry with no established players that possess the competencies required to compete in that industry. In this situation, the option of acquiring an established enterprise that possesses those competencies is ruled out, and the company may have no choice but to enter through an internal new venture. This was the position that Monsanto found itself in back in 1979 when it contemplated entering the biotechnology field to produce herbicide and pest-resistant crop seeds. The biotechnology field was young at that time, and there were no incumbent companies focused on applying biotechnology to agricultural products. Accordingly, Monsanto established an internal new venture to enter the field, even though at the time it lacked the required competencies. Indeed, Monsanto's whole venturing strategy was built around the notion that it needed to build competencies ahead of other potential competitors, thereby gaining a strong competitive lead in this newly emerging field.

Pitfalls of New Ventures

Despite the popularity of the internal new-venture strategy, its failure is reportedly high. The evidence on the failure rate of new products indicates the scope of the problem, because most internal new ventures are associated with new-product offerings. According to the evidence, somewhere between 33 and 60 percent of all new products that reach the marketplace do not generate an adequate economic return.[21] Three reasons are often given to explain the relatively high failure rate of internal new ventures: (1) market entry on too small a scale, (2) poor commercialization of the new-venture product, and (3) poor corporate management of the venture process.[22]

Scale of Entry. Research suggests that *on average,* large-scale entry into a new business is often a critical precondition of new-venture success. Although in the short run, large-scale entry means significant development costs and substantial losses, in the long run (which can be as long as five to twelve years, depending on the industry), it brings greater returns than small-scale entry.[23] The reasons include the ability of large-scale entrants to more rapidly realize scale economies, build brand loyalty, and gain access to distribution channels, all of which increase the probability of a new venture's succeeding. In contrast, small-scale entrants may find themselves handicapped by high costs due to a lack of scale economies and a lack of market presence that limits their ability to build brand loyalties and gain access to distribution channels. These scale effects are probably particularly significant when a company is entering an established industry with incumbent companies that possess scale economies, brand loyalties, and access to distribution channels, and the new entrant often has to match these in order to succeed.

Figure 10.5 plots the relationships among scale of entry and profitability over time for successful small-scale and large-scale ventures. The figure shows that successful small-scale entry incurs lower initial losses, but in the long run large-scale entry generates greater returns. However, perhaps because of the costs of large-scale entry and the potential losses if the venture fails, many companies prefer a small-scale entry strategy. Acting on this preference can be a mistake, for the company fails to build up the market share necessary for long-term success.

Commercialization. Many internal new ventures are high-technology operations. To be commercially successful, science-based innovations must be developed with market requirements in mind. Many internal new ventures fail when a company ignores the basic needs of the market. A company can become blinded by the

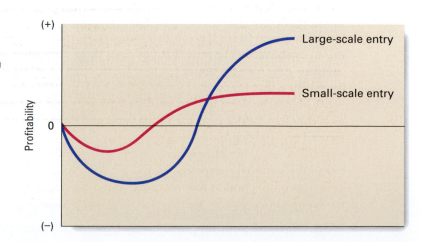

FIGURE 10.5

Scale of Entry, Profitability, and Cash Flow

technological possibilities of a new product and fail to analyze market opportunities properly.[24] Thus, a new venture may fail because of a lack of commercialization or because it is marketing a technology for which there is no demand.

For example, consider the desktop computer marketed by NeXT, the company started by the founder of Apple, Steven Jobs. The NeXT system failed to gain market share because the computer incorporated an array of expensive technologies that consumers simply did not want, such as optical disk drives and hi-fidelity sound. The optical disk drives, in particular, turned off customers because they made it tough to switch work from a PC with a floppy drive to a NeXT machine with an optical drive. In other words, NeXT failed because its founder was so dazzled by leading-edge technology that he ignored customer needs.

Poor Implementation.   Managing the new-venture process raises difficult organizational issues.[25] Although we deal with the specifics of implementation in later chapters, we must note some of the most common mistakes here.[26] The shotgun approach of supporting many different internal new-venture projects can be a major error, for it places great demands on a company's cash flow and can result in the best ventures being starved of the cash they need for success.

Another common mistake is failure by corporate management to set the strategic context within which new-venture projects should be developed. Simply taking a team of research scientists and allowing them to do research in their favorite field may produce novel results, but these results may have little strategic or commercial value. It is necessary to be very clear about the strategic objectives of the venture and to understand how the venture will seek to establish a competitive advantage.

Failure to anticipate the time and costs involved in the new-venture process constitutes a further mistake. Many companies have unrealistic expectations regarding the time frame. Reportedly, some companies operate with a philosophy of killing new businesses if they do not turn a profit by the end of the third year, clearly an unrealistic view, given the evidence that it can take five to twelve years before a venture generates substantial profits.

Guidelines for Successful Internal New Venturing

To avoid the pitfalls, a company should adopt a structured approach to managing internal new venturing. New venturing typically begins with R&D: *exploratory research* aimed at advancing basic science and technology (the "R" in R&D) and *development research* aimed at finding and refining the commercial applications for a technology (the "D" in R&D). Companies with a strong track record of internal new venturing often excel in both kinds of R&D: they help to advance the basic science, and then they find commercial applications for the science.[27] To advance the basic science, it is important for companies to (1) have strong links with universities, where much of the basic scientific knowledge underlying new technologies is discovered, and (2) to make sure that some basic research funding is left entirely in the hands of research personnel who are given the opportunity to pursue "blue-sky" projects that might ultimately yield unexpected and commercially valuable technologies and products. For example, 3M has close links with a number of universities, including the University of Minnesota in its hometown, and will fund basic research at those universities. 3M also allows (indeed encourages) its researchers to spend 15 percent of their time on projects of their own choosing, a good proportion of which are basic research projects.

However, if the pursuit of basic research (the "R" in R&D) is all that a company does well, it will probably generate very few successful commercial ventures. To translate good science into good products, it is critically important that a good chunk of R&D funding be directed toward commercial ventures. Companies can take a number of steps to make sure that this is the case. First, many companies with large, central research labs place a good proportion of the funding for central research in the hands of business unit managers, who presumably will fund only research projects that promise a commercial payoff (at the same time, some funds must be left for blue-sky projects). Second, to make effective use of its R&D capacity, a company's top managers must spell out key strategic objectives and then communicate them to its scientists and engineers. Much research should be made relevant to strategic goals.[28] For example, one of the biggest research projects at Microsoft Research has long been natural language recognition software, precisely because a central strategic objective of the company has been to make computers easy to use, and researchers reason that if computers can understand spoken language, then commands can be input by voice rather than through a keyboard, and this will make computers easier to use.

To increase the probability of commercial success, a company should foster close links between R&D and marketing personnel, for this is the best way to ensure that research projects address the needs of the market. The company should also foster close links between R&D and manufacturing personnel to ensure that the company has the capability to manufacture any proposed new products. Many companies successfully integrate different functions by setting up project teams, with representatives of the various functional areas, to oversee the development of new products. For example, Hewlett Packard's success in introducing new products in the personal computer industry has been linked to its use of project teams that oversee the development of a new product from its inception to its market introduction.

Another advantage of such teams is that they can significantly reduce the time to develop a new product. While R&D personnel are working on the design, manufacturing personnel can be setting up facilities, and marketing personnel can be developing its plans. Because of such integration, Compaq (now acquired by Hewlett Packard) needed only six months to take the first portable personal computer from an idea on the drawing board to a marketable product.

To use resources to the best effect, a company must also devise a selection process for choosing only the ventures that demonstrate the greatest probability of commercial success. Picking future winners is a tricky business, since by definition new ventures have an uncertain future. One study found the uncertainty surrounding new ventures to be so great that it usually took a company four to five years after launching the venture to reasonably estimate the venture's future profitability.[29] Nevertheless, a selection process is necessary if a company is to avoid spreading its resources too thinly over too many projects.

Once a project has been selected, management needs to monitor the progress of the venture closely. Evidence suggests that the most important criterion for evaluating a venture during its first four to five years is market share growth rather than cash flow or profitability. In the long run, the most successful ventures are those that increase their market share rapidly, for this gives them the volume required to gain scale economies and learning effects, which lead to superior profitability. A company should have clearly defined market share objectives for an internal new venture and decide to retain or kill it in its early years on the basis of its ability to achieve market share goals. Only in the medium term should profitability and cash flow begin to take on greater importance.

The association of large-scale entry with greater long-term profitability suggests that a company can increase the probability of success for an internal new venture by thinking big. This means constructing efficient-scale manufacturing facilities ahead of demand, making large marketing expenditures to build a market presence and brand loyalty, and a commitment by corporate management to accept initial losses as long as market share is expanding.

Entry Strategy: Acquisitions

As we saw in Chapter 9, acquisitions are the main vehicle that companies use to execute a horizontal integration strategy. In addition, acquisitions are an important part of vertical integration and diversification strategies. In the *Opening Case,* we saw how Tyco used acquisitions to grow the company tenfold in ten years. Similarly, between 1997 and 2001, Intel made some eighteen acquisitions valued at around $8 billion in order to execute its strategic decision to diversify into the communications chip business (see Strategy in Action 10.2). Companies rely on acquisitions because they have many advantages over internal new venturing. But as we first noted in Chapter 9, many acquisitions also fail to generate profitable returns for the acquiring company, so there are clearly considerable risks associated with acquisitions. Here we look at the benefits and risks of using acquisitions to execute a corporate-level strategy.

Attractions of Acquisitions

In the case of horizontal integration, acquisitions are the method of executing the strategy. With regard to diversification (or vertical integration), companies often use acquisition to enter a business area that is new to them when they lack important competencies (resources and capabilities) required to compete in that area, but can purchase an incumbent company that has those competencies at a reasonable price. Companies also have a preference for acquisitions when they feel the need to move fast. Building a new business through internal venturing can be a relatively slow process. In contrast, acquisition is a much quicker way to establish a significant market presence and generate profitability. A company can purchase a market leader with a strong position overnight rather than spend years building up a market leadership position through internal development. Thus, when speed is important, acquisition is the favored entry mode. Intel, for example, used acquisitions to build its communications chip business because it sensed that the market was developing very quickly, and it would take too long to develop all of the required competencies internally, so it acquired them by purchasing other companies (see Strategy in Action 10.2).

Acquisitions are also often perceived to be somewhat less risky than internal new ventures, primarily because there is a perception that they involve less uncertainty. Due to the nature of internal new ventures, large uncertainties are associated with projecting future profitability, revenues, and cash flows. In contrast, when a company makes an acquisition, it is acquiring known profitability, known revenues, and known market share, all of which reduce uncertainty. An acquisition allows a company to buy an established business with a track record, and for this reason, many companies favor acquisitions.

Finally, acquisitions may be the preferred entry mode when the industry to be entered is well established and incumbent enterprises enjoy significant protection from barriers to entry. As you recall from Chapter 2, barriers to entry arise from factors associated with product differentiation (brand loyalty), absolute cost advantages, and economies of scale. When such barriers are substantial, a company finds entering an industry through internal new venturing difficult. To enter, a company may have to construct an efficient manufacturing plant, undertake massive advertising to break down established brand loyalties, and quickly build up distribution outlets— all goals that are hard to achieve and likely to involve substantial expenditures. In contrast, by acquiring an established enterprise, a company can circumvent most entry barriers. It can purchase a market leader, which already benefits from substantial scale economies and brand loyalty. Thus the greater the barriers to entry are, the more likely it is that acquisitions will be the favored entry mode. (We should note here that the attractiveness of an acquisition is predicated on the assumption that an incumbent company can be acquired for less than it would cost to enter the same industry by an internal new venture. As we shall see in the next section, the validity of this assumption is often questionable.)

Acquisition Pitfalls   For the reasons just noted, acquisitions have long been a popular vehicle for executing corporate-level strategies. However, despite this popularity, there is ample evidence that many acquisitions fail to add value for the acquiring company and, indeed, often end up dissipating value. For example, a study by Mercer Management Consulting looked at 150 acquisitions worth more than $500 million each that were undertaken between January 1990 and July 1995.[30] The Mercer study concluded that 50 percent of these acquisitions ended up eroding, or substantially eroding, shareholder value, and another 33 percent created only marginal returns. Only 17 percent of these acquisitions were judged to be successful. Similarly, a study by KPMG, an accounting and management consulting company, looked at 700 large acquisitions between 1996 and 1998 and found that although some 30 percent of these actually created value for the acquiring company, 31 percent destroyed value, and the remainder had little impact.[31]

More generally, a wealth of evidence from academic research suggests that many acquisitions fail to realize their anticipated benefits.[32] In a major study of the postacquisition performance of acquired companies, David Ravenscraft and Mike Scherer concluded that the profitability and market shares of acquired companies often declined after acquisition.[33] They also noted that a smaller but substantial subset of acquired companies experienced traumatic difficulties, which ultimately led to their being sold off by the acquiring company. In other words, Ravenscraft and Scherer's evidence, like that presented by McKinsey & Company, suggests that many acquisitions destroy rather than create value.

Many acquisitions apparently fail to create value for four major reasons: (1) companies often experience difficulties when trying to integrate divergent corporate cultures, (2) companies overestimate the potential economic benefits from an acquisition, (3) acquisitions tend to be very expensive, and (4) companies often do not adequately screen their acquisition targets.

Postacquisition Integration. Having made an acquisition, the acquiring company has to integrate the acquired business into its own organizational structure. Integration can entail the adoption of common management and financial control systems, the joining together of operations from the acquired and the acquiring company, or the establishment of linkages to share information and personnel. Many unexpected problems can occur when integration is attempted. Often they stem from differences in corporate cultures. After an acquisition, many acquired companies experience high management turnover, possibly because their employees do not like the acquiring company's way of operating.[34] Research evidence suggests that the loss of management talent and expertise, to say nothing of the damage from constant tension between the businesses, can materially harm the performance of the acquired unit.[35] For an example of what can occur, see Strategy in Action 10.3, which examines the high management turnover at Boston Co. after it was acquired by Mellon Bank.

Strategy in Action 10.3

Postacquisition Problems at Mellon Bank

In the early 1990s, Frank Cahouet, the CEO of Philadelphia-based Mellon Bank, conceived of a corporate strategy that would reduce the vulnerability of Mellon's earnings to changes in interest rates. Cahouet's solution was to diversify into financial services to gain access to a steady flow of fee-based income from money management operations. As part of this strategy, in 1993 Mellon acquired Boston Co. for $1.45 billion. Boston is a high-profile money management company that manages investments for major institutional clients, such as state and corporate pension funds. In 1994, Mellon followed up its Boston acquisition with the acquisition of mutual fund provider Dreyfus Corp., for $1.7 billion. As a result, by 1995 almost half of Mellon's income was generated from fee-based financial services.

In 1995, Mellon hit some serious bumps on the road in its attempt to become a money market powerhouse. Problems at Boston Co. began to surface soon after the Mellon acquisition. From the start, there was a clear clash of cultures. At Mellon, many managers arrive at their mundane offices by 7 A.M. and put in twelve-hour days for modest pay by banking industry standards. They are also accustomed to a firm management hierarchy that is carefully controlled by Frank Cahouet, whose management style emphasized cost containment and frugality. Boston Co. managers also put in twelve-hour days, but they expected considerable autonomy, flexible work schedules, high pay, ample perks, and large performance bonuses. In most years, the top twenty executives at Boston earned between $750,000 and $1 million each. Mellon executives who visited the Boston Co. unit were dumb-struck by the country club atmosphere and opulence they saw. In its move to streamline Boston, Mellon insisted that Boston cut expenses and introduced new regulations for restricting travel, entertainment, and perks.

Things started to go wrong in October 1993 when the Wisconsin state pension fund complained to Mellon of lower returns on a portfolio run by Boston Co. In November, Mellon liquidated the portfolio, taking a $130 million charge against earnings. Mellon also fired the responsible portfolio manager, claiming that this manager was making "unauthorized trades." At Boston Co., however, many managers saw Mellon's action as violating guarantees of operating autonomy that it had given Boston at the time of the acquisition. They blamed Mellon for prematurely liquidating a portfolio whose strategy, they claimed, Mellon executives had approved and that, moreover, could still prove a winner if interest rates fell (which they subsequently did).

Infuriated by Mellon's interference in the running of Boston Co., in March seven managers at Boston Co.'s asset management unit, including the unit's CEO, Desmond Heathwood, proposed a management buyout to Mellon. This unit was one of the gems in Boston's crown, with over $26 billion in assets under management. Heathwood had been openly disdainful of Mellon's bankers, believing that they were out of their league in the investment business. In April, Mellon rejected the buyout proposal, and Heathwood promptly left to start his own investment management company. A few days later, Mellon asked employees at Boston to sign employment contracts that limited their ability to leave and work for Heathwood's competing business. Thirteen senior employees refused to sign and quit to join Heathwood's new money management operation.

The defection of Heathwood and his colleagues was followed by a series of high-profile client defections. The Arizona State Retirement System, for example, pulled $1 billion out of Mellon and transferred it to Heathwood's firm, and the Fresno County Retirement System transferred $400 million in assets over to Heathwood. As one client stated, "We have a relationship with the Boston Co. that goes back over 30 years, and the people who worked on the account are the people who left—so we left too."

Reflecting on the episode, Frank Cahouet noted, "We've clearly been hurt. . . . But this episode is very manageable. We are not going to lose out momentum." Others were not so sure. In this incident, they saw yet another example of how difficult it can be to merge two divergent corporate cultures and how the management turnover that results from such attempts can deal a serious blow to any attempt to create value out of an acquisition.

Sources: M. Murray and J. Rebello, "Mellon Bank Corp: One Big Unhappy Family," *Wall Street Journal,* April 28, 1995, pp. B1, B4. K. Holland, "A Bank Eat Bank World—with Indigestion," *Business Week,* October 30, 1995, p. 130.

Overestimating Economic Benefits. Even when companies achieve integration, they often overestimate the potential for creating value by joining together different businesses. They overestimate the strategic advantages that can be derived from the acquisition and thus pay more for the target company than it is probably worth. Richard Roll has attributed this tendency to hubris on the part of top management. According to Roll, top managers typically overestimate their ability to create value from an acquisition, primarily because rising to the top of a corporation has given them an exaggerated sense of their own capabilities.[36]

Coca-Cola's acquisition of a number of medium-sized wine-making companies illustrates the situation of a company that overestimates the economic benefits from an acquisition. Reasoning that a beverage is a beverage, Coca-Cola wanted to use its distinctive competence in marketing to dominate the U.S. wine industry. But after buying three wine companies and enduring seven years of marginal profits, Coca-Cola finally conceded that wine and soft drinks are very different products, with different kinds of appeal, pricing systems, and distribution networks. It subsequently sold the wine operations to Joseph E. Seagram & Sons for $210 million—the price it had paid for the purchases and a substantial loss when adjusted for inflation.[37]

The Expense of Acquisitions. Acquisition of companies whose stock is publicly traded tends to be very expensive. One reason is that shareholders of the acquired company are unlikely to sell out unless they are paid a significant premium over the current market value of the stock. Another is that the management of the target company is not likely to agree to an acquisition unless there is a substantial premium over the current market value. In general, premiums tend to run 30 to 50 percent over the market value prior to a takeover bid. This implies that if the prior market value was an accurate reflection of the future profit potential of a company, the acquiring company must be able to increase the value of the target company after the acquisition by at least the same amount to make the acquisition pay, a tall order.

Moreover, the price of acquisition targets can get bid up in the acquisition process. This is likely to occur in the case of contested bids, where two or more companies simultaneously bid for control of a single target company. In addition, when there is a lot of acquisition activity in an industry or sector, the price of *potential* target companies can get bid up by investors who are speculating that a bid will be made at some point, which further increases the cost of making an acquisition. This happened in the telecommunications sector between 1996 and 2000. There was a common perception at the time that demand for telecommunications equipment was accelerating rapidly. To make sure they could meet the needs of customers who were demanding leading-edge equipment, many of the larger telecommunications equipment suppliers went on acquisition binges. JDS Uniphase, Cisco Systems, Nortel, Corning, and Lucent all raced each other to buy up smaller telecommunications equipment suppliers that were developing promising technology. The result was that stock prices for such companies got bid up by investors who speculated that the companies they invested in would get bought out at a premium. In the end, the process got totally out of hand, with companies that had very few tangible assets being acquired for huge sums of money. When the telecommunications boom turned to bust, many of the acquiring companies found that they had overpaid for their acquisitions, which generated few revenues and even fewer profits, and they had to take large accounting write-downs. In 2001, Nortel Networks wrote down $12.3 billion in goodwill on its balance sheet to reflect a reduction in the value of the assets it had acquired during the boom. Another telecom equipment supplier, Corning, wrote down $4.8 billion, and JDS Uniphase wrote down a staggering $40 billion. Strategy in Action 10.4 provides the details.

Related to the high costs of acquisition is the debt that companies often take on to finance them. Many of the most aggressive acquirers of the 1990s, for example, took on large amounts of debt to finance their acquisitions. Tyco International used a mix of cash and its own stock to pay for its acquisitions. Although some of the cash it used came from internally generated funds, much of it came from issuing bonds (i.e., by adding debt). As a result, by decade's end, Tyco had $23 billion in debt on its balance sheet. The debt could easily have been financed had the economy continued to grow during 2000–2001, but a slowdown in economic activity made it difficult for

Strategy in Action 10.4

JDS Uniphase's $40 Billion Error

In 1999, it looked as if JDS Uniphase had the perfect storm at its back and was riding a wave of new orders for the optical gear that it made for telecommunications networks to financial nirvana. Only one problem seemed to stand in the way of the company's achieving this glittering future: it could not ramp up capacity fast enough. To meet the wall of orders before it and expand its portfolio of product offerings, JDS Uniphase decided to acquire any and all competitors it could get its hands on. The decision was made easy by the high price of JDS's own stock, which had soared to $150, valuing the company at almost $220 billion. To many, the valuation seemed excessive given that in June 2000, the company had revenues of $1.43 billion and was losing money. Nevertheless, JDS decided to use its own richly valued stock as "cheap currency" to finance its acquisitions.

Between November 1999 and July 2000, JDS made three acquisitions for $58.6 billion, including the $41 billion acquisition of SDL, a company with a book value of only $2 billion (SDL made voice, data, and Internet transmission technologies). The difference between SDL's book value of $2 billion and the purchase price of $41 billion was entered in JDS's balance sheet as "goodwill." **Goodwill** reflects the premium a company pays over and above the value of a target company's identifiable or tangible assets—in other words, it represents intangible assets such as technological knowledge, customer relationships, and brand loyalty.

By early 2001, it was becoming clear that JDS's acquisition strategy would not have a short-term payoff. Demand for telecommunications equipment had suddenly imploded, and JDS was confronted with revenues

that were estimated to hit $1.1 billion in the year ending June 2002, down from $3.2 billion a year earlier. The clear implication was that JDS had overpaid for its acquisitions. The recently acquired SDL unit, for example, was generating revenues of a few hundred million, losing money, and faced with a shrinking order book. It was now hard to construct any scenario under which SDL was worth $41 billion, or even $2 billion for that matter. On July 26, 2001, JDS announced that it would write down the value of goodwill on its balance sheet, taking a $44.8 billion noncash charge against earnings to do so. In the aftermath of the write-down, some analysts and several managers at JDS claimed that in a sense, it did not matter. After all, they said, no "real" money had been lost. JDS had not taken on any debt to finance its acquisitions; it had simply used its overvalued currency (high-priced stock) to buy assets that would have a tangible value going forward once the market for telecommunications equipment improved. Indeed, after the write-down, JDS had no debt at all and $440 million in cash on its balance sheet. Others questioned this logic, pointing out that the claim that there was no "real money" involved would seem absurd to long-term stockholders, who had seen the value of their stock decline from its high of over $150 to under $6 a share by April 2002. Real stockholder value had been destroyed because JDS had massively overpaid for its acquisitions during the telecom feeding frenzy.

Sources: C. Sewell, "When Boom Goes to Bust," *Telephony*, October 22, 2001, pp. 38–44. B. Ojo, "Wall Street, SEC Question Write Downs," *EBN*, July 23, 2001, p. G1. JDS Uniphase, 2001 10K Report.

Tyco to increase its own profits fast enough to generate the cash flow required to meet its debt obligations. Tyco was by no means the worst offender in this area. For example, George Pacific took on $12 billion in debt to spend $17 billion on acquiring other pulp and paper makers during the 1990s in an attempt to execute a horizontal integration strategy. By early 2002, with the economy weak and paper and pulp prices plunging, several analysts questioned whether George Pacific would be able to meet its debt obligations.[38]

Inadequate Preacquisition Screening. After researching acquisitions made by twenty different companies, a study by Philippe Haspeslagh and David Jemison came to the conclusion that one reason for acquisitions failure is management's inadequate attention to preacquisition screening.[39] They found that many companies decide to acquire other firms without thoroughly analyzing the potential benefits and costs. After the acquisition has been completed, many acquiring companies discover that instead of buying a well-run business, they have purchased a troubled organization.

That was the experience of the fast-growing insurance provider Conseco when it acquired Green Tree Financial Corp for $7.6 billion in 1998. Green Tree, the largest subprime and mobile home lender in the United States, specialized in lending money to low-income households. It charged high interest rates on its loans, which had a high risk of default. Green Tree was also highly leveraged, with a lot of debt on its balance sheet. At the time of the deal, Conseco's CEO, Stephen Hilbert, hailed the acquisition as "the deal of a lifetime," but to some observers, the margin for error seemed small. The skeptics were proved right in March 2000, when Hilbert announced that Conseco would take a $350 million charge against earnings to reflect significantly higher-than-expected loan losses. In other words, Green Tree's customers were defaulting on their loans at a high rate. The stock price plummeted, and Hilbert was forced to resign. Ultimately, Green Tree's loan portfolio was sold off for $1.5 billion, a substantial loss for Conseco.[40] In retrospect, it seems clear that Conseco did not adequately audit the financial statements and operations of Green Tree prior to completing the acquisition. If it had, it may well have discovered that Green Tree's customers were defaulting on their loans at a very rapid rate.

Guidelines for Successful Acquisition

To avoid pitfalls and make successful acquisitions, companies need to take a structured approach with four main components: (1) target identification and preacquisition screening, (2) bidding strategy, (3) integration, and (4) learning from experience.[41]

Identification and Screening. Thorough preacquisition screening increases a company's knowledge about potential takeover targets, leads to a more realistic assessment of the problems involved in executing an acquisition and integrating the new business into the company's organizational structure, and lessens the risk of purchasing a potential problem business. The screening should begin with a detailed assessment of the strategic rationale for making the acquisition and identification of the kind of enterprise that would make an ideal acquisition candidate.

Next, the company should scan a target population of potential acquisition candidates, evaluating each according to a detailed set of criteria, focusing on (1) financial position, (2) product market position, (3) competitive environment, (4) management capabilities, and (5) corporate culture. Such an evaluation should enable the company to identify the strengths and weaknesses of each candidate, the extent of potential economies of scope between the acquiring and the acquired companies, potential integration problems, and the compatibility of the corporate cultures of the acquiring and the acquired companies.

The company should then reduce the list of candidates to the most favored ones and evaluate them further. At this stage, it should sound out third parties, such as investment bankers, whose opinions may be important and who may be able to give valuable insights about the efficiency of target companies. The company that leads the list after this process should be the acquisition target.

After a target has been identified, there is still much that can be done before finalizing a deal. Tyco International, for example, routinely sent in a team of independent accountants to audit the books of an acquisition target to make sure that there were no skeletons in the accounting closet (see the *Opening Case*). This kind of detailed internal auditing of the books can be done only when the proposed acquisition is a friendly one in which the management team and board of the target company agree to the acquisition. If the bid is hostile, with the management team and board of the target company opposing the takeover bid, it is unlikely that the acquiring company will get the kind of access that it needs to do thorough due diligence. This is one reason that Tyco made only friendly acquisitions.

Bidding Strategy. The objective of bidding strategy is to reduce the price that a company must pay for an acquisition candidate. Probably the most effective thing that an acquirer can do is make only friendly takeover bids. In a hostile bid, the price of the target company often gets bid up by speculators who expect that the offer price will be raised by the acquirer, or that another company, sometimes called a *white knight*, might come in with a counteroffer more favorable to the management of the target company. It is this kind of reasoning that led Tyco International to eschew hostile takeover bids and make only friendly acquisitions.

Another essential element of a good bidding strategy is timing. For example, Hanson PLC, one of the most successful takeover machines of the 1980s, always looked for essentially sound businesses that were suffering from short-term problems due to cyclical industry factors or problems localized in one division. Such companies are typically undervalued by the stock market and thus can be picked up without payment of the standard 40 or 50 percent premium over current stock prices. With good timing, a company can make a bargain purchase. Tyco International also seemed to follow this practice, buying essentially sound businesses that were underperforming their peers due to short-term problems.

Integration. Despite good screening and bidding, an acquisition will fail unless positive steps are taken to integrate the acquired company into the organizational structure of the acquiring one quickly. Integration should center on the source of the potential strategic advantages of the acquisition—for instance, opportunities to share marketing, manufacturing, procurement, R&D, financial, or management resources. Integration should also be accompanied by steps to eliminate any duplication of facilities or functions. In addition, any unwanted activities of the acquired company should be sold. Finally, if the different business activities are closely related, they will require a high degree of integration. Again, it is clear from the *Opening Case* that Tyco International moved rapidly to integrate acquired units into its organization. Steps were taken immediately after an acquisition was completed to close or sell off duplicate or unwanted facilities and lay off excess employees. Tyco's incentive systems and internal financial controls were also introduced immediately after an acquisition closed. The reason Tyco was able to move so fast was that most of the groundwork was down *before* the acquisition closed.

Learning from Experience. There is quite a bit of evidence that although on average, most acquisitions fail to create value for the acquiring company, some repeat acquirers get very good at the process and generate significant value from acquisitions.[42] Tyco is an example of a repeat acquirer, as is General Electric. Although both have had their share of problems (and Tyco's are obviously serious), historically they do seem to have been able to make astute acquisitions. One reason may have been that they learned from their experience and developed a "playbook" of how to execute an acquisition. In Tyco's case, this playbook included not making hostile acquisitions, detailed auditing of the accounts of the target company, acquiring companies that would help Tyco achieve critical mass in an industry, moving quickly to realize cost savings after an acquisition, promoting managers one or two layers down to lead the newly acquired entity, and introducing profit-based incentive pay systems in the acquired unit.

Nevertheless, experience alone does not guarantee success.[43] It is important for managers to learn from their experience with acquisitions, performing postacquisition audits of the overall process to review what worked, what did not, and how things might be improved the next time.

Entry Strategy: Joint Ventures

Although joint ventures are not as widely used as acquisitions and internal new ventures for establishing new business activities, in certain circumstances they make a good deal of sense. A company may prefer internal new venturing to acquisition as an entry strategy into new business areas, yet hesitate to commit itself to an internal new venture because of the risks and costs of building a new operation up from the ground floor. Such a situation is most likely to occur when a company sees the possibility of establishing a new business in an embryonic or growth industry but the risks and costs associated with the project are more than it is willing to assume on its own. In these circumstances, the company may decide to enter into a joint venture with another company and use the joint venture as a vehicle for entering the new business area. Such an arrangement enables the company to share the substantial risks and costs posed by the new project. In addition, a joint venture makes sense when a company can increase the probability of successfully establishing a new business by joining forces with another company. For a company that has some of the skills and assets necessary to establish a successful new venture, teaming up with another company that has *complementary* skills and assets may increase the probability of success.

Consider the joint venture between United Technologies and Dow Chemical to build plastic-based composite parts for the aerospace industry. United Technologies was already involved in the aerospace industry (it built Sikorsky helicopters), and Dow Chemical had skills in the development and manufacture of plastic-based composites. The alliance called for United Technologies to contribute its advanced aerospace skills and for Dow to contribute its skills in developing and manufacturing plastic-based composites to a joint venture in which each company would have a 50 percent equity stake. The joint venture was to undertake the task of developing, manufacturing, and marketing a new line of plastic-based composite parts for the aerospace industry. Through the venture, both companies would become involved in new activities. They would, in short, be able to realize some of the benefits associated with related diversification without having to merge activities formally or bear the costs and risks of developing the new products on their own.

There are three main drawbacks to joint venture arrangements. First, a joint venture allows a company to share the risks and costs of developing a new business, but it also requires the sharing of profits if the new business succeeds. Second, the venture partners must share control. If the partners have different business philosophies, time horizons, or investment preferences, substantial problems can arise. Conflicts over how to run the joint venture can tear it apart and result in business failure. Third, a company that enters into a joint venture always runs the risk of giving critical know-how away to its joint venture partner, which might use that know-how to compete directly with the company in the future. For example, having gained access to Dow's expertise in plastic-based composites, United Technologies might dissolve the alliance and produce these materials on its own. However, such risk can be minimized if Dow gets a *credible commitment* from United Technologies. By entering into a formal joint venture rather than a more loosely structured alliance, United Technologies has given such a commitment because it has had to invest substantial amounts of capital. Thus if United Technologies tried to produce plastic-based composites on its own, it would essentially be competing against itself.

In sum, although joint ventures often have a distinct advantage over internal new venturing as a means of establishing a new business operation, they also have certain drawbacks. When deciding whether to go it alone or cooperate with another company in a joint venture, strategic managers need to assess the pros and cons of the alternatives carefully.

Restructuring

So far we have focused on strategies for expanding the scope of a company and entering into new business areas. We turn now to their opposite: strategies for reducing the scope of the company by *exiting* business areas. Reducing the scope of a company through restructuring has become an increasingly popular strategy, particularly among the companies that diversified their activities during the 1980s and 1990s. In most cases, companies that are engaged in restructuring are divesting themselves of diversified activities in order to concentrate on fewer businesses.[44] For example, in 1996 AT&T spun off its telecommunications equipment business (Lucent), and after acquiring two large cable TV companies in the late 1990s, AT&T sold its cable unit off to rival cable TV provider Comcast for $72 billion in 2002.

The first question that must be asked is why so many companies are restructuring at this time. After answering it, we examine the strategies that companies adopt for exiting from business areas. Then we discuss the various turnaround strategies that companies employ to revitalize their core business area.

Why Restructure?

A prime reason that extensively diversified companies restructure is that in recent years, the stock market has assigned a diversification discount to the stock of such enterprises.[45] The **diversification discount** refers to the empirical fact that the stock of highly diversified companies is often assigned a lower valuation relative to their earnings than the stock of less diversified enterprises. Investors apparently see highly diversified companies as less attractive investments than more focused enterprises. There are two reasons for this. First, investors are often put off by the complexity and lack of transparency in the consolidated financial statements of highly diversified enterprises, which do not give them a good picture of how the individual parts of the company are performing. In other words, they perceive the company as being a riskier investment than more focused companies, precisely because their financial statements are difficult to interpret. In such cases, restructuring tends to be an attempt to boost the returns to shareholders by splitting up the company into a number of parts.

A second reason for the diversification discount is that many investors have learned from experience that managers often have a tendency to pursue too much diversification, or diversify for the wrong reasons, such as the pursuit of growth for its own sake, rather than the pursuit of greater profitability.[46] We discussed this phenomenon earlier in the chapter. Suffice it to say that some senior managers have a tendency to expand the scope of their company beyond that point where the bureaucratic costs of managing extensive diversification exceed the additional value that can be created, and the performance of the company begins to decline. Restructuring in such cases is often a response to declining financial performance.

Restructuring can also be a response to failed acquisitions. This is true whether the acquisitions were made to support a horizontal integration, vertical integration, or diversification strategy. We noted earlier in the chapter that many acquisitions fail to deliver the anticipated gains. When this is the case, management often responds by cutting losses and exiting from the acquired business. Since there was a merger and acquisition boom between 1996 and 2000, if history is any guide we would expect to see this followed by a wave of restructurings as companies exit from businesses acquired during the boom, as indeed seems to be occurring.

A final factor of some importance in restructuring trends is that innovations in management processes and strategy have diminished the advantages of vertical integration or diversification. In response, companies have reduced the scope of their activities through restructuring and divestments. For example, ten years ago, there was little understanding of how long-term cooperative relationships between a company and its suppliers could be a viable alternative to vertical integration. Most companies considered only two alternatives for managing the supply chain: vertical integration or competitive bidding. As we noted in Chapter 9, however, if the conditions are right, a third alternative for managing the supply chain, *long-term contracting,* can be a superior strategy to both vertical integration and competitive bidding. Like vertical integration, long-term contracting facilitates investments in specialization. But unlike vertical integration, it does not involve high bureaucratic costs or dispense with market discipline. As this strategic innovation has spread throughout the business world, the relative advantages of vertical integration have declined.

Exit Strategies

Companies can choose from three main strategies for exiting business areas: divestment, harvest, and liquidation. You have already encountered all three in Chapter 6, where we discussed strategies for competing in declining industries. We review them briefly here.

Divestment. Of the three main strategies, divestment is usually favored. It represents the best way for a company to recoup as much of its initial investment in a business unit as possible. The idea is to sell the business unit to the highest bidder. Three types of buyers are independent investors, other companies, and the management of the unit to be divested. Selling off a business unit to independent investors, normally referred to as a **spinoff,** makes good sense when the unit to be sold is profitable and the stock market has an appetite for new stock issues (which is normal during market upswings but *not* during market downswings). Thus, for example, in 1992 the timber products company Weyerhaeuser successfully spun off its Paragon Trade

Brands to independent investors. Investors snapped up the stock of the new issue, which makes "own label" disposable diapers for supermarket chains and is highly profitable. Spinoffs do not work if the unit to be spun off is unprofitable and unattractive to independent investors or if the stock market is slumping and unresponsive to new issues.

Selling off a unit to another company is a strategy frequently pursued when a unit can be sold to a company in the same line of business as the unit. In such cases, the purchaser is often prepared to pay a considerable amount of money for the opportunity to substantially increase the size of its business virtually overnight.

Selling off a unit to its management is normally referred to as a **management buyout (MBO):** the unit is sold to its management, which often finances the purchase through the sale of high-yield bonds to investors. The bond issue is normally arranged by a buyout specialist, which along with management will typically hold a sizable proportion of the shares in the MBO. MBOs often take place when financially troubled units have only two other options: a harvest strategy or liquidation.

An MBO can be very risky for the management team, since its members may have to sign personal guarantees to back up the bond issue and may lose everything if the MBO ultimately fails. If the management team succeeds in turning around the troubled unit, its reward can be a significant increase in personal wealth. Thus, an MBO strategy can be characterized as a *high risk–high return* strategy for the management team. Faced with the possible liquidation of their business unit, many management teams are willing to take the risk. However, the viability of this option depends not only on a willing management team, but also on there being enough buyers of high yield–high risk bonds—so-called junk bonds—to be able to finance the MBO. In recent years, the general slump in the junk bond market has made the MBO strategy a more difficult one for companies to follow.

Harvest and Liquidation. A harvest or liquidation strategy is generally considered inferior to a divestment strategy because the company can probably best recoup its investment in a business unit by divestment. Second, a harvest strategy means halting investment in a unit in order to maximize short- to medium-term cash flow from that unit before liquidating it. Although this strategy seems fine in theory, it is often a poor one to apply in practice. Once it becomes apparent that the unit is pursuing a harvest strategy, the morale of the unit's employees, as well as the confidence of the unit's customers and suppliers in its continuing operation, can sink quickly. If this occurs, as it often does, the rapid decline in the unit's revenues can make the strategy untenable. Finally, a liquidation strategy is the least attractive of all to pursue since it requires the company to write off its investment in a business unit, often at a considerable cost. For a poorly performing business unit where a selloff or spinoff is unlikely and where an MBO cannot be arranged, it may be the only viable alternative.

Summary of Chapter

1. Managers often first consider diversification when their company is generating free cash flow, which are financial resources in excess of those necessary to maintain a competitive advantage in the company's original, or core, business.

2. A diversified company can create value by (a) transferring competencies among existing businesses, (b) leveraging competencies to create new businesses, (c) sharing resources to realize economies of scope, (d) using diversification as a means of managing rivalry in one or more industries, and (e) exploiting general organizational competencies that enhance the

performance of all business units within a diversified company. The bureaucratic costs of diversification are a function of the number of independent business units within the company and the extent of coordination between those business units.

3. Diversification motivated by a desire to pool risks or achieve greater growth is often associated with the dissipation of value.

4. There are three vehicles that companies use to enter new business areas: internal ventures, acquisition, and joint ventures.

5. Internal new venturing is typically employed as an entry strategy when a company has a set of valuable competencies in its existing businesses that can be leveraged or recombined to enter the new business area.

6. Many internal ventures fail because of entry on too small a scale, poor commercialization, and poor corporate management of the internal venture process. Guarding against failure involves a structured approach toward project selection and management, integration of R&D and marketing to improve commercialization of a venture idea, and entry on a significant scale.

7. Acquisitions are often favored as an entry strategy when the company lacks important competencies (resources and capabilities) required to compete in an area, but it can purchase an incumbent company that has those competencies and do so at a reasonable price. Acquisitions also tend to be favored when the barriers to entry into the target industry are high and the company is unwilling to accept the time frame, development costs, and risks of internal new venturing.

8. Many acquisitions fail because of poor postacquisition integration, overestimation of the value that can be created from an acquisition, the high cost of acquisition, and poor preacquisition screening. Guarding against acquisition failure requires structured screening, good bidding strategies, positive attempts to inte-

grate the acquired company into the organization of the acquiring one, and learning from experience.

9. Joint ventures may be the preferred entry strategy when (a) the risks and costs associated with setting up a new business unit are more than the company is willing to assume on its own and (b) the company can increase the probability of successfully establishing a new business by teaming up with another company that has skills and assets complementing its own.

10. Restructuring is often a response to (a) excessive diversification, (b) failed acquisitions, and (c) innovations in management process that have reduced the advantages of vertical integration and diversification.

11. Exit strategies include divestment, harvest, and liquidation. The choice of exit strategy is governed by the characteristics of the relevant business unit.

Discussion Questions

1. When is a company likely to choose related diversification and when unrelated diversification? Discuss with reference to an electronics manufacturer and an ocean shipping company.

2. Under what circumstances might it be best to enter a new business area by acquisition, and under what circumstances might internal new venturing be the preferred entry mode?

3. Imagine that IBM has decided to diversify into the cellular telecommunication provider business. What entry strategy would you recommend the company pursue? Why?

4. Look at Honeywell's portfolio of businesses (described in Honeywell's 10K statements, which can be accessed on the web at **www.honeywell.com**). How many different industries is Honeywell involved in? Would you describe Honeywell as a related or unrelated diversification company? How do you think that Honeywell's diversification strategy increases profitability?

Practicing Strategic Management

SMALL-GROUP EXERCISE: DUN & BRADSTREET

Break into small groups of three to five people, and appoint one group member as a spokesperson who will communicate your findings to the class when called on to do so by the instructor. Then read the following news release from Dun & Bradstreet. On the basis of this information, identify the strategic rationale for the split and evaluate how the

split might affect the performance three successor companies. If you were a stockholder in the old Dun & Bradstreet Corporation, would you approve of this split? Why?

Dun & Bradstreet CEO Robert E. Weissman today announced a sweeping strategy that will transform the 155-year-old business information giant into three publicly traded, global corporations. "This important action is designed to increase shareholder value by unlocking D&B's substantial underlying franchise strengths," said Weissman.

Building on preeminent Dun & Bradstreet businesses, the reorganization establishes three independent companies focused on high-growth information markets; financial information services; and consumer-product market research.

"Since the 1800s, D&B has grown by effectively managing a portfolio of businesses and gaining economies of scale," stated Weissman. "But the velocity of change in information markets has dramatically altered the rules of business survival. Today, market focus and speed are the primary drivers of competitive advantage. This plan is our blueprint for success in the 21st century," said Weissman.

The plan, approved today at a special meeting of D&B's board of directors, calls for D&B to create three separate companies by spinning off two of its businesses to shareholders. "D&B is the leader in business information," said Weissman. "By freeing our companies to tightly focus on our core vertical markets, we can more rapidly leverage this leadership position into emerging growth areas."

The three new companies are:

- Cognizant Corporation, a new high-growth company, including IMS International, the leading global supplier of marketing information to the pharmaceutical and healthcare industries; Nielsen Media Research, the leader in audience measurement for electronic media; and Gartner Group, the premier provider of advisory services to high-tech users, vendors and suppliers, in which Cognizant will hold a majority interest.
- The Dun & Bradstreet Corporation, consisting of Dun & Bradstreet Information Services, the world's largest source of business-to-business marketing and commercial-credit information; Moody's Investors Service, a global leader in rating debt; and Reuben H. Donnelley, a premier provider of Yellow Pages marketing and publishing.
- A. C. Nielsen, the global leader in marketing information for the fast-moving consumer packaged goods industry.

"These three separate companies will tailor their strategies to the unique demands of their markets, determining investments, capital structures and policies that will strengthen their respective global capabilities. This plan also clarifies D&B from an investor's perspective by grouping the businesses into three logical investment categories, each with distinct risk/reward profiles," said Weissman.

The Dun & Bradstreet Corporation is the world's largest marketer of information, software and services for business decision-making, with worldwide revenue of $4.9 billion in 1994.

ARTICLE FILE 10

Find an example of a company that has made an acquisition that apparently failed to create any value. Identify and critically evaluate the rationale that top management used

to justify the acquisition when it was made. Explain why the acquisition subsequently failed.

STRATEGIC MANAGEMENT PROJECT: MODULE 10

This module requires you to assess your company's use of acquisitions, internal new ventures, and joint ventures as strategies for entering a new business area or as attempts to restructure its portfolio of businesses.

A. If your company has entered a new business area during the past decade

1. Pick one new business area that your company has entered during the past ten years.
2. Identify the rationale for entering this business area.
3. Identify the strategy used to enter this business area.
4. Evaluate the rationale for using this particular entry strategy. Do you think that this was the best entry strategy to use? Justify your answer.
5. Do you think that the addition of this business area to the company has added or dissipated value? Again, justify your answer.

B. If your company has restructured its business during the past decade

1. Identify the rationale for pursuing a restructuring strategy.
2. Pick one business area that your company has exited from during the past ten years.
3. Identify the strategy used to exit from this particular business area. Do you think that this was the best exit strategy to use? Justify your answer.
4. In general, do you think that exiting from this business area has been in the company's best interest?

EXPLORING THE WEB
Visiting General Electric

Visit the web site of General Electric Company of the United States (**www.ge.com**). Using the information contained on that web site, answer the following questions.

1. Review GE's portfolio of major businesses. Does this portfolio make sense from a value creation perspective? Why?
2. What (if any) changes would you make to GE's portfolio of businesses? Why would you make these changes?
3. What (if any) core competencies do you think are held in common by one or more of GE's major business units? Is there any evidence that GE creates new businesses by leveraging its core competencies?

General Task: By searching through information sources on the Web, find an example of a company that has recently restructured its portfolio of businesses. Identify and evaluate the strategic rationale behind this restructuring to determine whether it makes sense.

Closing Case

The Changing Boundaries of AT&T, 1995–2002

On September 20, 1995, AT&T, the world's largest telecommunications company with annual revenues of $75 billion, announced that it would split itself into three independent companies. The largest of these, which was to retain the AT&T name, would manage the company's long-distance, international, and wireless telecommunications businesses. The new AT&T would retain its position as the largest provider of telecommunications service in the world, with 1995 revenues in excess of $50 billion. Second in size of the new companies was to be the network equipment business. Renamed Lucent Technologies, this business generated 1995 revenues of $21 billion and ranked as the third largest provider of telecommunication network equipment in the world after Germany's Alcatel and Motorola of the United States. The smallest of the new companies was AT&T's Global Information Solutions business, a manufacturer of computer systems with annual revenues of $9 billion. Global Information Solutions was built around NCR, a computer company that AT&T had acquired in 1991 for $7.5 billion.

The decision to break up AT&T into three parts was the result of a number of factors that came to a head in the mid-1990s. First was the impending deregulation of the U.S. telecommunications industry. After deregulation (which occurred in 1996), local and long-distance telephone companies would be free to enter each other's markets. AT&T would face more competition in its core long-distance business as the Regional Bell Operating Companies (RBOCs) tried to enter this market. At the same time, AT&T would be able to enter the local phone businesses and compete directly against the RBOCs. Second was the privatization of state-owned telephone companies around the world and the deregulation of many foreign telephone markets. These developments created enormous opportunities for AT&T, which for the first time saw the possibility of building a truly global telephone network by forming alliances with newly privatized telephone companies, and by entering foreign markets. Third was rapid change in the telecommunications business as new technologies, such as wireless communications and the Internet, created significant opportunities and threats for AT&T. Faced with such changes in its operating environment, AT&T's management decided that they needed to focus all their energies and resources on the company's core telecommunications business, unencumbered by the distractions presented by the network equipment and computer businesses.

There was also an understanding on the part of AT&T's management that the performance of the computer and network equipment businesses had suffered as a result of its association with AT&T. The equipment business was trying to sell products to companies that competed directly against AT&T, such as MCI and Sprint, or would compete against AT&T after deregulation, such as the RBOCs. These potential customers were increasingly reluctant to purchase equipment from a supplier that was also a competitor. For example, just before the breakup was announced, Motorola beat AT&T to an $800 million order for wireless telecommunications equipment from GTE. GTE had long been one of AT&T's largest equipment customers, but now it faced the threat of competing against AT&T in the local phone business. Freed from its association with AT&T, the network equipment business would have a greater chance of capturing business from other telephone service providers.

As for the computer business, this was forecast to lose around $1 billion in 1995. Although AT&T had always had some significant computer skills—after all, many network equipment products, such as digital switches, are essentially specialized computers—it had never been able to establish a profitable computer operation. During the 1980s, it had lost billions of dollars trying to establish a presence in the personal computer market through an internal new venture. Moreover, its 1991 acquisition of NCR, an attempt to strengthen this venture, turned out to be a disaster, partly because the computer market shifted away from the kind of customized equipment provided by NCR, and partly because there was a clash between the management cultures of the two companies that led to high management turnover in the acquired unit. Many now felt that AT&T's deep pockets had kept the computer operation in markets that it should have exited years ago, such as the personal computer market. They believed that an independent computer operation might be more responsive to market demands and would not be burdened by the clashing cultural heritage of AT&T and NCR.

Having completed its exit from the equipment and computer businesses, in 1999 AT&T purchased two large providers of cable TV: TCI and Media One. The theory behind the acquisitions was that AT&T would be able to use cable to offer local phone service to its customers, in addition to long-distance service, and just as important, to avoid paying access fees to local phone companies (the

RBOCs). Prior to the acquisitions, AT&T had no direct access to its customers and had to use the phone lines of local phone companies to *originate* and *terminate* calls for its long-distance customers. AT&T had to pay the local phone companies a *termination fee* for every phone call routed through their lines. The termination fee amounted to about 35 percent of the cost of every phone call made through AT&T's network. AT&T's hope was that it could use coaxial cable to originate and terminate calls to residential customers, thereby avoiding the termination fee and saving substantial costs.

The cable strategy did not work out as planned. After making the acquisition, AT&T discovered that it would cost billions of dollars to upgrade the cable TV systems so that they could also handle phone calls. Moreover, AT&T took on $56 billion in debt to finance the acquisitions of TCI and Media One. With billions more needing to be spent before it could offer phone service over cable, AT&T concluded that it would be years before it could generate sufficient income from these assets to cover the costs of serving existing and additional debt, so the CEO decided to cut the company's losses and sell the cable TV assets to the highest bidder. That turned out to be Comcast, another cable TV company, which paid AT&T $72 billion for these assets.

Case Discussion Questions

1. What changes in AT&T's operating environment triggered its 1995 decision to break the company up into three entities?

2. How might the breakup create value for shareholders?

3. Does the 1995 breakup imply that AT&T's pre-1995 strategic vision was seriously flawed?

4. Was the strategic rationale for acquiring TCI and Media One sound? If so, why did AT&T reverse course and sell off its cable assets in 2002? How might AT&T have handled this whole episode differently?

Sources: T. Jackson, "Giant Bows to Colossal Pressure," *Financial Times,* September 22, 1995, p. 13. "AT&T's Three Way Split," *Economist,* September 23, 1995, pp. 51–52. "Fatal Attraction," *Economist,* March 23, 1996, pp. 73–74. A. Ramirez, "Opportunity and New Risk for a Spinoff," *New York Times,* September 22, 1995, pp. C1, C4. J. Krause, "The Last AT&T Story," *Telephony,* February 4, 2002, pp. 32–40. "Comcast Hangs in to Win Auction for AT&T Cable," *Mergers and Acquisitions* (February 2002): 10–11.

Corporate Performance, Governance, and Business Ethics

11

Opening Case

The Fall of Enron

In early December 2001, the Enron Corporation filed for Chapter 11 bankruptcy protection. Enron, which started off as a natural gas pipeline operator and independent power producer, had emerged during the late 1990s as the principal player in the rapidly expanding market for energy trading. At its height in 2000, the company had boasted revenues of $101 billion, a stock market capitalization of $63 billion, and a chairman, Kenneth Lay, who was a high-profile confidant of then President-elect George W. Bush. The company was leveraging its expertise in energy trading to other market opportunities, including trading in paper, metals, water, and telecommunication capacity (or broadband). Enron believed that it could exploit the power of the Internet to create online markets in almost anything. The media loved the company. In 2000, *Fortune* magazine voted Enron "the most innovative company of the year." The *Economist* wrote

365

that Enron "has created what may be the most successful Internet venture of any company in any industry anywhere."

A few months after these words were written, Enron had ceased to exist as a functioning entity. On its last trading day, the stock stood at 61 cents per share, down from a high of $90 just a year earlier. Numbered among the stockholders who had seen their Enron holdings implode in value were many Enron employees, who had been obliged by company policies to hold Enron stock in their retirement accounts.

What made the collapse of Enron so disturbing was not just the size of the failure, but the manner in which the company unraveled. What bought Enron down so rapidly was an accumulation of more than $27 billion in off-balance-sheet debt held by partnerships hidden from the view of most investors, employees, and regulators. These partnerships were set up to exploit Enron's forays into ever more exotic online trading ventures, such as water and bandwidth trading. The partnerships were controlled by Enron managers but not owned by Enron, so the debt did not appear on Enron's balance sheets and thus did not affect the company's credit rating and borrowing costs. The partnerships were financed with debt raised from institutional investors. Using the company's high-flying stock as collateral, Enron guaranteed that debt. It often transferred its own assets to the partnerships, registering the transfer as revenues.

The partnerships were the brainchild of Enron's chief financial officer, Andrew Fastow, who used the partnership as a way of making Enron's balance sheet and earnings look stronger than they really were. Fastow also personally profited from the partnerships, many of which he controlled, reportedly making over $30 million from them. The partnership strategy, however, was very risky. If the aggressive investments the partnerships were making did not pan out, Enron, as the guarantor of partnership debt, would be on the hook. Moreover, if Enron's stock fell too far, guarantees backed by stock would have be replaced by cash, which would require Enron to raise more debt.

The first cracks in Enron's facade started to appear in August 2001 when the CEO, Jeffrey Skilling, suddenly and unexpectedly resigned, citing "personal reasons." Skilling had sold some $17.5 million of Enron stock in the months before he quit. Chairman Kenneth Lay, himself the former CEO, stepped back into the CEO position and reassured investors, spooked by Skilling's sudden departure. Then in October 2001, Enron recorded a third-quarter loss of $618 million and announced that it was reducing shareholder equity by $1.2 billion, primarily because of losses accumulated at partnerships. Enron's

stock, which had lost half its value since December 2000, suddenly plummeted. This created a death spiral in which Enron had to raise debt to guarantee debt accumulated at partnerships, a spiral that quickly led to bankruptcy.

When the existence of the partnerships was revealed, the financial community was stunned: there had been scarcely a reference to any of them in Enron's audited financial statements. By implication, investors were ignorant of the tremendous risks associated with the partnership strategy. It was difficult to escape the conclusion that Enron's management had deliberately played down the existence of the partnerships in order to mislead the financial markets about the true state of the company. Questions were also asked about Enron's auditor, Arthur Andersen. Why had it not drawn attention to the partnerships? Surely as auditor, it must have known about them? Why had Andersen apparently agreed with the tactic of keeping these partnerships hidden from public view? Was it to protect a lucrative financial relationship with an important client? Enron paid Andersen some $52 million in 2000—$25 million for auditing and $27 million for consulting services. The questions about Andersen's role became even sharper when it was revealed that the Andersen partner responsible for the Enron audit had instructed his staff to shred documents relating to the audit. Was Andersen trying to hide what it had known about the true financial state of the company?

The voices of critics grew louder when it was discovered that in August 2001, a midlevel Enron official, Sherron Watkins, had sent a memo to Kenneth Lay outlining the risks associated with the partnership strategy. Watkins warned Lay that Enron could implode in a wave of accounting scandals. Lay apparently expressed concern but continued to present a bullish face to the outside world and appears to have done nothing to rein in the CFO, Fastow. Lay moved to replace Fastow only on October 24, two days after the Securities and Exchange Commission announced that it had started an investigation into Enron's accounting practices. Worse still, throughout 2001, Enron's senior managers continued to sell millions of dollars of their own holdings in Enron's stock, while many employees were limited or prohibited from selling the Enron stock they held in their retirement accounts. Did the managers know something that they kept hidden from their own employees?

In the aftermath of Enron's collapse, the U.S. Congress announced that it would investigate allegations of financial misdealings at the company. Called before a House Committee, Lay and Fastow took the Fifth, while Skilling claimed ignorance of the details of the partnership dealings. Was the law broken? It looks that way. In August 2002, one senior Enron executive had pleaded guilty to money laundering and conspiracy charges, and agreed to cooperate with the government in bringing possible charges against other executives, including former CFO Fastow, whom the Justice Department named as an "unindicted co-conspirator in the fraud case." What seems clear is that billions of dollars in shareholder value evaporated and thousands of employees lost their jobs, while senior managers enriched themselves, because those same managers pursued very risky and highly leveraged strategies that were deliberately concealed from public view. Worse, this seems to have occurred with the blessing of the very people who were meant to expose the truth about a company's financial position to the public: the company's auditors, in this case Arthur Andersen.

Sources: "Why Honesty Is the Best Policy," *Economist,* March 9, 2002. "The Amazing Disintegrating Firm—Enron," *Economist,* December 8, 2001. Wendy Zellner et al., "The Fall of Enron," *Business Week,* December 17, 2001, pp. 30–40. Ken Brown et al., "Paper Trail: Andersen Fires Partner It Says Led Shredding of Enron Documents," *Wall Street Journal,* January 16, 2002, p. A1. Johnathan Weil, "Justice Department finds Building a Case Against Lay Tough," *Wall Street Journal,* August 26, 2002, p. A3.

Overview

The collapse of Enron raises troubling questions about corporate performance, corporate governance, and business ethics. It is now clear that at the very least, several senior managers at Enron behaved in an unethical manner, deliberately misleading shareholders and employees about the true state of the company's performance. It would seem that they did this to continue to meet the high financial performance expectations that they themselves had established for the company. By setting and then meeting these expectations, they hoped that Enron's stock price would continue to skyrocket, giving them the opportunity to exercise stock options for substantial personal gain. It is hard to escape the conclusion that senior managers at Enron deliberately misstated the true financial state of the company to enrich themselves. The losers in this process were key stakeholders in Enron: the company's stockholders, creditors, and employees.

Increasingly, the corporate scandals at companies like Enron and Arthur Andersen and the huge across-the-board decline in stock prices that occurred in 2001–2002 have the public asking, "What is happening in the world of business today?" Why is it that people like Ken Lay at Enron and Bernie Ebbers at WorldCom can take hundreds of millions in dollars out of their companies through their stock options, yet their shareholders have lost hundreds of billions of dollars in the value of their stock either directly or through their pension plans? Moreover, many thousands of hard-working Enron and WorldCom managers and employees have lost their jobs, and customers have received poorer-quality goods and services (customer complaints at WorldCom are increasing, and Enron is being investigated for its role in artificially manipulating the supply of electricity to California homes, which boosted its profits but contributed to the rolling blackouts experienced in California in 2001.)

This chapter examines the many important factors and issues that may prevent a company's strategies from being implemented in ways that raise corporate performance and lead to superior profitability. This chapter is concerned with how to ensure that managers implement strategies that are in the long-run interests of key stakeholders of the company, such as stockholders and employees. Corporate governance and business ethics are tools that can be put in place to make sure the interests of stakeholders are recognized and incorporated into the strategy-making process.

By the end of this chapter, you will understand why managers, when formulating and implementing strategies aimed at establishing a sustainable competitive advantage and superior profitability, should choose those that are legal and ethical and balance the claims of all its stakeholder groups.

The Causes of Poor Performance

Most of this book has been focused on what managers should do to maximize the long-run profitability of their company. The reality, however, is that many companies find it very difficult to earn a rate of return that exceeds their cost of capital—in other words, they are not very profitable. For example, in the air express industry, the cost of capital has been estimated at 12 percent (the cost of capital is the return that stockholders and bond holders expect on their investment of capital in the company). Between 1996 and 2001, UPS's average return on invested capital (ROIC) was 17.9 percent, Federal Express earned an average of 10.8 percent and Airborne Express 8 percent.[1] The implication is that neither Federal Express nor Airborne generated a return that exceeded their cost of capital. They were not good investments. This situation is not uncommon. In most industries, there are companies that are unable to generate a return on invested capital that exceeds their cost of capital and therefore are not performing up to the expectations of investors.

Sometimes poor performance is temporary, caused primarily by short-term declines in demand for an industry's product due to recessionary conditions; once demand recovers, so does company profitability. However, for other companies, poor performance is a persistent problem. Kmart, for example, has underperformed Wal-Mart for years and now is in Chapter 11 bankruptcy proceedings. DaimlerChrysler has been underperforming its primary rivals in the global automobile industry for several years.

Six causes of persistent poor performance stand out in most case studies of persistent poor performance:[2]

- Poor management
- A high cost structure
- A lack of adequate differentiation
- Overexpansion
- Structural shifts in demand and new competitors
- Organization inertia

Normally several, if not all, of these factors are present in a decline. For example, IBM's poor financial performance in the early 1990s was brought on by structural shifts in demand away from mainframe computers and toward client-server networks based on PCs, compounded by the emergence of powerful new competitors such as Compaq and Dell. IBM's slow response to these problems was due to poor senior management and organizational inertia.

Poor Management

Poor management covers a multitude of sins, ranging from sheer incompetence to neglect of core businesses and an insufficient number of good managers. One-person rule is not necessarily a bad thing, but it often seems to be at the root of poor management. One study found that the presence of a dominant and autocratic chief executive with a passion for empire-building strategies often characterizes many failing companies.[3] Another study of eighty-one turnaround situations found that in thirty-six cases, troubled companies suffered from an autocratic manager who tried to do it all and, in the face of complexity and change, could not.[4] In a review of the empirical studies of turnaround situations, Richard Hoffman identified a number of other management defects commonly found in poorly performing companies.[5] These included a lack of balanced expertise at the top (e.g., too many engineers), a lack of strong middle management, a failure to provide for orderly management succession by a departing CEO (which may result in an internal succession battle), and a failure by the board of directors to monitor management's strategic decisions adequately.

As we shall see later in the chapter, poor management also includes executives who pursue strategies designed to enrich themselves at the expense of stockholders, employees, and other stakeholders. Such strategic actions often depress the overall profitability of the company. In theory, the board of directors exists to hire, evaluate, and, if necessary, replace, the senior management of the company, and particularly the CEO. As such, the board should be in a position to make sure that such a situation does not occur. However, as we will see later in the chapter when we return to this issue and consider it in depth, many boards do not do their jobs.

High Cost Structure   A high cost structure will make it difficult for a company to earn a decent return on its invested capital. The two main causes of a high cost structure are low labor productivity and low capital productivity. Low labor productivity may stem from union-imposed restrictive working practices (as in the case of the auto and steel industries), management's failure to invest in labor-saving technologies or technologies that can boost the productivity of employees (such as information technology), and an organization that does not create incentives for employees to work productively. Low capital productivity can be due to failure to fully use the fixed assets of a company, such as its property, plant, and equipment. For example, a failure to use production capacity fully because of low market share can result in an inability to attain economies of scale and high unit costs. Low capital productivity can also be due to a failure to minimize working capital, by, for example, holding too much inventory.

Low employee and capital productivity can often be traced to deeper problems within an organization, such as inadequate financial controls. The most common aspect of inadequate financial controls is a failure to assign profit responsibility to key decision makers within the organization. A lack of accountability for the financial consequences of their actions can encourage middle-level managers to employ excess staff and spend resources beyond what is necessary for maximum efficiency. In such cases, bureaucracy may balloon and costs spiral out of control. In addition, a lack of adequate financial controls can lead managers to waste capital resources in unproductive investments. Just how this problem might be avoided is another topic that we return to later in the chapter.

Inadequate Differentiation   A lack of adequate differentiation can make it difficult for a company to earn a decent return on its invested capital. Inadequate differentiation has a number of sources, including poor product quality and a lack of compelling product attributes, such as superior features, performance, and styling. It means that a company will lack the ability to charge a premium price for its goods and services or the ability to hold prices low and use its superior differentiation as a tool for increasing sales volume and attaining scale economies. Either way, the net effect is to lower the profitability of the enterprise below what it might otherwise have been.

Inadequate differentiation can often be traced to deeper problems in the organization. For example, a failure to establish and properly manage cross-functional product development teams (see Chapter 4 for details) may mean that the company's product development efforts fall short, and its products lack the differential features and functions of those produced by competitors. Similarly, a failure to implement quality improvement processes, such as the Six Sigma quality improvement methodology discussed in Chapter 4, may result in poor product quality and, consequently, a negative perception of the company's products in the minds of consumers.

Overexpansion

The empire-building strategies of autocratic CEOs often involve rapid expansion and extensive diversification. Later in this chapter, we examine why a CEO might pursue empire-building strategies. For now, note that much of this diversification tends to be poorly conceived and adds little value to a company. As pointed out in Chapter 9, the consequences of too much diversification include loss of control and declining profitability. Moreover, companies that expand rapidly tend to do so by taking on large amounts of debt. This can subsequently place a huge financial burden on the company if economic conditions deteriorate and the company is no longer able to generate the cash flows required to service its debt payments.

Something like this happened to Tyco International, the acquisitive conglomerate profiled in the *Opening Case* to Chapter 10. Tyco expanded during the economic boom years of the 1990s, in part by using borrowed money (debt raised through bond issues) to finance ever larger acquisitions. As long as the economy remained strong, Tyco was able to generate the free cash flow required to service its debt commitments. However, as the economy weakened in 2000–2001, Tyco found itself struggling to generate the required cash flows and had to start selling off some of its previously acquired businesses, often at a considerable discount to their original purchase price, in order to raise the necessary cash. A similar problem beset WorldCom, profiled in the *Opening Case* to Chapter 9.

Structural Shifts in Demand and New Competitors

A **structural shift** in demand is one that is permanent, as opposed to a temporary cyclical shift due to short-term macroeconomic conditions. Structural shifts in demand can be brought about by major changes in technology, economic or political conditions, and social and cultural norms. Although such changes can open up market opportunities for new competitors, they also revolutionize industry structure and threaten the existence of many established enterprises, necessitating restructuring. For example, changing social habits have lead to a structural decline in consumption of breakfast cereal in the United States (people are substituting bagels and muffins for cereal). The result is that the profitability of major cereal companies such as Kellogg's has come under pressure in the face of declining revenue. In many cases, structural shifts in demand are difficult to anticipate, but once they occur, they can cause major problems for established companies. IBM's troubles in the early 1990s were in part due to a structural shift in demand away from mainframe computers and toward client server networks.

New competitors often go hand in hand with structural shifts in demand, particularly when the shift is caused by the arrival of a new technology. New competitors riding the wave of a new disruptive technology can revolutionize competition in an industry, making it very difficult for established enterprises to survive, a topic that we discussed in depth in Chapter 7.

Organizational Inertia

On their own, the emergence of powerful new competition and a structural shift in demand might not be enough to cause declining performance. What is also required is an organization that is slow to respond to such environmental changes. **Organizational inertia,** the inability of an organization to adapt in a timely manner to new circumstances, stands out as a major reason that companies are often so slow to respond to new competitive conditions.

Organizational inertia is complex and has a number of underlying causes.[6] One source is the existing distribution of power and influence within an organization.[7] The power and influence that individual managers enjoy is in part a function of their role in the organization hierarchy, as defined by structural position. By definition, most substantive changes in an organization require a change in structure and, by extension, a change in the internal distribution of power and influence. Some individuals will see their power and influence increase as a result of organization change, and some will see the converse. In general, managers whose power and influence is reduced as a consequence of organization change can be expected to resist it, primarily by arguing that the change might not work. To the extent that they are successful, this constitutes a source of organization inertia that might slow or stop change.

Another source of organization inertia is the existing culture of an organization, as expressed in norms and value systems. Value systems in particular reflect deeply held beliefs, and they can be very hard to change. If the formal and informal socialization mechanisms within an organization have been emphasizing a consistent set of values for a prolonged period of time, and if hiring, promotion, and incentive systems have all reinforced these values, then suddenly announcing that those values are no longer appropriate and need to be changed can quite naturally produce resistance and dissonance among the employees of an organization.

Organization inertia might also derive from preconceptions about the appropriate business model that is held in the heads of senior managers. The Icarus paradox explored in Chapter 3 notes the tendency of companies to continue to rely on the skills and capabilities that made them successful even when those capabilities do not match the new competitive environment.[8] When a particular business model has worked well in the past, managers might have difficulties accepting that it is no longer appropriate. Such cognitive myopia can result in an inability to accept the need for change until serious problems have already developed.

Strategic Change: Improving Performance

Improving the profitability of a company suffering from persistently low profitability usually involves a substantial turnaround in the way a company operates and the strategies it pursues. There is no standard model of how a company should respond to a decline in its profitability. Indeed, there can be no such model because every situation is unique. However, in most successful turnaround situations, a number of common features are present: changing the leadership, changing the strategy of the company, and changing the organization so that it can better implement the new strategy.

Changing the Leadership

Because the old leadership bears the stigma of failure, new leadership is an essential element of most turnaround situations. Often the new leader is from outside the company. For example, as the first step in implementing a turnaround, IBM replaced CEO John Akers with outsider Lou Gerstner. New leadership from outside may be necessary because the existing managers have been socialized into the long-established ways of operating within the company and might find it very difficult to see how things might be done differently. To resolve a crisis, the new leader should be able to make difficult decisions, motivate lower-level managers, listen to the views of others, and delegate power when appropriate.

Changing the Strategy

In many cases, poor profitability reflects a failed strategy that has left the company saddled with high costs, inadequate differentiation, and, perhaps, too many unprofitable lines of business. It follows that changing the strategy of the company is often a central ingredient of a successful turnaround. For a single-business enterprise, redefining strategic focus involves a reevaluation of the company's business-level strategy. A failed cost leader, for example, may reorient toward a more focused or differentiated strategy. For a diversified company, redefining strategic focus means identifying the businesses in the portfolio that have the best long-term profit and growth prospects and concentrating investment there.

Having redefined its strategic focus, a company should divest as many unwanted assets as it can find buyers for and liquidate whatever remains. It is important not to confuse unwanted assets with unprofitable assets. Assets that no longer fit in with the redefined strategic focus of the company may be very profitable. Their sale can bring the company much-needed cash, which it can invest in improving the operations that remain.

Improving the profitability of the operations that remain after asset sales and closures takes a number of steps to improve efficiency, quality, innovation, and customer responsiveness. (We discuss many of the functional-level strategies that companies can pursue to achieve these ends in Chapter 5, so you may want to review that chapter.) Note, though, that improving profitability typically involves one or more of the following: (1) laying off excess employees, (2) investing in productivity-enhancing equipment, (3) assigning profit responsibility to individuals and subunits within the company, by a change of organizational structure if necessary, (4) tightening financial controls, (5) cutting back on marginal products, (6) reengineering business process to cut costs and boost productivity, and (7) introducing total quality management processes.

Finally, a somewhat surprising but quite common turnaround strategy is to make acquisitions, primarily to strengthen the competitive position of a company's remaining core operations. For example, Champion International Corporation used to be a very diversified company, manufacturing a wide range of paper and wood products. After years of declining performance, Champion in the mid-1980s decided to focus on its profitable newsprint and magazine paper business. The company divested many of its other paper and wood products businesses, but at the same time it paid $1.8 billion for St. Regis Corp., one of the country's largest manufacturers of newsprint and magazine paper.

Changing the Organization

Changing leadership and strategy are by themselves not enough to improve the profitability of a poorly performing company. The organization itself must also be changed so that the company can better implement its strategy. The basic principles for successful organization change can be summarized as follows: (1) unfreeze the organization through shock therapy, (2) move the organization to a new state through change in the strategy and structure, and (3) refreeze the organization in its new state.

Unfreezing the Organization. Due to inertia forces, incremental change is often no change at all. Those whose power is threatened by a change effort can too easily resist incremental change. This leads to the big bang theory of change, which maintains that effective change requires taking bold action early on to "unfreeze" the established culture of an organization and change the distribution of power and influence. Shock therapy to unfreeze the organization might include closing down plants deemed uneconomic or planning and then announcing a dramatic structural reorganization. It is also important to realize that change will not take place unless senior managers are themselves committed to it. Senior managers must be able to articulate the need for change clearly so that employees understand both why it is being pursued and the benefits that will flow from successful change. Senior managers must also be willing to practice what they preach and take the necessary bold steps. If employees see senior managers preaching the need for change but not changing their own behavior or making substantive changes in the organization, they will soon loose faith in the change effort, which will flounder.

Movement. Once an organization has been unfrozen, it must be moved to its new state. Movement requires taking action, including closing down operations; reorganizing the structure; reassigning responsibilities; changing control, incentive, and reward systems; redesigning processes; and letting people go who are seen as an impediment to change. In other words, movement requires a substantial change in the form of a company's strategy and structure so that it matches the desired new strategic posture of the organization. For movement to be successful, it must be done with sufficient speed. Involving employees in the change effort is an excellent way to get them to appreciate and buy into the needs for change and to help with rapid movement. For example, a company might delegate substantial responsibility for designing operating processes to lower-level employees. If enough of their recommendations are then acted on, the employees will see the consequences of their efforts and consequently buy into the notion that change is really taking place.

Refreezing the Organization. Refreezing the organization takes longer. It may require that a new culture be established while the old one is being dismantled. Thus, refreezing requires that employees be socialized into the new way of doing things. Companies often use management education programs to achieve this effect. At General Electric, where long-time CEO Jack Welch instituted a major change in the culture of the company, management education programs were used to communicate new values to organization members. On its own, however, management education programs are not enough. Hiring policies must be changed to reflect the new realities, with an emphasis on hiring individuals whose own values are consistent with that of the new culture the firm is trying to build. Similarly, control and incentive systems must be consistent with the new realities of the organization, or change will never take hold. Equally important, senior management must recognize that changing culture takes a long time. Any let-up in the pressure to change may allow the old culture to reemerge as employees fall back into familiar ways of acting. The communication task facing senior managers therefore is a long-term endeavor that requires managers to be relentless and persistent in their pursuit of change. One of the striking features of Jack Welch's two-decade-long tenure at GE, for example, is that he never stopped pushing his change agenda. It was a consistent theme of his tenure. He was always thinking up new programs and initiatives to keep pushing the culture of the organization along the desired trajectory.

In sum, the successful turnaround of a persistently unprofitable organization requires new leadership, new strategy, and an extensive and ongoing effort to change the organization of the company so that it is aligned with the new strategic objectives. Successfully executing such an effort is perhaps one of the most difficult endeavors in management. However, there are some dramatic examples of companies and management teams that have been successful, including the team that ran IBM under Lou Gerstner and American Express under Harvey Golub. In both cases, these managers led teams that pushed through revolutionary changes in the strategy and organization of the respective companies, transforming them from failing enterprises into successful corporations once again.

Many companies have tried repeatedly to turn themselves around and failed. They either end up going bankrupt or being acquired by competitors for their remaining valuable assets. The big losers in such a process are the stakeholders of the company. In the next section, we look at how managers can reduce the probability of declining corporate performance by taking the interests of stakeholders into account when formulating and implementing strategies.

Stakeholders and Corporate Performance

A company's **stakeholders** are individuals or groups with an interest, claim, or stake in the company, in what it does, and in how well it performs.[9] They include stockholders, creditors, employees, customers, the communities in which the company does business, and the general public. Stakeholders can be divided into internal stakeholders and external stakeholders (see Figure 11.1). **Internal stakeholders** are stockholders and employees, including executive officers, other managers, and board members. **External stakeholders** are all other individuals and groups that have some claim on the company. Typically, this group comprises customers, suppliers, creditors (including banks and bondholders), governments, unions, local communities, and the general public.

All stakeholders are in an exchange relationship with the company. Each of the stakeholder groups listed in Figure 11.1 supplies the organization with important resources (or contributions), and in exchange each expects its interests to be satisfied (by inducements).[10] Stockholders provide the enterprise with risk capital and in exchange expect management to try to maximize the return on their investment. Creditors, and particularly bondholders, also provide the company with capital, and they expect that the interest due to them will be paid on time and in full. Employees provide labor and skills and in exchange expect commensurate income, job satisfaction, job security, and good working conditions. Customers provide a company with its revenues and in exchange want high-quality, reliable products that represent value for money. Suppliers provide a company with inputs and in exchange seek revenues and dependable buyers. Governments provide a company with rules and regulations that govern business practice and maintain fair competition and in exchange want companies that adhere to these rules. Unions help to provide a company with productive employees and in exchange they want benefits for their members in proportion to their contributions to the company. Local communities provide companies with local infrastructure and in exchange want companies that are responsible citizens. The general public provides companies with national infrastructure and in exchange seeks some assurance that the quality of life will be improved as a result of the company's existence.

FIGURE 11.1

Stakeholders and the Enterprise

A company must take these claims into account when formulating its strategies, or else stakeholders may withdraw their support. For example, stockholders may sell their shares, bondholders demand higher interest payments on new bonds, employees leave their jobs, and customers buy elsewhere. Suppliers may seek more dependable buyers. Unions may engage in disruptive labor disputes. Government may take civil or criminal action against the company and its top officers, imposing fines and in some cases jail terms. Communities may oppose the company's attempts to locate its facilities in their area, and the general public may form pressure groups, demanding action against companies that impair the quality of life. Any of these reactions can have a damaging impact on an enterprise. A detailed example is given in Strategy in Action 11.1, which looks at how Bill Agee, the former CEO of Morrison Knudson, lost his job because the strategies he pursued failed to satisfy the interests of two important stakeholder groups: the company's employees and its stockholders.

Strategy in Action   11.1

Bill Agee at Morrison Knudsen

Bill Agee made his name as a whiz kid who became the chief financial officer of paper maker Boise Cascade during the 1970s while he was in his early thirties. He left Boise Cascade after the company was forced to write down its profits by $250 million due to earlier overstatements of the value of timberland sales. At the time, the write-downs were the largest in corporate history, but this did not stop Agee from being appointed CEO of defense contractor Bendix in 1976 when he was only thirty-eight years old. At Bendix, Agee became involved in a famous corporate soap opera that began when he promoted a young manager, Mary Cunningham, to a senior post, over the heads of many other more experienced executives. At the time, many felt the promotion occurred because the two were romantically involved. Both denied this, but in 1982 Agee divorced his wife and married Cunningham, who by this time had left Bendix.

In 1988, Agee became CEO of Idaho-based Morrison Knudson (MK), a seventy-five-year-old construction company that had made its name as the prime contractor on a number of large western construction projects, including the Hoover Dam and the Trans Alaska pipeline. By the time Agee joined the company, MK was perceived as a venerable institution that wasn't quite living up to its performance potential. Agee's strategy for improving performance was to sell off certain of MK's assets and invest the proceeds in the securities of other companies. At the same time, he pushed MK to pursue large construction projects aggressively and to develop its rail car manufacturing business. At one time, the rail car manufacturing business had been a major success story at MK, but it had fallen on hard times, unable to hold its own in the face of aggressive competition.

On the surface, MK appeared to be prospering under Agee's leadership. In 1993, MK earned $35.8 million, and Agee proclaimed it a "banner year" and a "watershed period" for the company's drive into railroad and mass transit industries. Underneath the surface, however, things were unraveling for Bill Agee. For one thing, 62 percent of MK's profits in 1993 came from Agee's financial plays in securities trading and capital gains on asset sales. Strip out these one-time gains, and it was clear that the operating performance of MK was poor. A prime reason seems to have been Agee's insistence that in order to win new business, MK should be the low bidder on large contracts. For instance, when MK bid on a contract to build eighty transit cars for the Bay Area Rapid Transit District (BART) in Oakland, California, Agee knocked down the bid to $142 million. According to one insider, the result was that "we were looking at a $14 million loss on the contract the day we won it." In the second quarter of 1994, MK announced a $40.5 million loss after taking a $59.4 million charge for underbidding various transit car contracts. Similarly, in the third quarter of 1994, MK took a $9.2 million charge against profits for underbidding on a $100 million contract to rebuild locomotives for Southern Pacific.

To compound matters, there had been significant employee opposition to Agee's leadership. An anonymous letter sent to MK's board in November 1994 by a group of

MK executives calling themselves the MK Committee for Excellence leveled a whole slew of charges at Agee. Right off, they claimed, Agee irked subordinates by removing the portrait of MK's founder from the headquarters and replacing it with a near life-sized portrait of him and his wife, Mary Cunningham, paid for by the company. Agee further estranged insiders by quietly moving the CEO's office to his Pebble Beach estate in California and by scoffing at the company's engineering-oriented culture. Several old-hand MK engineering executives, who had top reputations in their field, were fired, usually after crossing swords with Agee over his policies.

There was also the matter of Agee's pay and perks. At $2.4 million, Agee's 1993 compensation was equal to 6.8 percent of MK's net income, more than any other CEO of a company with earnings in that range, according to a *Forbes* magazine list. According to insiders, MK paid $4 million a year for a corporate jet for Agee, equal to 13 percent of the company's general and administrative budget. The company also paid for landscaping services at Agee's Pebble Beach estate.

Things came to a head on February 1, 1995, when MK's board announced that the company would record a large loss for 1994. The board also announced that Agee would be stepping down as CEO, although initial indications were that he would stay on as chairman of the board. Preliminary figures suggested that MK would have to take a $179.6 million pretax charge in its 1994 fourth quarter, which would result in a net loss of $141 million for the quarter. At the same time, Standard & Poor's downgraded MK's long-term debt to junk bond rating, signaling that a significant risk of default existed.

The announcement gave rise to a blizzard of shareholder lawsuits and criticism, not only of Agee, but also of MK's board for acting so slowly. Many commentators wondered why it took a huge loss and an anonymous letter from MK employees to prod the board into action. Privately, several board members, most of whom were appointees and long-time friends of Agee, indicated that they were led astray by Agee, who repeatedly urged them not to worry about poor results. Still, many felt that the audit committee of the board of directors had not done a good job of vetting MK's financial accounts under Agee's leadership. Stung by this criticism, the growing evidence of financial mismanagement under Agee's leadership, and the downgrade of MK's debt by Standard & Poor's, the board reversed its earlier position and decided to strip Agee of all posts at MK.

The shareholder lawsuits were settled in September 1995. Under the agreement, MK was to pay out $63 million in cash and stock to shareholders. The settlement also required the company to strengthen its board by adding seven new directors over the next two years. As part of the settlement, Agee agreed to relinquish rights to about $3 million in severance pay and to a cut in his MK pension from $303,000 a year for life to $99,750 a year for life.

Sources: J. E. Rigdon and J. S. Lubin, "Why Morrison Board Fired Agee," *Wall Street Journal,* February 13, 1995, p. B1. C. McCoy. "Worst Five and One Year Performer: Morrison Knudson," *Wall Street Journal,* February 29, 1996, p. R2. "Morrison Knudson Settles Most Shareholder Lawsuits," *Wall Street Journal,* September 21, 1995, p. B8. J. E. Rigdon, "William Agee to Leave Morrison Knudson," *Wall Street Journal,* February 2, 1995, p. B1.

Stakeholder Impact Analysis

A company cannot always satisfy the claims of all stakeholders. The goals of different groups may conflict, and in practice few organizations have the resources to manage all stakeholders.[11] For example, union claims for higher wages can conflict with consumer demands for reasonable prices and stockholder demands for acceptable returns. Often the company must make choices. To do so, it must identify the most important stakeholders and give highest priority to pursuing strategies that satisfy their needs. Stakeholder impact analysis can provide such identification. Typically, stakeholder impact analysis follows these steps:

1. Identify stakeholders.

2. Identify stakeholders' interests and concerns.

3. As a result, identify what claims stakeholders are likely to make on the organization.

4. Identify the stakeholders who are most important from the organization's perspective.

5. Identify the resulting strategic challenges.[12]

Such an analysis enables a company to identify the stakeholders most critical to its survival and to make sure that the satisfaction of their needs is paramount. Most companies that have gone through this process quickly come to the conclusion that three stakeholder groups must be satisfied above all others if a company is to survive and prosper: customers, employees, and stockholders. Bill Agee, for example, lost his position because he failed to satisfy the demands of stockholders for a good return on their investment and the demands of employees for income, job satisfaction, job security, and good working conditions. More generally, companies that fail to satisfy the needs of its customers soon see their revenues fall and ultimately go out of business. Interestingly, Agee probably was satisfying the needs of customers since he was insisting on low prices; however, at the prices Agee was requiring, Morrison Knudsen could not possibly have been profitable.

The Unique Role of Stockholders

A company's stockholders are usually put in a different class from other stakeholder groups, and for good reason. Stockholders are legal owners and the providers of risk capital, a major source of the capital resources that allow a company to operate its business. The capital that stockholders provide to a company is seen as **risk capital** because there is no guarantee that stockholders will ever recoup their investment and or earn a decent return.

Recent history demonstrates all too clearly the nature of risk capital. Many investors who bought shares in companies that went public during the late 1990s and early 2000s through an initial public offering (IPO) subsequently saw the value of their holdings decline to zero, or something close to it. For example, in early 2000, Oniva.com, a provider of an online business-to-business marketplace aimed at small businesses, went public. On the first day of trading, the shares hit $25. They fell steadily afterward, and two years later, having lost 99 percent of their value, they were trading at $0.25, effectively wiping out the investment many made in the company. Of course, there are also some spectacular successes: investors who purchased shares of Dell, Microsoft, or Intel at their IPO have done extraordinarily well. But this is the nature of risk capital: the variance of returns is very high. To reward stockholders for providing the company with risk capital, management is obligated to pursue strategies that maximize the returns that stockholders get from their investment in the company's stock.

Over the past decade, maximizing returns to stockholders has taken on added importance as more and more employees have themselves become stockholders in the company for which they work through an employee stock ownership plan (ESOP). At Wal-Mart, for example, all employees who have served for more than one year are eligible for the company's ESOP. Under an ESOP, employees are given the opportunity to purchase stock in their company, sometimes at a discount to the market value of the stock. The company may also contribute to a certain proportion of the purchase price. By making employees stockholders, ESOPs tend to increase the already strong emphasis on maximizing returns to stockholders, for this now helps to satisfy two key stakeholder groups: stockholders and employees.

Profitability and Stakeholder Claims

Because of the unique position assigned to stockholders, managers normally seek to pursue strategies that maximize the returns that stockholders receive from holding shares in the company. As we noted in Chapter 1, stockholders receive a return on their investment in a company's stock in two ways: from dividend payments and from capital appreciation in the market value of a share (that is, by increases in stock market prices). The best way for managers to generate the funds for future dividend payments and to keep the stock price appreciating is for them to pursue strategies that maximize the company's long-run return on invested capital (ROIC).[13] As we saw in Chapter 3, ROIC is an excellent measure of the profitability of a company. It tells managers how efficiently they are using the capital resources of the company (including the risk capital provided by stockholders) to generate profits. A company that is generating a positive ROIC is covering all of its ongoing expenses and has money left over, which is then added to shareholders' equity, thereby increasing the value of a company, and thus the value of a share of stock in the company. Thus, maximizing long-run ROIC is the route to maximizing returns to stockholders.

In addition to maximizing returns to stockholders, boosting a company's profitability, as measured by its ROIC, is also consistent with satisfying the claims of several other key stakeholder groups. The more profitable a company is, the higher are the salaries that it can pay to productive employees, and the greater is the ability of the company to afford other benefits, such as health insurance coverage, all of which help to satisfy that stakeholder group. In addition, companies with a high level of profitability have no problem meeting their debt commitments, which provides creditors, including bondholders, with a measure of security. More profitable companies are also better able to undertake philanthropic investments, which can help to satisfy some of the claims that local communities and the general public place on a company. Pursuing strategies that maximize the long-run ROIC of the company is therefore generally consistent with satisfying the claims of various stakeholder groups.

There is an important cause-and-effect relationship here. It is pursuing strategies to maximize profitability that helps a company to better satisfy the demands that several stakeholder groups place on it, not the other way around. The company that overpays its employees in the current period, for example, may have very happy employees for a short while, but such action will raise the company's cost structure and limit its ability to attain a competitive advantage in the marketplace, thereby depressing its long-run profitability and hurting its ability to award future pay increases. As far as employees are concerned, the way many companies deal with this situation is to make future pay increases contingent on improvements in labor productivity. If labor productivity goes up, labor costs as a percentage of revenues will fall, profitability will rise, and the company can afford to pay its employees more and offer greater benefits.

The basic cause-and-effect relationship is summarized in Figure 11.2. This shows that strategies to increase long-run ROIC will, if successfully executed, lead to higher ROIC, which increases the ability of the company to satisfy key stakeholders. In turn, satisfied stakeholders are more likely to support the company: happy employees will work hard, satisfied customers will continue to buy the company's products, satisfied stockholders will support secondary stock offerings allowing the company to raise additional risk capital, and content bondholders will be more likely to purchase additional bonds at favorable interest rates—all of which can lead to higher long-term profitability.

Of course, not all stakeholder groups want the company to maximize its long-run ROIC. Suppliers are more comfortable about selling goods and services to profitable companies, because they can be assured that the company will have the funds to pay for those products. Similarly, customers may be more willing to purchase from profitable companies, because they can be assured that those companies will be around in the long run to provide after-sales services and support. But neither suppliers nor customers want the company to maximize its ROIC *at their expense*. Rather, they

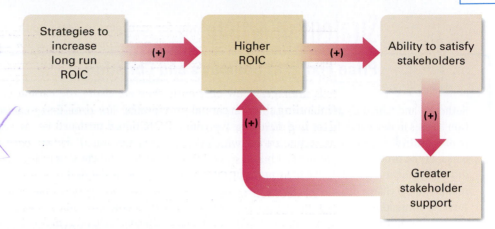

FIGURE 11.2

Relationship Between ROIC, Stakeholder Satisfaction, and Stakeholder Support

would like to capture some of these profits from the company in the form of higher prices for their goods and services (in the case of suppliers) or lower prices for the products they purchase from the company (in the case of customers). Thus, the company is in a bargaining relationship with some of its stakeholders, which was a phenomenon we discussed in Chapter 2.

Moreover, despite the argument that maximizing long-run ROIC is the best way to satisfy the claims of several key stakeholder groups, it should also be noted that a company has the obligation to do so within the limits set by the law and in a manner consistent with societal expectations. The unfettered pursuit of profit can lead to behaviors that are outlawed by government regulations, opposed by important public constituencies, or are simply unethical. Governments have enacted a wide range of regulations to govern business behavior, including antitrust laws, environmental laws, and laws pertaining to health and safety in the workplace. It is incumbent on managers to make sure that the company is in compliance with these laws when pursuing strategies.

Both illegal and unethical behavior seemed to have occurred at Enron. More generally, there is plenty of evidence that managers can be tempted to cross the line between the legal and illegal in their pursuit of greater profitability. The chief executive of Archer Daniels Midland, for example, was sent to jail after an FBI investigation revealed that the company had systematically tried to fix the price for lysine by colluding with other manufacturers in the global marketplace. In another example of price fixing, the seventy-six-year-old chairman of Sotheby's auction house was recently sentenced to a jail term and the former CEO to house arrest for fixing prices with rival auction house Christie's over a six-year period (see Strategy in Action 11.2).

Finally, it has been consistently emphasized that the goal of management should be to maximize *long-run* ROIC. This emphasis reflects two facts. First, investors, employees, and customers are generally interested only in companies that are going to be around for the long run. Employees, for example, are more likely to work for enterprises that can promise longer-term job security. Second, as noted in Chapter 1, maximizing short-run ROIC may not be consistent with maximizing long-run ROIC. A company can boost its ROIC in the current year by sharply curtailing capital investments. However, if such investments are required to maintain the long-run competitive position of the company, the result of reduced investment over several years may be a loss of competitive position and declining ROIC. Indeed, in more extreme cases, a focus on maximizing current ROIC can lead to actions that are entirely inappropriate and jeopardize the long-run survival of the company. This

Strategy in Action

Price Fixing at Sotheby's and Christie's

Sotheby's and Christie's are the two largest fine art auction houses in the world. In the mid-1990s, the two companies controlled 90 percent of fine art auction market, which at the time was worth some $4 billion a year. Traditionally, auction houses make their profit by the commission they charge on auction sales. In good times, these commissions can range as high as 10 percent on some items, but in the early 1990s, the auction business was in a slump, with the supply of art for auction drying up. With Sotheby's and Christie's desperate for works of art, sellers played the two houses off against each other, driving commissions down to 2 percent or even lower.

To try to control this situation, Sotheby's CEO, Dede Brooks, met with her opposite number at Christie's, Christopher Davidge, in a series of clandestine meetings held in car parking lots that began in 1993. Brooks claims that she was acting on behalf of her boss, Alfred Taubman, the chairman and controlling shareholder of Sotheby's. According to Brooks, Taubman had agreed with the chairman of Christie's, Anthony Tennant, to work together in the weak auction market and limit price competition. In their meetings, Brooks and Davidge agreed to a fixed and nonnegotiable commission structure. Based on a sliding scale, the commission structure would range from 10 percent on a $100,000 item to 2 percent on a $5 million item. In effect, Brooks and Davidge were agreeing to eliminate price competition between them, thereby guaranteeing both auction houses higher

profits. The price-fixing agreement started in 1993 and continued unabated for six years until federal investigators uncovered the arrangement and brought charges against Sotheby's and Christie's.

With the deal out in the open, lawyers filed several class action lawsuits on behalf of sellers who had been defrauded by Sotheby's and Christie's. Ultimately, some 100,000 sellers signed on to the class action lawsuits, which the auction houses settled with a $512 million payment. The auction houses also pleaded guilty to price fixing and paid $45 million in fines to U.S. antitrust authorities. As for the key players, the chairman of Christie's, as a British subject, was able to avoid prosecution in the United States (price fixing is not an offense for which someone can be extradited). Christie's CEO, Davidge, struck a deal with prosecutors and in return for amnesty handed over incriminating documents to the authorities. Brooks also cooperated with federal prosecutors and avoided jail (in April 2002 she was sentenced to three years' probation, six months' home detention, 1,000 hours of community service, and a $350,000 fine). Taubman, ultimately isolated by all his former co-conspirators, was sentenced to a year in jail and fined $7.5 million.

Sources: S. Tully, "A House Divided," *Fortune,* December 18, 2000, pp. 264–275. J. Chaffin, "Sotheby's Ex CEO Spared Jail Sentence," *Financial Times,* April 30, 2002, p. 10. T. Thorncroft, "A Courtroom Battle of the Vanities," *Financial Times,* November 3, 2001, p. 3.

seems to have occurred at Enron, where an obsession with maximizing current profitability led some managers to engage in risky (and fraudulent) actions that ultimately led to the collapse of the company. This rather begs the question of why managers would behave in such risky behavior. Agency theory provides an answer and an explanation for what went on at Enron and other companies.

Agency Theory

Agency theory looks at the problems that can arise in a business relationship when one person delegates decision making authority to another. Agency theory offers a way of understanding why managers do not always act in the best interests of stakeholders.[14] Although agency theory was originally formulated to capture the relationship between management and stockholders, the basic principles have also been extended to cover the relationship with other key stakeholders, such as employees, as well as between different layers of management within a corporation.[15] Although the focus of attention in this section is on the relationship between senior management and stockholders, it should not be forgotten that some of the same language can be applied to the relationship between other stakeholders and top managers and between top management and lower levels of management.

Principal-Agent Relationships

The basic propositions of agency theory are relatively straightforward. First, an **agency relationship** is held to arise whenever one party delegates decision-making authority or control over resources to another. The **principal** is the person delegating authority, and the **agent** is the person to whom authority is delegated. The relationship between stockholders and senior managers is the classic example of an agency relationship. Stockholders, who are the *principals,* provide the company with risk capital, but they delegate control over that capital to senior managers, and particularly the CEO, who as their *agent* is expected to use that capital in a manner that is consistent with the best interests of stockholders. As we have seen, this means using that capital to maximize the company's long-run ROIC.

The agency relationship continues on down within the company. For example, in the large, complex multibusiness company, top managers cannot possibly make all important decisions, so they delegate some decision-making authority and control over capital resources to business unit (divisional) managers. Thus, just as senior managers such as the CEO are the *agents* of stockholders, business unit managers are the *agents* of the CEO (and in this context, the CEO is the *principal*). The CEO entrusts business unit managers to use the resources over which they have control in the most effective manner so that they maximize the ROIC of their units, which helps the CEO to make sure that he or she maximizes the ROIC of the entire company, thereby discharging agency obligation to stockholders. More generally, whenever managers delegate authority to managers below them in the hierarchy and give them the right to control resources, an agency relation is established.

The Agency Problem

The essence of the **agency problem** is that agents and principals may have different goals, and consequently, agents may pursue goals that are not in the best interests of their principals. Agents may be able to do this because there is an **information asymmetry** between the principal and the agent; agents almost always have more information about the resources they are managing than the principal does. Unscrupulous agents can take advantage of any information asymmetry to mislead principals and maximize their own interests at the expense of principals.

In the case of stockholders, the information asymmetry arises because they delegate decision-making authority to the CEO, their agent, who by virtue of his or her position inside the company is likely to know far more than stockholders do about the company's operations. Indeed, there may be certain information about the company that the CEO is unwilling to share with stockholders because it would also help competitors. In such a case, withholding some information from stockholders may be in their best interests. More generally, the CEO, involved in the day-to-day running of the company, is bound to have an information advantage over stockholders, just as the CEO's subordinates may well have an information advantage over the CEO with regard to the resources under their control.

The information asymmetry between principals and agents is not necessarily a bad thing, but it can make it difficult for principals to measure how well an agent is performing, and thus hold the agent accountable for how well he or she is using the entrusted resources. There is a certain amount of performance ambiguity inherent in the relationship between a principal and agent: principals cannot know for sure if the agent is acting in his or her best interests. They cannot know for sure if the agent is using the resources to which he or she has been entrusted as effectively and efficiently as possible. To an extent, principals have to *trust* the agent to do the right thing.

Of course, this trust is not blind: principals do put mechanisms in place whose purpose is to monitor agents, evaluate their performance, and if necessary, take corrective action. As we shall see shortly, the board of directors is one such mechanism, for in part the board exists to monitor and evaluate senior managers on behalf of stockholders. Other mechanisms serve a similar purpose. In the United States, the requirement that publicly owned companies regularly file detailed financial statements with the Securities and Exchange Commission (SEC) that are in accordance with generally agreed accounting principles (GAAP) exists to give stockholders consistent and detailed information about how well management is using the capital to which they have been entrusted. Similarly, internal control systems within a company are there to help the CEO make sure that subordinates are using the resources to which they have been entrusted as efficiently and effectively as possible.

Despite the existence of governance mechanisms and comprehensive measurement and control systems, a degree of information asymmetry will always remain between principals and agents, and there is always an element of trust involved in the relationship. Unfortunately, not all agents are worthy of this trust, and a minority will deliberately mislead principals for personal gain. The interests of principals and agents are not always the same; they diverge, and some agents may take advantage of information asymmetries to maximize their own interests at the expense of principals.

For example, some authors have argued that like many other people, senior managers are motivated by desires for status, power, job security, and income.[16] By virtue of their position within the company, certain managers, such as the CEO, can use their authority and control over corporate funds to satisfy these desires at the cost of returns to stockholders. CEOs might use their position to invest corporate funds in various perks that enhance their status—executive jets, lavish offices, and expense-paid trips to exotic locations—rather than investing those funds in ways that increase stockholder returns. Economists have termed such behavior *on-the-job consumption*.[17] Bill Agee provides us with an example of a CEO who appeared to engage in excessive on-the-job consumption (see Strategy in Action 11.1).

Besides engaging in on-the-job-consumption, CEOs, along with other senior managers, might satisfy their desires for greater income by using their influence or control over the board of directors to get the compensation committee of the board to grant such pay increases. Critics of U.S. industry claim that extraordinary pay has now become an endemic problem and that senior managers are enriching themselves at the expense of stockholders and other employees. They point out that CEO pay has been increasing far more rapidly than the pay of average workers, primarily due to very liberal stock option grants that enable a CEO to earn huge pay bonuses in a rising stock market, even if the company underperforms the market and competitors.[18] In 1950, when *Business Week* started its annual survey of CEO pay, the highest-paid executive was General Motors CEO Charles Wilson, whose $652,156 pay packet translates into $4.4 million in inflation-adjusted dollars in 2001. In contrast, the highest-paid executive in *Business Week*'s 2001 survey, Larry Ellison, the CEO of Oracle Corporation, earned $706.1 million, primarily from exercising stock options.[19] In 1980, the average CEO earned 42 times what the average blue collar-worker earned. By 1990, this figure had increased to 85 times. Today, the average CEO earns more than 400 times the pay of the average blue collar worker.[20]

What rankles critics is the size of some CEO pay packages and their apparent lack of relationship to company performance.[21] In 1998, for example, Disney CEO Michael Eisner earned $575 million, mostly in the form of stock options, despite the fact that Disney did not do particularly well that year and the stock price fell 10 percent. Similarly, Larry Ellison's $706.1 million pay packet came in a year when Oracle's stock price plunged. Another big gainer in 2001, Jozef Straus, earned $150 million from stock options in a year when the company he serves as CEO, JDS Uniphase, recorded a $50 billion loss related to the writing down of goodwill for companies acquired at premium prices during the booming 1990s. Critics feel that the size of these pay awards was out of all proportion to the achievement of the CEOs.[22] If so, this represents a clear example of the agency problem.

A further concern is that in trying to satisfy a desire for status, security, power, and income, a CEO might engage in *empire building*, buying many new businesses in an attempt to increase the size of the company through diversification.[23] Although such growth may do little to enhance the company's profitability, and thus stockholder returns, it increases the size of the empire under the CEO's control and, by extension, the CEO's status, power, security, and income (there is a strong relationship between company size and CEO pay). To quote Carl Icahn, a famous financier:

> Make no mistake, a strongly knit corporate aristocracy exists in America. The top man, what's more, usually finds expanding his power more important than rewarding owners [stockholders]. When Mobil and USX had excess cash, did they enrich shareholders? Of course not. They bought Marcor and Marathon— disastrous investments, but major increases in the size of the manor.[24]

Thus, instead of maximizing stockholder returns, in an example of the agency problem, some senior managers may trade long-run profitability for greater company growth by buying new businesses. Figure 11.3 graphs profitability against the rate of growth in company revenues. A company that does not grow is probably missing out on some profitable opportunities.[25] A moderate revenue growth rate of G^* allows a company to maximize profitability, generating a return of Π^*. Thus, a growth rate of G_0 in Figure 11.3 is not consistent with maximizing profitability ($\Pi_1 < \Pi^*$). However, attaining growth in excess of G_1 requires diversification into areas that the company knows little about. Consequently, it can be achieved only by sacrificing

FIGURE 11.3

The Tradeoff Between Profitability and Revenue Growth Rates

profitability (that is, past G_1, the investment required to finance further growth does not produce an adequate return and the company's profitability declines). Yet G_2 may be the growth rate favored by an empire-building CEO, for it will increase his or her power, status, and income. At this growth rate, profits are equal only to Π_2. Because $\Pi^* > \Pi_2$, a company growing at this rate is clearly not maximizing its profitability or the wealth of its stockholders. However, a growth rate of G_2 may be consistent with attaining managerial goals of power, status, and income.

For an example of this kind of excessive growth, consider once more the example of Tyco International, the subject of the *Opening Case* in Chapter 10. Whatever the motivation of the CEO, with hindsight it is clear that Tyco grew too fast, paid too much for its acquisitions, and took on too much debt to finance those acquisitions. Tyco's revenue growth rate was impressive, but the resulting debt burden hurt the company's profitability and stock price.

The agency problem is not confined to the relationship between senior managers and stockholders. It can also bedevil the relationship between the CEO and subordinates and between them and their subordinates. A subordinate might use control over information to distort the true performance of the unit under his control in order to enhance his pay, increase his job security, or make sure that his unit gets more than its fair share of company resources.[26] In the Enron case, the former CEO, Jeffrey Skilling, has claimed that he was ignorant of the dealings of his CFO, Andrew Fastow, who used the creation of off-balance-sheet partnerships to net some $30 million. If true, this implies that Fastow deliberately misled his boss in order to profit for himself, and as such this would be an excellent example of the agency problem between a top manager and subordinate within a company. One of the most dramatic examples of an agency problem within a company during the last decade is given in Strategy in Action 11.3. This looks at how a rogue trader, Nick Leeson, took advantage of his superiors' ignorance to take extreme risks in an attempt to maximize his own personal wealth and ended up bankrupting his employer, Barings Bank.

Confronted with the possibility of the agency problem, the challenge for principals is to (1) shape the behavior of agents so that they act in accordance with the goals set by principles, (2) reduce the information asymmetry between agents and principles, and (3) develop mechanisms for removing agents who do not act in accordance with the goals of principles. Principals try to deal with these challenges through a series of governance mechanisms.

Strategy in Action 11.3

The Agency Problem and the Collapse of Barings Bank

In February 1995, the world was shaken by the revelation that unauthorized derivatives trading by a twenty-seven-year-old Englishman, Nick Leeson, employed at the Singapore Office of Britain's oldest bank, Barings Plc, had amassed losses that amounted to $1.33 billion. The debacle resulted in the collapse of Barings and its purchase, for one pound sterling, by a Dutch bank, ING. So ended the history of a 233-year-old bank whose clients at the time of its collapse included Queen Elizabeth II of England.

Despite his youth, Leeson had been a highly successful trader for Barings in Asia and was viewed as the senior Barings trader in Singapore. In September 1994, he started to speculate on the volatility of Japan's Nikkei 255 stock index. His motives were to maximize the size of his bonus, which could have easily run into seven figures had his strategy been successful, and solidify his position as a major trader. His strategy involved simultaneously writing uncovered put and call options on Nikkei 255 futures. This procedure will make money for the option writer provided that the market stays within a relatively narrow trading range. When Leeson began his trades, the Nikkei was trading at around 19,000. Leeson's strategy made Barings money so long as the Nikkei stayed between 18,500 and 19,500. Once the Nikkei went outside this range, Barings started to lose large amounts of money: about $70 million for every 1 percent move above or below these limits. The loss was exacerbated by Leeson's aggressive use of leverage: he was writing the options using borrowed money.

At first, the strategy worked. Leeson may have earned as much as $150 million for Barings from this strategy by the end of 1994. However, the strategy started to fall apart when the Kobe earthquake struck on January 17, 1995. Following the earthquake, the Nikkei fell below 18,500. In an attempt to push the market back above 18,500, Leeson purchased Nikkei futures, again using borrowed money, and increasing the size of his bet. It didn't work. Leeson's position deteriorated further on January 23 when the Nikkei fell 1,000 points to under 17,800. Increasingly desperate, Leeson responded to the crisis by borrowing more money to continue purchasing Nikkei futures in what was to prove to be a futile attempt to prop up the Nikkei index. By late February 1995, Barings had accumulated index positions that effectively amounted to a $7 billion highly leveraged bet that the Nikkei index would recover—a bet that was wrong.

Leeson's actions did not go unnoticed by other traders in Singapore or executives at Barings Bank in London. However, Barings executives and other traders were under the impression that Leeson was acting on behalf of a major client—perhaps a big hedge fund. No one could conceive that the positions belonged to Barings. As for the cash required to purchase Nikkei futures, apparently much of this came from an account for a fictitious client that Leeson had set up as early as 1992. Into this account went some of Barings's own cash, along with all of the proceeds of Leeson's option sales, and some fictitious profits from falsified arbitrage deals. He then used this fictitious account to pay the costs of borrowing money to finance his trading positions. When the account was exhausted, Leeson turned to Barings in London, saying that he was executing trades on behalf of a major client who would settle up in a few days. Barings proved willing to send more money to their star trader in Singapore.

Bolstered by the arrival of additional funds from London, Leeson kept up the charade until February 23 when the cash flowing out to cover borrowing costs exceeded Barings's preset limits. With the Nikkei continuing to decline, Leeson realized that he could no longer carry on with the game. He hurriedly faxed a letter to Barings in London tendering his resignation, adding that he was sorry for the trouble he had caused, and along with his wife boarded a plane out of Singapore. The next day, shocked Barings executives informed the Bank of England that they were technically bankrupt. The liabilities from Leeson's trades already exceeded $800 million and were growing by the hour as the Nikkei index continued to tumble.

The collapse of Barings had much to do with a lack of internal management controls, which allowed Leeson to speculate on a massive scale using borrowed money. Leeson was able to get away with this because of the poor monitoring of his activities by Barings's senior managers in England. In July 1995, the Bank of England issued a report on the collapse of Barings. According to the bank, "Significant amounts were regularly remitted to BFS without any clear understanding on the part of Barings' management on whose behalf these monies were to be applied, and without any real demur." The Bank of England's report also cited a number of senior managers at Barings for failing to apply proper controls.

Leeson was later tracked down, arrested in Malaysia, and ultimately sentenced to a four-year jail term for fraud. In an interview he gave to the BBC from his jail cell, Leeson gave more insight into the collapse of Barings. Leeson said that he got away with his trading for so long because of the failure of key executives at Barings's London headquarters to understand the business he was engaged in and to look more closely into his activities: "The first day that I asked for funding there should have been massive alarm bells ringing. But senior people in London that were arranging these payments didn't understand the basic administration of futures and options. . . . They wanted to believe in the profits being reported, and therefore they weren't willing to question."

In a spectacular example of the agency problem, Leeson exploited the information asymmetry that existed between himself and senior managers to pursue his own interests, placing risky bets on the Nikkei stock market index that could have netted Leeson millions but in the event plunged Barings into bankruptcy and sent Leeson to jail.

Sources: N. Bray and G. Whitney, "Barings Collapse Tied to Wide Cast," *Wall Street Journal,* July 19, 1995, p. A5. T. Shale, "Why Barings Was Doomed," *Euromoney* (March 1995): 38–41. "A Fallen Star," *Economist,* March 4, 1995, pp. 19–21.

Governance Mechanisms

Governance mechanisms are mechanisms that principals put in place to align incentives between principals and agents and to monitor and control agents. The purpose of governance mechanisms is to reduce the scope and frequency of the agency problem: to help ensure that agents act in a manner that is consistent with the best interests of their principals. In this section, the primary focus is on the governance mechanisms that exist to align the interests of senior managers (as agents) with their principals, stockholders. It should not be forgotten, however, that governance mechanisms also exist to align the interests of business unit managers with those of their superiors, and so on down within the organization.

Here we look at four main types of governance mechanisms for aligning stockholder and management interests: the board of directors, stock-based compensation, financial statements, and the takeover constraint. The section closes with a discussion of governance mechanism within a company to align the interest of senior and lower-level managers.

The Board of Directors

The board of directors is the centerpiece of the corporate governance system in the United States and the United Kingdom. Board members are directly elected by stockholders, and under corporate law they represent the stockholders' interests in the company. Hence, the board can be held legally accountable for the company's actions. Its position at the apex of decision making within the company allows it to monitor corporate strategy decisions and ensure that they are consistent with stockholder interests. If the board's sense is that corporate strategies are not in the best interest of stockholders, it can apply sanctions, such as voting against management nominations to the board of directors or submitting its own nominees. In addition, the board has the legal authority to hire, fire, and compensate corporate employees, including, most importantly, the CEO.[27] The board is also responsible for making sure that audited financial statements of the company present a true picture of its financial situation. Thus, the board exists to reduce the information asymmetry between stockholders and managers and to monitor and control management actions on behalf of stockholders.

The typical board of directors is composed of a mix of inside and outside directors. *Inside directors* are senior employees of the company, such as the CEO. They are required on the board because they have valuable information about the company's activities. Without such information, the board cannot adequately perform its monitoring function. But because insiders are full-time employees of the company, their interests tend to be aligned with those of management. Hence, outside directors are needed to bring objectivity to the monitoring and evaluation processes. *Outside directors* are not full-time employees of the company. Many of them are full-time professional directors who hold positions on the boards of several companies. The need to maintain a reputation as competent outside directors gives them an incentive to perform their tasks as objectively and effectively as possible.[28]

There is little doubt that many boards perform their assigned functions admirably. For example, one factor that led to the dismissal of Morrison Knudsen's CEO, Bill Agee, was that his strategies lost the support of the board (see Strategy in Action 11.1). Similarly, when the board of Sotheby's discovered that the company had been engaged in price fixing with Christie's, board members moved quickly to oust both the CEO and the chairman of the company (see Strategy in Action 11.2). But not all boards perform as well as they should. The board of Enron signed off on that company's audited financial statements, which were later shown to be grossly misleading.

Critics of the existing governance system charge that inside directors often dominate the outsiders on the board. Insiders can use their position within the management hierarchy to exercise control over what kind of company-specific information the board receives. Consequently, they can present information in a way that puts them in a favorable light. In addition, insiders have the advantage of intimate knowledge of the company's operations and because of their superior knowledge and control over information are sources of power, they may be better positioned than outsiders to influence boardroom decision making. The board may become the captive of insiders and merely rubber-stamp management decisions instead of guarding stockholder interests.

Some observers contend that many boards are dominated by the company CEO, particularly when the CEO is also the chairman of the board.[29] To support this view, they point out that both inside and outside directors are often the personal nominees of the CEO. The typical inside director is subordinate to the CEO in the company's hierarchy and therefore unlikely to criticize the boss. Because outside directors are frequently the CEO's nominees as well, they can hardly be expected to evaluate the CEO objectively. Thus, the loyalty of the board may be biased toward the CEO, not the stockholders. Moreover, a CEO who is also chairman of the board may be able to control the agenda of board discussions in such a manner as to deflect any criticisms of his or her leadership. This was a problem in the case of Bill Agee: he was both CEO and chairman of the board at Morrison Knudsen.

Today, there are clear signs that many corporate boards are moving away from merely rubber-stamping top management decisions and are beginning to play a much more active role in corporate governance. One catalyst has been an increase in the number of lawsuits filed by stockholders against board members. The trend started in the 1980s when a Delaware court ruled that the directors of Trans Union Corporation had been too quick to accept a takeover bid. The court held the directors personally liable for the difference between the offer they accepted and the price the company might have fetched in a sale. The directors then agreed to make up the $23.5 million difference. Since that ruling, a number of major lawsuits have been filed by stockholders against board members. Among them are suits directed against board members at Holly Farms, Northrop Corp., Lincoln Savings & Loan, Lotus Development Corp., and RJR Nabisco.[30]

Another catalyst has been the growing willingness of some institutional investors, such as the managers of large pension funds or index-linked mutual funds, to use their stockholding in a company, and the voting power it gives them, to gain seats on the board of directors, pressure managers to adopt policies that improve the performance of the company's stock, and pressure the board to replace the CEOs of poorly performing companies. For example, in the mid-1990s, officials of New York City's five major pension funds stated that they would nominate three candidates for seats on the board of Ethyl Corp., a maker of petroleum additives that has performed poorly in recent years. Their objective was to use these board seats to push management harder to improve the performance of Ethyl and, hence, the value of their stock in Ethyl. The pension funds were ultimately successful in getting their nominees on Ethyl's board.[31]

Spurred on by the threat of legal action and pressures from powerful institutional shareholders, an increasing number of boards have started to assert their independence from company management in general and from corporate CEOs in particular. Since the mid-1990s, boards of directors have engineered the removal or resignation of CEOs at a number of major companies, including American Express,

Compaq Computer, Digital Equipment, General Motors, IBM, and Sunbeam. Another trend of some significance is the increasing tendency for outside directors to be made chairs of the board. By the late 1990s, according to estimates from the National Association of Corporate Directors, 40 to 50 percent of big companies had an outside director as chair, up from less than half that figure in 1990.[32] Such appointments limit the ability of corporate insiders, and particularly of the CEO, to exercise control over the board. It is notable that the removal of Robert Stempel as the CEO of General Motors in the late 1990s followed the appointment of an outside director, John Smale, as chairman of the GM board. Still, when all is said and done, it must be recognized that boards of directors do not work as well as they should, and other mechanisms are need to align the interests of stockholders and managers.

Stock-Based Compensation

According to agency theory, one of the best ways to reduce the scope of the agency problem is for principals to establish incentives for agents to behave in their best interest through pay-for-performance systems. In the case of stockholders and top managers, stockholders can encourage top managers to pursue strategies that maximize a company's long-run ROIC, and thus the gains from holding its stock, by linking the pay of those managers to the performance of the stock price.

The most common pay-for-performance system has been to give managers stock options: the right to buy the company's shares at a predetermined (strike) price at some point in the future, usually within ten years of the grant date. Typically, the strike price is the price that the stock was trading at when the option was originally granted. The idea behind stock options is to motivate managers to adopt strategies that increase the share price of the company, for in doing so they will also increase the value of their own stock options.

Many top managers often earn huge bonuses from exercising stock options that were granted several years previously. While not denying that these options do motivate managers to improve company performance, critics claim that they are often too generous. A particular cause for concern is that stock options are often granted at such low strike prices that the CEO can hardly fail to make a significant amount of money by exercising them, even if the company underperforms the stock market by a significant margin.

Other critics, including the famous investor Warren Buffett, complain that huge stock option grants increase the outstanding number of shares in a company and therefore dilute the equity of stockholders; accordingly, they should be shown in company accounts as an expense against profits. However, under current accounting regulations, stock options, unlike wages and salaries, are not expensed. Buffett has noted that when his investment company, Berkshire Hathaway, "acquires an option issuing company, we promptly substitute a cash compensation plan having an economic value equivalent to that of the previous option plan. The acquiree's true compensation cost is therefore brought out of the closet and charged, as it should be, against earnings."[33] Buffett's point is that stock options are accounted for incorrectly in company financial statements. Table 11.1 details the amount that reported profits would have been reduced during the 1996–2000 period for several high-profile companies if stock options had been accounted for as an expense and deducted from profits. As can be seen, the impact would have been to depress profits severely at some of these companies, and by extension, ROIC.

Several academic studies suggest that stock-based compensation schemes for executives, such as stock options, can align management and stockholder interests. For instance, one study found that managers were more likely to consider the effects

TABLE 11.1

How Options Skew the Bottom Line

Company	Reduction in Net Profit If Options Had Been Expensed
AOL Time Warner	75 percent
Viacom	66 percent
NVIDIA	40 percent
MedImmune	31 percent
Lucent	30 percent
Pharmacia	28 percent
Cisco Systems	26 percent
Boise Cascade	17 percent

Source: D. Henry and M. Conlin, "Too Much of a Good Incentive?" *Business Week*, March 4, 2002, pp. 38–39.

of their acquisition decisions on stockholder returns if they themselves were significant shareholders.[34] According to another study, managers who were significant stockholders were less likely to pursue strategies that would maximize the size of the company rather than its profitability.[35] More generally, it is difficult to argue with the proposition that the chance to get rich from exercising stock options is the primary reason for the fourteen-hour days and six-day work weeks that many employees of fast-growing companies put in.

In summary, in theory, stock options and other stock-based compensation methods are a good idea; in practice, they have been abused. To limit the abuse, Alan Greenspan, chairman of the U.S. Federal Reserve, has joined Warren Buffett in arguing that accounting rules should be changed to treat options as an expense that must be charged against profits. Some companies have taken matters into their own hands even without a change in accounting rules. Microsoft, for example, routinely issues two sets of financial accounts: one in which options are expensed and one in which they are not. Boeing issues one set of accounts in which options are counted as an expense. The aerospace company has also gone an important step further in an effort to align management and stockholder interests, issuing what it calls "performance share" units that are convertible into common stock only if its stock appreciates at least 10 percent annually for five years. Similarly, Unilever has created a system in which stock options do not vest unless the company achieves total shareholder returns over a rolling three-year period that are above the median for the group of twenty peer companies, including Coca-Cola, Nestlé, and Procter & Gamble. What all of these companies are trying to do in their own way is to limit the free ride that many holders of stock options enjoyed during the boom of the 1990s, while continuing to maintain a focus on aligning management and stockholder interests through stock-based compensation schemes.[36]

Financial Statements and Auditors

Publicly trading companies in the United States are required to file quarterly and annual reports with the SEC that are prepared according to GAAP. The purpose of this requirement is to give consistent, detailed, and accurate information about how efficiently and effectively the agents of stockholders, the managers, are running the company. To make sure that managers do not misrepresent this financial information, the SEC also requires that the accounts be audited by an independent and accredited accounting firm. Similar regulations exist in most other developed nations. If the system works as intended, stockholders can have a lot of faith that the information contained in financial statements accurately reflects the state of affairs at a company. Among other things, such information can enable a stockholder to calculate the profitability (ROIC) of a company in which she invests and to compare its ROIC against that of competitors.

Unfortunately, in the United States at least, this system has not been working as intended. Although the vast majority of companies do file accurate information in their financial statements and although most auditors do a good job of reviewing that information, there is substantial evidence that a minority of companies have abused the system, aided in part by the compliance of auditors. This was clearly an issue at Enron, where the CFO and others misrepresented the true financial state of the company to investors by creating off-balance-sheet partnerships that hid the true state of Enron's indebtedness from public view. Enron's auditor, Arthur Andersen, also apparently went along with this deception in direct violation of its fiduciary duty.

There have been numerous examples in recent years of managers' gaming financial statements to present a distorted picture of their company's finances to investors. The typical motive has been to inflate the earnings or revenues of a company, thereby generating investor enthusiasm and propelling the stock price higher, which gives managers an opportunity to cash in stock option grants for huge personal gain, obviously at the expense of stockholders who have been mislead by the reports. Another alleged example of such behavior is given in Strategy in Action 11.4, which discusses how top managers at Computer Associates may have managed that company's financial statements in order to present a rosy picture and cash in very lucrative stock awards.

The gaming of financial statements by companies such as Enron and allegedly Computer Associates raises serious questions about the accuracy of the information contained in audited financial statements. First, it would appear that GAAPs are loose enough that unscrupulous managers can manipulate them to their advantage, at the expense of other stakeholder groups. Clearly, there may be need for reform here to tighten up regulations. For example, the regulation that allows companies to accumulate debt off balance sheet in special-purpose entities is clearly open to abuse, as the Enron debacle proves, and should be changed. Stockholders, bondholders, and employees have a right to know how indebted the company is, and managers have an obligation to report this, not hide debt in a special-purpose entity.

Second, the auditors are apparently not always doing their job. An explanation can be found in the conflict of interest that many auditing companies face, for in addition to an auditing business, many big accounting firms also have a lucrative consulting business with the very companies whose accounts they are required to audit in an impartial fashion. The desire to continue to cash in on lucrative consulting contracts, some claim, is why auditors may turn a blind eye to questionable accounting practices at a company. Again, fixing this problem may require reform, and in particular, the separation of auditing and consulting businesses into different companies.

Finally, the proliferation of accounting problems raises questions once more about how well boards of directors are discharging their fiduciary duty to stockholders. It is the board that appoints the auditors and is meant to ensure that the auditors are thorough. The problem is that many boards are still dominated by insiders, and when that is the case, the independence of the board can be questioned. Clearly, fix-

Strategy in Action   11.4

Did Computer Associates Inflate Revenues to Enrich Managers?

Computer Associates is one of the world's largest software companies. During the 1990s, its stock price appreciated at a rapid rate, driven in large part by surging revenues and a commensurate rise in profits. Because its revenues were growing more rapidly than those of rivals during the late 1990s, investors assumed that the company was gaining market share and that high profitability would follow, so they bid up the price of the company's stock. The senior managers of Computer Associates were major beneficiaries of this process.

Under a generous incentive program given to the company's three top managers by the board of directors—Charles Wang, then CEO and chairman of the board, Sanjay Kumar, the chief operating officer, and Russell Artzt, the chief technology officer—if the stock price stayed above $53.13 for sixty days, they would receive a special incentive stock award amounting to some 20 million shares. In May 1998, Kumar announced that Computer Associates had "record" revenues and earnings for the quarter. The stock price surged over the $53.13 trigger and stayed there long enough for all three to receive the special incentive stock award, then valued at $1.1 billion.

In late July 1998, after all three had received the award, Kumar announced that the effect of Asian economic turmoil and the year 2000 bug "leads us to believe that our revenue and earnings growth will slow over the next few quarters." The stock price promptly fell from the high 50s to under $40 a share. What followed was a series of class action lawsuits, undertaken on behalf of stockholders, that claimed that management had misled stockholders to enrich themselves. As a result of the lawsuits, the three were compelled to give back some of their gains, and the size of the award was reduced to 4.5 million shares. Wang stepped down as CEO, although he retained his position as chairman of the board, and Kumar became the CEO.

This was not the end of matters, however, for Computer Associates had attracted the attention of both the Justice Department and the SEC, which launched a joint investigation into the company's accounting practices. By 2002, they were reportedly focusing on a little-noticed action the company had taken in May 2000 to reduce its revenues by 10 percent, or $1.76 billion, below what it had previously reported for the three fiscal years that ended March 2000. The downward revisions, detailed in the company's 10K filings with the SEC, retroactively took hundreds of millions of dollars away from the top line in the fourteen months preceding the May 1998 stock award to senior managers, including some $513 million for the year ending March 1998. According to the company, earnings were unaffected by the revision because the lost revenue was offset by a commensurate downward revision of expenses. The downward revision reportedly came at the urging of auditor KPMG, which replaced Ernst & Young as the company's accountant in June 1999.

While the investigation was still ongoing in mid-2002, the implication that some observers were drawing was that Computer Associates deliberately overstated its revenues in the period prior to May 1998 to enrich the three top managers. The losers in this process were stockholders who purchased shares at the inflated price and longer-term shareholders who saw the value of their holdings diluted by the stock awarded to Wang, Kumar, and Artzt. In a statement issued after a report of the ongoing investigation was published in the *Wall Street Journal,* Computer Associates stated that it changed how it classified revenue and expenses at the advice of its auditors. "We continue to believe CA has acted appropriately," the company said. "This change in presentation had no impact on reported earnings, earnings per share, or cash flows."

Sources: J. Guidera, "Probe of Computer Associates Centers on Firm's Revenues," *Wall Street Journal,* May 20, 2002, pp. A3, 15. Ronna Abramson, "Computer Associates Probe Focus on 1998, 1999 Revenue," *The Street.Com,* May 20, 2002.

---

ing this problem requires the establishment of boards that are dominated by outside members and where the chairman of the board is not a company insider.

The government took some tentative steps toward reforming the corporate governance system in the United States in July 2002 when President Bush signed into law a measure that set up a new oversight board for accounting firms, required CEOs and CFOs to endorse their company's financial statements, and barred companies from hiring the same accounting firm for auditing and consulting services. However, many critics felt that this legislation did not go far enough and that it should have contained other elements, such as a requirement that stock options be treated as an expense. Others complained that the problem was not a lack of legislation, but that existing legislation had not been enforced aggressively enough by the Justice Department. To be fair though, by mid-2002 it was clear that the Justice Department was moving aggressively to bring criminal fraud charges against some of the key figures in corporate accounting scandals.

The Takeover Constraint

Given the imperfections in corporate governance mechanisms, it is clear that the agency problem may still exist at some companies. However, stockholders still have some residual power, for they can always sell their shares. If they start doing so in large numbers, the price of the company's shares will decline. If the share price falls far enough, the company might be worth less on the stock market than the book value of its assets. At this point, it may become an attractive acquisition target and runs the risk of being purchased by another enterprise, against the wishes of the target company's management.

The risk of being acquired by another company is known as the **takeover constraint.** The takeover constraint limits the extent to which managers can pursue strategies and take actions that put their own interests above those of stockholders. If they ignore stockholder interests and the company is acquired, senior managers typically lose their independence and probably their jobs as well. So the threat of takeover can constrain management action and limit the worst excesses of the agency problem.

During the 1980s and early 1990s, the threat of takeover was often enforced by **corporate raiders:** individuals or corporations that buy up large blocks of shares in companies that they think are pursuing strategies inconsistent with maximizing stockholder wealth. Corporate raiders argue that if these underperforming companies pursued different strategies, they could create more wealth for stockholders. Raiders buy stock in a company either to take over the business and run it more efficiently, or to precipitate a change in the top management, replacing the existing team with one more likely to maximize stockholder returns. Raiders are motivated not by altruism but by gain. If they succeed in their takeover bid, they can institute strategies that create value for stockholders, including themselves. Even if a takeover bid fails, raiders can still earn millions, for their stockholdings will typically be bought out by the defending company for a hefty premium. Called **greenmail,** this source of gain stirred much controversy and debate about its benefits. While some claim that the threat posed by raiders has had a salutary effect on enterprise performance by pushing corporate management to run their companies better, others claim there is little evidence of this.[37]

Although the incidence of hostile takeover bids has fallen off significantly since the early 1990s, this should not be taken to imply that the takeover constraint is no longer operating. Unique circumstances exist in the early 2000s that have made it more difficult to execute hostile takeovers. The boom years of the 1990s left many corporations with excessive debt (corporate America entered the new century with record levels of debt on its balance sheets), which limits the ability of companies to finance acquisitions, particularly hostile acquisitions, which are often particularly expensive. In addition, the market valuations of many companies got so out of line with underlying fundamentals during the stock market bubble of the 1990s that even after a substantial fall in certain segments of the stock market, such as the technology sector, valuations are still high relative to historic norms, making the hostile acquisition of even poorly run and unprofitable companies expensive. However, takeovers tend to go in cycles, and it seems likely that once excesses are worked out of the stock market and worked off corporate balance sheets, the takeover constraint will begin to reassert itself. It should be remembered that the takeover constraint is the governance mechanism of last resort and is often invoked only when other governance mechanisms have failed.

Governance Mechanisms Inside a Company

So far this section has focused on the governance mechanisms designed to reduce the agency problem that potentially exists between stockholders and managers. Agency relationships also exist within a company, and the agency problem can thus arise *between* levels of management. In this section, we explore how the agency problem can be reduced within a company by using two complementary governance mechanisms to align the incentives and behavior of employees with those of upper-level management: strategic control systems and incentive systems.

Strategic Control Systems. Strategic control systems are the primary governance mechanisms established within a company to reduce the scope of the agency problem between levels of management. These systems are the formal target setting, measurement, and feedback systems that allow managers to evaluate whether a company is executing the strategies necessary to maximize its long-run ROIC and, in particular, whether the company is achieving superior efficiency, quality, innovation, and customer responsiveness. They are discussed in more detail in subsequent chapters.

The purpose of strategic control systems is to (1) establish standards and targets against which performance can be measured, (2) create systems for measuring and monitoring performance on a regular basis, (3) compare actual performance against the established targets, and (4) evaluate results and take corrective action if necessary. In governance terms, their purpose is to make sure that lower-level managers, as the agents of top managers, are acting in a way that is consistent with top managers' goals, which should be to maximize the wealth of stockholders, subject to legal and ethical constraints.

One increasingly influential model that guides managers through the process of creating the right kind of strategic control systems to enhance organizational performance is the balanced scorecard model.[38] According to the **balanced scorecard model,** traditionally managers have primarily used financial measures of performance such as return on invested capital to measure and evaluate organizational performance. Financial information is extremely important, but it is not enough by itself. If managers are to obtain a true picture of organizational performance, financial information must be supplemented with performance measures that indicate how well an organization has been achieving the four building blocks of competitive advantage: efficiency, quality, innovation, and responsiveness to customers. This is so because financial results simply inform strategic managers about the results of decisions they have *already taken;* the other measures balance this picture of performance by informing managers about how accurately the organization has in place the building blocks that drive *future performance.*[39]

One version of the way the balanced scorecard operates is presented in Figure 11.4. Based on an organization's mission and goals, strategic managers develop a set of strategies to build competitive advantage to achieve these goals. They then establish an organizational structure to use resources to obtain a competitive advantage.[40] To evaluate how well the strategy and structure are working, managers develop specific

FIGURE 11.4

A Balanced Scorecard
Approach

performance measures that assess how well the four building blocks of competitive
advantage are being achieved:

- *Efficiency* can be measured by the level of production costs, the productivity of
  labor (such as the employee hours needed to make a product), the productivity of
  capital (such as revenues per dollar invested in property, plant, and equipment),
  and the cost of raw materials.

- *Quality* can be measured by the number of rejects, the number of defective products returned from customers, and the level of product reliability over time.

- *Innovation* can be measured by the number of new products introduced, the percentage of revenues generated from new products in a defined period, the time
  taken to develop the next generation of new products versus the competition, and
  the productivity of R&D (i.e., how much R&D spending is required to produce a
  successful product).

- *Responsiveness to customers* can be measured by the number of repeat customers,
  customer defection rates, level of on-time delivery to customers, and level of customer service.

As Kaplan and Norton, the developers of this approach suggest, "Think of the balanced scorecard as the dials and indicators in an airplane cockpit. For the complex
task of navigating and flying an airplane, pilots need detailed information about
many aspects of the flight. They need information on fuel, air speed, altitude, learning, destination, and other indicators that summarize the current and predicted environment. Reliance on one instrument can be fatal. Similarly, the complexity of
managing an organization today requires that managers be able to view performance
in several areas simultaneously."[41]

The way in which managers' ability to build a competitive advantage translates
into organizational performance is then measured using financial measures such as
the return on invested capital, the return on sales, and the capital turnover ratio (see
Chapter 3). Based on an evaluation of the complete set of measures in the balanced
scorecard, strategic managers are in a good position to reevaluate the company's mission and goals and take corrective action to rectify problems, limit the agency problem, or exploit new opportunities by changing the organization's strategy and
structure—which is the purpose of strategic control.

Employee Incentives. Control systems alone may not be sufficient to align incentives between stockholders, senior management, and the rest of the organization. To help do this, positive incentive systems are often put into place to motivate employees to work toward goals that are central to maximizing long-run ROIC. As already noted, employee stock ownership plans (ESOP) are one form of positive incentive, as are stock option grants. In the 1990s, ESOPs and stock ownership grants got pushed down deep within many organizations. At Microsoft, for example, all full-time employees receive stock options, and the amount of options they receive is determined by their performance evaluation in the prior year. In addition, all full-time employees are eligible to enroll in the company's ESOP. The logic behind such systems is straightforward: recognizing that the stock price, and therefore their own wealth, is dependent on the profitability of the company, employees will work toward maximizing profitability.

In addition to stock-based compensation systems, employee compensation can also be tied to goals that are linked to the attainment of superior efficiency, quality, innovation, and customer responsiveness. For example, the bonus pay of a manufacturing employee might depend on attaining quality and productivity targets, which if reached will lower the costs of the company, increase customer satisfaction, and boost the ROIC. Similarly, the bonus pay of a salesperson might be dependent on surpassing sales targets, and of an R&D employee on the success of new products she had a hand in developing.

Ethics and Strategy

The Enron story reviewed in the *Opening Case,* along with several other examples considered in this chapter, all underline the need for managers to behave in an ethical manner when making strategic decisions. From a management perspective, an **ethical decision** is one that reasonable or typical stakeholders would find acceptable because it aids stakeholders, the organization, or society. By contrast, an **unethical decision** is a decision a manager would prefer to disguise or hide from other people because it enables a company or a particular individual to gain at the expense of society or other stakeholders. There seems to be little question, for example, that by disguising the true state of the company to important stakeholders, such as stockholders, bondholders, and employees, some senior managers at Enron were able to push the value of the company's stock higher than would otherwise have been the case, enabling those same managers to profit from the sale of Enron stock they owned. This section looks at the issue of ethics and strategy and identifies some guiding principles that can help managers to make strategic decisions that are ethical.

The Purpose of Business Ethics

The purpose of business ethics is not so much to teach the difference between right and wrong as to give people the tools for dealing with moral complexity—tools that they use to identify and think through the moral implications of strategic decisions.[42] Most of us already have a good sense of what is right and wrong. The problem, however, is that although most managers rigorously adhere to such moral principles in their private life, some fail to apply them in their professional life, occasionally with disastrous consequences.

The sorry history of Manville Corporation illustrates such failure. Two decades ago, Manville (then Johns Manville) was solid enough to be included among the giants of U.S. industry. By 1989, 80 percent of the equity of Manville was owned by a trust representing people who had sued the company for liability in connection with one of its principal former products, asbestos. More than forty years ago, information began to reach the medical department of Johns Manville—and through it the company's managers—suggesting that inhalation of asbestos particles was a major cause of asbestosis, a fatal lung disease. Manville's managers suppressed the research. Moreover, as a matter of company policy, they apparently decided to conceal the information from affected employees, and the company's medical staff collaborated in the cover-up. Somehow, managers at Manville persuaded themselves that it was more important to cover up the situation than to take steps to improve working conditions and find safer ways to handle asbestos. They calculated that the cost of improving working conditions was greater than the cost of health insurance to cover those who became ill, and so the best "economic" decision was to conceal information from employees.[43]

The key to understanding the Manville story is the realization that the men and women at Manville who participated in the cover-up were not amoral monsters but just ordinary people. Most of them would probably never dream of breaking the law or of physically harming anyone. And yet they consciously made a decision that led directly to great human suffering and death. What seemed to have occurred was that the decision to suppress information was considered on purely economic grounds. Its moral dimension was ignored. Somehow the managers were able to convince themselves that they were engaged in making a rational business decision that should be subjected to an economic cost-benefit analysis. Ethical considerations never entered into this calculation. Such behavior is possible only in an environment where business decisions are viewed as having no ethical component. But as the Manville example shows, business decisions *do* have an ethical component.

The task of business ethics, therefore, is to make two central points: (1) business decisions have an ethical component and (2) managers must weigh the ethical implications of strategic decisions before choosing a course of action. Had managers at Manville been trained to think through the ethical implications of their decision, it is unlikely that they would have chosen the same course of action.

Shaping the Ethical Climate of an Organization

To foster awareness that strategic decisions have an ethical dimension, a company must establish an organizational climate that emphasizes the importance of ethics. This requires at least three steps. First, top managers have to use their leadership position to incorporate an ethical dimension into the values they stress. At Hewlett Packard, for example, Bill Hewlett and David Packard, the company's founders, propagated a set of values known as the HP Way. These values, which shape the way business is conducted both within and by the corporation, have an important ethical component. Among other things, they stress the need for confidence in and respect for people, open communication, and concern for the individual employee. Had these values been operational at Manville, they would have helped managers there avoid their catastrophic mistake.

Second, ethical values must be incorporated into the company's mission statement. Third—and this is most important—ethical values must be acted on. Top managers have to implement hiring, firing, and incentive systems that explicitly recognize the importance of adhering to ethical values in strategic decision making. At Hewlett Packard, for example, it has been said that although it is difficult for employees to lose their job (because of the concern for individual employees), nothing gets an employee fired more quickly than violating the ethical norms of the company as articulated in the HP Way.[44] In contrast, although Enron did have a code of ethics that explicitly incorporated ethical values into the company's mission statement, it is very clear that several of the senior managers did not act on those values, and in fact took actions that were directly counter to them.

Thinking Through Ethical Problems

Besides establishing the right kind of ethical climate in an organization, managers must be able to think through the ethical implications of strategic decisions in a systematic way. Philosophers have debated for centuries about the specific criteria that should be used to determine whether decisions are ethical or unethical. Three models of what determines whether a decision is ethical—the *utilitarian, moral rights,* and *justice* models—are summarized in Table 11.2. In theory, each model offers a different and complementary way of determining whether a decision or behavior is ethical, and all three models should be used to sort out the ethics of a particular course of action. Ethical issues, however, are seldom clear-cut, and the interests of different stakeholders often conflict, so it is frequently extremely difficult for a decision maker to use these models to ascertain the most ethical course of action. For this reason,

TABLE 11.2

Comparing Utilitarian, Moral Rights, and Justice

Model	Managerial Implications	Problems for Managers
Utilitarian model: An ethical decision is one that produces the greatest good for the greatest number of people.	Managers should compare and contrast alternative courses of action based on the benefits and costs of these alternatives for different organizational stakeholder groups. They should choose the course of action that provides the most benefits to stakeholders. For example, managers should locate a new manufacturing plant at the place that will most benefit its stakeholders.	How do managers decide on the relative importance of each stakeholder group? How are managers to measure the benefits and harms to each stakeholder group precisely? For example, how do managers choose among the interests of stockholders, workers, and customers?
Moral rights model: An ethical decision is one that best maintains and protects the fundamental rights and privileges of the people affected by it. For example, ethical decisions protect people's rights to freedom, life and safety, privacy, free speech, and freedom of conscience.	Managers should compare and contrast alternative courses of action based on the effect of these alternatives on stakeholders' rights. They should choose the course of action that best protects stakeholders' rights. For example, decisions that would involve significant harm to the safety or health of employees or customers are unethical.	If a decision will protect the rights of some stakeholders and hurt the rights of others, how do managers choose which stakeholder rights to protect? For example, in deciding whether it is ethical to snoop on an employee, does an employee's right to privacy outweigh an organization's right to protect its property or the safety of other employees?
Justice model: An ethical decision is one that distributes benefits and harm among stakeholders in a fair, equitable, or impartial way.	Managers should compare and contrast alternative courses of action based on the degree to which the action will promote a fair distribution of outcomes. For example, employees who are similar in their level of skill, performance, or responsibility should receive the same kind of pay. The allocation of outcomes should not be based on arbitrary differences such as gender, race, or religion.	Managers must learn not to discriminate among people because of observable differences in their appearance or behavior. Managers must also learn how to use fair procedures to determine how to distribute outcomes to organizational members. For example, managers must not give people they like bigger raises than they give to people they do not like or bend the rules to help their favorites.

many experts on ethics propose a practical guide to determine whether a decision or behavior is ethical.[45] A decision is probably acceptable on ethical grounds if a manager can answer yes to each of these questions:

1. Does my decision fall within the accepted values or standards that typically apply in the organizational environment?

2. Am I willing to see the decision communicated to all stakeholders affected by it—for example, by having it reported in newspapers or on television?

3. Would the people with whom I have a significant personal relationship, such as family members, friends, or even managers in other organizations, approve of the decision?

To think through ethical problems, several authors have recommended a four-step process.[46] In Step 1, managers must identify which stakeholders the decision would affect and in what ways. Most important, they need to determine whether the proposed decision would violate the rights of any stakeholders. The term **rights** refers to the fundamental entitlements of a stakeholder. For example, we might argue that the right to information about health risks in the workplace is a fundamental entitlement of employees. It is an entitlement that Manville ignored.

Step 2 involves judging the ethics of the proposed strategic decision given the information gained in Step 1. This judgment should be guided by various moral principles that should not be violated. The principles might be those articulated in a corporate mission statement or other company documents (such as Hewlett Packard's HP Way). In addition, certain moral principles that we have adopted as members of society—for instance, the prohibition on stealing—should not be violated. The judgment at this stage will also be guided by the decision rule that is chosen to assess the proposed strategic decision. Although long-run profit maximization is rightly the decision rule that most companies stress, it should be applied subject to the constraint that no moral principles are violated.

Step 3, establishing moral intent, means that the company must resolve to place moral concerns ahead of other concerns in cases where either the rights of stakeholders or key moral principles have been violated. At this stage, input from top management might be particularly valuable. Without the encouragement of top managers, middle-level managers might tend to place the narrow economic interests of the company before the interests of stakeholders. They might do so in the (usually erroneous) belief that top managers favor such an approach. Step 4 requires the company to engage in ethical behavior.

Summary of Chapter

1. The causes of persistently poor company performance include poor management, a high cost structure, inadequate differentiation, extensive diversification, structural shifts in demand, the emergence of powerful new competitors, and organization inertia.

2. Instituting a successful turnaround strategy requires new leadership, a change of strategy, and a change in organization.

3. Stakeholders are individuals or groups that have an interest, claim, or stake in the company, in what it does, and in how well it performs.

4. Stakeholders are in an exchange relationship with the company. They supply the organization with important resources (or contributions) and in exchange expect its interests to be satisfied (by inducements).

5. A company cannot always satisfy the claims of all stakeholders. The goals of different groups may conflict. The company must identify the most important

stakeholders and give highest priority to pursuing strategies that satisfy their needs.

6. A company's stockholders are its legal owners and the providers of risk capital, a major source of the capital resources that allow a company to operate its business. As such, they have a unique role among stakeholder groups.

7. Maximizing long-run ROIC is the route to maximizing returns to stockholders, and it is also consistent with satisfying the claims of several other key stakeholder groups.

8. Although maximizing long-run ROIC is the best way to satisfy the claims of several key stakeholder groups, a company has the obligation to do so within the limits set by the law and in a manner consistent with societal expectations.

9. An agency relationship is held to arise whenever one party delegates decision-making authority or control over resources to another.

10. The essence of the agency problem is that the interests of principals and agents are not always the same, and some agents may take advantage of information asymmetries to maximize their own interests at the expense of principals.

11. A number of governance mechanisms serve to limit the agency problem. These include the board of direc-

tors, stock-based compensation schemes, and the threat of a takeover.

12. Many strategic decisions have an ethical dimension. Any action by a company inevitably has an impact on the welfare of its stakeholders.

13. The purpose of business ethics is not so much to teach the difference between right and wrong, but to give people the tools for dealing with moral complexity– for identifying and thinking through the moral implications of strategic decisions.

Discussion Questions

1. How prevalent was the agency problem in corporate America during the late 1990s?

2. Who benefited the most from the late 1990s boom in initial public offerings of Internet companies: investors (stockholders) in those companies, managers, or investment bankers?

3. Why is maximizing return on invested capital consistent with maximizing returns to stockholders?

4. How might a company configure its strategy-making processes to reduce the probability that managers will pursue their own self-interest, at the expense of stockholders?

5. Should stock options be treated as an expense? If they were, what impact would this have on a company?

Practicing Strategic Management

SMALL-GROUP EXERCISE: EVALUATING STAKEHOLDER CLAIMS

Break up into groups of three to five people, and appoint one group member as a spokesperson who will communicate your findings to the class when called on by the instructor. Discuss the following:

1. Identify the key stakeholders of your educational institution. What claims do they place on the institution?

2. Strategically, how is the institution responding to those claims? Do you think the institution is pursuing the correct strategies in view of these claims? What might it do differently, if anything?

3. Prioritize the stakeholders in order of their importance for the survival and health of the institution. Do the claims of different stakeholder groups conflict with each other? If claims conflict, whose should be tackled first?

ARTICLE FILE 11

Find an example of a company that ran into trouble because it failed to take into account the rights of one of its stakeholder groups when making an important strategic decision.

STRATEGIC MANAGEMENT PROJECT: MODULE 11

This module deals with the relationships your company has with its major stakeholder groups. With the information you have at your disposal, perform the tasks and answer the questions that follow:

1. Identify the main stakeholder groups in your company. What claims do they place on the company? How is the company trying to satisfy those claims?

2. Evaluate the performance of the CEO of your company from the perspective of (a) stockholders, (b) employees, (c) customers, and (d) suppliers. What does this evaluation tell you about the ability of the

CEO and the priorities that he or she is committed to?

3. Try to establish whether the governance mechanisms that operate in your company do a good job of aligning the interests of top managers with those of stockholders.

4. Pick a major strategic decision made by your company in recent years, and try to think through the ethical implications of that decision. In the light of your review, do you think that the company acted correctly?

EXPLORING THE WEB
Visiting Merck

Visit the web site of Merck, the world's largest pharmaceutical company (**www.merck.com/overview/philosophy.html**), and read the mission statement posted there. Then answer the following questions:

1. Evaluate this mission statement in the light of the material contained in this chapter. Does the mission clearly state what Merck's basic strategic goal is? Do the values listed here provide a good guideline for managerial action at Merck? Do those values recognize stakeholder claims?

2. Follow the hypertext link "benefits humanity." Read the section on corporate responsibility. How does Merck attempt to balance the goals of providing stockholders with an adequate rate of return on their investment, while at the same time developing medicines that benefit humanity and that can be acquired by people in need at an affordable price? Do you think that Merck does a good job of balancing these goals?

General Task: Using the Web, find an example of a company where there was overt conflict between principals and agents over the future strategic direction of the organization.

Closing Case

Chainsaw Al Gets the Ax

In July 1996, Sunbeam, a troubled maker of small appliances, announced that it had hired Al Dunlap as its chief executive officer. Sunbeam's stock jumped 50 percent on the news to $18 5/8 as investors eagerly anticipated the gains that the legendary "Chainsaw Al" would bring to Sunbeam. Dunlap's reputation was built on a highly successful career as a turnaround specialist. Before joining Sunbeam, he had engineered a tough turnaround at Scott Paper. There he had laid off 31 percent of the workforce, including 70 percent of all upper-level managers. The stock market valuation of Scott tripled during his tenure. After only eighteen months at Scott, Dunlap walked away with $100 million in salary, bonus, stock gains, and perks, a richly deserved reward, he claimed, given the gains that he engineered in the stock of Scott Paper. Now investors hoped that he would work the same magic at Sunbeam.

Upon arrival at Sunbeam, Dunlap quickly fired seven of Sunbeam's top executives. Then he spent three months formulating his strategy, which he unveiled at an analyst meeting in November 1996. It was classic Dunlap: Sunbeam's workforce would be cut in half to just 6,000, eighteen of the company's twenty-six factories would be closed, four divisions would be disposed of, and the number of products Sunbeam offered would be reduced by 81 percent to 1,500. These measures were projected to produce annual savings of $225 million. Dunlap also laid out ambitious growth goals for Sunbeam, including doubling revenues to $2 billion (after divestitures), raising operating profit margins to 20 percent from 2.5 percent, launching at least thirty new products a year, and increasing international sales to $600 million. "Our growth mission," he proclaimed, "is to become the dominant and most profitable small household appliance and outdoor cooking company in North America, with a leading share of Latin American and Asian Pacific markets."

Right from the start, there were questions about the feasibility of this strategy. Several securities analysts that followed Sunbeam wondered how the company could possibly increase revenues given the depth of the cuts in employment and products, particularly since the North American market for small appliances was experiencing no growth. Nevertheless, Sunbeam's initial results seemed to suggest that Dunlap could pull off this trick. Revenues grew by 18 percent in 1997, while operating margins income rose to $109.4 million and the stock price surged to around $50 a share. It looked as if Dunlap was about to prove once again that tough guys finish first.

However, under the surface were problems. To increase revenues, Dunlap was urging Sunbeam's managers to engage in a "bill and hold" strategy with retailers. Under this arrangement, Sunbeam's products were purchased at large discounts and then held at third-party warehouses for delivery later. In effect, Dunlap was shifting sales from future periods into the current period. Although the approach was not illegal, the ethics of the approach were certainly questionable. Later, Dunlap defended the practice, claiming that it was an effort to extend the selling season and better meet surges in demand. Sunbeam's auditors, Arthur Andersen, also insisted that the practice met accounting standards.

In early March 1998, Dunlap announced that Sunbeam would acquire three companies, including Coleman, the manufacturer of outdoor camping stoves. The stock market responded enthusiastically, and the stock hit an all-time high of $53. Some critics wondered, however, if this implied that Sunbeam could not hit its growth goals from internally generated sales. Shortly afterward, Dunlap announced that the company would book a first-quarter loss of $44.6 million. Dunlap blamed the loss on underlings who had offered "stupid, low-margin deals" and insisted that it would "never happen again." To drive home his point, he fired a number of senior managers who, he claimed, were responsible for the "stupid, low-margin deals," including Donald Uzzi, Sunbeam's well-regarded executive vice president for worldwide consumer products. Around the same time, Dunlap announced that he would cut 5,100 more jobs at the acquired companies and at Sunbeam.

Dunlap's layoff announcement did not stop the fall in Sunbeam's stock price, which had been declining ever since the announcement of a first-quarter loss and now stood under $20. The decline in the stock price accelerated in late May 1998, when the highly regarded financial newspaper *Barron's* published a scathing analysis of Sunbeam. In the article, *Barron's* alleged that Dunlap had employed $120 million of artificial profit boosters in 1997, without which Sunbeam would have recorded a loss.

Dunlap was so concerned about the *Barron's* article that he called a special meeting of the company's board of directors on June 9, 1998. The board had been supportive of Dunlap to this point, and he could count several long-time friends among its number. What began as a straightforward meeting rebutting the *Barron's* article took a strange turn when one director asked Sunbeam's chief financial officer, Russ Kersh, if the company would make its next quarter's numbers. Kersh admitted that they were "challenging." At this point, Dunlap asked all of the outside advisers to step out and then told the board that he and the CFO would resign unless they got the right level of support from the board. "I have all of the necessary documents in my briefcase," Dunlap was reported to have said and then stormed out of the room.

Over the next few days, the board members started to dig deeper. One director placed a call to several top executives. He quickly discovered that many had lost confidence in Dunlap, whom they characterized as abusive and unethical. He was also disturbed to hear that not only would Sunbeam miss its growth goals in the coming quarter, but that revenues would probably come in $60 million *below* the $290 million recorded in the same quarter a year earlier.

Armed with this information, the board convened a second meeting on June 13. At that meeting, the directors all agreed that Dunlap had to go. Most of the directors were friends of Dunlap, but they felt betrayed by him, misled about the company's financial condition, its second-quarter earnings, and its yearly numbers. That day they placed a call to Dunlap and told him that he had been dismissed. Three days later, the board also fired Russ Kersh, the CFO. Commenting on Dunlap's demise, the CEO of a competitor to Sunbeam stated that Dunlap "is the logical extreme of an executive who has no values, no loyalty, no honor, no ethics. And yet he was held up as a corporate god in our culture. It greatly bothers me." A former plant manager whom Dunlap had fired remarked, "I guess the house of cards came tumbling down. When you reduce your workforce by 50 percent, you lose your ability to manage. You can survive like that for months, not years." Following the announcement that Dunlap had been fired, Sunbeam stock fell to under $8 a share, lower than it had been before Dunlap joined the company.

Case Discussion Questions

1. In whose best interests was Al Dunlap acting? Do you think he was honestly trying to discharge his obligation to key stakeholder groups, such as stockholders, employees, and customers?

2. Do you think the Sunbeam board exercised its fiduciary duty? What does this tell you about how boards can work?

3. In retrospect, what might Al Dunlap have done differently to engineer a turnaround at Sunbeam?

Sources: John Byrne, "How Al Dunlap Self-Destructed," *Business Week,* July 6, 1998, p. 58. G. DeGeorge, "Al Dunlap Revs Up His Chainsaw," *Business Week,* November 25, 1996, p. 37. "Exit Bad Guy," *Economist,* June 20, 1998, p. 70. Ellen Pollock and Martha Brannigan, "Mixed Grill: The Sunbeam Shuffle," *Wall Street Journal,* August 19, 1998, p. A1.

12

Implementing Strategy in Companies That Compete in a Single Industry

Opening Case

Strategy Implementation at Dell Computer

Dell Computer, was one of the fastest-growing companies of the 1990s, and its stock price increased at the rate of 100 percent a year, delighting its stockholders. Achieving this high return was a constant challenge for Michael Dell, and one of his biggest battles has been to manage and change Dell's organizational structure, control systems, and culture as his company grew.

Dell was nineteen when, in 1984, he took $1,000 and spent it on the computer parts he assembled himself into PCs that he then sold over the phone. Increasing demand for his PCs meant that within a few weeks, he needed to hire people to help him, and soon he found himself supervising three employees who worked together around a six-foot table to assemble computers while two more employees took orders over the phone.

By 1993, Dell employed 4,500 workers and was hiring over a hundred new workers each week just to keep pace with the demand for the computers. When he found himself working eighteen-hour days managing the company, he realized that he could not lead the company single-handedly. The company's growth had to be managed, and he knew that he had to recruit and hire strategic managers who had experience in managing different functional areas, such as marketing, finance, and manufacturing. He recruited executives from IBM and Compaq and with their help created a functional structure, one in which employees are grouped by the common skills they have or tasks they perform, for example, sales or manufacturing, to organize the value chain activities necessary to deliver his PCs to customers. As a part of this organizing process, Dell's structure also became taller, with more levels in the management hierarchy, to ensure he and his managers had sufficient control over the different activities of his growing business. Dell delegated authority to control Dell's functional value chain activities to his managers, which gave him the time he needed to perform his entrepreneurial task of finding new opportunities for the company.

Dell's functional structure worked well, and under its new management team, the company's growth continued to soar. By 1993, the company had sales of over $2 billion, twice as much as in 1992. Moreover, Dell's new structure had given functional managers the control they needed to squeeze out costs, and Dell had become the lowest-cost PC maker. Analysts also reported that Dell had developed a lean organizational culture, meaning that employees had developed norms and values that emphasized the importance of working hard to help each other find innovative new ways of making products to keep costs low and increase their reliability. Indeed, with the fewest customer complaints, Dell rose to the top of the customer satisfaction rankings for PC makers; its employees became known for the excellent customer service they give to PC buyers experiencing problems with setting up their computers.

Michael Dell realized that new and different kinds of problems were arising. Dell was now selling huge numbers of computers to different kinds of customers, for example, home, business, and educational customers and the different branches of government. Because customers now demanded computers with very different features or different amounts of computing power, its product line broadened rapidly. It started to become more difficult for employees to meet the needs of these different kinds of customers efficiently because each employee needed information about all product features or all of Dell's thousands of different sales offers across its product range.

In 1995, Dell moved to change his company to a market structure and created separate divisions, each geared to the needs of the different groups of customers—a consumer division, business division, and so on. In each division, teams of employees specialize in servicing the needs of one of these customer groups. This move to a more complex structure also allowed each division to develop a unique subculture that suited its tasks, and employees were able to obtain in-depth knowledge about the needs of their market that helped them to respond better to their customers' needs. So successful was this change in structure and culture that by 1999, Dell's revenues were over $30 billion, and its profits were in excess of $2.5 billion, a staggering increase from 1984.

Dell has continued to alter his company's structure to respond to the changing nature of its customers' needs and because its own distinctive competencies have increased over time. For example, Dell realized he could leverage his company's strengths in materials management, manufacturing, and Internet sales over a wider range of computer hardware products. So he decided to begin assembling servers, workstations, and storage devices to compete with IBM, Sun, and Compaq. The increasing importance of the Internet led him to split the market divisions into thirty-five smaller subunits that focus on more specialized groups of customers, and they all conduct the majority of their business over the Internet. Today, for example, Dell can offer large and small companies and private buyers a complete range of computers, workstations, and storage devices that can be customized to their needs.

To help coordinate its growing activities, Dell is increasingly making use of its corporate intranet and using information technology (IT) to standardize activities across divisions to integrate across functions. Dell's hierarchy is shrinking as managers are increasingly delegating everyday decision making to employees who have access, through IT, to the information they need to provide excellent customer service. To help reduce costs, it has also outsourced some of its customer service activities. As a result of these moves, Dell's workforce has become even more committed to sustaining its low-cost advantage, and its cost-conscious culture has become an important source of competitive advantage that is the envy of its competitors.

Sources: G. McWilliams, "Dell Looks for Ways to Rekindle the Fire It Had as an Upstart," *Wall Street Journal,* August 31, 2000, pp. A.1, A.8. "Dell Hopes to Lead Firm out of Desert," *Houston Chronicle,* September, 3, 2000, p. 4D. **www.dell.com,** 2002.

Overview

As the story of Dell suggests, this chapter examines how managers can best implement their strategies to achieve a competitive advantage and superior performance. A well-thought-out business model becomes profitable to pursue only if it can be implemented successfully. In practice, strategy implementation is a difficult and challenging task and a never-ending task. Managers cannot just create an organizing framework for a company's value chain activities and then assume it will keep working efficiently and effectively, just as they cannot select strategies and assume that these strategies will work as intended in the future when the environment is changing.

First, the main elements of strategy implementation and the way they work together to create an organizing framework for a company's people and activities are considered. Second, each of these elements—structure, control systems, and culture—is analyzed in detail. Third, the way strategic managers can use structure, control, and culture at the functional level to pursue functional-level strategies that create and build distinctive competencies is examined. The analysis then goes up to the industry level and the many different issues facing managers in implementing strategy to gain a competitive advantage in a single industry are addressed. The next chapter takes up where this one leaves off and examines strategy implementation across industries and across countries—that is, implementing corporate and global strategy.

By the end of this chapter and the next, you will understand the dynamics of strategy implementation and why the fortunes of a company often rest on its managers' abilities to design and manage its structure, control systems, and culture.

Implementing Strategy Through Organizational Structure, Control, and Culture

Strategy implementation refers to how a company should create, use, and combine organizational structure, control systems, and culture to pursue strategies that lead to a competitive advantage and superior performance. **Organizational structure** assigns employees to specific value creation tasks and roles and specifies how these tasks and roles are to be linked together in a way that increases efficiency, quality, innovation, and responsiveness to customers—the building blocks of competitive advantage. The purpose of organizational structure is to *coordinate and integrate* the efforts of employees at all levels—corporate, business, and functional—and across a company's functions and business units so that they work together in the way that will allow it to achieve the specific set of strategies in its business model.

Organizational structure does not by itself provide the set of incentives through which people can be *motivated* to make it work. Hence, there is a need for control systems. The purpose of a **control system** is to provide managers with (1) a set of incentives to motivate employees to work toward increasing efficiency, quality, innovation, and responsiveness to customers and (2) specific feedback on how well an organization and its members are performing and building competitive advantage so that managers can constantly take action to strengthen a company's business model. Structure provides an organization with a skeleton; control gives it the muscles, sinews, nerves, and sensations that allow managers to regulate and govern its activities.

Organizational culture, the third element of strategy implementation, is the specific collection of values, norms, beliefs, and attitudes shared by people and groups in an organization and that control the way they interact with each other and with stakeholders outside the organization.[1] As discussed in detail following, top managers can influence how and which beliefs and values develop in an organization, and values and beliefs are a third important determinant of how organizational members will work toward achieving organizational goals.[2] If organizational control has an impact on how a particular kind of organizational structure will work, so organizational culture determines how both structure and control will work in practice.

Figure 12.1 sums up the argument so far. Organizational structure, control, and culture are the means by which an organization motivates, coordinates, and "incentivizes" its members to work toward achieving the building blocks of competitive advantage. Top managers who wish to find out why it takes a long time for people to make decisions in a company, why there is a lack of cooperation between sales and manufacturing, or why product innovations are few and far between need to understand how the design of a company's structure and control system and the values and norms in its culture affect the way its employees are coordinated and motivated and rewarded by working together. *Organizational structure, control, and culture shape the way people behave, their values and attitudes, and determine how they will implement an organization's business model and strategies.*[3] On the basis of such an analysis, top managers can devise a plan to restructure or change their company's structure, control systems, and culture to improve coordination and motivation. Effective strategy implementation allows a company to obtain a competitive advantage and achieve above-average profitability.

Building Blocks of Organizational Structure

After formulating a company's business model and strategies, managers must make designing organizational structure its next priority. The value creation activities of organizational members are meaningless unless some type of structure is used to assign them to tasks and connect the activities of different people and functions.[4] Three basic choices are involved when managers design an organization's structure:

1. How best to group tasks into functions and group functions into business units or divisions to create distinctive competencies and pursue a particular strategy

2. How to allocate authority and responsibility to these functions and divisions

3. How to increase the level of coordination or integration between functions and divisions as a structure evolves and becomes more complex

The basic issues are discussed next and then taken up again when appropriate choices of structure at the different levels of strategy are considered.

FIGURE 12.1

Implementing Strategy

Grouping Tasks, Functions, and Divisions

Because, to a large degree, an organization's tasks are a function of its strategy, the dominant view is that companies choose a form of structure to match their organizational strategy. Perhaps the first person to address this issue formally was the Harvard business historian, Alfred D. Chandler.[5] After studying the organizational problems experienced in large U.S. corporations such as Du Pont and GM as they grew in the early decades of the twentieth century, Chandler reached two conclusions: (1) that in principle, organizational structure follows the range and variety of tasks that the organization chooses to pursue and (2) that U.S. companies' structures change as their strategy changes in a predictable way over time.[6] In general, this means that most companies first group people and tasks into functions, and functions into divisions.[7]

A *function* is a collection of people who work together and perform the same types of tasks or hold similar positions in an organization.[8] For example, the salespeople in a car dealership belong to the sales function. Together, car sales, car repair, car parts, and accounting are the set of functions that allow a car dealership to sell and maintain cars.

As organizations grow and produce a wider range of products, the amount and complexity of the handoffs or transfers between people, functions, and subunits necessary to create a product and deliver it to the customer increase. Recall from previous chapters that the communications and measurement problems surrounding transfers or handoffs are a major source of **bureaucratic costs,** the information distortion problems that increase the costs of negotiating, monitoring, and enforcing the exchanges necessary to add value to a product as it flows along a company's value chain to the final customer.[9]

The reasons that bureaucratic costs increase as companies pursue more complex strategies is discussed in detail following. For now, it is important to note that managers group tasks into functions and, when necessary, group functions into business units or divisions to reduce transaction costs. For example, as Dell Computer started to produce different kinds of products, it created separate divisions, each with its own marketing, sales, and accounting functions. A *division* is a group of functions created to allow an organization to better produce and dispose of its goods and services to customers. In developing an organizational structure, managers must decide how to group an organization's activities by function and division in a way that achieves organizational goals effectively, such as happened at Dell.[10]

Top managers can choose from among many kinds of structure to group their activities, with the choice made on the basis of its ability to meet the needs of their strategies best.

Allocating Authority and Responsibility

As organizations grow and produce a wider range of goods and services, the size and number of their functions and divisions increase. The number of handoffs or transfers between employees also increases, and to economize on transaction costs and effectively coordinate the activities of people, functions, and divisions, managers must develop a clear and unambiguous **hierarchy of authority:** an organization's chain of command—the relative authority that each manager has—extending from the CEO at the top down through the middle managers and first-line managers, to the nonmanagerial employees who actually make goods or provide services.[11] Every manager, at every level of the hierarchy, supervises one or more subordinates. The term **span of control** refers to the number of subordinates who report directly to a manager. When managers know exactly what their authority and responsibility is, information distortion problems are kept to a minimum, and handoffs and transfers can be negotiated and monitored in a way that economize on bureaucratic costs. For example, managers are less likely to risk invading another manager's turf and thus avoid the costly fights and conflicts that will inevitably result.

Tall and Flat Organizations. Companies choose the number of hierarchical levels they need on the basis of their strategy and the functional tasks necessary to achieve it.[12] As an organization grows in size or complexity (normally measured by the number of its employees, functions, and divisions), its hierarchy of authority normally lengthens, making the organizational structure taller. A tall organization has many levels of authority relative to company size; a flat organization has fewer levels relative to company size (see Figure 12.2). As a hierarchy becomes taller, problems that make the organization's structure less flexible and slow managers' response to changes in the organizational environment may result. It is vital that managers understand how these problems arise so they know how to change a company's structure to respond to them.

First, communication problems may arise. When an organization has many levels in the hierarchy, it can take a long time for the decisions and orders of upper-level managers to reach managers further down in the hierarchy, and it can take a long time for top managers to learn how well their decisions worked out. Feeling out of touch, top managers may want to verify that lower-level managers are following orders and may require written confirmation from them. Middle managers, who know they will be held strictly accountable for their actions, start devoting more time to the process of making decisions in order to improve their chances of being right. They might even try to avoid responsibility by making top managers decide what actions to take.

A second communication problem that can result is the distortion of commands and orders as they are transmitted up and down the hierarchy, which causes managers at different levels to interpret what is happening differently. Distortion of orders and messages can be accidental, occurring because different managers interpret messages from their own narrow functional perspectives. Or it can be intentional,

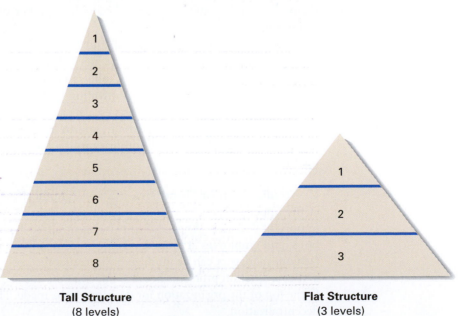

FIGURE 12.2

Tall and Flat Structures

Tall Structure
(8 levels)

Flat Structure
(3 levels)

occurring because managers low in the hierarchy decide to interpret information to increase their own personal advantage.

A third problem with tall hierarchies is that they usually indicate that an organization is employing many managers, and managers are expensive. Managerial salaries, benefits, offices, and secretaries are a huge expense for organizations. Large companies such as IBM and General Motors pay their managers billions of dollars a year. In the 2000s, hundreds of thousands of middle managers were laid off as dot-coms collapsed and high-tech companies like Hewlett Packard and Lucent attempted to reduce costs by restructuring and downsizing their workforces.

The Minimum Chain of Command. To ward off the problems that result when an organization becomes too tall and employs too many managers, top managers need to ascertain whether they are employing the right number of top, middle, and first-line managers and see whether they can redesign their hierarchies to reduce the number of managers. Top managers might well follow a basic organizing principle: the principle of the minimum chain of command states that a company should choose the hierarchy with the *fewest* levels of authority necessary to use organizational resources efficiently and effectively.

Effective managers constantly scrutinize their hierarchies to see whether the number of levels can be reduced—for example, by eliminating one level and giving the responsibilities of managers at that level to managers above and empowering employees below. This practice has become increasingly common in the United States as companies that are battling low-cost foreign competitors search for new ways to reduce costs. One manager who is constantly trying to empower employees and keep the hierarchy flat is Colleen C. Barrett, the number-two executive of Southwest Airlines.[13] Barrett, the highest-ranking woman in the airline industry, is well known for continually reaffirming Southwest's message that employees should feel free to go above and beyond their prescribed roles to provide better customer service. Her central message is that Southwest values and trusts its employees, who are empowered to take responsibility. Southwest employees are encouraged not to look to their superiors for guidance but rather to take responsibility to find ways to do the job better themselves. As a result, Southwest keeps the number of its middle managers to a minimum.

When companies become too tall and the chain of command too long, strategic managers tend to lose control over the hierarchy, which means that they lose control over their strategies. Disaster often follows because a tall organizational structure decreases, rather than promotes, motivation and coordination between employees, and functions and bureaucratic costs escalate as a result. One important way to overcome such problems, at least partially, and to lessen bureaucratic costs is to decentralize authority—that is, vest authority in the hierarchy's lower levels as well as at the top.

Centralization or Decentralization? Authority is centralized when managers at the upper levels of a company's hierarchy retain the authority to make the most important decisions. When authority is decentralized, it is delegated to divisions, functions, and employees at lower levels in the company. By delegating authority in this fashion, managers can economize on bureaucratic costs and avoid communication and coordination problems because information does not have to be constantly sent to the top of the organization for decisions to be made. There are three advantages to decentralization.

First, when strategic managers delegate operational decision-making responsibility to middle and first-level managers, they reduce information overload, enabling strategic managers to spend more time developing competitive strategy. Second, when managers in the bottom layers of the company become responsible for adapting strategy to suit local conditions, their motivation and accountability increase. The result is that decentralization promotes flexibility and reduces bureaucratic costs because lower-level managers are authorized to make on-the-spot decisions; handoffs are not needed. The third advantage is that when lower-level employees are given the right to make important decisions, fewer managers are needed to oversee their activities and tell them what to do. Consider some of the advantages set out in Strategy in Action 12.1 that Union Pacific experienced after it decentralized its operations.

If decentralization is so effective, why don't all companies decentralize decision making and avoid the problems of tall hierarchies? The answer is that centralization has its advantages too. Centralized decision making allows easier coordination of the organizational activities needed to pursue a company's strategy. If managers at all levels can make their own decisions, overall planning becomes extremely difficult, and the company may lose control of its decision making.

Centralization also means that decisions fit broad organization objectives. When its branch operations were getting out of hand, for example, Merrill Lynch increased centralization by installing more information systems to give corporate managers greater control over branch activities. Similarly, Hewlett Packard centralized R&D responsibility at the corporate level to provide a more directed corporate strategy. Furthermore, in times of crisis, centralization of authority permits strong leadership

Strategy in Action   12.1

Union Pacific Decentralizes to Increase Customer Responsiveness

Union Pacific, one of the biggest rail freight carriers in the United States, was experiencing a crisis in the late 1990s. The U.S. economic boom was causing a record increase in the amount of freight that the railroad had to transport, but at the same time, the railroad was experiencing record delays in moving the freight. Union Pacific's customers were irate and complaining bitterly about the problem, and the delays were costing the company millions of dollars in penalty payments—$150 million annually.

The problem stemmed from Union Pacific's very centralized management approach, devised in its attempt to cut costs. All scheduling and route planning was handled centrally at its headquarters office in the attempt to promote operating efficiency. The job of regional managers was largely to ensure the smooth flow of freight through their regions. Now, recognizing that efficiency had to be balanced by the need to be responsive to customers, Union Pacific's CEO, Dick Davidson, announced a sweeping reorganization to the company's customers. Henceforth, regional managers were to be given the authority to make operational decisions at the level at which it was most important: field operations. Regional managers could now alter scheduling and routing to accommodate customer requests even if this raised costs. The goal of the organization was now to "return to excellent performance by simplifying our processes and becoming easier to deal with." In making this decision, the company was following the lead of its competitors, most of which had already moved to decentralize their operations, recognizing its many advantages.

Sources: "Union Pacific to Reorganize," *cnnfn.com,* August 20, 1998, p. 20. **www.unionpacific.com,** press release, 1998.

because authority is focused on one person or group. This focus allows for speedy decision making and a concerted response by the whole organization. How to choose the right level of centralization for a particular strategy is discussed later.

Integration and Integrating Mechanisms

Much coordination takes place between people, functions, and divisions through the hierarchy of authority. Often, however, as a structure becomes complex, this is not enough, and top managers need to use various **integrating mechanisms** to increase communication and coordination among functions and divisions. The greater the complexity of an organization's structure, the greater is the need for coordination among people, functions, and divisions to make the organizational structure work efficiently.[14] Three kinds of integrating mechanisms that illustrate the kinds of issues involved are discussed next.[15] Once again, the issue is that these mechanisms are employed to economize on the information distortion problems that commonly arise when managing the handoffs or transfers between the ideas and activities of different people, functions, and divisions.

Direct Contact. Direct contact among managers creates a context within which managers from different functions or divisions can work together to solve mutual problems. However, several problems are associated with establishing contact among managers in different functions or divisions. Managers from different functions may have different views about what must be done to achieve organizational goals. But if the managers have equal authority (as functional managers typically do), the only manager who can tell them what to do is the CEO. If functional managers cannot reach agreement, no mechanism exists to resolve the conflict apart from the authority of the boss. In fact, one sign of a poorly performing organizational structure is the number of problems sent up the hierarchy for top managers to solve. The need to solve everyday conflicts and solve handoff or transfer problems raises bureaucratic costs. To reduce such conflicts and solve transfer problems, top managers use more complex integrating mechanisms to increase coordination among functions and divisions.

Liaison Roles. Managers can increase coordination among functions and divisions by establishing liaison roles. When the volume of contacts between two functions increases, one way to improve coordination is to give one manager in each function or division the responsibility for coordinating with the other. These managers may meet daily, weekly, monthly, or as needed to solve handoff issues and transfer problems. The responsibility for coordination is part of the liaison's full-time job, and usually an informal relationship forms between the people involved, greatly easing strains between functions. Furthermore, liaison roles provide a way of transmitting information across an organization, which is important in large organizations whose employees may know no one outside their immediate function or division.

Teams. When more than two functions or divisions share many common problems, direct contact and liaison roles may not provide sufficient coordination. In these cases, a more complex integrating mechanism, the **team,** may be appropriate. One manager from each relevant function or division is assigned to a team that meets to solve a specific mutual problem; members are responsible for reporting back to their subunits on the issues addressed and the solutions recommended. Teams are increasingly being used at all organizational levels.

Strategic Control Systems

Strategic managers choose the organizational strategies and structure they hope will allow the organization to use its resources most effectively to pursue its business model and create value and profit. Then they create **strategic control systems,** tools that allow them to monitor and evaluate whether, in fact, their strategy and structure are working as intended, how they could be improved, and how they should be changed if they are not working.

Strategic control is not just about monitoring how well an organization and its members are performing currently or about how well the firm is using its existing resources. It is also about how to create the incentives to keep employees motivated and focused on the important problems that may confront an organization in the future so that they work together to find solutions that can help an organization perform better over time.[16] To understand the vital importance of strategic control, consider how it helps managers to obtain superior efficiency, quality, innovation, and responsiveness to customers, the four basic building blocks of competitive advantage:

■ *Control and efficiency.* To determine how *efficiently* they are using organizational resources, managers must be able to measure accurately how many units of inputs (raw materials, human resources, and so on) are being used to produce a unit of output. They must also be able to measure the number of units of outputs (goods and services) they produce. A control system contains the measures or yardsticks that allow managers to assess how efficiently they are producing goods and services. Moreover, if managers experiment with changing the way they produce goods and services to find a more efficient way of producing them, these measures tell managers how successful they have been. Without a control system in place, managers have no idea how well their organizations are performing and how they can make it perform better, something that is becoming increasingly important in today's highly competitive environment.[17]

■ *Control and quality.* Today, competition often revolves around increasing the *quality* of goods and services. In the car industry, for example, within each price range, cars compete against one another in terms of their features, design, and reliability. So whether a customer buys a Ford Taurus, a GM Cavalier, a Chrysler Intrepid, a Toyota Camry, or a Honda Accord depends significantly on the quality of each company's product. Strategic control is important in determining the quality of goods and services because it gives managers feedback on product quality. If managers consistently measure the number of customers' complaints and the number of new cars returned for repairs, they have a good indication of how much quality they have built into their product.

■ *Control and innovation.* Strategic control can help to raise the level of *innovation* in an organization. Successful innovation takes place when managers create an organizational setting in which employees feel empowered to be creative and authority is decentralized to employees so that they feel free to experiment and take risks. Deciding on the appropriate control systems to encourage risk taking is an important management challenge, and, as discussed later in the chapter, an organization's culture becomes important in this regard.

■ *Control and responsiveness to customers.* Finally, strategic managers can help make their organizations more *responsive to customers* if they develop a control system that allows them to evaluate how well employees with customer contact are performing their jobs. Monitoring employees' behavior can help managers find ways to help increase employees' performance level, perhaps by revealing areas in which skills training can help employees or by finding new procedures that allow employees to perform their jobs better. When employees know their behaviors are being monitored, they may have more incentive to be helpful and consistent in the way they act toward customers.

Strategic control systems are the formal target-setting, measurement, and feedback systems that allow strategic managers to evaluate whether a company is achieving superior efficiency, quality, innovation, and customer responsiveness and implementing its strategy successfully. An effective control system should have three characteristics. It should be *flexible* enough to allow managers to respond as necessary to unexpected events; it should provide *accurate information*, giving a true picture of organizational performance; and it should supply managers with the information in a *timely manner* because making decisions on the basis of outdated information is a recipe for failure.[18] As Figure 12.3 shows, designing an effective strategic control system requires four steps:

Step 1: *Establish the standards and targets against which performance is to be evaluated.* General performance standards often derive from the goal of achieving superior efficiency, quality, innovation, or customer responsiveness. Specific performance targets are derived from the strategy pursued by the company. For example, if a company is pursuing a low-cost strategy, then reducing costs by 7 percent a year might be a target. If the company is a service organization such as Wal-Mart or McDonald's, its standards might include time targets for serving customers or guidelines for food quality.

Step 2: *Create the measuring and monitoring systems that indicate whether the standards and targets are being reached.* The company establishes procedures for assessing whether work goals at all levels in the organization are being achieved. In some cases, measuring performance is fairly straightforward. For example, managers can measure quite easily how many customers their employees serve by counting the number of receipts from the cash register. In many cases, however, measuring performance is a difficult task because the organization is engaged in many complex activities. How can managers judge how well their R&D department is doing when it may take five years for products to be developed? How can they measure the company's performance when the company is entering new

FIGURE 12.3

Steps in Designing an Effective Control System

Established standards and targets.

Create measuring and monitoring systems.

Compare actual performance against the established targets.

Evaluate result and take action if necessary.

markets and serving new customers? How can they evaluate how well divisions are integrating? The answer is that managers need to use the various types of control systems discussed below.

Step 3: *Compare actual performance against the established targets.* Managers evaluate whether and to what extent performance deviates from the standards and targets developed in Step 1. If performance is higher, management may decide that it has set the standards too low and may raise them for the next time period. If performance is too low, managers must decide whether to take remedial action. This decision is easy when the reasons for poor performance can be identified—for instance, high labor costs. More often, however, the reasons for poor performance are hard to uncover. They may stem from involved external factors, such as a recession. Alternatively, the cause may be internal. For instance, the R&D laboratory may have underestimated the problems it would encounter or the extra costs of doing unforeseen research. For any form of action, however, Step 4 is necessary.

Step 4: *Initiate corrective action when it is decided that the standards and targets are not being achieved.* Corrective action may mean changing any aspect of strategy or structure discussed in this book. For example, managers may invest more resources in improving R&D, or diversify, or even decide to change their organizational structure.

Levels of Strategic Control

Strategic control systems are developed to measure performance at four levels in a company: corporate, divisional, functional, and individual. Managers at all levels must develop the most appropriate set of measures to evaluate corporate-, business-, and functional-level performance. As the balanced scorecard approach discussed in Chapter 11 suggests, these measures should be tied as closely as possibly to the goals of achieving superior efficiency, quality, innovativeness, and responsiveness to customers. Care must be taken, however, to ensure that the standards used at each level do not cause problems at the other levels—for example, that a division's attempts to improve performance do not conflict with corporate performance. Furthermore, controls at each level should provide the basis on which managers at the levels below can select their control systems. Figure 12.4 illustrates these links.

Types of Strategic Control System

In Chapter 11, the balanced scorecard approach was discussed as a way of ensuring that managers complement the use of ROIC with other kinds of strategic controls to ensure they are pursuing strategies that maximize long-run performance. Here we consider three more types of control system: *personal control, output control, and behavior control.*

Personal Control. **Personal control** is the desire to shape and influence the behavior of a person in a *face-to-face interaction* in the pursuit of a company's goals. The most obvious kind of personal control is direct supervision from a manager further up in the hierarchy. The personal approach is useful because managers can question and probe subordinates about problems or new issues they are facing to get a better understanding of the situation, as well as to ensure that subordinates are performing their work effectively and not hiding any information that could cause problems down the line. Personal control also can come from a group of peers, such as occurs when people work in teams. Once again, personal control at the group level means that there is more possibility for learning to occur and competencies to develop, as well as greater opportunities to prevent free-riding or shirking.

FIGURE 12.4

Levels of Organizational Control

Output Control. **Output control** is a system in which strategic managers estimate or forecast appropriate performance goals for each division, department, and employee and then measure actual performance relative to these goals. Often a company's reward system is linked to performance on these goals, so output control also provides an incentive structure for motivating employees at all levels in the organization. Goals keep managers informed about how well their strategies are creating a competitive advantage and building the distinctive competencies that lead to future success. Goals exist at all levels in an organization.

Divisional goals state corporate managers' expectations for each division concerning performance on such dimensions as efficiency, quality, innovation, and responsiveness to customers. Generally, corporate managers set challenging divisional goals to encourage divisional managers to create more effective strategies and structures in the future. At Dell, for example, each division is given a clear performance goal to achieve, and divisional managers are given considerable autonomy in formulating a strategy to meet this goal.

Output control at the functional and individual levels is a continuation of control at the divisional level. Divisional managers set goals for functional managers that will allow the division to achieve its goals. As at the divisional level, functional goals are established to encourage development of competencies that provide the company with a competitive advantage. The four building blocks of competitive advantage act as the goals against which functional performance is evaluated. In the sales function, for example, goals related to efficiency (such as cost of sales), quality (such as number of returns), and customer responsiveness (such as the time needed to respond to customer needs) can be established for the whole function.

Finally, functional managers establish goals that individual employees are expected to achieve to allow the function to achieve its goals. Sales personnel, for example, can be given specific goals (related to functional goals) that they are required to achieve. Functions and individuals are then evaluated on the basis of achieving or not achieving their goals, and in sales, compensation is commonly pegged to achievement. The achievement of these goals is a sign that the company's strategy is working and meeting organizational objectives.

The inappropriate use of output control can promote conflict among divisions. In general, setting across-the-board output targets, such as return on investment targets, for divisions can lead to destructive results if divisions single-mindedly try to maximize divisional profits at the expense of corporate objectives. Moreover, to reach output targets, divisions may start to distort the numbers and engage in strategic manipulation of the figures to make their divisions look good.[19]

Behavior Control. **Behavior control** is control through the establishment of a comprehensive system of rules and procedures to direct the actions or behavior of divisions, functions, and individuals.[20] The intention of using behavior controls is not to specify the goals but to standardize the way of reaching them. Rules standardize behavior and make outcomes predictable. If employees follow the rules, then actions are performed and decisions handled the same way time and time again. The result is predictability and accuracy, the aim of all control systems. The main kind of behavior controls are operating budgets, standardization, and rules and procedures.

Once managers at each level have been given a goal to achieve, operating budgets that regulate how managers and workers are to attain those goals are established. An **operating budget** is a blueprint that states how managers intend to use organizational resources to achieve organizational goals most efficiently. Most commonly, managers at one level allocate to managers at a lower level a specific amount of resources to use to produce goods and services. Once they have been given a budget, managers must decide how they will allocate certain amounts of money for different organizational activities. These lower-level managers are then evaluated on the basis of their ability to stay inside the budget and make the best use of it. For example, managers at GE's washing machine division might have a budget of $50 million to develop and sell a new line of washing machines; they have to decide how much money to allocate to R&D, engineering, sales, and so on so that the division generates the most revenue and hence makes the biggest profit. Most commonly, large companies treat each division as a stand-alone profit center, and corporate managers evaluate each division's performance by its relative contribution to corporate profitability, something discussed in detail in the next chapter.

Standardization refers to the degree to which a company specifies how decisions are to be made so that employees' behavior becomes predictable.[21] In practice, there are three things an organization can standardize: *inputs, conversion activities,* and *outputs.*

When managers standardize, they screen *inputs* according to preestablished criteria or standards that determine which inputs to allow into the organization. If employees are the input in question, for example, then one way of standardizing them is to specify which qualities and skills they must possess and then to select only applicants who possess them. If the inputs in question are raw materials or component parts, the same considerations apply. The Japanese are renowned for the high quality and precise tolerances they demand from component parts to minimize problems with the product at the manufacturing stage. Just-in-time inventory systems also help standardize the flow of inputs.

The aim of standardizing *conversion activities* is to program work activities so that they are done the same way time and time again. The goal is predictability. Behavior controls, such as rules and procedures, are among the chief means by which companies can standardize throughputs. Fast-food restaurants such as McDonald's and Burger King standardize all aspects of their restaurant operations; the result is consistent fast food.

The goal of standardizing *outputs* is to specify what the performance characteristics of the final product or service should be—the dimensions or tolerances the product should conform to, for example. To ensure that their products are standardized, companies apply quality control and use various criteria to measure this standardization. One criterion might be the number of goods returned from customers or the number of customers' complaints. On production lines, periodic sampling of products can indicate whether they are meeting performance characteristics.

As with other kinds of controls, the use of behavior control is accompanied by potential pitfalls that must be managed if the organization is to avoid strategic problems. Top management must be careful to monitor and evaluate the usefulness of behavior controls over time. Rules constrain people and lead to standardized, predictable behavior. However, rules are always easier to establish than to get rid of, and over time the number of rules an organization uses tends to increase. As new developments lead to additional rules, often the old rules are not discarded, and the company becomes overly bureaucratized. Consequently, the organization and the people in it become inflexible and are slow to react to changing or unusual circumstances. Such inflexibility can reduce a company's competitive advantage by lowering the pace of innovation and reducing its responsiveness to customers.

Using Information Technology

Information technology is playing an increasing role in strategy implementation at all organizational levels. In fact, it is making it much easier for organizations to cost-effectively develop output and behavior controls that give strategic managers much more and much better information to monitor the many aspects of their strategies and to respond appropriately. IT, which provides a way of standardizing behavior through the use of a consistent, often cross-functional software platform, is a form of behavior control. IT is also a form of output control because when all employees or functions use the same software platform to provide up-to-date information on their activities, this codifies and standardizes organizational knowledge and makes it easier to monitor progress toward strategic objectives. IT is also a form of integrating mechanism because it provides people at all levels in the hierarchy and across all functions with more of the information and knowledge they need to perform their roles effectively. For example, today functional-level employees are able to access information easily from other functions using cross-functional software systems that keep them all informed about changes in product design, engineering, manufacturing schedules, and marketing plans that will have an impact on their activities. In this sense, IT overlays the structure of tasks and roles that is normally regarded as the "real" organizational structure. The many ways in which IT affects strategy implementation is discussed in the different sections of this and the next chapter. Strategy in Action 12.2 illustrates one way in which IT can help managers monitor and coordinate the effectiveness with which their strategies are being put into action.

Strategy in Action   12.2

Control at Cypress Semiconductor

In the fast-moving semiconductor business, a premium is placed on organizational adaptability. At Cypress Semiconductor, CEO T. J. Rodgers was facing a problem: How to control his growing 1,500-employee organization without developing a bureaucratic management hierarchy. Rodgers believed that a tall hierarchy hinders the ability of an organization to adapt to changing conditions. He was committed to maintaining a flat and decentralized organizational structure with a minimum of management layers. At the same time, he needed to control his employees to ensure that they perform in a manner consistent with company goals.

The solution that Rodgers adopted was to implement a computer-based information system through which he can manage what every employee and team is doing in decentralized organization. Each employee maintains a list of ten to fifteen goals, such as "Meet with marketing

for new product launch" or "Make sure to check with customer X." Noted next to each goal is when it was agreed on, when it is due to be finished, and whether it has been finished. All of this information is stored on a central computer. Rodgers claims that he can review the goals of all 1,500 employees in about four hours, and he does so each week. How is this possible? He manages by exception, looking only for employees who are falling behind. He then calls them—not to scold but to ask whether there is anything he can do to help them get the job done. It takes only about half an hour each week for employees to review and update their lists. This system allows Rodgers to exercise control over his organization without resorting to the expensive layers of a management hierarchy.

Sources: **www.cypress.com,** press release, 1998. B. Dumaine, "The Bureaucracy Busters," *Fortune,* June 17, 1991, p. 46.

Strategic Reward Systems

Organizations strive to control employees' behavior by linking reward systems to their control systems.[22] Based on its strategy (low cost or differentiation, for example), strategic managers must decide which behaviors to reward. They then create a control system to measure these behaviors and link the reward structure to them. Determining how to relate rewards to performance is a crucial strategic decision because it determines the incentive structure that affects the way managers and employees at all levels in the organization behave. As Chapter 11 points out, top managers can be encouraged to work in the shareholders' interests by being rewarded with stock options linked to the company's long-term performance. Furthermore, companies such as Kodak and GM require managers to buy company stock. When managers are made shareholders, they are more motivated to pursue long-term rather than short-term goals. Similarly, in designing a pay system for salespeople, the choice is whether to motivate them through straight salary or salary plus a bonus based on how much they sell. Neiman Marcus, the luxury retailer, pays employees a straight salary because it wants to encourage high-quality service but discourage a hard-sell approach. Thus, there are no incentives based on quantity sold. On the other hand, the pay system for rewarding car salespeople encourages high-pressure selling; it typically contains a large bonus for the number and price of cars sold.

Organizational Culture

The third element that goes into successful strategy implementation is managing *organizational culture,* the specific collection of values and norms shared by people and groups in an organization.[23] Organizational values are beliefs and ideas about what kinds of goals members of an organization *should* pursue and about the appropriate kinds or standards of behavior organizational members *should* use to achieve these goals. Bill Gates is a CEO who is famous for the set of organizational values that he emphasizes: entrepreneurship, ownership, creativity, honesty, frankness, and open communication. By stressing entrepreneurship and ownership, he strives to make Microsoft behave less like a big bureaucracy and more like a collection of smaller and very adaptive companies. Gates has emphasized giving lower-level managers considerable decision-making autonomy and encouraged them to take risks—that is, to be more like entrepreneurs and less like corporate bureaucrats. The stress he places on values such as honesty, frankness, and open communication is a reflection of his belief that an open internal dialogue is necessary for successful operations at Microsoft.[24]

From organizational values develop organizational norms, guidelines, or expectations that *prescribe* appropriate kinds of behavior by employees in particular situations and control the behavior of organizational members toward one another. The norms of behavior for software programmers at Microsoft include working long hours and weekends, wearing whatever clothing is comfortable (but never a suit and tie), consuming junk food, and communicating with other employees by email and the company's state-of-the-art intranet.

Organizational culture functions as a kind of control in that strategic managers can influence the kind of values and norms that develop in an organization—values and norms that specify appropriate and inappropriate behaviors and that shape and influence the way its members behave.[25] Strategic managers such as Gates deliberately cultivate values that tell their subordinates they should perform their roles in innovative, creative ways. They establish and support norms dictating that to be innovative and entrepreneurial, employees should feel free to experiment even if there is a significant chance of failure.

Other managers might cultivate values that say employees should always be conservative and cautious in their dealings with others, consult with their superiors before they make important decisions, and record their actions in writing so they can be held accountable for what happens. Managers of organizations such as chemical and oil companies, financial institutions, and insurance companies—any organization in which caution is needed—may encourage a conservative, cautious approach to making decisions.[26] In a bank or mutual fund, for example, the risk of losing investors' money makes a cautious approach to investing highly appropriate. Thus, we might expect that managers of different kinds of organizations will deliberately try to cultivate and develop the organizational values and norms that are best suited to their strategy and structure.

Organizational socialization is the term used to describe how people learn organizational culture. Through socialization, people internalize and learn the norms and values of the culture so that they *become* organizational members.[27] Control through culture is so powerful because once these values have been internalized, they become part of the individual's values, and the individual follows organizational values without thinking about them.[28] Often the values and norms of an organization's culture are transmitted to its members through the stories, myths, and language that people in the organization use, as well as by other means. This chapter's *Closing Case,* for example, discusses many of the stories and myths about Sam Walton and about how frugal he was (he used to drive a thirty-year-old pickup truck, for example, and lived in a very modest home) to reinforce Wal-Mart's low-cost strategy and frugal approach.

Culture and Strategic Leadership

Organizational culture is created by the strategic leadership provided by an organization's founder and top managers. The organization's founder is particularly important in determining culture because the founder imprints his or her values and management style on the organization. Walt Disney's conservative influence on the company he established continued until well after his death, for example. Managers were afraid to experiment with new forms of entertainment because they were afraid "Walt Disney wouldn't like it." It took the installation of a new management team under Michael Eisner to turn around the company's fortunes and allow it to deal with the realities of the new entertainment industry.

The leadership style established by the founder is transmitted to the company's managers, and as the company grows, it typically attracts new managers and employees who share the same values. Moreover, members of the organization typically recruit and select only those who share their values. Thus, a company's culture becomes more and more distinct as its members become more similar. The virtue of these shared values and common culture is that it *increases integration and improves coordination among organizational members.* For example, the common language that typically emerges in an organization because people share the same beliefs and values facilitates cooperation among managers. Similarly, rules and procedures and direct supervision are less important when shared norms and values control behavior and motivate employees. When organizational members buy into cultural norms and values, this bonds them to the organization and increases their commitment to find new ways to help it succeed. That is, employees are more likely to commit themselves to organizational goals and work actively to develop new skills and competencies to help achieve those goals. Strategy in Action 12.3 profiles how Ray Kroc built a strong culture at McDonald's.

Strategic leadership also affects organizational culture through the way managers design organizational structure, that is, the way they delegate authority and divide up task relationships. Michael Dell, for example, has tried to keep his company as flat as possible and has decentralized authority to lower-level managers and employees who are charged with striving to get "as close to the customer" as they can. As a result, he has created a cost-conscious customer service culture at Dell in which employees strive to provide high-quality customer service. Thus, the way an organization designs its structure affects the cultural norms and values that develop within the organization. Managers need to be aware of this fact when implementing their strategies.

Traits of Strong and Adaptive Corporate Cultures

Few environments are stable for any prolonged period of time. If an organization is to survive, managers must take actions that enable it to adapt to environmental changes. If they do not take such action, they may find themselves faced with declining demand for their products.

One way that managers can try is to create an **adaptive culture,** one that is innovative and encourages and rewards initiative taking by middle- and lower-level managers.[29] Managers in organizations with adaptive cultures are able to introduce changes in the way the organization operates, including changes in its strategy and structure that allow it to adapt to changes in the external environment. Organizations with adaptive cultures are more likely to survive in a changing environment and indeed should have higher performance than organizations with inert cultures.

Several scholars in the field have tried to uncover the common traits that strong and adaptive corporate cultures share and to find out whether there is a particular set of values that dominates adaptive cultures that is missing from weak or inert ones.

Strategy in Action

How Ray Kroc Established McDonald's Culture

In the restaurant business, maintaining product quality is all-important because the quality of the food, the service, and the restaurant premises vary with the chefs and waiters as they come and go. If a customer gets a bad meal, poor service, or dirty silverware, not only may that customer be lost but also other potential customers too, as negative comments travel by word of mouth. In this context, consider the problem Ray Kroc, the man who pioneered McDonald's growth, faced when McDonald's franchises began to open by the thousands throughout the United States. Kroc developed a sophisticated control system that specified every detail of how each McDonald's restaurant was to be operated and managed in order to create an organizational culture.

First, Kroc developed a comprehensive system of rules and procedures for franchise owners and employees to follow in running each restaurant. The most effective way to perform tasks from cooking burgers to cleaning tables was worked out in advance, written down in rule books, and then taught to each McDonald's manager and employee through a formal training process. Prospective franchise owners had to attend "Hamburger University," the company's training center in Chicago, where in an intensive, month-long program they learned all aspects of a McDonald's operation. They were expected to train their workforce and make sure that employees understood operating procedures thoroughly. Kroc's goal in establishing this system of rules and procedures was to build a common culture so that customers would always find the same level of quality in food and service. If customers always get what they expect from a restaurant, the restaurant has developed superior customer responsiveness.

Kroc also developed the McDonald's franchise system to help the company control its structure as it grew. He believed that a manager who is also a franchise owner (and thus receives a large share of the profits) is more motivated to buy into a company's culture than a manager paid on a straight salary. Thus, the McDonald's reward and incentive system allowed it to keep control over its operating structure as it expanded. Moreover, McDonald's was very selective in selling to its franchisees; they had to be people with the skills and capabilities that Kroc believed McDonald's managers should have.

Within each restaurant, franchise owners were instructed to pay particular attention to training their employees and instilling in them McDonald's concepts of efficiency, quality, and customer service. Shared norms, values, and an organizational culture also helped McDonald's standardize employees' behavior so that customers would know how they would be treated in a McDonald's restaurant. Moreover, McDonald's includes customers in its culture: customers bus their own tables, and it also shows concern for customers' needs by building playgrounds, offering Happy Meals, and organizing birthday parties for children. In creating its family-oriented culture, McDonald's ensures future customer loyalty because satisfied children are likely to become loyal adult customers.

An early but still influential attempt is T. J. Peters and R. H. Waterman's account of the values and norms characteristic of successful organizations and their cultures.[30] They argue that adaptive organizations show three common value sets. First, successful companies have values promoting a *bias for action*. The emphasis is on autonomy and entrepreneurship, and employees are encouraged to take risks—for example, to create new products—even though there is no assurance that these products will be winners. Managers are closely involved in the day-to-day operations of the company and do not simply make strategic decisions isolated in some ivory tower, and employees have a hands-on, value-driven approach.

The second set of values stems from the *nature of the organization's mission*. The company must stick with what it does best and develop a business model focused on its mission. A company can easily get sidetracked into pursuing activities outside its area of expertise just because they seem to promise a quick return. Management should cultivate values so that a company sticks to its knitting, which means strengthening its business model. A company must also establish close relationships with customers as a way of improving its competitive position. After all, who knows more about a company's performance than those who use its products or services? By emphasizing customer-oriented values, organizations are able to learn customers' needs and improve their ability to develop products and services that customers' desire. All of these management values are strongly represented in companies such as McDonald's, Wal-Mart, and Toyota, which are sure of their mission and take constant steps to maintain it.

The third set of values bears on *how to operate the organization*. A company should try to establish an organizational design that will motivate employees to do their best. Inherent in this set of values is the belief that productivity is obtained through people and that respect for the individual is the primary means by which a company can create the right atmosphere for productive behavior. An emphasis on entrepreneurship and respect for the employee leads to the establishment of a structure that gives employees the latitude to make decisions and motivates them to succeed. Because a simple structure and a lean staff best fit this situation, the organization should be designed with only the number of managers and hierarchical levels that are necessary to get the job done. The organization should also be sufficiently decentralized to permit employees' participation but centralized enough for management to make sure that the company pursues its strategic mission and that cultural values are followed.

In summary, these three main sets of values are at the heart of an organization's culture, and management transmits and maintains them through strategic leadership. Strategy implementation continues as managers build strategic control systems that help perpetuate a strong adaptive culture, further the development of distinctive competencies, and provide employees with the incentives to act in ways that build a company's competitive advantage. Finally, organizational structure contributes to the implementation process by providing the framework of tasks and roles that reduces transaction difficulties and allows employees to think and behave in ways that allow a company to achieve superior performance.

Building Distinctive Competencies at the Functional Level

Now that the main elements of strategy implementation have been outlined, the issue of creating the structure, control systems, and culture to put a company's strategies into action can be addressed. The first level of strategy to examine is the functional level because, as Chapter 3 discussed, a company's competitive advantage depends on its ability to use and develop distinctive competencies. Recall that an important aspect of *strategic intent* is the obsession that strategic managers have for building organizational resources and capabilities that will allow them to outperform their competitors; it means managers "focusing the organization's attention on the essence of winning, motivating people by communicating the value of the target, leaving room for individual and team contributions, sustaining enthusiasm . . . and using intent consistently to guide resource allocation."[31] Considering the three elements of strategy implementation in turn, what is the best way for managers to group people and tasks to build competencies? The answer for most companies is to group them by function and create a functional structure.

Grouping by Function: Functional Structure

On the quest to deliver a final product to the customer, two related value chain pressures mount. First, the range of value chain activities that must be performed expands, and it quickly becomes clear, as in Dell's case, that the expertise needed to perform them effectively is lacking. For example, it becomes apparent that the services of a professional accountant or a production manager or a marketing expert are needed to take control of specialized tasks. Second, it becomes clear that no one person can successfully perform more than one value chain activity without becoming overloaded. The company's founder, for instance, who may have been performing many value chain activities, realizes that he or she can no longer simultaneously make and sell the product. As most entrepreneurs discover, they have to decide how to group new employees to perform the various value chain activities most efficiently. Most choose the functional structure.

Functional structures group people on the basis of their common expertise and experience or because they use the same resources.[32] For example, engineers are grouped in a function because they perform the same tasks and use the same skills or equipment. Figure 12.5 shows a typical functional structure. Each of the rectangles represents a different functional specialization—R&D, sales and marketing, manufacturing, and so on—and each function concentrates on its own specialized task.

Functional structures have several advantages. First, if people who perform similar tasks are grouped together, they can learn from one another and become more specialized and productive at what they do. This can create capabilities and competencies in each function. Second, they can monitor each other to make sure that all are performing their tasks effectively and not shirking their responsibilities. As a result, the work process becomes more efficient, reducing manufacturing costs and increasing operational flexibility. A third important advantage of functional structures is that they give managers greater control of organizational activities. As already noted, many difficulties arise when the number of levels in the hierarchy increases. If people are grouped into different functions, each with their own managers, then *several different hierarchies are created,* and the company can avoid becoming too tall. There will be one hierarchy in manufacturing, for example, and another in accounting and finance. Managing the business is much easier when different groups specialize in different organizational tasks and are managed separately.

The Role of Strategic Control

Behind the concept of strategic intent is a vision of strategic control as a system that sets ambitious goals and targets for all managers and employees and then develops performance measures that *stretch and encourage managers and employees* to excel in their quest to raise performance. A functional structure promotes this goal because it promotes the ability of managers and employees to monitor and make constant improvements to operating procedures. It also allows for organizational learning,

FIGURE 12.5

Functional Structure

since managers, working closely with subordinates, can mentor them and help their technical development further.

Grouping by function also makes it easier to apply output control. Measurement criteria can be developed to suit the needs of each function to encourage members to stretch themselves. Each function knows how well it is contributing to overall performance, and indeed the part it plays in contributing to reductions in cost of good sold or gross margin. Managers can look closely to see if they are following the principle of the minimum chain of command and whether they need middle managers or perhaps could substitute this with control by **management by objectives,** a system in which employees are encouraged to help set their own goals so that managers, like Cypress's Rodgers, manage by exception, intervening only when they sense something is not going right. Given this increase in control, a functional structure also makes it possible to institute an effective strategic reward system in which pay can be closely linked to performance and managers can accurately assess the value of each person's contributions.

Developing Culture at the Functional Level

Often functional structures offer the easiest way for managers to build a cohesive culture. Consider Hewlett Packard (HP), a major provider of IT and computer infrastructure and services. Established in the 1940s, HP's culture is an outgrowth of the strong personal beliefs of the company's founders, Bill Hewlett and Dave Packard. Bill and Dave, as they were known within the company, created HP's culture in a formal statement of HP's basic values to serve everyone who had a stake in the company with integrity and fairness, including customers, suppliers, employees, stockholders, and society in general. They helped establish these values and build HP's culture by hiring like-minded people and letting these values guide their own actions as managers. Thus, the values developed by HP's founders helped guide managerial action at HP. In turn, the commitment to employees that this action signaled has helped foster a productive workforce that is willing to go to great lengths to help the company succeed. The result has been superior company performance over time.

In order to see how the different components of the strategy implementation process work together to implement functional strategy, consider how it works in three functions: manufacturing, R&D, and sales.

Manufacturing. In manufacturing, functional strategy usually centers on improving efficiency, quality, and responsiveness to customers. A company must create an organizational setting in which managers can learn how to economize on costs. In implementing functional strategies in a manufacturing setting, many companies today follow the lead of Japanese companies such as Toyota and Sony, which developed strong capabilities and competencies in manufacturing by operating total quality management (TQM) and flexible manufacturing systems (see Chapter 4).

With TQM, the inputs and involvement of all employees in the decision-making process are necessary to improve production efficiency and quality. Thus, it becomes necessary to decentralize authority to motivate employees to improve the production process. In TQM, work teams are created, and workers are given the responsibility and authority to discover and implement improved work procedures. Managers assume the role of coach and facilitator, and team members jointly take on the supervisory burdens. Work teams are often given the responsibility to control and discipline their own members and even to decide who should work in their team. Frequently, work teams develop strong norms and values, and work group culture becomes an important means of control; this type of control matches the new decentralized team approach. Quality control circles are created to exchange information and suggestions about problems and work procedures. A bonus system or employee stock ownership plan (ESOP) is frequently established to motivate workers and to allow them to share in the increased value that TQM often produces.

Nevertheless, to move down the experience curve quickly, most companies still exercise tight control over work activities and create behavior and output controls that standardize the manufacturing process. For example, human inputs are standardized through the recruitment and training of skilled personnel, the work process is programmed, often by computers, and quality control is used to make sure that outputs are being produced correctly. In addition, managers use output controls such as operating budgets to monitor costs and quality continuously. The extensive use of output controls and the continuous measurement of efficiency and quality ensure that the work team's activities meet the goals set for the function by management. Efficiency and quality increase as new and improved work rules and procedures are developed to raise the level of standardization. The aim is to find the match between structure and control and a TQM approach, so that manufacturing develops the distinctive competency that leads to superior efficiency and quality. However, control systems need to be chosen carefully, as the experience of Gateway, described in Strategy in Action 12.4, suggests.

R&D. The functional strategy for an R&D department is to develop a distinctive competency in innovation and technology that results in products that fit customers' needs. Consequently, the R&D department's structure, control, and culture should provide the coordination necessary for scientists and engineers to bring products quickly to market. Moreover, these systems should motivate R&D scientists to develop innovative products or processes.

In practice, R&D departments typically have a flat, decentralized structure that gives their members the freedom and autonomy to be innovative. Scientists and engineers are also grouped into teams because their performance can typically be judged only over the long term (it may take several years for a project to be completed). Consequently, extensive supervision by managers and the use of behavior control is a waste of managerial time and effort.[33] By letting teams manage their own transfer and handoff issues rather than using managers and the hierarchy of authority to coordinate work activities, managers implement R&D strategy in a way that avoids the information distortion problems that cause bureaucratic costs. Strategic managers take advantage of scientists' ability to work jointly to solve problems and to enhance each other's performance. In small teams too, the professional values and norms that highly trained employees bring to the situation promote coordination. A culture for innovation frequently emerges to control employees' behavior, as has occurred at Motorola and Intel, where the race to be first energizes the R&D teams. To create an innovative culture and speed product development, Intel uses a team structure in its R&D function. Intel has six teams that work on the next generation of chips so that each team's innovations can be put together to make the final product and ensure a state-of-the-art product. It also has six teams working simultaneously on the subsequent generation of chips and six teams working on the generation of chips to follow that one. In other words, to sustain its leading-edge technology, the company has created healthy competition between teams in which its scientists and engineers battle to be the one that produces the innovations that will allow Intel to control the technology of tomorrow.[34]

Strategy in Action   12.4

Gateway's New Rules Backfire

In 2001, Gateway, the personal computer maker, saw its customer satisfaction rating plummet as it dropped from third to fifth in consumer satisfaction among personal computer makers. This drop caused Gateway's managers considerable anxiety because they use this measure of customer satisfaction as an important indicator of their company's ongoing performance. A drop is very serious to a computer maker because the volume of its online sales depends on how easy it is for customers to put their mail order computer together when it reaches their homes and how easy it is for them to get advice and good service when they encounter a software or hardware problem. Customer satisfaction ratings also directly affect a company's profits, and as Gateway's computer shipments slipped by over 11 percent in 2001 compared to 2000, it began to lose money.

Gateway randomly surveys its customers thirty days after they receive their computer to inquire about the nature of their buying experience. Mike Ritter, director of Gateway consumer marketing, discovered that the source of customer dissatisfaction was a series of new rules and policies the company had instituted for its customer service reps to follow in its effort to reduce the escalating costs of after-sales service. As Gateway's product line had broadened and many different software and hardware options were made available to customers, so had the complexity of its customer service procedures. Employees had to have a great deal more information at their disposal to solve customer problems. These problems were often made more serious when customers installed other desired software on their computers, which then caused problems with the software already installed on the Gateway machine. As everybody who has installed new software knows, it can take considerable time to iron out the problems and get the new installation to work. This was costing Gateway millions of dollars in employee time spent on solving these problems—hence Gateway's desire to reduce these costs.

Ritter reported to Gateway CEO Ted Waitt that the fifteen rules and procedures that the company had insti-

tuted for its customer service reps to follow, and two rules in particular, were the source of customer dissatisfaction. The first problematic rule concerned the issue of customer-installed software. Gateway had told its service reps to inform customers that if they installed any other software on their machines, this would invalidate Gateway's warranty. This infuriated customers. The second policy was one of rewarding customer support reps on the basis of how quickly they handled customer calls, meaning that the more calls they handled in an hour or day, the higher the bonus they received.

The joint effect of these two rules was that customer reps were now motivated to minimize the length of a service call and in particular were unwilling to help solve customer problems that resulted from installation of "outlawed software" since this took a lot of time. Customers resented this treatment, and the result was the big decline in customer satisfaction. Moreover, customer reps were not happy because they felt they were violating Gateway's cultural values and norms about providing excellent customer service, and Gateway had prided itself on having a strong corporate culture.

Once Gateway's managers realized the source of the problem, they abolished the fifteen rules immediately. Within one month in 2001, the thirty-day survey saw customer satisfaction jump by over 10 percent. In retrospect, Gateway's managers described these new rules and policies as "misguided and stupid." They hope that the company's sales will start to increase and it will regain some market share it lost to Dell and Compaq. However, in July 2001, Gateway announced that it was closing its global computer-making operations and is in a tough race against Dell Computer, which now has over a 25 percent market share compared with less than 10 percent for Gateway. As Gateway's managers discovered, it is necessary to carefully choose and evaluate the rules and policies used to control employees' behavior to prevent unexpected problems from arising.

To spur teams to work effectively, the reward system should be linked to the performance of the team. If scientists, individually or in a team, do not share in the profits a company obtains from its new products or processes, they may have little motivation to contribute wholeheartedly to the team. To prevent the departure of their key employees and encourage high motivation, companies such as Merck, Intel, and Microsoft give their researchers stock options and rewards tied to their individual performance, their team performance, and the company's performance.

Sales. Salespeople work directly with customers, and when they are dispersed in the field, these employees are especially difficult to monitor. The cost-effective way to monitor their behavior and encourage high responsiveness to customers is usually to develop sophisticated output and behavior controls. Output controls, such as specific sales goals or goals for increasing responsiveness to customers, can be easily established and monitored by supervisors. Then output controls can be linked to a bonus reward system to motivate salespeople. Behavior controls, for instance, detailed reports that salespeople file describing their interactions with customers, can also be used to standardize salespeople's behavior and make it easier for supervisors to review their performance.[35]

Usually, few managers are needed to monitor their activities, and a sales director and regional sales managers can oversee even large sales forces because outputs and behavior controls are employed. Frequently, however, and especially when salespeople deal with complex products such as sales of pharmaceutical drugs or even luxury clothing, it becomes important to develop shared employee values and norms about the importance of patient safety or high-quality customer service, and managers spend considerable time training and educating employees to create such norms.

Similar considerations apply to the other functions, such as accounting, finance, engineering, and human resource management. Managers must implement functional strategy through the combination of structure, control, and culture that allows each function to create the competencies that lead to superior efficiency, quality, innovation, and responsiveness to customers. Strategic managers must also develop the incentive systems that motivate and align employees' interests with those of their companies.

Functional Structure and Bureaucratic Costs

No matter how complex their strategies become, most companies always retain a functional orientation because of the many advantages obtained by using a functional structure. Whenever different functions work together, bureaucratic costs inevitably arise because of the information distortions that lead to the communications and measurement problems discussed in Chapter 10. Often these problems arise from the transfers or handoffs across the different functions necessary to deliver the final product to the customer.[36] It is important that strategic managers understand when and how these problems arise because the need to implement more complex business- and corporate-level strategies only makes these information distortion problems worse. Indeed, it is the need to economize on the bureaucratic costs of solving such problems that lead to organizational arrangements that reduce the scope of information distortions. Most commonly, companies superimpose a more complex grouping on their activities to match their business model and strategy in a discriminating way. These more complex groupings are discussed later in the chapter. First, five factors that cancause information distortions—communications, measurement, customer, location, and strategic—are reviewed.

Communications Problems. As separate functional hierarchies evolve, functions can grow more remote from one another, and it becomes increasingly difficult to communicate across functions and to coordinate their activities. This communication problem stems from *differences in goal orientations,* noted in Chapter 11, that occur because the various functions develop distinct outlooks or understandings of the strategic issues facing a company.[37] Often, the different functions' pursuit of different competencies lead them to develop different time or goal orientations, for example. Some, such as manufacturing, have a short time frame and concentrate on achieving short-run goals, such as reducing manufacturing costs. Others, such as R&D, have a long-term point of view; their product development goals may have a time horizon of several years. These factors may cause each function to develop a different view of the strategic issues facing the company. Manufacturing, for example, may see the strategic issue as the need to reduce costs, sales may see it as the need to increase customer responsiveness, and R&D may see it as the need to create new products. These communication and coordination problems between functions increase bureaucratic costs.

Measurement Problems. Often a company's product range widens as it develops new competencies and enters new market segments, as happened to Dell. When this happens, a company may find it difficult to gauge or measure the contribution of a product or a group of products to its overall profitability—as noted in Chapter 10. Consequently, the company may turn out some unprofitable products without realizing it and may also make poor decisions about resource allocation. This means that the company's measurement systems are not complex enough to serve its needs. Dell Computer's explosive growth in the early 1990s, for example, caused it to lose control of its inventory management systems; hence, it could not accurately project supply and demand for the components that go into its personal computers. Problems with its organizational structure plagued Dell, reducing efficiency and quality. As one manager commented, designing its structure to keep pace with its growth was like "building a high performance car while going around the race track."[38] However, Dell succeeded and today enjoys a 10 to 20 percent cost advantage over competitors like Gateway and HP/Compaq.

Customer Problems. As the range and quality of an organization's goods and services increase, often more, and different kinds of, customers are attracted to its products. Servicing the needs of more customer groups and tailoring products to suit new kinds of customers cause increasing handoff problems between functions. It becomes increasingly difficult to coordinate the activities of value chain functions across the growing product range. Also, functions like production, marketing, and sales have little opportunity to differentiate products and increase value for customers by specializing in the needs of particular customer groups. Instead, they are responsible for servicing the complete product range. Thus, the ability to identify and satisfy customer needs may fall short in a functional structure.

Location Problems. Location factors may hamper coordination and control. If a growing company begins producing or selling in many different regional areas, then a functional structure may not be able to provide the flexibility needed for managers to respond to the different customer needs or preferences in the various regions. A functional structure is simply not the right way to handle regional diversity.

Strategic Problems. Sometimes the combined effect of all these factors is that long-term strategic considerations are ignored because managers are preoccupied with solving communication and coordination problems. As a result, a company may lose direction and fail to take advantage of new opportunities while bureaucratic costs escalate.

Experiencing one or more of these problems is a sign that bureaucratic costs are increasing and a company no longer has the correct approach to strategy implementation. Managers must change and adapt the organization's structure, control systems, and culture to economize on bureaucratic costs, strengthen distinctive competencies, and enhance its competitive advantage. These problems indicate that the company has outgrown its structure and managers need to develop a more complex structure that can meet the needs of its competitive strategy. They could also move to reduce some of these problems by adopting the outsourcing option as well. At this point, implementing strategy at the business level comes into focus.

The Outsourcing Option

Rather than move to a more complex, expensive structure, increasingly companies are turning to the outsourcing option and contracting with other companies to perform specific functional tasks for them. Obviously, it does not make sense to outsource activities in which a company has a distinctive competence because this would lessen its competitive advantage. But it does makes sense to outsource and contract with companies to perform such activities when they have a competitive advantage because they *specialize* in a particular value chain activity.

Thus, one way of avoiding the kinds of communication and measurement problems that arise when a company's product line becomes complex is to reduce the number of functional value chain activities it performs. This allows a company to focus on those competencies that are at the heart of its competitive advantage and economize on bureaucratic costs. Today, responsibility for activities such as a company's marketing, pension and health benefits, materials management, and information systems is being increasingly outsourced to companies that often specialize in the needs of a company in a particular industry. More outsourcing options such as using a global network structure are considered in Chapter 13.

Implementing Strategy in a Single Industry

Building capabilities in strategy implementation that allow a company to develop a competitive advantage starts at the functional level. However, to pursue its business-level strategy successfully, managers must find the right combination of structure, control, and culture that *links and combines* the competencies in a company's value chain functions in a way that enhances the ability to differentiate products and economizes on bureaucratic costs. In other words, the need to coordinate and integrate across functions and business units becomes of central importance at the business level. In this section, the strategy implementation issues for a company seeking to implement a successful competitive business-level strategy are considered.

There are two important issues that managers must address in strategy implementation at the business level: one concerns the revenue side of the profit equation and the other the cost side, as Figure 12.6 illustrates. First, effective strategy implementation improves the way in which people and groups choose strategies and make decisions that lead to increasing differentiation, more value for customers, and the opportunity to charge a premium price. Capabilities in managing its structure and culture allow a company to more rapidly and effectively combine its distinctive competencies or transfer or leverage competencies across business units to create new and improved differentiated products, for example.

Second, effective strategy implementation reduces the bureaucratic costs associated with solving the measurement and communications problems that derive from such things as transferring a product in progress between functions or a lack of cooperation between marketing and manufacturing or between business units. A poorly

FIGURE 12.6

How Organizational
Design Increases
Profitability

designed or inappropriate choice of structure or control system or a slow-moving bureaucratic culture (for example, a structure that is too centralized, an incentive system that causes functions to compete and not to cooperate, or a culture whose value and norms have little impact on employees) can cause the motivation, communication, measurement, and coordination problems that lead to high bureaucratic costs.

Effective strategy implementation, which often means the move to a more complex structure, economizes on bureaucratic costs, ultimately lowers a company's cost structure, and can give a company a low-cost advantage that raises profits. A more complex structure will cost more to operate because more highly paid managers will be needed, a more expensive IT system will be required, there may be a need for extra offices or even buildings, and so on. However, these are simply costs of doing business, and a company will happily bear this extra expense provided its new structure leads to increased revenues obtained from differentiating its products to attract more customers and new ways to lower its *overall* cost structure by obtaining scale economies from its expanded operations.

As discussed in Chapter 6, the most successful companies today are those that take great care to manage both the cost and differentiation sides of the profitability equation, although commonly one of these sides dominates their business model, such as Wal-Mart's low-cost approach and Sony's differentiation approach. The issue at the business level is that strategic managers must identify and implement the structure, control, and culture that coordinates and integrates its functions to achieve business-level strategy objectives. Because the focus at the business level is on managing cross-functional relationships, the issue of how to group organizational activities and functions and how to integrate them becomes vitally important.[39] Also, control systems must be selected and a culture managed with the need to coordinate cross-functional activities in mind.

Following, the strategy implementation issues involved in pursuing both a cost-leadership and a differentiation strategy are examined briefly. Then the way these approaches can be combined and an organizational structure chosen to allow companies to pursue business models oriented at (1) managing broad product lines, (2) being responsive to customers; (3) expanding nationally; (4) competing in a fast-changing high tech environment; and (5) focusing on a deep product line are considered.

Implementing a Cost-Leadership Approach

The aim of the cost-leadership strategy is to make the company pursuing it the lowest-cost producer in the market.[40] At the business level, this means reducing costs across *all* functions in the organization, including R&D and sales and marketing. If a company is pursuing a cost-leadership strategy, its R&D efforts probably focus on product and process development rather than on the more expensive product innovation, which carries no guarantee of success. In other words, the company stresses competencies that improve product characteristics or lower the cost of making existing products. Similarly, a company tries to decrease the cost of sales and marketing by offering a standard product to a mass market rather than different products aimed at different market segments, which is also more expensive.[41]

To implement a cost-leadership strategy, the company chooses a combination of structure, control, and culture compatible with the needs of the low-cost strategy. In practice, the functional structure is the most suitable provided that care is used to select the appropriate integrating mechanisms that reduce communications and measurement problems. For example, a TQM program can be effectively implemented when a functional structure is overlaid with cross-functional teams, for now team members can search for ways to improve operating rules and procedures that lower the cost structure or standardize and raise product quality.[42]

A cost-leadership approach also requires that strategic managers continuously monitor the way their structures and control systems are working to find ways to restructure or streamline it so that it operates more effectively. For example, managers need to be alert to ways to use IT to standardize operations and lower costs. To reduce costs further, cost-leadership companies use the cheapest and easiest forms of control available: output controls. For each function, a company adopts output controls that allow it to monitor and evaluate functional performance closely. In the manufacturing function, for example, the company imposes tight controls and stresses meeting budgets based on production, cost, or quality targets.[43] In R&D, too, the emphasis falls on the bottom line, and to demonstrate their contribution to cost savings, R&D teams focus their efforts on improving process technology. Cost-leadership companies are likely to reward employees through generous incentive and bonus plans to encourage high performance. Often their culture is based on values that emphasize the bottom line, such as those of Dell and McDonald's.

Implementing a Differentiation Approach

Effective strategy implementation can improve a company's ability to add value and to differentiate its products. To make its product unique in the eyes of the customer, for example, a differentiated company must design its structure, control, and culture around the *particular source* of its competitive advantage.[44] Specifically, companies implementing a differentiation approach need to design their structures around the source of their distinctive competencies, the differentiated qualities of their product, and the customer groups they serve.

Commonly, in pursuing differentiation, a company starts to produce a wider range of products and serve more market segments, which means it has to customize its products to the needs of different groups of customers. These factors make it more difficult to standardize activities and usually increase the bureaucratic costs associated with managing the handoffs or transfers between functions. Integration becomes much more of a problem; communications, measurement, location, and strategic problems increasingly arise; and the demands on functional managers increase.

To respond to these problems, strategic managers develop more sophisticated control systems, increasingly make use of IT, and focus on developing cultural norms and values that overcome problems associated with differences in functional orientations and focus on cross-functional objectives. The control systems used to match the structure are geared to a company's distinctive competency. For successful differentiation, it is important that the various functions do not pull in different directions; indeed, cooperation among the functions is vital for cross-functional integration. However, when functions work together, output controls become much harder to use. In general, it is much more difficult to measure the performance of people in different functions when they are engaged in cooperative efforts. Consequently, a company must rely more on behavior controls and shared norms and values when pursuing a strategy of differentiation.

That is why companies pursuing a differentiation strategy often have a markedly different kind of culture from those pursuing a low-cost strategy. Because human resources—good scientists, designers, or marketing people—are often the source of differentiation, these organizations have a culture based on professionalism or collegiality, a culture that emphasizes the distinctiveness of the human resource rather than the high pressure of the bottom line.[45] HP, Motorola, and Coca-Cola, all of which emphasize some kind of distinctive competency, exemplify companies with professional cultures.

In practice, the implementation decisions that confront managers who must simultaneously strive to increase the differentiated appeal of their products while being mindful of the need to manage its cost structure are dealt with together as strategic managers move to implement new, more complex kinds of organizational structure. As a company's business model and strategies evolve, strategic managers usually start to *superimpose* a more complex grouping of activities on its functional grouping and move to a new form of structure and control system that allows it to motivate employees better to coordinate its value chain activities.

Although more complex structures cost more to implement and operate than a simple functional structure, managers are willing to bear this extra cost so long as the new structure makes better use of functional competencies, increases its revenues, and lowers its overall cost structure. Recall from Chapter 10 that to economize on bureaucratic costs, organizational arrangements must be matched to the business model and strategy in a *discriminating way*.

Implementing a Broad Product Line—Product Structure

The structure that organizations most commonly adopt to solve the control problems that result from producing many different kinds of products for many different market segments is the *product structure*. The intent behind the change to a product structure is to break up a company's growing product line into a number of smaller, more manageable subunits within an organization to reduce bureaucratic costs due to communication, measurement, and the other problems noted earlier.

An organization that decides to group activities by product first decides how to group its overall product line into product groups or categories so that each product group can be developed, manufactured, distributed, and sold at the lowest cost consistent with permitting the differentiation needed to create value for customers. Each product group is targeted at satisfying the needs of a particular customer group and is managed by its own team of managers who focus their efforts on that group.

Second, to keep costs as low as possible, the decision is made to centralize support value chain functions such as R&D, marketing, sales, and accounting at the top of the organization, and the different product groups share their services. Each support function, in turn, is divided into product-oriented teams of functional specialists who focus on the needs of one particular product group. This arrangement allows each team to specialize and become expert in managing the needs of its product group. However, because all of the R&D teams belong to the same centralized function, they can share knowledge and information with each other that allows them to build their competence over time.

Strategic control systems can now be developed to measure the performance of each product group separately from the others. Thus, the performance of each product group is easy to monitor and evaluate, and corporate managers at the center can move more quickly to intervene if necessary. Also, the strategic reward system can be more closely linked to the performance of each product group, although top managers can still decide to make rewards based on corporate performance an important part of the incentive system. This will encourage the different product groups to share ideas and knowledge and promote the development of a corporate culture, as well as the product group culture that naturally develops inside each product group. A product structure is commonly used by food processors, furniture makers, personal and health products companies and large electronics companies. Strategy in Action 12.5 illustrates and describes how Kodak uses a product structure.

As the figure in Strategy in Action 12.5 shows, each of Kodak's product line uses the services of the central support functions and does not have its own support functions. The expense of creating separate support functions for each product line could be justified only if the needs of the different product lines were so different that *different sets of functional specialists* were required for each group of product. Normally, this happens only when a company enters new industries and markets and its range of product offerings becomes increasingly diverse and unrelated to each other. When this happens, a company requires an even more complex form of structure, a multidivisional structure, which is discussed in Chapter 13.

Increasing Responsiveness to Customer Groups—Market Structure

Suppose the source of competitive advantage in an industry depends on the ability to meet the needs of distinct and important sets of customers or different customer groups. What is the best way of implementing strategy now? Many companies develop a **market structure** that is conceptually quite similar to the product structure except that the focus is on customer groups instead of product groups.

For a company pursuing a strategy based on increasing responsiveness to customers, it is vital that the nature and needs of each different customer group be identified. Then people and functions are grouped by customer or market segment, and a different set of managers becomes responsible for developing the products that each group of customers wants and tailoring or customizing products to the needs of each particular customer group. In other words, to promote superior responsiveness to customers, companies design a structure around their customers and a market structure is adopted. A typical market structure is shown in Figure 12.7.

A market structure brings customer group managers and employees closer to specific groups of customers. These people can then take their detailed knowledge and feed it back to the support functions, which are kept centralized to reduce costs. For example, information about changes in customers' preferences can be quickly fed back to R&D and product design so that a company can protect its competitive advantage by supplying a constant stream of improved products for its installed

Strategy in Action

12.5

Kodak's Product Structure

The Eastman Kodak Company is one of the oldest and best-known companies in the world. The film used in the camera to capture Neil Armstrong's walk on the moon and John F. Kennedy, Jr.'s salute to his father's casket was Kodak film. For decades, Kodak monopolized the global film market, but starting in the 1970s, new low-cost competitors like Fuji began to take market share from Kodak.

To respond to these challenges, Kodak decided to strengthen its core photographic business by bringing out new and improved products, but it had to find a low-cost way to do so because it was already at a cost disadvantage compared to Fuji. Kodak's CEO, Daniel Carp, decided it would be necessary to move to a product structure, shown in the figure.

Carp decided to streamline Kodak's structure by dividing all its products into different product categories, such as consumer photographic products, digital imaging and digital cameras, health imaging products, and commercial imaging products. Each product group is headed by a separate team of managers responsible for managing the value chain functions necessary to develop advanced new products for customers. However, to reduce costs, each product line shares the services of R&D imaging, marketing, sales, accounting, and so on, which remain centralized. In essence, responsibility for strategy making is decentralized to managers inside each product line, but support value chain activities are kept centralized to defray costs and because developments can be quickly spread over and shared by Kodak's different imaging groups. For example, the R&D team that focuses on medical imaging can share discoveries about new methods for digitizing images with the R&D team for commercial products. As a result, Kodak is able to transfer its skills and leverage its competencies across product groups and market segments, and advances in digital imaging technology can be quickly communicated to each group to speed product development. Also, by keeping sales centralized, a single national sales force can sell the complete range of Kodak's imaging products. So far, this grouping of organizational activities by product as well as function has helped Kodak lower its cost structure and overcome many of its old problems of handing off or transferring its knowledge and skills across its many different product lines.

Sources: **www.kodak.com,** 2000. L. Johannes, "Kodak Streamlines Units to Be Nimbler in Digital Age," *Wall Street Journal,* November 3, 2000, p. B.1.

Kodak's Product Structure

FIGURE 12.7
Market Structure

customer base. This is especially important when a company serves well-identified customer groups such as Fortune 500 companies or small businesses. The *Opening Case* describes how Dell uses a market structure to maximize its responsiveness to important customer groups while at the same time keeping its overall cost structure as low as possible.

Expanding Nationally— Geographic Structure

Suppose a company starts to expand nationally through internal expansion or by engaging in horizontal integration and merging with other companies to expand its geographical reach. A company pursuing this competitive approach frequently moves to a **geographic structure** in which geographic regions become the basis for the grouping of organizational activities. A company may divide its manufacturing operations and establish manufacturing plants in different regions of the country, for example. This allows it to be responsive to the needs of regional customers and reduces transportation costs. Similarly, as a service organization such as a store chain or bank expands beyond one geographic area, it may begin to organize sales and marketing activities on a regional level to serve the needs of customers in different regions better.

A geographic structure provides more coordination and control than a functional structure because several regional hierarchies are created to take over the work, just as in a product structure, several product group hierarchies are created. A company such as FedEx clearly needs to operate a geographic structure to fulfill its corporate goal: next-day delivery. Large merchandising organizations, such as Neiman Marcus, Dillard's Department Stores, and Wal-Mart, have also moved to a geographic structure as they started building stores across the country. With this type of structure, different regional clothing needs (for example, sunwear in the South, down coats in the Midwest) can be handled as required. At the same time, because the information systems, purchasing, distribution, and marketing functions remain centralized, they can leverage their skills across all the regions. Thus, in using a geographic structure, a company can achieve economies of scale in buying, distributing, and selling and lower its costs structure while at the same time being more responsive (differentiated) to customer needs.

Neiman Marcus developed a geographic structure similar to the one shown in Figure 12.8 to manage its nationwide chain of stores. In each region, it established a team of regional buyers to respond to the needs of customers in each geographic area, for example, the western, central, eastern, and southern regions. The regional buyers then fed their information to the central buyers at corporate headquarters, who coordinated their demands to obtain purchasing economies and to ensure that Neiman Marcus's high-quality standards, on which its differentiation advantage depends, were maintained nationally.

FIGURE 12.8

FIGURE 12.8

Geographic Structure

The communication and measurement problems that lead to bureaucratic costs escalate quickly when technology is rapidly changing and industry boundaries are blurring. Frequently, competitive success depends on fast mobilization of a company's skills and resources, and managers face complex strategy implementation issues. A new grouping of people and resources becomes necessary, often one that is based on fostering a company's distinctive competencies in R&D, and managers need to make structure, control, and culture choices around the R&D function. At the same time, managers need to ensure that implementation will result in new products that meet customer needs and in a way that is cost-effective and will not result in high-priced products that are so expensive customers will not wish to buy them.

Competing in Fast-Changing, High-Tech Environments— Product-Team and Matrix Structures

Matrix Structure. To address these problems many companies choose a matrix structure.[46] In a **matrix structure,** value chain activities are grouped in two ways (see Figure 12.9). First, activities are grouped vertically by *function,* so that there is a familiar differentiation of tasks into functions such as engineering, sales and marketing, and R&D. In addition, superimposed on this vertical pattern is a horizontal pattern based on grouping by *product or project* in which people and resources are grouped to meet ongoing product development needs. The result is a complex network of reporting relationships among projects and functions designed to make R&D the focus of attention, as depicted in Figure 12.9.

Matrix structures are flat and decentralized, and employees inside a matrix have two bosses: a *functional boss,* who is the head of a function, and a *product or project boss,* who is responsible for managing the individual projects. Employees work on a project team with specialists from other functions and report to the project boss on project matters and the functional boss on matters relating to functional issues. All employees who work in a project team are called **two-boss employees** and are

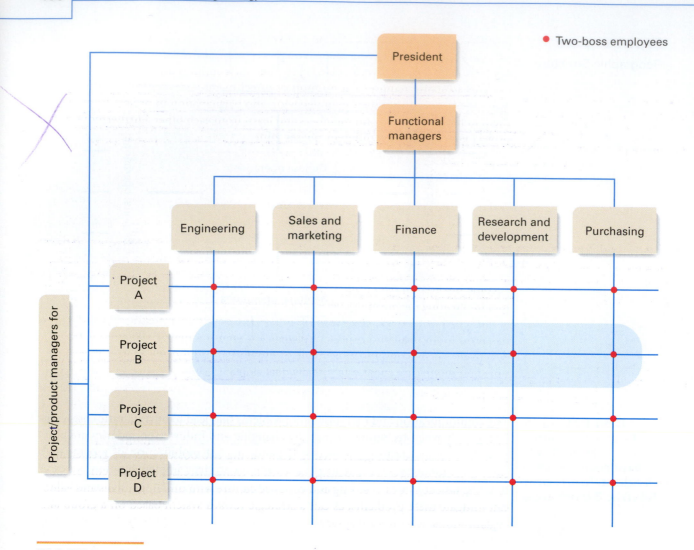

FIGURE 12.9

Matrix Structure

responsible for managing coordination and communication among the functions and projects.

Implementing a matrix structure promotes innovation and speeds product development, for this type of structure permits intensive cross-functional integration. Integrating mechanisms such as teams help transfer knowledge among functions and are designed around the R&D function. Sales, marketing, and production targets are geared to R&D goals; marketing devises advertising programs that focus on technological possibilities, and salespeople are evaluated on their understanding of new-product characteristics and their ability to inform potential customers about them.

Matrix structures were first developed by companies in high-technology industries such as aerospace and electronics; for example, TRW and Hughes. These companies were developing radically new products in uncertain, competitive environments, and speed of product development was the crucial consideration. They needed a structure that could respond to this need, but the functional structure was too inflexible to allow the complex role and task interactions necessary to meet new-product development requirements. Moreover, employees in these companies tend to be highly qualified and professional and perform best in autonomous, flexible working conditions. The matrix structure provides such conditions.

This structure requires a minimum of direct hierarchical control by supervisors. Team members control their own behavior, and participation in project teams allows them to monitor other team members and learn from each other. Furthermore, as the project goes through its different phases, different specialists from various functions are required. For example, at the first stage, the services of R&D specialists may be called for, and then at the next stage, engineers and marketing specialists may be needed to make cost and marketing projections. As the demand for the type of specialist changes, team members can be moved to other projects that require their services. Thus, the matrix structure can make maximum use of employees' skills as existing projects are completed and new ones come into existence. The freedom given by the matrix not only provides the autonomy to motivate employees but also leaves top management free to concentrate on strategic issues, since they do not have to become involved in operating matters. On all these counts, the matrix is an excellent tool for creating the flexibility necessary for quick reactions to competitive conditions.

In terms of strategic control and culture, the development of norms and values based on innovation and product excellence is vital if a matrix structure is to work effectively.[47] The constant movement of employees around the matrix means that time and money are spent establishing new team relationships and getting the project off the ground. The two-boss employee's role, balancing as it does the interests of the project with the function, means that cooperation between people is problematic and communication and conflict between both functions and between function and projects is possible and must be managed. Furthermore, the changing composition of product teams, the ambiguity arising from having two bosses, and the greater difficulty of monitoring and evaluating the work of teams increases the problems of coordinating task activities. A strong and cohesive culture with unifying norms and values can mitigate these problems, as can a strategic reward system based on a group and organizational level reward system.

Product-Team Structure. A major structural innovation in recent years has been the **product-team structure.** Its advantages are similar to those of a matrix structure, but it is much easier and far less costly to operate because of the way people are organized into permanent cross-functional teams, as Figure 12.10 illustrates. In the product-team structure, as in the matrix structure, tasks are divided along product or project lines. However, instead of being assigned only *temporarily* to different projects, as in the matrix structure, functional specialists become part of a *permanent* cross-functional team that focuses on the development of one particular range of products such as luxury cars or computer workstations. As a result, the problems associated with coordinating cross-functional transfers and handoffs are much lower than in a matrix structure, in which tasks and reporting relationships change rapidly. Moreover, cross-functional teams are formed at the beginning of the product development process, so that any difficulties that arise can be ironed out early, before they lead to major redesign problems. When all functions have direct input from the beginning, design costs and subsequent manufacturing costs can be kept low. Moreover, the use of cross-functional teams speeds innovation and customer responsiveness because when authority is decentralized, team decisions can be made more quickly.

A product-team structure groups tasks by product, and each product group is managed by a cross-functional product team that has all the support services

FIGURE 12.10

Product-Team Structure

necessary to bring the product to market. This is why it is different from the product structure, where support functions remain centralized. The role of the product team is to protect and enhance a company's differentiation advantage and at the same time coordinate with manufacturing to lower costs. John Fluke Manufacturing, a leader in electronic testing tools, is a good example of a company that makes use of product teams to speed product development. The company assembles "Phoenix teams," cross-functional groups that are given 100 days and $100,000 to identify a market need and a new product to fill it.[48] So far, these teams have led to the development of two successful new products.

Focusing on a Narrow Product Line

As Chapter 5 discusses, a focus strategy is directed at a particular market or customer segment. A company focuses on a narrow or deep product or range of products aimed at one type of customer or region. This strategy tends to have higher production costs than the other generic strategies because output levels are lower, making it harder to obtain substantial scale economies. As a result, a company using a focus strategy must exercise cost control. On the other hand, because some attribute of its product usually gives such a company its distinctive advantage—possibly its ability to provide customers with high-quality, personalized service—a company using a focus strategy has to develop some form of distinctive competency. For both reasons, the structure and control system adopted by a company following a focus strategy has to be inexpensive to operate but flexible enough to allow a distinctive competency to emerge.

A company using a focus strategy normally adopts a functional structure to meet these needs. This structure is appropriate because it is complex enough to manage the activities necessary to service the needs of a market segment or produce a narrow but deep range of products. At the same time, the handoff problems associated with pursuing a focused strategy are likely to be relatively easy to solve because a company remains small and specialized. Thus, a functional structure can provide all the integration necessary, provided that the focused firm has a strong, adaptive culture,

Strategy in Action   12.6

Restructuring at Lexmark

Lexmark, a printer and typewriter manufacturer, was one of IBM's many divisions, but IBM sold it after years of losses brought on by high operating costs and an inability to produce new products that could compete with Hewlett Packard and Japanese printer makers such as Canon and Epson.

Marvin Mann, an ex-IBM executive, was given the task of finding a way to restructure the company and turn it around. Mann realized at once the need for the company to focus its resources on producing a particular kind of printer to lower its out-of-control cost structure. One of the biggest contributors to its high cost structure was Lexmark's structure and control, so he decided to transform it. Then, he believed, he could begin to focus the company on producing a line of state-of-the-art laser and ink jet office printers.

Like the rest of IBM at that time, Lexmark had developed a tall, centralized structure, and all important decision making was made by top managers. This slowed decision making and made it very difficult to communicate across functions because so many managers at different levels and in different functions had to approve new plans. Moving quickly to change this system, Mann streamlined the company's hierarchy, which meant terminating 50 percent of its managers. This action cut out three levels in the hierarchy. He then decentralized authority to the managers of each of the company's four product groups and told them to develop their own plans and goals. In addition, to continue the process of decentralization, product managers were instructed to develop cross-functional teams comprising employees from all functions, with the goal of finding new and improved ways of organizing task activities to reduce costs. The teams were to use competitive benchmarking and evaluate their competitors' products in order to establish new performance standards to guide their activities. Finally, as an incentive for employees to work hard at increasing efficiency, innovation, and quality, Mann established a company stock ownership scheme to reward employees for their efforts.

Mann's strategy of restructuring Lexmark to focus on a narrow range of printer was successful. Within two years, the cost of launching new products went down by 50 percent and its new-product development cycle speeded up by 30 percent. In addition, by focusing the company's resources on a narrow range of products, he improved its R&D competence. Lexmark is a technology leader in the laser and ink jet industry. Its stock has performed well, and the company is enjoying considerable success against HP and Japanese competitors.

---

which is vital to the development of some kind of distinctive competency.[49] Additionally, because such a company's competitive advantage is often based on personalized service, the flexibility of this kind of structure lets the company respond quickly to customers' needs and change its products in response to customers' requests. The way in which Lexmark reorganized itself to focus on the production of office printers, examined in Strategy in Action 12.6, illustrates many of the issues in implementing a focus strategy.

The message of the preceding section is clear. Strategic managers must continually monitor the performance of their organizations as measured by its ability to increase differentiation, lower costs, and increase profitability and move to take action to change the way its people and activities are organized and controlled when managers sense declining performance or, indeed, when managers sense ways to increase performance. Combining and harmonizing structure, control, and culture is a demanding and difficult task but one that is crucial to promoting and sustaining competitive advantage and strengthening a company's business model.

Restructuring and Reengineering

Often, to improve corporate performance, the single business company employs restructuring and reengineering. **Restructuring** a company involves two steps: (1) streamlining the hierarchy of authority and reducing the number of levels in the hierarchy to a minimum and then (2) downsizing the work force by reducing the number of employees to reduce operating costs. When Jack Smith took over as the head of General Motors, for example, GM had more than twenty-two levels in the hierarchy and more than 20,000 corporate managers. Describing his organization as a top-heavy bureaucracy, Smith quickly moved to slash costs and restructure the company. Today, GM has only twelve levels in the hierarchy and half as many corporate managers.

There are many reasons that restructuring becomes necessary and an organization may need to downsize its operations.[50] Sometimes a change in the business environment occurs that could not have been foreseen; perhaps a shift in technology made the company's products obsolete, or a worldwide recession has reduced the demand for its products. Sometimes an organization has excess capacity because customers no longer want the goods and services it provides, perhaps because they are outdated or offer poor value for the money. Sometimes organizations downsize because they have grown too tall and inflexible and bureaucratic costs have become much too high. Sometimes they restructure even when they are in a strong position simply to build and improve their competitive advantage and stay on top.

All too often, however, companies are forced to downsize and lay off employees because they have not monitored the way they operate their basic business processes and have not made the incremental changes to their strategies and structures that allow them to adjust to changing conditions and keep bureaucratic costs under control. Advances in strategic management thinking, such as the development of new models of organizing work activities, or advances in information technology often offer managers the opportunity to implement their strategies in more effective ways.

One way of helping a company operate more effectively is to employ reengineering. **Reengineering** is the "fundamental rethinking and radical redesign of business processes to achieve dramatic improvements in critical, contemporary measures of performance such as cost, quality, service, and speed."[51] As this definition suggests, strategic managers who use reengineering must completely rethink how they organize their value chain activities. Instead of focusing on how a company's *functions* operate, strategic managers make business *processes* the focus of attention.

A **business process** is any activity that is vital to delivering goods and services to customers quickly or that promotes high quality or low costs (such as IT, materials management, or product development) that is not the responsibility of any *one* function but *cuts across functions*. Because reengineering focuses on business processes and not on functions, a company that reengineers always has to adopt a different approach to organizing its activities. Companies that take up reengineering deliberately ignore the existing arrangement of tasks, roles, and work activities. They start the reengineering process with the customer (not the product or service) and ask, "How can we reorganize the way we do our work, our business processes, to provide the best quality and the lowest-cost goods and services to the customer?"

Frequently, when companies ask this question, they realize that there are more effective ways to organize their value chain activities. For example, a business process that encompasses members of ten different functions working sequentially to provide goods and services might be performed by one person or a few people at a fraction of the cost after reengineering. Often individual jobs become increasingly complex, and people are grouped into cross-functional teams as business processes are reengineered to reduce costs and increase quality.

Hallmark Cards, for example, reengineered its card design process with great success. Before the reengineering effort, artists, writers, and editors worked separately in different functions to produce all kinds of cards. After reengineering, these same artists, writers, and editors were put in cross-functional teams, each of which now works on a specific type of card, such as birthday, Christmas, or Mother's Day. The result was that the time it took to bring a new card to market dropped from years to months, and Hallmark's performance increased dramatically.

Reengineering and total quality management (TQM), discussed in Chapter 4, are highly interrelated and complementary. After reengineering has taken place and value chain activities have been altered to speed the product to the final customer, TQM takes over, with its focus on how to continue to improve and refine the new process and find better ways of managing task and role relationships. Successful organizations examine both questions simultaneously and continuously attempt to identify new and better processes for meeting the goals of increased efficiency, quality, and customer responsiveness. Thus, they are always seeking to improve their visions of their desired future state.

Another example of reengineering is the change program that took place at IBM Credit, a wholly owned division of IBM that manages the financing and leasing of IBM computers, particularly mainframes, to IBM's customers. Before reengineering took place, when a financing request arrived at the division's headquarters in Old Greenwich, Connecticut, it went through a five-step approval process that involved the activities of five different functions. First, the IBM salesperson called the credit department, which logged the request and took details about the potential customer. Second, this information was taken to the credit-checking department, where a credit check on the potential customer was made. Third, when the credit check was complete, the request was taken to the contracts department, which wrote the contract. Fourth, from there it went to the pricing department, which determined the actual financial details of the loan, such as the interest rate and the term of the loan. Finally, the whole package of information was assembled by the dispatching department and delivered to the sales representative, who gave it to the customer.

This series of cross-functional activities took an average of seven days to complete, and sales representatives constantly complained that this delay resulted in a low level of customer responsiveness that reduced customer satisfaction. Also, potential customers were tempted to shop around for financing and even to look at competitors' machines. The delay in closing the deal caused uncertainty for all concerned.

The change process began when two senior IBM credit managers reviewed the finance approval process. They found that the time spent by different specialists in the different functions actually processing a loan application was only ninety minutes. The seven-day approval process was caused because of the delay in transmitting information and requests between departments. The managers also came to understand that the activities taking place in each department were not complex; each department had its own computer system containing its own work procedures, but the work done in each department was pretty routine.

Armed with this information, IBM managers realized that the approval process could be reengineered into one overarching process handled by one person with a computer system containing all the necessary information and work procedures to perform the five loan-processing activities. If the application were complex, a team of experts stood ready to help process it, but IBM found that after the reengineering effort, a typical application could be done in four hours rather than the previous seven days. A sales representative could go back to the customer the same day to close the deal, and all the uncertainty surrounding the transaction was removed.

As reengineering consultants Hammer and Champy note, this dramatic performance increase was brought about by a radical change to the process as a whole.[52] Change through reengineering requires managers to go back to the basics and pull apart each step in the work process to identify a better way to coordinate and integrate the activities necessary to provide customers with goods and services. As this example makes clear, the introduction of new IT is an integral aspect of reengineering. IT also allows a company to restructure its hierarchy since it provides more and better-quality information. IT today is an integral part of the strategy implementation process.

Summary of Chapter

1. Implementing a strategy successfully depends on selecting the right combination of organizational structure, control systems, and culture. Companies need to monitor and oversee the strategy implementation process to achieve superior profitability.

2. Effective strategy implementation can increase profitability in two ways. First, it economizes on bureaucratic costs and helps a company lower its cost structure. Second, it enhances the ability of a company's value creation functions to achieve superior efficiency, quality, innovativeness, and customer responsiveness and to obtain the advantages of differentiation.

3. The main issues in designing organization structure are how to group tasks, functions, and divisions; how to allocate authority and responsibility; and how to use integrating mechanisms to improve coordination between functions.

4. Strategic control provides the monitoring and incentive systems necessary to make an organizational structure work as intended and extends corporate governance down to all levels inside the company. The main kinds of strategic control system are output control and bureaucratic control, rewards systems, and control through information technology.

5. Organizational culture is the set of values, norms, beliefs, and attitudes that help to energize and motivate employees and control their behavior. A company's founder and top managers help determine which kinds of values emerge in an organization, and as such they should try to build a strong and adaptive culture to help increase performance over time.

6. At the functional level, each function requires a different combination of structure and control system to achieve its functional objectives.

7. At the business level, structure, control, and culture must be combined in a way that helps them implement their business-level strategy and manage the relationships among all the functions.

8. Cost-leadership and differentiation strategies each require a structure and control system that matches the source of their competitive advantage. Implementing a simultaneous cost-leadership and differentiation strategy is the problem facing many companies today.

9. Other specialized kinds of structures include the product, market, geographic, matrix, and product-team structures. Each has a specialized use and is implemented as a company's strategy warrants.

10. Restructuring and reengineering are two ways of improving the way a company's strategy is implemented.

Discussion Questions

1. What is the relationship of organizational structure, control, and culture? Give some examples of when and under what conditions a mismatch between these components might arise.

2. What kind of structure best describes the way your (a) business school and (b) university operate? Why is the structure appropriate? Would another structure fit better?

3. When would a company choose a matrix structure? What are the problems associated with managing this structure, and why might a product-team structure be preferable?

4. For each of the structures discussed in the chapter, outline the most suitable control systems.

5. What kind of structure, controls, and culture would you would be likely to find in (a) a small manufacturing company, (b) a chain store, (c) a high-tech company, and (d) a Big Four accounting firm?

Practicing Strategic Management

SMALL-GROUP EXERCISE: DECIDING ON AN ORGANIZATIONAL STRUCTURE

Break up into groups of three to five people. You are a group of managers of a major soft drinks company that is going head-to-head with Coca-Cola to increase market share. Your strategy is to increase your product range to offer a soft drink in every segment of the market to attract customers. Currently you have a functional structure. What you are trying to work out now is how best to implement your strategy in order to launch your new products. Should you move to a more complex kind of product structure, and, if so, which one? Alternatively, should you establish new-venture divisions, and spin off each kind of new soft drink into its own company so that it can focus its resources on its market niche? Thinking strategically, to improve your decision making, debate the pros and cons of the possible organizational structures, and decide which structure you will implement.

ARTICLE FILE 12

Find an example of a company that competes in one industry that has recently changed the way it implements its strategy. What changes did it make? Why did it make these changes? What effect did these changes have on the behavior of people and functions?

STRATEGIC MANAGEMENT PROJECT: MODULE 12

This module asks you to identify how your company implements its strategy. For this part of your project, you need to obtain information about your company's structure, control, systems, and culture. This information may be hard to obtain unless you can interview managers directly. But you can make many inferences about the company's structure from the nature of its activities, and if you write to the company, it may provide you with an organizational chart and other information. Also, published information, such as compensation for top management, are available in the company's annual reports or 10K. If your company is well known, magazines such as *Fortune* and *Business Week* frequently report on corporate culture or control issues. Nevertheless, you may be forced to make some bold assumptions to complete this part of the project.

1. How large is the company as measured by the number of its employees? How many levels in the hierarchy does it have from the top to the bottom? Based on

these two measures and any other information you may have, would you say your company operates with a relatively tall or a flat structure? Does your company have a centralized or a decentralized approach to decision making?

2. What changes (if any) would you make to the way the company allocates authority and responsibility?

3. Draw an organizational chart showing the main way in which your company groups its activities. Based on this chart, decide what kind of structure (functional, product, or divisional) your company operates with.

4. Why did your company choose this structure? In what ways is it appropriate for its business? In what ways is it not?

5. What kind of integration or integration mechanisms does your company use?

6. What are the main kinds of control systems your company is using? What kinds of behaviors is the organization trying to (a) shape and (b) motivate through the use of these control systems?

7. What role does the top management team play in creating the culture of your organization? Can you identify the characteristic norms and values that describe the way people behave in your organization? How does the design of the organization's structure affect its culture?

8. What are the sources of your company's distinctive competencies? Which functions are most important to it? How does your company design its structure, control, and culture at the *functional level* to enhance its (a) efficiency, (b) quality, (c) innovativeness, (d) and responsiveness to customers?

9. What is your company's business-level strategy? How does it design its structure and control systems to enhance and support its business-level strategy? For example, what steps does it take to further cross-functional integration? Does it have a functional, product, or matrix structure?

10. How does your company's culture support its strategy? Can you determine any ways in which its top management team influences its culture?

11. Based on this analysis, would you say your company is coordinating and motivating its people and subunits effectively? Why or why not? What changes (if any) would you make to the way your company's structure operates? What use could it make of restructuring or reengineering?

EXPLORING THE WEB
Visiting Home Depot

Go to **www.homedepot.com,** and examine corporate information such as the company overview, history, and press releases. Based on this information, what kind of structure, control systems, and culture do you think Home Depot has in place to implement its business model and strategies?

General Task: Search the Web for an example of a company that has been involved in changing the way it implements its strategy. What were its problems? How did it use structure, control, and culture to improve the way it operates?

Closing Case

Sam Walton's Approach to Implementing Wal-Mart's Strategy

Wal-Mart, headquartered in Bentonville, Arkansas, is the largest retailer in the world, with sales of almost $65 billion in 2002. Its success rests on the nature of the strategic control systems that its founder, the late Sam Walton, established for the company. Walton wanted all his managers and workers to have a hands-on approach to their jobs and to be totally committed to Wal-Mart's main goal, which he defined as total customer satisfaction. To motivate his employees, Walton created a strategic control system that gave employees at all levels continuous feedback about their and the company's performance.

First, Walton developed a financial control system that provided managers with day-to-day feedback about the performance of all aspects of the business. Through a sophisticated companywide satellite system, corporate managers at its Bentonville headquarters can evaluate the performance of each store, and even of each department in each store. Information about store profits and the rate of turnover of goods is provided to store managers daily, and store managers in turn communicate this information to Wal-Mart's 625,000 employees (who are called associates). By sharing such information, Walton's method encourages all associates to learn the fundamentals of the retailing business so they can work to improve it.

If any store seems to be underperforming, managers and associates meet to probe the reasons and to find solutions to help raise performance. Wal-Mart's top managers routinely visit stores having problems to lend their expertise, and each month top managers use the company's aircraft to fly to various Wal-Mart stores so they can keep their fingers on the pulse of the business. It is also customary for Wal-Mart's top managers to spend their Saturdays meeting together to discuss the week's financial results and their implications for the future.

Walton insisted on linking performance to rewards. Each manager's individual performance, measured by his or her ability to meet specific goals or output targets, is reflected in pay raises and chances for promotion (promotion to bigger stores in the company's 2,000-store empire and even to corporate headquarters, because Wal-Mart routinely promotes from within the company rather than hires managers from other companies). While top managers receive large stock options linked to the company's performance targets and stock price, even ordinary associates receive stock in the company. An associate who started with Walton in the 1970s would by now have accumulated more than $250,000 in stock because of the appreciation of Wal-Mart's stock over time.

Walton instituted an elaborate system of controls, such as rules and budgets, to shape employees' behavior. Each store performs the same activities in the same way, and all employees receive the same kind of training so they know how to behave toward customers. In this way, Wal-Mart is able to standardize its operations, which leads to major cost savings and allows managers to make storewide changes easily.

Finally, Walton was not content just to use output and behavior controls and monetary rewards to motivate his associates. To involve associates in the business and encourage them to develop work behaviors focused on providing quality customer service, he established strong cultural values and norms for his company. Some norms that associates are expected to follow include the *ten-foot attitude* that developed when Walton, during his visits to the stores, encouraged associates to "promise that whenever you come within 10 feet of a customer you will look him in the eye, greet him, and ask him if you can help him"; the *sundown rule,* which states that employees should strive to answer customers' requests by sundown on the day they receive them; and the *Wal-Mart cheer* ("Give me a *W,* give me an *A,*" and so on), which is used in all its stores.

The strong customer-oriented values that Walton created are exemplified in the stories its members tell one another about the company's concern for its customers. They include stories such as the one about Sheila, who risked her own safety when she jumped in front of a car to prevent a little boy from being struck; about Phyllis, who administered CPR to a customer who had suffered a heart attack in her store; and about Annette, who gave up the Power Ranger she had on layaway for her own son so a customer's son could have his birthday wish. The strong Wal-Mart culture also helps to control and motivate its

employees and helps associates to achieve the stringent output and financial targets the company has set for itself.

Case Discussion Questions

1. What were the main elements of the control system that Sam Walton created?

2. In what ways will this control system facilitate Wal-Mart's strategy of global expansion?

Sources: J. Pettet, "Wal-Mart Yesterday and Today," *Discount Merchandiser* (December 1995): 66–67. M. Reid, "Stores of Value," *Economist,* March 4, 1995, pp. ss5–ss7. M. Troy, "The Culture Remains the Constant," *Discount Store News,* June 8, 1998, pp. 95–98. **www.walmart.com.**

Implementing Strategy in Companies That Compete Across Industries and Countries

Opening Case

The "New HP" Gets Up to Speed

In May 2002, the merger between Hewlett Packard and Compaq to form the "new HP" was finally approved, and the two companies moved quickly to combine their skills and resources. The new HP is a leading global multibusiness IT-infrastructure provider, selling a complete range of computer hardware, software and solutions, information services, and imaging and printing products. HP currently serves more than 1 billion customers across 162 countries with 150,000 employees and generated almost $90 billion in 2001. The immediate task facing HP's managers is how to position the company to compete across industries against competitors like IBM, also a multibusiness IT infrastructure provider, and Dell, the leader in the fiercely competitive PC industry.

The justification for the merger to create the new HP would be the new company's ability to combine the former companies' cross-industry product lines and reap the benefits of both cost savings and differentiation. Joining both company's product lines would allow them to streamline the product range, eliminate the duplication of costly functional activities, and achieve billions in cost savings. Combining their joint operations would allow them to transfer, share, and leverage their competencies and achieve the value-creating benefits of increased product differentiation. Where will these gains come from?

First, the new HP is a leader in all the important industries in the computing and IT sector: servers, storage, management software, imaging and printing, personal computers and personal access devices, and so on. In other words, it will be able to provide customers with a *complete range* of totally compatible computing and IT products backed by a services group that will be able to provide the software and expertise to customize these products to the needs of customers. As a result, HP claims its products will provide better flexibility, better interoperability, and the lowest cost of ownership of any company in the industry.

To achieve these benefits, the two companies' many business units have been integrated and reorganized into four major product divisions, with a multidivisional structure selected to integrate the activities of its new four divisions: hardware, software, services, and imaging and printing. Each division will be treated as an independent profit center, and the divisions will be expected to work together to coordinate their new products and activities to make sure they are in keeping with its corporate strategy. The top executives in these divisions will report to Carly Fiorina, HP's CEO. Michael Capellas, the former CEO of Compaq and former HP president, was responsible for HP's global business groups, worldwide sales, supply chain management, and e-commerce operations. Capellas was totally committed to leveraging HP's competencies and capabilities in these areas because most of his time at Compaq was spent dealing with these critical issues.

Indeed, Capellas attributed Compaq's poor performance in the 1990s to a combination of factors that had affected HP as well. First, as it had grown through the 1990s, it had implemented a matrix structure to control its diverse businesses (as had the old HP at one time). Over time, however, the matrix structure resulted in increasingly slow decision making because *geography* rather than *product-line* considerations drove strategy making. The needs of the whole corporation were being ignored as the needs of each geographic business or division took precedence. Capellas scrapped the decentralized matrix structure and replaced it with a multidivisional one based on product line—for example, personal computers or high-end corporate workstations. At the same time, he instituted strict controls: each business was made

a profit center, and each division's managers were given clear sales and profit objectives and the responsibility to achieve those objectives.

Second, Capellas attributed Compaq's problems to its slowness in developing an Internet strategy and reaching out to customers, both corporate and individual. Capellas insisted that each division should integrate its activities and products around the Internet to streamline and integrate its own operations to reduce costs and speed decision making. He championed this idea and created an "Internet culture" at Compaq, and soon employees began to talk only about their division's business model in terms of its relationship to the Internet. Capellas charged a team of corporate managers with establishing a series of Internet teams to speed the development of Internet-based software systems to facilitate direct sales to all types of customers. Moreover, he demanded that these Internet systems be standardized across divisions in order to integrate their activities better and allow them to work together to provide large customers with a complete computer package consisting of mainframes and servers, as well as desktop and portable computers. Third, Capellas recognized how much of a competitive advantage Dell had gained over Compaq by its use of the Internet to facilitate the management of its value chain. He instructed managers to take all of Compaq's supply chain activities online to try to reduce Dell's 10 to 15 percent cost advantage.

Capellas was in charge of accomplishing these same things in the new HP while Fiorina, as CEO, was and is responsible for taking the broad view of HP's multibusiness model and forecasting how changes in IT might shift industry boundaries and affect the company in the future. Formulating HP's global multibusiness strategy will also be one of her major concerns, for the complexity of HP's global operations is staggering. The need to customize products to the needs of different world regions and to work out where to make them to lower HP's cost structure and increase the appeal of its products are major questions the whole of HP's top management is confronting right now.

Sources: M. Hays, "Compaq Maps Future," *Informationweek,* June 17, 1998, p. 14. A. Taylor III, "Compaq Looks Inside for Salvation," *Fortune,* August 16, pp. 124–128. **www.compaq.com,** press release, September 1999. **www.hp.com,** 2002.

Overview   The story of the new HP's efforts to develop a competitive multibusiness model to allow it to combine the old HP and Compaq's competencies to battle competitors like IBM and Dell suggests how complex strategic thinking can become at the corporate level. Companies have to continually examine how to improve the way they implement their multibusiness models to raise their performance.

This chapter takes off where the last one ends and examines how to implement strategy when a company decides to enter and compete in new industries, or countries when it expands globally, and when it chooses means such as merger or outsourcing to strengthen its multibusiness model. The strategy implementation issue remains the same: how to use organizational structure, control, and culture to allow a company to pursue its business model and strategies successfully. Once a company decides to compete across industries and countries, however, it confronts a new set of problems, some of them continuations of problems discussed in Chapter 12 and some of them a direct consequence of the more complex product and market choices it has made and hence which have to be implemented.

By the end of the chapter, you will appreciate the many complex issues and choices confronting managers with the task of managing multibusiness and global companies and the reasons that strategy implementation is an integral part of the process of achieving superior performance.

Managing Corporate Strategy Through The Multidivisional Structure

As Chapter 10 discusses, there are many ways in which corporate-level strategies such as vertical integration or diversification can be used to strengthen a company's competitive position in the industries in which it competes. However, substantial implementation problems arise as well, many of them due to the increasing bureaucratic costs associated with managing a larger collection of companies that operate in different industries. These costs are especially high when a company is seeking to gain the differentiation and low-cost advantages of transferring, sharing, or leveraging its distinctive competencies across industries. For companies pursuing a multibusiness model, the problems and costs of managing the handoffs or transfers between value chain functions across industries to obtain these benefits rise sharply. It is the need to economize on these costs that propels strategic managers to search for improved ways of implementing the corporate-level strategies necessary to pursue a multibusiness model.

As a company begins to enter new industries and produce completely different kinds of products for different markets, such as cars, fast food, and computers, the structures described in Chapter 12, such as the functional and product structure, are not up to the task. They cannot provide sufficient coordination between functions and motivation to employees that implementing a multibusiness model requires. As a result, the control problems (measurement, customer, location, strategic) that give rise to bureaucratic costs rise. Experiencing these problems is a sign that the company has outgrown its structure. Strategic managers need to invest more resources to develop a more complex structure—one that can meet the needs of its multibusiness strategy. The answer for most large, complex companies is to move to a multidivisional structure, design a cross-industry control system, and fashion a corporate culture to reduce these problems and economize on bureaucratic costs.

The multidivisional structure possesses two main innovations over a functional or product structure that allow a company to grow and diversify while reducing the coordination and control problems inherent in entering and competing in new industries. First, in each industry in which a company operates, strategic managers organize the companies in that industry into one or more subunits called *divisions*. Sometimes each division contains a full set of all the value chain functions it needs to pursue its business model; in this case, it is called a *self-contained division*. For example, GE competes in over 150 different industries, and in each industry, all of its divisions are self-sufficient and perform all the value creation functions. Sometimes the divisions inside an industry share value chain functions to obtain cost savings and because this often helps the divisions to benefit from leveraging competencies across divisions, as discussed in detail below. For example, PepsiCo has two major divisions in the soft drinks and snack foods industries; each has its own R&D and manufacturing functions, but they share the marketing and distribution functions to lower operating costs and achieve the gains from differentiation.

Second, the office of *corporate headquarters staff* is created to monitor divisional activities and to exercise financial control over each of the divisions.[1] This staff contains the corporate-level managers who oversee the activities of divisional managers. Hence, the organizational hierarchy is taller in a multidivisional structure than in a product or functional structure. The role of the extra managers is to develop strategic control systems that lower a company's overall cost structure, including finding ways to economize on the costs of controlling the handoffs and transfers between divisions. The extra cost of these corporate managers is more than justified if their actions lead to cost savings elsewhere or revenue-enhancing differentiation that boosts overall return on investment capital (ROIC) of the company.

In the multidivisional structure, day-to-day operations of a division are the responsibility of divisional management; that is, divisional management has *operating responsibility*. The corporate headquarters, which includes top executives as well as their support staff, is responsible for overseeing the company's long-term multibusiness model and for providing guidance for interdivisional projects. These executives have *strategic responsibility*. Such a combination of self-contained divisions with a centralized corporate management provides the extra coordination and control necessary to manage entry into new industries.

Figure 13.1 illustrates a typical multidivisional structure found in a large chemical company such as Du Pont. Although this company might easily have twenty different divisions, only three—the oil, pharmaceuticals, and plastics divisions—are represented here. Each division possesses some combination of the value chain functions it needs to pursue its own business model. Each is also normally treated by the corporate center as a profit center, and strategic control measures such as ROIC are used to monitor and evaluate each division's performance.[2] The use of this kind of output control makes it easier for corporate managers to identify high-performing and underperforming divisions and to take corrective action as necessary.

Because they have been separated into subunits by industry, each division is also able to develop the structure and culture that best suits its particular business model, for example, a product, matrix, or market structure. As a result, implementing a multidivisional structure allows a multibusiness company to take into account the need for each separate division to adopt the structure and control systems necessary to pursue its own business-level strategy effectively.

Figure 13.1 shows that the oil division has a functional structure because it is pursuing a low-cost approach, the pharmaceuticals division has a product-team structure to encourage speedy development of new drugs, and the plastics division has a matrix structure to allow it to quickly develop new kinds of customized plastic products to suit the changing needs of its customers. Sometimes size of operations alone is enough to compel a company to use a multidivisional structure. For example, inside one industry, the car industry, GM operates the whole corporation through a multidivisional structure, and each of its main car brands—Cadillac, Buick, and so on—is organized as separate divisions. Some issues in the way GM has operated its multidivisional structure over time are discussed in Strategy in Action 13.1.

FIGURE 13.1

Multidivisional Structure

As the GM story suggests, operating a multidivisional structure is a *continuing* challenge for managers. Because the multidivisional structure is so widely used, it is necessary to look closely at its advantages and disadvantages.

Advantages of a Multidivisional Structure

When managed effectively at both the corporate and the divisional levels, a multidivisional structure offers several advantages. Together, they can raise corporate profitability to a new peak because they allow the organization to implement the corporate-level strategies necessary to pursue the multibusiness model.

Enhanced Corporate Financial Control. The profitability of different business divisions is clearly visible in the multidivisional structure.[3] Because each division is its own profit center, financial controls can be applied to each business on the basis of profitability criteria such as ROIC. Typically, these controls cover establishing targets, monitoring performance on a regular basis, and selectively intervening when problems arise. Corporate headquarters is also in a better position to allocate corporate financial resources among competing divisions. The visibility of divisional performance means that corporate headquarters can identify the divisions in which investment of funds will yield the greatest long-term ROIC. In a sense, the corporate office is in a position to act as the investor or banker in an internal capital market, channeling funds to high-yield uses.

Enhanced Strategic Control. The multidivisional structure frees corporate managers from business-level responsibilities. Corporate managers have the time and scope for contemplating wider strategic issues and for developing responses to environmental changes, such as quickly changing industry boundaries. The multidivisional

Strategy in Action

GM's Multidivisional Structure Changes over Time

13.1

William C. Durant formed the General Motors Company on September 16, 1908. Into it, he brought about twenty-five different companies. Only four of them—Buick, Chevrolet, Pontiac, and Cadillac—survive as operating divisions today. Originally, each company retained its own operating identity, and the GM organization was simply a holding company, a central office surrounded by twenty-five satellites. When Alfred P. Sloan took over as president of GM in 1923, he inherited this collection of independently managed car companies, which made their own decisions, did their own R&D, and produced their own range of cars.

GM's principal competitor, the Ford Motor Car Company, was organized very differently. From the beginning, Henry Ford had emphasized the advantages of economies of scale and mass production and had designed a mechanistic structure to achieve them. He built a highly centralized hierarchy in which he had complete personal control over decision making. To reduce costs, Ford at first produced only one vehicle, the Model T, and gave enormous attention to finding improved ways of producing it. Because of its organizational design, Ford's company was initially much more profitable than GM. The problem facing Sloan was to compete with Ford not only in terms of product but in financial performance too.

Confronted with Ford's success, Sloan must have been tempted to close several of GM's small operations and concentrate production in a few locations where the company could enjoy the benefits of fewer models and cost savings from economies of scale. For example, he could have adopted a product division structure, created three product divisions to manufacture three kinds of car, and centralized support functions such as marketing, R&D, and engineering to reduce costs. Sloan, however, recognized the importance of the diverse sets of research, design, and marketing skills and competencies present in the small car companies. He realized that there was a great risk of losing this diversity of talent if he combined all these skills into one centrally located research and design department. Moreover, if the same set of support functions, such as engineering and design, worked for all of GM's divisions, there was a danger that all GM cars would begin to look alike. Nevertheless, Sloan also recognized the advantages of centralized control in achieving economies of scale, controlling costs, and providing for the development of a strategic plan for the company as a

whole rather than for each company separately. So he searched for an organizational structure that would allow him to achieve all these objectives simultaneously and found his answer in the multidivisional structure. In 1921, he instituted this change, noting that GM "needs to find a principle for coordination without losing the advantages of decentralization."

Each of GM's different businesses was placed in a self-contained operating division with support services like sales, production, engineering, and finance. Each division became a profit center and was evaluated on its return on investment. Sloan was quite clear about the main advantage of linking decentralization to return on investment: It raised the visibility of each division's performance. And, Sloan observed, it (1) "increases the morale of the organization by placing each operation on its own foundation, . . . assuming its own responsibility and contributing its share to the final result"; (2) "develops statistics correctly reflecting. . .the true measure of efficiency"; and (3) "enables the corporation to direct the placing of additional capital where it will result in the greatest benefit to the corporation as a whole."

Sloan recommended that transactions between divisions be set by a transfer-pricing scheme based on cost plus some predetermined rate of return. However, to avoid protecting a high-cost internal supplier, he also recommended a number of steps involving analysis of the operations of outside competitors to determine the fair price. Sloan established a strong, professional, centralized headquarters management staff to perform such calculations. Corporate management's primary role was to audit divisional performance and plan strategy for the total organization. Divisional managers were to be responsible for all product-related decisions.

In the 1980s, after fierce competition from the Japanese, GM took a hard look at its multidivisional structure. The duplication of R&D and engineering, and the purchasing of inputs by each division independently, was costing the company billions of extra dollars. In 1984, GM's five autonomous car divisions were combined into two groups: Chevrolet and Pontiac would concentrate on small cars and Buick, Oldsmobile, and Cadillac would focus on large cars.

GM hoped that the reorganization would reduce costs and speed product development, but it was a disaster. With control of design and engineering more centralized at the group level, the cars of the different divisions started to look the same. Nobody could tell a Buick from a Cadillac or an Oldsmobile. Sales plummeted. Moreover, the reorganization did not speed decision making. It increased the number of levels in the hierarchy by introducing the group level into the organization. As a result, GM had thirteen levels in its hierarchy; in comparison, Toyota had just five. Once again the company was in trouble. Before the reorganization, it had been too decentralized; now it was too centralized. What to do?

Realizing its mistake, GM moved to return control over product design to the divisions while continuing to centralize functions like engineering and purchasing to realize scale economies. This restructuring has had some success. Cadillac's management moved quickly to establish a new product identity and design new models. However, Oldsmobile never regained its differentiated appeal and the division was disbanded in 2001. Currently, GM is focusing on finding ways to lower its cost structure, which was one of the highest in the industry, and it has been successful. For example, it has reduced the number of cars in its product range and the number of different platforms used to make cars; it has also vertically disintegrated by spinning off high-cost internal suppliers and recentralized the purchasing of component parts using the car industry's B2B network to outsource more of its components. In 2002, it announced that its per unit costs of car making were down almost to the level of Ford and Chrysler, something it had to achieve to boost profitability and remain a major player in the global marketplace.

Sources: A. P. Sloan, *My Years at General Motors* (Garden City, N.Y.: Doubleday, 1946). A. Taylor III, "Can GM Remodel Itself?" *Fortune,* January 13, 1992, pp. 26–34; W. Hampton and J. Norman, "General Motors: What Went Wrong?" *Business Week,* March 16, 1987, pp. 102–110. **www.gm.com,** 2002. The quotations are on pp. 46 and 50 in Sloan, *My Years at General Motors.*

structure also enables corporate headquarters to obtain the proper information to perform long-run strategic and scenario planning for the entire corporation, including decisions about which businesses to expand and which to exit from.

Growth. The multidivisional structure lets the company overcome an organizational limit to its growth. By reducing information overload at the center, corporate managers can consider emerging opportunities for further growth and diversification. Communication problems are reduced because the same set of standardized accounting and financial output controls can be used for all divisions. Also, from a behavior control perspective, corporate managers are able to implement a policy of management by exception, which means that they intervene only when problems arise.

Stronger Pursuit of Internal Efficiency. Within a functional structure, the interdependence of functional departments means that the performance of each *individual* function inside a company cannot be measured by objective criteria. For example, the profitability of the finance function, marketing function, or manufacturing function cannot be assessed in isolation, because they are only part of the whole. This often means that within the functional structure, considerable degrees of organizational slack, that is, the unproductive use of functional resources, can go undetected. For example, the head of the finance function might employ a larger staff than required for efficiency to reduce work pressures inside the department and to bring the manager higher status. In a multidivisional structure, however, the individual efficiency of each autonomous division can be directly observed and measured in terms of the profit it generates. Thus, autonomy makes divisional managers accountable for their own performance; they can have no alibis for poor performance. The corporate office is thus in a better position to identify inefficiencies.

Problems in Implementing a Multidivisional Structure

Although research suggests that large companies that adopt a multidivisional structure outperform those that retain the functional structure, this structure has its disadvantages as well.[4] Good management can eliminate some of them, but others are inherent in the way the structure operates and require constant managerial attention, as the GM example in Strategy in Action 13.1 suggests.

Establishing the Divisional-Corporate Authority Relationship.

The authority relationship between corporate headquarters and the divisions must be correctly established. The multidivisional structure introduces a new level in the hierarchy: the corporate level. The problem lies in deciding how much authority and control to delegate to the operating divisions and how much authority to retain at corporate headquarters. This was the problem first noted by Sloan when he implemented the multidivisional structure into GM.[5] What Sloan found was that when headquarters retained too much power and authority, the operating divisions lacked sufficient autonomy to develop the business strategy that might best meet the needs of the division. On the other hand, when too much power was delegated to the divisions, they pursued divisional objectives, with little heed to the needs of the whole corporation. As a result, not all the potential gains from using this structure could be achieved.

Thus, the central issue in managing the multidivisional structure is how much authority should be *centralized* at corporate headquarters and how much should be *decentralized* to the divisions. This issue must be decided by each company in reference to the nature of its business- and corporate-level strategies. There are no easy answers, and as the environment changes or the company alters its strategies over time, the balance between corporate and divisional control will also change, as Strategy in Action 13.2 suggests.

Distortion of Information.

If corporate headquarters places too much emphasis on each division's individual profitability—for instance, by setting very high and stringent ROIC targets—divisional managers may choose to distort the information they supply top management and paint a rosy picture of it at the expense of future profitability. Bureaucratic costs now increase as divisions may attempt to make ROIC look better by cutting product development or new investments or marketing expenditures. Although such actions might boost short-run ROIC, they do so at the cost of cutting back on investments and expenditures that may be necessary to maintain the long-term profitability of the company. The problem stems from too tight financial control. GM suffered from this problem in recent years as declining performance prompted divisional managers to try to make their divisions look good to corporate headquarters to secure greater funds for future investment. Managing the corporate-divisional interface requires coping with subtle power issues.

Competition for Resources.

The third problem of managing a multidivisional structure is that the divisions themselves may compete for resources, and this rivalry can prevent gains from transferring, sharing, or leveraging distinctive competencies across businesses. For example, the amount of capital for investment that corporate managers have to distribute to the divisions is fixed. Generally, the divisions that can demonstrate the highest ROIC get the lion's share of the money. Because that large share strengthens them in the next time period, the strong divisions grow stronger. Consequently, divisions may actively compete for resources and thereby

Strategy in Action

13.2

Amoco, ARCO, and Burmah Castrol Become Part of BP

As with most other global oil companies, Amoco was engaged in three major activities: oil exploration, refining, and chemicals manufacturing. To manage these activities, it used a three-legged structure and created three independent operating subsidiaries to manage each of its three main activities. Each subsidiary had its own set of managers responsible for overseeing all the many different divisions inside each subsidiary; thus, there was an extra level of control: the subsidiary level. The managers of all three subsidiaries then reported to Amoco's corporate-level managers, who oversaw their activities and made the final decision on what each subsidiary should be doing. Because all important decision making at Amoco was centralized at the top, it often took a long time to make decisions because of the many managerial layers between Amoco's corporate managers and its divisional managers. The slow decision-making process hampered divisional managers' attempts to build a competitive advantage, but this situation was left unattended too during the prosperous oil industry of the 1980s.

By the 1990s, Amoco, like other global oil companies such as Exxon, British Petroleum, and Mobil, had experienced intense pressure to reduce costs because of flat gas prices. To try to boost profits, Amoco laid off more than one-quarter of its workforce, but this did not work. Amoco's managers then took a close look at its structure to see whether there was a way to increase its performance.

Amoco's chairman and CEO, H. Laurence Fuller, decided that a massive reorganization of Amoco's structure was necessary. Fuller eliminated Amoco's three-legged structure completely and removed all the managers at the subsidiary level. The three subsidiaries were divided into seventeen independent divisions according to their industry, and Amoco changed to a multidivisional structure. Henceforth, strategic responsibilities were decentralized to the managers of each division, who were free to choose their own business-level strategy. Each division was evaluated on the basis of its ability to reach certain ROIC targets set by corporate managers, but their own managers determined the way they achieved those targets.

By 1996, it was clear that Fuller's move to a multidivisional structure had worked. Managers were acting more entrepreneurially, and the company was operating more efficiently. However, in the late 1990s, oil industry companies began to consolidate further to make better use of their resources and lower their cost structure. Fuller agreed to merge Amoco with British Petroleum (BP). Because many of both companies' divisions were competing in the same industries, their activities overlapped and duplicated one another, so BP developed a value creation grid and then merged Amoco's seventeen divisions with its own thirty-three divisions. In 2001, BP acquired ARCO for its extensive gas reserves and Burmah Castrol, the well-known fuel oil maker. Once again, it integrated these companies into its existing operations, and from these mergers it strengthened its differentiated position in its major sectors of oil, gas, chemicals, and downstream activities such as retailing. BP also announced that it expected to achieve $5.9 billion in cost savings from these moves.

Sources: C. Soloman, "Amoco to Cut More Jobs and Radically Alter Its Structure," *Wall Street Journal,* July 22, 1995, p. B4. "Shell Reorganizes for Speed and Profit," *Oil and Gas Journal,* December 21, 1998, p. 31.

reduce interdivisional coordination. As a result, the potential gains from pursuing a multibusiness model will be lost.

Transfer Pricing. Divisional competition may lead to battles over **transfer pricing,** that is, conflicts over establishing the fair or "competitive" price of a resource or skill developed in one division that is to be transferred and sold to other divisions that require it. As discussed in Chapter 10, one of the origins of the problems of handoffs or transfers between divisions, and thus a major source of bureaucratic costs, is the problem of setting prices for resource transfers to obtain the benefits of the multibusiness models when pursuing a vertical integration or related diversification strategy.

Rivalry among divisions is common in the transfer pricing process because each supplying division has the incentive to set the highest price for its resources or skills to maximize its own revenues and profits. However, purchasing divisions view attempts to charge high prices as undermining their own profitability—hence the problem. Such competition can completely undermine the corporate culture and make a company a battleground. If such battles go unresolved, the benefits of the multibusiness model will not be achieved. Hence, there is a need for the sensitive design of incentive and control systems to make the multidivisional structure work.

Short-Term R&D Focus. If corporate headquarters sets extremely high and rigid ROIC targets, there is a danger that the divisions will cut back on R&D expenditures to improve their financial performance. Although this inflates divisional performance in the short term, it undermines a division's ability to develop new products and leads to a fall in the stream of long-term profits. Hence, corporate headquarters personnel must carefully control their interactions with the divisions to ensure that both the short- and long-term goals of the business are being achieved.

Duplication of Functional Resources. Because each division often possesses its own set of functions, such as finance or R&D, multidivisional structures are expensive to run and manage. R&D is an especially costly activity, and so some companies centralize such functions at the corporate level to serve all divisions. The duplication of specialist services is not a problem if the cost and differentiation gains from having separate specialist functions are substantial. Corporate managers decide whether duplication is financially justified and which services to centralize or decentralize to optimize short- and long-run profitability.

In sum, the advantages of divisional structures must be balanced against problems of implementing them, but an observant, professional management team that is aware of the issues involved can manage these problems. The increasing use of information technology is also making implementation easier and this is discussed after the issue of implementing structure, control, and culture for different kinds of multibusiness models has been addressed.

Structure, Control, Culture, and Corporate-Level Strategy

Once strategic managers select a multidivisional structure, they must then make choices about what kind of integrating mechanisms and control systems to use to make the structure work efficiently. Such choices depend on whether a company chooses to pursue a multibusiness model based on a strategy of unrelated diversification, vertical integration, or related diversification.

As discussed in Chapter 9, many possible differentiation and cost advantages derive from vertical integration. A company can coordinate resource-scheduling decisions among divisions operating in adjacent industries to reduce manufacturing costs and improve quality, for example.[6] This might mean locating a rolling mill next to a steel furnace to save the costs of reheating steel ingots and make it easier to control the quality of the final product. The many benefits from related diversification also come from transferring, sharing, or leveraging functional resources or skills across divisions, such as sharing distribution and sales networks to increase differentiation or lower the overall cost structure. With both strategies, the benefits to the company come from some *exchange of distinctive competencies* among divisions. To secure these benefits, the company must coordinate activities among divisions. Consequently, structure and control must be designed to handle the handoffs or transfers among divisions.

In the case of unrelated diversification, the multibusiness model is based on using capabilities in entrepreneurship, capabilities in managing organizational structure or culture effectively, or strategic capabilities—for example, through the ability to promote a culture that supports entrepreneurial behavior that leads to rapid product development or from restructuring an underperforming company and establishing an efficient internal capital market that allows corporate managers to make superior capital allocation decisions than would be possible using the external capital market. With this strategy, there are no exchanges among divisions, each operates separately and independently, and the exchanges that need to be coordinated take place between divisions and corporate headquarters. Structure and control must therefore be designed to allow each division to operate independently while giving corporate managers easy ability to monitor and to intervene if necessary.

The choice of structure and control mechanisms depends on the degree to which a company using a multidivisional structure needs to control the handoffs and interactions among divisions. The more interdependent the divisions—that is, the more they depend on each other for skills and resources—the greater are the bureaucratic costs associated with obtaining the potential benefits from a particular strategy.[7] Table 13.1 indicates what forms of structure and control companies should adopt to economize on the bureaucratic costs associated with the three corporate strategies.[8] We examine them in detail in the next sections.

Unrelated Diversification. Because there are *no exchanges or linkages* among divisions, unrelated diversification is the easiest and cheapest strategy to manage; it is associated with the lowest level of bureaucratic costs. The main requirement of the structure and control system is that it allows corporate managers to evaluate divisional performance easily and accurately. Thus, companies use a multidivisional

TABLE 13.1

Corporate Strategy and Structure and Control

Corporate Strategy	Appropriate Structure	Need for Integration	Type of Control		
			Financial Control	Behavior Control	Organizational Culture
Unrelated diversification	Multidivisional	Low (no exchanges between divisions)	Great use (e.g., ROI)	Some use (e.g., budgets)	Little use
Vertical integration	Multidivisional	Medium (scheduling resource transfers)	Great use (e.g., ROI, transfer pricing)	Great use (e.g., standardization, budgets)	Some use (e.g., shared norms and values)
Related diversification	Multidivisional	High (achieving synergies between divisions by integrating roles)	Little use	Great use (e.g., rules, budgets)	Great use (e.g., norms, values, common language)

structure, and each division is evaluated by output controls such as return on invested capital. A company also applies sophisticated accounting controls to obtain information quickly from the divisions so that corporate managers can readily compare divisions on several dimensions. Textron and Dover are good examples of companies that use sophisticated computer networks and accounting controls to manage their structures, which allow them almost daily access to divisional performance.

Divisions usually have considerable autonomy *unless* they fail to reach their ROIC goals. Generally, corporate headquarters will not intervene in the operations of a division unless there are problems. If problems arise, corporate headquarters may step in to take corrective action, perhaps replacing managers or providing additional financial resources, depending on the reason for the problem. If they see no possibility of a turnaround, they may decide to divest the division. The multidivisional structure allows the unrelated company to operate its businesses as a portfolio of investments that can be bought and sold as business conditions change. Often managers in the various divisions do not know one another; they may not even know what other companies are in the corporate portfolio. Hence, the idea of a corporate culture is meaningless.

The use of financial controls to manage a company means that no integration among divisions is necessary. This is why the bureaucratic costs of managing an unrelated company are low. The biggest problem facing corporate personnel is determining capital allocations to the various divisions so that the overall profitability of the portfolio is maximized. They also have to oversee divisional managers and make sure that divisions are achieving ROIC targets. Alco Standard's way of managing its businesses, described in Strategy in Action 13.3, demonstrates how to operate a strategy of unrelated diversification.

Strategy in Action   13.3

Alco Standard Gets It Right

Alco Standard, based in Valley Forge, Pennsylvania, is one of the largest office supply companies in the United States, distributing office and paper supplies and materials through a nationwide network of wholly owned distribution companies. It pursues a highly successful strategy of unrelated diversification. The policy of Alco's top management is that authority and control should be completely decentralized to the managers in each of the company's fifty divisions. Each division is left alone to make its own manufacturing or purchasing decisions even though some potential benefits, in the form of corporate-wide purchasing or marketing, are being lost. Top management pursues this nonintervention policy because it believes that the gains from allowing its managers to act as independent entrepreneurs exceed any potential cost savings that might result from coordinating interdivisional activities. It believes that a decentralized operating

system allows a big company to act in a way that is similar to a small company, avoiding the problem of growing bureaucracy and organizational inertia.

At Alco, top management interprets its role as relieving the divisions of administrative chores, such as bookkeeping and accounting, and collecting market information on competitive pricing and products, which allows divisional managers to improve their business-level strategy. Centralizing these information activities reduces each division's cost structure and provides the standardization that lets top management make better decisions about resource allocation. Alco's division heads are regarded as partners in the corporate enterprise and are rewarded through stock options linked to the performance of their divisions. So far, Alco has been very successful with its decentralized operating structure and has achieved a compound growth rate of 19 percent a year.

Vertical Integration. Vertical integration is a more expensive strategy to manage than unrelated diversification because *sequential resource flows* from one division to the next must be coordinated. Once again, the multidivisional structure economizes on the bureaucratic costs associated with achieving such coordination. This structure provides the centralized control necessary for the vertically integrated company to achieve benefits from the control of resource transfers. Corporate personnel assume the responsibility for devising output and behavior controls that solve the problems of transferring resources among divisions; for example, they are involved in solving transfer pricing problems. Also, complex rules and procedures are instituted that specify how exchanges are to be made to solve potential transaction problems. As previously noted, complex resource exchanges can lead to conflict among divisions, and corporate managers must try to minimize divisional conflicts.

Centralizing authority at corporate headquarters must be done with care in vertically related companies. It carries the risk of involving corporate managers in operating issues at the business level to the point at which the divisions lose their autonomy and motivation. These companies must strike the right balance of centralized control at corporate headquarters and decentralized control at the divisional level if it is to implement this strategy successfully.

Because their interests are at stake, divisions need to have input into scheduling and decisions regarding resource transfer. For example, the plastics division in a chemical company has a vital interest in the activities of the oil division, for the quality of the products it gets from the oil division determines the quality of its own products. Divisional integrating mechanisms can bring about direct coordination and information transfers among divisions.[9] To handle communication among divisions, a company sets up teams for the purpose; it can also use **integrating roles,** whereby an experienced senior manager assumes responsibility for managing complex transfers between two or more divisions. The use of integrating roles to coordinate divisions is common in high-tech and chemical companies, for example.

Thus, a strategy of vertical integration is managed through a combination of corporate and divisional controls. As a result, the organizational structure and control systems used for managing this strategy to economize on bureaucratic costs are more complex and more difficult to implement than those used for unrelated diversification. However, as long as the benefits that derive from vertical integration are realized, the extra expense in implementing this strategy can be justified.

Related Diversification. In the case of related diversification, the gains from pursuing this multibusiness model derive from the transfer, sharing, or leveraging of R&D knowledge, industry information, customer bases, and so on across divisions. Also, with this structure, the high level of resource sharing and joint production by divisions makes it hard for corporate managers to measure the performance of each individual division.[10] Thus, bureaucratic costs are substantial. The multidivisional structure helps to economize on these costs because it provides some of the extra coordination and control that is required. However, if a related company is to obtain the potential benefits from using its competencies efficiently and effectively, it has to adopt more complicated forms of integration and control at the divisional level to make the structure work.

First, output control is difficult to use because divisions share resources, so it is not easy to measure the performance of an individual division. Therefore, a company needs to develop a corporate culture that stresses cooperation among divisions and corporate rather than purely divisional goals. Second, corporate managers must establish sophisticated integrating devices to ensure coordination among divisions. Integrating roles and even integrating teams of managers are often essential because they provide the context in which managers from different divisions can meet and develop a common vision of corporate goals. The new HP, for instance, created a high-level integrating team composed of scores of managers to coordinate the merger process.[11]

An organization with a multidivisional structure must have the right mix of incentives and rewards for cooperation if it is to achieve gains from sharing skills and resources among divisions.[12] With unrelated diversification, divisions operate autonomously, and the company can quite easily reward managers on their division's individual performance. With related diversification, however, rewarding divisions is more difficult because they are engaged in so many shared activities and strategic managers must be sensitive and alert to achieve equity in rewards among divisions. The aim always is to design structure and control systems so that they can maximize the benefits from pursuing the strategy while economizing on bureaucratic costs.

The Role of Information Technology

The increasing use of IT is increasing the advantages and reducing the problems associated with implementing a multibusiness model effectively. IT does this because it facilitates output control, behavior control, and integration between divisions and between divisions and corporate headquarters.

On the advantage side, IT provides a common software platform that can make it much less problematic for divisions to share information and knowledge and obtain the benefits from leveraging their competencies. IT also facilitates output and financial control, making it easier for corporate headquarters to monitor divisional performance and decide when to intervene selectively. It also helps corporate managers better use their strategic and implementation skills because they can react more quickly given that they possess higher-quality, more timely information from the use of a sophisticated cross-organizational IT infrastructure.

In a similar fashion, IT makes it easier to manage the problems that occur when implementing a multidivisional structure. Because it provides both corporate and divisional managers with more and better information, it makes it easier for corporate managers to decentralize control to divisional managers and yet react quickly if the need arises. IT can also make it more difficult to distort information and hide bad news because divisional managers must provide standardized information that can be compared across divisions. Finally, IT eases the transfer pricing problem because divisional managers have access to detailed up-to-date information about how much a certain resource or skill would cost to buy in the external marketplace. Thus, a fair transfer price is easier to determine.

The multidivisional structure is ubiquitous for companies operating with a multibusiness model and pursuing corporate-level strategies to increase company profitability. This does not mean that they are easy to implement; however, they necessarily increase profitability, at least in the short run. Companies like HP and Compaq and AOL and Time Warner and Daimler and Chrysler justified their mergers on the basis that their combined operations will allow them to implement a multidivisional structure that will lead to substantial improvements in operational efficiency and an increased ability to innovate a stream of differentiated products.

Yet DaimlerChrysler has been unable to obtain the benefits it foresaw through combining its competencies in high quality with Chrysler's low-cost car making skills. AOL Time Warner's stock plunged in 2002 when the claimed cost savings and profitable new products expected from its merger were slow to appear. The stocks of WorldCom and Tyco profiled in Chapters 9 and 10 have also plunged as investors doubt these companies can in fact implement their multibusiness models to increase the value they can create. Will the new HP fare any better?

Implementing Strategy Across Countries

Global strategy can play a crucial role in strengthening the business model of both single-business and multibusiness companies. Indeed, few large companies that have expanded into new industries have not already expanded globally into new countries. Companies can use four basic strategies as they begin to market their products and establish production facilities abroad:

- A *multidomestic strategy* is oriented toward local responsiveness, and a company decentralizes control to subsidiaries and divisions in each country in which it operates to produce and customize products to local markets.

- An *international strategy* is based on R&D and marketing being centralized at home and all the other value creation functions being decentralized to national units.

- A *global strategy* is oriented toward cost reduction, with all the principal value creation functions centralized at the optimal global location.

- A *transnational strategy* is focused so that it can achieve local responsiveness and cost reduction. Some functions are centralized and others decentralized at the global location best suited to achieving these objectives.

The need to coordinate and integrate global value chain activities increases as a company moves from a multidomestic to an international to a global and then to a transnational strategy. To obtain the benefits of pursuing a transnational strategy, a company must transfer its distinctive competencies to the global location where they can create the most value and establish a global network to coordinate its divisions at home and abroad. The objective of such coordination is to obtain the benefits from transferring or leveraging competencies across a company's global business units. Thus, the bureaucratic costs associated with solving communications and measurement problems that arise in managing handoffs or transfers across countries to pursue a transnational strategy are much higher than those of pursuing the other strategies. The multidomestic strategy does not require coordinating activities on a global level because value creation activities are handled locally, by country or world region. The international and global strategies fit between the other two strategies: although products have to be sold and marketed globally, and hence global product transfers must be managed, there is less need to coordinate skill and resource transfers than for a transnational strategy.

The implication is that as companies change from a multidomestic to an international, global, or transnational strategy, they require a more complex structure, control system, and culture to coordinate the value creation activities associated with implementing that strategy. More complex structures economize on bureaucratic costs. In general, the choice of structure and control systems for managing a global business is a function of three factors:

1. The decision on how to distribute and allocate responsibility and authority between managers at home and abroad so that effective control over a company's global operations is maintained

2. The selection of the organizational structure that groups divisions both at home and abroad in a way that allows the best use of resources and serves the needs of foreign customers most effectively

3. The selection of the right kinds of integration and control mechanisms and organizational culture to make the overall global structure function effectively

Table 13.2 summarizes the appropriate design choices for companies pursuing each of these strategies.

Implementing a Multidomestic Strategy

When a company pursues a multidomestic strategy, it generally operates with a global-area structure (see Figure 13.2). When using this structure, a company duplicates all value creation activities and establishes an overseas division in every country or world area in which it operates. Authority is decentralized to managers in each overseas division, who devise the appropriate strategy for responding to the needs of the local environment. Managers at global headquarters use market and output controls, such as ROIC, growth in market share, and operation costs, to evaluate the performance of overseas divisions. On the basis of such global comparisons, they can make decisions about capital allocation and orchestrate the transfer of new knowledge among divisions.

A company that makes and sells the same products in many different countries often groups its overseas divisions into world regions to simplify the coordination of products across countries. Europe might be one region, the Pacific Rim another, and the Middle East a third. Grouping allows the same set of output and behavior controls to be applied across all divisions inside a region. Thus, global companies can reduce communications and transfer problems because information can be transmitted more easily across countries with broadly similar cultures. For example, consumers' preferences regarding product design and marketing are likely to be more similar among countries in one world region than among countries in different world regions.

TABLE 13.2
Global Strategy/Structure Relationships

	Multidomestic Strategy	International Strategy	Global Strategy	Transnational Strategy
	Low ← Need for Coordination → High			
	Low ← Bureaucratic Costs → High			
Centralization of Authority	Decentralized to national unit	Core competencies centralized, others decentralized to national units	Centralized at optimal global location	Simultaneously centralized and decentralized
Horizontal Differentiation	Global-area structure	International-division structure	Global product-group structure	Global-matrix structure, matrix in the mind
Need for Complex Integrating Mechanisms	Low	Medium	High	Very High
Organizational Culture	Not important	Quite important	Important	Very important

FIGURE 13.2

Global-Area Structure

Because the overseas divisions themselves have little or no contact with others in different regions, no integrating mechanisms are needed. Nor does a global organizational culture develop because there are no transfers of skills or resources or transfer of personnel among managers from the various world regions. Historically, car companies such as DaimlerChrysler, GM, and Ford used global-area structures to manage their overseas operations. Ford of Europe, for example, had little or no contact with its U.S. parent; capital was the principal resource exchanged.

One problem with a global-area structure and a multidomestic strategy is that the duplication of specialist activities across countries raises a company's overall cost structure. Moreover, the company is not taking advantage of opportunities to transfer, share, or leverage its competencies and capabilities on a global basis; for example, it cannot apply the low-cost manufacturing expertise that has developed in one world region in another. Thus, multidomestic companies lose the many benefits of operating globally. As Chapter 8 discusses, the popularity of this strategic orientation has decreased.

Implementing International Strategy

A company pursuing an international strategy adopts a different route to global expansion. Normally, the company shifts to this strategy when it decides to sell domestically made products in markets abroad. Until the 1990s, for example, companies such as Mercedes-Benz and Jaguar made no attempt to produce in a foreign market; instead, they distributed and sold their domestically produced cars internationally. Such companies usually just add a *foreign sales organization* to their existing structure and continue to use the same control system. If a company is using a functional structure, this department has to coordinate manufacturing, sales, and R&D activities with the needs of the foreign market. Efforts at customization are minimal. In overseas countries, a company usually establishes a subsidiary to handle local sales and distribution. For example, the Mercedes-Benz overseas subsidiaries allocate dealerships, organize supplies of spare parts, and, of course, sell cars. A system of behavior controls is then established to keep the home office informed of changes in sales, spare parts requirements, and so on.

A company with many different products or businesses operating from a multidivisional structure has the challenging problem of coordinating the flow of different products across different countries. To manage these transfers, many companies create an *international division,* which they add to their existing divisional structure (see Figure 13.3).[13] International operations are managed as a separate divisional business, with managers given the authority and responsibility for coordinating domestic product divisions with overseas markets. The international division also monitors and controls the overseas subsidiaries that market the products and decides how much authority to delegate to managers in these countries.

This arrangement of tasks and roles reduces the transaction of managing handoffs across countries and world regions. However, managers abroad are essentially

FIGURE 13.3

International Division
Structure

under the control of managers in the international division, and if domestic and overseas managers compete for control of strategy making, conflict and lack of cooperation may result. Many companies such as IBM, Citibank, and DaimlerChrysler have experienced this problem. Very often, significant strategic control has been decentralized to overseas divisions. When cost pressures force corporate managers to reassess their strategy and they decide to intervene, this frequently provokes resistance, much of it due to differences in culture—not just corporate but also country differences.

Implementing Global Strategy

When a company embarks on a global strategy today, it locates its manufacturing and other value chain activities at the global location that will allow it to increase efficiency, quality, and innovation. In doing so, it has to solve the problems of coordinating and integrating its global value chain activities. It has to find a structure that lowers the bureaucratic costs associated with resource transfers between corporate headquarters and its global divisions and provides the centralized control that a global strategy requires. The answer for many companies is a *global product division structure* (see Figure 13.4).

In this structure, a product division headquarters is created to coordinate the activities of its home and overseas operations. Within each division, headquarters

FIGURE 13.4

Global Product-
Division Structure

managers decide where to locate the different functions at the optimal global location for performing that activity. For example, Phillips has one division responsible for global R&D, manufacturing, marketing, and sales of its light bulbs, another for medical equipment, and so on. The headquarters of the medical division and its R&D is located in Bothell, Washington, manufacturing is done in Taiwan, and the products are sold by sales subsidiaries in each local market.

The product division structure allows managers to decide how best to pursue a global strategy—for example, to decide which value chain activities, such as manufacturing or product design, should be performed in which country to increase efficiency. Increasingly, U.S. and Japanese companies are moving manufacturing to low-cost countries such as China but establishing product design centers in Europe or the United States to take advantage of foreign skills and capabilities to obtain the benefits from this strategy.

Implementing Transnational Strategy

The main failing of the global product division structure is that although it allows a company to achieve superior efficiency and quality, it is weak when it comes to responsiveness to customers because the focus is still on centralized control to reduce costs. Moreover, this structure makes it difficult for the *different product divisions* to trade information and knowledge and to obtain the benefits from transferring, sharing, and leveraging their competencies. Sometimes the potential gains from sharing product, marketing, or R&D knowledge between product groups are high, but so too are the bureaucratic costs associated with achieving these gains. Is there a structure that can simultaneously economize on these costs and provide the coordination necessary to obtain these benefits?

In the 1990s, many companies implemented a *global matrix structure* to simultaneously lower their global cost structures *and* differentiate their activities through superior innovation and responsiveness to customers globally. Figure 13.5 shows such a structure that might be used by a company such as HP or a large oil and chemical company. On the vertical axis, instead of functions, there are the company's corporate *product groups,* which provide specialist services such as R&D, product design, and marketing information to its overseas divisions, which are often grouped by world region. These might be the petroleum, plastics, pharmaceuticals, or fertilizer product groups. On the horizontal axis are the company's *overseas divisions* in the various countries or world regions in which it operates. Managers at the regional or country level control local operations. Through a system of output and behavior controls, they then report to corporate product group personnel back in the United States and ultimately to the CEO or president; for example, Michael Capellas (before his recent departure from HP) was ultimately responsible for overseeing the way HP's global structure works. The heads of the world regions or country managers are also responsible for working with U.S. product group managers to develop the control and reward systems that will promote the transfer, sharing, or leveraging of competencies that will result in superior performance.

Implementing a matrix structure thus decentralizes control to overseas managers and provides them with considerable flexibility for managing local issues, but can still give product and corporate managers in the United States the centralized control they need to coordinate company activities on a global level. The matrix structure can allow knowledge and experience to be transferred among geographic regions, product divisions, and product divisions and regions. Because it offers many opportunities for face-to-face contact between managers at home and abroad, the matrix facilitates the transmission of a company's norms and values and, hence, the devel-

FIGURE 13.5

Global Matrix
Structure

● Individual operating companies

opment of a global corporate culture. This is especially important for a company with far-flung global operations for which lines of communication are longer. Club Med, for instance, uses a matrix to standardize high-quality customer service across its global vacation villages. Nestlé's experience with the global matrix structure is profiled in Strategy in Action 13.4.

Nestlé is not the only company to find the task of integrating and controlling a global matrix structure a difficult task. Some, like ABB, Ford, and Motorola, have dismantled their matrix structures and moved to a simplified global product group approach using IT to integrate across countries. If a matrix is chosen, however, other possible ways of making it work effectively include developing a strong cross-country organizational culture to facilitate communication and coordination among managers. For example, many companies are increasingly transferring managers between their domestic and overseas operations so they can implant the domestic culture in the new location and also learn by studying how their structure and systems work in the foreign country.

Toyota has made great efforts to understand how to manage car plants in overseas locations and how to transplant its culture into those plants. When it decided to enter and make cars in the United States, it first formed a joint venture with GM, and the companies combined their expertise in this car-making venture known as NUMMI. Toyota was responsible for implanting its knowledge of lean production in this plant; all the workers were cross-trained and taught how to monitor and benchmark their own performance and how to work in quality teams to improve it. Toyota then took all its learning from this venture and transferred it to its wholly owned car plant in Spartanburg, Virginia, where it turns out cars with as good a reliability record as those produced in its Japanese plants.

Every Toyota plant is under the control of Japanese managers, however, and managers from Toyota's Japanese headquarters are constantly monitoring its plant's performance and transferring and implanting Toyota's R&D innovations into its next car models. Toyota used a similar implementation strategy when it established car component and assembly operations in south Wales to serve the European Union market. Indeed, it chose south Wales and Virginia as locations for its plants because both

Strategy in Action   13.4

Using IT to Make Nestlé's Global Structure Work

Nestlé, based in Vevey, Switzerland, is the world's biggest food company, with global sales in excess of $50 billion in 2001. The company has been pursuing an ambitious program of global expansion by acquiring many famous companies—for instance, Perrier, the French mineral water producer, and Rowntree Mackintosh, the British candy maker. In the United States, Nestlé bought the giant Carnation Company, Stouffer Foods, Contadina, and Ralston Purina in 2002, which also made it the world's largest pet food maker.

Traditionally, Nestlé pursued a multidomestic strategy and managed its operating companies through a global area structure. In each country, each individual company (such as its Carnation division) was responsible for managing all aspects of its business-level strategy: in other words, companies were free to control their own product development and marketing and to manage all local operations. Nestlé's corporate executives decided acquisitions, expansions, and corporate resource decisions such as capital investment at the Vevey headquarters. Because all important decisions were made centrally, the size of the corporate staff increased dramatically. In the early 1990s, Nestlé realized it had major problems.

Corporate managers had become remote from the difficulties experienced by the operating companies, and the centralized operating structure slowed decision making. Nestlé had trouble responding quickly to the changing environment. Moreover, the company was forfeiting all the possible benefits from sharing and leveraging its distinctive competencies in food product development and marketing between operating companies and world regions. Because each subsidiary was operated separately, corporate executives had no ability to integrate their activities around the world. To raise its performance, Nestlé's managers sought to find a new way of organizing its activities.

Its CEO at the time, Helmut Maucher, started restructuring Nestlé from the top down. He stripped away the power of corporate management by decentralizing authority to the managers of seven global product groups that he created to oversee the company's major product lines (for example, coffee, milk, and candy) on a global level. The role of each global product group was to integrate the activities of the operating companies in their group to transfer and leverage distinctive competencies to create value. After the change, managers in the candy product group, for instance, began orchestrating the marketing and sale of Rowntree candy products, such as After Eight Mints and Smarties, throughout Europe and the United States, and sales climbed by 60 percent.

Maucher then grouped all operating companies within a country or region into one national or regional subsidiary and created a team of subsidiary managers to link and coordinate the activities of the various companies in that subsidiary. When the different companies or divisions started to share joint purchasing, marketing, and sales activities, major cost savings resulted. In the United States, the subsidiary management team reduced the number of sales officers nationwide from 115 to 22 and decreased the number of suppliers of packaging from 43 to 3.

Finally, Maucher decided to use a matrix structure to integrate the activities of the seven global product groups with the operations of Nestlé's country- or region-based subsidiaries. The goal of this matrix structure is to have the company pursue a transnational strategy, allowing it to obtain the gains from differentiation through global learning and cost reduction. For example, regional subsidiary managers now spend considerable time in Vevey with product division executives, discussing ways of exploiting and sharing the resources of the company on a global basis.

Although the new decentralized matrix structure improved Nestlé's ability to coordinate its structure, by 1998 it was clear that it still was not providing enough integration and coordination. Although more coordination was taking place between product groups *inside* a region such as the United States, little coordination was taking place across regions. Nestlé's top managers searched for ways to improve integration on a global scale. Their conclusion was that more output and behavior control was needed so that different product groups and different regions could learn from and understand what everyone else was doing—for example, what their product development plans were or how each product group handled its global supply chain.

Nestlé's solution was to sign, in June 2000, a $200 million contract with mySAP.com, with an extra $80 million for consulting and maintenance to install a standardized enterprise resource system (ERP) to integrate across *all* its global operations. Top managers hoped this system would give them the information they needed to exert centralized control of its operations that the matrix structure apparently did not provide. In essence, Nestlé began to use mySAP's value chain management software as a *substitute* for the matrix. With this IT, they would no longer need to rely on divisional managers to transfer information but henceforth could obtain it from mySAP's system. They would then be able to intervene at a global level as necessary.

To standardize Nestlé's IT system to ensure global compatibility, top managers decided to invest in a next-generation IT infrastructure and put this out for bid. Both IBM and HP bid for the contract to provide, install, program, and service the new network of computers so that they would work seamlessly with mySAP's software. IBM won this $500 million contract in March 2002 for what is now called Nestlé's "Globe Project" to create uniform business processes and computer systems around the world. Whether Nestlé will obtain the cost savings and differentiation advantages from using IT to integrate its global operations is still unclear. What is clear is that if the new IT works as expected, it will lead many other global companies to bolster their matrix or product group structures and use IT to improve their performance.

Sources: A. Edgecliffe-Johnson, "Nestle and Pillsbury Forge Ice Cream Alliance in U.S.," *Financial Times,* August 20, 1999, p. 2. B. Worthen, "Nestlé's ERP Odyssey," *CIO,* May 15, 2002, pp. 1–5. "Nestle Picks IBM over HP for $500 Million Contract," *Wall Street Journal,* March 7, 2002, p. B. 6. www.nestle.com, 2002.

regions have a strong local culture based on family and tradition that closely parallels Japan's culture. Toyota's managers felt that by choosing a similar local culture, they would have more chance of being able to implement its highly efficient work processes and procedures.

As the examples of Toyota and MTV (see the *Opening Case* in Chapter 8) suggest, companies that form global networks of managers who can move to and work in other countries so they can turn to each other for help are an important aspect of helping a company realize the benefits from its global operations. When managers can hold a "*matrix-in-the-mind,*" that is, learn to think about how they could transfer competencies around the company to create value, they can work to develop an information network that lets a company capitalize globally on the skills and capabilities of its employees.[14] To foster the development of the matrix-in-the-mind concept and promote cooperation, companies are increasingly making use of IT's integrating capability by using online teleconferencing, email, and global intranets among the parts of their global operations. For example, Hitachi coordinates its nineteen Japanese laboratories by means of an online teleconferencing system. Both Microsoft and HP make extensive use of global intranets to integrate their activities, and Nestlé hopes its Globe Project will accomplish the same goal.

These IT integration mechanisms help provide the coordination that is necessary for a global matrix structure to work effectively. However, the enormous number of global transfers and handoffs associated with achieving its benefits means that the bureaucratic costs associated with pursuing a transnational strategy are high. However, the potential gains for a company from using this strategy to share and leverage its competencies and capabilities to achieve superior efficiency, quality, innovation, and responsiveness to customers can easily outweigh these costs, making it a worthwhile strategy to pursue. Indeed, in most global industries today, there is usually one company—a Dell, Toyota, or McDonald's—that has learned how to pursue both a low-cost and a differentiation approach. In the complicated game of global competition, if companies do not at least strive to obtain these goals, they are likely to suffer at the hands of more agile rivals in the future.

Entry Mode and Implementation

As Chapter 10 noted, today many organizations are changing their corporate-level strategies and restructuring their organizations to find new ways to use their resources and capabilities to create value. This section focuses on the implementation issues that arise when companies use the three different modes of entry into new industries: internal new venturing, joint ventures, and mergers and acquisitions.

Internal New Venturing

Chapter 10 discusses how companies can enter new industries by transferring and leveraging their existing resources to create the set of value chain activities necessary to compete effectively in a new industry. Some of the benefits and pitfalls associated with internal new venturing were discussed there. Now we consider how structure, control, and culture can be used to increase the success of the new venturing process.

Most managers today are engaged full time in the effort to develop a competitive advantage in their existing product markets. Money and resources are always scarce, and employees are almost always overburdened, so how can managers create a setting in which employees are to be encouraged to act in ways that allow them to see how their functional competencies or products can be used in other industries?

At the heart of the issue is that corporate managers must treat the internal new-venturing process as a form of entrepreneurship and the people who are to pioneer and lead new ventures as **intrapreneurs,** or inside or internal entrepreneurs. This means that organizational structure, control, and culture must be designed to encourage creativity and give new-venture managers autonomy and freedom to develop and champion new products. At the same time, corporate managers want to make sure that the investment in new markets will be profitable and that a fit does exist between the new industry and the old one so that benefits can in fact be leveraged.[15] HP, for example, has worked hard to provide this balance between autonomy and constraint. To encourage innovation, its founders pioneered the idea of requiring its scientists and engineers to spend 15 percent of their time on projects of their own choosing; at the same time, scientists know that their ideas and the business models they developed to prove the value of their ideas will be scrutinized closely by divisional managers.[16]

3M also has carefully used structure, control, and culture to create a formal organization-wide new-venturing process that is one of the best known for promoting product innovation. 3M's goal is that at least 25 percent of its growth in sales each year should be attributed to new products developed within the past five years. To achieve this challenging goal, 3M has developed an implementation formula to ensure its employees are provided with the freedom and motivation to experiment and take risks.

On the structure side, 3M recognized early on the increasing importance of linking and coordinating the efforts of people in different functions to speed product development. As noted in the previous chapter, people in different functions tend to develop different subunit orientations and to focus their efforts on their own tasks to the exclusion of the needs of other functions. The danger of such tendencies is that each function will develop norms and values that suit its own needs but do little to promote organizational coordination and integration.

To avoid this problem, 3M established a system of cross-functional teams composed of members of product development, process development, marketing, manufacturing, packaging, and other functions to create organization-wide norms and values of innovation. So that all groups have a common focus, the teams work closely with customers; customers' needs become the platform on which the different functions can then apply their skills and capabilities.[17] For example, one of 3M's cross-functional teams worked closely with disposable diaper manufacturers to develop the right kind of sticky tape for their needs. To promote integration in the team and foster cooperative norms and values, each team is headed by a "product champion" who takes the responsibility for building cohesive team relationships and developing a team culture. In addition, one of 3M's senior managers becomes a "management sponsor" whose job is to help the team get resources and provide support when the going gets tough. After all, product development is a highly risky process; many projects do not succeed.

3M is also careful to use integrating mechanisms such as high-level product development committees to screen new ideas. Proven entrepreneurs and experienced managers from the other divisions and from R&D, marketing, sales, and manufacturing serve on this committee to screen the new ideas. New-product champions defend their products and projects before this committee to secure the resources for developing them. (Chapter 4 describes this development funnel.)

On the control side, 3M copied HP and developed a companywide norm that researchers should use 15 percent of their time on their own projects; it was this norm that helps to lead to the development of new products such as Post-it notes. In addition, 3M is careful to establish career ladders for its scientists in order to gain their long-term commitment, and it rewards successful product innovators. For example, it established the "Golden Step" program that gives employees substantial monetary bonuses to honor and reward the launch of successful new products and to develop norms and values that support and reward the sharing of information among scientists and people in different functions.

3M's structure and control systems have created an atmosphere in which employees know it is better to take a chance and risk making a mistake than do nothing at all. Managers understand that their job is to encourage creativity in their employees and teams and to foster a culture of innovation. However, the regular work of the organization goes on side by side with all this intrapreneurial activity.

The other main approach to internal new venturing has been championed by those who believe that the best way to encourage new-product development is to separate this effort from the rest of the organization. To provide new-venture managers with the autonomy to experiment and take risks, the company sets up a **new-venture division,** separate and independent from its other divisions, for the development of a new product. The logic behind this is that if a new-product team works from within a company's existing structure, its members will never have the freedom or autonomy to pursue radical new-product ideas. Away from the day-to-day scrutiny of top managers, new-venture managers will be able to pursue the creation of a new product and develop a new business model as though they were external entrepreneurs.

The new-venture division is controlled in a way that reinforces the entrepreneurial spirit. Thus, output controls are regarded as inappropriate because they can promote short-term thinking and inhibit risk taking. Instead, stock options are often used to reinforce a culture for entrepreneurship. Another issue with output controls is to keep top managers at bay. The thinking is that the up-front R&D costs of new venturing are high and its success uncertain. After spending millions of dollars, corporate managers might become concerned about the new-venture division's performance and might try to introduce tight output controls or strong budgets to increase accountability, measures that hurt the entrepreneurial culture.[18] Corporate managers may believe it is important to institute behavior and output controls that put some limits on freedom of action; otherwise, costly mistakes may be made and resources wasted on frivolous ideas.

Recently, there have been some indications that 3M's internal approach may be superior to the use of external new-venture divisions. This is because it appears that many new-venture divisions have failed to get successful new products to market. And even if they do, usually the new-venture division eventually begins to operate like any other division, and a company's cost structure rises because of the duplication of value chain activities.

Another issue is that scientists are often not the best people to develop successful business models because they lack formal training. Just as many medical doctors are earning MBAs today to understand the many strategic issues confronting their profession, so scientists need to be able to think strategically, and these skills may be lacking in a new-venture division.

HP illustrates many of these issues. Early in its history, HP used the new-venturing approach. As soon as a new self-supporting product was developed in one of HP's operating divisions, a new-venture division was spun off to develop and market the product. In this fashion, HP's goal was to keep its divisions small and entrepreneurial. Soon HP had over twenty-eight different divisions, each with its own value chain functions. At first, the value these divisions created exceeded their operating costs, but then problems emerged because of changing technological and industry conditions. Because they were operated separately, the divisions could not learn from each other, and because they all had separate R&D departments, sales forces, and so on, they began to compete for resources. For example, when one HP scientist pioneered what was to become biotechnology, the managers of other divisions could not see the logic of how it related to HP's existing activities and would not fund it. HP became saddled with high operating costs and missed-product opportunities. To solve the problem, it merged some divisions and brought their technologies and product lines together. It also sold off divisions to other companies to focus its activities and thus make it easier to transfer resources between its divisions.

Joint Venturing   Internal new venturing is an important means by which large, established companies can maintain their momentum and grow from within.[19] One alternative is to form strategic alliances, and even establish a formal joint venture with a company that has a valuable distinctive competency. Often in joint venturing, two or more companies agree to pool specific resources and capabilities that they believe will create more value for both companies and appoint managers from both companies to control the new operation. In this case, no separate entity is set up. Sometimes companies do establish a separate and independent company and agree to establish and share ownership of the new company, possibly with fifty-fifty ownership, or sometimes one company insists on having a 51 percent or more stake to give it the controlling interest. The companies then transfer to the new company whatever resources and capabilities they have agreed on to help it pursue the business model that will promote both companies' interests. This has been Microsoft's favored strategy in recent years as it enters industries with links to computing, such as the communications and entertainment industries. Normally, it takes a 51 percent stake to give it the right to buy out the company and integrate it into Microsoft should it have technology that proves vital to Microsoft's future interests.

Many of the advantages and pitfalls of joint venturing across industries and across cultures are discussed in Chapters 8 and 10. From an implementation perspective, important issues concern the way the venture is structured and controlled and the problems that frequently emerge in managing differences between the cultures of companies in a joint venture.

Allocating authority and responsibility is the first major implementation issue companies have to decide on. Both companies need to be able to monitor the progress of the joint venture so that they can learn from what goes on and benefit the most. One reason that some companies prefer to establish a new company and obtain a 51 percent ownership of it is to solve the problem of which company will have the ultimate authority and control over the new venture. The problem of a company's risking losing control of its core technology or competence when its enters into a strategic alliance was discussed in Chapter 8. The issue is that the future is unknown; it is not clear which company will benefit the most from whatever innovations the new company might develop.[20] Given this problem, steps must be taken up front to address this issue; this is why Microsoft normally insists on 51 percent ownership. Of course, to get the other company to agree to this, it pays a premium price for the other company.

Many companies form a contract to share skills and invest in each other and do not confront the issue of future ownership. Some of these have learned how dangerous this is, not only because their partners may take their learning and then go it alone and because the other party might be acquired by a competitor. For example, Compaq shared its technical knowledge with a company in the computer storage industry to promote joint product development, only to watch helplessly as that company was acquired by Sun Microsystems, which consequently obtained Compaq's knowledge.

The implementation issues are strongly dependent on whether the purpose of the joint venture is to share and develop technology, jointly distribute and market products and brands, or share access to customers. Whether the companies involved are competitors is also an important issue here. Some have claimed that Toyota received more benefit from the GM-Toyota venture discussed earlier because GM did not take Toyota's lean production knowledge and apply it quickly enough in its other divisions, while Toyota did and this put GM at a competitive disadvantage. Sometimes companies in different industries can simply realize joint benefits from collaboration. For example, in 2001, Nestlé and Coca-Cola announced a ten-year joint venture, to be called Beverage Partners Worldwide, through which Coca-Cola will distribute and sell Nestlé's Nestea ice tea, Nescafe, and other brands throughout the globe.[21] Similarly, Starbuck's Frappuccino is distributed by Pepsi. In this kind of joint venture, both companies can gain from sharing and pooling different competencies so that both realize value that would not otherwise be possible. In these cases, issues of ownership are less important, although the issue of allocating responsibility and monitoring performance remains.

Once the ownership issue has been settled, one company appoints the CEO, who is responsible for creating a cohesive top management team from the ranks of managers who have been transferred from the parent companies. The job of the top management team is to develop a successful business model. These managers then need to choose an organizational structure, such as the functional or product-team, that will make the best use of the resources and skills transferred from the parent. The need to provide a framework that combines their activities and integrates across people and functions is of paramount importance. So is the need to build a new company culture that can unite the members of the hitherto different cultures. In essence, solving all the implementation problems discussed in the previous chapter is on top managers' agenda.

Because solving these issues is expensive and time-consuming, it is not surprising that if the stakes are great and the future possibilities unknown, many companies decide that they might be better off by acquiring the other company and integrating it into their operations. Note also that this avoids the duplication of functional activities. If the stakes are less, however, and the future easier to forecast, as in the venture between Coca-Cola and Nestlé, then it makes sense to establish a new entity that can manage the transfers of complementary resources and skills between companies.

Mergers and Acquisitions

Mergers and acquisitions are the third, and most widely used, vehicle that companies can use to enter new industries or countries.[22] How to implement structure, control systems, and culture to manage a new acquisition is important because many acquisitions are unsuccessful. And one of the main reasons acquisitions perform poorly is that many companies do not anticipate the difficulties associated with merging or integrating new companies into their existing operations.[23]

At the level of structure, managers of both the acquiring and acquired companies have to confront the problem of how to establish new lines of authority and responsibility that will allow them to make the best use of both companies' competencies and capabilities. The *Opening Case* on the merger between HP and Compaq illustrates the issues. Before the merger Fiorina, Capellas, and their top management teams spent thousands of hours analyzing the range of both companies' activities, performing a value-chain grid analysis to determine how cost and differentiation advantages might be achieved. Based on this analysis, they merged all their divisions into four main product groups.

Imagine the problems in deciding who would control which group and which operating division and to whom these managers would report to: Fiorina or Capellas? In press releases, the companies' managers were careful to announce that the process of merging divisions was going smoothly and that battles over responsibilities and control of resources were being resolved to counter fears that infighting would prevent the benefits of the merger from being realized. One problem with a mishandled merger is that skilled managers who feel they have been demoted will leave the company, and if many do leave, this also may prevent its benefits from being realized.

Once the issue of lines of authority has been addressed, the issue of how to coordinate and integrate the merged companies to streamline and rationalize its operations to reduce costs and leverage competencies has to be addressed. For large companies, the answer, as for HP, is the multidivisional structure, but important control issues have to be resolved. In general, the more similar or related are the acquired companies' products and markets (a company has made a related acquisition, as in the HP case), the easier the job is of integrating their operations. Providing the acquiring company has an efficient control system, it can be adapted to the new company to standardize the way its activities are monitored and measured. Or managers can work hard to combine the best elements of each company's control systems and cultures or introduce a new IT system.

If managers make unrelated acquisitions, however, and then try to interfere with a company's strategy in an industry they know little about or apply inappropriate structure and controls to manage the new business, then major strategy implementation problems can arise. For example, if managers try to integrate unrelated companies with related ones in the search for some elusive benefits, apply the wrong kinds of controls at the divisional level, or interfere in business-level strategy, corporate performance can suffer as bureaucratic costs skyrocket. These mistakes explain why related acquisitions are sometimes more successful than unrelated ones.[24]

Even in the case of related diversification, the business processes of each company frequently are different, and their computer systems may be incompatible, as in the Nestlé case. The issue facing the merged company is how to use output and behavior controls to standardize business processes and reduce the cost of handing off and transferring resources. While installing the mySAP software, for example, managers in charge of the U.S. effort discovered that each of Nestlé's 150 different U.S. divisions was buying its own supply of the flavoring vanilla from the same set of suppliers. However, the divisions were not sharing information about how they were doing this, and vanilla suppliers, dealing with each Nestlé division separately, tried to charge each division as much as they could, with the result that each division paid a different price for the same input![25] How could this happen? Each division used a different code for its independent purchase, and managers at U.S. headquarters did not have the information to discover this. mySAP's software provides such information.

Finally, even when acquiring a company in a closely related industry, managers must realize that each company has a unique culture, or way of doing things. Such idiosyncrasies must be understood in order to manage the merged company effectively. Indeed, such idiosyncrasies are likely to be especially important when companies from different countries merge. Over time, top managers can change the culture and alter the internal workings of the company, but this is a difficult implementation task. The differences between HP and Compaq are a case in point. HP has a research-oriented culture and prizes its technology and the people who create it. Compaq is a marketing-driven organization and prizes a hands-on, value-driven approach. In June 2002, many analysts were waiting to see how the culture of the combined company would shake out. Would there be a departure of top Compaq managers given that HP is in control of the new company and its culture? Would it be possible to integrate their skills if they have such a different orientation? Where would most of the layoffs that would occur for cost-savings reason be coming from: HP's employees or Compaq's? The way the new HP deals with these issues is vital to determining its future culture.

In sum, managers' capability of managing structure, control, and culture and to integrating and connecting divisions to permit gains from leveraging competencies ultimately determines how well the new merged company will perform.[26] Some authors have argued that this is why the quality or capabilities of management is so important: Do Fiorina, and other HP managers have the skills to integrate the two companies? Analysts attribute Compaq's poor performance in the 1990s to its failure to integrate Digital Equipment's operations into Compaq's after it bought Digital in 1998. Will a similar fate befall HP? As discussed in Chapter 10 managers must have good entrepreneurial, strategic, and implementation capabilities to recognize opportunities for leveraging skills across different divisions to produce a new stream of products that customers want.[27] In 2002, AOL Time Warner, which defended their merger on their ability to accomplish just such a feat, was experiencing major problems because it turned out that customers were reluctant to buy such services as video on demand and online video game playing.

The path to merger and acquisition is fraught with dangers, which is why some companies claim that internal new venturing is the safest path, and it is best to grow organically from within. Yet with industry boundaries blurring and new global competitors emerging, companies often do not have the time to go it alone. How to enter a new industry or country is a complex implementation issue that requires thorough strategic analysis to make the right choice.

IT, the Internet, and Outsourcing

Understanding the many ways in which advances in information systems and technology are having an impact on strategy implementation is an important issue today. By improving the ability of managers to coordinate and control the activities of the organization and helping managers make more effective decisions, computer-based information systems have become an important aspect of strategy implementation. Evidence that capabilities in managing information systems can be a source of competitive advantage is growing; organizations that do not adopt leading-edge information systems are likely to be at a competitive disadvantage.

Information systems include many different varieties of software platforms and databases. These encompass companywide systems designed to manage all of a company's value chain activities provided by companies such as mySAP, PeopleSoft, JD Edwards, and others, to more general-purpose database products targeted toward specific uses, such as the products offered by Oracle, Microsoft, and many others. Information technologies encompass a broad array of communication media and devices that link information systems and people including voicemail, email, voice conferencing, videoconferencing, the Internet, groupware and corporate intranets, cell phones, fax machines, personal digital assistants, and so on. Information systems and information technologies are often inextricably linked and together are normally referred to as IT.[28]

IT and Strategy Implementation

At the level of organizational structure, control, and culture, IT has given strategic managers many new options in implementing their strategies. IT is instrumental in both shaping and integrating resources and capabilities. Moreover, its capabilities can be difficult to imitate since they are present not just in physical information systems but also in the organization-specific IT capabilities that develop inside a company over time. Wal-Mart legally protected what it regards as a core competency in IT by blocking the movement of some of its key programmers to dot-coms like Amazon.com.

Competitive strategy and the ability to pursue a low-cost and differentiation approach depend on a firm's ability to increase efficiency, quality, innovation, and customer responsiveness, and IT has a major impact on these sources of competitive advantage.[29] One advantage of IT is knowledge leveraging that involves sharing and integrating cross-functional expertise through appropriate forms of IT. Benefits include the delivery to customers of new differentiated goods and services. The way in which Citibank implemented an organization-wide IT to increase responsiveness to customers is instructive. In 2000, Citibank set as its goal to be the premier global international financial company. Studying its business model, it was clear that the main customer complaint was the amount of time customers had to wait for a response to their request, so it set out to solve this problem. Teams of managers examined the way Citibank's current IT worked and then redesigned it to empower employees and reduce the handoffs between people and functions. Employees were then given extensive training in operating the new IT system. Citibank has been able to document significant time and cost savings, as well as an increase in the level of personalized service it is able to offer its clients, which has led to a significant increase in the number of global customers.[30]

Indeed, IT has important effects on a company's ability to innovate. It improves the base of knowledge that employees draw on when they engage in problem solving and decision making and provides a mechanism to promote collaboration and information sharing both inside and across functions and business units. However, knowledge or information availability alone will not lead to innovation; it is the ability to use knowledge creatively that is the key to promoting innovation and creating competitive advantage. Prahalad and Hamel, for example, suggest that it is not the absolute level of knowledge a firm possesses that leads to competitive advantage, but the speed or velocity with which it is circulated in the firm.[31] IT transfers knowledge where it can add the highest value to the organization.

The project-based work characteristic of matrix structures provides a vivid example of this process. As a project progresses, the need for particular team members waxes and wanes. Some employees will be part of a project from beginning to end, and others will be asked to participate only at key times when their expertise is required. IT provides managers with the real-time capability to monitor project progress and needs and allocate resources accordingly to increase the value added of each employee. Traditionally, product design has involved sequential processing across functions, with handoffs as each stage of the process is completed (see Chapter 4). This linear process is being replaced by parallel, concurrent engineering made possible through the application of IT, allowing employees to work simultaneously with continual interaction through electronic communication, which can promote innovation.

IT has major effects on other aspects of a company's structure and control systems. The increasing use of IT has been associated with a flattening of the organizational hierarchy and a move toward greater decentralization and increased integration within organizations. By electronically providing managers with high-quality, timely, and relatively complete information, IT has reduced the need for a management hierarchy to coordinate organizational activities. Email systems and the development of organization-wide corporate intranets is breaking down the barriers that have traditionally separated departments and the result has been improved performance.[32] To facilitate the use of IT and to make organizational structure work, however, a company must create a control and incentive structure to motivate people and subunits, as Strategy in Action 13.5 suggests.

Some companies are taking full advantage of IT's ability to help them integrate their activities to simultaneously respond better to customer needs while making the most cost-effective use of their employees' skills by using a virtual organizational structure. The **virtual organization** is composed of people who are linked by computers, faxes, computer-aided design systems, and video teleconferencing and who may rarely, if ever, see one another face to face. People come and go as and when their services are needed, much as in a matrix structure.

Accenture, the global management consulting company, is becoming just such a virtual organization. Consultants are connected by laptops to an organization's **knowledge management system,** its company-specific information system that systematizes the knowledge of its employees and provides them with access to other employees who have the expertise to solve the problems that they encounter as they perform their jobs. The consultants pool their knowledge in a massive internal database they can easily access through computer and the company's intranet. The company's 40,000 consultants often work from their homes, traveling to meet the company's clients throughout the world and only rarely stopping in at one of Accenture's branch offices to meet their superiors and colleagues. CEO George Shaheen says the company's headquarters are wherever he happens to be at the time. (He spends 80 percent of his time traveling.)[33]

Strategy in Action   13.5

Oracle's New Approach to Control

Oracle is the second largest independent software company after Microsoft. Like Bill Gates, Microsoft's chairman, Oracle's cofounder and chairman, Larry Ellison, recognized that his company had a major problem in 1999: it was not using the latest Internet software—software it had developed itself—to control its activities even though its customers were! As a result, Oracle was having a difficult time understanding its customers' needs, and internally it was not experiencing the cost savings that result from implementing its own database and financial control software. Ellison moved quickly to change Oracle's control systems so that they were Internet based.

One of the main advantages of Internet-based control software is that it permits the centralized management of a company's widespread operations. Corporate managers can easily compare and contrast the performance of different divisions spread throughout the globe in real time and can quickly identify problems and take corrective action. However, to his embarrassment, Ellison discovered that Oracle's financial and human resource information was located on over seventy different computing systems across the world. It took a lot of time and effort to track such basic things as the size of the company's workforce and the sales of its leading products. As a result, it took a long time to take corrective action, and many opportunities were being missed.

Recognizing the irony of the situation, Ellison ordered his managers to change the way the company controlled—that is, monitored and evaluated—its activities and to implement its new Internet-based control systems as quickly as possible. His goal was to have all of Oracle's sales, cost, profit, and human resource information systems consolidated in two locations and to make this information available to managers throughout the company instantaneously with one click of a mouse. In addition, he instructed managers to investigate which kinds of activities were being monitored and controlled by people and wherever possible to substitute Internet-based control. For example, previously Oracle had over 300 people responsible for monitoring and managing such tasks as paper-based travel planning and expense report systems. These tasks were automated into software systems and put online, and employees were made responsible for filing their own reports. These 300 people were then transferred into sales and consulting positions. The savings was over $1 billion a year.

By using Internet software-based control systems, Oracle's managers are also able to get closer to their customers. In 1999, Oracle gave all its salespeople new customer relationship management software and instructed them to enter into the system detailed information about customers' purchases, future plans, web orders, and service requests. As a result, headquarters managers can track sales orders easily and if they see problems such as lost sales or multiple service requests can quickly contact customers to solve problems and so build better customer relations.

So amazed has Ellison been at the result of implementing Internet software systems that he has radically rethought Oracle's control systems. He now believes that because of the advances of modern computer information systems, Oracle's employees should be doing only one of three things: building its products, servicing its products, or selling its products. All other activities should be automated by developing new information control systems, and it should be the manager's job to use control only to facilitate one of these three front-line activities.

Source: M. Moeller, "Oracle: Practicing What It Preaches." *Business Week,* August 16, 1999, pp. 1–5.

Strategic Outsourcing and Network Structure   Another major impact of IT on strategy implementation has been its effects on a company's ability to pursue strategic outsourcing to strengthen its business model. As Chapter 9 discusses, the use of strategic outsourcing is increasing rapidly as organizations recognize the many opportunities it offers to promote differentiation, reduce costs, and increase their flexibility. U.S. companies spent $500 billion on outsourcing in 2000, and companies such as EDS, IBM, FedEx, and UPS are major beneficiaries of this increase.

Recall that outsourcing occurs as companies use short- and long-term contracts, joint ventures, and strategic alliances to link or form interorganizational relationships with other companies. IT increases the efficiency of such relationships. For example, it allows for the more efficient movement of raw materials and component parts between a company and its suppliers and distributors. It also promotes the transfer, share, and leveraging of competencies between companies, which can lead to design and engineering improvements that increase differentiation and lower costs.

As a consequence, there has been growing interest in electronic **business-to-business (B2B)** networks in which most or all of the companies in an industry (for example, car makers) use the same software platform to link to each other and establish industry specifications and standards. Then these companies jointly list the quantity and specifications of the inputs they require and invite bids from the thousands of potential suppliers around the world. Suppliers also use the same software platform so electronic bidding, auctions, and transactions are possible between buyers and sellers around the world. The idea is that high-volume standardized transactions can help drive down costs and raise quality at the industry level. The role Li & Fung plays in managing the global supply chain for companies in Southeast Asia is instructive in this regard, as Strategy in Action 13.6 shows.

Cross-company global electronic networks reduce the information costs associated with the search, evaluation, and monitoring of competing suppliers, often making global strategic alliances more attractive than vertical integration. In addition, firms that use electronic networks not only reduce costs; because they increase the pool of potential suppliers, they also reduce the bargaining power of suppliers. Similarly, beyond using IT to link backward with suppliers, companies can use IT to link forward in the value chain to connect its operations with those of customers, something that reduces their costs and creates a disincentive for customers to seek other suppliers.[34]

In order to implement outsourcing effectively, strategic managers must decide what organizational arrangements to adopt. Increasingly, a **network structure**—the set of strategic alliances that an organization creates with suppliers, manufacturers, and distributors to produce and market a product—is becoming the structure of choice to implement outsourcing. An example of a network structure is the series of strategic alliances that Japanese car companies such as Toyota and Honda formed with their suppliers of inputs, such as car axles, gearboxes, and air-conditioning systems. Members of the network work together on a long-term basis to find new ways to reduce costs and increase the quality of their products. Moreover, developing a network structure allows an organization to avoid the high costs of operating a complex organizational structure (the costs of employing many managers, for example). Finally, a network structure allows a company to form strategic alliances with foreign suppliers, which gives managers access to low-cost foreign sources of inputs, keeping costs low. The way Nike uses a global network structure to produce and market its sports, casual, and dress shoes is instructive.

Nike, located in Beaverton, Oregon, is the largest and most profitable sports shoe manufacturer in the world. The key to Nike's success is the network structure that Philip Knight, its founder and CEO, created to allow his company to produce and market shoes. The most successful companies today simultaneously pursue a low-cost and a differentiation strategy. Knight realized this early on and created an organizational structure to allow his company to achieve this goal.

By far, the largest function at Nike's headquarters in Beaverton is the design function, staffed by talented designers who pioneer innovations in sports shoe design

Strategy in Action   13.6

Li & Fung's Global Supply Chain Management

Finding the foreign suppliers that offer the lowest-priced and highest-quality products is an important task facing the managers of global organizations. These suppliers are located in thousands of cities in many countries around the world, so finding them is difficult. Often global companies use the services of foreign intermediaries or brokers, located near these suppliers, to find the one that best meets their input requirements. Li & Fung, now run by brothers Victor and William Fung, is one of these brokers that has helped hundreds of global companies to locate suitable foreign suppliers, especially suppliers in mainland China.

By 2001, managing global companies' supply chains became an even more complicated task. Foreign suppliers were increasingly specializing in just one part of the task of producing a product in their search for ways to reduce costs. For example, in the past, a company such as Target might have negotiated with a foreign supplier to manufacture 1 million units of a shirt at a certain cost per unit. But with specialization, Target might find it can reduce the costs of producing the shirt even further by splitting the operations involved in producing the shirt and having a different foreign supplier, often in different countries, perform each operation. For example, to get the lowest cost per unit, Target might first negotiate with a yarn manufacturer in Vietnam to make the yarn; then ship the yarn to a Chinese supplier to weave it into cloth; and then

to several different factories in Malaysia and the Philippines to cut the cloth and sew the shirts. Another foreign company might take responsibility for packaging and shipping the shirts to wherever in the world they are required. Since a company like Target has thousands of different clothing products under production and these change all the time, the problems of managing such a supply chain to get the full cost savings from global expansion are clear.

This is the opportunity that Li & Fung has capitalized on. Realizing that many global companies do not have the time or expertise to find such specialized low-price suppliers, they moved quickly to provide such a service. Li & Fung employs 3,600 agents who travel across thirty-seven countries to find new suppliers and inspect existing suppliers to find new ways to help their clients, global companies, get lower prices or higher-quality products. Global companies are happy to outsource their supply chain management to Li & Fung because they realize significant cost savings. And although they pay a hefty fee to Li & Fung, they avoid the costs of employing their own agents. As the complexity of supply chain management continues to increase, more and more companies like Li & Fung are appearing.

Source: "Business: Link in the Global Chain," *Economist,* June 2, 2001, pp. 62–63.

such as the air pump and Air Jordans that Nike introduced so successfully. Designers use computer-aided design (CAD) to design their shoes, and all new-product information, including manufacturing instructions, is stored electronically. When the designers have done their work, they relay the blueprints for the new products electronically to a network of suppliers and manufacturers throughout Southeast Asia with which Nike has formed strategic alliances.[35] Instructions for the design of a new sole, for example, may be sent to a supplier in Taiwan, and instructions for the leather uppers to a supplier in Malaysia. These suppliers produce the shoe parts, which are then sent for final assembly to a manufacturer in China with which Nike has established an alliance. From China, these shoes are shipped to distributors throughout the world. Of the 99 million pairs of shoes Nike makes each year, 99 percent are made in Southeast Asia.

There are three main advantages to this network structure for Nike. First, Nike's costs are very low because wages in Southeast Asia are a fraction of what they are in the United States, and this gives Nike a low-cost advantage. Second, Nike is able to respond to changes in sports shoe fashion very quickly. Using its global computer system, it can, literally overnight, change the instructions it gives to each of its suppliers so that within a few weeks, its foreign manufacturers are producing new kinds of shoes.[36] Any alliance partners that fail to perform up to Nike's standards are replaced with new partners, so Nike has great control over its network structure. In fact, the company works closely with its suppliers to take advantage of any new developments in technology that can help it reduce costs and increase quality. Third, the ability to outsource all its manufacturing abroad allows Knight to keep Nike's U.S. structure fluid and flexible. Nike uses a functional structure to organize its activities, and Knight decentralizes control of the design process to teams that are assigned to develop each of the new kinds of sports shoes for which Nike is known.

In conclusion, the implications of IT for strategy implementation are still evolving and will continue to do so as new software and hardware reshape a company's business model and its strategies. IT is changing the nature of value chain activities both inside and between organizations, affecting all four building blocks of competitive advantage: efficiency, quality, innovation, and responsiveness to customers. For the multibusiness company as for the single-business company, the need to be alert to such changes to strengthen its position in its core business has become a vital matter, and the success of companies like Dell and Wal-Mart and the failure of others such as Gateway and Kmart can be traced, in part, to their success in developing the IT capabilities that lead to sustained competitive advantage.

Summary of Chapter

1. At the corporate level, a company must choose the combination of structure, control systems, and culture that will allow it to operate a multibusiness model in a way that will lead to superior profitability.

2. As a company grows and diversifies, it adopts a multidivisional structure. Although this structure costs more to operate than a functional or product structure, it economizes on the bureaucratic costs associated with operating through a functional structure and gives a company the capability to handle its value creation activities more effectively.

3. As companies change their corporate strategies over time, they must change their structure because different strategies are managed in different ways. In particular, the move from unrelated diversification to vertical integration to related diversification increases the bureaucratic costs associated with managing a multibusiness model. Each requires a different combination on structure, control, and culture to economize on those costs.

4. As a company moves from a multidomestic to an international, global, and transnational strategy, it also needs to switch to a more complex structure that allows it to coordinate increasingly complex resource trans-

fers. Similarly, it needs to adopt a more complex integration and control system that facilitates resource sharing and the leverage of competencies around the globe. When the gains are substantial, companies frequently adopt a global matrix structure to share knowledge and expertise or implement control systems and culture to allow them to achieve its advantages.

5. To encourage internal new venturing, companies must design an internal venturing process that gives new-venture managers the autonomy they need to develop new products. Corporate managers need to provide the oversight that keeps new-venture managers motivated and on track.

6. The profitability of mergers and acquisitions depends on the structure and control systems that companies adopt to manage them and the way a company integrates them into its existing businesses.

7. IT is having increasingly important effects on the way multibusiness companies implement their strategies. Not only is it helping improve the efficiency with which the multidivisional structure operates, it also allows for the better control of complex value chain activities. The growth of outsourcing has also been promoted by IT and some companies have developed network structures to coordinate their global value chain activities.

Discussion Questions

1. When would a company decide to change from a functional to a multidivisional structure?
2. If a related company begins to buy unrelated businesses, in what ways should it change its structure or control mechanisms to manage the acquisitions?
3. What prompts a company to change from a global to a transnational strategy, and what new implementation problems arise as it does so?
4. How would you design a structure and control system to encourage entrepreneurship in a large, established corporation?
5. What are the problems associated with implementing a strategy of related diversification through acquisitions?

Practicing Strategic Management

SMALL-GROUP EXERCISE: DECIDING ON AN ORGANIZATIONAL STRUCTURE (Continued)

Break into the same groups used for the Chapter 12 Small Group Exercise. Reread the scenario in the Chapter 12 exercise and recall your group's debate about the appropriate organizational structure for your soft drinks company. Because it is your intention to compete with Coca-Cola for market share worldwide, there should also be a global dimension to your strategy, and you must consider what is the best structure globally as well as domestically. Debate the pros and cons of the types of global structures, and decide which is most appropriate and will best fit with your domestic structure.

ARTICLE FILE 13

Find an example of a company pursuing a multibusiness model that has changed its structure and control systems to manage its strategy better. What were the problems with the way it formerly implemented its strategy? What changes did it make to its structure and control systems? What effects does it expect these changes to have on performance?

STRATEGIC MANAGEMENT PROJECT: MODULE 13

Take the information you collected in the Chapter 12 on strategy implementation, and link it to the multibusiness model. You should collect information to determine if your company competes across industries or countries and also to see what role IT plays in allowing it to implement its business model.

1. Does your company use a multidivisional structure? Why or why not? What crucial implementation problems must your company manage to implement its strategy effectively? For example, what kind of integration mechanisms does it employ?
2. What is your company's corporate-level strategy? How does this affect the way it uses organizational structure, control, and culture?
3. What kind of international strategy does your company pursue? How does it control its global activities? What kind of structure does it use? Why?
4. Can you suggest ways of altering the company's structure or control systems to allow it to create more value? Would this change increase or decrease bureaucratic costs?
5. Does your company have a particular entry mode that it has used to implement its strategy?
6. In what ways does your company use IT to coordinate its value chain activities?
7. Assess how well you think your company has implemented its multibusiness (or business) model.

EXPLORING THE WEB
Visiting Sears

Go to **www.sears.com** and locate information for investors. Study the pattern in the history of Sears's diversification strategy in the 1980s, and look at its press releases. What have been the changes in its multibusiness model over time? How would you characterize its strategy today? What effects on its performance would you expect its recent strategic moves to have? Based on this analysis, how do you think Sears's structure, control systems, and culture have changed over time?

General Task: Search the Web for a multibusiness company that is in the process of modifying or changing the way it implements its strategy. What changes is it making to its structure or control systems? Does IT have a role in the changes? What structure is it moving toward? Why is this structure more appropriate than the old one?

Closing Case

Hughes Aircraft Changes Its Divisional Structure

Hughes Aircraft is one of the large U.S. defense companies battered by the end of the cold war and the decline in the defense budget. Hughes had been accustomed to a protected environment in which lavish government revenues allowed it to develop advanced technology for military uses, such as missiles, satellites, and radar systems. However, by 1990, Hughes was confronted with a major strategic problem. How could it compete in a new environment in which government revenues were scarce? To survive, Hughes had to find a new strategy based on diversifying and developing its technology for nonmilitary uses—and find it fast.

As a first step in changing direction, C. Michael Armstrong, an ex-IBM top manager, was appointed as CEO. In IBM's European division, Armstrong had developed a reputation as someone who could turn around a company and redeploy its resources quickly and effectively; investors hoped he could do so at Hughes. Armstrong began by analyzing the company's strategy and structure. What he found was a firm pursuing a differentiated strategy based on developing advanced technological products. To pursue its differentiated strategy, Hughes had developed a divisional structure to lead its development efforts. It had created seven separate technology divisions, each responsible for a different kind of product—missiles, radar, and so forth. Over time, the organization had become very tall and centralized as each technology division developed its own empire to support its efforts. The primary coordination between divisions took place at the top of the organization, where top divisional managers met regularly with corporate managers to report on and plan future product developments.

Armstrong recognized that this fit between strategy and structure might be appropriate for a company operating in a protected environment in which money was not a problem. However, it was not appropriate for a company facing intense pressure to lower costs and develop products for nonmilitary applications, such as consumer electronics and home satellites. The divisional structure duplicated expensive R&D activities, and no mechanism was in place to promote the sharing of knowledge and expertise among the different divisions. Moreover, there were few incentives for managers to cut costs because scarce resources had not been a problem, and managers had been rewarded mainly for the success of their product development efforts. Armstrong realized that to make

the company more competitive and improve the way it used its skills and resources, he had to find a new operating strategy and structure.

Armstrong began the process of change by focusing the company's strategy on customers and markets, not on technology and products. Henceforth, the needs of customers, not the needs of technology, would be the logic behind the organization of the company's activities. He changed the structure from a divisional one based on technology to one based on the needs of customers. The seven technology divisions were reengineered into five market groups according to the kinds of customers' needs they satisfied. Thus, consumer electronics became one market group, and industrial and commercial applications became another. Then technological expertise was reorganized to serve the needs of each kind of customer.

Continuing his reengineering program, Armstrong slashed the number of levels in the managerial hierarchy, eliminating two levels in order to bring managers closer to the customer. He continued this reengineering effort by decentralizing authority and pushing decision making down into the divisions, so that lower-level managers could better respond to customers' needs. In addition, he reorganized the company's international operations by transferring managers from the United States to foreign countries so that they would be closer to their customers.

To make this new customer-oriented structure work effectively, Armstrong also changed the organization's control systems. He created a system of output controls based on benchmarking competitors' costs to provide managers with standards against which to evaluate their performance and force them to pay attention to costs and quality. He then set up new incentive programs for managers and workers at all levels, linking the programs to achievement of the new targets for efficiency, quality, and responsiveness to customers. Finally, he worked hard with his top management team to establish and promote the norms and values of a customer-oriented organizational culture across the new market divisions. Henceforth, technology would be made to fit the customer, not vice versa.

Armstrong's efforts to engineer a new fit between strategy and structure at Hughes have been spectacularly successful. His top management team has fully bought into the new corporate culture, and divisional managers are adopting new entrepreneurial values based on meeting customers' needs. Some of the company's successes include the launch of its RCA minidisk satellite television system and the development of one of the largest private space-based satellite systems in the world. Its stock price has soared as Hughes uses its leading-edge technology to provide customers with quality products at competitive prices. With its new simultaneous differentiation and low-cost strategy, Hughes is performing well in the new competitive environment.

Case Discussion Questions

1. What problems did Armstrong discover with Hughes's strategy and structure?

2. What steps did he take to reengineer the company?

Source: J. Cole, "New CEO at Hughes Studied Its Managers, Got Them on His Side," *Wall Street Journal,* March 30, 1993, pp. A1, A8.

Notes

Chapter 1

1. There are several different ratios for measuring profitability, such as return on invested capital, return on assets, and return on equity. Although these different measures are highly correlated with each other, finance theorists argue that the return on invested capital is the most accurate measure of profitability. See Tom Copeland, Tim Koller, and Jack Murrin, *Valuation: Measuring and Managing the Value of Companies* (New York: Wiley, 1996).

2. Trying to estimate the relative importance of industry effects and firm strategy on firm profitability has been one of the most important areas of research in the strategy literature during the past decade. See Y. E. Spanos and S. Lioukas, "An Examination of the Causal Logic of Rent Generation," *Strategic Management Journal* 22:10 (October 2001): 907–934; and R. P. Rumelt, "How Much Does Industry Matter?" *Strategic Management Journal* 12 (1991): 167–185. See also A. J. Mauri and M. P. Michaels, "Firm and Industry Effects Within Strategic Management: An Empirical Examination," *Strategic Management Journal* 19 (1998): 211–219.

3. K. R. Andrews, *The Concept of Corporate Strategy* (Homewood, Ill.: Dow Jones Irwin, 1971); H. I. Ansoff, *Corporate Strategy* (New York: McGraw-Hill, 1965); C. W. Hofer and D. Schendel, *Strategy Formulation: Analytical Concepts* (St. Paul, Minn.: West, 1978).

4. **http://www.boeing.com/companyoffices/aboutus/mission/2016_VISION_8.5X11.**

5. **http://www.microsoft.com/mscorp/.**

6. These three questions were first proposed by P. F. Drucker, *Management—Tasks, Responsibilities, Practices* (New York: Harper & Row, 1974), pp. 74–94.

7. Derek F. Abell, *Defining the Business: The Starting Point of Strategic Planning* (Englewood Cliffs, N.J.: Prentice-Hall, 1980).

8. P. A. Kidwell and P. E.Ceruzzi, *Landmarks in Digital Computing* (Washington, D.C.: Smithsonian Institute, 1994).

9. J. C. Collins and J. I. Porras, "Building Your Company's Vision," *Harvard Business Review* (September–October 1996): 65–77.

10. **http://www.nucor.com/.**

11. See J. P. Kotter and J. L. Heskett, *Corporate Culture and Performance* (New York: Free Press, 1992). For similar work, see Collins and Porras, "Building Your Company's Vision."

12. E. Freeman, *Strategic Management: A Stakeholder Approach* (Boston: Pitman Press, 1984).

13. M. D. Richards, *Setting Strategic Goals and Objectives* (St. Paul, Minn.: West, 1986).

14. E. A. Locke, G. P. Latham, and M. Erez, "The Determinants of Goal Commitment," *Academy of Management Review* 13 (1988): 23–39.

15. R. E. Hoskisson, M. A. Hitt, and C. W. L. Hill, "Managerial Incentives and Investment in R&D in Large Multiproduct Firms," *Organization Science* 3 (1993): 325–341.

16. Robert H. Hayes and William J. Abernathy, "Managing Our Way to Economic Decline," *Harvard Business Review* (July–August 1980): 67–77.

17. Andrews, *Concept of Corporate Strategy*; Ansoff, *Corporate Strategy*; Hofer and Schendel, *Strategy Formulation*.

18. For details, see R. A. Burgelman, "Intraorganizational Ecology of Strategy Making and Organizational Adaptation: Theory and Field Research," *Organization Science* 2 (1991): 239–262; H. Mintzberg, "Patterns in Strategy Formulation," *Management Science* 24 (1978): 934–948; S. L. Hart, "An Integrative Framework for Strategy Making Processes," *Academy of Management Review* 17 (1992): 327–351; and G. Hamel, "Strategy as Revolution," *Harvard Business Review* 74 (July–August 1996): 69–83.

19. This is the premise of those who advocate that chaos theory should be applied to strategic management. See R. Stacey and D. Parker, *Chaos, Management and Economics* (London: Institute for Economic Affairs, 1994). See also H. Courtney, J. Kirkland, and P. Viguerie, "Strategy Under Uncertainty," *Harvard Business Review* 75 (November–December 1997): 66–79.

20. Hart, "Integrative Framework"; Hamel, "Strategy as Revolution."

21. See Burgelman, "Intraorganizational Ecology of Strategy Making and Organizational Adaptation," and Mintzberg, "Patterns in Strategy Formulation."

22. R. A. Burgelman and A. S. Grove, "Strategic Dissonance," *California Management Review* (Winter 1996): 8–28.

23. This story was related to the author by George Rathmann, who at the time was heading up 3M's research activities.

24. Richard T. Pascale, "Perspectives on Strategy: The Real Story Behind Honda's Success," *California Management Review* 26 (1984): 47–72.

25. This viewpoint is strongly emphasized by Burgelman and Grove, "Strategic Dissonance."

26. C. C. Miller and L. B. Cardinal, "Strategic Planning and Firm Performance: A Synthesis of More Than Two Decades of Research," *Academy of Management Journal* 37 (1994): 1649–1665. Also see P. R. Rogers, A. Miller, and W. Q. Judge, "Using Information Processing Theory to Understand Planning/Performance Relationships in the Context of Strategy," *Strategic Management Journal* 20 (1999): 567–577; and P. J. Brews and M. R. Hunt, "Learning to Plan and Planning to Learn," *Strategic Management Journal* 20: 889–913.

27. Courtney, Kirkland, and Viguerie, "Strategy Under Uncertainty."

28. P. J. H. Schoemaker, "Multiple Scenario Development: Its Conceptual and Behavioral Foundation," *Strategic Management Journal* 14 (1993): 193–213.

29. C. Kim and R. Mauborgne, "Procedural Justice, Strategic Decision Making, and the Knowledge Economy," *Strategic Management Journal* 19 (1998): 323–338; W. C. Kim and R. Mauborgne, "Fair Process: Managing in the Knowledge Economy," *Harvard Business Review* 75 (July–August 1997): 65–76.

30. G. Hamel and C. K. Prahalad, *Competing for the Future* (New York: Free Press, 1994).

31. See G. Hamel and C. K. Prahalad, "Strategic Intent," *Harvard Business Review* (May–June 1989): 64.

32. See C. R. Schwenk, "Cognitive Simplification Processes in Strategic Decision Making," *Strategic Management Journal* 5 (1984): 111–128; and K. M. Eisenhardt and M. Zbaracki, "Strategic Decision Making," *Strategic Management Journal* 13 (Special Issue, 1992): 17–37.

33. For a summary of research on strategic leadership, see D. C. Hambrick, "Putting Top Managers Back into the Picture," *Strategic Management Journal* 10 (Special Issue, 1989): 5–15. See also D. Goldman, "What Makes a Leader?" *Harvard Business Review* (November-December 1998): 92–105; H. Mintzberg, "Covert Leadership," *Harvard Business Review*

(November–December 1998): 140–148; and R. S. Tedlow, "What Titans Can Teach Us," *Harvard Business Review* (December 2001): 70–79.

34. N. M. Tichy and D. O. Ulrich, "The Leadership Challenge: A Call for the Transformational Leader," *Sloan Management Review* (Fall 1984): 59–68. F. Westley and H. Mintzberg, "Visionary Leadership and Strategic Management," *Strategic Management Journal* 10 (Special Issue, 1989): 17–32.

35. E. Wrapp, "Good Managers Don't Make Policy Decisions," *Harvard Business Review* (September–October 1967): 91–99.

36. J. Pfeffer, *Managing with Power* (Boston: Harvard Business School Press, 1992).

37. D. Goldman, "What Makes a Leader?" *Harvard Business Review* (November–December 1998): 92–105.

38. H. Simon, *Administrative Behavior* (New York: McGraw-Hill, 1957).

39. The original statement of this phenomenon was made by A. Tversky and D. Kahneman, "Judgment Under Uncertainty: Heuristics and Biases," *Science* 185 (1974): 1124–1131.

40. Schwenk, "Cognitive Simplification Processes," pp. 111–128.

41. B. M. Staw, "The Escalation of Commitment to a Course of Action," *Academy of Management Review* 6 (1981): 577–587.

42. R. Roll, "The Hubris Hypotheses of Corporate Takeovers," *Journal of Business* 59 (1986): 197–216.

43. Irvin L. Janis, *Victims of Groupthink,* 2nd ed. (Boston: Houghton Mifflin, 1982). For an alternative view, see S. R. Fuller and R. J. Aldag, "Organizational Tonypandy: Lessons from a Quarter Century of the Groupthink Phenomenon," *Organizational Behavior and Human Decision Processes* 73 (1998): 163–184.

44. See R. O. Mason, "A Dialectic Approach to Strategic Planning," *Management Science* 13 (1969): 403–414; R. A. Cosier and J. C. Aplin, "A Critical View of Dialectic Inquiry in Strategic Planning," *Strategic Management Journal* 1 (1980): 343-356; and I. I. Mintroff and R. O. Mason, "Structuring III—Structured Policy Issues: Further Explorations in a Methodology for Messy Problems," *Strategic Management Journal* 1 (1980): 331–342.

45. Mason, "A Dialectic Approach," pp. 403–414.

Chapter 2

1. M. E. Porter, *Competitive Strategy* (New York: Free Press, 1980).

2. Charles W. L. Hill has acted as an outside consultant to Tacoma City Light and evaluated the strategy on their behalf.

3. J. E. Bain, *Barriers to New Competition* (Cambridge Mass.: Harvard University Press, 1956). For a review of the modern literature on barriers to entry, see R. J. Gilbert, "Mobility Barriers and the Value of Incumbency," in R. Schmalensee and R. D. Willig, *Handbook of Industrial Organization,* vol. 1 (Amsterdam: North-Holland, 1989).

4. A detailed discussion of switching costs and lock in can be found in C. Shapiro and H. R. Varian, *Information Rules: A Strategic Guide to the Network Economy* (Boston: Harvard Business School Press, 1999).

5. Most of this information on barriers to entry can be found in the industrial organization economics literature. See especially the following works: Bain, *Barriers to New Competition;* M. Mann, "Seller Concentration, Barriers to Entry and Rates of Return in 30 Industries," *Review of Economics and Statistics* 48 (1966): 296–307; W. S. Comanor and T. A. Wilson, "Advertising, Market Structure and Performance," *Review of Economics*

and Statistics 49 (1967): 423–440; Gilbert, "Mobility Barriers"; and K. Cool, L.-H. Roller, and B. Leleux, "The Relative Impact of Actual and Potential Rivalry on Firm Profitability in the Pharmaceutical Industry," *Strategic Management Journal* 20 (1999): 1–14.

6. K. Fiewege, "Wall Street Hot on Airlines Despite 4th-Qtr Losses," Reuters Wire Report, January 15, 2002.

7. For a discussion of tacit agreements, see T. C. Schelling, *The Strategy of Conflict* (Cambridge, Mass.: Harvard University Press, 1960).

8. P. Ghemawat, *Commitment: The Dynamics of Strategy* (Boston: Harvard Business School Press, 1991).

9. A. S. Grove, *Only the Paranoid Survive* (New York: Doubleday, 1996).

10. In standard microeconomic theory, the concept used for assessing the strength of substitutes and complements is the cross elasticity of demand.

11. For details and further references, see Charles W. L. Hill, "Establishing a Standard: Competitive Strategy and Technology Standards in Winner Take All Industries," *Academy of Management Executive* 11 (1997): 7–25; and Shapior and Varian, *Information Rules.*

12. The development of strategic group theory has been a strong theme in the strategy literature. Important contributions include the following: R. E. Caves and Michael E. Porter, "From Entry Barriers to Mobility Barriers," *Quarterly Journal of Economics* (May 1977): 241–262; K. R. Harrigan, "An Application of Clustering for Strategic Group Analysis," *Strategic Management Journal* 6 (1985): 55–73; K. J. Hatten and D. E. Schendel, "Heterogeneity Within an Industry: Firm Conduct in the U.S. Brewing Industry, 1952–71," *Journal of Industrial Economics* 26 (1977): 97–113; Michael E. Porter, "The Structure Within Industries and Companies' Performance," *Review of Economics and Statistics* 61 (1979): 214–227. For more recent work, see K. Cool and D. Schendel, "Performance Differences Among Strategic Group Members," *Strategic Management Journal* 9 (1988): 207–233; C. S. Galbraith, G. B. Merrill, and G. Morgan. "Bilateral Strategic Groups," *Strategic Management Journal* 15 (1994): 613–626; and A. Nair and S. Kotha, "Does Group Membership Matter? Evidence from the Japanese Steel Industry," *Strategic Management Journal* (2001): 221–235.

13. For details on the strategic group structure in the pharmaceutical industry, see K. Cool and I. Dierickx, "Rivalry, Strategic Groups, and Firm Profitability," *Strategic Management Journal* 14 (1993): 47–59.

14. Charles W. Hofer has argued that life cycle considerations may be the most important contingency when formulating business strategy. See Hofer, "Towards a Contingency Theory of Business Strategy," *Academy of Management Journal* 18 (1975): 784–810. There is empirical evidence to support this view. See C. R. Anderson and C. P. Zeithaml, "Stages of the Product Life Cycle, Business Strategy, and Business Performance," *Academy of Management Journal* 27 (1984): 5–24; and D. C. Hambrick and D. Lei, "Towards an Empirical Prioritization of Contingency Variables for Business Strategy," *Academy of Management Journal* 28 (1985): 763–788. Also see G. Miles, C. C. Snow, and M. P. Sharfman, "Industry Variety and Performance," *Strategic Management Journal* 14 (1993): 163–177.

15. The characteristics of declining industries have been summarized by K. R. Harrigan, "Strategy Formulation in Declining Industries," *Academy of Management Review* 5 (1980): 599–604.

16. This perspective is associated with the Austrian school of economics, which goes back to Schumpeter. For a summary of this school and its implications for strategy, see R. Jacobson, "The Austrian School of Strategy," *Academy of Management Review* 17 (1992): 782–807. C. W. L. Hill and D. Deeds, "The Importance of Industry Structure for the Determination of Industry Profitability: A Neo-Austrian Approach," *Journal of Management Studies* 33 (1996): 429–451.

17. "A Tricky Business," *Economist,* June 30, 2001, pp. 55–56

18. D. F. Barnett and R. W. Crandall, *Up from the Ashes* (Washington, D.C.: Brookings Institute, 1986).

19. M. E. Porter, *The Competitive Advantage of Nations* (New York: Free Press, 1990).

20. The term *punctuated equilibrium* is borrowed from evolutionary biology. For a detailed explanation of the concept, see M. L. Tushman, W. H. Newman, and E. Romanelli, "Convergence and Upheaval: Managing the Unsteady Pace of Organizational Evolution," *California Management Review* 29:1 (1985): 29–44; and C. J. G. Gersick, "Revolutionary Change Theories: A Multilevel Exploration of the Punctuated Equilibrium Paradigm," *Academy of Management Review* 16 (1991): 10–36.

21. A. J. Slywotzky, *Value Migration: How to Think Several Moves Ahead of the Competition* (Boston: Harvard Business School Press, 1996).

22. R. D'Avani, *Hypercompetition* (New York: Free Press, 1994).

23. Hill and Deeds, "Importance of Industry Structure."

24. R. P. Rumelt, "How Much Does Industry Matter?" *Strategic Management Journal* 12 (1991): 167–185. See also A. J. Mauri and M. P. Michaels, "Firm and Industry Effects Within Strategic Management: An Empirical Examination," *Strategic Management Journal* 19 (1998): 211–219.

25. See R. Schmalensee, "Inter-Industry Studies of Structure and Performance," in Schmalensee and Willig (eds.), *Handbook of Industrial Organization.* Similar results were found by A. N. McGahan and M. E. Porter, "How Much Does Industry Matter, Really?" *Strategic Management Journal* 18 (1997): 15–30.

26. For example, see K. Cool and D. Schendel, "Strategic Group Formation and Performance: The Case of the U.S. Pharmaceutical Industry, 1932–1992," *Management Science* (September 1987): 1102–1124.

27. See M. Gort and J. Klepper, "Time Paths in the Diffusion of Product Innovations," *Economic Journal* (September 1982): 630–653. Looking at the history of forty-six products, Gort and Klepper found that the length of time before other companies entered the markets created by a few inventive companies declined from an average of 14.4 years for products introduced before 1930 to 4.9 years for those introduced after 1949.

28. The phrase was originally coined by J. Schumpeter, *Capitalism, Socialism and Democracy* (London: Macmillan, 1950), p. 68.

29. M. E. Porter, "Strategy and the Internet," *Harvard Business Review* (March 2001): 62–79.

30. U.S. Dept. of Labor, Bureau of Labor Statistics.

31. *Economist, The Economist Book of Vital World Statistics* (New York: Random House, 1990).

32. For a detailed discussion of the importance of the structure of law as a factor explaining economic change and growth, see D. C. North, Institutions, *Institutional Change and Economic Performance* (Cambridge: Cambridge University Press, 1990).

33. Charles W. L. Hill, *International Business* (New York: McGraw-Hill, 2003).

34. P. Dicken, *Global Shift* (New York: Guilford Press, 1992).

35. I. Metthee, "Playing a Large Part," *Seattle Post Intelligence,* April 9, 1994, p. 13.

36. T. Levitt, "The Globalization of Markets," *Harvard Business Review* (May–June 1983): 92–102.

37. Porter, *Competitive Advantage of Nations.* See also R. Grant, "Porter's Competitive Advantage of Nations: An Assessment," *Strategic Management Journal* 7 (1991): 535–548.

Chapter 3

1. M. Cusumano, *The Japanese Automobile Industry* (Cambridge, Mass.: Harvard University Press, 1989). S. Spear and H. K. Bowen, "Decoding the DNA of the Toyota Production System," *Harvard Business Review* (September–October 1999): 96–108.

2. The material in this section relies on the so-called resource-based view of the company. For summaries of this perspective, see J. B. Barney, "Company Resources and Sustained Competitive Advantage," *Journal of Management* 17 (1991): 99–120; J. T. Mahoney and J. R. Pandian, "The Resource-Based View Within the Conversation of Strategic Management," *Strategic Management Journal* 13 (1992): 63–380; R. Amit and P. J. H. Schoemaker, "Strategic Assets and Organizational Rent," *Strategic Management Journal* 14 (1993): 33–46; and M. A. Peteraf, "The Cornerstones of Competitive Advantage: A Resource-Based View," *Strategic Management Journal* 14 (1993): 179–191. B. Wernerfelt. "A Resource Based View of the Company," *Strategic Management Journal* 15 (1994): 171–180. K. M. Eisenhardt and J. A. Martin, "Dynamic Capabilities: What Are They?" *Strategic Management Journal,* 21 (2000): 1105–1121.

3. For a discussion of organizational capabilities, see R. R. Nelson and S. Winter, *An Evolutionary Theory of Economic Change* (Cambridge, Mass.: Belknap Press, 1982).

4. W. Chan Kim and R. Mauborgne, "Valu Innovation: The Strategic Logic of High Growth," *Harvard Business Review* (January–February 1997): 102–115.

5. The concept of consumer surplus is an important one in economics. For a more detailed exposition, see D. Besanko, D. Dranove, and M. Shanley, *Economics of Strategy* (New York: Wiley, 1996).

6. However, $P = V$ only in the special case when the company has a perfect monopoly and it can charge each customer a unique price that reflects the value of the product to that customer (i.e., where perfect price discrimination is possible). More generally, except in the limiting case of perfect price discrimination, even a monopolist will see most customers capture some of the value of a product in the form of a consumer surplus.

7. This point is central to the work of Michael Porter. See M. E. Porter, *Competitive Advantage* (New York: Free Press, 1985). See also P. Ghemawat, *Commitment: The Dynamic of Strategy* (New York: Free Press, 1991), chap. 4.

8. A. Priddle, "Efficiency by the Numbers," *Ward's Auto World* (July 2001): 57–59. D. C. Smith, "Power Surveys Set Standards for Measuring Quality," *Ward's Auto World* (July 2001): 34–35.

9. Porter, *Competitive Advantage.*

10. Ibid.

11. This approach goes back to the pioneering work by K. Lancaster: *Consumer Demand, a New Approach* (New York: 1971).

12. D. Garvin, "Competing on the Eight Dimensions of Quality," *Harvard Business Review* (November–December 1987): 101–119. P. Kotler. *Marketing Management* (Millennium ed.) (Upper Saddle River, N.J.: Prentice-Hall, 2000).

13. C. K. Prahalad and M. S. Krishnan, "The New Meaning of Quality in the Information Age," *Harvard Business Review* (September–October 1999): 109–118.

14. See D. Garvin, "What Does Product Quality Really Mean," *Sloan Management Review* 26 (Fall 1984): 25–44; P. B. Crosby, *Quality Is Free* (New York: Mentor, 1980); and A. Gabor, *The Man Who Discovered Quality* (New York: Times Books, 1990).

15. M. Cusumano, *The Japanese Automobile Industry* (Cambridge, Mass.: Harvard University Press, 1989). S. Spear and H. K. Bowen, "Decoding the DNA of the Toyota Production System," *Harvard Business Review* (September–October 1999): 96–108.

16. Kim and Mauborgne, "Valu Innovation."

17. G. Stalk and T. M. Hout, *Competing Against Time* (New York: Free Press, 1990).

18. Ibid.

19. Tom Copeland, Tim Koller, and Jack Murrin, *Valuation: Measuring and Managing the Value of Companies* (New York: Wiley, 1996). Also see S. F. Jablonsky and N. P. Barsky, *The Manager's Guide to Financial Statement Analysis* (New York: Wiley, 2001)

20. Copeland, Koller, and Murrin, *Valuation*.

21. This is done as follows. Signifying net profit by π, invested capital by K, and revenues by R, then $ROIC = \pi/K$. If we multiply through by revenues, R, this becomes $R \times (\pi/K) = (\pi \times R)/(K \times R)$, which can be rearranged as $\pi/R \times R/K$. π/R is the return on sales and R/K capital turnover.

22. Note that Figure 3.10 is a simplification and ignores some other important items that enter the calculation, such as depreciation/sales (a determinant of ROS) and other assets/sales (a determinant of capital turnover).

23. For examples of how to construct detailed profitability trees, see Copeland, Koller, and Murrin, *Valuation*. Also see Jablonsky and Barsky, *Manager's Guide to Financial Statement Analysis*.

24. This is the nature of the competitive process. For more detail, see C. W. L. Hill and D. Deeds, "The Importance of Industry Structure for the Determination of Company Profitability: A Neo-Austrian Perspective," *Journal of Management Studies, 33* (1996): 429–451.

25. As with resources and capabilities, so the concept of barriers to imitation is also grounded in the resource-based view of the company. For details, see R. Reed and R. J. DeFillippi, "Causal Ambiguity, Barriers to Imitation, and Sustainable Competitive Advantage," *Academy of Management Review* 15 (1990): 88–102.

26. E. Mansfield, "How Economists See R&D," *Harvard Business Review* (November–December 1981): 98–106.

27. S. L. Berman, J. Down, and C. W. L. Hill, "Tacit Knowledge as a Source of Competitive Advantage in the National Basketball Association," *Academy of Management Journal* (2002): 13–33.

28. P. Ghemawat, *Commitment: The Dynamic of Strategy* (New York: Free Press, 1991).

29. W. M. Cohen and D. A. Levinthal, "Absorptive Capacity: A New Perspective on Learning and Innovation," *Administrative Science Quarterly* 35 (1990): 128–152.

30. M. T. Hannah and J. Freeman, "Structural Inertia and Organizational Change," *American Sociological Review* 49 (1984): 149–164.

31. See "IBM Corporation," Harvard Business School Case #180-034.

32. Ghemawat, *Commitment*.

33. D. Miller, *The Icarus Paradox* (New York: HarperBusiness, 1990).

34. P. M. Senge, *The Fifth Discipline: The Art and Practice of the Learning Organization* (New York: Doubleday, 1990).

35. D. Kearns, "Leadership Through Quality," *Academy of Management Executive* 4 (1990): 86–89.

36. The classic statement of this position was made by A. A. Alchain, "Uncertainty, Evolution, and Economic Theory," *Journal of Political Economy* 84 (1950): 488–500.

Chapter 4

1. G. J. Miller, *Managerial Dilemmas: The Political Economy of Hierarchy* (Cambridge: Cambridge University Press, 1992).

2. H. Luft, J. Bunker, and A. Enthoven, "Should Operations Be Regionalized?" *New England Journal of Medicine* 301 (1979): 1364–1369.

3. G. Hall and S. Howell, "The Experience Curve from an Economist's Perspective," *Strategic Management Journal* 6 (1985): 197–212. M. Lieberman. "The Learning Curve and Pricing in the Chemical Processing Industries," *RAND Journal of Economics* 15 (1984): 213–228.

4. Boston Consulting Group, *Perspectives on Experience* (Boston: Boston Consulting Group, 1972); Hall and Howell, "The Experience Curve," pp. 197–212; W. B. Hirschmann, "Profit from the Learning Curve," *Harvard Business Review* (January–February 1964): 125–139.

5. A. A. Alchian, "Reliability of Progress Curves in Airframe Production," *Econometrica* 31 (1963): 679–693.

6. M. Borrus, L. A. Tyson, and J. Zysman, "Creating Advantage: How Government Policies Create Trade in the Semi-Conductor Industry," in P. R. Krugman (ed.), *Strategic Trade Policy and the New International Economics* (Cambridge, Mass.: MIT Press, 1986). S. Ghoshal and C. A. Bartlett, "Matsushita Electrical Industrial (MEI) in 1987," Harvard Business School Case #388-144 (1988).

7. Abernathy and Wayne, "Limits of the Learning Curve," pp. 109–119.

8. D. F. Barnett and R. W. Crandall, *Up from the Ashes: The Rise of the Steel Minimill in the United States* (Washington, D.C.: Brookings Institute, 1986).

9. See P. Nemetz and L. Fry, "Flexible Manufacturing Organizations: Implications for Strategy Formulation," *Academy of Management Review* 13 (1988): 627–638; N. Greenwood, *Implementing Flexible Manufacturing Systems* (New York: Halstead Press, 1986); and J. P. Womack, D. T. Jones, and D. Roos, *The Machine That Changed the World* (New York: Rawson Associates, 1990). R. Parthasarthy and S. P. Seith, "The Impact of Flexible Automation on Business Strategy and Organizational Structure," *Academy of Management Review* 17 (1992): 86–111.

10. B. J. Pine, *Mass Customization: The New Frontier in Business Competition* (Boston: Harvard Business School Press, 1993). S. Kotha, "Mass Customization: Implementing the Emerging Paradigm for Competitive Advantage," *Strategic Management Journal* 16 (1995): 21–42. J. H. Gilmore and B. J. Pine II, "The Four Faces of Mass Customization," *Harvard Business Review* (January–February 1997): 91–101.

11. "The Celling Out of America," *Economist,* December 17, 1994, pp. 63–64.

12. F. F. Reichheld and W. E. Sasser, "Zero Defections: Quality Comes to Service," *Harvard Business Review* (September–October 1990): 105–111.

13. The example comes from ibid.

14. Ibid.

15. R. Narasimhan and J. R. Carter, "Organization, Communication and Coordination of International Sourcing," *International Marketing Review* 7 (1990): 6–20.

16. H. F. Busch, "Integrated Materials Management," IJDP & MM 18 (1990): 28–39.

17. G. Stalk and T. M. Hout, *Competing Against Time* (New York: Free Press, 1990).

18. See Peter Bamberger and Ilan Meshoulam, *Human Resource Strategy: Formulation, Implementation, and Impact* (Thousand Oaks, Calif.: Sage, 2000). P. M. Wright and S. Snell, "Towards a Unifying Framework for Exploring Fit and Flexibility in Human Resource Management," *Academy of Management Review* 23 (October 1998): 756–772.

19. A. Sorge and M. Warner, "Manpower Training, Manufacturing Organization, and Work Place Relations in Great Britain and West Germany," *British Journal of Industrial Relations* 18 (1980): 318–333. R. Jaikumar, "Postindustrial Manufacturing," *Harvard Business Review* (November–December 1986): 72–83.

20. J. Hoerr, "The Payoff from Teamwork," *Business Week,* July 10, 1989, pp. 56–62.

21. "The Trouble with Teams," *Economist,* January 14, 1995, p. 61.

22. T. C. Powell and A. Dent-Micallef, "Information Technology as Competitive Advantage: The Role of Human, Business, and Technology Resource," *Strategic Management Journal* 18 (1997): 375–405. B. Gates, *Business @ the Speed of Thought* (New York: Warner Books, 1999).

23. "Cisco@speed," *Economist,* June 26, 1999, p. 12. S. Tully, "How Cisco Mastered the Net," *Fortune,* August 17, 1997, pp. 207–210. C. Kano, "The Real King of the Internet," *Fortune,* September 7, 1998, pp. 82–93.

24. Gates, *Business @ the Speed of Thought.*

25. K. J. Stiroh, "Investing in Information Technology: Productivity Payoffs in U.S. Industries," *Current Issues in Economic and Finance* 7 (June 2001): 1–7.

26. See the articles published in the special issue of the *Academy of Management Review on Total Quality Management* 19:3 (1994). The following article provides a good overview of many of the issues involved from an academic perspective: J. W. Dean and D. E. Bowen, "Management Theory and Total Quality," *Academy of Management Review* 19 (1994): 392–418. Also see T. C. Powell, "Total Quality Management as Competitive Advantage," *Strategic Management Journal* 16 (1995): 15–37.

27. For general background information, see "How to Build Quality," *Economist,* September 23, 1989, pp. 91–92; A. Gabor, *The Man Who Discovered Quality* (New York: Penguin, 1990); and P. B. Crosby, *Quality Is Free* (New York: Mentor, 1980).

28. W. E. Deming, "Improvement of Quality and Productivity Through Action by Management," *National Productivity Review* 1 (Winter 1981–1982): 12–22.

29. J. Bowles, "Is American Management Really Committed to Quality?" *Management Review* (April 1992): 42–46.

30. O. Port and G. Smith, "Quality," *Business Week,* November 30, 1992, pp. 66–75. See also "The Straining of Quality," *Economist,* January 14, 1995, pp. 55–56.

31. Bowles, "Is American Management Really Committed to Quality?" pp. 42–46. "The Straining of Quality," pp. 55–56.

32. Gabor, *The Man Who Discovered Quality.*

33. Deming, "Improvement of Quality and Productivity," pp. 12–22.

34. W. E. Deming, *Out of the Crisis* (Cambridge, Mass.: MIT Center for Advanced Engineering Study, 1986).

35. A. Ries and J. Trout, *Positioning: The Battle for Your Mind* (New York: Warner Books, 1982).

36. R. G. Cooper, *Product Leadership* (Reading, Mass.: Perseus Books, 1999).

37. E. Mansfield, "How Economists See R&D," *Harvard Business Review* (November–December 1981): 98–106.

38. Ibid.

39. Booz, Allen, and Hamilton, *New Products Management for the 1980's* (privately published research report, 1982).

40. A. L. Page, "PDMA's New Product Development Practices Survey: Performance and Best Practices" (paper presented at the PDMA Fifteenth Annual International Conference, Boston, October 16, 1991).

41. S. L. Brown and K. M. Eisenhardt, "Product Development: Past Research, Present Findings, and Future Directions," *Academy of Management Review* 20 (1995): 343–378. M. B. Lieberman and D. B. Montgomery, "First Mover Advantages," *Strategic Management Journal* 9 (Special Issue, Summer 1988): 41–58. D. J. Teece, "Profiting from Technological Innovation: Implications for Integration, Collaboration, Licensing and Public Policy," *Research Policy* 15 (1987): 285–305. G. J. Tellis and P. N. Golder, "First to Market, First to Fail?" *Sloan Management Review* (Winter 1996): 65–75.

42. G. Stalk and T. M. Hout, *Competing Against Time* (New York: Free Press, 1990).

43. K. B. Clark and S. C. Wheelwright, *Managing New Product and Process Development* (New York: Free Press, 1993). M. A. Schilling and C. W. L. Hill, "Managing the New Product Development Process," *Academy of Management Executive* 12:3 (August 1998): 67–81.

44. K. B. Clark and S. C. Wheelwright, *Managing New Product and Process Development* (New York: Free Press, 1993).

45. P. Sellers, "Getting Customers to Love You," *Fortune,* March 13, 1989, pp. 38–42.

46. O. Port, "Moving Past the Assembly Line," *Business Week,* (Special Issue, Reinventing America, 1992): 177–180.

47. G. P. Pisano and S. C. Wheelwright, "The New Logic of High Tech R&D," *Harvard Business Review* (September–October 1995): 93–105.

48. K. B. Clark and T. Fujimoto, "The Power of Product Integrity," *Harvard Business Review* (November–December 1990): 107–118. Clark and Wheelwright, *Managing New Product and Process Development.* Brown and Eisenhardt, "Product Development." Stalk and Hout, *Competing Against Time.*

49. C. Christensen, "Quantum Corporation—Business and Product Teams," Harvard Business School Case, #9-692-023.

50. S. Caminiti, "A Mail Order Romance: Lands' End Courts Unseen Customers," *Fortune,* March 13, 1989, pp. 43–44.

51. P. Sellers, "Getting Customers to Love You," *Fortune,* March 13, 1989, pp. 38–42.

52. Caminiti, "A Mail Order Romance: Lands' End Courts Unseen Customers," pp. 43–44.

53. Stalk and Hout, *Competing Against Time.*

Chapter 5

1. Derek F. Abell, *Defining the Business: The Starting Point of Strategic Planning* (Englewood Cliffs, N.J.: Prentice-Hall, 1980), p. 169.

2. R. Kotler, *Marketing Management,* 5th ed. (Englewood Cliffs, N.J.: Prentice-Hall, 1984). M. R. Darby and E. Karni, "Free Competition and the Optimal Amount of Fraud," *Journal of Law and Economics* 16 (1973): 67–86.

3. Abell, *Defining the Business,* p. 8.

4. Michael E. Porter, *Competitive Advantage: Creating and Sustaining Superior Performance* (New York: Free Press, 1985).

5. R. D. Buzzell and F. D. Wiersema, "Successful Share Building Strategies," *Harvard Business Review* (January–February 1981): 135–144. L. W. Phillips, D. R. Chang, and R. D. Buzzell, "Product Quality, Cost Position, and Business Performance: A Test of Some Key Hypotheses," *Journal of Marketing* 47 (1983): 26–43.

6. Michael E. Porter, *Competitive Strategy: Techniques for Analyzing Industries and Competitors* (New York: Free Press, 1980), p. 45.

7. Abell, *Defining the Business*, p. 15.

8. Some of the theoretical underpinnings for this approach can be found in G. R. Jones and J. Butler, "Costs, Revenues, and Business Level Strategy," *Academy of Management Review* 13 (1988): 202–213; and C. W. L. Hill, "Differentiation versus Low Cost or Differentiation and Low Cost: A Contingency Framework," *Academy of Management Review* 13 (1988): 401–412.

9. This section, and material on the business model, draw heavily on C. W. L. Hill and G. R. Jones, "The Dynamics of Business-Level Strategy" (unpublished paper, 2002).

10. Porter, *Competitive Advantage*.

11. Many authors have discussed cost leadership and differentiation as basic competitive approaches—for example, F. Scherer, *Industrial Market Structure and Economic Performance*, 10th ed. (Boston: Houghton Mifflin, 2000). The basic cost-leadership/differentiation dimension has received substantial empirical support; see, for example, D. C. Hambrick, "High Profit Strategies in Mature Capital Goods Industries: A Contingency Approach," *Academy of Management Journal* 26 (1983): 687–707.

12. Porter, *Competitive Advantage*, p. 37.

13. Ibid., pp. 13–14.

14. www.walmart.com (2002).

15. D. Miller, "Configurations of Strategy and Structure: Towards a Synthesis," *Strategic Management Journal* 7 (1986): 217–231.

16. Porter, *Competitive Advantage*, pp. 44–46.

17. Charles W. Hofer and D. Schendel, *Strategy Formulation: Analytical Concepts* (St. Paul, Minn.: West, 1978).

18. W. K. Hall, "Survival Strategies in a Hostile Environment," *Harvard Business Review* 58 (1980): 75–85. Hambrick, "High Profit Strategies," pp. 687–707.

19. J. Guyon, "Can the Savoy Cut Costs and Be the Savoy," *Wall Street Journal*, October 25, 1994, p. B1.

20. Porter, *Competitive Strategy*, p. 46.

21. Peter F. Drucker, *The Practice of Management* (New York: Harper, 1954).

22. Porter, *Competitive Advantage*, pp. 44–46.

23. G. Hamel and C. K. Prahalad, *Competing for the Future* (Boston: Harvard Business School Press, 1994), p. 129.

24. The development of strategic group theory has been a strong theme in the strategy literature. Important contributions include R. E. Caves and Michael Porter, "From Entry Barriers to Mobility Barriers," *Quarterly Journal of Economics* (May 1977): 241–262; K. R. Harrigan, "An Application of Clustering for Strategic Group Analysis," *Strategic Management Journal* 6 (1985): 55–73; K. J. Hatten and D. E. Schendel, "Heterogeneity Within an Industry: Company Conduct in the U.S. Brewing Industry, 1952–1971," *Journal of Industrial Economics* 26. pp. 97–113; and Michael E. Porter, "The Structure Within Industries and Companies' Performance," *Review of Economics and Statistics* 61 (1979): 214–227.

25. Hofer and Schendel, *Strategy Formulation*, pp. 102–104.

26. Our discussion of the investment, or posturing, component of business-level strategy draws heavily from ibid., especially Chap. 6.

27. Ibid., pp. 75–77.

28. K. R. Harrigan, "Strategy Formulation in Declining Industries," *Academy of Management Review* 5 (1980): 599–604.

29. Hofer and Schendel, *Strategy Formulation*, pp. 169–172.

30. L. R. Feldman and A. L. Page, "Harvesting: The Misunderstood Market Exit Strategy," *Journal of Business Strategy* 4 (1985): 79–85.

31. C. W. Hofer, "Turnaround Strategies," *Journal of Business Strategy* 1 (1980): 19–31.

32. For a basic introduction to game theory, see A. K. Dixit and B. J. Nalebuff, *Thinking Strategically* (New York: Norton, 1991). Also see A. M. Brandenburger and B. J. Nalebuff, "The Right Game: Using Game Theory to Shape Strategy," *Harvard Business Review* (July–August 1995): 59–71; and D. M. Kreps, *Game Theory and Economic Modeling* (Oxford: Oxford University Press, 1990).

Chapter 6

1. M. Porter, *Competitive Strategy: Techniques for Analyzing Industries and Competitors* (New York: Free Press, 1980), pp. 191–200.

2. S. A. Shane, "Hybrid Organizational Arrangements and Their Implications for Firm Growth and Survival: A Study of New Franchisors," *Academy of Management Journal* 1 (1996): 216–234.

3. Microsoft is often accused of not being an innovator, but the fact is that Gates and Allen wrote the first commercial software program for the first commercially available PC. Microsoft was the first mover in the industry. See P. Freiberger and M. Swaine, *Fire in the Valley* (New York: McGraw-Hill, 2000).

4. J. M. Utterback, *Mastering the Dynamics of Innovation* (Boston: Harvard Business School Press, 1994).

5. G. A. Moore, *Crossing the Chasm* (New York: HarperCollins, 1991), and *Living on the Fault Line* (New York: Harper Business, 2000).

6. Freiberger and Swaine, *Fire in the Valley*.

7. Moore, *Crossing the Chasm*.

8. Utterback, *Mastering the Dynamics of Innovation*.

9. Freiberger and Swaine, *Fire in the Valley*.

10. Everett Rogers, *Diffusion of Innovations* (New York: Free Press, 1995).

11. J. Brander and J. Eaton, "Product Line Rivalry," *American Economic Review* 74 (1985): 323–334.

12. P. Milgrom and J. Roberts, "Predation, Reputation, and Entry Deterrence," *Journal of Economic Theory* 27 (1982): 280–312. See also A. K. Dixit and B. J. Nalbuff, *Thinking Strategically* (New York: Norton, 1991).

13. Porter, *Competitive Strategy*, pp. 76–86.

14. O. Heil and T. S. Robertson, "Towards a Theory of Competitive Market Signaling: A Research Agenda." *Strategic Management Journal* 12 (1991): 403–418.

15. Robert Axelrod, *The Evolution of Cooperation* (New York: Basic Books, 1984).

16. F. Scherer, *Industrial Market Structure and Economic Performance*, 10th ed.(Boston: Houghton Mifflin, 2000), chap. 8.

17. The model differs from Ansoff's model for this reason.

18. H. Igor Ansoff, *Corporate Strategy* (London: Penguin Books, 1984), pp. 97–100.

19. Robert D. Buzzell, Bradley T. Gale, and Ralph G. M. Sultan, "Market Share—A Key to Profitability," *Harvard Business Review* (January–February 1975): 97–103. Robert Jacobson and David A. Aaker, "Is Market Share All That It's Cracked Up to Be?" *Journal of Marketing* 49 (1985): 11–22.

20. Ansoff, *Corporate Strategy*, pp. 98–99.

21. S. L. Brown and K. M. Eisenhardt, "Product Development: Past Research, Present Findings, and Future Directions," *Academy of Management Review* 20 (1995): 343–378.

22. The next section draws heavily on Marvin B. Lieberman, "Strategies for Capacity Expansion," *Sloan Management Review* 8 (1987): 19–27; and Porter, *Competitive Strategy*, pp. 324–338.

23. Jack Willoughby, "The Last Iceman," *Forbes,* July 13, 1987, pp. 183–202.

Chapter 7

1. Bureau of Economic Analysis, *Survey of United States Current Business, 2001.*

2. P. Woodall, "Survey: The New Economy: Untangling E-conomics," *Economist,* September 23, 2000, pp. S5–S7.

3. J. M. Utterback, *Mastering the Dynamics of Innovation* (Boston: Harvard Business School Press, 1994). H. R. Varian, *Information Rules: A Strategic Guide to the Network Economy* (Boston: Harvard Business School Press, 1999).

4. The layout is not universal, although it is widespread. The French, for example, use a different layout.

5. M. Craig, "Dueling DVD Recorder Formats," *Seattle Times,* January 9, 2002, p. C3.

6. For details, see Charles W. L. Hill, "Establishing a Standard: Competitive Strategy and Technology Standards in Winner Take All Industries," *Academy of Management Executive* 11 (1997): 7–25; Shapiro and Varian, *Information Rules;* B. Arthur, "Increasing Returns and the New World of Business," *Harvard Business Review* (July–August 1996): 100–109.

7. See Shapiro and Varian, *Information Rules.* Hill, "Establishing a Standard." M. A. Shilling, "Technological Lockout: An Integrative Model of the Economic and Strategic Factors Driving Technology Success and Failure," *Academy of Management Review* 23:2 (1998): 267–285.

8. Microsoft does not disclose the per unit licensing fee that it gets from original equipment manufacturers.

9. P. M. Romer, "The Origins of Endogenous Growth," *Journal of Economic Perspectives* 8:1 (1994): 3–22.

10. Data from **www.btechnews.com.**

11. Varian, *Information Rules.*

12. Business Software Association, *Sixth Annual Global Software Piracy Study* (May 2001).

13. International Federation of the Phonographic Industry, at **http://www.ifpi.org/.**

14. N. Ridgeway, "Let Them Burn," *Forbes,* March 4, 2002, p. 88.

15. Much of this section is based on Charles W. L. Hill, Michael Heeley, and Jane Sakson, "Strategies for Profiting from Innovation," in *Advances in Global High Technology Management* (Greenwich, Conn.: JAI Press, 1993), 3: 79–95.

16. M. Lieberman and D. Montgomery, "First Mover Advantages," *Strategic Management Journal* 9 (Special Issue, Summer 1988): 41–58.

17. J. Borzo, "Aging Gracefully," *Wall Street Journal,* October 15, 2001, p. R22.

18. The importance of complementary assets was first noted by D. J. Teece. See D. J. Teece, "Profiting from Technological Innovation," in D. J. Teece (ed.), *The Competitive Challenge* (New York: Harper & Row, 1986), pp. 26–54.

19. M. J. Chen and D. C. Hambrick, "Speed, Stealth, and Selective Attack: How Small Firms Differ from Large Firms in Competitive Behavior," *Academy of Management Journal* 38 (1995): 453–482.

20. E. Mansfield, M. Schwartz, and S. Wagner, "Imitation Costs and Patents: An Empirical Study," *Economic Journal* 91 (1981): 907–918.

21. E. Mansfield, "How Rapidly Does New Industrial Technology Leak Out?" *Journal of Industrial Economics* 34 (1985): 217–223.

22. This argument has been made in the game theory literature. See R. Caves, H. Cookell, and P. J. Killing, "The Imperfect Market for Technology Licenses," *Oxford Bulletin of Economics and Statistics* 45 (1983): 249–267; N. T. Gallini, "Deterrence by Market Sharing: A Strategic Incentive for Licensing," *American Economic Review* 74 (1984): 931–941; and C. Shapiro, "Patent Licensing and R&D Rivalry," *American Economic Review* 75 (1985): 25–30.

23. M. Christensen, *The Innovator's Dilemma* (Boston: Harvard Business School Press, 1997). R. N. Foster, *Innovation: The Attackers Advantage* (New York: Summit Books, 1986).

24. Foster, *Innovation.*

25. Ray Kurzweil, *The Age of the Spiritual Machines* (New York: Penguin Books, 1999).

26. See Christensen, *The Innovator's Dilemma,* and C. M. Christensen and M. Overdorf, "Meeting the Challenge of Disruptive Change," *Harvard Business Review* (March–April 2000): 66–77.

Chapter 8

1. M. E. Porter, *The Competitive Advantage of Nations* (New York: Free Press, 1990).

2. C. S. Tranger, "Enter the Mini-Multinational," *Northeast International Business* (March 1989): 13–14.

3. R. B. Reich, *The Work of Nations* (New York: Knopf, 1991).

4. "Matsushita Electrical Industrial in 1987," in C. A. Bartlett and S. Ghoshal (eds.), *Transnational Management* (Homewood, Ill.: Irwin, 1992).

5. J. P. Woomack, D. T. Jones, and D. Roos, *The Machine That Changed the World* (New York: Rawson Associates, 1990).

6. See J. Birkinshaw and N. Hood, "Multinational Subsidiary Evolution: Capability and Charter Change in Foreign Owned Subsidiary Companies," *Academy of Management Review* 23 (October 1998): 773–795. A. K. Gupta and Govindarajan, "Knowledge Flows Within Multinational Corporations," *Strategic Management Journal* 21 (2000): 473–496.

7. C. K. Prahalad and Yves L. Doz, *The Multinational Mission: Balancing Local Demands and Global Vision* (New York: Free Press, 1987). Also see J. Birkinshaw, A. Morrison, and J. Hulland, "Structural and Competitive Determinants of a Global Integration Strategy," *Strategic Management Journal* 16 (1995): 637–655.

8. Prahalad and Doz, *The Multinational Mission.*

9. "The Tire Industry's Costly Obsession with Size," *Economist,* June 8, 1993, pp. 65–66.

10. T. Levitt, "The Globalization of Markets," *Harvard Business Review* (May–June 1983): 92–102.

11. C. A. Bartlett and S. Ghoshal, *Managing Across Borders* (Boston: Harvard Business School Press, 1989).

12. C. J. Chipello, "Local Presence Is Key to European Deals," *Wall Street Journal,* June 30, 1998, p. A15.

13. Bartlett and Ghoshal, *Managing Across Borders.*

14. Ibid.

15. T. Hout, M. E. Porter, and E. Rudden, "How Global Companies Win Out," *Harvard Business Review* (September–October 1982): 98–108.

16. See Charles W. L. Hill, *International Business: Competing in the Global Marketplace* (New York: McGraw-Hill, 2000).

17. This can be reconceptualized as the resource base of the entrant, relative to indigenous competitors. For work that focuses on this issue, see W. C. Bogenr, H. Thomas, and J. McGee, "A Longitudinal Study of the Competitive Positions and Entry Paths of European Firms in the U.S. Pharmaceutical Market," *Strategic Management Journal* 17 (1996): 85–107. D. Collis, "A Resource Based Analysis of Global Competition," *Strategic Management Journal* 12 (1991): 49–68. S. Tallman, "Strategic Management Models and Resource Based Strategies Among MNE's in a Host Market," *Strategic Management Journal* 12 (1991): 69–82.

18. For a discussion of first-mover advantages, see M. Liberman and D. Montgomery, "First Mover Advantages," *Strategic Management Journal* 9 (Special Issue, Summer 1988): 41–58.

19. J. M. Shaver, W. Mitchell, and B. Yeung, "The Effect of Own Company and Other Company Experience on Foreign Direct Investment Survival in the U.S., 1987–92," *Strategic Management Journal* 18 (1997): 811–824.

20. S. Zaheer and E. Mosakowski, "The Dynamics of the Liability of Foreignness: A Global Study of Survival in the Financial Services Industry," *Strategic Management Journal* 18 (1997): 439–464.

21. Shaver, Mitchell, and Yeung, "The Effect of Own Company and Other Company Experience."

22. P. Ghemawat, *Commitment: The Dynamics of Strategy* (New York: Free Press, 1991).

23. This section draws on several studies, including: C. W. L. Hill, P. Hwang, and W. C. Kim, "An Eclectic Theory of the Choice of International Entry Mode," *Strategic Management Journal* 11 (1990): 117–128; C. W. L. Hill and W. C. Kim, "Searching for a Dynamic Theory of the Multinational Company: A Transaction Cost Model," *Strategic Management Journal* 9 (Special Issue on Strategy Content, 1988): 93–104. E. Anderson and H. Gatignon, "Modes of Foreign Entry: A Transaction Cost Analysis and Propositions," *Journal of International Business Studies* 17 (1986): 1–26; F. R. Root, *Entry Strategies for International Markets* (Lexington, Mass.: D. C. Heath, 1980). A. Madhok, "Cost, Value and Foreign Market Entry: The Transaction and the Company," *Strategic Management Journal* 18 (1997): 39–61.

24. F. J. Contractor, "The Role of Licensing in International Strategy," *Columbia Journal of World Business* (Winter 1982): 73–83.

25. O. E. Williamson, *The Economic Institutions of Capitalism* (New York: Free Press, 1985).

26. Andrew E. Serwer, "McDonald's Conquers the World," *Fortune,* October 17, 1994, pp. 103–116.

27. B. Kogut, "Joint Ventures: Theoretical and Empirical Perspectives," *Strategic Management Journal* 9 (1988): 319–332.

28. D. G. Bradley, "Managing Against Expropriation," *Harvard Business Review* (July–August 1977): 78–90.

29. C. W. L. Hill, "Strategies for Exploiting Technological Innovations," *Organization Science* 3 (1992): 428–441.

30. See K. Ohmae, "The Global Logic of Strategic Alliances," *Harvard Business Review* (March–April 1989): 143–154; G. Hamel, Y. L. Doz, and C. K. Prahalad, "Collaborate with Your Competitors and Win!" *Harvard Business Review* (January–February 1989): 133–139; and W. Burgers, C. W. L. Hill, and W. C. Kim, "Alliances in the Global Auto Industry," *Strategic Management Journal* 14 (1993): 419–432. P. Kale, H. Singh, and H. Perlmutter, "Learning and Protection of Proprietary Assets in Strategic Alliances: Building Relational Capital," *Strategic Management Journal* 21 (2000): 217–237.

31. "Asia Beckons," *Economist,* May 30, 1992, pp. 63–64.

32. Kale, Singh, and Perlmutter, "Learning and Protection of Proprietary Assets."

33. R. B. Reich and E. D. Mankin, "Joint Ventures with Japan Give Away Our Future," *Harvard Business Review* (March–April 1986): 78–90.

34. J. Bleeke and D. Ernst, "The Way to Win in Cross-Border Alliances," *Harvard Business Review* (November–December 1991): 127–135.

35. W. Roehl and J. F. Truitt, "Stormy Open Marriages Are Better," *Columbia Journal of World Business* (Summer 1987): 87–95.

36. K. McQuade and B. Gomes-Casseres, "Xerox and Fuji–Xerox," Harvard Business School Case #9-391-156.

37. T. Khanna, R. Gulati, and N. Nohria, "The Dynamics of Learning Alliances: Competition, Cooperation, and Relative Scope," *Strategic Management Journal* 19 (1998): 193–210. Kale, Singh, and Perlmutter, "Learning and Protection of Proprietary Assets."

38. Hamel, Doz, and Prahalad, "Collaborate with Your Competitors and Win!"

39. B. Wysocki, "Cross Border Alliances Become Favorite Way to Crack New Markets," *Wall Street Journal,* March 4, 1990, p. A1.

Chapter 9

1. Y. J. Dreazen, G. Ip, and N. Kulish, "Why the Sudden Rise in the Urge to Merge and Create Oligopolies?" *Wall Street Journal,* February 25, 2002, p. A1.

2. United Nations, *World Investment Report 2001* (New York: United Nations, November 2001).

3. Dreazen, Ip, and Kulish. "Why the Sudden Rise?"

4. For evidence on acquisitions and performance, see R. E. Caves, "Mergers, Takeovers, and Economic Efficiency," *International Journal of Industrial Organization* 7 (1989): 151–174; M. C. Jensen and R. S. Ruback, "The Market for Corporate Control: The Scientific Evidence," *Journal of Financial Economics* 11 (1983): 5–50; R. Roll, "Empirical Evidence on Takeover Activity and Shareholder Wealth," in J. C. Coffee, L. Lowenstein, and S. Rose (eds.), *Knights, Raiders and Targets* (Oxford: Oxford University Press, 1989); and A. Schleifer and R. W. Vishny, "Takeovers in the 60s and 80s: Evidence and Implications," *Strategic Management Journal* 12 (Special Issue, Winter 1991): 51–60. T. H. Brush, "Predicted Changes in Operational Synergy and Post Acquisition Performance of Acquired Businesses," *Strategic Management Journal* 17 (1996): 1–24.

5. "Few Takeovers Pay Off for Big Buyers," *Investors Business Daily,* May 25, 2001, p. 1.

6. K. R. Harrian, "Formulating Vertical Integration Strategies," *Academy of Management Review* 9 (1984): 638–652.

7. This is the essence of Chandler's argument. See Alfred D. Chandler, *Strategy and Structure* (Cambridge, Mass.: MIT Press, 1962). The same argument is also made by Jeffrey Pfeffer and Gerald R. Salancik, *The External Control of Organizations* (New York: Harper & Row, 1978). See also K. R. Harrigan, *Strategic Flexibility* (Lexington, Mass.: Lexington Books, 1985); K. R. Harrigan, "Vertical Integration and Corporate Strategy,"

Academy of Management Journal 28 (1985): 397–425; and F. M. Scherer, *Industrial Market Structure and Economic Performance* (Chicago: Rand McNally, 1981).

8. T. Chipty, "Vertical Integration, Market Foreclosure and Consumer Welfare in the Cable Television Industry," *American Economic Review* 91 (2001): 428–453. D. L. Rubinfeld and H. Singer, "Vertical Foreclosure in Broadband Access?" *Journal of Industrial Economics* 49 (2001): 299–318. This section is based on the transaction cost approach popularized by Oliver E. Williamson, *The Economic Institutions of Capitalism* (New York: Free Press, 1985).

9. Oliver E. Williamson, *The Economic Institutions of Capitalism.* For recent empirical work that uses this framework, see L. Poppo and T. Zenger, "Testing Alternative Theories of the Firm: Transaction Cost, Knowledge Based, and Measurement Explanations for Make or Buy Decisions in Information Services," *Strategic Management Journal* 19 (1998): 853–878.

10. Williamson, *Economic Institutions of Capitalism.*

11. A. D. Chandler, *The Visible Hand* (Cambridge, Mass.: Harvard University Press, 1977).

12. Julia Pitta, "Score One for Vertical Integration," *Forbes,* January 18, 1993, pp. 88–89.

13. Joseph White and Neal Templin, "Harsh Regimen: A Swollen GM Finds It Hard to Stick with Its Crash Diet," *Wall Street Journal,* September 9, 1992, p. A1.

14. Harrigan, *Strategic Flexibility,* pp. 67–87. See also Allan Afuah, "Dynamic Boundaries of the Firm: Are Firms Better Off Being Vertically Integrated in the Face of a Technological Change?" *Academy of Management Journal* 44 (2001): 1121–1228.

15. For a detailed theoretical rationale for this argument, see G. R. Jones and C. W. L. Hill, "A Transaction Cost Analysis of Strategy-Structure Choice," *Strategic Management Journal* 9 (1988): 159–172.

16. Kevin Kelly, Zachary Schiller, and James Treece, "Cut Costs or Else," *Business Week,* March 22, 1993, pp. 28–29.

17. X. Martin, W. Mitchell, and A. Swaminathan, "Recreating and Extending Japanese Automobile Buyer-Supplier Links in North America," *Strategic Management Journal* 16 (1995): 589–619. C. W. L. Hill, "National Institutional Structures, Transaction Cost Economizing, and Competitive Advantage," *Organization Science* 6 (1995): 119–131.

18. Standard & Poor's Industry Survey, Autos–Auto Parts, June 24, 1993.

19. See James Womack, Daniel Jones, and Daniel Roos, *The Machine That Changed the World* (New York: Rawson Associates, 1990). James Richardson, "Parallel Sourcing and Supplier Performance in the Japanese Automobile Industry," *Strategic Management Journal* 14 (1993): 339–350.

20. R. Mudambi and S. Helper, "The Close But Adversarial Model of Supplier Relations in the U.S. Auto Industry," *Strategic Management Journal* 19 (1998): 775–792.

21. Williamson, *Economic Institutions.* See also J. H. Dyer, "Effective Inter-Firm Collaboration: How Firms Minimize Transaction Costs and Maximize Transaction Value," *Strategic Management Journal* 18 (1997): 535–556.

22. Richardson, "Parallel Sourcing."

23. W. H. Davidow and M. S. Malone, *The Virtual Corporation* (New York: Harper & Row, 1992).

24. A. M. Porter, "Outsourcing Gains Popularity," *Purchasing,* March 11, 1999, pp. 22–24.

25. D. Garr, "Inside Outsourcing," *Fortune* 142:1 (2001): 85–92.

26. J. Krane, "American Express Hires IBM for $4 billion," *Columbian,* February 26, 2002, p. E2.

27. J. Vijayan, "The Outsourcing Boom," *Computerworld,* March 18, 2002, pp. 42–43.

28. Davidow and Malone, *The Virtual Corporation.*

29. Ibid. H. W. Chesbrough and D. J. Teece, "When Is Virtual Virtuous? Organizing for Innovation," *Harvard Business Review* (January–February 1996): 65–74. J. B. Quinn, "Strategic Outsourcing: Leveraging Knowledge Capabilities," *Sloan Management Review* (Summer 1999): 9–21.

Chapter 10

1. T. J. Peters and R. H. Waterman, *In Search of Excellence* (New York: Harper & Row, 1982).

2. G. Hamel and C. K. Prahalad, *Competing for the Future* (Boston: Harvard Business School Press, 1994).

3. Ibid.

4. D. Leonard Barton and G. Pisano, "Monsanto's March into Biotechnology," Harvard Business School Case #690-009 (1990). See Monsanto's home page for details of its genetically engineered seed products (**http://www.monsanto.com**).

5. This resource-based view of diversification can be traced to Edith Penrose's seminal book, *The Theory of the Growth of the Firm* (Oxford: Oxford University Press, 1959).

6. D. J. Teece, "Economies of Scope and the Scope of the Enterprise," *Journal of Economic Behavior and Organization* 3 (1980): 223–247. For recent empirical work on this topic, see C. H. St. John and J. S. Harrison, "Manufacturing Based Relatedness, Synergy and Coordination," *Strategic Management Journal* 20 (1999): 129–145.

7. For a detailed discussion, see C. W. L. Hill and R. E. Hoskisson, "Strategy and Structure in the Multiproduct Firm," *Academy of Management Review* 12 (1987): 331–341.

8. See, for example, G. R. Jones and C. W. L. Hill, "A Transaction Cost Analysis of Strategy Structure Choice," *Strategic Management Journal* (1988): 159–172; and Williamson, *Markets and Hierarchies* (New York: Free Press), pp. 132–175.

9. R. Buderi, *Engines of Tomorrow* (New York: Simon & Schuster, 2000).

10. C. W. L. Hill, "The Role of Headquarters in the Multidivisional Firm," in R. Rumelt, D. J. Teece, and D. Schendel, *Fundamental Issues in Strategy Research* (Cambridge, Mass.: Harvard Business School Press, 1994), pp. 297–321.

11. See, for example, Jones and Hill, "A Transaction Cost Analysis." Williamson, *Markets and Hierarchies.* Hill, "The Role of Headquarters in the Multidivisional Firm."

12. The distinction goes back to R. P. Rumelt, *Strategy, Structure and Economic Performance* (Boston: Harvard Business School Press, 1974).

13. For example, see C. W. L. Hill, "Diversified Growth and Competition," *Applied Economics* 17 (1985): 827–847. Rumelt, *Strategy, Structure and Economic Performance.* Jones and Hill, "A Transaction Cost Analysis."

14. See H. K. Christensen and C. A. Montgomery, "Corporate Economic Performance: Diversification Strategy Versus Market Structure," *Strategic Management Journal* 2 (1981): 327–343. Jones and Hill, "A Transaction Cost Analysis." G. Dess, J-F. Hennart, C. W. L. Hill, and A. Gupta, "Research Issues in Strategic Management," *Journal of Management* 21 (1995): 357–392. Hill. "The Role of Headquarters in the Multidivisional Company."

15. For reviews of the evidence, see V. Ramanujam and P. Varadarajan, "Research on Corporate Diversification: A Synthesis," *Strategic Management Journal* 10 (1989): 523–551; Dess, Hennart, Hill, and Gupta, "Research Issues in Strategic Management"; and David C. Hyland and J. David Diltz, "Why Companies Diversify: An Empirical Examination," *Financial Management* 31 (Spring 2002): 51–81.

16. M. E. Porter, "From Competitive Advantage to Corporate Strategy," *Harvard Business Review* (May–June 1987): 43–59.

17. For reviews of the evidence, see Ramanujam and Varadarajan, "Research on Corporate Diversification"; Dess, Hennart, Hill, and Gupta, "Research Issues in Strategic Management"; Hyland and Diltz, "Why Companies Diversify."

18. C. R. Christensen et al., *Business Policy Text and Cases* (Homewood, Ill.: Irwin, 1987), p. 778.

19. See H. K. Christensen and C. A. Montgomery, "Corporate Economic Performance: Diversification Strategy Versus Market Structure," *Strategic Management Journal* 2 (1981): 327–343; Jones and Hill, "A Transaction Cost Analysis"; Dess, Hennart, Hill, and Gupta, "Research Issues in Strategic Management"; Hill, "The Role of Headquarters."

20. For evidence, see C. W. L. Hill, "Conglomerate Performance over the Economic Cycle," *Journal of Industrial Economics* 32 (1983): 197–212; and D. T. C. Mueller, "The Effects of Conglomerate Mergers," *Journal of Banking and Finance* 1 (1977): 315–347.

21. See Booz, Allen, and Hamilton, *New Products Management for the 1980's* (privately published, 1982); A. L. Page, "PDMA's New Product Development Practices Survey: Performance and Best Practices" (presented at the PDMA Fifteenth Annual International Conference, Boston, October 16, 1991); and E. Mansfield, "How Economists See R&D," *Harvard Business Review* (November–December 1981): 98–106.

22. See R. Biggadike, "The Risky Business of Diversification," *Harvard Business Review* (May–June 1979): 103–111. R. A. Burgelman, "A Process Model of Internal Corporate Venturing in the Diversified Major Firm," *Administrative Science Quarterly* 28 (1983): 223–244. Z. Block and I. C. Macmillan, *Corporate Venturing* (Boston: Harvard Business School Press, 1993).

23. Biggadike, "The Risky Business of Diversification." Block and Macmillan, *Corporate Venturing.*

24. Buderi, *Engines of Tomorrow.*

25. I. C. MacMillan and R. George, "Corporate Venturing: Challenges for Senior Managers," *Journal of Business Strategy* 5 (1985): 34–43.

26. See R. A. Burgelman, M. M. Maidique, and S. C. Wheelwright, *Strategic Management of Technology and Innovation* (Chicago: Irwin, 1996), pp. 493–507. Also see Buderi, *Engines of Tomorrow.*

27. Buderi, *Engines of Tomorrow.*

28. See Block and Macmillan, *Corporate Venturing.* Burgelman, Maidique, and Wheelwright, *Strategic Management of Technology and Innovation.*

29. G. Beardsley and E. Mansfield, "A Note on the Accuracy of Industrial Forecasts of the Profitability of New Products and Processes," *Journal of Business* 23 (1978): 127–130.

30. J. Warner, J. Templeman, and R. Horn, "The Case Against Mergers," *Business Week,* October 30, 1995, pp. 122–134.

31. "Few Takeovers Pay Off for Big Buyers," *Investors Business Daily,* May 25, 2001, p. 1.

32. For evidence on acquisitions and performance, see R. E. Caves, "Mergers, Takeovers, and Economic Efficiency," *International Journal of Industrial Organization* 7 (1989): 151–174; M. C. Jensen and R. S. Ruback, "The Market for Corporate Control: The Scientific Evidence," *Journal of Financial Economics* 11 (1983): 5–50; R. Roll, "Empirical Evidence on Takeover Activity and Shareholder Wealth," in J. C. Coffee, L. Lowenstein, and S. Rose (eds.), *Knights, Raiders and Targets* (Oxford: Oxford University Press, 1989); and A. Schleifer and R. W. Vishny, "Takeovers in the 60s and 80s: Evidence and Implications," *Strategic Management Journal* 12 (Special Issue, Winter 1991): 51–60. T. H. Brush, "Predicted Changes in Operational Synergy and Post Acquisition Performance of Acquired Businesses," *Strategic Management Journal* 17 (1996): 1–24. T. Loughran and A. M. Vijh, "Do Long Term Shareholders Benefit from Corporate Acquisitions?" *Journal of Finance* 5 (1997): 1765–1787.

33. D. J. Ravenscraft and F. M. Scherer, *Mergers, Selloffs, and Economic Efficiency* (Washington, D.C.: Brookings Institution, 1987).

34. See J. P. Walsh, "Top Management Turnover Following Mergers and Acquisitions," *Strategic Management Journal* 9 (1988): 173–183.

35. See A. A. Cannella and D. C. Hambrick, "Executive Departure and Acquisition Performance," *Strategic Management Journal* 14 (1993): 137–152.

36. R. Roll, "The Hubris Hypothesis of Corporate Takeovers," *Journal of Business* 59 (1986): 197–216.

37. "Coca-Cola: A Sobering Lesson from Its Journey into Wine," *Business Week,* June 3, 1985, pp. 96–98.

38. D. Foust, "They Shopped—Now They've Dropped," *Business Week,* February 25, 2002, pp. 36–37.

39. P. Haspeslagh and D. Jemison, *Managing Acquisitions* (New York: Free Press, 1991).

40. D. Sparks, "No Money Grows Here," *Business Week,* April 17, 2000, pp. 174–176.

41. For views on this issue, see L. L. Fray, D. H. Gaylin, and J. W. Down, "Successful Acquisition Planning," *Journal of Business Strategy* 5 (1984): 46–55; C. W. L. Hill, "Profile of a Conglomerate Takeover: BTR and Thomas Tilling," *Journal of General Management* 10 (1984): 34–50; D. R. Willensky, "Making It Happen: How to Execute an Acquisition," *Business Horizons* (March–April 1985): 38–45; Haspeslagh and Jemison, *Managing Acquisitions;* and P. L. Anslinger and T. E. Copeland, "Growth Through Acquisition: A Fresh Look," *Harvard Business Review* (January–February 1996): 126–135.

42. M. L. A. Hayward, "When Do Firms Learn from Their Acquisition Experience? Evidence from 1990–1995," *Strategic Management Journal* 23 (2002): 21–39. K. G. Ahuja, "Technological Acquisitions and the Innovation Performance of Acquiring Firms: A Longitudinal Study," *Strategic Management Journal* 23 (2001): 197–220. H. G. Barkema and F. Vermeulen, "International Expansion Through Startup or Acquisition," *Academy of Management Journal* 41 (1998): 7–26.

43. Hayward, "When Do Firms Learn from Their Acquisition Experience?"

44. For a review of the evidence and some contrary empirical evidence, see D. E. Hatfield, J. P. Liebskind, and T. C. Opler, "The Effects of Corporate Restructuring on Aggregate Industry Specialization," *Strategic Management Journal* 17 (1996): 55–72.

45. A. Lamont and C. Polk, "The Diversification Discount: Cash Flows Versus Returns," *Journal of Finance* 56 (October 2001): 1693–1721. R. Raju, H. Servaes, and L. Zingales, "The Cost of

Diversity: The Diversification Discount and Inefficient Investment," *Journal of Finance* 55 (February 2000): 35–80.

46. For example, see Schleifer and Vishny, "Takeovers in the 60s and 80s."

Chapter 11

1. Salomon Smith Barney Research, 2001.

2. See J. Argenti, *Corporate Collapse: Causes and Symptoms* (New York: McGraw-Hill, 1976); R. C. Hoffman, "Strategies for Corporate Turnarounds: What Do We Know About Them?" *Journal of General Management* 14 (1984): 46–66; D. Schendel, G. R. Patton, and J. Riggs, "Corporate Turnaround Strategies: A Study of Profit Decline and Recovery," *Journal of General Management* 2 (1976): 1–22; and S. Siafter, *Corporate Recovery: Successful Turnaround Strategies and Their Implementation* (Harmondsworth, England: Penguin Books, 1984), pp. 25–60.

3. D. B. Bibeault, *Corporate Turnaround* (New York: McGraw-Hill, 1982).

4. Hoffman, "Strategies for Corporate Turnarounds," pp. 46–66.

5. Ibid.

6. M. T. Hannan and J. Freeman, "Structural Inertia and Organizational Change," *American Sociological Review* 49 (1984): 149–164. M. L. Tushman and C. A. O'Reilly, *Winning Through Innovation* (Boston: Harvard Business School Press, 1997).

7. J. Pfeffer, *Managing with Power: Politics and Influence Within Organizations* (Boston: Harvard Business School Press, 1992).

8. D. Miller, *The Icarus Paradox* (New York: Harper Business, 1990).

9. E. Freeman, *Strategic Management: A Stakeholder Approach* (Boston: Pitman Press, 1984).

10. C. W. L. Hill and T. M. Jones, "Stakeholder-Agency Theory," *Journal of Management Studies* 29 (1992): 131–154. J. G. March and H. A. Simon, *Organizations* (New York: Wiley, 1958).

11. Hill and Jones, "Stakeholder-Agency Theory."

12. I. C. Macmillan and P. E. Jones, *Strategy Formulation: Power and Politics* (St. Paul, Minn.: West, 1986).

13. Tom Copeland, Tim Koller, and Jack Murrin, *Valuation: Measuring and Managing the Value of Companies* (New York: Wiley, 1996).

14. M. C. Jensen and W. H. Meckling, "Theory of the Firm: Managerial Behavior, Agency Costs and Ownership Structure," *Journal of Financial Economics* 3 (1976): 305–360. E. F. Fama, "Agency Problems and the Theory of the Firm," *Journal of Political Economy* 88 (1980): 375–390.

15. Hill and Jones, "Stakeholder-Agency Theory."

16. For example, see R. Marris, *The Economic Theory of Managerial Capitalism* (London: Macmillan, 1964), and J. K. Galbraith, *The New Industrial State* (Boston: Houghton Mifflin, 1970).

17. E. F. Fama, "Agency Problems and the Theory of the Firm," *Journal of Political Economy* 88 (1980): 375–390.

18. A. Rappaport, "New Thinking on How to Link Executive Pay with Performance," *Harvard Business Review* (March–April 1999): 91–105.

19. L. Lavelle, F. F. Jespersen, and M. Arndt, "Executive Pay," *Business Week,* April 15, 2002, pp. 80–86.

20. John Byrne et al., "How to Fix Corporate Governance," *Business Week,* May 6, 2002, pp. 69–78.

21. For academic studies that look at the determinants of CEO pay, see M. C. Jensen and K. J. Murphy, "Performance Pay and Top Management Incentives," *Journal of Political Economy* 98 (1990): 225–264. Charles W. L. Hill and Phillip Phan, "CEO Tenure as a Determinant of CEO Pay," *Academy of Management Journal* 34 (1991): 707–717. H. L. Tosi and L. R. Gomez-Mejia, "CEO Compensation Monitoring and Firm Performance," *Academy of Management Journal* 37 (1994): 1002–1016. Joseph F. Porac, James B. Wade, and Timothy G. Pollock, "Industry Categories and the Politics of the Comparable Firm in CEO Compensation," *Administrative Science Quarterly* 44 (1999): 112–144.

22. Ellen Goodman, "CEO Pay Cap: Why Not Try It for Size?" *Houston Chronicle,* April 18, 1999, p. 6.

23. For recent research on this issue, see Peter J. lane, A. A. Cannella, and M. H. Lubatkin, "Agency Problems as Antecedents to Unrelated Mergers and Diversification: Amihud and Lev Reconsidered," *Strategic Management Journal* 19 (1998): 555–578.

24. Carl Icahn, "What Ails Corporate America—and What Should Be Done?" *Business Week,* October 27, 1986, p. 101.

25. E. T. Penrose, *The Theory of the Growth of the Firm* (London: Macmillan, 1958).

26. G. J. Miller, *Managerial Dilemmas: The Political Economy of Hierarchy* (Cambridge: Cambridge University Press, 1992).

27. O. E. Williamson, *The Economic Institutions of Capitalism* (New York: Free Press, 1985).

28. Fama, "Agency Problems and the Theory of the Firm."

29. S. Finkelstein and R. D'Aveni, "CEO Duality as a Double Edged Sword," *Academy of Management Journal* 37 (1994): 1079–1108. B. Ram Baliga and R. C. Moyer, "CEO Duality and Firm Performance," *Strategic Management Journal* 17 (1996): 41–53. M. L. Mace, *Directors: Myth and Reality* (Cambridge, Mass.: Harvard University Press, 1971). S. C. Vance, *Corporate Leadership: Boards of Directors and Strategy* (New York: McGraw-Hill, 1983).

30. Michele Galen, "A Seat on the Board Is Getting Hotter," *Business Week,* July 3, 1989, pp. 72–73.

31. J. S. Lublin. "Irate Shareholders Target Ineffective Board Members," *Wall Street Journal,* November 6, 1995, p. B1.

32. Gilbert Fuchsberg, "Chief Executives See Their Power Shrink," *Wall Street Journal,* March 15, 1993, pp. B1, B3.

33. Quoted in G. Morgenson, "Stock Options Are Not a Free Lunch," *Forbes,* May 18, 1998, pp. 212–217.

34. W. G. Lewellen, C. Eoderer, and A. Rosenfeld, "Merger Decisions and Executive Stock Ownership in Acquiring Firms," *Journal of Accounting and Economics* 7 (1985): 209–231.

35. C. W. L. Hill and S. A. Snell, "External Control, Corporate Strategy, and Firm Performance," *Strategic Management Journal* 9 (1988): 577–590.

36. D. Henry and M. Conlin, "Too Much of a Good Incentive?" *Business Week,* March 4, 2002, pp. 38–39.

37. J. P. Walsh and R. D. Kosnik, "Corporate Raiders and Their Disciplinary Role in the Market for Corporate Control," *Academy of Management Journal* 36 (1993): 671–700.

38. R. S. Kaplan and D. P. Norton, "The Balanced Scorecard—Measures That Drive Performance," *Harvard Business Review* (January–February 1992): 71–79.

39. R. S. Kaplan and D. P. Norton, "Using the Balanced Scorecard as a Strategic Management System," *Harvard Business Review* (January–February 1996): 75–85.

40. R. S. Kaplan and D. P. Norton, "Putting the Balanced Scorecard to Work," *Harvard Business Review* (September–October 1993): 134–147.

41. Kaplan and Norton, "The Balanced Scorecard," p. 72.

42. Robert C. Solomon, *Ethics and Excellence* (New York: Oxford University Press, 1992).

43. Saul W. Gellerman, "Why Good Managers Make Bad Ethical Choices," in Kenneth R. Andrews (ed.), *Ethics in Practice: Managing the Moral Corporation* (Boston: Harvard Business School Press, 1989).

44. Kirk O. Hanson and Manuel Velasquez, "Hewlett-Packard Company: Managing Ethics and Values," in *Business Roundtable, Corporate Ethics: A Prime Business Asset* (February 1988).

45. For example, see R. Edward Freeman and Daniel Gilbert, *Corporate Strategy and the Search for Ethics* (Englewood Cliffs, N.J.: Prentice-Hall, 1988). Thomas Jones, "Ethical Decision Making by Individuals in Organizations," *Academy of Management Review* 16 (1991): 366–395. J. R. Rest, *Moral Development: Advances in Research and Theory* (New York: Praeger, 1986).

46. For example, see Freeman and Gilbert, *Corporate Strategy and the Search for Ethics. Jones,* "Ethical Decision Making by Individuals in Organizations." Rest, *Moral Development.*

Chapter 12

1. L. Smircich, "Concepts of Culture and Organizational Analysis," *Administrative Science Quarterly* 28 (1983): 339–358.

2. G. R. Jones and J. M. George, "The Experience and Evolution of Trust: Implications for Cooperation and Teamwork," *Academy of Management Review* 3 (1998): 531–546.

3. Ibid.

4. J. R. Galbraith, *Designing Complex Organizations* (Reading, Mass.: Addison-Wesley, 1973).

5. Alfred D. Chandler, *Strategy and Structure* (Cambridge, Mass.: MIT Press, 1962).

6. The discussion draws heavily on ibid. and B. R. Scott, *Stages of Corporate Development* (Cambridge, Mass.: Intercollegiate Clearing House, Harvard Business School, 1971).

7. R. L. Daft, *Organizational Theory and Design,* 3rd ed. (St. Paul, Minn.: West, 1986), p. 215.

8. Child, *Organization,* pp. 52–70.

9. G. R. Jones and J. Butler, "Costs, Revenues, and Business Level Strategy," *Academy of Management Review* 13 (1988): 202–213; G. R. Jones and C. W. L. Hill, "Transaction Cost Analysis of Strategy-Structure Choice," *Strategic Management Journal* 9 1988): 159–172.

10. G. R. Jones, *Organizational Theory: Text and Cases* (Englewood Cliffs, N.J.: Prentice-Hall, 2000).

11. P. Blau, "A Formal Theory of Differentiation in Organizations," *American Sociological Review* 35 (1970): 684–695.

12. G. R. Jones, "Organization-Client Transactions and Organizational Governance Structures," *Academy of Management Journal* 30 (1987): 197–218.

13. S. McCartney, "Airline Industry's Top-Ranked Woman Keeps Southwest's Small-Fry Spirit Alive," *Wall Street Journal,* November 30, 1995, p. B.1.

14. P. R. Lawrence and J. Lorsch, *Organization and Environment* (Boston: Division of Research, Harvard Business School, 1967), pp. 50–55.

15. Galbraith, *Designing Complex Organizations,* chap. 1; J. R. Galbraith and R. K. Kazanjian, *Strategy Implementation: Structure System and Process,* 2nd ed. (St. Paul, Minn.: West, 1986), chap. 7.

16. R. Simmons, "Strategic Orientation and Top Management Attention to Control Systems," *Strategic Management Journal* 12 (1991): 49–62.

17. R. Simmons, "How New Top Managers Use Control Systems as Levers of Strategic Renewal," *Strategic Management Journal* 15 (1994): 169–189.

18. W. G. Ouchi, "The Transmission of Control Through Organizational Hierarchy," *Academy of Management Journal* 21 (1978): 173–192; and W. H. Newman, *Constructive Control* (Englewood Cliffs, N.J.: Prentice-Hall, 1975).

19. E. Flamholtz, "Organizational Control Systems as a Managerial Tool," *California Management Review* (Winter 1979): 50–58.

20. O. E. Williamson, *Markets and Hierarchies* (New York: Free Press, 1975); and W. G. Ouchi, "Markets, Bureaucracies, and Clans," *Administrative Science Quarterly* 25 (1980): 129–141.

21. H. Mintzberg, *The Structuring of Organizations* (Englewood Cliffs, N.J.: Prentice-Hall, 1979), pp. 5–9.

22. E. E. Lawler III, *Motivation in Work Organizations* (Monterey, Calif.: Brooks/Cole, 1973); and Galbraith and Kazanjian, *Strategy Implementation,* chap. 6.

23. L. Smircich, "Concepts of Culture and Organizational Analysis," *Administrative Science Quarterly* 28 (1983): 339–358.

24. General Electric, Harvard Business School Case #9-385-315 (1984).

25. Ouchi, "Markets, Bureaucracies, and Clans," p. 130.

26. Jones, *Organizational Theory.*

27. J. Van Maanen and E. H. Schein, "Towards a Theory of Organizational Socialization," in B. M. Staw (ed.), *Research in Organizational Behavior* (Greenwich, Conn.: JAI Press, 1979), pp. 1, 209–264.

28. G. R. Jones, "Socialization Tactics, Self-Efficacy, and Newcomers' Adjustments to Organizations," *Academy of Management Journal* 29 (1986): 262–279.

29. J. P. Kotter and J. L. Heskett, *Corporate Culture and Performance.*

30. T. J. Peters and R. H. Waterman, *In Search of Excellence: Lessons from America's Best-Run Companies* (New York: Harper & Row, 1982).

31. G. Hamel and C. K. Prahalad, "Strategic Intent," *Harvard Business Review* (May–June 1989): 64.

32. Galbraith and Kazanjian, *Strategy Implementation.* Child, *Organization;* R. Duncan, "What Is the Right Organization Structure?" *Organizational Dynamics* (Winter 1979): 59–80.

33. W. G. Ouchi, "The Relationship Between Organizational Structure and Organizational Control," *Administrative Science Quarterly* 22 (1977): 95–113.

34. R. Bunderi, "Intel Researchers Aim to Think Big While Staying Close to Development," *Research-Technology Management* (March–April 1998): 3–4.

35. K. M. Eisenhardt, "Control: Organizational and Economic Approaches," *Management Science* 16 (1985): 134–148.

36. O. E. Williamson, *Markets and Hierarchies: Analysis and Antitrust Implications* (New York: Free Press, 1975).

37. Lawrence and Lorsch, *Organization and Environment.*

38. K. Pope, "Dell Refocuses on Groundwork to Cope with Rocketing Sales," *Wall Street Journal,* June 18, 1993, p. B5.

39. Galbraith, *Designing Complex Organizations.* Lawrence and Lorsch, *Organization and Environment.* D. Miller, "Strategy Making and Structure: Analysis and Implications for Performance," *Academy of Management Journal* 30 (1987): 7–32.

40. Michael E. Porter, *Competitive Strategy: Techniques for Analyzing Industries and Competitors* (New York: Free Press, 1980). D. Miller, "Configurations of Strategy and Structure," *Strategic Management Journal* 7 (1986): 233–249.

41. D. Miller and P. H. Freisen, *Organizations: A Quantum View* (Englewood Cliffs, N.J.: Prentice-Hall, 1984).

42. J. Woodward, *Industrial Organization: Theory and Practice* (London: Oxford University Press, 1965). Lawrence and Lorsch, *Organization and Environment.*

43. R. E. White, "Generic Business Strategies, Organizational Context and Performance: An Empirical Investigation," *Strategic Management Journal* 7 (1986): 217–231.

44. Porter, *Competitive Strategy.* Miller, "Configurations of Strategy and Structure."

45. E. Deal and A. A. Kennedy, *Corporate Cultures* (Reading, Mass.: Addison-Wesley, 1985). "Corporate Culture," *Business Week,* October 27, 1980, pp. 148–160.

46. S. M. Davis and R. R. Lawrence, *Matrix* (Reading, Mass.: Addison-Wesley, 1977). J. R. Galbraith, "Matrix Organization Designs: How to Combine Functional and Project Forms," *Business Horizons* 14 (1971): 29–40.

47. Duncan, "What Is the Right Organizational Structure?" Davis and Lawrence, *Matrix.*

48. B. Saporito, "How to Revive a Fading Firm," *Fortune,* March 22, 1993, p. 80.

49. D. Miller, "Configurations of Strategy and Structure," in R. E. Miles and C. C. Snow (eds.), *Organizational Strategy, Structure, and Process* (New York: McGraw-Hill, 1978).

50. G. D. Bruton, J. K. Keels, and C. L. Shook, "Downsizing the Firm: Answering the Strategic Questions," *Academy of Management Executive* (May 1996): 38–45.

51. M. Hammer and J. Champy, *Reengineering the Corporation* (New York: HarperCollins, 1993).

52. Ibid., p. 39.

Chapter 13

1. Alfred D. Chandler, *Strategy and Structure* (Cambridge, Mass.: MIT Press, 1962). Williamson, *Markets and Hierarchies* (New York: Free Press). L. Wrigley, "Divisional Autonomy and Diversification" (Ph.D. diss., Harvard Business School, 1970).

2. R. P. Rumelt, *Strategy, Structure, and Economic Performance* (Boston: Division of Research, Harvard Business School, 1974). B. R. Scott, *Stages of Corporate Development* (Cambridge, Mass.: Intercollegiate Clearing House, Harvard Business School, 1971). Williamson, *Markets and Hierarchies.*

3. The discussion draws on each of the sources cited in endnotes 20–27 and on G. R. Jones and C. W. L. Hill, "Transaction Cost Analysis of Strategy-Structure Choice," *Strategic Management Journal* 9 (1988): 159–172.

4. H. O. Armour and D. J. Teece, "Organizational Structure and Economic Performance: A Test of the Multidivisional Hypothesis," *Bell Journal of Economics* 9 (1978): 106–122.

5. Alfred Sloan, *My Years at General Motors* (New York: Doubleday, 1983), chap. 3.

6. Jones and Hill, "Transaction Cost Analysis of Strategy."

7. Ibid.

8. R. A. D'Aveni and D. J. Ravenscraft, "Economies of Integration Versus Bureaucracy Costs: Does Vertical Integration Improve Performance?" *Academy of Management Journal* 5 (1994): 1167–1206.

9. Lawrence and Lorsch, *Organization and Environment.* J. R. Galbraith, *Designing Complex Organizations* (Reading, Mass.: Addison-Wesley, 1973). Michael Porter, *Competitive Advantage: Creating and Sustaining Superior Performance* (New York: Free Press, 1985).

10. P. R. Nayyar, "Performance Effects of Information Asymmetry and Economies of Scope in Diversified Service Firm," *Academy of Management Journal* 36 (1993): 28–57.

11. **www.hp.com,** 2002.

12. L. R. Gomez-Mejia, "Structure and Process of Diversification, Compensation Strategy, and Performance," *Strategic Management Journal* 13 (1992): 381–397.

13. J. Stopford and L. Wells, *Managing the Multinational Enterprise* (London: Longman, 1972).

14. C. A. Bartlett and S. Ghoshal, *Managing Across Borders: The Transnational Solution* (Cambridge, Mass.: Harvard Business School, 1991).

15. R. A. Burgelman, "Managing the New Venture Division: Research Findings and the Implications for Strategic Management," *Strategic Management Journal* 6 (1985): 39–54.

16. N. D. Fast, "The Future of Industrial New Venture Departments," *Industrial Marketing Management* 8 (1979): 264–279.

17. G. Imperato, "3M Expert Tells How to Run Meetings That Really Work," *Fast Company,* May 23, 1999, p. 18.

18. Burgelman, "Managing the New Venture Division."

19. R. A. Burgelman, "Corporate Entrepreneurship and Strategic Management: Insights from a Process Study," *Management Science* 29 (1983): 1349–1364.

20. R. Jones, "Towards a Positive Interpretation of Transaction Cost Theory: The Central Role of Entrepreneurship and Trust," in M. Hitt, R. E. Freeman, and J. S. Harrison (eds.), *Handbook of Strategic Management* (London: Blackwell, 2001), pp. 208–228.

21. M. Prendergast, "Is Coke Turning into a Mickey Mouse Outfit," *Wall Street Journal,* March 5, 2001, p. A.22.

22. M. S. Salter and W. A. Weinhold, *Diversification Through Acquisition* (New York: Free Press, 1979).

23. F. T. Paine and D. J. Power, "Merger Strategy: An Examination of Drucker's Five Rules for Successful Acquisitions," *Strategic Management Journal* 5 (1984): 99–110.

24. H. Singh and C. A. Montgomery, "Corporate Acquisitions and Economic Performance," unpublished manuscript, 1984.

25. B. Worthen, "Nestlé's ERP Odyssey," *CIO,* May 15, 2002, pp. 1–5.

26. G. D. Bruton, B. M. Oviatt, and M. A. White, "Performance of Acquisitions of Distressed Firms," *Academy of Management Journal* 4 (1994): 972–989.

27. C. K. Prahalad and R. A. Bettis, "The Dominant Logic: A New Linkage Between Diversity and Performance," *Strategic Management Journal* 7 (1986): 485–501. Porter, *Competitive Strategy.*

28. T. Dewett and G. R. Jones, "The Role of Information Technology in the Organization: A Review, Model, and Assessment," *Journal of Management* 27 (2001): 313–346.

29. Porter, 1996; Prahalad and Hamel, 1990.

30. Rucker, 2000.

31. Prahalad and Hamel.

32. Ibid.

33. "Andersen's Androids," *Economist,* May 4, 1996, p. 72.

34. Fulk and DeSanctis, 1995.

35. G. S. Capowski, "Designing a Corporate Identity," *Management Review* (June 1993): 37–38.

36. J. Marcia, "Just Doing It," *Distribution* (January 1995): 36–40.

Introduction: Analyzing a Case Study and Writing a Case Study Analysis

What Is Case Study Analysis?

Case study analysis is an integral part of a course in strategic management. The purpose of a case study is to provide students with experience of the strategic management problems that actual organizations face. A case study presents an account of what happened to a business or industry over a number of years. It chronicles the events that managers had to deal with, such as changes in the competitive environment, and charts the managers' response, which usually involved changing the business- or corporate-level strategy. The cases in this book cover a wide range of issues and problems that managers have had to confront. Some cases are about finding the right business-level strategy to compete in changing conditions. Some are about companies that grew by acquisition, with little concern for the rationale behind their growth, and how growth by acquisition affected their future profitability. Each case is different because each organization is different. The underlying thread in all cases, however, is the use of strategic management techniques to solve business problems.

Cases prove valuable in a strategic management course for several reasons. First, cases provide you, the student, with experience of organizational problems that you probably have not had the opportunity to experience firsthand. In a relatively short period of time, you will have the chance to appreciate and analyze the problems faced by many different companies and to understand how managers tried to deal with them.

Second, cases illustrate the theory and content of strategic management. The meaning and implications of this information are made clearer when they are applied to case studies. The theory and concepts help reveal what is going on in the companies studied and allow you to evaluate the solutions that specific companies adopted to deal with their problems. Consequently, when you analyze cases, you will be like a detective who, with a set of conceptual tools, probes what happened and what or who was responsible and then marshals the evidence that provides the solution. Top managers enjoy the thrill of testing their problem-solving abilities in the real world. It is important to re-member that no one knows what the right answer is. All that managers can do is to make the best guess. In fact, managers say repeatedly that they are happy if they are right only half the time in solving strategic problems. Strategic management is an uncertain game, and using cases to see how theory can be put into practice is one way of improving your skills of diagnostic investigation.

C1

Third, case studies provide you with the opportunity to participate in class and to gain experience in presenting your ideas to others. Instructors may sometimes call on students as a group to identify what is going on in a case, and through classroom discussion the issues in and solutions to the case problem will reveal themselves. In such a situation, you will have to organize your views and conclusions so that you can present them to the class. Your classmates may have analyzed the issues differently from you, and they will want you to argue your points before they will accept your conclusions, so be prepared for debate. This mode of discussion is an example of the dialectical approach to decision making. This is how decisions are made in the actual business world.

Instructors also may assign an individual, but more commonly a group, to analyze the case before the whole class. The individual or group probably will be responsible for a thirty- to forty-minute presentation of the case to the class. That presentation must cover the issues posed, the problems facing the company, and a series of recommendations for resolving the problems. The discussion then will be thrown open to the class, and you will have to defend your ideas. Through such discussions and presentations, you will experience how to convey your ideas effectively to others. Remember that a great deal of managers' time is spent in these kinds of situations: presenting their ideas and engaging in discussion with other managers who have their own views about what is going on. Thus, you will experience in the classroom the actual process of strategic management, and this will serve you well in your future career.

If you work in groups to analyze case studies, you also will learn about the group process involved in working as a team. When people work in groups, it is often difficult to schedule time and allocate responsibility for the case analysis. There are always group members who shirk their responsibilities and group members who are so sure of their own ideas that they try to dominate the group's analysis. Most of the strategic management takes place in groups, however, and it is best if you learn about these problems now.

Analyzing a Case Study

The purpose of the case study is to let you apply the concepts of strategic management when you analyze the issues facing a specific company. To analyze a case study, therefore, you must examine closely the issues confronting the company. Most often you will need to read the case several times—once to grasp the overall picture of what is happening to the company and then several times more to discover and grasp the specific problems.

Generally, detailed analysis of a case study should include eight areas:

1. The history, development, and growth of the company over time
2. The identification of the company's internal strengths and weaknesses
3. The nature of the external environment surrounding the company
4. A SWOT analysis
5. The kind of corporate-level strategy that the company is pursuing
6. The nature of the company's business-level strategy
7. The company's structure and control systems and how they match its strategy
8. Recommendations

To analyze a case, you need to apply the concepts taught in this course to each of these areas. To help you further, we next offer a summary of the steps you can take to analyze the case material for each of the eight points we just noted:

1. *Analyze the company's history, development, and growth.* A convenient way to investigate how a company's past strategy and structure affect it in the present is to chart the critical incidents in its history—that is, the events that were the most unusual or the most essential for its development into the company it is today. Some of the events have to do with its founding, its initial products, how it makes new-product market decisions, and how it developed and chose functional competencies to pursue. Its entry into new businesses and shifts in its main lines of business are also important milestones to consider.

2. *Identify the company's internal strengths and weaknesses.* Once the historical profile is completed, you can begin the SWOT analysis. Use all the incidents you have charted to develop an account of the company's strengths and weaknesses as they have emerged historically. Examine each of the value creation functions of the company, and identify the functions in which the company is currently strong and currently weak. Some companies might be weak in marketing; some might be strong in research and development. Make lists of these strengths and weaknesses. The SWOT Checklist (Table 1) gives examples of what might go in these lists.

3. *Analyze the external environment.* To identify environmental opportunities and threats, apply all the concepts on industry and macroenvironments to analyze the environment the company is confronting. Of particular importance at the industry level are Porter's five forces model and the stage of the life cycle model. Which factors in the macroenvironment will appear salient depends on the specific company being analyzed. Use each factor in turn (for instance, demographic factors) to see whether it is relevant for the company in question.

   Having done this analysis, you will have generated both an analysis of the company's environment and a list of opportunities and threats. The SWOT Checklist table also lists some common environmental opportunities and threats that you may look for, but the list you generate will be specific to your company.

4. *Evaluate the SWOT analysis.* Having identified the company's external opportunities and threats as well as its internal strengths and weaknesses, consider what your findings mean. You need to balance strengths and weaknesses against opportunities and threats. Is the company in an overall strong competitive position? Can it continue to pursue its current business- or corporate-level strategy profitably? What can the company do to turn weaknesses into strengths and threats into opportunities? Can it develop new functional, business, or corporate strategies to accomplish this change? *Never merely generate the SWOT analysis and then put it aside.* Because it provides a succinct summary of the company's condition, a good SWOT analysis is the key to all the analyses that follow.

5. *Analyze corporate-level strategy.* To analyze corporate-level strategy, you first need to define the company's mission and goals. Sometimes the mission and goals are stated explicitly in the case; at other times, you will have to infer them from available information. The information you need to collect to find out the company's corporate strategy includes such factors as its lines of business and the nature of

TABLE 1

A SWOT Checklist

Potential internal strengths	Potential internal weaknesses
Many product lines?	Obsolete, narrow product lines?
Broad market coverage?	Rising manufacturing costs?
Manufacturing competence?	Decline in R&D innovations?
Good marketing skills?	Poor marketing plan?
Good materials management systems?	Poor material management systems?
R&D skills and leadership?	Loss of customer good will?
Information system competencies?	Inadequate human resources?
Human resource competencies?	Inadequate information systems?
Brand name reputation?	Loss of brand name capital?
Portfolio management skills?	Growth without direction?
Cost of differentiation advantage?	Bad portfolio management?
New-venture management expertise?	Loss of corporate direction?
Appropriate management style?	Infighting among divisions?
Appropriate organizational structure?	Loss of corporate control?
Appropriate control systems?	Inappropriate organizational
Ability to manage strategic change?	structure and control systems?
Well-developed corporate strategy?	High conflict and politics?
Good financial management?	Poor financial management?
Others?	Others?
Potential environmental opportunities	Potential environmental threats
Expand core business(es)?	Attacks on core business(es)?
Exploit new market segments?	Increases in domestic competition?
Widen product range?	Increase in foreign competition?
Extend cost or differentiation advantage?	Change in consumer tastes?
Diversify into new growth businesses?	Fall in barriers to entry?
Expand into foreign markets?	Rise in new or substitute products?
Apply R&D skills in new areas?	Increase in industry rivalry?
Enter new related businesses?	New forms of industry competition?
Vertically integrate forward?	Potential for takeover?
Vertically integrate backward?	Existence of corporate raiders?
Enlarge corporate portfolio?	Increase in regional competition?
Overcome barriers to entry?	Changes in demographic factors?
Reduce rivalry among competitors?	Changes in economic factors?
Make profitable new acquisitions?	Downturn in economy?
Apply brand name capital in new areas?	Rising labor costs?
Seek fast market growth?	Slower market growth?
Others?	Others?

its subsidiaries and acquisitions. It is important to analyze the relationship among the company's businesses. Do they trade or exchange resources? Are there gains to be achieved from synergy? Alternatively, is the company just running a portfolio of investments? This analysis should enable you to define the corporate strategy that the company is pursuing (for example, related or unrelated diversification, or a combination of both) and to conclude whether the company operates in just one core business. Then, using your SWOT analysis, debate the merits of this strategy. Is it appropriate given the environment the company is in? Could a change in corporate strategy provide the company with new opportunities or transform a weakness into a strength? For example, should the company diversify from its core business into new businesses?

Other issues should be considered as well. How and why has the company's strategy changed over time? What is the claimed rationale for any changes? Often, it is a good idea to analyze the company's businesses or products to assess its situation and identify which divisions contribute the most to or detract from its competitive advantage. It is also useful to explore how the company has built its portfolio over time. Did it acquire new businesses, or did it internally venture its own? All of these factors provide clues about the company and indicate ways of improving its future performance.

6. *Analyze business-level strategy.* Once you know the company's corporate-level strategy and have done the SWOT analysis, the next step is to identify the company's business-level strategy. If the company is a single-business company, its business-level strategy is identical to its corporate-level strategy. If the company is in many businesses, each business will have its own business-level strategy. You will need to identify the company's generic competitive strategy—differentiation, low cost, or focus—and its investment strategy, given its relative competitive position and the stage of the life cycle. The company also may market different products using different business-level strategies. For example, it may offer a low-cost product range and a line of differentiated products. Be sure to give a full account of a company's business-level strategy to show how it competes.

Identifying the functional strategies that a company pursues to build competitive advantage through superior efficiency, quality, innovation, and customer responsiveness and to achieve its business-level strategy is very important. The SWOT analysis will have provided you with information on the company's functional competencies. You should investigate its production, marketing, or research and development strategy further to gain a picture of where the company is going. For example, pursuing a low-cost or a differentiation strategy successfully requires very different sets of competencies. Has the company developed the right ones? If it has, how can it exploit them further? Can it pursue both a low-cost and a differentiation strategy simultaneously?

The SWOT analysis is especially important at this point if the industry analysis, particularly Porter's model, has revealed threats to the company from the environment. Can the company deal with these threats? How should it change its business-level strategy to counter them? To evaluate the potential of a company's business-level strategy, you must first perform a thorough SWOT analysis that captures the essence of its problems.

Once you complete this analysis, you will have a full picture of the way the company is operating and be in a position to evaluate the potential of its strategy. Thus, you will be able to make recommendations concerning the pattern of its future actions. However, first you need to consider strategy implementation, or the way the company tries to achieve its strategy.

7. *Analyze structure and control systems.* The aim of this analysis is to identify what structure and control systems the company is using to implement its strategy and to evaluate whether that structure is the appropriate one for the company. Different corporate and business strategies require different structures. You

need to determine the *degree of fit between the company's strategy and structure.* For example, does the company have the right level of vertical differentiation (e.g., does it have the appropriate number of levels in the hierarchy or decentralized control?) or horizontal differentiation (does it use a functional structure when it should be using a product structure?)? Similarly, is the company using the right integration or control systems to manage its operations? Are managers being appropriately rewarded? Are the right rewards in place for encouraging cooperation among divisions? These are all issues to consider.

In some cases, there will be little information on these issues, whereas in others there will be a lot. In analyzing each case, you should gear the analysis toward its most salient issues. For example, organizational conflict, power, and politics will be important issues for some companies. Try to analyze why problems in these areas are occurring. Do they occur because of bad strategy formulation or because of bad strategy implementation?

Organizational change is an issue in many cases because the companies are attempting to alter their strategies or structures to solve strategic problems. Thus, as part of the analysis, you might suggest an action plan that the company in question could use to achieve its goals. For example, you might list in a logical sequence the steps the company would need to follow to alter its business-level strategy from differentiation to focus.

8. *Make recommendations.* The quality of your recommendations is a direct result of the thoroughness with which you prepared the case analysis. Recommendations are directed at solving whatever strategic problem the company is facing and increasing its future profitability. Your recommendations should be in line with your analysis; that is, they should follow logically from the previous discussion. For example, your recommendation generally will center on the specific ways of changing functional, business, and corporate strategies and organizational structure and control to improve business performance. The set of recommendations will be specific to each case, and so it is difficult to discuss these recommendations here. Such recommendations might include an increase in spending on specific research and development projects, the divesting of certain businesses, a change from a strategy of unrelated to related diversification, an increase in the level of integration among divisions by using task forces and teams, or a move to a different kind of structure to implement a new business-level strategy. Make sure your recommendations are mutually consistent and written in the form of an action plan. The plan might contain a timetable that sequences the actions for changing the company's strategy and a description of how changes at the corporate level will necessitate changes at the business level and subsequently at the functional level.

After following all these stages, you will have performed a thorough analysis of the case and will be in a position to join in class discussion or present your ideas to the class, depending on the format used by your professor. Remember that you must tailor your analysis to suit the specific issue discussed in your case. In some cases, you might completely omit one of the steps in the analysis because it is not relevant to the situation you are considering. You must be sensitive to the needs of the case and not apply the framework we have discussed in this section blindly. The framework is meant only as a guide, not as an outline.

Writing a Case Study Analysis

Often, as part of your course requirements, you will need to present a written case analysis. This may be an individual or a group report. Whatever the situation, there are certain guidelines to follow in writing a case analysis that will improve the evaluation your work will receive from your instructor. Before we discuss these guidelines and before you use them, make sure that they do not conflict with any directions your instructor has given you.

The structure of your written report is critical. Generally, if you follow the steps for analysis discussed in the previous section, *you already will have a good structure for your written discussion.* All reports begin with an *introduction* to the case. In it, outline briefly what the company does, how it developed historically, what problems it is experiencing, and how you are going to approach the issues in the case write-up. Do this sequentially by writing, for example, "First, we discuss the environment of Company X. . . . Third, we discuss Company X's business-level strategy. . . . Last, we provide recommendations for turning around Company X's business."

In the second part of the case write-up, the *strategic analysis* section, do the SWOT analysis, analyze and discuss the nature and problems of the company's business-level and corporate strategies, and then analyze its structure and control systems. Make sure you use plenty of headings and subheadings to structure your analysis. For example, have separate sections on any important conceptual tool you use. Thus, you might have a section on Porter's five forces model as part of your analysis of the environment. You might offer a separate section on portfolio techniques when analyzing a company's corporate strategy. Tailor the sections and subsections to the specific issues of importance in the case.

In the third part of the case write-up, present your *solutions and recommendations.* Be comprehensive, and make sure they are in line with the previous analysis so that the recommendations fit together and move logically from one to the next. The recommedations section is very revealing because your instructor will have a good idea of how much work you put into the case from the quality of your recommendations.

Following this framework will provide a good structure for most written reports, though it must be shaped to fit the individual case being considered. Some cases are about excellent companies experiencing no problems. In such instances, it is hard to write recommendations. Instead, you can focus on analyzing why the company is doing so well, using that analysis to structure the discussion. Following are some minor suggestions that can help make a good analysis even better:

1. Do not repeat in summary form large pieces of factual information from the case. The instructor has read the case and knows what is going on. Rather, use the information in the case to illustrate your statements, defend your arguments, or make salient points. Beyond the brief introduction to the company, you must avoid being *descriptive;* instead, you must be *analytical.*

2. Make sure the sections and subsections of your discussion flow logically and smoothly from one to the next. That is, try to build on what has gone before so that the analysis of the case study moves toward a climax. This is particularly important for group analysis, because there is a tendency for people in a group to split up the work and say, "I'll do the beginning, you take the middle, and I'll do the end." The result is a choppy, stilted analysis; the parts do not flow from one to the next, and it is obvious to the instructor that no real group work has been done.

3. Avoid grammatical and spelling errors. They make your work look sloppy.

4. In some instances, cases dealing with well-known companies end in 1998 or 1999 because no later information was available when the case was written. If possible, do a search for more information on what has happened to the company in subsequent years.

   Many libraries now have comprehensive web-based electronic data search facilities that offer such sources as *ABI/Inform*, *The Wall Street Journal Index*, the *F&S Index*, and the *Nexis-Lexis* databases. These enable you to identify any article that has been written in the business press on the company of your choice within the past few years. A number of nonelectronic data sources are also useful. For example, *F&S Predicasts* publishes an annual list of articles relating to major companies that appeared in the national and international business press. *S&P Industry Surveys* is a great source for basic industry data, and *Value Line Ratings and Reports* can contain good summaries of a firm's financial position and future prospects. You will also want to collect full financial information on the company. Again, this can be accessed from web-based electronic databases such as the Edgar database, which archives all forms that publicly quoted companies have to file with the Securities and Exchange Commission (SEC; e.g., 10-K filings can be accessed from the SEC's Edgar database). Most SEC forms for public companies can now be accessed from Internet-based financial sites, such as Yahoo's finance site (**http://finance.yahoo.com/**).

5. Sometimes instructors hand out questions for each case to help you in your analysis. Use these as a guide for writing the case analysis. They often illuminate the important issues that have to be covered in the discussion.

   If you follow the guidelines in this section, you should be able to write a thorough and effective evaluation.

The Role of Financial Analysis in Case Study Analysis

An important aspect of analyzing a case study and writing a case study analysis is the role and use of financial information. A careful analysis of the company's financial condition immensely improves a case write-up. After all, financial data represent the concrete results of the company's strategy and structure. Although analyzing financial statements can be quite complex, a general idea of a company's financial position can be determined through the use of ratio analysis. Financial performance ratios can be calculated from the balance sheet and income statement. These ratios can be classified into five subgroups: profit ratios, liquidity ratios, activity ratios, leverage ratios, and shareholder-return ratios. These ratios should be compared with the industry average or the company's prior years of performance. It should be noted, however, that deviation from the average is not necessarily bad; it simply warrants further investigation. For example, young companies will have purchased assets at a different price and will likely have a different capital structure than older companies do. In addition to ratio analysis, a company's cash flow position is of critical importance and should be assessed. Cash flow shows how much actual cash a company possesses.

Profit Ratios

Profit ratios measure the efficiency with which the company uses its resources. The more efficient the company, the greater is its profitability. It is useful to compare a company's profitability against that of its major competitors in its industry to determine whether the company is operating more or less efficiently than its rivals. In addition, the change in a company's profit ratios over time tells whether its performance is improving or declining.

A number of different profit ratios can be used, and each of them measures a different aspect of a company's performance. Here, we look at the most commonly used profit ratios.

Return on Invested Capital.   This ratio measures the profit earned on the capital invested in the company. It is defined as follows:

$$\text{Return on invested capital (ROIC)} = \frac{\text{Net profit}}{\text{Invested capital}}$$

Net profit is calculated by subtracting the total costs of operating the company away from its total revenues (total revenues − total costs). Total costs are the (1) costs of goods sold, (2) sales, general, and administrative expenses, (3) R&D expenses, and (4) other expenses. Net profit can be calculated before or after taxes, although many financial analysts prefer the before-tax figure. Invested capital is the amount that is invested in the operations of a company, that is, in property, plant, equipment, inventories, and other assets. Invested capital comes from two main sources: interest-bearing debt and shareholders' equity. Interest-bearing debt is money the company borrows from banks and from those who purchase its bonds. Shareholders' equity is the money raised from selling shares to the public, *plus* earnings that have been retained by the company in prior years and are available to fund current investments. ROIC measures the effectiveness with which a company is using the capital funds that it has available for investment. As such, it is recognized to be an excellent measure of the value a company is creating.[1] Remember that a company's ROIC can be decomposed into its constituent parts.

Return on Total Assets (ROA). This ratio measures the profit earned on the employment of assets. It is defined as follows:

$$\text{Return on total assests} = \frac{\text{Net profit}}{\text{Total assets}}$$

Return on Stockholders' Equity (ROE).   This ratio measures the percentage of profit earned on common stockholders' investment in the company. It is defined as follows:

$$\text{Return on stockholders' equity} = \frac{\text{Net profit}}{\text{Stockholders' equity}}$$

If a company has no debt, this will be the same as ROIC.

Liquidity Ratios   A company's liquidity is a measure of its ability to meet short-term obligations. An asset is deemed liquid if it can be readily converted into cash. Liquid assets are current assets such as cash, marketable securities, accounts receivable, and so on. Two liquidity ratios are commonly used.

---

[1] Tom Copeland, Tim Koller, and Jack Murrin, *Valuation: Measuring and Managing the Value of Companies* (New York: Wiley, 1996).

Current Ratio. The current ratio measures the extent to which the claims of short-term creditors are covered by assets that can be quickly converted into cash. Most companies should have a ratio of at least 1, because failure to meet these commitments can lead to bankruptcy. The ratio is defined as follows:

$$\text{Current ratio} = \frac{\text{Current assets}}{\text{Current liabilities}}$$

Quick Ratio. The quick ratio measures a company's ability to pay off the claims of short-term creditors without relying on selling its inventories. This is a valuable measure since in practice the sale of inventories is often difficult. It is defined as follows:

$$\text{Quick ratio} = \frac{\text{Current assets 2 inventory}}{\text{Current liabilities}}$$

Activity Ratios

Activity ratios indicate how effectively a company is managing its assets. Two ratios are particularly useful.

Inventory Turnover. This measures the number of times inventory is turned over. It is useful in determining whether a firm is carrying excess stock in inventory. It is defined as follows:

$$\text{Inventory turnover} = \frac{\text{Cost of goods sold}}{\text{Inventory}}$$

Cost of goods sold is a better measure of turnover than sales because it is the cost of the inventory items. Inventory is taken at the balance sheet date. Some companies choose to compute an average inventory, beginning inventory, and ending inventory, but for simplicity, use the inventory at the balance sheet date.

Days Sales Outstanding (DSO) or Average Collection Period. This ratio is the average time a company has to wait to receive its cash after making a sale. It measures how effective the company's credit, billing, and collection procedures are. It is defined as follows:

$$\text{DSO} = \frac{\text{Accounts receivable}}{\text{Total sales/360}}$$

Accounts receivable is divided by average daily sales. The use of 360 is the standard number of days for most financial analysis.

Leverage Ratios

A company is said to be highly leveraged if it uses more debt than equity, including stock and retained earnings. The balance between debt and equity is called the *capital structure*. The optimal capital structure is determined by the individual company. Debt has a lower cost because creditors take less risk; they know they will get their interest and principal. However, debt can be risky to the firm because if enough profit is not made to cover the interest and principal payments, bankruptcy can result. Three leverage ratios are commonly used.

Debt-to-Assets Ratio. The debt-to-assets ratio is the most direct measure of the extent to which borrowed funds have been used to finance a company's investments. It is defined as follows:

$$\text{Debt-to-assets ratio} = \frac{\text{Total debt}}{\text{Total assets}}$$

Total debt is the sum of a company's current liabilities and its long-term debt, and total assets are the sum of fixed assets and current assets.

Debt-to-Equity Ratio. The debt-to-equity ratio indicates the balance between debt and equity in a company's capital structure. This is perhaps the most widely used measure of a company's leverage. It is defined as follows:

$$\text{Debt-to-equity ratio} = \frac{\text{Total debt}}{\text{Total equity}}$$

Times-Covered Ratio. The times-covered ratio measures the extent to which a company's gross profit covers its annual interest payments. If this ratio declines to less than 1, the company is unable to meet its interest costs and is technically insolvent. The ratio is defined as follows:

$$\text{Times-covered ratio} = \frac{\text{Profit before interest and tax}}{\text{Total interest charges}}$$

Shareholder-Return Ratios

Shareholder-return ratios measure the return that shareholders earn from holding stock in the company. Given the goal of maximizing stockholders' wealth, providing shareholders with an adequate rate of return is a primary objective of most companies. As with profit ratios, it can be helpful to compare a company's shareholder returns against those of similar companies as a yardstick for determining how well the company is satisfying the demands of this particularly important group of organizational constituents. Four ratios are commonly used.

Total Shareholder Returns. Total shareholder returns measure the returns earned by time $t + 1$ on an investment in a company's stock made at time t. (Time t is the time at which the initial investment is made.) Total shareholder returns include both dividend payments and appreciation in the value of the stock (adjusted for stock splits) and are defined as follows:

$$\text{Total shareholder returns} = \frac{\substack{\text{Stock price } (t + 1) - \text{stock price } (t) \\ + \text{ sum of annual dividends per share}}}{\text{Stock price } (t)}$$

If a shareholder invests $2 at time t and at time $t + 1$ the share is worth $3, while the sum of annual dividends for the period t to $t + 1$ has amounted to $0.20, total shareholder returns are equal to $(3 - 2 + 0.2)/2 = 0.6$, which is a 60 percent return on an initial investment of $2 made at time t.

Price-Earnings Ratio. The price-earnings ratio measures the amount investors are willing to pay per dollar of profit. It is defined as follows:

$$\text{Price-earnings ratio} = \frac{\text{Market price per share}}{\text{Earnings per share}}$$

Market-to-Book Value. Market-to-book value measures a company's expected future growth prospects. It is defined as follows:

$$\text{Market-to-book value} = \frac{\text{Market price per share}}{\text{Earnings per share}}$$

Dividend Yield. The dividend yield measures the return to shareholders received in the form of dividends. It is defined as follows:

$$\text{Dividend yield} = \frac{\text{Dividend per share}}{\text{Market price per share}}$$

Market price per share can be calculated for the first of the year, in which case the dividend yield refers to the return on an investment made at the beginning of the year. Alternatively, the average share price over the year may be used. A company must decide how much of its profits to pay to stockholders and how much to reinvest in the company. Companies with strong growth prospects should have a lower dividend payout ratio than mature companies. The rationale is that shareholders can invest the money elsewhere if the company is not growing. The optimal ratio depends on the individual firm, but the key decider is whether the company can produce better returns than the investor can earn elsewhere.

Cash Flow

Cash flow position is cash received minus cash distributed. The net cash flow can be taken from a company's statement of cash flows. Cash flow is important for what it reveals about a company's financing needs. A strong positive cash flow enables a company to fund future investments without having to borrow money from bankers or investors. This is desirable because the company avoids paying out interest or dividends. A weak or negative cash flow means that a company has to turn to external sources to fund future investments. Generally, companies in strong-growth industries often find themselves in a poor cash flow position (because their investment needs are substantial), whereas successful companies based in mature industries generally find themselves in a strong cash flow position.

A company's internally generated cash flow is calculated by adding back its depreciation provision to profits after interest, taxes, and dividend payments. If this figure is insufficient to cover proposed new investments, the company has little choice but to borrow funds to make up the shortfall or to curtail investments. If this figure exceeds proposed new investments, the company can use the excess to build up its liquidity (that is, through investments in financial assets) or repay existing loans ahead of schedule.

Conclusion

When evaluating a case, it is important to be *systematic.* Analyze the case in a logical fashion, beginning with the identification of operating and financial strengths and weaknesses and environmental opportunities and threats. Move on to assess the value of a company's current strategies only when you are fully conversant with the SWOT analysis of the company. Ask yourself whether the company's current strategies make sense given its SWOT analysis. If they do not, what changes need to be made? What are your recommendations? Above all, link any strategic recommendations you may make to the SWOT analysis. State explicitly how the strategies you identify take advantage of the company's strengths to exploit environmental opportunities, how they rectify the company's weaknesses, and how they counter environmental threats. Also, do not forget to outline what needs to be done to implement your recommendations.

1

Vail Resorts, Inc.

This case was prepared by Herman L. Boschken, San Jose State University.

In 1962, Pete Seibert and Earl Eaton, along with several associates, opened the Vail Ski Resort, which is located in a long narrow valley known for its remoteness and spectacular alpine splendor. Previously home only to mountain ranchers and sheep herders, this area beckoned the ambitious developers because of its ideal ski terrain and a proposed interstate freeway, which was to traverse the valley floor on its way westward from Denver. The partnership would be called Vail Associates and over the remainder of the twentieth century, it would become a premier developer of world-class ski resorts. By the late 1990s, the firm had changed its name to Vail Resorts (VR) and had built or acquired three more Colorado ski resorts, all located within forty-five minutes of each other. In 2000, it expanded into summer venues with the acquisition of the Grand Teton Lodge Co. near Yellowstone, and in 2002, added Heavenly, its first ski resort outside Colorado, to its holdings.

By its fortieth anniversary season, the firm held the most-esteemed reputation in a mountain resort industry that included other prestigious names such as the Aspen Ski Co., Intrawest, and American Ski Co. But in many ways, VR had reached a crossroads by the turn of the century. The industry had been changing

for several years: an aging population was shrinking demand for skiing; snowboarding had encroached on the traditional alpine downhill skiing; competitors were making vast new investments in on-mountain and village facilities; several well-financed consolidations and mergers had reduced the field of resort providers to "the big four"; and newer resorts, like Whistler-Blackcomb (in Canada), were taking an increasing share of the maturing market.

Several things had happened internally as well. Over the course of thirty years, the firm Seibert and Eaton had founded was sold first to Texas oil entrepreneur Harry Bass in 1976 and then to Denver businessman George Gillett in 1985. Gillett, who had previously owned the Harlem Globetrotters, invested heavily in new ski facilities at Vail. His development plan led the resort to a commanding lead in customer popularity and growing profitability. By the early 1990s, however, bad management at Gillett's other enterprises led to his personal bankruptcy, which stranded Vail in a vicious struggle among his creditors. The spoils went to a New York investment firm led by junk-bond specialist Leon Black, who gained control of Vail in 1992. Black retained Gillett as the resort's chairman until the firm's IPO in 1997 installed a new chair and CEO: Adam Aron.

Aron came from the travel and leisure industry, where he had been president of Norwegian Cruise Lines and vice president of marketing for United Airlines. His reputation included recognition as one of the "100 best marketers in the U.S." Black also retained Andy Daly, Gillett's senior operations man, as the firm's president. Combined, the new leadership provided both "fresh eyes from the outside" and a topnotch seasoned industry professional to lead the firm into the new century. The two men wasted no time in setting an agenda. In the summer of 1996, the firm acquired the ski resort division of Ralcorp, which included Vail's primary competition—Breckenridge and Keystone, both located in adjacent Summit County. With a name change to Vail Resorts, the firm went public in early 1997 (NYSE ticker symbol: MTN) and opened its first corporate web site: www.snow.com.

Even with this rapid-fire agenda, it was clear nevertheless that it was time to ponder VR's strategy for the new century. How should the parts of this much larger firm fit together? How might the firm broaden its offerings to an all-season resort theme without losing the sense of an integrated product family? What alternatives lay ahead to maintain momentum, enhance profitability, and retain its world-class status in providing destination resort facilities?

Vail Resorts's Facilities

By the year 2000, the firm owned and operated four major destination winter resorts in Colorado, all located along the Rocky Mountain I-70 corridor in Eagle and Summit counties, and the Grand Teton summer resort in Jackson Hole, Wyoming. All the ski properties included long-term leases from the U.S. Forest Service for the mountain terrain, centrally located retail and commercial structures in the ski-in/ski-out villages, a few quaint hotels and hotel/convention centers, some golf courses, and other strategic facilities. Each resort is distinctive in theme and atmosphere, but all ascribe to Vail Resorts's reputation for quality service, all-season excellence, and trademark in providing a unique upscale experience to discerning customers.

As the firm's marquis resort, Vail is the largest single-mountain ski resort in North America. Built from the ground up, its village has the appearance and ambience of a traditional European alpine setting. Paralleling the interstate, the resort provides all the conveniences of a large rural town. It has two pedestrian-only village centers, which are connected to each other and the town's outer areas (some of which are four miles up or down the freeway) by a complimentary bus system. Vail has accommodations for over 30,000 people and contains over 100 restaurants and bars, 225 shops and markets, a skating arena, outdoor amphitheater, a PGA golf course, regional hospital, transportation center, schools, and a library. It is the primary or second home to professionals and executives from numerous blue-chip companies, "new economy" firms, and Wall Street investment houses. As a group, this clientele prefers anonymity outside their professional careers, and it has chosen Vail because of the resort's relaxed but discrete atmosphere.

With 12,500 acres under Forest Service permit, the resort has developed over 5,000 acres within its boundary of skiable terrain. Skiing is provided on both sides of a seven-mile ridge paralleling the village and interstate, and in an adjacent back-bowl called Blue Ski Basin. Within its skiable boundary, the mountain sports 174 trails serviced by thirty-two lifts with a capacity to handle 51,781 skiers per hour. Vertical drop (a measure of terrain steepness and ski-run length) is 3,330 feet, and the longest run is 4.5 miles. Snow is generally reliable January through April and averages 335 inches annually. Its vast size and varied terrain offer the most diversity of any resort in North America. In a week's stay, few are able to explore all its possibilities.

Ten miles to the west of Vail and located three miles off the interstate is the firm's smallest but most upscale resort, Beaver Creek. The resort actually contains three separate villages at different locations along the skirts of the mountain. Originally conceived as Colorado's location for the 1976 Olympics (which was aborted by a state referendum), the first of these is the core village of Beaver Creek. Opened in 1980, it was planned and designed by a state-of-the-art CAD system to fit a European elegance and environmental sophistication into the constrained setting of a tiny valley and stream. Emphasizing exclusivity, first-class accommodations, and "family friendliness," the alpine village sports twenty-five restaurants, over seventy shops, an outdoor ice-skating arena, the Hyatt Regency and Conference Center, the Vilar Performing Arts Center, and overnight capacity for 5,000 people. The second oldest village is Arrowhead, which VR purchased in the mid 1990s. Although it contains a couple of restaurants and some shopping, it is primarily residential, with condominiums for an additional 1,000 people. The third and newest village is Bachelor Gulch, located partway up the ski mountain between the other two villages.

It is an enclave of million-dollar homes and condominiums along ski runs and has gated-access to limit the nonskiing public. Like Arrowhead, it has limited public facilities, but the village is anchored with a prestigious Ritz-Carlton Hotel.

With over 1,600 acres of skiable terrain (most of which is under lease from the Forest Service), Beaver Creek Resort offers exceptional variety for families whose members exhibit different levels of skiing ability. Beginners can learn on gently sloping terrain at the very top of the mountain adjacent to intermediate and advanced runs (an unusual opportunity), while experts are challenged by some of the most difficult terrain in the industry. Its Birds of Prey downhill course is recognized by World-Cup skiers as the most challenging in North America. Within its official boundaries, the mountain contains 146 trails fed by thirteen lifts having a combined capacity of 24,739 skiers per hour. Vertical drop is 4,040 feet. Snowfall and winter conditions are similar to those at Vail, but the western part of the mountain (containing the Arrowhead and Bachelor Gulch villages) usually closes a few weeks earlier than the rest of the mountain.

VR's two other Colorado winter facilities are located off I-70 about an hour east of Vail and Beaver Creek along the Continental Divide. Opening as a ski resort in 1961, the largest of these is Breckenridge, which consists of a vast range of treeless peaks and an historical western mining town. Although being somewhat remolded to fit VR's family clientele, this resort community's reputation has emphasized the youthful exuberance of singles and couples seeking an active social life. As a consequence, it has more bars but fewer restaurants (totaling over fifty) than Vail and over 100 shops. In addition, the town has a performing-arts theater, museums, a golf course, and a large convention center. It has overnight accommodations for 25,000 people. The clientele of this historically preserved, year-round resort often cite the unique "sense of place and fabled Main Street experience" as a prime reason for coming.

The resort's linear sequence of mountain peaks contains 2,043 acres of skiable terrain, nearly all of which are leased from the Forest Service. As a craggy high-alpine backdrop to the town, the mountain offers 139 ski trails fed by twenty-five lifts, several of which provide direct access from different points in the town. Free buses also circulate from town to higher points on the mountain at peaks 7 and 8. Catering to all levels of skier proficiency, the moun-

tain has lift capacity for 30,656 skiers per hour, and a vertical drop of 3,398 feet. Being on the Continental Divide (the location of many of Colorado's highest elevations), Breckenridge gets slightly less snowfall (about 300 inches annually) than the Vail Valley resorts, but it comes earlier and is more reliable.

Vail Resort's forth winter resort is Keystone. Like Beaver Creek in origin and family focus, its off-mountain facilities were crafted along meadowland as a freestanding, planned unit development. Opened in 1970, the resort has steadily expanded over the years but has acquired a reputation for putting guests close to nature. Its trademark, "Nature of the Rockies," indicates more rustic facilities and accommodations than VR's other three winter resorts. It contains two main villages—the original Keystone Village and the new River Run (a joint partnership with Intrawest)—surrounded by residential areas containing homes and condominiums. The resort provides accommodations for about 5,000 people and contains about fifty shops and restaurants, a convention center for 1,800 people, and a PGA golf course. Additional housing and amenities are located about two miles away in the town of Dillon, the primary service area for Summit County.

Producing 1,861 acres of skiable terrain, Keystone has developed three successive on-mountain areas along a ridge emanating from the two adjacent village areas. With a focus on beginner and intermediate skiers, over 50 percent of the 116 trails are on more difficult slopes by Colorado standards. The three areas are serviced by twenty-two lifts having a combined capacity of 27,873 skiers per hour. Vertical drop is 2,900 feet. Although it receives less snowfall (about 230 inches) than the other three resorts, Keystone opens among the earliest and is one of the last to close during the season.

The four winter resorts are accessible by air and ground. Vail and Beaver Creek are located at the eastern edge of Eagle County, about 100 miles west of Denver. Breckenridge and Keystone are about sixty miles west of Denver. All are along or very near Interstate 70, which passes through the Denver metropolitan area on its way westward. Air transportation is available year-round through Denver International Airport (DIA) and seasonally through the Vail/Eagle County Airport. Ground transportation from both airports is provided by car-rental agencies, Greyhound Bus, and the Rocky Mountain Express van service. The ride from Denver traverses spectacular scenery but takes about two and one-half hours to Vail and Beaver Creek (the most distant). The ride from Eagle Airport is about forty-five minutes to the Vail Valley, but up to one and a half hours to the Summit County resorts.

The Recreation Resort Industry

With its emphasis on skiing and mountain sports, Vail Resorts operates in the "destination" segment of the recreation resort industry. As part of the sprawling vacation and leisure industry, this subindustry is itself a conglomerate of parts having no exact boundaries. According to the U.S. Department of Commerce, recreation resorts also overlap other related industries composed of segments such as amusement parks (e.g., Disney), gaming (e.g., Harrahs Entertainment), cruises (e.g., Princess Cruise Lines), and sporting events (e.g., the NFL). In this ill-defined industry category, competition therefore includes a vast assemblage of direct offerings and marginally substitutable products and services. With loosely segmented markets, strategic opportunities tend to be more elusive and potentially conflicting because they consist of different but partially overlapping customer profiles and product-market relationships.

Traditionally, customers in the recreation resort industry have been distinguished in the population by income, age, and family status (i.e., married/unmarried, with/without children). These factors often differentiated people inclined toward large-scale or mass recreational services coupled with less expensive accommodations (like the makeup of Disney World) from people seeking a more exclusive and intimate resort setting featuring high-value or high-status vacation venues (like those provided by Vail Resorts).

But in the opening years of the twenty-first century, a greater variety of demographic factors became determinants in customer demand analysis, which included educational level attained, occupational status (i.e., professional/managerial employment versus blue-collar/clerical jobs), lifestyle and other psychographic characteristics (cosmopolitan versus parochial awareness), and family makeup (i.e., singles/couples versus families), in addition to the traditional demographics. Looking forward, as industry producers figure out ways of assembling new customer profiles, novel services are likely to appear to keep this dynamic industry in flux.

Competition in the industry was also changing in dramatic ways. Ski resorts had divided into two types, partly the result of a maturing demand since the late 1980s. For those having limited access to capital, expansion into off-mountain amenities and overnight accommodations was sacrificed for development focused on mountain facilities like high-speed detachable chair lifts and snowmaking equipment. As result, most (the best known of which is Squaw Valley) became known as windshield resorts having principally day-use ski slopes with few accommodations on site, and usually requiring a daily roundtrip drive from home. For those resorts with deep pockets, investments in new "villages" with ski-in/ski-out access transformed the sites to "destination" resorts providing a complete experience, including not only accommodations but also "après-ski" activities for people who typically stay a week or longer. Extending this distinction, most of the better-financed destination resorts had also been shifting in the 1990s from a ski resort image to an integrated all-season setting offering winter recreation as well as golf and tennis, on-mountain summer activities, convention programs, world-class performing arts, and international festivals. A recent entry in this new approach is Squaw Valley, which is attempting a catch-up strategy in the destination market in a partnership with Intrawest and others.

With destination resorts having the most market reach demographically and geographically, Colorado claims several of the best known because of its central location in the scenic Rockies and between population centers on the East and West Coasts. Within the state, Vail Resorts competes with the Aspen Ski Company (which owns the three Aspen mountains and Snowmass, all proximally located in the Roaring Forks Valley), Intrawest (which owns controlling interest in Copper Mountain), American Ski Company (which owns Steamboat Springs), the city of Denver (which owns Winter Park), Telluride Golf and Ski, and several small destination operators (including Crested Butte and Purgatory).

Beyond Colorado, destination resort operators are spread out, with most having facilities in other parts of the Rockies, along the Pacific Crest/Sierras, in the northeastern United States, and southern Canada. In California, the major players until 2002 had been Intrawest (with interests at Squaw and Mammoth) and American Ski Company (which had owned Heavenly Valley until the resort's sale to VR). In Utah, most of the operators are small, privately held firms (which own Park City and Snowbird), with the exception of American Ski, which recently redeveloped a resort now called the Canyons. In Canada, Intrawest is the only major operator and owns Whistler-Blackcomb, Mt. Tremblant, and others.

Much of the current market structure of *destination* ski-resort competitors came about in the 1990s, when a rash of consolidations and mergers reduced the field to the "big four" and a few small specialized firms. Nearly all other firms that remain independent are operators of day-use resorts, which have lower capital costs because they offer few off-mountain activities. Figure 1 lists the principal firms and summarizes the site statistics for a selected list of their North American ski resorts.

During this period of consolidation, a technology-driven "arms race" in new development ensued. The target areas of primary investment included (1) thematic, planned-unit development villages at the ski-mountain base; (2) costly snowmaking equipment to guarantee visitors a quality skiing experience regardless of the vagaries of natural precipitation; (3) luxurious on-mountain restaurants to meet the cosmopolitan tastes of high-end skiers; and (4) state-of-the-art lift designs that provide faster, more comfortable access to the mountain top.

On the demand side of the market, destination-resort visitors were becoming more choosy at the turn of the century about the price-to-value of individual resorts. It had become clear that most destination visitors sought additional "creature comforts" both on and off the mountain, and they were willing to pay for exceptional luxury where quality was assured. VR's industry leadership in moving toward this high end market is reflected in an interfirm comparison of market position. Figure 2 compares market penetration for a selection of destination resorts according to each resort's annual skier days (calculated as one skier purchasing a lift ticket for one day).

For many years, VR's resorts have been ranked at or near the top of annual ski magazine surveys. Indeed, as the firm's flagship resort, Vail Mountain was ranked first for much of the 1990s and maintained that status into the twenty-first century. To a great extent, the firm's persistent market position is attributable to the fact that VR is the only firm in the industry that can achieve a cooperative administrative control over all aspects of the destination environment (i.e., mountain activities, local accommoda-

tions, village concessions, entertainment venues, airline and ground transportation), even though much of it is managed by a host of other firms acting as an integrated network of coproducers. As a result of its management of this multiple-partner strategic alliance, VR stood out among its competition in creating a superbly packaged product for the customer.

Nevertheless, the firm's market growth seemed to be stunted by events in the industry generally. As shown in Figure 3, the industry's long-term trend in skier-day visits had been persistently flat throughout the 1990s. An aging population of postwar baby boomers was thought to be a primary cause of this maturing demand. Skiing is a rigorous and potentially dangerous outdoor recreational activity and requires much physical stamina and a dose of youthful abandon. By contrast, baby boomers were moving into middle age during the 1990s and, as family responsibilities became more important in determining types of vacation venues, skiing's reputation as an expensive, singles-oriented, and physically exhausting sport came up short. Many former skiers and many others who might have tried skiing were moving to other segments of the vacation and leisure industry where less physical activity was required.

Besides aging of the population and intense, development-based competition, doing business in this industry had become more difficult because of a growing environmental ethic emerging among recreation and leisure customers. Over the thirty years since landmark legislation of the early 1970s, environmentalism not only had become institutionalized (by the inception of new laws, organizations, and processes) but also had acquired much broader appeal culturally. The impact of this growing respect for environmental concerns was especially felt by firms dealing with or affecting natural resources, a prime example of which were ski-resort operators.

Much of the public's awareness of a degraded environment came from individual experiences and knowledge of a loss in biodiversity and growing problems of pollution. But some public attention was heightened by protests made directly against target firms, some of it involving ecoterrorism. While most in the industry were subject to environmental litigation, varying degrees of nonviolent demonstrations, and media editorializing, Vail Resorts felt the full brunt of protestor anger. In the early morning hours of Monday, October 19, 1998, an ecoterrorist group firebombed Vail Mountain's premier restaurant

FIGURE 1

Destination Ski Resort Firms and Facilities (2000–2001 Summary of Resort Statistics)

Firm/Resort	Location	Lift Ticket Price	Skiable Acreage	Vertical Drop (Feet)	Number of Lifts	Number of Trails	Lift Capacity (Skiers/Hour)
Vail Resorts							
Vail Mountain	Colorado	$61	5,289	3,450	33	193	51,781
Breckenridge	Colorado	$57	2,043	3,398	25	139	30,656
Keystone	Colorado	$57	1,861	2,900	22	116	27,873
Beaver Creek	Colorado	$61	1,625	4,040	14	146	24,739
Aspen Ski and Golf							
Aspen/Snowmass	Colorado	$62	4,780	4,405	44	270	31,310
Intrawest							
Whistler/Blackcomb	British Columbia	$61CN	7,071	5,280	32	223	45,000
Mt. Tremblant	Quebec	$55CN	502	2,131	10	70	15,000
Mammoth Mountain	California	$54	3,500	3,100	28	150	42,100
Copper Mountain	Colorado	$55	2,433	2,601	23	125	31,000
American Ski Co.							
Steamboat Springs	Colorado	$58	2,500	3,668	20	107	30,000
Heavenly Valley	California	$56	4,800	3,500	27	82	40,000
Others							
Telluride	Colorado	$61	1,050	3,165	12	66	14,946
Winter Park	Colorado	$53	1,373	3,060	20	113	32,450
Park City	Utah	$60	2,200	3,100	14	83	19,700
Taos	New Mexico	$45	1,100	2,612	11	72	15,000

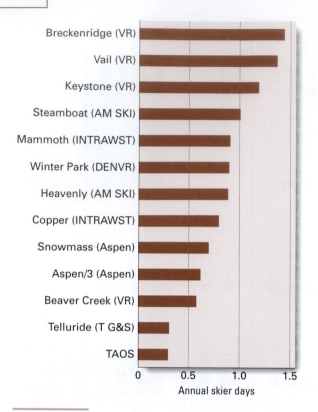

FIGURE 2

Annual Skier Days for Destination Resorts (Selected North American Resorts, 1999–2000 Season)

Sources: Colorado Ski Country; NSAA.

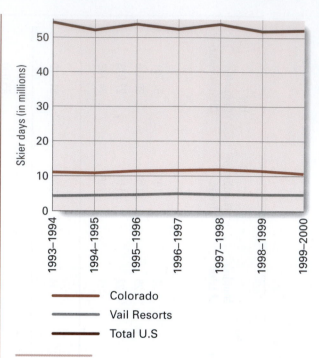

FIGURE 3

Trends in Skier Demand (Annual Skier Days, 1993–2000)

Sources: NSAA, Colorado Ski Country, Vail Resorts.

facility and damaged four ski lifts and the mountaintop headquarters of the Ski Patrol, all of which resulted in $12 million in damage.

Ostensibly done to protest Vail's development of Blue Ski Basin, a 650-acre addition to the mountain's skiable terrain, the act not only galvanized public disdain for the perpetrators, but also awakened a sense of urgency in VR's management. Although Aspen Ski and Golf was the industry's best-known firm for environmental sensitivity, VR had a far more substantial but unorganized environmental management ap-proach. In an effort to improve the firm's systematic handling of environmental issues, it began to give thought in 1999 to integrating the disparate components by drawing them together organizationally. What was taking form was a unifying, policy-driven approach to manage both the daily operations of resource sustainability and recycling and the longer-term planning requirements of the firm's continued development at its individual resorts.

The Vail Resorts Vision

Until its merger with Ralcorp and subsequent IPO in 1997, Vail Resorts had been a privately held firm made up of a closely knit family of managerial employees sharing a common interest in skiing. But under the new controlling ownership of Apollo Investors (Leon Black's holding company), the culture and leadership atmosphere changed dramatically. These corporate transitions raised several new managerial issues, but chief among them was the need for a fresh strategic outlook. During the firm's first year after the merger, the new executive team led by CEO Aron and president Daly articulated a long-term growth strategy to replace what Aron referred to as the "quick hits" of past years.

To launch the new vision, Aron set forth an explicit statement about strategic intent: "At Vail Resorts, we are focused on expanding and enhancing our core ski operations while increasing the scope, diversity and quality of the activities and services we offer our guests—skiers and nonskiers—throughout the year." Along with this declaration, he offered for the first time a set of five policy guidelines to drive the firm's strategic-action agenda: (1) create new attractions to enhance consumer appeal, (2) broaden participation in varied guest experiences (produce services previously provided by coproducers), (3) provide value through the firm's passion for quality, (4) leverage the firm's strong market position, and (5) capitalize on industry consolidation. All but one of these alluded unambiguously to a need for vertical integration of resort services and a development strategy involving significant on-mountain expansion and new venturing in the villages.

Although bringing greater strategic focus to development, for the most part, the guidelines sought to retain and buttress the firm's historical domain of customers and integrated product lines, which had been at the core of its past success as a destination resort provider. That strategic domain included a product image of world-class destination skiing, which imparted high status and upscale appeal to a youthful but financially well-off clientele. Unlike many other recreational sports, skiing invites the agile risk-taker. As shown in Figure 4, however, it is also associated with household wealth. In VR's case, more than 50 percent of customers have incomes exceeding $100,000, and 31 percent report incomes over $200,000. The firm's domination of the high-end segment of this income-driven market was central to making Vail number 1 in ski-magazine surveys during most of the 1980s and 1990s, as well as cultivating its image as a "playland of the rich."

During the 1990s, however, the Vail Resorts customer began to exhibit a more-accomplished set of demographic and psychological attributes. While income certainly still mattered, the typical VR customer was now also likely to be college educated, have a professional career (i.e., business executive, engineer, doctor, lawyer, academic, government official), and hold significant family responsibilities. As a result, VR's visitor today is more likely to be widely traveled, with global experience and a cosmopolitan outlook. Due in part to their professional responsibilities and institutional work environment, the firm's customer also tends to seek anonymity while on vacation and to prefer a resort environment that encourages others to share this desire. Indeed, this trait in the Vail customer is often mentioned in comparisons with Aspen's customer base, which reputedly is more likely to exhibit a want-to-be-seen Hollywood outlook.

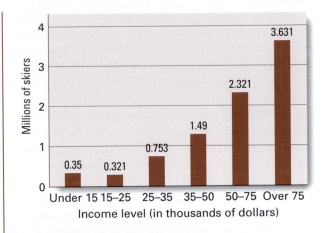

FIGURE 4

The Skiing Population, Distributed by Household Income (United States Population, 1997)

Source: U.S. Bureau of the Census.

In actual application, VR's strategic customer profile is an umbrella for different visitor subtypes. The largest of these are families (about 50 percent of visitations), many of which are multigenerational "boomer" families (i.e., a unit consisting of parents, children, and grandchildren). Although the exact mix varies from resort to resort, the remainder of visitations is about evenly divided among thirty-something couples, corporate and professional conference attendees, and college students. About 10 percent of visitations are made by foreign nationals who fit the demographic profile (especially those from Europe, South America, Japan, and Oceana, where skiing is very popular).

Such variety does not signal incompatible customer segments but rather variance in emphasis within the firm's multiple-attribute strategic profile. For example, although the multigenerational family perhaps represents the best all-round fit with the profile, college students are also a strategic fit. Even though typically lacking high-income professional employment, students often see a college degree as pursuant to the rewards of upper-middle-class status, suggesting even that this customer may become a quintessential replacement for aging boomers.

Until the 1990s, most in the destination ski-resort business saw little basis to differentiate the customer beyond household affluence and a passion for skiing. Providing faster ski lifts, well-manicured ski runs, and high-priced hotels seemed to be what the market recognized as a quality upscale product. As a result, the product most providers offered was *alpine skiing,* which focused primarily on ski-mountain hardware (mostly lifts and snowmaking) and opulent overnight accommodations. Although setting the terms for what president Daly called an "arms race" among industry competitors, this product vision did not directly account for some important emerging psychographic desires for friendly gathering places, spiritual renewal, novel adventure, stylistic flare, and cosmopolitan ambience.

While many in the industry ignored the implications and continued to promote the hardware-driven vision, VR began to cultivate skiing as a product of "luxurious pastoral serenity" and to offer an upscale opportunity to reconnect with the holistic self and valued friends, at least partially within the context of an international village setting. This new product vision was characterized as a *seamless experience,* blending together an uninterrupted progression of ski-resort pleasures while minimizing hassles and tradeoffs. For example, the pedestrian village (invented at Vail in the late 1970s) provides a ski-in/ski-out setting for visitors, placing stylistic ambience and the immediacy of mountain and village activities at the whim of customers without having to drive.

Although originally pioneered by Walt Disney half a century earlier, the emerging concept of seamlessness allowed VR to see opportunity in the threat of an aging population, and it resulted in the firm experiencing industry stability (even growth) in its financials. What many of the firm's competitors had missed in sticking with the old model was the opportunity to derive income from skier visits in ways other than the purchase of a lift ticket or an on-mountain sandwich. By upscaling its on-mountain restaurants, redefining ski school, buying some resort venues previously left to its network of coproducers (particularly classy hotels and resort retail and village commons), and becoming the primary on-line reservations agent for the four-resort packages, VR was able to generate a far greater revenue stream from each visitor than its competition. With the coming of the new millennium, the firm's refocus on an aging boomer as head of a multigenerational family was beginning to pay off. As Figure 5 shows, even though its skier visits followed the industry's flattened trend, the firm was generating revenues from each visitor that were as much as 50 percent greater than its destination-market competition.

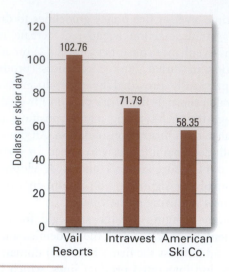

FIGURE 5

Ski Resort Revenue per Skier Day—Industry Comparison (Public Firms, 1999–2000 Ski Season)

During the 1990s, Vail Resorts had been a heavy investor in new facilities. It finished, for example, several eye-catching developments, including the well-known Beaver Creek village and launch of its sister village at Bachelor Gulch; a 650-acre north-face addition at Vail called Blue Sky Basin, along with Vail's redevelopment of the Eagle's Nest gondola and Adventure Ridge recreation area; and construction at Keystone of a new theme village called River Run, along with a golf community called River Ranch (both a joint venture with Intrawest).

Even with this sustained investment level, VR's new-found domain of product-market relationships spurred the firm to escalate substantially its investments into the twenty-first century. Although the firm doubled its size in 1997 with the Ralcorp resorts acquisition, as shown in Figure 6, it increased its capital development expenditures sixfold. Between 1997 and 2000, its capital improvement program for the four ski resorts (excluding acquisitions) averaged over $60 million annually and was allocated among projects such as redevelopment of the Lionshead gondola and pedestrian village at Vail, completion of Blue Sky Basin at Vail, completion of the outdoor ice-skating arena and Vilar performing arts center at Beaver Creek village, and launch of the Bachelor Gulch village and ski area at Beaver Creek.

Even though numerous environmental issues have been and continue to be voiced by local and national organizations concerned about pollution,

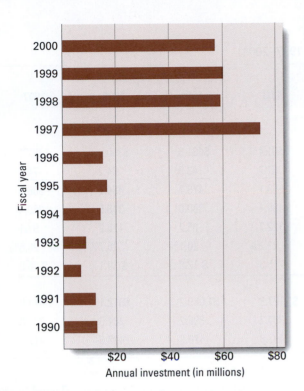

FIGURE 6

Four-Resort Capital Improvements Budget (Vail Resorts, Inc., 1990–2000)

biodiversity, and sustainability, the firm intends to continue its high level of capital investment for the strategic future (perhaps covering the next ten years). Current planning and environmental analysis, for example, is underway on a completely new 264-acre ski-in/ski-out village adjoining the firm's peaks 7 and 8 staging area above the town of Breckenridge. It will contain a mix of 430 "hot-bed" condominiums (individually owned rentals) and 110,000 square feet of retail space, which will be connected to the town center below by a twelve-passenger gondola. At Keystone, another development plan envisions a new base village and ski-mountain addition called Jones Gulch. At Beaver Creek, a new gondola is planned to connect the rapidly developing town of Avon to Bachelor Gulch and continue to the western ridge above Beaver Creek. Significant development is also underway at VR's summer-use Grand Teton resort, including a golf course and residential community. With the 2002 acquisition of Heavenly Resort, early planning is calling for major renewal of on-mountain facilities and new village initiatives.

The Firm's Financial Position

Vail Resorts is a mid-sized firm with assets of slightly over $1 billion and annual revenues of about $500 million (see Figure 7 for selected financial trends). Regarding contributions to revenue by the individual resorts, Vail accounts for about 33 percent of the total, Breckenridge and Keystone each about 25 percent, Beaver Creek 12 percent, and Grand Teton about 5 percent. As a result of varying year-to-year ski conditions (including two of the poorest winters on record), VR's recent financial results have been mixed. Revenues have consistently improved and operating margins are strong but have trended downward since the IPO. Compared with its public competitors, the firm has a far better record than American Ski Company (which merged in 2000 into Doral Corp due in part to its financial stress) but not as robust as that of Intrawest (which focuses more on real estate development than on resort operations). Although not a public firm (requiring SEC reporting), Aspen is rumored to be experiencing substantial financial problems and a declining market share.

To spread financial risk, VR has been diversifying its product line. Historically, more than 95 percent of its revenues came from the five-month ski season. With implementation of its all-season strategy at the ski resorts and its acquisition of summer resorts like the Grand Teton, the winter contribution was reduced in 2001 to about 70 percent. Risk of single-source income was also reduced in part from the firm's vertical integration of activities making up the seamless experience. As shown in Figure 8, nonlift-ticket sources of revenue (e.g., from ski school, on- and off-mountain dining, village retail/rental, hospitality management) represented more than 70 percent of the total in 2001 and have been steadily increasing over recent years. Real estate sales make up only about 10 percent of total revenues on average. They are important to the firm's growth strategy, however, because they feed future resort revenues by expanding the visitor bed base of the area (especially when it involves guest rental units, known as "hot beds").

The firm's 2001 asset base of $1.2 billion consists mainly of resort facilities (58 percent), which include retail/commercial buildings, corporation headquarters, lift and gondola terminals, on-mountain restaurants, land for facilities (such as golf courses, corporation yards, and village commons), and machinery and equipment (ski-lift towers and lines, snowmaking equipment, and snow-grooming

FIGURE 7

Trends in Selected Financial Data (Vail Resorts, Inc., 1997–2001)

Fiscal Year Ended July 31 (In Millions)	2001	2000	1999	1998	1997
Statement of operations					
Revenue					
From resorts	$524.1	$501.4	$431.8	$350.5	$292.1
From real estate	35.2	51.7	43.9	84.2	74.4
Total revenue	559.3	553.1	475.7	434.7	366.5
Operating expenses (excluding D&A)	430.7	430.4	380.0	318.5	269.4
Operating net (EBITDA)	128.6	122.7	95.7	116.2	97.1
Gross operating margin	23.0%	22.2%	20.1%	26.7%	26.5%
Net income	$ 18.7	$ 15.3	$ 12.8	$ 30.1	$ 26.0
Balance sheet data					
Total assets	$1,181.0	$1,127.8	$1,089.2	$912.1	$814.8
Long-term debt	388.4	394.2	398.2	284.0	236.3
Stockholders' equity	519.2	493.8	476.8	462.6	417.2

machines). The second largest asset category is intangibles (17 percent) and includes mostly trademarks and goodwill. The third major component is real estate held for sale (13 percent), which consists mostly of undeveloped or developing land. Nearly all of the on-mountain ski terrain is property leased for forty years from the U.S. Forest Service, which owns this land as part of the White River National Forest. Current assets account for slightly less than 10 percent of the firm's total asset base.

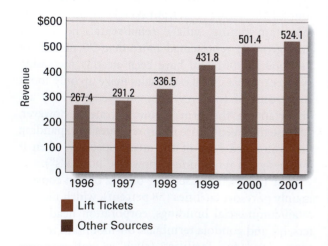

FIGURE 8

Lift Ticket Sales As a Percentage of Resort Revenues (Vail Resorts, Inc., 1997–2001)

Several recent acquisitions are not reflected in the 1997–2001 figures. They include the 2001 end-of-year purchase of Rock Resorts, owner of eleven small high-end resort hotels, and the 2002 purchase of the Heavenly Ski Resort in South Tahoe, California, for $96 million.

The Vail Resorts Organization

With Vail Resorts's new growth strategy, the ensuing changes unleashed a cascade of managerial events and consequences. Indeed, the sheer complexity of the combined resources from the 1997 merger made necessary a massive reorganization of authority. Over the years, the original organization structure provided well for the privately held Vail Valley firm. However, with the acquisition of Ralcorp's two Summit County resorts located an hour away, the purchase of Grand Teton Lodge Company in Wyoming, and the resultant doubling of the firm's asset size and employment base (at seasonal peak, the firm now employs over 12,000, of which half hold permanent year-round status), the existing structure was no longer suitable for the complex integration of diverse new resources, product markets, managerial cultures, personalities, and expertise.

By 2000, the reorganization was almost complete. As shown in Figure 9, the firm's new organization

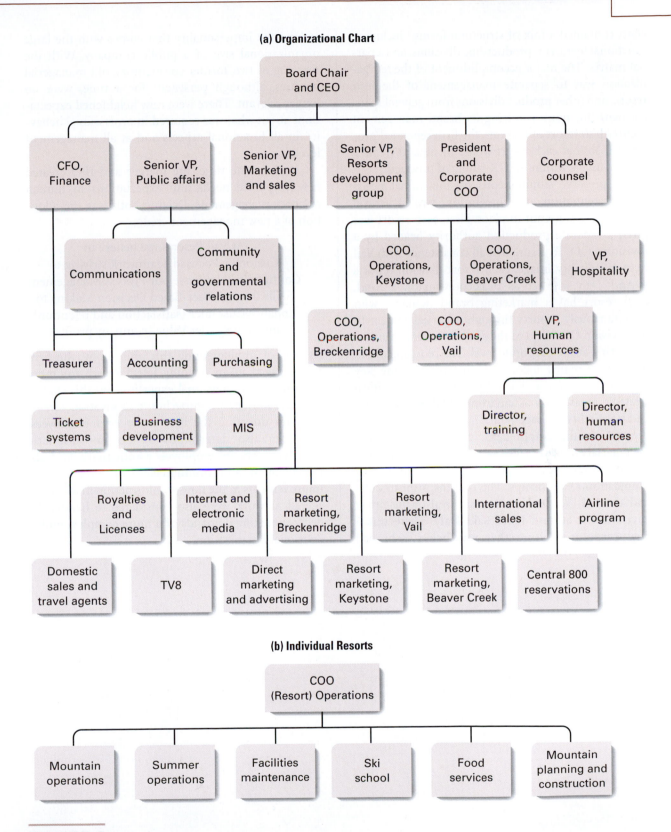

(a) Organizational Chart

(b) Individual Resorts

FIGURE 9

Vail Resorts, 2001 (Organization Chart)

chart contained a mix of structural forms, including functional hierarchy, product-line divisions, and a partial matrix. The major accomplishment of the reorganization was to separate management of the four resorts and other product divisions from general management functions. Applying its brand management approach to resort operations, the firm separated production so that each resort would be able to create a distinct image within the VR family of products.

To preserve simultaneous organizational needs for differentiation and integration, two structural components were put in place. First, each resort was given a separate production authority headed by a division COO. To assure overall consistency with Vail Resorts's quality image, each resort division reports to Andy Daly, who acts as "peak coordinator." Second, each resort has a marketing brand manager who simultaneously reports through a partial matrix to the division COO and to the senior vice president for marketing at the corporate level. The reorganization, however, remains incomplete regarding some key integration issues and insufficient in some critical strategic areas, such as environmental management and hospitality management.

At first, the comprehensive reorganization left managerial employees feeling ambiguous about what to expect in the new structure of authority and communication relationships. The months prior to 2000 had created "somewhat of a survival-of-the-fittest environment around here," said Daly. There was a new corporate culture that was being fashioned around the impersonality that comes with the large organizational size of a public company. With the merging of two former competitors, old managerial loyalties, although persistent for a time, were no longer relevant. There were now heightened expectations about what was required in professional behavior in all functional aspects and at all management levels.

At the same time, the merger and IPO created new corporate needs and expectations in human resource management. Driving both was the adoption of a new management credo:

> At Vail Resorts, we believe in
> Customer-Focused Teamwork striving to
> Continuously Improve our Process Management
> Skills through Fact-Based Decision Making to
> Enhance Customer (satisfaction and retention)
> and Shareholder Value (company profits).

As part of implementing this philosophy, the firm was engaged in an ongoing talent search for more and different professional expertise, and this change would require new approaches to motivating, retaining, and directing the best managerial employees. The firm also determined a need for dramatic improvements in employee productivity at both management and nonmanagement levels. Major improvements in the flow of information in the managerial network were also considered to handle the decisionmaking demands of a more complex, multidivisional organization.

Adrenaline Air Sports: Where the Speed Limit Is 120 Miles Per Hour ... or More

(condensed version)

This case was prepared by Larry D. Alexander (Associate Professor of Business Strategy at Virginia Tech), Billy Cockrell (owner of Adrenaline Air Sports, at Smith Mountain Lake Airport, Smith Mountain Lake, Virginia), and Jonathan Charlton (parachutist and Industrial and Systems Engineering student at Virginia Tech, Blacksburg, Virginia).

Billy Cockrell graduated from Botetourt High School in Roanoke, Virginia, on a Saturday in June 1990. His family had a small party for him later that day at their home to celebrate his graduation. At that gathering, his uncle J. C. Cockrell approached Billy and told him of the unique present he was giving Billy for graduation. He invited Billy to come to his parachute drop zone and take a tandem parachute jump free of charge. Billy's instant response to his uncle was, "No way I'm jumping out of a plane."

After High School

Billy did not feel mature enough to go on to college after high school. Instead, he enlisted for six years in the navy in December 1990, six months after graduating from high school. In the navy, he was trained and worked as a fire-control technician, radar operator, and, occasionally, a search-and-rescue swimmer.

At times in the navy, he would be out to sea on a cruise for three months at a stretch. In August 1992, he was stationed in Charleston, South Carolina. While many other sailors spent much of their spare time drinking in bars, Billy was looking for something different. One day while visiting on the telephone with his grandmother, Grosejean, she reminded him of the free tandem parachute jump that J. C., his uncle, had offered Billy two years before. This time Billy moved fast on the offer and made the jump the next Saturday at his uncle's drop zone in Greensboro, North Carolina.

Parachute drop-industry statistics show that only a few people who take a first parachute jump ever jump again. This was not the case with Billy Cockrell. He took his second jump the very next day, on Sunday. He became hooked on parachuting and thought he would like to someday work full-time at his own parachute drop zone.

Billy was transferred to various land and sea locations during his six-year navy stint. In 1993, he was sent to San Diego, California, for three months to go through more-advanced naval training. While there, he parachuted at Air Adventures, also located in San Diego, which was a fairly large drop zone operation. Billy was so enthused with his new-found sport that he recruited between forty and fifty people to take their first jump at that drop zone.

According to the United States Parachute Association (Exhibit 1), about 540,000 parachutists worldwide made about 5,563,000 jumps in 1998 alone. In the United States, 317,741 people made 3,500,000 combined jumps in the year 2000 and 34,217 people were members of the United States Parachute Association, headquartered in Alexandria, Virginia, near Washington, D.C. While approximately 300,000 people in the United States took a once-in-a-lifetime jump during 2000, other parachutists made multiple jumps in just one weekend. These veterans of the sport often took up to five or even ten jumps in a single day. At the extreme, Mike Zang made an amazing 500 parachute jumps in a 24-hour period in April of 2001. This amounted to one jump from a Porter type airplane at just 2,100 feet elevation every two minutes and 53 seconds.

A typical parachute jump by experienced jumpers can be described as follows. Four parachuters took off with a pilot in a small Cessna-type propeller airplane. It took about twenty to twenty-five minutes to reach 10,000 feet, where the pilot positioned the plane so that the jumpers could parachute and maneuver themselves back to the drop zone. When ready, the parachutists opened the Cessna's passenger door and briefly stood on a step outside the plane or jumped out from inside the plane.

The parachutist initially did a freefall—from 10,000 down to 3,000 feet, usually—with the main chute closed. The jumper's speed quickly accelerated to about 120 miles per hour. On average, a skydiver fell the first thousand feet in about ten seconds and then accelerated, falling each additional thousand feet in about six seconds. Thus, to freefall from 10,000 to 3,000 feet, it took only about forty-six seconds. At 3,000 feet, the jumper pulled a ripcord, which first opened the small pilot chute, then the large main parachute. At that point, the parachutist was "under canopy," slowly descending from the "adrenaline high" of freefall, enjoying the view, and pulling various steering cords to manuever his parachute back to the drop zone landing area.

All parachute gear was required to have a separate reserve chute in case the main chute did not open or opened incorrectly. Many jumpers paid $500 or more to have an optional automatic activation device attached to their packs so that their second, or reserve, chute opened at a preset altitude. The industry was so safety conscious that all reserve chutes had to be repacked by a rigger, a professional parachute packer, every four months even though it had not been used. This person also checked the two chutes for wear and tear and made any necessary repairs.

During freefall, some parachutists did what was called relative work with other parachutists before opening their parachutes. If four people were jumping together and doing relative work, they might start off in a star formation or point (all holding hands in a square with their feet farthest out), then go to a diamond for a second point, and then to a donut for a third point; if time permitted, they might form an open accordion for a fourth point.

The record number of skydivers to join hands and legs in a free fall pattern was 286 people, accomplished over Ottawa, Illinois in 1998. These very experienced skydivers jumped out of several different planes very quickly and then joined up in just one preplanned pattern. It was planned months in advance and rehearsed to accomplish it and to do it.

EXHIBIT 1

U.S. Parachute Association Skydiving Stats

Number of Skydivers worldwide (last reported in 1998 by FAI): 540,000

Number of Skydives worldwide (last reported in 1998 by FAI): 5,563,000

Number of people making a Skydive in the U.S., 2000: 317,741 [1999: 311,511]

Number of Skydives U.S., 2000: 3,500,000

USPA Members, end of 2000: 34,217

Number of Student Jumps:

Student Method	2000	1999
AFF	32,410	31,775
Tandem	185,410	181,775
Static Line	60,338	59,155
Total	278,158	277,366

Number of Members by Total Jump Numbers:

0–25	21.7%
26–250	33.2%
250+	45.1%

Members by Age Group:

0–29	21.0%
30–39	34.4%
40–49	25.7%
50–59	11.2%
60+	3.3%

Gender:

Male	82.0%
Female	14.7%
Unknown	3.3%

Other parachutists did free flying before they opened their parachutes. This was similar to the standard technique of "belly flying" except that the skydiver typically rotated through three positions: head down, feet first, and sitting. These skydivers often did relative work with other free flyers as they moved from one position to another in a choreographed plan. They might come together in a formation or spin and turn relative to each other without touching.

Free flyers going headfirst with their arms at their side could at times exceed 200 miles an hour. These speeds were measured by a Pro-Track helmet computer, which calculates the jumper's statistics, such as his elevation when jumping out of the plane, time in freefall, average speed in freefall, maximum speed in freefall, total elapsed time, and altitude at which the parachute opened.

Another activity performed by parachutists was canopy relative work. In this exercise, the parachutists opened their canopies quickly after exiting the airplane. Then they came together and hooked their feet into the lines of the parachute immediately beneath them. Thus, the parachuters were stacked on top of each other's canopy, the top parachutist controlling the direction of all those below him. This activity was riskier and was done at only a few drop zones throughout the United States, but Adrenaline Air Sports was not included.

Occasionally, some parachutists requested a "hop and pop" jump. This involved a shorter, and therefore, cheaper airplane ride to just 3,000 or 4,000 feet. The parachutists opened their chute a very short time after exiting the plane to test out equipment or to keep the costs down per jump.

The highest parachute jump ever made was by Captain Joseph Kittinger on August 16, 1960. He jumped using bottled oxygen from a balloon at an altitude of 102,800 feet, approximately 20 miles high. As he free fell down past about 80,000 feet in very thin air, he was traveling in excess of 600 miles an hour. Thus, he almost became the first person to break the speed of sound barrier without flying a plane or space vehicle. He also set another record for free falling 84,700 feet, some 16 miles, before opening his chute. As of 2002, Kittinger's records had never been broken, although recently several people were considering trying to break them.

Perhaps more amazing was the highest survived fall without a parachute by Vesna Vulovic on January 26, 1972. She was a stewardess on a DC-9 jet that blew up at 33,330 feet over Czechoslovakia. Everyone on the plane died. She was thrown free of the plane, fell some six miles, hit a snow drift, and amazingly lived.

Adrenaline Air Sports Opens for Business in November 1999

In the fall of 1999, Billy Cockrell signed a five-year lease to open his Adrenaline Air Sports drop zone at Smith Mountain Lake Airport. His rent paid for a hangar, a business office, an adjacent grassy area for parachutists to land on, and rights to take off and land on an unlimited basis from the airport, which was owned and operated by Joe Borgess.

The airport had an elevation of 940 feet and was located about a half mile from the beautiful and large Smith Mountain Lake, which offered boating, sailing, water skiing, swimming, fishing, golf, and parasailing. According to one statistic, up to 10,000 boats could be found on the lake on a busy weekend day. Billy Cockrell had heard from the local realtors that 10,000 new people came to stay at the lake each week during the busy, warm months.

Adrenaline Air Sports's scenic drop zone was located thirty-five miles southeast of Roanoke, Virginia, a city of 94,911 people that was adjacent to Salem to the west. Salem had a population of 24,747 people. Some forty-three miles west of downtown Roanoke (and further west of Salem) was Blacksburg, a college town of 39,573 people. It was the home of Virginia Tech, the largest college in the state, with an enrollment of 25,000 students.

Billy started getting his drop zone underway in fall of 1999. A major goal was to acquire an airplane to take jumpers up. In December 1999, he purchased a 1959 Cessna 182 for $45,000. He arranged to pay for it over a ten-year period with a loan from the Navy Credit Union, which he was eligible to borrow from as a navy veteran.

Billy used eBay and other Internet sources to get most of the equipment he needed to start up his operation. This included helmets and jump suits, which were both fairly expensive. From a Las Vegas supplier on the Internet, he purchased two tandem chutes and two student chutes, larger-sized parachutes used by parachutists starting to jump by themselves. In all, he paid some $15,000 for much of his equipment.

As the year 2000 approached, Billy gradually prepared to open for business and waited for the warm weather in March and April, during which, he hoped, he would attract more customers. As customers increased, Billy realized he needed more equipment.

In May 2000, he bought a third tandem chute, and then in August a fourth one.

In calendar year 2000, Adrenaline Air Sports's total sales amounted to about $90,000—a surprisingly good start for the first year of operations.

Adrenaline Air Sports in Summer 2001

The year 2001 was even better, particularly from April through October. Total sales for the year were $154,000.

Adrenaline Air Sports used part-time employees exclusively. Even Billy worked part-time for Adrenaline even though he might average forty hours a week. And that was on top of his regular full-time job at Luna Innovations in Blacksburg.

In addition, there was his weekend work at the Adrenaline Air Sports' drop zone. During the many bad-weather weekends from late fall to early spring, Billy often went down to his drop zone to get work done, even if no customers were likely to come in. Once the good weather arrived, he would put in a forty-hour weekend, beginning Friday night and ending Sunday night.

After work ended at Luna Innovations at 5 p.m. on Friday, Billy went home for a short time and then drove or flew the seventy miles to his drop zone at Smith Mountain Lake, usually arriving there between 7 and 8 p.m. He usually went first to Adrenaline's office building, which had lights, water, heat, lounge chairs, a bathroom, and some office space. As of March 2002, it also had a shower with hot and cold water, which Billy and some customers helped install. The term "customer" probably sounded strange to him because these people were fellow skydivers who were almost as committed to the sport as Billy.

The manifest on the computer listed all people who had reserved tandem-jump slots for Saturday or Sunday. Tandem jumps were made by first-time parachuters hooked to experienced and certified tandem instructors using one large canopy or parachute.

Most of these people made a reservation with Billy during the week, calling him either at his full-time job or at night at his home. Billy said that he got the most telephone calls on Mondays for parachuting the following weekend. He speculated that first-time jumpers convinced themselves and/or their friends the prior weekend to jump as something of a dare. Then they would call on Monday because if they waited beyond that day, they would often decide not to do it after all.

At Billy's office, he made sure that the various forms jumpers would have to complete were assembled. This included five pages of waivers of liability the jumpers would have to fill out before they were permitted to skydive.

Billy then went to the hangar. There was no heat in the hangar, but it did have lights. He cleaned the hangar and moved items to the wall so that parachuters could repack their chutes on the floor over the weekend or pay a packer to do it. Friday night Billy often repacked any parachutes that his customers would need for Saturday morning.

He owned eight parachutes, which he stored at Adrenaline Air Sports. In addition, some customers stored their own chutes in Billy's hangar when they were not using them. Billy's chutes included four tandem canopies, used for beginners who were attached to their instructor or tandem master, two for accelerated freefall for the next level of skydiving, and two used by just Billy himself. By late Sunday afternoon, nearly everyone was tired, so often nobody would repack these parachutes for the next weekend. Billy would therefore pack them Friday night if necessary. He would then sleep in his office, along with any parachuting customers and/or employees who had arrived early for the weekend. During warm months, they would sleep in the hangar. Everyone slept in sleeping bags, often on air mattresses for some added comfort.

Billy usually started working on Saturday morning by 7 a.m. The manifest was again rechecked and any additional paperwork for that day's jumpers assembled. Training aids were made available. First-time tandem jumpers started arriving by 8 a.m. or soon thereafter for their 8:30 jumps. As first-time jumpers arrived, they filled out forms and paid their $189 fee. They then met their instructor, who gave them ground training, and were asked if they wanted a videotape of their jump, which cost $60. The majority of first-time jumpers purchased the videotape so that they would have a souvenir of their skydiving adventure.

Marketing

Billy used a variety of strategies to get customers to try parachuting at his drop zone. They all helped, though it was hard to pinpoint which marketing approaches were the most effective.

One very helpful advertising technique involved using posters with the headline "Skydive Adrenaline Air Sports." The posters contained such statements as "Skydive at Virginia's Most Scenic Skydiving Center,"

"Specializing in Tandem and Accelerated Freefall," and "Your SAFETY is our FIRST PRIORITY!"

At the bottom of each sheet were tear-off strips of paper that had the name of Adrenaline Air Sports, a telephone number, and a web address. The posters were put up on bulletin boards, walls, and doors at colleges, grocery stores, strip shopping centers, and other places where likely first-time parachuters might see them. Billy also gave them to his loyal customers, asking them to put them up where they worked or near where they lived.

Another marketing strategy was advertising in the Yellow Pages of area telephone directories. Adrenaline Air Sports' ad in Verizon's November 2000 Yellow Pages for Montgomery County of Virginia, whose center was sixty-five miles from Billy's drop zone, read as follows:

SKYDIVE AT VIRGINIA'S MOST
SCENIC DROP ZONE
Located at Smith Mtn Lake Airport
LEARN TO SKYDIVE
WITH PROFESSIONALS
YOUR SAFETY
IS OUR #1 PRIORITY
Tandem AFF, Video
www.air-sports.com
Smith Mountain Lake . . . 296-1100

The problem with this was that since telephone directories covered such small geographic areas, a business had to spend a lot of money for ads if it was going to cover a large region. Billy paid approximately $18,000 for his numerous Yellow Pages ads per year.

Also appearing in this telephone directory were ads for two of Billy's main competitors, Skydive Orange and Skydive Virginia, both located northeast of Smith Mountain Lake and Charlottesville, 140 miles away from his drop zone.

Billy had tried radio advertising briefly, but never had run a television commercial. Because he had only used radio occasionally, he was not sure of its effectiveness.

Adrenaline Air Sports also placed a small monthly ad in the *Parachutist: Official Publication of the United States Parachute Association.* Adrenaline's three-line monthly ad usually read as follows:

Adrenaline Air Sports-Skydive Blue Ridge
Smith Mountain Lake Airport, Moneta
30 minutes southeast of Roanoke
(540) 296-1100
www.air-sports.com

Like all ads, this appeared along with six others from parachute drop zones in Virginia. Both Skydive Orange and Skydive Virginia were listed. Members of the U.S. Parachute Association automatically got this monthly magazine as part of their yearly membership dues. Over four hundred drop zones were listed in it by state and country.

Adrenaline Air Sports also had eye-catching bumper stickers. They contained one large A for both Adrenaline and Air. The stickers also said "SKYDIVE BLUE RIDGE" and gave a telephone number and web site address. They were given out free of charge to Billy's customers, their friends, and anyone who wanted one.

For first-time parachutists, another form of advertising was the videotape they could purchase as a souvenir of their adventure. Billy was convinced that these jumpers showed their videotapes to many of their friends, helping to stimulate an interest in parachuting. The cost of this advertising was free to Adrenaline Air Sports because beginners paid $60 to get their jumps videotaped.

Tracy Harris did almost all of the skydiving photography at Adrenaline Air Sports. He was about thirty-five years old and ran his own construction business during the week. On the weekends, he worked part-time for Billy with his video camcorder affixed to the top of his helmet. He would go up with every first-time jumper who wanted a videotape, and exited the plane just before the jumper and his tandem instructor. Tracy would record their exit, their freefall, the opening of the parachute (also called canopy), and some of their descent. He then quickly landed so that he could record the pair when they came in for their landing.

So popular were the videotapes that of Tracy Harris's four hundred jumps in 2001, about three hundred were made taking videos. Since Tracy was Adrenaline's sole skydive photographer, he could only handle one videotaping at a time.

Once Tracy finished recording one jumper's landing, he went up almost immediately in another plane with the next jumper. He stored his tapes and worked on them between jumps, on Saturday evenings, and on Sundays. Billy tried to deliver the finished videotapes by the end of Sunday night, if at all possible. Often, Billy or someone else would deliver the videotape to the jumper's home on Sunday night so he or she could have it almost immediately. Billy felt that the videotape was his best marketing tool because the proud first-time parachuter would want to show it to everyone he or she knew.

Flight Operations

Billy purchased his second Cessna 182 in April 2001 to handle the increased number of customers coming to his drop zone. Both planes were being purchased by him with bank loans he obtained from the Navy Credit Union and a local bank in southwest Virginia. With an average purchase price in excess of $40,000, these two small, single-engine propeller planes were a major investment.

Aviation fuel was another significant cost. During 2001, he purchased 11,000 gallons of aviation fuel, which cost almost $26,000, or $2.34 a gallon. On a busy weekend, each plane would consume about $400 in aviation fuel, or one refill every three flights.

Some simple maintenance Billy did on his own. For example, he replaced the oil on each plane frequently every twenty-five hours. Billy felt it was a cheap investment considering the age of the planes.

However, he had a problem getting his planes maintained on a regular basis. No one at his small airport did maintenance, so his planes had to be taken elsewhere to get maintenance. He couldn't ask his three pilots to fly his planes in the middle of the week because they all had regular jobs. One day in February 2001, Billy called the airport in Harrisonburg, Virginia. He said he needed to learn to fly for his business. He got started that day, and just seven days later, he had soloed and received his pilot's license. This changed one aspect of Billy's Adrenaline Air Sports operations.

At the end of a weekend of running his drop zone, Billy often flew one of his planes back to the Virginia Tech airport in Blacksburg, near where he lived and worked during the week. He left the plane there, got into his car, which was parked there for the weekend, and drove a few miles to his home. Then during the week, Billy would fly his plane late in the afternoon a hundred miles to Greensboro, North Carolina. There, his mechanic did routine maintenance on the plane and checked its airworthiness.

That same evening, Billy would fly the plane back to either Blacksburg or his drop zone. If he dropped it off at Adrenaline Air Sports, then someone—often one of his customers—would pick him up and take him back to the Blacksburg area. In this way, Billy's planes received regular maintenance checks in North Carolina during the week. While maintaining the planes took time, Billy was committed to running a very safe skydiving operation, and this started with safe airplanes.

On a busy weekend of good weather, both planes were used all day long. Each plane could take a maximum of four skydivers (or parachuters) and the pilot. Seats were removed from the planes, except for the pilot's seat, to accommodate the jumpers and their parachutes.

Billy recently changed the maximum altitude at which his planes would release skydivers. The new policy was that jumpers would be taken to a maximum of 10,000 feet. The Smith Mountain Airport was at an elevation of 1,130 feet, so jumpers could skydive and parachute a total of 8,870 feet. Previously, Billy would take jumpers up to 12,000 feet, charging them more. But he realized that it was not worth it because of the extra ten to fifteen minutes it took to climb to 12,000 feet. The new fee schedule was simple: $6 for a plane ride, plus $1 for each thousand feet. Thus, a ride to 10,000 feet cost $16 and a low-level "hop and pop" (hop out of the plane and pop the parachute) at, say, 4,000 feet would cost $10.

By 8 a.m., the two pilots had arrived to fly the jumpers. The strategy was to keep taking jumpers up as quickly as possible. Adrenaline Air Sports was lucky to have three competent part-time pilots:

J. D. Shumate—A 22-year-old full-time flight instructor at Averett College in Danville, Virginia. He had been a pilot at Adrenaline since it opened in 1999, and had approximately 40 jumps himself.

Jeff "Maverick" Perkins—A 26-year-old UPS (United Parcel Service) truck driver, who previously was a scheduler for U.S. Air Express. He also served as a paramedic in his hometown.

Bobby Bruch—A 42-year-old electrician who worked for Norfolk Southern railroad. He had been a pilot for Billy for one year.

After the first-time tandem jumpers, other parachuters went. This was based on the order in which they had signed up during the preceding week. Experienced jumpers usually had their own parachutes, gear, and clothing, so all they needed was a plane ride, which cost $16 and which took from twenty to twenty-five minutes. Some of these experienced jumpers had been in the sport for ten, twenty, or more years and had several thousand jumps to their credit.

This routine of taking jumpers up, letting them exit the plane, landing the plane, refueling when needed, and taking the next group up continued all morning. At 1 p.m., another set of first-time parachuters arrived.

Billy Cockrell paid approximately $8,000 for insurance each year. This covered his two Cessna planes and provided protection for lawsuits from customers that might get hurt.

Skydiving Instruction

Another key element of Billy's operations was skydiving instruction. Billy had several instructors, Richard Wagner being his lead one. Richard was an interesting person, like most of the people in the sport. He was forty-two years old, first started parachuting at age nineteen, and had over 2,500 jumps. He was vice president of a company in Mount Airy, North Carolina, that made steel reinforcing wire used in building construction.

Richard, who had been a friend of Billy's since 1993, usually came to the drop zone one day of the weekend. He was willing to do whatever Billy asked him to do, such as doing tandem jumps with beginners or coaching others doing accelerated-freefall jumps.

If Richard was not needed as a paid instructor, he would rehearse some four-way skydive patterns called relative work and then jump them. This so-called relative work was done during the fifty seconds or so that four jumpers were in freefall.

Billy had other part-time flight instructors. They included Miles Peters, aged thirty-five, who instructed tandem and accelerated freefall jumpers. Miles had over 1,900 jumps and had been skydiving for ten years. Randy Fields, aged thirty-three, also instructed accelerated freefall jumpers. Randy had over 2,000 jumps and had been with the sport over ten years. Tracy Gasperini, aged thirty-six, instructed tandem jumpers.

Beginning jumpers paid $189 for their tandem jump with an instructor. If they continued, the prices for the next set of jumps were as follows:

2nd jump – $	189	with tandem instructor
Before 3rd jump – $	100	for six-hour ground school
3rd jump – $	189	student with own chute, but two instructors jumping holding on to the student's sides until the student opens chute
4th jump – $	189	same as jumps 1 and 2
5th jump – $	189	jump with own chute with one coach with his own chute nearby
6th jump – $	179	jump with own chute with one coach nearby
7th jump – $	179	jump with own chute with one coach nearby
8th jump – $	179	jump with own chute with one coach nearby
9th jump – $	0	free jump for completing basic set of jumps; own chute and one coach nearby
	$1,582	total price for basic instructional jumps
10th jump – $	41	$16 to be taken to 10,000 feet and $25 to rent one parachute per jump; no charge for instructor or instructor's helper
11th–14th jump – $	41	same as jump 10 each
15th jump – $	41	first solo jump; one-way walkie-talkie provided to communicate with instructor on the ground who helps maneuver and land.

If a beginning jumper who was enthusiastic about the sport wanted to get his own equipment, he would probably purchase used equipment. Prices for good used parachute equipment might fall in the following range:

$ 750–$1,000	for main parachute
$ 750–$1,000	for reserve second chute
$ 750–$1,000	for pack containing both chutes
$ 750–$1,000	for automatic-activation device to open second parachute automatically (optional but good to have)
$ 3,000–$4,000	total price

If the skydiver wanted all new equipment, then the price range would be $4,000 to $6,000, depending on the quality of the parachute gear. Thus, if a parachuter made a significant investment in used or new equipment and packed his own chutes as well, the price per jump would be just $16.

After taking the twenty basic jumps, a parachuter could look forward to a solo jump and getting an A license. After that, a jumper could work toward getting B, C, and D licenses and then perhaps a coaching rating and an instructor's rating. How long it took to get these various licenses varied widely. Karen Alexander, aged eighteen, got all four licenses plus her coaching certificate in just ten months. Other jumpers might take several years to obtain their A and B licenses.

Another type of very unique parachuting was BASE jumping, which could not be done at Adrenaline Air Sports. BASE jumping involved parachuting off a building for *B*, off an antenna (radio tower or antenna on top of a building) for *A*, off a span of a bridge for *S*, and off the earth for *E*. A person who parachuted off all four was a true base jumper. Since many of these challenges were from low elevations, the jumper had no time to use a reserve chute if the first one failed. For example, on "Bridge Day" in October on the New River Valley Gorge Bridge, BASE jumpers can jump legally all day from the bridge, which is just 876 feet. On the high side was the Great Trango Tower, in Pakistan, which was BASE jumped by two people, Nicholas Feteris and Glen Singleman, from an elevation of 19,300. This mountain shaped like a pickle on its end required more vertical and difficult climbing than going up Mt. Everest. While BASE jumping could not be practiced at Billy's drop zone, one regular customer, Johnny Woody, was a qualified base jumper and was getting ready to jump into a 1,000 foot vertical cave in Mexico in the next few months.

Repacking Parachutes

Another support operation at Billy's drop zone was the repacking of parachutes so that someone else, or the same person, could make another jump. Experienced parachutists often repacked their own parachute, called the main chute.

For $5, they could have Karen Alexander or someone else at Adrenaline Air Sports pack their chute. Repacking of the larger tandem chute that all beginners used cost $10. Karen had learned to pack chutes from Billy and Billy's rigger, Buzz Conner, so she could earn enough money to take more jumps herself to pay for her new hobby. Other people were available to pack chutes if the demand was high enough.

It must be emphasized that each parachute pack had two chutes: the main chute and the backup chute. Only the main chute was repacked by an experienced parachuter or by a trained person, usually for a fee. The backup or reserve chute was packed only by a "rigger" who was certified by the Federal Aviation Administration to do this important, backup safety procedure. A malfunction with the main chute constituted an emergency situation; the parachutist would then cut away that chute, allowing it to drift down by itself, and open the backup chute. The U.S. Parachute Association standards required that only a rigger pack this life-saving, backup chute.

Finance

Billy Cockrell's sales for 2001 were $154,000. This marked a very good year, and an amazing increase in sales from 2001, which had only $90,000. The 2001 sales were the result of approximate 6,000 total jumps, of which about 500 were tandem jumps with beginners.

Human Resources

As briefly mentioned, all people who worked at Adrenaline Air Sports worked part-time. Furthermore, that work was done primarily on weekends when weather conditions made parachuting possible and enjoyable. Billy, as the owner, was the only one who came close to being a full-time employee.

The pilots and some of the instructors worked regularly for Billy. Most of the other employees came out to Adrenaline Air Sports not knowing if they would pay to jump for fun or if they would be paid to jump with others or if they would pack parachutes. Because they loved skydiving, liked Billy, and enjoyed the people at the drop zone, they would instantly switch from being a customer to an employee if asked to do so.

Competition
Skydive Orange

Located in Orange, Virginia, Skydive Orange was probably the largest parachute operation in the state of Virginia, which had seven major drop zones. Skydive Orange, which was about three hours from Billy's Adrenaline Air Sports, was usually open Friday, Saturday, and Sunday during the season. It also was open on Wednesdays from late April to midfall. During the colder months, it was only open on Saturday and Sunday, weather permitting. Some young, committed skydivers were there seven days a week, however, living in school buses that the drop zone rented out.

This drop zone operated two Cessna 182s and a Twin Otter (a twin-engine propeller plane). The Otter took approximately fourteen skydivers as high as 14,000 feet in just twenty minutes. More jumpers in less time generated much higher revenues per hour of operation. While Skydive Orange had this bigger plane, it also had higher prices for beginners and experienced jumpers. Videotapes also cost more.

Skydive Virginia

Somewhat close to Skydive Orange's operation was Skydive Virginia. It was located between Fredericksburg and Charlottesville, near Lake Anna, and was also about three hours from Adrenaline Air Sports. It was somewhat larger than Billy's operation and smaller than Skydive Orange's. It was usually open four days a week during the season: Friday, Saturday, Sunday, and Monday; during the colder months, it was open just on Saturday and Sunday.

Like Skydive Orange, Skydive Virginia had a couple of Cessnas capable of taking up four parachuters at once. This operation also used a King Air twin-engine plane (similar to Skydive Orange's Twin Otter) that could carry twelve jumpers at a time.

Skydive the Point

Skydive the Point was located in West Point, Virginia, forty miles east of Richmond, the state's capital. It was open Saturday and Sunday twelve months a year. For key weekends like Memorial Day, Skydive the Point would be open Thursday through Monday. It used a Twin Otter plane that fit twenty-two jumpers and flew up to 13,500 or 14,500 feet. The cost per jump for parachutists who owned their own gear was $20, or $19 if they were a member of the club. Since Skydive the Point was between Richmond and the greater Virginia Beach coastal area, and south of the Washington, D.C.–northern Virginia area, it drew upon a huge population base.

Skydive Suffolk

Skydive Suffolk was located at the Suffolk Airport, twenty-five miles west of Norfork and near the Atlantic Ocean. Like Skydive the Point, this drop zone was near a number of populated areas, particularly the Norfork–Virginia Beach area. Open Friday, Saturday, and Sunday year-round, Skydive Suffolk used a King Air, which took fourteen jumpers with their own parachute gear up to 14,000 feet for a price of $19. The company also had a Cessna, which took five jumpers up to 10,500 feet for $13.

Strategic Issues Facing Adrenaline Air Sports

A major issue facing Billy and all parachute drop zones was getting first-time jumpers to come back. According to statistics, only 3 percent of all first-time jumpers ever took a second jump even though most first-time jumpers had a favorable experience. The first jump cost $189 at Adrenaline Air Sports, and somewhat more at other drop zones. Furthermore, the cost for jump 2 was also $189, there was a $100 additional charge for ground school before jump 3 is made. By jump 6, the price reduced a little to $179. The ninth jump was thrown in free by Billy. Thus, the cost for the first nine jumps was about $1,582, or $175 per jump. After that, the price fell to $41 if the jumper was taken to 10,000 feet and rented a parachute.

Jared Campbell's first jump was taken in March 2001 and was somewhat typical of many first-time jumpers' experiences.

Jared had once told his friends that he wanted to take a parachute jump someday. His friend and past roommate Chris Sides therefore picked up one of Adrenaline Air Sports's cards from a poster on a bulletin board at Virginia Tech, where Jared was a student, eighty miles from Billy's drop zone. Chris then privately collected about $200 from Jared's friends to pay for one jump. Then on the Saturday after his twenty-second birthday, Chris and several of these "paying" friends told Jared they were taking him to see an air show that would include a flyby by the B2 Stealth Bomber.

Jared became suspicious after being driven for one and a half hours. Finally, when they turned onto a dirt road miles past Roanoke, he began to doubt that they were going to the air show.

His friend Chris said, "I guess by now you've guessed that there is no air show." Jared, while still puzzled, agreed. Chris then said, "The air show is you, Jared. We came here to see you parachute." So Jared received some training and went on a tandem jump with an instructor attached to him.

Most of the friends who had paid for Jared's jump came along to watch. While this meant a lot to him, little did he know that some of them had made informal bets on whether or not he would follow through. Chris chipped in an extra $60 to have the jump videotaped and then gave Jared the tape of his jump—before, during, and after—set to music.

A year after the jump, Jared was still interested in jumping again. However, he lacked funds to do so.

An unusual example of someone taking a second and third jump is former president George Bush senior. During World War II, he was a fighter pilot whose plane was shot down. Fortunately, he was able to parachute to safety and later get picked up by our troops. Amazingly, after being president from 1989 to 1993, at age 71 he took his second parachute jump in

March 1995 with the Golden Knights, the Army elite parachute team. Several years later, Bush did another jump, in 1999, at age 75. Still older is the record setter for age, Edwin Townsend, who parachuted with his own chute in 1987 at age 89.

Another strategic issue was determining how best to market this sport. What type of customer group should Adrenaline Air Sports target? What form of advertising would best reach these daredevils? Should Billy go after other sports enthusiasts, such as winter and summer skiiers, skateboarders, bicyclists, scuba divers, and cavers? Should he pursue more first-time jumpers, who often were young people in college, even though they almost never jumped again? (People had to be at least eighteen to parachute unless the drop zone allowed them to jump younger with their parents' written permission, in which case they had to be at least sixteen. Adrenaline Air Sports did not allow anyone under eighteen to jump at its drop zone.)

Other possible market segments existed. He could target married, childless men and women who were looking for some new excitement and challenge in their lives. Another possible target was men in their mid thirties to fifties facing midlife crises wanting a challenge to prove themselves. These and other groups continually came to mind when Billy considered which customer segments to focus on. Irrespective of the particular target, which marketing media would best reach them still needed to be determined.

A third issue facing Adrenaline Sports was what could be done, if anything, to make the sport more affordable for new skydivers. Once a person had an A license, after twenty or so jumps, the cost dropped considerably, but it was still an expensive sport. Billy's students paid for the first eight jumps, then received the ninth free. One parachutist at Billy's drop zone commented that people who had already taken eight jumps would undoubtedly pay for the ninth one. Billy considered offering a free jump earlier to encourage a person to continue.

At $189, Adrenaline Air Sports's fee for first-time jumpers was a little cheaper than most other drop zones'. And while the first jumps were expensive, Billy made money from these people, who often never jumped again; he claimed that he didn't make money off the veteran jumpers, who owned their own gear and paid just $16 a jump. Perhaps there was some way for Billy to lower the price of the instructors' jumps with new parachutists and increase rates for veteran jumpers. However, if rates were raised too much for the experienced jumpers, they might go elsewhere.

Another strategic issue was whether Billy could make Adrenaline Air Sports his job full-time. While Billy clearly was off to a good start with his drop zone, his location was not as suitable to year-round operations as locations in California or Florida, where mild winters made this possible. Still, some of the mid-Atlantic drop zones like Skydive Virginia were full-time businesses for the owners, even if they were open just on weekends during cold months.

What Billy needed to do was get more customers to come to his drop zone, which was beautiful when viewed from the air, during good-weather periods. Unfortunately, Billy had two small planes, Cessna 182s, which could only take up four jumpers at a time. Billy also lacked enough parachutes to rent if he were to get more customers during prime weekends and months. Finally, his location was far away from major metropolitan areas, such as Richmond, northern Virginia, and the Tidewater–Virginia Beach area. And while the Greensboro area of North Carolina was only eighty miles away, larger North Carolina cities like Durham, Raleigh, Winston-Salem, and Charlotte were further.

A final issue was safety. For most people, the thought of "jumping out of a perfectly good airplane," as military pilots like to put it, sends chills down their spine. The sport was, out of necessity, very safety conscious, but with speeds exceeding 120 miles an hour and no safety device resembling a seat belt, accidents were often fatal. Most nonjumpers felt parachuting was extremely dangerous. The type of people who were attracted to the sport were often outdoor types oriented to extreme sports. Jim Crouch, the safety and training coordinator of the U.S. Parachute Association, has noted that jumpers are "lacking in emergency canopy procedures, which causes accidents." He added that parachutists should not "downsize too quickly" to smaller-sized, higher-performance parachutes as this also increases risk.

Overall, expert opinion and industry statistics showed that skydiving was a safe, wholesome sport that had very loyal customers enjoying the sport.

General Aviation: an Industry Note

3

This case was prepared by Harold Dyck and Sue Greenfeld, California State University, San Bernardino.

General aviation is all "civil aviation activity except that of scheduled air carriers. This includes business transportation, air charter, air taxis, personal and recreational flying, emergency medical evacuation, agricultural flying, traffic and aerial observation, and flight training." The Federal Aviation Administration (FAA) counted 192,414 general aviation (GA) aircraft in the United States in 1997 and 612,298 active pilots in 1998. These pilots include student, recreational, private, commercial, airline-transport, helicopter, glider, and lighter-than-air ones. The FAA projects 231,000 active GA aircraft for 2011. Most GA aircraft are for personal use (34.8%); other uses are instructional (17.9%), business (10.8%), and corporate (10.4%) (**http://generalaviation.org/pages/faq.shtml,** January 22, 2001).

General aviation is part of the 1998–2002 National Plan of Integrated Airport Systems (NPIAS), which is "submitted to Congress. . . . The plan identifies 3,344 existing airports that are significant to national air transportation and contains estimates that $35.1 billion in infrastructure development is eligible for Federal aid . . . to meet the needs of all segments of civil aviation" (**www.faa.gov/arp/410home.htm,** January 26, 2001). There are 15,000 non-NPIAS "low activity landing areas," including private airstrips away from populated areas.

While GA pilots are allowed to land at large airports such as LAX or La Guardia, they rarely do. Of the 3,344 airports in the NPIAS, only twenty-nine are identified as "large hubs" that concentrate on airline passengers and freight operations. These hubs accounted for 67.3% of all passenger enplanments in 1998, but only 1.3% of active GA aircraft. Only five of them (Salt Lake City, Las Vegas, Honolulu, Miami, and Phoenix) have a significant number (averaging 343) of GA aircraft. The other twenty-four have fewer than thirty-four based aircraft each (**www.faa.gov/arp/410home.htm,** January 26, 2001).

Therefore, 69% of all active aircraft are based either at the 334 "reliever" airports or the 2,472 GA airports. Reliever airports are located in major metropolitan areas and allow pilots to avoid congested hub airports. They average 181 aircraft each, accounting for 32% of U.S. aircraft. Of the $35.1 billion in NPIAS development monies, reliever airports are allocated 7%, or $7.35 million each. GA airports are located in "communities that do not receive scheduled commercial service" and have "at least 10 locally owned aircraft." These GA airports receive 11% of the NPIAS development monies, or $1.56 million each (**www.faa.gov/arp/410home.htm,** January 26, 2001).

This case is presented as the basis for educational discussion rather than to illustrate either effective or ineffective handling of an administrative situation. Special appreciation is given to Ilia Adami for her research assistance. Reprinted by permission of the authors.

Those Who Fly

To become a pilot in the United States, a person must be at least sixteen years old, be in good health, and read, speak, and understand English. In 1998, there were around 618,000 certified pilots, including almost 98,000 student pilots, 247,000 private pilots, 122,000 commercial pilots, and 134,000 airline transport pilots (**http://www.api.faa.gov/airmen/toc.htm,** March 20, 2001, Table 1). For each type of certificate, a candidate must pass proficiency examinations as well as possess sufficient aeronautical experience.

Student pilots must pass a so-called Class III biannual medical exam given by an FAA-designated physician. This medical clearance lasts for three years for individuals under forty years and two years for those over forty. Students fly with their instructors until their instructors sign them off for their first solo fight usually after about ten to twelve hours of instruction. A student pilot earns his or her private-pilot's certificate with a minimum of thirty-five or forty hours, a written exam, and a check ride with an examiner. To earn a private-pilot's license, a person can expect to spend between $2,500 and $4,000. This includes plane rental at $45 to $60 per hour, an instructor's fee of $15 to $20 per hour, and $150 for ground-school instruction.

Commercial pilots can "fly for hire." They must be at least eighteen years old, should have an instrument rating, must hold a Class II annual medical certificate, must have at least 250 hours of flying time, and must pass a written exam and a check ride with an examiner. Airline-transport pilots can work for the major airlines, must be at least twenty-three years old, are required to log 1,500 hours of flight time, and must hold a Class I semiannual medical certificate, in addition to having to pass more stringent proficiency exams.

Pluses and Minuses of General Aviation Airports

Why would a community want a GA airport? GA airports provide a number of benefits and services to a community. Activities associated with GA airports include agriculture, firefighting, law enforcement, business, cargo, charter, corporate, disaster relief, glider, medical emergency, military, parachute, recreational flying, search and rescue, tourism, training, and ultralights (California Department of Transportation [DOT], 1998). The California DOT differentiates business from corporate activity in this way: business activity involves an individual who flies out of an airport for business without compensation to the pilot, while a corporate activity involves compensating a professional pilot who flies an aircraft owned or leased by the company.

In describing the economic impact of GA on the U.S. economy, Zuelsdorf and McClellan estimated that GA provided 638,000 jobs in 1998. These jobs include those directly related to GA as well as jobs that are indirectly related, such as restaurant workers at airports. They also estimated the total GA economic impact in the United States to be $64.5 billion in 1998, of which $21.8 billion was generated through GA airports (**http://api.hq.faa.gov/conference/procdoc2000/zuelsdor.pdf,** June 20, 2001).

On the other hand, the disadvantages of an airport in a community include noise, safety, air pollution, lower property values, and loss of tax revenue for the next-best use of the land. These affect a community's quality of life and excessive noise can affect children's learning. A study by Gary Evans and Lorraine Maxwell at Cornell University (1997) found that "children whose schools were affected by aircraft noise did not learn to read as well as those who were in quiet schools. The researchers compared children in a noisy school (in the flight path of a major international airport) with similar students in a quiet school and found that children in the noisy school had difficulty acquiring speech recognition skills, impacting on the ability to learn to read" (**http://www. lhh.org/noise/children/learning.htm,** May 7, 2001).

Airports also have certain inherent risks. Many airport neighbors have concerns about aircraft accidents, especially injuries and deaths to individuals on the ground. Table 1 shows data from the National Transportation Safety Board (NTSB) on GA accidents and fatalities from 1982 to 2000. The difference between total and onboard fatalities represents individuals killed on the ground by GA aircraft.

In terms of air pollution, the GA industry has made some movement towards a cleaner environment. For example, small GA aircraft now use low-lead gasoline. Lead has been identified as the second leading hazardous substance emitted into the environment. Lead poisoning can damage the central nervous system, the immune system, and kidneys (**http://www.atsdr.cdc.gov/cxcx3.html,** May 23, 2001). Another example of increased sensitivity to

TABLE 1

U.S. General Aviation Accidents, Fatalities, and Rates, 1982–2000

Year	Accidents		Fatalities		Flight Hours	Accidents Per 100,000 Flight Hours	
	All	Fatal	Total	Aboard		All	Fatal
1982	3,233	591	1,187	1,170	29,640,000	10.90	1.99
1983	3,077	556	1,069	1,062	28,673,000	10.73	1.94
1984	3,017	545	1,042	1,021	29,099,000	10.36	1.87
1985	2,739	498	956	945	28,322,000	9.66	1.75
1986	2,582	474	967	879	27,073,000	9.54	1.75
1987	2,495	447	838	823	26,972,000	9.25	1.65
1988	2,385	460	800	792	27,446,000	8.69	1.68
1989	2,232	431	768	765	27,920,000	7.98	1.53
1990	2,215	443	767	762	28,510,000	7.77	1.55
1991	2,175	433	786	772	27,678,000	7.85	1.56
1992	2,073	446	857	855	24,780,000	8.36	1.80
1993	2,039	398	736	732	22,796,000	8.94	1.74
1994	1,994	403	725	718	22,235,000	8.96	1.80
1995	2,053	412	734	727	24,906,000	8.23	1.64
1996	1,909	360	632	615	24,881,000	7.67	1.45
1997	1,851	352	641	635	25,464,000	7.27	1.38
1998	1,909	368	631	625	25,349,000	7.53	1.45
1999	1,913	342	630	622	29,496,000	6.49	1.16
2000	1,835	341	592	582	30,800,000	5.96	1.11

Notes: Data are preliminary for 2000. Flight hours are preliminary for 1999. Flight hours are estimated by the Federal Aviation Administration. Since April, 1995, the NTSB has been required by law to investigate all public-use accidents. The effect upon the number of general-aviation accidents has been an increase of about 1.75%.

Source: **http://www.ntsb.gov/aviation/Table10.htm,** May 7, 2001.

pollutants emitted into the air is the preflight safety test. Pilots are expected to inspect their fuel levels on the ground and drain fuel into a small gauge to check for water in the tanks. Water in the tanks could lead to carburetor ice, endangering the pilot and passengers if the engine should fail. A negative consequence of this safety test is the evaporation of discarded fuel, resulting in the pollutants benzene and 1,3-butadiene. However, pilots are now beginning to put this drained fuel back into the tanks.

According to the Aircraft Owners and Pilots Association (AOPA), "oftentimes property values are lower for residential areas surrounding an operating airport" (p. 8). The airport's master plan could affect development in the area. Government agencies may enforce zoning regulations. Building codes may require soundproofing for structures near airports. Real estate disclosures may be required to inform potential buyers of these land-use controls.

Also, a community-owned airport may reduce the tax base. This shows up as "in-lieu" property tax in the airport's accounting records, is an opportunity cost for the next-best use of the land, and can make the GA airport appear as a loss to the city. Other economic users, including developers and cities in search of new park land, have been increasing the pressure to close GA airports. Two recent examples include Meigs Field in Chicago and, in California, Santa

Monica's airport. Both of these GA airports are located in densely populated areas with high property values. Thus, a balanced approach would take into account GA's positive economic effects and the value of the next-best alternative.

Legislation Affecting General Aviation Airports

In the early days, aviation was largely unregulated. The passage of the Air Commerce Act of 1926 created the Department of Commerce Aeronautical Division to enforce Civil Air Regulations, the precursor of the Federal Aviation Regulations (FARs). The federal government became responsible for building airports, creating federal airways to separate aircraft, and testing pilots for aeronautical knowledge and physical capabilities for flying (**http://avstop.com/ news/ac.html,** June 20, 2001). In 1938, the federal government created the Civil Aeronautics Authority (CAA), which existed until 1958, when Congress passed the Federal Aviation Act and transferred administration and enforcement to the Federal Aviation Agency, later called the Federal Aviation Administration (FAA).

Today, in the twenty-first century, airways and pilots are highly regulated. For example, in the congested area around Los Angeles International Airport (LAX), there are special flight rules that a pilot must follow regarding the shoreline. The rules say the pilot must be flying at a specific altitude, airspeed, and direction, must be on a special radio frequency and transponder code, and must have a special chart in the aircraft. Special flight rules may also apply above unpopulated areas, such as the Grand Canyon. To help preserve the natural beauty and provide a true wilderness experience, the FAA limits flight over the Grand Canyon to narrow air corridors at precise altitudes. Except in an emergency, no aircraft may fly below the rim of the canyon.

The most recent major federal legislation, passed in 2000, is the Aviation Investment and Reform Act for the 21st Century, known as AIR-21. While this five-year authorization of funds is designed to address the issues of airport capacity, technological updates of air-traffic control, airline competition, and aviation safety, it also affects GA. For small airports, AIR-21 triples the funding from $500,000 to $1.5 million per year, provides them with entitle-

ment money based on their needs (up to $200,000 per year), and provides incentives to realize the benefits of air-traffic-control services. Finally, AIR-21 "creates a new funding program to help small underserved airports market and promote their air service" (**http://www.house.gov/transportation/press/ air21sum2.html,** July 3, 2001).

The Future of General Aviation

Today, GA pilots have computerized flight-management information systems with satellite-based GPS moving maps, sophisticated flight-planning software linked to real-time weather services through the Internet, and onboard radar storm displays. This is a far cry from 1927, when Charles Lindbergh flew across the Atlantic with "No parachute, no radio, no brakes, not even a forward-facing window (a small periscope would do)" (**http://www.acepilots.com/ lindbergh.html,** July 5, 2001). Despite the challenges of regulation, pollution, noise, increasing gas prices and insurance rates, and closing airports, the General Aviation Manufacturers Association forecasts increases through 2010 in the numbers of aircraft, pilots, flight hours, and fuel use, with only the number of hours per pilot decreasing:

	1999	2010	C (%)
Aircraft	219,500	229,100	4.4
Pilots	640,100	810,000	26.5
Flight Hours	31,800,000	38,100,000	19.8
Fuel (mil. gal.)	1,313	2,133	62.5
Hours per Pilot	49.7	47.0	−5.3

Source: General Aviation Manufacturers Association (GAMA), *General Aviation 2000 Statistical Databook* (Washington, D.C.: GAMA, 2000).

In addition, a wealth of information concerning GA and its future is available on the Web at the following addresses:

> **http://www.aopa.org/** AOPA (Airplane Owners and Pilots Association)

http://www.generalaviation.org/ GAMA (General Aviation Manufacturers Association

http://www.faa.gov/ FAA (Federal Aviation Administration)

http://www.nata-online.org/ NATA (National Air Transportation Association)

http://www.nbaa.org/ NBAA (National Business Aircraft Association)

Impact of the 9/11 Tragedy on General Aviation

Airport closures Numerous airports shut down nationwide, including the Redlands Municipal Airport for two weeks.

Airspace changes Both the FAA and the military upgraded their efforts to create and enforce temporary flight restrictions such as those protecting the president and vice president of the United States and nuclear reactors and other facilities of national importance.

Legislation Legislators passed a flurry of new legislation, including:

A massive victim's compensation and airline bailout bill

A major aviation and transportation security act affecting flight schools with increased screening of flight-instruction candidates and enhanced airspace restrictions

A bill making airport-security personnel employees of the federal government

The GA Industry Reparation Act of 2001 (Lobbyists claimed that small GA businesses were as adversely affected by the tragedy as the airlines.)

Industry forecasts The Airplane Owners and Pilots Association predicts a gradual increase in the number of student pilots over the next five years, but the FAA forecasts 15,000 fewer student pilots.

References

Aircraft Owners and Pilots Association (AOPA) (1999). *Airports, A Valuable Community Resource: A Guide to Obtaining Community Support for Your Local Airport.* Frederick, MD: AOPA.

California Department of Transportation (1998). *The California Aviation System: 1998 Inventory Element.*

Eckrose, Roy A., and William H. Green (1988). *How to Assure the Future of Your Airport.* Madison, WI: Ecrose/Green Associates.

Evans, G. W., and L. Maxwell (1997). Environment and Behavior, 29, Fay, T. W., Noise and health. New York, NY: The New York Academy of Medicine, in **http://www.lhh.org/noise/children/learning.htm,** May 7, 2001.

FAR/AIM 2001: Federal Aviation Regulations/Aeronautical Information Manual. Newcastle, WA: Aviation Supplies and Academics, Inc., 2000.

General Aviation Manufacturers Association (GAMA) (2000). *General Aviation 2000 Statistical Databook.* Washington, D.C.: GAMA.

Zuelsdorf, Robert J., and Eric B. McClellan "The Economic Impact of Civil Aviation on the U.S. Economy—2000," **http://api.hq.faa.gov/conference/procdoc2000/zuelsdor.pdf,** Wilbur Smith Associates, June 20, 2001.

http://generalaviation.org/pages/faq.shtml, January 22, 2001.

http://www.acepilots.com/lindbergh.html, July 5, 2001.

http://www.atsdr.cdc.gov/cxcx3.html, May 22, 2001.

http://www.api.faa.gov/airmen/toc.htm, March 20, 2001, Table 1.

http://www.faa.gov/arp/410home.htm, January 26, 2001.

http://www.house.gov/transportation/press/air21sum2.html, July 3, 2001.

http://www.ntsb.gov/aviation/Table10.htm, May 7, 2001.

Nomani, Asra Q., and Nancy Keates (1999), "A Tragedy Puts Small Planes in the Spotlight," *Wall Street Journal,* July 19, B1, B4.

Wells, Alexander T. (1996). *Airport Planning & Management.* 3d ed. New York: McGraw-Hill.

4 Redlands Municipal Airport

This case was prepared by Sue Greenfeld and Harold Dyck, California State University, San Bernardino.

Introduction and Background

Ron Mutter, public works director for the city of Redlands, reflects about broadening public use of the Redlands Municipal Airport. Acquired in 1962, the airport never quite lived up to expectations. While selling fuel and providing flight instruction, the airport did not succeed in establishing air ambulance services or charter flights or in enticing a Cessna pilot center to locate at the airport (Redlands City Council Minutes, 1962). However, the new mayor, Patricia (Pat) Gilbreath, a CPA-firm partner and pilot, sees the potential of the airport to be more economically viable and is working with Ron, the city council, and the city airport advisory board to encourage this to happen. In addition, an entrepreneur has approached the city with a three-phase plan to add new facilities to the airport.

Located in San Bernardino County, California, the 194-acre Redlands Municipal Airport is about sixty miles east of Los Angeles, four miles northeast of charming downtown Redlands, and three miles north of Interstate 10. The airport serves single- and small twin-engine general-aviation aircraft weighing less than 12,500 pounds. A few ultralights—hang gliders with motors—are also based at the airport. The air-port has no tower, but is served by an automated twenty-four-hour "unicom" radio frequency for advising pilots of landing conditions and allowing pilots to make position reports. This type of airport usually does not have a precision-instrument approach, but it recently acquired a geographic position system (GPS). The Redlands Municipal Airport bases 9%, or around 204 airplanes, of the county's 2,254 registered aircraft, is one of the county's eighteen paved airports, and is one of California's 257 airports (California Department of Transportation, 1998). In California, there are thirty-three primary and commercial-service airports and 176 reliever and general-aviation airports.

As city officials think about the airport, they wonder the following. Was purchasing the airport beneficial to the city of Redlands? Is the airport capable of generating enough resources to become self-supporting? Should the city be doing more to entice new business and/or pilots to the airport? Whose job is it to promote the airport? Are there important safety issues, such as allowing ultralights to land at the airport? Is the land surrounding the airport used to its potential? Is the airport capable of growing beyond the 204 aircraft now based there? How can the city predict changes in the demand for airport services? To what extent should the city consider the impact of nearby airports? And finally, how should the city balance the competing interests of the various public and private stakeholders?

City of Redlands

Founded in 1888, the city of Redlands sprang up around Assistencia Mission de San Gabriel, an outpost of Los Angeles's San Gabriel mission about fifty-five miles west of Redlands. According to "Redlands History" (**http://www.redlands-aor.com/history.htm,** May 8, 2000), Redlands was named for the color of its adobe soil. Most of the early settlers were from the Chicago area, including a few who were quite wealthy. The San Bernardino Mountains to the north provide a picturesque backdrop to the city, which flourished as a result of a burgeoning citrus industry until World War II—and then everything changed. The creation of a nearby army air corps depot (later Norton U.S. Air Force Base) led to a building boom.

In 1978, county Proposition R was passed to limit growth. Today, Redlands is known for its balanced approach to growth and its preservation of citrus acreage, which local residents refer to as the emerald necklace. This alludes to the dark-green citrus leaves and open-space areas that, when viewed from the air, look like emeralds encircling the city. The population in 1999 was 65,500 and has been fairly stable for the last ten years (**http://www.redlands-aor.com/main .htm,** May 8, 2000).

Exhibit 1 shows the relationships among the airport, the public works department of Redlands, and the city council. The citizens of Redlands elect all five city council members. The mayor is selected from the five by a vote of the city council. The city council appoints seven members to an airport advisory board. These nonpaid members are mostly pilots who meet monthly to discuss issues associated with the airport. According to the Redlands's web site, the

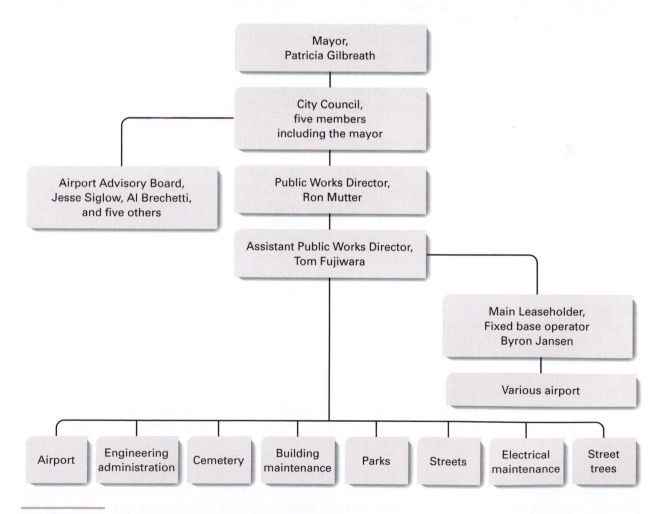

EXHIBIT 1

City Organizational Chart for Redlands Municipal Airport

airport advisory board shall have the power and duty to act in an advisory capacity to the city council in all matters pertaining to the administration, operation, development, improvement, and maintenance of the Redlands Municipal Airport (**http://www.alphais .com/redlands/3006.html#airport,** May 20, 2000). The assistant director and public works director serve as ex-officio members of this board.

History of the Airport

The history of the Redlands Airport can be divided into two periods. From 1945 to 1962 the airport was privately held, and from 1962 to the present it has been owned by the city of Redlands. In 1945, pilot Robert Kanaga, a returning U.S. Army Air Corps veteran of World War II, started laying plans for the Redlands Airport with the financial assistance of a Redlands optometrist, Austin Welch. The bulk of the land was leased from San Bernardino County for ten years at $150 a year. Kanaga was granted permission from the Civil Aeronautics Administration (the forerunner of the FAA) to operate an air agency facility. This business included training pilots, selling new Cessna aircrafts and repair.

When Kanaga was called back to active duty for the Korean War by the U.S. Air Force (formerly the U.S. Army Air Corps) in 1952, the airport was sold to the Southern California Turkey Growers Association, which used the hangar for turkey processing.

In 1955, Roy Haskins and Al Theos bought the airport and asked for help from their family members. . . . Denny Haskins started Red Aero Aviation, an aircraft-maintenance operation.

The Haskins family lengthened the runway twice, once in 1958 and again, in 1959, to the current length of 4,500 feet. Runway lights and fourteen **shade** hangars were also added. The Haskins set up a coffee shop, "but never made money," says Denny Haskins. Roy Haskins made an offer to sell the runway to the city of Redlands in October 1962 to enable the city to apply for federal-aid grants: city ownership of the airport was a prerequisite for obtaining funds for airport development. "It was free federal money," says Denny Haskins.

In 1964, the Redlands City Council authorized an FAA-recommended purchase of about ten acres of property adjoining the runway. A fire truck was added in 1965. Matching funds from the FAA and California State Aeronautics Division helped fund drainage, fencing, underground telephone lines, and other capital improvements in the 1960s. In 1967 and 1968, the city was engaged in promising talks with Golden West Airlines about offering flights, but these did not work out. In 1970, the airport added T-hangars (so-called because of the practice of alternating airplanes backwards and forwards in a long row).

The city continued to get funds from federal and state sources in the decades to follow. These funds were used for flood control, land acquisition, runway improvements, and a runway safety area, among other items. In 1985, a visual approach slope indicator was installed on Runway 8, the runway used for landings to the east. Additional improvements included security fencing and lighting, taxiway reconstruction, and paving an adjacent area for airplane tiedowns.

In order to receive federal and state funding, the city commissioned master plans for the airport in 1962, 1980, and 1991. The last plan, completed in November 1993 and costing $44,000, was financed in part by a grant from the U.S. Department of Transportation (DOT) and the FAA.

When the economic recession of the early 1990s hit California a year after the rest of the nation, the Redlands Airport was affected. Furthermore, nearby Norton U.S. Air Force base was slated for closure in 1994, which added to the uncertainty of the economic climate. Civic leaders did not know the extent to which a base closure would harm the local communities, but 4,250 military and 2,133 civilian jobs were expected to be lost. These figures did not include any indirect losses.

In 1996, the Redlands City Chamber of Commerce helped sponsor the fiftieth anniversary of the establishment of the Redlands Airport. Unfortunately, the June weekend selected for the air show was unseasonably warm; temperatures broke 100 degrees Fahrenheit, and the event lost over $10,000 for the Chamber.

Reflecting on the current situation, Ron Mutter states that in 1991, the Redlands Airport received almost $1,000,000 to create a ramp area to "tie down" airplanes adjacent to the taxiway, but, with the downturn of the economy, many pilots could no longer "afford their expensive toys. . . . Planes were sold, and the number of aircraft based in Redlands went down as much as 10%. . . . Right now we are renting only fifteen to twenty tiedowns out of 100, [but] all our hangars are rented out. We even have a waiting list. All we have available is outside tiedown spaces."

Another concern—mentioned by airport advisory-board members Jesse Siglow and Al Brechetti—revolves around the landing of ultralights at the airport. The Federal Aviation Regulations (FARs) define ultralights as powered or unpowered vehicles that are used in the air for recreational purposes by a single person and that do not need aircraft registration or an airworthiness certificate. The powered ultralights have less than five gallons of fuel and fly at speeds below fifty-five knots. The pilot does not need a license, medical certificate, or biennial flight review as would a general-aviation pilot. Ultralights may only be flown during daylight hours and never over populated areas (U.S. DOT, 1999). Due to the slow speed of ultralights, other pilots perceive them as a hazard. While there is some sentiment against allowing ultralights to be based at the airport, the FAA says they must be allowed to land, and some say that basing more ultralights at Redlands would benefit the airport by increasing the demand for tiedown space and services.

Existing Facilities

As visitors approach the airport, they pass by orange groves and a few scattered houses. They then see the airport's beacon light before parking outside the small terminal building (1,000 sq. ft.). This building has a lounge area with a few vending machines, restrooms, an office, and a counter, where a few pilot supplies are sold. The airport has no cafe or restaurant, but visitors can sit outside in the shade at picnic tables and watch planes take off and land on the east-west runway. Occasionally, a plane or two may taxi up to the fuel island. An "itinerant" or "transient" (i.e., a plane based at another airport) may tie down in the spaces provided for that purpose. The airport has 122 hangars, 349 outdoor tiedown spaces, and 185 additional spaces for transient planes. Hangars rent in the neighborhood of $250 per month.

In terms of future development, the south side of the airport has the most desirable terrain. Gil Brown and his partner, George Saliba, have petitioned the city to allow them to build sixteen new T-hangars. These would be larger than the existing hangars, would run between 1,300 and 1,600 square feet, have electric doors, and rent for around $300 per month. Brown and Saliba call their company Coyote Aviation and have a list of twenty-two people who want to buy or rent these hangars. The north side of the airport borders the Santa Ana Wash, which is part of a hundred-year floodplain. This is "difficult terrain with numerous slope changes, poor drainage and poor quality soil" (Coffman Associates, Inc., 1993).

Most of the airport's surrounding terrain is owned by the city, so municipal codes regulate or place restrictions on the height of buildings in the vicinity of plane takeoff and landing. New residential developments in the "airport influence area" are required to include an "avigation" easement: the homeowner must disclose to potential buyers the fact that the area has aircraft flights and/or noise.

Airport Businesses

Currently, one major leaseholder and three other fixed-base operators (FBOs) are leasing airport property from the city. The lease allows them to operate a private business at the airport as long it is related to the aviation industry. They can build hangars and rent those hangars out. They can operate offices that handle everything from flight training to selling airplane parts and avionics. They can run maintenance facilities for aircraft, operate emergency medical flight response facilities, and so forth.

The fifty-year leases are now about twenty years old, with three ten-year renewable options. The rates are very favorable to the leaseholders because the city wanted to attract businesses to develop the airport and generate revenue. In hindsight, says Mutter, there should have been other clauses of escalation factors (e.g., cost of living).

Redlands Municipal Airport houses sixteen organizations. Redlands Aviation holds the master lease, currently owned by the Jansen family: Byron and his father, mother, and two brothers. Byron Jansen's job is to open up the public lobby, rent out hangars and tiedown spaces, and sell fuel. With assistance, he staffs the lobby 8 a.m. to 5 p.m., Monday through Friday. Redlands Aviation feels the city is not compensating their company adequately for keeping the public lobby open.

The largest organization at the airport is Mission Aviation Fellowship (MAF), with ninety employees. MAF set up operations in Redlands in 1980 and has a fleet of seventy-five aircraft on forty-one bases flying in remote and isolated regions of twenty countries. Their literature describes their organization this way: "Serving God and responding to human needs since 1945, MAF US spans the globe to serve the needy with aviation and telecommunications service" (**http://www.maf.org/01_who.we.are/1-3who.html,** July 15, 1999). Previously, the technical support (flight and maintenance) was at Ramona, California, while administration was based one hundred miles away, in Fullerton, California.

According to Denny Hoekstra, director of aviation for MAF, the reason MAF selected Redlands as its main base was to merge the technical support with administration. "After doing a study and a matrix . . . , it was felt that Redlands was the best place to come to. Because of the local mountains here, we do a lot of mountain flying and training of our pilots . . . they go into third-world countries, [which] involves mountain flying, landing on unimproved airstrips on the sides of mountains, dirt strips with slope on them (Redlands' runway has a 3% slope). Some of them have peculiar approaches and some of them have illusions. The San Bernardino Mountains around here give us excellent opportunities for training."

Other businesses at the airport include Mercy Medical Airlift, a nonprofit organization whose mission is to "facilitate a charitable means of long distance medical air transport for all medically indigent,

low-income and financially vulnerable patients" (**http://www.mercymedical.org,** July 28, 2000). Another business is M.I. Air Corp., run by Masa and Marjo Mitsutomi. This organization specializes in providing flight training for airplane and helicopter pilots, especially students coming from Japan. Many international students train in the United States because it can cost three times or more to fly in their home countries. Exhibit 2 provides a complete list of businesses at the airport. Many of these are sole proprietorships.

Forecasting and Planning Issues Associated with the Airport

To receive federal funds for airport development and improvement, a city must submit a master plan. Redlands commissioned plans in 1962, 1980, and 1991. After commissioning the last plan, the city established the Planning Advisory Committee (PAC), which provided information to the airport consultants, Coffman Associates. The PAC members included "representatives of the City of Redlands, San Bernardino County, the Southern California Association of Government, the State of California, the FAA

EXHIBIT 2

Organizations Operating at Redlands Municipal Airport

Aero Tech Academy
  Flight training & aircraft rental

Aerodynamics, Inc.
  Fuel service & hangar rental

The Book Craftsman
  Custom binding, books/Bible restoration

Inland Aviation
  Aircraft maintenance & inspections

Mercy Medical Airlift
  Air medical transportation

Mission Aviation Fellowship
  Missionary pilot training

Redlands Aviation Corp.
  Aircraft maintenance & repair, annual inspections, flight training, aircraft rental, fuel, hangar & tiedown rentals

Redlands Propeller Service
  Aircraft maintenance & repair

Aerodrome Plane Rental & Flight Training
  Flight training & aircraft rental

Auto Pilot West, Inc.
  Aircraft electronics & avionics

City of Redlands
  Tiedown rental

Instrument Flight Simulation
  Flight training

M.I. Air Corp.
  Aircraft maintenance, repair, flight training & aircraft rental

Red Aero Aviation
  Aircraft maintenance & repair

Redlands Hangar Owners Association
  Hangar rental

Suhay Aircraft Co.
  Aircraft maintenance, repair, & annual inspections

and various aviation personnel, business and community leadership" (Coffman Associates, Inc., 1993). The consultants—located in Kansas City, Missouri, and Phoenix, Arizona—produced the 165-page report in November 1993.

The master plan covers facilities, socioeconomic characteristics (i.e., population, employment, and climate), aviation-demand forecasts, capacity analysis and facility requirements, development alternatives, environmental evaluation, airspace and land-use plans, and a financial program. The forecasts predict activity for the airport up through the year 2015. Among the tables and exhibits in the master plan is one showing the history of aircraft activity (see Exhibit 3).

The purpose of forecasting demand is to assist in planning for facilities, budgeting, and alternative development actions. The master plan provides ten identifying forecasts of the number of aircraft to be based at the Redlands Municipal Airport (see Exhibit 4). The first forecast shown is a trend line, which is a regression on the variable time. The next three forecasts (methods 2–4) are linear regressions, using expected city, county, and state population growth to predict the number of aircraft. The next two forecasts (methods 5–6) use population projections of 2.6% growth for the county and 1.1% for the state and assume a constant number of aircraft per capita and historical population growth. Methods 7 and 8 use a ratio of aircraft based at Redlands Municipal Airport in comparison to other markets, San Bernardino County and California. Methods 9 and 10 are used by two governmental agencies, the California Department of Transportation (CalTrans) and Southern California Association of Governments (SCAG). Using these methods of calculation, aircraft usage at the Redlands Municipal Airport for the year 2000 was

EXHIBIT 3

History of Aircraft Activity

	Based Aircraft				Operations			
Year	Single Engine	Multi-engine	Heli-copters	Total	Local	Itinerant	Air Taxi	Total
1961	44	1	3	48	3,600	3,600	0	7,200
1962	48	0	0	48	3,600	3,600	0	7,200
1963	48	0	0	48	6,000	4,000	0	10,000
1964	46	3	0	49	6,000	7,000	0	13,000
1965	59	3	0	62	6,000	7,000	0	13,000
1966	62	6	0	68	11,000	13,000	0	24,000
1967	60	6	0	66	11,000	12,000	0	23,000
1968	90	6	0	96	11,000	12,000	0	23,000
1970	80	6	0	86	30,000	6,000	0	36,000
1971	82	5	0	87	30,000	6,000	0	36,000
1975	95	5	0	100	24,150	3,000	0	27,150
1977	126	6	0	132	25,200	3,100	0	28,300
1984	N/A	N/A	N/A	320	N/A	N/A	N/A	N/A
1985	192	26	0	218	26,000	26,000	240	52,240
1986	204	26	0	230	26,000	26,000	240	52,240
1987	190	24	0	214	24,000	24,000	240	48,240
1988	190	24	0	214	24,000	24,000	240	48,240
1989	190	24	0	214	24,500	24,000	300	48,800
1990	200	30	0	230	33,600	31,200	300	65,100
1991	200	30	0	230	33,000	32,000	300	65,300

EXHIBIT 4

Ten Forecasts for the Number of Aircraft Based at Redlands Airport

Methods/Year	1995	2000	2005	2010	2015
Trend line	260	293	326	358	391
Pop. Regression, Redlands	294	325	357	388	419
Pop. Regression, San Bernardino County	301	345	388	431	497
Pop. Regression, CA	258	287	313	339	366
Per-capita based Aircraft, San Bernardino	239	267	295	323	366
Per-capita based Aircraft, CA	239	254	267	280	294
Market share, San Bernardino	238	247	256	267	274
Market share, CA	254	259	264	269	274
CalTrans	262	275	285	297	309
SCAG	298	325	352	378	405

Source: Coffman Associates, Inc. (1993).

estimated at between 247 and 345. By 1999, however, only about 230 aircraft were based at the airport.

In reviewing these forecasts, a statistician might ask the following questions: "Why were these ten forecasts so far off the mark? Why did no forecast include income as a variable? Or interest rates? Or some other aspect of the U.S. economy? Why were all the estimates assuming growth? And what about the supply of hangars? Could owners of airplanes prefer hangars that protect the airplane over tiedowns that leave the plane exposed to the elements? What about other competing airports in the vicinity?" Within twenty-five miles of the Redlands Airport, there are seven general-aviation airports: Flabob, Riverside, Rialto, Hesperia, Big Bear, Banning, and San Bernardino International (formerly, Norton U.S. Air Force Base).

The Relationship Between the Airport and the City of Redlands

As owner of the airport, the city is responsible for the runway, taxiway, and electrical beacon. The city grades the shoulders, paints markings on the runway, and keeps the weeds down. In addition, the city police patrol the premises, and city firefighters and paramedics respond to any emergency, such as when a pilot makes a wheel-up landing (when the pilot forgets to put the landing gear down).

Mayor Pat Gilbreath says, "One of the problems we have as a municipality is that Redlands is 'full service . . .' and part of that full service is operating parts of it . . . [without] good business sense. The airport is a classic case of that. . . . We can't let the airport get into terrible shape, and so it becomes an obligation of the General Fund." She notes that dollars spent by businesses at the airport have a multiplier effect on the city and believes that a number of intangibles help the airport be an economic generator. For example, she says, because she is a CPA, some of her clients will fly into Redlands to meet with her and she occasionally will fly out to meet them.

Whose job is it to create businesses at the airport, she wonders, noting that up to this point, the responsibility has been "entrepreneurial." "If somebody has an idea, they can bring it to the city council. . . . We need a restaurant, we need hangars . . . but the city should not really be running the airport, and that is why we are using these lease arrangements. It is like a franchise. We own it, but somebody else runs it."

Leaseholder Byron Jansen of Redlands Aviation remarks, "Our FBO is in sort of a unique position being that we have a public lobby. A lot of times we are thought of as running the Redlands Airport and we have a burden not to be seen that way. This is not our airport. We are not running this airport. We are leasing this building back to the city as a public lobby, but our business is simply to rent hangars and tiedowns and to sell some fuel, to enjoy flying our own airplanes, and we are not really very enthusiastic about politics or that end of things." Redlands Aviation's old lease expired in 1993, putting the arrangement with the city on a month-to-month basis. If a new lease is not negotiated, the lobby will close.

For many years, airport revenues closely matched expenses. The city deliberately kept expenses down so that they would not exceed revenues. In 1978, California passed Proposition 13, which tended to lock in property taxes and force cities to find other sources of revenue. In response to this, in 1989 the city drafted a new financial package, which created an in-lieu $40,000 property tax charged against airport revenues. This accounts for the opportunity cost of lost taxes from the next-best use of the land. Ron Mutter is expected to recover this lost tax revenue for the city. However, the revenues generated by the leases are fixed by their long-term (fifty-year) nature, and the airport now annually shows a loss.

In addition to the in-lieu property tax fee, the city has a general government overhead charge of 13.5%, which includes such items as time put in by the city attorney, finance department, director of public works, and so forth. Ron Mutter says, "Since I can't raise rates [on the long-term leases] or anything else, how do we deal with this? We did develop the west end of the runway some years ago. We built a number of tiedown spaces. We used a federal grant to do it. Our goal was to start renting some spaces and to open up a couple of leases down there. It would be used to start to make up this difference. No sooner did we finish the construction of that ramp than the [California] recession hit."

The Future

Mayor Pat Gilbreath is looking for reasons why both pilots and the general public would want to go to the airport. She wants to shake off the image of the airport as a **place for the rich to play with their toys—** an attitude expressed by a previous mayor, who even suggested the city council look at ways to get rid of the airport.

As the director of public works, Ron Mutter has a vision for the surrounding area. He has architectural plans for a nearby soccer field and restaurant. The emphasis would be on youth-oriented sports so that families could congregate, play sports, and eat at the airport restaurant. He also notes that the city of Redlands has never made a serious marketing effort, unlike the other local airports (such as Rialto, Banning, and Riverside). With all his other major responsibilities, he wonders how much he should get involved in promoting the airport.

Mayor Pat Gilbreath notes that Coyote Aviation originally proposed a three-phase project, only the first of which has been approved. This first phase consists of a fifty-year lease for the sixteen T-hangars being built. The city will break even for the first time, despite the $40,000 in-lieu tax, notes the mayor. Coyote Aviation also has a ten-year option to begin phase 2: constructing a restaurant/sandwich shop that may include a public lobby. Phase 3 would entail the construction of a large maintenance hangar, shade ports, and storage area. Other entrepreneurs are looking at aviation-based housing so that people could park their planes at the airport and live nearby.

Finally, the airport advisory board is proposing a committee to develop the airport. With all this renewed interest, the mayor wants to know how best to enhance the economic viability of the Redlands Airport while balancing the varied interests of her constituency.

REFERENCES

California Department of Transportation (1998). *The California Aviation System: 1998 Inventory Element*, September 7: 222, 268, 257–274.

Coffman Associates, Inc. (1993). *Master Plan for Redlands Municipal Airport, Redlands, California*, November.

http://www.alphais.com/redlands/3006.html#airport, May 20, 2000.

http://www.alphais.com/redlands/40737.html#9, August 10, 2000.

http://www.cedar.ca.gov/military/current_reuse/norton.htm, February 29, 2000.

http://www.faa.gov/arp/arphome.htm, July 19, 1999.

http://www.maf.org/01_who.we.are/1–3who.htm, July 15, 1999.

http://www.mercymedical.org, July 28, 2000.

http://www.redlands-aor.com/history.htm, May 8, 2000.

http://www.redlands-aor.com/main.htm, May 8, 2000.

Redlands City Council Minutes (1962), Book 20, June 6.

U.S. Department of Transportation (1999). *FAR/AIM 2000: Federal Aviation Regulations/Aeronautical Information Manual.* Newcastle, WA: Aviation Supplies & Academics, Inc.

5

Perdue Farms Inc.: Responding to Twenty-First-Century Challenges

This case was prepared by George C. Rubenson and Frank M. Shipper, Salisbury University.

I have a theory that you can tell the difference between those who have inherited a fortune and those who have made a fortune. Those who have made their own fortune forget not where they came from and are less likely to lose touch with the common man.

—Bill Sterling

Background and Company History

The history of Perdue Farms Inc. is dominated by seven themes: quality, growth, geographic expansion, vertical integration, innovation, branding, and service. Arthur W. Perdue, a Railway Express agent and descendant of a French Huguenot family named Perdeaux, founded the company in 1920 when he left his job with Railway Express and entered the egg business full-time near the small town of Salisbury, Maryland. Salisbury is located in a region immortalized in James Michener's *Chesapeake* and alternately known as the Eastern Shore or the DelMarVa peninsula. It includes parts of Delaware, Maryland, and Virginia. Arthur Perdue's only child, Franklin Parsons Perdue, was born in 1920, the year the company was founded.

Perdue Farms's mission statement (Exhibit 1) emphasizes quality. In the 1920s, Mr. Arthur, as he was called, bought leghorn breeding stock from Texas to improve the quality of his flock. He soon expanded his egg market and began shipments to New York. By practicing small economies such as mixing his own chicken feed and using leather from his old shoes to make hinges for his chicken coops, he stayed out of debt and prospered. He tried to add a new chicken coop every year.

By 1940, Perdue Farms was already known for quality products and fair dealing in a tough, highly competitive market. The company began offering chickens for sale when Mr. Arthur

The authors are indebted to Frank Perdue, Jim Perdue, and the numerous associates at Perdue Farms Inc., who generously shared their time and information about the company. In addition, the authors would like to thank the anonymous librarians at Blackwell Library, Salisbury State University, who routinely review area newspapers and file articles about the poultry industry—the most important industry on the DelMarVa peninsula. Without their assistance, this case study would not have been possible. This case is intended to be used as a basis for class discussion rather than as an illustration of either effective or ineffective handling of the situation. Reprinted by permission of George C. Rubenson and Frank M. Shipper.

EXHIBIT 1

Perdue Farms's Mission for the Year 2000

Stand on Tradition

Perdue was built upon a foundation of quality, a tradition described in our Quality Policy . . .

Our Quality Policy

**"We shall produce products and provide services
at all times that meet or exceed the expectations of our customers."**

**"We shall not be content to be of
equal quality to our competitors."**

"Our commitment is to be increasingly superior."

**"Contribution to quality is a responsibility
shared by everyone in the Perdue organization."**

Focus on Today

Our mission reminds us of the purpose we serve . . .

Our Mission

"Enhance the quality of life with great food and agricultural products."

While striving to fulfill our mission, we use our values to guide our decisions . . .

Our Values

- **Quality:** We value the needs of our customers. Our high standards require us to work safely, make safe food, and uphold the Perdue name.
- **Integrity:** We do the right thing and live up to our commitments. We do not cut corners or make false promises.
- **Trust:** We trust each other and treat each other with mutual respect. Each individual's skill and talent are appreciated.
- **Teamwork:** We value a strong work ethic and the ability to make each other successful. We care what others think and encourage their involvement, creating a sense of pride, loyalty, ownership, and family.

Look to the Future

Our vision describes what we will become and the qualities that will enable us to succeed . . .

Our Vision

"To be the leading quality food company with $20 billion in sales in 2020."

Perdue in the Year 2020

- **To our customers:** We will provide food solutions and indispensable services to meet anticipated customer needs.
- **To our consumers:** A portfolio of trusted food and agricultural products will be supported by multiple brands throughout the world.
- **To our associates:** Worldwide, our people and our workplace will reflect our quality reputation, placing Perdue among the best places to work.
- **To our communities:** We will be known in the community as a strong corporate citizen, trusted business partner, and favorite employer.
- **To our shareholders:** Driven by innovation, our market leadership and our creative spirit will yield industry-leading profits.

realized that the future lay in selling chickens, not eggs. In 1944, Mr. Arthur made his son, Frank, a full partner, calling the company A. W. Perdue and Son, Inc.

In 1950, Frank took over leadership of the company, which employed forty people. By 1952, revenues were $6 million from the sale of 2.6 million broilers. During this period, the company began to vertically integrate, operating its own hatchery, starting to create its own feed formulations, and operating its own feed mill. Perdue Farms also began to contract with others to grow chickens for them. By furnishing the growers with peeps (baby chickens) and feed, the company was able to maintain control of quality.

In the 1960s, Perdue Farms continued to vertically integrate by building its first grain-receiving and -storage facilities and Maryland's first soybean-processing plant. By 1967, annual sales had increased to about $35 million. By then, it became clear to Frank that profits lay in processing chickens. In an interview for *Business Week* (September 15, 1972), Frank recalled that "processors were paying us 10 cents a live pound for what cost us 14 cents to produce. Suddenly, processors were making as much as 7 cents a pound."

A cautious, conservative planner, Arthur Perdue had not been eager for expansion, and Frank was reluctant to enter poultry processing. But economics forced his hand, and, in 1968, the company bought its first processing plant, a Swift and Company operation in Salisbury.

From the first batch of chickens that it processed, Perdue's standards were higher than those of the federal government. The state grader on the first batch has often told the story of how he was worried that he had rejected too many chickens as not Grade A. As he finished his inspections for that first day, he saw Frank Perdue headed his way and he could tell that Frank was not happy. Frank started inspecting the birds and never argued over one that was rejected. Next, he saw Frank start to go through the ones that the state grader had passed and began to toss some of them over with the rejected birds. Finally, realizing that few met his standards, Frank put all of the birds in the reject pile. Soon, however, the facility was able to process 14,000 broilers per hour.

From the beginning, Frank Perdue refused to permit his broilers to be frozen for shipping, arguing that it resulted in unappetizing black bones and loss of flavor and moistness when cooked. Instead, Perdue chickens were—and some still are—shipped to the market packed in ice, justifying the company's advertisements at that time that it sold only "fresh, young broilers." However, this policy also limited the company's market to locations that could be serviced overnight from the Eastern Shore of Maryland. Thus, Perdue chose for its primary markets the densely populated towns and cities of the East Coast, particularly New York City, which consumes more Perdue chicken than all other brands combined.

Frank Perdue's drive for quality became legendary both inside and outside the poultry industry. In 1985, Frank and Perdue Farms Inc. were featured in the book *A Passion for Excellence,* written by Tom Peters and Nancy Austin.

In 1970, Perdue established its primary breeding and genetic-research programs. Through selective breeding, Perdue developed a chicken with more white breast meat than the typical chicken. Selective breeding has been so successful that Perdue's chickens are desired by other processors. Rumors have even suggested that Perdue chickens have been stolen on occasion in an attempt to improve competitor flocks.

In 1971, Perdue Farms began an extensive marketing campaign featuring Frank Perdue. In his early advertisements, he became famous for saying things like "If you want to eat as good as my chickens, you'll just have to eat my chickens." He is often credited with being the first to brand what had been a commodity product. During the 1970s, Perdue Farms expanded to areas north of New York City, such as Massachusetts, Rhode Island, and Connecticut.

In 1977, Mr. Arthur died at the age of ninety-one, leaving behind a company with annual sales of nearly $200 million, an average annual growth rate of 17% (compared to an industry average of 1%), the potential for processing 78,000 broilers per hour, and annual production of nearly 350 million pounds of poultry. Frank Perdue has said of his father, "I learned everything from him."

In 1981, Frank Perdue went to Boston for his induction into the Babson College Academy of Distinguished Entrepreneurs, an award established in 1978 to recognize the spirit of free enterprise and business leadership. Babson College president Ralph Z. Sorenson inducted Perdue into the academy, which then numbered eighteen men and women from four continents. Perdue had the following to say to the college students:

There are none, nor will there ever be, easy steps for the entrepreneur. Nothing, absolutely nothing, replaces the willingness to work earnestly, intelligently towards a goal. You have to be willing to pay the price. You have to have an insatiable appetite for detail, have to be willing to accept constructive criticism, to ask questions, to be fiscally responsible, to surround yourself with good people and, most of all, to listen.

The early 1980s saw Perdue Farms expand southward into Virginia, North Carolina, and Georgia. It also began to buy out other producers, such as Carroll's Foods, Purvis Farms, Shenandoah Valley Poultry Company, and Shenandoah Farms. The last two acquisitions diversified the company's markets to include turkey. New products included value-added items, such as "Perdue Done It!" a line of fully cooked chicken products.

James A. (Jim) Perdue, Frank's only son, joined the company as a management trainee in 1983 and became a plant manager. The latter half of the 1980s tested the mettle of the firm. Following a period of considerable expansion and product diversification, Perdue was told by a consulting firm to form several strategic business units that would be responsible for their own operations. In other words, the firm should decentralize. Soon after, the chicken market leveled off and then declined. In 1988, the firm experienced its first year in the red. Unfortunately, the decentralization had created duplication and enormous administrative costs. The firm's rapid plunge into the processing of turkey and other food it had little experience with contributed to the losses. As in the past, the company refocused, concentrating on efficiency of operations, improving communications throughout the company, and paying close attention to detail.

On June 2, 1989, Frank celebrated fifty years with Perdue Farms Inc. At a morning reception in downtown Salisbury, the governor of Maryland proclaimed it "Frank Perdue Day." The governors of Delaware and Virginia did the same. In 1991, Frank was named chairman of the executive committee and Jim Perdue became chairman of the board. Quieter, gentler, and more formally educated than his father, Jim Perdue focused on operations, renewing the company's commitment to quality control and strategic planning. Frank Perdue continued to do advertising and public relations. As Jim Perdue matured as the company leader, he took over the role of company spokesperson and began to appear in advertisements.

Under Jim Perdue's leadership, Perdue Farms expanded into Florida and west to Michigan and Missouri during the 1990s. In 1992, the international business segment was formalized as Perdue Farms and began serving customers in Puerto Rico, South America, Europe, Japan, and China. By 1998, international sales were $180 million per year. International markets are beneficial for the firm because U.S. customers prefer white meat, while customers in most other countries prefer dark meat.

Food-service sales to commercial consumers have also become a major market. New retail-product lines focus on value-added items, individually quick-frozen items, home-meal replacement items, and products for the delicatessen. The Fit 'n Easy label continues as part of a nutrition campaign using skinless, boneless chicken and turkey products.

The 1990s also saw the increased use of technology and the building of distribution centers. For example, all over-the-road trucks were equipped with satellite two-way communications and geographic positioning, allowing for real-time tracking, rerouting if needed, and accurate information for customers as to when products would arrive.

Nearly 20,000 employees have helped Perdue Farms increase revenues to more than $2.5 billion.

Management and Organization

From 1950 until 1991, Frank Perdue was the primary force behind Perdue Farms's growth and success. During Frank's years as the company leader, the poultry industry entered its high-growth period. Industry executives had typically developed professionally during the industry's infancy. Many had little formal education and started their careers in the barnyard, building chicken coops and cleaning them out. They often spent their entire careers with one company, progressing from supervisor of grow-out facilities to manager of processing plants to corporate executive. Perdue Farms was not unusual in that respect. An entrepreneur through and through, Frank lived up to his marketing image: "It takes a tough man to make a tender chicken." He mostly used a centralized management style that kept decision-making authority in his hands and those of a few trusted, senior executives, whom he had known for a lifetime. Workers were expected to do their jobs.

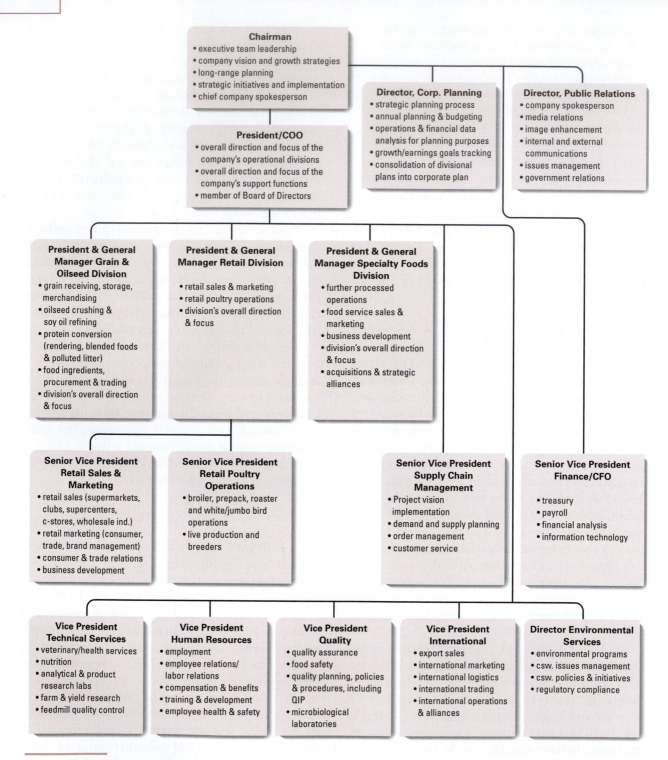

Chairman
- executive team leadership
- company vision and growth strategies
- long-range planning
- strategic initiatives and implementation
- chief company spokesperson

President/COO
- overall direction and focus of the company's operational divisions
- overall direction and focus of the company's support functions
- member of Board of Directors

Director, Corp. Planning
- strategic planning process
- annual planning & budgeting
- operations & financial data analysis for planning purposes
- growth/earnings goals tracking
- consolidation of divisional plans into corporate plan

Director, Public Relations
- company spokesperson
- media relations
- image enhancement
- internal and external communications
- issues management
- government relations

President & General Manager Grain & Oilseed Division
- grain receiving, storage, merchandising
- oilseed crushing & soy oil refining
- protein conversion (rendering, blended foods & polluted litter)
- food ingredients, procurement & trading
- division's overall direction & focus

President & General Manager Retail Division
- retail sales & marketing
- retail poultry operations
- division's overall direction & focus

President & General Manager Specialty Foods Division
- further processed operations
- food service sales & marketing
- business development
- division's overall direction & focus
- acquisitions & strategic alliances

Senior Vice President Retail Sales & Marketing
- retail sales (supermarkets, clubs, supercenters, c-stores, wholesale ind.)
- retail marketing (consumer, trade, brand management)
- consumer & trade relations
- business development

Senior Vice President Retail Poultry Operations
- broiler, prepack, roaster and white/jumbo bird operations
- live production and breeders

Senior Vice President Supply Chain Management
- Project vision implementation
- demand and supply planning
- order management
- customer service

Senior Vice President Finance/CFO
- treasury
- payroll
- financial analysis
- information technology

Vice President Technical Services
- veterinary/health services
- nutrition
- analytical & product research labs
- farm & yield research
- feedmill quality control

Vice President Human Resources
- employment
- employee relations/labor relations
- compensation & benefits
- training & development
- employee health & safety

Vice President Quality
- quality assurance
- food safety
- quality planning, policies & procedures, including QIP
- microbiological laboratories

Vice President International
- export sales
- international marketing
- international logistics
- international trading
- international operations & alliances

Director Environmental Services
- environmental programs
- csw. issues management
- csw. policies & initiatives
- regulatory compliance

EXHIBIT 2

Perdue Farms Senior-Management Organizational Chart

In later years, Frank increasingly emphasized the involvement of employees—or "associates," as they are referred to—in quality issues and operational decisions. This emphasis on employee participation undoubtedly eased the transfer of power in 1991 from Frank to his son, Jim. Although Jim grew up in the family business, he spent almost fifteen years earning an undergraduate degree in biology from Wake Forest University, a master's degree in marine biology from the University of Massachusetts at Dartmouth, and a doctorate in fisheries from the University of Washington in Seattle. Returning to Perdue Farms in 1983, he earned an MBA from Salisbury State University and was assigned the positions of plant manager, divisional quality-control manager, and vice president of quality improvement process prior to becoming chairman.

Company goals center on the three ps: people, products, and profitability. With a people-first management style, Jim believes that success rests on satisfying customer needs with quality products and putting associates first because "if they come first, they will strive to assure superior product quality—and satisfied customers." This view has had a profound impact on the company culture, which is based on Tom Peters's view that "nobody knows a person's twenty square feet better than the person who works there." In other words, management tries to gather ideas and information from everyone and to maximize productivity by transmitting these ideas throughout the organization.

Key to carrying out this policy is work force stability, a difficult goal in an industry that employs a growing number of associates working in physically demanding and sometimes stressful conditions. A significant number of associates are Hispanic immigrants who may have a poor command of the English language, are sometimes undereducated, and often lack basic health care. In order to increase these associates' opportunities for advancement, Perdue Farms focuses on helping them overcome their disadvantages.

For example, the firm provides English-language classes to help non–English-speaking employees assimilate and earn the equivalent of a high school diploma. To deal with physical stress, the company has an ergonomics committee in each plant that studies job requirements and seeks ways to redesign those jobs that put workers at the greatest risk. The company also has an impressive wellness program, which operates clinics at ten plants. The clinics are staffed by medical professionals working for medical-practice groups under contract to Perdue Farms. Employees can visit a doctor for anything from muscle strain to prenatal care to screening tests for a variety of diseases, and they have access to all Perdue-operated clinics. Care for dependents is also available. Benefits to the employees are obvious; the company also benefits through a reduction in time lost for medical office visits, lower turnover, and a happier, more productive, and more stable work force.

Marketing

In the early days, chicken was sold to butcher shops and neighborhood groceries as a commodity; that is, producers sold it in bulk, and butchers cut and wrapped it. The customer had no idea what firm grew or processed the chicken. Frank Perdue was convinced that higher profits could be made if the firm's products could be sold at a premium price. But the only reason a product can command a premium price is if customers ask for it by name—and that means the product must be differentiated and "branded." Hence, Perdue Farms emphasized superior quality, broader-breasted chickens, and a healthy golden color (the result of adding marigold petals in the feed to enhance the natural color of corn).

In 1968, Frank Perdue spent $50,000 on radio advertising. In 1969, he added $80,000 in TV advertising to his radio budget—against the advice of his advertising agency. Although his early TV ads increased sales, he decided the agency he was dealing with didn't match one of the basic Perdue tenets: "The people you deal with should be as good at what they do as you are at what you do." That decision set off a storm of activity on Frank's part. In order to select an ad agency that met his standards, Frank learned more about advertising than any poultry man before him and, in the process, catapulted Perdue Farms into the ranks of the top poultry producers in the country.

He began a ten-week immersion in the theory and practice of advertising. He read books and papers on advertising. He talked to sales managers of every newspaper, radio, and television station in the New York area, consulted experts, and interviewed forty-eight ad agencies. During April 1971, he selected Scali, McCabe, Sloves as his new advertising agency. As the agency tried to figure out how to successfully "brand" a chicken—something that had never been done—they realized that Frank Perdue was their greatest asset. "He looked a little like a chicken himself, and he sounded a little like one, and he squawked a lot!"

McCabe decided that Perdue should be the firm's spokesman. Frank initially resisted, but in the end, he accepted the role, and the campaign based on the slogan "It takes a tough man to make a tender chicken" was born. The firm's first TV commercial showed Frank on a picnic in the Salisbury City Park saying:

> A chicken is what it eats . . . And my chickens eat better than people do . . . I store my own grain and mix my own feed . . . And give my Perdue chickens nothing but pure well water to drink . . . That's why my chickens always have that healthy golden yellow color . . . If you want to eat as good as my chickens, you'll just have to eat my chickens.

Later ads touted high quality and the broader-breasted chicken:

> Government standards would allow me to call this a grade A chicken . . . but my standards wouldn't. This chicken is skinny . . . It has scrapes and hairs . . . The fact is, my graders reject 30% of the chickens government inspectors accept as grade A . . . That's why it pays to insist on a chicken with my name on it . . . If you're not completely satisfied, write me and I'll give you your money back . . . Who do you write in Washington? . . . What do they know about chickens?

> The Perdue roaster is the master race of chickens.

> Never go into a store and just ask for a pound of chicken breasts . . . Because you could be cheating yourself out of some meat . . . Here's an ordinary one-pound chicken breast, and here's a one-pound breast of mine . . . They weigh the same. But as you can see, mine has more meat, and theirs has more bone. I breed the broadest-breasted, meatiest chicken you can buy . . . So don't buy a chicken breast by the pound . . . Buy them by the name . . . and get an extra bite in every breast.

The ads paid off. In 1968, Perdue had about 3% of the New York market. By 1972, one out of every six chickens eaten in New York was a Perdue chicken, and 51% of New Yorkers recognized the label. Scali, McCabe, Sloves credited Perdue's "believability" for the success of the campaign. "This was advertising in

which Perdue had a personality that lent credibility to the product. If Frank Perdue didn't look and sound like a chicken, he wouldn't be in the commercials."

Frank had his own view. As he told a Rotary audience in Charlotte, North Carolina, in March 1989, "The product met the promise of the advertising and was far superior to the competition. Two great sayings tell it all: 'nothing will destroy a poor product as quickly as good advertising,' and 'a gifted product is mightier than a gifted pen!'"

Today, branded chicken is ubiquitous. The new task for Perdue Farms is to create a single theme for a wide variety of products (e.g., from fresh meat to fully prepared and frozen products) to a wide variety of customers (e.g., retail, food-service, and international markets). Industry experts believe that the market for fresh poultry has peaked and that sales of value-added and frozen products continue to grow at a healthy rate. Although domestic retail sales account for about 60% of Perdue Farms's revenues in 2000, food-service sales now account for 20%, international sales account for 5%, and grain and oilseed contribute the remaining 15%. The company expects food-service, international, and grain-and-oilseed sales to continue to grow as a percentage of total revenues.

Domestic Retail

Today's retail grocery customer is increasingly looking for ease and speed of preparation. To meet this need, Perdue Farms is concentrating on value-added products. The move toward value-added products has significantly changed the meat department in the modern grocery. There are now five distinct meat outlets for poultry:

1. The fresh meat counter—traditional, fresh meat; includes whole chicken and parts.

2. The delicatessen—processed turkey, rotisserie chicken.

3. The frozen counter—individually quick-frozen items such as frozen whole chickens, turkeys, and Cornish hens.

4. Home-meal replacement—fully prepared entrees, such as Perdue's Short Cuts and Deluca brand entrees, which are sold along with salads and desserts so that customers can assemble their own dinners. (The Deluca brand was acquired by Perdue Farms but is sold under its own name.)

5. Shelf stable—canned products.

Because Perdue Farms has always used the phrase "fresh young chicken" as the centerpiece of its marketing, value-added products and the retail frozen counter create a possible conflict for the company. Are these products compatible with the company's marketing image? If so, how does the company present the notion of quality in this broader product environment? To answer that question, Perdue Farms has been studying what "fresh young chicken" means to customers who consistently demand quicker and easier preparation and who admit that they freeze most of their fresh-meat purchases once they get home. One response is that "fresh young chicken" means that "quality" and "freshness" are closely associated. Thus, the real issue may be trust: the customer must believe that the product, whether fresh or frozen, is of the freshest, highest quality possible. Future marketing efforts must develop that concept.

Food Service

The food-service business consists of a wide variety of public and private customers, including restaurant chains, governments, hospitals, schools, prisons, transportation facilities, and the institutional contractors who supply meals to them. Historically, these customers have not been brand conscious, instead requiring the supplier to meet strict specifications at the lowest price, thus making this category a less than ideal fit for Perdue Farms. However, as Americans continue to eat a larger percentage of their meals away from home, traditional grocery sales have flattened and the food-service sector has shown strong growth. Across the domestic poultry industry, food service accounts for about 50% of total poultry sales; for Perdue Farms, about 20% of its revenues come from this category. Clearly, Perdue Farms is playing catch-up in this critical market.

Because Perdue Farms has neither strength nor expertise in the food-service market, management believes that acquiring companies with food-service expertise is the best strategy. One such acquisition is the purchase in September 1998 of Gol-Pak Corporation, based in Monterey, Tennessee. A further processor of products for the food-service industry, Gol-Pak had about 1,600 employees and revenues of about $200 million per year.

International

International markets have generally been a happy surprise. In the early 1990s, Perdue Farms began exporting specialty products such as chicken feet (known as paws) to customers in China. Although not approved for human consumption in the United States, paws are considered a delicacy in China. By 1992, international sales, which consisted principally of paws, had become a small but profitable business of about 30 million pounds per year. Building on this "toehold" over the next six years, Perdue Farms quickly had an international business of more than 500 million pounds per year (see Exhibit 3); annual revenues were more than $140 million from selling a wide variety of products to China, Japan, Russia, and the Ukraine.

In some ways, Japan is an excellent fit for Perdue Farms's products because customers there demand high quality. Furthermore, all Asian markets prefer dark meat, which means that what in America is excess meat can be sold in Asia at a premium price. On the downside, Perdue Farms gains much of its competitive advantage from branding (e.g., trademarks, processes, and technological and biological know-how), but this has little value internationally because most of Asia has not yet embraced the concept of branded chicken.

To better serve export markets, Perdue Farms has developed a portside freezing facility in Newport News, Virginia. This permits poultry to be shipped directly to the port, reducing processing costs and helping to balance ocean shipping costs to Asia, which are in the range of .66 cent per pound (contracting an entire ship is equal to contracting 300 to 500 truckloads).

EXHIBIT 3

Perdue Farms's International Sales, 1992–1998

Shipping poultry to Asia is not without problems. For example, in China delivery trucks are seldom refrigerated. Thus, the poultry can begin to thaw as it is being delivered, limiting the distance it can be transported prior to sale. One shipload of Perdue Farms chicken bound for Russia actually vanished and was later discovered to have been impounded using forged documents; eventually, most of its dollar value was recovered.

Initial demand for Perdue Farms's products in Russia, Poland, and eastern Europe was huge. By 1998, a significant portion of the international volume was going to Russia. Unfortunately, the crumbling of Russia's economy has had a devastating effect on imports, and sales have dropped significantly. Such instability of demand, coupled with rampant corruption, makes risking significant capital in Russia unacceptable.

Import duties and taxes for poultry are also a barrier. According to the U.S. Department of Agriculture (USDA), import duty rates in China are a whopping 45% for favored countries and 70% for unfavored countries; in addition, there is a 17% value-added tax for all countries. Import duties and taxes in Russia have been similarly high. Hence, profits can be expected to be slim.

Perdue Farms has created a joint partnership with the Jiang Nan Feng brand in order to develop a small processing plant in Shanghai. Brand recognition is being built with usual marketing tools. The products use the first "tray pack" wrapping available in Shanghai supermarkets. This new business shows promise because the sale in China of homegrown, fresh dark meat is a significant competitive advantage. Furthermore, government regulations do not permit exportation of foreign-grown poultry to the United States, but the possibility of importing white meat from Shanghai is attractive. Perdue Farms's management believes that investing in processing facilities in Asia requires the company to partner with a local firm. Attempting to do so by itself is simply too risky due to the significant cultural differences.

Operations

Two words sum up the Perdue approach to operations: quality and efficiency, with emphasis on the first. Perdue more than most companies embodies the total quality management slogan, "Quality: a journey without end." Some of the key events in this journey are listed in Exhibit 4.

EXHIBIT 4

Milestones in the Quality-Improvement Process at Perdue Farms

1924 – Arthur Perdue buys leghorn roosters for $25
1950 – Company adopts logo of a chick under a magnifying glass
1984 – Frank Perdue attends Philip Crosby's Quality College
1985 – Perdue recognized for its pursuit of quality in *A Passion for Excellence*
– Two-hundred Perdue managers attend Quality College
– Quality Improvement Process adopted
1986 – Corrective Action Teams established
1987 – Quality training for all associates established
– Error Cause Removal Process implemented
1988 – Steering committee formed
1989 – First annual quality conference held
– Team management implemented
1990 – Second annual quality conference held
– Values and corporate mission codified
1991 – Third annual quality conference held
– Customer satisfaction defined
1992 – Fourth annual quality conference held
– How to implement customer satisfaction explained to team leaders and quality improvement teams
– Quality index created
– Customer satisfaction index created
– "Farm to Fork" quality program created
1999 – Raw material quality index launched
2000 – High performance team process initiated

Both quality and efficiency are improved through the management of details. Exhibit 5 is a diagram of the structure and product flow of a generic, vertically integrated broiler company. This company can choose which steps in the process it wants to take and which it wants suppliers to take. For example, the company could purchase all grain, oilseed, meal, and other feed; or it could contract with hatcheries to supply primary breeders and hatchery-supply flocks.

Perdue Farms chose maximum vertical integration in order to control every detail. It breeds its own chickens and hatches its own eggs (nineteen hatcheries),

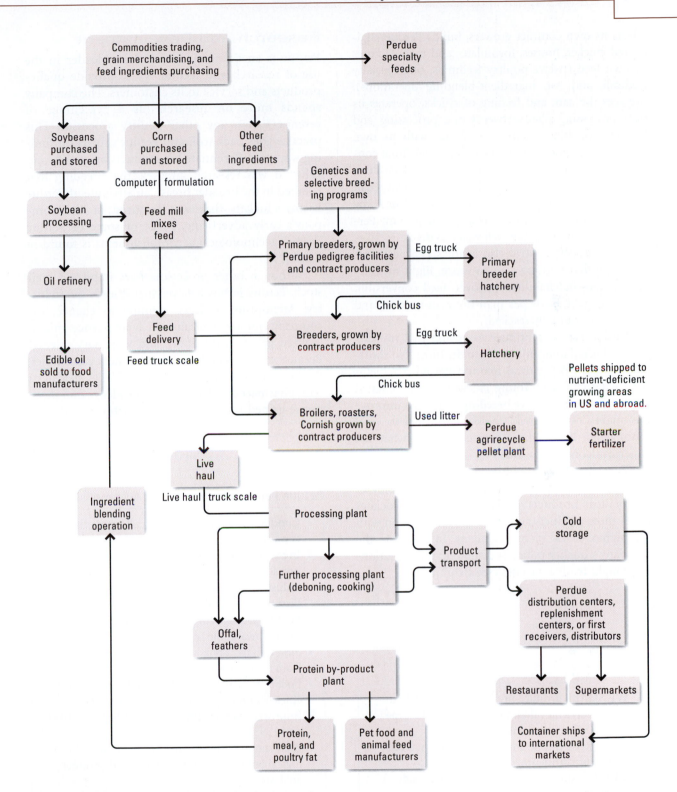

EXHIBIT 5

Perdue Farms's Integrated Operations

selects its own contract growers, builds Perdue-engineered chicken houses, formulates and manufactures its own feed (twelve poultry feedmills, one specialty feedmill, and two ingredient-blending operations), oversees the care and feeding of chicks, operates its own processing plants (twenty-one processing and further-processing plants), distributes with its own trucking fleet, and does its own marketing. Total control of this process formed the basis for Frank Perdue's early claims that his poultry was of higher quality than other poultry: "A chicken is what it eats . . . I store my own grain and mix my own feed . . . and give my Perdue chickens nothing but well water to drink.

Total process control also enables Perdue Farms to ensure that nothing goes to waste. Eight measurable items—hatchability, turnover, feed conversion, livability, yield, birds per man-hour, utilization, and grade—are routinely tracked.

Perdue Farms continues to ensure that nothing artificial is fed to or injected into the birds. No shortcuts are taken. A chemical-free and steroid-free diet is fed to the chickens. Young chickens are vaccinated against disease. Selective breeding is used to improve the quality of the stock: chickens are bred to yield more white breast meat because that is what the American consumer wants.

To ensure that its poultry continues to lead the industry in quality, Perdue Farms buys and analyzes competitors' products regularly. Inspection associates grade these products and share the information with the highest levels of management. In addition, the company's quality policy is displayed at all locations and taught to all associates (see Exhibit 6).

EXHIBIT 6

Quality Policy

- WE SHALL produce products and provide services at all times that meet or exceed the expectations of our customers.
- WE SHALL not be content to be of equal quality to our competitors.
- OUR COMMITMENT is to be increasingly superior.
- CONTRIBUTION TO QUALITY is a responsibility shared by everyone in the Perdue organization.

Research and Development

Perdue is an acknowledged industry leader in the use of research and technology to provide quality products and service to its customers. The company spends more on research (as a percentage of revenues) than any other poultry processor. This practice goes back to Frank Perdue's focus on finding ways to differentiate his products by quality and value. It was research into selective breeding that resulted in the broader breast, an attribute of Perdue Farms chicken that was featured in the company's early advertising. A list of some of Perdue Farms's technological accomplishments is found in Exhibit 7.

Although other processors have improved their stock, Perdue Farms believes that it leads the industry. Attempting to leave nothing to chance, the company employs specialists in avian science, microbiology, genetics, nutrition, and veterinary science. Because of its research and development capabilities, Perdue Farms is often involved in USDA field tests with pharmaceutical suppliers; knowledge and experience gained from these tests sometimes leads to a

EXHIBIT 7

Perdue Farms's Technological Accomplishments

- Conducts more research than all competitors combined
- Breeds chickens that consistently have more breast meat than any other bird produced in the industry
- First to use digital scales to guarantee weights
- First to package fully cooked chicken products in microwaveable trays
- First to have a box lab to define quality of boxes from different suppliers
- First to measure its chickens and competitors' chickens on fifty-two quality factors every week
- Improved 20% on time deliveries between 1987 and 1993
- Built state-of-the-art analytical and microbiological laboratories for feed and end-product analysis
- First to develop food-safety management practices for all areas of the company
- First to develop commercially viable litter pellets for poultry

competitive advantage. For example, Perdue has the most extensive and expensive vaccination program in the industry. The company is also working with, and studying the practices of, several European producers who use completely different methods.

The company has used research to significantly increase productivity. For example, in the 1950s, it took fourteen weeks to grow a 3-pound chicken; today, it takes only seven weeks to grow a 5-pound chicken. This gain in efficiency is due principally to improvements in the feed-to-chicken conversion rate. The current rate of conversion is about 2 pounds of feed to produce 1 pound of chicken, and feed represents about 65% of the cost of growing a chicken. Thus, if additional research can further improve the feed-to-chicken conversion rate by just 1%, the company would see additional income of $2.5 million to $3 million per week, or $130 million to $156 million per year.

Finance

Perdue Farms is privately held and considers financial information to be proprietary. Hence, available financial data are limited. Stock is primarily held by the family; a limited amount is held by management. Numbers commonly used by the media and the poultry industry peg Perdue Farms's revenues for 2000 at about $2.5 billion and the number of associates at nearly 20,000. *Forbes* magazine has estimated 2000 operating profits at about $160 million and net profits at about $22 million.

The firm's compound sales growth rate has been slowly decreasing during the past twenty years, mirroring the industry, which has been experiencing market saturation and overproduction. However, Perdue has compensated by using manpower more efficiently through such improvements as automation. For example, twenty years ago a 1% increase in associates resulted in a 1.6% increase in revenue; currently, a 1% increase in associates results in an 8.5% increase in revenues (see Exhibit 8).

Poultry operations can be divided into four segments: retail chicken (growth rate of 5%), food-service chicken and turkey (growth rate of 12%), international sales (growth rate of 64% over past six years), and grain and oilseed (growth rate of 10%). The bulk of sales continues to come from retail chicken, the sector with the slowest growth rate. The greatest opportunities appear to lie in food-service sales, where the

EXHIBIT 8

Annual Compound Growth Rate for Perdue Farms, 1980–2000

	Revenue	Associates	Sales/Associate
Past 20 years	10.60%	6.48%	3.87%
Past 15 years	8.45%	4.48%	4.48%
Past 10 years	7.39%	4.75%	2.52%
Past 5 years	8.39%	0.99%	7.33%

company is admittedly behind, and international sales, where political and economic instability in target countries makes the risk to capital significant.

Perdue Farms has been profitable every year since its founding, with the exception of 1988 and 1996. Company officials believe the loss in 1988 was caused by overproduction by the industry and higher administrative costs resulting from a decentralization effort begun during the mid eighties. At that time, there was a concerted effort to push decisions down through the corporate ranks to provide more autonomy. When the new strategy resulted in significantly higher administrative costs due to duplication of effort, the company responded quickly by returning to the basics, reconsolidating, and downsizing. The loss in 1996 was due to the impact of high corn prices. Currently, the goal is to constantly streamline in order to be cost effective.

Perdue Farms approaches financial management conservatively, using retained earnings and cash flow to finance most asset-replacement projects and normal growth. When planning expansion projects or acquisitions, long-term debt is used. The target debt limit is 55% of equity. Such debt is normally provided by domestic and international bank and insurance companies. The debt strategy is to match asset lives with liability maturities and have a mix of fixed-rate and variable-rate debt. Growth plans require about two dollars in projected incremental sales growth for each dollar invested.

Environment

Environmental issues present a constant challenge to all poultry processors. Growing, slaughtering, and processing poultry is a difficult and tedious process that demands absolute efficiency in order to keep operating costs at an acceptable level. Inevitably, detractors argue that the process is dangerous to workers, inhumane to the poultry, and hard on the environment and that it results in food that may not be safe. Thus, media headlines such as "Human Cost of Poultry Business Bared," "Animal Rights Advocates Protest Chicken Coop Conditions," "Processing Plants Leave a Toxic Trail," and "EPA Mandates Poultry Regulations" are routine.

Perdue Farms tries to be pro-active in managing environmental issues. In April 1993, the company created an environmental steering committee. Its mission is "to provide all Perdue Farms work sites with vision, direction, and leadership so that they can be good corporate citizens from an environmental perspective today and in the future." The committee is responsible for overseeing how the company is doing in such environmentally sensitive areas as waste water, storm water, hazardous waste, solid waste, recycling, bio-solids, and employee health and safety.

For example, disposing of dead birds has long been an industry problem. Perdue Farms developed small composters for use on each farm. Using this approach, carcasses resemble soil in a matter of a few days. The disposal of hatchery waste is another environmental challenge. Historically, manure and unhatched eggs were shipped to a landfill. However, Perdue Farms developed a way to reduce the waste by 50% by selling the liquid fraction to a pet-food processor that cooks it for protein. The other 50% is recycled through a rendering process. In 1990, Perdue Farms spent $4.2 million to upgrade its treatment facility with a state-of-the-art system at its Accomac, Virginia, and Showell, Maryland, plants. These facilities use forced air heated to 120 degrees, which causes the microbes to digest all traces of ammonia, even during the winter months.

More than ten years ago, North Carolina's Occupational Safety and Health Administration cited Perdue Farms for an unacceptable level of repetitive stress injuries at its Lewiston and Robersonville, North Carolina, processing plants. This sparked a major research program in which Perdue Farms worked with Health and Hygiene Inc., of Greensboro, North Carolina, to learn more about ergonomics: the repetitive movements required to accomplish specific jobs. Results have been dramatic. Launched in 1991 after two years of development, the program videotapes employees at all of Perdue Farms's plants in order to assign stress values to their tasks. Although the cost to Perdue Farms has been significant, results have been dramatic: workers' compensation claims went down 44%; lost-time recordables were just 7.7% of the industry average; serious repetitive-stress cases decreased by 80%, and there was a 50% reduction in lost time or surgery due to back injuries (Shelley Reese, "Helping Employees Get a Grip," *Business and Health,* August 1998).

Despite these advances, serious problems continue to develop. In 1997, the organism pfiesteria burst into media headlines when massive numbers of dead fish with lesions turned up along the Chesapeake Bay in Maryland. Initial findings pointed to manure runoff from the poultry industry as the cause. Political constituencies quickly called for increased regulation to insure proper manure storage and fertilizer use. Perdue Farms readily admits that "the poultry process is a closed system. There is lots of nitrogen and phosphorus in the grain, and it passes through the chicken and is returned to the environment as manure. Obviously, if you bring additional grain into a closed area such as the DelMarVa peninsula, you increase the amount of nitrogen and phosphorus in the soil unless you find a way to get rid of it." Nitrogen and phosphorus from manure normally make excellent fertilizer, which moves slowly in the soil. However, scientists speculate that erosion speeds up runoff, threatening the health of nearby streams, rivers, and larger bodies of water, such as the Chesapeake Bay. The problem for the industry is that proposals to control the runoff are sometimes driven more by politics and emotion than research, which is not yet complete.

Although it is not clear what role poultry-related nitrogen and phosphorus runoff played in the pfiesteria outbreak, regulators believe the microorganism feeds on the algae that grows when too much of these nutrients is present in the water. Thus, the EPA and various states are considering new regulations. Currently, contract growers are responsible for either using or disposing of the manure from their chicken houses. But some regulators and environmentalists believe that (1) it is too complicated to police the utilization-and-disposal practices of thousands of individual farmers, and (2) only the big poultry companies have the financial resources to properly dispose of the waste. Thus, they want to make poultry companies responsible for all waste disposal—a move that the industry strongly opposes.

Some experts have called for conservation measures that limit the density of chicken houses in a given area or require a percentage of chicken houses to be taken out of production periodically. Obviously this would be very hard on the farm families who own chicken houses, and the measure could result in fewer acres devoted to agriculture. Working with AgriRecycle Inc. of Springfield, Missouri, Perdue Farms has developed a possible solution: turn excess manure into pellets for use as fertilizer. This would permit sale outside the poultry-growing region, better balancing the input of grain. Spokesmen estimate that as much as 120,000 tons (nearly one-third of the surplus nutrients from manure produced each year on the DelMarVa peninsula) could be sold to corn growers in other parts of the country. Prices would be market driven but could be $25 to $30 per ton, suggesting a potential, small profit. Still, almost any attempt to control the problem potentially raises the cost of growing chickens, forcing poultry processors to look for locations where the chicken population is less dense.

In general, solving environmental problems attributable to the industry presents at least five major challenges to the poultry processor:

▌ how to maintain the trust of the poultry consumer

▌ how to ensure that the poultry remain healthy

▌ how to protect the safety of the employees and the integrity of the process

▌ how to satisfy legislators, who need to show their constituents that they are taking concrete action when environmental problems occur, and

▌ how to keep costs at an acceptable level.

Jim Perdue sums up Perdue Farms's position as follows: "We must not only comply with environmental laws as they exist today, but look to the future to make sure we don't have any surprises. We must make sure our environmental policy statement [see Exhibit 9] is real, that there's something behind it, and that we do what we say we're going to do."

Logistics and Information Systems

The recent explosion of poultry products and increase in customers placed a severe strain on Perdue Farms's logistical system, which was developed at a time when there were far fewer products, fewer delivery points, and lower volume. Hence, the company had limited ability to improve service levels, could not support further growth, and could not introduce services that might give it a competitive advantage.

In the poultry industry, companies are faced with two significant problems: time and forecasting. Fresh poultry has a limited shelf life, measured in days. Thus, forecasts must be extremely accurate and deliveries timely. On the one hand, estimating requirements too conservatively results in product shortages. High-volume customers such as Wal-Mart will not tolerate product shortages that lead to empty shelves and lost sales. On the other hand, if estimates are too high, the results are outdated products that cannot be sold and losses for Perdue Farms. A common expression in the poultry industry is "You either sell it or smell it."

Forecasting has always been extremely difficult in the poultry industry because the processor needs to know approximately eighteen months in advance how many broilers will be needed in order to size hatchery-supply flocks and contract with growers to provide live broilers. Most customers (e.g., grocers and food-service buyers) have a much smaller planning window. Additionally, Perdue Farms cannot know when rival poultry processors will discount a particular product reducing Perdue Farms sales, or when bad weather and other factors beyond the company's control may reduce demand.

Historically, poultry companies have based their estimates on past demand and information from industry networks and other contacts. Although product complexity has exacerbated the problem, the steady movement away from fresh product to frozen product (which has a longer shelf life) offers some relief.

Information technology (IT) has helped by shortening the distance between the customer and Perdue Farms. As far back as 1987, PCs were placed on the desks of customer-service associates, allowing each of them to enter customer orders directly. Next, a system was developed to put dispatchers in direct contact with every truck so that the dispatchers would have accurate information about product inventory and delivery at all times. Now, IT is moving to further shorten the distance between the customer and the Perdue Farms service representative by putting a PC on the customer's desk. All of these steps improve communication and shorten the time from order to delivery.

Today, poultry products fall into four channels of distribution:

1. Bulk fresh. **Timeliness and frequency of delivery are critical to ensure freshness.** Distribution requirements are high-volume and low-cost delivery.

EXHIBIT 9

Perdue Farms's Environmental Policy Statement

Perdue Farms is committed to environmental stewardship and shares that commitment with its farm family partners. We're proud of the leadership we're providing our industry in addressing the full range of environmental challenges related to animal agriculture and food processing. We've invested—and continue to invest—millions of dollars in research, new technology, equipment upgrades, and awareness and education as part of our ongoing commitment to protecting the environment.

■ Perdue Farms was among the first poultry companies with a dedicated Environmental Services department. Our team of environmental managers is responsible for ensuring that every Perdue facility operates with *100 percent compliance of all applicable environmental regulations and permits.*

■ Through our joint venture, Perdue AgriRecycle, Perdue Farms is investing $12 million to build in Delaware a first-of-its-kind pellet plant that will convert surplus poultry litter into a starter fertilizer that will be marketed internationally to nutrient deficient regions. The facility, which will serve the entire DelMarVa region, is scheduled to begin operation in April 2001.

■ We continue to explore new technologies that will reduce water usage in our processing plants without compromising food safety or quality.

■ We invested thousands of man-hours in producer education to assist our family farm partners in managing their independent poultry operations in the most environmentally responsible manner possible. In addition, all our poultry producers are required to have nutrient management plans and dead-bird composters.

■ Perdue Farms was one of four poultry companies operating in Delaware to sign an agreement with Delaware officials outlining our companies' voluntary commitment to help independent poultry producers dispose of surplus chicken litter.

■ Our Technical Services department is conducting ongoing research into feed technology as a means of reducing the nutrients in poultry manure. We've already achieved phosphorus reductions that far exceed the industry average.

■ We recognize that the environmental impact of animal agriculture is more pronounced in areas where development is decreasing the amount of farmland available to produce grain for feed and to accept nutrients. That is why we view independent grain *and* poultry producers as vital business partners and strive to preserve the economic viability of the family farm.

At Perdue Farms, we believe that it is possible to preserve the family farm; provide a safe, abundant, and affordable food supply; and protect the environment. However, we believe that can best happen when there is cooperation and trust between the poultry industry, agriculture, environmental groups, and state officials. We hope Delaware's effort will become a model for other states to follow.

2. Domestic frozen and further-processed products. **Temperature integrity is critical.** Distribution requirements are frequency and timeliness of delivery. This channel lends itself to dual-temperature trailer systems and load consolidation.

3. Export. **Temperature integrity, high volume, and low cost are critical.** This channel lends itself to inventory consolidation and custom loading of vessels.

4. Consumer-packaged goods (packaged-fresh, prepared, and deli products). **Differentiate via innovative products and services.** Distribution requirements are reduced lead time and low cost.

Thus, forecasting now requires the development of a sophisticated **supply-chain management system** that can efficiently integrate all facets of operations, including grain and oilseed activities, hatcheries and growing facilities, processing plants (which now produce more than four hundred products at more than twenty locations), distribution facilities and the distributors, supermarkets, food-service customers, and export markets (see Exhibit 5). Perdue Farms underlined the importance of the successful implementation of supply-chain management by creating a new executive position, senior vice president for supply-chain management.

A key step in overhauling the distribution infrastructure is building replenishment centers that will, in effect, be intermediaries between the processing plants and the customers. The portside facility in Norfolk, Virginia, which serves the international market, is being expanded and a new domestic freezer facility added.

Products are directed from the processing plants to the replenishment and freezer centers based on customer forecasts, which have been converted to an optimized production schedule. Perdue Farms trucks deliver these bulk products to the centers in finished or partly finished form. At the centers, finishing and packaging are completed. Finally, customer orders are custom-palletized and loaded on trucks (either Perdue owned or contracted) for delivery. All shipments are produced from replenishment-center inventory. Thus, the need for accurate forecasting by the distribution centers is critical.

In order to control the entire supply-chain management process, Perdue Farms purchased a multimillion-dollar IT system that represents the biggest nontangible expense in the company's history. This integrated, state-of-the-art information system required total process reengineering—a project that took eighteen months and required training 1,200 associates. Major goals of the system were to:

1. Make it easier and more desirable for the customer to do business with Perdue Farms.

2. Make it easier for Perdue Farms associates to do their jobs.

3. Reduce costs as much as possible.

Industry Trends

The poultry industry is affected by consumer and regulatory trends. Currently, chicken is the number-one meat consumed in the United States, with a 40% market share (Exhibits 10 and 11). A typical American consumes about 81 pounds of chicken, 69 pounds of beef, and 52 pounds of pork annually (USDA data). Chicken is also becoming the most popular meat in the world; in 1997, poultry set an export record of $2.5 billion. Although exports fell 6% in 1998—a decrease attributed to Russia's and

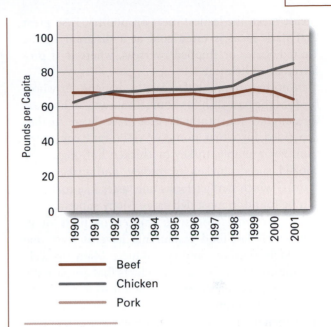

EXHIBIT 10

Consumption per Capita of Chicken, Beef, and Pork in the 1990s and Projected Consumption for 2000 and 2001

Asia's financial crises—food-industry experts expect this to be temporary. Hence, the world market is clearly a growth opportunity.

The popularity and growth of poultry products are attributed to both nutritional and economic issues. Poultry products contain significantly less fat and cholesterol than other meat products. In the United States, the demand for boneless, skinless

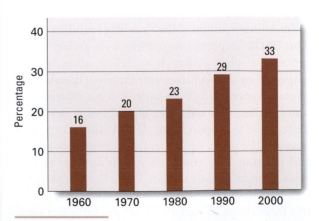

EXHIBIT 11

Chicken as a Percentage of Overall Meat, Poultry, and Fish Consumption, 1960–2000 breast meat, the leanest meat on poultry, is so great that dark meat is often sold at a discount in the United States or shipped overseas, where it is preferred to white meat.

Another trend is a decrease in demand for whole birds as the base dish for home meals and an increase in demand for products that have been further processed for either home or restaurant consumption. For example, turkey or chicken hot dogs, fully cooked sliced chicken or turkey, and turkey pastrami—which neither looks nor tastes like turkey—can be found in most deli cases. Many supermarkets sell either whole rotisserie chicken or parts of it. Almost all fast-food restaurants have at least one sandwich based on poultry products. Many up-scale restaurants feature poultry products that are partially prepared and then shipped to them frozen in order to simplify restaurant preparation. All these products have been further processed, adding value and potentially increasing the profit margin.

The industry is consolidating; that is, the larger companies in the industry are continuing to buy smaller firms. There are about thirty-five major poultry firms in the United States, but this number is expected to drop to twenty to twenty-five within the next ten years. There are several reasons for this. Stagnant U.S. demand and general product oversupply create downward price pressure, which makes it difficult for smaller firms to operate profitably. In addition, efficiency improvements require huge capital outlays. Finally, high-volume retailers such as Sam's Club and Royal Ahold (the Dutch owner of several U.S. supermarket chains) prefer to deal with large suppliers rather than many smaller processors.

The industry is heavily regulated. The Food and Drug Administration (FDA) monitors product safety. The USDA inspects live poultry as it arrives at the processing plant. After it is killed, each bird is inspected by a USDA inspector for avian diseases and contamination of feces or other foreign material. All poultry that does not meet regulations is destroyed under USDA supervision. USDA inspectors also examine the plant, equipment, operating procedures, and personnel for compliance with sanitary regulations. Congress has mandated that the USDA make this information available online. Additional intensive inspections of statistically selected product samples have been recommended by the National Academy of Sciences, so more FDA regulations are anticipated.

Although poultry produces less waste per pound of product than cattle or hogs, all meat industries are being scrutinized more closely by the EPA with regard to waste disposal. In general, waste generated at processing plants is well controlled by regulation, monitoring, and such penalties as fines. When an EPA violation occurs, the company that operates the plant may receive a substantial fine—potentially, millions of dollars.

Still, the most difficult problems to deal with are those that occur as a cumulative result of numerous processors operating in a relatively small area. For example, increasing poultry production in a given area intensifies the problem of disposal of manure. In manmade fertilizer, phosphorus and nitrogen exist in approximately a 1:8 ratio, whereas in poultry manure the ratio can be 1:1. Thus, the production of too much poultry manure can result in excessive phosphorus runoff into streams and rivers, potentially causing aquatic disease and degradation of water quality. This was the case in the 1997 outbreak of pfiesteria, a toxic microbe, in the tributaries of the Chesapeake Bay. Although the poultry industry insisted that there were many possible reasons for the problem, the media and most regulatory spokespersons attributed it primarily to phosphorus runoff from chicken manure. After much negative publicity and extensive investigation by both poultry processors and state regulatory agencies, Maryland passed the Water Quality Act of 1998, which required the industry to formulate nutrient-management plans. However, many environmentalists still believe that the EPA must create stricter regulations. Recent regulatory activity has continued to focus on Eastern Shore agriculture, especially the poultry industry. However, new studies from the U.S. Geological Survey suggest that the vast majority of nutrients affecting the Chesapeake Bay come from rivers that do not flow through the poultry-producing areas of the Eastern Shore. The studies also found that improved agricultural management practices have reduced nutrient runoff from farmlands. Jim Perdue says, "While the poultry industry must accept responsibility for its share of nutrients, public policy should view the watershed as a whole and address all the factors that influence water quality."

Other government agencies whose regulations impact the industry include the Occupational Safety and Health Administration (OSHA) and the Immigration and Naturalization Service (INS). OSHA enforces its employee-safety regulations via periodic inspections and levies fines when noncompliance is discovered. For example, a Hudson Foods poultry plant was fined more than a million dollars for alleged willful violations causing ergonomic injury to workers. The INS also uses periodic inspections to find undocumented workers. It estimates that the percentage of undocumented aliens working in the industry ranges from 3 to 78% of the work force, depending on the plant. Plants found to employ undocumented workers, especially those that are repeat offenders, can be heavily fined.

The Future

The marketplace for poultry in the twenty-first century will be very different from that of the past. Understanding the wants and needs of generation Xers and echo-boomers will be key to responding successfully to these differences.

Quality will continue to be essential. In the 1970s, quality was the cornerstone of Frank Perdue's successful marketing campaign to brand his poultry. However, in the twenty-first century, quality will not be enough. Today's customers expect—even demand—all products to be of high quality. Thus, Perdue Farms plans to use customer service to further differentiate the company from its competitors. The focus will be on learning how to become indispensable to the customer by reducing cost and delivering the product exactly the way the customer wants it, where and when the customer wants it. In short, as Jim Perdue says, "Perdue Farms wants to become so easy to do business with that the customer will have no reason to do business with anyone else."

In the poultry business, customer-purchase decisions, as well as company profitability, hinge on mere pennies. Thus, the location of processing facilities is critical. Historically, Perdue Farms has been an Eastern Shore company and has maintained major processing facilities there. However, it currently costs about 1.5 cents more per pound to grow poultry on the Eastern Shore than in Arkansas. This difference results from the cost of labor, compliance with federal and state environmental laws, resource costs (e.g., feed grain), and other variables. If regulations will permit the importation of foreign-grown poultry in the future, producers could even use inexpensive international labor markets to further reduce

costs. The opportunity for large growers to reduce costs in these ways puts increased pressure on small poultry companies, which suggests further consolidation of the industry.

Grocery companies are also consolidating in order to compete with huge food-industry newcomers, such as Wal-Mart and Royal Ahold. These new competitors increase efficiency by minimizing the number of their suppliers and buying huge amounts from each at the lowest possible price. In effect, suppliers and buyers become dependent on each other, and buyers expect their suppliers to do more for them. For example, Perdue Farms considers it possible that, using sophisticated distribution-information programs, they will soon be able to manage the entire meat-department requirements for several supermarket chains. Providing this service would support Perdue Farms's goal of becoming indispensable to its first-line retail customer, the grocer.

The twenty-first-century consumer will demand many options. Clearly, the demand for uncooked, whole chickens purchased at the meat counter has peaked. Demand is moving toward further-processed poultry. To support this trend, Perdue Farms plans to open several cooking plants. In addition, a criterion for future acquisitions will be whether they support value-added processing. Products from these plants will fill food-service requirements and grocery sales of prepared foods, such as delicatessen, frozen, home meal-replacement, and shelf-stable items. Additionally, the twenty-first-century customer will be everywhere. Whether at work, at a sports event, in school, or traveling on the highway, customers will expect to have convenient refreshment options and a wide selection of wholesome, ready-to-eat products.

Designing a distribution system that can handle all of these options is extremely difficult. For example, the system must be able to efficiently organize hundreds of customer orders for more than four hundred different products, which are processed and further prepared at more than twenty facilities throughout the southeast for delivery by one truck—a massive distribution task. As executives note, the company survived until now using distribution techniques created as long ago as the eighties, when there were a handful of products and processing facilities. However, the system approached gridlock during the late 1990s. Thus, Perdue Farms invested in a state-of-the-art information-processing system—a tough decision because "we could build two new processing plants for the price of this technology package."

International markets are a conundrum. On one hand, Perdue Farms's international market has grown from an insignificant side business in 1994 to one generating $140 million in 1999, about 5% of total revenues. Further, its contribution to profits is significant. Poultry is widely accepted around the world, providing opportunities for further growth. However, different places value different parts of the chicken and demand different meat color, preparation, and seasoning. Thus, products must be customized. Parts that are not in demand in one country must be sold at severely reduced prices, used as feed, or shipped frozen to a market where demand exists. While this can be done, it is a distribution problem that significantly complicates an already difficult forecasting model.

International markets can also be very unstable, exposing Perdue Farms to significant demand instability and potential losses. For example, in 1997, about 50% of Perdue Farms's international revenues came from Russia. However, political and economic problems there reduced 1999 revenues significantly. This high level of instability, coupled with the corruption that thrives in a country experiencing severe political and economic turmoil, introduces significant risk to investment.

Clearly, the future holds many opportunities. But none of them comes without risk, and Perdue Farms must carefully choose where it wants to direct its limited resources.

Wizards of the Coast 1990–2001

6

This case was prepared by Charles W. L. Hill, Suresh Kotha, and Richard Moxon, all from the University of Washington, and Frank Rothaermel from Michigan State University.

The excitement was high among the top managers of Wizards of the Coast, the world's leading adventure gaming company, as they sat down to review the company's progress during the first half of 1997. The company had just completed the acquisition of a major competitor, and with the opening of its first gaming entertainment center, it was pioneering a new retail concept. Fueled by one hit product, three years of tremendous growth had been followed by an unexpected downturn in revenues in 1996. Wizards now looked to be on the rebound, but everyone knew that the company still had to prove it had a sustainable-growth strategy for the future.

Creating the Magic

Wizards of the Coast was a privately held company best known for creating the world's leading adventure trading card game, Magic: The Gathering. Since its release in 1993, over five million consumers worldwide had embraced the game, which was available in nine languages and played in over fifty countries. See Exhibit 1 for a brief description of Magic.

This case is based primarily on field research and is intended to be used as a basis for class discussion rather than as an illustration of either effective or ineffective handling of the situation. Reprinted by permission of Frank T. Rothaermel, Suresh Kotha, and Charles W. L. Hill.

The Genesis

Wizards of the Coast was founded by Peter Adkison and a group of other young professionals in 1990 to develop role-playing games. Adkison had been intrigued by strategy and role-playing games ever since he was eleven, and in high school had developed a passion for the Dungeons & Dragons adventure role-playing game. He was working for Boeing as a computer-systems analyst, but was eager to start his own venture. Recalls Adkison, "I was a small cog in a huge machine that itself was a small cog in a huge machine." He and his friends kept their jobs but began developing role-playing games in their spare time.

In 1991, Adkison was introduced to Richard Garfield, a doctoral student in combinational mathematics at the University of Pennsylvania and an avid game player who had been designing his own games since he was a teenager. When the two got together at a game convention, the concept for Magic was born. Adkison had the idea that there was a need for a fantasy role-playing game that was portable and could be played anywhere in no more than an hour. He thought that it could be a card game. Garfield had also been interested in fantasy games since playing a game called Cosmic Encounter in the 1980s. One of the pieces in Cosmic Encounter had special powers. By invoking these powers, a player could change the rules of the game. This intrigued Garfield,

EXHIBIT 1

Magic: The Gathering

The game Magic: The Gathering combines elements of chess, bridge, and the role-playing game of Dungeons & Dragons. Magic is a trading-card game in which two players are rival wizards dueling for control of a magical "multiverse" called Dominia. Each player starts out with twenty life points. The goal is to reduce the opponent's life points to zero before the opponent can do the same—to kill the opponent.

Before starting the game, each player builds a deck of at least forty cards from his or her collection. Each player begins by shuffling the deck and drawing seven cards. Players alternate turns, with each turn a series of actions, such as attacking and defending. There are several types of illustrated cards. Lands are the most basic, providing the magical energy a player needs to play other cards. Others represent creatures, and still others represent spells that a player can cast. The basic strategy lies in choosing when to play what card and when to use what creatures for what purposes. Games usually last fifteen to thirty minutes, but some can last hours.

One of the key features of Magic is that each game played is unique: each player starts out with a deck of forty cards selected from among the more than four thousand sold. It is not uncommon for a player to own several hundred cards. This encourages players to buy or trade cards to enhance their powers and increase their strategic options.

The game is in perpetual evolution because new cards are released periodically and older ones retired by Wizards of the Coast. Retired cards gained instant status as collectibles and can be bought, sold, and traded between individuals, in hobby stores, and on the Internet. New cards are issued in different sets and limited editions. These expansions have kept the game novel and contributed to its phenomenal growth. Since the basic strategy in Magic is assembling the unassailable deck, serious players invest heavily in their collections.

In addition, with each edition of new cards the fantasy multiverse expands. Magic has undergone many extensions, and further expansion is limited only by the players' willingness to remain bewitched.

and he wondered what would happen if all the pieces were magic, each one altering the game in some unique way. He believed that this idea could lead to a fantasy board game, but Adkison persuaded him to focus on cards instead and to think about a format in which players could trade cards, buying and selling collectible cards similar to those of their sports heroes.

Garfield came back a few weeks later with a prototype of Magic: The Gathering. The idea was to combine trading cards and a fantasy game in which players controlled the acts of mystical characters. Recalls Garfield, "The concept of a trading-card game was one of the only 'Eureka!' experiences I've had."

Operating out of the basement of Adkison's home, Wizards of the Coast released Magic: The Gathering in August 1993. The game became an overnight success. The first printing of ten million cards, which was expected to last a year, sold out in six weeks. According to one game-store owner, "My initial was for 24 units, my second was for 572, and my third was, 'Send everything you've got in the warehouse.'" With sales success also came critical acclaim, Magic's winning several game and toy industry awards. Soon,

Adkison left Boeing, and Garfield a new teaching job, to work full-time on Wizards of the Coast.

Products and Customers

Magic cards were sold in starter decks of sixty randomly selected cards for about $8.95 and booster packs of eight or fifteen cards for about $2.95. Even though these were the recommended retail prices, it was not uncommon for retailers to unbundle decks and mark up the prices of cards in great demand. Because the cards also had original artwork that appealed to fantasy-game players and collectors, they were both collected and traded, their price determined by their strategic role and collector value. Each deck was unique, so no two players had identical sets of cards. Players traded cards in order to create a deck with desired characteristics.

According to the chief game developer for Wizards of the Coast, the typical Magic player was a person with a good education, a high household income, and an interest in computers. While the game was most popular with males in their teens or twenties, it had also caught on with younger teens and older men and women. College dormitories had been a breeding ground for new "gamers." Compared to the typical players of a board game such as Monopoly, the players of Magic saw the game more as a hobby—something on which they spent a significant amount of time and money.

Manufacturing and Distribution

Wizards contracted out the design, manufacturing, and packaging of its cards and other products. Most of its cards were designed by independent artists, who earned royalties from their Wizards' sales. In the beginning, the company relied on one supplier, Carta Mundi in Belgium, because no other firm could deliver the quality needed and do the sophisticated card sorting required. During the first two years of booming popularity, manufacturing capacity was the single biggest constraint on the growth of Wizards. Carta Mundi remained the largest supplier, but other suppliers were contracted as the game grew and they were able to meet Wizards' standards.

Wizards had built a widespread retail network to market its cards. Most adventure games were sold through small game, comic, or hobby shops, often mom-and-pop stores supplied by relatively small distributors. These shops were critical to reaching the serious gamers and accounted for about 75% of the company's sales. Wizards allocated new card series to these stores, and there was often a feeding frenzy as consumers rushed to get an advantage by buying the cards. With the popularity of Magic, Wizards was able to enter such national chains as Toys "R" Us, Barnes & Noble, and Target. These stores did not have the special atmosphere of the small retailers, but were more effective for reaching the mass market.

Growth Problems

The success of Magic put Wizards on an explosive growth trajectory. Sales of about $200,000 in 1993 rocketed to $57 million in 1994 and $127 million in 1995. Wizards and Adkison became entrepreneurial superstars. The company grew to about five hundred employees, moved in 1994 to new corporate offices, and opened several international sales offices.

Growth also brought problems. Many of the gamers who started with the company were not ready to move into managerial roles, and some managers who had been brought in could not work well with the gamers. In one case, Adkison found that someone who had been on the payroll for several months had never been hired by or reported to anybody. As Adki-son said, "I've made so many mistakes, it's not even funny."

But growth came to a sudden halt in 1996, when sales fell off to $117 million. Moving quickly to control costs, Wizards had its first layoffs. According to Adkison, part of the cause was the inevitable leveling off of Magic's customer base and another was the fragmentation of the retail game stores. The success of Magic had drawn too many entrepreneurs into the game-store business, and the resulting shakeout caused some distributors to go under, affecting Wizards too.

While sales in 1997 were expected to be about at the 1996 level, Adkison was aiming at future growth. "We certainly can operate in a slow-growth mode and make nice profits," he said. "But we are focused on growing the company more rapidly in the future." Part of the pressure for growth was coming from its original investors. Many of them were friends of the original entrepreneurs, came from modest backgrounds, and had become rich from their investment in Wizards; but this wealth was all on paper, and many wanted to cash out part of their investments. To take the company public at an attractive price, Wizards would need to have a good growth plan. Coming up with a sustainable-growth strategy was therefore critical.

The Wizards Culture

While developing the systems needed to manage a much larger enterprise, Adkison tried to preserve the creative culture in which the company had been formed. For many years, he refused to have his own office or even a cubicle. On his business cards and memos, his position and title were given as "CEO and janitor." He saw the company as a kind of small software firm with a casual, creative atmosphere that tolerated individualism and creativity—expressed, for example, in eccentric clothing, body piercing, and frequent nerf wars among the employees. Over the years, however, the atmosphere became more reserved and Peter even acquired a corner office.

Wizards executives and employees tended to be very committed to the gaming concept. Richard Garfield, the inventor of Magic, saw adventure games as the "intellectual counterpart of sports: they keep you mentally fit." He believed that with playing Magic came "a lot of stealth education," whether it was art appreciation because of the beautiful cards or enhanced literacy because of the occasional quote from Shakespeare. Garfield also believed that Magic was a strategic game that could be played successfully only when the player had a good understanding of strategy, probability, and chance.

However, Adkison recognized that devoted gamers did not always make good executives. "There's nobody in the company who's ever managed a company this size, including me," he said. "We're trying to balance the desire for top-notch people to take us to the next level with the desire to stay true to people who founded the company." The firm had hired experienced managers from established toy companies, used consultants on strategic and operational issues, and brought outsiders onto its board of directors. Adkison himself obtained a master's degree from the University of Washington Business School, knowing that he would need to continue strengthening the organization and help it develop a strategy for sustainable growth.

The Adventure Gaming Industry

Wizards executives defined the company as part of the adventure gaming industry, which was itself part of the much larger toy industry. They followed publications of the Toy Manufacturers of America, as well as the more specialized *Comics Retailer,* a monthly publication with in-depth reports on gaming developments. Total U.S. toy-industry sales in 1996 were estimated at over $17 billion, of which the biggest single category was video games. The games and puzzles category accounted for approximately $1.4 billion in sales. Role-playing, trading-card, and war games—the segments in which Wizards competed most directly—accounted for about $350 million to $500 million in 1996 sales, according to *Comics Retailer.* The Game Manufacturers Association estimated gaming sales at $750 million.

The adventure gaming industry began in the 1960s with the development of a number of war games. The industry was revolutionized in the early 1970s with the introduction of Dungeons & Dragons, the first popular role-playing game. The game attracted players by being complex and by giving players the opportunity to exercise their creativity. The industry was revolutionized once again in the early 1990s with the introduction of Magic. By 1997, Dungeons & Dragons and Magic were still the top-selling role-playing and trading-card games. Wizards' acquisition in 1977 of TSR, the developer of Dun-

geons & Dragons, brought the two largest game manufacturers under one roof. The rest of the industry consisted of companies that were much smaller. Industry observers predicted that the most serious competition would come from companies in other industries invading adventure games.

Although there was no clear distinction between adventure and family games, people pursued adventure games as a serious hobby, sometimes dedicating many hours a week to playing a certain game. This led some critics to characterize players of Dungeons & Dragons and Magic as members of a "cult." Industry executives felt that this was an unfair image and saw most "gamers" as devoted to the games' intellectual and creative challenges. According to a survey by the Game Manufacturers Association, adventure-game enthusiasts were young and literate and did well in school.

One issue facing the gaming industry was the rise of the Internet and computer-based games. While most people in the industry considered typical video games to represent either lonely quests through fantasy worlds or "shoot-'em-up" arcade-like games, the Internet offered the possibility of role-playing and trading cards in a virtual world. Whether or not games would prefer this to the face-to-face experiences of Dungeons and Magic was of concern to Wizards executives.

Growing the Magic

As the dominant adventure trading-card game, Magic did not have much potential for increasing its share of this market. Wizards focused instead on extending the Magic brand name into other products and targeting the mass market to increase the size of the adventure trading-card industry. At the same time, the company had begun promoting Magic tournaments in an effort to increase the game's legitimacy and defend it from its competition.

Extending the Brand

Adkison was now attempting through licensing, to leverage the Magic brand name into books, computer games, and other products. With the popularity of Magic, Wizards was able to pick and choose its opportunities.

Magic also appeared as a book series by Harper-Collins, selling over half a million copies, and came out as part of two CD-ROM computer games. Wizards executives felt that bookstores were a logical market for its products because Magic players tended to be heavy readers and the game was often played in bookstores.

Also through licensing agreements, Magic merchandise had been extended into prepaid phone cards, clothing, card albums and protectors, a Magic strategy guide and encyclopedia, and calendars. Wizards had also reached an agreement with an Internet development and design company to produce interactive CD-ROM products that would serve as guides to the fantasy worlds created by Wizards. The company also received movie and television offers, but no agreements were reached. Licensing revenues were estimated to be about $1 million annually.

Going for the Mass Market

The dream of Wizards and other adventure-game developers was the mass-market role-playing game. Selling a typical board game brought in revenue of less than $10 a game to a company, but customers could spend up to $500 per year on a role-playing game. A mass-market hit could easily generate a billion dollars.

Wizards introduced a more mainstream version of Magic named Portal, which was targeted at a broader audience (younger teens and families) and was launched with a media campaign costing nearly $5 million. This new game used card decks based on a variety of popular TV characters—such as Xena the Warrior Princess—and allowed these decks to be intermingled. The aim was to interest a consumer other than the gamer who had made Magic a success. Portal was to be distributed through mass-market retailers such as Toys "R" Us and Target.

But Wizards saw risks with the mass market also. Magic gamers were attracted to the atmosphere of game stores and to the experience of the game, not just the game itself. Mass-market retailers, on the other hand, saw games as "boxes." And with retailers' tremendous buying power, Wizards would not enjoy the same margins that it did on its Magic sales.

Developing Tournaments

To increase Magic sales, Wizards attempted to professionalize the activity of playing Magic, transforming it into a legitimate sport. Noted Adkison, "It's been proven that sports are very sustainable. They hold people's attention for a long time." One part of the strategy was to create players who had celebrity standing and who could popularize the game in the mass market.

Tournaments had been organized informally in the first years of Magic, many held in and sponsored by stores selling the game. Hundreds of these were held each year. In 1996, the company organized a six-city professional tournament series that offered $1 million in prizes and scholarships. Wizards also created a global-ranking system for all professional players that was accessible at its home page (**www.wizards.com**). In the United States, over fifty thousand tournament players competed in thirty leagues.

The Magic world-championship series generated such interest that in 1997 it was carried on television by ESPN. Players from over forty countries competed for individual and team titles and for $250,000 in prize money. Wizards was able to attract a corporate partner, MCI Telecommunications, to sponsor the series. According to one news analysis, the partnership gave legitimacy to Wizards and provided the game with a mass audience, while MCI was able to tap an attractive audience by associating itself with a "cool" event. According to the company that brokered the deal, Magic players were considered a good market due to their passion for the game and their desire to collect everything associated with it. "You've never seen loyalty like this. It's unrivaled across any other product or service category." MCI agreed to sponsor Wizards' Magic tournaments in exchange for exclusive worldwide rights to produce and distribute Magic prepaid telephone cards featuring the artwork of Magic cards.

Wizards also published a variety of magazines connected with its games. *The Duelist* contain articles, tips from celebrity players, and information on upcoming Magic tournaments. *Dragon* magazine, which came to Wizards with the acquisition of the Dungeons & Dragons game, had been published since the 1970s.

Defending the Brand

In addition to aggressively promoting Magic, Wizards of the Coast had applied for a patent covering not the design of the cards but the method of play. Entry barriers to the game industry were relatively low, and Wizards estimated that there were over one hundred games trying to compete with Magic. The company was set on collecting royalty payments from imitators.

Beyond Magic

The success of Magic had not blinded the Wizards executives to the need to seek new sources of revenue. As the leading trading-card game company, it was the target of game developers constantly looking for the next hit. Wizards's response was to develop new games and to acquire other game companies.

Product Development

Wizards developed and marketed what were considered to be great games, but none was able to replicate Magic. Adkison remained optimistic, but realized that repeating that success would be difficult. "We have several things we're working on in R&D that could turn out to be like Magic," he said. "But in the gaming business, you can't bank on past success. We have to learn to make money with smaller releases."

The adventure-game industry had developed largely as a result of two runaway hits: Dungeons & Dragons, then Magic. Adkison expected that another hit would again revolutionize the industry one day. But it seemed unlikely that the same company would be responsible. Wizards needed to position itself to succeed even if it was not the one to develop the next hit.

Acquisitions

After completing two major acquisitions, Wizards was considering others. One acquisition was Five Rings Publishing, developer of the Legends of the Five Rings trading-card game; the other was TSR Inc., creator of Dungeons & Dragons. Integrating these acquisitions had been a major challenge for Wizards. TSR had serious financial difficulties that Wizards had to sort out, and the company was in the process of moving TSR operations and many of TSR's staff from Wisconsin to its Seattle headquarters.

Wizards confirmed reports that it had held discussions with Westend Games, which had the licenses to a Star Wars role-playing game and a DC Comics role-playing game. Other small game companies also looked like attractive acquisition candidates.

Global Magic

Wizards estimated that Magic was played in over fifty countries by more than five million players. Successful, the company had international offices in Antwerp, London, Milan, and Paris and planned to open offices in Asia. Adkison noted that international sales had been very important to sustaining the company during the downturn in U.S. sales in 1996 and there was still a lot of expansion potential in the international market.

Game Centers

In May 1997, Wizards of the Coast opened its first retail and gaming store, a 34,000-square-foot Wizards of the Coast Game Center, located in Seattle close to the campus of the University of Washington. Designed as the first entertainment center for adventure gamers, it offered an extensive array of arcade video games, sold games and associated merchandise, offered food and beverages, and provided a place for trading-card gamers to meet and compete with others. It was also intended to be a site for tournaments.

According to Adkison, the game center was "sort of like Niketown or Planet Hollywood. We have the opportunity to create the ultimate gaming atmosphere. This is a club, a hangout, a place for the devoted game players to go and play anytime." Wizards hoped that game centers would create an even stronger game-playing community by encouraging people to consider games an entertainment choice, like going to the movies or dining out. Just as the cineplex concept broadened the movie-going public, Wizards hoped that "gameplexes" would encourage the growth of the game-playing community. The Seattle Game Center carried many competitive games, but Wizards games were featured most prominently.

Another function of the game centers was to improve the retail distribution of the Wizards' product line. The company was disappointed with the support given by traditional retailers to the games and felt that it knew better than retailers how to sell and support its games.

Wizards also knew that the success of game centers was not a sure thing. Companies like Gameworks had introduced family-entertainment centers with very limited success. Wizards was encouraged, however, by the success of Games Workshop—the developer of the popular Warhammer game—with a similar concept.

Lightning Strikes Twice: Pokemon

In 1998, Adkison recognized that Wizards of the Coast was still a one-product company whose future was tightly linked to the success of Magic. He said, "Magic provides over 90% of our cash flow. It is obviously our primary focus. The big strategic issue with Magic is to develop its potential to become a 'classic game' that yields steady profits year after year. I wouldn't mind being a $500 million to $1 billion company. We want to make games as big as the movies." As he thought about the company's future strategy, the possibility that Wizards would have another hit like Magic seemed highly unlikely.[1] How wrong he was, for within a year Wizards would be riding a wave much bigger than that generated by Magic.

Named after the endearing set of characters invented by Nintendo, Pokemon had begun life in Japan as a game for Nintendo's N64 and Game Boy video-game platforms. In 1997, one of Nintendo's employees developed the Pokemon trading-card game. The Nintendo employee was an avid player of Magic, and he had simply taken the underlying structure of the game—referred to in the industry as the "game mechanic"—and inserted a new set of characters: those of the Pokemon world. The resulting trading-card game was a sensation in Japan.

Seeing the potential, Nintendo decided to sell the trading-card game in the rest of the world. However, it faced two problems in selling Pokemon outside of Japan. First, it lacked the distribution required to sell the game; and second, Wizards of the Coast had applied for and received a patent on the game mechanic underlying Magic. Since the Pokemon trading-card game used the same game mechanic, Nintendo might be in violation of this patent. The obvious solution to this dilemma was for Nintendo to license the ex-Japanese rights to the Pokemon game to the company with the patent on the underlying game mechanic and with an established distribution system, brand name, and industry expertise: Wizards of the Coast.

The results of the deal soon exceeded the expectations of both companies. Pokemon quickly became a global phenomenon among the six- to twelve-year-old set. Sales of the trading cards rocketed, along with sales of the video games, and the growing popularity of an associated TV series. For Wizards, the result was an unexpected bonanza. The company's sales surged from $150 million in 1998 to an estimated $400 million in 1999. The popularity of Pokemon trading cards accounted for some $225 million of this increase.[2] As with Magic, Wizards quickly issued expansion sets that emphasized new themes and generated incremental sales revenues. The collectible aspect of Pokemon trading cards was, if anything, greater than that of Magic. Kids competed with each other to collect a full set of trading cards, including highly valued rare cards.

Another appealing aspect of the Pokemon phenomenon was that it broadened Wizards' appeal to a demographic that it had not been able to reach with Magic: six- to twelve-year-old kids. The "dark themes" of Magic had put off many parents, but appealed to fourteen- to twenty-five-year-olds with a passion for strategy games. At Wizards, the hope emerged that kids would cut their teeth on Pokemon and, when they grew older, move on to Magic. Moreover, Pokemon allowed Wizards to widen its distribution system, selling in mainstream locations that had not sold Magic.

The Hasbro Acquisition

With Pokemon emerging as *the* theme of the 1999/2000 Christmas season, the success of Wizards attracted the attention of major players in the toy industry, including, most notably, Hasbro. In September 1999, Hasbro made a $325 million bid to acquire Wizards, which the company quickly accepted.[3] Under the terms of the deal, Peter Adkison would continue as CEO of Wizards for at least four years, the company would remain at its current location, and it would be granted a high degree of operating autonomy. Hasbro was looking to Wizards to broaden its offering of Pokemon toys and games in advance of the holiday season. In addition, the growing presence of Wizards in the hobby niche of the gaming industry, along with its growing retail presence, appealed to Hasbro, which was suffering from stagnating sales of many of its traditional toy offerings.

From Wizards' perspective, the bid from Hasbro had a number of attractive features. Wizards had long planned to take the company public, but recognized that executing an Initial Public Offering (IPO) might be very difficult given the skeptical view of the hobby gaming industry held on Wall Street. Many of Wizards' key employees hold significant stock holdings in the company, but in the absence of an IPO, this stock was not very liquid. The market was very thin because there were only about three hundred stockholders. The Hasbro bid allowed these employees to turn their illiquid Wizards' stock into cash—a very appealing option to many. Moreover, an acquisition by Hasbro gave Wizards the opportunity to use

Hasbro's brand name to open certain doors, such as those of mass-market retailers who had traditionally been reluctant to stock the products of the hobby gaming industry. Hasbro's financial muscle could also help Wizards' to accelerate its retail-store strategy, to make further acquisitions in the industry, and to fund the advertising required to strengthen its brand.

Strategy Going Forward

The acquisition by Hasbro did not signal any big change in strategy at Wizards. The company continued to take steps to build its Magic and Pokemon trading-card games, hoping that like Monopoly and Risk, these games would become "classics." These steps included an extension of the organized-play concept to the Pokemon game, issuing of more expansion packs and new editions for Magic and Pokemon, television advertising campaigns, and broadening the distribution for Magic. In addition, the company continued to look for other opportunities to add to its franchise in the trading-card arena. In February 2000, Wizards announced that it had reached an agreement with Warner publishing to create a Harry Potter trading-card game that would employ a game mechanic similar to that of Magic and Pokemon and be marketed to ten- to fourteen-year-olds, the prime demographic for the best-selling Harry Potter books.[4] The game was scheduled to be released in late 2000. In February 2000, the company also announced that it had reached an agreement with the Major League Baseball Association and the Major League Baseball Players Association to create a trading-card game with a baseball theme, using league players as its central characters.

Wizards also continued to aggressively pursue its retail strategy, making a major strategic move prior to the Hasbro acquisition. In May 1999, Wizards acquired The Game Keeper Inc., which owned a chain of fifty-three retail stores that sold chess, puzzles, backgammon, dominoes, and family board games. Most of the stores were located in malls on the West Coast. The plan was to sell the full range of Wizards games in these stores and gradually convert them over to the Wizards brand name.[5] The company also continued to steadily expand the bigger game centers. In mid-1999, it had six game centers. By April 2000, the number had risen to eighteen and the company announced plans to open another thirty-four that year. Of these thirty-four, six would be converted from Game Keeper stores; the remaining game centers would be net additions. Not all of the game centers would be as large as the one in Seattle, but the average size would remain around 2,700 square feet, encompassing a retail store, an area for game play, and an area dedicated to coin-operated video games. The combination seemed to be a winning formula; the video-game and game-play areas drew in customers (and money, in the case of the video games), who would make purchases from the retail store.[6]

ENDNOTES

1. Charles Hill assisted in the facilitation of strategic planning sessions at Wizards that helped produce this strategy.
2. J. Milliot. Hasbro to acquire Wizards of the Coast. *Publishers Weekly,* September 20, 1999, p. 12.
3. J. Pereira and D. Golden. Games: With Wizards and Dragons, Hasbro expands its reach. *Wall Street Journal,* September 10, 1999, p. B1.
4. S. P. Chan. Wizards to make Harry Potter cards. *Seattle Times,* February 12, 2000, p. B1.
5. B. Ramsey. Wizard buys chain of stores. *Seattle Post Intelligencer,* May 6, 1999, p. D2.
6. D. Scheraga. Would you like to play a game? *Chain Store Age,* April 2000, pp. 50–51.

Napster

7

This case was prepared by Charles W. L. Hill, the University of Washington.

Lou Reed (artist): *"Artists, like anyone else, should be paid for their work."* [1]

Alanis Morissette (artist): *"Napster presents huge problems for the artists. It raises the question—which is positive—of where and how artists are compensated. But I don't agree with the model they have set up. The artist should be the person who's ultimately in a position to decide when and how something should be shared with whomever they choose to share it."* [2]

Eminem (artist): *"Whoever put my s**t on the Internet, I want to meet that mother****** and beat the s**t out of him."* [3]

Ted Cohen (record industry executive): *"I think it (Napster) is one of the coolest things to come around. I also thought the moment I saw it, 'My God! This could destroy the whole business.'"* [4]

Shawn Fanning (Napster founder) on hearing that the rock group Metallica had filed suit against Napster: *"Napster respects the role of artists and is very interested in working with Metallica and the music industry to develop a workable model that is fair to everyone while unleashing the power of the Internet to build enthusiasm for music."* [5]

Steven Wendell Isaacs (independent artist): *"I believe that Napster is a powerful promotional tool for the many artists and bands that want to reach large numbers of listeners but have not been able to get, or are disappointed by, the support provided by large recording labels."* [6]

James Breyer (venture capitalist): *"Napster is truly revolutionary—and it will be a precursor of some of the most important web applications over the next several years."* [7]

Introduction

Sometime in fall 1998, an indifferent eighteen-year-old student at Northeastern University in Boston had an epiphany. Wouldn't it be great, he thought, if people could share their music with each other over the Internet. [8] The student's name was Shawn Fanning, and the service that grew out of his epiphany, Napster, would shake the very foundations of the music recording industry. By 2000, Napster had taken

This case is intended to be used as a basis for class discussion rather than as an illustration of either effective or ineffective handling of the situation. Reprinted by permission of Charles W. L. Hill.

center stage in a pivotal struggle for the future of the industry. On one side was the Recording Industry Association of America (RIAA), the big five music recording labels, and several high profile recording artists, including Lars Ulrich of Metallica. On the other was a small company with less than fifty employees and limited funds, over thirty million users of Napster's service, and several artists who believed that supporting Napster was in their best interests, including Pearl Jam. In the middle was the U.S. judicial system.

The Music Industry

The music industry grew at a robust rate throughout the 1990s, registering global sales of $38.5 billion in 1999. The largest markets were the United States (37%), Japan (16.7%), the United Kingdom (7.6%), Germany (7.4%), France (5.2%), and Canada (2.3%). This growth came to an end in 2000, when global sales fell 5%, and again in 2001, when global sales slumped to $33.7 billion.

Despite the fall in sales, the International Federation of the Phonographic Industry (IFPI) claimed that demand for music was higher than ever, but that the decline in sales reflected the fact that "the commercial value of music is being widely devalued by mass copying and piracy."[9] According to the IFPA, one-third of all CDs and cassettes around the globe in 2000 were illegally produced and sold, suggesting that piracy cost the industry over $10 billion per annum.[10] Although illegal plants in Asia have long been the source of many pirated CDs and tapes, by 2001 the IFPI was getting increasingly concerned about consumers "burning" songs downloaded over the Internet onto CDs. In Germany, 18% of 10,000 consumers surveyed said burning CDs resulted in their buying less music. In the United States, nearly 70% of people who downloaded music burned the songs onto a CD-R disc, while 35% of people downloading more than twenty songs per month said they now buy less music as a result.[11]

As a result of consolidation, by 2001 the industry was dominated by five large recording companies that collectively accounted for over 90% of global recorded music sales. The five were Sony Music, Universal Music Group (which was owned by Vivendi, a French media conglomerate), EMI, Warner Music Group (owned by AOL Time Warner), and Bertelsmann Music Group or BMG (owned by Bertels-

mann, a large German media conglomerate). In 2000, Warner Music Group and EMI had attempted to merge their activities, but were prohibited from doing so by antitrust authorities in Europe, who believed that the merger would put too much market power in the hands of a small number of recording labels.

Music companies sign artists in return for royalties on units sold, which generally run between 12% and 16% of net revenues. The typical contract specifies that in return for royalties on future sales, the copyright of the artists' creations becomes the property of the music companies. The music companies then bear the costs of recording and producing the music, pressing the CDs, marketing, and distribution. It can cost around $1 million to produce and launch a new act, not counting the costs of manufacturing and distributing the CDs. These upfront costs are normally deducted from the artists' royalties. Although there are rare cases of instant hits, with an album selling over a million copies, the vast majority of new CDs are never profitable. Each year the major labels issue about 7,000 new CDs (and minor labels issue another 20,000). Most never recover the upfront recording and marketing costs. In the end, some 10% are profitable.[12] The low success rate implies that many artists never make a dime from their work. Moreover, under an industry practice known as cross-collateralization, the deficit from an artist's first album is added to the deficit from the second album, making it very difficult for some artists to ever make a profit on their work.

Since CDs were first introduced in 1983, their average price in real terms has fallen significantly. Between 1983 and 1996, the average price of a CD fell by more than 40%, while the consumer price index rose by nearly 60%. Despite the price fall, antitrust authorities on both sides of the Atlantic have investigated the music recording industry for alleged price fixing. In May 2000, the big five companies settled a suit with the United States Federal Trade Commission, agreeing to end a requirement that retail stores adhere to minimum prices in advertisements.[13] The agreement was expected to open the way for more price discounting of CDs in retail stores.[14] In August 2001, the European Union ended a similar investigation after three major recording companies agreed to end minimum price requirements.

Historically, the other big players in the music industry have been retailers. In 2000, 95% of CD sales in the United States were still made through music stores. However, the nature of distribution was changing, with discount stores such as Wal-Mart beginning to account for a larger proportion of total CD sales. **Amazon.com** was also emerging as an important distributor of CDs. In addition, experiments by the big five music companies in the online distribution of music were causing tensions with retailers, who started to fear that store sales might suffer.

Intellectual Property Rights and Technology

In the United States, the rights given to copyright holders are based on the Copyright Protection Act of 1976. (Similar legislation exists in other nations, and intellectual property is protected under World Trade Organization agreements, which over 120 countries have signed on to.) Under the 1976 act, copyright holders have the exclusive right to control the reproduction, modification, distribution, public performance, and public displays of their copyrighted material. This set of rights can be violated in three ways:[15]

1. **Direct copyright infringement:** The direct infringer violates any of the copyright holder's exclusive rights, for example, producing and selling a CD without obtaining permission from the copyright holder.

2. **Vicarious copyright infringement:** The vicarious infringer has the right and ability to control the direct infringer's actions and reap financial benefits from those actions. For example, the courts have held that swap meet organizers vicariously infringed if they knowingly created and administered a market in which bootleg music is bought and sold, and were paid a fee for admission.

3. **Contributory copyright infringement:** The infringer knowingly induced or caused the directly infringing conduct. For example, an electronic bulletin-board service was found liable when it encouraged subscribers to upload *Playboy* pictures so that other subscribers could download them.

Historically, the music industry has always been concerned about the potential for piracy of copyrighted material. New technology has often facilitated the low-cost copying and distribution of music. In the 1960s and 1970s, the advent of the audio cassette tape led to widespread illegal copying and distribution of music. In the early 1990s, the industry was deeply concerned about attempts by Sony to commercialize its Digital Audio Tape (DAT) technology, which they felt would facilitate high fidelity copying of recorded music and thus lead to greater piracy. Although the RIAA initially opposed Sony, they switched to supporting the technology once Sony agreed to incorporate software that would make it difficult to use DAT technology to make multiple copies of a music recording. In addition, in 1992 the Audio Home Recording Act required DAT manufacturers to pay a royalty on each blank tape they sold to compensate music companies for the piracy that would take place through DAT. DAT technology was not accepted by consumers, but it was clear the underlying copyright issues would not go away.

Another technology that raised the specter of copyright infringement was MP3. Originally developed in the 1980s, MP3 is a software technology for creating compressed digital music files which could be downloaded for free from the Internet. MP3 music files were created through a process known as "ripping," in which computer owners copy a CD into MP3's digital format, which is about one-twelfth the size of the original file. This compression was achieved by eliminating overlapping sound waves and digital audio signals that fell outside of human hearing range. The great virtue of compressed MP3 files is that they take up less space on a hard drive and can be transferred more easily over the Internet. Until the late 1990s, however, the speed of most Internet connections was so slow that there was little online demand for MP3 music files. Three things changed: the emergence of high-speed Internet connections, especially on college campuses; the growth of web sites such as **MP3.com,** which archived MP3 files; and the introduction of portable MP3 players.

In November 1997 **MP3.com** launched its site. **MP3.com** had purchased thousands of CDs and converted their contents into MP3 files which were stored on its web servers, where subscribers to **MP3.com**'s service could access and download them. In an attempt to protect itself from legal problems, **MP3.com** required a user to demonstrate that he owned the CD for which he was downloading MP3 files by inserting a copy of the CD into his computer

CD-Rom drive, where it could be detected by software **MP3.com** used. In the same year, Diamond Multimedia introduced the Rio, a small portable device that could play up to two hours of MP3s.

The music industry immediately saw the threat: consumers could use high-speed Internet connections to download MP3 files over the Internet and store them on their Rios, circumventing copyright in the process. The RIAA filed a temporary restraining order against Diamond in October 1998, but the U.S. Court of Appeals ruled that converting the digital content of a CD to other formats for personal use was protected by the so-called fair-use doctrine contained in the 1976 Copyright Act. (The fair-use doctrine basically allows individuals to make copies from copyright material they have purchased for their personal use—i.e. not for resale or distribution.)

Having failed to halt the sale of the Rio, Universal Music Group (UMG) immediately went after web sites from which MP3 files could be downloaded. **MP3.com** was the obvious first target. In May 2000, the U.S. District Court ruled that **MP3.com** had directly infringed on music companies' copyright, noting that in actuality, **MP3.com** was "replaying for the subscribers converted versions of the recordings it copied, without authorization, from plaintiffs' copyrighted CDs."[16] On September 6, Judge Jed Rakoff delivered his ruling that **MP3.com** would have to pay the music companies $25,000 for each of the CDs it had copied to stream to consumers who also owned those discs. It looked as if **MP3.com** would have to pay UMG between $118 million and $250 million. In making his judgment, Rakoff stated that "some companies operating in the area of the Internet seemed to believe that because their technology is somewhat novel, they are somehow immune from the ordinary application of the law."[17] Around the same time, the RIAA was also trying to shut down another Internet music service: Napster.

In addition to seeking legal recourse against copyright violators, the music industry tried to develop technology that would protect digital audio recordings from piracy and counterfeiting. The RIAA recruited Leonard Chiariglione, inventor of the MP3 format, to head up the effort. Chiariglione pulled together a consortium of 180 firms, including record companies and consumer electronics and software firms, in an attempt to create the Security Digital Music Initiative (SDMI), a set of technological guidelines that were intended to reduce the risk of copyright infringements of digital audio media. The SDMI tried to develop guidelines for two types of security measures:

1. Digital watermarks would be embedded in digital music, which then could only be played on SDMI compliant music players.

2. Digital rights management technology would embed digital music with an encrypted digital package that would limit the number of times a CD could be copied.

Unfortunately, the SDMI made little progress, reportedly because there were too many competing voices, all with veto power. Apparently, different sides in the industry kept vetoing each other's schemes for copyright protection.[18]

The Birth of Napster

While the music industry was struggling with the SDMI, Shawn Fanning was giving birth to its biggest challenge yet: Napster. There was nothing remarkable about Fanning that would lead one to believe that he would spawn a potentially world shattering idea.[19] One of five children, he grew up in Brockton, Massachusetts, a small town some twenty miles south of Boston. His family was solidly working class with one exception: his uncle, John Fanning, was a computer industry entrepreneur who ran a company called NetGames. During summers at high school, Shawn worked at John's company, where he picked up programming skills from other interns who were studying computer science at Carnegie Mellon. It was at this time that he also became a regular visitor to Internet chat rooms, and particularly Internet Rely Chat, or IRC, which had become a de facto meeting place in cyberspace for hackers, traders of copied software and music, and so on. To enter IRC rooms, Fanning had to give a user name, so he chose his nickname from high school, Napster.

Although Fanning tried to get into Carnegie Mellon, he had to settle for Northeastern. As luck would have it, one of Fanning's roommates was obsessed with MP3 technology, which he used to download music from Internet sites and play on his computer. What caught Fanning's interest was not so much the ability to trade music files over the Internet using MP3 technology, but his roommate's frequent complaints about the process. Internet music sites were not always easy to find, they were unreliable, the links were often broken, and the indices listing music on a site were out of date more often than not. At the time, Fanning was disenchanted with his courses at Northeastern, which he found to be pretty basic, and was looking around for something to do. Solving his roommate's problems seemed to fit the bill.

As it developed, Fanning's approach to fixing this problem was relatively straightforward. He envisioned an index managed by a central server that would list all of the MP3 music files that people had on their hard drives and were willing to share, along with the embedded web addresses of their location. The list could be created if people downloaded a piece of "client" software onto their PCs. This software would update the central list every time someone logged onto or off of the Internet. The MP3 files themselves would continue to reside on the hard drives of individual PCs. To download a file, a user simply had to click on the title of the song, and if the PC with that title was logged on, the file would be transferred from one PC to the other over the Internet.

In essence, Fanning was proposing to create a peer-to-peer network of personal computers, coordinated by a central server which managed the index of MP3 files. The idea itself was not that new, although Fanning's application was. The entire Internet is basically nothing more than a huge peer-to-peer network. In 1998, another attempt to utilize peer-to-peer technology, **SETI@home,** had caused a stir in the high-tech community. **SETI@home** was a program that harnessed the unused computing power of thousands of personal computers to analyze data from radio telescopes for evidence of signals from potential alien civilizations. The program that did this was embedded in a screensaver that could be downloaded from the **SETI@home** site. The basic idea was that when the computers were unused (and the screensaver was on), the SETI program would communicate with a central server, which would download data to the PC, where it would be analyzed and then uploaded back to the central server. After fifteen months, some two million volunteers had downloaded the screen saver; **SETI@home** had received the equivalent of 345,000 years' worth of computing time from its volunteers; and it was estimated that the distributed network of PCs allowed **SETI@home** to tap into computing power about ten times faster than that of a conventional supercomputer.[20]

It is not clear whether Fanning was aware of the parallel development of **SETI@home,** which demonstrated the remarkable potential of peer-to-peer computing. Fanning would provide an even more compelling demonstration. First of all, however, he had to get the program written, and he needed some help. Fanning roped in two friends, Jordan Ritter and Sean Parker, whom he had met through an online hacker group called w00w00. Together they would develop the core of Napster. As Ritter later commented, "At that stage, Napster was really just Shawn and a bunch of friends trying to help out. There were no venture capitalists, no uncles on the scene, and no shady hangers-on."[21] What drove Fanning on, according to another friend, was that people kept telling him it wouldn't work. They said that people would not be willing to share their music files. According to this friend, Fanning was "driven more by the desire to prove everyone that he was right than he was by any realization or recognition of a potential revolution."[22]

By early 1999, Shawn Fanning had dropped out of Northeastern and was working around the clock writing code for the server and client. To prove his doubters wrong, he decided to try out an early version of his software, which he had christened Napster, giving out the client software to around thirty friends. He asked them not to pass it on, an instruction that several ignored, and within a few days the software had been downloaded by some 3,000 to 4,000 people. Many of these early adopters proved to be an invaluable resource, providing feedback that helped Fanning to improve the software.

It was around this time that Shawn Fanning told his uncle, thirty-six-year-old John Fanning, what he was up to. John quickly saw the commercial potential of Napster. In May 1999 he incorporated Napster as a company and went looking for investors. According to *Business Week,* when the company was incorporated, John took 70% of the equity and Shawn 30%.[23] One insider reportedly commented, "I am told that this was done without Shawn Fanning's immediate knowledge or involvement. Newspapers have accurately reported the morally deplorable distribution of equity."[24]

Napster's Takeoff

The embryonic company clearly had a number of problems to solve. First, it needed capital; second, it had to develop a business model that would enable it to profit from the service it provided; and third, it needed to prepare itself for the inevitable challenge from the RIAA. Very early on, John Fanning began to explore the legal ramifications of Napster's business. Among others, he consulted with the law firm of Wilson, Sonsini, Goodrich & Rosati, which had successfully defended Diamond Multimedia against the RIAA. The conversations reportedly gave John the confidence to push the business forward, and the belief that if Napster were sued, the company would have a good shot at winning in court.[25] John seemed to think that because Napster did not actually copy and distribute MP3 files, but simply put people who wanted to swap files in touch with each other, it was not breaking the law.

In summer 1999, John Fanning started to get initial funding for Napster. His first calls were to high-net-worth individuals he knew personally. A friend, Yosi Amram, kicked in $250,000, and another added $100,000. By the end of the summer John had raised enough capital to keep Napster going through to the year's end. Napster moved to Silicon Valley in fall 1999, primarily on John's suggestion that being in the Valley would help in the quest to raise more capital. Shawn and his friends (now all Napster employees) were working sixteen- to twenty-hour days writing code while John was out looking for more venture capital.

In September, realizing that the company needed a CEO who could develop a business model, Eileen Richardson, who had ten years' experience in the venture capital world—but had never run a company—was hired. Richardson's main claim to fame was that she had led an investment in Firefly, an Internet service that recommends music, which was subsequently purchased by Microsoft. Her task was to help secure additional funding, develop a business model, and then hand off the job to her replacement. In October 1999, Napster had raised $2 million in series B venture capital funding from a number of wealthy Silicon Valley executives, including Angel Investors' founding partner, Ron Conway, and Joe Kraus, founder of **Excite@Home.** What helped to secure the funds for the fledgling company was the extraordinary growth of Napster over the previous few months.

Formally launched in June 1999, the program spread with unprecedented speed. There was no marketing or advertising to sell the service, which was given away for free. The service spread through word of mouth. The early adopters were students on university campuses with access to personal computers and high-bandwidth Internet connections. In the fall of 1999 Napster was featured on the web site **download.com,** helping to raise the service to new heights. In July 1999, the Napster community was estimated at 4.9 million. By October 2000, it was thirty-two million and the site was growing by a million users a week, with some 800,000 logged on at any one time.

Among the first to take notice were the administrators of university computing and communications resources. The utilization of their networks was skyrocketing as students used them to transfer MP3 files. By October 1999, Napster was already occupying 10% of the Internet bandwidth capacity at Oregon State University, which became the first to ban the service. At Florida State University, Napster was taking up 20% to 30% of the bandwidth, and at the University of Illinois, the figure at times soared to 75%–80%. Soon, university after university banned Napster. In almost all cases, the primary motive was not the protection of copyright, but a desire to protect scarce computing resources from being soaked up by Napster. By February 2000, for example, the popularity of Napster had pushed network utilization at New York University to 98%, slowing down access and impeding its value as an academic tool. Once Napster was banned, network utilization dropped immediately to 60% of capacity.[26] Not all universities banned Napster, however. Several Ivy League universities, including MIT and Harvard, continued to allow students to use the service, citing their commitment to providing Internet access for all of their community and noting that they did not regulate or monitor a user's choice of sites to visit. Moreover, in many universities that did ban Napster, students fought back, using 1960s-style rhetoric to claim that a ban on Napster amounted to censorship and a violation of free speech.

Why was Napster so attractive? The obvious appeal was that users could download music for free. Why pay $17.95 for a CD that contained ten tracks, only three of which you wanted, when you could download the best three from the Internet for free and leave out the rest? Others cite the convenience of the technology. To get new music, you didn't have to go down to a music store. You just booted up your computer, logged on to the service, and quickly downloaded what you wanted. Many also found it interesting to browse through the playlists of other users, finding music that they would not otherwise listen to. And you could find music on Napster that you could not find in a retail store: old music recordings, esoteric music, unpopular noncommercial music, and so on. Napster also seemed to go hand in hand with two other developments: the spread of portable MP3 players, and new technology that allowed PC users to burn or create customized CDs. In both cases, users could create personal collections or playlists of music tracks from Napster downloads.

According to an RIAA survey of 1,015 music consumers on the attractions of peer-to-peer file-sharing services, having access to a large selection and variety of artists ranked highest (87%), followed by the capability to download files quickly (84%), the ability to download individual songs (83%), a convenient search feature (81%), and the ability to get music for free (79%). Ability to access songs not commercially available ranked lowest (64%).[27]

Collision Course

It was soon apparent that Napster was on a collision course with the music industry. The core of the problem, according to the RIAA, was that Napster's service was violating copyright, facilitating massive piracy of intellectual property, and, consequently, stealing. The RIAA, along with executives from several music companies, started informal discussions with Napster during the late summer of 1999. Record-industry executives insisted that the talks were a sincere attempt to find some common ground. One idea being explored at the time was for Napster to sell a minority stake to the record companies, which in turn would allow Napster to license a host of content. However, many Napster insiders believed that the record-industry executives were never serious about negotiating a deal, and they were just biding time. Whatever the truth, many observers do agree that Napster's new CEO, Eileen Richardson, did nothing to help matters. By all reports, Richardson had an abrasive and combative manner in her dealings with the record companies and RIAA, which only served to distance the two sides.[28] The following exchange apparently occurred in a CNN online chat room:

RIAA: While there are many legitimate uses of MP3s, don't you feel that your service will be primarily used by music pirates?

Eileen Richardson: We are about enabling amateur and unknown artists to share their music on this new medium. Our job is not to stop pirating; that is your job.[29]

According to other sources, Richardson was once heard yelling on the phone to Frank Creighton, head of the RIAA's anti-piracy group. Richardson also had face-to-face meetings with Hilary Rosen, RIAA's president, that apparently did not go too well. One observer noted that "Eileen got into fights with Hilary. . . . Eileen was fairly arrogant and thought what they were doing was right."[30]

Whatever the truth of the situation, on December 7, 1999, with talks between Napster and the RIAA at an impasse, the RIAA filed suit against Napster on behalf of eighteen record companies, citing copyright infringement. Several songwriters filed suit a few days later, and others were to follow. The RIAA alleged that Napster was vicariously infringing copyright, and that it contributed to the direct infringement of copyright held by members of the music industry. The RIAA claimed damages of $100,000 for each copyrighted musical work that was copied with Napster's software. For its part, Napster contended that its users did not infringe copyright because they only made personal copies and used the service in a way that amounted to sampling. The fair-use section of the 1976 Copyright Protection Act stated: "The fair use of a copyrighted work, including such use by reproduction in copies or phonorecords or by any other means specified by that section, for purposes such as criticism, comment, news reporting, teaching (including multiple copies for class room use), scholarship, or research, is not an infringement of copyright."[31]

One of the most high profile suits filed by songwriters was that of the music group Metallica. Metallica had protested that Napster's users were engaged in the unauthorized copying and distribution of copyrighted material. Napster responded that if Metallica could identify users that were violating copyright law, it would remove them from the service. In April 2000, the band's attorney, Howard King, filed suit against Napster and several of the universities that allowed the service to continue, alleging that Napster and the universities were violating the Racketeering Influenced and Corrupt Organizations Act, legislation that was originally aimed at organized crime. King and the band's drummer, Lars Ulrich, also turned up at Napster's headquarters with thirteen boxes of computer print-outs that contained the names of 335,435 Napster users who had swapped Metallica MP3 files and asked Napster to take them off the service. According to Ulrich, their complaint was that "Napster hijacked our music without asking . . . my band authored the music which is Napster's lifeblood. We should decide what happens to it, not Napster—a company with no rights in our recordings which has never invested a penny in Metallica's music or had anything to do with its creation."[32] Shawn Fanning, a Metallica fan himself, was somewhat disturbed by the criticism made by one of his heroes. Thereafter, he would frequently appear in public wearing a Metallica T-shirt, most notably at the MTV Music Awards, where Ulrich sat in the audience.

One of the defenses often voiced by Napster at this time was that far from hurting CD, Napster actually encouraged them. The basic argument was that Napster was dispensing free samples. When something was appealing enough as a sound file on a home computer, people would go out to a record store and buy the entire CD, just as they would if they had heard the song on the radio.[33] In early 2000, 'N Sync, Britney Spears, and Eminem each had huge hits. In the weeks before their records came out, these were the three most heavily trafficked artists on Napster's services, causing some to wonder if marketing departments at their respective labels had seeded Napster with prerelease copies of their music as a promotional tool.[34] In contrast to Metallica, some musicians openly supported Napster. Smashing Pumpkins broke with its label, Virgin, and gave away the group's final album for free via Napster, a move that met with a massive response. Even some senior record-industry executives seemed to exhibit a degree of schizophrenia. Thomas Middlehoff, the CEO of Bertelsmann, owner of BMG, admitted, "Let's be honest; despite all the dangers, Napster is pretty cool." He thought that file sharing as a system was a great idea, but that Fanning's mistake was "not having developed a complementary system for the protection of intellectual property rights and combining the two."[35]

Roadblock

By late spring Napster had its back against the wall. Not only was the company the object of several lawsuits, but it was also fast running out of cash. Into the breach stepped Hummer Winblad, a high-profile Silicon Valley venture-capital firm. On May 21, Hummer Winblad announced that it would invest $15 million in Napster. A Hummer Winblad partner, Hank Barry, was brought in as CEO, replacing Richardson, while Hummer co-founder John Hummer joined Napster's board. Hank Barry was an interesting choice for CEO. A former lawyer with a strong background in intellectual property law, he promised to build a working business model for the company and to solve its legal problems. One of Barry's first actions was to bring in David Boies, who had led the Justice Department to victory in the Microsoft antitrust case, to defend Napster against the RIAA. He also hired two seasoned record-industry executives to round out the senior-management team.

However, Barry had little breathing room. The pace of the legal assault against Napster was quickening. On June 12, 2000, the RIAA filed for a preliminary injunction that would shut down Napster pending trial, citing ongoing and widespread copyright infringement that was causing the industry great harm. On July 26, 2000, Napster had its day in court. Inside Napster, there seemed to be a strong belief that the company would triumph. John Fanning sent around an internal e-mail stating that "if the motion is granted, the order will be stayed pending appeal to the Ninth Circuit, where the motion will be decided . . . and if they rule against us, which I view as a 10% chance, we would be appealing to the Supreme Court, where the future of the world will be hanging in the balance."[36] It was not to be. After a two-hour hearing and a brief fifteen-minute recess, the presiding judge dismissed virtually every argument that Boies could muster for Napster and granted the injunction. In making her ruling Judge Marilyn Patel noted that there was a big difference between making copies for friends, which might be protected by the fair-use section of the 1976 Act, and making copies available via Napster, where a music file could be downloaded by millions of anonymous users.[37]

With the injunction granted and the service shut down, Barry scrambled to develop a business model that would both make sense and facilitate an alliance with Napster's opponents: the music labels. With the cash burn rate running in excess of $500,000 a month, Barry realized that he needed to move as expeditiously as possible. Again, Napster considered selling a minority stake in the company to the music labels, and then splitting subscription, sponsorship, and advertising revenues. The economics seemed compelling; if 20 million users (half of Napster's total in mid 2000) paid $100 a year for subscriptions that would allow for unlimited downloads, that would be $2 billion a year for Napster and the record labels. One survey found that 68% of Napster users would be prepared to pay a $15 monthly subscription for the service. Barry himself was reportedly contemplating a subscription of $4.95 a month.[38]

In the interim, Napster continued to hope that it would ultimately win in court. That hope was dashed when on February 12, 2001, a three judge panel from the Ninth Circuit Court of Appeals issued its ruling. The appeals court upheld Patel's injunction and determined that Napster should be held liable for copyright infringement. The judges stated that using Napster to "get something for free they would ordinarily have to buy" was a commercial use, and thus copyright infringement. Although the appeals court did send the injunction back to Patel for clarification, it was clear that Napster would get little relief from the courts.

BMG to the Rescue?

While the court drama was still unfolding, on October 31, 2000, Bertelsmann (owner of BMG, the fifth biggest record label in the world) broke ranks with the other major labels and announced that it was forming an alliance with Napster to develop a subscription-based music-distribution service based on Napster's peer-to-peer technology. As part of the alliance, Bertelsmann provided Napster with a $60 million loan, buying the service much-needed time. In explaining the decision, Bertelsmann's CEO Thomas Middlehoff indicated that the genie was already out of the bottle with respect to file-swapping technology. Indeed, with two other Napster alternatives, Gnutella and FreeNet, already making an appearance, Middlehoff suggested that the industry needed to embrace the technology, not rail against it in the courts.

Middlehoff's goal was that BMG and Napster would introduce a paid-subscription service by mid 2001. However, progress was slow. In November 2001, with no subscription service in sight, Bertelsmann kicked in an additional $25 million loan to help Napster. By early 2002, Bertelsmann was reportedly contemplating a bid to buy out Napster for $15 million.[39] However, the bid was in risk of being derailed by internal strife at Napster. On March 25, board member John Fanning filed a lawsuit against two fellow directors, John Hummer and Hank Barry, claiming that the two venture capitalists were no longer directors because they were voted out on March 24, 2002. Napster's new CEO (the third), Konrad Hilbers, issued a statement calling the lawsuit "legally groundless." Observers speculated that the reason for the lawsuit was that Napster was running out of cash and might have to file for bankruptcy, leaving John Fanning (and very possibly Shawn Fanning) with no return from Napster. On April 12, Napster announced that it would lay off 30% of its work force, and this followed a 10% reduction in the previous month.[40]

In the interim, the major record labels continued to push ahead with plans to introduce their own online music service. In early 2002, the big five companies launched two services. Both services sell monthly subscriptions that allow users to listen to songs without downloading using streaming audio technology. Alternatively, subscribers can download versions of songs that in most cases cannot be burned onto a CD or transferred to a portable device. Each service only has songs from certain labels.

MusicNet, which offers songs from Warner Music, BMG, and EMI, has one subscription plan: $9.85 a month for 100 streams and 100 downloads. Downloads expire after thirty days and can't be played. Pressplay, which offers music from Sony, Universal, and EMI, offers four subscription plans, ranging in price from $9.95 to $24.95 a month, for up to 1,000 streams and 100 downloads. The higher subscription fee service from Pressplay will let users burn up to twenty songs a month onto CDs that will not expire, but no more than two songs from any one artist can be burned.[41]

ENDNOTES

1. Trevor Merriden. *Irresistible Forces.* Capstone Books, Oxford, U.K., 2001, p. 45.
2. Trevor Merriden. *Irresistible Forces.* Capstone Books, Oxford, U.K., 2001, p. 45.
3. John Alderman. *Sonic Boom.* Perseus Publishing, Cambridge Mass, 2001, p. 114.
4. John Alderman. *Sonic Boom.* Perseus Publishing, Cambridge Mass, 2001, p. 116.
5. John Alderman. *Sonic Boom.* Perseus Publishing, Cambridge Mass, 2001, p. 10.
6. Trevor Merriden. *Irresistible Forces.* Capstone Books, Oxford, U.K., 2001, p. 26.

7. S. P. Ante, S. V. Brull, D. K. Berman, and M. France. "How the music sharing phenomenon began, where it went wrong, and what happens next." *Business Week*, August 14, 2000, p. 114.

8. Trevor Merriden. *Irresistible Forces*. Capstone Books, Oxford, U.K., 2001.

9. IFPI News release. Global music sales down 5% in 2001. **www.ifpi.org.**

10. International Federation of the Phonographic Industry, Fighting Piracy, 2001. **www.ifpi.org.**

11. IFPI News release. Global music sales down 5% in 2001. **www.ifpi.org.**

12. RIAA. How much does it cost to make a CD? **www.riaa.org.**

13. J. R. Wilke. Music firms, U.S. hold settlement talks. *Wall Street Journal*, December 16, 1999, p. A3.

14. J. R. Wilke. FTC move expected to bring lower CD prices, *Wall Street Journal*, May 10, 2000, p. A3.

15. D. Kiron, C. E. Bagley, and M. J. Roberts. Napster. *Harvard Business School Case # 801–219*, March 29, 2001.

16. UMG Recordings v MP3.com Inc., 92 F. Supp 2d 349 (S.D.N.Y. 2000).

17. John Alderman. *Sonic Boom*. Perseus Publishing, Cambridge Mass, 2001, p. 143.

18. John Alderman. *Sonic Boom*. Perseus Publishing, Cambridge Mass, 2001, p. 91.

19. John Alderman. *Sonic Boom*. Perseus Publishing, Cambridge Mass, 2001.

20. Anonymous. Divide and Conquer. *The Economist*, July 29, 2002.

21. Trevor Merriden. *Irresistible Forces*. Capstone Books, Oxford, U.K., 2001, p. 6.

22. Trevor Merriden. *Irresistible Forces*. Capstone Books, Oxford, U.K., 2001, p. 7.

23. S. P. Ante, S. V. Brull, D. K. Berman, and M. France. "How the music sharing phenomenon began, where it went wrong, and what happens next." *Business Week*, August 14, 2000, pp. 112–120.

24. Trevor Merriden. *Irresistible Forces*. Capstone Books, Oxford, U.K., 2001, p. 9.

25. S. P. Ante, S. V. Brull, D. K. Berman, and M. France. "How the music sharing phenomenon began, where it went wrong, and what happens next." *Business Week*, August 14, 2000, pp. 112–120.

26. S. P. Ante, S. V. Brull, D. K. Berman, and M. France. "How the music sharing phenomenon began, where it went wrong, and what happens next." *Business Week*, August 14, 2000, p. 112–120.

27. RIAA. Market Data, **www.riaa.org.**

28. S. P. Ante, S. V. Brull, D. K. Berman, and M. France. "How the music sharing phenomenon began, where it went wrong, and what happens next." *Business Week*, August 14, 2000, p. 112–120.

29. Cited in D. Kiron, C. E. Bagley, and M. J. Roberts. Napster. *Harvard Business School Case # 801–219*, March 29, 2001.

30. S. P. Ante, S. V. Brull, D. K. Berman, and M. France. "How the music sharing phenomenon began, where it went wrong, and what happens next." *Business Week*, August 14, 2000, pp. 112–120.

31. Section 107 of the Copyright Act of 1976.

32. **Salon.com** magazine, May 1, 2000.

33. J. Selvin. Did Napster help boost record sales? *San Francisco Chronicle*, August 5, 2001.

34. John Alderman. *Sonic Boom*. Perseus Publishing, Cambridge Mass, 2001, p. 1117.

35. John Alderman. *Sonic Boom*. Perseus Publishing, Cambridge Mass, 2001, p. 116.

36. Quoted in S. P. Ante, S. V. Brull, D. K. Berman, and M. France. "How the music sharing phenomenon began, where it went wrong, and what happens next." *Business Week*, August 14, 2000, pp. 112–120.

37. Anonymous. Rewired for sound. *The Economist*, August 5, 2000, pp. 59–60.

38. S. Ante. Napster: Tune in, turn on, pay up. *Business Week*, November 13, 2000, p. 52.

39. L. Himelstein and T. Lowry. The sound at Napster: tick, tick, tick. *Business Week*, April 8, 2002, p. 73.

40. N. Wingfield. Napster lays off 30% of workers. *Wall Street Journal*, April 12, 2002, p. A16.

41. W. S. Mossberg. Record labels launch two feeble services to replace Napster. *Wall Street Journal*, February 7, 2002, p. B1.

AtomFilms

8

This case was prepared by Taz Pirmohamed (MBA '01) under the supervision of Professor Bharat Anand, Harvard Business School.

We are building an entertainment platform so that we can take advantage of any and all opportunities to lead the next-generation entertainment market. That is why I named the company Atom Corporation instead of AtomFilms or Atom Games—like an atom we are a building block in the entertainment space.

Mika Salmi, CEO, Atom Corporation—
December, 2000

Mika Salmi rushed into the "Holiday Romance" conference room carrying the term sheets from several different deals. In the past month, potential partners, including Hollywood studios, online entertainment start-ups, telecom companies, and peer-to-peer applications providers, had approached him. Now, he needed to determine which deals were critical to the long-term sustainability of the company.

In the past two years, Salmi had grown AtomFilms from an idea to a successful short-film distribution company. By December 2000, AtomFilms licensed and syndicated films to

hundreds of companies, including major airlines and cable television stations. In addition, AtomFilms had built a strong presence on the web with its award-winning consumer website. The business-to-business (B2B) film distribution business was growing quickly, and the business-to-consumer (B2C) website was one of the only remaining online entertainment sites on the web. Since 1997, almost all of the traditional Hollywood studios had either built or acquired an online entertainment property. But, many of their original business models had failed. Similarly, numerous online entertainment start-ups, without the backing of a Hollywood name, had either filed for bankruptcy or had initiated layoffs. By all accounts, "digital Hollywood"—the name given to the online entertainment industry—was a huge disappointment. With this in mind, Salmi wanted to ensure that both the B2C and B2B divisions of the business were profitable and sustainable in the long-term. Thus far, the B2C side of the business had been lagging.

In January 2001, after considering many alternative options to finance and grow the company, AtomFilms merged with Shockwave, a private company that supplied consumers with media players and entertainment content through its website. Shockwave's online advertising revenue model complemented AtomFilms' offline distribution revenue model. The combined entity would have several million users visiting its website, and Salmi wanted to employ a revenue model that could monetize site traffic without compromising growth. The options to do this included charging subscription fees to access site content, focusing solely on site advertising revenues, or selling the best short-film submissions to TV networks and movie studios so that they could be developed into a TV series or a feature film. Salmi was intent on selecting a revenue model that would best position the company in the rapidly evolving entertainment industry.

At the same time, AtomFilms viewed itself as uniquely positioned to take advantage of emerging content distribution channels, including mobile phones and personal digital assistants (PDAs). Short films were ideal for consumers seeking entertainment "on the go" since they could be compressed into files small enough to be downloaded and viewed in a few minutes. A few weeks earlier, a major European telecommunications company seeking to license AtomFilms content had approached Salmi. By enabling cellular subscribers to download short films onto their phones, the company would be able to increase airtime usage. Salmi had to decide whether or not this was the right deal to launch AtomFilms into the wireless space in Europe.

Finally, Salmi pondered the importance of emerging peer-to-peer (P2P) applications. P2P applications created by companies such as Napster and Scour had facilitated content distribution amongst users logged onto their networks. However, the increased popularity of P2P distribution networks might cause content sites such as AtomFilms to become redundant. Flycode—a new P2P start-up that specialized in both audio and visual (A-V) content transfer—wanted to license AtomFilms' content. In exchange, AtomFilms would be provided with a permanent space on Flycode's website. Even though Flycode lacked a working prototype or a clearly defined revenue model, the reputation of the founders was impressive. Salmi wondered whether the P2P space was an opportunity or threat to the B2C side of AtomFilms' business.

Salmi again examined the term sheets in his hands again. As he glanced at his watch, he realized how little time he had to act on each deal.

Landscape

Offline Entertainment Space

Movies Theatrical movies were a cornerstone of domestic entertainment spending. In 2000, U.S. consumers purchased 1.5 billion movie tickets worth approximately $7.8 billion at the box office. Although box office sales had been growing only at a moderate pace over the past decade, exhibition on the big screen was considered to be a key driver of film viewing in other channels—for example, television and home video.

Movie releases from six film distribution companies (see Exhibit 1a)—the Walt Disney Co., Viacom Inc., Sony Corp., Fox Entertainment Group (majority owned by News Corp. Ltd.), Time Warner Inc., and Universal Studios Group (majority owned by Seagram Co.)—typically accounted for at least 80% of box office revenues. These distributors provided some or all of the financing required to produce a film. In addition, the distribution company that handled the theatrical release often owned the rights to distribute the film through other channels such as pay-per-view television, cable television, and home video (Exhibit 1b). Disney's Buena Vista film business had consistently captured the highest theatrical market share (17% in 1999), followed by Warner Bros. (14%), Universal (13%), Paramount (11%), and Fox Entertainment (11%).[1] In addition, in 1999, U.S. films generated almost $7 billion in international box office sales—matching the size of domestic box office sales. The globalization of the film market, in turn, had helped bolster the independent film movement—since independent films often performed better in foreign markets.

Prior to 1989, the market for independent films was relatively small and fragmented. Independent films had trouble finding distribution outside the small circuit of "art-house" theatres across the country. Rarely would a major studio acquire and then distribute an independent film. However, in 1989 Miramax Films purchased the rights to Steven Soderbergh's *Sex, Lies and Videotape.* The film cost only $1.2 million to produce and grossed over $20 million at the box office, making it the first bona fide inde-

EXHIBIT 1A

Ownership of Properties by Media Conglomerates

Media Conglomerate	Film	TV	Music	Publishing	E-Commerce
Disney	Buena Vista Caravan Pictures Miramax Touchstone	ABC A&E ESPN Disney Channel		Hyperion Press	Go Network
Viacom	Paramount Pictures Blockbuster Ent.	MTV Nickelodeon VH1 TV Land Paramount TV Showtime Spelling Ent.		MacMillan Publishing	CBS Sportsline
Sony	Columbia/Tri-star Sony Pictures Studios	Columbia/Tri-star TV	Columbia Epic Relativity Red Inc.		
AOL/Time Warner	Castle Rock New Line Cinema Warner Brothers	HBO CNN TBS TNT Cartoon Network Comedy Central Cinemax	Atlantic Elektra Sire Records WB Records	Little, Brown Warner Books Time Magazine Fortune Sports Illustrated	AOL Hoover's
Bertelsmann		Largest radio/TV owner in Europe	BMG Arista	Random House Bantam	Barnes & Noble
Seagram	Universal Studios		Universal/Polygram		

pendent blockbuster. The success of the film marked the beginning of a mergers and acquisition frenzy as major studios either bought or merged with smaller production houses specializing in independent films. Independent films enabled studios to identify fresh talent for their studio divisions and create a more diverse portfolio of films. In 1994, Turner Entertainment acquired an independent film house called New Line Cinema. That same year, Twentieth Century Fox and Sony each created independent film divisions.

Television   Based on ratings data from Nielsen Media Research, Inc., the four major broadcast networks—ABC (owned by Walt Disney), CBS, FOX (majority owned by News Corp Ltd.) and NBC (owned by General Electric Co.) attracted close to 55% of U.S.

primetime viewers in 2000. Increasingly, major broadcast networks were taking an ownership interest in the shows they aired. By doing so, they could share the syndication revenues generated from reruns if a show turned out to be a hit.

Over-the-air broadcast stations not affiliated with any major network achieved roughly 10% market share. The remainder of the primetime audience was split between dozens of cable and satellite channels, none of which averaged more than 5% market share. Roughly 75% of all U.S. households subscribed to cable networks delivered through wired cable or satellite services. Cable networks fell into one of two categories. Most advertiser-supported networks, such as ESPN and CNN, were advertiser-supported and were delivered to the consumer via a cable system

EXHIBIT 1B

Typical Life Cycle of a
Motion Picture

Box Office Release (34%)
- Theatre sources of revenue
  - admissions
  - screen advertising
  - concessions
- Foreign release

Pay-per-view/Cable (8–10%)
- Seek continued growth in asset base (with return above COC)
  - expand product line
  - enter new geographies
  - increase penetration
- Invest to protect position

Television (6–8%)
- Improve returns through pricing, cost reductions and/or asset productivity enhancements
- Sell or exit if returns cannot be improved
- Television

Home Video (48%)
- Primary strategies
  - severe limits to growth in assets (investments)
  - improve returns through pricing and/or cost reductions, e.g., reduce complexity
- Secondary strategies
  - maintain growth if returns can be quickly raised above COC
  - sell or exit if returns cannot be improved

operator as part of a "basic" cable subscription package. Other networks, such as HBO, were pay-TV channels—to receive them, subscribers paid a fee in addition to the basic rates for cable or satellite service. ESPN and CNN had carved out a profitable niche with a relatively narrow range of programming, whereas USA Network and TBS SuperStation featured a broad sampling of broadcast network reruns, movies, and sports. Recently, many cable networks had invested more heavily in original program content. For example, Comedy Central won a sizeable audience when it aired the first-run series of *South Park* and HBO had garnered huge audience shares with *The Sopranos* and *Sex in the City*.

Video   The home video market was a major revenue source for movie distributors. Consumers were now spending nearly three times as much per year to watch films on videocassette or DVD as in the theatre. In 1999, the market for video rentals was $10 billion. Videotape and DVD purchases accounted for an additional $10 billion. Movie distributors often sold videos to video retailers. The two largest video retailers were Blockbuster Inc. (4,795 stores) and Hollywood Entertainment Corp. (1,615 stores). The rest of the video rental market was extremely fragmented and mainly comprised smaller, specialty video retailers with fewer than five locations.

Recently, movie distributors and video retailers were making greater use of revenue sharing agreements. Under this arrangement, distributors sold videos to a retailer for a lower price in exchange for sharing a portion of the future rental revenues. This practice had encouraged video retailers to carry more copies of popular titles in their stores to satisfy consumer demand, without the risk of inflating their inventory.

Online Entertainment

The world wide web   In 1991, Tim Berners-Lee, a researcher at the European Laboratory for Particle Physics, wrote the basic parameters of a new language for describing computer documents. The language, known as hypertext mark-up language or HTML, could describe text, data, graphics, video, and audio. As individual computer users wrote documents in HTML, and placed them on host computers that constituted the Internet, the World Wide Web emerged. In January 1999, more than 100 million individuals used the World Wide Web.

As World Wide Web usage increased, the variety of web sites appearing on the Internet also exploded. Early entertainment sites were furnished with only simple text-based content. By 2000, some websites featured live webcasts and interactive programming. However, in 1998, many major film studios were still

Digital Content

	Set-top Boxes/TV	PC
Type of Content	• Sit-up (active) and sit-back (passive) content • Original and existing • TV, film and interactive	• Sit-up (active) content • Original content • Existing content not well-suited to PC viewing • Interactive
Length	• Any	• <30 mins
Revenue Sources	• Contextual and traditional advertising • Subscription/PPV • E-commerce	• Advertising • E-commerce • Offline mass advertising if content adapted for TV/cable broadcast
Audience	• Broad	• Niche audiences • Primarily teen/college segments
Growth Levers	• Penetration of set-top boxes	• Broadband access • Production of content suitable for PC viewing

EXHIBIT 1C

Broadband and Convergence

wary of making a major web site investment, hoping that the Internet would not have a significant impact on their revenue streams for many years. Jake Winebaum, chairman of Disney's Buena Vista Internet Group, noted that "it took decades for a medium like cable television to economically sustain original programming. But after years of thriving on material repackaged from broadcast TV and movies, cable networks are increasingly producing original (content). You'll see the same thing on the Net that happened with cable TV—Disney wants to be there when it happens."

Moves by Hollywood

By 1999, despite the lack of compelling business models, the major film studios were financing online ventures. At the outset, studios simply transferred existing content and programming information to the Internet.

EXHIBIT 1D

Broadband Penetration

Projected Broadband Penetration	2000	2001	2002	2003	2004	2005
Number of PCs connected to BB	6.2	15.2	25.2	38.2	53.5	69.2
Satellite, web-enabled box	0.5	1.8	3.0	4.1	6.4	7.7
Satellite, advanced box	3.8	1.8	9.8	10.3	10.6	11.0
Cable, advanced digital box	0.1	1.8	4.0	10.6	23.8	36.4
Cable, basic digital box	4.1	1.8	7.4	7.1	2.6	1.9
Total BB consoles	—	1.8	7.4	16.2	30.9	43.5
	14.6	24.2	56.8	86.5	127.9	169.7

Source: Bruce Kasrel, "Broadband Content Splits," Forrester Research, Inc., October 2000.

DreamWorks SKG   In late 1999, Ron Howard of Imagine Entertainment and Steven Spielberg of DreamWorks SKG announced the creation of a new Internet-only entertainment company, POP.com. Funded by Paul Allen's Vulcan Ventures and launched in spring 2000, POP.com offered aspiring artists the opportunity to submit films that might be produced by POP.com, community-oriented features aimed at filmmakers, and short form content. Despite the fanfare that accompanied the site launch, POP.com announced major layoffs in September 2000 and a change in focus—from producing mass-market Internet content to running a movie news portal. POP.com was viewed as one of the several major start-up failures in the online entertainment space.

Sony   Mirroring its broad, offline entertainment-based revenue stream, Sony developed several online entertainment properties ranging from interactive gaming to multi-media content creation. The most profitable of Sony's online ventures was aimed at the 280,000 subscribers to the role-playing game *Everquest*. Subscribers would pay approximately $50 to buy the game on a CD-ROM and would then pay approximately $10 a month to play. In 2000, the *Everquest* site generated approximately $100 million in revenues.[2] Sony also planned to rollout an experimental online movie service in 2001, with a broader rollout once consumer broadband became more pervasive. The multi-media platform would enable users to download movies onto PCs, digital video recorders (for example, TiVo and Replay), cable set- top boxes, TV sets with built-in hard drives, and video game consoles like the Sony PlayStation. Meanwhile, a Sony unit called Sony Pictures Digital Entertainment had begun developing original, interactive content for the Internet. One example of Sony's content offering was an online show called *Dawson's Desktop*, an Internet brand extension of the popular teen drama *Dawson's Creek*. Fans could go deeper into the story by reading the lead character's e-mail or diary and by watching his home videos.

Disney   After launching its first major online property in 1995, Disney's Blast website quickly became the leading kids and family entertainment site, according to Media Metrix.[3] The site offered subscribers' access to games, stories, arts-and-crafts activities, message boards, and live events for $5.95 a month or $39.95 a year. Ken Goldstein, general manager of Disney Online, said that "Disney plans to revamp the site to add more sophisticated content, with a particular eye for collaborative activities aimed at children, such as a group treasure hunt." Disney also planned to add features to enable up to 24 players to collaborate in the same game and to allow them to type their comments into a chat layer of the game. The site also offered more free content in order to attract a larger base of users. Underlying all content on Disney's online property was the company's corporate philosophy—to develop the most innovative and parent-trusted content for both kids and families.

Warner Brothers   Warner Brothers created Warner Online in 1999 to develop a hallmark entertainment property called Entertaindom.com. The site was divided into four areas: Playdom, for online games; Toondom, for children's programming; Screendom, for television and movies; and Rhythmdom, for music. The site featured original programming produced by Warner Brothers and others. Warner Brothers planned to offer free content and to generate revenues from selling advertising, capturing a percentage of gross merchandise sales, and from pay-per-view events. It was also examining the feasibility of a subscription-based revenue model. Following the merger announcement of Time Warner with AOL in January 2000, the site was shut down.

Digital Entertainment Network (DEN)   In 1999, Marc Collins-Rector created DEN to develop and broadcast brief, episodic online shows aimed at 14- to 24-year-olds with a particular emphasis on gay, Christian, Hispanic, and Asian young adults. The online entertainment start-up attracted a blue-chip group of investors and partners before the site launch. By June 1999, over $33 million had been invested by Chase Capital Partners, Microsoft, and Dell Computer, and DEN was in production to create 13 online shows. At its peak, DEN employed more than 300 technical and creative staffers led by executives from Disney, Channel One, and other top-notch entertainment companies. However, after launching its website in late 1999, DEN ran into a series of financial difficulties and unfavorable press coverage regarding the conduct of its management team. In addition, DEN was criticized for freely using its venture capital dollars to pay huge management salaries and exorbitant program development costs. In early 2000, DEN failed to raise a new round of financing, withdrew its planned IPO, and ran out of cash. By May 2000, DEN had laid off its remaining 150 employees and announced it would file for bankruptcy reorganization or liquidation by the end of 2000.[4]

The Founding of AtomFilms
The European Market for Short Films

Short films or "shorts" were loosely defined as films that were shorter than a feature-length film. In general, shorts ranged from one to twenty minutes in length. Short films could be shown before feature films in theatres, as stand-alone films, or as a bundle of several shorts broadcast in one-half or one-hour time-slots. Short films were pervasive in Europe, because European television schedules offered more pockets of programming time that were ideal for broadcasting short content. By contrast, short films occupied a different niche in the U.S. entertainment market. There, short films were often used to showcase the talent of an actor, director, or producer in order to gain access to the financing or support required to produce a feature film. As a consequence of these differences, the commercial U.S. short-film industry was much smaller than its European counterpart.[5]

Discovery of Market Need

Mika Salmi, CEO and founder of AtomFilms, was the son of a professional hockey player from the National Hockey League in Finland. Growing up in Europe, Salmi acquired a passion for the entertainment industry while viewing innovative short-form content on Finnish television networks. From a very young age, Salmi demonstrated a keen interest in the entertainment industry. As a teen, he was a deejay, a rave promoter, and manager of a rock band. He recalled his instinct for identifying trends in popular culture: "I could always see where trends were moving, since I personally was always searching for the next new, new thing."

In 1992, Salmi was completing an MBA degree at INSEAD in Fontainebleau, France, when he discovered the French television station M6. M6 broadcast short-form entertainment of all kinds, including short films, music videos, and animation. Salmi, immediately struck by the innovative content that aired on the station, later recalled:

> My reasons for loving the content on M6 in the early 90s are the same reasons why I love MTV today. I can tune in anytime and be entertained. I don't have to commit myself to watching for half an hour, and I don't have to plan in advance when to tune in.

Although Salmi was convinced of the potential of providing short-form content to consumers, he was not sure how to leverage this idea into an entrepreneurial opportunity. In late 1994, Salmi moved to New York to work for Sony International Music and immediately noticed the lack of short-form content in the U.S. entertainment industry. He recounted:

> After I moved to New York, I felt deprived of the short-form content I was viewing in theatres and TV stations in Europe. There was a huge entertainment industry America, and yet short-form content was nowhere to be found in the mainstream U.S. market.

Salmi had dreamed of creating a cable channel similar to M6. Despite this, his first business plan was on a short-film distribution company that modeled itself on an independent label in the music industry. While writing the business plan, Salmi began to research the short film-industry by purchasing compilation videotapes of short films that had been published by local film festivals and distribution companies. He was amazed at what he found: "There were hundreds of distribution companies ranging in size from one-person shops to 100-person shops. I had no idea this was such a huge business and still invisible to the consumer."

The dearth of venture capital funding in the mid-nineties for film distribution companies led Salmi to realize that in order to build a sustainable revenue stream, any business model that focused on short-form content would need to encompass multiple distribution channels (e.g., theatre, TV, CD-ROM). But, still unsure about how to make the business plan a reality, Salmi moved to Seattle to join Real Networks as Director of Business Development for their entertainment division. After successfully launching *Real Audio*—a software "player" that enabled consumers to listen to digital music files on a PC—the company began to develop an audio-visual player. Salmi recalled:

> Our (market research) studies showed that people had very short attention spans while watching their PC, but they were actively engaged in the content. We also learned that the content

had to be unique, because consumers believed that if you could find it anywhere on the web, it couldn't be very good.

The dearth of web-friendly entertainment content led Real Networks to commission Spike Lee to create four short films specifically for the launch. Meanwhile, Salmi noticed that his clients also shared his frustration with the lack of unique content:

> Companies were trying to take movie trailers or live broadcasts and shoehorn them into the category of Internet entertainment. Neither the big studios nor the networks were set up to license, borrow, or lend content to web companies. There was no central clearinghouse for Internet-friendly entertainment content.

At this point, Salmi realized that his original business plan could deliver short-form entertainment using another channel—the Internet. So the AtomFilms business model was finally complete. His plan was further bolstered by the fact that "the U.S. market for short films was under-developed relative to Europe. Therefore, high-quality content would be more readily available in the United States and at a lower price." Salmi was finally ready to launch the company.

Visions of a B2B Company

Early on, Salmi recognized that AtomFilms could generate the most stable revenue stream from offline—not online—channels. Although consumer demand for online entertainment was growing, few entertainment companies had figured out how to build a viable entertainment business on the Internet. Salmi determined that the company needed to balance two critical issues—content acquisition and content distribution—to quickly reach profitability. With this in mind, Salmi hired Jannat Gargi and Brian Burke to build the content acquisition and content distribution departments.

The content acquisition side of the business was fueled by a grassroots public relations strategy that encompassed all the major film festivals:

> We tried to make a splash at every single film festival by giving away free stuff and by hosting big parties for our artists. One of our best publicity stunts was at the 1998 Sundance Film Festival when we rented a bus and showed short films inside. We built our brand, product recognition, and respect from industry professionals inside a bus! Everybody—including the press—loved it.

Soon, the AtomFilms brand became synonymous with short, independent filmmaking. The first film acquired by AtomFilms—entitled *Holiday Romance*—was nominated for an Academy Award for best short film in 1999. Recognition for AtomFilms products helped gain the trust and support of filmmakers across the globe. Salmi recalled that "pretty soon, our office was flooded with thousands of short-film reels from amateur and professional filmmakers."

The content distribution side of the business was also built using grassroots tactics. As Salmi described: "Brian was calling every single airline and TV station in the United States. He was attached to the telephone from morning until night calling every possible distribution channel to figure out who might buy our content."

In December 1998, Air Canada became the first paying customer of AtomFilms by purchasing five films for broadcast during their short-haul flights. Shortly afterward, several other airlines and cable television stations, such as the Sundance channel, also began to purchase content. Salmi noted: "All we needed was one customer in each channel to prove that the model worked. After that point, we were confident that we could raise enough money to build a larger sales force and really grow our business."

By mid 1999, AtomFilms' initial efforts had paid off. The company appeared to have created a cycle of growth: for every successful film it licensed, the company attracted more film submissions, more customers seeking to license its content, and more press detailing its success.

Incorporation of B2C

Although AtomFilms was a business-to-business (B2B) company, it built its first web site in November 1998 as a "live brochure" for its clients. Salmi recalled that: "the site was very functional—it simply detailed our company history and product line." However, in early 1999, Salmi spoke to several of his Internet clients, including @Home and the Go Network, to better understand how industry leaders were using A/V content over the web. He recalled: "I always thought we had the vision to use our content in much more innovative ways than our clients did. I was right. The web was full of lackluster entertainment sites that were *not* entertaining."

Armed with the belief that AtomFilms could create a superior web entertainment experience, Salmi prepared to launch a consumer web site. The site would showcase the company's best short films, create a community for short-film makers, and generate more public interest in short films. Salmi recalled that "on the day we launched the consumer web site, *USA Today* published an article about our innovative content, and we were instantly a huge hit . . . site traffic has been sky-rocketing ever since."

The traffic and registered users on the AtomFilms site experienced exponential growth. (See Exhibits 1–3.) However, the advertising and merchandise revenue stream from the website was still overshadowed by the licensing and syndication revenues generated from offline distribution channels. In addition, whereas the B2C revenue stream was small, the people and technology required to support site maintenance and development was substantial. Still, Salmi viewed the AtomFilms site as an important component of the company's brand identity, marketing strategy, and consumer outreach. With many people visiting the site and sharing AtomFilms content with their friends, the intangible impact of the site was significant.

Growth of AtomFilms

As the confidence of Salmi and his new management team began to grow, so did the revenues and client base of AtomFilms. By year-end 2000, AtomFilms had generated almost $5.8 million in revenues, including approximately $3 million in licensing and syndication revenue, $1.7M in advertising and sponsorship revenue and an additional $.1 million in revenue from merchandise sold through the company's web site. (Company financials for 1999, and projected figures for 2000–2001 are in Exhibit 2). The website was experiencing a similar level of success: by Q4 2000, AtomFilms had accumulated a total of 15.2M unique visitors and 1.8 million registered users or Atom "insiders." Users, who were spending an average of 15 minutes per session on the site, had viewed over 31 million films (see Exhibits 3a–d, 4, and 5 for additional information). Website visitors were mostly young, middle-income, males; about 21% of site visitors were females. Along the way, several major deals contributed to the rapid growth of AtomFilms.

Content Acquisition

By year-end 2000, AtomFilms had amassed more than 1,500 short-films sourced from 350 filmmakers worldwide. The acquisition cost per film had stabilized at approximately $2,400 per film, despite increased competition for short-form content in the marketplace. A series of partnership deals enabled AtomFilms to acquire a bundle of short films at a low cost. One such agreement was signed in February 2000 with the University of Southern California's (USC) film school. AtomFilms bought the online distribution rights for 100 films from USC's School Cinema and Television—including shorts made by George Lucas and Robert Zemeckis when they were film students.[6]

Another major deal involved the first Internet-only animated characters for exclusive viewing on the AtomFilms site. Aardman Animations—the production company that had created the film *Chicken Run* in early 2000—produced the *Angry Kid* series for AtomFilms. Within seven weeks, *Angry Kid*, watched by over one million people, set an Internet record as one of the most popular characters in the history of the Internet.

Syndication and Licensing

Creating a large client base of syndication clients in a nascent market for short films was one of the greatest challenges facing AtomFilms. Several unique syndication deals helped the company convince clients of the value of syndicating a short film. In November 1999, Intel had created the WebOutfitter site for exclusive use by purchasers of the Pentium III processor. The site demonstrated the potential of rich broadband content when coupled with broadband access and a high-speed microprocessor. Since high bandwidth was required to enjoy audio-visual content over the web, AtomFilms' shorts helped to demonstrate the power of Intel's microprocessors to its customers.

By late 2000, AtomFilms had tapped almost every entertainment distribution channel except movie theatres. In November 2000, Century Theatres—which owned and operated over 700 screens in 11 Western states—agreed to feature short films for the launch of their CineArts 6 multiplex in Evanston, Illinois. Since short films had not preceded a feature length film in a theatre for over 25 years, the deal represented an important victory for AtomFilms.

Advertising and Sponsorship

In 2000, AtomFilms' innovative deal with Volkswagen presented a unique model for advertising and sponsorship. Volkswagen (VW) developed a new site—vw.com—to expose young people to the carefree and fun lifestyle the company promoted. VW agreed to

EXHIBIT 2

AtomFilms Income Statement

	1999	2000E	2001E
Revenue			
Ads	136	1,488	1,081
Sponsorships	—	2,682	2,322
Total Ads and Sponsorships	—	4,170	3,404
Syndication—Business	187	3,954	5,681
Subscription—Consumer	—	71	225
Total Syndication and Subscription	—	4,025	5,906
Merchandise	67	354	—
Service	—	71	—
Total Merchandise and Service	—	424	—
Total Revenue	390	8,619	9,310
COGS—Royalties and Investments	88	2,396	630
COGS—Other Costs	87	2,239	2,105
Gross Margin	215	3,984	6,575
Operating Expenses			
Sales and Marketing			
Labor	670	3,002	3,031
Advertising	—	10,031	2,000
Other Costs	1,412	1,864	1,421
Total Sales and Marketing	2,082	14,897	6,453
Content Acquisition and Display	—	—	—
Labor	590	4,155	3,724
Content Acquisition Costs	—	1,021	600
Other Costs	693	1,937	1,858
Total Content Acquisition and Display	1,283	7,113	6,182
General, Administrative and IT	—	—	—
Labor	560	2,947	3,276
Other Costs	236	1,987	1,947
Total General, Administrative and IT	796	4,934	5,223
Facilities	520	1,776	2,550
Research and Development	—	445	—
Depreciation and Amortization	180	1,917	2,200
Total Operating Expenses	4,161	31,081	22,608
Income From Operations	(3,946)	(27,096)	(16,033)
Metrics			
Page Views		549,730	404,472
Total Content under Syndication		1,576	4,139

Source: AtomFilms. All numbers (except page views and total content under syndication) are in thousands of U.S. dollars.

EXHIBIT 3A

Site Traffic at AtomFilms

Source: AtomFilms 1999/2000.

[a]Registration wall on site removed in August 2000; data collected between May–August 2000.

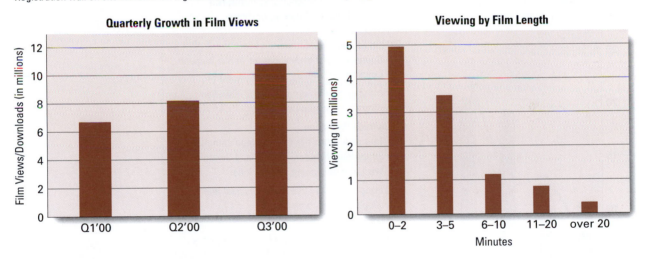

EXHIBIT 3B

Film Downloads on AtomFilms Website

Source: AtomFilms 1999/2000.

sponsor the "Journey Tour"—a cross-country tour in a VW van while showing Eric Saperston's short film entitled *The Journey*—at major college campuses in the United States. VW paid for a portion of the tour expenses, advertised on the AtomFilms site, and showed live webcasts of the trip on vw.com. In addition, VW mentioned the AtomFilms partnership in a series of national print and radio advertisements aimed at drawing traffic to the vw.com website.

Competition

IFILM   Created by Kevin Wendle, the founder of CNet and E Online, iFILM raised $37.5 million to host original short films by amateur filmmakers on its website. In 2000, however, iFILM changed its business model to become an online film directory while continuing to host original short films. The site also launched the iFILM Screening Network—a 14-day advance showcase where agencies could evaluate a

EXHIBIT 3C

User Demographics on AtomFilms Website

Source: AtomFilms 1999/2000.

Marketing/Promotions Reinforce Current Segment of Users

Film Festival Promotions
- Sponsorship of events, parties at film festivals
- Coverage in industry and popular press

Strong appeal to film-maker and indie film enthusiast communities

Journey Promotion
- Tour of Journey film to all college campuses
- Supporting sponsors are VW and Swatch, who wish to reach young, college kids

Strong appeal to indie film enthusiast and college student communities

Maverick Program
- Aimed at creating offline brand awareness
- Heavy users selected as 'Mavericks' to throw local Atom Film parties

Strong appeal to indie film enthusiast and college student communities

EXHIBIT 3D

Reviews and Referrals by AtomFilms Users

Source: AtomFilms 1999/2000.

filmmaker's work prior to the piece being viewed by a broader web audience. This portion of the site was created when the Creative Artists Agency (CAA) signed filmmakers Jeremy Hunt and Bruce Branit after their short film *405* appeared on iFILM. iFILM's revenue model involved securing 1% of the revenue from a successful filmmaker and agency relationship, instead of paying filmmakers directly for distribution rights. In December 2000, iFILM announced layoffs of 10% of total payroll for undisclosed reasons.[7]

Reelshort In partnership with Universal Pictures, Jeremy Bernard founded Reelshort in order to use short-film submissions to connect up-and-coming talent with big-name directors and actors. Reelshort paid filmmakers for the rights to a film and then

EXHIBIT 4

Management and Board Bios

Mika Salmi, CEO

Mika Salmi is CEO of AtomShockwave. In 1998, Salmi founded AtomFilms with the vision to discover and create new entertainment formats, marketed towards a wide array of distribution channels. Prior to AtomShockwave, Salmi was in charge of business development for media and entertainment at RealNetworks. He also spent seven years in the music industry for both Sony and EMI discovering bands such as Nine Inch Nails and Presidents of the United States of America. Salmi graduated Phi Beta Kappa with honors from the University of Wisconsin and earned his MBA from INSEAD in Fountainebleau, France.

Matt Hulett, President

Matt Hulett is President of AtomShockwave, responsible for operating and leading the business. Previously, as Chief Marketing and Online Officer for AtomFilms, Hulett led worldwide marketing, business, and online strategy. Prior to joining Atom, he was influential in the rise of RealNetworks. As group product manager, Hulett helped to make the RealPlayer streaming-media software the most popular non-browser product on the Web. Hulett was also responsible for founding the e-commerce and retail software distribution channels as well as popular consumer products, including RealPlayer Plus's and RealNetworks's subscription software services. Prior to RealNetworks, he spent five years as the worldwide marketing manager for WRQ's industry-leading Reflection PC-UNIX connectivity software. Hulett is a graduate of the University of Washington with a bachelor's degree in marketing and information systems.

Michael Comish, President, International

Based in London, Michael Comish manages AtomShockwave's international operations in Europe and Asia. Prior to joining AtomShockwave, Comish spent eight years in consulting, most recently as a partner in London with Mercer Management Consulting, one of the world's premier corporate strategy firms. At Mercer, he developed strategies for a number of leading technology and media companies such as Deutsche Telekom, Phillips, and Sprint, as well as branded-good companies such as Campbell's soups. Comish graduated with an honors degree in Business Administration from the University of Western Ontario, Canada, and earned his MBA from INSEAD in Fountainebleau, France.

Heather Redman, Executive Vice President, Corporate Strategy

Heather Redman leads corporate strategy and development at AtomShockwave. Prior to joining AtomShockwave, Redman was Senior Vice President, General Counsel and Secretary of Getty Images, Inc. Prior to its merger with Getty, she served as Vice President and General Counsel of digital photography pioneer PhotoDisc, Inc. Redman brings legal experience from the law firm Heller Ehrman White & McAuliffe. Redman graduated Phi Beta Kappa from Reed College and holds a law degree from Stanford Law School.

Eric Cansler, Senior Vice President, Finance and Operations

Eric Cansler is in charge of all financial operations at AtomShockwave. Cansler joins AtomShockwave from Headbone Interactive, where he was Vice President of Finance and Operations. At Headbone, Cansler worked to secure financing and led the company's transition from a CD-Rom to an Internet-focused content and entertainment company. Before Headbone, he was with Pantheon, Inc., a provider of software tools for Internet applications. Cansler spent six years with Arthur Andersen, LLP, as a consultant to high-tech clients. He graduated from the University of North Carolina and holds a Master degree in Accounting from the University of Colorado.

(continued)

EXHIBIT 4

Management and Board Bios *(continued)*

Michael Yanover, Senior Vice President, Entertainment

Michael Yanover heads the entertainment group at AtomShockwave. Since joining AtomShockwave, Yanover has initiated and is overseeing its key entertainment content, including some of its high profile Hollywood deals, such as that with acclaimed film director Tim Burton. Prior to joining AtomShockwave, Yanover started and ran independent TV, video game, and publishing companies, with some notable accomplishments being the creation of the "Men in Black" franchise and first prize at the 1999 Annecy International Animation Festival. Before that, he practiced as a transactional entertainment attorney in Los Angeles, representing clients such as Mel Gibson and Ridley Scott, and as a corporate and venture capital attorney in New York at Stroock, Stroock & Lavan, representing clients such as Warburg Pincus. Yanover holds an MBA in Finance from the University of Chicago and a J.D. from the University of Toronto.

Mike Edmunds, Senior Vice President, Interactive Products

Mike Edmunds leads AtomShockwave's Interactive Products Group, overseeing the acquisition and production of interactive entertainment content ranging from casual Web games to personal media creativity applications. Edmund has over eleven years experience in product development and technical management. As Vice President of Engineering at Macromedia, he was responsible for the Shockwave Player technology and Director multimedia authoring software. He also designed user interfaces and developed search engines at Verity, Inc. Edmunds holds a degree in computer science from the Massachusetts Institute of Technology.

Toni Marinovich, Chief Marketing Officer

Toni Marinovich leads the marketing and brand strategy for AtomShockwave. Marinovich joins AtomShockwave from Getty Images, where she held the position of Vice President of Global Marketing. While at Getty, she was responsible for the strategic direction and marketing of eight brands. She successfully developed marketing and creative services teams throughout Europe, resulting in several prestigious design awards. Marinovich has over twelve years of marketing experience working with Corbis Corporation, Apple Computer & Global Village Communications, among others. Marinovich holds a degree in Political Science from California State University in San Jose.

Seth Levenson, Vice President, Advertising Sales

Seth Levenson is responsible for driving AtomShockwave's advertising, sponsorship, and partnership revenue. Levenson joins AtomShockwave from Go.com, where he was Director of Advertising for the ESPN Internet Group. Having joined the Seattle-based Starwave Corporation in 1996, Levenson was the top revenue producer for the company's sites, such as ESPN.com, ABCNews.com, and Mr. Showbiz. Levenson has created and sold innovative cross-media advertising programs for major national advertisers, such as the Ford Motor Company, General Motors, MBNA, Intel, McDonald's and Universal Pictures. Levenson brings 14 years of media marketing and sales experience to AtomShockwave, including 5 years at Condé Nast Publications as Advertising Manager with Gourmet magazine and CondeNet. He earned his BA degree from Oberlin College and completed graduate programs at Harvard-Radcliffe College.

Lee Crawford, Vice President, Engineering

Lee Crawford leads Engineering and Operations teams at AtomShockwave and has over ten years experience directing the development of complex software systems. Prior to joining AtomShockwave, Crawford was Director of Engineering at Segasoft Networks, Inc., where he lead the Dreamcast Network project. Prior to Segasoft, he co-ran Twofish Technology, a consulting company guiding large, traditional corporations in shifting their applications to the web. Before that, he was a Senior Software Engineer at Thinking Machines Corporation. Crawford graduated from Florida State University with a degree in Computer Science.

EXHIBIT 5

AtomFilms Venture Financing

COMPANY OVERVIEW:

Business Brief:	Acquirer of exclusive licenses to films, animations, and digital content for distribution to a broad range of traditional and new media channels
Founded:	03/99
Status:	Private & Independent
Employees:	140
Stage:	Shipping Product
Industries:	Consumer & Business Services: Other

INVESTORS

Investment Firm	Participating Round
Warner Bros. Online	1
WaterView Advisors	1
Arts Alliance (London)	1, 2
Individual Investors	1, 2
Allen & Company Incorporated	1
Chase Capital Partners	2*
Intel Corporation	2
Trans Cosmos	2

* = Lead Investor

FINANCINGS TO DATE:

Round #	Round Type	Date	Amount Raised	Post $ Valuation (SMM)	Company Stage
1	Corp	5/99	5.0	NA	Product Development
2	First	12/99	20.0	NA	Shipping Product

EXECUTIVES AND BOARD MEMBERS:

Name	Title	Background/Former Employer
Heather Redman	SVP, Business Affair	SVP, General Counsel & Secretary, Getty Images; VP & General Counsel, PhotoDisc;
Eric Cansler	VP, Finance and Operations	CFO, Headbone Interactive; VP Finance, Pantheon
Irl Nathan	VP, Entertainment Technology	President & Cofounder, Pixel/Wave Entertainment
Frank Biondi	Board Member, Venture Investor	Senior Managing Director, Waterview Advisors
Robert Egan	Board Member, Venture Investor	Executive, Chase Capital Partners
Thomas Hoegh	Board Member, Venture Investor	Partner, Arts Alliance
Richard Barton	Board Member, Outsider	CEO, Expedia
Bill Heston	Board Member, Outsider	VP, Business Development, Getty Images
Mark Torrance	Board Member, Outsider	Chairman & Founder, Getty Images

Source: Compiled from VentureOne.

resold it through multiple distribution channels. Universal Pictures was one of the major investors in Reelshort. In return, Universal's development and production executives were given two weeks to view films on a private site prior to the work "going live" to the public. In addition, Reelshort could draw on the resources of Universal and its production partners to help nurture new talent.

Icebox   Icebox was launched in early 1999 by Steve Stanford, from Citysearch.com; Rob LaZebnik, a writer of *The Simpsons;* and Howard Gordon, a writer and producer of *The X-Files.* Icebox featured animated shorts that were both created in-house and submitted by amateur filmmakers. The site had signed over 100 established writers and producers hailing from *South Park, The Simpsons,* and *King of the Hill* to develop web-friendly animated content. Revenue was generated from three sources: advertising, merchandise sales, and licensing content to production studios and TV networks. In August 1999, Icebox announced a partnership with the Showtime cable network to produce a live action series based on the Icebox original animated series *Starship Regulars.*[8] In November 2000, Icebox laid off 50% of its staff for undisclosed reasons.[9] Then, in early 2001, Icebox officially closed down its site.

Pseudo programs   Created by Josh Harris, founder of the Internet market research firm Jupiter Communications, Pseudo produced and aired more than 40 non-mainstream, youth-oriented, interactive shows every week from its studio. Programming, which included games, music, fashion, and performing arts, featured interactive tools to facilitate communication between show hosts and web users. Pseudo generated revenues from advertising contracts with leading consumer brands, such as Arizona Jeans, Sprite, and Levi Strauss.[10] Pseudo.com closed its doors in December 2000. (See Exhibit 6).

Z.com   Z.com was a privately held company backed by the prolific Internet incubator Idealab! Z.com launched its site with original programming that included animation, short films, live events, and interactive games. Z.com was backed by several big-name Hollywood artists, including Brad Grey, the television producer of *The Sopranos* and Jerry Bruckheimer, one of Hollywood's top film producers whose credits included *Flashdance, Beverly Hills Cop,*

Top Gun, The Rock, and *Armageddon.* In late 2000, the company announced it had purchased the website Comedy.com and planned to integrate its programs with the Z.com offering.[11]

Emerging Technologies and Devices

Broadband

The term "broadband" was used to refer to a two-way, digital service that transmitted a minimum of 1.5 megabits per second (mbps) in at least one direction.[12] Narrowband devices, on the other hand, included an ordinary dial-up modem, which handled 28.8 or 56 kilobits per second (kbps). Still images and text could be adequately downloaded using narrowband devices. However, data-intensive applications like video-on-demand (VOD) required broadband connections. Broadband networks promised to unleash the Internet's full potential by providing high-speed data access to consumers' homes. In the United States, Internet access was expected to be a $13 billion business by 2002, and even larger if a portion of the $44 billion pay TV industry and the $110 billion local telephone market was included. The total addressable market was this large because broadband access could take place over one of three pipelines: high-speed telephone lines or DSL (Digital Subscriber Line), cable lines, or satellite connections.

DSL   By 1999, all the major local carriers were beginning to offer some form of DSL, since almost every household in the country had a phone line and roughly 60–70% could support DSL. The relatively slow rate at which consumers subscribed to DSL services, however, was attributed to three factors: limited geographic availability, difficulties in arranging installation, and high prices. In early 1999, the number of subscribers was roughly 75,000—a figure much lower than the local carriers had anticipated.

Cable   By 1999, 68% of U.S. households subscribed to cable television. Since the growth of cable subscribers had leveled out at 1% to 2% per year, the cable industry embraced high-speed Internet access as an opportunity to defend and grow its revenue base. All major cable operators were investors in one of two leading cable modem Internet service providers

(ISPs): @Home and Road Runner. @Home's service was available to 5.7 million of the 60 million homes reached by its cable partners' networks, whereas Road Runner was available to 3.6 million of the 27 million homes in its network. By 2000, fewer than 1.5 million homes subscribed to broadband services through either service. Despite the low adoption rates, cable companies also explored the possibility of offering telephone service over cable lines.

Satellite   Satellites provided a third alternative to new terrestrial fiber networks. However, whereas satellites were extremely efficient at broadcasting, they could transmit signals in one direction only. Although the technology for two-way communication was being developed, it was not ready for commercial introduction by early 2001. Hughes Network Systems used geo-stationary satellites to offer Internet access but required subscribers to use a dial-up modem and telephone line for upstream access. The difficulties in convincing consumers to purchase this complicated system had slowed the growth of satel-lite Internet access. By 2000, only 500,000 homes in the United States subscribed to this service.

Convergence

Nicholas Negroponte, a technology futurist and co-founder of the MIT Media Laboratory, had, in his description of convergence in 1995, declared that there would be no distinction between the TV and the PC in the future.[13] Nearly six years later, most U.S. households still did not use a "convergence" device in their homes. Although computers had persisted as a tool primarily associated with work, television was a tool used primarily for relaxation. Still, several companies and technologies had developed new devices that might help convergence take root in all households.[14]

Interactive television   The device created to facilitate convergence became more prolific once Microsoft bought Web TV—a Silicon Valley start-up—in 1997. Microsoft believed that Web TV devices could reach every American without a PC. But by 2000, Web TV

Technology Enablers	Pre-production	Online Film Distribution	Online Entertainment Content Distribution
Sightsound	ScriptShark	Atomfilms	Den
Shockwave	Medialive	Lemontv	Wirebreak
Real Networks	Idealive	Icebox	Pseudo
Windows Media Player	Patronet	Thebitscreen	Sputnik7
Apple Quick-time Player	Creativeplanet	Joecartoon	Movietv
		eveo	Metv
		Mediatrip	Regenerationtv
		iFILM	Broadcast
		Filmunderground	zchannel.net
		Raindance	Escreeningroom
		Shootingpeople	footage.net
		Alwaysindependentfilms	Internetv
		Movieflix	kkrs.net
		Thesync	
		Undergroundfilm	
		Zeroonefilms	
		Cinemanow	
		Bijoucafe	
		Pop	
		Scour	

EXHIBIT 6

Players in Online Entertainment

Source: Press clippings, web search; all underlined companies have filed for bankruptcy protection or closed site.

had sold only 1 million subscriptions and reached only 1% of U.S. households. In addition, many consumers seeking Internet access had purchased PCs— a trend aided by rapidly decreasing prices of personal computer hardware and software.

A recent example of a device the increased "interactivity" with the television was the Personal Video Recorder (PVR). PVRs performed the same functions as a videocassette recorder but used digital technology and a memory. PVRs allowed consumers to skip ads, pause live programming and then watch it later, and record programs on a particular topic so that consumers were able to program their own "channel." However, by year-end 2000, TiVo and Replay, two San Francisco-based start-ups that created PVR systems, had sold only 100,000 boxes between them. Microsoft had recently developed UltimateTV, an enhanced version of the PVR that was bundled with set-top boxes installed as part of a cable or satellite package. To date, several cable operators, including DirecTV and British satellite operator BskyB, had begun inserting PVRs into their boxes.

Game consoles   Using the PC as the primary game platform was expected to diminish because several game console manufacturers created convergence-oriented consoles with features such as Internet access, DVD, and CD players. These features were expected to transform gaming from a solitary to a group event, thus generating potential network effects in the retail gaming markets. These network effects, and the increased production of interactive game content, were expected to be the key drivers behind the projected 16.2 million U.S. households that would purchase Internet-connected consoles by 2003.[15] As delivery platforms evolved, revenue streams were expected to shift to advertising, pay-per-use, and product placement fees linked to Internet-based gaming.

The Sony Playstation2 (PS2)—released in the fall of 2000 was expected to capture nearly 90% of total new console sales. Sony, in a joint venture with Toshiba Corp., had spent more than $2 billion developing the PS2. The machine included a built-in video game console, DVD player, and CD-ROM drive. Even with all the accruements, it still had reserve space for a high-speed Internet connection and a hard drive for storing and playing music, movies and games. Sony Corporation envisioned the

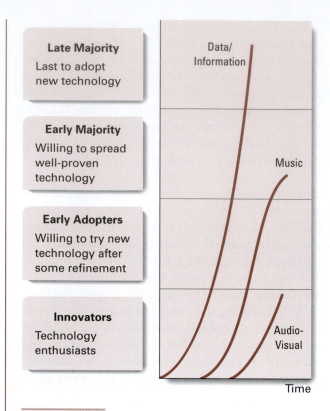

EXHIBIT 7

Adoption Curves for Data, Music, and Audio-Visual

PS2 emerging as the new "home-theatre-in-a-box" solution for families.[16]

Other game console makers had followed suit. The latest version of Sega's Dreamcast offered comparable graphics to the PS2 and a link to the Internet, but lacked a hard drive for storing media content. In 2001, Microsoft launched a new gaming console called X-Box that included an Internet connection and storage capacity similar to the PS2. However, without Sony or Sega's library of established games and characters, the X-Box was not expected to rival the sales of Sony's console for many years.[17]

Wireless   By 2000, total penetration of wireless devices was large enough that mobile phones were designed to function as convergence devices. Industry insiders envisioned mobile phones as devices for sending and receiving email messages, surfing the Internet, sending files from person-to-person, and storing digital music or audio-visual files. In several international markets that lacked the broadband infrastructure for cable or DSL connections, mobile

How?	*"A distributed computing architecture that allows client systems to communicate directly with other clients, with or without a single administrative server to coordinate and manage interactions between peers"*[a]
What?	• Documents sent via email • MP3 files with digital music • Budweiser "Wassup" video clip
Who?	• Napster (music) • Scour (A/V) • Gnutella/Freenet (all)
Why?	• Efficient sharing and distribution of content • Free, open to any user • Lack of external control/monitoring
Why not?	• Intellectual property rights • Security of data files on individual PCs

EXHIBIT 8A

Overview of Peer-to-Peer Networks

[a]"P2P: Publishing Computing Power to the Edge," Forrester Research, October 26, 2000.

phones were viewed as the ideal convergence device.[18]

By early 2000, Japan boasted mobile phone penetration rates of 46% in urban areas. NTT, Japan's largest local carrier, responded to this trend by developing a new wireless entertainment product. The i-Mode—an application developed in partnership with Sanyo and Liquid Audio Japan—sent top 10 music lists to i-Mode subscribers' cell phones. Subscribers could then purchase and burn an album onto a minidisk at the nearest music kiosk.

Emerging Applications: Peer-to-Peer Networks

A peer-to-peer (P2P) network was defined as a distributed computing architecture that allowed client systems to communicate directly with other clients, with or without a single administrative server to coordinate and manage interactions between peers.[19] (See Exhibits 8a–b.) In essence, P2P networking allowed peers to freely share files over an unregulated network. Following the rise of Napster, a communal music file-sharing application that became one of the most popular destinations on the web, P2P networks were being hailed as the next killer application for the web. By year-end 2000, Napster had attracted over 38 million users and had become the quintessential archetype for a successful P2P application.

Some observers argued that widespread usage of P2P technologies would be hampered by concerns regarding security and piracy. Although P2P networking enabled two disparate computers to communicate without a central server, it lacked the protection inherent in the traditional client/server model. Even with newly developed security measures, many individuals and companies distrusted applications that might make their PC vulnerable to outsiders.

B2C Applications of P2P Networking

The most profound P2P networking applications applied to sharing digital entertainment. In particular, many within the music industry felt the industry was undergoing a dramatic transformation as a result of an effective compression technology combined

EXHIBIT 8B

Applications of P2P Networks

Source: "P2P: Publishing Computing Power to the Edge," Forrester Research, October 26, 2000.

Advanced Search and File Sharing
Aimster and Centrata developing technology to search millions of peers and allow discovery of other users, instead of just data and Web pages

Harness Latent CPU Power
United Devices and Mojo Nation help to make users' systems available when not in personal use; likely applications in financial services industry

P2P Applications

Supply Chain Coordination
Consilient and Interbind developed applications for spot negotiations on price and delivery schedules to ease P2P interactions tied to supply chain

Real-Time P2P Collaboration
Groove Networks and CenterSpan developed new applications which use buddy lists to allow collaboration in real time on CAD tools, spreadsheets

with a file-sharing application. Although several different compression technologies had emerged via the Internet, MP3's technology enabled users to compress digital music files to an easily downloadable size while preserving the quality of the music file. Two companies, MP3 and Napster, had developed the most popular file sharing applications for Internet users. Their service was, in effect, a computer-based jukebox that allowed music fans to access songs, via the Internet, that they already possessed in physical compact disk form. Once the user logged in with a password, he or she could access the service from computers around the world.

P2P file-sharing applications posed several threats to the music industry. These included the prospects that music fans would access the Internet service with CDs borrowed from friends (i.e., for which they did not pay), that groups of fans would share passwords and be able to access one another's recordings via the Internet, and that copies of copyrighted music would be downloaded and stored from the Internet site and then passed along to others. The Recording Industry Association of America (RIAA), a trade group, had identified more than 4,500 music websites in the United States that illegally carried copyrighted recordings. Moreover, they predicted that by 2005 more than $3 billion of annual revenue would be lost as a result of illegal file sharing.[20] To

stem the tide, the RIAA filed copyright infringement litigation against MP3.com, calling for a halt to that firm's My.MPe.com service.[21]

Napster, the most successful file-sharing application with a community of 38 million users, had succeeded in creating so much consumer and media interest that the major music labels took notice. On October 31, 2000, Bertelsmann—the world's largest publishing and music company—announced a deal to offer a subscription service on Napster's site. Consumers would pay $4.95 per month to download music from Bertelsmann's BMG label alongside Napster's free download service. No other major music labels had signed up for a paid subscription service on Napster, although most offered secure paid downloads on their own sites (Exhibit 8c).

Recently, new companies had been created to replicate the Napster application for sharing audio-visual content rather than digital music. Scour, created in early 2000 and backed by Hollywood power broker Michael Ovitz, was the first of these companies. Despite strong consumer usage of the Scour application, the company filed for bankruptcy in November 2000 after being sued for copyright infringement by the film and music industries.[22]

Next, Bill Bales—a Napster co-founder and investor—created Flycode, a company whose seed money was obtained from senior managers at large

EXHIBIT 8C

Online Strategies of Major Music Companies

Distributor	Key Labels	Online Initiatives
BMG Entertainment	Arista RCA Zomba	▪ Offers secure downloads of 50+ albums and singles ▪ Retails CDs via GetMusic.com; a joint venture with UMG ▪ Acquired CDNow, July 2000 ▪ Partnership with Napster
EMI Recorded Music	Capitol Priority Virgin	▪ Offers secure downloads of 100 albums and 40 singles
Sony Music Entertainment	Columbia Epic	▪ Partnered with UMG to develop subscription services
Universal Music Group	Interscope MCA Mercury	▪ Partnered with UMG to develop subscription services ▪ Retails CDs via GetMusic.com; a joint venture with BMG ▪ Testing Bluematter multimedia format for downloads
Warner Music Group[a]	Atlantic Elektra Reprise Warner Bros	▪ Launching secure singles downloads in November 2000 ▪ Investments in ArtistDirect, Launch.com, and DiscoverMusic.com

[a] "Online Music: Napster and After," The Yankee Group, September 2000.

technology companies in Silicon Valley. Flycode aimed to develop a file-sharing application to enable distribution of video content and photographs with a more intelligent software interface. Having experienced the difficulty associated with controlling illegal content transfer while at Napster, Bales aimed to solve many of Napster's problems by using newly created technologies. Flycode intended to develop a new form of digital rights management software to protect copyrighted materials from piracy.

The Flycode business model differed from Napster. It planned to secure content from both amateur and professional artists and to provide artists with the option to give away ad-supported content, sell files individually, or sell subscriptions to Flycode's site. In addition, Flycode intended to collect ancillary revenue streams from site advertising, sponsorships, and by selling demographic user data to content providers. Flycode's target content partners included movie studios, television networks, and other content providers.

Recent Developments at AtomFilms

Deals

Wireless   As new wireless platforms emerged, Salmi realized that feature films and television shows required too much bandwidth to view on a wireless device. By

contrast, AtomFilms content was small enough to be transmitted at lower speeds. In April 2000, Microsoft and ActiveSky launched the new Windows-powered PocketPC devices. The ActiveSky Media Player was specifically developed to bring media streaming technology to small devices. AtomFilms entered into a partnership with Microsoft and ActiveSky that would enable short films to be pre-loaded into the new PDAs, to promote the viewing of short-form entertainment on large-screen mobile devices.

A second deal involved a telecommunications company. In November 2000, AtomFilms signed a syndication deal with Schibsted Telecom, the largest media company in Scandinavia. Schibsted, which attracted an estimated 50% of Scandinavian online traffic to its online properties, was seeking content for its new media portal. Schibsted syndicated 100 short films from AtomFilms for Internet distribution to its customers for their mobile and handheld devices.

Flycode   Flycode approached AtomFilms in the summer of 2000 with a content partnership opportunity. AtomFilms would supply content to the Flycode network for a small fee per file. AtomFilms' content would be wrapped in Flycode's proprietary technology to enable real-time tracking of content viewing. The data generated from the Flycode technology "wrapper" could be used to garner higher advertising dollars from companies that posted ads in Atom-Films content. Although a letter of intent had been signed, the final terms of the deal were undecided.

Financing

After witnessing a rather chilly climate for Internet start-ups following the precipitous drop in the NASDAQ in early 2000, Salmi was concerned about raising an additional $30M in a series D round of financing. Existing investors in AtomFilms contributed $5M in a bridge loan while Salmi sought other financing options. By Q4 2000, AtomFilms had attracted the attention of an Asian investor seeking to acquire the company to help develop its broadband and wireless platform in Asia; and interest in a merger with a leading online entertainment destination—Shockwave. After carefully considering both options, Salmi agreed to a merger between Atom-Films and Shockwave on December 15, 2000.

Shockwave was a private company with 57% of pre-merger ownership belonging to the online powerhouse Macromedia. The Shockwave site featured cutting-edge games, shows, music, and creativity applications, along with the Flash player—software required for viewing most animated works on the web. The revenue model of Shockwave stemmed from site advertising and totaled roughly three times AtomFilms' revenues in 2000. Monthly site traffic comparisons from Q4 2000 pegged Shockwave's traffic at approximately 12 million visits and AtomFilms' traffic at approximately 1.2 million visits.

Shockwave had accumulated a large roster of blue-chip advertisers and millions of site visitors seeking to download its free media player. However, the company was seeking to build both a global and offline channel presence. AtomFilms, on the other hand, had acquired the licensing rights to a massive content library, had developed many lucrative syndication relationships in offline channels, and had built offices and partnerships in the United States, Europe, and Asia. A merger with Shockwave would enable AtomFilms to reduce consumer marketing expenditures, to increase the breadth of content available on its site to include games and music, and to reach a much larger audience (See Exhibit 9). Although the cost-savings from the merger had not been fully explored, Salmi believed that the new entity could cut payroll from 300 to 200 persons, reduce lease costs by moving AtomFilms' staff to San Francisco, and decrease overall marketing costs by at least one-third.

Major Issues

Internal Resource Allocation

One of the key issues Salmi confronted, as he tried to steer the company to profitability, was financial and human resource allocation between the B2C and B2B sides of the business. The B2B licensing and syndication business generated sizeable revenues and profits for the company. Yet, Salmi believed that the size of the overall B2B film distribution market was relatively small. On the other hand, the B2C side of the business generated significant traffic and public relations for the company, but web surfers were notoriously difficult to monetize. This raised the question about which side of the AtomFilms business model was most sustainable in the long term. As the company expanded in size and scope, Salmi needed to decide where to focus precious time and resources.

Branding

The company also grappled with issues about its brand. So far, AtomFilms had built a strong brand connoting images such as "independent," "hip," and "short-form entertainment." It had also built a strong following among young, college-age males and the independent filmmaking community. However, the company now sought to broaden its viewer base in order to increase overall market demand for short-film entertainment. Salmi was uncertain about several issues regarding the company's brand. First, how could AtomFilms reposition its brand to appeal to a broad range of consumers? Second, which channels were most appropriate to reach out to new consumer segments? Third, should the online and offline channels deliver distinct messages to consumers? And, finally, what types of consumer marketing campaigns were appropriate for a company of this size and scope for each channel?

Wireless

Salmi was convinced that emerging wireless platforms were the ideal conduit for AtomFilms content. The company's vast library of short-form content was perfect for the new digital consumer. Consumers in Japan had already embraced technologies such as the I-Mode. However, the delivery of audio-visual content via wireless devices was largely untapped, and Salmi was not sure about how aggressively to tap this market.

EXHIBIT 9

AtomShockwave Fact Sheet

The Mission

To be the world's leading entertainment provider for businesses and consumers in emerging media formats.

The Company

AtomShockwave offers world-class entertainment, spanning games, films, and animations, driving distribution across the Internet, mobile devices, television, airlines and more. AtomShockwave is a pioneer and innovator in technology and content. The company is headquartered in San Francisco with regional offices in Los Angeles, New York, London and Tokyo. For more information, please visit **www.atomfilms.com** and **www.shockwave.com.**

The Catalog

The AtomShockwave catalog is as diverse as it is distinguished, offering groundbreaking games and interactive entertainment as well as an award-winning library of quality short films and animations from around the world, in every genre and style. With these original games, films, and animations, ranging from 30 seconds to 30 minutes in length, AtomShockwave is capable of offering entertainment anytime, everywhere.

Partnerships

AtomShockwave's breadth of advertising and sponsorship partners and syndication customers includes major television networks, theaters, Web sites broadband services, airlines, handheld and wireless devices and film institutes:

Acura	The Ford Motor Company	Palm IIIc
Adobe	F/X Networks	Real Networks
Altoids	HBO/Cinemax	Sci-Fi Channel
AMC Theaters	Hewlett-Packard	Sharper Image
Apple QuickTime	IBM	Showtime Networks
Blockbuster	Intel	Skyy Vodka
British Airways	Eastman Kodak	Sony
Camera World	Levi Strauss & Co.	Sony Playstation 2
Cartoon Network	Lexus	Swatch
Cathay Pacific	LucasFilm	Symantec
Century Theaters	Lugz	TiVo
Columbia Pictures	Maxim Online	United Airlines
Continental Airlines	Microsoft Pocket PC	Universal Pictures
Compaq	Microsoft Windows Media	20th Century Fox
Dell	New Line Cinema	Volkswagen
Delta Airlines	Nintendo	Warner Brothers
Finlandia Vodka	Nike	

Doing so might expose the AtomFilms brand to potential consumer dissatisfaction, owing to the slow speed or inefficiency of wireless content transfer. In addition, the telecom partners that had approached AtomFilms wanted to license its content but would not allow Salmi to decide how to market or deliver the content to consumers. How could he mitigate the risks of a poorly executed deal that exposed AtomFilms content to millions of European consumers?

Peer-to-Peer Networks

Despite the recently signed letter of intent to partner with Flycode on its audio-visual peer-to-peer net-work, Salmi wondered whether the evolution of new peer-to-peer models might make AtomFilms redundant in the consumer content distribution space. A successful P2P site could become the leading distribution platform for entertainment content—particularly if more intelligent applications could be developed that enabled consumers to navigate the vast array of content more efficiently. In addition, if filmmakers chose to distribute content via P2P networks, AtomFilms would find it increasingly difficult to search and secure high-quality content. The deal with Flycode had not yet been signed, and Salmi needed to determine the costs and benefits associated with joining forces with an unproven P2P networking company.

Future of the Company

Salmi also faced important strategic choices regarding the AtomFilms business model. During a recent senior management meetings, three models had been put on the table. First, AtomFilms could forge ahead with its current business model but place more emphasis on seeking several core corporate sponsors for its website. So far, several consumer products companies, including Ford and Volkswagen, had expressed interest in paying to maintain a constant presence on the AtomFilms site.

The second option was to introduce a subscription or pay-per-use fee on the AtomFilms website, in order to monetize consumer traffic on the site. However, fears of both radically diminished traffic and high consumer dissatisfaction upon the introduction of such a subscription fee had prevented the company from implementing this model in the past.

Finally, AtomFilms might leverage its relationships with filmmakers, talent agencies, production houses, and movie studios to gain a stronger foothold in the offline entertainment market. Under this scenario, AtomFilms would scan its thousands of film submissions to identify talent or scripts that might be useful to a talent agency or production house. In exchange, AtomFilms might participate in future revenue streams if the talent or scripts were used to produce a major feature film.

Ultimately, AtomFilms could not pursue all three strategies simultaneously. With a post-merger integration underway and with more announcements regarding failed online entertainment start-ups,

Salmi wanted to stay focused on his original mission—to create an entertainment company that delivered content to consumers anytime, anyplace, and through every channel imaginable.

ENDNOTES

1. "S&P Movies and Home Entertainment Industry Survey," May 2000.
2. Article in the October 9, 2000 issue of *Fortune* Magazine.
3. "Organization Profile: Disney Online," *PR Newswire,* December 27, 2000.
4. *Los Angeles Times,* May 18, 2000.
5. *The Wall Street Journal Europe,* August 14, 2000.
6. Bill Richards, Entertainment & Technology—Short and Sweet: "The Internet isn't quite ready for movies yet; But AtomFilms wants to be ready when it is," *The Wall Street Journal,* March 20, 2000.
7. Michelle Botwin, "Cybertainment 2000 Shakeout Hook Up Online Entertainment, " *Los Angeles Times,* December 29, 2000.
8. Red Herring Company Profile Icebox.com, October 2000.
9. Michelle Botwin, "Cybertainment 2000 Shakeout Hook Up Online Entertainment," *Los Angeles Times,* December 29, 2000.
10. Red Herring Company Profile: Pseudo Programs, August, 2000.
11. Article in the June 1, 2000 edition of the *Associated Press Newswires.*
12. Some of the information in this section is drawn from Mark Kwak and David Yoffie, "The Broadband Race: Industry Note," Harvard Business School note No. 799-106, May 3, 1999.
13. "A Survey of E-Entertainment," *The Economist,* October 7, 2000.
14. Ibid.
15. Ibid.
16. Christopher Stern, "Sony's Serious About PlayStation 2; Company Sees Console As the Centerpiece of Home Entertainment," *Washington Post,* October 28, 2000.
17. Ibid.
18. Japanese Market Primed for Subscriptions: Jupiter Concept Report, October 4, 2000.
19. "1 P2P: Pushing Computing Power to the Edge," Forrester Research, October 26, 2000.
20. Lee Bruno, "Peer Review," Red Herring, December 4, 2000.
21. "S&P Movies and Home Entertainment Industry Survey," May 2000.
22. *Los Angeles Times,* May 18, 2000.

ZOOTS—The Cleaner Cleaner

This case was prepared by Myra Hart and Research Associate Sharon I. Peyus, Harvard Business School.

When we did the research, we found that dry cleaning does not scream, "Opportunity!" All our interviews and our industry analysis indicated that people were willing to accept the mediocrity they were getting. They weren't particularly price sensitive; they weren't worried about the environment; all they wanted was to get their clothes back—clean, on time, and with all the buttons on.

Todd Krasnow, CEO, ZOOTS

On October 29, 1998, Todd Krasnow, CEO and co-founder of ZOOTS, welcomed the entire "clean team" staff, investors and friends to the company's grand opening. The "invitation only" party began in the late afternoon at ZOOTS' first retail dry cleaning establishment (Store #001) in Danvers, MA. It then moved on to ZOOTS' state-of-the-art central cleaning facility in Wilmington, MA. For the team, the party was an opportunity to share with family and friends the results of nine months of work that included securing funding, finding the right retail locations, staffing and training, and

designing the firm's Internet site. For Krasnow, it was the first time he was willing to provide anyone outside ZOOTS' immediate family a look at what they were doing.

Still, he was extremely cautious about calling attention to the new enterprise. Because of his high profile in the retail community, members of the press were very interested in learning what his new venture was all about. Krasnow, however, was not interested in the notoriety. He was determined to launch ZOOTS quietly so that he and his team could work out any operational issues in relative obscurity. His plans called for running in "stealth mode" until he had at least three ZOOTS stores open, so even as he acted the genial host of the party, he kept an eye out for uninvited guests. When he discovered some gatecrashers, he quietly escorted them out. It was clear they had not crashed for the "party experience."

Though the mood was festive, the celebration was deliberately kept simple. No champagne or chocolate truffles were served in the new 10,000-sq. ft. cleaning lab—only white wine, finger sandwiches, and packaged cookies. Nonetheless, the opening was a momentous event. On the one hand, it represented the culmination of extraordinary efforts. On the other hand, it marked the beginning of ZOOTS' "real work." Shortly after the party trimmings came down the next morning, the lab would be filled with thousands of pounds of dirty clothes that would have to be sorted, repaired, cleaned, packaged, and delivered back to their rightful owners within days.

Krasnow moved among the guests, chatting with employees and investors, laughing easily and congratulating each individual on his or her accomplishments. As he walked to the front of the room to offer the evening's few formal remarks, he chuckled to himself. He wondered what his Harvard Business School (HBS) classmates would think of his career in dry cleaning. Certainly, neither he nor they could have foreseen his choice when they graduated from HBS 15 years earlier.

Origins

Todd Krasnow

Todd Krasnow grew up in Westchester County, New York. He graduated from Cornell University in 1979 with a BS in Chemistry and, for the next 2 years, he applied his knowledge of chemistry as a food technologist at General Foods. His product line, Crispy Cookin', was intended to bring the taste of fast food into the home. His group patented a process that made it possible to retain the crispness of frozen fried food when heated in the oven. Krasnow himself received a patent for a quick frying process he developed that sealed a batter dipped piece of fish without cooking the fish itself. The finished frozen product bore a strong resemblance in taste, texture, and appearance to the fish served at the Arthur Treacher's restaurants.

Krasnow enjoyed the challenges of his work, but he was well aware that the technologists were not the key decision-makers in the company. After 2 years at General Foods, Krasnow left for Harvard Business School where he received his MBA in 1983. During his 2nd year at HBS, Krasnow took time out from his studies to co-author the school's annual musical. The 1983 spoof, *Soul Proprietors,* was a take off on *Damn Yankees,* in which two prospective HBS stu-

dents sold their souls to the devil to get into HBS. "It had a happy ending however," Krasnow recalled.

Krasnow worked at Star Market, a division of the Chicago-based Jewel Companies in the summer between his first and second years (1982). He joined the food and drug retailer after graduation, becoming one of the company's select group for fast track management trainees, informally (and somewhat irreverently) referred to as the "Jewel Jets." Krasnow's first 18 months on the job included a rotation through store operations areas including grocery, produce, deli, service, and store management.

He became Marketing and Media Coordinator in 1985. He worked closely with marketing director Myra Hart (HBS MBA '81) and took responsibility for preparing the weekly sales forecasts for the chain. After Hart told her marketing group that she would be leaving to join Tom Stemberg in the Staples start-up as vice president of operations, Krasnow approached her privately and indicated that he would be interested in joining the team. A few months later, in March 1986, he became Staples' Director of Marketing, charged with responsibility for selling the public on the office superstore's value proposition. His success with both traditional and direct marketing campaigns later earned him the title of Executive Vice President of Marketing. Krasnow maintained a strong role in setting the chain's marketing direction throughout his years at Staples, though his career path included several years in California helping to launch the west coast operations, an assignment running the company's international joint ventures, and the launch of the company's catalog operation. Along the way, Krasnow introduced many innovations, among them free *next day* delivery of office supplies.

For 10 years, Krasnow never considered looking outside the company for new opportunities. In 1996, the Executive Vice President of Sales and Marketing was completely committed to the company and to his longtime friend and mentor, Tom Stemberg who was the President and CEO of Staples. He was continually challenged by the work and, even more important, he was still having fun. However, when a group of investors approached him in late 1996 and asked him to consider joining their new venture as CEO, he found that he was tempted—not so much by the specific opportunity as by the idea of taking such a step. Stemberg was still young and deeply engaged in the leadership of Staples. It was unlikely that Krasnow would have the opportunity to lead Staples for many years to come, yet he was ready for such a challenge. He decided to discuss the offer with Stemberg.

Tom Stemberg

Tom Stemberg was a retailer through and through. After completing his education at Harvard (AB, 1971; MBA, 1973), he joined the Jewel Companies as a "mentored" management trainee. During his first months on the job, he spent his days bagging groceries, stocking shelves, and cleaning fish, but he also had regular meetings with a senior officer who had agreed to be his mentor during the training period. Assigned to Jewel's Star Market division in Boston, Stemberg quickly moved up the ladder. When he was named Vice President of Sales and Marketing just before his twenty-eighth birthday, he was the youngest senior officer in Jewel's history. His innovative marketing programs bolstered the supermarket's business and his aggressive leadership in marketing caught the attention of other major supermarket chains.

In late 1982, Stemberg joined Ohio-based First National Supermarkets (FNS) as Senior Vice President of Sales and Merchandising of its eastern division. In 1983, he was named president of the Connecticut-headquartered Edwards-Finast division. While at FNS, Stemberg concentrated his efforts on building a network of Edwards Food Warehouse stores, a high-volume, no-frills operation that offered low-priced merchandise, much of it under the Edwards-Finast label. In spite of his division's success, Stemberg decided to leave First National when, in January 1985, he realized that his differences with board chairman, Bob Samuels, were irreconcilable.

Stemberg conferred with his old friend and supermarketing colleague, Leo Kahn, as he sought the right opportunity. The two agreed to join forces and, with Kahn's encouragement, Stemberg wrote the business plan for Staples, the Office Superstore. Over the next 12 months, Stemberg recruited a senior management team, raised more than $4 million in initial funding, and opened the first of over 1000 retail stores in the US. His Staples concept and the team's execution of the concept changed the way small businesses and consumers bought office products. Initially, Stemberg was President and CEO and Kahn was Chairman of the Board. When Krasnow approached him in 1996 to discuss the possibility of leaving Staples to become the chief executive of another business, Stemberg was Chairman and Chief Executive Officer of Staples. He was also a director of both PETsMart and Cornerstone Brands. He served on the executive committees of the City of Hope, the National Office Products Council and was co-chair of the Friends of Harvard Basketball.

Searching for Opportunity

When Krasnow told him about the offer, Stemberg agreed that the time was right to consider such a move—Krasnow should either start his own venture or take over the helm of a substantial existing enterprise. Stemberg cautioned him, however, to think carefully about which opportunity to pursue, reminding him that there would be many good ones out there. Stemberg then went a step further, offering to help Krasnow develop a viable business concept, work with him to test the idea, write the plan, and secure funding.

Stemberg recalled the process he had used in 1985. When he decided to launch his own venture, he had started by taking a personal inventory of his skills and knowledge (which were in high-volume, low-margin retailing and distribution), then looked for market needs that could be served by these skills. After determining which areas of specialty retailing were growing the fastest, he conducted an industry analysis to determine what the size of the opportunity might be and what competitive action he could anticipate. Stemberg and Krasnow agreed to undertake a similar quest in February 1997, with Stemberg playing much the same role for Krasnow that Leo Kahn had done for him in 1985.

As a starting point, they determined that the new business venture should be in retail, should serve very basic needs, and should provide goods or services that required frequent "repeat" purchases. Krasnow was also committed to building a business that was based on strong customer relationships. As the two thought about the business models they might choose, they agreed that large-footprint category-killer stores (e.g., Staples, Home Depot, and Toys 'R Us) no longer represented the unique opportunity they had 10–15 years earlier. This decision freed them to explore business opportunities that would be profitable with much smaller scale operating units. One idea on which Stemberg had been keeping a file for several years was "dry cleaning."

They met frequently and compared notes on the retail experiences that they had personally found were less than satisfactory. They considered what it would take to change the way the products or services were delivered, then reviewed the industry structure and the likelihood of competitive or imitative responses. As Krasnow and Stemberg sifted through the many ideas they generated, they found that dry cleaning continued to intrigue them. Both had more than their share of frustrating dry cleaning experiences, with complaints ranging from missing shirt buttons to inconvenient hours, poor customer service, and cash only operations.

Each put up $250,000 to underwrite the research process and organized the new venture as a limited liability corporation that they called C.C., LLc (Limited Liability company). The "C.C." represented their commitment to building a Cleaner Cleaner, but their use of initials only was one of many steps they took to keep the focus of their new venture under wraps for as long as possible. A dozen years earlier, they had learned how quickly "me too" operations would spring up in the wake of a new concept introduction. Staples saw 22 office superstore operators open within 2 years of its launch. With both men even more visible in the retailing industry in 1997, they chose to delay the inevitable imitative flurry for as long as possible.

Defining the Territory

Krasnow began to research the dry cleaning universe, using both "bottom up" and "top down" approaches. He interviewed family and friends to get more information about their customer experiences. He was particularly interested in identifying individual hot buttons. He used the data he collected to build a profile of customer expectations about quality convenience service, and turnaround time. He also began to get a sense of the product mix his acquaintances had cleaned or laundered and what their heavy usage times were.

At the same time, Krasnow wanted to learn more about the business from the supplier's point of view. He convinced a local dry cleaner to help him understand all aspects of the business, particularly the marketing and operating issues. Using a year's worth of the cleaner's point-of-sale data provided, Krasnow

built a more robust model of usage, product mix, and general cleaning requirements. He also gained new insights about the demographics of heavy cleaning users. Though the research was conducted in Boston, he felt confident that he could extrapolate from these findings and make projections for other East Coast markets.

Krasnow also hired a consulting firm to survey 13 local area dry cleaners. In return for their cooperation, he agreed to share the survey results with all of them. He began to build a database of dry cleaning transactions in the greater Boston area with the expectation that he could use the information to develop more detailed demand and demographic information. He charted seasonality, consumer cycle times (time between drop-off and pick-up), and geographic concentration of customers. The survey corroborated his earlier findings and provided additional demographic data, product mix details, and even some information about individual business operating characteristics. He was pleased with the information he was able to amass through his own research and that of his consultants. He recalled:

> I'd never been a dry cleaner, but we were able to gather all kinds of knowledge—of how many shirts a dry cleaner does; how many and how often people come back (the next day, a week later, or more than six months later). We learned how often people come in only once and you never see them again. We determined how often high income people use dry cleaners versus low-income people, whether they were homeowners or renters, single or married, male or female. All of it was information that we could get our hands around. One thing that the research made clear was that customers were generally accepting of the status quo in the industry.

The Dry Cleaning Industry

For the most part, the business units in the highly fragmented industry were family owned. The low capital required for start-up and the relatively low level of skill needed made the industry particularly attractive to immigrants who often employed their entire families in the business. The International Fabricare Institute (IFI), a non-profit founded in 1883, was the industry association of dry cleaners, wet cleaners, launderers, apparel and textile manufacturers, suppliers, and other practitioners in the fabric-care industry that kept track of business growth and development. IFI estimated that in 1999 there were approximately 45,000 dry-cleaning stores generating approximately $8 billion in revenues. Projected sales for 2000 were $9 billion industry-wide (IFI). The 50 largest operators in the industry captured approximately 5% of total market share; 97% of all companies in the industry operated five stores or fewer.

One of the largest companies in the industry, Johnson Service Group PLC, operated dry cleaning companies in the UK and posted annual sales in 1999 close to $327 million.[1] The group also operated franchise dry cleaning outlets in the United States under the name Dryclean USA.

There were some newer venture capital backed companies that had national aspirations. For example, *Hangers of New England*, a retail franchise of professional garment care stores, operated one store in Wilmington, North Carolina and had announced plans to open up to 100 retail stores in 7 states (including Massachusetts) by the end of 2000. *Hangers* was unique because it used the patented and environmentally friendly Micare system developed by Micell Technologies. The cleaning process used no heat and relied on liquid carbon dioxide (CO_2)—a natural substance found in carbonated soft drinks—to remove spots and dirt rather than on traditional dry cleaning solvents.

Anton's Cleaners, a Tewksbury, MA–based chain of 40 stores was another potentially formidable competitor. Anton's was one of the largest dry cleaners operating stores and plants in Krasnow's target area of eastern Massachusetts and southern New Hampshire. Because Anton's provided on-site cleaning, it was able to offer same-day service to customers.

In spite of the fact that there were a few larger players, competition was generally assessed on a very local basis. Every dry cleaner within a three-minute radius of a retail outlet was considered a potential competitor. Because of this, each of the retail cleaning stores in a chain—even those within the radius of a single central cleaning plant—would operate in its own distinct competitive market. The fact that an individual dry cleaning establishment might be a part of a larger chain did not necessarily

make it any more formidable than a well-run "mom and pop" operation.

Building the Business
Defining the Business Concept

In spite of the fact that customers seemed to be willing to put up with inadequate dry cleaning service and that the dry cleaning industry appeared to defy rationalization, Krasnow was determined to go ahead. He planned to build a nationwide dry cleaning chain that focused on the customer experience. Though his new venture would use the web to attract customers and to track orders, the concept was, at its core a "brick and mortar" business. Stemberg and Krasnow believed that the hundreds of branded stores they envisioned would do for dry cleaning what Staples had done for office products—provide better service at reasonable prices.

The value proposition was simple. Their new venture would get the customers' cleaning done right, reliably, and conveniently. "We know that it's a winning formula and the customer is telling us that it's a winning formula," Krasnow emphasized. His cleaning team would not only meet, but also would surpass the expectations of the new economy's time-challenged consumers. It would offer customers a variety of convenient ways in which to take care of their dry cleaning needs.

Financing the Start-Up

Krasnow used the data he collected from customers, cleaners, consultants and industry information to build his financial assumptions. The revenues (pricing, average order size, customer counts, individual store volume) and operating costs (rents, store staffing, central facility operations) were estimates well documented by research. Krasnow relied on his own marketing experience and industry data to estimate other costs. He went so far as to have his team conduct time and motion studies of employee activities (shirt pressing, clothes sorting, as well as counter service at the retail stores) to provide the detail necessary for staffing and payroll models. He developed multiple scenarios that allowed comparison of revenues and profits for alternative operating models (e.g. on-site cleaning vs. centralized plant).

Though he did careful planning, Krasnow did not create a formal business plan. Since the first round of financing was provided by Stemberg, Krasnow, and a

---

1. Source: One Source

few selected associates, such a document was not required. "We had every important data point we needed in the plan that we circulated. We didn't include the market potential—but we thought we knew the answer based on our preliminary research."

In May 1998, Krasnow closed a $3.5 million series A round of financing. He and Stemberg contributed $1 million each and they raised an additional $1.5 million from a small group of family and friends. Krasnow also put in place a $5 million line of credit with a major Boston bank that was to be used to fund equipment purchases and working capital needs.

More Research

Krasnow hired independent marketing consultant, Phyllis Wasserman (HBS 1977), to conduct additional customer research. Wasserman, who had worked with Krasnow at Staples for seven years, had recently retired from her position as Sr. Vice President of Advertising and Communications. Krasnow had been deeply involved in creating and executing Staples' marketing strategy, but in his new venture, he found that his responsibilities as CEO consumed most of his time. His experience in working with Wasserman and his trust in her abilities led him to call her in on a consulting basis to take charge of several important marketing projects.

As Wasserman dug into the research, she found that dry cleaning was "a low-interest" category. Customers apparently gave little thought to choosing a dry cleaner, even though most expressed some dissatisfaction with the dry cleaning service they currently used. Wasserman noted that quality was a major weakness in the existing dry cleaning environment. "I pushed very hard on that score, and we wasted about a month trying to articulate our brand positioning statement—trying to define what we meant by quality and how we would communicate that to our potential customers," she recalled.

Krasnow recalled, "We started out thinking that we should emphasize environmental friendliness, convenience, and price, but the environmental piece didn't resonate with potential customers." The message that he believed would be most powerful was one of unequalled convenience and uncompromising quality. The C.C., Llc customer should be able to drop off or pick up clothes at any hour of the day or night and do so with the assurance that a favorite shirt or skirt wouldn't be missing any buttons when it was returned. If an item of clothing were missing a button,

it should be replaced automatically. The company's quality pledge would be, "Cleaning Done Right Or It's Free." In spite of his insistence on getting things done right, Krasnow believed it was most important to emphasize the convenience message, rather than quality. Wasserman agreed that convenience was a clearer and more concrete message around which she could build the brand. She elaborated:

> Building a brand name that would convey that message was critical. It was to be our unique selling proposition. Furthermore, convenience would be as our customers defined it—not as we defined it. We wanted to give our customers as many different ways to do business with us as they wanted, and we asked them to choose. Our message was, "We're not asking you to do business in our way, rather tell us how you want to do business with us."

Some of the conveniences the company would offer were extended hours, drive through drop off and pick up, and secure lockers that would provide the same kind of round-the-clock access that ATM's had introduced to banking customers. Computer systems would be built to provide customers order-tracking capabilities. Though there were still many logistical issues to work through, total customer convenience would be the company's defining difference.

Real Estate and Store Planning

Krasnow determined that centralized cleaning was the most efficient way to run the business. He planned to create regional "hub and spoke" networks of 7–10 retail stores serviced by a central cleaning plant. He anticipated that one of his prototype stores could produce three times the industry's average revenue, but he planned to use the Boston market to test his hypotheses and refine the operating model.

The store design would be kept clean and simple. Though not all locations would be built to exactly the same specifications, the prototype would include a 2400-sq. ft. facility with dedicated parking and space to accommodate a drive-through lane. In addition, each store would have a secure lobby area stocked with individual clothes lockers that would be accessible 24 hours a day. A proprietary system would enable customers to pick up and drop off clothes at any hour of the day or night using a key coded locker system and personalized garment bags. (See Exhibit 1.)

STORE CONFIGURATION

Floor Plan Prototype

Conveyors

Drive-Thru

Lobby Area

Detailing Area

Lockers

Exterior Store Design

Interior Store Design

EXHIBIT 1

Store Prototype

Densely populated, affluent areas, which had been identified as pockets of "heavy users" were targeted first. In early 1998, Krasnow signed leases for a retail store in Danvers and a site in Wilmington, MA, to be the "cleaning lab." He began looking for additional locations in metro Boston Nashua, NH, and Worcester and Springfield, MA. All of these stores were to be serviced by the Wilmington plant. The initial stores leased were in suburban locations. Once the Boston hub was functioning well, Krasnow planned to replicate it in other high volume markets.

Building the Brand

Krasnow and Stemberg had already selected a company name and logo, but they wanted Wasserman to take the next steps in developing the company's iden-

tity. She was delighted with the name, which she described as, "*in your face,* bold, different, yet likeable." She believed that people not only noticed, but also remembered **ZOOTS** because the name was short, playful, and easy to remember. It conjured up images of slightly zany "Zoot suits" and its individual components worked well. The letter "Z" was unusual both usually and audibly and the double "O's" lent themselves to bold graphics. Wasserman was confident that the ZOOTS name would translate well to electronic as well as print media.

She focused her energies on the challenge of store design. The operations group determined the physical layout of the facility, but she was responsible for creating ZOOTS' visual identity. She hired an experienced retail design firm and set out on her own to visit the best of branded retailers to see how they conveyed their messages through physical space. She and Krasnow spent hours discussing the image that they wanted ZOOTS to convey and ways in which they could express that image through the store design and décor. A dark wood interior would create a relaxed and comfortable store environment, but a minimalist approach with stark white surfaces would convey the "clean" image. Bold colors and powerful graphics would be more memorable. Wasserman argued for a clean and modern look— one that signaled fast and efficient service. "Everything we do needs to communicate *bold, different, revolutionary, modern,* and *fast,*" she told Krasnow.

Together, Wasserman and Krasnow reviewed design proposals, selecting elements they liked from each. Light colored woods, bold graphics, and crisp, bright colored signage were combined to create the ZOOTS image. Blue was the background color of choice because of its association with water and cleanliness. Once they agreed on the key elements, Wasserman and her design team completed a set of drawings for Krasnow. She dropped them off early on a Friday, then left for a long weekend on Nantucket with her family. When Stemberg looked over the package later that afternoon, he was disappointed because he thought the overall effect was "boring."

Wasserman had been at her "getaway retreat" only moments when the phone rang. When she picked up the receiver, she heard Krasnow's voice, in which she detected a note of barely controlled panic. He quickly brought her up to date on Stemberg's reaction and asked, "What can we do about it now?" Because the Danvers project was set to break ground on the following Monday, there was little time for making substantive changes. Wasserman looked down at the purple jacket that she had tossed on the bed when she came in. She told Krasnow to relax. She would have the problem solved by Monday. She called the design firm, described the color of her jacket, and asked them to change all the blue surfaces to purple in the drawings.

When she handed the revised drawings to Krasnow on Monday morning, his first response was, "Oh my God, they are really *purple.*" She tacked the drawings to his walls and suggested he live with them for a few hours. Twenty four hours later, he concurred, "We're going to be purple." "The color shouts,"

Wasserman declared. "The first thing that you see is a building that is different and announces, 'I'm here.'"

Wasserman selected an ad agency and began hiring staff. In the summer of 1999, Krasnow asked her to come on board as the full-time senior marketing person or to find her own replacement. She agreed to join the ZOOTS team because, as she recalled, "It was a marketer's dream opportunity to develop a brand that hasn't existed before as opposed to trying to communicate and enhance or change a brand that already has an image in customers' minds."

Operational Plans
Store Operations

Krasnow's decision to focus on convenience defined the kind of services that would be available. ZOOTS customers could expect courtesy and efficiency at the counter, as well as reliability and quality in cleaning services. However, the real ZOOTS' difference lay in extended store hours (7:00 am–8:00 pm daily, 8:00 am–6:00 pm Saturday, and 11:00 am–6:00 pm Sunday), drive-through drop off and pick up facilities, and 24 hour access through a secure personal locker system. ZOOTS planned to offer Internet access to track order information, web-based coupons and promotions, and automated credit card billing. ZOOTS also provided Goodwill Industries drop boxes in every store. Customers could bring in their discarded clothing and get a receipt for the donations. ZOOTS then cleaned and delivered the donated clothing free of charge.

Though some of these services were available at competing dry cleaning establishments, others were completely novel—for example, the 24-hour pick up service. Customers interested in the service pre-registered, then received a personalized, bar coded ZOOTS garment bag and a personal pin number. Clothes could be packed in the garment bag and deposited in store drop boxes at any hour. When customers wanted to pick up their orders, they could call the store (or enter the request through the web site) to request that their clothes be put in a locker. An electronic bulletin board inside the store vestibule/locker area would display the customer's name and locker number that could be accessed by keying in the pin number.

Drive-through accommodations provided a more conventional convenience alternative for customers who wanted to avoid the hassle of parking. A ZOOTS customer service representative came out to greet the customer and pick up any dirty clothing, then returned with finished cleaning orders and hung them up in the back seat. Consumers who rated this service particularly convenient were likely to have children or dogs in the car. In spite of the many alternatives available, the vast majority of customers preferred the more conventional way of doing business, taking the time to come inside so that they could point out spots and discuss special handling with the counter person.

Inside each ZOOTS store, large menu boards displayed available services and their costs. (ZOOTS services included laundering, clothing repair and alteration, professional wet cleaning, shoe polishing and repair, garment storage, wedding gown cleaning and boxing, drapery and curtain cleaning, and leather cleaning and restoration in addition to dry cleaning.) These menu board also informed customers what was included in normal processing and what was not. For example, repairing hems and cuffs was complimentary, but ironing a garment that had eight or more narrow pleats would cost an additional $4.

Home delivery service was one convenience that was *not* part of the business model that Krasnow crafted in 1998. Although he knew that some dry cleaners offered that amenity, he decided that he would not include that service, at least initially, choosing to focus all attention on opening retail stores.

Each store had a full time manager and several regular part time counter people who worked at least 20 hours per week. All went through a training program and were actively encouraged to make suggestions for operational improvements.

Store personnel greeted customers, cataloged and "detailed" the garments (entered a description of the garment and how each was to be cleaned or handled into the computer). They asked questions about any unusual fabrics, noticeable stains or damage, specific customer requests and preferences, and the date the items were required. While creating the customer invoice, the counter person also generated a "quick slip" with the detailed instructions that was inserted into an individual cleaning bag with the customer's order. The store clerks then sorted the individual orders according to the specific services required (cleaning, laundering, rush, repair) and bundled them in large transport bags marked with its own store number.

Plant Operations

ZOOTS' trucks picked up dirty laundry and returned finished orders to the retail stores twice daily, dropping dozens of clearly marked bags of dirty clothes at the central cleaning facility as it made its circuit. At the plant handlers opened the transport bags and removed the smaller detail bags, each of which included a copy of the "quick slip" with cleaning instructions, total number of pieces, and expected return date.

Approximately 20 people were stationed in booths tagging the garments individually. They used the quick slips inside each bag to determine what tags to affix. The tags denoted the originating store, special handling or repair instructions, and rush status. Because one garment could have multiple instructions, it was possible to have as many as 4 or 5 tags attached by staple, plastic tag, or safety pin through the manufacturer's label. Once the items were tagged, they were put into lots of approximately 100 garments, sorted by date needed and type of handling required.

After this initial tagging and sorting, the bins were moved to the cleaning area where there were five large (80 lb.) and three small hydrocarbon processing machines. Though the machines did a good job, many items had to pre-washed or pre-spotted before going into the machines. The plant team put pressure on the stores to tag spots more carefully so that they wouldn't be missed the first time around.

The cleaning process took approximately one hour. When it was completed, the clothes were again sorted. Shirts were batched for pressing while sweaters were sent through a steam tunnel on hangers. Approximately 40% of the items placed on hangers did not have to be pressed, including such items as silk blouses and dresses. These garments were placed on a conveyor rack that took them directly to the assembly area.

Suits, shirts, and pants generally required pressing. Once a garment had been pressed, it too was placed on the conveyor and sent to the assembly area where the garment was inspected for missing buttons, stains, or incorrect pressing. Experienced tailors were on hand to make repairs or mend any items that were discovered during the cleaning process whether or not the customer had pointed the problem out at the store. When process was completed, garments were sorted and hung on racks that corresponded to the tag color and delivery date.

An inspector then verified that the tags matched the garments and that the overall quality of the cleaned garments was acceptable. A "completion inspector" put a hole punch through the invoice and then a "bagger" bagged the garments using twist ties to secure all the items listed on the invoice. Depending on the number of steps required in the processing of a garment, as many as 10 or more people might handle a particular garment between drop off and pick up by the customer.

Running the Business
Off to a Rocky Start

When the last remains of the opening night party were swept away on the morning of October 30, 1998, the cleaning lab was ready "to let the games begin." The Danvers store was open and ready for business. All the systems were in place, the staff had been hired and trained, and the plant had already completed several test runs. However, all the best-laid plans quickly began to unravel. The office manager of ZOOTS headquarters failed to show up for work that morning. Not only had she decided to quit without giving notice, but she also drove off with all the cash register forms, garment tags, store coupons, and bank deposit slips in the trunk of her car. The Danvers store team had to scramble with manual back up systems while the plant had to make the best of a jerry-rigged tracking system.

Fortunately the business started slowly. Just as Krasnow had deliberately kept a low profile on the business start up, he also planned a very soft opening for the first store. No major fanfare, no radio or TV ads, only some local mailings with coupons. He wanted to start on a small scale so that he and the team could work through all the details. In the face of this minor opening disaster, he was relieved that they could make the necessary adjustments in relative obscurity. After a quick recovery from the opening fiasco, the ZOOTS team settled down to work on perfecting its systems for handling high volume and delivering on its promise of high quality service.

Quality and Efficiency Challenges

Soon after the cleaning lab opened, one of the cleaning lab employees stood at the entrance to the manager's door lamenting, "This shirt used to have sequins." The denuded shirt was one of many problems that surfaced as the crew learned the dry cleaning process—certain clothes just shouldn't be cleaned. What were occasional problems in "mom and pop" operations could easily become an almost daily occurrence at ZOOTS because of its anticipated high volume. "Rejects" or problem garments provided learning opportunities that enabled improvement, not only at the lab, but also at the retail store where garments were first received and inspected. The plant manager saw the sequined shirt as a call to action to develop a handbook for store personnel that would provide detailed instructions on what items should and should not be accepted for cleaning. Her goal was to eliminate unnecessary disappointment for the customers, but at the same time to control damage claims.

Claims were made because of damage to delicate fabrics or unusual materials, shrinkage, mysterious holes, fading, or missing buttons, but the most significant losses were those created by lost or missing items. If a tag fell off a garment or if the wrong tag was attached at the outset, it was extremely difficult for that garment to find its way back to its rightful owner. Because of the high volume at the ZOOTS plant, several new "orphaned" articles of clothing were created daily.

One member of the lab's management team took the initiative to create a spreadsheet of "orphan garments." He sent the sheet, which included detailed descriptions of the garments and their manufacturers, to the stores daily. Store personnel would then try to match up the items against specific customer complaints. Once the formal "orphan garment" program was organized, the average number of garments needing to be matched to their rightful owners was reduced from several full racks to approximately 15-20 at any given time. (Orphaned garments were donated to Goodwill Industries if they were unclaimed after 90 days.) Krasnow commented on how and why garments got lost in the first place:

One problem we had initially was losing garments. The computer system we had was a store-based system and it didn't allow us to split an order in the production facility. If a garment/order had 5 pieces and one piece got pulled out for a stain or extra treatment or something, we didn't have a good system for matching it back up with the original order. It would get into a different queue that might take a couple of days. By the time it got back to the re-assembly point, the lot number sequences were cycling through again. This "old" piece would come up and somebody assembling the order at 2:00 am in the morning would just look at a number and stick it on in with the next round of lot numbers. Then, off went the shirt to another customer who was expecting to get a dress back. We have fixed that, but it's the kind of problem you don't anticipate until it happens.

The operating part of the business is proving to be absolutely mind-boggling in terms of the challenge to have good service recovery and not make the mistakes in the first place. That's really where the opportunity . . . it's not like other dry cleaners have solved the problem—they just have it on a much smaller scale. We need to do it at scale.

A five-person team was established to identify critical problem areas and to develop solutions. Krasnow reviewed the store and plant problems daily and made frequent site visits as he and the team struggled to get the operations running smoothly. The items that topped their list included: accurate order assembly, increased efficiency and streamlined handling, improved handling of special care garments. The ZOOTS team regarded the customer complaints as a report card. Though they might be specific, they almost always raised issues that could be addressed and corrected across the board with all accounts, stores, and customers.

When there were damages, as in the case of the once-sequined shirt, ZOOTS used the Fabricare Institute's guide for determining claims or appropriate reimbursement to the customer. In some instances, a claim could be made against the manufacturer for faulty merchandise. As far as meeting efficiency goals, the cleaning lab still had a long way to go. Seasoned pressers could handle up to 50 shirts an hour, but the new pressers in the ZOOTS' lab averaged far less than that.

Cranking Up the Volume

The second and third ZOOTS stores opened in West Roxbury and South Attleboro, MA, in early 1999. When it had operated only one store, the ZOOTS team could overwhelm operating challenges with personal attention from the store manager, the plant supervisor, or headquarters staff. However, with multiple stores up and running, the systems had to take over.

ZOOTS ran its first major promotion, an insert ad in the Boston Globe with a $5 coupon, in late March 1999. At the same time, Krasnow granted his first newspaper interview to an old friend at the Boston Globe. At long last, he was willing to disclose the basic business concept and outline his plans for ZOOTS' growth (Exhibit 2).

The article was very positive and the $5 coupon that ran with the ad brought people into the stores in droves. However, the incredible spike in demand resulted in a ZOOTS systems meltdown. The Wilmington facility knew it was coming, but was simply not ready to handle the volume. Krasnow was the first to admit that, in spite of his retailing experience, the operations in this service-intensive business were quite different than they were in office supplies and food retailing. He recalled:

Many people in dry cleaning have run $1 million dry cleaners. The issues that we have with dry cleaning are not the actual dry cleaning or the pressing. It's the process management of thousands and thousands of garments a day that are all different, that have to go through the factory and come out on time— all while dealing with exceptions or premium service for special treatments—it adds to the complexity.

The marketing group immediately cut back on advertising and promotions. The challenge the ZOOTS team faced going forward was not in getting customers to try the service, but in figuring out how to get the dry cleaning done to their satisfaction. Krasnow admitted that the team underestimated the "manufacturing" process. He elaborated,

If I've made a mistake it's been in not being quick enough to bring in a full partner who was an operator, because we underestimated just how difficult the executional side of the cleaning production is. It is outside of my range of previous experience. We went in thinking that it was not that hard, but what has been hard is the execution.

EXHIBIT 2

Boston Globe Article

Source: Copyright © 1999 by Globe Newspaper Co (MA). Reproduced with permission of Globe Newspaper Co (MA) via Copyright Clearance Center.

Boston Globe newspaper clipping:

Business

THE BOSTON GLOBE • WEDNESDAY, MARCH 31, 1999

Looking to clean up

With Zoots, duo that helped create Staples aim to be national players in dry-cleaning business

Zoots CEO Todd Krasnow showed off some dry cleaning outside the West Roxbury store.

Another Option

The ZOOTS news item piqued the interest of Cliff Sirlin, a co-founder and owner of Cleaner Options. Sirlin's partner, Andy Applebaum, was on his honeymoon in Hawaii, but Sirlin was so intrigued by the article, which a Boston friend had faxed to him, that he picked up the phone and called Krasnow immediately. He explained that he and Applebaum owned a home delivery dry cleaning business that operated in joint ventures and franchising agreements with local dry cleaners. He wanted to know how the two companies could work together. Within 2 months, Krasnow had completed his due diligence, had acquired the business, and had introduced ZOOTS first home delivery route in the Boston market.

Growth Plans

ZOOTS raised a $9 million second round of angel funding in January 1999. Individual investors included Stemberg, Krasnow, and friends and family. By April 1999, Krasnow and Stemberg began to discuss raising a large round of venture capital to fund more aggressive growth. The first 3 stores were performing well against the targets that Krasnow had established, based on the performance data he had gleaned from the 13 dry cleaners included in his original research. The board urged him to accelerate the rollout of the business. Though Boston was a promising market and its expansion was a priority, finding good real estate was extremely difficult, so growth there would be slower than anticipated.

EXHIBIT 2 (continued)

Emerging**Business**

A REPORT ON NEW ENGLAND'S GROWING COMPANIES

Duo look to clean up with Zoots

Cindy La Pointe, manager of the West Roxbury Zoots, checked finished laundry.

Furthermore, once news of the ZOOTS concept was public knowledge, the board felt it was important to claim as many geographic markets as possible before competitors blossomed in every city. The Connecticut market was the most obvious next step. It would be a new hub with its own cleaning facility and a separate marketing umbrella, but it was proximate enough to headquarters for frequent site visits and close management supervision. Several sites were leased in the Hartford, CT, market and a central facility was underway in Wallingford, CT. The ZOOTS management team expected that the new stores would produce revenues and, eventually, profits at the same rate as the three stores already operating in Massachusetts.

Krasnow and his board began to push beyond the Connecticut borders to consider markets that were not so real estate-constrained. The goal was to locate profitable markets where more stores could be opened quickly. Krasnow, Stemberg, and other Staples board members pointed out that Staples had initially concentrated its growth in major metropolitan areas thinking that secondary markets would be more difficult to run efficiently and that they would be less profitable. When they opened those markets in later years, they discovered that, in fact, these investments were very profitable. That experience suggested that if ZOOTS ran into difficulties finding locations in the major metropolitan areas, it could move directly into secondary markets and build a profitable enterprise much more quickly.

When Boston Markets (formerly Boston Chicken) declared bankruptcy, it closed a number of stores and put the real estate on the block. Krasnow's team reviewed the list and found that there were sites available in the Virginia Beach, VA area that might provide ZOOTS a strong entry opportunity. Several members of the senior management team flew to Virginia Beach to investigate the potential of the Boston Market sites. Though the team rejected all of the Boston Market sites, they did find several other potential stores available that met their expansion criteria. They also found satisfactory space for the central plant. The operating economics looked good, and a large labor force was nearby.

In July 1999, Krasnow signed a lease for a new cleaning lab in Portsmouth, Virginia. The team spent the next few months working on getting permits, building the central facility, and securing store sites. Krasnow was closing in on his goal of creating a profitable business model that could be replicated in multiple geographic locations.

Krasnow was also making plans for entering the Philadelphia market. His real estate team located a site for the central cleaning facility and was scouting the neighborhoods for appropriate store locations.

Another major consideration was the purchase of a chain of dry cleaning stores in Ohio. Widmer's had both brick and mortar retail stores and a successful home delivery service. The Cleaner Options acquisition and integration had gone smoothly and Kras-

October 12, 1999

Dear valued shareholders,

The third quarter has been an active one for Zoots. We have seen our business develop in a number of important ways, but we have also missed several targets.

1   Acquisitions: On September 15th, we acquired Widmer's, the leading dry cleaning chain in Cincinnati. Widmer's operates 8 stores and 15 home delivery routes. In addition, they use a 30,000 square foot production facility for their cleaning, which is consistent with Zoots' centralized production philosophy. Given the excess capacity of this plant, we believe we can more than double the volume processed there, by opening Zoots stores and routes in areas not currently served by Widmer's.

2. Real Estate: We finished the quarter with 8 Zoots stores in operation, 2 fewer than our target. We believe that we will miss our year end target (20 stores) as 4 stores slide into early 2000. The delays have been caused by challenges in financing development sites and permitting. More importantly, the missed targets tell us we need a far more robust real estate pipeline to meet our 2000 objectives. In part, the pipeline is behind because of difficulty in staffing the real estate department. We anticipate resolving our staffing issues in the 4th quarter.

    During the quarter, we began construction on two 30,000 square foot cleaning laboratories: one in Portsmouth, Virginia and the other in Wallingford, Connecticut, just outside of Hartford. Both are scheduled to open late this year or early next year.

3. Operations: Store revenue has continued to exceed our expectations for the stores that are open, although, in total, store revenue is behind our budget due to the delayed openings. Home pick-up and delivery revenue is also exceeding our plans. At the end of the quarter nine routes were in operation in the Boston market. Store, cleaning lab and delivery expenses were in line with expectations.

    On October 4th, we began providing dry cleaning service for Streamline.com, a Boston based home delivery grocery service. Streamline.com is a publicly traded company that has offered dry cleaning as part of its service mix since its inception. We are providing the dry cleaning under the Clean'r Cleaner name (a trademark owned by Zoots).

4. Human resources: Bob Anarumo joined us in August as Chief Operating Officer. A copy of our internal announcement about Bob is attached.

EXHIBIT 3

October 1999 Letter to Shareholders

now saw acquisition of well-operated chains as another way to speed ZOOTS growth.

In June 1999, ZOOTS completed a confidential offering memorandum for 14,000,000 Class G shares at $2.50. Krasnow arranged his schedule to meet with venture capitalists around the country. In September 1999, ZOOTS closed a $38 million round of financing with Charlesbank Capital Partners, Chase Venture Capital, Weston Presidio Partners, and Dorset Capital as well as Krasnow, Stemberg and many of the individual investors who participated in the earlier rounds.

Getting Results

In August 1999, ZOOTS had broken ground for the Portsmouth/Virginia Beach cleaning facility and it was building out several retail store sites. The grand opening was planned for December 1999, but Krasnow was very uneasy about the decision long before the first store opened. He commented:

> The plan going into Portsmouth—it's almost laughable now—if it weren't so painful. We were going to open up 8 stores in the Virginia Beach/Portsmouth market by the end of 1999. That's how easy we thought the real estate was going to be. It turned out that getting the right real estate was every bit as hard as it was in New England. Our initial assessment of easy real estate was incorrect.
>
> Besides the real estate challenge, another important obstacle surfaced in mid-to-late August. We began to develop a new sales

Phyllis Wasserman joined us as Vice President, Marketing. Phyllis had been Senior Vice President, Advertising at Staples, where she successfully built a strong brand image through print, catalog and broadcast advertising. After leaving Staples, Phyllis consulted to a number of companies, including Zoots.

Paul Tritman joined us on October 11th, as Vice President, Production. Paul fills a critical position in which he will lead our efforts to improve cleaning quality and reliability while increasing efficiency. He was Director of Manufacturing and Controls Engineering for Kidde-Fenwal, Inc.

5. Financial: We recently closed a $38,000,000 equity financing, our first financing involving institutional investors. Our lead investor was Charlesbank Capital Partners. Other institutional investors include Chase Venture Capital Associates, Weston Presidio, and Dorset Capital. Mike Eisenson of Charlesbank and Steve Murray of Chase have joined our Board.

We expect to extend our bank credit facility from $5 million to $12 million in the coming month.

Finally, it is worth noting that our Danvers store celebrated its first anniversary last week. It has certainly been an exciting year since that first store opening day in October, 1998. On behalf of everyone at Zoots, thank you for giving us the support which has allowed us to build our business quickly.

Sincerely,

Todd Krasnow
C.E.O.

EXHIBIT 3 (*continued*)

EXHIBIT 3 (*continued*)

August, 1999

To the Zoots Family:

I am delighted to announce that Bob Anarumo will be joining Zoots on August 30th as Chief Operating Officer.

For the past six years, Bob has been President and CEO of the largest franchise group in Boston Market, with a territory spanning from Canada to Virginia and revenue of over $400 million. Bob opened or acquired 360 restaurants, and ran the most (and often only) profitable franchise group within the Boston Market network. Prior to Boston Market, Bob ran a 300 restaurant division of Pizza Hut. He also led the development of Pizza Hut delivery, which required the creation of locations and processes completely outside of the existing restaurant business. His drive to create well-run, customer focused operations are clearly demonstrated and fit our own culture exceptionally well.

As soon as Bob learns the Zoots business and gets to know our people, he will assume responsibility for all day-to-day operations. This includes store, home delivery and cleaning lab operations, as well as our distribution, logistics and human resource functions. This will allow me to spend more time with our marketing team to drive sales and our real estate team to explore significant real estate opportunities. Marketing and real estate will report to me. In addition, I shall focus on Zoots' long range development, including acquisition opportunities, financing, and other projects. Tom Sager and his team, along with JJ Pellegrino will report to me in these efforts. Larry Kennedy and the systems team will work closely with Bob, Tom and me to insure the continued development of systems that support our operation and enable rapid growth.

Bob and his family will be relocating from New Jersey. Please join me in welcoming him to Zoots.

Sincerely,

Todd Krasnow

Todd Krasnow

19 Needham Street, Suite #2, Newton, MA 02461-1622
Tel: 617-558-9666 Fax: 617-558-9667

projection model based on the data we were getting from our own stores and it really gave me cause to worry. Our initial real estate model was based on the 13 dry cleaners that we had gotten data from before we started ZOOTS. When we began to get reliable data from our own stores—which, by mid summer, included good and bad stores—we tightened up the criteria. The new model we built indicated that there was far less potential for building strong new stores in the Portsmouth market than we had anticipated. We ran the new model for the first time in mid-summer. We realized, 'Oops, because of the tight real estate market, we aren't going to have the number of stores we anticipated and the stores we do have aren't going to produce the sales we projected. How are we going to achieve the economies of scale we need in the plant?'

Based on our new info, it was clear that the Portsmouth and Virginia Beach sites didn't have as much potential as we had first thought. We did the math and discovered that we would not be able to fill the Portsmouth facility with the eight stores we had planned in the Virginia Beach and Norfolk markets.

We were under construction and couldn't turn the process around. We had just started the delivery business (the acquisition of Cleaner Options in NY), and had to ask the question of 'how are we ever going to get ourselves working properly in Virginia Beach?'

The original model had indicated that ZOOTS could open eight stores in the Portsmouth/Virginia Beach area, each of which would do "x" amount of business. By late August, Krasnow concluded that,

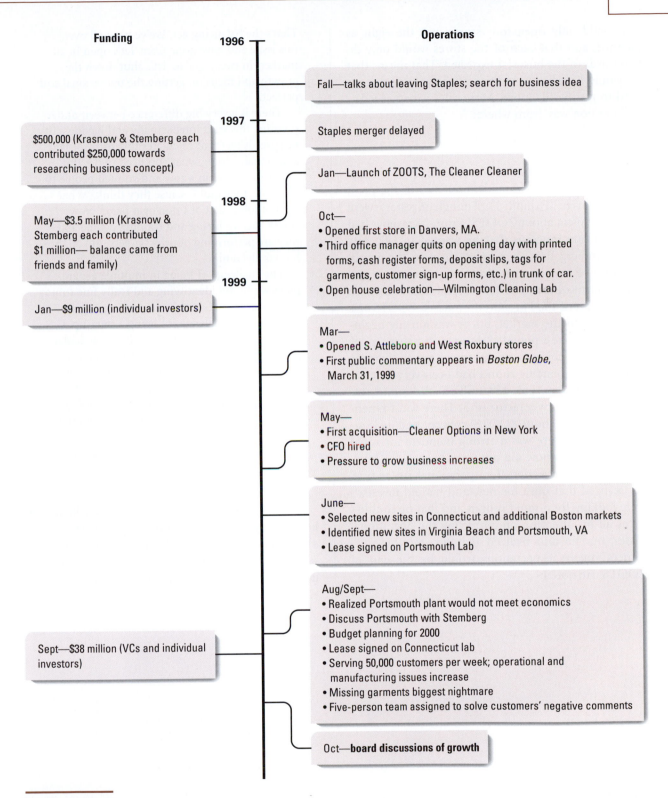

Funding

Operations

1996

Fall—talks about leaving Staples; search for business idea

1997

Staples merger delayed

$500,000 (Krasnow & Stemberg each contributed $250,000 towards researching business concept)

Jan—Launch of ZOOTS, The Cleaner Cleaner

1998

Oct—
• Opened first store in Danvers, MA.
• Third office manager quits on opening day with printed forms, cash register forms, deposit slips, tags for garments, customer sign-up forms, etc.) in trunk of car.
• Open house celebration—Wilmington Cleaning Lab

May—$3.5 million (Krasnow & Stemberg each contributed $1 million— balance came from friends and family)

1999

Jan—$9 million (individual investors)

Mar—
• Opened S. Attleboro and West Roxbury stores
• First public commentary appears in *Boston Globe*, March 31, 1999

May—
• First acquisition—Cleaner Options in New York
• CFO hired
• Pressure to grow business increases

June—
• Selected new sites in Connecticut and additional Boston markets
• Identified new sites in Virginia Beach and Portsmouth, VA
• Lease signed on Portsmouth Lab

Aug/Sept—
• Realized Portsmouth plant would not meet economics
• Discuss Portsmouth with Stemberg
• Budget planning for 2000
• Lease signed on Connecticut lab
• Serving 50,000 customers per week; operational and manufacturing issues increase
• Missing garments biggest nightmare
• Five-person team assigned to solve customers' negative comments

Sept—$38 million (VCs and individual investors)

Oct—**board discussions of growth**

EXHIBIT 4
ZOOTS Timeline

"we could only open four stores, not the eight as planned, and that each of the stores would only do two thirds of the business expected. That means that we would have only one third of the volume that we used to justify this move. More sales were needed—the question was 'from where?'"

October 1999

The shareholders letter of October 12, 1999 chronicled both the successes and the misses of the most recent quarter (Exhibit 3). Though investors were very optimistic about ZOOTS' future, Krasnow had some serious concerns that he wanted to talk over with Stemberg first, then bring them to the board. The first of his concerns was the quality of service and efficient operations. The second had to do with the specifics of the Portsmouth market. ZOOTS was committed to the market, but it was already beginning to look like a potential disaster on paper.

An overarching concern was how to manage growth. The financing round had been very successful. Though they took $38 million, the round was over-subscribed by a factor of 3. There was tremendous optimism about ZOOTS' concept and its leadership team. There was a strong mandate for rapid growth, but Krasnow did not want to grow the business without correcting the operational issues first. He realized that both his new and his old investors were looking for a rapid rollout and that he couldn't focus all his attention on correcting the operational issues, but he also realized that not meeting customers' quality expectations would be the end of ZOOTS. He noted:

That's the balancing act. We've been all over this issue and have gone from 'let's open in 20 markets in two years' to 'let's shut down the growth and focus on getting the operational stuff perfect.'

There is a very big difference between understanding this stuff intellectually and having a little spreadsheet that calculates this stuff for you and actually doing what you need to do. If it snows for 3 days in a row and you tell people to go home, they quit because they think, 'What kind of job is that, if I don't get paid?' Now you're back to hiring and training people and they are performing poorly—it gets into all those human dynamics.

The challenge of being in multiple geographies while still identifying and really fine tuning the business model, while also trying to grow, those are the challenges of being a start-up. I actually don't think there's anything particularly unique about these challenges. Individual elements are specific to my business, but this is what it means to be a start-up. I think that every business that has a lot of growth potential goes through this. My belief is even companies that are incredibly sexy from the outside, like e-Bay, etc. totally different type of business and workforce—everything is different—but they have the same issues.

Krasnow considered all the many challenges he had already overcome in launching ZOOTS (Exhibit 4) and knew that he would have to come up with some good answers about how to balance the operating challenges with the imperative for growth.

Nike: Sweatshops and Business Ethics

10

This case was prepared by Charles W. L. Hill, the University of Washington.

Introduction

Nike is in many ways the quintessential global corporation. Established in 1972 by former University of Oregon track star Phil Knight, Nike is now one of the leading marketers of athletic shoes and apparel on the planet. The company has $10 billion in annual revenues and sells its products in some 140 countries. Nike does not do any manufacturing. Rather, it designs and markets its products, while contracting for their manufacture from a global network of 600 factories scattered around the globe that employ some 550,000 people.[1] This huge corporation has made founder Phil Knight into one of the richest people in America. Nike's marketing phrase "Just do it!" and "swoosh" logo have become as recognizable in popular culture as the faces of its celebrity sponsors, such as Michael Jordan and Tiger Woods.

For all of its successes, the company has been dogged for more than a decade by repeated and persistent accusations that its products are made in "sweatshops" where workers, many of them children, slave away in hazardous conditions for below-subsistence wages. Nike's wealth, its detractors claim, has been built upon the backs of the world's poor. To many, Nike has become a symbol of the evils of globalization: a rich Western corporation exploiting the world's poor to provide expensive shoes and apparel to the pampered con-

This case is intended to be used as a basis for class discussion rather than as an illustration of either effective or ineffective handling of the situation. Reprinted by permission of Charles W. L. Hill.

sumers of the developed world. Nike's Niketown stores have become standard targets for anti-globalization protestors. Nike has been the target of repeated criticism and protests from several nongovernmental organizations, such as San Fransisco–based Global Exchange, a human-rights organization dedicated to promoting environmental, political, and social justice around the world.[2] News media have run exposés on working conditions in foreign factories that supply Nike. Students on the campuses of several major U.S. universities with which Nike has lucrative sponsorship deals have protested against the ties, citing Nike's use of sweatshop labor.

For its part, Nike has taken many steps to counter the protests. Yes, it admits, there have been problems in some overseas factories. But the company has signaled a commitment to improving working conditions. It requires that foreign subcontractors meet minimum thresholds for working conditions and pay. It has arranged for factories to be examined by independent auditors and terminated contracts with factories that do not comply with its standards. But for all this effort, the company continues to be a target of protests.

The Case Against Nike

Typical of the exposés against Nike was a *CBS 48 Hours* news report that aired on October 17, 1996.[3] Reporter Roberta Basin visited a Nike factory in Vietnam. With a shot of the factory, her commentary began:

The signs are everywhere of an American invasion in search of cheap labor. Millions of people who are literate, disciplined, and desperate for jobs. This is Niketown near what used to be called Saigon, one of four factories Nike doesn't own but subcontracts to make a million shoes a month. It takes 25,000 workers, mostly young women, to "Just Do It."

But the workers here don't share in Nike's huge profits. They work six days a week for only $40 a month, just 20 cents an hour.

Baskin interviews one of the workers in the factory, a young woman named Lap. Baskin tells the listener:

Her basic wage, even as a sewing team leader, still doesn't amount to the minimum wage. . . . She's down to 85 pounds. Like most of the young women who make shoes, she has little choice but to accept the low wages and long hours. Nike says that it requires all subcontractors to obey local laws; but Lap has already put in much more overtime than the annual legal limit: 200 hours.

Baskin then asks Lap what would happen if she wanted to leave, if she was sick or had to take care of a sick relative: could she leave the factory? Through a translator, Lap replies:

It is not possible if you haven't made enough shoes. You have to meet the quota before you can go home.

The clear implication of the story was that Nike was at fault for allowing such working conditions to persist in the Vietnamese factory (which, incidentally, was owned by a Korean company).

Another example of an attack on Nike's subcontracting practices occurred in June 1996. It was launched by USA, a foundation largely financed by labor unions and domestic-apparel manufacturers that oppose free trade with low-wage countries. According to Joel Joseph, chairman of the foundation, a popular line of high-priced Nike sneakers, the "Air Jordans," were put together by eleven-year-olds in Indonesia making 14 cents per hour. A Nike spokeswoman, Donna Gibbs, countered that this was false. According to Gibbs, the average worker made 240,000 *rupiah* ($103) a month working a maximum fifty-four-hour week, or about 45 cents per hour. Moreover, Gibbs noted, Nike had staff members in each factory monitoring conditions to make sure that they obeyed local minimum-wage and child-labor laws.[4]

Another example of the criticism against Nike is the following extracts from a newsletter published by Global Exchange:[5]

During the 1970s, most Nike shoes were made in South Korea and Taiwan. When workers there gained new freedom to organize and wages began to rise, Nike looked for "greener pastures." It found them in Indonesia and China, where Nike started producing in the 1980s, and most recently in Vietnam.

The majority of Nike shoes are made in Indonesia and China, countries with governments that prohibit independent unions and set the minimum wage at rock bottom. The Indonesian government admits that the minimum wage there does not provide enough to supply the basic needs of one person, let alone a family. In early 1997 the entry-level wage was a miserable $2.46 a day. Labor groups estimate that a livable wage in Indonesia is about $4.00 a day.

In Vietnam the pay is even less—20 cents an hour, or a mere $1.60 a day. But in urban Vietnam, three simple meals cost about $2.10 a day, and then of course there is rent, transportation, clothing, health care, and much more. According to Thuyen Nguyen of Vietnam Labor Watch, a living wage in Vietnam is at least $3 a day.

In another attack on Nike's practices, Global Exchange published a report in September 1997 on working conditions in four Nike and Reebok subcontractor's factories in southern China.[6] Global Exchange, in conjunction with two Hong Kong human-rights groups, had interviewed workers at the factories in 1995 and again in 1997. According to Global Exchange, in one factory, a Korean-owned subcontractor for Nike, workers as young as thirteen earned as little as 10 cents an hour and toiled up to seventeen hours daily in enforced silence. Talking during work was not allowed, and violators were fined $1.20 to $3.60, according to the report. The practices were in violation of Chinese labor law, which states that no child under sixteen may work in a factory, and the Chinese minimum-wage requirement of $1.90 for an eight-hour day. Nike condemned the study as "erroneous," charging that it incorrectly stated the wages of workers and made irresponsible accusations.

Global Exchange, however, continued to be a major thorn in Nike's side. In November 1997, the organization obtained and then leaked a confidential report by Ernst & Young of an audit that Nike had commissioned of a factory in Vietnam owned by a Nike subcontractor.[7] The factory had 9,200 workers and made 400,000 pairs of shoes a month. The Ernst & Young report painted a dismal picture of thousands of young women, most under age twenty-five, laboring ten and a half hours a day, six days a week, in excessive heat, noise, and foul air, for slightly more than $10 a week. The report also found that workers with skin or breathing problems had not been transferred to departments free of chemicals, and that more than half the workers who dealt with dangerous chemicals did not wear protective masks or gloves. It claimed workers were exposed to carcinogens that exceeded local legal standards by 177 times in parts of the plant and that 77% of the employees suffered from respiratory problems.

Put on the defensive yet again, Nike called a news conference and pointed out that it had commissioned the report, and had acted on it.[8] The company stated that it had formulated an action plan to deal with the problems cited in the report, and had slashed overtime, improved safety and ventilation, and reduced the use of toxic chemicals. The company also asserted that the report showed that Nike's internal monitoring system had performed exactly as it should have. According to one spokesman:

> This shows our system of monitoring works. . . . We have uncovered these issues clearly before anyone else, and we have moved fairly expeditiously to correct them.

Nike's Responses

Unaccustomed to playing defense, Nike formulated a number of strategies and tactics over the years to deal with the problems of working conditions and pay in subcontractor facilities. In 1996, Nike hired one-time U.S. ambassador to the United Nations, representative, and former Atlanta mayor Andrew Young to assess working conditions in subcontractors' plants around the world. The following year, after a two-week tour of three countries that included inspections of fifteen factories, Young released a mildly critical report. He informed Nike it was doing a good job in its treatment of workers, though it should do better. According to Young, he did not see:

> sweatshops, or hostile conditions. . . . I saw crowded dorms . . . but the workers were eating at least two meals a day on the job and making

what I was told were subsistence wages in those cultures.[9]

Young was widely criticized by human-rights and labor groups for not taking his own translators and for doing slipshod inspections, an assertion he repeatedly denied.

In 1996, Nike joined a presidential task force designed to find a way of banishing sweatshops in the shoe and clothing industries. The task force included industry leaders, representatives from human-rights groups, and labor leaders. In April 1997, they announced an agreement for workers' rights that U.S. companies could agree to when manufacturing abroad. The accord limited the work week to sixty hours, and called for paying at least the local minimum wage in foreign factories. The task force also agreed to establish an independent monitoring association—later named the Fair Labor Association (FLA)—to assess whether companies are abiding by the code.[10]

The FLA now includes among its members the Lawyers Committee for Human Rights, the National Council of Churches, the International Labor Rights Fund, 135 universities (universities have extensive licensing agreements with sports-apparel companies), and companies such as Nike, Reebok, and Levi Strauss.

In early 1997, Nike also began to commission independent organizations such as Ernst & Young to audit the factories of its subcontractors. In September 1997, Nike tried to show its critics that it was involved in more than just a public-relations exercise when it terminated its relationship with four Indonesian subcontractors, stating that they had refused to comply with the company's standards for wage levels and working conditions. Nike identified one of the subcontractors, Seyon, which manufactured specialty sports gloves for Nike, saying that Seyon refused to meet a 10.7% increase in the monthly wage, to $70.30, required by the Indonesian government in April 1997.[11]

On May 12, 1998, in a speech given at the National Press Club, Phil Knight spelled out in detail a series of initiatives designed to improve working conditions for the 500,000 people that make products for Nike at subcontractor facilities.[12] Among the initiatives Knight highlighted were the following:

> We have effectively changed our minimum age limits from the ILO (International Labor

Organization) standards of 15 in most countries and 14 in developing countries to 18 in all footwear manufacturing and 16 in all other types of manufacturing (apparel, accessories and equipment). Existing workers legally employed under the former limits were grandfathered into the new requirements.

During the past 13 months we have moved to a 100 percent factory audit scheme, where every Nike contract factory will receive an annual check by PricewaterhouseCoopers teams who are specially trained on our Code of Conduct Owner's Manual and audit/monitoring procedures. To date they have performed about 300 such monitoring visits. In a few instances in apparel factories they have found workers under our age standards. Those factories have been required to raise their standards to 17 years of age, to require three documents certifying age, and to redouble their efforts to ensure workers meet those standards through interviews and records checks.

Our goal was to ensure workers around the globe are protected by requiring factories to have no workers exposed to levels above those mandated by the permissible exposure limits (PELs) for chemicals prescribed in the OSHA indoor air quality standards.[13]

These moves were applauded in the business press, but they were greeted with a skeptical response from Nike's long-term adversaries in the debate over the use of foreign labor. While conceding that Nike's policies were an improvement, one critic writing in the *New York Times* noted that:

Mr. Knight's child labor initiative is . . . a smokescreen. Child labor has not been a big problem with Nike, and Philip Knight knows that better than anyone. But public relations is public relations. So he announces that he's not going to let the factories hire kids, and suddenly that's the headline.

Mr. Knight is like a three-card monte player. You have to keep a close eye on him at all times.

The biggest problem with Nike is that its overseas workers make wretched, below-subsistence wages. It's not the minimum age that needs raising, it's the minimum wage. Most of the workers in Nike factories in China and Vietnam make less than $2 a day, well below the subsistence levels in those countries. In Indonesia the pay is less than $1 a day.

The company's current strategy is to reshape its public image while doing as little as possible for the workers. Does anyone think it was an accident that Nike set up shop in human rights sink-holes, where labor organizing was viewed as a criminal activity and deeply impoverished workers were willing, even eager, to take their places on assembly lines and work for next to nothing?[14]

Other critics question the quality of Nike's auditors, PricewaterhouseCoopers (PwC). Dara O'Rourke, an assistant professor at MIT, followed the PwC auditors around several factories in China, Korea, and Vietnam. He concluded that although the auditors found minor violations of labor laws and codes of conduct, they missed major labor-practice issues, including hazardous working conditions, violations of overtime laws, and violation of wage laws. The problem, according to O'Rourke, was that the auditors had limited training and relied on factory managers for data and for setting up interviews with workers, all of which were performed in the factories. The auditors, in other words, were getting an incomplete and somewhat sanitized view of conditions in the factory.[15]

The Controversy Continues

Fueled perhaps by the unforgiving criticisms of Nike that continued after Phil Knight's May 1998 speech, a wave of protests against Nike occurred on many university campuses from 1998 to 2001. The moving force behind the protests was the United Students Against Sweatshops (USAS). The USAS argued that the Fair Labor Association (FLA), which grew out of the presidential task force on sweatshops, was an industry tool, and not a truly independent auditor of foreign factories. The USAS set up an alternative independent auditing organization, the Workers Rights Consortium (WRC), which they charged with auditing factories that produce products under collegiate licensing programs (under which Nike is a high-profile supplier of products). The WRC is backed, and partly funded, by labor unions and refuses to cooperate with companies, arguing that doing so would jeopardize its independence.

By mid 2000, the WRC had persuaded some forty-eight universities to join, including all nine campuses of the University of California systems, the University of Michigan, and the University of

Oregon, Phil Knight's alma mater. When Knight heard that the University of Oregon would join the WRC, as opposed to the FLA, he withdrew a planned $30 million donation to the university.[16] Despite this, in November 2000 another major northwest university, the University of Washington, announced that it too would join the WRC, although it would also retain its membership in the FLA.[17]

Nike continued to push forward with its own initiatives, updating progress on its web site. In April 2000, in response to accusations that it was still hiding conditions, it announced that it would release the complete reports of all independent audits of its subcontractors' plants. Global Exchange continued to criticize the company, arguing in mid 2001 that the company was not living up to Phil Knight's 1998 promises and that it was intimidating workers from speaking out about abuses.[18]

ENDNOTES

1. From Nike's corporate web site at **www.nikebiz.com.**
2. **www.globalexchange.org.**
3. "Boycott Nike," *CBS News 48 Hours,* October 17, 1996.
4. D. Jones. "Critics tie sweatshop sneakers to 'Air Jordan,'" *USA Today,* June 6, 1996, p. 1B.
5. Global Exchange Special Report: Nike Just Don't Do It. **http://www.globalexchange.org/education/publications/ newsltr6.97p2.html#nike.**
6. V. Dobnik. "Chinese workers abused making Nikes, Reeboks," *Seattle Times,* September 21, 1997, p. A4.
7. S. Greenhouse. "Nike shoeplant in Vietnam is called unsafe for workers," *New York Times,* November 8, 1997.
8. S. Greenhouse. "Nike shoeplant in Vietnam is called unsafe for workers," *New York Times,* November 8, 1997.
9. Quoted in: V. Dobnik. "Chinese workers abused making Nikes, Reeboks," *Seattle Times,* September 21, 1997, p. A4.
10. W. Bounds and H. Stout. "Sweatshop pact: Good fit or threadbare?" *Wall Street Journal,* April 10, 1997, p. A2.
11. Associated Press Reporter. "Nike gives four factories the boot," *Los Angeles Times,* September 23, 1997, p. 20.
12. Archived at **http://www.nikebiz.com/labor/speech_trans.shtml.**
13. OSHA is the United States Occupational Safety and Health Agency.
14. B. Herbert. "Nike Blinks," *New York Times,* May 21, 1998.
15. Dara O'Rourke. Monitoring the monitors: A critique of the PricewaterhouseCoopers (PwC) labor monitoring. Department of Urban Studies and Planning, MIT.
16. L. Lee and A. Bernstein. Who says student protests don't matter? *Business Week,* June 12, 2000, pp. 94–96.
17. R. Deen. UW to join anti-sweatshop group. *Seattle Post Intelligencer,* November 20, 2000, p. B2.
18. Anonymous. Rights group says Nike isn't fulfilling promises. *Wall Street Journal,* May 16, 2001.

11

WestJet Looks East[1]

In August 1999, the Canadian airline industry was taken by surprise when the Onex Corporation proposed to acquire and merge Canada's two large system carriers, Canadian Airlines and Air Canada. A long and debilitating rivalry between the two airlines was being pushed to a conclusion. Air Canada countered with a merger proposal of its own and ultimately prevailed in a high-profile takeover battle. With Onex out of the picture, the way was clear for Air Canada to achieve a near monopoly of domestic, regularly scheduled air travel. Meanwhile, the federal government, which had helped to begin the merger initiatives, insisted that it would sustain competition in the industry.

In light of these developments, the management of WestJet Airlines of Calgary were reviewing their growth plans and wondering, in particular, if they should shift from their focus on building and reinforcing their Western Canadian markets to expanding in the East. WestJet was a young, successful, low-fare airline patterned after Southwest Airlines, the most successful U.S. air carrier. WestJet had been profitable from its start-up in early 1996, and by 1999 was flying 13 Boeing 737s approximately 517 flights per week between 11 destinations in Western Canada. WestJet had just recently completed a $25 million initial public offering and planned to purchase three additional aircraft with the proceeds. At the time of the offering, WestJet's plan was to use the increased flight capacity for further penetration of the western market. A summary of WestJet's financial performance is given in Exhibit 1.

Industry Background: Domestic Warfare

The epic battle between Air Canada and Canadian had started with the deregulation of Canada's domestic airline industry in the mid-

One-time permission to produce Ivey cases granted by Ivey Management Services, 2002.

1. This case has been written on the basis of public sources only. Consequently, the interpretation and perspectives presented in this case are not necessarily those of WestJet or any of its employees.

EXHIBIT 1

Selected Financial Information for WestJet,
1998 and Projected 1999 ($000)

	12/31/1999	12/31/1998
Operating Revenues	$204,000	$125,000
Operating expenses	173,000	112,000
Operating income	30,000	13,000
Income before taxes	29,000	12,000
Net Income	16,000	7,000
Current assets	61,000	23,000
Capital and other assets	126,000	85,000
Total Assets	187,000	108,000
Current liabilities	50,000	29,000
Long-term debt	30,000	22,000
Deferred income tax	13,000	8,000
Shareholders equity	94,000	49,000
Total Liabilities and Shareholder Equity	187,000	108,000

Source: Company Financial Reports.

1980s.[2] At that time, Pacific Western Airlines, a successful regional carrier, spurned a potential marriage with Air Canada and set out to become a full-fledged national and international carrier. To achieve this, the company, renamed Canadian Airlines, acquired Canadian Pacific Airlines (which itself had just swallowed Eastern Provincial Airways, Nordair, and Quebecair) and a few years later, Wardair. As it emerged from this process, Canadian Airlines had assembled the essentials of an international air carrier; in particular, it held a strong position in Western Canada and important flag carrier routes across the Pacific and to Mexico and South America. On the other hand, Canadian was working from a relatively weak position in Eastern Canada and across the Atlantic. It was experiencing integration difficulties with the acquisitions, and it was saddled with significant debt. Canadian chose, nevertheless, to persist and to engage Air Canada in a winner-takes-all contest to

become Canada's dominant, regularly scheduled domestic and international carrier.

In the meantime, Air Canada was in transition from government ownership to publicly traded company. When full privatization was achieved in 1989, Air Canada was seen on the one hand as a carrier that was quite well-off in routes, equipment and finance, but, on the other hand, limited in its potential by overstaffing, low productivity and a pervasive attitude of entitlement.

A 10 Year Dog Fight

While cumbersome, Air Canada was the stronger airline. In a continuing war of attrition—marked by over-capacity in overlapping routes and frequencies, and corresponding price pressures—Canadian, with its burdensome debt, was soon in financial trouble. In 1992, with the economy in recession, Canadian posted a loss of over $500 million, reducing its accumulated equity to zero. Air Canada took note and pursued the possibility of a merger. The reaction from Canadian and its employees ranged from uncooperative to hostile, and Air Canada withdrew, reportedly to wait and pick up the pieces when Canadian fell into bankruptcy. Canadian soon got back into the thick of it, however, largely by way of a strategic alliance with AMR Corp., parent of American Airlines. The alliance provided for a critical $246 million equity investment in return for a service agreement that secured Canadian as a customer for AMR's Sabre information systems business and significant concessions by Canadian's employees, shareholders and creditors.

But, by 1995, Canadian was in serious trouble again. For that matter, Air Canada was suffering too—but it was somewhat better-off in scale, market position and financing. (Collectively, in their six fiscal years from 1990 through 1995, the two airlines posted cumulative losses of $2.15 billion, of which Canadian accounted for $1.26 billion.) Given the circumstances, Canadian management took a serious look at downsizing its domestic operations and retrenching to its more profitable international routes. As attractive as this idea looked in concept, there were serious obstacles to successful implementation, ranging from the maintenance of effective domestic feed and distribution for the international routes to absorbing the tangible and intangible costs of major layoffs and facility closings. Management chose instead to seek further payroll concessions and

2. After deregulation, the government would license airlines to fly any domestic route, any time, at any price, subject only to safety requirements. The government also retained provisions requiring that at least 75 per cent of the voting interests of air carrier license holders be owned and controlled by Canadians and that control of the airline be held in fact by Canadians.

productivity improvements to sustain their now-quixotic all-fronts contest with Air Canada.

Air Canada was not prepared to disengage, of course, and pressed on with the battle. The inevitable outcome was painfully slow to emerge. But over the next three years, Canadian lost a cumulative $3.19 million, and by late 1998, the airline was clearly having trouble assembling the cash needed to stay in the air. In March 1999, Canadian approached Federal Transport Department officials to explain its situation and to request that the government use Section 47 of the Transport Act to allow Canada's main airlines to enter into discussions that would normally be forbidden under competition regulations. Meanwhile, with the encouragement of Canadian, Onex Corporation and American Airlines executives were engaged in on and off talks about a venture to merge Canadian and Air Canada. When Section 47 was formally invoked in August, Air Canada was the first mover, with an offer to buy Canadian's international routes. Canadian rejected this out of hand. Then, in short order, Onex announced a plan to buy and merge both airlines in a deal that was heavily backed by American Airlines. Air Canada management was dismayed, to say the least, at the prospect of falling short so close to victory and outraged at the seeming complicity of the government in the process.

The Last Weeks of Canadian Airlines

A fierce takeover battle was joined, full of rancor, legal maneuvering, bids and counter-bids. The stakes were unprecedented. The competing proposals put forward by Onex and Air Canada were both structured such that the winner would emerge with control of a single airline serving over 80 per cent of Canada's regularly scheduled domestic air travel. Public relations programs were cranked up to a fever pitch. Both sides claimed that they would generate the greatest shareholder benefits, without, of course, abusing their monopoly position. One of Air Canada's promises—which seemed aimed at the not necessarily consistent goals of tying up yet another domestic market segment, while reassuring the public that price competition would continue—was that it would set up a separate low-fare carrier at Hamilton airport.[3] Just to make sure of its position, Air

3. Hamilton airport was located 60 kilometres south-west of Toronto's international airport. It was used by airfreight carriers, local air traffic and the occasional charter flight, but had no regularly scheduled passenger traffic.

Canada took a pre-emptive step in locking up all of Hamilton's available gates.

After 10 weeks of a very public contest, both sides were claiming that they would emerge the winner. Then, in early November, one of Air Canada's legal defenses came through: a judge in the Quebec Superior Court ruled that Onex's bid contravened the terms of the legislation under which Air Canada was privatized. Under the Air Canada Public Participation Act, no single party could control more than 10 per cent of Air Canada. Onex decided to withdraw, leaving Canadian hanging by a thread and looking for further backing from American Airlines and its Oneworld alliance partners. These last-ditch efforts were unsuccessful, and in early December, the Canadian board announced its approval of a $98 million takeover offer from Air Canada.

All that remained for the acquisition to proceed was approval from the federal government. This was expected, although some conditions would be imposed. The government was concerned about domestic competition, and as a condition for approving the merger, Air Canada would be required to hand over some gates at major airports.

Industry Background: Concurrent Developments

Passenger Traffic

From a historic high point reached in 1990, the number of passengers carried by Canada's domestic airlines dipped about 15 per cent in the recession of the early 1990s and did not recover to prerecession levels until 1995. Thereafter, growth was strong; overall, from 1990 through 1998, passenger counts grew 23 per cent, from 36.8 million to 45.4 million and the number of revenue passenger kilometres flown increased 41.5 per cent, from 66.8 billion to 94.5 billion. The distribution of demand by major airline and service is given in Table 1.

By Sector The components of passenger traffic growth over the 1990 to 1998 period reflected the increasing importance of transborder (United States) and other international traffic. Passenger traffic carried by domestic airlines grew 14 per cent over the period, transborder traffic grew 39 per cent and other international traffic grew 53 per cent. A particularly important event during the period was the signing of an "Open Skies" agreement with the United States in

TABLE 1

Passenger Kilometres Flown by Canadian Carriers—1990 and 1998 (millions)

	Air Canada	%	Canadian	%	Other Sch.*	%	Charter	%	Total	%
1990	25,504	37.6	21,624	31.9	3,975	5.9	16,675	24.6	67,778	100
1998	37,296	39.5	26,544	28.1	10,784	11.4	19,843	21.0	94,467	100

*The growth in "other scheduled" reflected the practice of most charter carriers in the 1990s to add some form of seasonal or peak-time scheduled carriage.

Source: Drawn from Transport Canada, Air Information in Canada, T-Facts. Includes domestic and international carriage.

1995. This treaty essentially removed pre-existing restrictions on air traffic between the two countries over a three-year period. It sustained the competitive status quo within each country, however, by not providing for cabotage—the right of an airline to carry local traffic within a foreign country. The revenue mix of the two major airlines in 1998, as shown in Table 2, reflected the results of these trends.

By Region   The distribution of passenger traffic carried by domestic carriers by region was six per cent for Atlantic Canada, 13 per cent for Quebec, 37 per cent for Ontario, 21 per cent for the Prairies and North, and 23 per cent for the Pacific.

By Airport   Passenger traffic in Canada was concentrated in relatively few airports. Toronto alone accounted for 31 per cent of the passenger traffic flown by Canadian carriers in 1998. Put together, the country's seven largest airports—Toronto, Vancouver, Montreal-Dorval, Calgary, Edmonton, Ottawa, Halifax, and Winnipeg—accounted for 83 per cent of all traffic flown by Canadian carriers. By sector, these same airports accounted for 75 per cent of the domestic, 97 per cent of the transborder and 90 per cent of the international passenger traffic flown by Canadian carriers.

By City Pair   Passenger traffic data for origin/destination traffic, or point-to-point traffic, further emphasizes the importance of the Toronto market in domestic air travel. The 10 highest-traffic domestic city pairs is presented in Table 3. Toronto anchored one end for seven of the top 10 city pairs.

Competition

The competitive context of the air travel market in Canada in the 1990s was a reflection of the seemingly irrational duel between Air Canada and Canadian. It was a hostile environment, marked by over-capacity, price-cutting and heavy losses for the two big airlines. It was remarkable that, under these circumstances, a number of relatively small carriers—namely, Royal Airlines, Canada 3000, AirTransat, Skyservice and WestJet—found viable market niches and were able to stay aloft and to grow. There were also notable failures—Greyhound, Vistajet and Astoria.

In the spring of 1996, Greyhound attempted to set up a low-fare, transcontinental service with its hubs in Winnipeg. Greyhound's low fares generated reasonable load factors and, interestingly, passenger profiles that were much further upscale than expected by industry observers. However, Greyhound was also saddled by costly delays in securing regulatory approvals, by inefficient secondhand 727 aircraft, by

TABLE 2

Passenger Revenue Mix for Major Airlines—1998 ($ millions)

	Domestic	Transborder	International	Total
Air Canada	2,294	1,426	1,257	4,977
Canadian	1,403	355	993	2,751

Source: Company Annual Reports.

TABLE 3

Point-to-Point Traffic for Selected City Pairs—1997 (thousands)*

Carriers	Scheduled	Charter	Total
Toronto to Montreal	1,182	NA	1,182
Toronto to Vancouver	830	233	1,063
Toronto to Ottawa	684	NA	684
Toronto to Calgary	495	95	590
Calgary to Vancouver	520	50	570
Toronto to Winnipeg	347	56	403
Toronto to Halifax	289	77	366
Edmonton to Vancouver	312	48	360
Calgary to Edmonton	308	NA	308
Toronto to Edmonton	282	44	326

*Excludes passengers flying the city pair as part of a connecting flight itinerary.

Source: Drawn from Transport Canada, Air Information in Canada, T-Facts Air Folder.

expensive aircraft lease arrangements, and by some questionable operating decisions, such as selling airline tickets in bus stations to avoid travel agent commissions. When the parent bus company was sold to Laidlaw Inc. in the summer of 1997, the airline was cut loose and quickly shut down.

Vistajet hardly got off the ground. It was to be a London, Ontario-based discount airline, but after four months of operation with one 30-year-old 737 and a bird strike that disabled the plane at a critical juncture, the new venture called it quits. Astoria, a two aircraft airline offering business class-only service between Toronto and Montreal, also folded after only four months of operation.

Competition and Government Policy

The federal government may have hoped that deregulation and the privatization of Air Canada would free it from some messy obligations. How wrong. By the early 1990s, Canadian's financial problems had become high-profile political issues. And, for the government, there were no easy solutions. Any significant effort to help Canadian—by, for example, providing financial assistance, moderating competition through reregulation, or dropping domestic ownership provisions—would fly in the face of the government's political and economic objectives to be and to be seen to be even-handed, to avoid interference with market mechanisms and to maintain a domestically controlled industry. Not helping Cana-

dian could result in an Air Canada monopoly, jeopardizing the government's goal of maintaining a healthy and competitive market, and, in the process, generating no small amount of criticism. Caught on the horns of a dilemma, the government tried to provide some aid to Canadian,[4] but it only bought some time for Canadian to pursue its own fate.

Faced with Canadian's failure, the government suspended competition rules, leading to the Air Canada—Onex takeover battle. In the furore that ensued, which included heated attacks on the government's actions and on the motives and intelligence of the transport minister, critics were nevertheless short on constructive alternatives. What the government did do was advise both Air Canada and Onex that it would be taking steps to protect the public interest, including provisions to:

▮ Prevent price gouging by any emerging monopoly carrier;

▮ Enhance competition in the domestic market, particularly by ensuring ease of entry and policing predatory practices;

▮ Maintain Canadian ownership and control of the industry;

▮ Maintain service to small communities;

▮ Ensure fair treatment of employees.

4. For example, the government purchased some of Canadian's aircraft in what some thought was a sweetheart deal.

The precise legislation to accomplish these aims was yet to be tabled, and some critics questioned whether these objectives could ever be achieved. In response, the government promised that if a competitive industry did not evolve in a reasonable time, it would have no hesitation about initiating further steps, such as the discussion of cabotage with the United States.

The Competitive Situation in Late 1999

As the new Air Canada took shape, the industry was rife with speculation about its strategic intentions and the consequences for travelers and industry players alike. Given the government's position on sustaining competition, it looked as if there would be opportunities for Canada's existing airlines and possibly for new entrants; the issues for the airlines were how and when to take advantage of these possibilities. Following is a brief review of the positions and apparent intentions of the incumbent and announced players.

The New Air Canada Despite the turmoil of the moment, complete with pending but uncertain government approvals and conditions, union clashes, and unresolved financial and operating issues at Canadian, there were some broad, if not settled, themes in Air Canada's positions. It was expected that as the air cleared the company would: Rationalize Air Canada's and Canadian's regional feeder carriers to eliminate gross duplication of capacity; Rationalize the domestic trunk routes of the two airlines to cut capacity by 15 per cent or more; Rationalize and expand its transborder operations (where it already held over 50 per cent of the market) and its other international operations, and use these dominant positions as forcefully as possible to influence domestic patronage and pricing; Increase prices and cut promotional spending as much as legally, politically and commercially feasible; Air Canada had already announced plans to create a stand-alone low fare airline based in Hamilton, and perhaps parallel stand-alone businesses for the leisure (charter) market and for cargo. This theme was a sore point with Air Canada's union since the company had made no secret of its desire for concessions in wages and work rules for the new entities. The initiatives for a separate low-fare airline within the Air Canada family remained unclear. Was it a public relations ploy to help gain approval for the acquisition of Canadian; or was it a strategic move to pre-empt other low-fare players, like WestJet?

Most observers doubted that Air Canada would be able, or would be allowed, to sustain all of the market share accrued through the merger. Air Canada clearly thought otherwise and appeared to be developing all segments of the industry.

Royal Airlines Royal was founded in 1979, and for many years operated as a Quebec-based charter carrier with additional cargo, water bombing and aircraft maintenance services. In the early 1990s, the company went public and expanded into charter operations in Canada and abroad. By 1999, Royal's fleet encompassed 11 large passenger aircraft. In anticipation of the opportunities that might be created by an Air Canada–Canadian merger, Royal added domestic scheduled services in October, 1999, with flights at peak times from Toronto, Montreal, Ottawa, Winnipeg, Halifax and Vancouver.

Canada 3000 Canada 3000 was a privately owned carrier that started business in 1988 as a dedicated charter carrier for international pleasure travel, and gradually added scheduled carrier operations in Canada and abroad. By 1999, the company's fleet of 15 large aircraft were focused on long-haul domestic and international routes that varied with seasonal traffic patterns. It was anticipated that Canada 3000 would expand its operations in response to industry restructuring, possibly with an IPO to finance fleet additions.

AirTransAt The parent of AirTransat, Transat A.T. Inc., operated an integrated vacation travel business encompassing every aspect of holiday travel organization and distribution. The airline's fleet of 20 large charter aircraft was dedicated to the vacation travel market in Canada and Europe. There were no indications that Transat intended to change its focus in response to the domestic market turmoil.

Skyservice Skyservice Airlines flew a charter fleet of four large aircraft mainly for two big tour operators, but also for incidental hire. The airline was a division of privately owned Skyservice Investments. This was an aggressive company and it was expected that it would attempt to expand its operations, possibly by way of long-haul scheduled domestic service.

CanJet The CanJet Corp. of Toronto had been working since the summer of 1999 on plans for a low-fare airline that would fly out of Hamilton to Montreal, Ottawa, Halifax and Winnipeg. Although the prospective venture was backed by a well-known industry figure, Kenneth Rowe, chairman of the IMP Group Ltd. of Halifax, as of early December it was still regarded as very much a paper airline.

Canadian Regional Airlines   There was an expectation the government would insist that Air Canada try to sell Canadian's regional feeder subsidiary as a condition of the acquisition. The airline consisted of 54 aircraft, most notably a fleet of 30 20-to-30-year-old, 60-to-85 passenger Fokker F 28 jets. These aircraft had been described uncharitably, but with some accuracy, by Robert Milton, Air Canada's CEO, as planes that "are rarely flown in the Third World anymore."

Although the strategic role of the regional airlines in Canada was to feed the hub-based trunk flights of their parents, up to 80 per cent of the passengers on regional airlines flew between cities without ongoing connections on the larger jet aircraft.[5] It was not clear in December 1999 whether or not there would be a buyer at an acceptable price, although one industry entrepreneur, Jim Deluce of Regional Airlines Holdings, had proposed purchasing both the Canadian and Air Canada regional subsidiaries.

WestJet and the 'Southwest' Business Model

WestJet commenced operations out of Calgary in 1996. The airline was the brainchild of several local businessmen unhappy with the price and service being provided in the West by the major carriers (and this at the height of a price and frequency battle!). The founders went into business with a strategy that copied the Southwest model, "rivet-for-rivet, stitch-for-stitch."

Other airlines had adopted this formula with varying degrees of success, including Morris Air (now part of Southwest) and Spirit Airlines in the United States, and easyJet, Ryanair and Virgin Express[6] in Europe. Interestingly, major system carriers on both continents had, by and large, experienced serious difficulties in their attempts to establish similar low-fare operating units.

The Southwest Low-Fare Airline Model

In the United States, Southwest Airlines had pioneered, developed, and exploited a low-fare airline model to the point of becoming the most consistently profitable airline in the world. Founded in 1971, with three planes serving three Texas cities, Southwest had overcome early problems and had steadily grown its fleet, route structure and financial record. Over the years, Southwest had become well known for its employee-oriented, irreverent, work-hard-play-hard culture which was epitomized in the iconoclastic management style of Herb Kelleher, chairman and CEO.

The Southwest business model departed from the conventional system-airline, hub-and-spoke model in three principal ways, by: (1) focusing on price-sensitive passengers; (2) employing a short-haul, point-to-point route system, and; (3) running a low-cost, no-frills operation. An outline of further differences in the conventional hub-and-spoke and Southwest models is presented in Table 4. There were, of course, other business models being pursued in the industry such as charter, scheduled charter, and full- or luxury-service medium- to long-haul point-to-point carriage, but these were less central to the WestJet situation.

The Competitive Features of the Southwest Model

The Southwest-style airlines took some pains to emphasize that their low-fare/short-haul operations were a complement to the traditional airlines in that they aimed primarily at budget-conscious travellers who might otherwise drive, use a bus or train, or not travel at all. While this was undoubtedly accurate as a point of focus, it was also true that as their systems expanded, low-fare airline routes overlapped city pairs served by the large system carriers, or by their subsidiary regional feeder operations. Indeed, the average length of a Southwest flight had been steadily increasing over the years and it was estimated that currently 40 per cent of passengers were either through or connecting.[7] As a result, the two airline system types invariably ended up in competition for at least part of the potential market. This was not a happy circumstance for the major carriers

5. Joe Randall, president of Air Canada's regional airline business, in The Globe and Mail, January 21, 2000.

6. Created when Virgin acquired EuroBelgian Express.

7. Connecting passengers landed at an intermediate airport and changed planes to complete their flight; through passengers landed at one or more intermediate airports but did not change planes to complete their flight.

TABLE 4

Comparison of the Hub-and-Spoke and Southwest Models

	Hub-and-Spoke	**Southwest**
Market Focus	Business travel	Personal travel
Value Proposition	Frequency, system, amenities	Low fare
Route System	Integrated hub-and-spoke	Point-to-point
Stage Length	Medium- and long-haul	Short-haul
Seating	Reserved	Open
Baggage	Transfer and interline	Check in/pick up only
Airport Requirements	Major metropolitan hubs	Secondary airports
Aircraft Turn Time (at gate)	30 to 60 minutes	15 to 20 minutes
Fleet	Multi-role/type	Single role/type 1 aircraft type
Ticketing	Travel Agents	Direct
Product	Multi-class, frills	Single class, no-frills
Promotional Focus	Service, loyalty programs, restricted price deals	Low price, few restrictions
Culture	Formal	Casual
Structure	Hierarchical, defined roles and relationships	Flat, multi-task
Personnel Systems	Union work rule driven	Task, enterprise success driven

who were already locked in a tough competitive battle with each other.

The response of the major carriers to the advent of low-fare competitors followed two avenues. First, they counter-attacked through their regular operations—by measures that included selective fare cuts, enhanced promotional incentives, and shifts in frequencies and equipment. Second, if low fare operators continued to grow, some of the majors tried the more direct counter of creating captive low-fare subsidiary operations. All these responses, however, were ultimately limited by the higher cost structures of the conventional airlines and by the difficulty of disentangling a subsidiary from the route structure and traditional practices, of the parent, including most notably union restrictions and cultural habits.

The Southwest formula was designed to achieve low cost. The key elements highlighted in Table 1 and other operational practices were designed to contribute to this end. The focus on one aircraft type, for example, contributed to lower employee-to-aircraft ratios, greater flexibility in crew assignments, and simplified maintenance, training programs and administrative procedures relative to the multi-air-

craft system carriers. The result of this dedication to low cost meant the low-fare carriers had substantially lower operating costs per unit of capacity than those of the conventional airlines. WestJet estimated, for example, that its operating costs, after equalization for stage length, were 40 per cent to 50 per cent lower than those of Canadian and Air Canada. This difference put conventional carriers at a terrific disadvantage if they chose to compete on price on any given city pair. Some comparative financial and operating statistics for selected airlines are presented in Exhibit 2.

Setting up a competitive, profitable, low-fare subsidiary had also proven to be a problematic endeavor for the traditional airlines. In the early 1990s, Continental Airlines launched Continental Life and closed it after a few years of substantial losses. Other entrants included, in the United States. United Airlines' United Shuttle, Delta Airlines' Delta Express and U.S. Airways' MetroJet, and in Europe, British Airways' GO. Although specific financial results were not available for these ventures, industry observers were generally skeptical about their profitability on any kind of fully allocated cost basis. United, for

EXHIBIT 2

Comparative Financial and Operating Performance for Selected Airlines*

	Southwest	WestJet	easyJet	Air Canada	Canadian	United
Financial Results						
Operating Revenues	6,226	126	184	5,932	3,171	26,257
Operating Expenses	5,203	112	181	5,788	3,173	24,016
Operating Income	1,022	14	3	144	(22)	2,209
Net Income	647	7	6	(16)	(138)	1,227
Operating Statistics**						
Average Stage Length (miles)***	450	378	NA	955	1,325	NA
Rev. Pass. Miles (RPM, millions)	31,419	639	1,302	23,212	16,695	124,609
Avail. Seat Miles (ASM, millions)	47,544	893	1,737	32,719	23,217	174,008
Load Factor (%)	66	72	75	71	72	72
Pass. Revenue/RPM (cents)****	19	19	NA	19	14	19
Pass. Revenue/ASM (cents)	13	13	NA	13	10	13
Oper. Revenue/ASM (cents)	13	14	11	16	11	15
Oper. Cost/ASM (cents)	11	13	10	16	11	14
Employees	25,844	629	394	23,000	14,123	91,000
ASM/Employee (millions)	1,840	1,420	4,410	1,430	1,640	1,910
Aircraft	280	11	8	157	81	577

* For fiscal year end, 1998.

** Air Canada, Canadian statistics exclude regional subsidiaries.

*** Typically, airline operating costs per mile decrease with longer flights. WestJet estimated, for example, that its operating costs per available seat mile if it operated with an average stage length of 1,113 miles (Calgary-Thunder Bay) would be about 8.2 cents per mile.

**** Simple passenger revenue comparisons are also confounded by stage length. As costs per mile fall with longer stage lengths, the tendency, under competition, is for prices per mile to fall as well.

Source: Company financial reports. All currencies converted to Canadian dollars.

example, had started United Shuttle to compete with Southwest in the Western United States, but had backed off from direct competition after reported losses of $200 million and repositioned the Shuttle as a feeder to its West Coast hubs. British Airways, which had launched GO in 1998 to compete with the challenge of Ryannair and easyJet, had reported operating losses of $32 million in GO's first year of operation—much to the delight of easyJet, which sponsored a contest offering prizes for the most accurate forecast of the losses.

Whatever their willingness to subsidize losses, whether it be on particular routes or with new entries, the conventional airlines faced the limitations of their own fiscal abilities and beyond this, the prospect of legal challenge for engaging in predatory competition. In the United Kingdom, for example, easyJet made a big thing of their underdog status by suing British Airways under Article 26 of the Treaty of Rome, which says that dominant players in a market should not operate below the cost of production.

WestJet's Progress

By late 1999, WestJet was on a roll. The company had overcome some early problems with safety regulations; acquired a fleet; established a route structure; built a reputation as an efficient and reliable, if unconventional operator; grown passenger volumes; fought off competitive challenges; completed a successful IPO; and was increasingly profitable.

TABLE 5

WestJet Service Coverage and Weekly Departures, Summer 1999

Airport Departures	Service Commenced	Aircraft in Service	Weekly Departures
Calgary	February, 1996	3	156
Vancouver	February, 1996		94
Kelowna	February, 1996		61
Edmonton	February, 1996		88
Victoria	March, 1996		27
Regina	June, 1996	4	21
Saskatoon	August, 1996		28
Abbotsford, B.C.	June, 1997	6	20
Winnipeg	March, 1998	8	27
Prince George	March, 1999		26
Thunder Bay	March, 1999	12	7

Source: WestJet Prospectus, April 1999.

Route Network

WestJet's route network focused on short-haul point-to-point service in Western Canada. This structure allowed WestJet to provide frequent service and dispense with many of the amenities usually provided on longer flights. The company's service coverage and departure frequencies as of late 1999 are summarized in Table 5. Whenever possible, WestJet picked niche routes where it could compete with non-stop jet service against the turbo-prop service of the majors' regional subsidiaries. On all its routes, WestJet sought to offer low everyday fares while maintaining a friendly service environment. Consistent with the Southwest model, WestJet offered a single class of service, did not interline baggage with other airlines, nor offer meal service, city ticket offices, frequent-flier programs, airport lounges or business class amenities.

Passenger Traffic

The impact of WestJet's entry, coupled with the competitive response of the majors, contributed to large increases in traffic on the targeted city pairs, as illustrated in Table 6. It appeared, indeed, that WestJet was correct in claiming that it was opening new demand segments for the industry.

Competitive Reaction

Air Canada and Canadian counter-attacked in predictable ways. They sought to match WestJet's everyday low prices—which were up to 60 per cent less than the nominal economy prices of the majors—but in doing so they raised "fences" to limit their overall revenue erosion—such as by limiting the number of seats available in varying discount ranges, by restricting the times when the low fares were available and by requiring minimum stay-overs. On the promotional

TABLE 6

Growth in Passenger Traffic for Largest City Pairs* (000 passengers)

	Cal-Van	Edm-Van	Cal-Edm	Kel-Van	Cal-Vic	Edm-Vic
1995	422	243	271	87	63	43
1997	674	438	375	192	162	123
% Inc.	60	80	38	119	155	186

Source: WestJet Prospectus, April 1999.

* For cities served by WestJet; all domestic carriers; traffic does not include domestic portion of international flights.

front, both airlines used occasional bonus point offers in their frequent-flyer programs to help stem the loss of high yield customers. Similarly, on occasion, the majors would price under on selected routes. Finally, the majors shuffled equipment and frequencies to try to improve their offering. At one point, for example, Air Canada attempted to compete in some city pairs by introducing its new 50-seat CRJ 700 regional jet, but had backed off after 10 months and little progress. Throughout these various forays, WestJet claimed that it made money on all routes.

In WestJet's assessment, Air Canada and Canadian were engaging in harassment and containment, rather than in trying to "blow 'em out of the sky"— although the two majors would no doubt have been happy to see this happen. The company was confident that, under these circumstances, it had room for continuing profitable growth.

WestJet's Options

In early September 1999, WestJet's CEO, Stephen Smith, reiterated the company's original plan: "We have a business plan we've been following and that plan contemplates the addition of three or four aircraft per year focused primarily on Western Canada . . . the company doesn't plan to fly further east than Thunder Bay for the foreseeable future . . . at least three to five years."[8] WestJet was, quite logically, concerned about not overextending itself. The airline had prospered in a tough market by following conservative policies with respect to growth and financing. It took pride, for example, in the fact that it had minimized the use of debt and owned 11 of its 13 aircraft.

As the events of the fall of 1999 unfolded, however, WestJet management was more or less compelled to take the possibility of eastern expansion into consideration. First, there was a matter of growth potential. If the company remained in Western Canada there was growth potential to perhaps 30 to 40 aircraft. A successful move to the East would more than double the potential. Second, there was a matter of timing, and particularly concerns about first-mover advantages. It was quite apparent that it would be just a matter of time before someone entered the East with a low-fare strategy—be it Air Canada or CanJet, or another start-up. As a condition of its merger with Canadian, Air Canada undertook not to start up a low-fare airline in eastern Canada until September 2001, provided there was a low-fare entrant within the next year.[9] If no other low-fare entrant stepped forward Air Canada could enter the eastern market as soon as September 2000. Air Canada also promised to facilitate gate access for newcomers at Hamilton airport. Finally, there was a chance that by remaining solely in the West, WestJet might become vulnerable to competition reaching out from their Eastern bases.

There was a strong temptation to push east, probably with an operation based at Hamilton airport. Beyond this, WestJet's management had to consider immediate and fundamental questions of pace—how fast and how significant an entry was necessary from a competitive standpoint, how fast and how significant an entry could the company digest, and how it would connect (if at all) to the company's routes in the West? And, finally, in the longer haul, what were WestJet's prospects against Air Canada and others?

---

8. The Globe and Mail, September 7, 1999.

9. There was no restriction of Air Canada launching a low-fare operation in Western Canada.

Avon Products, Inc.: The Personal-Care Industry

This case was prepared by Gabriela Del Carro and Marc E. Gartenfeld under the direction of Dr. Robert J. Mockler, St. John's University.

In spring 2000, Andrea Jung, president and CEO since November 1999 at Avon Products, Inc., faced the strategic decision of developing a growth strategy for the 115-year-old company. Avon Products, Inc., the world's largest direct seller of beauty and related personal-care products, sold to women in 137 countries via three million independent sales representatives who generated approximately $5.1 billion in annual revenues. Upon reviewing the financial statistics of Avon, Jung discovered that not only had earnings risen in the low-single digits in the past few years, but—also more disturbing—the growth rate had shrunk during the same time. In light of this problem, Jung faced significant strategic decisions in growing the company in lieu of its stagnant sales, limited distribution capabilities, and shifts in personal-care preferences and spending habits in this rapidly changing industry.

For 115 years, Avon had enjoyed worldwide success mainly due to its unique direct-selling distribution channel and worldwide brand-name recognition. However, recent single-digit growth indicated that the company needed to

This case is intended to be used as a basis for class discussion rather than as an illustration of either effective or ineffective handling of the situation. This case was prepared by Gabriella Del Carro, Marc E. Gartenfeld, and Robert J. Mockler, under whose supervision the case was written. Reprinted by permission of the authors.

make significant improvements in its overall operations. In 1999, sales increased approximately 1% as gains in fashion, jewelry and accessories, and noncore categories offset declines in cosmetics, fragrances, toiletries, and apparel. The single-digit growth rate had declined each year. Avon's direct-selling model generated 95% of the company's revenues. In 2000, Jung was deciding whether or not to enter Avon into a nonexclusive partnership with J C Penney and Sears to supplement its sales representatives, expand its distribution capabilities, and attract new customers in order to increase sales and earnings.

Under careful consideration was the type of products to be sold in these stores. The company was leaning towards higher-priced cosmetics, which would be sold exclusively in these department stores. By partnering with J C Penney and Sears, considered to be the weakest portion of the brand-name retail market, the company ran the risk of a possible further weakening of its brand image. Also, in marketing a higher-priced Avon line in those department stores, the company might be sending an unintentional message to consumers that the current Avon line was not of high enough quality to be sold in J C Penney and Sears. Avon had faced significant hard times in the past, and past efforts in diversifying products and distribution had put them at risk of debt and takeover.

Avon was also spending $30 million to re-launch **Avon.com,** in order to enable consumers to buy products from sales representatives online or directly through the company. The company was intending to allow each sales representative to customize his or her own web site, which would be linked to the company's home page. However, personalized inconsistent web sites could further erode Avon's already weakened image.

The global personal-care market was valued at $171.39 billion in 1999, with overall growth of 2.8% from 1995 through 1999 (Agos, 2000). The industry had had to deal with significant changes: shifting distribution channels and market demands as well as new consumer groups. Due to the ease of entry and aggressive competition in the industry, personal-care-product companies began to utilize the Internet as a distribution channel for their products. However, many of the well-established retail and direct-selling companies had been overly cautious in developing extensive web sites due to the fear of possible cannibalization. Younger companies, less-established retailers, and niche operators, however, recognized the opportunities of the Internet and were increasingly eroding the market share of major players. Expanding target markets had also restructured personal-care marketing and product plans. As a result of sustained marketing campaigns and greater product knowledge, consumers began to display more-sophisticated buying behavior. This trend was attributed to the rising spending power of the younger generations and their corresponding demand for high-quality beauty products. However, the young and affluent customer rarely shopped for personal-care products via the direct-selling channel. Other attractive customer segments in the industry included the Generation Y market, the ethnic market, and, increasingly, the men's personal-care market.

In light of Avon's disappointing financial situation and new retail initiatives, as well as changing market demands, Jung was considering the following strategic decisions. What type of product-line extensions or divestitures should Avon undertake? How should the company establish a successful Internet presence? If the company ventured into retail outlets, which would best suit the company's current structure and future goals? How could the company create a consistent and strong image? These and other decisions would have to be made if Avon was to grow, prosper, and triumph against competitors in the near, intermediate, and longer-term future.

The Personal-Care Industry and Competitive Market

Overall View of the Industry

The personal-care industry, as shown in Figure 1, was defined by the Food and Drug Administration (FDA) as all products intended to be applied to the body for cleansing, beautifying, promoting attractiveness, or altering the body's appearance (U.S. FDA, 2000A). The products in the personal-care industry were divided into skin care, makeup/color cosmetics, hair care, personal hygiene products, perfumes/fragrances, spa services, and other related items. The customers in the industry could be segmented according to their age (mature market, baby boomers, Generation X, Generation Y), by gender (male, female), and by ethnic origin (African American, Asian American, Latin American). Products in the industry were distributed and sold via three methods: direct selling, retail selling, and online selling. The personal-care industry was prominent in both the domestic and international markets and was regulated by the FDA, Federal Trade Commission, and Department of Transportation. Competition mainly came from Mary Kay Inc. and L'Oreal.

In 1999, the global market for personal-care products was valued at $171.39 billion, with overall growth of 2.8% from 1995 through 1999 (Agos, 2000). Overall, the market for personal-care products was expected to increase steadily in the future, reaching $197.97 billion in 2003, as seen in Figure 2.

Products/Services

Skin Care   Skin-care products, valued at $29.44 billion in 1999, were comprised of facial products, hand and body products, and cosmeceuticals (Agos, 2000). Approximately 39% of households purchased facial cleansers and lotions at least once a year with expenditures averaging $14.41; 22% of the purchases were attributed to perceived price savings (Grossman, 1999). Consumers tended to buy larger sizes and use larger quantities of hand and body lotion than the facial segment: approximately 73.7% of households bought skin and hand lotions, with yearly expenditures averaging $21.33 (Cooney-Curran, 2000). Consumers bought the products about four times a year, with 21.3% purchasing the products due to perceived price savings or deals (Cooney-Curran, 2000). Consumers were becoming increasingly price sensitive to hand and body lotion products, and at the same time,

FIGURE 1

The Personal-Care Industry

they demanded quality and effectiveness in the products they purchased.

Personal-care products considered to be drugs or "cosmeceuticals" were articles intended to cleanse, beautify, or promote attractiveness as well as treat or prevent disease or otherwise affect the structure or any function of the human body (U.S. FDA, 2000A). Skin cosmeceuticals comprised 25% of the total skin-care market in 1999 with sales of $1.5 billion (Bittar, 2000). The growth was driven by the introduction of cosmeceutical ingredients in mass products—once the exclusive domain of high-quality product manufacturers. It was projected that in the following years, the skin-care market would be dominated by cosmeceuticals, especially in the more-advanced economies. The entry of many mass companies into the market was likely to drive average prices up, which in turn would increase revenue growth (Bittar, 2000).

The most common skin cosmeceuticals were anti-wrinkle cosmeceuticals and sun cosmeceuticals.

Anti-wrinkle cosmeceuticals contained ingredients such as Retinal (a vitamin A derivative), which served to maintain the skin's youthful appearance. Product claims of "anti-aging," "wrinkle reduction," and "improves fine lines" dominated the skin-care segment, as consumers were eager to purchase products that delivered a glimmer of hope for healthier-looking skin and body. Sun cosmeceuticals came in two types: sunscreens and sun blocks. Sunscreens were creams, lotions, or oils that were SPF-rated and that reacted with chemicals in the skin to offer protection from the sun for a predetermined period without risking sunburn. Sun blocks were opaque creams or pastes containing zinc oxide or titanium dioxide, which prevented all ultraviolet radiation from reaching the skin, and, therefore, did not carry an SPF rating. Sunscreens with an SPF above 15 were sometimes referred to as sun blocks even though they still allowed some UV-light to pass through. Sun cosmeceuticals mainly protected individuals from sunlight-induced skin aging and melanoma, a form of skin cancer responsible for a 191% increase in mortality rates for men and 84% in women between 1950 and the mid 1990s (Altruis Biomedical Network, 2000C).

Keys to success with skin-care products were tailoring the products to specific needs and frequently introducing new products. Successful introduction of new skin-care products required strong company research and development. Other keys to success were strong brand loyalty and strong brand image, which made product claims viable.

Makeup/Color Cosmetics   The makeup/color cosmetic segment, valued at $19.1 billion in 1999, was the highest revenue-generating one in the personal-care industry. Figure 3 illustrates the components of the makeup/color cosmetic segment in order of sales volume.

Facial makeup/color cosmetic products included foundation, face powder, concealer, and rouge. Facial cosmetics were the highest revenue-generating segment in the makeup/color cosmetic market. Sales for foundation (a vanishing cream) were $602.7 million in 1999, a 19.1% gain over 1998. Foundation experienced the most growth of any color cosmetic cate-

gory, due in part to the use of sheer-skin effects (Sauer, 2000).

Eye makeup/color cosmetic products included mascara, eyeliner, eye shadow, and eyebrow pencil. Since eye cosmetics were used in a very sensitive area, product testing and safety were essential. Customers were increasingly demanding new products with an emphasis on all-in-one features, such as new brow products that emphasized definition and contour, mascara products with gel-based consistency to promote thickness and shine, and monochromatic and metallic colors for eye shadows.

Lip makeup/color cosmetic products were comprised of lipstick, lip gloss, and lip pencil. The trend in lip products was towards all-in-one products that provided color and moisturizing capabilities while also protecting the lips from harmful UV-rays and that contained SPF, vitamins, botanicals, antioxidants, and exfoliators.

Nail makeup/color cosmetic products consisted of nail varnish or enamel, nail varnish remover, and nail-treatment products. Nail cosmetics experienced the lowest growth in the personal-care industry due to fashion-related cycles and lack of new shades, colors, and product launches.

Growth in the overall makeup/color cosmetic segment was expected to remain strong in the future, especially as new products were expected to hit the market. Cosmetics were considered basic necessities and were purchased regardless of the health of the economy. Sales of cosmetics relied on disposable personal income, which was expected to increase 2.4% through 2003 (Sanabria, 2000A). However, the segment was heavily influenced by prevalent fashion trends, as shown at beauty web sites, in magazines, or at runway shows. Cosmetics were becoming more innovative and sophisticated; the popularity of multi-functional, all-in-one products was evidence of this trend. Consumers of makeup/color cosmetics were also seeking products tailored to their specific needs, and their increased product knowledge led to the demand for selection. Female consumers began to purchase cosmetics by the age of twelve. By the age of thirteen, 90% of them regularly used cosmetic products (Sanabria, 2000A).

Keys to success in the makeup/color cosmetics industry were developing products according to fashion trends, having a wide range of selection in each subcategory, and creating products according to needs. An additional key to success was developing product awareness and recognition among young consumers. Also, since makeup/color cosmetics were at times used on very sensitive areas of the body, strong quality control was required.

Hair Care   The hair-care segment was comprised of shampoo, conditioner, styling agents, and colorants. Shampoo was the most popular hair-care product. Due to consumer demand, special formulation shampoos were developed for particular hair types or for hair that had been subjected to a treatment such as coloring. Similarly, many new conditioning products offered a combination of benefits, such as protecting and strengthening the hair. Hair colorants were leading the hair-care segment, being driven by increased purchases by women, men, baby boomers, and Generation Y. It was reported that 50% of women colored their hair and 35% of them did it at home with a consistent growth rate projected for upcoming years (In Cosmetics99, 1999). Those who began to color their hair in their midthirties were likely to color it for life.

Additionally, there was social pressure for baby boomers to maintain a young-looking image, particularly for women of this age group who were pursuing careers. Hair colorants led to the introduction of styling products formulated for colored or UV-damaged hair that could intensify color and longevity. The hair-color category had grown 12% over the past year (Sanabria, 2000A). All hair types experienced problems to some degree. Thus, hair structure and physical properties of hair care were important factors to consider in developing new hair-care products, as were the specific needs for the hair types of different ethnic groups. Use of natural ingredients in

hair products was expected to drive growth in the hair-care segment for the next ten years, due to consumers' recognition that herbs had fewer side effects, promoted health, and were perceived to be cleaner and simpler (Altruis Biomedical Network, 2000A). In 1999, there were two to three times more brands than in 1990, causing market saturation in the hair-care segment (Sanabria, 2000B).

In order to succeed in this market, value-added products needed to be introduced in order to distinguish between the numerous products, and then a complete line of hair-care products would need to be developed in order to increase profits. Keys to success in marketing hair-care products were tailoring them to special needs, using natural ingredients, developing value-added products, and offering a complete line of products. Keys to success also included brand loyalty with existing consumers and awareness and recognition for younger consumers by offering trendy coloring products.

Personal Hygiene   The personal-hygiene segment included bath and shower products, deodorants, shaving products, and related items. Bath and shower products included bubble bath and cleansing products such as bar soap and body wash. Approximately 93% of the population used personal wash products, with above-average growth in shower gels and antibacterial products. However, bar soaps constituted two-thirds of bath product sales. Shaving products included razors, both electric and manual, and shaving creams. Competition among electric razors was expected to increase due to technological innovations. Manual razors were considered commodities that were easily interchangeable. As a result, many companies reduced prices and sustained smaller profit margins with this product in order to gain customer loyalty (Altruis Biomedical Network, 2000B). Other products in the personal-hygiene segment included oral-hygiene products and feminine-hygiene products.

In 1999, the total global market value of personal hygiene was $22.4 billion (Agos, 2000). Personal-hygiene products did not always follow the same trends as other personal-care items, since many personal-hygiene products were considered staples, as opposed to luxuries. Sales of personal-hygiene products designed exclusively for men were estimated at $1.7 billion in 1999 (NPD Group, 2000A). Manufacturers were increasingly targeting the "wellness" market, attempting to derive value from aromatherapeutic products advertised as relieving the stresses of modern life. These included essential oils like eucalyptus and menthol in bath additives, shower gels, and soaps. Many companies not primarily involved in personal-care products diversified their product line with personal-hygiene products, due to the non-cyclical market. Due to increased competition and number of products offered, a key to success was developing all-in-one products and utilizing aromatherapeutic ingredients. Most personal-hygiene products were distributed via retail outlets, and often the companies with the strongest brand names and largest profit margins would get premium shelf space. Many generic brands were available for price-conscious consumers.

Therefore, keys to success in this market were developing good relations with storeowners in order to obtain premium shelf space and increase sales and building strong brand loyalty.

Perfumes/Fragrances   The global fragrance market was valued at $22.2 billion in 1999 (NPD Group, 2000A). Sales of men's prestige fragrances rose to $960 million in 1999, a 6% increase from the previous year. Women's fragrances decreased by 1% in the same year (NPD Group, 2000A). Unisex fragrances were driving the market globally, growing from 6% of overall sales in 1995 to 8% in 1999 (NPD Group, 2000A). The fragrance market was highly sensitive to the marketing strategies of major fragrance houses.

The association with clothing and sports was expected to drive the market in the future. During the 1990s, a thousand new perfumes were launched (NPD Group, 2000A). Future trends included invisible scents which only reached the brain; microencapsulation, which would allow scents to remain on the skin for days; and natural aromatherapeutic scents, which stimulated mood, enhanced the senses, and reduced stress. Many companies offered single-use sprays in order to increase brand awareness. Also, companies were offering refillable perfumes, which were 20% to 40% cheaper than nonrefillables, in order to ensure repeat sales. Overall, companies participating in the fragrance industry were subjected to rising price competition, price transparency, and limited future-growth prospects. The fragrance market was heavily influenced by prevailing trends and further characterized by low-level brand loyalty. Consumers were becoming increasingly fashion and value conscious. Recent product launches indicated that mental well-being was having an impact on innovation, encouraging consumers to purchase value-added products (Anonymous, 2000).

Keys to success in the fragrance industry were new product introductions with an emphasis on mental well-being, increased brand awareness through the increased distribution of samples, and strong brand loyalty.

Figure 4 indicates the expected future sales growth of personal-care products from 1998 to 2005 segmented by type of product.

FIGURE 4

Expected Future Sales Growth of Personal-Care Products, 1998–2005

Low Growth (< 12%)	Premium women's fragrances, hand care, baby hair care, face masks, bath additives, styling agents, home perms, conditioners
Medium Growth (12–18%)	Facial makeup, baby toiletries, mass women's fragrances, baby skin care, premium's men's fragrances, 2-in-1 hair-care products, mass unisex fragrances, suntan products, after-sun products, bar soaps, toners, mass men's fragrances
High Growth (18–25%)	Shower products, eye makeup, post-shave products, salon hair care, body care, solid deodorants, talcum powder, premium unisex fragrances, cleansers, shampoo, spray deodorants
Exceptionally High Growth (> 25%)	Baby sun care, hair colorants, lip products, self-tanning products, cream deodorants, facial moisturizers

Source: F. Agos (2000). "State of the Industry: 2000," *Global Cosmetic Industry,* June 1, vol. 166, no. 6, p. 22.

Spa Services   Spas, also known as wellness centers, were places where individuals received therapeutic and beautifying services such as massages, body wraps, manicures, pedicures, and haircuts, hair colorants, and hair styling. Many spas sold a variety of prestigious, premium-priced personal-care products. Spas were becoming more commonplace for both men and women. Most consumers received samples of the products that were used in the services they received. As a result, many developed brand loyalty to products they perceived to be superior and specific to their needs.

Keys to success with spa services were offering samples of products used during the services, developing a strong brand image by developing and selling prestigious, high-priced products, and creating products tailored to needs.

Other Nonpersonal-Care Products   A few personal-care companies went beyond normal personal-care product line extensions and offered nonpersonal-care products such as jewelry, apparel, gift and decorative products, and home-entertainment items. The key to success with such products was to analyze each segment to see if it was profitable and fit the company's brand image.

Customers

Customers in the personal-care industry could be categorized according to age, gender, and ethnic origin.

Age   Customers could be segmented by age in four distinct markets: the mature market, baby boomers, Generation X, and Generation Y. Figure 5 illustrates the age ranges and size of each age segment.

Senior Citizens. The senior citizen segment was comprised of individuals aged fifty-four and over. The number of individuals in the United States aged sixty-five and older increased by over 3.7 million since 1990, reaching approximately 35 million people (Francese, 2000). The average household of senior citizens aged 65 to 74 spent nearly $30,000 a year on goods and services (Francese, 2000). However, as senior citizens aged, they tended to reduce their purchases of personal-care products. In recent years, department stores, malls, and specialty stores showed the greatest net declines in senior citizens' personal-care purchases. The preferred channels of distribution were drugstores, mass merchandisers, and, most

FIGURE 5

Customers in the Personal-Care Industry Segmented by Age

Senior Citizens 54 and above years old	34.8 million people (over age 65)
Baby Boomers 35–53 years old	81 million people 30% of the population
Generation X 23–34 years old	46 million people 17% of the population
Generation Y 5–22 years old	73 million people 28% of the population

Source: Global Cosmetic Industry (2000). "GENERATION GAPS: Global Cosmetic Industry Takes a Look at the Personal-Care Preferences, Spending Habits, and Power of Generation Y and X and Baby Boomers," [Online]. **http://www.findarticles.com/cf_0/m0HLW/6_166/63411614/p1/ article.jhtml**. Accessed November 1.

important, direct selling due to its convenience (Francese, 2000).

Baby Boomers. The baby-boomer segment, estimated at 81 million people or 30% of the population, was comprised of individuals aged 35 to 53 years old and the largest demographic segment (Global Cosmetic Industry, 2000). Within this segment, households headed by 45- to 53-year-olds had the highest median income and a median net worth of $57,755, higher than any other personal-care product customer age group, with increases expected (Global Cosmetic Industry, 2000). Their disposable income was valued at $930 billion in 1998, an increase of 7% in 1996. The boomers' spending power was expected to grow 16% over the next five years, reaching $1,080 billion by 2003 (Global Cosmetic Industry, 2000). This segment outspent all age groups in virtually every category, including categories not targeted to them (Brookman, 1999). Due to the age of this large demographic segment, they sought products that could reverse or halt the aging process, protect the skin from environmental stresses, and color gray hair.

Figure 6 portrays the personal-care items purchased regularly by baby boomers. The top five purchases in this segment were shampoo, deodorant, bath soap, hand and body lotion, and hair conditioner. Figure 7 illustrates the products that baby boomers were most likely to buy in the future. As

FIGURE 6

Personal-Care Items Purchased Regularly by Baby Boomers

Product	% Who Purchase Item Regularly
Shampoo	84
Deodorant	83
Bath soap	78
Hand and body lotion	53
Conditioner	46
Hair styling products	36
Men cologne	33
Lipstick	32
Facial moisturizer	32
Mascara	32
Facial cleanser	31
Eye makeup	28
Perfume—women's	25
Foundation	24
Nail polish	23
Hair colorant	22
Sunscreens	21
Blush	20
Face powder	17
OVERALL	98%

Source: Global Cosmetic Industry (2000). "GENERATION GAPS: Global Cosmetic Industry Takes a Look at the Personal-Care Preferences, Spending Habits, and Power of Generation Y and X and Baby Boomers," [Online]. **http://www.findarticles.com/cf_0/ m0HLW/6-166/63411614/p1/ article.jhtml.** Accessed November 1.

FIGURE 7

Personal-Care Products That Baby Boomers Were Most Likely to Buy

Category	Volume Index*
Feminine hygiene products	230
Pain remedies for back and leg	164
Hair colorants—women's	158
Ethnic hair products	155
Eyebrow and eyeliner cosmetics	155
Cream foundations	152
Dieting aids—appetite suppressants	150
Bath oil	147
Hand cream	146
Mascara	145
Perfume—women's	143
Skin cream—all purpose	141

*Volume indices above 120 indicate that dollar sales among households headed by women ages 45–54 were notably above expected levels.

Source: Global Cosmetic Industry (2000). "GENERATION GAPS: Global Cosmetic Industry Takes a Look at the Personal-Care Preferences, Spending Habits, and Power of Generation Y and X and Baby Boomers," [Online]. **http://www.findarticles.com/cf_0/m0HLW/ 6_166/63411614/p1/article.jhtml.** Accessed November 1.

indicated, personal-care-product purchases that were above expected levels and expected to increase in popularity were hair colorants, feminine-hygiene products, ethnic hair products, and various eye-makeup products.

Both men and women baby boomers were value- and quality-conscious, but not necessarily price-sensitive. Baby boomers were recreational shoppers and status-brand purchasers. Baby boomers shopped via numerous channels of distribution (including high-end specialty stores, department stores, full-line discount stores, and direct selling). Due to their hectic lifestyles and time constraints, keys to success were providing product information and education, creating products according to needs, and cultivating strong brand loyalty.

Generation X. The Generation X segment, averaging 46 million people, or 17% of the population, spent approximately $125 billion yearly (Global Cosmetic Industry, 2000). Figure 8 illustrates the most regularly purchased items by Generation X. The five most regular purchases by Generation X were shampoo, deodorant, bath soap, hair conditioner, and hand and body lotion. This age segment tended to purchase personal-care products they perceived to be unique and was expected to have increasing disposable income to spend in the coming years on luxury goods. In the future, they were expected to be loyal to the companies/brands from which they made purchases in the past (typically, well-known brand names). They also tended to be loyal to companies that demonstrated support of women's issues. Therefore, keys to success were a strong brand image, strong brand loyalty, offering of unique products, and sponsorship of women's issues.

FIGURE 8

FIGURE 8

Personal-Care Items Purchased Regularly by
Generation X

Product	% Who Purchase Item Regularly
Shampoo	83
Deodorant	79
Bath soap	77
Hair conditioner	52
Hand and body lotion	51
Hair styling products	40
Men's cologne	35
Deodorant soap	34
Lipstick	32
Facial cleanser	31
Mascara	29
Facial moisturizer	26
Women's Perfume	26
Eye makeup	25
Foundation	22
Nail polish	21
Face powder	19
Blush	17
Sunscreens	16
Hair colorant	14
OVERALL	97%

Source: Global Cosmetic Industry (2000). "GENERATION GAPS:
Global Cosmetic Industry Takes a Look at the Personal-Care
Preferences, Spending Habits, and Power of Generation Y and X and
Baby Boomers," [Online]. **http://www.findarticles.com/cf_0/m0HLW/
6_166/63411614/p1/article.jhtml**. Accessed November 1.

Generation Y. Generation Y was the 73 million
5- to 22-year-old people who comprised 28% of the
population. According to U.S. census projections,
Generation Y, nearly three times the size of Generation X, was expected to reach 33.6 million by 2005,
making for the largest teen population in U.S. history
(Anonymous, 1999). According to Teen Research
Unlimited, Generation Y spent $150 billion in 1999
and influenced $450 billion in purchases. Spending
in this segment centered mainly on food, clothing,
entertainment, and personal-care items (Anonymous, 1999). Generation Y purchased what they perceived to be quality yet affordable personal-care

products. They tended to prefer products created for
them and that addressed their needs. Most informed
of all the populations, they used the Internet for all of
their needs, including product information and purchasing, chatting with friends, and education. Generation Y was heavily influenced by the fashion and
music industries and was responsive to advertisements in these channels. However, they also developed brand loyalty to companies that subtly
marketed to them. Since they tended to value self-
expression and individualism, many experimented
with hair coloring and were inclined to purchase
nonpermanent hair colorants. Also, Generation Y
was expected to increase sales in the skin-care market. As their bodies began changing and developing,
skin-care issues, especially blemish concerns, were
expected to proliferate.

Keys to success with Generation Y were quality
products at affordable prices, products tailored to
their specific needs, and trendy, fashionable, youth-
oriented products. Keys to success were brand awareness and recognition, subtle marketing techniques,
and promotions targeted specifically to Generation Y.
The ability to distribute products through various distribution channels was an additional key to success.

Gender Females influenced an average of 90% of all
household purchase decisions and were the main
personal-care-product consumers (Mallory, 1995).
Approximately 72% of American women worked
full-time. The number of working wives with children under the age of six had risen by more than
400% since 1948, earning more than $1 trillion in
1994, a fivefold increase over 1975 (Mallory, 1995).
Working women spent less time shopping and were
more brand- and store-loyal than nonworking
women. Working women were less likely to shop during evening hours and on the weekend, as well as less
likely to buy through direct-mail catalogs. The key to
success in targeting to women in general was utilizing
various distribution channels.

The male consumer was increasingly purchasing
personal-care products, especially hair colorants
and fragrances. Although hair colorants for men
grew at a very slow pace from the 1950s to the
1990s, the last five years presented a 13.1% increase
in this sector (Sanabria, 2000B). The reason for this
growth was twofold: first, the stereotype that once
discouraged men from using products to enhance

their appearance was virtually nonexistent by 1999; second, the baby-boomer males, who were still in the work force, were striving to maintain a youthful appearance in their work environment. The growth in the male fragrance market had been attributed in part to aggressive advertising in magazines targeted at males, which were increasing in number. Male consumers were increasingly shopping for personal-care products in convenient retail locations. The most powerful driver for men was a brand name; while very loyal, they were also open to trying new products (NPD Group, 2000A). Nine out of ten men who wore a fragrance chose it and purchased it by themselves, which was a significant change from a decade earlier, when men were influenced by and reliant on women to make this decision. Men were increasingly purchasing hair-styling aids in hair-dressing salons. They were less price-sensitive than women and also more service-dependent. However, they demanded products created for them since they did not have an interest in purchasing personal-care products made for women.

Keys to success with males were promotions specifically targeting them, brand awareness through trials, masculine packaging, retail presence, and providing services to influence decisions. Additional keys to success were a strong brand name and brand loyalty.

Ethnic Origin   By the year 2050, nearly half of all Americans will be non-Caucasian (Herman, 2000). The three main segments in the personal-care ethnic market were African Americans, Asian Americans, and Latin Americans. African American growth figures had been fairly constant, while tremendous growth occurred in the Asian and Latin American segments. Consumers of non-Caucasian ethnicity spent more on personal-care products than any other consumer group, and subsequently demanded products tailored to their unique needs (Herman, 2000). Figure 9 illustrates personal-care products in greatest demand in this market: hair-care products dominated all other product segments in the personal-care industry. Figure 10 shows the top selling items in the ethnic hair-care market. Again, chemical hair products and hair stylants were the preferred items.

The second largest segment in the ethnic market was color cosmetics, though most ethnic users were limited to using products tailored for Caucasian skin and needed specialized skin-care products.

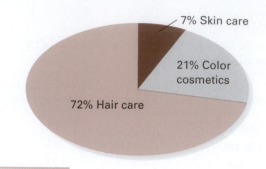

FIGURE 9

1999 Ethnic Market Expenditures in the Personal-Care Industry

Source: *Market Share Reporter 2000*. Detroit, MI: Gale Research.

African American Segment. The African American consumers, comprising approximately 34 million people, constituted the largest ethnic group in the United States and represented 12% of the population. With a growth rate of 11% annually, the African American segment was expected to grow to 45 million by 2020 (Kyriakos, 1999). Annual expenditures were expected to rise from $308 billion in 1990 to $532 billion in 1999, up 72.9% in nine years for a compound annual growth of 6.3%. About 50% of African Americans were considered middle class, up from only 16% in 1990 (Kyriakos, 1999). Unlike other ethnic groups that were clustered in a few geographic or metropolitan areas, African Americans drove the market in many U.S. cities (Herman, 2000).

FIGURE 10

1999 Ethnic Market Expenditures in the Hair-Care Segment

Source: *Market Share Reporter 2000*. Detroit, MI: Gale Research.

African American consumers tended to prefer popular or leading brands, were brand loyal, and were unlikely to purchase private-label and generic products. To satisfy the need in the marketplace, many personal-care companies developed products targeted to African American women, with an emphasis on hair care. It was noted that 64% of African Americans (compared to 51% of Caucasians) were willing to spend more for what they considered to be superior quality, which in turn led them to be 25% more likely to buy premium or brand names (Kyriakos, 1999). African American women spent three times more on hair-care products than the rest of the population. African American women were influenced by their individual lifestyles and required hair designs that were versatile. Because their hair was naturally fragile, to successfully target this market the industry needed to create products that were gentle and rich in moisturizing and conditioning agents. The biggest need in this industry was for a relaxer that did not damage hair, since 80% of African American women used chemicals on their hair, relaxers being most popular. Nearly 75% of African American women had six perfumes on average. African Americans demanded specialized skin products suited for their needs since dry skin was a common skin problem in this segment (Rocafort, 2000). In selling personal-care products, it was determined that mass media did not communicate well in the African American market. Many marketers supplemented their advertisements in magazines, newspapers, and media directed specifically to African Americans. African Americans were also more brand loyal to companies who sought to build relationships.

Keys to success with the African American segment were a premium brand name, products targeted to needs—specifically hair-care and skin-care products—specialized promotions, building relationships, and developing brand loyalty.

Asian American Segment. The Asian American population, at approximately 7 million and encompassing 3% of the population, was the fastest-growing minority in the United States (Shiffman, 1997). Asian Americans were considered to be better educated and more computer literate than the rest of the population. They spent more than $38 billion on consumer goods and services annually, and they valued quality and were willing to pay for it. This ethnic segment tended to be very loyal consumers, especially to retailers who made it known that they valued Asian American patronage. They were more responsive to advertisements featuring models of their ethnicity (Shiffman, 1997). Asian Americans sought products tailored specifically to their unique sensitive-skin needs, the reason many Asian immigrants continued to use products from Asia. Keys to success with Asian Americans were products targeted to needs, high-quality products, promotions targeted specifically to them, and developing brand awareness.

Latin American Segment. Latin Americans represented about 9% of the United States population, with a combined buying power of $205 billion. With a 53% population increase during the decade from 1980 to 1990 (and a 27% growth rate expected for the decade 2000 to 2010), Latin Americans were projected to surpass African Americans within twenty years as the largest American ethnic group (Shiffman, 1997). Latin Americans preferred well-known or familiar brands and purchased those they perceived to be more prestigious. They generally enjoyed shopping more than other ethnic groups did, but tended not to be impulse buyers and were increasingly utilizing promotions and price reductions offered by companies. They also appeared to be engaged in the process of acculturation, adopting the consumption patterns of the majority of U.S. consumers. Latin Americans also spent more time with mass media in their first language. Latin Americans were beginning to be targeted by some larger cosmetic companies.

Keys to success with Latin Americans were brand recognition, price reductions/discounts, and foreign-language advertisements.

Sales and Distribution

Personal-care products were sold and distributed via three main channels: direct, retail, and Internet.

Direct Selling Direct selling, which comprised face-to-face selling and remote selling, included both personal contact with consumers in their homes (and other non–store locations, such as offices) and telephone solicitations initiated by the retailer, emphasizing convenience and personalization. Consumers were often more relaxed in their homes than in retail stores, and were more likely to be attentive in the absence of competing brands. Senior citizens and those with children benefited from direct selling due to their limited mobility. For the company, direct selling presented lower overhead costs since store locations and fixtures were not necessary (Berman,

FIGURE 11

1999 Direct Selling—Percentage of Sales by Major Product Group

Source: The Direct Selling Industry (2000). "2000 Direct Selling Growth & Outlook Survey," [Online]. **http://www.dsa.org/factsht00.stm.** November 7.

FIGURE 12

Percentage of Sales by Type of Direct-Selling Medium

Source: The Direct Selling Industry (2000). "2000 Direct Selling Growth & Outlook Survey," [Online]. **http://www.dsa.org/factsht00.stm.** November 7.

1997). Figure 11 illustrates the major product groups involved in direct selling, with personal-care items the second most popular products sold via this channel. Figure 12 illustrates the popularity of face-to-face and remote selling.

Figures 13 and 14 indicate the percentage of sales attributed to the subsegments of face-to-face selling and remote selling.

However, in recent times, sales from direct selling—especially in the personal-care industry—were rising at a slow pace, for several reasons. More women were working and were not interested or available to purchase items at home. Improved job

opportunities in other fields and the interest in full-time, career-oriented positions reduced the number of people interested in direct-selling jobs. Sales productivity was low because the average transaction was small and consumers were increasingly unreceptive to this type of selling; many would not open their doors to salespeople or talk to telephone sales representatives (The Direct Selling Industry, 2000). Keys to success with direct selling were recruiting and maintaining quality and enthusiastic sales representatives. A key to success with current sales representatives was to offer incentives. Also, having strong internal relations was another important key to success.

FIGURE 13

Percentage of Sales by Face-to-Face Selling

Source: The Direct Selling Industry (2000). "2000 Direct Selling Growth & Outlook Survey," [Online]. **http://www.dsa.org/factsht00.stm.** November 7.

FIGURE 14

Percentage of Sales by Remote Selling

Source: The Direct Selling Industry (2000). "2000 Direct Selling Growth & Outlook Survey," [Online]. **http://www.dsa.org/factsht00.stm.** November 7.

Retail Selling   Personal-care products were sold mainly through four retail outlets: department stores, specialty stores, drugstores, and kiosks. Department stores had the greatest selection of any general-merchandise retailers, and often served as the anchor store in a shopping center or district, had strong credit-card penetration, and were usually part of a chain. Traditional department stores, such as Macy's and Bloomingdale's, merchandised average- to high-quality products with moderate to above-average pricing. Customer services ranged from medium to high levels of sales assistance, credit, and delivery. Macy's strategy was aimed at middle-class shoppers interested in a wide assortment and moderate prices, while Bloomingdale's aimed at upscale consumers through more trendy merchandise and higher prices.

During the past decade, sales growth in traditional department stores was behind that of the full-line discount stores. There were several reasons for this decline. Traditional department stores no longer had brand exclusivity for the items they sold because manufacturers' brands were also available at specialty and discount outlets. Many stores were too large and had too much unproductive selling space and low-turnover personal-care merchandise. Also, price-conscious consumers were increasingly attracted to discount retailers. Department stores, which represented approximately $80 billion in annual sales, cited a 1% decline in same-store sales from January 2000 to August 2000, despite a 7% increase in the overall retail industry (Berman, 1997). This was partly due to their high reliance on apparel, which comprised 75% of department stores' inventory, and their vulnerability to changes in consumer buying habits. In the past, consumers shopped at department stores for their merchandise selection and service; however, they now purchased at mass merchants for the same reasons—as well as for convenience and price. Traditional department stores were trying to target Generation Y by offering more fashion-conscious products combined with a more exciting decor. Keys to success with traditional department stores were offering medium- to high-priced quality products, having a wide assortment in the product mix, maintaining relationships with store managers for optimal displays and space, and hiring and maintaining qualified sales representatives for point-of-purchase assistance.

A full-line discount store was a high-volume, low-cost, fast-turnover outlet selling a broad range of merchandise for less than conventional prices. Its products were normally sold with minimal assistance in any single department, and catalogs were normally not available. Durable goods accounted for approximately 60% of all sales (Berman, 1997). In 1993, Wal-Mart, Kmart, and Target expanded operations to include almost 5,000 full-line discount stores that accounted for nearly $70 billion in sales that year. The average outlet tended to be smaller than the traditional department store, which improved productivity. The growth in most of the personal-care categories was stronger in full-line discount stores, since they were able to attract some of the drugstore customers. These locations were able to fuel growth by feeding off the heavy volume of customer traffic in their stores. Sales for facial cosmetics increased 15.7% in this outlet for 1999. Men's fragrances rose 12.5%, and women's fragrances rose 6.7%. Full-line discount stores catered to the middle- to lower-class consumer seeking average- to good-quality merchandise at competitive prices (Berman, 1997). Keys to success with full-line discount stores were products that required minimal assistance and stressed convenience and variety; average- to good-quality products that attracted more price-sensitive middle-class consumers; and creating strong relationships with store managers for optimal displays and space.

Specialty stores carried a narrow product line with a wide assortment of products within that category, and tailored their strategy to selected market segments. This method allowed the specialty store to maintain better selections, flexibility, and sales expertise than department stores. Specialty stores increased in popularity in the 1990s due to their image and their strong consumer focus. For the first half of 2000, specialty stores experienced a 4% increase in sales (D'Innocenzio, 2000). Specialty stores tended to target medium- to high-income baby-boomer and Generation X consumers. An example of a personal-care specialty store was Sephora, a company offering a hands-on shopping environment. Customers had the ability to browse through the various international, unique, and prestigious cosmetic selections that were organized alphabetically and by specific categories, and had the choice of shopping with no sales assistance or with detailed expert advice. The company was formed in 1993, and with 143 international stores, was the leading chain of perfume and cosmetic stores in France and the second in Europe. Keys to success in selling to specialty stores were unique and prestigious cosmetics and qualified sales representatives for point-of-purchase assistance.

Drugstores mainly sold mass-market personal-care products, with sales that increased steadily in 2000 and strong growth expected in the near future. New brands, such as Olay and Neutrogena, as well as advanced product formulations from established mass-market brands, helped drugstore chains gain loyalty from department-store shoppers. Although space remained tight in chain drugstore cosmetics departments, there was a growing trend to balance out the department with a product mix that was geared to a greater variety of consumers.

In addition to carrying traditional mainstream mass-market brands, drugstore chains were adding a broader assortment of products targeted toward professional, middle- to high-income women. In addition, chains were looking at brands targeting less affluent women or women looking for a broad selection of fashion shades in their cosmetics. Drugstores attributed their growth to strong marketing and merchandising initiatives, a marketing emphasis on cosmetics as a core department, and partnerships with manufacturers resulting in customized promotions (Parks, 1999B). Although full-line discount stores generated more customer traffic, drugstores were able to drive growth through prominent window displays, aggressive and consistent advertising, competitive prices, in-store service, and new products. Manufacturers were able to capitalize on these opportunities by maintaining good relations with storeowners. As a result, drugstores managed their marketing mix effectively while providing high levels of consumer satisfaction (Parks, 1999B). In 1999, chain drugstores experienced 9.6% gains in facial cosmetics. However, sales of nail cosmetics decreased 10.7% in the same year. Sales of men's and women's fragrances rose 5% and 2.2%, respectively. Other personal-care sales rose 3.9% to $1.42 billion, while unit volume fell 3.9% (Parks, 1999B).

Keys to success with drugstores were maintaining good relations with storeowners through a wide assortment of products in each category; gearing products towards both affluent and nonaffluent customers; introducing new products; advertising aggressively and consistently; and offering competitive prices.

A kiosk was an attractive freestanding structure located in malls, airports, and other high-traffic areas. A kiosk showcased a company's products and services and provided product information and, in some cases, purchasing opportunities. Mall owners had increasingly utilized kiosks as a strategic tool to raise sales-per-square-foot. Kiosks ranged in price from $4,000–$20,000, depending on the level of complexity and technology utilized in the design. The kiosk needed to be secure, well ventilated, and accessible to people of different sizes, physical abilities, and language skills. Currently, kiosks were becoming more computerized and offered video, audio, and interactivity, making the experience of using a kiosk more friendly and accessible. Although many personal-care companies did not utilize kiosks in malls, those that did stressed the need for exciting new products, enthusiastic and knowledgeable sales representatives, and samples and trials to distribute in order to increase brand awareness and product trial. These, along with strong brand image and prime location, were keys to success with kiosks.

Online Selling   With the emergence of the Internet as a shopping channel, many new personal-care companies developed web sites. This allowed them to utilize the Internet as a marketing tool by providing extensive company and product information on the site, as well as presenting brand images and advertising. However, many older companies had been cautious in using the Internet as a shopping channel since they considered it beyond their core competencies and were concerned that Internet sales might undermine their retail position and cannibalize product sales. Less-established companies were quicker in developing e-commerce sites, and as a result enjoyed increasing market share and international sales (Croft, 1997). Retail sales on the Internet were growing rapidly. In 1998, online retailers in the United States generated $14.9 billion in revenues, with a 140% increase expected for 1999 (NPD Group, 2000B). This trend was expected to continue as more consumers experimented with online access and e-commerce shopping. Unlike some other industries, the personal-care market was not yet saturated online. Therefore, personal-care companies could still develop loyal customer bases that could allow for stronger market dominance (Davis, 2000).

In 1998, there were two types of personal-care retailers online. Online-only retailers existed solely on the Internet and did not have physical locations.

Their advertising and marketing budget was directed towards customer acquisition and retention and brand awareness. Multi-channel retailers had established brands and a physical presence, and therefore did not need to spend as much as the online-only companies to build their brand online. Multi-channel retailers were able to leverage existing marketing efforts by adding their web address to promotions and encouraging customers to go online, an effort to capture an even larger share of their spending. Supplemental revenue accounted for less than half of 1% of their revenues, as opposed to 12% for online-only retailers (D'Innocenzio, 2000).

Online selling posed a major problem for direct-selling companies in general. Direct sellers' sales forces were usually partially or fully compensated based on a percentage of sales. With the introduction of online selling, sales representatives feared cannibalization of sales and loss of customers. As a result, many direct sellers were faced with strategic decisions on how to include the Internet as a channel of distribution while placating their sales representatives. At the end of 1999, more than 17 million households were shopping online, purchasing $20.2 billion over the Internet during the year. The number of online shoppers was expected to level off at about 50 million, but that trend was expected to be offset by a surge in average online spending per household, increasing from $1,167 in 1999 to $3,738 in 2004. At that point, online spending in the United States was expected to total $184 billion (NPD Group, 2000B).

Figure 15 illustrates the behavior of consumers when purchasing personal-care products via the Internet. In 1999, online personal-care sales accounted for 1% of the personal-care industry. Fragrance, makeup, and skin care accounted for 2% of all products sold online. A recent NPD report stated that 62% of polled consumers would consider purchasing personal-care products online and cited convenience as the most influential factor, as seen in Figure 16.

Only 31% of those polled considered price to influence shopping online versus in a retail store. In response to this, many online companies did not offer discounted prices, but rather coupons and other incentives to shop online. Another important factor influencing online purchasing decisions was brand names. Of those polled, 64% stated that they would buy products they had tried before. However, the type of products purchased influenced online pur-

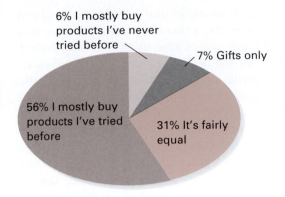

FIGURE 15

Types of Online Personal-Care Purchases

Source: NPD Group (2000C). "Media Metric Beauty Visory," [Online]. **http://www.npd.com/corp/content/special/ evisory.htm.** Accessed November 1.

chasing behavior. For example, those purchasing fragrance, makeup, and skin products were brand loyal when purchasing online. However, consumers seeking bath and body products tended to try to find the lowest price for their preferred brand. Another trend in online beauty retailing was the diminishing distinction between brands: prestige beauty products traditionally sold only in department stores were featured next to mass beauty products at some sites (NPD Group, 2000C).

FIGURE 16

Reasons for Purchasing Beauty Products Online Instead of in Traditional Stores

Shop any time	75%
Delivery of purchases	54%
Ease of comparison shopping	46%
Faster	42%
Avoid sales tax	38%
Find hard-to-find/exclusive brands	37%
Better prices	31%
Avoid interacting with salespeople	19%
Stores too far away	13%

Source: NPD Group (2000B). "NPD and Media Metrix e-Visory Report Anticipates Dramatic Growth of Online Beauty Sales," [Online]. **http://www.npd.com/corp/content/news/releases/press_000321.htm.** Accessed October 9.

The most successful and popular personal-care web sites were those that had existed for some time and had a high level of advertising. Web sites that featured health and beauty products were more visited than cosmetics-only web sites. Health-related sites typically carried mass-merchandise beauty brands. Cosmetics-only sites tended to carry only prestige or exclusive brands. Personal-care web sites offered value-added incentives to enhance their positions. All of the companies provided quick, easy returns; many offered free shipping, and some sent free samples with orders. Increasingly, most sites were also providing a wealth of consumer information in the form of magazine-type articles, reviews, directories for purchasing and service, and makeup tips (NPD Group, 2000C). However, almost two-thirds of consumers said they were unlikely or certain not to buy personal-care products or services from the Internet since it was stated to be difficult to purchase cosmetics without a trial or sample. This was most true with new product offerings.

In the future, the Internet is expected to become more popular and more acceptable among consumers as a shopping method. It was expected that conventional direct-selling personal-care companies would face exceptional competition in countries where computer use and penetration was high, such as in North America, Western Europe, and parts of the Asia-Pacific region. By the year 2003, the Internet is expected to account for 8.2% of overall home-shopping sales (NPD Group, 2000C).

Keys to success with the Internet were offering a convenient and easy-to-navigate site, having online selling capabilities, providing coupons and price incentives to shop online, providing enhanced features at the web site—such as product information and articles—offering samples and trials, and advertising to get the consumer to the web site. Additional keys to success were a strong brand name to generate traffic and encourage customer loyalty at an early stage.

Geographic Markets

Personal-care products were sold in both the domestic and international markets. The information provided in the following sections pertains to the domestic personal-care market. Overall, the largest continental market in the personal-care industry was North and South America in 1999, with total sales of $43 billion (Dutton, 1999). The increasing globalization of the world's economy presented significant opportunities for consumer-goods manufacturers. Barriers to investment in emerging markets were dropping, and disposable income in these regions was gradually increasing, bringing with it demand for staple consumer products (Dutton, 1999).

The global personal-care industry was expected to experience continued growth in the future, as levels of consumption in undeveloped markets were significantly lower than those in Western Europe and North America. However, personal-care companies in Western Europe were under increasing pressure to come up with new products to meet consumer demands for both wider choice and higher quality. In 1998, personal-care and cosmetics companies experienced the impact of the economic downturn in Asia in both regional and global sales. To help minimize declining profits, firms restructured, focused on their core businesses, and, in some cases, expanded to gain a foothold in Asian countries in preparation for their economic recovery. Asia and Latin America were considered to have huge growth potential even though they were subject to economic downturns. The products with the greatest global growth potential were basic items such as deodorant, shampoo, and soap, especially in developing regions. For example, since 1994, deodorant experienced an 18.2% sales growth globally, compared to only 11.6% growth for the personal-care and cosmetics market overall. New or improved formulas emphasizing health and well-being and cosmeceuticals were common among products launched in 1999 (Dutton, 1999). European consumers wanted more variety now that they had more outlets from which to buy personal-care products. Supermarket chains, which in some European countries had pharmacies inside their stores, had been anxious to establish themselves as providers of quality cosmetics and toiletries. In the global market, market share of the top twenty players grew from 68% in 1996 to 72% in 1998, with the top ten companies holding 54%. These top ten companies were L'Oreal, Unilever, Procter & Gamble, Johnson & Johnson, Avon, Shiseido, Colgate-Palmolive, Revlon, Amway, and Bristol-Myers Squibb (Dutton, 1999).

Keys to success in the international market were tailoring products to needs, utilizing various distribution outlets, and creating a presence in emerging countries.

Regulation

Cosmetics marketed in the United States need to comply with the provisions of the 1938 Federal Food, Drug, and Cosmetic Act (FD&C) and the Fair Packaging and Labeling Act (FPLA). The FD&C Act was passed by Congress to protect consumers from unsafe or deceptively labeled or packaged products by prohibiting the movement in interstate commerce of adulterated or misbranded food, drug devices, and cosmetics. The FPLA was passed by Congress to ensure that packages and their labels provided consumers with accurate information about the quantity of contents in order to facilitate value comparisons (U.S. FDA, 2000A). The FD&C Act prohibited the distribution of cosmetics that were adulterated or misbranded. A cosmetic was considered adulterated if it met one of the following conditions:

▍ Contained a substance that might have made the product harmful to consumers under typical conditions of use

▍ Contained a filthy, putrid, or decomposed substance

▍ Was manufactured or held under unsanitary conditions in which it might have become contaminated or harmful to consumers

▍ Was not a hair dye and contained an unpermitted color additive

A cosmetic was considered misbranded if it met one of the following conditions:

▍ Its labeling was false or misleading

▍ It did not bear the required labeling information

▍ Its container was made or filled in a deceptive manner (U.S. FDA, 2000B)

For enforcement of the law, the FDA conducted examinations and investigations of products, inspected establishments in which products were manufactured or held, and seized adulterated and misbranded products.

Another regulating agency was the Environmental Protection Agency (EPA), which regulated products so that they complied with the limitations on using and storing volatile organic compounds. The EPA also regulated the manufacturing process, including wastewater and toxic emissions. At the manufacturing level, the Department of Transportation controlled how raw materials were labeled and shipped.

Keys to success in regards to federal regulation were adherence to good manufacturing practices, effective self-inspections, and maintaining good relations with regulation authorities.

Competition

Mary Kay Inc.   Mary Kay Inc. was the number two direct seller of beauty products in the United States. It sold more than two hundred products in eight product categories—facial skin care, cosmetics, fragrances, wellness products, sun protection, nail care, body care, and men's skin care—with a fairly good brand name and loyalty. It sold quality products at affordable prices. In regards to its skin-care line, the company tended to have weak research and development capabilities and therefore had limited new product introductions and a weak brand image. Its skin-care and color-cosmetic product lines included all-in-one features and products tailored to meet needs. However, the company had a limited selection within each product category (Hoovers Online Network, 2000B).

The company's color-cosmetic line had products tailored to needs and developed according to fashion trends, but the selection of color cosmetics was limited. The company had a relatively weak personal-hygiene segment and did not have either a spa line or a hair-care line. Mary Kay had good brand awareness and loyalty with its fragrance line but was weak in the areas of new product introductions—particularly those promoting mental well-being—and distributing samples and trials.

Mary Kay had a limited customer base of women. Its most loyal customers were senior citizens due to the convenience of the company's direct-selling channel. Baby-boomer customers were attracted to the company's high-quality products, which were tailored to their needs, resulting in sufficient brand loyalty. However, boomers were not completely satisfied with shopping at Mary Kay since they desired product information and education and a variety of channels of distribution.

The company did not target Generation X or Generation Y. Although ethnic models were used in advertising and promotions, the company did not have products tailored to any ethnic segment. African Americans valued a premium brand name, products targeted to needs, specialized promotions, and strong internal relations—areas in which Mary Kay was weak. Its quality products appealed to Asian Americans, but the company was weak in targeting products to their needs, targeting them in its promotions, and developing brand awareness. Mary Kay did not have success with Latin Americans since the company was weak in brand recognition, price reductions and discounts, and foreign-language advertisements. It was attempting to reach the male market by selling fragrances, personal-hygiene, and skin products in masculine packaging, but it targeted women in its promotions and advertising for these products, resulting in a generally weak male customer base (Mary Kay Inc. Company Website, 2000).

Mary Kay's products were distributed via 600,000 direct-sales consultants in approximately thirty-six countries. Sales for the company reached $1 billion in 1999, and the company posted a one-year sales growth of 0.0% and a one-year employee growth of 7.1% (Hoovers Online Network, 2000B). Although Mary Kay was experiencing virtually no growth with its direct-selling model, the company decided not to expand into retail distribution in the near, intermediate, or long-term future in order to maintain strong internal relations. The company felt that expansion would affect their core sales representatives. The company successfully recruited and motivated their enthusiastic sales force through bonuses ranging from jewelry to the company's trademark pink Cadillac. The company did have a convenient and easy-to-navigate web site, but it did not offer a community site linking consumers to articles and advice on subjects related to personal-care products (Hoovers Online Network, 2000B).

The company did not advertise its web site because it was not being used for online selling. Consumers who reached the web site were directed to a page that allowed them to locate a consultant in their area. Consumers had the ability to order from the consultant's web site, allowing the company to develop a loyal customer base and a good brand name. Samples, trials, coupons, and price incentives were not readily available to customers either through the web site or direct selling (Mary Kay Inc. Company Website, 2000).

L'Oreal   L'Oreal was the world's largest beauty company, with products ranging from makeup and perfume to apparel leading to a very strong brand image in the personal-care market. L'Oreal was comprised of numerous brands, including L'Oreal and May-

belline, which were quality, unique, and affordable product lines; Lancôme, featuring more upscale, premium-priced products for more affluent customers; and Redken and Soft Sheen, which included hair products (L'Oreal Company Website, 2000).

L'Oreal's diverse product lines were sold in a variety of outlets, including department stores, full-line discount stores, drugstores, specialty stores, and the Internet. The company did not use kiosks or direct selling. L'Oreal sold its average- to good-quality products to attract more price-sensitive, middle-class consumers in full-line discount stores. These products required minimal assistance from sales people and stressed convenience and variety. The company was successful via this channel due to its strong relations with store managers, obtaining optimal displays and space. L'Oreal also distributed this type of product line via drugstores. The company enjoyed success due to its wide assortment of competitively priced products in each category, products geared to both affluent and non-affluent consumers, frequent new product introductions, and aggressive and frequent advertising.

L'Oreal conducted cosmetology and dermatology research and had a 19.5% stake in a pharmaceutical company. Its diverse product mix enabled the company to enjoy worldwide success and create strong customer bases in every category. The company's research department employed approximately 2,100 scientists and filed for about 400 patents a year—77 of them in 1999—with numerous product introductions each year. It devoted 3% of sales to cosmeceutical research (anti-aging products and sunscreen products). It sold its products in 150 countries, with products tailored according to regional needs and demands via various distribution channels. The company sold 56% of its products in Western Europe, 27% in North America, and 17% in the rest of the world (Hoovers Online Network, 2000C).

Almost 90% of the company's sales were generated from ten brands: Biotherm, Laboratoires GARNIER, Lancôme, L'Oreal, Maybelline, Redken, Helena Rubinstein, Vichy, and perfumes Giorgio Armani and Ralph Lauren. The Helena Rubinstein line consisted of products emphasizing natural ingredients and wellness targeted to the baby-boomer segment of the market. Lanvin, a subsidiary of the Group L'Oreal, developed a wide range of ready-to-wear fashion for men and women, made-to-measure fashion for men, and accessories and perfumes (Hoovers Online Network, 2000C).

Maybelline was a leader in quality, affordable, innovative, and trendy color cosmetics sold both in the United States and internationally. Maybelline products are distributed in 40,000 retail outlets, including drugstores, discount stores, supermarkets, and personal-care specialty stores, and are also carried in more than seventy countries worldwide. Due to its well-known brand name and good relations with store employees, the company was able to obtain optimal shelf space. Maybelline products were available on the Internet and featured trendy fashionable products in order to develop product awareness and recognition with Generation Y customers. The Maybelline web site offered content, community, price incentives, and purchasing options (Hoovers Online Network, 2000C).

In July 1998, L'Oreal acquired Soft Sheen Products, a large manufacturer of ethnic hair-care products. Soft Sheen, a major marketer in the United States, also had distribution in Africa. As a result, the company was considering distributing its numerous other brands in Africa. L'Oreal also owned Carson Inc., supposedly the largest marketer of ethnic hair- and skin-care products with global sales of $176 million. As a result, African Americans perceived the L'Oreal brands as having a premium brand name. They responded to the company's specialized promotions and efforts to build relationships. Asian Americans responded to the company's quality products. Latin Americans were also purchasers of L'Oreal products due to brand recognition, price reductions/discounts, and foreign-language advertisements.

L'Oreal also successfully launched a complete hair-care line both domestically and internationally. Its hair colorants, available in a variety of shades and including value-added features, targeted senior citizens, baby boomers, and Generation Y and men (L'Oreal Company Website, 2000). The company also had strong relations with male customers due to targeted promotions, creating brand awareness through trials, masculine packaging, having a retail presence, providing services to influence decisions, and having a strong brand name.

L'Oreal's convenient and easy-to-navigate main web site gives customers extensive product and company information. Not all its brands are available for online purchasing. It currently was expanding its L'Oreal web site internationally, which in turn developed customized web sites for each region, offering editorial content in the local language. At the time, only L'Oreal and Maybelline products could be purchased online. Through the samples and trials offered online as well as through advertisements to get customers to the site, L'Oreal was able to build a strong brand name and loyal customer base.

The Lancôme line was mainly distributed in traditional department stores due to its superior quality, premium pricing, wide assortment of product mix, relationships with store managers for optimal displays and space, and qualified sales representatives for point-of-purchase assistance. However, the product was available online and was highly successful. Approximately 52% of the visitors made a purchase and spent more than 30% more than consumers who bought via the traditional retail outlet (L'Oreal Company Website, 2000). This line was popular with affluent senior citizens, baby boomers, and Generation X customers. Its Lancôme line, which was a unique and prestigious cosmetic collection, was also sold via specialty stores since they provided qualified sales representatives for point-of-purchase assistance.

The company utilized a quality control department to ensure that all products were developed, designed, and delivered according to the highest standards. It conducted its own self-examinations to see if the company was growing and continuing according to specifications. The company advertised its numerous brands in various magazines and television spots according to its target market. For example, the company often sponsored events in order to develop brand awareness in its younger customers. Also, the company often issued samples and rebate coupons to develop brand awareness and recognition (L'Oreal Company Website, 2000).

Retail Competition   Traditional department stores offered a wide range of personal-care products with an emphasis on skin care, color cosmetics, personal hygiene, and perfumes/fragrances. The brands sold via this channel were usually prestigious, high-priced products geared toward medium- to highly affluent consumers: Christian Dior, Elizabeth Arden, Hard Candy, Lorac, and L'Ancome. They also appealed to affluent, young senior citizens. Department stores were strong in the baby-boomer market by offering high-quality and high-value products. Traditional department stores within themselves also sold via the Internet and were therefore strong in providing boomers with numerous channels of distribution. The department stores generally featured personal-care counters where consumers obtained personal assistance and product information via employees. Due to the higher price range of department stores' personal-care products, they were highly tailored to baby-boomer needs, thereby strengthening consumer loyalty. Traditional department store brands were also becoming increasingly popular with Generation X. Traditional department stores brands such as Polo Sport, Biotherm, Calvin Klein, and Nautica appealed to male customers since they contained masculine packaging, targeted promotions at the male sector, provided services to influence decisions, and created brand awareness through trials.

Full-line discount stores sold personal-care products in the skin-care, color-cosmetics, hair-care, personal-hygiene, and perfumes/fragrances categories. The brands sold via this channel included many private-label product lines such as My Generation and Sonia Kashuk, and affordable product lines including Vidal Sassoon, Pantene, Maybelline, Cover Girl, L'Oreal, and Revlon. The product lines were geared towards Generation X and Generation Y. The reason that full-line discount stores were so successful with Generation Y was due to its quality products at affordable prices, its trendy, fashionable, youth-oriented products tailored to needs, and strong brand awareness and recognition.

Specialty stores seemed to be in competition with traditional department stores since both channels carried high-quality, high-priced personal-care products. However, specialty stores such as Sephora tended to carry more obscure international brands such as Anna Sui, Benetton, Bvlgari, Nino Cerutti, and Poppy. As a result, specialty stores had high loyalty and recognition with both affluent baby boomers and Generation X. At a store like Sephora, customers had the ability to browse through the various unique and prestigious cosmetic selections that were organized alphabetically and by specific categories and had the choice to shop with no sales assistance or detailed expert advice.

Drugstores such as Genovese, CVS, and Rite Aid carried affordable mass-merchandise personal-care brands such as Oil of Olay, Neutrogena, Jane Cosmetics, Maybelline, and Revlon. Drugstores tended to compete with full-line discount stores in attracting Generation Y consumers, with quality products tailored to needs at affordable prices. However, drugstores also carried personal-care product lines geared towards both non-affluent and affluent male customers. Certain personal hygiene items, such as razors, toothpaste, and shampoo and conditioner, were nonelastic generic products purchased by both affluent or non-affluent men and women customers.

The Company
Overview of the Company

Avon Products, Inc. (Avon) was a manufacturer and marketer of personal-care products, including skin-care, hair-care, color cosmetics, fragrances, personal hygiene, and a limited line of nonpersonal-care products such as jewelry, apparel, decorative and home entertainment products and a provider of spa services. Avon commenced operations in 1886 and was incorporated on January 27, 1916. It provided one of the first opportunities for American women to be financially independent at a time when their place was traditionally at home. Avon distributed its products primarily through the direct-selling channel. It was considered the world's largest direct-seller of affordable, quality beauty products. However, the company also utilized kiosks and the Internet to increase its consumer base. The company marketed its products through its sales campaign brochures, sponsorship of women-related issues, and print and television advertisements.

Avon's main customers were women of all ethnic races with a concentration of those aged thirty-five and over. Avon had a prominent presence in the United States and 137 countries. The company had revenues of $5.3 billion in 1999 compared to $5.2 billion in 1998 (Avon, 2000). In 1999, through their three million representatives, Avon handled over one billion customer transactions and sold over two billion units, making it the sixth largest global beauty company (Avon, 2000). Figure 17 gives a detailed overview of Avon Products, Inc.

Products/Services

In the past, Avon carried various product lines targeted to specific regional needs. However, in doing so, the company obtained a fragmented brand image. To rectify this problem, Avon developed universal global brands. Avon had distinguished itself as the supplier of high-quality beauty products at affordable prices. More beauty products carried the Avon brand name than any other in the world (Avon,

FIGURE 17

Avon Products, Inc.

1999). Figure 18 illustrates Avon's product lines as a percentage of sales. It can be noted that skin care, hair care, color cosmetics, and fragrances were the largest grossing product lines. Figure 19 indicates the actual sales dollars generated by Avon's diverse product lines.

Major Product Lines   Avon was the creator of the first alpha-hydroxy skin-care products developed by a strong research and development department that was concurrently devising alternative skin-care regimes and anticipating frequent new product introductions (Parks, 2000). Its skin-care products were tailored to needs being demanded by the market, specifically those of aging consumers and female consumers by offering high-quality and high-value products at affordable prices. By developing its ANEW product line, Avon was able to tap into the growing cosmeceutical market. It also fulfilled skin-care market opportunities by offering products that included anti-aging features, natural ingredients, environmental protection lotions for the face, and complete skin-care regimes (Bittar, 2000). Due to this, Avon had a strong brand loyalty and brand image in the skin-care market.

Avon's line of value-added shampoos, conditioners, treatments, and styling products were somewhat tailored to consumer needs. The company developed many types of shampoos and conditioners to treat the major types of hair problems and colored or graying hair. It also had a line of hair-stylant products, although they were designed for normal (not ethnic-specific) hair types. Avon also sold an Herbal Care line that utilized natural ingredients to achieve healthier-looking hair (Hoovers Online Network, 2000A). The company did not have a hair-coloring product line and therefore did not successfully build brand recognition and awareness among younger consumers; nor did it capitalize on the need for this product by aging consumers. The company therefore

FIGURE 18

Avon Product Lines as a Percentage of
1999 Sales

Source: Hoovers Online Network (2000). "Avon Products, Inc.,"
[Online]. **http://www.hoovers.com/premium/profile/2/0,2147,10152,00
.htm.** Accessed October 11.

was weak in developing a complete hair-care line.
Since Avon's customers needed to shop elsewhere for
these products, the company had a weak brand image
and loyalty in the hair-care segment.

With the largest color palette in the world, Avon
had superior quality and quantity of makeup products. Its main cosmetic line, Avon Color, included a
wide range of face, eye, lip, and nail cosmetics, which
were customized according to various skin tones and
prevailing fashion trends. The line was the company's
largest global brand and the leading cosmetics brand
in the world (Avon, 1999). Beyond Color was Avon's
innovative anti-aging line, which combined anti-
aging treatments with color cosmetics. Color Trend

FIGURE 19

Avon Product Lines: Actual Sales in 1999

Product	$ Millions
Skin-care, hair-care, color cosmetics & fragrances	3,226
Gift & decorative	1,052
Apparel	556
Jewelry & accessories	455
Total	5,289

Source: Hoovers Online Network (2000A). "Avon Products, Inc.,"
[Online]. **http://www.hoovers.com/premium/profile/2/0,2147,10152,00
.htm.** Accessed October 11.

was Avon's global brand embracing trendy cosmetics
at affordable prices. Color Trend's full- and mini-
sized products were gradually becoming known.
However, they were not yet being aggressively purchased by the desired target market—Generation Y.
Currently, the line was offered only in Europe, Asia,
and Latin America (Avon, 1999).

Avon sold a number of personal-hygiene products, most of which fell into the bath-and-body category. It sold these products individually and as part of
a gift set, which allowed consumers to enjoy price
savings by purchasing more than one product. The
bath-and-body products included aromatherapeutic
ingredients and comprised all-in-one features. As a
result, the company had strong brand loyalty in this
segment (Avon, 2000). However, it was not established in the retail industry, so it did not yet have
strong relations with store managers, which was necessary for the long-term success of personal-hygiene
products. Skin-So-Soft, one of the company's best-
known brands, was first introduced in 1961. Currently, the Skin-So-Soft brand included products that
ranged from the original bath oil to Bug Guard Plus
with IR3535, a breakthrough technology that combined DEET-free bug repellent and PABA-free sunscreen. Naturals was a line of gentle and moisturizing
cleansers and bubble-bath products. The Aromatherapy line included candles, creams, lotions, bath products, and sprays that helped create a sense of mental
well-being and revitalization (Avon, 2000).

Avon was the world's leader in perfume sales, selling more units of fragrance than any other company
in the world. It released one global fragrance brand
per year, launched at the end of the year to coincide
with the holiday season. Avon's first new fragrance of
the millennium would be Incandessence, to be
launched worldwide in October. Incandessence also
would incorporate a unique perfume design. The
company developed a special time-released construction that changed the scent as the day progressed.
Each phase was composed of flowers, which reached
their peak of fragrance release in the given time
frame. The result was a prolonged experience and
enjoyment of the fragrance (Avon, 1999). The company's global fragrances, Women of Earth and Perceive, were the best-selling fragrance launches in the
world. Its Perceive fragrance included mood-enhanc-
ing pheromone technology, which was intended to
enhance feelings of confidence and well-being. The
company had a number of fragrances for both male

and female customers. However, Avon did not its issuing of samples throughout the years, which was imperative in the fragrance market. Despite this, it had good brand awareness and brand loyalty with its fragrance customers (Avon, 1999).

Limited Nonpersonal-Care Products Avon's limited nonpersonal-care products were considered to be part of the "Beyond Beauty" or "Beauty Plus" category. Avon specialized in exclusively designed fashion jewelry, including pierced and clip earrings, necklaces, bracelets, rings, and watches. Avon developed gold- and silver-tone costume jewelry, and genuine 925 sterling silver, featuring genuine and simulated stones and pearls. Jewelry designs were developed in small local markets before they were distributed globally, allowing the company to have the leading market share of costume jewelry worldwide (Avon, 2000). While jewelry represented approximately 13% of Avon's domestic business, it accounted for a much smaller percentage of the company's international sales. Sales of fashion jewelry and accessories rose significantly in 1999, reflecting the success of sterling silver and bolder jewelry designs, the introduction of licensed luggage, and a strong performance in watches and handbags (Avon, 2000).

Home entertainment and gift and decorative items also posted strong growth, which was due to the increased sales of inspirational and religious products. Avon's apparel line noted decreases in sales due to the underperformance of new product introductions (Avon, 1999). Not all the segments were profitable, and some contributed to Avon's fragmented brand image. Therefore, Avon was weak in analyzing each business segment in order to gauge profitability and brand-image development.

Spa Services Avon's spa services include hair care (cuts, style, and color), nail care (manicures and pedicures), personal hygiene (nutrition and lifestyle counseling, waxing), skin care (facials and body treatments), and cosmetics (makeup applications). New services include the opening of Eliza's Eyes at the Avon Centre, which was a boutique exclusively dedicated to the eyebrow. Also, in April 2000, the Avon Centre introduced Endermologie, a proven technique to reduce the appearance of cellulite, and Dermabrasion, a technique known to treat hyperpigmentation, acne scars, and fine lines and wrinkles (Byrnes, 2000). Avon developed a complete line of spa products, which complemented the services at the centre. These products were priced higher and were more value-driven than those featured in the brochure, resulting in an increase in more affluent consumers and brand image. These products, which were tailored to various customer needs, could be purchased either at the spa itself or on the company's web site. The company did not offer samples of the products it used in the services, which was a common practice in the industry.

Customers

Avon's customers included women—senior citizens, baby boomers, Generation X, and Generation Y—men, and consumers of ethnic origin.

Women Nearly half the women in the United States (48 million) relied on Avon and its personal-care products. Approximately 50% of American women had purchased from Avon in 1999 and 90% had purchased from Avon in their lifetime. The company was hoping to tap into the 59% of women who said they would purchase Avon products if they were more accessible (Nelson, 2000). Although some 70% of adult women in the United States said they would consider buying Avon through its direct-selling channel, nearly half of them were not served by a representative, while one million more would buy Avon's products but preferred not to shop through a representative. With women in general, Avon was weak in providing various distribution channels.

Avon had a strong senior-citizen customer base for two reasons. First, senior citizens had begun purchasing Avon products decades earlier and had developed strong loyalty to both the company and its product lines. Second, Avon's unique direct-selling channel was convenient for senior citizens due to their possible limited mobility.

Avon's customers included those of various ages and ethnic origins. Avon had fairly strong brand loyalty with older women consumers, since they had grown accustomed to purchasing Avon's products through a sales representative who visited them at home. Women in the baby-boomer segment were partial to Avon's high-quality, high-value products, wellness products, and products tailored specifically to their needs, and as a result had strong brand loyalty to the company. However, due to Avon's limited distribution channel and lack of extensive product information and education, the company did not provide an extremely satisfactory shopping experience to these customers.

Avon had good brand image and brand loyalty to Generation X due in part to its charitable sponsorship of women's issues and its unique products. With Generation Y, Avon had yet to establish brand recognition and awareness, since the company had not targeted this demographic segment with specific products tailored to their needs or with trendy, fashionable youth-oriented products. Those in this segment who did shop with Avon did so due to its quality products at affordable prices. Also, Avon was weak in advertising to this segment and in providing various distribution outlets in which to purchase products.

Men   Avon had extremely few male customers, since the company built its brand image as being a women's beauty and personal-care company. For male consumers, Avon was weak in targeting promotions specifically to them as well as generating brand awareness with trials and samples and creating a strong brand name and brand loyalty. The company did offer masculine packaging. Despite the fact that Avon was strong in providing services to influence decisions, it did not utilize the preferred male distribution outlet—retail stores.

Ethnic Customers   Avon was increasingly gaining foothold in the African American market. The company had just begun to develop color-cosmetic products targeted towards darker skin tones. As a result, the company had good brand loyalty with this customer segment. The company featured African American models in their sales brochures and found this to be an influencing factor in gaining brand recognition. It was building good relationships with those of this ethnic origin through its direct-selling model and sponsorships. Since it was one of the few personal-care companies to begin to develop products geared specifically towards African Americans, Avon was considered a premium brand name. Avon was not very focused on creating products specifically geared towards Latin Americans and Asian Americans, despite the fact that the company had developed some regional product modifications in Latin America and Asia in order to satisfy needs. The company did feature some Latin Americans in their promotions with copy written in Spanish at times. However, they were just beginning to include Asian models in their advertisements. Although the company offered quality products, which Asians considered pertinent, and price discounts, which were of value to Latin Americans, the company had not developed sufficient brand recognition and awareness with either of these consumer segments.

Sales and Distribution

Avon's products were distributed via three methods: direct selling, limited retail selling (kiosks), and online selling. To accelerate growth in the United States, Avon was seeking new channels to reach more customers and improve access to its products.

Direct Selling   Three million representatives, approximately 500,000 of whom worked in the United States, sold Avon's products worldwide (Byrnes, 2000). Almost all the representatives were women who sold on a part-time basis. Representatives were independent contractors or independent dealers, and were not agents or employees of Avon. Representatives purchased products directly from Avon and sold them to their customers, both in the home and in the workplace. In the United States, the representative contacted customers, selling primarily through the use of brochures, which highlighted new products and specially priced items, while also utilizing product samples, demonstration products, and selling aids such as makeup color charts. Through phone calls and personal visits Avon representatives built personal relationships with customers, issuing samples and brochures and making recommendations. Purchasing through Avon representatives allowed consumers the convenience of purchasing items beyond normal business hours and avoiding the lineups associated with retail shopping. Avon had strong monetary and flexibility incentives for its sales representatives, who generated 98% of the company's revenues. For independent Avon sales representatives, earnings were based on total sales, with total dollar amount increasing as the percentage increased. However, to encourage and motivate new representatives, Avon automatically guaranteed personal earnings of 40% on their first order, regardless of the dollar amount. Avon again guaranteed 40% personal earnings on the second, third, and fourth orders if the order was $50 or more. After the fifth order, earnings were based upon actual total dollar sales (Avon, 2000).

The company also built strong internal relations. In 1998, Avon launched its Leadership Representatives Program. Sales representatives were offered the opportunity to become leadership representatives, allowing them to receive significant cash bonuses for recruiting, training, and developing others in the field. Leadership representatives were able to earn from 2% to 14% of the sales of the representatives they successfully recruited and motivated. The United States had more than 12,000 leadership representatives, an increase of 6,000 in 1998. Sales districts with the highest level of leadership participation grew their sales in 1999 at more than double the rate of districts with the lowest participation (Byrnes, 2000). Also, since the representatives dedicated extensive time and energy into building their businesses, the company recognized individual achievements on all levels through its President's Recognition Program, which allowed representatives to set their own sales goals and rewarded them based on these achievements.

However, the company was weakening in its ability to recruit and retain quality employees since rumors of retail expansion proliferated throughout the company and the media.

Retail Selling—Beauty Centre Kiosks   Avon Beauty Centre kiosks, freestanding mini display stores measuring approximately 10 feet by 14 feet and located in select urban malls across the United States, were designed to display an upscale beauty image, showcase the company's beauty brands, and encourage customer trial of product. The kiosks, first developed in 1998, were mainly created to attract the approximately twenty to thirty million women who currently did not purchase Avon products (Parks, 1999). Each kiosk carried more than 350 Avon personal-care products and offered makeovers and beauty product advice from beauty consultants as well as samples and trials to increase brand awareness, thereby improving Avon's brand image. Avon was currently evaluating the performance of its approximate thirty-nine kiosk locations. Due to the infancy of the Beauty Centre kiosks, Avon did not have accurate sales figures and projections to utilize in measuring their performance (Parks, 1999). At this point, the kiosks only sold Avon color cosmetics, fragrances, and skin-care products. On average, each carried only 400 products out of more than 5,000 that constituted Avon's full line (Parks, 1999). By focusing on these three categories, Avon elevated its image as a beauty-care brand. The Beauty Centre personnel, who were enthusiastic and knowledgeable, were trained not to

place too much pressure on consumers to make a purchase after a makeover or manicure. And, unlike department-store brands, the Avon makeovers emphasized not only a trial of the product but a learning experience on applying cosmetics, thereby successfully increasing product knowledge and education (Parks, 1999). Thus far, Avon had done an average of 230 manicures and 250 makeovers per location. About 95% of kiosk consumers were new to Avon, and approximately 70% made a purchase, requested a brochure, and/or asked to be directed to a local Avon representative. The company planned to utilize the kiosks for new product launches in the future (Parks, 1999).

In 2000, Jung was deciding whether or not to enter Avon into a nonexclusive partnership with J C Penney and Sears to supplement its sales representatives, expand its distribution capabilities, and attract new customers in order to incite sales and earnings. Under careful consideration was the type of products to be sold in these stores. The company was leaning towards higher-priced cosmetics, which would be sold exclusively in the department stores. By partnering with J C Penney and Sears, considered to be the weakest portion of the brand retail market, the company ran the risk of the possible further reduction of its brand name. Also, in marketing a higher-priced Avon line in the department stores, the company might be sending an unintentional message to consumers that the current Avon line was not of high enough quality to be sold in J C Penney and Sears. Avon had faced significant hard times in the past. Past efforts at diversification in products and distribution had put them at risk of debt and takeovers (Nelson, 2000).

Online Selling   Avon's products were distributed online via the company's own web site, **Avon.com,** and with the emerging e-representatives. In 1997, the company attempted to create a basic web site and did so by offering only a small fraction of its products for sale. Management consciously downplayed the web site's role to avoid problems with its representatives. However, as the importance of the Internet in the industry became evident, the company struggled with a strategy that would capitalize on the advantages of online selling while placating their core sales representatives. Sales representatives even protested when the company attempted to print its web address on brochures; then covered up the address with stickers, thereby forcing the company to quickly remove it. They also voiced strong opinions regarding the fairness of Avon selling online while prohibiting its representatives to create their own sites (Hoovers Online Network, 2000A). The internal struggle with an Internet strategy spanned three years and, as a result, Avon lost its opportunity to be a market leader. Less-established companies immediately took advantage of the explosive growth of the Internet and secured approximately $1 billion online (Hoovers Online Network, 2000A).

Currently, the company offers online shopping in the United States, Brazil, Germany, Italy, and Japan. Domestically, since the company did not advertise the web site to a great extent, it was weak in driving consumers to the site. The company was slowly building a loyal customer base since its global brand name attracted consumers to the site. The company was strong in offering a simple and easy to navigate web site, but weak in offering samples or trials online. Also weak was its lack of community and content, which were further drivers to a web site. The company did not offer price incentives or coupons to shopping online. Prices for items online were relatively comparable to those offered in the bimonthly sales brochure.

In order to increase the company's Internet presence and appease its sales representatives, Avon planned to invest $60 million in the next three years to develop customized Internet sites for its sales representatives, thereby creating "e-representatives." The e-representatives would extend to consumers the opportunity to order Avon products twenty-four hours a day, seven days a week, while still offering free delivery and personal service. Visitors would connect to **Avon.com** and locate e-representatives within their zip code.

The cost to become an e-representative was $15, with commissions raging from 20% to 25% for orders shipped direct or 30% to 50% for ones the e-representative delivered. The program would significantly reduce organizational costs. Prior to the development of **Avon.com,** representatives completed a forty-page paper order form, which they submitted to the company via mail or fax. With the ability to complete online forms, the cost of processing the order would decrease from 90¢ per order to 30¢ per order (Avon, 2000). In total, e-representatives were expected to save the company $10 million by 2002 and were expected to add 1% to Avon's U.S.

sales growth annually. The e-representative initiative program seemed to be successful in placating the sales representatives and integrating Avon's channels of distribution. However, top managers at Avon struggled with the possibility that this chosen Internet strategy may not have been the best solution for the company. If every sales representative participated in the program, then Avon would have approximately 500,000 web sites. It was impossible to control the quality and content of each site, thereby leaving the possibility of an inconsistent and misrepresentative Avon brand image. As a result, the company was pondering alternative Internet strategies.

Marketing

Avon's products were marketed through sales campaign brochures during twelve to twenty-six individual sales campaigns each year. Each campaign was conducted using a brochure offering a wide assortment of products, many of which changed from campaign to campaign based on changing fashion trends and consumer tastes. Each year, Avon printed over 600 million sales brochures in more than twelve languages. In the United States alone, the brochure was distributed to fourteen million women every two weeks. Avon planned to allocate $20 million to upgrade the campaign sales brochure in order to project Avon's high-quality image to its varied customers (Avon, 1999), and $40 million to create a more successful television- and print-marketing plan for Avon in its domestic market. One idea was to target women over the age of 20 with an emphasis on cosmeceutical products. The company was also developing a global brand campaign featuring a new theme, "Let's Talk." Most of its advertising dollars were being planned for print ads in women's magazines such as *Ladies Home Journal, Glamour, O,* and *Cosmopolitan* and television advertising on networks (except ABC), syndicated programming, and cable. The idea of devoting about 15% of its budget to Hispanic advertisement efforts was under debate (Bittar, 2000).

Avon had sought to develop brand awareness through various charitable sponsorships devoted to women issues. Some activities included the Breast Cancer Awareness Crusade, the Avon Running—Global Women's Circuit (which promoted the importance of fitness in women's lives), Women of Enterprise Program (which recognized five women entrepreneurs who had overcome incredible obstacles to achieve business success), and the Avon

Worldwide Fund for Women's Health. These programs raised millions of dollars for health-related problems of concern to women (Hoovers Online Network, 2000A). Each of these initiatives had also been a lucrative incentive for the company to expand its product line by correlating the event with a profitable item. For example, Avon created an attractive **Avon Breast Cancer Crusade** from which part of the proceeds went to research. Avon was the official cosmetics, fragrance, and skin-care sponsor for the 1996 Summer Olympics Game and was the first major U.S. cosmetics company to announce a permanent end to animal testing (Hoovers Online Network, 2000A).

Geographic Markets

Avon was present in both the domestic and international personal-care markets. Avon's sales per geographic region are shown in Figure 20.

The company currently had operations in 51 markets and sold its products in 137 countries. Latin America posted strong results in 2000 with revenues from Brazil, Venezuela, and Central America offsetting declines in Argentina that were caused by economic conditions there. The Asia/Pacific regions had strong growths in China, which helped compensate for the weakening Philippine *peso*. Sales in Europe were not as strong as in other markets, due mainly to currency weaknesses (Company Sleuth, 2000). The company was aggressively pursuing new customers in emerging economies such as Taiwan, Malaysia, and Russia (Hoovers Online Network, 2000). Avon has a small retail presence in Asia and Latin America,

mainly in small boutiques sometimes run by its sales representatives. The success in the international sector could be partly attributed to Avon's ability to culturally adapt products according to regional needs. For example, Avon's Color Trend product line is featured mainly in Europe, Asia, and Latin America. The line features trendy and fashionable color cosmetics at affordable prices targeted specifically to younger personal-care customers. Several of its global brands were not available in the United States since they were created exclusively with a particular international market in mind.

Management

When Andrea Jung was promoted from Chief Operating Officer to Chief Executive Officer in November 1999, she became the first female CEO in the company's 115-year history. Jung emphasized open communication with all levels and sought to create a CEO advisory council of the ten top performers from every level of the company and from all around the world (Byrnes, 2000). Sixteen senior operating and other key executives comprised Avon Operating Council (AOC). With Andrea Jung as its leader, the AOC met bimonthly to review global operations and strategic initiatives in order to maximize shareholder wealth. The AOC's members represented an average of more than twenty years' experience with the company (Avon, 1999). Avon had more women in management positions (89%) than any other Fortune 500 company. Of Avon's officers, 47% were women, and five women sat on Avon's board of directors. The management of Avon was attempting to instill a sense of urgency around the need for decisive action and calculated risk taking. As one manager stated, "Pride, speed, and performance have become the watchwords for all of our associates as we strive to foster a high-performance culture around the Avon world" (Avon, 1999).

Avon's top managers were currently disputing strategic alternatives for growing the company. The most significant issues among management were Avon's slow earning growth, stagnant sales, limited distribution capabilities, and shifts in personal-care preferences and spending habits. The AOC members' views on how to expand the company differed: some favored Avon's gradual involvement in retail with a focus on current customers, while others preferred an aggressive retail growth strategy in order to obtain new and emerging personal-care customers. The

FIGURE 20

Avon's Sales by Geographic Region

Geographic Area	$ Millions	% of Total
North America		
United States	1,809	34
Other countries	274	5
Latin America	1,608	30
Europe	878	17
Asia/Pacific	720	14
Total	**5,289**	**100**

Source: Hoovers Online Network (2000A). "Avon Products, Inc.," [Online]. **http://www.hoovers.com/premium/profile/2/ 0,2147,10152,00.htm.** Accessed October 11.

company would remain in a stagnant position until a consensus could be reached.

Regulatory

Avon maintained strong relations with government officials through its strong adequate manufacturing practices and internal quality controls and self-inspections.

Financial

Figure 21 illustrates Avon's stock performance over the past five years.

The volatility evident in Figure 21 was due in part to earnings growth falling short of targets, unprecedented stock market volatility, and negative investor sentiment toward consumer-products companies in general. In 1999, the stock price dropped sharply in the second half and finished the year down 25% (Avon, 1999).

Avon's five-year net sales comparison is shown in Figure 22.

Although the company had positive net sales and earnings growth for the past five years, the increases were in the single digits and were declining each year. In fact, 1999's one-year revenue growth was a minute 1.5%. Most of Avon's product lines had single- to double-digit growth except apparel, which fell in the single digits. As Allan Mottus, a consultant to beauty

FIGURE 22

Avon's Five-Year Net Sales Comparison (in millions)

	1995	1996	1997	1998	1999
Net sales	$4,492	$4,814	$5,079	$5,213	$5,289

Source: Avon (1999). *Annual Report.*

and retail companies, stated in *Business Week,* "We're in one of the greatest economies of all times, and Avon's still finding it hard to increase sales" (Byrnes, 2000).

Towards the Future

At the bimonthly meeting of the Avon Operating Council, Andrea Jung decided to present her retail objectives to the other sixteen members of the board. She felt this was imperative since, although earnings were expected to remain positive for the future, the company's single-digit growth, volatile stock, and seemingly archaic and limited distribution channel did not bode well for the company's intermediate and long-term future. Avon needed a new strategic plan, emphasizing where to sell its products, who would be its target market, and which product lines best fit its brand image.

As she stood in front of the members, Andrea Jung articulated her retail idea to broaden Avon's reach in the United States. Jung stated her main objectives, which were to partner with Sears and J C Penney department stores and create a store-within-a-store, where it could introduce a new and more upscale exclusive product line. This retail initiative would be done in conjunction with direct selling. In implementing both strategies, Avon would benefit from increased profits, sales, and nationwide exposure, allowing the company to continue attracting the baby-boomer segment. The plan was financially appropriate, since the company would only invest $15 to $20 million to launch the products in these locations and a bulk of the expenses (such as advertising, overhead, and employee salary) would be carried by the department stores.

Jung argued that such a strategy was feasible since retail selling was on the rise, with an increase in customer traffic in virtually all traditional department stores. Baby boomers, whose spending power was

FIGURE 21

Avon's Stock Chart 1995–2000

Source: Bloomberg. "Avon Products Chart Center," [Online]. http://quote.bloomberg.com/gcenter/gcenter.cgi?iquote =AVP&PERIOD=5Y&equote1=&equote2=&equote3=&EXCH= US&T=markets_gcenter99.ht&x=36&y=6. Accessed November 30.

expected to grow 16% in the next five years, were among Avon's main customers and were seeking alternative channels of distribution with personal-care products, specifically traditional department stores. Direct selling was feasible since personal-care products were the second most popular product group sold via this channel. Also, face-to-face selling comprised 79.7% of direct selling. Through the years, Avon was able to recruit and maintain quality and enthusiastic sales representatives by offering incentives to employees and maintaining strong internal relations. Also, direct selling was the preferred shopping method for senior citizens, Avon's oldest and most loyal customers. The strategy was viable in light of the competition. Mary Kay Inc., Avon's direct-selling competitor, was also strong in recruiting and maintaining quality and enthusiastic sales representatives through its unique incentive program and strong employee relations. However, Avon's strategy would win against Mary Kay by diversifying its distribution channels into traditional retail department stores, where Mary Kay was weak, thereby increasing its baby-boomer customer base. The strategy would win also against L'Oreal, which had a strong market position in traditional department stores due to its medium- to high-priced quality products, a wide assortment in its product mix, relationships with store managers for optimal displays and space, and qualified sales representatives for point-of-purchase assistance. However, traditional department stores were still seeking new products to add to their mix as well as high-turnover personal-care merchandise, the exact qualities of Avon's new traditional-department-store product line. The strategy would also win against leading traditional department stores' competing brands. Avon would match the competitive medium- to high-priced products and have a competitive advantage with a globally recognized brand name and image.

After Jung finished the overview of her vision, the members of the board raised numerous objections. A senior member stated that in implementing such a plan, the company ran the risk of brand name erosion and sending mixed messages to consumers. If the retail products sold in stores were exclusive, consumers might deduce it to mean that the products sold in the brochure were of lesser quality. One of the newest inductees stated that Sears and J C Penney were recognized as the weakest portion of the mass retail market, tended to lack cosmetic consumers,

and did not currently have the selling cosmetic infrastructure such as beauty advisors. He also warned Jung that upon hearing this plan of retail expansion, the sales representatives, who would fear job security, would again be very irate.

To defend her strategy against the drawbacks presented, Jung stated that the company could allocate a portion of the following year's marketing budget to increase cosmetic traffic to J C Penney and Sears. Avon could promote its certified beauty advisors in order to build the traditional department stores' personal-care infrastructure. Avon could also increase monetary incentives in order to placate the sales representatives. Although Jung effectively defended her proposed strategy, the board, as a whole, advised Jung to obtain an outside opinion.

Jung decided to hire an outside consulting group to devise a strategic plan for Avon. Within two weeks, Jung was back in the same meeting room but listening to a different retail perspective. After carefully reviewing the industry and Avon's internal situation, the consultants advised Jung to take a three-step retail approach. First, the company would distribute its higher-priced and superior-quality spa products in specialty stores. Second, Avon should sell a more affordable line in full-line discount stores. And finally, the company should extend its unique kiosks in the domestic market. They informed Jung that the company would benefit from this strategy since it would attract diverse consumer groups, significantly increase sales and brand recognition across the nation, and placate both its unhappy shareholders and apprehensive sales representatives.

Specialty stores sold superior-quality and high-priced items to a selective market (medium- to highly affluent baby boomers) and were increasing in customer popularity, experiencing a 4% annual growth rate that was expected to continue. Selling via this channel was feasible since Avon currently had a prestigious, high-priced spa line with a strong brand image that attracted affluent consumers such as baby boomers seeking products targeted to their needs. Full-line discount stores had high customer traffic, were leaders in introducing new products, and attracted a less affluent personal-care customer segment, namely Generation Y. As a result, Avon would be a good fit for full-line discount stores since it would create a new and more affordable product line sold in an alternative selling channel which would appeal to younger personal-care customers.

The consultants pointed out that although there was not yet enough information to evaluate the performance of kiosks, expanding the structures was viable since their current performance showed strengths in increasing product knowledge and education and introducing new products to the general public. The expansion of kiosks was realistic since the start-up cost for a freestanding kiosk was reported to be approximately $6,000 and the selling concept was unique to the company, thereby giving Avon a competitive advantage. Also, since sales representatives would manage the kiosks, Avon would retain its enthusiastic and knowledgeable representatives, while also providing additional career expansion incentives. The consultants agreed with Jung that Avon would gain a competitive advantage over Mary Kay Inc. by expanding into retail distribution. Mary Kay did not have unique and prestigious cosmetic collections that could be sold via specialty stores; did not have a trendy and fashionable product line, which was imperative in full-line discount stores; and did not utilize kiosks as a channel of distribution. The proposal was also a winning strategy against L'Oreal: Although Avon would compete parallel to L'Oreal in specialty stores and full-line discount stores, Avon's kiosks would give the company a distinct competitive advantage by generating excitement and informing the public about Avon's new product lines. The strategy would also win against retail competition since Avon was a global brand name introducing new products backed by increased samples, trials, and product information.

As Jung listened she pointed out that there were three significant drawbacks to the solution. First, the plan to expand in all three channels simultaneously was not currently financially feasible. Second, Avon did not yet have strong relations in the retail market, which were necessary to gain placement in both the specialty stores and full-line discount stores. Third, even if 75% of Avon's 500,000 U.S. sales representatives decided to continue their direct-selling method, there would not be enough urban upscale retail space to accommodate that many kiosks. The consultants responded to Jung's first point by stating that the proposed retail strategy could be done in stages, beginning with the specialty stores and kiosks and followed by the full-line discount-store expansion. The time between the stages could be determined based on the success and profitability of the first stage. In response to point two: Avon would not have difficulty developing strong relations in the retail market. Managers were seeking high-quality products that carried a well-received brand name. Avon's personal-care items were high-margin products in a broad product category, thereby ensuring strong relations with retail managers. Third, in regards to the kiosk expansion problem, the consultants stated that as a longer-term strategy, the company could expand its kiosks into non-retail, high-customer traffic locations such as office buildings and airports. Jung thanked the consultants and left the boardroom.

Back in her office, Jung realized this was only the tip of the iceberg of the strategic decisions that needed to be made. There were still significant debates about which product lines should be expanded and divested and which consumer groups the company should focus on. Just the previous day, the marketing team presented a list of industry trends and opportunities, indicating that Avon was operating in a rapidly changing industry. A major opportunity that stood out in her mind was the positive impact of the Internet on the personal-care industry, and she wondered which would be the best way for Avon to capitalize on its success. These and many other strategic issues plagued Jung as she debated over the best way to grow the 115-year-old company. If Avon was to stay abreast of the competition, immediate action needed to be taken and Jung did not have much time left to decide.

REFERENCES

Agos, F. (2000). "State of the Industry: 2000," *Global Cosmetic Industry,* June 1, vol.166, no.6, p.22.

Altruis Biomedical Network (2000A). "Shampoos and Conditioners." [Online]. **http://www.hairless.net.** Accessed October 12.

Altruis Biomedical Network (2000B). "Products." [Online]. **http://e-shaving.net.** Accessed October 12.

Altruis Biomedical Network (2000C). "Sunburns and Sunscreens." [Online]. **http://sunscreens.net.** Accessed October 12.

Anonymous (2000). "Fragrances: Under Pressure?" *Global Cosmetic Industry,* September, vol. 167, iss. 3, p. 80.

Anonymous (1999). "Teens Push Aside the Boomers, Emerge as New Kings of Cool," *Times-Picayune,* April 1999.

Avon (1999). *Annual Report.*

Avon Company Website (2000). **http://www.avon.com.** Accessed October 1.

Berman, B. (1997). *Retail Management: A Strategic Approach.* New York, N.Y.: Prentice-Hall.

Bittar, C. (2000). "Anti-Aging Anew Gets a Makeover as Youthful Way to Skip Birthdays," *Brandweek,* September 4.

Bloomberg (2000). "Avon Products Chart Center." [Online]. **http://quote.bloomberg.com/gcenter/gcenter.cgi?iquote=AVP&PERIOD =5Y&equote1=&equote2=&equote3=&EXCH=US&T= markets_gcenter99.ht&x=36&y=6.** Accessed November 30.

Brookman, F. (1999). "Boomers Remain Formidable Force," *Drug Store News,* June 7.

Byrnes, N. (2000). "Avon: The New Calling," *Business Week,* September 18, iss. 3699, pp. 136–148.

Company Sleuth (2000). "Avon Reports Record Third Quarter Results." [Online]. **http://www.companysleuth.com.** Accessed October 22.

Cooney-Curran, J. (2000). "Deliveries of Hope," *Global Cosmetic Industry,* September, vol.167, iss.3, p. 6.

Croft, M. (1999). "Changing Face of Cosmetics; Consumers' Growing Ease with Internet Shopping Is Forcing Store-Based Cosmetic Companies to Tread the Home-Shopping Pathway," *Marketing Week,* May 27, pp. 40–41.

D'Innocenzio, A. (2000). "Specialty Retailers Gain More Customers Who Want Fresh Fashions and Good Service." *Associated Press.* [Online]. **http://www.mcall.com/html/business/news/d_g001_fistores.htm.** Accessed September 24.

Davis, D. (2000). "Cyberphobia! E-Commerce Poses a Serious Threat to Brick and Morter Retailers," *Global Cosmetics Industry,* March.

Dutton, G. (1999). "A Changing Landscape for Cosmetics and Personal Care," *Chemical Market Reporter,* April 5.

Francese, P. (2000). "With Senior Citizens, Population Growth Has Been a Gray Area," *Wall Street Journal,* NW3, May 24.

Global Cosmetic Industry (2000). "GENERATION GAPS: Global Cosmetic Industry takes a Look at the Personal-Care Preferences, Spending Habits, and Power of Generation Y and X and Baby Boomers." [Online]. **http://www.findarticles.com/cf_0/m0HLW/6_166/63411614/p1/article.jhtml.** Accessed November 1.

Grossman, A. (1999). "Facial Cleansers Trend Toward Ease, Quick Results," *Drug Store News,* February 1.

Herman, S. (2000). "Skin Deep," *Global Cosmetic Industry.* September 1, vol. 167, no.3, p. 50.

Hoovers Online Network (2000A). "Avon Products, Inc." [Online]. **http://www.hoovers.com/premium/profile/2/0,2147,10152,00.htm.** Accessed October 11.

Hoovers Online Network (2000B). "Mary Kay Inc." [Online]. **http://www.hoovers.com/co/capsul/8/0,2163,40298,00.html.** Accessed October 19.

Hoovers Online Network (2000C). "L'Oreal SA." [Online]. **http://www.hoovers.com/co/capsul/2/0,2163,41772,00.html.** Accessed October 19.

In Cosmetics99 (1999). "Shampoo and Styling Lead in the Hair Sector." [Online]. **http://www.dotfinechem.com/incos/s. . .atures/nov_dec99/sh ampoo/index.htm.** Accessed November 1.

Kyriakos, T. (1999). "Growing Wealth Creates Increased Spending," *Drug Store News,* June 7.

L'Oreal Company Website (2000). **http://www.loreal.com.** Accessed November 5.

Mallory, M. (1995). "Women on a Fast Track," *U.S. News and World Report,* November 6, vol. 119, no.18, p. 60.

Market Share Reporter (2000). Detroit, MI: Gale Research.

Mary Kay Inc. Company Website (2000). **http://www.marykay.com.** Accessed November 5.

Nelson, E. (2000). "Avon Expects Boutiques in Sears, Penneys to Break Even by 2002," *Wall Street Journal,* September 28, Eastern Edition, p. B14.

NPD Group (2000A). "NPD Fragrancetrack Reports Men Who Wear Fragrance Are Wearing It More Often." [Online]. **http://www.npd.com/corp/content/news/releases/press_000926.htm.** Accessed October 30.

NPD Group (2000B). "NPD and Media Metrix e-Visory Report Anticipates Dramatic Growth of Online Beauty Sales." [Online]. **http://www.npd.com/corp/content/news/releases/press_000321.htm;** Accessed October 9.

NPD Group (2000C). "Media Metrix NPD Beauty Visory, Summer 2000." [Online]. **http://www.npd.com/corp/content/special/evisory.htm.** Accessed November 1.

Parks, L. (1999A). "Avon Reaching Out to New Customers with Upscale Beauty Center Kiosks," *Drug Store News,* April 26.

Parks, L. (1999B). "Drug buyers optimistic about cosmetics sales.(New lines from Olay and Neutrogena helping)," *Drug Store Newsletter,* June 7.

Parks, L. (2000). "Beauty Makers Respond to Myriad of Needs, Creating Products Perfect for Everyone," *Drug Store Newsletter,* September 25, p. 37.

Rocafort, C. (2000). "Formulating for the Ethnic Hair Care Marketplace," *Soaps & Cosmetics.* [Online]. **http://www.wysiwyg://102/http://206.0.199.8/sc/mag/sc1.html.** Accessed November 9.

Sanabria, V. (2000A). "The Inner Hue: Self-Expression Dominates the Color Cosmetic Category," *Global Cosmetic Industry,* April.

Sanabria, V. (2000B). "Hair-Care Update: Innovative, Multifunctional Products and Emerging Market Segments Drive the Hair-Care Industry," *Global Cosmetic Industry,* May 1, vol.166, no. 5, p.18.

Sauer, P. (2000). "Varying Shades of Profitability Uncovered in Cosmetics and Personal Care," *Chemical Market Reporter,* May 8.

Schiffman, L. (1997). *Consumer Behavior.* Upper Saddle River, N.J. Prentice-Hall.

The Direct Selling Industry (2000). "2000 Direct Selling Growth & Outlook Survey." [Online]. **http://www.dsa.org/factsht00.stm.** November 7.

U.S. Food and Drug Administration (2000A). "Cosmetic Handbook." [Online]. **http://www.fda.org.** Accessed October 11.

U.S. Food and Drug Administration (2000B). "Cosmetic Labeling Manual." [Online]. **http://www.fda.org.** Accessed October 11.

13 The Body Shop International: U.S. Operations

This case was prepared by A. J. Almaney, Professor of Management at DePaul University.

Anita Roddick was instantly recognizable behind the wheel of a green Volkswagen Golf as she roared up to her Littlehampton headquarters in Sussex, England. With her hair flying and the sleeves of her shirt rolled like an army sergeant major's, the founder of the Body Shop International (BST), Britain's most successful global retailer, paused just long enough to admire her latest pet project: an enormous electronic sign that blared "STEER CLEAR OF SHELL—BOYCOTT NOW" at a Shell service station sitting across the road.

The question of the oil giant's responsibility for human-rights abuse in Nigeria was a current preoccupation of the perpetually crusading Roddick. But on this morning, she was scowling at some equally disquieting news from her board of directors: the profit figures from the United States were dismal. The company's U.S. division lost 3 million pounds in 1997, compared with a loss of 1.3 million pounds in 1996 and a profit of 4.9 million pounds in 1995. In addition, the company's share price, which was 365 pence in 1993, dropped to 121 pence in 1997.

Weak U.S. sales and a slumping share price were just two of the problems that threw the cosmetics concern into a midlife crisis. Competition was also increasing. A host of imitators, notably the Bath and Body Works, began to invade the company's market niche. On top of that, the company that boasted of putting principles before profits was accused of engaging in unethical practices. Its critics alleged that the company had misled the public about everything from its stand against animal testing to the ingredients in its products. Even though the company strenuously denied the allegation, the bad publicity had tarnished its image as one of the most glamorous growth stocks.[1]

The challenge facing the company was this: Did the entrepreneurial Roddick have what it would take to run a large company, and could it compete effectively against such aggressive and nimble competitors as the Bath and Body Works?

History

On a fact-finding trip Anita Roddick had made for the United Nations to study women in the Third World, she learned that for centuries women in underdeveloped countries had used organic potions to care for their skin, so she decided to open a cosmetics shop that would sell natural products in cheap containers. The shop, which later was named The BST, was started in 1976 in Brighton, England. The thirty-three-year-old housewife with two young daughters started the business to earn enough money to care for her family while her husband, Gordon Roddick, pursued a dream of horseback riding from Buenos Aires to New York.

With a bank loan of about 10 million British pounds, Roddick opened the first store carrying only twenty-five naturally based skin-care and hair-care products which were sold in clear urine sample bottles purchased from a local hospital. When supply of the bottles ran out, she began a refill policy. Handwritten labels with product information were pasted on the bottles. Before her husband had left for Buenos Aires, he told her she had to make 300 pounds a week in order to stay in business. "What happens, Gordon, if I don't?" she asked. He said, "Give it six months and then pack it up and meet me with the kids in Peru."[2]

The store proved to be so successful that another was opened within a year. When Gordon Roddick returned home in 1977, he joined his wife in the business. At first, he took over the tasks of filling bottles and handling the finances, teaching himself what he needed to learn as he went along. Although he later became the company's chairman, he continued to handle the financial side of the business while keeping a low profile. Gordon attributed the company's success to his wife. "Creatively, this is Anita's company entirely. She says what she wants, and we make all her dreams come true," he said.[3] A year later, they began to franchise the business.

The 1980s witnessed the company's explosive growth. Sales and profits grew on average 50% a year. In 1984, the company went public with the Roddicks' retaining 27.6% of the company's stock. Gordon continued to be the chairman while Anita served as managing director. In the same year, the company had 138 stores, 87 of which were located outside the United Kingdom. By the end of the decade, pretax profits climbed to an estimated 35 million pounds on sales of 212 million pounds despite the onset of a withering recession in British retailing.[4]

In 1988, the first Body Shop opened in the United States. All stores were owned by the company as franchising was not permitted until 1990. In 1992, a new U.S. headquarters opened in Raleigh, North Carolina, to make and distribute products to U.S. stores. In 1997, the number of stores reached 287; 138 of these were company owned. The Roddicks set as an objective increasing the number of stores in the United States to 500 by the year 2000.

Corporate Governance

The board of directors of the BST consisted of eleven members. As shown in Exhibit 1, all but three of them were company officers. While Anita held the chief executive officer's position, her husband was the chairman of the board.

The board met regularly throughout the year. Its functions included overall company strategy and future development, allocation of financial resources, acquisitions and divestitures, approval of major investments, annual budgets, senior executive appointments, budget policy, and risk management.

In 1997, the company came under criticism for not complying with The Code of Best Practices as defined in the United Kingdom by the Cadbury Committee. One of the recommendations of the Cadbury Committee was that an audit committee should consist of at least three non-executive directors. At the Body Shop, the committee consisted of only two such directors. A year later, however, the company complied with the committee's recommendation.

Profile of the CEO

Anita Roddick, the daughter of Italian immigrants, was born on October 23, 1942. She was educated at an all-girls high school in Littlehampton, Sussex, and graduated from Newton Park College of Education in Bath, England. When she was eighteen, Roddick learned from her mother that her much-loved stepfather was in fact her real father—a product of a love affair her mother had while she was still married to her first husband, whom she divorced when Roddick was eight.

As a young adult, Roddick traveled the world over. In a visit to Johannesburg, South Africa, she was arrested by the police for attending a jazz club on "black night." Upon her return home, she was introduced by her mother to her future husband, Gordon. The couple had two daughters.

For several years, she ran a cafe but became tired of the "crazy" hours. She began to look for a job with "sensible hours." That led her to open her own shop.

EXHIBIT 1

Board of Governance

Director	Age	Title
Anita L. Roddick	54	Chief executive officer
T. Gordon Roddick	55	Chairman
Stuart A. Rose	47	Managing director
Eric G. Helyer	61	Executive director
Jane Reid	44	Strategic development director and company secretary
Jeremy A. Kett	49	Finance director
Terry G. Hartin	51	Executive director
Ivan C. Levy	40	Executive director
Penny L. Houghes	37	Non-executive director
Aldo Papone	64	Non-executive director
Adrian D. Bellamy	55	Non-executive director

Source: The Body Shop International, *1998 Annual Report,* p. 40.

Anita Roddick was funny, provocative, and a great talker whose language was peppered with four-letter words. She attributed her bawdy language and feisty nature to her Italian heritage. When she was growing up, she felt different from her neighbors in Little-hampton. "We were noisy, always screaming and shouting. We played music loudly, ate pasta, and smelled of garlic," she said. She attributed her rebellious personality to her mother, who was not afraid to challenge the status quo.[5] She acquired a strong work ethic as a child, waiting tables in her parent's cafe. Highly emotional, she would jump up and down at board meetings and scream and clap her hands if she liked something. If she did not, she would dismiss it with a four-letter word.

Throughout her career, Roddick received many accolades. In 1985, for example, she was named Britain's Business Woman of the Year, and three years later she was awarded an Order of the British Empire by the royal family. In 1992, she won the Business Leader of the Year Award from the National Association of Women Business Owners in the United States.

Anita's Management Style

For many years, the BST was not managed professionally. It had no business plan and no job descriptions. In Roddick's own words, "You'd bury your head with laughter if you saw how unprofessional we were."[6] Working for Roddick, according to a former employee, was "like being in a circus parade. Your job is to follow behind the elephants and scoop up the dung."[7]

As a result, when the company expanded, it became difficult to retain managers who sought to run the organization more professionally. One such manager was Robert Cluckman, a retailing expert who had been recruited as the company's international general manager. He left in 1992, complaining about the BST's unstructured environment and lack of a strategic plan. Another manager, Janet Swaysland, lasted less than a year as vice president for communications and later said, "They were clueless about what they wanted."

Anita on Company Bigness

Roddick did not reconcile herself to the idea of having to run a big business. She thought that one could lose the sense of being remarkable by just being big. To her, wanting to be big was very much a male pathological trait. Roddick did not want the BST to be a McDonald's, where customer relationships would be lost. But she could not escape the fact that she was an entrepreneur who had created a big, bureaucratic organization. She was annoyed by the language being used: her staff talked about three-year plans, net income, and average sales, all of which she did not like. She was also annoyed with what she called the "obsession with meetings." "We are getting to a point where we can't fart without calling a meeting,"[8] she said.

She expressed concern over the fat-cat mentality that was creeping into her company. People would carelessly spill coffee on a new carpet, did not recycle newspapers, and left lights on after a meeting, all of which went against her philosophy of running a lean and green company.[9]

Anita on Profit

Ever since the company went public in 1984, Roddick struggled against what she described as "pressure from money men" who told her how to run the company and what she should be doing with her money. The sense of conflict kept growing, leading her to think seriously about taking the company private again. She thought financial figures were not unimportant, but to concentrate only on the figures was, in her view, "dumb." She also disputed the notion that shareholders should have more rights and influence on the company than employees, the community, and the environment.

Roddick had several reasons for taking the company public in the first place. For one thing, she felt that her business needed credibility to get good retail sites, and she was not being taken seriously by property owners who controlled retailing. For another, it was the "sexy" thing to do at the time. "When you have a crazy idea that should never have existed, all you want to do is push it to see how far it would go. It was a huge barometer of reassurance and a way of getting more money. It was like growing up."[10] She also admitted that vanity played a role in her decision.

Company Mission

In 1995, the BST retained a management consulting firm to undertake an appraisal of its structure, objectives, and methods of decision making and problem solving. One outcome of this process was the formulation of a mission statement (see Exhibit 2).

Company Vision

Roddick articulated the BST's vision in the following way:

> I believe quite passionately that there is a better way. I think you can rewrite the book on business. I think you can trade ethically; be committed to social responsibility, global

EXHIBIT 2

BST Mission Statement

> To dedicate our business to the pursuit of social and environmental change.
>
> To creatively balance the financial and human needs of our stakeholders: employees, customers, franchisees, suppliers, and shareholders.
>
> To courageously ensure that our business is ecologically sustainable: meeting the needs of the present without compromising the future.
>
> To meaningfully contribute to local, national and international communities in which we trade, by adopting a code of conduct which ensures care, honesty, fairness, and respect.
>
> To passionately campaign for the protection of the environment, human and civil rights, and against animal testing within the cosmetics and toiletries industry.
>
> To tirelessly work to narrow the gap between principle and practice, whilst making fun, passion, and care part of our daily lives.

Source: The Body Shop International, *1998 Annual Report*, p. 1.

responsibility; empower your employees without being afraid of them. I think you can really rewrite the book. That is the vision, and the vision is absolutely clear.[11]

Values

In addition to the mission and vision statements, the company also adopted a statement of values articulating its philosophy toward its stakeholders (see Exhibit 3).

1. To develop and build relationships with our shareholders and prospective shareholders, with the aim of creating a base of well-informed investors who fully understand the company's aims and objectives.

2. To operate a progressive dividend policy.[12]

Objectives

The BST set the following objectives, all of which pertained to the company's relations with its stakeholders:

1. To manage the business with the aim of maximizing shareholder interests, while also balancing the needs of other stakeholder groups.

EXHIBIT 3

Statement of Values

> We aim to ensure that human and civil rights, as set out in the Universal Declaration of Human Rights, are respected throughout our business activities. We will establish a framework based on this declaration to include criteria for workers' rights embracing a safe, healthy working environment, fair wages, no discrimination on the basis of race, creed, gender or sexual orientation, or physical coercion of any kind.
>
> We will support long-term, sustainable relationships with communities in need. We will pay special attention to those minority groups, women and disadvantaged peoples who are socially and economically marginalized.
>
> We will use environmentally sustainable resources wherever technically and economically viable. Our purchasing will be based on a system of screening and investigation of the ecological credentials of our finished products, ingredients, packaging, and suppliers.
>
> We will promote animal protection throughout our business activities. We are against animal testing in the cosmetics and toiletries industry. We will not test ingredients or products on animals, nor will we commission others to do so on our behalf. We will use our purchasing power to stop suppliers' animal testing.
>
> We will institute appropriate monitoring, auditing, and disclosure mechanisms to ensure our accountability and demonstrate our compliance with these principles.

Source: The Body Shop International, *The Body Shop Approach to Ethical Auditing.* Undated company document.

2. To develop and build relationships with our shareholders and prospective shareholders, with the aim of creating a base of well-informed investors who fully understand the company's aims and objectives.

3. To operate a progressive dividend policy.[13]

Strategy

In the mid 1980s, the company followed a strategy of growth through geographic expansion. With the UK market nearly saturated, Anita hoped that, in a decade, a map of the world would be dotted with the Body Shops.

Franchising served as a strategic tool for the company's growth. The first franchise shop opened in 1977

in Bognor Regis, West Sussex, in the United Kingdom. When Roddick entered the U.S. market in 1988, she opted to open her own stores instead of immediately franchise. She thought this would give the company time to adjust to the new market. When Roddick decided to franchise in the United States in 1990, she had more than 2,000 applicants. The BST's U.S. subsidiary acted as head franchisee in the United States. The head office, filling facilities, and main distribution center were based in Wake Forest, North Carolina. The subsidiary granted sub-franchise rights to individuals and organizations. In 1997, the company had 278 stores in the United States, 128 of which were company-owned.

Franchisees paid a flat fee of 60,000 pounds to buy into the business and then invested a minimum of 375,000 pounds to get the store built, stocked, and running. To determine whether the potential franchisees shared her passion for global issues, Roddick required them to take a comprehensive test that included questions about their taste in music, books, and film as well as their thoughts on how they would like to die. Because most of the franchisees had no formal business experience, Roddick had them work in a store where the existing staff could evaluate how they would fit in. Then the candidates went through extensive interviews at headquarters with Roddick and other top executives. Because of time constraints, Roddick had to develop ways to implement the same rigorous procedures in the United States without having to conduct the interviews personally. Once selected, the franchisees had to undergo extensive training in London or at one of the area development offices in the United States, where they learned the details of each product and the rules of merchandising and running the stores.

Organizational Structure

The BST was segmented into four divisions: the Body Shop UK, the Body Shop USA, the Singapore Operation, and Independent Overseas Franchisees. The Body Shop USA was broken down into Mail Order, Company Shops, Franchise Shops, and Area Distributors. Each of the Area Distributors was segmented into smaller units.

Strategy-Implementation Problems

Before long, the company's rapid expansion began to create difficulties. Instead of patiently learning the unique characteristics of the U.S. market and perfecting sales in its existing shops, the company charged into the top malls, to which it was not accustomed, in hopes of beating its competitors.[14]

Furthermore, Roddick's relationship with franchisees began to deteriorate. Some of them did not share her enthusiasm about certain causes. Although the typical franchisee—young, well educated, female—generally shared Anita's ideas and wanted to be part of the "family" structure, others were fearful that her radical ideas drove some customers away. They were also concerned that the company's rapid expansion had a cannibalizing effect, taking 4% away from their sales[15] and damaging the company's image by turning it into another McDonald's.[16] Some franchisees were unhappy about having to pay the 60,000 pounds purchase fee—something that their counterparts in the United Kingdom were exempted from.

Also, as the company expanded, its communication with its franchisees worsened. In a survey of the franchisees conducted by the company itself, it was found that 48% of them did not think the company's long-term strategy was clearly communicated to them.

Products

The company marketed over six hundred different products, which could be classified in seven broad groups:

1. Skin products: lotions and gels

2. Body products: bars and deodorants

3. Makeup products: lipstick, mascara, eye definer, and eye shadow

4. Fragrance products: body spray, perfume oil, and eau de toilettes

5. Hair products: shampoo, conditioners, and scalp treatment

6. Aromatherapy products: bath oil, massage oil, and relaxing body lotion

7. Hands and feet products: foot scrub, cooling leg gel, foot spray, hand cream, footsie roller, and file-a-foot

The BST's approach to packaging was to make it simple yet attractive.[17] All shampoos and lotions were sold in identical plastic bottles with black caps and green labels. The packing material was a vegetable-based starch, puffed into shape with no chemical binders. This material was biodegradable, dissolving in water in five minutes. The products were placed in clear containers with factual information of what was inside and what the product was good for.

Suppliers

In 1987, Roddick began the BST's Trade-Not-Aid program which involved purchasing natural ingredients from Third World countries, thus benefiting both the company and native communities. To find such ingredients, Anita traveled several times a year to remote areas of the Third World where she observed local customs and talked with native people about their methods of skin and hair care. Several indigenous groups signed agreements with BST to supply it with natural ingredients.

Industry

The personal-care products industry in the United States was about 39 billion pounds, which accounted for more than one-third of the total world market. In 1995, the industry grew by 11% to 3.3 billion pounds. The surge capped four years of strong industry growth that spawned scores of bath boutiques. Even retailers, such as the Gap, began to enter the market or expand their product line. By 1996, the number of soap and scent boutiques, which came to be known as The Body Shop Crowd reached 1,400, not counting such scent-purveying stores as Victoria's Secret, Fredrick's of Hollywood, and Banana Republic.[18]

Entry and exit barriers were relatively low because retail space was widely available and there were many suppliers of products for the industry. It was estimated that the average cost per store for leasehold improvement and furniture and fixtures was about 338,000 pounds, average pre-opening costs were about 7,500 pounds, and working capital requirements (mainly inventory purchases) were about 60,000 pounds.[19]

Being cyclical, with future growth expected to be 1% to 2% annually, and glutted with so many stores, the industry was ripe for a shakeout. Some stores were already beginning to slip, among them Nature's Elements, which filed for bankruptcy reorganization.

The one bright spot in this picture was the ethnic health and beauty aids market, which by 2001 was expected to grow by 6% to almost 3 billion pounds.

Competitors

The personal-care products market in the United States was highly segmented and included specialty stores, chains, and department stores. Packaging, price, selection, service, and quality were the principal attributes on which companies competed. Most competitors relied heavily on advertising that created unrealistic ideas of what people should look like and how their skin should feel and smell to others.

BST's major competitors included Bath and Body Works, Crabtree and Evelyn, Aveda, H2O plus, and Garden Botanika.

Bath and Body Works

The most successful of the competitors was Bath and Body Works, part of Intimate Brands, Inc., which itself was 83% owned by the Limited. Bath and Body Works benefited from the strength and experience of its parent company, the Limited.

The chief executive of Bath and Body Works (BBW) was Beth Pritchard, a hands-on executive who each month spent two days in one of her boutiques, wearing reindeer antlers and serving as a salesperson. To get a feel for her products, she tested them on herself, her daughter, and her friends. Pritchard's personal touch and her drive catapulted the company from being a blip in the personal-care product industry to being an industry leader. When she took over in 1991, the company had 95 stores and 30 million pounds in sales. By 1997, she expanded the chain to 750 stores with sales of 11 million pounds, leaving the BST a distant second (it had 287 U.S. stores). Like the BST, BBW did not advertise. Its success was attributed to word-of-mouth recommendations and in-store promotions, such as special offers.

The promotional theme BBW focused on was not natural products or animal protection but Americana. The shops were colorful places that evoked rural America and were designed to have a welcome, down-home feel. Checkered cloths covered the tables, and the merchandise sat in old barrels while the scents of fresh-baked pies emanated from the perfumes. Pritchard made innovation a priority. Roughly 30% of the company's products were new each season, far more than rivals'.[20]

In commenting on the ability of BBW to compete with BST in the United States, Leslie H. Wexner, the Limited's chairman, said his rival's background as a manufacturer and foreigner worked against her in the United States "They were not retailers," he said. "We have an advantage—we know the territory."[21]

Aveda

Aveda was founded by Horst Rechellbacher, an Austrian hairdresser, in 1977. Headquartered in Minneapolis, Minnesota, the company had 140 stores worldwide, 60 of them freestanding stores in the United States. Of its 80 international outlets, 50 were stores-within-stores in department stores and the rest were freestanding. Its sales in 1996 were estimated at 263 million pounds, an 80% increase over 1995.[22]

Aveda developed and marketed scent, hair, skin, makeup, and other lifestyle products created from flower and plant essences. Rechellbacher staked his company's existence on plants, believing that plants, if properly harvested and utilized, could offer powerful and complex ingredients for use in an unlimited range of products. Also, unlike petrochemically derived ingredients, plants were a renewable resource. The company established state-of-the-art research and manufacturing facilities in Minneapolis to develop technologies by which pure plant and flower essences could be extracted, and it was successful in targeting black consumers with such products as the Self Control Hair Styling Stick. These and other products were sold at thousands of beauty salons across the country.[23]

H2O Plus

A privately held company, H2O Plus opened its first store in Chicago in 1989, and within a year had 27 stores in mall locations stretching from San Francisco to Palm Beach, Florida. The company was created by Cindy Melk, a twenty-eight-year-old entrepreneur who said she wanted to offer a no-nonsense, affordable alternative to overpriced and overpackaged products sold in department stores.[24] The company distributed its products through fifty-eight company-owned stores, nine franchises, and four hundred department stores, including Marshall Field's, Dillard Department Stores, Macy's, and Federated Department Stores. Its target market consisted of women between the ages of 18 and 39, and its prices were about 15% to 20% lower than department-store designer lines of similar quality. Despite that, the company's sales volume dropped to 45 million pounds from 50 million. The decline was attributed to growing competition and lack of differentiation among the company's own products.[25]

Garden Botanika

Garden Botanika was established in 1990 in Redmond, Washington. The company sold high-quality, reasonably priced, botanically based personal-care products and cosmetics. The company began with three stores but grew to 196 stores by 1996. In 1997, it had 259 stores and planned to open 30 more that year. It introduced new products on a continuous basis, thus offering the customer an extensive product assortment. Its products, which targeted women between 30 and 49, ranged from makeup to perfume and bath gel. In 1997, the company mailed a thirty-six-page holiday catalog to nearly 3 million mail-order and retail customers. The catalog contained fragrance samples of some of the company's products. Although the company's sales increased from 9.6 million pounds in 1993 to over 138.6 million in 1997, its net losses rose from 2.1 million in 1993 to 7.4 million in 1997.

Crabtree and Evelyn

A private company, Crabtree and Evelyn had 115 stores. It tried to create the feel of an English sitting room in its stores. It sold British baked goods and china along with floral soaps. The company was acquired by Kepon Berhad (KLK), based in Kuala Lumpur, Malaysia. KLK had businesses in Malaysia, the United Kingdom, and Australia involving the production and processing of palm products, natural rubber, and cocoa. The acquisition was viewed as a means of expanding the company's retail outlets worldwide.[26]

Drugstores

Drugstore chains were initially slow to react to specialty stores such as the BST and BBW. As a result, they began to lose sales. To prevent further losses, the drugstore chains began to copy the specialty stores' concept. Their market research showed that consumers who shopped at drugstores cited familiarity with the store, its proximity to their home or workplace, and one-stop shopping as the main reasons for preferring their drugstore. Those who shopped at specialty stores did so when choosing gifts or when in a self-indulgent mood.[27]

Stores

Most of the BST's stores in the United States were small and had shelves too cluttered to appeal to American consumers. On the shelves were note cards with stories about the products or their ingredients. But there were also stacks of pamphlets with titles such as "Animal Testing and Cosmetics" and "What is natural?" The stores appeared dull and outdated and had shoddy-looking products such as spangly purses made out of bubble wrap, Day-Glo plastic hair clips, velvet alice bands, multicolored mascara, and pencil-case goodies. The stores were designed to be self-service: though the sales people were pleasant and knowledgeable about the products, they were trained not to be forceful with customers and to offer advice only when asked.[28]

Customers

The BST's target market consisted primarily of females over twenty-five years old. In 1997, females twenty-five to seventy-four years old numbered about 68 million and were expected to number 90 million by the year 2005.[29]

When the BST opened its stores in the United States, its counterculture approach to cosmetics appealed to many women. It aroused in them the feelings of enthusiasm, commitment, and loyalty more appropriate to a political movement than a store. Like missionaries selling Bibles, they even pitched its products to their friends.[30]

However, American consumers gradually grew lukewarm to the company's political messages, which continued to be popular in Europe. They were also not as loyal as the Europeans. More than European customers, Americans were influenced by price. Furthermore, Americans were used to shopping in malls, where storefronts tended to blur together and shopkeepers were not connected to the community, as was the case in Europe. Reflecting on the company's failure to relate to American consumers, Roddick said, "It was a different culture which we did not understand."[31]

Employees

The total number of employees at the Wake Forest, North Carolina, site was 240 including office, warehouse, and production personnel. In addition, the company employed 2,500 sales people in its stores.

Generally, the employees were very motivated and loyal to the company, often talking about the difficulty they would have working for an "ordinary company." Anita believed that employees of other companies were cynical about their employers and did not buy the argument that the companies cared about them. According to Anita, profits were "boring" to most employees even if they got a piece of the action.

The BST attacked employee cynicism in the same manner it attacked customers' cynicism about corporate advertising—with information. All employees could attend the company's training school where the emphasis was placed not on making profit but on the nature and uses of the products. They were encouraged to spend half a day each month volunteering in a community project—time for which they were paid. And after five years, they were also allowed a six-month sabbatical. Many of them used the time to travel or volunteer at the company-sponsored orphanages in Romania and Albania.

To find out employees' feelings about the company, the BST conducted surveys and focus groups. The results showed that 92% lauded the company's efforts on human rights, environmental protection, and animal welfare, and 75% were proud to tell others they were part of the BST family.

Communication

Anita attached a great deal of importance to communication as a means of getting the company's values across to its employees. She did that through face-to-face communication as well as through the company's newsletter. The newsletter, resembling an underground newspaper, devoted more space to the company's campaigns to save the rain forest and ban the ozone-depleting chemicals than to the opening of a new branch or the dropping of an old product. Anita was personally involved in determining the newsletter's content. She would suggest articles, check copy, choose illustrations, and change design. She viewed the newsletter as a direct line of communication from the leader to the rest of the organization.[32]

Advertising and Promotion

Anita Roddick learned how to use free publicity early on when her first store was threatened with a lawsuit by two neighboring funeral parlors which objected to having a store named The BST so near their corpses. She contacted the local paper with the sad story of a struggling mother about to lose her small shop and received generous press coverage. This resulted in a large number of sympathetic readers filing through her doors. Ever since, Anita chose not to market or advertise, believing it to be a waste of time and money that the consumer would end up paying for. This strategy also reflected her belief that customers were so overmarketed that they became increasingly cynical about advertising which told them half truths or untruths. That is why she was heavily criticized when she appeared in an American Express commercial to promote her Trade-Not-Aid program.[33]

Thus, instead of traditional advertising she relied on the generosity of the press which courted her company as it became the darling of the City (London's Wall Street). The BST actually racked up about 5.25 million pounds worth of free publicity a year from various articles about the entrepreneurial Anita. "I am always available to the press," Anita said. "I fervently believe that passion persuades, and I emit a lot of enthusiasm."[34] The only promotion the company used was limited to window displays, catalogs, and point-of-purchase displays. In such promotions, the marketing theme stressed the customer's "well-being" rather than glamor and instant rejuvenation as is the norm in this industry.[35] To strengthen its credibility with the customers, the company sought to educate them by telling them where the product came from, how it was made, what was in it, how it was tested, and what it could be used for."[36]

To generate more publicity for her company, Anita hired two public-relations firms, one in New York and one in London. Their job was to make sure Anita would keep a high profile in both the general and beauty press. In the United States she was written about in several publications, including *Time, Newsweek,* and *Inc.* She was also profiled on CBS television.

Research and Development

In the early 1990s, the company did not introduce any significant new products. It was too busy opening new stores in the United States. Instead of revamping the company's aging product line, top management devoted an increasing amount of time launching environmental projects. This provided its competitors with an opening to steal market share by offering new products.

In the mid 1990s, the company sought to introduce several new products and enhance existing products. The revamped product line, however, had mixed results. While a nonaerosol hair mousse flopped, a new line of cosmetics called "Colorings" did well.[37] In 1998, new products comprised 15% of the product mix. But that still fell below the industry average of 25%.

In developing new products, top management required that they should meet demanding safety and environmental standards, adopting a policy that opposed the use of animals in testing raw materials. The company used human volunteers to evaluate product safety prior to launch. The company also required suppliers of raw materials to provide written confirmation every six months that no raw materials were tested on animals.

Social Responsibility

Anita believed that business should do more than make money, create decent jobs, or sell good products. Rather, business should help solve major social problems by using its resources to come up with answers to such questions as: "How do we bring human fulfillment?" "How do we address mass unemployment?" "How do we prevent social alienation?"[38] In line with this philosophy, the company encouraged and contributed to social and environmental programs by helping such groups as Greenpeace, Amnesty International, and Friends of the Earth. All franchisees were asked to participate in the campaigns.

Anita also launched the Trade-Not-Aid program which included buying blue corn from the Pueblo Indians in New Mexico and Brazil's nut oil from the Kayapo Indians of the Amazon River Basis. The company also donated seed money to launch the *Big Issue*—a London weekly newspaper sold by the homeless.[39]

The company pursued a policy against animal testing. However, a 1992 British television documentary charged that the BST did use ingredients that had been tested on animals. In a public statement, the company asserted that its policy was never to use ingredients until five years after they had been tested on animals. A company spokesman said, "We are trying to give [suppliers] an incentive to stop testing on animals by telling them that if you stop testing and find other ways, we will buy your stuff."[40] The Roddicks sued for libel and won more than 800,000

pounds in damages. In 1994 an American journalist, writing in the magazine *Business Ethics,* broadened the charge of hypocrisy to include the BST's environmental standards, charitable contributions, and efforts to buy materials from the Third World. Anita dismissed the allegations as "recycled rubbish," and an independent research group later concluded that the charges were "broadly unfair."[41]

In response to these charges and to make sure that its values were adhered to, the company created a self-scrutinizing mechanism called the "Social Audit" to examine every aspect of the company such as corporate giving, community projects, animal testing, and trade-and-not aid programs. It also looked at human-resources issues such as staff conditions and family leave. The audit was verified by an outside auditor and released each year along with the company's financial results.

Finance

In 1997, the BST's share price dropped to 121 pence from its peak of 365 pence in 1993. This was due primarily to the poor performance of the company's U.S. division which lost 3 million pounds in 1997, compared with a loss of 1.3 million pounds in 1996 and a profit of 4.9 million pounds in 1995. Even though the total retail sales were 1% higher in 1997 than in 1996, comparable store sales showed a 4% decline.[42] (For the company's sales and profit by region, see Exhibit 4.)

EXHIBIT 4

BST Sales and Operating Profit for 1997

Region	Sales (in millions of British pounds)	Operating Profit (in millions of British pounds)
UK	106.1	13.6
USA	73.1	(3.0)
Europe	39.3	8.1
Asia	35.7	14.7
Americas (excluding USA)	9.9	3.1
Australia and New Zealand	6.7	2.0

Source: The Body Shop International, *1998 Annual Report,* p. 34.

The pressure on the company to place the bottom line ahead of its environmental concerns began to mount. It came not only from shareholders and franchisees who wanted to maximize their earnings but also from some employees and managers who were willing to sacrifice some of the company's ideals for the job security that profitability would allow.

The decline in profit was caused by higher overheads and an increase in the cost of promotion. Also contributing to the company's financial woes was the emergence of copycat retailers who stole some of the company's market share with aggressive discounting. Additionally, many customers were turned off by the company's politically correct message. "You can't be a flower child your whole life," said Allan Mottus, publisher of a cosmetics-

trade publication. "They have been relying on that friendly green message that worked well in Europe, but that wasn't enough in the States,"[43] he added. Reflecting on the company's poor performance in the United States, Gordon Roddick, the company's chairman, said, "The USA continues to pose our greatest challenge. The USA is one of the toughest marketplaces in the world."[44] (For the balance sheet and cash-flow statements, see appendixes A and B.)

The company's troubles in the U.S. market highlighted top management's lack of retail and marketing know-how. Although the company essentially pioneered the specialty bath-products concept, it faced agile competitors and high real-estate costs, something it was not accustomed to in the United Kingdom. In one Pennsylvania mall alone, the BST had eight direct competitors.[45]

APPENDIX A

BST Balance Sheet
(for the 52 weeks ended February 28, 1998)

	1998 (in millions of British pounds)	1997 (in millions of British pounds)
Fixed assets		
Tangible assets	50.7	52.7
Investments	50.5	15.8
	101.2	68.5
Current assets		
Stocks	28.5	21.2
Debtors	59.5	65.6
Cash at bank and in hand	21.3	39.0
	109.3	125.8
Creditors: amounts falling due within one year	59.3	44.9
Net current assets	50.0	80.9
Total assets less current liabilities	151.2	149.4
Creditors: amounts falling due after more than one year	—	0.1
Deferred tax	1.9	0.6
	149.3	148.7
Capital and reserves		
Called up share capital	9.7	9.7
Share premium account	42.8	42.1
Profit and loss account	96.8	96.9
Shareholders funds	149.3	148.7

Source: The Body Shop International, *1998 Annual Report,* p. 39.

APPENDIX B

BST Consolidated Cash Flow Statements
(for the 52 weeks ended February 28, 1998)

	1998 (in millions of British pounds)		1997 (in millions of British pounds)	
Net cash inflow from operating activities		41.5		51.7
Returns on investments and servicing of finance				
Interest received	1.5		1.7	
Interest paid	(1.6)	(0.1)	(1.7)	—
Taxation				
UK corporate tax	(16.3)		(14.7)	
Overseas corporate tax	(0.3)	(16.6)	(0.5)	(15.2)
Capital expenditure and financial investment				
Purchase of tangible fixed assets	(11.6)		(8.8)	
Purchase of EST shares	(1.5)		—	
Sale of tangible fixed assets	0.1	(13.0)	0.2	(8.6)
Acquisitions and disposals				
Cash consideration	(18.3)		(1.9)	
Cash and cash equivalents acquired	(0.7)		0.3	
Cash received on disposal	0.3	(18.7)	—	(1.6)
Equity dividends paid		(9.7)		(7.3)
Cash flow (outflow) before use of liquid resources and financing		(16.6)		19.0
Management of liquid resources				
Short-term deposits		5.3		(15.0)
Financing				
Issue of ordinary share capital	0.7		5.1	
Syndicated loan	18.3			
Loan repayments	(20.3)	(1.3)	(6.8)	(1.7)
Increase (decrease) in cash		(12.6)		2.3

Source: The Body Shop International, *1998 Annual Report,* p. 41

Economy

In 1997, the U.S. economy entered its seventh year of solid expansion, and the outlook remained optimistic. From 1997 through 2002, the economy would continue to grow, although at a more modest pace than in the past years.[46] Job growth would continue to be strong; and unemployment, inflation, and interest rates would continue to be relatively low. Until the year 2006, personal consumption expenditures were projected to increase by 2.1%, compared with 2.3% for 1986 to 1997. Personal income would increase by 4.8% and disposable income by 4.9%, compared with 5.9% and 5.8% for the previous ten years.[47]

Demographics

The growth rate of the total population was expected to slow down during 1997–2006 to an average annual rate of 0.8%, from 0.1% for the previous ten years.

The U.S. female population was projected to increase from about 137 million in 1997 to about 146 million in 2005 and to about 158 million in 2015.[48]

Ethnic diversity in the United States would become more pronounced. By the year 2001, nearly 30% of the population would be non–Anglo-Saxon. The number of Hispanic Americans was expected to double by 2010 to surpass African Americans as the largest ethnic group.[49] The Pacific Islander and Asian populations would quadruple by then. As a result, sales of ethnic hair-care products were expected to rise about 6% by 1999.

Culture

As baby boomers aged, the market for anti-aging products grew. This group numbered 43.2 million and accounted for the largest share of skin-care sales: almost 23%.

Widespread work stress contributed to the popularity of bath products. Customers, eager to soothe frazzled nerves and pamper themselves, began snapping up bath accessories ranging from shower puffs and bath salts to body scrubs and rubber duckies. The desire by baby boomers to spend more time at home and find more ways to relax would help feed the body-and-bath-products market. At the same time, new home designs that transformed bathrooms from closets into lounges promoted more leisure time in the bath. The bathing-as-leisure trend was expected to help the industry generate more sales in the foreseeable future.

Technology

Online sales of products of all types hit 1 billion in 1994 and 2.3 billion in 1995. Retail sales of products purchased on the Internet was expected to surpass 92 billion as the number of subscribers to the World Wide Web would reach 300 million by 2000. Beauty products accounted for an estimated 2% of all online sales but were predicted to reach 8% in five years.[50]

Conclusion

In the past, the BST stood alone in the U.S. natural-care-products market. However, as savvy competitors began to invade its turf and steal its market, key ques-

tions were raised about the company. For example, was the management style of the visionary and entrepreneurial Anita Roddick unsuitable for a large, publicly owned company? Why did the company stumble in the U.S. market? Should Anita be removed from her position and replaced with a professional manager? And how can the company regain its former competitive position?

ENDNOTES

1. Charles P. Wallace, "Can the Body Shop Shape Up?" *Fortune*, April 15, 1996, pp. 119–120.
2. Bo Burlingham, "This Woman Has Changed Business Forever," *Inc.*, June 1990, p. 46.
3. *Ibid.*
4. *Ibid.*, p. 34.
5. Adrienne Sanders, "Success Secrets of the Successful," *Forbes*, vol. 62, no. 10, November 2, 1998, pp. 22–24.
6. Tara Parket-Pope, "Body Shop Prepares U.S. Image Makeover," *Wall Street Journal*, November 12, 1996, p. B5.
7. "Anita Roddick," *Management Today*, March 1996, p. 45.
8. Burlingham, *op. cit.*, p. 34.
9. *Ibid.*
10. *Management Today, op. cit.*
11. Burlingham, *op. cit.*, p. 46.
12. The Body Shop International, *Our Agenda*. Undated company document.
13. *Ibid.*
14. Wallace, *op. cit.*
15. Jennifer Conlin, "Survival of the Fittest: Anita Roddick, Founder of the Body Shop," *Working Women*, vol. 19, no. 2, p. 28.
16. Wallace, *op. cit.*
17. Carolyn J. Poppe, "The New Look of Cosmetics Packaging," *Soap Cosmetics and Cosmetics Specialties*, vol. 72, no. 6, June 1996, p. 26.
18. Donald A. Davis, "Glut Indeed," *Drug and Cosmetic Industry*, vol. 159, no. 5, November 1996, p. 22. Also, see "Shoppers Just Want to Be Entertained," *Household and Personal Products Industry*, vol. 34, no. 11, November 1997, p. 12.
19. Intibrands, Inc., *1995 Annual Report*, p. 10.
20. Lori Bengiorno, "The McDonald's of the Toiletries," *Business Week*, August 4, 1997, pp. 79–80.
21. Wallace, *op. cit.*, p. 119.
22. "A Who's Who of Cosmetics—1997 . . . ," *Women's Wear Daily: Holiday Supplement*, vol. 34, September 1997.
23. "Aveda: Creating a Healthy Business," *Drug and Cosmetic Industry*, vol. 161, no. 2, August 1997, pp. 16–20.
24. Lauri Freeman, "Personal Care Products Fill Specialty Niche," *Stores*, vol. 73, no. 5, May 1991.
25. Cara Kagan, "H2O Dives into Relaunch Plans," *Women's Wear Daily*, vol. 171, no. 33, February 16, 1996, p. 6.
26. "Crabtree and Evelyn Sold," *European and Cosmetic Markets*, vol. 13, no. 8, August 1996, p. 277.
27. "Drugstores Turn Tide in Battle of the Bath," *Women's Wear Daily*, June 1997, p. 4.
28. Parker-Pope, *op. cit.*
29. U.S. Bureau of the Census, *Current Population Reports*, 1996, p. 17.
30. Burlingham, *op. cit.*, p. 36.
31. Earnest Beck, "Body Shop Founder Roddick Steps Aside As CEO," *Wall Street Journal*, May 13, 1998, p. B8.
32. Burlingham, *op. cit.*, pp. 40–41.

33. Connie Wallace, "Lessons in Marketing—from a Maverick, Anita Roddick," *Working Woman*, vol. 15, no. 10, October 1990, p. 81.

34. *Ibid.*

35. Burlingham, *op. cit.*, p. 37.

36. Conlin, *op. cit.*

37. Wallace, *op. cit.*

38. Eric Hollreiser, "The Body Shop Founder Seeks Site for Her Biz School with Heart," *Philadelphia Business Journal,* September 29, 1995, vol. 14, no. 31, p. 7.

39. Jennifer Conlin, *op. cit.*

40. *Ibid.*

41. Charles P. Wallace, *op. cit.*

42. The Body Shop International, *1997 Annual Report,* p. 33.

43. Parket-Pope, *op. cit.*

44. The Body Shop International, *1996 Annual Report,* p. 1.

45. Parke-Pope, *op. cit.*

46. Ray M. Perryman, "The Short-Term U.S. Outlook," *Journal of Business Forecasting and Methods,* vol. 6, no. 4, winter 1997, pp. 38–40.

47. Thomas Boustead, "The U.S. Economy to 2006," *Monthly Labor Review,* November 1997, pp. 6–22.

48. U.S. Bureau of the Census, *op. cit.*

49. "Demographic changes alter equation for chains," *Chain Drug Review,* vol. 18, no. 8, April 8, 1996, p. 35.

50. "Beware of the Web," *Non-Foods Merchandising,* vol. 38, no. 2, February 1996, p. 33.

14 J. P. Morgan Chase & Co.: The Credit Card Segment of the Financial Services Industry

This case was prepared by Steven Preziosi, Damon Swaner, and Marc E. Gartenfeld, all of St. John's University, and Dorothy G. Dologite, Baruch College, under the direction of Dr. Robert J. Mockler, St. John's University.

In January 2001, Chase Cardmember Services (CCS) executive Richard Srednicki was faced with the task of turning around the industry's fifth-largest credit card issuer. CCS's success over the next two years would determine its fate. While the U.S. credit card market had been saturated for several years, other firms had still managed to grow by introducing new products or finding profitable niches. CCS had done neither. Because the recent J. P. Morgan–Chase Manhattan merger involved pooling of interests, the newly created financial services giant was unable to sell off its credit card business for two years. This gave CCS twenty-four months to develop, implement, and begin to reap the benefits of a new long-term, enterprisewide, winning strategy.

All of the players in this industry faced the same problem: how to acquire and retain profitable customers. This made for a competitive, mostly zero-sum game. As a result, there had been rapid consolidation in the industry, with the largest firms controlling an increasing percentage of the total market.

CCS was in a unique position in the market. It had grown into a large player primarily as the result of combining other portfolios in several large bank mergers during the 1990s. Now it needed to find a way to grow internally. A new management team installed in early 2000 had reenergized the business and had worked diligently to build momentum and focus the employees on growth and profitability. However, the desired result of changing CCS into a long-term winner in the market was still far off.

In order to determine how it would position itself in the industry and convince customers that CCS could service them better than the other card issuers in the market, CCS management had to resolve a number of strategic questions. A strong customer service focus was an absolute necessity to retain customer loyalty. A focus on new products, underserved segments, new technologies, and value-added services was also required. Finally, a strong financial discipline and high return on investment were needed to continue to secure capital from its parent company. These and other strategic questions needed to be answered if CCS was to differentiate itself and so win against the competition in the near, intermediate, and long-term time frames.

Industry and Competitive Market

The Financial Services Industry

The financial services industry consists of investment banks, insurance companies, broker/dealers, asset managers, venture capital firms, and commercial banks, as shown in Figure 1. Investment banks provide services that include underwriting of public and private offerings, research, trading of advisory services for mergers and acquisitions, and financial engineering. Insurance companies provide a means of decreasing one's exposure to risk through policies that pay on the occurrence of some event. Broker/dealers perform two different functions: acting as agents bringing buyers and sellers of securities together and also acting as market makers standing ready to buy and sell securities by presenting a bid-ask spread at all times. Asset managers provide pension and mutual fund management services. Venture capital firms provide funding to start-up companies and firms looking to expand. Commercial banks include the traditional branch banking functions of deposit taking and lending. This sector also includes mortgage banking, small business and middle market banking activities, and credit card issuance.

Investment Banks   One of the many important roles of the investment bank is to assist companies in raising capital through its function as underwriter. Investment banks buy securities from a company and then sell them in secondary markets. Types of under-writing activities include initial public offerings; sale of bonds, commercial paper, and private debt; and equity offerings. Investment banks also play an important role in the creation of value for companies through mergers and acquisitions. In this capacity investment banks bring companies together with the end result of either combining the firms or facilitating the exchange of assets. Finally, one of the most important functions of the investment bank is to provide research and assessments of individual companies and sectors as a basis for its own investment or for sale to other investors.

Insurance Companies   Insurance companies provide a means of dealing with risk. They will pay out an agreed-upon sum contingent upon the occurrence of some event. Typical insurance policies include life insurance, auto insurance, medical insurance, and various types of disaster insurance. The insurance company is compensated for absorbing this risk by a premium that is paid periodically, usually monthly, by the insured.

Broker/Dealers   The broker/dealers, although usually the same firm, provide two different types of services. As a broker, the firm acts as an agent bringing buyers and sellers of securities together and executing transactions on their behalf in the over-the-counter markets and at the exchanges. Brokers are not participants in the transaction and do not take on any risk but rather are compensated exclusively

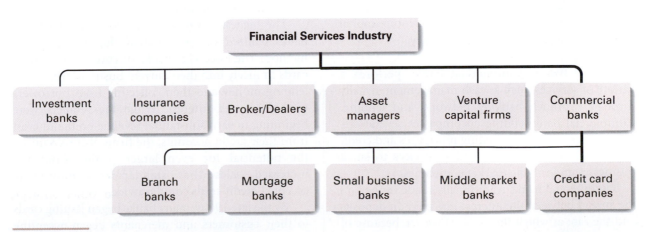

FIGURE 1

Structure of the Financial Services Industry

through commissions. As a dealer, the firm is party to the transactions in which it participates. Dealers must stand ready to buy and sell at any time and must provide a bid price, which is what the dealer is willing to pay for a certain security, and an ask price, which is the price at which the dealer is willing to sell. Dealers are compensated by the spread between the price paid for the security and the price at which it is sold.

Asset Managers   Asset managers include various large investors like pension funds, mutual funds, hedge funds, and 401(k)'s. All of these types of funds fall under the rubric of institutional investors. Institutional investors increasingly play a larger role in the secondary market by allowing small investors to diversify their portfolios into investments that they would not normally be able to afford. By pooling the assets of many investors, large funds are able to participate in IPOs, commercial paper markets, and bond markets, all of which are normally beyond the reach of the smaller investor.

Venture Capital Firms   Venture capital firms provide funding to start-up companies, expanding companies, and companies that are restructuring. Generally venture capitalists take on great risk in their investments. However, the venture capitalists ask much in return for their investment. They may take a large share in ownership of the company along with a seat on the board of directors. Investments are made by venture capital firms with one of three types of exit strategies in mind: taking the company public, selling to a larger company, or filing for bankruptcy. Although a large number of all investments fail, the remaining investments generally yield venture capital firms a very high return on their money.

Commercial Banks   Commercial banks perform a variety of services, such as cash management, usually through a branch banking network, and lending. Commercial bank lending encompasses several different types of credit, including mortgages and credit cards, and also provides banking services to small businesses and middle market companies.

Commercial banks traditionally made money on the spread between the interest rate paid on deposits and the rate at which they lent. However, because of the competitive pressures brought on by globalization and the Financial Services Modernization Act of

1999, the face of banking in the United States has dramatically changed. Under the old law (Glass-Steagall) the businesses of investment banking, commercial banking, and insurance were either not allowed to mix with each other or only allowed to mix in a very limited way. The passage of the Financial Services Modernization Act allowed these three businesses to operate under a new type of holding company and paved the way for much of the consolidation that was occurring in the financial services industry. In addition, the financial services industry, especially commercial banking, had been forced to change because of the arrival of the Internet. Every aspect of commercial banking operations had been modified in some way in order to accommodate Internet use.

This study focuses on the credit card segment of the commercial banking sector of the financial services industry.

The Credit Card Segment

History and Trends   The credit card industry in the United States can trace its roots to just prior World War I. In 1914, Western Union began to provide a deferred-payment service to its most credit-worthy customers. Over the next several decades, department stores and other retailers began to provide revolving credit accounts to many of their customers as well. In the 1950s, the popularity of revolving credit accounts grew and the retailers began using imprinted cards to help streamline the transaction process and identify customers. As customers made purchases using their cards, the charges were posted directly to the cardholders' accounts at the store, with bills being sent out monthly.

The biggest advances began to occur when the banks realized the potential of this new payment method. The large U.S. banks discovered that credit cards fit nicely into their current business, which was lending money and then collecting from borrowers over time with interest. While the retailers were beginning to earn substantial revenue on the interest from their credit accounts, the firms also recognized the potential for even larger profits from the increased sales that standardized, universally accepted credit cards could provide.

By the late 1960s, many banks began issuing cards to their customers and merchants began accepting them as payment. These early cards required payment in full within a short period of time, usually less than ninety days. However, banks quickly recognized the revenue potential of simply extending the repayment time while continuing to charge interest. Soon thereafter, banks, led by Bank of America, created associations to act as clearinghouses for credit card transactions. Some of these associations included BankAmericard, BankMark, and MasterCharge and were the forerunners of the current two associations, Visa and MasterCard.

Also in the late 1960s, another use for credit cards began to develop, the Travel and Entertainment (T&E) market. Cards issued by American Express, Diner's Club, and Carte Blanche, called charge cards as opposed to credit cards, became popular with traveling businesspeople. The difference between charge cards and the bank-issued credit cards was that charge cards did not involve the charging of interest, which was the banks' primary motivation for entering the industry. They were paid in full by the cardholder at the end of each billing cycle, which was usually one month. These firms derived revenue from charging the customers higher annual fees and the merchants higher transaction fees for accepting the cards.

By the late 1970s, card usage was commonplace. The bank-issued cards, T&E cards, and the original retailer-issued cards were all flourishing. Technological advances had helped ensure accuracy in the process, and most large merchants were accepting the cards.

In the 1980s Sears, the largest retailer issuer of cards, introduced its DiscoverCard, which included a unique value proposition, an annual rebate on the cardholder's total card purchases. Competition among credit card issuers began to accelerate rapidly. Citibank led the way with the development of the AAdvantage card, which offered American Airlines frequent flyer miles with each purchase. The use of direct mail campaigns increased dramatically as banks searched to expand their customer base beyond the reach of their traditional branch-banking network. During the 1980s the volume of outstanding credit card debt grew from $71 billion in 1980 to $242 billion by 1990 (Nilson Report, 2000).

The increase in credit card usage was even more dramatic in the 1990s, driven by a strong economy, aggressive marketing by credit card issuers, and changes in consumer spending preferences. Outstanding credit card debt grew to $675 billion by the end of the decade (Nilson Report, 2000).

By 2000, the industry had begun to consolidate. The smaller banks did not have the scale to compete with the few remaining large issuers. Competition in the market for credit-worthy customers had grown fierce, forcing banks to look for new niches. MBNA established a niche in an area ignored by large banks, affinity marketing. It focused on partnering with as many local partners as possible, including universities, organizations, and athletic teams. This allowed it to capitalize on the brand loyalty that customers had, not to MBNA, but to its affinity partners. Cap One found a niche with the lower-credit-quality customers offering higher-priced, or secured, lines of credit. Competition also began to come with substitute products, most notably debit cards, which provided the same payment features as credit cards but drew funds from the cardholder's deposit or checking account, as opposed to drawing upon a line of credit (History of the Credit Card, 2001; Credit Card History, 2001).

The growth in credit card usage was expected to continue. Established as the dominant payment method for Internet commerce, credit card usage would grow as web purchasing grew (Lowe, 2001). Also, as consumers' reliance on using cash for purchases continued to decrease, credit cards had additional opportunity for growth. The trend toward consolidation in the industry was likely to continue, as was the impact of technological advancement on credit cards. The credit card segment of the financial services industry is broken down further in Figure 2.

Functions of the Credit Card Segment   The credit card segment served two major functions for its customers (called cardholders). First, it was a payment mechanism that provided a means for cardholders to complete transactions for goods and services. Second, it was a debt access mechanism, allowing cardholders to borrow the funds used in competing transactions.

Payment Mechanism.   The credit card issuers provided cardholders with a means of paying for goods and services. The advantage over other forms of payments (cash, personal checks) was that customers could make purchases without having to physically interact with a merchant (i.e., telephone, Internet). Credit cards also allowed cardholders to keep track of all of their purchases with one monthly statement. In this arena, credit cards faced major competition from debit cards, which allowed cardholders the purchasing

FIGURE 2

Structure of the Credit Card Segment of the Commercial Banking Sector

advantages provided by credit cards but linked the payments to the cardholders' deposit accounts.

Trends in the technology area, such as greater Internet use and the change in lifestyle and buying habits that it had created, increased the average American's credit card use during the 1990s (Lowe, 2001). This created a great opportunity for payment method providers to increase market share. One major key to success in the payment mechanism role was to become the customer's first choice of payment mechanism by maintaining universal acceptance of cards and by using aggressive sales and advertising. Other keys to success were increasing card usage with value-added services like purchase protection or rebates, developing cardholder loyalty by deepening relationships through affinity or cross-selling other products, and developing aggressive advertising campaigns to attract new customers. Also important was leveraging the issuer's other business lines, particularly commercial bank segments, as a means of acquiring new customers.

Debt Access Mechanism.   In this role, cards allowed customers to pay for items with borrowed funds. This allowed cardholders to detach their purchasing from their income. With over $600 billion in credit card debt outstanding, credit card purchasing helped drive the U.S. economy. This volume of debt outstanding tripled during the 1990s and was eleven times the 1980 level by the end of the decade (Carney, 2000). The unique advantage of credit cards was the combination of these two functions: allowing cardholders to make all of their purchases when needed and to make payments when available (provided they make their nominal monthly minimum payments).

Credit card issuers earned revenue primarily from interest charged on debt outstanding. Customers that maintain outstanding debt on their credit card are called "revolvers," short for revolving credit users. Customers that use their credit cards primarily for transactions and do not maintain a debt balance are called "transactors." Transactors were much less profitable and were becoming a larger percentage of cardholders. In 1992, 29 percent of all cardholders were transactors; by 1998 the share was 42 percent (Mannix, 1998). This trend was forcing issuers to look for ways to increase customer profitability. One way to increase revenue from transactors was to charge an annual fee. However, given the multitude of choices available, annual fees were unattractive to customers unless they were associated with a value-added service for which customers were willing to pay (such as Citibank's AAdvantage card).

Opportunities had been created for making credits cards a debt access mechanism by increasing credit card usage as a payment mechanism. For example, in 1990 credit cards accounted for only 10.3 percent of total consumer payments, a number that is expected to increase to 23 percent by 2003. Credit card dollar volume is also expected to exceed $2.0 trillion by 2003 (Anonymous, 1998). The keys to success in this area were to attract and maintain debt by offering competitive rates to develop cardholder loyalty through affinity or depth of relationship and to limit loan losses through strong credit and collections policies.

Customers   The credit card industry can be broken down into the three main types of customers served: individuals, businesses, and corporations.

Individuals.   In the individual consumer market, the largest of the three, credit cards allowed cardholders to manage their finances. This market was fiercely competitive, with constant advertising and direct mail campaigns needed to sustain market share. Cardholders with outstanding debt could transfer balances to lower-interest-rate cards with increasing ease. Value-added services, including loyalty programs, rebates, and rewards, were required for customer retention because they increased cardholder attachment to the card and lessened the likelihood that they would switch to a competing card.

Customers were segmented by credit-worthiness. Customers that were considered credit-worthy were called the "prime" market. Issuers usually determined a customer's credit-worthiness by reviewing their credit bureau report, which contained a credit bureau score (FICO score). The higher the score, the more credit-worthy the customer. Customers that had derogatory credit bureau marks, usually caused by missed payments or loan defaults, were considered the "low prime" market. Customers that were the worst credit quality, including customers that had previously filed bankruptcy, were considered "subprime." The low and subprime markets had historically been underserved compared to the prime market in the United States.

The prime customer market had been the most competitive: the average U.S. household already had 2.4 credit cards by the end of 2000 (Coleman, 2001). All issuers were competing to be the card of choice for these customers since they were the most likely to have the means to pay back the borrowed funds. Loan losses were a concern in the credit card industry, and failure to control their level would have a large impact on an issuer's profitability. Opportunities in this area stemmed from trends in increased usage of credit cards (Anonymous, 1998). Additionally, opportunities had been created by the increase in the number of people shopping on the Internet. It was estimated that 17 million U.S. households would be shopping online by the end of 2001 and that 49 million households would be spending as much as $184 billion online by 2004 (Forrester Research, 2001). The keys to success in the prime market were increasing customer card usage by offering value-added services like purchase protection or frequent flyer programs, and attracting new customers through aggressive advertising. Also important was developing cardholder loyalty through affinity or depth of relationship, which made it less likely that cardholders would switch to a new card.

The low and subprime markets had been less saturated than the prime markets, but by 2001 they were becoming increasingly more competitive as issuers sought out new customers (Coleman, 2001). The trends that affected the prime market, including increased card usage and Internet purchasing, also affected this market. However, previously issuers were hesitant to enter this market for fear of high loan loss rates. Opportunities in this area, however, did exist because issuers like Cap One and Providian proved that credit cards to this segment could be issued profitably. Despite higher loan losses, these customers were more likely to revolve than prime customers and were thus incurring higher finance charges. The keys to success in this market were limiting loan losses by maintaining strong credit policies, attracting new customers through aggressive advertising, limiting losses by maintaining a strong collections department, and increasing profitability by selling charged-off accounts.

The loan loss rate, also called the charge-off rate, is shown for various credit card issuers in Table 1. Issuers charge off accounts after they reach 180 days past due. The charge-off rate is calculated by dividing total charge-offs by total average receivables. Companies

TABLE 1

Loan Loss Rates, 1999

Cap One	3.85%
MBNA	4.33
Citigroup	4.56
Amex	5.00
Bank One	5.23
Discover	5.42
Bank of America	5.57
J. P. Morgan Chase	5.66
Household	6.65
Fleet	6.78

Source: CardFlash Company Website (2001) [Online]. **http://www.cardflash.com.** Accessed April 24.

that continually add new accounts, like Cap One and MBNA, tend to have lower charge-off rates. Firms with more mature portfolios and fewer new accounts have higher loss rates. Acquiring new accounts especially in the prime market was the focus for most issuers.

Businesses. Credit cards served both functions, payments and debt access, for small businesses or merchants and organizations. This market was less competitive and smaller than the individual consumer market. Account acquisitions in this market were more heavily dependent upon the businesses' banking relationship with the parent company. Thus firms with a strong commercial bank presence had an advantage. Opportunities in this area stemmed from trends in the Internet's growth as a purchasing tool for consumers and a marketing tool for businesses. For example, 44 percent of U.S. companies were selling online in 2000 and 36 percent more said they would do so by the end of 2001 (Nua Internet Surveys, 2001). Additionally, small businesses that used the Internet had grown 46 percent faster than those that did not (Nua Internet Surveys, 2001). In terms of dollars and cents, Internet advertising generated $1.92 billion in 1998, which was double the 1997 figure, and small and home offices spent over $51 billion on high-tech goods in 1998 (Nua Internet Surveys, 2001).

The keys to success in the business market were maintaining customer loyalty by offering programs and promotions that rewarded businesses for using the card, such as rebates on purchases, and leveraging banking relationships that businesses had with the issuer's parent company to attract new business cardholders. Also important were attracting and maintaining debt by offering competitive rates and creating convenience for businesses through flexible payment arrangements.

Corporations. In the corporate card market, the focus was solely on the payment function of credit cards. Employees of major corporations carried credit cards for travel and entertainment purchases. At the end of each month, the employee submitted the expenses and the corporation paid the credit card bill. American Express had historically been the dominant player in this market. This market was less reliant on direct mail, the traditional form of account acquisition in the credit card segment, and instead relied on a sales force that sought out new corporate clients.

Opportunities in this market stemmed from the development of Internet technologies that allowed networking. One key to success was creating convenience for corporate cardholders through the creation of Intranet-type platforms that allowed online billing, reconciliation, and approval of charges within the corporate structure. Other keys to success were to leverage the parent company's investment bank by using relationships other firms had with the parent as a basis for winning these companies' corporate card business, and to maintain an aggressive sales force that would also seek out new corporate customers.

Products The major products of the credit card segment were Visa- and MasterCard-associated credit cards. However, these cards could also be cobranded cards, affinity cards, agent bank cards, or secured cards, among other types.

Visa and MasterCard controlled over 77 percent of the credit card market (*Star Ledger,* 2000). Most bank card issuers and monolines issued both Visa- and MasterCard-associated cards. Visa and MasterCard were associations on whose networks most credit card transactions were cleared. American Express and Discover each had their own networks and did not issue Visa- or MasterCard-associated cards. Members of the Visa and MasterCard associations were prohibited from issuing American Express or Discover cards but were allowed to issue both MasterCard and Visa cards.

A recent trend in the industry had been issuers choosing either Visa or MasterCard as a primary partner. Citibank and Chase had both chosen MasterCard, while NationsBank and Providian had chosen Visa. In doing so, the issuers were working out more favorable fee arrangements with their primary association. Issuers associated with either Visa or MasterCard in order to geographically extend the areas of acceptance of the issuing bank's cards. The key to success in this area was to create convenience for the cardholder by using the association with Visa or MasterCard to create wider acceptance of the issuing bank's card.

Cobranded Cards.   Cards partnered with large corporations also became an important part of the credit card industry. Partners included airlines, hotel chains, long-distance telephone companies, retailers, and gasoline companies. These cards generally offered cardholders some type of rebate or reward each time the card was used. For example, the Shell Oil card from J. P. Morgan Chase offered cardholders a 1 percent rebate for every dollar charged to the card, plus a 5 percent rebate on any Shell gasoline charged to the card. These rebates could then be used to offset future Shell gasoline purchases. However, the rewards paid to customers reduced the profitability of the relationship for card issuers. As a result, cobranded cards needed to strike a balance between offering attractive rewards to entice customers and remaining profitable. Cards with particularly rich rewards or with high levels of transactors, such as airline cobranded cards, generally charged annual fees.

Opportunities in this area stemmed from the issuers' ability to leverage cardholders' brand loyalty to the co-brand partner and to provide customers with value while remaining profitable. The keys to success were creating brand loyalty by offering discounts and promotions on products and services, increasing card usage by sending cardholders targeted offers or coupons for use with the co-brand partner, and creating value for co-brand partners by giving cardholders rebates when purchasing from the partner, thus increasing the likelihood that these customers would choose to purchase from the partner rather than the partner's competitors. Also important were partnering with large well-known national brands to gain market share and attract new customers, and attracting profitable customers through lucrative rewards programs that added significant

value to such a degree that customers would pay an annual fee for the card.

Affinity Cards.   These were also cards that were partnered with a company or organization, but the nature of the relationship was different than with cobranded cards. Affinity cards did not offer cardholders rewards. Instead, they were marketed to potential customers that were or wanted to be identified as being affiliated with the card's partner. Most universities, athletic teams, and professional organizations were currently in affinity partner relationships with card issuers. Since the target market for any affinity card was generally smaller than with cobranded cards, issuers needed to have numerous affinity partners to be successful in this market. Lasting brand loyalty could be created in this market by partnering with various organizations that cardholders were closely associated with.

One of the leading affinity card marketers was MBNA. MBNA had created affinity cards with various causes, such as the United Negro College Fund, developed affinity cards for over five hundred colleges and universities, and developed affinity cards with military and law enforcement agencies such as the U.S. Marine Corps and the National Association of Chiefs of Police. These kinds of affinity partnerships created greater loyalty among cardholders. MBNA lost only 2 percent of its profitable customers annually as compared to the industry average of 15 percent (Wherry, 2000).

A major key to success in this arena was having flexible systems and processes that allowed the issuer to manage thousands of affinity partners. Also important were maintaining an effective sales force that actively sought out new partners and a strong marketing team that was able to identify new segments.

Agent Bank Cards.   The trend in the financial services industry toward consolidation also affected the credit card segment. Many smaller credit card issuers were finding that they did not have the scale to manage a credit card portfolio profitably and were exiting the business. However, the small and mid-sized banks still wanted to be able to issue credit cards to their customers. In an agent banking relationship, a bank was able to provide its customers with a credit card without having to manage a credit card portfolio. An example of an agent banking transaction would be

MBNA's purchase of the credit card portfolio of First Tennessee Bank (Overdorf, 2000).

In an agent bank relationship, the smaller bank's customers were issued a card in the name of their bank, but the cards were owned and serviced by a larger card issuer. The advantage for the smaller company was that it could continue to meet the needs of its clientele. The advantage for the issuing company was the additional loans. The relationship was similar to that of a cobranded or affinity card, but in this case the partner was another financial institution. Since customers tended to be loyal to the bank where they had their accounts, the issuing firm was able to obtain loans from a population to which it would otherwise not have had access. Also, customers were less likely to default on loans to banks in which they had their other accounts. Thus agent banking cards generally had lower loan loss rates.

As the segment continued to consolidate, more portfolios were likely to come up for sale. For the issuers that had the capital to compete for these acquisitions and the ability to integrate new portfolios into their current business, this trend provided a substantial opportunity. Another key to success was to develop effective partnerships with the agent bank partners to ensure that the banks continued to solicit new customers for the agent bank card. Also, it was important to maintain an experienced agent bank team to service the portfolio and manage the relationship with the agent bank.

Since 78 percent of the $675 billion in outstanding credit card debt was controlled by the top ten issuers, the remaining 22 percent represented a lucrative cache of potential loyal customers (Nilson Report, 2000). This 22 percent, or approximately $150 billion, was more than double the portfolio of any one issuer other than Citibank at the end of 2000 (Cardflash, 2001).

Secured Cards.   Secured cards were offered to customers with poor credit quality. They required customers to keep cash on deposit with the card issuer. In return customers were given a card with a credit limit equal to the amount of their deposit. This allowed customers to whom issuers were not willing to grant credit to take advantage of the payment function of credit cards. Cap One successfully entered this market. As cardholders demonstrated their ability to use credit, Cap One would then convert them to a regular credit card. The key to success

with secured cards was to aggressively advertise to targeted customers or regions with lower credit quality in order to attract new cardholders.

Customer Services   Important to success in the credit card segment was maintaining customer loyalty. With all the brands of credit cards as well as other payment methods available, the one thing that a credit card issuer could do to distinguish itself from the competition was to provide greater convenience and value for its customers. The opportunities to create convenience and value stemmed from several different factors. Innovations in payment methods and the demand for a greater variety of payment methods had forced many payment method providers to create new ways to pay for goods and services. Additionally, technological advances, such as the Internet, had created new methods of buying goods and services and created demand for new and more secure ways to pay for those goods and services.

Creating Convenience.   Letting customers choose the way they wished to pay was an important part of creating convenience for customers and ultimately led to the kind of brand loyalty that was desired. One way to provide convenience and choice was to make a number of different payment systems available to the customer. Examples included credit cards; debit cards, which allowed customers to make payments that were directly withdrawn from the checking account; and stored value cards, which allowed customers to place a fixed amount of money on the card to make purchases. The stored value cards protected the customer in case the card was lost or stolen, since only the amount of money that had been placed electronically on the card would be lost. Another payment method, which was a product of the Internet age, was the smart card. The smart card contained an electronic chip that held a great deal of customer information and allowed for greater protection for purchases made over the Internet. Creating cards that combined the functionality of any or all of these types of cards presented a potential opportunity for issuers.

Creating Value.   Value for customers came in many forms: services or reward programs such as frequent flyer programs for individual customers, or ease of settlement and usage for business and corporate customers. For all customers a key to success was the development and creation of value-intensifying services in conjunction with payment methods. Examples were adding services to each type of card like extending warranties for goods bought with the card, offering cash back or insurance for goods bought with the card, and cobranding cards with retailers, restaurants, or airlines so that cardholders could get discounts or rebates from those partners.

Offering electronic bill payments created value to both corporate and individual customers. The bills were sent to individuals online and paid for online. This reduced the time and cost of bill collecting for many corporate customers while providing a convenient way to pay bills for individual customers. Additionally, electronic bill payments increased traffic on the payment method provider's web site, and from there a whole array of value-creating services could be provided. For example, purchasing platforms, which are electronic exchanges that connect buyers and sellers, could be linked to the payment provider's web site. These purchasing platforms would be commercial hubs for both business-to-business (B2B) and business-to-consumer (B2C) types of business. These platforms created value for businesses and convenience for their customers while extending the market share of the payment method.

Technology   Technological advances dramatically affected the credit card segment. The Internet and new payment methods like smart cards provided new opportunities for growth for card issuers.

Internet.   The growth of purchasing on the Internet was exponential, as shown in Figure 3. Credit cards were involved in 90 to 95 percent of Internet sales transactions (Lowe, 2001). Because of the Internet's increasing popularity, businesses of all kinds grew and gained access to new customer bases.

Although there had been tremendous growth in e-commerce and the Internet industry, many people who browsed online were still hesitant to shop online for fear of a security breach when placing personal information over the Internet. New security systems were in development but had not yet reached the majority of online consumers. The credit card had a substantial opportunity in this area.

The keys to success were to partner with highly trafficked web sites to attract potential customers, to create value-added services like online purchase protection or rebates for online purchases, and to main-

FIGURE 3

Growth of Internet Purchasing

Source: Nua Internet Surveys (2001). "The Internet and Businesses," [Online]. **http://www.nua.net/surveys/index**. Accessed March 1.

tain aggressive customer advertising targeted to online shoppers. It was also important to create a secure Internet environment by developing high-security systems for credit card use over the Internet and to create value and convenience for cardholders and merchants through the development of B2C web sites featuring merchants that accepted an issuer's cards and offered discounts to cardholders.

Payment Methods.   The technological advances that had changed banking and the credit card industry had affected payment methods. The creation and increasing popularity of various payment systems had created greater value and convenience for consumers. One innovation in electronic payments was the smart card, which contained a computer chip that activated a digital wallet when one was making purchases online. The chip contained a digital ID number that authenticated the cardholder and then launched the digital form-filling wallet when one was required to fill out forms to make purchases online.

The smart card gained rapid adoption in Europe and Asia, but growth in the United States was slow. In 2000, the total world market for smart cards was approximately $2.6 billion, but only $100 million was in the United States (Robinson, 2001). The U.S. had a well-developed infrastructure to accept magnetic-strip (traditional) credit cards and had been slow to make the investment to convert to smart cards. However, the potential increases in online purchasing suggested that an opportunity for issuers was to develop cards that contained both a magnetic strip and a smart chip like Amex's Blue card. These cards could still be used within the current infrastructure but also offered the Internet purchasing benefits of a smart card.

The keys to success for issuers in this area were to continuously develop technology, maintain strong advertising to make consumers aware of the technology, and maintain an aggressive sales force that would bring new payment systems to consumers and merchants. Also critical was to make the transition from regular credit cards to new payment methods as cost efficient as possible for merchants and to create convenience and choice for cardholders by offering various products, including dual cards.

Regulation   New laws and stricter application of regulations had an effect on the financial services industry, and on commercial banking in particular. In 1999, the Financial Services Modernization Act was passed, ushering in sweeping changes in the banking industry. This legislation, along with the application of antitrust laws and the bankruptcy reform act, had potential effects on the credit card segment.

Industry Modernization.   The Financial Services Modernization Act of 1999 repealed the Glass-Steagall Act, which prohibited cross-sector affiliation between the banking and securities industries. It also repealed the 1956 Bank Holding Company Act, which prohibited unions between the banking and insurance industries. The legislation established a new entity called a financial holding company. For a bank holding company to qualify as a financial holding company, all of its depository institution subsidiaries must be well managed and well capitalized and must have a satisfactory Community Reinvestment Act (CRA) rating. A financial institution seeking to become a multipurpose financial institution could structure itself in two ways. It could become a financial holding company and set up affiliates. This provided the most flexibility and greatest possibility for one-stop shopping. Alternatively, it could create subsidiaries. Although the federal government had issued an interim rule stating that those banks and their subsidiaries were allowed to operate many financial services, insurance underwriting, merchant banking, and real estate development were not allowed.

This legislation spurred a flood of mergers and acquisitions among financial institutions. One of the largest mergers in U.S. history resulted, the Travelers–Citigroup merger. This created a financial powerhouse that had operations in investment banking through its Solomon Smith Barney arm, insurance through Travelers, and commercial banking through Citibank.

Antitrust Laws.   The antitrust laws have also affected the credit card industry. In October of 1998 the Department of Justice (DOJ) brought an antitrust suit against Visa and MasterCard. The allegations were that Visa and MasterCard were not really competitors. The DOJ claimed that the two associations operated under a "duality" whereby member banks were allowed to issue both Visa- and MasterCard-branded plastic. According to the DOJ, this duality meant that these brands were in effect one business and that this one business held a dominant market position. This enabled them to stifle competition from rivals by forbidding banks from issuing rival cards like American Express or Discover.

The DOJ recommended that major card-issuing banks commit their credit and debit cards exclusively to either Visa or MasterCard. The implications of antitrust charges and subsequent recommendations by the DOJ caused a shift in the allegiance of many major banks. Since the lawsuit was initiated, many banks have chosen to focus their business with one brand or the other. For example, Citigroup and Chase chose to predominately use MasterCard, and Bank One and Bank of America chose to predominately use Visa. The result of this shift to either Visa or MasterCard meant another layer of competition between card issuers.

Bankruptcy Reform.   The Bankruptcy Reform Act could also have an impact on the industry. The new law would require all cardholders to meet certain income guidelines and seek out credit counseling before being allowed to file for bankruptcy. This could have long-term positive results for issuers, but it may also result in a short-term dramatic increase in loan losses as cardholders attempt to file before the new law takes effect (Cardflash, 2001). Issuers benefited in 1999 and 2000 from a declining bankruptcy trend, as shown in Table 2, but a dramatic increase, even short-term, would negatively affect issuers' profitability.

TABLE 2

U.S. Bankruptcy Filings

Year	Totals Filings	Business Filings	Consumer Filings
1991	943,987	71,549	872,438
1992	971,517	70,643	900,874
1993	875,202	62,304	812,898
1994	832,829	52,374	780,455
1995	926,601	51,959	874,642
1996	1,178,555	53,549	1,125,006
1997	1,404,145	54,027	1,350,118
1998	1,442,549	44,367	1,398,182
1999	1,319,465	44,367	1,281,581
2000	1,253,444	35,472	1,217,972

Source: ABI World (2001). "Filing Statistics," [Online]. **http://www.abiworld.org/stats/newstatsfront.html**. Accessed April 23.

Globalization   Globalization of the financial services industry has also an impact on the credit card sector. Globalization led to increased worldwide acceptance of credit cards and also led U.S. issuers to begin issuing cards to customers outside the United States.

Usage.   Visa and MasterCard expanded their networks globally, allowing U.S. customers to use their cards around the world. American Express and Discover built proprietary networks to also allow cardholders worldwide usage. Issuers without a proprietary network could take advantage of the Visa and MasterCard networks. This allowed credit cards to act as a universal payment mechanism, with the issuer handling the foreign exchange portion of the transactions. As a result, credit cards brought added convenience for customers traveling abroad.

Issuance.   Some U.S. issuers also built international credit card portfolios. Citibank and American Express were two of the largest U.S. issuers in the global market. American Express operated in the major markets in Europe and Japan, where it had over 1 million cards issued (Harner, 2000). Citibank was able to expand on the basis of its international consumer banking operations and looked to continue to grow in this business. Since international name recognition was required to be a successful international issuer, firms with a worldwide commercial banking presence had the advantage. Also

required was an international operational and legal infrastructure that enabled issuers to lend to customers in other countries. U.S. firms without an international consumer banking presence found it difficult to issue cards in foreign markets partly because of the lack of name recognition but also because of cultural differences (Levinshone, 2000).

Sales and Promotion   The primary account acquisition method used during the 1990s was direct mail. However, a new acquisition channel developed in the Internet, and issuers continued to look for other ways to attract customers.

Direct Mail.   Direct mail acquisitions helped fuel the growth in credit card issuance during the 1990s. By 2001 mailboxes were being stuffed with more credit card solicitations than ever, with the typical U.S. household receiving more than three card offers a month. In 2000, card issuers mailed a record 3.54 billion solicitations, up from 2.87 billion in 1999 (Coleman, 2001).

With this increase in solicitations also came a record-low response rate of 0.6 percent in 2000, compared with 1.0 percent in 1999 (Coleman, 2001). To be successful, issuers needed to develop creative campaigns to attract customers and to use technology to segment and target the base of potential customers. Also, issuers needed to seek out other means of acquiring customers.

Internet. The use of the Internet as an acquisition channel increased dramatically, with many issuers offering online applications and instant approval decisions. Partnering with or advertising on highly trafficked web sites was important to success. Also important was instant decision making, which allowed new cardholders to immediately begin using their new credit card number to make purchases on the Web. However, as this grew, the potential for fraudulent applications also grew.

Other. Other methods of account and customer acquisition included in-branch invitations and cross-selling customers from other businesses within the bank. In-branch invitation acquisitions stemmed from customers applying for credit through a firm's commercial banking branch network. Bank card issuers had an advantage over monolines in this area. Cross-selling also provided an acquisition channel. For firms that operated in other segments besides credit cards, customers of these other products provided acquisition targets. For example, banks that issued mortgages or auto loans could also issue credit cards to these customers.

Operations Credit card issuers needed to manage their operations effectively to remain profitable. One important area was the cost of doing business, including personnel cost. Another important operation was credit, which determined the firms' lending criteria.

Costs. Beyond the costs of acquiring customers, credit card issuers had other costs that needed to be managed effectively. The personnel cost of customer service and collections comprised a considerable portion of the issuer's expenses. The cost of printing and delivering monthly statements to customers was also substantial. The Internet provided an opportunity to reduce this particular cost. As issuers migrated customers to electronic statements, there could be reductions in paper, printing, and postage costs.

Credit. Another important operational area was credit underwriting. This involved determining who should be offered credit and how much they should be offered. Issuers usually developed risk criteria using an individual's credit bureau scores (otherwise called FICO scores). These scores took into account the individual's past credit and payment history.

Cardholders with missed payments or loan defaults would have lower FICO scores. Issuers offering credit to these low or subprime customers usually charged higher rates or fees to compensate for the increased risk of nonpayment.

Competition As a result of credit card industry consolidation, the largest issuers controlled an increasing percentage of the market. At the end of 2000, the top ten issuers controlled 78 percent of the total market (CardFlash, 2001). Competition among the leaders was fierce, and most of the country was saturated with cards and offers from all of the large firms on a regular basis. The growth of the top ten issuers is shown in Table 3.

Low introductory interest rates were common, with issuers content to issue loans for a time below their own cost of funds in hopes that the cardholders would stay long enough to become profitable customers. Value propositions also became increasingly important as issuers vied to become the card of choice, and retaining current cardholders became as important as acquiring new customers.

Bank Card Issuers. Banks historically made up the largest segment of the credit card industry. However, throughout the 1990s, companies whose sole business was credit cards began to take in increased share of the market. These firms, called monolines, used creative advertising and searched out new niches to win customers from the bank card issuers.

Citibank had historically been the largest player in the credit card market. Much of the innovation in the industry (cobranded cards, aggressive direct mail campaigns) began with Citibank. Many of the executives across the credit card industry began their careers with Citibank, including the CCS executive Richard Srednicki. In 1998, Citibank purchased the AT&T Universal Card portfolio, which allowed it to regain the leadership position that was briefly lost to Bank One after the latter's purchase of First USA. In 2000, Citibank purchased the Associates portfolio, signaling to the industry that it would continue to be an aggressive acquirer and would continue to use acquisitions to fuel its growth (McCafferty, 2001).

Citibank's greatest advantages were that it had the worldwide presence that made it attractive to business travelers and vacationers and that it had the scale to operate efficiently. It had credit card operations in forty-eight countries worldwide.

TABLE 3

Top Ten Credit Card Issuers (as of 12/31/00)

Rank/Issuer	4Q/00	4Q/99	Change
1. Citigroup	$87.7b	$72.4b	+21%
2. MBNA America	$70.4b	$58.8b	+20%
3. Bank One/FUSA	$67.0b	$69.4b	−18%
4. Discover	$47.1b	$38.0b	+24%
5. Chase Manhattan	$36.2b	$33.6b	+ 8%
6. American Express	$28.7b	$23.4b	+23%
7. Providian	$26.7b	$18.7b	+43%
8. Bank of America	$24.3b	$20.9b	+16%
9. Capital One	$22.7b	$15.7b	+45%
10. Household	$15.2b	$13.3b	+14%

Source: CardFlash (2001). "U.S. Payment Card Daily—Friday March 16, 2001," [Online]. **http://www.cardweb.com**. Accessed March 16.

Citibank had the top airline co-brand credit card with its partnership with American Airlines. It also had the top telecommunications co-brand from acquisition of the AT&T portfolio. Also, its over 100 million cardholders provided a substantial base from which to cross-sell other products in an attempt to deepen cardholders' relationships with the company and so make it less likely they would switch to another issuer's card (McCafferty, 2001).

Citibank attempted to limit its loan losses by maintaining strong collection departments and policies. It could also effectively integrate acquired portfolios, including agent banking portfolios. However, in 2001 it focused more on acquiring international credit card portfolios, which may have signaled a strategic decision to focus less on domestic portfolio acquisitions. Finally, Citibank had not made an effort to compete in the corporate card business and as a result had not developed the technological platform that would allow it to enter this market in the near term.

Other bank card issuers included most of the U.S. large and mid-sized banks. However, many of these banks did not have the scale to operate a credit card business efficiently, and as a result the trend had been toward exiting this business. Even large banks, like the Bank of New York and First Union, sold off their credit card portfolios.

Bank One became a large credit card issuer with its acquisition of the monoline First USA, which grew dramatically during the 1990s with aggressive direct

mail campaigns and very low introductory rates. It had an extensive co-brand network and an affinity relationship network of over 2,000 partners.

However, despite its size, Bank One ran into considerable financial trouble. In 2000, it was forced to take large write-offs associated with the credit quality of its credit card portfolio and then continued to struggle to remain profitable, with large numbers of customers accruing interest rates below the bank's cost of funds. Bank One had the scale to compete effectively but needed to work on strengthening its profitability, as well as its credit and collections policies.

Other bank card issuers faced similar problems. Because of size limitations, most did not have the international name recognition to compete in the international card issuance market, the capital to compete for portfolio acquisitions, or the technology to compete in the corporate card market.

Monoline Issuers. These firms had unique advantages and disadvantages over the bank card issuers. One disadvantage was that monolines did not have the same access to capital that the larger banks had. However, the credit card segments within the large banks had to compete for that capital with other, possibly more profitable, businesses within the bank. Monolines do not have this dilemma and as a result may be more flexible in their choices of investment projects.

MBNA had one of the most unique situations in the industry. In slightly over a decade, it built its company from a small Maryland bank into one of the largest credit card issuers in the United States. It held a competitive advantage in the sector of affinity marketing, an offshoot of cobranding, with over 4,000 affinity relationship partners.

MBNA built partnerships with thousands of small groups across the United States, from athletic teams to universities to professional groups. It also used its affinity relationship strategy to become a successful issuer in the United Kingdom, Ireland, and Canada.

MBNA's advantage was that it was able to use the affinity that individuals had for any one of its partners as a method for issuing them a credit card. Also, since people were less likely to default on a card that was associated with an organization that they were a part of or had affinity toward, the loan loss rates on MBNA's portfolio continued to be lower than the industry averages. Another advantage was its relentless focus on effective credit underwriting and customer service. Customer service was part of the MBNA culture and was imbued in each function, from account acquisitions through collections. MBNA had not opted to compete in the corporate card market and did not have the investment banking presence to leverage and win corporate card business.

American Express (Amex) was the leader in the corporate card market as well as in the charge card (nonrevolving credit) market. However, it also became an aggressive marketer of revolving credit cards, first with its Optima card and most recently with Blue. It had worldwide name recognition, partially because of the historical popularity of its traveler's check product. However, its worldwide card position is skewed more toward the charge card business than the credit card business.

Amex had several advantages over its competitors. First, it owned a global processing platform and thus did not use the MasterCard or Visa networks. This allowed it to build its brand name while other issuers' names often got lost behind the MasterCard or Visa brands. Amex also had a loyal customer base that paid their bills. As a result, Amex had a lower percentage of delinquent accounts (measured as accounts ninety or more days past due) than any of its competitors (McCafferty, 2001). Amex had also focused on customer service and had maintained a strong collections group that also helped to limit its loan losses. This base of loyal customers also provided a receptive audience for Amex to cross-sell

other products. For example, in 1999 Amex cardholders accounted for 30 percent of all new customers with American Express Financial Advisors (McCafferty, 2001). This helped build the depth of relationship needed to retain customers. Amex's strong brand name also provided a base from which to launch new products, like the Blue card.

The Blue card was unique in that it contained a "smart" chip as well as a magnetic strip as the means of identification. Amex had marketed it as the card for the new economy and had seen rapid growth in this portfolio. The Blue card was able to be marketed as the card for the new economy since the smart chip would allow for secure Internet transactions using a reader hooked up to the user's computer. However, as of early 2001, fewer than 1 percent of Blue cardholders were using the smart chip capability to make Internet purchases. This suggested that the success of the Blue launch was related more to a creative marketing campaign than to a fundamental change in the industry (Fargo, 2001).

In the corporate card market, Amex was the recognized leader. However, smaller competitors had built more flexible technology platforms for servicing corporate clients and had begun winning business away from Amex. In 2000, CCS purchased Paymentech, the largest of these competitors.

Historically, Amex had been an occasional acquirer of portfolios. However, by 2001 it had become a potential target for acquisition by larger financial services organizations like Citigroup and Morgan Stanley Dean Witter. It had run into some financial difficulty and so was less likely to be competing for agent bank acquisitions in the near term.

Other monoline issuers will have an impact on the future of the credit card industry. Discover rebounded after years of stagnation with a strong marketing campaign and its cash-back approach, which allowed cardholders to obtain a rebate in cash each year on a percentage of their purchases. Several other companies, including CCS, attempted a similar card without Discover's success.

Cap One became an aggressive marketer of credit cards during the latter part of the 1990s. It focused on lending to all levels across the credit spectrum, from "superprime," the most credit-worthy customers within the prime market, to subprime, the least credit-worthy customers. It had a very profitable secured card with which it served the subprime market. For a fee and a required up-front cash deposit, a high-credit-risk customer could obtain a low-credit-limit card with which he or she could build or rebuild credit. Once he or she had done so, Cap One would then offer a more flexible credit arrangement.

Cap One continued to grow rapidly using technology to segment the market of potential customers and to target offers specifically to their needs and preferences. During the fourth quarter of 2000, Cap One added three times as many new customers as any other issuer (Condon, 2001).

Providian Financial also grew through marketing to the subprime segment. It was also a buyer of distressed credit card assets, which were loans that other banks had charged off. However, Providian's loan loss rates were double those of Cap One (Condon, 2001).

Besides Amex, and to a lesser degree MBNA, the monolines did not have the international name recognition required to issue internationally. Nor did these firms have the commercial or investment banking presence to leverage for individual and corporate customer businesses. Also, although many of these companies were growing rapidly, they did not have the access to capital needed to be strong competitors for portfolio acquisitions.

The Company

Overview

Chase Cardmember Services (CCS) made up 29 percent of the cash operating earnings of J. P. Morgan Chase's commercial banking sector, as shown in Figure 4, but just over 7 percent of the earnings of the entire J. P. Morgan Chase company (J. P. Morgan Chase, 2000). CCS had benefited from the trend toward consolidation in the financial services industry during the 1990s. It had become one of the few remaining large issuers in the credit card segment as a result of two large bank mergers: Chemical Bank with Manufacturer's Hanover and this combined Chemical Bank with Chase Manhattan. The combination of these companies and the resultant combinations of the credit card portfolios helped CCS grow more than any of the individual firms had been able to do through internal growth or customer acquisitions.

CCS also benefited from the consolidation trend, specifically in the credit card segment, with numerous commercial banks exiting this segment. This was evidenced by its purchase of the entire credit card portfolio of the Bank of New York. While opportunity for CCS abounded as the number of

FIGURE 4

J. P. Morgan Chase Commercial Bank

Source: J. P. Morgan Chase (2000). *Annual Report.*

portfolios up for sale, including mid-sized and large portfolios, increased, CCS had still not proven it could expand its business via means other than portfolio acquisitions.

Products

CCS offered Visa and MasterCard products, including cobranded cards, agent bank cards, and a very minor secured card product, but it did not offer affinity cards. CCS also had a small but growing business and corporate card presence.

Cobranded Cards   Cobranded credit cards were one area in which CCS competed strongly, with offerings in various industries, including gasoline, airlines, and retailing.

Shell.   The Shell Oil card was the largest cobranded card that was part of the CCS portfolio. The CCS partnership with Shell began with Chemical Bank and had been maintained through several mergers. This was the one CCS credit card that advertised regularly on television. Advertisements could also be found at Shell gas stations around the United States. The card offered a 5 percent rebate on gas purchases made at Shell gas stations and a 1 percent rebate on all other purchases. These rebates could only be used at Shell gas stations to offset the cost of future gas purchases. The card was similar to cards offered by other oil companies.

The Shell card was the leading gasoline cobranded card. Gasoline cobranded cards developed as an offshoot to the gasoline cards that most oil companies had issued. The advantages for customers were that the cobranded card carried either a Master-Card or Visa logo, could be used for purchases other than gas, and allowed customers to earn rebates on their purchases. The advantage for Shell was the additional business from customers that would only want to buy gas from Shell so they could earn the rebates offered by the card. The advantages for CCS bank were the additional loans and becoming the card of choice for customers loyal to Shell.

The Shell card, like other cobranded cards offering rewards or rebates, tended to attract customers that charged frequently but also paid off their balance each month (called "transactors"). In general, CCS made most of its profits from customers that did not pay their balance each month, thus accruing finance charges (called "revolving"). Many cards that attracted "transactors" attached an annual fee to the card, but the Shell card remained attractive to customers since it did not have an annual fee.

Wal-Mart. The Wal-Mart card was CCS's second largest cobranded card. This card was launched with the nation's largest retailer in 1996. The card did not offer any value enhancement but carried a low fixed interest rate. This strategy was consistent with Wal-Mart's philosophy of everyday low prices. No value enhancement was added to the card because Wal-Mart did not want any customer to receive benefits not available to all of its customers.

This approach worked successfully for several years, and the portfolio grew steadily. However, competition in the industry had reduced interest rates across the board. In order to acquire new customers, most card issuers were offering very low introductory interest rates. Because of the nature of the relationship with Wal-Mart, CCS was prohibited from making similar offers. Thus the portfolio growth slowed considerably as customers became used to receiving low introductory offers.

Continental Airlines. The Continental Airlines card was CCS's airline cobranded card. Prior to 1997, CCS had been the issuer of the British Airways cobranded credit card. This card had a limited appeal outside of East Coast business travelers and wealthy individuals. At the same time, Marine Midland was struggling to maintain its credit card business and was looking for a buyer for the Continental Airlines portfolio. CCS decided to sell the British Airways portfolio and pur-

chase the Continental Airlines portfolio from Marine Midland. This card had a much broader appeal nationwide as a result of Continental's large U.S. presence.

The Continental Airlines card allowed cardholders to earn Continental frequent flyer miles for each dollar charged to the card. The card had a high annual fee compared with other CCS offerings, but it also offered bonus miles for opening the account, helping to overcome cardholders' aversion to annual fees.

The card was primarily marketed through direct mail, but it was also advertised on Continental Airlines flights and in airports at Continental terminals. The appeal was to business travelers, families looking to earn miles toward vacations, and anyone who flew often on Continental. The card was similar to offers by other airlines, particularly the Citibank AAdvantage card, which was partnered with American Airlines.

Toys "R" Us. The Toys "R" Us card was a small portfolio that was obtained when CCS purchased the credit card business of the Bank of New York in 1998. The card appealed primarily to parents with young children.

The card was relaunched in 1999 and allowed cardholders to earn rebate points that could be redeemed at Toys "R" Us and Toys "R" Us.com. The portfolio remained small and was marketed primarily at Toys "R" Us locations and on the Toys "R" Us.com web site.

Verizon. The Verizon card was the descendant of the Bell Atlantic cobranded card prior to the phone company's merger with GTE and its subsequent name change to Verizon. In 2001, CCS chose to terminate its relationship with the telecommunications company.

Like the Shell card and cobranded cards from other issuers, the Verizon card tended to appeal to "transactors," or customers who charged frequently, thus earning significant rebates, but who did not carry a balance monthly and did not accrue interest charges. CCS ending this relationship was possibly a signal that the industry was moving away from "transactor" cards that were unprofitable.

Agent Bank Cards CCS had agent banking relationships with two banks. The first was the Bank of New

York. This was a small portfolio of individuals and businesses that had Bank of New York credit cards that were issued and serviced by CCS. The other, larger relationship was with Huntington Bank. CCS purchased this portfolio in 1999, and it was the first all-agent bank portfolio that CCS purchased.

CCS continued to look to be a portfolio acquirer and recognized that many of the portfolio sales in the future would involve agent banking relationships. It had experience in integrating and managing two agent banking relationships and was looking to build on this experience. Other large firms, like Citibank and MBNA, had also been acquiring agent banking relationships, as evidenced by MBNA's purchase of the First Tennessee Bank portfolio. Agent banking relationships could also be sought out and developed without having to purchase portfolios, but this was less common.

This area represented an opportunity for growth for CCS since it gained experience from its two agent bank relationships, it had the capital to fund agent bank portfolio acquisitions, and portfolios continued to come up for sale.

Business and Corporate Cards   A growing and profitable segment of the CCS portfolio was the business and corporate card sector. The business card market involved cards issued to small businesses, many of them already having a banking relationship with Chase (or the Bank of New York and Huntington Bank, in the case of agent bank business cards).

However, a larger area for growth appeared to be the corporate card market. This involved issuing and servicing the credit cards issued to employees within large corporations. This sector was dominated by American Express. However, CCS had recently acquired the corporate card business of Paymentech. As part of this purchase, CCS acquired Paymentech's industry leading platform for acquiring and servicing corporate cards, and CCS president Richard Srednicki stated that this was a strategic growth area for the business (Dow Jones, 2000).

The corporate card business was less dependent on interest charges, since most corporations paid incurred expenses on a monthly basis. Also, since the corporation guaranteed payment on charges made by its employees, loan losses were not a concern. The revenue was derived mainly from fee income. This reduced CCS's reliance on interest rate–sensitive revenue. Also, J. P. Morgan Chase had a strong investment bank that CCS could leverage to acquire additional corporate clients.

Technology

CCS made several attempts to incorporate new technology into its business. It worked to incorporate the Internet and was also working to begin incorporating smart card technology.

The Internet   In 1999, CCS launched a cobranded card with the Internet retailer Shopnow.com. The card offered reward points for merchandise purchased at the site. However, in 2000 Shopnow.com realized that the value proposition for general purpose online retailers was limited and decided to change its name to Network Commerce and its business focus to B-to-B commerce (Boone, 2000). As a result, the Shopnow.com card never became the CCS entry into the new economy that it had hoped.

However, the Shopnow.com card was a good example of how CCS might fit into the core business of J. P. Morgan Chase going forward. It was developed after the Chase venture capital business funded Shopnow.com. This card was designed to help not only CCS but also Shopnow.com, which would in turn increase the value of Chase's investment in the company. Although it was unsuccessful, it set a precedent for potential future synergies within J. P. Morgan Chase.

CCS also developed an Internet presence as part of the www.chase.com site. The site allowed cardholders to check their current and previous statements online and, if they had a Chase checking account, pay their bill online.

Payment Methods   By the start of 2001, CCS had not issued a card that incorporated smart card technology. However, it was developing a smart card and was also looking into the possibility of combining smart card technology with its cobranded cards. The Continental Airlines card, which had a more affluent customer base than its other cobranded cards, was one possible alternative.

Regulation

The regulatory environment provided several opportunities and threats for CCS.

Financial Services Modernization   This legislation spurred a flood of mergers and acquisitions among financial institutions; among them was the merger of J. P. Morgan and Chase Manhattan. The resulting company, J. P. Morgan Chase, was a large multifaceted financial services company or one-stop shopping facility for financial services.

The creation of this large financial services conglomerate presented a challenge for CCS. CCS had now become a much smaller part of a larger company, and there was the possibility that it would not be deemed part of the core business of the new firm. The situation also presented an opportunity for CCS. CCS could present itself as an integral part of a financial services team that could provide a true one-stop-shopping financial services experience for customers. For example, for any business that did its investment banking, middle market banking, or branch network banking with J. P. Morgan Chase, CCS could add value by providing various payment methods for these customers. The key to success was to demonstrate to J. P. Morgan Chase that CCS could provide valuable services to existing clients by helping to create a true one-stop-shopping financial services experience for clients.

Antitrust Legislation The pending antitrust suit involving MasterCard and Visa was not likely to have a dramatic impact on CCS. Even if the government forced the Associations to drop the prohibition on member banks issuing American Express or other non-Visa or non-MasterCard cards, CCS would likely opt not to issue American Express cards because it was seen as an independent competitor. By 2000, CCS had already agreed to become primarily a MasterCard issuer.

Globalization

Since CCS cards were affiliated with Visa or Master-Card, its cardholders could use their cards worldwide. However, CCS opted to exit the international card issuance business.

Until mid 2000, CCS had a profitable and growing credit card business in Hong Kong, where it was the third largest credit card issuer. The Manhattan Card, as it was called, was considered the premier elite credit card in Hong Kong. This card portfolio was the largest part of J. P. Morgan Chase's international consumer banking operations, which also included branch banking networks in Hong Kong, Panama, and the Virgin Islands.

However, in 2000 the corporation made the strategic decision to exit the international commercial banking business. As a result, the Hong Kong credit card business was sold to Standard Chartered Bank for $1.32 billion and CCS became a domestic-only card issuer (ChinaOnline, 2000). After the merger with J. P. Morgan, CCS did have an internationally recognized brand name that it could leverage if it decided to reenter the international card issuance business. It also had the capital needed if it wanted to expand internationally via acquisition of foreign credit card businesses.

Finance

CCS had been a profitable and important segment of Chase Manhattan prior to the J. P. Morgan merger. However, as a result of the J. P. Morgan–Chase Manhattan merger, CCS's parent became primarily an investment bank. This could make it difficult for CCS to obtain capital from the corporation to fund portfolio acquisitions and other growth-oriented activities. CCS needed to focus on maintaining a high return on investment, since it has to compete for capital with profitable investment banking and venture capital projects in other parts of the corporation.

CCS made money primarily on interest charged to customers who borrowed money (revolved). It also made money on late fees charged to customers not making timely payments and overlimit fees charged to customers exceeding their credit limit. Another source of profit was insurance premiums

TABLE 4

CCS Charge-Off Rates (losses as % of total loans)

3Q00	4.97%
2Q00	5.09
1Q00	5.39
4Q99	5.25
3Q99	5.57
2Q99	5.85
1Q99	6.18
1999 (full year)	5.66
1998 (full year)	6.02
1997 (full year)	5.58

Source: Chase Manhattan (2000). *Third Quarter Earnings Release.*

charged to customers enrolling in payment insurance, which helped customers maintain their credit rating in the event they became unemployed.

Other CCS revenues included interchange income, which was a transaction-processing fee charged to merchants accepting credit cards as payment, cash advance fees, and annual fees. However, as more customers became transactors, CCS profitability was likely to become challenged as interest income decreased.

Another threat to CCS was the economy, since loan losses also affected its profitability. Bankruptcies had been on the decline during 1999 and 2000 because the economy had been strong. This had helped CCS reduce its overall loan losses. However, if this trend turned around, the credit card industry as a whole would be significantly affected (Lee, 2001). The Bankruptcy Reform Act currently before Congress could help offset some of this risk by making it difficult for some individuals to file bankruptcy. However, if the economy worsened, the volume of bankruptcies was still likely to increase dramatically.

Periodically, Chase securitized a portion of its credit card portfolio by selling a pool of credit card receivables to a trust, which issued securities to investors. The receivables underlying the securities that were sold to investors were not included in Chase's consolidated results. Securitization changed CCS's status from that of a lender to that of a servicer. When credit card receivables were securitized, CCS ceased to derive interest income on those receivables and instead received fees for continuing to service them. As a result, securitization did not significantly affect Chase's reported and operating net income. Table 5 shows CCS revenue for 1998–1999. Operating revenue is the revenue CCS

TABLE 5

CCS Revenue, Year Ended December 31, (in millions)

	1999	1998
Reported credit card revenue	$1,698	$1,474
Less impact of credit card securitizations	(318)	(299)
Operating credit card revenue	$1,380	$1,175

Source: Chase Manhattan (1999). *Annual Report.*

derives from its business activities. Reported revenue includes the additional income CCS derives from its securitization activities.

Management

Richard Srednicki began his career at Citibank and contributed to its growth into the leading U.S. credit card issuer during the 1980s. One of his more recent assignments was as an executive at AT&T in charge of the AT&T Universal Card. During his tenure, the AT&T card business was sold to Citibank as AT&T decided to exit the credit card business. CCS faced a similar situation: it was possible that its parent could possibly someday also want to exit the business.

David Coulter, the former CEO of Bank of America, was now running the J. P. Morgan Chase commercial bank, of which CCS was a major part. The success of CCS would likely be critical to Mr. Coulter's success as head of the commercial bank, and he had said that CCS was not for sale and would continue to look to be a portfolio acquirer (Moyer, 2001).

However, the decision about whether J. P. Morgan Chase would remain in the credit card segment probably rested with the CEO William Harrison and the board of directors. Mr. Harrison's experience had been more on the investment side of the banking industry, and the J. P. Morgan merger solidified that portion of the business without having a dramatic impact on the commercial banking operations. Analysts suggested that the slower-growing commercial banking business might not be a good fit with the expanding investment banking business.

Looking Toward the Future

Given the trends of consolidation and technological advance in the credit card segment, CCS management was exploring a number of strategic alternatives. The pressure was on to begin clarifying its strategic direction to both the investment community and the J. P. Morgan Chase board of directors. One decision that had to be made was the geographic scope CCS would take in expanding its business. Mr. Srednicki was considering two alternatives.

The first alternative for CCS was one centered on growth, both domestically and internationally. In this alternative, CCS would build a global credit card franchise and diversify its current business by expanding into other countries, particularly those countries where the J. P. Morgan and Chase names had substantial name recognition.

This alternative was feasible, since although J. P. Morgan Chase no longer had an international commercial banking presence, it did have a strong international presence in the investment banking sector. CCS could leverage this brand name recognition in countries like Canada, the United Kingdom, and Japan to expand to international consumers. CCS had the capital required to purchase portfolios anywhere in the world, which also made international expansion feasible. Finally, CCS could compete for international corporations' business for its corporate card business as well.

This alternative could win against the competition, because among its competitors, only Citibank and Amex had greater name recognition worldwide, and Amex was more focused on the charge card market. With the trend toward consolidation affecting the international financial services industry along with the domestic industry, the credit card segment worldwide was likely to consolidate faster than one firm alone could absorb. CCS had the capital required to acquire international portfolios as they came up for sale, and as a result, CCS was in a position to win against all of the other competitors except Citibank. If it participated during this consolidation, along with Citibank, it would build an international presence that could be leveraged in the future. If it did not participate in this consolidation in the near term, it would limit its ability to ever compete in this market. It could also win against all competition in the international corporate card business. It had the industry leading technology platform that could be applied to corporate card portfolios domestically and internationally and the worldwide investment banking presence to leverage for acquiring new business.

The main drawbacks to this strategy were CCS's lack of an international commercial banking presence to leverage for acquiring new customers, lack of an international infrastructure for servicing these customers, and Citibank's more dominant position in this area.

However, CCS could find ways around these problems. While Citibank did have a dominate position in this area, the industry was consolidating faster that Citibank alone could absorb. If CCS were to begin competing for and winning portfolios, it could participate with Citibank in absorbing this consolidation. Also, it could develop the required interna-

tional infrastructure through acquisition. Where Citibank might be more inclined just to purchase the portfolio of an international card issuer, CCS could look to also purchase the issuer's infrastructure.

A second alternative was one centered solely on domestic expansion. Mr. Srednicki had inherited a business that had already determined it would exit the international card business. In doing so it recognized that there was more opportunity domestically that it wished to focus on. This alternative would keep CCS on that path and allow it to focus its resources entirely on opportunities in the domestic market like corporate cards and agent banking cards.

This alternative was feasible, since CCS had the access to capital required to be an acquirer of domestic portfolios and could do so more frequently without having to also acquire the infrastructure that international expansion would require. Also, domestically CCS had a strong commercial banking presence, which was very helpful in acquiring loyal customers.

This alternative would allow CCS to win against the competition, since many competitors did not have the capital needed to be an aggressive acquirer. With this access to capital, and with Citibank focused on building its international business, CCS had a competitive advantage for domestic portfolio acquisitions. Also, most large U.S. corporations already had some relationship with J. P. Morgan Chase. As a result, CCS was in position to leverage these relationships, along with its industry leading technology platform for servicing corporate clients to win against the competition in the corporate card business. Internationally, CCS would have to compete for business with foreign banks whose relationship with foreign corporations might limit CCS's success in the corporate card market.

The major drawback to this alternative was the possibility that Citibank would change its focus from international expansion back to domestic expansion. Citibank's scale made it a difficult head-on competitor that could limit CCS's success in the domestic market.

However, CCS could find ways around this problem. As in the international market, the domestic credit card market was consolidating faster than one company could absorb. As a result, CCS could still succeed by participating along with Citibank in the segment's consolidation. It does have the advantage over Citibank in the corporate card segment, and could use this advantage to become the dominant acquirer of corporate card portfolios.

Mr. Srednicki needed to decide which strategic decision to implement. While CCS had a strong domestic presence and no international presence, the trend toward consolidation internationally made this a good time to build an international business. If he chose not to take advantage of this opportunity now, it was likely that CCS would not be able to enter this market successfully in the future. However, in both domestic and international markets, Citibank had advantages over CCS. With Citibank focusing internationally, this was a good time for CCS to focus on domestic opportunity. Mr. Srednicki's decision would determine what direction CCS would take to win against increasing competition in the near, intermediate, and long term.

REFERENCES

Anonymous (1998). "Expanding Economy Propels Credit Cards," *Industries in Transition,* vol. 25, p. 10.

Boone, R. (2000). "Shopnow.com Changes Name, Set Profit Goal," Local-Business.com. [Online]. **http://www.localbusiness.com/Story/0,1118,SEA_134552,00.html.** Accessed April 1, 2001.

CardFlash (2001). "U.S. Payment Card Daily—Friday March 16, 2001." [Online]. **http://www.cardweb.com.** Accessed March 16.

Carney, D. (2000). "Breaking Up the Old Card Game?" *Business Week,* June 12, vol. 3685, p. 98.

ChinaOnline (2001). "Hong Kong's Standard Chartered Bank Buys Chase Manhattan's Retail Credit Card Business." [Online]. **http://www.chinaonline.com/industry/financial/NewsArchive/Secure/2000/november/C00110101.asp.** Accessed March 30.

Coleman, C. (2001). "Credit Card Solicitations Get Record Low in Response Rate," *Wall Street Journal,* March 19.

Condon, B. (2001). "House of Cards," *Forbes.* [Online]. **http://www.forbes.com/forbes/2001/0402/077.html?_requestid=70916.** Accessed April 9.

Credit Card History (2001). "Credit Card History." [Online]. **http://www.worldwidebankcard.net/hist.htm.** Accessed March 1.

Dow Jones Newswire (2000). "Chase to Acquire Paymentech Unit," *Dallas Morning News,* November 21, p. 7D.

Fargo, J. (2001). "Bank Cards Heed the Smart Card Call," *Credit Card Management,* January 2, vol. 13, no. 10, p. 25.

Forrester Research (2001). [Online]. **http://www.forrester.com/ER/Press/Release/0,1769,164, FF.html.** Accessed March 1.

Harner, S. (2000). *Japan's Financial Revolution.* Armonk, N.Y.: M.E. Sharpe, Inc.

History of the Credit Card (2001). [Online]. **http://www.triumphant.com/history.htm.** Accessed March 1.

J. P. Morgan Chase (2000). *Annual Report.*

Lee, W. (2001). "Consumer Pinch Showing Up in Late Payments," *American Banker,* March 16.

Levinshone, A. (2000). "The Coming of a Financial Services Bazaar," *Strategic Finance,* April. [Online]. **http://www.mamag.com/strategicfinance/2000/04g.htm.** Accessed April 8, 2001.

Lowe, F. (2001). "Why Credit Will Still Rule the Web," *Credit Card Management,* February 2. [Online]. **http://www.cardforum.com/html/ccmissue/toc.htm.** Accessed April 8.

Mannix, M. (1998). "Goodbye to Debt," *U.S. News & World Report,* April 23, p. 63.

McCafferty, R. (2001). "Citigroup vs. American Express," *The Motley Fool.* [Online]. **http://www.fool.com/portfolios/rulemaker/2001/rulemaker010 319.htm?source=eheyhopop001101&ref=yhoolnk.** Accessed March 20.

Moyer, L. (2001). "JPM-Chase Retail Plan Goes Heavy on e-Tail," *American Banker,* February 21.

Nilson Report (2000). "The Future of Credit Cards in the United States," December, no. 730, pp. 6–7.

Nua Internet Surveys (2001). "The Internet and Businesses." [Online]. **http://www.nua.net/surveys/index.** Accessed March 1.

Overdorf, J. (2000). "First Tennessee Bank Sells Affinity/Co-Branded Programs." *Dow Jones Newswires,* November 30.

Robinson, Brian (2001). "Is It Too Late for Smart Cards?" Informationweek.com, March 19, pp. 61–64.

"U.S. Takes Visa, MasterCard to Court over Antitrust Concerns." *Star Ledger,* (2000) June 18.

Wherry, R. (2000). "Credit Check," *Forbes.* [Online]. **http://www.forbes.com/forbes/2000/1113/6613148a.html.** Accessed April 8, 2001.

15

Toyota: The Evolution of the Toyota Production System

This case was prepared by Charles W. L. Hill, the University of Washington.

Introduction

The growth of Toyota has been one of the great success stories of Japanese industry during the last half century. In 1947, the company was a little-known domestic manufacturer producing around 100,000 vehicles a year. Today it is the world's third largest automobile company with global production of 5.8 million vehicles and revenues of $108 billion. Toyota operates fifty-six plants in twenty-five countries and has a work force of more than 210,000. It is the market leader in Japan and is threatening to overtake Daimler Chrysler for the number three spot in the United States. In 2000, the Toyota Camry, with sales of 420,000, was the best-selling car in North America for the fourth consecutive year, while the Lexus, at 200,000 units sold, was the best-selling luxury brand in the United States.[1] Toyota's U.S. market share stood at 11 percent in 2000, up from 7.7 percent in 1996. In contrast, Daimler Chrysler's share was 14.7 percent in 2000, down from 16.2 percent in 1996.[2]

Toyota's vehicles consistently rank near the top in surveys of customer satisfaction and quality. As stated in the 2001 J. D. Power report on vehicle quality, "Toyota builds vehicles with more consistent quality levels across a platform than any other manufacturer."[3] Of sixteen vehicle segments looked at by J. D. Power, Toyota held the top spot for quality in seven J. D. Power gave the company's Kyushu plant in Japan the highest quality score of any car plant in the world. Moreover, Toyota's plant in Cambridge, Ontario, had the highest quality score of any plant in North America.

Not only does Toyota score well on quality metrics, but its plants also score well on productivity metrics. According to the 2001 Harbour Report, an annual survey of productivity in North American car plants, in 2000 it took Toyota 31.06 hours of employee time to build a car at its average North American plant. Although this is longer than the industry leading performance of Nissan, which can build a car in 27.63 hours, it is considerably less than the 39.94 hours it takes Ford to build a car, or the 40.52 hours at General Motors, or the more than 34 hours it takes Daimler Chrysler to build a car.[4]

This case describes the rise of Toyota from an obscure Japanese automobile company into the giant of today. It explains how the revolutionary production system developed at Toyota during the quarter of a century after 1950 paved the way for the company's current success.

The Origins of Toyota

The original idea behind the founding of the Toyota Motor Company came from the fertile mind of Toyoda Sakichi.[5] The son of a carpenter, Sakichi was an entrepreneur and inventor whose primary interest lay in the textile industry, but he had been intrigued by automobiles since a visit to the United States in 1910. Sakichi's principal achievement was the invention of an automatic loom that held out the promise of being able to lower the costs of weaving high-quality cloth. In 1926 Sakichi set up Toyoda Automatic Loom to manufacture this product. In 1930 Sakichi sold the patent rights to a British textile concern, Platt Brothers, for about 1 million yen, a considerable sum in those days. Sakichi urged his son, Toyoda Kiichiro, to use this money to study the possibility of manufacturing automobiles in Japan. A mechanical engineer with a degree from the University of Tokyo, in 1930 Kiichiro became managing director of loom production at Toyoda Automatic Loom.

Kiichiro was at first reluctant to invest in automobile production. The Japanese market was at that time dominated by Ford and General Motors, both of which imported knock-down car kits from the United States and assembled them in Japan. Given this, the board of Toyoda Automatic Loom, including Kiichiro's brother-in-law and the company's president, Kodama Risaburo, opposed the investment on the grounds that it was too risky. Kiichiro probably would not have pursued the issue further had not his father made a deathbed request in 1930 that Kiichiro explore the possibilities of automobile production. Kiichiro had to push, but in 1933 he was able to get permission to set up an automobile department within Toyoda Automatic Loom.

Kiichiro's belief was that he would be able to figure out how to manufacture automobiles by taking apart U.S.-made vehicles and examining them piece by piece. He also felt that it should be possible to adapt U.S. mass-production technology to manufacture cost efficiently at lower volumes. His confidence was based in large part upon the already considerable engineering skills and capabilities at his disposal through Toyoda Automatic Loom. Many of the precision engineering and manufacturing skills needed in automobile production were similar to the skills required to manufacture looms.

Kiichiro produced his first 20 vehicles in 1935, and in 1936 the automobile department produced 1,142 vehicles—910 trucks, 100 cars, and 132 buses. At this time, however, the production system was essentially craft-based rather than a modern assembly line. Despite some progress, the struggle might still have been uphill had not fate intervened in the form of the Japanese military. Japan had invaded Manchuria in 1931 and quickly found American-made trucks useful for moving men and equipment. As a result, the military felt that it was strategically important for Japan to have its own automobile industry. The result was the passage of an automobile manufacturing law in 1936 which required companies producing more than 3,000 vehicles per year in Japan to get a license from the government. Moreover, to get a license over 50 percent of the stock had to be owned by Japanese investors. The law also placed a duty on imported cars, including the knock-down kits that Ford and GM brought into Japan. As a direct result of this legislation, both GM and Ford exited from the Japanese market in 1939.

Once the Japanese government passed this law, Kodama Risaburo decided that the automobile venture could be profitable and switched from opposing to proactively supporting Kiichiro (in fact, Risaburo's wife, who was Kiichiro's elder sister, had been urging him to take this step for some time). The first priority was to attract the funds necessary to build a mass-production facility. In 1937 Risaburo and Kiichiro decided to incorporate the automobile department as a separate company in order to attract outside investors—which they were successful in doing. Kiichiro Toyoda was appointed president of the new company. The company was named the Toyota Motor Company. (The founding family's name, "Toyoda," means "abundant rice field" in Japanese. The new name had no meaning in Japanese.)

Upon incorporation, Risaburo and Kiichiro's vision was that Toyota should expand its passenger car production as quickly as possible. However, once again fate intervened in the form of the Japanese military. Toyota had barely begun passenger car production when war broke out; in 1939 the Japanese government, on advice from the military, prohibited passenger car production and demanded that the company specialize in the production of military trucks.

The Evolution of the Toyota Production System

After the end of World War II, Kiichiro was determined that Toyota should reestablish itself as a manufacturer of automobiles.[6] Toyota, however, faced a number of problems in doing this:

1. The Japanese domestic market was too small to support efficient-scale mass-production facilities such as those common in America by that time.

2. The Japanese economy was starved of capital, which made it difficult to raise funds to finance new investments.

3. New labor laws introduced by the American occupiers increased the bargaining power of labor and made it difficult for companies to lay off workers.

4. North America and Western Europe were full of large auto manufacturers eager to establish operations in Japan.

In response to the last point, in 1950 the new Japanese government prohibited direct foreign investment in the automobile industry and imposed high tariffs on the importation of foreign cars. This protection, however, did little to solve the other problems facing the company at this time.

From Mass Production to Flexible Production   At this juncture a remarkable mechanical engineer entered the scene: Ohno Taiichi. More than anyone else, it was Ohno who was to work out a response to the above problems. Ohno had joined Toyoda Spinning and Weaving in 1932 as a production engineer in cotton thread manufacture and entered Toyota when the former company was absorbed into the latter in 1943. Ohno worked in auto production for two years, was promoted and managed auto assembly and machine shops between 1945 and 1953, and in 1954 was appointed a company director.

When Ohno Taiichi joined Toyota the mass-production methods pioneered by Ford had become the accepted method of manufacturing automobiles. The basic philosophy behind mass production was to produce a limited product line in massive quantities to gain maximum economies of scale. The economies came from spreading the fixed costs involved in setting up the specialized equipment required to stamp body parts and manufacture components over as large a production run as possible. Since setting up

much of the equipment could take a full day or more, the economies involved in long production runs were reckoned to be considerable. Thus, for example, Ford would stamp 500,000 right-hand door panels in a single production run and then store the parts in warehouses until they were needed in the assembly plant, rather than stamp just those door panels that were needed immediately and then change the settings and stamp out left-hand door panels, or other body parts.

A second feature of mass production was that each assembly worker should perform only a single task, rather than a variety of tasks. The idea here was that as the worker became completely familiar with a single task, he could perform it much faster, thereby increasing labor productivity. Assembly line workers were overseen by a foreman who did not perform any assembly tasks himself, but instead ensured that the workers followed orders. In addition, a number of specialists were employed to perform nonassembly operations such as tool repair, die changes, quality inspection, and general "housecleaning."

After working in Toyota for five years and visiting Ford's U.S. plants, Ohno became convinced that the basic mass-production philosophy was flawed. He saw five problems with the mass-production system:

1. Long production runs created massive inventories that had to be stored in large warehouses. This was expensive both because of the cost of warehousing and because inventories tied up capital in unproductive uses.

2. If the initial machine settings were wrong, long production runs resulted in the production of a large number of defects.

3. The sheer monotony of assigning assembly line workers to a single task generated defects, since workers became lax about quality control. In addition, since assembly line workers were not responsible for quality control, they had little incentive to minimize defects.

4. The extreme division of labor resulted in the employment of specialists such as foremen, quality inspectors, and tooling specialists, whose jobs logically could be performed by assembly line workers.

5. The mass-production system was unable to accommodate consumer preferences for product diversity.

In addition to these flaws, Ohno knew that the small domestic market in Japan and the lack of capital for investing in mass-production facilities made the American model unsuitable for Toyota.

Reducing Setup Times.   Given these flaws and the constraints that Toyota faced, Ohno decided to take a fresh look at the techniques used for automobile production. His first goal was to try to make it economical to manufacture autobody parts in small batches. To do this, he needed to reduce the time it took to set up the machines for stamping out body parts. Ohno and his engineers began to experiment with a number of techniques to speed up the time it took to change the dies in stamping equipment. This included using rollers to move dies in and out of position along with a number of simple mechanized adjustment mechanisms to fine-tune the settings. These techniques were relatively simple to master, so Ohno directed production workers to perform the die changes themselves. This in itself reduced the need for specialists and eliminated the idle time that workers previously had enjoyed while waiting for the dies to be changed.

Through a process of trial and error, Ohno succeeded in reducing the time required to change dies on stamping equipment from a full day to fifteen minutes by 1962, and to as little as three minutes by 1971. By comparison, even in the early 1980s many American and European plants required anywhere between two and six hours to change dies on stamping equipment. As a consequence, American and European plants found it economical to manufacture in lots equivalent to ten to thirty days' supply and to reset equipment only every other day. In contrast, since Toyota could change the dies on stamping equipment in a matter of minutes, it manufactured in lots equivalent to just one day's supply, while resetting equipment three times per day.

Not only did these innovations make small production runs economical, but they also had the added benefit of reducing inventories and improving product quality. Making small batches eliminated the need to hold large inventories, thereby reducing warehousing costs and freeing up scarce capital for investment elsewhere. Small production runs and the lack of inventory also meant that defective parts were produced only in small numbers and entered the assembly process almost immediately. This had the added effect of making those in the stamping shops far more concerned about quality. In addition, once it became economical to manufacture small batches of components, much greater variety could be included into the final product at little or no cost penalty.

Organization of the Workplace.   One of Ohno's first innovations was to group the work force into teams. Each team was given a set of assembly tasks to perform, and team members were trained to perform each task that the team was responsible for. Each team had a leader who was himself an assembly line worker. In addition to coordinating the team, the team leader was expected to perform basic assembly line tasks and to fill in for any absent worker. The teams were given the job of housecleaning, minor tool repair, and quality inspection (along with the training required to perform these tasks). Time was also set aside for team members to discuss ways to improve the production process (the practice now referred to as "quality circles"). The immediate effect of this approach was to reduce the need for specialists in the workplace and to create a more flexible work force in which individual assembly line workers were not treated simply as human machines. All of this resulted in increased worker productivity.

None of this would have been possible, however, had it not been for an agreement reached between management and labor after a 1950 strike. The strike was brought on by management's attempt to cut the work force by 25 percent (in response to a recession in Japan). After lengthy negotiations, Toyota and the union worked out a compromise. The work force was cut by 25 percent as originally proposed, but the remaining employees were given two guarantees, one for lifetime employment and the other for pay graded by seniority and tied to company profitability through bonus payments. In exchange for these guarantees, the employees agreed to be flexible in work assignments. In turn, this allowed for the introduction of the team concept.

Improving Quality.   One of the standard practices in the mass-production automobile assembly plants was to fix any errors that occurred during assembly in a rework area at the end of the assembly line. Errors routinely occurred in most assembly plants either because bad parts were installed or because good parts were installed incorrectly. The belief was that stopping an assembly line to fix such errors would cause enormous bottlenecks in the production system. Thus it was thought to be more efficient to correct errors at the end of the line.

Ohno viewed this system as wasteful for three reasons: (1) since workers understood that any errors would be fixed at the end of the line, they had little incentive to correct errors themselves; (2) once a defective part had been embedded in a complex vehicle, an enormous amount of rework might be required to fix it; and (3) since defective parts were often not discovered until the end of the line when the finished cars were tested, a large number of cars containing the same defect may have been built before the problem was found.

In an attempt to get away from this practice, Ohno decided to look for ways to reduce the amount of rework at the end of the line. His approach involved two elements. First, he placed a cord above every workstation and instructed workers to stop the assembly line if a problem emerged that could not be fixed. It then became the responsibility of the whole team to come over and work on the problem. Second, team members were taught to trace every defect back to its ultimate cause and then to ensure that the problem was fixed so that it would not reoccur.

Initially, this system produced enormous disruption. The production line was stopping all the time and workers became discouraged. However, as team members began to gain experience in identifying problems and tracing them back to their root cause, the number of errors began to drop dramatically and stops in the line became much rarer, so that today in most Toyota plants the line virtually never stops.

Developing the _Kanban_ System   Once reduced setup times had made small production runs economical, Ohno began to look for ways to coordinate the flow of production within the Toyota manufacturing system so that the amount of inventory in the system could be reduced to a minimum. Toyota produced about 25 percent of its major components in-house (the rest were contracted out to independent suppliers). Ohno's initial goal was to arrange for components and/or subassemblies manufactured in-house to be delivered to the assembly floor only when they were needed, and not before (this goal was later extended to include independent suppliers).

To achieve this, in 1953 Ohno began experimenting with what came to be known as the _kanban_ system. Under the _kanban_ system, component parts are delivered to the assembly line in containers. As each

container is emptied, it is sent back to the previous step in the manufacturing process. This then becomes the signal to make more parts. The system minimizes work in progress by increasing inventory turnover. The elimination of buffer inventories also means that defective components show up immediately in the next process. This speeds up the processes of tracing defects back to their source and facilitates correction of the problem before too many defects are made. Moreover, the elimination of buffer stocks, by removing all safety nets, makes it imperative that problems be solved before they become serious enough to jam up the production process, thereby creating a strong incentive for workers to ensure that errors are corrected as quickly as possible. In addition, by decentralizing responsibility for coordinating the manufacturing process to lower-level employees, the _kanban_ system does away with the need for extensive centralized management to coordinate the flow of parts between the various stages of production.

After perfecting the _kanban_ system in one of Toyota's machine shops, Ohno had a chance to apply the system broadly in 1960 when he was made general manager of the Motomachi assembly plant. Ohno already had converted the machining, body stamping, and body shops to the _kanban_ system, but since many parts came from shops that had yet to adopt the system, or from outside suppliers, the impact on inventories was initially minimal. However, by 1962 he had extended the _kanban_ to forging and casting, and between 1962 and 1965 he began to bring independent suppliers into the system.

Organizing Suppliers   Assembly of components into a final vehicle accounts for only about 15 percent of the total manufacturing process in automobile manufacture. The remaining 85 percent of the process involves manufacturing more than ten thousand individual parts and assembling them into about one hundred major components, such as engines, suspension systems, transaxles, and so on. Coordinating this process so that everything comes together at the right time has always been a problem for auto manufacturers. The response at Ford and GM to this problem was massive vertical integration. The belief was that control over the supply chain would allow management to coordinate the flow of component parts into the final assembly plant. In addition, American firms held the view that vertical integration made them more efficient by reducing their dependence on other firms for materials and components and by limiting their vulnerability to opportunistic over-charging.

As a consequence of this philosophy, even as late as the mid 1990s General Motors makes 68 percent of its own components in-house, while Ford makes 50 percent. When they haven't vertically integrated, U.S. auto companies historically have tried to reduce the procurement costs that remain through competitive bidding—asking a number of companies to submit contracts and giving orders to suppliers offering the lowest price.

Under the leadership of Kiichiro Toyoda during the 1930s and 1940s, Toyota essentially followed the American model and pursued extensive vertical integration into the manufacture of component parts. In fact, Toyota had little choice in this matter, since only a handful of Japanese companies were able to make the necessary components. However, the low volume of production during this period meant that the scale of integration was relatively small. In the 1950s, however, the volume of auto production began to increase dramatically. This presented Toyota with a dilemma: should the company increase its capacity to manufacture components in-house in line with the growth in production of autos, or should the company contract out?

In contrast to American practice, the company decided that while it should increase in-house capacity for essential subassemblies and bodies, it would do better to contract out for most components. Four reasons seem to bolster this decision:

1. Toyota wanted to avoid the capital expenditures required to expand capacity to manufacture a wide variety of components.

2. Toyota wanted to reduce risk by maintaining a low factory capacity in case factory sales slumped.

3. Toyota wanted to take advantage of the lower wage scales in smaller firms.

4. Toyota managers realized that in-house manufacturing offered few benefits if it was possible to find stable, high-quality, and low-cost external sources of component supply.

At the same time, Toyota managers felt that the American practice of inviting competitive bids from suppliers was self-defeating. While competitive bidding might achieve the lowest short-run costs, the practice of playing suppliers off against each other did not guarantee stable supplies, high quality, or cooperation beyond existing contracts to solve design or engineering problems. Ohno and other Toyota managers believed that real efficiencies could be achieved if the company entered into long-term relationships with major suppliers. This would allow them to introduce the *kanban* system, thereby further reducing inventory holding costs and realizing the same kind of quality benefits that Toyota was already beginning to encounter with its in-house supply operations. In addition, Ohno wanted to bring suppliers into the design process since he believed that suppliers might be able to suggest ways of improving the design of component parts based upon their own manufacturing experience.

As it evolved during the 1950s and 1960s, Toyota's strategy toward its suppliers had several elements. First, the company spun off some of its own in-house supply operations into quasi-independent entities in which it took a minority stake, typically holding between 20 percent and 40 percent of the stock. It then recruited a number of independent companies with a view to establishing a long-term relationship with them for the supply of critical components. Sometimes, but not always, Toyota took a minority stake in these companies as well. All of these companies were designated as "first-tier suppliers." First-tier suppliers were responsible for working with Toyota as an integral part of the new product development team. Each first tier was responsible for the formation of a "second tier" of suppliers under its direction. Companies in the second tier were given the job of fabricating individual parts.

Both first- and second-tier suppliers were formed into supplier associations. Thus by 1986 Toyota had three regional supply organizations in Japan with 62, 135, and 25 first-tier suppliers. A major function of the supplier associations was to share information regarding new manufacturing, design, or materials management techniques among themselves. Concepts such as statistical process control, total quality control, and computer-aided design were rapidly diffused among suppliers by this means.

Toyota also worked closely with its suppliers, providing them with management expertise, engineering expertise, and sometimes capital to finance new investments. A critical feature of this relationship was the incentives that Toyota established to encourage its suppliers to focus on realizing continuous process improvements. The basic contract for a component would be for four to five years, with the price being agreed in advance. If by joint efforts the supplier and Toyota succeeded in reducing the costs of manufacturing the components, then the additional profit would be shared between the two. If the supplier by its own efforts came up with an innovation that reduced costs, the supplier would keep the additional profit that the innovation generated for the lifetime of the contract.

As a consequence of this strategy, today Toyota outsources more than almost any other major auto manufacturer. By the late 1980s Toyota was responsible for only about 27 percent of the value going into a finished automobile, with the remainder coming from outside suppliers. In contrast, General Motors was responsible for about 70 percent of the value going into a finished automobile. Other consequences included long-term improvements in productivity and quality among Toyota's suppliers that were comparable to the improvements achieved by Toyota itself. In particular, the extension of the *kanban* system to include suppliers, by eliminating buffer inventory stocks, in essence forced suppliers to focus more explicitly on the quality of their product.

Consequences   The consequences of Toyota's production system included a surge in labor productivity and a decline in the number of defects per car. Table 1 compares the number of vehicles produced per worker at General Motors, Ford, Nissan, and Toyota between 1965 and 1983.

These figures are adjusted for the degree of vertical integration pursued by each company. As can be seen, in 1960 productivity at Toyota already outstripped that of Ford, General Motors, and its main Japanese competitor, Nissan. As Toyota refined its production system over the next eighteen years, productivity doubled. In comparison, productivity essentially stood still at General Motors and Ford during the same period.

Table 2 provides another way to assess the superiority of Toyota's production system. Here the performance of Toyota's Takaoka plant is compared with that of General Motors's Framingham plant in 1987. As can be seen, the Toyota plant was more productive, produced far fewer defects per one hundred cars, and kept far less inventory on hand.

A further aspect of Toyota's production system is that the short setup times made it economical to manufacture a much wider range of models than is feasible at a traditional mass-production assembly plant. In essence, Toyota soon found that it could supply much greater product variety than its competitors with little in the way of a cost penalty. In 1990 Toyota was offering consumers around the world roughly as many products as General Motors (about 150), even though Toyota was still only half GM's size. Moreover, it could do this at a lower cost than GM.

Distribution and Customer Relations

Toyota's approach to its distributors and customers as it evolved during the 1950s and 1960s was in many ways just as radical as its approach toward suppliers. In 1950 Toyota formed a subsidiary, Toyota Motor Sales, to handle distribution and sales. The new subsidiary was headed by Kaymiya Shotaro from its inception until 1975. Kaymiya's philosophy was that dealers should be treated as "equal partners" in the Toyota family. To back this up, he had Toyota Motor Sales provide a wide range of sales training and service training for dealership personnel.

TABLE 1

Vehicles Produced per Worker (adjusted for vertical integration), 1965–1983

Year	General Motors	Ford	Nissan	Toyota
1965	5.0	4.4	4.3	8.0
1970	3.7	4.3	8.8	13.4
1975	4.4	4.0	9.0	15.1
1979	4.5	4.2	11.1	18.4
1980	4.1	3.7	12.2	17.8
1983	4.8	4.7	11.0	15.0

Source: M. A. Cusumano, *The Japanese Automotive Industry* (Cambridge, Mass.: Harvard University Press, 1989), Table 48, p. 197.

TABLE 2

General Motors's Framingham Plant Versus Toyota's Takaoka Plant, 1987

	GM Framingham	Toyota Takaoka
Assembly hours per car	31	16
Assembly defects per 100 cars	135	45
Inventories of parts (average)	2 weeks	2 hours

Source: J. P. Womack, D. T. Jones, and D. Roos, *The Machines That Changed the World* (New York: Macmillan, 1990), Figure 4.2, p. 83.

Kaymiya then used the dealers to build long-term ties with Toyota's customers. The ultimate aim was to bring customers into the Toyota design and production process. To this end, through its dealers, Toyota Motor Sales assembled a huge database on customer preferences. Much of these data came from monthly or semiannual surveys conducted by dealers. These asked Toyota customers their preferences for styling, model types, colors, prices, and other features. Toyota also used these surveys to estimate the potential demand for new models. This information was then fed directly into the design process.

Kaymiya began this process in 1952 when the company was redesigning its Toyopet model. The Toyopet was primarily used by urban taxi drivers. Toyota Motor Sales surveyed taxi drivers to try to find out what type of vehicle they preferred. They wanted something reliable, inexpensive, and with good city fuel mileage—which Toyota engineers then set about designing. In 1956 Kaymiya formalized this process when he created a unified department for planning and market research whose function was to coordinate the marketing strategies developed by researchers at Toyota Motor Sales with product planning by Toyota's design engineers. From this time on marketing information played a critical role in the design of Toyota's cars and, indeed, in the company's strategy. In particular, it was the research department at Toyota Motor Sales that provided the initial stimulus for Toyota to start exporting during the late 1960s after predicting, correctly, that growth in domestic sales would slow down considerably during the 1970s.

Overseas Expansion

Large-scale overseas expansion did not become feasible at Toyota until the late 1960s for one principal reason: despite the rapid improvement in productivity, Japanese cars were still not competitive.[7] In 1957, for example, the Toyota Corona sold in Japan for the equivalent of $1,694. At the same time the Volkswagen Beetle sold for $1,111 in West Germany, while Britain's Austin company was selling its basic model for the equivalent of $1,389 in Britain. Foreign companies were effectively kept out of the Japanese market, however, by a 40 percent value-added tax and shipping costs.

Despite these disadvantages, Toyota tried to enter the United States market in the late 1950s. The company set up a U.S. subsidiary in California in October 1957 and began to sell cars in early 1958, hoping to capture the American small car market (which at that time was poorly served by the U.S. automobile companies). The result was a disaster. Toyota's cars performed poorly in road tests on U.S. highways. The basic problem was that the engines of Toyota's cars were too small for prolonged high-speed driving and tended to overheat and burn oil, while poorly designed chassis resulted in excessive vibration. As a result, sales were slow and in 1964 Toyota closed down its U.S. subsidiary and withdrew from the market.

The company was determined to learn from its U.S. experience and quickly redesigned several of its models based on feedback from American consumer surveys and U.S. road tests. As a result, by 1967 the picture had changed considerably. The quality of Toyota's cars was now sufficient to make an impact in the U.S. market, while production costs and retail prices had continued to fall and were now comparable with international competitors in the small car market.

In the late 1960s Toyota reentered the U.S. market. Although sales were initially slow, they increased steadily. Then the OPEC-engineered fourfold increase in oil prices that followed the 1973 Israeli/Arab conflict gave Toyota an unexpected boost. U.S. consumers began to turn to small fuel-efficient cars in droves, and Toyota was one of the main beneficiaries. Driven primarily by a surge in U.S. demand, worldwide exports of Toyota cars increased from 157,882 units in 1967 to 856,352 units by 1974 and 1,800,923 units by 1984. Put another way, in 1967 exports accounted for 19 percent of Toyota's total output. By 1984 they accounted for 52.5 percent.

Success brought its own problems. By the early 1980s political pressures and talk of local content regulations in the United States and Europe were forcing an initially reluctant Toyota to rethink its exporting strategy. Toyota already had agreed to "voluntary" import quotas with the United States in 1981. The consequence for Toyota was stagnant export growth between 1981 and 1984. Against this background, in the early 1980s Toyota began to think seriously about setting up manufacturing operations overseas.

Transplant Operations

Toyota's first overseas operation was a 50/50 joint venture with General Motors established in February 1983 under the name New United Motor Manufacturing, Inc. (NUMMI). NUMMI, which is based in Fremont, California, began producing Chevrolet Nova cars for GM in December 1984.[8] The maximum capacity of the Fremont plant is about 250,000 cars per year.

For Toyota, the joint venture provided a chance to find out whether it could build quality cars in the United States using American workers and American suppliers. It also provided Toyota with experience dealing with an American union (the United Auto Workers Union) and with a means of circumventing "voluntary" import restrictions. For General Motors, the venture provided an opportunity to observe in full detail the Japanese approach to manufacturing. While General Motors's role was marketing and distributing the plant's output, Toyota designed the product and designed, equipped, and operated the plant. At the venture's start, thirty-four executives were loaned to NUMMI by Toyota and sixteen by General Motors. The chief executive and chief operating officer were both Toyota personnel.

By the fall of 1986 the NUMMI plant was running at full capacity and the early indications were that the NUMMI plant was achieving productivity and quality levels close to those achieved at Toyota's major Takaoka plant in Japan. For example, in 1987 it took the NUMMI plant nineteen assembly hours to build a car, compared to sixteen hours at Takaoka, while the number of defects per one hundred cars was the same at NUMMI as at Takaoka—forty-five.[9]

Encouraged by its success at NUMMI, in December 1985 Toyota announced that it would build an automobile manufacturing plant in Georgetown, Kentucky. The plant, which came on stream in May 1988, officially had the capacity to produce 200,000 Toyota Camrys a year. Such was the success of this plant, however, that by early 1990 it was producing the equivalent of 220,000 cars per year. This success was followed by an announcement in December 1990 that Toyota would build a second plant in Georgetown with a capacity to produce a further 200,000 vehicles per year.[10]

In 2001, Toyota had four vehicle assembly plants in North America with a total capacity to produce over 1 million vehicles per year. In addition, the company had two engine plants, an aluminum wheel plant, an aluminum casting plant, special parts and body parts plants, and an automatic transmission plant. In totally, these factories employed more than 123,000 Americans, more than Coca-Cola, Microsoft, and Oracle combined. Some 60 percent of all Toyota vehicles sold in the United States are now locally produced, and the company is aiming to add another U.S. plant capable of turning out an additional 250,000 vehicles a year by 2005.[11]

Although many of the senior managers at Toyota's U.S. plants were initially Japanese, increasingly they are American. The Americans are also starting to drive product development decisions. A pivotal event in the changing relationship occurred in the late 1990s, when Japanese managers resisted their U.S. colleagues' idea that the company should produce a V8 pickup truck for the American market. To change their minds, the U.S. executives took their Japanese counterparts to a Dallas Cowboys football game—with a pit stop in the Texas Stadium parking lot. There the Japanese saw row upon row of full-size pickups. Finally, it dawned on them that Americans see the pickup as more than a commercial vehicle, considering it primary transportation. The result of this was Toyota's best-selling V8 pickup truck, the Toyota Tundra.[12]

In addition to its North American transplant operations, Toyota moved to set up production in Europe in anticipation of the 1992 lowering of trade barriers among the twelve members of the European Economic Community. In 1989 the company announced that it would build a plant in England with the capacity to manufacture 200,000 cars per year by 1997.

In 2001, Toyota opened a second European plant in France, raising its total production capacity within the European Union to 370,000. Toyota's goal is to sell 800,000 cars a year in the EU by 2005, which would give the company a 5 percent share of the EU market.[13]

Despite Toyota's apparent commitment to expand U.S.- and European-based assembly operations, it has not all been smooth sailing. A major problem has been building an overseas supplier network that is comparable to Toyota's Japanese network. For example, in a 1990 meeting of Toyota's North American supplier's association, Toyota executives informed their North American suppliers that the defect ratio for parts produced by 75 North American and European suppliers was 100 times greater than the defect ratio for parts supplied by 147 Japanese suppliers— 1,000 defects per million parts versus 10 defects per million among Toyota's Japanese suppliers. Moreover, Toyota executives pointed out that parts manufactured by North American and European suppliers tend to be significantly more expensive than comparable parts manufactured in Japan.

Because of these problems, Toyota had to import many parts from Japan for its U.S. assembly operations. However, for political reasons Toyota was being pushed to increase the local content of cars assembled in North America. The company's plan was for 50 percent of the value of Toyota cars assembled in the United States to be locally produced by January 1991. Today the local content of cars produced in North America is over 70 percent. To improve the efficiency of its U.S.-based suppliers, Toyota embarked upon an aggressive supplier education process. In 1992, it established the Toyota Supplier Support Center to teach its suppliers the basics of the Toyota production system. By 2001, eighty-nine supplier companies had been through the center. Many have reportedly seen double- and triple-digit productivity growth as a result, as well as dramatic reductions in inventory levels.[14]

Product Strategy

Toyota's initial production was aimed at the small car/basic transportation end of the automobile market. This was true both in Japan and of its export sales to North America and Europe. During the 1980s, however, Toyota progressively moved up market and abandoned much of the lower end of the market to new entrants such as the South Koreans. Thus, the company's Camry and Corolla models, which initially were positioned toward the bottom of the market, have been constantly upgraded and now are aimed at the middle-income segments of the market. This upgrading reflects two factors: (1) the rising level of incomes in Japan and the commensurate increase in the ability of Japanese consumers to purchase mid-range and luxury cars and (2) a desire to hold onto its U.S. consumers, many of whom initially purchased inexpensive Toyotas in their early twenties and who have since traded up to more expensive models.

The constant upgrading of Toyota's models reached its logical conclusion in September 1989 when the company's Lexus division began marketing luxury cars to compete with Jaguars, BMWs, and the like. The Lexus range of cars includes the ES 250, which was initially priced at $22,000, and the LS 400, which comes fully loaded with a $43,000 price tag (for comparison, a Jaguar XJ6 costs $40,000). The initial purpose of Lexus was to go after America's luxury car market, which amounted to about 850,000 unit sales in 1989. The car is also being sold in Japan and Europe.

Encouraged by car testers who rated the Lexus LS 400 the best in its class, Toyota initially projected worldwide sales around 75,000 units for the Lexus models in 1990. The early results for Lexus fell short of expectations. Although the fully loaded LS 400 model appeared to be selling well, the ES 250 model was not, primarily because it was not enough of a luxury car to appeal to luxury buyers. Moreover, a slowdown in the U.S. auto market and the increasing specter of recession during 1990s cut into Lexus's potential sales. As a result, Toyota scaled back its projections for first-year sales from 75,000 to 60,000.[15] Toyota sold 57,162 Lexus models in North America during the 1990 model year.[16] By 2001, Toyota was selling over 200,000 Lexus models a year in the United States, making it the best-selling luxury brand in the country.

Another addition to Toyota's product range in recent years has been a minivan. As with the Lexus range, this vehicle was aimed at the North American market, where the minivan segment has grown most rapidly. Toyota first introduced a minivan in 1986, but it flopped. In typical Toyota fashion, the company dispatched product planners and design engineers to showrooms to find out why. Among the problems they identified were that the minivans lacked an aisle down the center, the short wheelbase gave them a pitchy ride, and the engine was not easy to service. Based on this feedback, Toyota designers completely redesigned the vehicle and reintroduced it in April 1990 as the Previa minivan. The early result exceeded expectations. Toyota sold 50,000 Previas in the first year and projected that it could easily sell 100,000 per year in the future.[17]

Toyota in 2001

As Toyota entered the new millennium, the company's managers could look back upon half a century of remarkable growth. The production system that it had pioneered was recognized as the standard to beat in the industry. From small beginnings in the mid 1980s, it had rapidly established a global production system. Toyota had become the third largest automobile company in the world, and it was still gaining market share in the United States and Europe.

Despite its successes, Toyota is not without problems. Most notably, while its business has blossomed in the United States, things have been tough in Japan for most of the last decade. Although Toyota has held onto its leadership position in Japan, sales have fallen as Japan has struggled with three recessions in ten years. For the first time ever, in 2001 Toyota sold more cars in the United States (1.74 million) than in Japan (1.71 million). More telling still, operating margins on U.S.-produced cars are estimated to run at around 13 percent, compared to 5 percent in Japan. The essence of the problem is that in Japan's shrinking market Toyota faces stiff competition from Nissan and Honda, while in the U.S. market, which is growing faster, Toyota is up against less efficient producers.

ENDNOTES

1. P. Strozniak, "Toyota Alters the Face of Production," *Industry Week*, August 13, 2001, pp. 46–48.
2. Standard & Poors, *Autos and Auto Parts*, December 27, 2001.
3. J. D. Power and Associates, "Toyota Motor Corporation Dominates Vehicle Quality," May 17, 2001, press release.
4. A. Priddle, "Efficiency by the Numbers," *Ward's AutoWorld*, July 2001, pp. 57–59.
5. This section is based primarily on the account given in M. A. Cusumano, *The Japanese Automobile Industry*.
6. The material in this section is drawn from three main sources: M. A. Cusumano, *The Japanese Automobile Industry*; Ohno Tai-ichi, *Toyota Production System* (Cambridge, Mass.: Productivity Press, 1990; Japanese Edition, 1978); J. P. Womack, D. T. Jones, and D. Roos, *The Machine That Changed the World* (New York: Macmillan, 1990).
7. The material in this section is based on M. A. Cusumano, *The Japanese Automobile Industry*.
8. Niland Powell, "U.S.-Japanese Joint Venture: New United Motor Manufacturing, Inc.," *Planning Review*, January–February 1989, pp. 40–45.
9. From J. P. Womack, D. T. Jones, and D. Roos, *The Machine That Changed the World*.
10. J. B. Treece, "Just What Detroit Needs: 200,000 More Toyotas a Year," *Business Week*, December 10, 1990, p. 29.
11. C. Dawson and L. Armstrong, "The Americanization of Toyota," *Business Week*, April 15, 2002, pp. 52–54.
12. Ibid., pp.
13. W. Kimberley, "Toyota Is Building in France," *Automotive Manufacturing and Production*, December 1999, p. 38.
14. P. Strozniak, "Toyota Alters the Face of Production," *Industry Week*, August 13, 2001, pp. 46–48.
15. "The Next Samurai," *The Economist*, December 23, 1989, pp. 69–72; M. Landler and W. Zellner, "No Joyride for Japan," *Business Week*, January 15, 1990, pp. 20–21.
16. "Elegant Nippon," *The Economist*, December 8, 1990, p. 73.
17. J. Flint, "The New Number Three?" *Forbes*, June 11, 1990, pp. 136–140.

Nucor in 2001

16

This case was prepared by Frank C. Barnes, University of North Carolina–Charlotte, and Beverly B. Tyler, North Carolina State University.

Nucor grew quickly in size, market share, and profits from 1975 to 1990. In spite of the economic recession in 1991, it appeared that the fastest-growing steel company in America was unstoppable. Customers liked Nucor's innovations and lower costs, investors were pleased with the high P/E ratio, and Nucor, with Ken Iverson as the model company president, was a media darling. But by the fall of 2001, just ten years later, much had changed. The steel industry worldwide was mired in one of its most unprofitable periods ever. The economic recession that hit Asia and Europe in the late 1990s reached the United States, speeded by the September 11 terrorist attack. The slowing economy affected major steel-consuming industries such as construction, automobiles, and farm equipment. Hamstrung by overcapacity, foreign companies with few markets abroad were dumping their steel in the United States. Although many competitors had copied Nucor's mini-mill production processes and reduced costs, over twenty U.S. steel companies had filed for bankruptcy protection since late 1997. As the company faced a new century, strategic thinking was never more important, expansion was not as simple, and opportunities in steel would be harder to come by. Nucor expected to become the largest steel

maker in the United States, but the challenges ahead were as great as at any period in the company's history.

Background

Nucor could be traced back to the company that manufactured the first Oldsmobile in 1897 and became the Reo Truck Company. As the company declined into bankruptcy in the postwar years, a 1955 merger created Nuclear Corp. of America. Following the "conglomerate" trend of the period, Nuclear acquired various "high-tech" businesses, such as radiation sensors, semiconductors, rare earths, and air conditioning equipment. However, the company lost money continually, and a fourth reorganization in 1965 put forty-year-old Ken Iverson in charge. The building of Nucor had begun.

Ken Iverson had joined the navy after high school in 1943 and had been transferred from officer training school to Cornell's Aeronautical Engineering Program. On graduation he selected mechanical engineering/metallurgy for a master's degree to avoid the long drafting apprenticeship in aeronautical engineering. His college work with an electron microscope earned him a job with International Harvester. After five years in their lab, his boss and mentor prodded him to expand his vision by going with a smaller company.

Over the next ten years, Iverson worked for four small metals companies, gaining technical knowledge and increasing his exposure to other

This case is intended to be used as a basis for class discussion rather than as an illustration of either effective and ineffective handling of the situation. Reprinted by permission of the authors.

C223

business functions. He enjoyed working with the presidents of these small companies and admired their ability to achieve outstanding results. Nuclear Corp., after failing to buy the company Iverson worked for, hired him as a consultant to find them another metals business to buy. In 1962, the firm bought a small joist plant in South Carolina that Iverson found, on the condition that he would run it.

Over the next four years Iverson built up the Vulcraft division as Nuclear Corp. struggled. The president, David Thomas, was described as a great promoter and salesman but a weak manager. A partner with Bear Stearns actually made a personal loan to the company to keep it going. In 1966, when the company was on the edge of bankruptcy, Iverson, who headed the only successful division, was named president and moved the headquarters to Charlotte, North Carolina, where he focused the company business first on the joist industry and soon moved into steel production.

He immediately began getting rid of the esoteric, but unprofitable, high-tech divisions and concentrated on the steel joist business he found successful. They built more joist plants and in 1968 built their first steel mill in South Carolina to "make steel cheaper than they were buying from importers." By 1984 Nucor had six joist plants and four steel mills, using the new "mini-mill" technology.

From the beginning, Iverson had the people running the various plants, called divisions, make all the major decisions about how to build and run Nucor. The original board was composed of Iverson; Sam Siegel, his financial chief; and Dave Aycock, who had been with the South Carolina joist company before Nuclear acquired it. Siegel had joined Nuclear as an accountant in 1961. He quit Nuclear but in their crisis agreed to return as treasurer if Iverson were named president. Aycock and Siegel were named vice presidents at the time Iverson was named president.

Dave Aycock was the last of eight children raised on a small farm in the poor Wadesboro, North Carolina, community. He attended the University of North Carolina at Chapel Hill for one month, before financial considerations convinced him to join the navy as an enlisted man. For the next three years and eight months his specialty was as a metalsmith. On leaving the service in 1954, he got a job at Vulcraft as a welder. Over the next six years he worked his way up to production supervisor and assistant plant manager, and then to sales manager.

Aycock had been very impressed with the owner of Vulcraft, Sanborn Chase. He described him as "the best person I've ever known" and as "a scientific genius." He said he was a man of great compassion who understood the atmosphere necessary to enable people to self-motivate. Chase, an engineer by training, invented a number of things in diverse fields. He also established the incentive programs for which Nucor later became known. With only one plant, he was still able to operate with a "decentralized" manner. Before his death in 1960, while still in his forties, the company was studying the building of a steel mill using newly developed mini-mill technology. His widow ran the company until it was sold to Nucor in 1962.

Aycock met Ken Iverson when Nuclear purchased Vulcraft, and they worked together closely for the next year and a half. Located in Phoenix at the corporate headquarters, he was responsible to Iverson for all the joist operations and was given the task of planning and building a new joist plant in Texas. In late 1963 he was transferred to Norfolk, where he lived for the next thirteen years and managed a number of Nucor's joist plants. Then in 1977 he was named the manager of the Darlington, South Carolina, steel plant.

Aycock had this to say about Iverson: "Ken was a very good leader, with an entrepreneurial spirit. He is easy to work with and has the courage to do things, to take lots of risks. Many things didn't work, but some worked very well." There is the old saying "failure to take risk is failure." This saying epitomizes a cultural value personified by the company's founder and reinforced by Iverson during his time at the helm. Nucor was very innovative in steel and joists. Their plant was years ahead in wire rod welding at Norfolk. In the late 1960s they had one of the first computer inventory management systems and design/engineering programs. They were very sophisticated in purchasing, sales, and managing, and they often beat their competition by the speed of their design efforts.

In 1984, Aycock became Nucor's president and chief operating officer, while Iverson became chairman and chief executive officer. Whereas Iverson was an enthusiastic spokesman for Nucor's story, Aycock took a more low keyed position. On one occasion he commented, "I was never as consumed by the excitement of making hot metal. To me Nucor is a company with lots of employees and investors." For him

Nucor's purpose was to create value for stockholders and employees. The fact that it did so by making steel was secondary.

By 1984, in just twenty years, a bankrupt conglomerate had become a leading steel company in America. It was a fairytale story. Tom Peters used Nucor's management style as an example of "excellence," while the barons of old steel ruled over creeping ghettos. NBC featured Nucor on television and *New Yorker* magazine serialized a book about how a relatively small American steel company built a team that led the whole world into a new era of steel making. As the NBC program asked: "If Japan Can, Why Can't We?" Nucor had! Iverson was rich, owning $10 million in stock, but with a salary which rarely reached $1 million, compared with some U.S. executives' $50 or $100 million. The forty-year-old manager of the South Carolina Vulcraft plant had become a millionaire. Stockholders chuckled, and non-unionized hourly workers, who had never seen a layoff in twenty years, earned more than the unionized workers of old steel and more than 85 percent of the people in the states where they worked. Many employees were financially quite secure.

Nucor owed much of its success to its benchmark organizational style and the empowered division managers. There were two basic lines of business. The first was the six steel joist plants that made the steel frames seen in many buildings. The second included four steel mills that utilized the innovative mini-mill technology to supply first the joist plants and later the outside customers. Nucor was still only the seventh largest steel company in America. Over its second twenty years, Nucor was to rise to become the second largest U.S. steel company. A number of significant challenges were to be met and overcome to get there, and once that horizon was reached even greater challenges would arise. The following describes the systems Nucor built and its organization, divisions, management, and incentive system.

Nucor's Organization

In the early 1990s, each of Nucor's twenty-two divisions, one for every plant, had a general manager who was also a vice president of the corporation. The divisions were of three basic types: joist plants, steel mills, and miscellaneous plants. The corporate staff consisted of less than twenty-five people. In the beginning Iverson had chosen Charlotte "as the new home base for what he had envisioned as a small cadre of executives who would guide a decentralized operation with liberal authority delegated to managers in the field," according to *South Magazine*. Iverson gave his views on keeping a lean organization:

> Each division is a profit center and the division manager has control over the day-to-day decisions that make that particular division profitable or not profitable. We expect the division to provide contribution, which is earnings before corporate expenses. We do not allocate our corporate expenses, because we do not think there is any way to do this reasonably and fairly. We do focus on earnings. And we expect a division to earn 25 percent return on total assets employed, before corporate expenses, taxes, interest or profit sharing. And we have a saying in the company—if a manager doesn't provide that for a number of years, we are either going to get rid of the division or get rid of the general manager, and it's generally the division manager.

A joist division manager commented on being in an organization with only four levels:

> I've been a division manager four years now and at times I'm still awed by it: the opportunity I was given to be a Fortune 500 vice president. . . . I think we are successful because it is our style to pay more attention to our business than our competitors. . . . We are kind of a "no nonsense" company.

The divisions did their own manufacturing, selling, accounting, engineering, and personnel management. A steel division manager, when questioned about Florida Steel, which had a large plant 90 miles away, commented, "I expect they do have more of the hierarchy. I think they have central purchasing, centralized sales, centralized credit collections, centralized engineering, and most of the major functions."

Nucor strengthened its position by developing strong alliances with outside parties. It did no internal research and development. Instead, it monitored others' work worldwide and attracted investors who brought it new technical applications at the earliest possible dates. Though Nucor was known for constructing new facilities at the lowest possible costs, its engineering and construction team consisted of only three individuals. They did not attempt to specify exact equipment parameters, but instead asked the equipment supplier to provide this information and then held the manufacturer accountable. They had alliances with selected construction companies around the country who knew the kind of work Nucor wanted. Nucor bought 95 percent of its scrap steel from an independent broker who followed the market and made recommendations regarding scrap purchases. It did not have a corporate advertising department, corporate public relations department, or corporate legal or environmental department. It had long-term relationships with outsiders to provide these services.

Because the steel industry had established a pattern of absorbing the cost of shipment, all users paid the same delivered price, regardless of the distance from the mill. Nucor broke with this tradition and stopped equalizing freight. It offered all customers the same sales terms. Nucor also gave no volume discounts, feeling that with modern computer systems there was no justification. Customers located next to the plant guaranteed themselves the lowest possible costs for steel purchases. Two tube manufacturers, two steel service centers, and a cold rolling facility had located adjacent to the Arkansas plant. These facilities accounted for 60 percent of the shipments from the mill. The plants were linked electronically to each other's production schedules and thus could function in a just-in-time inventory mode. All new mills were built on large enough tracks of land to accommodate collaborating businesses.

Iverson didn't feel greater centralization would be good for Nucor. Hamilton Lott, a Vulcraft plant manager, commented in 1997, "We're truly autonomous; we can duplicate efforts made in other parts of Nucor. We might develop the same computer program six times. But the advantages of local autonomy make it worth it." Joe Rutkowski, manager at Darlington steel, agreed, "We're not constrained; headquarters doesn't restrict what I spend. I just have to make my profit contribution at the end of year."

South Magazine observed that Iverson had established a characteristic organizational style described as "stripped down" and "no nonsense." "Jack Benny would like this company," observed Roland Underhill, an analyst with Crowell, Weedon and Co. of Los Angeles, and "so would Peter Drucker." Underhill pointed out that Nucor's thriftiness doesn't end with its "spartan" office staff or modest offices. "There are no corporate perquisites," he recited. "No company planes, no country club memberships, no company cars." *Fortune* noted, "Iverson takes the subway when he is in New York, a Wall Street analyst reports in a voice that suggests both admiration and amazement." The general managers reflected this style in the operation of their individual divisions. Their offices were more like plant offices or the offices of private companies, built around manufacturing rather than for public appeal. They were simple, routine, and businesslike.

Division Managers

The corporate personnel manager described management relations as informal, trusting, and not "bureaucratic." He felt there was a minimum of paperwork, that a phone call was more common than memos, and that no confirming memo was thought to be necessary.

A Vulcraft manager commented: "We have what I would call a very friendly spirit of competition from one plant to the next. And of course all of the vice presidents and general managers share the same bonus systems so we are in this together as a team even though we operate our divisions individually." He added: "When I came to this plant four years ago, I saw we had too many people, too much overhead. We had 410 people at the plant and I could see, from my experience at the Nebraska plant, we had many more than we needed. Now with 55 fewer men, we are still capable of producing the same number of tons as four years ago."

The divisions managed their activities with a minimum of contact with the corporate staff. Each day disbursements were reported to corporate office. Payments flowed into regional lockboxes. On a weekly basis, joist divisions reported total quotes, sales cancellations, backlog, and production. Steel mills reported tons rolled, outside shipments, orders, cancellations, and backlog.

Each month the divisions completed a two-page (11″ × 17″) "Operations Analysis" which was sent to all the managers. Its three main purposes were (1) financial consolidation, (2) sharing information among the divisions, and (3) corporate management examination. The summarized information and the performance statistics for all the divisions were then returned to the managers.

The general managers met three times a year. In late October they presented preliminary budgets and capital requests. In late February they met to finalize budgets and treat miscellaneous matters. Then, at a meeting in May, they handled personnel matters, such as wage increases and changes of policies or benefits. The general managers as a group considered the raises for the department heads, the next lower level of management for all the plants.

Vulcraft—Joist Divisions

One of Nucor's major businesses was the manufacture and sale of open web steel joists and joist girders at six Vulcraft divisions located in Florence, South Carolina; Norfolk, Nebraska; Ft. Payne, Alabama; Grapeland, Texas; St. Joe, Indiana; and Brigham City, Utah. Open web joists, in contrast to solid joists, were made of steel angle iron separated by round bars or smaller angle iron (Figure 1). These joists cost less, were stronger for many applications, and were used primarily as the roof support systems in larger buildings, such as warehouses and shopping malls.

The joist industry was characterized by high competition among many manufacturers for many small customers. With an estimated 40 percent of the market, Nucor was the largest supplier in the United States. It utilized national advertising campaigns and prepared competitive bids on 80 to 90 percent of the buildings using joists. Competition was based on price and delivery performance. Nucor had developed computer programs to prepare designs for customers and to compute bids based on current prices and labor standards. In addition, each Vulcraft plant maintained its own engineering department to help customers with design problems or specifications. The Florence manager commented, "Here on the East Coast we have six or seven major competitors; of course none of them are as large as we are. The competition for any order will be heavy, and we will see six or seven different prices." He added, "I think we have a strong selling force in the marketplace. It has been said to us by some of our competitors that in this particular industry we have the finest selling organization in the country."

Nucor aggressively sought to be the lowest-cost producer in the industry. Materials and freight were two important elements of cost. Nucor maintained its own fleet of almost 150 trucks to ensure on-time delivery to all of the states, although most business was regional because of transportation costs. Plants were located in rural areas near the markets they served. Nucor's move into steel production was a move to lower the cost of steel used by the joist business.

Joist Production   On the basic assembly line used at the joist divisions, three or four of which might make up any one plant, about six tons of joists per hour would be assembled. In the first stage eight people cut the angles to the right lengths or bent the round bars to the desired form. These were moved on a roller conveyer to six-man assembly stations, where the component parts would be tacked together for the next stage, welding. Drilling and miscellaneous work were done by three people between the lines. The nine-man welding station completed the welds before passing the joists on roller conveyers to two-man inspection teams. The last step before shipment was the painting.

The workers had control over and responsibility for quality. There was an independent quality control inspector who had the authority to reject the run of

(a)

(b)

FIGURE 1

Illustration of Joists

joists and cause them to be reworked. The quality control people were not under the incentive system and reported to the engineering department.

Daily production might vary widely, since each joist was made for a specific job. The wide range of joists made control of the workload at each station difficult; bottlenecks might arise anywhere along the line. Each workstation was responsible for identifying such bottlenecks so that the foreman could reassign people promptly to maintain productivity. Since workers knew most of the jobs on the line, including the more-skilled welding job, they could be shifted as needed. Work on the line was described by one general manager as "not machine type but mostly physical labor." He said the important thing was to avoid bottlenecks.

There were four lines of about twenty-eight people each on two shifts at the Florence division. The jobs on the line were rated on responsibility and assigned a base wage, from $11 to $13 per hour. In addition, a weekly bonus was paid on the total output of each line. Each worker received the same percent bonus on his base wage. The Texas plant was typical, with the bonus running at 225 percent, giving a wage of $27 an hour in 1999.

The amount of time required to make a joist had been established as a result of experience; the general manager had seen no time studies in his fifteen years with the company. As a job was bid, the cost of each joist was determined through the computer program. The time required depended on the number of panels and the length and depth of the joist. At the time of production, the labor value of production, the standard, was determined in a similar manner. The South Carolina general manager stated, "In the last nine or ten years we have not changed a standard."

The Grapeland plant maintained a time chart, which was used to estimate the labor required on a job. The plant teams were measured against this time for bonus. The chart was based on the historical time required on the jobs. Every few years the time chart was updated. Because some of the changes in performance were due to equipment changes, generally the chart would be increased by half the change and the employee would benefit in pay from the other half. The last change, two years ago, saw some departments' pay increased by as much as 10 percent. The production manager at Grapeland considered himself an example for the Nucor policy—"the sky is the limit." He had started in an entry position and risen to the head of this plant of two hundred people.

Table 1 shows the productivity of the South Carolina plant in tons per man-hour for a number of years. The year 1999 set a record for overall tonnage. The manager explained that the small drop in 2000 was due to managerial changes; he was new to the division and had brought two new managers with him.

Steel Divisions

Nucor moved into the steel business in 1969 to provide raw material for the Vulcraft plants. Iverson said, "We got into the steel business because we wanted to build a mill that could make steel as cheaply as we were buying it from foreign importers or from offshore mills." Thus they entered the industry using the new mini-mill technology after they took a task force of four people around the world to investigate new technological advancements. A case writer from Harvard recounted the development of the steel divisions:

> By 1967 about 60% of each Vulcraft sales dollar was spent on materials, primarily steel. Thus, the goal of keeping costs low made it imperative to obtain steel economically. In addition, in 1967 Vulcraft bought about 60% of its steel from foreign sources. As the Vulcraft Division grew, Nucor became concerned about its ability to obtain an adequate economical supply of steel and in 1968 began construction of its first steel mill in Darlington, South Carolina. By 1972 the Florence, South Carolina, joist plant was purchasing over 90% of its steel from this mill. The Fort Payne, Alabama plant bought about 50% of its steel from Florence. The other joist plants in Nebraska, Indiana and Texas found transportation costs prohibitive and continued to buy their steel from other

---

TABLE 1

Tons per Man-hour

1977—0.163	1982—0.208	1987—0.218
1978—0.179	1983—0.215	1988—0.249
1979—0.192	1984—0.214	1999—0.251
1980—0.195	1985—0.228	2000—0.241
1981—0.194	1986—0.225	

steel companies, both foreign and domestic. Since the mill had excess capacity, Nucor began to market its steel products to outside customers. In 1972, 75% of the shipments of Nucor steel was to Vulcraft and 25% was to other customers.

Between 1973 and 1981 they constructed three more bar mills and their accompanying rolling mills to convert the billits into bars, flats, rounds, channels, and other products. Iverson explained in 1984:

> In constructing these mills we have experimented with new processes and new manufacturing techniques. We serve as our own general contractor and design and build much of our own equipment. In one or more of our mills we have built our own continuous casting unit, reheat furnaces, cooling beds and in Utah even our own mill stands. All of these to date have cost under $125 per ton of annual capacity—compared with projected costs for large integrated mills of $1,200–1,500 per ton of annual capacity, ten times our cost. Our mills have high productivity. We currently use less than four man hours to produce a ton of steel. This includes everyone in the operation: maintenance, clerical, accounting, and sales and management. On the basis of our production workers alone, it is less than three man hours per ton. Our total employment costs are less than $60 per ton compared with the average employment costs of the seven largest U.S. steel companies of close to $130 per ton. Our total labor costs are less than 20% of our sales price.

In 1987 Nucor was the first steel company in the world to begin to build a mini-mill to manufacture steel sheet, the raw material for the auto industry and other major manufacturers. This project opened up another 50 percent of the total steel market. The first plant in Crawfordsville, Indiana, was successful, and three additional sheet mills were constructed between 1989 and 1990. Through the years these steel plants were significantly modernized and expanded until the total capacity was 3 million tons per year at a capital cost of less than $170 dollars per ton by 1999. Nucor's total steel production capacity was 5.9 million tons per year at a cost of $300 per ton of annual capacity. The eight mills sold 80 percent of their output to outside customers and the balance to other Nucor divisions. A new million-ton steel plate mill was under construction in Hartford County, North Carolina.

All four of the bar mills were actually two mills operating side by side. One mill concentrated on the larger bar products, which had separate production and customer demands, while the other mill concentrated on smaller-diameter bar stock. Throughout Nucor each operation was housed in its own separate building with its own staff. Nucor designed its processes to limit work-in-process inventory, to limit space, to utilize a pull approach to material usage, and to increase flexibility.

The Steel-Making Process   A steel mill's work is divided into two phases: preparation of steel of the proper "chemistry" and the forming of the steel into the desired products. The typical mini-mill utilized scrap steel, such as junk auto parts, instead of the iron ore, which would be used in larger, integrated steel mills. The typical bar mini-mill had an annual capacity of 200,000 to 600,000 tons, compared with the 7 million tons of Bethlehem Steel's Sparrow's Point, Maryland, integrated plant.

In the bar mills a charging bucket fed loads of scrap steel into electric arc furnaces. The melted load, called a heat, was poured into a ladle to be carried by overhead crane to the casting machine. In the casting machine the liquid steel was extruded as a continuous red-hot solid bar of steel and cut into lengths weighing some 900 pounds called "billets." In the typical plant the billet, about 4 inches in cross section and about 20 feet long, was held temporarily in a pit where it cooled to normal temperatures. Periodically billets were carried to the rolling mill and placed in a reheat oven to bring them up to 2,000 degrees Fahrenheit, at which temperance they would be malleable. In the rolling mill, presses and dies progressively converted the billet into the desired round bars, angles, channels, flats, and other products. After cutting to standard lengths, they were moved to the warehouse.

Nucor's first steel mill, which employed more than five hundred people, was located in Darlington, South Carolina. The mill, with its three electric arc furnaces, operated twenty-four hours per day, five and a half days per week. Nucor had made a number of improvements in the melting and casting operations. The general manager of the Darlington plant developed a system that involved preheating the ladles, which allowed for the faster flow of steel into the caster and resulted in better control of the steel characteristics. Thus less time and lower capital investment were required at Darlington than at other mini-mills at the time of its construction. The casting machines were "continuous casters," as opposed to the old batch method. The objective in the "front" of the mill was to keep the casters working. At the time the Darlington plant was also perhaps the only mill in the country that regularly avoided the reheating of billets. This saved $10 to $12 per ton in fuel usage and losses due to oxidation of the steel. The cost of developing this process had been $12 million. All research projects had not been successful. The company spent approximately $2 million in an unsuccessful effort to utilize resistance heating. It lost even more on an effort at induction melting. As Iverson told *Metal Producing,* "That costs us a lot of money. Timewise it was very expensive. But you have got to make mistakes and we've had lots of failures."

The Darlington design became the basis for plants in Nebraska, Texas, and Utah. The Texas plant had cost under $80 per ton of annual capacity. Whereas the typical mini-mill at the time cost approximately $250 per ton, the average cost of Nucor's four mills was under $135. An integrated mill was expected to cost between $1,200 and $1,500 per ton.

The Darlington plant was organized into twelve natural groups for the purpose of incentive pay. Two mills each had two shifts with three groups—melting and casting, rolling mill, and finishing. In melting and casting there were three or four different standards, depending on the material, that were established by the department manager years ago based on historical performance. The general manager stated, "We don't change the standards." The caster, key to the operation, was used at a 92 percent level—one percentage point greater than the claims of the manufacturer. For every good ton of billet above the standard hourly rate for the week, workers in the group received a 4 percent bonus. For example, with a common standard of 10 tons per run hour and an actual rate for the week of 28 tons per hour, the workers would receive a bonus of 72 percent of their base rate in the week's paycheck. In the rolling mill there were more than one hundred products, each with a different historical standard. Workers received a 4 to 6 percent bonus over the computed standard for every good ton sheared per hour for the week. A manager stated: "Meltshop employees don't ask me how much it costs Chaparral or LTV to make a billet. They want

to know what it costs Darlington, Norfolk, Jewitt to put a billet on the ground—scrap costs, alloy costs, electrical costs, refractory, gas, etc. Everybody from Charlotte to Plymouth watches the nickels and dimes."

Management Philosophy

Aycock, while still the Darlington manager, stated:

The key to making a profit when selling a product with no aesthetic value, or a product that you really can't differentiate from your competitors, is cost. I don't look at us as a fantastic marketing organization, even though I think we are pretty good; but we don't try to overcome unreasonable costs by mass marketing. We maintain low costs by keeping the employee force at the level it should be, not doing things that aren't necessary to achieve our goals, and allowing people to function on their own and judging them on their results.

To keep a cooperative and productive work force you need, number one, to be completely honest about everything; number two, to allow each employee as much as possible to make decisions about that employee's work, to find easier and more productive ways to perform duties; and number three, to be as fair as possible to all employees. Most of the changes we make in work procedures and in equipment come from the employees. They really know the problems of their jobs better than anyone else. We don't have any industrial engineers, nor do we ever intend to, because that's a type of specialist who tends to take responsibility off the top division management and give them a crutch.

To communicate with my employees, I try to spend time in the plant and at intervals have meetings with the employees. Usually if they have a question they just visit me. Recently a small group visited me in my office to discuss our vacation policy. They had some suggestions and, after listening to them, I had to agree that the ideas were good.

In discussing his philosophy for dealing with the work force, the Florence manager stated:

I believe very strongly in the incentive system we have. We are a nonunion shop and we all feel that the way to stay so is to take care of our people and show them we care. I think that's easily done because of our fewer layers of management. . . . I spend a good part of my time in the plant, maybe an hour or so a day. If a man wants to know anything, for example an insurance question, I'm there and they walk right up to me and ask me questions, which I'll answer the best I know how.

We don't lay our people off and we make a point of telling our people this. In the slowdown of 1994, we scheduled our line for four days, but the men were allowed to come in the fifth day for maintenance work at base pay. The men in the plant on an average running bonus might make $17 to $19 an hour. If their base pay is half that, on Friday they would only get $8 to $9 an hour. Surprisingly, many of the men did not want to come in on Friday. They felt comfortable with just working four days a week. They are happy to have that extra day off.

About 20 percent of the people took the fifth day at base rate, but still no one had been laid off, in an industry with a strong business cycle.

In an earlier business cycle the executive committee decided in view of economic conditions that a pay freeze was necessary. The employees normally received an increase in their base pay the first of June. The decision was made at that time to freeze wages. The officers of the company, as a show of good faith, accepted a 5 percent pay cut. In addition to announcing this to the workers with a stuffer in their pay envelopes, the executives held meetings. Each production line, or incentive group of workers, met in the plant conference room with all supervisory personnel—foreman, plant production manager, and division manager. The production manager explained the economic crisis the company was facing to the employees, and all of their questions were answered.

Personnel and Incentive Systems

The foremost characteristic of Nucor's personnel system was its incentive plan. Another major personnel policy was providing job security. Also, all employees at Nucor received the same fringe benefits. There was only one group insurance plan. Holidays and vacations did not differ by job. Every child of every Nucor employee received up to $1,200 a year for four years if he or she chose to go on to higher education, including technical schools. The company had no executive dining rooms or restrooms and no fishing lodges, company cars, or reserved parking places.

Jim Coblin, Nucor's vice president of human resources, described Nucor's systems for *HRMagazine* in a 1994 article: "No-frills HR at Nucor: a lean, bottom-line approach at this steel company empowers employees." Coblin, as benefits administrator, received part-time help from one of the corporate secretaries in the corporate office. The plants typically used someone from their finance department to handle compensation issues, although two plants had personnel generalists. Nucor plants did not have job descriptions; they found they caused more problems than they solved, given the flexible work force and nonunion status of Nucor employees. Surprisingly, Coblin also found performance appraisal a waste of time. If an employee was not performing well, the problem would be dealt with directly. He had observed that when promotional opportunities became available, the performance appraisals were not much help in filling the position. So he saw both of these as just more paperwork. The key, he believed, was not to put a maximum on what employees could earn and to pay them directly for productivity. Iverson firmly believed that the bonus should be direct and involve no discretion on the part of a manager.

Employees were kept informed about the company. Charts showing the division's results in return-on-assets and bonus payoff were posted in prominent places in the plant. The personnel manager commented that as he traveled around to all the plants, he found that everyone in the company could tell him the level of profits in his or her division. The general managers held dinners at least once but usually twice a year with their employees. The dinners were held with fifty or sixty employees at a time, resulting in as many as twenty dinners per year. After introductory remarks the floor was open for discussion of any work-related problems. There was a new employee orientation program and an employee handbook that contained personnel policies and rules. The corporate office sent all news releases to each division, where they were posted on bulletin boards. Each employee in the company also received a copy of the annual report. For the last several years the cover of the annual report had contained the names of all Nucor employees.

Absenteeism and tardiness were not a problem at Nucor. Each employee had four days of absences before pay was reduced. In addition to these, missing work was allowed for jury duty, military leave, or the death of close relatives. After this, a day's absence cost an employee bonus pay for that week, and lateness of more than a half hour meant the loss of bonus for that day.

Safety was a concern of Nucor's critics. With ten fatalities in the 1980s, Nucor was committed to doing better. Safety administrators were appointed in each plant, and safety improved in the 1990s. The company also had a formal grievance procedure, although the Darlington manager couldn't recall the last grievance he had processed.

The company had conducted attitude surveys every three years for over two decades. These provided management insight into employee attitudes on twenty issues and allowed comparisons across plants and divisions. There were some concerns and differences, but most employees appeared very satisfied with Nucor as an employer (see appendices 1 and 2). The surveys suggested that pay was not the only thing the workers liked about Nucor. The personnel manager said that an NBC interviewer, working on the documentary "If Japan Can, Why Can't We?" often heard employees say, "I enjoy working for Nucor because Nucor is the best, the most productive, and the most profitable company that I know of."

The average hourly worker's pay was over twice the average earnings paid by other manufacturing companies in the states where Nucor's plants were located. In many rural communities where Nucor had located, it provided better wages than most other manufacturers. The new plant in Hertford County illustrated this point in a June 21, 1998, article in the *Charlotte Observer,* entitled "Hope on the Horizon: In Hertford County, Poverty Reigns and Jobs are Scarce." Here the author wrote, "In North Carolina's forgotten northeastern corner, where poverty rates run more than twice the state average, Nucor's $300 million steel mill is a dream realized." The plant on the banks of the Chowan River in North Carolina's coastal district had their employees earning a rumored $60,000 a year, three times the local average manufacturing wage. Nucor had recently begun developing its plant sites with the expectation that other companies would colocate to save shipping costs. Four companies have announced plans to locate close to Nucor's property, adding another one to two hundred jobs. People couldn't believe such wages, but calls to the plant's chief financial officer got "We don't like to promise too much, but $60,000

might be a little low." The average wage for these jobs at Darlington was $70,000. The plant's CFO added that Nucor didn't try to set pay "a buck over Wal-Mart" but went for the best workers. The article noted that steel work is hot and often dangerous, and that turnover at the plant may be high as people adjust to this and to Nucor's hard-driving team system. He added, "Slackers don't last." The state of North Carolina had given $155 million in tax credits over twenty-five years. The local preacher said, "In fifteen years, Baron (a local child) will be making $75,000 a year at Nucor, not in jail. I have a place now I can hold in front of him and say 'Look, right here. This is for you.'"

The Incentive System   There were four incentive programs at Nucor, one each for (1) production workers, (2) department heads, (3) staff people such as accountants, secretaries, or engineers, and (4) senior management, which included the division managers. All of these programs were based on group performance.

Within the production program, groups ranged in size from twenty-five to thirty people and had definable and measurable operations. The company believed that a program should be simple and that bonuses should be paid promptly. "We don't have any discretionary bonuses—zero. It is all based on performance. Now we don't want anyone to sit in judgment, because it never is fair," said Iverson. The personnel manager stated: "Their bonus is based on roughly 90 percent of the historical time it takes to make a particular joist. If during a week they make joists at 60 percent less than the standard time, they receive a 60 percent bonus." This was paid with the regular pay the following week. The complete paycheck amount, including overtime, was multiplied by the bonus factor. A bonus was not paid when equipment was not operating: "We have the philosophy that when equipment is not operating everybody suffers and the bonus for downtime is zero." The foremen were also part of the group and received the same bonus as the employees they supervised.

The second incentive program was for department heads in the various divisions. The incentive pay here was based on division contribution, defined as the division earnings before corporate expenses and profit sharing are determined. Bonuses were reported to run between 0 and 90 percent (average 35–50 percent) of a person's base salary. The base salaries at this level were set at 75 percent of industry norms.

There was a third plan for people who were not production workers, department managers, or senior managers. Their bonus was based on either the division return-on-assets or the corporate return-on-assets, depending on the unit they were a part of. Bonuses were typically 30 percent or more of a person's base salary for corporate positions.

The fourth program was for the senior officers. The senior officers had no employment contracts, pension or retirement plans, or other perquisites. Their base salaries were set at about 75 percent of what an individual doing similar work in other companies would receive. Once return-on-equity reached 9 percent, slightly below the average for manufacturing firms, 5 percent of net earnings before taxes went into a pool, which was divided among the officers based on their salaries. "Now if return-on-equity for the company reaches, say 20 percent, which it has, then we can wind up with as much as 190 percent of our base salaries and 115 percent on top of that in stock. We get both." Half the bonus was paid in cash and half was deferred. Individual bonuses ranged from zero to several hundred percent, averaging 75 to 150 percent.

However, the opposite was true as well. In 1982 the return was 8 percent and the executives received no bonus. Iverson's pay in 1981 was approximately $300,000 but dropped the next year to $110,000. "I think that ranked by total compensation I was the lowest paid CEO in the Fortune 500. I was kind of proud of that, too." In his 1997 book, *Plain Talk: Lessons from a Business Maverick,* Iverson said, "Can management expect employees to be loyal if we lay them all off at every dip of the economy, while we go on padding our own pockets?" Even so, by 1986 Iverson's stock was worth over $10 million dollars and the once Vulcraft manager was a millionaire.

In lieu of a retirement plan, the company had a profit sharing plan with a deferred trust. Each year 10 percent of pretax earnings was put into profit sharing for all people below officer level. Twenty percent of this was set aside to be paid to employees in the following March as a cash bonus, and the remainder was put into trust for each employee on the basis of the percentage of their earnings as a percentage of total wages paid within the corporation. The employee was vested after the first year. Employees received a quarterly statement of their balance in profit sharing.

The company had an Employer Monthly Stock Investment Plan to which Nucor added 10 percent to the amount the employee contributed on the purchase of any Nucor stock, and paid the commission. After each five years of service with the company, the employee received a service award consisting of five shares of Nucor stock. Moreover, if profits were good, extraordinary bonus payments would be made to the employees. For example, in December 1998 each employee received a $800 payment. Iverson said:

> I think the first obligation of the company is to the stockholder and to its employees. I find in this country too many cases where employees are underpaid and corporate management is making huge social donations for self-fulfillment. We regularly give donations, but we have a very interesting corporate policy. First, we give donations where our employees are. Second, we give donations that will benefit our employees, such as to the YMCA. It is a difficult area and it requires a lot of thought. There is certainly a strong social responsibility for a company, but it cannot be at the expense of the employees or the stockholders.

Having welcomed a parade of visitors over the years, Iverson had become concerned with the pattern apparent at other companies' steel plants: "They only do one or two of the things we do. It's not just incentives or the scholarship program; it's all those things put together that results in a unified philosophy for the company."

Building on Success

Throughout the 1980s and 1990s Nucor continued to take the initiative and to be the prime mover in steel and the industries vertically related to steel. For example, in 1984 Nucor broke with the industry pattern of basing the price of an order of steel on the quantity ordered. Iverson noted, "Some time ago we began to realize that with computer order entry and billing, the extra charge for smaller orders was not cost justified." In a seemingly risky move in 1986, Nucor began construction of a $25 million plant in Indiana to manufacture steel fasteners. Imports had grown to 90 percent of this market as U.S. companies failed to compete. Iverson said, "We're going to bring that business back; we can make bolts as cheaply as foreign producers." A second plant, in 1995, gave Nucor 20 percent of the U.S. market for steel fasteners. Nucor also acquired a steel bearings manufacturer in 1986, which Iverson called "a good fit with our business, our policies and our people."

In early 1986 Iverson announced plans for a revolutionary plant at Crawfordsville, Indiana, which would be the first mini-mill in the world to manufacture flat-rolled or sheet steel, the last bastion of the integrated manufacturers. This market alone was twice the size of the existing market for mini-mill products. It would be a quarter of a billion dollar gamble on a new technology. The plant was expected to halve the integrated manufacturer's $3 of labor per ton and save $50 to $75 on a $400-a-ton selling price. If it worked, the profit from this plant alone would come close to the profit of the whole corporation. *Forbes* commented, "If any mini-mill can meet the challenge, it's Nucor. But expect the going to be tougher this time around." If successful, Nucor had the licensing rights to the next two plants built in the world with this technology.

Nucor had spent millions trying to develop the process when it heard of some promising developments at a German company. In the spring of 1986, Aycock flew to Germany to see the pilot machine at SMS Schloemann-Siemag AG. In December the Germans came to Charlotte for the first of what they thought would be many meetings to hammer out a deal with Nucor. Iverson shocked them when he announced Nucor was ready to build the first plant of its kind.

Kieth Busse was given the job of building the Crawfordsville, Indiana, sheet steel plant. Though an accountant by training, Busse had designed and built Nucor's state-of-the-art bolt factory. A midwesterner of German extraction, as a sideline he ran a gun supermarket in Fort Wayne and was the biggest machine gun dealer in northern Indiana. The process of bringing this plant online was so exciting that it became the basis for a best-selling book by Robert Preston, which was serialized in *New Yorker* magazine.

Preston reported on a conversation at dinner during construction between Iverson and Busse. Thinking about the future, Busse was worried that Nucor might someday become like Big Steel. He asked, "How do we allow Nucor to grow without expanding the bureaucracy?" He commented on the vice presidents stacked on vice presidents, research departments, assistants to assistants, and so on. Iverson agreed. Busse seriously suggested, "Maybe we're going to need group vice presidents." Iverson's heated response was "Do you want to ruin the company? That's the old Harvard Business School thinking. They would only get in the way, slow us down." He said the company could at least double, to $2 billion, before it added a new level of management. "I hope that by the time we have group vice presidents I'll be collecting Social Security."

The gamble on the new plant paid off and Busse, the general manager of the plant, became a key man within Nucor. The new mill began operations in August of 1989 and reached 15 percent of capacity by the end of the year. In June of 1990 it had its first profitable month, and Nucor announced the construction of a second plant in Arkansas.

In December 1992, Nucor signed a letter of intent with Oregon Steel Mills to build a sheet mill on the West Coast to begin in 1994. This project was later canceled. The supply and cost of scrap steel to feed the mini-mills was an important future concern to Iverson. So at the beginning of 1993 Nucor announced the construction of a plant in Trinidad to supply its mills with iron carbide pellets. The innovative plant would cost $60 million and take a year and a half to complete. In 1994 the two existing sheet mills were expanded and a new $500 million, 1.8-million-ton sheet mill in South Carolina was announced, to begin operation in early 1997.

In what the *New York Times* called their "most ambitious project yet," in 1987 Nucor had begun a joint venture with Yamato Kogyo, Ltd., to make structural steel products in a mill on the Mississippi River in a direct challenge to the Big Three integrated steel companies. He put John Correnti in charge of the operation.

John Correnti, born in the Finger Lakes region of western New York, received a degree in civil engineering from Clarkson University in 1969. He commented: "I was a C/F student my first two years and an A/B student my last two years." After seventeen offers, he accepted a job with U.S. Steel in their construction department. He was energetic and ambitious and became one of the youngest people to ever become a construction superintendent there. The construction group members were considered mavericks at U.S. Steel and specialized in overcoming the bureaucracy and paperwork. While employed by U.S. Steel, Correnti conducted projects in a wide range of steel operations across the country.

While working on a project in Texas in 1980, Correnti married a Texan and decided to leave U.S. Steel rather than move his wife out of Texas. A headhunter showed him a construction manager job with Nucor, a company he had never heard of. And Ken Iverson convinced him to join the company and move to Salt Lake City to build a bar plant at Plymoth, Utah. Correnti was used to being independent: "I just started doing things, and I figured that when they didn't want me to do something, I'd hear from somebody. I never heard from anybody."

In 1984 he moved to a more-challenging job of vice president and general manager of the Utah bar mill, which was not performing well. He wasted no time getting everyone focused on cost cutting, pointing out examples of wasted pens in one man's desk and the possibility of washing and reusing gloves. The plant office, dubbed the Taj Mahal by people in the plant, was too far from the main operations, so Correnti had it torn down and moved the staff into a nearby engineering building. He wouldn't let the salespeople have carpet until their sales reached the desired level. By the time he left in 1986 to build the Nucor-Yamato plant, the division was turning profitable.

Correnti built and then became the general manager of Nucor-Yamato when it started up in 1988. In 1991 he surprised many people by deciding to double Nucor-Yamato's capacity by 1994. It became Nucor's largest division and the largest wide flange producer in the United States. By 1995, Bethlehem Steel was the only other wide flange producer of structural steel products left and had plans to leave the business.

Nucor started up its first facility to produce metal buildings in 1987. A second metal buildings facility began operations in late 1996 in South Carolina, and a new steel deck facility, in Alabama, was announced for 1997. At the end of 1997 the Arkansas sheet mill was undergoing a $120 million expansion to include a galvanizing facility.

In 1995 Nucor became involved in its first international venture, an ambitious project with Brazil's Companhia Siderurgica National to build a $700 million steel mill in the state of Ceara. While other minimills were cutting deals to buy and sell abroad, Nucor was planning to ship iron from Brazil and process it in Trinidad.

Nucor set records for sales and net earnings in 1997 (see appendix 3 for financial reports and appendix 4 for financial ratios). In the spring of 1998, as Iverson approached his seventy-third birthday, he was commenting, "People ask me when I'm going to retire. I tell them our mandatory retirement age is ninety-five, but I may change that when I get there." It surprised the world when, in October 1998, Ken Iverson left the board. He retired as chairman at the end the year. Although sales for 1998 decreased 1 percent and net earnings were down 10 percent, the management made a number of long-term investments and closed draining investments. Start-up began at the new South Carolina steam mill and at the Arkansas sheet mill expansion. The plans for a North Carolina steel plate mill in Hertford were announced. This would bring Nucor's total steel production capacity to 12 million tons per year. The plant in Trinidad, which had proven much more expensive than was originally expected, was deemed unsuccessful and closed. Finally, directors approved the repurchase of up to 5 million shares of Nucor stock.

Still, the downward trends at Nucor continued. Sales and earnings were down 3 percent and 7 percent, respectively, for 1999. However, these trends did not seem to affect the company's investments. Expansions were under way in the steel mills, and a third building systems facility was under construction in Texas. Nucor was actively searching for a site for a joist plant in the Northeast. A letter of intent was signed with Australian and Japanese companies to form a joint venture to commercialize the strip casting technology. To understand the challenges facing Nucor, industry, technology, and environmental trends in the 1980s and 1990s must be considered.

The U.S. Steel Industry in the 1980s

The early 1980s had been the worst years in decades for the steel industry. Data from the American Iron and Steel Institute showed shipments falling from 100 million tons in 1979 to the mid-80 levels in 1980 and 1981. Slackening in the economy, particularly in auto sales, led the decline. In 1986, when industry capacity was at 130 million tons, the outlook was for a continued decline in per capita consumption and movement toward capacity in the 90- to 100-million-ton range. The chairman of Armco saw "millions of tons chasing a market that's not there: excess capacity that must be eliminated."

The large, integrated steel firms, such as U.S. Steel and Armco, that made up the major part of the industry, were the hardest hit. The *Wall Street Journal* stated, "The decline has resulted from such problems as high labor and energy costs in mining and processing iron ore, a lack of profits and capital to modernize plants, and conservative management that has hesitated to take risks."

These companies produced a wide range of steels, primarily from ore processed in blast furnaces. They had found it difficult to compete with imports, usually from Japan, and had given market share to imports. They sought the protection of import quotas. Imported steel accounted for 20 percent of the U.S. steel consumption, up from 12 percent in the early 1970s. The U.S. share of world production of raw steel declined from 19 to 14 percent over the period. Imports of light bar products accounted for less that 9 percent of the U.S. consumption of those products in 1981, according to the U.S. Commerce Department, while imports of wire rod totaled 23 percent of U.S. consumption.

Iron Age stated that exports, as a percentage of shipments in 1985, were 34 percent for Nippon, 26 percent for British Steel, 30 percent for Krupp, 49 percent for USINOR of France, and less than 1 percent for every American producer on the list. The consensus of steel experts was that imports would average 23 percent of the market in the last half of the 1980s.

Iverson was one of the very few in the steel industry to oppose import restrictions. He saw an outdated U.S. steel industry that had to change.

We Americans have been conditioned to believe in our technical superiority. For many generations a continuing stream of new inventions and manufacturing techniques allowed us to far outpace the rest of the world in both volume and efficiency of production. In many areas this is no longer true and particularly in the steel industry. In the last three decades, almost all the major developments in steel making were made outside the U.S. There were eighteen continuous casting units in the world before there was one in this country. I would be negligent if I did not recognize the significant contribution that the government has made toward the technological deterioration of the steel industry. Unrealistic depreciation schedules, high corporate taxes, excessive regulation and jaw-boning for lower steel prices have make it difficult for the U.S. steel industry to borrow or generate the huge quantities of capital required for modernization.

By the mid 1980s the integrated mills were moving fast to get back into the game: they were restructuring, cutting capacity, dropping unprofitable lines, focusing products, and trying to become responsive to the market. The industry made a pronounced move toward segmentation. Integrated producers focused on mostly flat-rolled and structural grades, reorganized steel companies focused on a limited range of products, mini-mills dominated the bar and light structural product areas, and specialty steel firms sought niches. There was an accelerated shutdown of older plants, elimination of products by some firms, and the installation of new product lines with new technologies by others. High-tonnage mills restructured to handle sheets, plates, structural beams, high-quality bars, and large pipe and tubular products, which allowed a resurgence of specialized mills: cold-finished bar manufacturers, independent strip mills, and mini-mills.

The road for the integrated mills was not easy. As *Purchasing* pointed out, tax laws and accounting rules slowed the closing of inefficient plants. Shutting down a ten-thousand-person plant could require a firm to hold a cash reserve of $100 million to fund health, pension, and insurance liabilities. The chairman of Armco commented: "Liabilities associated with a planned shutdown are so large that they can quickly devastate a company's balance sheet."

Joint ventures had arisen to produce steel for a specific market or region. The chairman of USX called them "an important new wrinkle in steel's fight for survival" and stated, "If there had been more joint ventures like these two decades ago, the U.S. steel industry might have built only half of the dozen or so hot-strip mills it put up in that time and avoided today's over capacity." *Purchasing* observed, "The fact is that these combined operations are the result of a laissez faire attitude within the Justice Department under the Reagan administration following the furor when government restrictions killed the planned USS takeover of National Steel."

The American Iron and Steel Institute reported steel production in 1988 of 99.3 million tons, up from 89.2 million in 1987, and the highest in seven years. As a result of modernization programs, 60.9 percent of production was from continuous casters. Exports for steel increased and imports fell. Some steel experts believed the United States was now cost-competitive with Japan. However, 1989 proved to be a year of "waiting for the other shoe to drop," according to *Metal Center News.* U.S. steel production was hampered by a new recession, the expiration of the voluntary import restraints, and labor negotiations in several companies. Declines in car production and consumer goods hit flat-rolled steel hard. AUJ Consultants told MCN, "The U.S. steel market has peaked. Steel consumption is tending down. By 1990, we expect total domestic demand to dip under 90 million tons."

The U.S. Steel Industry in the 1990s

The economic slowdown of the early 1990s did lead to a decline in the demand for steel through early 1993, but by 1995 America was in its best steel market in twenty years and many companies were building new flat-roll mini-mills. A *Business Week* article at the time described it as "the race of the Nucor look-alikes." Six years after Nucor pioneered the low-cost German technology in Crawfordsville, Indiana, the competition was finally gearing up to compete. Ten new projects were expected to add 20 million tons per year of the flat-rolled steel, raising U.S. capacity by as much as 40 percent by 1998. These mills opened in 1997, just as the industry was expected to move into a cyclical slump. It was no surprise that worldwide competition increased and companies that had previously focused on their home markets began a race to become global powerhouses. The foreign push was new for U.S. firms, which had focused on defending their home markets. U.S. mini-mills focused their international expansion primarily in Asia and South America.

Meanwhile, in 1994 U.S. Steel, North America's largest integrated steel producer, began a major business process reengineering project to improve order fulfillment performance and customer satisfaction on the heels of a decade of restructuring. According to *Steel Times International,* "U.S. Steel had to completely change the way it did business. Cutting labor costs, and increasing reliability and productivity took the company a long way towards improving profitability and competitiveness. However, it became clear that this leaner organization still had to implement new technologies and business processes if it was to maintain a competitive advantage." The goals of the business process reengineering project

included a sharp reduction in cycle time, greatly decreased levels of inventory, shorter order lead times, and the ability to offer real-time promise dates to customers. In 1995, the company successfully installed integrated planning/production/order fulfillment software, and the results were very positive. U.S. Steel believed that the reengineering project had positioned it for a future of increased competition, tighter markets, and raised customer expectations.

In late 1997 and again in 1998 the decline in demand prompted Nucor and other U.S. companies to slash prices to compete with the unprecedented surge of imports. By the last quarter of 1998 these imports had led to the filing of unfair trade complaints with U.S. trade regulators, causing steel prices in the spot market to drop sharply in August and September before they stabilized. A press release by the U.S. secretary of commerce, William Daley, stated, "I will not stand by and allow U.S. workers, communities and companies to bear the brunt of other nations' problematic policies and practices. We are the most open economy of the world. But we are not the world's dumpster." In early 1999 American Iron and Steel Institute reported in its Opinion section of its web page the following quotes by Andy Sharkey and Hank Barnette. Sharkey said, "With many of the world's economies in recession, and no signs of recovery on the horizon, it should come as no surprise that the United States is now seen as the only reliable market for manufactured goods. This can be seen in the dramatic surge of imports." Barnette noted, "While there are different ways to gauge the impact of the Asian crisis, believe me, it has already hit. Just ask the 163,000 employees of the U.S. steel industry."

The Commerce Department concluded in March 1999 that six countries had illegally dumped stainless steel in the United States at prices below production costs or home market prices. The Commerce Department found that Canada, South Korea, and Taiwan were guilty only of dumping, while Belgium, Italy, and South Africa also gave producers unfair subsidies that effectively lowered prices. However, on June 23, 1999, The *Wall Street Journal* reported that the Senate decisively shut off an attempt to restrict U.S. imports of steel, despite industry complaints that a flood of cheap imports was driving them out of business. Advisors of President Clinton were reported to have said that the president would likely veto the bill if it passed. Administrative officials opposed the bill because it would violate international trade law and leave the United States open to retaliation.

The American Iron and Steel Institute (AISI) reported that in May 1999 U.S. steel mills shipped 8,330,000 net tons, a decrease of 6.7 percent from the 8,927,000 net tons shipped in May 1998. They also stated that for the first five months of 1999 shipments were 41,205,000 net tons, down 10 percent from the same period in 1998. AISI president and CEO Andrew Sharkey III said, "Once again, the May data show clearly that America's steel trade crisis continues. U.S. steel companies and employees continue to be injured by high levels of dumping and subsidized imports. . . . In addition, steel inventory levels remain excessive, and steel operating rates continue to be very low." Table 2A compares the average import customs value per net ton of steel for May 1999 to the first quarter of 1998, and Table 2B compares U.S. imports of steel mill products by country of origin for the first five months in 1999 to those of 1998 and 1997.

As the 1990s ended, Nucor was the second largest steel producer in the United States, behind USX. The company's market capitalization was about two times that of the next smaller competitor. Even in a tight industry, someone can win. Nucor was in the best position because the industry was very fragmented and there are many marginal competitors.

Steel Technology and the Mini-Mill

A new type of mill, the "mini-mill," had emerged in the United States during the 1970s to compete with the integrated mill. The mini-mill used electric arc furnaces initially to manufacture a narrow product line from scrap steel. The leading U.S. mini-mills in the 1980s were Nucor, Florida Steel, Georgetown Steel, North Star Steel, and Chaparral. Between the late 1970s and 1980s, the integrated mills' market share fell from about 90 percent to about 60 percent, with the integrated steel companies averaging a 7 percent return on equity, the mini-mills averaging 14 percent, and some, such as Nucor, achieving about 25 percent. In the 1990s mini-mills tripled their output to capture 17 percent of domestic shipments. Moreover, integrated mills' market share fell to around 40 percent, while mini-mills' share rose to 23 percent, reconstructed mills' increased their share from 11 to 28 percent, and specialized mills increased their share from 1 to 6 percent.

Some experts believed that a relatively new technology, the twin shell electric arc furnace, would help mini-mills increase production, lower costs, and take market share. According to the *Pittsburgh Business Times*, "With a twin shell furnace, one shell—the chamber holding the scrap to be melted—is filled and heated. During the heating of the first shell, the

TABLE 2A

Average Import Customs Value per Net Ton (selected products)

Product	May 1999	1st Quarter 1998	% Change
Wire rods	$275	$350	−21.50%
Structural shapes	267	379	−29.60
Plates cut lengths	456	490	−6.90
Plates in coils	257	377	−31.70
Reinforcing bars	198	300	−33.90
Line pipe	429	524	−18.20
Black plate	551	627	−12.20
Sheets, hot rolled	242	304	−20.40
Sheets, cold rolled	400	549	−27.10
Sheet & strip galvanized electrolytic	483	609	−20.70
Total, all steel mill products	332	455	−27.00

Source: American Iron and Steel Press Release, June 24, 1999.

TABLE 2B

U.S. Imports of Steel Mill Products by Country of Origin (thousands of net tons)

Country	5 Mos 99 Prelim	5 Mos 98	5 Mos 97	5 Mos 99 vs. 5 Mos 98 % Change	5 Mos 99 vs. 5 Mos 97 % Change
European Union	2,569	2,634	3,048	−2.5%	−15.7%
Canada	2,157	2,146	2,035	0.5	6.0
Japan	1,452	2,099	1,015	−30.8	43.1
Mexico	1,444	1,263	1,432	14.3	0.8
Brazil	1,428	987	1,565	44.7	−8.8
Korea	1,330	1,064	643	25.0	106.8
Russia	343	1,583	1,680	−78.3	−79.6
Australia	316	366	121	−13.7	161.2
South Africa	252	214	120	17.8	110.0
China	243	177	274	37.3	−11.3
India	170	118	90	70.3	123.3
Indonesia	187	116	33	61.2	466.7
Turkey	148	232	209	−36.2	−29.2
Ukraine	105	392	290	−73.2	−63.8
Others	1,546	1,188	1,038	27.5	46.0
Total	**13,690**	**14,578**	**13,593**	**−6.1**	**0.7**

Source: American Iron and Steel Press Release, June 24, 1999.

second shell is filled. When the heating is finished on the first shell, the electrodes move to the second. The first shell is emptied and refilled before the second gets hot." This increased production by 60 percent. Twin shell production had been widely adopted in the last few years. For example, Nucor Steel began running a twin shell furnace in November 1996 in Berkeley, South Carolina, and installed another in Norfolk, Nebraska, which began operations in 1997. "Everyone accepts twin shells as a good concept because there's a lot of flexibility of operation," said Rodney Mott, vice president and general manager of Nucor-Berkeley. However, this move toward twin shell furnaces could mean trouble with scrap availability. According to an October 1997 quote in the *Pittsburgh Business Times* by Ralph Smaller, vice president of process technology at Kvaerner, "Innovations that feed the electric furnaces' production of flat-rolled [steel] will increase the demand on high quality scrap and alternatives. The technological changes are just beginning and will accelerate over the next few years."

According to a September 1997 *Industry Week* article, steel makers around the world are now closely monitoring the development of continuous "strip casting" technology, which may prove to be the next leap forward for the industry. "The objective of strip casting is to produce thin strips of steel (in the 1-mm to 4-mm range) as liquid steel flows from a tundish— the stationary vessel which receives molten steel from the ladle. It would eliminate the slab-casting stage and all of the rolling that now takes place in a hot mill." Strip casting was reported to have some difficult technological challenges, but companies in Germany, France, Japan, Australia, Italy, and Canada had strip-casting projects under way. In fact, all of the significant development work in strip casting was taking place outside the United States.

Larry Kavanaph, American Iron and Steel Institute vice president for manufacturing and technology, said, "Steel is a very high-tech industry, but nobody knows it." Today's most productive steel-making facilities incorporate advanced metallurgical practices, sophisticated process-control sensors, state-of-the-art computer controls, and the latest refinements in continuous casting and rolling mill technology. Michael Shot, vice president for manufacturing at Carpenter Technology Corp., Reading, Pennsylvania, a specialty steels and premium-grade alloys producer, said, "You don't survive in this industry unless you have the technology to make the best products in the world in the most efficient manner."

Environmental and Political Issues

Not all stakeholders have been happy with the way Nucor does business. In June 1998, *Waste News* reported that Nucor's mill in Crawfordsville, Indiana, was cited by the United States Environmental Protection Agency for alleged violations of federal and state clean air rules. The Pamlico–Tar River Foundation, the NC Coastal Federation, and the Environmental Defense Fund had concerns about the state's decision to allow the company to start building the plant before the environmental review was completed. According to the *News & Observer* web site, "The environmental groups charge that the mill will discharge 6,720 tons of pollutants into the air each year."

There were also concerns about the fast-track approval of the facility being built in Hertford County. First, this plant was located on the banks of one of the most important and sensitive stretches of the Chowan, a principal tributary to the national treasure Albemarle Sound and the last bastion of the state's once vibrant river-herring fishery. North Carolina passed a law in 1997 that required the restoration of this fishery through a combination of measures designed to prevent overfishing, restore spawning and nursery habitats, and improve water quality in the Chowan. "New federal law requires extra care in protecting essential habitat for the herring, which spawn upstream," stated an article in the *Business Journal.* Second, there were concerns regarding the excessive incentives the state gave to convince Nucor to build a $300 million steel mill in the state. Some questioned whether the promise of three hundred well-paying jobs in Hertford County was worth the $155 million in tax breaks the state was giving Nucor to locate there.

Management Evolution

As Nucor opened new plants, each was made a division and given a general manager who had complete responsibility for all aspects of the business. The corporate office did not involve itself in the routine functioning of the divisions. There was no centralized purchasing, hiring and firing, or division accounting. The total corporate staff was still less than twenty-five people, including clerical staff, when 1999 began.

In 1984, Dave Aycock moved into the corporate office as president. Ken Iverson was chief executive officer and chairman. Iverson, Aycock, and Sam Siegel operated as an executive board, providing overall direction to the corporation. By 1990 Aycock, who had invested his money wisely, owned over 600,000 shares of Nucor stock, five hotels and farms in three states, and was ready to retire. He was sixty, five years younger than Iverson, and was concerned that if he waited, he and Iverson might be leaving the company at the same time. Two people stood out as candidates for the presidency, Keith Busse and John Correnti. In November, Iverson called Correnti to the Charlotte airport and offered him the job. Aycock commented, "Keith Busse was my choice, but I got outvoted." In June 1991 Aycock retired and Keith Busse left Nucor to build an independent sheet mill in Indiana for a group of investors.

Thus Iverson, Correnti, and Siegel led the company. In 1993, Iverson had heart problems and major surgery. Correnti was given the CEO role in 1996. The Board of Directors had always been small, consisting of the executive team and one or two past Nucor vice presidents. Several organizations with large blocks of Nucor stock had been pressing Nucor to diversify its board membership and add outside directors. In 1996 Jim Hlavacek, head of a small consulting firm and friend of Iverson, was added to the board.

Only five, not six, members of the board were in attendance during the Board of Directors meeting in the fall of 1998, because of the death of Jim Cunningham. Near its end, Aycock read a motion, drafted by Siegel, that Ken Iverson be removed as chairman. It was seconded by Hlavacek and passed. It was announced in October that Iverson would be a chairman emeritus and a director, but after disagreements Iverson left the company completely. It was agreed that Iverson would receive $500,000 a year for five years. Aycock left retirement to become chairman.

The details of Iverson's leaving did not become known until June of 1999, when John Correnti resigned after disagreements with the board and Aycock took his place. All of this was a complete surprise to investors and brought the stock price down 10 percent. Siegel commented, "The board felt Correnti was not the right person to lead Nucor into the twenty-first century." Aycock assured everyone that he would be happy to move back into retirement as soon as replacements could be found.

In December 1999 Correnti became chairman of rival Birmingham Steel, with an astounding corporate staff of 156 people. With Nucor's organizational changes, he questioned their ability to move as fast in the future. "Nucor's trying to centralize and do more mentoring. That's not what grew the company to what it is today."

Aycock moved ahead with adding outside directors to the board. He appointed Harvey Gantt, principal in his own architectural firm and former mayor of Charlotte; Victoria Haynes, formally B. F. Goodrich's chief technology officer; and Peter Browning, chief executive of Sonoco (biographical sketches of board members and executive management are provided in appendices 5 and 6). Then he moved to increase the corporate office staff by adding a level of executive vice presidents over four areas of business and adding two specialist jobs in strategic planning and steel technology. When Siegel retired, Aycock promoted Terry Lisenby to CFO and treasurer, and hired a director of information technology to report to Lisenby (Figure 2 provides the organization chart).

Jim Coblin, vice president of human resources, believed the additions to management were necessary, saying, "It's not bad to get a little more like other companies." He noted that the various divisions did their business cards and plant signs differently; some did not even want a Nucor sign. Sometimes six different Nucor salesmen would call on the same customer.

FIGURE 2

Nucor Organization Chart

"There is no manager of human resources in the plants, so at least we needed to give additional training to the person who does most of that work at the plant," he stated. With these new additions there would be a director of information technology and two important committees, one for environmental issues and the second for audit.

Coblin believed that the old span of control of twenty people might have worked well when there was less competition. Aycock considered it "ridiculous," saying, "It was not possible to properly manage, to know what was going own. The top managers have totally lost contact with the company." Coblin was optimistic that the use of executive vice presidents (EVPs) would improve management. The three meetings of the general managers had slowly increased from about one and a half days to about two and a half days and had become more focused. The new EVP positions would add a perspective above the level of the individual plants. Instead of fifteen individual detailed presentations, each general manager would give a five-minute briefing and then there would be an in-depth presentation on the group, with team participation. After some training by Lisenby, the divisions had recently done a pretty good job with a SWOT analysis. Coblin thought these changes would make Nucor a stronger global player.

To **Jeff Kemp,** the new general manager of strategic planning and business development, the big issue was how to sustain earnings growth. In the U.S. steel industry there were too many marginal competitors. The U.S. government had recently added to the problem by giving almost a billion dollars to nine mills, which simply allowed them to limp along and weaken the industry. Kemp was looking for Nucor's opportunities within the steel industry. He asked why Nucor had bought a bearing company. His experience in the chemical industry suggested a need for Nucor to establish a position of superiority and grow globally, driving industry competition rather than reacting. He argued that a company should protect its overall market position, which could mean sacrifices for individual plants. Aycock liked Kemp's background in law and accounting and had specifically sought someone from outside the steel industry to head up Nucor's strategic planning. By June 2000 Kemp had conducted studies of other industries in the U.S. market and had developed a working document that identified opportunities worthy of further analysis.

"Every company hits a plateau," Aycock observed. "You can't just go out and build plants to grow. How do you step up to the next level? I wouldn't say it's a turning point but we have to get our strategic vision and strategic plans." He stated, "We are beginning Nucor's first ever strategic planning sessions; it was not necessary before." They had just received an image survey from a consulting firm (Exhibit 1).

EXHIBIT 1

Nucor's Image Survey

In early 2000, Nucor had an outside consulting firm conduct a survey of the company's image as seen by the top ten to fifteen managers, including the corporate office. They also gathered the views of a few analysts and media personnel. The managers still agreed that Nucor valued risk taking, innovation, and a lean management structure with aggressive, hard-working employees who accepted the responsibility of failure along with the opportunity for success. They seemed to see Nucor as a way of doing business—not just a way of making steel—in terms of values and personality, not just business terms. When asked to associate Nucor's persona with a public figure, John Wayne was the clear choice.

The managers in the field seemed to believe that the new layer of management was needed, and they were not concerned about a loss of decentralization. They liked the new management team and the changes so far, particularly the improved communications with the corporate office. However, the corporate managers thought the company was changing much faster than the division managers. They also held a more positive view of the company regarding how good the company was in their community or with the environment.

The people from the media had positive views of Nucor as hard-working and committed to its employees, and as an innovative risk-taking economic powerhouse. Some who were most familiar with the company believed that it needed to do a better job of communicating its vision during a period of transition.

Aycock believed Nucor needed to be quick to recognize developing technology in all production areas. He noted the joint venture to develop a new "strip caster" that would cast the current flat-rolled material in a more-finished form. The impact could be "explosive," allowing Nucor to build smaller plants closer to markets. This would be particularly helpful on the West Coast. Nucor would own the U.S. and Brazilian rights, and its partners would own the rest. Aycock was also looking forward to the next generation of steel mills and this time wanted to own the rights. He praised Iverson's skill at seeing new technology and committing the company to it.

Aycock was very interested in acquisitions, but he believed "they must fit strategically." A bar mill in the upper central Midwest and a flat-rolled plant in the Northeast would be good. A significant opportunity existed in preengineered buildings. Aycock intended to concentrate on steel for the next five to six years, achieving an average growth rate of 15 percent per year. In about seven years he would like to see Nucor ready to move into other areas. He said Nucor had already "picked the low-hanging grapes" and must be careful in its next moves.

Steel and Nucor in the Twenty-first Century

In September 2000, David Aycock stepped aside as he had planned, and Dan DiMicco was elected president and chief executive officer of Nucor. Peter Browning was elected chairman of the Board of Directors. Aycock retired from the board a year later.

Sales for 2000 increased 14 percent over 1999 to reach a record level. Earnings were also at record levels, 27 percent over 1999. The year had begun on a strong footing, but business had turned weak by the year's end. While Nucor remained profitable, other steel companies faced bankruptcy. A Vulcraft plant was under construction in New York. It was Vulcraft's first northeastern operation and expanded its geographical coverage into a new region. It was also attempting a breakthrough technological step in strip casting at Crawfordsville—the Castrip process. It sold its grinding ball process and the bearing products operation because they were not a part of Vulcraft's core business.

In the company's annual report DiMicco laid out its plans for 2000 and beyond: "Our targets are to deliver an average annual earnings growth of 10 to 15 percent over the next ten years, to deliver a return well in excess of our cost of capital, to maintain a minimum average return on equity of 14 percent, and to deliver a return on sales of 8 to 10 percent. Our strategy will focus on Nucor becoming a "market leader" in every product group and business in which we compete. This calls for significant increases in market share for many of our core products and the maintenance of market share where we currently enjoyed a leadership position." While pointing out that it would be impossible to obtain this success through the previous strategy of greenfield construction, he added, "There will now be a heavy focus on growth through acquisitions. We will also continue growing through the commercialization of new disruptive and leapfrog technologies."

In early 2001 the *Wall Street Journal* predicted that all but two of the United States's biggest steel makers would post fourth-quarter losses. AK Steel Holding Corp. and Nucor Corp. were expected to have profits for the quarter of 2000, while U.S. Steel Group, a unit of USX Corp., was expected to post a profit for the year but not for the fourth quarter. By October 1, more than twenty steel companies in the United States, including Bethlehem Steel Corp. and LTV Corp., the nation's third and fourth largest U.S. steel producers, respectively, had filed for bankruptcy protection. Over a dozen producers were operating under Chapter 11 bankruptcy-law protection, which allows them to maintain market share by selling steel cheaper than non–Chapter 11 steel makers. On October 20, *The Economist* noted that of the fourteen steel companies followed by Standard & Poor, only Nucor was indisputably healthy. In the fall of 2001, 25 percent of domestic steel companies were in bankruptcy proceedings, and the United States was the largest importer of steel in the world. Experts believed that close to half of the U.S. steel industry might be forced to close before conditions improved.

The world steel industry found itself in the middle of one of its most unprofitable and volatile periods, in part because of a glut of steel that has sent prices to twenty-year lows. While domestic steel producers found themselves mired in red ink, many foreign steel makers desperately needed to continue to sell in the relatively open U.S. market to stay profitable. The industry was hovering around 75 percent capacity, a level too low to be profitable for many companies. Three European companies—France's USINOR SA, Luxembourg's Arbed SA, and Spain's

Aceralia Corp.—were in the process of merging to form the world's largest steel company. Two Japanese companies—NKK Corp. and Kawasaki Steel Corp.—were in talks of a merger that would make them the world's second biggest steel maker. These new large steel makers could outmuscle U.S. competitors, which were less efficient, smaller, and financially weaker than their competitors in Asia and Europe. The largest U.S. steel maker, USX-U.S. Steel Group, was currently only the eleventh largest producer in the world, and consolidation in the industry could push it further down the list. In spite of these worsening conditions, global steel production increased 7 percent last year to a record 747 million tons, and efforts were under way to negotiate a worldwide reduction in steel production.

In addition to cheap imports, U.S. steel producers were facing higher energy prices, weakening demand by customer industries, increasingly tough environmental rules, and a changing cost structure among producers. With the declining economy, energy prices could begin to drop. However, so would the demand for construction, automobiles, and farm equipment. Environmental rules could lead to costly modifications and closings of old plants that produced coke along with vast clouds of ash and acrid green smoke. In 1990 mini-mills accounted for 36 percent of the domestic steel market, but by 2000 the more efficient mini-mills had seized 50 percent of the market and the resulting competition had driven prices lower.

In March 2001, Nucor made its first acquisition in ten years, purchasing a mini-mill in New York from Sumitomo Corp. Nucor had hired about five people to help plan for future acquisitions. DiMicco commented, "It's taken us three years before our team has felt this is the right thing to do." In the challenged industry, it would be cheaper to buy than to build plants. During this downturn Nucor was taking advantage of competitors' weaknesses to take market share and invest in new facilities.

In the first quarter, sales decreased 14 percent and earnings were cut in half, despite steel shipments' being at record levels. By the third quarter, sales were down 12 percent, profit was down 70 percent, and earnings per share were down 60 percent from the previous year. In the third quarter Nucor had $20.5 million in net income, compared to $67.8 million from the year before. The company shipped 3.04 million tons of steel, a 10.4 percent increase over the year before, setting a new tonnage record. DiMicco stated, "All the U.S. mills could close and there would still be excess capacity." The year 2001 would indeed be a year to test the metal of the new Nucor!

Appendix 1: Nucor Employee Survey

Question Description	Year*	Almost Never	Seldom	Sometimes	Often	Very Often
1. Meet schedule	5	1	4	22	47	26
	4	1	4	25	48	21
	3	4	10	39	37	9
	2	11	16	40	26	7
	1	10	15	0	0	75
2. Have tools	5	1	4	19	44	32
	4	1	3	21	47	28
	3	2	5	32	46	15
	2	6	10	36	37	10
	1	6	11	0	0	83
3. Open communication	5	7	14	34	29	16
	4	11	19	35	25	11
	3	11	19	37	26	7
	2	24	23	32	16	5
	1	24	25	0	0	51

(continued)

Appendix 1: Nucor Employee Survey *(continued)*

Question Description	Year*	Almost Never	Seldom	Sometimes	Often	Very Often
4. Maintenance	5	5	11	28	37	19
	4	6	11	31	36	16
	3	5	14	32	37	13
	2	13	16	34	28	10
	1	13	16	0	0	71
5. Drug test	5	2	3	9	34	53
	4	4	4	12	35	45
	3	5	4	13	33	44
	2					
	1					
6. Rules fair	5	8	13	24	30	25
	4	9	13	25	31	22
	3	10	11	23	31	25
	2					
	1					
7. Computer systems	5	8	14	32	29	16
	4	10	17	33	27	13
	3	13	18	32	27	10
	2	21	20	34	19	7
	1	23	21	0	0	57
8. Informed	5	5	9	21	34	31
	4	6	9	24	34	26
	3	9	14	27	33	17
	2	15	15	30	28	12
	1	16	16	0	0	69
9. Supervisor fair	5	4	7	20	36	34
	4	6	7	20	35	32
	3	6	9	26	38	21
	2	10	11	32	35	13
	1	13	12	0	0	74
10. Supervisor ideas	5	7	11	24	30	29
	4	8	12	29	30	21
	3	11	15	28	30	16
	2	17	18	31	24	10
	1	18	17	0	0	65
11. Division managers' actions	5	8	12	39	31	19
	4	7	14	33	33	13
	3	9	17	35	30	9
	2	20	21	34	20	6
	1	18	22	0	0	60
12. Division managers informed	5	7	12	27	34	20
	4	6	12	28	35	19
	3	8	15	31	32	14
	2	17	18	33	23	9
	1	15	20	0	0	65

(continued)

Appendix 1: Nucor Employee Survey (continued)

Question Description	Year*	Almost Never	Seldom	Sometimes	Often	Very Often
13. General managers' actions	5	6	9	27	35	23
	4	7	14	33	33	13
	3	9	17	35	30	9
	2	20	21	34	20	6
	1	18	22	0	0	60
14. General managers' response	5	8	13	31	30	18
	4	7	14	32	33	14
	3	12	19	34	28	8
	2	19	20	35	21	6
	1	20	22	0	0	58
15. General managers' information	5	4	8	25	38	25
	4	6	12	28	35	19
	3	8	15	31	32	14
	2	17	18	33	23	9
	1	15	20	0	0	65
16. Oa tm gd	5	2	5	19	42	32
	4	6	9	27	35	22
	3	8	11	29	35	17
	2	17	14	32	26	11
	1	13	12	0	0	74
17. Headquarter directions	5	2	3	18	44	33
	4	1	2	17	45	36
	3	1	3	19	47	29
	2					
	1					
18. Paid fr-out	5	6	9	21	31	32
	4	6	9	20	34	30
	3	10	13	24	33	20
	2	14	13	28	31	14
	1	11	13	0	0	75
19. Paid fr-in	5	10	13	24	29	24
	4	10	14	22	31	23
	3	16	16	25	29	14
	2	21	15	26	27	11
	1	19	15	0	0	66
20. Heal care	5	10	14	30	32	14
	4	8	12	31	35	14
	3	19	18	31	24	7
	2	11	13	33	31	12
	1	8	11	0	0	80

* The most recent survey was 5.

Appendix 2: Nucor Survey Plant Comparisons

Question*	Descrpt.	Total Company	Vulcraft Plants						Steel Plants					Other Plants					
			V1	V2	V3	V4	V5	V6	S1	S2	S3	S4	S5	01	02	03	04	05	06
1	Meet sche	5	4	6	5	6	5	5	5	6	5	4	1	5	11	2	18	6	3
2	Have tools	5	2	4	3	7	3	4	2	8	6	3	2	6	11	3	17	5	6
3	Open com	21	17	23	16	15	18	26	21	26	23	19	15	24	31	23	35	21	30
4	Maint	16	12	13	12	9	22	13	13	26	25	19	9	13	29	11	33	15	29
5	Drug test	5	5	6	5	3	3	5	8	7	4	5	2	4	9	3	4	5	11
6	Rules fair	21	15	24	19	13	12	20	21	31	16	26	15	22	26	32	36	19	37
7	Cmplt sys	22	16	22	18	20	19	31	20	27	28	24	15	28	26	18	55	24	40
8	Informed	14	8	22	12	15	18	17	12	18	19	10	8	22	16	15	23	17	11
9	Supv fair	11	9	21	13	11	12	15	10	13	10	10	4	15	14	13	9	11	10
10	Supv idea	18	14	32	19	20	18	24	15	18	18	13	9	26	25	18	25	20	13
11	Dmgr act	20	13	23	17	14	15	28	23	26	32	16	11	18	18	14	48	24	41
12	Dmgr infm	19	17	16	15	14	14	23	19	27	31	19	13	15	24	9	44	21	36
13	Gmgr act	15	9	17	8	15	9	25	16	17	15	19	5	29	20	4	43	10	43
14	Gmgr gets	21	15	22	12	18	14	24	22	25	24	28	12	30	25	9	45	25	43
15	Gmgr infm	12	11	8	7	14	7	17	15	13	15	18	4	11	15	2	35	13	34
16	Oa tm gd	7	3	7	3	4	7	8	7	9	13	6	1	8	5	2	22	15	13
17	Hq direct	5	3	7	3	2	2	10	6	11	16	4	3	3	4	1	11	4	2
18	Paid fr-out	15	16	26	19	20	19	20	16	15	14	10	6	42	25	8	11	11	19
19	Paid fr-in	23	18	33	21	28	23	26	24	22	25	23	12	45	29	20	28	20	33
20	Heal care	24	14	19	16	34	16	27	22	42	31	12	25	18	8	27	7	29	23

* For text of questions, see appendix 1.

Appendix 3: Financial Report

Annual Report: Consol. Inc Acct., Yrs End. Dec.31 (thousand $)

	12/31/2001	12/31/2000	12/31/1999	12/31/1998	12/31/1997
Net sales	$4,139,248	$4,586,146	$4,009,346	$4,151,232	$4,184,498
Costs and expenses					
Cost of products sold	$3,820,303	$3,925,478	$3,480,479	$3,591,783	$3,578,941
Marketing, administrative and other expenses	$138,559	$183,175	$154,774	$147,972	$145,410
Interest expense (income)	($6,525)	($816)	($5,095)	($3,832)	($35)
	$3,965,387	$4,107,838	$3,630,157	$3,735,924	$3,724,315
Earnings before federal income taxes	$173,861	$487,308	$379,189	$415,309	$460,182
Federal income taxes	$60,900	$167,400	$134,600	$151,309	$165,700
Net earnings	**$112,961**	**$310,908**	**$244,589**	**$263,709**	**$294,482**
Com. divds	—	—	45,354	42,129	35,154
Capital expenditures	$261,145	$415,405	$374,718	$502,910	$306,749
Average number of shares (thousands)	77,814	77,582	87,247	87,862	87,872
Operating income as calculated	—	—	$630,730	$664,595	$677,911
Depreciation	$289,063	$259,365	$256,637	$253,118	$217,764

Consolidated Balance Sheet (thousand $)

	12/31/2001	12/31/2000	12/3 1/1999	12/31/1998	12/31/1997
Assets					
Current assets	$1,373,666	$1,379,539	$1,538,509	$1,129,467	$1,125,508
Property, plant, and equipment	$2,365,655	$2,329,421	$2,191,339	$2,097,079	$1,858,875
Total assets	**$3,759,348**	**$3,710,867**	**$3,729,848**	**$3,226,546**	**$2,984,383**
Liabilities and Stockholders' Equity					
Total current liabilities	$484,159	$558,068	$531,031	$486,897	$524,454
Long-term debt after one year	$460,450	$460,450	$390,450	$215,450	$167,950
Total stockholders' equity	$2,201,460	$2,130,951	$2,262,248	$2,072,552	$1,876,426
Total liabilities	**$3,759,348**	**$3,710,867**	**$3,729,848**	**$3,226,546**	**$2,984,383**
Net working capital	$889,507	$821,460	$1,007,478	$642,570	$601,055
Equity per share	$28.29	$27.47	$25.96	$23.73	$21.32
Capital expenditures	$261,145	$415,405	$374,718	$502,910	$306,749
Number of common shares (thousands)			90,103	90,052	
Number of treasury shares (thousands)			2,969	2,699	

Source: Standard & Poor's Corporate Records.

Appendix 4: Financial Ratios

	1990	1991	1992	1993	1994	1995	1996	1997	1998	1999	2000
Net sales	1,481	1,465	1,619	2,253	2,975	3,462	3,647	4,184	4,151	4,009	4,586
Net earnings	75	65	79	123	227	275	248	294	264	245	311
Current assets	313	334	382	468	639	831	828	1,126	1,129	1,539	1,381
Current liabilities	203	229	272	350	382	447	466	524	487	531	558
Long-term debt > 1 year	29	73	247	352	173	107	153	168	215	390	460
Stockholders' equity	653	712	784	902	1,123	1,382	1,609	1,876	2,973	2,262	2,131
Total assets	1,036	1,182	1,507	1,829	2,002	2,296	2,620	2,984	3,227	3,730	3,722
COGS	1,293	1,303	1,417	1,966	2,492	2,900	3,139	3,579	3,591	3,480	3,925
Shares out, year end	86	86	87	87	87	88	88	88	88	87	78
Current ratio	1.54	1.46	1.40	1.34	1.67	1.86	1.78	2.15	2.32	2.90	2.47
Long-term debt : equity ratio	0.04	0.10	0.32	0.39	0.15	0.08	0.10	0.09	0.07	0.17	0.22
Profit margin	5.1%	4.4%	4.9%	5.5%	7.6%	7.9%	6.8%	7.0 %	6.4%	6.1%	6.8%
Return on equity	11.5%	9.1%	10.1%	13.6%	20.2%	19.9%	15.4%	15.7%	8.9%	10.8%	14.6%
Return on total assets	7.2%	5.5%	5.2%	6.7%	11.3%	12.0%	9.5%	9.9%	8.2%	6.6%	8.4%
Total asset turnover	143.0%	124.0%	107.0%	123.0%	149.0%	151.0%	139.0%	140.0%	129.0%	107.0%	123.0%
Gross profit margin	12.7%	11.1%	12.5%	12.7%	16.2%	16.2%	13.9%	14.5%	13.5%	13.2%	14.4%
Earning per share	$0.87	$0.76	$0.91	$1.41	$2.61	$3.13	$2.82	$3.34	$3.00	$2.82	$3.99

Appendix 5: Board of Directors and Executive Management

To 1990

Board: Iverson, Aycock, Siegel, Vandekieft
Executive Office: Iverson, Aycock, Siegel

1990

Board: Iverson, Aycock, Cunningham, Siegel, Vandekieft
Executive Office: Iverson, Aycock, Siegel

1991 to 1994

Board: Iverson, Aycock, Siegel, Cunningham, Correnti
Executive Office: Iverson, Siegel, Correnti, Lisenby, Prichard

1995 to 1996

Board: Iverson, Aycock, Siegel, Cunningham, Correnti, Hlavacek

Executive Office: Iverson, Siegel, Correnti, Doherty, Prichard

1997

Board: Iverson, Aycock, Siegel, Cunningham, Correnti, Hlavacek
Executive Office: Iverson, Siegel, Correnti, Lisenby, Prichard

1998

Board: Aycock, Siegel, Correnti, Hlavacek, Browning, Gantt, Haynes
Executive Office: Aycock, Siegel, Correnti, Parrish, Rutkowski, Lisenby, Prichard

1999 to 2000

Board: Aycock, Siegel, Hlavacek, Browning, Gantt, Haynes
Executive Office: Aycock, Lisenby, DiMicco, Lott, Parrish, Rutkowski, Coblin, Prichard

Appendix 6: Biographies of Board Members and Executive Managers

H. David Aycock joined the predecessor to Nucor in 1962 when it bought the Vulcraft plant in Florence, South Carolina, where he was sales manager. He became the general manager at the Vulcraft plant in Nebraska in 1963. He was instrumental in building and operating the plant, and he also managed the Texas plant. In 1981 he became general manager of the Nucor steel plant in South Carolina. In 1985 he became president and chief operating officer. He retired in June 1991 but remained on the board. In October 1998, Mr. Aycock became chairman and, in June 1999, chief executive officer. In September 2000 he stepped down as Nucor's CEO and chairman of the Board of Directors. He retired from the board in 2001.

Peter C. Browning has been the president and chief executive officer of Sonoco Products Company and was senior officer in 1993. He was previously the president, chairman, and chief executive officer of National Gypsum Company. He was elected chairman of Nucor's Board of Directors in September 2000.

James W. Cunningham was a vice president of Nucor and general manager of the research chemicals division in Phoenix from 1966 until the division was sold in 1998. He died on September 15, 1998, at seventy-seven years of age.

Daniel R. DiMicco was executive vice president of Nucor-Yamato, Nucor Steel Hertford (plate division), and Nucor Building Systems before becoming president. He graduated from Brown University in 1972 with a bachelor of science in engineering, metallurgy, and materials science. He received a master's in metallurgy from the University of Pennsylvania in 1975. He was with Republic Steel in Cleveland as a research metallurgy and project leader until he joined Nucor in 1982 as plant metallurgist and manager of quality control for Nucor Steel in Utah. In 1988 he became melting and castings manager. In 1991 he became general manager of Nucor-Yamato and a vice president in 1992. In September 2000 he was elected president and chief executive officer of Nucor.

John A. Doherty served as vice president and engineering consultant at Nucor.

Harvey B. Gantt was a partner in Gantt Huberman Architects for more than twenty-five years. He also served as mayor of the city of Charlotte, North Carolina, and was active in civic affairs. He was the first African American graduate of Clemson University. He joined Nucor's Board of Directors in 1998.

Victoria F. Haynes is the president of Research Triangle Institute in Chapel Hill, North Carolina. Until 2000, she was the chief technical officer of the B. F. Goodrich Co. and vice president of its advanced technology group. She started with Goodrich in 1992 as vice president of research and development. She joined Nucor's Board of Directors in 1998.

James D. Hlavacek is the managing director of Market Driven Management. Mr. Hlavacek was a neighbor and long-term friend of Mr. Iverson. He joined Nucor's Board of Directors in 1995.

Terry S. Lisenby is chief financial officer and an executive vice president of Nucor. He graduated from the University of North Carolina at Charlotte in 1976 with a bachelor of science in accounting. Mr. Lisenby held accounting and management positions with Seidman and Seidman, Harper Corporation of America, and Concept Development, Inc. He joined Nucor in September 1985 as manager of financial accounting. He became vice president and corporate controller in 1991 and assumed the role of chief financial officer on January 1, 2000.

Hamilton Lott, Jr., is executive vice president of the Vulcraft operations, cold-finished operations in Nebraska, and the Utah grinding ball plant. He graduated from the University of South Carolina in 1972 with a bachelor of science in engineering and then served in the United States Navy. He joined Nucor in 1975 as a design engineer at Florence. He later served as engineering manager and as sales manager of Nucor's Vulcraft division in Indiana. He was general manager of the Vulcraft division in Texas from 1987 to 1993 and general manager in Florence from 1993 to 1999. He became a vice president in 1988 and joined the Executive Office in 1999.

D. Michael Parrish is executive vice president for the four steel plants and Nucor Fastener. He graduated from the University of Toledo in 1975 with a bachelor of science in civil engineering. He joined Nucor in September 1975 as a design engineer for Vulcraft and became engineering manager at Vulcraft in 1981. In 1986 he moved to Alabama as manufacturing manager and in 1989 returned to Utah as vice president and general manager. In 1991 he took the top job with Nucor Steel Texas and in 1995 with Nucor Steel Arkansas. In January 1999 he moved into the corporate office as executive vice president.

Leroy C. Prichard is vice president, Steel Technologies, at Nucor.

Joseph A. Rutkowski is executive vice president of Nucor Steel in Indiana, Arkansas, Berkeley, and South Carolina and of Nucor Bearing Products. He graduated from Johns Hopkins University in 1976 with a bachelor of science in materials science engineering. He held metallurgical and management positions with Korf Lurgi Steeltec, North American Refractories, Georgetown Steel, and Bethlehem Steel. He joined Nucor in 1989 as manager of cold finish in Nebraska and became melting and casting manager in Utah before becoming vice president and general manager of Nucor Steel in Darlington in 1992. In 1998 he moved to Hertford as vice president and general manager to oversee the building of the new plate mill.

Richard N. Vandekieft is a former vice president of Nucor.

17 Digital Devices: Current and Future Market Opportunities

This case was prepared by Charles W. L. Hill, the University of Washington.

Introduction

The computer industry is now entering its third era.[1] The first era was characterized by the mainframe computer and was dominated by IBM with its proprietary hardware and software standards. The second era was characterized by the personal computer and was dominated by Microsoft with its proprietary software standards, MS-DOS and then Windows. The World Wide Web will characterize the third era of computing. The center of gravity in the vast computing and communications complex is now moving rapidly off the desktop and onto the Web. This shift is being driven by the emergence of web-based "killer applications" that deliver compelling value to users, including email, information retrieval and manipulation, and e-commerce and ebusiness applications. Many of these applications are still in their infancy, and there is the promise of continued rapid growth. For example, online sales in the United States, which reached $9 billion in 1998, are projected to reach anywhere from $75 billion to $147 billion by 2003, according to forecasts from a number of different firms.[2]

This case is intended to be used as a basis for class discussion rather than as an illustration of either effective or ineffective handling of the situation. Reprinted by permission of Charles W. L. Hill.

Unlike prior eras, it is unclear whether any one company will dominate this new era. Nor is it clear whether proprietary standards will play the central role in this era that they have in prior eras. After all, the key to the rapid growth of the Net has been the development of protocols that are in the public domain, such as TCP/IP, HTML, and XML, not proprietary standards. What does seem increasingly clear, however, is that in this new era users will be able to access and manipulate a vast amount of information and computing power that reside "out there" on the Web using a number of different digital devices in addition to the personal computer. These devices (often called information appliances) are characterized by specialized functionality, technological elegance, ergonomic simplicity, and low device costs (under $500). They include hand-held personal assistants; wireless phones with Internet functionality, including smart phones; web-enabled televisions; Internet-ready video game terminals; and web tablets. As with paradigm shifts in prior eras and other industries, the dominant enterprise in the personal computer era faces special challenges born of its prior dominance as it tries to overcome inertia forces and reposition itself to succeed in a world where the ground is shifting from under its feet and the rules are changing rapidly in ways that are only clear ex post facto. That enterprise, of course, is

Microsoft. The emergence of digital devices represents an important competitive arena in which many believe Microsoft must not only participate, but also win, if the company is to be successful going forward.

Technological Trends

The shift to the third era of computing is being facilitated by a number of technological trends that continue to increase the power of computing and drive down its cost, increase the supply and drive down the cost of communications bandwidth, and promise to provide persistent ubiquitous connectivity to the Web through wired and wireless conduits. These trends should ultimately allow individuals to access personal and business information anywhere anytime through any digital device and to draw upon the vast supply of computing power that resides remotely on the Web to manipulate that information and execute economic transactions.

Trends in computing power continue to be driven by the exponential logic of Moore's law. According to computer scientist, entrepreneur, author, and cyber poet Ray Kurzweil, if Moore's law persists for another ten years, a $1,000 personal computer will be able to perform about a trillion calculations a second, up from a "mere billion" today.[3] For sure, Moore's law will probably grind to a halt fifteen to twenty years from now because of the limitations placed on photolithographic technology by quantum physics and the physics of light. But by then, a $4,000 computing device in (1999) dollars will have approximately the same computational capability as the human brain (20 million billion calculations per second). Nor will progress in computing power stop when it becomes impossible to further shrink the geometry of features on a silicon chip. Before then, a new wave of computing devices based on molecular switches, photonic connections, DNA-based computing, and/or quantum computing principles will probably have replaced today's computing paradigm.[4]

But that's all in the future. For now, the point is that exponential progress will enable computer manufacturers to put significant computing power into very small devices within a few very years. When coupled with Internet connectivity, the exponential growth in computing power should be able to support business and consumer software applications that currently are beyond the reach not only of the desktop computer, but also of today's supercomputers, and that stretches our imagination. One example would be autonomous software agents or digital assistants that have the ability to recognize and communicate in natural language, learn from experience, and perform a variety of complex tasks for their owners. Another would be video conferencing using holographic three-dimensional (3D) technology, although for this to become a reality, massive increases in communications bandwidth would also be required; but then again, the supply of bandwidth is also increasing exponentially.

Advances in optical communications technology are driving forward the rapid increase in the supply of bandwidth, while simultaneously driving down the costs of that bandwidth. The speed of this advance is currently most evident in the fiber-optic core or backbone of telecommunications networks, where advances in laser technology coupled with the introduction of dense wave division multiplexing (DWDM) are generating rapid advances in the speed of data transmission. In 1999, the most powerful backbone system transmitted data at a rate of 10 gigabytes per second (a giga is a billion). In early 2000, Nortel Networks was marketing a 40-gigabyte-per-second system, capable of transmitting 90,000 volumes of an encyclopedia every second. By early 2002, Nortel plans to deploy a 6.4-terabit (trillion bit) system. If the current trajectory holds, bandwidth capacity will increase 200 times by 2004—and that may be just the beginning.[5]

Although this surge in bandwidth has yet to dramatically impact the experience of the average computer user, that too may change. Two impediments have limited the supply of bandwidth to end users— the last mile problem and the slow rate of wireless data transmission. The *last mile problem* refers to the inability of business and computer users to access high-bandwidth conduits (fiber-optic cables) at their offices and homes because of the high cost of building out such a network from its core to its periphery. While there is no immediate solution, the rollout of cable modems, DSL lines, and Internet links via satellite television receivers is now proceeding and will bring much faster access and download speeds to many small businesses and residences. More generally, fiber-optic connections are now included as a matter of course in new business construction, and developers are experimenting with the installation of fiber-optic outlets in new residential construction. As demand for bandwidth increases, over time we may see the emergence of all optical networks in which optical switching technology replaces today's electronic routers and most businesses and residences are linked by fiber or fiberless optical networks that rely upon shooting lasers through the air.[6] Such developments will make virtually limitless bandwidth available to the average user—even the residential user.

As for the slow rate of wireless data transmission, here too constraints are being pushed back. As that happens, the wireless Internet will become a technological and commercial reality. One key is the adoption of third-generation (or 3G) digital wireless networks that aim to increase data transmission rates from a paltry 9.5 K per second to a more respectable 2.5 M per second. DoCoMo is now rolling out the world's first 3G network in Japan. Europe should follow in 2002, and the United States, ever the laggard in wireless, sometime between 2003 and 2005.[7]

Although it is already possible to access information stored on the Internet through a wireless phone, the use of wireless phones as Internet terminals will be enhanced by the widespread adoption of another standard that is in the public domain, the emerging Wireless Application Protocol (WAP). Already endorsed by over eight hundred companies worldwide, WAP provides a common standard for developing web content for access by wireless-enabled digital devices with small screens, lower connection speeds, and less memory than a personal computer (PC). WAP is based on a programming language called Wireless Markup Language (WML) that is related to XML. Once companies produce versions of their web sites in WML, they can be accessed by anyone with a wireless-enabled digital device that uses WAP and a microbrowser. This is now beginning to untether much of the Internet, opening it up to the mobile user.

Another technology that feeds into the wireless Internet equation is Bluetooth. Named after a ninth-century Viking chief who united warring tribes, Bluetooth is a public communications protocol that seeks to enable a wide variety of digital devices to communicate with each other and exchange signals via radio waves. Although Bluetooth only works over short distances (no more than 100 feet), it will allow for seamless synchronization between an individual's personal digital devices—such as a smart phone, hand-held PC, and desktop PC—without the need for proprietary data synchronization software. Bluetooth is designed to be compatible with the WAP and

is currently supported by around one thousand companies, including all the major players in the computing and communications space.

Bluetooth may also help make the vision of ubiquitous computing proposed by the late Mark Weiser a reality. Before his untimely death in 1999, Weiser was the chief technologist at Xerox's Palo Alto Research Center. According to Weiser, the coming era of computing will be characterized by a profusion of inexpensive computers with which we will interact on an almost constant basis. Computers, in the form of special-purpose embedded processors, can already be found in watches, ovens, cars, wallets, and cell phones. Inevitably, these computers will become more pervasive, will talk to one another (via Bluetooth), and will form the invisible computational infrastructure of our lives. Ultimately, argued Weiser, "If your refrigerator watches you take the milk carton in and out every day, and if your refrigerator could talk to your wallet, then when you went to the store the wallet could tell the milk cartons that you need milk. And the milk cartons could then say to you, 'Hey buy me, you're out of milk.'"[8]

Some argue that another technological development needed if Weiser's vision is to become a reality is an overarching universal platform or distributed operating system that will allow the devices in a network to locate and work seamlessly with each other. Both Sun Microsystems and Microsoft are attempting to create such a system. Sun's prototype system is Jini, and Microsoft's is known as Universal Plug and Play (Upnp). Jini is the latest addition to Sun's Java vision. What Java aims to do for software Jini hopes to do for the machines that run it: provide a distributed operating system in which devices of every description can meet. Jini is about trying to create an architecture, a universal language, a set of super protocols—to knit together the emerging global computer and communications network and make everything work with, and be accessible by, everything else.[9]

The basic point of Jini is to simplify user interaction with the network. The key to Jini is Java's platform independence and its own innate ability to work over existing network software and protocols. As an extension of the Java code, along with the federation of Java Virtual Machines (JVMs), Jini becomes the universal language for disparate devices. The core of Jini's architecture lies in a "lookup service" knows as JavaSpace. The lookup service acts as an electronic bulletin board that monitors the devices attached to a network. So Java's ability to run on different computers, combined with the ability of Jini-enabled devices to send their own software code to the lookup service and receive instructions from other devices, is what gives a Jini network its potential magic.[10]

To consumers this means the ability to connect, power, and control through the network any appliance with an embedded processor, including hand-held devices, smart phones, set top boxes, and home thermostats. Once connected, the device announces itself to the network, indicates what it is there to do, and then carries out its task. On a corporate scale, Jini has potential for altering the way networks operate, without changing the underlying structure. Computing power would be distributed among devices connected to the computer, letting them share each other's resources. If Jini works, you will be able to sit with your laptop, and it will be able to reach out across the network; for the moments that you need the power, it will become the largest supercomputer in the world.[11] Instead of a platform designed to provide all capabilities in all cases, Jini provides only what is needed. And by using Java as the standard platform, you achieve interoperability. Basically, any device with a link to the network and a programmable ROM can be a network device with Jini.[12]

Microsoft's competing Universal Plug and Play platform was announced in June 1999. Upnp is based on the same open standards that underlie the Internet. To send commands among Upnp appliances, the software would use an in-house wired or wireless (e.g., Bluetooth) network. But like Jini, the software would tap into the Internet to perform more complex tasks. By mid June 2000, Sun reportedly had some 35 partners signed up to develop devices that are Jini-enabled, while Microsoft had about 125 partners working on products and technologies related to Upnp. However, neither company expects products to be commercially available for another twelve to eighteen months.[13]

So where is all this technology leading us? We cannot know for sure, but as science fiction writer William Gibson has pointed out, there is a sense in which the future is already with us; it's just unevenly distributed. Looking at current technological trends can help us discern the shape of things to come through the fog of our ignorance. Gazing dimly through the mist, what we think we see is a world

where computing power and communications bandwidth are both abundant and inexpensive, where computational devices surround us, and where these devices talk effortlessly to each other through wired and wireless connections using protocols that are in the public domain, and perhaps a distributed software in a platform such as Jini or Upnp. This does not look like the proprietary segmented world of the mainframe and personal computer eras, but it is a world of infinite profit opportunities waiting to be discovered.

Digital Devices

The term *digital devices* (or *information appliances*) covers a wide range of different devices including hand-held personal digital assistants (PDAs), PC companions, wireless phones with Internet functionality, set top boxes, video game terminals, and web tablets. What these devices have in common right now is that they are all computers, they are not PCs, they are inexpensive (most are priced under $500), and they have mass market potential. Unlike the PC, which is a general-purpose machine, these various devices are specialized appliances designed specifically to perform certain tasks. Their specialized functionality is both their strength and their limitation. While they lack the flexibility of the PC, they are better suited to performing specific tasks, from playing videogames to managing personal information for people not tied permanently to a desk (which means just about everyone). If current trends are any guide, within a very short time most if not all of these devices will be able to access the Internet. Moreover, they should be able to communicate directly with each other using technologies such as Bluetooth. At that point they will become specialized appliances with general-purpose web-browsing capabilities.

Since the early 1980s, the personal computer has been the growth engine of the computer industry. Although some have predicted the demise of the PC, this seems highly unlikely. However, it is true that the growth rate is slowing down in more-developed markets such as the United States, where sales in the first half of 2000 increased at single-digit rates, compared to a 15 percent growth outside the United States. One of the reasons for this is that home penetration now exceeds 50 percent in the United States and business penetration is much higher (International Data Corporation pegged home penetration in the United States at 52 percent in mid 2000 and predicted that it would surpass 60 percent in 2001).[14] Although replacement demand for PCs is likely to remain robust, and although many homes may ultimately have several PCs, the high growth rates of the past seem less likely to continue.

Hand-Held Personal Digital Assistants

While the PC market is maturing, the growth rate of digital devices is accelerating rapidly. Take the hand-held personal digital assistants (PDAs), such as those produced by Palm, Handspring, and Microsoft. These devices are designed to perform basic information management functions associated with scheduling, address books, note taking, email, word processing, and expense tracking. Although there have been experiments with several different form factors—some with miniature keyboards (so-called PC companions) and some without—the form factor that seems to be dominating is the one pioneered by Palm with its original Palm Pilot, which is the essence of simplicity. The Palm Pilot was the brain child of Jeff Hawkins and Donna Dubinsky (who subsequently left Palm to found Handspring). Their vision was to produce a simple electronic device that would function as a calendar, an address book, a to-do list, and a memo writer. They believed that the main competitor for the Pilot would be paper, not computers. Accordingly, they tried hard to make the Pilot a model of simplicity. For example, looking up the day schedule is no more difficult than opening a date book: one push of a button and there it is. They succeeded beyond their expectations.

First introduced in 1996, within eighteen months over 1 million Palm Pilots were shipped. By 1999, some 2.3 million PDAs had been shipped in the United States. IDC projected U.S. sales of 3.6 million PDAs in 2000 and 9.7 million in 2004. The worldwide figure is expected to grow from 4 million PDAs in 2000 to over 17 million devices in 2004, while average selling prices will decline somewhat to $320 a unit. If this comes to pass, worldwide sales will rise from $1.6 billion in 1999 to $5.5 billion in 2004, representing an annual compound growth rate of over 24 percent (see Table 1 for sales forecasts).[15] Following the lead set by the introduction of the Palm VII in mid 1999, an increasing proportion of these PDAs will have wireless functionality and an ability to access the Web through microbrowser technology.

TABLE 1A

Worldwide Unit Sales Forecasts for Digital Devices, 1999–2004 (000)

	1999	2000	2001	2002	2003	2004
Internet-enabled game consoles	1,933	8,400	16,005	25,410	25,603	22,638
Internet-enabled TVs	6,117	13,992	18,334	19,336	18,736	17,808
Smart hand-held devices*	1,723	3,348	6,619	12,592	21,599	33,176

* Includes PDAs, PC companions, and smart wireless phones.

Source: IDC, Review and Forecast of Worldwide Information Appliance Market, 2000.

TABLE 1B

Worldwide Unit Sales Installed Base for Digital Devices, 1999–2004 (000)

	1999	2000	2001	2002	2003	2004
Internet-enabled game consoles	2,841	11,241	27,246	51,809	75,418	85,731
Internet-enabled TVs	10,131	23,564	40,208	56,901	70,888	81,291
Smart hand-held devices*	3,414	6,150	11,691	22,560	40,811	67,367

* Includes PDAs, PC companions, and smart wireless phones.

Source: IDC, Review and Forecast of Worldwide Information Appliance Market, 2000.

Wireless Phones

Projected growth rates for wireless phones that can access the Internet using WAP protocols are similarly dramatic and, significantly, involve much larger unit volumes. Right now there are some 550 million wireless subscribers in the world. Penetration is over 30 percent in the United States and between 30 and 50 percent across much of Europe and Japan. In Finland, close to 70 percent of the population now have cell phones. According to estimates from Nokia, by 2004 the number of wireless subscribers will approach 1.4 billion worldwide. Moreover, an increasing proportion of these wireless subscribers will be using phones that are Internet-enabled and that incorporate larger display screens and microbrowsers that can read WML-formatted web pages. Nokia forecasts that by 2004 some 600 million web-enabled wireless phones will have been sold, surpassing by 50 to 100 million the number of PCs connected to the Internet.[16] The leading edge of this movement can be seen in Japan, where NTT's DoCoMo started a persistent (always-on) wireless Internet phone service in February 1999. By mid 2000, DoCoMo had signed 10 million subscribers and competitors offering similar services had signed another 5 million, so that 12 percent of the Japanese population now has access to persistent wireless data connections. At this rate, soon more Japanese will have Internet connections through wireless phones than via PCs.

IDC forecasts a much smaller number of "smart phone" sales than Nokia, but it defined *smart phones* narrowly to include just those phones that not only have Internet microbrowser functionality but also include personal information management functions in the device (as in a PDA) that work when the phone is not connected to the network. Clearly, such devices will be very close substitutes for the wireless-enabled PDA like the Palm VII. According to IDC, worldwide shipments of the "smart phones" segment will grow from around 1 million units in 2000 to 21.6 million units in 2004 and will generate sales of $7.5 billion at an average selling price of $350.[17]

Videogame Consoles

Videogame consoles represent yet another specialized digital device that is rapidly becoming Internet-enabled. Some 40 percent of United States households already own a videogame console. Videogame players have shown a tendency to upgrade to more powerful machines every time a new generation of hardware comes along. The next generation of videogame consoles now arriving are designed for 128-bit games and include Sega's Dreamcast, Sony's Playstation II, Microsoft's X-Box, and Nintendo's Dolphin. All of these consoles will probably have web-browsing capabilities, since they were initially included to facilitate multiplayer gaming over the Internet. Users will also be able to download games, movies, and music onto their consoles, as well as use their consoles to browse the Web, send email, execute e-commerce transactions, and so on. These capabilities have led some to speculate that videogame terminals are a Trojan horse in the living room that might ultimately hit PC sales.[18]

Sony is the current market leader in the videogame space. The total videogame market is huge, generating $20 billion in worldwide sales annually and $7.1 billion in the United States. U.S. videogame sales are closing in on Hollywood film revenues, and the industry is growing faster than either the music or film business. Sony has sold some 77 million units of its PlayStation console worldwide. It introduced the PlayStation 2 console in Japan in March 2000 and shipped 1.41 million units in just two months.[19] According to IDC, 1.9 million Internet-enabled videogame consoles were shipped in 1999 (primarily the Sega Dreamcast), 8.4 million would be shipped in 2000 (the Dreamcast and PlayStation 2), and 22.6 million would be shipped by 2004 (see Table 1).[20] If the videogame manufacturers are successful in their attempt to broaden the market appeal of their equipment to include a larger proportion of adults, these figures could prove quite conservative.

Set Top Boxes

Another category of digital devices that has garnered significant attention is the web-enabled television category. In the short to medium term, most of the growth here will involve the purchase of set top boxes. Set top boxes can be used to decode and encode digital signals, thereby transforming a standard TV into a more powerful and interactive Internet-enabled device. Set top boxes are needed because the average TV lasts twelve to fifteen years. Such legacy equipment lacks digital capabilities necessary to access Internet media. In the long run, fully integrated digital TVs are expected to reduce the need for set top boxes.

Although the concept of interactive TV has been around for decades and companies have been talking about set top boxes and associated services for some years now, sales have been slow to pick up. In part, this is because the reality of interactive TV has often lagged behind the hype. Microsoft's Web TV, launched in 1996, is one of the more successful attempts to introduce interactive TV services and has more than 1 million subscribers, but by mid 2000 the venture still had not offered users full integration with Microsoft services such as email and instant chat. However, an improved version was scheduled to roll out in fall 2000 with the introduction of Web TV's Ultimate TV platform. More generally, several industry analysts believe that the set top box market is now ready for prime time. For example, Jupiter Communications forecasted that by 2004, 29 percent of U.S. households should have access to some form of interactive television and interactive TV services could generate some $10 billion in revenues.[21] Forrester saw an even quicker ramp up, with 25 percent of U.S. homes having an interactive TV service by 2002.[22] IDC forecasted that between 2000 and 2004 some 45 million set top boxes would be sold in the United States and 90 million would be sold worldwide (see Table 1).[23]

The catalysts for projected growth in the set top box arena include several new service offerings announced in 2000. For example, in mid 2000, AOL announced plans to launch an interactive TV service, AOLTV. Around the same time, Blockbuster Entertainment announced that it had teamed up with Enron to provide video-on-demand service to U.S. households using set top box technology. Under this agreement, Enron would encode and stream movies over its nationwide fiber-optic network and store them on servers at Blockbuster locations as well as near customers' houses. To provide the "last mile" of transport to customers, Enron and Blockbuster signed on as affiliates several providers of high-speed access, including SBC Communications, Qwest, and Covad.[24]

Other Categories

Although PDAs, web-enabled wireless phones and TVs, and videogame consoles are at the leading edge of the digital device revolution, they by no means constitute the full range of actual or potential devices. Other consumer devices include hand-held PC companions, auto PCs, and stand-alone web

tablets or screen phones that offer Internet connectivity. So far, the most successful of these formats have been the hand-held PC companions. These compact clam shell devices come equipped with miniature keypads, versions of popular PC applications, and an ability to synchronize information with desktop PCs. However, sales of this category seem to have stalled, particularly in the United States, where shipments fell from 421,000 units in 1998 to a projected 235,000 units in 2000. Nor are things projected to get much better in the United States, where the category seems to be in danger of extinction. However, growth elsewhere, particularly in Europe, where Psion's PC companion offerings have a strong following, could lift worldwide unit sales from around 1 million in 2000 to 1.8 million by 2004.[25]

A number of vertical application devices used in business settings are also often included in the digital device category. Even though they are not mass market consumer devices, they share some features with consumer devices, including the utilization of similar operating systems, such as Windows CE, web functionality, and wireless capabilities. Such VADs include devices used to gather data from the field or in a mobile situation and transmit it to a central point. Familiar examples include the keypad-based handsets used by FedEx delivery and pickup drivers to collect tracking data for packages. Key- or pen-based vertical application devices are also used to collect inventory information from a warehouse, by physicians accessing patient records in a hospital, and so on. These specialized devices cost more than other digital devices—typically between $1,000 and $2,000 each. Worldwide unit sales are projected to grow from 2.25 million in 2000 to 4.66 million in 2004, representing $6.2 billion worth of potential revenues.[26]

Summary

Three points are worth emphasizing at this juncture. First, digital devices seem poised to emerge as a key *complement* to the personal computer. The PC is likely to retain its important role in the home and office, but increasingly consumers and businesses will also use other devises to manage their personal information and access the Web to gather and manipulate information, communicate, and perform economic transactions.

Second, in the consumer space at least, sales of digital devices will probably accelerate more rapidly than sales of PCs, with total shipments of such devices surpassing those of the PC by 2003. IDC projects shipments of PCs to consumers in the United States to grow from 16 million units in 1999 to 25 million units in 2003. Over the same time period, the combined U.S. unit sales to consumers of PDAs, set top boxes, Internet-ready videogame consoles, and smart phones (narrowly defined) are projected to rise from 3 million units in 1999 to around 30 million units in 2003 (see Figure 1).[27] If wireless phones with web-browsing capability are included in these figures, the gap becomes much greater, since many of the 130 million wireless service subscribers expected by then will own wireless phones with microbrowsers that can interpret WML-formatted web data.[28]

Third, in the digital device arena, no single form factor will dominate. If IDC's projections are anywhere close to the mark, there will be a worldwide installed base of some 270 million digital devices by the end of 2004, with Internet-ready game consoles, set top boxes, and a combined PDA/smart phone category, each accounting for roughly 30 percent of the total devices.[29] Again, it is important to emphasize that IDC does not include in its data web-enabled wireless phones that lack the personal information management functionality of smart phones. It is worth emphasizing yet again that Nokia forecasts that by 2004 some 600 million wireless phones will have been sold that contain some form of web functionality.

The Players

There are a large number of companies that play either directly or indirectly in the digital device space. The space itself can be broken down into several categories (see Figure 2), including hardware providers, operating system providers, application software providers, Internet service providers, and providers of Internet servers' software. The categories are broad and can be subdivided still further. For example, PDAs, wireless phones, set top boxes, videogame consoles, and vertical application devices are all subdivisions of the hardware category; operating system providers include providers of device operating systems, such as Palm with its Palm operating system (OS) and Microsoft with Windows CE, and providers of real-time operating systems for embedded microprocessors such as Wind River Systems; application providers include those producing applications aimed at the consumer space (such as Electronic Arts, which produces games that have online multiplayer functionality) and providers of business applications that can be accessed through Internet-enabled digital devices, be they wireless or wired (such as Microsoft, Oracle, SAP); and so on. Some companies play in just one segment. For example, Handspring is currently focused exclusively on the PDA space, while other companies play in multiple segments (such as Microsoft and Sony). Microsoft in particular is now participating in one form or another in all five major categories in the arena, making it the only company with such a broad spread of assets.

The remainder of this case focuses on just one segment of the device space illustrated in Figure 2: the operating system space. Moreover, it focuses on the providers of operating systems for relatively large consumer devices such as PDAs and smart phones (Palm, Microsoft, and Psion/Symbian), rather than providers of embedded real-time operating systems (Wind River Systems). It is important to keep the wider playing field in mind, however, when evaluating the strategy of companies competing in this space. Ultimately, an analysis of the wider arena should inform strategic decisions at the level of device operating systems.

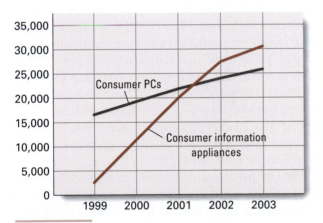

FIGURE 1

United States Sales of Consumer Personal Computers and Digital Devices, 1999–2003

Source: IDC Review and Forecast of Worldwide Information Appliance Market, 2000.

Note: Consumer information appliances include PDAs, PC companions, Internet-enabled TVs, Internet-enabled game consoles, and smart wireless phones.

FIGURE 2

Categories in the Digital Device Space

Palm

Palm began selling its pioneering Palm Pilot in 1996 when it was part of U.S. Robotics, which was acquired by 3Com in 1997.[30] Palm was subsequently spun out of 3Com in mid 2000 and now operates as an independent entity. Since the introduction of the Palm Pilot, Palm has emerged as the leader in the hand-held space. In 1999, Palm had a 66 percent share of the worldwide PDA market, and some 75 percent of the PDA's shipped worldwide used the Palm OS (Palm licenses its operating system to other vendors, which now include Handspring and Sony).[31] In the all-important United States market, Palm's lead was stronger still. Palm held 83.5 percent of the hand-held market in the United States in 1999, versus 9.8 percent for PDAs that utilized Microsoft's Windows CE operating system.[32] As of June 2000, Palm had sold over 7 million Palm devices worldwide and revenues had grown from around $1 million in 1995 to over $1 billion in 2000.

The appeal of the original Palm Pilot was based on a combination of functionality, simplicity, mobility, and an ability to synchronize data with a PC. Palm has tried to stay true to its original vision with its current PDA product line, which includes the Palm III, V, VII, and m100 product. The Palm VII comes with wireless capabilities, and the m100 is positioned as an entry-level device and is designed to appeal to a wide range of consumers. Prices range from $450 for the Palm VIIx to $150 for the entry-level m100. Most Palm models utilize monochrome screens—primarily to keep down power consumption—although the Palm IIIc comes with a color screen. Palm's PDAs run on low-speed (16–20 MHz) Motorola Dragon Ball microprocessors, again to keep power consumption down. The systems are shipped with between 2 and 8 MB of RAM and 2 MB of ROM that cannot be extended. Palm seems committed to a design philosophy that emphasizes simplicity, elegance, ease of use, and low power consumption.

To complement the Palm VII, in 1999 Palm introduced Palm.Net, a subscription-based wireless access service that enables Palm users to access web-clipping content on the Internet. Palm offers prepaid packages that provide for limited access to these data, for $9.99 or $24.99 per month (charging additional amounts for network usage in excess of the prepaid package). Unlimited access costs $44.99 a month. Using the Palm VII as a wireless-enabled Internet access device, Palm.Net subscribers can get stock quotes, read news clippings, check airline times, access online shops, and, increasingly, access enterprise data and applications. Palm.Net optimizes web data for display on Palm screens. Palm is also a supporter of the WAP.

Palm's stated strategy is to establish the Palm platform as the industry standard for hand-held devices.

The Palm platform consists of several key components. These include (1) the 16-bit operating system itself, (2) the user interface, (3) application programming interfaces that allow third-party developers to write applications that run on the Palm platform, (4) development tools, (5) HotSync data synchronization technology that allows the Palm to synchronize information with PCs or enterprise databases, (6) Graffiti script recognition technology that enables users to input data through a pen-based interface, and (7) web-clipping software that allows content providers to present, and users to receive, Internet and enterprise data in a format optimized for hand-held devices.

The Palm platform software code is designed to allow applications to run quickly and reliably and to minimize power, processing, and memory requirements without sacrificing performance. Palm designs separations between software layers, the underlying basic code or kernel, and the hardware reference design specific to the Palm devices. This means that the Palm platform can be broken into easily configurable components, allowing the Palm OS to run on a variety of different digital devices. Thus, in addition to the PDA form factor, elements of the Palm platform have been licensed to run on wireless phones, set top boxes, and vertical application devices.

In general, Palm seems committed to licensing its platform on a selective basis to other companies that make a wide range of digital devices. Symbol Technologies has licensed the Palm OS and has used it in a number of vertical application devices. Qualcomm has licensed the Palm OS and has used it in its pdQ digital smart phone. In late 1999, Palm announced a nonexclusive agreement with Nokia (the world's largest producer of wireless handsets) to work jointly on the development of wireless phones that use the Palm platform. Handspring licensed the Palm OS to run its own PDA offering, the Visor, a striking product developed by the inventors of the original Palm Pilot, Jeff Hawkins and Donna Dubinsky. In June 2000, Sony announced that it too would license the Palm OS to run its own line of hand-held PDAs, which were slated for market introduction in late 2000. Palm's decision to license its OS to competing manufacturers of PDAs is an interesting one and reflects the company's belief that it is more important to increase the total market for PDAs using the Palm OS than to monopolize the supply of those PDAs. It is worth noting that, after a slow start, Handspring's Visor seemed in 2000 to be gaining significant share from Palm in retail sales.[33]

Palm's early market lead and broad market adoption has helped to attract a large community of third-party developers who develop software applications that run on the Palm platform. Palm provides tools to this community to help them develop applications. As of June 2000, some 77,000 developers had registered to use Palm developer tools to create applications for the Palm platform, up from 5,000 in only eighteen months. Although Palm extracts no license revenue from these applications, the company believes that the spread of applications will further adoption of its platform and accordingly devotes considerable attention to nurturing third-party developers. Palm has also established a $150 million venture capital fund to invest in promising developers.

Palm sees the enterprise market as a significant opportunity. Most of Palm's devices have been used in professional settings, but historically they have been purchased by individual users rather than by corporations. The introduction of the Palm VII, with its ability to access enterprise data from remote locations, has considerably increased the value of the Palm platform from an enterprise perspective. Palm devices are now on the approved standards list of over three hundred companies, including eighty-nine *Fortune* 500 companies. To further the adoption of the Palm platform in corporate settings, Palm has established relationships with companies like Oracle, People Soft, Sap, Siebel, and Sybase to develop applications that provide access to enterprises databases using the Palm platform. For example, SAP's mobile R/3, introduced in mid 1998, runs on the Palm platform.[34] Similarly, in mid 1998, Oracle announced a partnership with Palm to integrate a 150-kbyte version of the Oracle Lite client database into Palm OS units. Oracle states that this integration will let Palm OS applications and data be replicated, synchronized, and shared with Oracle8 databases. However, most software companies are hedging their bets by developing applications for *both* the Palm OS and Windows CE platforms.

Microsoft

Microsoft competes in this space with its Windows CE operating system. Unlike Palm, Microsoft does not manufacture PDAs itself, but instead works with various computer companies who do, including

Hewlett Packard and Compaq. In April 2000, Microsoft introduced the third version of its operating system for digital devices, Windows CE 3.0. The prior versions had failed to garner significant sales. For example, in the PDA market, devices using the Windows CE OS slipped from 14.5 percent of the worldwide market in 1998 to 12.6 percent in 1999.[35]

Windows CE 3.0 is just part of Microsoft's offering in the device space. Windows NT Embedded, a derivative of Windows NT 4.0, is targeted at devices in the mid to high range of the spectrum that need a more powerful embedded operating system than Windows CE. These devices include office automation systems such as Xerox's Document Center Systems. In addition, the Microsoft Server Appliance Kit, an add-on to Windows 2000, enables development of server appliances based on Windows 2000 technology.[36]

Windows CE is a modular OS that can be configured for different devices. Version 3.0 includes an update of Microsoft's Platform Builder tool, which is used to configure the OS for each specific deployment environment. Using the Platform Builder technology, Microsoft contends that a build of the OS can range from as little as 300 KB to as much as 4 MB. The goal here is to enable an original equipment manufacturer to customized Windows CE to their particular device and application. For applications that can leverage it, Internet Explorer 4.0 is integrated with Windows CE 3.0 along with the Windows Media Player.

Compared to prior versions, Windows CE 3.0 also has improved real-time operating system (RTOS) capabilities. Potentially this extends the reach of Windows CE into a wide range of digital devices that need RTOS capabilities. These include manufacturing process controls, high-speed data acquisition devices, telecommunications switching equipment, medical monitoring equipment, aircraft "fly-by-wire" controls, and weapons delivery, space navigation and guidance, laboratory experiment control, automobile engine control, and robotics systems. While Microsoft's internal tests show that Windows CE 3.0 does now meet the minimum requirements for an RTOS, independent reviewers still believe that the response time of the OS is too slow for it to qualify as a true RTOS.[37]

Windows CE has been ported to twelve different processor architectures and 180 different CPUs. Unlike Palm's 16-bit OS, Windows CE is a 32-bit operating system. Microsoft contends that without a 32-bit processor, the complex graphical interfaces for Internet-connected devices that it expects developers to create using Windows CE would not be possible. A definite attraction of CE is that developers can use Microsoft Windows development tools and Win 32 APIs to write applications. This leverages the skill base of the large Windows development community. It is estimated that some 5 million developers around the world are currently writing software for Windows. Thus, in theory there is a huge reservoir of talent out there ready to write software for Windows CE while programs for other Windows systems can be quickly modified for CE.[38] To further help a developer, included with Platform Builder is Embedded Visual Tools, a development environment analogous to the Visual Studio product in the general-purpose product line that can be used to build applications on top of Windows CE 3.0.

One of the first Windows CE 3.0 products to hit the market is the Pocket PC, a line of PDAs produced by Hewlett Packard and Compaq, among others. HP's Jornada 548 is at the top end of the range. Priced at $550, it comes with a color screen, a 133-MHz, 32-bit Hitatchi processor, 32 MB of RAM, and 16 MB of ROM. Storage space can be increased using flash memory cards. The battery life is estimated at eight hours. For comparison, the battery life of the Palm VII is several weeks. The Jornada is longer, thicker, and heavier than Palm models (9.1 ounces versus 6.7 ounces for the Palm VIIx).

Most reviews suggest that the Pocket PC is strong in areas where Palm machines are weak and vice versa. The Pocket PCs contain all of the basic PIM (Personal Information Management) functions that come with Palm's devices. In addition, they also let users play games and MP3 digital music files, record voice notes, and read electronic books using Microsoft's Reader that includes Microsoft's Clear Type font display. The Pocket PC will also display Microsoft Word and Excel files, and thus enable the user to open many email attachments. The handwriting recognition software is less demanding than Palm's Graffiti. The Pocket PC offers a fast USB connection to a desktop machine, and, with a modem attached, the Pocket PC can access an Internet standard or AOL email account and surf the Web using pocket Internet Explorer. The device is suited for applications that need SQL, SSL (Secure Sockets Layer) with 128-bit encryption, Windows network authentication and access, guaranteed asynchronous message delivery, or remote procedure calls.

Clearly, Microsoft and its partners are targeting users that need more from a PDA than a basic organizer and are prepared to pay a premium price for that additional functionality. On the downside, the Pocket PC is a bulkier machine with much shorter battery life and less elegance than the minimalist Palm and Handspring devices. For those who want just the basic PIM functions of the Palm, the Pocket PC may prove to be a hard sell. Despite this, most observers now believe that the Pocket PC offers the Palm OS its first credible challenge. IDC, for example, forecasts that with the arrival of Windows CE 3.0, Microsoft's share of the world PDA operating system market will grow from an estimated 18 percent in 2000 to 39 percent in 2004, while Palm's share will slip from 75 percent to 50 percent.[39] Like Palm, Microsoft is committed to licensing Windows CE 3.0 widely. Microsoft has been quietly working with a number of equipment manufacturers and service providers in an attempt to get its technology incorporated into smart phones. In June 2000, the company announced that it would join forces with Samsung to provide a version of Windows CE 3.0 as the OS for Samsung smart phones, along with Microsoft Mobile Explorer, a microbrowser for Internet and email access.[40] Ericsson has also agreed to adopt Mobile Explorer for use in some of its smart phones.[41] Microsoft has also entered into a joint venture with Qualcomm to develop wireless devices and services based on CE and Qualcomm's CDMA digital cellular technology.[42]

Microsoft is pushing Windows CE in the set top box arena. As part of a broad agreement that included a $5 billion investment by Microsoft, AT&T agreed to use Microsoft's Windows CE software in at least 2.5 million set top boxes. This is in addition to a 1998 deal with TCI (now owned by AT&T) to put Windows CE in 5 million set top boxes. However, both deals were nonexclusive, and AT&T has been at pains to indicate that it will also use competing software, such as the Java OS promoted by Sun Microsystems.[43] These nonexclusive agreements reflect one of the biggest fears of device manufacturers and suppliers of complement services, such as cable— namely, that Microsoft will dominate the digital device world in much the same way as it has dominated the PC world. If this were to occur, Microsoft could conceivably capture much of the economic value in the marketplace, leaving device manufacturers and service providers to compete with each other in a commodity world. In the words of TCI president Leo Hinderly, many device manufacturers and complement suppliers "don't want to be a Bill Gates download."[44] This fear adds momentum behind any offering that is perceived as helping to keep Microsoft's ambitions in check. In other words, there is something of a presumption in favor of non-Microsoft solutions on the part of many other participants in the digital device value chain.

More generally, some critics of Microsoft's strategy argue that the company's attempt to modularize Windows CE so that it can be used across a very wide range of devices will not work. A frequently heard argument is that the digital device arena lacks the same compelling need for standardization that Microsoft exploited in the PC arena.[45] The world of digital devices is far more fragmented than that of the PC, so the argument goes; hence standards are naturally less important. This view is reflected in the following quote from Jerry Fidler, CEO of Wind River Systems, whose VxWorks operating system kernel for embedded processors competes in some of the same space as Windows CE. Fidler noted, "It's going to be tough for Microsoft. This isn't a one-size-fits-all market. Applications are specific, not standard like they are in the PC world. This world is chaos."[46]

Psion/Symbian/EPOC

Psion is a British company that was an early leader in the market for hand-held PC companions (which, unlike PDAs, combine a small form factor and screen with a keyboard for data input). Its Series 5 machine was introduced in mid 1997, a full six months before similar devices utilizing Windows CE. The Series 5 was greeted with critical and popular acclaim, especially in Europe. The Series 5, which is a derivative of Psion's popular Series 3 machine, uses Psion's EPOC operating system and a novel and highly usable keyboard that offers far more than the tiny-buttoned keyboards usually associated with hand-held computers. The Psion Series 5 comes with a set of built-in applications that share data formats with popular Microsoft desktop applications. These include a Word-compatible word processor. Psion provides excellent desktop connectivity with Windows through its PsiWin product.[47]

Psion has followed up its successful Series 5 machine with a more powerful Series 7 machine that comes equipped with a modem and has web-browsing functionality. Although the PC companion category is declining in the United States, Psion's strong following in Europe has led to predictions that the category will continue to grow in Western Europe. Moreover, Psion is preparing to introduce a Palm-type PDA in 2001. Because of these factors, IDC believes that Psion's EPOC operating system will continue to be a player in the hand-held computer space (PDAs plus PC companions), accounting for 13.2 percent of worldwide operating system sales for the category in 2004, up from 7.5 percent in 2000 (see Table 2).[48]

It is in the smart phone category, however, that Psion's EPOC is poised for the greatest potential gain. In 1998, Psion pulled an ace out of the hole in the form of Symbian: a joint venture with cellular telephone giants Ericsson, Nokia, and Motorola. The objective of the venture was to adapt Psion's EPOC operating system as the OS for the next generation of smart wireless phones. Subsequently, Matsushita also joined the venture, and Sony has licensed EPOC technology from Symbian for its future smart phone ventures. Collectively, Psion's partners in Symbian and licensees account for more than 80 percent of the global sales of mobile phones. If their share holds and smart phone sales grow as predicted, Psion's EPOC could emerge not only as a significant competitor to Windows CE and the Palm OS, but also as the market leader in the smart phone category.[49] In 2000, IDC predicted that some 60 percent of all smart phones sold in 2004 would utilize an EPOC operating system (see Table 3).[50]

Symbian will license EPOC to all comers for a fee of around $5 to $10 per phone, which compares favorably to the $25 per unit that Microsoft reportedly charges to license CE.[51] Psion claims that EPOC is better suited than CE to cell phones, where long battery life and efficient use of memory are more important than links to a PC desktop. Be this as it may, there is no doubt that EPOC has another attraction to Psion's partners and any potential licensees—it is not a Microsoft product. This point has been underlined by Psion's founder, David Potter, who in outlining the thinking behind Symbian explained that "we looked at the cellular industry, an industry selling 100 million units a year, and asked: 'Are these guys really going to allow the mighty Bill to come in and take their businesses?' It's absolutely obvious that there is no way they are going to do that. We looked at their needs and said, 'Let's make these guys secure.'"[52] Building on this success, Potter has announced his intentions to license EPOC to other electronic hardware manufacturers, such as set top box manufacturers.

However, for all of its promise, Symbian has its detractors and problems. Not least of these is that its EPOC-based Quartz operating system for smart phones is not yet ready for market introduction. More seriously perhaps, Psion's partners in the Symbian venture seem to be hedging their bets. Nokia has also signed a deal with Palm to license the Palm platform, and Ericsson is licensing OS technology from Microsoft. Wireless phone vendors also seem to be developing some of their own software technology, albeit around the Quartz platform, in an attempt to create some unique value. These fractures in the Symbian alliance have prompted some high-level defections from the venture, including that of former Psion and Symbian executive Juha Christensen, who

---

TABLE 2

Worldwide Market Share Forecasts for Hand-Held Computers (PDAs and PC Companions) by Operating System, 1999–2004 (% share)

	1999	2000	2001	2002	2003	2004
Win CE (PC companions)	9.3	7.1	5.6	4.5	3.8	3.1
Win CE (PDAs)	10.0	15.1	20.9	26.5	31.0	34.8
EPOC	8.5	7.5	10.4	11.2	12.3	13.2
Palm OS	60.6	62.3	56.9	52.8	48.9	45.7
Other	11.7	7.9	6.1	5.0	4.0	3.2

Source: IDC Review and Forecast of Worldwide Information Appliance Market, 2000.

TABLE 3

Worldwide Smart Phone Market Share Forecasts by Operating System, 1999–2004 (% share)

	1999	2000	2001	2002	2003	2004
EPOC	0	11.5	50.5	55.7	57.1	59.4
Win CE	0	0	9.8	13.4	16.1	20.0
GEOS	94.8	50	0	0	0	0
Palm OS	2.3	35.6	37.1	28.7	25.0	19.1
Other	3.1	2.9	2.6	2.2	1.8	1.5

Source: IDC Review and Forecast of Worldwide Information Appliance Market, 2000.

left Symbian in March to join rival Microsoft.[53] As a consequence, the most that can be said at this juncture is that Symbian is still in the game with a shot at getting an EPOC-based operating system established as the dominant format in the smart phone arena, but that the probability of this occurring is lower than it was when the venture was established.

Key Strategic Issues

The competitive situation in the digital device arena is still unfolding daily. Huge uncertainties abound as to the future direction of the market. How will the technology evolve? What are the attributes of the technology required to facilitate this development? Will standards be important in the digital device arena, or in segments of that arena? What kind of products will be demanded by mass-market consumers, as opposed to technophiles? Where will the growth be? What product attributes in terms of form factors and functions will be required to drive forward expansions of demand? What is the correct technological, product development and competitive strategy for Microsoft to pursue in order for the company to help the market grow and to position itself to profit from that growth, irrespective of how critical uncertainties resolve themselves? How can Microsoft gain a major share in a market where not only competitors, but also suppliers of important complements, have a vested interest in seeing the company's market share bounded?

ENDNOTES

1. Perhaps the most compelling statement of this was made by the late Mark Weiser, chief technologist at Xerox PARC. See Elizabeth Wasserman, "Electronics Guru Predicts Ubiquitous Computing," *Arizona Republic,* January 19, 1998, p. E1; and Mark Weiser, "The Future of Ubiquitous Computing on Campus," *Communications of the ACM* 41(1), January 1998, p. 41.
2. Kevin Werbach, "Analysts Only Guessing at E-commerce Sales Figures," *Seattle Post Intelligencer,* December 9, 1999, p. C2.
3. Ray Kurzweil, *The Age of Spiritual Machines* (New York: Penguin, 1999).
4. Stan Williams, "The Computer of the Future," *Technology Review,* September–October 1999, pp. 92–96.
5. Stephen Pizzo, "The Race for Fiberspace," *Forbes ASAP,* August 21, 2000, p. 73.
6. See Peter Fairley, "The Microphotonics Revolution," *Technology Review,* July–August 2000, pp. 38–44; and Jeff Hecht, "Light Signals Direct," *Technology Review,* July–August 2000, p. 27. George Gilder sees the emergence of all optical networks, complete with optical switches, fiber in the home, and laser-based local networks, as an inevitable development: Eric Pfeiffer, "Gilder on Optics," *Forbes ASAP,* August 21, 2000, p. 97.
7. M. Hamblem, "3G Wireless," *Computerworld,* p. 63.
8. Wasserman, "Eletronics Guru," p. E1.
9. Kevin Kelly and Spencer Reiss, "One Huge Computer," *Wired,* August 1998.
10. Izarek Shopper, Net Watch: Sun Microsystems and Jini Architecture, October 1998.
11. Ibid.
12. Aaron Goldberg, "I Dream of Jini, and So Should You," *PC Week,* August 3, 1998.
13. Peter Loftus, "Apples and Oranges,"*Wall Street Journal,* June 26, 2000, p. R28.
14. David Hamilton, "U.S. PC Sales Slowed During the Second Quarter," *Wall Street Journal,* July 24, 2000, p. A4.
15. Jill House, *Market Mayhem: The Smart Handheld Devices Market Forecast and Analysis* (IDC, 2000). Rex Crum, "Palm and Handspring: The Whole World in Their Hands?" *Upside Today,* August 18, 2000.
16. Jay Palmer, "Palmed Off," *Barron's,* February 28, 2000, pp. 31–34.
17. House, *Market Mayhem.*
18. Dean Takahashi, "Buying Decision, the Big Game: It's Sony Versus Sega Versus Nintendo Versus Microsoft," *Wall Street Journal,* June 26, 2000, p. R16.
19. Alex Pham, "Global Wars," *Boston Globe,* May 29, 2000, p. C1.
20. K. Hause, B. Ma, D. Hwang, and J. House, *Review and Forecast of the World Wide Information Appliance Market, 1999–2004* (IDC 2000).
21. A. E. Cha, "AOL to Meld TV and Internet Services," *Washington Post,* July 27, 2000, p. E1.
22. Mike Snider, "Your TV's Little Black Box Is Growing Up," *USA Today,* July 17, 2000, p. D3.

23. Hause et al., *Review and Forecast.*
24. Sallie Hofmeister, "Blockbuster in Pact with Enron to Offer Demanded Video," *Los Angeles Times,* July 20, 2000, p. C1.
25. House, *Market Mayhem.*
26. Ibid.
27. Hause et al., *Review and Forecast.*
28. C. Pottorf and C. Vyas, *U.S. Wireless Services and Devices Market Assessment, 1999–2004* (IDC, 2000).
29. Hause et al., *Review and Forecast.*
30. Much of the information in this section is derived from the June 2000 Palm 10K.
31. House, *Market Mayhem.*
32. Matt Hamblen, "Pocket PC May Help Microsoft Gain Handheld Market Share," *Computer World,* February 28, 2000.
33. Crum, "Palm and Handspring."
34. Richard Levin and Tom Davey, "Handhelds—Mobile Evolution," *Information Week,* June 15, 1998, p. 20.
35. House, *Market Mayhem.*
36. Al Gillen, *Windows as An Embedded OS: Where Does It Fit In?* (IDC, August 2000).
37. Ibid.
38. Jeff Jurvis, "Business Support Grows for Windows CE," *Information Week,* March 2, 1998.
39. House, *Market Mayhem.*
40. Pui-Wing Tam, "Microsoft, Samsung to Join on 'Smart Phones,'" *Wall Street Journal,* June 14, 2000, p. B6.
41. Matt Hamblen, "Microsoft, Ericsson Partner on Wireless," *Computerworld,* December 13, 1999, p. 30.
42. J. G. Spooner, "Alliance to Bolster CE," *PC Week,* November 9, 1998, p. 16.
43. Dave Bank and Din Clark, "Microsoft Windows Heads for TV Sets," *Wall Street Journal,* May 7, 1999, p. A3.
44. S. Hamm, "Microsoft's Future: A Band of Powerful Foes is Determined to Slow the Gates Juggernaut," *Business Week,* January 19, 1998, p. 58.
45. "Windows CE Falls Short," *Forrester Report* 5(1) May 1998.
46. E. W. Desmond, "Microsoft's Big Bet on Small Machines," *Fortune,* July 20, 1998, p. 86.
47. N. Clayton and S. Vogel, "Palmistry," *The Scotsman,* September 9, 1998, p. 8.
48. House, *Market Mayhem.*
49. C. P. Wallace, "The Man Bill Gates Fears Most," *Fortune,* November 23, 1998, p. 257.
50. House, *Market Mayhem.*
51. Dan Gillmor, "Formidable Force Aims at Microsoft," *San Jose Mercury News,* July 7, 1998, p. E1.
52. Wallace, "The Man Bill Gates Fears Most."
53. S. Baker and K. Capell, "So Much for This Microsoft Rival," *Business Week,* May 1, 2000, p. 66.

Treo: Handspring's Last Stand?

18

This case was prepared by Melissa A. Schilling, Chad Beaupierre, Scott Bevier, Roberto Ekesi, and Vicken Librarikian, New York University.

It was December 2001 and the cofounders of Handspring, Donna Dubinsky and Jeff Hawkins, were sitting on a plane on the way to the CTIA Wireless IT and Internet convention in Las Vegas. Dubinsky and Hawkins were about to unveil their latest product, the Treo Communicator, at the most-recognized trade show for wireless technologies. Unlike Handspring's previous personal digital assistant (PDA) offerings, this product was an integrated "smart phone" and represented Handspring's first attempt to enter the wireless communications market and a fundamental shift in corporate strategy.

Though Handspring was second only to Palm in the worldwide hand-held computer market share, it had yet to turn a profit. PDA price wars and slumping sales had decimated margins in the PDA industry and left producers with large quantities of rapidly obsolescing inventory. Economic conditions had forced Handspring to mark down even its more-advanced models. Facing increased economic pressures, a battered stock price, and increasing competition in the PDA market, Dubinsky and Hawkins were attempting to reinvent Hand-

This case is intended to be used as a basis for class discussion rather than as an illustration of either effective or ineffective handling of the situation. Reprinted by permission.

spring as a leader in the smart phone market (see appendix 1 for an excerpt of a Handspring management discussion on repositioning the company). Smart phone shipments were expected to grow to almost 5 million units in 2002, amounting to $2.3 billion in sales.[1] Smart phones also had higher margins. However, entering the smart phone market also meant pitting the company against very large and established rivals such as Nokia, Samsung, and Ericsson. Could Handspring convince enterprises and individual consumers that it was the right company to deliver a competitive product in the wireless communications market? Would it be able to compete with competitors that had more experience and scale in the telecommunications market? If Handspring was able to successfully penetrate the smart phone market, would that be enough to turn the company's financial situation around?

Background

Handspring was cofounded in July 1998 by Jeff Hawkins and Donna Dubinsky. Hawkins was the original founder of Palm Computing, a company that made handwriting recognition software for PDAs. US Robotics acquired Palm in 1995, bringing badly needed capital to fund development costs, and in 1996 the company introduced the first generation of Palm Pilot PDAs. However, after 3Com acquired US Robotics in 1997, Hawkins and Dubinsky decided to leave the company and start a new venture that would produce PDAs based on the Palm operating system: Handspring.[2] They completed their core management team with Ed Colligan, another former 3Com employee who had been responsible for marketing the Palm PDA devices (see appendix 2 for a full management team description). They positioned Handspring to the public and investors as the same people doing the same thing, this time just better. The executive team's mantra was "Innovate, innovate, and innovate. Yet keep it small, simple, affordable, and connected."

Handspring entered the PDA market in mid 1999 with its Visor device. The Visor was priced lower than Palm's PDAs, and with its Springboard module contained more functions than Palm's devices. The module allowed the PDA to be expanded by inserting a range of components, such as mobile phones, digital cameras, pagers, modems, MP3 players, and additional software applications.[3] Handspring launched a global marketing program for its Visor and Springboard modules, selling through a variety of distribution channels that included the World Wide Web, value-added resellers, international distribution agencies, and retailers. Handspring's largest retailers were Best Buy, Staples, and CompUSA, which accounted for 14, 13, and 10 percent of sales, respectively. Competing primarily on design and price, the consumer segment was Handspring's primary target, while the business segment received only a secondary focus.

Before long it became apparent that the Springboard modules, initially praised by consumers and feared by competitors, were not going to revolutionize the PDA market. The Springboard modules never achieved strong market acceptance because they were expensive and could only make the Visor devices imitate, and not replace, other devices. This lack of a compelling differentiating factor, combined with an increasingly competitive PDA market, had moved Handspring into a very vulnerable competitive position. Since the fall of 2000, investors had seen Handspring's stock price drop from a high of $95 to as low as $1.20. By December 2001, Handspring's stock was trading at just over $6 a share. Facing increasingly difficult economic conditions and a third straight year of increasing operating losses (see Figures 1, 2, and 3 for Handspring's financials), Handspring had

to do something drastic. Though it had already made one foray into merging cell phone and PDA capabilities with the VisorPhone (a Springboard module that acted as a cell phone), that product had received a lukewarm welcome. The module was expensive, and the combination of the module and the PC was bulky and awkward. This time around the company decided to commit fully to the smart phone concept by introducing a product that would put phone capability and styling first, with PDA functionality second: the Treo.

The Treo is a single device that integrates the functionality of a cell phone, PDA, and pager with "always on" capability.[4] Unlike regular cell phones that have some organizer capabilities, smart phones such as the Treo had larger, sharper screens that could display regular web pages rather than the small subset of web pages designed to be readable on cell phone displays.[5] At its launch, it was heralded as the smart phone with the tightest integration of these functions and capabilities. Handspring was betting that it could establish the Treo as the future in handheld communications.

Treo Communicator

The Treo was designed to fit in the palm of one's hand and combined three existing products (cell phone, PDA, and pager) into one small package without compromising functionality or ease of use. It was the first product to come close to realizing the product concept inspired by Gene Roddenberry's *Star Trek.* The Treo was equipped with a dual-band Global System for Mobile Communications (GSM) world phone that would be upgradeable to GPRS (General Packet Radio Service) networks when they became more widely available. Handspring was also developing a version that would run on Sprint's third-generation Code Division Multiple Access (CDMA) networks.

The Treo did not have the Springboard module, but it did feature a display (available in monochrome sixteen-shade gray scale or color) that was only slightly smaller than the standard Handspring Visor display and that acted as a touch screen. Like the Motorola StarTac or Ericsson World Phone (or *Star Trek*'s tricorders, for that matter), the Treo had a flip cover protecting the display and keyboard area. It also came with either a keyboard or writing area (both models were offered to suit different customer prefer-

FIGURE 1

Balance Sheet

Handspring, Inc. Consolidated Balance Sheets (in thousands, except share and per share amounts)

	June 30, 2001	July 1, 2000
Assets		
Current assets		
Cash and cash equivalents	$ 87,580	$196,548
Short-term investments	33,943	—
Accounts receivable, net of allowance for doubtful accounts of $2,239		
and $50 as of June 30, 2001, and July 1, 2000, respectively	12,850	20,484
Prepaid expenses and other current assets	19,473	1,776
Inventories	2,857	40
Total current assets	156,703	218,848
Long-term investments	80,237	2,664
Property and equipment, net	15,041	8,280
Intangibles and other assets	1,254	680
Total assets	$253,235	$230,472
Liabilities and Stockholders' Equity		
Current liabilities		
Accounts payable	$ 37,881	$ 20,152
Accrued liabilities	70,152	16,034
Total current liabilities	108,033	36,186
Long-term liabilities	—	57
Commitments and contingencies		
Stockholders' equity		
Preferred stock, $0.001 par value per share, 10,000,000 shares authorized;		
nil shares issued and outstanding at June 30, 2001, and July 1, 2000	—	—
Common stock, $0.001 par value per share, 1,000,000,000 shares authorized;		
129,949,768 and 125,436,978 shares issued and outstanding at June 30, 2001,		
and July 1, 2000, respectively	130	125
Additional paid-in capital	368,166	321,116
Deferred stock compensation	(29,445)	(58,268)
Accumulated other comprehensive income (loss)	994	(64)
Accumulated deficit	(194,643)	(68,680)
Total stockholders' equity	145,202	194,229
Total liabilities and stockholders' equity	$253,235	$230,472

Source: Handspring 10K, June 30, 2001.

ences), a built-in microphone, and an infrared port. It measured 4.3 inches by 2.7 inches by 0.7 inches and weighed only 5.2 ounces. Like other Handspring products, the backbone of the Treo was the Palm operating system. The Treo featured a 33-MHz Motorola Dragonball processor, 16 megabytes of memory, and a rechargeable Lithium Ion battery.

When the Treo model with the monochrome display was purchased with a one-year wireless service contract, the device sold for $399, but as a stand-alone product it was priced at $599 (prices were higher for color displays). To encourage existing Visor users to upgrade to the Treo, Handspring offered a $100 rebate to Treo customers who sent in the serial numbers from their Visors. Existing Visor users were a primary target for the Treo, since one of its key points of differentiation from other smart phones was the option to use the Graffiti handwriting recognition software used on Visor PDAs.

The communicator was fully integrated with the built-in Phone Book, allowing one to dial directly from the contact list. Moreover, the Treo had a

FIGURE 2

Statement of Operations

Handspring, Inc. Consolidated Statements of Operations (in thousands, except per share amounts)

	Year Ended June 30, 2001	Year Ended July 1, 2000	Period from July 29, 1998 (date of inception) to June 30, 1999
Revenue	$ 370,943	$101,937	$ —
Costs and operating expenses			
Cost of revenue	292,311	69,921	—
Research and development	23,603	10,281	2,738
Selling, general and administrative	145,132	42,424	2,451
In-process research and development	12,225	—	—
Amortization of deferred stock compensation and intangibles(*)	32,830	40,077	3,646
Total costs and operating expenses	506,101	162,703	8,835
Loss from operations	(135,158)	(60,766)	(8,835)
Interest and other income, net	12,195	675	446
Loss before taxes	(122,963)	(60,091)	(8,389)
Income tax provision	3,000	200	—
Net loss	**$ (125,963)**	**$ (60,291)**	**$ (8,389)**
Basic and diluted net loss per share	**$ (1.21)**	**$ (1.77)**	**$ (0.71)**
Shares used in calculating basic and diluted net loss per share	**103,896**	**34,015**	**11.772**
(*) Amortization of deferred stock compensation and intangibles			
Cost of revenue	$ 4,521	$ 5,904	$ 526
Research and development	6,926	8,059	1,217
Selling, general and administrative	21,383	26,114	1,903
	$ 32,830	$ 40,077	$ 3,646

Source: Handspring 10K, June 30, 2001.

speaker phone and was compatible with several external headset options. The Treo also possessed common PDA features such as Date Book Plus, Phone Book, To Do List, and Memo Pad, and it allowed its user to organize short-term and long-term schedules. The Treo's paging capabilities enabled users to send and receive email and short SMS text messages from virtually any location. Importantly, the Treo provided web access to its users using Handspring's "Blazer" wireless web browser. To go online, a user had only to push a button and the Treo would connect automatically. It could bookmark up to one hundred web sites and run a wide range of applications, such as one that provided maps of the New York City subway system or a program that translated between English, French, Spanish, German, and Italian. It could transfer data from various other Palm OS devices, and it could even run

applications that were not developed to run on the Palm OS.

Some analysts observed that Handspring's advantage might be that adding voice capabilities to a PDA would be simpler and more effective than adding PDA capabilities to a phone. John Troyer, chief strategy officer at Neomar, remarked, "I think it's a lot easier to put voice into a PDA than it is to jam a PDA into a phone. I think we're seeing the result of that." Critics were quick to point out, however, that the Treo's battery life was subpar, with only 2.5 hours of talk time. Additionally, though the Blazer browser had earned accolades, surfing the Web using GSM was "agonizingly slow," and thus web-surfing functionality was unlikely to become a particularly valuable feature until GPRS network upgrades became available.[6] Furthermore, though the email system shipped with the Treo at its launch was adequate for

FIGURE 3

Statement of Cash Flows

Handspring, Inc. Consolidated Statements of Cash Flows (in thousands)

	Year Ended June 30, 2001	Year Ended July 1, 2000	Period from July 29, 1998 (date of inception) to June 30, 1999
Cash flows from operating activities			
Net loss	$(125,963)	$ (60,291)	$ (8,389)
Adjustments to reconcile net loss to net cash used in operating activities			
Depreciation and amortization	7,104	2,668	70
Amortization of deferred stock compensation and intangibles	32,830	40,077	3,646
In-process research and development	12,225	—	—
Write-off of excess and obsolete inventories	26,811	—	—
Charitable contribution of common stock	—	900	—
Amortization of costs associated with financing agreement	—	568	31
Amortization of premium or discount on available-for-sale securities, net	(1,313)	(118)	(108)
Gain on sale of available-for-sale securities	(277)	—	—
Stock compensation to non-employees	—	815	15
Changes in assets and liabilities			
Accounts receivable	6,625	(20,484)	—
Prepaid expenses and other current assets	(18,219)	(1,751)	(48)
Inventories	(10,011)	(40)	—
Intangibles and other assets	(40)	(616)	(64)
Accounts payable	18,701	18,944	884
Accrued liabilities	34,584	15,941	67
Net cash used in operating activities	**(16,943)**	**(3,387)**	**(3,896)**
Cash flows from investing activities			
Purchases of available-for-sale securities	(244,972)	(4,474)	(10,965)
Sales and maturities of available-for-sale securities	186,866	10,424	4,833
Purchases of investments for collateral on operating leases	(51,287)	(2,106)	(150)
Purchases of property and equipment	(14,283)	(9,818)	(780)
Cash acquired from acquisition	29	—	—
Net cash used in investing activities	**(123,647)**	**(5,974)**	**(7,062)**
Cash flows from financing activities			
Proceeds from borrowings	—	6,000	—
Principal payments on borrowings	(83)	(6,000)	—
Issuance of redeemable convertible preferred stock, net	—	11,490	17,972
Net proceeds from initial public offering and exercise of underwriters' overallotment	27,969	184,928	—
Proceeds from issuance of common stock	3,109	2,012	519
Repurchase of common stock	(41)	—	—
Net cash provided by financing activities	**30,954**	**198,430**	**18,491**
Effect of exchange rate changes on cash	668	(54)	—
Net increase (decrease) in cash and cash equivalents	(108,968)	189,015	7,533
Cash and cash equivalents			
Beginning of period	196,548	7,533	—
End of period	**$ 87,580**	**$196,548**	**$ 7,533**
Supplemental disclosure of cash flow information			
Cash paid for interest	$ 6	$ 37	$ 1
Cash paid for taxes	$ 236	$ 1	$ 1

Source: Handspring 10K, June 30, 2001.

individual consumers, it lacked the security required by corporate users; thus third-party software was initially required for corporate customers. However, Handspring later joined forces with Visto, a leading provider of web-based email and synchronization services, to develop a software program ("Treo Mail") that would bring wireless email from any Microsoft Exchange or standard Internet account, thus meeting the needs of most mobile executives.[7]

Repositioning Handspring

"The theme for the company is Treo."

—*Ed Colligan, Chief Operating Officer, Handspring*

Treo represented more than just an additional product in Handspring's portfolio—Handspring was "betting the farm" on the success of the new device. As stated by CEO Donna Dubinsky, Handspring would be "transitioning out of the organizer business and into the communicator business."[8] Handspring would continue to support the Visor so long as there was demand, but it would direct all of its development and promotion effort toward the communicator. Some analysts wondered why Handspring would abandon the Visor platform, risking alienating third-party developers for the platform and rendering all Springboard development and inventory obsolete.[9]

Treo also represented a shift in market focus for Handspring. Though individual consumers would still be targeted, the Treo would be targeted primarily at the enterprise market. Management believed the integration of phone, PDA, and pager made the Treo an appealing corporate productivity tool and that the growth potential in the business-to-business (B2B) market was greater than that in the business-to-consumer (B2C) market. At a major corporate software convention in Las Vegas, Ed Colligan stated, "We believe that this is a really compelling enterprise device for wireless voice and data. I think as we build critical mass in the enterprise with the Treo, you'll see more applications. It takes a breakthrough device to get developers going."

To attract share in the enterprise market, the product would require great breadth in available software applications and supporting tools. To ensure that a wide range of applications for the device would be available, Handspring formed several comarketing agreements with software companies that had already developed widely used applications for Visor and Palm PDAs and cell phones, to produce applications for a myriad of purposes like personal use (email, maps, browsers), business use (groupware, sales force automation, CRM, spreadsheets), and entertainment (games, pictures, personal rings).

Handspring marketed and distributed the Treo to both consumers and businesses through various channels, including retail and online stores as well as B2B agreements. For example, Handspring formed sales and marketing relationships with Neomar and Infowave whereby the companies would jointly promote Handspring's Treo and their wireless data access platforms. In addition to its own direct sales, Handspring appointed the major wholesaler Ingram Micro to focus on the enterprise market, and D&H Distributing to promote its products on college campuses.

Because the Treo was the company's first cell phone–based product offering, GSM wireless service providers had become a new and significant retail channel. The company formed partnerships with Cingular Wireless and Voicestream to sell the Treo with wireless service plans. To unlock global markets, Handspring also established similar deals with foreign wireless networks in Europe and Asia. For example, Handspring formed a strategic distribution agreement with APE Telecom, one of Sweden's leading producers of mobile communication products, to cover the marketing and distribution of the Handspring Treo to the Swedish market.

Internal Development

Handspring's products were designed by its internal engineering, marketing, and manufacturing organizations. Technologies required to support product development were either created internally or licensed from external providers. Its internal staff included engineers from many disciplines—software architects, electrical engineers, mechanical engineers, radio specialists, user interface design specialists, and others. Once a project was approved, a cross-functional team was assembled to design the product and transition it into manufacturing. To develop innovative products while minimizing time to market, the company used parallel development teams working on multiple projects. Before products were released into production, they had to pass a series of quality benchmarks and manufacturing guidelines.

Handspring's research and development expenditures in 2001 totaled $23.6 million, up from

$10.3 million in 2000 and $2.7 million in 1999. As of August 31, 2001, it had ninety-three people engaged in research and development activities, and it planned to focus its development efforts on wireless communicators.[10]

Supply-Chain Management

Though design, marketing and sales were conducted primarily in-house, Handspring was the quintessential outsourcer when it came to manufacturing and service. External parties handled manufacturing and assembly, customer and technical support, and repair services. All production of the Visor hand-held computers had been outsourced to Flextronics and Solectron. Visor phones had been built in partnership with Option International of Leuven, Belgium. Motorola provided microprocessors, Wavecom supplied the Treo with its integrated dual-band GSM radio module for wireless voice and data communications, and Acura Tech Ltd. supplied connector systems. Several components (such as the microprocessors) were available only from a single source.

Outsourcing components and manufacturing enabled Handspring to focus on its core competencies and helped to minimize inventory levels. Handspring's supply-chain management techniques backfired, however, when component shortages delayed the Treo's introduction in the United States and prompted the company to lower its production targets.[11] Handspring consequently decided to route most of its early production to Europe, where the GSM standard is more widespread and customers are considered to be more ready for smart phones.[12]

Choosing Sides in Standards Battles

The developers of the Treo had to place bets on who would win in two separate standards battles: operating systems for hand-held computers, and wireless telecommunication standards for mobile phones. The Palm operating system (OS) was an obvious choice given Handspring's history. It also held a commanding 77 percent worldwide market share at the end of 1999, and though estimates indicated that the share declined to 66 percent by the end of 2001, that still represented a significant lead over the next leading contender, Microsoft's Windows CE. However, forecasts for future trends in hand-held operating systems were troubling. Microsoft's share was predicted to gain significantly, mostly at the expense of the Palm OS share (see Figure 4 for worldwide hand-held operating system shares).

In the wireless telecommunications standards battles, Treo had put its money on the Global System for Mobile Communications (GSM). The Treo utilized GSM technology on two bands—900/1,900 MHz in North America, and 900/1,800 MHz in Asia

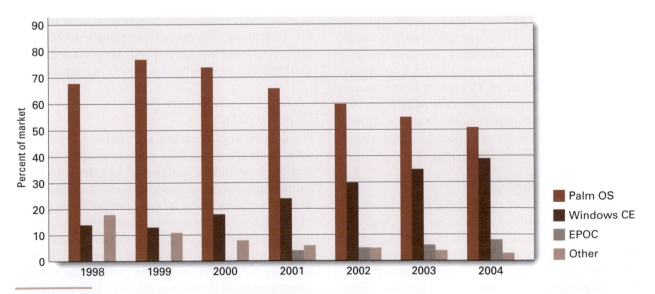

FIGURE 4

Worldwide Hand-Held Operating System Shares for 1998 and 1999, and Forecasts for 2000 to 2004

Source: Salomon Smith Barney, October 18, 2000.

and Europe.[13] Though GSM was the dominant standard globally, in the United States a wireless telecom standards battle was still unfolding. Following deregulation of the telecommunications industry in 1996, several national wireless networks had emerged (such as Cingular, Verizon, VoiceStream, Sprint PCS, and AT&T wireless), and industry players supported different digital voice wireless platforms. Of these platforms, the GSM served as the leading format for second-generation wireless communications with the largest worldwide installed base by 2000 (for an explanation of the various generations of wireless telecommunications service, see Exhibit 1).

GSM was developed in the 1980s to set a common standard for digital wireless voice communication in Europe as European markets began to unify.[14] However, by March 1999 all three of the largest wireless handset makers—Ericsson, Motorola, and Nokia—were also manufacturing wireless phones based on Qualcomm's Code Division Multiple Access (CDMA) second-generation (2G) wireless format.[15] Twenty-five percent of worldwide wireless subscribers were forecasted to have adopted CDMA technology by the end of 2002, making it the second most widely used 2G format.[16] The third most prevalent wireless platform technology, TDMA, was developed by AT&T. It was used primarily in North America and accounted for 9 percent of worldwide cellular subscribers in 2000. Most network system providers, like Ericsson, produced networks for all types of leading network technologies.

Globally, GSM was the dominant standard, and it was also better positioned for the transition to 2.5G and 3G GPRS service. However, in the United States in 2001, GSM only had an 11 percent market share; most U.S. wireless service providers adhered to the CDMA or TDMA standards. The Treo would thus function seamlessly in Europe and Asia, but coverage in the United States would be spotty.

Building a Web of Alliances

To ensure that the Treo would have a wide range of high-quality applications available for it, Handspring built a web of alliances with third-party software developers. In addition to the relationship with Visto described previously, Handspring also teamed with several leading wireless solution providers (including Aether Systems, Infowave, Neomar, Synchrologic, Wireless Knowledge, and others) to ensure that

email delivery would be secure. Handspring forged a relationship with Avantgo for its Internet ability, and with Pumatech for desktop synchronization.

Handspring also established marketing agreements with several other key software developers. It teamed with Extended Systems Inc. to comarket the Treo and other Handspring products with the latter's Xtnd Connect Server, which enabled wireless synchronization between corporate servers and hand-held devices. Handspring partnered with Synchrologic Inc. to market the Treo and other devices with Synchrologic's iMobile Suite software, which allowed wireless access to groupware, sales force automation, and customer relationship management data.

Handspring and Handango combined forces to build two online software stores. One store would be dedicated to individual consumers, while the other store would be dedicated to businesses. The stores would sell products ranging from productivity-enhancing software to games. In addition, each company would actively market the other's products via its company web sites, newsletters, and other media. Handspring also allied with Brightpoint, a large distributor of mobile phones, to distribute the Treo and provide integrated logistics services for the device.[17]

One of Handspring's most important alliance relationships was with Palm. Handspring had entered into a nonexclusive licensing agreement with Palm to use the Palm operating system. This agreement did not expire until the end of 2009, but because of its nonexclusive clause, Handspring would be able to migrate the Treo to another operating system if market demand warranted this. Given the dynamic nature of the marketplace, keeping the Treo flexible was a priority.

Competition

Handspring would be facing an expanded set of competitors in the hand-held communication devices market. It would be competing in a head-to-head battle with established mobile phone manufacturers to obtain market share. In spring of 2002, the global market share leaders in hand-held communications devices were Nokia, Motorola, Ericsson, and Samsung (see Figure 5 for comparative market shares). Whereas the market for mobile phones was mature, the smart phone market was relatively new and growing, and it was expected to attract the attention of most of the major mobile phone manufacturers. In

EXHIBIT 1

Three Generations of Wireless Telecommunications

Original cellular networks (now referred to as first generation) supported only analog voice communication. However, in the 1990s, the second generation (2G) of wireless communication emerged that supported voice and text transmission over digital networks.

2G Wireless. In 2G wireless communications, calls were established using an exclusive circuit so that the connection was lost as soon as such a call was ended. Networks were capable of handling only a certain number of such "circuit-switched" calls.

The 2G wireless industry underwent rapid change in the 1990s. The 1996 Telecommunications Act unleashed rapid increases in competition in the wireless industry, and several national wireless service providers emerged in the United States, including AT&T Wireless, Sprint PCS, Nextel Communications, Verizon Wireless, Cingular Wireless, and VoiceStream Wireless. On a global scale NTT DoCoMo, Vodafone, Telecom Italia, and France Telecom all emerged as leading wireless service providers. Additionally, many smaller carriers emerged in the industry to gain over 17 percent of the wireless market. With the increase in competition, pricing for voice wireless service fell to its most "attractive" prices ever, drawing more users to wireless phones. At the same time, revenue per subscriber had been declining in many countries, like the United States, due to the lingering effects of deregulation as the price of wireless services continued to fall. This shift toward marginal pricing as the wireless voice market matured drove wireless companies to continue differentiating their products through development of new technology. One of the primary areas targeted was the development of networks that would enable broadband Internet access. In the late 1990s, wireless service providers began planning to upgrade their existing networks and to build new wireless transmission systems to incorporate these new wireless technologies. To support the data needs of broadband wireless, networks needed to be updated to "packet-switching networks" that would allow a continuous connection for wireless users to send and receive data at any time.[18]

2.5G Wireless: The Bridge to the Future. Before entirely new 3G wireless systems were installed worldwide to support the needs of emerging wireless technology, many network providers planned to update existing networks to support packet-switching technology that would provide an "always-on" continuous connection, but at slower speeds than would be possible with 3G networks. These "bridging technologies" were known as 2.5G systems because they relied upon equipment from existing 2G networks. CDMA technology proved to be an initial leader in the move to 2.5G systems because the core CDMA technology was already based on an underlying packet-switching technology, requiring only a system upgrade. To upgrade GSM networks, General Packet Radio Service (GPRS) technology was planned to allow handsets an always-on connection by upgrading existing signals.

Most wireless companies saw 2.5G technologies only as a stepping stone to 3G, since 3G systems would ultimately be cheaper to operate and would offer data connection speeds up to ten times faster than 2.5G networks. However, as some industry researchers pointed out, 2.5G phones could "steal 3G's thunder" if users resisted 3G technology in favor of lower usage costs of 2.5G systems, thereby forestalling 3G indefinitely.[19] One of the first operational 2.5G wireless packet transmission networks was NTT DoCoMo's i-mode network that became operational in February 1999. By March 2000, the network, which ran on TDMA technology, had already achieved close to 21 million subscribers.[20]

Planning for 3G Wireless. By 2001 all major wireless manufacturers were active in the development of 3G wireless technologies, and planning had begun for installation of 3G wireless networks across the globe. These new networks would be able to fully support the broadband data needs of emerging wireless technologies, while providing a continuous connection to the wireless Internet.

As 3G wireless systems, based on new frequencies from their 2G predecessors, became closer to a reality, multinational wireless companies worked to band together to ensure compatibility among different 3G systems. By 2001, twenty-seven wireless service providers and vendors, including handset manufacturers Ericsson, Motorola, and Nokia, had joined together to form the 3G.IP group, focused on promoting a common IP-based wireless system for 3G mobile communications technology while ensuring rapid standards development. 3G.IP focused on 3G development using wireless CDMA technology that has CDMA technology at its core, but that could easily be added to the existing global GSM core network.[21] Wireless CDMA appeared to be a leading platform among competing 3G wireless technologies, although no clear standard had yet emerged by early 2001.

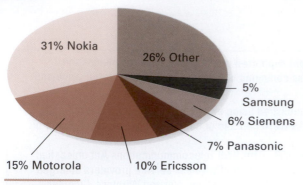

FIGURE 5

Worldwide Wireless Telecommunications
Market Share in 2001

Source: **www.cellular.co.za.**

fact, Nokia, Samsung, and Kyocera already had smart phones available on the market.

The three smart phones that offered the most direct competition for the Treo were the Kyocera QCP 6035, the Samsung SPH-1300, and the Nokia 9290. The functionality provided by each of these phones was nearly identical, offering few opportunities for differentiating the products to consumers. The major differences between the models were in size and weight, with the Treo being the smallest and lightest. It was 11 percent smaller and lighter than Samsung's SPH-I300, 35 percent lighter and 60 percent smaller than the Kyocera QCP 6035, and 20 percent lighter and 35 percent smaller than the Nokia 9290. Handspring hoped that the compact design would prove to be a critical factor in mobile phone purchases. The various models also differed in the included accessories, protective covers, and input methods, where a clear winning approach was not yet evident.

Because it was being heavily marketed as an employee productivity tool for the enterprise, the Treo would also be in competition with PDAs. It would be in most direct competition with products such as the Palm Pilot i705 and the RIM Blackberry 5810, which provided wireless connectivity. Though not nearly as large as the mobile phone competitors, Palm and RIM were both well-recognized and established competitors in the PDA market.

Both of these PDAs offered "always-on" connectivity, though the Palm i705 did not offer voice capability and thus was not truly a mobile phone. RIM's Blackberry 5810's phone capability was available only through an integrated headset jack. The device was

priced at $499 and was lighter (but larger) than the Treo, and like the Treo it used the GSM network but did not operate in Europe (a different model, the 5820, was required for use in Europe).[22]

The Future

Handspring shipped 47,000 units of the Treo in the first quarter of 2002, and Wall Street responded warmly, pushing Handspring's stock price up to 34 percent. But both Dubinsky and Hawkins knew that the Treo would be a key inflection point in Handspring's history. Like many young start-ups, Handspring still had not achieved profitability, and the patience of the investing public was wearing thin. The company desperately wanted to avoid the recent fate of many other bankrupt technology companies. Would Handspring have the resources necessary to battle giants like Nokia and Samsung? Would Handspring be able to effectively penetrate the enterprise market, and would this market shift pay off? Would the higher margins of smart phones rescue the company from its financial woes, or were smart phones destined for the same heavy price cutting that had afflicted PDAs? The company had made a serious gamble, and now all eyes were watching to see how the relatively new company would fare in the high-stakes battle to secure the next dominant design in personal computing and communicating technology.

Appendix 1: Excerpt from Management Discussion in Handspring 2001 10K

If we are unable to compete effectively with existing or new competitors, our resulting loss of competitive position could result in price reductions, fewer customer orders, reduced margins, and loss of market share.

The market for hand-held computing and wireless communication products is highly competitive, and we expect competition to increase in the future. Some of our competitors or potential competitors have significantly greater financial, technical, amd marketing resources than we do. These competitors may be able to respond more rapidly than we can to new or emerging technologies or changes in customer requirements. They may also devote greater resources to the development, promotion, and sale of the products than we do.

Our products compete with a variety of hand-held devices, including keyboard-based devices, sub-notebook computers, smart phones, and two-way pagers. Our principal competitors, and possible new competitors, include:

- Palm, from whom we license our operating system;

- licensees of the Microsoft's PocketPC operating system for hand-held devices such as Casio, Compaq, and Hewlett-Packard;

- licensees of Symbian EPOCH operating systems for wireless communication devices such as Panasonic and Siemens;

- other Palm OS operating system licensees, including Acer, Handera, Sony, and Symbol;

- smart phone manufacturers such as Ericsson, Kyocera, Motorola, Nokia, and Samsung;

- Research In Motion Limited, a leading provider of wireless E-mail, instant messaging, and Internet connectivity; and

- a variety of start-up companies looking to compete in our current and future markets.

We expect our competitors to continue to improve the performance of their current products and to introduce new products, services, and technologies. Successful new product introductions or enhancements by our competitors could reduce the sales and market acceptance of our products, cause intense price competition, and result in reduced gross margins and loss of market share.

Our failure to compete successfully against current or future competitors could seriously harm our business. To be competitive, we must continue to invest significant resources in research and development, sales, and marketing. We cannot be sure that we will have sufficient resources to make these investments or that we will be able to make the technological advances necessary to be competitive.

Appendix 2: Handspring Management Team

Jeff Hawkins

Currently chairman and chief product officer of the company, Jeff Hawkins cofounded Handspring with Donna Dubinsky in July 1998 after their incredibly successful run together at Palm Computing. In 1994, Hawkins invented the original PalmPilot products and founded Palm Computing, now a 3Com company. He is often credited as the designer who reinvented the hand-held market.

An industry veteran with nearly twenty years of technical expertise, Hawkins currently holds nine patents for various hand-held devices and features. His vision for hand-held computing dates back to the 1980s, when as vice president of research at GRiD Systems Corporation he served as principal architect and designer for the GRiDPad and GRiD Convertible. Prior to that, he held key technical positions with Intel Corporation. Hawkins earned his B.S. in electrical engineering from Cornell University.

Donna Dubinsky

Currently president and CEO, Donna Dubinsky cofounded Handspring with Jeff Hawkins in July 1998 to create a new breed of hand-held computers for consumers. As president and CEO of Palm Computing, Dubinsky helped make the PalmPilot the best-selling hand-held computer and the most rapidly adopted new computing product ever produced. When Dubinsky first joined Hawkins at Palm Computing in 1992, shortly after the company was founded, she brought with her more than ten years of marketing and logistics experience from Apple and Claris. Dubinsky and Hawkins introduced the original PalmPilot in February 1996, a move that revitalized the hand-held computing industry.

In addition to her position as CEO of Handspring, Dubinsky currently serves as a director of Intuit Corporation and is a trustee of the Computer Museum History Center. She earned her B.A. from Yale University and her M.B.A. from the Harvard Graduate School of Business Administration.

Ed Colligan

Currently chief operating officer, Ed Colligan joined Handspring to lead the development and marketing efforts for a new generation of hand-held computers. As the vice president of marketing for Palm Computing, Ed Colligan worked with Jeff Hawkins and Donna Dubinsky to lead the product marketing and marketing communications efforts for Palm, including the successful positioning, launch, and marketing of the popular Palm product family.

Prior to Palm, Colligan was vice president of strategic and product marketing at Radius Corporation. During his eight years there, Colligan helped make Radius the brand leader in Macintosh graphics, graphic imaging, and hardware development.

Colligan's multiple successes have earned him several marketing industry accolades. *Marketing Computers Magazine* named him the 1997 Marketer of the Year, and *Advertising Age* named him one of the Top 100 Marketers of 1997, an award that spanned all product categories. He holds a B.A. from the University of Oregon.

Bernard Whitney

Bernard Whitney joined Handspring as chief financial officer in June 1999. He comes to Handspring from Sanmina, Inc., an electronics manufacturing company, where he served as executive vice president and chief financial officer. A primary focus at Sanmina was leading the systems technology and strategic development effort that included eight successful acquisitions.

Prior to Sanmina, Whitney served as vice president of finance for Network General Corporation, a network fault tolerance and performance management solutions company.

From 1987 to 1995, Whitney held a variety of positions in corporate finance for mass storage manufacturer Conner Peripherals. He has an M.B.A from San Jose State University and a B.S. in business administration from the California State University at Chico.

ENDNOTES

1. Salomon Smith Barney, "Smart Handheld Device Market Segments, Worldwide, 1998–2004E," October 18, 2000.
2. P. Tjahyadikarta and M. A. Schilling, "Palm Economy," Boston University Teaching Case # 2001-01, and forthcoming in M. Hitt, D. Ireland, and B. Hoskisson, *Strategic Management: Competitiveness and Globalization*, 5th ed. (St. Paul, MN: West Publishing, 2001).
3. Stephanie Miles, "Is Palm Ready for the Handheld Challenge?" CNET News.com, September 13, 1999.
4. "Always on" refers to devices that are capable of remaining continuously connected to the Internet.
5. R. Pegoraro, "Even the Best of the Phone-PDA Combos Aren't Good Enough," *Washington Post*, January 27, 2002, p. H.07.
6. K. Shaw, "Handspring Treo: An End User Review," *Network World*, February 4, 2002: **www.nwfusion.com.**
7. S. Wildstrom, "An E-mailer Out to Squash Blackberry," *Business Week*, April 29, 2002, pp. 24ff.
8. M. Moore, "Treo Melds Phone, Wireless Net, PDA in 'Star Trek' Style," *Houston Chronicle*, January 24, 2002.
9. J. Sullivan, "Handspring Bets the Farm on Treo—Then Postpones It," *Wireless Data News*, January 30, 2002, pp. 1ff.
10. Handspring 10K, 2001.
11. Pegoraro, "Even the Best."
12. Sullivan, "Handspring Bets the Farm."
13. Moore, "Treo Melds Phone."
14. **www.nokia.com.**
15. P. Henning, "Qualcomm, Ericsson Unite over New Wireless Standard," *Red Herring*, 2000: **www.redherring.com.**
16. Anonymous, *S&P Telecommunications Wireless Industry Survey* (New York: McGraw-Hill, December 28, 2000), p. 5.
17. Matthew M. Nordan of Forrester Research, quoted in A. Reinhardt, S. Baker, W. Echikson, K. Carlisle, and P. Schmidt, "Who Needs 3G Anyway?" *Business Week: European Business*, March 26, 2001, p. 18.
18. **www.nttdocomo.com.**
19. **www.ericsson.com.**
20. "Brightpoint Signs Distribution Agreement with Handspring," *Wall Street Research Net*, February 27, 2002.
21. Anonymous, "Two Stumbling Steps Toward 3G," *Economist Technology Quarterly*. December 9, 2000: **www.economist.com.**
22. W. S. Mossberg, "Gadgets—The Mossberg Solution: Which Smart Phone Is the Smartest?" *Wall Street Journal*, April 10, p. D3.

The Home Video Game Industry: From Pong to X-Box

19

This case was prepared by Charles W. L. Hill, the University of Washington.

An Industry Is Born

In 1968, Nolan Bushell, the twenty-four-year-old son of a Utah cement contractor graduated from the University of Utah with a degree in engineering.[1] Bushnell then moved to California, where he worked briefly in the computer graphics division of Ampex. At home, Bushnell turned his daughter's bedroom into a laboratory. There, he created a simpler version of Space War, a computer game that had been invented in 1962 by an MIT graduate student, Steve Russell. Bushnell's version of Russell's game, which he called Computer Space, was made of integrated circuits connected to a 19-inch black-and-white television screen. Unlike a computer, Bushnell's invention could do nothing but play the game, which meant that, unlike a computer, it could be produced cheaply.

Bushnell envisioned video games like his standing next to pinball machines in arcades. With hopes of having his invention put into production, Bushnell left Ampex to work for a small pinball company that manufactured 1,500 copies of his video game. The game never sold, primarily because the player had to read a full page of directions before he or she could play the game—way too complex for an arcade game. Bushnell left the pinball company and with a friend, Ted Dabney, put up $500 to start a company that would develop a simpler video game. They wanted to call the company Syzygy, but the name was already taken, so they settled on Atari, a Japanese word that was the equivalent of "*check* in the *go*."

In his home laboratory, Bushnell built the simplest game he could think of. People knew the rules immediately, and it could be played with one hand. The game was modeled on table tennis, and players batted a ball back and forth with paddles that could be moved up and down sides of a court by twisting knobs. He named the game "Pong" after the sonarlike sound that was emitted every time the ball connected with a paddle.

In the fall of 1972, Bushnell installed his prototype for Pong in Andy Capp's tavern in Sunnyvale, California. The only instructions were "avoid missing the ball for a high score." In the first week, 1,200 quarters were deposited in the casserole dish that served for a coin box in Bushnell's prototype. Bushnell was ecstatic; his simple game had brought in $300 in a week. The pinball machine that stood next to it averaged $35 a week.

Lacking the capital to mass-produce the game, Bushnell approached established

This case is intended to be used as a basis for class discussion rather than as an illustration of either effective or ineffective handling of the situation. Reprinted by permission of Charles W. L. Hill.

amusement game companies, only to be repeatedly shown the door. Down but hardly out, Bushnell cut his hair, put on a suit, and talked his way into a $50,000 line of credit from a local bank. He set up a production line in an abandoned roller skating rink and he hired people to assemble machines while Led Zeppelin and the Rolling Stones were played at full volume over the speaker system of the rink. Among his first batch of employees was a skinny seventeen-year-old named Steve Jobs, who would latter found a few companies of his own, including Apple Computer, NeXT, and Pixar. Like others, Jobs had been attracted by a classified ad that read "Have Fun and Make Money."

In no time at all, Bushnell was selling all the machines that his small staff could make—about ten per day—but to grow, he needed additional capital. While the ambience at the rink, with its mix of rock music and marijuana fumes, put off most potential investors, Don Valentine, one of the country's most astute and credible venture capitalists, was impressed with the growth story. Armed with Valentine's money, Atari began to increase production and expand their range of games. New games included Tank and Breakout; the latter was designed by Jobs and a friend of his, Steve Wozniak, who had left Hewlett-Packard to work at Atari.

By 1974, 100,000 Ponglike games were sold worldwide. Although Atari manufactured only 10 percent of the games, the company still made $3.2 million that year. With the Pong clones coming on strong, Bushnell decided to make a Pong system for the home. In fact, Magnavox had been marketing a similar game for the home since 1972, although sales had been modest.[2] Bushnell's team managed to compress Atari's coin-operated Pong game down to a few inexpensive circuits that were contained in the game console. Atari's Pong had a sharper picture and more sensitive controllers than Magnavox's machine. It also cost less. Bushnell then went on a road show, demonstrating Pong to toy buyers, but he received an indifferent response and no sales. A dejected Bushnell returned to Atari with no idea of what to do next. Then the buyer for the sporting goods department at Sears came to see Bushnell, reviewed the machine, and offered to buy every home Pong game Atari could make. With Sears's backing, Bushnell boosted production. Sears ran a major television ad campaign to sell home Pong, and Atari's sales soared, hitting

$450 million in 1975. The home video game had arrived.

Boom and Bust

Nothing attracts competitors like success, and by 1976 about twenty different companies were crowding into the home video game market, including National Semiconductor, RCA, Coleco, and Fairchild. Recognizing the limitations of existing home video game designs, Fairchild came out in 1976 with a home video game system capable of playing multiple games. The Fairchild system consisted of three components—a console, controllers, and cartridges. The console was a small computer optimized for graphics processing capabilities. It was designed to receive information from the controllers, process it, and send signals to a television monitor. The controllers were hand-held devices used to direct on-screen action. The cartridges contained chips encoding the instructions for a game. The cartridges were designed to be inserted into the console.

In 1976, Bushnell sold Atari to Warner Communications for $28 million. Bushnell stayed on to run Atari. Backed by Warner's capital, in 1977 Atari developed and bought out its own cartridge-based system, the Atari 2600. The 2600 system was sold for $200, and associated cartridges retailed for $25–$30. Sales surged during the 1977 Christmas season. However, a lack of manufacturing capacity on the part of market leader Atari and a very cautious approach to inventory by Fairchild led to shortages and kept sales significantly below what they could have been. Fairchild's cautious approach was the result of prior experience in consumer electronics. A year earlier it had increased demand for its digital watches, only to accumulate a buildup of excess inventory that had caused the company to take a $24.5 million write-off.[3]

After the 1977 Christmas season, Atari claimed to have sold about 400,000 units of the 2600 VCA, about 50 percent of all cartridge-based systems in American homes. Atari had also earned more than $100 million in sales of game cartridges. By this point, second-place Fairchild sold around 250,00 units of its system. Cartridge sales for the year totaled about 1.2 million units, with an average selling price of around $20. Fresh from this success and fortified by market forecasts predicting sales of 33 million cartridges and an installed base of 16 million machines by 1980, Bushnell committed Atari to manufacturing 1 million units of the 2600 for the 1978 Christmas season. Atari estimated that total demand would reach 2 million units. Bushnell was also encouraged by signals from Fairchild that it would again be limiting production to around 200,000 units. At this point, Atari had a library of nine games. Fairchild had seventeen.[4]

Atari was not the only company to be excited by the growth forecasts. In 1978, a host of other companies, including Coleco, National Semiconductor, Magnavox, General Instrument, and a dozen other companies, entered the market with incompatible cartridge-based home systems. The multitude of choices did not seem to entice consumers, however, and the 1978 Christmas season brought unexpectedly low sales. Only Atari and Coleco survived an industry shakeout. Atari lost Bushnell, who was ousted by Warner executives. (Bushnell went on to start Chuck E. Cheese Pizza Time Theater, a restaurant chain that had 278 outlets by 1981.) Bushnell later stated that part of the problem was a disagreement over strategy. Bushnell wanted Atari to price the 2600 at cost and make money on sales of software; Warner wanted to continue making profits on hardware sales.[5]

Several important developments occurred in 1979. First, several game producers and programmers defected from Atari to set up their own firm, Activision, and to make games compatible with the Atari 2600. Their success encouraged others to follow suit. Second, Coleco developed an expansion module that allowed its machine to play Atari games. Atari and Mattel (which entered the market in 1979) did likewise. Third, the year 1979 saw the introduction of three new games to the home market—Space Invaders, Asteroids, and Pac Man. All three were adapted from popular arcade games and all three helped drive demand for players.

Demand recovered strongly in late 1979 and kept growing for the next three years. In 1981, U.S. sales of home video games and cartridges hit $1 billion. In 1982, they surged to $3 billion, with Atari accounting for half of this amount. It seemed as if Atari could do no wrong; the 2600 was everywhere. About 20 million units were sold, and by late 1982, a large number of independent companies, including Activision, Imagic, and Epyx, were now producing hundreds of games for the 2600. Second-place Coleco was also doing well, partly because of a popular arcade game,

Donkey Kong, which it had licensed from a Japanese company called Nintendo.

Atari was also in contact with Nintendo. In 1982, the company very nearly licensed the rights to Nintendo's Famicom, a cartridge-based video game system machine that was a big hit in Japan. Atari's successor to the 2600, the 5200, was not selling well and the Famicom seemed like a good substitute. The negotiations broke down, however, when Atari discovered that Nintendo had extended its Donkey Kong license to Coleco. This allowed Coleco to port a version of the game to its home computer, which was a direct competitor to Atari's 800 home computer.[6]

After a strong 1982 season, the industry hoped for continued growth in 1983. Then the bottom dropped out of the market. Sales of home video games plunged to $100 million. Atari lost $500 million in the first nine months of the year, causing the stock of parent company Warner Communications to drop by half. Part of the blame for the collapse was laid at the feet of an enormous inventory overhang of unsold games. About 15 to 20 million surplus game cartridges were left over from the 1982 Christmas season (in 1981, there were none). On top of this, around 500 new games hit the market in 1993. The average price of a cartridge plunged from $30 in 1979 to $16 in 1982, and then to $4 in 1983. As sales slowed, retailers cut back on the shelf space allocated to video games. It proved difficult for new games to make a splash in a crowded market. Atari had to dispose of 6 million ET: The Extraterrestrial games. Meanwhile, big hits from previous years, such as Pac Man, were bundled with game players and given away free to try to encourage system sales.[7]

Surveying the rubble, commentators claimed that the video game industry was dead. The era of dedicated game machines was over, they claimed. Personal computers were taking their place.[8] It seemed to be true. Mattel sold off its game business, Fairchild moved on to other things, Coleco folded, and Warner decided to break up Atari and sell its constituent pieces—at least, those pieces for which it could find a buyer. No one in America seemed to want to have anything to do with the home video game business; no one, that is, except for Minoru Arakawa, the head of Nintendo's U.S. subsidiary, Nintendo of America (NOA). Picking through the rubble of the industry, Arakawa noticed that there were people who still packed video arcades, bringing in $7 billion a year, more money than the entire movie industry. Perhaps it was not a lack of interest in home video games that had killed the industry. Perhaps it was bad business practice.

The Nintendo Monopoly

Nintendo was a century-old Japanese company that had built up a profitable business making playing cards before diversifying into the video game business. Based in Kyoto and still run by the founding Yamauchi family, the company started to diversify into the video game business in the late 1970s. The first step was to license video game technology from Magnavox. In 1977, Nintendo introduced a home video game system in Japan based on this technology that played a variation of Pong. In 1978, the company began to sell coin-operated video games. It had its first hit with Donkey Kong, designed by Sigeru Miyamoto.

The Famicom

In the early 1980s, the company's boss, Hiroshi Yamauchi, decided that Nintendo had to develop its own video game machine. He pushed the company's engineers to develop a machine that combined superior graphics-processing capabilities and low cost. Yamauchi wanted a machine that could sell for $75, less than half the price of competing machines at the time. He dubbed the machine the Family Computer, or Famicom. The machine that his engineers designed was based on the controller, console, and plug in the cartridge format pioneered by Fairchild. It contained two custom chips—an 8-bit central processing unit and a graphics-processing unit. Both chips had been scaled down to perform only essential functions. A 16-bit processor was available at the time, but to keep costs down, Yamauchi refused to use it.

Nintendo approached Ricoh, the electronics giant, which had spare semiconductor capacity. Employees at Ricoh said that the chips had to cost no more that 2,000 yen. Ricoh thought that the 2,000-yen price point was absurd. Yamauchi's response was to guarantee Ricoh a 3-million-chip order within two years. Since the leading companies in Japan were selling, at most, 30,000 video games per year at the time, many within the company viewed this as an outrageous commitment, but Ricoh went for it.[9]

Another feature of the machine was its memory—2,000 bytes of random access memory (RAM), compared to the 256 bytes of RAM in the Atari machine. The result was a machine with superior graphics-processing capabilities and faster action that could handle far more complex games than Atari games. Nintendo's engineers also built a new set of chips into the game cartridges. In addition to chips that held the game program, Nintendo developed memory map controller (MMC) chips that took over some of the graphics-processing work from the chips in the console and enabled the system to handle more complex games. With the addition of the MMC chips, the potential for more-sophisticated and more complex games had arrived. Over time, Nintendo's engineers developed more powerful MMC chips, enabling the basic 8-bit system to do things that originally seemed out of reach. The engineers also figured out a way to include a battery backup system in cartridges that allowed some games to store information independently—to keep track of where a player had left off or to track high scores.

The Games

Yamauchi recognized that great hardware that would not sell itself. The key to the market, he reasoned, was great games. Yamauchi had instructed the engineers, when they were developing the hardware, to make sure that "it was appreciated by software engineers." Nintendo decided that it would become a haven for game designers. "An ordinary man," Yamauchi said, "cannot develop good games no matter how hard he tries. A handful of people in this world can develop games that everyone wants. Those are the people we want at Nintendo."[10]

Yamauchi had an advantage in the person of Sigeru Miyamoto. Miyamoto had joined Nintendo at the age of twenty-four. Yamauchi had hired Miyamoto, a graduate of Kanazawa Munici College of Industrial Arts, as a favor to his father and an old friend, although he had little idea what he would do with an artist. For three years, Miyamoto worked as Nintendo's staff artist. Then in 1980, Yamauchi called Miyamoto into his office. Nintendo had started selling coin-operated video games, but one of the new games, Radarscope, was a disaster. Could Miyamoto come up with a new game? Miyamoto was delighted. He had always spent a lot of time drawing cartoons, and as a student, he had played video games constantly. Miyamoto believed that video games could be used to bring cartoons to life.[11]

The game Miyamoto developed was nothing short of a revelation. At a time when most coin-operated video games lacked characters or depth, Miyamoto created a game around a story that had both. Most games involved battles with space invaders or heroes shooting lasers at aliens; Miyamoto's game did neither. Based loosely on *Beauty and the Beast* and *King Kong*, Miyamoto's game involved a pet ape who runs off with his master's beautiful girlfriend. His master is an ordinary carpenter called Mario, who has a bulbous nose, a bushy mustache, a pair of large pathetic eyes, and a red cap (which Miyamoto added because he was not good at hairstyles). He does not carry a laser gun. The ape runs off with the girlfriend to get back at his master, who was not especially nice to the beast. The man, of course, has to get his girlfriend back by running up ramps, climbing ladders, jumping off elevators, and the like, while the ape throws objects at the hapless carpenter. Since the main character is an ape, Miyamoto called him Kong; because the main character is as stubborn as a donkey, he called the game Donkey Kong.

Released in 1981, Donkey Kong was a sensation in the world of coin-operated video arcades and a smash hit for Nintendo. In 1984, Yamauchi again summoned Miyamoto to his office. He needed more games, this time for Famicom. Miyamoto was made the head of a new research and development (R&D) group and told to come up with the most imaginative video games ever.

Miyamoto began with Mario from Donkey Kong. A colleague had told him that Mario looked more like a plumber than a carpenter, so a plumber he became. Miyamoto gave Mario a brother, Luigi, who was as tall and thin as Mario was short and fat. They became the Super Mario Brothers. Since plumbers spend their time working on pipes, large green sewer pipes became obstacles and doorways into secret worlds. Mario and Luigi's task was to search for the captive Princess Toadstool. Mario and Luigi are endearing bumblers, unequal to their tasks yet surviving. They shoot, squash, or evade their enemies—a potpourri of inventions that include flying turtles and stinging fish, man-eating flowers and fire-breathing dragons—while they collect gold coins, blow air bubbles, and climb vines into smiling clouds.[12]

Super Mario Brothers was introduced in 1985. For Miyamoto, this was just the beginning. Between 1985 and 1991, Miyamoto produced eight Mario games. About 60 to 70 million were sold worldwide, making Miyamoto the most successful game designer in the world. After adapting Donkey Kong for Famicom, he also went on to create other top-selling games, including another classic, The Legend of Zelda. While Miyamoto drew freely from folklore, literature, and pop culture, the main source for his ideas was his own experience. The memory of being lost among a maze of sliding doors in his family's home was re-created in the labyrinths of the Zelda games. The dog that attacked him when he was a child attacks Mario in Super Mario. As a child, Miyamoto had once climbed a tree to catch a view of far-off mountains and had become stuck. Mario gets himself in a similar fix. Once Miyamoto went hiking without a map and was surprised to stumble across a lake. In the Legend of Zelda, part of the adventure is in walking into new places without a map and being confronted by surprises.

Nintendo in Japan

Nintendo introduced Famicom into the Japanese market in May 1983. Famicom was priced at $100, more than Yamauchi wanted, but significantly less than the products of competitors. When he introduced the machine, Yamauchi urged retailers to forgo profits on the hardware because it was just a tool to sell software, and that is where they would make their money. Backed by an extensive advertising campaign, 500,000 units of Famicom were sold in the first two months. Within a year, the figure stood at 1 million, and sales were still expanding rapidly. With the hardware quickly finding its way into Japanese homes, Nintendo was besieged with calls from desperate retailers frantically demanding more games.

At this point Yamauchi told Miyamoto to come up with the most imaginative games ever. However, Yamauchi also realized that Nintendo alone could not satisfy the growing thirst for new games, so he initiated a licensing program. To become a Nintendo licensee, companies had to agree to an unprecedented series of restrictions. Licensees could issue only five Nintendo games per year, and they could not write those titles for other platforms. The licensing fee was set at 20 percent of the wholesale price of each cartridge sold (game cartridges wholesaled for around

$30). It typically cost $500,000 to develop a game and took around six months. Nintendo insisted that games not contain any excessively violent or sexually suggestive material and that they review every game before allowing it to be produced.[13]

Despite these restrictions, six companies (Bandai, Capcom, Konami, Namco, Taito, and Hudson) agreed to become Nintendo licensees, not least because millions of customers were now clamoring for games. Bandai was Japan's largest toy company. The others already made either coin-operated video games or computer software games. Because of these licensing agreements, they saw their sales and earnings surge. For example, Konami's earnings went from $10 million in 1987 to $300 million in 1991.

After the six licensees began selling games, reports of defective games began to reach Yamauchi. The original six licensees were allowed to manufacture their own game cartridges. Realizing that he had given away the ability to control the quality of the cartridges, Yamauchi decided to change the contract for future licensees. Future licensees were required to submit all manufacturing orders for cartridges to Nintendo. Nintendo charged licensees $14 per cartridge, required that they place a minimum order for 10,000 units, (later the minimum order was raised to 30,000), and insisted on cash payment in full when the order was placed. Nintendo outsourced all manufacturing to other companies, using the volume of its orders to get rock bottom prices. The cartridges were estimated to cost Nintendo between $6 and $8 each. The licensees then picked up the cartridges from Nintendo's loading dock and were responsible for distribution. In 1985, there were seventeen licensees. By 1987, there were fifty. By this point, 90 percent of the home video game systems sold in Japan were Nintendo systems.

Nintendo in America

In 1980, Nintendo established a subsidiary in America to sell its coin-operated video games. Yamauchi's American-educated son-in-law, Minoru Arakawa, headed the subsidiary. All of the other essential employees were Americans, including Ron Judy and Al Stone. For its first two years, Nintendo of America (NOA), based originally in Seattle, struggled to sell second-rate games such as Radarscope. The subsidiary seemed on the brink of closing. NOA could not even make the rent payment on the warehouse. Then they received a large shipment from Japan:

2,000 units of a new coin-operated video game. Opening the box, they discovered Donkey Kong. After playing the game briefly, Judy proclaimed it a disaster. Stone walked out of the building, declaring that "it's over."[14] The managers were appalled. They could not imagine a game less likely to sell in video arcades. The only promising sign was that a twenty-year employee, Howard Philips, rapidly became enthralled with the machine.

Arakawa, however, knew he had little choice but to try to sell the machine. Judy persuaded the owner of the Spot Tavern near Nintendo's office to take one of the machines on a trial basis. After one night, Judy discovered $30 in the coin box, a phenomenal amount. The next night there was $35, and $36 the night after that. NOA had a hit on its hands.

By the end of 1982, NOA had sold over 60,000 copies of Donkey Kong and had booked sales in excess of $100 million. The subsidiary had outgrown its Seattle location. They moved to a new site in Redmond, a Seattle suburb, where they located next to a small but fast-growing software company run by an old school acquaintance of Howard Philips, Bill Gates.

By 1984, NOA was riding a wave of success in the coin-operated video game market. Arakawa, however, was interested in the possibilities of selling Nintendo's new Famicom system in the United States. Throughout 1984, Arakawa, Judy, and Stone met with numerous toy and department store representatives to discuss the possibilities, only to be repeatedly rebuffed. Still smarting from the 1983 debacle, the representatives wanted nothing to do with the home video game business. They also met with former managers from Atari and Caloco to gain their insights. The most common response they received was that the market collapsed because the last generation of games were awful.

Arakawa and his team decided that if they were going to sell Famicom in the United States, they would have to find a new distribution channel. The obvious choice was consumer electronics stores. Thus, Arakawa asked the R&D team in Kyoto to redesign Famicom for the U.S. market so that it looked less like a toy (Famicom was encased in red and white plastic), and more like a consumer electronics device. The redesigned machine was renamed the Nintendo Entertainment System (NES).

Arakawa's big fear was that illegal, low-quality Taiwanese games would flood the U.S. market if NES was successful. To stop counterfeit games being played on NES, Arakawa asked Nintendo's Japanese engineers to design a security system into the U.S. version of Famicom so that only Nintendo-approved games could be played on NES. The Japanese engineers responded by designing a security chip to be embedded in the game cartridges. NES would not work unless the security chips in the cartridges unlocked, or shook hands with, a chip in NES. Since the code embedded in the security chip was proprietary, the implication of this system was that no one could manufacture games for NES without Nintendo's specific approval.

To overcome the skepticism and reluctance of retailers to stock a home video game system, Arakawa decided in late 1985 to make an extraordinary commitment. Nintendo would stock stores and set up displays and windows. Retailers would not have to pay for anything they stocked for ninety days. After that, retailers could pay Nintendo for what they sold and return the rest. NES was bundled with Nintendo's best-selling game in Japan, Super Mario Brothers. It was essentially a risk-free proposition for retailers, but even with this, most were skeptical. Ultimately, thirty Nintendo personnel descended on the New York area. Referred to as the Nintendo SWAT team, they persuaded some stores to stock NES after an extraordinary blitz that involved eighteen-hour days. To support the New York product launch, Nintendo also committed itself to a $5 million advertising campaign aimed at the seven- to fourteen-year-old boys who seemed to be Nintendo's likely core audience.

By December 1985, between 500 and 600 stores in the New York area were stocking Nintendo systems. Sales were moderate, about half of the 100,000 NES machines shipped from Japan were sold, but it was enough to justify going forward. The SWAT team then moved first to Los Angeles, then to Chicago, then to Dallas. As in New York, sales started at a moderate pace, but by late 1986 they started to accelerate rapidly, and Nintendo went national with NES.

In 1986, around 1 million NES units were sold in the United States. In 1987, the figure increased to 3 million. In 1988, it jumped to over 7 million. In the same year, 33 million game cartridges were sold. Nintendo mania had arrived in the United States. To expand the supply of games, Nintendo licensed the rights to produce up to five games per year to thirty-one American software companies. Nintendo contin-

ued to use a restrictive licensing agreement that gave it exclusive rights to any games, required licensees to place their orders through Nintendo, and insisted on a 30,000-unit minimum order.[15]

By 1990, the home video game market was worth $5 billion worldwide. Nintendo dominated the industry, with a 90 percent share of the market for game equipment. The parent company was, by some measures, now the most profitable company in Japan. By 1992, it was netting over $1 billion in gross profit annually, or more than $1.5 million for each employee in Japan. The company's stock market value exceeded that of Sony, Japan's premier consumer electronics firm. Indeed, the company's net profit exceeded that of all the American movie studios combined. Nintendo games, it seemed, were bigger than the movies.

As of 1991, there were over 100 licensees for Nintendo, and over 450 titles were available for NES. In the United States, Nintendo products were distributed through toy stores (30 percent of volume), mass merchandisers (40 percent of volume), and department stores (10 percent of volume). Nintendo tightly controlled the number of game titles and games that could be sold, quickly withdrawing titles as soon as interest appeared to decline. In 1988, retailers requested 110 million cartridges from Nintendo. Market surveys suggested that perhaps 45 million could have been sold, but Nintendo allowed only 33 million to be shipped.[16] Nintendo claimed that the shortage of games was in part due to a worldwide shortage of semiconductor chips.

Several companies had tried to reverse-engineer the code embedded in Nintendo's security chip, which competitors characterized as a lockout chip. Nintendo successfully sued them. The most notable was Atari Games, one of the successors of the original Atari, which in 1987 sued Nintendo of America for anticompetitive behavior. Atari claimed that the purpose of the security chip was to monopolize the market. At the same time, Atari announced that it had found a way around Nintendo's security chip and would begin to sell unlicensed games.[17] NOA responded with a countersuit. In a March 1991 ruling, Atari was found to have obtained Nintendo's security code illegally and was ordered to stop selling NES-compatible games. However, Nintendo did not always have it all its own way. In 1990, under pressure from Congress, the Department of Justice, and several lawsuits, Nintendo rescinded its exclusivity requirements, freeing up developers to write games for other platforms. However, developers faced a real problem: what platform could they write for?

Sega's Sonic Boom

Back in 1954, David Rosen, a twenty-year-old American, left the U.S. Air Force after a tour of duty in Tokyo.[18] Rosen had noticed that Japanese people needed lots of photographs for ID cards, but that local photo studios were slow and expensive. He formed a company, Rosen Enterprises, and went into the photo-booth business, which was a big success. By 1957, Rosen had established a successful nationwide chain. At this point, the Japanese economy was booming, so Rosen decided it was time to get into another business—entertainment. As his vehicle, he chose arcade games, which were unknown in Japan at the time. He picked up used games on the cheap from America and set up arcades in the same Japanese department stores and theaters that typically housed his photo booths. Within a few years, Rosen had 200 arcades nationwide. His only competition came from another American-owned firm, Service Games (SeGa), whose original business was jukeboxes and fruit machines.

By the early 1960s, the Japanese arcade market had caught up with the U.S. market. The problem was that game makers had run out of exciting new games to offer. Rosen decided that he would have to get into the business of designing and manufacturing games, but to do that he needed manufacturing facilities. SeGa manufactured its own games, so in 1965 Rosen approached the company and suggested a merger. The result was Sega Enterprise, a Japanese company with Rosen as its CEO.

Rosen himself designed Sega's first game, Periscope, in which the objective was to sink chain-mounted cardboard ships by firing torpedoes, represented by lines of colored lights. Periscope was a big success not only in Japan, but also in the United States and Europe, and it allowed Sega to build up a respectable export business. Over the years, the company continued to invest heavily in game development, always using the latest electronic technology.

Gulf and Western, a U.S. conglomerate, acquired Sega in 1969, with Rosen running the subsidiary. In 1975, Gulf and Western (G&W) took Sega public in the United States, but left Sega Japan as a G&W subsidiary. Hayao Nakayama, a former Sega distributor,

was drafted as president. In the early 1980s, Nakayama pushed G&W to invest more in Sega Japan so that the company could enter the then-booming home video game market. When G&W refused, Nakayama suggested a management buyout. G&W agreed, and in 1984, for the price of just $38 million, Sega became a Japanese company once more. (Sega's Japanese revenues were around $700 million, but by now the company was barely profitable.)

Sega was caught off guard by the huge success of Nintendo's Famicom. Although it released its own 8-bit system in 1986, the machine never commanded more than 5 percent of the Japanese market. Nakayama, however, was not about to give up. From years in the arcade business, he understood that great games drove sales. Nevertheless, he also understood that more powerful technology gave game developers the tools to develop more appealing games. This philosophy underlay Nakayama's decision to develop a 16-bit game system, Genesis.

Sega took the design of its 16-bit arcade machine and adapted it for Genesis. Compared to Nintendo's 8-bit machine, the 16-bit machine featured an array of superior technological features, including high-definition graphics and animation, a full spectrum of colors, two independent scrolling backgrounds that created an impressive depth of field, and near CD quality sound. The design strategy also made it easy to port Sega's catalog of arcade hits to Genesis.

Genesis was launched in Japan in 1989 and in the United States in 1990. In the United States, the machine was priced at $199. The company hoped that sales would be boosted by the popularity of its arcade games, such as the graphically violent Altered Beast. Sega also licensed other companies to develop games for the Genesis platform. In an effort to recruit licensees, Sega asked for lower royalty rates than Nintendo, and it gave licensees the right to manufacture their own cartridges. Independent game developers were slow to climb on board, however, and the $200 price tag for the player held back sales.

One of the first independent game developers to sign up with Sega was Electronic Arts. Established by Trip Hawkins, Electronic Arts had focused on designing games for personal computers and consequently had missed the Nintendo 8-bit era. Now Hawkins was determined to get a presence in the home video game market, and aligning his company's wagon with Sega seemed to be the best option. The Nintendo playing field was already crowded, and Sega offered a far less restrictive licensing deal than Nintendo. Electronic Arts subsequently wrote several popular games for Genesis, including John Madden football and several gory combat games.[19]

Nintendo had not been ignoring the potential of the 16-bit system. Nintendo's own 16-bit system, Super NES, was ready for market introduction in 1989—at the same time as Sega's Genesis. Nintendo introduced Super NES in Japan in 1990, where it quickly established a strong market presence and beat Sega's Genesis. In the United States, however, the company decided to hold back longer to reap the full benefits of the dominance it enjoyed with the 8-bit NES system. Yamauchi was also worried about the lack of backward compatibility between Nintendo's 8-bit and 16-bit systems. (The company had tried to make the 16-bit system so that it could play 8-bit games but concluded that the cost of doing so was prohibitive.) These concerns may have led the company to delay market introduction until the 8-bit market was saturated.

Meanwhile, in the United States, the Sega bandwagon was beginning to gain momentum. One development that gave Genesis a push was the introduction of a new Sega game, Sonic the Hedgehog. Developed by an independent team that was contracted to Sega, the game featured a cute hedgehog that impatiently tapped his paw when the player took too long to act. Impatience was Sonic's central feature—he had places to go, and quickly. He zipped along, collecting brass rings when he could find them, before rolling into a ball and flying down slides with loops and underground tunnels. Sonic was Sega's Mario.

In mid 1991, in an attempt to jump-start slow sales, Tom Kalinske, head of Sega's American subsidiary, decided to bundle Sonic the Hedgehog with the game player. He also reduced the price for the bundled unit to $150, and he relaunched the system with an aggressive advertising campaign aimed at teenagers. The campaign was built around the slogan "Genesis does what Nintendon't." The shift in strategy worked, and sales accelerated sharply.

Sega's success prompted Nintendo to launch its own 16-bit system. Nintendo's Super NES was introduced at $200. However, Sega now had a two-year head start in games. By the end of 1991, about 125 game titles were available for Genesis, compared to twenty-five for Super NES. In May 1992, Nintendo reduced the price of Super NES to $150. At this time Sega was claiming a 63 percent share of the 16-bit market in the United States, and Nintendo claimed a 60 percent share. By now, Sega was cool. It began to take more chances with mass media–defined morality. When Acclaim Entertainment released its bloody *Mortal Kombat* game in September 1992, the Sega version let players rip off heads and tear out hearts. Reflecting Nintendo's image of their core market, its version was sanitized. The Sega version outsold Nintendo's two to one.[20] Therefore, the momentum continued to run in Sega's favor. By January 1993, there were 320 titles available for Sega Genesis, and 130 for Super NES. In early 1994, independent estimates suggested that Sega had 60 percent of the U.S. market and Nintendo had 40 percent, figures Nintendo disputed.

3DO

Trip Hawkins, whose first big success was Electronic Arts, founded 3DO in 1991.[21] Hawkins's vision for 3DO was to shift the home video game business away from the existing cartridge-based format and toward a CD-ROM-based platform. The original partners in 3DO were Electronic Arts, Matsushita, Time Warner, AT&T, and the venture capital firm Kleiner Perkins. Collectively they invested over $17 million in 3DO, making it the richest start-up in the history of the home video game industry. 3DO went public in May 1993 at $15 per share. By October of that year, the stock had risen to $48 per share, making 3DO worth $1 billion—not bad for a company that had yet to generate a single dollar in revenues.

The basis for 3DO's $1 billion market cap was patented computer system architecture and a copyrighted operating system that allowed for much richer graphics and audio capabilities. The system was built around a 32-bit RISC microprocessor and proprietary graphics processor chips. Instead of a cartridge, the 3DO system stored games on a CD-ROM that was capable of holding up to 600 megabytes of content, sharply up from the 10 megabytes of content found in the typical game cartridge of the time. The slower access time of a CD-ROM compared to a cartridge was alleviated somewhat by the use of a double-speed CD-ROM drive.[22]

The belief at 3DO—a belief apparently shared by many investors—was that the superior storage and graphics-processing capabilities of the 3DO system would prove very attractive to game developers, allowing them to be far more creative. In turn, better games would attract customers away from Nintendo and Sega. Developing games that used the capabilities of a CD-ROM system altered the economics of game development. Estimates suggested that it would cost approximately $2 million to produce a game for the 3DO system and could take as long as twenty-four months to develop. However, at $2 per disc, a CD-ROM cost substantially less to produce than a cartridge.

The centerpiece of 3DO's strategy was to license its hardware technology for free. Game developers paid a royalty of $3 per disc for access to the 3DO operating code. Discs typically retailed for $40 each.

Matsushita introduced the first 3DO machine into the U.S. market in October 1993. Priced at $700, the machine was sold through electronic retailers that carried Panasonic high-end electronics products. Sega's Tom Kalinsky noted, "It's a noble effort. Some people will buy 3DO, and they'll have a wonderful experience. It's impressive, but it's a niche. We've done the research. It does not become a large market until you go below $500. At $300, it starts to get interesting. We make no money on hardware. It's a cut-throat business. I hope Matsushita understands that."[23] CD-ROM discs for the 3DO machine retailed for around $75. The machine came bundled with Crash n Burn, a high-speed combat racing game. However, only eighteen 3DO titles were available by the crucial Christmas period, although reports suggested that 150 titles were under development.[24]

Sales of the hardware were slow, reaching only 30,000 by January 1994.[25] In the same month, AT&T and Sanyo both announced that they would begin to manufacture the 3DO machine. In March, faced with continuing sluggish sales, 3DO announced that it would give hardware manufacturers two shares of 3DO stock for every unit sold at or below a certain retail price. Matsushita dropped the price of its machine to $500. About the same time, Toshiba, LG, and Samsung all announced that they would start to produce 3DO machines.

By June 1994, cumulative sales of 3DO machines in the United States stood at 40,000 units. Matsushita announced plans to expand distribution beyond the current 3,500 outlets to include the toy and mass merchandise channels. Hawkins and his partners announced that they would invest another $37 million in 3DO. By July, there were 750 3DO software

licensees, but only forty titles were available for the format. Despite these moves, sales continued at a very sluggish pace and the supply of new software titles started to dry up.[26]

In September 1996, 3DO announced that it would either sell its hardware system business or move it into a joint venture.[27] The company announced that about 150 people, one-third of the work force, would probably lose their jobs in the restructuring. According to Trip Hawkins, 3DO would now focus on developing software for online gaming. Hawkins stated that the Internet and Internet entertainment constituted a huge opportunity for 3DO. The stock dropped $1.375 to $6.75.

Sega's Saturn

3DO was not alone in moving to a CD-ROM-based format. Both Sega and Sony also introduced CD-ROM-based systems in the mid 1990s. Sega had in fact beaten 3DO to the market with its November 1992 introduction of the Sega CD, a $300 CD-ROM add-on for the 16-bit Genesis. Sega sold 100,000 units in its first month alone. Sales then slowed down, however, and by December 1993 were standing at just 250,000 units. One reason for the slowdown, according to critics, was a lack of strong games. Sega was also working on a 32-bit CD-ROM system, Saturn, which was targeted for a mid-1995 introduction in the United States. In January 1994, Sega announced that Microsoft would supply the operating system for Saturn.[28]

In March 1994, Sega announced the Genesis Super 32X, a $150 add-on cartridge designed to increase the performance of Genesis cartridge and CD-ROM games. The 32X contained the 32-bit Hitachi microprocessor that was to be used in Saturn. Sega called the 32X "the poor man's 32-bit machine" because it sold for a mere $149. Introduced in the fall of 1994, the 32X never lived up to its expectations. Most users appeared willing to wait for the real thing, Sega Saturn, promised for release the following year.

In early 1995, Sega informed the press and retailers that it would release Saturn on "Sega Saturn Saturday, Sept 2nd," but Sega released the 32-bit Saturn in May 1995. It was priced at $400 per unit and accompanied by the introduction of just ten games. Sega apparently believed that the world would be delighted by the May release of the Saturn. However, Saturn was released without the industry fanfare that normally greets a new game machine. Only four retail chains received the Saturn in May, while the rest were told they would have to wait until September. This move alienated retailers, who responded by dropping Sega products from their stores.[29] Sega appeared to have made a marketing blunder.[30]

Sony's PlayStation

In the fall of 1995, Sony entered the fray with the introduction of the Sony PlayStation.[31] PlayStation used a 32-bit RISC microprocessor running at 33 MHz and using a double-speed CD-ROM drive. PlayStation cost an estimated $500 million to develop. The machine had actually been under development since 1991, when Sony decided that the home video game industry was getting too big to ignore. Initially, Sony was in an alliance with Nintendo to develop the machine. Nintendo walked away from the alliance in 1992, however, after a disagreement over who owned the rights to any future CD-ROM games. Sony went alone.[32]

From the start, Sony felt that it could leverage its presence in the film and music business to build a strong position in the home video game industry. A consumer electronics giant with a position in the Hollywood movie business and the music industry (Sony owned Columbia Pictures and the Columbia record label), Sony believed that it had access to significant intellectual property that could form the basis of many popular games.

In 1991, Sony established a division in New York: Sony Electronic Publishing. The division was to serve as an umbrella organization for Sony's multimedia offerings. Headed by Iceland native Olaf Olafsson, then just twenty-eight years old, this organization ultimately took the lead role in both the market launch of PlayStation and in developing game titles.[33] In 1993, as part of this effort, Sony purchased a well-respected British game developer, Psygnosis. By the fall of 1995, this unit had twenty games ready to complement PlayStation: The Haldeman Diaries, Mickey Mania (developed in collaboration with Disney), and Johnny Mnemonic, based on the William Gibson short story. To entice independent game developers such as Electronic Arts, Namco, and Acclaim Entertainment, Olafsson used the promise of low royalty rates. The standard royalty rate was set at $9 per disc, although developers that signed on early enough were given a lower royalty rate. Sony also provided approximately 4,000 game development tools to licensees in an effort to help them speed games to market.[34]

To distribute PlayStation, Sony set up a retail channel separate from Sony's consumer electronics sales force. It marketed the PlayStation as a hip and powerful alternative to the outdated Nintendo and Sega cartridge-based systems. Sony worked closely with retailers before the launch to find out how it could help them sell the PlayStation. To jump-start demand, Sony set up in-store displays to allow potential consumers to try the equipment. Just before the launch, Sony had lined up an impressive 12,000 retail outlets in the United States.[35]

Sony targeted its advertising for PlayStation at males in the eighteen- to thirty-five-year age range. The targeting was evident in the content of many of the games. One of the big hits for PlayStation was Tomb Raider, whose central character, Lara Croft, combined sex appeal with savviness and helped to recruit an older generation to PlayStation.[36] PlayStation was initially priced at $299, and games retailed for as much as $60. Sony's Tokyo-based executives had reportedly been insisting on a $350–$400 price for PlayStation, but Olafsson pushed hard for the lower price. Because of the fallout from this internal battle, in January 1996, Olafsson resigned from Sony. By then, however, Sony was following Olafsson's script.[37]

Sony's prelaunch work was rewarded with strong early sales. By January 1996, more than 800,000 PlayStations had been sold in the United States, plus another 4 million games. In May 1996, with 1.2 million PlayStations shipped, Sony reduced the price of PlayStation to $199. Sega responded with a similar price cut for its Saturn. The prices on some of Sony's initial games were also reduced to $29.99. The weekend after the price cuts, retailers reported that PlayStation sales were up by between 350 percent and 1,000 percent over the prior week.[38] The sales surge continued through 1996. By the end of the year, sales of PlayStation and associated software amounted to $1.3 billion, out of a total for U.S. sales at $2.2 billion for all video game hardware and software. In March 1997, Sony cut the price of PlayStation again, this time to $149. It also reduced its suggested retail price for games by $10 to $49.99. By this point, Sony had sold 3.4 million units of PlayStation in the United States, compared to Saturn's 1.6 million units.[39] Worldwide, PlayStation had outsold Saturn by

13 million to 7.8 million units, and Saturn sales were slowing.[40] The momentum was clearly running in Sony's favor, but the company now had a new challenge to deal with: Nintendo's latest generation game machine, the N64.

Nintendo Strikes Back

In July 1996, Nintendo launched Nintendo 64 (N64) in the Japanese market. This release was followed by a late fall introduction in the United States. N64 is a 64-bit machine developed in conjunction with Silicon Graphics. Originally targeted for introduction a year earlier, N64 had been under development since 1993. The machine used a plug-in cartridge format rather than a CD-ROM drive. According to Nintendo, cartridges allow for faster access time and are far more durable than CD-ROMs (an important consideration with children).[41]

The most-striking feature of the N64 machine, however, was its 3D graphics capability. N64 provides fully rounded figures that can turn on their heels and rotate through 180 degrees. Advanced ray tracing techniques borrowed from military simulators and engineering workstations added to the sense of realism by providing proper highlighting, reflections, and shadows.

N64 was targeted at children and young teenagers. It was priced at $200 and launched with just four games. Despite the lack of games, initial sales were very strong. Indeed, 1997 turned out to be a banner year for both Sony and Nintendo. The overall U.S. market was strong, with sales of hardware and software combined reaching a record $5.5 billion. Estimates suggest that PlayStation accounted for 49 percent of machines and games by value. N64 captured a 41 percent share, leaving Sega trailing badly with less than 10 percent of the market. During the year, the average price for game machines had fallen to $150. By year-end there were 300 titles available for PlayStation, compared to forty for N64. Games for PlayStation retailed for $40, on average, compared to over $60 for N64.[42]

By late 1998, PlayStation was widening its lead over N64. In the crucial North American market, PlayStation was reported to be outselling N64 by a two-to-one margin, although Nintendo retained a lead in the under-twelve category. At this point, there were 115 games available for N64 versus 431 for PlayStation.[43] Worldwide, Sony had now sold close to

55 million PlayStations. The success of PlayStation had a major impact on Sony's bottom line. In fiscal 1998, PlayStation business generated revenues of $5.5 billion for Sony, 10 percent of its worldwide revenues, but accounted for $886 million, or 22.5 percent, of the company's operating income.[44]

The Next Generation

After almost vanishing from the marketplace in 1998, Sega made a bold attempt to retake a leadership position with the late 1998 introduction in Japan of its Dreamcast home video game machine. The Dreamcast is the most powerful home video game machine yet, with the capability to display advanced 3D graphics. The Dreamcast runs on a 128-bit microprocessor at 200 MHz and uses a Microsoft Windows CE operating system. The games are stored on a CD-ROM, and the machine comes equipped with a 56K modem to facilitate multiplayer online game playing. Priced at $240 and launched with only a handful of games, the Dreamcast still sold over 1 million units in its first few months on the Japanese market.

Sega has scheduled a September 1999 date for the U.S. launch of the Dreamcast. The machine is priced at $199. Up to twelve games will be available at launch, including a new version of Sonic the Hedgehog that cost an estimated $30 million to produce. By Christmas 1999, there should be thirty games, and 100 by mid 2000. Sega has licensed approximately 100 independent developers to work on Dreamcast games. The company has plans to spend some $100 million on advertising to launch the system in the United States. Sega has already struck distribution agreements with some of the largest chains in the United States, including Toys "R" Us, Wal-Mart, and Sears. About 20,000 stores should be carrying the Dreamcast. As of spring 1999, advanced orders for the Dreamcast stood at 300,000.[45]

Sony also has plans to launch a 128-bit machine, dubbed PlayStation 2, in 2000. Sony is reportedly investing $1 billion in development of PlayStation 2. The machine is expected to have graphics capabilities 200 times faster than the original PlayStation and will utilize a DVD disk for storage. In an attempt to leverage its huge global base, Sony plans to make its new machine backward compatible with the original PlayStation.[46] Nintendo is also reportedly working on a 128-bit machine, although details are sketchy.

The great unknown is the threat that the personal computer poses to the video game industry. The threat has been discussed for years, but until recently general-purpose PCs have lacked the capabilities of specialized game machines. This may now be changing. Microsoft has provided a direct interface between Windows applications and three-dimensional graphics technology with a variation on its Active X technology, Direct X. According to game developers, the combination of Direct X, fast Pentium microprocessors, faster CD-ROM drives, and graphics accelerator chips has made the PC a much more appealing platform for which to write games. Another attraction of writing for the PC is that game developers do not have to pay royalties to PC manufacturers for the privilege of supplying compatible games.

Since early 1997, most new PCs have been sold with 3D graphics capability. With prices dropping to under $1,000 for high-powered "entry level" PCs, industry estimates suggest that over 100 million PCs may be sold in 1998, all of them with a high enough specification to run advanced games. Indeed, many believe that game software is the only application that really stretches the modern PC.[47]

The New Millennium

In the history of the video game industry, each new chapter has been associated with a launch of a new generation of more powerful machines that can support faster processing, better graphics, and more compelling game play. In each era, a different company has risen to market dominance. The original video game consoles were produced by Atari and were based on 4-bit technology. Nintendo dominated the 8-bit era; Sega, the 16-bit era; and Sony, the 32-bit era. Nintendo launched a 64-bit machine in 1996, but its competitors didn't follow, preferring instead to focus on the development of 128-bit machines. Sega was the first to market a 128-bit video game console, which it launched in Japan in late 1998 and in the United States in late 1999. Sony launched its own 128-bit machine, Sony PlayStation 2, in 2000. Industry newcomer Microsoft and Nintendo are currently developing their own 128-bit machines.

With the possible exception of Nintendo's offering, all these machines will have web-browsing capabilities to facilitate multiplayer gaming over the Internet. Users will also be able to download games, movies, and music onto their consoles and use their consoles to browse the web, send email, execute ecommerce transactions, and so on. These capabilities have led some to speculate that video game consoles might ultimately hit personal computer sales.[48]

The prize that these competitors are going after is a $20-billion-a-year worldwide market that industry analysts say is growing more rapidly than the film or music industries. United States video game sales now rival Hollywood box-office revenues. More people than ever are playing video games and spending more time doing it. More than 40 percent of U.S. households now have at least one game console, according to estimates from International Data Corp.[49]

Sega Dreamcast

Sega introduced its 128-bit console, Sega Dreamcast, in the United States in September 1999 (the Japanese market launch was late 1998). The Dreamcast came equipped with a 56-kilobit modem to allow for online gaming over the Internet. By late 2000, Sega had sold around 6 million Dreamcasts worldwide, accounting for about 15 percent of console sales since its launch. The company has a goal of shipping 10 million units by March 2001.[50] Sega has nurtured Dreamcast sales by courting outside software developers who help keep the pipeline full of new games, including Crazy Taxi, Resident Evil, and Quake III Arena. Another 170 games are scheduled for the 2002 holiday season.

In April 2000, Sega announced that it would provide its Dreamcast video game console at no charge to customers who subscribe to a new Sega web service for two years at $21.95 a month. Customers who have already bought the Dreamcast console, which lists for $199, will get a free keyboard and a $200 check if they subscribe.[51] This represents something of a gamble by Sega. No one really knows whether there's a critical number of game players who want to hook their machines to their television sets and cruise the Web. The business potential of online games has received a lot of attention, but the usual game medium is still the personal computer. Still, by April 2000 company data showed that about 20 percent of Sega Dreamcast owners were already using the console's built-in modem. They were going online to cruise the Internet or send email. In March 2000, the company launched the first Internet game played from a video game console. In the simple game, Chu Chu Rocket, players help lead mice through mazes and escape from pursuing cats.

To run its online operation, Sega set up Sega.com, an independent company headed by Brad Huang, a thirty-five-year-old former hedge-fund manager who pitched the strategy to Sega chairman Isao Okawa a year ago. Sega's online gaming web site, SegaNet, made its debut in August 2000. The web site is Sega's portal to the Internet, providing a gathering place for Sega fans. During 2000, Sega planned to launch 12 online games, including versions of hits like Quake III Arena and Half-Life. In addition, Sega will offer multiplayer online console games like football and basketball. Gamers could play basketball over the Internet, for example, with as many as eight human players on two teams. Eventually, Sega hopes to provide games for which it will be able to charge a premium monthly fee.

Despite its position as first mover with a 128-bit machine, and despite a bold Internet strategy, as of late 2000 the company appeared to be struggling. Sega was handicapped first by product shortages due to constraints on the supply of component parts and then by a lack of demand as consumers waited to see whether PlayStation 2 would be a more attractive machine. In September 2000, Sega responded to the impending launch of Sony's PlayStation 2 by cutting the price for its console from $199 to $149. Then in late October, Sega announced that, due to this price cut, it would probably lose over $200 million for the fiscal year ending March 2001.[52]

Sony PlayStation 2

Sony's first video game console, the original PlayStation, has been a phenomenal success worldwide. Since its release in 1995, more than 27 million units have been sold in the United States and about 80 million worldwide. In 1999, Sony held a 53 percent share in the market for consoles. PlayStation 2 was launched in Japan in mid 2000, and in the United States at the end of October 2000. Initially priced at $299, PlayStation 2 is undoubtedly a powerful machine. At its core is a 300-megahertz graphics processing chip that was jointly developed with Toshiba and consumed about $1.3 billion in R&D. Referred to as the Emotion Engine processor, the chip allows the machine to display stunning graphic images previously found only on supercomputers. The chip makes the PlayStation 2 the most powerful video game machine yet.

The machine is set up to play different CD and DVD formats, as well as proprietary game titles. As is true with the original PlayStation, PlayStation 2 can play audio CDs. The system is also compatible with the original PlayStation: any PlayStation title can be played on the PlayStation 2. To help justify the price tag, the unit doubles as a DVD player with picture quality as good as current players. The PlayStation 2 does not come equipped with a modem, but it does have networking capabilities and a modem can be attached using one of two USB ports.[53]

Despite the raw power of PlayStation 2, a couple of things have blemished the market launch. First, Sony made far-reaching performance claims for PlayStation 2, but it is receiving some criticism from game experts who have suggested that the first games available for the new system have not matched the talk. Although Sony has sold 3 million PlayStation 2 consoles in Japan since the launch in March 2000, the devices have clearly fallen short of expectations. Programmers grumble that the machine is very hard to write games for. Game players in Japan have complained about blurry and "jagged" images. Designers still don't have a blockbuster PlayStation 2 software title after eighteen months on the job. Sony counters that most game developers have not had sufficient time to write games for the new system, and that the second generation of games written for PlayStation 2 should take better advantage if PlayStation's capabilities. Another problem arose in late October 2000, when Sony announced that it expects to ship just 500,000 machines—half the number previously announced—to the United States for the product's launch. Sony blamed the shortfall on a chip shortage. It plans to ship about 100,000 more PlayStations each week until Christmas. Sony's marketers had long anticipated that demand for the "PS 2," as the company calls PlayStation 2, would outstrip supply at first—but not by this much.[54]

Nintendo GameCube

Nintendo has garnered a solid position in the industry with its N64 machine by focusing on its core demographic, seven- to twelve-year-olds. In 1999, Nintendo took 33 percent of the hardware market and 28 percent of the game market. Nintendo's next generation video game machine, code named Dolphin and named GameCube, packs a modem and a powerful 400-megahertz, 128-bit processor made by IBM into a compact cube. GameCube marks a shift away from Nintendo's traditional approach of using proprietary cartridges to hold game software.

Instead, software for the new player will come on 8-centimeter compact disks, which are smaller than music compact disks. The new disks hold 1.5 gigabytes of data each, far greater storage capacity than the old game cartridges. Players will be able to control GameCube using wireless controllers.[55]

Nintendo has tried to make the GameCube easy for developers to work with rather than focusing on raw peak performance. While developers no doubt appreciate this, by the time GameCube hits store shelves, PlayStation 2 will have been on the market for eighteen months and may have a solid library of games. On the other hand, Nintendo's greatest asset is its intellectual property, which is instantly recognizable by its core demographic and includes Donkey Kong, Super Mario Brothers, and the Pokemon characters. Currently, Nintendo expects to introduce the GameCube in Japan in July 2001, and in the United States in October 2001.

Microsoft X-Box

Microsoft was first rumored to be developing a video game console in late 1999. In March 2000, Bill Gates made it official when he announced that Microsoft would enter the home video game market in fall 2001 with a console code named X-Box. In terms of sheer computing power, the 128-bit X-Box towers above its competitors. X-Box will have a 733-megahertz Pentium III processor, a high-powered graphics chip from Nvidia Corp, a built-in broadband cable modem to allow for online game playing and high-speed Internet browsing, 64 megabytes of memory, CD and DVD drives, and an internal hard disk drive, all features no other console has to date. The operating system will be a stripped-down version of its popular Windows system optimized for graphics-processing capabilities. Microsoft claims that because the X-Box will be based on familiar PC technology, it will be much easier for software developers to write games for. It should be relatively easy to convert games from the PC to run on the X-Box, and vice versa.[56]

Although Microsoft will be a new entrant to the video game industry, it is no stranger to games. Microsoft has long participated in the PC gaming industry and is one of the largest publishers of PC games, with hits such as Microsoft Flight Simulator and Age of Empires I and II to its credit. Sales of Microsoft's PC games have increased 50 percent annually over the past four years, and the company now controls about 10 percent of the PC game market. The company has also offered online gaming for some time, including its popular MSN Gaming Zone site. Started in 1996, the web site is the largest online PC gaming hub on the Internet. Nearly 12 million subscribers pay $9.95 a month to play premium games such as Asheron's Call or Fighter Ace. Or they can play traditional card and board games for free. Nor is Microsoft new to hardware; its joysticks and game pads outsell all other brands and it has an important mouse business.

Microsoft's entry into the home video game market was in part a response to the potential threat from companies like Sony and Sega. Microsoft worried that Internet-ready consoles like PlayStation 2 and Dreamcast might take over many web-browsing functions from the personal computer. Some in the company described Internet-enabled video game terminals as Trojan horses in the living room. In Microsoft's calculation, it made sense to get in the market to try and keep Sony and others in check. With annual revenues in excess of $20 billion worldwide, the home video game market is huge and an important source of potential growth for Microsoft. Still, by moving away from its core market, Microsoft is taking a huge risk, particularly given the scale of investments required to develop the X-Box, which could run as high as $1.5 billion.

ENDNOTES

1. A good account of the early history of Bushnell and Atari can be found in S. Cohen, *Zap! The Rise and Fall of Atari,* New York: McGraw-Hill, 1984.
2. Isaacs, R., "Video Games Race to Catch a Changing Market," *Business Week,* December 26, 1977, p. 44B.
3. Pagnano, P., "Atari's Game Plan to Overwhelm Its Competitors," *Business Week,* May 8, 1978, p. 50F.
4. Isaacs, R., "Video Games Race to Catch a Changing Market," *Business Week,* December 26, 1977, p. 44B.
5. Pagnano, P., "Atari's Game Plan to Overwhelm Its Competitors," *Business Week,* May 8, 1978, p. 50F; and Sheff, D., *Game Over,* New York: Random House, 1993.
6. Cohen, S., *Zap! The Rise and Fall of Atari,* New York: McGraw-Hill, 1984.
7. Kehoe, L., "Atari Seeks Way out of Video Game Woes," *Financial Times,* December 14, 1983, p. 23.
8. Schrage, M., "The High Tech Dinosaurs: Video Games, Once Ascendant, Are Making Way," *Washington Post,* July 31, 1983, p. F1.
9. Sheff, D., *Game Over,* New York: Random House, 1993.
10. Quoted in Sheff, D., *Game Over,* New York: Random House, 1993, p. 38.
11. Sheff, D., *Game Over,* New York: Random House, 1993.
12. Golden, D., "In Search of Princess Toadstool," *Boston Globe,* November 20, 1988, p. 18.
13. Gross, N., and Lewis, G., "Here Come the Super Mario Bros.," *Business Week,* November 9, 1987, p. 138.
14. Sheff, D., *Game Over,* New York: Random House, 1993.

15. Golden, D., "In search of Princess Toadstool," *Boston Globe,* November 20, 1988, p. 18.

16. Staff Reporter, "Marketer of the Year," *Adweek,* November 27, 1989, p. 15.

17. Lazzareschi, C., "No Mere Child's Play," *Los Angeles Times,* December 16, 1988, p. 1.

18. For a good summary of the early history of Sega, see Battle, J., and Johnstone, B., "The Next Level: Sega's Plans for World Domination," *Wired,* release 1.06, December 1993.

19. Sheff, D., *Game Over,* New York: Random House, 1993.

20. Battle, J., and Johnstone, B., "The Next Level: Sega's Plans for World Domination," *Wired,* release 1.06, December 1993.

21. For background details, see Flower, J., "3DO: Hip or Hype?" *Wired,* release 1.02, May/June 1993.

22. Brandt, R., "3DO's New Game Player: Awesome or Another Betamax?" *Business Week,* January 11, 1993, p. 38.

23. Flower, J., "3DO: Hip or Hype?" *Wired,* release 1.02, May/June 1993.

24. Jacobs, S., "Third Time's a Charm (They Hope)," *Wired,* release 2.01, January 1994.

25. Dunkin, A., "Video Games: The Next Generation," *Business Week,* January 31, 1994, p. 80.

26. Greenstein, J., "No Clear Winners, Though Some Losers; the Video Game Industry in 1995," *Business Week,* December 22, 1995, p. 42.

27. Staff Reporter, "3DO Says 'I Do' on Major Shift of Its Game Strategy," *Los Angeles Times,* September 17, 1996, p. 2.

28. Battle, J., and Johnstone, B., "The Next Level: Sega's Plans for World Domination," *Wired,* release 1.06, December 1993.

29. Greenstein, J., "No Clear Winners, Though Some Losers: The Video Game Industry in 1995," *Business Week,* December 22, 1995, p. 42.

30. Hamilton, D. P., "Sega Suddenly Finds Itself Embattled," *Wall Street Journal,* March 31, 1997, p. A10.

31. Taves, S., "Meet Your New Playmate," *Wired,* release 3.09, September 1995.

32. Kunni, I., "The Games Sony Plays," *Business Week,* June 15, 1998, p. 128.

33. Platt, C., "WordNerd," *Wired,* release 3.10, October 1995.

34. Kunni, I., "The Games Sony Plays," *Business Week,* June 15, 1998, p. 128.

35. Trachtenberg, J. A., "Race Quits Sony Just Before U.S. Rollout of Its PlayStation Video-Game System," *Wall Street Journal,* August 8, 1995, p. B3.

36. Beenstock, S., "Market Raider: How Sony Won the Console Game," *Marketing,* September 10, 1998, p. 26.

37. Trachtenberg, J. A., "Olafsson Calls It Quits as Chairman of Sony's Technology Strategy Group," *Wall Street Journal,* January 23, 1996, p. B6.

38. Greenstein, J., "Price Cuts Boost Saturn, PlayStation Hardware Sales," *Video Business,* May 31, 1996, p. 1.

39. Greenstein, J., "Sony Cuts Prices of PlayStation Hardware," *Video Business,* March 10, 1997, p. 1.

40. Hamilton, D., "Sega Suddenly Finds Itself Embattled," *Wall Street Journal,* March 31, 1997, p. A10.

41. Staff Reporter, "Nintendo Wakes Up," *The Economist,* August 3, 1996, pp. 55–56.

42. Takahashi, D., "Game Plan: Video Game Makers See Soaring Sales Now—And Lots of Trouble Ahead," *Wall Street Journal,* June 15, 1998, p. R10.

43. Takahashi, D., "Sony and Nintendo Battle for Kids Under 13," *Wall Street Journal,* September 24, 1998, p. B4.

44. Kunni, I., "The Games Sony Plays," *Business Week,* June 15, 1998, p. 128.

45. Takahashi, D., "Sega Is Pricing Game Machine on the Low Side," *Wall Street Journal,* April 16, 1999, p. B6.

46. Paradise, J., "Sony to Launch New PlayStation in Coming Year," *Wall Street Journal,* March 3, 1999, p. B1.

47. Fitzgerald, B., "Pieces of the Puzzle—Closer to Reality," *Wall Street Journal,* November 16, 1998, p. R33.

48. Takahashi, D., "Buying Decision, the Big Game: It's Sony Versus Sega Versus Nintendo Versus Microsoft," *Wall Street Journal,* June 26, 2000, p. R16.

49. Hause, K., Ma, B., Hwang, D., and House, J., *Review and Forecast of the World Wide Information Appliance Market,* 1999–2004, IDC, 2000.

50. Guth, R. A., "Sega Cites Dreamcast Price Cuts for Loss Amid Crucial Time for Survival of Firm," *Wall Street Journal,* October 30, 2000, p. A22.

51. Takahashi, D., "Sega Will Give Away Dreamcast Players to Lure Subscribers to the Web," *Wall Street Journal,* April 4, 2000, p. B1.

52. Guth, R. "Sega Cites Dreamcast Price Cuts for Loss Amid Crucial Time for Survival of Firm," *Wall Street Journal,* October 30, 2000, p. A22.

53. Oxford, T., and Steinberg, S. "Ultimate Game Machine Sony's PlayStation 2 Is Due on Shelves Oct. 26. It Brims with Potential—But at This Point Sega's Dreamcast Appears a Tough Competitor," *Atlanta Journal/Atlanta Constitution,* October 1, 2000, p. P1.

54. Hwang, S. "Sony Rolls Out PlayStation Ads Despite Shortage," *Wall Street Journal,* October 6, 2000, p. B1.

55. Guth, R. A., "New Players from Nintendo Will Link to Web," *Wall Street Journal,* August 25, 2000, p. B1.

56. Takahashi, D., "Microsoft's X-Box Impresses Game Developers," *Wall Street Journal,* March 13, 2000, p. B12.

Microsoft Windows Versus Linux

20

This case was prepared by Charles W. L. Hill, the University of Washington.

Windows is still a no-brainer for most people.
—*Linus Torvalds, August 2000*

Intellectual property is an artificial legal scheme. Companies that keep users from sharing software are antisocial.

—*Richard Stallman, unpaid head,*
Free Software Foundation, April 1998

Companies who think they can give away their products—or build them on the backs of those that have no intellectual-property value—will be unable to sustain their businesses.

—*Craig Mundie, Senior Vice President, Microsoft, May 2001*

Linux is a toy.
—*Steve Ballmer, Microsoft CEO, March 2001*[1]

Linux is a disruptive technology.

—*Michael Dell, CEO,*
Dell Computer Corporation,
Linux World Key Note Address, August 2000

The Accidental Entrepreneur

Linux is an operating system kernel that can be downloaded for free from the Internet. It is the creation not of a company, but of a self-organizing community of developers working together voluntarily over the Internet to improve the source code of the system. The source code is published on the Internet under a general public license. This specifies that licensees must agree to make any improvements or additions to the operating system freely available in the form of source code.

Linus Torvalds initiated the development of Linux in 1991.[2] At the time, Torvalds was a twenty-one-year old computer science student at the University of Helsinki, Finland. He was taking a class on programming for the UNIX operating system, a powerful commercial operating system originally developed by AT&T. Frustrated by the limited availability of UNIX hardware at the university, Torvalds purchased a PC with the intention of writing some basic UNIX-like code that would run on the low-powered machine. He

This case is intended to be used as a basis for class discussion rather than as an illustration of either effective or ineffective handling of the situation. Reprinted by permission of Charles W. L. Hill.

started by writing a task-switching protocol and then added other features as the need arose.

Within six months Torvalds had put together many of the elements of an operating system—task switching, a file management system, and device drivers. At this point, Torvalds realized that he had developed the basic elements of an operating system kernel. Torvalds christened his embryonic operating system Linux, a play on his first name and UNIX.

Torvalds was aided in the development of Linux by software available from the Free Software Foundation's GNU project. (GNU is a recursive acronym that stands for "Gnu's Not UNIX.") Richard Stallman, then a programmer at MIT's artificial intelligence lab, began the GNU project in 1984. The aim of the GNU project was to write a complete and free version of UNIX. Hardly wishing to reinvent the wheel, Torvalds tweaked Linux so that it fit GNU's preexisting library of programs. In his words, "I never ported programs, I ported the kernel to work with the programs."[3]

Torvalds also adopted another of Stallman's ideas, the general public license scheme (GPL), often referred to as a "copyleft" scheme. A GPL allows users to sell, copy, and change copyleft programs—but specifies that any modifications to the source code must be made freely available.

The Open-Source Software Paradigm

In mid-1991, Torvalds posted the source code of Linux on a University of Helsinki FTP server under a GPL so that others could download and use it. In return, he asked for advice on improving the system. Soon the emails started coming in with comments, suggestions, and software patches to improve Linux. Almost by accident, Torvalds had stumbled on a new paradigm for designing software: the open-source software paradigm. A distributed community of Linux users connected only by the Internet had spontaneously organized itself and was working cooperatively, for no pay, to improve the functionality of the operating system.

Like Torvalds, the development community was composed primarily of computer hobbyists whose main motivation was the ego gratification associated with solving complex technical challenges. Some developers cooperated to solve a problem. Others competed with each other for bragging rights, with the best codes winning through a process of Darwinian selection. If an author drifted away from the process, no longer improving his or her bit of code, other people would pick it up and work on it. Hovering over this entire process was the omnipresent Torvalds, whose role evolved into orchestrator and arbitrator of the "competition" that was emerging among developers to improve Linux.

Several advantages of the open source software development process soon became apparent. First, developers were free to choose what area they worked on, rather than being assigned to a task they might not want. The matching of programmer to task by self-selection increased the speed of development. Second, Linux reflected the diversity of the user base and was quickly adapted to run on a wide range of processor architectures, including processors from Intel (386 to Pentium), Digital Equipment (Alpha), Sun (SPARC), Silicon Graphics (MIPS), and Motorola (Power PC). Third, the open-source process meant that the code was rapidly tested by end users in a diverse range of environments and was quickly debugged, with patches appearing on a weekly basis.

In parallel to this somewhat anarchic process, there was always a stable release distribution that moved forward when new features had been thoroughly tested. Linux moved through a series of point releases—1.1, 1.2, etc.—and subpoint releases—1.2.12, 1.2.13, and so on. When a big enough jump in software functionality occurred, developers moved on to the next version, a process presided over by Torvalds. The result of this process was an operating system kernel that was efficient in its use of computer resources, could run in a diverse set of computer environments, was very stable, and improved at a rapid rate. And the kernel was free.

By 1994, Linux had matured to the point where Torvalds decided to release Linux 1.0. At this juncture, the grassroots movement was gaining momentum, the user base was already large, and the core Linux development team was substantial. Among the thousands of files in Linux 1.0, there was one simply called Credits. This file listed the names, addresses, and contributions of the main participants in the development of the operating system. The list included more than one hundred names scattered around the world.

Building Momentum

With the release of Linux 1.0, Linux began to gain momentum. As befits a grassroots movement, the early adopters of Linux were technically minded individuals and Linux evangelists who started using Linux in the workplace because it suited their individual needs. The early adopters were concentrated in higher education, government agencies such as NASA, and research institutions. Soon, however, the operating system started to penetrate corporations, typically entering individual departments under the radar screen of corporate information officers.

Two developments occurred together to give Linux adoption a big boost. The first was the formation of several companies designed to exploit the Linux phenomenon.[4] These included Caldera and Red Hat Software, both established in 1994. How do you make money out of an operating system that is free? The idea behind Caldera and Red Hat was to bundle Linux together with associated programs on a CD, such as a graphical user interface for Linux; sell it for a low price; and then build a large enough user base to profit by selling services such as installation, customization, and technical support—services that the distributed developers of Linux had no interest in offering, but which Linux would need if it was ever to be more than a cult phenomenon.

Another central idea behind these companies was to provide legitimacy for Linux, which in turn would overcome resistance from corporate information officers, who seemed unlikely to approve adoption of software that was free, written by "hackers," and not backed by any identifiable vendor who could be held accountable and offer help when things went wrong.

The second development that boosted Linux was the rapid growth of the World Wide Web in the mid 1990s. Designed and distributed through the medium of the Internet, Linux itself was a child of the Web. As early as 1995, research suggested that almost 50 percent of new Internet server implementations were Linux based.[5] Free, stable, and platform independent, and placing low demands on computing resources, Linux turned out to be the ideal operating system for an appliance server. (Appliance servers are network-enabled devices designed explicitly to provide a single dedicated service, such as email, file and print, or Internet access, or a predefined suite of services.)

By 1997, Red Hat claimed that Linux had gained a presence in many large organizations. Included among Red Hat's customers were NASA, Disney, Lockheed Martin, General Electric, UPS, NASDAQ, the IRS, and Boeing, as well as most leading U.S. universities. It must be said, however, that most of these customers were individuals or departments, and not the corporation or agency per se. Since the operating system could be downloaded for free from multiple sites, it was very difficult to determine how many people were actually using Linux. Red Hat estimated the number in 1997 to be between 3 and 5 million.[6] International Data Corporation estimated that about 150,000 servers were shipped with a Linux operating system in 1997.[7]

Equally important as adoptions by large organizations was the ability of Linux to gain a foothold among cost- and performance-conscious small and medium-sized businesses. Typical of these businesses was Mahaffey's Quality Printing, an offset and flexographic printer in Jackson, Mississippi. Mahaffey's got a T1 Internet connection in 1996 and originally used Windows NT to run the company's servers. The company was experiencing rapid growth, however, and its servers suffered frequent crashes and restarts running on NT. The production manager had read about Linux in an article in *Wired* magazine and decided to try it as an FTP server. The experience was so positive that Mahaffey's decided to stay with Linux for the FTP server, and the company also decided to stick with the operating system as its server solution. By 1999, the company had seven Linux servers for print-and-file serving: OPI, FTP, mail, DNS, Web, database, and fax serving. The decision gave Mahaffey's significant savings. They did not have to pay for an operating system license, plus the lower power requirements of Linux meant that they could run the operating system on aging Intel hardware. The company calculated that it saved approximately $60,000 and got a stable operating system too.[8]

Going Mainstream

In 1998, Linux started to penetrate the mainstream, but not through any mass-marketing campaign or direct sales effort. No player had the resources to carry out such a campaign. It had simply proved its value again and again in different computing environments, and thus generated support from a growing community of users, service providers, and application providers. The almost religious fervor of the open source movement aided adoption among those looking for an alternative to Microsoft.

On university campuses, courses on Linux were increasingly popular, thereby increasing the supply of developers eager to improve the operating system or work on Linux applications. The ability to look at the source code of an operating system, and manipulate it, was enormously attractive to students. Demand was given a boost by some high-profile implementations of Linux that began to increase its legitimacy, at least in the eyes of corporate information officers. For example, Digital Domain Inc. used workstations running Linux to render many of the stunning graphical images from the blockbuster movie *Titanic*. NASA's Goddard Space Flight Center built a supercomputer out of off-the-shelf PC components and chose Linux to run the machine. When they were reported in industry news media, such implementations helped to get the Linux bandwagon rolling.

The big driver of demand, however, remained the web or appliance server market. According to IDC data, approximately 500,000 copies of Linux were shipped as server operating systems during 1998, making Linux second to Microsoft's Windows NT, which shipped 1.2 million copies.[9] As the year progressed, a growing number of software companies added legitimacy to Linux by aligning themselves with the operating system. In July 1998, database providers Informix, Oracle, and Sybase all announced that they would offer Linux versions of their database software. In September 1998, Intel and Netscape announced that they would invest in Red Hat Software. In November 1998, at the annual Comdex computer trade show in Las Vegas, there was a sharp increase in the number of Linux-oriented companies showing their wares. In December 1998, media reports suggested that IBM would announce a broad service and support agreement for Red Hat's distribution of Linux. Also in December, Coral announced that it would distribute a limited-feature Linux version of its WordPerfect software for free.

Increasing recognition set up a virtuous circle in which growing demand elicited more recognition from software companies, who pledged to support Linux, which generated more demand for Linux and led to more pledges. The process was spurred on by the fact that Linux was not a Microsoft product, and many in the industry had an interest in seeing Microsoft dethroned from its commanding position.

Ironically, a backhanded complement from Microsoft in the form of a leaked internal confidential memo, dubbed the "Halloween memo" because of its release date, added to the growing hype surrounding Linux. In it, a Microsoft employee described Linux as a "direct short term revenue and platform threat to Microsoft, particularly in the server space." The memo also noted that case studies provided "dramatic" evidence that open-source software can match and exceed the quality of commercial software, and that open-source advocates "are making progressively more credible agreements that their products are at least as robust—if not more—than commercial alternatives."[10]

Linux Gets Hyped

In the supercharged economic environment of the late 1990s, it is perhaps not surprising that Linux too became the object of excessive hype. From being the obscure brainchild of one student in Finland, Linux was suddenly transformed in the eyes of certain media sources into a prime-time contender for Microsoft's operating system hegemony.

Calmer voices pointed out that while Linux might be a strong contender in segments of the server market, its appeal in the desktop arena was marginal. The key consideration was a lack of compelling applications, such as the ubiquitous Microsoft Office, financial management software, and games. Even with all of the strengths of the Linux development community, Microsoft could still count on an army of developers schooled in Win 32 API protocols to keep writing applications to run on Windows. Given a choice between writing applications for a platform that had yet to penetrate the desktop and writing for one that dominated the desktop, developers naturally acted according to their economic interests, even if their noneconomic preferences lay elsewhere. In addition, while graphical user interfaces (GUIs) were now available for Linux, it was still regarded by many as a technical system that was intimidating to the average user.

Immersed in the rhetoric of the new economy, however, many anti-Microsoft opinion leaders brushed aside such concerns in their desire to see Linux succeed. It was certainly true that many cost-conscious dot-com start-ups were adopting Linux as the operating system for their web servers precisely because it was free and stable. Since Linux was not the product of a company—a concept that was difficult for many to grasp—attention shifted to the growing list of Linux distributors and complementors, such as Red Hat, Caldera Systems, and VA Linux, several of which went public in 1999 and 2000, and saw dramatic increases in their share prices.

Red Hat was typical: it went public in August 2000 and closed on the first day of trading at $52.06 a share, a gain of 271.88 percent. The shares peaked a few months later at $150, valuing Red Hat at $25 billion. At the time, Red Hat had revenues of $52.8 million and an operating loss of $46.7 million. By mid 2001 the shares had fallen to $3.75, giving Red Hat a more modest market cap of $637 million. In the interim, the company had annual revenues of $102.65 million, but losses of $107.4 million. The Red Hat story and the similar experience of its Linux peers suggest that a profitable business model based on Linux may be difficult to achieve.

Beyond the Hype

Although the implosion of the dot-com bubble and the associated wreckage took some of the steam out of the Linux bandwagon, the underlying trends remained positive, particularly in the server market. Exhibit 1 summarizes the actual and forecasted worldwide server unit shipments by operating system over the 1997–2005 period, as presented by IDC.[11]

Exhibit 1 clearly shows the rapid rise of Linux between 1998 and 2000, and suggests that this growth will continue unabated through 2005, with a compound annual growth rate of 38.8 percent between 2000 and 2005. Also evident is the penetration of Windows NT and now Windows 2000 into the server space. Windows NT beat NetWare as the market leader in 1998, and Windows 2000 is expected to maintain this position for Microsoft through 2005, with a compound annual growth rate of 14.3 percent. The big loser is NetWare from Novell, which is rapidly losing ground to Windows 2000 and Linux. Unix too, is predicted to lose share.

Linux 2.4

The continual improvement in Linux is helping to drive adoption in the server arena. The current version, Linux 2.4, was released in early 2001. Linux 2.4 has many features designed for corporate enterprise computing. The kernel provides improvements in capacity, storage management, and symmetric multiprocessing. Linux 2.4 offers a logical volume manager subsystem to enhance its storage management capabilities. It allows system administrators to add and remove Linux storage disks, without the need for rebooting. It also produces file system snapshots for backup purposes. Linux can now support files larger than 2 GB and addresses up to 64 GB of physical memory on Intel-based servers.

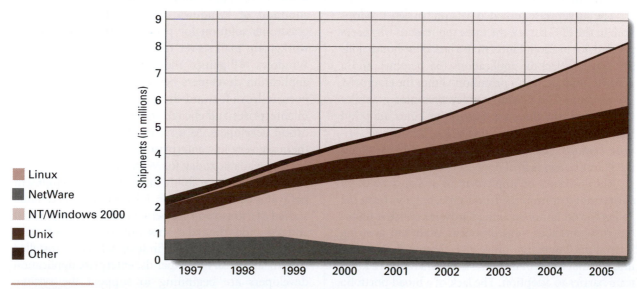

EXHIBIT 1

Worldwide Server Shipments by Operating System, 1997–2005

Linux 2.4 supports three new microprocessor architectures: Intel's Architecture 64 (IA64), which is also known as Itanium; IBM System/390 mainframes; and SuperH, which is the microprocessor used in Windows CE hand-held devices. It also provides support for a wide range of hardware devices, including universal serial bus (UBS) drivers for digital cameras, keyboards, mice, modems, network cards, printers, scanners, and zip drives.

Drivers and Barriers to Linux Adoption

Recent surveys by IDC and Gartner support the perception that the adoption of Linux in the server arena is being driven by a combination of low cost and reliability. In 2001, IDC asked IT managers in approximately 865 organizations to identify the three top reasons why they would consider adopting Linux as a server operating system.[12] Initial price was cited by 41 percent of those surveyed, followed by reliability (27 percent). Availability of specific applications was cited as the third reason for adoption (19 percent). The specific applications include other open source software, such as Apache Web server, Samba for print-and-file serving, and Sendmail for email and messaging solutions, and open-source development tools.

A mid 2000 Gartner survey of 709 decisionmakers for server operating systems yielded similar results.[13] About 54 percent cited the low initial price, 32 percent cited reliability, and 19 percent cited low ongoing operating costs. Interviews of Linux adopters tend to reinforce these results.

The surveys also provided data on barriers to adoption. In the IDC survey, the three top reasons why users decided not to adopt Linux were a lack of in-house skills (39 percent), lack of applications (36 percent), and a desire to limit platform profusion within the enterprise (34 percent). The Gartner survey presented a similar picture, with the three top barriers to Linux adoption identified by respondents being lack of service and support options (22 percent), lack of in-house skills (18 percent), and lack of applications (16 percent).

The low cost of implementing a Linux solution derives not just from the free license, but also from the ability to run Linux on aging hardware, which is a plus for cost-conscious organizations. With the growing interest in Linux on university campuses, it seems unlikely that a lack of in-house skills will remain a long-term barrier to adoption. The lack of a broad portfolio of enterprise applications is currently a problem for Linux both in the server arena and on the desktop.

Commenting on the results of its survey, IDC postulates that Linux is now crossing the chasm from technically minded early adopters to mainstream acceptance. The crossing is essentially summarized by a shift from a belief in the open-source paradigm as an "anything but Microsoft" grassroots movement to a more pragmatic and objective analysis of the economic benefits that Linux offers to adopters.

Linux Use on Servers

The lack of enterprise computing applications explains why most of Linux implementation is currently limited to the application server arena. Linux is still a niche product. Another IDC survey of Linux use reported that respondents overwhelmingly cited Internet/intranet application workloads as the most common use for Linux (78 percent).[14] Strong use was also reported for file and print (58 percent), software development (57 percent), and email messaging (57 percent). Internet service providers (ISPs) in particular are attracted to the low cost of Linux given their own operating environment, which is characterized by extreme pressure on profit margins. Only 7.5 percent of respondents indicated that they used Linux for enterprise applications such as enterprise resource planning, customer relationship management, supply chain management, and human resource functions.

Linux may currently be confined to a niche, but it is worth noting that when Windows NT was launched, it too was supported by very few enterprise grade server applications. As with Linux, the early adoption of Windows NT consisted mostly of a grassroots solution for print-and-file servers and a workgroup mail server for small groups of PCs. As Windows NT gained momentum, enterprise grade application developers began to support NT, which in turn drove forward the adoption of Windows NT in enterprises and elicited more support from application developers. As a result of this virtuous circle, there are very few enterprise server applications that are not available today for Windows 2000.

Could Linux be following a similar development path? It is certainly possible. Like Windows NT, Linux started as a grassroots movement in corporations that entered under the radar screen of corporate information managers. And like Windows NT, as the installed base of Linux servers expands, enterprise application developers are beginning to support the system. Among others, SAP, Oracle, and IBM began announcing applications for Linux in mid to late 2000.

Vendor Support for Linux on the Server

The bullish case for Linux is boosted by the growing list of hardware vendors and software providers that are supporting Linux. Major hardware vendors, including Compaq, Dell, Fujitsu, Hitachi, IBM, and NEC, have embraced Linux and ship the operating system on their servers. As noted earlier, Oracle, Sybase, and Informix have all ported their database management software to Linux. In 2001, Dell and Oracle announced a deal to put Oracle database software on its Linux servers. SAP has ported its enterprise software to Linux. Hewlett Packard offers worldwide support for Linux, and Computer Associates now provides a version of Unicenter TNG for Linux.[15]

IBM's Linux Push

In one of the single biggest commitments to Linux, IBM announced in December 2000 plans to invest nearly $1 billion in Linux software development, hardware, services, the open-source community, and partnerships during 2001.[16] IBM seems to be betting heavily that Linux will become a major operating sys-

tem in the enterprise and will drive IBM's eServer sales growth across all of the company's eServer platforms—from appliances to mainframes. IBM now has more than 1,500 employees focused on Linux hardware and software development. In addition, IBM chairman and CEO Lou Gerstner also announced a deal in which IBM would build what it claims is the world's largest Linux supercomputer. The system, now deployed by Royal Dutch/Shell Group, consists of 1,024 IBM X-series servers packaged in thirty-two racks and all running Linux. The system is designed to analyze seismic data.

IBM apparently sees Linux as a way to compete simultaneously with both Microsoft and Sun. An IBM spokesperson has stated that IBM will discontinue its AIX offerings when Linux contains the enterprise features that customers demand from commercial UNIX products. IBM seems willing to cannibalize its own UNIX business to beat Sun and Microsoft. To support this strategy, IBM has produced the diagram summarized in Exhibit 2, which illustrates how IBM Linux solutions can be used to replace Windows. Some comments from an IBM

EXHIBIT 2

Replacing Windows with IBM Linux Solutions[17]

EXHIBIT 3

Comments from an IBM Document

The outages in the MSN Messenger emphasize increasing concerns about Microsoft's ability to move from developing software to turning its products into rentable Web services through the .NET and Hailstorm strategies. This . . . is an early example of Microsoft's lack of technical infrastructure and capability to support a large scale, Web-based service and distribution model. This disadvantage for Microsoft is a key advantage for IBM in numerous ways.

Linux is highly stable and reliable—here are the facts: According to a Zona Research report published in October 2000, 80% of respondents replied that stability and reliability were the deciding factors when it came to choosing Linux as their operating system. The Standish group found that Linux servers are more reliable than Microsoft servers when it comes to peak operational downtime. This research shows that Linux servers have about 14 hours of unplanned downtime per year, amounting to 99.6% uptime during average peak operational periods. By comparison, Standish found the average Microsoft Enterprise Cluster to have just over 99% uptime or about 30 hours of downtime during the average peak operational period. Further, according to an article by Alan Radding published in *Information Week* in April 2001, in terms of actual hours, *the Microsoft server cluster will be down more than twice as long as a Linux server.*

Despite Microsoft Corp.'s continued contention that open-source operating systems don't make good business sense, the Transaction Processing Performance Council released new data in mid-May showing that IBM's upcoming DB2 7.2 release running on Linux 2.4.3 outperforms SQL Server 2000 running on Windows 2000 in the 100GB category, by the order of 2,733 queries per hour for DB2 on Linux versus 1,699 per hour on SQL Server 2000. [See complete results on **http://www.tpc.org**.—results are current as of 6/26/01.]

In addition to licensing and auditing costs . . . Microsoft Windows 2000 Advanced Server . . . starts at $4,000 per 25 users. That does not include add-on components and connectors. So, to run a moderately sized eBusiness application, supporting, say, 7,000 possible users, and entry level server costs could start at $1.1 million.

document attacking Microsoft and supporting Linux are given in Exhibit 3. The comments give some insights into IBM's likely sales strategy under its Linux initiative.

Despite the rising tide of third-party support from the likes of IBM, there is little sign yet that Linux is moving out of its niche in the server arena. For all of the high-profile announcements of Linux support, Windows 2000 still holds a huge lead in available enterprise applications. For Linux to grow outside its niche, this lead must obviously change.

Linux on the Client

Although Linux is making rapid headway in certain segments of the server market, it is currently a no-show on the desktop. The early hype promoted Linux as an alternative to Windows for the client, but at this point, Linux looks set to join Next OS and IBM's OS/2 as also-rans in a business Microsoft dominates almost completely. Accumulating evidence shows that Linux is making little headway. Eazel, considered by many to be one of the most promising developers of applications for Linux desktops, closed its doors in May 2001. Started by the team that had developed the

interface for the Apple Macintosh, Eazel had been trying to develop a similar interface for Linux. The company failed because it was unable to raise additional funding from venture capitalists.

Eazel's demise followed a similar retreat from the Linux market by Corel, the Canadian software company that owns both WordPerfect Office (a competitor to Microsoft Office) and Corel Draw. Corel had developed Linux versions of WordPerfect Office and Corel Draw and had entered the market as a distributor of the Linux operating system. Corel struggled to become profitable, however, and in October 2000 accepted a $135 million investment by Microsoft in return for a commitment to develop applications for Microsoft's .NET initiative. In January 2001, the company stepped back from its role as a Linux operating system distributor as part of a plan to "return to profitability."[18] In August 2001, Dell Computer announced that it would stop selling desktop and notebook computers pre-installed with the Linux operating system due to a lack of demand.[19]

One does not have to look hard to find reasons for the inability of Linux to establish itself on the desktop. There is no economic reason to switch. In fact, there are economic costs to doing so. The vast bulk of existing applications, including Microsoft Office, are written to run on Windows. Most users have invested in a library of Windows applications, are familiar with the Windows GUI, are content enough with the system they have, and see no compelling reason to bear the costs of switching to another system. Even if the operating system is free, the applications would not be, and there would be a cost involved in learning a new system. The GUIs for Linux, such as KDE and Gnome, are not as user friendly as Windows. Some Linux implementations still use the old command line interface, a format that most desktop users haven't seen since the heyday of MS-DOS in the 1980s.

Some argue that for Linux to start making inroads in mature PC markets such as the United States, new Linux applications would have to offer compelling economic reasons for bearing the costs of switching and installing a Linux operating system. For longtime Windows users, there is no sign of such applications anywhere on the horizon and no indication as to what they might be.

Linux is making some headway, however, in the K–12 educational market.[20] Cash-strapped schools are finding that they can build PC labs for students at a much lower cost by buying old Intel hardware and installing Linux. Applications for Linux, such as StarOffice and Mozilla, meet the bulk of basic educational needs—word processing, spreadsheets, presentation software, Web browsing, and email. Scoffing at the notion that Linux is a more difficult system, a representative of the Open Source Educational Foundation has noted, "We have kindergartners using it [Linux] on a daily basis without any problems."[21]

Linux appears to be gaining traction on the desktop in some foreign markets.[22] To varying degrees, this seems to be the case in Central and Eastern Europe and in China. In general, these markets are price sensitive and the level of PC penetration is currently very low, so widespread attachment to Windows is not a major issue. In these markets, the low cost of Linux is a real benefit to PC vendors and buyers. It is probably no coincidence that the growing popularity of Linux in price-sensitive developing markets is occurring at the same time that Microsoft is stepping up efforts to reduce the level of piracy of its products. Even in these markets though, the lack of Linux applications is hindering adoption. Unless this situation changes, these markets may default toward Windows standardization in the long run.

How Vulnerable Is Microsoft?
The Strengths of Linux

The picture of Linux that is emerging is one of a highly successful niche operating system that is valued in focused segments of the server market for its low cost and stability. ISPs in particular have embraced Linux as a choice for web servers. Outside this niche, however, Linux is currently limited by a lack of enterprise and desktop applications. While Linux supporters, including Linus Torvalds, concede that Linux has a long way to go before it becomes a threat to the hegemony of Windows on the desktop, the situation in the server arena is less clear.

Theoretically at least, the growing installed base of Linux servers, when coupled with the desire of many other enterprises to see a non-Microsoft solution, could trigger an increase in the supply of enterprise applications written to run on Linux. The trick is to get the process going. A larger number of enterprise applications could unleash a bandwagon effect, where the increasing availability of Linux applications drives forward adoption of more Linux servers and induces developers to write more applications based on Linux, which further increases demand for the servers, and so on. If it proceeds far enough, this virtuous circle could result in the market flipping from Microsoft dominated to Linux dominated. Once that happens in the server arena, downward migration of Linux onto the desktop (perhaps using a different computing paradigm where many Office applications reside on servers) could become a possibility.

The commitment of companies such as IBM to promoting Linux should be taken as a signal that this scenario is not entirely remote. Microsoft's history demonstrates that an operating system that enters corporations through a grassroots movement and establishes itself initially in selected niches or beachheads can become an enterprisewide system.

To bolster their case, supporters of Linux point out that in a recent test, Linux outperformed Windows 2000.[23] In May 2001, Transaction Processing Performance Council (TPPC) benchmarks revealed that IBM's DB2 7.2 on Linux 2.4.3 outperformed Microsoft SQL Server and Windows 2000 in a 100 GB database test. In prior TPPC tests, Microsoft has typically won with the SQL Server and Windows 2000 duo across various hardware configurations. Microsoft dismissed the results, arguing that the numbers were more reflective of database performance than of operating system capabilities.

Linux supporters also point to the strong interest in Linux on university campuses. The open-source software model allows students to look at and experiment with the source code of Linux, making it useful for courses on operating systems. In a campus bookstore, one is likely to see rows of books on Linux in the computer section. At the very least, the number of graduates with development talent and training in Linux will alleviate a perceived barrier to Linux adoption cited in corporate surveys—the lack of in-house talent.

Limitations of Linux and the Advantages of Microsoft

Questions about the value and long-term viability of Linux remain. The lack of enterprise and desktop applications remains a vexing problem. Linux may be cheap, and it may be able to take advantage of inexpensive aging hardware, but what about the total cost of ownership? Does the lack of Linux talent strain an organization and give rise to unanticipated costs? The open-source software paradigm may have worked well when the Linux code was relatively compact, but will the paradigm scale to a more complex and bulky code? Between release 1.0 and 2.4, the Linux kernel grew from a few thousand lines of code to over 1 million. At what point does the complexity of the development process overwhelm the open-source model? How practical is it to have a single individual, currently Torvalds, acting as final arbitrator? Can voluntary cooperation and coordination sustain the growth of a system that others are profiting from, including ISPs, Linux distributors, application developers, and service providers? Will developers motivated by ego gratification begin to question why they are working for free on a system so that others can get rich? When does the revolution run out of steam? And if key distributors such as Red Hat begin to take ownership of the system, will Linux splinter into several incompatible versions, as occurred with UNIX?

Then there is the tenacity of Microsoft to consider. Microsoft has also shown a willingness to experiment with licensing its own source code, although not in a manner that is similar to the GNU General Public License under which Linux source code is distributed.[24] During the second half of 2000, Microsoft launched a pilot program that gave a small number of large enterprise customers access to the source code—under strict nondisclosure agreements—for Windows operating environments. The goal was to allow customers to review the code, thereby boosting their confidence in areas such as security and encryption, and helping them to address deployment concerns. In March 2001, the program was expanded to include about 1,000 North American enterprise customers, and in May 2001 the program was expanded internationally. At the same time, Microsoft has licensed the source code for one or more Microsoft products to over 100 universities in the United States and abroad, giving students hands-on experience with Microsoft source code.

Microsoft has many other advantages. While Windows NT was prone to crashing, Windows 2000 has won praise for its stability, thereby reducing one of the factors that induced companies to try Linux in the first place. As noted, Windows has the clear advantage in terms of applications. A large development community is schooled in Win 32 API and ready to write more applications for Windows. Windows 2000 seems to be a secure system, while Microsoft charges that the Linux security model is weak. Microsoft has the advantage of a big support infrastructure, the cost of which can be spread over a vast installed base. Corporate information officers might want to standardize their enterprise software on a single platform for economic reasons. Microsoft is in a unique position to fulfill this need with its offerings from Windows 2000 Datacenter Server: Windows 2000 Server, Windows XP desktop offerings, and Windows CE. All of this suggests that while Linux may continue to make headway in segments of the server market, other market shifts will be required if Linux is to become a viable contender against Windows for enterprise applications and on the desktop.

ENDNOTES

1. Cited in S. Campbell, "Linux Debate," *Crn,* March 26, 2001, p. 3.
2. Background material for this section drawn from the following sources: G. Moody, "The Greatest OS That (N)ever Was," *Wired,* Release 5.08, August 1997; S. Davis, "Linux: Software with a License to Use," *Wall Street Journal,* April 3, 1998, p. B7F; G. Moody, *Rebel Code: Linux and the Open Source Revolution,* 2001.

3. G. Moody, "The Greatest OS That (N)ever Was," *Wired,* Release 5.08, August 1997.

4. J. Burke, "The Finnish Connection," *Red Herring,* August 1, 1996.

5. M. Bolzern, "Public Domain OS Catches On," *Software Magazine,* October 1995, pp. 8–9.

6. G. Moody, "The Greatest OS That (N)ever Was," *Wired,* Release 5.08, August 1997.

7. W. Wilson, "Linux Blazing into Tech Mainstream," *Seattle Post Intelligencer,* December 28, 1998, p. C1.

8. D. Greenlaw, "Linux Illuminations from an Early Adopter," *Printing Impressions,* May 2000, p. 76.

9. W. Wilson, "Linux Blazing into Tech Mainstream," *Seattle Post Intelligencer,* December 28, 1998, p. C1.

10. B. Ploskina, "Halloween Memo: Great Threat or Gobbledygook?" *Ent,* November 18, 1998, pp. 1, 52.

11. International Data Corporation. Worldwide Server Market Forecast and Analysis, 2001–2005, June 2001, IDC Report #25031.

12. International Data Corporation, "Users' Perceptions of Linux: Time to Start Crossing the Chasm," August 2001, IDC Bulletin #25269.

13. "What the Enterprise Thinks of Linux: Service Needs and Adoption Drivers," Garnter Advisory, October 16, 2000.

14. International Data Corporation, "Linux Usage: Enterprise Application Need Not Apply—Yet," IDC Bulletin #23876.

15. C. R. Lubrano, "Linux or Windows: What Should You Do?" *Datapro,* June 14, 2001; M. Hubley, "Major Service Vendors' Commitment to Linux and OSS," Gartner Advisory, June 15, 2001.

16. Anonymous, "IBM Invests Almost $1 Billion in Linux," *InfoWorld,* December 18, 2000.

17. Microsoft Field Bulletin, "Answering the 'Winning with Linux' Letter," August 2001.

18. E. Scannell. "Corel Steps Away from Linux to Focus on Being Profitable," *InfoWorld,* January 29, 2001, p. 24.

19. A. Krauss, "Dell Ends Linux Offering," *New York Times,* August 3, 2001, p. 4.

20. A. Gonzalez, "Penguin Enrolls in U.S. Schools," *Wired News,* August 20, 2001, www.wired.com.

21. A. Gonzalez, "Penguin Enrolls in U.S. Schools," *Wired News,* August 20, 2001, www.wired.com.

22. N. Spit and A. Jump, "Linux in Eastern Europe: More Than Just an Insurance Policy?" Gartner Advisory, September 19, 2000.

23. C. R. Lubrano, "Linux or Windows: What Should You Do?" *Datapro,* June 14, 2001.

24. A. Gillen, "Microsoft Extends Its Source Licensing Efforts," IDC Flash #24643, May 2001.

21

IBM Global Services: The Professional Computer Services Industry

This case was prepared by Vincent Pawlowski and Marc E. Gartenfeld, both of St. John's University, and Dorothy G. Dologite, Baruch College, under the direction of Dr. Robert J. Mockler, St. John's University.

In early 2001, John Joyce, chief financial officer of International Business Machines (IBM), in presenting the company's fourth-quarter and full-year 2000 results to industry securities analysts at the Investors Relations Meeting on January 17, 2001, commented that although IBM Global Services (IGS) had posted growth quarter to quarter and year to year, results for 2000 were not what they wanted (IBM, 2001a). IBM Global Services had not met the company's objectives for the full year or the last quarter in either revenue or pretax income (PTI), and its direct expense grew faster than its revenue. This certainly raised some concerns, considering IGS's position as IBM's growth engine and second largest contributor to the company's bottom line. Joyce was also very careful to remind analysts that a slowing economy and its potential impact on information technology spending were still wild cards for future growth. The main issue to be resolved was to create an enterprisewide strategy that

would differentiate IBM Global Services from its competition.

Since December 1996, when IBM established IBM Global Services (IGS), IGS had achieved outstanding business results. IGS had grown faster than the industry, and IBM Global Services was then widely recognized as the largest computer services company in the world, surpassing EDS. Prior to this period, Integrated Systems Solution Corporation (ISSC), an IBM subsidiary and the predecessor of IGS, had similar results. It was accepted that the success of IBM's services business was a major contributor to IBM's overall business recovery and that the future of IBM depended on the future success of IBM Global Services. Figure 1 identifies the segments of IBM (hardware, global services, software, global financing, enterprise investments/other) and the company's percentage of revenue by segment.

The computer services industry includes three broad categories of services: processing services (data entry, credit card authorization, billing payroll processing), network services (electronic data interchange services, electronic mail delivery, file transfer, and electronic funds transfer), and professional computer services (technology consulting, custom programming, systems integration, and outsourcing). The industry had experienced a prolonged period of

FIGURE 1

IBM Company's Percentage of Revenue
by Segment

	2000	1999	1998
Hardware	42.7	43.3	44.2
Global services	37.5	36.7	35.4
Software	14.3	14.5	14.5
Global financing	3.9	3.6	3.5
Enterprise Investments/other	1.6	1.9	2.4
Total	100	100	100

Source: IBM Annual Report (2001).

strong growth, which was expected to continue into 2001 and beyond primarily due to the service demands associated with the use of the Internet in business (Hoovers Online Network, 2001a). This rapid growth was stimulating increased competition as well as high acquisition and alliance activity. However, a major impediment to sustained growth was the shortage of computer professionals, including programmers and system designers. This shortage was also significantly increasing the labor costs within this industry.

Louis V. Gerstner, Jr., chairman and CEO of IBM, had driven IBM to follow an overall strategic focus to maintain a superior standing in the computer industry (hardware, software, services, and financing). However, as IBM entered the twenty-first century a smaller percentage of its customers was expected to buy an item with "IBM" stamped on it. Gerstner made this clear in a statement from late 1999 (IBM, 2001b):

> Sometime within the next five years, more than half of our revenues and workforce will come from services. This will mean that, very soon, revered IBM brand attributes like quality, reliability and innovation will primarily be descriptors of IBM people—their knowledge, ideas and behavior—just as today they describe IBM ThinkPads, servers and software.

The future of IBM was expected to be determined by its effectiveness in competing in the rapidly growing and highly competitive computer services industry, specifically in the professional computer services segment. The overall computer services industry is a segment of the computer industry. The computer industry is comprised primarily of hardware, software, and services.

In light of IGS's declining financials and its overall importance to the future success of the IBM Corporation, Gerstner was asking his IGS executive management team to consider changing the way IGS was doing business. IGS's immediate task was to make several strategic decisions in the areas of target customers, services to be offered, geographic market expansion, and changes to its management system to take advantage of the industry trends, and to attract and retain skilled resources. These and other specific strategic questions needed answering if IBM Global Services was to differentiate itself from its competition and so achieve a winning edge over competitors within intensively competitive, rapidly changing immediate, intermediate, and long-term time frames.

Computer Services Industry

The segment of focus, computer services, can be divided into three main categories: processing services, network services, and professional computer services, as shown in Figure 2.

Computer services firms typically enter long-term relationships with their customers. This is true of all three segments (professional computer, processing, and network services). These firms do so by signing contracts that specify the amount of time the designated services are to be provided and the monetary value of the services. Revenues derived from multiyear contracts can be accurately predicted by the computer services vendor and by financial analysts. Some computer services firms do business through annual or other short-term contracts that are renewed at expiration with great predictability. Computer services vendors undertake efforts to increase their retention rates, or percentage of contract renewals, which usually run well over 90 percent (U.S. Business Reporter, 2001a).

With a solid knowledge of revenues under multiyear contracts and past retention rates for contracts coming up for renewal, computer services firms can predict with a high degree of confidence the amount of revenues that they'll earn in a set time period. Based on these accurate revenue assessments, computer services companies can set and manage their expenses at the levels necessary to earn the required

FIGURE 2

The Computer Services Industry

return in each period. Rarely do computer services vendors post results that are materially different from those expected by the company or stock analysts.

According to Standard and Poor's Industry Survey, the computer services industry had experienced a prolonged period of strong growth, which was expected to continue into 2001 and beyond. Spending on computer services was forecasted to rise about 11 percent in 2001, to an estimated $429.9 billion. This figure was in addition to the 11 percent growth in 2000, when sales reached an estimated $387.5 billion (Standard and Poor's Industry Survey, 2001a).

A large percentage of growth in 2000 came in the second half of the year. This concentration reflected the year's having gotten off to a slow start, due to the lack of any year 2000 (Y2K) impact and a corresponding shortfall in spending, as well as a delay in spending by IT managers (Rosen, 2001). In 1999, the sector total of $349 billion represented 13 percent growth over 1998 (Standard & Poor's Industry Survey, 2001b).

According to Standard and Poor's Industry Survey, the global computer services industry would continue growing at a compound annual rate of 11 percent through 2004. The United States accounted for about 46 percent of the worldwide market for computer services in 1999, a percentage that was expected to remain steady over the next several years. The overall computer services business is a broad-based industry and is highly fragmented, with the ten largest firms accounting for about 33 percent of total worldwide services revenues (Standard & Poor's Industry Survey, 2001c).

According to the U.S. Department of Labor, 1.96 million people were employed in the computer and data processing services industry at the end of October 2000, a rise of 6.5 percent from the 1.84 million employed at the end of 1999. The figure in 1999 represented growth of 8.2 percent from the 1.7 million employed at the end of 1998. However, while industry employment has been growing significantly faster than the U.S. economy, a major impediment is a shortage in skilled technology labor (U.S. Business Reporter, 2001b).

The United States is the world's largest producer and consumer of computer products and services. As presented in the U.S. Department of Commerce's Industry Outlook '99, where it referenced a *Datamation* magazine's 1996 survey of computer companies worldwide, this survey indicated that eight of the top ten companies are U.S. companies. The survey results are shown in Figure 3. Within each specific product or service sector, the U.S. portion of leading companies is equally high. Additionally, most of the innovative and fastest growing computer services companies are in the United States. Because of the world dominance of U.S. companies, global trends and issues tend to be the same as those that affect the domestic industry.

One of the most significant trends in the computer services industry was convergence within the overall computer industry. Companies in diverse areas—computer hardware, software, information services, data communications, and telecommunications—were rapidly forming alliances with each other through joint ventures, mergers, and acquisitions. These alliances allowed companies to integrate computer technology products with computer services so that they could offer a greater selection of products and services (services within all three segments). A key objective of these alliances was to remain viable in an increasingly competitive national

FIGURE 3

Top Ten Global Service and Support Suppliers, 1996* (millions of dollars)

Company	Country	Revenues ($)
IBM	United States	22,785
Electronic Data Systems	United States	14,441
Hewlett Packard	United States	9,462
Digital Equipment	United States	5,988
Computer Science	United States	5,400
Accenture (Anderson Consulting)	United States	4,877
Fujitsu	Japan	4,160
Cap Gemini Sogeti	France	4,104
Unisys	United States	3,949
Automatic Data Processing	United States	3,567

*Services and support includes outsourcing, facilities management, systems integration, IT consulting, contract programming, and disaster recovery.

Source: U.S. Department of Commerce's U.S. (2001b), Industry Outlook '99: Information Services, p. 4.

and international marketplace by increasing the company's pool of resources with minimal training expense, increasing revenue growth, and increasing the breadth of service offerings.

In the past, alliances and acquisitions were common among hardware and software companies and hardware and communications equipment companies. In 2001, they were springing up among firms in much more diverse areas: hardware and software, data communications, Internet applications and World Wide Web development, graphics development, networking, and information publishing. Not only were large, well-known companies forming alliances among themselves, they were also forming them with smaller, more obscure companies. Small companies were forming alliances to keep a firm grip on their markets.

These alliances were designed to ensure the participating firm's competitiveness in the marketplace by offering business and residential consumers a broader range of high-quality products and services.

Alliances and acquisitions also gave companies the ability to increase skilled resources without the need for extensive training of existing or newly hired resources. This strategy also offered the opportunity to increase revenues by acquiring the other company's markets and service offerings.

All this was causing a blurring of traditional industry categories in computer information technology and communications. In the past, distinctions among hardware manufacturers, software developers, communication equipment producers, service providers, and telecommunications companies were relatively clear. However, computer companies were diversifying their operations to enter the more lucrative computer services industry. Hewlett-Packard is an example, with its introduction of eservices. Companies were branching out into a wide variety of activities through alliances with or acquisitions of other companies and diversification of their own internally developed services mixes.

Another factor in this increased spending was the trend toward client server architectures and away from traditional mainframe architectures. These factors were providing great opportunities for computer services providers to offer services such as systems integration, consulting, maintenance, outsourcing, and disaster recovery.

As previously stated, the computer services industry can be divided into three main categories: processing services, network services, and professional computer services.

The Processing Services Segment

This segment comprises vendors that process their customers' transactions and data using the vendor-owned computer systems (often with proprietary software). IDC estimates that the sector's revenues were $65.3 billion in 1999, with forecast growth of 6.6 percent in 2000, to $69.6 billion, and 6.5 percent in 2001, to $74.1 billion. IDC expects the sector to grow at about a 6 percent compound annual rate through 2004. The largest independent computer services processing vendor is Automatic Data Processing Inc. (ADP), a major supplier of employer, brokerage, dealer, and claims services, with revenues of $6.3 billion in fiscal 2000 (September) (Standard and Poor's Industry Survey, 2001d).

The outlook was very good for data processing services. Traditional data processing services had strong growth opportunities. These services include data entry, credit card authorization, billing, and payroll processing. They are commonly referred to as back-office functions because they are routine, high-volume, easily automated functions. Many service providers in this area are small companies that target local businesses as their clients. The demand for traditional data processing services is directly related to the strength of the local and national economies.

The Network Services Segment

Network services companies provide a broad range of value-added network services, including electronic interchange services, electronic mail delivery, file transfer, and electronic funds transfer. These firms are increasingly providing more-sophisticated forms of electronic commerce, including services that facilitate sales and customized research over the Internet.

The dominant factor in the growth of network services is the acceptance of the Internet as a business tool. In addition, the growth of the Internet as a means of electronic communications in residential markets will have a positive effect on certain network services companies.

The third segment of the computer services industry is professional computer services, the focus of this case.

The Professional Computer Services Segment

The broad professional services segment, which is the industry's largest, includes services, supported technology platforms, targeted customers, methods of sales and distribution, targeted markets, the competition, and the supportive management system, as shown in Figure 4. The professional computer services segment was expected to experience strong growth, except in certain areas such as custom programming. Growth in this area could level off as a result of the wide selection of sophisticated off-the-shelf hardware and software solutions. Other factors, such as greater hardware compatibility, the efficiencies offered by next-generation languages, and the growing standardization of data types, are contributing trends as well.

Numerous factors were to stimulate growth in this segment overall. Foremost among them are businesses' continued preference for client server architectures, the increased complexity of new information technology products, and the need to integrate them successfully into business operations. Additional factors contributing to the growth of this segment were the many information technology vendors, the convergence of information technology and communications technology products, and the need

FIGURE 4

The Professional Computer Services Industry

to integrate these products efficiently and effectively into business operations.

An additional trend in global professional computer services was the record levels at which foreign businesses have been purchasing computers, software, and data communication equipment. This buying rush had been stimulated in part by reduced tariffs on information technology products in many countries. This international expansion of the information technology infrastructure benefits the companies offering professional computer services by providing greater opportunities for related services.

Another important trend in this segment industry was the growing proportion of spending on professional services relative to spending in the information technology markets overall, both at the national and international levels. Expenditures on software and computer services have increased continuously compared with those on hardware, particularly in countries whose information technology and telecommunications infrastructure are relatively strong and developed. On average, one-fifth of information technology expenditures go to support services such as outsourcing, systems integration, consulting, customer programming, and disaster recovery. That share of spending was becoming the single largest segment of computer information technology spending (Hoovers Online Network, 2001b).

In a related trend, firms that traditionally specialized in computer products are developing new services and generating a higher proportion of their revenues from them. This has occurred as prices for computer components have fallen in a fiercely competitive environment. According to Standard and Poor's, IBM Corporation earned about $18.4 billion, about 24 percent of its revenues, in the twelve months ending in 1997, from computer-related services. And this figure has been steadily increasing each year since. Digital Equipment Corporation derived about 42 percent of its revenues from computer services, an amount totaling $6.2 billion in that same period ending in 1997. The database market leader Oracle Corporation has expanded its consulting business; in this same period, computer services accounted for $3 billion (51 percent) of the company's revenues. Its closest competitor, Sybase Inc., derived about 46 percent of its revenue from consulting, education, and other computer services associated with sales of its core software products (Standard and Poor's Industry Survey, 2001e).

This increase in spending was due to advances in technology and the growing complexity of computer information technology, communication, and telecommunications systems. In addition, maintaining, supporting, and integrating information technology, computer services, and telecommunications in a multivendor environment generate a greater demand for computer services, such as consulting or outsourcing. This was illustrated by an industry survey performed by Computer Science Corporation in which they surveyed information services executives from several countries. Figure 5 presents the top ten issues, many of which offer opportunities for professional computer services; for example, issues 2 and 3 can be addressed through consulting services; issue 4, through systems integration services; issues 6 and 8, through outsourcing services. Another significant trend was the prevalence of acquisitions as companies scrambled to increase their technical skills, increase their service offerings, enter new markets, or establish themselves in new geographic areas.

Perhaps the most important factor in the growth of professional computer services was the Internet. Businesses were attempting to take advantage of the Internet's potential while maintaining security and control over critical business data and information. This created great demand for systems integration and computer consulting to resolve these sometimes divergent goals.

FIGURE 5

Top Information Technology Issues Worldwide*

1. Organizing and utilizing data.
2. Aligning IS and corporate goals.
3. Connecting electronically to customers, suppliers, and/or partners.
4. Integrating systems.
5. Developing an electronic business strategy.
6. Capitalizing on advances in IT.
7. Instituting cross-functional information systems.
8. Cutting IS costs.
9. Using IT for competitive breakthroughs.
10. Improving IS human resources.

*Based on a November 1999 survey of information services executives.

Source: Standard and Poor's Industry Survey (2001f), Computers: Commercial Services, January 25, p. 9.

A troublesome trend in the industry that could slow future growth was the shortage of skilled professionals. This shortage was affecting the availability of programmers and systems designers. This shortage was also significantly increasing the labor costs within this industry. All service providers faced the challenge of attracting and retaining these highly sought-after skills. However, some studies suggested that this shortage was not as serious as it was being portrayed. These studies suggested that there was no shortage and that the industry created its own problems by using overly specific criteria for employment and by failing to make good use of older workers (Dr. Dobb's Journal, 2000).

Services The services offered in the professional computer services segment are consulting, custom programming, systems integration, and outsourcing. These services are applied across multiple technology platforms, which will be discussed later. The greatest opportunities were available in consulting, systems integration, and outsourcing. These areas had enjoyed the most significant growth and, as previously stated, this trend would continue because of the continued complexity of information technology.

Consulting. Computer consulting firms work with corporations to create and implement strategies to cope with the most complex business problems. Consultants combine their industry specific experience with technology expertise to help clients improve overall performance and competitiveness. These firms address a client's issues by assessing and defining long-term information technology (IT) systems management strategy, designing administrative processes and selecting tools to manage systems, and creating an organizational structure that supports ongoing evaluation of system performance against dynamic business needs.

Many of the same factors driving demand for other technology services are driving demand for consulting services. In the private sector, companies are struggling to deal with continual changes in the regulatory environment, increased global competition, postmerger integration issues, industry consolidation, the new digital economy, and growth strategies. This expected growth is presented in Figure 6.

In the public sector, pressure from taxpayers constantly requires governments to do more with less. The same pressures exist in the private sector as well. To compete more effectively, companies need to look for ways to expand revenues, cut costs, operate more efficiently, manage risk more effectively, and improve their customer service. Consulting organizations help their clients manage these major issues. These services are also crucial for a government agency or company seeking to pursue an Internet strategy.

The keys to success in the area of consulting are offering a wide range of consulting services, including both business and information technology services. Both require business and technical expertise because customers are taking a new look at how business and IT service help them achieve success. These two areas (business and technology) are now tightly integrated. It is equally important to have highly skilled consulting resources. These resources need to have strong consulting skills, technology, and industry knowledge and expertise.

FIGURE 6

Worldwide Consulting Services (millions of dollars)

	1998	1999	2000	2003*	Annual Percentage Growth 1998–2003
Business consulting	6,674	8,118	9,856	17,850	21.7
IT consulting	22,763	26,551	30,887	49,675	16.9
Total	29,437	34,669	40,743	67,525	18.1

*Forecast.

Source: Standard and Poor's Industry Survey (2001g), Computers: Commercial Services, January 25, p. 7.

Custom Programming. Professional services firms involved in custom programming provide clients with programmers on a temporary, per diem basis. Such firms are known as body shops. Fees typically correlate with the technical skill required for the project. Customers of professional services firms include organizations whose current personnel lack the needed expertise, as well as firms undertaking projects that require additional staff but not permanent new employees. Demand for professional computer services, such as custom programming, had been aided by a long-standing shortage of computer professionals, including programmers and systems designers, available to work in business and government.

The general demand for software applications had grown substantially faster than the productivity of computer programmers. Although such an environment should be positive for the computer services industry, revenue growth in the custom programming business was actually slowing. The proliferation of prepackaged software and new software application development tools had decreased the demand for custom programming services. In addition, customer attitudes were changing. Customers were now looking for total, integrated solutions from their service providers. They no longer wanted to purchase the hardware, software, and communications equipment and then have to manage the integration themselves through customer programming.

The keys to success in custom programming are computer programming expertise and a wide range of programming knowledge. Through this expertise, a firm can develop a reputation for quality code. Effective maintenance of the application is another key to success and is related to the overall quality of the code. This will ensure the profitability of the business relationship and continue to enhance the reputation of the custom programming provider.

Systems Integration. The systems integrator's role is to produce a unique computer system that meets a client's specific needs. The process is generally executed in various phases of a system's life cycle: planning, design, construction, implementation, and operation. A rapidly growing sector, systems integration owes its popularity to quickly advancing technology, a shortage of technical personnel, and the complexity of automating front-office processes. Its two major markets are government and the commercial market.

The outlook for the commercial systems integration market was bright; it was expected to expand significantly faster than the government market. With such attractive prospects, integration firms that traditionally served government agencies have entered the commercial arena. Hardware vendors and the major accounting firms, as well as dedicated systems integrators, all hoped to ride the wave of growth in commercial systems integration. This growth is illustrated in Figure 7.

The key to success in the area of systems integration is the ability to ascertain a client's requirements and to translate them into a total, end-to-end solution. Success requires a thorough knowledge and ability to execute a system's life cycle: planning, design, construction, implementation, and operation. A clear demonstration of these skills leads to another key to success, a reputation as a quality systems integrator.

FIGURE 7

Worldwide Systems Integration Services (millions of dollars)

	1998	1999	2000	2003*	Annual Percentage Growth 1998–2003
Application development	57,028	67,063	78,009	128,595	17.7
Integration	32,815	39,737	48,329	88,863	22.0
Deployment	21,527	25,320	29,718	45,919	16.4
Total	11,370	132,120	156,056	263,377	18.8

* Forecast.

Source: Standard and Poor's Industry Survey (2001h), Computers: Commercial Services, January 25, p. 7.

Outsourcing. In the computer services industry, outsourcing involves a client organization hiring a computer services firm (or outsourcing vendor) to perform a portion of its data processing and data management tasks. As part of the contract (which is often many years in length), the outsourcing vendor typically agrees to purchase the client's computer center facilities to execute the contract. This includes hiring the customer's data processing employees.

Outsourcing helps relieve companies of the task of managing computing resources and thus allows them to focus on their core business. It furnishes the flexibility needed to expand the customer's data processing capabilities on a seasonal or ongoing basis; adopt new technologies; migrate key applications to new platforms; and quickly develop, test, and deploy new applications. It also provides the technical skill and support to supplement the customer's in-house staff as needed. It matches computing resources to changing business requirements and helps minimize the customer's technology investment by leveraging the vendor's expertise. Outsourcing can also provide the flexibility to adopt and deploy new technology.

The outsourcing market is growing as a viable alternative to in-house information systems management. Major players include Andersen Consulting, Computer Sciences, Electronic Data Systems, and IBM. The widespread success of outsourcing is confirmed by the numerous megacontracts that large corporations from various industries have awarded in recent years. Valued at billions of dollars over several years, these megacontracts involve varied types of services. Growth in this segment is presented in Figure 8.

Outsourcing services can include facilities management (in which the outsourcing vendor operates the client's data center on-site); remote computing (in which processing is done off-site); and communications network management, contract software programming, and software maintenance. Because no company can depend on a single customer, vendors generally manage more than one megacontract at a time.

The key to success in this area is to assume quickly the IT support requirements of the client without disrupting its operations. This requires significant investment in data centers strategically placed within the chosen geographic markets and the ability to provide the required resources and/or absorb the resources (both hardware and human resources) transferred from the client to the vendor's operation. The overall key to success in the area of services is to achieve market presence and share by providing a wide range of service offerings and customizing the service to meet the needs of specific industries or businesses. A provider must also have the ability to offer a continuous flow of new services as IT trends evolve. This adaptability is accomplished through strong research and development. Another key to success is to achieve brand identification through

---

FIGURE 8

Worldwide Outsourcing Services (millions of dollars)

	1998	1999	2000	2003*	Annual Percentage Growth 1998–2003
Operational services	44,521	51,532	59,779	92,929	15.9
Application management	7,858	9,412	11,246	18,929	19.2
Help desk	4,178	4,873	5,696	8,926	16.4
Business continuation	6,197	7,264	8,595	14,666	18.8
Asset management	2,637	3,198	3,919	7,144	22.1
Transaction processing	17,874	19,340	21,221	30,544	11.3
Total	83,265	95,619	110,456	173,138	15.8

*Forecast.

Source: Standard and Poor's Industry Survey (2001i), Computers: Commercial Services, January 25, p. 7.

wide advertising. These services must be based on the current technology platforms being utilized by clients.

Supported Technology Platforms   These services cover all technology platforms: mainframe (enterprise systems), client/server, and ebusiness. Each of these platforms presents opportunities to professional computer services providers.

Mainframe.   The mainframe is the largest computer, a powerhouse with extensive memory and extremely rapid processing power. It is used for very large business, scientific, or military applications where a computer must handle massive amounts of data or many complicated processes. The death of the mainframe was prematurely announced in the late 1980s and early 1990s.

This technology made a resurgence due to its relatively cheap support costs compared to client/server technology, its ability to manage huge amounts of data and databases, and its scalability. IBM, the traditional leader in mainframe technology, led this effort by repositioning the mainframe as an enterprise server, which offered continued opportunity for this technology.

Client/Server.   The client/server platform is a model for computing that splits processing between clients and servers on a network and assigns functions to the machine most able to perform the function. The client is the user's point of entry for the required function and is normally a desktop computer, a workstation, or a laptop computer. The server provides the client with services or application access. The server can be a mainframe or a smaller specialized computer. Even though the relative support cost of client/server technology is high, its flexibility and cost of initial hardware investment is an advantage.

The high total cost of ownership, including initial purchase costs, the cost of hardware and software upgrades, maintenance, technical support, and training, is still relatively high for client/server technology. The advent of network computers is helping to address this issue and is a key component of the emerging "network economy."

Network computing utilizes a simplified desktop device that does not store software programs or permanent data. Users download whatever software or data they need from a central computer over the Internet or an organization's own internal network. The high total cost of ownership for client/server technology makes outsourcing of these services very attractive and offers professional computer service providers a clear opportunity. The emergence of network computing, driving the new network economy, offers significant opportunities for the computer industry overall, but especially for the professional computer services segment. Companies will be looking at computer servers as just another utility, with vast networks delivering applications, data, and computing capabilities to an estimated 1 trillion network-connected devices by the year 2005. Companies will be relying on computer services firms to provide all their IT needs. The network economy was expected to bring into question how companies acquire and manage information technology because the IT infrastructure will be moved out of the corporate data center and onto a global network. Companies will be renting it as a service, with the expectation that it will vastly increase a company's access to computing power, expertise, and innovation.

Ebusiness.   This is a suite of products (hardware, software, and services) that enables an organization to use the Internet and other digital mediums for communication and coordination, and the management of the firm. It is an enabler that extends the reach of existing management. It includes, but is not limited to, e-commerce—the process of buying and selling goods and services electronically and involving transactions using the Internet, networks and other digital technologies.

This technology was emerging as the primary technology platform for the new economy. It was revolutionizing the way business operated and was managed, and was providing professional computer service providers significant opportunity in the areas of outsourcing of web content hosting (a company hosting its web site on a vendor's infrastructure and having the vendor provide total management), consulting (providing a client advice and direction as it staked its claim in the ebusiness marketplace safely, quickly, and profitably), and custom programming (providing application development services that understand, use, and expand a client's intranet, extranet, and messaging potential through complex web application development).

This technology offered great opportunity for professional computer service companies because it was estimated that over 50 percent of large companies and 75 percent of small and medium businesses were still in the early stages of web adoption as of 2000. Early adoption is defined as having only a web presence. These companies were still not leveraging the full power of the Internet for transaction processing and delivery services (ebizchronicle.com, 2001). Therefore, these companies would be looking for various services to enable them to conduct business over the Internet.

The key to success in the technology area is to have excessive knowledge across all technology platforms. Although ebusiness was clearly the industry focus at this time, many companies had significant investment in large mainframes, and the client/server was still the predominant architecture used throughout the industry. The ability to build new solutions based on current and future technology was also crucial, and it required a strong research and development capability.

The Growth and Impact of the Internet   Originally, the Internet was an inexpensive and helpful communication device for academics and defense industry engineers. In the mid 1980s, after the invention of the World Wide Web, it began to be used for a broader purpose. The development in the early 1980s of graphic viewers to interface with the Web was the breakthrough that enabled a larger portion of the computer-using population to embrace the Internet. As the Internet grew through the mid 1990s, online transactions remained in its infancy. As the year 2000 approached, however, the ability to buy and sell electronically was refined, and a fundamental transformation occurred in the United States and the global market place.

Internet use became oriented more toward business needs: advertising, marketing, communication, and (to an extent) sales. The corporate world's use of the Internet has outpaced the earlier uses, such as file access and file transfer. Internet technology is having a profound effect on global trade of software products and on technical, financial, professional, and many other services, but especially computer services.

Customers   The customer base for the computer services industry includes a wide range of organizations. It offers services primarily to corporations, including large enterprises and medium and small businesses, as well as government institutions, and private institutions.

Corporations (Large Enterprises).   These companies (with more than 1,000 employees) offered the professional computer services segment an opportunity to provide its broad range of services to a company's management. The large enterprises had several motivations in seeking professional computer services. These companies clearly saw information technology (IT) as critical to their competitive advantage. Its IT executives were involved in business strategy, and the business executives were involved in IT decisions. These companies are typically not IT innovators, but they are fast followers. They are uncomfortable with the Internet but planned significant use of it. They preferred all-in-one solutions, which were often customized solutions, that bundle computer products and professional computer services. They usually preferred long-term relationships with one or two services providers.

The key to success in attracting and retaining large corporations was the ability of the service provider to provide a customized, all-in-one solution. The service provider needed to have a proven track record in providing services to meet the specific needs of the company's industry. Therefore, a broad range of service offerings, skilled resources with the ability to customize these offerings, and the knowledge of the customer's industry were crucial. These ingredients would enable a service provider to attract and retain large corporate customers because it could meet their specific requirements.

Corporations (Medium and Small).   These companies (with less than 1,000 employees) offer the professional computer services segment a significant opportunity because they are one of the untapped growth areas. However, they are very difficult to market to and support. Therefore, a company that can effectively market to and efficiently support medium and small corporations can have a strategic advantage over the competition.

These companies are comfortable with Internet technology and have widely deployed it. They prefer long-term, trusted advisors, and they often purchase services but are highly price sensitive. They typically cannot and do not meet their IT requirements internally (especially small businesses) and they do not want customized solutions. It is estimated that almost half (45 percent) of future opportunities in professional computer services will come from small and medium businesses. This market, for instance, was growing faster than either large enterprise or consumer markets. In the United States alone, there were 22 million small businesses. They typically have simpler business and IT processes. While they are highly diverse and costly to reach, many, but not all, understand that the Web can enable them to compete with much larger firms on an equal footing because everyone is just a click away on the Web.

The keys to success in attracting and retaining medium and small corporations and businesses is the ability to provide standardized solutions at a competitive price. In addition, because of the challenge of effectively marketing to and supporting this type of customer, a strong direct marketing capability is also crucial.

Government Institutions.   These organizations are as large as, if not larger than, large enterprise corporations and require high maintenance. Many government operations, such as NASA and NATO, are technology oriented and therefore present an opportunity for professional computer services providers. For example, the largest user of system integration services is the U.S. government. However, ongoing pressure to reduce government spending in general and to cut defense budgets in particular has produced uncertainties in this segment. This trend is truly global. But it may also have a reverse effect for some government institutions that seek to reduce their cost through efficiencies brought about by computer innovations. This could lead to an increased demand for professional computer services. The keys to success with government institutions is to have knowledge of and the ability to leverage the bureaucracy found in such organizations.

Nonprofit Organizations.   These organizations may be large or small. They include education providers, community organizations, and religious organizations, to name a few. They offer an opportunity because they require computer service solutions just like any other customer; however, they are typically very price sensitive. The key to success for nonprofit organizations is the ability to provide standardized solutions at the lowest cost possible, as it is for medium and small corporations. Overall keys to success in attracting and retaining customers is

knowing how to service customers through knowledge of their specific industry or business, and by targeting the customer segments with the greatest growth potential.

Sales/Distribution   The sales and distribution strategies within the professional computer services industry utilize professional sales forces, direct marketing, and/or working through business partners.

Professional Sales Force.   Typically professional computer service providers employ trained professionals to sell their services. These resources are usually trained to support a specific industry sector (for example, the manufacturing, financial, or entertainment sector). Industry knowledge is crucial in this services segment. Customers want and expect that their providers know their industry-specific requirements and can translate these requirements into meaningful solutions. They may also have skills for a specific technology or offering. These highly skilled and expensive resources are usually applied to the firm's largest customers. These customers require personalized, face-to-face support, and their contract values can support the cost of the sales force. The key to success for a professional sales force is their ability to market the company's services in the context of the client's industry or business. This requires in-depth industry and technology knowledge.

Direct Marketing.   The underlying logic of direct marketing is making direct contact with customers through alternate media (for example, telephone, telemarketing, mail, or the Internet). Many professional computer services companies employ telemarketing and the Internet to sell to customers, especially small to medium-sized customers.

The key to success with direct marketing as a channel is to ensure that customers have ready access to these sales resources. The ability to reach a person, with limited delay, is a must. Many telemarketing functions offer 24/7 coverage, and many firms are incorporating a "call me" facility from their web sites, which allows a customer to receive a call back within a specified period of time.

Business Partners.   Business partners are independent distributors who enter into agreements with professional computer services providers to market and distribute all or part of the provider's solutions. Business partners develop, market, influence, sell, deliver, and/or support solutions with components (hardware, software, and services) from the service company with whom they have partnered. The key to success with business partners is to develop strong relationships with this alternate channel by providing quality services for them to market and offering incentives to ensure your services are reaching the customers. An overall key to success in the area of sales and distribution is to control cost by applying appropriate sales channels to the customer segment.

Domestic and International Markets   Global demand for professional computer services was growing tremendously. The United States accounted for about 46 percent of the worldwide market for professional computer services in 1999. Significant growth was expected for the United States and for Europe and Asia, especially in the areas of system integration and outsourcing. Many leading professional computer services firms generate up to one-third of their revenue abroad, so their performance can be affected by growth trends in the real gross domestic product (GDP) of foreign economies. IT spending as a percentage of GDP was growing in every country, and was led by English-speaking countries. France and Germany were projected to join these leaders as well. Asia, including China, represented another growth area, even though it was behind the worldwide average for IT spending (Standard & Poor's, 2001j).

The size and growth opportunities available in international markets continue to attract professional computer services companies. With a significant percentage of revenues tied to foreign markets, many firms are subject to foreign currency risk. For U.S.-based firms, overseas sales are translated from local currencies into dollars. A strong dollar hurts reported earnings, while a weak dollar helps. The European and Asian markets represented significant opportunity for professional computer services providers. This was especially true for outsourcing opportunities across all technology platforms, but especially true for ebusiness.

The key to success in this area is to maintain and grow market share by servicing a diverse set of markets (geographic and industry specific). This is accomplished from a geographic perspective by having a presence in each of the major markets. A service provider should have data centers strategically located in the geographic areas to provide outsourcing services.

Management System   The sustained growth of computer services, and in particular, professional computer services, triggered a serious shortage of skilled IT professionals, and this has ignited a war for talent among IT service providers. By 2001, an estimated 800,000 IT positions in the United States and Europe were unfilled for lack of qualified candidates, and fewer college graduates were choosing computer sciences. Professional computer service providers faced the challenge of attracting and retaining these required resources. In an industry where skilled resources are the most important, professional computer services providers must have a management system that attracts and retains their employees by enabling them to realize their business and professional growth potential.

Competition   Each of the various computer services market segments is dominated by several large vendors that use their size, reputation, expertise, and marketing prowess to secure the largest contracts awarded by the largest organizations. These companies are likely to bid successfully on the largest contracts in this industry.

Computer services firms are entrusted to install, manage, or otherwise refine an organization's computer networks or perform crucial processing tasks. Therefore, it's rare for a small, unknown computer services firm with limited operating experience to win business with a Fortune 1000 company or other large organization. Opportunities do exist, however, for smaller vendors to service the computing needs of small office, home office, and personal computing markets, where the jobs are less complex.

Customer demand is attracting increasing competition from traditional services competitors and spawning new competition as services providers seek leadership positions across the full spectrum or in elements of the services value chain. The four prevalent types of competitors are:

- Consultants/systems integrators (like Accenture, formerly Andersen Consulting)
- Full-service providers (such as EDS and CSC)
- Local/niche providers (for example, NTT or ADP)
- Traditional IT providers (like HP or Oracle, Sybase)

In its most recent quarterly report, 4Q 2000, Computer Sciences (CSC) continued showing revenue growth in the 12 percent range. It signed $4.4 billion worth of new contracts in the quarter, with new deals up 45 percent in the first half of its fiscal year. Electronic Data Systems had been harder hit by the Y2K slump, but reported 8 percent growth in its most recent quarter. EDS is starting work on a $6.9 billion deal with the U.S. Navy, signed in the previous quarter. The other services industry news was no news at all: the planned takeover of Pricewaterhouse-Coopers's consulting business by HP was called off, mostly because of HP's inability to pay for the expensive deal with its slumping stock (Hoovers Online Network, 2001).

The following competitive analysis is based on the leader within each of the four types of competitors listed above.

Consultants/Systems Integrators (Accenture).   Accenture (formerly Andersen Consulting, a unit of Andersen Worldwide) is a global management and technology consulting organization generating $8.9 billion in fiscal year 1999, ending December 31, 1999. This represents an 8 percent increase over 1998 results and a 10 percent increase after removing the impact of international exchange rates (Accenture, 2001). The company's mission was to help its clients create the client's future. Accenture was repositioning itself by moving beyond consulting to become a network of businesses that will be a market maker of the new ebusiness economy. To execute this mission, Accenture integrated its various industry specializations with its competencies in strategic services, change management, processes, and technologies to provide a total solution for its customers. To serve its strategic deliverables, the company offers its customers various services addressing supply chain management, electronic commerce, customer relationship management, enterprise business solutions, and knowledge management. The partnership also provides outsourcing of business operations through its business process management operation, along with custom programming and system integration services. Accenture lacked the broad services offerings provided by a full services provider such as IBM Global Services.

After a prolonged two-and-a-half-year struggle, on August 7, 2000, an international arbitrator ruled that the links between accounting firm Arthur Andersen and Andersen Consulting be severed immediately. Under the ruling, the consulting arm lost the right to the Andersen name at the end of the 2000 calendar year, an outcome seen as a victory for the consulting group. Arthur Andersen had claimed that Andersen Consulting should pay a termination fee of $14.5 billion to leave the umbrella organization, a claim that was denied. However, Arthur Andersen retained the right to jointly developed software and gained $1 billion in undistributed funds. The split freed Andersen Consulting from an SEC ruling on conflict of interest between audit and consulting that now limits the kinds of consulting work permitted to Big Five accounting firms. Beginning January 1, 2001, Andersen Consulting operated under its new brand name, Accenture, a combination of "accent" and "future" that means to accelerate, to amplify, and to exceed expectations. This name change triggered a massive advertising campaign to achieve brand identification as a worldwide professional computer services provider.

Accenture announced record global revenue for the fiscal year ending August 31, 2000, a 15.4 percent increase over the previous year. The firm had achieved double-digit growth for the past seven consecutive years and eleven of the past twelve years (Accenture, 2001).

The company was known for the following strengths:

- *Global Presence.* Accenture had grown significantly from its formation in 1989, with $1.6 billion in revenue and 21,400 employees, to become a leading management and technology consulting firm, generating $8.9 billion in revenue in 1999, and employing approximately 65,000 people in forty-eight countries. The company claimed 85 percent of the Fortune 100 global companies as customers, which they market to via dedicated sales/consulting resources known for their skills and industry knowledge, and an Internet presence limited to presenting information only (no transactions), and good relationships with business partners. They had effectively marketed and serviced large, small, and medium businesses by providing all-in-one solutions and, to a limited extent, competitively priced standardized solutions. In the e-commerce area, Accenture claimed their clients include more than half of both the Fortune Global 500 and the Industry Standard 100, representing the most important companies of the Internet economy (Accenture, 2001).

■ *Broad Industry Coverage.* Accenture targeted sixteen industry segments, grouped into five global market units: financial services, products, communications and high tech, resources, and government. The firm's government and communications industries led all its industry sectors with 35 percent and 29 percent growth, respectively. The firm estimated its electronic commerce revenue to $1.5 billion in 1999, triple the firm's $500 million e-commerce revenue in 1998. Its consumer and pharmaceutical products, electronics/high-tech, and insurance industries also showed double-digit growth again in 1999. Financial services, which represented the fastest growing global market in 1998 at 33 percent, exhibited 0 percent growth in 1999 resulting from an 18 percent decline in health services that offset an 11 percent gain in insurance. While the communications and high-tech global market also showed significant growth in 1999 at 29 percent, overall it slowed from a 25 percent increase in 1998, reflecting a drop in media and entertainment revenue growth from 31 percent to 4 percent. Professionals in the company's industry form teams with representatives from the firm's competencies in technology, strategy, change management, and process (Accenture, 2001).

■ *Strong Research and Development (R&D) Effort.* Through R&D activities, Accenture assesses the business impact of new technologies and applies emerging technologies to create innovative business solutions. The company operated the Center for Strategic Technology Research (CSTaR) and conducted leading-edge research on technologies. Specifically, CSTaR continually investigates how the convergence of computing, communication, and content technologies changes how we work and live in the next three to five years.

Despite these strengths, Accenture exhibited some weaknesses and faced some risks:

■ *Change in Top Management.* In September 1999, Andersen Consulting managing partner and CEO George Shaheen resigned his position to join an Internet grocer, Webvan Group, with a compensation package estimated at more than $100 million. Shaheen had served as chief executive since the firm's formation in 1989, overseeing the firm's

increase in revenue from $1.3 billion in 1989 to $8.3 billion in 1998. Several industry analysts questioned Accenture's continued success with the departure of Shaheen. In November 1999, the partners appointed a longtime Andersen Consulting partner, Joe W. Forehand, as the new CEO and managing partner. Forehand, who had held leadership positions in eleven of the sixteen industries served by Andersen Consulting, planned to focus on taking Andersen Consulting to its "next level of marketplace leadership." Forehand faced the challenges of the transformation of Accenture into a profitable ebusiness consulting firm, the branding challenge of a name change, and industrywide alteration of the long-standing billing per-hour formula to a fixed-fee market.

■ *Competitive Market.* Accenture faced an increasingly competitive market as management consultants, systems integrators, and systems vendors continued to expand their operations into related technology consulting and outsourcing operations. In addition, the Big Five accounting firms now also relied on the profitable consulting within the professional computer services area. Smaller niche firms had also started to provide more-focused competition in localized markets. The company faced increased competition in the ebusiness area because many consulting firms established ebusiness strategies. In addition, the company competed with smaller firms, which were perceived as providing leading-edge knowledge while being flexible, and were increasingly attracting large corporate clients as well as experienced consultants. However, Accenture had strong market intelligence due to is worldwide network of consultants and the relationships it had developed as part of the Andersen Worldwide team.

■ *Employee Turnover.* Due to industry growth, Accenture faced a tight market for recruiting and retaining employees. While the company had improved its employee turnover rate somewhat, it still saw top employees in the IT field leaving to join Internet start-ups that offered large compensation packages, typically with significant stock options. IPO slowdowns were expected to temper this trend in 2001 but burnout from long hours and travel did remain issues. This was a sign that Accenture did not have an effective management system to attract and retain skilled resources.

Limited Service Offerings. Accenture had a distinct weakness because it was limited in the services it provided, focusing solely on consulting and systems integration. They did not provide outsourcing services, an area that presented significant opportunity, especially because businesses were implementing ebusiness solutions, and because of the emergence of network computing, both leading to the growth of outsourcing services.

Full Services Providers (EDS).   EDS, which takes credit for pioneering the concept of outsourcing nearly four decades ago, was among a handful of large outsourcers offering an end-to-end services portfolio, including management consulting, ebusiness solutions, business process management, and information solutions. Since entering the arena, EDS claimed to have become a global leader in providing ebusiness and information technology services to 9,000 business (large and small, providing all-in-one and standardized solutions) and government clients in approximately fifty-five countries around the world. EDS markets through a worldwide network with a direct sales force with an industry orientation, maintains a limited Internet presence (no transaction capability), and offers good business partner relationships. The company posted revenues of $18.53 billion in 1999 and signed new contracts in 1999 valued at more than $24.9 billion (EDS, 2001).

The company was known for the following strengths:

Global Presence and Broad Industry Coverage. The company has more than 121,000 employees worldwide and brings deep industry knowledge to solve challenges in a wide variety of industries, including communications, energy, finances, government, health care, manufacturing and retailing, and transportation. Business alliances with industry-leading organizations, including relationships with companies such as WebMethods, SeeBeyond, and SAP America, have been key to EDS's efforts to extend its clients' reach in the marketplace with new services.

Operational Efficiency. The company has recently set in motion changes designed to streamline its operations, including reducing its work force and rearranging its offerings, to make it a leaner, more efficient competitor and to update its image as a lumbering, stodgy behemoth. EDS increased its investment in research and development to enable a continuous flow of new services supporting current and future technologies.

The company was known for the following weakness:

Aggressive Buying of Market Share. Several industry analysts were questioning EDS's strategy for competing against outsourcing leader IBM Global Services. EDS was sacrificing profit margin by aggressively buying market share. The concern was that EDS was paying too much to win outsourcing contracts. EDS was paying several times what would have normally been a competitive rate, an example of which was the 2001 contract to assume management of the Sabre's air-travel infrastructure.

Local/Niche Providers (ADP). With nearly 500,000 clients across multiple industries, ADP was one of the largest companies in the world dedicated to providing computerized transaction processing, data communications, and information services for specific niche markets. However, ADP's services were very narrowly focused, allowing them to focus on the customer segments with the greatest growth potential for ADP's service offerings. The company's services included employer services, such as payroll, payroll tax, and human resource management; brokerage services, such as securities transaction processing and investor communication services; industry specific computing and consulting services for auto and truck dealers; and dealer services, such as computerized auto repair estimating and auto parts availability services. All of ADP's computing services enabled clients to process and/or distribute data (their own, ADP's, or that of third parties) and/or to access and utilize ADP and third-party databases and information through the use of ADP's batch, interactive, and client site systems. These services are marketed through a network of highly skilled direct sales force resources. ADP focused on providing custom and standardized solutions at a competitive price. The core services were supported by consulting services, custom programming, and systems integration. ADP's consultancy was very strong due to its narrow focus, which allowed for strong industry and technical expertise in the areas they serviced.

Employer services, brokerage services, dealer services, and claims services were the company's four largest businesses. Together, they represent over 95 percent of ADP's revenue and are the key strategic elements of the company's future growth. The company was very strong financially, with approximately $6.3 billion in annual revenues, over $4.5 billion in shareholders' equity, over 12 percent growth in revenue and earnings, about 20 percent return on equity, 156 consecutive quarters of record revenues and earnings per share, and 39 consecutive years of double-digit increases in EPS (ADP, 2001).

For fiscal 2000, which ended June 30, 2000, revenues grew 13 percent, to about U.S. $6.3 billion. Prior to nonrecurring charges in 1999, pretax earnings increased 21 percent, and diluted earnings per share increased 16 percent, to $1.31. During fiscal year 1999, the company sold several businesses and decided to leave several other businesses and contracts. It also recorded transaction costs and other adjustments related to Employer Services's acquisition of Vincam. The combination of these transactions resulted in nonrecurring charges of $0.03 in fiscal year 1999. Fiscal year 2000 was ADP's thirty-ninth consecutive year of double-digit earnings per share growth since becoming a public company in 1961 (ADP, 2001).

Strengths. ADP continued to operate from a position of solid financial results and liquidity. Standard & Poor's includes ADP among only ten companies to which it gives its highest AAA rating. The company remained very strong financially, with more than $6.3 billion in annual revenues, over $4.5 billion in shareholders' equity, over 12 percent growth in revenue and earnings, about 20 percent return on equity, 156 consecutive quarters of record revenues and earnings per share, and 39 consecutive years of double-digit increases in EPS. The market potential for the company was still excellent. Employer Services (ES) was its oldest business and was the leading provider of outsourced payroll and human resources management services. However, very good potential remained in every ES market segment as the outsourcing trend continued to gain momentum. For instance, ADP's business that provided payroll and other services to small and medium businesses in North America had over 370,000 clients, yet this represented only a fraction of the 11 million companies plus 24 million home-based businesses in the U.S. market that could potentially use the company's services. About 60 percent of middle-market companies still had not yet chosen to outsource payroll and human resources management. Also, although the company's National Accounts business in North America had grown to over $800 million annually, the market potential among ADP's existing large employer clients was over $11 billion. ADP did not fully leverage these relationships as a distribution channel.

Weaknesses. ADP had grown essentially through an ongoing strategic program of acquisitions rather than through internal growth. Some industry analysts believed that continued growth through acquisition for the company will become increasingly difficult over time and may ultimately lead to the need for costly restructuring. With the continued growth of other competitive organizations, and the advances made in the various technologies required to support customers in the markets in which ADP served, there was an expected increase in competition for the company to deal with in the future. These factors may, at some point, cause the company to be unable to report the same high levels of continuing growth as it had in the past. For example, increased competitive pressures may ultimately prevent ADP from maintaining its string of 156 consecutive quarters of double-digit earnings per share (EPS) growth. In addition, due to its narrow focus and the targeting of local and niche customers, it was weak in addressing the needs of large corporate customers and did not have or need a large Internet presence.

Traditional IT Providers (Hewlett Packard) Much of chairman, president, and CEO Carly Fiorina's tenure at Hewlett Packard (HP) had been focused on the reorganization of a company plagued by high overhead costs and the inability to respond to market conditions. Through a combination of layoffs, product line reorganizations, and a refocusing on the computer services sector, Fiorina transformed HP into a focused competitor. The company's financial results indicated that Hewlett Packard had some success in this area. After posting weak quarter-over-quarter results during much of 1998 and into 1999, results for the quarter ending June 2000 showed a 16 percent revenue increase (HP, 2001a).

However, during the first quarter of fiscal year 2001, revenue grew only 2 percent to $11.9 billion, from $11.6 billion the previous year. Consequently, HP missed the forecast of $12.4 billion on its top line by 4 percent. HP's earnings per share (EPS) for the first quarter of 2001 were $0.16, compared with $0.40 the previous year. HP's officials blamed a slowdown in the U.S. economy, execution issues, pricing pressure on the PC and printing businesses, and adverse currency effects when explaining why the company missed its forecast. The disparity between the contributions of earnings for each business unit was increasingly steady. Its image and printing segment was of increasing importance to HP. The computing system segment's top line increased 2 percent, representing 40 percent of the total revenue. The third major business division, computer services, posted the highest year-over-year growth rate of 13 percent, and represents 15.5 percent of revenue. However, computer services' operational results declined 19 percent, from $125 million to $101 million, when comparing the first quarter of 2000 to the first quarter of 2001 (HP, 2001b). HP should have been concerned with the fact that they were growing faster in this area with diminishing profitability.

HP credited part of its revenue growth to its eservices strategy, designed to highlight the way HP technology supports the growth of electronic services over the Internet. In general, the company's product strategy essentially utilizes all of the company's products, ranging from inkjet printers and consumer appliances to PCs, workstations, and high-end UNIX servers. This strategy had given Hewlett Packard a focused message that appeared to be winning over some customers. Previously, Hewlett Packard seemed to be outmaneuvered by rivals such as Sun Microsystems and IBM. HP had also implemented an industry orientation to its market strategy, but they were still fundamentally a hardware company. As a hardware company, they had a good ability to build new solutions based on current and future technologies due to their research and development capabilities.

As with all of the competitors within the traditional IT provider category, HP was limited in the range of services it provided. Typically these companies focused on their original core product and wrapped services around that competency. In the case of HP, it was equipment; for Oracle and Sybase, it was software, specifically database management software and services. All were seeking to provide ebusiness support and services but did not have the full range of services as did some of the other categories of competitors. They were weak in the areas of consulting, custom programming, systems integration, and outsourcing.

The Company

Since December 1996, when IBM established IBM Global Services (IGS), IGS had achieved outstanding business results. IBM Global Services had grown its business faster than the industry, and IGS was widely recognized as the largest services company in the world, surpassing EDS, as shown in Figure 9. Previously, ISSC, an IBM subsidiary, had similar results. It was accepted that the success of IBM's services business was a major contributor to IBM's overall business recovery.

IBM Global Services's results in 2000 were not what the company's executives wanted. IGS didn't meet its objectives for the full year or last quarter in

FIGURE 9

Top Five Service Providers in 1999

Company	Type of Services	Revenue (U.S.$ in billions)	Market Share (%)
IBM Global Services	Multisegment*	34.6	8.2
EDS	Multisegment	18.6	4.4
Accenture	Consultancy	10.3	2.5
Computer Sciences Corp.	Multisegment	8.9	2.1
Hewlett Packard	Multisegment	7.9	1.9

*Multisegment = full-service provider (consulting, custom programming, system integration, outsourcing).

Source: IBM (2001c), "Services," **http://www.ibm.com/services/fullservice.html#its**. Accessed: February 19, 2001.

either revenue or pretax income (PTI), and its direct expense grew faster than its revenue. IGS's investment in web hosting was showing promise, with revenue growth of more than 200 percent last year. Web hosting, part of ebusiness services, was a new business and had required significant investment, and it has not yet contributed to gross profit.

In the fourth quarter of 2000, IGS grew 5 percent (12 percent at a constant currency rate), to $9.2 billion, reflecting revenue growth across all services categories. Ebusiness services revenues grew more than 70 percent year over year. Revenue comparisons for IBM Global Services were adversely affected by a year-over-year decline in the Y2K services business and the sale of the IBM Global Network to AT&T in 1999, ending IGS's direct involvement in the network services segment. After adjusting for these factors, IBM Global Services revenues (excluding maintenance) increased 10 percent (17 percent at a constant currency rate) (IBM, 2001d).

IGS had been very successful in increasing its revenue, broadening its range of service offerings, and building its pool of resources through acquisitions and alliances. In the first quarter of 2001, they had acquired Mainspring Corporation, an ebusiness consulting firm, for $80 million; and Informix, a database application and consulting company, for $1 billion. They also entered into strategic alliances with Ariba, a provider of business-to-business (B2B) applications and services, and i2, a supply chain management and ebusiness consulting firm.

In light of the significant opportunities presented by the computer services industry and IBM's desire to transform itself into a service company (both IT and business services) through its IGS business unit, IGS will need to consider changing the way they conduct business. This services orientation will require them to answer the following questions: How can they convert the ebusiness mind share that they have developed to true market share? How will IGS expand its outsourcing service to include the other geographic areas, such as Europe and Asia? How can IGS take advantage of the services opportunities in the small and medium business market segment, and be profitable while doing so? And what management systems investments are necessary to support this business transformation? These and other strategic decisions will have to be made if IBM Global Services is to succeed and win against the competition.

Services

IBM Global Services offers consulting services, custom programming, systems integration, and outsourcing services through three lines of businesses (LOBs). Each line of business is segmented along industry lines, so they have an in-depth understanding of the customer's specific challenges and requirements.

Consulting and Custom Programming   Consulting and custom programming services are offered through IGS's Business Innovation Services (BIS) line of business. Business Innovation Services provides business and industry consulting and custom programming. By combining industry expertise with leading-edge technologies, BIS develops innovative solutions to help its customers solve complex challenges associated with business, such as growing revenue and profit, attracting and retaining customers, reducing costs and time to market in inventory, and enabling new business designs and processes.

Business Innovation Services had a network of worldwide consulting practices staffed with highly trained consultants. These practices had an industry orientation and focused on five main industry sectors: communications, distribution, financial services, industrial, and public. The revenue from the consulting practices was steadily increasing, while the revenue from the custom programming services offered by BIS remained flat year to year.

System Integration   This service is provided through IGS's Integrated Technology Services (ITS) LOB. ITS understands that improving the effectiveness and efficiency of computer systems is vital to business growth. It helps companies gain greater productivity and optimizes return on the companies' computer investments. ITS builds the technical infrastructure that enables new business initiatives and helps customers keep pace with rapidly changing technology. ITS can help assure the continued performance and value of a customer's systems and networks. They assess the customer's systems environment, define and prioritize initiatives for improvement, and provide support and training to the customer's IT department and end users.

IBM Global Services's integrated technology services had a proven track record of helping customers pull all their information technology systems together. ITS ensures the reliability of systems and networks, maximizes IT efficiency and flexibility, secures Internet transactions, provides support and training, and maintains server hardware, software, and networks. ITS experts helped companies worldwide to address the total IT picture, from architecture and proof of concept to network consulting and integration. ITS is very strong in providing true end-to-end solutions.

Outsourcing   This service is provided through IGS's Strategic Outsourcing (SO) LOB. SO understands that gaining a competitive advantage through outsourcing involves evaluating the customer's business strategy and differentiating core from noncore operations. SO provided its customers with a flexible management strategy, immediate technological improvements through world-class skills, infrastructure, and management processes, as well as ongoing, reliable, and secure management of business operations. SO takes over all aspects of running a customer's data center or companywide computer infrastructure.

IGS's strategic outsourcing was the world's largest and most-experienced outsourcing provider, with over 73,000 servers and mainframes under its management in 133 global data centers. Fifteen of these centers were focused exclusively on ebusiness (hosting a customer's Internet and/or intranet sites). Although IGS SO has this extensive global reach, they do not have a significant outsourcing market share in Europe and parts of Asia. When putting together an outsourcing deal, IGS believes it is imperative that they protect the interests of both IGS and the customer. They seek to maintain an acceptable level of profitability while guarding the customer's investment by ensuring IGS's ability to deliver a full range of quality services throughout the life of the contract.

Supported Technology Platforms

IGS, as well as IBM overall, offers solutions across all technology platforms: mainframe, client/server, and ebusiness. IGS had been the industry leaders and innovators in all three areas. IBM demonstrated this commitment to technology leadership and the rapid delivery of customer solutions incorporating this technology innovation through its extensive investment in research and development.

IBM had led all companies in the number of patents issued by the U.S. government patent office during the eight years leading up to 2000. IBM led all companies again in 2000 U.S. patents with 2,886 issued patents. As of 2000, IBM held nearly 34,000 patents worldwide, including about 19,000 in the United Sates. In addition, the company is one of the largest non-European patent holders in Europe and one of the largest non-Japanese patent holders in Japan. IBM's expenses in research and development were $5,151 million in 2000, $5,273 million in 1999, and $5,046 million in 1998. Although all of its major competitors had good R&D capabilities, no one matched IBM's investment or success, as illustrated by the number of patents held worldwide.

IBM was the leading manufacturer of mainframes and has successfully repositioned this technology, once thought to be a dinosaur and a dead-end technology, as an enterprise server and a mass-storage access device. Ebusiness spans many of IGS's offerings and contributed significantly to its performance in 2000. The company's total discrete ebusiness revenue grew more than 70 percent, to approximately $5 billion in 2000. This increase was driven by ebusiness consulting, ebusiness systems integration, and ebusiness hosting services (a form of outsourcing).

IBM had been focusing on the Internet, ebusiness, and the network economy enabling technology for several years. The network economy was defined as the expected shift of computing to the network, which represented the next major opportunity for IGS: the emerging model of delivering technology and services on an as-needed, pay-as-you-go basis. This was the basis for what was being called the future "network economy" or "e-utility." It was expected to drive a new emerging world economy, calling attention to the distinct economic behaviors that result from global interconnection of information systems.

IGS had sold IBM Global Network Services to AT&T, but just the network infrastructure, circuits, and switching equipment. That business was very competitive and required constant capital improvements and investment. IGS retained the centralized computing capability that would be the true driver of this next generation of computing.

Customers

IBM Global Services understands that customers are looking to professional computer services providers to guide them in transforming their businesses through the integration of business and information technology strategies. The customers expect to receive value for the dollars spent on information technology. IGS provides that value by helping customers enhance their global reach, strategy execution, competitive advantage, supplier relationship, and customer loyalty. IGS was achieving this once again through its industry orientation, segmenting its customers not only by size but also by the customer's industry (i.e., retail, manufacturing, transportation, and financial).

IGS's broad range of service offerings, industry orientation, extensive research and development capabilities, and strong market intelligence enables them to provide both customizable, all-in-one solutions for large customers and competitively priced standardized solutions for small and medium business customers. IGS services both large companies and small and medium businesses. However, IGS's services, known for their quality and innovation, were more in line with the needs of large companies because of cost and complexity. Therefore, they were not targeting a customer segment with significant revenue potential. However, there was a renewed emphasis on attracting small and medium businesses by including a small and medium sector to IGS's industry alignment.

Sales/Distribution

IBM, including IGS, was world renowned for its superior sales force. For many years, IBM was symbolized by its highly trained and aggressive sales force, known for their skills and trademark blue suits, white shirts, and wingtip shoes. By the mid 1990s, the company's image had softened and there was a more casual approach to sales to match the changing corporate environment, but IBM was still praised for its superior sales force.

IGS had the ability to call upon a wide network of industry specific sales force experts. These resources were also highly trained to market services across industry sectors. This dedicated sales force was skilled and knowledgeable in specific technologies and offerings. IGS ensured the effectiveness of its sales force by requiring them to be certified in specific technology and industry knowledge. The certification was a combination of internal and external education requirements and the successful certification from outside boards (i.e., Microsoft, CISCO, and the Project Management Institute's certifications).

IBM had a worldwide network of telemarketing centers. These centers were established to market specifically to medium-sized customers offering a limited product line (mid-range and personal systems). This strategy had proven successful in North America, so it was being expanded to all the major geographic areas (Latin America, Europe, and Asia).

IBM, including IGS, was also in the process of reinventing itself as an ebusiness. It was using the Internet to market, sell, and deliver certain products. IBM had successfully launched a business-to-consumer site, a business-to-business web site, and an online technical support site. However, these channels were focusing on particular products (mid-range and personal systems, and software that could be delivered electronically). Services were not being aggressively marketed or delivered through the Internet.

IBM had established a strong Business Partner Program. As of 2001, there were approximately 45,000 business partners comprising 90,000 program and contractual relationships across IBM technologies, products, services, and solutions. IGS understood that these relationships were invaluable in the ongoing creation and delivery of solutions that efficiently address customer requirements and market opportunities such as ebusiness. In 2000, revenue growth through business partners was up 11 percent year to year. Business partners generated nearly 35 percent of IBM's revenue in 2000, compared with 20 percent four years previously. A significant portion of this was in the services area. In 1998, business partners were responsible for more than 60 percent of the revenue derived from the medium and small business market, which, many agreed, was a rich services opportunity.

A major strength of IGS was the skills and expertise of its personnel. This is of paramount importance in a services business where a company's skills and expertise are its products. These skills include specific technology knowledge, but even more important, specific industry knowledge.

Markets

IGS's strength was its global reach, providing a customer with services locally and internationally. IGS could provide services consistently across many countries and could be available in multiple locations under a single contract. IGS is the industry's number 1 worldwide provider of professional computer services, with more than 136,000 employees in 160 countries. IGS markets all its services across these global markets. However, it had not fully leveraged its outsourcing capabilities to foreign markets. This was especially true in Europe and Asia.

A major weakness of IGS, which can also be a strength, was its size. It was often slow to bring new services to market due to the size and complexity of the company and its management system. An example of this slow responsiveness was its introduction of ebusiness colocation facilities. Colocation facilities offered Internet start-ups a low-cost hosting facility where they could manage their own application, providing them with the required flexibility, but they did not have to be concerned with the management of the network, infrastructure, and security. IGS introduced this offering at the end of the dot-com boom, thereby losing out on the explosive growth in this area and then being stuck with expensive data-center floor space.

Management System

For many years, perspective employees saw employment at IBM as a great opportunity. Several surveys had identified IBM as one of the best companies in the area of employee benefits. This distinction had eroded since the 1980s, due in part to the company's financial difficulties in the mid 1980s through the early 1990s. Part of the company's recovery plans included mass layoffs and reduction in benefits. Although these were harsh measures, they were effective. By the mid to late 1990s, IBM (in particular, IGS) was once again an industry leader. Other changes in the corporate culture, due to the hard times of the early 1990s, were a flattening of the management structure and the elimination of corporate bureaucracy, which had previously made the company slow to make decisions. The new, more casual management style was more attractive to the personnel the company was then trying to attract.

However, IGS still had not embraced many of the strategies other consulting and services firms were utilizing for some time. These strategies included aggressive stock option programs covering more than just the company's executive ranks, and attractive signing bonuses. A stock option program is an opportunity for employees to share in the company's success over the long term by establishing a financial link to the shareholder value they work to produce. Stock option and signing bonus programs can deliver a competitive edge in employee recruitment, retention, and motivation. In an industry where knowledge represents a key asset, IGS had to continue to recruit and retain top employees. This was a weakness across the industry due to the shortage of IT professionals.

Looking Toward the Future

IBM Global Services is well positioned in the professional computer services industry; however, the company was worried that this position would erode if it did not take advantage of the existing industry trends when making key strategic decisions. The recent financial performance was disappointing, although the company continued to show growth in this important segment for IBM Corporation.

Gerstner, IBM's CEO, stated that the future of IBM would depend on the performance and growth of services, especially in the area of ebusiness, and the emerging "network economy" or "e-utility" model. This would be accomplished by focusing its resources on expanding services across the entire spectrum of ebusiness solutions, and targeting nontraditional customer segments, markets, and geographic locations.

Key IGS executives were proposing one alternative, which was to concentrate solely on ebusiness service offerings. This would limit its expansion in traditional offerings such as client server and enterprise systems (mainframe). IGS's priorities would be to capture a wide set of service opportunities and to secure ebusiness leadership in the marketplace. They would achieve these goals by aggressively increasing ebusiness service offerings, including ebusiness consulting, ebusiness integration services, and ebusiness outsourcing services, while maintaining traditional services.

This strategy was feasible because the Internet and ebusiness services were viewed as the growth engine for this segment, and IBM already had significant brand recognition in this area. They had coined the term *ebusiness*. IGS could turn this ebusiness mind share into true market share by offering all the necessary services a company needs to be successful in the web-based economy. This targeted focus would not dilute IGS resources across multiple service lines, especially custom application development, which this alternative would abandon. This was supported by the fact that ebusiness revenue grew more than 70 percent, to approximately $5 billion in 2000, with expected strong growth in subsequent years.

This alternative could win against the competition because of IGS's existing reputation as a world leader in professional computer services. In addition, the shift of resources to focus on ebusiness service offerings would assist in addressing the shortage of skilled resources and would offer another advantage over its competition (consultants/system integrators, full service providers, local/niche providers, and traditional IT providers). IGS would be positioned as the leader of ebusiness services, the most rapidly growing segment of services. IGS was better than the competition in several areas. Although all the competition had embraced ebusiness (Accenture in the area of consulting services, EDS in the area of outsourcing, and HP in the area of hardware), none had the capability to provide IGS's broad range of ebusiness services. Plus, by focusing its vast resources solely on ebusiness, IGS could bring solutions to market more rapidly. This strategy also has the potential of laying the foundation for exploiting the emerging network economy or e-utility model. This is the reshaping of the IT infrastructure from one that is largely internally built and managed by a company to one that is built and managed by external service providers for on-demand use by a company. This could truly differentiate IGS from its competition. IGS's ability to market using all three challenges of a dedicated professional sales force, direct marketing, and business partners was another advantage.

A major drawback with this shift away from being a full professional services provider to one focusing solely on ebusiness offerings was that IGS would be losing potential future revenue from traditional professional computer services sources. In addition, customers contracted for other services often contract with their existing service provider as they migrate to ebusiness. A way around these drawbacks would be to ensure that IGS is truly positioned as the world leader in ebusiness, which would be accomplished through a worldwide promotion strategy.

Other IGS executives were proposing another alternative, which was to expand the service offerings to provide a full range of professional services, but with an emphasis on ebusiness, network computing, and the future network economy. IGS would offer consulting, systems integration, and outsourcing to accommodate a client's needs and once again abandon a significant focus on custom application development. This strategy was feasible because the Internet and ebusiness services were viewed as the growth engine for this segment, and IBM already had significant brand recognition in these areas. However, this strategy would not limit the targeted services. IGS would provide a full range of services from the traditional client/server and enterprise systems (mainframes) to the emerging ebusiness and the future network computing. This strategy is feasible because it would continue to attract clients with a broad range of requirements, many of whom have not embraced ebusiness or are at various stages of their migration to ebusiness and still require other services. It is also feasible because of IBM's extensive investment in research and development, which ensures a continuous flow of services needed to support this type of strategy.

This alternative could win against the competition because of IGS's existing reputation as a world leader in professional computer services. IGS's brand recognition and global reach provided them advantages in pursuing these opportunities. IGS's competition (consultants/system integrators, full service providers, local/niche providers, and traditional IT providers) did not have the same name recognition with ebusiness as IGS enjoyed. They all faced the increased demands of their large customers to provide all-in-one solutions and at the same time provide standardized solutions at a competitive price, an area in which IGS held an advantage. IGS was better than the competition in several areas, but especially in the ability to provide a continuous flow of new products and services through their extensive investment in research and development (over $5 billion per year) as compared to the research and development of competitors such as EDS and HP.

A drawback to this strategy is the overextension of the company's resources to attempt to be all things to all clients. The size of the company has been a weakness before; offering too broad a range of services can negatively affect IGS's speed in bringing new services to market. Another drawback of offering such a broad range of services is the cost required to build and maintain the required skills, central delivery centers, facilities, and equipment. Ways around these drawbacks are IBM's continued investment in research and development and a continued evolution of the company's management structure, allowing the large company to have the speed of a smaller firm.

Based on these arguments, it was difficult to decide which alternative to choose, or whether to consider a third alternative. In general, Gerstner and the IGS executive team needed to decide which strategic decisions to implement in many different areas. There were many significant decisions to be made relative to which customers, services, and geographic markets to focus on, to name just a few. IBM Global Services can provide a broad range of service choices for companies of all sizes in many different geographic areas. The challenge is to decide which combination of alternatives will take advantage of industry trends, differentiate them from the competition, and secure the continued growth and success of IBM Global Services.

REFERENCES

Accenture (2001), "About Us," http://www.accenture.com/xd/xd.asp?it=enWeb&xd=aboutus\about_home.xml. Accessed February 21, 2001.

ADP (2001), "About the Company," http://www.adp.com/corporate/about.html. Accessed February 21, 2001.

Dr. Dobb's Journal (2001), http://www.ddj.com/articles/2000/0004/0004k/0004k.htm. Accessed April 1, 2001.

ebizchronicle (2001), http://www.ebizchronicle.com/backgrounders/may/summary.htm. Accessed April 3, 2001.

Hoovers Online Network (2001a), "Computer Services Industry," http://www.hoovers.com/industry/snapshot/0,2204,58,00.html. Accessed February 19, 2001.

Hoovers Online Network (2001b), "Computer Services Industry," http://www.hoovers.com/industry/snapshot/0,2204,58,00.html. Accessed February 19, 2001.

HP (2001a), http://www.hp.com/country/us/eng/companyinfo.htm. Accessed February 22, 2001.

HP (2001b), http://www.hp.com/country/us/eng/companyinfo.htm. Accessed February 22, 2001.

IBM (2001a), "Investor Relations," http://www.ibm.com/Investor. Accessed February 19, 2001.

IBM (2001b), "About the Company," http://www.ibm.com/IBM. Accessed February 19, 2001.

IBM (2001c), "Services," http://www.ibm.com/services/fullservice.html#its. Accessed February 19, 2001.

IBM (2001d), "Worldwide Services," http://www.ibm.com/services/worldwide/. Accessed February 19, 2001.

IBM Annual Report (2001).

Rosen, Cheryl (2001), "The Shrinking IT Budget," *Information Week.Com,* March 5, pp. 22–24.

Standard & Poor's Industry Survey (2001a), Computers: Commercial Services, January 25, p. 6.

Standard & Poor's Industry Survey (2001b), Computers: Commercial Services, January 25, p. 7.

Standard & Poor's Industry Survey (2001c), Computers: Commercial Services, January 25, p. 7.

Standard & Poor's Industry Survey (2001d), Computers: Commercial Services, January 25, p. 15.

Standard & Poor's Industry Survey (2001e), Computers: Commercial Services, January 25, p. 9.

Standard & Poor's Industry Survey (2001f), Computers: Commercial Services, January 25, p. 6.

Standard & Poor's Industry Survey (2001g), Computers: Commercial Services, January 25, p. 7.

Standard & Poor's Industry Survey (2001h), Computers: Commercial Services, January 25, p. 7.

Standard & Poor's Industry Survey (2001i), Computers: Commercial Services, January 25, p. 7.

Standard & Poor's Industry Survey (2001j), Computers: Commercial Services, January 25, p. 7.

U.S. Business Reporter, Industry Overview (2001a), "Computer Services Industry," http://www.activemedia-guide.com/computer_services.htm. Accessed February 19, 2001.

U.S. Business Reporter, Industry Overview (2001b), "Computer Services Industry," http://www.activemedia-guide.com/computer_services.htm. Accessed February 19, 2001.

U.S. Department of Commerce's U.S. (2001a), Industry Outlook '99: Information Services, p. 15.

U.S. Department of Commerce's U.S. (2001b), Industry Outlook '99: Information Services, p. 4.

22

SAP and the Evolving Web Software ERP Market

This case was prepared by Gareth R. Jones, Texas A&M University.

In 1972, after the project they were working on for IBM's German subsidiary was abandoned, five German IBM computer analysts left the company and founded Systems Applications and Products in Data Processing, known today as SAP. These analysts had been involved in the provisional design of a software program that would allow information about cross-functional and cross-divisional financial transactions in a company's value chain to be coordinated and processed centrally—resulting in enormous savings in time and expense. They observed that other software companies were also developing software designed to integrate across value chain activities and subunits. Using borrowed money and equipment, the five analysts worked day and night to create an accounting software platform that could integrate across all the parts of an entire corporation. In 1973, SAP unveiled an instantaneous accounting transaction processing program called R/1, one of the earliest examples of what is now called an enterprise resource planning system (ERPS).

Today, ERP is an industry term for the multi-module applications software that allows a company to manage the set of activities and transactions necessary to manage the business processes for moving a product from the input stage, along the value chain, to the final customer. As such, ERPs can recognize, monitor, measure, and evaluate all the transactions involved in business processes such as product planning, the purchasing of inputs from suppliers, the manufacturing process, inventory and order processing, and customer service itself. Essentially, a fully developed ERP provides a company with a standardized Information Technology (IT) platform that gives complete information about all aspects of its business processes and cost structure across functions and divisions so that it can (1) constantly search for ways to perform these processes more efficiently and lower its cost structure, and (2) allow it to improve and service its products and raise their value to customers. For example, ERPs provide information that allows for the design of products that match customer needs and lead to superior responsiveness to customers.

To give one example, Nestlé installed SAP's newest ERP software across its more than 150 U.S. food divisions in 2001. It thus discovered that each division was paying a different price for the same flavoring, vanilla. The same small set of vanilla suppliers was charging each division as much as they could get, so all divisions paid widely different prices depending on their bargaining power with the supplier. Before the

This case is intended to be used as a basis for class discussion rather than as an illustration of either effective or ineffective handling of the situation. Reprinted by permission of the author.

SAP system was installed, managers had no idea this was happening because their IT system could not compare and measure the same transaction (e.g., purchasing vanilla) across divisions. SAP's standardized cross-company software platform revealed this problem, and hundreds of thousands of dollars in cost savings were achieved by solving this one transaction difficulty alone.

SAP focused its R/1 software on the largest multinational companies with revenues of at least $2.5 billion. Although relatively few in number, these companies, most of which were large manufacturers, stood to gain the most benefit from ERP, and they were willing to pay SAP a premium price for its product. Its focus on this influential niche of companies helped SAP develop a global base of leading companies. Its goal, as it had been from the beginning, was to create the global industry standard for ERP by providing the best business applications software infrastructure.

In its first years, SAP not only developed ERP software, it also used its own internal consultants to install it physically on-site at its customers' corporate IT centers, manufacturing operations, and so on. Determined to increase its customer base quickly, however, SAP switched strategies in the 1980s. It decided to focus primarily on the development of its ERP software and to outsource, to external consultants, more and more of the implementation services needed to install and service its software on-site in a particular company. It formed a series of strategic alliances with major global consulting companies such as IBM, Accenture, and Cap Gemini to install its R/1 system in its growing base of global customers.

ERP instillation is a long and complicated process. A company cannot simply adapt its information systems to fit SAP's software; it must use consultants to rework the way it performs its value chain activities so that its business processes, and the information systems that measure these business processes, became compatible with SAP's software. SAP's ERP system provides a company with the information needed to achieve best industry practices across its operations. The more a particular company wishes to customize the SAP platform to its particular business processes, the more difficult and expensive the implementation process and the harder it becomes to realize the potential gains from cost savings and value added to the product.

SAP's outsourcing consulting strategy allowed it to penetrate global markets quickly and eliminated the huge capital investment needed to provide this service on a global basis. For consulting companies, however, the installation of SAP's software became a major money-spinner, and SAP did not enjoy as much of the huge revenue streams associated with providing computer services, such as the design, installation, and maintenance of an ERP platform on an ongoing basis. It did earn some revenue by training consultants in the intricacies of installing and maintaining SAP's ERP system.

By focusing on ERP software development, SAP did not receive any profits from this highly profitable revenue stream, and made itself dependent on consulting companies that now became the experts in the installation/customization arena. This decision had unfortunate long-term consequences because SAP began to lose firsthand knowledge of its customers' problems and an understanding of the changing needs of its customers, especially when the Internet and cross-company integration became a major competitive factor in the ERP industry. For a company whose goal was to provide a standardized platform across functions and divisions, this outsourcing strategy seemed like a strange choice to many analysts. Perhaps SAP should have expanded its own consulting operations to run parallel with those of external consultants, rather than providing a training service to these consultants to keep them informed about its constantly changing ERP software.

To some degree, its decision to focus on software development and outsource at least 80 percent of installation was a consequence of its German founders' "engineering" mindset. Founded by computer program engineers, SAP's culture was built on values and norms that emphasized technical innovation, and the development of leading-edge ERP software was the key success factor in the industry. SAP poured most of its money into research and development (R&D) to fund projects that would add to its platform's capabilities; consequently, it had much less desire and money to spend on consulting. Essentially, SAP was a product-focused company and believed R&D would produce the technical advances that would be the source of its competitive advantage and allow it to charge its customers a premium price for its ERP platform. By 1988, SAP was spending more than 27 percent of gross sales on R&D.

As SAP's top managers focused on developing its technical competency, however, its marketing and sales competency was ignored because managers believed the ERP platform would sell itself. Many of its internal consultants and training experts began to feel they were second-class citizens, despite the fact that they brought in the business and were responsible for the vital role of maintaining good relationships with SAP's growing customer base. It seemed that the classic problem of managing a growing business from the entrepreneurial to the professional management phase was emerging. SAP's top managers were not experienced business managers who understood the problems of implementing a rapidly growing company's strategy on a global basis; the need to develop a sound corporate infrastructure was being shoved aside.

In 1981, SAP introduced its second-generation ERP software, R/2. Not only did it contain many more value-chain/business process software modules, but it also linked its ERP software to the databases and communication systems used on mainframe computers, thus permitting greater connectivity and ease of use of ERP throughout a company. The R/1 platform had been largely a cross-organizational accounting/financial software module; the new software modules could handle procurement, product development, and inventory and order tracking. Of course, these additional components had to be compatible with each other so that they could be seamlessly integrated together on-site, at a customer's operations. SAP did not develop its own database management software package; its system was designed to be compatible with Oracle's database management software, the global leader in this segment of the software industry. Once again, this was to have repercussions later, when Oracle began to develop its own ERP software, essentially moving from database software into ERP development.

As part of its push to make its R/2 software the industry standard, SAP had also been in the process of customizing its basic ERP platform to accommodate the needs of companies in different kinds of industries. The way value chain activities and business processes are performed differs from industry to industry because of differences in the manufacturing processes and other factors. ERP software solutions must be customized by industry to perform most effectively. Its push to become the ERP leader across industries, across all large global companies, and across all value chain business processes required a huge R&D investment. In 1988, the company went public on the Frankfurt stock exchange to raise the necessary cash. By 1990, with its well-received multi-lingual software, SAP had emerged as one of the leading providers of business applications software, and its market capitalization was soaring. SAP began to dominate ERP software sales in the high-tech and electronics, engineering and construction, consumer products, chemical, and retail industries. Its product was increasingly being recognized as superior to the other ERP software being developed by companies such as PeopleSoft, S. D. Edwards, and Oracle. One reason for SAP's increasing competitive advantage was that it could offer a broad, standardized, state-of-the-art solution to many companies' business process problems, one that spanned a wide variety of value chain activities spread around the globe. By contrast, its competitors, like PeopleSoft, offered more-focused solutions aimed at one business process, such as human resources management.

SAP Introduces the R/3 Solution

SAP's continuing massive investment in developing new ERP software resulted in the introduction of its R/3, or third-generation, ERP solution in 1992. Essentially, the R/3 platform expanded on its previous solutions; it offered seamless, real-time integration for over 80 percent of a company's business processes. It had also embedded in the platform hundreds and then thousands of industry best practice solutions, or templates, that customers could use to improve their operations and processes. The R/3 system was initially composed of seven different modules corresponding to the most common business processes. Those modules are production planning, materials management, financial accounting, asset management, human resources management, project systems, and sales and distribution.

R/3 was designed to meet the diverse demands of its previous global clients. It could operate in multiple languages and convert exchange rates, and so on, on a real-time basis. SAP, recognizing the huge potential revenues to be earned from smaller business customers, ensured that R/3 could now also be configured for smaller customers and be customized to suit the needs of a broader range of industries. Furthermore, SAP designed R/3 to be "open architecturally," meaning that it could operate with whatever kind of computer hardware or software (the legacy system) that a particular company was presently using. Finally, in response to customer concerns that SAP's standardized system meant huge implementation problems in changing their business processes to match SAP's standardized solution, SAP introduced some limited customization opportunity into its software. Using specialized software from other companies, SAP claimed that up to 20 percent of R/3 could now be customized to work with the company's existing operating methods and thus would reduce the problems of learning and implementing the new system. However, the costs of doing this were extremely high and became a huge generator of fees for consulting companies. SAP used a variable-fee licensing system for its R/3 system; the cost to the customer was based on the number of users within a company, on the number of different R/3 modules that were installed, and on the degree to which users utilized these modules in the business planning process.

SAP's R/3 far outperformed its competitors' products in a technical sense and once again allowed it to charge a premium price for its new software. Believing that competitors would take at least two years to catch up, SAP's goal was to get its current customers to switch to its new product and then it could rapidly build its customer base to penetrate the growing ERP market. In doing so, it was also seeking to establish R/3 as the new ERP market standard and lock in customers before competitors could offer a viable alternative. This strategy was vital to its future success because, given the way an ERP system changes the nature of a customer's business processes once it is installed and running, there are high switching costs involved in moving to another ERP product, costs that customers want to avoid.

R/3's growing popularity led SAP to decentralize more and more control of the marketing, sale, and installation of its software on a global basis to its foreign subsidiaries. While its R&D and software development remained centralized in Germany, it began to open wholly owned subsidiaries in most major country markets. By 1995, it had eighteen national subsidiaries; today, it has over fifty. In 1995, SAP established a U.S. subsidiary to drive sales in the huge U.S. market. Its German top managers set the subsidiary a goal of achieving $1 billion in revenues within five years. To implement this aggressive growth strategy, and given that R/3 software needs to be installed and customized to suit the needs of particular companies and industries, several different regional SAP divisions were created to manage the needs of companies and industries in different U.S. regions. Also, the regional divisions were responsible for training an army of consultants, both internal and external, from companies such as Accenture, on how to install and customize the R/3 software. For every internal lead SAP consultant, there were soon about nine to ten external consultants working with SAP's customers to install and modify the software.

The problems with a policy of decentralization soon caught up with SAP, however. Because SAP was growing so fast and there was so much demand for its product, it was hard to provide the thorough training consultants needed to perform the installation of its software. Once SAP had trained an internal consultant, that consultant would sometimes leave to join the company for which he or she was performing the work or even to start an industry-specific SAP consulting practice, with the result that SAP's customers' needs were being poorly served. Since the large external consulting companies made their money based on the time it took their consultants to install a particular SAP system, some customers were complaining that consultants were deliberately taking too long to implement the new software to maximize their earnings, and were even pushing inappropriate or unnecessary R/3 modules.

The word started to circulate that SAP's software was both difficult and expensive to implement, which hurt its reputation and sales. Some companies had problems implementing the R/3 software; for example, Chevron spent over $100 million and two years installing and getting its R/3 system operating effectively. In one well-publicized case, Foxmeyer Drug blamed SAP software for the supply chain problems that led to its bankruptcy. The firm's major creditors sued SAP in court, alleging that the company had promised R/3 would do more than it could. SAP responded that the problem was not the software but the way the company had tried to implement it, but SAP's reputation was harmed nevertheless.

SAP's policy of decentralization was also somewhat paradoxical because the company's mission was to supply software that linked functions and divisions rather than separated them, and the characteristic problems of too much decentralization of authority soon became evident throughout SAP. In its U.S. subsidiary, each regional SAP division started developing its own procedures for pricing SAP software, offering discounts, dealing with customer complaints, and even rewarding its employees and consultants. There was a total lack of standardization and integration inside SAP America and indeed between SAP's many foreign subsidiaries and their headquarters in Germany. This meant that little learning was taking place between divisions or consultants, there was no monitoring or coordination mechanism in place to share SAP's *own* best practices between its consultants and divisions, and organizing by region in the United States was doing little to build core competences. For example, analysts were asking, If R/3 has to be customized to suit the needs of a particular industry, why didn't SAP use a market structure and divide its activities by the needs of customers based in different industries? These problems slowed down the process of implementing SAP software and prevented quick and effective responses to the needs of potential customers.

SAP's R/3 was also criticized as being too standardized because it forced all companies to adapt to what SAP had decided were best industry practices. When consultants reconfigured the software to suit a particular company's needs, this process often took a long time and sometimes the system did not perform as well as had been expected. Many companies felt that the software should be configured to suit their business processes and not the other way around, but again SAP argued that such a setup would not lead to an optimal outcome. For example, SAP's retail R/3 system could not handle Home Depot's policy of allowing each of its stores to order directly from suppliers, based upon centrally negotiated contracts between Home Depot and those suppliers. SAP's customers also found that supporting their new ERP platform was expensive and that ongoing support cost three to five times as much as the actual purchase of the software, although the benefits they received from its R/3 system usually exceeded these costs substantially.

The Changing Industry Environment

Although the United States had become SAP's biggest market, the explosive growth in demand for SAP's software had begun to slacken by 1995. Competitors such as Oracle, Baan, PeopleSoft, and Marcum were catching up technically, often because they were focusing their resources on the needs of one or a few industries or on a particular kind of ERP module (for example, PeopleSoft's focus on the HRM module). Indeed SAP had to play catch-up in the HRM area and develop its own to offer a full suite of integrated business solutions. Oracle, the second largest software maker after Microsoft, was becoming a particular threat as it expanded its ERP offerings outward from its leading database knowledge systems and began to offer more and more of an Internet-based ERP platform. As new aggressive competitors emerged and changed the environment, SAP found it needed to change as well.

Competitors were increasing their market share by exploiting weaknesses in SAP's software. They began to offer SAP's existing and potential customers ERP systems that could be customized more easily to their situation; systems that were less expensive than SAP's, which still were charged at a premium price; or systems that offered less expensive module options. SAP's managers were forced to reevaluate their business model, and their strategies and the ways in which they implemented them.

New Implementation Problems

To a large degree, SAP's decision to decentralize control of its marketing, sales, and installation to its subsidiaries was due to the way the company had operated from its beginnings. Its German founders had emphasized the importance of excellence in innovation as the root value of its culture, and SAP's culture was often described as "organized chaos." Its top managers had operated from the beginning by creating as flat a hierarchy as possible to create an internal environment where people could take risks and try new ideas of their own choosing. If mistakes occurred or projects didn't work out, employees were given the freedom to try a different approach. Hard work, teamwork, openness, and speed were the norms of their culture. Required meetings were rare and offices were frequently empty because most of the employees were concentrating on research and development. The pressure was on software developers to create superior products. In fact, the company was proud of the fact that it was product driven, not service oriented. It wanted to be the world's leading innovator of software, not a service company that installed it.

Increasing competition led SAP's managers to realize that they were not capitalizing on its main strength—its human resources. In 1997, it established a human resources management (HRM) department and gave it the responsibility to build a more formal organizational structure. Previously it had outsourced its own HRM. HRM managers started to develop job descriptions and job titles, and put in place a career structure that would motivate employees and keep them loyal to the company. They also put in place a reward system, which included stock options, to increase the loyalty of their technicians, who were being attracted away by competitors or were starting their own businesses because SAP did not then offer a future: a career path. For example, SAP sued Siebel Systems, a niche rival in the customer relationship software business, in 2000 for enticing twelve of its senior employees, who it said took trade secrets with them. SAP's top managers realized that they had to plan long term, and that innovation by itself was not enough to make SAP a dominant global company with a sustainable competitive advantage.

At the same time that it started to operate more formally, it also became more centralized to encourage organizational learning and to promote the sharing of its own best implementation practices across divisions and subsidiaries. Its goal was to standardize the way each subsidiary or division operated across the company, thus making it easier to transfer people and knowledge where they were needed most. Not only would this facilitate cooperation, it would also reduce overhead costs, which were spiraling because of the need to recruit trained personnel as the company grew quickly and the need to alter and adapt its software to suit changing industry conditions. For example, increasing customer demands for additional customization of its software made it imperative that different teams of engineers pool their knowledge to reduce development costs, and that consultants should not only share their best practices but also cooperate with engineers so that the latter could understand the problems facing customers in the field.

The need to adopt a more standardized and hierarchical approach was also being driven by SAP's growing recognition that it needed more of the stream of income it could get from both the training and installation sector of the software business. It began to increase the number of its consultants. By having them work with its software developers, they became the acknowledged experts and leaders when it came to specific software installations and could command a high price. SAP also developed a large global training function to provide the extensive ERP training that consultants needed and charged both individuals and consulting companies high fees for attending these courses so that they would be able to work with the SAP platform. SAP's U.S. subsidiary also moved from a regional to a more market-based focus by re-aligning its divisions, not by geography, but by their focus on a particular sector or industry, for example, chemicals, electronics, pharmaceuticals, consumer products, and engineering.

Once again, however, the lines of authority between the new industry divisions and the software development, sales, installation, and training functions were not worked out well enough and the hoped-for gains from increased coordination and cooperation were slow to be realized. Globally too, SAP was still highly decentralized and remained a product-focused company, thus allowing its subsidiaries to form their own sales, training, and installation policies. Its subsidiaries continued to form strategic alliances with global consulting companies, allowing them to obtain the majority of revenues from servicing SAP's growing base of R/3 installations. SAP's top managers, with their engineering mindset, did not appreciate the difficulties involved in changing a company's structure and culture, either at the subsidiary or the global level. They were disappointed in the slow pace of change because their cost structure remained high, although their revenues were increasing.

New Strategic Problems

By the mid 1990s, despite its problems in implementing its strategy, SAP was the clear market leader in the ERP software industry and the fourth largest global software company because of its recognized competencies in the production of state-of-the-art ERP software. Several emerging problems posed major threats to its business model, however. First, it was becoming increasingly obvious that the development of the Internet and broadband technology would become important forces in shaping a company's business model and processes in the future. SAP's R/3 systems were specifically designed to integrate information about all of a company's value chain activities, across its functions and divisions, and to provide real-time feedback on its ongoing performance.

However, ERP systems focused principally on a company's internal business processes; they were not designed to focus and provide feedback on cross-company and industry-level transactions and processes on a real-time basis. The Internet was changing the way in which companies viewed their boundaries; the emergence of global ecommerce and online cross-company transactions was changing the nature of a company's business processes both at the input and output sides.

At the input side, the Internet was changing the way a company managed its relationships with its parts and raw materials suppliers. Internet-based commerce offered the opportunity of locating new, low-cost suppliers. Developing web software was also making it much easier for a company to cooperate and work with suppliers and manufacturing companies and to outsource activities to specialists who could perform the activities at lower cost. A company that previously made its own inputs or manufactured its own products could now outsource these value chain activities, which changed the nature of the ERP systems it needed to manage such transactions. In general, the changing nature of transactions across the company's boundaries could affect its ERP system in thousands of ways. Companies like Commerce One and Ariba, which offered this supply chain management (SCM) software, were growing rapidly and posing a major threat to SAP's "closed" ERP software.

At the output side, the emergence of the Internet also radically altered the relationship between a company and its customers. Not only did the Internet make possible new ways to sell to wholesalers, its largest customers, or directly to individual customers, it also changed the whole nature of the company–customer interface. For example, using new customer relationship management (CRM) software from software developers like Siebel systems, a company could offer its customers access to much more information about its products so that customers could make more-informed purchase decisions. A company could also understand customers' changing needs so it could develop improved or advanced products to meet those needs; and a company could offer a whole new way to manage after-sales service and help solve customers' problems with learning about, operating, and even repairing their new purchases. The CRM market was starting to boom.

In essence the Internet was changing both industry- and company-level business processes and pro-

viding companies and whole industries with many more avenues for altering their business processes at a company or industry level, so that they could lower their cost structure or increasingly differentiate their products. Clearly, the hundreds of industry best practices that SAP had embedded in its R/3 software would become outdated and redundant as e-commerce increased in scope and depth and offered improved industry solutions. SAP's R/3 system would become a dinosaur within a decade unless it could move quickly to develop or obtain competencies in the software skills needed to develop web-based software.

These developments posed a severe shock to SAP's management, who had been proud of the fact that, until now, SAP had developed all its software internally. They were not alone in their predicament. The largest software companies, Microsoft and Oracle, had been caught unaware by the quickly growing implications of web-based computing. The introduction of Netscape's web browser had led to a collapse in Microsoft's stock price because investors saw web-based computing, not PC-based computing, as the choice of the future. SAP's stock price also began to reflect the beliefs of many people that expensive, rigid, standardized ERP systems would not become the software choice as the Web developed. One source of SAP's competitive advantage was based on the high switching costs of moving from one ERP platform to another. However, if new web-based platforms allowed both internal and external integration of a company's business processes, and new platforms could be customized more easily to answer a particular company's needs, these switching costs might disappear. SAP was at a critical point in its development.

The other side of the equation was that the emergence of new web-based software technology allowed hundreds of new software industry start-ups, founded by technical experts equally as qualified as those at SAP and Microsoft, to enter the industry and compete for the wide-open web computing market. The race was on to determine which standards would apply in the new web computing arena and who would control them. The large software makers like Microsoft, Oracle, IBM, SAP, Netscape, Sun Microsystems, and Computer Associates had to decide how to compete in this totally changed industry environment. Most of their customers, companies large and small, were still watching developments before deciding how and where to commit their IT budgets. Hundreds of billions of dollars in future software sales were at stake, and it was not clear which company had the competitive advantage in this changing environment.

Rivalry among major software makers in the new web-based software market became intense. Rivalry between the major players and new players, like Netscape, Siebel Systems, Marcum, I2 Technology, and SSA, also intensified. The major software makers, each of which was a market leader in one or more segments of the software industry, such as SAP in ERP, Microsoft in PC software, and Oracle in database management software, sought to showcase their strengths to make their software compatible with web-based technology. Thus, Microsoft strove to develop its Windows NT network-based platform and its Internet Explorer web browser to compete with Netscape's Internet browser and Sun Microsystems's open-standard Java web software programming language, which was compatible with any company's proprietary software, unlike Microsoft's NT.

SAP also had to deal with competition from large and small software companies that were breaking into the new web-based ERP environment. In 1995, SAP teamed with Microsoft, Netscape, and Sun Microsystems to make its R/3 software Internet-compatible with any of their competing systems. Within one year, it introduced its R/3 Release 3.1 Internet-compatible system, which was most easily configured, however, when using Sun's Java web-programming language. SAP raised new funds on the stock market to undertake new rounds of the huge investment necessary to keep its web-based R/3 system up to date with the dramatic innovations in web software development and to broaden its product range to offer new, continually emerging web-based applications, for example, applications such as the corporate intranets, business-to-business (B2B) and business-to customer (B2C) networks, web site development and hosting, security and systems management, and streaming audio and video teleconferencing.

Because SAP had no developed competency in web software development, its competitors started to catch up. Oracle emerged as its major competitor; it had taken its core database management software used by thousands of large companies and overlaid it with web-based operating and applications software. Oracle could now offer its huge customer base a growing suite of web software, all seamlessly integrated. The suite of software also allowed them to perform Internet-based ERP value chain business processes. While Oracle's system was nowhere near as comprehensive as SAP's R/3 system, it allowed for cross-industry networking at both the input and output sides, it was cheaper and easier to implement quickly, and it was easier to customize to the needs of a particular customer. Oracle began to take market share away from SAP.

New companies like Siebel Systems, Commerce One, Ariba, and Marcum, which began as niche players in some software applications such as SCM, CRM, intranet, or web site development and hosting, also began to build and expand their product offerings so that they now possessed ERP modules that competed with some of SAP's most lucrative R/3 modules. Commerce One and Ariba, for example, emerged as the main players in the rapidly expanding business-to-business (B2B) industry supply chain management market. B2B is an industry-level ERP solution that creates an organized market and thus brings together industry buyers and suppliers electronically and provides the software to write and enforce contracts for the future development and supply of an industry's inputs. Although these niche players could not provide the full range of services that SAP could provide, they became increasingly able to offer attractive alternatives to customers seeking specific aspects of an ERP system. Also, companies like Siebel, Marcum, and I2 claimed that they had the ability to customize their low-price systems, and prices for ERP systems began to fall.

In the new software environment, SAP's large customers started to purchase software on a "best of breed" basis, meaning that customers purchased the best software applications for their specific needs from different, leading-edge companies rather than purchasing all of their software products from one company as a package—such as SAP offered. Sun began to promote a free Java computer language as the industry "open architecture" standard, which meant that, as long as each company used Java to craft their specific web-based software programs, they would all work seamlessly together and there would no longer be an advantage to using a single dominant platform like Microsoft's Windows or SAP's R/3. Sun was and is trying to break Microsoft's hold over the operating system industry standard, Windows. Sun wanted each company's software to succeed because it was "best of breed," not because it locked customers in and created enormous switching costs for them should they contemplate a move to a competitor's product.

All these different factors caused enormous problems for SAP's top managers. What strategies should they use to protect their competitive position? Should they forge ahead with offering their customers a broad, proprietary, web-based ERP solution and try to lock them in and continue to charge a premium price? Should they move to an open standard and make their R/3 ERP Internet-enabled modules compatible with solutions from other companies, and indeed forge alliances with those companies to ensure that their software operated seamlessly together? Since SAP's managers still believed they had the best ERP software and the capabilities to lead in the web software arena, was this the best long-run competitive solution? Should SAP focus on making its ERP software more customizable to its customers' needs and make it easier for them to buy selected modules to reduce the cost of SAP software? This alternative might also make it easier for them to develop ERP modules that could be scaled back to suit the needs of medium and small firms, which increasingly were becoming the targets of its new software competitors. Once these new firms got a toehold in the market, it would then be a matter of time before they improved their products and began to compete for SAP's installed customer base. SAP realized that it had to refocus its business model, especially because rivals were rapidly buying niche players and, at the same time, filling gaps in their product lines to be able to compete with SAP.

Opportunities and threats were emerging from all sides. The question was how to proceed, especially since the various major software companies were all supporting different industry standards to promote their own competitive advantage in the Internet world. Microsoft was fighting to preserve the dominance of its Windows platform from the encroachments made by Sun's Java platform and the free Linux platform, which was being championed by IBM as the operating platform of the future. Indeed, IBM recognized that lucrative revenues could be earned from computer services and consulting and had changed its strategy in the 1990s. No longer was its major focus the development of proprietary software but the design, installation, and servicing of whatever hardware and software system its customers chose to deploy. For IBM, championing and develop-

ing Linux was a way to increase revenues. By 2001, 7 to 10 percent of companies' operating systems were running on the free Linux system. For IBM, however, promoting Linux, as Sun was promoting Java, was also a way to frustrate Microsoft's aims to control the industry standard for personal computing operating software in a web-based software environment.

The mySAP.com Initiative

In 1997, SAP sought a quick fix to its problems by releasing new R/3 solutions for ERP Internet-enabled supply chain management (SCM) and customer relationship management (CRM) solutions, which converted its internal ERP system into an externally based network platform. SCM, now know as the "back end" of the business, integrates the business processes necessary to manage the flow of goods, from the raw material stage to the finished product. SCM programs forecast future needs, and plan and manage a company's operations, especially its manufacturing operations. CRM, known as the "frontend" of the business, provides companies with solutions and support for business processes directed at improving sales, marketing, customer service, and field service operations. CRM programs are rapidly growing in popularity because they lead to better customer retention and satisfaction and higher revenues. In 1998, SAP followed with industry solution maps, business technology maps, and service maps, all of which were aimed at making its R/3 system dynamic and responsive to changes in industry conditions. In 1998, recognizing that its future rested on its ability to protect its share of the U.S. market, it listed itself on the New York Stock Exchange and began to expand the scope of its U.S. operations.

In 1999, however, the full extent of the change in SAP's business model and strategies became clear when it introduced its mySAP.com (mySAP) initiative to gain control of the web-based ERP, SCM, and CRM markets, and to extend its reach into any e-commerce or Internet-based software applications. The mySAP initiative was a comprehensive ebusiness platform designed to help companies collaborate and succeed, regardless of their industry or network environment. It demonstrated several elements of SAP's changing strategic thinking for how to succeed in the 2000s.

First, to meet its customer's needs in a new electronic environment, SAP used the mySAP platform to change itself from a vendor of ERP components to a provider of ebusiness solutions. The platform was to be the online portal through which customers could view and understand the way its Internet-enabled R/3 modules could match their evolving needs. SAP recognized that its customers were increasingly demanding access to networked environments with global connectivity, where decisions could be executed in real time through the Internet. Customers wanted to be able to leverage new ebusiness technologies to improve basic business goals like increasing profitability, improving customer satisfaction, and lowering overhead costs. In addition, customers wanted total solutions that could help them manage their relationships and supply chains.

MySAP was to offer a total solutions ERP package, including SCM and CRM applications, which would be fundamentally different from the company's traditional business application software. SAP's software would no longer force the customer to adapt to SAP's standardized architecture; mySAP software could be adapted to facilitate a company's transition into an ebusiness. In addition, the solution would create value for a company by building on its already developed core competencies; mySAP would help to leverage those core competencies, thus building a company's competitive advantage from within, rather than by creating it solely through the installation of SAP's industry best practices. SAP created a full range of front- and back-end products such as SCM and CRM software, available through its mySAP.com portal, that are specific to different industries and manufacturing technologies. These changes meant that it could compete in niche markets and make it easier to customize a particular application to an individual company's needs.

Second, mySAP provided the platform that would allow SAP's product offerings to expand and broaden over time, an especially important feature because web-based software was evolving into ever more varied applications. SAP was essentially copying other software makers, who were branching out into more segments of the software industry to capitalize on higher growth software segments and to prevent obsolescence should demand for their core software erode because of technological developments. Henceforth, SAP was not offering product-based solutions but customer-based solutions. Its mySAP ebusiness platform solutions are designed to be a scalable and flexible architecture that supports data-bases, applications, operating systems, and hardware platforms from almost every major vendor.

Third, SAP realized that cost was becoming a more important issue because competition from low-cost rivals demonstrated that customers could be persuaded to shift vendors if they were offered good deals. Indeed, major companies like Oracle often offered their software at discount prices or even gave it away free to well-known companies to generate interest and demand for their product. SAP focused on making mySAP more affordable by breaking up its modules and business solutions into smaller, separate products. Customers could now choose which particular solutions best met their specific needs; they no longer had to buy the whole package. At the same time, all mySAP offerings were fully compatible with the total R/3 system so that customers could easily expand their use of SAP's products. SAP was working across its whole product range to make its system easier and cheaper to use. SAP realized that repeat business is much more important than a one-time transaction, so they began to focus on seeking out and developing new, related solutions for their customers to keep them coming back and purchasing more products and upgrades.

Fourth, mySAP was aimed at a wider range of potential customers. By providing a simpler and cheaper version of its application software coupled with the introduction of the many mySAP ebusiness solution packages, SAP broadened its offerings targeted not only to large corporations but also small and medium-sized companies. MySAP allowed SAP to provide a low-cost ERP system that could be scaled down for smaller firms. For example, for small to mid-sized companies that lack the internal resources to maintain their own business applications on-site, mySAP offered hosting for data centers, networks, and applications. Small businesses could benefit greatly from the increased speed of installation and reduced cost possible through outsourcing and by paying a fee to use mySAP in lieu of having to purchase SAP's expensive software modules. SAP also focused on making its R/3 mySAP offerings easier to install and use, and reduced implementation times and consulting costs in turn reduced the costs of supporting the SAP platform for both small and large organizations.

To support its mySAP initiative, SAP had continued to build in-house training and consulting capabilities to increase its share of revenues from the services side of its business. SAP's increasing web software services efforts paid off because the company was now better able to recognize the problems experienced by customers. This result led SAP to recognize both the needs for greater responsiveness to customers and customization of its products to make their installation easier. Its growing customer awareness had also led it to redefine its mission as a developer of business solutions, the approach embedded in mySAP, rather than as a provider of software products.

To improve the cost effectiveness of mySAP installations, SAP sought a better way to manage its relationships with consulting companies. It moved to a parallel sourcing policy, in which several consulting firms competed for a customer's business, and it made sure a SAP consultant was always involved in the installation and service effort to monitor external consultants' performance. This helped keep service costs under control for its customers. Because customer needs changed so quickly in this fast-paced market and SAP continually improved its products with incremental innovations and additional capabilities, it also insisted that consultants undertake continual training to update their skills, training for which it charged high fees. In 2000, SAP adopted a stock option program to retain valuable employees after losing many key employees—programmers and consultants—to competitors.

Fifth, SAP increasingly embraced the concept of open architecture, and its mySAP offerings are compatible with the products of most other software makers. It had already ensured that its mySAP platform worked with operating systems such as Microsoft NT, Sun's Java, and UNIX, for example. Now it focused on ensuring that its products were compatible with emerging web applications software from any major software maker—by 2001 SAP claimed to have over 1,000 partners.

Indeed, strategic alliances and acquisitions became increasingly important parts of its strategy to reduce its cost structure, enhance the functionality of its products, and build its customer base. Because of the sheer size and expense of many web-based software endeavors, intense competition, and the fast-paced dynamics of this industry, SAP's top managers began to realize they could not go it alone and produce everything in-house. SAP's overhead costs had rocketed in the 1990s as it pumped money into building its mySAP initiative. Intense competition seemed to indicate that continuing massive expenditures would be necessary. SAP's stock price had decreased because higher overhead costs meant falling profits despite increasing revenues. SAP had never seemed to be able to enjoy sustained high profitability because changing technology and competition had not allowed it to capitalize on its acknowledged position as the ERP industry leader.

Given existing resource constraints and time pressures and the need to create a more profitable business model, in the 2000s SAP's managers realized that they needed to partner with companies that now dominated in various niches of the software market. By utilizing already developed best of breed software, SAP would not have to deploy the capital necessary if it were to go it alone. In addition, synergies across partner companies might allow future development to be accomplished more efficiently and enable it to bring new mySAP products to the market more quickly.

One example of SAP reaping the benefits of such synergies was its alliance with Commerce One, a leading provider of B2B marketplace software and online procurement applications. The alliance created value for SAP, which obtained the skills of Commerce One's engineers and allowed it to share resources and development costs. In 2001, SAP solidified its alliance with Commerce One by making a $250 million investment in the company, and it launched a U.S. subsidiary, SAPMarkets, to compete in the business-to-business e-commerce services market. In another major alliance, it announced in 2002 that it was joining with IBM to speed the delivery of product life-cycle management (PLM) software and services to its growing base of manufacturing customers. PLM offers an integrated environment that ensures that all people involved in product development, manufacturing, and services have quick and secure access to all shared, current information so that they can plan appropriately on a global level. SAP will incorporate IBM's own industry specific solutions into its mySAP PLM software, and IBM will deliver consulting, integration, and implementation services around mySAP PLM solutions. This is a huge potential market; manufacturing companies have always been the main customer base for SAP's ERP systems.

Not only did SAP form alliances with other companies, it also used acquisitions to drive its entry into new segments of the web software market. For example, SAP acquired Top Tier Software Inc. in 2001 to gain access to its iView technology. This technology allows seamless integration between the web software of different companies and is critical for SAP because it lets customers drag-and-drop and mix information and applications from both SAP and non-SAP platform-based systems, and thus enables the open systems architecture SAP has increasingly supported. Top Tier was also an enterprise portal software maker, and in 2001 SAP teamed up with Yahoo to use these competencies to create a new U.S. subsidiary called SAP Portals, which would deliver state-of-the-art enterprise portal products that would enable people and companies to collaborate effectively and at any time. It also opened SAP hosting to provide hosting and web maintenance services.

By 2002, SAP believed that its partnerships and alliances had maneuvered it into a position of continued market dominance for the twenty-first century. Many of the major vendors of the databases, applications, operating systems, and hardware platforms that mySAP supports were once considered the competition, but the companies were now working together to create value by maximizing the range of web-based products that could be offered to customers through a common interface. MySAP adds value to its competitors products by decreasing the exclusivity between the applications of different companies. In essence, SAP was treating these other products as complementary products, which added to the value of its own, promoted mySAP as the industry standard, and increased its dominance of the ERP web software market.

SAP's managers were shocked when it became clear that Microsoft, also recognizing the enormous potential of web software ERP sales, particularly in the small and medium business segment of the market, might be planning to compete in this market segment in 2002. Microsoft had bought two companies that competed in this segment to bolster its own web software offerings. Also, when Microsoft introduced its new XP operating system in 2001, it had not included a Java applications package to allow web software developers to write ebusiness software that would be compatible with XP, undercutting its rival Sun's attempts to bypass the Window's platform using its Java language. However, this also undercut SAP's open architecture initiatives because many of its mySAP installations were based on Java, not Microsoft's NT platform. SAP's managers saw this move as an attempt by Microsoft to wipe out the competitive advantage SAP had been gaining since the introduction of mySAP in 1999. SAP challenged Microsoft to indicate its support for the Java language. Already under scrutiny and attack by Sun and other software companies for its anticompetitive trade practices, Microsoft seemed to step back when it announced in June 2002 that its next version of XP would contain support for Java-based programming. Clearly, however, an open architecture and industry standard for web-based software are not in Microsoft's interests, especially if word processing and other important office applications become available as part of any e-commerce platform such as mySAP.

Microsoft could well became a formidable potential competitor for SAP because of Microsoft's competencies in a wide area of software products and because it has the resources to develop quickly and easily an ERP system with web-based solutions. In the past, SAP tried to avoid this competition problem by partnering with Microsoft in a wide variety of endeavors and making sure its products were compatible with Microsoft's, thus making their interests mutual rather than divisive. However, if Microsoft sees its Windows platform coming under increasing threat, it could quickly move into SAP's and Oracle's market. The competitive battle over industry standards seems far from over.

The recession that started in 2000 has also increased competition in the ERP industry. SAP and Oracle, in particular, have battled to protect and increase their market share. The huge drop in spending on IT by major companies and the decrease in the number of new customers has hit the industry hard. The stock prices of all these companies have fallen dramatically, with some like I2 Systems, also a provider of SCM solutions, fighting to survive. Competition among software companies has been intense, and customers have taken advantage of this rivalry to demand price discounts from SAP as well as other companies, which hurts revenues and profits. Smaller competitors like I2 and Siebel lowered their prices to the point where they took a loss on a particular sale to gain market share. The weakest companies have been forced to fall back on their main strengths and reduce their range of product offerings. This strategy will help SAP because it has the resources to withstand the current downturn and therefore might emerge stronger as a result.

SAP's number of software installations and customers increased steadily between 1998 and 2002. The number of software installations grew at a faster pace than the number of customers, a characteristic of the lock-in feature of investment in one ERP platform. In 2002, SAP was still the number 1 vendor of standard business applications software, with a worldwide market share of over 30 percent. Oracle was next with a 16 percent share of the market. SAP claimed that it had 10 million users and 50,000 SAP installations in 18,000 companies in 120 countries in 2002, and that half of the world's top 500 companies used its software.

Implementing mySAP

SAP's problems were not just in the strategy area, however. Its mySAP initiative had increased its overhead costs, and it still could not find the appropriate organizational structure to make the best use of its resources and competencies. It continued to search for the right structure for servicing the growing range of its products and the increasing breadth of the companies, in terms of size, industry, and global location, it was now serving.

Recall that in the mid 1990s, SAP had began to centralize authority and control to standardize its own business processes and manage knowledge effectively across organizational subunits. While this reorganization resulted in some benefits, it had the unfortunate result of lengthening the time it took SAP to respond to the fast-changing web software ERP environment. To respond to changing customer needs and the needs for product customization, SAP now moved to decentralize control to programmers and its sales force to manage problems where and when they arose. SAP's managers felt that in an environment where markets are saturated with ERP vendors and where customers want service and systems that are easier to use, it was important to get close to the customer. SAP had now put in place its own applications software for integrating across its operating divisions and subsidiaries, allowing them to share best practices and new developments and thus avoid problems that come with too much decentralization of authority.

To speed the software development process, SAP divided its central German software development group into three teams in 2000. One team works on the development of new products and features, the second refines and updates functions in its existing products, and the third works on making SAP products easier to install. Also, to educate its customers and speed customer acceptance and demand for mySAP, SAP changed its global marketing operations in late 2000. Following its decentralized style, each product group once had its own marketing department that operated separately to market and sell its products. This decentralization had caused major problems because customers didn't understand how the various parts of mySAP fit together. It also wasted resources and slowed the sales effort. Announcing that "SAP had to develop a laserlike focus on marketing," a far cry from its previous focus on its engineering competency, SAP's top managers centralized control of marketing at its U.S. subsidiary and put control of all global marketing into the hands of one executive, who was now responsible for coordinating market efforts across all mySAP product groups and all world regions.

Soon after, in 2001, once again to speed up the implementation of the mySAP initiative, SAP folded the SAPMarkets and SAP Portals subsidiaries into SAP's other operations and split the SAP product line into distinct but related mySAP product groups, each of which was to be treated as an independent profit center, with the head of each product group reporting directly to SAP's chairperson. The type of web software application or ERP industry solution being offered to the customer differentiates each product group (see Exhibit 1).

SAP also changed the way its three German engineering groups worked with the different mySAP products groups. Henceforth, a significant part of the engineering development effort would take place inside each mySAP product group so that program engineers, who write and improve the specific new mySAP software applications, were joined with the sales force for that group. Now they could integrate their activities and provide better customized solutions. The software engineers at its German headquarters, besides conducting basic R&D, would be responsible for coordinating the efforts of the different mySAP engineering groups, sharing new software developments among groups, providing expert solutions, and ensuring all the different mySAP applications worked together seamlessly.

Each mySAP product group is now composed of a collection of cross-functional product development teams focused on their target markets. Teams are

EXHIBIT 1

mySAP.com Product Groups

mySAP.com Solutions	
▪ Industry solutions	▪ mySAP exchanges
▪ Solutions for small and mid-sized businesses	▪ mySAP business intelligence
▪ mySAP enterprise portals	▪ mySAP financials
▪ mySAP supply chain management	▪ mySAP human resources
▪ mySAP customer relationship management	▪ mySAP mobile business
▪ mySAP supplier relationship management	▪ mySAP hosted solutions
▪ mySAP product life cycle management	▪ mySAP technology

mySAP.com Industry Solutions	
▪ mySAP aerospace and defense	▪ mySAP media
▪ mySAP automotive	▪ mySAP mill products
▪ mySAP banking	▪ mySAP mining
▪ mySAP chemicals	▪ mySAP oil and gas
▪ mySAP consumer products	▪ mySAP pharmaceuticals
▪ mySAP engineering and construction	▪ mySAP public sector
▪ mySAP financial service provider	▪ mySAP retail
▪ mySAP health care	▪ mySAP service providers
▪ mySAP higher education and research	▪ mySAP telecommunications
▪ mySAP high tech	▪ mySAP utilities
▪ mySAP insurance	

given incentives to meet their specific sales growth targets and to increase operating effectiveness, including reducing the length of installation time. The purposes of the new product group/team approach was to decentralize control, make SAP more responsive to the needs of customers and to changing technical developments, and still give SAP centralized control of development efforts. To ensure that its broadening range of software was customizable to the needs of different kinds of companies and industries, SAP enlisted some of its key customers as "development partners" and as members of these teams. Customers from large, mid-sized, and small companies were used to test new concepts and ideas. Within every mySAP product group, cross-functional teams focused on customizing its products for specific customers or industries. SAP opened the development process to its competitors and allowed them to work with SAP teams to make their products compatible with SAP's products and with the computer

platforms or legacy systems already installed in their customers' operations. Through this implementation approach, SAP was striving to pull its actual and potential customers and competitors toward the single, open standard of SAP. The company also instituted stricter training and certification methods for consultants to improve the level of quality control and protect its reputation.

At the global level, SAP grouped is national subsidiaries into three main world regions: Europe, the Americas, and Asia/Pacific. This grouping made it easier to transfer knowledge and information between countries and serve the specific demands of national markets inside each region. Also, this global structure made it easier to manage relationships with consulting companies and to coordinate regional marketing and training efforts, both under the jurisdiction of the centralized marketing and training operations.

Thus, at present SAP operates with a loose form of matrix structure. To increase internal flexibility and responsiveness to customers while at the same time boosting efficiency and market penetration, the world regions, the national subsidiaries, and the sales people and consultants within them constitute one side of the matrix. The centralized engineering, marketing, and training functions and the twenty or so different mySAP product groups compose the other side. The problem facing SAP is to coordinate all these distinct subunits so they will lead to rapid acceptance of SAP's new mySAP platform across all the national markets in which it operates.

In practice, a salesperson in any particular country works directly with a client to determine what type of ERP system he or she needs. Once this system is determined, a project manager from the regional subsidiary or from one of the mySAP groups is appointed to assemble an installation team from members of the different product groups whose expertise is required to implement the new client's system. Given SAP's broad range of evolving products, the matrix structure allows SAP to provide those products that fit the customer's needs in a fast, coordinated way. SAP's policy of decentralizing authority and placing it in the hands of its employees enables the matrix system to work. SAP prides itself on its talented and professional staff who can learn and adapt to many different situations and networks across the globe.

The Future

In April 2002, SAP announced that its revenues had climbed 9.2 percent, but its first-quarter profit fell 40 percent because of a larger-than-expected drop in license revenue from the sale of new software. It seems that many customers have been reluctant to invest in the huge cost of moving to the mySAP system given the recession and continuing market uncertainty. Its rivals have fared worse, however, and SAP announced it had several orders for mySAP in the works, and that the 18,000 companies around the world using its flagship R/3 software would soon move to its new software once their own customers had started to spend more money. In the meantime, SAP announced it would introduce a product called R/3 Enterprise, which would be targeted at customers not yet ready to make the leap to mySAP. R/3 Enterprise is a collection of web software that can be added easily to the R/3 platform to provide a company with the ability to network with other companies and perform many

e-commerce operations. SAP hopes this new software will show its R/3 customers what mySAP can accomplish for them once it is running in their companies. SAP's managers believe the company is poised to jump from being the third largest global software company to being the second, ahead of Oracle, if it can use its mySAP open system architecture to overcome Microsoft's stranglehold on the software market and bypass the powerful Windows standard.

REFERENCES

Boudette, N. E., "E-Business: SAP Boosts Commerce One Stake," *Wall Street Journal,* July 2, 2001, p. B8.

Boudette, N. E., "Germany's SAP Reorganizes Its Marketing, Focuses on Web," *Wall Street Journal,* 2000, August 7, p. A8.

Boudette, N. E., "Results Show SAP Is Waiting to Benefit from Recovery," *Wall Street Journal,* April 19, 2002, p. A16.

"Burger King Corporation Selects SAP to Enable Information Technology Strategy," mySAP.com. Accessed June 25, 2002.

Collett, S., "SAP: Whirlpool's Rush to go Live Led to Shipping Snafus," *www.computerworld,* November 4, 1999.

Conlin, R., "SAP Teams with Yahoo! On Portal Venture," CRMDaily.com, April 4, 2001.

Conlin, R., "SAP Upgrades CRM App, Unveils New Strategy," CRMDaily.com, April 23, 2001.

Edmondson, G., and Baker, S., "Silicon Valley on the Rhine," *Business Week,* November 7, 1997.

Hill, S., "SAP 'Opens Up,'" *Msi,* Oak Brook, August 2001.

Jacobs, F., and Whybark, D. *Why ERP? A Primer on SAP Implementation.* New York: McGraw-Hill, 2000.

Kersteller, J., "Software," *Business Week,* January 8, 2001.

Key, P. "SAP Strategy: Displace All Competing Gateways," *Philadelphia Business Journal,* September 27, 1999.

King, J., "Commerce One Deal Reflects SAP Strategy Shift," Computerworld.com, June 15, 2000.

King, S., and Ohlson, K., "Update: Commerce One Deal Reflects SAP Strategy Shift," Computerworld.com, 2000.

Konicki, S., "Overwhelmed—SAP Regroups Software Business," *Information Week,* June 6, 2000.

Konicki, S., and Maselli, J., "SAP Touts Customers' Experiences," *Informationweek,* June 3, 2002.

Krill, P., "SAP Takes on Its CRM Rivals," *Infoworld,* September 10, 2001.

Maselli, J., "Analysts Steer Customers Away from SAP CRM Upgrade," *Information Week,* September 10, 2001.

Meissner, G. *Inside the Secret Software Power.* New York: McGraw-Hill, 2000.

O'Brien, K., "Many Blows to SAP Strength," http://www.it.mycareer.com.au/software/20000125/A39678-2000Jan21.html. Accessed January 25, 2000.

Pender, L., "SAP CEO: Don't Blame Us for Snafus," www.Zdnet.com, November 10, 1999.

SAP AG, "SAP Transforms E-Business with New mySAP Technology for Open Integration," *Business Wire,* November 6, 2001.

SAP Annual Reports and 10K Reports, 1998–2002.

Scannell, E., "Accenture, SAP Jump into Bed," *Infoworld,* July 9, 2001.

Standard and Poor's Industry Overview—Software, *Industry Survey,* April 26, 2001.

Weston, R., "SAP Strategy Extends Scope," CNETNews.com, September 15, 1998.

www.mySAP.com, 2002.

www.SAP.com, 2002.

Iridium: Communication for the New Millennium

23

This case was prepared by Min Yee Ji and Steven Angga-Prana under the supervision of Melissa A. Schilling, New York University.

The Ice Trek

In November 1998, the Iridium Ice Trek team—Eric Philips, Peter Hillary, and John Muira—set out from the coast of Antarctica to ski to the South Pole and back.[1] The journey was 1,742 miles and was one of the longest unsupported polar treks of any kind. The 100-day trek covered some of the most remote and inhospitable terrain in the world.

The Ice Trek team was the first private expedition to communicate via telephone direct from the Antarctic interior to the outside world. The team used two Kyocera telephones connected to the Iridium satellite system for broadcast of the expedition live to an audience of millions. For the trekkers, Iridium phones offered peace of mind in dangerous times; the ability to keep in touch with family during the Christmas season; and the ability to share the journey's other highs and lows with the outside world through phone calls to print, radio, television, and electronic media. The millions of listeners at home were kept up to date all the way to the end, when the three skiers reached the South Pole on January 26, 1999.

This case is intended to be used as a basis for class discussion rather than as an illustration of either effective or ineffective handling of the situation. The authors would like to acknowledge the help and support of Shawn Kuehn, Ryan Steele, Colin Blaney, Jay Margolis, and Frances Zeon. Reprinted by permission.

Despite the technological benefits of the Iridium system, there was a lack of subscribers using the global telecommunications service in the first year. By April 1999, the company reported 10,230 voice customers and just over 2,000 pager users, out of 200,000 projected for the end of 1998.[2] The future of global communication for trekkers and other adventurers who travel to remote locations was in jeopardy.

Birth of the Satellite Giant

Iridium was the first to market a service that allowed users to communicate anywhere, anytime. It took ten years of hard work and development to make this vision a reality. In 1987, three Motorola engineers—Ray Leopold, Ken Peterson, and Bary Bertiger—proposed a gateway concept costing $5 billion.[3] The gateway allowed the constellation of satellites to communicate with existing terrestrial telephone systems. The idea caught on with executives at Motorola and, in 1990, the Iridium system concept was unveiled at simultaneous press conferences in Beijing, London, Melbourne, and New York City. The press conferences created enough public and institutional confidence that Motorola spun off Iridium as a separate company in 1991. The fledgling company was in charge of deploying and developing the network, and in its first year reserved radio frequencies for the Iridium low earth orbit satellites (LEOs). The following year, the company took the first steps toward creating its constellation of satellites and secured a $3.37 billion contract with Motorola for system development, construction, and delivery.[4] Motorola became the prime contractor supplying satellites, gateways, and communication products for the system. The next four years progressed smoothly; with Motorola's backing, Iridium was able to raise $1.9 billion by 1996.[5] With finances secured, the terrestrial facilities used in operating and monitoring the satellites were completed. By May 1998, Iridium launched sixty-six satellites into orbit with 100 percent launch success, the best launch track record for any developer of low earth orbit satellites for voice communications.

The bad news was the lack of subscribers using the system after its completion. The lack of subscribers resulted in the resignation of Roy Grant, the chief financial officer, in April 1999, and the business was forced to seek an extension from creditors after failing to meet revenue and subscription goals.[6] A few weeks later, vice chairman and chief executive officer Edward Staiano resigned both his positions, as well as his post as chairman of Iridium World Communications Ltd.[7]

Satellite 101

The idea behind satellite communication was the ability to make a call anywhere in the world. While cellular networks covered the densely populated areas, 86 percent of the land remained outside a terrestrial cellular network. A global telecommunication device—one device that could work anywhere, even in the Amazon jungle, Gobi Desert, or Atlantic Ocean—was needed. So the Iridium concept was designed, not to replace or compete with existing cellular networks, but to fill in the holes between them.[8]

Before the Iridium concept was developed, satellite phones were as large and bulky as a briefcase. They had to be aligned with a compass and remain stationary while in use. These phones received transmissions from satellites called geosynchronous earth orbit (GEO). The satellites tracked the Earth at exactly its rotational speed to remain in the same position at 22,300 miles above the Earth.[9] The distance of these satellites from earth required only five GEOs operating in tandem to cover the whole globe. The result, however, was a noticeable delay of at least half a second in the transmitted sound from the GEOs.

The Iridium system, named after the atomic element iridium, used LEO satellites sitting 485 miles above earth. These satellites transmitted service in milliseconds to smaller, compact phones. Since LEOs were closer to earth, each satellite covered a much smaller area compared to GEOs. The Iridium system originally required seventy-seven satellites to cover the whole Earth.[10] The system was later decreased to sixty-six LEO satellites, with eleven spare satellites, to make the system more efficient and cheaper. Iridium's LEO divided the Earth into six orbital planes, eleven operational satellites, and one spare in each orbital plane.[11] Satellite controller stations, called gateways, controlled all of the LEOs, making the Iridium network incompatible with any other system.

Through these LEOs, Iridium provided voice, data, facsimile, and paging services to subscribers with hand-held wireless phones and pagers. The Iridium LEO system worked to provide these services using several frequencies, or bands. A call made from the Iridium handsets was connected directly to the satellites, which then either connected the call to another satellite or a gateway, depending on the receiver's location. This system was capable of handling a maximum of 1,100 simultaneous calls.[12] Calls made to Iridium handsets from landline phones were routed to the public network, the gateway, and then the satellite, which would then connect to the handsets. The system required the use of subscriber identity module (SIM) cards, which identified the caller with information such as phone number and country of origin. Due to the complexities of the Iridium structure, the system was smart enough to reject calls made in areas where no agreements or licensing had been established with the local government.

The Market: Calling Planet Earth!

Iridium was focused toward both the business traveler and workers in highly specialized industries that required connectivity in remote locations, such as mining, maritime, oil and gas exploration, humanitarian organizations, and aeronautics, as well as a list of other potential subscribers. The size of the target market involved in specialized industries was but a handful. In 1999, it was determined that barely 3 percent of America's work force was engaged in farming, mining, or other activities requiring people to live where Mother Nature put the resources.[13] The larger part of the target market was already situated in established centers, where terrestrial cellular networks satisfied their communication needs. Iridium's vice president of marketing and corporate communications, John Windolph, targeted this market as the "affluent business person, the international traveler who spends at least three weeks a year on the road and makes at least $70,000 per annum . . . [and who] use[s] 55 minutes of wireless service a day, and 70 percent of [whose] calling time is spent on international calls."[14] Iridium not only provided continuous satellite coverage but was also seen as a status symbol—an individual could be the first owner of a satellite phone on his or her block. Customers might also adopt satellite services out of fear of losing communication during vacations in areas where telephone service was inconvenient or nonexistent, such as on a sailboat. Iridium saw a market niche that had not been targeted and offered three communication services: world satellite service, world roaming service, and world page service to satisfy the market's needs.[15]

World Satellite Service   World satellite service enabled subscribers to make telephone calls via Iridium's satellite system. This service required the use of a satellite handset or fixed unit on ships, trucks, and airplanes. One satellite handset cost anywhere from $1,000 to $3,500. Unlike cellular, these phones weighed approximately 2 pounds and had nearly 2-foot-long antennas. Even with a huge pipe antenna attached to a brick-sized phone, Iridium's reception quality varied, especially when the phone was used inside a building. However, Iridium officials argued that these phones were not designed for urban use, which is why they teamed with Sprint to offer a world roaming service.[16] Per-minute charges varied depending on where the call was placed. Originally, each call cost anywhere from $2 to $7 per minute, in addition to the $69 monthly fee.[17] Due to the competition, Iridium was forced to reduce these rates by 65 percent. These per-minute charges varied for international satellite service, domestic satellite service, and international water service.[18]

World Roaming Service   World roaming service provided service extension to existing subscribers of cellular for times when they roamed to areas where cellular service was nonexistent or when the local cellular provider technology differed from the subscribers' technology. For example, a code division multiple access (CDMA) phone would not work in a

time division multiple access (TDMA) network. By using a cellular cassette inserted in the Iridium phone's back, Iridium world roam service subscribers could enjoy seamless coverage, even in areas where their cellular provider had no agreement to provide service. In such areas, the handset searched for a wireless network. When one was not available, the handset automatically switched to one of Iridium's satellites. This satellite handset differed, however, from the one required for the world satellite service. Without the rear cellular cassette, the phone acted like a normal cellular phone and, most important, was just as small as any other cellular phone.

Iridium's major partner in the world roaming service, Sprint, made Iridium's service available to all of Sprint's personal communication system (PCS) customers traveling internationally. These customers retained their Sprint PCS phone numbers and were billed to their Sprint PCS statements. Sprint was expected to charge the Iridium-based service at $1.49 a minute for worldwide roaming, $1.99 a minute for domestic satellite calls, and $3.99 a minute for international satellite service.[19]

World Page Service   Iridium's world page service provided global paging services, wireless messaging, and information services. Each pager cost about $500, with a monthly fee of $159. Customers received the benefit of alphanumeric services and could even receive up to 200-word messages emailed from Iridium's web site.[20]

Marketing Campaign

To sell its satellite services, Iridium needed a global advertising campaign appealing to markets worldwide. Iridium looked for an advertising agency that not only exhibited creativity and outstanding service but also achieved positive chemistry throughout the organization. Ammirati Puris Lintus was selected and given a budget of $180 million. In addition to direct mail campaigns in twenty markets and in twenty different languages, Iridium advertised in *Fortune,* the *Wall Street Journal,* the in-flight magazines of thirty-seven airlines, and other publications read by jet-setting business executives. Advertisements were designed to create product awareness and to emphasize that the phones would work anywhere. The marketing campaign's overall objective was to create an aspirational brand that would be associated with exclusive activities. The goal of this advertising was achieved: there were 1.5 million responses to advertisements that ran in the fourth quarter of 1998, which was right on target, according to John Windolph, vice president of marketing and corporate communications.[21] Iridium was creating a brand overnight and educating the market about the use of satellite phones. Iridium also sponsored sporting events in remote locations where the Iridium phones were needed and used as primary communication devices. For example, Iridium sponsored sailing events, road rallies, expeditions, and any activities located outside regular telecommunications services, such as Bitter End Road Rally and Eco Challenge.[22]

Demand

Iridium was a large-scale, technologically advanced system of low-orbit satellites that was conceived many years before cellular phones were used on a widespread basis. The company thus focused on the high end of the market. The consumers in this target market traveled frequently for business or pleasure. Iridium was confident in the growth of this market and forecasted that 240,000 subscribers would use their system in 1999. They also forecasted that this market would roughly double in scope every year thereafter, with 4.5 million subscribers and revenues of $5 billion in 2005 (Exhibit 1).[23] By 1999, however, it was clear that Iridium would not meet forecasted demand, with only 27,000 subscribers.[24]

EXHIBIT 1

Iridium Subscriber Forecasts, 1996–2007
(thousands of satellite voice subscribers)

Year	Old Forecasts	New Forecasts
1998	160	40
1999	796	400
2000	1,259	1,259
2001	1,852	1,852
2002	2,547	2,547
2003	3,226	3,226
2004	3,791	3,791
2005	4,261	4,261
2006	4,652	4,652

Source: Merrill Lynch.

Iridium's Operational Structure

Iridium's system comprised nineteen strategic partners from around the world. Seventeen of these partners participated in the operation and maintenance of twelve ground station gateways.[25] Those twelve gateway operators also served as regional distributors of Iridium services in their commercial territories (Exhibit 2). The gateway operators were segmented according to twelve regions, or territories, which they managed: (1) Iridium Africa Corporation, (2) SudAmerica Corporation, (3) Middle East Corporation, (4) Iridium Canada, (5) Iridium India Telecom Limited, (6) Iridium Italia S.p.A., (7) SK Telecom of Korea, (8) South Pacific Iridium Holding Limited of Indonesia and Thai Satellite Telecom Company, (9) Sprint Iridium of the United States, (10) Nippon Iridium of Bermuda, (11) Verbacom Holdings of Germany, and (12) Pacific Asia Communications Ltd. of Taiwan. Strategic partners not involved in the day-to-day operations of the Iridium system helped to develop the actual constellation. Khrunichev State

EXHIBIT 2

Iridium's Regional Gateways Operating Companies

Regional Gateway	Operating Company
Beijing, China	Iridium China (HK) Ltd.
Seoul, Korea	SK Telecom (Iridium Korea)
Nagano, Japan	Nippon Iridium Telecom Corp.
Taipei, Taiwan	Pacific Iridium Telecom Corp.
Bangkok, Thailand	Thai Satellite Telecom Iridium South Pacific
Tempe, Arizona, United States	Iridium North America Iridium Central America & Mexico
Hawaii, United States	U.S. Government Gateway
Rio de Janeiro, Brazil	Iridium SudAmerica Corp.
Rome, Italy	Iridium Italia Iridium Communications Germany
Moscow, Russia	Iridium Eurasia
Jeddah	Iridium Middle East Corp. Iridium Africa Corp.
Mumbai	Iridium India Telecom Ltd.

Source: C. A. Ingley & Co.

Research and Production Space Center manufactured launch vehicles and orbital stations. As a subcontractor, Khrunichev launched satellites for Iridium. Iridium China, a wholly owned subsidiary of China Aerospace, was responsible for launching satellites over China's air space.

Still other strategic partners developed the hardware and software for the global telecommunications giant. Lockheed Martin Corporation was a major subcontractor to Motorola for the construction of the Iridium satellites. And while Lockheed provided the parts for the satellites, Raytheon was primarily responsible for the design and construction of the main mission antennas of the satellites. Neither partner was involved with the operation of the Iridium gateways, however.

Operating Contracts

Motorola, which owned 19 percent of Iridium, was involved in several contracts amounting to $3.4 billion. Motorola provided overall coordination for several subcontractors for the design, development, production, and delivery in orbit of the space segment. Its terrestrial network development contract required the subcontractors to design the gateway hardware and software. The operations and maintenance contract ensured day-to-day management of the space segment after deployment: the subcontractors were obligated to monitor, upgrade, and replace hardware and software as necessary to maintain performance specifications.[26]

Regional Gateways

Fifteen franchises, which were subsidiaries of Iridium LLC, operated the regional gateways. The business offices of these gateway operators distributed service to end-users directly through cellular operators and regional telecommunications providers.[27] In addition to delivering satellite communication to the appropriate carriers, gateway operators were in charge of identifying and training service providers and their sales staff.[28] Besides marketing and distributing the products and services, each operator franchise was also responsible for negotiating communication rights with eighty nations around the world and developing interfaces with terrestrial phone networks.[29]

Production and Distribution

Production of handsets and pagers were outsourced to a Japanese firm, Kyocera, and to Motorola. Products had to meet stringent quality control standards imposed by Iridium. During the original rollout, Kyocera had difficulties meeting quality control standards and was unable to ship significant quantities of phones until early March 1999. Although Motorola's satellite phones and pagers were available since the commencement of commercial operations, the production of cellular cassettes for its dual-mode satellite/cellular phones and some other accessories were delayed.

Competition for Global Voice

Competition in the global voice market required developing a constellation of satellites that could cover the entire world at once. This setup meant launching enough satellites so that at least one satellite could be seen from every point on the Earth. Iridium faced twelve main contenders, but its closest competitors were Globalstar and ICO (Exhibits 3 and 4).

Globalstar

Globalstar, a global telecommunications service, commenced operations on October 13, 1999. Globalstar was established in 1991 as a consortium of leading international telecommunications companies providing wholesale mobile and fixed satellite-based telephone services. It offered voice calling, short messaging services, roaming, positioning, facsimile, and data transmission on the Globalstar satellite system. It had a constellation of forty-eight LEO satellites and offered services to existing cellular telephone networks in more than 100 countries on six continents.[30]

Products and Services   The competition was fierce for securing the largest market, what Globalstar called the "cellular extension market." This market was an all-encompassing segment that included voice services in vertical and unserved markets, such as industrial and maritime.[31] Globalstar's second largest target market was the market for fixed voice services. This market included rural telephony markets, which slightly overlap the cellular extension market. Globalstar considered the global roamer (Iridium's primary market) to be its smallest market.[32]

Like Iridium, Globalstar offered roaming features that incorporated cellular service. It required dual-mode handsets that were compatible with the

EXHIBIT 3

The Global Mobile Market—Who Owns What?

Iridium	ICO Global	Globalstar	Teledesic (Broadband)
Motorola	Inmarsat	Loral Space Systems	Boeing
Veba	TRW	Qualcomm	AT&T Wireless
RWE	British Telecom	Vodafone Airtouch	Craig McCaw
Bell Canada	Deutsche Telekom	Alcatel	Bill Gates
Telecom Italia	Swisscom	Alenia	Prince Alwaleed
Korea Mobile Telecom	Sonera	Motorola	George Soros
Nippon Iridium	Singapore Telecom	China Telecom	
UCOM	Telefónica de Espana	DACOM	
Lockheed Martin	T_Mobil	France Telecom	
Sprint	Telkom SA	General Electric	
		Daimler Chrysler	
		Aerospace	
		Hyundai	

Source: ArcChart at www.arcchart.com.

cellular network and the satellite network. Similar to Iridium, its services required the use of a cellular cassette, which extended the antennas to receive satellite signals. Globalstar gained a competitive edge through its price points. The Globalstar handsets retailed for $900.[33] The company also offered cheaper domestic pricing plans than did Iridium. Globalstar charged a monthly service charge and fees for satellite connection and use. Its "Beyond Basic" service was priced at $29.99 per month and $1.69 per minute of airtime; the "Beyond 100" plan included 100 minutes for $169.99, with additional minutes at $1.49 each; and the "Beyond 250" plan included 250 minutes for $369.99, with additional minutes at $1.39 each.[34] With its competitive price points and global partners, Globalstar believed it could generate 5,000 subscribers in 1999, 383,000 subscribers in 2000, and an impressive installed base of 850,000 users in 2001.[35]

Partnership   Globalstar's competitiveness in the market was enhanced by its reputable founders—Loral Corporation and Qualcomm, Inc.—and its strategic partners representing the world's leading telecommunications service providers and equipment manufacturers. Globalstar's strategic partners included telecommunications service providers AirTouch, Dacom, France Telecom, and Vodafone, who provided on-the-ground marketing and telephony experience, and telecommunications systems manufacturers Alcatel, Alenia, DASA, Hyundai, Loral, Qualcomm, and Space Systems/Loral.[36]

EXHIBIT 4

Cost of Satellite System—Amortized Total by Year, Day, Minute, and Second

System	Total Cost ($ billions)	Lifespan	Yearly Cost ($ millions)	Daily Cost ($)	Per-Minute Cost ($)	Per-Second Cost ($)
Globalstar	2.2	5	440	1,205,479	837	13.95
ICO Global	3.5	12	291.666	799,087	555	9.25
Iridium	5.0	5	1,000	2,739,726	1,903	31.71

Source: L. Swasey, "Sorting Through the Satellite Voice Market," *Advanstar Communications,* July 15, 1999.

ICO Global Communication

ICO Global Communications (ICO) was established in January 1995. It included a holding company and seventeen wholly owned direct and indirect subsidiaries formed to conduct its business worldwide.[37] By August 1999, ICO had filed a voluntary petition for reorganization under Chapter 11 due to insufficient capital before its satellite service started. In March 2000, however, a group of investors led by telecommunications pioneer Craig O. McCaw and his affiliated companies, Teledesic LLC and Eagle River Investments LLC, were talking about leading a group of international investors who would provide up to $1.2 billion to ICO.

Products and Services   ICO's proposed satellite service would commence in the first quarter of 2001 and would deliver digital voice, data, facsimile, and messaging services to users all over the world. In October 1998, ICO established ICO-roam, allowing customers of existing Global System for Mobile Communications (GSM) networks to roam into ANSI-41 cellular networks in North America using their home cellular number. The service was offered through customers' existing cellular network operators or service providers, and all charges were billed on their usual monthly invoices. The phones were similar to any GSM unit but had dual modes: cellular and satellite.

ICO forecasted a demand of 53 million subscribers, which would generate $47.4 billion by the end of 2010.[38] The target markets for ICO were similar to Iridium's and Globalstar's. ICO provided communication for mariners, people in remote areas requiring fixed units, mobile users, land transport operators, and government employees in military and relief agencies.

Unlike Iridium's system, ICO utilized medium Earth orbit (MEO) satellites that circled 6,494 miles above the Earth's surface.[39] This structure gave ICO global coverage with only ten satellites. The total infrastructure cost $3.5 billion, with $292 million in annual operating costs (Exhibit 5).[40] Furthermore, ICO's satellites lasted twelve years—twice the lifespan of Iridium's satellites.

Partnership   A team led by NEC Corporation and including Hughes Network Systems Inc. and Ericsson Limited was responsible for the design, manufacture, construction, installation, and testing of the ICONET ground network. Hughes Space and Communications International Inc. built ICO's satellites and supplied launch services. Mitsubishi, NEC, and Nera developed and manufactured ICO phones. Samsung Electronics supplied ICO with approximately $60 million worth of handsets.[41]

Alternatives for Global Travelers

Another option for international travelers was to use cellular services that operated in multiple countries and regions. In the past, various standards and frequencies, such as TDMA, CDMA, and global system for mobilization (GSM), hindered global roaming into different technological networks. However, cellular phones were becoming more adaptive to such differences through features such as multiple-band operation, which allowed phones to work in two different cellular technology networks.[42] Using their original phone numbers, cellular subscribers could roam into another country at a much lower price. A GSM handset with multiple-band features cost about $300 to $400, while the domestic charges cost $0.35 and roaming charges cost about $2.00 per minute.[43] The GSM network was available in over one hundred countries. Cellular providers had already begun to make mutual agreements to let subscribers roam in their territories.

The Future of Iridium

Although Iridium had a first-mover advantage, its management acknowledged that the transition from a development stage company to an operating stage company was not smooth. A key challenge that confronted Iridium was meeting subscriber forecasts. Iridium needed 27,000 subscribers by March 1999 to fulfill loan agreements with its creditors. In addition to its problems with financing, Iridium had difficulties coordinating its suppliers and service providers. One of its main suppliers, Kyocera, was unable to deliver quality phones on time during the first few months of operation, while its service providers were not trained properly for sales. Another challenge for the company was competing rivals, such as ICO and Globalstar, which were very aggressive in marketing their products through price cuts and services. As revenues began to lag far behind projections, Iridium's managers began to feel increasingly uneasy about Iridium's prospects.

EXHIBIT 5

Financial Statements, Iridium and Competitors, 1996–1998

Iridium—Balance Sheet

Fiscal Year End	12/31/1998	12/31/1997	12/31/1996
Cash	24,756,000	359,260,000	1,889,000
Receivables	93,000	NA	NA
Other current assets	32,052,000	20,216,000	10,630,000
Total current assets	56,901,000	379,476,000	12,519,000
Property/Plant/Equipment	3,584,209,000	3,151,380,000	2,390,385,000
Net property/Equipment	3,584,209,000	3,151,380,000	2,390,385,000
Depreciation and other assets	97,785,000	114,831,000	31,177,000
Total assets	3,738,895,000	3,645,687,000	2,434,081,000
Accounts payable	165,539,000	106,794,000	17,937,000
Other current liabilities	131,532,000	360,601,000	100,563,000
Total current liabilities	297,071,000	467,395,000	118,500,000
Long-term debt	2,530,735,000	1,264,288,000	505,000,000
Other long-term liabilities	433,926,000	279,367,000	238,552,000
Total liabilities	3,261,732,000	2,011,050,000	862,052,000
Retained earnings	−1,680,194,000	−427,393,000	−133,840,000
Other liabilities	2,157,357,000	2,062,030,000	1,705,869,000
Shareholders equity	477,163,000	1,634,637,000	1,572,029,000
Total liability/Net worth	3,738,895,000	3,645,687,000	2,434,081,000

Iridium—Income Statement

Fiscal Year End	12/31/1998	12/31/1997	12/31/1996
Net sales	186,000	NA	NA
Gross profit	186,000	NA	NA
Sell/Gen/Admin	749,162,000	177,474,000	70,730,000
Inc b/Dep & amort	−748,976,000	−177,474,000	−70,730,000
Depreciation and amortization	673,341,000	119,124,000	674,000
Nonoperating income	−249,906,000	3,045,000	2,395,000
Income before taxes	−1,672,223,000	−293,553,000	−69,009,000
Prov for inc tx	7,971,000	NA	4,589,000
N/I b/Ex-item	−1,680,194,000	−293,553,000	−73,598,000
Net income	−1,680,194,000	−293,553,000	−73,598,000

ICO Global—Balance Sheet

Fiscal Year End	12/31/1998	12/31/1997	12/31/1996
Cash	548,692,000	378,780,000	756,385,000
Market securities	228,005,000	NA	NA
Other current assets	11,253,000	59,093,000	8,064,000
Total current assets	787,950,000	437,873,000	764,449,000

(continued)

EXHIBIT 5 *(continued)*

ICO Global—Balance Sheet *(continued)*

Fiscal Year End	12/31/1998	12/31/1997	12/31/1996
Property/Plant/Equipment	1,818,568,000	860,929,000	301,271,000
Accumulated depreciation	NA	NA	NA
Net Property/Equipment	1,818,568,000	860,929,000	01,271,000
Depreciation and other assets	57,466,000	95,138,000	41,000,000
Total assets	2,663,984,000	1,393,940,000	1,106,720,000
Accounts payable	104,851,000	30,313,000	18,929,000
Other current liabilities	57,944,000	27,401,000	1,275,000
Total current liabilities	162,795,000	57,714,000	20,204,000
Long-term debt	533,021,000	4,432,000	NA
Other long-term liabilities	4,409,000	30,348,000	2,608,000
Total liabilities	700,225,000	92,494,000	22,812,000
Comm stock net	2,076,000	1,800,000	1,359,000
Capital surplus	2,305,681,000	1,934,512,000	1,438,848,000
Retained earnings	−342,964,000	−232,288,000	−44,311,000
Other liabilities	−1,034,000	−402,578,000	−311,988,000
Shareholders' equity	1,963,759,000	1,301,446,000	1,083,908,000
Total liability/Net worth	2,663,984,000	1,393,940,000	1,106,720,000

ICO Global—Income Statement

Fiscal Year End	12/31/1998	12/31/1997	12/31/1996
Net sales	142,000	NA	NA
Cost of goods sold	289,000	NA	NA
Gross profit	−147,000	NA	NA
Sell/Gen/Admin	142,189,000	67,569,000	48,913,000
Inc b/Dep & amort	−142,336,000	−67,569,000	−48,913,000
Depreciation and amortization	5,684,000	3,332,000	1,341,000
Nonoperating income	41,127,000	−114,494,000	20,639,000
Income before taxes	−106,893,000	−185,395,000	−29,615,000
Prov for inc tx	3,783,000	2,582,000	1,647,000
N/I b/Ex-item	−110,676,000	−187,977,000	−31,262,000
Net income	−110,676,000	−187,977,000	−31,262,000
Outstanding shares	207,647,618	180,567,513	186,867,513

Globalstar—Balance Sheet

Fiscal Year End	12/31/1998	12/31/1997	12/31/1996
Inv/Adv to subs	612,716,000	482,676,000	173,118,000
Total assets	612,716,000	482,676,000	173,118,000
Accrued expense	1,679,000	1,679,000	NA

(continued)

EXHIBIT 5 *(continued)*

Globalstar—Balance Sheet *(continued)*

Fiscal Year End	12/31/1998	12/31/1997	12/31/1996
Total current liabilities	1,679,000	1,679,000	NA
Total liabilities	1,679,000	1,679,000	NA
Preferred stock	301,410,000	300,358,000	NA
Comm stock net	30,638,000	10,000,000	10,000,000
Capital surplus	318,643,000	175,750,000	175,750,000
Retained earnings	−51,864,000	−27,712,000	−12,632,000
Other liabilities	12,210,000	22,601,000	NA
Shareholders' equity	611,037,000	480,997,000	173,118,000
Total liability/Net worth	612,716,000	482,676,000	173,118,000

Globalstar—Income Statement

Fiscal Year End	12/31/1998	12/31/1997	12/31/1996
Nonoperating income	−2,950,000	2,290,000	−12,632,000
Interest expense	21,202,000	17,370,000	NA
Income before taxes	−24,152,000	−15,080,000	−12,632,000
N/I b/Ex-item	−24,152,000	−15,080,000	−12,632,000
Net income	−24,152,000	−15,080,000	−12,632,000
Outstanding shares	30,638,152	10,000,000	10,000,000

Source: Disclosure Report.

ENDNOTES

1. www.icetrek.org.
2. C. Bulloch, 1999, "Trouble for Big LEOs," *Telecommunications,* Vol 33, Issue 9 (International Edition), pp. S132–S135.
3. www.iridium.com.
4. Ibid.
5. Ibid.
6. Anonymous, 1999, "DOD to Buy Gear for Iridium Use," *Electronic Engineering Times,* April 5, p. 8.
7. Anonymous. 1999, "Iridium's CEO Resigns Due to Dispute with Board of Directors," *Satellite News,* April 26, p. 1.
8. J. Meyers, 1997, "The Final Countdown," *Telephony,* November 17, p. 36.
9. D. Rohde, 1997, "Satellites: Are They for You?" *Network World,* September 8, p. 30.
10. W. Stallings and R. Van Slyke, 1998, *Business Data Communications.*
11. D. Larsen, 1999, "Iridium Takes to the Skies," *Utility Business,* March, pp. 41–45.
12. M. Warwick, 1999, "Up in Smoke," *Communication International,* October, pp. 72–75.
13. P. R. Krugman, 1999, "When Did the Future Get So Boring?" *Fortune,* September 27, pp. 42–44.
14. K. Higgins, 1999, "The Anytime, Anywhere Phone Company," *Marketing Management,* Vol. 8, Issue 1, pp. 4–8.
15. www.iridium.com.
16. J. Sheridan, 1999, "Bullish on Iridium," *Industry Week,* June 21, pp. 46–50.
17. L. Swasey, 1999, "Sorting Through the Satellite Voice Market," *Advanstar Communications,* July 15, pp. 24–26.
18. J. Sheridan, 1999, "Bullish on Iridium," *Industry Week.* June 21, pp. 46–50.
19. Ibid.
20. D. Larsen, 1999, "Iridium Takes to the Skies," *Utility Business,* March, pp. 41–45.
21. K. Higgins, 1999, "The Anytime, Anywhere Phone Company," *Marketing Management,* Vol. 8, Issue 1, pp. 4–8.
22. Ibid.
23. Merrill Lynch, 1999, "Iridium Faces Further Financing Difficulties," *Satellite International.*
24. Ibid.
25. www.iridium.com.
26. Iridium World Communications Ltd., 1998, Annual Report.
27. C. Ingley, 1999, "Global Vision: Making the Right Connections," *Satellite Communications,* February, pp. 38–44.
28. Iridium World Communications Ltd., 1998, Annual Report.
29. K. Higgins, 1999, "The Anytime, Anywhere Phone Company," *Marketing Management,* Vol. 8, Issue 1, pp. 4–8.
30. www.globalstar.com.
31. A. Cosper, 1999, "Globalstar's Grace Under Pressure," *Satellite Communications,* December, p. 26.
32. Ibid.

33. Baskerville Communications Corp., 1998, "Adjusted Capital Expenditures for Major Global MSS Providers," *Satellite International.*

34. K. Carroll, 2000, "Globalstar USA Goes Commercial," *Telephony,* June 19, p. 30.

35. Merrill Lynch, 1999, "Globalstar's Subscriber Forecast," *Satellite International.*

36. www.ee.surrey.ac.uk/Personal/L.Wood/constellations/background .html.

37. www.ico.com.

38. Dresdner Kleinwort Benson, 1998, "ICO Financial and Subscriber Forecasts," *BaskervilleCommunications.*

39. www.Lloyd.com.

40. L. Swasey, 1999, "Sorting Through the Satellite Voice Market," *Advanstar Communications, Inc.,* July 15, pp. 24–26.

41. www.ico.com.

42. C. Mason, 1999, "Does Your Phone Roam in Rome?" *America's Network,* October 1, pp. 51–54.

43. www.omnipoint.com.

24

A Hundred-Year War: Coke vs. Pepsi, 1890s—1990s

This case was prepared by Professor Chiaki Moriguchi and Research Associate David Lane, Harvard Business School. It is a rewrite of cases prepared by Professor Michael E. Porter and Professor David B. Yoffie.

For decades, competition between Coca-Cola and Pepsi-Cola has been labeled "the cola wars." The most intense battles were fought over the $56 billion industry in the United States, where the average American consumed 55 gallons of soft drinks per year. As the U.S. soft drink industry matured, however, the cola wars were moving increasingly to international markets. Coke, the world's largest soft drink company with a 51% share of the worldwide soft drink market, earned 75% of its 1998 profits outside of the United States. Pepsi, with only 15% of its beverage operating profits coming from overseas, continued to challenge Coke in international markets. According to Roger Enrico, CEO of Pepsi-Cola:

> The warfare must be perceived as a continuing battle without blood. Without Coke, Pepsi would have a tough time being an original and lively competitor. The more successful they are, the sharper we have to be. If the Coca-Cola Company

didn't exist, we'd pray for someone to invent them. And on the other side of the fence, I'm sure the folks at Coke would say that nothing contributes as much to the present-day success of the Coca-Cola Company [as] Pepsi.[1]

As the cola wars continued into a second century, Coke and Pepsi faced such perennial questions as: How could they maintain their growth at home? How would the industry's changing landscape affect their profitability? How should they redesign their strategies in response to diverse and constantly evolving market conditions abroad?

Economics of the U.S. Soft Drink Industry

Americans consumed 23 gallons of soft drinks a year in 1970 compared to 55 gallons in 1998 (see Exhibit 1). This growth was fueled by the increasing availability and affordability of soft drinks in the marketplace, and by the introduction and popularity of diet soft drinks. Over the past two decades, the real price of soft drinks fell, and consumer demand appeared responsive

1. Roger Enrico, *The Other Guy Blinked and Other Dispatches From the Cola Wars* (New York: Bantam Books, 1988).

EXHIBIT 1

U.S. Industry Consumption Statistics

	1970	1975	1981	1985	1990	1991	1992	1993	1994	1995	1996	1997	1998
Historical Soft Drink Consumption													
Cases (millions)	3,090	3,780	5,180	6,500	7,914	8,040	8,160	8,395	8,608	8,952	9,489	9,682	9,880
Gallons/capita	22.7	26.6	34.5	40.8	47.7	47.8	48.0	48.4	49.6	51.2	52.6	53.7	54.8
As a % of total beverage consumption	12.4	14.4	18.7	22.4	26.1	26.2	26.3	29.8	27.2	28.1	28.8	29.4	30.0
U.S. Liquid Consumption Trends (gallons/capita)													
Soft drinks	22.7	26.3	34.2	40.8	47.7	47.8	48.0	48.4	49.6	51.2	52.6	53.7	54.8
Coffee	35.7	33.0	27.2	26.8	26.4	26.5	26.1	28.4	29.5	29.9	29.8	29.3	28.9
Milk	18.5	21.6	24.3	23.8	24.1	23.3	23.1	25.1	25.0	24.8	24.5	24.3	24.0
Beer	22.8	21.8	20.6	19.8	19.4	19.4	19.2	22.8	22.7	22.4	22.2	22.1	22.1
Bottled water	—	1.2	2.7	5.2	9.2	9.6	9.9	9.5	10.3	10.9	11.4	11.4	11.3
Tea	5.2	7.3	7.3	7.3	7.0	6.7	6.8	6.9	6.9	6.6	6.6	6.7	6.8
Juices	6.5	6.8	6.9	7.4	6.2	6.4	6.6	6.5	6.5	6.4	6.4	6.4	6.3
Powdered drinks	—	4.8	6.0	6.3	5.7	5.9	5.6	5.2	5.2	5.2	5.1	5.1	5.0
Wine	1.3	1.7	2.1	2.4	2.0	1.9	1.8	1.7	1.8	1.8	1.9	1.9	1.9
Distilled spirits	1.8	2.0	2.0	1.8	1.5	1.4	1.3	1.3	1.3	1.2	1.2	1.2	1.2
Subtotal	114.5	126.5	133.3	141.6	149.2	148.9	148.4	155.8	158.8	160.4	161.7	162.1	162.3
Imputed water consumption	68.0	56.0	49.2	40.9	33.3	33.6	34.1	26.7	23.7	22.1	20.8	20.4	20.2
Total*	182.5	182.5	182.5	182.5	182.5	182.5	182.5	182.5	182.5	182.5	182.5	182.5	182.5

Source: John C. Maxwell, Jr., *Beverage Industry Annual Manual 1992/1993*, and *The Maxwell Consumer Report*, Feb. 3, 1994; *Adams Liquor Handbook*, casewriter estimates.

[a]This analysis assumes that each person consumes on average one-half gallon of liquid per day.

to declining prices.[2] Many alternatives to soft drinks existed, including coffee, beer, milk, tea, bottled water, juices, powdered drinks, wine, distilled spirits, and tap water. Yet Americans drank more soda than any other beverage, with the soft-drink category being the only one with rising consumption every year between 1970 and 1998. The cola segment of the soft drink industry held the dominant share (almost 70%) of the market in the 1990s, followed by lemon/lime, pepper, orange, root beer, and other flavors.

Soft drinks consisted of a flavor base, a sweetener, and carbonated water. Four major participants were involved in the production and distribution of soft drinks: 1) concentrate producers, 2) bottlers, 3) retail channels, and 4) suppliers.

Concentrate Producers

The concentrate producer blended raw material ingredients (excluding sugar or high fructose corn syrup), packaged it in plastic canisters, and shipped the blended ingredients to the bottler. The concentrate producer added artificial sweetener to make diet soda concentrate, while bottlers added sugar or high fructose corn syrup themselves. The process involved little capital investment in machinery, overhead, or labor. A typical concentrate manufacturing plant cost approximately $5–$10 million to build, and one plant could serve the entire United States.

A concentrate producer's most significant costs were for advertising, promotion, market research, and bottler relations. Marketing programs were jointly implemented and financed by concentrate producers and bottlers. Concentrate producers usually took the lead in developing the programs, particularly in product planning, market research, and advertising. They invested heavily in their trademarks over time, with innovative and sophisticated marketing campaigns (see Exhibit 2). Bottlers assumed a larger role in developing trade and consumer promotions, and paid an agreed percentage—typically 50% or more—of promotional and advertising costs. Concentrate producers employed extensive sales and marketing support staff to work with and help improve the performance of their bottlers, setting standards and suggesting operating procedures. Concentrate producers also negotiated directly with the bottlers' major suppliers—particularly sweetener and packaging suppliers—to encourage reliable supply, faster delivery, and lower prices.

Once a fragmented business with hundreds of local manufacturers, the landscape of the U.S. soft drink industry had changed dramatically over time. Among national concentrate producers, Coca-Cola and Pepsi-Cola, the soft drink unit of PepsiCo, claimed a combined 76% of the U.S. soft drink market in sales volume in 1998, followed by Dr Pepper/Seven-Up, Cadbury Schweppes, and Royal Crown (see Exhibit 3).[3] There were also private-label brand manufacturers and several dozen other national and regional producers. Exhibit 4 gives financial data for the leading American soft drink companies.

Bottlers

Bottlers purchased concentrate, added carbonated water and high-fructose corn syrup, bottled or canned the soft drink, and delivered it to customer accounts. Coke and Pepsi bottlers offered "direct store door" delivery (DSD), which involved route delivery sales people physically placing and managing the soft drink brand in the store. Smaller national brands, such as Shasta and Faygo, distributed through food store warehouses. DSD entailed managing the shelf space by stacking the product, positioning the trademarked label, cleaning the packages and shelves, and setting up point-of-purchase displays and end-of-aisle displays. The importance of the bottler's relationship with the retail trade was crucial to continual brand availability and maintenance. Cooperative merchandising agreements (CMAs) between retailers and bottlers were used to promote soft drink sales. Retailers agreed to specified promotional activity and discount levels in the CMA in exchange for a payment from the bottler.

The bottling process was capital-intensive and involved specialized, high-speed lines. Lines were interchangeable only for packages of similar size and construction. Bottling and canning lines cost from $4–$10 million each, depending on volume and package type. The minimum cost to build a small bottling plant, with warehouse and office space, was $20–$30 million. The cost of an efficient large plant, with four lines, automated warehousing, and a capacity of 40 million cases, was $75 million in 1998.[4]

---

2. Robert Tollison et al., *Competition and Concentration* (Lexington Books, 1991), p. 11.

3. Cadbury Schweppes acquired Dr Pepper and Seven-Up in 1994.

4. "Louisiana Coca-Cola Reveals Crown Jewel," *Beverage Industry,* January 1999.

EXHIBIT 2

Advertising Spending by Brand in the United States ($ millions)

	1975	1980	1985	1990	1995	1996	1997	1998
Coca-Cola Company								
Coca Cola	$25.3	$47.8	$71.6	$90.4	$82.4	$131.6	$112.9	$115.5
Diet Coke			40.6	69.1	72.2	60.4	39.7	39.7
Sprite	2.6	10.7	22.2	23.4	49.6	55.8	58.4	56.5
Diet Sprite			6.7	7.6	2.2	NA	NA	NA
Tab	6.5	12.6	15.6	NA	NA	NA	NA	NA
Pepsi-Cola Company								
Pepsi-Cola	17.9	40.2	56.9	79.4	112.2	90.4	106.0	106.0
Diet Pepsi	3.7	11.6	32.9	76.5	10.8	0.2	19.7	13.9
Mountain Dew	2.8	10.2	9.0	11.7	29.8	29.0	34.0	39.8
Dr Pepper Company								
Dr Pepper	6.2	16.1	9.6	24.1	37.7	40.9	48.5	55.2
Diet Dr Pepper	1.6	2.9	5.7	6.6	24.4	NA	NA	NA
Seven-Up Company								
7-Up	10.2	25.5	22.3	31.4	15.2	33.0	38.5	26.9
Diet 7-Up	3.3	7.9	15.6	8.5	NA	NA	NA	NA
Royal Crown Cola								
Royal Crown	10.9	6.6	5.1	1.4	2.5	NA	NA	NA
Diet Rite Cola	3.5	3.4	3.5	3.2	0.4	NA	NA	NA
Canada Dry	5.2	10.1	12.4	4.5	5.8	NA	NA	NA
All Others	10.5	26.3	30.4	58.3	55.0	112.0	90.1	116.1
Industry Total	**114.0**	**241.0**	**383.0**	**498.0**	**523.3**	**553.3**	**547.8**	**569.6**

Source: Advertising Age, Beverage Industry, company annual reports.

Roughly 80–85 plants were required for full distribution across the United States. Among top bottlers in 1998, packaging accounted for approximately half of bottlers' cost of goods sold, concentrate for one-third, and nutritive sweeteners for one-tenth.[5] Labor accounted for most of the remaining variable costs. Bottlers also invested capital in trucks and distribution networks. Bottlers' gross profits often exceeded 40%, but operating margins were razor thin. See Exhibit 5 for the cost structures of a typical concentrate producer and bottler.

The number of U.S. soft drink bottlers had fallen from over 2,000 in 1970 to less than 500 in 1998.[6] Historically, Coca-Cola was the first concentrate producer to build nation-wide franchised bottling networks, a move that Pepsi and Seven-Up followed. The typical franchised bottler owned a manufacturing and sales operation in an exclusive geographic territory, with rights granted in perpetuity by the franchiser. In the case of Coca-Cola, territorial rights did not extend to fountain accounts—Coke delivered to its fountain accounts directly, not through its bottlers. The rights

5. Calculated from M. Dolan et al., "Coca-Cola Beverages," Merrill Lynch Capital Markets, July 6, 1998.

6. Timothy Muris et al., *Strategy, Structure, and Antitrust in the Carbonated Soft-Drink Industry* (Quorum Books, 1993), p. 63.

EXHIBIT 3

U.S. Soft Drink Market Share by Case Volume (percent)

	1966	1970	1975	1980	1985	1990	1995	1998
Coca-Cola Company								
Classic					5.8	19.4	20.0	20.6
Coca-Cola	27.7	28.4	26.2	25.3	14.4	0.7	0.2	a
Cherry Coke					1.6	0.6	0.9	0.7
diet Coke					6.3	9.1	9.5	8.6
diet Cherry Coke						0.2	0.1	0.1
Tab	1.4	1.3	2.6	3.3	1.1	0.2	0.1	a
Caffeine-Free Coke, diet Coke, and Tab					1.8	3.1	2.5	3.0[a]
Sprite and diet Sprite	1.5	1.8	2.6	3.0	4.2	4.4	5.6	7.0
Others	2.8	3.2	3.9	4.3	1.9	2.7	4.1	4.3
Total	**33.4**	**34.7**	**35.3**	**35.9**	**37.1**	**40.4**	**42.9**	**44.6**
PepsiCo, Inc.								
Pepsi-Cola	16.1	17.0	17.4	20.4	18.2	17.3	15.4	14.5
Diet Pepsi	1.9	1.1	1.7	3.0	3.7	6.2	5.4	5.0
Caffeine-Free Pepsi, and Diet Pepsi					2.3	2.3	1.9	1.9
Mountain Dew	1.4	0.9	1.3	3.3	2.9	3.8	5.6	6.7
Diet Mountain Dew						0.5	0.7	0.8
Slice					0.7	0.9	0.9	0.6
Diet Slice					0.6	0.4	0.2	0.1
Others	1.0	0.8	0.7	1.1	0.2	0.4	0.5	1.3
Total	**20.4**	**19.8**	**21.1**	**27.8**	**28.6**	**31.8**	**30.6**	**31.0**
Seven-Up	6.9	7.2	7.6	6.3	5.7	4.0	2.7	2.1
Dr Pepper	2.6	3.8	5.5	6.0	4.7	5.8	6.0	6.1
Royal Crown Co.	6.9	6.0	5.4	4.7	2.9	2.6	2.0	1.3
Cadbury Schweppes	NA	NA	NA	NA	4.5	3.2	16.1[b]	14.4[b]
Other companies	29.8	28.5	25.1	19.3	16.5	12.2	8.4	8.7
Total (mil. cases)	**2,927**	**3,670**	**4,155**	**5,180**	**6,500**	**7,914**	**8,952**	**9,880**

Source: John C. Maxwell, Jr., *Beverage Industry Annual Manual 1992/1993; The Maxwell Consumer Report,* February 3, 1994; and the Beverage Marketing Corporation, cited in *Beverage World,* March 1996 and March 1999.

[a]For 1998, Coca-Cola ("New Coke") and Tab are included, along with Citra, in the caffeine-free category.
[b]After 1995, Cadbury-Schweppes's shares include the shares of Seven-Up and Dr. Pepper.

granted to the bottlers were subject to termination only in the event of default by the bottler. The original Coca-Cola franchise contract, written in 1899, was a fixed-price contract that did not provide for contract renegotiation even if ingredient costs changed. With considerable effort, often involving bitter legal disputes, Coca-Cola amended the contract in 1921 and again in 1978 to adjust concentrate price. In 1986, Coke won a further amendment to the bottling contract that pro-

vided the company with greater pricing flexibility. Pepsi negotiated concentrate prices with its bottler association, and normally based price increases on the Consumer Price Index. According to an industry report, the price of concentrate sold to bottlers had increased at an annual rate of 3%–4% during the 1990s.[7]

7. "Following Coke, Pepsi Will Raise Prices," *New York Times,* November 22, 1999.

Coca-Cola and Pepsi franchise agreements allowed bottlers to handle the non-cola brands of other concentrate producers. Franchise agreements also allowed bottlers to choose whether or not to market new beverages introduced by the concentrate producer. Some restrictions applied, however, as bottlers could not carry directly competitive brands. For example, a Coca-Cola bottler could not sell Royal Crown Cola, but it could distribute Seven-Up, if it decided not to carry Sprite. Franchised bottlers had the freedom to participate in or reject new package introductions, local advertising campaigns and promotions, and test marketing. The bottlers also had the final say in decisions concerning retail pricing, new packaging, selling, advertising, and promotions in its territory, though they could only use packages authorized by the franchiser. Historically, most franchised bottlers in the United States had been small, privately owned, and independent. More recently, the major concentrate producers had initiated consolidation among their bottlers and taken partial equity positions in large franchised bottlers based in urban areas. In addition to franchised bottlers, the major concentrate producers fully owned and operated a number of bottlers on their own.

Retail Channels

In the late 1990s, the distribution of soft drinks in the United States took place through food stores (40%), fountain outlets[8] (17%), convenience stores (14%), vending machines (8%), and other outlets (21%). Mass merchandisers, warehouse clubs, and drug stores made up most of the last category. Bottler's profitability by type of retail outlet is shown in Exhibit 6. Profits were affected by delivery method and frequency, drop size, advertising, and marketing.

The main distribution channel for soft drinks was the supermarket. Soft drinks were among the five largest selling product lines sold by supermarkets, traditionally yielding a 15%–20% gross margin (about average for food products) and accounting for 3%–4% of food store revenues.[9] Soft drinks represented a large percentage of a supermarket's business, and were also a big traffic draw. Bottlers fought for retail shelf space to ensure visibility and accessibility

for their products, and looked for new locations to increase impulse purchases, such as placing coolers at checkout counters. The proliferation of products and packaging types created intense shelf-space pressures. Supermarkets' share of soft drink sales fell in the 1990s due to the rise of new retail formats and widespread price discounting.

Discount retailers, warehouse clubs, and drug stores accounted for about 16% of soft drink sales in 1998.[10] These firms often had their own private label soft drink, or they sold a generic label such as President's Choice. One of the largest private label brand manufacturers was the Cott Corporation. Cott purchased concentrate from Royal Crown, bottled or canned the product, and sold it to more than forty retail chain stores, including Wal-Mart, Sam's Club, and Safeway. Private label soft drinks were usually delivered to a retailer's warehouse, while branded soft drinks were delivered directly to the store. With the warehouse delivery method the retailer was responsible for storage, transportation, merchandising, and stocking the shelves, thus incurring additional costs (see Exhibit 7 for a comparative profit margin analysis). Doug Ivester, Coca-Cola COO in 1993, had this to say, "Coke delivers and stocks its soda, while Cott drops its pop at retailers' warehouses. The trouble is, most retailers have never had a good understanding of what their costs really are."[11]

Historically, Pepsi had focused on sales through retail outlets, while Coke had dominated fountain sales. Coca-Cola had a 65% share of the fountain market in 1998, while Pepsi had 25%.[12] Competition for fountain sales was intense, and was characterized by "significant everyday discounting to national and local customers."[13] National fountain accounts were essentially "paid sampling," with soft drink companies earning pretax operating margins of around 2%. For restaurants, by contrast, fountain was extremely profitable—soft drinks were one of their highest margin products. Coke and Pepsi invested in the development of fountain equipment, such as service dispensers, and provided their fountain customers with cups, point-of-sale material, advertising, and in-store promotions to increase brand presence. After

---

8. The "fountain outlets" traditionally referred to soda fountains, but was later used also for restaurants, cafeterias, and other establishments that served soft drinks by the glass using fountain dispensers.

9. *Progressive Grocer 1998 Sales Manual Databook,* July 1998, p. 68.

10. Greg Johnson, "It's a Take-No-Prisoners Attitude in the Soft Drink Wars," *Los Angeles Times,* May 28, 1998.

11. Patricia Sellers, "Brands—It's Thrive or Die," *Fortune,* August 23, 1993.

12. Sanford C. Bernstein data, in *The Wall Street Journal,* May 8, 1998, p. A3.

13. *Beverage World,* 1989.

EXHIBIT 4

Financial Data for the Leading Soft Drink Companies ($ millions)

	1975	1980	1985	1986	1987	1988
Coca-Cola Company[a]						
Soft drinks, United States						
Sales	NA	1,486	1,865			
Operating profits/sales		11.1%	11.6%			
Soft drinks, International						
Sales	NA	2,349	2,677			
Operating profit/sales		21.0%	22.9%			
Consolidated						
Sales	2,773	5,475	5,879			
Net profit/sales	9.0%	7.7%	12.3%			
Net profit/equity	21.0%	20.0%	24.0%			
Long-term debt/assets	3.0%	10.0%	23.0%			
Coca-Cola Enterprises (CCE)[c]						
Sales						
Operating profit/sales						
Net profit/sales						
Net profit/equity						
Long-term debt/assets						
PepsiCo, Inc.[d]						
Soft drinks, United States						
Sales	1,065	2,368	2,725			
Operating profit/sales	10.4%	10.3%	10.4%			
Soft drinks, International						
Sales	NA	NA	NA			
Operating profit/sales						
Consolidated						
Sales	2,709	5,975	7,585			
Net profit/sales	4.6%	4.4%	5.6%			
Net profit/equity	18.0%	20.0%	30.0%			
Long-term debt/assets	35.0%	31.0%	36.0%			
Dr Pepper Company						
Sales	138	339	174	181	207	244
Net profit/sales	8.6%	7.8%	2.3%	2.5%	−0.1%	−4.5%
Net profit/equity	24.0%	24.0%	30.0%	NA	−1.0%	−30.6%
Long-term debt/assets	NA	38.0%	47.0%	50.0%	38.0%	80.1%
Seven-Up Company[f]						
Sales	214	353	678	271	297	
Net profit/sales	9.5%	NA	NA	−2.4%	2.5%	
Net profit/equity	24.0%	NA	NA	−2.5%	14.8%	
Long-term debt/assets	2.0%	NA	NA	42.0%	66.0%	
Dr Pepper/Seven-Up Companies[g]						
Sales						511
Operating profit/sales						11.7%
Net loss or profit						−79
Long-term debt/assets						140.6
Royal Crown Corporation[h]						
Sales	258	438	986	1,102	1,109	1,122
Net profit/sales	5.2%	2.3%	0.6%	−0.8%	1.6%	3.2%
Net profit/equity	17.0%	10.0%	5.0%	−9.0%	15.0%	23.0%
Long-term debt/assets	NA	38.0%	47.0%	50.0%	38.0%	46.0%

Source: Company annual reports.

[a]Coca-Cola's soft drink sales were comprised primarily of concentrate sales. Coke's 44% stake in CCE was accounted for by the equity method of accounting. Coke's share of CCE's net earnings was included in its consolidated net income figure.

[b]From 1994, Coca-Cola reported U.S. data as part of a North American category that included Canada and Mexico.

[c]CCE's net losses in 1991 and 1992 were due to debt transactions, which increased net income expense.

[d]PepsiCo's soft drink sales included sales by company-owned bottlers.

[e]In 1998, PepsiCo began reporting U.S. data as part of a North American category including Canada.

	1989	1990	1991	1992	1993	1994	1995	1996	1997	1998
		2,461	2,646	2,813	2,966	5,327[b]	5,513[b]	6,050[b]	6,443[b]	6,915[b]
		16.5%	17.7%	18.1%	20.8%	17.2%	15.5%	15.7%	20.3%	21.1%
		6,125	7,245	8,551	9,205	10,812	12,559	12,576	12,357	11,898
		29.4%	29.7%	29.5%	29.9%	29.3%	29.1%	28.4%	33.3%	29.5%
		10,236	11,572	13,074	13,957	16,264	18,127	18,673	18,868	18,813
		13.5%	14.0%	12.7%	15.6%	15.7%	16.5%	18.7%	21.9%	18.8%
		36.0%	38.0%	43.0%	51.7%	48.8%	55.4%	56.7%	56.5%	42.0%
		8.0%	10.0%	10.0%	11.9%	10.3%	7.6%	6.9%	4.7%	3.6%
		3,933	3,915	5,127	5,465	6,011	6,773	7,921	11,278	13,414
		8.3%	3.1%	6.0%	7.0%	7.3%	6.9%	6.9%	6.4%	6.5%
		2.4%	−2.1%	3.6%	0.3%	1.1%	1.2%	1.4%	1.5%	1.1%
		6.0%	−5.8%	−14.8%	−1.2%	5.2%	5.7%	7.4%	9.6%	5.8%
		39.0%	51.0%	43.4%	47.0%	47.9%	46.3%	47.2%	50.3%	45.5%
		5,035	5,172	5,485	5,918	7,045	7,427	7,734	7,852	8,266[e]
		13.4%	14.4%	14.6%	15.8%	15.7%	16.7%	18.3%	16.5%	14.7%
		1,489	1,744	2,120	2,720	2,609	3,040	2,853	2,689	2,385
		6.3%	6.7%	6.7%	6.3%	5.6%	3.9%	−29.1%	−5.1%	−9.2%
		17,515	19,292	21,970	25,021	17,984	19,067	20,337	20,917	22,348
		6.2%	5.6%	5.9%	6.4%	7.6%	7.5%	4.6%	7.1%	8.9%
		22.0%	19.5%	23.0%	25.1%	19.9%	19.4%	14.2%	21.5%	31.1%
		33.0%	42.0%	38.0%	31.4%	38.0%	35.9%	36.9%	24.6%	17.8%
	267	311	381							
	3.0%	5.7%	4.5%							
	18.1%	42.5%	−62.2							
	78.7%	74.7%	72.3%							
	514	540	601	659	707	769				
	22.2%	22.8%	23.0%	24.4%	25.9%	26.5%				
	−42	−33	−38	−140	78	66				
	149.0	152.2	138.5	163.4	116.3	113.9				
	1,175	1,231	1,027	1,075	1,058	150.8	214.6	309.1	555.7	736.4
	−0.1%	−0.9%	−1.6%	−0.7	−5.7%	2.2%	5.6%	0.3%	9.7%	12.9%
	−1.0%	−11.0%	−39.0%	−7.7%	NA					
	46.0%	46.0%	34.0%	35.3%	53.7%					

[f]Seven-Up was purchased by Philip Morris in 1978; in 1986, Seven-Up's domestic operation was sold to Hicks and Haas, and its international operation was sold to PepsiCo. Seven-Up had negative shareholders equity in 1988, 1989, and 1990.

[g]Dr Pepper/Seven-Up was formed in 1988. The company experienced net losses due to changes relating to new financial accounting rules and a company recapitalization plan. Cadbury Schweppes acquired the company in 1994, after which figures for Dr Pepper/Seven-Up became unavailable.

[h]Royal Crown was purchased by DWG Corporation in late 1984. Royal Crown Corporation was made up of RC Cola and Arby's, a franchised restaurant system. In 1994, Royal Crown was sold to Triarc Corporation, which acquired Mistic Beverages in 1995, and Snapple and Stewarts in 1997. From 1994, Royal Crown sales were reported jointly with those of Triarc's other beverage brands and net profit/sales is altered to Triarc's beverage operating profit/sales.

EXHIBIT 5

Comparative Cost and Financial Structure of a Typical U.S. Concentrate Producer and Bottler (per standard case of 24 8-ounce bottles), 1993

	Concentrate Producer		Bottler	
	Dollars per Case	**Percent of Sales**	**Dollars per Case**	**Percent of Sales**
Profit and Loss Data				
Net sales	.66	100%	2.99	100%
Cost of sales	.11	17	1.69	57
Gross profit	.55	83	1.30	43
Selling and delivery	.01	2	.85	28
Advertising and marketing	.26	39	.05	2
General and administration	.05	13	.13	4
Pretax profit	.23	29	.27	9
Balance Sheet Data				
Cash, investments	.12		.16	
Receivables	.32		.30	
Inventories	.02		.16	
Net property, plant & equipment	.07		.82	
Goodwill	.03		1.37	
Total assets	.56		2.81	
Pretax profit/total assets	.41		.10	

Source: Industry analysts and casewriter estimates.

EXHIBIT 6

U.S. Soft Drink Retail Outlets, 1993

	Food Stores	**Convenience Stores**	**Fountain**	**Vending**	**Other**	**Total**
Percent of industry volume	40.0%	14.0%	17.0%	8.0%	21.0%	100.0%
Share of channel:						
Coca-Cola (all brands)	32.8	29.6	58.9	48.6	45.4	40.7%
Pepsi-Cola (all brands)	28.5	37.4	27.0	40.6	32.5	31.3%
Other brands	38.7	33.0	14.1	10.8	22.1	28.0%
Bottling Profitability Per Case (192 ounces per case):						
Net Price	$3.14	$3.09	$1.52[b]	$6.05	$1.90	$3.13
NOPBT[a]	$0.25	$0.40	$0.05[b]	$0.69	$0.31	$0.34

Source: Industry analysts and casewriter estimates.

[a]Net Operating Profit Before Tax.
[b]Industry average, excluding Coca-Cola bottlers. The Coca-Cola Company supplies fountain outlets directly.

EXHIBIT 7

Comparative Profit Margin Analysis for Door-Store Delivery, Private Label, and Warehouse Delivered Soft Drinks in the United States, 1993

Category	Retail Price	Cost of Goods	Gross Profit	Handling Costs	Net Profit per Unit	Net Profit per Case	Net Margin
DSD	$1.01	$.86	$.15	$.07	$.08	$.48	7.9%
Private Label	.69	.55	.14	.17	(.03)	(.18)	N/A
Warehouse	.82	.65	.17	.17	.00	.00	.00

Source: Jesse Meyers' Beverage Digest, July 1993. Reprinted with permission. Copyright 1993 *Beverage Digest.*

Pepsi entered the first-food restaurant business with the acquisitions of Pizza Hut (1978), Taco Bell (1986), and Kentucky Fried Chicken (1986), Coca-Cola persuaded other chains such as Wendy's and Burger King to switch to Coke. PepsiCo spun its restaurant business off to the public in 1997, while retaining the Frito-Lay snack food business.

Concentrate produces offered bottlers rebates to encourage them to purchase and install vending machines. The owners of the property on which vending equipment was located usually received a sales commission. Coke and Pepsi were the largest suppliers of soft drinks to the vending channel. Juice, tea, and lemonade were also available through vending machines.

Suppliers

Concentrate producers and bottlers purchased two major inputs: packaging, which included $3.4 billion in cans, $1.3 billion in plastic bottles, and $0.6 billion in glass; and sweeteners, which included $1.1 billion in sugar and high fructose corn syrup, and $1.0 billion in artificial sweetener (predominantly aspartame). The majority of U.S. soft drinks were packaged in metal cans (55%), then plastic bottles (40%), and glass bottles (5%). Cans were an attractive packaging material because they were easily handled, stocked, and displayed, weighed little, and were durable and recyclable. Plastic bottles, introduced in 1978, boosted home consumption of soft drinks because of their larger 1-liter, 2-liter, and 3-liter sizes.

The concentrate producers' strategy towards can manufacturers was typical of their supplier relationships. Coke and Pepsi negotiated on behalf of their bottling networks, and were among the metal can industry's largest customers. Since the can constituted about 40% of the total cost of a packaged beverage, bottlers and concentrate producers often maintained relationships with more than one supplier. In the 1960s and 1970s, Coke and Pepsi backward integrated to make some of their own cans, but largely exited the business by 1990. In 1994, Coke and Pepsi instead sought to establish stable long-term relationships with their suppliers. Major can producers included American National Can, Crown Cork & Seal, and Reynolds Metals. Metal cans were viewed as commodities, and there was chronic excess supply in the industry. Often two or three can manufacturers competed for a single contract, which lowered their margins.

With the advent of diet soft drinks in the 1980s, Coke and Pepsi began purchasing aspartame, most notably from Nutrasweet Company, and selling presweetened diet soda concentrate to bottlers. After the expiration of Nutrasweet's U.S. aspartame patent in 1991, Coke amended its franchise bottler contract to pass along two-thirds of any increase or savings in the cost of artificial sweetener to its bottlers. Though not contractually obligated, Pepsi followed suit.

The Evolution of the U.S. Soft Drink Industry

Early History[14]

Coca-Cola was formulated in 1886 by John Pemberton, a pharmacist in Atlanta, Georgia, who sold it at drug store soda fountains as a "potion for mental and physical disorders." A few years later, Asa Candler acquired

14. See J. C. Louis and Harvey Yazijian, *The Cola Wars* (Everest House, 1980); Mark Pendergrast, *For God, Country, and Coca-Cola* (Charles Scribner's, 1993); David Greising, *I'd Like the World to Buy a Coke* (John Wiley & Sons, 1997).

the formula, established a sales force, and began brand advertising of Coca-Cola. Tightly guarded in an Atlanta bank vault, the formula for Coca-Cola syrup, known as "Merchandise 7X," remained a well-protected secret. Candler granted Coca-Cola's first bottling franchise in 1899 for a nominal one dollar, believing that the future of the drink rested with soda fountains. The company's bottling network grew quickly, however, reaching 370 franchisees by 1910.

In its early years, Coke was constantly plagued by imitations and counterfeits, which the company aggressively fought in court. In 1916 alone, courts barred 153 imitations of Coca-Cola, including the brands Coca-Kola, Koca-Nola, Cold-Cola, and the like. Coke introduced and patented a unique 6.5-ounce "skirt" bottle to be used by its franchisees that subsequently became an American icon.

Robert Woodruff, who became CEO in 1923, began working with franchised bottlers to make Coke available wherever and whenever a consumer might want it. He pushed the bottlers to place the beverage "in arm's reach of desire," and argued that if Coke were not conveniently available when the consumer was thirsty, the sale would be lost forever. During the 1920s and 1930s, Coke pioneered open-top coolers to store-keepers, developed automatic fountain dispensers, and introduced vending machines. Woodruff also initiated "lifestyle" advertising for Coca-Cola, emphasizing the role of Coke in a consumer's life.

Woodruff also developed Coke's international business. In the onset of World War II, at the request of General Eisenhower, he promised that "every man in uniform gets a bottle of Coca-Cola for five cents wherever he is and whatever it costs the company." Beginning in 1942, Coke was exempted from wartime sugar rationing whenever the product was destined for the military or retailers serving soldiers. Coca-Cola bottling plants followed the movements of American troops; sixty-four bottling plants were set up during the war—largely at government expense. This contributed to Coke's dominant market shares in most European and Asian countries, a lead that the company still retained in the 1990s.

Pepsi-Cola was invented in 1893 by a North Carolina pharmacist, Caleb Bradham. Like Coke, Pepsi adopted a franchise bottling system, and by 1910 it had built a network of 270 franchised bottlers. Pepsi struggled, however, declaring bankruptcy in 1923 and again in 1932. Business began to pick up in the midst of the Great Depression, when Pepsi lowered the price for its 12-ounce bottle to a nickel, the same price Coke charged for its 6.5-ounce bottle. When Pepsi tried to expand its bottling network in the late 1930s, its choices were small local bottlers striving to compete with wealthy Coke franchisees.[15] Pepsi nevertheless began to gain the market position.

In 1938, Coke filed suit against Pepsi, claiming that Pepsi-Cola was an infringement on the Coca-Cola trademark. The court ruled in favor of Pepsi in 1941, ending a series of suits and countersuits between the two companies. With its famous radio jingle, "Twice as Much, for Nickel Too," Pepsi's U.S. sales surpassed those of Royal Crown and Dr Pepper in the 1940s, trailing only Coca-Cola. In 1950, Coke's share of the U.S. soft drink market was 47% and Pepsi's was 10%; hundreds of regional soft drink companies continued to produce a wide assortment of flavors.

The Cola Wars Begin

In 1950, Alfred Steele, a former Coca-Cola marketing executive, became Pepsi's CEO. Steele made "Beat Coke" his theme and encouraged bottlers to focus on take-home sales through supermarkets. The company introduced the first 26-ounce bottles to the market, targeting family consumption, while Coke stayed with its 6.5-ounce bottle. Pepsi's growth soon began tracking the growth of supermarkets and convenience stores in the United States: There were about 10,000 supermarkets in 1945, 15,000 in 1955, and 32,000 at the peak in 1962.

In 1963, under the leadership of new CEO Donald Kendall, Pepsi launched its "Pepsi Generation" campaign that targeted the young and "young at heart." Pepsi's ad agency created an intense commercial using sports cars, motorcycles, helicopters, and a catchy slogan. The campaign helped Pepsi narrow Coke's lead to a 2-to-1 margin. At the same time, Pepsi worked with its bottlers to modernize plants and improve store delivery services. By 1970, Pepsi's franchise bottlers were generally larger compared to Coke bottlers. Coke's bottling network remained fragmented, with more than 800 independent franchised bottlers that focused mostly on U.S. cities of 50,000 or less.[16] Throughout this period, Pepsi sold concentrate to its

15. Louis and Yazijian, p. 23.
16. Pendergrast, p. 310.

bottlers at a price approximately 20% lower than Coke. In the early 1970s, Pepsi increased the price to equal that of Coca-Cola. To overcome bottlers' opposition, Pepsi promised to use the extra margin to increase advertising and promotion.

Coca-Cola and Pepsi-Cola began to experiment with new cola and noncola flavors and a variety of packaging options in the 1960s. Before then, the two companies had adopted a single product strategy, selling only their flagship brand. Coke introduced Fanta (1960), Sprite (1961), and low-calorie Tab (1963). Pepsi countered with Teem (1960), Mountain Dew (1964), and Diet Pepsi (1964). Each introduced non-returnable glass bottles and 12-ounce metal cans in various packages. Coke and Pepsi also diversified into non-soft drink industries. Coke purchased Minute Maid (fruit juice), Duncan Foods (coffee, tea, hot chocolate), and Belmont Springs Water. Pepsi merged with snack-food giant Frito-Lay in 1965 to become PepsiCo, claiming synergies based on shared customer targets, store-door delivery systems, and marketing orientations.

In the late 1950s, Coca-Cola, still under Robert Woodruff's leadership, began using advertising that finally recognized the existence of competitors, such as "American's Preferred Taste" (1955) and "No Wonder Coke Refreshes Best" (1960). In meetings with Coca-Cola bottlers, however, executives only discussed the growth of their own brand and never referred to its closest competitor by name. During the 1960s, Coke primarily focused on overseas markets, apparently believing that domestic soft drink consumption had neared saturation. Pepsi meanwhile battled aggressively in the United States, doubling its share between 1950 and 1970.

The Pepsi Challenge

In 1974, Pepsi launched the "Pepsi Challenge" in Dallas, Texas. Coke was the dominant brand in the city and Pepsi ran a distant third behind Dr Pepper. In blind taste tests hosted by Pepsi's small local bottler, the company tried to demonstrate that consumers in fact preferred Pepsi to Coke. After its sales shot up in Dallas, Pepsi started to roll out the campaign nationwide, although many of its franchise bottlers were initially reluctant to join.

Coke countered with rebates, rival claims, retail price cuts, and a series of advertisements questioning the tests' validity. In particular, Coke used retail price

discounts selectively in markets where the Coke bottler was company owned and the Pepsi bottler was an independent franchisee. Nonetheless, the Pepsi Challenge successfully eroded Coke's market share. In 1979, Pepsi passed Coke in food store sales for the first time with a 1.4 share point lead. Breaking precedent, Brian Dyson, president of Coca-Cola, inadvertently uttered the name "Pepsi" in front of Coke's bottlers at the 1979 bottlers conference.

During the same period, Coke was renegotiating its franchise bottling contract to obtain greater flexibility in pricing concentrate and syrups. Bottlers approved the new contract in 1978 only after Coke conceded to link concentrate price changes to the CPI, adjust the price to reflect any cost savings associated with a modification of ingredients, and supply unsweetened concentrate to bottlers who preferred to purchase their own sweetener on the open market.[17] This brought Coke's policies in line with Pepsi, which traditionally sold its concentrate unsweetened to its bottlers. Immediately after securing bottler approval, Coke announced a significant concentrate price hike. Pepsi followed with a 15% price increase of its own.

Coke's Reawakening

In 1980, Cuban-born Roberto Goizueta was named CEO and Don Keough president of Coca-Cola. In the same year, Coke switched from sugar to the lower-priced high fructose corn syrup, a move Pepsi emulated three years later. Coke also intensified its marketing effort, increasing advertising spending from $74 million to $181 million between 1981 and 1984. Pepsi elevated its advertising expenditure from $66 million to $125 million over the same period. Goizueta sold off most of the non-soft drink businesses he had inherited, including wine, coffee, tea, and industrial water treatment, while keeping Minute Maid.

Diet Coke was introduced in 1982 as the first extension of the "Coke" brand name. Much of Coca-Cola management referred to its brand as "Mother Coke," and considered it too sacred to be extended to other products. Despite internal opposition from company lawyers over copyright issues, Diet Coke was a phenomenal success. Praised as the "most successful consumer product launch of the eighties," it became within a few years not only the nation's most

---

17. Pendergrast, p. 323.

popular diet soft drink, but also the third-largest selling soft drink in the United States.

In April 1985, Coke announced the change of its 99-year-old Coca-Cola formula. Explaining this radical break with tradition, Goizueta saw a sharp depreciation in the value of the Coca-Cola trademark as "the product had a declining share in a shrinking segment of the market."[18] On the day of Coke's announcement, Pepsi declared a holiday for its employees, claiming that the new Coke tasted more like Pepsi. The reformulation prompted an outcry from Coke's most loyal customers, many of whom consumed large amounts of Coca-Cola daily. Bottlers joined the clamor. Three months later, the company brought back the original formula under the name Coca-Cola Classic, while retaining the new formula as the flagship brand under the name New Coke. Six months later, Coke announced that Coca-Cola Classic (the original formula) would henceforth be considered its flagship brand.

New soft drink brands proliferated in the 1980s. Coke introduced 11 new products, including Cherry Coke, Caffeine-Free Coke, and Minute-Maid Orange. Pepsi introduced 13 products, including Caffeine-Free Pepsi-Cola, Lemon-Lime Slice, and Cherry Pepsi. The number of packaging types and sizes also increased dramatically, and the battle for shelf space in supermarkets and other food stores grew fierce. By the late 1980s, both Coke and Pepsi offered more than ten major brands, using at least seventeen containers and numerous packaging options.[19] The struggle for market share intensified, and the level of retail price discounting increased sharply. Consumers were constantly exposed to cents-off promotions and a host of other supermarket discounts.

Throughout the 1980s, the smaller concentrate producers were shuffled from one owner to another. Over five years, Dr Pepper was sold (all and in part) several times, Canada Dry twice, Sunkist once, Shasta once, and A&W Brands once. Some of the deals were made by food companies, but several were leveraged buyouts by investment firms. Coke and Pepsi did not stand on the sidelines. Each tried to buy the most prominent American niche players. In January 1986,

Pepsi announced its intention to acquire Seven-Up from Philip Morris. One month later, Coca-Cola announced plans to acquire Dr Pepper. In June of that year, the Federal Trade Commission voted to oppose both acquisitions, although Pepsi eventually acquired Seven-Up's international operations. Acquisition effort continued. In June, 1998, Pepsi purchased Tropicana, a premium fruit juice producer, for $3.3 billion. In December 1998, Coca-Cola agreed to pay $1.8 billion for Cadbury Schweppes' soft drink brands for all markets but the U.S., France, and South Africa. Regulatory opposition, however, forced Coke to exclude much of Europe from the deal, and the acquisition remained unapproved by Australia, Canada, and Mexico as of December 1999.

Reorganizing the Bottling System

Relations between Coke and its franchised bottlers had been strained since the contract renegotiation of 1978. Coke struggled to persuade bottlers to cooperate in marketing and promotion programs, upgrade plant and equipment, and support new product launches.[20] The cola wars had particularly weakened small independent franchised bottlers. High advertising spending, product and packaging proliferation, and widespread retail price discounting raised capital requirements for bottlers, while lowering their margins. Many bottlers that had been owned by one family for several generations no longer had the resources or the commitment to be competitive.

At a July 1980 dinner with Coke's fifteen largest domestic bottlers, Goizueta announced a plan to refranchise bottling operations. Coke began buying up poorly managed bottlers, infusing capital, and quickly reselling them to better-performing bottlers. Refranchising allowed Coke's larger bottlers to expand outside their traditionally exclusive geographic territories.

When two of its largest bottling companies came up for sale in 1985, Coke moved swiftly to buy them for $2.4 billion preempting outside financial bidders. Together with other bottlers that Coke had recently bought, these acquisitions placed one-third of Coca-Cola's volume in company-owned bottlers. In 1986, Coke began to replace its 1978 franchise agreement with the Master Bottler Contract that afforded Coke much greater freedom to change concentrate price.

18. *The Wall Street Journal*, April 24, 1986.
19. Timothy Muris, David Scheffman, and Pablo Spiller, *Strategy, Structure, and Antitrust in the Carbonated Soft Drink Industry* (Quorum Books, 1993), p. 73.

20. Greising, p. 88.

Coke reportedly raised its concentrate price significantly under the new contract.[21]

Coke's bottler acquisitions had increased its long-term debt to approximately $1 billion. In 1986, on the initiative of Doug Ivester, who later became CEO, the company created an independent bottling subsidiary, Coca-Cola Enterprises (CCE), and sold 51% of its shares to the public, while retaining the rest. The minority equity position enabled Coke to separate its financial statements from CCE. As Coke's first so-called "anchor bottler," CCE consolidated small territories into larger regions, renegotiated with suppliers and retailers, merged redundant distribution and material purchasing, and cut its work force by 20%. CCE moved towards mega-facilities, investing in 50 million-case production lines with high levels of automation and massive warehouse and delivery capabilities.

Coke continued to acquire independent franchised bottlers and sell them to CCE.[22] "We became an investment-banking firm specializing in bottler deals," reflected Don Keough. In 1997 alone, Coke put together more than $7 billion in deals involving bottlers. By then, CCE was Coke's largest bottler with annual sales of $11 billion, handling over 60% of Coke's North American volume.[23] Some industry observers questioned Coke's accounting practice, as Coke retained substantial managerial influence in its arguably independent anchor bottler.[24]

In the late 1980s, Pepsi also acquired MEI Bottling for $591 million, Grand Metropolitan's bottling operations for $705 million, and General Cinema's bottling operations for $1.8 billion. The number of Pepsi bottlers decreased from more than 400 in the mid-1980s to less than 200 in the mid-1990s. Pepsi owned about half of these bottling operations outright and held equity positions in most of the rest. Experience in the snack food and restaurant businesses boosted Pepsi's confidence in its ability to manage the bottling business.

In 1998, Pepsi separated its bottling operations to form the Pepsi Bottling Group (PBG).[25] By the end of 1998, PBG handled 54% of Pepsi's domestic beverage volume, and 32% of its volume worldwide.[26] In April 1999, PBG went public, with Pepsi retaining a 35% equity stake.

The bottler consolidation of the 1990s made smaller concentrate producers increasingly dependent on the Pepsi and Coke bottling network to distribute their products. In response, Cadbury Schweppes in 1998 bought and merged two large U.S. bottlers to form its own bottler, American Beverage Corporation.

Toward the Total Beverage Company

Although Americans still consumed more soft drinks than any other beverage, the average annual growth of sales volume during the 1990s was 3%, compared to 6% in the previous decade. Some industry analysts argued that U.S. soft drink consumption had approached its limit, while others believed that innovations would continue to fuel consumption. Coke and Pepsi also faced challenges from private label brands and "new age" beverages. Private label brand cola, accounting for 11% of the U.S. soft drink market in 1998, was sold through expanding discount retailers and warehouse chains at up to 35% lower price compared to national brands.[27] New age beverages included naturally flavored soda and tea-based drinks introduced by firms such as Clearly Canadian and Snapple, among others, as well as fruit drinks and sports drinks. In 1998, some 3 billion gallons (11.1 gallons per capita) of new age beverages were consumed in the United States, garnering sales of $7.7 billion, up from $900 million in 1993.[28]

Coke and Pepsi launched new drinks throughout the 1990s, including Power Aide, All Sport, Nordic Mist, and Tropical Chill. Both companies predicted that future increases in market share would come from beverages other than carbonated soft drinks. Pepsi pronounced itself a "total beverage company," and Coca-Cola appeared to be moving in the same direction, recasting its performance metric from share of the soda market to "share of stomach." "If Americans want to drink tap water, we want it to be Pepsi tap water," said Pepsi's vice-president for new

21. Robert McGough, "No More Mr. Nice Guy," *Financial World,* July 25, 1989, pp. 30–34.
22. Greising, p. 292.
23. *Beverage Industry,* January 1999, p. 17.
24. Albert Meyer and Dwight Owsen, "Coca-Cola's Accounting," *Accounting Today,* September 28, 1998.
25. *Beverage World,* October 1998, p. 20.

26. M. Gramig, "Pepsi to Spin Off Bottling Group," *The Atlanta Journal and Constitution,* January 9, 1999, p. D1.
27. *Beverage World,* 1998.
28. *New Age Beverages,* 1998; *Beverage World,* March 1999.

business, describing the philosophy behind the new strategy.[29] Coke's Goizueta echoed that view: "Sometimes I think we even compete with soup."[30]

Internationalizing the Cola Wars

Coke and Pepsi also increasingly looked overseas for new growth. In the 1990s, new access to markets in China, India, and Eastern Europe stimulated some of the most intense battles of the cola wars. In many international markets, per capita consumption levels remained a fraction of those in the United States. For example, while the average American drank 878 eight-ounce cans of soft drinks in 1998, the average Chinese drank 23. In 1998, Coca-Cola held a world market share of 51%, compared to Pepsi's 21% and Cadbury Schweppes' less than 8%. Among major overseas markets, Coke dominated in Western Europe and much of Latin America, while Pepsi had marked presence in the Middle East and Southeast Asia (see Exhibit 8).

By the end of World War II, Coca-Cola was the largest international producer of soft drinks. Coke steadily expanded its overseas operations in the 1950s, and the name Coca-Cola soon became a synonym for American culture. Following Coke, Pepsi entered Europe soon after the war, and—benefiting from Arab and Soviet exclusion of Coke—into the Middle East and Soviet bloc in the early 1970s. However, Pepsi put less emphasis on its international operations during the subsequent decade. In 1980, international sales accounted for 62% of Coke's soft drink volume, in contrast to 20% of Pepsi's. Pepsi rejoined the international battles in the late 1980s, realizing that many of its foreign bottling operations were inefficiently run and "woefully uncompetitive."[31]

Coke and Pepsi approached international markets differently. Coke built brand presence in developing markets where soft drink consumption was low but potential was large, such as Indonesia: With 200 million inhabitants, a median age of 18, and per capita consumption of 9 eight-ounce cans of soda a year, one Coke executive noted that "they sit squarely on the equator and everybody's young. It's soft drink

heaven."[32] In order to penetrate Coke strongholds, Pepsi utilized a niche strategy with well-executed blitzes, targeting big cities in Latin America and other countries. At the same time, Pepsi moved broadly into markets where Coke had little or no presence.

Coke and Pepsi also organized their overseas bottlers differently. Coke appointed anchor bottlers—large and experienced bottlers—to swiftly enter new markets and organize local bottling networks. Like its U.S. practice, Coke typically held minority equity in anchor bottlers. By 1998, Coke had 10 anchor bottlers operating in 40 international markets, handling about 47% of its global volume.[33] In contrast, Pepsi formed alliances directly with a large number of local bottlers (through joint ventures, partial ownership, and direct control) and invested heavily with its own money to develop their business skills and infrastructure. Including wholly-owned bottlers, Pepsi maintained equity control in over 20% of its bottling system on a volume basis, or about 50% on a revenue basis. Following Coke's lead, however, Pepsi also began to establish anchor bottlers overseas.

Unlike the U.S. market, the bottling contracts for foreign franchisees were not perpetual but typically ran for 3 to 10 years with no guarantee of renewal. Foreign contracts usually did not contain restrictions on concentrate pricing, providing concentrate producers with more discretion to use the prices for strategic purposes. Coke and Pepsi made pricing decisions on a country-by-country basis, taking local conditions into account. Local bottlers set retail prices on the basis of retail channel development, growth in disposable income, and the availability of alternative beverages. Concentrate producers encountered various obstacles in international operations, including cultural differences, political instability, price controls, advertising restrictions, foreign exchange controls, and lack of infrastructure. Their operating margins, nevertheless, were considerably higher abroad on average than in the United States.[34] The following vignettes illustrate how the cola wars had played out in different foreign markets.

29. Marcy Magiera, "Pepsi Moving Fast To Get Beyond Colas," *Advertising Age,* July 5, 1993.
30. Greising, p. 233.
31. Larry Jabbonsky, "Room to Run," *Beverage World,* August 1993.

32. John Huey, "The World's Best Brand," *Fortune,* May 31, 1993.
33. Pendergrast, p. 280.
34. Greising, p. 180.

EXHIBIT 8

Soft Drink Industry—Selected International Market Shares, 1998

	Population (000)	8-oz Per Capita[a]	Coca-Cola[b]	PepsiCo[b]	Cadbury Schweppes[b]
Asia					
Australia	18,613	449	57.1%	9.8%	16.2%
China	1,236,915	23	33.0	15.5	0.1
India	984,004	6	53.0	41.4	1.4
Indonesia	212,942	9	87.0	5.1	3.2
Japan	125,932	96	55.9	8.2	2.1
Pakistan	135,135	10	27.4	64.7	0.1
Philippines	77,726	208	69.1	18.2	
South Korea	46,417	117	53.3	13.2	0.2
Thailand	60,037	133	50.3	45.7	0.2
Vietnam	76,236	10	61.1	34.0	3.4
Europe					
Czech Republic	10,286	255	34.5	16.5	1.4
France	58,805	161	59.2	7.5	5.1
Germany	82,079	353	55.2	4.9	0.9
Hungary	10,208	303	51.0	44.0	4.7
Italy	56,783	218	45.8	5.9	1.1
Netherlands	15,731	362	45.1	14.5	1.5
Poland	38,607	176	27.9	14.7	0.6
Romania	22,396	109	49.0	8.5	0.3
Russia	146,861	67	33.0	11.7	3.0
Spain	39,134	378	57.8	16.0	4.5
United Kingdom	58,970	360	33.3	11.7	6.3
Latin America					
Argentina	36,265	345	61.0	29.0	2.5
Brazil	169,807	277	48.4	5.8	0.7
Colombia	38,581	181	57.0	8.1	0.2
Mexico	98,553	580	68.4	19.7	4.2
Peru	26,111	115	40.0	15.8	3.5
Venezuela	22,803	321	72.4	22.0	1.5
North America					
Canada	30,675	493	39.4	34.3	9.7
United States	270,312	878	44.5	31.4	14.4
Africa					
Kenya	28,337	30	98.4	1.0	0.6
South Africa	42,835	210	81.7	0.0	16.1
Sudan	33,551	11	4.0	65.8	
Yemen	16,388	40	35.0	15.0	50.0
Zaire (Congo)	49,001	5	75.1	10.5	
Middle East					
Egypt	66,050	49	56.8	38.1	3.1
Israel	5,644	400	67.6	13.6	1.0
Morocco	29,114	78	91.0	4.0	5.0
Saudi Arabia	20,786	237	25.0	74.8	0.2
World Total	**5,927,000**	**125**	**51.0**	**20.8**	**7.4**

Source: Beverage Digest Company, *The Green Sheet,* September 24, 1999. Reprinted with permission. Copyright 1999 *Beverage Digest.*

[a]128 ounces = 1 gallon.
[b]Corporate share includes local brands, if owned or controlled by Coke, Pepsi, or Cadbury Schweppes.

Japan

Coca-Cola was first introduced to Japan in 1961. By the early 1970s, Japan had become Coke's largest market outside the United States, contributing 18% of Coke's total corporate earnings.[35] Coke took small equity stakes in bottling plants owned by well-connected Japanese business partners, including Mitsubishi, Mitsui, Kirin Brewery, and Kikkoman, a leading soy-source producer. Coca-Cola's direct distribution system, which bypassed the traditional Japanese layers of wholesalers, threw the beverage industry into an uproar. Yet the popularity of the product and Japan's early emulation of all things American promoted acceptance of the new methods.[36] Coke introduced vending machines to Japan, a channel that eventually accounted for more than half of Coke's Japanese sales.[37] Adjusting to local preference, Coke regularly introduced new products—as many as twenty per year—most of which were not carbonated soft drinks but varieties of teas, coffees, juices, and flavored water.

Pepsi had never had a notable presence in Japan until Suntory became its master franchisee in 1997. As Japan's second-largest beverage company, Suntory offered Pepsi access to its broad distribution system and was expected to double Pepsi's market share to about 16%.

Germany and Eastern Europe

Germany, although a profitable market for Coca-Cola, had been for many years a patchwork of 160 small and poorly capitalized bottlers. Under Goizueta's initiative, the bottling network was consolidated to 60 well-capitalized bottlers by the early 1990s. Pepsi went another route, taking control of all its independent German bottler in the mid-1980s. When Coke moved quickly into East Germany and Eastern Europe in 1989, Pepsi remained preoccupied with reorganizing its existing German bottlers.

Pepsi's pre-existing ties to government bureaucrats in Eastern Europe proved insufficient to preserve market dominance in the face of Coke's marketing efforts. By 1992, Coke's market share topped Pepsi's in every country except Poland and Czechoslovakia, and before long, those countries fell as well. Even in Russia, where Pepsi's 60% share led Coca-Cola's 38% as recently as 1994, a strategy focused on ties to the new capitalist elite brought Coca-Cola market supremacy by 1997.[38]

India

Strong nationalist sentiment once forced both Coca-Cola and Pepsi out of India in the 1970s. When the Indian government insisted that Coke disclose its secret formula in exchange for continuing operation, the company closed its business in that hot and thirsty country of 850 million souls.[39] Pepsi was permitted to return in 1988 only upon agreeing to export $5 of Indian-made products for every $1 of materials it imported. Coke returned two years later, agreeing to channel its investment through local joint venture partner Parle Exports. Coke invested $70 million in India's largest bottler, acquiring Parle's own brands as well as immediate access to Parle's 54 bottling plants. Parle, however, continued to bottle and sell its own brands, including local market leader "Thums Up," after having sold the right to do so to Coke. In protest, Coke concentrated marketing support on its own, rather than Parle's former brands. Even so, in 1996, Coca-Cola's own brands held just a 20% share, trailing both Thums Up's 40% share and Pepsi's 30% share of the Indian market.

Mexico

Mexico was the largest soft drink market outside the United States. In the early 1990s, as part of its strategy of attacking "Coke fortresses," Pepsi invested more than $750 million in marketing, bottling, and distribution infrastructure to boost its market share in Monterey.[40] Pepsi moved to refit several of its bottlers with state-of-the-art lines that filled disposable plastic containers, ignoring the fact that for Mexicans—as for most other Latin Americans—a soft drink was to be consumed on the spot in order to return the glass bottle and get a refund.[41] The blitz initially was a success, and Pepsi's local cola share

35. Pendergrast, p. 313.
36. Pendergrast, p. 282.
37. June Preston, "Things May Go Better for Coke amid Asia Crisis, Singapore Bottler Says," *Journal of Commerce,* June 29, 1998, p. A3.
38. Greising, p. 188 and p. 273.
39. Enrico, p. 5.
40. Elisabeth Malkin, Phillip L. Zweig, and Lori Bongiorno, "No Deposit, No Return," *Business Week,* September 23, 1996.
41. David Swafford, "The Fizz that Couldn't Last . . . Pepsi Goes Flat in Latin America," *Latin Finance,* November 1996.

tripled to 24% in four months. Coke, however, hit back with price discounting that reduced Pepsi's margins, and the campaign quickly faltered. Pepsi bottlers were left with expensive and ultramodern production lines running at about 30% capacity. As the peso devaluation hit the economy in 1994, Pepsi's local bottlers with costly dollar-denominated debt began defaulting in 1996.[42] In 1999, Pepsi took over and reorganized the bottlers, merging them into a Mexican anchor bottler, Gemex.

Venezuela

Venezuela was the only South American country in which Pepsi outsold Coke by a margin approaching 4-to-1. That changed overnight in August 1996 when Pepsi's long-time local bottler, Embotelladoros Hit de Venezuela (EHV), switched to Coca-Cola. Pepsi had franchised EHV as its sole Venezuelan bottler in 1940 but had held no equity. EHV had succeeded in selling Pepsi in Venezuela by sweetening the recipe to conform to local taste and by developing its own local advertising. Coke paid $500 million to acquire a 50%

share of the $400 million-per-year bottler. Pepsi filed a complaint with Venezuela's anti-monopoly commission for breach of franchise contract and won a $2 million fine from Coke. Separately, the International Court of Arbitration ordered EHV to pay Pepsi $94 million, the equivalent of a decade of Pepsi's Venezuelan profits. In the meantime, Pepsi found a new joint venture partner and responded to Coke with price discounting and heavy investment in retail distribution. Appealing to loyal customers cultivated over five decades, Pepsi recovered a 29% share of the Venezuelan market by year-end 1998.[43]

As the cola wars continued overseas, the management of Coke and Pepsi faced new and old questions: Could Pepsi catch up with Coke in global market share as it had in the U.S. markets? Would overseas soft drink markets evolve into a duopoly, as in the United States, or might other patterns emerge, with different players, different organizational structures, and different levels of profitability?

42. Malkin et al, "No Deposit, No Return."

43. Constance L. Hays, "Coca-Cola Is Battling to Consolidate its Recent Gains over PepsiCo in a Turf War in Venezuela," *New York Times,* December 18, 1998, p. C3.

25 Wal-Mart Stores, Inc.: Strategies for Dominance in the New Millennium

This case was prepared by James W. Camerius, Northern Michigan University.

David Glass had recently announced that he was stepping down from his role as president and chief executive officer (CEO) at Wal-Mart Stores, Inc. He stepped to the podium in early 2000 at a Kansas City convention of the company's store managers to introduce Wal-Mart's new CEO, Lee Scott, fifty-one, to a crowd of cheering executives. "I'm not going anywhere; I'll be around to give everyone more help than they probably would like," Glass suggested. At sixty-four years old, he would remain chairman of the firm's executive committee.

Lee Scott was only the third CEO in the entire history of Wal-Mart. Sam Walton had built the company from the ground up. During the twelve years that David Glass held the position, sales grew from $16 billion to $165 billion. Lee Scott had been personally recruited by David Glass twenty-one years before from a Springdale, Arkansas, trucking company to come to Wal-Mart as manager of the truck fleet. In his years at Wal-Mart he had established himself as a leader, innovator, and team player. Over the last four years he served as chief operating officer (COO) and vice chairman of the company. He was aware that there were

This case is intended to be used as a basis for class discussion rather than as an illustration of either effective or ineffective handling of the situation. Reprinted by permission of James W. Camerius.

tremendous opportunities to serve new markets with the company's stores. His management mandate was to drive the company to a new level of success in domestic and international markets.

A Maturing Organization

In 2000, Wal-Mart Stores, Inc., Bentonville, Arkansas, operated mass merchandising retail stores under various names and retail formats including Wal-Mart discount department stores; Sam's Wholesale Clubs, wholesale/retail membership warehouses; and Wal-Mart Supercenters, large combination grocery and general merchandise stores in all fifty states. In the international division, it operated stores in Canada, Mexico, Argentina, Brazil, Germany, South Korea, the United Kingdom, and Puerto Rico, and stores through joint ventures in China. It was not only the nation's largest discount department store chain, it had surpassed the retail division of Sears, Roebuck, & Co. in sales volume as the largest retail firm in the United States. It was also considered the largest retailer in the world, with sales of $165 billion in 1999. The McLane Company, Inc., a Wal-Mart subsidiary, sold a wide variety of grocery and nongrocery products to different retailers, including selected Wal-Marts, Sam's Clubs, and

Supercenters. In 1999, *Discount Store News* honored Wal-Mart as "Retailer of the Century" with a commemorative issue of the periodical.

A financial summary of Wal-Mart Stores, Inc., for the fiscal years ended January 31, 1999, and January 31, 2000, is shown in appendixes A and B. An eleven-year financial summary for the fiscal years January 31, 1990, to January 31, 2000, is shown in appendix C. Appendix D lists the Wal-Mart Board of Directors and Executive Officers on January 31, 2000.

The Sam Walton Spirit

Much of the success of Wal-Mart was attributed to the entrepreneurial spirit of its founder and chairman of the board, Samuel Moore Walton (1918–1992). Many considered him one of the most influential retailers of the century. Sam Walton (or "Mr. Sam," as some referred to him) traced his down-to-earth, old-fashioned, homespun, evangelical ways to growing up in rural Oklahoma, Missouri, and Arkansas. Although he was remarkably blasé about his roots, some suggested that it was the simple belief in hard work and ambition that had "unlocked countless doors and showered upon him, his customers, and his employees . . . , the fruits of . . . years of labor in building [this] highly successful company."

"Our goal has always been in our business to be the very best," Sam Walton said in an interview, "and, along with that, we believe that in order to do that, you've got to make a good situation and put the interests of your associates first. If we really do that consistently, they in turn will cause . . . our business to be successful, which is what we've talked about and espoused and practiced. The reason for our success," he said, "is our people and the way that they're treated and the way they feel about their company." Many have suggested it was this people-first philosophy, which guided the company through the challenges and setbacks of its early years, that allowed the company to maintain its consistent record of growth and expansion in later years.

There was little about Sam Walton's background that reflected his amazing success. He was born in Kingfisher, Oklahoma, on March 29, 1918, to Thomas and Nancy Walton. Thomas Walton was a banker at the time and later entered the farm mortgage business and moved to Missouri. Sam Walton, growing up in rural Missouri in the depths of the Great Depression, discovered early that he "had a fair amount of ambition and enjoyed working," he once noted. He completed high school at Columbia, Missouri, and received a Bachelor of Arts degree in economics from the University of Missouri in 1940. "I really had no idea what I would be," he once said, "At one point in time," adding as an afterthought, "I thought I wanted to become president of the United States."

A unique, enthusiastic, and positive individual, Sam Walton was "just your basic homespun billionaire," a columnist once suggested. "Mr. Sam is a life-long small-town resident who didn't change much as he got richer than his neighbors," he noted. Walton had tremendous energy, enjoyed bird hunting with his dogs, and flew a corporate plane. When the company was much smaller he could boast that he personally visited every Wal-Mart store at least once a year. A store visit usually included Walton leading Wal-Mart cheers that began, "Give me a W, give me an A . . . ." To many employees he had the air of a fiery Baptist preacher. Paul R. Carter, a Wal-Mart executive vice president, was quoted as saying, "Mr. Walton has a calling." He became the richest man in America, and by 1991 had created a personal fortune for his family in excess of $21 billion. In 1999, despite a division of wealth, five family members were still ranked among the richest individuals in the United States.

Sam Walton's success was widely chronicled. He was selected by the investment publication, *Financial World* in 1989 as the "CEO of the Decade." He had honorary degrees from the University of the Ozarks, the University of Arkansas, and the University of Missouri. He also received many of the most-distinguished professional awards of the industry like "Man of the Year," "Discounter of the Year," and "Chief Executive Officer of the Year," and was the second retailer to be inducted into the Discounting Hall of Fame. He was a recipient of the Horatio Alger Award in 1984 and acknowledged by *Discount Stores News* as "Retailer of the Decade" in December 1989. "Walton does a remarkable job of instilling near-religious fervor in his people," said analyst Robert Buchanan of A. G. Edwards. "I think that speaks to the heart of his success." In late 1989 Sam Walton was diagnosed with multiple myeloma, or cancer of the bone marrow. He planned to remain active in the firm as chairman of the board of directors until his death. He died in 1992.

The Marketing Concept

Genesis of an Idea

Sam Walton started his retail career in 1940 as a management trainee with the JC Penney Co. in Des Moines, Iowa. He was impressed with the Penney method of doing business and later modeled the Wal-Mart chain on "The Penney Idea" (see Exhibit 1). The Penney Company found strength in calling employees associates rather than clerks. Founded in Kemerer, Wyoming, in 1902, Penney's located stores on the main streets of small towns and cities throughout the United States. Early Walton 5 & 10s were on main streets and served rural areas.

Following service in the U.S. Army during World War II, Sam Walton acquired a Ben Franklin variety store franchise in Newport, Arkansas. He operated this store successfully with his brother, James L. "Bud" Walton (1921–1995), until losing the lease in 1950. When Wal-Mart was incorporated in 1962, the firm was operating a chain of fifteen stores. Bud Walton became a senior vice president of the firm and concentrated on finding suitable store locations, acquiring real estate, and directing store construction.

The early retail stores owned by Sam Walton in Newport and Bentonville, Arkansas, and later in other small towns in adjoining southern states, were variety store operations. They were relatively small

---

EXHIBIT 1

The Penney Idea, 1913

1. To serve the public, as nearly as we can, to its complete satisfaction.

2. To expect for the service we render a fair remuneration and not all the profit the traffic will bear.

3. To do all in our power to pack the customer's dollar full of value, quality, and satisfaction.

4. To continue to train ourselves and our associates so that the service we give will be more and more intelligently performed.

5. To improve constantly the human factor in our business.

6. To reward men and women in our organization through participation in what the business produces.

7. To test our every policy, method, and act in this wise: "Does it square with what is right and just?"

Source: Trimble, Vance H., *Sam Walton: The Inside Story of America's Richest Man,* New York: Dutton, 1990.

---

operations of 6,000 square feet, were located on main streets, and displayed merchandise on plain wooden tables and counters. Operated under the Ben Franklin name and supplied by Butler Brothers of Chicago and St. Louis, they were characterized by a limited price line, low gross margins, high merchandise turnover, and concentration on return on investment. The firm, operating under the Walton 5 & 10 name, was the largest Ben Franklin franchisee in the country in 1962. The variety stores were phased out by 1976 to allow the company to concentrate on the growth of Wal-Mart discount department stores.

Foundations of Growth

The original Wal-Mart discount concept was not a unique idea. Sam Walton became convinced in the late 1950s that discounting would transform retailing. He traveled extensively in New England, the cradle of off-pricing. After he had visited just about every discounter in the United States, he tried to interest Butler Brothers executives in Chicago in the discount store concept. The first Kmart, as a "conveniently located one-stop shopping unit where customers could buy a wide variety of quality merchandise at discount prices," had just opened in Garden City, Michigan. Walton's theory was to operate a similar discount store in a small community and in that setting, he would offer name brand merchandise at low prices and would add friendly service. Butler Brothers executives rejected the idea. The first "Wal-Mart Discount City" opened in late 1962 in Rogers, Arkansas.

Wal-Mart stores would sell nationally advertised, well-known brand merchandise at low prices in austere surroundings. As corporate policy, they would cheerfully give refunds, credits, and rain checks. Management conceived the firm as a "discount department store chain offering a wide variety of general merchandise to the customer." Early emphasis was placed on opportunistic purchases of merchandise from whatever sources were available. Heavy emphasis was placed upon health and beauty aids (H&BA) in the product line and "stacking it high" in a manner of merchandise presentation. By the end of 1979, there were 276 Wal-Mart stores located in eleven states.

The firm developed an aggressive expansion strategy. New stores were located primarily in communities of 5,000 to 25,000 in population. The stores' sizes ranged from 30,000 to 60,000 square feet, with

45,000 being the average. The firm also expanded by locating stores in contiguous geographic areas. When its discount operations came to dominate a market area, it moved to an adjoining area. While other retailers built warehouses to serve existing outlets, Wal-Mart built the distribution center first and then spotted stores all around it, pooling advertising and distribution overhead. Most stores were less than a six-hour drive from one of the company's warehouses. The first major distribution center, a 390,000-square-foot facility, opened in Searcy, Arkansas, outside Bentonville, in 1978.

National Perspectives

At the beginning of 1991, the firm had 1,573 Wal-Mart stores in thirty-five states, with expansion planned for adjacent states. Wal-Mart became the largest retailer and the largest discount department store in the United States.

As a national discount department store chain, Wal-Mart Stores, Inc., offered a wide variety of general merchandise to the customer. The stores were designed to offer one-stop shopping in thirty-six departments that included family apparel, health and beauty aids, household needs, electronics, toys, fabric and crafts, automotive supplies, lawn and patio, jewelry, and shoes. At certain store locations, a pharmacy, automotive supply and service center, garden center, or snack bar was also operated. The firm operated its stores with "everyday low prices" as opposed to putting heavy emphasis on special promotions, which called for multiple newspaper advertising circulars. Stores were expected to "provide the customer with a clean, pleasant, and friendly shopping experience."

Although Wal-Mart carried much the same merchandise, offered similar prices, and operated stores that looked much like the competition, there were many differences. In the typical Wal-Mart store, employees wore blue vests to identify themselves, aisles were wide, apparel departments were carpeted in warm colors, a store employee followed customers to their cars to pick up their shopping carts, and the customer was welcomed at the door by a "people greeter" who gave directions and struck up conversations. In some cases, merchandise was bagged in brown paper sacks rather plastic bags because customers seemed to prefer them. A simple Wal-Mart logo in white letters on a brown background on the front of the store served to identify the firm. Yellow smiley faces were used on in-store displays. Consumer studies determined that the chain was particularly adept at striking the delicate balance needed to convince customers its prices were low without making people feel that its stores were too cheap. In many ways, competitors like Kmart sought to emulate Wal-Mart by introducing people greeters, upgrading interiors, developing new logos and signage, and introducing new inventory response systems.

A "satisfaction guaranteed" refund and exchange policy was introduced to allow customers to be confident of Wal-Mart's merchandise and quality. Technological advancements like scanner cash registers, hand-held computers for ordering of merchandise, and computer linkages of stores with the general office and distribution centers improved communications and merchandise replenishment. Each store was encouraged to initiate programs that would make it an integral part of the community in which it operated. Associates were encouraged to "maintain the highest standards of honesty, morality, and business ethics in dealing with the public."

The External Environment

Industry analysts labeled the 1980s and early 1990s as eras of economic uncertainty for retailers. Many retailers were negatively affected by increased competitive pressures, sluggish consumer spending, slower-than-anticipated economic growth in North America, and recessions abroad. In 1995, Wal-Mart management felt the high consumer debt level caused many shoppers to reduce or defer spending on anything other than essentials. Management also felt that the lack of exciting new products or apparel trends reduced discretionary spending. Fierce competition resulted in lower margins, and the lack of inflation stalled productivity increases.

By 1998, the country had returned to prosperity. Unemployment was low, total income was relatively high, and interest rates were stable. Combined with a low inflation rate, buying power was perceived to be high and consumers were generally willing to buy. At the beginning of the year 2000, the United States had experienced one of the longest periods of economic expansion in its history.

Many retail enterprises confronted heavy competitive pressure by restructuring. Sears, Roebuck & Company, based in Chicago, became a more-focused retailer by divesting itself of Allstate Insurance

Company and its real estate subsidiaries. In 1993, the company announced it would close 118 unprofitable stores and discontinue the unprofitable Sears general merchandise catalog. It eliminated 50,000 jobs and began a $4 billion, five-year remodeling plan for its remaining multiline department stores. After unsuccessfully experimenting with an everyday low-price strategy, management chose to re-align its merchandise strategy to meet the needs of middle market customers, who were primarily women, by focusing on product lines in apparel, home, and automotive. The new focus on apparel was supported with the advertising campaign, "The Softer Side of Sears." A later companywide campaign broadened the appeal: "The many sides of Sears fit the many sides of your life." Sears completed its return to its retailing roots by selling off its ownership in Dean Witter Financial Services, Discovery Card, Coldwell Banker Real Estate, and Sears mortgage banking operations. In 1999, Sears refocused its marketing strategy with a new program that was designed to communicate a stronger whole-house and event message. A new advertising campaign was introduced with the slogan, "The good life at a great price. Guaranteed." In 2000, a new store format was introduced that concentrated on five focal areas: appliances, home fashions, tools, kids, and electronics. Other departments, including men's and women's apparel, assumed a support role in these stores.

By the early 1990s, the discount department store industry had changed in several ways and was thought to have reached maturity by many analysts. Several formerly successful firms like E. J. Korvette, W. T. Grant, Atlantic Mills, Arlans, Federals, Zayre, Heck's, and Ames had declared bankruptcy and either liquidated or reorganized as a result. Venture announced liquidation in early 1998. Firms like Target Stores and Shopko Stores began carrying more fashionable merchandise in more attractive facilities and shifted their emphasis to more national markets. Specialty retailers such as Toys "R" Us, Pier 1 Imports, and Oshmans had matured and were no longer making big inroads in toys, home furnishings, and sporting goods. The superstores of drug and food chains were rapidly discounting increasing amounts of general merchandise. Some firms, like May Department Stores Company with Caldor and Venture, and Woolworth Corporation with Woolco, had withdrawn from the field by either selling their discount divisions or closing them down entirely. Woolworth's

remaining 122 Woolco stores in Canada were sold to Wal-Mart in 1994. All remaining Woolworth variety stores in the United States were closed in 1997.

Several new retail formats had emerged in the marketplace to challenge the traditional discount department store format. The superstore, a 100,000- to 300,000-square-foot operation, combined a large supermarket with a discount general-merchandise store. Originally a European retailing concept, these outlets where known as "malls without walls." Kmart's Super Kmart, American Fare, and Wal-Mart's Supercenter Store were examples of this trend toward large operations. Warehouse retailing, which involved some combination of warehouse and showroom facilities, used warehouse principles to reduce operating expenses and thereby offer discount prices as a primary customer appeal. Home Depot combined the traditional hardware store and lumberyard with a self-service home improvement center to become the largest home-center operator in the nation.

Some retailers responded to changes in the marketplace by selling goods at price levels (20 to 60 percent) below regular retail prices. These off-price operations appeared as two general types: (1) factory outlet stores like Burlington Coat Factory Warehouse, Bass Shoes, and Manhattan's Brand Name Fashion Outlet, and (2) independents like Loehmann's, T. J. Maxx, Marshall's, and Clothestime, which bought seconds, overages, closeouts, or leftover goods from manufacturers and other retailers. Other retailers chose to dominate a product classification. Some super specialists like Sock Appeal; Little Piggie, Ltd; and Sock Market offered a single, narrowly defined classification of merchandise with an extensive assortment of brands, colors, and sizes. Niche specialists, like Kids Mart, a division of Venator (Woolworth) Corporation, targeted an identified market with carefully selected merchandise and appropriately designed stores. Some retailers like Silk Greenhouse (silk plants and flowers), Office Club (office supplies and equipment), and Toys "R" Us (toys) were called "category killers" because they had achieved merchandise dominance in their respective product categories. Stores like The Limited, Limited Express, Victoria's Secret, and The Banana Republic became minidepartment specialists by showcasing new lines and accessories alongside traditional merchandise lines.

Kmart Corporation, headquartered in Troy, Michigan, became the industry's third largest retailer after Sears, Roebuck & Co. and second largest discount department store chain in the United States in 1990. Kmart had 2,171 stores and $35,925 million in sales at the beginning of 2000. The firm was perceived by many industry analysts and consumers in several independent studies as a laggard. It had been the industry sales leader for several years and had recently announced a turnaround in profitability. In the same studies, Wal-Mart was perceived as the industry leader, even though, according to the *Wall Street Journal*, "they carry much the same merchandise, offer prices that are pennies apart and operate stores that look almost exactly alike." "Even their names are similar," noted the newspaper. The original Kmart concept of a "conveniently located, one-stop shopping unit where customers could buy a wide variety of quality merchandise at discount prices" had lost its competitive edge in a changing market. As one analyst noted in an industry newsletter: "They had done so well for the past 20 years without paying attention to market changes, now they have to." Kmart acquired a new president and chief executive officer in 2000. Wal-Mart and Kmart sales growth over the period 1990–1999 is reviewed in Exhibit 2. A competitive analysis is shown of four major retail firms in Exhibit 3.

Some retailers like Kmart had initially focused on appealing to professional, middle-class consumers who lived in suburban areas and who were likely to be price sensitive. Other firms like Target, which had adopted the discount concept early, attempted to go generally after an upscale consumer. Some firms such as Fleet Farm and Pamida served the rural consumer, while firms like Value City and Ames Discount Department Stores chose to serve the urban consumer.

In rural communities, Wal-Mart's success often came at the expense of established local merchants and units of regional discount store chains. Hardware stores, family department stores, building supply outlets, and stores featuring fabrics, sporting goods, and shoes were among the first either to close or to relocate. Regional discount retailers in the Sunbelt states like Roses, Howard's, T.G.&Y., and Duckwall-ALCO, which once enjoyed solid sales and earnings, were forced to reposition themselves by renovating stores, opening bigger and more modern units, re-merchandising assortments, and offering lower prices. In many cases, stores like Coast-to-Coast and Ben Franklin closed after a Wal-Mart announcement that it was planning to build in a specific community. "Just the word that Wal-Mart was coming made some stores close up," indicated one local newspaper editor.

Domestic Corporate Strategies

The corporate and marketing strategies that emerged at Wal-Mart were based on a set of two main objectives that had guided the firm through its growth years. In the first objective, the customer was featured:

EXHIBIT 2

Competitive Sales and Store Comparison, 1990–1999

Year	Kmart		Wal-Mart	
	Sales (000)	Stores*	Sales (000)	Stores*
1999	$35,925,000	2,171	$165,013,000	3,989
1998	33,674,000	2,161	137,634,000	3,999
1997	32,183,000	2,136	117,958,000	3,406
1996	31,437,000	2,261	104,859,000	3,054
1995	34,389,000	2,161	93,627,000	2,943
1994	34,025,000	2,481	82,494,000	2,684
1993	34,156,000	2,486	67,344,000	2,400
1992	37,724,000	2,435	55,484,000	2,136
1991	34,580,000	2,391	43,886,900	1,928
1990	32,070,000	2,350	32,601,594	1,721

*Number of general merchandise stores.

EXHIBIT 3

An Industry Comparative Analysis, 1999

	Wal-Mart	Sears	Kmart	Target
Sales (millions)	$165,013	$41,071	$35,925	$33,702
Net income (thousands)	$ 5,377	$ 1,453	$ 403	$ 1,144
Net income per share	$ 1.21	$ 3.83	$ 1.29	$ 2.45
Dividends per share	$ .14	$ n/a	$ n/a	$ .40
Percentage sales change	20.0%	2.7%	6.6%	9.9%

Number of stores:

Wal-Mart, United States
  Discount Stores—1,801
  Sam's Clubs—463
  Supercenters—721

Wal-Mart International
  Discount stores—572
  Sam's Clubs—49
  Supercenters—383

Sears Roebuck & Company (all divisions)
  Sears Merchandise Group
    Full-line department stores—858
    Hardware stores—267

Sears dealer stores—738
Sears Auto Centers stores—798
NTB National Tire & Battery stores—310

Kmart Corporation
  Big Kmart—1,860
  Traditional Kmart—206
  Super Kmart—105

Target Corporation
  Target—912
  Mervyn's—267
  Department stores—64

Source: Corporate annual reports.

"customers would be provided what they want, when they want it, all at a value." In the second objective, the team spirit was emphasized: "treating each other as we would hope to be treated, acknowledging our total dependency on our Associate-partners to sustain our success." The approach included aggressive plans for new store openings; expansion to additional states; upgrading, relocating, refurbishing, and remodeling of existing stores; and opening new distribution centers. For Wal-Mart management, the 1990s were considered an era in which the firm grew to become a truly nationwide retailer that operated in all fifty states. At the beginning of 2000, Wal-Mart management predicted that over the next five years, 60 to 70 percent of sales and earnings growth would come from domestic markets with Wal-Mart stores and supercenters, and another 10 to 15 percent from Sam's Club and McLane. The remaining 20 percent of the growth would come from planned growth in international markets. As David Glass once noted, "We'll be fine as long as we never lose our responsiveness to the customer."

In the 1980s, Wal-Mart developed several new retail formats. The first Sam's Club opened in Oklahoma City, Oklahoma, in 1983. The wholesale club was an idea that had been developed earlier by other firms but found its greatest success and growth in acceptability at Wal-Mart. Sam's Clubs featured a vast array of product categories with limited selection of brand and model; cash-and-carry business with limited hours; large (100,000-square-foot), bare-bones facilities; rock-bottom wholesale prices; and minimal promotion. The limited membership plan permitted wholesale members who bought membership and others who usually paid a percentage above the ticket price of the merchandise. A revision in merchandising strategy resulted in fewer items in the inventory mix with more emphasis on lower prices. A later acquisition of 100 Pace warehouse clubs, which were converted into Sam's Clubs, increased that division's units by more than one-third. At the beginning of 2000, there were 463 Sam's Clubs in operation.

Wal-Mart Supercenters were large combination stores. They were first opened in 1988 as Hypermarket*USA, a 222,000-square-foot superstore that combined a discount store with a large grocery store, a food court of restaurants, and other service businesses such as banks or videotape rental stores. A scaled-down version of Hypermarket*USA was called the Wal-Mart Supercenter, and was similar in merchandise offerings, but with about 180,000 to 200,000 square feet of space. These expanded store concepts also included convenience stores and gasoline distribution outlets to "enhance shopping convenience." The company proceeded slowly with these plans and later suspended its plans for building any more hypermarkets in favor of the supercenter concept. At the beginning of 2000, Wal-Mart operated 721 supercenters. The name, Hypermarket*USA, was no longer used to identify these large stores.

Wal-Mart also tested a new concept called the neighborhood market in several locations in Arkansas. Identified by the company as "small-marts," these green-and-white stores were stocked with fresh fruits and vegetables, a drive-up pharmacy, a twenty-four-hour photo shop, and a selection of classic Wal-Mart hard goods. Management elected to move slowly on this concept, planning to open no more than ten a year. The goal was to ring the superstores with these smaller stores to attract customers who were in a hurry and wanted only a few items.

The McLane Company, Inc., a provider of retail and grocery distribution services for retail stores, was acquired in 1991. It was not considered a major segment of the total Wal-Mart operation.

Several programs were launched in Wal-Mart stores to highlight popular social causes. The "buy American" program was a Wal-Mart retail program initiated in 1985. The theme was "Bring It Home to the USA" and its purpose was to communicate Wal-Mart's support for American manufacturing. In the program, the firm exerted substantial influence to encourage manufacturers to produce goods in the United States rather than import them from other countries. Vendors were encouraged to initiate the process by contacting the company directly with proposals to sell goods that were made in the United States. Buyers also targeted specific import items in their assortments on a state-by-state basis to encourage domestic manufacturing. According to Haim Dabah, president of Gitano Group, Inc., a maker of fashion discount clothing that imported 95 percent of its clothing and now makes about 20 percent of its

products here: "Wal-Mart let it be known loud and clear that if you're going to grow with them, you sure better have some products made in the U.S.A." Farris Fashion, Inc. (flannel shirts); Roadmaster Corporation (exercise bicycles); Flanders Industries, Inc. (lawn chairs); and Magic Chef (microwave ovens) were examples of vendors that chose to participate in the program.

From the Wal-Mart standpoint, the "Buy American" program centered around value—producing and selling quality merchandise at a competitive price. The promotion included television advertisements featuring factory workers, a soaring American eagle, and the slogan: "We buy American whenever we can, so you can too." Prominent in-store signage and store circulars were also included. One store poster read: "Success Stories—These items formerly imported, are now being purchased by Wal-Mart in the U.S.A."

Wal-Mart was one of the first retailers to embrace the concept of "green" marketing. The program offered shoppers the option of purchasing products that were better for the environment in three respects: manufacturing, use, and disposal. The program was introduced through full-page advertisements in the *Wall Street Journal* and *USA Today*. In-store signage identified products that were environmentally safe. As Wal-Mart executives saw it, "Customers are concerned about the quality of land, air, and water, and would like the opportunity to do something positive." To initiate the program, 7,000 vendors were notified that Wal-Mart had a corporate concern for the environment and asked for their support in various ways. Wal-Mart television advertising showed children on swings, fields of grain blowing in the wind, and roses. Green-and-white store signs, printed on recycled paper, marked products or packaging that had been developed or redesigned to be more environmentally sound.

The Wal-Mart private brand program began with the "Ol' Roy" brand, the private-label dog food named for Sam Walton's favorite hunting companion. Introduced to Wal-Mart stores in 1982 as a low-price alterative to national brands, Ol' Roy became the biggest seller of all dog-food brands in the United States. "We are a [national] brand-oriented company first," noted Bob Connolly, executive vice president of merchandising at Wal-Mart. "But we also use private labels to fill value or pricing voids that, for whatever reason, the brands left behind. Wal-Mart's private label program included thousands of products that had brand names such as Sam's Choice, Great Value, Equate, and Spring Valley.

Wal-Mart had become the channel commander in the distribution of many brand-name items. As the nation's largest retailer and in many geographic areas the dominant distributor, it exerted considerable influence in negotiation for the best price, delivery terms, promotion allowances, and continuity of supply. Many of these benefits could be passed on to consumers in the form of quality name-brand items available at lower than competitive prices. As a matter of corporate policy, management often insisted on doing business only with producers' top sales executives rather than going through a manufacturer's representative. Wal-Mart had been accused of threatening to buy from other producers if firms refused to sell directly to it. In the ensuing power struggle, Wal-Mart executives refused to talk about the controversial policy or admit that it existed. As a spokesperson of an industry association of sales agencies' representatives suggested, "In the Southwest, Wal-Mart's the only show in town." An industry analyst added, "They're extremely aggressive. Their approach has always been to give the customer the benefit of a corporate saving. That builds up customer loyalty and market share."

Another key factor in the mix was an inventory control system that was recognized as the most sophisticated in retailing. A high-speed computer system linked almost all the stores to headquarters and the company's distribution centers. It logged electronically every item sold at the checkout counter, automatically kept the warehouses informed of merchandise to be ordered, and directed the flow of goods to the stores and even to the proper shelves. Most important for management, it helped detect sales trends quickly and speeded up market reaction time substantially. According to Bob Connolly, executive vice president of merchandising, "Wal-Mart has used the data gathered by technology to make more inventory available in the key items that customers want most, while reducing inventories overall."

At the beginning of 2000, Wal-Mart set up a separate company for its web site, with plans to go public. Wal-Mart.com Inc., based in Palo Alto, California, was jointly owned by Wal-Mart and Accel Partners, a Silicon Valley venture-capital firm. The site included a wide range of products and services that ranged from shampoo to clothing to lawn mowers, as well as airline, hotel, and rental car bookings. After launching and then closing a Sam's Club web site, Wal-Mart had plans to reopen the site in mid-June 2000 with an emphasis on upscale items such as jewelry, housewares, and electronics and full product lines for small business owners. SamsClub.com would be run by Wal-Mart from the company's Bentonville, Arkansas, headquarters.

International Corporate Strategies

In 1994, Wal-Mart entered the Canadian market with the acquisition of 122 Woolco discount stores from Woolworth Corporation. When acquired, the Woolco stores were losing millions of dollars annually, but operations became profitable within three years. At the end of 1999, the company had 166 Wal-Mart discount stores in Canada and planned to open seventeen new stores in fiscal 2000. The company's operations in Canada were considered a model for Wal-Mart's expansion into other international markets. With 35 percent of the Canadian discount and department store market, Wal-Mart was the largest retailer in that country.

With a tender offer for shares and mergers of joint ventures in Mexico, the company in 1997 acquired a controlling interest in Cifra, Mexico's largest retailer. Cifra, later identified as Wal-Mart de Mexico, operated stores with various concepts in every region of Mexico, ranging from the nation's largest chain of sit-down restaurants to a softline department store. Retail analysts noted that the initial venture involved many costly mistakes. Time after time it sold the wrong products, including tennis balls that wouldn't bounce in high-altitude Mexico City. Large parking lots at some stores made access difficult because many people arrived by bus. In 2000, Wal-Mart operated 397 Cifra outlets in Mexico, in addition to twenty-seven Wal-Mart Supercenters and thirty-four Sam's Club stores.

When Wal-Mart entered Argentina in 1995, it initially faced challenges adapting its United States–based retail mix and store layouts to the local culture. Although globalization and American cultural influences had swept through the country in the early 1990s, the Argentine market did not accept American cuts of meat, bright-colored cosmetics, and jewelry that gave prominent placement to emeralds, sapphires, and diamonds, even though most Argentine women preferred wearing gold and silver. The first stores even had hardware departments full of tools wired for 110-volt electric power; the standard throughout Argentina was 220. Compounding the challenges were store layouts that featured narrow aisles; stores appeared crowded and dirty.

Wal-Mart management concluded that Brazil, with the fifth largest population in the world and people who had a tendency to follow U.S. cultural cues, offered great opportunities for Wal-Mart. Although financial data were not broken out on South American operations, retail analysts cited the accounts of Wal-Mart's Brazilian partner, Lojas Americanas SA, to suggest that Wal-Mart lost $100 million in start-up costs of the initial sixteen stores. Customer acceptance of Wal-Mart stores was mixed. In Canada and Mexico, many customers were familiar with the company from cross-border shopping trips. Many Brazilian customers were not familiar with the Wal-Mart name. In addition, local Brazilian markets were already dominated by savvy local and foreign competitors such as Grupo Pao de Acucar SA of Brazil and Carrefour SA of France. And Wal-Mart's insistence on doing things "the Wal-Mart way" initially alienated many local suppliers and employees. The country's continuing economic problems also presented a challenge. In 2000, Wal-Mart planned to expand its presence by opening three more Sam's Clubs in Brazil.

Because of stubborn local regulations, management felt it would be easier for Wal-Mart to buy existing stores in Europe than to build new ones. The acquisition of twenty-one "hypermarkets" in Germany at the end of 1997 marked the company's first entry into Europe, which management considered "one of the best consumer markets in the world." These large stores offered one-stop shopping facilities similar to Wal-Mart supercenters. In early 1999, the firm also purchased seventy-four Interspar hypermarket stores. All of these German stores were identified with the Wal-Mart name and restocked with a new and revamped selection of merchandise. In response to local laws that forced early store closings and banned Sunday sales, the company simply opened stores earlier to allow shopping to begin at 7 A.M.

Wal-Mart acquired ASDA, Britain's third largest supermarket group, for $10.8 billion in July 1999. With its own price rollbacks, people greeters, "permanently low prices," and even smiley faces, ASDA had emulated Wal-Mart's store culture for many years. Based in Leeds, England, the firm had 232 stores in England, Scotland, and Wales. While the culture and pricing strategies of the two companies were nearly identical, there were differences, primarily in the size and product mix of the stores. The average Wal-Mart Supercenter in 1999 was 180,000 square feet in size and had about 30 percent of its sales in groceries. In contrast, the average ASDA store had only 65,000 square feet and did 60 percent of sales in grocery items.

The response in Europe to Wal-Mart was immediate and dramatic. Competitors scrambled to match Wal-Mart's low prices, long hours, and friendly service. Some firms combined to strengthen their operations. For example, France's Carrefour SA chain of hypermarkets combined forces with competitor, Promodes, in a $16.5 billion deal. In 1999, Carrefour dominated the European market with 9,089 locations. It was also one of the world's largest retailers with market dominance in Europe and in Latin America and Asia.

Wal-Mart's initial effort to enter China fell apart in 1996 when Wal-Mart and Thailand's Charoen Pokphand Group terminated an eighteen-month-old joint venture because of management differences. Wal-Mart decided to consolidate its operations with five stores in the Hong Kong border city of Shenzhen, one in Dalian, and another in Kumming. Although management had plans to open ten additional stores in China by the end of 2000, analysts concluded that the company was taking a low-profile approach because of possible competitive response and government restrictions. Beijing restricted the operations of foreign retailers in China, requiring them, for instance, to have government-backed partners. In Shenzhen, it limited the number of stores Wal-Mart could open. Planned expansion in the China market came as China prepared to enter the World Trade Organization and its economy showed signs of accelerating. At the beginning of 2000, Wal-Mart operated five supercenters in South Korea.

The international expansion accelerated management's plans for the development of Wal-Mart as a global brand along the lines of Coca-Cola, Disney, and McDonald's. "We are a global brand name," said Bobby Martin, an early president of the international division of Wal-Mart. "To customers everywhere it means low cost, best value, greatest selection of quality merchandise and highest standards of customer service," he noted. Some changes were mandated in Wal-Mart's international operations to meet local tastes and intense competitive conditions. "We're building companies out there," said Martin. "That's like starting Wal-Mart all over again in South America or Indonesia or China." Although stores in different international markets would coordinate purchasing to gain leverage with suppliers, developing new technology and planning overall strategy would be done from Wal-Mart headquarters in Bentonville, Arkansas. At the beginning of 2000, the international division of Wal-Mart operated 572 discount stores, 383 supercenters, and forty-nine Sam's Clubs. Wal-Mart's international unit accounted for $22.7 billion in sales in 1999. Exhibit 4 shows the countries in which stores were operated and the number of units in each country.

Decisionmaking in a Market-Oriented Firm

One principle that distinguished Wal-Mart was the unusual depth of employee involvement in company affairs. Corporate strategies put emphasis on human resources management. Wal-Mart employees became associates, a name borrowed from Sam Walton's early association with the JC Penney Co. Input was encouraged at meetings at both the store and corporate level. The firm hired employees locally and provided training programs. Through a "letter to the president" program, management encouraged employees to ask questions, and made words like *we, us,*

EXHIBIT 4

Wal-Mart International Division, 1999

Country	Stores
Mexico	460
United Kingdom	236
Canada	166
Germany	95
Brazil	16
Puerto Rico	15
Argentina	10
China	8
South Korea	5

Source: Wal-Mart, Hoover's Online.

and *our* part of the corporate language. Several special award programs recognized individual, department, and division achievement. Stock ownership and profit-sharing programs were introduced as part of a partnership concept

The corporate culture was complimented by the editors of the trade publication, *Mass Market Retailers,* when they recognized all 275,000 associates collectively as the "Mass Market Retailers of the Year." "The Wal-Mart associate," the editors noted, "in this decade that has come to symbolize all that is right with the American worker, particularly in the retailing environment and most particularly at Wal-Mart." The "store within a store" concept, as a Wal-Mart corporate policy, trained individuals to be merchants by being responsible for the performance of their own departments as if they were running their own businesses. Seminars and training programs afforded them opportunities to grow within the company. "People development, not just a good program for any growing company but a must to secure our future," is how Suzanne Allford, vice president of the Wal-Mart people division, explained the firm's decentralized approach to retail management development.

"The Wal-Mart way" was a phase that was used by management to summarize the firm's unconventional approach to business and the development of the corporate culture. As noted in a report referring to a recent development program: "We stepped outside our retailing world to examine the best managed companies in the United States in an effort to determine the fundamentals of their success and to 'benchmark' our own performances." "The name 'total quality management' (TQM) was used to identify this vehicle for proliferating the very best things we do while incorporating the new ideas our people have that will assure our future." In 1999, *Discount Store News* honored Wal-Mart Stores, Inc., as "Retailer of the Century" with a commemorative 200-page issue of the magazine.

The Growth Challenge

H. Lee Scott, Jr., indicated that he would never forget his first meeting with Sam Walton. "How old are you?" Walton asked the then thirty-year-old Scott, who had just taken a job overseeing the Wal-Mart trucking fleet. "Do you think you can do this job?" asked Walton. When Scott said yes, Walton agreed and said, "I reckon you can." More than twenty years later, as Wal-Mart's new CEO, Scott was facing his toughest challenge yet: keeping the world's biggest retailer on its phenomenal roll and delivering the huge sales and earnings increases that investors had come to expect from Wal-Mart over the years. Analysts had correctly projected that Wal-Mart would surpass General Motors to be ranked number 1 in revenue on the Fortune 500 list in 2000. The combination of growth and acquisition had caused revenue to make huge leaps every year. In 1999, revenues went up 20 percent, from $139 billion in 1998 to $165 billion. Earnings also increased in 1999 by 21 percent, to nearly $5.4 billion. Industry analysts noted that this growth was in addition to an 18 percent compound annual growth rate over the past decade.

Wal-Mart Stores, Inc., revolutionized American retailing with its focus on low costs, efficient customer service, and everyday low pricing to drive sales. Although the company had suffered though some years of lagging performance, it had experienced big gains from its move into the grocery business with one-stop supercenters and in international markets with acquisitions and new ventures. To keep it all going and growing was a major challenge. As the largest retailer in the world, the company and its leadership were challenged to find new areas to continue to increase sales and profits into the future. H. Lee Scott knew that an ambitious expansion program was necessary to allow the company to meet these objectives.

Appendix A: Wal-Mart Stores, Inc., Consolidated Balance Sheets and Operating Statements, 1998–1999*

Consolidated Statements of Income

	Fiscal years ended January 31		
	2000	1999	1998
Revenues			
Net sales	$ 165,013	$ 137,634	$117,958
Other income—net	1,796	1,574	1,341
	166,809	139,208	119,299
Costs and expenses			
Cost of sales	129,664	108,725	93,438
Operating, selling, and general and administrative expenses	27,040	22,363	19,358
Interest costs			
Debt	756	529	555
Capital leases	266	268	229
	157,726	131,885	113,580
Income before income taxes, minority interest, equity in unconsolidated subsidiaries, and cumulative effect of accounting change	9,083	7,323	5,719
Provision for income taxes			
Current	3,476	3,380	2,095
Deferred	(138)	(640)	20
	3,338	2,740	2,115
Income before minority interest, equity in unconsolidated subsidiaries, and cumulative effect of accounting change	5,745	4,583	3,604
Minority interest and equity in unconsolidated subsidiaries	(170)	(153)	(78)
Income before cumulative effect of accounting change	5,575	4,430	3,526
Cumulative effect of accounting change, net of tax benefit of $119	(198)	—	—
Net income	$ 5,377	$ 4,430	$ 3,526
Net income per common share			
Basic net income per common share			
Income before cumulative effect of accounting change	$ 1.25	$ 0.99	$ 0.78
Cumulative effect of accounting change, net of tax	(0.04)	–	–
Net income per common share	$ 1.21	$ 0.99	$ 0.78
Average number of common shares	4,451	4,464	4,516
Diluted net income per common share			
Income before cumulative effect of accounting change	$ 1.25	$ 0.99	$ 0.78
Cumulative effect of accounting change, net of tax	(0.04)	0.00	0.00
Net income per common share	$ 1.20	$ 0.99	$ 0.78
Average number of common shares	4,474	4,485	4,533
Pro forma amounts assuming accounting change had been in effect in fiscal 2000, 1999, and 1998			
Net income	$ 5,575	$ 4,393	$ 3,517
Net income per common share, basic and diluted	$ 1.25	$ 0.98	$ 0.78

*Amounts in millions except per-share data.

Appendix B: Wal-Mart Stores, Inc., Consolidated Balance Sheets and Operating Statements, 1998–1999*

Consolidated Balance Sheets

	January 31	
	2000	**1999**
Assets		
Current assets		
Cash and cash equivalents	$ 1,856	$ 1,879
Receivables	1,341	1,118
Inventories		
At replacement cost	20,171	17,549
Less LIFO reserve	378	473
Inventories at LIFO cost	19,793	17,076
Prepaid expenses and other	1,366	1,059
Total current assets	24,356	21,132
Property, plant, and equipment, at cost		
Land	8,785	5,219
Building and improvements	21,169	16,061
Fixtures and equipment	10,362	9,296
Transportation equipment	747	553
	41,063	31,129
Less accumulated depreciation	8,224	7,455
Net property, plant, and equipment	32,839	23,674
Property under capital lease		
Property under capital lease	4,285	3,335
Less accumulated amortization	1,155	1,036
Net property under capital leases	3,130	2,299
Other assets and deferred charges		
Net goodwill and other acquired intangible assets	9,392	2,538
Other assets and deferred charges	632	353
Total assets	$70,349	$49,996
Liabilities and shareholders' equity		
Current liabilities		
Commercial paper	$ 3,323	$ —
Accounts payable	13,105	10,257
Accrued liabilities	6,161	4,998
Accrued income taxes	1,129	501
Long-term debt due within one year	1,964	900
Obligations under capital leases due within one year	121	106
Total current liabilities	25,803	16,762
Long-term debt	13,672	6,908
Long-term obligations under capital leases	3,002	2,699
Deferred income taxes and other	759	716
Minority interest	1,279	1,799
Shareholders' equity		
Preferred stock ($.10 par value; 100 shares authorized, none issued)		
Common stock ($.10 par value; 5,500 shares authorized, 4,457 and 4,448 issued and outstanding in 2000 and 1999, respectively)	446	445
Capital in excess of par value	714	435
Retained earnings	25,129	20,741
Other accumulated comprehensive income	(455)	(509)
Total shareholders' equity	25,834	21,112
Total liabilities and shareholders' equity	$70,349	$49,996

*Amounts in millions.

Appendix C: Wal-Mart Stores, Inc., Financial Summary, 1990–2000*

Eleven-Year Financial Summary

	2000	1999	1998
Net sales	$165,013	$137,634	$ 117,958
Net sales increase	20%	17%	12%
Comparative store sales increase	8%	9%	6%
Other income—net	1,796	1,574	1,341
Cost of sales	129,664	108,725	93,438
Operating, selling, and general and administrative expenses	27,040	22,363	19,358
Interest costs			
Debt	756	529	555
Capital leases	266	268	229
Provision for income taxes	3,338	2,740	2,115
Minority interest and equity in unconsolidated subsidiaries	(170)	(153)	(78)
Cumulative effect of accounting change, net of tax	(198)	—	—
Net income	5,377	4,430	3,526
Per share of common stock			
Basic net income	1.21	0.99	0.78
Diluted net income	1.20	0.99	0.78
Dividends	0.20	0.16	0.14
Financial position			
Current assets	$ 24,356	$ 21,132	$ 19,352
Inventories at replacement cost	20,171	17,549	16,845
Less LIFO reserve	378	473	348
Inventories at LIFO cost	19,793	17,076	16,497
Net property, plant and equipment, and capital leases	35,969	25,973	23,606
Total assets	70,349	49,996	45,384
Current liabilities	25,803	16,762	14,460
Long-term debt	13,672	6,908	7,191
Long-term obligations under capital leases	3,002	2,699	2,483
Shareholders' equity	25,834	21,112	18,503
Financial ratios			
Current ratio	.9	1.3	1.3
Inventories/working capital	(13.7)	3.9	3.4
Return on assets†	9.8%§	9.6%	8.5%
Return on shareholders' equity‡	22.9%	22.4%	19.8%
Other year-end data			
Number of domestic Wal-Mart stores	1,801	1,869	1,921
Number of domestic Supercenters	721	564	441
Number of domestic Sam's Club units	463	451	443
International units	1,004	715	601
Number of associates	1,140,000	910,000	825,000
Number of shareholders	341,000	261,000	246,000

*Dollar amounts in millions except per-share data.

†Net income before minority interest, equity in unconsolidated subsidiaries, and cumulative effect of accounting change/average assets.

‡Net income/average shareholders' equity.

§Calculated without giving effect to the amount by which a lawsuit settlement exceeded established reserves.

The effects of the change in accounting method for Sam's Club membership revenue recognition would not have a material impact on this summary prior to 1998. Therefore, pro forma information as if the accounting change had been in effect for all years presented has not been provided.

Acquisition of the ASDA Group PLC and the company's related debt issuance had a significant impact on the fiscal 2000 amounts in this summary.

1997	1996	1995	1994	1993	1992	1991	1990
$104,859	$ 93,627	$ 82,494	$ 67,344	$ 55,484	$ 43,887	$ 32,602	$ 25,811
12%	13%	22%	21%	26%	35%	26%	25%
5%	4%	7%	6%	11%	10%	10%	11%
1,319	1,146	914	645	497	404	262	175
83,510	74,505	65,586	53,444	44,175	34,786	25,500	20,070
16,946	15,021	12,858	10,333	8,321	6,684	5,152	4,070
629	692	520	331	143	113	43	20
216	196	186	186	180	153	126	118
1,794	1,606	1,581	1,358	1,171	945	752	632
(27)	(13)	4	(4)	4	(1)	—	—
—	—	—	—	—	—	—	—
3,056	2,740	2,681	2,333	1,995	1,609	1,291	1,076
0.67	0.60	0.59	0.51	0.44	0.35	0.28	0.24
0.67	0.60	0.59	0.51	0.44	0.35	0.28	0.24
0.11	0.10	0.09	0.07	0.05	0.04	0.04	0.03
$ 17,993	$ 17,331	$ 15,338	$ 12,114	$ 10,198	$ 8,575	$ 6,415	$ 4,713
16,193	16,300	14,415	11,483	9,780	7,857	6,207	4,751
296	311	351	469	512	473	399	323
15,897	15,989	14,064	11,014	9,268	7,384	5,808	4,428
20,324	18,894	15,874	13,176	9,793	6,434	4,712	3,430
39,604	37,541	32,819	26,441	20,565	15,443	11,389	8,198
10,957	11,454	9,973	7,406	6,754	5,004	3,990	2,845
7,709	8,508	7,871	6,156	3,073	1,722	740	185
2,307	2,092	1,838	1,804	1,772	1,556	1,159	1,087
17,143	14,756	12,726	10,753	8,759	6,990	5,366	3,966
1.6	1.5	1.5	1.6	1.5	1.7	1.6	1.7
2.3	2.7	2.6	2.3	2.7	2.1	2.4	2.4
7.9%	7.8%	9.0%	9.9%	11.1%	12.0%	13.2%	14.8%
19.2%	19.9%	22.8%	23.9%	25.3%	26.0%	27.7%	30.9%
1,960	1,995	1,985	1,950	1,848	1,714	1,568	1,399
344	239	147	72	34	10	9	6
436	433	426	417	256	208	148	123
314	276	226	24	10	—	—	—
728,000	675,000	622,000	528,000	434,000	371,000	328,000	271,000
257,000	244,000	259,000	258,000	181,000	150,000	122,000	80,000

Appendix D: Wal-Mart Stores, Inc., Board of Directors and Executive Officers, January 31, 2000

Directors

John A. Cooper, Jr.	H. Lee Scott
Stephen Friedman	Jack C. Shewmaker
Stanley C. Gault	Donald G. Soderquist
David D. Glass	Dr. Paula Stern
Roland Hernandez	Jose Villarreal
Dr. Frederick S. Humphries	John T. Walton
E. Stanley Kroenke	S. Robson Walton
Elizabeth A. Sanders	

Officers

S. Robson Walton
Chairman of the Board

H. Lee Scott
President and CEO

David D. Glass
Chairman, Executive Committee of the Board

Donald G. Soderquist
Senior Vice Chairman

Paul R. Carter
Executive Vice President and Vice President, Wal-Mart Realty

Bob Connolly
Executive Vice President, Merchandise

Thomas M. Coughlin
Executive Vice President and President and CEO, Wal-Mart Stores Division

David Dible
Executive Vice President, Speciality Division

Michael Duke
Executive Vice President, Logistics

Thomas Grimm
Executive Vice President and President and CEO, Sam's Club

Don Harris
Executive Vice President, Operations

John B. Menzer
Executive Vice President, President, and CEO, International Division

Coleman Peterson
Executive Vice President, People Division

Thomas M. Schoewe
Executive Vice President and Chief Financial Officer

Robert K. Rhoads
Senior Vice President, General Counsel, and Secretary

J. J. Fitzsimmons
Senior Vice President, Finance, and Treasurer

Source: Wal-Mart Stores, Inc., 2000 Annual Report.

REFERENCES

Albright, Mark, "Changes in Store," *New York Times,* May 17, 1999, pp. 10, 12.

Bergman, Joan, "Saga of Sam Walton," *Stores,* January 1988, pp. 129–130+.

Boudette, Neil E., "Wal-Mart Plans Major Expansion in Germany," *Wall Street Journal,* July 20, 2000, p. A21.

Cummins, Chip, "Wal-Mart's Net Income Increases 28%, but Accounting Change Worries Investors," *Wall Street Journal,* August 10, 2000, p. A6.

"David Glass's Biggest Job Is Filling Sam's Shoes," *Business Month,* December 1988, p. 42.

Feldman, Amy, "How Big Can It Get?" *Money,* December 1999, pp. 158+.

Friedland, Johnathan, and Louise Lee, "The Wal-Mart Way Sometimes Gets Lost in Translation Overseas," *Wall Street Journal,* October 8, 1997, pp. A1, A12.

Gustke, Constance, "Smooth Operator," *Worth,* March 2000, pp. 41+.

Helliker, Kevin, "Wal-Mart's Store of the Future Blends Discount Prices, Department-Store Feel," *Wall Street Journal,* May 17, 1991, pp. B1, B8.

Helliker, Kevin, and Bob Ortega, "Falling Profit Marks End of Era at Wal-Mart," *Wall Street Journal,* January 18, 1996, p. B1.

"How the Stores Did," *Wall Street Journal,* May 5, 2000, p. B4.

Huey, John, "America's Most Successful Merchant," *Fortune,* September 23, 1991, pp. 46–48+.

Johnson, Jay L., "The Supercenter Challenge," *Discount Merchandiser,* August 1989, pp. 70+.

Komarow, Steven, "Wal-Mart Takes Slow Road in Germany," *USA Today,* May 5, 2000, p. 3B.

Krauss, Clifford, "Wal-Mart Learns a Hard Lesson," *International Herald Tribune,* December 6, 1999, p. 15.

Larrabee, John, "Wal-Mart Ends Vermont's Holdout," *USA Today,* September 19, 1995, p. 4B.

Lee, Louise, "Discounter Wal-Mart Is Catering to Affluent to Maintain Growth," *Wall Street Journal,* February 7, 1996, p. A1.

Lee, Louise, and Joel Millman, "Wal-Mart to Buy Majority Stake in Cifra," *Wall Street Journal,* June 4, 1997, pp. A3+.

Loomis, Carol J., "Sam Would Be Proud," *Fortune,* April 17, 2000, pp. 131+.

"Management Style: Sam Moore Walton," *Business Month,* May 1989, p. 38.

Marsch, Barbara, "The Challenge: Merchants Mobilize to Battle Wal-Mart in a Small Community," *Wall Street Journal,* June 5, 1991, pp. A1, A4.

Mason, Todd, "Sam Walton of Wal-Mart: Just Your Basic Homespun Billionaire," *Business Week,* October 14, 1985, pp. 142–143+.

Mitchener, Brandon, and David Woodruff, "French Merger of Hypermarkets Gets a Go-Ahead," *Wall Street Journal,* January 26, 2000, p. A19.

Nelson, Emily, "Wal-Mart to Build a Test Supermarket in Bid to Boost Grocery-Industry Share," *Wall Street Journal,* June 19, 1998, p. A4.

Nelson, Emily, and Kara Swisher, "Wal-Mart Eyes Public Sale of Web Unit," *Wall Street Journal,* January 7, 2000, p. A3.

"Our People Make the Difference: The History of Wal-Mart," video cassette, Bentonville, Arkansas: Wal-Mart Video Productions, 1991.

Peters, Tom J., and Nancy Austin, *A Passion For Excellence,* New York: Random House, pp. 266–267.

Rawn, Cynthia Dunn, "Wal-Mart vs. Main Street," *American Demographics,* June 1990, pp. 58–59.

"Retailer Completes Purchase of Wertkauf of Germany," *Wall Street Journal,* December 31, 1997, p. B3.

Rudnitsky, Howard, "How Sam Walton Does It," *Forbes,* August 16, 1982, pp. 42–44.

"Sam Moore Walton," *Business Month,* May 1989, p. 38.

Schwadel, Francine, "Little Touches Spur Wal-Mart's Rise," *Wall Street Journal,* September 22, 1989, p. B1.

Sears, Roebuck & Co., *Annual Report,* Chicago, Illinois: Sears, 1999.

Sheets, Kenneth R., "How Wal-Mart Hits Main St.," *U.S. News & World Report,* March 13, 1989, pp. 53–55.

Target Corporation, *Annual Report,* Minneapolis, Minnesota: Target, 1999.

"The Early Days: Walton Kept Adding a Few More Stores," *Discount Store News,* December 9, 1985, p. 61.

Tomlinson, Richard, "Who's Afraid of Wal-Mart?" *Fortune,* June 26, 2000, p. 186.

Trimble, Vance H., *Sam Walton: The Inside Story of America's Richest Man,* New York: Dutton, 1990.

Voyle, Susanna, "Asda Criticised for Price Claims," *Financial Times,* December 8, 1999, p. 3.

"Wal-Mart's Asda Says CEO to Head Europe Expansion," *Wall Street Journal Europe,* December 3, 1999, p. 6.

"Wal-Mart Spoken Here," *Business Week,* June 23, 1997, pp. 138+.

Wal-Mart Stores, Inc., *Annual Report,* Bentonville, Arkansas: Wal-Mart, 2000.

"Wal-Mart Takes a Stand," *The Economist,* May 22, 1999, p. 31.

"Wal-Mart: The Model Discounter," *Dun's Business Month,* December 1982, pp. 60–61.

"Wal-Mart Wins Again," *The Economist,* October 2, 1999, p. 33.

Walton, Sam, with John Huey, *Sam Walton Made in America,* New York: Doubleday Publishing Company, 1992.

Wonacott, Peter, "Wal-Mart Finds Market Footing in China," *Wall Street Journal,* July 17, 2000, p. A31.

"Work, Ambition—Sam Walton," press release, Corporate and Public Affairs, Wal-Mart Stores, Inc.

Zellner, Wendy, "Someday, Lee, This May All Be Yours," *Business Week,* November 15, 1999, pp. 84+.

Zimmerman, Ann, "Wal-Mart Posts 19% Profit Rise, Exceeding Analysts' Expectations," *Wall-Street Journal,* May 10, 2000, p. B8.

Zimmerman, Ann, "Wal-Mart to Open Reworked Web Site for Sams-Club.com, June 6, 2000, p. B8.

26 Wal-Mart's Mexican Adventure

This case was prepared by Charles W. L. Hill, the University of Washington.

Introduction

Wal-Mart is America's and the world's largest retailer. It was founded by the legendary Sam Walton in the 1960s, and by 2001, Wal-Mart generated over $100 billion in annual sales from 4,000 stores, more than 1,000 of which were now located outside the United States. The company operates three basic store formats: the traditional Wal-Mart stores, which sell a wide range of basic consumer merchandise, from household products to clothes and electronics; Wal-Mart supercenters, which are larger stores that have groceries added to the basic merchandising mix; and Sam's Clubs, which are deep discount stores that carry a limited range of low-priced merchandise and food. Although the company was still opening new stores in the United States in 2001, it had recognized since the early 1990s that its U.S. growth prospects were ultimately limited by market saturation. Believing that its unique culture, format, and operating systems would give it a competitive edge in many foreign markets, Wal-Mart embarked on an international expansion strategy in 1991, when it opened the first Sam's Club store in Mexico City. A decade later, Mexico is the brightest star in the company's international division, with over 500 Mexican stores generating $9 billion in sales. Getting to this point, however, was not easy. Wal-Mart had suf-

This case is intended to be used as a basis for class discussion rather than as an illustration of either effective or ineffective handling of the situation. Reprinted by permission of Charles W. L. Hill.

fered several setbacks along the way that might have discouraged a less ambitious and near-sighted rival from continuing.

Wal-Mart's Competitive Advantage

Wal-Mart's spectacular four-decade growth from a small Arkansas retailer to a national powerhouse was based on a first-class management team that pursued several innovative operations strategies. These strategies backed up the company's commitment to deliver a large selection of high-value merchandise at low cost to consumers.

The firm's early success was based partly on a strategy of locating in small southern towns that had no other major retail presence. When Wal-Mart entered most of these towns, its primary competitors were small mom-and-pop stores that had a much higher cost structure than the discounter. Wal-Mart quickly gained significant share in these towns and did not have to face competition from other discounters, such as Kmart, which were focused on large urban areas.

As the number of stores grew, Wal-Mart pioneered the development of a hub-and-spoke distribution system, where central distribution warehouses were strategically located to serve clusters of stores. This system allowed Wal-Mart to replenish stock in its stores rapidly and to keep the amount of store space that needed to be dedicated to inventory to a minimum. The results included higher sales per square foot and more rapid inventory turnover. This combination helped to increase store sales and drive down inventory and logistics costs. The firm was also one of the first to utilize computer-based information systems to track in-store sales and transmit this information to suppliers. The information provided by these systems was used to determine pricing and stocking strategy and to manage inventories better. The combination of state-of-the art information systems and the hub-and-spoke distribution system allowed Wal-Mart to build the leanest supply chain in the industry. Wal-Mart is still a leader today in information systems. All Wal-Mart stores, distribution centers, and suppliers are linked together via sophisticated information systems and satellite-based communications systems that allow for daily adjustments to orders, inventories, and prices.

Wal-Mart is also famous for a dynamic and egalitarian culture that grants major decisionmaking authority to store managers, department managers, and individual employees (who Wal-Mart refers to as "associates"). Wal-Mart is renowned for treating its employees extremely well, but at the same time, for demanding commitment and excellent performance from them. This culture is backed up with generous profit sharing and stock ownership plans for all employees, including associates, which makes every employee "think and behave like an owner of the company." Wal-Mart has thus developed a culture and a control system that create incentives for associates and managers to give their best for the company. The result is higher employee productivity, which again translates into lower cost.

As Wal-Mart has grown, it has also garnered significant leverage with its suppliers, whether they are small manufacturers or global enterprises, such as Procter & Gamble, for whom Wal-Mart is the largest single account. Wal-Mart has used this leverage to demand lower prices from its suppliers, and it passes the savings on to its customers in the form of "everyday low prices."

Mexican Genesis

By 1990, Wal-Mart was concerned that its growth rate in the United States would inevitably slow down. This trend would slow stock price appreciation for Wal-Mart, which would be bad news for the thousands of Wal-Mart associates who were also stockholders. The company embarked on two strategies to recharge its growth rate. The first was expansion into the grocery business with the opening of Wal-Mart supercenters that would stock food products in addition to Wal-Mart's traditional merchandise. The second strategy was international expansion.

At the time that Wal-Mart was considering going international, the United States was entering negotiations with Mexico and Canada for creating a North American free-trade area (subsequently called NAFTA). This piqued Wal-Mart's interest in Mexico. Historically, significant barriers to cross-border trade and investment, substantial state involvement in business activity, and high inflation had characterized the Mexican economy. Under the government of Carlos Salinas, a Harvard trained economist, however, Mexico had embraced free-market reforms. State-owned enterprises were being privatized. Barriers to trade and investment with the United States had already been lowered significantly by Salinas and would fall much further under the NAFTA proposal. Tariffs on goods imported from the United States had come down from as much as 100 percent in the mid 1980s, to a maximum of 20 percent by the early 1990s. Under NAFTA, many of these tariffs would fall to zero. Many barriers to cross-border investment had been eliminated. Salinas had also imposed a tight monetary policy, which had lowered Mexico's inflation rate into the single digits. The country's economy was growing at a 4 to 5 percent annual rate by the early 1990s, faster than that of the United States, while disposable income had increased by some 70 percent since Salinas took office in 1988. Although Mexico was still a very poor country by U.S. standards, approximately 30 million of its 80 million people could now be classified as middle class. This segment was concentrated in three main urban areas: Mexico City, Guadalajara, and Monterrey.

Although the Mexican retail market was still fragmented and dispersed, four national supermarket chains had emerged and accounted for over 30 percent of the retail market. The largest of these, Cifra, operated about 120 discount and grocery stores in 1991 and generated sales of approximately $2.2 billion. Wal-Mart founder Sam Walton had first met one of Cifra's three founding brothers, Jeronimo Arango, in 1990. The two men immediately hit it off, and both agreed that the free-trade deal being negotiated among Canada, Mexico, and the United States opened opportunities for Wal-Mart to cooperate with Cifra in Mexico.

Having decided that Mexico would be a good proving ground for its foreign growth strategy, Wal-Mart employees debated several options for expansion, including licensing its brand name to franchisees, expanding via wholly owned subsidiaries, or entering into a joint venture with a Mexican company such as Cifra. The company quickly concluded that its competitive advantage was based on the combination of corporate culture and its supporting information and logistics systems, and that such a combination would be difficult to transfer to franchisees. The management know-how that underlay Wal-Mart's culture and systems was simply not amenable to franchising. At the same time, Wal-Mart realized that it knew little about the culture and business systems in Mexico, so the company decided to enter into a fifty-fifty joint venture agreement with Cifra.

Teething Problems

Wal-Mart's Mexican expansion began with the establishment of a single Sam's Club store in Mexico City in 1991. In 1992, Wal-Mart established six more stores, all Sam's Clubs, in Mexico. In 1993, the company began to open stores under the Wal-Mart name. When the first store in Mexico City opened its doors, an enormous crowd showed up, and all seventy-two cash registers were ringing constantly. It didn't last. Within months, the sales rate at Wal-Mart's Mexican stores had slowed down considerably, not surprising perhaps in a country where per-capita income was only about $2,000 per year. But according to critics, the problems had more to do with missteps by Wal-Mart than low income levels.

When Wal-Mart opened its first store in Monterrey in 1993, it had to bar the doors to control the crowds. Soon the local press was lambasting the company, however, for charging 15 to 20 percent more for merchandise than it did at its Wal-Mart store across the border in Laredo, Texas, a two-hour drive to the north. A Wal-Mart spokesperson pointed out that the higher prices reflected the transportation costs between the Wal-Mart distribution center in Laredo and its Monterrey store. In addition, the NAFTA agreement had not yet been implemented, and high tariffs contributed to the higher prices. But Wal-Mart also conceded that it was having problems replicating its U.S. distribution system in Mexico. Poor infrastructure, crowded roads, and a lack of leverage with local suppliers (many of whom would not or could not deliver directly to Wal-Mart's stores or distribution centers, as was common in the United States), all led to higher prices and lower margins for Wal-Mart.

Another problem was getting the right selection of merchandise. Many of the first Wal-Mart stores in Mexico carried items that were popular in the United States but were rarely used in Mexico, like ice skates, riding lawn mowers, leaf blowers, and fishing tackle. Managers would slash prices on these items to move the inventory, only to find that Wal-Mart's automated information systems ordered more to replenish the depleted inventory.

Then there were problems with government bureaucrats. After the implementation of NAFTA in January 1994, Wal-Mart believed that things would get easier, but it was not to be. In the summer of 1994, Mexican government inspectors made a surprise visit to Wal-Mart's new superstore in Mexico City. The inspectors found thousands of products that they claimed were improperly labeled or lacked instructions in Spanish. The store was ordered shut for seventy-two hours while the oversights were corrected. This brush with what they saw as overzealous inspectors sobered Wal-Mart's managers. The 200,000-square-foot supercenter that was inspected carried about 80,000 products. Each now had to be labeled in Spanish to indicate the country of origin, contents, instructions, and, in some cases, an import permit number. The inspectors charged that about 11,700 pieces of merchandise lacked such labels. Wal-Mart's managers responded by pointing out that many of the targeted goods—about 40 percent or more—were purchased from a local Mexican distributor. Nevertheless, the regulators insisted that the retailer had ultimate responsibility for the labeling. Some Wal-Mart managers wondered if this kind of bureaucratic red tape was a deliberate attempt by government officials to raise the costs of doing business in Mexico and thereby frustrate Wal-Mart's expansion plans.

The 1994 Peso Crisis

As if these problems were not enough, in late 1994 the Mexican economy took a sharp turn for the worse. The Mexican currency, the peso, had been pegged to the value of the U.S. dollar since the early 1980s and was allowed to depreciate by only about 4 percent per year against the dollar. Since the mid

1980s, prices in Mexico had risen by about 45 percent more than had prices in the United States, making the current exchange rate increasingly difficult to maintain. In 1993 and 1994, the Mexican economy responded to the drop in tariff barriers by importing products at a rapid rate. By late 1994, Mexico was running a $17 billion annual deficit on merchandised trade, which amounted to about 6 percent of the country's GDP. Currency traders began to place large bets that the Mexican government would be forced to devalue the peso against the dollar. Fearing this outcome, foreign investors who had rushed into the country in 1993 and early 1994, buying Mexican stocks and pushing the stock market up to record levels, reversed their course and moved a lot of money out of the country.

The Mexican government stepped into the foreign exchange market to defend its currency, using its foreign exchange reserves to buy pesos. But the outward flow of funds was so great that Mexico soon realized that its strategy would only deplete its foreign exchange reserves. Accepting the inevitable, in December 1994 the Mexican government announced that it would no longer peg the peso against the dollar and would let it float freely on the foreign exchange market. Immediately the peso plunged, losing about 40 percent of its value against the dollar in a matter of days. The Mexican economy plunged into an economic recession.

For Wal-Mart and other American firms that had moved into Mexico to take advantage of NAFTA, this was a severe blow. By this time, Wal-Mart had sixty-three stores in Mexico, but many of them were still stocked with goods imported from the United States. The fall in the value of the peso meant that it now cost even more to bring in goods from the United States, while the economic recession that now gripped Mexico meant that consumers had even less to spend. Over the next two years, retail sales in Mexico were to fall by 16 percent. Wal-Mart, which had planned to open another twenty-five stores in 1995, quickly put its Mexican expansion plans on hold.

Expansion Resumes

Although Mexico was to experience a two-year economic slowdown, the United States economy continued to grow. With Mexican goods now costing less in the United States and with trade barriers reduced or eliminated under NAFTA, Mexican exports boomed.

Foreign companies began to invest heavily in the country, seeing it as a low-cost location from which to export to its giant neighbor next door. The combination of an export boom and rapid foreign direct investment created jobs and helped to lift the Mexican economy out of its slump. Seeing that the corner was being turned, Wal-Mart's expansion plans were back on track by late 1995.

By mid 1997, Wal-Mart had about 145 stores in Mexico. Unlike several other foreign retailers, it had decided to take advantage of the economic slump to build its market share. The company was also making strong improvements in its operating efficiency. It had opened a distribution center in Mexico City, and it rapidly became the most efficient in the entire Wal-Mart system, in part due to very low labor costs. This allowed Wal-Mart to start reducing its inventory and logistics costs. Wal-Mart had also struck a three-way partnership with EASO, a Mexican trucking company, and MS Carriers Corp, a U.S. trucking company that does significant work for Wal-Mart in the United States. Under the agreement, MS Carriers shared its fleet of modern trucks, as well as its satellite systems designed to help plan delivery times, with EASO. This arrangement helped EASO cut its costs by 25 percent, and it passed the savings on to Wal-Mart, which now uses 200 of EASO's trucks to run its Mexican logistics system.

Wal-Mart also started to sell far more Mexican goods, in part because many of its suppliers had themselves located in Mexico to take advantage of lower production costs and the advantages under NAFTA. In an example of the savings this strategy produced, Wal-Mart officials cite the case of a Vega television from Sony. Imported from Japan, the combination of transportation costs and a 23 percent tariff meant that the television retailed for $1,600 in Wal-Mart's Mexican store, out of the reach of all but the most affluent Mexican consumers. But in 1999, Sony built a Vega television factory in Mexico to take advantage of NAFTA. The television now costs about $600 in Mexico, and sales are picking up.

Wal-Mart had also learned from its early mistakes and thus improved the mix of product offerings at its Mexican stores. Slow-moving items such as leaf blowers had been replaced by items that sold well in Mexico but would not in the United States, such as maids' uniforms. As its scale of operations in Mexico grew, Wal-Mart was also able to use its purchase volume to gain leverage with suppliers and bargain down prices in return for large purchase volumes. Wal-Mart then passed these prices on to consumers, enabling the company to gain market share and remain profitable even as total retail spending in Mexico shrank during 1995 and 1996. In contrast, Sears and Kmart, two U.S. competitors that had entered Mexico at the same time, left the country.

In mid 1997, Wal-Mart signaled its continuing commitment to Mexico by purchasing a controlling interest in its joint venture partner, Cifra. By combining Cifra's stores with the stores established by the joint venture, Wal-Mart now had 373 stores in Mexico, making it the largest retailer in the country by far. The new company was then listed on Mexico's stock exchange, the Bolsa, as Wal-Mart de Mexico (it soon become known as WalMex). The listing allowed Wal-Mart to begin introducing the same stock-based incentive plans for its associates in Mexico that had worked so well in the United States. Wal-Mart retained a 54 percent stake in WalMex, which it raised to 60 percent in April 2000.

By 1999, Wal-Mart felt that it had improved its cost structure in Mexico to such an extent that it could now start to be more aggressive about passing on cost savings to Mexican consumers. In August 1999, it closed down a supercenter in Mexico City for a single day and marked down all prices by 16 percent. It then reopened under the banner of "everyday low pricing." Sales surged, with the growth in volume more than making up for the lower prices. The experiment was such a success that Wal-Mart rolled out the program in all of its Mexican supercenters a month later. In May 2000, the program was extended to cover all Wal-Mart stores in Mexico. By July 2001, WalMex same-store sales growth exceeded that of competitors for eight out of the last twelve months, and for seven months in a row.

REFERENCES

DePalma, A., "Big Companies in Mexico Among the Peso's Worst Victims," *New York Times,* January 30, 1995, p. D4.

Ginns, J. J., "Wal-Mart Ventures into Mexico," Harvard Business School Case # 9-793-071, December 1992.

Luhnow D., "How NAFTA Helped Wal-Mart Reshape the Mexican Market," *Wall Street Journal,* August 31, 2001, pp. A1, A2.

Smith, G., "NAFTA: A Green Light for Red Tape," *Business Week,* July 25, 1994, p. 48.

"Wal-Mart: Mexico's Largest Retailer," *Chain Store Age,* June 2001, pp. 52–54.

Wal-Mart 10K reports, 1996–2000, news releases, and other information posted on the company's web site (www.wal-mart.com).

Walton, S., *Made in America,* New York: Bantam Books, 1992.

Kmart Corporation: Seeking Customer Acceptance and Preference

27

This case was prepared by James W. Camerius, Northern Michigan University.

On June 1, 2000, the search for the new chairman and chief executive officer of Kmart Corporation was over. Charles C. Conaway, a thirty-nine-year-old drugstore chain executive, was selected to fill the position. His appointment meant that the strategic direction of Kmart would come from a man who was previously unknown outside the drugstore industry. He would have to provide an answer to a crucial question: How can Kmart respond to the challenges of industry leader Wal-Mart Stores, Inc., in the extremely competitive arena of discount retailing?

As president and chief operating officer of CVS Corporation, Conaway was the number 2 executive at the nation's largest drugstore chain, whose annual sales were about half those of Kmart's annual revenues of $36 billion. By all accounts, Conaway had made a sizable contribution in sales, earnings, and market value at CVS, Inc., headquartered in Woonsocket, Rhode Island. CVS had 1999 sales of $18 billion, with 4,100 stores. Conaway, who became president and chief operating officer of CVS in 1998, was responsible for merchandising, advertising, store operations, and logistics. After joining the firm in 1992, he helped engi-neer the restructuring of the then parent Melville Corporation, a diversified retailer, into a successful drugstore chain. Conaway said in an interview upon assuming his new position with Kmart that his primary task would be to improve customer service, productivity of resources, and problems with out-of-stock merchandise. Setting the stage for a new direction, Conaway said, "Customer service is going to be at the top. We're going to measure it and we're going to tie incentives around it."

Floyd Hall, the previous chairman, president, and chief executive officer of Kmart since June 1995, appeared pleased with the appointment. He had announced two years earlier that he wanted to retire, and now he would be able to do so. In the last five years, Hall had restored Kmart profitability and made improvements in store appearance and merchandise selection. Analysts had noted, however, that the firm lacked a definable niche in discount retailing. Studies had shown that number 1 ranked Wal-Mart, originally a rural retailer, had continued to be known for lower prices. Target Corporation, number 3 in sales, had staked out a niche as a merchandiser of discounted upscale products. Kmart was left without a feature that would give it competitive distinction in the marketplace.

Kmart's financial results in the first quarter of fiscal 2000 reported that net income fell 61 percent, to $22 million. The decline ended a string of fifteen consecutive quarters of profit increases that Hall felt had signaled a turnaround at the discount chain. Hall was very optimistic, however, about the company's future. The financial information over the previous periods had convinced him that a new corporate strategy that he introduced would revitalize Kmart's core business, its 2,171 discount stores, and would put the company on the road to recovery. Industry analysts had noted that Kmart, once an industry leader, had posted eleven straight quarters of disappointing earnings prior to 1998 and had been dogged by persistent bankruptcy rumors. Analysts cautioned that much of Kmart's recent growth reflected the strength of the consumer economy and that uncertainty continued to exist about the company's future in a period of slower economic growth.

Kmart Corporation was one of the world's largest mass-merchandise retailers. After several years of restructuring, it was composed largely of general merchandise businesses in the form of traditional Kmart discount department stores and Big Kmart stores (general merchandise and convenience items) as well as Super Kmart Centers (food and general merchandise). It operated in all fifty states of the United States and in Puerto Rico, Guam, and the U.S. Virgin Islands. It also had equity interests in Meldisco subsidiaries of Footstar, Inc., which operated Kmart footwear departments. Measured in sales volume, it was the third largest retailer and the second largest discount department store chain in the United States.

The discount department store industry was perceived by many to have reached maturity. As part of that industry, Kmart had a retail management strategy that was developed in the late 1950s and revised in the early 1990s. The firm was in a dilemma in terms of corporate strategy. The problem was how to lay a foundation for providing a new direction that would reposition the firm in a fiercely competitive environment.

The Early Years

Kmart was the outgrowth of an organization founded in 1899 in Detroit by Sebastian S. Kresge. The first S. S. Kresge store represented a new type of retailing that featured low-priced merchandise for cash in low-budget, relatively small (4,000- to 6,000-

square-foot) buildings with sparse furnishings. The adoption of the "5¢ and 10¢" or "variety store" concept, pioneered by F. W. Woolworth Company in 1879, led to rapid and profitable development of what was then the S. S. Kresge Company.

Kresge believed it could substantially increase its retail business by centralizing buying and control, developing standardized store operating procedures, and expanding into heavy traffic areas with new stores. In 1912, the firm was incorporated in Delaware. It had eighty-five stores with sales of $10,325,000, and, next to Woolworth's, was the largest variety chain in the world. In 1916, it was reincorporated in Michigan. Over the next forty years, the firm experimented with mail-order catalogs, full-line department stores, self-service, several price lines, and the opening of stores in planned shopping centers. It continued its emphasis, however, on variety stores.

By 1957, corporate management became aware that the development of supermarkets and the expansion of drugstore chains into general merchandise lines had made inroads into market categories previously dominated by variety stores. It also became clear that a new form of store with a discount merchandising strategy was emerging.

The Cunningham Connection

In 1957, in an effort to regain competitiveness and possibly save the company, Frank Williams, then president of Kresge, nominated Harry B. Cunningham as general vice president. This maneuver was undertaken to free Cunningham, who had worked his way up the ranks in the organization, from operating responsibility. He was being groomed for the presidency and was given the assignment of studying existing retailing businesses and recommending marketing changes.

In his visits to Kresge stores and those of the competition, Cunningham became interested in discounting—particularly the discounting operations of a new store in Garden City, Long Island. Eugene Ferkauf had recently opened large discount department stores called E. J. Korvette. The stores had a discount mass-merchandising emphasis that featured low prices and margins, high turnover, large freestanding departmentalized units, ample parking, and a location typically in the suburbs.

Cunningham was impressed with the discount concept, but he knew he first had to convince the Kresge board of directors, whose support would be necessary for any new strategy to succeed. He studied E. J. Korvette for two years and presented Kmart with the following recommendation:

> We can't beat the discounters operating under the physical constraints and the self-imposed merchandise limitations of variety stores. We can join them—and not only join them, but with our people, procedures, and organization, we can become a leader in the discount industry.

In a speech delivered at the University of Michigan, Cunningham made his management approach clear by concluding with an admonition from the British author, Sir Hugh Walpole: "Don't play for safety, it's the most dangerous game in the world."

The board of directors at Kmart had a difficult job. Change is never easy, especially when the company has established procedures in place and a proud heritage. Before the first presentation to the board could be made, rumors were circulating that one shocked senior executive had said:

> We have been in the variety business for sixty years—we know everything there is to know about it, and we're not doing very well in that, and you want to get us into a business we don't know anything about.

The board of directors eventually accepted Cunningham's recommendations. When president Frank Williams retired, Cunningham became the new president and chief executive officer and was directed to proceed with his recommendations.

The Birth of Kmart

Management conceived the original Kmart as a conveniently located, one-stop shopping unit where customers could buy a wide variety of quality merchandise at discount prices. The typical Kmart store was 75,000 square feet, all on one floor. It generally stood by itself in a high-traffic, suburban area, with plenty of parking. All stores had a similar floor plan.

The firm made an $80 million commitment in leases and merchandise for thirty-three stores before the first Kmart opened in 1962 in Garden City, Michigan. As part of this strategy, management decided to rely on the strengths and abilities of its own people to make decisions rather than employing outside experts for advice.

The original Kresge 5¢ & 10¢ variety store operation was characterized by low gross margins, high turnover, and concentration on return on investment. The main difference in the Kmart strategy would be the offering of a much wider merchandise mix.

The company had the knowledge and ability to merchandise 50 percent of the departments in the planned Kmart merchandise mix, and contracted for operation of the remaining departments. In the following years, Kmart took over most of those departments originally contracted to licensees. Eventually, all departments, except shoes, were operated by Kmart.

By 1987, the twenty-fifth anniversary year of the opening of the first Kmart store in America, sales and earnings of Kmart Corporation were at all-time highs. The company was the world's largest discount retailer, with sales of $25,627 million, and operated 3,934 general merchandise and specialty stores. On April 6, 1987, Kmart Corporation announced that it agreed to sell most of its remaining Kresge variety stores in the United States to McCrory Corporation, a unit of the closely held Rapid American Corporation of New York.

The Nature of the Competitive Environment

A Changing Marketplace

The retail sector of the United States economy went through several dramatic and turbulent changes during the 1980s and early 1990s. Retail analysts concluded that many retail firms were negatively affected by increased competitive pressures, sluggish consumer spending, slower than anticipated economic growth in North America, and recessions abroad. As one retail consultant noted:

> The structure of distribution in advanced economies is currently undergoing a series of changes that are as profound in their impact and as pervasive in their influence as those that occurred in manufacturing during the nineteenth century.

This changing environment affected the discount department store industry. Nearly a dozen firms, like

E. J. Korvette, W. T. Grant, Arlans, Atlantic Mills, and Ames, filed for bankruptcy or planned a reorganization. Some firms, like Woolworth (Woolco Division), had withdrawn from the field entirely after years of disappointment. St. Louis–based May Department Stores sold its Caldor and Venture discount divisions, each with annual sales of more than $1 billion. Venture announced liquidation in early 1998.

Senior management at Kmart felt that most of the firms that had difficulty in the industry faced the same situation. First, they were very successful five or ten years ago but had not changed and therefore had become somewhat dated. Management that had a historically successful formula, particularly in retailing, was perceived as having difficulty adapting to change, especially at the peak of success. Management would wait too long when faced with a threat in the environment and then would have to scramble to regain competitiveness.

Wal-Mart Stores, Inc., based in Bentonville, Arkansas, was an exception. It was especially growth oriented and had emerged in 1991 as the nation's largest retailer as well as the largest discount department store chain in sales volume, and continued in that position through 2000. Operating under various names and formats, nationally and internationally, it included Wal-Mart stores, Wal-Mart supercenters, and Sam's Warehouse Clubs. The firm found early strength in cultivating rural markets, merchandise restocking programs, "everyday low pricing," and the control of operations through companywide computer programs that linked cash registers to corporate headquarters.

Sears, Roebuck & Co., in a state of stagnated growth for several years, completed a return to its retailing roots by spinning off to shareholders its $9 billion controlling stake in its Allstate Corporation insurance unit and the divestment of financial services. After unsuccessfully experimenting with an everyday low price strategy, management chose to refine its merchandising program to meet the needs of middle market customers, who were primarily women, by focusing on product lines in apparel, home, and automotive.

Many retailers, such as Target Corporation (formerly Dayton Hudson), which adopted the discount concept, attempted generally to go after an upscale customer. The upscale customer tended to have an annual household income of $25,000 to $44,000. Other segments of the population were served by firms like Ames Department Stores, Rocky Hill, Connecticut which appealed to outsized, older, and lower-income workers, and by Shopko Stores, Inc., Green Bay, Wisconsin, which attempted to serve the upscale rural consumer.

Kmart executives found that discount department stores were being challenged by several other retail formats. Some retailers were assortment oriented, with a much greater depth of assortment within a given product category. Toys "R" Us was an example of a firm that operated 20,000-square-foot toy supermarkets. Its prices were very competitive within an industry that was very competitive. When the consumers entered a Toys "R" Us facility, there was usually no doubt in their minds that if the product wasn't there, no one else had it. In the late 1990s, however, Toys "R" Us was challenged by Wal-Mart and other firms that offered higher service levels, more aggressive pricing practices, and more-focused merchandise selections.

Some retailers were experimenting with the off-price apparel concept, where name brands and designer goods were sold at 20 to 70 percent discounts. Others, such as Home Depot and Menards, operated home improvement centers that were warehouse-style stores with a wide range of hard-line merchandise for both do-it-yourselfers and professionals. Still others opened drug supermarkets that offered a wide variety of high-turnover merchandise in a convenient location. In these cases, competition was becoming more risk oriented by putting $3 or $4 million in merchandise at retail value in an 80,000-square-foot facility and offering genuinely low prices. Jewel-Osco stores in the Midwest, Rite Aid, CVS, and a series of independents were examples of organizations employing the entirely new concept of the drug supermarket.

The competition was offering something that was new and different in terms of depth of assortment, competitive price image, and format. Kmart management perceived this as a threat because these were viable businesses that hindered the firm in its ability to improve and maintain market share in specific merchandise categories. An industry competitive analysis is shown in Exhibit 1.

Expansion and Contraction

When Joseph E. Antonini was appointed chairman of Kmart Corporation in October 1987, he was charged with the responsibility of maintaining and eventually

EXHIBIT 1

An Industry Competitive Analysis, 1999

	Kmart	Wal-Mart	Sears	Target
Sales (millions)	$35,925	$165,013	$41,071	$33,702
Net income (millions)	403	5,575	1,453	1,144
Sales growth	6.6%	20%	2.7%	10%
Profit margin	1.1%	3.4%	2.8%	3.4%
Sales/square feet	233	374	318	242
Return/equity	6.4%	22.9%	23%	19.5%

Number of stores

Kmart Corporation
  Kmart Traditional Discount Stores—202
  Big Kmart—1,860
  Super Kmart Centers—105

Wal-Mart Stores, Inc. (includes international)
  Wal-Mart Discount Stores—2,373
  Supercenters—1,104
  Sam's Clubs—512

Sears, Roebuck & Company
  Full-line stores—858
  Hardware stores—267

Sears dealer stores—738
Sears automotive stores:
    Sears Auto Centers—798
    National Tire and Battery stores—310
Contract sales
The Great Indoors (prototype decorating)—2

Target Corporation
  Target—912
  Mervyn's—267
  Department store division—64

Source: Company annual reports.

accelerating the chain's record of growth, despite a mature retail marketplace. He moved to string experimental formats into profitable chains. As he noted:

Our vision calls for the constant and never-ceasing exploration of new modes of retailing, so that our core business of U.S. Kmart stores can be constantly renewed and reinvigorated by what we learn from our other businesses.

In the mid 1970s and throughout the 1980s, Kmart became involved in the acquisition or development of several smaller new operations. Kmart Insurance Services, Inc., acquired as Planned Marketing Associates in 1974, offered a full line of life, health, and accident insurance centers located in twenty-seven Kmart stores, primarily in the South and Southwest.

In 1982, Kmart initiated its own off-price specialty apparel concept called Designer Depot. A total of twenty-eight Designer Depot stores were opened in 1982 to appeal to customers who wanted quality upscale clothing at budget prices. A variation of this concept, called Garment Rack,

was opened to sell apparel that normally would not be sold in Designer Depot. A distribution center was added in 1983 to supplement both. Neither venture was successful.

Kmart also attempted an unsuccessful joint venture with the Hechinger Company of Washington, D.C., a warehouse home-center retailer. After much deliberation, however, Kmart chose instead in 1984 to acquire Home Centers of America of San Antonio, Texas, which operated 80,000-square-foot warehouse home centers. The new division, renamed Builders Square, had grown to 167 units by 1996. It capitalized on Kmart's real estate, construction, and management expertise and on Home Centers of America's merchandising expertise. Builders Square was sold in 1997 to the Hechinger Company. On June 11, 1999, Hechinger filed for Chapter 11 bankruptcy protection. As a result, Kmart recorded a noncash charge of $354 million that reflected the impact of lease obligations for former Builders Square locations that were guaranteed by Kmart.

Waldenbooks, a chain of 877 bookstores, was acquired from Carter, Hawley, Hale, Inc., in 1984. It was part of a strategy to capture a greater share of the market with a product category that Kmart already had in its stores. Kmart management had been interested in the book business for some time and took advantage of an opportunity in the marketplace to build on its common knowledge base. Borders Books and Music, an operator of fifty large-format superstores, became part of Kmart in 1992 to form the "Borders Group," a division that would include Waldenbooks. The Borders Group, Inc., was sold during 1995.

The Bruno's, Inc., a joint venture formed a partnership with Kmart in 1987 to develop large combination grocery and general merchandise stores, or "hypermarkets," called American Fare. The giant, one-stop-shopping facilities of 225,000 square feet traded on the grocery expertise of Bruno's and the general merchandise of Kmart to offer a wide selection of products and services at discount prices. A similar venture, called Super Kmart Center, represented later thinking on combination stores with a smaller size and format. In 2000, Kmart operated 105 Super Kmart Centers, all in the United States.

In 1988, the company acquired a controlling interest in Makro Inc., a Cincinnati-based operator of warehouse club stores. With annual sales of about $300 million, Makro operated member-only stores that were stocked with low-priced fresh and frozen groceries, apparel, and durable goods in suburbs of Atlanta, Cincinnati, Washington, D.C., and Philadelphia. Pace Membership Warehouse, Inc., a similar operation, was acquired in 1989. The club stores were sold in 1994.

PayLess Drug Stores, a chain that operated super-drugstores in several western states, was sold in 1994 to Thrifty PayLess Holdings, Inc., an entity in which Kmart maintained a significant investment. Interests in the Sports Authority, an operator of large-format sporting goods stores that Kmart acquired in 1990, were disposed of during 1995.

On the international level, an interest in Coles Myer, Ltd., Australia's largest retailer, was sold in November 1994. Interests in thirteen Kmart general merchandise stores in the Czech and Slovak republics were sold to Tesco PLC, one of the United Kingdom's largest retailers, at the beginning of 1996. In February 1998, Kmart stores in Canada were sold to Hudson's Bay Co., a Canadian chain of historic full-service department stores. The interest in Kmart Mexico, S.A. de C.V., was disposed of in fiscal year 1997.

Founded in 1988, OfficeMax, with 328 stores, was one of the largest operators of high-volume, deep-discount office products superstores in the United States. It became a greater-than-90-percent-owned Kmart unit in 1991. Kmart's interest in OfficeMax was sold during 1995. In November 1995, Kmart also sold its auto service center business to a new corporation controlled by Penske Corporation. In connection with the sale, Kmart and Penske entered into a sublease arrangement concerning the operation of Penske Auto Service Centers.

During 1999, Kmart signed agreements with Supervalu, Inc., and Fleming Companies, Inc., under which both would assume responsibility for the distribution and replenishment of grocery-related products to all Kmart stores. Kmart also maintained an equity interest in Meldisco subsidiaries of Footstar, Inc., operators of footwear departments in Kmart stores.

The Maturation of Kmart

Early corporate research revealed that, on the basis of convenience, Kmart served 80 percent of the population. One study concluded that one out of every two adults in the United States shopped at a Kmart at least once a month. Despite this popular appeal, strategies that had allowed the firm to have something for everybody were no longer felt to be appropriate for the new millennium. Kmart found that it had a broad customer base because it operated on a national basis. Its early strategies had assumed the firm was serving everyone in the markets where it was established.

Kmart was often perceived as aiming at the low-income consumer. The financial community believed the original Kmart customer was blue collar, low-income, and upper lower class. The market served, however, was more professional and middle class because Kmart stores were initially built in suburban communities where that population lived.

Although Kmart had made a major commitment in more recent years to secondary or rural markets, these areas had previously not been cultivated. In its initial strategies, the firm perceived the rural consumer as different from the urban or suburban customer. In re-addressing the situation, it discovered that its product assortments in rural areas were too limited and there were too many preconceived notions about what the Nebraska farmer really wanted. The firm discovered that the rural consumer didn't always shop for bib overalls and shovels but for microwave ovens, in other words, the same things that everyone else shopped for.

One goal was not to attract more customers but to get the customer coming in the door to spend more. Once in the store, the customer was thought to demonstrate more divergent tastes. The upper-income consumer would buy more health and beauty aids, cameras, and sporting goods. The lower-income consumer would buy toys and clothing. In the process of trying to capture a larger share of the market and get people to spend more, the firm began to recognize a market that was more upscale. When consumer research was conducted and management examined the profile of the trade area and the profile of the person who shopped at Kmart in the past month, they were found to be identical. Kmart was predominately serving the suburban consumer in suburban locations. In 1997, Kmart's primary target customers were women between the ages of twenty-five and forty-five years, with children at home and with annual household incomes between $20,000 and $50,000. The core Kmart shopper averaged 4.3 visits to a Kmart store per month. The purchase amount per visit was $40. The purchase rate was 95 percent during a store visit. The firm estimated that 180 million people shopped at Kmart in an average year.

In lifestyle research in markets served by the firm, Kmart determined there were more two-income families, families were having fewer children, there were more working wives, and customers tended to be homeowners. Customers were very careful about how they spent their money and were perceived as wanting quality. This was in distinct contrast to the 1960s and early 1970s, which tended to have the orientation of a throwaway society. The customer now said, "What we want are products that will last longer. We'll have to pay more for them but we still want them and at the lowest price possible." Customers wanted better quality products but still demanded competitive prices. According to a Kmart annual report, "Consumers today are well educated and informed. They want good value and they know it when they see it. Price remains a key consideration, but the consumer's new definition of value includes quality as well as price."

Corporate management at Kmart considered the discount department store to be a mature idea. Although maturity was sometimes looked on with disfavor, Kmart executives felt that naturity did not mean a lack of profitability or lack of opportunity to increase sales. The industry was perceived as being "reborn." In this context, in the 1990s a series of new retailing strategies designed to upgrade the Kmart image were developed.

The 1990 Renewal Program

The strategies that emerged to confront a changing environment were the result of an overall reexamination of existing corporate strategies. This program included accelerated store expansion and refurbishing, capitalization on dominant lifestyle departments, centralized merchandising, more capital investment in retail automation, an aggressive and focused advertising program, and continued growth through new specialty retail formats. The initial 1990, five-year, $2.3 billion program involved almost all Kmart discount stores. There would be approximately 250 new full-size Kmart stores, 620 enlargements, 280 relocations, and thirty closings. In addition, 1,260 stores would be refurbished to bring their layout and fixtures up to new-store standards. Another program introduced in 1996 resulted in an additional $1.1 billion being spent to upgrade Kmart stores. By year-end 1999, 1,860 new Big Kmart stores offered more pleasant shopping experiences thanks to the updated and easy-to-shop departmental adjacencies, better signing and lighting, wider aisles, and more attractive in-store presentations.

One area receiving initial attention was improvement in the way products were displayed. The traditional Kmart layout was by product category. Often the locations for departments were holdovers from the variety store. Many departments would not give up prime locations. As part of the new marketing strategy, the shop concept was introduced. Management recognized that it had a sizable "do-it-yourself" store. As planning management discussed the issue, "nobody was aware of the opportunity. The hardware department was right smack in the center of the store because it was always there. The paint department was over here and the electrical department was over there. All we had to do," management contended, "was put them all in one spot and everyone could see that we had a very respectable 'do-it-yourself' department." The concept resulted in several new departments such as "Soft Goods for the Home," "Kitchen

Korners," and "Home Electronic Centers." The goal behind each department was to sell an entire lifestyle-oriented concept to consumers, making goods complementary so shoppers would want to buy several interrelated products rather than just one item.

Name brands were added in soft and hard goods because management recognized that the customer transferred the product quality of branded goods to perceptions of private label merchandise. In the eyes of Kmart management, "If you sell Wrangler, there is good quality. Then the private label must be good quality." The company increased its emphasis on trusted national brands, such as Rubbermaid, Procter & Gamble, and Kodak, and on major strategic vendor relationships. In addition it began to enhance its private-label brands such as Kathy Ireland, Jaclyn Smith, Route 66, and Sesame Street in apparel. Additional private-label merchandise included K Gro in home gardening, American Fare in grocery and consumables, White-Westinghouse in appliances, and Penske Auto Centers in automotive services. Some private labels were discontinued following review.

Kmart hired Martha Stewart, an upscale Connecticut author of lavish best-selling books on cooking and home entertaining, as its lifestyle spokesperson and consultant. Martha Stewart was featured as a corporate symbol for housewares and associated products in advertising and in-store displays. Management visualized her as the next Betty Crocker, a fictional character created some years ago by General Mills, Inc., and a representative of its interest in lifestyle trends. The Martha Stewart Everyday home fashion product line was introduced in 1995 and was expanded in 1996 and 1997. A separate division was established to manage strategy for all Martha Stewart–label goods and programs. Merchandise was featured in the redesigned once-a-week Kmart newspaper circular, which carried the advertising theme: "The quality you need, the price you want."

Several thousand prices were reduced to maintain "price leadership across America." As management noted, "It is absolutely essential that we provide our customers with good value—quality products at low prices." Although lowering of prices hurt margins and contributed to an earnings decline, management felt that unit turnover of items with lowered prices enabled "Kmart to maintain its pricing leadership [and] will have a most positive impact on our business in the years ahead."

A centralized merchandising system was introduced to improve communication. A computerized, highly automated replenishment system tracked how quickly merchandise sold and, just as quickly, put fast-moving items back on the shelves. Satellite capability and a point-of-sale (POS) scanning system were introduced as part of the program. Regular, live satellite communication from Kmart headquarters to the stores allowed senior management to communicate with store managers and facilitated questions and answers. The POS scanning system allowed a record of every sale and transmission of the data to headquarters. This system enabled Kmart to respond quickly to what's new, what's in demand, and what would keep customers coming back.

The company opened its first Super Kmart Center in 1992. The format combined general merchandise and food with an emphasis on customer service and convenience. The stores ranged in size from 135,000 to 190,000 square feet, with more than 40,000 grocery items. The typical Super Kmart operated seven days a week, twenty-four hours a day, and generated high traffic and sales volume. The centers also featured wider shopping aisles, appealing displays, and pleasant lighting to enrich the shopping experience. Super Kmarts featured in-house bakeries, USDA fresh meats, fresh seafood, delicatessens, cookie kiosks, cappuccino bars, in-store eateries and food courts, and fresh-food carry-out salad bars. In many locations, the center provided customer services like video rental, dry cleaning, shoe repair, beauty salons, optical shops, express shipping services, and a full line of traditional Kmart merchandise. To enhance the appeal of the merchandise assortment, emphasis was placed on "cross-merchandising." For example, toasters were featured above the fresh baked breads, kitchen gadgets were positioned across the aisle from produce, and baby centers featured everything from baby food to toys. At the end of 1999, the company operated 105 Super Kmart stores.

The Planning Function

Corporate planning at Kmart was the result of executives, primarily the senior executive, recognizing change. The role played by the senior executive was to get others to recognize that nothing is good forever. "Good planning" was the result of getting involved. "Poor planning" was done by those who didn't recognize the need for it, and once they did, it was too late to survive. Good planning, if done regularly, was assumed to result in improved performance. Kmart's Michael Wellman, then director of planning and research, said, "Planning, as we like to stress, is making decisions now to improve performance tomorrow. Everyone looks at what may happen tomorrow, but the planners are the ones who make decisions today. That's where I think too many firms go wrong. They think they are planning because they are writing reports and are aware of changes. They don't say, 'because of this, we must decide today to spend this money to do this to accomplish this goal in the future.'"

Kmart management believed that the firm had been very successful in the area of strategic planning. "When it became necessary to make significant changes in the way we were doing business," Michael Wellman suggested, "that was accomplished on a fairly timely basis." When the organization made the change in the 1960s, it recognized there was a very powerful investment opportunity and capitalized on it—far beyond what anyone else would have done. We just opened stores at a great, great pace. Management, when confronted with a crisis, would state, 'It's the economy, or it's this, or that, but it's not the essential way we are doing business.'" He also noted, "Suddenly management would recognize that the economy may stay like this forever. We need to improve the situation and then do it." Strategic planning was thought to arise out of some difficult times for the organization.

Kmart had a reasonably formal planning organization that involved a constant evaluation of what was happening in the marketplace, what competition was doing, and what kinds of opportunities were available. Management felt a need to diversify because Kmart would not be a viable company unless it was growing. Management felt it was not going to grow with the Kmart format forever. It needed growth and opportunity, particularly for a company that was able to open 200 stores on a regular basis. Wellman felt that, "Given a 'corporate culture' that was accustomed to challenges, management would have to find ways to expend that energy. A corporation that is successful has to continue to be successful. It has to have a basic understanding of corporate needs and be augmented by a much more rigorous effort to be aware of what's going on in the external environment."

A planning group at Kmart represented several functional areas of the organization. Management described it as an "in-house consulting group" with some independence. It was made up of (1) financial planning, (2) economic and consumer analysis, and (3) operations research. The chief executive officer (CEO) was identified as the primary planner of the organization.

Reorganization and Restructuring

Kmart's financial performance for 1993 was disappointing. The company announced a loss of $974 million on sales of $34,156,000 for the fiscal year ended January 26, 1994. Antonini, noting the deficit, felt it occurred primarily because of lower margins in the U.S. Kmart stores division. "Margin erosion," he said, "stemmed in part from intense industrywide pricing pressure throughout 1993." He was confident, however, that Kmart was on track with its renewal program to make the more than 2,350 U.S. Kmart stores "competitive, on-trend, and cutting merchandisers." Tactical Retail Solutions, Inc., estimated that during Antonini's seven-year tenure with the company, Kmart's market share in the discount arena fell to 23 percent, from 35 percent. Other retail experts suggested that because the company had struggled for so long to have the right merchandise in the stores at the right time, it had lost customers to competitors. An aging customer base was also cited.

In early 1995, following the posting of its eighth consecutive quarter of disappointing earnings, Kmart's board of directors announced that Antonini would be replaced as chairman. It named Donald S. Perkins, former chairman of Jewel Companies, Inc., and a Kmart director, to the position. Antonini relinquished his position as president and chief executive officer in March. After a nationwide search, Floyd Hall, fifty-seven, former chairman and CEO of the Target discount store division of the Dayton-Hudson Corporation, was appointed chairman, president, and chief executive officer of Kmart in June 1995.

The company concluded the disposition of many noncore assets in 1996, including the sale of the Borders group, OfficeMax, the Sports Authority, and Coles Myer. During the 1990s, it also closed a large number of underperforming stores in the United States and cleared out $700 million in aged and discontinued inventory in the remaining stores.

In 1996, Kmart converted 152 of its traditional stores to feature a new design that was referred to as the high-frequency format. These stores were named Big Kmart. The stores emphasized the departments deemed the most important to core customers and offered an increased mix of high-frequency, everyday basics and consumables in the pantry area located at the front of each store. These items were typically priced at a one- to three-percentage differential from the leading competitors in each market and served to increase inventory turnover and gross margin dollars. In addition to the pantry area, Big Kmart stores featured improved lighting, new signage that was easier to see and read, and adjacencies that created a smoother traffic flow. In 1999, 588 stores were converted to the new Big Kmart format, bringing the total to 1,860. Other smaller stores would be updated to a "best of Big Kmart" prototype.

Kmart launched its first e-commerce site in 1998. The initial Kmart.com offered a few products and was not considered a successful venture. In 1999, Kmart partnered with Softbank Venture Capital, who provided technical expertise, experienced personnel, and initial capital, to create an Internet site 60 percent owned by Kmart. BlueLight.com increased the number of Kmart products it offered online to about 65,000, from 1,250. It planned to boost the number to 100,000 by year-end 2000 and possibly to millions of items in the future.

Major changes were made to the management team. In total, twenty-three of the company's thirty-seven corporate officers were new to the company's team since 1995. The most dramatic restructuring had taken place in the merchandising organization, where all four of the general merchandise managers responsible for buying organizations joined Kmart since 1995. In addition, fifteen new divisional vice presidents joined Kmart during 1997. Significant changes were also made to the board of directors, with nine of fifteen directors new to the company since 1995. A list of the board of directors and corporate officers from March 2000 is shown in appendix D.

At the end of his tenure, Floyd Hall announced that the company mandate in the year and century ahead was to create sustained growth that would profitably leverage all of the core strengths of the firm. The corporate mission in 2000 was "to become the discount store of choice for low- and middle-income households by satisfying their routine and seasonal shopping needs as well as or better than the competition." Management believed that the actions taken by Charles Conaway, the new president, would have a dramatic impact on how customers perceived Kmart, how frequently they shopped in the stores, and how much they would buy on each store visit. Increasing customers' frequency and the amount they purchased during each store visit were seen as having a dramatic impact on the company's efforts to increase its profitability.

Appendix A: Kmart Corporation, Consolidated Balance Sheets and Operating Statements, 1998–1999

	Years Ended January 26, 2000; January 27, 1999; and January 28, 1998		
	1999	**1998**	**1997**
Sales	$35,925	$33,674	$32,183
Cost of sales, buying, and occupancy	28,102	26,319	25,152
Gross margin	7,823	7,355	7,031
Selling, general, and administrative expenses	6,523	6,245	6,136
Voluntary early retirement programs	—	19	114
Continuing income before interest, income taxes, and dividends on convertible preferred securities of subsidiary trust	1,300	1,091	781
Interest expense, net	280	293	363
Income tax provision	337	230	120
Dividends on convertible preferred securities of subsidiary trust, net of income taxes of $27, $27, and $26	50	50	49
Net income from continuing operations	633	518	249
Discontinued operations, net of income taxes of $(124)	(230)	—	—
Net income	$ 403	$ 518	$ 249
Basic earnings per common share			
Net income from continuing operations	$ 1.29	$ 1.05	$ .51
Discontinued operations	(.47)	—	—
Net income	$ .82	$ 1.05	$ .51
Diluted earnings per common share			
Net income from continuing operations	$ 1.22	$ 1.01	$ .51
Discontinued operations	(.41)	—	—
Net income	$ .81	$ 1.01	$ .51
Basic weighted average shares (millions)	491.7	492.1	487.1
Diluted weighted average shares (millions)	561.7	564.9	491.7

	As of January 26, 2000, and January 27, 1999	
	1999	**1998**
Current assets		
Cash and cash equivalents	$ 344	$ 710
Merchandise inventories	7,101	6,536
Other current assets	715	584
Total current assets	8,160	7,830
Property and equipment, net	6,410	5,914
Other assets and deferred charges	534	422
Total assets	$15,104	$14,166
Current Liabilities		
Long-term debt due within one year	$ 66	$ 77
Trade accounts payable	2,204	2,047
Accrued payroll and other liabilities	1,574	1,359
Taxes other than income taxes	232	208
Total current liabilities	4,076	3,691
Long-term debt and notes payable	1,759	1,538

(continued)

Appendix A: Kmart Corporation, Consolidated Balance Sheets and Operating Statements, 1998–1999 *(continued)*

	As of January 26, 2000, and January 27, 1999	
	1999	1998
Current assets *(continued)*		
Capital lease obligations	1,014	1,091
Other long-term liabilities	965	883
Company obligated mandatorily redeemable convertible preferred securities of a subsidiary trust holding solely 7¾% convertible junior subordinated debentures of Kmart (redemption value of $1,000)	986	984
Common stock, $1 par value, 1,500,000,000 shares authorized; 481,383,569 and 493,358,504 shares issued, respectively	481	493
Capital in excess of par value	1,555	1,667
Retained earnings	4,268	3,819
Total liabilities and shareholders' equity	$15,104	$14,166

Appendix B: Kmart Corporation, Financial Performance, 1990–1999*

Year	Sales (000)	Assets (000)	Net Income (000)	Net Worth (000)
1990	$32,070,000	$13,899,000	$756,000	$5,384,000
1991	34,580,000	15,999,000	859,000	6,891,000
1992	37,724,000	18,931,000	941,000	7,536,000
1993	34,156,000	17,504,000	(974,000)	6,093,000
1994	34,025,000	17,029,000	296,000	6,032,000
1995†	31,713,000	15,033,000	(571,000)	5,280,000
1996†	31,437,000	14,286,000	(220,000)	6,146,000
1997†	32,183,000	13,558,000	249,000	6,445,000
1998	33,674,000	14,166,000	518,000	6,963,000
1999	35,925,000	15,104,000	403,000	7,290,000

Source: Fortune financial analysis and Kmart annual reports.

*After taxes and extraordinary credit or charges.
†Data from 1995, 1996, and 1997 reflect disposition of subsidiaries.

Appendix C: Financial Performance, Wal-Mart Stores, Inc., 1990–1999

Year	Sales (000)	Assets (000)	Net Income (000)	Net Worth (000)
1990	$32,601,594	$11,388,915	$1,291,024	$ 5,365,524
1991	43,886,900	15,443,400	1,608,500	6,989,700
1992	55,484,000	20,565,000	1,995,000	8,759,000
1993	67,344,000	26,441,000	2,333,000	10,753,000
1994	82,494,000	32,819,000	2,681,000	12,726,000
1995	93,627,000	37,541,000	2,740,000	14,756,000
1996	104,859,000	39,604,000	3,056,000	17,143,000
1997	117,958,000	45,384,000	3,526,000	18,503,000
1998	137,634,000	49,996,000	4,393,000	21,112,000
1999	165,013,000	70,349,000	5,575,000	25,834,000

Source: Wal-Mart annual reports/*Fortune* financial analysis.

Appendix D: Board of Directors and Corporate Officers, Kmart Corporation, March 27, 2000

Board of Directors

James B. Adamson,[1]
Chairman, President, and
Chief Executive Officer,
Advantica Restaurant Group

Lilyan H. Affinito[1,3,5]
Former Vice Chairman of the Board,
Maxxam Group Inc.

Stephen F. Bollenbach[4]
President and Chief Executive Officer,
Hilton Hotels Corporation

Joseph A. Califano, Jr.[4]
Chairman and President,
The National Center on Addiction and
Substance Abuse at Columbia University

Richard G. Cline[2,3,5]
Chairman, Hawthorne Investors, Inc.,
Chairman, Hussmann International, Inc.

Willie D. Davis[2]
President,
All Pro Broadcasting, Inc.

Joseph P. Flannery[3,4,5]
Chairman of the Board, President,
and Chief Executive Officer,
Uniroyal Holding, Inc.

Floyd Hall[3]
Chairman of the Board, President,
and Chief Executive Officer,
Kmart Corporation

Robert D. Kennedy[2]
Former Chairman of the Board and
Chief Executive Officer,
Union Carbide Corporation

J. Richard Munro[3,4,5]
Former Co-Chairman of the Board and
Co-Chief Executive Officer,
Time Warner Inc.

Robin B. Smith[1,5]
Chairman and Chief Executive Officer,
Publishers Clearing House

Thomas Stallkamp[4]
Vice Chairman and Chief Executive
Officer, MSX International

James O. Welch, Jr.[2]
Former Vice Chairman, RJR
Nabisco Inc. and Chairman,
Nabisco Brands, Inc.

Committees:
1 = Audit
2 = Compensation and incentives
3 = Executive
4 = Finance
5 = Directors and corporate governance
* = Committee chair

Corporate Officers

Floyd Hall
Chairman of the Board, President,
Chief Executive Officer

Michael Bozic
Vice Chairman

Andrew A. Giancamilli
President and General Merchandise
Manager, U.S. Kmart

Donald W. Keeble
President, Store Operations, U.S. Kmart

Warren F. Cooper
Executive Vice President, Human
Resources and Administration

Ernest L. Heether
Senior Vice President, Merchandise
Planning and Replenishment

Paul J. Hueber
Senior Vice President, Store Operations

Cecil B. Kearse
Senior Vice President, General
Merchandise Manager—Home

Larry E. Carlson
Vice President, Real Estate Market Strategy

Ronald J. Chomiuk
Vice President, General Merchandise
Manager—Pharmacy/HBC/
Cosmetics/Photo Finishing

Timothy M. Crow
Vice President, Compensation, Benefits,
Workers Compensation and HRIS

Larry C. Davis
Vice President, Advertising

David R. Fielding
Vice President, Northwest Region

Larry J. Foster
Vice President, Training and
Organizational Development

G. William Gryson, Jr.
Vice President, Special Projects

Walter E. Holbrook
Vice President, Southeast Region

Shawn M. Kahle
Vice President, Corporate Affairs

Harry Meeth, III
Vice President, Design and Construction

Douglas M. Maissner
Vice President, Northeast Region

(continued)

Appendix D: Board of Directors and Corporate Officers, Kmart Corporation, March 27, 2000 (continued)

Corporate Officers (continued)

James L. Misplon
Vice President, Taxes

Ann A. Morgan
Vice President, Field Human Resources

Lorna E. Nagler
Vice President, General Merchandise
Manager—Kidsworld and Menswear

Gary J. Ruffing
Vice President, Merchandise
Presentation and Communication

Lucinda C. Sapienza
Vice President, General Merchandise
Manager—Ladieswear, Fashion
Accessories, and Lingerie

David L. Schuvie
Vice President, Electronic Sales
and Services

Brent C. Scott
Vice President, Grocery Operations

Jerome J. Kuske
Senior Vice President, General
Merchandise Manager—Hardlines

James P. Mixon
Senior Vice President, Logistics

Joseph A. Osbourn
Senior Vice President and Chief Information
Officer

E. Jackson Smailes
Senior Vice President, General
Merchandise Manager—Apparel

Martin E. Welch III
Senior Vice President and Chief Financial
Officer

Lorrence T. Kellar
Vice President, Real Estate

Nancie W. LaDuke
Vice President and Secretary

Ronald Laila
Vice President, Merchandise Controller

Thomas W. Lemke
Vice President, Data Base Marketing

Michael P. Lynch
Vice President, Southwest Region

Michael T. Macik
Vice President, Human Resources and
Labor and Associate Relations

Leo L. Maniago
Vice President, Mideast Region

David R. Marsico
Vice President, Store Operations

Stephen E. Sear
Vice President, Facilities Management
and Corporate Purchasing

Stephen W. St. John
Vice President, Great Lakes Region

E. Anthony Vaal
Vice President, Global Operations,
Corporate Brands, and Quality
Assurance

John S. Valenti
Vice President, Southern Region

Leland M. Viliborghi
Vice President, Central Region

Michael J. Viola
Vice President and Treasurer

Francis J. Yanak
Vice President, General Merchandise
Manager—Food and Consumables

REFERENCES

Berner, Robert, "Kmart's Earnings More Than Tripled in First Quarter," *Wall Street Journal,* May 14, 1998, p. A13.

Brauer, Molly, "Kmart in Black 'in 6 Months,' " *Detroit Free Press,* p. E1.

Business Week, "Where Kmart Goes Next Now That It's No. 2," June 2, 1980, pp. 109–110, 114.

Bussey, John, "Kmart Is Set to Sell Many of Its Roots to Rapid-American Corp's McCrory," *Wall Street Journal,* April 6, 1987, p. 24.

Carruth, Eleanore, "Kmart Has to Open Some New Doors on the Future," *Fortune,* July 1977, pp. 143–150, 153–154.

Coleman, Calmetta, "BlueLight.com Aims to Coax Kmart Shoppers Online," *Wall Street Journal,* June 19, 2000, p. B4.

Coleman, Calmetta, "Kmart Lease Pledge May Slow Rebound," *Wall Street Journal,* May 24, 1999, p. A3.

Coleman, Calmetta, "Kmart's New CEO Outlines Plans for Fast Changes," *Wall Street Journal,* July 27, 2000, p. B4.

Coleman, Calmetta, "Kmart Sees $740 Million Pretax Charge from Closing 72 Stores, Other Changes," *Wall Street Journal,* July 26, 2000, p. B10.

Coleman, Calmetta, "Kmart Selects CVS President to Be Its CEO," *Wall Street Journal,* June 1, 2000.

Coleman, Calmetta, "Kmart's Wave of Insider Sales Continues Amid Questions About Retailer's Plans," *Wall Street Journal,* June 23, 1999, p. A4.

Dewar, Robert E., "The Kresge Company and the Retail Revolution," *University of Michigan Business Review,* July 2, 1975, p. 2.

Duff, Christina, and Joann S. Lubin, "Kmart Board Ousts Antonini As Chairman," *Wall Street Journal,* January 18, 1995, p. A3.

Elmer, Vickie, and Joann Muller, "Retailer Needs Leader, Vision," *Detroit Free Press,* March 22, 1995, pp. 1A, 9A.

Frankel, Mark, "Attention, Kmart Grocery Shoppers," *Business Week,* August 2, 1999, p. 49.

Guiles, Melinda G., "Attention, Shoppers: Stop That Browsing and Get Aggressive," *Wall Street Journal,* June 16, 1987, pp. 1, 21.

Guiles, Melinda G., "Kmart, Bruno's Join to Develop 'Hypermarkets,' " *Wall Street Journal,* September 8, 1987, p. 17.

Ingrassia, Paul, "Attention Non Kmart Shoppers: A Blue-Light Special Just for You," *Wall Street Journal,* October 6, 1987, p. 42.

Kmart Corporation, *Annual Report,* Troy, Michigan, 1990.

Kmart Corporation, *Annual Report,* Troy, Michigan, 1995.

Kmart Corporation, *Annual Report,* Troy, Michigan, 1996.

Kmart Corporation, *Annual Report,* Troy, Michigan, 1997.

Kmart Corporation, *Annual Report,* Troy, Michigan, 1999.

Kmart Corporation, *Kmart Fact Book,* Troy, Michigan, 1997.

Kranhold, Kathryn, "Kmart Hopes to Steer Teens to Route 66," *Wall Street Journal,* July 27, 2000, p. B14.

Main, Jerry, "Kmart's Plan to Be Born Again," *Fortune,* September 21, 1981, pp. 74–77, 84–85.

Rice, "Why Kmart Has Stalled," *Fortune,* October 9, 1989, p. 79.

Saporito, Bill, "Is Wal-Mart Unstoppable?" *Fortune,* May 6, 1991, pp. 50–59.

Schwadel, Francine, "Kmart to Speed Store Openings, Renovations," *Wall Street Journal,* February 27, 1990, p. 3.

Sternad, Patrica, "Kmart's Antonini Moves Far Beyond Retail 'Junk' Image," *Advertising Age,* July 25, 1988, pp. 1, 67.

Talaski, Karen, "Kmart Profits Plunge Sharply," *Detroit News,* May 12, 2000, p. 1B.

Talaski, Karen, "Kmart to Invest $2 Billion," *Detroit News,* August 11, 2000, p. 1C.

Wellman, Michael, Interview with Director of Planning and Research, Kmart Corporation, August 6, 1984.

Woodruff, David, "Will Kmart Ever Be a Silk Purse?" *Business Week,* January 22, 1990, p. 46.

28

Tosco and the New Millennium

This case was prepared by M. Edgar Barrett with the assistance of Andrew Kimbrough, Research Assistant, Thunderbird, The American Graduate School of International Management.

> . . . the refiner that Thomas D. O'Malley built into the nation's largest independent from a tiny base a decade ago still has trouble getting respect. Though the company has higher profits than any of its independent competitors as well as some of the lowest costs, the oil world has largely viewed Tosco as a garage-sale groupie on the prowl for major companies' castaways.[1]

Much to the consternation of Tosco's senior management, this quote seemed to capture the sentiments of many in both the worldwide oil community and the overall financial market. Tosco Corporation had annualized revenues approaching $25 billion (U.S.), was the third-largest refiner and the second-largest C-store chain in the United States, and easily ranked ahead of such firms as Phillips and Sunoco in retail gasoline sales (see Exhibits 1 and 2 for data on Tosco and its relative position prior to the major acquisitions of 2000).

Despite the existence of this data, Tosco's common shares traded at a price earnings (P/E) ratio of approximately nine during the latter half of 2000, whereas the domestic oil refining and marketing industry was selling at an average multiple of fourteen and the overall U.S. market was selling at a multiple of 30.[2]

Company Background

Hein Koolsbergen and a group of investors created The Oil Shale Corporation in Los Angeles, California, in 1955, a company formed specifically to develop oil shale reserves worldwide. Oil shale is a hard, porous substance that can contain oil deposits but requires specialized, and expensive, oil extraction techniques. Koolsbergen hoped to capitalize on the oil shale development processes available at the time to extract oil and gas from these difficult-to-develop deposits.

The Oil Shale Corporation's first project was in Brazil, where it hoped to profitably develop the country's oil shale reserves and assist the country in reducing its reliance on oil imports. The project fell through due to lack of financial support. In 1965, the company formed the Colony Shale Oil Project in partnership with Atlantic Richfield Corporation (Arco), a large oil company (which became part of BP in 2000)

1. Alexei Barrionuevo, "Tosco Ready to Join Big Leagues with Exxon Mobil Deal—Refiner's Purchase of Gasoline-Station Network Makes It a Major Player," *Wall Street Journal*, February 29, 2000.

2. Price earnings data taken from Charles Schwab Equity Report Card, August 24, 2000.

EXHIBIT 1

Relative Capacity: U.S.-Based Refineries

Rank	1 July 00[1]		1 January 00[2]		1 January 99[3]		1 January 97[3]		1 January 95[3]	
	Firm	000 bpd	Firm	000 bpd	Firm	000 bpd	Firm	000 bpd	Firm	000 bpd
1	ExxonMobil[4]	1,785	ExxonMobil	1,913	BP Amoco	1,419	Chevron	1,047	Chevron	1,206
2	BP[4,5]	1,640	BP Amoco	1,430	Exxon	1,119	Exxon	1,017	Amoco	998
3	Tosco[4]	1,300	Chevron	1,049	Chevron	969	Amoco	1,010	Exxon	992
4	Chevron	1,050	Marathon	935	Marathon	935	Mobil	952	Mobil	929
5	Marathon	935	Tosco	920	Tosco	910	Shell	897	Shell	761
6	Motiva	850	Motiva	852	Motiva	849	Sunoco	704	BP America	701
7	Valero[4]	800	Equilon	748	Equilon	837	Star Enterprise[6]	605	Sunoco	700
8	Sunoco	725	Sunoco	724	Sunoco	724	Marathon	570	Star Enterprise	600
9	UDS[4]	568	Koch	557	Mobil	705	BP America	564	Marathon	570
10	Koch	557	Conoco	523	Koch	557	Koch	514	Citgo	503
11	Conoco	525	Clark	518	Clark	510	Citgo	506	Koch	485
12	Clark	520	Arco	512	Conoco	507	Conoco	491	Tosco	470
13	Citgo	470	Valero	494	Arco	486	Arco	484	Arco	453
14	Equilon	460	Citgo	473	Citgo	470	Tosco	466	Conoco	438
15	Phillips	384	UDS	412	UDS	465	Texaco	357	Texaco	351
Top 5		6,730 (40.8%)		6,267 (38.4%)		5,382 (33.5%)		4,923 (31.9%)		4,886 (31.7%)
Top 15		12,569 (76.2%)		12,060 (73.9%)		11,462 (71.5%)		10,184 (65.9%)		10,157 (65.8%)
Total U.S.		16,485 Est.[1]		16,312 Est.[1]		16,057		15,452		15,435

[1] *Source:* Casewriter estimates.

[2] *Source:* U.S. Energy Information data taken from website.

[3] *Source:* U.S. Energy Information Administration data as cited in *NPN Market Facts*, 1996 through 2000.

[4] Includes acquisitions or disposition completed or announced since 1/1/00.

[5] BP, Amoco, and Arco.

[6] Joint Venture of Texaco and Saudi Aramco.

EXHIBIT 2

Relative Market Share: U.S. Motor Gasoline Sales[1]

Rank	1999[2] Firm	SOM[4]	Outlets[5]	States[6]	1998[3] Firm	SOM	Outlets	States	1997[3] Firm	SOM	Outlets	States
1	ExxonMobil[7]	18.61	15,913	36	BP Amoco[8]	10.40	15,500	37	Mobil	10.00	7,436	30
2	BP Amoco[8]	10.73	16,300	37	Mobil	9.97	7,413	34	Shell	9.83	9,300	39
3	Marathon[9]	8.24	3,482	16	Exxon	8.65	8,500	36	Citgo	9.53	14,885	48
4	Equilon LLC[10]	8.22	9,400	32	Marathon[9]	7.98	3,117	12	Exxon	8.53	8,500	40
5	Citgo	7.98	13,813	47	Shell	7.86	N.A.	N.A.	Amoco	8.26	9,184	33
6	Chevron	7.70	7,980	29	Chevron	7.77	8,126	28	Texaco	8.19	13,859	41
7	Sunoco	4.45	3,538	18	Texaco	6.96	N.A.	N.A.	Chevron	7.23	7,752	30
8	Motiva LLC[11]	4.35	14,200	26	Citgo	6.92	15,079	48	Marathon[9]	5.53	3,088	12
9	Arco[8]	3.63	1,760	5	A-H	4.90	637	N.A.	Sunoco	4.55	3,789	19
10	Phillips	3.58	5,913	32	Sunoco	4.43	3,721	18	Phillips	4.08	6,530	32
11	Tosco	3.35	4,143	36	Phillips	3.81	5,916	31	Arco	3.45	1,547	5
12	Conoco	3.34	4,958	20	Arco	3.68	1,760	5	Tosco	3.32	4,786	37
13	A-H[12]	3.28	701	N.A.	Tosco	3.48	4,527	36	Conoco	3.04	4,968	19
14	Shell	2.14	N.A.	N.A.	Conoco	3.12	4,897	20	BP America	N.A.	6,775	21
15	UDS[13]	1.96	3,779	17	Coastal	2.80	1,540	32	A-H	N.A.	N.A.	N.A.
Top 15 Share		**91.56**				**92.73**				**N.A.**		

[1] *Source: NPN Market Facts*, 1995 through 2000 and various annual reports.
[2] Preliminary data.
[3] Revised data, including firms in existence at that date.
[4] SOM = Share of Market
[5] Outlets = Branded Retail Outlets
[6] States = Number of States
[7] Exxon and Mobil merged in late 1999. They divested approximately 2,400 outlets in 2000.
[8] BP and Amoco merged in late 1998. BP acquired Arco in April 2000.
[9] Includes joint venture operations with Ashland since January, 1998.
[10] Shell/Texaco joint venture in 31 Western and Midwestern States, with Shell holding 56%.
[11] Shell/Texaco/Saudi Aramco joint venture, in 26 Eastern and Southern States; Shell: 35%, Texaco and Saudi Aramco. each 32.5%.
[12] AH = Amerada Hess.
[13] UDS = Ultramar Diamond Shamrock.

EXHIBIT 2 (continued)

Relative Market Share: U.S. Motor Gasoline Sales

Rank	1996				1995				1994			
	Firm	SOM	Outlets	States	Firm	SOM	Outlets	States	Firm	SOM	Outlets	States
1	Mobil	9.67	7,589	29	Mobil	9.90	7,689	32	Shell	8.85	8,609	41
2	Exxon	9.58	8,400	41	Shell	9.83	8,767	40	Mobil	8.75	7,705	27
3	Shell	9.36	8,609	41	Citgo	9.46	14,054	46	Citgo	8.22	13,116	46
4	Citgo	9.17	14,529	48	Exxon	8.44	8,250	37	Exxon	8.07	8,700	37
5	Texaco	8.10	13,785	25	Texaco	8.27	13,023	45	Chevron	7.95	7,903	27
6	Amoco	7.85	9,184	33	Amoco	8.04	9,600	30	Texaco	7.92	13,746	27
7	Chevron	6.92	8,614	25	Chevron	7.23	7,988	26	Amoco	7.91	9,608	30
8	Marathon	5.83	2,392	11	Marathon	5.83	2,380	11	Marathon	5.73	2,356	11
9	Phillips	4.08	6,888	32	Sunoco	4.70	3,861	19	BP America	5.32	6,750	27
10	BP America	3.51	6,752	21	BP America	4.60	6,800	25	Sunoco	4.01	4,115	19
11	Sunoco	3.33	3,806	19	Phillips	4.21	7,106	32	Phillips	3.98	7,247	33
12	Arco	3.31	1,547	5	Arco	3.40	1,700	5	Arco	3.27	1,547	5
13	Conoco	2.91	5,196	41	Conoco	3.11	5,017	37	Conoco	2.84	5,017	37
14	Unocal	1.88	1,421	7	Unocal	1.89	1,325	7	Unocal	2.26	1,421	7
15	Total	1.75	2,106	19	Total	1.87	1,991	18	Total	1.81	1,767	17
Top 15 Share		87.25				90.78				86.85		

Source: NPN Market Facts, 1995 through 2000 and various annual reports.

with substantial operations on the West Coast of the United States. The partnership acquired, and then attempted to develop, 7,000 acres of oil shale reserves in Colorado. This project had to be abandoned when U.S. environmental restrictions of the 1960s rendered it unprofitable.

Koolsbergen then decided to de-emphasize oil shale development and diversify The Oil Shale Corporation's operations. In 1970, the company purchased the Signal Oil and Gas refinery in Bakersfield, California, and in 1972 expanded its refining presence further by purchasing all of Monsanto's petroleum operations. In 1976, long-time Oil Shale executive Morton Winston became CEO of the company and renamed the firm Tosco, an acronym formed from The Oil Shale Corporation. Under Winston, Tosco purchased Phillips Petroleum's West Coast assets and became the largest petroleum product supplier to independent marketers in the United States.

When the increase in oil prices of the 1970s once again made oil shale development financially attractive, Tosco refocused on its oil shale business by making substantial investments in its Colony Shale partnership with Arco. Arco, however, was fearful of escalating costs in the partnership and sold its 60% partnership interest to Exxon in 1980.

When Colony Shale was unable to secure government funding to support the high cost of oil shale development, Exxon withdrew its support. The partnership was effectively terminated in 1982. Tosco's large investments in its oil shale subsidiary, however, left the company in serious financial distress. In 1983, Morton Winston resigned as CEO and was replaced by Matthew Talbot.

Talbot's tenure at the helm was reasonably short-lived. In 1988, by increasing its ownership interest in Tosco to 40%, Thomas O'Malley's Argus Energy investment company was in a position to install O'Malley as the company's Chief Executive Officer. Following his arrival in 1989, O'Malley initiated a series of moves to reorient the company toward refining and marketing.

Thomas O'Malley began his career as a trader after graduating from Manhattan College in 1968 and was initially employed by Phillip Brothers Inc. He later moved to Salomon Brothers Inc., where he rose to the position of Vice Chairman and CEO of Salomon Brothers Phibro Energy subsidiary. In the 1980s, O'Malley formed the Argus Energy investment partnership and in the mid-1980s took a 20% stake in

Tosco. In 1988, the partnership increased its stake to 40% and, near the end of 1989, took over management of the company, naming O'Malley CEO.

By early 1990, Tosco was a financially struggling, independent oil exploration and production firm with a modest refining presence on the U.S. West Coast. Its sole revenue-producing asset was its Avon refinery, which was located in the San Francisco Bay area and served the wholesale petroleum market in Northern California. The company also retained ownership of oil shale properties in Utah and Colorado.

Growth Through Acquisitions

During the early 1990s, both the domestic and worldwide oil and gas industries were well into a period of restructuring and consolidation. The decade of the 1980s had not been kind to the overall industry, with both falling and volatile crude oil prices and a general situation of over-capacity in virtually all aspects of the industry. While this scenario did not bode well for healthy, robust industry profits, it did provide a number of opportunities to buy assets at a discount to their replacement cost.

In addition, most refineries that were operating in the early 1990s were designed to process a particular crude oil feed of a relatively uniform chemical composition. Processing crude from a single field or region meant that the refining processes could be optimized for both maximum production output and, often, minimum operating costs. O'Malley, however, wanted to allow his refinery managers to vary their crude oil inputs so that they would have more flexibility in choosing a supply source. He believed that this would allow his managers to exercise more control over refining margins by being more selective with inputs. Additionally, he wanted to give his refinery managers more autonomy in choosing the products to be produced so that each refinery could produce the highest margin product mix for its particular market.

1993–1994   Tosco's first acquisition under O'Malley was the April 1993 purchase of Exxon's Bayway refinery in Linden, New Jersey. The addition of this refinery, which had a capacity of over 250,000 barrels per day (bpd), gave the firm a presence on both U.S. coasts and access to the retail and wholesale gasoline markets in both Northern California and the Greater New York City area. Within a year or so, O'Malley's team was able to increase daily production runs at the refinery by about 12%, contributing to a substantial per-unit cost saving.

Tosco also expanded into the retail gasoline marketing business in December 1993 with its acquisition of British Petroleum's (BP's) refining and marketing network in the Pacific Northwest region of the United States. Tosco made an initial payment of $125 million and committed to pay BP a portion of the profits earned from the acquired assets over the succeeding five years. This contingent payment was capped at $150 million.

The deal gave Tosco a refinery in Ferndale, Washington (on Puget Sound approximately 100 miles north of Seattle), and a retail marketing network of 105 company-owned stations, 27 leased stations, and a marketing structure serving 377 independently owned BP outlets located almost entirely in Oregon and Washington. One product tanker and product terminals in Renton and Tacoma, Washington, were also included. The acquisition gave Tosco an immediate 16% share of the retail gasoline market in the two states and an 85,000 bpd capacity refinery complex.

Tosco further expanded its U.S. West Coast petroleum products marketing presence in August 1994 when it acquired BP's Northern California operations under long-term lease arrangements. A total of 414 company-owned, company-leased, or independently owned outlets bearing the BP name were included in this transaction.[3] In December of the

same year, Tosco used a similar arrangement to acquire all 100 of the Exxon stations in Arizona. By early 1995, Tosco's refining and marketing operations included three refineries and approximately 1,050 owned, leased, or franchised service station sites in four states (see Exhibit 3).

1995–1996   Two significant acquisitions occurred during this two-year period, both of which were finalized in 1996. In early February, the firm acquired the U.S. Northeast refining and marketing assets of BP for $64.4 million, plus the value of the related inventories. Assets acquired included a 150,000 bpd (non-operating) refinery in Trainer, Pennsylvania, seven product terminals, and approximately 500 retail service station sites.

Later, in May 1996, the company completed its $772 million acquisition of the Circle K Corporation. This brought about 2,400 company-controlled convenience stores, approximately 2,000 of which sold gasoline, into the Tosco organization. The Circle K operations were located in a 28-state region, primarily across the southern half of the country.

Circle K Corporation was a Phoenix, Arizona-based firm that was originally founded in El Paso, Texas, in 1951. The company expanded dramatically

3. According to some industry observers at the time, BP shed its U.S. West Coast refining and marketing operations due, in part, to an inability to compete effectively against Arco. Ironically, BP Amoco acquired Arco in April, 2000.

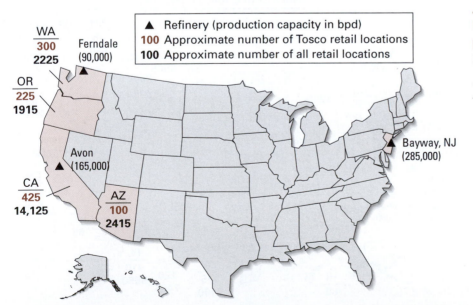

▲ Refinery (production capacity in bpd)
100 Approximate number of Tosco retail locations
100 Approximate number of all retail locations

WA
300
2225
Ferndale
(90,000)

OR
225
1915

Avon
▲ (165,000)

CA
425
14,125

AZ
100
2415

Bayway, NJ
(285,000)

EXHIBIT 3

Early 1995 Refining and Marketing Operations

Source: Casewriter Estimates and Annual Reports.

during the late 1980s, a period during which many other C-store chains were growing and many of the major oil firms were adding merchandise offerings to their own gasoline retailing locations. The heightened competition, when combined with the heavy debt load incurred in financing a rapid expansion, led to a bankruptcy filing in 1990. The company shed approximately one-half of its assets while going through a court-supervised reorganization and emerged from the bankruptcy process in the mid 1990s. The company continued to struggle, however, as the competitive landscape remained difficult.[4]

Finally, in December 1996, Tosco entered into a definitive agreement to acquire the U.S. West Coast refining and marketing operations of Unocal Corporation at a price of approximately $1.4 billion. The assets in question included four California-based refineries, approximately 1,350 Union 76-branded retail outlets, and a variety of product distribution-related assets. By early 1997, Tosco was the largest independent refiner in the country. Its refining and marketing operations included seven refineries,

approximately 5,000 retail outlets (of which about half were company operated), 25 company-controlled wholesale terminals, and 1,300 miles of pipelines, and a lubricant blending, packaging and marketing business (see Exhibit 4).

1997–1998   The Unocal acquisition was finalized in late March 1997. With control of the additional set of assets, Tosco became the fifth-largest refiner in the United States and the second- or third-largest gasoline retailer in all of the major market areas within the state of California. The deal's primary benefits, however, appeared to lie in the increased operating efficiencies made possible with Tosco's now-enlarged asset base in California and the fact that it now had nearly total control over two nationally recognized brand names—Circle K in merchandise and 76 in petroleum products marketing.[5]

This two-year period also saw the continuation of Tosco's high-grading of individual operating assets. Various sources, including Hoover's Online and Paine Webber, reported the acquisition and disposition of assets such as product terminals, retail outlets,

---

4. In what later proved to be a precursor to future events, Circle K and Unocal seriously considered forming a co-branding joint venture which would have involved all Circle K stores in the Phoenix, Tucson, and Las Vegas metropolitan areas.

5. There were a few pre-existing license grants relating to 76 truck stops and the Uno-Ven joint venture with Petroleos de Venezuela S.A. in the U.S. Middle West.

EXHIBIT 4

Early 1997 Refining and Marketing Operations

Source: Casewriter Estimates, Annual Reports, and *NPN Market Facts,* Mid-July 2000.

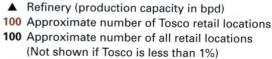

▲ Refinery (production capacity in bpd)
100 Approximate number of Tosco retail locations
100 Approximate number of all retail locations
(Not shown if Tosco is less than 1%)

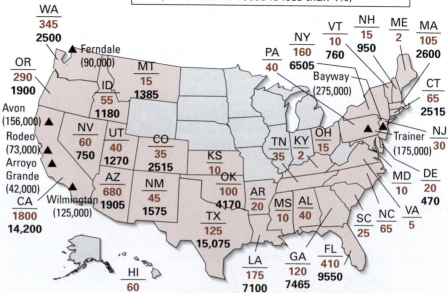

and various pieces of vacant land. In general, the acquisitions were in geographic areas where Tosco already had a major presence, and the dispositions related to either overlapping assets from the recent large acquisitions or retail operations in areas where Tosco did not have a significant presence.

1999   The year 1999 contained no blockbuster deals. It did, however, see significant events occur in several diverse areas. In February, a fire at the Avon refinery near San Francisco resulted in four fatalities and a lengthy closure of the facility—which was not fully operating again until late July. The incident led to a flurry of negative press coverage, a thorough safety review, extensive employee training, and a public statement by the CEO that "We are not going to run a refinery that cannot be operated safely."[6] The firm also paid fines and other related payments totaling nearly $3 million and agreed to pay $21 million to settle wrongful death lawsuits filed by relatives of three of the workers killed. Two other lawsuits, one by the family of a fourth person killed and one by a worker disabled by the accident, were still pending in mid-2000.

In February, Tosco also signed a memorandum of understanding with Union Carbide Corp. to create a 50/50 joint venture to produce and market polypropylene (PP). Tosco would construct a $200 million, 775 million pounds-per-year (lb/yr) polypropylene plant at its Bayway refinery in Linden, New Jersey. Production from the new refinery would be combined with output from its existing propylene output at Bayway and production from Union Carbide's Seadrift, Texas, and Norco, Louisiana, refineries. The joint venture was scheduled to begin on the day that Tosco's new refinery began production, sometime in early 2001. Tosco was to use Union Carbide's Unipol PP process at its plant in exchange for payments to be made to Union Carbide over the life of the joint venture.

Polypropylene is a plastic used in products such as car bumpers, baby diapers, and plastic bottles and provides higher margins than most other refined petroleum products. Previous to the joint venture arrangement, Tosco produced 400 million lb./yr. of propylene and assumed substantial transportation costs to have it shipped to third-party refiners for conversion to polypropylene. The Tosco/Union Car-

bide venture would be one of the five-largest polypropylene suppliers in North America with a combined annual capacity (among the three plants) of approximately 1.6 billion lb./yr.

The year also saw an acceleration of Tosco's rebranding program with an increasing number of retail sites converted to the Circle K/76 format (Circle K merchandise and 76 petroleum products). In April, for example, it was announced that the BP name was being given up in the U.S. Pacific Northwest with all sites moving to the Circle K/76 format.

The retail site acquisitions and dispositions for the year continued the general theme of the prior several years, with the following transactions being the most prominent:

- March—Announced the sale of 320 retail sites in Colorado, Utah, Texas, and the U.S. Midwest.
- June—Sold 45 locations in Idaho to Jackson's Food Stores, making them the largest C-store operator in that state.
- July—Announced the acquisition of 137 sites in Pittsburgh and the U.S. Southeast from BP Amoco.
- October—Announced the acquisition of 87 sites in the U.S. Southeast from Boardman Petroleum.

Finally, Tosco was added to the Standard and Poor's 500 Index (S&P 500) in September 1999. Exhibit 5 provides data on Tosco's refining and marketing operations in mid-2000.

2000   Tosco returned to the large-deal mode in 2000. The largest of the year's deals was closed in February for $860 million and resulted in Tosco acquiring the Exxon system of retail gasoline and convenience store outlets from New York through Maine in the Northeastern U.S. and the Mobil system from New Jersey through Virginia in the Middle Atlantic region.[7]

Collectively, Tosco's acquisition consisted of 1,740 retail gasoline and C-store outlets as well as some undeveloped sites and distribution terminals. Tosco also acquired exclusive rights to the Exxon and Mobil brands in the applicable areas for a period of ten years. Many industry observers believed that Tosco

---

6. Tosco Corporation, 1999 Annual Report.

7. As a condition of approval for the merger of Exxon and Mobil in December 1999, the U.S. Federal Trade Commission required the combined firm to divest itself of approximately 2,450 service stations and the Benicia (California) refinery, among other items. The Tosco deal was closed less than 90 days after the finalization of the ExxonMobil merger.

EXHIBIT 5

Tosco: Mid-2000 Refining
and Marketing
Operations

Source: Casewriter Estimates,
Annual Reports and *NPN Market
Facts,* Mid-July 2000; and Tosco
press releases and Investor Relations presentations.

▲ Refinery (production capacity in bpd)
100 Approximate number of Tosco retail locations
100 Approximate number of all retail locations
(Not shown if Tosco is less than 1%)

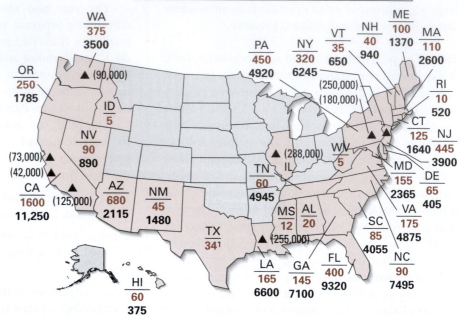

¹ All located in Far West Texas

would gradually re-brand its new Mobil and Exxon locations with the Circle K and 76 brands.

Tosco moved again in the second quarter of the year with the $420 million acquisition of the Wood River Refinery and Chemical Complex from Equilon Enterprises LLC (a joint venture of Texaco, Inc. and Royal Dutch Shell). Equilon had been reported to be trying to focus primarily on its refining operations on the U.S. West Coast, and the disposition of the Wood River Refinery was consistent with this theme.[8] The 295,000 bpd facility raised Tosco's total refining capacity to 1.245 million bpd, making it the third-largest U.S. refiner after ExxonMobil (approximately 1.8 million bpd) and BP (approximately 1.7 million bpd). It also represented Tosco's initial refining foray into the Midwestern region of the country, where the Roxana, Illinois, facility was located. Initial estimates were that the refinery and chemical complex would add three billion dollars (U.S.) of revenue to Tosco on an annualized basis.

The Wood River acquisition was seen as an attractive one by most industry analysts. The price

agreed upon was reported to be significantly lower than the price Clark Refining and Marketing Company offered for the complex in 1999. The Clark deal fell apart due to the prospective buyer's inability to secure high-yield debt financing at the time. Tosco was also expected to be able to improve the returns at the refinery by broadening and varying the crude slate—with an emphasis upon more use of high sulfur crude.

Avon Refinery Sale In early July 2000, Tosco announced that it had entered into an agreement to sell its Avon (California) refinery to Ultramar Diamond Shamrock (UDS), another independent refiner and marketer, for $730 million. The $730 million net present value included a $650 million payment at closing and a participation payment of $150 million spread over the next eight years.[9] This deal closed in early September.

As noted by the Associated Press, the decision to sell the Avon Refinery Complex represented Tosco "throwing in the towel" on a long-troublesome asset.

8. "Tosco Fills Gap Between East, West Coasts with Acquisition of Wood River Refinery," *The Oil Daily,* April 2000, as reported by Northern Light Technology.

9. The Avon Refinery Complex was also expected to require capital investments of $300 million over the next three years to cover such things as complying with various environmental mandates.

"We retreated. That's the beginning, middle, and end of it. I think a new owner will do better with it," said Thomas O'Malley.[10]

UDS already owned a 125,000 bpd refinery in the Los Angeles area, which meant that they immediately became the fifth-largest refiner on the U.S. West Coast. Tosco, in turn, dropped to fourth-largest behind Chevron, BP, and Equilon Enterprise. It was expected that UDS would both invest heavily in the refinery to increase production and comply with environmental mandates and initiate a program to expand their retail presence in Northern California via the addition of more Beacon branded sites.

BP Amoco Alliance Refinery   Also in early July, Tosco announced a deal to acquire the BP Amoco Alliance Refinery on the U.S. Gulf Coast in Louisiana. The transaction, which was for approximately $760 million ($660 million, plus $100 million in working capital), closed in early September.

The Alliance refinery provided Tosco entry into the Gulf Coast market and (via product pipelines) allowed it to serve the Middle Atlantic and New York harbor region as well. The 250,000 bpd refinery, which was described as "world class" by one investment banking firm,[11] was more technologically sophisticated than most of its Gulf Coast peers with lower operating costs as well. In addition, near-term requirements for capital expenditures were believed to be quite modest.

Finally, in late July 2000, Tosco made a move into the international arena with the announcement that it intended to buy substantially all of the assets of the Irish National Petroleum Corporation Limited (INPCL) for $100 million, plus the cost of the crude oil and petroleum products at the time of closing. The main assets of INPCL were a modern 75,000 bpd refinery located in Cork and an 8.5 million barrel, deepwater crude oil and oil products complex located in Bantry Bay. The refinery had been upgraded, at a cost of $100 million over the past three years, so that it could meet the European Union requirements for low sulfur gasoline and diesel fuels.

Tosco was reported to be planning to lease half of the facilities at Bantry Bay on a long-term basis to the Irish government for their use as storage for the country's strategic petroleum reserves. It was also planning to use some of the refinery output, some 30,000 bpd of low sulfur fuel oil, as feedstock for the surplus upgrading facility at their Bayway and Trainer refinery complexes.

Other Sizeable Independents

The refining and marketing segments of the overall oil and gas industry in the United States had historically been dominated by large, integrated firms. For example, in early 2000, the five largest players in the domestic retail gasoline business were reported to hold about 57% of the overall market—and all five were portions (or affiliates) of major integrated firms.[12] Nonetheless, at least three independents[13] had been competing effectively with the integrated majors over the past few years. These three included Sun Oil Company (Sunoco), Tosco, and Ultramar-Diamond Shamrock (UDS) (see Exhibit 2).

On the refining side, however, the story was slightly different. Five of the ten largest refiners in the United States were independents, led by Tosco in the number three position.[14] The other four large independents included Valero, Sunoco, UDS, and Koch Industries (see Exhibit 1).

Over the next few pages, some brief background data is provided on two of these independents (UDS and Valero), as well as another major C-store chain (7-Eleven) and two alliance networks—one formed by Marathon and Ashland (MAP and Speedway SuperAmerica) and one formed by Shell and Texaco (Equilon and Motiva).

Ultramar-Diamond Shamrock

Ultramar-Diamond Shamrock (UDS) was the third-largest independent oil refiner and marketer in the United States, behind Tosco and Sunoco. The firm owned five refineries located in California, Oklahoma, and Texas with a combined capacity of

10. Associated Press Newswires, "Tosco, Ultramar execs see sale of Martinez refinery as 'classic win-win'," July 6, 2000.
11. Douglas T. Terreson, Paul J. Coppola and Jacques H. Rousseau, "Tosco Company Update: Tosco Strikes Again, Raising Estimates, PT $40/Sh.," Morgan Stanley Dean Witter, July 13, 2000, pg. 2.
12. BP Amoco and Arco presentation, 16 March 2000, as shown on BP: Alive: Alaska-Gas-Downstream (http://www.bpamoco.com).
13. Defined here to be primarily refining and marketing, as opposed to integrated oil and gas, firms.
14. Data is taken from *NPN Market Facts*, Mid-July 2000, pp. 110–111, and is based on refining capacity.

550,000 bpd and operated roughly 5,000 gas station/C-stores under the Diamond Shamrock, Ultramar, Beacon, and Total brand names in eighteen states. The company also owned a home heating oil business which served 236,000 households in New England and Eastern Canada and produced petrochemicals and natural gas liquids. Ultramar-Diamond Shamrock rounded out its marketing business with 4,000 wholesale branded outlets that sold diesel, jet fuel, lube oil, and asphalt to commercial customers and the military.

The National Convenience Stores chain, with 661 convenience stores in Texas, was purchased by Diamond Shamrock in 1995 for $260 million. By 1996, the firm had gained a 16% market share, making it the largest gasoline retailer in Texas, and operated 2,700 Corner Store, Stop-N-Go, and Diamond Shamrock C-stores. The company was also the second-largest gasoline retailer in New Mexico and Colorado. Its refineries in Three Rivers and Dumas, Texas, had a total capacity of 225,000 bpd. In 1996, Diamond Shamrock merged with Ultramar Corporation to form Ultramar Diamond Shamrock.

At the time of the merger with Diamond Shamrock, Ultramar operated refineries in Wilmington, California, and Quebec, Canada, with a combined capacity of 250,000 bpd. The company also sold gasoline at 360 California locations and 1,400 Eastern Canadian locations under the Ultramar and Beacon brands.

The Ultramar-Diamond Shamrock (UDS) merger was finalized in January 1997, creating what was then the fourth-largest refining and marketing firm in North America with $9 billion in revenue, 17,000 workers and 4,400 retail gasoline outlets.

In November 1997 UDS acquired Total Petroleum North American Ltd. for approximately $880 million in UDS stock and assumed debt. Total Petroleum operated three refineries (combined capacity 150,000 bpd) and owned eleven terminals, 1,136 miles of pipeline and 2,127 Total-branded gasoline stations. The deal gave Ultramar Diamond Shamrock a network of 6,381 retail outlets in 19 states and six Canadian provinces, a total refining capacity of 650,000 bpd, and boosted its total pipeline holdings to 5,679 miles.

In 1998, UDS signed a letter of intent to form the Diamond 66 joint venture with Phillips Petroleum. The highly publicized joint venture would have created a petroleum retailing organization with 12,000 gas station/C-stores and ten refineries in 36 states and six Canadian provinces. The original agreement had given UDS a 55% controlling interest in Diamond 66 in exchange for a $500 million cash payment to Phillips at the deal's close and an additional $300 million one year later. In the end, though, the two companies were unable to come to terms on the final agreement and the transaction was cancelled.

Valero Energy Corporation

Valero Energy Corporation, a San Antonio, Texas-based firm, was also one of the leading independent refiners of motor fuels in the United States. The company owned four refineries in Texas and Louisiana, one refinery in New Jersey, and a refinery in the San Francisco Bay area. Valero's products were marketed in 31 states and selected export markets. The company was transitioning into gasoline retail marketing with its acquisition of 340 Exxon-branded retail sites in Northern California.

Like Tosco, Valero had benefited from the asset divestitures of major oil companies in recent years. Valero bought Mobil's Paulsboro, New Jersey, refinery in 1998 and, most recently, purchased the Exxon-Mobil Benicia refinery in the San Francisco Bay area. Valero became one of the top five-to-seven refiners as measured by refining capacity in the United States and, with its acquisition of the Benicia refinery, obtained access to the large market for motor fuels in California. A summary of Valero's refining capacity as of mid-2000 is presented in Table 1.

Throughout Valero's growth period in the 1990s, the firm remained focused on upgrading its refineries to both increase overall output and to increase refining complexity and flexibility. This approach allowed Valero's refineries to process a wide slate of feedstocks that sold at a discount to the benchmark West Texas Intermediate crude oil.

On March 2, 2000, Valero agreed to purchase ExxonMobil's Benicia, California, refinery and all of the Exxon-branded California retail assets for a purchase price of $895 million, plus the value of inventories at the close of the transaction. This deal came as a result of the Federal Trade Commission and State of California Consent Decrees requiring divestiture of certain assets by Exxon and Mobil in order to satisfy antitrust issues associated with their merger. The Benicia Refinery, located on the Carquinez Straits of the San Francisco Bay, northeast of

TABLE 1

U.S. Refining Capacity (in bpd), Mid-2000, Valero

Refinery	Location	Capacity[1]	Capacity[2]
Corpus Christi Refinery	Corpus Christi, Texas	215,000	215,000[3]
Texas City Refinery	Texas City, Texas	200,000	152,000
Paulsboro Refinery	Paulsboro, New Jersey	170,000	152,000
Benicia Refinery	Benicia, California	160,000	129,500
Houston Refinery	Houston, Texas	120,000	72,500
Krotz Springs Refinery	Krotz Springs, Louisiana	85,000	78,000
Total		**950,000**	**799,000**

[1] As reported by Valero Energy Corporation on their website, www.valero.com (Benicia Slideshow Outline, 3/10/2000).
[2] As shown in *NPN Market Facts,* mid-July 2000. This report was based on US EIA data from 1998.
[3] Amended to reflect actual capacity as the cited source appeared to have inaccurate data.

the city of San Francisco, was a highly complex refinery with a rated crude oil capacity of 130,000 bpd.

The retail assets portion of the acquisition included 80 company-owned retail sites, 75 of which were in the San Francisco Bay Area. The Consent Decrees' requirements that ExxonMobil withdraw the Exxon brand name from these 75 stations allowed Valero to develop its own brand by rebranding these locations with the Valero name. Another 260 independently owned and operated retail facilities outside the Bay area included in the transaction were allowed to retain rights to the Exxon brand, continue to accept the Exxon credit cards and receive Exxon brand support. Valero received exclusive rights to the Exxon brand throughout California for a ten-year period, except in the San Francisco Bay area.

7-Eleven Incorporated

7-Eleven Incorporated was the Dallas, Texas-based operator of the 7-Eleven convenience store chain. In 1999, the company generated $8.3 billion in revenue through merchandise and gasoline sales at its outlets. The company also owned or had interests in stores in Canada and Mexico and licensed the 7-Eleven brand worldwide. Tosco became 7-Eleven's primary C-store competitor when it purchased the Circle-K convenience store chain in 1997.

7-Eleven purchased Citgo Gasoline Refining and Marketing Company in 1983. The deal included 300 Citgo service stations and use of the Citgo brand at its 7-Eleven outlets. In 1986, 7-Eleven sold a 50% interest in Citgo to the Venezuelan national oil company, Petroleos de Venezuela (PDVSA) in order to raise cash for other acquisitions. Following an attempted leveraged buyout, 7-Eleven filed for bankruptcy in 1990.

Ito-Yokado, 7-Eleven's Japanese partner and franchisee, entered the picture in 1991 when it purchased 70% of the company and named Clark Matthews as the new CEO. Matthews rationalized operations by closing under-performing stores, renovating the remaining stores and upgrading merchandise offerings. In 1992, the company's distribution system was sold to Wal-Mart, making Wal-Mart the nation's largest supplier to C-stores. In 1998, the company implemented an electronic Retail Information System (RIS) similar to that in use at its licensed outlets in Japan. The RIS connected all of the retail stores to a central network, allowing managers to optimize inventory management and product mix. 7-Eleven also introduced daily merchandise deliveries to 3,700 of its 5,800 retail outlets.

By late 1999, 7-Eleven, was positioning its U.S. retail outlets as an order fulfillment destination for online transactions initiated within its stores and at consumers' homes. The V.com, or virtual machine strategy, was established in 1998 as a pilot program for developing in-store product delivery and payment systems similar to those used successfully by Ito-Yokado's stores in Japan. Their long-term plan for V.com seemed to consist of a complete set of e-commerce services similar to those offered by 7-Eleven in Japan.

Marathon Ashland Petroleum LLC

Marathon Ashland Petroleum (MAP) was a 62/38 percent ownership joint venture between USX Corporation's USX-Marathon and Ashland Corporation. The venture was formed in 1998 to reduce costs and obtain economies of scale for the companies' refining and marketing assets. MAP operated seven refineries in the Midwestern states and Texas, representing a combined 935,000 bpd of crude oil capacity. MAP was the fifth-largest refiner in the U.S. with 6% of total U.S. refining capacity. The firm also sold motor gasoline through its 3,500 Marathon and Ashland-branded retail outlets. MAP had a retail presence in twelve primarily Midwestern states and had a 20% or greater market share in several of those states. MAP also had an interest in 8,000 miles of pipeline and operated over ninety asphalt and light product terminals in the Midwest and Southeast.

In addition to MAP, a related subsidiary of USX-Marathon, Speedway SuperAmerica LLC, owned and operated 2,300 locations in 19 states located in the Midwestern and Southeastern sections of the United States. Speedway SuperAmerica ranked first in the nation in company owned and operated truck stops (150 in a 12-state region) and third in the nation in company owned and operated convenience stores and gasoline outlets.

The Alliance Companies

The alliance companies were a collection of four related partnerships among Shell, Texaco, and the national oil company of the Kingdom of Saudi Arabia, Saudi Arabian Oil Company (Saudi Aramco). The three companies formed the alliance in 1998 by combining major portions of each participant's downstream operations (petroleum refining, distribution, and marketing) in the United States. The two major firms within the alliance were:

▌ Equilon Enterprises LLC

▌ Motiva Enterprises LLC

Both companies were based in Houston, Texas. The alliance companies posted combined gross revenues of $33.4 billion and controlled $17.1 billion in total assets in 1998. The overall enterprise was large, but each of the organizations operated semi-autonomously.

Equilon Enterprises LLC

Shell Oil Company and Texaco Incorporated combined major elements of their Western and Midwestern U.S. petroleum refining businesses to form Equilon. Shell and Texaco owned 56% and 44%, respectively. Equilon refined and marketed gasoline and petroleum products under both the Shell and Texaco brand names in 31 Western states and was responsible for the national transporation and lubricants businesses of the partner firms. The firm provided products to about 9,000 Shell and Texaco retail and wholesale outlets and had an 8.2% market share nationally. It was reported to have a 12% market share in the 31 states in which it operated and to be either number one or two in 14 of those states. Company assets included four refineries with a combined capacity of 563,000 bpd as of mid-2000. Three of them were located in California and one near Seattle.

Not long after Equilon was formed, Jim Morgan, president and CEO of the Equilon partnership, began looking for asset sale opportunities that would boost the firm's bottom line. In 1999 and early 2000, the company announced the sale of two of its then-owned refineries, representing almost half of Equilon's refining capacity. Equilon's intent was said to include a de-emphasis on refining and an expansion of its marketing, terminal, pipeline, lubricants, and trading businesses.[15]

Motiva Enterprises LLC

Motiva combined significant elements of Shell, Texaco, and Saudi Aramco's Eastern and Gulf Coast petroleum refining and marketing businesses. The previous Star Enterprise joint venture between Texaco and Saudi Aramco was dissolved and the assets from that partnership were rolled into Motiva Enterprises. The ownership split among the listed partners was 35%, 32.5%, and 32.5%, with Shell controlling the largest share of the company. Similar to Equilon, Motiva refined and marketed gasoline and petroleum products under the Shell and Texaco brand names. It operated in 26 states and Washington, D.C., providing product to 14,600 branded retail and wholesale

15. Former President of Shell Global Solutions International BV in the Netherlands, Rob J. Routs, succeeded Jim Morgan as Equilon's President and CEO in March 2000. Although it was officially stated that Mr. Morgan had chosen to retire, suspicion existed that the change was precipitated by dissatisfaction with Equilon's performance.

outlets. Motiva claimed to have a 15.4% market share in its operational region and to be either number one or two in 17 of its 26 states. The company's assets included four refineries with a combined capacity of 850 million bpd.

Turbulence in Refining and Marketing

By late 2000, the refining and marketing sector of the domestic oil and gas business had evolved such that it was quite different from what had prevailed as recently as a decade earlier. The independent refiners with Tosco leading the parade, had steadily increased their presence (see Exhibit 1). On the East Coast, for example, Tosco and Sun Oil Company (Sunoco) together controlled approximately 55% of the refining capacity. On the West Coast, the story was similar—but less dramatic—with Tesoro, Tosco, UDS, and Valero holding about 35% of industry capacity.[16]

Large, independent retail gasoline marketers such as Sunoco, Tosco, and UDS were providing meaningful competition for the majors in virtually every region of the country as well—with Tosco dominating in Arizona and UDS leading in Texas. British Petroleum (BP), meanwhile, had acquired both Amoco and Arco and reemerged as a major North American gasoline retailer. As of early 2000, they claimed to be the number one retailer in the United States, with 18,000 gas stations, a 15% share of the national market, and a 20% or greater market share in eight states including Washington, California, Nevada, Georgia, North and South Carolina, and Tennessee.[17]

Meanwhile, the C-store and retail gasoline industries had, for all practical purposes, converged to form an ill-defined, but sizeable, industry of his own. As of late 1999, the U.S. C-store industry had topped $160 billion in sales with nearly 100,000 locations nationwide. (See Exhibit 6 for more data on the U.S. C-store industry.)

The C-store industry, perhaps due to its relatively high gross margins and relatively stable return-on-

equity performance over the past few years, attracted a diverse set of companies. It counted majors, independents, and non-oil players among its largest firms. The top 20 firms, for example, included Tosco, Marathon-USX, UDS, and 7-Eleven as well as Exxon-Mobil, BP, Chevron, and Kampgrounds of America, Inc. (with 522 locations in 47 states).[18]

Despite the rosy picture that one might infer from the growth shown by some of the faster-changing players in the refining and marketing sector, the financial markets had not been looking favorably upon either the industry sector or its individual participants. In January 2000, for example, the average Price-to-Equity (P/E) and Price-to-Cash Flow (P/CF) ratios across Sunoco, Tosco, Valero, and UDS were 10.8 and 4.8, respectively.[19]

Among all the turbulence, however, some underlying truths appeared to have been present for some time in this sector of the overall oil and gas industry. The refining and marketing sector, for example, was still largely a game dominated by relatively large firms. Tosco's annualized revenues were running at approximately $25 billion (U.S.), when one considered its acquisitions and divestitures during 2000. Sunoco, UDS, and Valero, none of whom were among the top five refiners or gasoline marketers in the country, were all multibillion-dollar operations nonetheless. (See Exhibit 7 for data on the major geographic regions in terms of refinery capacity and utilization.) Finally, at least some of the independent players in this sector—and, in particular, Tosco—were reporting results that compared favorably with those of many of the so-called majors. (See Exhibit 8 for comparative financial and operating data across eight different firms for the 1995 to 1998 period.)

Tosco in the New Millennium

By late 2000, Toscos operations extended across 31 states encompassing all of the East, West and Gulf Coast states, as well as a few in the interior. The firm was also in a number of different segments of the overall oil and gas industry—ranging from petrochemicals at one extreme to pure C-store operations, with no gasoline retailing involved, at the other. As such, the firm competed with a wide range of firms

16. Michael Mayer, and Craig Ellis, *Tosco Corporation: Investment Conclusion and Valuation,* Schroder & Co., Inc., January 31, 2000, pp. 7 and 9, and *NPN Market Facts,* Mid-July 2000, pp. 110–111 and 114–115.

17. BP Amoco, "Alaska-Gas-US Downstream," BP Amoco and Arco Presentation, 16 March 2000, pp. 2 and 3, as reported on the BP website (http://www.bp.com).

18. "Top 50 U.S. Convenience Store Companies," *NPN Market Facts,* Mid-July 2000, p. 134.

19. The average for the S&P Industrials for the same time period was 29.2 and 17.7, respectively. Mayer, *Tosco Corporation,* p. 15.

EXHIBIT 6

Statistical Data on U.S. C-Stores: 1995–1999

	1999	1998	1997	1996	1995
Total Industry Sales	N.A.	$ 164B	$ 156.2B	$151.9B	$144.1B
In-Store	N.A.	$ 75.1B	$ 72.4B	$ 70.7B	$ 69.7B
Motor Fuel	N.A.	$ 88.9B	$ 83.8B	$ 81.2B	$ 74.4B
Total C-Stores	N.A.	96,700	95,700	94,200	93,200
Selling Motor Fuel	75.0%	77.0%	73.0%	73.0%	73.0%
Avg. Gallons/Month	110,500	95,100	84,500	82,000	81,000
Gross Margin/Gallon	13.4¢	12.6¢	13.4¢	13.1¢	13.4¢
Gross Margin	19.6%	20.8%	20.9%	20.3%	20.8%
In-Store	30.0%	31.2%	32.0%	31.2%	30.4%
Motor Fuel	11.7%	12.0%	11.3%	10.7%	11.8%
Average Store Sales/Year	N.A.	$ 1970m	$ 1876m	$1932m	$1842m
In-Store	$ 856m	$ 777m	$ 757m	$ 751m	$ 748m
Motor Fuel	N.A.	$ 1193m	$ 1199m	$1181m	$1094m
EBITDA[1]/Store	$ 83,500	$ 74,600	$ 65,300	N.A.	N.A.
Top Quartile	$140,200	$112,300	$101,400	N.A.	N.A.
Bottom Quartile	$ 31,400	$ 39,200	$ 26,000	N.A.	N.A.
Pre-Tax Profit/Store	2.0%	2.1%	1.6%	1.6%	2.2%
Top Quartile	2.9%	3.7%	3.0%	N.A.	N.A.
Bottom Quartile	(0.1%)	(0.1%)	(0.7%)	N.A.	N.A.
Performance Ratios					
Pre-Tax ROA	N.A.	10.5%	8.3%	6.1%	8.6%
Pre-Tax ROE	N.A.	24.9%	34.9%	21.5%	28.2%
Accts Pay. To Inventory	N.A.	1.5X	1.5X	1.3X	1.4X
Merchandise Shrinkage	N.A.	1.5%	1.8%	1.2%	1.4%

[1]EBITDA = Earnings Before Interest, Taxes, Depreciation and Amortization.

Source: Convenience Store Industry Fact Book, National Association of Convenience Stores; Alexandria, Virginia, 12th Edition, 1999, pp. 6–9, 24–27, 30, 46, 58, 59, and 104; and 2000 NACS/CS News Industry Databank as cited in *NPN Market Facts* 2000.

from ExxonMobil and BP at one extreme to Travel Centers of America and Stewart's Ice Cream Company, Inc. (both C-store chains with more than 150 units each) at the other. Finally, Tosco had become a rather sizeable firm as well (see Exhibit 9 for financial and operating data).

On the refining side, Tosco had become a significant player by almost any standard. They now controlled about 8% of the capacity available in the United States and were ranked behind only ExxonMobil and BP. On a worldwide basis, they had moved up to about the number 12 position—just above Texaco and the Kuwait National Petroleum Company.[20]

While they had built no new refineries on their own, Tosco's most recent acquisitions had all been purchased at a discount to replacement cost.[21] Each of them, in addition, was technologically sophisticated in terms that provided benefits at both the input process level and the outgoing products slate level. All of their refineries except one (Wood River) were located in or near a retail marketing region in which Tosco was a significant player.

The near-term outlook for refinery profits appeared to be quite positive as well. After a disastrous period during the late 1990s, the fundamentals seemed to have improved markedly. The incremental

20. Based on Year 2000 data used to update the rankings shown in "Worldwide Refining: How the World's Largest Refiners Rank," *Data Book 1999, Oil and Gas Journal,* 1999, p. 202.

21. The INPC acquisition, for example, involved paying $100 million for a facility that had been upgraded at that cost over the past three years. See Tosco press release dated July 31, 2000.

EXHIBIT 7

Refinery Capacity and Utilization: Selected Regions (barrels per calendar day, in thousands)

	1998	1997	1996	1995	1994	1993	1992	1991
TOTAL WORLD								
Refinery Capacity	80,440	79,845	77,800	76,885	75,575	74,240	73,390	74,830
Refinery Throughput	67,490	67,145	64,740	63,320	62,270	62,195	61,650	61,685
Capacity Utilization	83.9%	84.1%	83.2%	82.4%	82.4%	83.8%	84.0%	82.4%
UNITED STATES								
Refinery Capacity	16,155	15,705	15,450	15,335	15,435	15,030	15,120	15,700
Refinery Throughput	14,835	14,660	14,195	13,975	13,865	13,615	13,410	13,300
Capacity Utilization	91.8%	93.3%	91.9%	91.1%	89.8%	90.6%	88.7%	84.7%
Domestic Demand	18,917	18,620	18,309	17,725	17,718	17,237	17,033	16,714
WESTERN EUROPE								
Refinery Capacity	16,305	16,425	16,225	16,285	16,440	16,485	16,655	16,480
Refinery Throughput	15,265	14,835	14,670	14,430	14,370	14,245	13,975	13,800
Capacity Utilization	93.6%	90.3%	90.4%	88.6%	87.2%	86.4%	83.9%	83.7%
ASIA & AUSTRALASIA								
Refinery Capacity	19,390	18,755	17,860	17,110	15,945	15,385	14,575	13,740
Refinery Throughput	16,245	16,460	15,410	14,490	13,815	12,765	11,950	11,190
Capacity Utilization	83.8%	87.8%	86.3%	81.8%	86.6%	83.0%	82.0%	81.4%
MIDDLE EAST								
Refinery Capacity	5,935	5,835	5,660	5,555	5,335	5,020	4,680	4,450
Refinery Throughput	5,720	5,645	5,370	5,320	4,920	4,810	4,300	3,790
Capacity Utilization	96.4%	96.7%	94.9%	95.8%	92.2%	95.8%	91.9%	85.2%
CENTRAL & SOUTH AMERICA								
Refinery Capacity	6,465	6,555	6,145	6,210	6,090	6,110	6,140	6,075
Refinery Throughput	5,365	5,235	4,895	4,800	4,915	4,835	4,735	4,665
Capacity Utilization	83.0%	79.9%	79.7%	77.3%	80.7%	79.1%	77.1%	76.8%

Source: National Petroleum New Market Facts, Mid-July 2000, Adams Trade Press, Inc., Arlington Heights, Illinois, pp. 69 and 74.

EXHIBIT 8

Summary Performance Data for Selected Industry Firms

| | Revenues | | Net Income | | Ident. Assets[2] | | Return on Sales | | Return on Assets[3] | | Firm-Wide | | Refinery |
	Firm ($ Millions)	R&M[1]	Firm ($ Millions)	R&M	Firm ($ Millions)	R&M	Firm (Percent)	R&M	Firm (Percent)	R&M	ROE[4] (Percent)	D/E[5] (Percent)	Cap. Util.[6] (Percent)
ARCO													
1995	15,819	5,555	1,376	200	23,999	3,165	8.70	3.60	5.73	6.32	20.36	99.26	104.0
1996	14,580	6,932	1,663	287	25,715	3,380	11.80	4.14	6.47	8.49	21.32	71.70	98.3
1997	14,757	6,853	1,771	325	22,425	3,564	12.35	4.74	7.90	9.12	20.40	41.69	97.9
1998	10,809	5,470	452	281	25,199	3,826	4.39	5.14	1.79	7.34	5.96	57.15	97.3
CHEVRON													
1995	36,310	N.A.	930	N.A.	34,330	N.A.	2.56	N.A.	2.72	N.A.	6.48	31.49	88.6
1996	43,893	29,580	2,607	419	34,854	N.A.	5.94	1.42	7.48	N.A.	16.69	25.53	91.1
1997	41,963	28,946	3,256	899	35,473	11,895	7.76	3.11	9.18	7.55	18.64	25.36	89.2
1998	30,557	21,070	1,339	600	36,540	11,643	4.38	2.84	3.66	5.15	7.86	25.79	83.1
EXXON													
1995	123,920	N.A.	6,470	1,272	91,296	N.A.	5.22	N.A.	7.09	N.A.	16.00	19.24	98.3
1996	134,249	106,755	7,510	885	95,527	32,538	5.59	0.83	7.86	2.72	17.25	16.67	95.2
1997	137,242	109,772	8,460	2,063	96,064	32,591	6.16	1.88	8.81	6.33	19.38	16.15	100.2
1998	117,772	95,216	6,370	2,458	92,630	33,752	5.41	2.58	6.88	7.28	14.56	10.35	95.4
MOBIL													
1995	75,370	62,362	2,376	894	42,138	22,463	3.15	1.43	5.64	3.98	13.24	25.79	92.0
1996	81,503	70,796	2,964	913	46,408	23,520	3.64	1.29	6.39	3.88	15.54	23.33	89.1
1997	65,906	55,871	3,272	1,025	43,559	20,212	4.96	1.83	7.51	5.07	16.81	18.86	105.5
1998	53,531	45,233	1,704	1,016	42,754	18,532	3.18	2.25	3.99	5.48	9.28	20.24	110.5

[1]R&M: Refining and Marketing
[2]Identifiable Assets
[3]Net income as a percentage of closing assets.
[4]Net income as a percentage of closing equity.
[5]Long-term debt as a percentage of stockholders' equity.
[6]Refinery capacity utilization for U.S.-based refineries only.

Source: U.S. Oil and Gas Company Performance Report, Third Edition, PennWell Publishing, July 1999, and Tosco and Valero annual reports.

EXHIBIT 8 *(continued)*

Summary Performance Data for Selected Industry Firms

	Revenues		Net Income		Ident. Assets[2]		Return on Sales		Return on Assets[3]		Firm-Wide		Refinery
	Firm ($ Millions)	R&M[1]	Firm ($ Millions)	R&M	Firm ($ Millions)	R&M	Firm (Percent)	R&M	Firm (Percent)	R&M	ROE[4] (Percent)	D/E[5] (Percent)	Cap. Util.[6] (Percent)
SHELL (U.S.)													
1995	24,650	18,355	1,520	778	27,021	8,763	6.17	4.24	5.63	8.88	10.97	9.39	95.9
1996	29,151	22,944	2,021	336	28,709	9,326	6.93	1.46	7.04	3.60	14.06	5.52	99.3
1997	28,959	22,236	2,104	410	29,601	9,277	7.27	1.84	7.11	4.42	14.22	3.95	99.5
1998	15,451	4,193	(1,727)	169	26,543	5,970	(11.18)	4.03	(6.51)	2.83	(15.17)	4.30	96.2
TEXACO													
1995	36,787	19,411	607	486	24,937	N.A.	1.65	2.50	2.43	N.A.	6.38	57.81	101.7
1996	45,500	22,997	2,018	691	26,963	5,297	4.44	3.00	7.48	13.05	19.46	49.41	105.2
1997	46,667	24,322	2,664	789	29,600	5,861	5.71	3.24	9.00	13.46	20.87	43.14	108.4
1998	31,707	20,263	578	537	28,570	3,351	1.82	2.65	2.02	16.03	4.88	53.68	108.9
TOSCO													
1995	7,284	7,284	77	77	2,003	N.A.	1.06	1.06	3.84	N.A.	12.29	92.33	115.6[8]
1996	9,923	9,923	146	146	3,555	3,432	1.47	1.47	4.10	4.25	13.67	77.25	114.8[8]
1997	13,282	13,282	213	213	5,975	5,832[7]	1.60	1.60	3.56	3.65	10.94	72.80	102.2[8]
1998	12,022	12,022	106	106	5,843	5,755[7]	0.88	0.88	1.81	1.84	5.55	71.02	103.8[8]
[1999]	14,362	14,362	442	442	6,212	6,120[7]	3.07	3.07	7.11	7.22	20.95	64.17	92.4[8]
UDS													
1995	8,084	7,706	117	90	4,217	3,840	1.45	1.17	2.77	2.34	8.81	117.24	N.A.
1996	10,208	9,747	(36)	(44)	4,420	3,922	(0.35)	(0.45)	(0.81)	(1.12)	(2.89)	132.63	N.A.
1997	10,882	10,410	155	142	5,595	5,231	1.47	1.36	2.86	2.71	9.18	110.61	92.4[8]
1998	11,133	10,877	(78)	(72)	5,315	4,964	(0.70)	(0.66)	(1.47)	(1.45)	(5.64)	139.96	109.6[8]
[1999]	13,971	13,826	173	172	4,936	4,548	1.24	1.24	3.50	3.78	11.60	88.90	112.6[8]

[1]R&M: Refining and Marketing
[2]Identifiable Assets
[3]Net income as a percentage of closing assets.
[4]Net income as a percentage of closing equity.
[5]Long-term debt as a percentage of stockholders' equity.
[6]Refinery capacity utilization for U.S.-based refineries only.
[7]Does not include non-operating segment assets, which is consistent with other firms.
[8]Refinery input from annual report divided by US EIA data on capacity.

Source: U.S. Oil and Gas Company Performance Report, Third Edition, PennWell Publishing, July 1999, and Tosco and Valero annual reports.

EXHIBIT 9

Summary Financial and Operating Data for Tosco: 1991 to 1999

	1999	1998	1997	1996	1995	1994	1993	1992	1991
FINANCIAL DATA									
Total Sales ($ millions)	$ 14,362	$ 12,022	$ 13,282	$ 9,923	$ 7,284	$ 6,366	$ 3,559	$ 1,861	$ 1,609
Refining	8,550	6,796	7,654	6,960	N.A.	N.A.	N.A.	N.A.	N.A.
Marketing	5,812	5,226	5,628	2,963	N.A.	N.A.	N.A.	N.A.	N.A.
Merchandise	2,040	2,098	2,003	1,173	29	N.A.	N.A.	N.A.	N.A.
Motor Fuel	3,772	3,128	3,625	1,790	N.A.	N.A.	N.A.	N.A.	N.A.
Pre-Tax Income[1] ($ millions)									
Corporate	$ 766	$ 199	$ 381	$ 248	$ 127	$ 134	$ 132	$ (74.4)	$ 75.4
Refining[2]	566	60	233	243	N.A.	N.A.	N.A.	N.A.	N.A.
Marketing[2]	216	154	163	19	N.A.	N.A.	N.A.	N.A.	N.A.
Pre-Tax ROA[3]									
Corporate	12.7%	3.4%	8.0%	8.9%	6.7%	N.A.	N.A.	N.A.	N.A.
Refining[2]	15.9%	1.7%	9.0%	N.A.	N.A.	N.A.	N.A.	N.A.	N.A.
Marketing[2]	9.1%	6.7%	8.0%	N.A.	N.A.	N.A	N.A.	N.A.	N.A.
Net Income ($ millions)	$ 441.7	$ 106.2	$ 212.7	$ 146.3	$ 77.1	$ 83.8	$ 80.6	$ (74.4)	$ 75.4
EPS (Diluted)	2.83	0.67	1.37	1.16	0.69	0.76	0.79	(0.96)	0.79
Closing Share Price (Year End)	27.06	25.47	36.88	25.53	12.15	9.11	8.92	6.13	7.46
OPERATING DATA									
Refining									
Capacity[4]	920,000	910,000	764,000	466,000	468,000	470,000	387,000	150,000	150,000
Throughput (bpd)	850,900	944,800	793,400	535,000	540,900	503,680	425,560	152,510	139,980
Gasoline Output—Tosco	53.7%	53.7%	52.4%	50.4%	50.4%	48.9%	53.8%	60.5%	57.3%
All U.S. Refineries[5]	43.2%	42.0%	41.6%	43.1%	44.0%	43.1%	43.0%	43.0%	43.1%
OTHER									
Retail Fuel Volume (million gallons)	4,452	4,490	4,159	2,061	1,047	769	N.A.	—	—
Gross Margin/Gallon	11.4¢	12.1¢	12.8¢	11.6¢	10.0¢	N.A.	N.A.	—	—
Gas Stations	4,143	4,476	4,652	3,270	1,015	995	520	—	—
C-Stores	2,070	2,313	2,395	2,400	115	75	N.A.	—	—
Employees[6]	24,600	26,300	26,200	24,300	4,000	3,600	3,000	1,000	900

[1]This number is also before distributions on Trust Preferred Securities

[2]Ignores those (relatively minor) expenses and assets shown in a non-operating segment.

[3]Based on average of opening and closing asset balance.

[4]Derived from EIA data, annual report data, and acquisition data for refineries purchased.

[5]Derived from *NPN Market Facts 2000,* Mid-July 2000, p. 145.

[6]Includes part-time employees at retail locations.

Source: Tosco Corporation Annual Reports (unless otherwise noted).

increase in refining capacity on a worldwide basis was expected to fall well below the increase in demand during both 2000 and 2001.[22] This, when combined with the regulatory move toward cleaner burning fuels in both the United States and the European Union,[23] was expected to mean that there could be shortages of both motor gasoline and distillate (primarily fuel oil) in the United States over the next 12 to 18 months. In fact, both motor gasoline stocks and distillate stocks were reported to be at the low end of the normal range by mid-2000.[24]

On the retail gasoline marketing side, Tosco had significantly enhanced their competitive position over the past few years. In addition to their strong West Coast operations, the recent acquisition of ExxonMobil properties on the East Coast had provided them with some areas of relatively high market share in the Middle Atlantic states. A recent presentation by Jay Allen, Tosco's president and CFO, had noted the following local market shares on a post-acquisition basis (see Table 2).

The same presentation had been used to assert that the U.S.-based refining and marketing earnings of Tosco had exceeded more of both Exxon and Chevron over the nine-month period ending 30 September 1999 and those of Exxon, Mobil, or Chevron for the three-month period ending on the same date.[25] This data, however, did not negate the overall volatility of refining and marketing earnings—where another observer noted that gasoline retailing margins had been nearly three times as high in California during the second quarter of 1999 (23.7¢ per gallon) as they were in the third quarter (8.9¢ per gallon).[26]

On the merchandise side, Tosco was now the first or second-largest C-store chain in the United States, depending on which source was cited, with over two billion dollars in annual revenue. While the margins in this business were quite positive (see Exhibit 6), there were a lot of players—some 22 of them had more than 500 locations each as of October 1999.[27]

TABLE 2

Projected Local Market Share in Selected Locations

Geographic Location	Share of Market
Greater Philadelphia	22.5%
Washington, D.C.	11.7%
Northern New Jersey	17.2%
New York City and Long Island	8.3%

Source: Jay Allen, Paine Webber presentation, February 15, 2000.

In terms of the newer ventures of Tosco, the firm was both moving up the value chain with its new polypropylene joint venture with Union Carbide and broadening its geographic reach with its acquisition of INPCL. The former was forecast to produce after-tax returns on capital of about 15% based on mid-cycle margins. The latter provided Tosco with an English-language entry point to the European Union as well as a source of 30,000 bpd of low sulfur fuel oil for use in the surplus upgrading capacity at the Bayway and Trainer refineries.[28]

Conclusion

Tosco, clearly, had changed markedly over the last few years. From a struggling firm with one significant asset, it evolved into a major player with operations in 31 states and plans to be in one European country as well. Yet, in some ways, the firm's approach toward its business had not changed much over the past decade. As its CEO, Thomas D. O'Malley, was quoted as saying:

> We are a patient buyer of assets, . . . the biggest opportunities for us will remain in the same areas that we've become expert in, and that's buying assets at reasonable prices, reorganizing them and then running them at a profit.[29]

The financial community, while not pricing Tosco's shares as high as its management would prefer, did nonetheless view that team in a fairly positive light. The firm had built a reputation with Wall Street

22. Douglas T. Terreson, Paul J. Coppola and Jacques H. Rousseau, "Tosco Company Update: Tosco Asset Sale Positive, Maintain Strong Buy, PT $40," Morgan Stanley Dean Witter, July 6, 2000, pp. 4 and 5.
23. Meaning that some smaller refineries would probably prove to be uneconomic in terms of cost required to upgrade (Editor).
24. Terreson, "Tosco Company Update," July 6, 2000.
25. Jay Allen, Paine Webber presentation, February 15, 2000.
26. Mayer, *Tosco Corporation*, p. 10.
27. "Top 50 U.S. Convenience Store Companies," p. 134.
28. "Tosco Corporation Announces Agreement to Buy the Operating Assets of the Irish National Petroleum Corporation Limited," Tosco Corporation Press Release, July 31, 2000.
29. "CEO Interview: Thomas D. O'Malley, Tosco Corporation," *The Wall Street Transcript*, DLJ Energy Supplement, March, 1999.

as having a very disciplined, even tight-fisted, approach to its operations. As one analyst described them: "O'Malley has simply done it leaner and meaner than the competition."[30]

The more positive among the analysts, particularly on the sell side of the industry,[31] were quite upbeat on the prospects for the firm over the next 12 to 18 months. Doug Terreson and his colleagues at Morgan Stanley Dean Witter (MSDW) for example,

were predicting earnings-per-share figures of $3.10 and $4.05 for calendar 2000 and 2001, respectively, with a price target (PT) of $40 per share.[32] Attaining such a share price would represent a 35% improvement over that recorded on the date that MSDW released this particular company update.

O'Malley, quite clearly would be pleased with such a turn of events—particularly as he was reported to be holding some three million shares of the firm's stock. As he put it: "I own over three million shares of stock in this company. My interests are parallel with the shareholders."[33]

---

30. Fadel Gheit (Fahnestock & Co.) as quoted in Barrionuevo, "Tosco Ready to Join Big Leagues."
31. "Sell side" analysts work for firms that tend to underwrite or "sell" securities issues for corporate customers. "Buy side" analysts, on the contrary, work for large institutions such as insurance firms which tend to acquire ("buy") securities for their investment portfolios.

32. Terreson, "Tosco Company Update," July 21, 2000.
33. "CEO Interview," *The Wall Street Transcript.*

The Evolution of the Air Express Industry, 1973—2002

29

This case was prepared by Charles W. L. Hill, the University of Washington.

Introduction

The air express industry is that segment of the broader air cargo industry that specializes in rapid (normally overnight) delivery of small packages. It is generally agreed that the air express industry in the United States began with Fred Smith's vision for Federal Express Company, which started operations in 1973. Federal Express transformed the structure of the existing air cargo industry and paved the way for rapid growth in the overnight package segment of that industry. A further impetus to the industry's development was the 1977 deregulation of the U.S. air cargo industry. This deregulation allowed Federal Express (and its emerging competitors) to buy large jets for the first time. The story of the industry during the 1980s was one of rapid growth and new entry. Between 1982 and 1989, air express cargo shipments in the United States grew at an annual average rate of 31 percent. In contrast, shipments of air freight and air mail grew at an annual rate of only 2.7 percent.[1] This rapid growth attracted new entrants such as United Parcel Service (UPS) and Airborne Freight (which operates under the name Airborne Express). The entry of UPS triggered severe price cutting, which ultimately drove some of the weaker competitors out of the market and touched off a wave of consolidation in the industry.

By the mid 1990s, the industry structure had stabilized with three firms—Federal Express, UPS, and Airborne Express—accounting for approximately 70 percent of U.S. air express shipments. (See Table 1 for a comparison of the three companies.) During the first half of the 1990s, the air express industry continued to grow at a healthy rate, with express shipments expanding from 4,404 million ton miles in 1990 to 7,042 ton miles in 1994, an annual growth rate of slightly more than 16 percent.[2] Despite this growth, the industry was hit by repeated rounds of price cutting as the three biggest firms battled to capture major accounts. In addition to price cutting, the big three also competed vigorously on the basis of technology, service offerings, and the global reach of their operations. By the late 1990s and early 2000s, however, the intensity of price competition in the industry had moderated, with a degree of pricing discipline being maintained, despite the fact that the growth rate for the industry slowed down. Between 1995 and 2000, the industry grew at 9.8 percent per year. In 2001, however, the volume of express parcels shipped by air fell by 5.9 percent, partly due to an economic slowdown, and partly due to the aftereffects of the September 11 terrorist attack on the United States.[3]

This case is intended to be used as a basis for class discussion rather than as an illustration of either effective or ineffective handling of the situation. Reprinted by permission of Charles W. L. Hill.

TABLE 1

Main U.S. Air Express Operators, 2001

	Federal Express	UPS	Airborne
U.S. market share*	26%	53%	9%
Revenues	$18.3 billion	$29.7 billion	$2.85 billion
Average return on invested capital (ROIC), 1996–2001	17.9%	10.8%	8%
Aircraft fleet	662	560	118
Employees	215,000	359,000	22,500
Delivery vehicles	43,500	152,000	14,900

Sources: Standard & Poor's Airlines, *Industry Surveys,* March, 2002; Salomon Smith Barney Research; company 10K statements.

*Market share figures are for combined air and ground business.

The Industry in 1973

In 1973, roughly 1.5 billion tons of freight were shipped in the United States. Most of this freight was carried by surface transport, with air freight accounting for less than 2 percent of the total.[4] While shipment by air freight was often quicker than shipment by surface freight, the high cost of air freight had kept down demand. The typical users of air freight at this time were suppliers of time-sensitive, high-priced goods, such as computer parts and medical instruments, which were needed at dispersed locations but which were too expensive for their customers to hold as inventory.

The main cargo carriers in 1973 were major passenger airlines, which operated several all-cargo planes and carried additional cargo in their passenger planes, along with a handful of all-cargo airlines such as Flying Tiger. From 1973 onward, the passenger airlines moved steadily away from all-cargo planes and began to concentrate cargo freight in passenger planes. This change was a response to increases in fuel costs, which made the operation of many older cargo jets uneconomical.

With regard to distribution of cargo to and from airports, in 1973 about 20 percent of all air freight was delivered to airports by the shipper and/or picked up by the consignee. The bulk of the remaining 80 percent was accounted for by three major intermediaries: (1) Air Cargo Incorporated, (2) freight forwarders, and (3) the U.S. Postal Service. Air Cargo Incorporated was a trucking service, wholly owned by twenty-six airlines, which performed pickup and delivery service for the airlines' direct customers. Freight forwarders were trucking carriers who consolidated cargo going to the airlines. They purchased cargo space from the airlines and retailed this space in small amounts. They dealt primarily with small customers, providing pickup and delivery services in most cities, either in their own trucks or through contract agents. The U.S. Postal Service used air service for transportation of long-distance letter mail and air parcel post.[5]

The Federal Express Concept

Founded by Fred Smith, Jr., Federal Express was incorporated in 1971 and began operations in 1973. At that time, a significant proportion of small-package air freight flew on commercial passenger flights. Smith believed that there were major differences between packages and passengers, and he was convinced that the two had to be treated differently. Most passengers moved between major cities and wanted the convenience of daytime flights. Cargo shippers preferred nighttime service to coincide with late-afternoon pickups and next-day delivery. Because small-package air freight was subservient to the requirements of passengers' flight schedules, it was often difficult for the major airlines to achieve next-day delivery of air freight.

Smith's aim was to build a system that could achieve next-day delivery of small-package air freight (less than seventy pounds). He set up Federal Express with his $8 million family inheritance and $90 million in venture capital. Federal Express established a hub-and-spoke route system, the first airline to do so. The hub of the system was Memphis, chosen for its good weather conditions, central location, and the fact that it was Smith's hometown. The spokes were regular routes between Memphis and shipping facilities at public airports in the cities serviced by Federal Express. Every weeknight, aircraft would leave their home cities with a load of packages and fly down the spokes to Memphis (often with one or two stops on the way). At Memphis, all packages were unloaded, sorted by destination, and reloaded. The aircraft then returned back to their home cities in the early hours of the morning. Packages were ferried to and from airports by Federal Express couriers driving the company's vans and working to a tight schedule. Thus, from door to door, the package was in Federal Express's hands. This system guaranteed that a package picked up from a customer in New York at 5 P.M. would reach its final destination in Los Angeles (or any other major city) by noon the following day. It enabled Federal Express to realize economies in sorting and to utilize its air cargo capacity efficiently. Federal Express also pioneered the use of standard packaging with an upper weight limit of seventy pounds and a maximum length plus girth of 108 inches. This standard helped Federal Express to gain further efficiencies from mechanized sorting at its Memphis hub. Later entrants into the industry copied Federal Express's package standards and hub-and-spoke operating system.

To accomplish overnight delivery, Federal Express had to operate its own planes. Restrictive regulations enforced by the Civil Aeronautics Board (CAB), however, prohibited the company from buying large jet aircraft. To get around this restriction, Federal Express bought a fleet of twin-engine executive jets, which it converted to minifreighters. These planes had a cargo capacity of 6,200 pounds, which enabled Federal Express to get a license as an air taxi operator.

After 1973, Federal Express quickly built up volume. By 1976, it had an average daily volume of 19,000 packages, a fleet of thirty-two aircraft, 500 delivery vans, and 2,000 employees, and it had initiated service in seventy-five cities. After three years of posting losses, the company turned in a profit of $3.7 million on revenues of $75 million.[6] However, volume had grown so much that Federal Express desperately needed to use larger planes to maintain operating efficiencies. As a result, Smith's voice was added to those calling for Congress to deregulate the airline industry and allow greater competition.

Deregulation and Its Aftermath

In November 1977, Congress relaxed regulations controlling competition in the air cargo industry, one year before passenger services were deregulated. This involved a drastic loosening of standards for entry into the industry. The old CAB authority of naming the carriers that could operate on the various routes was changed to the relatively simple authority of deciding which among candidate carriers was fit, willing, and able to operate an all-cargo route. In addition, CAB controls over pricing were significantly reduced. The immediate effect was an increase in rates for shipments, particularly minimum- and high-weight categories, suggesting that prices had been held artificially low by regulation. As a result, the average yield (revenue per ton mile) on domestic airfreight increased 10.6 percent in 1978 and 11.3 percent in 1979.[7]

Freed from the constraints of regulation, Federal Express immediately began to purchase larger jets and quickly established itself as a major carrier of small-package air freight. Despite the increase in yields, however, new entry into the air cargo industry was limited, at least initially. This was mainly due to the high capital requirements involved in establishing an all-cargo carrier. Indeed, by the end of 1978, there were only four major all-cargo carriers serving the domestic market: Airlift International, Federal Express, Flying Tiger, and Seaboard World Airlines. While all of these all-cargo carriers had increased their route structure following deregulation, only Federal Express specialized in next-day delivery for small packages. Demand for a next-day delivery service continued to boom. Industry estimates suggest that the small-package priority market had grown to about 82 million pieces in 1979, up from 43 million in 1974.[8]

At the same time, in response to increasing competition from the all-cargo carriers, the passenger airlines continued their retreat from the all-cargo business (originally begun in 1973 as a response to high fuel prices). Between 1973 and 1978, there was a 45 percent decline in the mileage of all-cargo flights by the airlines. This decrease was followed by a 14 percent decline between 1978 and 1979. Instead of all-cargo flights, the airlines concentrated their attentions on carrying cargo in passenger flights. This practice hurt the freight forwarders badly. The freight forwarders had long relied on the all-cargo flights of major airlines to achieve next-day delivery. Now the freight forwarders were being squeezed out of this segment by a lack of available lift at the time needed to ensure next-day delivery.

This problem led to one of the major postderegulation developments in the industry: the acquisition and operation by freight forwarders of their own fleets of aircraft. Between 1979 and 1981, five of the six largest freight forwarders became involved in this activity. The two largest were Emery Air Freight and Airborne Express. Emery operated a fleet of sixty-six aircraft at the end of 1979, the majority of which were leased from other carriers. In mid 1980, this fleet was providing service to approximately 129 cities, carrying both large-volume shipments and small-package express.

Airborne Express acquired its own fleet of aircraft in April 1980 with the purchase of Midwest Charter Express, an Ohio-based all-cargo airline. Then, in 1981, Airborne opened a new hub in Ohio, which became the center of its small-package express operation. This enabled Airborne to provide next-day delivery for small packages to 125 cities in the United States.[9] Other freight forwarders that moved into the overnight mail market included Purolator Courier and Gelco, both of which offered overnight delivery by air on a limited geographic scale.

Industry Evolution, 1980–1986
New Products and Industry Growth
In 1981, Federal Express expanded its role in the overnight market with the introduction of an overnight letter service, with a limit of two ounces. This guaranteed overnight delivery service was set up in direct competition with the U.S. Postal Service's Priority Mail. The demand for such a service was illustrated by its expansion to about 17,000 letters per day within its first three months of operation.

More generally, the focus of the air express industry was changing from being predominantly a conduit for goods to being a distributor of information—particularly company documents, letters, contracts, drawings, and the like. As a result of the growth in demand for information distribution, new product offerings such as the overnight letter, and Federal Express's own marketing efforts, the air express indus-

try enjoyed high growth during the early 1980s, averaging more than 20 percent per year.[10] Indeed, many observers attribute most of the growth in the overnight delivery business at this time to Federal Express's marketing efforts. According to one industry participant, "Federal Express pulled off one of the greatest marketing scams in the industry by making people believe they absolutely, positively, had to have something right away."[11]

Increasing Price Competition
Despite rapid growth in demand, competitive intensity in the industry increased sharply in 1982 following the entry of UPS into the overnight-delivery market. UPS was already by far the largest private package transporter in the United States, with an enormous ground-oriented distribution network and revenues in excess of $4 billion per year. In addition, for a long time, UPS had offered a second-day air service for priority packages, primarily by using the planes of all-cargo and passenger airlines. In 1982, UPS acquired a fleet of twenty-four used Boeing 727-100s and added four DC-8 freighters from Flying Tiger. These purchases allowed UPS to introduce next-day air service in September 1982—at roughly half the price Federal Express was charging at the time.[12]

Federal Express countered almost immediately by announcing that it would institute 10:30 A.M. priority overnight delivery (at a cost to the company of $18 million). None of the other carriers followed suit, however, reasoning that most of their customers are usually busy or in meetings during the morning hours, so delivery before noon was not really that important. Instead, by March 1983, most of the major carriers in the market (including Federal Express) were offering their high-volume customers contract rates that matched the UPS price structure. Then three new services introduced by Purolator, Emery, and Gelco Courier pushed prices even lower. A competitive free-for-all followed, with constant price changes and volume discounts being offered by all industry participants. These developments hit the profit margins of the express carriers. Between 1983 and 1984, Federal Express saw its average revenue per package fall nearly 14 percent, while Emery saw a 15 percent decline in its yield on small shipments.[13]

Beginning around this time, customers began to group together and negotiate for lower prices. For example, Xerox set up accounts with Purolator and

Emery that covered not only Xerox's express packages but also those of fifty other companies, including Mayflower Corp., the moving company, and the Chicago Board of Trade. By negotiating as a group, these companies could achieve prices as much as 60 percent lower than those they could get on their own.[14]

The main beneficiary of the price war was UPS, which by 1985 had gained the number 2 spot in the industry, with 15 percent of the market. Federal Express, meanwhile, had seen its market share slip to 37 percent from about 45 percent two years earlier. The other four major players in the industry at this time were Emery Air Freight (14 percent of market share), Purolator (10 percent of market share), Airborne Express (8 percent of market share), and the U.S. Postal Service (8 percent of market share).[15] The survival of all four of these carriers in the air express business was in question by 1986. Emery, Purolator, and the U.S. Postal Service were all reporting losses on their air express business, while Airborne had seen its profits slump 66 percent in the first quarter of 1986 and now had razor-thin margins.

Industry Evolution, 1987–1996
Industry Consolidation

A slowdown in the growth rate of the air express business due to increasing geographic saturation and inroads made by electronic transmission (primarily fax machines) stimulated further price discounting in 1987 and early 1988. Predictably, this discounting created problems for the weakest companies in the industry. The first to go was Purolator Courier, which had lost $65 million during 1985 and 1986. Purolator's problems stemmed from a failure to install an adequate computer system. The company was unable to track shipments, a crucial asset in this industry, and some of Purolator's best corporate customers were billed 120 days late.[16] In 1987, Purolator agreed to be acquired by Emery. Emery was unable to effect a satisfactory integration of Purolator, and it sustained large losses in 1988 and early 1989.

Consolidated Freightways was a major trucking company and parent of CF Air Freight, the third largest heavy shipment specialist in the United States. In April 1989, Consolidated Freightways acquired Emery for $478 million. However, its shipment specialist, CF Air Freight, soon found itself struggling to cope with Emery's problems. In its first eleven

months with CF, Emery lost $100 million. One of the main problems was Emery's billing and tracking system, described as a "rat's nest" of conflicting tariff schedules, which caused overbilling of customers and made tracking packages en route a major chore. In addition, CF enraged corporate customers by trying to add a "fuel surcharge" of 4 to 7 percent to prices in early 1989. Competitors held the line on prices and picked up business from CF/Emery.[17]

As a result of the decline of the CF/Emery/Purolator combination, the other firms in the industry were able to pick up market share. By 1994, industry estimates suggested that Federal Express accounted for 35 percent of domestic air freight and air express industry revenues; UPS had 26 percent; Airborne Express was third with 9 percent; and Emery, DHL (a large Brussels-based international air express carrier), and the U.S. Postal Service each held onto 4 percent of the market. The remainder of the market was split among numerous small cargo carriers and several combination carriers, such as Evergreen International and Atlas Air. (Combination carriers specialize mostly in heavy freight but do carry some express mail.)[18]

The other major acquisition in the industry during this time was the purchase of Flying Tiger by Federal Express for $880 million in December 1988. Although Flying Tiger had some air express operations in the United States, its primary strength was as a heavy cargo carrier with a global route structure. The acquisition was part of Federal Express's goal of becoming a major player in the international air express market. However, the acquisition had its problems. Many of Flying Tiger's biggest customers, including UPS and Airborne Express, were Federal Express's competitors in the domestic market. These companies had long paid Tiger to carry packages to those countries where they had no landing rights. It seemed unlikely that these companies would continue to give international business to their biggest domestic competitor. Additional problems arose in the process of trying to integrate the two operations. These problems included the scheduling of aircraft and pilots, the servicing of Tiger's fleet, and the merging of Federal's nonunionized pilots with Tiger's unionized pilots.[19]

During the late 1980s and early 1990s, there were also hints of further consolidations. TNT Ltd., a large Australian-based air cargo operation with a global network, made an unsuccessful attempt to acquire

Airborne Express in 1986. TNT's bid was frustrated by opposition from Airborne and by the difficulties inherent in getting around U.S. law, which currently limits foreign firms from having more than a 25-percent stake in U.S. airlines. In addition, DHL Airways, the U.S. subsidiary of DHL International, was reportedly attempting to enlarge its presence in the United States and was on the lookout for an acquisition.[20]

Pricing Trends

In October 1988, UPS offered new discounts to high-volume customers in domestic markets. For the first time since 1983, competitors declined to match the cuts. Then in January 1989, UPS announced a price increase of 5 percent for next-day air service, its first price increase in nearly six years. Federal Express, Airborne, and Consolidated Freightways all followed suit with moderate increases. Additional rate increases of 5.9 percent on next-day air letters were announced by UPS in February 1990. Federal Express followed suit in April, and Airborne also implemented selective price hikes on noncontract business of 5 percent, or 50 cents, per package on packages up to twenty pounds.

Just as prices were stabilizing, however, the 1990–1991 recession came along. For the first time in the history of the U.S. air express industry, there was a decline in year-on-year shipments, with express freight falling from 4,455 million ton miles in 1989 to 4,403 million ton miles in 1990. This decline triggered off another round of competitive price cuts, and yields plummeted. Although demand rebounded strongly, repeated attempts to raise prices in 1992, 1993, and 1994 simply did not stick.[21]

Much of the price cutting was focused on large corporate accounts, which by this time accounted for 75 percent by volume of express mail shipments. For example, as a result of deep price discounting in 1994, UPS was able to lure home shopping programmer QVC and computer mail-order company Gateway 2000 away from Federal Express. At about the same time, however, Federal Express used discounting to capture retailer Williams-Sonoma away from UPS.[22] This prolonged period of price discounting depressed profit margins and contributed to losses at all three major carriers during the early 1990s. Bolstered by a strong economy, prices finally began to stabilize during late 1995, when price increases announced by UPS were followed by similar announcements at Federal Express and Airborne.[23]

Product Trends

Second-Day Delivery   Having seen a slowdown in the growth rate of the next-day document delivery business during the early 1990s, the major operators in the air express business began to look for new product opportunities to sustain their growth and margins. One trend was a move into the second-day delivery market, or deferred services, as it is called in the industry. The move toward second-day delivery was started by Airborne Express in 1991, and it was soon imitated by its major competitors. Second-day delivery commands a substantially lower price point than next-day delivery. In 1994, Federal Express made an average of $9.23 on second-day deliveries, compared to $16.37 on priority overnight service. The express mail operators see deferred services as a way to utilize excess capacity at the margin, thereby boosting revenues and profits. Since many second-day packages can be shipped on the ground, the cost of second-day delivery can more than compensate for the lower price.

In some ways, however, the service has been almost too successful. During the mid 1990s, the growth rate for deferred services was significantly higher than for priority overnight mail because many corporations came to the realization that they could live with a second-day service. At Airborne Express, for example, second-day delivery accounted for 42 percent of total volume in 1996, up from 37 percent in 1995.[24]

Premium Services   Another development was a move toward a premium service. In 1994, UPS introduced its Early AM service, which guaranteed delivery of packages and letters by 8:30 A.M. in select cities. UPS tailored Early AM toward a range of businesses that needed documents or materials before the start of the business day, including hospitals, who are expected to use the service to ship critical drugs and medical devices; architects, who need to have their blueprints sent to a construction site; and salespeople. Although demand for the service is predicted to be light, the premium price makes for high profit margins. In 1994, UPS's price for a letter delivered at 10:30 A.M. was $10.75, while it charged $40 for an equivalent Early AM delivery. UPS believes that it can provide the service at little extra cost because most of its planes arrive in their destination cities by 7:30 A.M. Federal Express and Airborne initially declined to follow UPS's lead.[25]

Logistics Services   Another development of some note was the move by all major operators into third-party logistics services. Since the latter half of the 1980s, more and more companies have been relying on air express operations as part of their just-in-time inventory control systems. As a result, the content of packages carried by air express operators has been moving away from letters and documents and toward high-value, low-weight products. By 1994, less than 20 percent of Federal Express's revenues came from documents.[26] To take advantage of this trend, all of the major operators have been moving into logistics services that are designed to assist business customers in their warehousing, distribution, and assembly operations. The emphasis of this business is on helping their customers reduce the time involved in their production cycles and gain distribution efficiencies.

In the late 1980s, Federal Express set up a Business Logistics Services (BLS) division. The new division evolved from Federal Express's Parts Bank. The Parts Bank stores critical inventory for clients, most of whom are based in the high-tech electronics and medical industries. On request, Federal Express will ship this inventory to its client's customers. The service saves clients from having to invest in their own distribution systems. It also allows their clients to achieve economies of scale by making large production runs and then storing the inventory at the Parts Bank.

The BLS division has expanded this service to include some assembly operations and customs brokerage and to assist in achieving just-in-time manufacturing. Thus, for example, one U.S. computer company relies on BLS to deliver electronic subassemblies from the Far East as a key part of its just-in-time system. Federal Express brings the products to the United States on its aircraft, clears them through customs with the help of a broker, and manages truck transportation to the customer's dock.

UPS moved into the logistics business in 1993 when it established UPS Worldwide Logistics, which it positioned as a third-party provider of global supply chain management solutions, including transportation management, warehouse operations, inventory management, documentation for import and export, network optimization, and reverse logistics. UPS's logistics business is based at its Louisville, Kentucky, hub. In 1995, the company announced that it would invest $75 million to expand the scope of this facility, bringing total employment in the facility to 2,200 by the end of 1998.[27]

Airborne Express also made a significant push into this business. Several of Airborne's corporate accounts utilize a warehousing service called Stock Exchange. As with Federal Express's Parts Bank, clients warehouse critical inventory at Airborne's hub in Wilmington, Ohio, and then ship those items on request to their customers. In addition, Airborne has set up a commerce park on 1,000 acres around its Wilmington hub. The park is geared toward companies that want to outsource logistics to Airborne and can gain special advantages by locating at the company's hub. Not the least of these advantages is the ability to make shipping decisions as late as 2 A.M. Eastern time.

Information Systems

Since the late 1980s, the three major U.S. air express carriers have devoted more and more attention to competing on the basis of information technology. The ability to track a package as it moves through an operator's delivery network has always been an important aspect of competition in an industry where reliability is so highly valued. Thus, all the major players in the industry have invested heavily in bar-code technology, scanners, and computerized tracking systems. More recently, UPS, Federal Express, and Airborne have all invested in Internet-based technology that allows customers to schedule pickups, print shipping labels, and track deliveries online.

Globalization

Perhaps the most important development for the long-run future of the industry has been the increasing globalization of the air freight industry. The combination of a healthy U.S. economy, strong and expanding East Asian economies, and the move toward closer economic integration in Western Europe all offer opportunities for growth in the international air cargo business. The increasing globalization of companies in a whole range of industries from electronics to autos, and from fast food to clothing, is beginning to dictate that the air express operators follow suit.

Global manufacturers want to keep inventories at a minimum and deliver just in time as a way of keeping down costs and fine-tuning production, which requires speedy supply routes. Thus, some electronics companies will manufacture key components in one location, ship them by air to another for final assembly, and then deliver them by air to a third location for sale. This setup is particularly convenient for industries producing small high-value items (for example, electronics, medical equipment, and computer software) that can be economically transported by air and for whom just-in-time inventory systems are crucial for keeping down costs. It is also true in the fashion industry, where timing is crucial. For example, the clothing chain The Limited manufactures clothes in Hong Kong and then ships them by air to the United States to keep from missing out on fashion trends.[28] In addition, an increasing number of wholesalers are beginning to turn to international air express as a way of meeting delivery deadlines.

The emergence of integrated global corporations is also increasing the demand for the global shipment of contracts, confidential papers, computer printouts, and other documents that are too confidential for Internet transmission or that require real signatures. Major U.S. corporations are increasingly demanding the same kind of service that they receive from air express operators within the United States for their far-flung global operations.

As a consequence of these trends, rapid growth is predicted in the global arena. According to forecasts, the market for international air express is expected to grow at approximately 18 percent annually from 1996 to 2016.[29] Faced with an increasingly mature market at home, the race is on among the major air cargo operators to build global air and ground transportation networks that will enable them to deliver goods and documents between any two points on the globe within forty-eight hours.

The company with the most extensive international operations by the mid 1990s was DHL. In 1995, DHL enjoyed a 44 percent share of the worldwide market for international air express services (see Table 2).[30] Started in California in 1969 and now based in Brussels, DHL is smaller than many of its rivals, but it has managed to capture as much as an 80 percent share in some markets, such as documents leaving Japan, by concentrating solely on international air express. The strength of DHL was enhanced in mid 1992 when Lufthansa, Japan Airlines, and the Japanese trading company Nisho Iwai announced that they intended to invest as much as $500 million for a 57.5 percent stake in DHL.

TABLE 2

International Air Express Market Shares, 1995

Company	Market Share
DHL International	44%
Federal Express	21%
UPS	12%
TNT	12%
Others	11%

Source: Standard & Poor's, "Aerospace and Air Transport," *Industry Surveys,* February 1996.

Although Lufthansa and Japan Airlines are primarily known for their passenger flights, they are also among the top five air freight haulers in the world, both because they carry cargo in the holds of their passenger flights and because they each have a fleet of all-cargo aircraft.[31]

TNT Ltd., a $6 billion Australian conglomerate, is another big player in the international air express market, with courier services from 184 countries as well as package express and mail services. In 1995, its share of the international air express market was 12 percent, down from 18 percent in 1990.[32]

Among U.S. carriers, Federal Express was first in the race to build a global air express network. Between 1984 and 1989, Federal Express purchased seventeen other companies worldwide in an attempt to build its global distribution capabilities, culminating in the $880 million purchase of Flying Tiger. The main asset of Flying Tiger was not so much its aircraft, but its landing rights overseas. The Flying Tiger acquisition gave Federal Express service to 103 countries, a combined fleet of 328 aircraft, and revenues of $5.2 billion in fiscal year 1989.[33]

However, Federal Express has had to suffer through years of losses in its international operations. Start-up costs were heavy, due in part to the enormous capital investments required to build an integrated air and ground network worldwide. Between 1985 and 1992, Federal Express spent $2.5 billion to build an international presence. Faced also with heavy competition, Federal Express found it difficult to generate the international volume required to fly its planes above the break-even point on many international routes. Because the demand for outbound service from the United States is greater than the demand for inbound service, planes that left New York full often returned half empty.

Trade barriers have also proved very damaging to the bottom line. Customs regulations require a great deal of expensive and time-consuming labor, such as checking paperwork and rating package contents for duties. These regulations obviously inhibit the ability of international air cargo carriers to effect express delivery. Federal Express has been particularly irritated by Japanese requirements that each inbound envelope be opened and searched for pornography, a practice that seems designed to slow down the company's growth rate in the Japanese market.

Federal Express has also found it extremely difficult to get landing rights in many markets. For example, it took three years to get permission from Japan to make four flights per week from Memphis to Tokyo, a key link in the overseas system Then in 1988, just three days before the service was due to begin, the Japanese notified Federal Express that no packages weighing more than 70 pounds could pass through Tokyo. To make matters worse, until 1995 Japan limited Federal Express's ability to fly on from Tokyo and Osaka to other locations in Asia. The Japanese claimed, with some justification, that due to government regulations, the U.S. air traffic market is difficult for foreign carriers to enter, so they see no urgency to help Federal Express build a market presence in Japan and elsewhere in Asia.[34]

After heavy financial losses, Federal Express abruptly shifted its international strategy in 1992, selling off its expensive European ground network to local carriers to concentrate on intercontinental deliveries. Under the strategy, Federal Express relies on a network of local partners to deliver its packages. Also, Federal Express entered into an alliance with TNT to share space on Federal Express's daily trans-Atlantic flights. Under the agreement, TNT flies packages from its hub in Cologne, Germany, to Britain, where they are loaded onto Federal Express's daily New York flight.[35]

UPS has also built up an international presence. In 1988, UPS bought eight smaller European air freight companies and Hong Kong's Asian Courier Service, and it announced air service and ground delivery in 175 countries and territories. However, it has not been all smooth sailing for UPS either. UPS had been using Flying Tiger for its Pacific shipments. The acquisition of Flying Tiger by Federal Express left UPS in the difficult situation of shipping its parcels on a competitor's plane. UPS was concerned that its shipments would be pushed to the back of the aircraft. Since there were few alternative carriers, UPS pushed for authority to run an all-cargo route to Tokyo, but approval was slow in coming. "Beyond rights," to carry cargo from Tokyo to further destinations (such as Singapore and Hong Kong), were also difficult to gain.

In March 1996, UPS sidestepped years of frustrations associated with building an Asian hub in Tokyo by announcing that it would invest $400 million in a Taiwan hub, which would henceforth be the central node in its Asian network. The decision to invest in an Asian hub followed closely on the heels of a 1995 decision by UPS to invest $1.1 billion to build a ground network in Europe. In September 1996, UPS went one step further toward building an international air express service when it announced that it would start a pan-European next-day delivery service for small packages. UPS hopes that its recent moves will finally push the international operations of the carrier into the black after eight years of losses.[36]

The other U.S. carrier that is making a determined push overseas is Airborne Express. From the start, however, Airborne's strategy differed from that of Federal Express and UPS because it decided not to invest in its own international air fleet and ground operations. Airborne's strategy has two components. First, it will continue to fly its own planes in the United States but will book space on other air carriers for shipments going overseas. Second, it has been looking for strategic alliances with foreign companies that would give it market access and ground operations overseas. In 1989, the company announced an alliance with Mitsui & Co., a $125 billion-a-year Japanese trading and finance firm, and Tonami Transportation Co., operators of a ground-based express delivery service in Japan called Panther Express. The deal called for Mitsui to purchase $40 million worth of Airborne's stock and to provide $100 million in aircraft financing over five years and for the partners to collaborate in building volume in the Japan–U.S. air express market.

Industry Evolution, 1997–2002
Competitive Trends

The industry continued to grow at a solid rate through 2000, which helped to establish a stable pricing environment. In 2001, things took a turn for the worse, with recessionary conditions in the United States triggering a 7.6 percent decline in the number of domestic packages shipped by air. Even though the economy started to rebound in 2002, analysts were predicting only a 3 percent increase in the number of packages shipped by air.[37] Despite the weak environment, pricing discipline remained solid. Unlike the 1990–1991 recession, there was no price war. Indeed, in early 2002, UPS pushed through a 3.5 percent increase in prices, which was quickly followed by the other carriers. The carriers were also successful in tacking on a fuel surcharge to the cost of packages to make up for sharply higher fuel costs in 2001.[38]

During 1997–2002, several notable trends occurred in the industry. First, all three players continued to build their logistics services. UPS was reportedly the most successful in this area. By 2000, UPS's logistics business was the largest in the industry, with revenues of over $1 billion, an increase of 58 percent over the prior year. Growth forecasts were as high as 40 percent per year.[39] UPS was reportedly stealing share from FedEx in this area. (Federal Express changed its name to FedEx in 2000.) Most analysts expected logistics services to continue to be a growth area.

Second, all three carriers focused on supplementing their air networks with extensive ground networks and ground hubs to ship packages overnight. With more customers moving from overnight mail to deferred services, such as second-day delivery, this shift in emphasis has become a necessity. Demand for deferred services help up reasonably well during 2001, even as demand for overnight packages slumped. Prices for deferred and ground services are considerably lower than are prices for air services, but so are the costs (see Table 3). UPS has been the most

aggressive in building ground delivery capabilities (of course, it already had extensive ground capabilities before its move into the air). In 1999, UPS decided to integrate overnight delivery into its huge ground transportation network. The company spent about $700 million to strengthen its ground delivery network by setting up regional ground hubs. By doing so, it found it could ship packages overnight on the ground within a 500-mile radius. Because ground shipments are cheaper than air shipments, the result was a significant cost savings for UPS. The company also deferred delivery of about 123 aircraft that were on order, reasoning that they would not be needed as quickly because more of UPS's overnight business was moved to the ground.[40]

FedEx has also accelerated the buildup of its ground network. In 1997, FedEx spent $500 million to acquire an established ground shipping company, supplementing its existing capability. It spent an additional $150 million in 2001 to strengthen the system and hopes to be able to provide ground service to all U.S. homes by the end of 2002, giving it a similar capability to UPS. In addition, FedEx struck a deal in 2001 with the U.S. Postal Service (USPS), under which FedEx will provide airport-to-airport transportation for 250,000 pounds of USPS Express Mail packages nightly and about 3 million pounds of USPS Priority Mail packages. The Priority Mail will be moved on FedEx planes that normally sit idle during the day. The deal could reportedly be worth $7 billion in additional revenues to FedEx over the seven-year term of the agreement. In addition, FedEx should reap cost savings from the better utilization of its lift capacity.[41]

The third trend has been a move toward selling various product offerings—including air delivery, ground package offerings, and logistics services—to business customers as a bundle. The basic idea behind bundling is to offer complementary products at a bundled price that is less than would have been the case if each item had been purchased separately. Yet again, UPS has been the most aggressive in offering bundled services to corporate clients. UPS is clearly aiming to set itself up as a one-stop shop offering a broad array of transportation solutions to customers. FedEx has also made moves in this area, and most recently, Airborne Express started to bundle its product offerings in mid 2001.[42]

The fourth trend of note has been ongoing speculation that further consolidation is likely in the

TABLE 3

Product Yield Comparisons, 2001

Company	Overnight Air	Deferred Air	Ground
Airborne	$9.16	$7.03	$5.60
FedEx	$14.96	$10.88	$5.98
UPS	$19.32	$12.52	$6.03

Source: Salomon Smith Barney Research, *Wrap It Up—Bundling and the Air Express Sector,* May 3, 2002.

industry. The source of most of the rumors has been Deutsche Post (DP). The recently privatized German postal service acquired in the late 1990s a 51 percent interest in DHL, whose U.S. airline, DHL Airways, has a small position in the U.S. air express market (remember, DHL is a major player in the international market). DP has made no secret about its desire to build a strong position in the global parcel express, forwarding, and third-party logistics businesses. DP spent approximately $5 billion to acquire several companies in the logistics business between 1997 and 1999. In November 2000, Deutsche Post went private with an initial public offering that raised $5.5 billion. In 2001 and 2002, it was rumored to be considering bids for two U.S. companies, Airborne Express and BAX Global, a freight forwarder. Other possible takeover candidates include Consolidated Freightways, another small player in the air express industry but one with a large ground network.

Currently, DP is theoretically constrained in its ability to operate an airline in the United States by the law that limits foreign ownership of a U.S. airline to 25 percent (air express operators are considered airlines for the purposes of this law). However, DP seems to have circumvented this law in the case of DHL by establishing a complex ownership structure. DP owns 51 percent of DHL, which in turn owns 23 percent of DHL Airways, the U.S. airline operations of DHL. The belief is that DP will use DHL Airways as the vehicle for any U.S. acquisitions, such as the rumored acquisition of Airborne Express. In early 2001, USPS and FedEx filed petitions against Deutsche Post with the U.S. Department of Transportation, contending that DP's ownership of DHL Airways was against the law (they argued that DP in effect controlled DHL Airways). However, the U.S. Department of Transportation rejected the petitions, potentially opening the way for DP to acquire Airborne Express under a similar ownership and control arrangement.[43]

ENDNOTES

1. Standard & Poor's, "Aerospace and Air Transport," *Industry Surveys,* February 1996.
2. Ibid.
3. Standard & Poor's, Airlines, *Industry Surveys,* March 2002.
4. Christopher H. Lovelock, "Federal Express (B)," Harvard Business School Case No. 579–040, 1978.
5. Standard & Poor's, "Aerospace and Air Transport," *Industry Surveys,* January 1981.
6. Lovelock, "Federal Express (B)."
7. Standard & Poor's, "Aerospace and Air Transport," *Industry Surveys,* January 1981.
8. Ibid.
9. Ibid.
10. Standard & Poor's, "Aerospace and Air Transport," *Industry Surveys,* January 1984.
11. Carol Hall, "High Fliers," *Marketing and Media Decisions,* August 1986, p. 138.
12. Standard & Poor's, "Aerospace and Air Transport," *Industry Surveys,* January 1984.
13. Standard & Poor's, "Aerospace and Air Transport," *Industry Surveys,* December 1984.
14. Brian Dumaine, "Turbulence Hits the Air Couriers," *Fortune,* July 21, 1986, pp. 101–106.
15. Ibid.
16. Chuck Hawkins, "Purolator: Still No Overnight Success," *BusinessWeek,* June 16, 1986, pp. 76–78.
17. Joan O'C. Hamilton, "Emery Is One Heavy Load for Consolidated Freightways," *BusinessWeek,* March 26, 1990, pp. 62–64.
18. Standard & Poor's "Aerospace and Air Transport," *Industry Surveys,* February 1996.
19. "Hold That Tiger: FedEx Is Now World Heavyweight," *Purchasing,* September 14, 1989, pp. 41–42.
20. Standard & Poor's, "Aerospace and Air Transport," *Industry Surveys,* April 1988.
21. Standard & Poor's, "Aerospace and Air Transport," *Industry Surveys,* February 1996.
22. David Greising, "Watch Out for Flying Packages," *BusinessWeek,* November 1994, p. 40.
23. Staff reporter, "UPS to Raise Its Rates for Packages," *Wall Street Journal,* January 9, 1995, p. C22.
24. Marilyn Royce, "Airborne Freight," *Value Line Investment Survey,* September 20, 1996.
25. Robert Frank, "UPS Planning Earlier Delivery," *Wall Street Journal,* September 29, 1994, p. A4.
26. Frank, "Federal Express Grapples with Changes in U.S. Market."
27. Company press releases (http://www.ups.com/news/).
28. Joan M. Feldman, "The Coming of Age of International Air Freight," *Air Transport World,* June 1989, pp. 31–33.
29. Standard & Poor's, "Aerospace and Air Transport," *Industry Surveys,* February 1996.
30. Ibid.
31. Peter Greiff, "Lufthansa, JAL, and a Trading Firm Acquire a Majority Stake in DHL," *Wall Street Journal,* August 24, 1992, p. A5.
32. Standard & Poor's, "Aerospace and Air Transport," *Industry Surveys,* February 1996.
33. "Hold That Tiger: FedEx Is Now a World Heavyweight."
34. Douglas Blackmon, "FedEx Swings from Confidence Abroad to a Tightrope," *Wall Street Journal,* March 15, 1996, p. B4.
35. Daniel Pearl, "Federal Express Plans to Trim Assets in Europe," *Wall Street Journal,* March 17, 1992, p. A3.
36. Company press releases (http://www.ups.com/news/).
37. C. Haddad and M. Arndt, "Saying No Thanks to Overnight Air," *Business Week,* April 1, 2002, p. 74.
38. Salomon Smith Barney Research, *Wrap It Up—Bundling and the Air Express Sector,* May 3, 2002.
39. C. Haddad and J. Ewing, "Ground Wars," *Business Week,* May 21, 2001, p. 64.
40. C. Haddad and M. Arndt, "Saying No Thanks to Overnight Air," *Business Week,* April 1, 2002, p. 74.
41. E. Walsh, "Package Deal," *Logistics,* February 2001, pp. 19–20.
42. Salomon Smith Barney Research, *Wrap It Up—Bundling and the Air Express Sector,* May 3, 2002.
43. P. Needham, "Coming to America," *Journal of Commerce,* April 22, 2002, p. 12.

30 Airborne Express in 2002

This case was prepared by Charles W. L. Hill, the University of Washington.

Introduction

Airborne Inc., which operates under the name Airborne Express, is an air-express transportation company that provides express and second-day delivery of small packages (less than seventy pounds) and documents throughout the United States and to and from many foreign countries. The company owns and operates an airline and a fleet of ground-transportation vehicles to provide complete door-to-door service. It is also an air freight forwarder, moving shipments of any size on a worldwide basis. As of 2002, Airborne Express held third place in the U.S. air express industry, with 9 percent of the market for small package deliveries. Its main domestic competitors are Federal Express, which has 26 percent of the market, and United Parcel Service (UPS), which has 53 percent of the market. There are several small players, including DHL Airways, Consolidated Freightways (CF), and the U.S. Postal Service, each of which holds less than 5 percent of the market share.[1]

This case was made possible by the generous assistance of Airborne Express. The information given in this case was provided by Airborne Express. Unless otherwise indicated, Airborne Express and the Securities and Exchange Commission's 10-K filings are the sources of all information contained within this case. The case is based on an earlier case, which was prepared with the assistance of Daniel Bodnar, Laurie Martinelli, Brian McMullen, Lisa Mutty, and Stephen Schmidt. The case is intended as a basis for classroom discussion rather than as an illustration of either effective or ineffective handling of an administrative situation. Reprinted by permission of Charles W. L. Hill.

The evolution of the air express industry and the current state of competition in the industry were discussed in a companion case: Case 29, "The Evolution of the Air Express Industry, 1973–2002." The current case (Case 30) focuses on the operating structure, competitive strategy, organizational structure, and cultures of Airborne Express.

History of Airborne Express

Airborne Express was originally known as Pacific Air Freight when it was founded in Seattle at the close of World War II by Holt W. Webster, a former Army Air Corps officer. (See Exhibit 1 for a list of major milestones in the history of Airborne Express.) The company was merged with Airborne Freight Corporation of California in 1968, taking the name of the California company but retaining management direction by the former officers of Pacific Air Freight. Airborne was initially an exclusive air freight forwarder. Freight forwarders such as Airborne arrange for the transportation of air cargo between any two destinations. They purchase cargo space from the airlines and retail this space in small amounts. They deal primarily with small customers, providing pickup and delivery services in most cities, either in their own trucks or through contract agents.

Following the 1977 deregulation of the airline industry, Airborne entered the air express industry by leasing the airplanes and pilots of Midwest Charter, a small airline operating out of its own airport in Wilmington, Ohio.

EXHIBIT 1

Major Milestones at Airborne Express[2]

1946: Airborne Flower Traffic Association of California is founded to fly fresh flowers from Hawaii to the mainland.

1968: Airborne of California and Pacific Air Freight of Seattle merge to form Airborne Freight Corporation. Headquarters are in Seattle, Washington.

1979–1981: Airborne Express is born. After purchasing Midwest Air Charter, Airborne buys Clinton County Air Force Base in Wilmington, Ohio, becoming the only carrier to own and operate an airport. The package sort center opens, creating the "hub" for the hub-and-spoke system.

1984–1986: Airborne is first carrier to establish a privately operated foreign trade zone in an air industrial park.

1987: Airborne opens the Airborne Stock Exchange, a third-party inventory management and distribution service. In the same year, service begins to and from more than 8,000 Canadian locations.

1988: Airborne becomes the first air express carrier to provide same-day delivery, through its purchase of Sky Courier.

1990: The International Cargo Forum and Exposition names Airborne the carrier with the most-outstanding integrated cargo system over the previous two years.

1991: Airborne is the first transportation company to receive Volvo-Flyg Motors' Excellent Performance Award. *Computerworld* ranks Airborne the "most effective user of information systems in the U.S. transportation industry." In addition, Airborne receives the "Spread the Word!" Electronic Data Interchange (EDI) award for having the largest number of EDI users worldwide in the air express and freight forwarding industry.

1992: Airborne introduces Flight-ReadySM—the first prepaid Express Letters and Packs.

1993: Airborne introduces Airborne Logistics Services (ALS), a new subsidiary providing outsourced warehousing and distribution services. IBM consolidates its international shipping operation with Airborne.

1994: Airborne opens its Ocean Service Division, becoming the first express carrier to introduce ocean shipping services. Airborne Logistics Services (ALS) establishes the first new film distribution program for the movie industry in fifty years. Airborne also becomes the first company to provide online communication to Vietnam.

1995: Airborne Alliance Group, a consortium of transportation, logistics, third-party customer service operations, and high-tech companies providing value-added services, is formed. Airborne opens a second runway at its hub, which is now the United States's largest privately owned airport. Airborne also expands its fleet, acquiring Boeing 767-200 aircraft.

1996: Airborne Express celebrates fifty years of providing value-added distribution solutions to business.

1997: Airborne Express has its best year ever, with net earnings increasing three-and-a-half-fold over the previous year. Airborne's stock triples, leading to a two-for-one stock split in February 1998.

1998: Airborne posts record profits and enters the Fortune 500. The first of thirty Boeing 767s is introduced to its fleet. *The Business Consumer Guide* rates Airborne as the Best Air Express Carrier for the fourth consecutive year.

1999: Airborne@home, a unique alliance with the United States Postal Service, is introduced. It enables etailers, catalog companies, and similar businesses to ship quickly and economically to the residential marketplace. Optical Village is created. Part of Airborne Logistics Services, this new division brings together some of the biggest competitors in the optical industry to share many costs and a single location for their assembly, storage, inventory, logistics, and delivery options.

2000: Airborne announces several changes in senior management, including a new president and chief operating officer, Carl Donaway. Several new business initiatives are announced, most notably a ground service scheduled to begin April 1, 2001. Airborne also wins the Brand Keys Customer Loyalty Award, edging out the competition for the second consecutive year.

2001: Airborne launches ground delivery service and 10:30 A.M. service, giving it a comprehensive, full-service industry competitive capability. Airborne.com launches its Small Business Center, as well as various enhancements to help all business customers speed and simplify the shipping process. Airborne also releases the Corporate Exchange shipping application, simplifying desktop shipping for customers while giving them greater control. Advanced tracking features are added to airborne.com and Airborne eCourier is released, enabling customers to send confidential, signed documents electronically.

Airborne quickly became dissatisfied, however, with the limited amount of control they were able to exercise over Midwest, which made it difficult to achieve the kind of tight coordination and control of logistics that was necessary to become a successful air express operator. Instead of continuing to lease Midwest's planes and facility, Airborne decided in 1980 to buy "the entire bucket of slop: company, planes, pilots, airport and all."

Among other things, the Midwest acquisition put Airborne in the position of being the only industry participant to own an airport. Airborne immediately began the job of developing a hub-and-spoke system capable of supporting a nationwide distribution system. An efficient sorting facility was established at the Wilmington hub. Airborne upgraded Midwest's fleet of prop and propjet aircraft by buying a modern fleet of DC-8s, DC-9s, and YS-11 aircraft. These planes left major cities every evening, flying down the spokes and carrying letters and packages to the central sort facility in Wilmington, Ohio. There, the letters and packages were unloaded, sorted according to their final destination, and then reloaded and flown to their final destination for delivery before noon the next day.

During the late 1970s and early 1980s, dramatic growth in the industry attracted many competitors. As a consequence, competition became intense, despite a high-growth rate price, forcing several companies to the sidelines by the late 1980s. Between 1984 and 1990, average revenues per domestic shipment at Airborne fell from around $30 to under $15 (today, they run at just under $9). Airborne was able to survive this period by pursuing several strategies that increased productivity and drove costs down to the lowest levels in the industry. Airborne's operating costs per shipment fell from $28 in 1984 to about $14 by 1990 (they fell to $9.79 by 2001). As a consequence, by the late 1980s, Airborne had pulled away from a pack of struggling competitors to become one of the top three companies in the industry, a position it still held in 2002.

Air Express Operations
The Domestic Delivery Network

As of 2002, Airborne Express had 305 ground stations within the United States. The stations are essentially the ends of the spokes in Airborne's hub-and-spoke system. The distribution of stations allows Airborne to reach all major population centers in the country. In each station are about fifty to fifty-five drivers plus staff. About 80 percent of Airborne's 115,300 full-time and 7,200 part-time employees work at this level. The stations are the basic units in Airborne's delivery organization. Their primary task is to ferry packages between clients and the local air terminal. Airborne utilizes approximately 14,900 radio-dispatch delivery vans and trucks to transport packages, of which 6,000 are owned by the company. Independent contractors under contract with the company provide the balance of the company's pickup and delivery services.

Airborne's drivers make their last round of major clients at 5 P.M. The drivers either collect packages directly from clients or from one of the company's more than 15,300 drop boxes. The drop boxes are placed at strategic locations, such as in the lobbies of major commercial buildings. To give clients a little more time, in most major cities there are also a few central drop boxes that are not emptied until 6 P.M. If a client needs still more time, the package can be delivered to the airport by 7 P.M. so it will make the evening flight.

When a driver picks up a package, he or she uses a hand-held scanner to read a bar code that is attached to the package. This information is then fed directly into Airborne's proprietary FOCUS (Freight, On-Line Control and Update System) computer system. FOCUS, which has global coverage, records shipment status at key points in the life cycle of a shipment. Thus, a customer can call Airborne on a twenty-four-hour basis to find out where their package is in Airborne's system. FOCUS also allows a customer direct access to shipment information through the Internet. All a customer needs to do is access Airborne's web site and key the code number assigned to a package, and FOCUS will tell the customer where the package is currently in Airborne's system.

When the driver has completed the pickup route, she or he takes the load to Airborne's loading docks at the local airport. (Airborne serves all ninety-nine major metropolitan airports in the United States.) There, the packages are loaded into C-containers (discussed later in this case study).

Several C-containers are then towed by hand or by tractor to a waiting aircraft, where they are loaded onto a conveyor belt and they pass through the passenger door of the aircraft. Before long, the aircraft is loaded and takes off. It will either fly directly to the company's hub at Wilmington or make one or two stops along the way to pick up more packages.

Sometime between midnight and 2 A.M., most of the aircraft will have landed at Wilmington. An old strategic air command base, Wilmington's location places it within a 600-mile radius (an overnight drive or one-hour flying time) of 60 percent of the U.S. population. Wilmington also has the advantage of good weather. In all the years that Airborne has operated at Wilmington, air operations have been fogged in on only a handful of days. In 1995, Airborne opened a second runway at Wilmington. Developed at a cost of $60 million, the second runway makes Wilmington the largest privately owned airport in the country. The runway expansion was part of a $120 million upgrade of the Wilmington sort facility.

After arrival at Wilmington, the plane taxis down the runway and parks alongside a group of aircraft that are already disgorging their load of C-containers. Within minutes the C-containers are unloaded from the plane down a conveyor belt and towed to the sort facility by a tractor. The sort facility has the capacity to handle 1.2 million packages per night. At the end of 2001, the facility handled an average of 1 million packages a night. The bar codes on the packages are read, and then the packages are directed through a labyrinth of conveyor belts and sorted according to final destination. The sorting is partly done by hand and partly automated. At the end of this process, packages are grouped together by final destination and loaded into a C-container. An aircraft bound for the final destination is then loaded with C-containers, and by 5 A.M. most aircraft have taken off.

Upon arrival at the final destination, the plane is unloaded and the packages are sorted according to their delivery points within the surrounding area. Airborne couriers then take the packages on the final leg of their journey. Packages have a 75 percent probability of being delivered to clients by 10:30 A.M., and a 98 percent probability of being delivered by noon.

Regional Trucking Hubs

Although about 71 percent of packages are transported by air and pass through Wilmington, Airborne has also established ten regional trucking hubs that deal with the remaining 29 percent of the company's domestic volume. These hubs sort shipments that originate and have a destination within approximately a 300-mile radius. The first one was opened in Allentown, Pennsylvania, which is centrally located on the East Coast. This hub handles packages that are being transported between points within the Washington, D.C.–Boston area. Instead of transporting packages by air, packages to be transported within this area are sorted by the drivers at pickup and delivered from the driver's home station by scheduled truck runs to the Allentown hub. There, they are sorted according to destination and taken to the appropriate station on another scheduled truck run for final delivery.

One advantage of ground-based transportation through trucking hubs is that operating costs are much lower than for air transportation. The average cost of a package transported by air is more than five times greater than the cost of a package transported on the ground. This cost differential is transparent to the customer, however, who assumes that all packages are flown. Thus, Airborne can charge the same price for ground-transported packages as for air-transported packages, but the former yields a much higher return. The trucking hubs also have the advantage of taking some of the load off the Wilmington sorting facility, which is currently operating at about 90 percent capacity.

International Operations

In addition to its domestic express operations, Airborne is also an international company providing service to more than 200 countries worldwide. International operations accounted for about 11 percent of total revenues in 2001. Airborne offers two international products: freight products and express products. Freight products are commercial-sized, larger-unit shipments. This service provides door-to-airport service. Goods are picked up domestically from the customer and then shipped to the destination airport. A consignee or an agent of the consignee gets the paperwork and must clear the shipment through customs. Express packages are small packages, documents, and letters. This service is door to door, and all shipments are cleared through customs by Airborne. Most of Airborne's international revenues come from freight products.

Airborne does not fly any of its own aircraft overseas. Instead, it contracts for space on all-cargo airlines or in the cargo holds of passenger airlines. Airborne owns facilities overseas in Japan, Taiwan, Hong Kong, Singapore, Australia, New Zealand, and London. These facilities function in a manner similar to Airborne's domestic stations (that is, they have their own trucks and drivers and are hooked into the FOCUS tracking system). The majority of foreign distribution, however, is carried out by foreign agents. Foreign agents are large, local, well-established surface delivery companies. Recently, Airborne has entered into several exclusive strategic alliances with large foreign agents. Currently it has alliances in Japan, Thailand, Malaysia, and South Africa. (The rationale for entering strategic alliances, along with Airborne's approach to global expansion, is discussed in greater detail later in this case.)

Another aspect of Airborne's international operations has been the creation at its Wilmington hub of the only privately certified foreign trade zone (FTZ) in the United States. While in an FTZ, merchandise is tax free and no customs duty is paid on it until it leaves. Thus, a foreign-based company may store critical inventory in the FTZ and have Airborne deliver it just in time to U.S. customers. This allows the foreign company to hold inventory in the United States without having to pay customs duty on it until the need arises.

Aircraft Purchase and Maintenance

As of 2001, Airborne Express owned a fleet of 118 aircraft, including twenty-four DC-8s, seventy-four DC-9s, and twenty Boeing 767s. In addition, approximately seventy smaller aircraft are chartered nightly to connect smaller cities with company aircraft that then operate to and from the Wilmington hub. To keep capital expenditures down, Airborne has traditionally purchased only used planes. Airborne converts the planes to suit its specifications at a maintenance facility based at its Wilmington hub. Once it gets a plane, Airborne typically guts the interior and installs state-of-the-art electronics and avionics equipment. The company's philosophy is to get all of the upgrades that it can into an aircraft.

Although this kind of overhaul can cost a lot up front, the payback is increased aircraft reliability and a reduction in service downtime. Airborne also standardizes cockpits as much as possible, which makes it easier for crews to switch from one aircraft to another if the need arises. According to the company, the total purchase and modification of a secondhand DC-9 costs about $10 million, compared with the cost of an equivalent new plane of $40 million. An additional factor reducing operating costs is that Airborne's DC-9 aircraft require only a two-person cockpit crew, as opposed to the three-person crews required in most Federal Express and UPS aircraft.

After conversion of the aircraft, Airborne strives to keep aircraft maintenance costs down by carrying out almost all of its own fleet repairs. (It is the only all-cargo carrier to do so.) The Wilmington maintenance facility can handle everything except major engine repairs and has the capability to machine critical aircraft parts if needed. The company sees this in-house facility as a major source of cost savings. It estimates that maintenance labor costs are 50 to 60 percent below the costs of having the same work performed outside.

In December 1995, Airborne announced a deal to purchase twelve used Boeing 767-200 aircraft between the years 1997 and 2000, and it announced plans to purchase an additional ten to fifteen used 767-200s between the years 2000 and 2004. These were the first wide-bodied aircraft in Airborne's fleet. The cost of introducing the first twelve aircraft was about $290 million, and the additional aircraft will cost another $360 million. The shift to wide-bodied aircraft was promoted by an internal study, which concluded that with growing volume, wide-bodied aircraft would lead to greater operating efficiencies.

During 2001, Airborne was using about 66.6 percent of its lift capacity on a typical business day. This compares with 76.7 percent capacity utilization in 1997, and 70 percent utilization in 2000. In late 2001, Airborne reduced its total lift capacity by approximately 100,000 pounds to about 4 million pounds a day, in an attempt to reduce excess capacity of certain routes and better match supply with demand conditions.

C-Containers

C-containers are uniquely shaped 60-cubic-foot containers developed by Airborne Express in 1985 at a cost of $3.5 million. They are designed to fit through the passenger doors of DC-8 and DC-9 aircraft. They replaced the much larger A-containers widely used in the air cargo business. At six times the size of a C-container, A-containers can be loaded only through specially built cargo doors and require specialized loading equipment. The loading equipment required for C-containers is a modified belt loader, similar to that used for loading baggage onto a plane, and about 80 percent less expensive than the equipment needed to load A-containers. The use of C-containers also means that Airborne does not have to bear the $1 million per plane cost required to install cargo doors that will take A-containers. The C-containers are shaped to allow maximum utilization of the planes' interior loading space. Fifty of the containers fit into a converted DC-9, and about eighty-three fit into a DC-8-62. A C-container filled with packages can be moved by a single person, making it easy to load and unload. Airborne Express has taken out a patent on the design of the C-containers.

Information Systems

Airborne utilizes three information systems to help boost productivity and improve customer service. The first of these systems is referred to as the LIBRA II system. LIBRA II equipment, which includes a metering device and PC computer software, is installed in the mailroom of clients. With minimum data entry, the metering device weighs the package, calculates the shipping charges, generates the shipping labels, and provides a daily shipping report. By December 2001, the system was in use at approximately 9,900 domestic customer locations. The use of LIBRA II not only benefits the customers but also lowers Airborne's operating costs because LIBRA II shipment data are transferred into Airborne's FOCUS shipment tracking system automatically, thereby avoiding duplicate data entry.

FOCUS is the second of Airborne's three main information systems. As discussed earlier, FOCUS is essentially a worldwide tracking system. The bar code on each package is read at various points (for example, at pickup, at sorting in Wilmington, at arrival, and so forth) with hand-held scanners, and this information is fed into Airborne's computer system. Using FOCUS, Airborne can track the progress of a shipment through its national and international

logistics system. The major benefit is in terms of customer service. Through an Internet link, Airborne's customers can track their own shipments through Airborne's system on a twenty-four-hour basis.

For its highest-volume corporate customers, Airborne has developed Customer Linkage, an electronic data interchange (EDI) program and the third information system. The EDI system is designed to eliminate the flow of paperwork between Airborne and its major clients. The EDI system allows customers to create shipping documentation at the same time they enter orders for their goods. At the end of each day, shipping activities are transmitted electronically to Airborne's FOCUS, where they are captured for shipment tracking and billing. Customer Linkage benefits the customer by eliminating repetitive data entry and paperwork. It also lowers the company's operating costs by eliminating manual data entry. (In essence, both LIBRA II and Customer Linkage push a lot of the data-entry work into the hands of customers.) The EDI system also includes electronic invoicing and payment remittance processing. Airborne also offers its customers a program known as Quicklink, which significantly reduces the programming time required by customers to take advantage of linkage benefits.

Strategy

Market Positioning

In the early 1980s, Airborne Express tried hard to compete head-to-head with Federal Express with an attempt to establish broad market coverage, including both frequent and infrequent users. Frequent users are shippers that generate more than $20,000 of business per month, or more than 1,000 shipments per month. Infrequent users generate less than $20,000 per month, or less than 1,000 shipments per month.

To build broad market coverage, Airborne followed Federal Express's lead of funding a television advertising campaign designed to build consumer awareness. By the mid 1980s, however, Airborne decided that this method of building market share was expensive. The advertising campaign bought recognition but little penetration. One of the principal problems was that it was expensive to serve infrequent users. Infrequent users demanded the same level of service as frequent users, but Airborne would typically get only one shipment per pickup with an infrequent user compared with ten or more shipments per pickup with a frequent user. Far more pickups were required to generate the same volume of business. Given the extremely competitive nature of the industry at this time, such an inefficient utilization of capacity was of great concern to Airborne.

Consequently, in the mid 1980s, Airborne decided to become a niche player in the industry and focused on serving the needs of high-volume corporate accounts. The company slashed its advertising expenditure, pulling the plug on its television ad campaign, and invested more resources in building a direct sales force, which is now 460. By focusing on high-volume corporate accounts, Airborne could establish scheduled pickup routes and use its ground capacity more efficiently. This enabled the company to achieve significant reductions in its unit cost structure. Partly due to this factor, Airborne executives estimate that their cost structure is as much as $3 per shipment less than that of FedEx. Another estimate suggests that Airborne's strategy reduced labor costs by 20 percent per unit for pickup and 10 percent for delivery.

Of course, there is a downside to this strategy. High-volume corporate customers have a great deal more bargaining power than infrequent users, so they can and do demand substantial discounts. For example, in March 1987 Airborne achieved a major coup when it won an exclusive three-year contract to handle all of IBM's express packages weighing less than 150 pounds. To win the IBM account, however, Airborne had to offer rates up to 84 percent below Federal Express's list prices. Nevertheless, the strategy seems to have worked. As of 1995, approximately 80 percent of Airborne's revenues come from corporate accounts, most of them secured through competitive bidding. The concentrated volume that this business represents has helped Airborne to drive down costs.

Delivery Time, Reliability, and Flexibility

Another feature of Airborne's strategy was the decision not to try to compete with Federal Express on delivery time. Federal Express and UPS have long guaranteed delivery by 10:30 A.M. Airborne guarantees delivery by midday, although it offers a 10:30 guarantee to some very large corporate customers. Guaranteeing delivery by 10:30 A.M. would mean

stretching Airborne's already tight scheduling system to the limit. To meet its 10:30 A.M. deadline, FedEx has to operate with a deadline for the previous day's pickups of 6:30 P.M. Airborne can afford to be a little more flexible and can arrange pickups as late as 7:00 P.M. if that suits a corporate client's particular needs. Later pickups clearly benefit the shipper, who is, after all, the paying party.

In addition, Airborne executives feel that a guaranteed 10:30 A.M. delivery is unnecessary. The extra hour and a half does not make a great deal of difference to most clients, and they are willing to accept the extra time in exchange for lower prices. In addition, Airborne stresses the reliability of its delivery schedules. As one executive put it, "A package delivered consistently at 11:15 A.M. is as good as delivery at 10:30 A.M." This reliability is enhanced by Airborne's ability to provide shipment tracking through its FOCUS.

Deferred Services

With a slowdown in the growth rate of the express mail market toward the end of the 1980s, Airborne decided in 1990 to enter the deferred-delivery business with its Select Delivery Service (SDS) product. SDS provides for next-afternoon or second-day delivery. Packages weighing 5 pounds or less are generally delivered on a next-afternoon basis, with packages of more than 5 pounds being delivered on a second-day basis. SDS shipments comprised approximately 42 percent of total domestic shipments in 1995. They are priced lower than overnight express products, reflecting the less time-sensitive nature of these deliveries. The company will utilize any spare capacity on its express flights to carry SDS shipments. In addition, Airborne will use other carriers, such as passenger carriers with spare cargo capacity in their planes, to carry less urgent SDS shipments.

Early in 1996, Airborne began to phase in two new services to replace SDS. Next Afternoon Service is available for shipments weighing 5 pounds or less, and Second Day Service is offered for shipments of all weights. By 2001, deferred shipments accounted for 46 percent of total domestic shipments.

Ground Delivery Service

In April 2001, Airborne launched a ground delivery service (GDS) in response to similar offerings from

FedEx and UPS. Airborne concluded that it was important to offer this service to retain parity with its principal competitors and to be able to offer bundled services to its principal customers (that is, to offer them air, ground, and logistics services for a single bundled price). Airborne also felt that they could add the service with a relatively minor initial investment, $30 million, because it leveraged existing assets, including trucks, tracking systems, and regional ground hubs and sorting facilities.

The new service has initially been introduced on a limited basis and is targeted at large corporate customers. GDS is priced less than deferred services, reflecting the less time-sensitive nature of the GDS offering. GDS accounted for 1.5 percent of domestic shipments in 2001, and 4 percent in the fourth quarter of 2001.

Logistics Services

Although small-package express mail remains Airborne's main business, the company is increasingly promoting a range of third-party logistics services through its Advanced Logistics Services Corp. (ALS) subsidiary. These services provide customers with the ability to maintain inventories in a 1-million-square-foot "stock exchange" facility located at Airborne's Wilmington hub or at sixty smaller stock exchange facilities located around the country. The inventory can be managed either by Airborne or by customer's personnel. Inventory stored at Wilmington can be delivered utilizing either Airborne's airline system or, if required, commercial airlines on a next-flight-out basis. ALS's central print computer program allows information on inventories to be sent electronically to customers' computers located at Wilmington, where Airborne's personnel monitor prints output and ships inventories according to customers' instructions.

For example, consider the case of Data Products Corp., a producer of computer printers. Data Products takes advantage of low labor costs to carry out significant assembly operations in Hong Kong. Many of the primary component parts for its printers, such as microprocessors, are manufactured in the United States and have to be shipped to Hong Kong. The finished product is then shipped back to the United States for sale. In setting up a global manufacturing system, Data Products had a decision to make: either consolidate the parts from its hundreds of suppliers in-house and then arrange for shipment to Hong Kong, or contract someone to handle the whole logistics process. Data Products decided to contract, and they picked Airborne Express to consolidate the component parts and arrange for shipments.

Airborne controls the consolidation and movement of component parts from the component part suppliers to the Hong Kong assembly operation so that inventory-holding costs are minimized. The key feature of Airborne's service is that all of Data Products's materials are collected at Airborne's facility at Los Angeles International Airport. Data Products's Hong Kong assembly plants can then tell Airborne what parts to ship by air as they are needed. Thus, Airborne can provide inventory control for Data Products. In addition, by scheduling deliveries so that year-round traffic between Los Angeles and Hong Kong can be guaranteed, Airborne can negotiate a better air rate from Japan Air Lines (JAL) for the transportation of component parts.

International Strategy

One of the major strategic challenges currently facing Airborne (along with the other express mail carriers) is how best to establish an international service that is comparable to their domestic service. Many of Airborne's major corporate clients are becoming more global in their strategic orientation. They are increasingly demanding a compatible express mail service. In addition, the rise of companies with globally dispersed manufacturing operations that rely on just-in-time delivery systems to keep their inventory holding costs down has created a demand for a global air express service that can transport critical inventory between operations located in different areas of the globe (consider the example of Data Products discussed earlier in this case study).

The initial response of FedEx and UPS to this challenge was to undertake massive capital investments to establish international airlift capability and international ground operations based on the U.S. model. Their rationale was that a wholly owned global delivery network was necessary to establish the tight control, coordination, and scheduling required for a successful air express operation. More recently, however, FedEx pulled out of its European ground operations while continuing to fly its own aircraft overseas.

Airborne has decided on a quite different strategy. In part born of financial necessity (Airborne lacks the capital necessary to imitate FedEx and UPS), Airborne has decided to pursue what they refer to as a "variable cost strategy." This strategy involves two main elements: (1) the utilization of international airlift on existing air cargo operators and passenger aircraft to get their packages overseas, and (2) entry into strategic alliances with foreign companies that already have established ground delivery networks. With this strategy, Airborne hopes to be able to establish global coverage without having to undertake the kind of capital investments that Federal Express and UPS have.

Airborne executives defend their decision to continue to purchase space on international flights rather than fly their own aircraft overseas by making several points. First, Airborne's international business is currently 70 percent outbound and 30 percent inbound. If Airborne were to fly its own aircraft overseas, some would have to fly back half-empty. Second, on many routes, Airborne simply doesn't yet have the volume necessary to justify flying its own planes. Third, national air carriers are currently giving Airborne good prices. If Airborne began to fly directly overseas, the company would be seen as a competitor and might no longer be given price breaks. Fourth, getting international airlift space is currently not a problem. While space can be limited in the third and fourth quarters of the year, Airborne is such a big customer that it usually has few problems getting lift. On the other hand, the long-term viability of this strategy is questionable given the rapid evolution in the international air express business. Flying Tiger was once one of Airborne's major providers of international lift. Following the purchase of Flying Tiger by FedEx, however, Airborne has reduced its business with Flying Tiger. Apart from concerns about giving business to a competitor, Airborne fears that its packages will be pushed to the back of the plane whenever Flying Tiger has problems of capacity overload.

With regard to strategic alliances, Airborne currently has joint venture operations in Japan, Thailand, Malaysia, and South Africa. The alliance with Mitsui was announced in December 1989. Mitsui is one of the world's leading trading companies. Together with Tonami Transportation Co., Mitsui owns Panther Express, one of the top five express carriers in Japan and a company with a substantial ground network. The deal called for the establishment of a joint venture among Airborne, Mitsui, and Tonami. Known as Airborne Express Japan, the joint venture combined Airborne's existing Japanese operations with Panther Express. Airborne handles all the shipments to and from Japan. The joint venture is 40 percent owned by Airborne, 40 percent owned by Mitsui, and 20 percent owned by Tonami. The agreement specifies that board decisions must be made by consensus among the three partners. A majority of two cannot outvote the third. In addition, the deal called for Mitsui to invest $40 million in Airborne Express through the purchase of a new issue of nonvoting, 6.9 percent cumulative, convertible preferred stock and a commitment to Airborne from Mitsui of up to $100 million for aircraft financing. Airborne executives saw the Mitsui deal as a major coup, both financially and in terms of market penetration into the Japanese market. The primary advantage claimed by Airborne executives for expanding via strategic alliances is that the company gets an established ground-based delivery network overseas without having to make capital investments.

Organization

In 2001, Carl Donaway became CEO, replacing the longtime top management team of Robert Cline, the CEO, and Robert Brazier, the president and COO. Both had been with the company since the early 1960s. Prior to becoming CEO, Donaway was responsible for airline operations, including managing the Wilmington hub, the package sorting facility, and all aircraft and flight maintenance operations. The philosophy at Airborne is to keep the organizational structure as flat as possible, shorten the lines of communication, and allow for a free flow of ideas within the managerial hierarchy. The top managers generally feel that they are open to ideas suggested by lower-level managers. At the same time, the decision-making process is fairly centralized. The view is that interdependence between functions makes centralized decision making necessary. To quote one executive, "Coordination is the essence of this business. We need centralized decision making in order to achieve this."

Control at Airborne Express is geared toward boosting productivity, lowering costs, and maintaining a reliable high-quality service. These goals are achieved through a combination of budgetary controls, pay-for-performance incentive systems, and a corporate culture that continually stresses key values. For example, consider the procedure used to control stations (where about 80 percent of all employees work). Station operations are reviewed on a quarterly basis using a budgetary process. Control and evaluation of station effectiveness stress four categories. The first is service, measured by the time between pickup and delivery. The goal is to achieve 95 to 97 percent of all deliveries before noon. The second category is productivity, measured by total shipments per employee hour. The third category is controllable cost, and the fourth is station profitability. Goals for each of these categories are determined each quarter in a bottom-up procedure that involves station managers in the goal-setting process. These goals are then linked to an incentive pay system whereby station managers can earn up to 10 percent of their quarterly salary just by meeting their goals with no maximum on the upside if they go over the goals.

The direct sales force also has an incentive pay system. The target pay structure for the sales organization is 70 percent base pay and a 30 percent commission. There is no cap, however, on the commissions for salespeople. So in theory, there is no limit to what a salesperson can earn. There are also contests designed to boost performance. For example, there is a so-called top gun competition for the sales force in which the top salesperson for each quarter wins a $20,000 prize.

Incentive pay systems apart, however, Airborne is not known as a high payer. The company's approach is not to be the compensation leader. Rather, the company tries to set its salary structure to position it in the middle of the labor market. Thus, according to a senior human resources executive, "We target our pay philosophy [total package—compensation plus benefits] to be right at the 50th percentile plus or minus 5 percent."

A degree of self-control is also achieved by trying to establish a corporate culture that focuses employees' attention on the key values required to maintain a competitive edge in the air express industry. The values continually stressed by top managers at Airborne, and communicated throughout the organization by the company's newspaper and a quarterly video, emphasize serving customers' needs, maintaining quality, doing it right the first time around, and excellent service. There is also a companywide emphasis on productivity and cost control. One executive, when describing the company's attitude to expenditures, said, "We challenge everything. . . . We're the toughest sons of bitches on the block." Another noted, "Among managers I feel that there is a universal agreement on the need to control costs. This is a very tough business, and our people are aware of that. Airborne has an underdog mentality—a desire to be a survivor."

Airborne in 2002

The late 1990s and early 2000s were very difficult years for Airborne Express. A combination of weak volume growth (and an absolute decline in 2001); high fuel costs; a switch from premium overnight service to lower-margin deferred services; and strong competition from FedEx and UPS, both of whom had a superior capability to bundle products, pounded the company. After recording record earnings of $137 million in 1997, Airborne saw its profits slide over the next four years (see Exhibits 2–5 for details on Airborne's financial performance). In 2001, the company lost $19 million on revenues of $3.2 billion, even though this number represented an increase from the $2.9 billion revenues generated in 1997. For years, Airborne's niche strategy had served the company well and allowed it to make a return in a very competitive industry, but now analysts questioned whether Airborne could survive as an independent entity. The company, they said, simply lacked the global scale and scope of its larger rivals.

There was persistent speculation that Airborne would ultimately be acquired by DHL, which is 51 percent owned by Germany's Deutsche Post. DHL had a small position inside the United States but was the largest global shipper of express packages. Acquiring Airborne would give Deutsche Post the U.S. delivery network that it currently lacked to round out the global delivery and logistics business it is building. However, U.S. law currently prevents a foreign entity from owning more than 25 percent of a U.S. airline. Deutsche Post may be able to get around this restriction by using DHL Airways, a U.S.

EXHIBIT 2

Airborne Express Income Statement, 1997–2001 (in $ millions)

	Year Ended December 31				
	2001	**2000**	**1999**	**1998**	**1997**
Revenues:					
Domestic	$2,850,798	$2,895,818	$2,772,782	$2,712,344	$2,514,737
International	360,291	380,132	366,342	361,440	397,672
	3,211,089	3,275,950	3,139,124	3,073,784	2,912,409
Operating Expenses:					
Transportation purchased	1,046,954	1,042,541	965,722	944,357	922,885
Station and ground operations	1,067,764	1,055,142	975,669	914,919	858,238
Flight operations and maintenance	557,412	588,582	513,337	477,799	431,474
General and administrative	265,545	258,149	240,089	248,497	234,366
Sales and marketing	90,390	82,512	77,196	71,354	70,346
Depreciation and amortization	208,355	206,406	209,390	184,526	169,845
Federal legislation compensation	(13,000)	—	—	—	—
	3,223,420	3,233,332	2,981,403	2,841,452	2,687,154
Earnings (Loss) from Operations	(12,331)	42,618	157,721	232,332	225,255
Other Income (Expense):					
Interest, net	(19,868)	(23,425)	(17,262)	(12,882)	(27,790)
Discount on sales of receivables	(9,293)	(96)	—	—	—
Other	12,588	4,129	6,929	2,135	—
Earnings (Loss) Before Income Taxes	(28,904)	23,226	147,388	221,585	197,465
Income Taxes	(9,446)	8,940	56,187	84,300	77,393
Net Earnings (Loss) Before Change in Accounting	(19,458)	14,286	91,201	137,285	120,072
Cumulative Effect of Change in Accounting	—	14,206	—	—	—
Net Earnings (Loss)	($19,458)	$28,492	$91,201	$137,285	$120,072
Net Earnings (Loss) per Share:					
Basic					
Before change in accounting	($0.40)	$0.30	$1.88	$2.77	$2.68
Cumulative effect of change in accounting	—	0.29	—	—	—
Net earnings (loss)	($0.40)	$0.59	$1.88	$2.77	$2.68
Diluted					
Before change in accounting	($0.40)	$0.30	$1.85	$2.72	$2.44
Cumulative effect of change in accounting	—	0.29	—	—	—
Net earnings (loss)	($0.40)	$0.59	$1.85	$2.72	$2.44
Dividends per Share:	$0.16	$0.16	$0.16	$0.16	$0.15
Performance as a Percentage of Revenues:					
Operating margin	−0.4%	1.4%	5.0%	7.6%	7.8%
Pretax margin	−0.9%	0.7%	4.7%	7.2%	6.8%
Effective tax rate	32.7%	38.5%	38.1%	38.0%	39.2%
Net margin before change in accounting	−0.6%	0.4%	2.9%	4.5%	4.1%

EXHIBIT 3

Airborne Express, Shipment Revenue Statistics, 1997–2001

	Year Ended December 31				
	2001	**2000**	**1999**	**1998**	**1997**
Average Revenue per Pound:					
Domestic					
Overnight	$ 2.58	$ 2.45	$ 2.42	$ 2.36	$ 2.26
Next-afternoon service	3.65	3.61	3.34	3.05	3.03
Second-day service	1.26	1.23	1.24	1.19	1.18
Ground delivery service	0.57	—	—	—	—
100 lbs. and over	0.94	0.94	0.90	0.79	0.81
Total domestic	$ 2.02	$ 2.03	$ 2.03	$ 1.96	$ 1.89
International					
Express	$ 3.78	$ 3.83	$ 3.97	$ 4.02	$ 4.47
Freight	0.77	0.79	0.82	0.96	1.05
Total international	$ 1.03	$ 1.10	$ 1.17	$ 1.31	$ 1.35
Total shipments	$ 1.82	$ 1.89	$ 1.90	$ 1.85	$ 1.79
Average Revenue per Shipment:					
Domestic					
Overnight	$ 9.83	$ 9.74	$ 9.44	$ 9.26	$ 9.33
Next-afternoon service	6.99	6.63	6.43	6.27	5.86
Second-day service	7.03	7.45	7.49	7.22	7.15
Ground delivery service	5.60	—	—	—	—
100 lbs. and over	176.63	198.24	189.82	163.47	184.74
Total domestic	$ 8.76	$ 8.92	$ 8.76	$ 8.56	$ 8.45
International					
Express	$ 18.48	$ 19.00	$ 20.34	$ 20.72	$ 21.26
Freight	622.47	607.08	571.04	540.07	592.41
Total international	$ 57.33	$ 57.96	$ 52.05	$ 56.03	$ 69.78

EXHIBIT 4

Airborne Express Shipment Volume Statistics, 1997–2001

	Year Ended December 31				
	2001	**2000**	**1999**	**1998**	**1997**
Annual Growth Rates:					
Domestic					
Overnight	−8.1%	−0.5%	0.0%	7.8%	18.0%
Next-afternoon service	−4.1%	−3.5%	−3.4%	8.2%	92.5%
Second-day service	15.4%	12.3%	2.6%	2.3%	−11.8%
Ground delivery service	—	—	—		
100 lbs. and over	−15.5%	−3.4%	−19.8%	5.9%	13.8%
Total domestic	0.1%	1.9%	−0.1%	6.6%	16.8%
International					
Express	−4.3%	−7.3%	10.3%	15.2%	16.1%
Freight	−2.5%	0.5%	−8.1%	−8.8%	−11.2%
Total international	−4.2%	−6.8%	9.1%	13.2%	13.2%
Total shipments	0.1%	1.7%	0.1%	6.7%	16.8%
Shipments by Category as a Percentage of Total Shipments:					
Domestic					
Overnight	51.7%	56.3%	57.6%	57.7%	57.1%
Next-afternoon service	15.8%	16.5%	17.4%	18.0%	17.8%
Second-day service	29.0%	25.1%	22.7%	22.2%	23.2%
Ground delivery service	1.5%	—	—		
100 lbs. and over	0.1%	0.1%	0.1%	0.1%	0.1%
Total domestic	98.1%	98.0%	97.8%	98.0%	98.1%
International					
Express	1.8%	1.9%	2.1%	1.9%	1.7%
Freight	0.1%	0.1%	0.1%	0.1%	0.2%
Total international	1.9%	2.0%	2.2%	2.0%	1.9%
Total shipments	100.0%	100.0%	100.0%	100.0%	100.0%

EXHIBIT 5

Work Force and Productivity Statistics

	Year Ended December 31				
	2001	**2000**	**1999**	**1998**	**1997**
Labor:					
Number of employees					
Full-time	15,300	16,000	15,200	14,300	13,500
Part-time	7,200	8,100	8,300	8,700	9,000
Total employees	22,500	24,100	23,500	23,000	22,500
Labor Productivity:					
Total salaries, wages, and benefits (in thousands)	$1,212,122	$1,189,051	$1,098,557	$1,029,180	$945,562
Labor cost as a percentage of total revenues	37.7%	36.3%	35.0%	33.5%	32.5%
Labor cost as a percentage of operating expenses	37.6%	36.8%	36.8%	36.2%	35.2%
Labor cost per shipment	$3.68	$3.61	$3.40	$3.19	$3.12
Labor cost per FTE *	$ 60,354	$ 56,781	$ 53,963	$ 51,796	$ 50,100
Shipments per employee hour *	7.9	7.6	7.6	7.8	7.7
Shipments per FTE *	16,394	15,713	15,887	16,258	16,040
Full-time equivalents	20,084	20,941	20,358	19,870	18,874

*Computed on the basis of paid full-time equivalents and employee hours.

airline that is 23 percent owned by DHL, to acquire Airborne Express.

Meanwhile, Airborne went about its business, and in the first quarter of 2002 showed that it may be down but is not yet out. The company surprised analysts by earning a $5.3 million profit in the quarter (analysts had expected a $5 million loss). This profit was achieved despite a decline in the volume of overnight deliveries. The key to the performance was the new ground delivery service (GDS), which averaged 92,000 shipments a day, well above the company's own forecasts of 60,000 shipments a day.

Commenting on this performance, one analyst noted that the GDS is the key "to stopping the market share declines in the overnight express business, and it's the key to [Airborne] being more competitive in the bundling of freight services to fight back against FedEx and UPS."[3]

ENDNOTES

1. Standard and Poor's Industry Survey, Airlines, March, 2002.
2. Source: http://www.airborne.com/Company/History .asp?nav5AboutAirborne/CompanyInfo/History.
3. M. Schlangenstein, "Unexpected Delivery from Airborne," *Seattle Times*, April 30, 2002, p. C2.

31

Blockbuster in 2002

This case was prepared by Gareth R. Jones, Texas A&M University.

In June 2002, John Antioco, Blockbuster Inc.'s CEO, was reflecting on the challenges facing the company in the next five years. DVDs were increasingly becoming the rental medium of choice, and the video game market was booming. How long would the VHS market remain profitable, and how quickly would the threat of video-on-demand (VOD) bite into Blockbuster's revenues? With its nearly 8,000 global stores, 5,400 in the United States alone, Blockbuster had an enviable brand name and enormous marketing clout, but how could Antioco use it in a way to increase revenues and prevent the return of the problems that had plagued the company when he took over in 1997? What strategies needed to be developed to strengthen Blockbuster's business model in the coming years?

Blockbuster's History

David Cook, the founder of Blockbuster, formed David P. Cook & Associates, Inc., in 1978 to offer consulting and computer services to the petroleum and real estate industries. He created programs to analyze and evaluate oil and gas properties and to compute oil and gas reserves. When oil prices began to decline in 1983 due to the breakdown of the OPEC cartel, his business started to decline and Cook began evaluating alternative businesses in which he

could apply his skills. He decided to leave his current business by selling his company and to enter the video-rental business based on a concept for a video superstore. He opened his first superstore, called Blockbuster Video, in October 1985 in Dallas, Texas.

Cook developed his idea for a video superstore by analyzing the trends in the video industry occurring at that time. During the 1980s, the number of households that owned VCRs was increasing rapidly and so were the number of video-rental stores set up to serve their needs. In 1983, 7,000 video-rental stores were in operation; by 1985, there were 19,000; and by 1986, there were over 25,000, of which 13,000 were individually owned. These mom-and-pop video stores generally operated for a limited number of hours, offered customers only a limited selection of videos, and were often located in out-of-the-way strip shopping centers. These small stores often charged a membership fee in addition to the tape rental charge, and generally, customers brought an empty box to the video-store clerk, who would exchange it for a tape if it was available—a procedure that was often time-consuming, particularly at peak times such as evenings and weekends.

Cook realized that, as VCRs became more widespread and the number of available film titles steadily increased, customers would begin to demand a larger and more-varied selection of titles from video stores. They would also demand more convenient store locations and quicker in-store service than mom-and-pop stores could offer. He realized that the time was right for the development of the next generation of video stores, and he used this opportunity to implement his video superstore concept, which is still the center of Blockbuster's strategy.

The Video Superstore Concept

Cook's superstore concept was based on several components. First, Cook decided that, to give his video superstores a unique identity that would appeal to customers, the stores should be highly visible, stand-alone structures rather than part of a shopping center. In addition, his superstores would be large (between 3,800 and 10,000 square feet), well lit, and brightly colored (for example, each store has a bright blue sign with "Blockbuster Video" displayed in huge white letters). Each store would have ample parking and would be located in the vicinity of a large urban population to maximize potential exposure to customers.

Second, each superstore would offer a wide variety of tapes, such as adventure, children's, instructional, and video game titles. Believing that movie preferences differ in different locations, Cook decided to have each store offer a different selection of between 7,000 and 13,000 film titles organized alphabetically in over thirty categories. New releases were arranged alphabetically against the back wall of each store to make it easier for customers to make their selections.

Third, he created the concept of a three-day rental period for $3, based on the belief that many customers, particularly those with children, wanted to keep tapes for longer than a one-day period. (In 1991, a two-evening rental program was implemented, making new releases only $2.50 for two evenings during the first three weeks after release; after this period, the usual $3 for three evenings applied.) If the tape is available, it is behind the cover box. The customer takes the tape to the checkout line and hands the cassette and his or her membership card to the clerk, who scans the bar codes on both the tape and the card. The customer is then handed the tape and told that it is due back by midnight three days later. For example, if the tape were rented Thursday afternoon, it would be due back Saturday at midnight.

Fourth, Cook's superstores targeted the largest market segments, adults in the eighteen- to forty-nine-year-old group and children in the six- to twelve-year-old group. Cook believed that if his stores could attract children, then the rest of the family would probably follow. Blockbuster carries no X-rated movies and its goal is to be "America's Family Video Store." New releases are carefully chosen based on reviews and box-office success to maximize their appeal to families.

Finally, Cook decided that his superstores would offer customers the convenience of long operating hours and quick service, generally from 10:00 A.M. to midnight seven days a week, because he believed that customers want to choose a movie and get out of the store quickly. Members receive a plastic identification card that is read by the point-of-sale equipment developed by the company. This system uses a laser bar-code scanner to read important information from both the rental cassette and the ID card. The rental amount is computed by the system and due at the time of rental. Movie returns are scanned by laser, and any late or rewind fees are recorded on the account and automatically recalled the next time the member rents a tape. This system reduced customer checkout time and increased convenience. In addition, it provided Blockbuster with data on customer demographics, cassette rental patterns, and the number of times each cassette had been rented, all of which resulted in a database that increased in value over time as it grew bigger.

These five elements of Blockbuster's approach were successful, and customers responded well. Wherever Blockbuster opened, the local mom-and-pop stores usually closed down, unable to compete with the number of titles and the quality of service that a Blockbuster store could provide. By 1986, Blockbuster owned eight stores and had franchised eleven more to interested investors who could see the potential of this new approach to video rental. Initially, the company opened stores in markets with a minimum population of 100,000. Franchises were located in Atlanta, Chicago, Detroit, Houston, San Antonio, and Phoenix. New stores, which cost about $500,000 to $700,000 to equip, grossed an average of $70,000 to $80,000 a month.

Early Growth and Expansion

John Melk, an executive at Waste Management Corp. who had invested in a Blockbuster franchise in Chicago, would change the history of the company. He contacted H. "Wayne" Huizenga, a former Waste Management colleague, in February 1987 to tell him of the enormous revenue and profits his franchise was making. Huizenga had experience in growing small companies in fragmented industries. In 1955, he had quit college to manage a three-truck trash-hauling operation; in 1962, he bought his own operation, Southern Sanitation. In 1968, Southern Sanitation merged with Ace Partnership, Acme Disposal, and Atlas Refuse Service to form Waste Management. In succeeding years, Huizenga borrowed against Waste Management stock to buy over 100 small companies that provided services such as auto-parts cleaning, dry cleaning, lawn care, and portable-toilet rentals. He used their cash flows to purchase yet more firms. By the time Huizenga, vice chairman, resigned in 1984, Waste Management was a $6 billion Fortune 500 company and Huizenga was a wealthy man.

Although Huizenga had a low opinion of video retailers, he agreed to visit a Blockbuster store. Expecting a dingy store renting X-rated films, he was pleasantly surprised to find a brightly lit, family video supermarket. Detecting the opportunity to make Cook's superstore concept national, Huizenga, Melk, and Donald Flynn (another Waste Management executive) agreed to purchase 33 percent of Blockbuster from Cook for $18.6 million in 1986. (They also became directors at this time.) In 1987, CEO David Cook decided to take his money and leave Blockbuster to pursue another venture at Amtech Corporation. With the departure of the founder, Huizenga took over as CEO in April 1987, with the goal of making Blockbuster a national company and the industry leader in the video-rental market.

Recognizing his inexperience in retailing and franchising, Huizenga hired top managers who knew how to develop and grow a retail chain. First, he hired Luigi Salavaneschi, a former McDonald's executive who had gained considerable expertise in facility location during his involvement in the rapid expansion of McDonald's. He also hired Thomas Gruber, a former McDonald's marketing executive, as the chief marketing officer. Through their experience at McDonald's, these men had the background to orchestrate Blockbuster's rapid growth.

Blockbuster's Explosive Growth

Blockbuster's new top management team mapped out the company's growth strategy, the elements of which are discussed in this section.

Location

Store location is a critical issue to a video-rental store, and Huizenga moved quickly with Salavaneschi to obtain the best store locations in each geographic area into which Blockbuster expanded. They developed a "cluster strategy," whereby they targeted a particular geographic market, such as Dallas, Boston, or Los Angeles, and then opened new stores one at a time until they had saturated the market. Thus, within a few years, the local mom-and-pop stores found themselves surrounded and many, unable to compete with Blockbuster, closed down. Video superstores were always located near busy, well-traveled routes to establish a broad customer base. The cluster strategy eventually brought Blockbuster into 133 television markets (the geographic area that television reaches), where it reached 75 to 85 percent of the U.S. population.

Marketing

On the marketing side, Blockbuster's chief marketing officer, Tom Gruber, applied his knowledge of McDonald's family-oriented advertising strategy to strengthen Cook's original vision of the video-rental business. In 1988, he introduced Blockbuster Kids to strengthen the company's position as a family video store. This promotion, aimed at the six- to twelve-year-old age group, introduced four characters and a dog to appeal to Blockbuster's young customers. To demonstrate additional commitment to families, each store stocked forty titles recommended for children and provided a kids' clubhouse equipped with televisions and toys so that children could amuse themselves while their parents browsed for videos. In addition, Blockbuster allowed its members to specify what rating category of tapes (such as PG or R) may be rented through their account. A policy called Youth-Restricted Viewing forbade R-rated tape rentals to children under seventeen. Blockbuster also implemented the free Kidprint Program: a child's name, address, and height are recorded on a videotape given to parents and local police for identification purposes. In addition, Blockbuster has a program called America's Most Important Videos Are Free, which offers free rental of public-service tapes about topics such as fire safety and parenting. Finally, to attract customers and to build brand recognition, Gruber initiated joint promotions between Blockbuster and companies like Domino's Pizza, McDonald's, and Pepsi-Cola—something it continues to do today.

Operations

Blockbuster also made great progress on the operations side of the business. As discussed earlier, the operation of a Blockbuster superstore is designed to provide fast checkout and effective inventory management. The company designed its point-of-sale computer system, which is available only to company-owned and franchised stores, to make rental and return transactions easy.

Rapid expansion strains a company's operating systems. To support its stores, Blockbuster opened a 25,000-square-foot distribution center in Dallas in 1986. The distribution center has the capacity to store 200,000 cassette tapes that are removed from the original container. A label with a security device is affixed to the cassette. Each videotape is then bar-coded and placed into a hard plastic rental case. The facility has the capacity to process the initial inventory requirement of about 10,000 tapes for up to three superstores per day. In addition, Blockbuster supplies the equipment and fixtures, such as computer software and hardware, shelving, signs, and cash registers, needed to operate a new store. In 1987, the physical facilities of the distribution center were expanded to double capacity, to 400,000 videocassettes.

Blockbuster's growing buying power also gave it another operations advantage. As the largest single purchaser of prerecorded videotapes in the U.S. market, it could negotiate discounts off retail price. Cassettes are bought at an average of $40 per tape and rented for three nights at $3. Thus, the cash investment on hit videotapes is recovered in forty-five to sixty days, and the investment on nonhit titles is regained in two-and-a-half to three months. In its early days, Blockbuster could use its efficient distribution system to send extra copies of films declining in popularity to new stores, where demand is increasing. This ability to transfer tapes to locations where they are most demanded is very important for customers who want new tapes on the shelves when they are first released. It also allows the company to use its inventory to the best advantage and to receive the maximum benefit from each videotape.

Management and Structure

For Blockbuster, as for any company, rapid growth poses the risk of losing control over daily operations and allowing costs to escalate. Recognizing this predicament, Blockbuster established three operating divisions to manage the functional activities necessary to retain effective control over its operations as it grew. Blockbuster Distribution Corp. was created to handle the area licensing and franchising of new stores, and to service their start-up and operation—offering assistance with the selection, acquisition, assembly, packaging, inventory, and distribution of videocassettes, supplies, and computer equipment. Blockbuster Management Corp. was established to assist with the training of new store management, facility location and acquisition, and employee training. Finally, Blockbuster Computer Systems Inc. was formed to install, maintain, and support the software programs for the inventory and point-of-sale equipment. These three divisions provide all the support services necessary to manage store expansion.

Rapid growth also led Blockbuster to oversee store operations through a regional- and district-level organizational structure. In 1988, responsibility for store development and operations was decentralized to the regional level. However, corporate headquarters is kept fully informed of developments in each regional area, even in each store, through the computerized inventory and sales system. For example, Blockbuster's corporate inventory and point-of-sale computer systems track sales and inventory in each store and each region. The role of regional management is to oversee the stores in their regions, providing advice and monitoring stores' performance to make sure that they keep up Blockbuster's high standards of operation as its chain of superstores grow.

New-Store Expansion

With Blockbuster's functional-level competencies in place, the next step for Huizenga was to begin a rapid program of growth and expansion. Huizenga believed that expanding rapidly to increase revenue and market share was crucial for success in the video-rental industry. Under his leadership, Blockbuster opened new stores quickly, developed a franchising program, and began to acquire competitors to increase the number of its stores.

To facilitate rapid expansion, Blockbuster began to use its skills in store location, distribution, and sales. At first, Blockbuster focused on large markets, preferring to enter a market with a potential capacity for 500 stores—normally a large city. Later, Blockbuster decided to enter smaller market segments, like towns with a minimum of 20,000 people within driving distance. All stores were built and operated using the superstore concept described earlier. Using the services of its three divisions, it steadily increased its number of new-store openings until, by 1993, it owned over 2,500 video stores.

Blockbuster's rapid growth was also attributable to Huizenga's skills in acquisitions. Beginning in 1986, the company began to acquire many smaller regional video chains to gain a significant market presence in a city or region. In 1987, for example, the twenty-nine video stores of Movies to Go were acquired to expand Blockbuster's presence in the Midwest. Blockbuster then used this acquisition as a starting point for opening many more stores in the region. Similarly, in 1989, it acquired 175 video stores from Major Video Corp. and Video Library to develop a presence in southern California. In 1991, it took over 209 Erol's Inc. stores to obtain the stronghold that Erol's previously held in the mid-Atlantic states. All acquired stores were made to conform to Blockbuster's standards. Any store that could not was closed down. Most acquisitions were financed by existing cash flow or by issuing new shares of stock rather than by taking on new debt. These deals reflect Huizenga's reluctance to borrow money.

Licensing and Franchising

Recognizing the need to build market share rapidly and develop a national brand name, Huizenga also recruited top management to start an ambitious franchise program. Franchising, in which the franchisee is solely responsible for all financial commitments connected with opening a new store, allowed Blockbuster to expand rapidly without incurring debt. The downside of franchising is that Blockbuster had to share profits with the franchise owners. When franchising, it is important to maintain consistency in stores. Thus, the franchisees were required to operate their stores in the same way as company-owned stores and to follow the same store format for rental selection and the use of proprietary point-of-sale equipment.

Blockbuster's current method of franchising was established in January 1988. Under this plan, a franchisee is granted the right to open a store for twenty years, with renewal rights of an additional five years if the store is in compliance with agreements. All franchise owners pay an initial fee of up to $55,000 for the privilege of using the Blockbuster Video trademark. The capital investment required to open a store generally ranges from $425,000 to $650,000. All licensed and franchised stores must meet Blockbuster's design criteria and use its standardized operating systems so customers have no problems identifying and using the company's stores. A charge of up to $36,000 is assessed for software, and the monthly software-maintenance fee varies from $500 to $650. Franchise owners pay royalty fees from 3 to 8 percent of gross revenue, as determined by their agreement with Blockbuster; remit a certain percentage for marketing and promotions; and contribute 1 percent of gross receipts for national advertising. Contributions to national advertising began in 1989 when the five hundredth store was opened. All rental transactions must be recorded in the point-of-sale inventory control program, and any inventory must be approved by Blockbuster. Franchise owners are also required to buy from Blockbuster at least 5,000 videotapes of the required initial inventory of 7,000. In addition, the franchise owner must complete Blockbuster's training program or hire a manager who has completed Blockbuster's training program to run the store. Assistance with activities such as site selection and employee training are available for a fee.

Franchising facilitated the rapid expansion of Blockbuster Video. By 1992, the company had over 1,000 franchised stores, compared to 2,000 company-owned stores. Recognizing the long-term profit advantages of owning its own stores, however, Blockbuster began to repurchase attractive territories from franchisees. In 1993, the company spent $248 million to buy the 400 stores of its two largest franchisees and, with a new store opening every day, it owned over 2,500 stores by the end of 1993.

By the end of 1992, however, despite its rapid growth, Blockbuster still controlled only about 15 percent of the market—its 27,000 smaller rivals shared the rest. Consequently, in 1993, Blockbuster announced plans for a new round of store openings and acquisitions that would give it a 25 to 30 percent market share within two or three years.

The Home-Video Industry

By 1990, revenues from video rentals exceeded the revenues obtained in movie theaters. For example, video-rental revenues rose to $11 billion in 1991, compared to movie theater revenues of $4.8 billion and cable movie channel (like HBO) revenues of

$5.2 billion. The huge growth in industry revenues led to increased competition for customers, and as noted above, 28,000 video stores operated in the United States in 1990.

Blockbuster's rapid growth put it in a commanding position. In 1990, it had no national competitor and was the only company operating beyond a regional level. The next largest competitor, West Coast Video, had only $120 million in 1991 revenues, while Blockbuster had revenues of $868 million. However, Blockbuster faced many competitors at the local and regional levels. For example, various supermarket chains across the United States, such as Kroger and Winn Dixie, also expanded their video-rental operations and had video-rental revenues of $1.35 billion in 1991. In some markets, however, price wars started to break out. In the San Antonio market, for example, competition among video stores resulted in Blockbuster reducing its prices to $2.00, but then HEB (a supermarket chain) responded by dropping its price to $1.50 and offering $.99 specials, which started a new price war.

Mature Market

As the video-rental market matured, the level of competition in the industry changed. During the 1980s, video rentals grew rapidly due to the proliferation of VCRs. By 1990, however, 70 percent of households had VCRs, compared to 2 percent in 1980, and industry growth dropped from the previous double digits to 7 percent. The slow growth in VCR ownership and rentals made competition more severe. To a large degree, competition in the video-rental industry was fierce because new competitors could enter the market with relative ease; the only purchase necessary is videotapes. Unlike small video-rental companies, however, Blockbuster could negotiate discounts with tape suppliers because it buys new releases in such huge volumes.

New Technology

One growing problem facing Blockbuster by the early 1990s was the variety of new ways in which customers could view movies and enjoy other kinds of entertainment. Blockbuster has always felt competition both from other sources of movies—such as cable television and movie theaters—and from other forms of entertainment—such as bowling, baseball games, and outdoor activities. In the 1990s, technology began to give customers more ways to watch movies. New technological threats included pay-per-view or video-on-demand systems, digital compression, and direct broadcast satellites.

Pay-per-view movies could become a major competitive threat to video-rental stores. Currently, with pay-per-view systems, cable customers can call their local cable company and pay a fee to have a scheduled movie, concert, or sporting event aired on their television. Soon, a cable customer could call up their local "video company" and choose any movie to be aired on his or her television for a fee; the cable company would make the movie available when the customer wanted it. Telephone companies are becoming interested in the potential for pay-for-view because the networks of fiber-optic cable they are installing in ordinary households can transmit movies as well. Huizenga claims Blockbuster is not overly concerned about pay-per-view systems because only one-third of U.S. households have access to pay-per-view, and fiber-optic cables are expensive. It also claimed that home video rental is cheaper than pay-per-view and new releases are obtained thirty to forty-five days before pay-per-view.

Video-on-demand takes the pay-per-view concept further. Bellcore, the research branch of the regional Bell companies, invented video-on-demand. With this system (still in the trial stage), a customer will use an interactive box to select a movie from a list of thousands. The choice will be transmitted to an information warehouse that will store thousands of tapes in digital formats. The selected video will then be routed back to the customer's house through a series of switches, and a signal splitter will send the movie into the home through the phone lines. This technology bypasses the local video-rental store because the movies are stored on digital tape at the cable company's headquarters.

Movie companies or video stores like Blockbuster could function as the information warehouses from which the video selections are made. Blockbuster is interested in acting as the warehouse so that it can control the video-on-demand market, which could become a direct threat to video rental as the technology is refined. Blockbuster began discussions with Bell Atlantic Corporation, which developed a video-on-demand system for customers in northern Virginia. Bell hopes to offer between thirty and one hundred films, which would be instantly available to customers. Blockbuster, which would provide the movies for the video-on-demand system, views this move as an expansion of its business rather than a cannibalization of video rentals.

U.S. West, one of the baby bells, also announced plans to build a video-on-demand network to serve 13 million homes in fourteen states. With its partner, Time Warner, it planned eventually to reach 23 percent of the viewing market. The linking of phone companies with other entertainment companies could become a direct threat to Blockbuster, but Huizenga believes the local Blockbuster store could become the center or hub of the video-on-demand network. He feels that phone companies would prefer to deal with Blockbuster rather than with companies like Time Warner or Paramount, both of which lack Blockbuster's skills in video retailing and its established customer base—the 30 million customers who make 600 million trips per year to the local video store. Note that if Blockbuster did become the information warehouse of video-on-demand systems, videotape rentals would decrease, hurting Blockbuster's own rental revenues and likely finishing off the local mom-and-pop stores. If all worked out the way Huizenga envisions, in the long run, Blockbuster would seize control of both the video-rental and video-on-demand market.

Other new technologies include digital compression and direct broadcast satellites. Digital compression allows up to five television channels to be sent on the same bandwidth that can be used to carry only one channel. This provides more space for movies to be sent to customers. Direct broadcast satellites (DBS) were also an emerging threat because cable service could be obtained anywhere in the United States by installing a small, 2-foot-diameter satellite dish. The dishes, which first cost between $500 and $700, soon fell in price as companies like Hughes mass-produced them. Existing land-based cable companies responded by installing vast networks of fiber-optic cable also capable of carrying hundreds of channels. These new technologies allowed companies to transmit movies directly into people's homes, which would harm the video-rental industry because customers would no longer have to go to video-rental stores to get a movie.

Blockbuster's Emerging Strategies

Blockbuster also took advantage of its great size and secure financial position (provided by the large growth in its domestic revenues) to diversify into new industries and into global markets. It believed it could transfer the skills and capabilities it had developed in the domestic video-rental market to new markets and countries.

Global Expansion

Seventy percent of the world's VCRs are in countries outside the United States, and foreign countries account for half of total world video-rental revenues. In 1991, the United States was the largest video market, with revenues of $11 billion; Japan was second, with $2.6 billion, followed by the United Kingdom, with $1.4 billion, and Canada, with $1.2 billion. Blockbuster began to expand into international markets in 1989 when it saw the opportunity to exploit its marketing expertise, superstore concept, operating knowledge, financial strength, and ability to attract franchisees abroad.

Just as it did in the United States, Blockbuster started a program both to build new video superstores and to acquire foreign competitors abroad. Planning to be a leader in home entertainment around the world, Blockbuster's objective was to obtain a 25 percent share of international revenue by 1995 and to have 2,000 stores in international markets by 1996. In 1989, stores were opened in Canada and the United Kingdom. In 1990, Blockbuster opened its first store in Puerto Rico. It continued its expansion into the United Kingdom, Canada, the Virgin Islands, Venezuela, and Spain. Franchise agreements were also signed in Japan, Australia, and Mexico.

In Japan, Blockbuster formed a joint venture in March 1991 with Den Fujita & Co., Ltd., which runs McDonald's Co. Japan and has a stake in Toys "R" Us Japan Ltd. This venture opened fifteen stores in Japan in 1992, thirty stores in l993, and 1,000 stores within ten years. Due to fierce price competition, the Japan stores are meeting only 90 percent of sales projections. Under the terms of this fifty-fifty joint venture agreement with Fujita & Co., Ltd., Blockbuster can franchise more stores in Japan. Blockbuster is importing its video concepts to a market that is very interested in video rentals. By forming a joint venture, Blockbuster can benefit from the expertise of Japanese locals in running a business in Japan.

To expand in the United Kingdom, in 1992 Blockbuster purchased Cityvision PLC, the United Kingdom's largest video retailer, for $81 million cash and 3.9 million shares of stock. At this time, Cityvision ran 875 stores in Britain and Austria under the name Ritz. Blockbuster transformed the Ritz outlets into Blockbuster stores and used the chain as a start for additional expansion into Europe, just as it had taken over large video chains in the United States on its way to becoming the national leader. Joint ventures were also negotiated in France, Germany, and Italy. Blockbuster increased the number of franchise stores in Mexico, Chile, Venezuela, and Spain. By the end of 1992, the company had 952 stores in nine foreign countries, with plans to establish at least 1,200 more by 1995.

Blockbuster created an international home-video division to oversee and manage its expansion into foreign markets. Besides having expertise in international operations, marketing, merchandising, product purchasing, distribution, franchising, real estate, and field support, this division is proficient at dealing with differences in entertainment, language, and business cultures in different countries and is successfully implementing Blockbuster's domestic strategy in its foreign operations.

Diversification

Blockbuster became a national video-rental chain because of the way it positioned itself in the market as a family-oriented store with a wide selection of videos, convenient hours and locations, and fast checkout. Blockbuster began to expand its entertainment concept into several new markets or industries, such as film entertainment programming and music retailing. To increase its revenue, Blockbuster also made deals to broaden its range of product offerings.

To enter the entertainment programming market, Blockbuster invested in Spelling Entertainment Group and Republic Pictures. Both companies have large film libraries—a source of inexpensive movies for Blockbuster's retail operations. For example, Blockbuster gained access to Spelling's library of 600 feature films and fifty-five television shows, including *Beverly Hills 90210*. The deal also provided Blockbuster with access to the broadcast and cable television markets. Spelling's proficiency in cable network programming could help Blockbuster, which was contemplating building its own cable channel. Republic's programming library includes classics such as *High Noon, The Quiet Man,* and *The Bells of St. Mary's.* This investment also strengthened Block-

buster's hold on the programming side of the entertainment industry because Republic has ongoing deals with the television, home-video, and theatrical markets.

Blockbuster also chose the music retail business as an area into which it could expand its entertainment concept. As in the video-rental industry, many music stores were mom-and-pop businesses or part of small, regional chains. Music stores had begun to market videos such as the Walt Disney collection, musicals, and family movies. Blockbuster saw a fit between selling records, cassettes, and compact discs (CDs) and renting or selling videos. So it decided to employ the same strategy it had used in the video-rental market: opening new stores and acquiring chains of music stores using the revenues from its video superstores. However, Blockbuster decided not to sell CDs and cassettes in its video stores. Instead, its music business was to be operated independently, with stores using the same superstore concept that was so successful in the video-rental business. The planned stores would be large and would offer a wide selection of music products such as recorded music, computer software, games, and even books. The proposed new name for the music-store chain was Chartbusters.

As part of its plan to diversify into the $8 billion record industry, Blockbuster agreed to buy Sound Warehouse and Music Plus, two record-store chains, for $185 million. At the time, Sound Warehouse was the seventh largest music retailer and Music Plus was the twelfth largest. These two retail chains had a total of 236 stores in thirty-five states, primarily in California and the South. This acquisition made Blockbuster the seventh largest music chain.

With 30 million video customers, Blockbuster felt it could transfer and share its resources and capabilities. For example, it could introduce joint promotions and advertising between its music and video stores, giving a customer a 15 percent discount on a CD for renting two videos. Customers who visit one of the video stores would be encouraged to visit Blockbuster's music stores, and vice versa. Because of its ability to attract families and young people, Blockbuster believed it had a considerable advantage. In 1991, 64 percent of record sales were made to people age fifteen to thirty-four, Blockbuster's main customer group.

The company also branched its entertainment concept. In 1990, it sponsored the first Blockbuster

Bowl—Florida State University versus Penn State. The company also saw an opportunity in themed, family-oriented entertainment centers, which would have batting cages, miniature golf, a high-tech video arcade, virtual-reality computer simulators, play areas for children, food service, and merchandising. It planned to open the first center in 1993. In June 1990, Blockbuster formed a joint venture to develop and operate three amphitheaters, circular outdoor arenas for rock concerts and other entertainment events. The first amphitheater was opened in Phoenix, Arizona, in November 1990. Other entertainment deals include gaining exclusive rights to distribute the 1990 World Series and other major-league baseball video productions and exclusive retail rights to the 1992 Summer Olympics from NBC. These events would be distributed on video.

In an effort to manage the companies it acquired and in its quest to become a full-service home entertainment retailer, Blockbuster reorganized in 1993, and split into several divisions: domestic home video, international home video, music retailing, international music retailing, new-technology ventures, and other entertainment ventures.

Huizenga Sells Blockbuster to Viacom

Blockbuster's stated goal in 1992 was to increase net income by at least 20 percent a year over the next five years. In October 1992, Blockbuster Video opened its three thousandth store and its one thousandth international store. Although Blockbuster, with its rapid growth and large positive cash flow, seemed poised to become an entertainment powerhouse, Huizenga knew that there were clouds ahead. The rapid advance in digital technology, including the Internet and broadband, meant that video-on-demand, a service in which customers could download new movies directly from their cable company or some other outlet, was a growing reality. Some analysts were even suggesting that Blockbuster was a dinosaur. And Huizenga soon found out that the music retailing industry was also highly competitive and that he faced fierce competition from large music retail chains. The music retail industry had many more experienced competitors than the video-rental industry. Some major competitors, like Sam Goody's and Tower Records, also had plans to accelerate the development of their own music megastores. Profit margins in music retailing were narrow, and large merchandisers like Wal-Mart were starting to lower the prices of CDs. Price wars were flaring up as a result. Even in the video-rental business, entrepreneurs who had watched Blockbuster's rapid growth still felt there was an opportunity for entry. Chains such as Hollywood Video began to expand rapidly, and increased competition seemed imminent in the video-rental business, too.

Huizenga decided that the time was ripe to sell the Blockbuster chain, just as he had sold other chains before, and an opportunity came when Sumner Redstone, chairman of Viacom, become involved in an aggressive bidding war to buy Paramount Studios, the movie company.

Redstone recognized the value of Blockbuster's huge cash flow in helping to fund the debt needed to take over Paramount. Ignoring the risks involved in taking over Blockbuster, Viacom acquired the company in 1994 for $8.4 billion in stock. (Further details about the logic behind the acquisition are found in the Viacom case later in the book.) Huizenga left the company and took his huge stockholdings with him.

Just the next year, in 1995, a tidal wave of problems hit the Blockbuster chain. First, a brutal price war broke out in the video-rental industry as new video chain start-ups fought for a niche in major markets and for some of the lucrative industry revenues. Second, movie studios started to lower the price of tapes, realizing that they could make more money by selling them directly to customers rather than letting companies like Blockbuster make the money through tape rentals. Third, as both Blockbuster's video and music operations expanded, it became obvious that the company did not have the materials management and distribution systems needed to manage the complex flow of products to its stores. Overhead costs started to soar. Combined with declines in revenues, the company turned from making a profit to incurring a loss. Blockbuster's cash flow was much less useful to Redstone now, burdened as he was by the huge debt for Paramount. Blockbuster's declining performance led to Viacom's stock price dropping sharply, and Redstone reacted by firing its top managers and searching for an experienced executive to turn the Blockbuster division around.

Blockbuster, 1996–1998

Given Blockbuster's soaring overhead costs, Redstone naturally looked for an executive who had experience in low-cost merchandising and information systems. In 1996, he pulled off a coup by hiring William Fields, the heir apparent to David Glass, Wal-Mart's CEO, and an information systems and logistics expert. Redstone saw Fields as the ideal person to turn Blockbuster's now 4,500 stores into broad-based entertainment retail outlets. Understanding Wal-Mart's sophisticated distribution system, Fields began planning a huge state-of-the-art distribution facility that would serve all Blockbuster's U.S. stores and replace its outdated facility. He also started the development of a new state-of-the-art point-of-sale merchandising information system that would give Blockbuster real-time feedback on which videos were generating the most money and when they should be transferred to stores in other regions to make the most of Blockbuster's stock of videos—its most important physical resource. Third, Fields added more retail merchandise, such as candy, comics, and audio books, to Blockbuster's product mix. The results of these efforts would take a couple of years to bear fruit, however. So to reduce debt, Viacom also scaled back expansion plans for the company, cutting by 25 percent the number of new video stores it planned to open in 1997 to 600, from the 800 it opened in 1996.

Some analysts believed that, by 1997, Redstone recognized the negative impact of Blockbuster's operations on its stock price and was trying to cut costs and thus boost short-term profits and harvest the company so that he could spin off Blockbuster. Redstone may also have sensed that the troubled division was not going to be fixed fast. Sales were expected to be flat in 1997.

Apparently, Fields and Redstone disagreed over Blockbuster's future in the Viacom empire. Its performance continued to decline in the first quarter of 1997, with a drop in profit of 20 percent. Only thirteen months after taking over at Blockbuster, Fields resigned in April 1997. Viacom's stock fell to a three-year low. Redstone argued that this was absurd because Blockbuster generated $3 billion in revenue and $800 million in cash flow for Viacom. In 1996, he argued it was due for a rebound in profitability. However, the specter of video-on-demand and increased price competition in the music and video business made analysts wonder if Blockbuster was going to recover. Furthermore, Fields was the expert in distribution and logistics. They wondered if Blockbuster would now be able to use its new distribution facility to cut costs when it opened. So many retail chains had filed for Chapter 11 bankruptcy in the 1990s, and many wondered if Blockbuster would be next on the list.

Once again, Redstone searched for an executive who could help turn Blockbuster around. John Antioco, the chief of PepsiCo's Taco Bell restaurants, was in the news at the time. In just eight months, Antioco introduced a new menu, new pricing, and a new store setup, thus engineering an about-face in Taco Bell's performance. A mounting loss was turned into rising profit. Antioco seemed to be the perfect choice as Blockbuster's CEO.

After Antioco took the helm, he assessed the situation. The video-rental market was still flat. Satellite services, with hundreds of movie channels, were becoming an increasingly popular way of watching new movies; sales of movie videos were soaring as their price came down in outlets such as Wal-Mart. Fields's strategy of enlarging the entertainment product lines carried in Blockbuster stores seemed like a logical move, but it had failed as costs continued to rise. Products had a short shelf life because changing fads and fashions made the value of Blockbuster's inventory unpredictable. What should Antioco do?

In fact, Antioco had once orchestrated a strategy similar to Fields's when he was in charge of taking the convenience store operator, CircleK, out of bankruptcy. At CircleK, Antioco had attempted to generate increased sales by encouraging customers who stopped for gas to enter the store and buy lottery tickets, prepared food, and so on. He had also redecorated the chain to attract customers and installed the then-new credit-card fuel machines to speed the fueling process. It seemed that Fields's basic approach was not wrong; the problem was defining Blockbuster's merchandising mix. And how should Antioco manage the purchase and distribution of Blockbuster's biggest ongoing expense, videotapes, to create a value chain that would lead to increased profitability?

Antioco realized that he needed to focus on reorganizing Blockbuster's value chain to reduce costs and generate more revenues simultaneously. Blockbuster's biggest expense and asset was its inventory of videos, so this was the logical place to start. Antioco and Redstone examined the way Blockbuster obtained its movies: from the big studios, MGM, Disney, and so on, at the high price of $65. Because it had to pay this high price, Blockbuster could not purchase enough copies of a particular hit movie to satisfy customer demand when the videotape was released. The result was that customers left unsatisfied and revenues were being lost. Perhaps there was a better way of managing the process for both the movie studios and Blockbuster to raise revenues from video rental.

Antioco and Redstone proposed that Blockbuster and the movie studios enter into a revenue-sharing agreement, whereby the movie studios would supply Blockbuster with tapes at cost, at around $8. This price would allow it to purchase 800 percent more copies of a single title. Blockbuster then would split rental revenues with the studios fifty-fifty. The hoped-for result would be growth in the market for rental tapes by 20 to 30 percent a year. Thus, both Blockbuster's and the movie studios' revenues would grow. This would also counter the threat from satellite programming, which was taking away all their revenues. Six million households were now subscribing to direct satellite services. While this deal was being negotiated in 1997, video rentals at Blockbuster dropped 4 percent more, and the studios that had been hesitating to enter into this radically different kind of sales agreement quickly signed. This agreement came at a crucial point for Blockbuster because its cash flow continued to drop as it faced higher write-off costs for outdated tapes. With the new revenue-sharing agreement signed, however, the profitability of its new business model would increase dramatically. (Blockbuster's market share increased from something less than 30 percent to over 40 percent in the next five years, and after a few years the division returned to profitability.) The movie studios also benefited because their stream of income increased.

Antioco's second major change in strategy was to abandon the attempt to transform Blockbuster's stores into general entertainment outlets and refocus on its core movie-rental business. In October 1998, it sold its 378 Blockbuster music chains to Wherehouse Entertainment for $115 million. Antioco still believed, however, as in case of CircleK, that it was a question of deciding what kinds of products would best fit the Blockbuster model, and how again to manage the value chain to keep operating expenses as low as possible while increasing revenues. In 1998,

one answer to this dilemma arrived when Citibank and Blockbuster announced a strategic alliance to install automated teller machines in up to 3,000 Blockbuster stores nationwide. Citibank would bear the costs of operating these machines and would pay Blockbuster a hosting fee, putting no drain on Blockbuster's resources, and helping cash-strapped customers. In 1998, Blockbuster also announced that it was testing home delivery of rental tapes to homes in the Boston area through a local distributor, Streamline. This strategy did not turn out to be successful, however.

Nevertheless, all these changes hurt Blockbuster's performance in the short term. In 1998, Viacom announced that it would record a $437 million charge in the second quarter to write down the value of its Blockbuster videotape inventory because it now had to revise the accounting method it adopted when it entered the new revenue-sharing agreement for tapes from Hollywood studios. (In 1997, it also had to take a charge of $323 million because of the problems noted above.) These charges wiped out Viacom's profits, and Redstone once again announced that a spinoff or initial public offering (IPO) of Blockbuster was likely because the unit was punishing Viacom's stock price and threatening Viacom's future profitability.

On the plus side, however, the revenue-sharing agreement resulted in a sharp increase in revenues; some video-store rentals increased by 13 percent in the second quarter of 1998, compared to a year earlier. Since rental tapes would now be amortized over only a three-month period—the time of greatest rental sales—not the old six to twenty-six months, the new business model seemed poised finally to increase cash flows. One good year for Blockbuster would allow Redstone, who had been increasingly criticized for his purchase of Blockbuster, to go forward with his desire to pursue an "IPO carve out," whereby Viacom would sell between 10 and 20 percent of the Blockbuster stock to the public in an IPO. This move would create a public market for the stock and make an eventual spinoff possible.

By the end of 1998, there were continuing signs of recovery. The revenue-sharing agreement had allowed Blockbuster's managers to develop strategies for increasing responsiveness to customers and allowed them to pursue their business model in a profitable way. With the huge increase in the supply of new videotapes made possible by the revenue-sharing agreement, Blockbuster was now able to offer the Blockbuster Promise to its customers: their chosen title would be in stock or next time it's free. Also, lower prices could now be charged for older video titles to generate additional revenues without threatening profitability. It turned out that the real threat to Blockbuster in the 1990s was not from new technology like video-on-demand, but from the lack of the right strategies to keep customers happy—having the products in stock that they wanted—and from a failure to understand the important dynamics behind the value chain, such as revenue sharing, that would grow the market.

Outside the United States, Blockbuster had been increasing the scope of its international operations. In 1994, it opened its first stores in Italy and New Zealand. In 1995, it entered Israel, Brazil, Peru, Columbia, and Thailand. In 1996, it entered Ecuador, Portugal, El Salvador, Panama, and Scandinavia, where it purchased Christianshavn Video in Denmark. In 1996, in entered Taiwan and Uruguay. In 1998, it acquired Video Flick's stores in Australia. In 1999, it entered Hong Kong as a gateway to China. In 1999, it opened its two hundredth store in Mexico, and in 2000, it expanded its operations in Central America to include Costa Rica and Guatemala. By 2002, it operated almost 2,600 stores outside the United States. The main advantage of its global operations is that it can constantly distribute copies of tapes that are less in demand domestically to other countries overseas, where they will appear as new releases and customers will be willing to pay the highest rental prices for them. In turn, the tapes will trickle down to other countries so that, even though revenues might be less, the cost of the tape has already been amortized and operations will still be profitable. On the other hand, it can also identify foreign-made movies that might attract a large U.S. viewing audience.

In 1998, Blockbuster finally opened its 820,000-square-foot distribution center in Kinney, Texas; now it was in a position to reduce costs and speed delivery of tapes to locations where they were most in demand, and to move them again when demand dropped. Also in 1998, Blockbuster began to offer Neighborhood Favorites, a program where each store would stock tapes customized to local tastes. In keeping with this differentiation approach, Blockbuster developed Blockbuster Rewards, its frequent renters program. The rewards program is designed to keep Blockbuster customers returning regularly to its stores with a coupon for a free video every month.

Blockbuster, 1999–2002

The year 1999 turned out to be a major turning point for Blockbuster. With its business model reestablished, Antioco orchestrated a successful IPO in August 1999. It was also the first of four consecutive years of increasing store sales as Antioco set about changing the entertainment mix in stores to increase revenues. It was clear to Antioco that by 1999, DVDs would become the next entertainment media of choice, and DVDs were a natural product-line extension for Blockbuster. In 1999, Blockbuster introduced DVDs into 3,000 of its stores to assess their promise; customer reaction was favorable because sales of DVD players and other digital media were soaring. In 2000, Blockbuster increased the number of DVD titles it carried because they had higher profit margins than tapes. Blockbuster also began to stock video game CDs and DVDs because the success of the Sony Playstation 2 made it clear that the video game rental business was becoming increasingly lucrative.

Recognizing the growing importance of satellite programming, Blockbuster also formed an alliance with DIRECTTV in 2000 to provide a cobranded pay-per-view service on DIRECTV. Blockbuster also became a new distribution channel for DIRECTV because it began to train its salespeople to sell dishes in its stores. Blockbuster receives a fee for each dish it sells and a share of future monthly payments, and every time a DIRECTV customer orders pay-per-view movies, Blockbuster will receive a payment that is higher than the net profit it makes from each current VHS rental. Antioco argued that this arrangement would give Blockbuster entry into the new technology, and would add between 5 and 15 percent to Blockbuster's revenues. Even a 5 percent increase each year over the next decade would have a substantial impact on its bottom line. DIRECTV gains because Blockbuster will use its database of 42 million households—an important asset—and its $200 million advertising budget to help guide DIRECTV's programming choices, increase market penetration, and increase its monthly pay-per-view order rate. Of course, this arrangement may reduce the number of customers coming into a Blockbuster store; however, Antioco wanted to become involved in in-house entertainment, regardless of the delivery channel.

In another attempt to get more control of the content, or entertainment software, end of the business, Blockbuster announced in 2000 an agreement with MGM to digitally stream and download recent theatrical releases, films, and television programming from the MGM library to Blockbuster's web site for pay-per-view consumption. Initial testing of the program started at the end of 2000. Blockbuster announced that it planned to have similar agreements in place with other movie studios shortly. In 2000, it also signed a deal with TiVo, a maker of set-top digital recorders, to offer a video-on-demand service through broadband using TiVo recorders. TiVo agreed to put demonstration kiosks in over 4,000 Blockbuster stores for its 65 million customers. The push toward video-on-demand was increasing.

The pace of change speeded up in 2001 when Blockbuster abandoned attempts to customize tape offerings to local markets and eliminated 25 percent of the company's less productive VHS tapes to focus on the booming market for DVDs. Once again, it took a loss to amortize these tapes, but then shipped them to its stores overseas to capitalize on growing global demand for these products. The result was that, by the end of 2001, the company achieved record revenues, strong cash flow, and increased profitability while it lowered its debt by more than $430 million. Since 1997, Antioco had increased Blockbuster's revenues from $3.3 billion to over $5 billion and had turned free cash flow from a negative position to over $250 million for 2001. Blockbuster's stock rose as investors realized that the company now had a business model that generated cash.

In August 2000, Antioco once again reaffirmed Blockbuster's goal to lessen its dependence on video rental by focusing more on delivering home entertainment. It started to roll out its "Blockbuster on demand" pay-per-view. He argued that video rental and pay-per-view could exist side by side. In 2001, as sales of DVDs soared, Antioco tried to repeat the success he had had in revenue-sharing with movie studios by arguing that falling DVD prices would not generate the highest long-term returns, and he lobbied for higher DVD wholesale prices to protect future DVD rental revenues. No revenue-sharing agreement was negotiated for DVDs, however, and Antioco did not see the rise in the wholesale price he had hoped for because of strong customer demand for DVDs.

In August 2001, however, five major movie studios—Sony, AOL Time Warner, Universal, MGM, and Paramount (also a Viacom division)—announced a plan to bypass powerful middlemen like Blockbuster and HBO and offer their own pay-per-view service directly to customers. In addition, it was reported that Disney and 20th Century Fox were planning their own pay-per-view service. All of a sudden, the threat of the new digital technology had become a reality because the studios sought to find the right platform on which to launch the service to customers. It had been Antioco's goal, just as it was Huizenga's before, that Blockbuster should provide this pivotal role. However, its own slow attempts to roll out pay-per-view revealed that it had no special competencies in the digital arena. It was still not clear how broadband downloads to customers would be handled in the future, nor was it clear which companies—movie studios, cable operators, satellite providers, and so on—would control the process.

All movies would be licensed to any video-on-demand service on a nonexclusive basis, so there would be no antitrust issues. Thus, in theory, Blockbuster could still operate its own pay-per-view through its stores. Each studio would control the pricing and availability of its films. To some degree, the studios were trying to limit digital piracy of their films and to prevent the emergence of a movie Napster. Service was planned to start sometime in 2002, after encryption and software problems were resolved. Consumers will pay a $3.99 fee similar to that charged by HBO and Blockbuster, and they will download an encrypted, digitally compressed film that can be stored on their hard drive for up to thirty days. The broadband download time would be twenty to forty minutes. Once the downloaded file is opened, however, it has to be watched in twenty-four hours. The file will play through a medium such as Real Networks or Microsoft Media Player.

In the short run, Antioco felt that the threat to Blockbuster posed by this development would be limited. Business travelers were expected to be the biggest customers for this kind of service. In the future, however, when PCs and televisions converge into one unit, the market could be huge and could annihilate Blockbuster's niche. The news hit Blockbuster's share price hard. Once again, the company seemed to be in trouble, although Antioco argued that Blockbuster would be able to license the rights to show pay-per-view movies on the same terms as any other distributor and that video-on-demand would not be a real threat for another five years. Anything could happen in that time, given the pace of technological change—perhaps Blockbuster might then have a viable format and be at the center of video-on-demand changes.

Nevertheless, realizing that the future is unclear, Antioco wondered again how to broaden the product line to keep revenues increasing and ward off any possible future declines in rental revenues. His answer came at the end of 2001, when Microsoft introduced its XBox video game console to compete with the Playstation 2 and Game Cube. The robust sales in the video game market became clear—it is a $15-billion-a-year revenue market. Blockbuster decided to carry a full line of Game Cube, XBox, and Playstation software and hardware for rental and to sell video games in its stores. It also began to work exclusive deals with game makers for old gaming systems and software because of the huge base of older generation video games. The attraction of these products to customers is that they can try any game they want before they must pay the high price for a game that they may not like. Also, rental makes variety possible. In the summer of 2002, Blockbuster began to offer $19.95 monthly rental service for unlimited video game rental. Also, this strategy fits Blockbuster's family profile because parents might come to the store to rent a DVD while their children can pick out a video game. Video games seemed to be a natural complementary product line. In May 2002, Blockbuster announced that it wanted to become "[g]amers' most comprehensive rental and retail resource."

In 2002, Blockbuster announced that it was switching even more quickly to high-margin DVDs and phasing out even more of its VHS. DVDs would thus account for 40 percent of the chain's rental inventory. Together, DVDs and video games now constitute more than half of Blockbuster's product offerings, and this percentage is expected to rise as DVDs sweep away VHS tapes much as CDs have swept away vinyl records. DVD rentals increased 115 percent in 2001 and the spring of 2002, and Blockbuster made $66 million in net income in the first quarter of 2002. During Memorial Day weekend in 2002, Blockbuster unveiled a new look for its video

game section and added products in the push to double its video game rentals by 2003.

Finally, in June 2002, Blockbuster went to court to confront independent video retailers who claimed that its VHS revenue-sharing agreement, which had saved the company in 1999, violated antitrust laws by discriminating against them because they did not obtain preferential price treatment. Independents argued that before the revenue-sharing deals were negotiated, Blockbuster had only 24 percent of the market, while the independents had 55 percent. Today, Blockbuster has 40 percent and has real market power. Antioco argued that the outcome of the trial would have no real impact on his company because revenue-sharing deals do not exist for DVDs, and DVDs and video games were the key to the company's future.

The following question remains, however; how will video-on-demand and pay-per-view affect Blockbuster in the coming years if movie studios continue to increase their efforts to go directly to customers? Will the power of the Blockbuster brand name and huge store chain empire be enough to give it the bargaining power it needs to deal with that new competitive environment? Or will Blockbuster simply become a video game retail and rental chain?

REFERENCES

Apar, Bruce, "Ruminations on Burstyn, Bezos & Blockbuster," *Video Store,* January 14–January 20, 2001, p. 6.

Arnold, Thomas K., "Broadbuster," *Video Store,* August 6–August 12, 2000, pp. 1, 38.

Blockbuster 10Ks and annual reports, 1988–2001.

"Citibank Reaches Pact to Install Its ATMs in Blockbuster Stores," *Wall Street Journal,* May 28, 1998, p. A11.

Clarkin, Greg, "Fast Forward," *Marketing and Media Decisions,* March, 1990, pp. 57–59.

DeGeorge, G., *Business Week,* January 22, 1990, pp. 47–48.

DeGeorge, Gail, Jonathan Levine, and Robert Neff, "They Don't Call It Blockbuster for Nothing," *Business Week,* October 19, 1992, pp. 113–114.

Desjardins, Doug, "Blockbuster Scores with Games, DVDs," *DSN Retailing Today,* May 6, 2002, p. 5.

Fabrikant, Geraldine, "Blockbuster President Resigns: Video Chain Revamps to Adapt to New Units," *New York Times,* January 5, 1993, p. D6.

Frankel, Daniel, "Blockbuster Revamps Play Areas," *Video Business,* May 27, 2002, p. 38.

Gaudiosi, John, "Blockbuster Pushes PS2," *Video Store,* December 2–December 8, 2001, pp. 1, 38.

"Global Notes: Focus 1-Blockbuster Entertainment Corp. (BV)," *Research Highlights,* October 26, 1990, p. 9.

Grossman, Laurie, and Gabriella Stern, "Blockbuster to Buy Controlling Stake in Spelling in Swap," *Wall Street Journal,* March 9, 1993, p. B9.

Heller, Laura, "Radio Shack, Blockbuster Put Synergies to the Test," *DSN Retailing Today,* June 4, 2001, p. 5.

Hume, Scott, "Blockbuster Means More Than Video," *Advertising Age,* June 1, 1992, p. 4.

Kadlec, Daniel, "How Blockbuster Changed the Rules," *New York Times,* August 3, 1998, pp. 48–49.

Kirkwood, Kyra, "Blockbuster Moves into Used DVDs," *Video Store,* March 25, 2000, p. 1.

McCarthy, M., *Wall Street Journal,* March 22, 1991, pp. Al, A6.

Orwall, Bruce, "Five Studios Join Venture for Video on Demand," *Wall Street Journal,* August 17, 2001, p. A3.

QRP Merrill Lynch Extended Company Comment, November 16, 1990.

Roberts, Johnnie, "Blockbuster Officials Envision Superstores for Music Business," *Wall Street Journal,* October 28, 1992, p. B10.

Rosenblum, Trudi M., "Blockbuster to Add Audiobooks," *Publishers Weekly,* June 19, 2000, p. 14.

Sandomir, S., *New York Times,* June 19, 1991, pp. S22–S25.

Savitz, Eric, "An End to Fast Forward?" *Barron's,* December 11, 1989, pp. 13, 43–46.

Shapiro, Eben, "Heard on the Street: Chief Redstone Tries to Convince Wall Street There's Life Beyond Blockbuster at Viacom," *Wall Street Journal,* April 24, 1997, p. C2:3.

Shapiro, Eben, "Movies: Blockbuster Seeks a New Deal with Hollywood," *Wall Street Journal,* March 25, 1998, p. B1.

Shapiro, Eben, "Viacom Net Drops 70% as Cash Flow Slips on Weakness at Blockbuster Unit," *Wall Street Journal,* October 30, 1997, p. B8.

Shapiro, Eben, "Viacom Sets Major Charge Tied to Blockbuster," *Wall Street Journal,* July 23, 1998, p. A3.

Shapiro, Eben, "Viacom Trims Blockbuster's Expansion, Igniting Speculation of Eventual Spinoff," *Wall Street Journal,* March 28, 1997, p. B5:1.

Shapiro, Eben, and Nikhil Deogun, "Antioco Takes Top Job at Troubled Blockbuster," *Wall Street Journal,* June 4, 1997, p. A3:1.

Shapiro, Eben, and Susan Pulliam, "Heard on the Street: Viacom to Name Wal-Mart's Heir Apparent, William Fields, to Head Blockbuster Video," *Wall Street Journal,* March 29, 1996, p. C2.

Sweeting, Paul, "Big Blue Trimming Tapes," *Video Business,* September 17, 2001, p. 1.

Tarr, Greg, "DirecTV Teams with Blockbuster," *Twice,* May 15, 2000, p. 1.

Tedesco, Richard, "MGM, Blockbuster to Stream TV, Films," *Broadcasting & Cable,* January 24, 2000, p. 128.

"TiVo, Blockbuster Ink Cross-Promo Deal," *Twice,* January 17, 2000, p. 24.

"Video Stocks Stumbled," *Video Business,* September 3, 2001, p. 4.

Villa, Joan, "Blockbuster Game Exclusive," *Video Store,* January 20–January 26, 2002, pp. 1, 40.

Warren, Audrey, and Martin Peers, "Video Retailers Have Day in Court—Plaintiffs Say Supply Deals Between Blockbuster Inc. and Studios Violate Laws," *Wall Street Journal,* June 13, 2002, p. B10.

www. Blockbuster.com.

Video Concepts, Inc.

32

This case was prepared by John Dunkelberg and Tom Goho, Wake Forest University.

As Chad Rowan, the owner of Video Concepts, Inc., looked over his monthly income statement, he could only shake his head over how it could have been so much different. In many ways, he was a very successful entrepreneur, having started and grown a profitable business. In other ways, he felt trapped in a long-term, no-win situation. The question now was: what should he do given the current business environment? Basically, Rowan had a profitable business, but the profits were relatively small and had stopped growing since a strong competitor, Blockbuster Video, had moved into town. The profits, however, were not enough to pay off his long-term debts and provide him with any more than a subsistence living. In addition, the chances of selling his business for enough to pay off his debts and then start another business were not good. In reflecting on what might have been, Rowan commented:

> I had really hoped to expand Video Concepts into several similar-sized towns within a couple of hours' driving distance from here. The financial projections, which had been fairly accurate until Blockbuster arrived, indicated expansion was possible. I thought I was growing fast and had put

about as much capital into the business as I could afford. I had even hoped to get a partner to go into this business with me, and one was very interested. Right now, however, I do not feel that I'm getting a very good return on my time and capital.

Talking about the current situation, Rowan said:

> I guess I'm getting a taste of my own medicine. As I grew, several local businesses went out of business, but the good news is that the total market has grown since Blockbuster opened its store. Their marketing clout has brought more people into the market.

To compete with Blockbuster, Rowan has tried everything he can think of to get market share. He has said, "The only way to increase revenues seems to be to raise the rental price, but my lower price is the best marketing strategy I have. If I raise the price, I'm afraid I will lose a lot of market share."

Background

Chad Rowan had been interested in having his own business since he had started and operated a lawn service business in high school. Rowan had started in the ninth grade mowing lawns for his neighbors using his family's lawn mower. By the time he had graduated from high school, his business had grown to a service that had purchased its own equipment: a riding mower, two smaller mowers, two blowers, a

This case is intended to be used as a basis for class discussion rather than as an illustration of either effective or ineffective handling of the situation. This case was presented at the 1993 North American Case Research Association (NACRA) case workshop. Copyright © 1993 by John Dunkelberg, Tom Goho, and the North American Case Research Association. Reprinted with permission. All rights reserved.

lawn aerator, an edger, and a trimmer. His business grew to the point that he employed three of his high school friends. The profits from this business were enough to pay his tuition to college, and he continued the business throughout his four college years.

Rowan majored in business and took the only two courses available in entrepreneurship and small-business management. During his senior year, he researched the video-rental business, which at that time was a relatively new industry. His research resulted in a paper on the video-rental business. The paper included a business plan for the start-up of a small video-rental store with an inventory of about 500 videotapes. By the middle of his senior year, Rowan knew he wanted to start in the video-rental business, and he had already chosen the site, a vacant retail store in the downtown business district of his hometown.

Starting a Business

After graduation in 1987, Rowan opened Video Concepts, a video-rental store with 200 square feet of retail space and a 500-tape rental library in Lexington, North Carolina, a town of about 28,000 people. Video Concepts started slowly but was profitable within six months. Rowan tried several innovative marketing techniques, including home delivery, a free rental after ten rentals, and selling soft drinks and popcorn both at the store and with the delivered videos. To help reduce the expense of the start-up business, Rowan lived at home with his parents and took only $500 a month for his own wages. Revenues that first year were $64,000, with all surplus cash flows used to buy additional videotapes. At the end of the first year's operation, Rowan decided to expand to a larger store.

A 1,000-square-foot retail store was available in a small shopping center that served a major neighborhood area. Using the value of some corporate stocks that he owned as collateral, Rowan borrowed $80,000 from his banker to open this store. The loan was a seven-year note with only interest due during the term of the loan and the entire principal due in seven years. The new store had 3,000 videotapes. Rowan purchased all his new releases through Major Video, one of the top three wholesale distributors in the United States. To increase the size of his video library, he purchased more than 2,000 used tapes from a firm that purchased tapes from bankrupt firms for resale.

Over the next two years, Video Concepts continued to grow rapidly and remained profitable. Rowan continued to put all profits into the purchase of additional tapes, however. Revenues during the second year increased to $173,000 and to $278,000 in the third year.

Growth Continues

The chance to open a third store became a reality when a furniture retail store, originally located in Lexington's busiest shopping district, decided to move to its own, larger building on the outskirts of town. The store contained 3,000 square feet of space, enough to hold more than 12,000 tapes on display. Rowan obtained a three-year lease on the store and opened his third video-rental store in the fall of 1990. Video Concepts now had stores in the three main shopping areas of Lexington.

The new Video Concepts store used open display racks for the videotapes, and customers could quickly and easily locate the type of movies they wanted by going to the appropriate section (for example, new releases, horror, science fiction, action, classic, and so forth) and walking down the aisle. Checking out was quick and easy thanks to a new computer software program that reduced checkout time to less than thirty seconds per customer. In addition, the software program allowed Rowan to keep track of the number of times each tape was rented, how many tapes each customer rented, and who had past-due tapes. The system also allowed Rowan to track sales easily on a daily, weekly, or monthly basis. The new store and the more efficient operation enabled Video Concepts to become a growing and fairly profitable business.

During the next year, growth at the three Video Concepts stores continued, with the majority of the growth coming from the new store. Rowan continued the policy of a free rental after ten rentals, reduced the price per rental to $1.99 per night, and introduced some advertising, which was centered primarily on local high school promotional events. The original two stores saw little growth in sales but remained profitable.

As his business had grown, the number of competitors had steadily decreased, and by the summer of 1991, only six of the original seventeen competitors were still operating. Rowan thought his aggressive pricing strategy, high-quality service, and good selection of new releases were factors in the demise of some of his smaller competitors. His six competitors averaged a tape inventory of less than 1,000 videos, and none had more than 1,600 videos. Rowan estimated that the annual revenues from video rentals in Lexington at the time was about $600,000.

The increase in video-rental chain stores nationally had not gone unnoticed by Rowan, and he had visited several competitors' stores in nearby cities. During his visits, Rowan primarily had tried to see what the competition was doing and learn what he must do to be more efficient and stay competitive. Although he had visited Blockbuster Video stores in several nearby cities, Rowan estimated that their stores would require annual revenues of at least $600,000 a store to be profitable. For this reason, Rowan believed that Lexington was too small to attract a major video-rental chain store. He also believed that he had a store operation that was as well stocked and efficiently operated as a chain-store operation.

With these thoughts in mind, he began paying himself a modest annual salary of $15,000. In addition, he was ready to start paying off the second loan of $200,000 that he had borrowed to open the new store. To obtain this last loan, Rowan had used all his assets as collateral because he believed that these stores were an excellent investment. In the summer of 1991, with sales increasing in every month, Rowan had reason to think that he had built a successful business.

Serious Competition Arrives

In August 1991, Blockbuster Entertainment announced that it would open a store in Lexington. Although a very young corporation, Blockbuster was the largest video-rental chain store in the United States. Blockbuster had grown from nineteen stores in 1986 to 2,028 (1,025 company-owned and 1,003 franchises) in 1991, with total revenues over $1.2 billion in 1992. The typical Blockbuster store carried 8,000 to 14,000 tapes, and the stores ranged in size from 4,000 to 10,000 square feet. In 1991 the 1,248 company-owned stores that had been in operation for more than a year were averaging monthly revenues of $74,984.

Although U.S. growth in consumer spending on video rentals seemed to have slowed, Blockbuster believed it had the opportunity to take market share away from the smaller competitors through its strategy of building large stores with a greater selection of tapes than most of its competitors. As the largest video-rental chain in the United States, Blockbuster also had advantages in marketing and in the purchase of inventory. Blockbuster's standard pricing was $3.50 per tape for two nights, but local stores had some pricing discretion.

In the fall of 1991, Blockbuster built a new store almost across the street from the main Video Concepts store. It purchased a vacant lot for $310,000 and then leased a 6,400-square-foot building that was built to its specifications under a long-term lease agreement for $8.50 per square foot for the first three years. The cost of completely furnishing the building, including stocking it with videotapes, was about $375,000, and Blockbuster spent more than $150,000 on the grand-opening promotions. Thus, Blockbuster spent about $835,000 to open its store, compared with the slightly more than $200,000 that Video Concepts had spent to open its similar-sized store. Blockbuster's operating costs were very similar to those of Video Concepts because the computer checkout equipment was similar and both firms had approximately the same personnel costs. Both firms depreciated their tapes over twelve months.

Blockbuster's Impact on Video Concepts

Rowan decided not to try to meet the grand-opening blitz by Blockbuster with an advertising promotion of his own, but he did start including brochures on Video Concepts with each rental. The brochure noted that the rental fee at Video Concepts was lower than Blockbuster's, that Video Concepts had a new game section with Nintendo games, that Video Concepts was a family entertainment store (that is, no X-rated videos), and that Video Concepts was a locally owned store that supported local school events. Rowan felt his past reputation for low prices ($1.99 versus $3.50 at Blockbuster), his hometown ownership, and courteous service were the appropriate responses to a well-financed competitor. He did not believe that he should even attempt to match Blockbuster's advertising budget and that he should not try to beat Blockbuster at its game. That is, he must continue to do what he did best and not try to match Blockbuster's marketing strategy. He did, however, increase the number of tapes purchased for each new release.

With the opening of the new Blockbuster store and its attendant grand-opening marketing campaign,

Video Concepts' revenues dropped about 25 percent for two months and then started slowly climbing back to its pre-opening levels. During this two-month period, Rowan had worked even harder to provide excellent customer service through brief training sessions for his employees. He had always had employee training sessions, but these new sessions emphasized the competitive threat from Blockbuster and the need to provide the best customer service possible. The primary points of these sessions were directed toward informing customers, as they checked out, of how many rentals they had before they could obtain a free rental, of the customer's ability to reserve videos, and of Video Concepts' willingness to deliver videos to a customer's home at no extra charge. (These were all services that Blockbuster did not offer.)

Unfortunately, Video Concepts' revenues hit a plateau of just under $40,000 per month and stayed there, with the normal minor seasonal variations, for the next twelve months. During this time, Rowan attempted several marketing promotions, including rent-one-get-one-free on the normally slow nights (Mondays, Tuesdays, and Wednesdays), mailing brochures to all Video Concepts customers that briefly highlighted the advantages of shopping at Video Concepts over Blockbuster (lower prices and additional services), and a free rental coupon.

The promotions seemed to help Video Concepts maintain the current revenue level, but they also decreased the profitability of the operation. To improve profitability, Rowan examined his operation for ways of making it more efficient. By studying the hour-by-hour sales patterns, he was able to schedule his employees more efficiently. He also used the information provided by the software program to determine when the rentals of hit and/or new releases had peaked. Rowan learned that there was a fairly good market for used tapes for a short period of time, but if the tapes were not sold during this time, he would end up with a tape that had very little rental demand and little resale value.

The problem with the hit videos was twofold. The first was the determination of how many tapes to purchase. There seemed to be little correlation between a hit at the box office and a hit from rentals. When the video was first released for rental, Rowan would buy forty to fifty videotapes at a cost of about $60 each. The demand for these videos would be very high for about six weeks to three months, after which the demand would drop significantly. The second

problem, therefore, was the determination of when and how many of the tapes to sell before the demand would drop to the level of nonhit videos. Rowan believed that he had solved the second problem by carefully watching the sales figures for the tapes. Analysis of this information helped to minimize his investment in the inventory of tapes, which marginally improved cash flow.

The Dilemma

Two years after Blockbuster had opened its store, Rowan carefully analyzed the financial statements for Video Concepts (see Tables 1 and 2). The company was profitable and had been able to maintain its market share. What was evident was the fact that the arrival of Blockbuster had increased the demand for video rentals in Lexington to an estimated $1,300,000 a year. Blockbuster's share was estimated to be about $700,000 a year, and the few remaining independents had approximately $100,000 a year in revenues.

To Rowan, the current situation was fairly straightforward. Video Concepts had a store that was comparable to Blockbuster's in tape selection, per-

TABLE 1

Video Concepts, Inc., Income Statement
One Year Ending June 30, 1993

Revenues		$465,958
Cost of goods*		192,204
Gross profit		$273,754
Expenses		
Salaries[†]	$108,532	
Payroll taxes	11,544	
Utilities	20,443	
Rent	23,028	
Office expenses	26,717	
Maintenance	6,205	
Advertising expenses	4,290	
Interest expenses	27,395	
Total expenses		228,154
Income before taxes		45,600
Taxes		10,944
Net income		$ 34,656

*Cost of goods = purchase price minus market value of tapes. This method is used because most of the tapes purchased are depreciated over a twelve-month period.
[†]Salaries include Chad's salary of $15,000.

TABLE 2

Video Concepts, Inc.
Balance Sheet, June 30, 1993

Cash	$ 15,274	Accounts payable	$ 15,429
Inventory	4,162	Sales taxes payable	2,415
Prepaid expenses	1,390	Withholding/FICA payable	3,270
Total current assets	$ 20,826	Total current liabilities	$ 21,114
Office equipment	$ 48,409	Bank term loan	$247,518
Furniture and fixtures	53,400	Common stock	20,800
Videocassette tapes	303,131	Retained earnings	24,153
Leasehold improvements	39,800		
Accumulated depreciation*	(151,981)		
Total assets	$ 313,585	Total liabilities and equity	$313,585

*Includes the depreciation of tapes.

sonnel costs, and efficiency of operation. Video Concepts had a cost advantage, with lower store leasing costs ($3.50 per square foot versus $8.50), but Blockbuster had a bigger advantage in the use of its purchasing power to purchase videotapes at a much lower cost. Video Concepts' major marketing strength was its lower rental price ($1.99 versus $3.00), but Blockbuster utilized a much larger advertising budget to attract customers. All of the Blockbuster stores in that region charged $3.50 for rental, except for the one in Lexington.

As had happened nationwide, the growth of video-rental revenue leveled off in the Lexington area starting in 1992. Nationwide in 1992, sales increased only 4.7 percent for Blockbuster stores that had been in operation more than one year. Future growth did not look bright. Advances in cable television technology could render video-store rentals obsolete because fiber optics allowed cable subscribers to order a wide variety of movies at home through pay-per-view services. This technology is still in development stages, however, and its spread to small towns is certainly many years away.

Looking to the future, Rowan felt that, for all his efforts, the net income from the Video Concepts operation would not provide him as high a return on his time and capital as he had expected. He was still paying only the interest on his long-term loans, and paying off the debt seemed several years away. From Rowan's viewpoint, he had several options. He considered raising the price of an overnight rental to $2.49 to make the business more profitable, but he was afraid of what the consequences of such a move might be. He also considered hiring someone to manage the business and find another job for himself. He had received offers of corporate jobs in the past and was considering exploring this option again. Another alternative was to try to sell the business. As Rowan pondered these alternatives, he tried to think of a solution that he might have overlooked. What he was sure of, however, was that he did not wish to keep working twelve-hour days at a business that did not seem to have a bright future.

REFERENCES

"Blockbuster Goes After a Bigger, Tougher Rep," *Variety,* January 25, 1993, p. 151.

"Blockbuster, IBM Plans Set Retailers Spinning," *Variety,* May 17, 1993, p. 117.

"Blockbuster Idea Might Work for Computer Industry," *Mac Week,* May 24, 1993, p. 62.

"Blockbuster Sizes Up PPV Potential: Talks Home Delivery with Bell Atlantic," *Billboard,* January 30, 1993, p. 11.

"Changes in Distribution Landscape Have Players Scouting Claims," *Billboard,* May 16, 1993, p. 52.

"Oscar Noms Mean Gold for Video Industry," *Variety,* February 24, 1992, p. 79.

"Play It Again and Again, Sam," *Newsweek,* December 16, 1991, p. 57.

"Recording Industry Hits Blockbuster," *Advertising Age,* May 17, 1993, p. 46.

"Record Store of Near Future: Computers Replace the Racks," *New York Times,* May 12, 1993, p. A1.

"Stretching the Tape," *New York Times,* April 22, 1993, p. B5.

"Video and Laser Hot Sheet," *Rolling Stone,* March 4, 1993, p. 72.

"VSDA Regaining Its Sense of Direction," *Variety,* June 8, 1992, p. 19.

33 AOL Time Warner: Creating a Colossus

This case was prepared by Charles W. L. Hill, the University of Washington.

Introduction

On January 10, 2000, America Online (AOL) and Time Warner stunned the business world by announcing plans to merge the two companies together into a powerhouse that would span both online and traditional media. The merger, which at the time was valued at $156 billion, was the largest ever. The plan called for AOL shareholders to get 55 percent of the stock in the combined company. Time Warner CEO Gerald Levin would become CEO of the new company. AOL's CEO, Steve Case, would become chairman, and Bob Pittman, AOL's president, would become copresident of the combined company and, in the view of many, heir apparent to Levin. The company would be called AOL Time Warner (AOL TW). The proposed merger would combine the largest online service provider of the Internet era with one of the blue chip companies of the old media world. Founded in 1923, Time Warner has a vast array of magazine, TV broadcasting, film, music, and cable service properties. These include *Time* and *Life* magazines, Warner's film and music properties, CNN, TNT, and HBO, and cable systems that serve 20 percent of the United States. AOL, founded only fifteen years ago, had just 20 percent of the revenue and 15 percent of the employees of Time Warner. However, most observers commented that, in this "marriage of

equals," it was the upstart that was in effect acquiring the older company.[1]

In explaining why they were merging, executives from both companies cited a wide range of synergies. They claimed that Time Warner's cable system would help AOL to roll out a broadband version of its service, that AOL would be able to offer Time Warner content to its online subscribers, thereby enhancing the value of the service and guaranteeing continued growth, and that there were huge possibilities for cross-selling between AOL and Time Warner subscribers. They predicted that the combined company would be able to grow revenues at 12 to 15 percent per annum, earnings before interest, taxes, depreciation, and amortization (EBITDA) by 25 percent per annum, and free cash flow by 50 percent per annum.[2]

It took a year for the merger to close, primarily because the companies had to deal with a range of difficult antitrust issues. In the intervening period, the stock price of AOL fell from $68 to $47 a share, reflecting a slowdown in economic activity in the United States, and thus in advertising spending, a major component of revenue for both AOL and Time Warner. Still, the management of the new company stuck to their optimistic forecasts, predicting that they would grow EBITDA by 33 percent in 2001. It was not to be. Hit by weak advertising spending, AOL TW's EBITDA grew by only 18 percent and revenues by 5 percent.

In April 2002, AOL TW stock, which had hit a high of $56 in May 2001, was trading at $19 a share. The company announced that it would

This case is intended to be used as a basis for class discussion rather than an illustration of either effective of ineffective handling of the situation. Reprinted by permission of Charles W. L. Hill.

take a massive $54 billion charge against earnings, writing down the goodwill taken on as a result of the merger and essentially recognizing that the merger was based on an unrealistic valuation of the combined entity. CEO Gerald Levin had retired and was replaced not by AOL's Bob Pitman, as many initially expected, but by a Time Warner man, Richard Parsons. Parsons scaled back the bullish forecasts and stated that AOL TW would grow revenues by maybe 5 to 8 percent in 2002 and EBITDA by 8 to 12 percent. Even these scaled-back figures were viewed with suspicion by critics, who cited slow subscriber growth at the AOL division and a weak rollout of AOL's broadband offerings. Some were even speculating that AOL might be spun out of AOL TW.

The Rise of AOL

When AOL went public in 1992, it had fewer than 200,000 subscribers and revenues of just $27 million. By the time its merger was announced with Time Warner, the company was closing in on 22 million subscribers and was generating revenues of around $6 billion. The rise of the company had been dramatic and often controversial. It was initially seen as a distant third to two well-funded rivals, Prodigy and CompuServe, but by 2000 Prodigy had exited the industry, and AOL had acquired CompuServe in 1997. In addition, AOL acquired ICQ's instant messaging service in 1998, and shortly afterwards purchased Netscape, the company that had pioneered the Internet browser. Microsoft's MSN Network had emerged as a competitor mid decade, but in 2000 it was still a distant second to AOL, with just 3 million subscribers.

AOL offered subscribers access to a proprietary network that could be used to send and receive email, read bulletin boards, enter chat rooms, browse a wide range of media content, and purchase goods from e-commerce providers with a "storefront" on the network. In addition, from 1994 onward, AOL incorporated a web browser into its software, giving subscribers access to the rapidly growing World Wide Web (WWW). Much of AOL's success was attributed to the ease with which its software could be installed and used; the software organized content and features in a graphical user interface that was intuitively easy for computer neophytes to navigate. What also helped was the popularity of key features of the service such as email and chat rooms, the wide range of content that could be found on the service, and the company's own relentless and savvy marketing that had made AOL one of the best-known brands in America. For example, AOL "you've got mail" sound bite quickly became a signature of popular culture and the title of a highly successful film. Although sophisticated users of the Internet had derided AOL as the "Internet on training wheels," apparently that was what the mass market wanted—and AOL was, if nothing else, determined to give customers what they wanted.

AOL's Evolving Business Model

Over the course of the decade, AOL's business model had changed a number of times. Originally revenues were generated almost entirely from subscriptions, with usage being charged by the hour. In 1996, some 91 percent of AOL's revenues came from subscription fees, with the balance coming from advertising and commerce transactions. Through December 31, 1994, the standard monthly membership fee for AOL was $9.95 for five hours of access and $3.50 per hour thereafter. In January 1995, AOL reduced the per hour fee to $2.95, although it left the base fee unchanged. In May 1996, AOL announced an additional pricing plan for heavy users of the service. This included twenty hours of service for $19.95 per month and an hourly fee of $2.95 for use in excess of that.

However, by 1996 the Internet was becoming increasingly well organized due to the emergence of portals such as Yahoo.com, leading some critics to question the need for a proprietary online service like AOL. Internet service providers (ISPs) from small "mom-and-pop" operations to telecommunications giants like AT&T and MCI had sprung up and were starting to offer unlimited access to the Internet for $19.95 a month. Under AOL's pricing plan, the heaviest users could run up bills anywhere from $50 to $300 per month. Partly as a result, AOL's subscriber churn rate was unacceptably high. Estimates suggested that by mid 1996 the monthly churn rate was running at around 6 percent, implying that over 70 percent of AOL's customers would leave the service within one year of joining.[3] Since it cost AOL at least $45 in marketing expenses to get a new subscriber onto the service, the implication was that many subscribers were leaving before AOL had the chance to recoup the cost of acquiring them.[4] Moreover, among the customers who were leaving were longtime heavy users who were AOL's biggest spenders. Although representing only one-third of the subscriber base, these heavy users were accounting for two-thirds of AOL's revenues.

On October 10, 1996, Microsoft's MSN announced that it would adopt a flat rate pricing scheme of $19.95 per month for unlimited access to MSN's "proprietary content" and the Web. The move forced AOL's hand. On October 29, AOL announced that from December 1 it too would offer unlimited access for $19.95 per month.[5] Following the announcement of the move to flat rate pricing and unlimited access, AOL's membership surged. The service added over half a million new members in December alone. By early January, close to 8 million people were using the service, exceeding both the company's expectations and the capacity of its network. Hundreds of thousands of new members were joining the service—only to be greeted by busy signals! Complaints from irritated members overwhelmed the capacity of AOL's customer service operation. On January 16, AOL responded by announcing that it would invest an additional $100 million in its dial-up network over the next few months. The company also pledged to reduce its marketing expenditures and pull its TV ad campaign until the capacity of its network had been upgraded. The busy signals continued. A number of state attorneys general banded together and announced that they would sue AOL for deceptive selling practices, false advertising, and even fraud. By the end of January, AOL agreed to give a refund to any member who requested it as compensation for the inability to access the network. In return, the states agreed to drop their lawsuit.[6]

With revenue growth from subscribers now constrained by flat rate pricing, CEO Steve Case decided it was time to leverage the brand in order to maximize revenues from advertising and e-commerce—and AOL had to move quickly. Although it had already embarked on this road a year ago, the move to flat rate pricing gave the strategy new urgency. In October 1996, Case hired Bob Pittman as president of AOL Networks. It was to be Pittman's job to leverage the AOL brand and diversify the company's revenue sources. Then forty-two years old, Pittman had already left his mark on global pop culture. A one-time radio disk jockey, in 1981, together with John Lack, Pittman started an all-music cable TV channel called Music television, or MTV. Charismatic, photogenic, and charming, Pittman was in many ways the ultimate marketing *wunderkind*. In addition to MTV, Pittman also had a hand in the creation of VH1 and the Nike at Nite cable TV channels.[7]

Pittman sharpened the focus of the strategy. Prior to Pittman's arrival, AOL had been considering entering all sorts of businesses itself, from selling books to long-distance telephone service. Pittman's view was that AOL had the most valuable real estate on the Internet and that AOL should leverage that, helping other organizations sell their goods and services to AOL members.

On February 25, 1997, Pittman announced the first of what was to become a steady stream of deals. Under this deal, Tel-Save Holdings, a long-distance telephone service reseller, paid AOL $100 million for the privilege of being able to sell long-distance services to AOL's members. Prior to the deal, Tel-Save had 500,000 customers. The $100 million was an advance on future commission payments that would be due to AOL for members Tel-Save signed up. For Tel-Save, the deal had two big attractions. It was a cost-effective way of reaching 8 million potential customers, and AOL would bill Tel-Save customers electronically and charge their credit cards for calls made using Tel-Save. Tel-Save estimated that electronic billing and credit card payments would reduce its unit costs by 30 percent, enabling it to offer customers long-distance rates 20 percent below those offered by rivals.[8] By March 1998, AOL and Tel-Save announced that the long-distance reseller had added 500,000 customers from AOL.[9]

On March 4, 1997, AOL opened to advertisers its 14,000 chat rooms, which logged 1 million hours daily. On June 10, CUC International agreed to pay AOL an advance of $50 million against future commissions in order to market its range of discount services directly to AOL subscribers. CUC expected to generate more than 1 million new interactive memberships per year from its AOL connection.[10] On July 7, Amazon.com, the Internet bookseller, agreed to pay AOL at least $19 million over three years in advances on commissions to be the featured bookseller on AOL's web site, aol.com. If Amazon.com sales through AOL exceeded targets, this figure would be increased. Barnes and Noble paid a similar amount (later increased to $40 million) to be the bookseller on AOL's proprietary service. Also in July 1997, 1–800-FLOWERS agreed to pay AOL at least $25 million in advances on commissions over four years to sell on the service. The flower company expected the deal to produce $250 million in sales over four years.[11]

Around the same time, AOL began to charge retailers "rents" of at least $250,000 per year for their spots on AOL, in addition to commissions. This represented a shift from the old practice by which AOL simply took a cut of the sales generated from sales over AOL. Revenues from this source had been disappointing, but Pittman felt that the change in incentive structure implied by the imposition of rents would yield significant dividends down the road.

In addition to taking a cut out of e-commerce transactions, AOL also began to change its relationship with content providers during this period. Under the old pricing scheme, AOL *paid* content providers a fee based on the time members spent at their sites. With the hourly fee now gone, AOL had no incentive to pay content providers. Instead, the company started requiring content providers to pay it a fee in exchange for the privilege of being able to offer content through AOL. In one of the first deals, announced in July 1997, AOL stated that it had signed CBS Sportsline to serve as an "anchor tenant" for the service's sports channel.[12] In addition to demanding fees, AOL started to weed out weak content providers, refusing to renew their contracts when they came due.

The fruits of this change in strategy started to become apparent by 1998. In fiscal 1995, AOL generated some $6 million in revenues from advertising and commercial fees. This increased to $100.2 million in 1996, $180 million in 1997, and $511 million in 1998. The figure for 1999 looked set to exceed $1 billion out of total AOL revenues of more than $4 billion. Moreover, there was no sign of a slowdown in the flow of deals bringing cash into AOL's coffers. In early 1999, AOL entered into a five-year agreement valued at $500 million with First USA under which First USA became the exclusive marketer of credit card products and service on AOL. Similarly, in July 1999 drkoop.com, an Internet-based health care site established by Dr. Everett Koop, the former surgeon general of the United States, agreed to pay AOL $89 million over four years. This was an advance on commissions for the chance to sell to AOL's members, which by then exceeded 19 million.[13] As of March 31, 1999, AOL's *backlog* of advertising and commerce revenues exceeded $1.3 billion (the *backlog* refers to future revenues guaranteed to AOL under the terms of agreements with content providers and online retailers).[14]

The Quest for Bandwidth

As 1999 progressed, it became increasingly clear that AOL needed to be able to offer its members greater bandwidth. *Bandwidth* refers to the rate at which digital data can be transferred between two points (the term *broadband* refers to a high-bandwidth connection). Currently most consumers only have relatively low-bandwidth connections to the Internet over standard telephone lines (a typical computer modem can transmit and receive data at 56 kilobytes per second). AOL CEO Steve Case had long argued that greater bandwidth connections would allow high-resolution video and audio data to be transmitted effectively to consumers over the Internet. In turn, this would dramatically expand the range of interactive service that consumers could access over the Internet, which could drive forward the growth in demand for AOL's various offerings.

There are various ways of delivering high-bandwidth connections to the home, all of which are in the early stages of being rolled out.[15] One way utilizes DSL (digital subscriber line) technology to increase the bandwidth of standard copper telephone lines. DSL technology typically moves data at between 128 K and 1.5 megabytes per second, with 640 K being the norm. This is the solution favored by telephone companies. By mid 1999 there were about 180,000 DSL subscribers in the United States. But DSL signals degrade with distance and typically won't work more than 3 miles from a phone switch.

Another solution involves adapting the coaxial cable used to transmit cable TV signals to carry two-way Internet traffic. Consumers with cable modems attached to their personal computers (PCs) would then be able to access the Internet at speeds up to five hundred times faster than with a standard 56-K telephone modem. TV cables run past 95 percent of homes in the United States. By mid 1999, 750,000 people in the United States were using services based on cable modems.

A third solution is to use digital satellite technology to beam down data at very high bandwidth rates. The problem with this solution right now is that the consumers can't beam data back at similar rates. Rather, they have to communicate requests for data through conventional telephone lines operating at 56 K. By mid 1999, some 25,000 consumers were using satellite services to connect to the Internet.

Steve Case is not the only one who believes that high-bandwidth connectivity is the key to expanding demand for interactive services over the Internet. Microsoft's Bill Gates also believes that high-bandwidth connectivity is crucial, and he sees high bandwidth driving forward demand for Microsoft software and services, including AOL rival MSN.[16] In 1998, Microsoft began to invest in cable TV companies as part of a strategy to create incentives for the cable companies to speed up their moves to upgrade their coaxial cable networks so that they could carry Internet traffic.

Microsoft started the ball rolling with a $5 billion investment in Comcast, a nationwide cable operator. Soon thereafter, AT&T jumped into the fray when it acquired the number one cable operator in the United States, TCI, for $75 billion. AT&T announced that it intended to provide phone service and Internet access over cable. Along with TCI came @Home, in which TCI had a controlling ownership stake. @Home was a leader in offering Internet access over coaxial cable. Then on May 10, 1999, AT&T acquired another major cable company, MediaOne, for $60 billion. MediaOne happened to be part owner of Roadrunner, which was a major competitor to @Home. As part of the AT&T-MediaOne deal, Microsoft agreed to invest $5 billion in AT&T and to purchase a 30 percent stake in MediaOne's European cable TV operating subsidiary, TeleWest (at one point, Microsoft was rumored to be preparing a rival bid for MediaOne).[17]

This flurry of deals led to speculation that AOL might be shut out of high-bandwidth access to the Internet via cable. Up to this point the cable networks had been closed to AOL because federal regulators had ruled that cable operators have the exclusive right to market data services to their own subscribers. AOL challenged this ruling, but met with little success. It lobbied regulators to allow it access to AT&T's now extensive cable network, which was reserved for AT&T's cable ISP, @Home, but again got nowhere. As an alternative, in early 1999 AOL entered into strategic alliances with two of America's telephone giants, Bell Atlantic and SBC Communications, to use DSL technology to make available a high-speed upgrade connection to AOL subscribers starting summer 1999.

This was followed by a May 12 announcement that AOL would make a record $1.5 billion investment in Hughes Electronics and jointly introduce new consumer offerings with Hughes's DirecTV

satellite service.[18] The proposed offerings include AOL-Plus, which will provide high-speed Internet connection over satellite, and AOL TV for such television-based functions as interactive shopping, web surfing, email, and electronic chat, more commonly performed over the Internet. A set-top box, which the partners are developing jointly, will allow TV viewers to chat with friends, check their email, and engage in e-commerce. Although this deal put AOL back in the broadband race and positioned the company to enter the interactive TV market, the shortcomings of current satellite systems still left AOL at a potential disadvantage.

Time Warner

Time Warner, created in 1990 by the merger of Warner Communications and Time, was the world's largest media conglomerate.[19] In 2000 the company comprised six major segments: *cable networks,* principally interests in cable television programming; *publishing,* principally interests in magazine publishing, book publishing, and direct marketing; *music,* principally interests in recorded music and music publishing; *filmed entertainment,* principally interests in filmed entertainment, television production, and television broadcasting; *cable,* principally interests in cable television systems; and *digital media,* consisting principally of interests in Internet-related and digital media businesses.

In 1999, the year prior to the merger announcement, Time Warner had revenues of $27 billion and a net income of $1.95 billion. The revenue split between different businesses is given in Exhibit 1. The earnings split, measured by earnings before interest,

EXHIBIT 1

Time Warner Revenue Breakdown

Source: AOL Time Warner Form 10K, 2000.

tax, and amortization, is given in Exhibit 2. The digital media business was a start-up operation at this time; it generated no revenues and registered a loss.

Cable Networks

Time Warner owned a portfolio of cable television networks that included three of the top five networks in the United States, which accounted for 26 percent of all basic cable subscription revenue in the country and around 28 percent of basic cable advertising revenues. These networks included Turner Networks, which was acquired earlier in the decade when Time Warner bought Ted Turner's Turner Broadcasting (the acquisition left Ted Turner with a substantial shareholding in Time Warner and a seat on the board). Turner Networks included CNN, TBS, and TNT. CNN, the pioneering twenty-four-hour-a-day cable news service, had more than 77 million subscribers in the United States at the time of the merger announcement. Together with CNN International, CNN reached more than 200 million locations in 212 countries and territories by December 2001. When the merger was announced, TBS had approximately 77 million subscribers in the United States, and TNT approximately 75 million subscribers.

In addition, Time Warner owned HBO, which was the leading pay television service in the world and which together with its sister service, Cinemax, had approximately 36 million subscribers. A majority of HBO's programming and a large portion of that on Cinemax consist of recently released, uncut, and uncensored theatrical motion pictures. However, HBO was also gaining a reputation for developing its own compelling programming content. Two series,

The Sopranos and Sex in the City, had helped to boost HBO's rating and garnered the network a number of industry awards.

Time Warner also owned the Cartoon Network and a 50 percent interest in Comedy Central and Court TV. The Cartoon Network, which was number two to Nickelodeon, had around 61 million subscribers, and Court TV reached some 36 million.

Publishing

Time Warner's publishing interests were conducted primarily by Time Incorporated, which was a wholly owned subsidiary of the company. Time Inc. publishes some of the world's best-known magazines, including *Time, People, Sports Illustrated, Fortune, Money, Entertainment Weekly,* and *In Style,* and it accounted for 40 percent of magazine industry profits when the merger was announced. In 1999, Time magazines accounted for a leading 22.6 percent of the total advertising revenue in consumer magazines. *People, Time,* and *Sports Illustrated* were ranked 1, 2, and 3, respectively, in advertising revenue, and Time had eight of the thirty leading magazines in terms of advertising dollars. Advertising rates are a function of circulation, with high-circulation publications being able to demand higher rates from advertisers. Time has been experimenting, with considerable success, with brand extension strategies, publishing new offerings, such as *Teen People* and *Time for Kids,* that have swelled the overall circulation of Time publications.

Although single copies of magazines are sold through retail news dealers and other outlets that are supplied by wholesalers or directly by Time, most magazines are sold by subscription and delivered through the mail. Subscriptions are sold by direct mail and online solicitation, subscription sales agencies, television and telephone solicitation, and insert cards in magazines and other publications. Time was generally recognized as having one of the best subscription selling machines in the industry.

Time also has two major trade publishing houses, Warner Books and Little, Brown. In 1999, Time Warner Trade Publishing placed thirty-six books on the *New York Times* bestseller lists.

Music

Time Warner's music interests are run through Warner Music Group (WMG), whose record labels include Warner Bros., Atlantic, Elektra, and London-Sire. WMG is one of the five largest record labels in

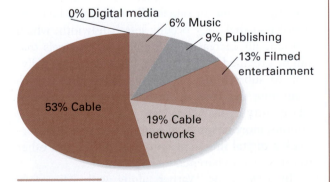

EXHIBIT 2

Earnings Breakdown (EBITA)

Source: AOL Time Warner Form 10K, 2000.

the world, with a 13 percent share of the U.S. music sales in 2000. WMG's artists include Madonna, Matchbox Twenty, Eric Clapton, Red Hot Chili Peppers, Brandy, Kid Rock, Goo Goo Dolls, Missy Elliot, Tim McGraw, Bare Naked Ladies, and Don Henley. However, WMG's market share had slipped from more than 20 percent just five years previously. Moreover, the entire recording industry was entering troubled waters, with the ease of distributing and swapping music files over the Internet potentially starting to disrupt the industry. The recording industry argued that the rise of file-sharing services such as Napster led to an increase in digital piracy rates in the United States and falling sales.

WMG is a vertically integrated music company. After an artist has entered into a contract with a WMG label, a master recording of the artist's music is produced and provided to WMG's manufacturing operation, which replicates the music primarily on CDs and audiocassettes. A WMG subsidiary, Ivy Hill, prints material that is included with CDs and audiocassettes and creates packaging for them. WMG's distribution arms sell product and deliver it, either directly or through subdistributors and wholesalers, to thousands of record stores, mass merchants, and other retailers throughout the country. CDs and audiocassettes are also increasingly being sold directly to consumers through Internet retailers such as CDnow and Amazon.com.

On January 24, 2002, just two weeks after the AOL–Time Warner merger had been announced, Time Warner announced that WMG and EMI's recording business would merge, forming a fifty-fifty joint venture, although Warner would control the board of the venture. The venture would create the largest music company in the world, with a huge catalog of around 2 million songs. In a news conference announcing the proposed venture, Time Warner executives argued that the combined company would be better positioned to deal with the opportunities and threats posed by the rise of the Internet as a primary medium for distributing music.

Filmed Entertainment

Time Warner's filmed entertainment businesses operate under the Warner Brothers, New Line Cinema, and Castle Rock film production names. The businesses produce and distribute theatrical motion pictures, television shows, animation, and other programming; distribute home videos; operate the WB Television Network; license rights to the company's characters; operate retail stores featuring consumer products based on the company's characters and brands; and operate motion picture theaters.

Warner Bros. Pictures's strategy includes building movie franchises, which will continue with the planned expansion of *The Matrix* into a series of films. In 2001 the first of a series of Harry Potter motion pictures and the first of the Lord of the Rings trilogy were introduced.

The WB Television Network (the WB) was established in 1995. During the 1999–2000 broadcast season, the WB expanded its prime-time program line-up to six nights and started airing thirteen hours of series programming from Sunday to Friday nights. The network's line-up includes the family series *7th Heaven*, as well as programming aimed at a teen and young adult audience, such as *Dawson's Creek, Charmed, Buffy the Vampire Slayer, Felicity, Roswell, Popular,* and *Angel*. Total TV household coverage of the WB was 83 percent in 2000.

Cable

In 2000 Time Warner was the second-largest operator of cable TV systems in the United States, behind AT&T Broadband and ahead of Comcast. The company's cable business served some 12.6 million subscribers in 2000. These included approximately 6.7 million subscribers in a joint venture between TWE and Advance/Newhouse, a family-owned cable TV system. The joint venture is 66 percent owned by Time Warner.

During 1999, Time Warner Cable began an aggressive rollout of digital cable service in many of its cable systems. As of 2000, Time Warner Cable had approximately 430,000 digital service subscribers. The digitalization of signals allows them to be compressed so that they occupy less bandwidth, which substantially increases the number of channels that can be provided over a system. Digital set-tops delivered to subscribing customers offer a digital programming tier with up to one hundred networks, CD-quality music services, more pay-per-view options, more channels of multiplexed premium services, a digital interactive program guide, and other features such as parental lockout options.

In 1998 Time Warner, along with Microsoft, Compaq, and MediaOne, formed a joint venture, Road Runner, to operate and expand Time Warner Cable's and MediaOne's high-speed online service business (MediaOne was subsequently acquired by AT&T Broadband). Time Warner, through its various subsidiaries, has a 54.9 percent interest in Road Runner, which provides high-speed Internet access and also offers content optimized for broadband-capable networks. Road Runner affiliates with local cable television system operators, principally Time Warner Cable and MediaOne, in exchange for a percentage of the cable operator's retail revenue from subscribers for the Road Runner service. In early 2000, Road Runner had approximately 550,000 subscribers (of which approximately 330,000 were in Time Warner Cable systems).

Digital Media

In 1999 Time Warner created Time Warner Digital Media (TW Digital Media) to develop and implement a companywide digital media strategy, to fund and oversee digital media initiatives across Time Warner's divisions, and to identify and pursue digital media-related investment opportunities. The Digital Media business funds and participates in the oversight of the company's significant Internet sites, including CNN.com and CNNfn.com.

Merger Synergies

The management's of both AOL and Time Warner claimed that the merger was justified on the basis of the substantial synergies that the combined company could realize. In a show of editorial independence, an article in *Fortune* magazine, a Time Warner publication, quickly pointed out that the synergies would indeed have to be substantial, enormous actually, if the merger were to pay.[20] At the time, the combined market value of the two companies was around $290 billion, while the combined earnings were $2.7 billion, implying a price-to-earnings ratio of over 100. To make the merger pay, according to the article, the combined company would have to grow earnings at 22 percent per annum for the next fifteen years—not exactly an easy task even in the very best of times. Indeed, the article concluded that "getting there would be like pushing a boulder up an alp"! So how did the management of AOL and Time Warner plan to pull off this?

Distribution Synergies: Broadband Access

The merger would at a stroke help solve one of AOL's biggest problems, how to offer high-speed Internet service to its 22 million subscribers. As many Internet users have found out, downloading graphics-intensive web content over telephone lines using 56-K modems can be a very slow process, to say nothing of the wait required to download streaming video data. If the Internet is to fulfill its potential, the speed of Internet connections (the bandwidth) must be increased. Although AOL had made some headway with DSL and satellite systems, so far it had been shut out of the most-promising broadband distribution conduit, the coaxial cable used by cable TV. The merger would give AOL access to Time Warner's cable TV system with its 12.6 million subscribers. AOL could then offer these customers high-speed access to the Internet over Time Warner's cable TV systems. In effect, the merger allowed AOL to integrate forward into the distribution of its content.[21]

Content Synergies: Enhancing the Value of AOL

A second benefit claimed for the merger was that AOL would be able to offer Time Warner's rich array of content to its subscribers, thereby enhancing the value of its service. AOL has always seen itself as a media company offering compelling content to its customers. If content is indeed king on the Internet, the combination of AOL's web savvy and Time Warner's magazine and broadcasting properties opens up the potential for delivering a wide range of innovative content over the Internet to AOL's subscriber base. In addition to existing Time Warner services, such as CNN.com, these might include an ability to access TNT's vast film library on demand (assuming a cable modem), archived CNN news clips, web versions of *Time* magazine, and a range of web properties that have yet to be imagined. If the online version of this content were proprietary to AOL, it would help to justify a premium price for AOL's service, or growing subscriptions at a faster rate.

Operating Synergies: Cutting Costs

There were also some concrete operating synergies to be had from the merger. The two companies could combine sales and back-office functions such as customer support call centers. Managers claimed that these combinations alone could yield cost savings of $1 billion a year, according to the two companies, although a detailed breakdown of exactly where such savings would come from was hard to get. Then there was the potential for enhanced cross-selling between the subscribers of the two companies. Taken together, the two companies have access to more than 100 million subscribers. So in theory, for example, AOL installation CDs could be sold with Time publications, and AOL could use its service to market Time Warner's magazines, cable services, music, and so forth.[22]

Venture Synergies: The Creation of New Business

In addition to the above, there was also a belief that an AOL–Time Warner combination would be better positioned to create new businesses in the era of digital distribution of media, including films, magazines, and music. This would lead to much faster revenue growth than either AOL or Time Warner could achieve by themselves. It was music that was the focus on the most immediate speculation. The proposed merger between WMG and EMI's music interests would make AOL Time Warner the largest music company in the world, with access to a library of 2 million songs. The rapid rise of Napster, a company that was pioneering the digital distribution of music using peer-to-peer computer technology, was shaking the very foundations of the music industry. Although all of the big music companies were suing Napster for copyright infringement, and it seemed highly likely that the service would run into substantial legal problems, most observers still felt that the future of the music industry lay in the digital distribution of titles over the Internet. Not only would digital distribution cut significant costs out of the music industry, but it would also allow users to make their own music compellations, downloading choice content over the Internet. The massive popularity of Napster's service was a testament to this (although it must be admitted that getting music for free also had something to do with the popularity of the service).

Combine AOL's strong position in cyberspace, and its technology savvy, with WMG-EMI's music list, and the optimists argued that there should be a business model that would allow AOL Time Warner to profit from the disruptive technology represented by peer-to-peer computing and file-swapping technology. Exactly what such a business model might look like was not clear, but surely with all of the talent at its disposal, AOL Time Warner could solve the puzzle. Moreover, once AOL Time Warner had solved this puzzle for music, it could turn its attention to other areas where the technology promised both opportunities and threats—the digitalization and digital distribution of film and books. Again, AOL Time Warner's strong position in publishing and filmed entertainment positioned the company ideally for this brave new world.

Antitrust Issues

Before the proposed merger could be consummated, there were some thorny antitrust issues that had to be resolved. Regulators harbored fears that AOL Time Warner would deny competing providers—such as Earthlink, Juno, and Microsoft's MSN service—of Internet service access to its cable TV subscribers. To guard against this possibility, as a condition for approving the merger, officials at the Federal Trade Commission (FTC) required that AOL Time Warner commit to giving its cable customers the choice of three Internet service providers other than AOL. In addition, the FTC wanted AOL Time Warner to sign a deal with at least one competing provider as a precondition for the merger being approved. The reason that the FTC gave for taking this hard-line stance is that they did not want AOL Time Warner to offer its service first, before opening up the Time Warner cable system to competing providers. The irony in the FTC's stance was that a different government agency, the Federal Communication Commission (FCC), had not required that existing cable companies open up access to multiple Internet service providers!

On November 20, 2000, Time Warner announced that it had struck a deal with Earthlink that would allow this provider to offer Internet service to Time Warner's cable customers. The deal, which was contingent upon final approval of the merger, was aimed at satisfying the concerns of the FTC. Apparently satisfied, the FTC gave the merger the green light.

The FTC was not the only antitrust agency that AOL and Time Warner had to deal with, however. Since both companies were multinational concerns with substantial European interests, they also had to get approval from the European Union's (EU) Competition Commission. In recent years, the commission had not been shy about ruling on mergers between U.S.-based companies with substantial European activities. It had blocked a proposed merger between General Electric and Honeywell on antitrust grounds, and now it was making noises about the proposed combination between AOL and Time Warner. Its objection centered not on AOL and Time Warner per se, but on the potential market power that the WMG-EMI merger would give AOL Time Warner in the music industry, particularly given AOL's strong position in the online market.

A second concern of the EU was that AOL Europe was a joint venture with Germany's largest media company, Bertelsmann AG. The creation of AOL Time Warner would thus indirectly lead to greater concentration in the online distribution of media in Europe, with two of the world's largest media companies being effectively joined at the hip through AOL Europe.

After intense negotiation with the commission, the managements of AOL and Time Warner realized that they would have to make concessions on both of these issues if the merger was to win approval. They thus dropped the proposed linkup between WMG and EMI and agreed to buy out Bertelsmann's stake in AOL Europe. With this commitment in hand, on October 12, 2000, the commission gave its blessing to the merger.

Prework

Even before the merger was officially approved, AOL's Robert Pittman, who was slated to become copresident of the combined company with Time Warner's Richard Parsons, moved into Time Warner's head office and took the lead in integrating the two companies.[23] During 2000 the two companies signed between 150 and 200 commercial agreements. As an example, Warner music helped to sell AOL subscriptions by embedding AOL software on the latest CD from the rock group Match Box 20. AOL also generated 500,000 new subscribers for *Time* magazine. Perhaps most importantly, Pittman started holding regular meetings between AOL and Time Warner managers. For Time Warner, which has traditionally operated in a decentralized manner, this represented a big change. Reportedly, prior to Pittman's arrival many of the heads of Time Warner's divisions had not seen each other in years. Pittman told them to look at the potential for integration to produce cost savings and cross-selling both within Time Warner and between Time Warner and AOL. Pittman also told them that he would change the company's compensation system for senior executives. Historically, the compensation of divisional executives at Time Warner was based exclusively on the performance of their divisions. Pittman stated that he would link a

good portion of it to the performance of the entire company after the merger.

Another Pittman initiative was the formation of a group loosely called the "Advertising Council." This group comprised every division's top people in sales, marketing, product licensing, and merchandising. Following final approval of the merger, the group planned to meet every two weeks to identify and monitor attempts for cross-selling. In 2000, one of the key collaborations between the two companies involved AOL TV, a device similar to Microsoft's Web TV that allows users to surf the Web and send email and instant messaging from their TV sets. Eventually, it will probably be integrated with Time Warner's set-top boxes to provide high-speed Internet access and allow users to interact with TV shows. AOL TV started promoting various Time Warner magazines and cable networks in 2000, and AOL did online promotions for various Warner music artists.

The First Year and Beyond

With approval from the FTC and EU Competition Commission in hand, the merger was formally consummated on January 11, 2001. The AOL unit was set up as a stand-alone division within AOL Time Warner's corporate structure (see Exhibit 3). The new company began 2001 by setting some high expectations. Revenues were expected to grow 10.5 percent in 2001 to $40 billion, while AOL Time Warner's preferred profit measure, EBITDA, was forecast by management to grow 33 percent to $11 billion. Although CEO Gerald Levin laid out the financial forecasts, Bob Pittman was widely regarded as the man behind them.

Initially, things seemed to be heading on the right track at the new company. In the first quarter of 2001, AOL Time Warner's EBITDA earnings measure grew by 20 percent, ahead of the company's 18 to 19 percent target for that quarter. The performance of the AOL unit was particularly strong. AOL overcame widespread softness in the online advertising market to post a 10 percent growth in online ad revenues, increasing its market share at the expense of competitors like Yahoo. In May 2001, with its subscriber base exceeding 23 million, AOL took advantage of its strong market position to raise the price of its online service 9 percent to $23.90 from $21.95 a month. The last time AOL increased prices was in 1998, when it had 11 million members. That time, it raised prices from $19.95. Its two largest competitors, Earthlink

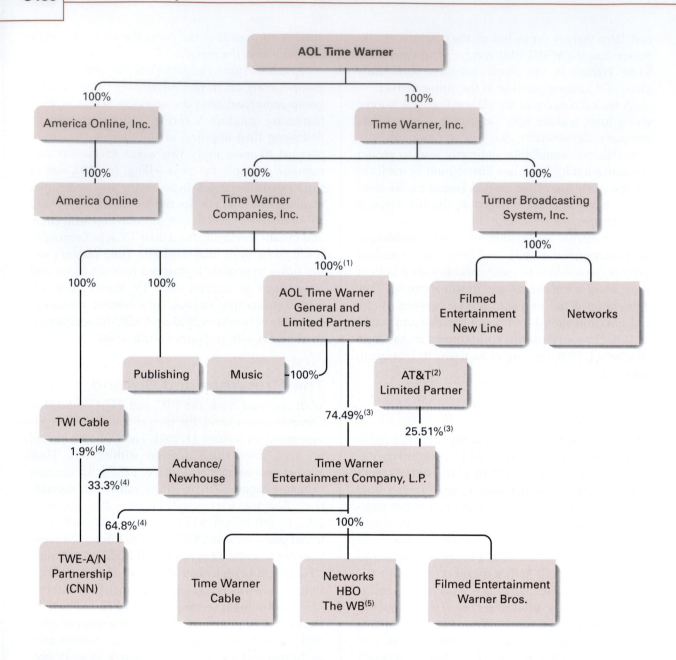

EXHIBIT 3

AOL Time Warner's Organization Structure

1. Time Warner Companies, Inc. directly or indirectly owns 100% of the capital stock of each of the AOL Time Warner General and Limited Partners.
2. Interest held by AT&T Corp.'s subsidiary, MediaOne TWE Holdings, Inc.
3. Pro rata priority capital and residual equity interests. In addition, the AOL Time Warner General Partners own 100% of the priority capital interests that are junior to the pro rata priority capital interests.
4. Direct or indirect common equity interests. In addition, TWI Cable indirectly owns preferred partnership interests.
5. Tribune Broadcasting owns a 22.25% interest in The WB.

Source: AOL Time Warner Form 10K, 2001.

and Microsoft's MSN network, did not announce plans to change their prices. Earthlink, with 4.8 million subscribers, charged $19.95 a month, and MSN, with 5 million subscribers, charged $21.95 a month.[24]

Several other divisions also registered strong performance as the year progressed. The filmed entertainment division had a banner year with several blockbuster films, including *Harry Potter and the Sorcerer's Stone,* the first of the *Lord of the Rings* trilogy, and *Oceans Eleven,* all registering impressive box-office numbers. The Harry Potter film was on track to become the highest grossing film of all time. Moreover, the strategy of building franchises in the movie business was looking as if it might pay long-term dividends. In 2002, there would be another *Harry Potter* and another *Lord of the Rings* film, plus a new *Austin Powers* movie and a new *Matrix* film. *Harry Potter and the Sorcerer's Stone* also provided investors with an early example of the enormous power of AOL Time Warner to leverage content across its divisions. The movie was made by Warner Brothers, and the soundtrack was recorded by WMG's Atlantic label. The film was on the cover of *Entertainment Weekly,* a Time Inc. publication, and AOL's web sites promoted the film through games, competitions, sneak previews, and advanced bookings. As Richard Parsons put it, the Harry Potter movie was an example of driving synergy both ways: "We use the different platforms to drive the movie, and the movie to drive business across the platforms."[25]

However, as the year lengthened it became increasingly clear that business conditions had deteriorated for AOL Time Warner, and in the end the ambitious goals set for the first year of the merger, and perhaps beyond, proved to be too much of a stretch (see Exhibit 4). For 2001, AOL Time Warner registered EBITDA of $7.43 billion on revenues of $38.2 billion. The stock price, which traded at $47.23 a share on the day of the merger, peaked at $56.60 on May 22, before falling to $32.10 by year end. As 2002 progressed, things got worse still for the company.

In April 2002, Time Warner announced that it would take a $54 billion charge against earnings to write down the goodwill on its books due to the merger. In effect, the company was admitting that when the merger was consummated, AOL's stock had been massively overvalued. Although this writedown impacted AOL's balance sheet, it did not impact the earnings potential of the company. However, the company also sharply reduced its long-term growth forecasts from 12 to 15 percent per annum for EBITDA to 8 to 12 percent per annum. What was going wrong?

Advertising Slowdown

The most obvious problem AOL Time Warner encountered in its first year was a sharp slowdown in

---

EXHIBIT 4

Revenue and EDITDA for AOL Time Warner, 2001 and 2000 Pro Forma ($ millions)

Segment	Revenue 2001	Revenue 2000	EBITDA 2001	EBITDA 2000
AOL	8,718	7,703	2,945	2,350
Cable	6,992	6,054	3,199	2,859
Filmed entertainment	8,759	8,119	1,017	796
Cable networks	7,050	6,802	1,797	1,502
Music	3,929	4,148	419	518
Publishing	4,810	4,645	909	747
Corporate	—	—	(294)	(304)
Merger related costs	—	—	(250)	(155)
Intersegment elimination	(2,024)	(1,258)	(86)	(46)
Total revenues and EBITDA	38,234	36,213	9,656	8,267
Depreciation and amortization	—	—	(9,203)	(8,650)
Total revenues and operating income (loss)	38,234	36,213	453	(383)

Source: AOL Time Warner Form 10K, 2001.

advertising expenditure in the United States, which entered a recession in 2001. Advertising spending tends to be very sensitive to the overall level of economic activity, and consequently very cyclical. It is often said that advertising spending is the first to feel the effects of an economic slowdown, and the last to recover. In 2000, with the United States enjoying its longest economic expansion in history, advertising spending in the United States surged 9.6 percent, partly thanks to advertising spending by dot.com companies. In 2001 the other shoe dropped, and U.S. advertising spending fell by 6.8 and 5.4 percent in the worlds' seven largest advertising markets. For 2002, forecasts suggested that advertising spending would slip by a further 3.3 percent in the United States and 1.9 percent globally.[26]

This slowdown presented an obvious problem for AOL Time Warner, which, as the world's largest media company, depends critically upon advertising spending for a good portion of its revenues and profits. As a whole, the company continued to grow revenues from advertising, but the rate of growth was slower than anticipated. Moreover, as 2001 turned to 2002, it began to look as if the rate of growth in advertising revenue at the AOL unit might fall. The problem for AOL was twofold. First, much of its advertising was from other dot.com's, and as they ran out of cash in 2001 this began to dry up. Second, Internet advertising in general fell out of favor with traditional companies in 2001, as many questioned the returns from banner ads.

Exhibit 5 shows the rise in advertising spending on the Internet from early 1996 through the first quarter of 2002. As can be seen, total online ad spending peaked at $2 billion in the first quarter of 2000 and started to fall of sharply after that, primarily because of the implosion of dot.com advertising. AOL was isolated from this effect for a while because it had signed many three-year ad deals in 1996–1999. As these deals expired, however, many were not renewed, and by late 2001 AOL was feeling the impact. In the first quarter of 2001, advertising and commerce revenue at AOL fell by 31 percent compared to the period a year earlier, to $501 million.[27]

AOL Subscription Growth Slows Down

Although subscriptions at AOL continued to grow, by late 2001 the rate of growth was slowing, and this trend continued in 2002. By March 2002, AOL had 34.6 million subscribers, a 20 percent year-to-year

EXHIBIT 5

Total Online Advertising Spending, 1996–2002

Source: Salomon Smith Barney estimates.

increase. While this might look impressive, the 5.8 million net gain year to year was 10 percent lower than the yearly gain to December 2001. Put another way, AOL added 1.3 million subscribers in the first quarter of 2002, 40 percent fewer than it added in the first quarter of 2001. The bulk of new subscribers came from outside the United States. The slowdown in the subscription growth rate was particularly bothersome given that the decline on online advertising spending meant that AOL now had to rely more on subscription revenue to hit its revenue and EBITDA targets (subscriptions accounted for 68 percent of AOL's revenue in the first quarter of 2002, the fourth consecutive quarter in which its share had grown).

AOL's Broadband Problem

A source of frustration for AOL throughout 2001 and early 2002 was its inability to make rapid headway in the broadband access market. Although the merger gave AOL access to Time Warner's cable system, and although AOL started to roll out broadband offerings on this system, it was unable to get access to other cable systems. Even though AOL Time Warner had to agree to open up its cable system to three competing Internet providers as a precondition for the merger, no such condition was placed on other cable systems. AOL had to convince other cable operators, such as Comcast and AT&T Broadband, to carry its service, and that proved difficult. The main sticking points were twofold: (1) whether the cable operators got any share of AOL's advertising revenue generated from high-speed business, and (2) who "controlled" the customer, meaning who would be responsible for selling the service to customers, billing them, and so on.[28] The cable companies wanted to retain control, primarily out of fear that if AOL customers could jump between cable and telephone companies' DSL offerings, they would have no loyalty to cable.

The impasse was serious, given that cable was fast emerging as the favored means to access the Internet at high speeds (see Exhibit 6).[29] By the end of 2001 there were 7 million cable customers in the United States using cable to access the Internet at high speeds, a 7 percent household penetration rate. This compared to 2.8 million DSL subscribers, a 3 percent penetration rate. While both cable and DSL Internet usage are growing at the same rate, cable is doing so from a much higher base. The most recent forecasts suggest that by 2006 broadband will account for 40 percent of all online households.[30]

AOL's problems were compounded in 2001 when it lost out to Comcast in an attempt to acquire AT&T Broadband, the cable unit of AT&T. AT&T had decided to exit the cable business and sold AT&T Broadband via an auction. Comcast was backed by Microsoft (which is an investor in both Comcast and AT&T). Assuming the merger is approved by regulators, Comcast will now be the largest cable provider in the United States, with 23 million subscribers. Given its relationship with Microsoft, there is an obvious fear that MSN will be given preferential access to Comcast's network and that AOL will have to pay a heavy price for access. Further clouding the situation, in March 2002 the FCC ruled that high-speed Internet access over cable pipes is an "information service," keeping it free from government oversight and effectively ensuring that cable companies did not have to open up access to competitors. It is still possible, however, that federal regulators might require Comcast to open up its cable network to other Internet service providers as a precondition for approving the proposed merger.

To further complicate issues, AT&T Broadband held a 25.5 percent stake in Time Warner Entertainment. That stake will now fall into Comcast's hands, which has indicated that it would like to unload the stake. Analysts have valued it at $10 billion, and some speculate that AOL Time Warner may have to buy the stake in order to get access to Comcast's network.[31] Compounding issues even further, the Newhouse family, which owns a cable network and is a partner in AOL Time Warner's cable system, has indicated that it is considering withdrawing from the partnership, effectively taking 2.3 million of AOL Time Warner's 12.8 million cable subscribers with it.[32]

Finally, there were signs that when AOL customers did switch to cable broadband offerings, they frequently dropped their AOL service. This was a particular problem in those regions where AOL Time Warner had no cable presence. Having to pay $40 a month for fast Internet access over a cable modem, consumers saw no reason to pay another $23.95 a month for AOL's slow dial-up network.

Strategic Issues in Mid 2002

With the performance of AOL Time Warner falling below expectations and the AOL unit, far from being the jewel in the crown, suddenly looking like a millstone around AOL Time Warner's neck, the company had to deal with some major strategic issues. First, there were management changes. In December 2001 Gerald Levin announced that he would step down in May, to be replaced not by Bob Pittman, as many had expected, but by Richard Parsons, a Time Warner man. Parsons immediately lowered expectations going forward, stating that "we will underpromise and overdeliver." Pittman would stay on as COO. This was followed by an announcement in April that Barry Schuler, the head of AOL, would step aside and

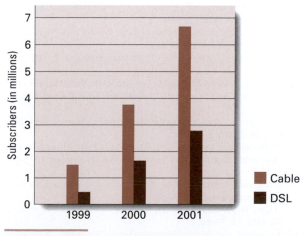

EXHIBIT 6

Broadband Internet Access in the United States

concentrate on developing digital services such as home networking and digital music delivery. Bob Pittman would once again head the AOL unit, while retaining his title as COO of the combined company. Pittman's job was clear—solve the emerging problems at AOL.

Meanwhile, speculation swirled about the company's strategy going forward. While Parsons stated that AOL would remain part of the company and that the Internet was central to the future of AOL Time Warner, outside voices called for the company to spin out the AOL unit.[33] The logic behind this suggestion was as follows: Time Warner's assets are worth between $16 and $20 a share, according to several Wall Street analysts. With AOL Time Warner stock trading at $18 a share in late April 2002, the stock market was effectively valuing the AOL unit at zero. In fact, analysts value the AOL unit at anywhere between $3 and $8 a share (which is down from a high of $83 a share immediately prior to the merger announcement). So by spinning off AOL, the combined value of the two companies would immediately trade higher (between $19 and $28 a share, according to these estimates).

Another issue concerned AOL Time Warner's financial position. The prospect of having to pay $10 billion to purchase Comcast's stake in Time Warner Entertainment (assuming that Comcast's bid for AT&T Broadband is approved by regulators) raised questions about AOL Time Warner's financial resources. Moreover, as part of the merger agreement with the FTC the company was still on the hook to pay $7 billion to acquire Bertelsmann's stake in AOL Europe. How was AOL Time Warner to finance this, particularly since the recent $54 billion writedown of its goodwill had reduced the strength of its balance sheet and would raise the costs of financing any debt offering? Potentially, AOL Time Warner also needed capital to purchase smaller cable TV providers to bolster its flagging broadband strategy. How could all of this be achieved?

There were also major concerns about the AOL unit going forward. Was the service now entering a slow-growth phase? How could the unit stop customers from defecting when they switched to high-speed Internet access over cable modems? What kind of concessions should AOL make to cable companies to get access to their pipes? Should it give up control over customers? When would advertising revenue come back, and how strong would the recovery be?

Finally, management had to grapple with how best to realize the potential gains from the merger. Were the synergies real? How might AOL Time Warner best realize them? What should AOL Time Warner do in the music businesses, where the online distribution of music seemed inevitable?

ENDNOTES

1. C. Yang et al., "Welcome to the 21st Century," *Business Week,* January 24, 2000, pp. 36–38.
2. C. J. Loomis, "AOL Time Warner's New Math," *Fortune,* February 4, 2002, pp. 98–102.
3. Kara Swisher, *AOL.COM: How Steve Case Beat Bill Gates, Nailed the Netheads, and Made Millions in the War for the Web* (New York: Random House, 1998).
4. Gene Koprowski, "AOL CEO Steve Case," *Forbes ASAP,* October 7, 1996, pp. 94–95.
5. David Hilzenrath, "Emergency Overhaul for AOL," *Washington Post,* October 30, 1996, p. A1.
6. Swisher, *AOL.COM.*
7. David Hilzenrath, "Turnaround Task at AOL," *Washington Post,* October 31, 1996, p. E1.
8. Jared Sandberg, "Firm Pays AOL $100 Million in Phone Pact," *Wall Street Journal,* February 26, 1997, pp. B4, B6.
9. "AOL and Tel-Save Approach Half a Million Long Distance Lines," AOL press release, March 25, 1998.
10. "AOL and CUC Announce Online Partnership," AOL press release, June 10, 1997.
11. Jared Sandberg, "Retailers Pay Big for Internet Space," *Houston Chronicle,* July 13, 1997, 2 STAR Edition, p. 8.
12. "AOL/SportsLine Deal," *New Media Age,* July 10, 1997, p. 6.
13. Paul Tolme, "AOL, Koop in $89 Million Alliance," *Associated Press,* July 8, 1999.
14. "America Online Reports FY99 Third Quarter Income," AOL press release, April 27, 1999.
15. Andy Reinhardt, "As the Web Spins," *Business Week,* May 24, 1999, p. 30.
16. Bill Gates interview with Charles W. L. Hill, June 1998.
17. Allan Sloan, "AT&T-MediaOne Soap Opera Has Just About Everything," *Business Week,* May 11, 1999, p. 3.
18. Sallie Hofmeister, "AOL, Hughes Link Up to Challenge Cable," *Los Angeles Times,* June 22, 1999, p. 1.
19. The following section draws on Time Warner's 1999 and 2000 10K reports filed with the SEC.
20. C. J. Loomis, "AOL+TWX=?" *Fortune,* February 7, 2000, pp. 81–84.
21. M. Peers, N. Wingfield, and L. Landro, "AOL, Time Warner, Leap Borders to Plan a Mammoth Merger," *Wall Street Journal,* January 11, 2000, p. A1.
22. C. Yang et al., "Welcome to the 21st Century," *Business Week,* January 24, 2000, pp. 36–38.
23. M. Peers and J. Angwin, "AOL, Time Warner Are Already Putting Operations Together," *Wall Street Journal,* November 10, 2000, p. A1.
24. J. Angwin, "America Online Boosts Price for Flagship Service," *Wall Street Journal,* May 23, 2001, p. A3.
25. "Harry Potter and the Synergy Test," *The Economist,* November 10, 2001, pp. 59–60.
26. A. Galloni, "Ad Report Suggests Delayed Recovery," *Wall Street Journal,* April 16, 2002, p. B5.

27. Salomon Smith Barney Research, *Internet–Online Media and eCommerce,* March 1st, 2002.

28. J. Angwin and M. Peers, "AOL Rethinks Its Game Plan on Internet Access," *Wall Street Journal,* April 19, 2002, p. A3.

29. Salomon Smith Barney Research, *Internet–Online Media and eCommerce.*

30. Ibid.

31. D. Henry. T. Lowery, and C. Yang, "AOL, You've Got Misery," *Business Week,* April 8, 2002, pp. 58–60.

32. D. Mermigas, "It's Getting Worse for AOL TW," *Electronic Media,* April 1, 2002, p. 16.

33. J. Angwin and M. Peers," AOL Breakup? Parlor Game for Wall Street," *Wall Street Journal,* April 22, 2002, p. C1.

34 | The Viacom Empire

This case was prepared by Gareth R. Jones, Texas A&M University.

CBS Broadcasting established Viacom as in independent company in 1970 to comply with regulations set forth by the U.S. Federal Communications Commission (FCC) barring television networks from owning cable TV systems or from syndicating their own programs in the United States. The increasing spread of cable television and the continuing possibility of conflicts of interest between television networks and cable television companies made the spinoff necessary, and Viacom separated formally from CBS in 1971 when CBS distributed Viacom's stock to its shareholders at the rate of one share for every seven shares of CBS stock.

Viacom quickly became one of the largest cable operators in the United States, with over 90,000 cable subscribers. It also owned the syndication rights to a large number of popular, previously run CBS television series that it made available for syndication to cable TV stations. Revenue from these rights accounted for a sizable percentage of Viacom's income.

In 1976, to take advantage of Viacom's experience in syndicating programming to cable TV stations, its managers decided to establish the Showtime movie network to compete directly with HBO, the leading outlet for films on cable television. In 1977, Viacom earned $5.5 million on sales of $58.5 million. Most of its earnings represented revenues from the syndication of its television series, but they also reflected

growth of its own cable TV systems, which at this time had about 350,000 subscribers. Recognizing that both producing and syndicating television programming could earn greater profits, Viacom's managers decided to produce their own television programs in the late 1970s and early 1980s. Their efforts produced only mixed results, however, no hit series resulted from their work, and the Big Three television networks of ABC, NBC, and CBS continued to dominate the airwaves.

During the early 1980s, the push to expand the cable television side of its business became Viacom's managers' major priority. Cable television is a highly capital-intensive business, and Viacom made a large investment to build its cable infrastructure; for example, it spent $65 million on extending its customer base in 1981 alone. By 1982, Viacom had added 450,000 subscribers to the 90,000 it inherited from CBS, making it the ninth largest cable operator in the United States. Also, by 1982 Viacom sales had grown to $210 million, with about half its revenues coming from program syndication and about half from its cable operations.

Viacom's managers, however, continued to feel that its cable operations were not a strong enough engine for future growth. One reason was that cable TV prices were regulated at this time, and cable companies were limited in how much they could charge customers. Its managers continued to believe that real growth in earnings would come not from providing cable television service but providing the *content* of cable programming—television programs.

Given their previous failure in making their own programs, Viacom's managers sought to make acquisitions in the content side of the business—in companies that made entertainment programs. In 1981, Viacom started in a small way by buying a minority stake in Cable Health Network, a new advertiser-supported television network. Then, in September 1985, it made the acquisition that would totally change the company's future. Viacom purchased the MTV Networks from Warner Bros., a company that desperately needed cash because Warner's own cable TV system was suffering from a lack of investment.

The MTV Networks included MTV, a new popular music video channel geared toward the fourteen-to-twenty-four-age group; Nickelodeon, a channel geared toward children; and VH-1, a music video channel geared toward an older twenty-five-to-forty-four-age audience. MTV was the most popular property in the MTV Network. Its quick pace and flashy graphics were popular among young television viewers, and its young audience was a major target of large advertisers. The popularity of a station's programming determines how many advertisers it will attract and how much it can charge them. While MTV was performing well, Nickelodeon had been less successful and had not achieved any notable following among young viewers, which limited the revenues it could earn from advertisers. Viacom moved quickly to revamp Nickelodeon, giving it the slick, flashy look of MTV and developing unique programming that appealed to children, programming that was very different from that offered by competitors like the Disney Channel. In the next few years, Nickelodeon went from being the least popular channel on basic cable among children to being the most popular, and Viacom's managers were confident that they had in place the beginning of a new programming strategy to complement Viacom's cable TV interests and to guide the company to long-term profitability.

Enter Sumner Redstone

Viacom's hopes were shattered when its Showtime channel lost about 300,000 customers between March 1985 and March 1986 because of intense competition from HBO. HBO, under its then CEO Frank Biondi, was making itself the dominant pay movie channel by producing its own innovative programming and by forming exclusive agreements with major movie studios like Paramount to offer their movies to HBO first. As a result of the loss of customers, Viacom's cash flow dropped dramatically, and the company lost $9.9 million on sales of $919.2 million in 1986. Further weakened by the $2 billion debt load it had incurred to fund its cable expansion program and make its programming acquisitions, Viacom became a takeover target.

After a competitive six-month battle to acquire the company, Sumner M. Redstone bought Viacom for $3.4 billion in March 1986. Redstone was the owner of a closely held corporation, National Amusements Inc. (NAI), that owned and operated 675 movie screens in fourteen states in the United States and the United Kingdom. Redstone became chairman of Viacom's board and moved quickly to take control of the company. He had built NAI from fifty drive-in movie theaters to a modern theater chain. He is credited with pioneering the development of the multiplex movie theater concept, which offers moviegoers a choice of a dozen or more screens to choose from. However, running a chain of movie theaters was very different from running a debt-laden media conglomerate as complicated as Viacom.

Many analysts felt that Redstone had overpaid for Viacom, but he saw a great potential for growth. Besides its cable television systems and syndication rights, which now included the popular TV series *The Cosby Show*, Redstone recognized the potential of its MTV and Nickelodeon channels. Moreover, over the years Viacom had acquired five television and eight radio stations in major markets, which he saw as valuable investments. Redstone moved quickly to solve Viacom's problems, and with the "hands-on" directive management style for which he is well known, he fired Viacom's top managers and began the search for capable managers who would be loyal and obedient to him. To turn Showtime around, he immediately hired Frank Biondi, the chief executive who had made HBO the dominant movie channel, as CEO of Viacom.

Frank Biondi was just a few days away from moving to Hollywood to run Columbia Pictures when Redstone called and asked him to take over as CEO of Viacom. The forty-nine-year-old Biondi was known for his strong financial, deal-making, and strategic skills and a knack for managing a diverse group of young executives and building them into a cooperative unit. Unlike Redstone, who likes to be directly involved in the day-to-day operations of a business, however, Biondi felt that his job was to set challenging goals, find the resources—both capital and people—to achieve them, and then get out of the way to let his managers achieve them. His approach was to decentralize control to his managers and to let them get the job done. Analysts felt the combination of Redstone's hands-on approach and Biondi's future thinking style made them a very effective team to head the growing entertainment conglomerate.

Viacom Speeds Up

Redstone's takeover of Viacom was fueled by his belief that cable television programming would become the dominant means of providing consumers with their entertainment content in the future. With the acquisition of Viacom, Redstone now owned 76 percent of MTV and Nickelodeon, which together gave Viacom access to millions of viewers aged two to twenty-four. Redstone believed Viacom's cable networks were its "crown jewels" because they provided half the company's revenues and profits, which came both from subscribers (the cable companies that bought the programming) and from advertisers (who advertised on these channels). To strengthen the cable channel franchise and build its brand name, Redstone restructured MTV and installed a more aggressive advertising and sales staff. Against the expectations of many industry analysts, MTV and Nickelodeon experienced continued growth and profitability. In 1989, for example, the MTV Networks won 15 percent of all dollars spent on cable advertising. MTV was expanding throughout the world, broadcasting to Western Europe, Japan, Australia, and large portions of Latin America.

Despite the success of the MTV channels, Redstone still faced the problem of paying off the debt that he had incurred to acquire Viacom—debt that amounted to $450 million in interest in the first two years following the takeover. Several fortuitous events aided him. First, shortly after the buyout, Viacom began to earn millions of dollars from television stations wanting to show reruns of the blockbuster *Cosby Show*. Second, in 1987 Congress deregulated cable television and allowed cable television companies to charge what they liked for their programming. The result was that the prices charged for cable television service soared, and so did the price of cable television franchises. Redstone took full advantage of this situation to sell off some of Viacom's cable assets to help reduce debt. In February 1989, Viacom's Long

Island and suburban Cleveland cable systems were sold to Cablevision Systems Corp. for $545 million, or about twenty times their annual cash flow. Cablevision also bought a 5 percent stake in Showtime for $25 million, giving it an interest in promoting the channel to Cablevision's customers and helping Showtime get back in competition with HBO. These events enabled Redstone to significantly cut Viacom's debt and negotiate more favorable terms on its loans. However, it was rough going, and Viacom lost $154.4 million in 1987, even though its sales increased to almost $1 billion.

With Viacom's finances on a firmer footing and Showtime showing some renewed vigor, Redstone and Biondi began to plan how to make Viacom a leader in the production of creative entertainment. In a strategic alliance with the Hearst Corp. and Capital Cities/ABC Inc., Viacom introduced Lifetime, a channel geared toward women. Viacom Pictures was started in 1989 so that the company could make its own movies. Viacom Pictures produced ten feature films in its first year at a cost of about $4 million a film—a very low cost compared to the money the major studios like Paramount and Universal spent. Under Biondi, Viacom's television production operations, which had always achieved mixed results, started to achieve great success with programs like *Matlock* for NBC and *Jake and the Fatman* for CBS. To increase subscribers to the important Showtime channel, Redstone sold 50 percent of Showtime to TCI, a major cable systems operator, for $225 million in 1989. In November of 1989, Viacom bought five more radio stations for $121 million to add to the nine it already owned.

Together with the five television stations and the fourteen cable systems it owned, Viacom's many different properties and assets earned revenues of $1.4 billion in 1989 and generated profits of $131 million. In 1990 and 1991, however, while Viacom's sales continued to increase, Viacom experienced losses of $89 million and $49 million on sales of $1.6 billion and $1.7 billion, respectively, because of increased costs associated with developing new programming and the lackluster performance of its Showtime network.

Viacom in the Early 1990s

The problem facing Redstone and Biondi was how to position Viacom for profitable growth in the 1990s.

Both executives felt that developing and expanding Viacom's strengths in content programming—often referred to as entertainment software—were the key to its future success, despite how costly such programming was. They believed that the message or content that is sent is what really matters, not the medium or distribution channels that carry it. As Biondi put it, "In the end, a pipe is just a pipe. The customer doesn't care how the information is obtained; all that matters is the message."

To build its content programming strengths, Biondi worked hard to build and expand on the success of Viacom's MTV channels. His goal was to promote the MTV networks as global brands that were perceived as having something unique to offer. Since MTV's viewers dominate the record-buying audience, Biondi sought to negotiate exclusive contracts that give MTV the first crack at playing most major record companies' music videos—thus making it unique. At the same time, under Redstone and Biondi's control MTV went from being a purely music video channel to a channel that championed new kinds of programming to appeal to a young audience. The result was innovative programming such as *Beavis and Butthead, Road Stories,* and other kinds of youth-oriented programming interspersed with music videos. In addition, Redstone and Biondi did not neglect the lucrative licensing market that accompanies hit television series, such as the slew of activity toys made by Mattel for new Nickelodeon characters that hit the shelves in 1992. The *Beavis and Butthead* phenomenon also generated many lucrative spinoff products.

In developing its programming strategy, however, Viacom's interest was not in promoting certain specific programs or stars—all of which may have short-lived popularity of fame—but in building its networks as unique brands. For example, on the MTV channel, the goal was to attract viewers because of what the channel as a whole personifies—an appeal to youth. Its success is based not on any particular person but on what MTV stands for. Under its new management, MTV prospered and its franchise was extended into Europe, Asia, and Latin America. Soon, MTV reached 250 million households in seventy-four countries. Viacom began to perform much better: in 1992 it made profits of $48 million on sales of $1.86 billion, and in 1993 it made profits of $70 million on sales of $2 billion.

While the development of innovative new programming was one reason for Viacom's return to profitability, a second, very important reason was

Redstone's emphasis on keeping costs under control. Redstone is well known for his frugal way of doing business. He runs Viacom in a cost-conscious manner, and this trend is evident throughout the organization, from the top executives to the lower levels of management. For example, Redstone has his office not in a prestigious Park Avenue, New York, location like the large networks, but in a small unimposing building a couple of blocks from New York's "red light" district. Despite his huge personal net worth, he was still walking to work every morning.

Redstone tries to instill his cost-conscious attitude down through the organization and across its many properties into specific business projects. For example, in the last decade costs have spiraled at many Hollywood studios and television networks because the producers are at the mercy of talent agencies that demand high prices for their stars, writers, and production companies. Not so with Viacom. Redstone demanded that all its own programming be produced by its own employees using low-cost, homegrown talent. An example of this is the production of its MTV shows. All of its hosts are virtually unknown and are paid little relative to network hosts like Dan Rather or Barbara Walters, who are paid millions of dollars a year. When one of the series produced by Viacom became a hit, the agent for the star of the show demanded that the actor receive a big increase in pay. Redstone decided not to pay the price and hired a new actor at a much lower cost. In 1990, Viacom opened a state-of-the-art production facility in Orlando, Florida—Nickelodeon Studios Florida—to produce its own programming for its kid's network and thus keep its costs down.

Changes in the Media and Entertainment Industry

In their efforts to build their companies' programming strengths, Redstone and Biondi realized that the environment around them was rapidly changing and that it was not at all clear how programming would be delivered to customers in the future. First, by the mid 1990s the U.S. cable television industry was in a state of flux. Emerging technologies such as wireless microwave transmission and satellite, and eventually broadband, threatened to bypass traditional cable systems, rendering Viacom's investment in wired cable much less valuable. Second, pressures were building to deregulate the telecommunications industry, and eventually companies in different industries, for example, cable companies, telephone companies, and Internet service providers (ISPs), were allowed to enter each other's markets. A number of regional phone companies interested in supplying television programming to their phone customers through new fiber-optic phone lines contacted Redstone. These companies wanted to take advantage of Viacom's programming capabilities and transit its channels through their phone lines.

This trend reinforced Redstone and Biondi's belief that during the coming decade the most successful companies would not be those that offered customers a channel into the home by cable, telephone wire, or wireless transmission. Instead, they believed that to prosper in this fast-changing environment an entertainment company should be the provider of the entertainment to all these channels. In other words, the most successful companies would be those that could offer the programming to go on the channels—the software providers. With its MTV, Nickelodeon, Showtime, and Cinemax channels, as well as its syndicated programming and ability to make its own programming, Viacom was in a good position to form alliances with the companies that provided the channels into the home. It would provide the software (the programming) to the companies that provided the hardware (the wired and wireless cable companies and telephone companies). Viacom's revenues would come both from the fees it charged to the hardware providers and most importantly from the advertising revenues it would obtain from selling spots on its many channels, revenues that are determined by the extent of the viewing audience. However, Redstone and Biondi had discovered how expensive it is to develop innovative programming and how devastating the effects of a flop of several movies or programs can be for profitability. The question was how to obtain high-quality programming at the right price, especially in an entertainment and media industry in which the value of companies was rocketing as stock prices increased.

The Paramount and Blockbuster Mergers

Viacom now had a new mission: it should become a software-driven company with a goal of driving its entertainment software through every distribution system, to every multimedia application, and to every region on earth. To achieve Viacom's mission, Redstone began to search for a company that possessed the software strengths that could produce the programming content for worldwide distribution. In particular, he went looking for an entertainment company that had an already established film studio that would round out Viacom's programming portfolio by supplying feature films and TV shows to its television channels. Paramount Pictures provided Redstone with his opportunity.

Paramount's many businesses include both entertainment and publishing. Its entertainment businesses include the production, financing, and distribution of motion pictures, television programming, and prerecorded videocassettes; and the operation of motion picture theaters, independent television stations, regional theme parks, and Madison Square Garden. Paramount also owned a large library of movies. Its publishing interests included Simon & Schuster, which publishes and distributes hardcover and paperback books for the general public and textbooks for elementary schools, high schools, and colleges; it also provides information services for businesses and professions.

Redstone and Biondi began to picture the extensive synergies that a merger with Paramount would provide Viacom in the future. As Redstone told reporters, "This merger is not about two plus two equaling four, but six, or eight, or ten." Redstone believed that together Viacom and Paramount would be a much more efficient and profitable organization. He had a vision, for example, of Paramount making films that featured MTV characters like Beavis and Butthead and new cable TV channels supported by Paramount's library of 1,800 films and 6,100 television programs. Both Redstone and Biondi believed that Paramount was a priceless asset for an entertainment company hoping to provide a broad range of programming content for future distribution to global customers. With its strengths not just in visual programming but also in publishing books and magazines, Viacom would become a multimedia entertainment powerhouse that could redraw the competitive map in the entertainment industry.

On September 12, 1993, after behind-the-scene talks between Redstone and Paramount executives, Paramount announced an $8.2 billion merger with Viacom. Soon, however, a bidding war for Paramount started. Barry Diller, the CEO of QVS Network Inc., another large entertainment company and the owner of the home shopping network, recognized the logic behind Viacom's strategy and announced a hostile bid for Paramount. On September 20, 1993, QVC announced an $80 per share or $9.5 billion bid for Paramount, and the battle between Viacom and QVC for ownership of Paramount Communications Inc. was on.

This unwelcome bid from QVS presented a significant problem for Redstone: Viacom still had substantial debt because of his original 1987 acquisition of Viacom and the rapid development of its own television programming. Redstone could not afford to counter QVS's bid unless he obtained other sources of financing, and he had to search around for partners to support his bid. After a career of financing deals with his own pocketbook, including the 1987 Viacom takeover, the seventy-year-old tycoon was forced to turn to other companies to rescue the Paramount deal. Redstone found two potential partners in Nynex and Blockbuster.

Nynex, one of the Baby Bell companies, anticipated that deregulation would allow it to enter the cable television market and wanted an alliance with a company that could supply it with programming content. Blockbuster, under its own energetic CEO Wayne Huizenga, had grown to become the largest chain of video stores in the nation. Blockbuster was cash rich as a result of its recent rapid growth. Huizenga, recognizing the threat that the growth in electronic movie mediums (such as video pay per view, wireless cable, and videos through fiber-optic phone lines) could pose to the sale and rental of videocassettes, was on the lookout for a way to reduce this risk. He agreed to support Redstone's bid for Paramount as a way to diversify Blockbuster's interests.

Redstone was not anxious to forge alliances with these companies, commenting that alliances are tricky: "No one who is not a hypocrite or a liar can guarantee how a relationship will look in the future." Moreover, Redstone also saw that Blockbuster's future was in doubt as a result of the growth in electronic means of providing home movie videos. However, his need for cash to outbid QVS for ownership of Paramount was stronger than his worries about forming the alliances. On October 21, 1993, after having aligned himself with these partners, Redstone obtained $600 million cash from Blockbuster and a $1.2 billion commitment from Nynex Corp. He then used this money to match QVS's offer of $80 per share for 51 percent of Paramount stock with the rest in Viacom stock. Furthermore, anticipating a higher offer by QVC, Viacom raised its bid to $85 a share for 51 percent of the stock. Many analysts argued that this bidding war had become a personal battle between Redstone and QVC chairman Barry Diller and that whoever was the winner was doomed to pay much too much for Paramount—so much for low-cost programming.

On December 20, QVC raised its offer to $92 a share in cash for 50.1 percent, topping Viacom, which asked for more time to raise cash. On December 22, Paramount signed a merger agreement with QVC, but the bidding could continue, with a deadline for final bids on February 1, 1994. Redstone, desperate for more cash, went to Blockbuster CEO Wayne Huizenga for more money. Huizenga, increasingly convinced that it was in Blockbuster's shareholders' best interests to merge with Viacom, suggested that Viacom should take over Blockbuster for a hefty stock price. Redstone, recognizing the value of Blockbuster's cash reserves and huge cash flow from current operations, agreed.

On January 7, 1994, Viacom announced an $8.4 billion merger with Blockbuster; it also announced a new bid for Paramount for $105 a share in cash. After the bruising battle with QVC, Viacom gained full ownership of Paramount on July 7, 1994. Redstone hailed the new Viacom as an "entertainment colossus" and "a massive global media company."

Explosive Growth

In a few short years, Redstone had gone from controlling several hundred movie theaters to controlling the properties and franchises of three Fortune 500 companies; Viacom, Blockbuster, and Paramount. By engineering the three-way merger of Viacom, Paramount, and Blockbuster Entertainment, Redstone created one of the three largest media empires in the United States (the others being the Disney/Capital Cities ABC, and AOL Time Warner), with annual revenues in excess of $10 billion. This was a large jump from the $2 billion revenue that Viacom had just before these mergers. However, Redstone and Biondi faced several major challenges in managing Viacom's new entertainment empire.

Engineering Synergies

To justify the expensive purchase of Paramount and Blockbuster, it became essential that Redstone and

Biondi engineer synergies between Viacom's different entertainment properties, each of which was organized as a separate business division. Several efforts were immediately begun. Paramount executives were instructed to evaluate the potential of new shows developed by MTV for sale to television networks and TV stations. Viacom launched its new channel, the United Paramount Network (UPN), in January 1995 to take advantage of all the programming resources across its entertainment divisions. For example, MTV executives were instructed to quickly begin developing programming for the new network channel, which in 1996 was on the air only a few hours a day but today is on the air five days a week and through its TV broadcasting affiliates can reach almost all U.S. television households.

In another attempt to create synergies, Paramount executives were instructed to make their moviemaking skills available to the MTV Network and to help it make inexpensive movies that could be distributed through Paramount. One result of this was a Beavis and Butthead movie produced by Paramount and scheduled for late 1996. This was a first step in Redstone's strategy to boost the output of movies at the Paramount studio without having to finance a big increase in the studio's own movie budget and to find ways of making low-budget movies.

Redstone and Biondi also searched for synergies between Blockbuster and Viacom's other divisions. They hoped that Blockbuster could link its retail stores with Viacom's cable networks and Paramount's extensive film library. Perhaps Blockbuster could sell copies of Paramount's vast library of movies to encourage people to create their own video collections. Also, the release of a new Paramount movie on video could be timed to coincide with a major advertising campaign in Blockbuster stores to promote the launch. In addition, Viacom's publishing division, Simon & Schuster, would be able to release paperback books to coincide with the release, and perhaps even a multimedia CD-ROM product could be introduced to boost sales. Finally, the launch of new movies could be timed to coincide with a major advertising blitz on the MTV channel—something that happened when Paramount released *Mission Impossible,* a youth-oriented movie, in the summer of 1996.

Viacom's top executives also planned to use Blockbuster's massive database of 50 million video-rental customers to "reverse-engineer" Paramount movies. The idea was to look at the entertainment tastes of consumers in this database and tailor Paramount films to appeal to the customer—right down to the casting of actors. As Redstone said, "Viacom through its new combination of assets is poised to participate in, and in many ways define, the entertainment and information explosion about to engulf the globe." Clearly, there was potential for synergies to emerge between Viacom's various divisions.

Reducing Debt

While obtaining synergies was one major challenge facing Viacom's top managers, so too was the need to reduce debt. After the Paramount deal, Viacom had nearly $12 billion in debt against just $4.8 billion in equity, and Redstone realized the need to sell off some assets to reduce this debt. In keeping with Viacom's new strategy of being a provider of programming content, Redstone sought to protect his creative entertainment assets and decided to sell Viacom's distribution assets—some of Paramount's properties and its extensive cable system. The first asset to be put on the block was Madison Square Garden, which was sold to ITT and Cablevision for $1.08 billion in March 1995. Redstone also sold Viacom's 33 percent interest in the Lifetime cable network to its other partners, Capital Cities and Hearst, for about $318 million, the television station WTXF-TV in Philadelphia to Fox for $200 million, and various noncore television stations.

Redstone had no intention to sell Paramount's seven television stations, however, which distributed the new United Paramount Network (UPN) to many major markets. Simon & Schuster, Viacom's publishing division, was also instructed to sell nonessential assets, and six professional book divisions were sold off because they did not fit the publisher's strategy of focusing on consumer, education, business, reference, and international publishing. Also, Viacom did attempt to sell Spelling Entertainment for $1 billion in late 1994, but then withdrew from the sale after it could not find a buyer at this price. Then, in January 1995, Viacom announced that it would sell its cable television systems division to TCI Cable, one of the five biggest cable companies in the United States, for $1.6 billion. These asset sales reduced Viacom's debt by a few billion but still left it with a huge debt burden.

Structure and Management Challenges

As discussed previously, Sumner Redstone enjoys hands-on control of the day-to-day running of the company and is constantly involved in managing the problems facing the various divisions. To jump-start the process of leveraging competencies across divisions and reduce costs, he moved quickly to develop a hand-picked team of executives across Viacom's new divisions to install his cost-conscious frugal values in divisional managers. Before being acquired, Paramount was run by an all-powerful boss, Martin S. Davis, and a group of executives who indulged in luxuries like flying in corporate jets and spending company funds lavishly. Redstone sold Paramount's two corporate jets and installed his own cost-conscious managers to change Paramount's free-spending habits. In 1994, Viacom dismissed Richard E. Snyder, the headstrong chairman of Simon & Schuster, also an executive known for his free-spending ways, and replaced him with Jonathan Newcomb, who made his name as a competent administrator rather than as a visionary publisher. Newcomb still plans to continue Snyder's strategy of overseas expansion and technological innovation, however.

Media and Entertainment Industry Challenges

The fast-changing entertainment and media industry also created many new challenges for Redstone and Biondi. The major Hollywood players were changing rapidly. In the old Hollywood, seven major studios dominated film and TV production, while the Big Three networks—ABC, CBS, and NBC—delivered the programming to mass audiences. Now, the number of distribution channels was exploding and the well-established relationship between producers and distributors was eroding.

Government regulations that prevented broadcast networks from owning TV programs were phased out, and the competitive dynamics of the industry began to change dramatically. Viacom's strategy to develop a full line of entertainment programming fitted well with the changes occurring in the industry. Also, as discussed previously, the regulations that prohibit telephone and cable companies from invading each other's turf were eliminated. Many phone companies formed alliances with Viacom to obtain access to its innovative programming and network channels. Similarly, digital and wireless technology vastly expanded the carrying capacity of cable and television networks, and the operators of these distribution channels were also anxious to carry high-impact programming, such as that offered by Viacom's networks, to break through the clutter.

The media and entertainment industry was also experiencing rapid globalization as U.S. movies, news, and TV shows spread around the world. The U.S. market is still the largest indigenous market for entertainment, but as the standard of living rises in many other countries, opportunities for expansion abroad also grow quickly. A major challenge facing Viacom was to obtain access to the global marketplace—with a potential market of 900 million viewers in India and a billion-plus in China. As an example of Viacom's global push, in March 1995 Viacom won a cable television license to launch its Nickelodeon and VH-1 channels in Germany, Europe's biggest and potentially most lucrative media market, to complement the MTV pop music network, which has operated in Europe since 1987.

Technology challenges also confronted the media industry. Advances in digital and information technology, including streaming audio and video, began to offer viable new ways to distribute software content to customers. Just as the dominance of the Big Three networks—ABC, NBC, and CBS—has been eroded by the growth of companies like Viacom with its assorted networks, so now many new avenues for distributing content to consumers were emerging with the growth of the Internet and advances in broadband technology. Digital piracy was also becoming evident, as web sites were springing up to exchange digital files, and companies like Napster were just a few years away.

Finally, the growing strength of Viacom spurred the consolidation of the entertainment industry. In 1995, Time Warner announced that it would merge with Turner Broadcasting, and Disney announced that it would merge with Capital Cities/ABC. As a result, the industry was now composed of four major players: Disney, Viacom, Time Warner, and News Corp., which owns the Fox channel.

Problems for Viacom

Soon after Redstone's expensive decision to buy Paramount, the Paramount movie *Forrest Gump* became a surprise hit, generating over $250 million for Viacom and silencing those Redstone critics who had argued that he had spent too much to buy the movie company. Viacom's managers began to feel like Forrest Gump, with his philosophy that "life is like a box of chocolates: You never know what you're going to get." It seemed that Redstone and Viacom had been in the right place at the right time and had made a profitable acquisition. Just as Redstone had sensed the potential of MTV, so too had he sensed the potential of Paramount and Blockbuster.

By summer 1995, however, the selection of chocolates in Viacom's box did not seem as good as in 1994. Many of the hoped-for synergies had not been obtained or were taking longer to happen than Redstone and Biondi had thought. For example, before the merger Redstone claimed that Blockbuster would be valuable to Viacom as a distributor of its creative programming; however, few benefits of this kind had been achieved. Similarly, analysts argued that Paramount had to cooperate much more closely with Viacom's cable TV channels and with Blockbuster Video if synergies were to be forthcoming. Moreover, the performance of both the Paramount and Blockbuster divisions had been disappointing.

The Gump smash hit had been followed by a string of expensive failures. Redstone and Biondi had begun to realize that making movies is a very risky business and that past successes are no indication of future success. Paramount's share of the box office dropped from 14 percent in 1994 to 10 percent in 1995. Moreover, Redstone was annoyed about the high marketing and production costs of the movies that Paramount was making, and after a string of failures, including *Jade, Sabrina,* and *Home for the Holidays,* wanted to know why the studio had spent $20 million advertising another flop, *Nick of Time,* which was clearly a loser. Hit movies are vital to a movie studio because they provide the cash flow that pays for the flops and bankrolls the future. Paramount's poor performance was hurting Viacom's cash flow and ability to service its debt. Moreover, box-office hits are crucial because they drive the rest of a movie studio's profits from international markets to home video and television.

To compound the Paramount problem, the Blockbuster division was also not doing well. Viacom had bought Blockbuster at the peak of its success—when its revenues were doubling every year and its free cash flow was a valuable asset. After the acquisition Blockbuster began to run into intense competition from two sources. First, a number of new rival video chains such as Hollywood Video had recently sprung up that were giving it intense competition and creating a price war in some markets. Second, pay-per-view television was spreading rapidly, especially in large urban markets, and the emergence of electronically transmitted video—which could then be taped (illegally) for future use—was taking away its customers. Blockbuster's revenues were flat, and the hoped-for growth in cash flow to help service Viacom's debts had not occurred; indeed, Blockbuster's costs were increasing as it got into the music retailing business and began to expand its product line.

To make matters worse, Redstone had a falling-out with the top management teams of Paramount and Blockbuster, who he thought were doing a poor job. He forced the resignations of many key executives and went in search of new leadership talent. Then, in January 1996 he stunned the entertainment world when he announced that he was firing his second-in-command Frank Biondi, who was well respected throughout Hollywood, because he believed Biondi did not have the "hands-on skills" needed to manage the kinds of problems that Viacom was facing. Redstone felt that Biondi's decentralized management style was out of place in a company actively searching for synergies and cost reductions. In place of Biondi he promoted his two lieutenants, Phillipe Dauman and Tom Dooley, to orchestrate Viacom's strategy, even though they had little direct experience with the entertainment business.

Viacom's New Moves

In March 1996, Redstone hired William Fields, a senior Wal-Mart manager who had extensive experience in running efficient retail operations through advanced IT, to be the CEO of Blockbuster. Redstone hoped he could find a way to transform the Blockbuster Video stores into more broad based entertainment-software stores, given that it currently seemed likely that the video rental business would be swept away by the new wireless cable and direct broadcasting technologies.

Redstone himself became more involved in the day-to-day running of Paramount, spending more time with its marketing and production executives to understand the workings of the business. Many analysts wondered how good a job the seventy-year-old Redstone would do without the aid of a seasoned entertainment executive. Analysts also pointed to Viacom's lack of a strong global presence or any executives who had experience globally. They noted that Redstone did not have any personal international experience.

In the spring of 1996 Viacom's stock price plunged from a high of $54.50 to $35 as investors fled the stock because of problems at Blockbuster and Paramount. In the summer of 1996, after a string of flops (with the exception of one movie, *Mission Impossible*), Redstone announced plans to cut back the number of movies Paramount would make and to reduce their production costs as he searched for a new strategy. Chief among Viacom's problems was its huge debt, which had to be pruned by more asset sales. In addition, Redstone and his managers had to find ways to reduce rising operating costs and overheads as well as to find new ways of leveraging resources and competences across divisions to increase revenues and build cash flow.

On the cost side, flat revenues and soon-to-be losses at Blockbuster and Paramount were pulling down the performance of the whole corporation. Blockbuster was now a growing liability, and Field's efforts were not bearing quick results. In fact, Blockbuster's revenues were falling. In 1997, Fields left and Redstone brought in a new CEO, John Antioco. In 1998 they streamlined Blockbuster's operations and sold off its new music store business for $115 million in cash. (The Blockbuster case provides detailed information on Blockbuster's new strategy.) They also introduced the radical idea of video-rental revenue sharing with the movie studios, and within a few years Blockbuster's revenues were increasing again. Also, in 1998 Redstone sold off all the rest of Paramount Studios's publishing interests, except for its lucrative consumer publishing group, to Pearson for $4.6 billion and used this money to reduce debt.

On the revenue side, there were signs that some potential synergies were emerging. For example, an alliance between MTV and Simon & Schuster resulted in a successful line of "Beavis and Butthead" titles, and Paramount did produce a successful Beavis and Butthead movie. Also, Viacom's global presence was widening as Redstone formed alliances overseas and as its television studios were developing new channels, including a second MTV channel to be called MTV2, which would focus exclusively on music videos, since the regular MTV channel had become more involved in regular programming. In 1997 growing demand for its entertainment content led Viacom to offer to buy the rest of Spelling entertainment with its Star Trek franchise and Big Ticket Television Unit. Its content was perfect for Viacom's growing UPN network, although that network had

yet to make a profit. Redstone integrated Spelling into Paramount's television operations to obtain economies of scale and scope in the production of new television programming. He was clearly focused on reaping the long-term benefits from his entertainment empire, although the poor performance of Viacom's stock was a big personal embarrassment to him as his acquisitions were continually being criticized.

By 1999, Blockbuster's recovering revenues and cash flow allowed Redstone to announce an initial offering of Blockbuster stock so that the performance of that division could be separated from the rest of the company. Redstone believed it was impossible to assess Viacom's true value until a real market value was put on this unit. About 18 percent of Blockbuster's stock was sold at $16 to $18 a share, and the over $250 million raised was used to pay off its debt.

Also in 1999, Redstone hired the experienced media and entertainment manager and former head of CBS, Mel Karmazin, as Viacom's chief operating officer to help solve its ongoing problems. Karmazin was well known for his ability to select and manage hit programming and for his hands-on ability to find ways to leverage resources to improve operational effectiveness. He set to work restructuring Viacom's businesses to engineer cross-divisional synergies, create new programming content, and enhance its revenue and earnings stream.

Both Redstone and Karmazin also understood that one of the most important reasons to build an entertainment empire was to achieve economies of scale that arise from being able to offer potential advertisers the opportunity to advertise their products across multiple channels that attract different kinds of viewers. In other words, a potential advertiser could produce one or more themed commercials to run across all of Viacom's different TV networks as well as with its movies or in its books, theme parks, and so on. Redstone had also watched Disney merge with the ABC networks to provide it with a major new distribution channel for its Disney franchise, a move that also had made DisneyABC the biggest entertainment and media company in the world.

Since the majority of Viacom's future revenue stream would come from advertising, Redstone established a new unit, Viacom Plus, to provide a centralized advertising service that deals directly with large advertisers and handles advertising for *all* of Viacom's divisions. For example, in 2001 Procter &

Gamble and Viacom Plus negotiated a ground-breaking cross-platform deal whereby P&G would pay $300 million for advertising spread across nine of Viacom's major divisions; the success of this deal led it to pay $350 million in 2002 for advertising spread across fourteen of Viacom's divisions. P&G obtained a better deal than if it had negotiated with each Viacom property individually, and Viacom Plus reduced the costs associated with managing the vital advertising process. In 2002, Monster.com, the online job site, signed a $15 million deal with Viacom Plus to put all its "scatter money"—the money a company has to scatter across different channels and demographic groups—into the Viacom platform.

A new opportunity arose in 1999. CBS networks were in trouble because CBS ratings were dropping, and the company was interested in a merger in the consolidating entertainment industry. Redstone realized that with CBS's assets Viacom would reach the greatest number of viewers and listeners (CBS-owned Infinity Radio Broadcasting) of any media enterprise, spanning all ages and demographics from "cradle to cane." As such, it would become a premier outlet for advertisers around the world because it could now offer them the opportunity to achieve huge economies of scale and scope in their advertising efforts. Advertising content could be driven and promoted across virtually all media segments, including broadcast and cable television, radio, and outdoor advertising and new digital media. Also, channels such as MTV, MTV2, VH-1, and CMT could now be broadcast over Trinity's radio stations and over the Internet, and CBS's high-quality content, such as its news and sports programming, could be broadcast over all Viacom's properties. The huge scale would also give the combined company bargaining power with programming suppliers and allow it to maximize the effectiveness of its sales force across all its divisions—a major source of potential extra revenue and cost savings. Perhaps a part of Viacom's problems was that it was simply not big enough?

In September 1999 Viacom and CBS Corporation announced that they would merge the two companies in the largest media transaction to that date. All operations of the company would report to Mel Karmazin. The range of Viacom's properties was now staggering in its scope, especially because at the time of the merger CBS was in the process of taking control of radio station owner Infinity Broadcasting and King World productions, which syndicated such shows as *Jeopardy* and the *Oprah Winfrey Show.* Moreover, the merger was achieved through a stock swap so that no debt needed to be incurred to fund it, something Viacom could still little afford to do because its revenues and performance were still only slowly increasing.

Karmazin now gave his full attention to structuring and managing Viacom's assets to realize the gains from sharing and leveraging the competencies of its division across all its operations. It began to seem that with the CBS acquisition Viacom had achieved the critical mass that made such gains realizable. In May 2000, Karmazin announced the integration of the company's theme parks, Paramount Parks, into the Viacom entertainment group. This move would grow the parks faster by linking them to Viacom's other properties, such as its Nickelodeon and MTV cast of characters. In 2000, Karmazin integrated Paramount's and CBS's television groups, and the new division consisted of thirty-five television stations reaching eighteen of the top twenty television markets in the United States. This led to major operational and sales efficiencies, especially because all advertising and promotion could be linked to the company's Infinity radio stations and outdoor advertising operations, creating the "advertising bundle" mentioned above. CBS now could act as a local as well as a national broadcaster, and it could leverage its news, sports, and other programming across many more markets. In 2000, Viacom's television studios also formed a unit called MTV Films to produce movies for Paramount. Most of the low-budget movies, which generally cost around $30 million to make (less than half the normal Hollywood budget), have made a profit, including the rugrats movies and *Beavis and Butthead Do America.*

In 2001, in yet another move to make it the number one advertising platform in the world for advertisers with programming that appealed to every demographic category, Viacom acquired Black Entertainment Television (BET) for $3 billion. The BET network reaches 63.4 million U.S. households, and its other channels, like BET on Jazz and BET International, reach thirty countries in Europe and thirty-six in Africa. The BET acquisition was just one part of Viacom's push to become the dominant global media company. Continuing its strategy of leveraging value from its properties, BET is seeking more ways to integrate its activities with other Viacom properties, both by customizing various Viacom TV programming for BET's channels and vice versa, not only popular shows but also news and sports.

All of Viacom's networks were also instructed to follow MTV's lead and develop a global strategy to produce content locally in each country in which they were broadcast to increase the company's global viewing audience. MTV, for example, has a presence in most of the world's major markets; it reaches 125 million households and is a major revenue generator for Viacom. And, while it broadcasts its U.S. programming in countries abroad, it had also produced successful shows in countries abroad that are customized to local tastes; these have proved so popular that they have been transferred successfully to the United States and other countries. In 2001, Redstone met China's president Jaing in Beijing to affirm Viacom's commitment to China, and in May 2001 channels such as MTV and Nickelodeon started to be broadcast in China, also with extensive programming customized to the Chinese market.

Throughout the 2000s, Karmazin has continued his push to find the best way to integrate Viacom's many properties to realize economies of scale and scope. Appendix 1 describes Viacom's entertainment empire in 2002.

In 2001, the increasingly popular UPN and CBS broadcast networks were put under the CBS television unit. This linked the distribution and programming arms of the CBS television business, also making it easier to leverage resources and competencies across all business units and, once again, making it easier to sell services to advertisers. In 2002, Viacom integrated its Simon & Schuster consumer book operations into the Viacom Entertainment Group for similar reasons. By closely aligning its publishing and entertainment operations, managers could discover more revenue-enhancing opportunities to cross-develop and promote entertainment content. Viacom's organizational structure in 2002 is shown in Exhibit 1.

Talented leaders were continuing to emerge in the new Viacom divisions, and managers who had the ability to recognize these opportunities were being put in charge of bigger chunks of the Viacom empire. In 2001 Simon & Schuster had fourteen No.1 *New York Times* bestsellers, and it publishes more than two thousand books annually. Also, by 2002, the importance of the Infinity Radio division to Viacom was becoming increasingly apparent, since it contributed more and more revenue and earnings to Viacom through its 183 radio stations as it became linked into Viacom's multichannel advertising strategy and enjoyed the benefits of carrying content from Viacom's MTV and country and western channels.

Viacom's stock climbed in the spring of 2002, despite the huge fall in advertising revenues caused by the recession in 2000 and the following September 11 tragedy—a fall that caused the earnings of its broadcast networks to drop by 20 percent. The over 10 percent fall in advertising revenues affected all entertainment and media companies and caused a plunge in the stock price of companies like Yahoo and AOL Time Warner. Indeed, the latter's stock price fell so far that Viacom became the number two global media company in 2002. Analysts now felt that Viacom was the best-positioned media company to benefit from the upswing in advertising that was expected in the latter half of 2002 because of its combination of large-scale operations, leading brands, and diverse revenue streams. While the broadcast groups' earnings fell by 20 percent, for example, the earnings of the cable network division rose by 12 percent, largely because of greater broadcasting in the United States and abroad. Redstone claimed in the summer of 2002 that the worst was over.

Still reeling from the downturn in advertising, Redstone and Karmazin continued to seek ways to counter future threats to the Viacom empire, particularly the threat from digital and broadband technology, which had hurt the Blockbuster unit and which might in the future threaten Viacom's distribution channels as TVs and computers would merge and more and more households would gain broadband connections to the Internet. Recognizing that Viacom and its Blockbuster unit had no particular competencies in digital technology, in May 2002 Viacom announced a major new initiative when it signed an agreement with IBM for IBM to build a companywide computing platform to support digital management of software content, wireless content delivery, and media applications delivered on demand, such as video-on-demand. The contract called on IBM to help properties such as Paramount pictures, MTV networks, CBS, and BET develop new computing initiatives that would help them leverage their resources and promote the cross-sharing of ideas. At the same time a standardized digital platform would help lower its cost structure and provide it with all the benefits of advanced IT in producing significant cost savings.

EXHIBIT 1

Viacom's Organizational Structure, 2002

There have been many reports since the hiring of Mel Karmazin that he and Redstone have locked heads on many occasions and that Karmazin was especially critical of Redstone's expensive acquisitions, which increased debt but had no clear future benefits. However, by June 2002, with the CBS merger and BET acquisition showing the value of Viacom's growth strategy, Karmazin was joking that their management styles were complementary and that he was in no rush to assume leadership of Viacom, especially since the seventy-nine-year-old Redstone was "good for another thirty to forty years—at least!" Redstone, however, joked that when Karmazin's contract expired in 2003, Karmazin "might want to retire." Karmazin's response, of course, was "never, never, never." After all, what COO would not want to control the Viacom empire?

REFERENCES

www.viacom.com.

Viacom Annual Reports and 10Ks, 1991–2001.

International Directory of Company Histories, vol. 7 (St. James Press, 1994,) pp. 560–562.

"The Paramount Takeover: The Drama Ended, Two Stars Get New Scripts; Viacom's Biondi Has to Stretch to Fill Big Role," *Wall Street Journal,* February 16, 1994, p. B1.

"The MTV Tycoon—Sumner Redstone is Turning Viacom into the Hottest Global TV Network," *Business Week,* September 21, 1992, pp. 56–62.

Matthew Schifrin, "I Can't Even Remember the Old Stars' Names," *Forbes,* March 16, 1992, pp. 44–45.

Nancy Hass, "The Message Is the Medium," *Financial World,* June 8, 1993, pp. 24–25.

"Redstone in Motion," *Financial World,* December 6, 1994, pp. 36–38.

"Paramount: Do I Hear $11 Billion?" *Business Week,* November 8, 1993, p. 36.

"The Ending of Paramount's Script May Not Be Written Yet," *Business Week,* September 27, 1993, pp. 38–39.

"Sumner Redstone Gets a Little Help from His Friends," *Business Week,* October 11, 1993, p. 36.

"The Paramount Takeover: Wall Street's Final Analysis: Might Made Right," *Wall Street Journal,* February 16, 1994, p. B1.

"Viacom Now Is a Full Owner of Paramount After Vote," *Wall Street Journal,* July 8, 1994, p. B9.

"Viacom Inc.: Paramount Gets 'First Look' at MTV Unit's TV Shows," *Wall Street Journal,* November 11, 1994.

"Viacom Firms Up Plans for Movies Produced by MTV," *Wall Street Journal,* Jun 14, 1994, p. B8.

"Sumner at the Summit," *Business Week,* February 28, 1994, p. 32.

"Deals Give Viacom Even More Muscle," *Wall Street Journal,* September 30, 1994, p. B1.

"Viacom Unit Continues Sell-off of Business That Don't Fit Strategy," *Wall Street Journal,* November 22, 1994, p. B4.

"Hollywood Scuffle," *Business Week,* December 12, 1994, pp. 38–38.

"Frank Biondi—A Media Tycoon's Take on the 21st Century," *Business Week,* 21st Century Capitalism, p. 190.

"Viacom Inc. Wins German License for Nickelodeon," *Wall Street Journal,* March 1, 1995, p. B10.

"Remaindered at Simon & Schuster," *Business Week,* June 27, 1994, p. 32.

"Gump Happens—and Viacom Is Thanking Its Lucky Stars," *Business Week,* August 8, 1994, p. 29.

Karissa S. Wang, "Mel Sez: CBS 'Pretty Darn Good,'" *Electronic Media,* June 3, 2002, p. 37.

Steve McClellan, "Viacom: Flat and Happy," *Broadcasting & Cable,* February 18, 2002, p. 8.

Martin Peers, "Viacom Posts $1.11 Billion Loss Largely Due to Goodwill Charge," *Wall Street Journal,* April 26, 2002, p. B4.

Marc Gunther, "MTV Films: It's a Sleeper," *Fortune,* April 29, 2002, pp. 24–28.

Dyan Machan, "Redstone Rising," *Forbes,* May 13, 2002, pp. 46–48.

Wayne Friedman, "Viacom Snares Monster TV Deal," *Advertising Age,* April 29, 2002, p. 1.

Jack Neff and Wayne Friedman, "P&G Broadens Deal with Viacom Plus," *Advertising Age,* June 17, 2002, p. 3.

Shirley Brady, "BET Seeks More Ways to Work with Viacom Family," *Cable World,* June 10, 2002, p. 24.

"IBM Thrusts into Entertainment via Viacom," *Communications Today,* May 8, 2002, p. 1.

Martin Peers, "Viacom Passes AOL in Market Value—CBS Acquisition Has Brought Shareholder Value to Media Company," *Wall Street Journal,* June 6, 2002, p. B3.

Appendix 1: The Viacom Empire in 2002

Broadcast and Cable Television

The CBS Television Network of more than two hundred affiliated stations provides viewers with some of the nation's best entertainment, news, and sports programming. Popular programs include *Everybody Loves Raymond,* the *Late Show* with David Letterman, and *60 Minutes.* Sports franchises include the NFL and the NCAA Basketball Championship. The daytime drama *The Young and the Restless* leads a daytime programming line-up that has been number one for more than twelve years.

MTV Networks owns and operates many of the most popular basic cable television programming services, including MTV: Music Television, the world's most widely distributed television network, reaching almost 400 million households in 164 countries and territories; Nickelodeon, which is seen in over 300 million households worldwide via localized channels, branded blocks, and individual programs; VH1, reaching over 96 million households around the world; and TNN, which serves 87 million homes in North America with the tops in pop culture programming. Other services include MTV2, Nick at Nite, TV Land, CMT, and the Digital Suite from MTV Networks. MTVN is also involved in a variety of entertainment businesses that extend its brands, including films, books, and online and consumer products.

BET comprises Black Entertainment Television, the largest national cable network serving African Americans, reaching 67 million U.S. households; BET on Jazz: The Jazz Channel, the country's only twenty-four-hour network devoted to jazz music; BET's publishing unit, BET Books; BET Pictures, which produces made-for-TV movies and documentaries; and BET.com, the leading online destination for African Americans.

Paramount Television is one of the largest suppliers of television programming for the broadcast, first-run syndication and cable markets, with over 55,000 hours of programming in its library. Its six production units are Paramount Network Television, Viacom Productions, Spelling Television, Big Ticket Television, Paramount Domestic Television, and Paramount International Television.

CBS Enterprises is a global leader in distribution. Its domestic syndication arm, King World Productions Inc., sells first-run programming such as *Wheel of Fortune, Jeopardy!,* and the *Oprah Winfrey Show.* Its off-network slate includes the hit CBS series *Everybody Loves Raymond.* Outside the United States, CBS Broadcast International is one of the premier distributors of U.S. network series programming, while its subsidiary, King World International Productions, is a leader in format sales and local production worldwide.

The United Paramount Network (UPN) reaches more than 86 percent of U.S. television homes through its affiliated stations, and it broadcasts ten hours of on-time, primetime programming each week. Popular programs include *Buffy the Vampire Slayer; Enterprise,* the latest installment in the Star Trek franchise; and *Roswell.*

Showtime Networks Inc. (SNI) owns the premium television networks Showtime, the Movie

Channel, and FLIX. SNI operates and manages the premium television network Sundance Channel, which is owned by SNI, Robert Redford, and Universal Studios. SNI also markets and distributes sports and entertainment events for exhibition to subscribers on a pay-per-view basis.

Viacom Television Stations Group consists of thirty-four television stations, reaching nine of the top ten television markets in the United States. The division includes sixteen owned and operated CBS stations and eighteen UPN-affiliated stations.

The CBS Television Stations Division includes duopolies in seven major markets, with CBS and UPN stations in Philadelphia, Boston, Dallas, Detroit, Miami, and Pittsburgh.

Comedy Central, the country's only all-comedy network, is jointly owned by Viacom and HBO and presents the biggest comedy stars from the past and present along with today's hottest newcomers.

Viacom Plus is the company's integrated sales and marketing arm. The group's mission is to create long-term marketing partnerships that build brands and drive revenue for both clients and the company.

Radio and Outdoor Advertising

Infinity Broadcasting is the radio and outdoor advertising unit of Viacom. Infinity Radio, the unit's radio division, operates over 180 radio stations, the majority of which are in the nation's largest markets. Infinity also manages and holds an equity position in Westwood One, Inc. Viacom Outdoor, Infinity's outdoor advertising division, has properties across North America and Europe, including the top one hundred markets in the United States.

Motion Pictures and Theatrical Exhibition

Paramount Pictures, one of the original major motion picture studios, has been a leading producer and distributor of feature films since 1912. Its more-than-2,500-title library includes Oscar winners such as *Forrest Gump, Braveheart,* and *Titanic* (the highest-grossing motion picture of all time) and recent releases *Jimmy Neutron: Boy Genius, Vanilla Sky,* and *Lara Croft: Tomb Raider.* Paramount Home Entertainment, a global leader in the distribution of filmed entertainment on videocassette and DVD, distributes theatrical releases from Paramount Pictures, Paramount Classics, Nickelodeon Movies, and MTV Films as well as nontheatrical releases both in the United States

and abroad. Recent successes include *Save the Last Dance* and *What Women Want.*

Famous Players, founded in 1920, is Canada's top-grossing, fastest-growing, and longest-operating theatrical exhibitor. The Toronto-based company offers audiences the best possible theatrical film experience through its 102 locations with 884 screens throughout Canada, including theaters in its joint venture with IMAX and its partnership with Alliance Atlantis. United International Pictures (UIP), in which Viacom has a 33 percent interest, handles general distribution of Paramount Pictures's films outside the United States and Canada. United Cinemas International (UCI), a joint venture between Viacom and Universal, operates approximately 970 screens in 113 theaters in the United Kingdom, Ireland, Germany, Austria, Spain, Japan, Italy, Taiwan, Poland, Argentina, Brazil, and Panama and is one of the largest operators of multiplex theaters outside the United States.

Viacom Consumer Products is a leader in the entertainment-licensing arena, merchandising properties on behalf of Paramount Pictures, Paramount Television, Viacom Productions, and Spelling Television, as well as third-party properties.

Famous Music Publishing is one of the top ten music publishers in the United States and one of the world's major suppliers of music to all mediums. Its diversified catalog of over 100,000 copyrights spans seven decades and includes music from Oscar-winning motion pictures such as *The Godfather, Forrest Gump,* and *Titanic* as well as every genre of contemporary music, including hits written or recorded by Blon-die, Bush, Montell Jordan, Garth Brooks, Ricky Martin, Eric Clapton, Whitney Houston, and Barbra Streisand.

Video

Blockbuster is the world's leading renter of videos, DVDs, and videogames, with nearly 7,800 stores throughout the Americas, Europe, Asia, and Australia. More than 3 million customers visit a Blockbuster store each day.

Internet

MTV.com is one of the leading music entertainment destinations on the Web, giving fans unlimited access and an intimate connection to their favorite artists, shows, and other fans. The site delivers unparalleled online programming with popular features like Radio

MTV.com, News, and unique community features, including MTV member profiles, instant messaging, and more. CBS.com and CBSNews.com, CBS's branded online offerings, promote and complement on-air programming, including *Survivor, CSI, Everybody Loves Raymond,* and *60 Minutes.* Nickelodeon Online is the leading portfolio of kids' and parents' destinations, featuring Nick.com, Nickjr.com, nick-at-nite.com, tvland.com, teachers.nick.com, and gas.nick.com. Viacom Interactive Ventures manages an Internet portfolio that includes equity relationships with over a dozen web sites, including CBS.MarketWatch.com, CBS.SportsLine.com, Hollywood.com, Switchboard.com, and the free-cash Internet portal iWon.com. VH1.com is a leading online destination for new music, entertainment, and artist information while serving as the online extension for the network's news and entertainment programming and its award-winning community-based initiative VH1 Save the Music.

Publishing

Simon & Schuster publishes more than 2,100 titles annually under thirty-eight well-known trade, mass market, children's, and new media imprints. The division published ninety-nine *New York Times* best-sellers in 2001, including fourteen at No. 1.

Parks

Paramount Parks is one of the largest theme park companies in the world and entertains approximately 13 million visitors annually at its five North American theme parks and its interactive attraction Star Trek: The Experience at the Las Vegas Hilton.

35

Monsanto (A): Building a Life Sciences Company

This case was prepared by Charles W. L. Hill, the University of Washington.

Introduction

As Monsanto entered the new millenium, Bob Shapiro, Monsanto's CEO, reflected on how much the company had changed during the last quarter of a century and on the vast opportunities and daunting challenges now confronting the enterprise. Monsanto was established in 1901 when John Queeny, a chemicals salesman, invested $5,000 in manufacturing facilities to produce saccharin, a synthetic sweetener. Over the next half a century, Monsanto moved into raw materials production, becoming an integrated chemical manufacturer. By the early 1970s, St. Louis–based Monsanto was one of the world's largest producers of high-volume, commodity chemical products. Then the first OPEC oil shock hit and Monsanto saw its margins drastically compressed by rising raw material prices and plunging demand.

It was at this point that Monsanto began on a journey that was to transform the company into a life sciences behemoth. From small beginnings, the company had grown to become one of the world's leading producers of agricultural and animal biotechnology products. Along the way it had acquired G. D. Searle, a second-tier pharmaceutical firm, thereby add-ing human life sciences to its animal and agricultural life science businesses. By the late 1990s, twenty years of investment in life sciences seemed to be paying off. Monsanto had introduced genetically altered cotton, potatoes, canola, corn, and soybean seeds, engineered to produce natural herbicides and/or to resist damage from Roundup, Monsanto's best-selling chemical herbicide. Sales of these seeds were growing rapidly as farmers recognized their potential to boost crop yields. Furthermore, Monsanto had plans to roll out forty new genetically altered seed products during the 1999–2002 period.[1] Meanwhile, under Monsanto's tutelage, Searle had assembled one of the best new product pipelines in the pharmaceutical industry, and he expected to launch more than two dozen new products between 1999 and 2002, led by Celebrex, the first in a class of new painkillers.[2] To complete the transformation of Monsanto from a chemical to a life sciences company, in September 1997 Monsanto spun off its chemical operations as an independent company, Solutia. What remained was a company with sales of more than $9 billion that analysts thought could grow its earnings at an annual compound rate of 20 percent per annum for years to come.

Despite the growth potential of the new Monsanto, however, Shapiro had more than a few worries. Getting Monsanto to this position had been an expensive endeavor that had left the company straining under an $8.2 billion debt load, a debt-to-equity ratio of 1.25, and a $360 million annual interest bill. Given its debt, some analysts questioned whether Monsanto had the financial resources and the marketing and sales muscle to maximize the potential of its pharmaceutical and agricultural biotechnology pipelines. To address these concerns, in June 1998 Monsanto announced an agreement to merge with American Home Products (AHP). Many saw the potential merger as an ideal marriage of complementary assets, with AHP's financial resources and strengths in pharmaceutical distribution being a good match for Monsanto's bulging new product pipeline. However, in October 1998 the merger talks broke down, reportedly because of disagreements between senior executives at the two companies over operations and strategy. Now Shapiro had to devise an alternative strategy to maximize the value of Monsanto's pipeline.

If this were not enough, in September 2000 Monsanto's U.S. patent on glyphosate, the key ingredient in Roundup, would expire. Roundup was Monsanto's best-selling product, accounting for over $1.5 billion of its $4 billion in 1998 sales to agricultural markets. In countries outside of the United States where the patent had already expired, prices for Roundup had been cut in half. Many analysts believed that the same was about to occur in the United States. Of course, Shapiro's hope was that the slack would be taken up by the increased sales of Roundup-ready seeds, which should also boost demand for Roundup. Here too, however, there was a problem, for there was growing opposition to genetically engineered foodstuffs among the environmental community, which referred to transgenic crops as a form of "genetic pollution."[3] The resistance was strongest in Europe, where, in response to public disquiet, the European Union considered blocking imports of genetically altered agricultural products.[4]

Building Life Sciences at Monsanto

The life science business at Monsanto was constructed over a quarter of a century during the tenure of three CEOs: John Hanley, Richard Mahoney, and Robert Shapiro. At the outset of this twenty-five-year odyssey Monsanto was a major chemical company with substantial sales from low-margin, capital-intensive, commodity chemical operations that pro-duced fibers, plastics, and agricultural chemicals. The main raw material input for these products was petrochemicals, leaving Monsanto highly vulnerable to fluctuations in the price of oil. Pushed by the OPEC oil price hikes of 1973 and 1979, both Hanley and Mahoney repeatedly emphasized the need for Monsanto to migrate its revenues away from low-margin commodity business toward proprietary, high-margin businesses. In the words of Richard Mahoney in a 1989 article:

> Our current strategy at Monsanto began to emerge in the mid 1970s, undertaken because we realized that, after thirty years of growth, many of our traditional chemical markets were maturing. In addition, oil companies and oil-producing nations were crowding into these markets. Not wanting to become a me-too player, we began to evaluate potential new directions. That decision liberated us to look at other technologies. Underlying that search was a determination to find technologies that would present whole new families of opportunities to exploit. We dedicated ourselves to becoming one of the truly great industrial enterprises by the early 1990s. In financial terms that means a 20 percent return on equity consistently, year after year.[5]

Hanley, who ran Monsanto from 1972 to 1983, made the first moves into biotechnology. Mahoney, his successor, built on this over the next ten years and in addition steered the company toward human pharmaceuticals with the 1985 acquisition of G. D. Searle. Shapiro, who succeeded Mahoney in 1993, completed the process.

Establishing Competencies in Biotechnology

The genesis of life sciences at Monsanto can be traced back to a 1973 decision to fund a small biotechnology skunkworks to carry out cellular research.[6] The skunkworks was the brain child of Ernie Jaworski, a senior research scientist at Monsanto. Jaworski had been following developments in plant genetics among the academic community. Like many other scientists, he had been stunned by the news in early 1973 that two California scientists, Stanley Cohn and Herbert Boyer, had managed to isolate fragments of a gene from one bacterium and insert them into another to create a bit of living cellular material that had never before existed.[7] Jaworski reasoned that it might be possible to use the Cohn-Boyer method—referred to as recombinant DNA technology—to genetically alter crop seeds to make them resistant to herbicides. The herbicides could then be used to kill the weeds around the crops as they were growing, without fear of harming the crops. This would help boost demand for one of Monsanto's newest products, the herbicide Roundup. Approved for market introduction in 1974, Roundup was a proprietary environmentally friendly herbicide developed by Monsanto. At the time, it could only be applied before crop growth, since it failed to discriminate between weeds and crops. Another possibility might have been to genetically alter crops so that they would express proteins that function as "natural" insecticides, repelling harmful pests. An example would be the cotton bollworm, which ate cotton plants and forced cotton farmers to spend significant sums on insecticides.

Jaworski proposed his idea to John Hanley, Monsanto's new CEO who joined Monsanto from Procter & Gamble in 1972. Hanley agreed to fund the establishment of the skunkworks, and Jaworski set up the operation with a staff of thirty-five scientists. The main focus of Jaworski's skunkworks, was on understanding cell biology with a view to creating crops with innate herbicide resistance. At the same time, Jaworski was cognizant of the opportunities that might exist if animal proteins could be produced using recombinant DNA technology. Back in the 1930s, Russian scientists had extracted growth hormone from the pituitary glands of slaughtered pigs and cows. They found that by injecting the hormone into a live animal, they could accelerate growth and, in the case of cows, increase milk production. However, the process was too expensive, and the technology required to mass-produce growth hormone proteins did not exist at that point in time, so for decades growth hormone remained little more than a scientific curiosity.[8] Now Jaworski realized that recombinant DNA technology might be used to mass-produce animal growth hormones, so he authorized research into growth hormones. However, progress was hindered by a lack of resources.

In 1976, Jaworski tried to persuade Monsanto to invest in Genentech, one of the first biotechnology start-ups. Herbert Boyer, one of the inventors of recombinant DNA technology, was one of the two founders of the company. At the time Genentech was seeking initial venture capital to finance basic research aimed at producing human proteins using recombinant DNA technology. Jaworski believed that Genentech might be an interesting way for Monsanto to get a foothold in this emerging field. However, Monsanto's top management was not enamoured by the growth possibilities that had them producing silicon for semiconductors, and expressed no interest in the possibility. In retrospect, this proved to be a mistake.

In 1978, Genentech produced the first human protein (somatostatin) in a microorganism (*E. coli* bacteria). Also in 1978, it succeeded in cloning human insulin using the same technology. The method involved using recombinant DNA technology to insert the piece of human DNA that carries instructions for producing the desired human protein (such as the gene to produce insulin) into the DNA of a microorganism (usually *E. coli* bacteria or some form of yeast). Because it now contained the gene for making the human protein, the microorganism expressed (produced) this protein. Cultures of the microorganism were then placed in fermentation tanks, where they multipled and produced more of the desired protein. The microorganism was then harvested, and the desired protein was removed and converted into a drug, such as human insulin, that could be injected into people who lacked the protein (such as diabetics in the case of insulin).[9] In 1979, Genentech used this technology to engineer microorganisms to produce human growth hormone. The company went public in 1980 with an offering that leapt from $35 a share to a high of $88 after less than an hour on the market. At the time, this was one the largest stock run-ups ever.[10]

Against the background of rising interest in biotechnology, in 1979 Hanley hired Howard Schneiderman to head Monsanto's research and development (R&D) efforts. At the time he was hired, Schneiderman was the dean of biological sciences at the University of California, Irvine. As a member of the National Academy of Science and a recognized expert in the techniques of genetic engineering, Schneiderman struck Hanley as the ideal person to oversee Monsanto's biotechnology efforts. As Schneiderman later recalled it, Hanley posed a question to Schneiderman: "We spent $170 million on research in 1978. We probably should have spent $275 million. Do you have any good ideas?"[11] Schneiderman was instantly sold. "If you are a red-blooded American who has chosen research as a career, and a guy comes along and says, 'Do you have any good ideas for $100 million worth of research?' it's a fantastic temptation."[12] At Irvine, Schneiderman had administered an $8 million budget.[13] Hanley made Schneiderman senior vice president for research and development and gave him the charter to make Monsanto a "significant world force in molecular biology."[14]

Schneiderman moved quickly. Jaworski's group was transferred into central R&D under Schneiderman's direction. Jaworski was made the director of biological sciences within the corporate R&D staff and was given free rein to go on a hiring spree to attract brilliant young researchers. It wasn't easy; a surge of new biotechnology start-ups offering attractive stock option contracts to scientists were competing with Monsanto for scarce talent. Monsanto had an advantage, however. Its financial resources offered scientists the opportunity to engage in long-term research projects, free from financial worries. Schneiderman's reputation also helped, and the company hired 135 Ph.D.s in the first three years of his tenure. What also helped was the company's decision to invest $165 million to build a Life Sciences Research Center on a 210-acre campus 25 miles west of downtown St. Louis. Referred to within Monsanto as "the house that Howard built," the research center was a powerful symbol of Monsanto's commitment to basic biotechnology research. By 1990, the facility had 250 laboratories and 900 research scientists, making it one of the most powerful concentrations of life science research effort anywhere in the world.[15]

Research Alliances

Despite Monsanto's aggressive investment in R&D, Schneiderman was the first to admit that Monsanto could not do it all alone. Within three months of joining the company, Schneiderman entered into an alliance with Genentech. By this time, Genentech had already figured out how to use recombinant DNA technology to mass-produce human growth hormone. Monsanto was interested in using the same technology to mass-produce animal growth hormones. In return for the rights to the bovine somatotropin growth hormone (BST), Monsanto paid Genentech $990,000, agreed to make several subsequent milestone payments, and promised royalties on future sales of BST. Genentech delivered the first 600 milligrams of BST in December 1981, and initial tests showed that the product worked like natural BST.[16]

In 1982, Monsanto forged an alliance with nearby Washington University to get access to leading-edge academic research on molecular biology. This was Monsanto's second big involvement with a university. Back in 1974 the company had entered into a twelve-year, $23 million agreement with Harvard Medical School for research on the molecular basis of organ development. However, Monsanto was not satisfied with this arrangement. A major problem had been that the Harvard researchers refused to give Monsanto access to research findings until they had been published in academic journals. Moreover, the company had found it was unable to direct or influence the course of research at Harvard.[17]

This time, Monsanto structured the agreement to give the company greater access to research results and a greater ability to direct the research process. The agreement called for Monsanto to invest $23.5 million over five years for biomedical research into proteins and peptides, small proteins that modify the behavior of cells. About one-third of the effort was to be directed toward basic research, and the rest directed toward new pharmaceutical products aimed at treating a variety of ailments, including allergies. The contract specified that faculty members participating in projects funded by Monsanto would be free to publish all results of their findings and that Washington University would hold any resulting patents. Monsanto, on the other hand, would have exclusive marketing rights to such patents. Projects to receive funding would be selected by a committee that included four university and four Monsanto scientists. Monsanto scientists would be able to work side by side with university researchers in university laboratories, and vice versa.

This agreement raised concerns in some quarters that it might violate fundamental principles of academic research and freedom. Albert Gore, Jr., then a Democratic representative from Tennessee and chairman of the Investigation and Oversight Subcommittee of the House Committee on Science and Technology, commented, "You don't have to know algebra to figure out how that committee works. No research can be done unless the company gives permission."[18] In reply, Schneiderman insisted that "everything is carefully designed to enable the university to be true to its fundamental purpose."[19]

The Washington University deal was followed by a series of other research deals structured along similar lines. These included a $5 million five-year agreement with Oxford University in the United Kingdom to sequence the structure of certain plant proteins and a $4 million five-year agreement with Rockefeller

University to investigate the structure and regulation of plant genes involved in photosynthesis. Smaller agreements were also signed with the California Institute of Technology, the University of California (San Francisco), and Harvard University. In 1985, the Washington University agreement was extended to cover eight and a half years, and the total funds committed increased to $62 million, making it the largest collaborative agreement of its kind.[20] According to Schneiderman, such contracts provide "a powerful insight into the future," fund research that is "more likely to make a leap," keep Monsanto researchers "in the front line of academic research," and "can be a magnet for attracting good people to Monsanto."[21]

Acquiring Searle

As Monsanto embarked on its journey into the life sciences business, it was not altogether clear what the focus of the company would ultimately be. Jaworski's skunkworks, and many of the scientists hired after Schneiderman arrived, focused primarily on applying the principles of molecular biology to plants. This made good sense given Monsanto's strong position in agricultural herbicides, a position that was getting stronger all the time due to the success of Roundup, which by the early 1980s was generating over $500 million a year in sales and was Monsanto's most profitable product.[22] On the other hand, the alliance with Genentech signaled an interest in animal proteins, and the agreement with Washington University was in large part directed at producing human pharmaceuticals.

Within Monsanto, the debate was not so much about whether the company should leverage its growing life science expertise to enter the human pharmaceutical business, as it was about how best to achieve this. By 1983, Monsanto, in collaboration with its university partners, was beginning to identify some interesting candidates for clinical investigation. An example was atrial peptide, a human protein that had been isolated from the atrium of the heart by researchers at Washington University. The protein dilates the vascular system, and Monsanto believed that it might have value as a drug for controlling blood pressure.[23] However, Monsanto lacked both the regulatory experience with the FDA and the distribution network required to maximize the potential of such pharmaceuticals.

The slow pace of Monsanto's move away from its low-margin commodity chemicals business added

urgency. By 1984, the company was still generating 60 percent of its sales from its traditional chemical operations, even though 65 percent of its operating profits came from agricultural chemicals, and most of those could be attributed to just two products, Roundup and another herbicide, Lasso (the patent on Lasso was set to expire in 1988). Monsanto's new CEO, Richard Mahoney, wanted to accelerate the shift away from commodity chemicals and simultaneously gain a pharmaceutical distribution network. To further attainment of these objectives, in 1983 Monsanto hired the investment banker Goldman, Sachs & Co. to identify acquisition candidates in the pharmaceutical business. In 1984, Monsanto acquired a small Belgian drug company, Continental Pharma, but a large acquisition candidate eluded it. G. D. Searle was on the list compiled by Goldman, Sachs & Co., but the company was 34 percent owned by the Searle family, and they seemed unlikely to sell. This changed in 1984 when the Searle family indicated that they wanted to sell their stake, effectively putting Searle on the block. Searle's pharmaceutical business had been a lackluster performer in recent years. The company had not introduced a significant new drug for eight years. It did, however, have a powerful antiulcer drug, Cytotec, in late-stage clinical trials. There were also a number of interesting drug candidates further down the product development pipeline. Searle also had aspartame (NutraSweet), the artificial sweetener that generated $600 million in annual sales—roughly half of Searle's total revenues. However, the patent on aspartame was due to expire in 1992. Initially, Monsanto wanted to purchase Searle's pharmaceutical business, leaving Searle with NutraSweet, but Searle refused to deal and negotiations broke down.

In 1985, Monsanto approached Searle again, this time with an offer to buy the entire company. The change in Monsanto's position was in part due to a reassessment of the value of NutraSweet. Searle had just won regulatory approval to use 100 percent NutraSweet in diet soda. Mahoney believed that this would expand sales for NutraSweet to close to $1 billion before the patent expired, throwing off significant free cash flow in the process. In Mahoney's words, "NutraSweet brings a very interesting earnings stream in the time between now and when our biotechnology begins to pay off."[24]

In July 1985, Monsanto announced that it had agreed to purchase Searle for $2.7 billion, or about seventeen times Searle's estimated 1985 earnings. While many analysts commented that the acquisition was too expensive and that Monsanto was paying a hefty premium for a mediocre drug company that had not introduced any significant new products for some time, Monsanto seemed pleased with its purchase. One business development executive in the company noted that "Searle's marketing and distribution operations will be the vehicle by which we can go forward and commercialize new products worldwide. Now Monsanto has the infrastructure to realize the benefits of biotechnology."[25] Mahoney also noted that "Searle has done a very good job of finding product leads of its own. We are engaged in a long-term strategic move to have Searle's and Monsanto's strengths melded together."[26] In fact, by mid 1986, Searle had twenty-one new chemical or biological entities in various stages of clinical development, one of the best pipelines in the pharmaceutical industry. These included cardiovascular drugs for hypertension and irregular heartbeat; central nervous system drugs for depression, epilepsy, and pain; immunoinflammatory drugs for arthritis; and an ulcer medication.[27] However, most of these products were still in the early stages of clinical testing, there was no guarantee that they would show the desired combination of efficacy and manageable side effects in clinical trials, and even if they did, they were years from market introduction.

Developing Products

With the 1985 acquisition of Searle, Monsanto had assembled the main building blocks required to embark on the transformation from a major chemical company into a life sciences concern. At the time, Ernest Jaworski commented that "by 1990 Monsanto will be the greatest biotechnology company in the world."[28] Executives in other biotechnology firms characterized such comments as "absolutely ridiculous" and an "extraordinary boast."[29] They noted that it was small entrepreneurial biotechnology enterprises such as Amgen, Genentech, and Biogen that had succeeded in moving biotechnology products to market, not large corporations like Monsanto. Large companies, the critics noted, lacked the required sense of urgency, drive, and creativity of smaller biotechnology enterprises. In 1986, only two biotechnology products were on the market, insulin and human growth hormone. Genentech, not a large

pharmaceutical firm, produced both of these. Moreover, all five biotechnology products then in phase III (final-stage) clinical trials belonged to entrepreneurial biotechnology companies, not large pharmaceutical enterprises. More than anything else, the critics felt that Monsanto was underestimating the problems involved in developing biotechnology products and bringing them to market.

Ps-3732

By 1986 Monsanto was already beginning to get a taste for the problems involved in developing biotechnology products. On May 20 of that year the Environmental Protection Agency (EPA) turned down an application from the company to field-test its first genetically altered microbe, dealing a body blow to one of the company's most-advanced agricultural biotechnology research projects.[30] The microbe in question was a genetically engineered bacteria that produced a protein that functioned as a natural insecticide and was capable of killing insects that fed on corn. In denying the company's request to proceed with field testing, the EPA was bowing to pressure from environmental activists, who had criticized Monsanto's testing procedures and questioned the safety of releasing genetically altered organisms into the environment.

The research project that produced the bacteria was begun in 1980 when a twenty person team of scientists, led by thirty-two-year-old Robert Kaufman, received approval to develop microbes that produced "natural" insecticides. The thinking was straightforward; farmers around the world were spending about $7 billion on chemical pesticides, but these pesticides also killed animals, polluted ground water and rivers, and showed up in traces in foods. Surely, Monsanto executives believed, farmers would buy a genetically engineered product that was cheaper, easier to use, and did not harm the environment or human health.

By late 1982, after collecting and analyzing hundreds of bacteria that colonized the roots of corn, Dr. Kaufman and his team isolated a single microbe, dubbed Ps-3732, that was capable of mass reproduction and able to compete with other microorganisms for space around the roots of corn plants. The team had also identified a natural toxin capable of killing caterpillar-type pests and generated by one of the three to five thousand genes in the chromosomes in another common bacterium, *Bacillus thuringiensis*. By the end of 1983, the team had isolated the gene and had succeeded in inserting it into the chromosomes of Ps-3732 using recombinant DNA technology.

The team now believed that they had a means to deliver a natural insecticide. The plan was to sell corn seeds coated with the genetically modified bacteria. After the farmer planted the seeds, the bacteria would multiple in the soil and form a barrier around the roots of the corn, preventing damage from cutworms, a common pest. Before field testing the bacteria, Kaufman's team undertook seventeen safety studies designed to establish the environmental impact of the genetically modified Ps-3732. The bacteria were fed to mice, quail, fish, and bees, and a wide variety of other plants were exposed to it. No adverse effects were observed. Armed with these data, Monsanto submitted a request to the EPA to move forward with a field test.

At this point, Jeremy Rifkin entered the picture. A well-known radical activist, Rifkin was president of the Foundation for Economic Trends, a policy study group largely funded from sales of Rifkin's own books. Rifkin had already established a reputation as a vocal and effective critic of the imperialism of modern science in general, and biotechnology in particular. In Monsanto's request, he saw an opportunity to nip the emerging agricultural biotechnology movement in the bud.

Rifkin's attack on Monsanto had two thrusts. First, he argued that once released into the environment, genetically altered bacteria could spread uncontrollably. Such "genetic pollution" might cause problems that had not yet been identified. Second, he requested from the EPA access to all of Monsanto's data on safety studies. He then had these data reviewed and critiqued by several ecologists and microbiologists that he had worked with for several years. These experts criticized Monsanto's safety studies as poorly conducted and scientifically inconclusive. Armed with this finding, Rifkin formally petitioned the EPA to deny Monsanto a permit to field-test Ps-3732.

The EPA subsequently issued a report on Monsanto's safety study tests. Written by microbiologists on the EPA's staff, the report stated that thirteen of the seventeen studies were either inconclusive or scientifically flawed. Kaufman acknowledged that some of the safety studies were scanty, but he argued that Monsanto was breaking new ground, that many of the tests were the first of their kind, and that the EPA ignored a lot of good data and instead simply focused on those tests where there was some question about the sample design. Kaufman subsequently met with the EPA's advisory panel—which was composed of independent academic advisors—after which the panel indicated that it would "reverse" the staff evaluation and recommend that the EPA allow Monsanto to proceed with the experiment. In reaching its decision, the panel acknowledged that some of Monsanto's safety studies were poorly designed, but it added that it had enough data from other sources to know that if Monsanto's microbe were released into the environment, it would not be a hazard.

Unfortunately for Monsanto, the panel's advice is not binding, although reversal of the panel's recommendation is a rare event. Alerted by EPA insiders as to what the panel recommendation would be, Rifkin continued to put pressure on the EPA, indicating that he would sue the agency if it approved the field test. This put Dr. John Moore, the head of the EPA, in a difficult position. Although privately he acknowledged that Monsanto's microbe was in all probability not harmful, he recognized that a lawsuit would give Rifkin the opportunity to probe Monsanto and the EPA in public. Cognizant of Rifkin's eloquence and his influence among certain U.S. Congress members, and aware of the holes in some of Monsanto's studies, Moore decided to deny the request, although he urged the company to undertake several safety studies and resubmit the request. In a short letter to the company, Moore noted, "I believe that it is in the best interests of Monsanto and the EPA that the general public develop a feeling of trust and confidence that all decisions to permit experiments of this sort be based on expert evaluation of reliable data." Later Moore commented that "we do not have the knowledge to completely understand the interactions of organisms in the environment. I think caution is absolutely justified."[31] Commenting on the decision, Rifkin stated that "we owe it to ourselves and the next generation to raise these issues and ask these questions. We are talking about the ability to change the genetic code of life, and that's ominous power. We ought to have a thorough, reasonable, and well thought out public debate. It ought not to be left in the hands of Monsanto."[32]

In the aftermath of the EPA's decision, Kaufman resigned from Monsanto to join a start-up biotechnology company, his team was reassigned, and Monsanto decided to shelve the project and pursue other avenues in the agricultural biotechnology research arena.

Genetically Altering Plants

One of the other avenues that the company was pursuing was the genetic manipulation of plant DNA. Unknowingly, human beings have been manipulating plant DNA since the dawn of the agricultural revolution thousands of years ago, but they have done it through the slow and highly imprecise methods of selective breeding and hybridization. By harnessing biotechnology, Monsanto hoped to dramatically reduce the time required to produce new varieties of crops and to design crops that had specific desirable traits. To this end, in 1981 a twenty-eight-year-old scientist within Monsanto, Robert Fraley, was put in charge of the plant molecular biology group and given the task of developing better crops through genetic engineering.[33]

Fraley's group first had to confront the problem of how to alter a plant's DNA. They settled on the novel approach of harnessing bacteria that have the natural ability to invade plant cells without destroying the cells. The bacterium they chose, *Agrobacterium tumefaciens,* invades a plant's cell and produces tumorous crown galls on infected species. The utility of this bacterium as a gene transfer system was first recognized when it was demonstrated that the crown galls were actually produced as a result of the transfer and integration of genes from the bacterium into the genome of the plant cells. The scientists theorized that if they could disable the disease-causing genes in *Agrobacterium,* it would prove to be a useful vector for transporting foreign genes into the DNA of a plant.[34]

It took two years to disassemble *Agrobacterium's* genetic code and remove the regions of DNA that produced crown gall. They then took another bacteria, *E. coli,* and isolated the gene that made *E. coli* resistant to an antibiotic called kanamycin. They cut the kanamycin-resistant gene out of the *E. coli* and spliced it into the DNA of the *Agrobacterium.* They then infected cells from a petunia plant with the modified *Agrobacterium.* The significance of this is that kanamycin is normally lethal to petunias. When they exposed *Agrobacterium*-infected petunia cells to kanamycin, however, the petunia cells continued to divide. In 1983, Fraley announced that Monsanto had produced a kanamycin-resistant petunia that was the world's first genetically engineered plant.[35] Subsequent experiments found that traits introduced into the DNA of host plants were stable over multiple generations during crossbreeding.[36]

Fraley then used the same methodology for more elaborate, and commercially important, plant transformations. The first successful gene-altering experiment with a staple crop came in 1987, when Fraley's group succeeded in modifying soybeans to resist damage from glyphosate, the active ingredient in the company's best-selling herbicide, Roundup. The glyphosate gene had been isolated from bacteria and then inserted into the soybean cells' genetic structure using recombinant DNA technology.

While Monsanto claimed Roundup-resistant plants would boost yields, critics in the environmental community opposed Monsanto's attempt to create crops resistant to Roundup. Because Roundup does not discriminate between weeds and crops, farmers must use it with extreme care and avoid it altogether in soybean, corn, and cotton fields. The development of Roundup-resistant crops, however, allowed farmers to spray the herbicide freely, a fact that troubled environmentalists. As one put it: "Monsanto's rhetoric is low or no pesticide agriculture, but in fact what they are delivering is a whole new generation of herbicide-tolerant plants that will shackle us to chemicals for the foreseeable future."[37] For its part, Monsanto pointed out that Roundup is an environmentally friendly herbicide. Glyphosate becomes inert on contact with the soil, breaking down into nitrogen and other nontoxic elements that are naturally found in the soil.

A series of other crop modifications followed the creation of Roundup-resistant soybeans. These included the engineering of an array of crops—tomatoes, potatoes, alfalfa, tobacco, and cucumber—that were resistant to viral infections. By 1990, the company had also succeeded in engineering transgenic cotton, tomato, and potato plants that contain genes from bacteria that produce proteins fatal to budworms, bollworms, and other common farm pests.[38] The insect-resistant crops were based on genes from a family of bacteria called *Bacillus thuringiensis,* commonly referred to as Bt. The Bt genes are a code for assembling proteins that can kill certain pests while having no effect on beneficial insects and animals. Bts have been used in sprays for decades, mostly by organic farmers, who forgo the use of manmade chemicals. But the sprays were not effective enough to make much of a dent in the chemical-pesticides market. Monsanto wanted to change that, in the process saving farmers millions of dollars per year in spending on insecticides. Once more, however, the environmental community protested loudly. A big concern was that over time common pests would develop resistance to the Bt protein. In particular, they worried that insects and weeds would quickly build up resistance to the transgenic plants and the herbicides used in conjunction with them, possibly leaving farmers worse off than before after a short burst of extra productivity.[39]

BST

Monsanto licensed the rights to bovine somatotropin growth hormone (BST) from Genentech in 1981 and received the first batch of BST in December of that year. Monsanto planned to perfect BST so that it could be used to boost milk production in dairy cattle (subsequently, studies at universities and at dairy farms have found that the drug increases milk production 10 to 20 percent in well-managed herds). It took twelve years and an estimated $300 million in R&D before the company finally won approval to sell BST in the marketplace.[40]

Monsanto's product is produced by inserting the BST gene from cows into *E. coli* bacteria, which are then multiplied in fermentation tanks. The bacteria are then harvested and the BST protein is removed, purified, and converted into the drug that can be injected into cows. This process might sound straightforward, but it is not. It took several years for Monsanto's scientists to find the ideal environment in fermentation vats for the care and feeding of the BST-producing *E. coli*. *E coli* turned out to be difficult to mass-produce, requiring just the right amount of oxygen and nutrients and the correct temperature. If any one of these variables was not right, other bacteria could swamp *E. coli*, dramatically lowering BST yields from the fermentation process. Then researchers ran into problems when they tried to kill the bacteria and "crack open" the organisms. Cracking open bacteria involves submitting the organisms to very high pressure and then releasing that pressure. The sudden drop in pressure causes the bacteria to pop open and release their contents. Monsanto found that the BST-laden bacteria quickly wore down the stainless steel valves on pressure equipment. The reason: BST protein particles have the consistency of superhard grains of sand. As a result, the pressure equipment was breaking down constantly. Solving the problem

required the invention of ceramic valves that could withstand the wear and tear from BST. After cracking, Monsanto found that it needed to conduct seven more purification steps to separate the BST molecules from thousands of other proteins, fats, and carbohydrates in the *E. coli* mix. To perfect the purification process, Monsanto had to develop special filters that prevented BST from becoming contaminated.

Another problem was finding the correct formulation of the drug. Early BST tests required scientists to inject cows every day, but Monsanto concluded that such a regime would be too expensive and cumbersome for farmers, and it developed a formulation that only needed to be injected weekly. Then there was also the issue of where to produce BST. United States regulations prohibit the export of drugs that have not been approved for marketing by the FDA in the United States. Monsanto reasoned that it might get approval to market BST from foreign regulators before it received FDA approval (correctly, as it turned out), so the company decided to locate the manufacturing facilities in Austria.

Difficult as they were, however, solving all of these production problems was minor compared to the political and regulatory problems that Monsanto had to solve before BST could be marketed. The problems started in 1985, when researchers at Cornell University reported that the results of early field trials found that the drug increased milk production by as much as 40 percent. The widely publicized results dismayed dairy farmers in New York, Wisconsin, Minnesota, and other milk-producing states. They came at a time when large dairy surpluses were pushing prices down, forcing family farms out of business. Thousands of farmers in the Upper Middle West joined with Jeremy Rifkin in a grassroots campaign that in 1990 succeeded in persuading the state legislatures of Wisconsin and Minnesota to enact temporary moratoriums on the use of the drug in the event it was approved. The moratoriums expired in 1991. In the same year, an unprecedented review by a panel of experts convened by the National Institutes of Health declared the drug safe.

In November 1993, the FDA got its turn. After extensive testing and review, the FDA approved Monsanto's BST. This represented the first time the government would allow food to be produced using a genetically engineered drug. The decision was made by Dr. David A. Kessler, the commissioner of food and drugs, who noted, "There is virtually no difference in milk from treated and untreated cows. In fact, it's not possible using current scientific techniques to tell them apart. We have looked carefully at every single question raised, and we are confident this product is safe for consumers, for cows and for the environment." Jeremy Rifkin was defiant in response. To quote: "We have said since 1986 that if the F.D.A. ever approved this drug that the final battleground would be the grocery stores, restaurants and convenience stores. This is the beginning of food politics in this country. If Monsanto succeeds with this product, they open the floodgates on the biotechnology age. If we succeed, it will send a chilling message through the agricultural business that people don't want genetically engineered foods."[41]

COX-2 Inhibitor

In 1999, Monsanto's Searle unit introduced Celebrex, the first in a new class of pain treatments for arthritis that offers the same benefit as existing pain relief medications for arthritis (such as aspirin), but with a sharp reduction in the harmful—and often dangerous—side effects of stomach irritation, ulcers, and internal bleeding. The product was the result of a fifteen-year quest by Philip Needleman to understand the role of cyclo-oxygenase (COX) enzymes in the regulation of prostaglandins, hormonelike fatty acids that are crucial to the body's maintenance.[42] As a researcher in the medical school at Washington University, Needleman studied complex chemicals that act as on-off switches in the body. Needleman and a colleague discovered a chemical inhibitor that affects prostaglandins. He learned more from an English researcher, who discovered that aspirin and aspirinlike drugs block the production of prostaglandins and thus reduce pain. But too much blocking is dangerous. Prostaglandins help regulate blood flow through the kidneys and aid in blood clotting. Without prostaglandins producing a protective coating, the stomach would eat itself because of the acid it secretes during digestion. As a result of this effect, patients taking drugs that block COX enzymes, such as aspirin, can suffer from serious stomach lesions. The resulting internal bleeding contributed to the death of some sixteen thousand people a year in the United States alone.

Needleman found that there are two COX enzymes: COX-1 handles the body's housekeeping; injury or disease triggers COX-2. Aspirin and other similar painkillers, referred to as nonsteroidal anti-inflammatory drugs (NSAIDs), block both enzymes—hence the side effects. Needleman wanted to block just COX-2. If that could be achieved, it would be possible to develop a pain medicine that lacked the side effect profile of NSAIDs. By the late 1980s, Needleman was convinced that this was possible, but he did not have the resources to do much about it. At this point he was also chair of the Department of Pharmacology at Washington University. In this role he had helped negotiate the original Monsanto–Washington University research agreement and now helped the company to allocate funds to Washington University researchers. The company was looking for a successor to Schneiderman and was favorably disposed towards hiring another academic. Needleman had the combination of scientific credentials and leadership skills that Monsanto was looking for, and he was also a known quantity to the company. Like Schneiderman before him, Needleman found the possibilities enticing: "I became enthralled with the idea of what it's like to have all of the people and resources to attack a problem."[43] In 1989, he joined the company as chief scientist.

At Monsanto's Searle division, Needleman found a company that had a long history of household-name products, but the new product pipeline seemed relatively bare to him, and he found the research effort to be diffused. Moreover, Needleman was aware of the costs and risks involved in bringing a new drug to market. Producing human pharmaceuticals is if anything a more expensive and risky business than producing transgenic crops. On average, it can take twelve years and cost $300 million to take a drug from the laboratory to the marketplace. To make matters worse, some 80 percent of products that enter clinical trials fail to make it to the market. A drug candidate must go through three sets of increasingly expensive clinical trials to test for safety, dosage, and efficacy (referred to as phase I, II, and III trials). It then faces a rigorous review at the hands of the FDA. On average, 70 percent of drug candidates that enter into phase I trials make it through to phase II, 47 percent entering phase II make it to phase III, and 82 percent entering phase III make it to the FDA, where 74 percent are approved.[44]

Realizing that Searle lacked the resources of its larger pharmaceutical industry rivals, Needleman developed a two-pronged strategy for Searle's R&D.[45] First, he directed research effort toward three main therapeutic areas: arthritis, oncology, and cardiovascular problems. By concentrating resources,

Searle could match or exceed the dollars spent per therapeutic area by larger rivals. In 1998, for example, Searle spent $280 million per therapeutic area, compared to $250 million at Pfizer and $200 million at Merck.[46] Second, he developed the discipline of killing off drug development projects early if they didn't survive what he characterized as "killer experiments."

As part of this strategy, Needleman "exploded the budget for COX-2." The search for a COX-2 inhibitor became the biggest project Searle had ever undertaken. For three years a team of thirty chemists and thirty biologists examined two thousand chemical compounds in the quest to find a COX-2 inhibitor. Urgency was added to the quest by the fact that Merck was also racing to develop a COX-2 inhibitor. When the Searle team found the compound that eventually became Celebrex, they submitted it to a "killer experiment" while it was being tested in a phase I trial as an arthritis treatment. The killer experiment was to discover whether the drug relieved severe tooth pain. Needleman reasoned that if the drug alleviated dental pain, it would also get arthritis. Celebrex survived the experiment, and the phase I and II trials suggested that the drug not only relieved pain, but also had none of the dangerous side effects associated with other treatments. After a 8,000-patient phase III trial produced favorable results, Searle filed with the FDA for approval to market the drug in August of 1998. Because the drug was the first COX-2 inhibitor to come up for review, the FDA granted Celebrex a propriety review, which meant that it would announce a decision within six months (normally, FDA approval can take as long as twelve months). Approval was granted in December 1998, and Celebrex was launched in mid January, 1999, the first in a new class of "superaspirin" painkillers.

Product Launches

Monsanto launched BST in February 1994. It was to be the first in a series of new product launches over the next five years that was to finally generate significant revenues for the company, almost a quarter of a century after Jaworski's skunkworks started Monsanto down the biotechnology road.

BST

By early 1999, BST, which Monsanto sold under the brand name Posilac, was being regularly injected in some 30 percent of dairy herds in the United States. Follow-up data showed that BST boosted milk production by about 10 percent on average. Robust demand for milk and milk products in the United States meant that the supply glut feared by dairy farmers did not materialize. Monsanto and the FDA continued to monitor BST for possible adverse effects. As of 1999, the FDA continued to state that milk from BST-treated cows posed no health risks. The American Medical Association, the World Health Organization, and the National Institutes of Health have issued similar findings. According to Monsanto, BST has enjoyed robust sales gains and in 1998 passed 100 million doses—at $5.80 per dose.[47]

Despite its success in the United States, however, Monsanto has still not been able to get the product approved for sale in either Canada or the European Union (EU). In early 1999, Health Canada, the Canadian version of the FDA, rejected Monsanto's application to market BST. While a review of existing data by Canadian scientists found no significant risk to human beings who ingest products from animals treated with BST, they noted that short-term tests on lab rats suggest that further study is needed. Health Canada concluded that there was sufficient concern to warrant not approving the drug.[48]

In 1989, the European Union imposed a moratorium on the use of animal growth hormones, or the sale of products produced by those hormones, on the grounds that European farmers were already producing too much milk and beef, and there was no need for greater production. The moratorium was extended in 1996 and 1997 and was due to expire at the end of 1999. In early 1999, the animal health and welfare committee of the EU concluded that BST should not be injected into cattle. Its report cited increased likelihood of mastitis, foot problems, and injection site reactions, which would also lead to welfare problems besides human health risks. In contrast, another EU committee, the committee for veterinary medicinal products, had ruled in 1998 that BST was perfectly safe.[49] More generally, public opinion in the EU seemed to be strongly against not just BST, but genetically modified foods in general. In the United States, the Clinton administration considered appealing to the World Trade Organization (WTO) on the grounds that the EU ban on BST represented an unfair restraint of trade that was at variance with WTO rules, of which the EU was a signatory.

Genetically Modified Crops

Following regulatory approval, in 1996 Monsanto introduced the first wave of its genetically modified crops: Roundup Ready Soybeans, Bollgard Insect Protected Cotton, and New Leaf Insect Protected Potatoes. Getting to this point had required sixteen years of research and, according to various estimates, cost between $300 million and $500 million in R&D spending. A series of other products were scheduled to follow over the next few years, including Roundup-ready canola, cotton, and oil seed rape, Yield Guard insect-protected corn, insect-protected tomatoes, corn rootworm–protected cotton, and Roundup Ready insect-protected soybeans (which adds Bt to Roundup Ready soybeans to provide both insect resistance and herbicide tolerance).

Although it was acknowledged as a technology leader and the first to bring a substantial number of products to market, Monsanto did not have the field entirely to itself. It faced the prospect of competition from several large companies, including DuPont and Swiss-based Novartis. DuPont had developed soybeans that tolerated the company's powerful Synchrony herbicide. Novartis had genetically altered corn seed so that it produced a protein that killed a common pest, the European corn borer. Both companies also had active research programs that promised to produce a range of genetically modified crops over the next decade.

Several smaller agricultural biotechnology companies had also been developing genetically altered crops, including DeKalb Genetics and Calgene. Calgene had introduced the first genetically engineered crop the previous year, a tomato that ripened more slowly and would stay fresh longer on supermarket shelves. Calgene was also developing a variety of soybean that was resistant to glyphosate, the active ingredient in Roundup. Similarly, DeKalb was developing corn seed that was resistant to glyphosate. Monsanto purchased Calgene in April 1997 for $240 million.

Distribution Agreements   The delivery vehicle for all of Monsanto's genetic improvements was seed. However, the company had not traditionally been a strong player in the seed business. Thus, to produce and deliver genetically modified seed to farmers, Monsanto needed to find a way to participate in the seed industry. Companies in this industry grow seeds and then distribute them to farmers. The issue was further complicated by the fact that the genes that Monsanto created provided only one specific trait to the farmer. It was crucial that Monsanto's genes be incorporated in the best germplasm available, necessitating that Monsanto find some way to cooperate with leading seed companies. In its 1998 annual report, the company explained the issue as follows:

> Seed is the delivery vehicle for biotechnology traits. Integrating seed into our life sciences system will accelerate the development of new traits and their introduction into new varieties. The combination of breeding and genomics will accelerate the development of new varieties with better quality. Germplasm, the basic genetic structure of a plant, determines the characteristics of that variety, such as yield potential or drought resistance. Germplasm is crucial to grower acceptance; our traits must be available in the varieties that growers prefer. While we license our technology for use in other companies' germplasm—and that's an integral part of our overall strategy—we need to be involved from the start in developing new varieties that include the best traits.

The seed industry itself was highly concentrated, with a small number of players dominating the market. Different seed companies also focused on different product and vertical segments of the seed market. For example, Delta & Pine Land had a 55 percent share of the U.S. market for cotton seeds, but a zero percent share of the market for corn seeds, and only 1 percent of the market for soybean seeds. In contrast, Pioneer Hi-Bred had a 44 percent share of the market for corn seeds, a 19 percent share of the soybean market, and no position in the market for cotton seeds. Other large seed companies included DeKalb Genetics, Northrup King (owned by Sandoz), Cargill, Ciba Seeds (owned by Ciba Geigy), Asgrow (owned by ELM of Mexico), and Holden's Foundation Seeds. DeKalb Genetics and Holden's were among the companies that focused on producing seeds, which they then sold to distributors.

Monsanto's initial approach was to explore a variety of relationships with seed companies. It decided to license its Roundup Ready Soybean technology to a broad range of seed companies. It also entered into an exclusive licensing agreement with Delta Pine & Land to produce and market Bollgard Cotton. In early 1996, the company acquired a minority position in DeKalb, which would produce Monsanto's Yield Guard corn. Independent of Monsanto, DeKalb Genetics had developed a strain of corn that was resistant to glyphosate. In September 1996 Monsanto acquired one of its Roundup Ready Soybean technology licensees, Asgrow, for $240 million. At the time of the acquisition, Asgrow ranked second among U.S. soybean seed companies, with an 18 percent market share for licensed and proprietary products. Monsanto stated that it would continue to license its technology to other soybean seed companies.

In January 1997, Monsanto acquired Holden's Foundation Seeds and Corn States Hybrid Service and Corn States International, which marketed Holden's products worldwide, for around $1 billion. Like DeKalb, Holden's specializes in developing corn germ plasma, the genetic foundation for seed corn varieties. It licenses the germ plasma to independent companies, which in turn create corn hybrids for commercial use. Although Holden's doesn't sell seeds directly to farmers, it supplies one-third of the corn seed parent stock planted in the United States every year. Along with DeKalb and leading corn seed seller Pioneer Hi-Bred International, Holden's owns one of the three largest pools of corn genetics in the world. It's stored in the form of millions of kernels in cooled storage rooms. According to Monsanto's CEO, Holden's would give Monsanto "an excellent delivery mechanism for our biotechnology innovations in corn. These acquisitions mean the latest technological advances will be made available to the greatest possible number of seed companies of all sizes with unparalleled speed."[50] Holden's had been the subject of acquisition rumors for months before the Monsanto takeover. The company reportedly got bids or inquiries from several multinational companies that were moving into agricultural biotechnology, including DuPont, Dow-Elanco, AgrEvo, and Novartis.[51]

The acquisition spree continued in 1998 when Monsanto purchased DeKalb Genetics outright for $2.3 billion, Delta Pine & Land for $1.3 billion, wheat seed company AgriPro, and the international seed business of Cargill. As a result of these acquisitions, Monsanto controlled an estimated 86 percent of the U.S. cotton seed market and nearly 50 percent of the corn and soybean seed markets.[52] To finance these acquisitions, Monsanto offered about $1.5 billion in common and preferred stock and took on $2.5 billion in long-term debt, adding significant leverage to its balance sheet.[53] Monsanto's view of the industry value chain in early 1999 and its position in it are summarized in Figure 1. The companies listed under the "seed" box in Figure 1 are biotechnology companies with which Monsanto had research alliances in 1999.

Monsanto was not alone is buying its way into the seed business. In May 1997, DuPont invested $1.7 billion to acquire a 20 percent stake in Pioneer High Breeds, the largest seed producer in the United States. Like Monsanto, DuPont made the purchase to speed up the process of commercializing its discoveries in agricultural biotechnology and bring genetically altered seeds to the market more rapidly. Many independent observers worried that in their race to become the Coke and Pepsi of agricultural biotechnology, Monsanto and DuPont were fast creating an oligopolistic situation in the seed business.[54] Their fears intensified in March 1999 when DuPont offered $7.7 billion to purchase all of Pioneer. If regulators approve the DuPont-Pioneer deal, three companies—DuPont, Monsanto, and Novartis—will control two-thirds of the North American seed corn market, 45 percent of the soybean seed market, and 85 percent of the U.S. cotton seed market.[55]

Pricing Strategy A big issue for Monsanto was how to price genetically altered seeds to capture the value implied by its proprietary position and its years of heavy investment in R&D. With regard to Bollgard cotton, which was distributed by Delta Pine & Land, Monsanto decided to price the seed at market rates but to tack on a separate technology fee of $32 per acre that the farmers had to pay directly to Monsanto. The pricing strategy presented farmers with something of a gamble; would it cost more to fight pests using traditional methods, or should they pay the fee to Monsanto? And would the cotton survive if they didn't use Bollgard? Depending on the year, most farmers estimate that they spend anywhere from $20 to $100 per acre spraying against pests. While some of this cost is saved if they plant Bollgard cotton, they might still have to use some sprays to fight other pests.[56]

According to Monsanto, in its first full year, 1996, more than 5,700 U.S. farmers purchased Bollgard cotton and planted 1.8 million acres, or 13 percent of the total cotton acres in the United States. Approximately 60 percent of Bollgard users were able to

FIGURE 1

The Value Chain for Transgenic Crops

*Pending closure
Source: Monsanto Investment Conference, May 3, 1999.

Global Platform Spans Value Chain

totally eliminate insecticides, saving the average grower $33 per acre on land planted with Bollgard. Crop yields from fields planted with Bt cotton increased by 8 to 10 percent. Four out of five users said they were either satisfied or very satisfied with the cotton's overall performance. Only 2 percent said that they would not use it again.[57]

With regard to Roundup-ready soybeans, Monsanto decided to charge a technology fee of $5 per 50-pound bag of seed. A 50-pound bag of soybean seeds was selling for between $13 and $15 in 1996. Roundup-ready soybeans cost between $18 and $20 per bag, depending on the seed company (Monsanto did not control the retail price; distributors did). Monsanto also required farmers to sign an agreement promising not to reuse the patented seed—which annoyed many farmers who were in the habit of doing so. The farmers also had to agree to use Roundup, and not any competing glyphosate-based herbicide. The contract also allowed Monsanto to visit their farms for three years to make sure they kept their promise. In response to numerous complaints, Monsanto later dropped the requirement that farmers allow the com-

pany to inspect their operations, but it raised the technology fee to $6.50 per bag in 1998.[58]

Monsanto's marketing pitch for Roundup-ready soybeans emphasized two things. First, the company extolled the virtues of being able to use the environmentally friendly broad-spectrum Roundup herbicide to control weeds *after* crops began to sprout, rather than more expensive crop-specific herbicides. The company estimated that this would save farmers $12 to $16 per acre in reduced weed control costs, which of course had to be offset against the $5 technology fee. Second, Monsanto emphasized that if farmers made greater use of Roundup, they could reduce their use of traditional deep tillage weed control methods. This would have a long-term benefit in terms of reduced soil erosion. Put differently, it would facilitate the adoption of conservation tillage methods.

Roundup Strategy If Monsanto's push into Roundup ready crops generated the sales that the company hoped for, the result would be a substantial surge in demand for Roundup that should expand sales past the expiration of its U.S. patent on glyphosate in

September 2000. By 1996, Roundup was generating over $1 billion in annual sales for Monsanto. To ensure that revenue growth was not held back by volume constraints, in 1996 Monsanto embarked on a $200 million project to expand production capacity for Roundup over three years. To help protect its proprietary position, the company developed a new formulation of Roundup, Roundup Ultra, and applied for a patent on Ultra. Roundup Ultra contained surfactants and additives that improved the herbicide's absorption by weeds. This means that Ultra has less chance of being washed away by rain—it is absorbed by weeds in one to two hours, whereas basic Roundup takes six hours. The company estimated that 90 percent of Roundup users would switch to Ultra by 1997, primarily because of the convenience (prior to Ultra, they had to purchase surfactants and additives separately and add them to Roundup).[59]

At the same time, Monsanto continued a move begun ten years previously to price Roundup aggressively. Between 1992 and 1998, Monsanto reduced the price of Roundup by 9 percent in the United States market. This, coupled with the tie-in to sales of Monsanto's genetically altered crops, produced a 201 percent increase in the volume of Roundup sales. Even larger volume increases were observed in other nations, where Monsanto's patent had already expired. In Brazil, for example, Monsanto cut the price of Roundup by 45 percent between 1992 and 1998 and was rewarded by a 685 percent surge in volume. In Canada, a 34 percent reduction in price over the same time period led to a 310 percent increase in Roundup volume.[60]

In 1998 and 1999, Monsanto took additional steps to deal with the increased threat of competition after the U.S. patent on glyphosate expired. The catalyst was an attempt by Zeneca to test its own brand of glyphosate-based herbicide, Touchdown, on Monsanto's Roundup-ready soybeans. Zeneca already sold Touchdown outside of the United States and was preparing to sell in the United States after September 2000. In mid 1998, Monsanto sued Zeneca, saying it had illegally acquired Roundup-ready soybean seed for testing Touchdown. The British company responded by suing Monsanto, charging that the company's requirement that farmers use its brand of glyphosate on Roundup-ready crops was anticompetitive. In March 1999 the companies dropped their lawsuits against each other. Monsanto agreed to allow Zeneca to use its Touchdown on seeds using Monsanto's Roundup-ready herbicide-tolerant technology. In return, Zeneca agreed to pay Monsanto an unspecified licensing fee.[61]

While the lawsuits were still pending, Monsanto entered into a number of separate agreements to sell glyphosate to five other agricultural chemical companies, including Dow Chemicals and Novartis. Under the terms of these agreements, which extended for five years and could be renewed thereafter, Monsanto also agreed to allow U.S. farmers to use glyphosate herbicides from these companies on Roundup-ready cotton and soybeans in 2000, and on corn in 2001. Commenting on the Dow deal, a Monsanto spokesman noted, "We were concerned that Dow would go and build glyphosate plants and engage in a price war. By having Monsanto provide supplies of glyphosate, Dow will have better costs of production."[62]

Early Results and Looking Ahead Since 1996, the use of transgenic seeds has increased exponentially, from 4 million acres planted in 1996 to 70 million acres in 1998. In 1997, sales of transgenic crops totaled $4 billion. The worldwide market was projected to double by 2002. In 1996, only 1 million acres of Monsanto's Roundup-ready soybeans were planted. In 1998, around half of the United States's 75-million-acre soybean crop would be Roundup-ready. If growth continued, in 1999 Monsanto would earn almost $300 million in royalties from sales of soybean seeds alone. Bt cotton was also expected to be used on more than half of the U.S. cotton acreage planted in 1999. Moreover, adoption was also occurring quickly overseas. China used Monsanto's Bt cotton for about a quarter of its planting in 1999. Of the nearly 70 million acres planted with genetically modified crops worldwide in 1998, Monsanto varieties accounted for over 70 percent. Monsanto claims that they could have sold a lot more if they had had the seed (see Figure 2 for details).[63]

Human Pharmaceuticals

During the 1990s Monsanto's Searle unit launched a number of products, culminating in the launch of Celebrex, the COX-2 inhibitor, in early 1999. The first of these, Ambien, a treatment for insomnia, was introduced in 1993 and by 1998 was generating over $450 million in annual revenues. This was followed by Daypro, a once-a-day NSAID treatment for osteoarthritis and rheumatoid arthritis that generated annual sales of $308 million in 1998, and Arthrotec, another NSAID drug that also has ulcer prevention properties, which generated revenues of $346 million in 1998. Revenues from all three of these drugs, however, could well be dwarfed by sales of Celebrex.[64]

Aware that Merck's competing COX-2 inhibitor, Vioxx, would probably be on the market by mid 1999, Searle entered into a comarketing agreement with Pfizer. The goal was to leverage the reach of Pfizer's large sales force, reckoned by many to be among the best in the industry. To jump-start market adoption, Searle and Pfizer sent 45,000 "patient starter kits" to physicians and pharmacies. In each free kit there were ten bottles, each containing a twenty-five-day supply of Celebrex. Using a sophisticated database, Searle gave its samples to doctors who most often prescribe arthritis-related painkillers (NSAIDs)—rheumatologists, orthopedic surgeons, and podiatrists. Searle also aimed the kits at physicians in big medical practices who prescribe large amounts of NSAIDs.[65]

As might be expected, the marketing pitch emphasized that Celebrex offers the same pain relief as traditional NSAIDs but causes fewer side effects, such as intestinal bleeding and ulcers. Pricing was perhaps the most difficult issue. Searle and Pfizer tested some seven hundred different pricing models before settling on a cost to consumers of about $2.42 per day. This was significantly more than generic NSAIDs, which can cost as little as 10 cents per day, but less than most analysts had initially expected. In part, the lower price was a concession to managed care organizations that were trying to get control of soaring prescription costs. Following a formal launch meeting of February 22, hundreds of sales representatives from both companies fanned out to doctors' offices in what was one of the most intense marketing efforts ever. The aim was to acquaint the nation's 150,000 doctors with the virtues of Celebrex within six months. This was to be followed by a consumer advertising blitz. The cost of this effort was forecasted to exceed $100 million.[66]

The initial results from this launch effort were nothing short of spectacular. By April, Searle was reporting that it had already directly contacted 70 percent of the nation's doctors. According to independent research data, two months after the launch some 100 percent of rheumatologists surveyed were aware of the drug and 98 percent had prescribed it. This compared with averages of 85 percent and 54 percent for new arthritis treatments.[67] It was soon apparent that Celebrex was experiencing the second fastest sales ramp-up of any drug product launch in U.S. history, outpaced only by sales of

FIGURE 2

Major Players in the Agricultural Seed and Chemical Industry: Projected 1999 Revenues

Source: Monsanto Investment Conference, May 3 1999.

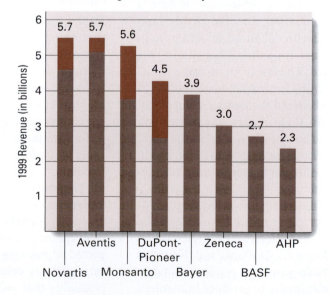

Pfizer's male impotence drug, Viagra. Two months after the launch, analysts predicted first-year sales in excess of $550 million and sales of $3 billion annually by 2002. To put this in context, in 1998 Monsanto's total sales were $8.65 billion, and those of its Searle unit $2.42 billion.

Looking Ahead

In September 1997, Monsanto confirmed its commitment to life sciences when it spun off its commodity chemical businesses to stockholders as an independent unit with sales of close to $3 billion. What remained of Monsanto was focused on agricultural and human life sciences. In both areas, the company had ambitious long-term plans.

Agriculture

The success of the first wave of Monsanto's transgenic crops was based on the benefits farmers gained in the form of improved yield and economies in the use of inputs. Although these products offered no direct benefits to consumers, there was an indirect benefit from the increase in productivity; consumers needed to spend less of their disposable incomes on food. The second wave of transgenic crops, which Monsanto and others were set to introduce in the 1999–2004 time period, offered quality and nutrition traits; in other words, valued-added outputs. Examples include oilseed rape with high lauric, stearate, oleic, and GLA contents (all nutritionally beneficial); soybeans containing proteins that reduce cholesterol or have a medical value in combating osteoporosis or hormonal cancer; maize with enhanced oil and protein contents; and high-starch potatoes that would take up less fat when fried. The last of these was a Monsanto product scheduled for market introduction in 2000. Monsanto had altered the genetic sequence of the potatoes to make them higher in starches and lower in water. When cut into french fries, the potatoes absorbed less fat in the deep fryer. The result: the fries tasted the same, but they had fewer calories and a better texture.[68]

A third wave of genetically modified crop products further down the pipeline could best be described as "plants as factories." Examples under development at Monsanto, DuPont, and Novartus included using tobacco plants to produce albumin and growth hormones, maize to produce humanized

monoclonal antibodies for treating diseases, and transgenic oilseed rape for producing modified fatty acids. Rape could also be modified to produce high levels of beta carotene, much greater than the amounts produced in crops such as carrots. This could be significant for meeting dietary deficiencies in some developing countries. There is also research under way to engineer plants that produce fibers, polymers, or intermediaries that otherwise could come from petrochemicals.

To accelerate the process of developing new transgenic crop varieties, in 1997 Monsanto entered into an alliance with Millenium, a biotechnology firm with expertise in screening genes to identify the causes of diseases—an area known as genomics. The terms of the deal called for Monsanto to pay Millenium $118 million over five years for *exclusive* access to Millennium's gene research in agriculture. In addition, Monsanto stated that it would start a gene research unit in Cambridge, Millenium's base, which would employ up to 150 scientists by the end of 1998. Millennium would hire most of the staff. According to a Monsanto spokesman, "By greatly increasing the speed and precision with which we can analyze new product leads, this agreement will help us rapidly bring future Monsanto life sciences products to market."[69] The Millennium announcement came one day after Monsanto said it was extending an existing collaboration with another genomics firm, Incyte Pharmaceutical, also in agricultural genetics.

Pharmaceuticals

In pharmaceuticals, Monsanto set itself the goal of continuing to grow its product portfolio and development pipeline in arthritis, oncology, and cardiovascular diseases by adding one new chemical or biological entity to the pipeline every year (on average) and one new "technology platform" every three years. A technology *platform* refers to the notion of adding multiple indications for the same drug or using an understanding of a basic biological process to develop a family of drugs.

The concept of a technology platform can best be understood by considering how Monsanto hoped to exploit its technology platform in COX-2 inhibitors (see Figure 3). COX-2 enzyme expression is suspected of playing a role in Alzheimer's and some cancers, such as colon cancer (FAP). This raises the possibility that a COX-2 inhibitor, such as Celebrex, might be a useful treatment for these diseases. Searle conducted phase III trials to explore the use of Celebrex in treating FAP, had data from a phase II trial using Celebrex to treat Alzheimer patients, and on the basis of this intended to move forward with a phase III Alzheimer trial. Searle was also looking at producing different COX-2 inhibitors, such as deracoxib for the veterinary market or valdecoxib, a second-generation COX-2 inhibitor.

The Concerns of Analysts

While impressed by Monsanto's plans, analysts worried that the company lacked the resources required to grow its business given its debt load. Of particular concern was the pharmaceutical area, where Monsanto was still a small player relative to industry leaders. With a smaller research budget and sales force presence, there were fears that the Searle company would not be able to fully exploit and extend its strong product pipeline.

In mid 1998, the company seemed to have found a solution to these issues when it announced a merger with American Home Products (AHP). AHP had a world-class pharmaceutical sales force and a strong financial position, but lacked Monsanto's deep product pipeline. However, the merger talks collapsed in October 1998, reportedly because of clashes between the top management of both companies over layoffs and attitudes toward R&D spending and risk taking. In the aftermath of the collapse, Monsanto's management vowed to go it alone.[70]

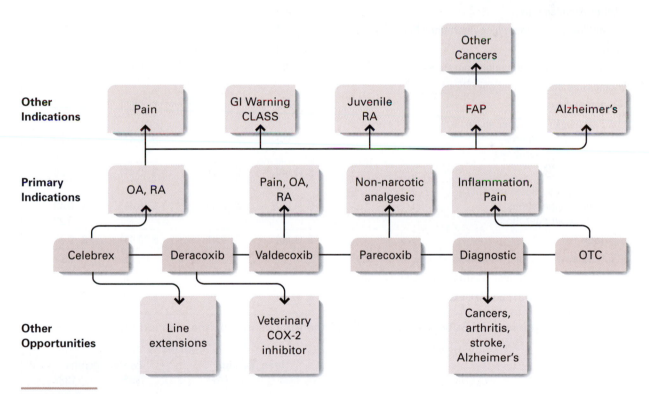

FIGURE 3

COX-2 Inhibitor Technology Platform

Source: Monsanto.

Appendix 1: Monsanto's Financial Position, 1996–1998

Monsanto Company and Subsidiaries Statement of Consolidated Income (dollars in millions, except per share), Unaudited

	Three Months Ended December 31,		Twelve Months Ended December 31,	
	1998	1997	1998	1997
Net sales	$ 2,148	$ 1,820	$ 8,648	$ 7,514
Costs, expenses and other				
Cost of goods sold	971	749	3,593	3,091
Selling, general and administrative expenses	675	557	2,421	2,023
Technological expenses	391	326	1,358	1,044
Acquired in-process research and development	213	75	402	684
Amortization of intangible assets	281	59	487	173
Restructuring and other special charges—net	307		272	
Interest expense	98	59	312	170
Interest income	(11)	(9)	(50)	(45)
Other expense—net	69	7	96	8
Income (loss) from continuing operations before taxes	(846)	(3)	(243)	366
Income taxes	(243)	(8)	7	72
Income (loss) from continuing operations	(603)	5	(250)	294
Income from discontinued operations				176
Net income (loss)	$ (603)	$ 5	$ (250)	$ 470
Basic earnings / (loss) per share				
Continuing operations	$ (1.00)	$ 0.01	$ (0.41)	$ 0.50
Discontinued operations				0.30
Total	$ (1.00)	$ 0.01	$ (0.41)	$ 0.80
Diluted earnings / (loss) per share				
Continuing operations	$ (1.00)	$ 0.01	$ (0.41)	$ 0.48
Discontinued operations				0.29
Total	$ (1.00)	$ 0.01	$ (0.41)	$ 0.77
Weighted average common shares—basic (in millions)			603.5	590.2
Weighted average common shares—diluted (in millions)			603.5	610.5
Earnings before interest and tax expense (EBIT)	$ (748)	$ 56	$ 69	$ 536

Monsanto Companies and Subsidiaries Segment Data (dollars in millions), Unaudited

	EBITDA *			
	Three Months		Twelve Months	
	1998	1997	1998	1997
Segment				
Agricultural products	$ 35	$ (11)	$ 1,092	$ 939
Nutrition and Consumer products	88	109	405	440
Pharmaceuticals	222	197	451	422
Corporate and other	(25)	(26)	(183)	(94)
Total	$ 320	$ 269	$ 1,765	$1,707

* EBITDA (earnings before interest expense, taxes, depreciation and amortization excluding unusuals) is EBIT excluding depreciation, amortization, and the effects of unusual items.

Appendix 1: Monsanto's Financial Position, 1996–1998 *(continued)*

Monsanto Company and Subsidiaries Statement of Consolidated Financial Position
(dollars in millions), Unaudited

	Dec. 31, 1998	Dec. 31, 1997
Assets		
Current assets		
Cash and cash equivalents	$ 89	$ 134
Trade receivables	2,404	1,823
Prepaid assets and other Receivables	1,141	692
Deferred income tax benefit	567	243
Inventories	2,004	1,374
Total current assets	6,205	4,266
Net property, plant and equipment	3,254	2,400
Intangible assets	6,047	2,837
Investment and other assets	1,233	1,271
Total assets	$16,739	$10,774
Liabilities and Shareowners' Equity		
Current liabilities		
Payables and accruals	$ 2,998	$ 1,813
Short-term debt	1,069	1,726
Total current liabilities	4,067	3,539
Long-term debt	6,259	1,979
Postretirement liabilities	871	735
Other liabilities	536	417
Shareowners' equity	5,006	4,104
Total liabilities and shareowners' equity	$16,739	$10,774
Working capital	$ 2,138	$ 727
Debt to capital ratio	59%	47%

ENDNOTES

1. J. Vorman, "China Seen Swiftly Adopting Transgenic Cotton," *Reuters*, April 26, 1999.

2. Monsanto, "In the Pipeline," www.monsanto.com.

3. J. Rifkin, "Perils of Unnatural Science," *Financial Times*, June 20, 1998, p. 9.

4. C. Blackledge, "Benefits That Go Against the Grain," *Financial Times*, March 15, 1999, p. 4.

5. R. J. Mahoney, "The Player's Point of View," *Institutional Investor*, June 1989, p. 23.

6. D. Leonard Barton and G. Pisano, "Monsanto's March Into Biotechnology," Harvard Business School Case 9-690-009.

7. K. Schneider, "Betting the Farm on Biotechnology," *New York Times*, June 10, 1990, section 3, part 2, p. 26.

8. R. Steyer, "BST Is Monsanto's Splice of Life," *St. Louis Post-Dispatch*, April 25, 1994, p. 12.

9. K. Drlica, *Understanding DNA and Gene Cloning* (New York: Wiley, 1997).

10. Company history summarized at www.gene.com.

11. Schneider, "Betting the Farm."

12. Ibid.

13. "Offer of Top R&D Post Lured Him Off Campus," *Chemical Week*, January 23, 1980, p. 48.

14. "The Reworking of Monsanto," *Chemical Week*, January 12, 1983, p. 42.

15. K. Schneider, "Betting the Farm."

16. Steyer, "BST."

17. E. B. Fiske, "Monsanto Research Pact Aims to Cut Academic Controversy," *New York Times*, June 4, 1982, p. 21A; D. Sanger, "Corporate Links Worry Scholars," *New York Times*, October 17, 1982, Late City Final Edition, section 3, p. 4.

18. Sanger, "Corporate Links."

19. Fiske, "Monsanto Research Pact."

20. B. J. Spalding, "Monsanto's Bid for the Lead in Biotechnology," *Chemical Week*, June 11, 1986, p. 41.

21. Ibid.

22. "Reworking of Monsanto."

23. "Monsanto-Searle: A Biotech Coupling," *Chemical Engineering*, August 19, 1985, p. 26.

24. J. E. Ellis, and E. K. Spragius, "Why Monsanto Is Bucking the Odds," *Business Week*, August 5, 1985, p. 76.

25. "Monsanto-Searle."

26. Ibid.

27. Spalding, "Monsanto's Bid."

28. Ibid.

29. Ibid.

30. K. Schneider, "Biotech's Stalled Revolution," *New York Times*, November 16, 1986, section 6, p. 43.

31. Ibid.

32. Ibid.

33. Schneider, "Betting the Farm."

34. C. S. Gasser and R. T. Fraley, "Genetically Engineering Plants for Crop Improvement," *Science*, June 16, 1989, vol. 244, no. 4910, p. 1293.

35. "Plant-Genetics Advance: Antibiotic-Resistant Petunias," *Popular Science*, April 1983, vol. 222, p. 19.

36. Gasser and Fraley, "Genetically Engineering Plants."

37. Schneider, "Betting the Farm."

38. Ibid.

39. B. J. Feder, "Out of the Lab, a Revolution on the Farm," *New York Times*, March 3, 1996, p. 3.

40. Steyer, "BST."

41. K. Schneider, "U.S. Approves Use of Drug to Raise Milk Production," *New York Times*, November 6, 1993, p. 1.

42. R. Steyer, "Discovery of Arthritis Drug Began in WU Lab." *St. Louis Post-Dispatch*, April 6, 1998, p. A1.

43. Ibid.

44. These figures come from the FDA's own database and were compiled by Analysis Group Economics, a drug industry consulting firm.

45. T. M. Burton, "A Pharmaceutical Plumb in Monsanto's Basket," *Wall Street Journal*, June 2, 1998, p. B1.

46. Figures come from Monsanto's May 3, 1999, presentation to securities analysts, posted at www.monsanto.com.

47. M. Groves, "Canada Rejects Hormone That Boosts Cow's Milk Output," *Los Angeles Times*, January 15, 1999, p. C1.

48. Ibid.

49. K. O'Sullivan, "EU Scientific Committee Casts Doubt on Safety of Injected Hormone Used to Boost Milk Yield," *Irish Times*, March 17, 1999, p. 2.

50. J. Swiatek, "Business of Seeds Changing in Big Ways," *Indianapolis Star*, January 12, 1997, p. E1.

51. R. Steyer, "Monsanto Buys Seed Corn Firm," *St. Louis Post-Dispatch*, January 7, 1977, p. C6.

52. P. Downs, "Badseed; Company Has Near Monopoly on the Seed Industry," *The Progressive*, February, 1999, vol. 63, no. 2, p. 36.

53. T. M. Burton, "Monsanto's Cost Cutting Steps to Raise Cash for Seed Company Acquisitions," *Wall Street Journal*, November 12, 1998, p. A4.

54. S. Kilman and S. Warren, "Old Rivals Fight for New Turf Biotechnology Crops," *Wall Street Journal*, May 27, 1998, p. A4.

55. R. Steyer, "DuPont's Purchase of Pioneer Validates Big Bet Monsanto Made on Seed Companies," *St. Louis Post-Dispatch*, March 21, 1999, p. E1.

56. S. J. Willis, "Farmers Torn over Use of Pest Fighter," *Arizona Business Gazette*, May 29, 1997, p. 16.

57. Monsanto, Bollgard Cotton Update, March 1997.

58. R. Steyer, "Super Soybean," *St. Louis Post-Dispatch*, February 25, 1996, p. E1.

59. R. Steyer, "Monsanto Reports Success for New Roundup," *St. Louis Post-Dispatch*, December 22, 1996, p. 1E.

60. Figures come from Monsanto's May 3, 1999, presentation to securities analysts, posted at www.monsanto.com.

61. R. Steyer, "Monsanto, British Firm End War over Herbicides," St. Louis Post-Dispatch, March 19, 1999, p. C9.

62. R. Steyer, "Monsanto Will License Roundup Rights to Dow," *St. Louis Post-Dispatch*, January 20, 1999, p. C1.

63. R. F. Service, "Chemical Industry Rushes Toward Greener Pastures," *Science*, October 23, 1998, vol. 282, p. 608; J. Vorman, "China Seen Swiftly Adopting Transgenic Cotton," *Reuters*, April 26, 1999.

64. Data from Monsanto's May 3, 1999, presentation to securities analysts, posted at www.monsanto.com.

65. "Safe Painkiller Set to Launch Pharmaceuticals World War," *Financial Times*, February 5, 1999, p. 26.

66. A. Barrett and R. A. Melcher, "Why Searle Is Feeling No Pain," *Business Week*, February 15, 1999, p. 36.

67. Data from Monsanto's May 3, 1999, presentation to securities analysts, posted at www.monsanto.com.

68. R. Lenzner and B. Upbin, "Monsanto v Malthus," *Forbes*, March 10, 1997, pp. 58–60.

69. R. Rosenberg, "Millennium Inks Pact Worth as Much as $218 m," *Boston Globe*, October 29, 1997, p. C2.

70. T. M. Burton and E. Tanouye, "Another Drug Industry Megamerger Goes Bust," *Wall Street Journal*, October 14, 1998, p. B1.

Monsanto (B): Merger and Rebirth

36

This case was prepared by Charles W. L. Hill, the University of Washington.

Introduction

On December 20, 1999, the boards of Pharmacia and Monsanto formally approved a merger between the two enterprises, valued at $27 billion. For Pharmacia's CEO, Fred Hassan, the merger represented the latest and most dramatic move in his quest to transform Pharmacia from a perennial "also ran" into one of the leading growth companies in the pharmaceutical industry. Hassan had joined Pharmacia in 1997 after holding a high-ranking position at rival American Home Products. In the two and a half years since he had become CEO, Hassan had received accolades from Wall Street for reducing costs at Pharmacia and rationalizing the company's product pipeline. But Hassan knew that if the company was to grow, it needed some blockbuster drugs. There were not enough of those in Pharmacia's product development pipeline, but Monsanto's Searle unit had several, including its recently approved COX-2 inhibitor, Celebrex.[1]

As for Monsanto and its CEO, Robert Shapiro, the merger came at the end of a tough year during which the value of the company's stock was cut in half. What ailed Monsanto was a combination of high debt and environmental protests against its genetically modified seeds. In 1997 and 1998, Monsanto built up some $6 billion in debt as it acquired six seed companies. The debt would not have mattered had demand for Monsanto's genetically modified seeds continued to grow as forecasted, but a rising wave of environmental protests scuttled growth projections. Responding to continent-wide protests against genetically modified foodstuffs, in 1998 the European Union placed a moratorium on the approval of any more genetically engineered crops. At the same time, many large European food companies bowed to public opinion and announced that they would not use any genetically modified ingredients in their foods.[2]

For Monsanto, which had pioneered the use of biotechnology to produce genetically modified seeds, this was a major setback. Monsanto had naively believed that environmentalists would embrace its "feed the world" vision in which it promised to use the wonders of biotechnology to produce "environmentally friendly" crops that did not need to be treated so often with harmful chemical pesticides and would produce better yields. Instead, environmentalists fretted about the unknown risks of growing and consuming genetically modified food. They argued that Monsanto's genetically modified seed corn, which was engineered to produce natural herbicides, would lead to the evolution of "superbugs" that would soon be immune to the natural herbicides. They expressed fears that genetically modified foodstuffs could have yet unknown adverse consequences on human health, including a rise in cancers. They argued that the introduction of genetically modified crops might lead to "genetic pollution," with engineered traits that seem to be desirable in crops producing unanticipated harmful side effects. When a species of rare and harmless butterfly was apparently killed by the herbicide that Monsanto had engineered into some of its seed corn, the environmentalists thought they had found the smoking gun.

Monsanto asserted that these fears were unfounded. The company produced reams of scientific data to back up its position, but in the court of public opinion this received short shift. While the American consumer apparently cared little about all of this, things got worse for Monsanto when some American food companies that exported products to Europe, such as Gerber and Archer Daniels Mills (ADM), also began to reduce their demand for genetically modified crops. While agreeing with Monsanto that there was no evidence that genetically modified crops produced any harmful effects, they were apparently mindful of the need to cater to public opinion. This raised the specter that American farmers, who had been among the most enthusiastic adopters of Monsanto's genetically altered food stuffs, would reduce their demand for the seeds too; this would effectively blow a hole right through the heart of Monsanto's growth assumptions.[3]

Gains from the Merger

Hassan's justification for the merger was straightforward. Pharmacia was too small a player to compete effectively in the global pharmaceutical industry. It needed the scale of a larger firm to support the R&D, marketing, and sales expenses required to discover, produce, and market new pharmaceuticals. It also needed a pipeline of promising drugs under development, and Monsanto's Searle unit had one of the best in the industry. As for Monsanto, it too needed a better sales and marketing presence to leverage its drug pipeline. Shapiro had realized this for some time. In 1998 he had unsuccessfully pursued a merger proposal with American Home Products that would have achieved this goal. According to unofficial company sources, that merger was scuttled by personality clashes between Shapiro and the CEO of American Home Products. This did not seem to be a problem this time around. Hassan would be the CEO of the new company and Shapiro would be the chairman.

Hassan told investors that the new Pharmacia would have pharmaceutical sales of $9 billion, a strong development pipeline, a $2 billion R&D budget, and the potential to achieve a 20 percent annual growth rate in pharmaceuticals. He also believed that some $600 million in annual cost savings could be realized by eliminating duplication between the two businesses. As for Monsanto's agricultural biotechnology business, Hassan agreed that this had problems, although he also stated that in the long run he thought that the world would come round to Monsanto's view. Monsanto, he said, was simply five to ten years ahead of its time.

Still, recognizing the drag on Pharmacia that Monsanto's agriculture business might produce, he announced that this part of Monsanto would be spun out of the merged company within a year. The plan was to initially offer about 20 percent of the agricultural company for sale to the public and to spin out the remainder two years later. This would leave two companies, a pure-play pharmaceutical enterprise that combined the old Pharmacia and Monsanto's Searle unit, and a pure-play agricultural biotechnology unit that would trade under the Monsanto name.

The New Monsanto

In preparation for the partial spinoff of Monsanto from the new Pharmacia, in mid 2000 the Monsanto unit sold off its NutraSweet and Equal artificial sweetener businesses for $1.7 billion, using the proceeds to pay down some of Monsanto's debt load. In October 2000, Pharmacia sold 14 percent of Monsanto via an initial public offering, raising some $700 million in the process. This would be used to further pay down Monsanto's debt. Pharmacia planned to spin off the remainder of Monsanto's agricultural unit in late 2002, while holding onto the Searle unit.[4]

The new Monsanto is the second largest seed company in the world and the third largest agrochemical company, and it remains the leader in genetically engineered seed corn. Despite the debate over genetically modified foods, sales of food made from genetically modified crops material surged from some $4 billion in 1997 to $19 billion in 1999.[5] Monsanto is a major beneficiary of this shift. Going forward, Monsanto plans to reduce operating costs by $225 million per annum by integrating the operations of six seed companies bought during the 1997–1998 period. Monsanto has also scaled back its R&D spending on agricultural biotechnology from $700 million to $600 million and refocused attention on a limited number of major areas such as corn, wheat, cotton, and soybeans, where returns promise to be largest, while dropping potatoes, vegetables, and other crops.

Clearly, the new Monsanto faces significant challenges going forward. One of the biggest is to convince a skeptical public and Wall Street that agricultural biotechnology is not a dead end. Although genetically modified seeds have been widely accepted in the United States, Canada, and Argentina, serious problems are evident elsewhere. The situation in Europe is a difficult one for Monsanto, but at least it was contained to that region in 1998 and 1999. The task became harder in late 2000 when a court in Brazil, a key developing market for Monsanto and one of the world's largest agricultural producers, blocked the sale of Monsanto's genetically altered soybeans. The court was ruling on a suit filed by environmental activists in Brazil. Although Monsanto may still ultimately win the case on appeal, the development is a serious one. Licensing genetically modified soybean seeds to Brazil was projected to add at least $1 billion to Monsanto's annual revenues. That would have been just the beginning, since Monsanto has plans to introduce at least another ten genetically engineered crops into Brazil, which is already the company's largest export market. It is also worth noting that a range of countries, including Australia and Japan, have recently announced plans to regulate the sale of genetically modified foodstuffs. Moreover, some U.S. farmers are reportedly having second thoughts about genetically modified crops, primarily because the export market for such crops is now limited by actions taken in Europe and elsewhere.

Monsanto's other major problem is the expiration in late 2000 of its patent on Roundup, its single biggest product, with global sales of over $3.2 billion. Sales of Roundup have been robust in recent years, growing at 20 percent per annum, thanks in large part to the tie-in with Roundup-ready seeds. However, the combination of a backlash against genetically modified seeds, a slowing farm economy, and the emergence of close substitutes for Roundup seemed likely to reduce the growth rate for Roundup sales going forward to closer to 5 percent.[6]

The First Year

Monsanto's first year as an independent unit was better than many expected. The stock rose some 75 percent since Pharamacia listed the company. Net profits increased 8 percent in 2001, and were projected to increase another 5 percent in 2002. While hardly spectacular, this increase was achieved against the background of a weak economy.

More importantly for the long run, there were signs that things were beginning to turn in Monsanto's favor. A turning point seemed to come in mid 2001, when StarLink, a Monsanto genetically modified corn approved only for animal feed, found its way into taco shells and other U.S. foods. Critics expected the incident to become a rallying cry in the United States against genetically modified foodstuffs, but the American consumer just shrugged and went on eating tacos. This was followed by a report from the United Nations that came out in support of biotechnology crops, stressing the benefits for the 800 million people worldwide who suffer from malnutrition. In October, the Environmental Protection Agency in the United States approved the sale of Monsanto's genetically modified corn seed for another seven years after finding that it posed no risk to humans or animals. Perhaps even more importantly, in the 2001 growing season U.S. farmers planted 11 percent more genetically modified seeds from Monsanto than in 2000. Biotech soybean planting rose 16 percent, and some 63 percent of the total U.S. soybean crop came from biotech seeds. Despite progress, problems still remain. Monsanto still cannot market its biotech soybean seeds in Brazil, the second largest soybean producer in the world behind the United States. Moreover, in Europe resistance to genetically modified foodstuffs remains strong, with no new biotech seeds or food stuffs having received regulatory approval since 1998.[7]

As for Roundup, as expected, sales started to fall in 2001 and 2002 as the expiration of patent protection resulted in greater competition and lower prices. Despite this, in the first quarter of 2002 Monsanto's sales grew 7 percent as a 17 percent increase in sales of Monsanto's seeds offset a fall in Roundup revenues. Going forward, the company's CEO, Hendrik Verfaillie, has stated that Monsanto is poised to deliver significant shareowner value by growing earnings and increasing cash flow. According to Verfaillie, "Monsanto is uniquely positioned to deliver integrated solutions to farmers today. Our strong core businesses are complemented by a leadership position in biotechnology solutions, seeds and genomics. These strengths, together with a disciplined approach that focuses on the growth segment of the agricultural industry, will add even more value in the medium to long term as we realize global expansion of current and future products."[8]

According to Verfaillie, Monsanto is continuing its transformation from a traditional chemical company to a company offering high-tech, value-added solutions. In 2001, nearly 70 percent of the company's revenues were from traditional agricultural products such as Roundup, but by 2007 Verfaillie expects that more than half of Monsanto's revenues will come from its seeds and genomics segment. Likewise, the company continues to focus the vast majority of its R&D investment in the seeds and technology solutions, while most competitors spend their R&D dollars on agricultural chemicals.

ENDNOTES

1. R. Langreth, "Monsanto Merger Is Just Latest of Bold Moves by Pharmacia CEO," *Wall Street Journal,* December 20, 1999, p. A3.
2. A. Barrett, "Rocky Ground for Monsanto?" *Business Week,* June 12, 2000, pp. 72–76.
3. S. Kilman and T. M. Burton, "Farm and Pharm: Monsanto Boss's Vision of 'Life Sciences' Firm Now Confronts Reality," *Wall Street Journal,* December 21, 1999, p. A1.
4. "Monsanto Raises $700 Million in IPO," *Los Angeles Times,* October 18, 2000, p. C4.
5. J. Epstein, "Brazilians Boil over Ban on Altered Beans," *Christian Science Monitor,* August 25, 2000, p. 1.
6. A. Barrett, "Rocky Ground?"
7. J. Forster and G. Smith, "A Genetically Modified Comeback," *Business Week,* December 24, 2001, pp. 60–61.
8. Taken from CEO statement on Monsanto's web site. See: **http://www.monsanto.com/monsanto/media/02/02May1_Shareowners.html.**

Eli Lilly & Company: The Global Pharmaceutical Industry

37

This case was prepared by Elizabeth Petrovski and Marc E. Gartenfeld under the direction of Dr. Robert J. Mockler, St. John's University.

The company under study was Eli Lilly & Company, a major pharmaceutical company within the health care industry. Eli Lilly, which had previously suffered from a sloppy, unfocused strategy and had recovered strongly in the mid 1990s due its highly successful antidepressant Prozac, was facing another bout of corporate depression in 1998–1999. Eli Lilly was fighting to keep patent protection on Prozac, which was to expire in 2003, and was involved in legal battles to stop the encroachment of generic drug companies into the antidepressant market. Prozac sales were almost $3 billion, or 30 percent of Lilly's total revenues, and a loss of the patent would seriously hurt company earnings. In February 1999, management at Eli Lilly had to design a strategy to protect future earnings in the case of losing the Prozac patent.

Eli Lilly was a research-based, global pharmaceutical firm that concentrated on research, development, and marketing in the following areas: neuroscience, endocrinology, oncology, cardiovascular disease, infectious diseases, and women's health. In addition to the Prozac patent woes, the company entered into

This case is intended to be used as a basis for class discussion rather than as an illustration of either effective or ineffective handling of the situation. This case was prepared by Elizabeth Petrovski, Marc E. Gartenfeld, and Robert J. Mockler, under whose supervision the case was written. Reprinted by permission of the authors.

an agreement with Sepracor Inc. to allow it to acquire exclusive rights to market a new form of Prozac. This would allow Lilly to keep the drug patented and thus keep a monopoly on the antidepressant market for another fifteen years. For this they were under investigation by the Federal Trade Commission (FTC) for alleged antitrust activity. Future Prozac sales were also being challenged by new antidepressant compounds entering the market. Lastly, sales for Evista, a postmenopausal osteoporosis drug rolled out in early 1998, had been disappointing. These more or less represented Lilly's major issues at home.

Prozac was not alone in its pending expirations; in the U.S. industry, there were a number of blockbuster drugs nearing expiration around the year 2000 that would create an assault on earnings not easily overcome. On the upside, the U.S. market itself was still offering great growth potential, and the late 1990s trends of globalization, an aging worldwide population, longer life expectancy, opening of new markets, and increased demand from Third World nations experiencing rising standards of living offered pharmaceutical firms worldwide continued sales growth.

Research and development (R&D) had been said to be the lifeblood of the pharmaceutical industry (Gerstein, 1997; Sharpe and Keelin, 1998). Those firms able to innovate and bring new drugs to the market were those that prospered. In an arena of rapidly increasing R&D costs, pharmaceutical firms that wished to remain competitive had been finding merger partners throughout the 1990s to spread these costs over a broader base of sales. U.S. pharmaceutical firms concerned about future growth in the United States increased their sales of drugs in foreign markets fourfold between 1980 and 1998. European-based companies attracted by the high growth of U.S. pharmaceuticals wanted a piece of the pie and thus were seeking U.S. merger partners.

In the midst of globalization across all industries where firms looked to capture new geographical markets to remain competitive—and specifically in the pharmaceutical industry, where there was talk of a global launch being a byproduct of industry consolidation—Eli Lilly's percent of revenues derived from sales abroad decreased dramatically, from 44 percent in 1995 to 36 percent in 1998. The company's U.S. sales remained strong after a revamped strategy in the early 1990s; however, the U.S. market's future was uncertain in light of the dominance of managed care companies and an ever-expanding generics market.

With 30 percent of their revenues at stake, Eli Lilly's short-term future partially lay in the hands of the U.S. court system and simultaneously in the company's ability to bring new products to the market. Did Lilly have enough R&D and marketing muscle to go it alone in an industry in the midst of a consolidation trend? Should Lilly have considered the option of purchasing or teaming up with a generic subsidiary to fend off the encroachment of an expanding generic market? Would the addition of over-the-counter medicines be an appropriate hedge against patent losses? What kind of product mix in terms of therapeutic class, the area of disease for which a drug was created, was optimal? In light of pressures at home from generic drug companies and specifically Lilly's being threatened with the loss of Prozac's patent or at least its approaching expiration, could the company afford to allow foreign sales as a percent of total revenues to continue to decrease? The main question to be resolved was how to differentiate Eli Lilly & Company from its competition and so achieve a winning edge over competitors in intensely competitive, rapidly changing immediate, intermediate, and long-term time frames.

Industry and Competitive Market

The health care industry, as shown Figure 1, consisted primarily of the following entities: not-for-profit and for-profit health benefit providers, governments, research institutions, biotechnology companies, and foreign markets. For-profit health care benefit providers were broken down into service organizations, which provide hospital management, health care plans, or long-term care; and product organizations such as drug companies (drugmakers) and medical products and supplies companies. Drugmakers collaborated with research institutes, including universities, national agencies, and biotechnology companies, to develop therapeutic medicines. They were also one of the most-regulated industries on the globe and had to answer to government regulatory bodies with regard to drug approval as well as industry practices. The amount of government interference depended on the country's political system and tended to vary around the globe.

The dynamics surrounding the industry in the United States had changed in the 1990s. Previously, pharmaceutical companies sunk massive funds into R&D of new drugs and heavily emphasized the sales to physicians. The companies and their one-sided pricing strategy were protected by patents and the public's general indifference to pricing due to reimbursement from health insurance programs. Managed care's emergence changed all this, since it provided service to entire companies for fixed fees and thus was highly sensitive to pricing. Also entering the picture were pharmacy benefits management companies (PBMs), which processed prescription drug claims for managed-care companies and large employers. In this way, buyers of drugs were able to decide which drug purchases to reimburse based on volume discounts provided by drug companies, putting pressure on the prices that pharmaceutical companies charge (Anonymous, 1999B).

The Pharmaceutical Industry

The pharmaceutical industry, as shown in Figure 2, consisted then of the product organizations, such as drug companies (drugmakers), and product and supplies organizations. Also included in this group were diversified companies, those that combined different aspects of the production end of health care benefit providers.

FIGURE 1

Health Care Industry

Industry growth rates had been gargantuan since the end of World War II due to an ever-increasing demand for pharmaceuticals worldwide, with the world per capita consumption of drugs increasing 70 percent between 1975 and 1990. The industry had actually grown dramatically during the time of the war in response to demand for penicillin and anti-infectives. Impressive growth rates at the end of the 1990s were tied to several factors both external and internal. External factors included increased demand due to the aging population and a large untreated population; a highly distinct internal factor was the tendency for firms to use cooperation (joint ventures and alliances) as a business strategy, which often resulted in increased margins. The most pervasive industry trend at the end of the 1990s, however, was the tendency for companies to combine forces. Mostly the merging craze was said to be the result of quickly escalating R&D costs, and in an industry whose major preoccupation was bringing new drugs to market, this was seen as a means to beef up research capabilities and seize economies of scale, thereby protecting future profits. Thus at this point in time, size was often considered to be a key to success.

The size of the global industry was $250 billion in 1999, and 6 to 7 percent annual worldwide sales growth was predicted for the years 1999–2003, shown in Figure 3. In addition, discoveries in rational drug design and molecular biology were cited as contributing to industry growth (Standard & Poor's, 1998). Rational drug design involves the use of computer technology to study cellular targets in order to modify them in the treatment of disease. In the United States toward the end of the 1990s, the Food and Drug Administration (FDA) adopted practices that allowed for the swifter passage of new drugs to market while the European Union established its own FDA counterpart.

The pharmaceutical industry in general was not subject to the fluctuations of the business cycle from which other companies' sales suffered. Related was the fact that the price of pharmaceuticals was relatively inelastic; that is, individuals would not decrease consumption of a particular drug because of an increase in price.

Participants

The participants consisted of producers and marketers of ethical, proprietary, and generic types of

FIGURE 2

Pharmaceutical Industry

drugs. Ethical drugs were those sold to patients only through a prescription, while proprietary were those sold over the counter without the consultation of a physician. Ethical drugs fell into either the branded or generic categories. The major pharmaceutical companies primarily produced ethical products, and this end of the producing groups was fairly concentrated at the end of the 1990s; that is, the top ten companies accounted for almost 40 percent of world retail sales, as shown in Figure 4. Another trend during this period was that drug companies that were making headway into the lifestyle drug segment were actually creating new markets with new drug discoveries, such as Merck's Proscar treatment for enlarged prostrate glands and Pharmacia & Upjohn's Rogaine hair growth stimulant (Standard & Poor's, 1998). A

key to success then was the ability to direct research toward not only therapeutic treatment for disease but also lifestyle improvement drugs.

Major Pharmaceuticals Major pharmaceuticals or research-based firms included those companies whose most distinguishing characteristic was their ability to devote a significant portion of their earnings to research and development. Most of the largest firms were spending between 14 and 18 percent of their earnings on R&D in the late 1990s, as opposed to the average U.S. manufacturing firm, which spent less than 4 percent of its revenues on R&D (Standard & Poor's, 1998). These firms concentrated primarily on the research, development, manufacture, and marketing of ethical/prescription products. Thus a

FIGURE 3

Projected World Pharmaceutical Market
by Region by 2002

Market/Region	Projected Market Size (U.S.$ billions)
North America	169.9
Europe	100.8
Japan	45.8
Latin America & Caribbean	30.5
South-East Asia & China	20.1
Middle East	10.6
Eastern Europe	7.4
Indian subcontinent	7.3
Australasia	5.4
Africa	5.3
CIS	3.2

Source: IMS Health (1999), "Global Pharma Forecast 1998–2002"
[Online]. ***http://ims-global.com/insight/report/generics/report.htm.***
Accessed March 20.

key to success in this sector was the ability to devote
a significant portion of earnings to R&D.

Diversified Companies Other pharmaceutical companies produced combinations of ethical and propri-

etary drugs, and still some others also manufactured
medical devices. In this latter case, company revenues
were normally equally divided between ethical and
proprietary pharmaceuticals and medical devices.
Proprietary or over-the-counter drugs were consumer oriented in that they tended to be mass
marketed and thus carried much lower margins than
the ethical category. Most over-the-counter medications had their start as prescription drugs and came
into being as the result of the expiration of the patent.
Thus R&D was no longer the most crucial aspect in
this sector; instead it was the ability of the firm to support large schemes of advertising and promotion.

Generic Companies Lastly, other companies produced primarily generic products and thus, in the
interest of competition, provided the customer with
added choices of medications. Generic drugs were
compounds that contained the same active ingredient as the branded counterpart. Moreover, they acted
as the motivating force for innovation by the ethical
producers, since once a product patent expired, its
profit potential was all but finished. The modern
generic industry evolved in the United States by 1984
legislation that gave any generic company challenging a branded drug the right to sell their version for
six months before other generics were allowed to
compete (Sherrid, 1999). Thus a key to success for

FIGURE 4

Leading Companies in 1998 Global Pharmaceutical Sales*

Companies	Sales (U.S.$ billions)	World Market Share(%)	Growth from Previous Year (%)
Novartis	$10.6	4.2%	5.0%
Merck & Co.	10.6	4.2	8.0
Glaxo Wellcome	10.5	4.2	1.0
Pfizer	9.9	3.9	21.0
Bristol-Myers Squibb	9.8	3.9	11.0
Johnson & Johnson	9.0	3.6	8.0
American Home Products	7.8	3.1	1.0
Roche	7.6	3.0	6.0
Lilly	7.4	2.9	17.0
SmithKline Beecham	7.3	2.9	6.0
Leading 10 Corporations	*90.7*	*36.1*	*8.0*

*Proposed mergers not included.

Source: IMS Health (1999), "Global Pharma Forecast 1998–2002" [Online]. *http://ims-global.com/insight/report/generics/report.htm.* Accessed
March 20.

ethical producers was the ability of a company to defend patents against the encroachment of generic substitutes.

Glaxo Wellcome's Zantac was a shining example of how a company's profits could be eroded upon the entrance of a generic substitute. When the patent on this drug expired in July of 1997, generic rivals entered the market at prices 80 percent less than the original. This brought the company's sales from $3 billion in 1996 to 2.1 billion in 1997 (Standard & Poor's, 1998). Thus in order to stay profitable, the ethical producers had to continue to bring innovation to the market. Some ethical producers owned a generic-producing subsidiary as a means of protecting their earnings from patent losses.

The top ten world generic markets were valued at $14.3 billion in 1997, with growth rates almost double that of the total retail sector. Between 1997 and 2002, 120 patented molecules representing $15 billion were scheduled to expire, including top sellers Prozac, Losec, and Renitec. Some loss of market share was imminent in all cases of patent expiration; however, the exact loss would depend on specific conditions in the market. The United States, United Kingdom, and Germany were all considered to have relatively sophisticated generic markets at the end of the 1990s, attested to by high volume and low prices (IMS Health, 1999).

Customers

With an industry such as this, customers ranged from individuals who purchased pharmaceutical products over the counter to those hospital patients who were administered medications where choice might not have played a role in the decision. The importance of these varied by geographical market in the late 1990s, since countries were in the midst of altering public health care systems, and thus the dynamics in certain markets were going through a process of change. For example, in countries where direct-to-consumer (DTC) advertising was gaining in acceptance and practice, such as in the United States, individual customers were being increasingly targeted. In other markets where governments heavily subsidized pharmaceutical care, governments were the customer and in 1999 were still strongly influencing the practices of drug manufacturers.

Individual Patients   Individual patients purchased ethical pharmaceuticals on the recommendation of a physician whose counsel they sought or received through treatment of a debilitating illness. Through the growing use of DTC advertising, buyers of ethical products were becoming more informed, and therefore were playing a larger role in the drug purchase decision process. The decision being only on the part of a physician was occurring less often. Individuals selected over-the-counter drugs, sometimes termed self-medications, and thus personal decision and marketing constituted a much larger role in this sector.

Growth in the pharmaceutical industry beyond 1999 took into account a lengthening of life expectancy in Western cultures and an aging of the world population (the over-sixty-five population was expected to rise from 380 million in 1997 to 800 million by the year 2025) (World Health Organization, 1998), translating to greater demand for pharmaceuticals. Long life expectancy would not necessarily translate, however, to healthier geriatric-age individuals. Pharmaceutical companies that would be able to target conditions such as heart disease, stroke, arthritis, cancer, depression, impotence, osteoporosis, and Alzheimer's disease would experience the strongest growth. In addition, the World Health Organization (WHO) was predicting a doubling of cancer cases in many countries during the period 2000–2025, with a 33 percent increase in lung cancer in women and a 40 percent increase in prostate cancer for men in Europe by the year 2005 (Standard & Poor's, 1998). A key to success therefore was the ability of companies to identify and develop treatments for future widespread maladies.

Physicians   In the United States, physicians were typically the target of pharmaceutical marketing practices prior to the 1990s and thus carried much influence in treatment decisions affecting the final customer, the patient. The emergence and dominance of managed care in the health care industry was reducing the influence of the physician in the purchase decision.

Large-Scale Purchasers   Large-scale buyers such as hospitals and managed care health providers received discounted pricing due to the size of their purchases. In the United States during the 1990s, the dominance of managed care in the health care provider industry was changing the way pharmaceutical firms reaped profits. Sixty-five percent of all prescriptions by mid

1998 were for persons covered by managed care organizations, an increase from 30 percent at the beginning of the 1990s. This percentage was expected to reach 75 in the year 2000 (Standard & Poor's, 1998). Because of increased large-scale purchases by managed care companies, pharmaceutical companies had to provide discounting while increasing their volumes to stay profitable. This would support size as being another key to success.

Governments   Governments also acted as customers when they purchased for different government agencies and public health care systems. In the United States, Medicare and Medicaid, the two major government health care programs, were expected to account for almost one-fifth of drug sales. In countries with public health care systems, governments were the customers and therefore had much more control over industry practices, contracts, and, most importantly, pricing. In Europe, government interference in the industry in the form of price controls was the norm in order to keep national drug budgets under control. Attempts at deregulation by the European Union were unsuccessful in 1998.

Pricing

Pricing of pharmaceutical products varies by geographical market, but mainly followed two paths: pricing set by the market (in the United States and the United Kingdom) and prices set by governments (most others) (Vilas-Boas and Tharp, 1997). Other governments were taking part in efforts to reduce regulation including that of pricing; however, prices set by the market were still mainly prevalent in the United States and the United Kingdom. In the U.S. market specifically, prices were being put under pressure in the 1990s by large purchasers who could command volume discounts; however, volume sales were still providing strong revenue growth. This obviously was expected to have a profound effect on geographical choices of marketing by drug manufacturers. In countries with a national health plan that covered pharmaceutical care, pharmaceutical companies had practically no influence over product decisions by governments. In terms of pricing, then, access to the U.S. market was a key to success. However, having acute awareness of deregulation in other markets around the globe in order to make wise market-entry decisions was also considered a key to success.

Distribution

Distribution of pharmaceutical products was accomplished through wholesalers, physicians, hospitals, and retailers (pharmacists). In the United States, approximately 70 percent of prescription pharmaceuticals were distributed through wholesalers to hospitals, health maintenance organizations (HMOs), and retail pharmacies. The remaining were sold by manufacturers to physicians, hospitals, retailers, and others (Standard & Poor's, 1998).

In the United States, wholesalers could potentially wield much power, as they were able to influence the breadth of a product's distribution through exclusive agreements with drug manufacturers to distribute specific drugs in specific regions.

Pharmaceutical firms worldwide counted on salespeople to market their products through relationship building with doctors and pharmacists and dissemination of literature. This practice was taking on a more multidimensional twist in the United States, and as the industry went through transformation, marketing was also directed toward managed care organizations, including HMOs, and directly to patients. At the end of 1998, several companies were greatly increasing their sales forces, otherwise known as "detail people" within the industry, in order to handle the introduction of new products. Thus a key to success involved a company's possession of a sizable sales force.

Pharmaceutical Benefits Management Companies (PBMs)   PBMs acted as intermediaries between pharmaceutical manufacturers and large drug purchasers by means of aiding large drug purchasers in managing pharmaceutical costs. They sold pharmaceuticals to large employers, HMOs, hospitals, and other large health benefit providers. Thus they carried immense purchasing clout and were able to pass on savings to large customers. Specifically, their principal aim was to process prescription drug claims for managed care companies and large employers. In this way, drug buyers could choose which prescriptions they wanted to reimburse based on volume discounts (Anonymous, 1999B). They emerged in the United States as an offshoot of managed care and thus were partly responsible for the altering of pharmaceutical distribution in the 1990s. As a result of their intermediary role, they were able to wrestle away some of the drugmakers' profits. To counteract this profit-squeezing phenomenon, some pharmaceutical manufacturers acquired PBMs as part of their business portfolios. This approach had mixed success.

Because of major differences in health care systems around the globe, the role of PBMs outside the United States was limited. However, as early as 1997, U.S. PBM companies were seeking ways to enter pharmaceutical markets abroad (Edlin, 1997). At this point in time, it appeared that their role would be slightly different in a place such as Europe. PBMs had more of the role of medical care information coordinator in order to provide European patients with more informed decision making capability in terms of choosing medicines (Edlin, 1997). It was also apparent in the late 1990s that the European system of health care was on the verge of being changed, since countries could not afford to continue the systems they had enjoyed. Some European firms were involved in ventures with U.S. companies in the interest of introducing a type of managed care to Europe.

Products

Products in the industry could be classified by their therapeutic benefit—the class of disease they treated. They could also be classified by how they were prescribed: through a doctor's prescription only or through over-the-counter sales. Further, prescription drugs could be either branded products, which were the direct result of lengthy and costly R&D trials, or of the generic type, those that mimiced their branded counterpart in terms of therapeutic benefit and thus emerged when patents expired.

Ethical (Prescription) Drugs: Branded and Generic   At the end of the 1990s, prescription drugs fell into these five main therapeutic sectors: central nervous system, cardiovascular, gastrointestinal/metabolism agents, anti-infective, and respiratory drugs. Most major pharmaceutical producers concentrated their efforts in selected areas because of the high cost of research and development. For example, Merck & Co. traditionally had specialized in antihypertensive and cholesterol-lowering products, while Glaxo-Wellcome had dominated the respiratory drug category. With managed care service providers dominating the U.S. market, there was speculation that offering wider spectrums of products would increasingly become a key to success.

These therapeutic sectors could be further classified into therapeutic classes, that is, by the specific maladies that they treated. For example, the central nervous system sector included the classes of sedatives, antidepressants, drugs for Alzheimer's disease, Parkinson's disease, and ALS (Lou Gehrig's disease). The top ten therapeutic classes accounted for 30 percent of total revenues worldwide in 1998, and three of these leading ten were experiencing 20 percent sales growth per year and more (IMS Health, 1999), as shown in Figure 5.

FIGURE 5

Leading Therapy Classes in 1998 Global Pharmaceutical Sales

Class	Sales (U.S.$ billions)	% of Market	1998 Growth (%)
1. Antiulcerants	$12.9	5.1%	3.0%
2. Cholesterol and triglyceride reducers	9.6	3.8	20.0
3. Antidepressants	9.4	3.7	21.0
4. Calcium antagonists plain	8.7	3.4	1.0
5. Cephalosporins and combinations	6.8	2.7	−1.0
6. ACE inhibitors plain (antihypertensive)	6.5	2.6	4.0
7. Non-narcotic analgesics	6.2	2.5	−4.0
8. Antirheumatics	6.0	2.4	4.0
9. Antipsychotics	3.9	1.6	30.0
10. Broad-spectrum penicillins	3.8	1.5	4.0

Source: IMS Health (1999), "Global Pharma Forecast 1998–2002" [Online]. *http://ims-global.com/insight/report/generics/report.htm.* Accessed March 20.

An industry trend gaining momentum in the late 1990s in response to the higher R&D cost was the tendency for drug companies to seek second and third therapeutic benefits from a previously marketed drug. This practice helped to bring down a company's R&D expenditure. There were several success stories, including Glaxo-Wellcome's discovery that their antidepressant drug marketed under the name Zyban had been found to be an effective smoking cessation treatment (Morrow, 1999), while Viagra, Pfizer's blockbuster impotence drug, had been originally tested to treat angina (heart drug).

In general, when assessing the strength of a pharmaceutical company, the product portfolio was one of the main focuses, in addition to R&D capabilities. One had to appraise not only the sales potential of current products, but the future potential of those products, including pending patent registrations, and finally, products in the company's pipeline. What new drugs would it be bringing to market in the future? These were all keys to success in the 1990s.

Related to this was the actual business portfolio, which companies had to design from a strategic point of view quite carefully. The merger and acquisition situation reflected a need to increase company size; however, attention had to be paid to the types of business in which a company participated. At the end of the 1990s, among the firms that had experienced success, there existed varying types of business portfolio strategies, which included areas of ethical drugs, over-the-counter drugs, animal products, pharmacy benefit management, and medical devices, all related businesses. Within pharmaceutical units, companies had to choose among therapeutic areas. A company's business unit portfolio depended on its known strengths and its management's preferences. One common denominator was having a clear and defined focus. That is, the choice of areas in which to concentrate was not necessarily vital, but recognizing where the company could succeed and then moving in that direction was. Firms whose focus was unclear, such as SmithKline Beecham, ended up having to defend weak earnings reports and to make excuses to shareholders. Thus a key to success was the ability to select and effectively manage the combination of business units in operation under any one firm's control.

Generic Drugs   Also relevant in this sector of producers was the participation of generic drug companies.

In the United States, growth in generics had been spurred by a growth in the service sector of managed care and the number of branded drugs that were to lose patents around the year 2000. The former situation was a response to a larger trend of cost control within the health care industry in general. The philosophy behind managed care was preventative maintenance to keep costs down, that is, treating patients before any serious type of malady occurred. Generic drugs, which were chemical equivalents to branded drugs, entered the market at a time when a patent on a branded drug expired. Generic drugmakers avoided the costs of R&D, FDA approval, and advertising, necessary investments by their counterpart brand producers. They were able to pass these cost savings (50–90 percent) on to customers, and thus generics were highly appropriate for the cost-conscious managed care service sector. This obviously did not bode well for the brand producer who had lost the patent.

Over-the-Counter Drugs   Over-the-counter drugs came into existence when the patent on an ethnic/prescription drug expired. In fact, in the United States most of the ethical products on the market started out as ethical products (Standard & Poor's, 1998). After the expiration of an ethical drug's patent, a company might apply to the FDA for over-the-counter status, which could be a very lucrative road to take. Over-the-counter drugs faced a very different market than the ethical sector, since they more or less responded to the forces of supply and demand. They could actually be considered part of the consumer products industry, where heavy spending on marketing was essential to build brand recognition and customer loyalty to retain market share. Companies had often used line extensions to increase sales in other segments, such as children's versions of adult medicines. Further, like consumer products, over-the-counter drugs had low margins. All these characteristics were dissimilar to the ethical sector. Over-the-counter drugs did not have the heavy FDA reporting requirements characteristic of the ethical sector. A key to success in this sector was therefore the company's portfolio of recognizable brands.

Research and Development/Manufacturing

There were three main stages in the life cycle of a prescription drug: research and development, patent protection, and FDA approval/product launch.

Research and Development   The development of new drugs, which required years of laborious research, started in either an academic or an industrial laboratory and might have been an accidental discovery but most often was the result of work completed with a specific objective in sight. Raw materials used in the production of drugs included plant substances, animal substances, and inorganic compounds (Standard & Poor's, 1998). The work involved the screening of multitudinous combinations of compounds, most of which in the end were discarded. Compounds that looked successful began the long process of animal tests for useful properties, potency, and toxicity (Gerstein, 1997). If the compound was proven to be effective with animals, it began the process of human trials, which could take from one to five years. The FDA identified three phases through which a new drug had to pass before it was brought to market.

▌ Phase I: Drug was given to a small number of healthy people to test its safety.

▌ Phase II: Drug was administered to people with the disease that it was intended to treat.

▌ Phase III: Rigorous tests were performed involving larger groups of ill patients.

Out of twenty drugs passing through these three stages, one or two actually gained approval for marketing. More staggering perhaps was the fact that only one in five thousand compounds discovered ever reached the pharmacy shelf, and fewer than one-third of companies recouped their R&D investment (Hoover's Online: Pharm. & Medical Equip.,1999).

A new drug was given three designations: (1) a chemical name based on the structure of the compound, (2) a generic name, simpler than the chemical name, and (3) a brand name used to identify it to the public as well as for registering for trademarks (Gerstein, 1997).

Above all, R&D—specifically, a company's product portfolio and pipeline—was said to indicate the health of a company, not to mention direct its strategic objectives (Saldanha, Pesanello, and Harrington, 1997), as shown in Figure 6.

R&D in the industry in the late 1990s was attracting major attention because companies were under continuous pressure to innovate. R&D expenditures more than doubled between 1991 and 1998, while the industry was expected to grow approximately 7 percent beyond 1998. This translated to a requirement of twenty-four to thirty-six new products launched by 2005, earning over $1 billion each, in order to support this growth. Thus, the pressures on companies with regard to R&D investment were tremendous approaching the year 2000 (Anonymous, 1999D).

Patent Protection   Patent protection usually began after the compound had been discovered and had a duration of twenty years. This was stipulated under the rules of the World Trade Organization (WTO) for protection of intellectual property. Since the process

---

FIGURE 6

Pipeline Importance*

	Company A (Multinational)	Company B (Global)	Company C (Regional/Transnational)
Organization	Decentralized	Centralized	Integrated teams
Strategy	Locally driven and implemented	Established globally Implemented locally	Established globally Refined regionally Implemented locally
Communication	Bottom up	Top down	Team based
Product portfolio	Aging; me-too	Narrow & innovative	Broad & innovative
Pipeline (five-year horizon)	Limited potential for innovation	High potential for innovation	High to moderate potential for innovation

*The quality of a company's product portfolio and its R&D pipeline affect its global marketing strategy and organizational structure.

Source: G. Saldanha, P. Pesanello, and E. Harrington (1997), "Building Value Through Global Markets," *Pharmaceutical Executive,* December 17(12): 72–78 [Online]. *http://proquest.umi.com.* Accessed April 14, 1999.

of clinical development and human trials was taking up to ten years in the 1990s, the shelf life of a drug would normally be ten or twelve years (Moran, 1999). Some industry analysts put it another way—companies would have to create five new drugs per year to keep up with industry growth rates (Moran, 1999).

By the end of the 1990s, companies were facing a changing environment in the area of intellectual property protection due to intended global streamlining of patent protection from country to country, especially under the efforts of the WTO. In many cases, patent protection outside the United States, however, was still much weaker than that inside the United States and companies had to guard their intellectual property well.

In the late 1990s, an industry trend involved not only protecting patented drugs from generics entering the market, but also trying to extend a patent in some form or another to protect the earnings captured by a particular drug, especially for those that had so-called blockbuster status. One way for companies to do this was to change the drug product ever so slightly, just enough to require a new patent: for example, changing a drug from injectable to tableted form. In the United States, this was a major complaint by generic companies. Upon the entrance of a generic drug, it was more important then for ethical producers to turn to marketing for product differentiation. When a drug arrived on the market, its therapeutic benefit was its selling point; however, with the arrival of generic challengers, it now became more important to distinguish the branded drug from competitors, and therefore marketing and product differentiation were the new goals. Thus a key to success was the ability of companies to protect patents, find creative ways to extend patent protection, and lastly, in the event of competitors entering the market, creatively differentiate a drug from those of competitors.

Approval/Product Launch   In the United States, a drug had to be approved by the FDA before it could be brought to market, which involved the company filing complete information about the new compound, including its material composition, formulation materials, manufacturing methods, controls, packaging, and proposed text for the label (Gerstein, 1997). It also had to be proven to be effective for the treatment for which it was intended. Outside the United States, a regulatory body within the country where the drug would be marketed must give approval. At the end of the 1990s, the FDA was still considered the world's drug approval organization, since many drugs were being developed in the United States, where pharmaceutical firms were strongest and R&D was successful. Many drugs started their existences here and would be marketed overseas after a successful U.S. launch.

In general, when assessing the value of a drug company, the number of drugs in the research and development pipeline was critical. Furthermore, much attention was given to the phase (I, II, or III) in the development cycle that drugs had achieved, this being an indication of a company's success in terms of future profit growth potential.

Marketing and Promotion

Marketing and promotion (DTC) played a significant role in the over-the-counter sector of the pharmaceutical industry, whereas within the ethical sector, research and development had traditionally been the lifeblood for survival. This distinguishing factor between the two sectors started to become somewhat blurred in the 1990s in the United States. Within the ethical sector, total advertising expenditures between 1993 and 1997 went from $183 million to $875 million. Underlying factors included a loosening of advertising regulations in the ethical sector by the FDA, customers' desire to be informed about health care and medications, and the widespread use of the Internet.

With the growth in DTC marketing, the dynamics of industry distribution were somewhat altered. In the past, doctors were alone in being able to prescribe drugs, with pharmacists being the only ones to distribute them. With the increase in DTC advertising, patients began to request name brands from their physicians. Ethical producers found DTC advertising to be extremely effective because it served not only as a selling device but also as a means of keeping the medical profession abreast about specific drugs. The use of DTC advertising could also create a stronger association between ethical product brand names and company names in the eyes of consumers—now more than ever, patients themselves. This would make a company's image even more critical as a part of marketing and promotion.

The trend toward DTC advertising in the ethical sector, however, had not yet arrived in Europe, where health care was still mostly not privatized. It was clear, however, that DTC practices were beginning to spread outside the United States. In the United Kingdom, DTC advertising was still illegal; however, to overcome this DTC advertising had taken the form of centering ads around a disease with only a mention of a drug company for the cure (Yates, 1999). The International Federation of Pharmaceutical Manufacturers Association (IFPMA), an agency that promoted cooperation between countries in terms of health care and pharmaceutical practices and whose members were regional and national associations representing research-based pharmaceutical companies, required all members and those they represented to accept the association's provisions in the *IFPMA Code of Pharmaceutical Marketing Practices.*

Publicity, as with other industries, especially adverse publicity, could influence markets more powerfully than any form of paid advertising or promotion, and this industry was very sensitive to any negative publicity because of the nature of the products. Negative publicity in the past had usually been the result of ineffective drugs or, worse-case scenario, drugs that had a strong debilitating effect on patients. Thus a key to success was efficacy and safety of products.

Regulation

The FDA had always been considered the world's "gold standard" in terms of safely approving drugs for marketing. With a newly unified Europe, the European Medicines Evaluations Agency (EMEA) was created by the European Council in 1995 to streamline practices among countries within the EU, which then seriously challenged the stand-alone authority of the FDA. In the early 1990s the FDA moved to bring drugs to market more swiftly, shortening approval times from thirty-five months in 1992 to twenty-two months in 1997.

Further steps were being taken to deregulate the European licensing system in the mid 1990s. Greatly affecting the European market were regulations on pricing within the industry. Price controls enforced by European governments, which were usually footing the health care bills, ensured that prices did not get out of control and put increased pressure on European companies' profits. As late as December 1998, the European Council was still not willing to pass deregulation laws and was more concerned with

cost containment (Moore, 1998). With center-left governments dominating the environment in Europe, there was not much hope for deregulation in the late 1990s.

Regulation streamlining at the end of the 1990s was one of the dynamics changing the global industry as well. Worldwide, regulation existed to accomplish two main objectives: allow the entrance of pharmaceutical products into markets and protecting the health of the public. Regulation and compliance in different markets had always led to difficulty for drug marketers seeking to expand outside their home markets. Specifically, regulation systems in the United States, Europe, and Japan varied greatly and profoundly affected the means of achieving profitability by outsiders in those markets.

Japan's Ministry of Health and Welfare (the Koseisho), responsible for operation of Japan's health care system, including the surveillance and regulation of drugs, traditionally did not allow companies to submit foreign clinical studies on drug treatments, but only those studies carried out on Japanese patients.

The International Conference on Harmonization (ICH) was founded in 1991. Since its inception, it concentrated its efforts on streamlining and bringing uniformity to drug approval processes across the three geographical markets, which happened to be the three largest pharmaceutical markets at the end of the 1990s: the United States, Japan, and Europe. This effort had a profound effect on marketing practices within the global pharmaceutical industry because approval times between these three countries varied considerably, with the EMEA having the shortest guaranteed completion of an application. In addition, the application and market maintenance fee structures for drugs varied across these markets, with those of the European Union being the least costly. It thus appeared that testing, manufacturing, and marketing a new drug in Europe had its advantages over doing the same in other markets. Therefore, a key to success was having a presence in Europe in order to benefit from these advantages, as well as to participate in a region comprising 30 percent of the global pharmaceutical market. In addition, firms had to be in an optimal position to participate in these three geographical markets in time for harmonization of drug approval laws, which were expected to have a profound effect on the industry.

Joint Ventures/Strategic Alliances to Mergers and Acquisitions

Since the 1980s, combining forces, in agreements ranging from joint ventures, or strategic alliances, to the most extreme form of union, mergers and acquisitions, had been a common strategy in the industry that was used to put more muscle behind costly research, development, and scientific breakthrough. The marketing arm of the business also became a factor, since firms would join forces in order to have a more extensive sales force.

Joint Ventures and Strategic Alliances Joint ventures and alliances had long been a common strategy because pharmaceutical firms did well to create alliances with smaller biotechnology or biopharmaceutical companies that were possibly developing new drugs. Conversely, smaller pharmaceutical firms sought alliances with larger firms that had more marketing muscle in order to bring a new discovery to the market. In addition, companies often had relationships with university scientists and, in the United States, with the National Institutes of Health, which had the power to forward products still in the research chain of development to drug companies. As with joint venture strategy in many industries, the advantages of having a foreign partner when entering foreign markets lie in the foreign partner's familiarity with business practices in a particular country. Lastly, alliances between foreign companies allowed drugmakers to license drugs discovered in foreign countries in the home market. In the late 1990s, U.S. drugmakers were increasingly collaborating with biotechnology firms to develop therapeutic compounds through genomics (genetics) research. Thus a key to success was a company's ability to create joint ventures and strategic alliances.

Mergers and Acquisitions Mergers and acquisitions, the most extreme form of joint ventures, had been increasingly evident in the business environment of the pharmaceutical industry since the beginning of the 1990s. One study states that in the first six months of 1990 alone, 151 mergers in this industry were announced. Some of the more famous mergers had been Beecham with Smithkline, Merrell Dow with Marion, Bristol-Myers with Squibb, and Upjohn with Pharmacia (Agrawal, 1997).

During the late 1990s, a new wave toward consolidation appeared with mergers and acquisitions. This trend had the same catalyst seen in joint ventures, but it incorporated other factors into the equation. In general, the new European single market and the recent entrance of the euro ushered in a flood of mergers and acquisitions in Europe. Specifically, the pharmaceutical industry was ripe for these unions because of the steep costs of R&D, said to be the lifeblood of any pharmaceutical company. In 1999 the cost of bringing a new drug to market was estimated to be $350 to $500 million, and the process generally took fifteen years. Therefore, there were many who supported the argument that "size mattered" when it came to pharmaceuticals. The industry's global revenues of $250 billion in 1999 were expected to reach $400 billion by the year 2003, yet no one company had been able to boast more than 5 percent of total market share.

Prior to 1980, pharmaceutical companies had as their strengths innovation, patent protection of drugs, and pricing flexibility. While U.S. pharmaceutical firms had been able to boast strong growth over the years, as reflected in high equity drug stock prices, this growth (once in double-digit figures) was expected to slow in 1999 to a level of 9 percent (IMS Health, 1999). European firms' growth rates were at a level of approximately 6 percent and were expected to remain flat, along with those of Japan. U.S. growth was boosted by the increase in managed care facilities, while in Europe national governments were mainly responsible for health care systems and thus used price controls. No movement toward privatization was necessarily in sight. In the United States, managed care represented 50 percent of the medical products market and was expected to reach 90 percent by the end of the year 2000. Thus European players were seeking U.S. partners to gain exposure in the strong U.S. market and to realize economies of scale.

Initially, the move toward consolidation was driven by weakness in comparison to U.S. companies. Specifically, this indicated that companies might not have enough projects in the R&D arena to protect future earnings. With the surge in mergers and acquisitions, average company size was on the increase, and thus the optimum company size for this industry would likely have to be redefined. This was exemplified by the fact that the largest pharmaceutical firm in 1997, Glaxo Wellcome, boasted $11.6 billion in sales;

the proposed mergers, if realized, would put the top company, AHP-SmithKline Beecham, at $27.0 billion in sales, as Figure 7 indicates.

All mergers were not necessarily successful. Three large mergers in 1998 did not happen as intended, and although the real issues were not disclosed, there appeared to be unwillingness on the part of management in all three cases to give up the reins. Moreover, despite the presence of the single European market, many practices still varied from country to country, including tax, accounting, and auditing standards; pension provisions; corporate and shareholding structures; culture and language; industry structure; and regulatory requirements (Curwen, 1999). At one point it appeared that these failures would put a damper on future unions, but in late 1998, Hoechst and Rhone-Poulenc, Sanofi SA and Synthelabo, and Zeneca and Astra all announced their intention to join forces. European companies were said to be looking for American partners to seize a part of the massive U.S. market; however, lofty equity prices in early 1999 kept them at bay.

In general, global consolidation in this industry protected future earnings through cost cutting, which in turn gave companies more time for development of new drugs. It also insured against earnings risk when patents expired. Lastly, it enhanced a company's research and development prospects and expanded its global market reach. However, the benefits of mergers and acquisitions even during the consolidation trend of the late 1990s were in contin-

FIGURE 7

Proposed Mergers
(combined pro forma sales)

Drug Deals	
AHP-SmithKline Beecham (canceled)	$27.0 billion
AHB-Monsanto (canceled)	23.0 billion
Glaxo Wellcome-SmithKline Beecham (canceled)	19.0 billion
Zeneca-Astra	15.9 billion
Hoechst-RP	13.0 billion
Sanofi-Synthélabo	6.1 billion

Source: A. Scott, (1999), "Drug Makers Consolidate," *Chemical Week,* January 6, 161(1): 29 [Online]. *http://proquest.umi.com.* Accessed March 23.

uous debate. It was noted that size did not always contribute to strength, while it could certainly contribute to logistical headaches. Past success stories exemplified the fact that smaller entities could be just as valid. An example was the European division of Pfizer, which was responsible for three-quarters of the company's output with a mere one-third of the R&D resources (LLY NEWS, 1999). In the late 1990s, it appeared that on mergers the jury was still out.

Markets

Typically, one of the main difficulties in marketing pharmaceuticals abroad was considered to be the differing regulatory environments, which appeared to be moving toward convergence at the end of the 1990s.

North America (U.S.)   The North American market boasted 40 percent of world market share as of early 1999, as well as the highest growth rates among all the regions worldwide. This rate was supported by product innovation and volume sales to managed care facilities. It was the market that European companies had their eyes on for expansion and was partially responsible for the great industry consolidation in progress in 1998. European and smaller firms looked for merger partners to compete with stronger U.S. players or actually sought U.S. merger partners in order to capture part of the U.S. market. In various research studies on the U.S. pharmaceutical industry in the 1980s, predictions varied on the future competitiveness of American companies. One study cited the fact that FDA regulations and longer regulatory review periods would hamper future competitiveness, but by 1999 this issue had already been addressed and perhaps rectified by new FDA regulation passed in 1998, which shortened the average review period for new drugs. Essentially, the U.S. market was extremely attractive, and healthy pharmaceutical firms derived significant portions of their earnings from it. Thus strong operations and sales in this market were keys to success.

Foreign Markets (Non-U.S.)   Between 1999 and 2004, in addition to North America, the fastest-growing markets in the industry were predicted to be the Middle East, Australasia, and Southeast Asia, including China (IMS Health, 1999) (see Figure 8). Europe was expected to continue to be plagued by price controls. Southeast Asia, which was experiencing rapid growth

FIGURE 8

Five-Year Forecast of the Global Pharmaceutical Markets (1998–2002)

Regions	CAGR %	Regions	CAGR %
North America	9.8%	Eastern Europe	8.6%
Europe	5.8	Middle East	10.6
Japan	4.9	Africa	3.3
Latin America and Caribbean	8.4	Indian Subcontinent	8.6
Southeast Asia/China	11.0	Australasia	9.8
Eastern Europe	8.6	CIS	6.7
Total World Market	**8.0%**		

Source: IMS Health (1999), "Global Pharma Forecast 1998–2002" [Online]. *http://ims-global.com/insight/report/generics/report.htm.* Accessed March 20.

before the Asian crisis, was expected to return to that phase by 2001–2002.

U.S. and foreign markets varied by the ways in which drugs were brought to market, by regulatory procedures, and by ways in which market forces worked. Outside the United States, even though it was less difficult and costly to move a drug through the phases of development, actual sales practices between the drug company and the customer, usually the government, involved more relationship building, covert pacts, and price controls. Thus market forces took a backseat position.

Europe   At the same time that the American market was experiencing strong growth at the end of the 1990s, Europe's growth was expected to be approximately 7 percent. The European market was considered to be lagging at the end of the 1990s and not necessarily the place to be for pharmaceutical players. The fault lay partially with the European socialized health care system, which, in maintaining price controls and other government intervention tools, squeezed drug company budgets. The hope in Europe was for deregulation to take hold, which would unleash price controls and increase volume. European companies in the midst of this situation speculated that they would not be sought out for merger partners, but rather as takeover candidates.

China and Asia   As with other industries in China, the pharmaceutical industry faced large prospects for growth due to current small per-capita consumption, an already rapidly growing industry, and the tendency

for Chinese consumers to switch to Western-style medicines in lieu of traditional Chinese medicines (homeopathic). A major drawback of marketing in China lay in the fact that although China had laws protecting intellectual property, the laws did not cover pharmaceuticals; the law specifically permitted copying of patented medicines (Mauer Fron and Smith, 1998). In the past, companies for whom this had been an issue had registered complaints with Chinese authorities without necessarily achieving success (Mauer Fron and Smith, 1998). Even with this major impediment, China's market was considered to be too great to overlook. In 1999 this market was expected to grow by 14 percent; however, because of the continuing Asian financial crisis, products planned for export were to be offered in the domestic market, adding to severe competition pressures. Profits earned in the industry in China were expected to decrease by 250 million yuan in the same year. A key to success therefore in this market was to establish a presence, with the expectation that rewards would not necessarily be near term (Anonymous, 1999A).

Japan   Japan boasted the highest per-capita prescription drug market outside the United States in 1998, and thus was the second largest market in the world. However, at that time Japan's government still exercised stiff control over drug prices, including required across-the-board price cuts on drugs every few years (Standard & Poor's, 1998). In the mid 1990s, Japan was seen as an ideal geographical location to facilitate expansion into Asia, specifically into South Korea and China (Yoshida, 1995).

Competitors

Because of the business structure of the pharmaceutical industry, the structure of competition was also unique. One could witness a strategy dichotomy. On the one hand, the high cost of R&D bore witness that size was important and specialization of R&D in certain therapeutic areas would help to keep costs down. On the other hand, being able to offer various types of products allowed companies to offer one-stop shopping to customers, that is, drug wholesalers and hospitals. The competition appeared to be more focused on the former situation and thus concentrated in certain therapeutic areas. Geographies were also an important consideration, since not only did therapeutic area dictate competitive strength, but breadth of sales and marketing—strength in specific geographical areas—would also indicate more or less the type of competition, direct or nondirect.

Another important consideration was the fact that drug companies, as in other industries, could decide how to design their business portfolios. Some companies concentrated solely on ethical products, often including some participation in the animal health care market, which was seen as providing synergies with human health care. Some firms included over-the-counter product manufacturing in their portfolios; thus they were also participating in the consumer products industry, where emphasis was on brand recognition and consumer loyalty. Even though the emphasis in this sector was different, it was a way to protect earnings when patents for strong-selling products expired.

Because of the nature and structure of the pharmaceutical industry at the end of the 1990s, competition in a particular therapeutic area could emerge from any corner of the industry. Companies could seek out alliances for product development and marketing, and thus competition could emerge from companies that previously might not have had a strength in a particular area. Once a product entered the market, even nongeneric companies could try to mimic the product by studying its patent application.

Major Competitors   By classifying competition according to therapeutic strengths, one can identify the following competitors: Novo Nordisk A/S, Pfizer, Inc., and SmithKline Beecham plc.

Novo Nordisk A/S   This Danish company was still the world's leading producer of insulin and industrial enzymes. Health care products comprised 75 percent of the company's sales in 1997. The company also produced insulin injection and monitoring systems, treatments for osteoporosis and menopause, growth hormones, antidepressants, and epilepsy treatments. More than half of the company's sales were within Europe at the end of the 1990s.

The company's most prevalent strengths were its health products for diabetes, which, until 1998, were mainly marketed in Europe. In 1998, the company signed an agreement with Schering-Plough to make inroads into the U.S. market with their diabetes drugs. This move proved to be successful, since the company experienced a 20 percent increase in insulin sales in the United States in 1998 (Moore, 1999). Prevalent products included Seroxat, introduced in 1992 for depression, and Gabitril for epilepsy and NovoSeven for hemophilia, both introduced in 1995.

The company portfolio's inclusion of industrial enzymes represented another way that pharmaceutical firms diversified to take advantage of manufacturing synergies. In early 1999, however, the company embarked on a major strategy shift when it revealed that the two businesses would be split into separate legal entities. This decision was a result, in part, of the industry's merger mania, which created powerful rivals with which Nordisk felt it could not compete with its business portfolio. The company was also following an industry trend of sharpening its focus around core strengths. It also caused massive speculation that the pharmaceutical entity would be seeking a merging partner.

The merger speculation about Novo Nordisk was also born out of the fact that the company had a relatively small size in terms of annual sales ($2.5 billion in 1997), and smaller firms like Nordisk, seeking out R&D and marketing muscle, were ripe to merge with other firms. Novo Nordisk had been strong in terms of R&D expenditure as a percentage of sales—in 1997, the company spent 16.3 percent of earnings on R&D.

Pfizer, Inc.   Pfizer was one of the leaders in the production of ethical drugs (number one in the U.S.) and was a producer of animal health treatments and consumer health products sold over the counter. Pfizer was the creator of the anti-impotence drug Viagra, launched in 1998. Prescription drugs produced included treatment for cardiovascular disease, antidepressants, antibiotics, and cholesterol-lowering drugs. Health care products accounted for 85 percent of the company's revenues. Pfizer's strength lay in its R&D capabilities, and the company had 170 drugs in its research pipeline in 1999. It also had a strong presence in the consumer products market with such known brands as BenGay muscle rub, Visine eyedrops, and Bain de Soleil sunscreens.

Pfizer was an example of a company that had both ethical and over-the-counter products in its business portfolio. It was considered one of the powerhouses in the industry, with a formidable R&D team that consistently used 15 percent of the company's revenues. Its drug pipeline was the envy of the industry, with sixty new drugs in the early stages of development and an approximate total of 170 drugs in the pipeline in 1998 (Moran, 1999). Pfizer had overcome hard times during the 1980s when it experienced gaps in the product pipeline. After suffering through years of weak earnings due to strong investment in R&D and a vast sales force, the company came back with a vengeance and during the early 1990s had moved from number thirteen in terms of worldwide prescription drug sales to number four. Pfizer's sales force reached 14,500 in 1998 (Stipp, 1998). The company had a few top-selling drugs in its portfolio at the end of the 1990s, including Viagra, Norvasc, a hypertension drug that had sales of $2.2 billion in 1997, and Zoloft, an antidepressant that was a strong competitor to Prozac.

SmithKline Beecham plc. SmithKline Beecham, based in the United Kingdom, produced both prescription and over-the-counter treatments. Prescription drugs included antidepressants and vaccines for illnesses such as diphtheria, tetanus, and hepatitis. It was also a leader in workplace drug testing. Planned mergers with Glaxo Wellcome and American Home Products failed; however, the company was still actively seeking a merger partner in 1998–1999.

The company's total revenues in 1998 were over $13 billion, 60 percent of which were derived from pharmaceutical sales and 30 percent from consumer products. The antidepressant Paxil/Seroxat was the company's second best-selling drug in that year, behind the antibiotic Augmentin. In 1998, Smith-Kline found itself continuing on a path of strategic missteps. Previously, CEO Mr. Jan Leschly had tried to lead the company toward more broadened strategic goals, which included the purchase of a pharmacy benefit management business. A mere increase of 4 percent in sales in 1998 was proof that this approach had failed. Other players in the industry had been doing just the opposite at the end of the 1990s—streamlining businesses and focusing their strategies. Other signs of difficulty included the closing of excess manufacturing plants and layoffs of approximately three thousand people. Smith-Kline's R&D expenditure, reduced to 10 percent in 1998 from 17 percent in the previous year, also demonstrated a sign of trouble.

Other competitors Other competitors produced both ethical drugs for humans and animals, over-the-counter drugs, and generic drugs. They included Schering-Plough Corporation, Merck & Co., Inc. (tied for the number one selling company by worldwide sales with Novartis AG), Scheim Pharmaceutical, Inc., a producer of generic drugs, Bristol-Myers Squibb Co., Glaxo Wellcome plc, and Novartis AG.

In general, competition dynamics were unique within this industry in the sense that in any given period, companies could be direct competitors because of the products they were developing or marketing at a particular time. Other companies would be considered indirect competitors, since their business portfolios could contain drug treatments for different therapeutic areas. Competition pressures could change instantly, since even drugs in the late stages of development did not necessarily "make it" into the market and thus could completely change a company's therapeutic strengths. Given the consolidation trend in the 1990s, the composition of the industry was changing, and consequently the dynamics of competition were changing.

The Company

Colonel Eli Lilly, pharmacist and Union officer in the Civil War, founded Eli Lilly & Company in 1876, and the company remained family owned until 1953. Eli Lilly expanded into the world market in the 1950s and 1960s, and over the years experimented with different business portfolio strategies, including diversifying with the purchase of Elizabeth Arden in 1971 (it was sold in 1987) and of IVAC (a medical instruments manufacturer) in 1977. Lilly's launch of Humulin (synthetic insulin) in 1982 made it the first pharmaceutical firm to market a genetically engineered drug.

Prior to the 1990s, drugmakers used a common strategy in the eternal struggle for profit growth.

Heavy emphasis was placed on R&D in the interest of developing new drugs, while the nurturing of strong sales forces enabled companies to move products by selling to physicians. Drugs protected by patents were not vulnerable to price competition. Further, patients covered by traditional health insurance plans were unaffected by price in general.

In the 1990s, in a move sanctioned by the Clinton administration, managed care became the approach to low-cost health care and changed the dynamics of the American industry. Pharmacy benefits management firms (PBMs) emerged to help large companies control the costs of pharmacy benefits programs. They emphasized use of alternatives to branded pharmaceuticals carrying lofty prices and thus put earnings pressure on pharmaceutical firms. In the early 1990s, weakened equity prices of pharmaceutical firms reflected this pressure. Lilly lost $11 billion in market capitalization in eighteen months (Eli Lilly, 1998).

Some U.S. firms responded by beating the PBMs at their own game—they purchased them. In 1994, Lilly purchased PCS Health Systems for $4 billion. However, the distinct strategic advantage that Lilly anticipated, funneling its own products through PCS, did not happen. Partially responsible were perceived conflicts of interest by drug customers as well as by the U.S. Federal Trade Commission (FTC). Lilly sold off PCS Health Systems in 1997, which resulted in a substantial write-off. Since PBMs had proven to be profitable entities, other pharmaceutical companies such as Merck were willing to retain them as part of their business portfolios.

Selling PCS was to be part of a general transformational strategy that Randall Tobias, then CEO of Lilly, implemented in the mid 1990s. After an evaluation of the business portfolio of the company, Mr. Tobias realized that Lilly's strength was in its core business: pharmaceuticals. As a result he divested some of the noncore entities, including medical device businesses, cosmetics, agricultural products, and a hard gelatin capsule business. In addition, acquisitions were made and relationships fostered to strengthen the core business, including a strategic alliance to develop and market a blood substitute product; ownership of Sphinx Pharmaceuticals, primarily a research and development division; and a stake in a biotechnology firm to have access to the testing of cutting-edge chemical substances.

It appeared that some of these efforts had paid off by the end of the 1990s. In 1997 Lilly's earnings per share boasted growth of 21 percent versus 20 percent for Merck and 13 percent for Pfizer (Stipp, 1998).

Products

In the mid to late 1990s, Lilly's structure was revamped around the five core therapeutic areas in which it had already carried a strong presence by that time: infectious diseases, cancer, cardiovascular products, endocrinology, and neuroscience. Between 1995 and 1998, new Lilly products accounted for 78 percent of the company's sales growth. Some of the major drugs are shown in Figure 9.

Prozac   This product accounted for almost 30 percent of company sales. It was used for treatment of depression and bulimia. Prozac (fluoxetine) was part of the company's group of neuroscience products, their largest-selling product group. The pending expiration on the patent for this product in the year 2003 was making company executives nervous and sent them scrambling for ways to hang onto its success, including an agreement with Sepracor to develop a new version of Prozac minus the side effects. Prozac's success was challenged in some geo-

FIGURE 9

Eli Lilly & Company Net Sales in 1998 (U.S.$ millions)

Class	Sales	% Change from 1997	% of Total
Prozac	$2,811.5	10%	30%
Zyprexa	1,442.7	98	16
Anti-infectives	1,160.9	(9)	13
Insulins	1,154.9	8	13
Animal health	614.4	4	7
Axid	418.0	(20)	4
ReoPro	365.4	44	4
Gemzar	306.8	76	3
Humatrope	268.0	3	3
Evista	144.1	N/M	1

Source: Eli Lilly and Company (1999), 10K report for the fiscal year ended December 31, 1998 [Online]. *http://www.sec.gov/Archives/edgar/data/59478/0000950131-99-001772.txt.* Accessed April 17.

graphic markets, such as in Australia and Canada, where generic competition had made some inroads, and in France, where competition had put pressure on sales.

Lilly's impressive results at the end of 1998 were due mostly to Prozac, whose sales grew 8 percent worldwide, mostly supported by U.S. sales, which grew by 10 percent. International sales of Prozac remained essentially flat due to competition in foreign markets. Prozac had been the company's savior, responsible for Lilly's turnaround in the mid 1990s. But in April of 1999, Lilly reported first-quarter Prozac sales down 4 percent from the previous year, with U.S. sales down 6 percent and a 2 percent rise in world sales (Anonymous, 1999C).

One way Lilly tried to protect its patent on Prozac was to market the drug in other forms, such as a once-a-week pill. This new form of Prozac was submitted to the FDA for approval in early 1999.

Even if Lilly were able to retain patent protection on Prozac until 1993, there were competitors producing other antidepressants that were showing promise, such as Celexa, marketed by Warner-Lambert and Forest Laboratories, Inc., and Pfizer's Zoloft and SmithKline Beecham's Paxil, which were second and third, respectively, in terms of sales in the antidepressant market. In addition, even though Prozac had shown strong sales growth overseas and sales had increased 10 percent in the United States in 1998, some experts were not necessarily optimistic about its future with Lilly. Lilly stock suffered a blow in March 1999, dropping over 5 percent after one securities analyst lowered estimates for Prozac sales in 1999 (Anonymous, 1999E).

During February 1999, Lilly and Barr Laboratories Inc. reached a partial settlement with regard to Barr's patent-rights lawsuit, which was a victory for Lilly in that it barred Barr from manufacturing generic versions of Prozac. However, the case was not completely resolved because of appeals filed by Barr.

Anti-infectives (Antibiotics)   Comprising 15 percent of company sales in 1997, Lilly's sales of anti-infectives decreased 13 percent. This was one therapeutic area where strong competition from generics in the United States and overseas led to a sales decline. Sales outside the United States accounted for approximately 75 percent of anti-infectives sales.

Insulins   Insulins included Humulin and Humalog. The production of insulins constituted 13 percent of the company's sales in 1998.

Other   The following newer products (launched in 1996) accounted for 13 percent of company sales in 1997:

- *Zyprexa.* This product was an antischizophrenic—a treatment for schizophrenia and related psychoses. Zyprexa boasted sales of $1.4 billion, 16 percent of the company's sales, in its first year of existence on the world market. Whether it would become another Prozac remained to be seen.

- *Gemzar.* This was a product treating cancer.

- *ReoPro.* This was a cardiovascular agent.

- *Evista.* An estrogenlike compound that prevented osteoporosis and perhaps breast cancer, representing Lilly's late 1990s efforts toward moving into women's health care, this had disappointing sales in the first year of only $144 million, or 1 percent of the company's sales in 1998. The British drug company Zeneca Inc. sued Lilly in February 1999 for making claims about Evista as a treatment for breast cancer, since research in this area had not been completed. Lilly executives responded by saying that this had been identified as part of the company's long-term strategy for Evista, but as of yet they said Lilly had not made such claims.

All other products in addition to the ones discussed above comprised 13 percent of company sales.

Lilly also had devoted a portion of its efforts to the animal health sector, which comprised 7 percent of the company's sales in 1998 (Eli Lilly, 1998).

Patent protection of a company's products was a good indicator of the strength of future profits, especially in the light of high R&D costs. Lilly's product patent expiration scenario at the end of the 1990s was centered around Prozac, whose patent was due to expire in 2001; the patent for how it functioned was to expire in 2003, as shown in Figure 10.

Distribution

Within the United States, Lilly used two hundred independent wholesale outlets to distribute its pharmaceutical products. The company's primary objective in distribution was ensuring that customers—physicians, pharmacies, hospitals, and health care

FIGURE 10

Eli Lilly & Company Patent Expirations
for Major Therapeutic Products

Product	Year	Product	Year
Prozac	2001, 2003	ReoPro	2015
Axid	2002	Gemzar	2006*
Zyprexa	2011	Evista	2012*
Humalog	2013		

Source: Eli Lilly and Company (1999), 10K report for the fiscal year ended December 31, 1998 [Online]. *http://www.sec.gov/Archives/edgar/data/59478/0000950131-99-001772.txt.* Accessed April 17.

professionals—had immediate access to its products. In 1998, four primary wholesale distributors were responsible for 55 percent of the company's consolidated net sales; the remainder was distributed by smaller wholesalers, none of which accounted for more than 7 percent of consolidated net sales (Eli Lilly, 1998).

Distribution outside the United States was accomplished through salaried sales representatives. Neuroscience products made up the largest therapeutic class of drugs marketed outside the United States. In the late 1990s, Lilly stepped up marketing efforts in certain emerging markets, such as Central and Eastern Europe, Latin America, Asia, and Africa. However, sales outside the United States remained at 37 percent of company sales, down from 44 percent in 1995.

Alliances

Consistent with the strategic industry-wide business model, Lilly was heavily involved in alliances to perform research. At the end of 1997, the company was involved in fifty significant research alliances, thirty of which were signed in 1997 (Eli Lilly, 1999).

Other alliances and agreements involved crucial aspects of drug marketing and served to lengthen Lilly's so-called monopoly on patented drugs. In late 1998, Lilly signed an agreement with Sepracor, a company that specialized in removing side effects from drugs currently on the market and licensing the rights to market the new product back to the original company. In this case, Sepracor was researching a new form of Prozac, which, if successful, would allow Lilly to continue with their exclusive rights to Prozac, the blockbuster drug that in 1998 was responsible for

30 percent of Lilly's revenues. It was not without opposition from other industry participants that Lilly was proceeding with this agreement. The U.S. FTC was investigating the agreement in early 1999 because of a lawsuit against Lilly by Barr Laboratories, a generic drugmaker, which stood to lose the marketing of a generic form of Prozac and thus the entry of competition if the Lilly-Sepracor deal was allowed to proceed. Other research alliances included collaboration with Takeda Chemical Industries, Ltd., a Japanese pharmaceutical company, to comarket the company's oral diabetes treatment, which was still under regulatory approval in 1999. In 1998, Lilly made an agreement with ICOS Corporation to enter into an eventual joint venture for the study of treatments for sexual dysfunction.

Overseas Markets

In the late 1990s, Lilly was selling in 159 countries. The company had R&D facilities in nine countries, including North America, Europe, and Japan. It had manufacturing facilities in twenty countries, including locations in Australia, South America, China, the Middle East, Europe, and the United States.

In 1997, while the company's overall sales increased 16 percent, sales in the United States increased 28 percent and outside the United States by merely 1 percent. The weakness in overseas sales was in part due to unfavorable exchange rates and price decreases. In 1998, overseas sales experienced a turnaround because of the successes of some of the new drugs, but foreign sales as a percentage of total sales still remained at approximately 36 percent of total revenues in 1998, as shown in Figures 11 and 12.

FIGURE 11

Eli Lilly & Company Overseas Sales
(U.S.$ millions)

Year	Amount	Year	Amount
1989	1,335.7	1994	2,430.2
1990	1,636.9	1995	2,950.9
1991	1,807.0	1996	3,081.0
1992	1,996.2	1997	3,105.9
1993	2,097.5	1998	3,400.6

Source: Eli Lilly and Company (1999), 10K report for the fiscal year ended December 31, 1998 [Online]. *http://www.sec.gov/Archives/edgar/data/59478/0000950131-99-001772.txt.* Accessed April 17.

FIGURE 12

Eli Lilly & Company Sales, 1998,
by Geographic Area

Region	U.S.$ millions	% of Total
U.S.	5,837	63
Western Europe	1,692	18
Other regions	1,708	18
Total	9,237	100

Source: Hoover's Online (1999), Company Capsules [Online].
http://www.hoovers.com. Accessed March 29.

Research and Development

Lilly Research Laboratories (LRL) was the division of the company responsible for R&D for pharmaceutical products and animal health products. In 1997, Lilly's expenditures for R&D were $1.3 billion, or 16 percent of sales. This was in line with major competitors, for whom the percentage spent on R&D ranged from 14 to 18 percent. In 1998, research and development costs increased by 27 percent. The company stated that the increase was due to greater R&D efforts as well as the development of external R&D collaborations. One of the industry benchmarks was comparing the rate of sales growth to the rate of R&D expenditure growth. When R&D growth was higher, pressure was put on earnings. In Lilly's case, although sales growth had been strong, R&D expenditures were increasing at a faster rate. This might have been the result of Prozac earnings being directed toward new research and development.

Toward the Future

The most prevalent industry factor at work at the end of the 1990s was the quickly escalating R&D costs, which necessitated choosing core businesses wisely in order to enjoy higher margins. The tendency for companies to join forces to confront this phenomenon was beginning to change the average size of pharmaceutical manufacturing organizations. Lilly had already experienced some success with reorganizing its business around its core competencies, five specific therapeutic categories in the mid 1990s, after the entrance of a new CEO, Randall Tobias, in 1993. It was through this reorganization that the blockbuster product Prozac emerged, boosting the company's sales and making Lilly a top ten contender within the industry. Lilly realized that Prozac had boosted it into this prestigious group of players; however, it had to design a new strategy to continue strong growth post Prozac in light of market and internal conditions.

The U.S. market, which had usually boasted strong growth rates throughout the second half of the century, had once again been booming because of product innovation and strong volume sales. Smaller pharmaceutical firms, especially those outside the United States wanting to get a piece of the action, looked for merger partners with whom they could join either to increase their R&D muscle or to have immediate access to the American market. However, even the U.S. market's strong growth rates could not be counted on because of the dominance of managed care, which was changing the dynamics of the industry and putting downward pressure on prices. The industry also had to focus on global launching, even though markets outside the United States appeared to be less attractive with socialist governments and price controls.

An additional prevailing external factor was the aging of the world population and the lengthening of life expectancy. Experts had cited several conditions from which the oldest age groups would suffer in this environment, and a key to success in the future would be the ability to address these particular areas with treatment.

Lilly realized that it was in a middle-of-the-road position. In the current environment of rising R&D costs, its pipeline of drugs contained some decent candidates to create strong future sales growth. However, it remained to be seen whether the company could manage the loss of Prozac and still provide excellent growth and shareholder value. Wall Street analysts were on the fence about Lilly, and some recommendations were: yes, buy pharmaceuticals, but hold off on Lilly. Internally, Lilly was going through some of its own transitions. Randall Tobias, who had led the company through the mid 1990s reorganization and had guided the Prozac success story, decided to retire in 1998. The new CEO, Sidney Taurel, had to decide on a strategic direction toward which to carry the company into the new millennium in light of industry and company conditions.

At a meeting of the Board of Directors in the spring of 1999, Mr. Laurel was evaluating possible alternatives provided by various directors. Mr. Charles E. Golden, executive vice president and chief financial officer, realized that Lilly had already tightened its therapeutic focus onto five basic areas that would help it capture and take advantage of an aging world population—it already had a presence here. Mr. Golden recognized that Lilly, like many other pharmaceutical firms, was at the mercy of its drug pipeline, since at the time it was approaching a possible loss of Prozac. There were some promising drugs in its pipeline, specifically, Zyprexa, which had blossomed in its second year of sales to a USD 1.4 billion selling drug. The other promising candidates were ReoPro and Gemzar, but neither of these looked like it would have the strength of Prozac. Thus the company had to devise a way to maintain its main contender status within the industry by continuing the growth rates it had achieved with Prozac. It did not want this success story to be a onetime deal.

Mr. Golden felt that he had to expand the company by locating a merger partner by which he could enter a compatible sector that would provide earnings with a type of insurance when the drug pipeline had possible gaps. In this way, Lilly could continue to pursue pharmaceuticals and use its strength in R&D, as it had done previously, but would have the added protection of consumer products that focused more on marketing and sales, an area in which Lilly had been strong. While both consumer product and pharmaceutical demand were considered to be relatively insensitive to swings in the business cycle, a consumer goods unit would equal revenues minus the pipeline problem. Golden cited Pfizer, the powerhouse company whose drug pipeline had been formidable against the competition but which at the same time had been able to focus on building strong brand recognition with consumer products. The fact was that strength in one sector had not deterred Pfizer from performing well in the other. In other words, the businesses were compatible, and this addition could be strategically beneficial. In addition, since most over-the-counter medicines had their beginnings as ethical products, Lilly would be able to make this transition on its own upon expiration of patents. It seemed a logical move on the part of Mr. Golden.

Mr. Taurel listened carefully to these arguments. The idea of making strides toward becoming a powerhouse like Pfizer had always attracted him, and the theory behind Mr. Golden's presentation was certainly logical. Pfizer was living proof that this strategy of having varying business units could work; however, he felt rather uneasy about such a radical strategy change. After all, his predecessor had refocused Lilly's strategy around the company's core competencies and had sold off other business units, making strong focus one of the company's strengths. He felt that although the loss of Prozac might have serious consequences for earnings, Lilly's pipeline was still promising and had been effective against competition in similar therapeutic areas. He added that the company should perhaps be keeping its eggs in this strategic basket and not be so quick to reverse the internal trend of the mid 1990s. He was willing to listen to other proposals.

Another officer at Lilly, Mr. Gerhard N. Mayr, president of intercontinental operations, although not opposed to finding a merger partner, had a different idea. He noted that Lilly had excellent success in the United States, a market that had provided strong growth potential and the most attractive market in the industry. However, he recognized that other competitors were experiencing higher sales percentages overseas and that Lilly, if it wanted to retain its status in the industry, could not necessarily rely only on the U.S. market for future growth. Secondly, the company size in terms of sales was changing because of the trend toward mergers and acquisitions, and at least in the near term, it was losing its position as a top contender in terms of sales.

Lilly's success story with Prozac had become, in 1998, mostly a U.S. phenomenon. That is, Prozac sales overseas had been basically flat because of competition from European firms. Even though Lilly was already operating in some 150 countries, sales outside the United States did not well represent the company's investment in those markets. If it had better representation in those markets, perhaps in the form of a European partner with compatible therapeutic competencies, it would be able to accomplish a threefold objective: further strengthen its R&D capabilities, since R&D in Europe was highly respected; pick up synergies with a foreign partner while increasing its capital base in an environment of mergers and acquisitions that were quickly expanding the average size of firms in the industry; and increase its presence in Europe so it could participate in more opening markets in the future. In this way, the company could also remain focused on its core competencies, an industry key to success in the late 1990s. Mayr noticed that companies like SmithKline Beecham were experiencing problems because of too broadly designed strategies. Thus Lilly had to stick with its therapeutic competencies—however, with a partner.

Mr. Laurel had listened to both of these arguments intently, but he was not necessarily intent on making an immediate decision. Both his board members had put forth ideas that had strategic sense; however, he felt that the situation merited deeper thought and analysis.

REFERENCES

Agrawal, M. (1997). "Global Competitiveness in the Pharmaceutical Industry: An Examination of the Factors." Center for Global Education, St. John's University, September.

Anonymous (1999A). "Boost for China's Pharmaceutical Industry for 1999," Intelli-Health, Inc. [Online]. *http://www.intelihealth.com/IH/ihtIH*. Accessed April 20.

Anonymous (1999B). "Business: Pill Pushing." *Economist*, February 13, 350(8106): 66 [Online]. *http://proquest.umi.com*. Accessed March 23.

Anonymous (1999C). "Eli Lilly Sales Higher but Prozac Down." *Financial Times*, April 1999 [Online]. *http://www.ft.com/hippocampus/qb266e.htm*. Accessed April 19.

Anonymous (1999D). "Experts Predict Growing Revenue, Greater Expense in Global Market." *Medical Marketing and Media*, February, 34(2): 18 [Online]. *http://proquest.umi.com*. Accessed April 14.

Anonymous (1999E). "Lilly Shares Drop on Concern About Prozac." *New York Times*, March 18: C4 [Online]. *http://proquest.umi.com*. Accessed April 14; Curwen, A. (1999). "Acquisitions in Europe," *European Venture Capital Journal*, March 1 [Online]. *http://proquest.umi.com*. Accessed March 18.

Edlin, M. (1997). "Pharmacy Benefits Go Global." *Managed Healthcare*, December, 7(12): 30 [Online]. *http://proquest.umi.com*. Accessed March 18, 1999.

Eli Lilly & Company (1998). Annual Report [Online]. *http://www.elililly.com*. Accessed March 15, 1999.

Eli Lilly & Company (1999). 10K report for the fiscal year ended December 31, 1998 [Online]. *http://www.sec.gov/Archives/edgar/data/59478/0000950131-99-001772.txt*. Accessed April 17.

Gerstein, A. (1997). "Pharmaceutical Industry." *Collier's Encyclopedia* [Online]. *http://web7.infotrac-custom.com/*. Accessed March 10, 1999.

Hoover's Online (1999). Company Capsules [Online]. *http://www.hoovers.com*. Accessed March 29.

IMS Health (1999). "Global Pharma Forecast 1998–2002" [Online]. *http://ims-global.com/insight/report/generics/report.htm*. Accessed March 20.

LLY NEWS (1999). *Corporate Communications Internal Publication*, March 12.

Mauer Fron, J., and Craig S. Smith (1998). "Drugs: Prozac's Maker Confronts China over Knockoffs." *Wall Street Journal*, March 25: B1 [Online]. *http://proquest.umi.com*. Accessed April 19, 1999.

Moran, C. (1999). "Industry Snapshot: Pharmaceuticals and Medical Equipment." *Hoover's Online Industry Zone* [Online]. *http://www.hoovers.com/features/industry/pharm.html*. Accessed April 19.

Moore, S. D. (1998). "Hopes Dwindle That EU Would Dismantle Draconian Price Controls on Medicines." *Wall Street Journal*, December 7: 1 [Online]. *http://proquest.umi.com*. Accessed March 10, 1999.

Moore, S. D. (1999). "Novo Nordisk, Following Rivals' Path, Opts to Split into Two Separate Entities." *Wall Street Journal*, February 24: 1 [Online]. *http://proquest.umi.com*. Accessed April 12.

Morrow, D. J. (1999). "Companies Find Bonus in Drugs That Cure Several Ills." *New York Times*, March 19: C1 [Online]. *http://proquest.umi.com*. Accessed April 12.

Saldanha, G., P. Pesanello, and E. Harrington (1997). "Building Value Through Global Markets." *Pharmaceutical Executive*, December, 17(12): 72–78 [Online]. *http://proquest.umi.com*. Accessed April 14, 1999.

Scott, A. (1999). "Drug Makers Consolidate." *Chemical Week*, January 6, 161(1): 29 [Online]. *http://proquest.umi.com*. Accessed March 23.

Sharpe, P., and Tom Keelin (1998). "How SmithKline Beecham Makes Better Resource-Allocation Decisions." *Harvard Business Review*, March–April, 76(2): 45–52 [Online]. *http://proquest.umi.com*. Accessed April 12, 1999.

Sherrid, P. (1999). "A Big Downer for Prozac." *U.S. News and World Report*, February 1, 126(4): 42–43 [Online]. *http://proquest.umi.com*. Accessed March 15.

Standard & Poor's Industry Surveys (1998). "Healthcare: Facilities, Managed Care, Pharmaceuticals, Products and Supplies," December 17.

Stipp, D. (1998). "Why Pfizer was So Hot." *Fortune*, May 11 [Online]. *http://www.pfizer.com/pfizerinc/about/fortune2.html*. Accessed April 10, 1999.

Vilas-Boas, I. M., and C. Patrick Tharp (1997). "Practitioner Update: The Drug Approval Process in the U.S., Europe, and Japan: Some Marketing and Cost Implications." *Journal of Managed Care Pharmacy*, July–August, 3(4) [Online]. *http://www.amcp.org/public/pubs/journal/vol3/num4/drug.html*. Accessed April 13, 1999.

Yates, K. (1999). "Fit for the World." *Campaign*, January 8: 3–5 [Online]. *http://proquest.umi.com*. Accessed April 14.

Yoshida, M, (1995). "Pharmaceuticals: West Meets East in the Asian Markets." *Tokyo Business Today*, August, 63(8): 36–37 [Online]. *http://proquest.umi.com*. Accessed April 12, 1999.

38 Kikkoman Corporation in the Mid 1990s: Market Maturity, Diversification, and Globalization

This case was prepared by Norihito Tanaka, Kanagawa University, Marilyn L. Taylor, University of Missouri at Kansas City, Joyce A. Claterbos, University of Kansas, and NACRA.

In early 1996, Mr. Yuzaburo Mogi, president of Kikkoman Corporation, faced a number of challenges. Analysts indicated concern with Kikkoman's slow sales growth and noted that the company's stock had underperformed on the Nikkei Exchange in relation to the market

The authors express deep appreciation to Kikkoman Corporation, which provided encouragement to this study, including access to the U.S. manufacturing and marketing facilities in addition to time in the corporate offices in Japan. The authors also gratefully acknowledge the support for this study provided by the Japanese Department of Education and the Institute for Training and Development in Tokyo. Quotes and data in this case study were drawn from a variety of personal interviews in the United States and Japan, company documents, and public sources. Documents and public sources appear in the list of references at the conclusion of the case.

This case is intended to be used as a basis for class discussion rather than as an illustration of either effective or ineffective handling of the situation.

and to its peers for several years. Throughout the world, ongoing changes in taste preferences and dietary needs presented threats to the company's traditional food lines. The company marketed its branded products in ninety-four countries and had to consider which products and markets to emphasize as well as which new markets to enter. As Mr. Mogi described the company's focus, "We are now concentrating on further enhancing our ability to serve consumers in Japan and overseas. The basic keynotes of this effort are expansion of soy sauce markets, diversification, and globalization."

In Japan, Kikkoman had long dominated the soy sauce market, and its mid 1990s market share position of 27 percent was well beyond the 10 percent of its next closest competitor. However, its share of the soy sauce market had continued to decline from its high of 33 percent in 1983, falling from 28 percent in 1993 to 27.2 percent in 1994. Further, although the company's worldwide sales had increased slightly overall from 1994 to 1995, sales of soy sauce in Japan had decreased over 1 percent during that period.

The U.S. market had provided significant opportunity in the post–World War II period. However, the company's U.S. market share for soy and other company products was essentially flat. In addition, three competitors had built plants in the United States beginning in the late 1980s. Mr. Mogi was aware that Kikkoman's choices in the U.S. market would provide an important model for addressing higher income mature markets.

With a market capitalization of nearly ¥160 billion,[1] Kikkoman Corporation was the world's largest soy sauce producer, Japan's nineteenth largest food company, and also Japan's leading soy sauce manufacturer. The company was the oldest continuous enterprise among the two hundred largest industrials in Japan. It began brewing shoyu, or naturally fermented soy sauce, in the seventeenth century and had dominated the Japanese soy industry for at least a century. The company held 50 percent of the U.S. soy sauce market and 30 percent of the world market. Kikkoman had thirteen manufacturing facilities in Japan and one each in the United States, Singapore, and Taiwan. The company was one of the few traditional manufacturers

to successfully establish a presence worldwide. (Exhibits 1 and 2 have the locations of and information on the company's principal subsidiaries. Exhibits 3 and 4 list the consolidated financial statements.)

Kikkoman in Japan

The Beginnings in Noda

In 1615, the widow of a slain samurai warrior fled three hundred miles from Osaka to the village of Noda near Edo (now called Tokyo). With her five children, the widow Mogi embarked upon rice farming and subsequently began brewing shoyu, or soy sauce. The quality of the Mogi family's shoyu was exceptional almost from its beginnings. At the time, households produced shoyu for their own use, or local farmers made and sold excess shoyu as a side enterprise to farming. As more people moved to the urban areas in the seventeenth and eighteenth centuries, there was increased demand for nonhome production. Households developed preferences for the product of a particular brewer. (See Appendix A: The Making of Soy Sauce.)

EXHIBIT 1

Locations of Principal Subsidiaries

Source: "Flavors That Bring People Together," Kikkoman Corporation Brochure, 1994.

EXHIBIT 2

Consolidated Subsidiaries as of FY 1995

Subsidiary	Country	Paid-In Capital ((¥)m/$m)	Kikkoman Equity (%)
Japan Del Monte	Japan	900	99.7%
Mann's Wine	Japan	900	100.0
Pacific Trading	Japan	72	66.7
Morishin	Japan	30	66.7
Kikkoman Foods, Inc.	U.S.	U.S.$ 6	100.0
Kikkoman International	U.S.	U.S.$ 3.5	92.6
JFC International	U.S.	U.S.$ 1.2	98.0
Kikkoman Trading Europe	Germany	DM 1.5	75.0
Kikkoman Pte	Singapore	S$ 7.5	100.0
Kikkoman Trading Pte	Singapore	S$ 0.4	100.0
Tokyo Food Processing	U.S.	U.S.$ 0.02	100.0
Hapi Products	U.S.	U.S.$ 0.05	100.0
Rex Pacific	U.S.	U.S.$ 1.5	100.0

Source: Table 4: Consolidated Subsidiaries, UBS Securities Limited, May 28, 1996, as reported by *Investext.*

Shoyu had come to Japan with the arrival of Buddhism in the sixth century. The teachings of Buddhism prohibited eating meat and fish. Residents of the Japanese islands turned from meat-based to vegetable-based flavorings. One of the favorites became a flavorful seasoning made from fermented soybeans. A Japanese Zen Buddist priest who had studied in China brought the recipe to Japan. The Japanese discovered that adding wheat gave the sauce a richer, more mellow flavor.

Over the eighteenth century, Noda became a major center for shoyu manufacturing in Japan. Shoyu's major ingredients, soybeans and wheat, grew readily in the rich agricultural Kanto plain that surrounded Noda. The trip to the major market of Edo took only one day on the Edo River. The various shoyu-producing families in the Noda area actively shared their knowledge of fermentation. The Mogi family and another Noda area family, the Takanashi family, were especially active in the industry. By the late eighteenth century, the two families had become interrelated through marriage. Their various enterprises made considerable investment in breweries, and family members began ancillary enterprises such as grain brokering, keg manufacture, and transportation.

Japan's Shoyu Distribution System and Industry Structure

Japan's neophyte and fragmented shoyu industry had two distribution systems during this time. In the rural areas, the shoyu breweries sold their products directly to households. In the cities, urban wholesalers distributed shoyu, vinegar, and sake. The wholesalers purchased bulk shoyu and established their own brands. The wholesalers controlled pricing, inventory, distribution, and marketing knowledge. They would distribute branded shoyu only on consignment. During the 1800s, the wholesalers formed alliances that gave them near monopolistic power over the Tokyo market. As the shoyu manufacturers became more efficient, they found it impossible to lower prices or make other adjustments to increase their market share.

The Mogi and Takanashi families took several steps to counteract the wholesalers' dominance. The Takanashi family had diversified into wholesaling some years prior and were part of the wholesalers' alliance. One Mogi family intermarried with a wholesaler's family—a traditional strategy in Japan for cementing strategic alliances. In addition, the Mogi and Takanashi families worked to increase brand recognition and dominance. In 1838, Mogi Saheiji

EXHIBIT 3

Consolidated Profit and Loss Statement ((¥) m)

	1989	1990	1991	1992	1993	1994	1995
Sales	195,851	196,925	206,861	211,671	203,491	200,976	203,286
COGS	117,062	118,808	122,872	124,882	118,504	117,809	119,656
Gross profit	78,789	78,117	83,989	86,789	84,987	83,167	83,629
Gross profit margin (%)	40.2	39.7	40.6	41	41.8	41.4	41.1
SG&A expenses	71,227	71,876	74,181	76,019	74,320	72,689	72,836
SG&A exp. (%)	36.4	36.5	35.9	35.9	36.5	36.2	35.8
Operating profit	7,562	6,240	9,807	10,769	10,666	10,477	10,792
Operating margin (%)	3.9	3.2	4.7	5.1	5.2	5.2	5.3
Net non-op. income	−572	−1,042	−1,564	−1,895	−2,282	−2,197	−2,305
Recurring profit	6,990	5,197	8,243	8,873	8,384	8,280	8,487
Recurring margin (%)	3.6	2.6	4	4.2	4.1	4.1	4.2
Net extraordinary income	181	1,165	1,317	59	108	1,434	−1,177
Pretax profit	7,170	6,363	9,559	8,932	8,493	9,714	7,310
Tax	3,327	3,299	4,726	5,178	4,597	4,157	3,569
Tax rate (%)	46.4	50.7	49.4	58	54.1	42.8	48.8
Minority interest	56	78	37	34	1	−52	46
Amortization of consol. dif.	0	0	−35	1	5	0	−314
Equity in earnings	1,097	1,464	1,188	1,245	887	1,002	996
Net profit	4,697	4,694	6,166	4,928	4,688	6,614	4,447
Shares outstanding (m)	169.08	169.71	169.97	178.61	187.62	187.77	197.2
EPS	27.8	27.7	31.3	25	23.8	33.5	22.6
EPS change (%)	80	−0.4	13.3	−20.2	−4.9	41	−32.8
Cash flow per share	20.8	46.5	48	41.9	44.4	58.5	46.8
Average exchange rate (¥/USD)	137.96	144.79	134.71	126.65	111.20	102.21	94.06

Sources: Table 9: UBS Securities Limited, May 28, 1996; *The World Almanac,* 1998 (original source: IMF).

applied for and received the shogunate's recognition of his family's premier brand, named Kikkoman. He aggressively promoted the brand by sponsoring professional storytellers and sumo wrestlers, embossing paper lanterns and umbrellas with the Kikkoman trademark, and putting ornate gold labels from Paris on his Kikkoman shoyu kegs. In the latter part of the nineteenth century, Kikkoman shoyu won recognition in several world's fairs.

In reaction to depressed market prices and fluctuating costs of inputs, a number of the Noda shoyu brewers formed the Noda Shoyu Brewers' Association in 1887. The association purchased raw materials, standardized wages, and regulated output quality. The members' combined efforts resulted in the largest market share at the time, 5 to 10 percent of the Tokyo market, and widespread recognition of the high quality of Noda shoyu.

Noda brewers, and especially the Mogi and Takanashi families, began research and development activities early. The Japanese government encouraged the Noda shoyu brewers to conduct research in the recovery and processing of the two byproducts of shoyu manufacture, shoyu oil and shoyu cake. In the early 1900s, the association began to fund a joint research and development laboratory.

The Shoyu Industry in the Twentieth Century

In 1910, there were still fourteen thousand known makers of shoyu in Japan. However, a number of

EXHIBIT 4

Consolidated Balance Sheet ((¥) m)

	1990	1991	1992	1993	1994	1995
Current Assets	81,611	88,092	89,705	103,152	105,220	107,339
Cash and deposits	13,254	17,570	18,261	28,826	36,381	37,366
Accounts receivable	43,579	44,661	44,503	46,009	44,246	44,439
Securities	315	1,012	1,316	3,310	3,306	3,307
Inventories	21,769	21,300	22,484	21,469	18,579	19,258
Fixed assets	94,631	97,999	105,231	113,940	112,183	119,411
Tangible assets	52,087	53,254	59,276	67,649	65,795	72,684
Land	11,768	12,011	11,910	15,156	15,613	11,540
Investments	26,371	29,597	31,771	33,051	34,083	35,006
Total Assets	177,583	187,316	195,955	218,561	218,805	228,308
Liabilities and Owner's Equity						
Current liabilities	48,040	52,626	54,014	50,272	46,663	63,400
Short-term borrowings	18,846	18,908	19,046	17,462	14,838	15,741
Fixed liabilities	58,374	58,850	62,351	85,532	85,143	71,710
Long-term borrowings	4,457	4,549	4,723	3,274	3,091	2,312
Bonds and CBs[a]	26,565	26,346	26,231	46,170	44,776	29,921
Minority interest	1,223	1,166	1,157	1,103	1,024	427
Total liabilities	107,638	112,643	117,522	136,909	132,832	135,538
Shareholders' equity	69,945	74,673	78,434	81,651	85,973	92,770
Total Liabilities and Equity	177,583	187,316	195,955	218,561	218,805	228,308

[a]There were two CBs issued January 90 exercisable at (¥) 1,522. The other two were issued July 93 and were exercisable at (¥) 969. With the share price at approximately (¥) 100, the total dilution factor was about 18 percent, with 80 percent of that dependent on the two CBs exercisable at (¥) 969. Of 228 ((¥) m) in 1995, about 170 belonged to the parent (i.e., Japan corporation) company.

Source: Nikkei Needs as reported in Table 12: Consolidated Balance Sheet, UBS Securities Limited, May 28, 1996.

changes led to consolidation. Manufacturing shifted from a small-batch, brewmaster-controlled production process to a large-batch, technology-controlled process. Mogi families in Noda invested in modernized plants, and a fifth-grade Japanese geography reader featured a state-of-the-art Kikkoman facility. A national market also developed, thanks to the development of a railway system throughout most of the country. In addition, consumer tastes shifted to the Tokyo-style shoyu produced by eastern manufacturers such as the Noda Shoyu Brewers' Association.

Consumers also began to purchase shoyu in smaller glass bottles rather than in the traditional large wooden barrels that sometimes leaked and were expensive to build and difficult to store. Raw materials also became more expensive as the brewers increasingly sought higher-quality imported soybeans (from Manchuria, China, and Korea) and salt (from England, Germany, and China). The association members controlled costs by purchasing in bulk and demanding high-quality materials from suppliers.

The Noda Shoyu Company: 1918–1945—A Family *Zaibatsu*[2]

In 1918, seven Mogi families and a related Takanashi family combined their various enterprises into a joint stockholding company called the Noda Shoyu Company. The merger was in reaction to the market upheaval caused by World War I. The new company was a small *zaibatsu* with nearly a dozen companies in manufacturing fermented grain-based products, transportation, and finance. Unlike early shoyu manufacturing, where ownership, management, and operations were clearly separated, the Mogi and Takanashi families owned, managed, and operated their firm. Initially, the family produced thirty-four different brands of shoyu at various price points. The Kikkoman brand had a history of heavy promotion for over forty years, greater Tokyo market share, and a higher margin than the company's other brands. The Kikkoman brand became the company's flagship brand. The new corporation continued its long-standing emphasis on research and development and aggressively pursued new manufacturing processes, increased integration, and acquisition of other shoyu companies.

After the Mogi Takanashi coalition, the company aggressively pursued a strong nationwide sole agent system and direct distribution. The combined company also continued Kikkoman's well-known advertising activities. Kikkoman had carried out the first newspaper advertising in 1878. In 1922, the company carried out the firm's first advertising on the movie screen.

During the 1920s, the company aggressively modernized with machines such as hydraulic presses, boilers, conveyors, and elevators. The company's modernization efforts were emulated by competitors, and the results were increased supply and heightened industry competition. The changes brought about by increased automation led to severe labor unrest. One particularly long strike against the Kikkoman company in the late 1920s almost destroyed the participating labor union. After the strike ended, Kikkoman rehired about a third of the striking employees. The company centralized and reorganized the work processes to accommodate improved technology, restructured work practices, and established methods to monitor and reward workers for their performance. However, the company also established efforts to improve the identity of the workers with the company. Internal communications carried the message that all employees were members of one family, or ikka, united in a common purpose—the production of shoyu. The Noda Shoyu Company was also heavily involved in the city of Noda and supported many of its cultural and charitable activities as well as the local railroad, bank, town hall, cultural center, library, fire station, elementary school, hospital, recreation facilities and association, and much of the city's water system.

Kikkoman's International Activities

Kikkoman's initial export activities began in the late seventeenth century with Dutch and Chinese traders. The Dutch began to export shoyu to Holland and the rest of Europe, while the Chinese served the southeast Asian markets. The shoyu brewers relied on agents for these early export transactions. During the nineteenth century, one Mogi patriarch opened a factory in Inchon, Korea. Demand for the increasing export, marketing, and direct investment continued to come primarily from Japanese and other peoples living abroad whose traditional cuisines called for shoyu. In 1910, the Noda city brewers' international activities were recognized when the Japanese government selected Noda shoyu to appear in a public relations publication introducing Japan's industries overseas.

Noda Shoyu Company continued to expand internationally between World War I and World War II. Acquisition of raw materials from abroad continued. The company added a manufacturing facility for shoyu and miso in Manchuria and two shoyu factories in North America. Other facilities in Japan were expanded or updated to support increasing international sales.

The company established sales offices in China and Korea to market shoyu, miso, and sake. By the late 1930s, the company exported 10 percent of its output, about half to the Asian region—especially Korea, China, and Indonesia—and half to Hawaii and California. Almost all of the exports were the Kikkoman brand and were sold through food import/export firms to the company's traditional customers.

Post–World War II Kikkoman in Japan

At the end of World War II, Kikkoman operated only in Japan. Activities elsewhere had been closed. To meet the need for capital, Kikkoman issued publicly traded stock in 1946, reducing family ownership markedly. (Exhibit 5 shows the changes in ownership from 1917 to 1993.) The post–World War II period brought a number of social changes to Japanese society. Japanese families began the change to nuclear- rather than extended-family formation. Food tastes changed, leading among other trends, to a decline in per-capita consumption of shoyu. Compared with other industries, demand for soy sauce grew very slowly. In 1942, demand for soy sauce in Japan was 1.7 times greater than in 1918. Demand in the 1960s was expected to be 2.2 times greater than that in 1918. However, modernization led to increased output.

EXHIBIT 5

Noda Shoyu Company and Kikkoman Corporation Ownership

Shareholder Name	Holdings (% of total shares or assets)			
	1917	1925	1955	1993
Mogi-Takanashi-Horikiri brewing families	100.0%[a]	34.6%	15.0%[b]	2.3%
Senshusha holding company		62.0	3.1	3.4
Insurance and banking companies			9.9[c]	20.5[c]
All others		3.6	71.1	73.6

[a]Eight holdings ranging from 1.4 percent to 29.3 percent.
[b]Five holdings ranging from 1.5 percent to 4.4 percent.
[c]In 1955 and 1993, including Meiji Mutual Insurance Co., Mitsubishi Trust Bank; in 1955, including Kofukan Foundation and Noda Institute of Industrial Science; in 1993, including Nitsuit Trust Bank, Nippon Life Insurance, Sumitomo Trust, and Yasuda Trust.

Sources: W. Mark Fruin, *Kikkoman—Company, Clan, and Community* (Cambridge, MA: Harvard University Press, 1983), pp. 98, 121, 249; *Japan Company Handbook,* Toyo Keizai, Inc., 1993, p. 207.

Kikkoman had received considerable recognition for its advertising efforts prior to World War II. After the war, the company began to market even more aggressively in Japan. These efforts included establishing the company's strong nationwide distribution system throughout Japan; mounting aggressive activities in marketing research, advertising, and consumer education; and changing to a new and more Western image. As a result of Kikkoman's marketing efforts, the company's market share rose sharply. (Exhibit 6 shows the national output of shoyu and the company's market share from 1893 to 1994.) In 1964 the company officially changed its name to Kikkoman Shoyu, and in 1980 it became Kikkoman Corporation. The word *Kikkoman* is a combination of "kikko" (the shell of a tortoise) and "man" (ten thousand). It was taken from an old Japanese saying, "A crane lives a thousand years and a tortoise ten thousand years" (implying, in other words, "May you live as long!"). In essence, the Kikkoman brand connotes a long-lasting living thing. Kikkoman had become well known for its advertising skill in Japan and had found that the word *Kikkoman* was easy for Americans to pronounce.

The company also diversified its product line using its expertise in shoyu manufacture, fermentation, brewing, and foods marketing. This diversification included a 1963 venture to market Del Monte products in Japan. In 1990, the company bought the Del Monte assets and marketing rights for the Del Monte brand name in the Asia–Pacific region.

EXHIBIT 6

National Output and Company Market Share of Shoyu (in kiloliters)[a]

Year	National Output (Japan)	Noda Shoyu Share (%)
1893	230,360	3.5%
1903	317,500	4.5
1913	430,435	6.1
1923	624,764	5.1
1933	576,026	10.1
1943	680,955	12.0
1953	822,179	14.1
1963	1,051,730	21.4
1973	1,277,887	31.4
1983	n.a.	33.0
1993	n.a.	28.0
1994	1,323,529[b]	27.2

[a]1 kiloliter = 264 gallons.
[b]Derived from Kikkoman's production of 360,000 kl and its 27.2 percent market share. Residents of Japan consumed about 2.6 gallons of soy sauce per capita yearly. In contrast, U.S. citizens consumed about 10 tablespoons.
[c]As reported by UBS Securities Limited, May 28, 1996, in *Investext.* This source also reported that demand for soy sauce was flat in Japan and production between 1984 and 1994 had declined about 5.1 percent.

Source: W. Mark Fruin, *Kikkoman—Company, Clan, and Community* (Cambridge, MA: Harvard University Press, 1983), pp. 40–41.

(Exhibit 7 shows Kikkoman Corporation's product lists as of 1949, 1981, and 1994.) Kikkoman's R&D expertise led to activities in biotechnology and products such as enzymes, diagnostic reagents, and other biologically active substances used to test for microorganisms in water samples in hospitals, food-processing factories, and semiconductor plants. The company also developed a number of patents at home and overseas. The company became involved in both the import and export of wines. It also undertook activities in food-processing machinery. In spite of the diversification, Kikko-

man's domestic sales were still about 55 percent soy sauce related.

In the 1990s, soy sauce continued as a perennial favorite in Japan's cuisine, although demand was essentially flat. Among the remaining three thousand shoyu companies in Japan, Kikkoman produced 360,000 kl in Japan, or about 27 percent of the country's output. (Exhibit 6.) The company faced price pressures, especially on its base product of soy sauce, mainly because of the competitive pressures at the retail level in Japan and the aggressive introduction of private brands. Sales in the Del Monte line also

EXHIBIT 7

Kikkoman Corporation Products and Product Lines

1949	1981	1994
Kikkoman Brand soy sauce, sauce, memmi and tsuyu (soup bases)	**Kikkoman Brand** soy sauce, mild soy sauce (lower salt, 8%), light color soy sauce (usu-kuchi), teriyaki barbecue marinade and sauce, Worcestershire sauce, tonkatsu sauce, memmi and tsuyu (soup bases), sukiyaki sauce, instant soy soup mix, instant osumono (clear broth soup mix)	**Kikkoman Brand** soy sauce, mild soy sauce (lower salt, 8%), light color soy sauce (usu-kuchi), teriyaki sauce, Worcestershire sauce, tonkatsu sauce, memmi (soup base), sukiyaki sauce, sashimi soy sauce, lemon-flavored soy sauce, mirin (sweet rice wine), Aji-Mirin, plum wine, instant miso (soybean paste) soups, egg flower soup mixes, rice crackers, tofu, neo-genmai (puffed brown rice), genmai soups, oolong tea, tsuyu-dakono (soup base), ponzu soy sauce, soy sauce dressing, oyster sauce, bonito stock
Manjo Brand mirin (sweet rice wine), sake, shochu, whiskey	**Manjo Brand** mirin (sweet rice wine), shochu, plum wine	**Manjo Brand** triangle, komaki
	Yomonoharu Brand sake	**Yomonoharu Brand**
	Del Monte Brand tomato ketchup, juice, puree, paste, chili sauce, Mandarin orange juice	**Del Monte Brand** tomato ketchup, juice, fruit drinks, Mandarin orange juice
	Disney Brand fruit juice (orange, pineapple, grape), nectar (peach, orange)	
	Mann's Brand[a] wine and sparkling wine, brandy	**Mann's Brand** koshu, koshu (vintage), zenkoji, blush, brandy
	Higeta Brand shoyu, tsuyu, Worcestershire sauce	
	Ragu Brand spaghetti sauces	
	Kikko's Brand tomato ketchup	**Beyoung** protein powder, wheat germ
	Monet Brand cognac	**Imported Wines** aujoux, chateau tatour, boriemanoux, franz reh and sohn, pol roger

*Marketed, not manufactured, by Kikkoman.
[a]The company established its Mann Wine subsidiary in 1964.

Sources: W. Mark Fruin, *Kikkoman—Company, Clan, and Community* (Cambridge, MA: Harvard University Press, 1983), pp. 275–276; "Flavors That Bring People Together," Kikkoman Corporation Brochure, 1994.

decreased in the early 1990s. To improve performance, Kikkoman began to reduce its product line from a high of 5,000 items to an expected eventual 2,500. One bright spot was the growth in wines and spirits. In addition, Kikkoman also introduced successful new soy-sauce-related products in 1993, 1994, and 1995 in the form of two soup stocks and Steak Soy Sauce. Profit increases in the early 1990s came primarily from higher-priced luxury products. (Exhibits 8 and 9 display the parent company financial statements.) The company recognized that continuing success in its mature domestic market would depend on continuous development of new applications and variations of its older products as well as development of new products.

Kikkoman in the United States in the Post–World II Era

U.S. Market Potential

The various Mogi family branches and Noda Shoyu Company had been expanding company efforts beyond Japan since the early 1800s. Japanese expatriates living in various countries and other peoples whose traditional cuisine used shoyu constituted the company's primary pre–World War II markets. By the end of World War II, however, the various family enterprises and the Noda Shoyu Company had ended all activities outside Japan. Then in 1949 Kikkoman started to export soy sauce, mainly to the United States. In the 1950s, consumption of soy sauce began to decline in Japan. Noda Shoyu Company decided to invest heavily in expanding the international sales of Kikkoman brand shoyu to overseas markets. Whereas prior to World War II, Noda Shoyu's major overseas

markets were Asia and Hawaii, after the war, the company decided to focus on the mainland United States because (1) political and economic conditions in Asia were very unstable, (2) the Japanese community in Hawaii had relearned shoyu brewing during World War II, and there were many small Hawaiian shoyu breweries that would have made competition intense in that market, and (3) the United States had a healthy and rapidly growing economy.

Several changes in the U.S. market made that market attractive to Noda Shoyu Company. First, Americans who had been in Asia during or just after World War II developed a taste for Japanese goods, including food. Second, the company expected that as Asians in the United States became more Americanized, their consumption of traditional foods including soy sauce would decline. Third, American eating habits were shifting to more natural foods and to food that could be prepared quickly. Noda Shoyu Company moved to target both Asians and non-Asians in its marketing efforts.

During the 1956 U.S. presidential election, Noda Shoyu bought air time to advertise Kikkoman brand products. Yuzaburo Mogi, son of the head of the company's planning department, urged this move to U.S. television advertising.

U.S. Distribution Activities

During the years immediately after World War II, Japanese companies in general relied on a small group of internationalized and entrepreneurial Japanese and Japanese-American individuals. Sale of food products in the United States involved a complex distribution system with heavy reliance on food brokers as promoters to local wholesalers and retail-

EXHIBIT 8

Parent Company Revenues by Product Line ((¥) m)

	1994	1995	% Change	1996E	% Change
Soy sauce	74,666	73,843	−1.1%	75,000	1.6%
Food	15,091	16,310	8.1	18,500	13.4
Del Monte	24,692	19,857	−19.6	19,000	−4.3
Alcohol	24,993	25,925	3.7	27,000	4.1
Others	4,159	4,285	3	4,500	5
Total	143,601	140,220	−2.4	144,000	2.7

Source: Table 5: UBS Securities Limited, May 28, 1996, as reported by *Investext.*

EXHIBIT 9

Parent Company Balance Sheet ((¥) m)

	1993	1994	1995
Current assets	78,463	81,805	80,749
Fixed assets	88,007	86,029	89,599
Total	166,802	168,000	170,348
Short-term liabilities	33,469	32,033	46,762
Long-term liabilities	79,898	79,527	66,567
Equity	53,434	56,440	57,019
Total liabilities and equity	166,802	168,000	170,348

Source: Table 11: UBS Securities Limited, May 28, 1996, as reported by *Investext.*

ers. Food brokers required careful training by a knowledgeable sales team in how to use the product, especially where the product was unusual or unfamiliar to consumers. Food brokers marketed the product to wholesalers and large retailers, took orders for the product, and relayed the orders to the manufacturer or, in the case of foreign manufacturers, the manufacturer's agent. The manufacturer or agent then made delivery of the product to the wholesaler or retailer and handled all billing and accounts, paying the broker a commission for his or her marketing representation. The food broker was an important link between the manufacturer and the wholesaler or retailer. Food brokers were evaluated based on their ability to persuade retailers and wholesalers to carry products and to feature them prominently.

In 1957, the company formed Kikkoman International, Inc. (KII), a joint venture between Noda Shoyu Company in Japan and Pacific Trading of California. KII was incorporated in San Francisco to serve as the marketing and distribution center for Kikkoman products in the United States. Most of the products were produced by Noda Shoyu Company, but some were purchased from other manufacturers and sold under the Kikkoman label.

Over the next ten years, sales grew 20 to 30 percent a year. In 1960, the Safeway grocery store chain agreed to have some of its stores carry Kikkoman Soy Sauce. Noda Shoyu opened regional sales offices for KII in Los Angeles (1958), New York City (1960), Chicago (1965), and Atlanta (1977). Retail marketing activities included in-store demonstrations, advertis-

ing campaigns in women's magazines that emphasized soy sauce use in American cuisine, and limited television commercials. The company used brokers as their distribution channels to supermarkets and wholesalers for the small oriental retail stores. It encouraged food brokers through contests and training. For the food service and industrial market segments, the company carried out industrial magazine ad campaigns and special educational programs. It also formed partnerships with the American Veal Manufacturers' Association and the Avocado Association to feature Kikkoman Soy Sauce in their product advertisements.

Other major international companies had to modify their products for the United States. However, Kikkoman marketed the same soy sauce in the United States as in Japan. The company's experience in its campaign to "Westernize" soy sauce for the Japanese market applied to the campaign in the United States. In the United States, Kikkoman provided traditional, low-sodium preservative-free, and dehydrated soy sauce. The company also marketed tailor-made sauces, other food extracts, and agents.

Exploration of Potential U.S. Manufacturing Capacity

As early as 1965, Kikkoman Corporation began to explore the possibility of manufacturing in the United States. However, the company determined that sales in North America were insufficient to support the economies of scale required for a minimum efficient scale production facility. Instead, in 1968 Kikkoman Corporation contracted with a subsidiary of Leslie Salt Company of Oakland, California, to bottle the Kikkoman soy sauce shipped in bulk from Japan and to blend and bottle teriyaki sauce, a major ingredient of which was soy sauce. These bottling efforts constituted Kikkoman's first post–World War II manufacturing efforts in the United States. Bottling in the United States reduced customs and tariff costs. However, moving goods back and forth from the United States and Japan added considerably to the company's costs. In the mid 1980s, Japan imported 95 percent and 88 percent of its soybeans and wheat, respectively. The United States was Japan's major source of supply. Transportation of raw materials (such as soybeans and wheat) to Japan was between 5 and 20 percent of preproduction costs; transportation costs of brewed soy sauce from Japan to the United States was 25 percent of production costs. Various import/export restrictions and tariffs increased the risk and expense of importing raw materials to Japan and exporting finished goods to the United States.

The North American market was potentially much larger than the Japanese market, and Kikkoman had a greater share of the North American market than the company had in Japan. Yuzaburo Mogi hired a Columbia University classmate as a consultant, and the company formed a team to work with him to consider a U.S. plant. By 1970, the analyses, in spite of higher U.S. labor costs, favored construction of a U.S. manufacturing facility. As Yuzaburo Mogi put the company's motivation, "We made a decision to go after the American consumer."

Selection of Walworth, Wisconsin

The team considered over sixty potential sites in the East, West, and Midwest. The team chose the Midwest because of its central location and crop production. Ultimately, the team selected a 200-acre dairy farm site in Walworth, Wisconsin. Walworth provided the best fit with the five criteria established by the company: (1) access to markets (it was close to Milwaukee and Chicago, and the geographic convenience of a midway point between the East and West Coasts made shipping relatively efficient); (2) ample supplies of wheat and soybeans (soybeans came from Wisconsin, wheat from North Dakota, and salt from Canada); (3) a dedicated work force; (4) a strong community spirit; and (5) an impeccable supply of water. Kikkoman also appreciated Wisconsin's emphasis on a clean environment.

Walworth, Wisconsin, was situated about two hours northwest of Chicago and about one hour west of Milwaukee. A community of about 1,100, Walworth was surrounded by some of the most productive farmland in the United States. The area included a number of other smaller communities whose economies depended primarily on farming and summer vacation home residences. The company hired a local consultant, lawyer Milton Neshek, who ultimately became general counsel of Kikkoman Foods, Inc. Mr. Neshek described the original reaction to Kikkoman's purchase of prime farmland as mixed, "with a small faction on the town board opposed to the company coming in." Yuzaburo Mogi described the opposition as strong. Residents of the small, rural, close-knit farming community expressed concerns about the impact of a large, especially foreign,

corporation in a small community, the potential inflation of land values, and the possibility of industrial pollution.

One of Neshek's partners, Thomas Godfrey, visited Kikkoman facilities in Noda City, Japan. "When Kikkoman called me in 1971," said Godfrey, "and asked me to create a Wisconsin corporation for them so they could make soy sauce, I didn't even know what the hell soy sauce was. Nobody else around here did either." Walworth's plant manager, Bill Wenger, recalled his introduction to the company. In 1972, he was stationed with the U.S. Marines in Hawaii. His mother sent a newspaper clipping about the soy sauce plant, suggesting that it might be a good place to begin his return to civilian life. Wenger and his wife didn't know what soy sauce was either, but his wife went to the local grocery store and bought a bottle. As Wenger described it, the purchase was "some horrible local Hawaiian brand. She brought it home and opened it. We looked at one another and said, '*@& . . . , this stuff is terrible.'" Another of the three American production managers employed at the plant had a similar tale. The production manager said, "The first year I worked here, we never had any soy sauce in my home. My wife wouldn't buy it, wouldn't even allow it in the house. I finally brought home a bottle and put it on some meatloaf. Now we use it on just about everything. I put it on peaches. And we even have a local minister who puts it on his ice cream. . . . I do too. It's good."

No other Japanese-owned manufacturing facility had been constructed in the United States at the time. Neshek's partner, Godfrey, visited Noda because, as he put it, "I had to see for myself what it was they were talking about. I had to make sure the factory wasn't going to pollute the air and water and stink up the place." Local Kikkoman representatives met with organizations such as the local Grange, Farm Bureau groups, church groups, Rotary, and ladies' clubs. Wisconsin's governor, Patrick Lucey, came to one of the seven town meetings held to discuss the plant and explain the state's role and position. Yuzaburo Mogi described the process as "removing the fears of the local people and local council about the building of the new factory." The company was able to convince area residents that Kikkoman would not pollute the environment and would use local labor and other resources. The final vote of the county zoning board was 53 for, 13 against. The town board declined to oppose the zoning board's action. Among other issues, Kikkoman put a great deal of effort into reducing potential pollution. In talking about this process of "nemawashi," or root tending, Mr. Mogi emphasized the importance of a prosperous coexistence between the company and the local community. He said, "We've been doing business in Noda for 360 years. We learned a long time ago that to survive you need to coexist with the surrounding community."

Opening the New Plant

In January 1971, Kikkoman executives along with Japanese, Walworth, and Wisconsin officials held a ceremonial ground breaking on the 200-acre site. A Cleveland, Ohio, design and construction firm built the plant. Other American companies, many located in the region, built many of the critical components. The initial investment in the 10,000-kiloliter facility was $8 million, and the plant was finished just in time to avoid the 1973 American embargo on the sale of soybeans to Japan. Kikkoman's Walworth plant was the first Japanese investment in production capacity in the United States in the post–World War II period and the first plant Kikkoman built outside Japan after World War II. Opening ceremonies included dignitaries and officials from Wisconsin, Kikkoman, Japan, and the United States. The seven hundred invited guests heard the texts of telegrams from the Japanese prime minister and President Richard Nixon. President Nixon referred to the plant as a "visionary step (that) will mean meaningful trade relations and balance of trade and will enhance further friendships between our two countries."

From its opening in 1972 through the mid 1990s, the company expanded the Walworth facility eight times to 500,000 square feet. Kikkoman invested in facilities or equipment every year, with production increasing 8 to 10 percent per year. Originally, the plant produced two products, soy sauce and teriyaki sauce. In the mid 1990s, the plant produced eighteen products, including regular and light soy sauce, teriyaki steak sauce, sweet and sour sauce, and tempura dip. All but one used a soy base. The company had been very careful about pollution, treating its wastewater carefully so that there was no threat to nearby popular Geneva Lake. The Walworth town clerk said, "There's no noise, no pollution. I live about three-quarters of a mile from them, and once a day, I get a whiff of something that's like a sweet chocolate odor. It's no problem." The company marketed the plant's output in all fifty states plus Canada and Mexico. Soy sauce was shipped in many varieties, including bottles ranging from 5 to 40 ounces, 1- to 5-gallon pails, and sometimes in stainless steel tank trucks for large customers. McDonald's, for example, used soy sauce in one of the Chicken McNuggets condiments.

Management of the Walworth Plant

The company maintained a state-of-the-art laboratory at the Walworth facilities. However, plant management pointed out that the most accurate test during production was the human nose. "Our people have worked with the product for so long, a whiff can tell them something is not quite right," said one Kikkoman director. The venture was described as "a prime example of the best combination of Japanese and American business and industrial savvy." As the plant's general manager, Michitaro Nagasawa, a Ph.D. in biochemistry from the University of Wisconsin, put it, "The productivity of this plant is the highest of all our plants. . . . It's an exceptional case in Kikkoman history. We took the sons and daughters of farmers, trained them and taught them about total quality management. They were raw recruits with no experience in making soy sauce. People with farm backgrounds are very diligent workers. They will work 7 days a week, 24 hours a day if necessary. They understand what hard work is."

The plant opened with fifty employees. Originally, fourteen Japanese Kikkoman employees and their families came to Walworth to train employees and get the plant functioning. The Japanese families scattered in groups of two or three to settle in Walworth and various nearby communities. Local women's community organizations "adopted" the Japanese wives, formed one-to-one friendships, and helped the Japanese wives become acclimated to the communities, including learning to drive, using the local supermarkets, and hiring baby sitters for their children. The Japanese husbands joined local service clubs. "That helped achieve an understanding between the Americans and Japanese and helped them to assimilate faster. It exposed Japanese people to a farming town that had had no Asian people before," noted Bill Nelson, Kikkoman Foods vice president. Kikkoman established the practice of rotating its Japanese employees back to Japan after an average of five years in the United States. In the mid 1990s, only seven Japanese families remained in the Walworth area, still spread throughout the local communities.

Community Contributions

Kikkoman Foods, Inc., was an active and contributing member of the community. The company donated time and funds on three levels. At the local level, the company established Kikkoman Foods Foundation in 1993. The foundation, which was to be ultimately funded at the $3 million level, was formed to support area charitable activities. The company supported as many as thirty local projects a year, including college scholarships for area students, local hospital activities, a vocational program that assisted people in developing employment-related skills, and a nearby facility that preserved circus-related items. As Walworth's town clerk put it, "They sponsor just about everything—Community Chest (an organization similar to the United Way), Boy Scouts, Girl Scouts, all the way down the line. They're very good neighbors." The clerk treasurer from a nearby town said, "You see their name in the paper almost every week, helping out some organization."

At the state level, Kikkoman Foods, Inc., supported the University of Wisconsin educational system, established up to four Beloit College scholarships to honor Governor Lucey at his alma mater, and funded a Mogi Keizaburo scholarship at the Milwaukee School of Engineering. Members of the board of directors served on several public service boards and commissions. At the national level, Kikkoman Corporation, through its U.S. subsidiary Kikkoman Foods, Inc., supported Youth for Understanding exchange programs. At the fifth anniversary celebration, Kikkoman's chairman reported that the plant had developed better than had been anticipated. At the tenth anniversary celebration of the Kikkoman plant, the local Walworth paper reported, "In the 10 years that Kikkoman Foods, Inc., has been located here, it has become an integrated part of the community. The company has truly become a part of the Walworth community, and not only in a business sense." In 1987, reflecting Kikkoman's contributions, Wisconsin's governor appointed Yuzaburo Mogi as Wisconsin's honorary ambassador to Japan.

Kikkoman's Japanese–American Management in the United States

In the mid 1990s, Kikkoman operated its U.S. activities through two subsidiaries, Kikkoman Foods, Inc. (KFI), and Kikkoman International, Inc. (KII). KFI owned and operated the Walworth manufacturing plant. KII in San Francisco, California, undertook marketing responsibilities, including wholesaler and distributor activities throughout the United States. The boards of directors for both subsidiaries had several members from the parent corporation but were primarily Americans from among local operations officers or local Walworth citizens (for KFI) or the broader U.S. community (for KII). The KFI board met as a whole once a year and rotated the site of its annual stockholders' meeting between Japan and Wisconsin. An executive committee met monthly to consider operational decisions. The executive committee included Yuzaburo Mogi, who attended two to three meetings in the United States every year, and the head of Kikkoman Corporation's International Division. The remaining members of the executive committee included American and Japanese officers from the U.S. corporation. The KII board operated in a similar manner but met only in the United States.

Yuzaburo Mogi believed that a long-term commitment was essential for international success. A 1961 alumnus of Columbia University's Graduate School of Business, Mr. Mogi was the first Japanese to graduate from a U.S. university with an M.B.A. degree. In the years following graduation, he worked in various departments in Kikkoman, including accounting, finance, computers, long-range planning, and new product development. In time, he took on other roles, including member of Kikkoman's board of directors (1979), managing director of the company (1982), executive management director (1989), and executive vice president (1994). The seventeenth generation of his family to brew soy sauce, Mr. Mogi had become Kikkoman's president in early 1995. He explained his view regarding the necessity of a long-term perspective: "We should do business from a longer range viewpoint. It will be very difficult to expect fruitful results in the short run under different and difficult circumstances. Failure will be inevitable in foreign countries if one proceeds with a short-range view. In fact, it took Kikkoman 16 years to become established in the United States."

Of the five senior managers at the Walworth facility, three were Japanese and two were American. The plant manager, the finance manager, and the laboratory manager were Japanese. It was expected that these three positions would continue to be Japanese appointments. One American manager described the situation: "We know we will only attain a certain level, but that's OK, though. I can accept that. Soy sauce has been made in Japan for centuries. It's their product, their technology. They have the history, the research."

The general manager, that is, the plant manager, was the most senior person in authority at the plant and was responsible directly to headquarters in Japan. The appointment would be a person who had been with the company for many years. The finance manager's position required someone who was familiar with Japanese accounting systems and who was steeped in the Japanese emphasis on long-range profits. Japanese corporate headquarters controlled their foreign branches through their accounting and finance sections.

Mr. Mogi explained the Japanese appointment to the position of laboratory manager: "The production of soy sauce is very sophisticated. Normally, we recruit graduates with a master's degree in Japan who have gone to universities that have specialized programs in soy sauce production. In America, there is no university that teaches soy sauce production techniques, so it is difficult to promote Americans into general manager positions." As Dr. Magasawa, general manager at the Walworth plant, put it in explaining the discriminating tastes the Japanese have developed since childhood, "The sensory system, passion, feeling, or sensitivity can't transfer. That is based on just experience. Our vice president is a kind of god in this plant because he recognizes (even) a slight difference. . . . I don't have that. That's why I can't be manufacturing vice president. I am a general manager—nothing special. I am a biochemist (with) 39 years in Kikkoman, mostly in research."

Decisions at the Walworth plant, when possible, were made by consensus. KFI vice president Bill Nelson described the plant management as American in content and Japanese in style, with decisions arrived at from the bottom up and most matters of importance needing a consensus of employees. "It's hard, really, to get at because of the fact that nothing . . . here should run in an American style or a Japanese style or what have you. It was just simply—let's see what happens when you have both parties participate," he said. Nelson gave the example of an idea for changing summer working hours to start at 7 A.M. instead of 8 A.M. so that workers could leave earlier and enjoy more daylight. It was, Nelson, pointed out, unusual for a company to even entertain the idea. Nelson explained the process: "Instead of simply exploring it on a management level, here we started the process by asking individual employees what per-

sonal inconvenience would be experienced if the hours were changed."

Milton Neshek observed that Japanese management and the middle management at the Walworth plant worked well together with long-range budgeting and strategic planning carried out by the Japanese executive team. He described the situation: "Our 30 employees feel like part of our family. That makes management more responsive to employees. Decisions, whenever possible, are made by consensus." The fact that the plant has no labor union was no surprise to Nelson. As he put it, a union "has never been an issue here."

Yuzaburo Mogi summarized Kikkoman's approach to its U.S. operations and, in particular, its Walworth plant as a five-point approach:

Kikkoman has been successful doing business in the United States by adapting to American laws, customers, and most importantly, its culture. . . . (An) important matter to consider, especially when establishing a manufacturing plant in a foreign country, is the maintenance of what has come to be called "harmony" with society and the local community. A foreign concern should try to prosper together with society and the local community. . . . It is important to try to localize the operation. . . . (Our) . . . first commitment is the employment of as many local people as possible. Second we try to participate in local activities . . . trying to be a good corporate citizen (in Wisconsin) and contributing to society through our business activities. Third, we have been trying to avoid the so-called "Japanese-village" . . . by advising our people from Japan not to live together in one single community, but to spread out and live in several separate communities in order to become more familiar with the local people. Fourth, we try to do business with American companies. The fifth commitment is our practice of delegating most authority to local management in order to better reflect local circumstances. Through this process we are better able to make the most responsible decision. If we have an opinion, for example, we discuss it with other members at a local meeting in our American plant before reaching a decision. Kikkoman attempts to avoid a remote-control situation with letters or telephone calls from Japan. . . . If we have an opinion, we discuss it with other members at a local meeting in our American plant before reaching a decision.

The plant did encounter intercultural issues, however. For example, plant manager Bill Wenger pointed out, "Communication can be a problem sometimes. The language barrier is one reason. Then there's the problem of saving face. If a mistake is made, the Japanese tend to cover up for one another so the person who made the mistakes doesn't lose face."

The company was a popular local employer in Walworth. Local unemployment was phenomenally low at 2 percent, but the Walworth plant had over one thousand active applications on file for the plant's 136 positions. However, turnover among plant employees was negligible. "No one quits unless it is a move by a spouse. Our absenteeism is minimal and as for tardiness—we just don't have it. We offer competitive wages and good benefits. . . . [E]mployees feel like part of our family," said general counsel Neshek. Company officials stated that they paid about 10 percent more than the state average of $9.71 per hour, and employees did not have to contribute to the cost of their health insurance. As the company's vice president Shin Ichi Sugiyama put it, "In management, our primary concern is always the employee." The employees reported, "We feel like they listen to us. Our opinion counts, and we have the ability to make change, to better the company."

Mr. Sugiyama pointed out that the Walworth plant's productivity and quality had been about equal to that of Japanese plants. Productivity improved following the plant opening and by 1993 was actually the best of all the company's plants.

The U.S. Market in the 1990s[3]
U.S. Demand in the 1990s

After the opening of the Walworth plant, Kikkoman's U.S. sales growth slowed somewhat. However, Ken Saito, Kikkoman's brand manager for the Midwest, summarized the company's hopes: "Americans are more adventurous than Japanese when it comes to trying new foods. That's why we have developed some products only for the American market. But most Americans still are not familiar with how to use soy sauce." Thus, the company developed a number of nonoriental recipes that call for soy sauce and other Kikkoman products, for example, teriyaki chicken wings and Pacific Rim pizza with sweet and sour sauce, beef and chicken fajitas, and grilled salmon with confetti salsa flavored with "lite" soy sauce. Kikkoman clearly expected Americans to increasingly use soy sauce for applications beyond oriental foods and expected significant growth in the company's base product in the United States. According to Saito, "We figure the market in the United States will increase 100 times in the next decade." Kikkoman marketing coordinator, Trisha MacLeod, articulated the goal as "to get consumers to realize soy sauce is the oldest man-made condiment, and that it can also be used in meatloaf, barbecue—across the spectrum."

MacLeod pointed out, "Americans eat a lot more soy sauce than they realize." However, America's per-capita consumption was barely ten tablespoons, translating into $300 million in North American-sales. In contrast, Japanese per-capita consumption was about 10.5 quarts per person, which translated into about $1.4 billion in annual sales in Japan.

The population of Asian immigrants and families of Asian descent was projected to grow significantly in the United States. The California population increased 127 percent to 2.8 million during the 1980s. The total population of Asian Americans in the United States was estimated at 7.3 million in 1990, up 108 percent over the 1980s. Asian peoples represented the traditional mainstay market for oriental foods. Asians had higher income and educational levels than any other ethnic groups in the United States. However, each country represented a different cuisine, and the different Asian ethnic groups required different marketing approaches. Asian populations had spread throughout many parts of the United States, and retail outlets were learning how to highlight and display oriental foods to spur sales. Restaurants greatly influenced American food-buying habits. One industry executive observed that almost all U.S. restaurant kitchens in the 1990s had soy sauce. A 1996 National Restaurant Association study indicated that ethnic foods were increasing in popularity. Thus, oriental food manufacturers and distributors expected that oriental food sales would increase sharply.

Some information in the mid 1990s suggested strong and increasing popularity for oriental foods. U.S. sales of oriental foods had slowed considerably. The most recent aggregate information regarding the demand for oriental food in the United States in the mid 1990s is shown in Exhibit 10.

EXHIBIT 10

U.S. Oriental Food Sales ($000,000)

	1992	1993	1994
Sales	$275	$305	$301

Source: Information Resources, Inc., Chicago, Illinois.

By the late 1980s, consumers began to indicate dissatisfaction with canned entrees, at $81 million in sales the second largest subcategory of oriental foods. Sales of this subcategory had declined as much as 10 percent (1991 to 1992) and showed no signs of abating. Competition was intense, with a third of all products sold on the basis of feature, price, and/or display promotion.

U.S. Major Competitors

Kikkoman's two major competitors in the United States were Chun King and LaChoy. Both companies made soy sauce by hydrolyzing vegetable protein. This European-derived method was faster and less expensive than the six-month fermentation process Kikkoman used. By 1971, Kikkoman had surpassed Chun King in supermarket sales of soy sauce, becoming number two in the American marketplace. In 1976, Kikkoman outsold LaChoy brand soy sauce and became the number one retailer of soy sauce in the United States, a position it continued to hold in the mid 1990s. However, the company faced strong competitors in the oriental foods category and in the sauces and condiments subcategory.

The new consumer focus was on oriental food ingredients that individuals could add to home-cooked dishes. "People are cooking more oriental foods at home," said Chun King's vice president of marketing. "Over 40 percent of U.S. households stir-fry at least once a month. Sauces are an opportunity to get away from the canned image." Indeed, sauces were the only growth area on the oriental food category, with 1992 sales rising 11 percent over the previous year. Rivals Chun King and LaChoy were flooding the oriental foods aisle in American supermarkets with new products. LaChoy had about 40 percent of the shelf products in oriental foods, and Chun King had about 20 percent.

However, there were more changes than just new products. In the early 1990s, LaChoy and Chun King had revved up their marketing efforts under new ownership. LaChoy was owned by ConAgra's Hunt-Wesson division. Among other initiatives, ConAgra, a major U.S. food company, hired a new advertising firm for LaChoy.

A Singapore-based firm purchased Chun King in 1989 and brought in a new management team. As one observer put it, "The brand had really been neglected as part of Nabisco (its previous owner). It was just a small piece of a big pie." The new management team introduced a line of seasoned chow mein noodles and another of hot soy sauces. The firm's marketing plan included consumer promotions and a print ad campaign in women's magazines. Chun King's 1992 oriental food sales were estimated at $30 million. In mid 1995, ConAgra purchased Chun King from the Singapore company and added the brand to its Hunt-Wesson division. ConAgra was no stranger to the Chun King brand. The large U.S. competitor had purchased Chun King's frozen food line in 1986 from Del Monte. It was expected that Hunt-Wesson would eventually consolidate manufacturing but continue to aggressively advertise the two brands separately. As a Hunt-Wesson executive put it, "They're both established leaders in their field, and they both have brand strength."

LaChoy advertised itself as "the world's largest producer of oriental foods created for American tastes." The company led the oriental foods category with sales (excluding frozen) of $87 million in 1992 and $104.4 million in 1994. Its products included chow mein noodles, bamboo shoots, sauces, and miscellaneous foods. About $28 million of the 1992 sales came from sauce and marinade sales. La Choy's manager of corporate communications indicated that the Chicago-based firm planned no increase in marketing spending in reaction to the new Chun King initiatives. However, the company did plan to advertise two new lines—Noodle Entrees and Stir-Fry Vegetables 'N Sauce. The company expected to expend most of its marketing support for the latter product line, a set of vegetables in four sauces formulated for consumers to stir-fry with their choice of meat.

Kikkoman and Other Competitors

Kikkoman remained the one bright spot in the oriental food category of sauces and marinades. It controlled $63 million of the $160 million sauces/marinades segment and supported its position with a moderate amount of advertising—$3.2 million in 1992, about the same as in 1991. In its major product lines, Kikkoman controlled about two-thirds of the California market and had about one-third market share in other major U.S. sales regions. The company was test-marketing a new line of sauces for addition to the consumer's own vegetables and meat.

Kikkoman also had to consider recent moves by several other competitors. Yamasa Shoyu Co., Ltd., Japan's second largest soy sauce maker, had announced plans to build a factory in Oregon in mid 1994. This multigenerational company was founded in 1645 in Choshi City, Japan. Estimates on the cost of the Oregon factory ranged from $15 million to $20 million, and the plant was expected to eventually employ fifty workers. Yamasa intended to produce soy sauce for the U.S. market by using soybeans shipped from the midwest. It took Yamasa four years to select the final site for its new plant. The company produced a number of products in addition to soy sauce, including other food and drugs made from biological raw materials such as soybean protein and wheat starch.

Hong Kong–based Lee Kum Kee was a producer and importer of Chinese-oriented sauces and condiments. Lee Kum Kee had opened a sauce-manufacturing plant in Los Angeles in 1991 to keep up with rising U.S. demand and to reduce dependence on imports, thus avoiding payment of import duties, which could be as high as 20 percent. The company was a Hong Kong subsidiary of one of Japan's leading soy sauce brewers. Lee Kum Kee retailed its sauces in big supermarket chains in all fifty states. Historically, the company imported its soy sauce through an independent U.S.-based importer of the same name. The U.S. importer also imported about forty other food products, mostly marinades, curries, and sauces from the East. Lee Kum Kee found its sales propelled by the population doubling of Americans of Asian or Pacific Island descent.

Competitor San-J International of the San-Jirushi Corporation of Kuwana, Japan, built a soy sauce plant in Richmond, Virginia, in 1988. Hawaiian competitor Noh Foods of Hawaii innovated a line of oriental dried seasonings and powdered mixes. In reaction, other manufacturers, including Kikkoman, produced copycat products. Noh Foods distributed its products in the United States, Europe, and Australia through distributors and trade show activities.

Kikkoman's International Position

The Kikkoman Vision

In the mid 1990s, Kikkoman manufactured in four countries and marketed its brand products in over ninety countries. (Exhibit 11 compares domestic and non-Japan sales and operating profits.) Of the company's 3,200 employees, over 1,000 were in international subsidiaries, and only 5 percent of those were Japanese. The company saw at least part of its mission as contributing to international cultural exchange. Yuzaburo Mogi explained,

> Kikkoman believes that soy sauce marketing is the promotion of the international exchange of food culture. In order to create a friendlier world, I believe we need many types of cultural exchanges. Among these, there is one that is most closely related to our daily lives—the eating of food. Soy sauce is one of the most important food cultures in Japan. Hence, the overseas marketing of soy sauce means the propagation of Japanese food culture throughout the world.

As one U.S. scholar who had studied the company extensively in the 1980s put it, "There is an evident willingness on the part of Kikkoman to experiment with new products, production techniques, management styles, and operational forms in the international arena." Yuzaburo Mogi put it similarly when he said, "It should be understood that adjustment to different laws, customs, and regulations is imperative, instead of complaining about those differences."

Kikkoman in Europe

Kikkoman began its marketing activities in Europe in 1972. It found Europeans more conservative and slower to try new tastes than Americans. The firm

EXHIBIT 11

Consolidated Results FY 1995 ((¥) m)

	Domestic	Non-Japan
Sales	162,426	40,860
Operating profit	6,640	4,152
Operating margin	4.0	10.1

Source: Table 7: UBS Securities Limited, May 28, 1996, as reported by *Investext.*

found Germany the least conservative and opened restaurants there in 1973. By the early 1990s, the company had opened six Japanese steak houses in Germany. The restaurants gave their customers, over 90 percent of who were non-Asian, the opportunity to try new cuisine. The Kikkoman trading subsidiary in Germany was the company's European marketing arm. Said the managing director for Kikkoman's European marketing subsidiary located in Germany, "Germany and Holland are big business for us, as both countries are very much into interesting sauces and marinades." Kikkoman's managing director of Europe made it clear that he had aggressive plans to grow sales both by increasing the sales of soy sauce as well as by extending the markets in which the company operated. The massive ready-made meal business in both the United States and Europe had huge potential for Kikkoman. The firm would need to market to end consumers at the retail level as well as to food manufacturers.

The company established its second overseas manufacturing facility in 1983. This facility supplied soy sauce to Australian and European markets. By the early 1990s, Kikkoman had about 50 percent of the Australian soy sauce market. The United Kingdom brand debut occurred in 1986, and the 1992 U.K. market was estimated at 1 billion pounds. In 1993, the firm opened a 25,000-square-foot warehouse in London. With $1.66 billion (U.S.) in sales, Kikkoman had come a long way with "just" soy sauce. Overall, analysts noted that the United States had experienced about 10 percent annual growth in soy sauce demand and expected Europe to expand similarly.

Kikkoman in Asia

In Asia, the company opened a production facility in Singapore in 1983 and incorporated a trading company in 1990. Industry observers expected the company to enter the soy sauce market in China in the near future. In addition, other Asian countries offered various opportunities in sauces, condiments, and foods.

Kikkoman—The Challenges

The company the Mogi family had headed for nearly four hundred years confronted a number of challenges on the global stage in the latter part of the 1990s. Kikkoman executives realized that the company's future could depend primarily on its mature

domestic market. The multigeneration family firm would have to change its image as a maker of a mature product. As Mr. Mogi stated, "We . . . take pride in our ability to contribute to the exchange of cultures by using some of the world's most familiar flavors. We are now concentrating on further enhancing our ability to serve consumers in Japan and overseas. Kikkoman continues as a company that is proud of its heritage, but nevertheless willing and able to adapt to the constantly evolving requirements of our customers and markets."

ENDNOTES

1. In early 1996, the exchange rate was about 95 yen per U.S. dollar. Thus, in U.S. dollars, Kikkoman's market value was about $1.7 billion. Sales at year end 1995 for the consolidated company were ¥203 billion, or slightly less than $2 billion (see Exhibits 2 and 3 for consolidated financial data and Exhibits 8, 9, and 11 for parent company and domestic versus non-Japan revenues plus other selected financial information).

2. *Zaibatsu:* Industrial and financial combines dissolved by occupation fiat after World War II, but which have reemerged as somewhat weaker entities. Some of these *zaibatsu* have developed into large conglomerates such as Mitsubishi. However, they should be distinguished from *keiretsu* (of which Mitsubishi is also one of largest). *Keiretsu* are informal enterprise group-based associations of banks, industrials, and so forth.

3. Information on the market and competitors was drawn primarily from InfoScan.

REFERENCES

Allen, Sara Clark. "Kikkoman, a Good Neighbor in Wisconsin," *Business,* Tuesday, June 11, 1996.

Bergsman, Steve. "Patience and Perseverance in Japan," *Global Trade,* Vol. 109, Issue 8 (August 1989), pp. 10, 12.

Campbell, Dee Ann. "Del Monte Foods to See European Foods Business," *Business Wire,* April 17, 1990.

Demestrakakes, Pan. "Quality for the Ages," *Food Processing,* Vol. 70, No. 6 (September 1996).

"Fireflies Help Kill Germs," *Times Net Asia,* January 1, 1996.

Forbish, Lynn. "Grand Oriental Celebration Held for Opening of Kikkoman Foods," *Janesville Gazette,* June 18, 1973.

Forrest, Tracy. "Kikkoman: a Way of Life," *Super Marketing,* January 28, 1994.

Fruin, W. Mark. *Kikkoman: Company, Clan, and Community* (Cambridge, MA: Harvard University Press, 1983).

Hewitt, Lynda. "Liquid Spice," *Food Manufacture,* February, 1993, p. 23.

Hostveldt, John. "Japan's Kikkoman Corp. Brews Success Story in Walworth," *Business Dateline: The Business Journal—Milwaukee,* Vol. 3, No. 31, Sec. 3 (May 19, 1986), p. 17.

"In-Store: Happy New Year's Feast," (Article on Kikkoman's In-Store Promotion), *Brandsweek,* Vol. 37 (January 1, 1996), pp. 14–15.

Jansen, Leah. "Kikkoman Spices Up Walworth's Quality of Life," *Janesville Gazette,* January 21, 1984.

Jensen, Debra. "Kikkoman Executive Lauds Wisconsin, Lucey," *Gazette,* January 13, 1989, p. 1B.

Jensen, Don. "A Stainless Success Story," *Kenosha News,* Business Section, August 1, 1993.

"The Joy of Soy: How a Japanese Sauce Company Found a Happy Home in Walworth, Wisc.," *Chicago Tribune Magazine,* January 31, 1993, p. 13.

Kikkoman Corporation: Flavors That Bring People Together (Company Brochure).

Kinugasa, Dean. "Kikkoman Corporation," 1979 (Private Translation by Norihito Tanaka and Marilyn Taylor, 1994).

La Choy's home page (**www.hunt-wesson.com/lachoy/main/mission/**).

LaGrange, Maria L. "RJR Sells Del Monte Operations for $1.4 Billion," *Los Angeles Times,* September 26, 1989, p. 2.

Mogi, Yuzaburo. "The Conduct of International Business: One Company's Credo—Kikkoman, Soy Sauce and the U.S. Market" (available from Company).

Mogi, Yuzaburo. *"Masatsunaki Kokusai Senryaku"* (Tokyo, Japan: Selnate Publishing Co., Ltd., 1988—in English translation).

Ostrander, Kathleen. "Kikkoman's Success Tied to Proper Blend," *Business Datelines (Wisconsin State Journal),* March 1, 1992 p. 29.

Plett, Edith. "Kikkoman Foods Marks Fifth Year," *Janesville Gazette,* January 26, 1979.

Redman, Russell. "Hunt-Wesson Acquires Chun King," *Supermarket News,* Vol. 45, No. 19 (May 8, 1995), p. 101.

SBA home page, Wisconsin Gallery.

Schoenburg, Lorraine. "Governor Supports Kikkoman," *Janesville Gazette,* September 14, 1989.

Shima, Takeshi. "Kikkoman's Thousand-Year History," *Business JAPAN,* January, 1989, p. 65.

Wilkins, Mira. "Japanese Multinational in the United States: Continuity and Change, 1879–1990," *Business History Review,* Vol. 64, Issue 4 (Winter 1990), pp. 585–629.

Yates, Ronald E. "Wisconsin's Other Brew," *Chicago Tribune Magazine,* January 31, 1993, p. 14.

In addition to personal interviews in Tokyo, Walworth, Wisconsin, and San Francisco, information and quotations were also drawn from these references. This list is part of a much broader set of sources that the authors consulted.

Appendix A:
The Making of Soy Sauce

The Chinese began making jiang, a precursor of soy sauce, about 2,500 years ago. The most likely story of soy sauce's origins relates how Kakushin, a Japanese Zen priest who studied in China, returned to Japan in the middle of the thirteenth century and began preparing a type of miso, or soybean paste produced through fermentation, that became a specialty of the area. By the end of the thirteenth century, the liquid was called *tamari* and sold commercially along with the miso. Experimentation with the raw ingredients and methods of fermentation began. Vegetarianism also became popular in Japan during this time, and people were eager for condiments to flavor their rather bland diet. Soldiers also found the transportability of the seasonings useful.

Soy sauce evolved from tamari and miso by adding wheat to the soybean fermentation mash. The Japanese modified the shoyu to include wheat to gentle the taste so that it did not overwhelm the delicate flavors of Japanese cuisine. Most households made their shoyu during the slack time in agricultural cycles. Families harvested grains in the fall and processed them into mash. The mash fermented from October–December to January–March, when the shoyu was pressed from the mash.

Regional differences among the soy sauces developed depending upon the mix of soybean, wheat, and fermentation techniques. Even in the last decade of the twentieth century, there were hundreds of local varieties of soy sauce available commercially in Japan.

Produced in the traditional way, soy sauce was a natural flavor enhancer. In the later part of the twentieth century, ingredient-conscious consumers shied away from artificial flavor enhancers. Soy sauce responded to the challenge of finding ingredients to flavor foods. For vegetarian manufacturers, the "beefy" taste provided by the soy sauce without any meat extract was highly desirable.

There were two methods of manufacturing soy sauce—the traditional fermentation process used by Kikkoman and the chemical method.

Soy Sauce Through Fermentation—Kikkoman's Traditional Method

Kikkoman's process was the traditional one and involved processing soy and wheat to a mash. Kikkoman had developed an innoculum of seed mold that the company added. The seed mold produced a growth, the development of which was controlled by temperature and humidity. The resulting mash (*koji*) was discharged into fermentation tanks where selected microorganism cultures and brine were added. The product (*moromi* mash) was aerated and mixed, then aged. During this process, enzymes formed in the cells of the *koji* and provided the characteristics of the brewed sauce. The soybean protein changed to amino acid, and the enzymatic reaction that occurred between the sugar and amino acids produced the taste and color. Enzymes changed the wheat starch to sugars for sweetness, and a special yeast developed, changing some of the sugars to alcohol. Fermentation changed other parts of the sugars to alcohol that produced tartness. The brewing process determined flavor, color, taste, and aroma. The brine added to the *koji* mixture stimulated the enzymes and produced the reddish brown liquid mash. This process resulted in *umami*—or flavor-enhancing—abilities, as well as the brewed flavor components. The final mash was pressed between layers of cloth under constant pressure. After a pasteurization process to intensify color and aromas, the shoyu was filtered again and bottled. There were no flavorings, coloring, additives, or artificial ingredients in the product. According to produce developers, these complex flavors were not present in brewed soy sauce.

Chemically Produced Soy Sauce

Nonbrewed soy sauce could be made in hours. Soybeans were boiled with hydrochloric acid for fifteen to twenty hours. When the maximum amount of amino acid was removed from the soybeans, the mixture was cooled to end the hydrolysis action. The amino acid liquid was then neutralized, mixed with charcoal, and finally purified through filtration. Color and flavor were introduced via varying amounts of corn syrup, salt, and caramel coloring. The resulting soy sauce was then refined and bottled.

39

CenturyTel in a Bear Hug

This case was prepared by Lawrence R. Jauch and Melissa V. Melancon, University of Louisiana at Monroe.

Glen Post, CEO of CenturyTel (CTL), was in his office at company headquarters in Monroe, Louisiana, on a hot day in late August, 2001, when word arrived that AllTel had given him a "bear hug." "Bear hug" acquisitions are unsolicited, publicly announced offers to buy a company. They have been turning up recently in communications-related industries. Companies sometimes resort to bear hugs after being rejected through traditional channels out of the public eye. Even if the private offer includes a significant premium to a company's current stock price, top executives and directors may turn it down if they believe the stock market is putting an unduly cheap price on the shares. That could be why CTL spurned AllTel, despite the potential of a 40 percent premium above CTL's current market price. Alternatively, it could be just a matter of wanting to stay independent. AllTel and CenturyTel are regional rivals. Offered one analyst, "I think it's pride, rather than price. . . . It's understandable."

A CEO can easily turn down an offer made in private, but a bear hug forces a corporate board to consider any reasonable bid because directors have a responsibility to provide shareholders with the best financial returns. It steps up the pressure. Sometimes, the only way to get past unwilling board members is to use public pressure. Alltel and its advisers have to convince large shareholders of CenturyTel to pressure the board. Bear hug acquisitions require massive public relations offensives directed at institutional shareholders and other board members besides the chair and CEO. "It's PR directed toward people whose decision making matters." Despite the pressure, companies can and do adopt takeover defenses. One of the key defenses is voting rights. In the case of CenturyTel, owners of stock prior to 1988 have 10 votes per share. The founder of CTL, Clarke Williams, controls the board so tightly that it may be impossible to win a proxy fight.

Some bear hug announcements are mainly designed to be disruptive to rivals. The communications industry has been ravaged over the past year, and its companies have been left vulnerable to mergers and acquisitions. Competitive local exchange carriers face potential problems, since many observers believe there are too many companies chasing the same customers. Many overbuilt, leaving themselves stuck with unused networks. Therefore, the industry is ripe for consolidation, and wireless services companies will be among the first to merge or buy each other.

CenturyTel had been shopping around for its wireless unit and had approached AllTel as a potential buyer of its wireless operations. However, apparently AllTel wanted the whole company, because the rural fixed-wire business was highly profitable and having a ready customer base made CTL's wireless business more valuable. (See Table 1 for financial data on CenturyTel and AllTell.)

Now Glen and CTL were faced with some key decisions. Should CTL counteroffer AllTel? How could he get rid of the bear hug? Should he continue to try to sell the wireless operations? Should CTL continue its past strategy?

A Brief History of CenturyTel

William and Marie Williams gave the Oak Ridge Telephone Company as a gift to their son Clarke on his return from World War II (see Table 2). The sleepy little local exchange telephone company began its first of many acquisitions in 1972. After forays in and out of larger metropolitan areas, Century decided to stay focused mainly in rural and suburban areas. It was first listed on the New York Stock Exchange in 1978; the firm became one of the S&P 500 companies in 1999. Mainly through acquisitions, the company has added long-distance, Internet, data transmission, and cellular services to its local exchange offerings.

As of June 30, 2001, CenturyTel was the eighth largest local exchange telephone company in the United States based on access lines (1,807,950). Its network was 100 percent digital [Centrex; Integrated Services Digital Network (ISDN); Advanced Intelligent

---

TABLE 1

Selected Financial Results (9/01/2001)

	CenturyTel	AllTel	Industry Average	Industry High	Industry Low	S&P 500
Growth rates						
Revenue—5-year growth rate	23.4%	17.8%	15.6%	1,857.6%	(100.0)%	15.2%
EPS—5-year growth rate	13.4%	27.3%	11.5%	171.8%	(71.0)%	17.4%
Dividend—5-year growth rate	5.3%	5.7%	(0.8)%	463.7%	(100.0)%	8.7%
Capital spending—5-year growth rate	18.0%	31.9%	29.4%	2,662.8%	(100.0)%	7.2%
Financial strength						
Quick ratio (MRQ)	0.5	0.9	0.8	21.2	0.0	1.1
Current ratio (MRQ)	0.6	1.0	1.0	32.2	0.0	1.7
LT debt/equity (MRQ)	1.3	0.8	1.2	25.2	0.0	0.7
Total debt/equity (MRQ)	1.3	0.8	1.2	25.2	0.0	0.7
Interest coverage (TTM)	2.4	5.0	4.4	481.6	(7,039.5)	9.1
Management effectiveness						
Return on assets—5-year average	5.6%	9.4%	5.5%	26.9%	(4,884.2)%	8.3%
Return on investment—5-year average	6.1%	10.7%	7.8%	190.1%	(800.3)%	13.2%
Return on equity—5-year average	15.6%	25.2%	21.2%	743.0%	(518.5)%	22.2%
Profitability ratios						
Gross margin—5-year average	49.3%	37.2%	44.4%	100.0%	(95.2)%	47.9%
EBITD margin—5-year average	49.3%	35.1%	29.9%	82.5%	(98.2)%	21.9%
Operating margin—5-year average	29.7%	21.4%	14.4%	58.0%	(99.0)%	18.4%
Profit margin—5-year average	17.4%	14.4%	7.4%	58.6%	(99.9)%	11.5%
Effective tax rate—5-year average	39.8%	41.4%	40.9%	94.9%	0.0%	35.5%
Operating efficiency						
Revenue/employee	$298,070	$269,399	$299,080	$3,335,333	$118	$718,012
Net income/employee	$ 47,421	$ 49,184	$ 30,998	$ 985,194	$ 0	$ 96,034
Asset turnover	0.3×	0.6×	0.4×	7.6×	0.0×	1.0×
Stock prices						
High, 52 weeks	39.87	68.68				
Low, 52 weeks	25.45	49.43				
Capital structure—debt	57%	43%				
Capital structure—equity	43%	57%				
Beta	.81	.80				

TABLE 2

CenturyTel Highlights

1930	William Clarke and Marie Williams purchase Oak Ridge Telephone Company in Oak Ridge, Louisiana.
1946	The Williams's son, Clarke McRae, today chairman of the board, assumes management of CTL.
1972	Century acquires La Crosse Telephone Corporation in Wisconsin.
1978	Century's common stock first traded on the New York Stock Exchange as CTL. (Later also listed on the Berlin Stock Exchange.) Century begins replacing mechanical switches with digital computer technology.
1983	Century files for FCC approval to operate cellular systems in three areas in Michigan.
1989–92	Acquires Universal Telephone and Central Telephone Company of Ohio.
1993	Acquires San Marcos Telephone Company; provides long-distance and operator services. Acquires Interactive Communications, Inc; provides interactive information services nationwide. Forms competitive access provider (CAP)—Metro Access Networks (MANs) to compete with local exchange carriers in metropolitan areas.
1994	Acquires Celutel (five cellular systems in metropolitan areas in Mississippi and Texas); renamed Century Cellunet. Acquires Kingsley Telephone Company; 2,400 in northern Michigan near other Century properties. Acquires Pine Bluff, Arkansas, Metropolitan Statistical Area (MSA), and buys additional ownership in a cellular system operated by Century in Michigan.
1995	Acquires Tele-Max, Inc., in Denton County, Texas, that owns part of a limited cellular partnership operating a cellular system in Dallas MSA. Acquires cellular operations in Michigan RSA, adjacent to cellular properties Century operates. Acquires cellular systems serving Mississippi RSAs adjacent to Century's Jackson, Mississippi, cellular market.
1996	Acquires Ringgold (Louisiana) Telephone Co.; ownership in North LA Cellular Partnership increases to 87 percent. Surpasses the half-million customer mark in its local exchange operations. Surpasses the 100,000-customer milestone in its long-distance operations. Acquires Mississippi RSA in central Mississippi, adjacent to Century's Jackson MSA and cellular systems.
1997	Acquires Pecoco, Inc., in Randolph, Wisconsin; minority interest in two cellular partnerships serving Madison and Milwaukee representing approximately 35,000 pops. Divested Metro Access Networks, Inc. (MAN). Created a strategic alliance with Brooks Fiber Properties, Inc.; became Brooks Fiber's largest shareholder; alliance consisted of developing CLEC networks in seven Texas cities; opportunity for Century and Brooks to develop additional CLEC networks in Century's wireless markets in Michigan on a 50-50 joint venture basis. Largest acquisition to date with purchase of Pacific Telecom, Inc. (PTI); gained about 660,000 telephone access lines in twelve states, bringing access lines to nearly 1.2 million. Acquired nearly 1.9 million cellular pops in six states.
1998	Introduced the name CenturyTel to communicate CTL's ability to offer multiple services in a bundled or packaged manner. Purchase of Ameritech's telephone operations and directory publishing business in twenty-one communities in Wisconsin.
1999	Declared a 3-for-2 stock split. CenturyTel was added to the Standard & Poor's (S&P) 500 Index. Closed the sale of its Alaska-based operations to Fox Paine Capital. Acquired the cellular system serving the Vicksburg and Greenville, Mississippi, markets. Sold the assets of its wireless operations in the Brownsville and McAllen, Texas, markets. Purchased the Internet service provider DigiSys, Inc., in Kalispell, Montana.

(continued)

TABLE 2 *(continued)*

CenturyTel Highlights

2000	Acquired GTE properties in Arkansas and Missouri; added 230,500 access lines to its existing 46,000 in Arkansas; partnered with Spectra Communications to service 127,000 access lines. Completed two transactions to purchase seventy-seven Wisconsin local exchange properties from Verizon; paid Verizon about $195 million in cash to purchase 70,000 access lines; in a joint venture with Telephone USA of Wisconsin, LLC, bought an additional 62,650 access lines in thirty-five Wisconsin exchanges for $170 million.
2001	Acquisition pending of ninety-eight exchanges in Missouri and ninety in Alabama for $2.159 billion from Verizon. Announced an increase in common dividends for a twenty-eighth consecutive year.

Network (AIN)]. Services offered included local number Internet access, custom local area signaling services (CLASS), videoconferencing, and long distance (414,000 subscribers).

The latest Verizon acquisition, if approved, would increase CenturyTel's wireline ownership 37 percent, from 1.8 million to 2.5 million access lines, and add 369,000 access lines in Missouri as well as 306,000 in Alabama, taking CTL into its twenty-second state. Glen Post commented, "This advances our strategy to expand our wireline business in rural and suburban areas that cluster with our existing operations. We're still in the process of considering separation of our wireless business in some form."

Through acquisitions and internal development, CenturyTel also became the eighth largest cellular operator in the United States based on population equivalents owned. Operating in six states, CTL had 779,958 cellular units in service (majority-owned markets), with 9,512,571 pops (the portion of the population of the service areas based on ownership interest). Using digital-ready platforms and a nationwide Signaling System 7 (SS7) network, CTL operated 855 cell sites (including personal communications services, or PCS). CTL cellular distribution was based on company-owned retail locations, agents, and Wal-Mart Kiosks.

The Telecommunications (Telecom) Services Industry

The telecommunications industry encompasses the movement of voice, video, and data over distances long or short. The broad industry comprises local exchange, wireless service of all types (including cel-

lular phones, pagers, and palm-type devices), satellite broadcast, fiber optics, copper wire, undersea and coaxial cable, the Internet, microwave, private networks, long-distance service, and videoconferencing. In telecom services, some of the most important influences come from government action, technological change, and competitor behavior.

Government Influence on Competition

Twenty years ago, there was AT&T the Great. This firm reigned supreme over the entire telecom system of the United States. AT&T owned the long-distance business, most of the local phone companies, the labs that created the latest telephone technology, and the companies that manufactured much of the industry's equipment. It was the largest employer in the United States, with about 1 million workers. Telephone service was excellent but relatively expensive.

In a bout of deregulation during the 1980s, the U.S. government's antitrust people stepped in and made AT&T spin off its seven "Baby Bells," the local phone companies, into independent regional corporations (such as Verizon, Bellsouth). Deregulation allowed intense competition in long-distance services from MCI (WorldCom), Sprint, and an increasingly long list of upstarts. As a result, the cost of making a long-distance call plummeted. However, deregulation was far from complete; AT&T was restrained from offering local phone services while the Baby Bells were restrained from offering long-distance services, keeping their monopolies on local phone lines.

Congress enacted sweeping deregulation with the Telecommunications Act of 1996. It was anticipated that this act would lead to vigorous competition in local telephone services. The theory was that allowing cable television companies and long-distance carriers to serve local markets while allowing the former Bell companies to enter the domestic long-distance and international markets would spur innovation and competition that would benefit consumers.

The 1996 act created a new breed of company called competitive local exchange carriers (CLECs). The nascent CLEC industry competes with the Baby Bells in the $100+ billion local telecommunications market, providing voice and data services to business and residential consumers alike. CLECs have competed vigorously with the Baby Bells and now claim 6 to 8 percent of the local telecom market. The Baby Bell phone companies were allowed to sell long-distance phone services to compete against AT&T, WorldCom/MCI, and Sprint. However, the Baby Bells had to give up their monopolies on local phone services. The former Baby Bells and other existing local phone companies became known as incumbent local exchange carriers (ILECs).

ILECs have operated as monopolies regulated by the Federal Communications Commission (FCC) and various state agencies (public service commissions or public utility commissions). Most of such commissions have regulated pricing and intrastate access charges through "rate of return" regulation that allows authorized levels of earnings. Most of these commissions also (1) regulate the purchase and sale of ILECs, (2) prescribe depreciation rates and certain accounting procedures, and (3) regulate various other matters, including certain service standards and operating procedures. Legislatures and regulatory commissions in most states have reduced the regulation of ILECs or intend to do so. Such reduced oversight may allow ILECs to offer new and competitive services faster.

The 1996 act also focused especially on advanced services in rural and high-cost areas. Section 254 of the act specifies that "consumers in all regions of the nation, including low-income consumers and those in rural, insular, and high cost areas, should have access to telecommunications and information services, including interexchange services and advanced telecommunications." The act authorized the establishment of new federal and state "universal service funds" to provide support to eligible carriers. Some allege that the act established contradictory objectives of promoting universal service by maintaining billions of dollars of industry subsidies for local telephone service while encouraging competition in the same market, where the costs of service have been skewed in favor of rural and residential users. In areas where prices have been subsidized historically, competition can result in an increase, not a decrease, in prices as they rise toward the true costs. If the FCC implements new universal support mechanisms for rural carriers based on forward-looking cost models (as it did for nonrural carriers in October 1999), revenues of ILECs could be negatively impacted. (The federal Universal Service Fund represented 7.9 percent of CenturyTel's year 2000 revenue.)

FCC and FAA Regulation The FCC regulates interstate services by regulating the access charges that are billed to long-distance companies for use of a local network in connection with the origination and termination of interstate telephone calls. Additionally, the FCC prescribes certain rules and regulations for telephone companies, including regulations regarding the use of radio frequencies; a uniform system of accounts; and the separation of costs between jurisdictions and, ultimately, between interstate services.

During the 1980s and early 1990s, the FCC awarded two ten-year licenses to provide cellular service in each MSA and RSA market (metropolitan or rural statistical areas). Initially, one license was reserved for companies offering local telephone service in the market (the wireline carrier), and one license was available for firms unaffiliated with the local telephone company (the nonwireline carrier). The FCC has permitted telephone companies to acquire control of nonwireline licenses in markets in which they do not hold interests in the wireline license. The completion of an acquisition involving a cellular system requires prior FCC approval and, in certain cases, receipt of other federal and state regulatory approvals.

The FCC has also taken steps to (1) require certain cellular towers and antennas to comply with radio frequency radiation guidelines, (2) require cellular carriers to work with public safety or law enforcement officials to process 911 calls and conduct electronic surveillance, and (3) enable cellular subscribers to retain their existing telephone numbers when they change service providers. These increase the cost of providing cellular service.

In 1997, the FCC established new programs to provide discounted telecom services to schools, libraries, and rural health care providers. Local, cellular, and long-distance operators are required to contribute to these programs. Firms recover their contributions in their rates for interstate services (passing charges on to their customers). Other FCC initiatives have resulted in the allocation of additional radio spectrum or the issuance of licenses for emerging mobile communications technologies that are competitive with cellular and telephone operations. In late 2001 the FCC decided to phase out limits as to how much of the airwaves mobile phone companies can hold in a single market. Such action could lead to greater industry consolidation. Carriers say this allows service improvements, but critics fear this will dampen competition and lead to higher prices.

Cellular systems are subject to certain Federal Aviation Administration (FAA) tower height regulations as well as state or local zoning and land use regulations concerning transmitters and antennas. Moreover, there is an increasing possibility of local community opposition to new towers.

Technology

Improvement in telecom infrastructure has made distance irrelevant to the cost of an in-country phone call. Speed advantages are possible in new phone technology. For example, ATM (asynchronous transfer mode) allows voice, video, and data signals to be transmitted digitally over advanced phone switches at speeds from 25 million to 1 billion bits per second, much faster than traditional analog phone lines, which only move at 2 million bits per second.

However, new technologies—wireless phones, email, instant messaging, and cable modems—are siphoning business off the old telephone networks. New technologies account for 10 to 15 percent of communications that would have traveled over the traditional phone network two to three years ago. A reduction in access lines may begin to characterize the industry. Before, when consumers started using the Internet, they often bought second and third phone lines. Now, as households sign up for high-speed access, about half of these disconnect their second phone lines.

An important development to watch is "instant messaging" on America Online and other Internet services. Currently a method of chatting in real time, online, with friends and associates via sophisticated email, this technology will evolve into a voice-based system as broadband access increases and more PCs become equipped for Internet telephony. At that point, instant voice-based chatting will be a no-cost,

viable alternative to some telephone calls. Because of its base of registered subscribers, AOL provides instant text messaging to 100 million people worldwide.

Telephone service and email are beginning to converge. Companies such as jfax.com offer local telephone numbers all over the world for customers who spend a lot of time traveling. The customer gets a personalized phone number in the area code of choice. Fax and voice messages are translated into email. The user then checks email to get faxes, voice mail, and email all in one place. Net2Phone, using voice over Internet protocol (IP) technology, allows people to place inexpensive telephone calls over a computer, telephone, or fax machine to any telephone or fax machine worldwide, allowing a savings of up to 95 percent when calling internationally. IP telephony is efficient because the line is used for other purposes when people are not talking. Moreover, it does not need costly phone switches to route calls to a particular line. That would make IP telephony cheaper and more profitable than today's phone technology.

Several large wireless carriers have taken initial steps to provide wireless data, short messaging, and other enhanced "next generation" digital wireless services. Several large domestic carriers that currently use the TDMA (time division multiple access) standard either have announced their intention to abandon TDMA or have begun to overlay their TDMA systems with additional network elements permitting packet data transmissions. Functions that might require a $5 million circuit switch can be done by a Cisco router that costs $20,000. Some cable companies have considered this as a substitute technology.

However, the leading supporter of phone via cable—AT&T Broadband—is in limbo. Comcast and AOL Time Warner have their home phone plans on hold. They are waiting for perfection of cheaper Internet call-handling technology to replace today's costly circuit switch system. Too many digital packets still take too long to arrive, creating delays and interruptions, and garble like a bad cell phone call. The cable industry also must hammer out standards for IP telephony so it can provide the security and features required for a company to offer primary phone service. To be sold as a home's only phone, for example, the line must be able to connect directly to 911 emergency centers. Cox, the only other cable provider committed to phone, still believes cable is the next best technology for telecom services. "We have always thought that being able to offer voice, video, and data was the Holy Grail." Some research indicates that the most attractive piece of the bundle is high-speed data. If a goal is to make the customer relationship deeper, then high-speed data may perform better than phone lines. However, consumers may trust their phone companies more than they trust cable operators to carry their conversations.

The cellular telephone industry has been in existence for over sixteen years in the United States. The industry has grown significantly during this period, and cellular service is now available in substantially all areas of the United States. In June 2000 there were estimated to be over 97 million wireless customers across the United States.

Technological developments involving the application of digital radio technology offer certain advantages over analog technologies, including expanding the capacity of mobile communications systems, improving voice clarity, permitting the introduction of new services, and making such systems more secure.

Competition

Competition is rising as the lines between telecom, computing, and data networking blur. The Telecommunications Act of 1996 opened the door for competition in the marketplace, but few consumers are aware of all the options now at their disposal. Competition is generally restricted to large urban business markets. Competition in the rural and suburban areas has not developed or at least does not yet benefit residential customers. ILECs increasingly face competition from CLECs, particularly in high-population areas. CLECs provide competing services through reselling the ILECs' local services, through use of the ILECs' unbundled network elements, or through their own facilities.

ILECs increasingly face competition from alternative communication systems constructed by long-distance carriers, large customers (private networks), or alternative access vendors. These systems are capable of originating or terminating calls without use of the ILECs' networks. Customers may also use wireless or Internet voice service to bypass ILECs' switching services.

There are two thousand companies and subsidiaries providing local telephone services in the United States. One hundred fifty (150) firms offer long-distance services over network facilities of which they own at least a part. Another 350 companies provide toll services by reselling the long-distance services of the large carriers that have built their own nationwide networks. About 300 CLECs have built fiber networks in urban business districts that connect with the networks of long-distance carriers. The precise number of firms providing telecommunications services in the United States is unknown, since many are unregulated, small, privately held enterprises. The total probably is around 4,100. Although well over 90 percent of wireline service revenues are controlled by a few large companies, new services based on new or improved technologies provide ample scope for niche market players in telecom services. Competition between providers of wireless communications services is conducted principally on the basis of price, services, and enhancements offered, the technical quality and coverage of the system, and the quality and responsiveness of customer service.

Mergers continue to occur at all levels of the telecommunications industry, and that trend is expected to continue in the absence of sharp antitrust or regulatory opposition. The antitrust environment under President Bush is expected to be easier. With a weak economy and overcapacity evident, consolidation is more likely. For those with financial muscle, assets can be acquired more cheaply since stocks of weaker companies are often available at bargain prices. Changes in the accounting rules ending the practice of amortizing goodwill will spur hostile offers since earnings of the takeover firms will no longer be diluted. Some predict that ultimately only three of the original seven Bell regional companies may remain, each allied or merged with one of the two or three big U.S. long-distance carriers or with a foreign carrier. In a few years, there may only be a handful of truly global telecommunications carriers.

Market capitalization in the telecommunications services industry ranges from a high of $62.3 billion (AT&T) to less than $1 billion. By way of comparison, AllTel's market capitalization was about $17.7 billion, and CenturyTel had about $4.8 billion in market capital as of September 2001.

Table 3 shows selected economic data and company data from CenturyTel and AllTel.

The number of companies that have requested authorization to provide local exchange service in CenturyTel's service areas has increased substantially,

TABLE 3

Selected Economic and Company Data

P E	1996	1997	1998	1999	2000	2001*
AllTel	16.0	16.1	21.6	29.6	23.1	20.20
CenturyTel	15.3	14.8	22.1	25.6	21.3	20.1

EPS	1996	1997	1998	1999	2000	
AllTel	1.92	2.12	2.09	2.39	2.70	
CenturyTel	0.98	1.89	1.67	1.72	1.65	1.50

Bond rating	Coupon	Maturity	YTM*			
AllTel (selected issues)**						A
Debenture	7.25	2004	5.12*			
Debenture	6.75	2005	5.46*			
Debenture	6.50	2013	6.80*			
Debenture	7.00	2016	6.72*			
Debenture	6.80	2029	7.77*			
CenturyTel (selected issues)						BBB+
Sr. note A	7.75	2004	5.58*			
Sr. note B	8.25	2024	8.14*			
Sr. note C	6.55	2005	5.79*			
Sr. note D	7.20	2025	8.03*			
Sr. note E	6.15	2005	5.33*			
Sr. note F	6.30	2008	6.13*			
Sr. note G	6.875	2028	8.02*			

	1996	1997	1998	1999	2000	2001
AAA corporate	7.37%	7.26%	6.53%	7.04%		
BAA	8.05%	7.86%	7.22%	7.87%		
GDP growth		3.20%	4.77%	4.41%	2.81%	
Unemployment rate		4.95%	4.51%	4.23%	4.01%	
Rf (10-year treasury)	6.44%	6.35%	5.26%	5.64%	6.03%	5.17%
S&P 500 Index returns	17.2%	23.4%	26.7%	19.5%	−10.1%	−11.3%
S&P 500 P/E	19.1	24.2	32.6	30.5		26.2
S&P 500 yield	1.97	1.60	1.32	1.14		1.8%
S&P 500 index	740.43	970.43	1229.2	1469.3		
Prime rate	8.27%	8.44%	8.36%	7.97%	9.23%	7.81%

*Figures through July 2001.
**Figures as of September 2001.

especially in CTL's newly acquired Verizon markets. Others may take similar action in the future.

Economic Outlook

When the economic bubble burst during the latter half of 2000, one of the hardest hit industry sectors was the dot-com industry. The telecommunications industry followed the decline foreshadowed by the dot-coms. This downturn in the economy spread to all sectors of the economy. Stock values declined 20 to 40 percent during this time, and the Federal Reserve cut interest rates eleven times, suggesting that there was grave concern about the economic future. Pessimists in the economy suggest that the current trend presages the advent of another recessionary period in the United States.

Industry Trends and Outlook

With the demand for communications more insatiable than ever, the U.S. market reached a value of $285 billion in 2000. High-volume business customers account for 43 percent of the market, with residential users accounting for 30 percent of the market. The number of telephone access lines in the United States was estimated to exceed 180 million in the year 2000. A healthy overall 4 percent annual growth rate can be anticipated because of continued increases in the number of households with demand for second or third lines, unless wireless and broadband offset this. The number of business access lines has been growing 7 percent annually.

Wireline telecommunications services generated 85 percent of telecom services revenue in 1998. Wireless could increase from the current 15 percent to 20 percent of total revenues in 2004. Analysts agree that wireless will continue to draw significant amounts of voice telephony traffic from wireline, especially in highly penetrated markets. An increasing percentage of consumers are using wireless handsets as a primary, as opposed to secondary, means of communication.

Growth in total long-distance use should continue to increase at a 10 percent annual rate, but prices may decline somewhat, particularly when the Baby Bells enter the market. Toll services represent fewer than 4 percent and should be close to 3 percent of total industry revenues; toll revenues could reach $118 billion in 2004.

Several plausible scenarios facing the industry have been suggested by different industry analysts. According to optimists, the industry future is very positive. They see:

1. Continued rapid growth in wireless communications;

2. Convergence of wireless phones and the Internet;

3. Deregulation and the breaking down of barriers among telecommunications industries;

4. Bundling of cable TV, telephone, Internet, and wireless services for consumers;

5. "Instant messaging" online as an alternative to telephone calls;

6. Companies offering flat-rate pricing, eliminating the need for separate sales staffs and offices.

With broadband service now available to over half of the nation's consumers, analysts predict that almost 40 percent of U.S. households may subscribe to broadband services in 2003. As consumers use more-advanced Internet applications that require greater bandwidth, carriers will rush to meet the insatiable demand for high-speed connectivity. It took the United States almost fifty years to achieve 30 percent penetration for electric service, almost forty years for telephone service, and almost twenty years for television. On the other hand, it has taken only seven years to achieve such penetration for the Internet, and it is estimated that broadband service will achieve a 30 percent penetration rate in only five years.

Such a scenario could result in greater consolidation in the industry. Merger inquiries are not unusual in a competitive industry facing an uncertain economy, and some expect more mergers between long-distance and local phone carriers. Traditional telecom companies (providing basic voice and data services) would become information and communications companies (offering integrated voice, enhanced data, video, and multimedia services) and would look for partners that could increase the ability of the combined firms to compete in the global marketplace. Telecom companies would likely seek partners that offered different types of services in adjacent markets or that had developed expertise in new technologies to offer "bundling." Bundling is the practice of offering a bundle of services for one price. Customers may get multiple services such as an Internet connection, local and long-distance wireline service, and wireless phone or cable TV, all from the same company. A typical middle-income family in the United States may be willing to spend $100 to $150 monthly for cable TV, telephone service, and Internet access. Bundled services provide simplified billing as the customer only has to pay one monthly bill for a range of services. A company that wants to provide its customers with one-stop shopping for all their communications needs is unlikely to have the necessary resources and expertise in-house and will need to buy or form a joint venture with other companies.

However, some pessimists view the future another way. Some consolidation that has already created "one-stop shops" in telecom has slowed. The meltdown in Internet stocks created a profound change in market psychology. Cash-strapped carriers have found it difficult to raise money, especially as revenue growth slowed. Hence, carriers may begin to cut back on capital spending. The optical revolution that began transforming the long-distance network in the 1980s is about to go local to speed data transfer; but this requires large capital investments, even as telecom revenue growth is likely to slow. Smaller companies are being forced into alliances with larger corporations for access to capital and customers. Still, a volatile market makes it difficult to value a takeover target. Hence, "focus" instead of "bundling" may be the new mantra, and the leaders could be companies such as Vodafone (which concentrates on wireless). Players in the high-growth wireless market and carriers in the dying long-distance phone business may both be at risk, especially as falling prices and the routing of more traffic over private line networks and the Internet take place.

Like everything else, the terrorist attacks and their aftermath will impact the telecom industry. Immediately following September 11, many travelers used videoconferencing instead of airplanes to make business connections. The attacks changed the perceptions of many that a cell phone was no longer a luxury, but a necessity. Some expect that growth rates of wireless may be up 30 percent annually for several years because of this. Security and privacy concerns will affect the ways in which people communicate thereby affecting the development and use of the telecom system. Therefore, the forecasts and scenarios will be altered in as yet unforeseen ways.

Corporate Governance

Top Management

Most of CenturyTel top management has been with the firm for over fifteen years. The key personnel include the following:

- **Clarke M. Williams,** founder and chairman of the board; mother and father gave him Oak Ridge Telephone Company.

- **Glen F. Post III,** president, chief executive officer, and vice chairman of the board, joined CenturyTel in 1976. Senior vice president and treasurer 1984; executive vice president and chief operating officer 1988; president, chief executive officer, and vice chairman of the board 1992; M.B.A.

- **Karen A. Puckett,** executive vice president and chief operating officer, joined CenturyTel in 2000; M.B.A., directs all of CTL's telecommunications operations, including sales, marketing, engineering, and other support functions: twenty years of communications experience; served as area president of GTE's Texas wireless region.

- **R. Stewart Ewing, Jr.,** executive vice president and chief financial officer, joined CenturyTel in 1983; vice president and controller 1984; executive vice president and chief financial officer 1999; B.S. in business; certified public accountant (CPA); key role in CenturyTel's acquisition strategy by negotiating all stages of purchase agreements from legal and regulatory to folding new companies into CenturyTel's corporate structure and philosophy.

- **Harvey P. Perry,** executive vice president and chief administrative officer, joined CenturyTel in 1984; general counsel 1984; executive vice president and chief administrative officer 1999; J.D.; Bar Association; responsible for the human resources and administrative services functions within CenturyTel as well as the operation of CenturyTel Air.

- **David D. Cole,** senior vice president, operations support, joined CenturyTel in 1982; director of regulatory affairs 1982; president, Wireless Group 1996; senior vice president, Operations Support 1999; M.B.A.; operational finance, billing and revenue assurance, government relations, revenues, and customer service areas.

- **Mike Maslowski,** senior vice president and chief information officer, joined CenturyTel in 1999; responsible for all of CTL's information systems activities; thirty years of experience working in the telecommunications business with Illinois Bell, AT&T, and Lucent Technologies; focus is on developing information systems that identify customer needs, help package products and services, and enhance ease of acquisition.

Board of Directors

Six of the fourteen board members are present or former executives of CenturyTel. Ten of the fourteen have served on the board for fifteen years or more. The composition of the board is as follows:

- **William R. Boles, Jr.,** age 44; a director since 1992; an executive officer, director, and practicing attorney.

- **Virginia Boulet,** age 47; a director since January 1995; partner, Phelps Dunbar, L.L.P., a law firm.

- **Ernest Butler, Jr.,** age 72; a director since 1971; chairman, president, and a director of I. E. Butler Securities Inc., an investment banking firm, since February 1998; for over thirty years prior to such time, Mr. Butler served as an executive officer of Stephens Inc., an investment banking firm.

- **Calvin Czeschin,** age 65; a director since 1975; president and chief executive officer of Yelcot Telephone Company and Czeschin Motors.

- **James B. Gardner,** age 66; a director since 1981; managing director of the capital markets division of Service Asset Management Company, a financial services firm; a director of Ennis Business Forms, Inc.; prior to April 1994, Mr. Gardner served as an executive officer of various financial institutions or other financial service companies.

- **W. Bruce Hanks,** age 46; a director since 1992; interim athletic director of the University of Louisiana at Monroe; vice president–strategic issues; executive vice president–chief operating officer; senior vice president–corporate development and strategy; president–telecommunications services.

- **R. L. Hargrove, Jr.,** age 69; a director since 1985; retired as executive vice president of CTL in 1987 after twelve years of service as an officer.

- **Johnny Hebert,** age 72; a director since 1968; president of family-owned electrical contracting business.

- **F. Earl Hogan,** age 79; a director since 1968; managing partner of EDJ Farms Partnership, a farming enterprise, for several years prior to his retirement in December 1997.

- **C. G. Melville, Jr.,** age 60; a director since 1968; private investor since 1992; retired executive officer of an equipment distributor.

- **Harvey P. Perry,** age 56; a director since 1990; executive vice president and chief administrative officer of CTL since May 1999; senior vice president of CTL; general counsel and secretary of CTL since 1984 and 1986, respectively.

- **Glen F. Post III,** age 48; a director since 1985; vice chairman of the board, president and chief executive officer of CTL.

- **Jim D. Reppond,** age 59; a director since 1986; retired; vice president of Telephone Group of CTL from January 1995 to July 1996; president of Telephone Group of CTL from May 1987 to December 1994.

- **Clarke M. Williams,** age 79; a director since 1968; chairman of the board of CTL. Mr. Williams, who is the father-in-law of Harvey P. Perry, founded CTL's telephone business in 1946.

Stock Ownership and Control

CenturyTel's Articles of Incorporation specify that each share of common stock beneficially owned continuously by the same person since May 30, 1987, generally entitles the holder thereof to ten votes per share. The holders of 10.6 million shares of common stock were entitled to ten votes per share. Seven hundred twenty-eight (728) institutions own 71.1 percent of the 141 million CTL common shares outstanding. The average institutional ownership of the Communications Services Industry is 35.0 percent, and the average institutional ownership of the S&P 500 as a whole is 58.6 percent. Table 4 identifies the distribution and voting power of selected common shareholders.

CenturyTel Business Operations (as of the end of fiscal year 2000)

CenturyTel's local exchange telephone subsidiaries operated over 1.8 million telephone access lines, primarily in rural, suburban, and small urban areas in twenty-one states, with the largest customer bases located in Wisconsin, Arkansas, Washington, Missouri, Michigan, Louisiana, and Colorado. CTL is the eighth largest local exchange telephone company in the United States based on the number of access lines served (see Table 5).

CenturyTel's cellular systems (1) served approximately 751,000 customers in nineteen metropolitan

TABLE 4

Nature and Amount of Ownership of Common Shares

	Number of Shares	Percent of Shares	Percent of Voting Power
Capital Research and Management Company	10,597,250	7.5%	4.5%
Regions Bank, as trustee of the Stock Bonus Plan and ESOP (the "Benefit Plans")	8,460,064	6.0%	28.1%
	310,582	—	—
	202,922	—	—
All directors and executive officers as a group (18 persons)	3,581,604	2.5%	2.9%

statistical areas (MSAs) and twenty-two rural service areas (RSAs) in Michigan, Louisiana, Arkansas, Mississippi, Wisconsin, and Texas and (2) had access to approximately 7.6 million cellular pops (the estimated population of licensed cellular telephone markets multiplied by CTL's proportionate equity interest in the licensed operators). CTL also owned minority equity interests in ten MSAs and sixteen RSAs representing approximately 1.9 million cellular pops. CTL's 9.5 million aggregate pops make it the eighth largest cellular telephone company in the United States (see Table 6).

CTL also provides long-distance, Internet access, competitive local exchange carrier, broadband data, security monitoring, and other communications and business information services in certain local and regional markets.

CEO Glen Post says CenturyTel's vision is to be the leading provider of integrated communications services to rural areas and smaller cities in America.

CenturyTel continually evaluates the possibility of acquiring additional telecom assets and at any given time may be engaged in discussions or negotiations regarding additional acquisitions. CTL generally does not announce its acquisitions until it has entered into a preliminary or definitive agreement. Over the past few years the number and size of communications properties on the market have increased substantially. Although CTL's primary focus will continue to be on acquiring telephone and wireless interests that are proximate to its properties or that serve a customer base large enough for CTL to operate efficiently, other communications interests may also be acquired.

CTL had approximately 6,860 employees, approximately 1,270 of whom were members of seventeen different bargaining units, including the International Brotherhood of Electrical Workers and the Communications Workers of America. Relations with employees are generally good.

TABLE 5

CenturyTel Access Lines (6/30/2001)

Arizona	1,920	Arkansas	274,783	Colorado	96,696	Idaho	6,331
Indiana	5,471	Iowa	2,060	Louisiana	103,948	Michigan	117,406
Minnesota	31,114	Mississippi	23,520	Missouri	130,493	Montana	66,345
Nevada	486	New Mexico	6,369	Ohio	85,328	Oregon	79,696
Tennessee	27,967	Texas	50,947	Washington	190,869	Wisconsin	500,818
Wyoming	5,383						
				Total	**1,807,950**		

TABLE 6

CenturyTel Wireless Operations

	Year Ended December 31		
	2000	1999	1998
Majority-owned and operated MSA and RSA systems			
Cellular systems operated	41	42	44
Cell sites	743	711	644
Population of systems operated	8,219,411	8,267,140	9,026,150
Customers			
At beginning of period	707,486	624,290	569,983
Gross units added internally	339,247	240,084	214,767
Disconnects	284,880	146,325	160,460
Net units added internally	54,367	93,759	54,307
Effect of property dispositions	(10,653)	(10,563)	
At end of period	751,200	707,486	642,290
Market penetration at end of period	9.1%	8.6%	6.9%
Churn rate	1.95%	2.02%	2.23%
Average monthly service revenue per customer	$ 49	$ 53	$ 57
Construction expenditures (in thousands)	$58,468	$58,760	$57,326

Telephone Operations

CTL's local exchange telephone subsidiaries derive revenue from providing (1) local telephone services (33 percent), (2) network access services (58 percent), and (3) other related services (9 percent) (see Table 7). Network access revenues primarily relate to services provided by CTL to long-distance carriers, wireless carriers, and other customers in connection with the use of CTL's facilities to originate and terminate interstate and intrastate long-distance telephone calls. Other revenues include revenues related to (1) leasing, selling, installing, maintaining, and repairing customer premise telecommunication equipment and wiring, (2) providing billing and collection services for long-distance companies, and (3) participating in the publication of local directories.

CTL has experienced growth in its telephone operations over the past several years, a substantial portion of which was attributable to the acquisitions of telephone properties from Verizon and PTI and the expansion of services (see Table 8). A portion of CTL's access line growth was offset by the sale of CTL's Alaska telephone operations. CTL expects future growth in telephone operations from (1) acquiring additional telephone properties, (2) providing service to new customers, (3) increas-ing network usage, and (4) providing additional services made possible by advances in technology, improvements in CTL's infrastructure, and changes in regulation.

All of CTL's access lines are digitally switched. The installation of digital switches, high-speed data circuits, and related software has been an important component of CTL's growth strategy. This allows CTL to offer enhanced voice services (such as call forwarding, conference calling, caller identification, selective call ringing, and call waiting) and data services. This increases utilization of access lines. CTL has expanded its list of premium services (such as voice mail) offered in certain service areas and has aggressively marketed these services. CTL is installing fiber-optic cable in certain of its high-traffic routes and provides alternative routing of phone service over fiber-optic cable networks in several strategic operating areas. Subsidiaries had over ten thousand miles of fiber-optic cable in use.

Certain large communications companies for which CTL currently provides billing and collection services continue to indicate their desire to reduce their expenses, which has resulted and may continue to result in future reductions of CTL's billing and collection revenues.

TABLE 7

CenturyTel Income Sources (dollars in thousands)

	Year Ended December 31		
	2000	**1999**	**1998**
Operating Revenues			
Local service	$ 408,538	$ 353,534	$ 331,736
Network access*	727,797	654,003	629,583
Other	117,634	118,575	116,024
Total	**$1,253,969**	**$1,126,112**	**$1,077,343**
Operating Expenses			
Plant operations	$ 290,062	$ 251,704	$ 233,896
Customer operations	105,950	88,552	90,331
Corporate and other	163,761	160,631	157,142
Depreciation and amortization	317,906	273,666	261,370
Total	**$ 877,679**	**$ 774,553**	**$ 742,739**
Operating Income	**$ 376,290**	**$ 351,559**	**$ 334,604**

*Network access revenues increased due to the following factors:	**2000**	**1999**
Acquisitions	$75,938	17,645
Increased recovery from the federal Universal Service Fund (USF)	15,753	8,193
Disposition of Alaska properties	(23,348)	(39,985)

Wireless Operations

The development strategy for wireless operations is to secure operating control of service areas that are geographically clustered. This aids CTL's marketing efforts and provides various operating and service advantages. Because most cellular markets are located in rural, suburban, or small urban areas, CTL believes that most of its customers typically require only local or regional services. CenturyTel lacks the facilities and national brand name necessary to compete effectively for business customers requiring nationwide services, and CTL does not actively target these customers in its marketing campaigns. CTL has targeted roaming service revenues, but there is no formal roaming venture with any national carrier.

CTL has access to approximately 9.5 million cellular pops, of which 65 percent were applicable to MSAs and 35 percent were RSA pops. Approximately

TABLE 8

CenturyTel Growth in Telephone Operations (dollars in thousands)

	Year Ended December 31			
	2000	**1999**	**1998**	**1997**
Access lines	1,800,565	1,272,867	1,346,567	1,203,000
% residential	76	75	74	74
% business	24	25	26	26
Operating revenues	$1,253,969	$1,126,112	$1,077,343	$526,000
Capital expenditures	$ 275,523	$ 233,512	$ 233,190	$115,000

19 percent of cellular customers currently subscribe to digital services. Revenue results from charges to subscribers for access to its systems, for minutes of use, and for enhanced services, such as voice mail (see Table 9). A subscriber may purchase rate plans that bundle these services in different ways and are designed to fit different customer requirements. Average monthly cellular revenue per customer declined to $49 in 2000 from $53 in 1999 and $57 in 1998. Average revenue per customer is expected to further decline as additional lower-usage customers are activated, as CTL continues to receive pressure from other cellular operators to reduce roaming rates, and as competitive pressures intensify.

CTL markets its wireless services through several distribution channels, including its direct sales force, retail outlets owned by CTL, and independent agents. Advertising includes direct mail, billboard, magazine, radio, television, and newspaper advertisements. The sales and marketing costs of obtaining new subscribers include advertising and a direct expense applicable to most new subscribers, in the form of either a commission payment to an agent or an incentive payment to a direct sales employee. CTL typically purchases cellular phones in bulk and typi-

cally resells them at a loss to meet competition or to stimulate sales by reducing the cost of becoming a cellular customer. The average cost of acquiring each new customer ($289 in 2000) remains one of the larger expenses in conducting wireless operations. CenturyTel seeks to lower this average cost by focusing on its direct distribution channels. CTL opened its first retail outlet in 1994 and currently operates 143 such outlets.

Churn rate (the average percentage of cellular customers that terminate service each month) is an industrywide concern. A significant portion of the churn in CTL's markets is due to disconnecting service to cellular customers for nonpayment of their bills. In addition, CTL faces substantial competition from other wireless providers, including PCS providers. CTL's average monthly churn rate, excluding prepaid customers, in its majority-owned and -operated markets was 1.95 percent in 2000 and 2.02 percent in 1999. CTL is attempting to lower its churn rate by increasing its proactive customer service efforts and implementing additional customer retention programs.

The construction and maintenance of cellular systems are capital intensive. CTL has continued to

TABLE 9

CenturyTel Wireless Income (dollars in thousands)

	Year Ended December 31		
	2000	**1999**	**1998**
Operating revenues*			
Service	$328,956	$305,006	$302,468
Roaming	99,791	106,486	96,271
Equipment sales	14,822	10,777	9,088
	$443,569	$422,269	$407,827
Operating expenses			
Cost of equipment sold	$ 30,064	$ 21,408	$ 16,992
System operations	69,641	56,866	60,049
General, administrative	78,087	79,569	81,350
Sales and marketing	82,673	61,903	57,967
Depreciation and amortization	65,239	68,593	62,345
	$325,704	$288,339	$278,703
Operating income	$117,865	$133,930	$129,124
Minority interest—wireless operations	(11,598)	(12,911)	(12,635)
Income from unconsolidated cellular entities	26,986	27,675	32,869
	$133,253	$148,694	$149,358

*All of CTL's wireless customers are located in Michigan, Louisiana, Wisconsin, Mississippi, Texas, and Arkansas.

add cell sites to increase coverage, provide additional capacity, and improve the quality of these systems. CTL operated 743 cell sites in its majority-owned markets.

CTL owned licenses to provide PCSs representing approximately 3.0 million pops and thirty-six local multipoint distribution system (LMDS) licenses representing approximately 12.2 million pops. CenturyTel plans to use a portion of its LMDS licenses in connection with its new competitive local exchange business. CTL is currently evaluating its options with respect to the remainder of these licenses, some of which will lapse if not used by specified dates.

A substantial number of the cellular systems in MSAs and RSAs operated by CTL are owned by limited partnerships in which CTL is a general partner. Partnership agreements include customary provisions concerning capital contributions, sharing of profits and losses, and dissolution and termination of the partnership. Most of these agreements vest complete operational control with the general partner.

Other Operations

CenturyTel expects that the growth of operating income for its other operations will slow in future periods as it incurs increasingly larger expenses in connection with expanding its fiber network and competitive local exchange carrier businesses (see Table 10). CTL expects to incur a combined operat-ing loss ranging from $15 to $20 million in 2001 in its fiber network and competitive local exchange carrier businesses.

CenturyTel Financial Activities

CenturyTel's financial statements appear in Tables 11–13. A few explanations may help in the interpretation of the data.

The interest expense increase in FY 2000 was primarily related to the Verizon acquisition and higher interest rates. CTL acquired over 490,000 telephone access lines and related assets from Verizon in four separate transactions for approximately $1.5 billion in cash. To finance these acquisitions on a short-term basis, CTL borrowed $1.157 billion on a floating-rate basis under its new $1.5 billion credit facility with Bank of America, N.A., and Citibank, and borrowed $300 million on a floating-rate basis under its existing credit facility with Bank of America. CenturyTel then issued $500 million of 8.375 percent Notes and $400 million of 7.75 percent Notes. Net proceeds were used to repay a portion of debt in connection with the Verizon acquisitions. Because the Wisconsin Public Service Commission rejected CenturyTel's request to increase the access rates previously charged by Verizon, these acquisitions would dilute CTL's 2001 earnings more than expected.

Excluding acquisitions, CenturyTel relies on cash provided by operations to provide for its cash needs.

TABLE 10

CenturyTel Other Operations (dollars in thousands)

	Year Ended December 31		
	2000	**1999**	**1998**
Operating revenues			
Long distance	$ 104,435	$ 83,087	$53,027
Internet	23,491	16,818	14,267
Call center	3,765	11,749	9,701
Other	116,697	16,634	14,920
Total	$ 148,388	$128,288	$91,915
Operating expenses			
Cost of sales and operating expenses	$ 112,219	$ 99,151	$70,993
Depreciation and amortization	4,911	6,557	4,839
Total	$ 117,130	$105,708	$75,832
Operating income	$ 31,258	$ 22,580	$16,083

TABLE 11

CenturyTel, Inc., Annual Income Statement (in thousand U.S. dollars, except per share amounts)

	Year Ended December 31				
	1996	**1997**	**1998**	**1999**	**2000**
Telephone	$451,538	$530,597	$1,077,343	$1,126,112	$1,253,969
Mobile communication	250,243	307,742	407,827	422,269	443,569
Paging/other	47,896	63,182	91,915	128,288	148,388
Total revenues	**$749,677**	**$901,521**	**$1,577,085**	**$1,676,669**	**$1,845,926**
Cost-sales/operating	$394,360	$474,256	$768,720	$819,784	$932,457
Depreciation/amortization	132,021	159,495	328,554	348,816	388,056
Total expenses	**$526,381**	**$633,751**	**$1,097,274**	**$1,168,600**	**$1,320,513**
Interest expense	(44,662)	(56,474)	(167,552)	(150,557)	(183,302)
Other, net	25,008	197,045	75,199	71,760	44,074
Income before taxes	**$203,642**	**$408,341**	**$ 387,458**	**$ 429,272**	**$ 386,185**
Income taxes	74,565	152,363	158,701	189,503	154,711
Income after taxes	**$129,077**	**$255,978**	**$ 228,757**	**$ 239,769**	**$ 231,474**
Preferred dividend	(420)	(460)	(408)	(403)	(399)
Common dividend/share	$ 0.16	$ 0.1647	$ 0.1733	$ 0.18	$ 0.19

Phone operations are a stable source of cash flow and help the long-term program of capital improvements. Budgeted capital expenditures for 2001 are projected to be $400 million for telephone operations, $70 million for wireless operations, and $80 million for other operations. This includes the installation of fiber-optic cable and the upgrading of plant and equipment, including digital switches, to provide enhanced services, particularly in newly acquired markets. Expenditures in wireless focus on constructing additional cell sites. Capital expenditures for other operations include $20 million for construction of competitive local exchange networks.

CenturyTel continually evaluates the possibility of acquiring additional telecommunications properties. The firm has 4.6 million shares of common, and 200,000 shares of CenturyTel preferred are available for future acquisitions.

AllTel (AT)

AllTel is aiming to become a dominant rural communications carrier. Its ILEC operations (second largest in the United States) accounted for 38.6 percent of FY 2000 profit. AT's wireless telephone services (50.8 percent) are the sixth largest in the United States. All-Tel is leveraging strong cash flows from its ILEC operations to fund Emerging Businesses (generating operating losses of $23.9 million in 2000), including competitive local exchange (CLEC) operations outside its incumbent service territory and long-distance services. AT expanded its CLEC service into seventeen additional markets in four new states, bringing its total CLEC presence to forty-three markets covering ten states. At the end of 2000, AllTel had approximately 1.1 million long-distance customers, up about 20 percent from 1999.

AT's goal for its Emerging Businesses unit is to expand margins through cross-selling of additional services to existing customers. In AT's ILEC service territory (including 2.6 million customer lines), about 44 percent of all local phone customers also subscribed to CTL's long-distance phone service at the end of 2000. Approximately 50 percent of AT's ILEC service territory is covered by its wireless phone services, with 13 percent of covered local customers also subscribing to wireless services. In its CLEC markets, AllTel provides bundled services (including local, long-distance, and wireless) to higher-volume medium and small business customers. These bundled services are provided at a discount and are billed on a single, consolidated billing statement.

TABLE 12

CenturyTel, Inc., Annual Balance Sheet (in thousand U.S. dollars)

	Year Ended December 31				
	1996	1997	1998	1999	2000
Assets					
Cash/ST investments	$ 8,402	$ 26,017	$ 5,742	$ 56,640	$ 19,039
Receivable—customers	86,444	143,613	130,289	128,338	182,454
Other accounts receivable	0	83,659	55,109	64,719	124,711
Materials/supplies	8,222	21,994	23,709	28,769	38,532
Other	6,166	8,197	11,389	7,607	11,768
Total current assets	$ 109,234	$ 283,480	$ 226,238	$ 286,073	$ 376,504
Property/plant/equipment	$1,685,693	$3,845,498	$4,289,658	$0	$0
Telephone	0	0	0	3,439,469	4,999,808
Wireless	0	0	0	472,725	522,684
Other properties	0	0	0	281,713	392,024
Depreciation	(536,681)	(1,586,935)	(1,938,205)	(1,937,449)	(2,955,223)
Goodwill	532,410	1,767,352	1,956,701	1,644,884	2,509,033
Other assets	237,849	400,006	401,063	517,992	548,460
Total assets	$2,028,505	$4,709,401	$4,935,455	$4,705,407	$6,393,290
Liabilities					
Note payable	$0	$0	$0	$0	$276,000
Current portion long-term debt	19,919	55,244	53,010	62,098	149,962
Accounts payable	60,548	83,378	87,627	78,450	127,287
Accrued salaries	0	38,225	36,900	34,570	33,859
Other current liabilities	63,677	124,340	90,381	96,827	104,251
Accrued interest	0	20,821	36,926	37,232	52,011
Total current liabilities	$ 144,144	$ 322,008	$ 304,844	$ 309,177	$ 743,370
Total Long-Term Debt	$ 625,930	$2,609,541	$2,558,000	$2,078,311	$3,050,292
Deferred liabilities	230,278	477,580	541,129	469,927	567,549
Total liabilities	$1,000,352	$3,409,129	$3,403,973	$2,857,415	$4,361,211
Shareholder Equity					
Preferred stock	$10,041	$8,106	$8,106	$7,975	$7,975
Common stock	59,859	91,104	138,083	139,946	140,667
Paid in capital	474,607	469,586	451,535	493,432	509,840
Retained earnings	494,726	728,033	932,611	1,146,967	1,351,626
Treas. Stk/Other	0	11,893	0	0	0
Other equity	(11,080)	(8,450)	1,147	59,672	21,971
Total equity	$1,028,153	$1,300,272	$1,531,482	$1,847,992	$2,032,079
Total Liabilities and Shareholder Equity	$2,028,505	$4,709,401	$4,935,455	$4,705,407	$6,393,290
Shares outstanding	134,682	136,656	138,083	139,946	140,667

TABLE 13

CenturyTel, Inc., Annual Cash Flow Statement (in thousand U.S. dollars)

	Year Ended December 31				
	1996	**1997**	**1998**	**1999**	**2000**
Cash from (Used by) Operations					
Net income	$129,077	$ 225,978	$228,757	$239,769	$ 231,474
Depreciation	132,021	159,495	328,554	348,816	388,056
Cellular entities	(26,952)	(27,794)	(32,869)	(27,675)	(26,986)
Minority interest	6,675	5,498	12,797	27,913	10,201
Deferred taxes	7,935	16,230	17,713	(17,139)	41,820
Property sales	(815)	(169,640)	(49,859)	(62,808)	(20,593)
Accounts receivable	(4,353)	7,649	(15,277)	(15,181)	(82,252)
Accounts payable	5,103	(25,440)	4,249	(11,469)	48,653
Accrued expenses	1,285	58,205	(34,908)	(59,571)	(967)
Current assets	6,220	7,263	15,033	(1,354)	3,605
Noncurrent assets	0	0	0	0	(46,026)
Other noncurrent liabilities	4,305	2,173	(1,706)	(5,311)	4,087
Other, net	4,151	7,702	(4,760)	(7,288)	11,394
Cash from operations	**$264,652**	**$ 297,319**	**$467,774**	**$408,702**	**$ 562,466**
Plus: Cash from (Used by) Investment Activities					
Acquisitions	($ 46,327)	($1,543,814)	($222,569)	($ 20,972)	($1,540,856)
Capital expenditures	(222,885)	(181,225)	(310,919)	(389,908)	(449,537)
Property sales	0	202,705	132,307	484,467	29,495
Minority/cellular	14,904	16,015	26,515	22,219	35,842
Insurance, investment	(5,944)	(12,962)	(2,786)	(2,545)	(5,753)
Note receivable	1,667	22,500	0	0	0
Other	(2,106)	(6,346)	4,807	(23,416)	(3,267)
Other investing	18,900	0	0	0	20,000
Cash from investing	**($241,791)**	**($1,503,127)**	**($375,645)**	**$ 69,773**	**($1,914,076)**
Plus: Cash from (Used by) Financing Activities					
Debt issuance	$ 59,649	$1,312,546	$957,668	$ 15,533	$2,715,852
Debt, net	(71,220)	(79,203)	(1,015,015)	(438,399)	(1,375,895)
Common stock issue	10,089	14,156	15,033	19,182	7,996
Dividends (paid)	(21,775)	(22,671)	(24,179)	(25,413)	(26,815)
Other	258	(1,405)	951	1,520	1,490
Hedge contracts	0	0	(40,237)	0	(4,345)
Debt issuance costs	0	0	(6,625)	0	(4,274)
Cash from financing	**($ 22,999)**	**$1,223,423**	**($112,404)**	**($427,577)**	**$1,314,009**
Equals: Increase (Decrease) in Cash					
Net Change in Cash	**($ 138)**	**$ 17,615**	**($ 20,275)**	**$ 50,898**	**($ 37,601)**
Free cash flow	$ 19,992	$ 93,423	$132,676	($ 6,691)	$ 86,114

In addition to communications, AT has an Information Services division (10.7 percent of 2000 operating profit) that provides data processing and account management services to financial institutions and telecommunications industries. The unit's clients include forty-eight of the fifty leading U.S. banks. During FY 2000, Information Services processed 50 percent of all U.S. residential mortgages and 34 percent of all U.S. consumer loans. To improve the operating efficiency of its information services business, AllTel recorded a restructuring charge of $10.1 million to account for severance and employee benefit costs related to a planned work force reduction and for lease termination costs related to the consolidation of operating locations.

Recent AllTel Transactions and Agreements

During FY 1999, AllTel completed mergers with Liberty Cellular Inc., Aliant Communications Inc., Standard Group, Inc., Advanced Information Resources, Ltd., and Southern Data Systems. In connection with these mergers, about 6.5 million shares of AllTel common stock were issued.

During FY 2000, AT and the Georgia Public Service Commission reached a settlement to resolve all pending litigation, requiring AllTel to issue a one-time credit of about $25 to approximately 450,000 wireline customers in Georgia. Also in FY 2000, AllTel, Bell Atlantic Corporation, GTE Corporation, and Vodafone Airtouch agreed to exchange wireless properties in thirteen states. The companies also signed a new national roaming agreement that allows their customers to roam on one another's networks at reduced rates across a footprint covering almost 95 percent of the U.S. population. These agreements required AllTel to sell its Personal Communications Services operations in Mobile, Alabama, and Pensacola, Florida. The sale of these PCS assets was necessary in order for AT to meet the U.S. Department of Justice guidelines regarding the overlap of wireless properties. In connection with the exchange of wireless assets with Bell Atlantic and GTE, AllTel also recorded integration expenses and other charges consisting of severance and employee benefit costs related to work force reduction and branding and signage costs.

AllTel's Results

AllTel has acquired interests in twenty-seven wireless markets representing about 14.6 million pops and approximately 1,467,000 wireless customers, while divesting interests in 42 wireless markets representing 6.9 million pops and approximately 778,000 customers. Thus, at the end of FY 2000, the wireless division had more than 6.3 million customers in twenty-one states. The unit is undergoing two important transitions. The first is an effort to move analog customers to digital service. AllTel projects that more than 70 percent of its subscriber base will be digital by the end of 2001, up from nearly 40 percent in 2000 and 10 percent in 1999. The second transition is to eliminate roaming fees and move toward simple, one-rate pricing plans.

For telephone operations as a whole, average revenue per customer per month was $49.32 in FY 2000. Reductions in average revenue per customer per month reflect expansion of local, regional, and national calling plans, decreased roaming rates, and continued penetration into competitive market segments. New roaming agreements with Bell Atlantic, GTE, and Vodafone offer new rate plans that provide customers with national wireless coverage with no toll or roaming charges. AllTel expects that these national rate plans will increase customer usage and increase its ability to compete effectively for the high-volume, roaming customer.

A financial snapshot for AllTel is found in Tables 14 and 15.

The Future

When the latest acquisition from Verizon is completed, CenturyTel expects that its new properties will generate revenues of up to $550 million and produce a cash flow of up to $300 million during the first full year of operations. The properties experienced more than 19 percent population growth between 1990 and 2000. CenturyTel will absorb about 950 Verizon employees after the sale closes in 2002.

The acquisition may signal that CenturyTel executives believe that the wireline business offers better long-term growth prospects in rural markets. It can serve as the distribution pipe for business and residential customers. Says one analyst, "I believe there is greater value to be seen for CenturyTel by separating its wireless." CenturyTel's wireless business has come under some pressure since it lacks a roaming arrangement with a larger carrier. AllTel has such an agreement with Verizon Wireless.

TABLE 14

AllTel Corporation Annual Income Statement (in thousand U.S. dollars, except per share amounts)

	Year Ended December 31				
	1996	**1997**	**1998**	**1999**	**2000**
Total revenue	$4,239,467	$4,906,958	$5,780,700	$6,461,400	$7,067,000
Total expenses	$3,427,997	$3,777,767	$4,754,800	$4,936,300	$5,399,500
Interest expense	(237,196)	(274,917)	(278,400)	(280,200)	(310,800)
Other, net	4,514	232,157	357,400	85,900	1,994,000
Income before taxes	$ 578,788	$1,086,431	$1,104,900	$1,330,800	$3,350,700
Income taxes	227,532	433,950	501,800	547,200	1,385,300
Income after taxes	$ 351,256	$ 652,481	$ 603,100	$ 783,600	$1,965,400
Preferred dividend	(1,071)	(1,233)	(1,200)	(900)	(100)
Common dividends/share	$1.055	$1.115	$1.175	$1.235	$1.29

Glen Post still faces the $8.75 billion acquisition bear hug from AllTel. The open letter from AllTel's CEO, Scott Ford, said he was "mystified by CenturyTel's refusal to negotiate." Ford's letter called CenturyTel's wireless business "subscale," saying that it had underperformed regional cellular peers, including AllTel, over the past eighteen months. Alltel also said a successful sale of the wireless business could leave CenturyTel with large tax liabilities. CenturyTel officials in the past have asserted that separation of the business could be done in a tax-friendly way.

Ford has commented that CenturyTel's board was out of touch with its shareholder base and was denying the group a fair return on their investments. Glen Post released a letter to Ford stating, "There is no reason to reconsider [our] decision. While we believe your letter is clearly misleading, we have no intention of engaging in your public letter-writing campaign." CenturyTel later revealed that it had considered and rejected takeover offers from AllTel twice before.

Shareholders said they might be more supportive of CenturyTel's planned separation of its wireless and traditional telephone businesses if the firm

TABLE 15

AllTel Corporation Annual Balance Sheet (in thousand U.S. dollars)

	Year Ended December 31				
	1996	**1997**	**1998**	**1999**	**2000**
Total current assets	$ 709,468	$ 880,791	$ 1,102,561	$ 1,167,200	$ 1,780,700
Depreciation	(2,072,789)	(2,904,507)	(3,814,390)	(4,556,400)	(5,564,400)
Total assets	$5,359,183	$8,570,405	$10,155,454	$10,774,200	$12,182,000
Total current liabilities	$ 590,696	$1,004,492	$ 1,301,841	$ 1,194,000	$ 1,515,900
Total long-term debt	$1,756,142	$3,699,519	$ 3,678,626	$ 3,750,400	$ 4,611,700
Deferred taxes	$ 674,887	$ 710,723	$ 1,001,143	$ 917,500	$217,000
Other long-term liabilities	233,896	437,864	541,812	706,600	742,000
Total liabilities	$3,255,621	$5,852,598	$ 6,523,422	$ 6,568,500	$ 7,086,600
Total equity	$2,103,562	$2,717,807	$ 3,632,032	$ 4,205,700	$ 5,095,400
Total liabilities and shareholder equity	$5,359,183	$8,570,405	$10,155,454	$10,774,200	$12,182,000
Shares outstanding	187,200	273,411	306,015	314,258	312,984

explained adequately why that plan was more attractive financially. A survey of roughly a dozen large CenturyTel shareholders supports AllTel's claim that it is gaining support among CTL's large investors. Victory Capital Management earlier in 2001 owned as many as 2 million CenturyTel shares, but reduced that to more than 300,000 shares over concern that CTL's main growth vehicles were slowing down. "To have a company just place their stake in the sand and say CTL is not for sale and we're just going to pursue this wireless spinoff without coming to the table one more time. I'm still at a loss as to why."

However, many shareholders find AllTel's current offer far too low. Scott Mayo, comanager of John Hancock's Large Cap Value Fund, who manages around a million CenturyTel shares, says, "Putting these two companies together really makes a lot of sense. But I think they could sweeten the offer a little bit." CTL is worth closer to $55 per share. AllTel's current bid values CTL at about $41.38 per share. (This was before the CTL acquisition announcement.) If the acquisition were to be consummated, excellent synergies between the companies could contribute to long-term EPS growth and enhance the value of AllTel's wireless unit. Ford would not comment on whether his company would sweeten its offer, and said he has never been told it was inadequate in the first place. "They've said we don't want to talk. They've said we've talked to our bankers and our lawyers and CTL is not for sale. Do they think it's inadequate? If that's what they're saying, then they need to say that."

Growing animosity between the two firms makes friendly talks unlikely—even if AllTel sweetens its bid. CenturyTel filed a lawsuit seeking to keep its rival from unfairly promoting its unsolicited bid, asking the U.S. district court to keep AllTel from interfering with the auction of its wireless business. Investors and analysts concede that it would take an enormous amount of shareholder pressure to bring the two parties to the table; and given the preventative takeover measures, they believe the merger is unlikely to take place.

Therefore, Glen Post was pondering several options. Should CenturyTel keep its wireless operation or seek another buyer? How much would the wireless operation be worth to a buyer? If AllTel sweetens the bid, how high would the offer have to be for the board to approve it? Would a suitor other than AllTel be friendlier?

Appendix: A Glossary of Telecommunications Terminology

access charge   A fee charged subscribers or other telephone companies by a local exchange carrier for the use of its local exchange networks.

analog signal   A signaling method that uses continuous changes in the amplitude or frequency of a radio transmission to convey information.

bandwidth   The capacity of a telecom line to carry signals. The necessary bandwidth is the amount of spectrum required to transmit the signal without distortion or loss of information. FCC rules require suppression of the signal outside the band to prevent interference.

broadband   A descriptive term for evolving digital technologies that provide consumers with a signal switched facility offering integrated access to voice service, high-speed data service, video-demand services, and interactive delivery services.

cellular technology   Term often used for all wireless phones regardless of the technology they use, derives from cellular base stations that receive and transmit calls. Both cellular and PCS phones use cellular technology.

common carrier   In the telecommunications arena, the term used to describe a telephone company.

cramming   Practice by which customers are billed for enhanced features such as voice mail, caller-ID, and call-waiting that they have not ordered.

dial around   Long-distance services that require consumers to dial a long-distance provider's access code (or "10-10" number) before dialing a long-distance number to bypass or "dial around" the consumer's chosen long-distance carrier in order to get a better rate.

landline   Traditional wired phone service.

land mobile service   A public or private radio service providing two-way communication, paging, and radio signaling on land.

network   Any connection of two or more computers that enables them to communicate. Networks may include transmission devices, servers, cables, routers, and satellites. The phone network is the total infrastructure for transmitting phone messages.

personal communications services (PCS) Any of several types of wireless, voice, and/or data communications systems, typically incorporating digital technology. PCS licenses are most often used to provide services similar to advanced cellular mobile or paging services. However, PCS can also be used to provide other wireless communications services, including services that allow people to place and receive communications while away from their home or office, as well as wireless communications to homes, office buildings, and other fixed locations.

pops Portion of the population of the service area.

service provider A telecommunications provider that owns circuit-switching equipment.

spectrum The range of electromagnetic radio frequencies used in the transmission of sound, data, and television.

subscriber line charge (SLC) A monthly fee paid by telephone subscribers that is used to compensate the local telephone company for part of the cost of installation and maintenance of the telephone wire, poles, and other facilities that link your home to the telephone network. These wires, poles, and other facilities are referred to as the "local loop." The SLC is one component of access charges.

telephony Word used to describe the science of transmitting voice over a telecommunications network.

unbundling The access provided by a local exchange carrier so that other service providers can buy or lease portions of its network elements, such as interconnection loops, to serve subscribers.

REFERENCES

AllTel Corporation. *Standard & Poor's Stock Report.* September 8, 2001.

CenturyTel Corporation. *Standard & Poor's Stock Report.* October, 2001.

CenturyTel, 10-K, U.S. Securities and Exchange Commission. 2001.

CenturyTel Notice of Annual Meeting and Proxy Statement. May 10, 2001.

"CenturyTel History." Retrieved 9/24/01 from **www.centurytel.com/ index.cfm?action=About%20Us&subaction=History.**

Centurytel, Inc., ProVestor Plus Company Report. September 17, 2001.

"CenturyTel Increases Quarterly Cash Dividend." February 28, 2001. Retrieved 9/24/01 from **www.centurytel.com/index.cfm?action= News&subaction=Financial%20News&pr_id=126.**

"CenturyTel Leadership." Retrieved 9/24/01 from **www.centurytel .com/index.cfm?action=About%20Us&subaction=CenturyTel %20Leadership.**

"CenturyTel Media Contacts." Retrieved September 21, 2001, from **http://centurytel.com/index.cfm?action=About%20Us& subaction= Media%20Contacts.**

"CenturyTel to Acquire 675,000 Access Lines from Verizon for $2.159 Billion." Retrieved October 22, 2001, from **www.centurytel .com/index.cfm?action=News&details=Acquisitions&pr_id=305.**

"FCC Votes to Cut Airwaves Phone Limits." *USA Today,* November 9, 2001, p. B1.

Haddad, Charles. "The Bells Aren't Ringing." *Business Week,* November 12, 2001, pp. 118–120.

Hilburn, Greg. "CenturyTel to Buy Verizon Lines." *News-Star,* October 23, 2001, p. A1.

Johnson, Tom. "Alltel Renews Public Pressure on CenturyTel." Retrieved September 17, 2001, from **http://tools.fidelity.com/ news/RM/index.cfm?story=RM-20010828-N28299487.**

Johnson, Tom. "CenturyTel Investors Ready to Talk, but Want Higher Price." Retrieved September 17, 2001, from **http://tools.fidelity .com/news/rc/index.cfm?story=rc-20010831-n31328542.**

Kagan, Jeffrey. "Analysts Predict AT&T Merger Talk May Set Off New Trend." *News-Star.* October 7, 2001, p. D1.

Lieberman, David. "Cost Break from Phone, Cable Link Creeps Along." *USA Today,* October 8, 2001, p. B1.

"Management Discussion: Alltel Corp (AT)." Retrieved 9/18/01 from **http://excite.elogic.com/sec_mgmt.asp?defview=FULL&ticker= at&Submit2=Go.**

Non, Sergio G. "Embracing an Acquisition Trend: The Bear Hug." *CNET News.com,* August 22, 2001. Retrieved from **http://quickenexcite .cnet.com/news/0-1007-200-6943204.html.**

"Overview of the Telecommunications Industry." Retrieved September 24, 2001, from **http://www.plunkettresearch.com/ telecommunications/telecom_trends.htm.**

Rosenbush, Steve. "Telecommunications." *Business Week Online,* January 8, 2001. Retrieved September 24, 2001, from **http://www .businessweek.com:2001/01_02/b3714089.htm.**

"Telecommunications Services." *U.S. Industry & Trade Outlook 2000.* New York: McGraw-Hill Companies, Inc., 1999, pp. 30–1 to 30–26.

Thomton, Emily. "It Sure Is Getting Hostile." *Business Week,* January 14, 2002, pp. 28–30.

U.S. Department of Commerce, Bureau of Economic Analysis.

Wolcott, David A. "An ALTS Analysis: Local Competition Policy & The New Economy." February 2, 2001. Retrieved from **http://www. alts.org/Filings/020201Analysis.pdf.**

Whirlpool Corporation's Global Strategy

40

This case was prepared by Meredith Martin, Simon Algar, and Vipon Kumar under the supervision of Professor Andrew C. Inkpen, Thunderbird, the Graduate School of International Management.

We want to be able to take the best capabilities we have and leverage them in all our companies worldwide.

—*David Whitman, Whirlpool CEO, 1994*
Quoted in the Harvard Business Review

In 1989, Whirlpool Corporation (Whirlpool) embarked on an ambitious global expansion with the objective of becoming the world market leader in home appliances. Beginning with the purchase of a majority stake in an appliance company owned by Philips, the Dutch electronics firm, Whirlpool purchased a majority stake in an Indian firm, established four joint ventures in China, and made significant new investments in its Latin America operations.

However, by the mid-1990s, serious problems had emerged in the company's international operations. In 1995, Whirlpool's European profit fell by 50% and in 1996, the company reported a $13 million loss in Europe. In Asia, the situation was even worse. Although the region accounted for only 6% of corporate sales, Whirlpool lost $70 million in Asia in 1996 and $62 million in 1997. In Brazil, Whirlpool found

itself a victim in 1997, and again in 1998, of spiraling interest rates. Despite the company's investments of hundreds of millions of dollars throughout the 1990s to modernize operations there, appliance sales in Brazil plummeted by 25% in 1998. Whirlpool expected that 1999 would be the third straight year of declining sales for the Brazilian subsidiary.

In response to these problems, Whirlpool began a global restructuring effort. In September 1997, the company announced that it would cut 10% of its global workforce over the next two years and pull out of two joint ventures in China. In announcing the cuts, Whirlpool's CEO David Whitwam said, "We are taking steps to align the organization with the marketplace realities of our industry."[1] In Latin America, 3,500 jobs were abolished, and significant investments were made to upgrade plants and product lines.

After the optimism of the early 1990s, what went wrong with Whirlpool's global strategy? Was the company overly ambitious? Was there

1. C. Quintanilla and J. Carlton, "Whirlpool Announces Global Restructuring Effort," *Wall Street Journal,* 19 Sept. 1997: A3, A6.

a lack of understanding about how to create an integrated global strategy? Or, were the problems the result of changes in the competitive and economic environments in Europe, Asia, and Latin America? Should Whirlpool have foreseen the problems and reacted earlier?

The Appliance Industry in the late 20th Century

Approximately 120 million home appliances are sold in developed countries each year.[2] The appliance industry is generally classified into four categories: laundry, refrigeration, cooking, and other appliances. Appliances are constructed in capital intensive plants, and design usually varies among countries and regions.

The North American Industry

Although it was estimated that 46 million appliances were sold in North America annually, the market was expected to grow little in the late 1990s. Saturation levels were high, with virtually 100% of households owning refrigerators and cookers and over 70% owning washers. Because of the limited growth opportunities, competition was fierce. In the United States, the industry had consolidated in the 1980s, leaving four major competitors: Whirlpool, General Electric, Electrolux, and Maytag (see Exhibit 1 for more detail). These four firms controlled about 80% of the market.[3] Each firm offered a variety of products and brands segmented along price lines. Distribution of these appliances was generally through sales to builders for new houses or to retailers, such as department stores and specialty resellers.

In a *Harvard Business Review* article in 1994 called "The Right Way to Go Global," David Whitwam, Whirlpool's CEO, described the competitive situation that existed in the early 1990s:

> Even though we had dramatically lowered costs and improved product quality, our profit margins in North America had been declining because everyone in the industry was pursuing the same course and the local market was mature. The four main players—Whirlpool,

General Electric, Maytag, and White Consolidated, which had been acquired by Electrolux—were beating one another up everyday.[4]

With limited growth opportunities and a handful of major players in the United States, it was critical that firms focus on cost reduction, productive efficiency, and product quality. Product innovation was also critical, although few major innovations had occurred in recent years. The appliance firms segmented their products according to different consumers' needs, and each strived to achieve greater economies of scale. Still, by the end of the 1990s, the competitive landscape remained unattractive. Profit margins continued to decline for most firms. Many analysts believed that the market for appliances was saturated and that there would be little increase in growth rates. This saturation had left the distributors focusing primarily on replacement purchases and purchases for new housing developments.

The European Industry

In the early 1980s, there were approximately 350 producers of household appliances in Europe. With consolidation in the industry, by the late 1980s the number had shrunk to about one hundred.[5] By early 1995, it was estimated that five of the companies, including Electrolux (with a 25% market share), Philips Bauknecht, and Bosche-Siemens, controlled over 70% of the market.[6] The industry was highly regionalized, with many of the companies producing a limited number of products for a specific geographic area.

The European market consisted of more than 320 million consumers whose preferences varied by country and by region. For example, Swedes preferred galvanized washing machines to withstand the damp salty air.[7] The British washed their clothes more often than the Italians did, and wanted quieter machines. The French liked to cook on gas at high temperatures, splattering grease on cooking surfaces, and so preferred self-cleaning ovens, while the Ger-

2. Weiss, David D. and Andrew C. Gross, "Industry Corner: Major Household Appliances in Western Europe," *Business Economics*, Vol. 30, Issue 3, July 1995: 67.

3. Echikson, William. "The Trick to Selling in Europe," *Fortune*, 20 Sept. 1993: 82.

4. Maruca, Regina Fazio. "The Right Way to Go Global: An Interview with Whirlpool CEO David Whitwam," *Harvard Business Review*, March–April 1994: 137.

5. Weiss and Gross.

6. Jancsurak, Joe, "Holistic Strategy Pays Off," *Appliance Manufacturer*, Feb. 1995: W-3, W-4.

7. Steinmetz, Greg and Carl Quintanilla. "Tough Target: Whirlpool Expected Easy Going in Europe, and It Got a Big Shock," *Wall Street Journal*, 10 April 1998: Sec. A:1.

EXHIBIT 1

Major Competitors in the United States

GE Appliance	General Electric Appliance was the second-largest manufacturer of household appliances in the U.S. (behind Whirlpool). Other brand names produced by the company included Monogram, Profile, Profile Performance, Hotpoint, and some private brands for retailers. GE Appliance comprised approximately 6% of the parent company's sales and had the top market share position in India and Mexico. In addition, the company had a 50-50 joint venture with General Electric Co., the leading appliance firm in the United Kingdom.
Maytag	Maytag's products were generally aimed at the mid-to-high end of the market and commanded a premium price based on product quality and reliability. Other brand names produced by Maytag included Jenn-Air, Magic Chef, Performa, and Hoover. Maytag entered the European market in 1989, but after a decline in profits, pulled out of Europe in 1995. Maytag had a limited presence in China.
AB Electrolux	AB Electrolux was the world's largest producer of household appliances. Other Electrolux brand names included Frigidaire, Tappan, and Kelvinator. The Swedish company had the number one market share in Europe and number four market share in North America. Electrolux entered the United States when it bought White Consolidated Industries in 1986. The firm was actively expanding overseas into Eastern Europe, China, India, South East Asia, and Latin America.

Sources: Hoovers Online. Accessed 2/9/00. Remich/Norman C. "A Kentucky Thoroughbred that is Running Strong," *Appliance Manufacturer,* July 1995: GEA-3. Steinmetz, Greg and Carl Quintanilla. Tough Target: Whirlpool Expected Easy Going in Europe, and It Got a Big Shock," *Wall Street Journal,* 10 April 1998; Sec. A:1.

mans liked to cook on electric stoves at lower temperatures and did not need such features.[8]

Distribution of the appliances in Europe was different than in the United States. Most appliances were sold through independent retailers, who had become organized in buying groups or as multiple store chains.[9] A smaller channel was through independent kitchen specialists who sold complete kitchen packages, including appliances.[10]

The Asian Industry

Asia, the world's second largest home appliance market, was also the fastest growing market of the 1980s. By the mid-1990s, it was growing at a rate of between 8% and 12% annually, a rate that was expected to continue well past the year 2000.[11] The industry was highly fragmented, consisting of manufacturers primarily from Japan, Korea, and Taiwan. Matsushita,

the market leader, held less than 10% market share outside Japan.

Asian consumer preferences were different from those in Europe or North America. Kitchen appliances needed to be smaller to fit in Asian kitchens. Lack of space sometimes required the consumer to store the appliance in an outside hallway and transport it into the kitchen for use.[12] Therefore, high value was placed on appliances that were portable, usually lightweight and on wheels, and easily hooked up to electrical and water supplies. Refrigerators also tended to be smaller and more colorful. Indeed, when Asian countries first began to experience significant economic growth, some East Asians viewed their refrigerators as status symbols and liked to display them prominently, perhaps even in the sitting room. Clothes dryers and dishwashers were uncommon in most Asian countries, but most homes had microwaves.

Appliances in Asia were traditionally sold through small retail shops. However, the industry was beginning to witness a shift away from these small

8. Schiller, Zachary, et al., "Whirlpool Plots the Invasion of Europe," *Business Week,* 5 Sept. 1988: 70.

9. Jancsurak, Joe, "Group Sales: Channel Focused," *Appliance Manufacturer,* Feb. 1995: W-14.

10. "Group Sales," W-14.

11. Babyak, Richard J, "Strategic Imperative," *Appliance Manufacturer,* Feb. 1995: W-21.

12. Babyak, Richard J, "Demystifying the Asian Consumer," *Appliance Manufacturer,* Feb. 1995: W26.

shops and towards distribution through national, power retailer organizations, especially in China and parts of Southeast Asia.

The Latin American Industry

The economic stability in Latin America in the 1990s made the region an attractive growth proposition. The appliance makers hoped that the days of hyper-inflation and economic mismanagement were over, and they were pleased to see that governments were reducing tariffs. Distributors in Latin America were generally responsible for marketing a company's appliances to small independent retailers in the region.[13] In 1994, there were over 65 competitors in the Latin American market, many of them sub-sidiaries of U.S. parents.

Whirlpool Corporation

Whirlpool was founded in 1911 as The Upton Machine Co. in St Joseph, Michigan, to produce an electric motor-driven wringer washer. The company merged with The Nineteen Hundred Washer Company in 1929 and began to sell their first automatic washing machine through Sears, Roebuck & Co. in 1947. The Whirlpool brand was introduced in 1948 and steadily built a strong retail relationship with Sears. Through a series of acquisitions and mergers, the company emerged as a leading force in the U.S. appliance industry with annual revenue reaching $2 billion in 1978 (see Exhibit 2 for more detail on Whirlpool's history). Whirlpool's headquarters was in Benton Harbor, Michigan.

As of 1998, Whirlpool Corporation claimed to be the world's leading manufacturer of major home appliances. The company manufactured in thirteen countries and marketed its products under eleven major brand names (including Kenmore, Sears, KitchenAid, Roper, Inglis, and Speed Queen) to over 140 countries. Whirlpool's sales were $8.2 billion in fiscal year 1997.

The Globalization of Whirlpool

Whirlpool's first international investment was in 1957 when the firm acquired an equity interest in Multibras S.A., a Brazilian manufacturer of white

goods. In 1969, the company entered the Canadian market by purchasing an equity interest in Inglis Ltd. and acquired sole ownership in 1990.

By the mid-1980s, Whirlpool saw that, despite increasing efficiencies and product quality, its profit margins were rapidly decreasing in North America. Top management believed that if the company continued to follow its current path, the future would be "neither pleasant nor profitable."[14] They considered restructuring the company financially or diversifying into related businesses but eventually settled on further global expansion for two main reasons: the company wished to take advantage of less mature markets around the world and it did not want to be left behind by its competitors, which had already begun to globalize.

Whitwam's Vision and Platform Technology

David Whitman joined Whirlpool in 1968 as a marketing management trainee and rose through the sales and marketing ranks to succeed Jack Sparks as CEO in 1987. Although Whitwam admitted that he had never actually run a multinational company until Whirlpool bought Philips in 1989, he believed that:

> The only way to gain lasting competitive advantage is to leverage your capabilities around the world, so that the company as a whole is greater than the sum of its parts. Being an international company—selling globally, having global brands or operations in different countries—isn't enough.[15]

Whitwam was convinced that most companies with international divisions were not truly global at all, as their various regional and national divisions still operated as autonomous entities rather than working together as a single company. He believed that the only way to achieve his vision of an integrated international company, or one company worldwide, was through intensive efforts to understand and respond to genuine customer needs and through products and services that earn long-term customer loyalty.

Whitwam talked about his vision of integrating Whirlpool's geographical businesses so that the company's expertise would not be confined to one location or product. He forecast appliances such as a World Washer, a single machine that could be sold anywhere,

13. Janesurak, Joe, "South American Sales Co.: Linking the Americas, Europe," *Appliance Manufacturer*, Feb. 1995: W-39.

14. Maruca, p. 136.
15. Maruca, p. 137.

EXHIBIT 2

Whirlpool History

1911	Upton Machine Co. is founded in St. Joseph, Michigan, to produce electric motor-driven wringer washers.
1916	First order for washers is sold to Sears, Roebuck and Co.
1929	Upton Machine merges with Nineteen Hundred Washer Company of Binghamton, New York. The new firm, Nineteen Hundred Corp., operates plants in Michigan and New York until Binghamton is closed in 1939.
1942	All facilities are converted to wartime production until end of World War II in 1945.
1947	The company's first automatic washer is introduced to the market by Sears.
1948	A Whirlpool brand automatic washer is introduced, thus establishing dual distribution—one line of products for Sears, another for Nineteen Hundred.
1950	Nineteen Hundred Corporation is renamed Whirlpool Corporation. Automatic dryers are added to the product line.
1951	LaPorte, Indiana, plant is acquired. It will become the company's parts distribution center. Whirlpool merges with Clyde (Ohio) Porcelain Steel and converts the plant to washer production. All washers eventually will be produced here.
1955	Manufacturing facilities are purchased in Marion, Ohio, from Motor Products Corp., and dryer production is transferred there. Whirlpool merges with Seeger Refrigerator Co. of St. Paul, Minnesota, and the Estate range and air conditioning divisions of R.C.A. RCA Whirlpool is established as the brand name; Whirlpool-Seeger Corporation, as the company name. A refrigeration plant is acquired in Evansville, Indiana, from International Harvester.
1956	First full line of RCA Whirlpool home appliances is introduced. RCA will be used with the Whirlpool brand name until 1967. New administrative center is completed on 100-acre site in Benton Harbor.
1957	Company name is changed back to Whirlpool Corporation. Appliance Buyers Credit Corporation is established as a wholly owned finance subsidiary. It will be renamed Whirlpool Financial Corporation in 1989.
1957	Whirlpool invests in Brazilian appliance market through purchase of equity interest in Multibrás S.A. It is renamed Brastemp S.A. in 1972.
1966	The Norge plant in Fort Smith, Arkansas, is acquired, adding more than one million sq. ft. of refrigeration manufacturing space.
1967	Toll-free Cool-Line® Telephone Service begins. Renamed the Consumer Assistance Center in 1990, it gives customers direct, 24-hour access to Whirlpool. The company's first totally new manufacturing facility is completed in Findlay, Ohio. Dishwashers and, later, ranges will be manufactured there.
1968	The Elisha Gray II Research & Engineering Center is completed in Benton Harbor. For the first time, annual revenues reach $1 billion.
1969	The company enters the Canadian appliance market through purchase of an equity interest in Inglis Ltd. Sole ownership is established in 1990.
1970	Construction is completed on a new plant in Danville, Kentucky. Production of trash compactors and, later, vacuum cleaners is transferred there.
1976	Whirlpool increases its investment in the Brazilian market through purchase of equity interests in Consul S.A., an appliance manufacturer, and Embraco S.A., a maker of compressors.
1978	Annual revenues reach $2 billion.
1983	The company announces a phaseout of washer assembly at St. Joseph. All washers will be made at Clyde.
1984	The St. Paul Division is closed. Production of freezers and ice makers moves to Evansville.
1986	Whirlpool purchases the KitchenAid division of Hobart Corporation. A majority interest is purchased in Aspera s.r.l., an Italian compressor manufacturer. Whirlpool will become sole owner before the business is sold to Embraco of Brazil in 1994. Whirlpool closes most of its St. Joseph Division. The remaining machining operation is renamed the Benton Harbor Division.

(continued)

EXHIBIT 2 *(continued)*

Whirlpool History

1987	Whirlpool and Sundaram-Clayton Limited of India form TVS Whirlpool Limited to make compact washers for the Indian market. Whirlpool will acquire majority ownership in 1994.
1988	A joint venture company, Vitromatic S.A. de C.V., is formed with Vitro, S.A. of Monterrey, to manufacture and market major home appliances for Mexican and export markets. Whirlpool acquires the Roper brand name, which it will use to market a full line of value-oriented home appliances.
1989	Whirlpool and N.V. Philips of the Netherlands form a joint venture company, Whirlpool Europe B.V., from Philips major domestic appliance division, to manufacture and market appliances in Europe. Whirlpool will become sole owner in 1991. Appliance operations in the United States, Canada, and Mexico are brought together to form the North American Appliance Group (NAAG). Annual revenues catapult over the $6 billion mark.
1990	A program is launched to market appliances in Europe under the dual brands Philips and Whirlpool. Whirlpool Overseas Corporation is formed as a subsidiary to conduct marketing and industrial activities outside North America and Western Europe. An Estate brand of appliances targeted to national accounts is introduced.
1991	The company commits globally to its Worldwide Excellence System, a total quality management program dedicated to exceeding customer expectations. NAAG repositions its refrigeration business. The Port Credit, Ontario, plant is closed. Top- and bottom-mount refrigerators are consolidated at Evansville, side-by-side refrigerators at Fort Smith.
1992	Whirlpool assumes control of SAGAD S.A., of Argentina. Whirlpool Hungarian Trading Ltd. is formed to sell and service appliances in Hungary. Whirlpool Tatramat is formed to make and sell washing machines and market other major home appliances in Slovakia. Whirlpool will take controlling interest in 1994. A Small Appliance Business Unit is formed to operate on a global basis. Revenues top $7 billion. The South American Sales Co. (SASCo), a joint venture with Whirlpool's Brazilian affiliates, begins directing export sales to 35 Latin American countries.
1993	Whirlpool Overseas Corporation is replaced by two separate regional organizations: Whirlpool Asia and Whirlpool Latin America. Whirlpool Asia sets up headquarters in Tokyo with regional offices in Singapore, Hong Kong, and Tokyo. Sales subsidiaries are opened in Poland and the Czech Republic, adding to Whirlpool Europe's growing presence in Eastern Europe. Whirlpool wins the $30 million Super Efficient Refrigerator Program sponsored by 24 U.S. utilities. Inglis Ltd. becomes Canada's leading home appliance manufacturer.
1994	Whirlpool Asia and Teco Electric & Machinery Co. Ltd. form Great Teco Whirlpool Co. Ltd. to market and distribute home appliances in Taiwan. Whirlpool becomes a stand-alone brand in Europe. Brazilian affiliates Consul and Brastemp merge to form Multibrás S.A. Electrodomésticos. Whirlpool breaks ground in Tulsa, Oklahoma, for a new plant to make freestanding gas and electric ranges. Whirlpool's Asian headquarters is moved to Singapore, and the number of operating regions is increased from three to four. Whirlpool exits vacuum cleaner business. To strengthen competitiveness, a major restructuring is announced in North America and Europe. One U.S. and one Canadian plant close. Total revenues top $8 billion.
1995	An executive office is formed in Whirlpool Asia to lead the company's rapid growth and manage strategic deployment in the region. Whirlpool acquires controlling interest in Kelvinator of India Ltd., one of India's largest manufacturers and marketers of refrigerators. TVS Whirlpool Ltd. changes name to Whirlpool Washing Machines Ltd. (WWML). Construction is completed on a new plant in Greenville, Ohio. KitchenAid small appliances will be manufactured there. Whirlpool begins to sell appliances to Montgomery Ward. Whirlpool Europe opens representative office in Russia. Whirlpool Financial Corporation (WFC) is established in India. Whirlpool assumes control of Beijing Whirlpool Snowflake Electric Appliance Group Co. Ltd., a refrigerator and freezer manufacturing joint venture. Beijing Embraco Snowflake Compressor Co. Ltd., a compressor manufacturing joint venture, is formed between Embraco and Beijing Snowflake. Whirlpool has a minority position in the joint venture. Whirlpool acquires controlling interest in

(continued)

EXHIBIT 2 *(continued)*

Whirlpool History

1995 (continued)	Whirlpool Narcissus (Shanghai) Co. Ltd., a washing machine manufacturing joint venture. Whirlpool acquires majority ownership of SMC Microwave Products Co. Ltd., a microwave oven manufacturing joint venture. Shenzhen Whirlpool Raybo Air-Conditioner Industrial Co. Ltd., an air conditioner manufacturing joint venture, is formed with Whirlpool having a majority stake. Whirlpool investments in Asia increase to over US$350 million, and employees total more than 9,300.
1996	Whirlpool Europe opens sales subsidiaries in Romania and Bulgaria. Production of electric and gas ranges officially begins in Whirlpool's new plant in Tulsa, Oklahoma. The company's new Greenville, Ohio, plant, which manufactures KitchenAid small appliances, begins production. The Ft. Smith Division in Arkansas begins production of trash compactors. Whirlpool Asia employees total more than 12,000. Whirlpool Europe acquires the white goods business of Gentrade of South Africa. The acquisition provides Whirlpool a sales and manufacturing base in this country.

Source: <http://www.whirlpool.com>

and he wanted to standardize the company's manufacturing processes. According to Whitwam,

> Today products are being designed to ensure that a wide variety of models can be built on the same basic platform. . . . Varying consumer preferences require us to have regional manufacturing centers. But even though the features . . . vary from market to market, much of the technology and manufacturing processes involved are similar.[16]

Given this view that standardization should be the focus, Whirlpool planned to base all its products, wherever they were built or assembled, on common platforms. These platforms would produce the technological heart of the product, the portion of the product which varied little across markets. The products could then be diversified to suit individual and regional preferences. In this way, the parts that the customer sees—the dimensions of the appliance, the metal case, and the controls—could be varied by segment or market to fulfill consumers' needs. The products would also have to meet rigorous quality and environmental standards to ensure that they could be used in different countries around the world.

Whitwam believed that the platform technology would bring a $200 million annual savings in design and component costs by the time it was fully implemented in the year 2000.[17] In addition, management was convinced that the platform strategy would put the company two to three years ahead of its competitors.

Platform technology, however, represented only the beginning of Whirlpool's globalization strategy.

According to Whitwam in the 1994 interview, Whirlpool could not truly achieve its goal of globalization until:

> . . . we have cross-border business teams . . . running all of our operations throughout the world . . . There will also come a day when we'll identify a location where the best skills in a certain product area should be concentrated, and that place will become the development center for that type of product . . . [but] while we may have only one major design center for a given product, not everyone associated with that product will have to be located there.[18]

Developing and Implementing the Global Strategy

By 1987 Whirlpool had adopted a five-year plan to develop a new international strategy. The company's 1987 Annual Report included the following statement:

> The U.S. appliance industry has limited growth opportunities, a high concentration of domestic competitors, and increasing foreign competition. Further, the United States represents only about 25% of the worldwide potential for major appliance sales. Most importantly, our vision can no longer be limited to our national borders because national borders no longer define market boundaries. The marketplace for products and services is more global than ever before and growing more so every day.

16. Maruca, p. 136.
17. Whirlpool Corporation, Annual Report, 1997.
18. Maruca, p. 145.

Recent industry forecasts indicated that approximately three-quarters of the growth in domestic appliance sales between 1995 and 2000 would be in East Asia (including Australia), Eastern Europe, and South and Central America. According to the forecasts, by 2000 these three regions (excluding Japan) would account for about 34% of sales.

European Expansion

In 1989, Whirlpool bought a major stake in N.V. Philips, a struggling Dutch appliance operation, and then purchased the remaining equity in 1991 for a total of $1.1 billion.[19] Whitwam believed that the U.S. and European markets were very similar and hoped that Whirlpool would be able to replicate their successes in the United States in the new market through implementation of a pan-European strategy. Whirlpool management also believed that the European market was becoming more "American." Research performed by the company indicated that European integration was making it more difficult for smaller companies to survive and that the industry was ripe for consolidation. Whirlpool's plan was to be one of the big players following this consolidation, and Whitwam was expecting a 20% share of the $20 billion market by the year 2000.[20] Whirlpool's strategy was to focus on brand segmentation and operational efficiency. It was believed that the company that produced the most innovative products while reducing costs would capture the market.

The European subsidiary, Whirlpool Europe BV (WEBV), created a brand portfolio segmented by price. Bauknecht (Philip German brand) served as the company's high-end product while Ignis served as the lower-end, value brand. The Philips/Whirlpool brand filled the middle range.[21] However, the company decided to heavily market the Whirlpool brand name at the expense of managing its other European brands. Managers at Bauknecht in Germany saw their marketing budgets slashed, and Bauknecht's market share fell from 7% to 6%.[22] By 1995, however, consumer research showed Whirlpool to be the most recognized appliance brand name in Europe, despite the fact that many Germans, Italians, and French had a problem pronouncing the name.

To better manage sales and service throughout the region, Whirlpool set up two centralized distribution centers: one in Cassinetta, Italy, and one in Schorndorf, Germany. Operations were streamlined in order to achieve reduced costs through economies of scale and considerable efforts were put toward product innovation and increasing operational efficiency. This strategic focus was overlaid with a global outlook, and managers were regularly rotated between Europe and the United States. The rotation generated a crossover of ideas but annoyed retail clients who felt that they had no continuity when dealing with senior managers.

The early years of European expansion were successful. Sales and profits increased steadily, and Whirlpool made a profit of $129 million in Europe in 1993. The company was able to cut costs by reducing the number of suppliers it dealt with and by using common parts in its appliances.

However, Whirlpool was not the only company aggressively attacking the market, and competition subsequent to Whirlpool's entry grew fierce. Electrolux and Bosch-Siemens both greatly improved their efficiency, along with many of the smaller European companies. The European companies laid off large numbers of workers, built up their core businesses, and concentrated on generating profits. Bosch-Siemens expanded its overseas operations while keeping production local and the company managed to raise its non-German revenue by more than 30% in five years. Electrolux shed all of its non-appliance businesses and cut its workforce by 15,000, closing 25 factories. Electrolux invested in new factories and achieved higher efficiency. Both Electrolux and Bosch-Siemens increased their profitability.

Across the industry, European plants doubled their output from 1990 to 1998 and cut the time needed to build a washing machine from five days to eight hours. Companies embraced computer-aided design techniques to speed the development of products. In 1997, it was reported that a new washing machine could move from the ideas stage to the shops in just 2-1/2 years, twice as fast as only a few years before. The "value gap" which existed between appliances in the United States and Europe also closed by an estimated 15% to 20% for all appliances.[23]

19. Steinmetz and Quintanilla, A:6.
20. Steinmetz and Quintanilla, A:1, A:6.
21. "Holistic Strategy," W-3.
22. Steinmetz and Quintanilla, A:6.

23. Jancsurak, Joe, "Marketing: Phase 2," *Appliance Manufacturer,* Feb. 1995: W-10.

The state of the retail sector also changed. Traditionally, the producers had determined price in the European appliance industry. These producers had been able to reduce their costs through greater operational efficiencies and had allowed the retailers to keep their margins constant. However, by the 1990s, the number of retail outlets across Europe had fallen significantly, giving the larger surviving retailers more power when dealing with manufacturers. Recession in Europe also caused consumers to become more cost-conscious, and brands such as the low-price firm Indesit won considerable market share.

With all companies becoming more efficient as producers, there was a shift towards product innovation as the basis for competition. For example, Whirlpool increased the size of the entrance of its front-loading washing machines, thus allowing clothes to be pushed into the machine more easily and contributing to increased sales. Companies also attempted to improve customer service and to create appliances that were more friendly to the environment. Such changes were not going unnoticed, but the industry appeared to be extremely mature. Not only were new entrants, such as Whirlpool, GE, Daewoo of South Korea, and Malaysia's Sime Datby, trying to build up sales from a small base, but the traditional European producers had become more aggressive. More than that, few were making tactical or strategic errors. Seeing the increased costs of competition and the growing intensity of rivalry, Maytag left the European market in 1995, selling its Hoover unit at a $130 million loss. Leonard Hadley, Maytag's chairman, commented, "Europe isn't an attractive place to try to go in and dislodge the established players."[24]

Eastern Europe was seen as the next great battleground and Whirlpool expanded its operations in 1996 to newly developing countries in Eastern and Central Europe. In 1997, Whirlpool opened new offices in Romania, Bulgaria, Turkey, Morocco, and South Africa from its European headquarters. Sales in the initial years were disappointing.

Problems for Whirlpool

Whirlpool's sales leveled off in the mid-1990s and profits began to fall. Sales only increased 13% from 1990 to 1996, which was far from the levels management had expected. The company initiated a major restructuring in 1995 and laid off 2,000 employees. The restructuring did not solve the problems and in 1996, the company's European operations recorded a loss of $13 million. Between 1995 and 1997 the company also witnessed a rise in materials and labor costs. Exhibit 3 shows Whirlpool's stock prices versus the S&P 500. Exhibits 4 and 5 show Whirlpool corporate and business unit financial information.

24. Steinmetz and Quintanilla, A:6.

EXHIBIT 3

Whirlpool Share Price*

*The Whirlpool share price is on the bottom.

— WHR
— S&P 500

EXHIBIT 4

Whirlpool Financial Statements

Balance Sheet	Dec-98 US$MM	Dec-97 US$MM	Dec-96 US$MM	Dec-95 US$MM
Cash	636	578	129	149
Securities	0	0	0	0
Receivables	1,711	1,565	2,366	2,117
Allowances	116	156	58	81
Inventory	1,100	1,170	1,034	1,029
Current Assets	3,882	4,281	3,812	3,541
Property and Equipment, Net	5,511	5,262	3,839	3,662
Depreciation	3,093	2,887	2,041	1,883
Total Assets	7,935	8,270	8,015	7,800
Current Liabilities	3,267	3,676	4,022	3,829
Bonds	1,087	1,074	955	983
Preferred Mandatory	0	0	0	0
Preferred Stock	0	0	0	0
Common Stock	83	82	81	81
Other Stockholders' Equity	1,918	1,689	1,845	1,796
Total Liabilities and Equity	7,935	8,270	8,015	7,800

Income Statement	Dec-98 US$MM	Dec-97 US$MM	Dec-96 US$MM	Dec-95 US$MM
Total Revenues	10,323	8,617	8,696	8,347
Cost of Sales	9,596	8,229	8,331	6,311
Other Expenses	39	377	65	31
Loss Provision	45	160	63	50
Interest Expense	260	168	165	141
Income Pre Tax	564	−171	130	242
Income Tax	209	−9	81	100
Income Continuing	310	−46	156	209
Discontinued	15	31	0	0
Extraordinary	0	0	0	0
Changes	0	0	0	0
Net Income	325	−15	156	209
EPS Primary	$4.09	($0.20)	$2.08	$2.80
EPS Diluted	$4.06	($0.20)	$2.07	$2.76

Sources: Whirlpool Annual Reports

EXHIBIT 5

Whirlpool Business Unit Sales and Operating Profit

	Sales (in millions of US dollars)			
	Dec-97	**Dec-96**	**Dec-95**	**Dec-94**
North America	5263	5310	5093	5048
Europe	2343	2494	2428	2373
Asia	400	461	376	205
Latin America	624	268	271	329
Other	−13	−10	−5	−6
Total	8617	8523	8163	7949

	Operating Profit (in millions of US dollars)			
	Dec-97	**Dec-96**	**Dec-95**	**Dec-94**
North America	546	537	445	522
Europe	54	−13	92	163
Asia	−62	−70	−50	−22
Latin America	28	12	26	49
Restructuring charge	343	−30		−248
Business dispositions	−53			60
Other	159	−158	−147	−154
Total	11	278	366	370

Sources: Whirlpool Annual Reports

Whirlpool announced a second restructuring in 1997. The company planned to cut a further 4,700 jobs worldwide, or about 15% of its workforce, mostly in Europe. In 1998, WEBV had a 12% market share and held the number three market position. However, in 1998, the profit margin had reduced further to 2.3%, compared to 10% in the U.S.

Whirlpool's managers blamed a number of causes—reduced consumer demand, poor economic growth, the rising Italian lira, intense competition, and even the European Monetary Union—for its poor performance in Europe but shareholders were unimpressed. Indeed, Scott Graham, analyst at CIBC Oppenheimer, commented in 1998, "The strategy has been a failure. Whirlpool went in big [into overseas markets] and investors have paid for it."

In 1998, Whirlpool's goals remained the same, but the timeframes for delivery grew. Whitwam attributed the performance to temporary problems in the newer regions of activity and believed that Whirlpool was now coming through the challenges." He and the rest of his management team remained resolute.

> We were convinced when we first bought [the Philips operation] and we're convinced now. The benefits from Europe have begun to flow. But they have yet to be recognized.[25]

Asian Expansion

Whirlpool's strategy in Asia consisted of five main points: partnering to build win-win relationships; attracting, retaining, and developing the best people; ensuring quality in all aspects of the business; exceeding customer needs and expectations; and offering four key products (refrigerators, washers, microwaves, and air conditioners). Although Whirlpool announced in 1987 a full-scale cooperation with Dai-ichi, a department store retailer in Japan, the company

25. Steinmetz and Quintanilla, A:6.

decided to focus its efforts in Asia primarily on India and China. There were two main reasons for this decision. First, recent changes in government regulations in both countries made it possible for foreign corporations to own a controlling interest in a manufacturing company. Second, the large populations of India and China reduced the risk of establishing large-scale operations there.

Whirlpool decided that the best way to enter the Asian market was through joint ventures, as they would allow the company to quickly establish a manufacturing presence in Asia. Once it had accomplished this goal, Whirlpool planned to build its own manufacturing facilities in the region. In 1987, Whirlpool announced an agreement with Sundram Clyton of India to manufacturer compact washers for the Indian market, a joint venture which later became known as Whirlpool Washing Machines Limited. In 1993, the Asian group established regional headquarters in Tokyo and a pan-Asian marketing, product development, and technology center in Singapore.

Whirlpool intensified its Asian acquisition strategy in 1995 with various acquisitions and joint ventures in both India and China. The company bought controlling interest in Kelvinator in India, combined it with Whirlpool Washing Machines Limited, and renamed the new entity Whirlpool of India (WOI). In addition to giving Whirlpool a 56% interest in WOI, the Kelvinator purchase gave the company direct access to more than 3,000 trade dealers in India. Between 1994 and 1995, the company also set up four joint ventures in China, as it believed that China's market for appliances was likely to equal or surpass that of North America within ten years. By 1996, Whirlpool's investment in Asia had reached $350 million and they employed over 12,000 people. In 1997, the Asian businesses generated over $400 million in sales.

Despite its investments, however, the company suffered operating losses in Asia of $70 million in 1996 and $62 million in 1997. In 1997, Whirlpool decided to restructure its Chinese operations when overcapacity in the refrigerator and air-conditioning markets drove prices down significantly. In 1997, Whirlpool decided to find strategic alternatives for the two money-losing joint ventures which catered to these two markets.

Smaller Chinese companies were also seizing considerable market share away from the multinational foreign competition. Haier, a Chinese producer of air conditioners, microwave ovens, refrigerators, and

dishwashers publicly announced plans to become a global brand by 2002 and had already expanded into Indonesia and the Philippines. In addition, the Chinese government was strongly encouraging consumers to "buy Chinese."[26] Too many producers were making similar goods, and production soon outpaced demand. For example, although Whirlpool believed it would take approximately five to six years for the market to become saturated, the refrigerator and air conditioning markets were deemed saturated just two years after Whirlpool established its joint ventures in China. In addition, the company's Asian operations produced products of poorer quality than its Japanese rivals.[27]

Competition and overcapacity were not the only problems for Whirlpool. The company had overestimated the size of the market. The Chinese middle class that could afford new home appliances numbered only about 120 million, and there was no tradition in China of changing appliances that worked properly.

Once in China, Whirlpool also realized that it had not properly understood the distribution system. The company discovered that there were huge geographical distances between Chinese cities and that the country lacked strong distribution channels. The company had not expected to face major problems with telecommunications and, despite the country's huge labor supply, Whirlpool had difficulties finding qualified people for its factories.

The situation in India was similar. Despite having invested heavily in advertising and promotions, Whirlpool blamed overcapacity and difficult trading conditions in the refrigerator sector for its losses. Nevertheless, Whitwam remained confident:

> Our lower cost structure and focus on the remaining majority-owned joint ventures in China, combined with our strong market position in India and Asia-Pacific sales subsidiaries, leave Whirlpool well positioned for future growth and profitability in this region . . . Our growing knowledge of Asia and ability to draw on the other global resources of Whirlpool will lead to continued improvement in our operating performance in 1998 and beyond, especially as we manage through a difficult market and economic environment.[28]

26. Shuchman, Lisa, "Reality Check," *Wall Street Journal,* 1998 April 30: Global Investing Section: 1.
27. Vlasic, Bill and Zachary Schiller. "Did Whirlpool Spin Too Far Too Fast?" *Business Week,* 24 June 1996: 136.
28. Whirlpool Corporation. Annual Report, 1997.

Whirlpool continued to invest money in India and committed over $100 million to build a new plant near Pune to produce chlorofluorocarbon-free and frost-free refrigerators for the Indian market. The company began construction of the new facility in 1997 and the factory began commercial production in the first quarter of 1998.

Latin American Expansion

Throughout most of the 1990s, Brazil was Whirlpool's most profitable foreign operation.[29] The company first bought into the Brazilian market in 1957 and held equity positions in three companies: Brasmotor S.A., Multibras, and Embraco. These companies held a 60% market share and after 40 years of operating in Brazil, had extremely high brand recognition and brand loyalty. Whirlpool took over Philips Argentine subsidiary, SAGAD, in 1992. In the mid-90s, sales and profit figures were good, with sales up 28% in 1994–1995, and 15% in 1996. In 1997, Brazilian operations recorded approximately $78 million in earnings.

Because Latin America had lower appliance penetration rates than Europe and the United States (e.g., only 15% of Brazilian homes owned microwaves, compared with 91% in the United States), the region appeared to be a good target for expansion. By the mid-1990s, Latin America was beginning to achieve economic stability, and growth was sure to follow. Consumers felt the same way. Many consumers were now able to replace old and worn-out appliances using budget plans and credit arrangements.

In 1997 in Brazil, Whirlpool spent $217 million to increase its equity share in Brasmotor from 33% to 66%. Whirlpool then invested another $280 million in 1997 and 1998 to renew plants and product lines. The company introduced data transfer systems, flexible production lines, and launched new products. Shortly after Whirlpool made these large investments in Brazil, however, interest rates in the country began to climb. The Brazilian government doubled interest rates in October 1997 and again in 1998. As a result, the currency depreciated and the economy suffered. In real terms, the *real* fell more than 50% in the six months

prior to January 1999. Total foreign investment in Brazil slumped, and the country was eventually forced to request a $41.5 billion credit line from the International Monetary Fund in order to help rescue the economy.

Worse yet, Whirlpool's market research told them that consumers had reacted quickly to the economic problems. Many were afraid of job cuts in the worsening economy and were wondering whether Brazil would resort to the traditional solution of printing money to solve the economic problems. Consumers foresaw inflation and realized that they would not be able to afford to purchase Whirlpool's appliances, especially on credit. As Antonio da Silva, a thirty-seven-year-old maintenance worker said, "I'm afraid to pay over many months because you don't know if interest rates or inflation will rise again."[30]

In 1998, Whirlpool's Brazilian sales fell by 25%, or $1 billion.[31] Equally important, Whirlpool's *real* reserves had shrunk in value against the dollar, and the company was expecting inflationary pressures. As a result, in late 1998 the company announced more restructuring to its Latin American operations. Whirlpool immediately cut 3,200 jobs (about 25% of the workforce) to improve efficiency, and the company planned to cut out levels in the production chain in its seven factories in Brazil, Argentina, and Chile. At the same time, the company increased its marketing efforts in the region.

As of 1998, Whirlpool was still confident of a return to profitability in Latin America. The company believed that industry shipments to Brazil in 1999 would equal those in 1997. *Business Week* characterized the company as bullish:

> The experience of surviving Brazil's many debt crises, bouts of hyperinflation, and military governments has given Whirlpool a been-there, done-that aura of confidence.[32]

But, given Whirlpool's poor showing in the earlier phases of its globalization plan, it still had far to go in convincing the many sceptics and disappointed shareholders that globalization was the best strategy. Many analysts were unsure whether Whirlpool's self-confidence was actually deserved or if it was little more than self-delusion.

29. Katz, Ian, "Whirlpool: In the Wringer," *Business Week*, 14 Dec. 1998: 83.

30. Katz, 83.
31. Katz, 83.
32. Katz, 87.

41 "You Push the Button, We Do the Rest": From Silver Halide to Infoimaging at Eastman Kodak

---

This case was prepared by Gareth R. Jones, Texas A&M University.

In April 2002, Daniel Carp, the chief executive officer (CEO) of the Eastman Kodak Company, was reflecting on Kodak's situation. Kodak had just reported a 74 percent drop in first-quarter earnings on a 9 percent decline in sales, with no growth in sales for 2002 in sight, and Kodak's stock had dropped by 10 percent. Was Kodak's new "infoimaging" business model—based on strategies to counter the threats posed to Kodak's traditional silver halide–based technology by the convergence of imaging and digital information technology—working? Did the company have the digital products in place to rebuild its profitability and fulfill its "You press the button, we do the rest" promise? Or, after ten years of declining sales and profits, was the company just on the verge of another downward slope in the face of intense global competition on all its product fronts? Carp, a thirty-year Kodak veteran, thought it was a pity that Colby Chandler, Kodak's CEO in the late 1980s, had chosen to lessen Kodak's dependence on the photo-

This case is intended to be used as a basis for class discussion rather than as an illustration of either effective or ineffective handling of the situation. Reprinted by permission of the author.

graphic products industry and counter competition from other imaging techniques by engaging in an ambitious program of diversification. If only that money had been invested early in digital photographic technology . . .

Kodak's History

Eastman Kodak Company was incorporated in New Jersey on October 24, 1901, as successor to the Eastman Dry Plate Company, the business originally established by George Eastman in September 1880. The Dry Plate Company had been formed to develop a dry photographic plate that was more portable and easier to use than other plates in the rapidly developing photography field. To mass-produce the dry plates uniformly, Eastman patented a plate-coating machine and began to manufacture the plates commercially. Eastman's continuing interest in the infant photographic industry led to his development in 1884 of silver halide paper–based photographic roll film. Eastman capped this invention with his introduction of the first portable camera in 1888. This camera used his own patented film, which was developed using his own proprietary method. Thus Eastman had gained control of all the stages of the photographic process. His breakthroughs made possible the development of photography as a mass leisure activity. The popularity of the "recorded images" business was immediate, and sales boomed. Eastman's inventions revolutionized the photographic industry, and his company was uniquely placed to lead the world in the development of photographic technology.

From the beginning, Kodak focused on four primary objectives to guide the growth of its business: (1) mass production to lower production costs, (2) maintaining the lead in technological developments, (3) extensive product advertising, and (4) the development of a multinational business to exploit the world market. Although common now, those goals were revolutionary at the time. In due course, Kodak's yellow boxes could be found in every country in the world. Preeminent in world markets, Kodak operated research, manufacturing, and distribution networks throughout Europe and the rest of the world. Kodak's leadership in the development of advanced color film for simple, easy-to-use cameras and in quality film processing was maintained by constant research and development in its many research laboratories. Its huge volume of production allowed it to obtain economies of scale. Kodak was also its own supplier of the plastics and chemicals needed to produce film, and it made most of the component parts for its cameras.

Kodak became one of the most profitable American corporations, and its return on shareholders' equity averaged 18 percent for many years. To maintain its competitive advantage, it continued to invest heavily in research and development in silver halide photography, remaining principally in the photographic business. In this business, as the company used its resources to expand sales and become a global business, the name *Kodak* became a household word signifying unmatched quality. By 1990, approximately 40 percent of Kodak's revenues came from sales outside the United States.

Starting in the early 1970s, however, and especially in the 1980s, Kodak ran into major problems, reflected in the drop in return on equity. Its preeminence was being increasingly threatened as the photographic industry and industry competition changed. Major innovations had taken place within the photography business, and new methods of recording images and memories beyond silver halide technology, most noticeably digital imaging, were emerging.

The New Industry Environment

In the 1970s, Kodak began to face an uncertain environment in all its product markets. First, the color film and paper market from which Kodak made 75 percent of its profits experienced growing competition from Japanese companies, led by Fuji Photo Film Co. Fuji invested in huge, low-cost manufacturing plants, using the latest technology to mass-produce film in large volume. Fuji's low production costs and aggressive, competitive price cutting squeezed Kodak's profit margin. Finding no apparent differences in quality and obtaining more vivid colors with the Japanese product, consumers began to switch to the cheaper Japanese film, and this shift drastically reduced Kodak's market share.

Besides greater industry competition, another liability for Kodak was that it had done little internally to improve productivity to counteract rising costs. Supremacy in the marketplace had made Kodak complacent, and it had been slow to introduce productivity and quality improvements. Furthermore, Kodak (unlike Fuji in Japan) produced film in many different countries in the world rather than in a single country, and this also gave Kodak a cost disadvantage. Thus the combination of Fuji's efficient production and Kodak's own management style allowed the Japanese to become the cost leaders—to charge lower prices and still maintain profit margins.

Kodak was also facing competition on other product fronts. Its cameras had an advantage because of their ease of use as compared with complex 35-mm single-lens reflex models. They were also inexpensive. However, the quality of their prints could not compare with those of 35-mm cameras. In 1970 Kodak had toyed with the idea of producing a simple-to-use 35-mm camera but had abandoned it. In the late 1970s, however, the Japanese did develop an easy-to-use 35-mm pocket camera featuring such innovations as auto flash, focus, and rewind. The quality of the prints produced by these cameras was far superior to the grainy prints produced by the smaller Instamatic and disk cameras, and consumers began to switch to these products in large numbers.

This shift led to the need for new kinds of film, which Kodak was slow to introduce, thus adding to its product problems.

Shrinking market share due to increased competition from the Japanese was not Kodak's only problem. In the early 1980s, it introduced several less-than-successful products. In 1982 it introduced a new disk camera as a replacement for the pocket Instamatic. The disk camera used a negative even smaller than the negative of the Instamatic and was smaller and easier to use. Four and a half million units were shipped to the domestic market by Christmas, but almost a million of the units still remained on retailers' shelves in the new year. The disk cameras had been outsold by pocket 35-mm cameras, which produced higher-quality pictures. The disk camera also sold poorly in the European and Japanese markets. Yet Kodak's research showed that 90 percent of disk camera users were satisfied with the camera and especially liked its high "yield rate" of 93 percent printable pictures, compared with 75 percent for the pocket Instamatic.

A final blow on the camera front came when Kodak lost its patent suit with Polaroid Corp. Kodak had forgone the instant photography business in the 1940s when it turned down Edwin Land's offer to develop his instant photography process. Polaroid developed it, and instant photography was wildly successful, capturing a significant share of the photographic market. In response, Kodak set out in the 1960s to develop its own instant camera to compete with Polaroid's. According to testimony in the patent trial, Kodak spent $94 million perfecting its system, only to scrub it when Polaroid introduced the new SX-70 camera in 1972. Kodak then rushed to produce a competing instant camera, hoping to capitalize on the $6.5 billon in sales of instant cameras. However, on January 9, 1986, a federal judge ordered Kodak out of the instant photography business for violating seven of Polaroid's patents in its rush to produce an instant camera. The cost to Kodak for closing its instant photography operation and exchanging the 16.5 million cameras sold to consumers was over $800 million. In 1985 Kodak reported that it had exited the industry at a cost of $494 million. However, the total costs of this misadventure were finally realized on July 15, 1991, when Kodak agreed to pay Polaroid a sum of $925 million to settle out of court a suit that Polaroid had brought against Kodak for patent infringement.

On its third product front, photographic processing, Kodak also experienced problems. It faced stiff competition from foreign manufacturers of photographic paper and from new competitors in the film-processing market. Increasingly, film processors were turning to cheaper sources of paper to reduce the costs of film processing. Once again the Japanese had developed cheaper sources of paper and were eroding Kodak's market share. At the same time, many new independent film-processing companies had emerged and were printing film at far lower rates than Kodak's own official developers. These independent laboratories had opened to serve the needs of drugstores and supermarkets, and many of them offered twenty-four-hour service. They used the less expensive paper to maintain their cost advantage and were willing to accept lower profit margins in return for a higher volume of sales. As a result, Kodak lost markets for its chemical and paper products—products that had contributed significantly to its revenues and profits.

The photographic industry surrounding Kodak had changed dramatically. Competition had increased in all product areas, and Kodak, while still the largest producer, faced increasing threats to its profitability as it was forced to reduce prices to match the competition. To cap the problem, by 1980 the market was all but saturated: 95 percent of all U. S. households owned at least one camera. Facing increased competition in a mature market was not an enviable position for a company used to high profitability and growth.

The second major problem that Kodak had to confront was due not to increased competition in existing product markets but to the emergence of new industries that provided alternative means of producing and recording images. The introduction of videotape recorders, and later video cameras, gave consumers an alternative way to use their dollars to produce images, particularly moving images. Video basically destroyed the old, film-based home movie business on which Kodak had a virtual monopoly. After Sony's introduction of the Betamax machine in 1975, a video industry grew into a multibillion-dollar business. VCRs and 16-mm video cameras became increasingly hot-selling items as their prices fell with the growth in demand and the standardization of technology. The development of compact 8-mm video cameras that were much smaller than the 16-mm version, and then the later introduction of laser disks, compact disks, and, in the 1990s, DVDs were also significant developments. The vast amount of data that can be recorded on these disks gave them a great advantage in reproducing images through electronic means. It was increasingly apparent that the whole nature of the imaging and recording process was changing from chemical methods of reproduction to electronic, digital methods. Kodak's managers should have perceived this transformation to digital-based methods as a disruptive technology because its technical preeminence was based on sliver halide photography. However, as is always the case with such technologies, the real threat lies in the future.

These changes in the competitive environment caused enormous difficulties for Kodak. Between 1972 and 1982 profit margins from sales declined from 15.7 to 10.7 percent. Kodak's glossy image lost its luster. It was in this declining situation that Colby Chandler took over as chairman in July 1983.

Kodak's New Strategy

Chandler saw the need for dramatic changes in Kodak's businesses and quickly pioneered four changes in strategy: (1) he strove to increase Kodak s control of its existing chemical-based imaging businesses; (2) he aimed to make Kodak the leader in electronic imaging; (3) he spearheaded attempts by Kodak to diversify into new businesses to increase profitability; and (4) he began on major efforts to reduce costs and improve productivity. To achieve the first three objectives, he began a huge program of acquisitions, realizing that Kodak did not have the time to venture new activities internally. Because Kodak was cash rich and had low debt, financing these acquisitions was easy.

For the next six years. Chandler acquired businesses in four main areas, and by 1989 Kodak had been restructured into four main operating groups: imaging, information systems, health, and chemicals. In a statement to shareholders at the annual meeting in 1988, Chandler announced that with the recent acquisition of Sterling Drug for $5 billion the company had achieved its objective: "With a sharp focus on these four sectors, we are serving diversified markets from a unified base of science and manufacturing technology. The logical synergy of the Kodak growth strategy means that we are neither diversified as a conglomerate nor a company with a one-product family."

The way these operating groups developed under Chandler's leadership is described in the following text.

The Imaging Group

Imaging comprised Kodak's original businesses, including consumer products, motion picture and audiovisual products, photo finishing, and consumer electronics. The unit was charged with strengthening Kodak's position in its existing businesses. Kodak's strategy in its photographic imaging business has been to fill gaps in its product line by introducing new products either made by Kodak or bought from Japanese manufacturers and sold under the Kodak name. For example, in attempting to maintain market share in the camera business, Kodak introduced a new line of disk cameras to replace the Instamatic lines. However, in addition, Kodak bought a minority stake and entered into a joint venture with Chinon of Japan to produce a range of 35-mm automatic cameras that would be sold under the Kodak name. This arrangement would capitalize on Kodak's strong brand image and give Kodak a presence in this market to maintain its camera and film sales. That venture succeeded; Kodak sold 500,000 cameras and gained 15 percent of the market. In addition, Kodak invested heavily in developing new and advanced film. It introduced a whole new range of "DX" coded film to match the new 35-mm camera market film that possesses the vivid color qualities of Fuji film. Kodak had not developed vivid film color earlier because of its belief that consumers wanted "realistic" color.

Kodak also made major moves to solidify its hold on the film-processing market. It attempted to stem the inflow of foreign low-cost photographic paper by gaining control over the processing market. In 1986 it acquired Texas-based Fox Photo Inc. for $96 million and became the largest national wholesale photograph finisher. In 1987, it acquired the laboratories of American Photographic Group. In 1989, it solidified its hold on the photo-finishing market by forming a joint venture between its operations and the photo-finishing operations of Fuqua industries. The new company, Qualex Inc., had ninety-four laboratories nationwide. These acquisitions provided Kodak with a large, captive customer for its chemical and paper products as well as control over the photo-finishing market. Also, in 1986 Kodak introduced new improved one-hour film-processing labs to compete with other photographic developers. To accompany the new labs, Kodak popularized the Kodak "Color Watch" system that requires these labs to use only Kodak paper and chemicals. Kodak hoped that this would stem the flow of business to one-hour mini-labs and also establish the industry standard for quality processing.

New and improved film products, including Kodak Gold Label film and Ektachrome film, were announced during 1988, as were new types of 35-mm cameras. Kodak also formed a battery venture with Matsushita to produce a range of alkaline batteries for Kodak. A gold-topped battery was introduced to compete with Duracell's copper-top battery. Moreover, Kodak internally ventured a new lithium battery that lasted six times as long as conventional batteries. As a result of these moves, Kodak regained control over the processing end of the market and made inroads into the camera, film, and battery ends as well. In 1988, Kodak earnings were helped by the decline in value of the dollar, which forced Fuji Photo, its main competitor, to raise its prices. Consequently, Kodak was able to increase its prices. All these measures increased Kodak's visibility in the market; Kodak was protecting its mission of "You push the button, we do the rest."

Kodak also engaged in a massive internal cost-cutting effort to improve the efficiency of the photographic products group. Beginning in 1984 it introduced more and more stringent efficiency targets aimed at reducing waste while increasing productivity. In 1986, it established a baseline for measuring the total cost of waste incurred in the manufacture of film and paper throughout its worldwide operations. By 1987 it had cut that waste by 15 percent, and by 1989 it announced total cost savings worth $500 million annually.

Despite these strategic moves, the net earnings of Kodak's photographic business dropped dramatically in 1989. Although Kodak's volume and sales of its products were up, profit margins were down. Polaroid with its new One Film product was advertising aggressively to capture market share. Fuji, realizing the strong threat posed by Kodak's reassertion of industry control, responded with an intense competitive push. Both Fuji and Kodak were spending massive amounts to advertise their products in order to increase market share. In 1989, Kodak had 80 percent of the $7 billion film market while Fuji had 11 percent, but Fuji increased its advertising budget by 65 percent in 1989 to increase its market share and

simultaneously offered discount coupons on its film products. Moreover, Fuji announced plans for a major new filmmaking plant in Europe—a plant the size of its Japanese plant, which by itself can produce enough film for one-quarter of the world market. The result was a huge amount of excess capacity in global film production as Fuji, the cost leader, went all out to build global market share through aggressive pricing.

Kodak's losses mounted as it was forced to reduce prices to counter Fuji's attempts to build market share and to give multipack discounts on its products. Also to fight back, Kodak announced a fifteen-year agreement with the Walt Disney Company to use Disney characters in its advertising. However, these moves were very expensive for Kodak and slashed profits. They also offset most of the benefits from Kodak's cost-cutting effort, and the slow growth in Kodak's core photographic imaging business meant that there was little prospect of increasing profitability.

It was because of this slow industry growth that Chandler saw the need for diversification. Because sales increased only 5 percent a year and Kodak already had 80 percent of the market, it was tied to the fortunes of one industry. While this made Kodak cash-rich when competition was weak, it made Kodak poor when competition increased. This fact, plus the increasing use and growing applications of digital imaging techniques, led to Chandler's second strategic thrust: an immediate policy of acquisition and diversification into the electronic imaging business with the stated goal of being "first in both industries"—imaging and digital.

The Information Systems Group

In 1988, when Sony introduced an electronic camera that could take still pictures and then transmit them back to a television screen, it became increasingly obvious that the threat to Kodak from new electronic imaging techniques would continue to increase. Although pictures taken with video film could not match the quality achieved with chemical reproduction, the advent of compact disks offered the prospect of an imaging medium that could meet such standards in the future. To survive and prosper in the imaging business, Kodak's managers began to realize that it required expertise in a broad range of technologies to satisfy customers' recording and imaging needs—they began to see the threat posed by the disruptive technology. Kodak's managers saw that a large number of different types of electronic markets were emerging. Electronic imaging had become important in the medical sciences and in all business, technical, and research activities, driven by the advent of powerful personal computers. However, Kodak's managers did not choose to focus on imaging products and markets close to "photographs." They began to target any kind of imaging applications in communications, computer science, and various hard-copy-output technologies that they felt might be important in the imaging markets of the future. Since Kodak had no expertise in digital imaging, it began to buy companies its managers perceived did have these skills, and then pursued its strategy of marketing the products of these companies under its own famous brand name—for instance, an electronic publishing system for corporate documents and an automated microfilm-imaging system.

Kodak thus began a strategy of acquisitions and joint ventures to invest its excess cash in new imagining technologies that it hoped, somehow, would lead to increased future profitability. In the new Information Systems group several acquisitions were made, including Atex Inc., Eikonix Corp., and Disconix Inc. Atex, acquired in 1981, made newspaper and magazine electronic publishing and text-editing systems to newspapers and magazines worldwide as well as to government agencies and law firms. Eikonix Corp. was a leader in the design, development, and production of precision digital imaging systems. Further growth within the Information Systems group came with the development of the Ektaprint line of copier-duplicators. The copiers achieved good sales growth and reached new standards for quality, reliability, and productivity in the very competitive high-volume segment of the copier marketplace. In 1988, Kodak announced another major move into the copier service business. It purchased IBM's copier service business and copier sales agreements in the United States. Kodak also announced that it would market copiers manufactured by IBM while continuing to market its own Ektaprint copiers. This service agreement was eventually extended to sixteen countries outside the United States.

Kodak also announced two new image management packages: the Kodak Ektaprint Electronic Publishing System (KEEPS) and the Kodak Imaging Management System (KIMS). KIMS electronically scans, digitizes, and stores film images and transmits image information electronically. The system enables users with large, active databases to view and manipulate information stored on microfilm and magnetic or optical disks. KEEPS was a high-quality electronic publishing package that had the ability to edit, print, and update text and graphics for publications. However, the KEEPS package included a computer made by Sun Microsystems, software produced by Interleaf Inc. and just enhanced by Kodak, and a printer manufactured by Canon. In 1988, Kodak announced that it would begin marketing a "VY-P1" printer developed in a joint venture with Hitachi to make high-quality still images from VCRs and camcorders. Although Kodak had begun to spend more and more of its R&D budget on digital imaging, it still had not internally ventured any important new products.

Moreover, these new markets did not overlap much with its core photography business. With these moves, Kodak extended its activities into the electronic areas of artificial intelligence, computer systems, consumer electronics, peripherals, telecommunications, and test and measuring equipment. Kodak was hoping to gain a strong foothold in these new businesses to make up for losses in its traditional business—not to strengthen its core business.

Soon, Kodak's managers began to purchase imaging companies that made products as diverse as computer workstations and floppy disks. It aggressively acquired companies to fill in its product lines and obtain technical expertise in information systems. After taking more than a decade to make its first four acquisitions, Kodak completed seven acquisitions in 1985 and more than ten in 1986. Among the 1985 acquisitions—for $175 million—was Verbatim Corporation, a major producer of floppy disks. This acquisition made Kodak one of the three big producers in the floppy disk industry.

Entry into the information systems market, like the expansion in its core photographic products business, produced new competitive problems for Kodak. In entering office information systems, Kodak entered areas where it faced strong competition from established companies such as IBM, Apple, and Sun. The Verbatim acquisition brought Kodak into direct competition with 3M. Entering the copier market brought Kodak into direct competition with Japanese firms such as Canon that competitively marketed their own lines of advanced, low-cost products. Kodak was entering new businesses where it had little expertise, where it was unfamiliar with the competitive problems, and where there was already strong competition.

Thus Kodak was forced to retreat from some of these markets. In 1990, it announced that it would sell Verbatim to Mitsubishi. (Mitsubishi was immediately criticized by Japanese investors for buying a company with an old, outdated product line.) Kodak was soon forced to withdraw from many other areas of business by selling assets or closing operations and taking a write-off. For example, to reduce costs it sold Sayett Technology, Kodak Video programs and videocassettes, and Aquidneck Data Corporation. The decline in the performance of the Information Systems group, attributed to increased competition, a flat office systems market, and delays in bringing out new products, reduced earnings from operations from a profit of $311 million in 1988 to a loss of $360 million in 1989.

The Health Group

Kodak's interest in health products emerged from its involvement in the design and production of film for medical and dental x-rays. The growth of imaging in medical sciences offered Kodak an opportunity to apply its skills in new areas, and it began to develop such products as Kodak Ektachem—clinical blood analyzers. It developed other products—Ektascan laser imaging films, printers, and accessories—for improving the display, storage, processing, and retrieval of diagnostic images.

However, Kodak did not confine its interests in medical and health matters to imaging-based products. In 1984, it established within the health group a life sciences division to develop and commercialize new products deriving from Kodak's distinctive competencies in chemistry and biotechnology. One of the division's objectives was to focus on product opportunities in markets with relatively few competitors and high profit potential—products such as nutritional supplements that can be delivered orally or intravenously, as well as nutrition products for sale over the counter to consumers. Another objective was to develop innovative ways to control the absorption of pharmaceutical drugs into the body so that a drug would remain therapeutically effective for the optimum amount of time. A third objective involved developing new applications for existing products and processes. Kodak had in its files about 500,000 chemical formulations on which it could base new products.

Within life sciences was the bioproducts division, which engaged in joint research with biotechnology companies such as Cetus Corporation, Amgen, and Immunex. Bioproducts pursued an aggressive strategy to scale up and commercialize products based on biotechnology derived from in-house as well as outside contract research. Ventures entered into by the bioproducts division included an agreement with Advanced Genetic Sciences for the commercial production of SNOW-MAX, a product useful in making artificial snow for ski areas.

Kodak began to enter into joint ventures in the biotechnical industry, both to build its business and to enter new businesses. In April 1985 Kodak and ICN Pharmaceuticals jointly announced the formation of a research institute that would explore new biomedical compounds aimed at stopping the spread of viral infections and slowing the aging process. Kodak and ICN were to invest $45 million over six years to form and operate the Nucleic Acid Research Institute, a joint venture located at ICN's Costa Mesa, California, facility. The institute would dedicate much of its research exclusively to preclinical studies of new antiviral and anti-aging substances.

However, these advances into biotechnology proved expensive, and the uncertainty of the industry caused Kodak to question the wisdom of entering this highly volatile area. In 1988, to reduce the costs of operating the bioproducts division, a joint venture incorporating bioproducts was formed between Kodak and Cultor Ltd. of Finland, and Kodak essentially left the market. The remaining parts of the life sciences division were then folded into the health group in 1988, when Chandler completed Kodak's biggest acquisition, the purchase of Sterling Drug for more than $5 billion.

The Sterling acquisition once again totally altered Kodak's strategy for the health group. Sterling Drug is a worldwide manufacturer and marketer of prescription drugs, over-the-counter medicine, and consumer products. It has such familiar brand names as Bayer aspirin, Phillips' milk of magnesia, and Panadol. Chandler thought this merger would provide Kodak with the marketing infrastructure and international drug registration that it needed to become a major player in the pharmaceuticals industry. With this acquisition Kodak's health group became pharmaceutically oriented, its mission being to develop a full pipeline of major prescription drugs and a world-class portfolio of over-the-counter medicine.

Analysts, however, questioned the acquisition. Once again Chandler was taking Kodak into an industry where competition was intense and the industry itself was consolidating because of the massive cost of drug development. Kodak had no expertise in this area, despite its forays into biotechnology, and the acquisition was unrelated to the other activities of the health group. Some analysts claimed that the acquisition was aimed at deterring a possible takeover of Kodak and that it was too expensive.

The acquisition of Sterling dramatically increased the sales of the health group but dampened Kodak's earnings and helped lead to a reversal in profits in 1989. Moreover, by purchasing Sterling, Kodak had obtained Sterling's Lehn & Fink products division, which produced products as diverse as Lysol and Minwax wood-care products. Far from wishing to sell this division, Kodak believed that this acquisition would lead to long-term profits. Analysts asked whether this was growth without profitability.

The Chemicals Group

Established more than sixty-five years ago as a supplier of raw materials for Kodak's film and processing businesses, the Eastman Chemical Company has been responsible for developing many of the chemicals and plastics that have made Kodak the leader in the photographic industry. The company has also been a major supplier of chemicals, fibers, and plastics to thousands of customers worldwide. Kodak has been enjoying increased growth in its plastic material and resins unit because of outstanding performance and enthusiastic customer acceptance of Kodak PET (polyethylene terephthalate), a polymer used in soft-drink bottles and other food and beverage containers. The growth in popularity of 16-ounce PET bottles spurred a record year for both revenue and volume in 1985. Kodak announced the opening of a major new PET facility in England in 1988. In 1986, three new businesses were established within the chemicals group: specialty printing inks, performance plastics, and animal nutrition supplements. They all had the common objective of enabling the chemicals group to move quickly into profitable new market segments where there is the potential for growth.

In its chemical business, too, Kodak ran into the same kinds of problems experienced by its other operating groups. There is intense competition in the plastics industry, not only from U.S. firms like Du-Pont but also from large Japanese and European firms like Imperial Chemical Industries PLC and Hoech, which compete directly with Kodak for sales. In specialty plastics and PET, for example, volume increased but Kodak was forced to reduce prices by 5 percent to compete with other firms in the industry. This squeeze in profit margins also contributed to the reversal in earnings in 1989.

Logical Synergies?

With the huge profit reversal in 1989 after all the years of acquisition and internal development, analysts were questioning the existence of the "logical synergy" that Chandler claimed for Kodak's businesses. Certainly, the relative contributions of the various operating groups to Kodak's total sales differed from the past, and Kodak was somewhat less dependent on the photographic industry. But was Kodak positioned to compete successfully in the 1990s? What was the rationale for Kodak's entry into different businesses? What were the synergies that Chandler was talking about? Wasn't the improvement on profits in 1990 due to corporate restructuring to reduce costs?

Corporate Restructuring and Cost Reduction

As Chandler tackled changes in strategy, he also directed his efforts at reshaping Kodak's management style and organizational structure to (1) reduce costs and (2) make the organization more flexible and attuned to the competitive environment. Because of its dominance in the industry, in the past Kodak had not worried about outside competition. As a result, the organizational culture at Kodak emphasized traditional, conservative values rather than entrepreneurial values. Kodak was often described as a conservative, plodding monolith because all decision making had been centralized at the top of the organization among a clique of senior managers. Furthermore, the company had been operating along functional lines. Research, production, and sales and marketing had operated separately in different units at corporate headquarters and dispersed to many different global locations. Kodak's different product groups also operated separately. The result of these factors was a lack of communication and slow, inflexible decision making that led to delays in making new product decisions. When the company attempted to transfer resources between product groups, conflict often resulted, and the separate functional operations also led to poor product group relations, for managers protected their own turf at the expense of corporate goals. Moreover, there was a lack of attention to the bottom line, and management failed to institute measures to control waste.

Another factor encouraging Kodak's conservative orientation was its promotion policy. Seniority and loyalty to "mother Kodak" counted nearly as much as ability when it came to promotions. Only twelve presidents had led the company since its beginnings in the 1880s. Long after George Eastman's suicide in 1932, the company followed his cautious ways: "If George didn't do it, his successors didn't either."

Kodak's technical orientation also contributed to its problems. Traditionally, its engineers and scientists had dominated decision making, and marketing had been neglected. The engineers and scientists were perfectionists who spent enormous amounts of time developing, analyzing, testing, assessing, and retesting new products. Little time, however, was spent determining whether the products satisfied consumer needs. As a result of this technical orientation, management passed up the invention of xerography, leaving the new technology to be developed by a small Rochester firm named Haloid Company (later Xerox). Similarly, Kodak had passed up the instant camera business. Kodak's lack of a marketing orientation allowed competitors to overtake it in several areas that were natural extensions of the photography business, such as 35-mm cameras and video recorders.

Kodak's early management style, while profitable throughout the 1960s because of the company's privileged competitive position, was thus creating difficulties. With its monopoly in the photographic film and paper industry gone, Kodak was in trouble. Chandler had to alter Kodak's management orientation. He began with some radical changes in the company's culture and structure.

Firmly committed to cost cutting, Chandler orchestrated a massive downsizing of the work force to eliminate the fat that had accumulated during Kodak's prosperous past. Traditionally, Kodak had prided itself on being one of the most "Japanese" of all U.S. companies, hiring college graduates and giving them a permanent career. Now it had to go against one of its founding principles and reduce its work force. Kodak's policy of lifetime employment

was swept out the door when declining profitability led to a large employee layoff. Chandler instituted a special early retirement program, froze pay raises, and ordered the company's first layoffs in more than a decade. By 1985, the "yellow box factory" had dropped 12,600 of its 136,000 employees. To further reduce costs in 1986, divisions were required to cut employment by an additional 10 percent and to cut budgetary expenditures by 5 percent. These measures helped, but because of Kodak's deteriorating performance, new rounds of cost cutting came in 1988 and 1989. Additional 5 percent reductions in employment aimed at saving $1 billion. The effect of these huge cuts was seen in 1990 when profits rebounded; however, it was not clear whether their effect on earnings would be short run or long run.

Although these measures had an effect on Kodak's culture, Chandler still needed to reshape Kodak's structure. In 1985 he began by shedding the old, stratified corporate structure for what he called an "entrepreneurial" approach. The first step was to reorganize the imaging group into seventeen operating units. Each of the seventeen lines of business contained all the functions necessary for success, including marketing, financial, planning, product development, and manufacturing. Each unit was treated as an independent profit center and was managed by a young executive with authority over everything from design to production. All units had the common goal of improving quality and efficiency and eliminating problems in the transfer of resources and technology among operating groups. The purpose behind this change was to eliminate the old divisional orientation, which had led to competition and reduced integration within the company. Chandler hoped the changes in organizational control and structure would promote innovation, speed reaction time, and establish clear profit goals. With this restructuring, Chandler also reduced Kodak's top-heavy management to decentralize decision making to lower levels in the hierarchy. This reorganization was a sign that the company was at last shedding its paternalistic approach to management.

With its new risk-taking attitude, Kodak also attempted to create a structure and culture to encourage internal venturing. It formed a "venture board" to help underwrite small projects and make conventional venture capital investments. In addition, the company created an "office of submitted ideas" to screen outside projects. Kodak received more than three thousand proposals, but only thirty survived the screening process. This aggressive research program led to a breakthrough in tubular silver halide grains, which improve the light-gathering capability of film. The discovery resulted in the new line of 35-mm products. However, Kodak's attempts at new venturing were generally unsuccessful. Of the fourteen ventures that Kodak created, six were shut down, three were sold, and four were merged into other divisions. One reason was Kodak's management style, which also affected its new businesses. Kodak's top managers never gave operating executives real authority or abandoned the centralized, conservative approach of the past. One example is Kodak's managing of Atex Inc., the manufacturer of desktop publishing systems that Kodak bought in 1981. Because of Kodak's overbearing management style, the top executives and employees of Atex resigned, creating serious management problems for Kodak. The Atex executives claimed that Kodak executives were hardworking but bureaucratic and did not understand the competitive nature of computer technology. Kodak managers should have been reacting to the computer marketplace weekly. They did not, and Atex executives could not handle Kodak's slow pace.

Another reason for the failure at managing new ventures and acquisitions was that Kodak did not give managers an equity stake in the new ventures, so they felt that they had no stake in the ventures' success. Having learned its lesson, Kodak announced that throughout the company pay would be more closely related to performance. For example, in 1990 up to 40 percent of a manager's annual compensation was to be based on corporate performance. Even at the middle-manager level, 15 percent of compensation was to be linked to company results. Kodak hoped by these measures to make the company more entrepreneurial and to move it along the cost reduction path.

Kodak also reorganized its worldwide facilities to reduce costs. International divisions were turning out identical products at higher cost than their counterparts in the United States. In a plan to coordinate worldwide production to increase productivity and lower costs, Kodak streamlined European production by closing duplicate manufacturing facilities and centralizing production and marketing operations, and it also brought some foreign manufacturing home. As a result, Kodak gained $55 million in productivity savings. However, Fuji's new European facility posed a severe challenge. Starting from scratch and employing production techniques learned from low-cost Japanese operations, Fuji remained the clear cost leader with the ability to start a price war to increase market share.

George Fisher Changes Kodak

Chandler retired as CEO in 1989 and was replaced by his chief operating officer, Kay Whitmore, another Kodak veteran. Whitmore immediately was forced to confront the problem of dealing with the poor performance of Chandler's misguided acquisitions. As Kodak's performance continued to plunge under his leadership, however, he came under intense scrutiny from analysts, who began to question the whole logic behind Kodak's aggressive diversification efforts. Whitmore responded by hiring managers from outside Kodak to help him restructure the company, but when they proposed selling off most of Kodak's new acquisitions and laying off many more thousands of employees to reduce costs, Whitmore resisted. He, too, was entrenched in the old Kodak culture and was unwilling to take such drastic steps. Finally, after continued criticism from analysts, Kodak's board of directors ousted Whitmore as CEO and in 1993 George Fisher, the first outsider to lead Kodak in 117 years, became the new CEO. George Fisher left his job as CEO of Motorola to join Kodak. At Motorola, he had been credited with leading that company into the digital age, and it was his expertise in the digital sector that led to his appointment. Fisher was given 2 million Kodak stock options at around $90 a share, Kodak's then stock price, to reward him for what many felt would be a fast turnaround in Kodak's fortunes.

Fisher's strategy was to reverse Chandler's diversification into any industry in the digital sector. Kodak's principal thrust, Fisher decided, should be to strengthen its competencies in the digital photography industry. However, given that Kodak had spent so much money on making its acquisitions, the question was what to do about its other businesses, especially as the company was now burdened with increasing debt from its acquisitions and falling profits. Fisher's solution was dramatic.

Looking at Kodak's four business groups, he decided that the over-the-counter drugs component of the Health Products Group was doing nothing to add value to Kodak's profitability, and he decided to divest Sterling Drugs to pay off debt. Soon, all that was left of this group was the health imaging business. Fisher also decided that the Chemicals Group, despite its expertise in the invention and manufacture of chemicals, no longer fitted with his new digital strategy. Henceforth Kodak would buy its chemicals in the open market, and in 1995 he spun this group off and gave each Kodak shareholder a share in the new company, Eastman Chemicals, whose stock price soon increased rapidly. The Information Systems Group with its diverse businesses was a more difficult challenge; the issue was which components would help promote Kodak's new digital strategy and which were superfluous and could be sold off. In the end, Fisher decided that Kodak would focus on building its presence in the document imaging industry with a focus on photocopiers, commercial inkjet printers, and commercial digital imaging and either sold or closed down the various other parts of the business that did not fit this theme. However, he also decided to outsource the sales and service end of the business, and in 1995 Kodak announced an agreement with Danka Business Systems for them to sell and service Kodak's high-volume copiers throughout the United States and Canada.

With these actions, within two years Fisher had pared down Kodak's debt by $7 billion, dumped chemicals and health, and boosted Kodak's stock price—all this signaled good times ahead. However, Fisher still had to confront the problems inside Kodak's core photographic imaging group, and here the solution was neither easy nor quick. Kodak was still plagued by high operating costs that were still 27 percent of annual revenue, and Fisher knew he needed to get these costs down to about 15 to 20 percent to compete effectively in the digital world. Kodak's work force had shrunk to 95,000 by 1993, and he wanted to avoid further layoffs, which would demoralize an already shaken work force. But with Kodak's current revenue in 1995 of $16 billion, this would mean finding ways to squeeze another couple of billion out of operating costs.

At the same time, Fisher also knew that Kodak had to invest more and more of its R&D budget into digital imaging. Kodak had no particular competency in making either digital cameras or the software necessary to allow them to operate efficiently. Soon Kodak was spending over $400 million a year on digital projects. However, new digital products were slow to come on line. Also, consumers were slow to embrace digital photography, the cameras were expensive and bulky, the software was complicated to use, and printing digital photographs was both expensive and difficult at this time. Neither Kodak nor its customers had ramped up the digital photography learning curve, and by 1997 its digital business was still losing over $100 million a year.

To compound matters, in 1995 Fuji Film decided to open up a state-of-the-art filmmaking operation in the United States to further attack the $6 billion film market with "home-grown" products. Fuji also snatched the biggest photo-finishing contract in the United States, the Wal-Mart account, away from Kodak in 1995, and soon after sales of Fuji film in Wal-Mart started to rocket. Through 1995–1997 Fuji also lowered its prices and started a price war, and by 1997 Kodak's share of the U.S. film market had fallen to 78 percent, down a further 4 percent from 1996, while Fuji's had risen to 14 percent. This loss of four points cost Kodak about $125 million in lost sales, and sales of private-label film were beginning to increase, putting more pressures on revenues and costs.

To speed product development, Fisher reorganized Kodak's product groups into fourteen autonomous business units based on serving the needs of distinct groups of customers, such as those for its health products or commercial products. The idea was to decentralize decision making, thus putting managers closer to their major customers and escaping from Kodak's suffocating centralized style of decision making. Fisher also changed the top managers in charge of the film and camera units; however, he did not bring in many outsiders to spearhead the new digital efforts. This new emphasis on customer groups also meant that overhead costs rose because each unit had its own complement of functions; thus sales forces and so on were duplicated.

Fisher had been performing the roles of Kodak's chairman, CEO, president, *and* COO—something that analysts now started to complain about bitterly. How could Kodak get rid of its centralized decision-making style when its new leader apparently wanted to centralize all important decision making in his own hands? The reorganization into fourteen autonomous business units had not decentralized control to business unit leaders, and Fisher and his top management team were still overseeing all important strategy decisions. This explained the slow pace of change at Kodak. Thus while Fisher had brought Kodak's focus back to its core photography business, he had not put in place the infrastructure that would allow its managers to achieve its new digital mission.

In 1996, Fisher finally realized his dilemma, and with pressure from the board Daniel A. Carp was named Kodak's president and COO, the appointment to COO meaning that he was Fisher's heir apparent as Kodak's CEO. Carp was a Kodak veteran who had spearheaded the global consolidation of its operations and its entry into major new international markets such as China. He was widely credited with having had a major impact on Kodak's attempts to fight Fuji on a global level and help it to maintain its market share. Henceforth, Kodak's Digital and Applied Imaging, Business Imaging, and Equipment manufacturing—almost all its major operating groups—would now report to Carp. Carp also retained control of the Greater China region, where potential future film sales were seen as crucial to Kodak's future in its battle with arch-rival Fuji.

However, Kodak's revenues and profits continued to decline during the mid to late 1990s. It was slowly but steadily losing market share in its core film business to Fuji, but now generic film brands were also attracting customers and putting squeezes on profit margins. By 2000 analysts estimated it only had 66 percent percent of the U.S. market. Although the major price war with Fuji was over, sales of private-label film were still rising, and Kodak was periodically forced to use tactics such as multipack price discounts and rebates to prevent even further erosions to its market share, even at the cost of profits. Fisher knew that Kodak must preserve its market share to protect its future profitability and to give time both for it to develop its own digital competencies and for customers to develop an understanding and appetite for digital cameras. Meanwhile, the quality of the pictures taken by digital cameras was advancing rapidly as more and more pixels were being crammed into them. Also, at the low end, the price of a basic digital camera was falling rapidly because of economies of scale in production. Perhaps, finally, the digital photography market was taking off, but would Kodak be able to meet the challenge?

Despite early enthusiasm from analysts, Kodak's slow progress on all fronts and Fisher's leadership had become a major disappointment. When in July 1997 Fisher announced poor second-quarter results, many analysts and shareholders who had bought into his new strategy for Kodak began to bail out. Its share price soon tumbled to below $70 from $90, and Fisher's stock options that had been granted at $90 were now valueless at this price. Many analysts wondered if Kodak's board had been right in February 1997 to extend Fisher's contract for three more years to December 31, 2000.

Carp's Growing Influence

With Carp now in control of both Kodak's digital and global operations, the pace of change started to quicken. In 1997, Kodak announced it would open an office of the COO in Hong Kong to capitalize on trends in emerging markets, especially because of China's low-cost manufacturing advantages. In addition, in April 1997 Kodak increased its stake in the Japanese camera manufacturer Chinon to 50.1 percent effectively taking control of the company that now was making its advanced digital cameras and scanners. In 1997, Kodak announced it would operate the largest photo lab in the world in Fuji's home territory at the 1998 Olympic Winter Games in Nagano, Japan. It would loan all journalists its new digital cameras and provide them with the ability to scan ordinary negatives, convert their pictures into digital form, and send them anywhere around the world. This was a major advertising coup for Kodak and promoted its rapidly developing digital capabilities.

In 1998, Kodak announced its lowest-priced-yet digital camera with "megapixel" (million pixels per inch) image quality. This camera also, looked and operated like a conventional point-and-shoot camera. In the same month Kodak bought Picturevision Inc., whose digital Photonet online network products, combined with Kodak's brand name, would attract more customers who could now scan their pictures into its digital network, transmit the images and share them with others, and also receive outputs ranging from reprints to enlargements. Photo retailers also named Kodak's digital picture–maker kiosks the "top product of the year." Customers could take their ordinary photographs and use the kiosks to remove red eye, do quick and easy color corrections, and zoom or crop to select and print the best part of a photo. Essentially, Kodak was using these kiosks and to help customers learn about the advantages of digital photography and to help develop the market.

Kodak and Intel also formed an agreement to use Intel digital scanning equipment in Kodak's Qualex photo-finishing labs to make it easy for customers to put photos onto CD-ROM for use in home computers. In 1998, America Online and Kodak announced a strategic alliance to offer AOL members an exclusive online service, "You've Got Pictures," whereby AOL members could have their regular processed pictures delivered in digital format to their AOL mailbox. Customers were becoming increasingly familiar with how the new digital products worked, and Kodak was in the forefront of online efforts to capture customers and promote the Internet for transmission of digital images.

Thus Kodak was beginning to make steady progress in its "infoimaging mission." Under Carp's leadership its digital cameras were growing in popularity, in large part because of its developing competencies in making easy-to-use camera-printer software. Also, its digital kiosks and photo-finishing operations were being increasingly visited by customers, and their number was increasing rapidly both in the United States and globally. In recognition of his progress, in June 1999 Kodak's board named Carp as new CEO of Kodak, and he was to keep his other roles of president and COO. Fisher was to remain chairman until January 2001.

In the next few years Kodak's developing digital skills led to new products in all its major businesses. In 1999, its Health Imaging group announced the then fastest digital image management system for echocardiography labs. It also entered the digital radiography market with three state-of-the-art digital systems for capturing x-ray images. Its Document Imaging group announced several new electronic document management systems. It also teamed up with inkjet maker Lexmark to introduce the stand-alone Kodak Personal Picture Maker by Lexmark, which could print color photos from both compact flash cards and Smart Media. Its Commercial and Government Systems group announced advanced new high-powered digital cameras for uses such as in space and in the military. This group also became increasingly involved with Japanese Sanyo in developing full-color, active-matrix, organic electroluminescent (OEL) displays, which are much easier to view than conventional liquid crystal displays (LCDs). OEL displays are also as thin as a dime and require much less power. Since they are perfectly matched to mobile digital devices such as Smart Phones and personal digital assistants (PDAs), they had a huge market potential.

With these developments, Kodak's net earnings shot up between 1998 and 2000, and its stock price recovered somewhat. However, one reason for the increase in net revenues was that the devastating price war with Fuji that had raged from 1979 to 1999 had ended as both companies saw that continuing to offer price discounts simply reduced both companies' profits. Kodak also was still not getting quickly to the market the range of new digital imaging products it needed to drive its future profitability, since there was intense competition in the core film businesses, which had traditionally given it 30 to 40 percent of its profits. Here, as in film products, Kodak's high operating costs overwhelmed the benefits it obtained from its new product introductions and hurt its bottom line—its profits were not increasing.

Kodak in the 2000s

New digital product developments and changing industry conditions in most of its markets began to punish Kodak as it entered the 2000s. In the Consumer Imaging group, for example, Kodak launched a new camera, the EasyShare, in 2001. Over 4 million digital cameras were sold in 2000 and over 6 million in 2001, and over a half-million of the easy-to-use new Kodak camera were sold. However, given the huge development costs and intense competition from Japanese companies like Sony and Canon, who also make advanced cameras and "digicams," Kodak has not yet made any money from its digital cameras. Moreover, every time it sells one it reduces demand for its high-margin film; thus Kodak is cannibalizing a profitable product for an unprofitable one!

Kodak argued that it would make more money in the future from sales of the paper necessary to print these images and from its photo-finishing operations. However, it is becoming increasingly obvious that consumers are not printing out many of the photographs they take, preferring to save many in disk form and only selecting and printing out the few best ones to send to their friends. With chemical films, one could not pick and choose; the whole roll had to be developed. So revenues are not increasing on this front. Moreover, it is the ink sellers such as Hewlett-Packard (HP) and Lexmark, who have been charging monopoly prices for ink cartridges, that have been making the money in printing images, and Kodak has failed to use its strengths in chemicals to get into the printer ink business.

On the photo-finishing end, Kodak's future revenues and profits depend on it maximizing the number of its in-store kiosks or the number of photo-finishing contracts with large chain stores. After Kodak lost the Wal-Mart contract to Fuji, it signed new agreements with Walgreen's (the second largest U.S. film processor, with over three thousand stores) and with Kmart. It also operated its own Fox and Qualex photo-finishing labs. However, in 2001, Kmart declared Chapter 11 bankruptcy, and the Fox photo store chain, which was primarily finishing traditional roll film, went bankrupt, causing a large loss to Kodak. To compound matters, in June 2002 it was reported that Walgreen's was testing Fuji's new photo-finishing laboratory system in thirty of its stores and that it might award this important contract to Fuji when it came up for renewal sometime in 2002.

While Kodak is fighting back with its own advanced digital finishing labs, by 2002 advances in digital photo-finishing technology had brought down the price of digital kiosks so far that in the future an easy-to-use kiosk is expected to be found in every corner store. However, there are other major players in the market. Hewlett-Packard, long a leader in printing, has also developed state-of-the-art consumer photo-finishing products. Indeed, Kodak has teamed up with HP to unveil Phogenix, a joint partnership program for on-site photo finishing using HP's print technology, which will provide a product indistinguishable from the silver halide product. Fuji and Olympus have also developed their own systems that they are aggressively marketing.

In fact, in June 2002, recognizing that Fuji was gaining a competitive edge in the vital photo-finishing systems market, Kodak announced that it was buying key components of its new digital system from Agfa, a European imaging firm, since it did not have the time to develop them itself. This suggests that Kodak's technology is no better than that of competitors, and it might be even behind that of competitors like Fuji. Thus it is not clear that Kodak has a lead in all the activities—cameras, software, paper, and photo finishing—necessary to dominate the photography market as it had in the past. It does have its powerful brand name going for it, however,

which is why it has been so concerned to protect its market share at any cost to its profits.

At the industry level, the emergence of powerful buyers in many markets has seriously hurt Kodak's performance. In photo finishing, large store chains like Wal-Mart and Walgreen's are in a strong bargaining position and can threaten Kodak's profitability (it has been estimated that 10 percent of Kodak's photo-finishing operations are with Walgreen's). This same situation occurred in the health imaging industry. Here, Kodak's state-of-the-art imaging products were widely expected to generate large revenues and boost its profitability. However, after a good start, in 2000 Kodak faced the problem of bargaining over prices with Novation Group Purchasing organization, a major buyer of health equipment, and therefore a powerful buyer as well. Kodak was forced to slash its prices to win the contract against agile competitors, and this experience was repeated with many other large health care providers. So intense was competition in this segment that in 2001 sales of laser printers and health-related imagining products, which make up Kodak's second biggest business, fell 7 percent while profit in the segment fell 30 percent, causing a large drop in Kodak's share price.

While in 2001 Kodak had over $19 billion in revenues, in 2002 it was expected to earn around $13 billion, and its profits have stagnated. By early 2002, analysts were once again beginning to wonder if Kodak under Carp was really faring any better than Kodak under Fisher. In an embarrassing turn of events, Kodak's new COO, Patricia Russo, a well-respected executive who had left Lucent to take over the important job of restructuring Kodak, abruptly left the company and returned to Lucent. Analysts once again attributed this to Kodak's entrenched, inbred, and unresponsive management that persists in doing all it can to frustrate real efforts to reduce costs and streamline its operations. For despite all the advances in its digital skills, Kodak is still burdened with high operating costs, well out of proportion with its declining revenues. In 2000, after its profits fell drastically, it announced another two thousand job cuts, and in 2001 it announced another five thousand, for a total of seven thousand, bringing Kodak's work-force down to about seventy-eight thousand.

In 2001 Carp also announced another major reorganization of Kodak's businesses in line with a plan suggested by Russo before her departure. To give it a sharper focus on its products and customers, Kodak announced that it was moving from a structure based on customer groups to one based on strategic product lines. It disbanded its three global area groups and moved Entertainment Imaging into the Photography group, which now contains all its silver halide and digital photography operations. Health Imaging was to be operated as a totally self-contained stand-alone business. Commercial Imaging continues to manage its document systems and inkjet business. The Components group handles Kodak's display products and its new OLE optics business, which Kodak hopes will allow it to diversify into a high-growth product market. Thus, with this reorganization Kodak is once again involved in four distinct lines of business that appear to have little in common, as in the Chandler era.

Analysts are still wondering if the layoffs or reorganization will be enough to turn the company's performance around. The bottom line is that Kodak's film business is a huge generator of cash, but the company has so far failed either to reduce costs or to use that cash to fund entry into businesses that will generate a future stream of profits. Perhaps Kodak should sell off or spin off its health, commercial, and optics operations, eliminate its debt, and focus on reducing costs and building its digital presence in its core photography group. Amazingly enough, it still pays shareholders one of the top ten dividends of all companies in the Fortune 500. Analysts argue that it should be run for profit now, not in the future. Kodak's managers reply that the economic recession and events of 2000–2002 are to blame for a large part of its problems and that it has all the pieces in place for a sustained recovery and for dominance in the digital arena using its powerful brand name once the market has recovered. Its other businesses will only boost its future profitability. Only time will tell, but Kodak's stock price plunged in 2002 and was selling in the $30s in June—a far cry from the $90s when Fisher took over and a continuing sign of the fall of this once economic powerhouse.

REFERENCES

www.Kodak.com, *2002.*
Kodak Annual Reports, 1980–2001.
Thomas Moore, "Embattled Kodak Enters the Electronic Age," *Fortune,* August 22,1983, pp. 120–128.
"Kodak's New Lean and Hungry Look," *Business Week,* May 30, 1983, p. 33.
Charles K. Ryan, Eastman Kodak, Company Outline, Merrill Lynch, Pierce, Framer & Smith Incorporated, May 7, 1986.
John Greenwald, "Aiming for a Brighter Picture," *Time,* January 9, 1984, p. 49.
Barbara Buell, "Kodak Is Trying to Break Out of Its Shell," *Business Week,* June 10, 1985, pp. 92–95.
Barbara Buell, "Kodak Scrambles to Fill the Gap," *Business Week,* February 8, 1986, p.30.
"Kodak's New Image: Electronic Imaging," *Electron Business,* January 1986, pp. 38–43.
Barbara Buell, "A Gust of Fresh Air for the Stodgy Giant of Rochester," *Business Week,* June 10, 1985, p. 93.
"Yellow at the Edges," *Economist,* December 7, 1984, p. 90.
James S. Hirsch, "Kodak Effort at 'Intrapreneurship' Fails," *Wall Street Journal,* August 17, 1990, p. 32.
"Agfa to Supply Kodak with Lab Equipment," Yahoo.com, Friday, June 7, 2002.
Franklin Paul, "Sony to Muscle into Kodak's Digital Printing Arena," Yahoo.com, Wednesday, June 5, 2002.
"Citigroup Moves to Stress Global Products," Yahoo.com, Tuesday, June 11, 2002.
Daniel P. Palumbo, "Kodak Embraces Disruptive Technology," *Journal of Business Strategy,* July–August 2001, p. 11.
Franklin Paul, "Kodak Digital Camera, Software Sims to Ease Printing," Yahoo.com, Tuesday, May 21, 2002.
"Kodak, Walt Disney Sign Multiyear Alliance Agreement," Yahoo.com, Tuesday, May 28, 2002.
Daniel Eisenburg, "Kodak's Photo Op," *Time,* April 30, 2001, p. 46.
Emily Nelson and Joseph B. White, "Blurred Image: Kodak Moment Came Early for CEO Fisher, Who Takes a Stumble—Bet on Digital Photography Has Been a Money Loser; Fuji Is Gaining Ground—Dennis Rodman's Film Flop," *Wall Street Journal,* July 25, 1997, p. A1.
James Bandler, "Kodak Will Acquire Ofoto in a Move to Expand Services," *Wall Street Journal,* May 1, 2001, p. B9.
"Business Brief—Kmart Corp.: Retailer Teams with Kodak in an Online Photo," *Wall Street Journal,* May 9, 2001.
James Bandler, "Kodak's Net Fell 93% in Second Quarter on Weakness in Film," *Medical Divisions," Wall Street Journal,* July 18, 2001, p. B4.
Fauziah Muhtar, "Kodak Zooms In with New Digital Cameras," *Computimes Malaysia,* May 2, 2002, p. 1.
"Moody's Downgrades Kodak's Debt Rating on Digital Concerns," *Wall Street Journal,* March 20, 2002, p. B5.
Laura Heller, "PMA Highlights Print Kiosks, but Digital Imaging Steals Show," *DSN Retailing Today,* March 11, 2002, p. 6.
"Business Brief—Eastman Kodak Co.: Suit Is Filed Charging Sun with Infringement of Patents," *Wall Street Journal,* February 15, 2002, p. B8.
Andy Serwer, "Kodak: In the Noose," *Fortune,* February 4, 2002, pp. 147–148.
Adrienne Carter, "Kodak's Promising Developments," *Money,* February 2002, p. 39.
Geoffrey Smith and Faith Keenan, "Kodak Is the Picture of Digital Success," *Business Week,* January 14, 2002, p. 39.
James Bandler and Joann Lublin, "Russo's Departure Is a Blow to Kodak as It Seeks to Move into the Digital Age," *Wall Street Journal,* January 8, 2002, p. B4.
James Bandler, "Kodak Advances in Market Share of Digital Cameras," *Wall Street Journal,* December 21, 2001, p. B2.
Doug Olenick, "Kodak, Sanyo Plan to Produce OEL Flat-Panel Displays," *Twice,* December 17, 2001, p. 90.
James Bandler, "Kodak, Sanyo Agree to Make New Type of Screen Display," *Wall Street Journal,* December 4, 2001, p. B7.

James Bandler, "Kodak Will Offer Its Staff a Chance to Upgrade Options," *Wall Street Journal,* November 30, 2001, p. B7.

"Business Brief—Eastman Kodak Co.: Photo Concern Is Shutting Its Picture Vision Operation," *Wall Street Journal,* November 20, 2001.

"Eastman Kodak to Acquire Encad," *Daily Deal,* November 16, 2001.

John Hechinger, "Kodak to Reorganize Its Business Again," *Wall Street Journal,* November 15, 2001, p. B12.

James Bandler, "Kodak Stock Falls on Credit Downgrade, Signs Film Market Share Is Decreasing," *Wall Street Journal,* November 1, 2001, p. B8.

James Bandler, "Kodak Net Plumments 77% on Weak Sales," *Wall Street Journal,* October 25, 2001, p. B9.

James Bandler, "Kodak Slashes Earnings Forecast, Citing Weak Sales," *Wall Street Journal,* September 20, 2001, p. B4.

"Eastman Kodak Rating May Fall a Rung Lower," *Wall Street Journal,* July 24, 2001.

42 Restructuring Exide

This case was prepared by Charles W. L. Hill, the University of Washington.

Introduction

In March 1999, Exide Corporation announced that Robert Lutz, the flamboyant sixty-seven-year-old former Chrysler executive who helped turn that company around in the early 1990s, would become chairman, president, and chief executive officer of Exide. Lutz, an outspoken former marine known for his love of good cigars, fine wine, and flying jet fighters, would have his work cut out for him. Exide was a company in trouble. The world's largest manufacturer of lead acid batteries, the company had reportedly sacrificed profitability in its quest for market share leadership. For the financial year ending March 1999, Exide lost $9 million on global sales of $2.37 billion. A series of bank-financed acquisitions during the 1990s had left the company with a weak balance sheet, including $1.3 billion in debt that cost $100 million in annual interest payments to serve. Moreover, a price war in the lead battery industry was squeezing profit margins.

Exide's Business

Market Segments and Customers

Exide manufactures batteries for customers in two broad areas: industrial and automotive. The industrial area, which accounts for around 37 percent of Exide's revenues, is broken down

This case is intended to be used as a basis for class discussion rather than as an illustration of either effective or ineffective handling of the situation. Reprinted by permission of Charles W. L. Hill.

into two segments. One, the motive power business, is engaged in the manufacture of batteries for electric vehicles, including fork lift trucks, golf carts, wheel chairs, and electric floor cleaning equipment. The other industrial segment, network power, makes standby batteries used for backup power applications, to ensure continuous power supply in case of main (primary) power failure or outage. The largest customers here are manufacturers of telecommunications equipment, who incorporate the batteries in their equipment to ensure that it continues to function in the case of a power outage (which is why you can still make phone calls, even if you do not have power at home). A second customer group is businesses that use standby batteries in computer installations so that the computer system stays up even if the power goes down.

In the industrial motive power business, most of Exide's batteries are sold through independent lift truck dealers or sold directly to large users of lift trucks, such as Wal-Mart and Kroger. Exide's customers in the industrial network power business include manufacturers of telecommunications equipment, as well as telecommunications service providers. Customers include Lucent, Motorola, and Nokia, all major global producers of telecommunications equipment, and AT&T, British Telecom, China Telecom, Deutsche Telekom, GTE, and Nippon Telephone and Telegraph, all service providers.

The automotive area of Exide's business, which accounts for 67 percent of global revenues, is composed primarily of the manufacture and sale of lead acid batteries to automobile manufacturers and to "aftermarket" distributors. Principal OEM customers include Daimler-Chrysler, for whom Exide is the primary global battery supplier, Ford, Toyota, Mack Trucks, John Deere, Volvo, the Renault Group, Volkswagen, and BMW. Aftermarket batteries are sold principally though retail automotive parts chains and mass merchandisers. Customers in the United States include NAPA Distribution Centers, Wal-Mart, Kmart, and Les Schwab Tire. Customers in Europe include large national distributors such as Kwik Fit in the United Kingdom. In the United States, Exide batteries are sold in the aftermarket under the Exide and Champion brand names. In Europe the brand names in the aftermarket vary from country to country and include Exide, Fulmen, DETA, Tudor, SONNAK, and Centra.

Competition

Exide is the global market share leader in both the motive power and network power segments of the industrial area. Major competitors include U.K.-based Invensys's Hawker battery group, C&D Technologies (another U.S. firm), and Yuasa of Japan. In the automotive area, Exide again leads with a 36 percent share of the global market for automobile batteries (both OEM and aftermarket). Exide's largest competitors in the United States automotive segment include Delphi Automotive and Johnson Controls. In Europe, Exide faces a number of strong local competitors, including Varta, Fiamm, and Hoppeke. Price competition has long been intense in all markets, with major customers using their buying power to bargain down battery prices. Exide's financial troubles in the late 1990s, however, were due in part to an outbreak of extremely aggressive price competition in Europe.

Manufacturing, Employees, and Facilities

Lead is the principal material used in the manufacturing of batteries, accounting for about one-fifth of the cost of goods sold. Exide operates a number of lead recycling plants in both the United States and Europe. It reclaims lead from used batteries that end users returned to distributors. Exide fulfills most of its lead requirements from its recycling plants. Other key raw materials include lead oxide and bulk chemicals.

Exide employs some 20,000 people, 8,500 in the United States and approximately 10,900 in Europe.

The company operates some fifty facilities, the bulk of which are in Europe and North America, where most of the company's sales are concentrated. Exide has some fourteen manufacturing facilities in North America, sixteen in Western Europe, two in Australia, one in New Zealand, and one in Turkey. In Western Europe, there are manufacturing and lead recycling facilities in each major national market.

Lutz's Changes

Lutz moved rapidly to make a number of changes in Exide's business. One of his first decisions was to pull out of a supply agreement with Sears. Exide sold over 4.5 million batteries per year to Sears, but to get the agreement the company had to slash prices. The result was that Exide was making less from the Sears deal than it was from deals one-fifth the size. Lutz also pushed the company to shift demand from low-priced battery models to higher-priced branded products, particularly in the automotive segment. Consistent with this theme, in June 1999 Exide introduced a new lead acid battery, the Select Orbital battery. While the battery cost $125, Exide claimed that it was based on a radically new design and would retain its charge for over a year, substantially longer than a conventional battery. Moreover, while a conventional battery has a life of around thirty to forty months, Exide claimed that the Orbital would last five years and stand up to far more abuse.

Lutz also pushed the company to quickly solve its legal problems. The company was being sued in the United States for recycling old batteries and selling them as new through distributors such as Sears. Under Lutz's direction, instead of fighting the lawsuits, Exide quickly settled them for a few million dollars and took a one-time charge against earnings.

Within some fifteen months of his arrival, Lutz had replaced the entire board of directors and the majority of senior executives in both Europe and North America. Worldwide battery product capacity had been cut by some 20 percent through plant closures, the company's debt load had been substantially pared back by issuing additional stock and using the proceeds to pay down debt, and Exide had made a major acquisition, paying $368 million in stock and cash for GNB Technologies, a major supplier in the fast-growing market for standby batteries in telecommunications and computer equipment. Perhaps the most difficult change Lutz initiated, however, was one in the organization structure of Exide's business.

Changing the Organization Structure: Product or Geography?

When he arrived at Exide, Lutz found a structure that was based on geography with ten different country organizations. The genesis of this structure was rooted in history. Many of the country organizations had previously been independent businesses that Exide had acquired in its rush to gain global market share. After being acquired, the majority continued to function as self-contained operations with their own brands, manufacturing facilities, and distribution systems. Exide managed the different subsidiaries on an arms-length basis, setting profit goals for each and awarding local executives big bonuses if they exceeded those goals.

It soon became apparent to Lutz that this structure was causing problems for Exide, particularly in Europe. When Lutz arrived, Exide's European business was losing money. The various country managers in Europe blamed the losses on significant price discounting. After talking to competitors and customers, Lutz found that there indeed was significant price discounting in Europe, but in many cases this was because different Exide subsidiaries were competing against each other for major customers. They were exporting into each other's territories or competing aggressively for a share in third countries. Thus, for example, the British subsidiary was gaining share in Australia from the German subsidiary by underselling the latter by 10 to 15 percent. Part of the blame for this competition could be laid at the feet of an incentive system that rewarded country managers for increasing the performance of their unit, irrespective of whether that was at the expense of another Exide unit.

Convinced that the structure had to change, Lutz held five management retreats between June 1999 and January 2000. "Where does our future lie?" Lutz asked the thirty senior executives assembled for the first meeting. "Does it lie in country management or in global business units?" Many of the country managers reacted with apprehension to the question. Several argued that their regions were in good shape and that any problems that existed were due to weaknesses elsewhere or to general industry conditions.

Between retreats managers working in teams were assigned to grapple with the various dilemmas con-fronting the company, using existing and alternative models of the organization as solutions. In a typical assessment, one team looked at Exide's Asian expansion strategy. It concluded that the geographic focus encouraged construction of manufacturing plants in each country Exide entered, even though it was not profitable to keep putting up plants like that. On the third retreat, the teams started to report their findings, and it quickly became apparent that many were concluding that only a product line structure could cure Exide's ills. After a vigorous debate, Lutz stood up and announced, "We don't have consensus yet. . . . But I'm going to make a decision, and we are going to a global business unit structure."

Under the proposed structure that Lutz revealed at the next meeting, six global business units replaced the geographic organization. Each business unit was built around a distinct product line, such as network power, industrial motive power, and so on. It was the global business units that were now given responsibility for major strategic and operational decisions, such as what to produce where, how much to charge customers, and selling to major regional or global customers. Country managers were given a coordinating role and the responsibility for local sales efforts and distribution.

Although by now expected, the announcement was a severe blow for many country managers. Effectively, it meant a demotion. When one country manager frowned at the announcement, Lutz looked at him and asked, "Why don't you give this a try?" "No," the manager replied, "I'm out of here!" Another country manager told a consultant: "Being a country manager is my life. It's something I've worked for my entire life. I don't see how I'll have a role going forward." Subsequently, the manager was given the option of moving from Naples to Frankfurt, for less money, or leaving the company. He chose the former option, but his family refused to move and stayed in Naples. Other country managers came out of the process quite well. Albrecht Leuschner, the head of the German unit, found himself promoted to lead the global network power business unit, which was to be headquartered in Germany.

The Acquisition of GNB Technologies

Leuschner found himself in this position for just six weeks. In May 2000, Exide acquired GNB Technologies for its fast-growing network power business and industrial motive power businesses. The acquisition gave Lutz a problem; he feared that Mitchell Bregman, the well-regarded president of GNB's operation, might leave once Exide folded his industrial battery business into its global network power and industrial motive power business units. Instead, Lutz approached Bregman and told him that after the acquisition he would retain control over the North American industrial battery business. In effect, after only six weeks, the global business unit structure was being amended. There was now a European business unit for network power headed by Leuschner, a European business unit for industrial motive power that was run out of the United Kingdom, and a North American industrial battery business headed by Bregman.

Initially, the decision gave rise to a turf battle between Leuschner and Bregman. The point of contention was over who should run China for Exide. Bregman wanted to form and direct a Chinese subsidiary, because China represented his unit's fastest-growing market. Leuschner lobbied to form a joint venture in China that would be under his command. Bregman was finally persuaded to give in to Leuschner, but only after he had been given control over South American operations and had been guaranteed control over operations in Korea, Japan, and Taiwan.

Now all parties claim that the structure is working well. The company still maintains separate industrial battery sales forces in North America and Europe, in what has become a de facto regional structure. However, teams from the European and North American units have begun making joint pitches to global customers such as Ford and Lucent.

REFERENCES

L. Chappell, "Lutz Put Exide in Recovery," *Automotive News,* August 6, 2001, p. 49.

Exide 2000 and 2001 10K filed with Securities and Exchange Commission.

J. S. Lublin, "Place vs Product: It's Tough to Choose a Management Model," *Wall Street Journal,* June 27, 2001, pp. A1, A4.

M. Maynard, "Lutz Gets a Charge Out of a New Career: Exide CEO Achieves a Dream," *USA Today,* June 1, 1999, p. 12B.

D. W. Nauss, "Ex-Chrysler Exec Robert Lutz to Head Troubled Exide Corporation," *Los Angeles Times,* November 17, 1998, p. 3.

A. Puchalsky, "Exide Makes Tough Choices in Comeback," *Wall Street Journal,* March 26, 1999.

R. Sherefkin, "New One Two Punch at Exide," *Automotive News,* June 12, 2000, p. 22.

A. Taylor, "Getting Back in the Fast Lane," *Fortune,* March 6, 2000.

43

First Greyhound, Then Greyhound Dial, Then Dial: What Will Happen in 2002?

This case was prepared by Gareth R. Jones, Texas A&M University.

It was June 2002 and Herbert Baum, Dial's CEO, was reflecting on the performance of the company since he had been brought in to engineer a turnaround in 2000. He had sold off underperforming product lines and invested heavily in building Dial's core products like Dial soap. By April 2002 he had been happy to report a rebound in Dial's earnings, which sent its share soaring from the lows it had reached in April 2001, when its earnings plunged by 69 percent due to the poor strategic decisions of his predecessor. Now the question was what to do? Should he continue to build Dial's portfolio of brand name products and strive to keep the company independent? Or, should he sell off the company, either as a whole or in parts, to other companies that would now be prepared to pay a high price for its strong brand name products? While pondering this question, Baum thought that the history of the company, which had started out as Greyhound, might provide him with some important clues.

Greyhound's Early History and Growth

Greyhound was founded in Hibbing, Minnesota, in 1914. Its first business was providing bus transportation to carry miners to work at the Mesabi Iron Range. Because Greyhound was the sole provider of bus service for these workers, it was immediately successful. In its very first year, the new corporation started expanding its routes and acquiring interests in bus companies operating near Chicago. For the next sixteen years, the young company continued purchasing interests in bus companies, extending its route structure from New York to Kansas City. In 1930, the name *Greyhound Corporation* was adopted, and the now-familiar running-dog logo was painted on the buses.

For the next twenty-seven years, Greyhound continued to acquire bus interests in order to consolidate its routes and link its various bus operations. Growth proceeded sometimes by purchase, sometimes by stock swaps, and sometimes by merger. However, the result was always the same to the traveling public: it saw more and more of the familiar running dog. By 1960, Greyhound had substantially achieved its objective of operating a bus system that could carry passengers to most destinations in the continental United States and Canada.

By 1962, however, Greyhound was facing the prospect of increasingly limited opportunities to expand its route system; in the company's favor was the fact that bus operations were generating large sums of excess cash, which could fund expansion into new businesses. So Greyhound's board of directors decided to diversify into operations outside the bus transportation industry.

This case is intended to be used as a basis for class discussion rather than as an illustration of either effective or ineffective handling of the situation. Reprinted by permission of the author.

In that same year, Greyhound began the program of acquisition that turned it into a conglomerate. It solidified its bus-manufacturing operations into Motor Coach Industries, which became the foundation of Greyhound Dial's transportation manufacturing operating division. Also in 1962, the corporation acquired Boothe Leasing Company, an enterprise that specialized in equipment leasing. Boothe Leasing was renamed Greyhound Leasing and became the core business around which Greyhound's financial services division was to be built. Thus, by the end of 1963, Greyhound Corporation was operating in three major businesses: bus transportation, bus manufacturing, and financial services. Bus manufacturing supplied buses to bus transportation as well as to other bus companies.

Acquisitions Between 1966 and 1970

Gerry Trautman was appointed CEO in 1966, and he wasted no time in accelerating Greyhound's new strategy for expansion and growth. From Trautman's installation as CEO until 1970, Greyhound acquired more than thirty widely different companies and formed a new operating division—services—that specialized in managing transportation-related businesses, such as Border Brokerage Company, which operated two duty-free shops at the Canadian border, and Florida Export Group, which also handled duty-free commerce. In addition, the services division included Manncraft Exhibitors, a company that specialized in building displays for major exhibitions; Nassau Air Dispatch, a Caribbean shipping company; and Freeport Flight Services, a Bahamian aircraft-servicing business. Trautman also brought in a line of cruise ships in the Caribbean, the Bahama Cruise Line Company. Then he added companies as diverse as Ford Van Lines of Lincoln, Nebraska, a company specializing in furniture moving; Red Top Sedan Service, a Florida limousine service; two regional intercity bus lines; Washington Airport Transport, a commuter carrier from the Washington, D.C., suburbs to Dulles Airport; and Gray Line New York Tours Corporation, a sightseeing bus line. Furthermore, he added Hausman Bus Parts to the bus-manufacturing unit.

Not all the companies that Trautman acquired proved to be as profitable or as manageable as he had hoped. What he was looking for was value as well as some synergy with Greyhound's existing transportation activities. However, as the acquisition process continued, synergy became a secondary objective. When Trautman became dissatisfied with an acquisition, he would divest it as quickly as he had acquired it, and many companies were spun off. Near the end of his tenure as CEO, Trautman would boast that Greyhound had achieved "diversification within diversification." What he meant was that in his view the operating groups had become diversified, so that each individually was recession-proof and all were enhancing the financial strength of the holding company.

Trautman's boldest maneuver and biggest acquisition came in 1970. He acquired Armour & Co., another large conglomerate that had many diverse business interests in food and consumer products. Trautman paid $400 million in cash, notes, and stock to take over Armour, which was primarily a large meat-packing company with more than $2 billion of sales in marginally profitable businesses. However, Armour also had interests in pharmaceuticals, cosmetics, and consumer products such as soap, through its very profitable Dial division. Trautman knew that it appeared as though he had overpaid for Armour-Dial. However, he soon reduced the price of the acquisition by selling off, for some $225 million, a number of Armour's divisions that he considered to be peripheral to Armour's core food and consumer businesses. In 1977, he sold off Armour's pharmaceutical division for $87 million, reducing Greyhound's net investment to $88 million. What remained after the divestitures were Armour's food operations and Armour's Dial division, from which would emerge Greyhound Dial's consumer products operating division.

Trautman hoped that his new acquisition would be more recession-proof than the bus business, if not countercyclical to it. However, the Armour acquisition brought to Greyhound new businesses that had management problems of their own in areas in which Greyhound had no experience, such as the price of pork bellies, cycles for meat packers' contracts, and foreign competition.

Trautman's Acquisitions and Divestitures Between 1970 and 1978

For the next eight years, Greyhound under Trautman continued buying businesses and increasing the size of the operating divisions in its corporate portfolio. By 1978, Greyhound's holding company consisted of five operating divisions: transportation, bus manufacturing, food and consumer products, financial, and services/food service. Each of these operating divisions acquired many new businesses, so that Greyhound was still undergoing "diversification within diversification." Many of the new acquisitions, however, were failures. Businesses as diverse as a chicken hatchery, a European acquisition to expand the financial services group, and various transportation businesses (Caribbean Gray Cruise Line, Ltd., VAVO Greyhound N.V. of Schoonhoven, Netherlands, Shannon-Greyhound Coaches, and Hausman Bus Parts) proved unprofitable.

Greyhound's portfolio of businesses kept changing during this period, and Trautman continued to feel that he was shaping a diversified company that would have a powerful base in many lines of business. He was willing to take the risk of acquiring some companies that would be failures as long as the overall health of the company was strengthened. However, Greyhound became more and more distant from its core business—bus transportation.

In April 1978, Trautman engineered another major acquisition by acquiring 97 percent of the stock of Verex Corporation, the largest private insurer of residential mortgages in the United States. The Verex acquisition was intended to strengthen the operations of Greyhound's financial operating division. Verex insured first mortgages on residential real estate generally having loan-to-value ratios in excess of 80 percent.

By 1978, Greyhound had grown nearly as large as it would grow under Trautman's leadership. The collection of businesses that he had assembled—some by acquisition, some by internal growth, and some by selling off pieces of larger businesses—was designed to make Greyhound more resistant to economic downturns. The activities of Greyhound's five major operating divisions are summarized below.

▎ *Transportation.* This operating division comprised the intercity services division and the travel services division. Transportation operated regularly scheduled passenger bus service between most metropolitan areas in North America and engaged in related operations, such as package shipping, sightseeing services, airport ground transportation, and deluxe tour and charter bus services.

▎ *Bus manufacturing.* The largest maker of intercity buses in North America, the bus-manufacturing division had operations that were vertically integrated to fabricate bus shells of intercity design, assemble buses, and manufacture bus parts for final assembly. In addition, this operating division warehoused and distributed replacement parts to meet its own requirements and the larger requirements of the bus industry. Greyhound bus manufacturing was the principal U.S. supplier of buses to charter operators and sightseeing companies.

▎ *Food and consumer products.* The companies in this operating group manufactured and marketed products to independent retailers under private-label arrangements and distributed several products under their own trademarks. These trademarks included Dial, Tone, and Pure & Natural soaps, Armour Star and Armour Tree canned meat and meat food products, Dial antiperspirants and shampoos, Appian Way pizza mixes, Parsons' ammonia, Bruce floor care products, Magic sizing and prewash, and Malina handknitting yarns and needle products.

▎ *Services/food service.* Companies in this operating division provided a broad range of services directed primarily to business markets, although duty-free shops located at airports and on cruise ships were targeted toward the consumer market. Greyhound convention services (GCS) specialized in designing, fabricating, warehousing, shipping, and setting up exhibits for trade shows, conventions, and exhibitions. GCS also served as a decorating contractor at conventions and trade show sites. The food service division, generally known as Greyhound food management (GFM), served approximately 2,400 locations in industrial plants, bus terminals, airports, office buildings, schools, colleges, and other facilities.

▎ *Financial.* This operating division consisted of Greyhound Computer Corporation, a company specializing in computer leasing and sales in the United States, Canada, Mexico, and Europe; Greyhound Leasing and Financial Corporation, a company specializing in worldwide industrial equipment leasing; Pine Top Insurance, an entity that reinsured commercial property and provided excess casualty insurance for large policyholders; and Verex Corporation, the leading private insurer of highly leveraged residential mortgages for primary lenders. Travelers Express Company, Inc., another company in the financial division, specialized in providing travelers' checks and check-cashing services in 32,000 retail establishments and financial institutions in the mainland United States and Puerto Rico.

Together, those five operating divisions were generating combined revenues of nearly $4.5 billion. Trautman had accomplished his objective of using profits from the bus operations to move Greyhound into other businesses.

Trautman Selects Teets to Take over Greyhound

Serious problems became apparent at Armour when the food and consumer products operating division went from a profit of $22 million in 1979 to a loss of $1.7 million in 1980. Armour's problems came at a very inconvenient time for Trautman because he had planned to retire in 1980. Trautman wanted to solve Armour's difficulties while he kept business rolling at Greyhound's other groups and prepared a successor to take over the collection of companies that he had assembled. That successor was to be John Teets.

Teets was very different from Trautman. His background did not include Harvard Business School or law practice. Instead, Teets had learned to be an effective hands-on manager by staying as close to the action as possible. He had worked for his father's construction company but decided that he wanted to operate a restaurant. He borrowed money, started his own restaurant, and quickly made it successful. However, soon after he had paid back his loan money and his restaurant was earning a profit, it burned to the ground. In search of a new business opportunity, Teets answered a newspaper advertisement about a position managing a Greyhound food service concession stand at the New York World's Fair in 1964.

After joining the services/food service operating group, Teets quickly distinguished himself as a tight-fisted cost cutter who could make money on a miserly budget. He seemed to have a talent for squeezing every last penny out of everything he managed. Teets moved up quickly, gaining a reputation as an extremely effective manager. By 1975, he was put in charge of the food service group, which primarily operated a conglomeration of marginally profitable, obscure, franchised restaurants. His aggressive management style produced quick results, and in 1980 he

was named the outstanding executive in the food industry. Also in 1980, in addition to Teets's responsibilities as CEO of the food service group, Trautman named Teets to head Armour and turn around the division's performance.

In 1981, Armour's major problem, as Teets saw it, was that it was paying 30 to 50 percent more in wages and fringe benefits than its competitors. Teets asked Armour's unions for immediate wage concessions. He told the unions that if he failed to get the concessions, he would have to start closing plants. After a bitter strike, wage concessions in excess of 15 percent were obtained. Given these concessions, the cost cutting from plant closings, and more efficient operating procedures, it looked as though Armour had bought itself some time.

With Armour running more efficiently, the bus business cruising along on excess profits because of the recession and energy crunch in 1979–1980, and high profits in its financial operating division generated by high interest rates in the early 1980s, it seemed that the stage was set for Trautman's retirement. In fact, all that remained was to formally select a successor. It was not difficult for Trautman to make up his mind about who that should be. He was impressed with Teet's successes in managing the services/food service group and also with the way in which Teets had dominated Armour's labor unions.

Teets Seeks Solutions

In 1981, John Teets succeeded Gerry Trautman as the chief executive officer of the Greyhound Corporation. The challenge facing Teets was to manage Greyhound's diverse businesses so that he would be able to achieve at least a 15 percent return on equity. However, many problems on the horizon might hinder the achievement of this goal. Some were the direct consequence of Trautman's ambitious expansion and diversification efforts. Others resulted from changes in environmental factors and consumer preferences. Still others stemmed from internal inefficiencies that Teets hoped he would be able to remedy.

Two challenges in particular caused Teets to feel uneasy about the corporation's overall profit picture. The first problem was Armour's high production costs, which made it a weak competitor. The second was the challenge faced by Greyhound Bus Lines: the need to compete in a newly deregulated bus transportation market. He knew that if he did not find solutions for these two problems, they would seriously diminish the Greyhound Corporation's earnings. The contribution of each operating division to Greyhound's total sales revenues in 1981 is presented in Figure 1.

Dealing with Armour's High Production Costs

Having been president of Armour, Teets was very familiar with the division's problems: its high production costs, the reluctance of union leadership and rank-and-file workers to agree with Greyhound's assessment of Armour's problems, and its utter inability to successfully change its marketing orientation to compete effectively. In addition, Teets was concerned about Armour's inefficient plants and the volatility of hog and pork-belly prices, which cyclically depressed Armour's 1981 profit of $9 million and represented a profit margin of less than 0.39 percent on sales of more than $2.3 billion. Teets sensed that it was not going to be easy to make Armour a low-cost leader. Thus, he decided to divest Armour.

In preparation for the sale, he separated the Armour Food Company from Armour-Dial. On December 18, 1983, the food company was sold to ConAgra, Inc., for $166 million. With the Armour sale, Teets was chopping off nearly half of Greyhound's business. Nevertheless, even with Greyhound's revenues dropping from $5 billion in 1982 to less than $3 billion in 1984 without Armour, the sale gave Teets the opportunity to put Greyhound in better shape than it had been in years.

The Bus Line Divestiture

Teets was also concerned about the 1981 passage of House bill H.R. 3663, which deregulated the intercity

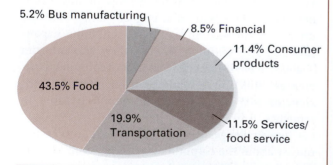

FIGURE 1

Greyhound in 1981

Source: Data from Greyhound Dial Corporation, Annual Report, 1990.

bus business. Greyhound Bus Lines had based its route system on the competitive conditions that had existed in the earlier business environment. Teets, however, sensed that future success in the bus business would be based not on the extensiveness of Greyhound's route system or its fifty years of experience in operating in a regulated industry but on its ability to make money by charging competitive fares.

With the beginning of deregulated competition in the intercity bus business and declining passenger revenues resulting from the end of the energy crunch, Greyhound found itself paying wages and benefits that were 30 to 50 percent higher than those paid by its competitors. Furthermore, its chief competitor, Trailways, having negotiated significant wage concessions from the Amalgamated Transit Union, had immediately passed the savings on to customers in the form of lower fares. Trailways's action was a frontal assault on Greyhound's most lucrative routes in an attempt to gain market share. Greyhound's response was to match every one of Trailways's price cuts. Although Greyhound preserved its market share, it lost millions of dollars.

For Greyhound Bus Lines, the legacy of deregulation was a total inability to be a low-cost provider of bus transportation. Deregulation had brought about the emergence of lower-cost competitors in regional markets, competitors that were able to be responsive and flexible in pricing and in reacting to Greyhound's actions. As a result, Greyhound lost its competitive edge. In 1986, in an effort to save the bus lines, Teets converted 120 company-owned terminals to commission agencies, trimming a huge overhead burden. He also created four stand-alone regional bus companies and a new travel and charter company. Finally, he franchised several of Greyhound's least profitable routes to independent operators, licensing them to use the Greyhound logo and trademark.

However, the one factor that Teets could not control was winning a new labor contract. In February 1986, an offer to freeze wages was rejected by the union. In October, in a deteriorating market, a second offer involving concessions was presented with the understanding that its rejection would prompt the sale of the company. The offer was subsequently rejected, and fifteen days later Teets announced the sale of Greyhound Bus Lines for approximately $350 million to an investor group headquartered in Dallas. Teets claimed that the actions taken by management in an effort to salvage the bus business were exactly the ones that made it an attractive acquisition for the Currey Group in Dallas.

The sale of Greyhound Bus Lines brought in $290 million in cash and equivalents, including a 22.5 percent interest in a new holding company established by the Dallas investor group.

Divestitures in the Financial Operating Division

Besides selling Greyhound Bus Lines in 1987, Teets also sold Greyhound Capital Corporation (GCC). The decision to sell GCC reportedly reflected Teets's conviction that "some businesses just fit better into Greyhound's plans than others." What this statement really meant was that GCC had become an underperformer in the face of lowered interest rates and changes in the tax laws that disallowed investment tax credits. GCC was sold for $140 million, realizing a one-time gain of $79.7 million for Greyhound.

In early 1987, Greyhound announced its intention to sell Verex. The timing of the acquisition had been a disaster, given the recession in the real estate market caused by the oil bust in the early 1980s. Verex suffered huge losses generated by insurance claims from business generated before 1985. These claims were originating in states where severe downturns in farming, auto production, and oil drilling had led to a widespread inability to keep up with mortgage payments.

Not surprisingly, Teets could not find a buyer for Verex. In January 1988, Greyhound announced that it had stopped taking applications for new mortgage insurance and that it was discontinuing its mortgage insurance business. It also announced that 1987 results would reflect a one-time after-tax charge of $45 million as a result of reclassifying Verex as a discontinued operation; then Greyhound would manage Verex's existing portfolio to minimize continuing losses from the company's operations. Management hoped the remnants of Verex would not be a drain on corporate resources.

With the sale of Greyhound Bus Lines, Greyhound Capital Corporation, and Armour, and with the discontinuation of Verex, Teets announced that he was near the end of his mammoth task of restructuring Greyhound and shedding businesses that seemed to lack sufficient growth potential. By late 1987, Greyhound Corporation was primarily a consumer products and services company. Figure 2 sum-

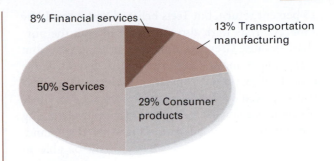

FIGURE 2

Total Revenues: 3.3 Billion

Source: Data from Greyhound Dial Corporation, Annual Report, 1990.

marizes the contribution of the different operating groups to total revenues in 1988. Compare the Greyhound Corporation that Teets structured (Figure 2) with the corporation he inherited in 1982 (Figure 1).

With the restructuring in place, Wall Street looked for an improvement in Greyhound's performance. However, it soon became obvious that the stack of businesses created by Teets was not proving much more profitable than the ones he had divested. There was only an 8.8 percent return on equity in 1987, and net income after nonrecurring losses was $25.1 million, the lowest for many years. Revenue was $2.5 billion. Teets maintained that the problems with Greyhound's various divisions could not have been foreseen as the restructuring was taking place but that Greyhound was set for "substantial profits in the future." Teets began a program of acquisitions and new product developments to strengthen Greyhound's presence in the four business areas identified in Figure 2 and to begin the turnaround process.

Consumer Products

In the midst of the divestiture of Armour and Greyhound Bus Lines, Teets had made one major acquisition. On February 21, 1985, he announced the purchase of Purex Industries and its thirty household cleaning products for $264 million. Teets's aim with this acquisition was to boost profits in Greyhound's Consumer Products operating division (principally composed of the old Dial division) by using the Dial sales force and marketing expertise to sell Purex products—Purex bleach, Brillo soap pads, Old Dutch cleanser, and Sweetheart and Fels-Naptha soap, among others.

The Purex acquisition drew mixed reviews from Wall Street. It did not meet Teets's goal of a

15 percent return, but Teets believed that it would by 1988. Analysts were also unimpressed with the purchase because Greyhound had not been successful in managing Armour. Teets responded that Dial was capable of marketing consumer products, although it had not been successful at developing its own lines. He cited as evidence the fact that Dial was marketing the number one deodorant soap in its Dial brand. Analysts did concede that Teets should be able to realize increased profitability by using the same sales force to sell Purex and Dial products. Along with Purex's household cleaners, Greyhound also got Elio's Pizza as part of the Purex acquisition. Teets was enthusiastic about expanding this frozen pizza business nationwide from its East Coast base. This was to be done by means of the Dial sales force.

The Dial operating division, as it was now known, became the center of Teets's attention and the flagship of the Greyhound Corporation. In the past Dial had not had much success in launching new products, but Teets was determined to change the situation, recognizing that growth in revenue had to come from the manufacture and marketing of new products. The first product introduced by the Dial division was Lunch Buckets, a range of microwavable meals with a stable shelf life of two years. This was a new market segment. Previously all microwavable meals had been frozen. Lunch Buckets meals were very successful and surpassed early expectations by a wide margin. By 1988, they had national distribution. By 1990, they had seized a 30 percent market share, becoming the market leader. In 1990, Dial announced new low-calorie Lunch Buckets.

Another new product introduced in 1987 was Liquid Dial antibacterial soap. This product, too, was very successful, and by 1990 it had achieved a 20 percent market share and was the second-best-selling liquid soap in the market, after Procter & Gamble's Ivory liquid. Another successful new product was Mountain Fresh Dial, a highly scented version of Dial's deodorant soap. Additional developments were liquid Purex detergent and other cleaning products.

In 1988, Teets acquired the household products and industrial specialties businesses of the 20 Mule Team division of United States Borax and Chemical Corporation. Teets announced a new advertising campaign to reestablish the market presence of Borax bleaches and cleaning powders. Teets's formula for increasing the Dial division's market share called for further extensions of the Dial brand, further extensions of the Purex brand name, and Parsons' ammonia.

Greyhound Dial, Then Dial

On June 4, 1990, Teets learned that Greyhound Bus lines, the bus transportation company that he had sold in 1987, had declared bankruptcy and Greyhound's stake was now valueless. To distance his "new" company from Greyhound, he changed the company's name to Greyhound Dial in February 1990, and the next year it became simply Dial. The name change also marked the company's new focus on its consumer products division. However, the price of Dial's stock, which had been more or less unchanged for the last six years, started to plunge in 1990 after Dial reported a loss. Analysts wondered whether Teets would ever be able to improve the company's profitability.

In September 1990, another consumer products acquisition was announced: Breck hair care products. Breck had 1989 revenues of $60 million. Teets announced that integrating Breck into Dial would result in annual sales of more than $1 billion for the Dial division. Teets said that "Breck has been a household name for 60 years. It's a perfect fit with our other Dial products and under Dial management the power of the Breck name will flourish." Under its previous owners, Breck had languished. Teets hoped to turn the product around by applying Dial's marketing skills.

From the changes he had orchestrated, Teets was hoping for sizable revenue growth and profit from the Dial division, and in March 1991, as an indication of the company's future strategy, the company's name was again changed, to the Dial Corporation.

Services

By 1987, the restaurant food services division was contributing the most to total revenues. It was natural, therefore, that Teets should seek to strengthen food operations. In 1987, Dial purchased the nation's second biggest airline catering and airline retailing business. The new operation had three units: Dobbs International Services, the nation's second largest provider of in-flight meals for airlines; Dobbs Houses, the operator of restaurants at many airports; and Carson International, which operated the food and beverage concession at Chicago's O'Hare Airport. In 1990, Teets announced that Dobbs had had a record year—the company had served sixty scheduled airlines in forty cities. Moreover, it had added five new accounts, including Houston International Airport.

Teets strengthened Dial's Travelers Express money order business with the purchase of Republic Money Orders, Inc., of Dallas. This acquisition made Dial the leader in the money order business, ahead of the U.S. Postal Service. Teets had returned to the cruise ship industry in 1984 with the takeover of Premier Cruise Lines. In 1986, he negotiated an agreement with the Walt Disney Company that made Dial's Premier Cruise Line Disney's exclusive cruise ship line, with three- and four-day sailing to the Bahamas from Cape Canaveral in Florida. The cruise line business enjoyed record sales, and in 1989 another line was added.

The New Look of the Dial Corporation

The new look of Dial's businesses after the acquisitions and divestitures is shown in Table 1. Teets acknowledged the wide diversity of businesses in the

TABLE 1
Greyhound's Businesses

Consumer Products	Services	Transportation Manufacturing	Financial Services
The Dial Corporation	Brewster Transport Company, Ltd.	Motor Coach Industries (MCI)	Greyhound Financial Corporation
Food	Consultants and Designers, Inc.	Transportation Manufacturing Corporation (TMC)	Greyhound Financial and Leasing
Personal care	Carson International, Inc.	• Custom Coach	Greyhound Financial Services, Ltd.
Laundry and household	Dobbs Houses, Inc.		Greyhound Bank PLC
	Dobbs International Services, Inc.		

Greyhound Airport Services Companies	Greyhound International Travel, Inc. (GITI)
Greyhound Exhibitgroup Inc.	Greyhound Leisure Services, Inc. (GLSI)
Greyhound Exposition Services, Inc.	• Florida Export Warehouse
Greyhound Food Management, Inc.	• International Cruise Shops
• Faber Enterprises, Inc.	• Greyhound Leisure Services Duty-Free Shops
• Glacier Park, Inc.	• Premier Cruise Lines, Ltd.
• GFM Engineering and Design Group	Greyhound Lines of Canada, Ltd.
• GFM Fast Food Division	Travelers Express Company, Inc.
• GFM Public Service Division	• Republic Money Orders, Inc.
• GFM Truckstop Systems	Universal Coach Parts, Inc.
• Restaura	
• Restaura, S.A.	

Source: Greyhound Dial Corporation, Annual Report, 1990.

company's portfolio. However, he contended that the businesses did fit together. In his words, "We are a multiservice business. We operate in niches and were number one or two in most of these niches. From a recession standpoint, I think we're going to feel it less than most major companies." Teets argued that Dial was making acquisitions to strengthen its presence in existing niches. By concentrating on a niche, the corporation avoided going head-to-head with major competitors. Moreover, the niches were recession-proof, small-ticket items such as Lunch Buckets and soap, not refrigerators and cars. Teets argued that Dial was positioned for growth and that management expected revenues to increase steadily over the next few years. See Table 2.

Some analysts, however, felt that the organization was still a hodgepodge of different businesses in need of rationalization. They pointed to the lack of fit between a cruise ship line and hotel operations in Glacier National Park and contract catering, saying that Dial was still a collection of companies with no real connection. They also argued that Greyhound Dial's breakup value was more than $60 a share, while its stock price had been in the range of $25 to $35 for years. Teets agreed that some minor divestitures were necessary, but he believed that the best way to proceed was to stay in the same niches and manage the existing businesses more efficiently.

Dial, 1990–1996

In 1991, it appeared that, at last, things were going Dial's way. Dial's share price, which had plummeted to less than $10 a share at the end of 1990, rose to almost $25 a share by the end of 1992. This turnaround occurred for several reasons. First, Dial had finally spun off its loss-making financial services group to stockholders so that the liabilities no longer affected its balance sheet. Second, its consumer products group, and in particular the Dial soap division, was performing strongly. Dial had become the number one selling deodorant soap in the United States, with more than 20 percent of the market. Third, Teets had orchestrated a major downsizing, or what he had called "rightsizing," reducing the number of corporate managers from four hundred to three hundred. Also, all of Dial's different businesses were subjected to close scrutiny to try to reduce costs, and employment was reduced across the board, even in the successful Dial division. Teets also reduced corporate debt from a high of $850 million to $550 million

through the sales of certain assets such as Dobbs House, its airport catering company. Analysts hoped that all these events were the first signs of a turnaround in the company's performance.

These hopes were doomed, however, by a series of problems that emerged in Dial's various businesses. In the 1990s, businesses in Dial's transportation manufacturing unit began to perform poorly, draining the company's profits. In 1993, Teets decided to dispose of it. Also, its Purex bleach business was doing poorly and losing money. It began to seem that just when Dial was making strides in one of its businesses, problems in another were wiping out the effects of the improvement. Investors began to wonder again about Teets's claims for his recession-proof niche strategy.

By 1995, major problems were affecting many areas of the company, including the pivotal Dial division. Teets, desperate to increase the company's return on equity and stock price, which had been flat since its high in 1992, began again to slash costs. One way he did this was by reducing the advertising budget for Dial soap products from $8.7 million to $4.9 million. However, this was something that no niche player could afford to do when battling such industry giants as Procter & Gamble and Unilever, whose new soap Lever 2000 made major inroads into sales of Dial soap. Dial soap's market share dropped to 17.6 percent from 19.7 percent of the market in 1995, which was a severe blow to the Dial Corporation's most important product line and a disaster for the company.

The Purex division also was not performing well. The Purex bleach line was phased out in 1995 because of mounting losses. Late in 1995, Purex detergent, the low-priced detergent that had been selling well, came under intense pressure from Procter & Gamble, which introduced a competing low-priced brand, Ultra Bonus, that was aimed directly at Purex. Dial was forced to slash the price of Purex by 10 percent to compete, further cutting into the company's profits. Furthermore, Dial's successful Lunch Buckets, the line of microwave products, had generated a host of imitators from major food companies that quickly introduced their own competing products. Having lost this niche and no longer able to compete, Dial phased out Lunch Buckets in 1995. It began to seem to Dial's managers that even when they found a winning strategy their larger competitors just stole the idea away from them.

TABLE 2

The Dial Corporation: Consolidated Balance Sheet
(000 omitted, except per-share data)

	Year-ended December 31		
	1995	**1994**	**1993**
Revenues	$ 3,575,070	$ 3,546,847	$ 3,000,342
Costs and expenses			
Costs of sales and services	$ 3,271,151	$ 3,216,627	$ 2,725,049
Restructuring charges and asset write downs	191,100		
Unallocated corporate expense and other items, net	43,194	43,938	42,734
Interest expense	75,994	61,195	57,292
Minority interests	4,346	3,392	3,618
	$ 3,585,785	$ 3,325,152	$ 2,828,693
Income (loss) before income taxes	$ (10,715)	$ 221,695	$ 171,649
Income taxes (benefit)	(11,852)	81,384	61,376
Income from Continuing Operations	$ 1,137	$ 140,311	$ 110,273
Income from discontinued operations			32,120
Income before extraordinary charge and cumulative effect of change in accounting principle	$ 1,137	$ 140,311	$ 142,393
Extraordinary charge for early retirement of debt net of tax benefit of $11,833			(21,908)
Cumulative effect net of tax benefit of $7,544 to January 1, 1995 of initial application of SFAS No. 121, "Accounting for the Impairment of Long-Lived Assets and for Long-Lived Assets to Be Disposed Of"	(17,696)		
Net income (loss)	$ (16,559)	$ 140,311	$ 120,485
Income (Loss) per Common Share			
Continuing operations	$ 0.00	$ 1.61	$ 1.28
Discontinued operations			0.38
Income before extraordinary charge and cumulative effect of change in accounting principle	$ 0.00	$ 1.61	$ 1.66
Extraordinary charge			(0.26)
Cumulative effect, to January 1, 1995, of initial application of SFAS No. 121	(0.20)		
Net income (loss) per common share	$ (0.20)	$ 1.61	$ 1.40

Dial's other businesses were also suffering problems. Its cruise ship line, Premier Cruise Lines, which had formed an agreement with the Walt Disney Company to operate Disney's theme cruises on the Big Red Boat, lost its license in 1995 when Disney decided that it would launch its own cruise line. With four aging ships, and lacking any differentiated appeal in the increasingly competitive cruise ship industry in the 1990s, the company put its ships up for sale and withdrew from the cruise ship business—one more recession-proof niche gone.

Then, Dial's airline food business began to suffer in the 1990s when, to cut down on costs in an increasingly competitive airline industry, the major airlines cut back on the quality of the food they offered their customers. Airlines that had offered full meals began to offer snacks, and airlines such as Southwest offered passengers nothing. In airports, too, there had been a move to allow fast-food chains to set up their franchises on site to increase the variety of foods offered to customers. All this hurt Dial's catering businesses.

It was becoming increasingly obvious to industry analysts that Dial was nothing more than a hodge-podge of different businesses that had nothing in common, were not recession-proof, and did not even have a secure niche.

Dial, 1996–2002

With its profits flat or eroding and no turnaround in sight, the question became how to create new value from Dial's different businesses. The movement of many diversified companies to break up their operations and let individual businesses go it alone in the early 1990s gave Teets his answer. He would split apart Dial's consumer products and services operations—thus dismantling the empire he had built since 1984—into two different companies. One, which would still be known as the Dial Corp., would consist of all its consumer product interests and would have revenues of about $1.3 billion. The other, to be called Viad Corp., would manage its remaining financial, catering, and exhibition businesses and have revenues of about $2.2 billion.

Initially, analysts thought that the breakup would allow the two new companies to realize more value. For example, since they operated separately, a downturn in the business of one division would no longer hurt the performance of the other. Moreover, after the breakup managers would be able to make decisions that could promote their own businesses, not corporate interests. However, analysts later came to realize that in the future there would be two sets of managers who would have to be paid to manage the two companies and two sets of overhead costs. Moreover, the question arose as to whether there was any value to be created by the breakups, because all of Dial's businesses were under threats from more efficient and aggressive competitors such as Procter & Gamble, Colgate-Palmolive, and Unilever. Analysts came to believe increasingly that more value could be made for shareholders if the company dismantled itself and sold off its assets separately to the highest bidder. A bidder could then merge a particular Dial business into its own operations and thus reduce manufacturing, distribution, or marketing costs or even use its skills to increase the division's differentiation advantage.

In July 1996, John Teets's plan came under increasing attack from Michael Price, president of Heine Securities Corp. Price was the advisor to Mutual Series Funds, a large mutual fund company that owned 9.9 percent of Dial's stock. Price, along with other analysts, however, argued that Teet's plan would reduce, not increase, value for shareholders and that what Teets should do was to divest Dial's many different businesses and return the proceeds to shareholders. Of course, the selloff would mean that many of Dial's managers might find themselves out of well-paying jobs, including Teets, who had earned many millions of dollars over the years. On the other hand, these managers had not created much value for their shareholders.

In 1996, Teets answered his critics with half-page ads in the *Wall Street Journal* arguing that his strategy was a "strategy for empowered growth" that would allow each of the two new companies to "aggressively pursue acquisition opportunities without worry about upsetting the balance in Dial's existing mix of business." However, he did not explain how new value would be created by the two companies or how the proposed acquisitions might create value. Since Teets's acquisition strategy had met with little success for the last twelve years, what reason would shareholders have to suppose it would improve in the future?

This question remained unanswered, but in 1996 Viad was spun off to stockholders, Teets stepped down as CEO, and a new CEO, Malcolm Jozoff, was appointed to head what was now a consumer products company, albeit one that sold canned beef and shampoo. Jozoff was recruited from Procter & Gamble because Dial's board believed that a P&G veteran would understand how to fashion a business model to promote the profitability of a soap and detergent maker. What they forgot was that P&G is a differentiator whose claim to fame is developing new and improved products and marketing them successfully to consumers. While it is true that Dial, the best-selling antibacterial soap, was their flagship differentiated product, Dial's other main products, such as Purex detergent, Breck Shampoo, and even Armour corned beef, were not bought for their differentiated qualities but because of their low price. Even Dial soap did not command much of a premium price compared to P&G's and Unilever's brands; it sold because of the advertising expenditures used to promote its brand name.

Jozoff, however, given his immersion in P&G's "differentiation" culture, saw Dial's problems as the lack of a differentiated appeal of its products, not the fact that its high-cost structure was eroding the profitability of a low-price cost leadership strategy. Jozoff's efforts were thus directed toward increasing customer demand by differentiating Dial's brands. To promote Purex washing powder, he entered into a joint venture with Germany's Henkel group to use that company's expertise in stain removal to boost Purex's cleaning power (not its strong point); he proposed to call the new powder "Purex Advanced," and to recoup the extra costs it would cost a few dollars more a pack. He felt these moves would position it against Tide, the leading brand. Knowing that P&G was entering the home dry-cleaning market, he introduced a new Purex home dry-cleaning kit, and also knowing that P&G and Unilever were introducing washing powder in tablet form, he put in motion Purex Tablets. To push Dial into higher-end personal care products, he bought two companies, Sarah Michaels and Freeman Cosmetics, that specialized in producing upscale soaps, bath powders, and oils for gift boxes, although he did not propose to sell these under the Dial name. Also, knowing that rivals were developing new kinds of antibacterial soap with more fragrant scents and better foaming qualities, he reformulated Dial soap to position it against tough future competition. Jozoff also agreed to acquire the Plusbelle brand hair care business from Revlon for $46.5 million. Plusbelle was the leader in the Argentinean market. These acquisitions cost over $300 million and pushed up Dial's debt to over $550 million. Teets had left Dial saddled with a $300 million debt during the Viad spinoff, whereas Viad emerged virtually debt free.

In changing Dial's business-level strategy, Jozoff plunged the company into a whole new set of problems. First, the movement to a differentiation strategy raised Dial's cost structure, especially because of the extra debt it had to assume, so he was betting the company's future on consumers' acceptance of Dial's new products and higher-pricing structure. At the same time, Jozoff brought the company into more direct competition with the rivals such as P&G and Unilever that had much more money to spend on the expensive business of promoting new brand products. For example, it was estimated that in 1994 it would cost $5 million in fees to retailers to promote a new consumer product in the greater New York area; that figure had risen to $25 million by 1999 because

of increasing competition for shelf space caused by the consolidation both of consumer product companies and of retailers and supermarkets such as Kroger's.

When Dial's new products started to be manufactured and introduced in 1998 and 1999, at first things looked good; sales increased by 12 percent in 1998 and by 13 percent in 1999 to $1.7 billion, and operating profits grew 13 percent in 1998 and 17 percent in 1999. However, it turned out that things were not as good as they seemed. While sales did increase in 1998, largely as the result of a big increase in marketing expenditures to sell the new, wider product range, by 1999 consumers were turning away from Dial's brands. By the middle of 1999 Dial's top managers knew there were problems, but to disguise the issue from the board, the company's sales team was instructed to boost the end-of-year sales figures by "stuffing the channel" with Dial products, that is, sending huge inventories of products, particularly Dial soap, to retailers that counted as sales in the company's books, and by offering retailers big promotions to sell its products at discounted prices to move them off the shelves.

Major errors were also made. First, expecting customers to stock up on canned goods because of Y2K glitches, the company loaded up stores with extra Armor Star Vienna Sausage and then raised prices hoping its competitors would follow. When there was no Y2K panic and competitors didn't raise prices, most of this product was left unsold and was either returned or sold at cost. Second, although it seemed to Jozoff that the Sarah Michaels and Freeman Cosmetics acquisitions were natural, albeit "upmarket," extensions to Dial's product line, Dial was not prepared for the huge manufacturing challenges involved in custom-packing gift boxes and matching them to the needs of the customers. As Baum (see next section) later said, upmarket products such as scented lotions, bath oils, and aromatherapy products are "fashion products," whereas Dial's business was "bread-and-butter" products where low-cost production and distribution were vital. Third, it turned out that the market for home dry cleaning was far smaller than anticipated, and Dial's dry-cleaning product was simply left on the shelf because of its rivals' higher advertising budgets.

Even in the vital soap business, problems arose. Because Dial had stuffed the channels with its old soap product, when its new improved scented moisturizing soap came out in late 1999, retailers would not sell it until they had sold the old soap product. This gave a leg up to P&G and Unilever, which had also introduced a new range of soap to compete with Dial. Finally, Dial discovered that customers didn't understand the properties of the new improved Purex washing powder or why they should spend a lot more for it. As Baum later commented, he pleaded with Jozoff to introduce it under another upmarket name to differentiate it, but this was not done, and the powder was left stuck in the middle—not differentiated and not low cost.

Dial Gets a New CEO

As a result of all these problems, estimates for Dial's 2000 operating profits dropped from $73 million to $60 million in the summer of 2000, wiping out all its previous gains. The board became increasingly aware of the problems that had been taking place, and in August 2000 they ousted Jozoff as CEO and replaced him with a vocal board member, Herbert M. Baum. Baum, a former Campbell Soup executive and CEO of Quaker State (which he had sold to Pennzoil) and then the COO of Hasbro, the toy maker, was surprised to be asked to take over yet one more turnaround effort at Dial, but he accepted the challenge. Since his experience was with bread-and-butter products—canned soups and oil—he was familiar with the problems of managing a company's cost structure to get the most value out of its products. He also recognized the importance of finding the right strategy to compete against rivals like P&G and powerful retail chains like Kroger and Wal-Mart, both of which were launching private-label low-price washing powders and soaps at the low end of the market. The problem was that he had to move fast because Dial's performance and stock price were collapsing.

Baum took a close look at how Dial's brands were managed internally. He reorganized them into a product structure with five product groups—personal cleansing, washing powders, air fresheners, food products, and Dial International. For the first time, Baum made the product line managers accountable for their own inventory management and profit-and-loss figures. Previously, these had been spread across brands so that each line's relative performance had been hidden. Now it was possible to identify specific underperforming brands and decide

what to do about them—turn them around, sell them off, or close them down.

Baum then turned his attention to the various problems that emerged in launching Dial's new products. Recognizing the importance of protecting Dial soap's market share, he pumped money into advertising its improved products to regain their momentum and build their profitability. With Purex, he decided to go ahead with the introduction of Purex tablets, but ended the joint venture with Henkel and went back to the old low-cost strategy. He also decided to sell off the Sarah Michaels and Freeman upscale lines, which had only resulted in losses, and he used the money to reduce Dial's debt. He also withdrew from the home dry-cleaning market and took Purex's product off the shelf. The savings in operating costs from abandoning these product lines both provided money to fund Dial's core soap, Purex, and Renuzit air freshener products and lowered its cost structure.

In September 2001, Baum announced that, given the increasing competitive pressures in all its brand categories from companies like P&G and Unilever, he and the board felt that it would be better if Dial were part of a larger enterprise. Various possible acquirers came forward to look at the company's books in the next months, but it appeared that none of them wanted to buy the whole company. In the meantime, Baum's business model and strategies began to pay off for Dial. Its inventory stocking and manufacturing problems were gone; brand managers were squeezing out costs now that they were directly responsible for their brand's performance; and top managers were not distracted by searching for elusive new product opportunities but were focusing, perhaps for the first time, on managing all aspects of the value chain to reduce costs. With its well-known products, sold at the right price, there was no reason why Dial should not be able to increase revenues and profits and build cash flow.

In fact, the company astounded analysts when in April 2002, only six months after it put itself up for sale, it raised its first-quarter earnings estimates, citing stronger-than-expected domestic sales. Dial's share reached $20, up from just $12 only a year before. Since no buyer for Dial had emerged, Baum also announced in April that Dial itself, to strengthen and protect its core businesses, would be looking to make acquisitions in the coming year. However, recognizing that nobody wanted to buy the whole of

Dial because of its many different product lines, Baum emphasized that Dial would be buying brands, not companies—those with high volumes and those that used the same sales channels as Dial to make better use of the company's resources.

It seems that the future of the company depends on how quickly Baum can build up Dial's competencies in product development and brand management on the one hand, and on manufacturing and inventory control on the other. If these improve as time goes on, then Dial with its pruned and cleaner product lines will become an even more attractive takeover target; indeed, if Baum can find a buyer for Armor foods, its divestiture is almost certain. However, the meat-packing business is notoriously risky, and its low profit margins are not attractive. The question is which course of action—remaining independent or a effecting a breakup—will Baum, Dial's board, and outside analysts think will create most value for shareholders?

REFERENCES

Moody's Transportation Manual, 1987.

A. Stuart, "Greyhound Gets Ready for a New Driver," *Fortune,* March 3, 1966, pp. 34–38.

Greyhound Corporation, Annual Reports, 1966–1990.

Dial Corporation, Annual Reports and 10K Reports, 1971–2002.

"Greyhound: A Big Sell-off Leaves It Built for Better Speed," *Business Week,* July 25, 1983, pp. 88–90.

"Greyhound's New Strategy: Slimmed Down and Decentralized, It's After More Market Share, 15% on Equity," *Dun's Business Month,* February 1984, pp. 66–68.

S. Toy and J. H. Dobrzynski, "Will More Soap Help Greyhound Shine?" *Business Week,* March 11, 1985, pp. 73–78.

"The Greyhound Corporation," *Wall Street Journal Transcript,* February 5, 1990, pp. 96, 204.

"Dial Corp.: Firm's Loss of $26.2 Million Is Due to Special Charges," *Wall Street Journal,* October 25, 2000, p. B8.

Jack Neff and Kate MacArthur, "Beleaguered Dial Cuts Product Lines," *Advertising Age,* September 25, 2000, p. 128.

"Dial Corp.: Loss of $7.5 Million Posted, Partly from a Restructuring," *Wall Street Journal,* January 25, 2001, p. B5.

Rebecca Flass, "Dial Shifts Direction," *Adweek,* May 21, 2001, p. 8.

"Dial Agrees to Buy Plusbelle," *Wall Street Journal,* March 30, 2000, p. C14.

Steven Lipin and Anna W. Mathews, "Dial Board, Hit by New Profit Shortfall, Ousts Top Executives and Turns to Baum," *Wall Street Journal,* August 8, 2000, p. A3.

Arlene Weintraub and Christopher Palameri, "Wish Everyone Used Dial? Dial Does," *Business Week,* September 25, 2000, pp. 132–134.

Kerri Walsh, "Dial Raises First-Quarter Earnings Estimates; Eyes Brand Acquisitions," *Chemical Week,* April 17, 2002, p. 36.

"Dial Jettisons Underperforming Unit," *SPC Soap, Perfumery, and Cosmetics,* London, September, 2001, p. 4.

Brent Shearer, "Under Competitive Pressures, Dial Puts Itself Up for Sale," *Mergers and Acquisitions,* October 2001, p. 23.

"Dial Corp.: Earnings Forecast Climbs Again to as Much as 25 Cents a Share," *Wall Street Journal,* April 10, 2002, p. A8.

Jack Neff, "Clorox, Dial Exit Dry Cleaning Biz," *Advertising Age,* September 10, 2001, p. 4.

Kerri Walsh, "Dial May Be Broken Up," *Chemical Week,* August 15, 2001, p. 25.

"Dial Puts Itself Up for Sale Despite Portfolio, Analysts Say Company Could Fetch $2 Billion," *Chemical Market Reporter,* August 13, 2001, p. 3.

"Dial Corp.: Quarterly Earnings Surge, Outlook for Year Is Raised," *Wall Street Journal,* July 26, 2001.

Gene G. Marcial, "With Dial, Clorox Could Clean Up," *Business Week,* October 4, 1999, p. 247.

"Dial Corp.: Laundry-Products Venture to Tap Henkel Technology," *Wall Street Journal,* April 21, 1999.

Index